123RD YEAR

# WISDEN

## CRICKETERS' ALMANACK

## 1986

EDITED BY JOHN WOODCOCK

PUBLISHED BY JOHN WISDEN & CO LTD
6 WARWICK COURT
LONDON WC1R 5DJ

A MEMBER OF THE
McCORQUODALE GROUP OF COMPANIES

COVER EDITION £12.50 CASED EDITION £14.50

John Wisden & Co Ltd
6 Warwick Court
London WC1R 5DJ



ISBN
Cased edition 0 947766 04 9
Soft cover edition 0 947766 05 7



Computer typeset by SB Datagraphics, Colchester

Printed in Great Britain by Spottiswoode Ballantyne Printers Ltd

# PREFACE

This 123rd edition of *Wisden* shows no significant changes from the 122nd, though it has been, as usual, a struggle keeping it to its present length.

I am especially pleased that Sir Donald Bradman is among the contributors. His only previous article for the Almanack, in 1939, was headed "Cricket at the Crossroads". He chose that title himself (as he did this), saying that it was "intended to convey a meaning but not to be misunderstood". It was written after what he felt had been a singularly happy series of Test matches between England and Australia. Last summer's, also between England and Australia, was the same; but it is now another world we live in, as the great batsman observes. "Little did I appreciate [in 1938] what a revolution would engulf cricket before another 50 years had passed", he writes.

Mike Brearley extols Alan Knott upon his retirement. No-one's game, he says, with the possible exception of Ian Botham's, has given him more pleasure. There is an article on the finances of cricket and cricketers by Jack Bannister, who knows all there is to know about them in his capacity as Secretary of the Cricketers' Association. My old friend, John Kitchin, writes of even wetter summers than 1985, though at the time it seemed hardly possible that there could ever have been one. E. M. Wellings, once the most polemical of cricket writers, traces the history of the covering of pitches over the last 100 years.

When an Australian team is in England they normally provide two or three of the Five Cricketers of the Year. In 1948 they supplied all five (Hassett, Johnston, Lindwall, Miller and Tallon). This time only Craig McDermott is included, Allan Border, their captain, having been chosen before. There was no opposing Tim Robinson, who had such a prolific first year in Test cricket. Richard Ellison's major contribution to England's two innings victories over Australia, at Edgbaston and The Oval, is also recognised. It seemed fitting to have a representative of the Gloucestershire side, in view of their strong and unexpected challenge for the County Championship, and no-one batted more consistently for them than Phil Bainbridge. Neal Radford, the only bowler to take 100 first-class wickets in the 1985 English season, completes the list.

The Cricket Records section is back with Bill Frindall, who looked after it from 1971 to 1978. My thanks are due to Barry McCaully, who filled the breach when Michael Fordham died so suddenly in 1982, but found, with his other commitments, that the days were insufficiently long. As the best known of all cricket statisticians, and one of the few whose full-time work it is, Bill Frindall is the recipient of every fact and figure from the world of cricket. For the first time space has been found for some of the more significant records of one-day international cricket.

Unless otherwise stated in the scores, wides and no-balls have been debited to the bowlers all the way through this edition. It will be seen, too, that certain full scores are printed again from Pakistan. This was not done last year, when it was really not possible to vouch for their accuracy.

The overseas section continues to expand. Being the venue for official visits from full members of the International Cricket Conference, Sharjah now qualifies for its own entry. Cricket in Denmark appears for the first time, and Sri Lanka crop up with increasing regularity. Simultaneously, of course, the list of contributors grows. To them all, whether professional journalists and photographers, county secretaries, schoolmasters, members of the secretariats at Lord's or just willing assistants, I am most grateful for their help. I would also thank all those who write to me each year, many of them from distant parts.

John Arlott (Books), R. L. Arrowsmith (Obituaries) and Robert Brooke (Births and Deaths) are always a source of strength, and once again Christine Forrest and Graeme Wright have done a huge share of the work. Much of the credit for the book belongs to these two.

JOHN WOODCOCK

Longparish,
Hampshire.

## LIST OF CONTRIBUTORS

The Editor acknowledges with gratitude the assistance afforded in the preparation of the Almanack by the following:

Jack Arlidge (Sussex)
John Arlott (Books)
R. L. Arrowsmith (Obituaries)
Chris Aspin (Lancashire Leagues)
B. J. Aspital
Philip August
J. D. Bannister (Warwickshire)
Brian Bearshaw (Lancashire)
Michael Berry
John Billot (Glamorgan)
J. Watson Blair (Scotland)
Sir Donald Bradman
Mike Brearley
R. T. Brittenden
Robert Brooke (Births and Deaths)
Kenneth R. Bullock (Canada)
C. R. Buttery (New Zealand)
John Callaghan (Yorkshire)
M. J. Carey
D. B. Carr
Terry Cooper (Middlesex)
Geoffrey Copinger
Mike Coward
Tony Cozier (West Indies)
Patrick Eagar
D. A. Ellman-Brown
Matthew Engel
Paton Fenton (Oxford University)
David Field (Surrey)
David Foot
Bill Frindall (Records)
D. E. J. Frith
Nigel Fuller (Essex)
M. E. Gear
Trevor Grant
David Hallett (Cambridge University)
Les Hatton
Brian Hayward (Hampshire)
Brian Heald
Eric Hill (Somerset)
Grenville Holland (UAU)
Brian Hunt
Ken Ingman (ESCA)
Vic Isaacs
Martin Johnson (Leicestershire)
Abid Ali Kazi
Ken Kelly
John Kitchin
Brian Langley
Stephanie Lawrence
John Lawson (Nottinghamshire)
Alan Lee
Edward Liddle
Peter Lush
John Mackinnon (Australia)
Alison Mann
Michael Melford
John Minshull-Fogg
Chris Moore (Worcestershire)
Dudley Moore (Kent)
John Morris
Gerald Mortimer (Derbyshire)
David Munden
Rod Nicholson
Graham Otway
A. L. A. Pichanick
Qamar Ahmed
Andrew Radd (Northamptonshire)
Netta Rheinberg
Geoffrey Saulez
Derek Scott (Ireland)
Brian Scovell
Peter Sichel (South Africa)
Bill Smith
P. A. Snow
Fred Speakman (Northamptonshire)
J. R. Stephenson
P. N. Sundaresan (India)
John Thicknesse
Gerry Vaidyasekera (Sri Lanka)
D. R. Walsh (HMC Schools)
E. M. Wellings
Geoffrey Wheeler (Gloucestershire)
A. S. R. Winlaw

# CONTENTS

Preface .......... 2
Index .......... 7
Notes by the Editor .......... 48
Five Cricketers of the Year .......... 57
Whither Cricket Now? By Sir Donald Bradman .......... 65
Alan Knott – A Thorough Genius by J. M. Brearley .......... 69
A Financial Revolution by Jack Bannister .......... 74
1903 – The Wettest Summer of Them All? by John Kitchin .......... 77
Covering by Degrees by E. M. Wellings .......... 81
Test Cricketers 1877-1985 .......... 85
Cricket Records .......... 125
Features of 1985 .......... 256
First-Class Averages, 1985 .......... 260
Individual Scores of 100 and Over .......... 267
Ten Wickets in a Match .......... 271
Six Wickets in an Innings .......... 271
The Australians in England, 1985 .......... 273
The Zimbabweans in England, 1985 .......... 309
The Cricket Council, TCCB and NCA .......... 317
Marylebone Cricket Club .......... 318
Other Matches at Lord's, 1985 .......... 322
Rules of Qualification .......... 330
Britannic Assurance County Championship, 1985 .......... 333
The First-Class Counties in 1985 .......... 340
Oxford and Cambridge Universities in 1985 .......... 613
Other Matches, 1985 .......... 643
NatWest Bank Trophy, 1985 .......... 647
Benson and Hedges Cup, 1985 .......... 669
John Player League, 1985 .......... 701
Minor County Championship, 1985 .......... 781
Second Eleven Championship, 1985 .......... 799
Warwick Under-25 Championship, 1985 .......... 816
The UAU Championship, 1985 .......... 818
The Lancashire Leagues, 1985 .......... 820
Irish and Scottish Cricket in 1985 .......... 822
Schools Cricket in 1985 .......... 826
England in India (and Sri Lanka), 1984-85 .......... 878
The Australians in India, 1984-85 .......... 900
The Indians in Pakistan, 1984-85 .......... 904
The West Indians in Australia, 1984-85 .......... 909
The New Zealanders in Sri Lanka and Pakistan, 1984-85 .......... 926
The Pakistanis in New Zealand, 1984-85 .......... 938
The Sri Lankans in Australia, 1984-85 .......... 950
The New Zealanders in West Indies, 1984-85 .......... 953
Benson and Hedges World Series Cup, 1984-85 .......... 967
Benson and Hedges World Championship of Cricket, 1984-85 .......... 979
Rothmans Trophy in Sharjah, 1984-85 .......... 990
England Young Cricketers in West Indies, 1984-85 .......... 994
Overseas Domestic Cricket in 1984-85 .......... 998
Women's Cricket, 1985 .......... 1154
Births and Deaths of Cricketers .......... 1162
Obituaries .......... 1206
The Laws of Cricket .......... 1222
International Cricket Conference .......... 1250
Rules of Limited-Overs Competitions .......... 1253
Meetings in 1985 .......... 1258
Cricket Books, 1985 by John Arlott .......... 1261
Fixtures, 1986 .......... 1283

# INDEX

*Note:* For reasons of space, certain entries which appear in alphabetical order in sections of the Almanack are not included in this index. These include names that appear in Test Cricketers, Births and Deaths of Cricketers, Individual batting and bowling performances in the 1985 first-class season, and Oxford and Cambridge Blues.

*c. = catches; d. = dismissals; p'ship = partnership; r. = runs; w. = wickets.*

** Signifies not out or an unbroken partnership*

## A


Aamer Malik (Lahore):– 2 hundreds on début, *131*.

Abdul Kadir (Pak.):– Test p'ship record, *227*.

Abdul Qadir (Pak.): 114 w. in Tests, *181;* 103 w. in Pakistan season, *157;* 10 w. or more in Test (1), *227;* Test p'ship record, *213*.

Abel, R. (Eng.):– 33,124 r., *134;* 3,309 r. in season, *146;* Highest for Surrey, *130;* 74 hundreds, *131;* 357* v Somerset, *128, 130;* 2 Test hundreds, *190, 199;* Carrying bat in Test, *174;* 379 for 1st wkt, *142*.

Abrahams, J. (Lancs.):– Captain of Lancashire, *437*.

Adcock, N. A. T. (SA):– 104 w. in Tests, *180;* 26 w. in series, *202;* Test p'ship record, *229*.

Addresses of representative bodies, *1160*.

Adhikari, H. R. (Ind.):– Test captain, *232;* 1 Test hundred, *233;* Test p'ship records, *225, 242*.

Afaq Hussain (Pak.):– Test p'ship record, *227*.

Aftab Baloch (Pak.):– Test début at 16, *186;* 428 v Baluchistan, *128*.

Agha Zahid (HBL):– 2 hundreds in match (2), *132*.

Agnew, J. P. (Eng.):– 9 w. in innings, *258*.

Ahad Khan (Pak. Rlwys):– 9 w. for 7 r., *153*.

Alabaster, J. C. (NZ):– Test p'ship records, *231, 237*.

Alderman, T. M. (Aust.):– 79 w. in Tests, *180;* 42 w. in series, *183, 196;* Test p'ship record, *227*.

Alexander, F. C. M. (WI):– Test captain, *202, 232, 234;* 1 Test hundred, *219;* 23 d. in series, *184;* 5 c. in Test innings, *185*.

Alim-ud-Din (Pak.):– 2 Test hundreds, *213, 242*.

Allan, P. J. (Aust.):– 10 w. in innings, *152*.

Allcott, C. F. W. (NZ):– 190* for 8th wkt, *145;* Test p'ship record, *229*.

Allen, D. A. (Eng.):– 122 w. in Tests, *179;* Test p'ship records, *213*.

Allen, G. O. (Eng.):– Test captain, *189, 202, 209;* Test cricket at 45, *187;* 1 Test hundred, *207;* 81 w. in Tests, *179;* 10 w. in innings, *152;* 10 w. or more in Test (1), *211;* Test p'ship record, *208*.

Alletson, E. B. (Notts.):– Fast scoring, *138;* 34 r. in over, *139*.

Alley, W. E. (Som.):– 3,019 r. in season, *146*.

Allom, M. J. C. (Eng.):– Test hat-trick, *183, 208*.

Allott, P. J. W. (Eng.):– 115 for 10th wkt, *258;* Test p'ship record, *211*.

Altaf Shah (HBFC):– 355 for 5th wkt, *144*.

Amarnath, L. (Ind.):– Test captain, *223, 232, 241;* Hundred on Test début, *171, 210;* 410 for 3rd wkt, *143*.

Amarnath, M. (Ind.):– 3,241 r. in Tests, *169;* 8 Test hundreds, *224, 233, 242;* 2,234 r. in overseas season, *147;* Test p'ship records, *225, 234, 242*.

Amarnath, S. (Ind.):– Hundred on Test début, *172, 237;* Test p'ship record, *238*.

Amerasinghe, A. M. J. G. (SL):– Test p'ship record, *244*.

Ames, L. E. G. (Kent):– 37,248 r., *134;* 2,434 r. in Tests, *167;* 1,000 r. (17), *136;* 3,058 r. in season, *146;* 102 hundreds, *131;* 8 Test hundreds, *190, 199, 203, 207;* 2 hundreds in match, *132;* 1,113 d., *161;* 127 d. in season, *161;* 8 d. in Test, *185;* 2,482 r. and 100 d. in season, 1,919 r. and 121 d. in season, 1,795 r. and 127 d. in season, *158;* Test p'ship records, *200, 208*.

Amin Lakhani (Pak. Univs):– Double hat-trick, *151*.

Amir Elahi (Ind. and Pak.):– Test p'ship record, *243*.

Amiss, D. L. (Eng.):– 40,673 r., *134;* 3,612 r. in Tests, *167;* 1,379 Test r. in year, *173;* 1,000 r. (22), *136;* 96 hundreds,

Amiss, D. L. (Eng.):– *contd*
*131;* 11 Test hundreds, *203, 207, 210, 212;* 2 hundreds in match, *132;* 262* v West Indies, *170, 203;* Batting through Test innings, *174;* Highest aggregate in 1978, *146.*

Anderson, J. H. (SA):– Test captain, *215.*

Anderson, R. W. (NZ):– Test p'ship record, *239.*

Andrew, K. V. (Eng.):– 7 d. in innings, *162.*

Andrews, C. W. (Qld):– 335 for 7th wkt, *144.*

Anil Dalpat (Pak.):– Test p'ship record, *240.*

Antarctica, Cricket in, *825.*

Anwar Iqbal (H'bad):– Hit the ball twice, *149.*

Anwar Miandad (IDBP):– Hit the ball twice, *149.*

Appearances in Test cricket:– As captain, *124;* Most, *124*; Most consecutive, *187.*

Appleyard, R. (Eng.):– 200 w. in season, *155.*

Apte, M. L. (Ind.):– 1 Test hundred, *233.*

Archer, R. G. (Aust.):– 1 Test hundred, *219;* Test p'ship records, *220.*

Arkwright, H. A.:– 18 w. v Gentlemen of Kent, *154.*

Arif Butt (Pak.):– Test p'ship record, *240.*

Arif-ud-Din (UBL):– 10 d. in match, *161.*

Armstrong, N. F. (Leics.):– 36 hundreds, *132.*

Armstrong, W. W. (Aust.):– Test captain, *189;* All-round, *158;* 2,863 r. in Tests, *168;* 2,172 r. v England, *197;* 45 hundreds, *132;* 6 Test hundreds, *192, 216;* Hundred and double-hundred, *133;* 303* v Somerset, *129;* Carrying bat in Test, *174;* 87 w. in Tests, *180;* 428 for 6th wkt, *144;* Test p'ship record, *217.*

Arnold, E. G. (Eng.):– All-round, *158;* 393 for 5th wkt, *144.*

Arnold, G. G. (Eng.):– 115 w. in Tests, *179.*

Arnold, J. (Eng.):– 37 hundreds, *132.*

Arshad Ali (Sukkur):– Obstructing the field, *149.*

Arshad Pervez (HBL):– 426 for 2nd wkt, *143.*

Asda Challenge, *644;* Fixtures 1986, *1288.*

Ashdown, W. H. (Kent):– Highest for Kent, *130;* 332 v Essex, *128;* 307* in day, *140;* 305* v Derbyshire, *129;* 39 hundreds, *132.*

Ashes, The:– *188-97;* History of, *1034.*

Ashraf Ali (Pak.):– Test p'ship record, *243.*

Asif Iqbal (Pak.):– Test captain, *241;* 3,575 r. in Tests, *169;* 45 hundreds, *132;* 10 Test hundreds, *213, 226, 239, 242;* 350 for 4th wkt, *144;* 190 for 9th wkt, *145, 176, 213;* Test p'ship records, *213, 227, 236, 240.*

Asif Masood (Pak.):– Test p'ship record, *213.*

Aslam Ali (UBL):– 456 for 3rd wkt, *141, 143.*

Aslett, D. G. (Kent):– Hundred on début, *130;* 263 for 2nd wkt, *257.*

Astill, W. E. (Eng.):– All-round, *158;* 2,431 w., *156;* 100 w. (9), *157.*

Athar Khan (Allied Bank):– Handled the ball, *149.*

Athey, C. W. J. (Eng.):– 10,000 r., *259;* 305 for 3rd wkt, *257.*

Atkinson, D. St E. (WI):– Test hundred, *219;* 347 for 7th wkt, *144, 220;* Test p'ship records, *220, 231.*

Atkinson, G. (Som.):– 1st wkt hundreds, *142.*

Attewell, W. (Eng.):– 100 w. (10), *157.*

Australia:– Australia in Test cricket (*see p. 127*)*;* B & H World Championship of Cricket, *979-86;* B & H World Series Cup, *967-78;* Definition of first-class matches, *1252;* Domestic season 1984-85, *998-1033;* Highest individual Test innings, *170;* Highest Test innings, *176;* Leading batsmen in Tests, *168;* Leading bowlers in Tests, *180;* Lowest Test innings, *178*; Most consecutive Test appearances, *187;* Most Test appearances, *124;* Most Test appearances as captain, *124;* Oldest Test player, *187;* Representative body, *1160;* Summary of Tests, *188;* Test cricketers (1877-1985), *96-103;* Youngest and oldest on Test début, *186.*

Australia v England, 1985, *289, 292, 295, 300, 303, 305.*

Australia v England (women), 1984-85, *1154-60.*

Australia v New Zealand, 1985-86, *952.*

Australia v West Indies, 1984-85, *916, 918, 920, 922, 924.*

Australians in England, 1985, *273-307.*

Australians in India, 1984-85, *900-3.*

Australian Under-19 in Sri Lanka, 1984-85, *1142.*

Azad, K. (Ind.):– Handled the ball, *149*.
Azhar Abbas (B'pur):– 10 d. in match, *161*.
Azharuddin, M. (Ind.):– 3 Test hundreds, *172, 210;* Hundred on Test début, *172, 210*; Test p'ship record, *211*.
Aziz Malik (Lahore Div.):– Hit the ball twice, *149*.

## B

Bacchus, S. F. A. F. (WI):– 250 v India, *170, 232*.
Bacher, A. (SA):– Test captain, *215*.
Badcock, C. L. (Aust.):– 325 v Victoria, *128;* 1 Test hundred, *192*.
Badcock, F. T. (NZ):– Test p'ship record, *229*.
Baichan, L. (WI):– Hundred on Test début, *172, 235;* Hundred and double-hundred, *133*; 2 hundreds in match (2), *132*.
Baig, A. A. (Ind.):– Hundred on Test début, *172, 210;* Test p'ship record, *225*.
Bailey, T. E. (Eng.):– All-round, *158;* 28,642 r., *135;* 2,290 r. in Tests, *167;* 1,000 r. (17), *136;* 1 Test hundred, *207;* 2,082 w., *156;* 132 w. in Tests, *179;* 100 w. (9), *157;* 10 w. in innings, *152;* 10 w. or more in Test (1), *205;* Test p'ship record, *213*.
Bainbridge, P. (Glos.):– Cricketer of the Year, *57*; 305 for 3rd wkt, *257*.
Bairstow, D. L. (Eng.):– Captain of Yorkshire, *597*; Hundred before lunch, *256;* 11 c. in match, *161;* 7 c. in innings, *162*.
Bakewell, A. H. (Eng.):– 1 Test hundred, *203;* 8 c. in match, *163*.
Balaskas, X. C. (SA):– 1 Test hundred, *229*.
Balderstone, J. C. (Leics.):– 253 for 2nd wkt, *257*.
Banerjee, S. N. (Ind.):– 249 for 10th wkt, *145*.
Banks, D. A. (Worcs.):– Hundred on début, *130*.
Bannerman, C. (Aust.):– Hundred on Test début, *171, 192*.
Bannister, J. D. (Warwicks.):– "A Financial Revolution", *74-6;* 10 w. in innings, *152*.
Baptiste, E. A. E. (WI):– Test p'ship record, *205*.
Barber, R. W. (Eng.):– 1 Test hundred, *190;* Test p'ship record, *213*.
Barclay, J. R. T. (Sussex):– Captain of Sussex, *548*. All-round, *159*.
Bardsley, W. (Aust.):– Test captain, *190;* 2,469 r. in Tests, *168;* 53 hundreds, *132;* 6 Test hundreds, *192, 216;* 2 hundreds in same Test, *172, 192;* Carrying bat in Test, *174;* Test p'ship record, *217*.
Barker, G. (Essex):– 1,000 r. (15), *137;* Hundred on début, *130*.
Barlow, E. J. (SA):– 2,516 r. in Tests, *168;* 43 hundreds, *132;* 6 Test hundreds, *199, 216;* 341 for 3rd wkt, *143, 217*.
Barlow, R. G. (Eng.):– Hit the ball twice, *149;* 4 hat-tricks, *151*.
Barnes, S. F. (Eng.):– 189 w. in Tests, *179;* 106 w. v Australia, *197;* 104 w. in overseas season, *157;* 49 w. and 34 w. in series, *183, 202;* 17 w. in Test, *154, 181;* 14 w. in Test, *181;* 10 w. or more in Test (7), *195, 201;* 9 w. in Test innings, *182;* 8 w. in Test innings (2), *182*.
Barnes, S. G. (Aust.):– 3 Test hundreds, *192, 224;* 405 for 5th wkt, *144, 176;* Test p'ship records, *195, 224*.
Barnes, W. (Eng.):– 1 Test hundred, *190*.
Barnett, C. J. (Eng.):– 48 hundreds, *132;* 2 Test hundreds, *190;* 11 sixes in innings, *139*.
Barnett, K. J. (Derbys.):– Captain of Derbyshire, *340*.
Barratt, E. (Surrey):– 10 w. in innings, *151*.
Barrett, J. E. (Aust.):– Carrying bat in Test, *174*.
Barrington, K. F. (Eng.):– 31,714 r., *134;* 6,806 r. (avge 58.67) in Tests, *167, 171;* 2,111 r. v Australia, *197;* 1,039 Test r. in year, *173;* 1,000 r. (15), *137;* 76 hundreds, *131;* 20 Test hundreds, *171, 190, 199, 203, 207, 210, 212;* 256 v Australia, *170, 190;* 64 c. in season, *162;* Test p'ship records, *200, 208, 213*.
Barrow, I. (WI):– 1 Test hundred, *204*.
Bartlett, G. A. (NZ):– Test p'ship records, *229*.
Barton, P. T. (NZ):– 1 Test hundred, *229*.
Bates, W. (Eng.):– Test hat-trick, *183;* 14 w. in Test, *181, 195*.
Beaumont Cup (WI), *1077-8*.
Beck, J. E. F. (NZ):– Test p'ship record, *229*.
Bedfordshire, *646, 782-3, 784-5*.

Bedi, B. S. (Ind.):– Test captain, *209, 223, 232, 236, 241;* 1,560 w., *157;* 266 w. in Tests, *181;* 10 w. or more in Test (1), *225;* Most w. in 1973, *155;* Test p'ship records, *234, 238.*

Bedser, A. V. (Eng.):– 236 w. in Tests, *179;* 104 w. v Australia, *197;* 100 w (11), *157;* 39 w. in series, *183;* 14 w. in Test, *181, 195;* 10 w. or more in Test (5), *195, 201, 211.*

Bell, A. J. (SA):– Test p'ship record, *201.*

Benaud, J. (Aust.):– 1 Test hundred, *226.*

Benaud, R. (Aust.):– Test captain, *189, 215, 218, 223, 225;* Fast scoring, *174;* 11 sixes in innings, *139;* 2,201 r. in Tests, *168;* 3 Test hundreds, *216, 219;* 248 w. in Tests, *180;* 106 w. in overseas season, *157;* 10 w. or more in Test (1), *225;* All-round in Tests, *181;* Test p'ship records, *217, 220.*

Benjamin, S. (Rajasthan):– 7 d. in innings, *162.*

Benson and Hedges Cup:– *669-99;* Fixtures, 1986, *1283-6;* Rules, *1253-5.*

Benson and Hedges World Championship of Cricket, 1984-85, *979-89.*

Benson and Hedges World Series Cup, 1984-85, *967-78.*

Bensted, E. C. (Qld):– 335 for 7th wkt, *144.*

Berkshire, *649, 781, 783, 785-6.*

Berry, L. G. (Leics.):– 30,225 r., *134;* 1,000 r. (18), *136;* 45 hundreds, *132.*

Berry, R. (Eng.):– 10 w. in innings, *152.*

Bestwick, W. (Derbys.):– 10 w. in innings, *152.*

Betancourt, N. (WI):– Test captain, *202;* Oldest West Indian on début, *186.*

Bhandarkar, K. V. (M'tra):– 455 for 2nd wkt, *141, 143.*

Binks, J. G. (Eng.):– 1,071 d., *161;* 107 d. in season, *161;* 5 c. in Test innings, *186;* 412 consecutive Championship appearances, *255.*

Binny, R. M. H. (Ind.):– 451 for 1st wkt, *141, 143;* Test p'ship records, *242.*

Bird, M. C. (Eng.):– Test p'ship record, *200.*

Bisset, M. (SA):– Test captain, *198.*

Blackham, J. McC. (Aust.):– Test captain, *189-90;* Test p'ship record, *195.*

Blackie, D. D. (Aust.):– Test cricket at 46, *187;* Oldest Australian Test début, 186.

Bland, C. H. G. (Sussex):– 10 w. in innings, *151*.
Bland, K. C. (SA):– 3 Test hundreds, *199, 216;* Test p'ship record, *229*.
Bligh, Hon. Ivo (Lord Darnley) (Eng.):– Test captain, *188;* The Ashes, *1034*.
Blues, List of (1946-85):– Cambridge, *638;* Oxford, *635*.
Blunt, R. C. (NZ):– 338* v Canterbury, *128, 140;* 184 for 10th wkt, *145*.
Blythe, C. (Eng.): 2,506 w., *156;* 215 w. in season, *154;* 100 w. (14), *157;* 100 w. in Tests, *179;* 17 w. in day, *154;* 17 w. in match, *153, 154;* 15 w. in Test, *181, 201;* 10 w. or more in Test (4), *195, 201;* 10 w. in innings, *152;* 8 w. in Test innings, *182*.
Board, J. H. (Eng.):– 1,206 d., *160*.
Bolus, J. B. (Eng.): 39 hundreds, *132*.
Bonnor, G. J. (Aust.):– 1 Test hundred, *192*.
Boon, D. C. (Aust.):– 206* v Northamptonshire, *256*.
Booth, B. C. (Aust.):– Test captain, *190;* 5 Test hundreds, *192, 215, 219*.
Booth, R. (Worcs.):– 1,122 d., *160;* 100 d. in season (2), *161*.
Borde, C. G. (Ind.):– Test captain, *223;* 3,061 r. in Tests, *169;* 1,604 r. in Indian season, *147;* 5 Test hundreds, *233, 237, 242;* Test p'ship record, *225*.
Border, A. R. (Aust.):– Test captain, *189, 218;* 69 consecutive Tests, *187;* 11,821 r. (avge 52.30), *136;* 5,332 r. (avge 50.78) in Tests, *168, 171;* 1,073 Test r. in year, *173;* 14 Test hundreds, *192, 219, 224, 226;* 4 hundreds in succession, *137*, 2 hundreds in same Test, *173;* Test p'ship records, *224, 227, 228*.
Borland, A. F. (Natal):– 4 w. with consecutive balls, *150*.
Bosanquet, B. J. T. (Eng.):– 2 hundreds in match, *132;* 8 w. in Test innings, *183*.
Botham, I. T. (Eng.):– Test captain, *190, 202;* Captain of Somerset, *516;* 65 consecutive Tests, *187;* 4,409 r. in Tests, *167;* 1,095 Test r. in year, *173*; 13 Test hundreds, *190, 207, 210, 212;* Fast Test hundreds, *174;* Fastest hundred in 1985, *256;* 30 r. in over, *140;* 80 sixes in season, *139;* 12 sixes in innings, *139;* 343 w. in Tests, *179;* 136 w. v Australia, *197;* 100 w. in one-day ints, *245;* 10 w. or more in Test (4), *195, 208, 211;* 8 w. in Test innings (2), *182-3;* All-round, *159, 181, 246;* All-round in Tests, *172, 181;* Test p'ship record, *211*.
Bowden, M. P. (Eng.):– Test captain, *198*.
Bowes, W. E. (Eng.):– 1,639 w., *157;* 100 w. (9), *157*.
Bowley, E. H. (Eng.):– 28,378 r., *135;* 1,000 r. (15), *137;* 52 hundreds, *132;* 1 Test hundred, *207;* 490 for 1st wkt, *141*.
Bowley, F. L. (Worcs.):– 38 hundreds, *132*.
Boyce, K. D. (WI):– All-round, *159;* 10 w. or more in Test (1), *205;* Test p'ship record, *234*.
Boycott, G. (Eng.):– Test captain, *206, 212;* Testimonial, *612;* 47,434 r. (avge 56.94), *134, 135;* 8,114 r. in Tests, *167;* 2,945 r. v Australia, *197;* 1,000 r. (26), *136-7;* 149 hundreds, *131;* 22 Test hundreds, *171, 190, 199, 203, 207, 210, 212;* 13 hundreds in season, *137;* 2 hundreds in match (3), *132;* Avge of 102.53 in English season, *147;* Carrying bat in Test, *174;* Carrying bat in 1985, *257;* Highest aggregate in 1971, 1975, *146;* 1st wkt hundreds, *142;* 351 for 1st wkt, *257;* Test p'ship record, *195*.
Boyd-Moss, R. J. (CUCC and Northants):– 2 hundreds in match (2), *132;* 3 hundreds v Oxford, *324*; 255 for 2nd wkt, *257*.
Bradley, W. M. (Eng.):– 3 hat-tricks, *151*.
Bradman, Sir D. G. (Aust.):– "Whither Cricket Now?" *65-8;* Test captain, *189, 223;* Fast scoring, *175;* 28,067 r. (avge 95.14), *135;* 6,996 r. (avge 99.94) in Tests, *168, 170;* 5,028 r. v England, *197;* 1,690 r. in Australian season, *147;* 1,025 Test r. in year, *173;* 1,000 r. (April 30-May 31), *148;* 1,000 r. (16), *136-7;* 974 r. in series, *173, 195;* 452* v Queensland, *128;* 369 v Tasmania, *128, 138;* 357 v Victoria, *128;* 340* v Victoria, *128;* 334 v England, *128, 130, 170, 192;* 309* in day, *140;* 304 v England, *129, 170, 192;* 300 r. in 213 min., *138;* 299* v South Africa, *170, 216;* 278 at Lord's, *252;* 270 and 254 v England, *170, 192;* 117 hundreds, *131;* 29 Test hundreds, *172, 192, 216, 219, 224;* 13 hundreds in season, *137;* 6 hundreds in succession, *137;* 4 hundreds in succession, *137;* 2 hundreds in same Test, *172, 224;* 2 hundreds in match, *132;* Hundred and double-hundred, *133;* 10 successive fifties, *137;* Average of 115.66 in English season, *147;* 50 boundaries in

Bradman, Sir D. G. (Aust.):– *contd* innings, *139;* 30 r. in over, *140;* 451 for 2nd wkt, *141, 143, 176, 195;* 405 for 5th wkt, *144, 176, 195;* 346 for 6th wkt, *176, 195;* Test p'ship records, *195, 217, 224.*
Bradburn, W. P. (NZ):– Test p'ship record, *229.*
Brain, W. H. (Glos.):– w-k hat-trick, *151, 162.*
Braund, L. C. (Eng.):– All-round, *158;* 3 Test hundreds, *190, 199;* 8 w. in Test innings, *182.*
Brayshaw, I. J. (W. Aust.):– 10 w. in innings, *152.*
Brearley, J. M. (Eng.):– "Alan Knott – A Thorough Genius", *69-73;* Test captain, *189, 206, 209, 212;* 25,185 r., *135;* 312* v North Zone in day, *129, 140*; 45 hundreds, *132.*
Brearley, W. (Eng.):– 17 w. in match, *153;* 4 w. with consecutive balls, *150.*
Briasco, P. S. (C. Dist.):– 317 for 2nd wkt, *143.*
Briggs, J. (Eng.):– 1 Test hundred, *190;* Test hat-trick, *183;* 2,221 w., *156;* 118 w. in Tests, *179;* 100 w. (12), *157;* 15 w. in Test, *181, 201;* 10 w. or more in Test (4), *195, 201;* 10 w. in innings, *151;* 8 w. for 11 r. in Test innings, *182.*
Bright, R. J. (Aust.):– 10 w. or more in Test (1), *227.*
Britannic Assurance Championship, *see* County Championship.
Brockwell, W. (Eng.):– 379 for 1st wkt, *142.*
Bromfield, H. D. (SA):– Test p'ship record, *229.*
Bromley-Davenport, H. R. (Eng.):– Test p'ship record, *200.*
Brookes, D. (Eng.):– 30,874 r., *134;* 1,000 r. (17), *136;* 71 hundreds, *131.*
Brown, A. S. (Glos.):– 7 c. in innings, *163.*
Brown, D. J. (Eng.):– 79 w. in Tests, *179.*
Brown, F. R. (Eng.):– Test captain, *189, 198, 202, 206.*
Brown, G. (Eng.):– 37 hundreds, *143.*
Brown, J. T. (Eng.):– 1 Test hundred, *190;* 311 v Sussex, *129;* 300 v Derbyshire, *129;* 554 and 378 for 1st wkt, *141, 141-2.*
Brown, S. M. (Middx):– 1st wkt hundreds, *142.*
Brown, W. A. (Aust.):– Test captain, *221;* 13,840 r. (avge 51.44), *136;* 39 hundreds, *132;* 4 Test hundreds, *192, 216;* Carrying bat in Test, *174;* Test p'ship record, *217.*
Buckinghamshire, *654, 781-2, 783, 786.*
Burge, P. J. (Aust.):– Handled the ball, *148;* 2,290 r. in Tests, *168;* 38 hundreds, *132;* 4 Test hundreds, *192.*
Burgess, M. G. (NZ):– Test captain, *206, 221, 238;* 2,684 r. in Tests, *169;* 5 Test hundreds, *207, 231, 239;* Test p'ship records, *208, 222, 237, 239.*
Burke, J. W. (Aust.):– 3 Test hundreds, *192, 216, 224;* Hundred on Test début, *171, 192.*
Burke, S. F. (SA):– 10 w. or more in Test (1), *229.*
Burki, J. (Pak.):– Test captain, *212;* 3 Test hundreds, *213;* Test p'ship records, *213.*
Burns, W. B. (Worcs.):– 102* and hat-trick v Gloucestershire, *160;* 8 c. in match, *163;* 393 for 5th wkt, *144.*
Burton, G. (Eng.):– 10 w. in innings, *151.*
Buss, M. A. (Sussex):– All-round, *159.*
Butcher, B. F. (WI):– 3,104 r. in Tests, *169;* 7 Test hundreds, *204, 219, 232;* 335 for 5th wkt, *144.*
Butler, H. J. (Eng.):– 3 hat-tricks, *151.*
Butler, S. E. (OUCC):– All 10 Cambridge w., *151, 324;* 15 Cambridge w., *324.*
Butt, H. R. (Eng.):– 1,262 d., *160.*

## C

Cairns, B. L. (NZ):– 130 w. in Tests, *181;* 10 w. or more in Test (1), *208;* Test p'ship record, *208.*
Calthorpe, Hon. F. S. G. (Eng.):– Test captain, *202.*
Camacho, G. S. (WI):– Slow scoring, *175.*
Cambridge University 1985:– *624-34;* Blues, *638-42* (*Also see Oxford v Cambridge*).
Cambridgeshire, *782, 783, 786-7.*
Cameron, F. J. (NZ):– Test p'ship record, *229.*
Cameron, H. B. (SA):– Test captain, *198;* Test p'ship record, *229.*
Canada v USA, *1152.*
Canadian cricket, *1151-2*; Tour by MCC, *1153.*
Captains in Test cricket, *124* (*Also see individual series*).
Career records, *259;* of players not retained, *899.*
Carew, G. M. (WI):– 1 Test hundred, *204.*
Carew, M. C. (WI):– 1 Test hundred, *230;* Test p'ship record, *220.*

Carr, A. W. (Eng.):– Test captain, *189, 198*; 45 hundreds, *132*.
Carr, D. B. (Eng.):– Test captain, *209*.
Carrying bat through innings:– in a Test match, *174;* in 1985, *257*.
Carson, W. N. (Auck.):– Fast scoring, *138;* 445 for 3rd wkt, *138, 143*.
Cartwright, T. W. (Eng.):– 1,536 w., *157;* 100 w. (8), *157;* Most w. in 1972, *155*.
Castle Bowl (SA):– *1035-6, 1057-9*.
Catches in 1985, *355*.
Catterall, R. H. (SA):– 3 Test hundreds, *199-200*.
Cave, H. B. (NZ):– Test captain, *230, 236, 238;* 239 for 9th wkt, *145*.
Central Lancashire League, 1985, *820-1*.
Chaman Lal (Mehandra College):–502* v Government College, *253*.
Chandrasekhar, B. S. (Ind.):– 242 w. in Tests, *181;* 35 w. in series, *183;* 10 w. or more in Test (2), *225, 234;* 8 w. in Test innings, *182;* Test p'ship records, *211, 225*.
Chapman, A. P. F. (Eng.):– Test captain, *189-90, 198, 202;* 1 Test hundred, *190;* Hundreds at Lord's, *324*.
Chapman, J. (Derbys.): 283 for 9th wkt, *145*.
Chappell, G. S. (Aust.):– Test captain, *124, 189, 218, 221, 223, 225, 227;* 24,535 r. (avge 52.20), *136;* 7,110 r. (avge 53.86) in Tests, *168, 171;* 2,619 r. v England, *197;* 51 consecutive Tests, *187;* 74 hundreds, *131;* 24 Test hundreds, *171, 192-3, 219, 222, 224, 226;* 2 hundreds in same Test, *173, 219, 222;* 2 separate hundreds (4), *132-3;* Hundred and double-hundred, *133;* Hundred on Test début, *172, 192;* 122 c. in Tests, *185;* 14 c. in series, *185;* 7 c. in Test, *185;* All-round, *246;* Test p'ship records, *222, 227*.
Chappell, I. M. (Aust.):– Test captain, *189-90, 218, 221, 225;* 5,345 r. in Tests, *168;* 2,138 r. v England, *197;* 71 consecutive Tests, *187;* 59 hundreds, *131;* 14 Test hundreds, *193, 219, 222, 224, 226;* 2 hundreds in same Test, *172, 222;* 2 hundreds in match (3), *132-3;* 105 c. in Tests, *185;* 6 c. in Test, *186;* Test p'ship records, *220, 222*.
Chapple, M. E. (NZ):– Test captain, *206;* Test p'ship record, *229*.
Chatfield, E. J. (NZ):– 10 w. or more in Test (1), *231*.
Chatterjee, P. (Bengal):– 10 w. in innings, *152*.
Chauhan, C. P. S. (Ind.):– 2,084 r. in Tests, *169;* 405 for 1st wkt, *141;* Test p'ship records, *211, 225, 234, 242*.
Cheetham, J. E. (SA):– Test captain, *198, 215, 228;* Test p'ship records, *229*.
Cheshire, *647-8, 781, 783-4, 787-8*.
Chidgey, G. J. (Free Foresters):– Hundred on début, *130*.
Chipperfield, A. G. (Aust.):– 1 Test hundred, *216;* Test p'ship record, *217*.
Christiani, R. J. (WI):– 1 Test hundred, *232*.
Christy, J. A. J. (SA):– 1 Test hundred, *229;* Test p'ship records, *229*.
Chubb, G. W. A. (SA):– Oldest South African Test début, *187*.
Clark, E. A. (Middx):– Hundred on début, *130*.
Clarke, S. T. (WI):– Test p'ship record, *235*.
Claughton, J. A. (OUCC):– Hundred on début, *130*.
Clay, J. C. (Eng.):– 17 w. in match, *153*.
Clift, P. B. (Leics.):– Hat-trick, *258*.
Close, D. B. (Eng.):– Test captain, *202, 209, 212;* Test cricket at 45, *187;* Youngest English Test player, *186;* 34,968 r., *134;* 1,000 r. (20), *136;* 52 hundreds, *132;* 813 c., *162;* XI v Rest of the World XI, *645*.
Club Cricket Championship (William Younger Cup), *327-8*.
Club Cricket Conference, *877*.
Coe, S. (Leics.):– Highest for Leicestershire, *130*.
Coen, S. K. (SA):– 305 for 2nd wkt, *143*.
Collinge, R. O. (NZ):– 116 w. in Tests, *181;* Test p'ship records, *176, 237, 239*.
Collins, A. E. J. (Clifton Coll.):– 628* v North Town, *253*.
Collins, G. C. (Kent):– 10 w. in innings, *152*.
Collins, H. L. (Aust.):– Test captain, *189, 215;* 4 Test hundreds, *193, 216;* Hundred on Test début, *171*.
Combined Services:– Address, *1161;* v NCA Young Cricketers, *327;* v Zimbabweans, *311*.
Commaille, J. M. M. (SA):– 305 for 2nd wkt, *143;* 244* for 6th wkt, *144*.
Compton, D. C. S. (Eng.):– Fast scoring, *138, 175;* 38,942 r. (avge 51.85), *134,*

Compton, D. C. S. (Eng.):– *contd* *136;* 5,807 r. (avge 50.06) in Tests, *167, 171;* 3,816 r. in season, *146;* 1,159 Test r. in year, *173;* 1,000 r. (17), *136;* 753 r. in series, *201;* 123 hundreds, *131;* 18 hundreds in season, *137;* 17 Test hundreds, *190, 199, 203, 207, 212;* 4 successive hundreds, *137;* 2 hundreds in same Test, *172, 190;* 2 hundreds in match (3), *132;* 300 v NE Transvaal in 181 min., *129, 138;* 278 v Pakistan, *170, 212;* 273 r. in day v Pakistan, *175;* Avge of 90.85 in English season, *147;* 424* for 3rd wkt, *143;* Test p'ship records, *195, 200, 213.*

Coney, J. V. (NZ):– Test captain, *238;* 2,094 r. in Tests, *169;* 2 Test hundreds, *207, 239;* Test p'ship records, *208, 222, 231, 241.*

Congdon, B. E. (NZ):– Test captain, *206, 221, 230, 238;* 3,448 r. in Tests, *169;* 61 Test appearances, *124;* 7 Test hundreds, *207, 222, 231;* Test p'ship records, *208, 223, 231, 237.*

Connolly, A. N. (Aust.):– 102 w. in Tests, *180.*

Consecutive Test appearances, *187.*

Constantine, Lord Learie (WI):– 107 and hat-trick, *160.*

Contractor, N. J. (Ind.):– Test captain, *209, 232, 241;* 1 Test hundred, *224;* 4 successive hundreds, *137;* 152 and 102* on début, *131.*

Contributors, List of, *4.*

Cook, C. (Eng.):– 100 w. (9), *157.*

Cook, G. (Northants):– Captain of Northamptonshire, *483.*

Cope, G. A. (Eng.):– Most w. in 1976, *155.*

Copson, W. H. (Derbys.):– 5 w. in 6 balls, *150;* 4 w. with consecutive balls, *150;* 3 hat-tricks, *151.*

Cornford, W. L., (Eng.):– 1,000 d., *161.*

Cornwall, *781, 783, 788.*

Corrall, P. (Leics.):– 10 d. in match, *161.*

Cosier, G. J. (Aust.):– 2 Test hundreds, *219, 226;* Hundred on Test début, *172, 219;* Test p'ship records, *227.*

Cosstick, S. (Vic.):– 6 w. for 1 r., *153.*

Cottam, R. M. H. (Eng.):– Most w. in 1969, *155.*

Cotter, A. (Aust.):– 89 w. in Tests, *180.*

County caps in 1985, *815.*

County Championship:– *332-9;* Appearances, *255;* Champion counties, *336;* Constitution of, *255;* Fixtures, 1986, *1283-8;* Match results 1864-1985, *337;* Over-rate and run-rate, *1061;* Positions 1890-1985, *338-9.*

Cowdrey, C. S. (Kent):– Captain of Kent, *420.*

Cowdrey, M. C. (Eng.):– Test captain, *189-90, 198, 202, 209, 212;* 42,719 r., *134;* 7,624 r. in Tests, *167;* 2,433 r. v Australia, *197;* 1,000 r. (27), *136-7;* 114 Tests, *124;* 107 hundreds, *131;* 23 Test hundreds, *171, 190-1, 199, 203, 207, 210, 212;* 2 hundreds in match (3), *132;* 307 v South Australia, *129;* 120 c. in Tests, *185;* 6 c. in Test, *186;* 411 for 4th wkt v West Indies, *176, 205;* Test p'ship records, *205, 208, 213.*

Cowie, J. (NZ):– 10 w. or more in Test (1), *208;* Test p'ship records, *208.*

Cowley, N. G. (Hants):– All-round, *159.*

Cowper, R. M. (Aust.):– 10,595 r. (avge 53.78), *136;* 2,061 r. in Tests, *168;* 5 Test hundreds, *193, 219, 224;* 307 v England, *129, 170, 193;* Test p'ship records, *227.*

Cox, G. (Sussex):– 50 hundreds, *132.*

Cox, G. R. (Surrey):– 17 w. in match, *153;* 5 w. for 0 r., *153.*

Craig, I. D. (Aust.):– Test captain, *215;* Youngest Australian Test player, *186.*

Cranston, K. (Eng.):– Test captain, *202.*

Crapp, J. F. (Eng.):– 38 hundreds, *132.*

Crawford, W. P. A. (Aust.):– Test p'ship record, *224.*

Cricket associations and societies, *876-7.*

Cricket Council, *317, 1160.*

Cricket Society Award, *826.*

Cricketer Cup winners, *1205.*

Cricketers' Association, The, *1205.*

Cricketers of the Year (*See* Births and Deaths of Cricketers), *1162-1204.*

Crisp, R. J. (SA):– 4 w. with consecutive balls (2), *150;* 3 hat-tricks, *151.*

Croft, C. E. H. (WI):– Slow scoring, *175;* 125 w. in Tests, *180;* 8 w. in Test innings, *182;* Test p'ship records, *205, 220, 235.*

Cromb, I. B. (NZ):– Test p'ship record, *229.*

Crowe, J. J. (NZ):– 2 Test hundreds, *207, 231;* Test p'ship records, *208, 231.*

Crowe, M. D. (NZ):– 2 Test hundreds, *207, 231;* Slow scoring, *175;* Test p'ship records, *231.*

Cumberland, *651, 782, 783, 788-9.*

Cunis, R. S. (NZ):– Test p'ship records, *231, 239.*

Currie Cup (SA), *1035, 1037-56.*
Curtis, T. S. (Worcs.):– 227 for 5th wkt, *258.*

## D

Dacre, C. C. (Auck.):– 2 hundreds in match (2), *132.*
Dalton, E. L. (SA):– 2 Test hundreds, *200;* Test p'ship record, *201.*
Darling, J. (Aust.):– Test captain, *189, 215;* 3 Test hundreds, *193.*
Dates of Formation of County Clubs, including Minor Counties, *254-5.*
Davidson, A. K. (Aust.):– 186 w. in Tests, *180;* 10 w. or more in Test (2), *221, 225;* Test p'ship record, *220.*
Davidson, G. (Derbys.):– Highest for Derbyshire, *130.*
Davies, D. E. (Glam.):– All-round, *158;* Highest for Glamorgan, *130;* 1,000 r. (16), *136;* 139 and hat-trick v Leicestershire, *160;* 1st wkt hundreds, *142.*
Davies, J. G. W. (CUCC and Kent):– President of MCC, *318.*
Davis, C. A. (WI):– 4 Test hundreds, *204, 230, 232;* Test avge of 54.20, *171;* Test p'ship record, *231.*
Davis, I. C. (Aust.):– 1 Test hundred, *226;* Test p'ship records, *222, 227.*
Davison, B. F. (Leics. and Tas.):– 26,923 r., *135;* 53 hundreds, *132.*
Dawkes, G. O. (Derbys.):– 1,042 d., *161;* w-k hat-trick, *151, 162.*
Dean, H. (Eng.):– 100 w. (8), *157;* 17 w. in match, *153.*
Deed, J. A. (Kent II):– 252 v Surrey II, *253.*
de Mel, A. L. F. (SL):– Test p'ship record, *244.*
Dempster, C. S. (NZ):– 35 hundreds, *132;* 2 Test hundreds, *207;* Test p'ship record, *208.*
Denmark, Cricket in, *1061.*
Denness, M. H. (Eng.):– Test captain, *189-90, 202, 206, 209, 212;* 25,886 r., *135;* 1,000 r. (15), *137;* 4 Test hundreds, *191, 207, 210;* Test p'ship record, *208.*
Dennett, G. E. (Glos):– 2,147 w., *156;* 201 w. in season, *155;* 100 w. (12), *157;* 10 w. in innings, *152.*
Denton, D. (Eng.):– 36,479 r., *134;* 1,000 r. (21), *136;* 69 hundreds, *131;* 1 Test hundred, *199;* 2 hundreds in match (3), *132.*
Depeiza, C. C. (WI):– 1 Test hundred, *219;* 347 for 7th wkt v Australia, *144, 220.*
Derbyshire:– *333, 340-55;* Championship positions, *338-9;* Highest score, *163;* Highest individual score, *130;* Lowest score, *164.*
Derbyshire II, *799, 801-2.*
Desai, R. B. (Ind.):– Test p'ship records, *238, 242.*
Desai, S. (Karn.):– 451* for 1st wkt, *141, 143.*
de Silva, D. S. (SL):– Test captain, *240;* 12 Tests, *124;* 9 w. in Test, *182;* Oldest Sri Lankan Test début, *187;* Test p'ship records, *244.*
de Silva, G. R. A. (SL):– Test p'ship record, *244.*
Devon, *655-6, 781, 783, 789.*
Dexter, E. R. (Eng.):– Test captain, *189, 202, 206, 209, 212;* 4,502 r. in Tests, *167;* 1,038 Test r. in year, *173;* 51 hundreds, *132;* 8 Test hundreds, *191, 199, 203, 207, 210, 213;* Test p'ship records, *213.*
Dias, R. L. (SL):– 2 Test hundreds, *241, 244;* Test p'ship records, *241, 243, 244.*
Dick, A. E. (NZ):– 23 d. in series, *184;* Test p'ship record, *229.*
Dilley, G. R. (Eng.):– Hat-trick, *258.*
Dipper, A. E. (Glos.):– 1,000 r. (15), *137;* 53 hundreds, *132.*
Doggart, G. H. G. (Eng.):– 215* on début, *130.*
D'Oliveira, B. L. (Eng.):– 2,484 r. in Tests, *167;* 43 hundreds, *132;* 5 Test hundreds, *191, 207, 210, 213.*
Dollery, H. E. (Eng.):– 1,000 r. (15), *137;* 50 hundreds, *132.*
Donnelly, M. P. (NZ):– 1 Test hundred, *207;* Hundreds at Lord's, *324.*
Dorreen, N. (Cant.):– 265 for 7th wkt, *145.*
Dorset, *781, 783, 784, 790.*
Doshi, D. R. (Ind.):– 114 w. in Tests, *181.*
Double, The, *158-9, 181, 246, 258.*
Double hundreds in 1985, *256.*
Double internationals, *250.*
Douglas, J. (Middx):– 1st wkt hundreds, *142.*
Douglas, J. W. H. T. (Eng.):– Test captain, *189-90, 198;* All-round, *158;* 1 Test hundred, *199;* 3 hat-tricks, *151;* 1,893 w., *156;* Test p'ship record, *200.*
Dowling, G. T. (NZ):– Test captain, *206, 230, 236, 238;* 2,306 r. in Tests, *169;* 3 Test hundreds, *237;* Test p'ship records, *237.*

Downes, A. D. (Otago):– 4 w. with consecutive balls, *150*.
Downton, P. R. (Eng.):– 20 d. in series, *184*; 289 for 5th wkt, *258*.
Drake, A. (Yorks):– 10 w. in innings, *152;* 4 w. with consecutive balls, *150*.
Ducat, A. (Eng.):– 52 hundreds, *132;* 306* v Oxford Univ., *129;* 50 boundaries in innings, *139*.
Duchess of Norfolk's XI:– v Australians, *278;* v Zimbabweans, *314;* 1986 fixtures, *1288, 1289*.
Duckworth, G. (Eng.):– 1,090 d., *160;* 107 d. in season, *161*.
Duff, R. A. (Aust.):– 2 Test hundreds, *193;* Hundred on Test début, *171*.
Dujon, P. J. L. (WI):– 4 Test hundreds, *204, 219, 232;* 110 d. in Tests, *184;* 93 d. in one-day ints, *246;* 20 d. in series, *184*.
Duleep Trophy (Ind.), *1103, 1117-20*.
Duleepsinhji, K. S. (Eng.):– Highest for Sussex, *130;* 50 hundreds, *132;* 4 successive hundreds, *137;* 3 Test hundreds, *191, 207;* 2 hundreds in match (3), *132;* Hundred and double-hundred, *133;* 333 v Northamptonshire, *128, 130*.
Dunell, O. R. (SA):– Test captain, *198*.
Durani, S. A. (Ind.):– 1 Test hundred, *233;* 75 w. in Tests, *181;* 10 w. or more in Test (1), *211*.
Durham, *648, 658, 782, 783, 784, 790-1*.
Dymock, G. (Aust.):– 78 w. in Tests, *180;* 10 w. or more in Test (1), *225*.
Dyson, A. H. (Glam.):– 305 consecutive Championship appearances, *255;* 1st wkt hundreds, *142*.
Dyson, J. (Aust.):– 2 Test hundreds, *193, 219*.

## E

Eady, C. J. (Tas.):– 566 v Wellington, *253*.
East, D. E. (Essex):– 8 c. in innings, *162, 259;* 186 for 8th wkt, *258*.
Edgar, B. A. (NZ):– 3 Test hundreds, *222, 231, 239;* Slow scoring, *175;* Test p'ship record, *222*.
Edmonds, P. H. (Eng.):– 88 w. in Tests, *179;* Test p'ship record, *211*.
Edrich, J. H. (Eng.):– Test captain, *190;* 39,790 r., *134;* 5,138 r. in Tests, *167;* 2,644 r. v Australia, *197;* 1,000 r. (21), *136;* 103 hundreds, *131;* 12 Test hundreds, *191, 203, 207, 210;* 2 hundreds in match (4), *132;* 310* v New Zealand, *129, 170, 207;* 57 boundaries in innings, *139;* Highest aggregate in 1969, *146;* 1st wkt hundreds, *142;* Test p'ship record, *208*.
Edrich, W. J. (Eng.):– 36,965 r., *134;* 3,539 r. (avge 80.43) in season, *146, 147;* 2,440 r. in Tests, *167;* 1,010 r. (April 30/May 31), *148;* 1,000 r. (15), *137;* 86 hundreds, *131;* 6 Test hundreds, *191, 199, 207;* 424* for 3rd wkt, *143;* Test p'ship records, *200*.
Edwards, R. (Aust.):– 2 Test hundreds, *193*.
Elliott, G. (Vic.):– 9 w. for 2 r., *153*.
Elliott, H. (Eng.):– 1,206 d., *160;* 10 d. in match, *161*.
Ellison, R. M. (Eng.):– Cricketer of the Year, *58;* 10 w. or more in Test (1), *195;* Test p'ship record, *214*.
Emburey, J. E. (Eng.):– 75 w. in Tests, *179*.
Emmett, G. M. (Eng.):– 37 hundreds, *132;* 2 hundreds in match (2), *132*.
Emmett, T. (Eng.):– 16 w. in day, *154*.
Endean, W. R. (SA):– Handled the ball, *148;* 3 Test hundreds, *200, 216, 229;* Test p'ship records, *217, 229*.
Engineer, F. M. (Ind.):– 2,611 r. in Tests, *169;* 2 Test hundreds, *210, 233;* Test p'ship records, *211, 238*.
England:– B & H World Championship of Cricket, *979-86;* Definition of first-class matches, *642;* England in Test cricket (*see p. 127*); England v Rest of the World, *215;* Highest individual Test innings, *170;* Highest Test innings, *176;* Hon. MCC members, *321;* Leading batsmen in Tests, *167;* Leading bowlers in Tests, *179;* Lowest Test innings, *178;* Most consecutive Test appearances, *187*, Most Test appearances, *124;* Most Test appearances as captain, *124;* Oldest Test player, *187;* Qualification and registration of players, *330-1;* Representative body, *317;* Summary of Tests, *188;* Test cricketers (1877-1985), *85-96;* Youngest and oldest on Test début, *186*.
England v Australia, 1985, *289, 292, 295, 300, 303, 305*.
England in Australia (women), 1984-85, *1154-60*.
England in India and Sri Lanka, 1984-85, *878-98*.
England Young Cricketers in West Indies, 1984-85, *994-7*.

English Counties XI in Zimbabwe, 1984-85, *1147-50*.
English Estates Trophy, *784*.
English Schools Cricket Association:– Address, *1161;* 1985 season, *826-8*.
Errata in *Wisden*, 1985, *1296*.
Essex: *333, 356-72;* Championship positions, *338-9;* Highest score, *163;* Highest individual score, *130;* Lowest score, *164*.
Essex II, *799, 801, 802*.
Esso Scholarships, *307*.
Eton v Harrow, *325-6*.
Evans, T. G. (Eng.):– 2,439 r. in Tests, *167;* 2 Test hundreds, *203, 210;* 1,066 d. *161;* 219 d. in Tests, *184;* 75 d. v Australia, *197;* 20 d. in series, *184*.

**F**

Fagg, A. E. (Eng.):– 27,291 r., *135;* 58 hundreds, *131;* 2 double-hundreds, *132-3;* 2 hundreds in match (2), *132*.
Fairbairn, A. (Middx):– Hundred on début, *130*.
Falkner, N. J. (Surrey):– Hundred on début, *130*.
Family connections, *248-9*.
Fane, F. L. (Eng.):– Test captain, *190, 198;* 1 Test hundred, *199*.
Farnes, K. (Eng.):– 10 w. or more in Test (1), *195*.
Farrimond, W. (Eng.):– 7 d. in innings, *162*.
Faulkner, G. A. (SA):– 4 Test hundreds, *200, 216;* 82 w. in Tests, *180*.
Favell, L. E. (Aust.):– 1 Test hundred, *224;* 2 hundreds in match (2), *132*.
Fazal Mahmood (Pak.):– Test captain, *225, 234, 241;* 139 w. in Tests, *181;* 10 w. or more in Test (3), *214, 227, 236*.
Features of 1985, *256-9*.
Fender, P. G. H. (Eng.):– All-round, *158;* Hundred in 35 minutes, *138*.
Ferguson, W. (WI):– 10 w. or more in Test (1), *205*.
Fernandes, M. P. (WI):– Test captain, *202*.
Ferreira, A. M. (Warwicks.):– 500 w., *259*.
Ferris, J. J. (Aust. and Eng.):– 10 w. or more in Test (1), *201*.
Fielder, A. (Eng.):– 10 w. in innings, *152;* 235 for 10th wkt, *145*.
Fielding statistics, 1985, *355*.
Findlay, T. M. (WI):– Test p'ship record, *231*.
Fingleton, J. H. (Aust.):– 5 Test hundreds, *193, 216;* Test p'ship records, *195, 217*.
First-class match defined, *642, 1251-3*.
First-wicket hundreds, *142*.
First-wicket partnerships, *141-2*.
Fisher, H. (Yorks.):– LBW hat-trick, *151*.
Fishlock, L. B. (Eng.):– 56 hundreds, *131;* 2 hundreds in match (4), *132*.
Five Cricketers of the Year:– *Wisden* 1986, *57-64;* Prior to 1986, *see Births and Deaths of Cricketers*.
Flavell, J. A. (Eng.):– 1,529 w., *157;* 100 w. (8), *157;* 3 hat-tricks, *151;* LBW hat-trick, *151*.
Fleetwood-Smith, L. O'B. (Aust.):– 10 w. or more in Test (1), *195*.
Fletcher, K. W. R. (Eng.):– Test captain, *209, 214;* Captain of Essex, *356;* 35,701 r., *134;* 3,272 r. in Tests, *167;* 1,090 Test r. in year, *173;* 1,000 r. (20), *136;* 62 hundreds, *131;* 7 Test hundreds, *191, 203, 207, 210, 213;* Slow Test hundred, *176;* 186 for 8th wkt, *258;* Test p'ship records, *208, 211*.
Forbes, W. F.:– Throwing record, *254*.
Formation of counties, *254-5*.
Foster, D. G. (Warwicks.):– Throwing record, *254*.
Foster, F. R. (Eng.):– Highest for Warwickshire, *130;* 305* for Warwickshire, *129, 130*.
Foster, M. L. C. (WI):– 1 Test hundred, *219;* Test p'ship record, *220*.
Foster, N. A. (Eng.):– 10 w. or more in Test (1), *211*.
Foster, R. E. (Eng.):– Test captain, *198;* 2 hundreds in match (3), *132, 133;* 287 v Australia on Test début, *129, 171, 172, 191;* Test p'ship record, *195*.
Foster, W. L. (Worcs.):– 2 hundreds in match, *133*.
Four w. with consecutive balls, *150*.
Fourth innings highest totals, *165*.
Fowler, G. (Eng.):– 3 Test hundreds, *203, 207, 210;* Fast scoring, *138;* Test p'ship records, *208, 211*.
Frank, C. N. (SA):– 1 Test hundred, *216;* Test p'ship record, *217*.
Fredericks, R. C. (WI):– 4,334 r. in Tests, *168;* 40 hundreds, *132;* 8 Test hundreds, *204, 219, 230, 232, 235;* 2 hundreds in match (3), *132;* Fast Test hundred, *175;* Test p'ship records, *205, 231, 235*.
Freeman, A. P. (Eng.):– 3,776 w., *156;* 2,090 w. in eight seasons, *155;* 1,122 w.

Freeman, A. P. (Eng.):– *contd* in four seasons, *155;* 304 w. in season, *154;* 200 w. (8), *154-5;* 100 w. (17), *157;* 100 w. by June 13, *155;* 17 w. in match (2) *153;* 10 w. in innings (3), *152;* 10 w. or more in Test (3), *201, 205;* 3 hat-tricks, *151.*

Freeman, D. L. (NZ):– Youngest New Zealand Test player, *186.*

French, B. N. (Notts.):– 500 d., *259;* 10 d. in match, *161;* 6 d. in innings, *259.*

Fry, C. B. (Eng.):– Test captain, *189, 198;* 30,886 r. (avge 50.22), *134, 136;* Aggregate of 3,147 r., *146;* 94 hundreds, *131;* 13 hundreds in season, *137;* 6 successive hundreds, *137;* 2 Test hundreds, *191, 199;* 2 hundreds in match (5), *132;* Hundred and double-hundred, *133;* Avge of 81.30 in English season, *147;* 1st wkt hundreds, *142.*

Funston, K. J. (SA):– Test p'ship record, *229.*

Future tours, *1034.*

## G

Gaekwad, A. D. (Ind.):– 2 Test hundreds, *233, 242;* Slowest double-hundred, *176, 242;* Test p'ship records, *234, 242.*

Gaekwad, D. K. (Ind.):– Test captain, *209.*

Game, W. H.:– Throwing record, *254.*

Ganteaume, A. G. (WI):– Hundred on Test début, *171, 204.*

Garner, J. (WI):– 220 w. in Tests, *180;* 116 w. in one-day ints, *245;* Test p'ship records, *220, 231, 235.*

Gatting, M. W. (Middx):– Captain of Middlesex, *467*; 15,000 r., *259;* 2,246 r. in Tests, *167;* 36 hundreds, *132;* 4 Test hundreds, *191, 210*; Test p'ship record, *211.*

Gavaskar, S. M. (Ind.):– Test captain, *124, 209, 223, 232, 236, 241, 243;* 106 Tests, *124;* 90 consecutive Tests, *187;* 23,539 r. (avge 51.39), *136;* 8,654 r. (avge 50.60) in Tests, *169, 171;* 2,121 r. in overseas season, *147;* 1,555 Test r. in year, *173*; 774 r. in series, *173;* 74 hundreds, *131;* 30 Test hundreds, *171, 210, 224, 233, 237, 242, 243;* 2 hundreds in same Test (3), *132, 172, 233, 242;* Hundred and double-hundred, *133;* 236* v West Indies, *170, 233;* Carrying bat in Test, *174;* 340 v Bengal, *128;* 421 for 1st wkt, *141;* Test p'ship records, *211, 225, 234, 238, 242, 243.*

Geary, G. (Eng.):– 2,063 w., *156;* 100 w. (11), *157;* 10 w. in innings, *152;* 10 w. or more in Test (1), *201.*

Geddes Grant/Harrison Line Trophy (WI), *1063, 1078.*

Ghavri, K. D. (Ind.):– 109 w. in Tests, *181;* Test p'ship records, *225.*

Ghosh, A. (Bihar):– 10 d. in match, *161.*

Ghulam Ahmed (Ind.):– Test captain, *232, 236;* 10 w. or more in Test (1), *225;* Test p'ship record, *243.*

Gibb, P. A. (Eng.):– 2 Test hundreds, *199;* Hundred on Test début, *171;* Test p'ship record, *200.*

Gibb, P. J. M. (Tvl):– 342 for 4th wkt, *144.*

Gibbons, H. H. I. (Worcs.):– 44 hundreds, *132.*

Gibbs, G. L. R. (WI):– 390 for 1st wkt, *141, 143.*

Gibbs, L. R. (WI):– 309 w. in Tests, *180;* 10 w. or more in Test (2), *205;* 8 w. in Test innings, *182;* Hat-trick v Australia, *183;* Most w. in 1971, *155.*

Giffen, G. (Aust.):– Test captain, *189;* All-round, *158;* 1 Test hundred, *192;* 113 and hat-trick v Lancashire, *160;* 103 w. in Tests, *180, 197;* 17 w. in match, *153;* 10 w. in innings, *151;* 10 w. or more in Test (1), *196;* 3 hat-tricks, *151.*

Gifford, N. (Eng.):– Captain of Warwickshire, *564;* 1,935 w., *156;* Test p'ship records, *208, 211.*

Gillette Cup, winners and records, *666-8.*

Gilligan, A. E. R. (Eng.):– Test captain, *189, 198;* 10 w. or more in Test (1), *201;* Test p'ship record, *200.*

Gilligan, A. H. H. (Eng.):– Test captain, *206.*

Gilmour, G. J. (Aust.):– 1 Test hundred, *222;* Test p'ship records, *222.*

Gimblett, H. (Eng.):– 310 v Sussex, *129;* 50 hundreds, *132;* 2 hundreds in match (2), *132.*

Gladwin, C. (Eng.):– 100 w. (12), *157.*

Glamorgan:– *333, 373-87;* Championship positions, *338-9;* Highest score, *163;* Highest individual score, *130;* Lowest score, *164.*

Glamorgan II, *799, 801, 803.*

Gleeson, J. W. (Aust):– 93 w. in Tests, *180.*

Gloucestershire:– *333, 388-402;* Championship positions, *338-9;* Highest

Gloucestershire:– *contd*
score, *163*; Highest individual score, *130*; Lowest score, *164*.

Gloucestershire II, *799, 801, 803-4*.

Goddard, J. D. C. (WI):– Test captain, *202, 218, 230, 232*; 502* for 4th wkt, *141*; Test p'ship record, *231*.

Goddard, T. L. (SA):– Test captain, *198, 215, 228*; 2,516 r. in Tests, *168*; 1 Test hundred, *200*; Carrying bat in Test, *174*; 123 w. in Tests, *180*.

Goddard, T. W. (Eng.):– 2,979 w., *156*; 200 w. (4), *154-5*; 100 w. (16), *157*; 17 w. in day, *154*; 17 w. in match, *153*; 10 w. in innings, *152*; 6 hat-tricks, *151*; Test hat-trick, *183*.

Goel, R. (Haryana):– 7 w. for 4 r., *153*.

Gomes, H. A. (WI):– 2,841 r. in Tests, *169*; 9 Test hundreds, *204, 219, 232*; Test p'ship records, *205, 220*.

Gomez, G. E. (WI):– Test captain, *202*; 1 Test hundred, *232*; 10 w. or more in Test (1), *221*; 434 for 3rd wkt, *143*; Test p'ship record, *234*.

Gooch, G. A. (Eng.):– Captain of Essex, *356*; 20,000 r., *259*; 3,027 r. in Tests, *167*; 54 hundreds, *132*; 5 Test hundreds, *191, 203, 210*; Highest aggregate in 1984, 1985, *146*; 202 v Nottinghamshire, *256*; 30 r. in over, *140*; Record score in B & H Cup, *698*; in JPL, *779*; 351 for 2nd wkt, *257*.

Goonatillake, H. M. (SL):– Test p'ship record, *244*.

Gover, A. R. (Eng):– 200 w. (2), *155*; 100 w. (8), *157*; 4 w. with consecutive balls, *150*.

Gower, D. I. (Eng):– Test captain, *189, 202, 209, 212, 214*; Captain of Leicestershire, *452*; 15,000 r., *259*; 5,385 r. in Tests, *167*; 2,075 r. v Australia, *197*; 1,061 Test r. in year, *173*; 12 Test hundreds, *191, 203, 207, 210, 213*; 7 one-day int. hundreds, *245*; 351, 331 and 253 for 2nd wkt, *257*; Test p'ship record, *213*.

Grace, Dr E. M. (Eng):– 192* and 10 w., *151, 160*.

Grace, Dr W. G. (Eng.):– Test captain, *189-90*; All-round, *158*; Highest for Gloucestershire, *130*; Test cricket at 50, *187*; Throwing the cricket ball, *254*; 54,896 r., *134, 135, 158*; 2,739 r. in season, *146*; 1,000 r. (28), *136*; 1,000 r. in May, *148*; 126 hundreds, *131*; 2 Test hundreds, *191*; Hundred on Test début, *171*; 2 hundreds in match (3), *132-3*; 344 v Kent, *128*; 318* v Yorkshire, *129, 130*; 301 v Sussex, *129*; 130 and 102* at Canterbury, *133*; 123 and hat-trick v Kent, *160*; 104 and 10 w., *160*; 51 boundaries in innings, *139*; 2,876 w., *156, 157, 158*; 100 w. (10), *157*; 17 w. in match, *153*; 10 w. in innings, *151*; 877 c., *162*; 1st wkt hundreds, *142*.

Graham, H. (Aust.):– 2 Test hundreds, *193*; Hundred on Test début, *171*.

Grant, G. C. (WI):– Test captain, *202, 218*.

Grant, R. S. (WI):– Test captain, *202*.

Graveney, D. A. (Glos.):– Captain of Gloucestershire, *388*.

Graveney, J. K. (Glos.):– 10 w. in innings, *152*.

Graveney, T. W. (Eng.):– Test captain, *190*; 47,793 r., *134*; 4,882 r. in Tests, *167*; 1,000 r. (22), *136*; 122 hundreds, *131*; 11 Test hundreds, *191, 203, 210, 213*; 2 hundreds in match (3), *132*; 258 v West Indies, *170, 203*; Test p'ship records, *205, 213*.

Gray, A. H. (Surrey):– Hat-trick, *258*; 8 w. in innings, *258*; 4 w. in 5 balls, *258*.

Gray, E. J. (NZ):– 226 for 6th wkt, *144*.

Gray, J. R. (Hants):– 1st wkt hundreds, *142*.

Greenidge, C. G. (WI):– 28,461 r., *135*; 4,816 r. in Tests, *168*; 1,149 Test r. in year, *173*; 65 hundreds, *132*; 12 Test hundreds, *204, 219, 230, 232, 235*; 6 one-day int. hundreds, *245*; 2 hundreds in match (3), *132*; 2 hundreds in same Test, *173, 204*; Hundred on Test début, *172, 232*; 1,000 r. (15), *136*; Avge of 82.23 in English season, *147*; 204 v Warwickshire, *256*; 13 sixes in innings (2), *139*; Test p'ship records, *205, 220, 231, 234, 235*.

Gregory, C. W. (Aust.):– 383 v Queensland, *128*; 318 r. in day, *140*; 55 boundaries in innings, *139*.

Gregory, D. W. (Aust.):– Test captain, *188*.

Gregory, J. M. (Aust.):– 2 Test hundreds, *193, 217*; Fastest Test hundred, *174-5*; 85 w. in Tests, *180*.

Gregory, R. J. (Surrey):– 39 hundreds, *132*.

Gregory, S. E. (Aust.):– Test captain, *189, 215*; 2,282 r. in Tests, *168*; 2,193 r. v

Gregory, S. E. (Aust.):– *contd* England, *197;* 4 Test hundreds, *193;* Test p'ship record, *195.*

Greig, A. W. (Eng.):– Test captain, *189, 202, 209;* 3,599 r. in Tests, *167;* 58 consecutive Tests, *187;* 8 Test hundreds, *191, 203, 207, 210;* 141 w. in Tests, *179;* 10 w. or more in Test (2), *205, 208;* 8 w. in Test innings, *182;* All-round, *159;* 6 c. in Test, *186;* Test p'ship records, *205, 211.*

Grieves, K. J. (Lancs.):– 63 c. in season, *162;* 8 c. in match, *163.*

Griffin, G. M. (SA):– Hat-trick v England, *183.*

Griffith, C. C. (WI):– 94 w. in Tests, *180.*

Griffith, H. C. (WI):– 138 for 10th wkt, *145.*

Griffith, S. C. (Eng.):– Hundred on Test début, *171, 203.*

Grimmett, C. V. (Aust.):– 216 w. in Tests, *180;* 44 w. in series, *183;* 14 w. v South Africa, *181;* 10 w. in innings, *152;* 10 w. or more in Test (7), *195, 217, 221;* Test p'ship record, *217.*

Grounds, Test match, *250-1.*

Grout, A. T. W. (Aust.):– 187 d. in Tests, *184;* 76 d. v England, *197;* 23 d. in series, *184;* 8 c. in innings, *162;* 8 d. in Test, *185;* 6 c. in Test innings, *185.*

Gulfraz Khan (Pak. Rlwys):– 12 sixes in innings, *139;* 240 for 8th wkt, *145.*

Gunn, G. (Eng.):– Test cricket at 50, *187;* 35,208 r., *134;* 1,000 r. (20), *136;* 62 hundreds, *131;* 2 Test hundreds, *191;* 2 hundreds in match (3), *132, 133;* Hundred on Test début, *171;* (and G. V. Gunn) Hundreds in same match, *133;* 1st wkt hundreds, *142.*

Gunn, J. (Eng.):– All-round, *158;* 40 hundreds, *132.*

Gunn, W. (Eng.):– 25,791 r., *135;* 48 hundreds, *132;* 1 Test hundred, *191.*

Gupte, M. S. (M'tra), 405 for 1st wkt, *141.*

Gupte, S. P. (Ind.):– 149 w. in Tests, *181;* 10 w. in innings, *152;* 10 w. or more in Test (1), *234;* 9 w. in Test innings, *182, 234.*

Guy, J. W. (NZ):– 1 Test hundred, *237;* Test p'ship record, *237.*

Guystac Trophy (WI), *1076-7.*

## H

Hadlee, D. R. (NZ):– Test p'ship records, *222, 239.*

Hadlee, R. J. (NZ):– All-round, *158, 181;* 1,000 w., *259;* 2,088 r. in Tests, *169;* 1 Test hundred, *231;* 266 w. in Tests, *181;* 100 w. in one-day ints, *245;* 10 w. or more in Test (3), *182, 208, 231, 238;* 9 w. in Test innings, *952;* 8 w. in innings, *258;* 7 w. in Test innings, *183;* Most w. in 1981, 1984, *155;* All-round, *159, 181,* Test p'ship records, *222, 239.*

Hadlee, W. A. (NZ):– Test captain, *206, 221.*

Hafeez, A. (Ind. and Pak.), *see* Kardar, A. H.

Haig, N. E. (Eng.):– All-round, *158.*

Haig, W. S. (Otago):– 266 for 5th wkt, *144.*

Haigh, S. (Eng.):– 2,012 w., *156;* 100 w. (11), *157;* 5 hat-tricks, *151;* 4 w. with consecutive balls, *150.*

Hall, A. E. (SA):– 10 w. or more in Test (1), *201.*

Hall, W. W. (WI):– 192 w. in Tests, *180;* 10 w. or more in Test (1), *234;* Hat-trick v Pakistan, *183;* Test p'ship record, *234.*

Hallam, M. R. (Leics.):– 2 hundreds in match (3), *132, 133;* Hundred and double-hundred (2), *133.*

Halliwell, E. A. (SA):– Test captain, *198, 215;* Test p'ship record, *217.*

Hallows, C. (Eng.):– 1,000 r. in May, *148;* 55 hundreds, *131;* 2 hundreds in match (2), *132;* 1st wkt hundreds, *142.*

Hamence, R. A. (Aust.):– 2 hundreds in match (2), *132.*

Hammond, W. R. (Eng.):– Test captain, *189, 198, 202, 206, 209;* 50,551 r. (avge 56.10), *134, 136;* 7,249 r. (avge 58.45) in Tests, *167, 171;* 3,323 r. in season, *146;* 2,852 r. v Australia, *197;* 1,042 r. in May, *148;* 1,000 r. (22), *136;* 905 r. in series, *173, 195;* 167 hundreds, *131;* 22 Test hundreds, *171, 191, 192, 199, 203, 207, 210;* 15 and 13 hundreds in season, *137;* 4 successive hundreds, *137;* 2 hundreds in match (7), *132;* 2 hundreds and 10 c. in match, *163;* 2 hundreds in same Test, *172, 191;* 336* v New Zealand, *128, 170, 207;* 317 v Nottinghamshire, *129;* 302* and 302 v Glamorgan, *129;* 295 r. in day in Test, *175;* 251 v Australia, *170;* Avge of 84.90 in English season, *147;* 83 w. in Tests, *179;* 819 c., *162;* 78 c. and 65 c. in season, *162;* 10 c. in match, *163;* Test p'ship records, *194, 200, 205, 208, 211.*

Hampshire:– *333, 403-19;* Championship positions, *338-9;* Highest score, *163;*

Hampshire:– *contd*
Highest individual score, *130;* Lowest score, *164.*
Hampshire II, *799, 801, 804-5.*
Hampshire, J. H. (Eng.):– 28,059 r., *135;* 1,000 r. (15), *137;* 43 hundreds, *132;* Hundred on Test début, *171, 203.*
Handled the ball, Instances in first-class cricket, *148-9.*
Hanif Mohammad (Pak.):– Test captain, *212, 225, 238;* Test début at 17, *186;* Longest first-class innings, *128, 129;* 17,059 r. (avge 52.32), *136;* 3,915 r. in Tests, *169;* 55 hundreds, *131;* 12 Test hundreds, *213, 226, 235, 239, 242;* 2 hundreds in match (3), *132;* 2 hundreds in same Test, *172, 213;* 499 v Bahawalpur, *128;* 337 v West Indies, *128, 170, 235;* 64 boundaries in innings, *139;* Test p'ship records, *213, 236, 240, 243.*
Hanumant Singh (Ind.):– Hundred on Test début, *172, 210;* Hundred and double-hundred, *133;* Test p'ship record, *238.*
Hardie, B. R. (Essex):– NatWest Bank Trophy final Man of the Match, *665.*
Hardinge, H. T. W. (Eng.):– 33,519 r., *134;* 1,000 r. (18), *136;* 75 hundreds, *131;* 4 successive hundreds, *137;* 2 hundreds in match (4), *132;* Hundred and double-hundred, *133.*
Hardstaff, J. jun. (Eng.):– 31,847 r., *134;* 83 hundreds, *131;* 4 Test hundreds, *191, 207, 210;* Test p'ship records, *195, 208.*
Haroon Rashid (Pak.):– 3 Test hundreds, *213, 244;* Test p'ship record, *213.*
Harris, 4th Lord (Eng.):– Test captain, *188.*
Harris, C. B. (Notts.):– 1st wkt hundreds, *142.*
Harris, M. J. (Middx and Notts.):– 41 hundreds, *132;* 2 hundreds in match (3), *132.*
Harris, P. G. Z. (NZ):– Test p'ship record, *229.*
Harrogate Festival, *644.*
Hart, R. T. (C. Dist.):– 317 for 2nd wkt, *143.*
Hartigan, R. J. (Aust.):– Hundred on Test début, *171, 193;* Test p'ship record, *195.*
Harvey, R. N. (Aust.):– Test captain, *190;* 21,699 r. (avge 50.93), *136;* 6,149 r. in Tests, *168;* 2,416 r. v England, *197;* 834 r. in series, *173;* 67 hundreds, *131;* 21 Test hundreds, *171, 193, 216, 219, 224;* 6 c. in Test, *186;* Test p'ship records, *217, 220, 224.*
Harvey-Walker, A. J. (Derbys.):– Hundred on début, *130.*
Hassan, B. (Notts.):– Career figures, *899.*
Hassett, A. L. (Aust.):– Test captain, *189, 215, 218;* 16,890 r. (avge 58.24), *135;* 3,073 r. in Tests, *168;* 59 hundreds, *131;* 10 Test hundreds, *193, 216, 219, 224;* 2 hundreds in match (2), *132;* Test p'ship records, *195, 216.*
Hastings, B. F. (NZ):– 4 Test hundreds, *222, 231, 239;* Test p'ship records, *176, 208, 222, 231, 239.*
Hathorn, C. M. H. (SA):– 1 Test hundred, *200.*
Hat-tricks:– *150-1;* Double, *150;* in Test matches, *183;* All caught, *151;* All LBW, *151;* All stumped, *151;* Three and more, *151;* in 1985, *258.*
Havewalla, D. R. (BB and CI Rlwys):– 515 v St Xavier's, *253.*
Hawke, 7th Lord (Eng.):– Test captain, *198;* 292 for 8th wkt, *145.*
Hawke, N. J. N. (Aust.):– 91 w. in Tests, *180;* 10 w. or more in Tests (1), *221.*
Hawkesworth, W. (Otago):– 184 for 10th wkt, *145.*
Hayes, E. G. (Eng.):– 27,318 r., *135;* 1,000 r. (16), *136;* 48 hundreds, *132.*
Hayes, F. C. (Eng.):– Hundred on Test début, *172, 203;* 34 r. in over, *139.*
Hayes, J. A. (NZ):– Obstructing the field, *149.*
Haynes, D. L. (WI):– 3,348 r. in one-day ints, *245;* 3,234 r. in Tests, *169;* 8 one-day int. hundreds, *245;* 7 Test hundreds, *204, 219, 230, 232;* Batting through Test innings (2), *174;* Handled the ball, *149;* Test p'ship records, *220, 231, 234.*
Hayward, T. W. (Eng.):– 43,551 r., *134;* 3,518 r. in season, *146;* 1,000 r. (20), *136;* 1,000 r. (April 16-May 31), *148;* 104 hundreds, *131;* 13 hundreds in season, *137;* 4 successive hundreds, *132-3, 137;* 3 Test hundreds, *191, 199;* 2 hundreds in match (3), *132;* 315* v Lancashire, *129;* 1st wkt hundreds, *142.*
Hazare, V. S. (Ind.):– Test captain, *209, 232;* 18,569 r. (avge 58.02), *135;* 2,192 r. in Tests, *169;* 60 hundreds, *131;* 7 Test hundreds, *210, 224, 233, 242;* 2 hundreds in same Test, *172, 224;* 2 hundreds in match (3), *132;* 316* v Baroda, *129;* 309

Hazare, V. S. (Ind.):– *contd*
v Hindus, *129;* 577 for 4th wkt, *141, 144;* 245 for 9th wkt, *145;* Test p'ship records, *211, 225, 242.*

Headley, G. A. (WI):– Test captain, *202;* 2,190 r. (avge 60.83) in Tests, *169, 170;* 10 Test hundreds, *204, 219;* 2 hundreds in same Test, *172, 204;* 2 hundreds in match (2), *132;* 344* v Lord Tennyson's Team, *128;* 270* v England, *170, 204;* Hundred on Test début, *171;* 487* for 6th wkt, *141, 144.*

Headley, R. G. A. (WI):– 1st wkt hundreds, *142.*

Hearn, P. (Kent):– Hundred on début, *130.*

Hearne, J. T. (Eng.):– 3,061 w., *156;* 200 w. (3), *154-5;* 100 w. (15), *157;* 100 w. by June 12, *155;* 10 w. or more in Test (1), *195;* 4 hat-tricks, *151;* Hat-trick v Australia, *183;* Test p'ship record, *200.*

Hearne, J. W. (Eng.):– All-round, *158;* 37,252 r., *134;* 1,000 r. (19), *136;* 96 hundreds, *131;* 1 Test hundred, *191.*

Hemmings, E. E. (Eng.):– 10 w. in innings, *152.*

Henderson, S. P. (CUCC, Worcs. and Glam.):– Career figures, *899.*

Henderson, W. A. (NE Tvl):– 7 w. for 4 r., *153;* 5 w. in 6 balls, *150;* 4 w. with consecutive balls, *150.*

Hendren, E. H. (Eng.):– Test cricket at 46, *187;* 57,611 r. (avge 50.80), *134, 136;* 3,525 r. in Tests, *167;* 3,311 r. in season, *146;* 1,765 r. in West Indies, *147;* 1,000 r. (25), *136;* 170 hundreds, *131;* 13 hundreds in season, *137;* 7 Test hundreds, *191, 199, 203;* 2 hundreds in match (4), *132;* 301* v Worcestershire, *129;* 277* at Lord's, *252;* 755 c., *162;* Test p'ship record, *195.*

Hendrick, M. (Eng.):– 87 w. in Tests, *179.*

Hendriks, J. L. (WI):– Test p'ship record, *220.*

Hendry, H. L. (Aust.):– 1 Test hundred, *193;* 325* v New Zealanders, *128.*

Hertfordshire, *650, 782, 783, 791-2.*

Hick, G. A. (Zimb. and Worcs.):– 230 v Oxford University, *256, 310-1;* 277 for 4th wkt, *258.*

Hickton, W. (Lancs.):– 10 w. in innings, *151.*

Hide, J. B. (Sussex):– 4 w. with consecutive balls, *149.*

Higgs, J. D. (Aust.):– Test p'ship record, *224.*

Higgs, K. (Eng.):– 1,531 w., *157;* 3 hat-tricks, *151;* Test p'ship record, *205.*

Highest aggregates:– Individual, *146;* Team, *165, 176, 247.*

Highest individual scores:– *128-30, 253;* in Tests, *170.*

Highest innings totals:– in Tests, *176-7;* in one-day ints, *246.*

Highest partnerships, *141-5.*

Highest total for each county:– Individual, *130;* Team, *163.*

Hilditch, A. M. J. (Aust.):– 2 Test hundreds, *193, 219;* Handled the ball, *149.*

Hill, A. (Eng.):– 3 hat-tricks, *151.*

Hill, A. J. L. (Eng.):– 1 Test hundred, *199.*

Hill, C. (Aust.): – Test captain, *189, 215;* 3,412 r. in Tests, *168;* 2,660 r. v England, *197;* 1,061 Test r. in year, *173;* 45 hundreds, *132;* 7 Test hundreds, *193, 216;* 365* v NSW, *128;* 232 for 9th wkt, *145;* Test p'ship records, *195.*

Hinds, F. (A. B. St Hill's XI):– 10 w. in innings, *152.*

Hinkly, E. (Kent):– 10 w. in innings, *151.*

Hirst, G. H. (Eng.):– All-round, *158;* Highest for Yorkshire, *130;* 36,323 r., *134;* 1,000 r. (19), *136;* 60 hundreds, *131;* 341 v Leicestershire, *128, 130;* 54 boundaries in innings, *139;* 2,739 w., *156;* 208 w. in season, *154;* 100 w. (15), *157.*

Hit the ball twice, Instances in first-class cricket, *149.*

HMC Schools in 1985, *826 8.*

Hoad, E. L. G. (WI):– Test captain, *202;* 138 for 10th wkt, *145.*

Hobbs, Sir J. B. (Eng.):– Test cricket at 47, *187;* 61,237 r. (avge 50.65), *134, 136;* 5,410 r. (avge 56.94) in Tests, *167, 171;* 3,636 r. v Australia, *197;* 3,024 r. in season, *146;* 1,000 r. (26), *136;* 197 hundreds, *131;* 16 hundreds in season, *137;* 15 Test hundreds, *191, 199, 203;* 4 successive hundreds, *137;* 2 hundreds in match (6), *132;* 316* v Middlesex at Lord's, *129, 252;* Avge of 82 in English season, *147;* 428 for 1st wkt, *141;* 1st wkt hundreds, *142;* Test p'ship record, *194.*

Hobbs, R. N. S. (Eng.):– Hundred in 44 minutes, *138.*

Hogan, T. G. (Aust.):– Test p'ship record, *220*.

Hogg, R. M. (Aust.):– 123 w. in Tests, *180;* 41 w. in series, *183, 196;* 10 w. or more in Test (2), *196;* Test p'ship record, *220*.

Holder, V. A. (WI):– 109 w. in Tests, *180;* Test p'ship record, *235*.

Holding, M. A. (WI):– 500 w., *259;* 233 w. in Tests, *180;* 122 w. in one-day ints, *245*; 14 w. in Test (1), *181, 206;* 11 w. in Test (1), *221;* 8 w. in Test innings, *182, 206;* Test p'ship record, *205*.

Holford, D. A. J. (WI):– 1 Test hundred, *204;* Test p'ship records, *205, 220*.

Holland, R. G. (Aust.):– 10 w. or more in Test (1), *221*.

Hollies, W. E. (Eng.):– 2,323 w., *156;* 100 w. (14), *157;* 10 w. in innings, *152*.

Holmes, G. C. (Glam.):– 250* for 1st wkt, *257*.

Holmes, P. (Eng.):– Test cricket at 45, *187;* 30,574 r., *134;* 1,000 r. (15), *137;* 67 hundreds, *131;* 315* v Middlesex at Lord's, *129, 252;* 302* v Hampshire, *129;* 555 for 1st wkt, *141;* 1st wkt hundreds, *142*.

Holt, J. K. (WI):– 2 Test hundreds, *204, 232;* Test p'ship record, *205*.

Honours' List in 1985, *1257*.

Hooker, J. E. H. (NSW):– 4 w. with consecutive balls, *150;* 307 for 10th wkt, *145*.

Hookes, D. W. (Aust.):– 1 Test hundred, *228;* 4 successive hundreds, *137;* 2 hundreds in match (3), *132-3;* Hundred in 43 minutes off 34 balls, *138;* Test p'ship records, *228*.

Hopkins, J. A. (Glam.):– 250* for 1st wkt, *257*.

Horan, T. (Aust.):– Test captain, *188;* 1 Test hundred, *193*.

Hornby, A. N. (Eng.):– Test captain, *188, 190*.

Hordern, H. V. (Aust.):– 10 w. or more in Test (2), *196*.

Horner, N. F. (Warwicks.):– 377* for 1st wkt, *142*.

Houghton, D. L. (Zimb.):– 277 for 4th wkt, *258*.

Howard, N. D. (Eng.):– Test captain, *209*.

Howarth, G. P. (NZ):– Test captain, *206, 221, 230, 236, 238, 240;* Captain of Surrey, *532;* 2,531 r. in Tests, *169;* 6 Test hundreds, *207, 231, 237, 239;* 2 hundreds in same Test, *173, 207;* Test p'ship records, *222, 231, 239*.

Howarth, H. J. (NZ):– 86 w. in Tests, *181;* Test p'ship records, *222*.

Howell, H. (Eng.):– 10 w. in innings, *152*.

Howell, W. P. (Aust.):– 17 w. in match, *153;* 10 w. in innings, *151*.

Howorth, R. (Eng.):– All-round, *158;* 100 w. (9), *157*.

Hubble, J. C. (Kent):– 10 d. in match, *161*.

Hughes, K. J. (Aust.):– Test captain, *189, 218, 223, 225;* 4,415 r. in Tests, *168;* 1,163 Test r. in year, *173;* 53 consecutive Tests, *187;* 9 Test hundreds, *193, 219, 224, 226;* Test p'ship records, *224, 227*.

Huish, F. H. (Kent):– 1,328 d., *160;* 102 d. in season, *161;* 10 d. in match, *161*.

Humpage, G. W. (Warwicks.):– 500 d., *259;* 13 sixes in innings, *139;* 470 for 4th wkt, *141, 144*.

Humphries, D. J. (Worcs.):– Career figures, *899*.

Hundreds:– In 1985, *267-70;* Before lunch in 1985, *256;* Fastest in 1985, *256;* Fastest in Tests, *174;* Most individual (35 or more), *131-2;* Most in season, *137;* Most in Tests, *171;* On début, *130-1, 171-2;* Slowest in Tests, *175;* 4 or more in succession, *137;* 2 in match, *132-3, 256*.

Hundred and double-hundred in match, *133;* in a Test, *173*.

Hunte, C. C. (WI):– 3,245 r. in Tests, *169;* 8 Test hundreds, *204, 219, 232, 235;* Hundred on Test début, *172;* 260 v Pakistan, *170, 235;* Carrying bat in Test, *174;* 446 for 2nd wkt, *143;* Test p'ship record, *235*.

Hunter, D. (Yorkshire):– 1,327 d., *161*.

Hutchings, K. L. (Eng.):– 1 Test hundred, *191*.

Hutton, Sir Leonard (Eng.):– Test captain, *189, 202, 206, 209, 212;* 40,140 r. (avge 55.51), *134, 135;* 6,971 r. (avge 56.67) in Tests, *167, 171;* 3,429 r. in season, *146;* 2,428 r. v Australia, *197;* 1,294 r. and 1,050 r. in month, *148;* 1,000 r. (17), *136;* 129 hundreds, *131;* 19 Test hundreds, *191, 199, 203, 207, 210;* 2 hundreds in match (3), *132;* 364 v Australia, *128, 129, 170, 191;* Carrying bat in Test (2), *174;* Obstructing the field, *149;* 1st wkt hundreds, *142;* Test p'ship records, *194-5, 200, 205*.

Hutton R. A. (Eng.):– All round, *159*.

## I

Ibadulla, Khalid (Pak.):– Hundred on Test début, *172, 226;* Obstructing the field, *149;* 377* for 1st wkt, *142;* Test p'ship record, *227.*

Ibrahim, K. C. (Ind.):– 274 for 7th wkt, *145.*

ICC Trophy, 1986:– Fixtures, *1289-90.*

Iddon, J. (Eng.):– 46 hundreds, *132.*

Ijaz Ahmed (Lahore Greens):– Obstructing the field, *149.*

Ikin, B. J. (Griq. West):– LBW hat-trick, *151.*

Illingworth, R. (Eng.):– Test captain, *189, 202, 206, 209, 212;* All-round, *158;* 2 Test hundreds, *203, 210;* 2,072 w., *156;* 122 w. in Tests, *179;* 100 w. (10), *157;* Test p'ship record, *211.*

Imran Khan (Pak.):– Test captain, *212, 225, 241;* All-round, *159, 181, 246;* All-round in Tests, *172, 181;* 2,023 r. in Tests, *170;* 2 Test hundreds, *235, 242;* 1,000 w., *259;* 232 w. in Tests, *181;* 40 w. in series, *183;* 14 w. in Test, *181, 244;* 10 w. or more in Test (4), *227, 243, 244;* 8 w. in Test innings (2), *182, 243, 244;* Test p'ship records, *227, 236, 243.*

Imtiaz Ahmed (Pak.):– Test captain, *212, 225;* 2,079 r. in Tests, *170;* 300* v Commonwealth XI, *129;* 3 Test hundreds, *235, 239, 242;* 308 for 7th wkt, *145, 240;* Test p'ship records, *240, 243.*

India:– B & H World Championship of Cricket, *979-89;* Definition of first-class matches, *1252*; Domestic season 1984-85, *1102-20;* Highest individual Test innings, *170;* Highest Test innings, *177;* India in Test cricket (*see p. 127*); Leading batsmen in Tests, *169;* Leading bowlers in Tests, *181;* Lowest Test innings, *178;* Most consecutive Test appearances, *187;* Most Test appearances, *124;* Most Test appearances as captain, *124;* Representative body, *1160;* Summary of Tests, *188;* Test cricketers (1932-85), *116-20;* Youngest and oldest on Test début, *186.*

India v England, 1984-85, *885, 888, 891, 893, 897.*

India v Sri Lanka, 1985-86, *952.*

Indians in England, 1986:– Tour fixtures, *1288-9.*

Indians in Pakistan, 1984-85, *904-8.*

Individual hundreds (35 or more), *131-2.*

Inman, C. C. (Leics.):– 57 in 8 min, *137;* 32 r. in over, *140.*

Insole, D. J. (Eng.):– 25,237 r., *135;* 54 hundreds, *132;* 1 Test hundred, *199.*

International Cricket Conference:– Addresses of members, *1160-1;* Constitution and Membership, *1250-3;* Meeting, *1258-9.*

Inter-Services Tournament, *1260.*

Intikhab Alam (Pak.):– Test captain, *212, 225, 234, 238;* Test début at 17, *186;* 1 Test hundred, *213;* 1,571 w., *157;* 125 w. in Tests, *181;* 10 w. or more in Test (2), *240;* 190 for 9th wkt, *145, 176, 213;* Test p'ship records, *213, 227, 240.*

Iqbal Qasim (Pak.):– 137 w. in Tests, *181;* 10 w. or more in Test (2), *227, 243;* Test p'ship records, *227, 240, 243.*

Iqtidar Ali (Allied Bank):– Hit the ball twice, *149.*

Irani Trophy (Ind.), *1116.*

Iredale, F. A. (Aust.):– 2 Test hundreds, *193.*

Ireland:– v Australians, *301-2;* v MCC, *321;* v Scotland, *643-4;* in NatWest Bank Trophy, *655.*

Irish Cricket in 1985, *822-3.*

Ironmonger, H. (Aust.):– Oldest Australian Test player, *187;* Test début at 46, *186;* 10 w. or more in Test (2), *217, 221.*

Irvine, B. L. (SA):– 1 Test hundred, *216.*

Israr Ali (B'pur):– 6 w. for 1 r., *153.*

I Zingari results, 1985, *1260.*

## J

Jackman, R. D. (Eng.):– Most w. in 1980, *155;* 3 hat-tricks, 151.

Jackson, A. A. (Aust.):– Hundred v England on Test début, *171, 193.*

Jackson, Hon. Sir F. S. (Eng.):– Test captain, *189;* 5 Test hundreds, *191.*

Jackson, H. L. (Eng.):– 1,733 w., *156;* 100 w. (10), *157.*

Jaisimha, M. L. (Ind.):– 2,056 r. in Tests, *169;* 3 Test hundreds, *210, 224.*

Jalal-ud-Din (Pak.):– Hat-trick in one-day int., *246;* Handled the ball, *149.*

James, K. D. (Hants):– 6 for 22 v Australians, *292;* 227 for 8th wkt, *258.*

Jameson, J. A. (Eng.):– 465* for 2nd wkt, *141, 143.*

Jamshedji, R. J. D. (Ind.):– Oldest Indian Test début, *186.*

Jardine, D. R. (Eng.):– Test captain, *189, 202, 206, 209;* 35 hundreds, *132;* 1 Test hundred, *203;* Avge of 91.09 in English season, *147;* Test p'ship record, *194.*

Jarman, B. N. (Aust.):– Test captain, *190;* 10 d. in match, *161;* Test p'ship record, *224.*

Jarvis, P. W. (Yorks.):– Hat-trick, *258.*

Jarvis, T. W. (NZ):– 1 Test hundred, *231;* 387 for 1st wkt, *142, 143, 231;* Test p'ship record, *231.*

Javed Miandad (Pak.):– Test captain, *225, 234, 238, 244;* 22,534 r. (avge 53.27), *136;* 5,044 r. (avge 54.92) in Tests, *169, 171;* 53 consecutive Tests, *187;* 63 hundreds, *132;* 13 Test hundreds, *226, 239, 242;* 2 hundreds in match (4), *132;* 2 hundreds in same Test, *173, 239;* Hundred on Test début, *172, 239;* 311 v National Bank, *129;* 280* v India, *170, 242;* 200* v Australians, *256, 297-8;* 8 c. in match, *163;* 451 for 3rd wkt, *141;* 306* for 4th wkt, *258;* Test p'ship records, *227, 240, 243, 244.*

Jenkins, R. O. (Eng.):– Double hat-trick, *150;* 3 hat-tricks, *151.*

Jessop, G. L. (Eng.):– All-round, *158;* Fastest English Test hundred, *174, 191;* 26,698 r., *135;* 53 hundreds, *132;* 2 hundreds in match (4), *132;* 1 Test hundred, *174, 191*; 200 r. in 120 min. and 130 min., *138.*

Jesty, T. E. (Hants):– 32 r. in over, *140.*

John Player League:– *700-80;* Fixtures, 1986, *1290-1*; Rules, *1253-4, 1255-6.*

John, V. B. (SL):– Test p'ship record, *244.*

Johnson, G. W. (Kent):– Career figures, *899.*

Johnson, H. H. H. (WI):– 10 w. or more in Test (1), *206.*

Johnson, I. W. (Aust.):– Test captain, *189, 218, 223, 225;* 109 w. in Tests, *180;* Test p'ship records, *220, 224.*

Johnson, J. S. (Shropshire):– Hundred on début, *130.*

Johnson, L. A. (Northants):– 10 d. in match (2), *161.*

Johnston, W. A. (Aust.):– Avge of 102 in English season, *147;* 160 w. in Tests, *180.*

Jones, A. (Glam.):– 36,049 r., *134;* 1,000 r. (23), *136;* 56 hundreds, *131;* 2 hundreds in match (3), *132.*

Jones, A. O. (Eng.):– Test captain, *189;* 391 for 1st wkt, *141.*

Jones, E. (Aust.):– 10 w. or more in Test (1), *195.*

Jones, E. W. (Glam.):– 7 d. in innings, *162.*

Jones Cup (WI), *1076.*

Jordon, R. C. (Vic):– 10 c. in match, *161.*

Joshi, P. G. (Ind.):– Test p'ship record, *242.*

Julien, B. D. (WI):– 2 Test hundreds, *204, 235;* Test p'ship records, *205, 235.*

Jupp, V. W. C. (Eng.):– All-round, *158;* 1,658 w., *156;* 102 and hat-trick, *160;* 100 w. (10), *157;* 5 hat-tricks, *151.*

## K

Kallicharran, A. I. (WI):– Test captain, *218, 232;* 29,771 r., *134;* 4,399 r. in Tests, *168;* 78 hundreds, *131;* 12 Test hundreds, *204, 219, 230, 232, 235;* Hundred on Test début, *172, 230;* Highest aggregate in 1982, *146;* Record score in NatWest Bank Trophy, *666;* 470 for 4th wkt, *141, 144;* Test p'ship records, *220, 231, 234.*

Kamal Najamuddin (Kar.):– 10 d. in match, *161;* 418 for 1st wkt, *141.*

Kanhai, R. B. (WI):– Test captain, *202, 218;* 28,774 r., *135;* 6,227 r. in Tests, *168;* 61 consecutive Tests, *187;* 83 hundreds, *131;* 15 Test hundreds, *204, 219-20, 233, 235;* 256 v India, *170, 233;* 2 hundreds in match (2), *132;* 2 hundreds in same Test, *172, 219;* Hundred and double-hundred, *133;* Avge of 82.53 in English season, *147;* 465* for 2nd wkt, *141, 143;* Test p'ship records, *220, 234, 235.*

Kapil Dev (Ind.):– Test captain, *232, 241;* 2,788 r. in Tests, *169;* 67 consecutive Tests, *187;* 3 Test hundreds, *210, 233;* 500 w., *259;* 258 w. in Tests, *181;* 10 w. or more in Test (2), *234, 243;* 9 w. in Test innings, *182, 234;* 8 w. in Test innings, *182;* All-round in one-day ints, *246;* All-round in Tests, *181;* Test p'ship record, *211.*

Kardar, A. H. (Ind. and Pak.):– Test captain, *124, 212, 225, 234, 238, 241;* Test p'ship record, *236.*

Keeton, W. W. (Eng.):– Highest for Notts., *130;* 54 hundreds, *132;* 312* v Middlesex, *129, 130;* 1st wkt hundreds, *142.*

Kelleway, C. (Aust.):– 3 Test hundreds, *193, 216;* Test p'ship records, *217*.
Kelly, J. J. (Aust.):– 8 d. in Test, *185*.
Kennedy, A. S. (Eng.):– All-round, *158;* 2,874 w., *156;* 205 w. in season, *155;* 100 w. (15), *157;* 10 w. in innings, *152;* 3 hat-tricks, *151*.
Kenny, R. B. (Ind.):– Test p'ship record, *225*.
Kent:– *333, 420-36;* Championship positions, *338-9;* Highest score, *163;* Highest individual score, *130;* Lowest score, *164*.
Kent II, *799, 801, 805*.
Kenyon, D. (Eng.):– 37,002 r., *134;* 1,000 r. (19), *136;* 74 hundreds, *131*.
Kerr, R. B. (Qld):– 388 for 1st wkt, *141*.
Khalid Alvi (Kar.):– 418 for 1st wkt, *141*.
Khalid Hassan (Pak.):– Test début at 16, *186*.
Khalid Irtiza (UBL):– 456 for 3rd wkt, *141, 143*.
Killick, E. H. (Sussex):– 344 consecutive Championship appearances, *255*.
Kilner, R. (Eng.):– All-round, *158*.
King, C. L. (WI):– 1 Test hundred, *230*.
King, J. H. (Eng.):– Hit the ball twice, *149;* 25,121 r., *135;* 2 hundreds in match (2), *132*.
Kinneir, S. P. (Eng.):– Test début at 40, *186*.
Kippax, A. F. (Aust.):– 12,747 r. (avge 57.67), *135;* 43 hundreds, *132;* 2 Test hundreds, *193, 219;* 2 hundreds in match (2), *132;* 315* v Queensland, *129;* 307 for 10th wkt, *145*.
Kirmani, S. M. H. (Ind.):– 2,717 r. in Tests, *169;* 2 Test hundreds, *210, 224;* 193 d. in Tests, *184;* 6 d. in Test innings, *185*, Test p'ship records, *211, 225, 234, 238, 242*.
Kirsten, N. (Border):– 7 d. in innings, *162*.
Kirsten, P. N. (Derbys. and W. Prov.):– 41 hundreds, *132;* 4 successive hundreds, *137;* 2 hundreds in match (2), *132;* Highest aggregate in 1980, *146*.
Kline, L. F. (Aust.):– Test hat-trick, *183*.
Knight, B. R. (Eng.):– All-round, *158;* 2 Test hundreds, *207, 210;* Test p'ship record, *208*.
Knott, A. P. E. (Eng.):– "Alan Knott – A Thorough Genius" (and career figures), *69-73;* 4,389 r. in Tests, *167;* 65 consecutive Tests, *187;* 5 Test hundreds, *191, 203, 207, 213;* 1,344 d. in career, *160;* 269 d. in Tests, *184;* 105 d. v Australia, *197;* 24 d. in series, *184;* 5 d. in Test innings, *185;* Test p'ship records, *195, 205, 208*.
Kripal Singh, A. G. (Ind.):– Hundred on Test début, *172, 237;* Test p'ship record, *238*.
Kunderan, B. K. (Ind.):– 2 Test hundreds, *210*.

## L

Lacey, Sir F. E. (Hants):– 323* v Norfolk, *253*.
Laird, B. M. (Aust.):– Test p'ship record, *222*.
Laker, J. C. (Eng.):– 1,944 w., *156;* 193 w. in Tests, *179;* 100 w. (11), *157;* 46 w. in series, *183, 196;* 19 w. in Test, *153, 181, 195;* 10 w. in innings (2), *152;* 10 w. in Test innings, *152, 182;* 10 w. or more in Test (3), *195, 201;* 9 w. in Test innings, *182;* 8 w. for 2 r., *153;* 4 hat-tricks, *151*.
Lamb, A. J. (Eng.):– 2,211 r. in Tests, *167;* 41 hundreds, *132;* 7 Test hundreds, *203, 207, 210, 214;* 6 c. in Test, *186;* 30 r. in over, *140;* Test p'ship record, *214*.
Lambert, W. (Sussex):– 107 and 157 v Epsom (1817), *133*.
Lancashire:– *333, 437-51;* Championship positions, *338-9;* Highest score, *163;* Highest individual score, *130;* Lowest score, *164*.
Lancashire II, *799, 801, 806*.
Lancashire League, 1985, *820-1*.
Lance, H. R. (SA):– 174 for 10th wkt, *145;* Test p'ship record, *217*.
Langley, G. R. A. (Aust.):– 21 d. in series, *184;* 9 d. in Test, *185*.
Langridge, James (Eng.):– All-round, *158;* 31,716 r., *134;* 1,000 r. (20), *136;* 42 hundreds, *132;* 1,530 w., *157*.
Langridge, J. G. (Sussex):– 34,380 r., *134;* 1,000 r. (17), *136;* 76 hundreds, *131;* 4 successive hundreds, *137;* 2 hundreds in match (2), *132;* 786 c., *162;* 69 c. in season, *162;* 490 for 1st wkt, *141*.
Langton, A. B. C. (SA):– Test p'ship record, *201*.
Larkins, W. (Eng.):– 15,000 r., *259;* 37 hundreds, *132*; 255 for 2nd wkt, *257*.
Larwood, H. (Eng.):– 100 w. (8), *157;* 78 w. in Tests, *179;* 10 w. or more in Test (1), *195;* Test p'ship record, *195*.
Laver, F. (Aust.):– 8 w. in Test innings, *182*.

Lawrence, G. B. (SA):– 8 w. in Test innings, *182*.

Lawry, W. M. (Aust.):– Test captain, *189, 215, 218, 223;* 18,734 r. (avge 50.90), *136;* 5,234 r. in Tests, *168;* 2,233 r. v England, *197;* 1,056 Test r. in year, *173;* 50 hundreds, *132;* 13 Test hundreds, *193, 216, 219, 224;* Carrying bat in Test (2), *174;* 382 for 1st wkt, *142;* Test p'ship records, *195, 220, 224*.

Laws of Cricket, *1222-50*.

Lawson, G. F. (Aust.):– 140 w. in Tests, *180;* 10 w. or more in Test (2), *196, 221;* 8 w. in Test innings, *183;* Test p'ship record, *227*.

League Cricket Conference:– v Zimbabweans, *314*.

Lee, F. S. (Som.):– 1st wkt hundreds, *142*.

Lee, H. W. (Eng.):– Test début at 40, *187;* 38 hundreds, *132;* 2 hundreds in match (2), *132*.

Lee, I. S. (Vic.):– 424 for 4th wkt, *144*.

Lee, J. W. (Som.):– 1st wkt hundreds, *142*.

Lee, P. G. (Eng.):– Most w. in 1975, *155*.

Lees, W. K. (NZ):– 1 Test hundred, *239;* 8 c. in Test, *185;* Test p'ship record, *239*.

Leggat, I. B. (NZ):– 239 for 9th wkt, *145*.

Legge, G. B. (Eng.):– 1 Test hundred, *207*.

Leicestershire:– *333, 452-66;* Championship positions, *338-9;* Highest score, *163;* Highest individual score, *130;* Lowest score, *164*.

Leicestershire II, *799, 801, 807*.

Lester, E. (Yorks.):– 2 hundreds in match (2), *132*.

Lethbridge, C. (Warwicks.):– Career figures, *899*.

Lever, J. K. (Eng.):– 1,549 w., *157;* 10 w. or more in Test (1), *211;* Most w. in 1979, 1983, *155*.

Lever, P. (Eng.):– Test p'ship records, *208, 211*.

Leveson Gower, Sir H. D. G. (Eng.):– Test captain, *198*.

Lewis, A. R. (Eng.):– Test captain, *209, 212;* 1 Test hundred, *210;* 1st wkt hundreds, *142*.

Leyland, M. (Eng.):– Fast scoring, *138;* 33,659 r., *134;* 2,764 r. in Tests, *167;* 1,000 r. (17), *136;* 80 hundreds, *131;* 9 Test hundreds, *191, 199;* Test p'ship record, *194*.

Lillee, D. K. (Aust.):– 355 w. in Tests, *180;* 167 w. v England, *197;* 103 w. in one-day ints, *245;* 39 w. in series, *183;* 10 w. or more in Test (7), *196, 221, 223, 227;* Test p'ship record, *227*.

Lilley, A. A. (Eng.):– Hit the ball twice, *149*; 84 d. v Australia, *197*.

Lilley, A. W. (Essex):– Hundred on début, *130*.

Lillywhite, James jun. (Eng.):– Test captain, *188;* 10 w. in innings, *151*.

Lincolnshire, *782, 783, 792*.

Lindsay, D. T. (SA):– 3 Test hundreds, *216;* 30 r. in over, *140;* 24 d. in series, *184;* 8 c. in Test, *185;* 6 c. in Test innings, *185;* Test p'ship records, *217, 229*.

Lindsay, N. V. (SA):– 221 for 9th wkt, *145*.

Lindwall, R. R. (Aust.):– Test captain, *223;* 2 Test hundreds, *193, 219;* 228 w. in Tests, *180;* 114 w. v England, *197*.

Llewellyn, C. B. (SA):– All-round, *158;* 10 w. or more in Test (1), *217;* 2 hundreds in match (2), *132;* Test p'ship record, *217*.

Lloyd, C. H. (WI):– Test captain, *124, 202, 218, 230, 232, 234;* Captain of Lancashire, *437;* 110 Tests, *124;* 30,885 r., *134;* 7,515 r. in Tests, *168;* 78 hundreds, *131;* 19 Test hundreds, *204, 220, 233, 235;* 200 r. in 120 min., *138;* 161 for 9th wkt, *145, 234;* 335 for 5th wkt, *144;* Test p'ship records, *234, 235*.

Lloyd, D. (Eng.):– 38 hundreds, *132;* Double-hundred v India, *210*.

Loader, P. J. (Eng.):– Hat-trick v West Indies, *183*.

Lock, G. A. R. (Eng.):– 2,844 w., *156;* 200 w. in season (2), *154;* 174 w. in Tests, *179;* 100 w. (14), *157;* 10 w. in innings, *152;* 10 w. or more in Test (3), *205, 208;* 4 hat-tricks, *151;* 830 c., *162;* 64 c. in season, *162;* 8 c. in match, *163*.

Lockwood, W. H. (Eng.):– 10 w. or more in Test (1), *195;* 3 hat-tricks, *151*.

Logie, A. L. (WI):– 1 Test hundred, *233*.

Lohmann, G. A. (Eng.):– Hat-trick v South Africa, *183;* 1,805 w., *156;* 200 w. (3), *154-5;* 112 w. in Tests, *179;* 100 w. (8), *157;* 35 w. in series, *183;* 15 w. in Test, *181;* 10 w. or more in Test (5), *195, 201;* 9 w. in Test innings, *182;* 8 w. in Test innings (3), *182*.

Long, A. (Surrey and Sussex):– 1,046 d., *161;* 11 c. in match, *161;* 7 c. in innings, *162*.

Lords and Commons Cricket, 1985, *1296*.

Lord's Cricket Ground:– *252-3;* Matches in 1985, *319-29.*

Lowest innings totals:– in Tests, *178;* in one-day ints, *247.*

Lowest match aggregates, *165, 178.*

Lowry, T. C. (NZ):– Test captain, *206.*

Loxton, S. J. E. (Aust.):– 1 Test hundred, *216;* Test p'ship record, *224.*

Luckhurst, B. W. (Eng.):– 48 hundreds, *132;* 2 Test hundreds, *210, 213.*

Lumb, R. G. (Yorks.):– 1st wkt hundreds, *142.*

Lynch, M. A. (Surrey):– 3 successive sixes, *257;* 252 for 5th wkt, *258.*

Lyons, J. J. (Aust.):– 1 Test hundred, *193.*

## M

Macartney, C. G. (Aust.):– 2,131 r. in Tests, *168;* 49 hundreds, *132;* 7 Test hundreds, *193, 216;* 4 successive hundreds, *137;* 2 hundreds in match (2), *132;* 345 v Nottinghamshire, *128, 130, 138, 140;* 300 r. in 205 min., *138;* 51 boundaries in innings, *139;* 10 w. or more in Test (1), *196.*

Macaulay, G. G. (Eng.):– 1,837 w., *156;* 211 w. in season, *154;* 100 w. (10), *157;* 4 hat-tricks, *151.*

McCabe, S. J. (Aust.):– 2,748 r. in Tests, *168;* 6 Test hundreds, *193, 216.*

McCool, C. L. (Aust.):– 1 Test hundred, *193.*

McCosker, R. B. (Aust.):– 4 Test hundreds, *193, 219, 226;* 2 hundreds in match (3), *132.*

McCubbin, G. R. (Tvl):– 221 for 9th wkt, *145.*

McDermott, C. J. (Aust.):– Cricketer of the Year, *60*; 8 w. in Test innings, *183, 258.*

McDonald, C. C. (Aust.):– 3,107 r. in Tests, *168;* 5 Test hundreds, *193, 217, 219;* Test p'ship records, *217, 220.*

McDonald, E. A. (Aust.):– 205 w. in season, *155;* 3 hat-tricks, *151.*

McDonald's Cup (Aust.), *1032-3.*

McDonnell, P. S. (Aust.):– Test captain, *188;* 3 Test hundreds, *193.*

McEwan, K. S. (Essex and W. Prov.):– 61 hundreds, *131;* Career figures, *899;* Hundred before lunch, *256;* Highest aggregate in 1983, *146.*

McFarlane, L. L. (Northants, Lancs. and Glam.):– Career figures, *899.*

McGibbon, A. R. (NZ):– Test p'ship record, *237.*

McGirr, H. M. (NZ):– Oldest New Zealand Test début, *187.*

McGlew, D. J. (SA):– Test captain, *198, 215, 228;* 2,440 r. in Tests, *168;* 7 Test hundreds, *200, 216, 229;* Slow Test hundred, *176;* 255* v New Zealand, *170, 229;* Carrying bat in Test, *174;* Test p'ship records, *217, 229.*

McGregor, S. N. (NZ):– 1 Test hundred, *239;* Test p'ship record, *229.*

Mackay, K. D. (Aust.):– Test p'ship records, *217, 220.*

Mackay-Coghill, D. (Tvl):– 174 for 10th wkt, *145.*

McKenzie, G. D. (Aust.):– 246 w. in Tests, *180;* 10 w. or more in Tests (3), *221, 225;* 8 w. in Test innings, *182;* Test p'ship records, *217, 224.*

MacLaren, A. C. (Eng.):– Test captain, *189-90;* Highest for Lancashire, *130;* 47 hundreds, *132;* 5 Test hundreds, *191;* 424 v Somerset, *128, 130;* 65 boundaries in innings, *139.*

Maclean, J. A. (Aust.):– 7 d. in innings, *162.*

McLean, R. A. (SA):– 2,120 r. in Tests, *168;* 5 Test hundreds, *200, 229;* Test p'ship records, *229.*

McLeod, C. E. (Aust.):– 1 Test hundred, *193.*

McMorris, E. D. A. (WI):– 1 Test hundred, *233;* Test p'ship record, *234.*

McWatt, C. A. (WI):– Test p'ship record, *205.*

Madan Lal (Ind.):– Test p'ship records, *211, 242.*

Madugalle, R. S. (SL):– 12 Tests, *124;* Test p'ship record, *244.*

Mahmood Rashid (UBL):– Obstructing the field, *149.*

Mailey, A. A. (Aust.):– 99 w. in Tests, *180;* 36 w. in series, *183, 196;* 10 w. in innings, *152;* 10 w. or more in Test (2), *196;* 9 w. in Test innings,. *182;* Test p'ship record, *195.*

Majid J. Khan (Pak.):– Test captain, *212;* 27,328 r., *135;* 3,931 r. in Tests, *169;* 73 hundreds, *131;* 8 Test hundreds, *226, 235, 239;* 30 r. in over, *140;* 13 sixes in innings, *139;* Highest aggregate in 1972, *146;* 389 for 1st wkt, *141;* Test p'ship records, *227, 236, 240.*

Makepeace, H. (Eng.):– 25,799 r., *135;* 43 hundreds, *132;* 1 Test hundred, *191.*

Mallett, A. A. (Aust.):– 132 w. in Tests, *180;* 10 w. or more in Test (1), *225;* 8 w. in Test innings, *182.*

Malone, S. J. (Essex, Hants and Glam.):– Career figures, *899.*

Maninder Singh (Ind.):– Test cricket at 17, *186.*

Manjrekar, V. L. (Ind.):– 3,208 r. in Tests, *169;* 38 hundreds, *132;* 7 Test hundreds, *210, 233, 237;* Test p'ship records, *211, 238.*

Mankad, V. (Ind.):– Test captain, *232, 241;* 2,109 r. in Tests, *169;* 5 Test hundreds, *210, 224, 237;* 162 w. in Tests, *181;* 10 w. or more in Test (2), *211, 243;* 8 w. in Test innings (2), *182, 211, 243;* 413 for 1st wkt v New Zealand, *141, 176, 238.*

Mann, A. L. (Aust.):– 1 Test hundred, *224.*

Mann, F. G. (Eng.):– President of MCC, *318;* Test captain, *198, 206;* 1 Test hundred, *199.*

Mann, F. T. (Eng.):– Test captain, *198.*

Mansoor Akhtar (Pak.):– 1 Test hundred, *226;* 561 for 1st wkt, *141, 143;* 389 for 1st wkt, *141;* Test p'ship record, *227.*

Maqsood Kundi (MCB):– 196* for 10th wkt, *145.*

Marks, V. J. (Eng.):– All-round, *159;* 500 w., *259;* 8 w. in innings, *258;* Test p'ship record, *213.*

Marriott, C. S. (Eng.):– 10 w. or more in Test (1), *205.*

Marsh, R. W. (Aust.):– 3,633 r. in Tests, *168;* 96 Tests, *124;* 52 consecutive Tests, *187;* 3 Test hundreds, *193, 222, 226;* 355 d. in Tests, *184;* 148 d. v England, *197;* 1,220 r. and 123 d. in one-day ints, *246*; 28 d., 26 d., 23 d. and 21 d. in series, *184;* 11 c. in match, *161;* 10 c. in match, *161;* 9 c. in Test, *185;* 8 c. in Test (3), *185;* 6 c. in Test innings, *185;* Test p'ship records, *222.*

Marshall, M. D. (WI):– 188 w. in Tests, *180;* 10 w. or more in Test (2), *221, 231;* Most w. in 1982, *155;* Test p'ship records, *231, 234.*

Marshall, R. E. (WI):– 35,725 r., *134;* 1,000 r. (18), *136;* 68 hundreds, *131;* 1st wkt hundreds, *142.*

Martin, F. (Eng.):– 10 w. or more in Test (1), *195;* 4 w. with consecutive balls, *150.*

Martin, F. R. (WI):– 1 Test hundred, *220.*

Martin, J. W. (Aust.):– Test p'ship records, *220, 224.*

Martindale, E. A. (WI):– 255 for 8th wkt, *145.*

Marx, W. F. E. (Tvl):– 240 on début, *131.*

Marylebone Cricket Club, The:– *317, 318-21;* v Australians, *282-3.*

MCC in Canada, 1985, *1153.*

MCC Schools v National Association of Young Cricketers, *326-7.*

Masood Anwar (R'pindi):– 8 c. in match, *163.*

Masood Iqbal (HBL):– 7 d. in innings, *162.*

Massie, H. H. (Aust.):– Test captain, *190.*

Massie, R. A. L. (Aust.):– 16 w. in Test, *181, 196;* 10 w. or more in Test (1), *196;* 8 w. in Test innings (2), *182, 196;* Test p'ship record, *227.*

Matthews, F. C. L. (Notts.):– 17 w. in match, *153.*

Matthews, G. R. J. (Aust.):– Test p'ship record, *227.*

Matthews, T. J. (Aust.):– Double hat-trick in Test, *150, 183;* 4 hat-tricks, *151.*

May, P. B. H. (Eng.):– Test captain, *124, 189, 198, 202, 206, 209;* 27,592 r. (avge 51.00), *135, 136;* 4,537 r. in Tests, *167;* 52 consecutive Tests, *187;* 85 hundreds, *131;* 13 Test hundreds, *191, 199, 204, 207, 210;* 4 successive hundreds, *137;* 2 hundreds in match (3), *132;* Hundred on Test début, *171, 199;* 285* v West Indies, *170, 204;* Test p'ship record, *176, 205.*

Maynard, M. P. (Glam.):– Hundred on début, *130, 385;* 3 successive sixes, *257, 385.*

Mayne, E. R. (Aust.):– 456 for 1st wkt, *141, 143.*

Mead, C. P. (Eng.):– 55,061 r., *134;* 3,179 r. in season, *146;* 1,000 r. (27), *136-7;* 665 Championship appearances, *255;* 153 hundreds, *131;* 13 hundreds in season, *137;* 4 Test hundreds, *191, 199;* 2 hundreds in match (3), *132;* Hundred and double-hundred, *133.*

Mead, W. (Eng.):– 1,916 w., *156;* 100 w. (10), *157;* 17 w. in match, *153.*

Meckiff, I. (Aust.):– Test p'ship record, *217.*

Medlycott, K. T. (Surrey):– Hundred on début, *130.*

Meetings in 1985:– International Cricket Conference, *1258-9;* MCC, *318-9;* TCCB, *1258-9*.
Mehra, M. (Ind. Rlwys):– Obstructing the field, *149*.
Mehra, V. L. (Ind.):– Youngest Indian Test player, *186*.
Melville, A. (SA):– Test captain, *198;* 4 Test hundreds, *200;* 2 hundreds in same Test, *172, 200;* 299 for 7th wkt, *145;* Test p'ship record, *200*.
Mendis, G. D. (Sussex):– 10,000 r., *259;* 4 hundreds in 4 days, *412;* 2 hundreds in same match, *256*.
Mendis, L. R. D. (SL):– Test captain, *124, 214, 227, 240, 244;* 3 Test hundreds, *214, 243;* 2 hundreds in same Test, *173, 243;* Test p'ship records, *214, 228, 243, 244*.
Mercer, J. (Sussex, Glam. and Northants):– 1,593 w., *157;* 100 w. (9), *157;* 10 w. in innings, *152*.
Merchant, Uday (Bombay):– 360 for 5th wkt, *144*.
Merchant, V. M. (Ind.):– 12,876 r. (avge 72.74), *135;* 4 successive hundreds, *137;* 44 hundreds, *132;* 3 Test hundreds, *210;* 359* v Maharashtra, *128;* 142 and hat-trick, *160;* 371 for 6th wkt, *144*.
Metcalfe, A. A. (Yorks.):– Hundred on début, *130*.
Middlesex:– *333, 467-82;* Championship positions, *338-9;* Highest score, *163;* Highest individual score, *130;* Lowest score, *164*.
Middlesex II, *799-800, 801, 807-8*.
Milburn, C. (Eng.):– 2 Test hundreds, *204, 213;* Test p'ship record, *205*.
Miller, G. (Eng.):– 10,000 r., *259*.
Miller, K. R. (Aust.):– 2,958 r. in Tests, *168;* 41 hundreds, *132;* 7 Test hundreds, *193, 219;* 170 w. in Tests, *180;* 10 w. or more in Test (1), *196;* Test p'ship records, *217, 220*.
Mills, J. E. (NZ):– Hundred on Test début, *171, 207;* 190* for 8th wkt, *145;* Test p'ship record, *208*.
Mills, P. T. (Glos.):– 5 w. for 0 r., *153*.
Milton, C. A. (Eng.):– 32,150 r., *134;* 1,000 r. (16), *136;* 56 hundreds, *131;* 2 hundreds in match (2), *132;* Hundred on Test début, *172, 207;* 755 c., *162;* 63 c. in season, *162;* 8 c. in match, *163*.
Milton, W. H. (SA):– Test captain, *198*.
Minor Counties:– *781-98;* B & H Cup, *669, 699;* Championship winners, *798;* Fixtures, 1986, *1291-3;* Formation, *254-5;* Highest individual scores, *253;* Representative body, *877;* Umpires, *1257*; v Australians, *297;* v Zimbabweans, *313-4*.
Miran Bux (Pak.):– Test début at 47, *186;* Oldest Pakistan Test player, *187*.
Mitchell, A. (Eng.):– 44 hundreds, *132;* 4 successive hundreds, *137*.
Mitchell, B. (SA):– 3,471 r. in Tests, *168;* 8 Test hundreds, *200, 229;* 2 hundreds in same Test, *172, 200;* 6 c. in Test, *185;* 299 for 7th wkt, *145;* Test p'ship records, *200-1, 229*.
Mitchell, F. (Eng. and SA):– Test captain, *198, 215*.
Mitchell, T. B. (Eng.):– 100 w. (10), *157;* 10 w. in innings, *152*.
Modi, R. S. (Ind.):– 1 Test hundred, *233;* 410 for 3rd wkt, *143;* 371 for 6th wkt, *144*.
Mohammad Farooq (Pak.):– Test p'ship record, *240*.
Mohammad Ilyas (Pak.):– 1 Test hundred, *239;* Test p'ship record, *240*.
Mohammad Iqbal (Muslim Model HS):– 475* v Islamia HS, *253*.
Mohol, S. N. (M'tra):– 4 w. with consecutive balls, *150*.
Mohsin Khan (Pak.):– 2,468 r. in Tests, *170;* 1,029 Test r. in year, *173;* 7 Test hundreds, *213, 226, 242, 244;* Handled the ball, *149;* 426 for 2nd wkt, *143;* Test p'ship records, *213, 227*.
Mold, A. W. (Eng.):– 1,673 w., *156;* 200 w. (2), *154;* 100 w. (9), *157;* 4 w. with consecutive balls, *150*.
Moloney, D. A. R. (NZ):– Test p'ship record, *208*.
Mooney, F. L. H. (NZ):– Test p'ship record, *208*.
Moore, R. H. (Hants):– Highest for Hampshire, *130;* 316 v Warwickshire, *129, 130*.
Morgan, H. E. (Glam.):– 254 v Monmouthshire, *253*.
Morkel, D. P. B. (SA):– 222 for 8th wkt, *145*.
Moroney, J. R. (Aust.):– 2 hundreds in same Test, *172, 216*.
Morris, A. R. (Aust.):– Test captain, *190, 218;* 12,614 r. (avge 53.67), *136;* 3,533 r. in Tests, *168;* 2,080 r. v England, *197;* 46 hundreds, *132;* 12 Test hundreds, *193, 216, 219, 224;* 2 hundreds in same

Morris, A. R. (Aust.):– *contd*
Test, *172, 193;* 2 hundreds in match (2), *131, 132;* 148 and 111 on début, *131;* Test p'ship record, *224.*
Morrison, J. F. M. (NZ):– 1 Test hundred, *222;* Test p'ship record, *222.*
Mortimore, J. B. (Eng.):– All-round, *158;* 1,807 w., *156.*
Moss, A. E. (Cant.):– 10 w. in innings on first-class début, *151.*
Moss, J. K. (Aust.):– 390* for 3rd wkt, *143.*
Motz, R. C. (NZ):– 100 w. in Tests, *181.*
Moxon, M. D. (Yorks.):– Hundred on début, *130*; 351 for 1st wkt, *257.*
Mudassar Nazar (Pak.):– 3,099 r. in Tests, *169;* 38 hundreds, *132;* 8 Test hundreds, *213, 239, 242;* Slowest Test hundred, *176;* 761 r. in series, *173;* Carrying bat in Test, *174*; All-round in one-day ints, *246;* Average of 82.50 in English season, *147;* 451 for 3rd wkt, *141;* 389 for 1st wkt, *141;* Test p'ship records, *213, 240, 243.*
Murdoch, W. L. (Aust. and Eng.):– Test captain, *188-190;* 2 Test hundreds, *193;* 321 v Victoria, *129.*
Murray, A. R. A. (SA):– 1 Test hundred, *229;* Test p'ship record, *229.*
Murray, B. A. G. (NZ):– Test p'ship record, *237.*
Murray, D. A. (WI):– 10 d. in match, *161;* 9 d. in Test, *185.*
Murray, D. L. (WI):– Test captain, *218;* 189 d. in Tests, *184;* 24 d. in series, *184;* Test p'ship records, *220, 234, 235.*
Murray, J. T. (Eng.):– 1,025 r. and 104 d. in season, *158;* 1 Test hundred, *203;* 1,527 d., *160;* 100 d. in season (2), *161;* 6 c. in Test innings, *185;* Test p'ship record, *205.*
Mushtaq Ali (Ind.):– 2 Test hundreds, *210, 233.*
Mushtaq Mohammad (Pak.):– Test captain, *225, 234, 238, 241;* Youngest Test player, *186;* 31,091 r., *134;* 3,643 r. in Tests, *169;* 1,000 r. (15), *137;* 72 hundreds, *131;* 10 Test hundreds, *213, 226, 235, 239, 242;* 303* v Karachi Univ., *129;* 79 w. in Tests, *181;* All-round, *159;* 350 for 4th wkt, *144;* Test p'ship records, *213, 236, 240.*
Mycroft, W. (Derbys.):– 17 w. in match, *153.*

## N

Nadeem Yousuf (MCB):– 196* for 10th wkt, *145.*
Nadkarni, R. G. (Ind.):– 1 Test hundred, *210;* 88 w. in Tests, *181;* 10 w. or more in Test (1), *225;* Test p'ship records, *211, 238.*
Nagarwalla, N. D. (M'tra):– 245 for 9th wkt, *145.*
Nanan, R. (WI):– Test p'ship record, *235.*
Nash, G. (Lancs.):– 4 w. with consecutive balls, *149.*
Nasim-ul-Ghani (Pak.):– Test début at 16, *186;* 1 Test hundred, *213;* Test p'ship record, *213.*
National Association of Young Cricketers:– v MCC Schools, *326-7.*
National Club Championship, *327-8.*
National Cricket Association:– *317;* Address, *1161;* Young Cricketers v Combined Services, *327.*
National Village Championship, *328-9.*
NatWest Bank Trophy:– *647-68;* Fixtures, 1986, *1285-8;* Rules, *1253-5.*
Nayudu, C. K. (Ind.):– Test captain, *209;* 11 sixes in innings, *139.*
Nazar Mohammad (Pak.):– 1 Test hundred, *242;* Carrying bat in Test, *174.*
Neale, P. A. (Worcs.):– Captain of Worcestershire, *580.*
Needham, A. (Surrey):– Hundred before lunch, *256.*
Newham, W. (Eng.):– Slow batting in Test, *175;* 344 for 7th wkt, *144.*
Newman, J. A. (Hants):– All-round, *158;* 2,032 w., *156;* 100 w. (9), *157.*
New Zealand:– B & H World Championship of Cricket, *980-8;* Definition of first-class matches, *1252;* Domestic season 1984-85, *1080-101;* Highest individual Test innings, *170;* Highest Test innings, *177;* Leading batsmen in Tests, *169;* Leading bowlers in Tests, *181;* Lowest Test innings, *178;* Most consecutive Test appearances, *187;* Most Test appearances, *124;* Most Test appearances as captain, *124;* New Zealand in Test cricket (*see p. 127*); Representative body, *1160;* Summary of Tests, *188;* Test cricketers (1929-85), *112-6;* Youngest and Oldest on Test début, *186.*
New Zealand v Australia, 1985-86, *952.*
New Zealand v Pakistan, 1984-85, *943, 944, 947.*

New Zealanders in England, 1986, Fixtures, *1289*.

New Zealanders in Sri Lanka and Pakistan, 1984-85, *926-37*.

New Zealanders in West Indies, 1984-85, *953-66*.

New Zealanders (Young) in Zimbabwe, 1984-85, *1143-7*.

Nicholls, R. B. (Glos.):– 1,000 r. (15), *137;* 395 for 1st wkt, *141*.

Nichols, M. S. (Eng.):– All-round, *158;* 1,841 w., *156;* 100 w. (11), *157*.

Nicolson, J. F. W. (Natal):– 424 for 1st wkt, *141, 143*.

Nicholas, M. C. J. (Hants):– Captain of Hampshire, *403;* 259 for 4th wkt, *258*.

Nimbalkar, B. B. (M'tra):– 443* v Western Indian States, *128;* 50 boundaries in innings, *139;* 455 for 2nd wkt, *141, 143*.

Nissan Shield (SA), *1036, 1059-60*.

Noble, M. A. (Aust.):– Test captain, *188;* 37 hundreds, *132;* 1 Test hundred, *193;* 121 w. in Tests, *180;* 10 w. or more in Test (2), *196;* 428 for 6th wkt, *144*.

Noreiga, J. M. (WI):– 9 w. in Test innings, *182*.

Norfolk, *651-2, 782, 783, 792-3*.

Northamptonshire:– *333, 483-98;* Championship positions, *338-9;* Highest score, *163;* Highest individual score, *130;* Lowest score, *164*.

Northamptonshire II, *800, 801, 808-9*.

Northumberland, *782, 783, 793*.

Nottinghamshire:– *333, 499-515;* Championship positions, *338-9;* Highest score, *163;* Highest individual score, *130;* Lowest score, *164*.

Nottinghamshire II, *800, 801, 809-10*.

Nourse, A. D. (SA):– Test captain, *198, 215;* 12,472 r. (avge 51.53), *136;* 2,960 r. (avge 53.81) in Tests, *168, 171;* 621 r. in series, *201;* 41 hundreds, *132;* 9 Test hundreds, *200, 216;* Test p'ship record, *200*.

Nourse, A. W. (SA):– Handled the ball, *148;* Oldest South African Test player, *187;* 2,234 r. in Tests, *168;* 38 hundreds, *132;* 1 Test hundred, *216;* 304* v Transvaal, *129;* 53 boundaries in innings, *139;* Test p'ship records, *217*.

Nunes, R. K. (WI):– Test captain, *202*.

Nupen, E. P. (SA):– Test captain, *198;* 10 w. or more in Test (1), *201;* Test p'ship record, *201*.

Nurse, S. M. (WI):– 2,523 r. in Tests, *169;* 6 Test hundreds, *204, 220, 230;* 258 v New Zealand, *170, 230;* Test p'ship record, *205*.

## O

Oates, T. W. (Notts.):– 10 d. in match, *161*.

O'Brien, Sir T. C. (Eng.):– Test captain, *198*.

Obstructing the field: Instances in first-class cricket, *149*.

Ochse, A. E. (SA):– Youngest South African Test player, *186*.

O'Connor, J. (Eng.):– 28,875 r., *134;* 1,000 r. (16), *136;* 72 hundreds, *131*.

O'Keeffe, K. J. (Aust.):– Test p'ship records, *222, 227*.

Old, C. M. (Eng.):– Career figures, *899;* Fast scoring, *138;* 143 w. in Tests, *179;* 4 w. in 5 balls v Pakistan, *214*.

Oldest players on Test début, *186*.

Oldest Test players, *187*.

Oldfield, N. (Eng.):– 38 hundreds, *132*.

Oldfield, W. A. (Aust.):– 130 d. in Tests, *184;* 90 d. v England, *197*.

Oldroyd, E. (Yorks.):– 36 hundreds, *132*.

Ollis, R. L. (Som.):– Career figures, *899*.

O'Neill, N. C. (Aust.):– 13,859 r. (avge 50.95), *136;* 2,779 r. in Tests, *168;* 45 hundreds, *132*; 6 Test hundreds, *193, 219, 224, 226*.

Ontong, R. C. (Glam.):– Captain of Glamorgan, *373;* All-round, *159*; 100 and 10 wkts in match, *258*.

O'Reilly, W. J. (Aust.):– 144 w. in Tests, *180;* 102 w. v England, *197;* 10 w. or more in Test (3), *196;* Test p'ship record, *217*.

Ormiston, R. W. (Wgtn):– 226 for 6th wkt, *144*.

Ormrod, J. A. (Worcs. and Lancs.):– Career figures, *899*.

O'Shaughnessy, S. J. (Lancs.):– Hundred in 35 minutes, *138;* Fast scoring, *138*.

Over-rates in County Championship, *1061*.

Owen-Smith, H. G. (SA):– 1 Test hundred, *200;* Test p'ship record, *201*.

Oxford v Cambridge, *322-5*.

Oxford & Cambridge Universities:– v Australians, *291;* in B & H Cup, *669*.

Oxford University 1985:– *613-24;* Blues, *635-8;* v Zimbabweans, *310-1*.

Oxfordshire, *649, 781, 783, 794*.

## P


PACO Cup (Pak.), *1121-2, 1129-38.*

Page, M. L. (NZ):– Test captain, *206, 228;* 1 Test hundred, *207.*

Pairaudeau, B. H. (WI):– Hundred on Test début, *172, 233;* Test p'ship record, *234.*

Pakistan:– B & H World Championship of Cricket, *981-9;* Definition of first-class matches, *1252-3;* Domestic season 1984-85, *1121-38;* Highest individual Test innings, *170;* Highest Test innings, *177;* Leading batsmen in Tests, *169;* Leading bowlers in Tests, *181;* Lowest Test innings, *178;* Most Test appearances, *124;* Most Test appearances as captain, *124;* Oldest Test player, *187;* Pakistan in Test cricket (*see p. 127*); Representative body, *1160;* Summary of Tests, *188;* Test cricketers (1952-85), *120-3;* Youngest and oldest on Test début, *186.*

Pakistan v India, 1984-85, *906, 907, 908.*

Pakistan v New Zealand, 1984-85, *931, 933, 937.*

Pakistan Under-23 in Sri Lanka, 1984-85, *1140-2.*

Pakistanis in New Zealand, 1984-85, *938-49.*

Palm, A. W. (SA):– 244* for 6th wkt, *144.*

Palmer, G. E. (Aust.):– 78 w. in Tests, *180;* 10 w. or more in Test (2), *196.*

Pandya, A. (Saurashtra):– Handled the ball, *148.*

Parfitt, P. H. (Eng.):– 26,924 r., *135;* 1,000 r. (15), *137;* 58 hundreds, *131;* 7 Test hundreds, *199, 207, 210, 213;* 2 hundreds in match (2) *132;* Test p'ship records, *208, 213.*

Parkar, G. A. (Ind.):– 421 for 1st wkt, *141.*

Parkar, Z. A. (Bombay):– 10 d. in match, *161.*

Parker, C. W. L. (Glos.):– 3,278 w., *156;* 200 w. (5), *154-5;* 100 w. (16), *157;* 100 w. by June 12, *155;* 17 w. in match, *153;* 10 w. in innings, *152;* 6 hat-tricks, *151;* Double hat-trick, *150.*

Parker, J. M. (NZ):– Test captain, *238;* 3 Test hundreds, *207, 222, 237;* Test p'ship records, *222.*

Parker, P. W. G. (Eng.):– 32 r. in over, *140.*

Parkhouse, W. G. A. (Eng.):– 1,000 r. (15), *137.*

Parkin, C. H. (Eng.):– 200 w. (2), *154-5.*

Parks, H. W. (Sussex):– 42 hundreds, *132.*

Parks, J. H. (Eng.):– All-round, *158;* 3,003 r. in season, *146;* 41 hundreds, *132.*

Parks, J. M. (Eng.):– 36,673 r., *134;* 1,000 r. (20), *136;* 51 hundreds, *132;* 2 Test hundreds, *199, 203;* 1,182 d., *160;* 114 d. in Tests, *184;* 8 c. in Test, *185;* Test p'ship records, *200, 205.*

Parks, R. J. (Hants):– 10 d. in match, *161.*

Parsons, Rev. J. H. (Warwicks.):– 38 hundreds, *132.*

Partnerships:– First-wicket, *141-2;* Highest, *141;* Highest for each country, *143-5;* Highest in Tests, *176* (*see individual series for records v countries*).

Pascoe, L. S. (Aust.):– Test p'ship record, *222.*

Passailaigue, C. C. (WI):– 487* for 6th wkt, *141, 144.*

Pataudi (Sen.), Nawab of (Eng. and Ind.):– Test captain, *209;* 4 successive hundreds, *137;* Hundred on Test début, *171, 191.*

Pataudi (Jun.), Nawab of (Ind.):– Test captain, *124, 209, 223, 232, 236;* 2,793 r. in Tests, *169;* 6 Test hundreds, *210, 224, 237;* 2 hundreds in match (2), *132.*

Patel, B. P. (Ind.):– 1 Test hundred, *233;* Test p'ship records, *234, 238.*

Patel, D. N. (Worcs.):– All-round, *159.*

Patel, J. M. (Ind.):– 14 w. in Test, *181, 225;* 9 w. in Test innings, *182, 225.*

Patil, S. M. (Ind.):– 4 Test hundreds, *210, 224, 242;* Test p'ship record, *242.*

Patron's Trophy (Pak.), *1121, 1123-6.*

Paynter, E. (Eng.):– 653 r. in series, *201;* 45 hundreds, *132;* 4 Test hundreds, *191, 199;* 2 hundreds in match (2), *132;* 2 hundreds in same Test, *172, 199;* 322 v Sussex, *128;* Test avge of 59.23, *170;* Test p'ship records, *194-5.*

Payton, W. R. D. (Notts.):– 39 hundreds, *132.*

Peach, H. A. (Surrey):– Fast scoring, *138;* 4 w. with consecutive balls, *150.*

Pearse, D. K. (Natal):– Handled the ball, *149.*

Pearson, A. J. G. (CUCC and Som.):– 10 w. in innings, *152.*

Peate, E. (Eng.):– 214 w. in season, *154;* 8 w. for 5 r., *153.*

Peel, R. (Eng.):– 1,754 w., *156;* 102 w. in Tests, *179;* 100 w. (8), *157;* 10 w. or more in Test (2), *195;* 292 for 8th wkt, *145.*

Pegler, S. J. (SA):– Test p'ship record, *217*.
Pellew, C. E. (Aust.):– 2 Test hundreds, *193*.
Perks, R. T. D. (Worcs.):– 2,233 w., *156;* 100 w. (16), *157*.
Perrin, P. A. (Essex):– Highest for Essex, *130;* 29,709 r., *134;* 1,000 r. (18), *136;* 66 hundreds, *131;* 2 hundreds in match (4), *132;* 343* v Derbyshire, *128, 130;* 68 boundaries in innings, *139*.
Pervez Akhtar (Pak. Rlwys):– 337* v Dera Ismail Khan, *128*.
Petherick, P. J. (NZ):– Hat-trick v Pakistan, *183*.
Phadkar, D. G. (Ind.):– 2 Test hundreds, *210, 224;* Test p'ship record, *225*.
Phillip, N. (WI):– Career figures, *899*.
Phillips, H. (Sussex):– 10 d. in match, *161*.
Phillips, R. B. (Qld):– 7 d. in innings, *162*.
Phillips, W. B. (Aust.):– Hundred on Test début, *172, 226;* 2 Test hundreds, *219, 226;* Test p'ship record, *227*.
Pickett, H. (Essex):– 10 w. in innings, *151*.
Pilling, H. (Lancs.):– Career figures, *899*.
Pinch, C. (S. Aust.):– 2 hundreds in match (2), *132*.
Pithey, A. J. (SA):– 1 Test hundred, *200;* Test p'ship record, *201*.
Place, W. (Eng.):– 36 hundreds, *132;* 1 Test hundred, *204*.
Pocock, P. I. (Eng.):– 1,577 w., *157;* 5 w. in 6 balls, *150;* 4 w. with consecutive balls, *150;* Test p'ship record, *205*.
Pollard, V. (NZ):– 2 Test hundreds, *207;* Test p'ship records, *208, 231, 237*.
Pollock, P. M. (SA):– 116 w. in Tests, *180;* 10 w. or more in Test (1), *201;* Test p'ship records, *217, 229*.
Pollock, R. G. (SA):– Handled the ball, *148;* 19,813 r. (avge 54.58), *136;* 2,256 r. (avge 60.97) in Tests, *168, 170;* 60 hundreds, *131;* 7 Test hundreds, *200, 216;* 2 hundreds in match (2), *132;* 274 v Australia, *170, 216;* 341 for 3rd wkt and 338 for 5th wkt, *143, 144;* Test p'ship records, *217*.
Ponsford, W. H. (Aust.):– 13,819 r. (avge 65.18), *135;* 2,122 r. in Tests, *168;* 47 hundreds, *132;* 7 Test hundreds, *193, 219;* Hundred on Test début, *171;* 437 v Queensland, *128;* 429 v Tasmania, *128;* 352 v New South Wales, *128;* 336 v South Australia, *128;* 334 r. in day, *140;* 281* at Lord's, *252;* 266 v England, *170, 193;* 456 for 1st wkt, *141;* 375 for 1st wkt, *141;* 451 for 2nd wkt, *141, 143, 176, 195;* Test p'ship records, *176, 195*.
Pooley, E. (Surrey):– 12 d. and 10 d. in matches, *161*.
Poore, M. B. (NZ):– Test p'ship record, *229*.
Poore, R. M. (Hants):– 304 v Somerset, *129;* Avge of 91.23 in English season, *147;* 411 for 6th wkt, *144*.
Popplewell, N. F. M. (Som.):– Career figures, *899*; Hundred in 41 minutes, *138*.
Pougher, A. D. (Eng.):– 5 w. for 0 r., *153*.
Powell, J. L. (Cant.):– 265 for 7th wkt, *145*.
Prasanna, E. A. S. (Ind.):– 189 w. in Tests, *181;* 10 w. or more in Tests (2), *225, 238;* 8 w. in Test innings, *182, 238*.
Price, W. F. F. (Eng.):– 7 c. in innings, *162*.
Prideaux, R. M. (Eng.):– 25,136 r., *135;* 41 hundreds, *132;* 2 hundreds in match (2), *132;* 1st wkt hundreds, *142*.
Pritchard, T. L. (Warwicks.):– 3 hat-tricks, *151*.
Procter, M. J. (SA):– All-round, *159;* 48 hundreds, *132;* 6 successive hundreds, *137;* Hundred and hat-trick (2), *160;* 4 hat-tricks, *151;* LBW hat-trick (2), *151;* Most w. in 1977, *155*.
Prodger, J. M. (Kent):– 8 c. in match, *163*.
Prout, J. A. (Wesley Coll.):– 459 v Geelong College, *253*.
Prudential World Cup finals, *247*.
Public Schools, highest score, *253*.
Pullar, G. (Eng.):– 41 hundreds, *132;* 4 Test hundreds, *199, 210, 213;* Test p'ship record, *213*.

## Q

Qasim Omar (Pak.):– 2 Test hundreds, *226, 242;* 2 hundreds in match (2), *132;* Hundred and double-hundred, *133;* Test p'ship records, *227, 243*.
Quaid-e-Azam Trophy (Pak.), *1121, 1126-9*.
Quaife, Wm (Eng.):– 36,012 r., *134;* 1,000 r. (24), *136;* 72 hundreds, *131*.
Qualification of players for England, *330-1; 1259*.
Quin, S. O. (Vic.):– 424 for 4th wkt, *144*.
Quirk, T. (N. Tvl):– Obstructing the field, *149*.

## R

Rabone, G. O. (NZ):– Test captain, 206, 228; 1 Test hundred, 229; Test p'ship record, 229.

Rackemann, C. G. (Aust.):– 10 w. or more in Test (1), 227.

Radford, N. V. (Worcs.):– Cricketer of the Year, 61; First to 100 w. in 1985, 258; Most w. in 1985, 155.

Radley, C. T. (Eng.):– 25,276 r., 135; 44 hundreds, 132; 2 Test hundreds, 207, 213; 1,000 r. (16), 136; 200 v Northamptonshire, 256; 289 for 5th wkt, 258.

Rae, A. F. (WI):– 4 Test hundreds, 204, 233.

Raiji, M. N. (Bombay):– 360 for 5th wkt, 144.

Raja Sarfraz (R'pindi):– 240 for 8th wkt, 145.

Ramadhin, S. (WI):– Most balls in single innings, 184; Most balls in Test match, 184; 188 w. in Tests, 180; 10 w. or more in Test (1), 206; Test p'ship record, 231.

Ramaswami, C. (Ind.):– Test début at 40, 187.

Ramchand, G. S. (Ind.):– Test captain, 223; 2 Test hundreds, 224, 237; Test p'ship record, 238.

Ranasinghe, A. N. (SL):– Test p'ship records, 244.

Ranatunga, A. (SL):– Youngest Sri Lankan Test player, 186; Test p'ship records, 228, 244.

Randall, D. W. (Eng.):– 20,000 r., 259; 2,470 r. in Tests, 167; 37 hundreds, 132; 7 Test hundreds, 191, 207, 210, 213; Hundred and double-hundred, 133; Test p'ship record, 211.

Rangnekar, K. M. (Ind.):– 274 for 7th wkt, 145.

Ranji Trophy (Ind.), 1102-3, 1104-16.

Ranjitsinhji, K. S. (HH the Jam Sahib of Nawanagar) (Eng.):– 24,692 r. (avge 56.37), 136; 3,159 r. in season, 146; 72 hundreds, 131; 2 Test hundreds, 191; Hundred on Test début, 171, 191; Avge of 87.57 in English season, 147; 344 for 7th wkt, 144.

Ransford, V. S. (Aust.):– 1 Test hundred, 193; Test p'ship records, 217.

Rao, J. S. (Ind. Serv.):– Double hat-trick, 150; 3 hat-tricks, 151.

Rashid Israr (HBL):– 350 v National Bank, 128.

Ratnayeke, J. R. (SL):– 5 w. in Test innings, 183; Test p'ship record, 244.

Read, W. W. (Eng.):– Test captain, 189, 198; 338 v Oxford Univ., 128; 38 hundreds, 132; 1 Test hundred, 191; Test p'ship record, 195.

Record hit, 254.

Redmond, R. E. (NZ):– Hundred on Test début, 172, 239; Test p'ship record, 239.

Redpath, I. R. (Aust.):– 4,737 r. in Tests, 168; 8 Test hundreds, 193, 219, 222, 226; Carrying bat in Test, 174; 32 r. in over, 140; Test p'ship records, 222.

Registration of players, 330-1, 1259.

Reid, J. F. (NZ):– 5 Test hundreds, 237, 239, 241; Test avge of 53.85, 171; Test p'ship records, 239, 241.

Reid, J. R. (NZ):– Test captain, 124, 206, 228, 230, 236, 238; 3,428 r. in Tests, 169; 2,188 r. in overseas season, 147; 1,915 r. in South African season, 147; 58 consecutive Tests, 187; 39 hundreds, 132; 6 Test hundreds, 207, 229, 237, 239; 50 boundaries in innings, 139; 15 sixes in innings, 139; 85 w. in Tests, 181; 324 for 4th wkt, 144; Test p'ship records, 208, 229, 237, 239.

Relations in Test cricket, 248-9.

Relf, A. E. (Eng.):– All-round, 158; 1,897 w., 156; 100 w. (11), 157.

Representative Bodies, Addresses of, 1160-1.

Rest of the World v England:– 215; England players, 124.

Rhodes, A. E. G. (Derbys.):– 5 hat-tricks, 151.

Rhodes, W. (Eng.):– All-round, 158; Oldest Test player, 187; 39,802 r., 134; 2,325 r. in Tests, 167; 1,000 r. (21), 136; 763 Championship appearances, 255; 58 hundreds, 131; 2 hundreds in match (2), 132; 2 Test hundreds, 191, 199; 4,187 w., 156; 200 w. (3), 154; 127 w. in Tests, 179; 109 w. v Australia, 197; 100 w. (23), 157; 15 Australian w. in match, 181, 195; 10 w. or more in Test (1), 195; 8 w. in Test innings, 182, 195; Test p'ship records, 194-5.

Rice, C. E. B. (Notts. and Tvl):– Captain of Nottinghamshire, 499; All-round 159; 20,000 r., 259; 40 hundreds, 132.

Richards, A. R. (SA):– Test captain, 198

Richards, B. A. (SA):– 28,358 r. (avge 54.74), 135, 136; 1,000 r. (15), 137; 80 hundreds, 131; 2 Test hundreds, 216; 2

Richards, B. A. (SA):– *contd*
hundreds in match (2), *132;* 356 v Western Australia, *128;* 325* in day, *140.*

Richards, I. V. A. (WI):– Test captain, *202, 218, 230;* Highest for Somerset, *130;* 26,841 r. (avge 50.26), *135, 136;* 5,889 r. (avge 54.02) in Tests, *168, 171;* 4,071 r. in one-day ints, *245;* 1,710 Test r. in year, *173;* 829 r. in series, *173;* 86 hundreds, *131;* 19 Test hundreds, *204, 220, 230, 233, 235;* 8 one-day int. hundreds, *245;* 322 v Warwickshire, *128, 130, 140, 256;* 291 v England, *170, 204;* Highest one-day int. score, *245;* Highest aggregate in 1977, *146;* 50 boundaries in innings, *139, 257;* All-round, *246;* Test p'ship records, *220, 231, 234.*

Richardson, A. J. (Aust.):– 280 v MCC, *130;* 1 Test hundred, *193.*

Richardson, D. W. (Eng.):– 65 c. in season, *162.*

Richardson, P. E. (Eng.):– 26,055 r., *135;* 2,061 r. in Tests, *167;* 44 hundreds, *132;* 5 Test hundreds, *191, 199, 204, 207;* Slow Test hundred, *176;* Test p'ship record, *205.*

Richardson, R. B. (WI):– 4 Test hundreds, *220, 230;* Test p'ship records, *220, 231.*

Richardson, T. (Eng.):– 2,105 w., *156;* 1,005 w. in four seasons, *155;* 200 w. (3), *154;* 100 w. (10), *157;* 88 w. in Tests, *179;* 10 w. or more in Test (4), *195-6;* 10 w. in innings, *151;* 8 w. in Test innings, *183;* 4 hat-tricks, *151.*

Richardson, V. Y. (Aust.):– Test captain, *215;* 1 Test hundred, *193;* 6 c. in Test, *185;* 5 c. in Test innings, *186.*

Ridgway, F. (Eng.):– 4 w. with consecutive balls, *150.*

Rigg, K. E. (Aust.):– 1 Test hundred, *217.*

Ritchie, G. M. (Aust.):– 2 Test hundreds, *194, 226.*

Rixon, S. J. (Aust.):– 22 d. in series, *184.*

Roach, C. A. (WI):– 2 Test hundreds, *204.*

Roberts, A. M. E. (WI):– 202 w. in Tests, *180;* 10 w. or more in Test (2), *206, 234;* Most w. in 1974, *155;* 161 for 9th wkt, *145, 234;* Test p'ship record, *220, 234.*

Roberts, A. W. (NZ):– Test p'ship record, *208.*

Robertson, J. D. (Eng.):– Highest for Middlesex, *130;* 31,914 r., *134;* 1,000 r. (15), *137;* 67 hundreds, *131;* 2 Test hundreds, *204, 207;* 331* v Worcestershire, *128, 130;* 331 r. in day, *140;* 1st wkt hundreds, *142.*

Robins, R. W. V. (Eng.):– Test captain, *206;* 1 Test hundred, *199.*

Robinson, R. T. (Eng.):– Cricketer of the Year, *63;* 3 Test hundreds, *191, 210;* 2 hundreds in same match, *256;* 331 for 2nd wkt, *257;* Test p'ship record, *211*

Roebuck, P. M. (Som.):– Captain of Somerset, *516;* 10,000 r., *259;* Carrying bat in 1985, *257.*

Roller, W. E. (Surrey):– 204 and hat-trick v Sussex, *160.*

Root, C. F. (Eng.):– 1,512 w., *157;* 219 w. in season, *154;* 100 w. (9), *157.*

Rothmans Trophy (Sharjah), *990-3.*

Rowan, E. A. B. (SA):– 3 Test hundreds, *200, 216;* 306* v Natal, *129;* 342 for 4th wkt, *144;* Test p'ship record, *200.*

Rowe, L. G. (WI):– 2,047 r. in Tests, *169;* 7 Test hundreds, *204, 220, 230;* 4 successive hundreds, *137;* 2 hundreds on Test début, *133, 172-3, 230;* Hundred and double-hundred, *133;* 302 v England, *129, 170, 204;* Test p'ship records, *205, 220, 231.*

Roy, Pankaj (Ind.):– Test captain, *209;* 2,442 r. in Tests, *169;* 5 Test hundreds, *210, 233, 237;* 4 successive hundreds, *137;* 2 hundreds in match (2), *132;* 413 for 1st wkt v New Zealand, *141, 176, 238.*

Run-rate in County Championship, *1061.*

Rushby, T. (Surrey):– 10 w. in innings, *152.*

Russell, A. C. (Eng.):– 27,545 r., *135;* 71 hundreds, *131;* 5 Test hundreds, *191-2, 199;* 2 hundreds in match (3), *132;* 2 hundreds in same Test, *172, 199;* Test p'ship record, *200.*

Russell, W. E. (Eng.):– 25,525 r., *135*; 41 hundreds, *132.*

Ryder, J. (Aust.):– Test captain, *189;* 3 Test hundreds, *194, 216;* Test avge of 51.62, *171.*

## S

Saadat Ali (Income Tax):– Hundred and double-hundred, *133;* 1,649 r. in Pakistan season, *147.*

Sadiq Mohammad (Pak.):– 2,579 r. in Tests, *170;* 50 hundreds, *132;* 5 Test hundreds, *213, 226, 239;* 4 successive hundreds, *137;* 2 hundreds in match (3), *132;* Test p'ship record, *240.*

Saeed Ahmed (Pak.):– Test captain, *212;* 2,991 r. in Tests, *170;* 5 Test hundreds, *226, 235, 239, 242;* 4 successive hundreds, *137;* Test p'ship records, *236, 240.*
Saggers, R. A. (Aust.):– 21 d. in series, *184;* 10 d. in match, *161;* 7 d. in innings, *162.*
Salah-ud-Din (Pak.):– Hundred and double-hundred, *133;* 353 for 6th wkt, *144;* Test p'ship record, *240.*
Salim Malik (Pak.):– 5 Test hundreds, *213, 239, 242, 244;* Hundred on Test début, *172, 244;* Test p'ship records, *213, 227, 242, 244.*
Sandham, A. (Eng.):– 41,284 r., *134;* 1,000 r. (20), *136;* 107 hundreds, *131;* 2 Test hundreds, *204;* 325 v West Indies, *128, 170, 204;* 219 v Australians, *129;* 428 for 1st wkt, *141;* 1st wkt hundreds, *142.*
Sandhu, B. S. (Ind.):– Test p'ship record, *234.*
Sardesai, D. N. (Ind.):– 2,001 r. in Tests, *169;* 5 Test hundreds, *233, 237;* Test p'ship records, *234, 238.*
Sarfraz Nawaz (Pak.):– 177 w. in Tests, *181;* 10 w. or more in Test (1), *227;* 9 w. in Test innings, *182, 227;* Test p'ship records, *213, 236.*
Sarwate, C. T. (Ind.):– 236 for 8th wkt, *145;* 249 for 10th wkt, *145.*
Saunders, J. V. (Aust.):– 79 w. in Tests, *180.*
Scarborough Festival, *644-5;* Address of Secretary, *1161;* Fixtures, 1986, *1288.*
Schofield, R. M. (C. Dist.):– 7 c. in innings, *162.*
Scotland:– v Ireland, *643-4;* v MCC, *643;* v Zimbabweans, *313;* in B & H Cup, *669;* in NatWest Bank Trophy, *652-3.*
Scott, H. J. H. (Aust.):– Test captain, *189;* 1 Test hundred, *194.*
Scott, M. S. (Worcs. and Sussex):– Career figures, *899.*
Scottish Cricket in 1985, *823-5.*
Scotton, W. H. (Eng.):– Handled the ball, *148;* Test p'ship record, *195.*
Sealy, J. E. D. (WI):– Youngest West Indian Test player, *186.*
Second XI Championship:– *799-815;* Championship winners, *815;* Fixtures, 1986, *1293-5.*
Serjeant, C. S. (Aust.):– 1 Test hundred, *219.*
Services Tournament, *1260.*
Seymour, James (Kent):– 27,238 r., *135;* 1,000 r. (16), *136;* 53 hundreds, *132;* 2 hundreds in match (2), *132.*
Shackleton, D. (Eng.):– 2,857 w., *156;* 100 w. (20), *157;* 8 w. for 4 r., *153.*
Shacklock, F. J. (Notts.):– 4 w. with consecutive balls, *150.*
Shafiq Ahmed (Pak.):– 43 hundreds, *132;* Hundred and double-hundred, *133;* 389 for 1st wkt, *141.*
Shahid Israr (Pak.):– 7 d. in innings, *162.*
Shahid Mahmood (Pak.):– 10 w. in innings, *152.*
Sharma, C. (Ind.):– Test p'ship record, *211.*
Sharp, G. (Northants):– Career figures, *899.*
Sharp, J. (Eng.):– 38 hundreds, *132;* 1 Test hundred, *192.*
Sharp, J. C. (Melb. GS):– 506* v Geelong College, *253.*
Sharpe, P. J. (Eng.):– 1 Test hundred, *207;* 71 c. in season, *162.*
Shastri, R. J. (Ind.):– 5 Test hundreds, *210, 233, 242;* 200 r. in 113 min., *138, 1108;* 36 r. in over, *139, 1108;* 13 sixes in innings, *139, 1108;* Man of Series, B & H World Championship of Cricket, *989;* Test p'ship records, *211, 234, 242.*
Shaw, A. (Eng.):– Test captain, *188;* 2,021 w., *156;* 201 w. in season, *155;* 100 w. (9), *157;* 10 w. in innings, *151;* Double hat-trick, *150;* 3 hat-tricks, *151.*
Sheahan, A. P. (Aust.):– 2 Test hundreds, *224, 226.*
Sheffield Shield (Aust.), *998-1032.*
Shell Shield (WI), *1062-3, 1064-76.*
Shell Trophy (NZ), *1080-1, 1082-101.*
Shepherd, D. J. (Glam.):– 2,218 w., *156;* 100 w. (12), *157;* Most w. in 1970, *155.*
Shepherd, D. R. (Glos.):– Hundred on début, *130.*
Shepherd, J. N. (WI):– All-round, *159.*
Shepherd, T. F. (Surrey):– 42 hundreds, *132.*
Sheppard, Rt Rev. D. S. (Eng.):– Test captain, *212;* 45 hundreds, *132;* 3 Test hundreds, *192, 210.*
Sherwell, P. W. (SA):– Test captain, *198, 215;* 1 Test hundred, *200.*
Shillingford, G. C. (WI):– Test p'ship record, *231.*
Shillingford, I. T. (WI): 1 Test hundred, *235.*

Shoaib Mohammad (Pak.):– Test p'ship record, *213*.
Shodhan, D. H. (Ind.):– Hundred on Test début, *171, 242*.
Shrewsbury, A. (Eng.):– Test captain, *188-9;* 26,439 r., *135;* 59 hundreds, *131;* 3 Test hundreds, *192;* 6 c. in Test, *185;* 391 for 1st wkt, *141*.
Shropshire, *653, 782, 783, 794-5*.
Siedle, I. J. (SA):– 1 Test hundred, *200;* 424 for 1st wkt, *141, 143;* Test p'ship record, *200*.
Sikander Bakht (Pak.):– 10 w. or more in Test (1), *243;* 8 w. in Test innings, *182*.
Silk Cut Challenge, 1985, *1256*.
Silva, S. A. R. (SL):– 1 Test hundred, *214;* Test p'ship record, *244*.
Simpson, R. B. (Aust.):– Test captain, *189, 215, 218, 223, 225;* 21,029 r. (avge 56.22), *136;* 4,869 r. in Tests, *168;* 2,063 r. in overseas season, *147;* 1,381 Test r. in year, *173;* 60 hundreds, *131;* 10 Test hundreds, *194, 216, 219, 224, 226;* 2 hundreds in same Test, *172, 226;* 2 hundreds in match (2), *132;* 359 v Queensland, *128;* 311 v England, *129, 170, 194;* 110 c. in Tests, *185;* 13 c. in series (2), *185;* 382 for 1st wkt, *142, 220;* Test p'ship records, *195, 220, 224*.
Simpson, R. T. (Eng.):– 30,546 r., *134;* 64 hundreds, *131;* 4 Test hundreds, *192, 199, 207, 213;* Test p'ship records, *205, 208*.
Sims, Sir Arthur:– 433 for 8th wkt, *145*.
Sims, J. M. (Eng.):– 1,582 w., *157;* 100 w. (8), *157;* 10 w. in innings, *152*.
Sinclair, B. W. (NZ):– Test captain, *206, 236;* 3 Test hundreds, *207, 229, 239;* Test p'ship records, *229, 239*.
Sinclair, J. H. (SA):– 3 Test hundreds, *200, 217*.
Singh, R. P. (Holkar):– 236 for 8th wkt, *145*.
Sivaramakrishnan, L. (Ind.):– Test cricket at 17, *186;* 10 w. or more in Test (1), *211*.
Slack, J. K. E. (CUCC):– Hundred on début, *130*.
Slack, W. N. (Middx):– 201* v Australians, *256, 302;* Carrying bat in 1985, *257*.
Smailes, T. F. (Eng.):– 10 w. in innings, *152*.
Smales, K. (Notts.):– 10 w. in innings, *152*.
Smart, C. C. (Glam.):– 32 r. in over, *140*.
Smith, A. C. (Eng.):– Test p'ship record, *208*.
Smith, C. Aubrey (Eng.):– Test captain, *198*.
Smith, C. L. (Eng.):– 2 hundreds in same match, *256*; First to 1,000 r., *256*.
Smith, E. J. (Eng.):– 7 d. in innings, *162*.
Smith, I. D. S. (NZ):– 1 Test hundred, *207;* Test p'ship record, *231*.
Smith, K. D. (Warwicks.):– Career figures, *899*.
Smith, M. J. (Middx):– 40 hundreds, *132*.
Smith, M. J. K. (Eng.):– Test captain, *189, 198, 202, 206, 209;* 39,832 r., *134;* 3,245 r. in season, *146;* 2,278 r. in Tests, *167;* 1,000 r. (20), *136;* 69 hundreds, *131;* 3 Test hundreds, *199, 204, 210;* 3 hundreds v Cambridge, *324;* Test p'ship records, *205, 211*.
Smith, M. S. (Natal):– 7 c. in innings, *162*.
Smith, O. G. (WI):– 4 Test hundreds, *204, 220, 233;* Hundred on Test début, *172, 220;* Test p'ship records, *231, 235*.
Smith, R. (Essex):– All-round, *158*.
Smith, R. A. (Hants):– 259 for 4th wkt, *258*.
Smith, S. G. (Northants):– All-round, *158;* 4 w. with consecutive balls, *150*.
Smith, T. P. B. (Eng.):– 1,697 w., *156*.
Smith, V. I. (SA):– 6 w. for 1 r., *153*.
Smith, W. C. (Surrey):– 247 w. in season, *154*.
Snooke, S. J. (SA):– Test captain, *198;* 1 Test hundred, *217;* 10 w. or more in Test (1), *201;* 8 w. in Test innings, *182*.
Snow, J. A. (Eng.):– 202 w. in Tests, *179;* 10 w. or more in Test (1), *205;* Test p'ship record, *205*.
Sobers, Sir G. S. (WI):– Test captain, *202, 218, 230, 232;* Test début at 17, *186;* 85 consecutive Tests, *187;* 28,315 r. (avge 54.87), *135, 136;* 8,032 r. (avge 57.78) in Tests, *168, 171;* 1,193 Test r. in year, *173*; 1,000 r. (15), *137;* 824 r. in series, *173;* 86 hundreds, *131;* 26 Test hundreds, *171, 204, 220, 230, 233, 235;* 2 hundreds in same Test, *172, 235;* 2 hundreds in match (2), *132;* 365* v Pakistan, *128, 170, 235;* 36 r. in over, *139;* All-round, *159, 181;* 235 w. in Tests, *180;* 109 c. in Tests, *185;* 6 c. in Test, *186;* 446 for 2nd wkt, *143;* Test p'ship records, *205, 231, 235*.
Solkar, E. D. (Ind.):– 1 Test hundred, *233;* 6 c. in Test, *186;* Test p'ship record, *234*.

Solomon, J. S. (WI):– 1 Test hundred, *233;* Hundreds in first three first-class innings, *131.*

Somerset:– *333, 516-31;* Championship positions, *338-9;* Highest score, *163;* Highest individual score, *130;* Lowest score, *164.*

Somerset II, *781, 783, 795, 800, 801, 810-1.*

South Africa:– Definition of first-class matches, *1253;* Domestic season 1984-85, *1035-60;* Highest individual Test innings, *170;* Highest Test innings, *177;* Leading batsmen in Tests, *168;* Leading bowlers in Tests, *180;* Lowest Test innings, *178;* Most Test appearances, *124;* Most Test appearances as captain, *124;* Oldest Test player, *187;* Representative bodies, *1160;* South Africa in Test cricket (*see p. 127*); Summary of Tests, *188;* Test cricketers (1888-1970), *104-8;* Youngest and oldest on Test début, *186.*

Southerton, J. (Eng.):– Oldest Test début, *186;* Test cricket at 49, *187;* 1,680 w., *156;* 210 w. in season, *154;* 100 w. (9), *157;* 16 w. in day, *154.*

Spofforth, F. R. (Aust.):– 207 w. in season, *154;* 94 w. in Tests, *180;* 14 England w. in match, *181, 196;* 10 w. or more in Test (4), *196;* 7 w. for 3 r., *153;* Test hat-trick, *183;* 4 hat-tricks, *151.*

Spooner, R. H. (Eng.):– 1 Test hundred, *199.*

Squires, H. S. (Surrey):– 37 hundreds, *132.*

Sri Lanka:– B & H World Championship of Cricket, *981-6;* B & H World Series Cup, *967-76;* Definition of first-class matches, *1253;* Domestic season 1984-85, *1139-42;* Highest individual Test innings, *170;* Highest Test innings, *177;* Lowest Test innings, *178;* Most Test appearances, *124;* Most Test appearances as captain, *124;* Representative body, *1160;* Sri Lanka in Test cricket (*see p. 127*); Summary of Tests, *188;* Test cricketers (1982-85), *123-4;* Oldest and youngest on Test début, *186-7.*

Sri Lanka v India, 1985-86, *952.*

Sri Lankans in Australia, 1984-85, *950-1.*

Stackpole, K. R. (Aust.):– 2,807 r. in Tests, *168;* 7 Test hundreds, *194, 216, 219, 222, 224.*

Staffordshire, *652, 782, 783, 795-6.*

Stanworth, J. (Lancs.):– 115 for 10th wkt, *258.*

Stanyforth, Lt.-Col. R. T. (Eng.):– Test captain, *198.*

Statham, J. B. (Eng.):– 2,260 w., *156;* 252 w. in Tests, *179;* 100 w. (13), *157;* 10 w. or more in Test (1), *201;* 3 hat-tricks, *151.*

Status of matches in UK, *642, 1252.*

Stead, B. (Notts.):– Most w. in 1972, *155.*

Steel, A. G. (Eng.):– Test captain, *189-90;* 2 Test hundreds, *192.*

Steele, D. S. (Eng.):– 1 Test hundred, *204.*

Steele, J. F. (Leics. and Glam.):– 390 for 1st wkt, *141.*

Stephenson, H. W. (Som.):– 1,084 d., *160.*

Stevens, G. T. S. (Eng.):– Test captain, *198;* 466* v Lambda, *253;* 10 w. or more in Test (1), *205.*

Stewart, A. J. (Surrey): 252 for 5th wkt, *258.*

Stewart, M. J. (Eng.):– 26,492 r., *135;* 1,000 r. (15), *137;* 49 hundreds, *132;* 77 c. in season, *162;* 7 c. in innings, *163.*

Stewart, W. J. (Warwicks.):– 17 sixes in match, *139.*

Steyn, S. S. L. (W. Prov.):– 222 for 8th wkt, *145.*

Stimpson, P. J. (Worcs.):– 1st wkt hundreds, *142.*

Stocks, F. W. (Notts.):– Hundred on début, *130.*

Stoddart, A. E. (Eng.):– Test captain, *189-90;* 2 Test hundreds, *192;* 485 v Stoics *253;* 1st wkt hundreds, *142.*

Stollmeyer, J. B. (WI):– Test captain, *202, 218, 232;* 2,159 r. in Tests, *169;* 4 Test hundreds, *220, 230, 233;* 324 v British Guiana, *128;* 355 for 1st wkt, *142.*

Storie, A. C. (Northants):– Hundred on début, *130.*

Stricker, L. A. (SA):– Test p'ship record, *217.*

Strudwick, H. (Eng.):– Test cricket at 46, *187;* 1,468 d., *160;* 21 d. in series, *184.*

Stumpings in 1985, *355.*

Subba Row, R. (Eng.):– Highest for Northamptonshire, *130;* 3 Test hundreds, *192, 204;* 300 v Surrey, *129, 130;* Test p'ship record, *211.*

Suffolk, *654-5, 782, 783-4, 796-7.*

Surrey:– *333, 532-47;* Championship positions, *338-9;* Highest score, *163;* Highest individual score, *130;* Lowest score, *164.*

Surrey II, *800, 801, 811-2.*

Sussex:- *333, 548-63;* Championship positions, *338-9;* Highest score, *163;* Highest individual score, *130;* Lowest score, *164.*

Sussex II, *800, 801, 812.*

Sutcliffe, B. (NZ):- Test captain, *228, 230;* 2,727 r. in Tests, *169;* 44 hundreds, *132;* 5 Test hundreds, *207, 237;* 2 hundreds in match (4), *132;* Hundred and double-hundred, *133;* 385 v Canterbury, *128;* 355 v Auckland, *128;* 1st wkt hundreds, *142;* 266 for 5th wkt, *144;* Test p'ship records, *208, 229, 237.*

Sutcliffe, H. (Eng.):- Fast scoring, *138;* 50,138 r. (avge 51.95), *134, 136;* 4,555 r. (avge 60.73) in Tests, *167, 170;* 3,336 r. in season, *146;* 2,741 r. v Australia, *197;* 1,000 r. (24), *136;* 149 hundreds, *131;* 16 Test hundreds, *192, 199, 207;* 13 and 14 hundreds in season, *137;* 4 successive hundreds, *137;* 2 hundreds in same Test (2), *172, 192, 199;* 2 hundreds in match (4), *132;* 313 v Essex, *129;* Avge of 96.96 in English season, *147;* 1st wkt hundreds, *142;* 555 for 1st wkt, *141, 143.*

Suttle, K. G. (Sussex):- 30,225 r., *134;* 1,000 r. (17), *136;* 49 hundreds, *132;* 423 consecutive Championship appearances, *255.*

## T

Taber, H. B. (Aust.):- 20 d. in series, *184;* 12 d. in match, *161;* 8 d. in Test, *185;* 7 d. in innings, *162.*

Taberer, H. M. (SA):- Test captain, *215.*

Tahir Naqqash (Pak.):- Test p'ship record, *243.*

Talat Ali (Pak.):- Hundred and double-hundred, *133.*

Tallon, D. (Aust.):- 20 d. in series, *184;* 12 d. in match, *161;* 7 d. in innings, *162.*

Tancred, A. B. (SA):- Carrying bat in Test, *174.*

Tancred, L. J. (SA):- Test captain, *198, 215;* Test p'ship record, *217.*

Tarilton, P. H. (B'dos):- 304* v Trinidad, *129.*

Tariq Bashir (HBFC):- 355 for 5th wkt, *144.*

Tarrant, F. A. (Vic. and Middx):- All-round, *158;* 182* and 10 w., *160;* 100 w. (8), *157;* 10 w. in innings, *152;* 5 hat-tricks, *151;* 4 w. with consecutive balls, *150.*

Taslim Arif (Pak.):- 1 Test hundred, *226;* 10 d. in match, *161;* 7 d. in innings, *162;* Test p'ship record, *227.*

Tate, M. W. (Eng.):- All-round, *158;* 1 Test hundred, *199;* 2,784 w., *156;* 200 w. (3), *154-5;* 155 w. in Tests, *179;* 116 w. in overseas season, *157;* 100 w. (14), *157;* 38 w. in series, *196;* 10 w. or more in Test (1), *196;* 3 hat-tricks, *151.*

Tattersall, R. (Eng.):- 100 w. (8), *157;* 10 w. or more in Test (1), *201.*

Tavaré, C. J. (Eng.):- 2 Test hundreds, *207, 210;* Slow scoring, *175;* 49 c. in season, *162;* Test p'ship record, *208.*

Tayfield, H. J. (SA):- 170 w. in Tests, *180;* 37 w. in series, *183, 202;* 26 w. in series, *202;* 13 w. in Test (2), *181, 201, 217;* 9 w. in Test innings, *182;* 8 w. in Test innings, *182;* Test p'ship record, *229.*

Taylor, B. (Essex):- 1,294 d., *160;* 301 consecutive Championship appearances, *255.*

Taylor, B. R. (NZ):- 2 Test hundreds, *231, 237;* Hundred on Test début, *172, 237;* 111 w. in Tests, *181;* Test p'ship record, *237.*

Taylor, D. D. (NZ):- 1st wkt hundreds, *142.*

Taylor, D. J. S. (Som.):- Obstructing the field (JPL), *149.*

Taylor, H. W. (SA):- Test captain, *124, 198, 215;* 2,936 r. in Tests, *168;* 582 r. in series, *201;* 7 Test hundreds, *200;* Test p'ship record, *201.*

Taylor, J. M. (Aust.):- 1 Test hundred, *194;* Test p'ship record, *195.*

Taylor, N. R. (Kent):- Hundred on début, *130*; 263 for 3rd wkt, *257.*

Taylor, R. W. (Eng.):- 1,646 d., *160;* 174 d. in Tests, *184;* 20 d. in series, *184;* 10 c. in Test, *185;* 10 c. in match (2), *161;* 7 c. in Test innings, *185;* 7 c. in innings (3), *162;* Test p'ship records, *211, 213.*

Tennyson, Hon. L. H. (Lord Tennyson) (Eng.):- Test captain, *189.*

Test and County Cricket Board:- Meetings, *1258-9;* Officers, *317.*

Test match grounds, *250-1.*

Test matches, duration of and qualification for, *1251.*

Texaco Trophy matches:- in 1985, *284-7;* in 1986, *1284, 1286.*

Thompson, G. J. (Eng.):- 1,591 w., *157;* 100 w. (8), *157.*

Thomson, J. R. (Aust.):– 200 w. in Tests, *180;* 100 w. v England, *197*.
Thomson, K. (NZ):– Test p'ship record, *237*.
Thomson, N. I. (Eng.):– 1,597 w., *157;* 100 w. (12), *157;* 10 w. in innings, *152*.
Thousand runs in May, *148*.
Throwing records, *254*.
Tied matches, *166, 247*.
Tilcon Trophy:– *644;* Fixtures, 1986, *1284*.
Titmus, F. J. (Eng.):– All-round, *158;* 2,830 w., *156;* 153 w. in Tests, *179;* 100 w. (16), *157*.
Todd, L. J. (Kent):– 38 hundreds, *132*.
Tolchard, R. W. (Eng.):– 1,037 d., *161;* Obstructing the field (JPL), *149*.
Toogood, G. J. (OUCC):– 149 and 10 w. v Cambridge, *258, 322-3, 324*.
Toohey, P. M. (Aust.):– 1 Test hundred, *219*.
Toshack, E. R. H. (Aust.):– 10 w. or more in Test (1), *225*.
Tours, Future, *1034*.
Townsend, L. F. (Eng.):– All-round, *158*.
Tremlett, T. M. (Hants):– 227 for 8th wkt, *258*.
Tribe, G. E. (Aust.):– All-round, *158;* 100 w. (8), *157*.
Troup, G. B. (NZ):– 10 w. or more in Test (1), *231*.
Trott, A. E. (Aust. and Eng.):– All-round, *158;* Double hat-trick, *150;* Hit over Lord's Pavilion, *253;* 1,674 w., *156;* 200 w. (2), *154;* 10 w. in innings, *152;* 8 w. in Test innings, *182;* 4 w. with consecutive balls, *150*.
Trott, G. H. S. (Aust.):– Test captain, *189;* 1 Test hundred, *194*.
Trueman, F. S. (Eng.):– 2,304 w., *156;* 307 w. in Tests, *179;* 100 w. (12), *157;* 10 w. or more in Test (3), *196, 205;* 8 w. in Test innings, *182;* 4 hat-tricks, *151;* Test p'ship record, *213*.
Trumble, H. (Aust.):– Test captain, *190;* 141 w. in Tests, *180;* 10 w. or more in Test (3), *196;* 8 w. in Test innings, *182;* 2 Test hat-tricks, *183;* 3 hat-tricks, *151;* Test p'ship record, *195*.
Trumper, V. T. (Aust.):– 3,163 r. in Tests, *168;* 2,263 r. v England, *197;* 42 hundreds, *132*; 8 Test hundreds, *194, 216;* 300* v Sussex, *129;* 200 r. in 131 min., *138;* 433 for 8th wkt, *145;* Test p'ship record, *217*.
Tuckett, L. (SA):– Test p'ship record, *201*.
Tunnicliffe, J. (Yorks.):– 70 c., 65 c. and 64 c. in season, *162;* 554 and 378 for 1st wkt, *141, 142*.
Turner, A. (Aust.):– 1 Test hundred, *219;* Test p'ship record, *227*.
Turner, C. T. B. (Aust.):– 283 w. in season, *154;* 106 w. in Australian season, *155, 157;* 101 w. in Tests, *180, 197;* 17 w. in match, *153;* 10 w. or more in Test (2), *196*.
Turner, G. M. (NZ):– Test captain, *221, 236, 238;* Highest for Worcestershire, *130;* 34,346 r., *134;* 2,991 r. in Tests, *169;* 1,244 r. in NZ season, *147;* 1,000 r. (18), *136;* 1,000 r. (April 24-May 31), *148;* 103 hundreds, *131;* 7 Test hundreds, *222, 231, 237, 239;* 2 hundreds in same Test, *173, 222;* 2 hundreds in match (6), *132;* 311* v Warwickshire in day, *129, 130, 140;* 259 v West Indies, *170, 231;* Avge of 90.07 in English season, *147;* Carrying bat in Test (2), *174;* Highest aggregate in 1970, 1973, *146;* 387 for 1st wkt, *142, 143, 231;* Test p'ship records, *222, 231, 239*.
Turner, J. B. (Minor Counties):– Hundred on début, *130*.
Tyldesley, E. (Eng.):– 38,874 r., *134;* 3,024 r. in season, *146;* 1,000 r. (19), *136;* 102 hundreds, *131;* 3 Test hundreds, *199, 204;* 4 successive hundreds, *137;* 2 hundreds in match (2), *132;* 10 successive fifties, *137;* Test avge of 55.00, *171*.
Tyldesley, J. T. (Eng.):– 37,897 r., *134;* 3,041 r. in season, *146;* 1,000 r. (19), *136;* 86 hundreds, *131;* 4 Test hundreds, *192, 199;* 2 hundreds in match (3), *132*.
Tyldesley, R. K. (Eng.):– 1,509 w., *157;* 100 w. (10), *157;* 5 w. for 0 r., *153;* 4 w. with consecutive balls, *150*.
Tyler, E. J. (Som.):– 10 w. in innings, *151*.
Tyson, F. H. (Eng.):– 76 w. in Tests, *179;* 10 w. or more in Test (1), *196*.

## U

UAU Championship, 1985, *818-9*.
Ulyett, G. (Eng.):– 1 Test hundred, *192;* 4 w. with consecutive balls, *149*.
Umpires for 1986, 1257.
Umpires, Association of Cricket, *1161*.
Umrigar, P. R. (Ind.):– Test captain, *223, 232, 236;* 16,155 r. (avge 52.28), *136;* 3,631 r. in Tests, *169;* 49 hundreds, *132;*

Umrigar, P. R. (Ind.):– *contd*
12 Test hundreds, *210-1, 233, 237, 242;* Test p'ship records, *238, 242.*

Underwood, D. L. (Eng.):– 2,368 w., *156;* 297 w. in Tests, *179;* 105 w. v Australia, *197;* 100 w. (10), *157;* 10 w. or more in Test (6), *196, 208, 214;* 8 w. in Test innings, *182;* Most w. in 1978, 1979, 1983, *155.*

USA v Canada, *1152.*

## V

Valentine, A. L. (WI):– 139 w. in Tests, *180;* 10 w. or more in Test (2), *206;* 8 w. in Test innings, *183, 206.*

Valentine, B. H. (Eng.):– 35 hundreds, *132;* 2 Test hundreds, *199, 210;* Hundred on Test début, *171, 210.*

van der Bijl, P. G. V. (SA):– 1 Test hundred, *200.*

van der Merwe, P. L. (SA):– Test captain, *198, 215;* Test p'ship record, *217.*

Van Ryneveld, C. B. (SA):– Test captain, *198, 215;* Test p'ship record, *200.*

Veivers, T. R. (Aust.):– Test p'ship records, *224, 227.*

Vengsarkar, D. B. (Ind.):– 4,328 r. in Tests, *169;* 1,174 Test r. in year, *173*; 9 Test hundreds, *211, 224, 233, 242;* Test p'ship records, *225, 234, 242.*

Venkataraghavan, S. (Ind.):– Test captain, *209, 232;* 156 w. in Tests, *181;* 10 w. or more in Test (1), *238;* 8 w. in Test innings, *182, 238.*

Verity, H. (Eng.):– 1,956 w., *156;* 200 w. (3), *154-5;* 144 w. in Tests, *179;* 100 w. (9), *157;* 17 w. in day, *154;* 17 w. in match, *153;* 15 Australian w. in match, *181, 196;* 10 w. in innings (2), *152;* 10 w. or more in Test (2), *181, 196, 211;* 8 w. in Test innings, *182, 196.*

Viljoen, K. G. (SA):– 2 Test hundreds, *200, 217.*

Village Championship, *328-9.*

Vincent, C. L. (SA):– 84 w. in Tests, *180.*

Vine, J. (Eng.):– 25,171 r., *135;* 399 consecutive Championship appearances, *255;* 1st wkt hundreds, *142;* Test p'ship record, *195.*

Virgin, R. T. (Som. and Northants):– 37 hundreds, *132;* Highest aggregate in 1974, *146;* 1st wkt hundreds, *142.*

Viswanath, G. R. (Ind.):– Test captain, *209, 241;* 87 consecutive Tests, *187;* 6,080 r. in Tests, *169;* 1,388 Test runs in year, *173;* 43 hundreds, *132;* 14 Test hundreds, *211, 224, 233, 237, 242;* Hundred on début, *131;* Hundred on Test début, *131, 172, 224;* 415 for 3rd wicket, *176, 211;* Test p'ship records, *211, 225, 234.*

Vivian, G. E. (NZ):– Test p'ship record, *237.*

Vivian, H. G. (NZ):– 1 Test hundred, *229;* Test p'ship record, *229.*

Vizianagram, Maharaj of (Ind.):– Test captain, *209.*

Voce, W. (Eng.):– 1,558 w., *157;* 98 w. in Tests, *179;* 10 w. or more in Test (2), *196, 205.*

Vogler, A. E. E. (SA):– 36 w. in series, *183;* 16 w. in day, *154;* 10 w. in innings, *152;* 10 w. or more in Test (1), *201;* 6 c. in Test, *185.*

## W

Wade, H. F. (SA):– Test captain, *198, 215.*

Wade, W. W. (SA):– 1 Test hundred, *200.*

Wadekar, A. L. (Ind.):– Test captain, *209, 232;* 2,113 r. in Tests, *169;* 36 hundreds, *132;* 1 Test hundred, *237;* 323 v Mysore, *128;* Test p'ship record, *211.*

Wadsworth, K. J. (NZ):– 96 d. in Tests, *184;* Test p'ship records, *222, 231.*

Waheed Mirza (Sind):– 324 v Quetta, *128;* 561 for 1st wkt, *141, 143.*

Waite, J. H. B. (SA):– 2,405 r. in Tests, *168;* 50 Tests, *124;* 4 Test hundreds, *200, 217, 229;* 141 d. in Tests, *184;* 26 d. in series, *184;* Test p'ship records, *201, 217.*

Walcott, C. L. (WI):– 11,820 r. (avge 56.55), *136;* 3,798 r. (avge 56.68) in Tests, *169, 171;* 827 r. in series, *173;* 40 hundreds, *132;* 15 Test hundreds, *204, 220, 230, 233, 235;* 2 hundreds in same Test, *172, 220;* 2 hundreds in match (2), *132;* 314* v Trinidad, *129;* 574* for 4th wkt, *141, 144;* Test p'ship records, *231, 234, 235.*

Wales v MCC, *644;* v Zimbabweans, *314.*

Walker, A. K. (Notts.):– 4 w. with consecutive balls, *150.*

Walker, M. H. N. (Aust.):– 138 w. in Tests, *180;* 8 w. in Test innings, *183;* Test p'ship record, *227.*

Walker, P. M. (Eng.):– 73 c., 69 c. and 65 c. in season, *162;* 8 c. in match, *163.*

Walker, V. E. (Middx):– 108 and 10 w., *160;* 10 w. in innings (2), *151.*
Walkley, E. (S. Aust.):– 232 for 9th wkt, *145.*
Wall, T. W. (Aust.):– 10 w. in innings, *152.*
Wallace, W. M. (NZ):– Test captain, *228;* 324 for 4th wkt, *144.*
Walters, C. F. (Eng.):– Test captain, *190;* 1 Test hundred, *210.*
Walters, K. D. (Aust.):– 5,357 r. in Tests, *168;* 45 hundreds, *132;* 15 Test hundreds, *194, 219, 222, 224, 226;* 2 hundreds in same Test, *172, 219;* Hundred and double-hundred, *133;* Hundred on Test début, *172, 194;* 250 v New Zealand, *170, 222;* Test p'ship records, *220, 222.*
Waqar Hassan (Pak.):– 1 Test hundred, *239;* 308 for 7th wkt v New Zealand, *145, 240.*
Ward, A. (Eng.):– 1 Test hundred, *192.*
Ward, J. T. (NZ):– Test p'ship record, *237.*
Ward, W. (MCC):– 278 at Lord's, *252.*
Wardle, J. H. (Eng.):– 1,846 w., *156;* 102 w. in Tests, *179;* 100 w. (10), *157;* 10 w. or more in Test (1), *201.*
Warnapura, B. (SL):– Test captain, *214, 243, 244.*
Warner, Sir Pelham F. (Eng.):– Test captain, *189, 198;* 29,028 r., *134;* 60 hundreds, *131;* Hundred on Test début, *171, 199;* Carrying bat in Test, *174.*
Warren, A. (Eng.), 283 for 9th wkt, *145.*
Warwick Under-25 Competition:– *816-7;* Fixtures, 1986, *1294-5.*
Warwickshire:– *333, 564-79;* Championship positions, *338-9;* Highest score, *163;* Highest individual score, *130;* Lowest score, *164.*
Warwickshire II, *800, 801, 812-3.*
Washbrook, C. (Eng.):– 34,101 r., *134;* 2,569 r. in Tests, *167;* 1,000 r. (20), *136;* 76 hundreds, *131;* 6 Test hundreds, *192, 199, 204, 207;* 359 for 1st wkt v South Africa, *200;* 1st wkt hundreds, *142.*
Wasim Akram (Pak.):– 10 w. or more in Test (1), *240.*
Wasim Bari (Pak.):– Test captain, *212;* 81 Tests, *124;* 228 d. in Tests, *184;* 62 d. in one-day ints, *246;* 8 c. in Test, *185;* 7 c. in Test innings, *162, 185;* Test p'ship records, *227, 236, 243.*
Wasim Raja (Pak.):– 2,821 r. in Tests, *170;* 4 Test hundreds, *213, 235, 242;* Test p'ship records, *236, 243, 244.*
Wass, T. G. (Notts.):– 1,666 w., *156;* 100 w. (10), *157;* 16 w. in day (2), *154.*
Wasu, H. (Vidarbha):– Obstructing the field, *149.*
Watkins, A. J. (Eng.):– 2 Test hundreds, *199, 210.*
Watkins, J. R. (Aust.):– Test p'ship record, *227.*
Watson, F. B. (Lancs.):– 50 hundreds, *132;* 300* v Surrey, *129;* 1st wkt hundreds, *142.*
Watson, W. (Eng.):– 25,670 r., *135;* 55 hundreds, *131;* 2 Test hundreds, *192, 204.*
Watson-Smith, R. (Border):– 183* and 125* in first two first-class innings, *131.*
Watts, E. A. (Surrey):– 10 w. in innings, *152.*
Wazir Mohammad (Pak.):– Test p'ship records, *236.*
Webb, M. G. (NZ):– Test p'ship record, *223.*
Weekes, E. D. (WI):– 12,010 r. (avge 55.34), *136;* 4,455 r. (avge 58.61) in Tests, *168, 171;* 779 r. in series, *173;* 36 hundreds, *132;* 15 Test hundreds, *204, 220, 230, 233, 235;* 5 successive hundreds, *137;* 2 hundreds in same Test, *172, 233;* 304* v Cambridge Univ., *129;* Avge of 79.65 in English season, *147;* Test p'ship records, *205, 231, 234, 235.*
Weekes, K. H. (WI):– 1 Test hundred, *204.*
Wellard, A. W. (Eng.):– All-round, *158;* 1,614 w., *157;* 66 sixes in season, *139;* 30 r. and 31 r. in over, *140;* 100 w. (8), *157.*
Wellham, D. M. (Aust.):– Hundred on début, *131;* Hundred on Test début, *131, 172, 194.*
Wells, C. M. (Sussex):– All-round, *159.*
Wells, P. (Kent):– 4 w. with consecutive balls, *149.*
Wessels, K. C. (Aust.):– 4 Test hundreds, *194, 219, 226, 228;* Hundred on Test début, *172, 194;* Highest aggregate in 1979, *146;* 388 for 1st wkt, *141;* Test p'ship record, *228.*
West Indies:– B & H World Championship of Cricket, *980-8;* B & H World Series Cup, *967-78;* Definition of first-class matches, *1253;* Domestic season 1984-85, *1062-79;* Highest

West Indies:- *contd*
individual Test innings, *170;* Highest Test innings, *176;* Leading batsmen in Tests, *168-9;* Leading bowlers in Tests, *180;* Lowest Test innings, *178;* Most consecutive Test appearances, *187;* Most Test appearances, *124;* Most Test appearances as captain, *124;* Oldest Test player, *187;* Representative body, *1160;* Summary of Tests, *188;* Test cricketers (1928-85), *108-12;* West Indies in Test cricket (*see p. 127*); Youngest and oldest on Test début, *186-7*.

West Indies in Australia, 1984-85, *909-25*.

West Indies v New Zealand, 1984-85,

Weston, M. J. (Worcs.):- 227 for 5th wkt, *258*.

Wettimuny, S. (SL):- 2 Test hundreds, *214, 244;* 190 v England, *170, 214, 252;* Carrying bat in Test, *174;* Longest innings in Lord's Test, *252;* Test p'ship records, *214, 241, 244*.

Whatmore, D. F. (Aust.):- 6 c. in Test, *185*.

Whitbread Scholarships, *989*.

White, G. C. (SA):- 2 Test hundreds, *200*.

White, J. C. (Eng.):- Test captain, *190, 198;* 2,356 w., *156;* 100 w. (14), *157;* 16 w. in day, *154;* 10 w. in innings, *152;* 10 w. or more in Test (1), *196;* 8 w. in Test innings, *183*.

Whitehead, H. (Leics.):- 380 for 1st wkt, *142*.

Whitehouse, J. (Warwicks.):- Hundred on début, *130*.

Whitelaw, P. E. (Auck.):- Fast scoring, *138;* 445 for 3rd wkt, *138, 143*.

Whittaker, G. J. (Surrey):- 253* v Gloucestershire II, *253*.

Whitty, W. J. (Aust.):- 37 w. in series, *183;* Test p'ship record, *217*.

Whysall, W. W. (Eng.):- 51 hundreds, *132;* 4 successive hundreds, *137;* 2 hundreds in match (2), *132;* 1st wkt hundreds, *142*.

Wicket-keeping records:- *160-2, 184-5;* in 1985, *355*.

Wicket records (1st to 10th), *143-5*.

Wiener, J. M. (Aust.):- 390* for 3rd wkt, *143*.

Wight, G. L. (British Guiana):- 390 for 1st wkt, *141, 143*.

Wiles, C. A. (WI):- Test début at 40, *186*.

Willey, P. (Eng.):-All-round, *159;* 2 Test hundreds, *204;* B & H Cup final Man of the Match, *698*.

William Younger Cup (National Club Championship), *327-8*.

Williams, A. B. (WI):- 2 Test hundreds, *220, 233;* Hundred on Test début, *172, 220*.

Williams, E. A. V. (WI):- 255 for 8th wkt, *145*.

Willis, R. G. D. (Eng.):- Test captain, *189, 206, 209, 212;* 325 w. in Tests, *179;* 128 w. v Australia, *197;* 8 w. in Test innings, *182;* Test p'ship records, *211, 213*.

Wills Cup (Pak.), *1122*.

Wilmot, A. L. (E. Prov.):- 338 for 5th wkt, *144*.

Wilson, A. E. (Glos.):- 10 c. in match, *161*.

Wilson, D. (Eng.):- 30 r. in over, *140;* 3 hat-tricks, *151*.

Wilson, E. R. (Eng.):- Test début at 41, *186*.

Wilson, G. A. (Worcs.):- 3 hat-tricks, *151*.

Wiltshire, *782, 783, 797*.

Winslow, P. L. (SA):- 1 Test hundred, *200;* 30 r. in over, *140;* Test p'ship record, *201*.

Wisden, J. (Sussex):- 10 w. in innings, *151*.

Wisden Trophy, *202*.

Women's Cricket, 1985, *1154*.

Women's Cricket Association, Address of Secretary, *1161*.

Wood, C. J. B. (Leics.):- 37 hundreds, *132;* 2 separate hundreds, *132;* 380 for 1st wkt, *142*.

Wood, G. M. (Aust.):- 3,109 r. in Tests, *168*, 8 Test hundreds, *194, 219, 222, 224, 226;* Test p'ship record, *222*.

Wood, H. (Eng.):- 1 Test hundred, *199;* Test p'ship record, *200*.

Woodfull, W. M. (Aust.):- Test captain, *189, 215, 218;* 13,392 r. (avge 65.00), *135;* 2,300 r. in Tests, *168;* 49 hundreds, *132;* 7 Test hundreds, *194, 216;* Carrying bat in Test (2), *174;* 375 for 1st wkt, *142*.

Woods, S. M. J. (Eng. and Aust.):- 10 w. in innings, *151*.

Woolley, C. N. (Northants):- 326 consecutive Championship appearances, *255*.

Woolley, F. E. (Eng.):– All-round, *158;* Test cricket at 47, *187;* 58,969 r., *134;* 3,352 r. in season, *146;* 3,283 r. in Tests, *167;* 1,000 r. (28), *136-7;* 707 Championship appearances, *255;* 52 consecutive Test matches, *187;* 145 hundreds, *131;* 5 Test hundreds, *192, 199;* 4 successive hundreds, *137;* 305* v Tasmania, *129, 138;* 300 r. in 205 min., *138;* 2,068 w., *156;* 100 w. (8), *157;* 83 w. in Tests, *179;* 10 w. or more in Test (1), *196;* 1,018 c., *162;* 6 c. in Test, *185;* 235 for 10th wkt, *145;* Test p'ship record, *195*.

Woolmer, R. A. (Eng.):– 3 Test hundreds, *192*.

Wootton, G. (Notts.):– 10 w. in innings, *151*.

Worcestershire:– *333, 580-96;* Championship positions, *338-9;* Highest score, *163;* Highest individual score, *130;* Lowest score, *164*.

Worcestershire II, *800, 801, 813-4*.

World Cup:– Finals, *247;* 1987, *1138*.

Worrell, Sir F. M. M. (WI):– Test captain, *202, 218, 232;* 15,025 r. (avge 54.24), *136;* 3,860 r. in Tests, *169;* 39 hundreds, *132;* 9 Test hundreds, *204-5, 220, 230, 233;* 308* v Trinidad, *129;* 261 v England, *170, 204;* Carrying bat in Test, *174;* 574* and 502* for 4th wkt, *141, 144;* Test p'ship records, *205, 231, 234*.

Worrell, Frank, Trophy, *218*.

Worthington, T. S. (Eng.):– 1 Test hundred, *210;* Test p'ship record, *211*.

Wright, C. W. (Eng.):– Test p'ship record, *200*.

Wright, D. V. P. (Eng.):– 2,056 w., *156;* 108 w. in Tests, *179;* 100 w. (10), *157;* 10 w. or more in Test (1), *201;* 7 hat-tricks, *151*.

Wright, J. G. (NZ):– 15,000 r., *259;* 2,133 r. in Tests, *169;* 40 hundreds, *132;* 4 Test hundreds, *207, 222, 237, 239;* Test p'ship records, *208, 239*.

Wright, K. J. (Aust.):– Test p'ship record, *224*.

Wyatt, R. E. S. (Eng.):– Test captain, *189-90, 198, 202, 206;* 39,405 r., *134;* 1,000 r. (18), *136;* 85 hundreds, *131;* 2 Test hundreds, *199;* 124 and hat-trick v Ceylon, *160*.

Wynyard, E. G. (Eng.):– 411 for 6th wkt, *144*.

## Y

Yadav, N. S. (Ind.):– Test p'ship record, *238*.

Yajurvindra Singh (Ind.):– 7 c. in Test, *185;* 5 c. in Test innings, *186*.

Yallop, G. N. (Aust.):– Test captain, *189, 225;* 2,756 r. in Tests, *168;* 8 Test hundreds, *194, 224, 226;* 2 hundreds in match (2), *132;* 268 v Pakistan, *170, 226;* Test p'ship records, *227, 228*.

Yardley, B. (Aust.):– 126 w. in Tests, *180;* 10 w. or more in Test (1), *221*.

Yardley, N. W. D. (Eng.):– Test captain, *189-90, 198, 202;* Test p'ship record, *200*.

Yardley, W. (CUCC and Kent):– Throwing record, *254*.

Yarnold, H. (Worcs.):– 110 d. in season, *161;* 7 d. in innings, *162*.

Yashpal Sharma (Ind.):– 2 Test hundreds, *211, 224;* Test p'ship records, *211, 234, 242*.

Yorkshire:– *333, 597-612;* Championship positions, *338-9;* Highest score, *163;* Highest individual score, *130;* Lowest score, *164*.

Yorkshire II, *800, 801, 814-5*.

Young Cricketer of the Year, *634*.

Young, D. M. (Worcs. and Glos.):– 40 hundreds, *132;* 395 for 1st wkt, *141*.

Young, J. A. (Eng.):– 100 w. (8), *157*.

Youngest Test players, *186*.

Younis Ahmed (Pak.):– 43 hundreds, *132;* 306* for 4th wkt, *258*.

Yuile, B. W. (NZ):– Test p'ship record, *239*.

## Z

Zaheer Abbas (Pak.):– Test captain, *212, 225, 238, 241;* 34,285 r. (avge 52.18), *134, 136;* 5,058 r. in Tests, *169;* 1,000 r. (17), *136;* 107 hundreds, *131;* 12 Test hundreds, *213, 226, 239, 242, 244;* 7 one-day int. hundreds, *245;* 4 successive hundreds, *137;* 2 hundreds in match (8), *132-3;* Hundred and double-hundred (4), *133;* 274 v England, *170, 213;* Avge of 88.69 in English season, *147;* 30 r. in over, *140;* Highest aggregate in 1976, 1981, *146;* Hit the ball twice, *149;* 353 for 6th wkt, *144;* Test p'ship records, *213, 227, 236, 243*.

Zimbabwe in 1984-85, *1143-50*.

Zimbabwe v English Counties XI, 1984-85, *1148, 1149*.
Zimbabwe v Young New Zealanders, 1984-85, *1143, 1145, 1146, 1147*.
Zimbabweans in England, 1985, *308-16*.
Zulch, J. W. (SA):- 2 Test hundreds, *217*; Carrying bat in Test, *174*.
Zulfiqar Ahmed (Pak.):- 10 w. or more in Test (1), *240;* Test p'ship record, *242*.

## INDEX OF ADVERTISERS

Association of Cricket Statisticians *1265*.
BBC Video, IV.
Britannic Assurance, *332*.
Bryan Grasshopper, *1298*.
Collins Willow, *1268-9*.
Cornhill Insurance, *1299*.
Cricket Society, *1273*.
Esso, II.
Gunn & Moore, *6*.
Lakeland Investments, *11*.
J. W. McKenzie, III.
National Westminster Bank, *646*.
Pelham Books, *1277*.
John Player, *700*.
Readersport, *9*.
Southern Booksellers, *1265*.
Texaco, *286*.
Wisden Cricket Monthly, *1297*.
Martin Wood, *1273*.

## INDEX OF FILLERS

Addresses of Representative Bodies, *1160*.
Antarctica, Cricket in, *825*.
Ashes, The, *1034*.
Australia v New Zealand, 1985-86, *952*.
Ban on Australian Players, *1033*.
Cancelled Tour, *1153*.
Career Figures of Players Retiring or Not Being Retained, *899*.
County Caps Awarded in 1985, *815*.
Cricket Associations and Societies, *876-7*.
Cricketer Cup Winners, 1967-1985, *1205*.
Cricketers' Association, The, *1205*.
Denmark, Cricket in, *1061*.
Errata in Wisden, *1296*.
Esso Scholarships, *307*.
Fielding in 1985, *355*.
Fine Tribute, *1120*.
Future Tours, *1034*.
Getty's Donation, *321*.
Honours' List, *1257*.
International Ambassadors, *899*.
Inter-Services Tournament, 1985, *1260*.
I Zingari Results, 1985, *1260*.
Lords and Commons Cricket, 1985, *1296*.
MCC in Canada, 1985, *1153*.
Over-rate and Run-rate in Britannic Assurance Championship, 1985, *1061*.
Record Testimonial, *612*.
Silk Cup Challenge, 1985, *1256*.
Sri Lanka v India, 1985-86, *952*.
Status of Matches in UK, *642*.
Umpires for 1986, *1257*.
Whitbread Scholarships, *989*
World Cup, 1987, *1138*.
Young Cricketer of the Year, *634*.

# NOTES BY THE EDITOR

As I write these Notes, England's leading cricketers, having regained the Ashes, are taking a well-earned rest. They have four months in which to enjoy a complete break from the game before leaving, in January 1986, for the Caribbean and another crack at the West Indians.

With an escalating number of Test matches and particularly of one-day internationals – in 1985 alone there were 94, exactly twice as many as in 1980 – players are in danger of becoming disenchanted and each country's domestic competitions of being seriously devalued. No-one was in any doubt, therefore, that David Gower's England side would benefit from the respite that came their way in the autumn of 1985, as should the game as a whole.

But not even an excess of representative cricket had prevented England from rallying with great heart from their heavy defeat at the hands of Clive Lloyd's West Indians in 1984. They won first in India, coming from behind to do so, and then got the better of the old enemy in England. Australia's cricket was known to be at a low ebb, but Allan Border's side still had to be beaten, and by winning three of the six Test matches, the last two by an innings, England made a good job of it.

I am not among those who maintain that there is no such thing as a weak Australian side. Nor, I think, was their captain by the time he flew home last September. He said as much at The Oval, after Australia had been beaten for the ninth time in their last fourteen Test matches. When they took the field next, back in Australia, it was to be beaten by an innings by New Zealand, which prompted Border to question his side's attitude as well as their ability. Some of them, he believed, had "forgotten the reason for playing Test cricket, the feeling of national pride". In other words, some were too concerned about money to give of their best. I doubt, in fact, whether the 1985 Australians would have finished in the first four in the County Championship. As a consequence of playing so much one-day cricket – they did nothing else for the first nine weeks of last year – they seemed to have lost the knack of taking wickets themselves and of selling their own wickets dearly. They were also handicapped, as England had been from 1982 until last spring, by the loss of senior players down the South African chute. All this left England with a great chance, especially their batsmen, and they took it with a vengeance.

## A Batting Bonanza

In all the years since England and Australia first met, there is no remote precedent for either side averaging 60 runs per 100 balls throughout a series, as England did last summer. In the original Test match, played at Melbourne in 1877, both sides averaged below 30. Even Bradman's Australians in England in 1948 were kept to 46.6. In 1930, when Bradman himself scored 974 runs at a rattling rate, Australia's overall average was 45.2. In 1928-29 in Australia, one of the best of all England batting sides (the first six in the order were Hobbs, Sutcliffe, Hammond, Jardine, Hendren and Chapman) averaged only 38.53, albeit in a series of timeless Tests. Only once in 25 years after the last war did

England average more than 40. Yet here they were in 1985 making their runs at 60.67 per 100 balls, or getting on for 4 an over, at once an indication of the range and belligerence of their own batting and the unfitness of some of the Australian bowling. Being covered the pitches, too, were immune from the vagaries of a wet, wretchedly grey summer; but that has applied for some years now.

### Gower runs into Form

It became a source of great joy watching England come together as a team. Much of the credit for this belonged to Gower and his vice-captain, Gatting. Once Gower had started to make runs against Australia – he had had a thin time of it with the bat in India – he grew visibly in authority in the field. His 166 at Trent Bridge, 215 at Edgbaston and 157 at The Oval amounted to a personal triumph. It was being widely said before Trent Bridge that his best batting form would continue to elude him so long as he retained the England captaincy. In the event, his alliance with Gatting, established in India while Botham was taking the winter of 1984-85 off, went from strength to strength and absorbed without difficulty Botham's rumbustious return last summer. The emergence of Robinson as a batsman capable of scoring 934 runs at an average of 62 in his first year of Test cricket was another major bonus. But the ultimate test of England's revival and Robinson's mettle lay ahead – in the West Indies in early 1986.

### The Spirit of the Game

The series against Australia was contested in a conspicuously good spirit, with Gower and Border setting the tone. In this respect it may, across the board, have been a better year, though it is difficult to be certain of that. In Pakistan, New Zealand's captain still had to be restrained from taking his side off the field, such was his despair at the umpires' interpretation of the Laws. Nor was there any love lost between the Australian and West Indian sides by the end of their series in Australia, though that was partly, at least, because they had been meeting each other so much too often. They fought out ten Test matches in as many months, which was far too many. Upon succeeding Lloyd as captain of West Indies, Vivian Richards said that nothing would change so far as his side's use of short-pitched bowling was concerned. But it was a step in the right direction when, soon after West Indies and New Zealand had finished a series of Test matches by exchanging a sickening fusillade of bouncers in Jamaica, Australia agreed at the annual meeting of the International Cricket Conference to produce a new draft to Law 42 (8) for consideration in 1986.

### Need for Strong Government

Although there was a time in the season when hardly a week seemed to pass without their meeting, the Disciplinary Committee of the Test and County Cricket Board gave the impression of preferring acquiescence to action. More than one umpire, after being called to Lord's to give evidence, left without having been seen to receive the backing he and his colleagues must have hoped for. Within the space of a fortnight, three past or present Test captains (Botham, Fletcher and Imran Khan), charged with bringing the game into disrepute, were merely "warned as to their future conduct". I will say only that games in general never needed strong government more than they do today, nor umpires and referees more sympathetic support. Cricket is not exempt from this. It was more as an administrative adjustment, I think, than as a threat that the TCCB, at their Winter Meeting, introduced a system of instant fines for misconduct by players appearing for England, to be imposed jointly by the captain and the chairman of selectors (or his nominee). It was done to avoid a repetition of the hiatus there had been after Botham became involved in an incident during the third Test match against Australia in July. Forty-six days were allowed to pass then before the matter was resolved. During an over in which nothing went right for him, Botham had displayed what the Board referred to as "public dissent". To all the world that is what it was, and all the world was watching, play being on television at the time – and what Botham does on television one day, his countless fans do on the recreation ground or the school playing field the next. Had he been up before the Professional Golfers' Association or the Jockey Club he would have paid for it. Had it been tennis he would probably not, and we know what tennis has come to. After much agonising, Lord's just admonished him.

## A Mountain of a Man

Botham was never out of the news for long. Not since W. G. Grace can a cricketer, by his physical presence and remarkable exploits, have so caught the attention of the sporting world. Bradman's feats were, of course, more phenomenal, Sobers's more effortlessly versatile; but off the field they maintained a lower, more urbane profile than Botham. Bernard Darwin, in a vintage profile of W.G., wrote of his "schoolboy love for elementary and boisterous jokes . . . his desperate and undisguised keenness, his occasional pettishness and pettiness, his endless power of recovering his spirits" – all of which could apply equally to Botham.

No-one can ever have sent the ball such huge distances as frequently as Botham did last summer. His 80 6s, most of them hit with the full face of the bat, often over extra-cover, were a record for an English first-class season. He scored at something like a run a ball for Somerset, yet still averaged 100 for them, and in the six Test matches he took 31 Australian wickets and held eight catches, some of them quite breathtaking. Wherever he played he added substantially to the gate, and when the winter came he tested a recent operation on a knee by walking from John O'Groats to Land's End and raising over £600,000 for charity, an astonishing achievement. There was much else, not all of it quite so admirable. There are times when Botham needs to be saved from his unrestraint, as well perhaps as from those who would exploit him. Somerset, for their part, decided at the end of the season that they needed to be saved from his captaincy. For him, no less than anyone else, England's tour of

West Indies presented a challenge – and one that he would relish. Of all the Test-playing countries, only they had not felt the full weight of his remarkable game.

## Worthy Champions

To be fair to Botham, it is no easy business being a county captain while having to miss as many as ten or twelve Championship matches through playing for England. It was no coincidence that while Somerset were finishing last in 1985, Leicestershire under Gower were only one place above them. That Middlesex should have won the title for the third time in six years, despite losing their own captain, Gatting, as well as Downton, Edmonds, Emburey and occasionally Cowans on England duty, made them most worthy champions. Gatting's forthright leadership still had a lot to do with their winning, but no more than their host of fast bowlers, most of them of Caribbean origin. Gloucestershire's third place, after coming last in 1984, represented a spectacular improvement, though it was at the cost of £8,000 in fines for the slowest over-rate of any county. Essex were pre-eminent as a one-day side, Fletcher's experience, Gooch's batting and a generally pragmatic style accounting for this. McEwan, a tower of strength since joining Essex in 1974, has returned to his native South Africa to farm. His place will be taken in 1986 by Border, one of very few distinguished Australian batsmen ever to join an English county.

## Looking for Loopholes

Despite replacing a South African with an Australian, Essex make a point of acting strictly within the TCCB's guidelines, aimed at reducing the overseas influence in county cricket. Other counties tend to look for loopholes in the rules of qualification and to find them. Gloucestershire are a case in point. Their challenge for the Championship last year, though it reawakened interest in the game within the county, could be traced to their signing, before the start of the season, two Zimbabweans (one, Curran, whose eligibility was tenuously based on the discovery that he possessed an Irish grandparent) and a Jamaican. Hampshire ran into second place on the backs of two brilliant West Indians and the Smith brothers from South Africa (both, it is true, qualified to play for England), but without including in their side, from the start of the season to the finish, a single Hampshire-born player. I should be sorry to see the English game without any overseas players – their contribution is often dazzling – but it is as well, in view of the ambivalence that exists, that the TCCB have further tightened the rules of qualification. Someone such as Curran will have in future to accomplish a period of four years' residence within a member country of the EEC. Insisting even upon that needed care, so fine is the line between what is best for English cricket and a cricketer's legal rights.

## The Case for Natural Pitches

Regulations concerning the covering of pitches are also under review, which is good news. Since full covering was introduced into county cricket in 1981 (it has come to stay in Test matches, in the interests, for better or worse, of uniformity and thrift) the game has lost in variety. There can be no doubt of that. One felt deprived last season of some absorbing cricket, wherein, but for the covers, batsmen could regularly have been seen using their defensive skills against a turning ball on a drying pitch. Instead, on a succession of "plastic" pitches, all the life taken out of them by constant covering, runs were as plentiful as they have ever been. Only once before, in 1928, have as many as nineteen batsmen averaged over 50, and never before have as few as four regular bowlers taken their wickets at under 20 runs apiece – and this in a summer when it always *seemed* to be raining.

When games follow as predictable a pattern as they often did in 1985, captains are drawn into the most detailed collusion in search of a result, introducing an element of pretence and culminating as a rule in an agreement on the last morning upon the precise terms of any target to be set. All being well the covers will have been removed, if only partially, by the start of the 1986 season, or by 1987 at the latest, enabling the county game to regain some of its former diversity. I am inclined to think, too, that the system of allocating points in the Championship needs further revision. It was not only because of full covering and foul weather that there was a higher percentage (62.7) of drawn games in 1985 than at any time in the history of the competition. It must have been partly because of the exaggerated significance of bonus points, which reduces the incentive to aim for outright victory. Something is surely wrong when 2,034 bonus points are awarded, as in 1985, and only 1,216 points for actually winning games.

## Subba Row Takes Over

As 1985 ended, the report of the working party that had been sitting for a year under the chairmanship of C. H. Palmer, investigating the standards of English cricket, was still awaited. Some felt their deliberations had become academic, even irrelevant, in view of England's much-improved fortunes, but there was not really much question of that. The time had come for the English game to take another good look at itself, not only from the playing angle. If the working party had been seeking evidence from the Australian tour, for or against the introduction of four-day Championship cricket, they must have been disappointed. Although the Australians did play several four-day games against the counties, these made no significant impact. In October, Mr Palmer was succeeded by Raman Subba Row as Chairman of the TCCB. Now in new offices at Lord's, the Board has the widest responsibilities, and there is no more influential figure in the English game than its chairman.

A feeling of well-being greeted Mr Subba Row, Australia having just been beaten and a good season rescued from a wet summer. But he is not one to be complacent. He would have had reason to reprove those counties which put out much less than their best sides against the Australians, other than in the event of illness or injury. More than once the Australians were upset by this, even to the point of resenting it. He needed to be concerned, too, at the licence given to players in writing for the national press, and also about the effect the teachers' strike was having on cricket in the schools, where it is already played much less than it used to be.

On the other hand, an official England B tour in the New Year of 1986 was a new and welcome departure. The second best side was chosen, rather than one with the accent on youth, and for a tour which, as originally planned, would have prevented the players from taking up any other worthwhile cricketing engagement during the winter, a fee of £3,000, or just over, seemed meagre. With the lure of South Africa, and talk, however fanciful, of an entrepreneur, who is also Botham's agent, attempting to set up his own programme of one-day "exhibition" matches, as Mr Packer did with such unhappy consequences for cricket in Australia, it is important that players should not feel ill-used. In the ordinary way they are not, at any rate in England.

## A Healthy Budget

In Australia too little of the vast revenue which cricket produces has been going back into the game. The players know it and it has become a cause of discontent. In England it all does. The TCCB central fund, upon which the counties depend for their very existence, was well topped up at the end of last summer with the result that most of the counties declared useful profits. Border's Australians may not have been a great side, but they helped swell the coffers most abundantly. From the Tests and one-day internationals alone the takings were £2,468,322.

## Sponsors Galore

Being still of good report, cricket continues to attract the sponsors it needs, not only those whose names are widely identified with the game but hundreds that are not. As an illustration of this, let me quote from one of Surrey's many informative news letters: "A lot of work has been put in by our marketing department at The Oval in organising various sponsorships. You will see Surrey players this year displaying the British Airways Poundstretcher on their shirts, sweaters and track suits, and the Mazda Company has supplied us with cars. We are delighted that Nescafé have continued their sponsorship of our youth development scheme, which also involves Poundstretcher sponsorship in the form of an Under-18 youth tour to Australia for four weeks in December and January. In addition Alfred Marks have again provided player-incentive sponsorship in the Britannic Assurance Championship and George Brittain are this season's sponsors of the Player of the Month awards." Companies making the heaviest investments in the game hope for, indeed expect, some degree of television coverage in return. That is the quid pro quo, and because the John Player League no longer has BBC2 mostly to itself on Sunday afternoons the competition may not have quite the attraction for the sponsors that it did. The whole business of tobacco sponsorship is fast becoming a vexed question.

### Another Good Finish

The two cigarette competitions, the John Player and the Benson and Hedges, were won in 1985 by Essex and Leicestershire respectively. The NatWest, which also went to Essex, provided a last-ball finish for the third time in the last four years. A diversion from the more sober business of Test and Championship cricket, the NatWest final at Lord's makes a theatrical climax to the season. This time Randall, no longer a regular member of the England side but still a great favourite with the public, set up a memorable finish by scoring 18 of the 20 runs Nottinghamshire needed from the last over to beat Essex. At 34, and despite thoughts of retirement, Randall still personifies the sunny side of the game.

### Crowd Control

To guard against the hooliganism that has so harmed the image and marred the enjoyment of association football, the cricketing authorities are having to restrict licensing hours on grounds and to make special appeals for orderly behaviour. After the field at Headingley had been prematurely invaded at the end of the first Test match, in anticipation of the winning hit, steps were taken to avoid the same thing happening in the remaining Tests. It is a pity when many have to be denied their ordinary pleasures in order to restrain the few, but it was for the best. The one-day finals are also having to be more tightly controlled, while even in Derbyshire it was considered necessary to express publicly the county's concern at "the type of people" who were being attracted to Sunday games. The dreadful fire at Bradford City's football ground in April 1985 had repercussions in the cricket world, several clubs being obliged to take extra precautionary measures.

### Coveted Victories

In more distant parts Sri Lanka's first Test victory, against India in Colombo in September, provided them with a famous landmark. It had taken them three and a half years and fourteen Test matches to achieve. India's first, against England in Madras in 1952, came in their 25th Test and after nearly twenty years of trying, the war intervening; New Zealand's, against West Indies in Auckland in 1956, came only in their 45th Test match. New Zealand's victory over Australia in Australia at the end of last year, by two Tests to one, also fulfilled a long-coveted ambition. Richard Hadlee's bowling had most to do with it. Only the great S. F. Barnes, for England against South Africa in the Triangular Tournament in 1912, has taken more wickets in a three-Test series in this century than Hadlee did now. Barnes took 34 at the age of 39, Hadlee 33 at the age of 34. With a classical action and superb versatility, Hadlee holds back the years.

## A Melbourne Jamboree

India's victory in Melbourne in March, in the so-called "World Championship of Cricket", a one-day tournament arranged to mark the 150th anniversary of the founding of the state of Victoria, was as much of a surprise as their triumph over West Indies at Lord's in the final of the 1985 World Cup. The tournament itself was no more than a qualified success, the Australian public having by that stage of their season had more than enough one-day cricket. "They are killing a good product", said Border on the over-exposure of the one-day game, a warning all countries would do well to heed. Having flown on to Australia from India, where they did so well, England made disappointingly little contribution to this Melbourne jamboree, though they did share with Australia the privilege of playing in the first match under the new Melbourne floodlights, watched by 84,494 people.

## Eastern Magic

India also gave us the brightest new star of 1985 in Mohammad Azharuddin, who scored 110 in his first Test match, against England in Calcutta, 105 in his next in Madras, and 122 in his third in Kanpur. No-one had ever done that before, and Azharuddin made his runs with a charm, touch and instinct in keeping with the very best of the orientals. In the same series another young man, Sivaramakrishnan, bowled, if only for a while, some magically effective leg-breaks. With him helping India to win a Test match in Bombay, Holland doing the same for Australia at Lord's and Abdul Qadir for Pakistan against Sri Lanka in Karachi, this was a more reassuring year for those who fear for the leg-spinner's survival. Also overseas, the game took a firmer hold in an unlikely outpost, Sharjah in the Arabian Desert, where two one-day tournaments attracted sides officially chosen by their Boards of Control.

## The Forbidden Land

Never a year goes by without South Africa making its presence felt. With no chance of being voted back into membership of the ICC, and aware of the need for international competition to sustain their own game, the South African Cricket Union managed to arrange a full tour, starting in November, by a useful side of Australians, who accepted to go to South Africa in the certain knowledge that they would be banned forthwith from official Australian cricket. The team, led by the former Australian captain, Kim Hughes, was more experienced and arguably stronger than that which had lost the Ashes in England. They went at a time when South Africa was in ferment, and unlike the English side of 1982, the first of the "rebels", their tour coincided with their own domestic season. It thus presented the Australian authorities with a dilemma similar to that in 1977, when they encountered widespread defections to Mr Packer, and they had little alternative but to impose the bans they did. This is not to say that the Australian Board's own handling of the matter had been entirely plausible.

Then, as *Wisden* was going to press, England's two winter tours came under heavy and damaging political pressure. By insisting at the last minute that four of the England players should cut themselves off altogether from South Africa, where they had played and coached, the governments of Bangladesh and Zimbabwe prompted the TCCB to cancel the B side's visits to both these countries. This was in accordance with the policy of ICC, who passed a resolution in 1981, subsequently reconfirmed, that there must be no political interference by one member country in the selection of another country's team. More sympathy was felt for the Bangladesh Board of Cricket Control, whose contrition was manifest, than for the Zimbabwe Cricket Union, who, as if under pain of death from their government, blamed the TCCB for the impasse.

With the Sri Lankans alone managing to stand by their original commitment, England's B team were left in the end with only the middle leg of their projected tour, and soon it was looking as though the Test side, due to leave for West Indies a few weeks later, might have no tour at all. The threats came now not so much from the politicians of the Caribbean, who had had their say earlier, but from the more militant trade unions, particularly those in Trinidad. It was they who warned of serious disruptions unless four more England players, who had also visited South Africa for cricketing purposes, undertook not to do so in future.

Although deeply concerned to save the game from a split between white and non-white countries, the TCCB again saw the legal and moral implications of binding their players in this way. Their refusal to do so came as a relief to those who believed that in the past they had allowed themselves to be rather too easily manipulated by political propagandists. There need, in fact, be no doubt whatever that an abhorrence of apartheid is shared by all the world's cricketers. If the Cricketers' Association were to ask their members for a profession of this, no-one, I am sure, would abstain. There exists among them a fellowship which transcends politics, and one that until now has helped to make such a politically vulnerable game so wonderfully resilient.

# FIVE CRICKETERS OF THE YEAR

## PHIL BAINBRIDGE

In 1985 PHILIP BAINBRIDGE scored 1,644 runs at an average of 56.68. It was indisputably his best season and he must have come under close consideration for a place on one of England's winter tours. His runs were scored with some style. He is neat and mostly orthodox, having got an earlier penchant for whipping the ball through mid-wicket out of his system, and he can play off the back foot better than most of his contemporaries.

His captain, David Graveney, values him for the way he compiles his runs "when they matter most". He has the analytical approach to be expected from an erstwhile schoolteacher (he still lectures on PE to students at Brunel Technical College, Bristol, during the winter months). When he discerns the early signs of a technical flaw, he works tirelessly to eradicate it. In the early days of his county cricket, he used regularly to be ensnared by Eddie Hemmings, off bat and pad. The solution was something "Bains" puzzled out for himself.

Graveney calls him a well-organised batsman. Most players – teammates and opponents – call him competitive. The phlegmatic exterior reveals that he does not like giving his wicket away. Nor does he relish batting down the order. In 1985 he was number four and he knows how greatly he benefited from that, although he was not sure where he would end up when Brian Davison arrived on the Gloucestershire staff. Bainbridge was on the point of leaving Gloucestershire when, not so long ago, he seemed destined for permanent middle-order status.

But with a wise, psychological touch, the county made him vice-captain for 1985. "It was good for me. I thrive on responsibility." He became a wise counsellor, though still only 27, when the tactical triumvirate of Graveney, Davison and himself huddled pensively on the edge of the square. Bainbridge has many sound qualities as a player, quite apart from the driving will to win. He is a thinker, strong on the exploitation of an opponent's Achilles' heel. He is also a loyal team man with an ability and willingness, if necessary, to improvise.

Furthermore he is ambitious, and, while realistically accepting the standard of the competition among similarly talented batsmen, strives each season to add a refinement to his batting or an extra wile to his seam bowling in the pursuit of Test recognition. There were four centuries and eleven half-centuries from him last season, following a successful tour to Zimbabwe with the English Counties XI. "He shows a high level of concentration and doesn't from inclination ease off when he reaches his hundred", said Graveney.

As a medium-paced bowler he has diligently practised to move the ball away from the bat; he had no high regard for what used to be his natural in-swing. There were fewer wickets for him in 1985; fewer overs, too. That was because the county had three strike bowlers ahead of him – Lawrence, Walsh and Curran. But he feels he still took "important wickets". So he did – seven in the match against Worcestershire, and Cowdrey's and Benson's against Kent at Tunbridge Wells.

Bainbridge is smallish in stature, sharp and agile. Not too much gets past him in the covers. He has always wanted to be involved in every aspect of the game. Born at Stoke-on-Trent on April 16, 1958, he took early to cricket. At school he liked to open the batting and the bowling. His first hundred came when he was fourteen. He played for his school (Hanley HS), his county and Young England (against Australia in 1977) at schoolboy level. After leaving the Sixth Form College at Stoke, he had trials with four Second XIs: Derbyshire and Northamptonshire offered him a contract, in addition to Gloucestershire.

As a young soccer player he briefly appeared in the same side as Garth Crooks. Even more briefly he played scrum-half for one of Clifton's less prestigious XVs. But his winter sport is now confined to romantic nostalgia. As a result of breaking his wrist playing football, he batted in a special splint last season. Then, against Leicestershire at Cheltenham, he suffered a broken finger. "That's six to date. I'm going for the full set", he said, a smile creasing that slightly doleful expression. Even by his standards, he had quite an injury-prone summer. He fractured his cheekbone against Lancashire, while fielding at slip, and was concussed and carried off on a stretcher after losing sight of a ball from Surrey's Graham Monkhouse at The Oval.

Bainbridge is fundamentally a private person, though less so than he used to be. He likes a drink but is unlikely to dominate the post-match bar in gregarious bonhomie. At home with his wife, a qualified teacher, and their two young children, he conscientiously takes his photographs, does the husband's obligatory amount of DIY and says that he is starting out on golf. He claims to be a frustrated businessman; and he looks it as he turns up at the county ground, complete with executive case, in his new role of part-time marketing man.

With his unostentatious skills, Phil Bainbridge made a vital contribution to Gloucestershire's climb up the Championship table in 1985, thus strengthening the view held at Bristol, Gloucester and Cheltenham that he may well be his county's next captain. – D.F.

## RICHARD ELLISON

Family opinions are divided on the age at which Richard Ellison developed the ability to bowl the out-swinger that devastated Australia in the final two Tests of the 1985 Ashes series. His mother, Bridget, is convinced the talent was spotted when he was just seven years old. Ellison insists that when he took eight for 3 for Friars Preparatory School, Ashford, he was merely bowling straight up and down. "If they missed them I got a wicket, but I don't think I could move the ball then", he says.

He gives the credit for his development into a swing bowler to Alan Dixon, his coach at Tonbridge School, who later recommended the young all-rounder to his own former county, Kent. Richard's mother, however, is not a lady to be argued with. Her records of family cricketing achievements show that his great-grandfather played against the Grace brothers in the nineteenth century and that his grandfather captained Derbyshire Second XI at the age of 60.

With that background it was hardly surprising that RICHARD MARK ELLISON, born at Ashford, Kent, on September 21, 1959, the second of four children, was playing cricket on a local village green with his father Peter, an RAF officer, by the time he was three years old.

Peter Ellison died when Richard was only eight, but the encouragement to play sport was maintained when his mother married John Lendrum, the headmaster of Friars School. By the time Ellison moved on to Tonbridge, making the First XI in his first year, he was also playing football, hockey, rugby, fives and rackets. Later, while studying for a Bachelor of Education degree at St Luke's College, Exeter, he was chosen to represent the Southern Universities at hockey, and his powerful physique helped him to acquire a golf handicap of ten.

At Tonbridge, where he played alongside Christopher Cowdrey, later to be his county captain, Ellison was considered mainly as a left-handed batsman, making a highest score of 124 not out against Westminster School. During the holidays he played cricket for Malmesbury, his family having moved to the Wiltshire village of Grittleton. His first appearances for Kent were with the club and ground side in 1978. On his first-class début, in 1981, he scored 55 not out and figured in a century stand with Derek Underwood; but Kent had a rich crop of young batsmen at the time and he spent most of his early career down the order. Nevertheless, he had a batting average of 47.40 at the end of his first season, whereas his four wickets cost 144 runs apiece.

In the next two years he tuned his medium-paced bowling to become an integral part of Kent's attack, and in 1984, with England facing the humiliation of a five-nil whitewash at the hands of West Indies, he was called up for the final Test at The Oval. His match haul of five for 94 earned him a second cap against Sri Lanka at Lord's, a fortnight later, and then a place on England's tour to India.

With Ian Botham "resting" for the winter, Ellison was hailed as his natural successor, but while his bowling progressed his batting went in the opposite direction. In the opening game in India he made a powerful 83 not out at Jaipur, after which he went into the first Test at Bombay batting at number six. By the time of the third Test at Calcutta he was down to number ten. With the ball, however, he contributed a vital four for 66 in India's first innings as England won the second Test at Delhi, and he deserved greater reward for a marathon 55-over spell in the heat at Calcutta. Although he returned nought for 117, he beat the bat regularly. A combination of his batting failures, injury, and the selectors' desire to play Neil Foster, cost Ellison his place for the fourth Test at Madras, and he was to miss five more before earning a recall.

Although Ellison was arguably the pick of England's bowlers in the "World Championship of Cricket" in Melbourne and Sydney, which followed the Indian visit, his aspirations for the 1985 English season suffered a setback when he sprained ankle ligaments in a wet foothold in April and was out of the game for two months. While his brother, Charles, a Cambridge Blue at both cricket and golf, stole Richard's thunder by having Graham Gooch lbw for 99 on the opening day of the season, Richard's own future looked none too rosy. "With such a long injury, I didn't give myself a chance of playing against the Australians, nor of being picked for the tour to the West Indies. I thought they only picked quick bowlers and spinners for out there."

England, however, were struggling to find the right combination of faster bowlers to beat the Australians, and by the fourth Test Ellison was back as twelfth man. His re-inclusion came for the fifth Test at Edgbaston, when he grabbed his opportunity with both hands. After easing up on his two favourite pastimes – eating and drinking beer – he was eighteen pounds lighter and bowling a yard faster as the Australians tumbled to an innings defeat. While Richard's first ten Test wickets had cost him 48 runs each, at Edgbaston he was now Man of the Match with figures of ten for 104, at one stage taking four for 2 in five overs.

As England lifted the Ashes with another innings victory at The Oval, Ellison captured seven more wickets. Most importantly, he consistently penetrated the defences of Allan Border, capturing the Australian captain's valuable wicket in three out of four innings after he had shown earlier in the series that he was the biggest barrier in England's way. This startling turn-around in Ellison's fortunes also saw him finish top of the first-class bowling averages with 65 wickets at 17.20. His batting, however, was a potential still to be fulfilled. – G.O.

## CRAIG McDERMOTT

From the 1985 Australian tour of England, sufficient positive factors emerged to ward off the gloom and despair "down under" which would normally accompany such a conclusive loss in an Ashes series. There was a display of unforeseen leadership skills from Allan Border, the rapid maturing of Greg Ritchie, and, certainly not least, the rise of Craig McDermott, the young fast bowling hope.

McDermott came to England in May as a recent discovery in a team still feeling the effects of the retirement of the greatest wicket-taker in Test history, Dennis Lillee. He departed in September having reinforced the widespread belief that one day in the not-too-distant future he will lead his country's attack with the same devilish intent as Lillee. For the quiet young Queenslander with the serious and, at times, surly countenance bowled with outstanding application and vigour on pitches hardly made to order for a genuine fast bowler. That he finished as Australia's leading wicket-taker – 30 wickets in the six Test matches from 234.2 overs at a cost of 30.03 each – is a tribute to his undoubted skill and evidence that he should be ready to assume the role of Australia's number one strike bowler in the next couple of years. The current holder of that position, Geoff Lawson, may have something to say about such a forecast, but his poor tour placed a much greater workload on McDermott's shoulders than was expected at the start of the series.

There were times when the twenty-year-old ginger-haired speedster fell short of these increased expectations, as on the opening day of the third Test at Trent Bridge, when his first four overs cost 28 runs, but from such a young and inexperienced fast bowler, lapses were to be expected. He certainly balanced the books, first with a withering display in England's first innings of the second Test at Lord's, which brought him six for 70 and set Australia on the way to a series-levelling victory, and then with his eight for 141 in the first innings of the fourth Test at Old Trafford. That performance put him in exalted company as the tenth Australian to have taken eight wickets or more in a Test innings. He was also the youngest Australian and the third youngest from any country to take eight wickets in a Test innings.

Applying all his youthful enthusiasm to the task of achieving maximum pace on unhelpful pitches, McDermott literally ran into trouble several times. He was warned for following through on the pitch during the Lord's Test match and his subsequent efforts to correct this were a contributing factor to his occasional waywardness in later Tests. But rather than allow this to eat into his confidence he worked long and hard in the nets and county matches to overcome it, the kind of attitude which gave rise to the assessment that he looked set for a long and distinguished Test career.

CRAIG JOHN McDERMOTT was born in Ipswich, near Brisbane, on April 14, 1965, and first played cricket at the age of eight in grade three at Silkstone State School in Ipswich. At the same age he also played with the under-twelve team at the Warwick Road Cricket Club. But it was not till much later that he decided that cricket was for him. Throughout his schooling, first at Silkstone and then at Ipswich Grammar School, McDermott was an active all-round sportsman. Apart from cricket, his interests included athletics, rugby union, tennis and squash, all of which he played at club representative level. Though he was a promising fullback and wing three-quarter for Ipswich Grammar's rugby team, it was athletics which many thought would eventually lure him. He was school athletics champion for three successive years, his specialities being the triple jump, 400 metres and javelin. His talent as a triple jumper was confirmed when he finished third in the open division of the Queensland state titles.

He pursued all three interests through his early and mid teens, and it was not until he was chosen in the Australian under-nineteen team in the 1981-82 season that he decided to restrict himself to cricket. In that season he played in three junior "Tests" against Pakistan in Sydney, Perth and Hobart, the highlight being an eight-wicket haul in the second of them. Several of his team-mates in that series have also gone on to play Sheffield Shield cricket, including Mike Veletta (Western Australia), Tony Dodemaide (Victoria), Glen Trimble (Queensland) and Craig Bradley (South Australia). McDermott also toured England with the Australian under-nineteen team in 1983.

During his junior days at Ipswich he had a reputation as an all-rounder. But since coming into first-class cricket this has diminished as he has concentrated on improving his bowling. He made his first-class début soon after returning from the 1983 under-nineteen tour of England. Representing Queensland in the Sheffield Shield for the first time, he acquitted himself well, taking four for 75 in Victoria's first innings at Brisbane in December, 1983. It did not take long after that for his name to be prominent in Test selection discussions and twelve months later, with the Australian team in desperate need of fresh blood to contend with the rampant West Indians, he was brought into the team for the fourth Test in Melbourne. He had a memorable début, with match figures of six for 183 from 48 overs, including Vivian Richards, lbw for a duck in West Indies' second innings after scoring a double-century in the first. The Australians had good reason for celebration, and perhaps optimism, after this Test, apart from the promise shown by McDermott: it provided them with their first draw of the series, and they went on to achieve a stirring victory in the final Test at Sydney a few days later. – T.G.

## NEAL RADFORD

These days, precious few bowlers achieve the traditional target of 100 wickets in a season. In 1983, four reached the milestone (Lever, Emburey, Underwood and Gifford); in 1984 only two (Lever and Hadlee) did so; and in the wretchedly wet summer of 1985 there was just one bowling centurion, a man whose odds, when the season began, to be the only bowler to complete the feat would have been astronomical.

NEAL VICTOR RADFORD was, it would be true to say, largely unknown in England outside the cloistered confines of the county dressing-rooms. He had spent five seasons with Lancashire, taking a modest number of wickets and attracting minimal attention, and the fact that he continued, each winter, to play with some distinction in South Africa's Currie Cup meant little to the average English cricket-watcher.

In 1985, all this was to change quite dramatically. Radford took 100 wickets in Championship cricket alone and made such an impression on the people in power that he was named, in September, as bowling standby for England's two winter tours, the full trip to the West Indies and the B team mission to Bangladesh, Sri Lanka and Zimbabwe. Even Radford himself, who flew back to South Africa for another term with the formidable Transvaal side, was hard put to explain why his English career had undergone such a transformation at the relatively advanced age of 28. There were, however, several contributory factors.

The first, oddly enough, was his sacking by Lancashire at the end of the 1984 season. Perhaps Radford, who was born in Luanshya, Northern Rhodesia (now Zambia) on June 7, 1957, and has a degree of the native southern African confidence about him, did not quite hit it off with the earthier temperaments at Old Trafford. Certainly, after five seasons in which he never once totalled 50 wickets, let alone 100, Lancashire appeared to have few regrets about letting him go. But hereabouts events began to conspire in Radford's favour. He was now officially considered English, having completed his qualification period. He was a free agent of the right age and bowling type to suit any number of counties. Offers began to filter through. Hampshire and Warwickshire pursued their interest in him, but Radford chose Worcestershire. He had chosen well.

After the almost inevitable lean spell which followed the adoption of an ambitious youth policy, Worcestershire began last summer to fulfil the air of promise which had persisted for some while around New Road. Radford became an important link in a thriving and ambitious young outfit.

Michael Vockins, Secretary of the county, explains: "We had been building a side over a period of years and Neal seemed ideal. Clearly, he had ability and potential which had not been fully justified. We took a chance on the theory that a change of county would provide him with the right stimulus, and we soon found that we had a great worker and a super chap."

Radford, who had married a Lancashire girl, Lynne, in the close-season, moved into a new home in Worcester and began his English cricket career all over again: he was a new bowler. Mike Gatting, the Middlesex captain, recalls: "I had faced him before when he was with Lancashire but he was nothing like as dangerous. When we played Worcestershire he consistently moved the ball off the seam. He is not very quick but he does enough with the ball to be dangerous."

Radford, thriving on the emergence alongside him of such talents as Steve Rhodes, Graeme Hick and David Smith, began to play an increasingly significant role in the Worcestershire side as the season progressed. The story was told by his bowling returns. Vockins says: "Neal is the type who wants to bowl every day and is not happy unless he is involved. We were able to give him a lot of bowling, which did wonders for his confidence and showed through in his figures."

Consistently, he would take three or four wickets in an innings. Then, on a late-July Eastbourne pitch which helped him just enough, he took six for 76 against Sussex, impressing all those who faced him with his ability to move the ball. August was even more successful, launched by probably the most satisfying of all games as he scored runs (57 not out) and took wickets in a comprehensive defeat of his former employers, Lancashire. Many at Old Trafford now understandably felt aggrieved that a bowler of such capabilities had been released, but the question persists: would he have shown such an advance without a change of scene?

Later in August, Radford was to cause more devastation, taking five wickets against Essex and then crowning his season in the Bank Holiday matches against Worcestershire's local rivals, Warwickshire. He came to the crease on the Saturday morning with his side in ruins at 41 for six, rescued the innings with a top score of 34, and then bowled Warwickshire out for 94 with his Championship-best figures of six for 45. Worcestershire won that game, and won also in the John Player League on the Sunday, when the now buoyant Radford took four for 24.

Dark-haired, a little under six feet tall and with an economical build for one who bowls so many overs, Radford was undoubtedly county cricket's success story of 1985. His parents, Edith and Victor, would have been proud, and so too his brother Wayne, who has played for Glamorgan's second team and as a professional in the South Wales leagues. What is more, Worcestershire deserve to be proud: this was an instance of a county taking a chance with a discarded player whose talent and temperament had been questioned, backing their judgement by giving him ample opportunity, and then being richly rewarded. – A.L.

## TIM ROBINSON

For years English cricket followers watched jealously as other countries produced batsmen from nowhere, fully cooked and ready to play major Test innings, while England players had to marinate for years before they could match them. Then came ROBERT TIMOTHY ROBINSON, for whom everything went right from the moment he was chosen for the Indian tour in September 1984 until he got married in November 1985. And one trusts he lives happily ever after as well.

In his first eleven Test matches, against India and Australia, Robinson scored 934 runs at an average of 62.26, statistics which, a pedant might have argued, made him the best batsman of all time besides Bradman. No sane person believed that, least of all a down-to-earth fellow like Robinson; the greatest trial, against West Indies, was still to come. Beyond dispute, though, England have unearthed an opening bat of surprising ability, with a beautiful big-match temperament, whose advent played a major part in the team's revival after the disasters of 1984.

Robinson's triumphs included three major centuries: 160 at Delhi, 175 at Headingley and 148 at Edgbaston. On top of that he was Best Supporting Actor in the great Gatting-Fowler show at Madras: and if he had a few cheap runs when the awful Trent Bridge Test was at the embalmers, they were cancelled out by a widespread suspicion that, on début at Bombay, he was victim of the umpires' double – caught missing and lbw hitting.

In a sense, Robinson began the England resurgence. His innings at Delhi set up the win that ended the thirteen-match blank sequence. But for people at home that was barely more than a long-distance rumour. Acceptance came only when he made a spectacular impact on his first home Test at Headingley. As Robinson walked out to bat there, his eye was caught by a banner reading: "Where is Geoff Boycott?" When he was finally out, applauded to the pavilion by 20,000 Yorkshire converts after one of the great English Test Saturdays, and patted on the head by Botham, who had briefly overshadowed him, he was told he had a visitor. "I didn't know what to say or what to call him", Robinson recalled later. "Geoffrey or Mr Boycott. I'd never spoken to him before except to say good morning. He just wanted to say congratulations, and that meant a lot to me."

For Robinson, Boycott has always been the model. At Rajkot, when he scored the century in a drab game against West Zone that ensured his Test place, there was a point where he had already done enough and the cool of the pavilion began to seem overwhelmingly inviting. Robinson just began muttering to himself: "I mustn't get out now. Boycott wouldn't get out now." The Boycott influence goes back a long way. Between the ages of five and ten – he was born on November 21, 1958 – just as Geoffrey's every move was becoming a local obsession, Robinson lived near Sheffield. He went back there to university, and his wife is a Rotherham girl. He realised he might be winning when her family started looking for his score before Boycott's.

You can see evidence, too, in the bottom-handed square driving – but Robinson has learned to play long innings without making enemies, without forgetting cricket is a team game or subordinating run-getting to crease-occupation. "If I see a bad ball I hit it", he says. "If it is the first ball of a Test match, so be it." The master's mantle may not fit him perfectly yet, but it has certainly been to the dry cleaners.

It has taken a while for Robinson to grow into it. He was both precocious and a slow starter, having turned down Nottinghamshire at eighteen to do a degree in accountancy and financial management. The family are purest Nottinghamshire, from Sutton-in-Ashfield, and mostly colliers; the divisions caused by the miners' strike hit close to home. But Robinson's father escaped the pits and went into computing. After the Sheffield interlude, he moved to Dunstable, and his teenage son's serious cricket began there: first for the grammar school and then for the local club, who advertised for players to start a colts' team and got 50 replies. The applicants had to queue up and tell the coach, Pat Feakes, what they did. Robinson, having heard nearly all the others say they were batsmen, thought he had better fib. Fortunately, the club quickly cottoned on.

So did the nearest county, Northamptonshire. Their coach, Brian Reynolds, had Robinson in for a trial at sixteen and he went straight into the second team. But his mother had never liked the south and the Robinsons went back to Nottingham, where Frank Woodhead, the Trent Bridge coach, stepped in. In 1978, while still an undergraduate, Robinson made the first team.

His progress thereafter was not entirely serene. Nottinghamshire knew he had ability, but he did not make enough runs and those he did score mostly came on the leg side. By 1982 some thought he was going backwards. Robinson worked on his technique by borrowing the raised-bat stance from his captain, Clive Rice, which he is convinced helps keep him sideways-on. The off-side runs started flowing: in 1983 he passed 1,500 runs and won his county cap; in 1984 he scored 2,000 and made the tour.

Against the West Indians in 1984, Robinson's Nottinghamshire opening partner, Chris Broad, was chosen ahead of him, despite a steady undercurrent from Trent Bridge that the selectors had picked the wrong man. Broad was unlucky not to tour, having had to face the fire; but the doubts at Trent Bridge largely concerned Robinson's ability against top-class spin, not pace. His ability to deal with both is helped by his obvious level-headedness. When he saw videos of himself batting against Australia in the one-day internationals, he was not so much taken by the sight of himself on telly as distressed by signs that he was getting out of position on the front foot. He immediately got his pal Eddie Hemmings to help him sort out the problem in the nets.

He is determined to go on that way. One of his main satisfactions in 1985 was that he kept making runs for Nottinghamshire in between Tests. But he enjoys being famous: "It's still a great thrill for a stranger to come up and say 'Well done'. I don't think I'll ever get bored with that." After all the blasé superstars of recent years, Robinson is a tonic. Over the years to come the congratulations might well become just a little more routine – M.E.

## AS LUCK WOULD HAVE IT

[*Ken Kelly*

A crucial moment in the Ashes series. Australia looked to be saving the fifth Test at Edgbaston when Phillips, who had made 59, forced a short ball from Edmonds hard to the off-side. As Lamb took evasive action, the ball ricochetted gently from his right ankle to Gower, standing alongside him at silly point. This was a misfortune from which Australia never recovered.

THE GAME GOES ON

[*Adrian Murrell*

England's eventually successful tour of India had a most distressing start. On the day of the team's arrival in the country, Mrs Indira Gandhi was assassinated. Less than a month later the British Deputy High Commissioner in Bombay was murdered on his way to his office, the morning after entertaining the England players. Here, before the start of the first Test match soon afterwards, the England players stand in silent tribute. The first two Test matches drew disappointing crowds.

## INDIA'S NEW IDOL

[*Adrian Murrell*

Mohammad Azharuddin made a brilliant start to his Test career, scoring a century in each of his first three Test matches, all against England. Here, upon reaching the third of them in Kanpur, he is congratulated by Edmonds, as he soon will be by a young admirer.

ENGLAND'S SUCCESSFUL TEAM

[*Patrick Eagar*

The same team played for England in the last two Test matches against Australia, winning both by an innings. It was: *Back row:* P. R. Downton, J. E. Emburey, R. M. Ellison, L. B. Taylor, P. H. Edmonds, R. T. Robinson, B. W. Thomas (*physiotherapist*). *Front row:* A. J. Lamb, M. W. Gatting, D. I. Gower (*captain*), I. T. Botham, G. A. Gooch.

# KILTS AT LORD'S

[*Bill Smith*

Exactly 200 years after cricket is recorded as having first been played in Scotland, Freuchie, from Fifeshire, won the National Village Cricket Championship, organised by *The Cricketer*. Their team, photographed before the final, was: *Back row:* Pipe Major A. Pirnie, A. S. Duncan, F. Irvine, M. Wilkie, G. Wilson, D. Y. F. Christie (*captain*), D. Cowan, P. Hepplewhite, B. Y. F. Christie, L. Horne (*scorer*). *Front row:* G. Crichton, A. N. Crichton, A. N. McNaughton, T. Trewartha, J. S. Irvine.

THE CARES OF CAPTAINCY

[*Patrick Eagar*
Allan Border had much on his mind during 1985, Australian cricket being in turmoil; but as a batsman, even as a captain, he enhanced his reputation.

vii

SIX MORE

[*Patrick Eagar*

Coming in when England were 572 for four in the fifth Test match, Botham drove his first ball into the Edgbaston pavilion. Of the record 80 6s which he hit during the season, this was one of the most spectacular. The bowler was McDermott, the wicket-keeper is Phillips.

FIVE CRICKETERS OF THE YEAR

[*David Munden*/*Bill Smith*

P. Bainbridge (Gloucestershire)

FIVE CRICKETERS OF THE YEAR

[*Patrick Eagar*

R. M. Ellison (Kent and England)

FIVE CRICKETERS OF THE YEAR

[*Patrick Eagar*

C. J. McDermott (Australia)

FIVE CRICKETERS OF THE YEAR

[*Ken Kelly*

N. V. Radford (Worcestershire)

## FIVE CRICKETERS OF THE YEAR

[*Patrick Eagar*

R. T. Robinson (Nottinghamshire and England)

# WHITHER CRICKET NOW?

By SIR DONALD BRADMAN

At the request of the Editor I wrote a short piece for the 1939 *Wisden*. My main theme then was a plea for cricket to adapt itself to the quickening tempo of modern life, for administrators to consider ways of speeding up the game, to provide more modern scoreboards (especially in England), to face up to financial problems, and so on. Little did I appreciate at the time what a revolution would engulf cricket before another 50 years had passed.

The great stadiums of Sydney and Melbourne now display huge electronic scoreboards costing millions of dollars and giving a wealth of information to the spectators. The enormous electric light towers turn night into day at the flick of a switch. That, in turn, demands the use of a white ball, and to satisfy the television and marketing moguls the players turn out in a variety of coloured outfits.

The whole scene stirs up human emotions ranging from those of a largely new and young audience (more liberally sprinkled with females than of yore), who yell and scream their support, to those of the dyed-in-the-wool lovers of Test cricket, who yearn for more peaceful, bygone days. As with so many things, it becomes well-nigh impossible to bring about a reconciliation between the opposing attitudes.

But where does the truth lie and what about the future?

Despite my deep feeling for the traditional game, and my conviction that a vast majority of players and the public still regard Test cricket as the supreme contest, we must accept that we live in a new era. If Sir Neville Cardus were alive today, I can well imagine how eloquently he would bemoan the huge attendances at pop concerts compared with the lack of support for opera or a Beethoven evening. But I am sure he would also admit that, irrespective of the quality of the music or the musicians, the public are primarily interested in entertainment. Perhaps he would throw in his well-known reference to an eagle, no matter how beautiful in flight, being no match for the Concorde. I am satisfied that one-day cricket, especially day/night cricket, is here to stay. If there is a threat to the survival of the game of cricket, that threat lies in the first-class arena, and it behoves the administrators to understand the challenge and face up to it.

I confess to a love for both types of game. Nothing can match the continuous cut and thrust of a Test match, where the advantage see-saws and the result is unpredictable to the last ball. I can't imagine any sporting event being more exciting than the tied Test between West Indies and Australia. It wasn't only the finish. Here you had two teams of great players, led by imaginative and intelligent captains determined from the first ball to pursue victory by adhering to the principles upon which the game was founded. The match had spin and speed, superb batting and fielding; every facet of the game was manifested as both sides strove for victory.

It starkly revealed the Achilles' heel of the limited-overs match, namely the premium placed on defensive bowling and negative and defensive field-placing. One can get bored to death watching countless singles being taken when even the world's fastest bowler may be operating with no slips and five men on the boundary.

But let me turn to the good things about one-day cricket.

It rids the game of the unutterable bore who thinks occupancy of the crease and his own personal aggrandisement are all that matter. It demands fieldsmen

[*The Advertiser, Adelaide*

Sir Donald Bradman, taken in 1984.

of great speed and agility with good throwing arms. The standard of fielding at all levels of cricket has undoubtedly been lifted. Running between the wickets, too, has taken on a new dimension. Risks must be taken to maintain the essential run-rate. Umpires are put under enormous pressure, having to adjudicate frequently on split-second issues: to their credit, I believe they have responded in a very positive manner and improved their standards.

Inevitably one sees the odd umpiring mistake, graphically portrayed by the modern marvel of the instant replay on television. With this new aid available, I should see no loss of face or pride if umpires were to agree, when in doubt about a decision, to seek arbitration from "the box". This could never apply to LBW, but for run-outs, and, on odd occasions, for stumpings or a disputed catch, it would seem logical.

My first-class playing career began in 1927, and I remain a Trustee of the Adelaide Oval and a member of the main South Australian Cricket Association committee. Having watched first-class cricket in 1921, I have seen as observer, player or administrator, all the great players of the last 65 years. Indeed, I can probably claim to span 75 years because many of the 1920-21 players also played before the Great War. It is still absolutely fascinating to me to watch and compare players of different generations.

How often I was asked in 1985 whether Clive Lloyd's West Indians were the best team of all time! Unhesitatingly I replied that they were the best fielding combination I have seen. But no matter how competent their batting, bowling and fielding, they were so reliant on fast bowlers that they became out of balance on a slow, turning pitch. In addition, their batting became vulnerable, which was proved in Sydney when Australia's two spinners, Bennett and Holland, tore the heart out of the West Indian batting to win a convincing victory for Australia. And without detracting from the skill of Bennett and Holland, it was clear to any knowledgeable observer that they were not of the quality of O'Reilly and Grimmett. To me these facts are indisputable and tend to place matters in their proper perspective. Australia's victory confirmed my view that my 1948 side was the best I ever saw, with Lloyd's 1984-85 team and Armstrong's 1920-21 Australian side not far behind. And my reading of history causes me to think Joe Darling's 1902 Australians were perhaps equal to any.

How lovely to be able to speculate without having to prove the answer!

Many cricket enthusiasts claim that the one-day game has brought in its wake a decline in batting technique. This may have some validity, but it is not necessarily true. People get confused between a normal mode of play and the essential improvisation needed to circumvent defensive fields. Vivian Richards and Clive Lloyd are marvellous examples of batsmen capable of coping quite adequately in both types of cricket without sacrificing any basic soundness of technique. The main difference in their one-day attitude has been a willingness to take the risk of lofting the ball over fieldsmen's heads. I doubt if modern players in general cut or pull quite as well as some of their forbears did, but I attribute this largely to the ultra-heavy bats they use. These hinder shots other than those of the perpendicular kind, such as the drive.

Undeniably the limited-overs game caters for a plethora of fast and medium-pace bowlers who tend to bowl just short of a length. In general it discourages, in fact it almost tolls the knell of, the slow leg-spinner. But here again one must acclaim the marvellous leg-spin bowling of the young Indian, Sivaramakrishnan, who proved against the best batting in the world in Sydney and Melbourne early in 1985 that he could bowl his ten-overs stint, get wickets, and still be economical. I don't doubt that O'Reilly, Grimmett, Benaud, Verity and others would have done the same. So perhaps, after all, the game is highlighting the fact that *top-quality* spinners can and will survive any challenge.

An interesting facet of the limited-overs game is the general rule governing bouncers. It unquestionably controls them in a sensible and practical way, and is a rule which I believe should be adopted in all grades of cricket without delay. It clearly reveals the way experimental laws could be used in one-day games to ascertain their effectiveness and/or desirability in first-class matches.

I also believe we have now reached the stage when some limitation in the length of a bowler's run-up is warranted. It would be the first and most logical step towards speeding up the over-rate. In Australia that magnificent player, Malcolm Marshall (excluding Frank Tyson, the fastest bowler I have seen since Larwood), has repeatedly shown us that a short run-up is sufficient to generate maximum speed.

The money now being paid to players has spawned professionalism beyond anything dreamed of 50 years ago. With so much money at stake I doubt if the modern professionals enjoy their cricket as much as did the players who were financially independent of the game and played purely for the love of it. Perhaps, too, monetary reward is responsible for some of the theatrical performances and even bad manners occasionally portrayed in recent years on the field. Happily I feel this unhealthy phase is on the wane, as players understand that good sportsmanship and keen competitiveness are not incompatible.

Most people agree that too much cricket was played during the Australian summer of 1984-85, owing to the Melbourne anniversary tournament being added to the schedule. It highlighted the need to strike a proper balance between one-day games and normal first-class matches. The attendances at Sheffield Shield matches were adversely affected. Indeed, the mounting losses on Shield games, now amounting to hundreds of thousands of dollars annually, constitute the most seemingly intractable problem confronting Australian cricket today. We need the Shield to produce Test cricketers, but can receipts from sponsorship, television rights etc, continue to make up the losses? The current threat to the legality of certain sponsorships compounds the problem.

Looking on the bright side, 1984-85 produced the best Indian and Pakistan teams of my lifetime, and that is a great gain for the future of cricket in the international sphere. The advance of these two coincided with some lack-lustre efforts from England and Australia.

Lovers of cricket will find in the pages of *Wisden* plenty of evidence that cricket has had its problems for a century past. Things have not changed much. Problems are still there – they are just different. It remains for players and administrators to accept the challenge to keep cricket alive and vibrant, and not to shrink from the decisions needed to ensure that end.

# ALAN KNOTT – A THOROUGH GENIUS

By J. M. BREARLEY

Alan Knott was a great cricketer. In my view he was also the best wicket-keeper of his time. He had a good physique for the job – short, low-to-the-ground, agile and quick (though he himself foresees a new breed of tall 'keepers by analogy with tall goalkeepers, and maintains that he had to stretch so much because he was not particularly supple, especially in the hips). He had marvellous hands. Physically he kept himself extremely fit, and was an assiduous practiser. His technique was not classical; he took catches with one hand when he might have got two to the ball, and he sometimes dived when he could have reached the ball without falling. He had a sound reason for both – simply that for him these methods were more natural and more effective. His judgement about what to go for was unerring. As a first slip I always seemed to know when Alan would go for a catch in front of me, and I was never baulked by him or distracted by any tentativeness on his part. Standing up, he took the low ball without bending his knees and with his legs together. This gave him the right amount of give, against his legs. Moreover, if he missed it with his hands, the ball would not go for byes, and if the edge beat the gloves, there was no knee or elbow sticking out to obscure first slip's view, or to deflect the ball.

His constant exercising was a reflection of his perfectionism, as was the care he took to have essential equipment in perfect order. He kept and rehabilitated a favourite old bat specially for Tests; he spent the afternoon before the Melbourne Centenary Test in town getting a loose stitch from the webbing of a glove repaired, just in case he should uncharacteristically have to rely on it to make a catch.

He was also prepared to be unconventional in his gear, if it helped the job in hand. He once saw the New Zealand wicket-keeper, Ken Wadsworth, struck on the inside of the knee by an awkward throw-in; his pad had swivelled round as he moved towards the ball and had left the knee unprotected. As a result, Knott took to taping his pads to his trousers rather than using the middle strap and buckle; he thereby also reduced chafing. He did not mind at all that the effect was untidy: I have never known a cricketer who was less concerned with style for its own sake. He could never earn a living as a cosmetics salesman!

Though brilliant, he eschewed the flamboyant. He stood back to medium-pacers more than his predecessors, not at all for safety-first or to avoid error, but as the result of a cool calculation as to the overall effectiveness to the side.

As I say, he would have been in my book a more or less automatic selection for any team on the strength of his 'keeping alone. When his batting was put in the scales, all doubt fell away. For he was also a genius – a minor genius – with the bat. Here too, he was no purist for the sake of orthodoxy. Against fast bowling he realised that he had a better chance of playing a lifting delivery if he changed his grip so as to have his top hand behind the handle; this enables the batsman to hold his hands in front of his face and keep the bat straight. He evolved a kind of French cricket technique for use when he first went in against the quickest bowlers; but soon took every opportunity to attack, clipping the ball square on either side of the wicket and cutting deftly, often, intentionally, over the slips' heads. He reckons that if he were starting his career now he would learn to hook fast bowling, and cites the hours of practice Viv Richards went through, after a disastrous tour of Australia, with Andy Roberts bowling bouncers at him in Antigua.

Against fast bowlers, Knott's grip, stance and technique were totally different from those he adopted against medium-pacers and especially against

*Left:* ". . . he would have been in my book a more or less automatic selection for any team on the strength of his 'keeping alone. When his batting was put in the scales, all doubt fell away. For he was a genius – a minor genius – with the bat."

*Below:* Rodney Marsh is the victim of Alan Knott's leg-side catch at Headingley in 1977. Ian Botham was the bowler.

[*Patrick Eagar*

spinners. He might start an innings in an orthodox vein but quickly ventured into the unusual. He played a sort of off-glide to good effect, particularly against off-spinners. His sweeping was unique; on a drying pitch at Canterbury, he once played fifteen consecutive balls from Edmonds and Emburey with this shot and never missed or mis-hit one. His secret was to get low, watch the ball, and not try to hit it too hard. But many of us could follow all those instructions and still make a hash of it! I remember an innings against India at Bangalore in 1977. The pitch had deteriorated to the point where good spinners were almost unplayable. Yet "the flea" kept dancing down the pitch to Bedi and Prasanna and chipping them over mid-wicket or extra-cover. The cheek and verve of this innings (he finished with 81 not out) were unmatched in my experience.

Behind all his extravagances as a batsman – as with his idiosyncracies as a 'keeper – there were the basic skills. His head was always steady, and he was capable of a long defensive innings as well as of impish aggression. He was completely unselfish.

He was courageous too. But the courage that marked him out, for me, was of a more broad-based kind. He had the guts, the confidence and occasionally the stubbornness to stick to his method if he felt that he was right.

Personal health was one area in which these attitudes were expressed. Alan was no hypochondriac, but he was keenly interested in the state of his own body. He fell ill one evening in Delhi and in the middle of the night knocked on the physiotherapist's door, bearing a sample of what had recently been in his stomach. He wanted no sketchily based diagnosis. He was equally fussy about what went *into* his stomach. No cheese and meat at the same meal, for example. He drank little, and avoided parties. He needed eight hours of sleep, yet had to have a couple of hours clear for ablutions and exercises before breakfast (so it was not always easy to find room-partners for him on tour). After hurting his neck in two car accidents in the mid-seventies, he had his car seat remodelled. And he was so chary of draughts that he would come away from a day's play in India wearing three sweaters, an anorak with the hood up, and dark glasses. The lack of a surgical mask must have been an oversight. He was never unfit for a Test, though once, in 1976 against West Indies, he played too soon, he thought, after breaking a finger.

Tactically he was sound, though not without his biases. He had an exaggerated respect for pace, and would usually advise his captain to keep the seamers on. He sometimes overrated the players he knew best, though he was capable of hard judgements (as when he said of a colleague that he had learned nothing during his years in the game).

Politically, he was involved in both the major cricketing rebellions of our time, Packer's in 1977 and the South African Breweries' tour of 1982. Typically, his views were well thought out, courteously expressed and tenaciously held.

The man is all-of-a-piece, and at the heart of his life lie his close family ties and religious conviction. Leaving his wife and son behind for four months at a time became an insupportable wrench; and one of the attractions of World Series Cricket for him was the welcome given to families. He was able to take a flat in Sydney with his family, and use it as his home base for the season, whereas the English establishment were less sympathetic. Their attitude often represented an unwarranted suspicion based on their inability to understand him. Some felt it outrageous that a cricketer should lay down conditions about his wife's accompanying him during an England tour. He was not, it is true, ever "one of the boys"; but he was a complete professional and team-man. Even his stretching exercises on the field were viewed in some quarters with a surprising hostility, as if they were for show. Nothing could have been further from the truth.

As for religion, he became a Christian in 1974. This, he has said, changed his whole attitude to life. He came to see his behaviour during the rather ill-tempered series in India in 1972-73 as reprehensible. From then on, he was on the field an unfailing example to us all. He was generous to others: Paul Downton acknowledges the many tips and kindnesses he received from Alan while on the Kent staff and since. In 1977, when we won the Ashes at Headingley, "Knotty" seized a bail as a souvenir for the young Ian Botham, playing in his second Test, who was off the field injured at the end of the match.

His religious beliefs also helped him to a more philosophical attitude to his own performance. He became less concerned about the *outcome* of his play, and focused more on simply trying as hard as he could in the way he felt was most likely to succeed. His view is that it is the inner attitude that counts; the results will then look after themselves. He is utterly modest, and equally without false modesty.

Alan Knott has retired from the game while still playing it at a very high standard. In 1985 he was regarded by virtually all the top players as the best 'keeper in England. His decision to go was based, partly, on an ankle injury which he was told could get worse if he carried on. He reaches 40 in April of this year, not long after Les Ames's 80th birthday and Godfrey Evans's 65th. He hopes to coach, to help produce, perhaps, a successor to this line of Kent and England wicket-keepers. He will be a splendid coach, wise, thoughtful, kindly and occasionally controversial.

I cannot think of any cricketer, with the possible exception of Ian Botham, whose game has given me more pleasure.

## A. P. E. KNOTT – TEST CAREER

| | *T* | *I* | *NO* | *Runs* | *HI* | *Avge* | *50s* | *100s* | *Ct* | *St* |
|---|---|---|---|---|---|---|---|---|---|---|
| 1967 v Pakistan | 2 | 2 | 0 | 28 | 28 | 14.00 | – | – | 12 | 1 |
| 1967-68 v West Indies | 2 | 3 | 2 | 149 | 73* | 149.00 | 2 | – | 4 | 0 |
| 1968 v Australia | 5 | 8 | 1 | 116 | 34 | 16.57 | – | – | 11 | 4 |
| 1968-69 v Pakistan | 3 | 4 | 1 | 180 | 96* | 60.00 | 2 | – | 6 | 0 |
| 1969 v West Indies | 3 | 5 | 0 | 139 | 53 | 27.80 | 1 | – | 10 | 1 |
| 1969 v New Zealand | 3 | 4 | 0 | 54 | 21 | 13.50 | – | – | 9 | 2 |
| 1970-71 v Australia | 6 | 9 | 2 | 222 | 73 | 31.71 | 1 | – | 21 | 3 |
| 1970-71 v New Zealand | 1 | 2 | 0 | 197 | 101 | 98.50 | 1 | 1 | 0 | 0 |
| 1971 v Pakistan | 3 | 4 | 1 | 137 | 116 | 45.66 | – | 1 | 10 | 1 |
| 1971 v India | 3 | 5 | 0 | 223 | 90 | 44.60 | 2 | – | 10 | 1 |
| 1972 v Australia | 5 | 8 | 0 | 229 | 92 | 28.62 | 2 | – | 17 | 0 |
| 1972-73 v India | 5 | 8 | 0 | 168 | 56 | 21.00 | 1 | – | 11 | 1 |
| 1972-73 v Pakistan | 3 | 5 | 1 | 199 | 71 | 49.75 | 2 | – | 4 | 0 |
| 1973 v New Zealand | 3 | 5 | 0 | 72 | 49 | 14.40 | – | – | 12 | 0 |
| 1973 v West Indies | 3 | 5 | 1 | 35 | 21 | 8.75 | – | – | 7 | 0 |
| 1973-74 v West Indies | 5 | 9 | 1 | 365 | 87 | 45.62 | 3 | – | 4 | 0 |
| 1974 v India | 3 | 2 | 0 | 26 | 26 | 13.00 | – | – | 15 | 1 |
| 1974 v Pakistan | 3 | 4 | 0 | 132 | 83 | 33.00 | 1 | – | 7 | 0 |
| 1974-75 v Australia | 6 | 11 | 1 | 364 | 106 | 36.40 | 3 | 1 | 22 | 1 |
| 1974-75 v New Zealand | 2 | 1 | 1 | 29 | 29* | – | – | – | 3 | 0 |
| 1975 v Australia | 4 | 8 | 1 | 261 | 69 | 37.28 | 2 | – | 4 | 0 |
| 1976 v West Indies | 5 | 9 | 0 | 270 | 116 | 30.00 | 2 | 1 | 5 | 1 |
| 1976-77 v India | 5 | 8 | 1 | 268 | 81* | 38.28 | 2 | – | 13 | 2 |
| 1976-77 v Australia | 1 | 2 | 0 | 57 | 42 | 28.50 | – | – | 4 | 0 |
| 1977 v Australia | 5 | 7 | 0 | 255 | 135 | 36.42 | 1 | 1 | 12 | 0 |
| 1980 v West Indies | 4 | 7 | 0 | 36 | 9 | 5.14 | – | – | 11 | 0 |
| 1981 v Australia | 2 | 4 | 1 | 178 | 70* | 59.33 | 2 | – | 6 | 0 |
| TOTALS | 95 | 149 | 15 | 4,389 | 135 | 32.75 | 30 | 5 | 250 | 19 |

* *Signifies not out.*

**In 20 one-day internationals**, Alan Knott's record is as follows: **Batting:** 14 innings, 4 not out innings, 200 runs, HI 50, average 20.00; **Dismissals:** 15 catches, 1 stumping.

## A. P. E. KNOTT – FIRST-CLASS CAREER

| | *M* | *I* | *NO* | *Runs* | *HI* | *Avge* | *50s* | *100s* | *Ct* | *St* |
|---|---|---|---|---|---|---|---|---|---|---|
| 1964 ......... | 10 | 16 | 4 | 160 | 55 | 13.33 | 1 | – | 26 | 4 |
| 1964-65 ...... | 4 | 7 | 3 | 182 | 66 | 45.50 | 1 | – | 6 | 3 |
| 1965 ......... | 32 | 44 | 8 | 630 | 57 | 17.50 | 1 | – | 74 | 10 |
| 1966 ......... | 31 | 46 | 11 | 761 | 48* | 21.74 | – | – | 73 | 8 |
| 1966-67 ...... | 7 | 9 | 0 | 326 | 101 | 36.22 | 2 | 1 | 11 | 11 |
| 1967 ......... | 27 | 38 | 5 | 732 | 74 | 22.18 | 4 | – | 90 | 8 |
| 1967-68 ...... | 7 | 10 | 7 | 267 | 73* | 89.00 | 3 | – | 17 | 3 |
| 1968 ......... | 28 | 44 | 4 | 1,033 | 73 | 25.82 | 6 | – | 58 | 12 |
| 1968-69 ...... | 7 | 6 | 2 | 273 | 96* | 68.25 | 3 | – | 7 | 5 |
| 1969 ......... | 21 | 32 | 1 | 644 | 102 | 20.77 | 2 | 1 | 46 | 9 |
| 1969-70 ...... | 2 | 2 | 0 | 53 | 51 | 26.50 | 1 | – | 6 | 0 |
| 1970 ......... | 22 | 29 | 7 | 519 | 51* | 23.59 | 2 | – | 62 | 2 |
| 1970-71 ...... | 12 | 17 | 5 | 539 | 101 | 44.91 | 2 | 1 | 24 | 4 |
| 1971 ......... | 23 | 35 | 6 | 1,209 | 128* | 41.68 | 6 | 3 | 59 | 4 |
| 1972 ......... | 15 | 23 | 5 | 765 | 127* | 42.50 | 4 | 2 | 33 | 2 |
| 1972-73 ...... | 13 | 20 | 3 | 666 | 156 | 39.17 | 3 | 1 | 23 | 2 |
| 1973 ......... | 18 | 28 | 8 | 719 | 87 | 35.95 | 6 | – | 59 | 1 |
| 1973-74 ...... | 10 | 17 | 1 | 474 | 87 | 29.62 | 3 | – | 14 | 0 |
| 1974 ......... | 15 | 21 | 1 | 254 | 83 | 12.70 | 1 | – | 41 | 4 |
| 1974-75 ...... | 14 | 21 | 4 | 723 | 106* | 42.52 | 6 | 1 | 44 | 2 |
| 1975 ......... | 16 | 27 | 7 | 799 | 105* | 39.95 | 4 | 1 | 43 | 2 |
| 1976 ......... | 17 | 29 | 4 | 938 | 144 | 37.52 | 7 | 2 | 35 | 3 |
| 1976-77 ...... | 12 | 19 | 4 | 563 | 108* | 37.53 | 3 | 1 | 30 | 2 |
| 1977 ......... | 16 | 20 | 2 | 771 | 135 | 42.83 | 4 | 2 | 47 | 3 |
| 1979 ......... | 10 | 11 | 2 | 243 | 63 | 27.00 | 1 | – | 15 | 1 |
| 1980 ......... | 20 | 28 | 4 | 540 | 85* | 22.50 | 1 | – | 39 | 3 |
| 1981 ......... | 21 | 32 | 5 | 795 | 70* | 29.44 | 6 | – | 45 | 8 |
| 1981-82 ...... | 4 | 6 | 0 | 63 | 27 | 10.50 | – | – | 17 | 0 |
| 1982 ......... | 21 | 32 | 5 | 942 | 115* | 34.88 | 6 | 1 | 46 | 7 |
| 1983 ......... | 23 | 30 | 9 | 848 | 92* | 40.38 | 6 | – | 39 | 8 |
| 1984 ......... | 14 | 22 | 2 | 295 | 43 | 14.75 | – | – | 29 | 1 |
| 1985 ......... | 20 | 24 | 5 | 379 | 87* | 19.94 | 2 | – | 53 | 1 |
| TOTALS | 512 | 745 | 134 | 18,105 | 165* | 29.63 | 97 | 17 | 1,211 | 133 |

## LIMITED-OVERS MATCHES FOR KENT

| | *M* | *I* | *NO* | *Runs* | *HI* | *Avge* | *50s* | *Ct* | *St* |
|---|---|---|---|---|---|---|---|---|---|
| John Player League .... | 170 | 127 | 27 | 1,628 | 60 | 16.28 | 3 | 183 | 35 |
| Benson and Hedges Cup. | 68 | 58 | 7 | 888 | 65 | 17.41 | 2 | 79 | 9 |
| Gillette Cup .......... | 31 | 25 | 5 | 362 | 46 | 18.10 | – | 38 | 5 |
| NatWest Bank Trophy . | 15 | 11 | 0 | 93 | 24 | 8.45 | – | 21 | 1 |

# A FINANCIAL REVOLUTION

By JACK BANNISTER

Whatever the rights and wrongs of the Packer issue, it accelerated changes in English first-class cricket, some of which were already in the pipeline, so rapidly that within a decade there has taken place the biggest financial revolution in the history of the game. Starting from the top, the Test match payments to players and umpires have increased roughly sevenfold, and even at the bottom end of the scale, the successful introduction of a minimum wage in 1979 has more or less tripled county players' salaries. For players with the affluent clubs it may have done even more, and for very few has it done any less.

At the beginning of the 1977 season, an England player received £74 for a one-day international, £210 for a five-day Test match, and around £3,000 for an overseas tour. Add to that a county salary of £3,500, and a top regular England player in a year containing six home Test matches could earn directly from his skills a maximum of £4,500 from Test cricket and £8,000 in all, the equivalent of, say, £20,000 today.

Comparative figures for last year were £500 for a one-day international, £1,500 for a five-day Test, a touring fee of at least £12,000, and a county salary of only marginally less. That adds up to nearly £35,000, and the extra awards available from Cornhill, Texaco and the domestic sponsors mean that the top half-dozen England players earned in 1985 around £40,000 from actually playing cricket. Other spin-offs, including individual sponsorship and advertising contracts, as well as the loan of a car, vary according to the individual.

Nor have umpires been left behind, the ratio increase in their big-match fees being similar to that of the players. Ten years ago the fee for standing in a one-day international was £68 and in a full Test match £173. The corresponding figures are now £400 and £1,200 respectively, and a study of the difference in basic salaries available in 1977 and 1986 explains why there is now an umpires' waiting list, compared with a decade ago, when, annually, there was the threat of a shortage. By last year their annual basic salary had moved from £1,740 to £7,300, with a likely increase of around five per cent for 1986. For a top Test match umpire, standing in two Test matches and a one-day international, the marked improvement in the game's finances has brought an increase in annual salary from £2,154 to £10,460. Again, obviously, the improvement is less in real terms, after inflation has been evaluated, but it still marks a considerable upgrading, and the salary is for only about 90 days' work. Also, like the players, umpires live for most of the summer off an overnight expense figure, from which they would not make a loss, and they have their meals provided during matches. The seven-month close-season affords other earning opportunities, either through businesses they have established at the end of their playing careers, the majority of umpires being ex-players, or through other employment including coaching at home or overseas.

As a result of this increased remuneration, there is now a reserve list of three umpires in addition to the full list of 24, and there was no shortage of applicants last winter even for the reserve list. Another point is that the average age of the arbiters has been dramatically reduced in the last few years: only one umpire is now near the retiring age of 65, and with one exception the remainder are under 55.

And what about the average county player? Here, too, there has been a considerable improvement; but before the comparative figures are given for

[Patrick Eagar

"There has been a remarkable increase in the income from sponsorship generated at Board level." Here Mike Gatting, as captain of Middlesex, the 1985 county champions, receives the winners' prize of £20,000.

now and 1979, the progress towards the reluctant acceptance of a minimum wage by the clubs should be explained. The year of its introduction was 1979, and the arguments against it were many. No two clubs paid the same salaries, or even by the same method. Widely differing loyalty bonuses and appearance fees were paid, with expenses particularly variable. Another argument was that few clubs could afford the big increase in their overall wage bill: this would be inevitable, particularly for the younger players. There was also the implied threat that reductions in county staffs would have to be made with so much extra money to be found. The argument *for* the introduction of a minimum scale was that in 1977 one reserve county wicket-keeper received £400.

Another consideration in favour of a minimum scale was that it would lessen the chances of wealthier clubs luring away the more promising youngsters from other clubs. By persuading those clubs to generate more income and pay higher wages, fears of increased movement by players between clubs would accordingly be reduced. The counties finally agreed to dip their toes into the water in 1979, but only on a voluntary basis for the first year. Experience showed that some clubs were already meeting or exceeding the agreed target figure of £4,500 as a minimum wage. Others had shortfalls to meet of varying amounts, in one case £18,000.

Tribute must be paid to the late Edmund King of Warwickshire, who walked the tightrope between allaying the fears of the players that the voluntary scheme might be abused by the clubs, and those of the clubs who feared that a minimum wage was the thin end of a wedge which would eventually push the weaker counties out of existence. Thanks to Mr King's efforts, an annual platform of negotiation was established which has benefited everyone. The players have moved from a non-mandatory £4,500, inclusive of sponsors' awards and bonuses, to £7,665, exclusive of those monies. This effectively means that in 1986 an ordinary capped player (in his third year of being capped, because there are two annual steps between the awarding of a cap and the progression to the full minimum wage) will receive a minimum of £8,000, with at least five counties paying more than that, in one case considerably more.

The Test and County Cricket Board also fund a Group Retirement Scheme for players, in which fourteen clubs participate. Leicestershire, Kent and Nottinghamshire provide alternative schemes. Of a player's annual cricket earnings, $5\frac{1}{4}$ per cent go into this fund, which will amount this year to at least another tax-free £400 for each of them.

Uncapped players are treated according to age up to 23. Over that they receive a minimum of £4,250, plus, for a lot of them, rewards for length of service. In addition, a mandatory minimum payment will be made this year to uncapped players of £10 for each day played in the first team, whether in one-day matches or Championship games.

Many argue that despite this improvement the gap between the Test star and the "bread-and-butter" county cricketer is too wide to be explained satisfactorily by the argument that extra skills merit extra rewards. Indeed, because senior England players in the early eighties agreed with this, there have been only nominal increases in Test fees in the last four years.

The result of this wage explosion is that the overall county wage bill in 1978 of £700,000 has risen to at least £2,000,000. Yet the argument that such an increase would bring about a reduction in the size of county staffs has been rebutted by an increase in the number of registered and contracted players from 300 eight years ago to a current 350. It is also irrefutable that the introduction of a regularised minimum scale has made the game financially more attractive to youngsters as a profession. The other fear, held by some clubs, that cricket would follow soccer into bankruptcy is unfounded because, unlike the winter game where players make their wage demands individually and with little concern for football's financial structure, negotiators for the Cricketers' Association, being aware of the TCCB's overall annual income, know what can and cannot be afforded.

But how have the counties found so much extra money? A greater awareness of the need to maximise the use of their facilities all the year round would not alone have sufficed. There has been, as well, a remarkable increase in the income from sponsorship generated at Board level. At the beginning of the 1977 season, the TCCB's Marketing Committee had contracts worth £476,000. In 1985 these totalled £2,321,000. Therein lies one of the satisfactory effects of the Packer "revolution". Although such a process was already slowly evolving in English cricket, it was undoubtedly accelerated.

Umpires' complaints that, with so much extra money to be won, their job is being made nearly intolerable have to be tempered by the commensurate increase in their own rewards. But on-field behaviour does seem to have declined marginally, accompanied by more attempts to pressurise umpires. With money comes power and responsibility, and the players must make a conscious effort to prevent the first-class game from travelling even the shortest step down the wrong path, as would seem to have happened in Australia. There, the extra rewards have driven players and umpires apart. First-class cricket in England provides the only full-time professional circuit in the world, and in that it is unique. In its standards of on-field behaviour it is also unique, and to see that that continues to be so is the responsibility of everyone, particularly the players. Having got the rewards they asked for, they must show that they deserve them.

# 1903 – THE WETTEST SUMMER OF THEM ALL?

By JOHN KITCHIN

Loud roar'd the dreadful thunder,
The rain a deluge shower'd.

Andrew Cherry (1762-1822)

Surveys of cricket in England in this century tend to be focused on the commanding heights of the period. Such peaks as 1921, 1934 and 1947 come under frequent scrutiny, because cricket evolved as a pastime to be played and enjoyed ideally under blue skies and a blazing sun, and these were beautiful summers. This survey, though, must plumb the depths and walk the valleys, rain and yet more rain being its theme. In making a study of the wet seasons, I have allowed the testimony of contemporary witnesses to colour the scene. As will be seen, they have been inclined to pronounce their verdicts on a summer as "the worst ever" without, perhaps, due regard to objective judgement.

The curtain rises in 1903, a year overshadowed by a dramatic series between England and Australia twelve months earlier. "Never", according to the 1904 *Wisden*, "has county cricket been so much affected by rain as in 1903. The summer was the wettest within the experience of anyone now playing first-class cricket, worse even than 1879, and in nearly all parts of the country the game had to contend with overwhelming disadvantages. As was inevitable under such conditions, the various county clubs suffered severely in pocket . . . ."

Thereafter, the splendours of the Golden Age were not again dimmed until 1912. Then, "the Championship was more seriously affected than in any previous season; Yorkshire, the champions, had their matches interfered with to such a terrible extent that they lost £1,000." The Triangular Tournament was condemned by the Fates to fight against a combination of adverse conditions "which could hardly be imagined".

In 1924 even H. S. Altham's enthusiasm was chilled by his experiences as a coach at Winchester. He opened his review of Public School cricket: "Few even of the most zealous of enthusiasts can have been altogether sorry when the season of 1924 came to an end. A season of cloud and rain, of ruined wickets, of abandoned matches, and of disappointed hopes. Up and down the country cricketers of every category had a sorry time; the county clubs saw match after match make inroads into their funds or pile a balance even greater against them; the weekend player was again and again cheated of his jealously expected games, and the school cricketer was, perhaps, the hardest hit of all." In short, the summer of 1924 was without question "the worst since 1879" according to Mr Altham, who emphasised the point by quoting H. H. Stephenson of Surrey, and himself a great coach, who referred to 1879 as being "impossible" for coaching. The wet summers of 1903 and 1912 were either discounted or overlooked in an understandable desire not to minimise the traumas of the year just past.

Next come the summers of 1930, 1931 and 1932, which were all declared by contemporaries to be wetter than normal, though the scoring of Don Bradman in 1930 (2,960 runs at 98.66) and Herbert Sutcliffe in the two subsequent years (3,006 at 96.96 in 1931 and 3,336 at 74.13 in 1932) was still phenomenal. Most damaging to finances and morale was their cumulative effect. In a shrill complaint about the climate, C. Stewart Caine in his Notes in the 1933 *Wisden* was convinced that such a succession of wet summers was without parallel,

1985 – RAIN STOPS PLAY

[Patrick Eagar

"this conclusion being based upon recollections covering a period of more than fifty years". The May of 1932 seems to have been the last straw. Lord's was awash, and over the country as a whole 63 days' first-class cricket were lost during the month. The severe damage done to the finances of some of the poorer counties posed the threat of extinction, but salvation was at hand. The summers of 1933 and 1934 were both exceptionally fine.

The years before the outbreak of the Second World War produced one notably poor summer – 1936 – when nearly half the Championship matches played were left drawn. Even so, Hammond, with 1,281 runs in August, was able to eclipse W. G. Grace's long-standing record for the month. In 1938 the complete wash-out of the third Test match against Australia at Old Trafford was an isolated blemish on a fine summer.

In 1946 the gods did anything but smile upon the revival of the first-class game; but this did not deter the public from flocking to the matches amid the discomforts of dilapidated and sodden grounds. *Wisden's* editor, Hubert Preston, whose experience stretched back to 1895, described the weather as "execrable" and declared the conditions to be "the worst ever experienced in our notoriously uncertain summers". He even sheds a faint ray of light on the summer of 1888, by implying direct comparison with 1946. In 1888 "June was detestable and July indescribable".

Interest and enthusiasm marched hand in hand in 1947 with the glorious deeds of Compton and Edrich. Sadly the year proved to be a false dawn to what many were tempted to see as a new Golden Age. The Ashes were not finally recovered until 1953, and in general the flow of runs slowed to a trickle as the pitches deteriorated. To make matters worse, in 1954 the summer turned out to be one of the vilest on record. This was no way to greet the infant cricketing nation of Pakistan, and the counties between them made a loss of £75,000, Lancashire being the worst hit. "It is necessary to go back to 1903 to find such a disastrous summer", said *Wisden*.

Although 1955 brought a short reprieve, 1956 was rated as "the wettest summer in memory". There were no Australian centuries in the Tests of that year, and only Peter May managed an average of 50. The season's meagre total of 189 centuries was the lowest since 1924. Not content with this, the summers continued their sport of ducks and drakes, producing an even more disastrous 1958 for the young and soon forlorn New Zealand tourists. Indeed 1958 embodied all the features of a classically wet summer. The total of centuries sank to 146, two fewer than in 1903 when considerably less first-class cricket was played. As many as 43 bowlers, with Lock and Laker much to the fore, took their wickets at less than 20 runs apiece, one fewer, in fact, than in 1903. Worse still, there was a drop of more than 500,000 in attendances compared with the previous year, and the sum for distribution among the seventeen first-class counties shrank to £51,000 – a mere half of the 1957 surplus. Desperate remedies were called for and increased covering was tried in the Championship in 1959, which turned out to be one of the best summers for years.

The sixties were relatively dry, though 1965, the first year of twin tours, was wetter than normal, and an article in the 1969 *Wisden* by Jack Fingleton was entitled "Watery Reflections from Australia". To him, 1968 had "seemed to be a repetition of rain, delays, drawn games and disappointing cricket". It was, he wrote, "an abominable summer and cricketers cannot do themselves justice if the sun does not shine".

But never has a summer been subjected to so much public execration as last year's. On night after night Messrs Macaskill and Fish filled our television screens with rings of densely packed isobars foreboding ill. Yet a series of six Test matches against "the old enemy", comprising exactly one month of cricket, remained relatively unscathed. It is true that storms and "bursts" of rain pursued the tourists relentlessly in their other first-class matches, but what of the two splendid days at Lord's for the two cup finals, or of the Saturday of the second Test, enjoyed by a full house, or Ian Botham's prodigious feats of hitting?

How then can we reconcile the misfortunes of farmers and those engaged in the tourist industry in such a year with the general averages boasting nineteen batsmen exceeding 50 and only four bowlers under 20? The answer, it seems to me, is simple – covered pitches, well-protected approaches and damp outfields. The balance has been too heavily tilted in favour of the batsman. This must surely be so when the two best spin bowlers in the land, Emburey and Edmonds, have to bowl 79 and 82 balls respectively to earn a wicket.

But was 1985 really the worst this century? By no means, I think. This invidious distinction belongs to 1903, 1924 or 1958, three summers with hardly a trace of a silver lining – and that could certainly not be said of 1985.

In the following table the rainfall figures were supplied by the Meteorological Office at Hampstead. It is not an unreasonable assumption that they may well be lower than an average based on Manchester, Leeds, Nottingham or Birmingham. They show last season as having been the eighth wettest this century. The consequences of full pitch covering, as operating in 1985 but in none of the other years, are brought sharply into focus by the batting and bowling figures.

| | *Rainfall in May, June, July and August* | *Batsmen averaging between 40 and 50* | *Batsmen averaging over 50* | *Bowlers averaging under 20* | *First-class 100s* |
|---|---|---|---|---|---|
| 1903 | 17.89 inches | 11 | 2 | 44 | 148 |
| 1924 | 16.85 inches | 10 | 3 | 41 | 164 |
| 1958 | 14.00 inches | 3 | 1 | 43 | 146 |
| 1946 | 13.41 inches | 11 | 7 | 30 | 257 |
| 1956 | 13.33 inches | 10 | 0 | 29 | 189 |
| 1931 | 12.63 inches | 7 | 9 | 22 | 266 |
| 1954 | 12.00 inches | 5 | 6 | 31 | 231 |
| 1985 | 11.37 inches | 25 | 19 | 4 | 309 |
| 1912 | 11.26 inches | 8 | 3 | 41 | 164 |

# COVERING BY DEGREES

By E. M. WELLINGS

England's cricket authorities moved so cautiously in the matter of pitch covering that more than a century separated the first move in 1872 and total protection. The start was made at Lord's with pre-match covering of the prepared pitch. The game then spent 38 years digesting the implications of that before the protection of pitch ends during playing hours was introduced in 1910. Nearly another 70 years passed before the ultimate point, for good or ill, was reached with authorisation of total pitch protection against rain at all times for Test matches in 1979, and for all first-class games in 1982. Now, a further four years on, many counties are again of the opinion that it is a better Championship when pitches are partly open to the elements.

Overseas progress towards full covering was so much quicker that England's touring players first experienced all-dry Test match pitches in Australia in 1954-55. Australia had already legislated, by then, for all-embracing protection in state matches.

Between 1872 and 1985 administrators in England were not always consistent. The regulations issued were sometimes vague, even contradictory, and hedged around by such cumbersome phrasing as "prior to the commencement". Moreover, although the same representatives sat on both the Advisory County Cricket Committee and the Board of Control for Test Matches at Home, before the TCCB was formed, the two bodies were apt to take diametrically opposed courses. This inevitably made life awkward for umpires, who were bombarded with Instructions for Umpires, Additional Instructions, Further Additional Instructions and Special Instructions, plus Notes for Scorers and Umpires.

In 1907, for example, the Further Additional Instructions stated that "Counties should be advised to instruct their groundsman not to cover a pitch within 24 hours of a County match". Was that an advice or an instruction? Again, in 1924 the Advisory Committee moved to help insolvent counties with covering legislation designed to produce more play in wet weather. The regulation issued, however, must have been confusing to groundsmen and umpires. It stated that total covering "*may* be adopted" from 11.00 am on the previous day until the start of a match, and went on to say that subsequently the ground "*may* be again protected when necessary". If that seemed to give the go-ahead for full pitch protection against rain, even during the hours of play, it was promptly contradicted. The regulation went on to deal further with the playing hours, laying down that only an area of eighteen by twelve feet could be covered at each end, not extending more than three feet six inches in front of the popping crease. In the late 1930s the area restriction was removed to allow much more of the bowler's run-up to be protected. Later still, the projection in front of the crease was increased to four feet.

Not only did the Board of Control tend to move in the opposite direction from the Advisory Committee; at times it moved in both directions at once. While its Rule 28 stated that the covering practice in vogue at each ground should be "adhered to", it stipulated, in 1928, that for the Tests against West Indies the pitch "shall not be completely covered *before* [my italics] or during a Test Match". This was repeated for the New Zealand Tests the following year, still without Rule 28 being amended.

Before the Second World War, limited pitch covering did not materially change the character of the game in England, though total protection before

## COVERING YESTERDAY AND TODAY

[*Sport & General*

*Above:* For the Test match between England and Australia at Headingley in 1953 one small cover has to suffice at each end of the pitch, primarily to protect the creases. *Below:* Almost the whole of the Edgbaston ground is covered in 1983, leaving pitch and outfield ready for a prompt resumption of play.

[*Ken Kelly*

the start increased the importance of winning the toss and hence first innings. Before pitch ends were covered in 1910 there was no question about who should bowl on "stickies". With the ground in that condition only slow bowlers could enjoy a secure foothold. If the pitch was fit to play, umpires and players largely ignored the soggy state of the surrounding ground, as they were still doing, at times, many years later. In 1952 Jim Laker slipped while fielding on wet ground at Old Trafford, after bowling only two overs in the third Test against India, and dropped out of the attack. It was different abroad, where grounds generally dried more rapidly. During the 1936-37 MCC tour of Australia Verity was kept from the spinner's traditional "Tom Tiddler's" pitches while Voce and Allen bowled fast and with success. Even after restrictions on the covering of run-ups were lifted, the quicker bowlers still had to be careful when following through beyond the three feet six inches mark or the four feet mark. When, finally, unrestricted covering was introduced, all hazards were removed for such bowlers – but there were now no more "stickies" for them to exploit!

After the second war, cricket continued to move cautiously in the matter of covering. The 1947 Code contained the first actual *Law* on the subject. Law 11 stated "The pitch shall not be completely covered during a match unless special regulations so provide". The three feet six inches stipulation remained, but no limit was set to the ground behind the stumps which could be protected. In 1958 Special Instructions for Umpires in first-class matches laid down that if both captains and umpires were in agreement that a pitch was already so saturated that more rain could substantially delay resumption, then the whole pitch could be covered. The umpires then had to decide when to uncover. To expect such agreement was the height of optimism, for the trickiest decision, which umpires had to make frequently, came after captains had disagreed about pitch and ground fitness following rain. A year later the ICC – then the Imperial Cricket Conference – decided to allow complete covering as soon as a decision was taken to abandon play for the day.

The voluminous Regulations for First-Class Matches, 1962, carried one astonishing entry. At the end of the section on Test match covering came: "In 1963 the pitch to be covered only at weekends or perhaps when saturation point is reached." Cricket, as may be seen, was still some way from making up its mind on the matter after nearly a century of deliberation. Indeed there was hope among some and fear among others that the whole process might be reversed. In 1966 the Advisory Committee, noting support in the counties for a move back to uncovered pitches, decided that, while allowing weekend and night pitch protection, there should be "discretion for home counties to adopt less covering". But in 1969 it was back to a standard regulation.

The march towards full covering seemed to have been resumed, but in 1971 there was a hiccup. The Test match conditions were unaffected, but for other first-class games only covering of the ends was allowed, at all times including nights and weekends. However, total covering throughout was eventually authorised in 1979, 107 years after the first move in this intricate and wavering affair.

Sir Donald Bradman is numbered among those in favour of protecting pitches, a formidable advocate convinced that cricket is a game to be played exclusively on dry ground. Most batsmen who have not experienced the challenge of a "sticky dog" probably feel the same way. That total covering enables play to be resumed more quickly after rain and so provides more play is certain, though whether quantity can compensate for some loss of quality is not so certain.

Today, supporters of a fielding side in one-day cricket are excited in a tight finish by each ball bowled without a run conceded. Spectators used to be similarly thrilled by each ball successfully countered by a skilled batsman fighting the turning, lifting ball on a drying pitch. None present at The Oval on August 17, 1926, can ever have forgotten the feat of Hobbs and Sutcliffe in defying Australian spin on a pitch made spiteful by a thunderstorm the previous night. In particular there were ten heart-stopping overs of kicking off-spin from Arthur Richardson, most of them played by Hobbs, from which just one single was scored. An ordinary side could have been dismissed entirely that morning. Yet England's openers played through to the comparative calm of the afternoon and scored 172 together. I very much doubt whether such resourceful batting skill as shown that day could ever be developed by players batting only on the dry.

That the regulations have been changed so regularly indicates the strength of conflicting views about whether or not to cover. Those in favour argue that more play becomes possible when grounds are protected. The opposition prefer less, but more gripping, cricket on pitches made testing by rain. Both as player and spectator I am in the uncovering lobby. In the former capacity I treasure the memory of batting against George Macaulay and Verity on a "sticky" at Oxford, and lasting long enough to savour the excitement.

When looking back, I find that many of my watching highlights relate to games played on the wet, including the Hobbs-Sutcliffe epic at The Oval. In Brisbane in 1950 we marvelled at the craft of Len Hutton in similar conditions as he hit 62 not out while England were being routed for 122. Verity's match at Lord's in 1934, when he took fourteen for 80 in one day, also brought out the best in the obdurate Woodfull, who held up Verity for two hours and scored 43 in a total of 118. That match, heading for an inconclusive result, was reborn by rain. After two of the four days England had made 440 and Australia 192 for two. No excitement was anticipated until, on the Sunday night, rain fell.

Cricket on the wet is more engrossing to me than on the green-tops, which succeeded the "sticky" as the bowler's best friend when total covering was introduced.

# TEST CRICKETERS

## FULL LIST FROM 1877 TO SEPTEMBER 2, 1985*

These lists have been compiled on a home and abroad basis, appearances abroad being printed in *italics*.

**Abbreviations.** E: England. A: Australia. SA: South Africa. WI: West Indies. NZ: New Zealand. In: India. P: Pakistan. SL: Sri Lanka.

All appearances are placed in this order of seniority. Hence, any England cricketer playing against Australia in England has that achievement recorded first and the remainder of his appearances at home (if any) set down before passing to matches abroad. Although the distinction between amateur and professional was abolished in 1963, initials of English professionals before that date are still given in brackets. The figures immediately following each name represent the total number of appearances in *all* Tests.

Where the season embraces two different years, the first year is given; i.e. 1876 indicates 1876-77.

*When South Africa left the British Commonwealth in 1961 they ceased membership of the Imperial Cricket Conference, which in 1965 was renamed the International Cricket Conference. The rules of membership were changed then so that, although Pakistan have left the Commonwealth, they remain members of ICC.*

* *The lists for India and Sri Lanka do not include the three Test matches played between those countries in August and September, 1985.*

## ENGLAND

Number of Test cricketers: 513

Abel (R.) 13: v A 1888 (3) 1896 (3) 1902 (2); *v A 1891 (3); v SA 1888 (2)*
Absolom, C. A. 1: *v A 1878*
Agnew, J. P. 3: v A 1985 (1); v WI 1984 (1); v SL 1984 (1)
Allen (D. A.) 39: v A 1961 (4) 1964 (1); v SA 1960 (2); v WI 1963 (2) 1966 (1); v P 1962 (4); *v A 1962 (1) 1965 (4); v SA 1964 (4); v WI 1959 (5); v NZ 1965 (3); v In 1961 (5); v P 1961 (3)*
Allen, G. O. 25: v A 1930 (1) 1934 (2); v WI 1933 (1); v NZ 1931 (3); v In 1936 (3); *v A 1932 (5) 1936 (5); v WI 1947 (3); v NZ 1932 (2)*
Allom, M. J. C. 5: *v SA 1930 (1); v NZ 1929 (4)*
Allott, P. J. W. 13: v A 1981 (1) 1985 (4); v WI 1984 (3); v In 1982 (2); v SL 1984 (1); *v In 1981 (1); v SL 1981 (1)*
Ames (L. E. G.) 47: v A 1934 (5) 1938 (2); v SA 1929 (1) 1935 (4); v WI 1933 (3); v NZ 1931 (3) 1937 (3); v In 1932 (1); *v A 1932 (5) 1936 (5); v SA 1938 (5); v WI 1929 (4) 1934 (4); v NZ 1932 (2)*
Amiss, D. L. 50: v A 1968 (1) 1975 (2) 1977 (2); v WI 1966 (1) 1973 (3) 1976 (1); v NZ 1973 (3); v In 1967 (2) 1971 (1) 1974 (3); v P 1967 (1) 1971 (3) 1974 (3); *v A 1974 (5) 1976 (1); v WI 1973 (5) v NZ 1974 (2); v In 1972 (3) 1976 (5); v P 1972 (3)*
Andrew (K. V.) 2: v WI 1963 (1); *v A 1954 (1)*
Appleyard (R.) 9: v A 1956 (1); v SA 1955 (1); v P 1954 (1); *v A 1954 (4); v NZ 1954 (2)*
Archer, A. G. 1: *v SA 1898*
Armitage (T.) 2: *v A 1876 (2)*
Arnold (E. G.) 10: v A 1905 (4); v SA 1907 (2); *v A 1903 (4)*
Arnold, G. G. 34: v A 1972 (3) 1975 (1); v WI 1973 (3); v NZ 1969 (1) 1973 (3); v In 1974 (2); v P 1967 (2) 1974 (3); *v A 1974 (4); v WI 1973 (3); v NZ 1974 (2); v In 1972 (4); v P 1972 (3)*
Arnold (J.) 1: v NZ 1931
Astill (W. E.) 9: *v SA 1927 (5); v WI 1929 (4)*
Athey, C. W. J. 3: v A 1980 (1); *v WI 1980 (2)*
Attewell (W.) 10: v A 1890 (1); *v A 1884 (5) 1887 (1) 1891 (3)*

Bailey, T. E. 61: v A 1953 (5) 1956 (4); v SA 1951 (2) 1955 (5); v WI 1950 (2) 1957 (4); v NZ 1949 (4) 1958 (4); v P 1954 (3); *v A 1950 (4) 1954 (5) 1958 (5); v SA 1956 (5); v WI 1953 (5); v NZ 1950 (2) 1954 (2)*

Bairstow, D. L. 4: v A 1980 (1); v WI 1980 (1); v In 1979 (1); *v WI 1980 (1)*

Bakewell (A. H.) 6: v SA 1935 (2); v WI 1933 (1); v NZ 1931 (2); *v In 1933 (1)*

Balderstone J. C. 2: v WI 1976 (2)

Barber, R. W. 28: v A 1964 (1) 1968 (1); v SA 1960 (1) 1965 (3); v WI 1966 (2); v NZ 1965 (3); *v A 1965 (5); v SA 1964 (4); v In 1961 (5); v P 1961 (3)*

Barber (W.) 2: v SA 1935 (2)

Barlow, G. D. 3: v A 1977 (1); *v In 1976 (2)*

Barlow (R. G.) 17: v A 1882 (1) 1884 (3) 1886 (3); *v A 1881 (4) 1882 (4) 1886 (2)*

Barnes (S. F.) 27: v A 1902 (1) 1909 (3) 1912 (3); v SA 1912 (3); *v A 1901 (3) 1907 (5) 1911 (5); v SA 1913 (4)*

Barnes (W.) 21: v A 1880 (1) 1882 (1) 1884 (2) 1886 (2) 1888 (3) 1890 (2); *v A 1882 (4) 1884 (5) 1886 (1)*

Barnett (C. J.) 20: v A 1938 (3) 1948 (1); v SA 1947 (3); v WI 1933 (1); v NZ 1937 (3); v In 1936 (1); *v A 1936 (5); v In 1933 (3)*

Barratt (F.) 5: v SA 1929 (1); *v NZ 1929 (4)*

Barrington (K. F.) 82: v A 1961 (5) 1964 (5) 1968 (3); v SA 1955 (2) 1960 (4) 1965 (3); v WI 1963 (5) 1966 (2); v NZ 1965 (2); v In 1959 (5) 1967 (3); v P 1962 (4) 1967 (3); *v A 1962 (5) 1965 (5); v SA 1964 (5); v WI 1959 (5) 1967 (5); v NZ 1962 (3); v In 1961 (5) 1963 (1); v P 1961 (2)*

Barton (V. A.) 1: *v SA 1891*

Bates (W.) 15: *v A 1881 (4) 1882 (4) 1884 (5) 1886 (2)*

Bean (G.) 3: *v A 1891 (3)*

Bedser (A. V.) 51: v A 1948 (5) 1953 (5); v SA 1947 (2) 1951 (5) 1955 (1); v WI 1950 (3); v NZ 1949 (2); v In 1946 (3) 1952 (4); v P 1954 (2); *v A 1946 (5) 1950 (5) 1954 (1); v SA 1948 (5); v NZ 1946 (1) 1950 (2)*

Berry (R.) 2: v WI 1950 (2)

Binks, J. G. 2: *v In 1963 (2)*

Bird M. C. 10: *v SA 1909 (5) 1913 (5)*

Birkenshaw J. 5: *v WI 1973 (2); v In 1972 (2); v P 1972 (1)*

Bligh, Hon. I. F. W. 4: *v A 1882 (4)*

Blythe (C.) 19: v A 1905 (1) 1909 (2); v SA 1907 (3); *v A 1901 (5) 1907 (1); v SA 1905 (5) 1909 (2)*

Board (J. H.) 6: *v SA 1898 (2) 1905 (4)*

Bolus, J. B. 7: v WI 1963 (2); *v In 1963 (5)*

Booth (M. W.) 2: *v SA 1913 (2)*

Bosanquet, B. J. T. 7: v A 1905 (3); *v A 1903 (4)*

Botham, I. T. 79: v A 1977 (2) 1980 (1) 1981 (6) 1985 (6); v WI 1980 (5) 1984 (5); v NZ 1978 (3) 1983 (4); v In 1979 (4) 1982 (3); v P 1978 (3) 1982 (3); v SL 1984 (1); *v A 1978 (6) 1979 (3) 1982 (5); v WI 1980 (4); v NZ 1977 (3) 1983 (3); v In 1979 (1) 1981 (6); v P 1983 (1); v SL 1981 (1)*

Bowden, M. P. 2: *v SA 1888 (2)*

Bowes (W. E.) 15: v A 1934 (3) 1938 (2); v SA 1935 (4); v WI 1939 (2); v In 1932 (1) 1946 (1); *v A 1932 (1); v NZ 1932 (1)*

Bowley (E. H.) 5: v SA 1929 (2); *v NZ 1929 (3)*

Boycott, G. 108: v A 1964 (4) 1968 (3) 1972 (2) 1977 (3) 1980 (1) 1981 (6); v SA 1965 (2); v WI 1966 (4) 1969 (3) 1973 (3) 1980 (5); v NZ 1965 (2) 1969 (3) 1973 (3) 1978 (2); v In 1967 (2) 1971 (1) 1974 (1) 1979 (4); v P 1967 (1) 1971 (2); *v A 1965 (5) 1970 (5) 1978 (6) 1979 (3); v SA 1964 (5); v WI 1967 (5) 1973 (5) 1980 (4); v NZ 1965 (2) 1977 (3); v In 1979 (1) 1981 (4); v P 1977 (3)*

Bradley, W. M. 2: v A 1899 (2)

Braund (L. C.) 23: v A 1902 (5); v SA 1907 (3); *v A 1901 (5) 1903 (5) 1907 (5)*

Brearley, J. M. 39: v A 1977 (5) 1981 (4); v WI 1976 (2); v NZ 1978 (3); v In 1979 (4); v P 1978 (3); *v A 1976 (1) 1978 (6) 1979 (3); v In 1976 (5) 1979 (1); v P 1977 (2)*

Brearley, W. 4: v A 1905 (2) 1909 (1); v SA 1912 (1)

Brennan, D. V. 2: v SA 1951 (2)

Briggs (John) 33: v A 1886 (3) 1888 (3) 1893 (2) 1896 (1) 1899 (1); *v A 1884 (5) 1886 (2) 1887 (1) 1891 (3) 1894 (5) 1897 (5); v SA 1888 (2)*

Broad, B. C. 5: v WI 1984 (4); v SL 1984 (1)

Brockwell (W.) 7: v A 1893 (1) 1899 (1); *v A 1894 (5)*

Bromley-Davenport, H. R. 4: *v SA 1895 (3) 1898 (1)*

Brookes (D.) 1: *v WI 1947*

Brown (A.) 2: *v In 1961 (1); v P 1961 (1)*

Brown, D. J. 26: v A 1968 (4); v SA 1965 (2); v WI 1966 (1) 1969 (3); v NZ 1969 (1); v In 1967 (2): *v A 1965 (4); v WI 1967 (4); v NZ 1965 (2); v P 1968 (3)*

Brown, F. R. 22: v A 1953 (1); v SA 1951 (5); v WI 1950 (1); v NZ 1931 (2) 1937 (1) 1949 (2); v In 1932 (1); *v A 1950 (5); v NZ 1932 (2) 1950 (2)*

Brown (G.) 7: v A 1921 (3); *v SA 1922 (4)*

Brown (J. T.) 8: v A 1896 (2) 1899 (1); *v A 1894 (5)*

Buckenham (C. P.) 4: *v SA 1909 (4)*

Butcher, A. R. 1: v In 1979

Butcher, R. O. 3: *v WI 1980 (3)*

Butler (H. J.) 2: v SA 1947 (1); *v WI 1947 (1)*

Butt (H. R.) 3: *v SA 1895 (3)*

Calthorpe, Hon. F. S. G. 4: *v WI 1929 (4)*

Carr, A. W. 11: v A 1926 (4); v SA 1929 (2); *v SA 1922 (5)*

Carr, D. B. 2: *v In 1951 (2)*

Carr, D. W. 1: v A 1909

Cartwright, T. W. 5: v A 1964 (2); v SA 1965 (1); v NZ 1965 (1); *v SA 1964 (1)*

Chapman, A. P. F. 26: v A 1926 (4) 1930 (4); v SA 1924 (2); v WI 1928 (3); *v A 1924 (4) 1928 (4); v SA 1930 (5)*

Charlwood (H. R. J.) 2: *v A 1876 (2)*

Chatterton (W.) 1: *v SA 1891*

Christopherson, S. 1: v A 1884

Clark (E. W.) 8: v A 1934 (2); v SA 1929 (1); v WI 1933 (2); *v In 1933 (3)*

Clay, J. C. 1: v SA 1935

Close (D. B.) 22: v A 1961 (1); v SA 1955 (1); v WI 1957 (2) 1963 (5) 1966 (1) 1976 (3); v NZ 1949 (1); v In 1959 (1) 1967 (3); v P 1967 (3); *v A 1950 (1)*

Coldwell (L. J.) 7: v A 1964 (2); v P 1962 (2); *v A 1962 (2); v NZ 1962 (1)*

Compton (D. C. S.) 78: v A 1938 (4) 1948 (5) 1953 (5) 1956 (1); v SA 1947 (5) 1951 (4) 1955 (5); v WI 1939 (3) 1950 (1); v NZ 1937 (1) 1949 (4); v In 1946 (3) 1952 (2); v P 1954 (4); *v A 1946 (5) 1950 (4) 1954 (4); v SA 1948 (5) 1956 (5); v WI 1953 (5); v NZ 1946 (1) 1950 (2)*

Cook (C.) 1: v SA 1947

Cook, G. 7: v In 1982 (3); *v A 1982 (3); v SL 1981 (1)*

Cook, N. G. B. 9: v WI 1984 (3); v NZ 1983 (2); *v NZ 1983 (1); v P 1983 (3)*

Cope, G. A. 3: *v P 1977 (3)*

Copson (W. H.) 3: v SA 1947 (1); v WI 1939 (2)

Cornford (W. L.) 4: *v NZ 1929 (4)*

Cottam, R. M. H. 4: *v In 1972 (2); v P 1968 (2)*

Coventry, Hon. C. J. 2: *v SA 1888 (2)*

Cowans, N. G. 19: v A 1985 (1); v WI 1984 (1); v NZ 1983 (4); *v A 1982 (4); v NZ 1983 (2); v In 1984 (5); v P 1983 (2)*

Cowdrey, C. S. 5: *v In 1984 (5)*

Cowdrey, M. C. 114: v A 1956 (5) 1961 (4) 1964 (3) 1968 (4); v SA 1955 (1) 1960 (5) 1965 (3); v WI 1957 (5) 1963 (2) 1966 (4); v NZ 1958 (4) 1965 (3); v In 1959 (5); v P 1962 (4) 1967 (2) 1971 (1); *v A 1954 (5) 1958 (5) 1962 (5) 1965 (4) 1970 (3) 1974 (5); v SA 1956 (5); v WI 1959 (5) 1967 (5); v NZ 1954 (2) 1958 (2) 1962 (3) 1965 (3) 1970 (1); v In 1963 (3); v P 1968 (3)*

Coxon (A.) 1: v A 1948

Cranston, J. 1: v A 1890

Cranston, K. 8: v A 1948 (1); v SA 1947 (3); *v WI 1947 (4)*

Crapp (J. F.) 7: v A 1948 (3); *v SA 1948 (4)*

Crawford J. N. 12: v SA 1907 (2); *v A 1907 (5); v SA 1905 (5)*

Cuttell (W. R.) 2: *v SA 1898 (2)*

Dawson, E. W. 5: *v SA 1927 (1); v NZ 1929 (4)*

Dean (H.) 3: v A 1912 (2); v SA 1912 (1)

Denness, M. H. 28: v A 1975 (1); v NZ 1969 (1); v In 1974 (3); v P 1974 (3); *v A 1974 (5); v WI 1973 (5); v NZ 1974 (2); v In 1972 (5); v P 1972 (3)*

Denton (D.) 11: v A 1905 (1); *v SA 1905 (5) 1909 (5)*

Dewes, J. G. 5: v A 1948 (1); v WI 1950 (2); *v A 1950 (2)*

Dexter, E. R. 62: v A 1961 (5) 1964 (5) 1968 (2); v SA 1960 (5); v WI 1963 (5); v NZ 1958 (1) 1965 (2); v In 1959 (2); v P 1962 (5); *v A 1958 (2) 1962 (5); v SA 1964 (5); v WI 1959 (5); v NZ 1958 (2) 1962 (3); v In 1961 (5); v P 1961 (3)*

Dilley, G. R. 18: v A 1981 (3); v WI 1980 (3); v NZ 1983 (1); *v A 1979 (2); v WI 1980 (4); v In 1981 (4); v P 1983 (1)*

Dipper (A. E.) 1: v A 1921
Doggart, G. H. G. 2: v WI 1950 (2)
D'Oliveira, B. L. 44: v A 1968 (2) 1972 (5); v WI 1966 (4) 1969 (3); v NZ 1969 (3); v In 1967 (2) 1971 (3); v P 1967 (3) 1971 (3); *v A 1970 (6); v WI 1967 (5); v NZ 1970 (2); v P 1968 (3)*
Dollery (H. E.) 4: v A 1948 (2); v SA 1947 (1); v WI 1950 (1)
Dolphin (A.) 1: *v A 1920*
Douglas, J. W. H. T. 23: v A 1912 (1) 1921 (5); v SA 1924 (1); *v A 1911 (5) 1920 (5) 1924 (1); v SA 1913 (5)*
Downton, P. R. 21: v A 1981 (1) 1985 (6); v WI 1984 (5); v SL 1984 (1); *v WI 1980 (3); v In 1984 (5)*
Druce, N. F. 5: *v A 1897 (5)*
Ducat (A.) 1: v A 1921
Duckworth (G.) 24: v A 1930 (5); v SA 1924 (1) 1929 (4) 1935 (1); v WI 1928 (1); v In 1936 (3); *v A 1928 (5); v SA 1930 (3); v NZ 1932 (1)*
Duleepsinhji, K. S. 12: v A 1930 (4); v SA 1929 (1); v NZ 1931 (3); *v NZ 1929 (4)*
Durston (F. J.) 1: v A 1921

Edmonds, P. H. 33: v A 1975 (2) 1985 (5); v NZ 1978 (3) 1983 (2); v In 1979 (4) 1982 (3); v P 1978 (3); *v A 1978 (1); v NZ 1977 (3); v In 1984 (5); v P 1977 (2)*
Edrich, J. H. 77: v A 1964 (3) 1968 (5) 1972 (5) 1975 (4); v SA 1965 (1); v WI 1963 (3) 1966 (1) 1969 (3) 1976 (2); v NZ 1965 (1) 1969 (3); v In 1967 (2) 1971 (3) 1974 (3); v P 1971 (3) 1974 (3); *v A 1965 (5) 1970 (6) 1974 (4); v WI 1967 (5); v NZ 1965 (3) 1970 (2) 1974 (2); v In 1963 (2); v P 1968 (3)*
Edrich, W. J. 39: v A 1938 (4) 1948 (5) 1953 (3); v SA 1947 (4); v WI 1950 (2); v NZ 1949 (4); v In 1946 (1); v P 1954 (1); *v A 1946 (5) 1954 (4); v SA 1938 (5); v NZ 1946 (1)*
Elliott (H.) 4: v WI 1928 (1); *v SA 1927 (1); v In 1933 (2)*
Ellison, R. M. 7: v A 1985 (2); v WI 1984 (1); v SL 1984 (1); *v In 1984 (3)*
Emburey, J. E. 28: v A 1980 (1) 1981 (4) 1985 (6); v WI 1980 (3); v NZ 1978 (1); *v A 1978 (4); v WI 1980 (4); v In 1979 (1) 1981 (3); v SL 1981 (1)*
Emmett (G. M.) 1: v A 1948
Emmett (T.) 7: *v A 1876 (2) 1878 (1) 1881 (4)*
Evans, A. J. 1: v A 1921
Evans (T. G.) 91: v A 1948 (5) 1953 (5) 1956 (5); v SA 1947 (5) 1951 (3) 1955 (3); v WI 1950 (3) 1957 (5); v NZ 1949 (4) 1958 (5); v In 1946 (1) 1952 (4) 1959 (2); v P 1954 (4); *v A 1946 (4) 1950 (5) 1954 (4) 1958 (3); v SA 1948 (3) 1956 (5); v WI 1947 (4) 1953 (4); v NZ 1946 (1) 1950 (2) 1954 (2)*

Fagg (A. E.) 5: v WI 1939 (1); v In 1936 (2); *v A 1936 (2)*
Fane, F. L. 14: *v A 1907 (4); v SA 1905 (5) 1909 (5)*
Farnes, K. 15: v A 1934 (2) 1938 (4); *v A 1936 (2); v SA 1938 (5); v WI 1934 (2)*
Farrimond (W.) 4: v SA 1935 (1); *v SA 1930 (2); v WI 1934 (1)*
Fender, P. G. H. 13: v A 1921 (2); v SA 1924 (2) 1929 (1); *v A 1920 (3); v SA 1922 (5)*
Ferris, J. J. 1: *v SA 1891*
Fielder (A.) 6: *v A 1903 (2) 1907 (4)*
Fishlock (L. B.) 4: v In 1936 (2) 1946 (1); *v A 1946 (1)*
Flavell (J. A.) 4: v A 1961 (2) 1964 (2)
Fletcher, K. W. R. 59: v A 1968 (1) 1972 (1) 1975 (2); v WI 1973 (3); v NZ 1969 (2) 1973 (3); v In 1971 (2) 1974 (3); v P 1974 (3); *v A 1970 (5) 1974 (5) 1976 (1); v WI 1973 (4); v NZ 1970 (1) 1974 (2); v In 1972 (5) 1976 (3) 1981 (6); v P 1968 (3) 1972 (3); v SL 1981 (1)*
Flowers (W.) 8: v A 1893 (1); *v A 1884 (5) 1886 (2)*
Ford, F. G. J. 5: *v A 1894 (5)*
Foster, F. R. 11: v A 1912 (3); v SA 1912 (3); *v A 1911 (5)*
Foster, N. A. 9: v A 1985 (1); v WI 1984 (1); v NZ 1983 (1); *v NZ 1983 (2); v In 1984 (2); v P 1983 (2)*
Foster, R. E. 8: v SA 1907 (3); *v A 1903 (5)*
Fothergill (A. J.) 2: *v SA 1888 (2)*
Fowler, G. 21: v WI 1984 (5); v NZ 1983 (2); v P 1982 (1); v SL 1984 (1); *v A 1982 (3); v NZ 1983 (2); v In 1984 (5); v P 1983 (2)*
Freeman (A. P.) 12: v SA 1929 (3); v WI 1928 (3); *v A 1924 (2); v SA 1927 (4)*
Fry, C. B. 26: v A 1899 (5) 1902 (3) 1905 (4) 1909 (3) 1912 (3); v SA 1907 (3) 1912 (3); *v SA 1895 (2)*

Gatting, M. W. 41: v A 1980 (1) 1981 (6) 1985 (6); v WI 1980 (4) 1984 (1); v NZ 1983 (2); v P 1982 (3); *v WI 1980 (1); v NZ 1977 (1) 1983 (2); v In 1981 (5) 1984 (5); v P 1977 (1) 1983 (3)*

Gay, L. H. 1: *v A 1894*
Geary (G.) 14: v A 1926 (2) 1930 (1) 1934 (2); v SA 1924 (1) 1929 (2); *v A 1928 (4); v SA 1927 (2)*
Gibb, P. A. 8: v In 1946 (2); *v A 1946 (1); v SA 1938 (5)*
Gifford, N. 15: v A 1964 (2) 1972 (3); v NZ 1973 (2); v In 1971 (2); v P 1971 (2); *v In 1972 (2); v P 1972 (2)*
Gilligan, A. E. R. 11: v SA 1924 (4); *v A 1924 (5); v SA 1922 (2)*
Gilligan, A. H. H. 4: *v NZ 1929 (4)*
Gimblett (H.) 3: v WI 1939 (1); v In 1936 (2)
Gladwin (C.) 8: v SA 1947 (2); v NZ 1949 (1); *v SA 1948 (5)*
Goddard (T. W.) 8: v A 1930 (1); v WI 1939 (2); v NZ 1937 (2); *v SA 1938 (3)*
Gooch, G. A. 48: v A 1975 (2) 1980 (1) 1981 (5) 1985 (6); v WI 1980 (5); v NZ 1978 (3); v In 1979 (4); v P 1978 (2); *v A 1978 (6) 1979 (2); v WI 1980 (4); v In 1979 (1) 1981 (6); v SL 1981 (1)*
Gover (A. R.) 4: v NZ 1937 (2); v In 1936 (1) 1946 (1)
Gower, D. I. 76: v A 1980 (1) 1981 (5) 1985 (6); v WI 1980 (1) 1984 (5); v NZ 1978 (3) 1983 (4); v In 1979 (4) 1982 (3); v P 1978 (3) 1982 (3); v SL 1984 (1); *v A 1978 (6) 1979 (3) 1982 (5); v WI 1980 (4); v NZ 1983 (3); v In 1979 (1) 1981 (6) 1984 (5); v P 1983 (3); v SL 1981 (1)*
Grace, E. M. 1: v A 1880
Grace, G. F. 1: v A 1880
Grace, W. G. 22: v A 1880 (1) 1882 (1) 1884 (3) 1886 (3) 1888 (3) 1890 (2) 1893 (2) 1896 (3) 1899 (1); *v A 1891 (3)*
Graveney (T. W.) 79: v A 1953 (5) 1956 (2) 1968 (5); v SA 1951 (1) 1955 (5); v WI 1957 (4) 1966 (4) 1969 (1); v NZ 1958 (4); v In 1952 (4) 1967 (3); v P 1954 (3) 1962 (4) 1967 (3); *v A 1954 (2) 1958 (5) 1962 (3); v WI 1953 (5) 1967 (5); v NZ 1954 (2) 1958 (2); v In 1951 (4); v P 1968 (3)*
Greenhough (T.) 4: v SA 1960 (1); v In 1959 (3)
Greenwood (A.) 2: *v A 1876 (2)*
Greig, A. W. 58: v A 1972 (5) 1975 (4) 1977 (5); v WI 1973 (3) 1976 (5); v NZ 1973 (3); v In 1974 (3); v P 1974 (3); *v A 1974 (6) 1976 (1); v WI 1973 (5); v NZ 1974 (2); v In 1972 (5) 1976 (5); v P 1972 (3)*
Greig, I. A. 2: v P 1982 (2)
Grieve, B. A. F. 2: *v SA 1888 (2)*
Griffith, S. C. 3: *v SA 1948 (2); v WI 1947 (1)*
Gunn (G.) 15: v A 1909 (1); *v A 1907 (5) 1911 (5); v WI 1929 (4)*
Gunn (J.) 6: v A 1905 (1); *v A 1901 (5)*
Gunn (W.) 11: v A 1888 (2) 1890 (2) 1893 (3) 1896 (1) 1899 (1); *v A 1886 (2)*

Haig, N. E. 5: v A 1921 (1); *v WI 1929 (4)*
Haigh (S.) 11: v A 1905 (2) 1909 (1) 1912 (1); *v SA 1898 (2) 1905 (5)*
Hallows (C.) 2: v A 1921 (1); v WI 1928 (1)
Hammond, W. R. 85: v A 1930 (5) 1934 (5) 1938 (4); v SA 1929 (4) 1935 (5); v WI 1928 (3) 1933 (3) 1939 (3); v NZ 1931 (3) 1937 (3); v In 1932 (1) 1936 (2) 1946 (3); *v A 1928 (5) 1932 (5) 1936 (5) 1946 (4); v SA 1927 (5) 1930 (5) 1938 (5); v WI 1934 (4); v NZ 1932 (2) 1946 (1)*
Hampshire, J. H. 8: v A 1972 (1) 1975 (1); v WI 1969 (2); *v A 1970 (2); v NZ 1970 (2)*
Hardinge (H. T. W.) 1: v A 1921
Hardstaff (J.) 5: *v A 1907 (5)*
Hardstaff (J. jun.) 23: v A 1938 (2) 1948 (1); v SA 1935 (1); v WI 1939 (3); v NZ 1937 (3); v In 1936 (2) 1946 (2); *v A 1936 (5) 1946 (1); v WI 1947 (3)*
Harris, Lord 4: v A 1880 (1) 1884 (2); *v A 1878 (1)*
Hartley, J. C. 2: *v SA 1905 (2)*
Hawke, Lord 5: *v SA 1895 (3) 1898 (2)*
Hayes (E. G.) 5: v A 1909 (1); v SA 1912 (1); *v SA 1905 (3)*
Hayes, F. C. 9: v WI 1973 (3) 1976 (2); *v WI 1973 (4)*
Hayward (T. W.) 35: v A 1896 (2) 1899 (5) 1902 (1) 1905 (5) 1909 (1); v SA 1907 (3); *v A 1897 (5) 1901 (5) 1903 (5); v SA 1895 (3)*
Hearne (A.) 1: *v SA 1891*
Hearne (F.) 2: *v SA 1888 (2)*
Hearne (G. G.) 1: *v SA 1891*
Hearne (J. T.) 12: v A 1896 (3) 1899 (3); *v A 1897 (5); v SA 1891 (1)*
Hearne (J. W.) 24: v A 1912 (3) 1921 (1) 1926 (1); v SA 1912 (2) 1924 (3); *v A 1911 (5) 1920 (2) 1924 (4); v SA 1913 (3)*
Hemmings, E. E. 5: v P 1982 (2); *v A 1982 (3)*
Hendren (E. H.) 51: v A 1921 (2) 1926 (5) 1930 (2) 1934 (4); v SA 1924 (5) 1929 (4); v WI 1928 (1); *v A 1920 (5) 1924 (5) 1928 (5); v SA 1930 (5); v WI 1929 (4) 1934 (4)*

Hendrick, M. 30: v A 1977 (3) 1980 (1) 1981 (2); v WI 1976 (2) 1980 (2); v NZ 1978 (2); v In 1974 (3) 1979 (4); v P 1974 (2); *v A 1974 (2) 1978 (5); v NZ 1974 (1) 1977 (1)*
Heseltine, C. 2: v SA 1895 (2)
Higgs, K. 15: v A 1968 (1); v WI 1966 (5); v SA 1965 (1); v In 1967 (1); v P 1967 (3); *v A 1965 (1); v NZ 1965 (3)*
Hill (A.) 2: *v A 1876 (2)*
Hill, A. J. L. 3: *v SA 1895 (3)*
Hilton (M. J.) 4: v SA 1951 (1); v WI 1950 (1); *v In 1951 (2)*
Hirst (G. H.) 24: v A 1899 (1) 1902 (4) 1905 (3) 1909 (4); v SA 1907 (3); *v A 1897 (4) 1903 (5)*
Hitch (J. W.) 7: v A 1912 (1) 1921 (1); v SA 1912 (1); *v A 1911 (3) 1920 (1)*
Hobbs (J. B.) 61: v A 1909 (3) 1912 (3) 1921 (1) 1926 (5) 1930 (5); v SA 1912 (3) 1924 (4) 1929 (1); v WI 1928 (2); *v A 1907 (4) 1911 (5) 1920 (5) 1924 (5) 1928 (5); v SA 1909 (5) 1913 (5)*
Hobbs, R. N. S. 7: v In 1967 (3); v P 1967 (1) 1971 (1); *v WI 1967 (1); v P 1968 (1)*
Hollies (W. E.) 13: v A 1948 (1); v SA 1947 (3); v WI 1950 (2); v NZ 1949 (4); *v WI 1934 (3)*
Holmes, E. R. T. 5: v SA 1935 (1); *v WI 1934 (4)*
Holmes (P.) 7: v A 1921 (1); v In 1932 (1); *v SA 1927 (5)*
Hone, L. 1: *v A 1878*
Hopwood (J. L.) 2: v A 1934 (2)
Hornby, A. N. 3: v A 1882 (1) 1884 (1); *v A 1878 (1)*
Horton (M. J.) 2: v In 1959 (2)
Howard, N. D. 4: *v In 1951 (4)*
Howell (H.) 5: v A 1921 (1); v SA 1924 (1); *v A 1920 (3)*
Howorth (R.) 5: v SA 1947 (1); *v WI 1947 (4)*
Humphries (J.) 3: *v A 1907 (3)*
Hunter (J.) 5: *v A 1884 (5)*
Hutchings, K. L. 7: v A 1909 (2); *v A 1907 (5)*
Hutton (L.) 79: v A 1938 (3) 1948 (4) 1953 (5); v SA 1947 (5) 1951 (5); v WI 1939 (3) 1950 (3); v NZ 1937 (3) 1949 (4); v In 1946 (3) 1952 (4); v P 1954 (2); *v A 1946 (5) 1950 (5) 1954 (5); v SA 1938 (4) 1948 (5); v WI 1947 (2) 1953 (5); v NZ 1950 (2) 1954 (2)*
Hutton, R. A. 5: v In 1971 (3); v P 1971 (2)

Iddon (J.) 5: v SA 1935 (1); *v WI 1934 (4)*
Ikin (J. T.) 18: v SA 1951 (3) 1955 (1); v In 1946 (2) 1952 (2); *v A 1946 (5); v NZ 1946 (1); v WI 1947 (4)*
Illingworth (R.) 61: v A 1961 (2) 1968 (3) 1972 (5); v SA 1960 (4); v WI 1966 (2) 1969 (3) 1973 (3); v NZ 1958 (1) 1965 (1) 1969 (3) 1973 (3); v In 1959 (2) 1967 (3) 1971 (3); v P 1962 (1) 1967 (1) 1971 (3); *v A 1962 (2) 1970 (6); v WI 1959 (5); v NZ 1962 (3) 1970 (2)*
Insole, D. J. 9: v A 1956 (1); v SA 1955 (1); v WI 1950 (1) 1957 (1); *v SA 1956 (5)*

Jackman, R. D. 4: v P 1982 (2); *v WI 1980 (2)*
Jackson, F. S. 20: v A 1893 (2) 1896 (3) 1899 (5) 1902 (5) 1905 (5)
Jackson (H. L.) 2: v A 1961 (1); v NZ 1949 (1)
Jameson, J. A. 4: v In 1971 (2); *v WI 1973 (2)*
Jardine, D. R. 22: v WI 1928 (2) 1933 (2); v NZ 1931 (3); v In 1932 (1); *v A 1928 (5) 1932 (5); v NZ 1932 (1); v In 1933 (3)*
Jenkins (R. O.) 9: v WI 1950 (2); v In 1952 (2); *v SA 1948 (5)*
Jessop, G. L. 18: v A 1899 (1) 1902 (4) 1905 (1) 1909 (2); v SA 1907 (3) 1912 (2); *v A 1901 (5)*
Jones, A. O. 12: v A 1899 (1) 1905 (2) 1909 (2); *v A 1901 (5) 1907 (2)*
Jones, I. J. 15: v WI 1966 (2); *v A 1965 (4); v WI 1967 (5); v NZ 1965 (3); v In 1963 (1)*
Jupp (H.) 2: *v A 1876 (2)*
Jupp, V. W. C. 8: v A 1921 (2); v WI 1928 (2); *v SA 1922 (4)*

Keeton (W. W.) 2: v A 1934 (1); v WI 1939 (1)
Kennedy (A. S.) 5: *v SA 1922 (5)*
Kenyon (D.) 8: v A 1953 (2); v SA 1955 (3); *v In 1951 (3)*
Killick, E. T. 2: v SA 1929 (2)
Kilner (R.) 9: v A 1926 (4); v SA 1924 (2); *v A 1924 (3)*
King (J. H.) 1: v A 1909
Kinneir (S. P.) 1: *v A 1911*
Knight (A. E.) 3: *v A 1903 (3)*
Knight (B. R.) 29: v A 1968 (2); v WI 1966 (1) 1969 (3); v NZ 1969 (2); v P 1962 (2); *v A 1962 (1) 1965 (2); v NZ 1962 (3) 1965 (2); v In 1961 (4) 1963 (5); v P 1961 (2)*
Knight, D. J. 2: v A 1921 (2)

Knott, A. P. E. 95: v A 1968 (5) 1972 (5) 1975 (4) 1977 (5) 1981 (2); v WI 1969 (3) 1973 (3) 1976 (5) 1980 (4); v NZ 1969 (3) 1973 (3); v In 1971 (3) 1974 (3); v P 1967 (2) 1971 (3) 1974 (3); *v A 1970 (6) 1974 (6) 1976 (1); v WI 1967 (2) 1973 (5); v NZ 1970 (1) 1974 (2); v In 1972 (5) 1976 (5); v P 1968 (3) 1972 (3)*
Knox, N. A. 2: v SA 1907 (2)

Laker (J. C.) 46: v A 1948 (3) 1953 (3) 1956 (5); v SA 1951 (2) 1955 (1); v WI 1950 (1) 1957 (4); v NZ 1949 (1) 1958 (4); v In 1952 (4); v P 1954 (1); *v A 1958 (4); v SA 1956 (5); v WI 1947 (4) 1953 (4)*
Lamb, A. J. 38: v A 1985 (6); v WI 1984 (5); v NZ 1983 (4); v In 1982 (3); v P 1982 (3); v SL 1984 (1); *v A 1982 (5); v NZ 1983 (3); v In 1984 (5); v P 1983 (3)*
Langridge (James) 8: v SA 1935 (1); v WI 1933 (2); v In 1936 (1) 1946 (1); *v In 1933 (3)*
Larkins, W. 6: v A 1981 (1); v WI 1980 (3); *v A 1979 (1); v In 1979 (1)*
Larter (J. D. F.) 10: v SA 1965 (2); v NZ 1965 (1); v P 1962 (1); *v NZ 1962 (3); v In 1963 (3)*
Larwood (H.) 21: v A 1926 (2) 1930 (3); v SA 1929 (3); v WI 1928 (2); v NZ 1931 (1); *v A 1928 (5) 1932 (5)*
Leadbeater (E.) 2: *v In 1951 (2)*
Lee (H. W.) 1: *v SA 1930*
Lees (W. S.) 5: *v SA 1905 (5)*
Legge G. B. 5: *v SA 1927 (1); v NZ 1929 (4)*
Leslie, C. F. H. 4: *v A 1882 (4)*
Lever, J. K. 20: v A 1977 (3); v WI 1980 (1); v In 1979 (1); *v A 1976 (1) 1978 (1) 1979 (1); v NZ 1977 (1); v In 1976 (5) 1979 (1) 1981 (2); v P 1977 (3)*
Lever, P. 17: v A 1972 (1) 1975 (1); v In 1971 (1); v P 1971 (3); *v A 1970 (5) 1974 (2); v NZ 1970 (2) 1974 (2)*
Leveson Gower, H. D. G. 3: *v SA 1909 (3)*
Levett, W. H. V. 1: *v In 1933*
Lewis, A. R. 9: v NZ 1973 (1); *v In 1972 (5); v P 1972 (3)*
Leyland (M.) 41: v A 1930 (3) 1934 (5) 1938 (1); v SA 1929 (5) 1935 (4); v WI 1928 (1) 1933 (1); v In 1936 (2); *v A 1928 (1) 1932 (5) 1936 (5); v SA 1930 (5); v WI 1934 (3)*
Lilley (A. A.) 35: v A 1896 (3) 1899 (4) 1902 (5) 1905 (5) 1909 (5); v SA 1907 (3); *v A 1901 (5) 1903 (5)*
Lillywhite (James jun.) 2: *v A 1876 (2)*
Lloyd, D. 9: v In 1974 (2); v P 1974 (3); *v A 1974 (4)*
Lloyd, T. A. 1: v WI 1984
Loader (P. J.) 13: v SA 1955 (1); v WI 1957 (2); v NZ 1958 (3); v P 1954 (1); *v A 1958 (2); v SA 1956 (4)*
Lock (G. A. R.) 49: v A 1953 (2) 1956 (4) 1961 (3); v SA 1955 (3); v WI 1957 (3) 1963 (3); v NZ 1958 (5); v In 1952 (2); v P 1962 (3); *v A 1958 (4); v SA 1956 (1); v WI 1953 (5) 1967 (2); v NZ 1958 (2); v In 1961 (5); v P 1961 (2)*
Lockwood (W. H.) 12: v A 1893 (2) 1899 (1) 1902 (4); *v A 1894 (5)*
Lohmann (G. A.) 18: v A 1886 (3) 1888 (3) 1890 (2) 1896 (1); *v A 1886 (2) 1887 (1) 1891 (3); v SA 1895 (3)*
Lowson (F. A.) 7: v SA 1951 (2) 1955 (1); *v In 1951 (4)*
Lucas, A. P. 5: v A 1880 (1) 1882 (1) 1884 (2); *v A 1878(1)*
Luckhurst, B. W. 21: v A 1972 (4); v WI 1973 (2); v In 1971 (3); v P 1971 (3); *v A 1970 (5); 1974 (2); v NZ 1970 (2)*
Lyttelton, Hon. A. 4: v A 1880 (1) 1882 (1) 1884 (2)

Macaulay (G. G.) 8: v A 1926 (1); v SA 1924 (1); v WI 1933 (2); *v SA 1922 (4)*
MacBryan, J. C. W. 1: v SA 1924
McConnon (J. E.) 2: v P 1954 (2)
McGahey, C. P. 2: *v A 1901 (2)*
MacGregor, G. 8: v A 1890 (2) 1893 (3); *v A 1891 (3)*
McIntyre (A. J. W.) 3: v SA 1955 (1); v WI 1950 (1); *v A 1950 (10*
MacKinnon, F. A. 1: *v A 1878*
MacLaren, A. C. 35: v A 1896 (2) 1899 (4) 1902 (5) 1905 (4) 1909 (5); *v A 1894 (5) 1897 (5) 1901 (5)*
McMaster, J. E. P. 1: *v SA 1888*
Makepeace (H.) 4: *v A 1920 (4)*
Mann, F. G. 7: v NZ 1949 (2); *v SA 1948 (5)*
Mann, F. T. 5: *v SA 1922 (5)*
Marks, V. J. 6: v NZ 1983 (1); v P 1982 (1); *v NZ 1983 (1); v P 1983 (3)*

Marriott, C. S. 1: v WI 1933
Martin (F.) 2: v A 1890 (1); *v SA 1891 (1)*
Martin, J. W. 1: v SA 1947
Mason, J. R. 5: *v A 1897 (5)*
Matthews (A. D. G.) 1: v NZ 1937
May, P. B. H. 66: v A 1953 (2) 1956 (5) 1961 (4); v SA 1951 (2) 1955 (5); v WI 1957 (5); v NZ 1958 (5); v In 1952 (4) 1959 (3); v P 1954 (4); *v A 1954 (5) 1958 (5); v SA 1956 (5); v WI 1953 (5) 1959 (3); v NZ 1954 (2) 1958 (2)*
Mead (C. P.) 17: v A 1921 (2); *v A 1911 (4) 1928 (1); v SA 1913 (5) 1922 (5)*
Mead (W.) 1: v A 1899
Midwinter (W. E.) 4: *v A 1881 (4)*
Milburn, C. 9: v A 1968 (2); v WI 1966 (4); v In 1967 (1); v P 1967 (1); *v P 1968 (1)*
Miller, A. M. 1: *v SA 1895*
Miller, G. 34: v A 1977 (2); v WI 1976 (1) 1984 (2); v NZ 1978 (2); v In 1979 (3) 1982 (1); v P 1978 (3) 1982 (1); *v A 1978 (6) 1979 (1) 1982 (5); v WI 1980 (1); v NZ 1977 (3); v P 1977 (3)*
Milligan, F. W. 2: *v SA 1898 (2)*
Millman (G.) 6: v P 1962 (2); *v In 1961 (2); v P 1961 (2)*
Milton (C. A.) 6: v NZ 1958 (2); v In 1959 (2); *v A 1958 (2)*
Mitchell (A.) 6: v SA 1935 (2); v In 1936 (1); *v In 1933 (3)*
Mitchell, F. 2: *v SA 1898 (2)*
Mitchell (T. B.) 5: v A 1934 (2); v SA 1935 (1); *v A 1932 (1); v NZ 1932 (1)*
Mitchell-Innes, N. S. 1: v SA 1935
Mold (A. W.) 3: v A 1893 (3)
Moon, L. J. 4: *v SA 1905 (4)*
Morley (F.) 4: v A 1880 (1); *v A 1882 (3)*
Mortimore (J. B.) 9: v A 1964 (1); v In 1959 (2); *v A 1958 (1); v NZ 1958 (2); v In 1963 (3)*
Moss (A. E.) 9: v A 1956 (1); v SA 1960 (2); v In 1959 (3); *v WI 1953 (1) 1959 (2)*
Murdoch, W. L. 1: *v SA 1891*
Murray, J. T. 21: v A 1961 (5); v WI 1966 (1); v In 1967 (3); v P 1962 (3) 1967 (1); *v A 1962 (1); v SA 1964 (1); v NZ 1962 (1) 1965 (1); v In 1961 (3); v P 1961 (1)*

Newham (W.) 1: *v A 1887*
Nichols (M. S.) 14: v A 1930 (1); v SA 1935 (4); v WI 1933 (1) 1939 (1); *v NZ 1929 (4); v In 1933 (3)*

Oakman (A. S. M.) 2: v A 1956 (2)
O'Brien, T. C. 5: v A 1884 (1) 1888 (1); *v SA 1895 (3)*
O'Connor (J.) 4: v SA 1929 (1); *v WI 1929 (3)*
Old, C. M. 46: v A 1975 (3) 1977 (2) 1980 (1) 1981 (2); v WI 1973 (1) 1976 (2) 1980 (1); v NZ 1973 (2) 1978 (1); v In 1974 (3); v P 1974 (3) 1978 (3); *v A 1974 (2) 1976 (1) 1978 (1); v WI 1973 (4) 1980 (1); v NZ 1974 (1) 1977 (2); v In 1972 (4) 1976 (4); v P 1972 (1) 1977 (1)*
Oldfield (N.) 1: v WI 1939

Padgett (D. E. V.) 2: v SA 1960 (2)
Paine (G. A. E.) 4: *v WI 1934 (4)*
Palairet, L. C. H. 2: v A 1902 (2)
Palmer, C. H. 1: *v WI 1953*
Palmer, K. E. 1: *v SA 1964*
Parfitt (P. H.) 37: v A 1964 (4) 1972 (3); v SA 1965 (2); v WI 1969 (1); v NZ 1965 (2); v P 1962 (5); *v A 1962 (2); v SA 1964 (5); v NZ 1962 (3) 1965 (3); v In 1961 (2) 1963 (3); v P 1961 (2)*
Parker (C. W. L.) 1: v A 1921
Parker, P. W. G. 1: v A 1981
Parkhouse (W. G. A.) 7: v WI 1950 (2); v In 1959 (2); *v A 1950 (2); v NZ 1950 (1)*
Parkin (C. H.) 10: v A 1921 (4); v SA 1924 (1); *v A 1920 (5)*
Parks (J. H.) 1: v NZ 1937
Parks (J. M.) 46: v A 1964 (5); v SA 1960 (5) 1965 (3); v WI 1963 (4) 1966 (4); v NZ 1965 (3); v P 1954 (1); *v A 1965 (5); v SA 1964 (5); v WI 1959 (1) 1967 (3); v NZ 1965 (2); v In 1963 (5)*
Pataudi, Nawab of, 3: v A 1934 (1); *v A 1932 (2)*
Paynter (E.) 20: v A 1938 (4); v WI 1939 (2); v NZ 1931 (1) 1937 (2); v In 1932 (1); *v A 1932 (3); v SA 1938 (5); v NZ 1932 (2)*
Peate (E.) 9: v A 1882 (1) 1884 (3) 1886 (1); *v A 1881 (4)*
Peebles, I. A. R. 13: v A 1930 (2); v NZ 1931 (3); *v SA 1927 (4) 1930 (4)*
Peel (R.) 20: v A 1888 (3) 1890 (1) 1893 (1) 1896 (1); *v A 1884 (5) 1887 (1) 1891 (3) 1894 (5)*

Penn, F. 1: v A 1880
Perks (R. T. D.) 2: v WI 1939 (1); *v SA 1938 (1)*
Philipson, (H.) 5: *v A 1891 (1) 1894 (4)*
Pigott, A. C. S. 1: *v NZ 1983*
Pilling (R.) 8: v A 1884 (1) 1886 (1) 1888 (1); *v A 1881 (4) 1887 (1)*
Place (W.) 3: *v WI 1947 (3)*
Pocock, P. I. 25: v A 1968 (1); v WI 1976 (2) 1984 (2); v SL 1984 (1); *v WI 1967 (2) 1973 (4); v In 1972 (4) 1984 (5); v P 1968 (1) 1972 (3)*
Pollard (R.) 4: v A 1948 (2); v In 1946 (1); *v NZ 1946 (1)*
Poole (C. J.) 3: *v In 1951 (3)*
Pope (G. H.) 1: v SA 1947
Pougher (A. D.) 1: *v SA 1891*
Price, J. S. E. 15: v A 1964 (2) 1972 (1); v In 1971 (3); v P 1971 (1); *v SA 1964 (4); v In 1963 (4)*
Price (W. F. F.) 1: v A 1938
Prideaux, R. M. 3: v A 1968 (1); *v P 1968 (2)*
Pringle, D. R. 10: v WI 1984 (3); v In 1982 (3); v P 1982 (1); *v A 1982 (3)*
Pullar (G.) 28: v A 1961 (5); v SA 1960 (3); v In 1959 (3); v P 1962 (2); *v A 1962 (4); v WI 1959 (5); v In 1961 (3); v P 1961 (3)*

Quaife (Wm) 7: v A 1899 (2); *v A 1901 (5)*

Radley, C. T. 8: v NZ 1978 (3); v P 1978 (3); *v NZ 1977 (2)*
Randall, D. W. 47: v A 1977 (5); v WI 1984 (1); v NZ 1983 (3); v In 1979 (3) 1982 (3); v P 1982 (3); *v A 1976 (1) 1978 (6) 1979 (2) 1982 (4); v NZ 1977 (3) 1983 (3); v In 1976 (4); v P 1977 (3) 1983 (3)*
Ranjitsinhji, K. S. 15: v A 1896 (2) 1899 (5) 1902 (3); *v A 1897 (5)*
Read, H. D. 1: v SA 1935
Read (J. M.) 17: v A 1882 (1) 1890 (2) 1893 (1); *v A 1884 (5) 1886 (2) 1887 (1) 1891 (3); v SA 1888 (2)*
Read, W. W. 18: v A 1884 (2) 1886 (3) 1888 (3) 1890 (2) 1893 (2); *v A 1882 (4) 1887 (1); v SA 1891 (1)*
Relf (A. E.) 13: v A 1909 (1); *v A 1903 (2); v SA 1905 (5) 1913 (5)*
Rhodes (H. J.) 2: v In 1959 (2)
Rhodes (W.) 58: v A 1899 (3) 1902 (5) 1905 (4) 1909 (4) 1912 (3) 1921 (1) 1926 (1); v SA 1912 (3); *v A 1903 (5) 1907 (5) 1911 (5) 1920 (5); v SA 1909 (5) 1913 (5); v WI 1929 (4)*
Richardson (D. W.) 1: v WI 1957
Richardson (P. E.) 34: v A 1956 (5); v WI 1957 (5) 1963 (1); v NZ 1958 (4); *v A 1958 (4); v SA 1956 (5); v NZ 1958 (2); v In 1961 (5); v P 1961 (3)*
Richardson (T.) 14: v A 1893 (1) 1896 (3); *v A 1894 (5) 1897 (5)*
Richmond (T. L.) 1: v A 1921
Ridgway (F.) 5: *v In 1951 (5)*
Robertson (J. D.) 11: v SA 1947 (1); v NZ 1949 (1); *v WI 1947 (4); v In 1951 (5)*
Robins, R. W. V. 19: v A 1930 (2); v SA 1929 (1) 1935 (3); v WI 1933 (2); v NZ 1931 (1) 1937 (3); v In 1932 (1) 1936 (2); *v A 1936 (4)*
Robinson, R. T. 11: v A 1985 (6); *v In 1984 (5)*
Roope, G. R. J. 21: v A 1975 (1) 1977 (2); v WI 1973 (1); v NZ 1973 (3) 1978 (1); v P 1978 (3); *v NZ 1977 (3); v In 1972 (2); v P 1972 (2) 1977 (3)*
Root (C. F.) 3: v A 1926 (3)
Rose, B. C. 9: v WI 1980 (3); *v WI 1980 (1); v NZ 1977 (2); v P 1977 (3)*
Royle, V. P. F. A. 1: *v A 1878*
Rumsey, F. E. 5: v A 1964 (1); v SA 1965 (1); v NZ 1965 (3)
Russell (A. C.) 10: v A 1921 (2); *v A 1920 (4); v SA 1922 (4)*
Russell, W. E. 10: v SA 1965 (1); v WI 1966 (2); v P 1967 (1); *v A 1965 (1); v NZ 1965 (3); v In 1961 (1); v P 1961 (1)*

Sandham (A.) 14: v A 1921 (1); v SA 1924 (2); *v A 1924 (2); v SA 1922 (5); v WI 1929 (4)*
Schultz, S. S. 1: *v A 1878*
Scotton (W. H.) 15: v A 1884 (1) 1886 (3); *v A 1881 (4) 1884 (5) 1886 (2)*
Selby (J.) 6: *v A 1876 (2) 1881 (4)*
Selvey, M. W. W. 3: v WI 1976 (2); *v In 1976 (1)*
Shackleton (D.) 7: v SA 1951 (1); v WI 1950 (1) 1963 (4); *v In 1951 (1)*
Sharp (J.) 3: v A 1909 (3)
Sharpe (J. W.) 3: v A 1890 (1); *v A 1891 (2)*

Sharpe, P. J. 12: v A 1964 (2); v WI 1963 (3) 1969 (3); v NZ 1969 (3); *v In 1963 (1)*
Shaw (A.) 7: v A 1880 (1); *v A 1876 (2) 1881 (4)*
Sheppard, Rev. D. S. 22: v A 1956 (2); v WI 1950 (1) 1957 (2); v In 1952 (2); v P 1954 (2) 1962 (2); *v A 1950 (2) 1962 (5); v NZ 1950 (1) 1963 (3)*
Sherwin (M.) 3: v A 1888 (1); *v A 1886 (2)*
Shrewsbury (A.) 23: v A 1884 (2) 1886 (3) 1890 (2) 1893 (3); *v A 1881 (4) 1884 (5) 1886 (2) 1887 (1)*
Shuter, J. 1: v A 1888
Shuttleworth, K. 5: v P 1971 (1); *v A 1970 (2); v NZ 1970 (2)*
Sidebottom, A. 1: v A 1985
Simpson, R. T. 27: v A 1953 (3); v SA 1951 (3); v WI 1950 (3); v NZ 1949 (2); v In 1952 (2); v P 1954 (3); *v A 1950 (5) 1954 (1); v SA 1948 (1); v NZ 1950 (2) 1954 (2)*
Simpson-Hayward, G. H. 5: *v SA 1909 (5)*
Sims (J. M.) 4: v SA 1935 (1); v In 1936 (1); *v A 1936 (2)*
Sinfield (R. A.) 1: v A 1938
Smailes (T. F.) 1: v In 1946
Smith, A. C. 6: *v A 1962 (4); v NZ 1962 (2)*
Smith, C. A. 1: *v SA 1888*
Smith (C. I. J.) 5: v NZ 1937 (1); *v WI 1934 (4)*
Smith, C. L. 7: v NZ 1983 (2); *v NZ 1983 (2); v P 1983 (3)*
Smith (D.) 2: v SA 1935 (2)
Smith (D. R.) 5: *v In 1961 (5)*
Smith (D. V.) 3: v WI 1957 (3)
Smith (E. J.) 11: v A 1912 (3); v SA 1912 (3); *v A 1911 (4); v SA 1913 (1)*
Smith (H.) 1: v WI 1928
Smith, M. J. K. 50: v A 1961 (1) 1972 (3); v SA 1960 (4) 1965 (3); v WI 1966 (1); v NZ 1958 (3) 1965 (3); v In 1959 (2); *v A 1965 (5); v SA 1964 (5); v WI 1959 (5); v NZ 1965 (3); v In 1961 (4) 1963 (5); v P 1961 (3)*
Smith (T. P. B.) 4: v In 1946 (1); *v A 1946 (2); v NZ 1946 (1)*
Smithson (G. A.) 2: *v WI 1947 (2)*
Snow, J. A. 49: v A 1968 (5) 1972 (5) 1975 (4); v SA 1965 (1); v WI 1966 (3) 1969 (3) 1973 (1) 1976 (3); v NZ 1965 (1) 1969 (2) 1973 (3); v In 1967 (3) 1971 (2); v P 1967 (1); *v A 1970 (6); v WI 1967 (4); v P 1968 (2)*
Southerton (J.) 2: *v A 1876 (2)*
Spooner, R. H. 10: v A 1905 (2) 1909 (2) 1912 (3); v SA 1912 (3)
Spooner (R. T.) 7: v SA 1955 (1); *v In 1951 (5); v WI 1953 (1)*
Stanyforth, R. T. 4: *v SA 1927 (4)*
Staples (S. J.) 3: *v SA 1927 (3)*
Statham (J. B.) 70: v A 1953 (1) 1956 (3) 1961 (4); v SA 1951 (2) 1955 (4) 1960 (5) 1965 (1); v WI 1957 (3) 1963 (2); v NZ 1958 (2); v In 1959 (3); v P 1954 (4) 1962 (3); *v A 1954 (5) 1958 (4) 1962 (5); v SA 1956 (4); v WI 1953 (4) 1959 (3); v NZ 1950 (1) 1954 (2); v In 1951 (5)*
Steel, A. G. 13: v A 1880 (1) 1882 (1) 1884 (3) 1886 (3) 1888 (1); *v A 1882 (4)*
Steele, D. S. 8: v A 1975 (3); v WI 1976 (5)
Stevens, G. T. S. 10: v A 1926 (2); *v SA 1922 (1) 1927 (5); v WI 1929 (2)*
Stevenson, G. B. 2: *v WI 1980 (1); v In 1979 (1)*
Stewart (M. J.) 8: v WI 1963 (4); v P 1962 (2); *v In 1963 (2)*
Stoddart, A. E. 16: v A 1893 (3) 1896 (2); *v A 1887 (1) 1891 (3) 1894 (5) 1897 (2)*
Storer (W.) 6: v A 1899 (1); *v A 1897 (5)*
Street (G. B.) 1: *v SA 1922*
Strudwick (H.) 28: v A 1921 (2) 1926 (5); v SA 1924 (1); *v A 1911 (1) 1920 (4) 1924 (5); v SA 1909 (5) 1913 (5)*
Studd, C. T. 5: v A 1882 (1); *v A 1882 (4)*
Studd, G. B. 4: *v A 1882 (4)*
Subba Row, R. 13: v A 1961 (5); v SA 1960 (4); v NZ 1958 (1); v In 1959 (1); *v WI 1959 (2)*
Sugg (F. H.) 2: v A 1888 (2)
Sutcliffe (H.) 54: v A 1926 (5) 1930 (4) 1934 (4); v SA 1924 (5) 1929 (5) 1935 (2); v WI 1928 (3) 1933 (2); v NZ 1931 (2); v In 1932 (1); *v A 1924 (5) 1928 (4) 1932 (5); v SA 1927 (5); v NZ 1932 (2)*
Swetman (R.) 11: v In 1959 (3); *v A 1958 (2); v WI 1959 (4); v NZ 1958 (2)*

Tate (F. W.) 1: v A 1902
Tate (M. W.) 39: v A 1926 (5) 1930 (5); v SA 1924 (5) 1929 (3) 1935 (1); v WI 1928 (3); v NZ 1931 (1); *v A 1924 (5) 1928 (5); v SA 1930 (5); v NZ 1932 (1)*

Tattersall (R.) 16: v A 1953 (1); v SA 1951 (5); v P 1954 (1); *v A 1950 (2); v NZ 1950 (2); v In 1951 (5)*
Tavaré, C. J. 30: v A 1981 (2); v WI 1980 (2) 1984 (1); v NZ 1983 (4); v In 1982 (3); v P 1982 (3); v SL 1984 (1); *v A 1982 (5); v NZ 1983 (2); v In 1981 (6); v SL 1981 (1)*
Taylor (K.) 3: v A 1964 (1); v In 1959 (2)
Taylor, L. B. 2: v A 1985 (2)
Taylor, R. W. 57: v A 1981 (3); v NZ 1978 (3) 1983 (4); v In 1979 (3) 1982 (3); v P 1978 (3) 1982 (3); *v A 1978 (6) 1979 (3) 1982 (5); v NZ 1970 (1) 1977 (3) 1983 (3); v In 1979 (1) 1981 (6); v P 1977 (3) 1983 (3); v SL 1981 (1)*
Tennyson, Hon. L. H. 9: v A 1921 (4); *v SA 1913 (5)*
Terry, V. P. 2: v WI 1984 (2)
Thompson (G. J.) 6: v A 1909 (1); *v SA 1909 (5)*
Thomson, N. I. 5: *v SA 1964 (5)*
Titmus (F. J.) 53: v A 1964 (5); v SA 1955 (2) 1965 (3); v WI 1963 (4) 1966 (3); v NZ 1965 (3); v P 1962 (2) 1967 (2); *v A 1962 (5) 1965 (5) 1974 (4); v SA 1964 (5); v WI 1967 (2); v NZ 1962 (3); v In 1963 (5)*
Tolchard, R. W. 4: *v In 1976 (4)*
Townsend, C. L. 2: v A 1899 (2)
Townsend, D. C. H. 3: *v WI 1934 (3)*
Townsend (L. F.) 4: *v WI 1929 (1); v In 1933 (3)*
Tremlett (M. F.) 3: *v WI 1947 (3)*
Trott (A. E.) 2: *v SA 1898 (2)*
Trueman (F. S.) 67: v A 1953 (1) 1956 (2) 1961 (4) 1964 (4); v SA 1955 (1) 1960 (5); v WI 1957 (5) 1963 (5); v NZ 1958 (5) 1965 (2); v In 1952 (4) 1959 (5); v P 1962 (4); *v A 1958 (3) 1962 (5); v WI 1953 (3) 1959 (5); v NZ 1958 (2) 1962 (2)*
Tufnell, N. C. 1: *v SA 1909*
Turnbull, M. J. 9: v WI 1933 (2); v In 1936 (1); *v SA 1930 (5); v NZ 1929 (1)*
Tyldesley (E.) 14: v A 1921 (3) 1926 (1); v SA 1924 (1); v WI 1928 (3); *v A 1928 (1); v SA 1927 (5)*
Tyldesley (J. T.) 31: v A 1899 (2) 1902 (5) 1905 (5) 1909 (4); v SA 1907 (3); *v A 1901 (5) 1903 (5); v SA 1898 (2)*
Tyldesley (R. K.) 7: v A 1930 (2); v SA 1924 (4); *v A 1924 (1)*
Tylecote, E. F. S. 6: v A 1886 (2); *v A 1882 (4)*
Tyler (E. J.) 1: *v SA 1895*
Tyson (F. H.) 17: v A 1956 (1); v SA 1955 (2); v P 1954 (1); *v A 1954 (5) 1958 (2); v SA 1956 (2); v NZ 1954 (2) 1958 (2)*

Ulyett (G.) 25: v A 1882 (1) 1884 (3) 1886 (3) 1888 (2) 1890 (1); *v A 1876 (2) 1878 (1) 1881 (4) 1884 (5) 1887 (1); v SA 1888 (2)*
Underwood, D. L. 86: v A 1968 (4) 1972 (2) 1975 (4) 1977 (5); v WI 1966 (2) 1969 (2) 1973 (3) 1976 (5) 1980 (1); v NZ 1969 (3) 1973 (1); v In 1971 (1) 1974 (3); v P 1967 (2) 1971 (1) 1974 (3); *v A 1970 (5) 1974 (5) 1976 (1) 1979 (3); v WI 1973 (4); v NZ 1970 (2) 1974 (2); v In 1972 (4) 1976 (5) 1979 (1) 1981 (6); v P 1968 (3) 1972 (2); v SL 1981 (1)*

Valentine, B. H. 7: *v SA 1938 (5); v In 1933 (2)*
Verity (H.) 40: v A 1934 (5) 1938 (4); v SA 1935 (4); v WI 1933 (2) 1939 (1); v NZ 1931 (2) 1937 (1); v In 1936 (3); *v A 1932 (4) 1936 (5); v SA 1938 (5); v NZ 1932 (1); v In 1933 (3)*
Vernon, G. F. 1: *v A 1882*
Vine (J.) 2: *v A 1911 (2)*
Voce (W.) 27: v NZ 1931 (1) 1937 (1); v In 1932 (1) 1936 (1) 1946 (1); *v A 1932 (4) 1936 (5) 1946 (2); v SA 1930 (5); v WI 1929 (4); v NZ 1932 (2)*

Waddington (A.) 2: *v A 1920 (2)*
Wainwright (E.) 5: v A 1893 (1); *v A 1897 (4)*
Walker (P. M.) 3: v SA 1960 (3)
Walters, C. F. 11: v A 1934 (5); v WI 1933 (3); *v In 1933 (3)*
Ward, A. 5: v WI 1976 (1); v NZ 1969 (3); v P 1971 (1)
Ward (A.) 7: v A 1893 (2); *v A 1894 (5)*
Wardle (J. H.) 28: v A 1953 (3) 1956 (1); v SA 1951 (2) 1955 (3); v WI 1950 (1) 1957 (1); v P 1954 (4); *v A 1954 (4); v SA 1956 (4); v WI 1947 (1) 1953 (2); v NZ 1954 (2)*
Warner, P. F. 15: v A 1909 (1) 1912 (1); v SA 1912 (1); *v A 1903 (5); v SA 1898 (2) 1905 (5)*
Warr, J. J. 2: *v A 1950 (2)*
Warren (A. R.) 1: v A 1905
Washbrook (C.) 37: v A 1948 (4) 1956 (3); v SA 1947 (5); v WI 1950 (2); v NZ 1937 (1) 1949 (2); v In 1946 (3); *v A 1946 (5) 1950 (5); v SA 1948 (5); v NZ 1946 (1) 1950 (1)*

Watkins (A. J.) 15: v A 1948 (1); v NZ 1949 (1); v In 1952 (3); *v SA 1948 (5); v In 1951 (5)*
Watson (W.) 23: v A 1953 (3) 1956 (2); v SA 1951 (5) 1955 (1); v NZ 1958 (2); v In 1952 (1); *v A 1958 (2); v WI 1953 (5); v NZ 1958 (2)*
Webbe, A. J. 1: *v A 1878*
Wellard (A. W.) 2: v A 1938 (1); v NZ 1937 (1)
Wharton (A.) 1: v NZ 1949
White (D. W.) 2: *v P 1961 (2)*
White, J. C. 15: v A 1921 (1) 1930 (1); v SA 1929 (3); v WI 1928 (1); *v A 1928 (5); v SA 1930 (4)*
Whysall (W. W.) 4: v A 1930 (1); *v A 1924 (3)*
Wilkinson (L. L.) 3: *v SA 1938 (3)*
Willey, P. 21: v A 1980 (1) 1981 (4) 1985 (1); v WI 1976 (2) 1980 (5); v In 1979 (1); *v A 1979 (3); v WI 1980 (4)*
Willis, R. G. D. 90: v A 1977 (5) 1981 (6); v WI 1973 (1) 1976 (2) 1980 (4) 1984 (3); v NZ 1978 (3) 1983 (4); v In 1974 (1) 1979 (3) 1982 (3); v P 1974 (1) 1978 (3) 1982 (2); *v A 1970 (4) 1974 (5) 1976 (1) 1978 (6) 1979 (3) 1982 (5); v WI 1973 (3); v NZ 1970 (1) 1977 (3) 1983 (3); v In 1976 (5) 1981 (5); v P 1977 (3) 1983 (1); v SL 1981 (1)*
Wilson, C. E. M. 2: *v SA 1898 (2)*
Wilson, D. 6: *v NZ 1970 (1); v In 1963 (5)*
Wilson, E. R. 1: *v A 1920*
Wood (A.) 4: v A 1938 (1); v WI 1939 (3)
Wood, B. 12: v A 1972 (1) 1975 (3); v WI 1976 (1); v P 1978 (1); *v NZ 1974 (2); v In 1972 (3); v P 1972 (1)*
Wood, G. E. C. 3: v SA 1924 (3)
Wood (H.) 4: v A 1888 (1); *v SA 1888 (2) 1891 (1)*
Wood (R.) 1: *v A 1886*
Woods S. M. J. 3: *v SA 1895 (3)*
Woolley (F. E.) 64: v A 1909 (1) 1912 (3) 1921 (5) 1926 (5) 1930 (2) 1934 (1); v SA 1912 (3) 1924 (5) 1929 (3); v NZ 1931 (1); v In 1932 (1); *v A 1911 (5) 1920 (5) 1924 (5); v SA 1909 (5) 1913 (5) 1922 (5); v NZ 1929 (4)*
Woolmer, R. A. 19: v A 1975 (2) 1977 (5) 1981 (2); v WI 1976 (5) 1980 (2); *v A 1976 (1); v In 1976 (2)*
Worthington (T. S.) 9: v In 1936 (2); *v A 1936 (3); v NZ 1929 (4)*
Wright, C. W. 3: *v SA 1895 (3)*
Wright (D. V. P.) 34: v A 1938 (3) 1948 (1); v SA 1947 (4); v WI 1939 (3) 1950 (1); v NZ 1949 (1); v In 1946 (2); *v A 1946 (5) 1950 (5); v SA 1938 (3) 1948 (3); v NZ 1946 (1)*
Wyatt, R. E. S. 40: v A 1930 (1) 1934 (4); v SA 1929 (2) 1935 (5); v WI 1933 (2); v In 1936 (1); *v A 1932 (5) 1936 (2); v SA 1927 (5) 1930 (5); v WI 1929 (2) 1934 (4); v NZ 1932 (2)*
Wynyard, E. G. 3: v A 1896 (1); *v SA 1905 (2)*

Yardley, N. W. D. 20: v A 1948 (5); v SA 1947 (5); v WI 1950 (3); *v A 1946 (5); v SA 1938 (1); v NZ 1946 (1)*
Young (H. I.) 2: v A 1899 (2)
Young (J. A.) 8: v A 1948 (3); v SA 1947 (1); v NZ 1949 (2); *v SA 1948 (2)*
Young, R. A. 2: *v A 1907 (2)*

## AUSTRALIA

Number of Test cricketers: 330

A'Beckett, E. L. 4: v E 1928 (2); v SA 1931 (1); *v E 1930 (1)*
Alderman, T. M. 22: v E 1982 (1); v WI 1981 (2) 1984 (3); v P 1981 (3); *v E 1981 (6); v WI 1983 (3); v NZ 1981 (3); v P 1982 (1)*
Alexander, G. 2: v E 1884 (1); *v E 1880 (1)*
Alexander, H. H. 1: v E 1932
Allan, F. E. 1: v E 1878
Allan, P. J. 1: v E 1965
Allen, R. C. 1: v E 1886
Andrews, T. J. E. 16: v E 1924 (3); *v E 1921 (5) 1926 (5); v SA 1921 (3)*
Archer, K. A. 5: v E 1950 (3); v WI 1951 (2)
Archer, R. G. 19: v E 1954 (4); v SA 1952 (1); *v E 1953 (3) 1956 (5); v WI 1954 (5); v P 1956 (1)*
Armstrong, W. W. 50: v E 1901 (4) 1903 (3) 1907 (5) 1911 (5) 1920 (5); v SA 1910 (5); *v E 1902 (5) 1905 (5) 1909 (5) 1921 (5); v SA 1902 (3)*

Badcock, C. L. 7: v E 1936 (3); *v E 1938 (4)*
Bannerman, A. C. 28: v E 1878 (1) 1881 (3) 1882 (4) 1884 (4) 1886 (1) 1887 (1) 1891 (3); *v E 1880 (1) 1882 (1) 1884 (3) 1888 (3) 1893 (3)*
Bannerman, C. 3: v E 1876 (2) 1878 (1)
Bardsley, W. 41: v E 1911 (4) 1920 (5) 1924 (3); v SA 1910 (5); *v E 1909 (5) 1912 (3) 1921 (5) 1926 (5); v SA 1912 (3) 1921 (3)*
Barnes, S. G. 13: v E 1946 (4); v In 1947 (3); *v E 1938 (1) 1948 (4); v NZ 1945 (1)*
Barnett, B. A. 4: *v E 1938 (4)*
Barrett, J. E. 2: *v E 1890 (2)*
Beard, G. R. 3: *v P 1979 (3)*
Benaud, J. 3: v P 1972 (2); *v WI 1972 (1)*
Benaud, R. 63: v E 1954 (5) 1958 (5) 1962 (5); v SA 1952 (4) 1963 (4); v WI 1951 (1) 1960 (5); *v E 1953 (3) 1956 (5) 1961 (4); v SA 1957 (5); v WI 1954 (5); v In 1956 (3) 1959 (5); v P 1956 (1) 1959 (3)*
Bennett, M. J. 3: v WI 1984 (2); *v E 1985 (1)*
Blackham, J. McC. 35: v E 1876 (2) 1878 (1) 1881 (4) 1882 (4) 1884 (2) 1886 (1) 1887 (1) 1891 (3) 1894 (1); *v E 1880 (1) 1882 (1) 1884 (3) 1886 (3) 1888 (3) 1890 (2) 1893 (3)*
Blackie, D. D. 3: v E 1928 (3)
Bonnor, G. J. 17: v E 1882 (4) 1884 (3); *v E 1880 (1) 1882 (1) 1884 (3) 1886 (2) 1888 (3)*
Boon, D. C. 7: v WI 1984 (3); *v E 1985 (4)*
Booth, B. C. 29: v E 1962 (5) 1965 (3); v SA 1963 (4); v P 1964 (1); *v E 1961 (2) 1964 (5); v WI 1964 (5); v In 1964 (3); v P 1964 (1)*
Border, A. R. 72: v E 1978 (3) 1979 (3) 1982 (5); v WI 1979 (3) 1981 (3) 1984 (5); v In 1980 (3); v NZ 1980 (3); v P 1978 (2) 1981 (3) 1983 (5); *v E 1980 (1) 1981 (6) 1985 (6); v WI 1983 (5); v NZ 1981 (3); v In 1979 (6); v P 1979 (3) 1982 (3); v SL 1982 (1)*
Boyle, H. F. 12: v E 1878 (1) 1881 (4) 1882 (1) 1884 (1); *v E 1880 (1) 1882 (1) 1884 (3)*
Bradman, D. G. 52: v E 1928 (4) 1932 (4) 1936 (5) 1946 (5); v SA 1931 (5); v WI 1930 (5); v In 1947 (5); *v E 1930 (5) 1934 (5) 1938 (4) 1948 (5)*
Bright, R. J. 16: v E 1979 (1); v WI 1979 (1); *v E 1977 (3) 1980 (1) 1981 (5); v P 1979 (3) 1982 (2)*
Bromley, E. H. 2: v E 1932 (1); *v E 1934 (1)*
Brown, W. A. 22: v E 1936 (2); v In 1947 (3); *v E 1934 (5) 1938 (4) 1948 (2); v SA 1935 (5); v NZ 1945 (1)*
Bruce, W. 14: v E 1884 (2) 1891 (3) 1894 (4); *v E 1886 (2) 1893 (3)*
Burge, P. J. 42: v E 1954 (1) 1958 (1) 1962 (3) 1965 (4); v SA 1963 (5); v WI 1960 (2); *v E 1956 (3) 1961 (5) 1964 (5); v SA 1957 (1); v WI 1954 (1); v In 1956 (3) 1959 (2) 1964 (3); v P 1959 (2) 1964 (1)*
Burke, J. W. 24: v E 1950 (2) 1954 (2) 1958 (5); v WI 1951 (1); *v E 1956 (5); v SA 1957 (5); v In 1956 (3); v P 1956 (1)*
Burn, K. E. 2: *v E 1890 (2)*
Burton, F. J. 2: v E 1886 (1) 1887 (1)

Callaway, S. T. 3: v E 1891 (2) 1894 (1)
Callen, I. W. 1: v In 1977
Carkeek, W. 6: *v E 1912 (3); v SA 1912 (3)*
Carlson, P. H. 2: v E 1978 (2)
Carter, H. 28: v E 1907 (5) 1911 (5) 1920 (2); v SA 1910 (5); *v E 1909 (5) 1921 (4); v SA 1921 (2)*
Chappell, G. S. 87: v E 1970 (5) 1974 (6) 1976 (1) 1979 (3) 1982 (5); v WI 1975 (6) 1979 (3) 1981 (3); v NZ 1973 (3) 1980 (3); v In 1980 (3); v P 1972 (3) 1976 (3) 1981 (3) 1983 (5); *v E 1972 (5) 1975 (4) 1977 (5) 1980 (1); v WI 1972 (5); v NZ 1973 (3) 1976 (2) 1981 (3); v P 1979 (3); v SL 1982 (1)*
Chappell, I. M. 75: v E 1965 (2) 1970 (6) 1974 (6) 1979 (2); v WI 1968 (5) 1975 (6) 1979 (1); v NZ 1973 (3); v In 1967 (4); v P 1964 (1) 1972 (3); *v E 1968 (5) 1972 (5) 1975 (4); v SA 1966 (5) 1969 (4); v WI 1972 (5); v NZ 1973 (3); v In 1969 (5)*
Chappell, T. M. 3: *v E 1981 (3)*
Charlton, P. C. 2: *v E 1890 (2)*
Chipperfield, A. G. 14: v E 1936 (3); *v E 1934 (5) 1938 (1); v SA 1935 (5)*
Clark, W. M. 10: v In 1977 (5); v P 1978 (1); *v WI 1977 (4)*
Colley, D. J. 3: *v E 1972 (3)*
Collins, H. L. 19: v E 1920 (5) 1924 (5); *v E 1921 (3) 1926 (3); v SA 1921 (3)*
Coningham, A. 1: v E 1894
Connolly, A. N. 29; v E 1965 (1) 1970 (1); v SA 1963 (3); v WI 1968 (5); v In 1967 (3); *v E 1968 (5); v SA 1969 (4); v In 1964 (2); 1969 (5)*

Cooper, B. B. 1: v E 1876
Cooper, W. H. 2: v E 1881 (1) 1884 (1)
Corling, G. E. 5: *v E 1964 (5)*
Cosier, G. J. 18: v E 1976 (1) 1978 (2); v WI 1975 (3); v In 1977 (4); v P 1976 (3); *v WI 1977 (3); v NZ 1976 (2)*
Cottam, W. J. 1: v E 1886
Cotter, A. 21: v E 1903 (2) 1907 (2) 1911 (4); v SA 1910 (5); *v E 1905 (3) 1909 (5)*
Coultard, G. 1: v E 1881
Cowper, R. M. 27: v E 1965 (4); v In 1967 (4); v P 1964 (1); *v E 1964 (1) 1968 (4); v SA 1966 (5); v WI 1964 (5); v In 1964 (2); v P 1964 (1)*
Craig, I. D. 11: v SA 1952 (1); *v E 1956 (2); v SA 1957 (5); v In 1956 (2); v P 1956 (1)*
Crawford, W. P. A. 4: *v E 1956 (1); v In 1956 (3)*

Darling, J. 34: v E 1894 (5) 1897 (5) 1901 (3); *v E 1896 (3) 1899 (5) 1902 (5) 1905 (5); v SA 1902 (3)*
Darling, L. S. 12: v E 1932 (2) 1936 (1); *v E 1934 (4): v SA 1935 (5)*
Darling, W. M. 14: v E 1978 (4); v In 1977 (1); v P 1978 (1); *v WI 1977 (3); v In 1979 (5)*
Davidson, A. K. 44; v E 1954 (3) 1958 (5) 1962 (5); v WI 1960 (4); *v E 1953 (5) 1956 (2) 1961 (5); v SA 1957 (5); v In 1956 (1) 1959 (5); v P 1956 (1) 1959 (3)*
Davis, I. C. 15: v E 1976 (1); v NZ 1973 (3); v P 1976 (3); *v E 1977 (3); v NZ 1973 (3) 1976 (2)*
De Courcy, J. H. 3: *v E 1953 (3)*
Dell, A. R. 2: v E 1970 (1); v NZ 1973 (1)
Donnan, H. 5: v E 1891 (2); *v E 1896 (3)*
Dooland, B. 3: v E 1946 (2); v In 1947 (1)
Duff, R. A. 22: v E 1901 (4) 1903 (5); *v E 1902 (5) 1905 (5); v SA 1902 (3)*
Duncan, J. R. F. 1: v E 1970
Dymock, G. 21: v E 1974 (1) 1978 (3) 1979 (3); v WI 1979 (2); v NZ 1973 (1); v P 1978 (1); *v NZ 1973 (2); v In 1979 (5); v P 1979 (3)*
Dyson, J. 30: v E 1982 (5); v WI 1981 (2) 1984 (3); v NZ 1980 (3); v In 1977 (3) 1980 (3); *v E 1981 (5); v NZ 1981 (3); v P 1982 (3)*

Eady, C. J. 2: v E 1901 (1); *v E 1896 (1)*
Eastwood, K. H. 1: v E 1970
Ebeling, H. I. 1: *v E 1934*
Edwards, J. D. 3: *v E 1888 (3)*
Edwards, R. 20: v E 1974 (5); v P 1972 (2); *v E 1972 (4) 1975 (4); v WI 1972 (5)*
Edwards, W. J. 3: v E 1974 (3)
Emery, S. H. 4: *v E 1912 (2); v SA 1912 (2)*
Evans, E. 6: v E 1881 (2) 1882 (1) 1884 (1); *v E 1886 (2)*

Fairfax, A. G. 10: v E 1928 (1); v WI 1930 (5); *v E 1930 (4)*
Favell, L. E. 19: v E 1954 (4) 1958 (2); v WI 1960 (4); *v WI 1954 (2); v In 1959 (4); v P 1959 (3)*
Ferris, J. J. 8: v E 1886 (2) 1887 (1); *v E 1888 (3) 1890 (2)*
Fingleton, J. H. 18: v E 1932 (3) 1936 (5); v SA 1931 (1); *v E 1938 (4); v SA 1935 (5)*
Fleetwood-Smith, L. O'B. 10: v E 1936 (3); *v E 1938 (4); v SA 1935 (3)*
Francis, B. C. 3: *v E 1972 (3)*
Freeman, E. W. 11: v WI 1968 (4); v In 1967 (2); *v E 1968 (2); v SA 1969 (2); v In 1969 (1)*
Freer, F. W. 1: v E 1946

Gannon, J. B. 3: v In 1977 (3)
Garrett, T. W. 19: v E 1876 (2) 1878 (1) 1881 (3) 1882 (3) 1884 (3) 1886 (2) 1887 (1); *v E 1882 (1) 1886 (3)*
Gaunt, R. A. 3: v SA 1963 (1); *v E 1961 (1); v SA 1957 (1)*
Gehrs, D. R. A. 6: v E 1903 (1); v SA 1910 (4); *v E 1905 (1)*
Giffen, G. 31: v E 1881 (3) 1882 (4) 1884 (3) 1891 (3) 1894 (5); *v E 1882 (1) 1884 (3) 1886 (3) 1893 (3) 1896 (3)*
Giffen, W. F. 3: v E 1886 (1) 1891 (2)
Gilbert, D. R. 1: *v E 1985*
Gilmour, G. J. 15: v E 1976 (1); v WI 1975 (5); v NZ 1973 (2); v P 1976 (3); *v E 1975 (1); v NZ 1973 (1) 1976 (2)*
Gleeson, J. W. 29: v E 1970 (5); v WI 1968 (5); v In 1967 (4); *v E 1968 (5) 1972 (3); v SA 1969 (4); v In 1969 (3)*
Graham, H. 6: v E 1894 (2); *v E 1893 (3) 1896 (1)*
Gregory, D. W. 3: v E 1876 (2) 1878 (1)

Gregory, E. J. 1: v E 1876
Gregory, J. M. 24: v E 1920 (5) 1924 (5) 1928 (1); *v E 1921 (5) 1926 (5); v SA 1921 (3)*
Gregory, R. G. 2: v E 1936 (2)
Gregory, S. E. 58: v E 1891 (1) 1894 (5) 1897 (5) 1901 (5) 1903 (4) 1907 (2) 1911 (1); *v E 1890 (2) 1893 (3) 1896 (3) 1899 (5) 1902 (5) 1905 (3) 1909 (5) 1912 (3); v SA 1902 (3) 1912 (3)*
Grimmett, C. V. 37: v E 1924 (1) 1928 (5) 1932 (3); v SA 1931 (5); v WI 1930 (5); *v E 1926 (3) 1930 (5) 1934 (5); v SA 1935 (5)*
Groube, T. U. 1: *v E 1880*
Grout, A. T. W. 51: v E 1958 (5) 1962 (2) 1965 (5); v SA 1963 (5); v WI 1960 (5); *v E 1961 (5) 1964 (5); v SA 1957 (5); v WI 1964 (5); v In 1959 (4) 1964 (1); v P 1959 (3) 1964 (1)*
Guest, C. E. J. 1: v E 1962

Hamence, R. A. 3: v E 1946 (1); v In 1947 (2)
Hammond, J. R. 5: *v WI 1972 (5)*
Harry, J. 1: v E 1894
Hartigan, R. J. 2: v E 1907 (2)
Hartkopf, A. E. V. 1: v E 1924
Harvey, M. R. 1: v E 1946
Harvey, R. N. 79: v E 1950 (5) 1954 (5) 1958 (5) 1962 (5); v SA 1952 (5); v WI 1951 (5) 1960 (4); v In 1947 (2); *v E 1948 (2) 1953 (5) 1956 (5) 1961 (5); v SA 1949 (5) 1957 (4); v WI 1954 (5); v In 1956 (3) 1959 (5); v P 1956 (1) 1959 (3)*
Hassett, A. L. 43: v E 1946 (5) 1950 (5); v SA 1952 (5); v WI 1951 (4); v In 1947 (4); *v E 1938 (4) 1948 (5) 1953 (5); v SA 1949 (5); v NZ 1945 (1)*
Hawke, N. J. N. 27: v E 1962 (1) 1965 (4); v SA 1963 (4); v In 1967 (1); v P 1964 (1); *v E 1964 (5) 1968 (2); v SA 1966 (2); v WI 1964 (5); v In 1964 (1); v P 1964 (1)*
Hazlitt, G. R. 9: v E 1907 (2) 1911 (1); *v E 1912 (3); v SA 1912 (3)*
Hendry, H. L. 11: v E 1924 (1) 1928 (4); *v E 1921 (4); v SA 1921 (2)*
Hibbert, P. A. 1: v In 1977
Higgs, J. D. 22: v E 1978 (5) 1979 (1); v WI 1979 (1); v NZ 1980 (3); v In 1980 (2); *v WI 1977 (4); v In 1979 (6)*
Hilditch, A. M. J. 17: v E 1978 (1); v WI 1984 (2); v P 1978 (2); *v E 1985 (6); v In 1979 (6)*
Hill, C. 49: v E 1897 (5) 1901 (5) 1903 (5) 1907 (5) 1911 (5); v SA 1910 (5); *v E 1896 (3) 1899 (3) 1902 (5) 1905 (5); v SA 1902 (3)*
Hill, J. C. 3: *v E 1953 (2); v WI 1954 (1)*
Hoare, D. E. 1: v WI 1960
Hodges, J. H. 2: v E 1876 (2)
Hogan, T. G. 7: v P 1983 (1); *v WI 1983 (5); v SL 1982 (1)*
Hogg, R. M. 38: v E 1978 (6) 1982 (3); v WI 1979 (2) 1984 (4); v NZ 1980 (2); v In 1980 (2); v P 1978 (2) 1983 (4); *v E 1981 (2); v WI 1983 (4); v In 1979 (6); v SL 1982 (1)*
Hole, G. B. 18: v E 1950 (1) 1954 (3); v SA 1952 (4); v WI 1951 (5); *v E 1953 (5)*
Holland, R. G. 7: v WI 1984 (3); *v E 1985 (4)*
Hookes, D. W. 19: v E 1976 (1) 1982 (5); v WI 1979 (1); *v E 1977 (5); v WI 1983 (5); v P 1979 (1); v SL 1982 (1)*
Hopkins, A. J. Y. 20: v E 1901 (2) 1903 (5); *v E 1902 (5) 1905 (3) 1909 (2); v SA 1902 (3)*
Horan, T. P. 15: v E 1876 (1) 1878 (1) 1881 (4) 1882 (4) 1884 (4); *v E 1882 (1)*
Hordern, H. V. 7: v E 1911 (5); v SA 1910 (2)
Hornibrook, P. M. 6: v E 1928 (1); *v E 1930 (5)*
Howell, W. P. 18: v E 1897 (3) 1901 (4) 1903 (3); *v E 1899 (5) 1902 (1); v SA 1902 (2)*
Hughes, K. J. 70: v E 1978 (6) 1979 (3) 1982 (5); v WI 1979 (3) 1981 (3) 1984 (4); v NZ 1980 (3); v In 1977 (2) 1980 (3); v P 1978 (2) 1981 (3) 1983 (5); *v E 1977 (1) 1980 (1) 1981 (6); v WI 1983 (5); v NZ 1981 (3); v In 1979 (6); v P 1979 (3) 1982 (3)*
Hunt, W. A. 1: v SA 1931
Hurst, A. G. 12: v E 1978 (6); v NZ 1973 (1); v In 1977 (1); v P 1978 (2); *v In 1979 (2)*
Hurwood, A. 2: v WI 1930 (2)

Inverarity, R. J. 6: v WI 1968 (1); *v E 1968 (2) 1972 (3)*
Iredale, F. A. 14: v E 1894 (5) 1897 (4); *v E 1896 (2) 1899 (3)*
Ironmonger, H. 14: v E 1928 (2) 1932 (4); v SA 1931 (4); v WI 1930 (4)
Iverson, J. B. 5: v E 1950 (5)

Jackson, A. 8: v E 1928 (2); v WI 1930 (4); *v E 1930 (2)*
Jarman, B. N. 19: v E 1962 (3); v WI 1968 (4); v In 1967 (4); v P 1964 (1); *v E 1968 (4); v In 1959 (1); 1964 (2)*

Jarvis, A. H. 11: v E 1884 (3) 1894 (4); *v E 1886 (2) 1888 (2)*
Jenner, T. J. 9: v E 1970 (2) 1974 (2); v WI 1975 (1); *v WI 1972 (4)*
Jennings, C. B. 6: *v E 1912 (3); v SA 1912 (3)*
Johnson I. W. 45: v E 1946 (4) 1950 (5) 1954 (4); v SA 1952 (1); v WI 1951 (4); v In 1947 (4); *v E 1948 (4) 1956 (5); v SA 1949 (5); v WI 1954 (5); v NZ 1945 (1); v In 1956 (2); v P 1956 (1)*
Johnson, L. J. 1: v In 1947
Johnston W. A. 40: v E 1950 (5) 1954 (4); v SA 1952 (5); v WI 1951 (5); v In 1947 (4); *v E 1948 (5) 1953 (3); v SA 1949 (5); v WI 1954 (4)*
Jones, D. M. 2: *v WI 1983 (2)*
Jones, E. 19: v E 1894 (1) 1897 (5) 1901 (2); *v E 1896 (3) 1899 (5) 1902 (2); v SA 1902 (1)*
Jones, S. P. 12: v E 1881 (2) 1884 (4) 1886 (1) 1887 (1); *v E 1882 (1) 1886 (3)*
Joslin, L. R. 1: v In 1967

Kelleway, C. 26: v E 1911 (4) 1920 (5) 1924 (5) 1928 (1); v SA 1910 (5); *v E 1912 (3); v SA 1912 (3)*
Kelly, J. J. 36: v E 1897 (5) 1901 (5) 1903 (5); *v E 1896 (3) 1899 (5) 1902 (5) 1905 (5); v SA 1902 (3)*
Kelly, T. J. D. 2: v E 1876 (1) 1878 (1)
Kendall, T. 2: v E 1876 (2)
Kent, M. F. 3: *v E 1981 (3)*
Kippax, A. F. 22: v E 1924 (1) 1928 (5) 1932 (1); v SA 1931 (4); v WI 1930 (5); *v E 1930 (5) 1934 (1)*
Kline L. F. 13: v E 1958 (2); v WI 1960 (2); *v SA 1957 (5); v In 1959 (3); v P 1959 (1)*

Laird, B. M. 21: v E 1979 (2); v WI 1979 (3) 1981 (3); v P 1981 (3); *v E 1980 (1); v NZ 1981 (3); v P 1979 (3) 1982 (3)*
Langley, G. R. A. 26: v E 1954 (2); v SA 1952 (5); v WI 1951 (5); *v E 1953 (4) 1956 (3); v WI 1954 (4); v In 1956 (2); v P 1956 (1)*
Laughlin, T. J. 3: v E 1978 (1); *v WI 1977 (2)*
Laver, F. 15: v E 1901 (1) 1903 (1); *v E 1899 (4) 1905 (5) 1909 (4)*
Lawry, W. M. 67: v E 1962 (5) 1965 (5) 1970 (5); v SA 1963 (5); v WI 1968 (5); v In 1967 (4); v P 1964 (1); *v E 1961 (5) 1964 (5) 1968 (4); v SA 1966 (5) 1969 (4); v WI 1964 (5); v In 1964 (3) 1969 (5); v P 1964 (1)*
Lawson, G. F. 34: v E 1982 (5); v WI 1981 (1) 1984 (5); v NZ 1980 (1); v P 1983 (5); *v E 1981 (3) 1985 (6); v WI 1983 (5); v P 1982 (3)*
Lee, P. K. 2: v E 1932 (1); v SA 1931 (1)
Lillee, D. K. 70: v E 1970 (2) 1974 (6) 1976 (1) 1979 (3) 1982 (1); v WI 1975 (5) 1979 (3) 1981 (3); v NZ 1980 (3); v In 1980 (3); v P 1972 (3) 1976 (3) 1981 (3) 1983 (5); *v E 1972 (5) 1975 (4) 1980 (1) 1981 (6); v WI 1972 (1); v NZ 1976 (2) 1981 (3); v P 1979 (3); v SL 1982 (1)*
Lindwall, R. R. 61: v E 1946 (4) 1950 (5) 1954 (4) 1958 (2); v SA 1952 (4); v WI 1951 (5); v In 1947 (5); *v E 1948 (5) 1953 (5) 1956 (4); v SA 1949 (4); v WI 1954 (5); v NZ 1945 (1); v In 1956 (3) 1959 (2); v P 1956 (1) 1959 (2)*
Love, H. S. B. 1: v E 1932
Loxton, S. J. E. 12: v E 1950 (3); v In 1947 (1); *v E 1948 (3); v SA 1949 (5)*
Lyons, J. J. 14: v E 1886 (1) 1891 (3) 1894 (3) 1897 (1); *v E 1888 (1) 1890 (2) 1893 (3)*

McAlister, P. A. 8: v E 1903 (2) 1907 (4); *v E 1909 (2)*
Macartney, C. G. 35: v E 1907 (5) 1911 (1) 1920 (2); v SA 1910 (4); *v E 1909 (5) 1912 (3) 1921 (5) 1926 (5); v SA 1912 (3) 1921 (2)*
McCabe, S. J. 39: v E 1932 (5) 1936 (5); v SA 1931 (5); v WI 1930 (5); *v E 1930 (5) 1934 (5) 1938 (4); v SA 1935 (5)*
McCool, C. L. 14: v E 1946 (5); v In 1947 (3); *v SA 1949 (5) v NZ 1945 (1)*
McCormick, E. L. 12: v E 1936 (4); *v E 1938 (3); v SA 1935 (5)*
McCosker, R. B. 25: v E 1974 (3) 1976 (1) 1979 (2); v WI 1975 (4) 1979 (1); v P 1976 (3); *v E 1975 (4) 1977 (5); v NZ 1976 (2)*
McDermott, C. J. 8: v WI 1984 (2); *v E 1985 (6)*
McDonald, C. C. 47: v E 1954 (2) 1958 (5); v SA 1952 (5); v WI 1951 (1) 1960 (5); *v E 1956 (5) 1961 (3); v SA 1957 (5); v WI 1954 (5); v In 1956 (2) 1959 (5); v P 1956 (1) 1959 (3)*
McDonald, E. A. 11: v E 1920 (3); *v E 1921 (5); v SA 1921 (3)*
McDonnell, P. S. 19: v E 1881 (4) 1882 (3) 1884 (2) 1886 (2) 1887 (1); *v E 1880 (1) 1884 (3) 1888 (3)*
McIlwraith, J. 1: *v E 1886*
Mackay K. D. 37: v E 1958 (5) 1962 (3); v WI 1960 (5); *v E 1956 (3) 1961 (5); v SA 1957 (5); v In 1956 (3) 1959 (5); v P 1959 (3)*

McKenzie, G. D. 60: v E 1962 (5) 1965 (4) 1970 (3); v SA 1963 (5); v WI 1968 (5); v In 1967 (2); v P 1964 (1); *v E 1961 (3) 1964 (5) 1968 (5); v SA 1966 (5) 1969 (3); v WI 1964 (5); v In 1964 (3) 1969 (5); v P 1964 (1)*
McKibbin, T. R. 5: v E 1894 (1) 1897 (2); *v E 1896 (2)*
McLaren, J. W. 1: v E 1911
Maclean, J. A. 4: v E 1978 (4)
McLeod, C. E. 17: v E 1894 (1) 1897 (5) 1901 (2) 1903 (3); *v E 1899 (1) 1905 (5)*
McLeod, R. W. 6: v E 1891 (3); *v E 1893 (3)*
McShane, P. G. 3: v E 1884 (1) 1886 (1) 1887 (1)
Maddocks, L. V. 7: v E 1954 (3); *v E 1956 (2); v WI 1954 (1); v In 1956 (1)*
Maguire, J. N. 3: v P 1983 (1); *v WI 1983 (2)*
Mailey, A. A. 21: v E 1920 (5) 1924 (5); *v E 1921 (3) 1926 (5); v SA 1921 (3)*
Mallett, A. A. 38: v E 1970 (2) 1974 (5) 1979 (1); v WI 1968 (1) 1975 (6) 1979 (1); v NZ 1973 (3); v P 1972 (2); *v E 1968 (1) 1972 (2) 1975 (4) 1980 (1); v SA 1969 (1); v NZ 1973 (3); v In 1969 (5)*
Malone, M. F. 1: *v E 1977*
Mann, A. L. 4: v In 1977 (4)
Marr, A. P. 1: v E 1884
Marsh, R. W. 96: v E 1970 (6) 1974 (6) 1976 (1) 1979 (3) 1982 (5); v WI 1975 (6) 1979 (3) 1981 (3); v NZ 1973 (3) 1980 (3); v In 1980 (3); v P 1972 (3) 1976 (3) 1981 (3) 1983 (5); *v E 1972 (5) 1975 (4) 1977 (5) 1980 (1) 1981 (6); v WI 1972 (5); v NZ 1973 (3) 1976 (2) 1981 (3); v P 1979 (3) 1982 (3)*
Martin, J. W. 8: v SA 1963 (1); v WI 1960 (3); *v SA 1966 (1); v In 1964 (2); v P 1964 (1)*
Massie, H. H. 9: v E 1881 (4) 1882 (3) 1884 (1); *v E 1882 (1)*
Massie, R. A. L. 6: v P 1972 (2); *v E 1972 (4)*
Matthews, G. R. J. 5: v WI 1984 (1); v P 1983 (2); *v E 1985 (1); v WI 1983 (1)*
Matthews, T. J. 8: v E 1911 (2); *v E 1912 (3); v SA 1912 (3)*
Mayne, E. R. 4: *v E 1912 (1); v SA 1912 (1) 1921 (2)*
Mayne, L. C. 6: *v SA 1969 (2); v WI 1964 (3); v In 1969 (1)*
Meckiff, I. 18: v E 1958 (4); v SA 1963 (1); v WI 1960 (2); *v SA 1957 (4); v In 1959 (5); v P 1959 (2)*
Meuleman, K. D. 1: *v NZ 1945*
Midwinter, W. E. 8: v E 1876 (2) 1882 (1) 1886 (2); *v E 1884 (3)*
Miller, K. R. 55: v E 1946 (5) 1950 (5) 1954 (4); v SA 1952 (4); v WI 1951 (5); v In 1947 (5); *v E 1948 (5) 1953 (5) 1956 (5); v SA 1949 (5); v WI 1954 (5); v NZ 1945 (1); v P 1956 (1)*
Minnett, R. B. 9: v E 1911 (5); *v E 1912 (1); v SA 1912 (3)*
Misson, F. M. 5: v WI 1960 (3); *v E 1961 (2)*
Moroney, J. R. 7: v E 1950 (1); v WI 1951 (1); *v SA 1949 (5)*
Morris, A. R. 46: v E 1946 (5) 1950 (5) 1954 (4); v SA 1952 (5); v WI 1951 (4); v In 1947 (4); *v E 1948 (5) 1953 (5); v SA 1949 (5); v WI 1954 (4)*
Morris, S. 1: v E 1884
Moses, H. 6: v E 1886 (2) 1887 (1) 1891 (2) 1894 (1)
Moss, J. K. 1: v P 1978
Moule, W. H. 1: *v E 1880*
Murdoch, W. L. 18: v E 1876 (1) 1878 (1) 1881 (4) 1882 (4) 1884 (1); *v E 1880 (1) 1882 (1) 1884 (3) 1890 (2)*
Musgrove, H. 1: v E 1884

Nagel, L. E. 1: v E 1932
Nash, L. J. 2: v E 1936 (1); v SA 1931 (1)
Nitschke, H. C. 2: v SA 1931 (2)
Noble, M. A. 42: v E 1897 (4) 1901 (5) 1903 (5) 1907 (5); *v E 1899 (5) 1902 (5) 1905 (5) 1909 (5); v SA 1902 (3)*
Noblet, G. 3: v SA 1952 (1); v WI 1951 (1); *v SA 1949 (1)*
Nothling, O. E. 1: v E 1928

O'Brien, L. P. J. 5: v E 1932 (2) 1936 (1); *v SA 1935 (2)*
O'Connor, J. D. A. 4: v E 1907 (3); *v E 1909 (1)*
O'Donnell, S. P. 5: *v E 1985 (5)*
Ogilvie, A. D. 5: v In 1977 (3); *v WI 1977 (2)*
O'Keeffe, K. J. 24: v E 1970 (2) 1976 (1); v NZ 1973 (3); v P 1972 (2) 1976 (3); *v E 1977 (3); v WI 1972 (5); v NZ 1973 (3) 1976 (2)*
Oldfield, W. A. 54: v E 1920 (3) 1924 (5) 1928 (5) 1932 (4) 1936 (5); v SA 1931 (5); v WI 1930 (5); *v E 1921 (1) 1926 (5) 1930 (5) 1934 (5); v SA 1921 (1) 1935 (5)*

O'Neill, N. C. 42: v E 1958 (5) 1962 (5); v SA 1963 (4); v WI 1960 (5); *v E 1961 (5) 1964 (4); v WI 1964 (4); v In 1959 (5) 1964 (2); v P 1959 (3)*
O'Reilly, W. J. 27: v E 1932 (5) 1936 (5); v SA 1931 (2); *v E 1934 (5) 1938 (4); v SA 1935 (5); v NZ 1945 (1)*
Oxenham, R. K. 7: v E 1928 (3); v SA 1931 (1); v WI 1930 (3)

Palmer, G. E. 17: v E 1881 (4) 1882 (4) 1884 (2); *v E 1880 (1) 1884 (3) 1886 (3)*
Park, R. L. 1: v E 1920
Pascoe, L. S. 14: v E 1979 (2); v WI 1979 (1) 1981 (1); v NZ 1980 (3); v In 1980 (3); *v E 1977 (3) 1980 (1)*
Pellew, C. E. 10: v E 1920 (4); *v E 1921 (5); v SA 1921 (1)*
Phillips, W. B. 18: v WI 1984 (2); v P 1983 (5); *v E 1985 (6); v WI 1983 (5)*
Philpott, P. I. 8: v E 1965 (3); *v WI 1964 (5)*
Ponsford, W. H. 29: v E 1924 (5) 1928 (2) 1932 (3); v SA 1931 (4); v WI 1930 (5); *v E 1926 (2) 1930 (4) 1934 (4)*
Pope, R. J. 1: v E 1884

Rackemann, C. G. 5: v E 1982 (1); v WI 1984 (1); v P 1983 (2); *v WI 1983 (1)*
Ransford, V. S. 20: v E 1907 (5) 1911 (5); v SA 1910 (5); *v E 1909 (5)*
Redpath, I. R. 66: v E 1965 (1) 1970 (6) 1974 (6); v SA 1963 (1); v WI 1968 (5) 1975 (6); v In 1967 (3); v P 1972 (3); *v E 1964 (5) 1968 (5); v SA 1966 (5) 1969 (4); v WI 1972 (5); v NZ 1973 (3); v In 1964 (2) 1969 (5); v P 1964 (1)*
Reedman, J. C. 1: v E 1894
Renneberg, D. A. 8: v In 1967 (3); *v SA 1966 (5)*
Richardson, A. J. 9: v E 1924 (4); *v E 1926 (5)*
Richardson, V. Y. 19: v E 1924 (3) 1928 (2) 1932 (5); *v E 1930 (4); v SA 1935 (5)*
Rigg, K. E. 8: v E 1936 (3); v SA 1931 (4); v WI 1930 (1)
Ring, D. T. 13: v SA 1952 (5); v WI 1951 (5); v In 1947 (1); *v E 1948 (1) 1953 (1)*
Ritchie, G. M. 15: v WI 1984 (1); *v E 1985 (6); v WI 1983 (5); v P 1982 (3)*
Rixon, S. J. 13: v WI 1984 (3); v In 1977 (5); *v WI 1977 (5)*
Robertson, W. R. 1: v E 1884
Robinson, R. D. 3: *v E 1977 (3)*
Robinson, R. H. 1: v E 1936
Rorke, G. F. 4: v E 1958 (2); *v In 1959 (2)*
Rutherford, J. W. 1: *v In 1956*
Ryder, J. 20: v E 1920 (5) 1924 (3) 1928 (5); *v E 1926 (4); v SA 1921 (3)*

Saggers, R. A. 6: *v E 1948 (1); v SA 1949 (5)*
Saunders, J. V. 14: v E 1901 (1) 1903 (2) 1907 (5); *v E 1902 (4); v SA 1902 (2)*
Scott, H. J. H. 8: v E 1884 (2); *v E 1884 (3) 1886 (3)*
Sellers, R. H. D. 1: *v In 1964*
Serjeant, C. S. 12: v In 1977 (4); *v E 1977 (3); v WI 1977 (5)*
Sheahan, A. P. 31: v E 1970 (2); v WI 1968 (5); v NZ 1973 (2); v In 1967 (4); v P 1972 (2); *v E 1968 (5) 1972 (2); v SA 1969 (4); v In 1969 (5)*
Shepherd, B. K. 9: v E 1962 (2); v SA 1963 (4); v P 1964 (1); *v WI 1964 (2)*
Sievers, M. W. 3: v E 1936 (3)
Simpson, R. B. 62: v E 1958 (1) 1962 (5) 1965 (3); v SA 1963 (5); v WI 1960 (5); v In 1967 (3) 1977 (5); v P 1964 (1); *v E 1961 (5) 1964 (5); v SA 1957 (5) 1966 (5); v WI 1964 (5) 1977 (5); v In 1964 (3); v P 1964 (1)*
Sincock, D. J. 3: v E 1965 (1); v P 1964 (1); *v WI 1964 (1)*
Slater, K. N. 1: v E 1958
Sleep, P. R. 4: v P 1978 (1); *v In 1979 (2); v P 1982 (1)*
Slight, J. 1: *v E 1880*
Smith, D. B. M. 2: *v E 1912 (2)*
Smith, S. B. 3: *v WI 1983 (3)*
Spofforth, F. R. 18: v E 1876 (1) 1878 (1) 1881 (1) 1882 (4) 1884 (3) 1886 (1); *v E 1882 (1) 1884 (3) 1886 (3)*
Stackpole, K. R. 43: v E 1965 (2) 1970 (6); v WI 1968 (5); v NZ 1973 (3); v P 1972 (1); *v E 1972 (5); v SA 1966 (5) 1969 (4); v WI 1972 (4); v NZ 1973 (3); v In 1969 (5)*
Stevens, G. B. 4: *v In 1959 (2); v P 1959 (2)*

Taber, H. B. 16: v WI 1968 (1); *v E 1968 (1); v SA 1966 (5); 1969 (4); v In 1969 (5)*
Tallon, D. 21: v E 1946 (5) 1950 (5); v In 1947 (5); *v E 1948 (4) 1953 (1); v NZ 1945 (1)*

Taylor, J. M. 20: v E 1920 (5) 1924 (5); *v E 1921 (5) 1926 (3); v SA 1921 (2)*
Thomas, G. 8: v E 1965 (3); *v WI 1964 (5)*
Thompson, N. 2: v E 1876 (2)
Thoms, G. R. 1: v WI 1951
Thomson, A. L. 4: v E 1970 (4)
Thomson, J. R. 51: v E 1974 (5) 1979 (1) 1982 (4); v WI 1975 (6) 1979 (1) 1981 (2); v In 1977 (5); v P 1972 (1) 1976 (1) 1981 (3); *v E 1975 (4) 1977 (5) 1985 (2); v WI 1977 (5); v NZ 1981 (3); v P 1982 (3)*
Thurlow, H. M. 1: v SA 1931
Toohey, P. M. 15: v E 1978 (5) 1979 (1); v WI 1979 (1); v In 1977 (5); *v WI 1977 (3)*
Toshack, E. R. H. 12: v E 1946 (5); v In 1947 (2); *v E 1948 (4); v NZ 1945 (1)*
Travers, J. P. F. 1: v E 1901
Tribe, G. E. 3: v E 1946 (3)
Trott, A. E. 3: v E 1894 (3)
Trott, G. H. S. 24: v E 1891 (3) 1894 (5) 1897 (5); *v E 1888 (3) 1890 (2) 1893 (3) 1896 (3)*
Trumble, H. 32: v E 1894 (1) 1897 (5) 1901 (5) 1903 (4); *v E 1890 (2) 1893 (3) 1896 (3) 1899 (5) 1902 (3); v SA 1902 (1)*
Trumble, J. W. 7: v E 1884 (4); *v E 1886 (3)*
Trumper, V. T. 48: v E 1901 (5) 1903 (5) 1907 (5) 1911 (5); v SA 1910 (5); *v E 1899 (5) 1902 (5) 1905 (5) 1909 (5); v SA 1902 (3)*
Turner, A. 14: v WI 1975 (6); v P 1976 (3); *v E 1975 (3); v NZ 1976 (2)*
Turner, C. T. B. 17: v E 1886 (2) 1887 (1) 1891 (3) 1894 (3); *v E 1888 (3) 1890 (2) 1893 (3)*

Veivers, T. R. 21: v E 1965 (4); v SA 1963 (3); v P 1964 (1); *v E 1964 (5); v SA 1966 (4); v In 1964 (3); v P 1964 (1)*

Waite, M. G. 2: *v E 1938 (2)*
Walker, M. H. N. 34: v E 1974 (6); 1976 (1); v WI 1975 (3); v NZ 1973 (1); v P 1972 (2) 1976 (2); *v E 1975 (4); 1977 (5); v WI 1972 (5); v NZ 1973 (3) 1976 (2)*
Wall, T. W. 18: v E 1928 (1) 1932 (4); v SA 1931 (3); v WI 1930 (1); *v E 1930 (5) 1934 (4)*
Walters, F. H. 1: v E 1884
Walters, K. D. 74: v E 1965 (5) 1970 (6) 1974 (6) 1976 (1); v WI 1968 (4); v NZ 1973 (3) 1980 (3); v In 1967 (2) 1980 (3); v P 1972 (1) 1976 (3); *v E 1968 (5) 1972 (4) 1975 (4) 1977 (5); v SA 1969 (4); v WI 1972 (5); v NZ 1973 (3) 1976 (2); v In 1969 (5)*
Ward, F. A. 4: v E 1936 (3); *v E 1938 (1)*
Watkins, J. R. 1: v P 1972
Watson, G. D. 5: *v E 1972 (2); v SA 1966 (3)*
Watson, W. 4: v E 1954 (1); *v WI 1954 (3)*
Wellham, D. M. 5: v WI 1981 (1); v P 1981 (2); *v E 1981 (1) 1985 (1)*
Wessels, K. C. 23: v E 1982 (4); v WI 1984 (5); v P 1983 (5); *v E 1985 (6); v WI 1983 (2); v SL 1982 (1)*
Whatmore, D. F. 7: v P 1978 (2); *v In 1979 (5)*
Whitney, M. R. 2: *v E 1981 (2)*
Whitty, W. J. 14: v E 1911 (2); v SA 1910 (5); *v E 1909 (1) 1912 (3); v SA 1912 (3)*
Wiener, J. M. 6: v E 1979 (2); v WI 1979 (2); *v P 1979 (2)*
Wilson, J. W. 1: *v In 1956*
Wood, G. M. 53: v E 1978 (6) 1982 (1); v WI 1981 (3) 1984 (5); v NZ 1980 (3); v In 1977 (1) 1980 (3); v P 1978 (1) 1981 (3); *v E 1980 (1) 1981 (6) 1985 (5); v WI 1977 (5) 1983 (1); v NZ 1981 (3); v In 1979 (2); v P 1982 (3); v SL 1982 (1)*
Woodcock, A. J. 1: v NZ 1973
Woodfull, W. M. 35: v E 1928 (5) 1932 (5); v SA 1931 (5); v WI 1930 (5); *v E 1926 (5) 1930 (5) 1934 (5)*
Woods, S. M. J. 3: *v E 1888 (3)*
Woolley, R. D. 2: *v WI 1983 (1); v SL 1982 (1)*
Worrall, J. 11: v E 1884 (1) 1887 (1) 1894 (1) 1897 (1); *v E 1888 (3) 1899 (4)*
Wright, K. J. 10: v E 1978 (2); v P 1978 (2); *v In 1979 (6)*

Yallop, G. N. 39: v E 1978 (6); v WI 1975 (3) 1984 (1); v In 1977 (1); v P 1978 (1) 1981 (1) 1983 (5); *v E 1980 (1) 1981 (6); v WI 1977 (4); v In 1979 (6); v P 1979 (3); v SL 1982 (1)*
Yardley, B. 33: v E 1978 (4) 1982 (5); v WI 1981 (3); v In 1977 (1) 1980 (2); v P 1978 (1) 1981 (3); *v WI 1977 (5); v NZ 1981 (3); v In 1979 (3); v P 1982 (2); v SL 1982 (1)*

## SOUTH AFRICA

Number of Test cricketers: 235

Adcock, N. A. T. 26: v E 1956 (5); v A 1957 (5); v NZ 1953 (5) 1961 (2); *v E 1955 (4) 1960 (5)*
Anderson, J. H. 1: v A 1902
Ashley, W. H. 1: v E 1888

Bacher, A. 12: v A 1966 (5) 1969 (4); *v E 1965 (3)*
Balaskas, X. C. 9: v E 1930 (2) 1938 (1); v A 1935 (3); *v E 1935 (1); v NZ 1931 (2)*
Barlow, E. J. 30: v E 1964 (5); v A 1966 (5) 1969 (4); v NZ 1961 (5); *v E 1965 (3); v A 1963 (5); v NZ 1963 (3)*
Baumgartner, H. V. 1: v E 1913
Beaumont, R. 5: v E 1913 (2); *v E 1912 (1); v A 1912 (2)*
Begbie, D. W. 5: v E 1948 (3); v A 1949 (2)
Bell, A. J. 16: v E 1930 (3); *v E 1929 (3) 1935 (3); v A 1931 (5); v NZ 1931 (2)*
Bisset, M. 3: v E 1898 (2) 1909 (1)
Bissett, G. F. 4: v E 1927 (4)
Blanckenberg, J. M. 18: v E 1913 (5) 1922 (5); v A 1921 (3); *v E 1924 (5)*
Bland, K. C. 21: v E 1964 (5); v A 1966 (1); v NZ 1961 (5); *v E 1965 (3); v A 1963 (4); v NZ 1963 (3)*
Bock, E. G. 1: v A 1935
Bond, G. E. 1: v E 1938
Botten, J. T. 3: *v E 1965 (3)*
Brann, W. H. 3: v E 1922 (3)
Briscoe, A. W. 2: v E 1938 (1); v A 1935 (1)
Bromfield, H. D. 9: v E 1964 (3); v NZ 1961 (5); *v E 1965 (1)*
Brown, L. S. 2: *v A 1931 (1); v NZ 1931 (1)*
Burger, C. G. de V. 2: v A 1957 (2)
Burke, S. F. 2: v E 1964 (1); v NZ 1961 (1)
Buys, I. D. 1: v E 1922

Cameron, H. B. 26: v E 1927 (5) 1930 (5); *v E 1929 (4) 1935 (5); v A 1931 (5); v NZ 1931 (2)*
Campbell, T. 5: v E 1909 (4); *v E 1912 (1)*
Carlstein, P. R. 8: v A 1957 (1); *v E 1960 (5); v A 1963 (2)*
Carter, C. P. 10: v E 1913 (2); v A 1921 (3); *v E 1912 (2) 1924 (3)*
Catterall, R. H. 24: v E 1922 (5) 1927 (5) 1930 (4); *v E 1924 (5) 1929 (5)*
Chapman, H. W. 2: v E 1913 (1); v A 1921 (1)
Cheetham, J. E. 24: v E 1948 (1); v A 1949 (3); v NZ 1953 (5); *v E 1951 (5) 1955 (3); v A 1952 (5); v NZ 1952 (2)*
Chevalier, G. A. 1: v A 1969
Christy, J. A. J. 10: v E 1930 (1); *v E 1929 (2); v A 1931 (5); v NZ 1931 (2)*
Chubb, G. W. A. 5: *v E 1951 (5)*
Cochran, J. A. K. 1: v E 1930
Coen, S. K. 2: v E 1927 (2)
Commaille, J. M. M. 12: v E 1909 (5) 1927 (2); *v E 1924 (5)*
Conyngham, D. P. 1: v E 1922
Cook, F. J. 1: v E 1895
Cooper, A. H. C. 1: v E 1913
Cox, J. L. 3: v E 1913 (3)
Cripps, G. 1: v E 1891
Crisp, R. J. 9: v A 1935 (4); *v E 1935 (5)*
Curnow, S. H. 7: v E 1930 (3); *v A 1931 (4)*

Dalton, E. L. 15: v E 1930 (1) 1938 (4); v A 1935 (1); *v E 1929 (1) 1935 (4); v A 1931 (2); v NZ 1931 (2)*
Davies, E. Q. 5: v E 1938 (3); v A 1935 (2)
Dawson, O. C. 9: v E 1948 (4); *v E 1947 (5)*
Deane, H. G. 17: v E 1927 (5) 1930 (2); *v E 1924 (5) 1929 (5)*
Dixon, C. D. 1: v E 1913
Dower, R. R. 1: v E 1898
Draper, R. G. 2: v A 1949 (2)

Duckworth, C. A. R. 2: v E 1956 (2)
Dumbrill, R. 5: v A 1966 (2); *v E 1965 (3)*
Duminy, J. P. 3: v E 1927 (2); *v E 1929 (1)*
Dunell, O. R. 2: v E 1888 (2)
Du Preez, J. H. 2: v A 1966 (2)
Du Toit, J. F. 1: v E 1891
Dyer, D. V. 3: *v E 1947 (3)*

Elgie, M. K. 3: v NZ 1961 (3)
Endean, W. R. 28: v E 1956 (5); v A 1957 (5); v NZ 1953 (5); *v E 1951 (1) 1955 (5); v A 1952 (5); v NZ 1952 (2)*

Farrer, W. S. 6: v NZ 1961 (3); *v NZ 1963 (3)*
Faulkner, G. A. 25: v E 1905 (5) 1909 (5); *v E 1907 (3) 1912 (3) 1924 (1); v A 1910 (5) 1912 (3)*
Fellows-Smith, J. P. 4: *v E 1960 (4)*
Fichardt, C. G. 2: v E 1891 (1) 1895 (1)
Finlason, C. E. 1: v E 1888
Floquet, C. E. 1: v E 1909
Francis, H. H. 2: v E 1898 (2)
Francois, C. M. 5: v E 1922 (5)
Frank, C. N. 3: v A 1921 (3)
Frank, W. H. B. 1: v E 1895
Fuller, E. R. H. 7: v A 1957 (1); *v E 1955 (2); v A 1952 (2); v NZ 1952 (2)*
Fullerton, G. M. 7: v A 1949 (2); *v E 1947 (2) 1951 (3)*
Funston, K. J. 18: v E 1956 (3); v A 1957 (5); v NZ 1953 (3); *v A 1952 (5); v NZ 1952 (2)*

Gamsy, D. 2: v A 1969 (2)
Gleeson, R. A. 1: v E 1895
Glover, G. K. 1: v E 1895
Goddard, T. L. 41: v E 1956 (5) 1964 (5); v A 1957 (5) 1966 (5) 1969 (3); *v E 1955 (5) 1960 (5); v A 1963 (5); v NZ 1963 (3)*
Gordon, N. 5: v E 1938 (5)
Graham, R. 2: v E 1898 (2)
Grieveson, R. E. 2: v E 1938 (2)
Griffin, G. M. 2: *v E 1960 (2)*

Hall, A. E. 7: v E 1922 (4) 1927 (2) 1930 (1)
Hall, G. G. 1: v E 1964
Halliwell, E. A. 8: v E 1891 (1) 1895 (3) 1898 (1); v A 1902 (3)
Halse, C. G. 3: *v A 1963 (3)*
Hands, P. A. M. 7: v E 1913 (5); v A 1921 (1); *v E 1924 (1)*
Hands, R. H. M. 1: v E 1913
Hanley, M. A. 1: v E 1948
Harris, T. A. 3: v E 1948 (1); *v E 1947 (2)*
Hartigan, G. P. D. 5: v E 1913 (3); *v E 1912 (1); v A 1912 (1)*
Harvey, R. L. 2: v A 1935 (2)
Hathorn, C. M. H. 12: v E 1905 (5); v A 1902 (3); *v E 1907 (3); v A 1910 (1)*
Hearne, F. 4: v E 1891 (1) 1895 (3)
Hearne, G. A. L. 3: v E 1922 (2); *v E 1924 (1)*
Heine, P. S. 14: v E 1956 (5); v A 1957 (4); v NZ 1961 (1); *v E 1955 (4)*
Hime, C. F. W. 1: v E 1895
Hutchinson, P. 2: v E 1888 (2)

Ironside, D. E. J. 3: v NZ 1953 (3)
Irvine, B. L. 4: v A 1969 (4)

Johnson, C. L. 1: v E 1895
Jones, P. S. T. 1: v A 1902

Keith, H. J. 8: v E 1956 (3); *v E 1955 (4); v A 1952 (1)*
Kempis, G. A. 1: v E 1888
Kotze, J. J. 3: v A 1902 (2); *v E 1907 (1)*

Kuys, F. 1: v E 1898

Lance, H. R. 13: v A 1966 (5) 1969 (3); v NZ 1961 (2); *v E 1965 (3)*
Langton, A. B. C. 15: v E 1938 (5); v A 1935 (5); *v E 1935 (5)*
Lawrence, G. B. 5: v NZ 1961 (5)
Le Roux, F. le S. 1: v E 1913
Lewis, P. T. 1: v E 1913
Lindsay, D. T. 19: v E 1964 (3); v A 1966 (5) 1969 (2); *v E 1965 (3); v A 1963 (3); v NZ 1963 (3)*
Lindsay, J. D. 3: *v E 1947 (3)*
Lindsay, N. V. 1: v A 1921
Ling, W. V. S. 6: v E 1922 (3); v A 1921 (3)
Llewellyn, C. B. 15: v E 1895 (1) 1898 (1); v A 1902 (3); *v E 1912 (3); v A 1910 (5) 1912 (2)*
Lundie, E. B. 1: v E 1913

Macaulay, M. J. 1: v E 1964
McCarthy, C. N. 15: v E 1948 (5); v A 1949 (5); *v E 1951 (5)*
McGlew, D. J. 34: v E 1956 (1); v A 1957 (5); v NZ 1953 (5) 1961 (5); *v E 1951 (2) 1955 (5) 1960 (5); v A 1952 (4); v NZ 1952 (2)*
McKinnon, A. H. 8: v E 1964 (2); v A 1966 (2); v NZ 1961 (1); *v E 1960 (1) 1965 (2)*
McLean, R. A. 40: v E 1956 (5) 1964 (2); v A 1957 (4); v NZ 1953 (4) 1961 (5); *v E 1951 (3) 1955 (5) 1960 (5); v A 1952 (5); v NZ 1952 (2)*
McMillan, Q. 13: v E 1930 (5); *v E 1929 (2); v A 1931 (4); v NZ 1931 (2)*
Mann, N. B. F. 19: v E 1948 (5); v A 1949 (5); *v E 1947 (5) 1951 (4)*
Mansell, P. N. F. 13: *v E 1951 (2) 1955 (4); v A 1952 (5); v NZ 1952 (2)*
Markham, L. A. 1: v E 1948
Marx, W. F. E. 3: v A 1921 (3)
Meintjes, D. J. 2: v E 1922 (2)
Melle, M. G. 7: v A 1949 (2); *v E 1951 (1); v A 1952 (4)*
Melville, A. 11: v E 1938 (5) 1948 (1); *v E 1947 (5)*
Middleton, J. 6: v E 1895 (2) 1898 (2); v A 1902 (2)
Mills, C. 1: v E 1891
Milton, W. H. 3: v E 1888 (2) 1891 (1)
Mitchell, B. 42: v E 1930 (5) 1938 (5) 1948 (5); v A 1935 (5); *v E 1929 (5) 1935 (5) 1947 (5); v A 1931 (5); v NZ 1931 (2)*
Mitchell, F. 3: *v E 1912 (1); v A 1912 (2)*
Morkel, D. P. B. 16: v E 1927 (5); *v E 1929 (5); v A 1931 (5); v NZ 1931 (1)*
Murray, A. R. A. 10: v NZ 1953 (4); *v A 1952 (4); v NZ 1952 (2)*

Nel, J. D. 6: v A 1949 (5) 1957 (1)
Newberry, C. 4: v E 1913 (4)
Newson, E. S. 3: v E 1930 (1) 1938 (2)
Nicholson, F. 4: v A 1935 (4)
Nicolson, J. F. W. 3: v E 1927 (3)
Norton, N. O. 1: v E 1909
Nourse, A. D. 34: v E 1938 (5) 1948 (5); v A 1935 (5) 1949 (5); *v E 1935 (4) 1947 (5) 1951 (5)*
Nourse, A. W. 45: v E 1905 (5) 1909 (5) 1913 (5) 1922 (5); v A 1902 (3) 1921 (3); *v E 1907 (3) 1912 (3) 1924 (5); v A 1910 (5) 1912 (3)*
Nupen, E. P. 17: v E 1922 (4) 1927 (5) 1930 (3); v A 1921 (2) 1935 (1); *v E 1924 (2)*

Ochse, A. E. 2: v E 1888 (2)
Ochse, A. L. 3: v E 1927 (1); *v E 1929 (2)*
O'Linn, S. 7: v NZ 1961 (2); *v E 1960 (5)*
Owen-Smith, H. G. 5: *v E 1929 (5)*

Palm, A. W. 1: v E 1927
Parker, G. M. 2: *v E 1924 (2)*
Parkin, D. C. 1: v E 1891
Partridge, J. T. 11: v E 1964 (3); *v A 1963 (5); v NZ 1963 (3)*
Pearse, O. C. 3: *v A 1910 (3)*
Pegler, S. J. 16: v E 1909 (1); *v E 1912 (3) 1924 (5); v A 1910 (4) 1912 (3)*
Pithey, A. J. 17: v E 1956 (3) 1964 (5); *v E 1960 (2); v A 1963 (4); v NZ 1963 (3)*
Pithey, D. B. 8: v A 1966 (2); *v A 1963 (3); v NZ 1963 (3)*
Plimsoll, J. B. 1: *v E 1947*

Pollock, P. M. 28: v E 1964 (5); v A 1966 (5) 1969 (4); v NZ 1961 (3); *v E 1965 (3); v A 1963 (5); v NZ 1963 (3)*
Pollock, R. G. 23: v E 1964 (5); v A 1966 (5) 1969 (4); *v E 1965 (3); v A 1963 (5); v NZ 1963 (1)*
Poore, R. M. 3: v E 1895 (3)
Pothecary, J. E. 3: *v E 1960 (3)*
Powell, A. W. 1: v E 1898
Prince, C. F. H. 1: v E 1898
Procter, M. J. 7: v A 1966 (3) 1969 (4)
Promnitz, H. L. E. 2: v E 1927 (2)

Quinn, N. A. 12: v E 1930 (1); *v E 1929 (4); v A 1931 (5); v NZ 1931 (2)*

Reid, N. 1: v A 1921
Richards, A. R. 1: v E 1895
Richards, B. A. 4: v A 1969 (4)
Richards, W. H. 1: v E 1888
Robertson, J. B. 3: v A 1935 (3)
Rose-Innes, A. 2: v E 1888 (2)
Routledge, T. W. 4: v E 1891 (1) 1895 (3)
Rowan, A. M. B. 15: v E 1948 (5); *v E 1947 (5) 1951 (5)*
Rowan, E. A. B. 26: v E 1938 (4) 1948 (4); v A 1935 (3); 1949 (5); *v E 1935 (5) 1951 (5)*
Rowe, G. A. 5: v E 1895 (2) 1898 (2); v A 1902 (1)

Samuelson, S. V. 1: v E 1909
Schwarz, R. O. 20: v E 1905 (5) 1909 (4); *v E 1907 (3) 1912 (1); v A 1910 (5) 1912 (2)*
Seccull, A. W. 1: v E 1895
Seymour, M. A. 7: v E 1964 (2); v A 1969 (1); *v A 1963 (4)*
Shalders, W. A. 12: v E 1898 (1) 1905 (5); v A 1902 (3); *v E 1907 (3)*
Shepstone, G. H. 2: v E 1895 (1) 1898 (1)
Sherwell, P. W. 13: v E 1905 (5); *v E 1907 (3); v A 1910 (5)*
Siedle, I. J. 18: v E 1927 (1) 1930 (5); v A 1935 (5); *v E 1929 (3) 1935 (4)*
Sinclair, J. H. 25: v E 1895 (3) 1898 (2) 1905 (5) 1909 (4); v A 1902 (3); *v E 1907 (3); v A 1910 (5)*
Smith, C. J. E. 3: v A 1902 (3)
Smith, F. W. 3: v E 1888 (2) 1895 (1)
Smith, V. I. 9: v A 1949 (3) 1957 (1); *v E 1947 (4) 1955 (1)*
Snooke, S. D. 1: *v E 1907*
Snooke, S. J. 26: v E 1905 (5) 1909 (5) 1922 (3); *v E 1907 (3) 1912 (3); v A 1910 (5) 1912 (2)*
Solomon, W. R. 1: v E 1898
Stewart, R. B. 1: v E 1888
Stricker, L. A. 13: v E 1909 (4); *v E 1912 (2); v A 1910 (5) 1912 (2)*
Susskind, M. J. 5: *v E 1924 (5)*

Taberer, H. M. 1: v A 1902
Tancred, A. B. 2: v E 1888 (2)
Tancred, L. J. 14: v E 1905 (5) 1913 (1); v A 1902 (3); *v E 1907 (1) 1912 (2); v A 1912 (2)*
Tancred, V. M. 1: v E 1898
Tapscott, G. L. 1: v E 1913
Tapscott, L. E. 2: v E 1922 (2)
Tayfield, H. J. 37: v E 1956 (5); v A 1949 (5) 1957 (5); v NZ 1953 (5); *v E 1955 (5) 1960 (5); v A 1952 (5); v NZ 1952 (2)*
Taylor, A. I. 1: v E 1956
Taylor, D. 2: v E 1913 (2)
Taylor, H. W. 42: v E 1913 (5) 1922 (5) 1927 (5) 1930 (4); v A 1921 (3); *v E 1912 (3) 1924 (5) 1929 (3); v A 1912 (3) 1931 (5); v NZ 1931 (1)*
Theunissen, N. H. G. de J. 1: v E 1888
Thornton, P. G. 1: v A 1902
Tomlinson, D. S. 1: *v E 1935*
Traicos, A. J. 3: v A 1969 (3)
Trimborn, P. H. J. 4: v A 1966 (3) 1969 (1)
Tuckett, L. 9: v E 1948 (4); *v E 1947 (5)*
Tuckett, L. R. 1: v E 1913

van der Bijl, P. G. V. 5: v E 1938 (5)

Van der Merwe, E. A. 2: v A 1935 (1); *v E 1929 (1)*
Van der Merwe, P. L. 15: v E 1964 (2); v A 1966 (5); *v E 1965 (3); v A 1963 (3); v NZ 1963 (2)*
Van Ryneveld, C. B. 19: v E 1956 (5); v A 1957 (4); v NZ 1953 (5); *v E 1951 (5)*
Varnals, G. D. 3: v E 1964 (3)
Viljoen, K. G. 27: v E 1930 (3) 1938 (4) 1948 (2); v A 1935 (4); *v E 1935 (4) 1947 (5); v A 1931 (4); v NZ 1931 (1)*
Vincent, C. L. 25: v E 1927 (5) 1930 (5); *v E 1929 (4) 1935 (4); v A 1931 (5); v NZ 1931 (2)*
Vintcent, C. H. 3: v E 1888 (2) 1891 (1)
Vogler, A. E. E. 15: v E 1905 (5) 1909 (5); *v E 1907 (3); v A 1910 (2)*

Wade, H. F. 10: v A 1935 (5); *v E 1935 (5)*
Wade, W. W. 11: v E 1938 (3) 1948 (5); v A 1949 (3)
Waite, J. H. B. 50: v E 1956 (5); 1964 (2); v A 1957 (5); v NZ 1953 (5) 1961 (5); *v E 1951 (4) 1955 (5) 1960 (5); v A 1952 (5) 1963 (4); v NZ 1952 (2) 1963 (3)*
Walter, K. A. 2: v NZ 1961 (2)
Ward, T. A. 23: v E 1913 (5) 1922 (5); v A 1921 (3); *v E 1912 (2) 1924 (5); v A 1912 (3)*
Watkins, J. C. 15: v E 1956 (2); v A 1949 (3); v NZ 1953 (3); *v A 1952 (5); v NZ 1952 (2)*
Wesley, C. 3: *v E 1960 (3)*
Westcott, R. J. 5: v A 1957 (2); v NZ 1953 (3)
White, G. C. 17: v E 1905 (5) 1909 (4); *v E 1907 (3) 1912 (2); v A 1912 (3)*
Willoughby, J. T. I. 2: v E 1895 (2)
Wimble, C. S. 1: v E 1891
Winslow, P. L. 5: v A 1949 (2); *v E 1955 (3)*
Wynne, O. E. 6: v E 1948 (3); v A 1949 (3)

Zulch, J. W. 16: v E 1909 (5) 1913 (3); v A 1921 (3); *v A 1910 (5)*

## WEST INDIES

Number of Test cricketers: 184

Achong, E. 6: v E 1929 (1) 1934 (2); *v E 1933 (3)*
Alexander, F. C. M. 25: v E 1959 (5); v P 1957 (5); *v E 1957 (2); v A 1960 (5); v In 1958 (5); v P 1958 (3)*
Ali, Imtiaz 1: v In 1975
Ali, Inshan 12: v E 1973 (2); v A 1972 (3); v In 1970 (1); v P 1976 (1); v NZ 1971 (3); *v E 1973 (1); v A 1975 (1)*
Allan, D. W. 5: v A 1964 (1); v In 1961 (2); *v E 1966 (2)*
Asgarali, N. 2: *v E 1957 (2)*
Atkinson, D. St E. 22: v E 1953 (4); v A 1954 (4); v P 1957 (1); *v E 1957 (2); v A 1951 (2); v NZ 1951 (1) 1955 (4); v In 1948 (4)*
Atkinson, E. St E. 8: v P 1957 (3); *v In 1958 (3); v P 1958 (2)*
Austin, R. A. 2: v A 1977 (2)

Bacchus, S. F. A. F. 19: v A 1977 (2); *v E 1980 (5); v A 1981 (2); v In 1978 (6); v P 1980 (4)*
Baichan, L. 3: *v A 1975 (1); v P 1974 (2)*
Baptiste, E. A. E. 9: v A 1983 (3); *v E 1984 (5); v In 1983 (1)*
Barrow, I. 11: v E 1929 (1) 1934 (1); *v E 1933 (3) 1939 (1); v A 1930 (5)*
Barrett, A. G. 6: v E 1973 (2); v In 1970 (2); *v In 1974 (2)*
Bartlett, E. L. 5: *v E 1928 (1); v A 1930 (4)*
Betancourt, N. 1: v E 1929
Binns, A. P. 5: v A 1954 (1); v In 1952 (1); *v NZ 1955 (3)*
Birkett, L. S. 4 *v A 1930 (4)*
Boyce, K. D. 21: v E 1973 (4); v A 1972 (4); v In 1970 (1); *v E 1973 (3); v A 1975 (4); v In 1974 (3); v P 1974 (2)*
Browne, C. R. 4: v E 1929 (2); *v E 1928 (2)*
Butcher, B. F. 44: v E 1959 (2) 1967 (5); v A 1964 (5); *v E 1963 (5) 1966 (5) 1969 (3); v A 1968 (5); v NZ 1968 (3); v In 1958 (5) 1966 (3); v P 1958 (3)*
Butler, L. 1: v A 1954
Butts, C. G. 1: v NZ 1984
Bynoe, M. R. 4: *v In 1966 (3); v P 1958 (1)*

Camacho, G. S. 11: v E 1967 (5); v In 1970 (2); *v E 1969 (2); v A 1968 (2)*
Cameron, F. J. 5: *v In 1948 (5)*
Cameron, J. H. 2: *v E 1939 (2)*
Carew, G. M. 4: v E 1934 (1) 1947 (2); *v In 1948 (1)*
Carew, M. C. 19: v E 1967 (1); v NZ 1971 (3); v In 1970 (3); *v E 1963 (2) 1966 (1) 1969 (1); v A 1968 (5); v NZ 1968 (3)*
Challenor, G. 3: *v E 1928 (3)*
Chang, H. S. 1: *v In 1978*
Christiani, C. M. 4: v E 1934 (4)
Christiani, R. J. 22: v E 1947 (4) 1953 (1); v In 1952 (2); *v E 1950 (4); v A 1951 (5); v NZ 1951 (1); v In 1948 (5)*
Clarke, C. B. 3: *v E 1939 (3)*
Clarke, S. T. 11: v A 1977 (1); *v A 1981 (1); v In 1978 (5); v P 1980 (4)*
Constantine, L. N. 18: v E 1929 (3) 1934 (3); *v E 1928 (3) 1933 (1) 1939 (3); v A 1930 (5)*
Croft, C. E. H. 27: v E 1980 (4); v A 1977 (2); v P 1976 (5); *v E 1980 (3); v A 1979 (3) 1981 (3); v NZ 1979 (3); v P 1980 (4)*

Da Costa, O. C. 5: v E 1929 (1) 1934 (1); *v E 1933 (3)*
Daniel, W. W. 10: v A 1983 (2); v In 1975 (1); *v E 1976 (4) v In 1983 (3)*
Davis, B. A. 4: v A 1964 (4)
Davis, C. A. 15: v A 1972 (2); v NZ 1971 (5); v In 1970 (4); *v E 1969 (3); v A 1968 (1)*
Davis, W. W. 11: v A 1983 (1); v NZ 1984 (2); v In 1982 (1); *v E 1984 (1); v In 1983 (6)*
De Caires, F. I. 3: v E 1929 (3)
Depeiza, C. C. 5: v A 1954 (3); *v NZ 1955 (2)*
Dewdney, T. 9: v A 1954 (2); v P 1957 (3); *v E 1957 (1); v NZ 1955 (3)*
Dowe, U. G. 4: v A 1972 (1); v NZ 1971 (1); v In 1970 (2)
Dujon, P. J. L. 33: v A 1983 (5); v NZ 1984 (4); v In 1982 (5); *v E 1984 (5); v A 1981 (3) 1984 (5); v In 1983 (6)*

Edwards, R. M. 5: *v A 1968 (2); v NZ 1968 (3)*

Ferguson, W. 8: v E 1947 (4) 1953 (1); *v In 1948 (3)*
Fernandes, M. P. 2: v E 1929 (1); *v E 1928 (1)*
Findlay, T. M. 10: v A 1972 (1); v NZ 1971 (5); v In 1970 (2); *v E 1969 (2)*
Foster, M. L. C. 14: v E 1973 (1); v A 1972 (4) 1977 (1); v NZ 1971 (3); v In 1970 (2); v P 1976 (1); *v E 1969 (1) 1973 (1)*
Francis, G. N. 10: v E 1929 (1); *v E 1928 (3) 1933 (1); v A 1930 (5)*
Frederick, M. C. 1: v E 1953
Fredericks, R. C. 59: v E 1973 (5); v A 1972 (5); v NZ 1971 (5); v In 1970 (4) 1975 (4); v P 1976 (5); *v E 1969 (3) 1973 (3) 1976 (5); v A 1968 (4) 1975 (6); v NZ 1968 (3); v In 1974 (5); v P 1974 (2)*
Fuller, R. L. 1: v E 1934
Furlonge, H. A. 3: v A 1954 (1); *v NZ 1955 (2)*

Ganteaume, A. G. 1: v E 1947
Garner, J. 51: v E 1980 (4); v A 1977 (2) 1983 (5); v NZ 1984 (4); v In 1982 (4); v P 1976 (5); *v E 1980 (5) 1984 (5); v A 1979 (3) 1981 (3) 1984 (5); v NZ 1979 (3); v P 1980 (3)*
Gaskin, B. B. M. 2: v E 1947 (2)
Gibbs, G. L. R. 1: v A 1954
Gibbs, L. R. 79: v E 1967 (5) 1973 (5); v A 1964 (5) 1972 (5); v NZ 1971 (2); v In 1961 (5) 1970 (1); v P 1957 (4); *v E 1963 (5) 1966 (5) 1969 (3) 1973 (3); v A 1960 (3) 1968 (5) 1975 (6); v NZ 1968 (3); v In 1958 (1) 1966 (3) 1974 (5); v P 1958 (3) 1974 (2)*
Gilchrist, R. 13: v P 1957 (5); *v E 1957 (4); v In 1958 (4)*
Gladstone, G. 1: v E 1929
Goddard, J. D. C. 27: v E 1947 (4); *v E 1950 (4) 1957 (5); v A 1951 (4); v NZ 1951 (2) 1955 (3); v In 1948 (5)*
Gomes, H. A. 49: v E 1980 (4); v A 1977 (3) 1983 (2); v NZ 1984 (4); v In 1982 (5); *v E 1976 (2) 1984 (5); v A 1981 (3) 1984 (5); v In 1978 (6) 1983 (6); v P 1980 (4)*
Gomez, G. E. 29: v E 1947 (4) 1953 (4); v In 1952 (4); *v E 1939 (2) 1950 (4); v A 1951 (5); v NZ 1951 (1); v In 1948 (5)*
Grant, G. C. 12: v E 1934 (4); *v E 1933 (3); v A 1930 (5)*
Grant, R. S. 7: v E 1934 (4); *v E 1939 (3)*

Greenidge, A. E. 6: v A 1977 (2); *v In 1978 (4)*

Greenidge, C. G. 66: v E 1980 (4); v A 1977 (2) 1983 (5); v NZ 1984 (4); v In 1982 (5); v P 1976 (5); *v E 1976 (5) 1980 (5) 1984 (5); v A 1975 (2) 1979 (3) 1981 (2) 1984 (5); v NZ 1979 (3); v In 1974 (5) 1983 (6)*

Greenidge, G. A. 5: v A 1972 (3); v NZ 1971 (2)

Grell, M. G. 1: v E 1929

Griffith, C. C. 28: v E 1959 (1) 1967 (4); v A 1964 (5); *v E 1963 (5) 1966 (5); v A 1968 (3); v NZ 1968 (2); v In 1966 (3)*

Griffith, H. C. 13: v E 1929 (3); *v E 1928 (3) 1933 (2); v A 1930 (5)*

Guillen, S. C. 5: *v A 1951 (3); v NZ 1951 (2)*

Hall, W. W. 48: v E 1959 (5) 1967 (4); v A 1964 (5); v In 1961 (5); *v E 1963 (5) 1966 (5); v A 1960 (5) 1968 (2); v NZ 1968 (1); v In 1958 (5) 1966 (3); v P 1958 (3)*

Harper, R. A. 14: v A 1983 (4); v NZ 1984 (1); *v E 1984 (5); v A 1984 (2); v In 1983 (2)*

Haynes, D. L. 54: v E 1980 (4); v A 1977 (2) 1983 (5); v NZ 1984 (4); v In 1982 (5); *v E 1980 (5) 1984 (5); v A 1979 (3) 1981 (3) 1984 (5); v NZ 1979 (3); v In 1983 (6); v P 1980 (4)*

Headley, G. A. 22: v E 1929 (4) 1934 (4) 1947 (1) 1953 (1); *v E 1933 (3) 1939 (3); v A 1930 (5); v In 1948 (1)*

Headley, R. G. A. 2: *v E 1973 (2)*

Hendriks, J. L. 20: v A 1964 (4); v In 1961 (1); *v E 1966 (3) 1969 (1); v A 1968 (5); v NZ 1968 (3); v In 1966 (3)*

Hoad, E. L. G. 4: v E 1929 (1); *v E 1928 (1) 1933 (2)*

Holder, V. A. 40: v E 1973 (1); v A 1972 (3) 1977 (3); v NZ 1971 (4); v In 1970 (3) 1975 (1); v P 1976 (1); *v E 1969 (3) 1973 (2) 1976 (4); v A 1975 (3); v In 1974 (4) 1978 (6); v P 1974 (2)*

Holding, M. A. 55: v E 1980 (4); v A 1983 (3); v NZ 1984 (3); v In 1975 (4) 1982 (5); *v E 1976 (4) 1980 (5) 1984 (4); v A 1975 (5) 1979 (3) 1981 (3) 1984 (3); v NZ 1979 (3); v In 1983 (6)*

Holford, D. A. J. 24: v E 1967 (4); v NZ 1971 (5); v In 1970 (1) 1975 (2); v P 1976 (1); *v E 1966 (5); v A 1968 (2); v NZ 1968 (3); v In 1966 (1)*

Holt, J. K. 17: v E 1953 (5); v A 1954 (5); *v In 1958 (5); v P 1958 (2)*

Howard, A. B. 1: v NZ 1971

Hunte, C. C. 44: v E 1959 (5); v A 1964 (5); v In 1961 (5); v P 1957 (5); *v E 1963 (5) 1966 (5); v A 1960 (5); v In 1958 (5) 1966 (3); v P 1958 (1)*

Hunte, E. A. C. 3: v E 1929 (3)

Hylton, L. G. 6: v E 1934 (4); *v E 1939 (2)*

Johnson, H. H. H. 3: v E 1947 (1); *v E 1950 (2)*

Johnson, T. F. 1: *v E 1939*

Jones, C. M. 4: v E 1929 (1) 1934 (3)

Jones, P. E. 9: v E 1947 (1); *v E 1950 (2); v A 1951 (1); v In 1948 (5)*

Julien, B. D. 24: v E 1973 (5); v In 1975 (4); v P 1976 (1); *v E 1973 (3) 1976 (2); v A 1975 (3); v In 1974 (4); v P 1974 (2)*

Jumadeen, R. R. 12: v A 1972 (1) 1977 (2); v NZ 1971 (1); v In 1975 (4); v P 1976 (1); *v E 1976 (1); v In 1978 (2)*

Kallicharran, A. I. 66: v E 1973 (5); v A 1972 (5) 1977 (5); v NZ 1971 (2); v In 1975 (4); v P 1976 (5); *v E 1973 (3) 1976 (3) 1980 (5); v A 1975 (6) 1979 (3); v NZ 1979 (3); v In 1974 (5) 1978 (6); v P 1974 (2) 1980 (4)*

Kanhai, R. B. 79: v E 1959 (5) 1967 (5) 1973 (5); v A 1964 (5) 1972 (5); v In 1961 (5) 1970 (5); v P 1957 (5); *v E 1957 (5) 1963 (5) 1966 (5) 1973 (3); v A 1960 (5) 1968 (5); v In 1958 (5) 1966 (3); v P 1958 (3)*

Kentish, E. S. M. 2: v E 1947 (1) 1953 (1)

King, C. L. 9: v P 1976 (1); *v E 1976 (3) 1980 (1); v A 1979 (1); v NZ 1979 (3)*

King, F. M. 14: v E 1953 (3); v A 1954 (4); v In 1952 (5); *v NZ 1955 (2)*

King, L. A. 2: v E 1967 (1); v In 1961 (1)

Lashley, P. D. 4: *v E 1966 (2); v A 1960 (2)*

Legall, R. 4: v In 1952 (4)

Lewis, D. M. 3: v In 1970 (3)

Lloyd, C. H. 110: v E 1967 (5) 1973 (5) 1980 (4); v A 1972 (3) 1977 (2) 1983 (4); v NZ 1971 (2); v In 1970 (5) 1975 (4) 1982 (5); v P 1976 (5); *v E 1969 (3) 1973 (3) 1976 (5) 1980 (4) 1984 (5); v A 1968 (4) 1975 (6) 1979 (2) 1981 (3) 1984 (5); v NZ 1968 (3) 1979 (3); v In 1966 (3) 1974 (5) 1983 (6); v P 1974 (2) 1980 (4)*

Logie, A. L. 13: v A 1983 (1); v NZ 1984 (4); v In 1982 (5); *v In 1983 (3)*

McMorris, E. D. A. 13: v E 1959 (4); v In 1961 (4); v P 1957 (1); *v E 1963 (2) 1966 (2)*
McWatt, C. A. 6: v E 1953 (5); v A 1954 (1)
Madray, I. S. 2: v P 1957 (2)
Marshall, M. D. 40: v E 1980 (1); v A 1983 (4); v NZ 1984 (4); v In 1982 (5); *v E 1980 (4) 1984 (4); v A 1984 (5); v In 1978 (3) 1983 (6); v P 1980 (4)*
Marshall, N. E. 1: v A 1954
Marshall, R. E. 4: *v A 1951 (2); v NZ 1951 (2)*
Martin, F. R. 9: v E 1929 (1); *v E 1928 (3); v A 1930 (5)*
Martindale, E. A. 10: v E 1934 (4); *v E 1933 (3) 1939 (3)*
Mattis, E. H. 4: v E 1980 (4)
Mendonca, I. L. 2: v In 1961 (2)
Merry, C. A. 2: *v E 1933 (2)*
Miller, R. 1: v In 1952
Moodie, G. H. 1: v E 1934
Murray, D. A. 19: v E 1980 (4); v A 1977 (3); *v A 1981 (2); v In 1978 (6); v P 1980 (4)*
Murray, D. L. 62: v E 1967 (5) 1973 (5); v A 1972 (4) 1977 (2); v In 1975 (4); v P 1976 (5); *v E 1963 (5) 1973 (3) 1976 (5) 1980 (5); v A 1975 (6) 1979 (3); v NZ 1979 (3); v In 1974 (5); v P 1974 (2)*

Nanan, R. 1: *v P 1980*
Neblett, J. M. 1: v E 1934
Noreiga, J. M. 4: v In 1970 (4)
Nunes, R. K. 4: v E 1929 (1); *v E 1928 (3)*
Nurse, S. M. 29: v E 1959 (1) 1967 (5); v A 1964 (4); v In 1961 (1); *v E 1966 (5); v A 1960 (3) 1968 (5); v NZ 1968 (3); v In 1966 (2)*

Padmore, A. L. 2: v In 1975 (1); *v E 1976 (1)*
Pairaudeau, B. H. 13: v E 1953 (2); v In 1952 (5): *v E 1957 (2); v NZ 1955 (4)*
Parry, D. R. 12: v A 1977 (5); *v NZ 1979 (1); v In 1978 (6)*
Passailaigue, C. C. 1: v E 1929
Phillip, N. 9: v A 1977 (3); *v In 1978 (6)*
Pierre, L. R. 1: v E 1947

Rae, A. F. 15: v In 1952 (2); *v E 1950 (4); v A 1951 (3); v NZ 1951 (1); v In 1948 (5)*
Ramadhin, S. 43: v E 1953 (5) 1959 (4); v A 1954 (4); v In 1952 (4); *v E 1950 (4) 1957 (5); v A 1951 (5) 1960 (2); v NZ 1951 (2) 1955 (4); v In 1958 (2); v P 1958 (2)*
Richards, I. V. A. 77: v E 1980 (4); v A 1977 (2) 1983 (5); v NZ 1984 (4); v In 1975 (4) 1982 (5); v P 1976 (5); *v E 1976 (4) 1980 (5) 1984 (5); v A 1975 (6) 1979 (3) 1981 (3) 1984 (5); v In 1974 (5) 1983 (6); v P 1974 (2) 1980 (4)*
Richardson, R. B. 15: v A 1983 (5); v NZ 1984 (4); *v A 1984 (5); v In 1983 (1)*
Rickards, K. R. 2: v E 1947 (1); *v A 1951 (1)*
Roach, C. A. 16: v E 1929 (4) 1934 (1); *v E 1928 (3) 1933 (3); v A 1930 (5)*
Roberts, A. M. E. 47: v E 1973 (1) 1980 (3); v A 1977 (2); v In 1975 (2) 1982 (5); v P 1976 (5); *v E 1976 (5) 1980 (3); v A 1975 (5) 1979 (3) 1981 (2); v NZ 1979 (2); v In 1974 (5) 1983 (2); v P 1974 (2)*
Roberts, A. T. 1: *v NZ 1955*
Rodriguez, W. V. 5: v E 1967 (1); v A 1964 (1); v In 1961 (2); *v E 1963 (1)*
Rowe, L. G. 30: v E 1973 (5); v A 1972 (3); v NZ 1971 (4); v In 1975 (4); *v E 1976 (2); v A 1975 (6) 1979 (3); v NZ 1979 (3)*

St Hill, E. L. 2: v E 1929 (2)
St Hill, W. H. 3: v E 1929 (1); *v E 1928 (2)*
Scarlett, R. O. 3: v E 1959 (3)
Scott, A. P. H. 1: v In 1952
Scott, O. C. 8: v E 1929 (1); *v E 1928 (2); v A 1930 (5)*
Sealey, B. J. 1: *v E 1933*
Sealy, J. E. D. 11: v E 1929 (2) 1934 (4); *v E 1939 (3); v A 1930 (2)*
Shepherd, J. N. 5: v In 1970 (2); *v E 1969 (3)*
Shillingford, G. C. 7: v NZ 1971 (2); v In 1970 (3); *v E 1969 (2)*
Shillingford, I. T. 4: v A 1977 (1); v P 1976 (3)
Shivnarine, S. 8: v A 1977 (3); *v In 1978 (5)*
Singh, C. K. 2: v E 1959 (2)

Small, J. A. 3: v E 1929 (1); *v E 1928 (2)*
Small, M. A. 2: v A 1983 (1); *v E 1984 (1)*
Smith, C. W. 5: v In 1961 (1); *v A 1960 (4)*
Smith, O. G. 26: v A 1954 (4); v P 1957 (5); *v E 1957 (5); v NZ 1955 (4); v In 1958 (5); v P 1958 (3)*
Sobers, G. S. 93: v E 1953 (1) 1959 (5) 1967 (5) 1973 (4); v A 1954 (4) 1964 (5); v NZ 1971 (5); v In 1961 (5); 1970 (5); v P 1957 (5); *v E 1957 (5) 1963 (5) 1966 (5) 1969 (3) 1973 (3); v A 1960 (5) 1968 (5); v NZ 1955 (4) 1968 (3); v In 1958 (5) 1966 (3); v P 1958 (3)*
Solomon, J. S. 27: v E 1959 (2); v A 1964 (4); v In 1961 (4); *v E 1963 (5); v A 1960 (5); v In 1958 (4); v P 1958 (3)*
Stayers, S. C. 4: v In 1961 (4)
Stollmeyer, J. B. 32: v E 1947 (2) 1953 (5); v A 1954 (2); v In 1952 (5); *v E 1939 (3) 1950 (4); v A 1951 (5); v NZ 1951 (2); v In 1948 (4)*
Stollmeyer, V. H. 1: *v E 1939*

Taylor, J. 3: v P 1957 (1); *v In 1958 (1); v P 1958 (1)*
Trim, J. 4: v E 1947 (1); *v A 1951 (1); v In 1948 (2)*

Valentine, A. L. 36: v E 1953 (3); v A 1954 (3); v In 1952 (5) 1961 (2); v P 1957 (1); *v E 1950 (4) 1957 (2); v A 1951 (5) 1960 (5); v NZ 1951 (2) 1955 (4)*
Valentine, V. A. 2: *v E 1933 (2)*

Walcott, C. L. 44: v E 1947 (4) 1953 (5) 1959 (2); v A 1954 (5); v In 1952 (5); v P 1957 (4); *v E 1950 (4) 1957 (5); v A 1951 (3); v NZ 1951 (2); v In 1948 (5)*
Walcott, L. A. 1: v E 1929
Walsh, C. A. 6: v NZ 1984 (1); *v A 1984 (5)*
Watson, C. 7: v E 1959 (5); v In 1961 (1); *v A 1960 (1)*
Weekes, E. D. 48: v E 1947 (4) 1953 (4); v A 1954 (5) v In 1952 (5); v P 1957 (5); *v E 1950 (4) 1957 (5); v A 1951 (5); v NZ 1951 (2) 1955 (4); v In 1948 (5)*
Weekes, K. H. 2: *v E 1939 (2)*
White, W. A. 2: v A 1964 (2)
Wight, C. V. 2: v E 1929 (1); *v E 1928 (1)*
Wight, G. L. 1: v In 1952
Wiles, C. A. 1: *v E 1933*
Willett, E. T. 5: v A 1972 (3); *v In 1974 (2)*
Williams, A. B. 7: v A 1977 (3); *v In 1978 (4)*
Williams, E. A. V. 4: v E 1947 (3); *v E 1939 (1)*
Wishart, K. L. 1: v E 1934
Worrell, F. M. M. 51: v E 1947 (3) 1953 (4) 1959 (4); v A 1954 (4); v In 1952 (5) 1961 (5); *v E 1950 (4) 1957 (5) 1963 (5); v A 1951 (5) 1960 (5); v NZ 1951 (2)*

## NEW ZEALAND

Number of Test cricketers: 155

Alabaster, J. C. 21: v E 1962 (2); v WI 1955 (1); v In 1967 (4); *v E 1958 (2); v SA 1961 (5); v WI 1971 (2); v In 1955 (4); v P 1955 (1)*
Allcott, C. F. W. 6: v E 1929 (2); v SA 1931 (1); *v E 1931 (3)*
Anderson, R. W. 9: v E 1977 (3); *v E 1978 (3); v P 1976 (3)*
Anderson, W. M. 1: v A 1945
Andrews, B. 2: *v A 1973 (2)*

Badcock, F. T. 7: v E 1929 (3) 1932 (2); v SA 1931 (2)
Barber, R. T. 1: v WI 1955
Bartlett, G. A. 10: v E 1965 (2); v In 1967 (2); v P 1964 (1); *v SA 1961 (5)*
Barton, P. T. 7: v E 1962 (3); *v SA 1961 (4)*
Beard, D. D. 4: v WI 1951 (2) 1955 (2)
Beck, J. E. F. 8: v WI 1955 (4); *v SA 1953 (4)*
Bell, W. 2: *v SA 1953 (2)*
Bilby, G. P. 2: v E 1965 (2)
Blair, R. W. 19: v E 1954 (1) 1958 (2) 1962 (2); v SA 1952 (2) 1963 (3); v WI 1955 (2) *v E 1958 (3); v SA 1953 (4)*

Blunt, R. C. 9: v E 1929 (4); v SA 1931 (2); *v E 1931 (3)*
Bolton, B. A. 2: v E 1958 (2)
Boock, S. L. 25: v E 1977 (3) 1983 (2); v WI 1979 (3); v P 1978 (3) 1984 (2); *v E 1978 (3); v WI 1984 (3); v P 1984 (3); v SL 1983 (3)*
Bracewell, B. P. 6: v P 1978 (1) 1984 (1); *v E 1978 (3); v A 1980 (1)*
Bracewell, J. G. 13: v In 1980 (1); *v E 1983 (4); v A 1980 (3); v WI 1984 (1); v P 1984 (2); v SL 1983 (2)*
Bradburn, W. P. 2: v SA 1963 (2)
Burgess, M. G. 50: v E 1970 (1) 1977 (3); v A 1973 (1) 1976 (2); v WI 1968 (2); v In 1967 (4) 1975 (3); v P 1972 (3) 1978 (3); *v E 1969 (2) 1973 (3) 1978 (3); v A 1980 (3); v WI 1971 (5); v In 1969 (3) 1976 (3); v P 1969 (3) 1976 (3)*
Burke, C. 1: v A 1945
Burtt, T. B. 10: v E 1946 (1) 1950 (2); v SA 1952 (1); v WI 1951 (2); *v E 1949 (4)*
Butterfield, L. A. 1: v A 1945

Cairns, B. L. 42: v E 1974 (1) 1977 (1) 1983 (3); v A 1976 (1) 1981 (3); v WI 1979 (3); v In 1975 (1) 1980 (3); v P 1978 (3) 1984 (3); v SL 1982 (2); *v E 1978 (2) 1983 (4); v A 1973 (1) 1980 (3); v WI 1984 (2); v In 1976 (2); v P 1976 (2); v SL 1983 (2)*
Cameron, F. J. 19: v E 1962 (3); v SA 1963 (3); v P 1964 (3); *v E 1965 (2); v SA 1961 (5); v In 1964 (1); v P 1964 (2)*
Cave, H. B. 19: v E 1954 (2); v WI 1955 (3); *v E 1949 (4) 1958 (2); v In 1955 (5); v P 1955 (3)*
Chapple, M. E. 14: v E 1954 (1) 1965 (1); v SA 1952 (1) 1963 (3); v WI 1955 (1); *v SA 1953 (5) 1961 (2)*
Chatfield, E. J. 23: v E 1974 (1) 1977 (1) 1983 (3); v A 1976 (2) 1981 (1); v P 1984 (3); v SL 1982 (2); *v E 1983 (3); v WI 1984 (4); v P 1984 (1); v SL 1983 (2)*
Cleverley, D. C. 2: v SA 1931 (1); v A 1945 (1)
Collinge, R. O. 35: v E 1970 (2) 1974 (2) 1977 (3); v A 1973 (3); v In 1967 (2) 1975 (3); v P 1964 (3) 1972 (2); *v E 1965 (3) 1969 (1) 1973 (3) 1978 (1); v In 1964 (2) 1976 (1); v P 1964 (2) 1976 (2)*
Colquhoun, I. A. 2: v E 1954 (2)
Coney, J. V. 40: v E 1983 (3); v A 1973 (2) 1981 (3); v WI 1979 (3); v In 1980 (3); v P 1978 (3) 1984 (3); v SL 1982 (2); *v E 1983 (4); v A 1973 (2) 1980 (2); v WI 1984 (4); v P 1984 (3); v SL 1983 (3)*
Congdon, B. E. 61: v E 1965 (3) 1970 (2) 1974 (2) 1977 (3); v A 1973 (3) 1976 (2); v WI 1968 (3); v In 1967 (4) 1975 (3); v P 1964 (3) 1972 (3); *v E 1965 (3) 1969 (3) 1973 (3) 1978 (3); v A 1973 (3); v WI 1971 (5); v In 1964 (3) 1969 (3); v P 1964 (1) 1969 (3)*
Cowie, J. 9: v E 1946 (1); v A 1945 (1); *v E 1937 (3) 1949 (4)*
Cresswell G. F. 3: v E 1950 (2); *v E 1949 (1)*
Cromb, I. B. 5: v SA 1931 (2); *v E 1931 (3)*
Crowe, J. J. 20: v E 1983 (3); v P 1984 (3); v SL 1982 (2); *v E 1983 (2); v WI 1984 (4); v P 1984 (3); v SL 1983 (3)*
Crowe, M. D. 23: v E 1983 (3); v A 1981 (3); v P 1984 (3); *v E 1983 (4); v WI 1984 (4); v P 1984 (3); v SL 1983 (3)*
Cunis, R. S. 20: v E 1965 (3) 1970 (2); v SA 1963 (1); v WI 1968 (3); *v E 1969 (1); v WI 1971 (5); v In 1969 (3); v P 1969 (2)*

D'Arcy, J. W. 5: *v E 1958 (5)*
Dempster, C. S. 10: v E 1929 (4) 1932 (2); v SA 1931 (2); *v E 1931 (2)*
Dempster, E. W. 5: v SA 1952 (1); *v SA 1953 (4)*
Dick, A. E. 17: v E 1962 (3); v SA 1963 (2); v P 1964 (2); *v E 1965 (2); v SA 1961 (5); v P 1964 (3)*
Dickinson, G. R. 3: v E 1929 (2); v SA 1931 (1)
Donnelly, M. P. 7: *v E 1937 (3) 1949 (4)*
Dowling, G. T. 39: v E 1962 (3) 1970 (2); v In 1967 (4); v SA 1963 (1); v WI 1968 (3); v P 1964 (2); *v E 1965 (3) 1969 (3); v SA 1961 (4); v WI 1971 (2); v In 1964 (4) 1969 (3); v P 1964 (2) 1969 (3)*
Dunning, J. A. 4: v E 1932 (1); *v E 1937 (3)*

Edgar, B. A. 30: v E 1983 (3); v A 1981 (3); v WI 1979 (3); v In 1980 (3); v P 1978 (3); v SL 1982 (2); *v E 1978 (3) 1983 (4); v A 1980 (3); v P 1984 (3)*
Edwards, G. N. 8: v E 1977 (1); v A 1976 (2); v In 1980 (3); *v E 1978 (2)*
Emery, R. W. G. 2: v WI 1951 (2)

Fisher, F. E. 1: v SA 1952
Foley, H. 1: v E 1929

Franklin, T. J. 1: *v E 1983*
Freeman, D. L. 2: v E 1932 (2)

Gallichan, N. 1: *v E 1937*
Gedye, S. G. 4: v SA 1963 (3); v P 1964 (1)
Gray, E. J. 4: *v E 1983 (2); v P 1984 (2)*
Guillen, S. C. 3: v WI 1955 (3)
Guy, J. W. 12: v E 1958 (2); v WI 1955 (2); *v SA 1961 (2); v In 1955 (5); v P 1955 (1)*

Hadlee, D. R. 26: v E 1974 (2) 1977 (1); v A 1973 (3) 1976 (1); v In 1975 (3); v P 1972 (2); *v E 1969 (2) 1973 (3); v A 1973 (3); v In 1969 (3); v P 1969 (3)*
Hadlee, R. J. 57: v E 1977 (3) 1983 (3); v A 1973 (2) 1976 (2) 1981 (3); v WI 1979 (3); v In 1975 (2) 1980 (3); v P 1972 (1) 1978 (3) 1984 (3); v SL 1982 (2); *v E 1973 (1) 1978 (3) 1983 (4); v A 1973 (3) 1980 (3); v WI 1984 (4); v In 1976 (3); v P 1976 (3); v SL 1983 (3)*
Hadlee, W. A. 11: v E 1946 (1) 1950 (2); v A 1945 (1); *v E 1937 (3) 1949 (4)*
Harford, N. S. 8: *v E 1958 (4); v In 1955 (2); v P 1955 (2)*
Harford, R. I. 3: v In 1967 (3)
Harris, P. G. Z. 9: v P 1964 (1); *v SA 1961 (5); v In 1955 (1); v P 1955 (2)*
Harris, R. M. 2: v E 1958 (2)
Hastings, B. F. 31: v E 1974 (2); v A 1973 (3); v WI 1968 (3); v In 1975 (1); v P 1972 (3); *v E 1969 (3) 1973 (3); v A 1973 (3); v WI 1971 (5); v In 1969 (2); v P 1969 (3)*
Hayes, J. A. 15: v E 1950 (2) 1954 (1); v WI 1951 (2); *v E 1958 (4); v In 1955 (5); v P 1955 (1)*
Henderson, M. 1: v E 1929
Hough, K. W. 2: v E 1958 (2)
Howarth, G. P. 47: v E 1974 (2) 1977 (3) 1983 (3); v A 1976 (2) 1981 (3); v WI 1979 (3); v In 1980 (3); v P 1978 (3) 1984 (3); v SL 1982 (2); *v E 1978 (3) 1983 (4); v A 1980 (2); v WI 1984 (4); v In 1976 (2); v P 1976 (2); v SL 1983 (3)*
Howarth, H. J. 30: v E 1970 (2) 1974 (2); v A 1973 (3) 1976 (2); v In 1975 (2); v P 1972 (3); *v E 1969 (3) 1973 (2); v WI 1971 (5); v In 1969 (3); v P 1969 (3)*

James, K. C. 11: v E 1929 (4) 1932 (2); v SA 1931 (2); *v E 1931 (3)*
Jarvis, T. W. 13: v E 1965 (1); v P 1972 (3); *v WI 1971 (4); v In 1964 (2); v P 1964 (3)*

Kerr, J. L. 7: v E 1932 (2); v SA 1931 (1); *v E 1931 (2) 1937 (2)*

Lees, W. K. 21: v E 1977 (2); v A 1976 (1); v WI 1979 (3); v P 1978 (3); v SL 1982 (2); *v E 1983 (2); v A 1980 (2); v In 1976 (3); v P 1976 (3)*
Leggat, I. B. 1: *v SA 1953*
Leggat, J. G. 9: v E 1954 (1); v SA 1952 (1); v WI 1951 (1) 1955 (1); *v In 1955 (3); v P 1955 (2)*
Lissette, A. F. 2: v WI 1955 (2)
Lowry, T. C. 7: v E 1929 (4); *v E 1931 (3)*

MacGibbon, A. R. 26: v E 1950 (2) 1954 (2); v SA 1952 (1); v WI 1955 (3); *v E 1958 (5); v SA 1953 (5); v In 1955 (5); v P 1955 (3)*
McEwan, P. E. 4: v WI 1979 (1); *v A 1980 (2); v P 1984 (1)*
McGirr, H. M. 2: v E 1929 (2)
McGregor, S. N. 25: v E 1954 (2) 1958 (2); v SA 1963 (3); v WI 1955 (4); v P 1964 (2); *v SA 1961 (5); v In 1955 (4); v P 1955 (3)*
McLeod E. G. 1: v E 1929
McMahon T. G. 5: v WI 1955 (1); *v In 1955 (3); v P 1955 (1)*
McRae, D. A. N. 1: v A 1945
Matheson, A. M. 2: v E 1929 (1); *v E 1931 (1)*
Meale, T. 2: *v E 1958 (2)*
Merritt, W. E. 6: v E 1929 (4); *v E 1931 (2)*
Meuli, E. M. 1: v SA 1952
Milburn, B. D. 3: v WI 1968 (3)
Miller, L. S. M. 13: v SA 1952 (2); v WI 1955 (3); *v E 1958 (4); v SA 1953 (4)*
Mills, J. E. 7: v E 1929 (3) 1932 (1); *v E 1931 (3)*
Moir, A. M. 17: v E 1950 (2) 1954 (2) 1958 (2); v SA 1952 (1); v WI 1951 (2) 1955 (1); *v E 1958 (2); v In 1955 (2); v P 1955 (3)*
Moloney D. A. R. 3: *v E 1937 (3)*
Mooney, F. L. H. 14: v E 1950 (2); v SA 1952 (2); v WI 1951 (2); *v E 1949 (3); v SA 1953 (5)*

Morgan, R. W. 20: v E 1965 (2) 1970 (2); v WI 1968 (1); v P 1964 (2); *v E 1965 (3); v WI 1971 (3); v In 1964 (4); v P 1964 (3)*
Morrison, B. D. 1: v E 1962
Morrison, J. F. M. 17: v E 1974 (2); v A 1973 (3) 1981 (3); v In 1975 (3); *v A 1973 (3); v In 1976 (1); v P 1976 (2)*
Motz, R. C. 32: v E 1962 (2) 1965 (3); v SA 1963 (2); v WI 1968 (3): v In 1967 (4); v P 1964 (3); *v E 1965 (3) 1969 (3); v SA 1961 (5); v In 1964 (3); v P 1964 (1)*
Murray, B. A. G. 13: v E 1970 (1); v In 1967 (4); *v E 1969 (2); v In 1969 (3); v P 1969 (3)*

Newman J. 3: v E 1932 (2); v SA 1931 (1)

O'Sullivan, D. R. 11: v In 1975 (1); v P 1972 (1); *v A 1973 (3); v In 1976 (3); v P 1976 (3)*
Overton, G. W. F. 3: *v SA 1953 (3)*

Page, M. L. 14: v E 1929 (4) 1932 (2); v SA 1931 (2); *v E 1931 (3) 1937 (3)*
Parker, J. M. 36: v E 1974 (2) 1977 (3); v A 1973 (3) 1976 (2); v WI 1979 (3); v In 1975 (3); v P 1972 (1) 1978 (2); *v E 1973 (3) 1978 (2); v A 1973 (3) 1980 (3); v In 1976 (3); v P 1976 (3)*
Parker, N. M. 3: *v In 1976 (2); v P 1976 (1)*
Petherick, P. J. 6: v A 1976 (1); *v In 1976 (3); v P 1976 (2)*
Petrie, E. C. 14: v E 1958 (2) 1965 (3); *v E 1958 (5); v In 1955 (2); v P 1955 (2)*
Playle, W. R. 8: v E 1962 (3); *v E 1958 (5)*
Pollard, V. 32: v E 1965 (3) 1970 (1); v WI 1968 (3); v In 1967 (4); v P 1972 (1); *v E 1965 (3) 1969 (3) 1973 (3); v In 1964 (4) 1969 (1); v P 1964 (3) 1969 (3)*
Poore, M. B. 14: v E 1954 (1); v SA 1952 (1); *v SA 1953 (5); v In 1955 (4); v P 1955 (3)*
Puna, N. 3: v E 1965 (3)

Rabone, G. O. 12: v E 1954 (2); v SA 1952 (1); v WI 1951 (2); *v E 1949 (4); v SA 1953 (3)*
Redmond, R. E. 1: v P 1972
Reid, J. F. 13: v In 1980 (3); v P 1978 (1) 1984 (3); *v P 1984 (3); v SL 1983 (3)*
Reid, J. R. 58: v E 1950 (2) 1954 (2) 1958 (2) 1962 (3); v SA 1952 (2) 1963 (3); v WI 1951 (2) 1955 (4); v P 1964 (3); *v E 1949 (2) 1958 (5) 1965 (3); v SA 1953 (5) 1961 (5); v In 1955 (5) 1964 (4); v P 1955 (3) 1964 (3)*
Roberts, A. D. G. 7: v In 1975 (2); *v In 1976 (3); v P 1976 (2)*
Roberts, A. W. 5: v E 1929 (1); v SA 1931 (2); *v E 1937 (2)*
Rowe, C. G. 1: v A 1945
Rutherford, K. R. 4: *v WI 1984 (4)*

Scott, R. H. 1: v E 1946
Scott, V. J. 10: v E 1946 (1) 1950 (2); v A 1945 (1); v WI 1951 (2); *v E 1949 (4)*
Shrimpton, M. J. F. 10: v E 1962 (2) 1965 (3) 1970 (2); v SA 1963 (1); *v A 1973 (2)*
Sinclair, B. W. 21: v E 1962 (3) 1965 (3); v SA 1963 (3); v In 1967 (2); v P 1964 (2); *v E 1965 (3); v In 1964 (2); v P 1964 (3)*
Sinclair, I. M. 2: v WI 1955 (2)
Smith, F. B. 4: v E 1946 (1); v WI 1951 (1); *v E 1949 (2)*
Smith, H. D. 1: v E 1932
Smith, I. D. S. 25: v E 1983 (3); v A 1981 (3); v In 1980 (3); v P 1984 (3); *v E 1983 (2); v A 1980 (1); v WI 1984 (4); v P 1984 (3); v SL 1983 (3)*
Snedden, C. A. 1: v E 1946
Snedden, M. C. 10: v E 1983 (1); v A 1981 (3); v In 1980 (3); v SL 1982 (2); *v E 1983 (1)*
Sparling, J. T. 11: v E 1958 (2) 1962 (1); v SA 1963 (2); *v E 1958 (3); v SA 1961 (3)*
Stirling, D. A. 4: *v WI 1984 (1); v P 1984 (3)*
Sutcliffe, B. 42: v E 1946 (1) 1950 (2) 1954 (2) 1958 (2); v SA 1952 (2); v WI 1951 (2) 1955 (2); *v E 1949 (4) 1958 (4) 1965 (1); v SA 1953 (5); v In 1955 (5) 1964 (4); v P 1955 (3) 1964 (3)*

Taylor, B. R. 30: v E 1965 (1); v WI 1968 (3); v In 1967 (3); v P 1972 (3); *v E 1965 (2) 1969 (2) 1973 (3); v WI 1971 (4); v In 1964 (3) 1969 (2); v P 1964 (3) 1969 (1)*
Taylor, D. D. 3: v E 1946 (1); v WI 1955 (2)
Thomson, K. 2: v In 1967 (2)
Tindill, E. W. T. 5: v E 1946 (1); v A 1945 (1); *v E 1937 (3)*
Troup, G. B. 13: v A 1981 (2); v WI 1979 (3); v In 1980 (2); v P 1978 (2); *v A 1980 (2); v WI 1984 (1); v In 1976 (1)*
Truscott, P. B. 1: v P 1964

Turner, G. M. 41: v E 1970 (2) 1974 (2); v A 1973 (3) 1976 (2); v WI 1968 (3); v In 1975 (3); v P 1972 (3); v SL 1982 (2); *v E 1969 (2) 1973 (3); v A 1973 (2); v WI 1971 (5); v In 1969 (3) 1976 (3); v P 1969 (1) 1976 (2)*

Vivian, G. E. 5: *v WI 1971 (4); v In 1964 (1)*
Vivian, H. G. 7: v E 1932 (1); v SA 1931 (1); *v E 1931 (2) 1937 (3)*

Wadsworth, K. J. 33: v E 1970 (2) 1974 (2); v A 1973 (3); v In 1975 (3); v P 1972 (3); *v E 1969 (3) 1973 (3); v A 1973 (3); v WI 1971 (5); v In 1969 (3); v P 1969 (3)*
Wallace, W. M. 13: v E 1946 (1) 1950 (2); v A 1945 (1); v SA 1952 (2); *v E 1937 (3) 1949 (4)*
Ward, J. T. 8: v SA 1963 (1); v In 1967 (1); v P 1964 (1); *v E 1965 (1); v In 1964 (4)*
Watt, L. 1: v E 1954
Webb, M. G. 3: v E 1970 (1); v A 1973 (1); *v WI 1971 (1)*
Webb, P. N. 2: v WI 1979 (2)
Weir, G. L. 11: v E 1929 (3) 1932 (2); v SA 1931 (2); *v E 1931 (3) 1937 (1)*
Whitelaw, P. E. 2: v E 1932 (2)
Wright, J. G. 41: v E 1977 (3) 1983 (3); v A 1981 (3); v WI 1979 (3); v In 1980 (3); v P 1978 (3) 1984 (3); v SL 1982 (2); *v E 1978 (2) 1983 (3); v A 1980 (3); v WI 1984 (4); v P 1984 (3); v SL 1983 (3)*

Yuile, B. W. 17: v E 1962 (2); v WI 1968 (3); v In 1967 (1); v P 1964 (3); *v E 1965 (1); v In 1964 (3) 1969 (1); v P 1964 (1) 1969 (2)*

## INDIA

### Number of Test cricketers: 170

Adhikari, H. R. 21: v E 1951 (3); v A 1956 (2); v WI 1948 (5) 1958 (1); v P 1952 (2); *v E 1952 (3); v A 1947 (5)*
Ali, S. Abid, 29: v E 1972 (4); v A 1969 (1); v WI 1974 (2); v NZ 1969 (3); *v E 1971 (3) 1974 (3); v A 1967 (4); v WI 1970 (5); v NZ 1967 (4)*
Ali, S. Nazir, 2: v E 1933 (1); *v E 1932 (1)*
Ali, S. Wazir, 7: v E 1933 (3); *v E 1932 (1) 1936 (3)*
Amarnath, L. 24: v E 1933 (3) 1951 (3); v WI 1948 (5); v P 1952 (5); *v E 1946 (3); v A 1947 (5)*
Amarnath, M. 49: v E 1976 (2) 1984 (5); v A 1969 (1) 1979 (1); v WI 1978 (2) 1983 (3); v NZ 1976 (3); v P 1983 (2); *v E 1979 (2); v A 1977 (5); v WI 1975 (4) 1982 (5); v NZ 1975 (3); v P 1978 (3) 1982 (6) 1984 (2)*
Amarnath, S. 10: v E 1976 (2): *v WI 1975 (2); v NZ 1975 (3); v P 1978 (3)*
Amar Singh 7: v E 1933 (3); *v E 1932 (1) 1936 (3)*
Amir Elahi 1: *v A 1947*
Apte, A. L. 1: *v E 1959*
Apte, M. L. 7: v P 1952 (2); *v WI 1952 (5)*
Arun Lal 4: v SL 19821; *v P 1982 (3)*
Azad, K. 7: v E 1981 (3); v WI 1983 (2); v P 1983 (1); *v NZ 1980 (1)*
Azharuddin, M. 3: v E 1984 (3)

Baig, A. A. 10: v A 1959 (3); v WI 1966 (2); v P 1960 (3); *v E 1959 (2)*
Banerjee, S. A. 1: v WI 1948
Banerjee, S. N. 1: v WI 1948
Bedi, B. S. 67: v E 1972 (5) 1976 (5); v A 1969 (5); v WI 1966 (2) 1974 (4) 1978 (3); v NZ 1969 (3) 1976 (3); *v E 1967 (3) 1971 (3) 1974 (3) 1979 (3); v A 1967 (2) 1977 (5); v WI 1970 (5) 1975 (4); v NZ 1967 (4) 1975 (2); v P 1978 (3)*
Bhandari, P. 3: v A 1956 (1); v NZ 1955 (1); *v P 1954 (1)*
Bhat, A. R. 2: v WI 1983 (1); v P 1983 (1)
Binny, R. M. H. 18: v E 1979 (1); v WI 1983 (6); v P 1979 (6) 1983 (2); *v A 1980 (1); v NZ 1980 (1); v P 1984 (1)*
Borde, C. G. 55: v E 1961 (5) 1963 (5); v A 1959 (5) 1964 (3) 1969 (1); v WI 1958 (4) 1966 (3); v NZ 1964 (4); v P 1960 (5); *v E 1959 (4) 1967 (3); v A 1967 (4); v WI 1961 (5); v NZ 1967 (4)*

Chandrasekhar, B. S. 58: v E 1963 (4) 1972 (5) 1976 (5); v A 1964 (2); v WI 1966 (3) 1974 (4) 1978 (4); v NZ 1964 (2) 1976 (3); *v E 1967 (3) 1971 (3) 1974 (2) 1979 (1); v A 1967 (2) 1977 (5); v WI 1975 (4); v NZ 1975 (3); v P 1978 (3)*
Chauhan, C. P. S. 40: v E 1972 (2); v A 1969 (1) 1979 (6); v WI 1978 (6); v NZ 1969 (2); v P 1979 (6); *v E 1979 (4); v A 1977 (4) 1980 (3); v NZ 1980 (3); v P 1978 (3)*
Chowdhury, N. R. 2: v E 1951 (1); v WI 1948 (1)
Colah, S. H. M. 2: v E 1933 (1); *v E 1932 (1)*
Contractor, N. J. 31: v E 1961 (5); v A 1956 (1) 1959 (5); v WI 1958 (5); v NZ 1955 (4); v P 1960 (5); *v E 1959 (4); v WI 1961 (2)*

Dani, H. T. 1: v P 1952
Desai, R. B. 28: v E 1961 (4) 1963 (2); v A 1959 (3); v WI 1958 (1); v NZ 1964 (3); v P 1960 (5); *v E 1959 (5); v A 1967 (1); v WI 1961 (3); v NZ 1967 (1)*
Dilawar Hussain 3: v E 1933 (2); *v E 1936 (1)*
Divecha, R. V. 5: v E 1951 (2); v P 1952 (1); *v E 1952 (2)*
Doshi, D. R. 33: v E 1979 (1) 1981 (6); v A 1979 (6); v P 1979 (6) 1983 (1); v SL 1982 (1); *v E 1982 (3); v A 1980 (3); v NZ 1980 (2); v P 1982 (4)*
Durani, S. A. 29: v E 1961 (5) 1963 (5) 1972 (3); v A 1959 (1) 1964 (3); v WI 1966 (1); v NZ 1964 (3); *v WI 1961 (5) 1970 (3)*

Engineer, F. M. 46: v E 1961 (4) 1972 (5); v A 1969 (5); v WI 1966 (1) 1974 (5); v NZ 1964 (4) 1969 (2); *v E 1967 (3) 1971 (3) 1974 (3); v A 1967 (4); v WI 1961 (3); v NZ 1967 (4)*

Gadkari, C. V. 6: *v WI 1952 (3); v P 1954 (3)*
Gaekwad, A. D. 40: v E 1976 (4) 1984 (3); v WI 1974 (3) 1978 (5) 1983 (6); v NZ 1976 (3); v P 1983 (3); *v E 1979 (2); v A 1977 (1); v WI 1975 (3) 1982 (5); v P 1984 (2)*
Gaekwad, D. K. 11: v WI 1958 (1); v P 1952 (2) 1960 (1); *v E 1952 (1) 1959 (4); v WI 1952 (2)*
Gaekwad, H. G. 1: v P 1952
Gandotra, A. 2: v A 1969 (1); v NZ 1969 (1)
Gavaskar, S. M. 106: v E 1972 (5) 1976 (5) 1979 (1) 1981 (6) 1984 (5); v A 1979 (6); v WI 1974 (2) 1978 (6) 1983 (6); v NZ 1976 (3); v P 1979 (6) 1983 (3); v SL 1982 (1); *v E 1971 (3) 1974 (3) 1979 (4) 1982 (3); v A 1977 (5) 1980 (3); v WI 1970 (4) 1975 (4) 1982 (5); v NZ 1975 (3) 1980 (3); v P 1978 (3) 1982 (6) 1984 (2)*
Ghavri, K. D. 39: v E 1976 (3) 1979 (1); v A 1979 (6); v WI 1974 (3) 1978 (6); v NZ 1976 (2); v P 1979 (6); *v E 1979 (4); v A 1977 (3) 1980 (3); v NZ 1980 (1); v P 1978 (1)*
Ghorpade, J. M. 8: v A 1956 (1); v WI 1958 (1); v NZ 1955 (1); *v E 1959 (3); v WI 1952 (2)*
Ghulam Ahmed 22: v E 1951 (2); v A 1956 (2); v WI 1948 (3) 1958 (2); v NZ 1955 (1); v P 1952 (4); *v E 1952 (4); v P 1954 (4)*
Gopalan, M. J. 1: v E 1933
Gopinath, C. D. 8: v E 1951 (3); v A 1959 (1); v P 1952 (1); *v E 1952 (1); v P 1954 (2)*
Guard, G. M. 2: v A 1959 (1); v WI 1958 (1)
Guha, S. 4: v A 1969 (3); *v E 1967 (1)*
Gul Mahomed 8: v P 1952 (2); *v E 1946 (1); v A 1947 (5)*
Gupte, B. P. 3: v E 1963 (1); v NZ 1964 (1); v P 1960 (1)
Gupte, S. P. 36: v E 1951 (1) 1961 (2); v A 1956 (3); v WI 1958 (5); v NZ 1955 (5); v P 1952 (2) 1960 (3); *v E 1959 (5); v WI 1952 (5); v P 1954 (5)*

Hafeez, A. 3: *v E 1946 (3)*
Hanumant Singh 14: v E 1963 (2); v A 1964 (3); v WI 1966 (2); v NZ 1964 (4) 1969 (1); *v E 1967 (2)*
Hardikar, M. S. 2: v WI 1958 (2)
Hazare, V. S. 30: v E 1951 (5); v WI 1948 (5); v P 1952 (3); *v E 1946 (3) 1952 (4); v A 1947 (5); v WI 1952 (5)*
Hindlekar, D. D. 4: *v E 1936 (1) 1946 (3)*

Ibrahim, K. C. 4: v WI 1948 (4)
Indrajitsinhji, K. S. 4: v A 1964 (3); v NZ 1969 (1)
Irani, J. K. 2: *v A 1947 (2)*

Jai, L. P. 1: v E 1933
Jaisimha, M. L. 39: v E 1961 (5) 1963 (5); v A 1959 (1) 1964 (3); v WI 1966 (2); v NZ 1964 (4) 1969 (1); v P 1960 (4); *v E 1959 (1); v A 1967 (2); v WI 1961 (4) 1970 (3); v NZ 1967 (4)*
Jamshedji, R. J. 1: v E 1933

Jayantilal, K. 1: *v WI 1970*
Jilani, M. Baqa 1: *v E 1936*
Joshi, P. G. 12: v E 1951 (2); v A 1959 (1); v WI 1958 (1); v P 1952 (1) 1960 (1); *v E 1959 (3); v WI 1952 (3)*

Kanitkar, H. S. 2: v WI 1974 (2)
Kapil Dev 68: v E 1979 (1) 1981 (6) 1984 (4); v A 1979 (6); v WI 1978 (6) 1983 (6); v P 1979 (6) 1983 (3); v SL 1982 (1); *v E 1979 (4) 1982 (3); v A 1980 (3); v WI 1982 (5); v NZ 1980 (3); v P 1978 (3) 1982 (6) 1984 (2)*
Kardar, A. H. (*see* Hafeez)
Kenny, R. B. 5: v A 1959 (4); v WI 1958 (1)
Khan, M. Jahangir, 4: *v E 1932 (1) 1936 (3)*
Kirmani, S. M. H. 85: v E 1976 (5) 1979 (1) 1981 (6) 1984 (5); v A 1979 (6); v WI 1978 (6) 1983 (6); v NZ 1976 (3); v P 1979 (6) 1983 (3); v SL 1982 (1); *v E 1982 (3); v A 1977 (5) 1980 (3); v WI 1975 (4) 1982 (5); v NZ 1975 (3) 1980 (3); v P 1978 (3) 1982 (6) 1984 (2)*
Kischenchand, G. 5: v P 1952 (1); *v A 1947 (4)*
Kripal Singh, A. G. 14: v E 1961 (3) 1963 (2); v A 1956 (2) 1964 (1); v WI 1958 (1); v NZ 1955 (4); *v E 1959 (1)*
Krishnamurthy, P. 5: *v WI 1970 (5)*
Kulkarni, U. N. 4: *v A 1967 (3); v NZ 1967 (1)*
Kumar, V. V. 2: v E 1961 (1); v P 1960 (1)
Kunderan, B. K. 18: v E 1961 (1) 1963 (5); v A 1959 (3); v WI 1966 (2); v NZ 1964 (1); v P 1960 (2); *v E 1967 (2); v WI 1961 (2)*

Lall Singh 1: *v E 1932*

Madan Lal 38: v E 1976 (2) 1981 (6); v WI 1974 (2) 1983 (3); v NZ 1976 (1); v P 1983 (3); v SL 1982 (1); *v E 1974 (2) 1982 (3); v A 1977 (2); v WI 1975 (4) 1982 (2); v NZ 1975 (3); v P 1982 (3) 1984 (1)*
Maka, E. S. 2: v P 1952 (1); *v WI 1952 (1)*
Malhotra, A. 7: v E 1981 (2) 1984 (1); v WI 1983 (3); *v E 1982 (1)*
Maninder Singh 13: v WI 1983 (4); *v WI 1982 (3); v P 1982 (5) 1984 (1)*
Manjrekar, V. L. 55: v E 1951 (2) 1961 (5) 1963 (4); v A 1956 (3) 1964 (3); v WI 1958 (4); v NZ 1955 (5) 1964 (1); v P 1952 (3) 1960 (5); *v E 1952 (4) 1959 (2); v WI 1952 (4) 1961 (5); v P 1954 (5)*
Mankad, A. V. 22: v E 1976 (1); v A 1969 (5); v WI 1974 (1); v NZ 1969 (2) 1976 (3); *v E 1971 (3) 1974 (1); v A 1977 (3); v WI 1970 (3)*
Mankad, V. 44: v E 1951 (5); v A 1956 (3); v WI 1948 (5) 1958 (2); v NZ 1955 (4); v P 1952 (4); *v E 1946 (3) 1952 (3); v A 1947 (5); v WI 1952 (5); v P 1954 (5)*
Mansur Ali Khan (*see* Pataudi)
Mantri, M. K. 4: v E 1951 (1); *v E 1952 (2); v P 1954 (1)*
Meherhomji, K. R. 1: *v E 1936*
Mehra, V. L. 8: v E 1961 (1) 1963 (2); v NZ 1955 (2); *v WI 1961 (3)*
Merchant, V. M. 10: v E 1933 (3) 1951 (1); *v E 1936 (3) 1946 (3)*
Milkha Singh, A. G. 4: v E 1961 (1); v A 1959 (1); v P 1960 (2)
Modi, R. S. 10: v E 1951 (1); v WI 1948 (5); v P 1952 (1); *v E 1946 (3)*
Muddiah, V. M. 2: v A 1959 (1); v P 1960 (1)
Mushtaq Ali 11: v E 1933 (2); 1951 (1); v WI 1948 (3); *v E 1936 (3) 1946 (2)*

Nadkarni, R. G. 41: v E 1961 (1) 1963 (5); v A 1959 (5) 1964 (3); v WI 1958 (1) 1966 (1); v NZ 1955 (1) 1964 (4); v P 1960 (4); *v E 1959 (4); v A 1967 (3); v WI 1961 (5); v NZ 1967 (4)*
Naik, S. S. 3: v WI 1974 (2); *v E 1974 (1)*
Naoomal Jeoomal 3: v E 1933 (2); *v E 1932 (1)*
Narasimha Rao, M. V. 4: v A 1979 (2); v WI 1978 (2)
Navjot Singh 2: v WI 1983 (2)
Navle, J. G. 2: v E 1933 (1); *v E 1932 (1)*
Nayak, S. V. 2: *v E 1982 (2)*
Nayudu, C. K. 7: v E 1933 (3); *v E 1932 (1) 1936 (3)*
Nayudu, C. S. 11: v E 1933 (2) 1951 (1); *v E 1936 (2) 1946 (2); v A 1947 (4)*
Nissar, Mahomed 6: v E 1933 (2); *v E 1932 (1) 1936 (3)*
Nyalchand, S. 1: v P 1952

Pai, A. M. 1: v NZ 1969

Palia, P. E. 2: *v E 1932 (1) 1936 (1)*
Parkar, G. A. 1: *v E 1982*
Parkar, R. D. 2: v E 1972 (2)
Parsana, D. D. 2: v WI 1978 (2)
Patankar, C. T. 1: v NZ 1955
Pataudi sen., Nawab of, 3: *v E 1946 (3)*
Pataudi jun., Nawab of (now Mansur Ali Khan) 46: v E 1961 (3) 1963 (5) 1972 (3); v A 1964 (3) 1969 (5); v WI 1966 (3) 1974 (4); v NZ 1964 (4) 1969 (3); *v E 1967 (3); v A 1967 (3); v WI 1961 (3); v NZ 1967 (4)*
Patel, B. P. 21: v E 1976 (5); v WI 1974 (3); v NZ 1976 (3); *v E 1974 (2); v A 1977 (2); v WI 1975 (3); v NZ 1975 (3)*
Patel, J. M. 7: v A 1956 (2) 1959 (3); v NZ 1955 (1); *v P 1954 (1)*
Patiala, Yuvraj of, 1: v E 1933
Patil, S. M. 29: v E 1979 (1) 1981 (4) 1984 (2); v WI 1983 (2); v P 1979 (2) 1983 (3); v SL 1982 (1); *v E 1982 (2); v A 1980 (3); v NZ 1980 (3); v P 1982 (4) 1984 (2)*
Patil, S. R. 1: v NZ 1955
Phadkar, D. G. 31: v E 1951 (4); v A 1956 (1); v WI 1948 (4) 1958 (1); v NZ 1955 (4); v P 1952 (2); *v E 1952 (4); v A 1947 (4); v WI 1952 (4); v P 1954 (3)*
Prabhakar, M. 2: v E 1984 (2)
Prasanna, E. A. S. 49: v E 1961 (1) 1972 (3) 1976 (4); v A 1969 (5); v WI 1966 (1) 1974 (5); v NZ 1969 (3); *v E 1967 (3) 1974 (2); v A 1967 (4) 1977 (4); v WI 1961 (1) 1970 (3) 1975 (1); v NZ 1967 (4) 1975 (3); v P 1978 (2)*
Punjabi, P. H. 5: *v P 1954 (5)*

Rai Singh, K. 1: *v A 1947*
Rajinder Pal 1: v E 1963
Rajindernath, V. 1: v P 1952
Ramaswami, C. 2: *v E 1936 (2)*
Ramchand, G. S. 33: v A 1956 (3) 1959 (5); v WI 1958 (3); v NZ 1955 (5); v P 1952 (3); *v E 1952 (4); v WI 1952 (5); v P 1954 (5)*
Ramji, L. 1: v E 1933
Rangachary, C. R. 4: v WI 1948 (2); *v A 1947 (2)*
Rangnekar, K. M. 3: *v A 1947 (3)*
Ranjane, V. B. 7: v E 1961 (3) 1963 (1); v A 1964 (1); v WI 1958 (1); *v WI 1961 (1)*
Reddy, B. 4: *v E 1979 (4)*
Rege, M. R. 1: v WI 1948
Roy, A. 4: v A 1969 (2); v NZ 1969 (2)
Roy, Pankaj 43: v E 1951 (5); v A 1956 (3) 1959 (5); v WI 1958 (5); v NZ 1955 (3); v P 1952 (3) 1960 (1); *v E 1952 (4) 1959 (5); v WI 1952 (4); v P 1954 (5)*
Roy, Pranab 2: v E 1981 (2)

Sandhu, B. S. 8: v WI 1983 (1); *v WI 1982 (4); v P 1982 (3)*
Sardesai, D. N. 30: v E 1961 (1) 1963 (5) 1972 (1); v A 1964 (3) 1969 (1); v WI 1966 (2); v NZ 1964 (3); *v E 1967 (1) 1971 (3); v A 1967 (2); v WI 1961 (3) 1970 (5)*
Sarwate, C. T. 9: v E 1951 (1); v WI 1948 (2); *v E 1946 (1); v A 1947 (5)*
Saxena, R. C. 1: *v E 1967*
Sekar, T. A. P. 2: *v P 1982 (2)*
Sen, P. 14: v E 1951 (2); v WI 1948 (5); v P 1952 (2); *v E 1952 (2); v A 1947 (3)*
Sengupta, A. K. 1: v WI 1958
Sharma, C. 5: v E 1984 (3); *v P 1984 (2)*
Sharma, G. 1: v E 1984
Sharma, P. 5: v E 1976 (2); v WI 1974 (2); *v WI 1975 (1)*
Shastri, R. J. 34: v E 1981 (6) 1984 (5); v WI 1983 (6); v P 1983 (2); *v E 1982 (3); v WI 1982 (5); v NZ 1980 (3); v P 1982 (2) 1984 (2)*
Shinde, S. G. 7: v E 1951 (3); v WI 1948 (1); *v E 1946 (1) 1952 (2)*
Shodhan, R. H. 3: v P 1952 (1); *v WI 1952 (2)*
Shukla, R. C. 1: v SL 1982
Sivaramakrishnan, L. 6: v E 1984 (5); *v WI 1982 (1)*
Sohoni, S. W. 4: v E 1951 (1); *v E 1946 (2); v A 1947 (1)*
Solkar, E. D. 27: v E 1972 (5) 1976 (1); v A 1969 (4); v WI 1974 (4); v NZ 1969 (1); *v E 1971 (3) 1974 (3); v WI 1970 (5) 1975 (1)*
Sood, M. M. 1: v A 1959

Srikkanth, K. 8: v E 1981 (4) 1984 (2); *v P 1982 (2)*
Srinivasan, T. E. 1: *v NZ 1980*
Subramanya, V. 9: v WI 1966 (2); v NZ 1964 (1); *v E 1967 (2); v A 1967 (2); v NZ 1967 (2)*
Sunderram, G. 2: v NZ 1955 (2)
Surendranath, R. 11: v A 1959 (2); v WI 1958 (2); v P 1960 (2); *v E 1959 (5)*
Surti, R. F. 26: v E 1963 (1); v A 1964 (2) 1969 (1); v WI 1966 (2); v NZ 1964 (1) 1969 (2); v P 1960 (2); *v E 1967 (2); v A 1967 (4); v WI 1961 (5); v NZ 1967 (4)*
Swamy, V. N. 1: v NZ 1955

Tamhane, N. S. 21: v A 1956 (3) 1959 (1); v WI 1958 (4); v NZ 1955 (4); v P 1960 (2); *v E 1959 (2); v P 1954 (5)*
Tarapore, K. K. 1: v WI 1948

Umrigar, P. R. 59: v E 1951 (5) 1961 (4); v A 1956 (3) 1959 (3); v WI 1948 (1) 1958 (5); v NZ 1955 (5); v P 1952 (5) 1960 (5); *v E 1952 (4) 1959 (4); v WI 1952 (5) 1961 (5); v P 1954 (5)*

Vengsarkar, D. B. 76: v E 1976 (1) 1979 (1) 1981 (6) 1984 (5); v A 1979 (6); v WI 1978 (6) 1983 (5); v P 1979 (5) 1983 (1); v SL 1982 (1); *v E 1979 (4) 1982 (3); v A 1977 (5) 1980 (3); v WI 1975 (2) 1982 (5); v NZ 1975 (3) 1980 (3); v P 1978 (3) 1982 (6) 1984 (2)*
Venkataraghavan, S. 57: v E 1972 (2) 1976 (1); v A 1969 (5) 1979 (3); v WI 1966 (2) 1974 (2) 1978 (6); v NZ 1964 (4) 1969 (2) 1976 (3); v P 1983 (2); *v E 1967 (1) 1971 (3) 1974 (2) 1979 (4); v A 1977 (1); v WI 1970 (5) 1975 (3) 1982 (5); v NZ 1975 (1)*
Viswanath, G. R. 91: v E 1972 (5) 1976 (5) 1979 (1) 1981 (6); v A 1969 (4) 1979 (6); v WI 1974 (5) 1978 (6); v NZ 1976 (3); v SL 1982 (1); v P 1979 (6); *v E 1971 (3) 1974 (3) 1979 (4) 1982 (3); v A 1977 (5) 1980 (3); v WI 1970 (3) 1975 (4); v NZ 1975 (3) 1980 (3); v P 1978 (3) 1982 (6)*
Vizianagram, Maharaj Sir Vijaya 3: *v E 1936 (3)*

Wadekar, A. L. 37: v E 1972 (5); v A 1969 (5); v WI 1966 (2); v NZ 1969 (3); *v E 1967 (3) 1971 (3) 1974 (3); v A 1967 (4); v WI 1970 (5); v NZ 1967 (4)*

Yadav, N. S. 23: v E 1979 (1) 1981 (1) 1984 (4); v A 1979 (5); v WI 1983 (3); v P 1979 (5); *v A 1980 (2); v NZ 1980 (1); v P 1984 (1)*
Yajurvindra Singh 4: v E 1976 (2); v A 1979 (1); *v E 1979 (1)*
Yashpal Sharma 37: v E 1979 (1) 1981 (2); v A 1979 (6); v WI 1983 (1); v P 1979 (6) 1983 (3); v SL 1982 (1); *v E 1979 (3) 1982 (3); v A 1980 (3); v WI 1982 (5); v NZ 1980 (1); v P 1982 (2)*
Yograj Singh 1: *v NZ 1980*

*Note: Hafeez, on going later to Oxford University, took his correct name, Kardar.*

## PAKISTAN

Number of Test cricketers: 102

Abdul Kadir 4: v A 1964 (1); *v A 1964 (1); v NZ 1964 (2)*
Abdul Qadir 33: v E 1977 (3) 1983 (3); v A 1982 (3); v WI 1980 (2); v NZ 1984 (3); v In 1982 (5) 1984 (1); *v E 1982 (3); v A 1983 (5); v NZ 1984 (2); v In 1979 (3)*
Afaq Hussain 2: v E 1961 (1); *v A 1964 (1)*
Aftab Baloch 2: v WI 1974 (1); v NZ 1969 (1)
Aftab Gul 6: v E 1968 (2); v NZ 1969 (1); *v E 1971 (3)*
Agha Saadat Ali 1: v NZ 1955
Agha Zahid 1: v WI 1974
Alim-ud-Din 25: v E 1961 (2); v A 1956 (1) 1959 (1); v WI 1958 (1); v NZ 1955 (3); v In 1954 (5); *v E 1954 (3) 1962 (3); v WI 1957 (5); v In 1960 (1)*
Amir Elahi 5: *v In 1952 (5)*
Anil Dalpat 9: v E 1983 (3); v NZ 1984 (3); *v NZ 1984 (3)*
Anwar Hussain 4: *v In 1952 (4)*
Anwar Khan 1: *v NZ 1978*
Arif Butt 3: *v A 1964 (1); v NZ 1964 (2)*
Ashraf Ali 4: v In 1984 (2); v SL 1981 (2)
Asif Iqbal 58: v E 1968 (3) 1972 (3); v A 1964 (1); v WI 1974 (2); v NZ 1964 (3) 1969 (3) 1976 (3); v In 1978 (3); *v E 1967 (3) 1971 (3) 1974 (3); v A 1964 (1) 1972 (3) 1976 (3) 1978 (2); v WI 1976 (5); v NZ 1964 (3) 1972 (3) 1978 (2); v In 1979 (6)*

Asif Masood 16: v E 1968 (2) 1972 (1); v WI 1974 (2); v NZ 1969 (1); *v E 1971 (3) 1974 (3); v A 1972 (3) 1976 (1)*

Azeem Hafeez 18: v E 1983 (2); v NZ 1984 (3); v In 1984 (2); *v A 1983 (5); v NZ 1984 (3); v In 1983 (3)*

Azhar Khan 1: v A 1979

Azmat Rana 1: v A 1979

Burki, J. 25: v E 1961 (3); v A 1964 (1); v NZ 1964 (3) 1969 (1); *v E 1962 (5) 1967 (3); v A 1964 (1); v NZ 1964 (3); v In 1960 (5)*

D'Souza, A. 6: v E 1961 (2); v WI 1958 (1); *v E 1962 (3)*

Ehtesham-ud-Din 5: v A 1979 (1); *v E 1982 (1); v In 1979 (3)*

Farooq Hamid 1: *v A 1964*

Farrukh Zaman 1: v NZ 1976

Fazal Mahmood 34: v E 1961 (1); v A 1956 (1) 1959 (2); v WI 1958 (3); v NZ 1955 (2); v In 1954 (4); *v E 1954 (4) 1962 (2); v WI 1957 (5); v In 1952 (5) 1960 (5)*

Ghazali, M. E. Z. 2: *v E 1954 (2)*

Ghulam Abbas 1: *v E 1967*

Gul Mahomed 1: v A 1956

Hanif Mohammad 55: v E 1961 (3) 1968 (3); v A 1956 (1) 1959 (3) 1964 (1); v WI 1958 (1); v NZ 1955 (3) 1964 (3) 1969 (1); v In 1954 (5); *v E 1954 (4) 1962 (5) 1967 (3); v A 1964 (1); v WI 1957 (5); v NZ 1964 (3); v In 1952 (5) 1960 (5)*

Haroon Rashid 23: v E 1977 (3); v A 1979 (2) 1982 (3); v In 1982 (1); v SL 1981 (2); *v E 1978 (3) 1982 (1); v A 1976 (1) 1978 (1); v WI 1976 (5); v NZ 1978 (1)*

Haseeb Ahsan 12: v E 1961 (2); v A 1959 (1); v WI 1958 (1); *v WI 1957 (3); v In 1960 (5)*

Ibadulla, K. 4: v A 1964 (1); *v E 1967 (2); v NZ 1964 (1)*

Ijaz Butt 8: v A 1959 (2); v WI 1958 (3); *v E 1962 (3)*

Ijaz Faqih 2: v WI 1980 (1); *v A 1981 (1)*

Imran Khan 51: v A 1979 (2) 1982 (3); v WI 1980 (4); v NZ 1976 (3); v In 1978 (3) 1982 (6); v SL 1981 (1); *v E 1971 (1) 1974 (3) 1982 (3); v A 1976 (3) 1978 (2) 1981 (3) 1983 (2); v WI 1976 (5); v NZ 1978 (2); v In 1979 (5)*

Imtiaz Ahmed 41: v E 1961 (3); v A 1956 (1) 1959 (3); v WI 1958 (3); v NZ 1955 (3); v In 1954 (5); *v E 1954 (4) 1962 (4); v WI 1957 (5); v In 1952 (5) 1960 (5)*

Intikhab Alam 47: v E 1961 (2) 1968 (3) 1972 (3); v A 1959 (1) 1964 (1); v WI 1974 (2); v NZ 1964 (3) 1969 (3) 1976 (3); *v E 1962 (3) 1967 (3) 1971 (3) 1974 (3); v A 1964 (1) 1972 (3); v WI 1976 (1); v NZ 1964 (3) 1972 (3); v In 1960 (3)*

Iqbal Qasim 41: v E 1977 (3); v A 1979 (3) 1982 (2); v WI 1980 (4); v NZ 1984 (3); v In 1978 (3) 1982 (2); v SL 1981 (3); *v E 1978 (3); v A 1976 (3) 1981 (2); v WI 1976 (2); v NZ 1984 (1); v In 1979 (6) 1983 (1)*

Israr Ali 4: v A 1959 (2); *v In 1952 (2)*

Jalal-ud-Din 5: v A 1982 (1); v In 1982 (2) 1984 (2)

Javed Akhtar 1: *v E 1962*

Javed Miandad 68: v E 1977 (3); v A 1979 (3) 1982 (3); v WI 1980 (4); v NZ 1976 (3) 1984 (3); v In 1978 (3) 1982 (6) 1984 (2); v SL 1981 (3); *v E 1978 (3) 1982 (3); v A 1976 (3) 1978 (2) 1981 (3) 1983 (5); v WI 1976 (1); v NZ 1978 (3) 1984 (3); v In 1979 (6) 1983 (3)*

Kardar, A. H. 23: v A 1956 (1); v NZ 1955 (3); v In 1954 (5); *v E 1954 (4); v WI 1957 (5); v In 1952 (5)*

Khalid Hassan 1: *v E 1954*

Khalid Wazir 2: *v E 1954 (2)*

Khan Mohammad 13: v A 1956 (1); v NZ 1955 (3); v In 1954 (4); *v E 1954 (2); v WI 1957 (2); v In 1952 (1)*

Liaqat Ali 5: v E 1977 (2); v WI 1974 (1); *v E 1978 (2)*

Mahmood Hussain 27: v E 1961 (1); v WI 1958 (3); v NZ 1955 (1); v In 1954 (5); *v E 1954 (2) 1962 (3); v WI 1957 (3); v In 1952 (4) 1960 (5)*

Majid Khan 63: v E 1968 (3) 1972 (3); v A 1964 (1) 1979 (3); v WI 1974 (2) 1980 (4); v NZ 1964 (3) 1976 (3); v In 1978 (3) 1982 (1); v SL 1981 (1); *v E 1967 (3) 1971 (2) 1974 (3) 1982 (1); v A 1972 (3) 1976 (3) 1978 (2) 1981 (3); v WI 1976 (5); v NZ 1972 (3) 1978 (2); v In 1979 (6)*

Mansoor Akhtar 13: v A 1982 (3); v WI 1980 (2); v In 1982 (3); v SL 1981 (1); *v E 1982 (3); v A 1981 (1)*

Manzoor Elahi 2: v NZ 1984 (1); v In 1984 (1)

Maqsood Ahmed 16: v NZ 1955 (2); v In 1954 (5); *v E 1954 (4); v In 1952 (5)*

Mathias, Wallis 21: v E 1961 (1); v A 1956 (1) 1959 (2); v WI 1958 (3); v NZ 1955 (1); *v E 1962 (3); v WI 1957 (5); v In 1960 (5)*

Miran Bux 2: v In 1954 (2)

Mohammad Aslam 1: *v E 1954*

Mohammad Farooq 7: v NZ 1964 (3); *v E 1962 (2); v In 1960 (2)*

Mohammad Ilyas 10: v E 1968 (2); v NZ 1964 (3); *v E 1967 (1); v A 1964 (1); v NZ 1964 (3)*

Mohammad Munaf 4: v E 1961 (2); v A 1959 (2)

Mohammad Nazir 14: v E 1972 (1); v WI 1980 (4); v NZ 1969 (3); *v A 1983 (3); v In 1983 (3)*

Mohsin Kamal 1: v E 1983

Mohsin Khan 40: v E 1977 (1) 1983 (3); v A 1982 (3); v NZ 1984 (2); v In 1982 (6) 1984 (2); v SL 1981 (2); *v E 1978 (3) 1982 (3); v A 1978 (1) 1981 (2) 1983 (5); v NZ 1978 (1) 1984 (3); v In 1983 (3)*

Mudassar Nazar 52: v E 1977 (3) 1983 (1); v A 1979 (3) 1982 (3); v NZ 1984 (3); v In 1978 (2) 1982 (6) 1984 (2); v SL 1981 (1); *v E 1978 (3) 1982 (3); v A 1976 (1) 1978 (1) 1981 (3) 1983 (5); v NZ 1978 (1) 1984 (3); v In 1979 (5) 1983 (3)*

Mufasir-ul-Haq 1: *v NZ 1964*

Munir Malik 3: v A 1959 (1); *v E 1962 (2)*

Mushtaq Mohammad 57: v E 1961 (3) 1968 (3) 1972 (3); v WI 1958 (1) 1974 (2); v NZ 1969 (2) 1976 (3); v In 1978 (3); *v E 1962 (5) 1967 (3) 1971 (3) 1974 (3); v A 1972 (3) 1976 (3) 1978 (2); v WI 1976 (5); v NZ 1972 (2) 1978 (3); v In 1960 (5)*

Nasim-ul-Ghani 29: v E 1961 (2); v A 1959 (2) 1964 (1); v WI 1958 (3); *v E 1962 (5) 1967 (2); v A 1964 (1) 1972 (1); v WI 1957 (5); v NZ 1964 (3); v In 1960 (4)*

Naushad Ali 6: v NZ 1964 (3); *v NZ 1964 (3)*

Nazar Mohammad 5: *v In 1952 (5)*

Nazir Junior (*see* Mohammad Nazir)

Niaz Ahmed 2: v E 1968 (1); *v E 1967 (1)*

Pervez Sajjad 19: v E 1968 (1) 1972 (2); v A 1964 (1); v NZ 1964 (3) 1969 (3); *v E 1971 (3); v NZ 1964 (3) 1972 (3)*

Qasim Omar 17: v E 1983 (3); v NZ 1984 (3); v In 1984 (2); *v A 1983 (5); v NZ 1984 (3); v In 1983 (1)*

Ramiz Raja 2: v E 1983 (2)

Rashid Khan 4: v SL 1981 (2); *v A 1983 (1); v NZ 1984 (1)*

Rehman, S. F. 1: *v WI 1957*

Rizwan-uz-Zaman 3: v SL 1981 (2); *v A 1981 (1)*

Sadiq Mohammad 41: v E 1972 (3) 1977 (2); v WI 1974 (1) 1980 (3); v NZ 1969 (3) 1976 (3); v In 1978 (1); *v E 1971 (3) 1974 (3) 1978 (3); v A 1972 (3) 1976 (2); v WI 1976 (5); v NZ 1972 (3); v In 1979 (3)*

Saeed Ahmed 41: v E 1961 (3) 1968 (3); v A 1959 (3) 1964 (1); v WI 1958 (3); v NZ 1964 (3); *v E 1962 (5) 1967 (3) 1971 (1); v A 1964 (1) 1972 (2); v WI 1957 (5); v NZ 1964 (3); v In 1960 (5)*

Salah-ud-Din 5: v E 1968 (1); v NZ 1964 (3) 1969 (1)

Saleem Altaf 21: v E 1972 (3); v NZ 1969 (2); v In 1978 (1); *v E 1967 (2) 1971 (2); v A 1972 (3) 1976 (2); v WI 1976 (3); v NZ 1972 (3)*

Salim Malik 24: v E 1983 (3); v NZ 1984 (3); v In 1982 (6) 1984 (2); v SL 1981 (2); *v A 1983 (3); v NZ 1984 (3); v In 1983 (2)*

Salim Yousuf 1: v SL 1981

Sarfraz Nawaz 55: v E 1968 (1) 1972 (2) 1977 (2) 1983 (3); v A 1979 (3); v WI 1974 (2) 1980 (2); v NZ 1976 (3); v In 1978 (3) 1982 (6); *v E 1974 (3) 1978 (2) 1982 (1); v A 1972 (2) 1976 (2) 1978 (2) 1981 (3) 1983 (3); v WI 1976 (4); v NZ 1972 (3) 1978 (3)*

Shafiq Ahmad 6: v E 1977 (3); v WI 1980 (2); *v E 1974 (1)*

Shafqat Rana 5: v E 1968 (2); v A 1964 (1); v NZ 1969 (2)
Shahid Israr 1: v NZ 1976
Shahid Mahmood 1: *v E 1962*
Sharpe, D. 3: v A 1959 (3)
Shoaib Mohammad 5: v E 1983 (1); v NZ 1984 (1); *v NZ 1984 (1); v In 1983 (2)*
Shuja-ud-Din 19: v E 1961 (2); v A 1959 (3); v WI 1958 (3); v NZ 1955 (3); v In 1954 (5); *v E 1954 (3)*
Sikander Bakht 26: v E 1977 (2); v WI 1980 (1); v NZ 1976 (1); v In 1978 (2) 1982 (1); *v E 1978 (3) 1982 (2); v A 1978 (2) 1981 (3); v WI 1976 (1); v NZ 1978 (3), v In 1979 (5)*

Tahir Naqqash 15: v A 1982 (3); v In 1982 (2); v SL 1981 (3); *v E 1982 (2); v A 1983 (1); v NZ 1984 (1); v In 1983 (3)*
Talat Ali 10: v E 1972 (3); *v E 1978 (2); v A 1972 (1); v NZ 1972 (1) 1978 (3)*
Taslim Arif 6: v A 1979 (3); v WI 1980 (2); *v In 1979 (1)*
Tauseef Ahmed 10: v E 1983 (2); v A 1979 (3); v NZ 1984 (1); v In 1984 (1); v SL 1981 (3)

Waqar Hassan 21: v A 1956 (1) 1959 (1); v WI 1958 (1); v NZ 1955 (3); v In 1954 (5); *v E 1954 (4); v WI 1957 (1); v In 1952 (5)*
Wasim Akram 2: *v NZ 1984 (2)*
Wasim Bari 81: v E 1968 (3) 1972 (3) 1977 (3); v A 1982 (3); v WI 1974 (2) 1980 (2); v NZ 1969 (3) 1976 (2); v In 1978 (3) 1982 (6); *v E 1967 (3) 1971 (3) 1974 (3) 1978 (3) 1982 (3); v A 1972 (3) 1976 (3) 1978 (2) 1981 (3) 1983 (5); v WI 1976 (5); v NZ 1972 (3) 1978 (3); v In 1979 (6); 1983 (3)*
Wasim Raja 57: v E 1972 (1) 1977 (3) 1983 (3); v A 1979 (3); v WI 1974 (2) 1980 (4); v NZ 1976 (1) 1984 (1); v In 1982 (1) 1984 (1); v SL 1981 (3); *v E 1974 (2) 1978 (3) 1982 (1); v A 1978 (1) 1981 (3) 1983 (2); v WI 1976 (5); v NZ 1972 (3) 1978 (3) 1984 (2); v In 1979 (6) 1983 (3)*
Wazir Mohammad 20: v A 1956 (1) 1959 (1); v WI 1958 (3); v NZ 1955 (2); v In 1954 (5); *v E 1954 (2); v WI 1957 (5); v In 1952 (1)*

Younis Ahmed 2: v NZ 1969 (2)

Zaheer Abbas 76: v E 1972 (2) 1983 (3); v A 1979 (2) 1982 (3); v WI 1974 (2) 1980 (3); v NZ 1969 (1) 1976 (3) 1984 (3); v In 1978 (3) 1982 (6) 1984 (2); v SL 1981 (1); *v E 1971 (3) 1974 (3) 1982 (3); v A 1972 (3) 1976 (3) 1978 (2) 1981 (2) 1983 (5); v WI 1976 (3); v NZ 1972 (3) 1978 (2) 1984 (2); v In 1979 (5) 1983 (3)*
Zulfiqar Ahmed 9: v A 1956 (1); v NZ 1955 (3); *v E 1954 (2); v In 1952 (3)*

## SRI LANKA

Number of Test cricketers: 27

Amerasinghe, A. M. J. G. 2: v NZ 1983 (2)
de Alwis, R. G. 5: v A 1982 (1); v NZ 1983 (3); *v NZ 1982 (1)*
de Mel, A. L. F. 7: v E 1981 (1); v A 1982 (1); *v E 1984 (1); v In 1982 (1); v P 1981 (3)*
de Silva, D. S. 12: v E 1981 (1); v A 1982 (1); v NZ 1983 (3); *v E 1984 (1); v NZ 1982 (2); v In 1982 (1); v P 1981 (3)*
de Silva, G. R. A. 4: v E 1981 (1); *v In 1982 (1); v P 1981 (2)*
de Silva, P. A. 1: *v E 1984*
Dias, R. L. 9: v E 1981 (1); v A 1982 (1); v NZ 1983 (2); *v E 1984 (1); v In 1982 (1); v P 1981 (3)*

Fernando, E. R. N. S. 5: v A 1982 (1); v NZ 1983 (2); *v NZ 1982 (2)*

Goonatillake, H. M. 5: v E 1981 (1); *v In 1982 (1); v P 1981 (3)*
Gunasekera, Y. 2: *v NZ 1982 (2)*
Guneratne, R. P. W. 1: v A 1982

Jayasekera, R. S. A. 1: *v P 1981*
Jeganathan, S. 2: *v NZ 1982 (2)*
John, V. B. 6: v NZ 1983 (3); *v E 1984 (1); v NZ 1982 (2)*

Kaluperuma, L. W. 2: v E 1981 (1); *v P 1981 (1)*
Kaluperuma, S. M. S. 3: v NZ 1983 (3)

Madugalle, R. S. 12: v E 1981 (1); v A 1982 (1); v NZ 1983 (3); *v E 1984 (1); v NZ 1982 (2); v In 1982 (1); v P 1981 (3)*
Mendis, L. R. D. 10: v E 1981 (1); v A 1982 (1); v NZ 1983 (3); *v E 1984 (1); v In 1982 (1); v P 1981 (3)*

Ranasinghe, A. N. 2: *v In 1982 (1); v P 1981 (1)*
Ranatunga, A. 9: v E 1981 (1); v A 1982 (1); v NZ 1983 (3); *v E 1984 (1); v In 1982 (1); v P 1981 (2)*
Ratnayake, R. J. 4: v A 1982 (1); v NZ 1983 (1); *v NZ 1982 (2)*
Ratnayeke, J. R. 8: v NZ 1983 (2); *v E 1984 (1); v NZ 1982 (2); v In 1982 (1); v P 1981 (2)*

Silva, S. A. R. 2: *v E 1984 (1); v NZ 1982 (1)*

Warnapura, B. 4: v E 1981 (1); *v In 1982 (1); v P 1981 (2)*
Wettimuny, M. D. 2: *v NZ 1982 (2)*
Wettimuny, S. 11: v E 1981 (1); v A 1982 (1); v NZ 1983 (3); *v E 1984 (1); v NZ 1982 (2); v P 1981 (3)*
Wijesuriya, R. G. C. E. 1: *v P 1981*

## TWO COUNTRIES

Twelve cricketers have appeared for two countries in Test matches, namely:

Amir Elahi, *India and Pakistan.*
J. J. Ferris, *Australia and England.*
S. C. Guillen, *West Indies and NZ.*
Gul Mahomed, *India and Pakistan.*
F. Hearne, *England and South Africa.*
A. H. Kardar, *India and Pakistan.*
W. E. Midwinter, *England and Australia.*
F. Mitchell, *England and South Africa.*
W. L. Murdoch, *Australia and England.*
Nawab of Pataudi, sen., *England and India.*
A. E. Trott, *Australia and England.*
S. M. J. Woods, *Australia and England.*

## MOST TEST APPEARANCES FOR EACH COUNTRY

England: M. C. Cowdrey 114.
Australia: R. W. Marsh 96.
South Africa: J. H. B. Waite 50.
West Indies: C. H. Lloyd 110.
New Zealand: B. E. Congdon 61.
India: S. M. Gavaskar 106.
Pakistan: Wasim Bari 81.
Sri Lanka: D. S. de Silva and R. S. Madugalle 12.

## MOST TEST APPEARANCES AS CAPTAIN FOR EACH COUNTRY

England: P. B. H. May 41.
Australia: G. S. Chappell 48.
South Africa: H. W. Taylor 18.
West Indies: C. H. Lloyd 74.
New Zealand: J. R. Reid 34.
India: S. M. Gavaskar 46.
Pakistan: A. H. Kardar 23.
Sri Lanka: L. R. D. Mendis 6.

## ENGLAND v REST OF THE WORLD

The following were awarded England caps for playing against the Rest of the World in England in 1970, although the five matches played are now generally considered not to have rated as full Tests: D. L. Amiss (1). G. Boycott (2), D. J. Brown (2), M. C. Cowdrey (4), M. H. Denness (1), B. L. D'Oliveira (4), J. H. Edrich (2), K. W. R. Fletcher (4), A. W. Greig (3), R. Illingworth (5), A. Jones (1), A. P. E. Knott (5), P. Lever (1), B. W. Luckhurst (5), C. M. Old (2), P. J. Sharpe (1), K. Shuttleworth (1), J. A. Snow (5), D. L. Underwood (3), A. Ward (1), D. Wilson (2).

# CRICKET RECORDS

## Amended by BILL FRINDALL to end of 1985 season in England

Unless stated to be of a minor character, all records apply only to first-class cricket including some performances in the distant past which have always been recognised as of exceptional merit.

* Denotes not out or an unbroken partnership.

(A), (SA), (WI), (NZ), (I), (P) or (SL) indicates either the nationality of the player, or the country in which the record was made.

## INDEX

### BATTING

Individual Scores of 300 or More ... 128
Highest Individual Scores in England and Australia ... 129
Highest Innings for Each First-class County ... 130
Hundred on Début in England ... 130
Most Individual Hundreds ... 131
Two Separate Hundreds in a Match ... 132
Hundred and Double-Hundred in a Match ... 133
Batsmen who have Scored 25,000 Runs ... 134
Career Batting Average over 50 ... 135
1,000 Runs in a Season Fifteen Times or More ... 136
Four Hundreds or More in Succession ... 137
Most Fifties in Consecutive Innings ... 137
Most Hundreds in a Season ... 137
Fast Scoring ... 137
Most Personal Sixes in a Season ... 139
Most Personal Sixes in an Innings ... 139
Most Personal Boundaries in an Innings ... 139
Most Runs Scored off One Over ... 139
300 Runs in One Day ... 140
Highest Partnerships ... 141
Partnerships for First Wicket ... 141
First-Wicket Hundreds in Both Innings ... 142
Partnership Records for All Countries ... 143
Highest Aggregate in Each Season ... 146
Highest Batting Averages in an English Season ... 147
Highest Aggregates Outside England ... 147
1,000 Runs in May ... 148
1,000 Runs in Two Separate Months ... 148
Out Handled the Ball ... 148
Out Obstructing the Field ... 149
Out Hit the Ball Twice ... 149

### BOWLING AND FIELDING

Four Wickets with Consecutive Balls ... 149
Double Hat-Trick ... 150
Five Wickets with Six Consecutive Balls ... 150
Most Hat-Tricks ... 151
Unusual Hat-Tricks ... 151
Ten Wickets in One Innings ... 151
Most Wickets in a Match ... 153
Outstanding Analyses ... 153

Sixteen or More Wickets in a Day ..... 154
200 or More Wickets in a Season ..... 154
Most Wickets in Each Season ..... 155
1,500 Wickets or More in a Career ..... 156
100 Wickets in a Season Eight Times ..... 157
100 Wickets in a Season Overseas ..... 157

## ALL-ROUND CRICKET

20,000 Runs and 2,000 Wickets in a Career ..... 158
The Double ..... 158
1,000 Runs and 50 Wickets in a Season ..... 159
Hundred and Hat-trick ..... 160
Hundred and Ten Wickets in One Innings ..... 160
Hundred in Each Innings and Five Wickets Twice ..... 160
Wicket-keeping Records ..... 160
Most Catches – Excluding Wicket-keepers ..... 162

## THE SIDES

Highest Totals ..... 163
Highest for Each First-class County ..... 163
Lowest Totals ..... 164
Lowest for Each First-class County ..... 164
Highest Match Aggregates ..... 165
Lowest Match Aggregate ..... 165
Highest Fourth Innings Totals ..... 165
Largest Victories ..... 165
Tied Matches ..... 166
Matches Begun and Finished in One Day ..... 167

## TEST MATCH RECORDS

Scorers of 2,000 Runs in Tests ..... 167
Highest Individual Test Innings ..... 170
Test Batting Average over 50 ..... 170
Most Hundreds ..... 171
Hundred on Test Début ..... 171
300 Runs in First Test Match ..... 172
Hundred and Ten Wickets in a Test Match ..... 172
Two Separate Hundreds in a Test Match ..... 172
Hundred and Double-hundred in Same Test ..... 173
Most Runs in a Test Series ..... 173
1,000 Test Runs in a Calendar Year ..... 173
Carrying Bat Through Test Innings ..... 174
Fastest Test Fifties ..... 174
Fastest Test Hundreds ..... 174
Fastest Test Double-Hundreds ..... 175
Fastest Test Triple-Hundreds ..... 175
Most Runs in a Day by a Batsman ..... 175
Slowest Individual Test Batting ..... 175
Slowest Test Hundreds ..... 176
Highest Test Wicket Partnerships ..... 176
Highest Match Aggregates ..... 176
Highest Innings Totals in Tests ..... 176
Most Runs in a Day (Both Sides and One Side) ..... 177
Highest Fourth Innings Totals ..... 177
Lowest Match Aggregates ..... 178
Lowest Innings Totals in Tests ..... 178

Lowest Test Scores in Full Day's Play ........ 178
Bowlers with 75 Wickets in Tests ........ 179
Most Wickets in a Test, a Test Innings, and a Test Series ........ 181
Test Hat-Tricks ........ 183
Most Balls Bowled in a Test Match ........ 184
Wicket-keeping Records ........ 184
Most Catches – Excluding Wicket-keepers ........ 185
Youngest and Oldest Test Players ........ 186
Most Consecutive Test Appearances ........ 187
Summary of All Test Matches ........ 188
England v Australia ........ 188
England v South Africa ........ 198
England v West Indies ........ 202
England v New Zealand ........ 206
England v India ........ 209
England v Pakistan ........ 212
England v Sri Lanka ........ 214
England v Rest of the World ........ 215
Australia v South Africa ........ 215
Australia v West Indies ........ 218
Australia v New Zealand ........ 221
Australia v India ........ 223
Australia v Pakistan ........ 225
Australia v Sri Lanka ........ 227
South Africa v New Zealand ........ 228
West Indies v New Zealand ........ 230
West Indies v India ........ 232
West Indies v Pakistan ........ 234
New Zealand v India ........ 236
New Zealand v Pakistan ........ 238
New Zealand v Sri Lanka ........ 240
India v Pakistan ........ 241
India v Sri Lanka ........ 243
Pakistan v Sri Lanka ........ 244
Sri Lankan Record Partnerships for Each Wicket ........ 244

## ONE-DAY INTERNATIONAL CRICKET RECORDS

3,000 or More Runs ........ 245
Highest Individual Score for Each Country ........ 245
Five or More Hundreds ........ 245
Highest Partnership for Each Wicket ........ 245
100 or More Wickets ........ 245
Best Bowling for Each Country ........ 246
Hat-trick ........ 246
Career Dismissals ........ 246
All-round ........ 246
Highest Innings Totals ........ 246
Highest Totals Batting Second ........ 247
Highest Match Aggregates ........ 247
Lowest Innings Totals ........ 247
Tied Match ........ 247
World Cup Finals ........ 247

## MISCELLANEOUS

Relations in Test Cricket ........ 248
Double Internationals ........ 250
Test Match Grounds ........ 250

Large Attendances .......... 252
Lord's Cricket Ground .......... 252
Highest in Minor Counties and Other Matches .......... 253
Record Hit .......... 254
Throwing the Cricket Ball .......... 254
Formation Dates of County and Minor County Clubs .......... 254
Constitution of County Championship .......... 255
Most County Championship Appearances .......... 255
Most Consecutive County Championship Appearances .......... 255

# BATTING RECORDS

## INDIVIDUAL SCORES OF 300 OR MORE

| | | | |
|---|---|---|---|
| 499 | Hanif Mohammad | Karachi v Bahawalpur at Karachi | 1958-59 |
| 452* | D. G. Bradman | NSW v Queensland at Sydney | 1929-30 |
| 443* | B. B. Nimbalkar | Maharashtra v Kathiawar at Poona | 1948-49 |
| 437 | W. H. Ponsford | Victoria v Queensland at Melbourne | 1927-28 |
| 429 | W. H. Ponsford | Victoria v Tasmania at Melbourne | 1922-23 |
| 428 | Aftab Baloch | Sind v Baluchistan at Karachi | 1973-74 |
| 424 | A. C. MacLaren | Lancashire v Somerset at Taunton | 1895 |
| 385 | B. Sutcliffe | Otago v Canterbury at Christchurch | 1952-53 |
| 383 | C. W. Gregory | NSW v Queensland at Brisbane | 1906-07 |
| 369 | D. G. Bradman | South Australia v Tasmania at Adelaide | 1935-36 |
| 365* | C. Hill | South Australia v NSW at Adelaide | 1900-01 |
| 365* | G. S. Sobers | West Indies v Pakistan at Kingston | 1957-58 |
| 364 | L. Hutton | England v Australia at The Oval | 1938 |
| 359* | V. M. Merchant | Bombay v Maharashtra at Bombay | 1943-44 |
| 359 | R. B. Simpson | NSW v Queensland at Brisbane | 1963-64 |
| 357* | R. Abel | Surrey v Somerset at The Oval | 1899 |
| 357 | D. G. Bradman | South Australia v Victoria at Melbourne | 1935-36 |
| 356 | B. A. Richards | South Australia v W. Australia at Perth | 1970-71 |
| 355 | B. Sutcliffe | Otago v Auckland at Dunedin | 1949-50 |
| 352 | W. H. Ponsford | Victoria v NSW at Melbourne | 1926-27 |
| 350 | Rashid Israr | Habib Bank v National Bank at Lahore | 1976-77 |
| 345 | C. G. Macartney | Australians v Nottinghamshire at Nottingham | 1921 |
| 344* | G. A. Headley | Jamaica v Lord Tennyson's XI at Kingston | 1931-32 |
| 344 | W. G. Grace | MCC v Kent at Canterbury | 1876 |
| 343* | P. A. Perrin | Essex v Derbyshire at Chesterfield | 1904 |
| 341 | G. H. Hirst | Yorkshire v Leicestershire at Leicester | 1905 |
| 340* | D. G. Bradman | NSW v Victoria at Sydney | 1928-29 |
| 340 | S. M. Gavaskar | Bombay v Bengal at Bombay | 1981-82 |
| 338* | R. C. Blunt | Otago v Canterbury at Christchurch | 1931-32 |
| 338 | W. W. Read | Surrey v Oxford University at The Oval | 1888 |
| 337* | Pervez Akhtar | Railways v Dera Ismail Khan at Lahore | 1964-65 |
| 337† | Hanif Mohammad | Pakistan v West Indies at Bridgetown | 1957-58 |
| 336* | W. R. Hammond | England v New Zealand at Auckland | 1932-33 |
| 336 | W. H. Ponsford | Victoria v South Australia at Melbourne | 1927-28 |
| 334 | D. G. Bradman | Australia v England at Leeds | 1930 |
| 333 | K. S. Duleepsinhji | Sussex v Northamptonshire at Hove | 1930 |
| 332 | W. H. Ashdown | Kent v Essex at Brentwood | 1934 |
| 331* | J. D. Robertson | Middlesex v Worcestershire at Worcester | 1949 |
| 325* | H. L. Hendry | Victoria v New Zealanders at Melbourne | 1925-26 |
| 325 | A. Sandham | England v West Indies at Kingston | 1929-30 |
| 325 | C. L. Badcock | South Australia v Victoria at Adelaide | 1935-36 |
| 324 | J. B. Stollmeyer | Trinidad v British Guiana at Port-of-Spain | 1946-47 |
| 324 | Waheed Mirza | Karachi Whites v Quetta at Karachi | 1976-77 |
| 323 | A. L. Wadekar | Bombay v Mysore at Bombay | 1966-67 |
| 322 | E. Paynter | Lancashire v Sussex at Hove | 1937 |
| 322 | I. V. A. Richards | Somerset v Warwickshire at Taunton | 1985 |

| | | | |
|---|---|---|---|
| 321 | W. L. Murdoch | NSW v Victoria at Sydney | 1881-82 |
| 319 | Gul Mahomed | Baroda v Holkar at Baroda | 1946-47 |
| 318* | W. G. Grace | Gloucestershire v Yorkshire at Cheltenham | 1876 |
| 317 | W. R. Hammond | Gloucestershire v Nottinghamshire at Gloucester | 1936 |
| 316* | J. B. Hobbs | Surrey v Middlesex at Lord's | 1926 |
| 316* | V. S. Hazare | Maharashtra v Baroda at Poona | 1939-40 |
| 316 | R. H. Moore | Hampshire v Warwickshire at Bournemouth | 1937 |
| 315* | T. W. Hayward | Surrey v Lancashire at The Oval | 1898 |
| 315* | P. Holmes | Yorkshire v Middlesex at Lord's | 1925 |
| 315* | A. F. Kippax | NSW v Queensland at Sydney | 1927-28 |
| 314* | C. L. Walcott | Barbados v Trinidad at Port-of-Spain | 1945-46 |
| 313 | H. Sutcliffe | Yorkshire v Essex at Leyton | 1932 |
| 312* | W. W. Keeton | Nottinghamshire v Middlesex at The Oval‡ | 1939 |
| 312* | J. M. Brearley | MCC Under 25 v North Zone at Peshawar | 1966-67 |
| 311* | G. M. Turner | Worcestershire v Warwickshire at Worcester | 1982 |
| 311 | J. T. Brown | Yorkshire v Sussex at Sheffield | 1897 |
| 311 | R. B. Simpson | Australia v England at Manchester | 1964 |
| 311 | Javed Miandad | Karachi Whites v National Bank at Karachi | 1974-75 |
| 310* | J. H. Edrich | England v New Zealand at Leeds | 1965 |
| 310 | H. Gimblett | Somerset v Sussex at Eastbourne | 1948 |
| 309 | V. S. Hazare | The Rest v Hindus at Bombay | 1943-44 |
| 308* | F. M. M. Worrell | Barbados v Trinidad at Bridgetown | 1943-44 |
| 307 | M. C. Cowdrey | MCC v South Australia at Adelaide | 1962-63 |
| 307 | R. M. Cowper | Australia v England at Melbourne | 1965-66 |
| 306* | A. Ducat | Surrey v Oxford University at The Oval | 1919 |
| 306* | E. A. B. Rowan | Transvaal v Natal at Johannesburg | 1939-40 |
| 305* | F. E. Woolley | MCC v Tasmania at Hobart | 1911-12 |
| 305* | F. R. Foster | Warwickshire v Worcestershire at Dudley | 1914 |
| 305* | W. H. Ashdown | Kent v Derbyshire at Dover | 1935 |
| 304* | A. W. Nourse | Natal v Transvaal at Johannesburg | 1919-20 |
| 304* | P. H. Tarilton | Barbados v Trinidad at Bridgetown | 1919-20 |
| 304* | E. D. Weekes | West Indians v Cambridge University at Cambridge | 1950 |
| 304 | R. M. Poore | Hampshire v Somerset at Taunton | 1899 |
| 304 | D. G. Bradman | Australia v England at Leeds | 1934 |
| 303* | W. W. Armstrong | Australians v Somerset at Bath | 1905 |
| 303* | Mushtaq Mohammad | Karachi Blues v Karachi University at Karachi | 1967-68 |
| 302* | P. Holmes | Yorkshire v Hampshire at Portsmouth | 1920 |
| 302* | W. R. Hammond | Gloucestershire v Glamorgan at Bristol | 1934 |
| 302 | W. R. Hammond | Gloucestershire v Glamorgan at Newport | 1939 |
| 302 | L. G. Rowe | West Indies v England at Bridgetown | 1973-74 |
| 301* | E. H. Hendren | Middlesex v Worcestershire at Dudley | 1933 |
| 301 | W. G. Grace | Gloucestershire v Sussex at Bristol | 1896 |
| 300* | V. T. Trumper | Australians v Sussex at Hove | 1899 |
| 300* | F. B. Watson | Lancashire v Surrey at Manchester | 1928 |
| 300* | Imtiaz Ahmed | PM's XI v Commonwealth XI at Bombay | 1950-51 |
| 300 | J. T. Brown | Yorkshire v Derbyshire at Chesterfield | 1898 |
| 300 | D. C. S. Compton | MCC v N. E. Transvaal at Benoni | 1948-49 |
| 300 | R. Subba Row | Northamptonshire v Surrey at The Oval | 1958 |

† *Hanif Mohammad batted for 16 hours 10 minutes – the longest innings in first-class cricket.*
‡ *Played at The Oval because Lord's was required for Eton v Harrow.*

## HIGHEST INDIVIDUAL SCORES FOR TEAMS

*For English Teams in Australia*

| | | | |
|---|---|---|---|
| 307 | M. C. Cowdrey | MCC v South Australia at Adelaide | 1962-63 |
| 287 | R. E. Foster | England v Australia at Sydney | 1903-04 |

*Against Australians in England*

| | | | |
|---|---|---|---|
| 364 | L. Hutton | England v Australia at The Oval | 1938 |
| 219 | A. Sandham | Surrey at The Oval (record for any county) | 1934 |

*For Australian Teams in England*

| | | | |
|---|---|---|---|
| 345 | C. G. Macartney | v Nottinghamshire at Nottingham | 1921 |
| 334 | D. G. Bradman | Australia v England at Leeds | 1930 |

*Against English Teams in Australia*

| | | | |
|---|---|---|---|
| 307 | R. M. Cowper | Australia v England at Melbourne | 1965-66 |
| 280 | A. J. Richardson | South Australia v MCC at Adelaide | 1922-23 |

*For Each First-Class County*

| | | | |
|---|---|---|---|
| Derbyshire | 274 | G. Davidson v Lancashire at Manchester | 1896 |
| Essex | 343* | P. A. Perrin v Derbyshire at Chesterfield | 1904 |
| Glamorgan | 287* | D. E. Davies v Gloucestershire at Newport | 1939 |
| Gloucestershire | 318* | W. G. Grace v Yorkshire at Cheltenham | 1876 |
| Hampshire | 316 | R. H. Moore v Warwickshire at Bournemouth | 1937 |
| Kent | 332 | W. H. Ashdown v Essex at Brentwood | 1934 |
| Lancashire | 424 | A. C. MacLaren v Somerset at Taunton | 1895 |
| Leicestershire | 252* | S. Coe v Northamptonshire at Leicester | 1914 |
| Middlesex | 331* | J. D. Robertson v Worcestershire at Worcester | 1949 |
| Northamptonshire | 300 | R. Subba Row v Surrey at The Oval | 1958 |
| Nottinghamshire | 312* | W. W. Keeton v Middlesex at The Oval† | 1939 |
| Somerset | 322 | I. V. A. Richards v Warwickshire at Taunton | 1985 |
| Surrey | 357* | R. Abel v Somerset at The Oval | 1899 |
| Sussex | 333 | K. S. Duleepsinhji v Northamptonshire at Hove | 1930 |
| Warwickshire | 305* | F. R. Foster v Worcestershire at Dudley | 1914 |
| Worcestershire | 311* | G. M. Turner v Warwickshire at Worcester | 1982 |
| Yorkshire | 341 | G. H. Hirst v Leicestershire at Leicester | 1905 |

† *Played at The Oval because Lord's was required for Eton v Harrow.*

## HUNDRED ON DEBUT IN ENGLAND

(The following list does not include instances of players who have previously appeared in first-class cricket outside England or who performed the feat before 1946. Particulars of the latter are in *Wisdens* prior to 1984.)

| | | | |
|---|---|---|---|
| 114 | F. W. Stocks | Nottinghamshire v Kent at Nottingham | 1946 |
| 108 | A. Fairbairn | Middlesex v Somerset at Taunton | †‡1947 |
| 124 | P. Hearn | Kent v Warwickshire at Gillingham | 1947 |
| 215* | G. H. G. Doggart | Cambridge University v Lancashire at Cambridge | 1948 |
| 107* | G. Barker | Essex v Canadians at Clacton | †1954 |
| 135 | J. K. E. Slack | Cambridge University v Middlesex at Cambridge | 1954 |
| 100* | E. A. Clark | Middlesex v Cambridge University at Cambridge | 1959 |
| 113 | G. J. Chidgey | Free Foresters v Cambridge University at Cambridge | 1962 |
| 108 | D. R. Shepherd | Gloucestershire v Oxford University at Oxford | 1965 |
| 110* | A. J. Harvey-Walker | Derbyshire v Oxford University at Burton upon Trent | †1971 |
| 173 | J. Whitehouse | Warwickshire v Oxford University at Oxford | 1971 |
| 106 | J. B. Turner | Minor Counties v Pakistanis at Jesmond | 1974 |
| 112 | J. A. Claughton | Oxford University v Gloucestershire at Oxford | †1976 |
| 100* | A. W. Lilley | Essex v Nottinghamshire at Nottingham | 1978 |
| 146* | J. S. Johnson | Minor Counties v Indians at Wellington | 1979 |
| 110 | N. R. Taylor | Kent v Sri Lankans at Canterbury | 1979 |
| 146* | D. G. Aslett | Kent v Hampshire at Bournemouth | 1981 |
| 116 | M. D. Moxon | Yorkshire v Essex at Leeds | †1981 |
| 100 | D. A. Banks | Worcestershire v Oxford University at Oxford | 1983 |
| 122 | A. A. Metcalfe | Yorkshire v Nottinghamshire at Bradford | 1983 |
| 117* | K. T. Medlycott | Surrey v Cambridge University at Banstead | §1984 |
| 101* | N. J. Falkner | Surrey v Cambridge University at Banstead | §1984 |
| 106 | A. C. Storie | Northamptonshire v Hampshire at Northampton | †1985 |
| 102 | M. P. Maynard | Glamorgan v Yorkshire at Swansea | 1985 |

† *In his second innings.*

‡ *A. Fairbairn (Middlesex) in 1947 scored hundreds in the second innings of his first two matches in first-class cricket: 108 as above, 110* Middlesex v Nottinghamshire at Nottingham.*

§ *The only instance in England of two players performing the feat in the same match.*

*Notes:* A number of players abroad have also made a hundred on a first appearance.

The highest innings on début was hit by W. F. E. Marx when he made 240 for Transvaal against Griqualand West at Johannesburg in 1920-21.

There are three instances of a cricketer making two separate hundreds on début: A. R. Morris, New South Wales, 148 and 111 against Queensland in 1940-41, N. J. Contractor, Gujarat, 152 and 102* against Baroda in 1952-53, and Aamer Malik, Lahore "A", 132* and 110* against Railways in 1979-80.

J. S. Solomon, British Guiana, scored a hundred in each of his first three innings in first-class cricket: 114* v Jamaica; 108 v Barbados in 1956-57; 121 v Pakistanis in 1957-58.

R. Watson-Smith, Border, scored 310 runs before he was dismissed in first-class cricket, including not-out centuries in his first two innings: 183* v Orange Free State and 125* v Griqualand West in 1969-70.

G. R. Viswanath and D. M. Wellham alone have scored a hundred on both their début in first-class cricket and in Test cricket. Viswanath scored 230 for Mysore v Andhra in 1967-68 and 137 for India v Australia in 1969-70. Wellham scored 100 for New South Wales v Victoria in 1980-81 and 103 for Australia v England in 1981.

## MOST INDIVIDUAL HUNDREDS

(35 or More)

| | *Hundreds Total* | *Abroad* | *100th 100* | | *Hundreds Total* | *Abroad* | *100th 100* |
|---|---|---|---|---|---|---|---|
| J. B. Hobbs | 197 | 22 | 1923 | T. W. Graveney | 122 | 31 | 1964 |
| E. H. Hendren | 170 | 19 | 1928-29 | D. G. Bradman | 117 | 41† | 1947-48 |
| W. R. Hammond | 167 | 33 | 1935 | M. C. Cowdrey | 107 | 27 | 1973 |
| C. P. Mead | 153 | 8 | 1927 | A. Sandham | 107 | 20 | 1935 |
| G. Boycott | 149 | 27 | 1977 | Zaheer Abbas | 107 | 70† | 1982-83 |
| H. Sutcliffe | 149 | 14 | 1932 | T. W. Hayward | 104 | 4 | 1913 |
| F. E. Woolley | 145 | 10 | 1929 | J. H. Edrich | 103 | 13 | 1977 |
| L. Hutton | 129 | 24 | 1951 | G. M. Turner | 103 | 85† | 1982 |
| W. G. Grace | 126 | 1 | 1895 | L. E. G. Ames | 102 | 13 | 1950 |
| D. C. S. Compton | 123 | 31 | 1952 | E. Tyldesley | 102 | 8 | 1934 |

*† "Abroad" for D. G. Bradman is outside Australia; for Zaheer Abbas, outside Pakistan; for G. M. Turner, outside New Zealand.*

*E. H. Hendren and D. G. Bradman scored their 100th hundreds in Australia, Zaheer Abbas scored his in Pakistan.*

| | | | | | |
|---|---|---|---|---|---|
| D. L. Amiss | 96 | G. S. Chappell | 74 | K. W. R. Fletcher | 62 |
| J. W. Hearne | 96 | S. M. Gavaskar | 74 | G. Gunn | 62 |
| C. B. Fry | 94 | D. Kenyon | 74 | K. S. McEwan | 61 |
| W. J. Edrich | 86 | Majid J. Khan | 73 | V. S. Hazare | 60 |
| I. V. A. Richards | 86 | Mushtaq Mohammad | 72 | G. H. Hirst | 60 |
| G. S. Sobers | 86 | J. O'Connor | 72 | R. G. Pollock | 60 |
| J. T. Tyldesley | 86 | Wm. Quaife | 72 | R. B. Simpson | 60 |
| P. B. H. May | 85 | K. S. Ranjitsinhji | 72 | P. F. Warner | 60 |
| R. E. S. Wyatt | 85 | D. Brookes | 71 | I. M. Chappell | 59 |
| J. Hardstaff, jun. | 83 | A. C. Russell | 71 | A. L. Hassett | 59 |
| R. B. Kanhai | 83 | D. Denton | 69 | A. Shrewsbury | 59 |
| M. Leyland | 80 | M. J. K. Smith | 69 | A. E. Fagg | 58 |
| B. A. Richards | 80 | R. E. Marshall | 68 | P. H. Parfitt | 58 |
| A. I. Kallicharran | 78 | R. N. Harvey | 67 | W. Rhodes | 58 |
| C. H. Lloyd | 78 | P. Holmes | 67 | L. B. Fishlock | 56 |
| K. F. Barrington | 76 | J. D. Robertson | 67 | A. Jones | 56 |
| J. G. Langridge | 76 | P. A. Perrin | 66 | C. A. Milton | 56 |
| C. Washbrook | 76 | C. G. Greenidge | 65 | C. Hallows | 55 |
| H. T. W. Hardinge | 75 | R. T. Simpson | 64 | Hanif Mohammad | 55 |
| R. Abel | 74 | Javed Miandad | 63 | W. Watson | 55 |

G. A. Gooch . . . . . . . . . 54
D. J. Insole . . . . . . . . . . 54
W. W. Keeton . . . . . . . 54
W. Bardsley . . . . . . . . . 53
B. F. Davison . . . . . . . . 53
A. E. Dipper . . . . . . . . . 53
G. L. Jessop . . . . . . . . . 53
James Seymour . . . . . . . 53
E. H. Bowley . . . . . . . . 52
D. B. Close . . . . . . . . . . 52
A. Ducat . . . . . . . . . . . . 52
E. R. Dexter . . . . . . . . . 51
J. M. Parks . . . . . . . . . . 51
W. W. Whysall . . . . . . . 51
G. Cox jun. . . . . . . . . . . 50
H. E. Dollery . . . . . . . . 50
K. S. Duleepsinhji . . . . 50
H. Gimblett . . . . . . . . . 50
W. M. Lawry . . . . . . . . 50
Sadiq Mohammad . . . . 50
F. B. Watson . . . . . . . . 50
C. G. Macartney . . . . . 49
M. J. Stewart . . . . . . . . 49
K. G. Suttle . . . . . . . . . 49
P. M. Umrigar . . . . . . . 49
W. M. Woodfull . . . . . . 49
C. J. Barnett . . . . . . . . . 48
W. Gunn . . . . . . . . . . . . 48
E. G. Hayes . . . . . . . . . 48
B. W. Luckhurst . . . . . . 48
M. J. Procter . . . . . . . . 48
A. C. MacLaren . . . . . . 47
W. H. Ponsford . . . . . . 47
J. Iddon . . . . . . . . . . . . . 46
A. R. Morris . . . . . . . . . 46
W. W. Armstrong . . . . 45
Asif Iqbal . . . . . . . . . . . 45
L. G. Berry . . . . . . . . . . 45
J. M. Brearley . . . . . . . . 45
A. W. Carr . . . . . . . . . . 45
C. Hill . . . . . . . . . . . . . . 45
N. C. O'Neill . . . . . . . . 45
E. Paynter . . . . . . . . . . . 45
Rev. D. S. Sheppard . . 45
K. D. Walters . . . . . . . . 45
H. H. I. Gibbons . . . . . 44
V. M. Merchant . . . . . . 44
A. Mitchell . . . . . . . . . . 44
C. T. Radley . . . . . . . . . 44
P. E. Richardson . . . . . 44
B. Sutcliffe . . . . . . . . . . 44
E. J. Barlow . . . . . . . . . 43
B. L. D'Oliveira . . . . . . 43
J. H. Hampshire . . . . . . 43
A. F. Kippax . . . . . . . . 43
H. Makepeace . . . . . . . 43
Shafiq Ahmed . . . . . . . . 43
G. R. Viswanath . . . . . 43
Younis Ahmed . . . . . . . 43
James Langridge . . . . . 42
H. W. Parks . . . . . . . . . 42
T. F. Shepherd . . . . . . . 42
V. T. Trumper . . . . . . . 42
M. J. Harris . . . . . . . . . 41
P. N. Kirsten . . . . . . . . 41
A. J. Lamb . . . . . . . . . . 41
K. R. Miller . . . . . . . . . 41
A. D. Nourse . . . . . . . . 41
J. H. Parks . . . . . . . . . . 41
R. M. Prideaux . . . . . . 41
G. Pullar . . . . . . . . . . . . 41
W. E. Russell . . . . . . . . 41
R. C. Fredericks . . . . . . 40
J. Gunn . . . . . . . . . . . . . 40
C. E. B. Rice . . . . . . . . 40
M. J. Smith . . . . . . . . . 40
C. L. Walcott . . . . . . . . 40
J. G. Wright . . . . . . . . . 40
D. M. Young . . . . . . . . 40
W. H. Ashdown . . . . . . 39
J. B. Bolus . . . . . . . . . . 39
W. A. Brown . . . . . . . . 39
R. J. Gregory . . . . . . . . 39
W. R. D. Payton . . . . . 39
J. R. Reid . . . . . . . . . . . 39
F. M. M. Worrell . . . . . 39
F. L. Bowley . . . . . . . . . 38
P. J. Burge . . . . . . . . . . 38
J. F. Crapp . . . . . . . . . . 38
H. W. Lee . . . . . . . . . . . 38
D. Lloyd . . . . . . . . . . . . 38
V. L. Manjrekar . . . . . . 38
Mudassar Nazar . . . . . . 38
A. W. Nourse . . . . . . . . 38
N. Oldfield . . . . . . . . . . 38
Rev. J. H. Parsons . . . . 38
W. W. Read . . . . . . . . . 38
J. Sharp . . . . . . . . . . . . . 38
L. J. Todd . . . . . . . . . . . 38
J. Arnold . . . . . . . . . . . . 37
G. Brown . . . . . . . . . . . 37
G. M. Emmett . . . . . . . 37
W. Larkins . . . . . . . . . . 37
M. A. Noble . . . . . . . . . 37
D. W. Randall . . . . . . . 37
H. S. Squires . . . . . . . . . 37
R. T. Virgin . . . . . . . . . 37
C. J. B. Wood . . . . . . . 37
N. F. Armstrong . . . . . 36
M. W. Gatting . . . . . . . 36
E. Oldroyd . . . . . . . . . . 36
W. Place . . . . . . . . . . . . 36
A. L. Wadekar . . . . . . . 36
E. D. Weekes . . . . . . . . 36
C. S. Dempster . . . . . . . 35
D. R. Jardine . . . . . . . . 35
B. H. Valentine . . . . . . 35

## TWO SEPARATE HUNDREDS IN A MATCH

**Eight times:** Zaheer Abbas.

**Seven times:** W. R. Hammond.

**Six times:** J. B. Hobbs, G. M. Turner.

**Five times:** C. B. Fry.

**Four times:** D. G. Bradman, G. S. Chappell, J. H. Edrich, L. B. Fishlock, T. W. Graveney, H. T. W. Hardinge, E. H. Hendren, Javed Miandad, G. L. Jessop, P. A. Perrin, B. Sutcliffe, H. Sutcliffe.

**Three times:** L. E. G. Ames, G. Boycott, I. M. Chappell, D. C. S. Compton, M. C. Cowdrey, D. Denton, K. S. Duleepsinhji, R. E. Foster, R. C. Fredericks, S. M. Gavaskar, W. G. Grace, C. G. Greenidge, G. Gunn, M. R. Hallam, Hanif Mohammad, M. J. Harris, T. W. Hayward, V. S. Hazare, D. W. Hookes, L. Hutton, A. Jones, R. B. McCosker, P. B. H. May, C. P. Mead, A. C. Russell, Sadiq Mohammad, J. T. Tyldesley.

**Twice:** Agha Zahid, D. L. Amiss, L. Baichan, B. J. T. Bosanquet, R. J. Boyd-Moss, C. C. Dacre, G. M. Emmett, A. E. Fagg, L. E. Favell, H. Gimblett, C. Hallows, R. A. Hamence, A. L. Hassett, G. A. Headley, A. I. Kallicharran, J. H. King, A. F. Kippax, P. N. Kirsten, J. G. Langridge, H. W. Lee, E. Lester, C. B. Llewellyn, C. G. Macartney, C. A. Milton, A. R. Morris, P. H. Parfitt, Nawab of Pataudi jun., E. Paynter, C. Pinch, R. G. Pollock, R. M. Prideaux, Qasim Omar, W. Rhodes, B. A. Richards, Pankaj Roy, James Seymour, R. B. Simpson, G. S. Sobers, E. Tyldesley, C. L. Walcott, W. W. Whysall, G. N. Yallop.

*Notes:* W. Lambert scored 107 and 157 for Sussex v Epsom at Lord's in 1817 and it was not until W. G. Grace made 130 and 102* for South of the Thames v North of the Thames at Canterbury in 1868 that the feat was repeated.

T. W. Hayward (Surrey) set up a unique record in 1906 when in one week – six days – he hit four successive hundreds, 144 and 100 v Nottinghamshire at Nottingham and 143 and 125 v Leicestershire at Leicester.

D. W. Hookes (South Australia) scored four successive hundreds in eleven days at Adelaide in 1976-77: 185 and 105 v Queensland (tied match) and 135 and 156 v New South Wales.

A. E. Fagg alone has scored two double-hundreds in the same match: 244 and 202* for Kent v Essex at Colchester, 1938.

L. G. Rowe is alone in scoring hundreds in each innings on his first appearance in Test cricket: 214 and 100* for West Indies v New Zealand at Kingston in 1971-72.

Zaheer Abbas (Gloucestershire) set a unique record in 1976 by twice scoring a double hundred and a hundred in the same match without being dismissed: 216* and 156* v Surrey at The Oval and 230* and 104* v Kent at Canterbury. In 1977 he achieved this feat for a third time, scoring 205* and 108* v Sussex at Cheltenham, and in 1981 for a fourth time, scoring 215* and 150* v Somerset at Bath.

M. R. Hallam (Leicestershire), opening the batting each time, achieved the following treble: 210* and 157 v Glamorgan at Leicester, 1959; 203* and 143* v Sussex at Worthing, 1961; 107* and 149* v Worcestershire at Leicester, 1965. In the last two matches he was on the field the whole time, as was C. J. B. Wood when he scored 107* and 117* for Leicestershire against Yorkshire at Bradford, 1911.

W. L. Foster, 140 and 172*, and R. E. Foster, 134 and 101*, for Worcestershire v Hampshire at Worcester in July 1899, were the first brothers each to score two separate hundreds in the same first-class match.

The brothers I. M. Chappell, 145 and 121, and G. S. Chappell, 247* and 133, for Australia v New Zealand at Wellington in 1973-74, became the first players on the same side each to score a hundred in each innings of a Test match.

G. Gunn, 183, and G. V. Gunn, 100*, for Nottinghamshire v Warwickshire at Birmingham in 1931, provide the only instance of father and son each hitting a century in the same innings of a first-class match.

## HUNDRED AND DOUBLE-HUNDRED IN A MATCH

| | | | |
|---|---|---|---|
| C. B. Fry | 125 and 229 | Sussex v Surrey at Hove | 1900 |
| W. W. Armstrong | 157* and 245 | Victoria v South Australia at Melbourne | 1920-21 |
| H. T. W. Hardinge | 207 and 102* | Kent v Surrey at Blackheath | 1921 |
| C. P. Mead | 113 and 224 | Hampshire v Sussex at Horsham | 1921 |
| K. S. Duleepsinhji | 115 and 246 | Sussex v Kent at Hastings | 1929 |
| D. G. Bradman | 124 and 225 | Woodfull's XI v Ryder's XI at Sydney | 1929-30 |
| B. Sutcliffe | 243 and 100* | New Zealanders v Essex at Southend | 1949 |
| M. R. Hallam | 210* and 157 | Leicestershire v Glamorgan at Leicester | 1959 |
| M. R. Hallam | 203* and 143* | Leicestershire v Sussex at Worthing | 1961 |
| Hanumant Singh | 109 and 213* | Rajasthan v Bombay at Bombay | 1966-67 |
| Salah-ud-Din | 256 and 102* | Karachi v East Pakistan at Karachi | 1968-69 |
| K. D. Walters | 242 and 103 | Australia v West Indies at Sydney | 1968-69 |
| S. M. Gavaskar | 124 and 220 | India v West Indies at Port-of-Spain | 1970-71 |
| L. G. Rowe | 214 and 100* | West Indies v New Zealand at Kingston | 1971-72 |
| G. S. Chappell | 247* and 133 | Australia v New Zealand at Wellington | 1973-74 |
| L. Baichan | 216* and 102 | Berbice v Demerara at Georgetown | 1973-74 |
| Zaheer Abbas | 216* and 156* | Gloucestershire v Surrey at The Oval | 1976 |
| Zaheer Abbas | 230* and 104* | Gloucestershire v Kent at Canterbury | 1976 |
| Zaheer Abbas | 205* and 108* | Gloucestershire v Sussex at Cheltenham | 1977 |
| Saadat Ali | 141 and 222 | Income Tax v Multan at Multan | 1977-78 |
| Talat Ali | 214* and 104 | PIA v Punjab at Lahore | 1978-79 |
| Shafiq Ahmed | 129 and 217* | National Bank v MCB at Karachi | 1978-79 |
| D. W. Randall | 209 and 146 | Nottinghamshire v Middlesex at Nottingham | 1979 |
| Zaheer Abbas | 215* and 150* | Gloucestershire v Somerset at Bath | 1981 |
| Qasim Omar | 210* and 110 | MCB v Lahore at Lahore | 1982-83 |
| A. I. Kallicharran | 200* and 117* | Warwickshire v Northamptonshire at Birmingham | 1984 |

## BATSMEN WHO HAVE SCORED 25,000 RUNS

| | Career | R | I | NO | HI | 100s | Avge |
|---|---|---|---|---|---|---|---|
| J. B. Hobbs | 1905-34 | 61,237 | 1,315 | 106 | 316* | 197 | 50.65 |
| F. E. Woolley | 1906-38 | 58,969 | 1,532 | 85 | 305* | 145 | 40.75 |
| E. H. Hendren | 1907-38 | 57,611 | 1,300 | 166 | 301* | 170 | 50.80 |
| C. P. Mead | 1905-36 | 55,061 | 1,340 | 185 | 280* | 153 | 47.67 |
| †W. G. Grace | 1865-1908 | 54,896 | 1,493 | 105 | 344 | 126 | 39.55 |
| W. R. Hammond | 1920-51 | 50,551 | 1,005 | 104 | 336* | 167 | 56.10 |
| H. Sutcliffe | 1919-45 | 50,138 | 1,088 | 123 | 313 | 149 | 51.95 |
| T. W. Graveney | 1948-72 | 47,793 | 1,223 | 159 | 258 | 122 | 44.91 |
| G. Boycott | 1962-85 | 47,434 | 994 | 161 | 261* | 149 | 56.94 |
| T. W. Hayward | 1893-1914 | 43,551 | 1,138 | 96 | 315* | 104 | 41.79 |
| M. C. Cowdrey | 1950-76 | 42,719 | 1,130 | 134 | 307 | 107 | 42.89 |
| A. Sandham | 1911-38 | 41,284 | 1,000 | 79 | 325 | 107 | 44.82 |
| D. L. Amiss | 1960-85 | 40,673 | 1,048 | 117 | 262* | 96 | 43.68 |
| L. Hutton | 1934-60 | 40,140 | 814 | 91 | 364 | 129 | 55.51 |
| M. J. K. Smith | 1951-75 | 39,832 | 1,091 | 139 | 204 | 66 | 41.84 |
| W. Rhodes | 1898-1930 | 39,802 | 1,528 | 237 | 267* | 58 | 30.83 |
| J. H. Edrich | 1956-78 | 39,790 | 979 | 104 | 310* | 103 | 45.47 |
| R. E. S. Wyatt | 1923-57 | 39,405 | 1,141 | 157 | 232 | 85 | 40.04 |
| D. C. S. Compton | 1936-64 | 38,942 | 839 | 88 | 300 | 123 | 51.85 |
| E. Tyldesley | 1909-36 | 38,874 | 961 | 106 | 256* | 102 | 45.46 |
| J. T. Tyldesley | 1895-1923 | 37,897 | 994 | 62 | 295* | 86 | 40.60 |
| J. W. Hearne | 1909-36 | 37,252 | 1,025 | 116 | 285* | 96 | 40.98 |
| L. E. G. Ames | 1926-51 | 37,248 | 951 | 95 | 295 | 102 | 43.51 |
| D. Kenyon | 1946-67 | 37,002 | 1,159 | 59 | 259 | 74 | 33.63 |
| W. J. Edrich | 1934-58 | 36,965 | 964 | 92 | 267* | 86 | 42.39 |
| J. M. Parks | 1949-76 | 36,673 | 1,227 | 172 | 205* | 51 | 34.76 |
| D. Denton | 1894-1920 | 36,479 | 1,163 | 70 | 221 | 69 | 33.37 |
| G. H. Hirst | 1891-1929 | 36,323 | 1,215 | 151 | 341 | 60 | 34.13 |
| A. Jones | 1957-83 | 36,049 | 1,168 | 72 | 204* | 56 | 32.89 |
| Wm. Quaife | 1894-1928 | 36,012 | 1,203 | 186 | 255* | 72 | 35.38 |
| R. E. Marshall | 1945-72 | 35,725 | 1,053 | 59 | 228* | 68 | 35.95 |
| K. W. R. Fletcher | 1962-85 | 35,701 | 1,090 | 158 | 228* | 62 | 38.30 |
| G. Gunn | 1902-32 | 35,208 | 1,061 | 82 | 220 | 62 | 35.96 |
| D. B. Close | 1949-85 | 34,968 | 1,223 | 173 | 198 | 52 | 33.30 |
| J. G. Langridge | 1928-55 | 34,380 | 984 | 66 | 250* | 76 | 37.45 |
| G. M. Turner | 1964-83 | 34,346 | 792 | 101 | 311* | 103 | 49.70 |
| Zaheer Abbas | 1965-85 | 34,285 | 746 | 39 | 274 | 107 | 52.18 |
| C. Washbrook | 1933-64 | 34,101 | 906 | 107 | 251* | 76 | 42.67 |
| M. Leyland | 1920-48 | 33,659 | 932 | 101 | 263 | 80 | 40.50 |
| H. T. W. Hardinge | 1902-33 | 33,519 | 1,021 | 103 | 263* | 75 | 36.51 |
| R. Abel | 1881-1904 | 33,124 | 1,007 | 73 | 357* | 74 | 35.46 |
| C. A. Milton | 1948-74 | 32,150 | 1,078 | 125 | 170 | 56 | 33.73 |
| J. D. Robertson | 1937-59 | 31,914 | 897 | 46 | 331* | 67 | 37.50 |
| J. Hardstaff, jun. | 1930-55 | 31,847 | 812 | 94 | 266 | 83 | 44.35 |
| James Langridge | 1924-53 | 31,716 | 1,058 | 157 | 167 | 42 | 35.20 |
| K. F. Barrington | 1953-68 | 31,714 | 831 | 136 | 256 | 76 | 45.63 |
| Mushtaq Mohammad | 1957-85 | 31,091 | 843 | 104 | 303* | 72 | 42.07 |
| C. B. Fry | 1892-1921 | 30,886 | 658 | 43 | 258* | 94 | 50.22 |
| C. H. Lloyd | 1963-85 | 30,885 | 722 | 95 | 242* | 78 | 49.25 |
| D. Brookes | 1934-59 | 30,874 | 925 | 70 | 257 | 71 | 36.10 |
| P. Holmes | 1913-35 | 30,574 | 810 | 84 | 315* | 67 | 42.11 |
| R. T. Simpson | 1944-63 | 30,546 | 852 | 55 | 259 | 64 | 38.32 |
| L. G. Berry | 1924-51 | 30,225 | 1,056 | 57 | 232 | 45 | 30.25 |
| K. G. Suttle | 1949-71 | 30,225 | 1,064 | 92 | 204* | 49 | 31.09 |
| A. I. Kallicharran | 1966-85 | 29,771 | 739 | 77 | 243* | 78 | 44.97 |
| P. A. Perrin | 1896-1928 | 29,709 | 918 | 91 | 343* | 66 | 35.92 |
| P. F. Warner | 1894-1929 | 29,028 | 875 | 75 | 244 | 60 | 36.28 |
| J. O'Connor | 1921-39 | 28,875 | 906 | 80 | 248 | 72 | 34.95 |

| | Career | R | I | NO | HI | 100s | Avge |
|---|---|---|---|---|---|---|---|
| R. B. Kanhai ........ | 1955-82 | 28,774 | 669 | 82 | 256 | 83 | 49.01 |
| T. E. Bailey ......... | 1945-67 | 28,642 | 1,072 | 215 | 205 | 28 | 33.42 |
| C. G. Greenidge ..... | 1970-85 | 28,461 | 695 | 59 | 273* | 65 | 44.75 |
| E. H. Bowley ....... | 1912-34 | 28,378 | 859 | 47 | 283 | 52 | 34.94 |
| B. A. Richards ...... | 1964-83 | 28,358 | 576 | 58 | 356 | 80 | 54.74 |
| G. S. Sobers ........ | 1953-74 | 28,315 | 609 | 93 | 365* | 86 | 54.87 |
| A. E. Dipper ........ | 1908-32 | 28,075 | 865 | 69 | 252* | 53 | 35.27 |
| D. G. Bradman ...... | 1927-49 | 28,067 | 338 | 43 | 452* | 117 | 95.14 |
| J. H. Hampshire ..... | 1961-84 | 28,059 | 924 | 112 | 183* | 43 | 34.55 |
| P. B. H. May ....... | 1948-63 | 27,592 | 618 | 77 | 285* | 85 | 51.00 |
| A. C. Russell ........ | 1908-30 | 27,545 | 719 | 59 | 273 | 71 | 41.73 |
| Majid J. Khan ...... | 1961-83 | 27,328 | 697 | 60 | 241 | 73 | 42.90 |
| E. G. Hayes ........ | 1896-1926 | 27,318 | 896 | 48 | 276 | 48 | 32.21 |
| A. E. Fagg ......... | 1932-57 | 27,291 | 803 | 46 | 269* | 58 | 36.05 |
| James Seymour ...... | 1900-26 | 27,238 | 911 | 62 | 218* | 53 | 32.08 |
| P. H. Parfitt ........ | 1956-74 | 26,924 | 845 | 104 | 200* | 58 | 36.33 |
| B. F. Davison ....... | 1967-85 | 26,923 | 745 | 78 | 189 | 53 | 40.36 |
| I. V. A. Richards .... | 1971-85 | 26,841 | 572 | 38 | 322 | 86 | 50.26 |
| G. L. Jessop ........ | 1894-1914 | 26,698 | 855 | 37 | 286 | 53 | 32.63 |
| D. E. Davies ........ | 1924-54 | 26,566 | 1,033 | 79 | 287* | 32 | 27.84 |
| M. J. Stewart ....... | 1954-72 | 26,492 | 898 | 93 | 227* | 49 | 32.90 |
| A. Shrewsbury ...... | 1875-1902 | 26,439 | 811 | 90 | 267 | 59 | 36.66 |
| P. E. Richardson .... | 1949-65 | 26,055 | 794 | 41 | 185 | 44 | 34.60 |
| M. H. Denness ...... | 1959-80 | 25,886 | 838 | 65 | 195 | 33 | 33.48 |
| H. Makepeace ....... | 1906-30 | 25,799 | 778 | 66 | 203 | 43 | 36.23 |
| W. Gunn ........... | 1880-1904 | 25,791 | 850 | 72 | 273 | 48 | 33.15 |
| W. Watson ......... | 1939-64 | 25,670 | 753 | 109 | 257 | 55 | 39.86 |
| G. Brown .......... | 1908-33 | 25,649 | 1,012 | 52 | 232* | 37 | 26.71 |
| G. M. Emmett ...... | 1936-59 | 25,602 | 865 | 50 | 188 | 37 | 31.41 |
| J. B. Bolus .......... | 1956-75 | 25,598 | 833 | 81 | 202* | 39 | 34.03 |
| W. E. Russell ....... | 1956-72 | 25,525 | 796 | 64 | 193 | 41 | 34.87 |
| C. J. Barnett ........ | 1927-54 | 25,389 | 821 | 45 | 259 | 48 | 32.71 |
| L. B. Fishlock ....... | 1931-52 | 25,376 | 699 | 54 | 253 | 56 | 39.34 |
| C. T. Radley ........ | 1964-85 | 25,276 | 834 | 125 | 200 | 44 | 35.65 |
| D. J. Insole ......... | 1947-63 | 25,237 | 743 | 72 | 219* | 54 | 37.61 |
| J. M. Brearley ....... | 1961-83 | 25,185 | 768 | 102 | 312* | 45 | 37.81 |
| J. Vine ............. | 1896-1922 | 25,171 | 920 | 79 | 202 | 34 | 29.92 |
| R. M. Prideaux ...... | 1958-75 | 25,136 | 808 | 75 | 202* | 41 | 34.29 |
| J. H. King .......... | 1895-1926 | 25,122 | 988 | 69 | 227* | 34 | 27.34 |

† *In recent years some statisticians have removed from W. G. Grace's record a number of matches which they consider not to have been first-class. The above figures are those which became universally accepted upon appearance in W. G. Grace's obituary in the* Wisden *of 1916. Some works of reference give his career record as being 54,211–1,478–104–344–124–39.45. These figures also appeared in the 1981 edition of* Wisden.

## CAREER BATTING AVERAGE OVER 50

(Qualification: 10,000 runs)

| Avge | | Career | I | NO | R | HI | 100s |
|---|---|---|---|---|---|---|---|
| 95.14 | D. G. Bradman | 1927-49 | 338 | 43 | 28,067 | 452* | 117 |
| 72.74 | V. M. Merchant | 1929-51 | 221 | 44 | 12,876 | 359* | 43 |
| 65.18 | W. H. Ponsford | 1920-35 | 235 | 23 | 13,819 | 437 | 47 |
| 65.00 | W. M. Woodfull | 1921-35 | 245 | 39 | 13,392 | 284 | 49 |
| 58.24 | A. L. Hassett | 1932-54 | 322 | 32 | 16,890 | 232 | 59 |
| 58.02 | V. S. Hazare | 1934-67 | 366 | 46 | 18,569 | 316* | 59 |
| 57.67 | A. F. Kippax | 1918-36 | 254 | 33 | 12,747 | 315* | 43 |
| 56.94 | G. Boycott | 1962-85 | 994 | 161 | 47,434 | 261* | 149 |

| Avge | | Career | I | NO | R | HI | 100s |
|---|---|---|---|---|---|---|---|
| 56.55 | C. L. Walcott | 1941-64 | 238 | 29 | 11,820 | 314* | 40 |
| 56.37 | K. S. Ranjitsinhji | 1893-1920 | 500 | 62 | 24,692 | 285* | 72 |
| 56.22 | R. B. Simpson | 1952-78 | 436 | 62 | 21,029 | 359 | 60 |
| 56.10 | W. R. Hammond | 1920-51 | 1,005 | 104 | 50,551 | 336* | 167 |
| 55.51 | L. Hutton | 1934-60 | 814 | 91 | 40,140 | 364 | 129 |
| 55.34 | E. D. Weekes | 1944-64 | 241 | 24 | 12,010 | 304* | 36 |
| 54.87 | G. S. Sobers | 1952-74 | 609 | 93 | 28,315 | 365* | 86 |
| 54.74 | B. A. Richards | 1964-83 | 576 | 58 | 28,358 | 356 | 80 |
| 54.58 | R. G. Pollock | 1960-85 | 414 | 51 | 19,813 | 274 | 60 |
| 54.24 | F. M. M. Worrell | 1941-64 | 326 | 49 | 15,025 | 308* | 39 |
| 53.78 | R. M. Cowper | 1959-70 | 228 | 31 | 10,595 | 307 | 26 |
| 53.67 | A. R. Morris | 1940-64 | 250 | 15 | 12,614 | 290 | 46 |
| 53.27 | Javed Miandad | 1973-85 | 505 | 82 | 22,534 | 311 | 63 |
| 52.32 | Hanif Mohammad | 1951-76 | 371 | 45 | 17,059 | 499 | 55 |
| 52.30 | A. R. Border | 1976-85 | 267 | 41 | 11,821 | 200 | 33 |
| 52.28 | P. R. Umrigar | 1944-68 | 350 | 41 | 16,155 | 252* | 49 |
| 52.20 | G. S. Chappell | 1966-84 | 542 | 72 | 24,535 | 247* | 74 |
| 52.18 | Zaheer Abbas | 1965-85 | 746 | 39 | 34,285 | 274 | 107 |
| 51.95 | H. Sutcliffe | 1919-45 | 1,088 | 123 | 50,138 | 313 | 149 |
| 51.85 | D. C. S. Compton | 1936-64 | 839 | 88 | 38,942 | 300 | 123 |
| 51.53 | A. D. Nourse | 1931-53 | 269 | 27 | 12,472 | 260* | 41 |
| 51.44 | W. A. Brown | 1932-50 | 284 | 15 | 13,840 | 265* | 39 |
| 51.39 | S. M. Gavaskar | 1966-85 | 515 | 57 | 23,539 | 340 | 74 |
| 51.00 | P. B. H. May | 1948-63 | 618 | 77 | 27,592 | 285* | 85 |
| 50.95 | N. C. O'Neill | 1955-68 | 306 | 34 | 13,859 | 284 | 45 |
| 50.93 | R. N. Harvey | 1946-63 | 461 | 35 | 21,699 | 231* | 67 |
| 50.90 | W. M. Lawry | 1955-72 | 417 | 49 | 18,734 | 266 | 50 |
| 50.80 | E. H. Hendren | 1907-38 | 1,300 | 166 | 57,611 | 301* | 170 |
| 50.65 | J. B. Hobbs | 1905-34 | 1,315 | 106 | 61,237 | 316* | 197 |
| 50.26 | I. V. A. Richards | 1971-85 | 572 | 38 | 26,841 | 322 | 86 |
| 50.22 | C. B. Fry | 1892-1922 | 658 | 43 | 30,886 | 258* | 94 |

## 1,000 RUNS IN A SEASON

(Includes Overseas Tours and Seasons)

**28 times:** W. G. Grace 2,000 (6); F. E. Woolley 3,000 (1), 2,000 (12).

**27 times:** M. C. Cowdrey 2,000 (2); C. P. Mead 3,000 (2), 2,000 (9).

**26 times:** G. Boycott 2,000 (3); J. B. Hobbs 3,000 (1), 2,000 (16).

**25 times:** E. H. Hendren 3,000 (3), 2,000 (12).

**24 times:** Wm. Quaife 2,000 (1); H. Sutcliffe 3,000 (3), 2,000 (12).

**23 times:** A. Jones.

**22 times:** D. L. Amiss 2,000 (3); T. W. Graveney 2,000 (7); W. R. Hammond 3,000 (3), 2,000 (9).

**21 times:** D. Denton 2,000 (5); J. H. Edrich 2,000 (6); W. Rhodes 2,000 (2).

**20 times:** D. B. Close; K. W. R. Fletcher; G. Gunn; T. W. Hayward 3,000 (2), 2,000 (8); James Langridge 2,000 (1); J. M. Parks 2,000 (3); A. Sandham 2,000 (8); M. J. K. Smith 3,000 (1), 2,000 (5); C. Washbrook 2,000 (2).

**19 times:** J. W. Hearne 2,000 (4); G. H. Hirst 2,000 (3); D. Kenyon 2,000 (7); E. Tyldesley 3,000 (1), 2,000 (5); J. T. Tyldesley 3,000 (1), 2,000 (4).

**18 times:** L. G. Berry 2,000 (1); H. T. W. Hardinge 2,000 (5); R. E. Marshall 2,000 (6); P. A. Perrin; G. M. Turner 2,000 (3); R. E. S. Wyatt 2,000 (5).

**17 times:** L. E. G. Ames 3,000 (1), 2,000 (5); T. E. Bailey 2,000 (1); D. Brookes 2,000 (6); D. C. S. Compton 3,000 (1), 2,000 (5); L. Hutton 3,000 (1), 2,000 (8); J. G. Langridge 2,000 (11); M. Leyland 2,000 (3); K. G. Suttle 2,000 (1), Zaheer Abbas 2,000 (2).

**16 times:** D. G. Bradman 2,000 (4); D. E. Davies 2,000 (1); E. G. Hayes 2,000 (2); C. A. Milton 2,000 (1); J. O'Connor 2,000 (4); C. T. Radley; James Seymour 2,000 (1).

**15 times:** G. Barker; K. F. Barrington 2,000 (3); E. H. Bowley 2,000 (4); M. H. Denness; A. E. Dipper 2,000 (5); H. E. Dollery 2,000 (2); W. J. Edrich 3,000 (1), 2,000 (8); C. G. Greenidge; J. H. Hampshire; P. Holmes 2,000 (7); Mushtaq Mohammad; R. B. Nicholls 2,000 (1); P. H. Parfitt 2,000 (3); W. G. A. Parkhouse 2,000 (1); B. A. Richards 2,000 (1); J. D. Robertson 2,000 (9); G. S. Sobers; M. J. Stewart 2,000 (1).

*Notes:* F. E. Woolley reached 1,000 runs in 28 consecutive seasons (1907-1938). C. P. Mead did so 27 seasons in succession (1906-1936).

Outside England, 1,000 runs in a season has been reached most times by D. G. Bradman (in 12 seasons in Australia).

Three batsmen have scored 1,000 runs in a season in each of four different countries: G. S. Sobers in West Indies, England, India and Australia; M. C. Cowdrey and G. Boycott in England, South Africa, West Indies and Australia.

## FOUR HUNDREDS OR MORE IN SUCCESSION

**Six in succession:** C. B. Fry 1901; D. G. Bradman 1938-39; M. J. Procter 1970-71.

**Five in succession:** E. D. Weekes 1955-56.

**Four in succession:** A. R. Border 1985; D. G. Bradman 1931-32, 1948-49; D. C. S. Compton 1946-47; N. J. Contractor 1957-58; K. S. Duleepsinhji 1931; C. B. Fry 1911; W. R. Hammond 1936-37, 1945-46; H. T. W. Hardinge 1913; T. W. Hayward 1906; J. B. Hobbs 1920, 1925; D. W. Hookes 1976-77; P. N. Kirsten 1976-77; J. G. Langridge 1949; C. G. Macartney 1921; K. S. McEwan 1977; P. B. H. May 1956-57; V. M. Merchant 1941-42; A. Mitchell 1933; Nawab of Pataudi sen. 1931; L. G. Rowe 1971-72; P. Roy 1962-63; Sadiq Mohammad 1976; Saeed Ahmed 1961-62; H. Sutcliffe 1931, 1939; E. Tyldesley 1926; W. W. Whysall 1930; F. E. Woolley 1929; Zaheer Abbas 1970-71, 1982-83.

## MOST FIFTIES IN CONSECUTIVE INNINGS

10 . . . . . . E. Tyldesley in 1926 and D. G. Bradman in 1947-48 and 1948.

## MOST HUNDREDS IN A SEASON

**Eighteen:** D. C. S. Compton in 1947. These included six hundreds against the South Africans in which matches his average was 84.78. His aggregate for the season was 3,816, also a record.

**Sixteen:** J. B. Hobbs in 1925, when aged 42, played 16 three-figure innings in first-class matches. It was during this season that he exceeded the number of hundreds obtained in first-class cricket by W. G. Grace.

**Fifteen:** W. R. Hammond in 1938.

**Fourteen:** H. Sutcliffe in 1932.

**Thirteen:** G. Boycott in 1971, D. G. Bradman in 1938, C. B. Fry in 1901, W. R. Hammond in 1933 and 1937, T. W. Hayward in 1906, E. H. Hendren in 1923, 1927 and 1928, C. P. Mead in 1928, and H. Sutcliffe in 1928 and 1931.

## FAST FIFTIES

| *Minutes* | | | |
|---|---|---|---|
| 8† | C. C. Inman (57) | Leicestershire v Nottinghamshire at Nottingham . . . | 1965 |
| 11 | C. I. J. Smith (66) | Middlesex v Gloucestershire at Bristol . . . . . . . . . . . | 1938 |
| 14 | S. J. Pegler (50) | South Africans v Tasmania at Launceston . . . . . . . . | 1910-11 |
| 14 | F. T. Mann (53) | Middlesex v Nottinghamshire at Lord's . . . . . . . . . . | 1921 |
| 14 | H. B. Cameron (56) | Transvaal v Orange Free State at Johannesburg . . . | 1934-35 |
| 14 | C. I. J. Smith (52) | Middlesex v Kent at Maidstone . . . . . . . . . . . . . . . . . | 1935 |

† *Full tosses were bowled to expedite a declaration.*

## FASTEST HUNDREDS

| *Minutes* | | | |
|---|---|---|---|
| 35 | P. G. H. Fender (113*) | Surrey v Northamptonshire at Northampton .. | 1920 |
| 35† | S. J. O'Shaughnessy (105) | Lancashire v Leicestershire at Manchester .... | 1983 |
| 37 | C. M. Old (107) | Yorkshire v Warwickshire at Birmingham .... | 1977 |
| 40 | G. L. Jessop (101) | Gloucestershire v Yorkshire at Harrogate ..... | 1897 |
| 41 | N. F. M. Popplewell (143) | Somerset v Gloucestershire at Bath .......... | 1983 |
| 42 | G. L. Jessop (191) | Gentlemen of South v Players of South at Hastings .............................. | 1907 |
| 43 | A. H. Hornby (106) | Lancashire v Somerset at Manchester ........ | 1905 |
| 43 | D. W. Hookes (107) | South Australia v Victoria at Adelaide ....... | 1982-83 |
| 44 | R. N. S. Hobbs (100) | Essex v Australians at Chelmsford ........... | 1975 |

*Note:* The fastest known hundred in terms of balls received is off 34 balls by D. W. Hookes (above). P. G. H. Fender is calculated to have made his hundred off not fewer than 40 balls and not more than 46.

† *Scored on the last day of the season against a deliberate succession of long hops and full tosses bowled by D. I. Gower and J. J. Whitaker in the hope they might expedite a declaration.*

## FASTEST DOUBLE-HUNDREDS

| *Minutes* | | | |
|---|---|---|---|
| 113 | R. J. Shastri (200*) | Bombay v Baroda at Bombay ................ | 1984-85 |
| 120 | G. L. Jessop (286) | Gloucestershire v Sussex at Hove ........... | 1903 |
| 120 | C. H. Lloyd (201*) | West Indians v Glamorgan at Swansea ....... | 1976 |
| 130 | G. L. Jessop (234) | Gloucestershire v Somerset at Bristol ......... | 1905 |
| 131 | V. T. Trumper (293) | Australians v Canterbury at Christchurch ..... | 1913-14 |

## FASTEST TRIPLE-HUNDREDS

| *Minutes* | | | |
|---|---|---|---|
| 181 | D. C. S. Compton (300) | MCC v N. E. Transvaal at Benoni .......... | 1948-49 |
| 205 | F. E. Woolley (305*) | MCC v Tasmania at Hobart ............... | 1911-12 |
| 205 | C. G. Macartney (345) | Australians v Nottinghamshire at Nottingham . | 1921 |
| 213 | D. G. Bradman (369) | South Australia v Tasmania at Adelaide ...... | 1935-36 |

## FAST SCORING

P. G. H. Fender, for Surrey v Northamptonshire at Northampton in 1920, scored 113* out of 171 in forty-two minutes. He reached 50 in nineteen minutes and 100 in thirty-five minutes. Fender and H. A. Peach added 171 (unfinished) in forty-two minutes for the sixth wicket.

E. B. Alletson, for Nottinghamshire v Sussex at Hove in 1911, scored 189 out of 227 runs obtained while at the wicket in ninety minutes. He went from 50 to 189 in thirty minutes.

For Auckland v Otago at Dunedin in 1936-37, P. E. Whitelaw and W. N. Carson added 445 runs for the third wicket in 268 minutes – a world record.

H. Sutcliffe (194) and M. Leyland (45) hit 102 off six consecutive overs for Yorkshire v Essex at Scarborough, 1932.

G. Fowler and S. J. O'Shaughnessy put on 201 in 43 minutes for the first wicket for Lancashire v Leicestershire at Manchester in 1984, the fastest-recorded double-hundred partnership – but see † footnote to Fast Hundreds.

## MOST PERSONAL SIXES IN A SEASON

| | | | | | |
|---|---|---|---|---|---|
| 80 | I. T. Botham | 1985 | 66 | A. W. Wellard | 1935 |

*Note:* A. W. Wellard hit 50 or more sixes in a season four times. His number of 6s in 1935 has in the past been given as 72, but recent research has caused this to be adjusted.

## MOST PERSONAL SIXES IN AN INNINGS

| | | | |
|---|---|---|---|
| 15 | J. R. Reid (296) | Wellington v N. Districts at Wellington | 1962-63 |
| 13 | Majid J. Khan (147*) | Pakistanis v Glamorgan at Swansea | 1967 |
| 13 | C. G. Greenidge (273*) | D. H. Robins' XI v Pakistanis at Eastbourne | 1974 |
| 13 | C. G. Greenidge (259) | Hampshire v Sussex at Southampton | 1975 |
| 13 | G. W. Humpage (254) | Warwickshire v Lancashire at Southport | 1982 |
| 13 | R. J. Shastri (200*) | Bombay v Baroda at Bombay | 1984-85 |
| 12 | Gulfraz Khan (207) | Railways v Universities at Lahore | 1976-77 |
| 12 | I. T. Botham (138*) | Somerset v Warwickshire at Birmingham | 1985 |
| 11 | C. K. Nayudu (153) | Hindus v MCC at Bombay | 1926-27 |
| 11 | C. J. Barnett (194) | Gloucestershire v Somerset at Bath | 1934 |
| 11 | R. Benaud (135) | Australians v T. N. Pearce's XI at Scarborough | 1953 |

*Note:* W. J. Stewart (Warwickshire) hit seventeen 6s in the match v Lancashire, at Blackpool, 1959; ten in his first innings of 155 and seven in his second innings of 125.

## MOST PERSONAL BOUNDARIES IN AN INNINGS

| | | | |
|---|---|---|---|
| 68 | P. A. Perrin (343*) | Essex v Derbyshire at Chesterfield | 1904 |
| 65 | A. C. MacLaren (424) | Lancashire v Somerset at Taunton | 1895 |
| 64 | Hanif Mohammad (499) | Karachi v Bahawalpur at Karachi | 1958-59 |
| 57 | J. H. Edrich (310*) | England v New Zealand at Leeds | 1965 |
| 55 | C. W. Gregory (383) | NSW v Queensland at Brisbane | 1906-07 |
| 54 | G. H. Hirst (341) | Yorkshire v Leicestershire at Leicester | 1905 |
| 53 | A. W. Nourse (304*) | Natal v Transvaal at Johannesburg | 1919-20 |
| 51 | W. G. Grace (344) | MCC v Kent at Canterbury | 1876 |
| 51 | C. G. Macartney (345) | Australians v Nottinghamshire at Nottingham | 1921 |
| 50 | D. G. Bradman (369) | South Australia v Tasmania at Adelaide | 1935-36 |
| 50 | A. Ducat (306*) | Surrey v Oxford University at The Oval | 1919 |
| 50 | B. B. Nimbalkar (443*) | Maharashtra v Kathiawar at Poona | 1948-49 |
| 50 | J. R. Reid (296) | Wellington v N. Districts at Wellington | 1962-63 |
| 50 | I. V. A. Richards (322) | Somerset v Warwickshire at Taunton | 1985 |

*Note:* Boundaries include sixes.

## MOST RUNS SCORED OFF ONE OVER

(All instances refer to six-ball overs)

| | | | |
|---|---|---|---|
| 36 | G. S. Sobers | off M. A. Nash, Nottinghamshire v Glamorgan at Swansea (six 6s) | 1968 |
| 36 | R. J. Shastri | off Tilak Raj, Bombay v Baroda at Bombay (six 6s) | 1984-85 |
| 34 | E. B. Alletson | off E. H. Killick, Nottinghamshire v Sussex at Hove (46604446; including two no-balls) | 1911 |
| 34 | F. C. Hayes | off M. A. Nash, Lancashire v Glamorgan at Swansea (646666) | 1977 |

| | | | |
|---|---|---|---|
| 32 | C. C. Inman | off N. W. Hill, Leicestershire v Nottinghamshire at Nottingham (466664; full tosses were provided for him to hit) | 1965 |
| 32 | T. E. Jesty | off R. J. Boyd-Moss, Hampshire v Northamptonshire at Southampton (666662) | 1984 |
| 32 | P. W. G. Parker | off A. I. Kallicharran, Sussex v Warwickshire at Birmingham (466664) | 1982 |
| 32 | I. R. Redpath | off N. Rosendorff, Australians v Orange Free State at Bloemfontein (666644) | 1969-70 |
| 32 | C. C. Smart | off G. Hill, Glamorgan v Hampshire at Cardiff (664664) | 1935 |
| 31 | M. H. Bowditch (1) and M. J. Procter (30) | off A. A. Mallett, Western Province v Australians at Cape Town (Procter hit five 6s) | 1969-70 |
| 31 | A. W. Wellard | off F. E. Woolley, Somerset v Kent at Wells (666661) | 1938 |
| 30 | I. T. Botham | off P. A. Smith, Somerset v Warwickshire at Taunton (4466460 including one no-ball) | 1982 |
| 30 | D. G. Bradman | off A. P. Freeman, Australians v England XI at Folkestone (466464) | 1934 |
| 30 | H. B. Cameron | off H. Verity, South Africans v Yorkshire at Sheffield (444666) | 1935 |
| 30 | G. A. Gooch | off S. R. Gorman, Essex v Cambridge U. at Cambridge (662664) | 1985 |
| 30 | A. J. Lamb | off A. I. Kallicharran, Northamptonshire v Warwickshire at Birmingham (644664) | 1982 |
| 30 | D. T. Lindsay | off W. T. Greensmith, South African Fezela XI v Essex at Chelmsford (066666 to win the match) | 1961 |
| 30 | Majid J. Khan | off R. C. Davis, Pakistanis v Glamorgan at Swansea (606666) | 1967 |
| 30 | A. W. Wellard | off T. R. Armstrong, Somerset v Derbyshire at Wells (066666) | 1936 |
| 30 | D. Wilson | off R. N. S. Hobbs, Yorkshire v MCC at Scarborough (466266) | 1966 |
| 30 | P. L. Winslow | off J. T. Ikin, South Africans v Lancashire at Manchester (446646) | 1955 |
| 30 | Zaheer Abbas | off D. Breakwell, Gloucestershire v Somerset at Taunton (466626) | 1979 |

*Note:* The greatest number of runs scored off an eight-ball over is 34 (40446664) by R. M. Edwards off M. C. Carew, Governor-General's XI v West Indians at Auckland, 1968-69.

## 300 RUNS IN ONE DAY

| | | | |
|---|---|---|---|
| 345 | C. G. Macartney | Australians v Nottinghamshire at Nottingham | 1921 |
| 334 | W. H. Ponsford | Victoria v New South Wales at Melbourne | 1926-27 |
| 333 | K. S. Duleepsinhji | Sussex v Northamptonshire at Hove | 1930 |
| 331* | J. D. Robertson | Middlesex v Worcestershire at Worcester | 1949 |
| 325* | B. A. Richards | S. Australia v W. Australia at Perth | 1970-71 |
| 322† | E. Paynter | Lancashire v Sussex at Hove | 1937 |
| 322 | I. V. A. Richards | Somerset v Warwickshire at Taunton | 1985 |
| 318 | C. W. Gregory | New South Wales v Queensland at Brisbane | 1906-07 |
| 316† | R. H. Moore | Hampshire v Warwickshire at Bournemouth | 1937 |
| 315* | R. C. Blunt | Otago v Canterbury at Christchurch | 1931-32 |
| 312* | J. M. Brearley | MCC Under 25 v North Zone at Peshawar | 1966-67 |
| 311* | G. M. Turner | Worcestershire v Warwickshire at Worcester | 1982 |
| 309* | D. G. Bradman | Australia v England at Leeds | 1930 |
| 307* | W. H. Ashdown | Kent v Essex at Brentwood | 1934 |
| 306* | A. Ducat | Surrey v Oxford University at The Oval | 1919 |
| 305* | F. R. Foster | Warwickshire v Worcestershire at Dudley | 1914 |

† *E. Paynter's 322 and R. H. Moore's 316 were scored on the same day: July 28, 1937.*

## HIGHEST PARTNERSHIPS

| | | |
|---|---|---|
| 577 | V. S. Hazare (288) and Gul Mahomed (319), fourth wicket, Baroda v Holkar at Baroda | 1946-47 |
| 574* | F. M. M. Worrell (255*) and C. L. Walcott (314*), fourth wicket, Barbados v Trinidad at Port-of-Spain | 1945-46 |
| 561 | Waheed Mirza (324) and Mansoor Akhtar (224*), first wicket, Karachi Whites v Quetta at Karachi | 1976-77 |
| 555 | P. Holmes (224*) and H. Sutcliffe (313), first wicket, Yorkshire v Essex at Leyton | 1932 |
| 554 | J. T. Brown (300) and J. Tunnicliffe (243), first wicket, Yorkshire v Derbyshire at Chesterfield | 1898 |
| 502* | F. M. M. Worrell (308*) and J. D. C. Goddard (218*), fourth wicket, Barbados v Trinidad at Bridgetown | 1943-44 |
| 490 | E. H. Bowley (283) and J. G. Langridge (195), first wicket, Sussex v Middlesex at Hove | 1933 |
| 487* | G. A. Headley (344*) and C. C. Passailaigue (261*), sixth wicket, Jamaica v Lord Tennyson's XI at Kingston | 1931-32 |
| 470 | A. I. Kallicharran (230*) and G. W. Humpage (254), fourth wicket, Warwickshire v Lancashire at Southport | 1982 |
| 465* | J. A. Jameson (240*) and R. B. Kanhai (213*), second wicket, Warwickshire v Gloucestershire at Birmingham | 1974 |
| 456 | W. H. Ponsford (248) and E. R. Mayne (209), first wicket, Victoria v Queensland at Melbourne | 1923-24 |
| 456 | Khalid Irtiza (290) and Aslam Ali (236), third wicket, United Bank v Multan at Karachi | 1975-76 |
| 455 | B. B. Nimbalkar (443*) and K. V. Bhandarkar (205), second wicket, Maharashtra v Kathiawar at Poona | 1948-49 |
| 451 | D. G. Bradman (244) and W. H. Ponsford (266), second wicket, Australia v England, Fifth Test, at The Oval | 1934 |
| 451* | S. Desai (218*) and R. M. H. Binny (211*), first wicket, Karnataka v Kerala at Chikmagalur | 1977-78 |
| 451 | Mudassar Nazar (231) and Javed Miandad (280*), third wicket, Pakistan v India, Fourth Test, at Hyderabad | 1982-83 |

## PARTNERSHIPS FOR FIRST WICKET

| | | |
|---|---|---|
| 561 | Waheed Mirza and Mansoor Akhtar, Karachi Whites v Quetta at Karachi | 1976-77 |
| 555 | P. Holmes and H. Sutcliffe, Yorkshire v Essex at Leyton | 1932 |
| 554 | J. T. Brown and J. Tunnicliffe, Yorkshire v Derbyshire at Chesterfield | 1898 |
| 490 | E. H. Bowley and J. G. Langridge, Sussex v Middlesex at Hove | 1933 |
| 456 | E. R. Mayne and W. H. Ponsford, Victoria v Queensland at Melbourne | 1923-24 |
| 451* | S. Desai and R. M. H. Binny, Karnataka v Kerala at Chikmagalur | 1977-78 |
| 428 | J. B Hobbs and A. Sandham, Surrey v Oxford University at The Oval | 1926 |
| 424 | J. F. W. Nicholson and I. J. Siedle, Natal v Orange Free State at Bloemfontein | 1926-27 |
| 421 | S. M. Gavaskar and G. A. Parkar, Bombay v Bengal at Bombay | 1981-82 |
| 418 | Kamal Najamuddin and Khalid Alvi, Karachi v Railways at Karachi | 1980-81 |
| 413 | V. Mankad and Pankaj Roy, India v New Zealand at Madras (world Test record) | 1955-56 |
| 405 | C. P. S. Chauhan and M. S. Gupte, Maharashtra v Vidarbha at Poona | 1972-73 |
| 395 | D. M. Young and R. B. Nicholls, Gloucestershire v Oxford University at Oxford | 1962 |
| 391 | A. O. Jones and A. Shrewsbury, Nottinghamshire v Gloucestershire at Bristol | 1899 |
| 390 | G. L. Wight and G. L. R. Gibbs, B. Guiana v Barbados at Georgetown | 1951-52 |
| 390 | B. Dudleston and J. F. Steele, Leicestershire v Derbyshire at Leicester | 1979 |
| 389 | Majid J. Khan and Shafiq Ahmed, Punjab A v Sind A at Karachi | 1974-75 |
| 389 | Mudassar Nazar and Mansoor Akhtar, United Bank v Rawalpindi at Lahore | 1981-82 |
| 388 | K. C. Wessels and R. B. Kerr, Queensland v Victoria at St Kilda, Melbourne | 1982-83 |

| | | |
|---|---|---|
| 387 | G. M. Turner and T. W. Jarvis, New Zealand v West Indies at Georgetown | 1971-72 |
| 382 | R. B. Simpson and W. M. Lawry, Australia v West Indies at Bridgetown . | 1964-65 |
| 380 | H. Whitehead and C. J. B. Wood, Leicestershire v Worcestershire at Worcester | 1906 |
| 379 | R. Abel and W. Brockwell, Surrey v Hampshire at The Oval ............ | 1897 |
| 378 | J. T. Brown and J. Tunnicliffe, Yorkshire v Sussex at Sheffield .......... | 1897 |
| 377* | N. F. Horner and Khalid Ibadulla, Warwickshire v Surrey at The Oval ... | 1960 |
| 375 | W. H. Ponsford and W. M. Woodfull, Victoria v New South Wales at Melbourne ........................................ | 1926-27 |

## FIRST-WICKET HUNDREDS IN BOTH INNINGS

B. Sutcliffe and D. D. Taylor, for Auckland v Canterbury in 1948-49, scored for the first wicket 220 in the first innings and 286 in the second innings. This is the only instance of two double-century opening stands in the same match.

T. W. Hayward and J. B. Hobbs in 1907 accomplished a performance without parallel by scoring over 100 together for Surrey's first wicket four times in one week: 106 and 125 v Cambridge University at The Oval, and 147 and 105 v Middlesex at Lord's.

L. Hutton and C. Washbrook, in three consecutive Test match innings which they opened together for England v Australia in 1946-47, made 138 in the second innings at Melbourne, and 137 and 100 at Adelaide. They also opened with 168 and 129 at Leeds in 1948.

J. B. Hobbs and H. Sutcliffe, in three consecutive Test match innings which they opened together for England v Australia in 1924-25, made 157 and 110 at Sydney and 283 at Melbourne. On 26 occasions – 15 times in Test matches – Hobbs and Sutcliffe took part in a three-figure first-wicket partnership. Seven of these stands exceeded 200.

G. Boycott and J. H. Edrich, in three consecutive Test match innings which they opened together for England v Australia in 1970-71, made 161* in the second innings at Melbourne, and 107 and 103 at Adelaide.

In 1971 R. G. A. Headley and P. J. Stimpson of Worcestershire shared in first-wicket hundred partnerships on each of the first four occasions they opened the innings together: 125 and 147 v Northamptonshire at Worcester, 102 and 128* v Warwickshire at Birmingham.

J. B. Hobbs during his career, which extended from 1905 to 1934, helped to make 100 or more for the first wicket in first-class cricket 166 times – 15 of them in 1926, when in consecutive innings he helped to make 428, 182, 106 and 123 before a wicket fell. As many as 117 of the 166 stands were made for Surrey. In all first-class matches Hobbs and A. Sandham shared 66 first-wicket partnerships of 100 or more runs.

P. Holmes and H. Sutcliffe made 100 or more runs for the first wicket of Yorkshire on 69 occasions; J. B. Hobbs and A. Sandham for Surrey on 63 occasions; W. W. Keeton and C. B. Harris of Nottinghamshire on 46; T. W. Hayward and J. B. Hobbs of Surrey on 40; G. Gunn and W. W. Whysall of Nottinghamshire on 40; J. D. Robertson and S. M. Brown of Middlesex on 34; C. B. Fry and J. Vine of Sussex on 33; R. E. Marshall and J. R. Gray of Hampshire on 33; D. E. Davies and A. H. Dyson of Glamorgan on 32; and G. Boycott and R. G. Lumb of Yorkshire on 27.

J. Douglas and A. E. Stoddart in 1896 scored over 150 runs for the Middlesex first wicket three times within a fortnight. In 1901, J. Iremonger and A. O. Jones obtained over 100 for the Nottinghamshire first wicket four times within eight days, scoring 134 and 144* v Surrey at The Oval, 238 v Essex at Leyton, and 119 v Derbyshire at Welbeck.

J. W. Lee and F. S. Lee, brothers, for Somerset in 1934, scored over 100 runs thrice in succession in the County Championship.

W. G. Grace and A. E. Stoddart, in three consecutive innings against the Australians in 1893, made over 100 runs for each opening partnership.

C. Hallows and F. B. Watson, in consecutive innings for Lancashire in 1928, opened with 200, 202, 107, 118; reached three figures twelve times, 200 four times.

H. Sutcliffe, in the period 1919-1939 inclusive, shared in 145 first-wicket partnerships of 100 runs or more.

There were four first-wicket hundred partnerships in the match between Somerset and Cambridge University at Taunton in 1960. G. Atkinson and R. T. Virgin scored 172 and 112 for Somerset and R. M. Prideaux and A. R. Lewis 198 and 137 for Cambridge University.

# PARTNERSHIP RECORDS FOR ALL COUNTRIES

## Best First-Wicket Stands

| | | | |
|---|---|---|---|
| Pakistan | 561 | Waheed Mirza (324) and Mansoor Akhtar (224*), Karachi Whites v Quetta at Karachi | 1976-77 |
| English | 555 | P. Holmes (224*) and H. Sutcliffe (313), Yorkshire v Essex at Leyton | 1932 |
| Australian | 456 | W. H. Ponsford (248) and E. R. Mayne (209), Victoria v Queensland at Melbourne | 1923-24 |
| Indian | 451* | S. Desai (218*) and R. M. H. Binny (211*), Karnataka v Kerala at Chikmagalur | 1977-78 |
| South African | 424 | J. F. W. Nicolson (252*) and I. J. Siedle (174), Natal v Orange Free State at Bloemfontein | 1926-27 |
| West Indian | 390 | G. L. Wight (262*) and G. L. R. Gibbs (216), British Guiana v Barbados at Georgetown | 1951-52 |
| New Zealand | 387 | G. M. Turner (259) and T. W. Jarvis (182), New Zealand v West Indies at Georgetown | 1971-72 |

## Best Second-Wicket Stands

| | | | |
|---|---|---|---|
| English | 465* | J. A. Jameson (240*) and R. B. Kanhai (213*), Warwickshire v Gloucestershire at Birmingham | 1974 |
| Indian | 455 | B. B. Nimbalkar (443*) and K. V. Bhandarkar (205), Maharashtra v Kathiawar at Poona | 1948-49 |
| Australian | 451 | W. H. Ponsford (266) and D. G. Bradman (244), Australia v England at The Oval | 1934 |
| West Indian | 446 | C. C. Hunte (260) and G. S. Sobers (365*), West Indies v Pakistan at Kingston | 1957-58 |
| Pakistan | 426 | Arshad Pervez (220) and Mohsin Khan (220), Habib Bank v Income Tax Dept at Lahore | 1977-78 |
| New Zealand | 317 | R. T. Hart (167*) and P. S. Briasco (157), Central Districts v Canterbury at New Plymouth | 1983-84 |
| South African | 305 | S. K. Coen (165) and J. M. M Commaille (186), Orange Free State v Natal at Bloemfontein | 1926-27 |

## Best Third-Wicket Stands

| | | | |
|---|---|---|---|
| Pakistan | 456 | Khalid Irtiza (290) and Aslam Ali (236), United Bank v Multan at Karachi | 1975-76 |
| New Zealand | 445 | P. E. Whitelaw (195) and W. N. Carson (290), Auckland v Otago at Dunedin | 1936-37 |
| West Indian | 434 | J. B. Stollmeyer (324) and G. E. Gomez (190), Trinidad v British Guiana at Port-of-Spain | 1946-47 |
| English | 424* | W. J. Edrich (168*) and D. C. S. Compton (252*), Middlesex v Somerset at Lord's | 1948 |
| Indian | 410† | L. Amarnath (262) and R. S. Modi (156), India in England v The Rest at Calcutta | 1946-47 |
| Australian | 390* | J. M. Wiener (221*) and J. K. Moss (200*), Victoria v Western Australia at St Kilda, Melbourne | 1981-82 |
| South African | 341 | E. J. Barlow (201) and R. G. Pollock (175), South Africa v Australia at Adelaide | 1963-64 |

*† 415 runs were added for this wicket for India v England at Madras in 1981-82 in two separate partnerships. See Highest Test Wicket Partnerships for details.*

## Best Fourth-Wicket Stands

| | | | |
|---|---|---|---|
| Indian | 577 | V. S. Hazare (288) and Gul Mahomed (319), Baroda v Holkar at Baroda | 1946-47 |
| West Indian | 574* | C. L. Walcott (314*) and F. M. M. Worrell (255*), Barbados v Trinidad at Port-of-Spain | 1945-46 |
| English | 470 | A. I. Kallicharran (230*) and G. W. Humpage (254), Warwickshire v Lancashire at Southport | 1982 |
| Australian | 424 | I. S. Lee (258) and S. O. Quin (210), Victoria v Tasmania at Melbourne | 1933-34 |
| Pakistan | 350 | Mushtaq Mohammad (201) and Asif Iqbal (175), Pakistan v New Zealand at Dunedin | 1972-73 |
| South African | 342 | E. A. B. Rowan (196) and P. J. M. Gibb (203), Transvaal v N. E. Transvaal at Johannesburg | 1952-53 |
| New Zealand | 324 | J. R. Reid (188*) and W. M. Wallace (197), New Zealanders v Cambridge University at Cambridge | 1949 |

## Best Fifth-Wicket Stands

| | | | |
|---|---|---|---|
| Australian | 405 | S. G. Barnes (234) and D. G. Bradman (234), Australia v England at Sydney | 1946-47 |
| English | 393 | E. G. Arnold (200*) and W. B. Burns (196), Worcestershire v Warwickshire at Birmingham | 1909 |
| Indian | 360 | Uday Merchant (217) and M. N. Raiji (170), Bombay v Hyderabad at Bombay | 1947-48 |
| Pakistan | 355 | Altaf Shah (276) and Tariq Bashir (196), House Building Finance Corporation v Multan at Multan | 1976-77 |
| South African | 338 | R. G. Pollock (194) and A. L. Wilmot (152), Eastern Province v Natal at Port Elizabeth | 1975-76 |
| West Indian | 335 | B. F. Butcher (151) and C. H. Lloyd (201*), West Indians v Glamorgan at Swansea | 1969 |
| New Zealand | 266 | B. Sutcliffe (355) and W. S. Haig (67), Otago v Auckland at Dunedin | 1949-50 |

## Best Sixth-Wicket Stands

| | | | |
|---|---|---|---|
| West Indian | 487* | G. A. Headley (344*) and C. C. Passailaigue (261*), Jamaica v Lord Tennyson's XI at Kingston | 1931-32 |
| Australian | 428 | M. A. Noble (284) and W. W. Armstrong (172*), Australians v Sussex at Hove | 1902 |
| English | 411 | R. M. Poore (304) and E. G. Wynyard (225), Hampshire v Somerset at Taunton | 1899 |
| Indian | 371 | V. M. Merchant (359*) and R. S. Modi (168), Bombay v Maharashtra at Bombay | 1943-44 |
| Pakistan | 353 | Salah-ud-Din (256) and Zaheer Abbas (197), Karachi v East Pakistan at Karachi | 1968-69 |
| South African | 244* | J. M. M. Commaille (132*) and A. W. Palm (106*), Western Province v Griqualand West at Johannesburg | 1923-24 |
| New Zealand | 226 | E. J. Gray (126) and R. W. Ormiston (93), Wellington v Central Districts at Wellington | 1981-82 |

## Best Seventh-Wicket Stands

| | | | |
|---|---|---|---|
| West Indian | 347 | D. St E. Atkinson (219) and C. C. Depeiza (122), West Indies v Australia at Bridgetown | 1954-55 |
| English | 344 | K. S. Ranjitsinhji (230) and W. Newham (153), Sussex v Essex at Leyton | 1902 |
| Australian | 335 | C. W. Andrews (253) and E. C. Bensted (155), Queensland v New South Wales at Sydney | 1934-35 |

| | | | |
|---|---|---|---|
| Pakistan | 308 | Waqar Hassan (189) and Imtiaz Ahmed (209), Pakistan v New Zealand at Lahore | 1955-56 |
| South African | 299 | B. Mitchell (159) and A. Melville (153), Transvaal v Griqualand West at Kimberley | 1946-47 |
| Indian | 274 | K. C. Ibrahim (250) and K. M. Rangnekar (138), Bijapur XI v Bengal XI at Bombay | 1942-43 |
| New Zealand | 265 | J. L. Powell (164) and N. Dorreen (105*), Canterbury v Otago at Christchurch | 1929-30 |

## Best Eighth-Wicket Stands

| | | | |
|---|---|---|---|
| Australian | 433 | A. Sims (184*) and V. T. Trumper (293), An Australian XI v Canterbury at Christchurch | 1913-14 |
| English | 292 | R. Peel (210*) and Lord Hawke (166), Yorkshire v Warwickshire at Birmingham | 1896 |
| West Indian | 255 | E. A. V. Williams (131*) and E. A. Martindale (134), Barbados v Trinidad at Bridgetown | 1935-36 |
| Pakistan | 240 | Gulfraz Khan (207) and Raja Sarfraz (102), Railways v Universities at Lahore | 1976-77 |
| Indian | 236 | C. T. Sarwate (235) and R. P. Singh (88), Holkar v Delhi and District at Delhi | 1949-50 |
| South African | 222 | D. P. B. Morkel (114) and S. S. L. Steyn (261*), Western Province v Border at Cape Town | 1929-30 |
| New Zealand | 190* | J. E. Mills (104*) and C. F. W. Allcott (102*), New Zealanders v Civil Service at Chiswick | 1927 |

## Best Ninth-Wicket Stands

| | | | |
|---|---|---|---|
| English | 283 | A. Warren (123) and J. Chapman (165), Derbyshire v Warwickshire at Blackwell | 1910 |
| Indian | 245 | V. S. Hazare (316*) and N. D. Nagarwalla (98), Maharashtra v Baroda at Poona | 1939-40 |
| New Zealand | 239 | H. B. Cave (118) and I. B. Leggat (142*), Central Districts v Otago at Dunedin | 1952-53 |
| Australian | 232 | C. Hill (365*) and E. Walkley (53), South Australia v New South Wales at Adelaide | 1900-01 |
| South African | 221 | N. V. Lindsay (160*) and G. R. McCubbin (97), Transvaal v Rhodesia at Bulawayo | 1922-23 |
| Pakistan | 190 | Asif Iqbal (146) and Intikhab Alam (51), Pakistan v England at The Oval | 1967 |
| West Indian | 161 | C. H. Lloyd (161*) and A. M. E. Roberts (68), West Indies v India at Calcutta | 1983-84 |

## Best Tenth-Wicket Stands

| | | | |
|---|---|---|---|
| Australian | 307 | A. F. Kippax (260*), and J. E. H. Hooker (62), New South Wales v Victoria at Melbourne | 1928-29 |
| Indian | 249 | C. T. Sarwate (124*) and S. N. Banerjee (121), Indians v Surrey at The Oval | 1946 |
| English | 235 | F. E. Woolley (185) and A. Fielder (112*), Kent v Worcestershire at Stourbridge | 1909 |
| Pakistan | 196* | Nadeem Yousuf (202*) and Maqsood Kundi (109*) Muslim Commercial Bank v National Bank at Lahore | 1981-82 |
| New Zealand | 184 | R. C. Blunt (338*) and W. Hawkesworth (21), Otago v Canterbury at Christchurch | 1931-32 |
| South African | 174 | H. R. Lance (168) and D. Mackay-Coghill (57*), Transvaal v Natal at Johannesburg | 1965-66 |
| West Indian | 138 | E. L. G. Hoad (149*) and H. C. Griffith (84), West Indians v Sussex at Hove | 1933 |

*Note:* All the English record wicket partnerships were made in the County Championship.

## HIGHEST AGGREGATES IN A SEASON: OVER 3,000

| | Season | I | NO | R | HI | 100s | Avge |
|---|---|---|---|---|---|---|---|
| D. C. S. Compton | 1947 | 50 | 8 | 3,816 | 246 | 18 | 90.85 |
| W. J. Edrich | 1947 | 52 | 8 | 3,539 | 267* | 12 | 80.43 |
| T. W. Hayward | 1906 | 61 | 8 | 3,518 | 219 | 13 | 66.37 |
| L. Hutton | 1949 | 56 | 6 | 3,429 | 269* | 12 | 68.58 |
| F. E. Woolley | 1928 | 59 | 4 | 3,352 | 198 | 12 | 60.94 |
| H. Sutcliffe | 1932 | 52 | 7 | 3,336 | 313 | 14 | 74.13 |
| W. R. Hammond | 1933 | 54 | 5 | 3,323 | 264 | 13 | 67.81 |
| E. H. Hendren | 1928 | 54 | 7 | 3,311 | 209* | 13 | 70.44 |
| R. Abel | 1901 | 68 | 8 | 3,309 | 247 | 7 | 55.15 |
| W. R. Hammond | 1937 | 55 | 5 | 3,252 | 217 | 13 | 65.04 |
| M. J. K. Smith | 1959 | 67 | 11 | 3,245 | 200* | 8 | 57.94 |
| E. H. Hendren | 1933 | 65 | 9 | 3,186 | 301* | 11 | 56.89 |
| C. P. Mead | 1921 | 52 | 6 | 3,179 | 280* | 10 | 69.10 |
| T. W. Hayward | 1904 | 63 | 5 | 3,170 | 203 | 11 | 54.65 |
| K. S. Ranjitsinhji | 1899 | 58 | 8 | 3,159 | 197 | 8 | 63.18 |
| C. B. Fry | 1901 | 43 | 3 | 3,147 | 244 | 13 | 78.67 |
| K. S. Ranjitsinhji | 1900 | 40 | 5 | 3,065 | 275 | 11 | 87.57 |
| L. E. G. Ames | 1933 | 57 | 5 | 3,058 | 295 | 9 | 58.80 |
| J. T. Tyldesley | 1901 | 60 | 5 | 3,041 | 221 | 9 | 55.29 |
| C. P. Mead | 1928 | 50 | 10 | 3,027 | 180 | 13 | 75.67 |
| J. B. Hobbs | 1925 | 48 | 5 | 3,024 | 266* | 16 | 70.32 |
| E. Tyldesley | 1928 | 48 | 10 | 3,024 | 242 | 10 | 79.57 |
| W. E. Alley | 1961 | 64 | 11 | 3,019 | 221* | 11 | 56.96 |
| W. R. Hammond | 1938 | 42 | 2 | 3,011 | 271 | 15 | 75.27 |
| E. H. Hendren | 1923 | 51 | 12 | 3,010 | 200* | 13 | 77.17 |
| H. Sutcliffe | 1931 | 42 | 11 | 3,006 | 230 | 13 | 96.96 |
| J. H. Parks | 1937 | 63 | 4 | 3,003 | 168 | 11 | 50.89 |
| H. Sutcliffe | 1928 | 44 | 5 | 3,002 | 228 | 13 | 76.97 |

*Note:* W. G. Grace scored 2,739 runs in 1871 – the first batsman to reach 2,000 runs in a season. He made ten hundreds and twice exceeded 200, with an average of 78.25 in all first-class matches. At the time, the over consisted of four balls.

## HIGHEST AGGREGATE IN EACH SEASON

### Since Reduction of Championship Matches in 1969

| Season | | I | NO | R | HI | 100s | Avge |
|---|---|---|---|---|---|---|---|
| 1969 | J. H. Edrich | 39 | 7 | 2,238 | 181 | 8 | 69.93 |
| 1970 | G. M. Turner | 46 | 7 | 2,379 | 154* | 10 | 61.00 |
| 1971 | G. Boycott | 30 | 5 | 2,503 | 233 | 13 | 100.12 |
| 1972 | Majid J. Khan | 38 | 4 | 2,074 | 204 | 8 | 61.00 |
| 1973 | G. M. Turner | 44 | 8 | 2,416 | 153* | 9 | 67.11 |
| 1974 | R. T. Virgin | 39 | 5 | 1,936 | 144* | 7 | 56.94 |
| 1975 | G. Boycott | 34 | 8 | 1,915 | 201* | 6 | 73.65 |
| 1976 | Zaheer Abbas | 39 | 5 | 2,554 | 230* | 11 | 75.11 |
| 1977 | I. V. A. Richards | 35 | 2 | 2,161 | 241* | 7 | 65.48 |
| 1978 | D. L. Amiss | 41 | 3 | 2,030 | 162 | 7 | 53.42 |
| 1979 | K. C. Wessels | 36 | 2 | 1,800 | 187 | 6 | 52.94 |
| 1980 | P. N. Kirsten | 36 | 6 | 1,895 | 213* | 6 | 63.16 |
| 1981 | Zaheer Abbas | 36 | 10 | 2,306 | 215* | 10 | 88.69 |
| 1982 | A. I. Kallicharran | 37 | 5 | 2,120 | 235 | 8 | 66.25 |
| 1983 | K. S. McEwan | 39 | 5 | 2,176 | 189* | 8 | 64.00 |
| 1984 | G. A. Gooch | 45 | 7 | 2,559 | 227 | 8 | 67.34 |
| 1985 | G. A. Gooch | 33 | 2 | 2,208 | 202 | 7 | 71.22 |

## HIGHEST BATTING AVERAGES IN AN ENGLISH SEASON

(Qualification: 12 innings)

| | Season | I | NO | R | HI | 100s | Avge |
|---|---|---|---|---|---|---|---|
| D. G. Bradman ...... | 1938 | 26 | 5 | 2,429 | 278 | 13 | 115.66 |
| G. Boycott .......... | 1979 | 20 | 5 | 1,538 | 175* | 6 | 102.53 |
| W. A. Johnston ...... | 1953 | 17 | 16 | 102 | 28* | 0 | 102.00 |
| G. Boycott .......... | 1971 | 30 | 5 | 2,503 | 233 | 13 | 100.12 |
| D. G. Bradman ...... | 1930 | 36 | 6 | 2,960 | 334 | 10 | 98.66 |
| H. Sutcliffe .......... | 1931 | 42 | 11 | 3,006 | 230 | 13 | 96.96 |
| R. M. Poore ........ | 1899 | 21 | 4 | 1,551 | 304 | 7 | 91.23 |
| D. R. Jardine ....... | 1927 | 14 | 3 | 1,002 | 147 | 5 | 91.09 |
| D. C. S. Compton .... | 1947 | 50 | 8 | 3,816 | 246 | 18 | 90.85 |
| G. M. Turner ....... | 1982 | 16 | 3 | 1,171 | 311* | 5 | 90.07 |
| D. G. Bradman ...... | 1948 | 31 | 4 | 2,428 | 187 | 11 | 89.92 |
| Zaheer Abbas ....... | 1981 | 36 | 10 | 2,306 | 215* | 10 | 88.69 |
| K. S. Ranjitsinhji .... | 1900 | 40 | 5 | 3,065 | 275 | 11 | 87.57 |
| D. R. Jardine ....... | 1928 | 17 | 4 | 1,133 | 193 | 3 | 87.15 |
| W. R. Hammond .... | 1946 | 26 | 5 | 1,783 | 214 | 7 | 84.90 |
| D. G. Bradman ...... | 1934 | 27 | 3 | 2,020 | 304 | 7 | 84.16 |
| R. B. Kanhai ........ | 1975 | 22 | 9 | 1,073 | 178* | 3 | 82.53 |
| Mudassar Nazar ..... | 1982 | 16 | 6 | 825 | 211* | 4 | 82.50 |
| C. G. Greenidge ..... | 1984 | 16 | 3 | 1,069 | 223 | 4 | 82.23 |
| J. B. Hobbs ......... | 1928 | 38 | 7 | 2,542 | 200* | 12 | 82.00 |
| C. B. Fry ........... | 1903 | 40 | 7 | 2,683 | 234 | 9 | 81.30 |
| W. J. Edrich ........ | 1947 | 52 | 8 | 3,539 | 267* | 12 | 80.43 |

## HIGHEST AGGREGATES OUTSIDE ENGLAND

| | Season | I | NO | R | HI | 100s | Avge |
|---|---|---|---|---|---|---|---|
| *In Australia* | | | | | | | |
| D. G. Bradman ...... | 1928-29 | 24 | 6 | 1,690 | 340* | 7 | 93.88 |
| *In South Africa* | | | | | | | |
| J. R. Reid .......... | 1961-62 | 30 | 2 | 1,915 | 203 | 7 | 68.39 |
| *In West Indies* | | | | | | | |
| E. H. Hendren | 1929-30 | 18 | 5 | 1,765 | 254* | 6 | 135.76 |
| *In New Zealand* | | | | | | | |
| G. M. Turner ....... | 1975-76 | 20 | 4 | 1,244 | 177* | 5 | 77.75 |
| *In India* | | | | | | | |
| C. G. Borde ......... | 1964-65 | 28 | 3 | 1,604 | 168 | 6 | 64.16 |
| *In Pakistan* | | | | | | | |
| Saadat Ali .......... | 1983-84 | 27 | 1 | 1,649 | 208 | 4 | 63.42 |

*Note:* In more than one country, the following aggregates of over 2,000 runs have been recorded.

| | Season | I | NO | R | HI | 100s | Avge |
|---|---|---|---|---|---|---|---|
| M. Amarnath (P/I/WI) | 1982-83 | 34 | 6 | 2,234 | 207 | 9 | 79.78 |
| J. R. Reid (SA/A/NZ) | 1961-62 | 40 | 2 | 2,188 | 203 | 7 | 57.57 |
| S. M. Gavaskar (I/P) . | 1978-79 | 30 | 6 | 2,121 | 205 | 10 | 88.37 |
| R. B. Simpson (I/P/A/WI) ........ | 1964-65 | 34 | 4 | 2,063 | 201 | 8 | 68.76 |

## 1,000 RUNS IN MAY

Three batsmen have scored 1,000 runs in May, and four others – D. G. Bradman twice – have made 1,000 runs before June. Their innings-by-innings records are as follows:

| | *Runs* | *Avge* |
|---|---|---|
| W. G. Grace, May 9 to May 30, 1895 (22 days): | | |
| 13, 103, 18, 25, 288, 52, 257, 73*, 18, 169 | 1,016 | 112.88 |
| "W.G." was within two months of completing his 47th year. | | |
| W. R. Hammond, May 7 to May 31, 1927 (25 days): | | |
| 27, 135, 108, 128, 17, 11, 99, 187, 4, 30, 83, 7, 192, 14 | 1,042 | 74.42 |
| Hammond scored his 1,000th run on May 28, thus equalling "W.G.'s" record of 22 days. | | |
| C. Hallows, May 5 to May 31, 1928 (27 days): | | |
| 100, 101, 51*, 123, 101*, 22, 74, 104, 58, 34*, 232 | 1,000 | 125.00 |
| T. W. Hayward, April 16 to May 31, 1900: | | |
| 120*, 55, 108, 131*, 55, 193, 120, 5, 6, 3, 40, 146, 92 | 1,074 | 97.63 |
| D. G. Bradman, April 30 to May 31, 1930: | | |
| 236, 185*, 78, 9, 48*, 66, 4, 44, 252*, 32, 47* | 1,001 | 143.00 |
| On April 30 Bradman scored 75 not out. | | |
| D. G. Bradman, April 30 to May 31, 1938: | | |
| 258, 58, 137, 278, 2, 143, 145*, 5, 30* | 1,056 | 150.85 |
| Bradman scored 258 on April 30, and his 1,000th run on May 27. | | |
| W. J. Edrich, April 30 to May 31, 1938: | | |
| 104, 37, 115, 63, 20*, 182, 71, 31, 53*, 45, 15, 245, 0, 9, 20* | 1,010 | 84.16 |
| Edrich scored 21 not out on April 30. All his runs were scored at Lord's. | | |
| G. M. Turner, April 24 to May 31, 1973: | | |
| 41, 151*, 143, 85, 7, 8, 17*, 81, 13, 53, 44, 153*, 3, 2, 66*, 30, 10*, 111 | 1,018 | 78.30 |

## 1,000 RUNS IN TWO SEPARATE MONTHS

Only four batsmen, C. B. Fry, K. S. Ranjitsinhji, H. Sutcliffe and L. Hutton, have scored over 1,000 runs in each of two months in the same season. L. Hutton, by scoring 1,294 in June 1949, made more runs in a single month than anyone else. He also made 1,050 in August 1949.

## OUT HANDLED THE BALL

| | | |
|---|---|---|
| J. Grundy | MCC v Kent at Lord's | 1857 |
| G. Bennett | Kent v Sussex at Hove | 1872 |
| W. H. Scotton | Smokers v Non-Smokers at East Melbourne | 1886-87 |
| C. W. Wright | Nottinghamshire v Gloucestershire at Bristol | 1893 |
| E. Jones | South Australia v Victoria at Melbourne | 1894-95 |
| A. W. Nourse | South Africans v Sussex at Hove | 1907 |
| E. T. Benson | MCC v Auckland at Auckland | 1929-30 |
| A. W. Gilbertson | Otago v Auckland at Auckland | 1952-53 |
| W. R. Endean | South Africa v England at Cape Town | 1956-57 |
| P. J. Burge | Queensland v New South Wales at Sydney | 1958-59 |
| Dildar Awan | Services v Lahore at Lahore | 1959-60 |
| Mahmood-ul-Hasan | Karachi University v Railways-Quetta at Karachi | 1960-61 |
| Ali Raza | Karachi Greens v Hyderabad at Karachi | 1961-62 |
| Mohammad Yusuf | Rawalpindi v Peshawar at Peshawar | 1962-63 |
| A. Rees | Glamorgan v Middlesex at Lord's | 1965 |
| Pervez Akhtar | Multan v Karachi Greens at Sahiwal | 1971-72 |
| Javed Mirza | Railways v Punjab at Lahore | 1972-73 |
| R. G. Pollock | Eastern Province v Western Province at Cape Town | 1973-74 |

| | | |
|---|---|---|
| C. I. Dey | Northern Transvaal v Orange Free State at Bloemfontein | 1973-74 |
| Nasir Valika | Karachi Whites v National Bank at Karachi | 1974-75 |
| Haji Yousuf | National Bank v Railways at Lahore | 1974-75 |
| Masood-ul-Hasan | PIA v National Bank 'B' at Lyallpur | 1975-76 |
| D. K. Pearse | Natal v Western Province at Cape Town | 1978-79 |
| A. M. J. Hilditch | Australia v Pakistan at Perth | 1978-79 |
| Musleh-ud-Din | Railways v Lahore at Lahore | 1979-80 |
| Jalal-ud-Din | IDBP v Habib Bank at Bahawalpur | 1981-82 |
| Mohsin Khan | Pakistan v Australia at Karachi | 1982-83 |
| D. L. Haynes | West Indies v India at Bombay | 1983-84 |
| K. Azad | Delhi v Punjab at Amritsar | 1983-84 |
| Athar A. Khan | Allied Bank v HBFC at Sialkot | 1983-84 |
| A. Pandya | Saurashtra v Baroda at Baroda | 1984-85 |

## OUT OBSTRUCTING THE FIELD

| | | |
|---|---|---|
| C. A. Absolom | Cambridge University v Surrey at The Oval | 1868 |
| T. Straw | Worcestershire v Warwickshire at Worcester | 1899 |
| T. Straw | Worcestershire v Warwickshire at Birmingham | 1901 |
| J. P. Whiteside | Leicestershire v Lancashire at Leicester | 1901 |
| L. Hutton | England v South Africa at The Oval | 1951 |
| J. A. Hayes | Canterbury v Central Districts at Christchurch | 1954-55 |
| D. D. Deshpande | Madhya Pradesh v Uttar Pradesh at Benares | 1956-57 |
| M. Mehra | Railways v Delhi at Delhi | 1959-60 |
| K. Ibadulla | Warwickshire v Hampshire at Coventry | 1963 |
| Qaiser Khan | Dera Ismail Khan v Railways at Lahore | 1964-65 |
| Ijaz Ahmed | Lahore Greens v Lahore Blues at Lahore | 1973-74 |
| Qasim Feroze | Bahawalpur v Universities at Lahore | 1974-75 |
| T. Quirk | Northern Transvaal v Border at East London | 1978-79 |
| Mahmood Rashid | United Bank v Muslim Commercial Bank at Bahawalpur | 1981-82 |
| Arshad Ali | Sukkur v Quetta at Quetta | 1983-84 |
| H. Wasu | Vidarbha v Rajasthan at Akola | 1984-85 |

*Note:* This method of dismissal has occurred twice in the *John Player League:*

| | | |
|---|---|---|
| R. W. Tolchard | Leicestershire v Middlesex at Lord's | 1972 |
| D. J. S. Taylor | Somerset v Warwickshire at Birmingham | 1980 |

## OUT HIT THE BALL TWICE

| | | |
|---|---|---|
| H. E. Bull | MCC v Oxford University at Lord's | 1864 |
| H. R. J. Charlwood | Sussex v Surrey at Hove | 1872 |
| R. G. Barlow | North v South at Lord's | 1878 |
| P. S. Wimble | Transvaal v Griqualand West at Kimberley | 1892-93 |
| G. B. Nicholls | Somerset v Gloucestershire at Bristol | 1896 |
| A. A. Lilley | Warwickshire v Yorkshire at Birmingham | 1897 |
| J. H. King | Leicestershire v Surrey at The Oval | 1906 |
| A. P. Binns | Jamaica v British Guiana at Georgetown | 1956-57 |
| K. Bavanna | Andhra v Mysore at Guntur | 1963-64 |
| Zaheer Abbas | PIA 'A' v Karachi Blues at Karachi | 1969-70 |
| Anwar Miandad | IDBP v United Bank at Lahore | 1979-80 |
| Anwar Iqbal | Hyderabad v Sukkur at Hyderabad | 1983-84 |
| Iqtidar Ali | Allied Bank v Muslim Commercial Bank at Lahore | 1983-84 |
| Aziz Malik | Lahore Division v Faisalabad at Sialkot | 1984-85 |

# BOWLING AND FIELDING RECORDS

## FOUR WICKETS WITH CONSECUTIVE BALLS

| | | |
|---|---|---|
| J. Wells | Kent v Sussex at Brighton | 1862 |
| G. Ulyett | Lord Harris's XI v New South Wales at Sydney | 1878-79 |
| G. Nash | Lancashire v Somerset at Manchester | 1882 |

| | | |
|---|---|---|
| J. B. Hide | Sussex v MCC and Ground at Lord's | 1890 |
| F. J. Shacklock | Nottinghamshire v Somerset at Nottingham | 1893 |
| A. D. Downes | Otago v Auckland at Dunedin | 1893-94 |
| F. Martin | MCC and Ground v Derbyshire at Lord's | 1895 |
| A. W. Mold | Lancashire v Nottinghamshire at Nottingham | 1895 |
| W. Brearley† | Lancashire v Somerset at Manchester | 1905 |
| S. Haigh | MCC v Army XI at Pretoria | 1905-06 |
| A. E. Trott‡ | Middlesex v Somerset at Lord's | 1907 |
| F. A. Tarrant | Middlesex v Gloucestershire at Bristol | 1907 |
| A. Drake | Yorkshire v Derbyshire at Chesterfield | 1914 |
| S. G. Smith | Northamptonshire v Warwickshire at Birmingham | 1914 |
| H. A. Peach | Surrey v Sussex at The Oval | 1924 |
| A. F. Borland | Natal v Griqualand West at Kimberley | 1926-27 |
| J. E. H. Hooker† | New South Wales v Victoria at Sydney | 1928-29 |
| R. K. Tyldesley† | Lancashire v Derbyshire at Derby | 1929 |
| R. J. Crisp | Western Province v Griqualand West at Johannesburg | 1931-32 |
| R. J. Crisp | Western Province v Natal at Durban | 1933-34 |
| A. R. Gover | Surrey v Worcestershire at Worcester | 1935 |
| W. H. Copson | Derbyshire v Warwickshire at Derby | 1937 |
| W. A. Henderson | N.E. Transvaal v Orange Free State at Bloemfontein | 1937-38 |
| F. Ridgway | Kent v Derbyshire at Folkestone | 1951 |
| A. K. Walker§ | Nottinghamshire v Leicestershire at Leicester | 1956 |
| S. N. Mohol | Board of Control President's XI v Minister for Small Savings' XI at Poona | 1965-66 |
| P. I. Pocock | Surrey v Sussex at Eastbourne | 1972 |

† *Not all in the same innings.*

‡ *Trott achieved another hat-trick in the same innings of this, his benefit match.*

§ *Walker dismissed Firth with the last ball of the first innings and Lester, Tompkin and Smithson with the first three balls of the second innings, a feat without parallel.*

*Notes:* In their match with England at The Oval in 1863, Surrey lost four wickets in the course of a four-ball over from G. Bennett.

Sussex lost five wickets in the course of the final (six-ball) over of their match with Surrey at Eastbourne in 1972. P. I. Pocock, who had taken three wickets in his previous over, captured four more, taking in all seven wickets with eleven balls, a feat unique in first-class matches. (The eighth wicket fell to a run-out.)

P. G. H. Fender (Surrey) took six Middlesex wickets with eleven balls (including five with seven) at Lord's in 1927.

## HAT-TRICKS

### Double Hat-Trick

Besides Trott's performance, which is given in the preceding section, the following instances are recorded of players having performed the hat-trick twice in the same match, Rao doing so in the same innings.

| | | |
|---|---|---|
| A. Shaw | Nottinghamshire v Gloucestershire at Nottingham | 1884 |
| T. J. Matthews | Australia v South Africa at Manchester | 1912 |
| C. W. L. Parker | Gloucestershire v Middlesex at Bristol | 1924 |
| R. O. Jenkins | Worcestershire v Surrey at Worcester | 1949 |
| J. S. Rao | Services v Northern Punjab at Amritsar | 1963-64 |
| Amin Lakhani | Combined XI v Indians at Multan | 1978-79 |

### Five Wickets with Six Consecutive Balls

| | | |
|---|---|---|
| W. H. Copson | Derbyshire v Warwickshire at Derby | 1937 |
| W. A. Henderson | NE Transvaal v Orange Free State at Bloemfontein | 1937-38 |
| P. I. Pocock | Surrey v Sussex at Eastbourne | 1972 |

## Most Hat-Tricks

**Seven times:** D. V. P. Wright.
**Six times:** T. W. Goddard, C. W. L. Parker.
**Five times:** S. Haigh, V. W. C. Jupp, A. E. G. Rhodes, F. A. Tarrant.
**Four times:** R. G. Barlow, J. T. Hearne, J. C. Laker, G. A. R. Lock, G. G. Macaulay, T. J. Matthews, M. J. Procter, T. Richardson, F. R. Spofforth, F. S. Trueman.
**Three times:** W. M. Bradley, H. J. Butler, W. H. Copson, R. J. Crisp, J. W. H. T. Douglas, J. A. Flavell, A. P. Freeman, G. Giffen, K. Higgs, A. Hill, W. A. Humphries, R. D. Jackman, R. O. Jenkins, A. S. Kennedy, W. H. Lockwood, E. A. McDonald, T. L. Pritchard, J. S. Rao, A. Shaw, J. B. Statham, M. W. Tate, H. Trumble, D. Wilson, G. A. Wilson.

## Unusual Hat-Tricks

| | | |
|---|---|---|
| All "Stumped": | by W. H. Brain off C. L. Townsend, Gloucestershire v Somerset at Cheltenham | 1893 |
| All "Caught": | by G. J. Thompson off S. G. Smith, Northamptonshire v Warwickshire at Birmingham | 1914 |
| | by Cyril White off R. Beesly, Border v Griqualand West at Queenstown | 1946-47 |
| | by G. O. Dawkes (wicket-keeper) off H. L. Jackson, Derbyshire v Worcestershire at Kidderminster | 1958 |
| All "LBW": | H. Fisher, Yorkshire v Somerset at Sheffield | 1932 |
| | J. A. Flavell, Worcestershire v Lancashire at Manchester | 1963 |
| | M. J. Procter, Gloucestershire v Essex at Westcliff | 1972 |
| | B. J. Ikin, Griqualand West v OFS at Kimberley | 1973-74 |
| | M. J. Procter, Gloucestershire v Yorkshire at Cheltenham | 1979 |

# TEN WICKETS IN ONE INNINGS

| | *O* | *M* | *R* | | |
|---|---|---|---|---|---|
| E. Hinkly (Kent) | | | | v England at Lord's | 1848 |
| *J. Wisden (North) | | | | v South at Lord's | 1850 |
| V. E. Walker (England) | 43 | 17 | 74 | v Surrey at The Oval | 1859 |
| E. M. Grace (MCC) | 32.2 | 7 | 69 | v Gents of Kent at Canterbury | 1862 |
| V. E. Walker (Middlesex) | 44.2 | 5 | 104 | v Lancashire at Manchester | 1865 |
| G. Wootton (All England) | 31.3 | 9 | 54 | v Yorkshire at Sheffield | 1865 |
| W. Hickton (Lancashire) | 36.2 | 19 | 46 | v Hampshire at Manchester | 1870 |
| S. E. Butler (Oxford) | 24.1 | 11 | 38 | v Cambridge at Lord's | 1871 |
| James Lillywhite (South) | 60.2 | 22 | 129 | v North at Canterbury | 1872 |
| W. G. Grace (MCC) | 46.1 | 15 | 92 | v Kent at Canterbury | 1873 |
| A. Shaw (MCC) | 36.2 | 8 | 73 | v North at Lord's | 1874 |
| E. Barratt (Players) | 29 | 11 | 43 | v Australians at The Oval | 1878 |
| G. Giffen (Australian XI) | 26 | 10 | 66 | v The Rest at Sydney | 1883-84 |
| W. G. Grace (MCC) | 36.2 | 17 | 49 | v Oxford University at Oxford | 1886 |
| G. Burton (Middlesex) | 52.3 | 25 | 59 | v Surrey at The Oval | 1888 |
| †A. E. Moss (Canterbury) | 21.3 | 10 | 28 | v Wellington at Christchurch | 1889-90 |
| S. M. J. Woods (Cambridge U.) | 31 | 6 | 69 | v Thornton's XI at Cambridge | 1890 |
| T. Richardson (Surrey) | 15.3 | 3 | 45 | v Essex at The Oval | 1894 |
| H. Pickett (Essex) | 27 | 11 | 32 | v Leicestershire at Leyton | 1895 |
| E. J. Tyler (Somerset) | 34.3 | 15 | 49 | v Surrey at Taunton | 1895 |
| W. P. Howell (Australians) | 23.2 | 14 | 28 | v Surrey at The Oval | 1899 |
| C. H. G. Bland (Sussex) | 25.2 | 10 | 48 | v Kent at Tonbridge | 1899 |
| J. Briggs (Lancashire) | 28.5 | 7 | 55 | v Worcestershire at Manchester | 1900 |

| | O | M | R | | |
|---|---|---|---|---|---|
| A. E. Trott (Middlesex) | 14.2 | 5 | 42 | v Somerset at Taunton | 1900 |
| F. Hinds (A. B. St Hill's XI) | 19.1 | 6 | 36 | v Trinidad at Port-of-Spain | 1900-01 |
| A. Fielder (Players) | 24.5 | 1 | 90 | v Gentlemen at Lord's | 1906 |
| E. G. Dennett (Gloucestershire) | 19.4 | 7 | 40 | v Essex at Bristol | 1906 |
| A. E. E. Vogler (E. Province) | 12 | 2 | 26 | v Griqualand West at Johannesburg | 1906-07 |
| C. Blythe (Kent) | 16 | 7 | 30 | v Northamptonshire at Northampton | 1907 |
| A. Drake (Yorkshire) | 8.5 | 0 | 35 | v Somerset at Weston-super-Mare | 1914 |
| F. A. Tarrant (Maharaja of Cooch Behar's XI) | 35.4 | 4 | 90 | v Lord Willingdon's XI at Poona | 1918-19 |
| W. Bestwick (Derbyshire) | 19 | 2 | 40 | v Glamorgan at Cardiff | 1921 |
| A. A. Mailey (Australians) | 28.4 | 5 | 66 | v Gloucestershire at Cheltenham | 1921 |
| C. W. L. Parker (Glos.) | 40.3 | 13 | 79 | v Somerset at Bristol | 1921 |
| T. Rushby (Surrey) | 17.5 | 4 | 43 | v Somerset at Taunton | 1921 |
| J. C. White (Somerset) | 42.2 | 11 | 76 | v Worcestershire at Worcester | 1921 |
| G. C. Collins (Kent) | 19.3 | 4 | 65 | v Nottinghamshire at Dover | 1922 |
| H. Howell (Warwickshire) | 25.1 | 5 | 51 | v Yorkshire at Birmingham | 1923 |
| A. S. Kennedy (Players) | 22.4 | 10 | 37 | v Gentlemen at The Oval | 1927 |
| G. O. Allen (Middlesex) | 25.3 | 10 | 40 | v Lancashire at Lord's | 1929 |
| A. P. Freeman (Kent) | 42 | 9 | 131 | v Lancashire at Maidstone | 1929 |
| G. Geary (Leicestershire) | 16.2 | 8 | 18 | v Glamorgan at Pontypridd | 1929 |
| C. V. Grimmett (Australians) | 22.3 | 8 | 37 | v Yorkshire at Sheffield | 1930 |
| A. P. Freeman (Kent) | 30.4 | 8 | 53 | v Essex at Southend | 1930 |
| H. Verity (Yorkshire) | 18.4 | 6 | 36 | v Warwickshire at Leeds | 1931 |
| A. P. Freeman (Kent) | 36.1 | 9 | 79 | v Lancashire at Manchester | 1931 |
| V. W. C. Jupp (Northants) | 39 | 6 | 127 | v Kent at Tunbridge Wells | 1932 |
| H. Verity (Yorkshire) | 19.4 | 16 | 10 | v Nottinghamshire at Leeds | 1932 |
| T. W. Wall (South Australia) | 12.4 | 2 | 36 | v New South Wales at Sydney | 1932-33 |
| T. B. Mitchell (Derbyshire) | 19.1 | 4 | 64 | v Leicestershire at Leicester | 1935 |
| J. Mercer (Glamorgan) | 26 | 10 | 51 | v Worcestershire at Worcester | 1936 |
| T. W. Goddard (Glos.) | 28.4 | 4 | 113 | v Worcestershire at Cheltenham | 1937 |
| T. F. Smailes (Yorkshire) | 17.1 | 5 | 47 | v Derbyshire at Sheffield | 1939 |
| E. A. Watts (Surrey) | 24.1 | 8 | 67 | v Warwickshire at Birmingham | 1939 |
| *W. E. Hollies (Warwickshire) | 20.4 | 4 | 49 | v Nottinghamshire at Birmingham | 1946 |
| J. M. Sims (East) | 18.4 | 2 | 90 | v West at Kingston | 1948 |
| T. E. Bailey (Essex) | 39.4 | 9 | 90 | v Lancashire at Clacton | 1949 |
| J. K. Graveney (Glos.) | 18.4 | 2 | 66 | v Derbyshire at Chesterfield | 1949 |
| R. Berry (Lancashire) | 36.2 | 9 | 102 | v Worcestershire at Blackpool | 1953 |
| S. P. Gupte (Bombay) | 24.2 | 7 | 78 | v Combined XI at Bombay | 1954-55 |
| J. C. Laker (Surrey) | 46 | 18 | 88 | v Australians at The Oval | 1956 |
| J. C. Laker (England) | 51.2 | 23 | 53 | v Australia at Manchester | 1956 |
| G. A. R. Lock (Surrey) | 29.1 | 18 | 54 | v Kent at Blackheath | 1956 |
| K. Smales (Nottinghamshire) | 41.3 | 20 | 66 | v Gloucestershire at Stroud | 1956 |
| P. Chatterjee (Bengal) | 19 | 11 | 20 | v Assam at Jorhat | 1956-57 |
| J. D. Bannister (Warwickshire) | 23.3 | 11 | 41 | v Comb. Services at Birmingham | 1959 |
| A. J. G. Pearson (Cambridge University) | 30.3 | 8 | 78 | v Leicestershire at Loughborough | 1961 |
| N. I. Thomson (Sussex) | 34.2 | 19 | 49 | v Warwickshire at Worthing | 1964 |
| P. J. Allan (Queensland) | 15.6 | 3 | 61 | v Victoria at Melbourne | 1965-66 |
| I. J. Brayshaw (W. Australia) | 17.6 | 4 | 44 | v Victoria at Perth | 1967-68 |
| Shahid Mahmood (Karachi Whites) | 25 | 5 | 58 | v Khairpur at Karachi | 1969-70 |
| E. E. Hemmings (International XI) | 49.3 | 14 | 175 | v West Indies XI at Kingston | 1982-83 |

* *J. Wisden and W. E. Hollies achieved the feat without the direct assistance of a fielder. Wisden's ten were all bowled; Hollies bowled seven and had three leg-before-wicket.*

† *On debut in first-class cricket.*

## MOST WICKETS IN A MATCH

| | | | |
|---|---|---|---|
| 19-90 | J. C. Laker | England v Australia at Manchester | 1956 |
| 17-48 | C. Blythe | Kent v Northamptonshire at Northampton | 1907 |
| 17-50 | C. T. B. Turner | Australians v England XI at Hastings | 1888 |
| 17-54 | W. P. Howell | Australians v Western Province at Cape Town | 1902-03 |
| 17-56 | C. W. L. Parker | Gloucestershire v Essex at Gloucester | 1925 |
| 17-67 | A. P. Freeman | Kent v Sussex at Hove | 1922 |
| 17-89 | W. G. Grace | Gloucestershire v Nottinghamshire at Cheltenham | 1877 |
| 17-89 | F. C. L. Matthews | Nottinghamshire v Northants at Nottingham | 1923 |
| 17-91 | H. Dean | Lancashire v Yorkshire at Liverpool | 1913 |
| 17-91 | H. Verity | Yorkshire v Essex at Leyton | 1933 |
| 17-92 | A. P. Freeman | Kent v Warwickshire at Folkestone | 1932 |
| 17-103 | W. Mycroft | Derbyshire v Hampshire at Southampton | 1876 |
| 17-106 | G. R. Cox | Sussex v Warwickshire at Horsham | 1926 |
| 17-106 | T. W. Goddard | Gloucestershire v Kent at Bristol | 1939 |
| 17-119 | W. Mead | Essex v Hampshire at Southampton | 1895 |
| 17-137 | W. Brearley | Lancashire v Somerset at Manchester | 1905 |
| 17-159 | S. F. Barnes | England v South Africa at Johannesburg | 1913-14 |
| 17-201 | G. Giffen | South Australia v Victoria at Adelaide | 1885-86 |
| 17-212 | J. C. Clay | Glamorgan v Worcestershire at Swansea | 1937 |

*Notes:* H. A. Arkwright took eighteen wickets for 96 runs in a 12-a-side match for Gentlemen of MCC v Gentlemen of Kent at Canterbury in 1861.

W. Mead took seventeen wickets for 205 runs for Essex v Australians at Leyton in 1893, the year before Essex were raised to first-class status.

F. P. Fenner took seventeen wickets for Cambridge Town Club v University of Cambridge at Cambridge in 1844.

## OUTSTANDING ANALYSES

(Also see Ten Wickets in One Innings)

| | *O* | *M* | *R* | *W* | | |
|---|---|---|---|---|---|---|
| H. Verity (Yorkshire) | 19.4 | 16 | 10 | 10 | v Nottinghamshire at Leeds | 1932 |
| G. Elliott (Victoria) | 19 | 17 | 2 | 9 | v Tasmania at Launceston | 1857-58 |
| Ahad Khan (Railways) | 6.3 | 4 | 7 | 9 | v Dera Ismail Khan at Lahore | 1964-65 |
| J. C. Laker (England) | 14 | 12 | 2 | 8 | v The Rest at Bradford | 1950 |
| D. Shackleton (Hampshire) | 11.1 | 7 | 4 | 8 | v Somerset at Weston-super-Mare | 1955 |
| E. Peate (Yorkshire) | 16 | 11 | 5 | 8 | v Surrey at Holbeck | 1883 |
| F. R. Spofforth (Australians) | 8.3 | 6 | 3 | 7 | v England XI at Birmingham | 1884 |
| W. A. Henderson (N.E. Transvaal) | 9.3 | 7 | 4 | 7 | v Orange Free State at Bloemfontein | 1937-38 |
| Rajinder Goel (Haryana) | 7 | 4 | 4 | 7 | v Jammu and Kashmir at Chandigarh | 1977-78 |
| V. I. Smith (South Africans) | 4.5 | 3 | 1 | 6 | v Derbyshire at Derby | 1947 |
| S. Cosstick (Victoria) | 21.1 | 20 | 1 | 6 | v Tasmania at Melbourne | 1868-69 |
| Israr Ali (Bahawalpur) | 11 | 10 | 1 | 6 | v Dacca U. at Bahawalpur | 1957-58 |
| A. D. Pougher (MCC) | 3 | 3 | 0 | 5 | v Australians at Lord's | 1896 |
| G. R. Cox (Sussex) | 6 | 6 | 0 | 5 | v Somerset at Weston-super-Mare | 1921 |
| R. K. Tyldesley (Lancashire) | 5 | 5 | 0 | 5 | v Leicestershire at Manchester | 1924 |
| P. T. Mills (Gloucestershire) | 6.4 | 6 | 0 | 5 | v Somerset at Bristol | 1928 |

## SIXTEEN OR MORE WICKETS IN A DAY

| | | | |
|---|---|---|---|
| 17-48 | C. Blythe | Kent v Northamptonshire at Northampton | 1907 |
| 17-91 | H. Verity | Yorkshire v Essex at Leyton | 1933 |
| 17-106 | T. W. Goddard | Gloucestershire v Kent at Bristol | 1939 |
| 16-38 | T. Emmett | Yorkshire v Cambridgeshire at Hunslet | 1869 |
| 16-52 | J. Southerton | South v North at Lord's | 1875 |
| 16-69 | T. G. Wass | Nottinghamshire v Lancashire at Liverpool | 1906 |
| 16-38 | A. E. E. Vogler | E. Province v Griqualand West at Johannesburg | 1906-07 |
| 16-103 | T. G. Wass | Nottinghamshire v Essex at Nottingham | 1908 |
| 16-83 | J. C. White | Somerset v Worcestershire at Bath | 1919 |

## 200 OR MORE WICKETS IN A SEASON

| | *Season* | *O* | *M* | *R* | *W* | *Avge* |
|---|---|---|---|---|---|---|
| A. P. Freeman | 1928 | 1,976.1 | 423 | 5,489 | 304 | 18.05 |
| A. P. Freeman | 1933 | 2,039 | 651 | 4,549 | 298 | 15.26 |
| T. Richardson | 1895‡ | 1,690.1 | 463 | 4,170 | 290 | 14.37 |
| C. T. B. Turner** | 1888† | 2,427.2 | 1,127 | 3,307 | 283 | 11.68 |
| A. P. Freeman | 1931 | 1,618 | 360 | 4,307 | 276 | 15.60 |
| A. P. Freeman | 1930 | 1,914.3 | 472 | 4,632 | 275 | 16.84 |
| T. Richardson | 1897‡ | 1,603.4 | 495 | 3,945 | 273 | 14.45 |
| A. P. Freeman | 1929 | 1,670.5 | 381 | 4,879 | 267 | 18.27 |
| W. Rhodes | 1900 | 1,553 | 455 | 3,606 | 261 | 13.81 |
| J. T. Hearne | 1896 | 2,003.1 | 818 | 3,670 | 257 | 14.28 |
| A. P. Freeman | 1932 | 1,565.5 | 404 | 4,149 | 253 | 16.39 |
| W. Rhodes | 1901 | 1,565 | 505 | 3,797 | 251 | 15.12 |
| T. W. Goddard | 1937 | 1,478.1 | 359 | 4,158 | 248 | 16.76 |
| W. C. Smith | 1910 | 1,423.3 | 420 | 3,225 | 247 | 13.05 |
| T. Richardson | 1896‡ | 1,656.2 | 526 | 4,015 | 246 | 16.32 |
| A. E. Trott | 1899‡ | 1,772.4 | 587 | 4,086 | 239 | 17.09 |
| T. W. Goddard | 1947 | 1,451.2 | 344 | 4,119 | 238 | 17.30 |
| M. W. Tate | 1925 | 1,694.3 | 472 | 3,415 | 228 | 14.97 |
| J. T. Hearne | 1898‡ | 1,802.2 | 781 | 3,120 | 222 | 14.05 |
| C. W. L. Parker | 1925 | 1,512.3 | 478 | 3,311 | 222 | 14.91 |
| G. A. Lohmann | 1890‡ | 1,759.1 | 737 | 2,998 | 220 | 13.62 |
| M. W. Tate | 1923 | 1,608.5 | 331 | 3,061 | 219 | 13.97 |
| C. F. Root | 1925 | 1,493.2 | 416 | 3,770 | 219 | 17.21 |
| C. W. L. Parker | 1931 | 1,320.4 | 386 | 3,125 | 219 | 14.26 |
| H. Verity | 1936 | 1,289.3 | 463 | 2,847 | 216 | 13.18 |
| G. A. R. Lock | 1955 | 1,408.4 | 497 | 3,109 | 216 | 14.39 |
| C. Blythe | 1909 | 1,273.5 | 343 | 3,128 | 215 | 14.54 |
| E. Peate | 1882† | 1,853.1 | 868 | 2,466 | 214 | 11.52 |
| A. W. Mold | 1895‡ | 1,629 | 598 | 3,400 | 213 | 15.96 |
| W. Rhodes | 1902 | 1,306.3 | 405 | 2,801 | 213 | 13.15 |
| C. W. L. Parker | 1926 | 1,739.5 | 556 | 3,920 | 213 | 18.40 |
| J. T. Hearne | 1893‡ | 1,741.4 | 667 | 3,492 | 212 | 16.47 |
| A. P. Freeman | 1935 | 1,503.2 | 320 | 4,562 | 212 | 21.51 |
| G. A. R. Lock | 1957 | 1,194.1 | 449 | 2,550 | 212 | 12.02 |
| A. E. Trott | 1900 | 1,547.1 | 363 | 4,923 | 211 | 23.33 |
| G. G. Macaulay | 1925 | 1,338.2 | 307 | 3,268 | 211 | 15.48 |
| H. Verity | 1935 | 1,279.2 | 453 | 3,032 | 211 | 14.36 |
| J. Southerton | 1870† | 1,876.5 | 709 | 3,074 | 210 | 14.63 |
| G. A. Lohmann | 1888† | 1,649.1 | 783 | 2,280 | 209 | 10.90 |
| C. H. Parkin | 1923 | 1,356.2 | 356 | 3,543 | 209 | 16.94 |
| G. H. Hirst | 1906 | 1,306.1 | 271 | 3,434 | 208 | 16.50 |
| F. R. Spofforth | 1884† | 1,577 | 653 | 2,774 | 207 | 13.25 |
| A. W. Mold | 1894‡ | 1,288.3 | 456 | 2,548 | 207 | 12.30 |
| C. W. L. Parker | 1922 | 1,294.5 | 445 | 2,712 | 206 | 13.16 |

| | Season | O | M | R | W | Avge |
|---|---|---|---|---|---|---|
| A. S. Kennedy ........ | 1922 | 1,346.4 | 366 | 3,444 | 205 | 16.80 |
| M. W. Tate ........... | 1924 | 1,469.5 | 465 | 2,818 | 205 | 13.74 |
| E. A. McDonald ....... | 1925 | 1,249.4 | 282 | 3,828 | 205 | 18.67 |
| A. P. Freeman ........ | 1934 | 1,744.4 | 440 | 4,753 | 205 | 23.18 |
| C. W. L. Parker ....... | 1924 | 1,303.5 | 411 | 2,913 | 204 | 14.27 |
| G. A. Lohmann ....... | 1889‡ | 1,614.1 | 646 | 2,714 | 202 | 13.43 |
| H. Verity ............. | 1937 | 1,386.2 | 487 | 3,168 | 202 | 15.68 |
| A. Shaw ............. | 1878† | 2,630 | 1,586 | 2,203 | 201 | 10.96 |
| E. G. Dennett ......... | 1907 | 1,216.2 | 305 | 3,227 | 201 | 16.05 |
| A. R. Gover .......... | 1937 | 1,219.4 | 191 | 3,816 | 201 | 18.98 |
| C. H. Parkin .......... | 1924 | 1,162.5 | 357 | 2,735 | 200 | 13.67 |
| T. W. Goddard ........ | 1935 | 1,553 | 384 | 4,073 | 200 | 20.36 |
| A. R. Gover .......... | 1936 | 1,159.2 | 185 | 3,547 | 200 | 17.73 |
| T. W. Goddard ........ | 1939§ | 819 | 139 | 2,973 | 200 | 14.86 |
| R. Appleyard ......... | 1951 | 1,313.2 | 391 | 2,829 | 200 | 14.14 |

† *Indicates 4-ball overs;* ‡ *5-ball overs. All others were 6-ball overs except* § *8-ball overs.*
** *Exclusive of matches not reckoned as first-class.*

*Notes:* In four consecutive seasons (1928-31), A. P. Freeman took 1,122 wickets, and in eight consecutive seasons (1928-35), 2,090 wickets. In each of these eight seasons he took over 200 wickets.

T. Richardson took 1,005 wickets in four consecutive seasons (1894-97).

In 1896, J. T. Hearne took his 100th wicket as early as June 12. In 1931, C. W. L. Parker did the same and A. P. Freeman obtained his 100th wicket a day later.

C. T. B. Turner is the only bowler to take over 100 wickets in first-class matches in a season in Australia – 106 wickets in twelve matches, 1887-88.

## MOST WICKETS IN EACH SEASON

### Since Reduction of Championship Matches in 1969

| Season | | O | M | R | W | Avge |
|---|---|---|---|---|---|---|
| 1969 | R. M. H. Cottam ...... | 989.1 | 252 | 2,294 | 109 | 21.04 |
| 1970 | D. J. Shepherd ......... | 1,123.3 | 420 | 2,031 | 106 | 19.16 |
| 1971 | L. R. Gibbs ........... | 1,024.1 | 295 | 2,475 | 131 | 18.89 |
| 1972 | T. W. Cartwright ...... | 863 | 373 | 1,827 | 98 | 18.64 |
| | B. Stead .............. | 747 | 173 | 1,998 | 98 | 20.38 |
| 1973 | B. S. Bedi ............ | 864.2 | 307 | 1,884 | 105 | 17.94 |
| 1974 | A. M. E. Roberts ...... | 727.4 | 198 | 1,621 | 119 | 13.62 |
| 1975 | P. G. Lee ............ | 799.5 | 199 | 2,067 | 112 | 18.45 |
| 1976 | G. A. Cope .......... | 916.4 | 288 | 2,245 | 93 | 24.13 |
| 1977 | M. J. Procter ......... | 777.3 | 226 | 1,967 | 109 | 18.04 |
| 1978 | D. L. Underwood ...... | 815.1 | 359 | 1,594 | 110 | 14.49 |
| 1979 | J. K. Lever .......... | 700 | 166 | 1,834 | 106 | 17.30 |
| | D. L. Underwood ...... | 799.2 | 335 | 1,575 | 106 | 14.85 |
| 1980 | R. D. Jackman ........ | 746.2 | 220 | 1,864 | 121 | 15.40 |
| 1981 | R. J. Hadlee .......... | 708.4 | 231 | 1,564 | 105 | 14.89 |
| 1982 | M. D. Marshall ........ | 822 | 225 | 2,108 | 134 | 15.73 |
| 1983 | J. K. Lever .......... | 569 | 137 | 1,726 | 106 | 16.28 |
| | D. L. Underwood ...... | 936.3 | 358 | 2,044 | 106 | 19.28 |
| 1984 | R. J. Hadlee .......... | 772.2 | 248 | 1,645 | 117 | 14.05 |
| 1985 | N. V. Radford ........ | 779.4 | 130 | 2,493 | 101 | 24.68 |

*Note:* D. L. Underwood has taken 100 wickets 5 times and J. K. Lever 4 times in this period.

## 1,500 WICKETS OR MORE IN A CAREER

| | *Career* | *W* | *R* | *Avge* |
|---|---|---|---|---|
| W. Rhodes | 1898-1930 | 4,187 | 69,993 | 16.71 |
| A. P. Freeman | 1914-36 | 3,776 | 69,577 | 18.42 |
| C. W. L. Parker | 1903-35 | 3,278 | 63,821 | 19.46 |
| J. T. Hearne | 1888-1923 | 3,061 | 54,342 | 17.75 |
| T. W. Goddard | 1922-52 | 2,979 | 59,116 | 19.84 |
| †W. G. Grace | 1865-1908 | 2,876 | 51,545 | 17.92 |
| A. S. Kennedy | 1907-36 | 2,874 | 61,044 | 21.24 |
| D. Shackleton | 1948-69 | 2,857 | 53,303 | 18.65 |
| G. A. R. Lock | 1946-71 | 2,844 | 54,710 | 19.23 |
| F. J. Titmus | 1949-82 | 2,830 | 63,313 | 22.37 |
| M. W. Tate | 1912-37 | 2,784 | 50,567 | 18.16 |
| G. H. Hirst | 1891-1929 | 2,739 | 51,300 | 18.72 |
| C. Blythe | 1899-1914 | 2,506 | 42,136 | 16.81 |
| W. E. Astill | 1906-39 | 2,431 | 57,781 | 23.76 |
| D. L. Underwood | 1963-85 | 2,368 | 47,327 | 19.98 |
| J. C. White | 1909-37 | 2,356 | 43,759 | 18.57 |
| W. E. Hollies | 1932-57 | 2,323 | 48,656 | 20.94 |
| F. S. Trueman | 1949-69 | 2,304 | 42,154 | 18.29 |
| J. B. Statham | 1950-68 | 2,260 | 36,995 | 16.36 |
| R. T. D. Perks | 1930-55 | 2,233 | 53,770 | 24.07 |
| J. Briggs | 1879-1900 | 2,221 | 35,390 | 15.93 |
| D. J. Shepherd | 1950-72 | 2,218 | 47,298 | 21.32 |
| E. G. Dennett | 1903-26 | 2,147 | 42,568 | 19.82 |
| T. Richardson | 1892-1905 | 2,105 | 38,794 | 18.42 |
| T. E. Bailey | 1945-67 | 2,082 | 48,170 | 23.13 |
| R. Illingworth | 1951-83 | 2,072 | 42,023 | 20.28 |
| F. E. Woolley | 1906-38 | 2,068 | 41,066 | 19.85 |
| G. Geary | 1912-38 | 2,063 | 41,339 | 20.03 |
| D. V. P. Wright | 1932-57 | 2,056 | 49,305 | 23.98 |
| J. Newman | 1906-30 | 2,032 | 51,211 | 25.20 |
| A. Shaw | 1864-97 | 2,021 | 24,496 | 12.12 |
| S. Haigh | 1895-1913 | 2,012 | 32,091 | 15.94 |
| H. Verity | 1930-39 | 1,956 | 29,146 | 14.90 |
| J. C. Laker | 1946-65 | 1,944 | 35,789 | 18.40 |
| N. Gifford | 1960-85 | 1,935 | 45,097 | 23.30 |
| W. Attewell | 1881-1900 | 1,932 | 29,745 | 15.39 |
| A. V. Bedser | 1939-60 | 1,924 | 39,281 | 20.41 |
| W. Mead | 1892-1913 | 1,916 | 36,388 | 18.99 |
| A. E. Relf | 1900-21 | 1,897 | 39,724 | 20.94 |
| P. G. H. Fender | 1910-36 | 1,894 | 47,457 | 25.05 |
| J. W. H. T. Douglas | 1901-30 | 1,893 | 44,159 | 23.32 |
| J. H. Wardle | 1946-58 | 1,846 | 35,027 | 18.97 |
| G. R. Cox | 1895-1928 | 1,843 | 42,138 | 22.86 |
| M. S. Nichols | 1924-39 | 1,841 | 39,845 | 21.64 |
| J. W. Hearne | 1909-36 | 1,839 | 44,927 | 24.43 |
| G. G. Macaulay | 1920-35 | 1,837 | 32,440 | 17.65 |
| J. B. Mortimore | 1950-75 | 1,807 | 41,904 | 23.18 |
| G. A. Lohmann | 1884-98 | 1,805 | 25,110 | 13.91 |
| C. Cook | 1946-64 | 1,782 | 36,578 | 20.52 |
| R. Peel | 1882-99 | 1,754 | 28,446 | 16.21 |
| H. L. Jackson | 1947-63 | 1,733 | 30,101 | 17.36 |
| T. P. B. Smith | 1929-52 | 1,697 | 45,059 | 26.55 |
| J. Southerton | 1854-79 | 1,680 | 24,257 | 14.43 |
| A. E. Trott | 1892-1911 | 1,674 | 35,316 | 21.09 |
| A. W. Mold | 1889-1901 | 1,673 | 26,012 | 15.54 |
| T. G. Wass | 1896-1920 | 1,666 | 34,091 | 20.46 |
| V. W. C. Jupp | 1909-38 | 1,658 | 38,166 | 23.01 |
| C. Gladwin | 1939-58 | 1,653 | 30,265 | 18.30 |

| | *Career* | *W* | *R* | *Avge* |
|---|---|---|---|---|
| W. E. Bowes | 1928-47 | 1,639 | 27,470 | 16.76 |
| A. W. Wellard | 1927-50 | 1,614 | 39,302 | 24.35 |
| N. I. Thomson | 1952-72 | 1,597 | 32,866 | 20.57 |
| J. Mercer | 1919-47 | 1,593 | 37,302 | 23.41 |
| G. J. Thompson | 1897-1922 | 1,591 | 30,060 | 18.89 |
| T. Emmett | 1866-88 | 1,582 | 21,147 | 13.36 |
| J. M. Sims | 1929-53 | 1,582 | 39,401 | 24.90 |
| P. I. Pocock | 1964-85 | 1,577 | 41,553 | 26.34 |
| Intikhab Alam | 1957-82 | 1,571 | 43,472 | 27.67 |
| B. S. Bedi | 1961-82 | 1,560 | 33,843 | 21.69 |
| W. Voce | 1927-52 | 1,558 | 35,961 | 23.08 |
| A. R. Gover | 1928-48 | 1,555 | 36,753 | 23.63 |
| J. K. Lever | 1967-85 | 1,549 | 36,827 | 23.77 |
| T. W. Cartwright | 1952-77 | 1,536 | 29,357 | 19.11 |
| K. Higgs | 1958-82 | 1,531 | 36,196 | 23.64 |
| James Langridge | 1924-53 | 1,530 | 34,524 | 22.56 |
| J. A. Flavell | 1949-67 | 1,529 | 32,847 | 21.48 |
| C. F. Root | 1910-33 | 1,512 | 31,933 | 21.11 |
| R. K. Tyldesley | 1919-35 | 1,509 | 25,980 | 17.21 |

† *In recent years some statisticians have removed from W. G. Grace's record a number of matches which they consider not to have been first-class. The above figures are those which became universally accepted upon appearance in W. G. Grace's obituary in the* Wisden *of 1916. Some works of reference give his career record as being 2,809–50,999–18.15. These figures also appeared in the 1981 edition of* Wisden.

## 100 WICKETS IN AN ENGLISH SEASON EIGHT TIMES OR MORE

**23 times:** W. Rhodes 200 wkts (3).

**20 times:** D. Shackleton.

**17 times:** A. P. Freeman 300 wkts (1), 200 wkts (7).

**16 times:** T. W. Goddard 200 wkts (4), C. W. L. Parker 200 wkts (5), R. T. D. Perks, F. J. Titmus.

**15 times:** J. T. Hearne 200 wkts (3), G. H. Hirst 200 wkts (1), A. S. Kennedy 200 wkts (1).

**14 times:** C. Blythe 200 wkts (1), W. E. Hollies, G. A. R. Lock 200 wkts (2), M. W. Tate 200 wkts (3), J. C White.

**13 times:** J. B. Statham.

**12 times:** J. Briggs, E. G. Dennett 200 wkts (1), C. Gladwin, D. J. Shepherd, N. I. Thomson, F. S. Trueman.

**11 times:** A. V. Bedser, G. Geary, S. Haigh, J. C. Laker, M. S. Nichols, A. E. Relf.

**10 times:** W. Attewell, W. G. Grace, R. Illingworth, H. L. Jackson, V. W. C. Jupp, G. G. Macaulay 200 wkts (1), W. Mead, T. B. Mitchell, T. Richardson 200 wkts (3), R. K. Tyldesley, D. L. Underwood, J. H. Wardle, T. G. Wass, D. V. P. Wright.

**9 times:** W. E. Astill, T. E. Bailey, W. E. Bowes, C. Cook, R. Howorth, J. Mercer, A. W. Mold 200 wkts (2), J. Newman, C. F. Root 200 wkts (1), A. Shaw 200 wkts (1), J. Southerton 200 wkts (1), H. Verity 200 wkts (3).

**8 times:** T. W. Cartwright, H. Dean, J. A. Flavell, A. R. Gover 200 wkts (2), H. Larwood, G. A. Lohmann 200 wkts (3), R. Peel, J. M. Sims, F. A. Tarrant, R. Tattersall, G. J. Thompson, G. E. Tribe, A. W. Wellard, F. E. Woolley, J. A. Young.

## 100 WICKETS IN A SEASON OVERSEAS

| *W* | | *Season* | *Country* | *R* | *Avge* |
|---|---|---|---|---|---|
| 116 | M. W. Tate | 1926-27 | India | 1,599 | 13.78 |
| 106 | C. T. B. Turner | 1887-88 | Australia | 1,441 | 13.59 |
| 106 | R. Benaud | 1957-58 | South Africa | 2,056 | 19.39 |
| 104 | S. F. Barnes | 1913-14 | South Africa | 1,117 | 10.74 |
| 103 | Abdul Qadir | 1982-83 | Pakistan | 2,367 | 22.98 |

# ALL-ROUND CRICKET

## 20,000 RUNS AND 2,000 WICKETS IN A CAREER

| | *Career* | *R* | *Avge* | *W* | *Avge* | *'Doubles'* |
|---|---|---|---|---|---|---|
| W. E. Astill ....... | 1906-39 | 22,726 | 22.54 | 2,431 | 23.76 | 9 |
| T. E. Bailey ....... | 1945-67 | 28,642 | 33.42 | 2,082 | 23.13 | 8 |
| W. G. Grace ...... | 1865-1908 | 54,896 | 39.55 | 2,876 | 17.99 | 8 |
| G. H. Hirst ....... | 1891-1929 | 36,323 | 34.13 | 2,739 | 18.72 | 14 |
| R. Illingworth ...... | 1951-83 | 24,134 | 28.06 | 2,072 | 20.28 | 6 |
| W. Rhodes ........ | 1898-1930 | 39,802 | 30.83 | 4,187 | 16.71 | 16 |
| M. W. Tate ....... | 1912-37 | 21,717 | 25.01 | 2,784 | 18.16 | 8 |
| F. J. Titmus ....... | 1949-82 | 21,588 | 23.11 | 2,830 | 22.37 | 8 |
| F. E. Woolley ...... | 1906-38 | 58,969 | 40.75 | 2,068 | 19.85 | 8 |

# THE DOUBLE

## 2,000 RUNS AND 200 WICKETS IN A SEASON

1906 G. H. Hirst 2,385 runs and 208 wickets

## 3,000 RUNS AND 100 WICKETS IN A SEASON

1937 J. H. Parks 3,003 runs and 101 wickets

## 2,000 RUNS AND 100 WICKETS IN A SEASON

| | *Season* | *R* | *W* |
|---|---|---|---|
| W. G. Grace ..... | 1873 | 2,139 | 106 |
| W. G. Grace ..... | 1876 | 2,622 | 129 |
| C. L. Townsend ... | 1899 | 2,440 | 101 |
| G. L. Jessop ...... | 1900 | 2,210 | 104 |
| G. H. Hirst ...... | 1904 | 2,501 | 132 |
| G. H. Hirst ...... | 1905 | 2,266 | 110 |
| W. Rhodes ....... | 1909 | 2,094 | 141 |
| W. Rhodes ....... | 1911 | 2,261 | 117 |
| F. A. Tarrant ..... | 1911 | 2,030 | 111 |
| J. W. Hearne ..... | 1913 | 2,036 | 124 |
| J. W. Hearne ..... | 1914 | 2,116 | 123 |
| F. E. Woolley ..... | 1914 | 2,272 | 125 |
| J. W. Hearne ..... | 1920 | 2,148 | 142 |
| V. W. C. Jupp .... | 1921 | 2,169 | 121 |
| F. E. Woolley ..... | 1921 | 2,101 | 167 |
| F. E. Woolley ..... | 1922 | 2,022 | 163 |
| F. E. Woolley ..... | 1923 | 2,091 | 101 |
| L. F. Townsend ... | 1933 | 2,268 | 100 |
| D. E. Davies ...... | 1937 | 2,012 | 103 |
| James Langridge .. | 1937 | 2,082 | 101 |
| T E Bailey ....... | 1959 | 2,011 | 100 |

## 1,000 RUNS AND 200 WICKETS IN A SEASON

| | *Season* | *R* | *W* |
|---|---|---|---|
| A. E. Trott ....... | 1899 | 1,175 | 239 |
| A. E. Trott ....... | 1900 | 1,337 | 211 |
| A. S. Kennedy .... | 1922 | 1,129 | 205 |
| M. W. Tate ....... | 1923 | 1,168 | 219 |
| M. W. Tate ....... | 1924 | 1,419 | 205 |
| M. W. Tate ....... | 1925 | 1,290 | 228 |

The double feat of scoring 1,000 runs and taking 100 wickets in one season of first-class cricket has been accomplished as follows:

**Sixteen times:** W. Rhodes.

**Fourteen times:** G. H. Hirst.

**Ten times:** V. W. C. Jupp.

**Nine times:** W. E. Astill.

**Eight times:** T. E. Bailey, W. G. Grace, M. S. Nichols, A. E. Relf, F. A. Tarrant, M. W. Tate, F. J. Titmus, F. E. Woolley.

**Seven times:** G. E. Tribe.

**Six times:** P. G. H. Fender, R. Illingworth, James Langridge.

**Five times:** J. W. H. T. Douglas, J. W. Hearne, A. S. Kennedy, J. Newman.

**Four times:** E. G. Arnold, J. Gunn, R. Kilner, B. R. Knight.

**Three times:** W. W. Armstrong (Australians), L. C. Braund, G. Giffen (Australians), N. E. Haig, R. Howorth, C. B. Llewellyn, J. B. Mortimore, Ray Smith, S. G. Smith, L. F. Townsend, A. W. Wellard.

*Note:* R. J. Hadlee in 1984 was the first player to perform the feat since the reduction of County

Championship matches. A complete list of those performing the feat before then will be found on p. 202 of the 1982 *Wisden*.

## WICKET-KEEPERS DOUBLE

| | Season | R | D |
|---|---|---|---|
| L. E. G. Ames | 1928 | 1,919 | 121 |
| L. E. G. Ames | 1929 | 1,795 | 127 |
| L. E. G. Ames | 1932 | 2,482 | 100 |
| J. T. Murray | 1957 | 1,025 | 104 |

## 1,000 RUNS AND 50 WICKETS IN A SEASON

### Since Reduction of Championship Matches in 1969

| Season | | R | Avge | W | Avge |
|---|---|---|---|---|---|
| 1969 | A. W. Greig | 1,130 | 27.56 | 69 | 23.60 |
| | Mushtaq Mohammad | 1,831 | 59.06 | 78 | 24.38 |
| | G. S. Sobers | 1,023 | 42.62 | 54 | 24.42 |
| 1970 | A. W. Greig | 1,008 | 24.00 | 59 | 27.69 |
| | Mushtaq Mohammad | 1,482 | 36.14 | 58 | 28.50 |
| | G. S. Sobers | 1,742 | 75.73 | 64 | 24.06 |
| | P. M. Walker | 1,049 | 24.39 | 60 | 26.65 |
| 1971 | M. A. Buss | 1,337 | 31.83 | 62 | 26.59 |
| | A. W. Greig | 1,242 | 27.00 | 77 | 29.07 |
| | R. A. Hutton | 1,009 | 31.53 | 80 | 20.35 |
| | Mushtaq Mohammad | 1,660 | 33.87 | 52 | 27.25 |
| | M. J. Procter | 1,786 | 45.79 | 65 | 18.95 |
| | G. S. Sobers | 1,485 | 46.40 | 53 | 30.96 |
| 1972 | K. D. Boyce | 1,023 | 30.08 | 82 | 20.20 |
| | Mushtaq Mohammad | 1,949 | 59.06 | 57 | 19.82 |
| | M. J. Procter | 1,219 | 40.63 | 58 | 16.55 |
| 1974 | Imran Khan | 1,016 | 36.28 | 60 | 30.13 |
| 1975 | A. W. Greig | 1,699 | 47.19 | 56 | 33.41 |
| | C. E. B. Rice | 1,155 | 33.00 | 53 | 25.98 |
| 1976 | I. T. Botham | 1,022 | 34.06 | 66 | 28.48 |
| | Imran Khan | 1,092 | 40.44 | 65 | 23.41 |
| | M. J. Procter | 1,209 | 34.54 | 68 | 28.05 |
| 1977 | C. E. B. Rice | 1,300 | 35.13 | 50 | 22.26 |
| 1978 | M. J. Procter | 1,655 | 50.15 | 69 | 23.89 |
| 1979 | J. R. T. Barclay | 1,093 | 32.14 | 52 | 24.03 |
| | M. J. Procter | 1,241 | 38.78 | 81 | 18.91 |
| | C. E. B. Rice | 1,297 | 41.83 | 58 | 19.63 |
| | P. Willey | 1,109 | 41.07 | 52 | 32.63 |
| 1980 | M. J. Procter | 1,081 | 34.87 | 51 | 18.25 |
| 1981 | C. E. B. Rice | 1,462 | 56.23 | 65 | 19.20 |
| 1982 | I. T. Botham | 1,241 | 44.32 | 66 | 22.98 |
| | R. C. Ontong | 1,204 | 31.68 | 64 | 32.17 |
| | D. N. Patel | 1,104 | 26.92 | 50 | 30.62 |
| | P. Willey | 1,783 | 50.94 | 51 | 26.88 |
| 1983 | R. C. Ontong | 1,310 | 38.52 | 56 | 36.66 |
| | J. N. Shepherd | 1,025 | 36.60 | 67 | 30.55 |
| 1984 | N. G. Cowley | 1,042 | 30.64 | 56 | 31.76 |
| | R. J. Hadlee | 1,179 | 51.26 | 117 | 14.05 |
| | V. J. Marks | 1,262 | 52.58 | 86 | 25.96 |
| | R. C. Ontong | 1,320 | 35.67 | 74 | 29.12 |
| | D. N. Patel | 1,348 | 33.70 | 61 | 33.81 |
| | C. M. Wells | 1,389 | 43.40 | 59 | 23.66 |
| 1985 | R. C. Ontong | 1,121 | 48.73 | 64 | 27.76 |

## HUNDRED AND HAT-TRICK

W. G. Grace, MCC v Kent at Canterbury; 123, five for 82, and six for 47 including hat-trick (12-a-side) .......... 1874
G. Giffen, Australians v Lancashire at Manchester; 13, 113, and six for 55 including hat-trick .......... 1884
W. E. Roller, Surrey v Sussex at The Oval; 204, four for 28 including hat-trick, and two for 16. (Unique instance of 200 and hat-trick.) .......... 1885
W. B. Burns, Worcestershire v Gloucestershire at Worcester; 102*, three for 56, including hat-trick, and two for 21 .......... 1913
V. W. C. Jupp, Sussex v Essex at Colchester; 102, six for 61, including hat-trick, and six for 78 .......... 1921
R. E. S. Wyatt, MCC v Ceylon at Colombo; 124 and five for 39 including hat-trick. 1926-27
L. N. Constantine, West Indians v Northamptonshire at Northampton; seven for 45, including hat-trick, 107 (five 6s), and six for 67 .......... 1928
D. E. Davies, Glamorgan v Leicestershire at Leicester; 139, four for 27, and three for 31 including hat-trick .......... 1937
V. M. Merchant, Dr C. R. Pereira's XI v Sir Homi Mehta's XI at Bombay; 1, 142, three for 31 including hat-trick, and no wicket for 17 .......... 1946-47
M. J. Procter, Gloucestershire v Essex at Westcliff-on-Sea; 51, 102, three for 43, and five for 30 including hat-trick (all lbw) .......... 1972
M. J. Procter, Gloucestershire v Leicestershire at Bristol; 122, no wkt for 32, and seven for 26 including hat-trick .......... 1979

## HUNDRED AND TEN WICKETS IN ONE INNINGS

V. E. Walker, England v Surrey at The Oval; ten for 74, four for 17, 20* and 108. 1859
E. M. Grace, MCC v Gentlemen of Kent at Canterbury; five for 77, ten for 69, and 192* .......... 1862
W. G. Grace, MCC v Oxford University at Oxford; two for 60, ten for 49, and 104. 1886
F. A. Tarrant, Maharaja of Cooch Behar's XI v Lord Willingdon's XI at Poona; ten for 90, one for 22, 182* and 8* .......... 1918-19

## HUNDRED IN EACH INNINGS AND FIVE WICKETS TWICE

G. H. Hirst, Yorkshire v Somerset at Bath; six for 70, five for 45, 111 and 117*. 1906

## WICKET-KEEPING RECORDS

## MOST DISMISSALS IN A CAREER

| | *Ct* | *St* | *Total* |
|---|---|---|---|
| R. W. Taylor (1960-84) | 1,471 | 175 | 1,646 |
| J. T. Murray (1952-75) | 1,270 | 257 | 1,527 |
| H. Strudwick (1902-27) | 1,215 | 253 | 1,468 |
| A. P. E. Knott (1965-85) | 1,211 | 133 | 1,344 |
| F. H. Huish (1895-1914) | 952 | 376 | 1,328 |
| D. Hunter (1889-1909) | 955 | 372 | 1,327 |
| B. Taylor (1949-73) | 1,082 | 212 | 1,294 |
| H. R. Butt (1890-1912) | 971 | 291 | 1,262 |
| J. H. Board (1891-1915) | 852 | 354 | 1,206 |
| H. Elliott (1920-47) | 904 | 302 | 1,206 |
| J. M. Parks (1949-76) | 1,089 | 93 | 1,182 |
| R. Booth (1951-70) | 946 | 176 | 1,122 |
| L. E. G. Ames (1926-51) | 698 | 415 | 1,113 |
| G. Duckworth (1923-47) | 751 | 339 | 1,090 |
| H. W. Stephenson (1948-64) | 752 | 332 | 1,084 |

| | *Ct* | *St* | *Total* |
|---|---|---|---|
| J. G. Binks (1955-69) | 895 | 176 | 1,071 |
| T. G. Evans (1939-69) | 816 | 250 | 1,066 |
| A. Long (1960-80) | 922 | 124 | 1,046 |
| G. O. Dawkes (1937-61) | 896 | 146 | 1,042 |
| R. W. Tolchard (1965-83) | 912 | 125 | 1,037 |
| W. L. Cornford (1921-47) | 656 | 344 | 1,000 |

## 100 OR MORE DISMISSALS IN A SEASON

| | | |
|---|---|---|
| 127 (79ct, 48st) | L. E. G. Ames, Kent | 1929 |
| 121 (69ct, 52st) | L. E. G. Ames, Kent | 1928 |
| 110 (62ct, 48st) | H. Yarnold, Worcestershire | 1949 |
| 107 (77ct, 30st) | G. Duckworth, Lancashire | 1928 |
| 107 (96ct, 11st) | J. G. Binks, Yorkshire | 1960 |
| 104 (82ct, 22st) | J. T. Murray, Middlesex | 1957 |
| 102 (70ct, 32st) | F. H. Huish, Kent | 1913 |
| 102 (95ct, 7st) | J. T. Murray, Middlesex | 1960 |
| 101 (85ct, 16st) | R. Booth, Worcestershire | 1960 |
| 100 (62ct, 38st) | F. H. Huish, Kent | 1911 |
| 100 (36ct, 64st) | L. E. G. Ames, Kent | 1932 |
| 100 (91ct, 9st) | R. Booth, Worcestershire | 1964 |

## TEN OR MORE DISMISSALS IN A MATCH

| | | | |
|---|---|---|---|
| 12 (8ct, 4st) | E. Pooley | Surrey v Sussex at The Oval | 1868 |
| 12 (9ct, 3st) | D. Tallon | Queensland v New South Wales at Sydney | 1938-39 |
| 12 (9ct, 3st) | H. B. Taber | New South Wales v South Australia at Adelaide | 1968-69 |
| 11 (all ct) | A. Long | Surrey v Sussex at Hove | 1964 |
| 11 (all ct) | R. W. Marsh | Western Australia v Victoria at Perth | 1975-76 |
| 11 (all ct) | D. L. Bairstow | Yorkshire v Derbyshire at Scarborough | 1982 |
| 10 (5ct, 5st) | H. Phillips | Sussex v Surrey at The Oval | 1872 |
| 10 (2ct, 8st) | E. Pooley | Surrey v Kent at The Oval | 1878 |
| 10 (9ct, 1st) | T. W. Oates | Nottinghamshire v Middlesex at Nottingham | 1906 |
| 10 (1ct, 9st) | F. H. Huish | Kent v Surrey at The Oval | 1911 |
| 10 (9ct, 1st) | J. C. Hubble | Kent v Gloucestershire at Cheltenham | 1923 |
| 10 (8ct, 2st) | H. Elliott | Derbyshire v Lancashire at Manchester | 1935 |
| 10 (7ct, 3st) | P. Corrall | Leicestershire v Sussex at Hove | 1936 |
| 10 (9ct, 1st) | R. A. Saggers | New South Wales v Combined XI at Brisbane | 1940-41 |
| 10 (all ct) | A. E. Wilson | Gloucestershire v Hampshire at Portsmouth | 1953 |
| 10 (7ct, 3st) | B. N. Jarman | South Australia v New South Wales at Adelaide | 1961-62 |
| 10 (all ct) | L. A. Johnson | Northamptonshire v Sussex at Worthing | 1963 |
| 10 (all ct) | R. W. Taylor | Derbyshire v Hampshire at Chesterfield | 1963 |
| 10 (8ct, 2st) | L. A. Johnson | Northamptonshire v Warwickshire at Birmingham | 1965 |
| 10 (9ct, 1st) | R. C. Jordon | Victoria v South Australia at Melbourne | 1970-71 |
| 10 (all ct) | R. W. Marsh† | Western Australia v South Australia at Perth | 1976-77 |
| 10 (6ct, 4st) | Taslim Arif | National Bank v Punjab at Lahore | 1978-79 |
| 10 (9ct, 1st) | Arif-ud-Din | United Bank v Karachi 'B' at Karachi | 1978-79 |
| 10 (all ct) | R. W. Taylor | England v India at Bombay | 1979-80 |
| 10 (all ct) | R. J. Parks | Hampshire v Derbyshire at Portsmouth | 1981 |
| 10 (9ct, 1st) | A. Ghosh | Bihar v Assam at Bhagalpur | 1981-82 |
| 10 (8ct, 2st) | Z. A. Parkar | Bombay v Maharashtra at Bombay | 1981-82 |
| 10 (9ct, 1st) | Kamal Najamuddin | Karachi v Lahore at Multan | 1982-83 |
| 10 (all ct) | D. A. Murray | West Indies XI v South Africa at Port Elizabeth | 1983-84 |
| 10 (7ct, 3st) | Azhar Abbas | Bahawalpur v Lahore City Greens at Bahawalpur | 1983-84 |
| 10 (7ct, 3st) | B. N. French | Nottinghamshire v Oxford University at Oxford | 1984 |

† *Marsh also scored a hundred (104), a unique "double".*

## SEVEN OR MORE DISMISSALS IN AN INNINGS

| | | | |
|---|---|---|---|
| 8 (all ct) | A. T. W. Grout | Queensland v Western Australia at Brisbane | 1959-60 |
| 8 (all ct) | D. E. East | Essex v Somerset at Taunton | †1985 |
| 7 (4ct, 3st) | E. J. Smith | Warwickshire v Derbyshire at Birmingham | 1926 |
| 7 (6ct, 1st) | W. Farrimond | Lancashire v Kent at Manchester | 1930 |
| 7 (all ct) | W. F. F. Price | Middlesex v Yorkshire at Lord's | 1937 |
| 7 (3ct, 4st) | D. Tallon | Queensland v Victoria at Brisbane | 1938-39 |
| 7 (all ct) | R. A. Saggers | New South Wales v Combined XI at Brisbane | 1940-41 |
| 7 (1ct, 6st) | H. Yarnold | Worcestershire v Scotland at Dundee | 1951 |
| 7 (4ct, 3st) | J. W. Brown | Scotland v Ireland at Dublin | 1957 |
| 7 (6ct, 1st) | N. Kirsten | Border v Rhodesia at East London | 1959-60 |
| 7 (all ct) | M. S. Smith | Natal v Border at East London | 1959-60 |
| 7 (all ct) | K. V. Andrew | Northamptonshire v Lancashire at Manchester | 1962 |
| 7 (all ct) | A. Long | Surrey v Sussex at Hove | 1964 |
| 7 (all ct) | R. M. Schofield | Central Districts v Wellington at Wellington | 1964-65 |
| 7 (all ct) | R. W. Taylor | Derbyshire v Glamorgan at Derby | 1966 |
| 7 (6ct, 1st) | H. B. Taber | New South Wales v South Australia at Adelaide | 1968-69 |
| 7 (6ct, 1st) | E. W. Jones | Glamorgan v Cambridge University at Cambridge. | 1970 |
| 7 (6ct, 1st) | S. Benjamin | Central Zone v North Zone at Bombay | 1973-74 |
| 7 (all ct) | R. W. Taylor | Derbyshire v Yorkshire at Chesterfield | 1975 |
| 7 (6ct, 1st) | Shahid Israr | Karachi Whites v Quetta at Karachi | 1976-77 |
| 7 (all ct) | J. A. Maclean | Queensland v Victoria at Melbourne | 1977-78 |
| 7 (5ct, 2st) | Taslim Arif | National Bank v Punjab at Lahore | 1978-79 |
| 7 (all ct) | Wasim Bari | Pakistan v New Zealand at Auckland | 1978-79 |
| 7 (all ct) | R. W. Taylor | England v India at Bombay | 1979-80 |
| 7 (all ct) | D. L. Bairstow | Yorkshire v Derbyshire at Scarborough | 1982 |
| 7 (6ct, 1st) | R. B. Phillips | Queensland v New Zealanders at Brisbane | 1982-83 |
| 7 (3ct, 4st) | Masood Iqbal | Habib Bank v Lahore at Lahore | 1982-83 |

† *The first eight wickets to fall.*

## WICKET-KEEPERS' HAT-TRICKS

W. H. Brain, Gloucestershire v Somerset at Cheltenham, 1893 – three stumpings off successive balls from C. L. Townsend.

G. O. Dawkes, Derbyshire v Worcestershire at Kidderminster, 1958 – three catches off successive balls from H. L. Jackson.

## MOST CATCHES – EXCLUDING WICKET-KEEPERS

### In a Career

| | | | |
|---|---|---|---|
| 1,018 | F. E. Woolley (1906-38) | 813 | D. B. Close (1949-85) |
| 877 | W. G. Grace (1865-1908) | 786 | J. G. Langridge (1928-55) |
| 830 | G. A. R. Lock (1946-71) | 755 | E. H. Hendren (1907-38) |
| 819 | W. R. Hammond (1920-51) | 755 | C. A. Milton (1948-74) |

### In a Season

| | | | | | |
|---|---|---|---|---|---|
| 78 | W. R. Hammond | 1928 | 65 | W. R. Hammond | 1925 |
| 77 | M. J. Stewart | 1957 | 65 | P. M. Walker | 1959 |
| 73 | P. M. Walker | 1961 | 65 | D. W. Richardson | 1961 |
| 71 | P. J. Sharpe | 1962 | 64 | J. Tunnicliffe | 1904 |
| 70 | J. Tunnicliffe | 1901 | 64 | K. F. Barrington | 1957 |
| 69 | J. G. Langridge | 1955 | 64 | G. A. R. Lock | 1957 |
| 69 | P. M. Walker | 1960 | 63 | K. J. Grieves | 1950 |
| 65 | J. Tunnicliffe | 1895 | 63 | C. A. Milton | 1956 |

*Note:* The most catches by a fielder since the reduction of County Championship matches in 1969 is 49 by C. J. Tavaré, 1979.

### In a Match

| | | | |
|---|---|---|---|
| 10 | W. R. Hammond | Gloucestershire v Surrey at Cheltenham | †1928 |
| 8 | W. B. Burns | Worcestershire v Yorkshire at Bradford | 1907 |
| 8 | A. H. Bakewell | Northamptonshire v Essex at Leyton | 1928 |
| 8 | W. R. Hammond | Gloucestershire v Worcestershire at Cheltenham | 1932 |
| 8 | K. J. Grieves | Lancashire v Sussex at Manchester | 1951 |
| 8 | C. A. Milton | Gloucestershire v Sussex at Hove | 1952 |
| 8 | G. A. R. Lock | Surrey v Warwickshire at The Oval | 1957 |
| 8 | J. M. Prodger | Kent v Gloucestershire at Cheltenham | 1961 |
| 8 | P. M. Walker | Glamorgan v Derbyshire at Swansea | 1970 |
| 8 | Javed Miandad | Habib Bank v Universities at Lahore | 1977-78 |
| 8 | Masood Anwar | Rawalpindi v Lahore Division at Rawalpindi | 1983-84 |

† *Hammond also scored a hundred in each innings.*

### In an Innings

| | | | |
|---|---|---|---|
| 7 | M. J. Stewart | Surrey v Northamptonshire at Northampton | 1957 |
| 7 | A. S. Brown | Gloucestershire v Nottinghamshire at Nottingham | 1966 |

## THE SIDES

## HIGHEST TOTALS

| | | |
|---|---|---|
| 1,107 | Victoria v New South Wales at Melbourne | 1926-27 |
| 1,059 | Victoria v Tasmania at Melbourne | 1922-23 |
| 951-7 dec. | Sind v Baluchistan at Karachi | 1973-74 |
| 918 | New South Wales v South Australia at Sydney | 1900-01 |
| 912-8 dec. | Holkar v Mysore at Indore | 1945-46 |
| 910-6 dec. | Railways v Dera Ismail Khan at Lahore | 1964-65 |
| 903-7 dec. | England v Australia at The Oval | 1938 |
| 887 | Yorkshire v Warwickshire at Birmingham | 1896 |
| 849 | England v West Indies at Kingston | 1929-30 |
| 843 | Australians v Oxford and Cambridge Universities Past and Present at Portsmouth | 1893 |

## HIGHEST FOR EACH FIRST-CLASS COUNTY

| | | | |
|---|---|---|---|
| Derbyshire | 645 | v Hampshire at Derby | 1898 |
| Essex | 692 | v Somerset at Taunton | 1895 |
| Glamorgan | 587-8 | v Derbyshire at Cardiff | 1951 |
| Gloucestershire | 653-6 | v Glamorgan at Bristol | 1928 |
| Hampshire | 672-7 | v Somerset at Taunton | 1899 |
| Kent | 803-4 | v Essex at Brentwood | 1934 |
| Lancashire | 801 | v Somerset at Taunton | 1895 |
| Leicestershire | 701-4 | v Worcestershire at Worcester | 1906 |
| Middlesex | 642-3 | v Hampshire at Southampton | 1923 |
| Northamptonshire | 557-6 | v Sussex at Hove | 1914 |
| Nottinghamshire | 739-7 | v Leicestershire at Nottingham | 1903 |
| Somerset | 675-9 | v Hampshire at Bath | 1924 |
| Surrey | 811 | v Somerset at The Oval | 1899 |
| Sussex | 705-8 | v Surrey at Hastings | 1902 |
| Warwickshire | 657-6 | v Hampshire at Birmingham | 1899 |
| Worcestershire | 633 | v Warwickshire at Worcester | 1906 |
| Yorkshire | 887 | v Warwickshire at Birmingham | 1896 |

## LOWEST TOTALS

| | | |
|---|---|---|
| 12 | Oxford University v MCC and Ground at Oxford | †1877 |
| 12 | Northamptonshire v Gloucestershire at Gloucester | 1907 |
| 13 | Auckland v Canterbury at Auckland | 1877-78 |
| 13 | Nottinghamshire v Yorkshire at Nottingham | 1901 |
| 14 | Surrey v Essex at Chelmsford | 1983 |
| 15 | MCC v Surrey at Lord's | 1839 |
| 15 | Victoria v MCC at Melbourne | †1903-04 |
| 15 | Northamptonshire v Yorkshire at Northampton | †1908 |
| 15 | Hampshire v Warwickshire at Birmingham (Following on, Hampshire scored 521 and won by 155 runs.) | 1922 |
| 16 | MCC and Ground v Surrey at Lord's | 1872 |
| 16 | Derbyshire v Nottinghamshire at Nottingham | 1879 |
| 16 | Surrey v Nottinghamshire at The Oval | 1880 |
| 16 | Warwickshire v Kent at Tonbridge | 1913 |
| 16 | Trinidad v Barbados at Bridgetown | 1942-43 |
| 16 | Border v Natal at East London (first innings) | 1959-60 |
| 17 | Gentlemen of Kent v Gentlemen of England at Lord's | 1850 |
| 17 | Gloucestershire v Australians at Cheltenham | 1896 |
| 18 | The 'B's v England at Lord's | 1831 |
| 18 | Kent v Sussex at Gravesend | †1867 |
| 18 | Tasmania v Victoria at Melbourne | 1868-69 |
| 18 | Australians v MCC and Ground at Lord's | †1896 |
| 18 | Border v Natal at East London (second innings) | 1959-60 |
| 19 | Sussex v Surrey at Godalming | 1830 |
| 19 | Sussex v Nottinghamshire at Hove | †1873 |
| 19 | MCC and Ground v Australians at Lord's | 1878 |
| 19 | Wellington v Nelson at Nelson | 1885-86 |

† *Signifies that one man was absent.*

*Note:* At Lord's in 1810, The 'B's, with one man absent, were dismissed by England for 6.

## LOWEST TOTAL IN A MATCH

| | | |
|---|---|---|
| 34 | (16 and 18) Border v Natal at East London | 1959-60 |
| 42 | (27 and 15) Northamptonshire v Yorkshire at Northampton | 1908 |

*Note:* Northamptonshire batted one man short in each innings.

## LOWEST FOR EACH FIRST-CLASS COUNTY

| | | | |
|---|---|---|---|
| Derbyshire | 16 | v Nottinghamshire at Nottingham | 1879 |
| Essex | 30 | v Yorkshire at Leyton | 1901 |
| Glamorgan | 22 | v Lancashire at Liverpool | 1924 |
| Gloucestershire | 17 | v Australians at Cheltenham | 1896 |
| Hampshire | 15 | v Warwickshire at Birmingham | 1922 |
| Kent | 18 | v Sussex at Gravesend | 1867 |
| Lancashire | 25 | v Derbyshire at Manchester | 1871 |
| Leicestershire | 25 | v Kent at Leicester | 1912 |
| Middlesex | 20 | v MCC at Lord's | 1864 |
| Northamptonshire | 12 | v Gloucestershire at Gloucester | 1907 |
| Nottinghamshire | 13 | v Yorkshire at Nottingham | 1901 |
| Somerset | 25 | v Gloucestershire at Bristol | 1947 |
| Surrey | 14 | v Essex at Chelmsford | 1983 |
| Sussex | 19 | v Nottinghamshire at Hove | 1873 |
| Warwickshire | 16 | v Kent at Tonbridge | 1913 |
| Worcestershire | 24 | v Yorkshire at Huddersfield | 1903 |
| Yorkshire | 23 | v Hampshire at Middlesbrough | 1965 |

## HIGHEST MATCH AGGREGATES

| | | |
|---|---|---|
| 2,376 for 38 wickets | Maharashtra v Bombay at Poona | 1948-49 |
| 2,078 for 40 wickets | Bombay v Holkar at Bombay | 1944-45 |
| 1,981 for 35 wickets | England v South Africa at Durban | 1938-39 |
| 1,929 for 39 wickets | New South Wales v South Australia at Sydney | 1925-26 |
| 1,911 for 34 wickets | New South Wales v Victoria at Sydney | 1908-09 |
| 1,905 for 40 wickets | Otago v Wellington at Dunedin | 1923-24 |

### In England

| | | |
|---|---|---|
| 1,723 for 31 wickets | England v Australia at Leeds | 1948 |
| 1,601 for 29 wickets | England v Australia at Lord's | 1930 |
| 1,507 for 28 wickets | England v West Indies at The Oval | 1976 |
| 1,502 for 28 wickets | MCC v New Zealanders at Lord's | 1927 |
| 1,499 for 31 wickets | T. N. Pearce's XI v Australians at Scarborough | 1961 |
| 1,496 for 24 wickets | England v Australia at Nottingham | 1938 |
| 1,494 for 37 wickets | England v Australia at The Oval | 1934 |

## LOWEST MATCH AGGREGATE

| | | |
|---|---|---|
| 105 for 31 wickets | MCC v Australians at Lord's | 1878 |

*Note:* The lowest aggregate since 1900 is 158 for 22 wickets, Surrey v Worcestershire at The Oval, 1954.

## HIGHEST FOURTH INNINGS TOTALS

(Unless otherwise stated, the side making the runs won the match.)

| | | |
|---|---|---|
| 654-5 | England v South Africa at Durban<br>(After being set 696 to win. The match was left drawn on the tenth day.) | 1938-39 |
| 604 | Maharashtra v Bombay at Poona<br>(After being set 959 to win.) | 1948-49 |
| 576-8 | Trinidad v Barbados at Port-of-Spain<br>(After being set 672 to win. Match drawn on fifth day.) | 1945-46 |
| 572 | New South Wales v South Australia at Sydney<br>(After being set 593 to win.) | 1907-08 |
| 529-9 | Combined XI v South Africans at Perth<br>(After being set 579 to win. Match drawn on fourth day.) | 1963-64 |
| 518 | Victoria v Queensland at Brisbane<br>(After being set 753 to win.) | 1926-27 |
| 507-7 | Cambridge University v MCC and Ground at Lord's | 1896 |
| 502-6 | Middlesex v Nottinghamshire at Nottingham<br>(Game won by an unfinished stand of 271; a county record.) | 1925 |
| 502-8 | Players v Gentlemen at Lord's | 1900 |
| 500-7 | South African Universities v Western Province at Stellenbosch | 1978-79 |

## LARGEST VICTORIES

### Largest Innings Victories

| | | |
|---|---|---|
| Inns and 851 runs: | Railways (910-6 dec.) v Dera Ismail Khan (Lahore) | 1964-65 |
| Inns and 666 runs: | Victoria (1,059) v Tasmania (Melbourne) | 1922-23 |
| Inns and 656 runs: | Victoria (1,107) v New South Wales (Melbourne) | 1926-27 |
| Inns and 605 runs: | New South Wales (918) v South Australia (Sydney) | 1900-01 |
| Inns and 579 runs: | England (903-7 dec.) v Australia (The Oval) | 1938 |
| Inns and 575 runs: | Sind (951-7 dec.) v Baluchistan (Karachi) | 1973-74 |
| Inns and 527 runs: | New South Wales (713) v South Australia (Adelaide) | 1908-09 |
| Inns and 517 runs: | Australians (675) v Nottinghamshire (Nottingham) | 1921 |

## Largest Victories by Runs Margin

685 runs: New South Wales (235 and 761-8 dec.) v Queensland (Sydney) ..... 1929-30
675 runs: England (521 and 342-8 dec.) v Australia (Brisbane) .............. 1928-29
638 runs: New South Wales (304 and 770) v South Australia (Adelaide) ...... 1920-21
625 runs: Sargodha (376 and 416) v Lahore Municipal Corporation (Faisalabad) 1978-79
609 runs: Muslim Commercial Bank (575 and 282-0 dec.) v WAPDA (Lahore) 1977-78
571 runs: Victoria (304 and 649) v South Australia (Adelaide) .............. 1926-27
562 runs: Australia (701 and 327) v England (The Oval) .................. 1934

## Victory Without Losing a Wicket

Lancashire (166-0 dec. and 66-0) beat Leicestershire by ten wickets (Manchester) 1956
Karachi 'A' (277-0 dec.) beat Sind 'A' by an innings and 77 runs (Karachi) .... 1957-58
Railways (236-0 dec. and 16-0) beat Jammu and Kashmir by ten wickets (Srinagar) 1960-61
Karnataka (451-0 dec.) beat Kerala by an innings and 186 runs (Chikmagalur) . 1977-78

# TIED MATCHES IN FIRST-CLASS CRICKET

There have been 32 tied matches since the First World War.

Somerset v Sussex at Taunton ........................................ 1919
(The last Sussex batsman not allowed to bat under Law 45 [subsequently Law 17 and now Law 31])
Orange Free State v Eastern Province at Bloemfontein .................. 1925-26
(Eastern Province had two wickets to fall.)
Essex v Somerset at Chelmsford ...................................... 1926
(Although Essex had one man to go in, MCC ruled that the game should rank as a tie. The ninth wicket fell half a minute before time.)
Gloucestershire v Australians at Bristol ............................ 1930
Victoria v MCC at Melbourne ......................................... 1932-33
(Victoria's third wicket fell to the last ball of the match when one run was needed to win.)
Worcestershire v Somerset at Kidderminster .......................... 1939
Southern Punjab v Baroda at Patiala ................................. 1945-46
Essex v Northamptonshire at Ilford .................................. 1947
Hampshire v Lancashire at Bournemouth ............................... 1947
D. G. Bradman's XI v A. L. Hassett's XI at Melbourne ................ 1948-49
Hampshire v Kent at Southampton ..................................... 1950
Sussex v Warwickshire at Hove ....................................... 1952
Essex v Lancashire at Brentwood ..................................... 1952
Northamptonshire v Middlesex at Peterborough ........................ 1953
Yorkshire v Leicestershire at Huddersfield .......................... 1954
Sussex v Hampshire at Eastbourne .................................... 1955
Victoria v New South Wales at Melbourne ............................. 1956-57
T. N. Pearce's XI v New Zealanders at Scarborough ................... 1958
Essex v Gloucestershire at Leyton ................................... 1959
Australia v West Indies (First Test) at Brisbane .................... 1960-61
Bahawalpur v Lahore 'B' at Bahawalpur ............................... 1961-62
Hampshire v Middlesex at Portsmouth ................................. 1967
England XI v England Under-25 XI at Scarborough ..................... 1968
Yorkshire v Middlesex at Bradford ................................... 1973
Sussex v Essex at Hove .............................................. 1974
South Australia v Queensland at Adelaide ............................ 1976-77
Central Districts v England XI at New Plymouth ...................... 1977-78
Victoria v New Zealanders at Melbourne .............................. 1982-83
Muslim Commercial Bank v Railways at Sialkot ........................ 1983-84
Sussex v Kent at Hastings ........................................... 1984
Northamptonshire v Kent at Northampton .............................. 1984

*Note:* Since 1948 a tie has been recognised only when the scores are level with all the wickets down in the fourth innings. This ruling applies to all grades of cricket, and in the case of a one-day match to the second innings, provided that the match has not been brought to a further conclusion.

## MATCHES BEGUN AND FINISHED IN ONE DAY

*Since 1900. A fuller list may be found in the Wisden of 1981 and preceding editions.*

Yorkshire v Worcestershire at Bradford, May 7 .......... 1900
MCC and Ground v London County at Lord's, May 20 .......... 1903
Transvaal v Orange Free State at Johannesburg, December 30 .......... 1906
Middlesex v Gentlemen of Philadelphia at Lord's, July 20 .......... 1908
Gloucestershire v Middlesex at Bristol, August 26 .......... 1909
Eastern Province v Orange Free State at Port Elizabeth, December 26 .......... 1912
Kent v Sussex at Tonbridge, June 21 .......... 1919
Lancashire v Somerset at Manchester, May 21 .......... 1925
Madras v Mysore at Madras, November 4 .......... 1934
Ireland v New Zealanders at Dublin, September 11 .......... 1937
Derbyshire v Somerset at Chesterfield, June 11 .......... 1947
Lancashire v Sussex at Manchester, July 12 .......... 1950
Surrey v Warwickshire at The Oval, May 16 .......... 1953
Somerset v Lancashire at Bath, June 6 (H. T. F. Buse's benefit) .......... 1953
*Auckland v Fiji at Auckland, March 9 .......... 1953-54
Kent v Worcestershire at Tunbridge Wells, June 15 .......... 1960

* *After three declarations on the third day, no play having been possible on the first two days.*

## TEST MATCH RECORDS

### SCORERS OF 2,000 RUNS IN TESTS

FOR ENGLAND

| | *T* | *I* | *NO* | *R* | *HI* | *100s* | *Avge* |
|---|---|---|---|---|---|---|---|
| G. Boycott | 108 | 193 | 23 | 8,114 | 246* | 22 | 47.72 |
| M. C. Cowdrey | 114 | 188 | 15 | 7,624 | 182 | 22 | 44.06 |
| W. R. Hammond | 85 | 140 | 16 | 7,249 | 336* | 22 | 58.45 |
| L. Hutton | 79 | 138 | 15 | 6,971 | 364 | 19 | 56.67 |
| K. F. Barrington | 82 | 131 | 15 | 6,806 | 256 | 20 | 58.67 |
| D. C. S. Compton | 78 | 131 | 15 | 5,807 | 278 | 17 | 50.06 |
| J. B. Hobbs | 61 | 102 | 7 | 5,410 | 211 | 15 | 56.94 |
| D. I. Gower | 76 | 129 | 11 | 5,385 | 215 | 12 | 45.63 |
| J. H. Edrich | 77 | 127 | 9 | 5,138 | 310* | 12 | 43.54 |
| T. W. Graveney | 79 | 123 | 13 | 4,882 | 258 | 11 | 44.38 |
| H. Sutcliffe | 54 | 84 | 9 | 4,555 | 194 | 16 | 60.73 |
| P. B. H. May | 66 | 106 | 9 | 4,537 | 285* | 13 | 46.77 |
| E. R. Dexter | 62 | 102 | 8 | 4,502 | 205 | 9 | 47.89 |
| I. T. Botham | 79 | 125 | 3 | 4,409 | 208 | 13 | 36.13 |
| A. P. E. Knott | 95 | 149 | 15 | 4,389 | 135 | 5 | 32.75 |
| D. L. Amiss | 50 | 88 | 10 | 3,612 | 262* | 11 | 46.30 |
| A. W. Greig | 58 | 93 | 4 | 3,599 | 148 | 8 | 40.43 |
| E. H. Hendren | 51 | 83 | 9 | 3,525 | 205* | 7 | 47.63 |
| F. E. Woolley | 64 | 98 | 7 | 3,283 | 154 | 5 | 36.07 |
| K. W. R. Fletcher | 59 | 96 | 14 | 3,272 | 216 | 7 | 39.90 |
| G. A. Gooch | 48 | 84 | 4 | 3,027 | 196 | 5 | 37.83 |
| M. Leyland | 41 | 65 | 5 | 2,764 | 187 | 9 | 46.06 |
| C. Washbrook | 37 | 66 | 6 | 2,569 | 195 | 6 | 42.81 |
| B. L. D'Oliveira | 44 | 70 | 8 | 2,484 | 158 | 5 | 40.06 |
| D. W. Randall | 47 | 79 | 5 | 2,470 | 174 | 7 | 33.37 |
| W. J. Edrich | 39 | 63 | 2 | 2,440 | 219 | 6 | 40.00 |
| T. G. Evans | 91 | 133 | 14 | 2,439 | 104 | 2 | 20.49 |
| L. E. G. Ames | 47 | 72 | 12 | 2,434 | 149 | 8 | 40.56 |
| W. Rhodes | 58 | 98 | 21 | 2,325 | 179 | 2 | 30.19 |
| T. E. Bailey | 61 | 91 | 14 | 2,290 | 134* | 1 | 29.74 |
| M. J. K. Smith | 50 | 78 | 6 | 2,278 | 121 | 3 | 31.63 |
| M. W. Gatting | 41 | 70 | 10 | 2,246 | 207 | 4 | 37.43 |
| A. J. Lamb | 38 | 64 | 6 | 2,211 | 137* | 7 | 38.12 |
| P. E. Richardson | 34 | 56 | 1 | 2,061 | 126 | 5 | 37.47 |

## FOR AUSTRALIA

| | *T* | *I* | *NO* | *R* | *HI* | *100s* | *Avge* |
|---|---|---|---|---|---|---|---|
| G. S. Chappell ...... | 87 | 151 | 19 | 7,110 | 247* | 24 | 53.86 |
| D. G. Bradman ...... | 52 | 80 | 10 | 6,996 | 334 | 29 | 99.94 |
| R. N. Harvey ....... | 79 | 137 | 10 | 6,149 | 205 | 21 | 48.41 |
| K. D. Walters ....... | 74 | 125 | 14 | 5,357 | 250 | 15 | 48.26 |
| I. M. Chappell ...... | 75 | 136 | 10 | 5,345 | 196 | 14 | 42.42 |
| A. R. Border ........ | 72 | 127 | 22 | 5,332 | 196 | 14 | 50.78 |
| W. M. Lawry ....... | 67 | 123 | 12 | 5,234 | 210 | 13 | 47.15 |
| R. B. Simpson ....... | 62 | 111 | 7 | 4,869 | 311 | 10 | 46.81 |
| I. R. Redpath ....... | 66 | 120 | 11 | 4,737 | 171 | 8 | 43.45 |
| K. J. Hughes ........ | 70 | 124 | 6 | 4,415 | 213 | 9 | 37.41 |
| R. W. Marsh ........ | 96 | 150 | 13 | 3,633 | 132 | 3 | 26.51 |
| A. R. Morris ........ | 46 | 79 | 3 | 3,533 | 206 | 12 | 46.48 |
| C. Hill ............. | 49 | 89 | 2 | 3,412 | 191 | 7 | 39.21 |
| V. T. Trumper ....... | 48 | 89 | 8 | 3,163 | 214* | 8 | 39.04 |
| G. M. Wood ........ | 53 | 101 | 5 | 3,109 | 172 | 8 | 32.38 |
| C. C. McDonald ..... | 47 | 83 | 4 | 3,107 | 170 | 5 | 39.32 |
| A. L. Hassett ....... | 43 | 69 | 3 | 3,073 | 198* | 10 | 46.56 |
| K. R. Miller ........ | 55 | 87 | 7 | 2,958 | 147 | 7 | 36.97 |
| W. W. Armstrong .... | 50 | 84 | 10 | 2,863 | 159* | 6 | 38.68 |
| K. R. Stackpole ...... | 43 | 80 | 5 | 2,807 | 207 | 7 | 37.42 |
| N. C. O'Neill ....... | 42 | 69 | 8 | 2,779 | 181 | 6 | 45.55 |
| G. N. Yallop ........ | 39 | 70 | 3 | 2,756 | 268 | 8 | 41.13 |
| S. J. McCabe ........ | 39 | 62 | 5 | 2,748 | 232 | 6 | 48.21 |
| W. Bardsley ......... | 41 | 66 | 5 | 2,469 | 193* | 6 | 40.47 |
| W. M. Woodfull ..... | 35 | 54 | 4 | 2,300 | 161 | 7 | 46.00 |
| P. J. Burge .......... | 42 | 68 | 8 | 2,290 | 181 | 4 | 38.16 |
| S. E. Gregory ....... | 58 | 100 | 7 | 2,282 | 201 | 4 | 24.53 |
| R. Benaud .......... | 63 | 97 | 7 | 2,201 | 122 | 3 | 24.45 |
| C. G. Macartney ..... | 35 | 55 | 4 | 2,131 | 170 | 7 | 41.78 |
| W. H. Ponsford ...... | 29 | 48 | 4 | 2,122 | 266 | 7 | 48.22 |
| R. M. Cowper ....... | 27 | 46 | 2 | 2,061 | 307 | 5 | 46.84 |

## FOR SOUTH AFRICA

| | *T* | *I* | *NO* | *R* | *HI* | *100s* | *Avge* |
|---|---|---|---|---|---|---|---|
| B. Mitchell .......... | 42 | 80 | 9 | 3,471 | 189* | 8 | 48.88 |
| A. D. Nourse ........ | 34 | 62 | 7 | 2,960 | 231 | 9 | 53.81 |
| H. W. Taylor ........ | 42 | 76 | 4 | 2,936 | 176 | 7 | 40.77 |
| E. J. Barlow ........ | 30 | 57 | 2 | 2,516 | 201 | 6 | 45.74 |
| T. L. Goddard ....... | 41 | 78 | 5 | 2,516 | 112 | 1 | 34.46 |
| D. J. McGlew ....... | 34 | 64 | 6 | 2,440 | 255* | 7 | 42.06 |
| J. H. B. Waite ....... | 50 | 86 | 7 | 2,405 | 134 | 4 | 30.44 |
| R. G. Pollock ....... | 23 | 41 | 4 | 2,256 | 274 | 7 | 60.97 |
| A. W. Nourse ....... | 45 | 83 | 8 | 2,234 | 111 | 1 | 29.78 |
| R. A. McLean ....... | 40 | 73 | 3 | 2,120 | 142 | 5 | 30.28 |

## FOR WEST INDIES

| | *T* | *I* | *NO* | *R* | *HI* | *100s* | *Avge* |
|---|---|---|---|---|---|---|---|
| G. S. Sobers ......... | 93 | 160 | 21 | 8,032 | 365* | 26 | 57.78 |
| C. H. Lloyd ......... | 110 | 175 | 14 | 7,515 | 242* | 19 | 46.67 |
| R. B. Kanhai ........ | 79 | 137 | 6 | 6,227 | 256 | 15 | 47.53 |
| I. V. A. Richards .... | 77 | 116 | 7 | 5,889 | 291 | 19 | 54.02 |
| C. G. Greenidge ..... | 66 | 111 | 13 | 4,816 | 223 | 12 | 49.14 |
| E. D. Weekes ....... | 48 | 81 | 5 | 4,455 | 207 | 15 | 58.61 |
| A. I. Kallicharran .... | 66 | 109 | 10 | 4,399 | 187 | 12 | 44.43 |
| R. C. Fredericks ..... | 59 | 109 | 7 | 4,334 | 169 | 8 | 42.49 |

| | *T* | *I* | *NO* | *R* | *HI* | *100s* | *Avge* |
|---|---|---|---|---|---|---|---|
| F. M. M. Worrell .... | 51 | 87 | 9 | 3,860 | 261 | 9 | 49.48 |
| C. L. Walcott ....... | 44 | 74 | 7 | 3,798 | 220 | 15 | 56.68 |
| C. C. Hunte ......... | 44 | 78 | 6 | 3,245 | 260 | 8 | 45.06 |
| D. L. Haynes ........ | 54 | 88 | 7 | 3,234 | 184 | 7 | 39.92 |
| B. F. Butcher ........ | 44 | 78 | 6 | 3,104 | 209* | 7 | 43.11 |
| H. A. Gomes ........ | 49 | 75 | 10 | 2,841 | 143 | 9 | 43.70 |
| S. M. Nurse .......... | 29 | 54 | 1 | 2,523 | 258 | 6 | 47.60 |
| G. A. Headley ....... | 22 | 40 | 4 | 2,190 | 270* | 10 | 60.83 |
| J. B. Stollmeyer ...... | 32 | 56 | 5 | 2,159 | 160 | 4 | 42.33 |
| L. G. Rowe ......... | 30 | 49 | 2 | 2,047 | 302 | 7 | 43.55 |

## FOR NEW ZEALAND

| | *T* | *I* | *NO* | *R* | *HI* | *100s* | *Avge* |
|---|---|---|---|---|---|---|---|
| B. E. Congdon ....... | 61 | 114 | 7 | 3,448 | 176 | 7 | 32.22 |
| J. R. Reid ........... | 58 | 108 | 5 | 3,428 | 142 | 6 | 33.28 |
| G. M. Turner ....... | 41 | 73 | 6 | 2,991 | 259 | 7 | 44.64 |
| B. Sutcliffe .......... | 42 | 76 | 8 | 2,727 | 230* | 5 | 40.10 |
| M. G. Burgess ....... | 50 | 92 | 6 | 2,684 | 119* | 5 | 31.20 |
| G. P. Howarth ...... | 47 | 83 | 5 | 2,531 | 147 | 6 | 32.44 |
| G. T. Dowling ....... | 39 | 77 | 3 | 2,306 | 239 | 3 | 31.16 |
| J. G. Wright ........ | 41 | 71 | 2 | 2,133 | 141 | 4 | 30.91 |
| J. V. Coney ......... | 40 | 67 | 12 | 2,094 | 174* | 2 | 38.07 |
| R. J. Hadlee ........ | 57 | 96 | 12 | 2,088 | 103 | 1 | 24.85 |

## FOR INDIA

| | *T* | *I* | *NO* | *R* | *HI* | *100s* | *Avge* |
|---|---|---|---|---|---|---|---|
| S. M. Gavaskar ...... | 106 | 185 | 14 | 8,654 | 236* | 30 | 50.60 |
| G. R. Viswanath ..... | 91 | 155 | 10 | 6,080 | 222 | 14 | 41.93 |
| D. B. Vengsarkar .... | 76 | 124 | 11 | 4,328 | 159 | 9 | 38.30 |
| P. R. Umrigar ....... | 59 | 94 | 8 | 3,631 | 223 | 12 | 42.22 |
| M. Amarnath ....... | 49 | 83 | 7 | 3,241 | 120 | 8 | 42.64 |
| V. L. Manjrekar ..... | 55 | 92 | 10 | 3,208 | 189* | 7 | 39.12 |
| C. G. Borde .......... | 55 | 97 | 11 | 3,061 | 177* | 5 | 35.59 |
| Nawab of Pataudi jun. | 46 | 83 | 3 | 2,793 | 203* | 6 | 34.91 |
| Kapil Dev .......... | 68 | 101 | 9 | 2,788 | 126* | 3 | 30.30 |
| S. M. H. Kirmani .... | 85 | 122 | 22 | 2,717 | 102 | 2 | 27.17 |
| F. M. Engineer ...... | 46 | 87 | 3 | 2,611 | 121 | 2 | 31.08 |
| Pankaj Roy ......... | 43 | 79 | 4 | 2,442 | 173 | 5 | 32.56 |
| V. S. Hazare ........ | 30 | 52 | 6 | 2,192 | 164* | 7 | 47.65 |
| A. L. Wadekar ...... | 37 | 71 | 3 | 2,113 | 143 | 1 | 31.07 |
| V. Mankad ......... | 44 | 72 | 5 | 2,109 | 231 | 5 | 31.47 |
| C. P. S. Chauhan .... | 40 | 68 | 2 | 2,084 | 97 | 0 | 31.57 |
| M. L. Jaisimha ...... | 39 | 71 | 4 | 2,056 | 129 | 3 | 30.68 |
| D. N. Sardesai ...... | 30 | 55 | 4 | 2,001 | 212 | 5 | 39.23 |

## FOR PAKISTAN

| | *T* | *I* | *NO* | *R* | *HI* | *100s* | *Avge* |
|---|---|---|---|---|---|---|---|
| Zaheer Abbas ....... | 76 | 123 | 11 | 5,058 | 274 | 12 | 45.16 |
| Javed Miandad ...... | 68 | 108 | 16 | 5,044 | 280* | 13 | 54.92 |
| Majid J. Khan ....... | 63 | 106 | 5 | 3,931 | 167 | 8 | 38.92 |
| Hanif Mohammad ... | 55 | 97 | 8 | 3,915 | 337 | 12 | 43.98 |
| Mushtaq Mohammad . | 57 | 100 | 7 | 3,643 | 201 | 10 | 39.17 |
| Asif Iqbal .......... | 58 | 99 | 7 | 3,575 | 175 | 11 | 38.85 |
| Mudassar Nazar ..... | 52 | 81 | 5 | 3,099 | 231 | 8 | 40.77 |

| | T | I | NO | R | HI | 100s | Avge |
|---|---|---|---|---|---|---|---|
| Saeed Ahmed ....... | 41 | 78 | 4 | 2,991 | 172 | 5 | 40.41 |
| Wasim Raja ......... | 57 | 92 | 14 | 2,821 | 125 | 4 | 36.16 |
| Sadiq Mohammad .... | 41 | 74 | 2 | 2,579 | 166 | 5 | 35.81 |
| Mohsin Khan ....... | 40 | 65 | 5 | 2,468 | 200 | 7 | 41.13 |
| Imtiaz Ahmed ....... | 41 | 72 | 1 | 2,079 | 209 | 3 | 29.28 |
| Imran Khan ......... | 51 | 77 | 12 | 2,023 | 123 | 2 | 31.12 |

## HIGHEST INDIVIDUAL TEST INNINGS

| | | |
|---|---|---|
| 365* | G. S. Sobers, West Indies v Pakistan at Kingston | 1957-58 |
| 364 | L. Hutton, England v Australia at The Oval | 1938 |
| 337 | Hanif Mohammad, Pakistan v West Indies at Bridgetown | 1957-58 |
| 336* | W. R. Hammond, England v New Zealand at Auckland | 1932-33 |
| 334 | D. G. Bradman, Australia v England at Leeds | 1930 |
| 325 | A. Sandham, England v West Indies at Kingston | 1929-30 |
| 311 | R. B. Simpson, Australia v England at Manchester | 1964 |
| 310* | J. H. Edrich, England v New Zealand at Leeds | 1965 |
| 307 | R. M. Cowper, Australia v England at Melbourne | 1965-66 |
| 304 | D. G. Bradman, Australia v England at Leeds | 1934 |
| 302 | L. G. Rowe, West Indies v England at Bridgetown | 1973-74 |
| 299* | D. G. Bradman, Australia v South Africa at Adelaide | 1931-32 |
| 291 | I. V. A. Richards, West Indies v England at The Oval | 1976 |
| 287 | R. E. Foster, England v Australia at Sydney | 1903-04 |
| 285* | P. B. H. May, England v West Indies at Birmingham | 1957 |
| 280* | Javed Miandad, Pakistan v India at Hyderabad | 1982-83 |
| 278 | D. C. S. Compton, England v Pakistan at Nottingham | 1954 |
| 274 | R. G. Pollock, South Africa v Australia at Durban | 1969-70 |
| 274 | Zaheer Abbas, Pakistan v England at Birmingham | 1971 |
| 270* | G. A. Headley, West Indies v England at Kingston | 1934-35 |
| 270 | D. G. Bradman, Australia v England at Melbourne | 1936-37 |
| 268 | G. N. Yallop, Australia v Pakistan at Melbourne | 1983-84 |
| 266 | W. H. Ponsford, Australia v England at The Oval | 1934 |
| 262* | D. L. Amiss, England v West Indies at Kingston | 1973-74 |
| 261 | F. M. M. Worrell, West Indies v England at Nottingham | 1950 |
| 260 | C. C. Hunte, West Indies v Pakistan at Kingston | 1957-58 |
| 259 | G. M. Turner, New Zealand v West Indies at Georgetown | 1971-72 |
| 258 | T. W. Graveney, England v West Indies at Nottingham | 1957 |
| 258 | S. M. Nurse, West Indies v New Zealand at Christchurch | 1968-69 |
| 256 | R. B. Kanhai, West Indies v India at Calcutta | 1958-59 |
| 256 | K. F. Barrington, England v Australia at Manchester | 1964 |
| 255* | D. J. McGlew, South Africa v New Zealand at Wellington | 1952-53 |
| 254 | D. G. Bradman, Australia v England at Lord's | 1930 |
| 251 | W. R. Hammond, England v Australia at Sydney | 1928-29 |
| 250 | K. D. Walters, Australia v New Zealand at Christchurch | 1976-77 |
| 250 | S. F. A. F. Bacchus, West Indies v India at Kanpur | 1978-79 |

**The highest individual innings for other countries are:**

| | | |
|---|---|---|
| 236* | S. M. Gavaskar, India v West Indies at Madras | 1983-84 |
| 190 | S. Wettimuny, Sri Lanka v England at Lord's | 1984 |

## TEST BATTING AVERAGE OVER 50

(Qualification: 20 innings)

| Avge | | T | I | NO | R | HI | 100s |
|---|---|---|---|---|---|---|---|
| 99.94 | D. G. Bradman (*A*) ....... | 52 | 80 | 10 | 6,996 | 334 | 29 |
| 60.97 | R. G. Pollock (*SA*) ........ | 23 | 41 | 4 | 2,256 | 274 | 7 |
| 60.83 | G. A. Headley (*WI*) ....... | 22 | 40 | 4 | 2,190 | 270* | 10 |
| 60.73 | H. Sutcliffe (*E*) ........... | 54 | 84 | 9 | 4,555 | 194 | 16 |
| 59.23 | E. Paynter (*E*) ........... | 20 | 31 | 5 | 1,540 | 243 | 4 |

| Avge | | T | I | NO | R | HI | 100s |
|---|---|---|---|---|---|---|---|
| 58.67 | K. F. Barrington (*E*) | 82 | 131 | 5 | 6,806 | 256 | 20 |
| 58.61 | E. D. Weekes (*WI*) | 48 | 81 | 5 | 4,455 | 207 | 15 |
| 58.45 | W. R. Hammond (*E*) | 85 | 140 | 16 | 7,249 | 336* | 22 |
| 57.78 | G. S. Sobers (*WI*) | 93 | 160 | 21 | 8,032 | 365* | 26 |
| 56.94 | J. B. Hobbs (*E*) | 61 | 102 | 7 | 5,410 | 211 | 15 |
| 56.68 | C. L. Walcott (*WI*) | 44 | 74 | 7 | 3,798 | 220 | 15 |
| 56.67 | L. Hutton (*E*) | 79 | 138 | 15 | 6,971 | 364 | 19 |
| 55.00 | E. Tyldesley (*E*) | 14 | 20 | 2 | 990 | 122 | 3 |
| 54.92 | Javed Miandad (*P*) | 68 | 108 | 16 | 5,044 | 280* | 13 |
| 54.20 | C. A. Davis (*WI*) | 15 | 29 | 5 | 1,301 | 183 | 4 |
| 54.02 | I. V. A. Richards (*WI*) | 77 | 116 | 7 | 5,889 | 291 | 19 |
| 53.86 | G. S. Chappell (*A*) | 87 | 151 | 19 | 7,110 | 247* | 24 |
| 53.85 | J. F. Reid (*NZ*) | 13 | 22 | 2 | 1,077 | 180 | 5 |
| 53.81 | A. D. Nourse (*SA*) | 34 | 62 | 7 | 2,960 | 231 | 9 |
| 51.62 | J. Ryder (*A*) | 20 | 32 | 5 | 1,394 | 201* | 3 |
| 50.78 | A. R. Border (*A*) | 72 | 127 | 22 | 5,332 | 196 | 14 |
| 50.60 | S. M. Gavaskar (*I*) | 106 | 185 | 14 | 8,654 | 236* | 30 |
| 50.06 | D. C. S. Compton (*E*) | 78 | 131 | 15 | 5,807 | 278 | 17 |

## MOST TEST HUNDREDS

| Total | | E | A | SA | WI | NZ | I | P | SL |
|---|---|---|---|---|---|---|---|---|---|
| 30 | S. M. Gavaskar (*India*) | 4 | 5 | — | 13 | 2 | — | 5 | 1 |
| 29 | D. G. Bradman (*Australia*) | 19 | — | 4 | 2 | 0 | 4 | — | — |
| 26 | G. S. Sobers (*West Indies*) | 10 | 4 | 0 | — | 1 | 8 | 3 | — |
| 24 | G. S. Chappell (*Australia*) | 9 | — | 0 | 5 | 3 | 1 | 6 | 0 |
| 22 | W. R. Hammond (*England*) | — | 9 | 6 | 1 | 4 | 2 | — | — |
| 22 | M. C. Cowdrey (*England*) | — | 5 | 3 | 6 | 2 | 3 | 3 | — |
| 22 | G. Boycott (*England*) | — | 7 | 1 | 5 | 2 | 4 | 3 | 0 |
| 21 | R. N. Harvey (*Australia*) | 6 | — | 8 | 3 | 0 | 4 | 0 | — |
| 20 | K. F. Barrington (*England*) | — | 5 | 2 | 3 | 3 | 3 | 4 | — |

## HUNDRED ON TEST DEBUT

| | | |
|---|---|---|
| C. Bannerman (165*) | Australia v England at Melbourne | 1876-77 |
| W. G. Grace (152) | England v Australia at The Oval | 1880 |
| H. Graham (107) | Australia v England at Lord's | 1893 |
| †K. S. Ranjitsinhji (154*) | England v Australia at Manchester | 1896 |
| †P. F. Warner (132*) | England v South Africa at Johannesburg | 1898-99 |
| †R. A. Duff (104) | Australia v England at Melbourne | 1901-02 |
| R. E. Foster (287) | England v Australia at Sydney | 1903-04 |
| G. Gunn (119) | England v Australia at Sydney | 1907-08 |
| †R. J. Hartigan (116) | Australia v England at Adelaide | 1907-08 |
| †H. L. Collins (104) | Australia v England at Sydney | 1920-21 |
| W. H. Ponsford (110) | Australia v England at Sydney | 1924-25 |
| A. A. Jackson (164) | Australia v England at Adelaide | 1928-29 |
| †G. A. Headley (176) | West Indies v England at Bridgetown | 1929-30 |
| J. E. Mills (117) | New Zealand v England at Wellington | 1929-30 |
| Nawab of Pataudi (102) | England v Australia at Sydney | 1932-33 |
| B. H. Valentine (136) | England v India at Bombay | 1933-34 |
| †L. Amarnath (118) | India v England at Bombay | 1933-34 |
| †P. A. Gibb (106) | England v South Africa at Johannesburg | 1938-39 |
| S. C. Griffith (140) | England v West Indies at Port-of-Spain | 1947-48 |
| A. G. Ganteaume (112) | West Indies v England at Port-of-Spain | 1947-48 |
| †J. W. Burke (101*) | Australia v England at Adelaide | 1950-51 |
| P. B. H. May (138) | England v South Africa at Leeds | 1951 |
| R. H. Shodhan (110) | India v Pakistan at Calcutta | 1952-53 |

| | | |
|---|---|---|
| B. H. Pairaudeau (115) | West Indies v India at Port-of-Spain | 1952-53 |
| †O. G. Smith (104) | West Indies v Australia at Kingston | 1954-55 |
| A. G. Kripal Singh (100*) | India v New Zealand at Hyderabad | 1955-56 |
| C. C. Hunte (142) | West Indies v Pakistan at Bridgetown | 1957-58 |
| C. A. Milton (104*) | England v New Zealand at Leeds | 1958 |
| †A. A. Baig (112) | India v England at Manchester | 1959 |
| Hanumant Singh (105) | India v England at Delhi | 1963-64 |
| Khalid Ibadulla (166) | Pakistan v Australia at Karachi | 1964-65 |
| B. R. Taylor (105) | New Zealand v India at Calcutta | 1964-65 |
| K. D. Walters (155) | Australia v England at Brisbane | 1965-66 |
| J. H. Hampshire (107) | England v West Indies at Lord's | 1969 |
| †G. R. Viswanath (137) | India v Australia at Kanpur | 1969-70 |
| G. S. Chappell (108) | Australia v England at Perth | 1970-71 |
| ‡L. G. Rowe (214, 100*) | West Indies v New Zealand at Kingston | 1971-72 |
| A. I. Kallicharran (100*) | West Indies v New Zealand at Georgetown | 1971-72 |
| R. E. Redmond (107) | New Zealand v Pakistan at Auckland | 1972-73 |
| †F. C. Hayes (106*) | England v West Indies at The Oval | 1973 |
| †C. G. Greenidge (107) | West Indies v India at Bangalore | 1974-75 |
| †L. Baichan (105*) | West Indies v Pakistan at Lahore | 1974-75 |
| G. J. Cosier (109) | Australia v West Indies at Melbourne | 1975-76 |
| S. Amarnath (124) | India v New Zealand at Auckland | 1975-76 |
| Javed Miandad (163) | Pakistan v New Zealand at Lahore | 1976-77 |
| †A. B. Williams (100) | West Indies v Australia at Georgetown | 1977-78 |
| †D. M. Wellham (103) | Australia v England at The Oval | 1981 |
| †Salim Malik (100*) | Pakistan v Sri Lanka at Karachi | 1981-82 |
| K. C. Wessels (162) | Australia v England at Brisbane | 1982-83 |
| W. B. Phillips (159) | Australia v Pakistan at Perth | 1983-84 |
| §M. Azharuddin (110) | India v England at Calcutta | 1984-85 |

† *In his second innings of the match.*
‡ *L. G. Rowe is the only batsman to score a hundred in each innings on début.*
§ *M. Azharuddin is the only batsman to score hundreds in each of his first three Tests.*

## 300 RUNS IN FIRST TEST MATCH

| | | | |
|---|---|---|---|
| 314 | L. G. Rowe (214, 100*) | West Indies v New Zealand at Kingston | 1971-72 |
| 306 | R. E. Foster (287, 19) | England v Australia at Sydney | 1903-04 |

## HUNDRED AND TEN WICKETS IN A TEST MATCH

| | | | |
|---|---|---|---|
| I. T. Botham | 114 and thirteen for 106 | England v India at Bombay | 1979-80 |
| Imran Khan | 117 and eleven for 180 | Pakistan v India at Faisalabad | 1982-83 |

## TWO SEPARATE HUNDREDS IN A TEST MATCH

**Three times:** S. M. Gavaskar v West Indies (1970-71), v Pakistan (1978-79), v West Indies (1978-79).

**Twice in one series:** C. L. Walcott v Australia (1954-55).

**Twice:** H. Sutcliffe v Australia (1924-25), v South Africa (1929); G. A. Headley v England (1929-30 and 1939); G. S. Chappell v New Zealand (1973-74), v West Indies (1975-76).

**Once:** W. Bardsley v England (1909); A. C. Russell v South Africa (1922-23); W. R. Hammond v Australia (1928-29); E. Paynter v South Africa (1938-39); D. C. S. Compton v Australia (1946-47); A. R. Morris v England (1946-47); A. Melville v England (1947); B. Mitchell v England (1947); D. G. Bradman v India (1947-48); V. S. Hazare v Australia (1947-48); E. D. Weekes v India (1948-49); J. Moroney v South Africa (1949-50); G. S. Sobers v Pakistan (1957-58); R. B. Kanhai v Australia (1960-61); Hanif Mohammad v England (1961-62); R. B. Simpson v Pakistan (1964-65); K. D. Walters v West Indies (1968-69); †L. G. Rowe v

New Zealand (1971-72); I. M. Chappell v New Zealand (1973-74); G. M. Turner v Australia (1973-74); C. G. Greenidge v England (1976); G. P. Howarth v England (1977-78); ‡A. R. Border v Pakistan (1979-80); L. R. D. Mendis v India (1982-83); Javed Miandad v New Zealand (1984-85).

† *L. G. Rowe's two hundreds were on his Test début.*

‡ *A. R. Border scored 150* and 153 to become the first batsman to score 150 in each innings of a Test match.*

## HUNDRED AND DOUBLE-HUNDRED IN SAME TEST

| | | |
|---|---|---|
| K. D. Walters (Australia) | 242 and 103 v West Indies at Sydney | 1968-69 |
| S. M. Gavaskar (India) | 124 and 220 v West Indies at Port-of-Spain | 1970-71 |
| †L. G. Rowe (West Indies) | 214 and 100* v New Zealand at Kingston | 1971-72 |
| G. S. Chappell (Australia) | 247* and 133 v New Zealand at Wellington | 1973-74 |

† *On Test début.*

## MOST RUNS IN A TEST SERIES

| | *T* | *I* | *NO* | *R* | *HI* | *100s* | *Avge* | | |
|---|---|---|---|---|---|---|---|---|---|
| D. G. Bradman | 5 | 7 | 0 | 974 | 334 | 4 | 139.14 | A v E | 1930 |
| W. R. Hammond | 5 | 9 | 1 | 905 | 251 | 4 | 113.12 | E v A | 1928-29 |
| R. N. Harvey | 5 | 9 | 0 | 834 | 205 | 4 | 92.66 | A v SA | 1952-53 |
| I. V. A. Richards | 4 | 7 | 0 | 829 | 291 | 3 | 118.42 | WI v E | 1976 |
| C. L. Walcott | 5 | 10 | 0 | 827 | 155 | 5 | 82.70 | WI v A | 1954-55 |
| G. S. Sobers | 5 | 8 | 2 | 824 | 365* | 3 | 137.33 | WI v P | 1957-58 |
| D. G. Bradman | 5 | 9 | 0 | 810 | 270 | 3 | 90.00 | A v E | 1936-37 |
| D. G. Bradman | 5 | 5 | 1 | 806 | 299* | 4 | 201.50 | A v SA | 1931-32 |
| E. D. Weekes | 5 | 7 | 0 | 779 | 194 | 4 | 111.28 | WI v I | 1948-49 |
| †S. M. Gavaskar | 4 | 8 | 3 | 774 | 220 | 4 | 154.80 | I v WI | 1970-71 |
| Mudassar Nazar | 6 | 8 | 2 | 761 | 231 | 4 | 126.83 | P v I | 1982-83 |
| D. G. Bradman | 5 | 8 | 0 | 758 | 304 | 2 | 94.75 | A v E | 1934 |
| D. C. S. Compton | 5 | 8 | 0 | 753 | 208 | 4 | 94.12 | E v SA | 1947 |

† *Gavaskar's aggregate was achieved in his first Test series.*

## 1,000 TEST RUNS IN A CALENDAR YEAR

| | *T* | *I* | *NO* | *R* | *HI* | *100s* | *Avge* | *Year* |
|---|---|---|---|---|---|---|---|---|
| I. V. A. Richards (*West Indies*) | 11 | 19 | 0 | 1,710 | 291 | 7 | 90.00 | 1976 |
| S. M. Gavaskar (*India*) | 18 | 27 | 1 | 1,555 | 221 | 5 | 59.80 | 1979 |
| G. R. Viswanath (*India*) | 17 | 26 | 3 | 1,388 | 179 | 5 | 60.34 | 1979 |
| R. B. Simpson (*Australia*) | 14 | 26 | 3 | 1,381 | 311 | 3 | 60.04 | 1964 |
| D. L. Amiss (*England*) | 13 | 22 | 2 | 1,379 | 262* | 5 | 68.95 | 1974 |
| G. S. Sobers (*West Indies*) | 7 | 12 | 3 | 1,193 | 365* | 5 | 132.55 | 1958 |
| D. B. Vengsarkar (*India*) | 18 | 27 | 4 | 1,174 | 146* | 5 | 51.04 | 1979 |
| K. J. Hughes (*Australia*) | 15 | 28 | 4 | 1,163 | 130* | 2 | 48.45 | 1979 |
| D. C. S. Compton (*England*) | 9 | 15 | 1 | 1,159 | 208 | 6 | 82.78 | 1947 |
| C. G. Greenidge (*West Indies*) | 14 | 22 | 4 | 1,149 | 223 | 4 | 63.83 | 1984 |
| I. T. Botham (*England*) | 14 | 22 | 0 | 1,095 | 208 | 3 | 49.77 | 1982 |
| K. W. R. Fletcher (*England*) | 13 | 22 | 4 | 1,090 | 178 | 2 | 60.55 | 1973 |
| A. R. Border (*Australia*) | 14 | 27 | 3 | 1,073 | 162 | 3 | 44.70 | 1979 |
| C. Hill (*Australia*) | 12 | 21 | 2 | 1,061 | 142 | 2 | 55.78 | 1902 |
| D. I. Gower (*England*) | 14 | 25 | 2 | 1,061 | 114 | 1 | 46.13 | 1982 |
| W. M. Lawry (*Australia*) | 14 | 27 | 2 | 1,056 | 157 | 2 | 42.24 | 1964 |
| S. M. Gavaskar (*India*) | 9 | 15 | 2 | 1,044 | 205 | 4 | 80.30 | 1978 |
| K. F. Barrington (*England*) | 12 | 22 | 2 | 1,039 | 132* | 3 | 51.95 | 1963 |
| E. R. Dexter (*England*) | 11 | 15 | 1 | 1,038 | 205 | 2 | 74.14 | 1962 |
| K. F. Barrington (*England*) | 10 | 17 | 4 | 1,032 | 172 | 4 | 79.38 | 1961 |
| Mohsin Khan (*Pakistan*) | 10 | 17 | 3 | 1,029 | 200 | 4 | 73.50 | 1982 |
| D. G. Bradman (*Australia*) | 8 | 13 | 4 | 1,025 | 201 | 5 | 113.88 | 1948 |
| S. M. Gavaskar (*India*) | 11 | 20 | 1 | 1,024 | 156 | 4 | 53.89 | 1976 |

## CARRYING BAT THROUGH TEST INNINGS

(Figures in brackets show side's total)

| | | | | |
|---|---|---|---|---|
| A. B. Tancred | 26* | (47) | South Africa v England at Cape Town | 1888-89 |
| J. E. Barrett | 67* | (176) | Australia v England at Lord's | 1890 |
| R. Abel | 132* | (307) | England v Australia at Sydney | 1891-92 |
| P. F. Warner | 132* | (237) | England v South Africa at Johannesburg | 1898-99 |
| W. W. Armstrong | 159* | (309) | Australia v South Africa at Johannesburg | 1902-03 |
| J. W. Zulch | 43* | (103) | South Africa v England at Cape Town | 1909-10 |
| W. Bardsley | 193* | (383) | Australia v England at Lord's | 1926 |
| W. M. Woodfull | 30* | (66)‡ | Australia v England at Brisbane | 1928-29 |
| W. M. Woodfull | 73* | (193)† | Australia v England at Adelaide | 1932-33 |
| W. A. Brown | 206* | (422) | Australia v England at Lord's | 1938 |
| L. Hutton | 202* | (344) | England v West Indies at The Oval | 1950 |
| L. Hutton | 156* | (272) | England v Australia at Adelaide | 1950-51 |
| Nazar Mohammad | 124* | (331) | Pakistan v India at Lucknow | 1952-53 |
| F. M. M. Worrell | 191* | (372) | West Indies v England at Nottingham | 1957 |
| T. L. Goddard | 56* | (99) | South Africa v Australia at Cape Town | 1957-58 |
| D. J. McGlew | 127* | (292) | South Africa v New Zealand at Durban | 1961-62 |
| C. C. Hunte | 60* | (131) | West Indies v Australia at Port-of-Spain | 1964-65 |
| G. M. Turner | 43* | (131) | New Zealand v England at Lord's | 1969 |
| W. M. Lawry | 49* | (107) | Australia v India at Delhi | 1969-70 |
| W. M. Lawry | 60* | (116)† | Australia v England at Sydney | 1970-71 |
| G. M. Turner | 223* | (386) | New Zealand v West Indies at Kingston | 1971-72 |
| I. R. Redpath | 159* | (346) | Australia v New Zealand at Auckland | 1973-74 |
| G. Boycott | 99* | (215) | England v Australia at Perth | 1979-80 |
| S. M. Gavaskar | 127* | (286) | India v Pakistan at Faisalabad | 1982-83 |
| Mudassar Nazar | 152* | (323) | Pakistan v India at Lahore | 1982-83 |
| S. Wettimuny | 63* | (144) | Sri Lanka v New Zealand at Christchurch | 1982-83 |

† *One man absent.* ‡ *Two men absent.*

*Notes:* G. M. Turner (223*) holds the record for the highest score by a player carrying his bat through a Test innings. He is also the youngest player to do so, being 22 years 63 days old when he first achieved the feat (1969).

Nazar Mohammad and Mudassar Nazar are the only instance of father and son carrying their bat through a Test innings.

D. L. Amiss (262*) batted throughout England's second innings of 432 for nine v West Indies at Kingston, 1973-74, the tenth wicket adding 40, unbroken, in fifty-three minutes.

D. L. Haynes (55 and 105) opened the batting and was last man out in each innings for West Indies v New Zealand at Dunedin, 1979-80.

## FASTEST TEST FIFTIES

| *Minutes* | | | |
|---|---|---|---|
| 28 | J. T. Brown | England v Australia at Melbourne | 1894-95 |
| 29 | S. A. Durani | India v England at Kanpur | 1963-64 |
| 30 | E. A. V. Williams | West Indies v England at Bridgetown | 1947-48 |
| 30 | B. R. Taylor | New Zealand v West Indies at Auckland | 1968-69 |
| 33 | C. A. Roach | West Indies v England at The Oval | 1933 |
| 34 | C. R. Browne | West Indies v England at Georgetown | 1929-30 |

## FASTEST TEST HUNDREDS

| *Minutes* | | | |
|---|---|---|---|
| 70 | J. M. Gregory | Australia v South Africa at Johannesburg | 1921-22 |
| 75 | G. L. Jessop | England v Australia at The Oval | 1902 |
| 78 | R. Benaud | Australia v West Indies at Kingston | 1954-55 |
| 80 | J. H. Sinclair | South Africa v Australia at Cape Town | 1902-03 |
| 86 | B. R. Taylor | New Zealand v West Indies at Auckland | 1968-69 |

*Note:* The fastest known hundred in a Test match in terms of balls received is off 67 balls by J. M. Gregory for Australia v South Africa at Johannesburg, 1921-22. R. C. Fredericks, for West Indies v Australia at Perth, 1975-76, reached his hundred off 71 balls. I. T. Botham, for England v Australia in 1981, reached three figures off 87 balls in the third Test match and off 86 balls in the fifth.

## FASTEST TEST DOUBLE-HUNDREDS

| *Minutes* | | | |
|---|---|---|---|
| 214 | D. G. Bradman | Australia v England at Leeds | 1930 |
| 223 | S. J. McCabe | Australia v England at Nottingham | 1938 |
| 226 | V. T. Trumper | Australia v South Africa at Adelaide | 1910-11 |
| 234 | D. G. Bradman | Australia v England at Lord's | 1930 |
| 240 | W. R. Hammond | England v New Zealand at Auckland | 1932-33 |
| 241 | S. E. Gregory | Australia v England at Sydney | 1894-95 |
| 245 | D. C. S. Compton | England v Pakistan at Nottingham | 1954 |

## FASTEST TEST TRIPLE-HUNDREDS

| *Minutes* | | | |
|---|---|---|---|
| 287 | W. R. Hammond | England v New Zealand at Auckland | 1932-33 |
| 336 | D. G. Bradman | Australia v England at Leeds | 1930 |

## MOST RUNS IN A DAY BY A BATSMAN

| | | | |
|---|---|---|---|
| 309 | D. G. Bradman | Australia v England at Leeds | 1930 |
| 295 | W. R. Hammond | England v New Zealand at Auckland | 1932-33 |
| 273 | D. C. S. Compton | England v Pakistan at Nottingham | 1954 |
| 271 | D. G. Bradman | Australia v England at Leeds | 1934 |

## SLOWEST INDIVIDUAL TEST BATTING

| | | |
|---|---|---|
| 2* in 80 minutes | C. E. H. Croft, West Indies v Australia at Brisbane | 1979-80 |
| 3* in 100 minutes | J. T. Murray, England v Australia at Sydney | 1962-63 |
| 5 in 102 minutes | Nawab of Pataudi jun, India v England at Bombay | 1972-73 |
| 8 in 120 minutes | T. E. Bailey, England v South Africa at Leeds | 1955 |
| 9 in 120 minutes | W. Newham, England v Australia at Sydney | 1887-88 |
| 9 in 125 minutes | T. W. Jarvis, New Zealand v India at Madras | 1964-65 |
| 10* in 133 minutes | T. G. Evans, England v Australia at Adelaide | 1946-47 |
| 18 in 194 minutes | W. R. Playle, New Zealand v England at Leeds | 1958 |
| 19 in 220 minutes | M. D. Crowe, New Zealand v Sri Lanka at Colombo (SSC) | 1983-84 |
| 20 in 193 minutes | Hanif Mohammad, Pakistan v England at Lord's | 1954 |
| 21 in 210 minutes | P. G. Z. Harris, New Zealand v Pakistan at Karachi | 1955-56 |
| 28* in 250 minutes | J. W. Burke, Australia v England at Brisbane | 1958-59 |
| 31 in 264 minutes | K. D. Mackay, Australia v England at Lord's | 1956 |
| 35 in 332 minutes | C. J. Tavaré, England v India at Madras | 1981-82 |
| 55 in 336 minutes | B. A. Edgar, New Zealand v Australia at Wellington | 1981-82 |
| 57 in 346 minutes | G. S. Camacho, West Indies v England at Bridgetown | 1967-68 |
| 58 in 367 minutes | Ijaz Butt, Pakistan v Australia at Karachi | 1959-60 |
| 68 in 458 minutes | T. E. Bailey, England v Australia at Brisbane | 1958-59 |
| 99 in 505 minutes | M. L. Jaisimha, India v Pakistan at Kanpur | 1960-61 |
| 105 in 575 minutes | D. J. McGlew, South Africa v Australia at Durban | 1957-58 |
| 114 in 591 minutes | Mudassar Nazar, Pakistan v England at Lahore | 1977-78 |
| 197* in 682 minutes | F. M. M. Worrell, West Indies v England at Bridgetown | 1959-60 |
| 259 in 705 minutes | G. M. Turner, New Zealand v West Indies at Georgetown | 1971-72 |
| 337 in 970 minutes | Hanif Mohammad, Pakistan v West Indies at Bridgetown | 1957-58 |

*Note:* C. J. Tavaré scored 147 in 710 minutes in two innings (69 in 287 minutes and 78 in 423 minutes) for England v Australia at Manchester, 1981.

## SLOWEST TEST HUNDREDS

| | | |
|---|---|---|
| 557 minutes | Mudassar Nazar, Pakistan v England at Lahore | 1977-78 |
| 545 minutes | D. J. McGlew, South Africa v Australia at Durban | 1957-58 |
| 488 minutes | P. E. Richardson, England v South Africa at Johannesburg | 1956-57 |

*Notes:* The slowest for any Test in England is 458 minutes by K. W. R. Fletcher, England v Pakistan, The Oval, 1974.

The slowest double-hundred in a Test took 652 minutes (426 balls): A. D. Gaekwad, India v Pakistan at Jullundur, 1983-84. It is also the slowest-ever first-class double-hundred.

## HIGHEST TEST WICKET PARTNERSHIPS

| | | |
|---|---|---|
| 413 for 1st | V. Mankad (231) and Pankaj Roy (173) for India v New Zealand at Madras | 1955-56 |
| 451 for 2nd | W. H. Ponsford (266) and D. G. Bradman (244) for Australia v England at The Oval | 1934 |
| 451 for 3rd | Mudassar Nazar (231) and Javed Miandad (280*) for Pakistan v India at Hyderabad | 1982-83 |
| 411 for 4th | P. B. H. May (285*) and M. C. Cowdrey (154) for England v West Indies at Birmingham | 1957 |
| 405 for 5th | S. G. Barnes (234) and D. G. Bradman (234) for Australia v England at Sydney | 1946-47 |
| 346 for 6th | J. H. W. Fingleton (136) and D. G. Bradman (270) for Australia v England at Melbourne | 1936-37 |
| 347 for 7th | D. St E. Atkinson (219) and C. C. Depeiza (122) for West Indies v Australia at Bridgetown | 1954-55 |
| 246 for 8th | L. E. G. Ames (137) and G. O. Allen (122) for England v New Zealand at Lord's | 1931 |
| 190 for 9th | Asif Iqbal (146) and Intikhab Alam (51) for Pakistan v England at The Oval | 1967 |
| 151 for 10th | B. F. Hastings (110) and R. O. Collinge (68*) for New Zealand v Pakistan at Auckland | 1972-73 |

## HIGHEST MATCH AGGREGATES

| *Runs* | *Wkts* | | | *Days played* |
|---|---|---|---|---|
| 1,981 | 35 | South Africa v England at Durban | 1938-39 | 10† |
| 1,815 | 34 | West Indies v England at Kingston | 1929-30 | 9‡ |
| 1,764 | 39 | Australia v West Indies at Adelaide | 1968-69 | 5 |
| 1,753 | 40 | Australia v England at Adelaide | 1920-21 | 6 |
| 1,723 | 31 | England v Australia at Leeds | 1948 | 5 |
| 1,661 | 36 | West Indies v Australia at Bridgetown | 1954-55 | 6 |

† *No play on one day.* ‡ *No play on two days.*

## HIGHEST INNINGS TOTALS IN TESTS

| | | |
|---|---|---|
| 903-7 dec. | England v Australia at The Oval | 1938 |
| 849 | England v West Indies at Kingston | 1929-30 |
| 790-3 dec. | West Indies v Pakistan at Kingston | 1957-58 |
| 758-8 dec. | Australia v West Indies at Kingston | 1954-55 |
| 729-6 dec. | Australia v England at Lord's | 1930 |
| 701 | Australia v England at The Oval | 1934 |
| 695 | Australia v England at The Oval | 1930 |
| 687-8 dec. | West Indies v England at The Oval | 1976 |
| 681-8 dec. | West Indies v England at Port-of-Spain | 1953-54 |

| | | |
|---|---|---|
| 674-6 | Pakistan v India at Faisalabad | 1984-85 |
| 674 | Australia v India at Adelaide | 1947-48 |
| 668 | Australia v West Indies at Bridgetown | 1954-55 |
| 659-8 dec. | Australia v England at Sydney | 1946-47 |
| 658-8 dec. | England v Australia at Nottingham | 1938 |
| 657-8 dec. | Pakistan v West Indies at Bridgetown | 1957-58 |
| 656-8 dec. | Australia v England at Manchester | 1964 |
| 654-5 | England v South Africa at Durban | 1938-39 |
| 652-7 dec. | England v India at Madras | 1984-85 |
| 652-8 dec. | West Indies v England at Lord's | 1973 |
| 652 | Pakistan v India at Faisalabad | 1982-83 |
| 650-6 dec. | Australia v West Indies at Bridgetown | 1964-65 |

**The highest innings for the countries not mentioned above are:**

| | | |
|---|---|---|
| 644-7 dec. | India v West Indies at Kanpur | 1978-79 |
| 622-9 dec. | South Africa v Australia at Durban | 1969-70 |
| 551-9 dec. | New Zealand v England at Lord's | 1973 |
| 491-7 dec. | Sri Lanka v England at Lord's | 1984 |

## MOST RUNS IN A DAY (BOTH SIDES)

| | | |
|---|---|---|
| 588 | England (398 for six), India (190 for no wkt) at Manchester | 1936 |
| 522 | England (503 for two), South Africa (19 for no wkt) at Lord's | 1924 |
| 508 | England (221 for two), South Africa (287 for six) at The Oval | 1935 |

## MOST RUNS IN A DAY (ONE SIDE)

| | | |
|---|---|---|
| 503 | England (503 for two) v South Africa at Lord's | 1924 |
| 494 | Australia (494 for six) v South Africa at Sydney | 1910-11 |
| 475 | Australia (475 for two) v England at The Oval | 1934 |
| 471 | England (471 for eight) v India at The Oval | 1936 |
| 458 | Australia (458 for three) v England at Leeds | 1930 |
| 455 | Australia (455 for one) v England at Leeds | 1934 |

## HIGHEST FOURTH INNINGS TOTALS

### To win

| | | |
|---|---|---|
| 406-4 | India v West Indies at Port-of-Spain | 1975-76 |
| 404-3 | Australia v England at Leeds | 1948 |
| 362-7 | Australia v West Indies at Georgetown | 1977-78 |
| 348-5 | West Indies v New Zealand at Auckland | 1968-69 |
| 344-1 | West Indies v England at Lord's | 1984 |

### To draw

| | | |
|---|---|---|
| 654-5 | England (needing 696 to win) v South Africa at Durban | 1938-39 |
| 429-8 | India (needing 438 to win) v England at The Oval | 1979 |
| 423-7 | South Africa (needing 451 to win) v England at The Oval | 1947 |
| 408-5 | West Indies (needing 836 to win) v England at Kingston | 1929-30 |

### To lose

| | | |
|---|---|---|
| 445 | India (lost by 47 runs) v Australia at Adelaide | 1977-78 |
| 440 | New Zealand (lost by 38 runs) v England at Nottingham | 1973 |
| 417 | England (lost by 45 runs) v Australia at Melbourne | 1976-77 |
| 411 | England (lost by 193 runs) v Australia at Sydney | 1924-25 |

## LOWEST MATCH AGGREGATES

(For a completed match)

| *Runs* | *Wkts* | | | *Days played* |
|---|---|---|---|---|
| 234 | 29 | Australia v South Africa at Melbourne | 1931-32 | 3† |
| 291 | 40 | England v Australia at Lord's | 1888 | 2 |
| 295 | 28 | New Zealand v Australia at Wellington | 1945-46 | 2 |
| 309 | 29 | West Indies v England at Bridgetown | 1934-35 | 3 |
| 323 | 30 | England v Australia at Manchester | 1888 | 2 |

† *No play on one day.*

## LOWEST INNINGS TOTALS IN TESTS

| | | |
|---|---|---|
| 26 | New Zealand v England at Auckland | 1954-55 |
| 30 | South Africa v England at Port Elizabeth | 1895-96 |
| 30 | South Africa v England at Birmingham | 1924 |
| 35 | South Africa v England at Cape Town | 1898-99 |
| 36 | Australia v England at Birmingham | 1902 |
| 36 | South Africa v Australia at Melbourne | 1931-32 |
| 42 | Australia v England at Sydney | 1887-88 |
| 42 | New Zealand v Australia at Wellington | 1945-46 |
| 42† | India v England at Lord's | 1974 |
| 43 | South Africa v England at Cape Town | 1888-89 |
| 44 | Australia v England at The Oval | 1896 |
| 45 | England v Australia at Sydney | 1886-87 |
| 45 | South Africa v Australia at Melbourne | 1931-32 |
| 47 | South Africa v England at Cape Town | 1888-89 |
| 47 | New Zealand v England at Lord's | 1958 |

**. lowest innings for the countries not mentioned above are:**

| | | |
|---|---|---|
| 76 | West Indies v Pakistan at Dacca | 1958-59 |
| 62 | Pakistan v Australia at Perth | 1981-82 |
| 93 | Sri Lanka v New Zealand at Wellington | 1982-83 |

† *Batted one man short.*

## LOWEST TEST SCORES IN FULL DAY'S PLAY

95 At Karachi, October 11, 1956. Australia 80 all out; Pakistan 15 for two (first day, 5½ hours).

104 At Karachi, December 8, 1959. Pakistan 0 for no wicket to 104 for five v Australia (fourth day, 5½ hours).

106 At Brisbane, December 9, 1958. England 92 for two to 198 all out v Australia (fourth day, 5 hours). *England were dismissed five minutes before the close of play, leaving no time for Australia to start their second innings.*

112 At Karachi, October 15, 1956. Australia 138 for six to 187 all out; Pakistan 63 for one (fourth day, 5½ hours).

117 At Madras, October 19, 1956. India 117 for five v Australia (first day, 5½ hours).

117 At Colombo (SSC), March 21, 1984. New Zealand 6 for no wicket to 123 for four (fifth day, 5 hours, 47 minutes).

122 At Port Elizabeth, March 4, 1957. England's last wicket fell after the first twenty minutes without addition. South Africa then made 122 for seven in five and a half hours (third day, 6 hours).

122 At Brisbane, December 8, 1958. Australia 156 for six to 186 all out; England 92 for two (third day, 5 hours).

122 At Melbourne, January 3, 1959. Australia 282 for seven to 308 all out and 9 for one; England 87 all out (fourth day, 5 hours). *There were two intervals between innings, amounting to twenty minutes.*

122 At Melbourne, December 30, 1978. Australia 243 for four to 258 all out; England 107 for eight (second day, 6 hours).

123 At Hyderabad, January 4, 1978. England 123 for two to 191 all out; Pakistan 55 for one (third day, 5½ hours).

124 At Dacca, November 17, 1959. Pakistan 74 for four to 134 all out; Australia 64 for one (fourth day, 5½ hours).

124 At Kanpur, December 23, 1959. India 226 for six to 291 all out; Australia 59 for two (fourth day, 5½ hours).

128 At Bridgetown, February 9, 1954. England 53 for two to 181 for nine v West Indies (third day, 5 hours).

## In England

151 At Lord's, August 26, 1978. England 175 for two to 289 all out; New Zealand 37 for seven (third day, 6 hours).

159 At Leeds, July 10, 1971. Pakistan 208 for four to 350 all out; England 17 for one (third day, 6 hours).

## BOWLERS WITH 75 WICKETS IN TESTS

### FOR ENGLAND

| | *T* | *Balls* | *R* | *W* | *Avge* | *5 W/i* | *10 W/m* |
|---|---|---|---|---|---|---|---|
| I. T. Botham | 79 | 18,391 | 9,046 | 343 | 26.37 | 25 | 4 |
| R. G. D. Willis | 90 | 17,357 | 8,190 | 325 | 25.20 | 16 | — |
| F. S. Trueman | 67 | 15,178 | 6,625 | 307 | 21.57 | 17 | 3 |
| D. L. Underwood | 86 | 21,862 | 7,674 | 297 | 25.83 | 17 | 6 |
| J. B. Statham | 70 | 16,056 | 6,261 | 252 | 24.84 | 9 | 1 |
| A. V. Bedser | 51 | 15,918 | 5,876 | 236 | 24.89 | 15 | 5 |
| J. A. Snow | 49 | 12,021 | 5,387 | 202 | 26.66 | 8 | 1 |
| J. C. Laker | 46 | 12,027 | 4,101 | 193 | 21.24 | 9 | 3 |
| S. F. Barnes | 27 | 7,873 | 3,106 | 189 | 16.43 | 24 | 7 |
| G. A. R. Lock | 49 | 13,147 | 4,451 | 174 | 25.58 | 9 | 3 |
| M. W. Tate | 39 | 12,523 | 4,055 | 155 | 26.16 | 7 | 1 |
| F. J. Titmus | 53 | 15,118 | 4,931 | 153 | 32.22 | 7 | — |
| H. Verity | 40 | 11,143 | 3,510 | 144 | 24.37 | 5 | 2 |
| C. M. Old | 46 | 8,858 | 4,020 | 143 | 28.11 | 4 | — |
| A. W. Greig | 58 | 9,802 | 4,541 | 141 | 32.20 | 6 | 2 |
| T. E. Bailey | 61 | 9,712 | 3,856 | 132 | 29.21 | 5 | 1 |
| W. Rhodes | 58 | 8,220 | 3,425 | 127 | 26.96 | 6 | 1 |
| D. A. Allen | 39 | 11,297 | 3,779 | 122 | 30.97 | 4 | — |
| R. Illingworth | 61 | 11,934 | 3,807 | 122 | 31.20 | 3 | — |
| J. Briggs | 33 | 5,332 | 2,094 | 118 | 17.74 | 9 | 4 |
| G. G. Arnold | 34 | 7,650 | 3,254 | 115 | 28.29 | 6 | — |
| G. A. Lohmann | 18 | 3,821 | 1,205 | 112 | 10.75 | 9 | 5 |
| D. V. P. Wright | 34 | 8,135 | 4,224 | 108 | 39.11 | 6 | 1 |
| R. Peel | 20 | 5,216 | 1,715 | 102 | 16.81 | 6 | 2 |
| J. H. Wardle | 28 | 6,597 | 2,080 | 102 | 20.39 | 5 | 1 |
| C. Blythe | 19 | 4,438 | 1,863 | 100 | 18.63 | 9 | 4 |
| W. Voce | 27 | 6,360 | 2,733 | 98 | 27.88 | 3 | 2 |
| P. H. Edmonds | 33 | 8,232 | 2,866 | 88 | 32.56 | 2 | — |
| T. Richardson | 14 | 4,485 | 2,220 | 88 | 25.22 | 11 | 4 |
| M. Hendrick | 30 | 6,208 | 2,248 | 87 | 25.83 | — | — |
| W. R. Hammond | 85 | 7,967 | 3,138 | 83 | 37.80 | 2 | — |
| F. E. Woolley | 64 | 6,495 | 2,815 | 83 | 33.91 | 4 | 1 |
| G. O. Allen | 25 | 4,390 | 2,379 | 81 | 29.37 | 5 | 1 |
| D. J. Brown | 26 | 5,098 | 2,237 | 79 | 28.31 | 2 | — |
| H. Larwood | 21 | 4,969 | 2,212 | 78 | 28.35 | 4 | 1 |
| F. H. Tyson | 17 | 3,452 | 1,411 | 76 | 18.56 | 4 | 1 |
| J. E. Emburey | 28 | 6,473 | 2,240 | 75 | 29.86 | 3 | — |

## FOR AUSTRALIA

| | *T* | *Balls* | *R* | *W* | *Avge* | *5 W/i* | *10 W/m* |
|---|---|---|---|---|---|---|---|
| D. K. Lillee ......... | 70 | 18,467 | 8,493 | 355 | 23.92 | 23 | 7 |
| R. Benaud .......... | 63 | 19,108 | 6,704 | 248 | 27.03 | 16 | 1 |
| G. D. McKenzie ..... | 60 | 17,681 | 7,328 | 246 | 29.78 | 16 | 3 |
| R. R. Lindwall ...... | 61 | 13,650 | 5,251 | 228 | 23.03 | 12 | — |
| C. V. Grimmett ...... | 37 | 14,573 | 5,231 | 216 | 24.21 | 21 | 7 |
| J. R. Thomson ...... | 51 | 10,535 | 5,601 | 200 | 28.00 | 8 | — |
| A. K. Davidson ...... | 44 | 11,587 | 3,819 | 186 | 20.53 | 14 | 2 |
| K. R. Miller ........ | 55 | 10,461 | 3,906 | 170 | 22.97 | 7 | 1 |
| W. A. Johnston ...... | 40 | 11,048 | 3,826 | 160 | 23.91 | 7 | — |
| W. J. O'Reilly ....... | 27 | 10,024 | 3,254 | 144 | 22.59 | 11 | 3 |
| H. Trumble ......... | 32 | 8,099 | 3,072 | 141 | 21.78 | 9 | 3 |
| G. F. Lawson ....... | 34 | 7,776 | 4,040 | 140 | 28.85 | 10 | 2 |
| M. H. N. Walker .... | 34 | 10,094 | 3,792 | 138 | 27.47 | 6 | — |
| A. A. Mallett ........ | 38 | 9,990 | 3,940 | 132 | 29.84 | 6 | 1 |
| B. Yardley .......... | 33 | 8,909 | 3,986 | 126 | 31.63 | 6 | 1 |
| R. M. Hogg ......... | 38 | 7,633 | 3,499 | 123 | 28.44 | 6 | 2 |
| M. A. Noble ........ | 42 | 7,109 | 3,025 | 121 | 25.00 | 9 | 2 |
| I. W. Johnson ....... | 45 | 8,780 | 3,182 | 109 | 29.19 | 3 | — |
| G. Giffen ........... | 31 | 6,325 | 2,791 | 103 | 27.09 | 7 | 1 |
| A. N. Connolly ...... | 29 | 7,818 | 2,981 | 102 | 29.22 | 4 | — |
| C. T. B. Turner ...... | 17 | 5,195 | 1,670 | 101 | 16.53 | 11 | 2 |
| A. A. Mailey ........ | 21 | 6,117 | 3,358 | 99 | 33.91 | 6 | 2 |
| F. R. Spofforth ...... | 18 | 4,185 | 1,731 | 94 | 18.41 | 7 | 4 |
| J. W. Gleeson ....... | 29 | 8,857 | 3,367 | 93 | 36.20 | 3 | — |
| N. J. N. Hawke ..... | 27 | 6,974 | 2,677 | 91 | 29.41 | 6 | 1 |
| A. Cotter ........... | 21 | 4,633 | 2,549 | 89 | 28.64 | 7 | — |
| W. W. Armstrong .... | 50 | 8,052 | 2,923 | 87 | 33.59 | 3 | — |
| J. M. Gregory ....... | 24 | 5,581 | 2,648 | 85 | 31.15 | 4 | — |
| T. M. Alderman ..... | 22 | 5,373 | 2,597 | 79 | 32.87 | 5 | — |
| J. V. Saunders ....... | 14 | 3,565 | 1,796 | 79 | 22.73 | 6 | — |
| G. Dymock ......... | 21 | 5,545 | 2,116 | 78 | 27.12 | 5 | 1 |
| G. E. Palmer ........ | 17 | 4,519 | 1,678 | 78 | 21.51 | 6 | 2 |

## FOR SOUTH AFRICA

| | *T* | *Balls* | *R* | *W* | *Avge* | *5 W/i* | *10 W/m* |
|---|---|---|---|---|---|---|---|
| H. J. Tayfield ....... | 37 | 13,568 | 4,405 | 170 | 25.91 | 14 | 2 |
| T. L. Goddard ....... | 41 | 11,736 | 3,226 | 123 | 26.22 | 5 | — |
| P. M. Pollock ....... | 28 | 6,522 | 2,806 | 116 | 24.18 | 9 | 1 |
| N. A. T. Adcock ..... | 26 | 6,391 | 2,195 | 104 | 21.10 | 5 | — |
| C. L. Vincent ....... | 25 | 5,863 | 2,631 | 84 | 31.32 | 3 | — |
| G. A. Faulkner ...... | 25 | 4,227 | 2,180 | 82 | 26.58 | 4 | — |

## FOR WEST INDIES

| | *T* | *Balls* | *R* | *W* | *Avge* | *5 W/i* | *10 W/m* |
|---|---|---|---|---|---|---|---|
| L. R. Gibbs ......... | 79 | 27,115 | 8,989 | 309 | 29.09 | 18 | 2 |
| G. S. Sobers ......... | 93 | 21,599 | 7,999 | 235 | 34.03 | 6 | — |
| M. A. Holding ....... | 55 | 11,842 | 5,414 | 233 | 23.23 | 13 | 2 |
| J. Garner ........... | 51 | 11,769 | 4,792 | 220 | 21.78 | 6 | — |
| A. M. E. Roberts .... | 47 | 11,135 | 5,174 | 202 | 25.61 | 11 | 2 |
| W. W. Hall ......... | 48 | 10,421 | 5,066 | 192 | 26.38 | 9 | 1 |
| M. D. Marshall ...... | 40 | 8,864 | 4,157 | 188 | 22.11 | 13 | 2 |
| S. Ramadhin ........ | 43 | 13,939 | 4,579 | 158 | 28.98 | 10 | 1 |
| A. L. Valentine ...... | 36 | 12,953 | 4,215 | 139 | 30.32 | 8 | 2 |
| C. E. H. Croft ....... | 27 | 6,165 | 2,913 | 125 | 23.30 | 3 | — |
| V. A. Holder ........ | 40 | 9,095 | 3,627 | 109 | 33.27 | 3 | — |
| C. C. Griffith ........ | 28 | 5,631 | 2,683 | 94 | 28.54 | 5 | — |

## FOR NEW ZEALAND

| | T | Balls | R | W | Avge | 5 W/i | 10 W/m |
|---|---|---|---|---|---|---|---|
| R. J. Hadlee | 57 | 14,292 | 6,341 | 266 | 23.83 | 19 | 4 |
| B. L. Cairns | 42 | 10,388 | 4,170 | 130 | 32.07 | 6 | 1 |
| R. O. Collinge | 35 | 7,689 | 3,393 | 116 | 29.25 | 3 | — |
| B. R. Taylor | 30 | 6,334 | 2,953 | 111 | 26.60 | 4 | — |
| R. C. Motz | 32 | 7,034 | 3,148 | 100 | 31.48 | 5 | — |
| H. J. Howarth | 30 | 8,833 | 3,178 | 86 | 36.95 | 2 | — |
| J. R. Reid | 58 | 7,725 | 2,835 | 85 | 33.35 | 1 | — |

## FOR INDIA

| | T | Balls | R | W | Avge | 5 W/i | 10 W/m |
|---|---|---|---|---|---|---|---|
| B. S. Bedi | 67 | 21,364 | 7,637 | 266 | 28.71 | 14 | 1 |
| Kapil Dev | 68 | 14,522 | 7,406 | 258 | 28.70 | 18 | 2 |
| B. S. Chandrasekhar | 58 | 15,963 | 7,199 | 242 | 29.74 | 16 | 2 |
| E. A. S. Prasanna | 49 | 14,353 | 5,742 | 189 | 30.38 | 10 | 2 |
| V. Mankad | 44 | 14,686 | 5,236 | 162 | 32.32 | 8 | 2 |
| S. Venkataraghavan | 57 | 14,877 | 5,634 | 156 | 36.11 | 3 | 1 |
| S. P. Gupte | 36 | 11,284 | 4,403 | 149 | 29.55 | 12 | 1 |
| D. R. Doshi | 33 | 9,322 | 3,502 | 114 | 30.71 | 6 | — |
| K. D. Ghavri | 39 | 7,042 | 3,656 | 109 | 33.54 | 4 | — |
| R. G. Nadkarni | 41 | 9,165 | 2,559 | 88 | 29.07 | 4 | 1 |
| S. A. Durani | 29 | 6,446 | 2,657 | 75 | 35.42 | 3 | 1 |

## FOR PAKISTAN

| | T | Balls | R | W | Avge | 5 W/i | 10 W/m |
|---|---|---|---|---|---|---|---|
| Imran Khan | 51 | 12,551 | 5,316 | 232 | 22.91 | 16 | 4 |
| Sarfraz Nawaz | 55 | 13,926 | 5,798 | 177 | 32.75 | 4 | 1 |
| Fazal Mahmood | 34 | 9,834 | 3,434 | 139 | 24.70 | 13 | 4 |
| Iqbal Qasim | 41 | 10,787 | 3,995 | 137 | 29.16 | 5 | 2 |
| Intikhab Alam | 47 | 10,474 | 4,494 | 125 | 35.95 | 5 | 2 |
| Abdul Qadir | 33 | 8,777 | 4,003 | 114 | 35.11 | 8 | 2 |
| Mushtaq Mohammad | 57 | 5,260 | 2,309 | 79 | 29.22 | 3 | — |

*Note:* G. S. Sobers (West Indies), R. Benaud (Australia), I. T. Botham (England), Kapil Dev (India), Imran Khan (Pakistan) and R. J. Hadlee (New Zealand) have scored 2,000 runs and taken 200 wickets.

# MOST WICKETS IN A TEST MATCH

| | | | |
|---|---|---|---|
| 19-90 | J. C. Laker | England v Australia at Manchester | 1956 |
| 17-159 | S. F. Barnes | England v South Africa at Johannesburg | 1913-14 |
| 16-137† | R. A. L. Massie | Australia v England at Lord's | 1972 |
| 15-28 | J. Briggs | England v South Africa at Cape Town | 1888-89 |
| 15-45 | G. A. Lohmann | England v South Africa at Port Elizabeth | 1895-96 |
| 15-99 | C. Blythe | England v South Africa at Leeds | 1907 |
| 15-104 | H. Verity | England v Australia at Lord's | 1934 |
| 15-124 | W. Rhodes | England v Australia at Melbourne | 1903-04 |
| 14-90 | F. R. Spofforth | Australia v England at The Oval | 1882 |
| 14-99 | A. V. Bedser | England v Australia at Nottingham | 1953 |
| 14-102 | W. Bates | England v Australia at Melbourne | 1882-83 |
| 14-116 | Imran Khan | Pakistan v Sri Lanka at Lahore | 1981-82 |
| 14-124 | J. M. Patel | India v Australia at Kanpur | 1959-60 |
| 14-144 | S. F. Barnes | England v South Africa at Durban | 1913-14 |
| 14-149 | M. A. Holding | West Indies v England at The Oval | 1976 |
| 14-199 | C. V. Grimmett | Australia v South Africa at Adelaide | 1931-32 |

† *On Test début.*

*Notes:* The best for South Africa is 13-165 by H. J. Tayfield against Australia at Melbourne, 1952-53.

The best for New Zealand is 11-58 by R. J. Hadlee against India at Wellington, 1975-76.

The best bowling for Sri Lanka is 9-162 by D. S. de Silva against Pakistan at Faisalabad, 1981-82.

## MOST WICKETS IN A TEST INNINGS

| | | | |
|---|---|---|---|
| 10-53 | J. C. Laker | England v Australia at Manchester | 1956 |
| 9-28 | G. A. Lohmann | England v South Africa at Johannesburg | 1895-96 |
| 9-37 | J. C. Laker | England v Australia at Manchester | 1956 |
| 9-69 | J. M. Patel | India v Australia at Kanpur | 1959-60 |
| 9-83 | Kapil Dev | India v West Indies at Ahmedabad | 1983-84 |
| 9-86 | Sarfraz Nawaz | Pakistan v Australia at Melbourne | 1978-79 |
| 9-95 | J. M. Noreiga | West Indies v India at Port-of-Spain | 1970-71 |
| 9-102 | S. P. Gupte | India v West Indies at Kanpur | 1958-59 |
| 9-103 | S. F. Barnes | England v South Africa at Johannesburg | 1913-14 |
| 9-113 | H. J. Tayfield | South Africa v England at Johannesburg | 1956-57 |
| 9-121 | A. A. Mailey | Australia v England at Melbourne | 1920-21 |
| 8-7 | G. A. Lohmann | England v South Africa at Port Elizabeth | 1895-96 |
| 8-11 | J. Briggs | England v South Africa at Cape Town | 1888-89 |
| 8-29 | S. F. Barnes | England v South Africa at The Oval | 1912 |
| 8-29 | C. E. H. Croft | West Indies v Pakistan at Port-of-Spain | 1976-77 |
| 8-31 | F. Laver | Australia v England at Manchester | 1909 |
| 8-31 | F. S. Trueman | England v India at Manchester | 1952 |
| 8-34 | I. T. Botham | England v Pakistan at Lord's | 1978 |
| 8-35 | G. A. Lohmann | England v Australia at Sydney | 1886-87 |
| 8-38 | L. R. Gibbs | West Indies v India at Bridgetown | 1961-62 |
| 8-43† | A. E. Trott | Australia v England at Adelaide | 1894-95 |
| 8-43 | H. Verity | England v Australia at Lord's | 1934 |
| 8-43 | R. G. D. Willis | England v Australia at Leeds | 1981 |
| 8-51 | D. L. Underwood | England v Pakistan at Lord's | 1974 |
| 8-52 | V. Mankad | India v Pakistan at Delhi | 1952-53 |
| 8-53 | G. B. Lawrence | South Africa v New Zealand at Johannesburg | 1961-62 |
| 8-53† | R. A. L. Massie | Australia v England at Lord's | 1972 |
| 8-55 | V. Mankad | India v England at Madras | 1951-52 |
| 8-56 | S. F. Barnes | England v South Africa at Johannesburg | 1913-14 |
| 8-58 | G. A. Lohmann | England v Australia at Sydney | 1891-92 |
| 8-58 | Imran Khan | Pakistan v Sri Lanka at Lahore | 1981-82 |
| 8-59 | C. Blythe | England v South Africa at Leeds | 1907 |
| 8-59 | A. A. Mallett | Australia v Pakistan at Adelaide | 1972-73 |
| 8-60 | Imran Khan | Pakistan v India at Karachi | 1982-83 |
| 8-65 | H. Trumble | Australia v England at The Oval | 1902 |
| 8-68 | W. Rhodes | England v Australia at Melbourne | 1903-04 |
| 8-69 | H. J. Tayfield | South Africa v England at Durban | 1956-57 |
| 8-69 | Sikander Bakht | Pakistan v India at Delhi | 1979-80 |
| 8-70 | S. J. Snooke | South Africa v England at Johannesburg | 1905-06 |
| 8-71 | G. D. McKenzie | Australia v West Indies at Melbourne | 1968-69 |
| 8-72 | S. Venkataraghavan | India v New Zealand at Delhi | 1964-65 |
| 8-76 | E. A. S. Prasanna | India v New Zealand at Auckland | 1975-76 |
| 8-79 | B. S. Chandrasekhar | India v England at Delhi | 1972-73 |
| 8-81 | L. C. Braund | England v Australia at Melbourne | 1903-04 |
| 8-84† | R. A. L. Massie | Australia v England at Lord's | 1972 |
| 8-85 | Kapil Dev | India v Pakistan at Lahore | 1982-83 |
| 8-86 | A. W. Greig | England v West Indies at Port-of-Spain | 1973-74 |
| 8-92 | M. A. Holding | West Indies v England at The Oval | 1976 |

| | | | |
|---|---|---|---|
| 8-94 | T. Richardson | England v Australia at Sydney | 1897-98 |
| 8-103 | I. T. Botham | England v West Indies at Lord's | 1984 |
| 8-104† | A. L. Valentine | West Indies v England at Manchester | 1950 |
| 8-107 | B. J. T. Bosanquet | England v Australia at Nottingham | 1905 |
| 8-112 | G. F. Lawson | Australia v West Indies at Adelaide | 1984-85 |
| 8-126 | J. C. White | England v Australia at Adelaide | 1928-29 |
| 8-141 | C. J. McDermott | Australia v England at Manchester | 1985 |
| 8-143 | M. H. N. Walker | Australia v England at Melbourne | 1974-75 |

† *On Test début.*

*Note:* The best for New Zealand is 7-23 by R. J. Hadlee against India at Wellington, 1975-76.
The best for Sri Lanka is 5-42 by J. R. Ratnayeke against New Zealand at Colombo (SSC), 1983-84.

## MOST WICKETS IN A TEST SERIES

| | *T* | *R* | *W* | *Avge* | | |
|---|---|---|---|---|---|---|
| S. F. Barnes | 4 | 536 | 49 | 10.93 | England v South Africa | 1913-14 |
| J. C. Laker | 5 | 442 | 46 | 9.60 | England v Australia | 1956 |
| C. V. Grimmett | 5 | 642 | 44 | 14.59 | Australia v South Africa | 1935-36 |
| T. M. Alderman | 6 | 893 | 42 | 21.26 | Australia v England | 1981 |
| R. M. Hogg | 6 | 527 | 41 | 12.85 | Australia v England | 1978-79 |
| Imran Khan | 6 | 558 | 40 | 13.95 | Pakistan v India | 1982-83 |
| A. V. Bedser | 5 | 682 | 39 | 17.48 | England v Australia | 1953 |
| D. K. Lillee | 6 | 870 | 39 | 22.30 | Australia v England | 1981 |
| M. W. Tate | 5 | 881 | 38 | 23.18 | England v Australia | 1924-25 |
| W. J. Whitty | 5 | 632 | 37 | 17.08 | Australia v South Africa | 1910-11 |
| H. J. Tayfield | 5 | 636 | 37 | 17.18 | South Africa v England | 1956-57 |
| A. E. E. Vogler | 5 | 783 | 36 | 21.75 | South Africa v England | 1909-10 |
| A. A. Mailey | 5 | 946 | 36 | 26.27 | Australia v England | 1920-21 |
| G. A. Lohmann | 3 | 203 | 35 | 5.80 | England v South Africa | 1895-96 |
| B. S. Chandrasekhar | 5 | 662 | 35 | 18.91 | India v England | 1972-73 |

## TEST HAT-TRICKS

| | | |
|---|---|---|
| F. R. Spofforth | Australia v England at Melbourne | 1878-79 |
| W. Bates | England v Australia at Melbourne | 1882-83 |
| J. Briggs | England v Australia at Sydney | 1891-92 |
| G. A. Lohmann | England v South Africa at Port Elizabeth | 1895-96 |
| J. T. Hearne | England v Australia at Leeds | 1899 |
| H. Trumble | Australia v England at Melbourne | 1901-02 |
| H. Trumble | Australia v England at Melbourne | 1903-04 |
| T. J. Matthews†<br>T. J. Matthews | Australia v South Africa at Manchester | 1912 |
| M. J. C. Allom‡ | England v New Zealand at Christchurch | 1929-30 |
| T. W. Goddard | England v South Africa at Johannesburg | 1938-39 |
| P. J. Loader | England v West Indies at Leeds | 1957 |
| L. F. Kline | Australia v South Africa at Cape Town | 1957-58 |
| W. W. Hall | West Indies v Pakistan at Lahore | 1958-59 |
| G. M. Griffin | South Africa v England at Lord's | 1960 |
| L. R. Gibbs | West Indies v Australia at Adelaide | 1960-61 |
| P. J. Petherick‡ | New Zealand v Pakistan at Lahore | 1976-77 |

† *T. J. Matthews did the hat-trick in each innings of the same match.*
‡ *On Test début.*

## MOST BALLS BOWLED IN A TEST MATCH

S. Ramadhin (West Indies) sent down 774 balls in 129 overs against England at Birmingham, 1957. It was the most delivered by any bowler in a Test, beating H. Verity's 766 for England against South Africa at Durban, 1938-39. In this match Ramadhin also bowled the most balls (588) in any single first-class innings, including Tests.

It should be noted that six balls were bowled to the over in the Australia v England Test series of 1928-29 and 1932-33, when the eight-ball over was otherwise in force in Australia.

## WICKET-KEEPING RECORDS

### Most Dismissals in a Test Career

| | *T* | *Ct* | *St* | *Total* |
|---|---|---|---|---|
| R. W. Marsh (Australia) | 96 | 343 | 12 | 355 |
| A. P. E. Knott (England) | 95 | 250 | 19 | 269 |
| Wasim Bari (Pakistan) | 81 | 201 | 27 | 228 |
| T. G. Evans (England) | 91 | 173 | 46 | 219 |
| S. M. H. Kirmani (India) | 85 | 157 | 36 | 193 |
| D. L. Murray (West Indies) | 62 | 181 | 8 | 189 |
| A. T. W. Grout (Australia) | 51 | 163 | 24 | 187 |
| R. W. Taylor (England) | 57 | 167 | 7 | 174 |
| J. H. B. Waite (South Africa) | 50 | 124 | 17 | 141 |
| W. A. Oldfield (Australia) | 54 | 78 | 52 | 130 |
| J. M. Parks (England)† | 46 | 103 | 11 | 114 |
| P. J. L. Dujon (West Indies) | 33 | 108 | 2 | 110 |

† *J. M. Parks's figures include two catches taken in three Tests in which he did not keep wicket.*

*Note:* K. J. Wadsworth (92ct, 4st) made most dismissals for New Zealand.

### Most Dismissals in a Test Series

(*Played in 5 Tests unless otherwise stated*)

| | | | |
|---|---|---|---|
| 28 (all ct) | R. W. Marsh | Australia v England | 1982-83 |
| 26 (all ct) | R. W. Marsh | Australia v West Indies (6 Tests) | 1975-76 |
| 26 (23ct, 3st) | J. H. B. Waite | South Africa v New Zealand | 1961-62 |
| 24 (21ct, 3st) | A. P. E. Knott | England v Australia (6 Tests) | 1970-71 |
| 24 (all ct) | D. T. Lindsay | South Africa v Australia | 1966-67 |
| 24 (22ct, 2st) | D. L. Murray | West Indies v England | 1963 |
| 23 (22ct, 1st) | F. C. M. Alexander | West Indies v England | 1959-60 |
| 23 (21ct, 2st) | A. E. Dick | New Zealand v South Africa | 1961-62 |
| 23 (20ct, 3st) | A. T. W. Grout | Australia v West Indies | 1960-61 |
| 23 (22ct, 1st) | A. P. E. Knott | England v Australia (6 Tests) | 1974-75 |
| 23 (21ct, 2st) | R. W. Marsh | Australia v England | 1972 |
| 23 (all ct) | R. W. Marsh | Australia v England (6 Tests) | 1981 |
| 23 (16ct, 7st) | J. H. B. Waite | South Africa v New Zealand | 1953-54 |
| 22 (all ct) | S. J. Rixon | Australia v India | 1977-78 |
| 21 (20ct, 1st) | A. T. W. Grout | Australia v England | 1961 |
| 21 (16ct, 5st) | G. R. A. Langley | Australia v West Indies | 1951-52 |
| 21 (all ct) | R. W. Marsh | Australia v Pakistan | 1983-84 |
| 21 (13ct, 8st) | R. A. Saggers | Australia v South Africa | 1949-50 |
| 21 (15ct, 6st) | H. Strudwick | England v South Africa | 1913-14 |
| 20 (19ct, 1st) | P. R. Downton | England v Australia (6 Tests) | 1985 |
| 20 (19ct, 1st) | P. J. L. Dujon | West Indies v Australia | 1983-84 |
| 20 (18ct, 2st) | T. G. Evans | England v South Africa | 1956-57 |
| 20 (17ct, 3st) | A. T. W. Grout | Australia v England | 1958-59 |
| 20 (16ct, 4st) | G. R. A. Langley | Australia v West Indies (4 Tests) | 1954-55 |
| 20 (19ct, 1st) | H. B. Taber | Australia v South Africa | 1966-67 |
| 20 (16ct, 4st) | D. Tallon | Australia v England | 1946-47 |
| 20 (18ct, 2st) | R. W. Taylor | England v Australia (6 Tests) | 1978-79 |

## Most Dismissals in One Test

| | | | |
|---|---|---|---|
| 10 (all ct) | R. W. Taylor | England v India at Bombay | 1979-80 |
| 9 (8ct, 1st) | G. R. A. Langley | Australia v England at Lord's | 1956 |
| 9 (all ct) | R. W. Marsh | Australia v England at Brisbane | 1982-83 |
| 9 (all ct) | D. A. Murray | West Indies v Australia at Melbourne | 1981-82 |
| 8 (6ct, 2st) | L. E. G. Ames | England v West Indies at The Oval | 1933 |
| 8 (6ct, 2st) | A. T. W. Grout | Australia v Pakistan at Lahore | 1959-60 |
| 8 (all ct) | A. T. W. Grout | Australia v England at Lord's | 1961 |
| 8 (all ct) | J. J. Kelly | Australia v England at Sydney | 1901-02 |
| 8 (all ct) | G. R. A. Langley | Australia v West Indies at Kingston | 1954-55 |
| 8 (all ct) | W. K. Lees | New Zealand v Sri Lanka at Wellington | 1982-83 |
| 8 (all ct) | D. T. Lindsay | South Africa v Australia at Johannesburg | 1966-67 |
| 8 (all ct) | R. W. Marsh | Australia v West Indies at Melbourne | 1975-76 |
| 8 (all ct) | R. W. Marsh | Australia v New Zealand at Christchurch | 1976-77 |
| 8 (all ct) | R. W. Marsh | Australia v England at Adelaide | 1982-83 |
| 8 (all ct) | J. M. Parks | England v New Zealand at Christchurch | 1965-66 |
| 8 (7ct, 1st) | H. B. Taber | Australia v South Africa at Johannesburg | 1966-67 |
| 8 (all ct) | Wasim Bari | Pakistan v England at Leeds | 1971 |

## Most Dismissals in a Test Innings

| | | | |
|---|---|---|---|
| 7 (all ct) | Wasim Bari | Pakistan v New Zealand at Auckland | 1978-79 |
| 7 (all ct) | R. W. Taylor | England v India at Bombay | 1979-80 |
| 6 (all ct) | A. T. W. Grout | Australia v South Africa at Johannesburg | 1957-58 |
| 6 (5ct, 1st) | S. M. H. Kirmani | India v New Zealand at Christchurch | 1975-76 |
| 6 (all ct) | D. T. Lindsay | South Africa v Australia at Johannesburg | 1966-67 |
| 6 (all ct) | R. W. Marsh | Australia v England at Brisbane | 1982-83 |
| 6 (all ct) | J. T. Murray | England v India at Lord's | 1967 |

# MOST CATCHES – EXCLUDING WICKET-KEEPERS

## In a Test Career

| | |
|---|---|
| G. S. Chappell (Australia) | 122 in 87 matches |
| M. C. Cowdrey (England) | 120 in 114 matches |
| R. B. Simpson (Australia) | 110 in 62 matches |
| W. R. Hammond (England) | 110 in 85 matches |
| G. S. Sobers (West Indies) | 109 in 93 matches |
| I. M. Chappell (Australia) | 105 in 75 matches |

## In a Test Series

| | | | |
|---|---|---|---|
| 15 | J. M. Gregory | Australia v England | 1920-21 |
| 14 | G. S. Chappell | Australia v England (6 Tests) | 1974-75 |
| 13 | R. B. Simpson | Australia v South Africa | 1957-58 |
| 13 | R. B. Simpson | Australia v West Indies | 1960-61 |

## In One Test

| | | | |
|---|---|---|---|
| 7 | G. S. Chappell | Australia v England at Perth | 1974-75 |
| 7 | Yajurvindra Singh | India v England at Bangalore | 1976-77 |
| 6 | A. Shrewsbury | England v Australia at Sydney | 1887-88 |
| 6 | A. E. E. Vogler | South Africa v England at Durban | 1909-10 |
| 6 | F. E. Woolley | England v Australia at Sydney | 1911-12 |
| 6 | J. M. Gregory | Australia v England at Sydney | 1920-21 |
| 6 | B. Mitchell | South Africa v Australia at Melbourne | 1931-32 |
| 6 | V. Y. Richardson | Australia v South Africa at Durban | 1935-36 |

| | | | |
|---|---|---|---|
| 6 | R. N. Harvey | Australia v England at Sydney | 1962-63 |
| 6 | M. C. Cowdrey | England v West Indies at Lord's | 1963 |
| 6 | E. D. Solkar | India v West Indies at Port-of-Spain | 1970-71 |
| 6 | G. S. Sobers | West Indies v England at Lord's | 1973 |
| 6 | I. M. Chappell | Australia v New Zealand at Adelaide | 1973-74 |
| 6 | A. W. Greig | England v Pakistan at Leeds | 1974 |
| 6 | D. F. Whatmore | Australia v India at Kanpur | 1979-80 |
| 6 | A. J. Lamb | England v New Zealand at Lord's | 1983 |

### In a Test Innings

| | | | |
|---|---|---|---|
| 5 | V. Y. Richardson | Australia v South Africa at Durban | 1935-36 |
| 5 | Yajurvindra Singh | India v England at Bangalore | 1976-77 |

## YOUNGEST TEST PLAYERS

| *Years* | *Days* | | | |
|---|---|---|---|---|
| 15 | 124 | Mushtaq Mohammad | Pakistan v West Indies at Lahore | 1958-59 |
| 16 | 191 | Aftab Baloch | Pakistan v New Zealand at Dacca | 1969-70 |
| 16 | 248 | Nasim-ul-Ghani | Pakistan v West Indies at Bridgetown | 1957-58 |
| 16 | 352 | Khalid Hassan | Pakistan v England at Nottingham | 1954 |
| 17 | 118 | L. Sivaramakrishnan | India v West Indies at St John's, Antigua | 1982-83 |
| 17 | 122 | J. E. D. Sealy | West Indies v England at Bridgetown | 1929-30 |
| 17 | 193 | Maninder Singh | India v Pakistan at Karachi | 1982-83 |
| 17 | 239 | I. D. Craig | Australia v South Africa at Melbourne | 1952-53 |
| 17 | 245 | G. S. Sobers | West Indies v England at Kingston | 1953-54 |
| 17 | 265 | V. L. Mehra | India v New Zealand at Bombay | 1955-56 |
| 17 | 300 | Hanif Mohammad | Pakistan v India at Delhi | 1952-53 |
| 17 | 341 | Intikhab Alam | Pakistan v Australia at Karachi | 1959-60 |

*Note:* The youngest Test players for countries not mentioned above are: England – D. B. Close, 18 years 149 days, v New Zealand at Manchester, 1949; New Zealand – D. L. Freeman, 18 years 197 days, v England at Christchurch, 1932-33; South Africa – A. E. Ochse, 19 years 1 day, v England at Port Elizabeth, 1888-89; Sri Lanka – A. Ranatunga, 18 years 78 days, v England at Colombo, 1981-82.

## OLDEST PLAYERS ON TEST DEBUT

| *Years* | *Days* | | | |
|---|---|---|---|---|
| 49 | 119 | J. Southerton | England v Australia at Melbourne | 1876-77 |
| 47 | 284 | Miran Bux | Pakistan v India at Lahore | 1954-55 |
| 46 | 253 | D. D. Blackie | Australia v England at Sydney | 1928-29 |
| 46 | 237 | H. Ironmonger | Australia v England at Brisbane | 1928-29 |
| 42 | 242 | N. Betancourt | West Indies v England at Port-of-Spain | 1929-30 |
| 41 | 337 | E. R. Wilson | England v Australia at Sydney | 1920-21 |
| 41 | 27 | R. J. D. Jamshedji | India v England at Bombay | 1933-34 |
| 40 | 345 | C. A. Wiles | West Indies v England at Manchester | 1933 |
| 40 | 216 | S. P. Kinneir | England v Australia at Sydney | 1911-12 |

| Years | Days | | | |
|---|---|---|---|---|
| 40 | 110 | H. W. Lee | England v South Africa at Johannesburg | 1930-31 |
| 40 | 56 | G. W. A. Chubb | South Africa v England at Nottingham | 1951 |
| 40 | 37 | C. Ramaswami | India v England at Manchester | 1936 |

*Note:* The oldest Test player on début for New Zealand was H. M. McGirr, 38 years 101 days, v England at Auckland, 1929-30; for Sri Lanka, D. S. de Silva, 39 years 251 days, v England at Colombo (PSO), 1981-82.

## OLDEST TEST PLAYERS

(Age on final day of their last Test match)

| Years | Days | | | |
|---|---|---|---|---|
| 52 | 165 | W. Rhodes | England v West Indies at Kingston | 1929-30 |
| 50 | 327 | H. Ironmonger | Australia v England at Sydney | 1932-33 |
| 50 | 320 | W. G. Grace | England v Australia at Nottingham | 1899 |
| 50 | 303 | G. Gunn | England v West Indies at Kingston | 1929-30 |
| 49 | 139 | J. Southerton | England v Australia at Melbourne | 1876-77 |
| 47 | 302 | Miran Bux | Pakistan v India at Peshawar | 1954-55 |
| 47 | 249 | J. B. Hobbs | England v Australia at The Oval | 1930 |
| 47 | 87 | F. E. Woolley | England v Australia at The Oval | 1934 |
| 46 | 309 | D. D. Blackie | Australia v England at Adelaide | 1928-29 |
| 46 | 206 | A. W. Nourse | South Africa v England at The Oval | 1924 |
| 46 | 202 | H. Strudwick | England v Australia at The Oval | 1926 |
| 46 | 41 | E. H. Hendren | England v West Indies at Kingston | 1934-35 |
| 45 | 245 | G. O. Allen | England v West Indies at Kingston | 1947-48 |
| 45 | 215 | P. Holmes | England v India at Lord's | 1932 |
| 45 | 140 | D. B. Close | England v West Indies at Manchester | 1976 |

## MOST CONSECUTIVE TEST APPEARANCES

| | | |
|---|---|---|
| 90 | S. M. Gavaskar, India | Bombay 1974-75 to Kanpur 1984-85 |
| 87 | G. R. Viswanath, India | Georgetown 1970-71 to Karachi 1982-83 |
| 85 | G. S. Sobers, West Indies | Port-of-Spain 1954-55 to Port-of-Spain 1971-72 |
| 71 | I. M. Chappell, Australia | Adelaide 1965-66 to Melbourne 1975-76 |
| 69 | A. R. Border, Australia | Melbourne 1978-79 to The Oval 1985 |
| 67 | Kapil Dev, India | Faisalabad 1978-79 to Delhi 1984-85 |
| 65 | I. T. Botham, England | Wellington 1977-78 to Karachi 1983-84 |
| 65 | A. P. E. Knott, England | Auckland 1970-71 to The Oval 1977 |
| 61 | R. B. Kanhai, West Indies | Birmingham 1957 to Sydney 1968-69 |
| 58† | A. W. Greig, England | Manchester 1972 to The Oval 1977 |
| 58† | J. R. Reid, New Zealand | Manchester 1949 to Leeds 1965 |
| 53 | K. J. Hughes, Australia | Brisbane 1978-79 to Sydney 1982-83 |
| 53 | Javed Miandad, Pakistan | Lahore 1977-78 to Sydney 1983-84 |
| 52 | R. W. Marsh, Australia | Brisbane 1970-71 to The Oval 1977 |
| 52 | P. B. H. May, England | The Oval 1953 to Leeds 1959 |
| 52 | F. E. Woolley, England | The Oval 1909 to The Oval 1926 |
| 51 | G. S. Chappell, Australia | Perth 1970-71 to The Oval 1977 |

† *Indicates complete Test career.*

## SUMMARY OF ALL TEST MATCHES

To end of 1985 season in England

| | | Tests | Won by | | | | | | | | Tied | Drawn |
|---|---|---|---|---|---|---|---|---|---|---|---|---|
| | | | *E* | *A* | *SA* | *WI* | *NZ* | *I* | *P* | *SL* | | |
| **England** | v Australia | 257 | 86 | 96 | – | – | – | – | – | – | – | 75 |
| | v South Africa | 102 | 46 | – | 18 | – | – | – | – | – | – | 38 |
| | v West Indies | 85 | 21 | – | – | 30 | – | – | – | – | – | 34 |
| | v New Zealand | 60 | 30 | – | – | – | 3 | – | – | – | – | 27 |
| | v India | 72 | 30 | – | – | – | – | 9 | – | – | – | 33 |
| | v Pakistan | 39 | 13 | – | – | – | – | – | 3 | – | – | 23 |
| | v Sri Lanka | 2 | 1 | – | – | – | – | – | – | – | – | 1 |
| **Australia** | v South Africa | 53 | – | 29 | 11 | – | – | – | – | – | – | 13 |
| | v West Indies | 62 | – | 27 | – | 19 | – | – | – | – | 1 | 15 |
| | v New Zealand | 15 | – | 8 | – | – | 2 | – | – | – | – | 5 |
| | v India | 39 | – | 20 | – | – | – | 8 | – | – | – | 11 |
| | v Pakistan | 28 | – | 11 | – | – | – | – | 8 | – | – | 9 |
| | v Sri Lanka | 1 | – | 1 | – | – | – | – | – | – | – | – |
| **South Africa** | v New Zealand | 17 | – | – | 9 | – | 2 | – | – | – | – | 6 |
| **West Indies** | v New Zealand | 21 | – | – | – | 7 | 3 | – | – | – | – | 11 |
| | v India | 54 | – | – | – | 22 | – | 5 | – | – | – | 27 |
| | v Pakistan | 19 | – | – | – | 7 | – | – | 4 | – | – | 8 |
| **New Zealand** | v India | 25 | – | – | – | – | 4 | 10 | – | – | – | 11 |
| | v Pakistan | 27 | – | – | – | – | 3 | – | 10 | – | – | 14 |
| | v Sri Lanka | 5 | – | – | – | – | 4 | – | – | – | – | 1 |
| **India** | v Pakistan | 35 | – | – | – | – | – | 4 | 6 | – | – | 25 |
| | v Sri Lanka | 1 | – | – | – | – | – | – | – | – | – | 1 |
| **Pakistan** | v Sri Lanka | 3 | – | – | – | – | – | – | 2 | – | – | 1 |
| | | 1,022 | 227 | 192 | 38 | 85 | 21 | 36 | 33 | – | 1 | 389 |

| | *Tests* | *Won* | *Lost* | *Drawn* | *Tied* | *Toss Won* |
|---|---|---|---|---|---|---|
| England | 617 | 227 | 159 | 231 | – | 303 |
| Australia | 455 | 192 | 134 | 128 | 1 | 228 |
| South Africa | 172 | 38 | 77 | 57 | – | 80 |
| West Indies | 241 | 85 | 60 | 95 | 1 | 130 |
| New Zealand | 170 | 21 | 74 | 75 | – | 83 |
| India | 226 | 36 | 82 | 108 | – | 113 |
| Pakistan | 151 | 33 | 38 | 80 | – | 80 |
| Sri Lanka | 12 | – | 8 | 4 | – | 5 |

## ENGLAND v AUSTRALIA

| *Season* | Captains *England* | *Australia* | *T* | *E* | *A* | *D* |
|---|---|---|---|---|---|---|
| 1876-77 | James Lillywhite | D. W. Gregory | 2 | 1 | 1 | 0 |
| 1878-79 | Lord Harris | D. W. Gregory | 1 | 0 | 1 | 0 |
| 1880 | Lord Harris | W. L. Murdoch | 1 | 1 | 0 | 0 |
| 1881-82 | A. Shaw | W. L. Murdoch | 4 | 0 | 2 | 2 |
| 1882 | A. N. Hornby | W. L. Murdoch | 1 | 0 | 1 | 0 |

### THE ASHES

| *Season* | Captains *England* | *Australia* | *T* | *E* | *A* | *D* | *Held by* |
|---|---|---|---|---|---|---|---|
| 1882-83 | Hon. Ivo Bligh | W. L. Murdoch | 4* | 2 | 2 | 0 | E |
| 1884 | Lord Harris[1] | W. L. Murdoch | 3 | 1 | 0 | 2 | E |
| 1884-85 | A. Shrewsbury | T. Horan[2] | 5 | 3 | 2 | 0 | E |

| Season | Captains: England | Australia | T | E | A | D | Held by |
|---|---|---|---|---|---|---|---|
| 1886 | A. G. Steel | H. J. H. Scott | 3 | 3 | 0 | 0 | E |
| 1886-87 | A. Shrewsbury | P. S. McDonnell | 2 | 2 | 0 | 0 | E |
| 1887-88 | W. W. Read | P. S. McDonnell | 1 | 1 | 0 | 0 | E |
| 1888 | W. G. Grace[3] | P. S. McDonnell | 3 | 2 | 1 | 0 | E |
| 1890† | W. G. Grace | W. L. Murdoch | 2 | 2 | 0 | 0 | E |
| 1891-92 | W. G. Grace | J. McC. Blackham | 3 | 1 | 2 | 0 | A |
| 1893 | W. G. Grace[4] | J. McC. Blackham | 3 | 1 | 0 | 2 | E |
| 1894-95 | A. E. Stoddart | G. Giffen[5] | 5 | 3 | 2 | 0 | E |
| 1896 | W. G. Grace | G. H. S. Trott | 3 | 2 | 1 | 0 | E |
| 1897-98 | A. E. Stoddart[6] | G. H. S. Trott | 5 | 1 | 4 | 0 | A |
| 1899 | A. C. MacLaren[7] | J. Darling | 5 | 0 | 1 | 4 | A |
| 1901-02 | A. C. MacLaren | J. Darling[8] | 5 | 1 | 4 | 0 | A |
| 1902 | A. C. MacLaren | J. Darling | 5 | 1 | 2 | 2 | A |
| 1903-04 | P. F. Warner | M. A. Noble | 5 | 3 | 2 | 0 | E |
| 1905 | Hon. F. S. Jackson | J. Darling | 5 | 2 | 0 | 3 | E |
| 1907-08 | A. O. Jones[9] | M. A. Noble | 5 | 1 | 4 | 0 | A |
| 1909 | A. C. MacLaren | M. A. Noble | 5 | 1 | 2 | 2 | A |
| 1911-12 | J. W. H. T. Douglas | C. Hill | 5 | 4 | 1 | 0 | E |
| 1912 | C. B. Fry | S. E. Gregory | 3 | 1 | 0 | 2 | E |
| 1920-21 | J. W. H. T. Douglas | W. W. Armstrong | 5 | 0 | 5 | 0 | A |
| 1921 | Hon. L. H. Tennyson[10] | W. W. Armstrong | 5 | 0 | 3 | 2 | A |
| 1924-25 | A. E. R. Gilligan | H. L. Collins | 5 | 1 | 4 | 0 | A |
| 1926 | A. W. Carr[11] | H. L. Collins[12] | 5 | 1 | 0 | 4 | E |
| 1928-29 | A. P. F. Chapman[13] | J. Ryder | 5 | 4 | 1 | 0 | E |
| 1930 | A. P. F. Chapman[14] | W. M. Woodfull | 5 | 1 | 2 | 2 | A |
| 1932-33 | D. R. Jardine | W. M. Woodfull | 5 | 4 | 1 | 0 | E |
| 1934 | R. E. S. Wyatt[15] | W. M. Woodfull | 5 | 1 | 2 | 2 | A |
| 1936-37 | G. O. Allen | D. G. Bradman | 5 | 2 | 3 | 0 | A |
| 1938† | W. R. Hammond | D. G. Bradman | 4 | 1 | 1 | 2 | A |
| 1946-47 | W. R. Hammond[16] | D. G. Bradman | 5 | 0 | 3 | 2 | A |
| 1948 | N. W. D. Yardley | D. G. Bradman | 5 | 0 | 4 | 1 | A |
| 1950-51 | F. R. Brown | A. L. Hassett | 5 | 1 | 4 | 0 | A |
| 1953 | L. Hutton | A. L. Hassett | 5 | 1 | 0 | 4 | E |
| 1954-55 | L. Hutton | I. W. Johnson[17] | 5 | 3 | 1 | 1 | E |
| 1956 | P. B. H. May | I. W. Johnson | 5 | 2 | 1 | 2 | E |
| 1958-59 | P. B. H. May | R. Benaud | 5 | 0 | 4 | 1 | A |
| 1961 | P. B. H. May[18] | R. Benaud[19] | 5 | 1 | 2 | 2 | A |
| 1962-63 | E. R. Dexter | R. Benaud | 5 | 1 | 1 | 3 | A |
| 1964 | E. R. Dexter | R. B. Simpson | 5 | 0 | 1 | 4 | A |
| 1965-66 | M. J. K. Smith | R. B. Simpson[20] | 5 | 1 | 1 | 3 | A |
| 1968 | M. C. Cowdrey[21] | W. M. Lawry[22] | 5 | 1 | 1 | 3 | A |
| 1970-71† | R. Illingworth | W. M. Lawry[23] | 6 | 2 | 0 | 4 | E |
| 1972 | R. Illingworth | I. M. Chappell | 5 | 2 | 2 | 1 | E |
| 1974-75 | M. H. Denness[24] | I. M. Chappell | 6 | 1 | 4 | 1 | A |
| 1975 | A. W. Greig[25] | I. M. Chappell | 4 | 0 | 1 | 3 | A |
| 1976-77‡ | A. W. Greig | G. S. Chappell | 1 | 0 | 1 | 0 | — |
| 1977 | J. M. Brearley | G. S. Chappell | 5 | 3 | 0 | 2 | E |
| 1978-79 | J. M. Brearley | G. N. Yallop | 6 | 5 | 1 | 0 | E |
| 1979-80‡ | J. M. Brearley | G. S. Chappell | 3 | 0 | 3 | 0 | — |
| 1980‡ | I. T. Botham | G. S. Chappell | 1 | 0 | 0 | 1 | — |
| 1981 | J. M. Brearley[26] | K. J. Hughes | 6 | 3 | 1 | 2 | E |
| 1982-83 | R. G. D. Willis | G. S. Chappell | 5 | 1 | 2 | 2 | A |
| 1985 | D. I. Gower | A. R. Border | 6 | 3 | 1 | 2 | E |
| | In Australia | | 134 | 49 | 66 | 19 | |
| | In England | | 123 | 37 | 30 | 56 | |
| | Totals | | 257 | 86 | 96 | 75 | |

** The Ashes were awarded in 1882-83 after a series of three matches which England won 2-1. A fourth unofficial match was played, each innings being played on a different pitch, and this was won by Australia.*

*† The matches at Manchester in 1890 and 1938 and at Melbourne (Third Test) in 1970-71 were abandoned without a ball being bowled and are excluded.*

*‡ The Ashes were not at stake in these series.*

*Notes:* The following deputised for the official touring captain or were appointed by the home authority for only a minor proportion of the series:

[1]A. N. Hornby (First). [2]W. L. Murdoch (First), H. H. Massie (Third), J. McC. Blackham (Fourth). [3]A. G. Steel (First). [4]A. E. Stoddart (First). [5]J. McC. Blackham (First). [6]A. C. MacLaren (First, Second and Fifth). [7]W. G. Grace (First). [8]H. Trumble (Fourth and Fifth). [9]F. L. Fane (First, Second and Third). [10]J. W. H. T. Douglas (First and Second). [11]A. P. F. Chapman (Fifth). [12]W. Bardsley (Third and Fourth). [13]J. C. White (Fifth). [14]R. E. S. Wyatt (Fifth). [15]C. F. Walters (First). [16]N. W. D. Yardley (Fifth). [17]A. R. Morris (Second). [18]M. C. Cowdrey (First and Second). [19]R. N. Harvey (Second). [20]B. C. Booth (First and Third). [21]T. W. Graveney (Fourth). [22]B. N. Jarman (Fourth). [23]I. M. Chappell (Seventh). [24]J. H. Edrich (Fourth). [25]M. H. Denness (First). [26]I. T. Botham (First and Second).

## HIGHEST INNINGS TOTALS

| | | |
|---|---|---|
| For England | in England: 903-7 dec. at The Oval | 1938 |
| | in Australia: 636 at Sydney | 1928-29 |
| For Australia | in England: 729-6 dec. at Lord's | 1930 |
| | in Australia: 659-8 dec. at Sydney | 1946-47 |

## LOWEST INNINGS TOTALS

| | | |
|---|---|---|
| For England | in England: 52 at The Oval | 1948 |
| | in Australia: 45 at Sydney | 1886-87 |
| For Australia | in England: 36 at Birmingham | 1902 |
| | in Australia: 42 at Sydney | 1887-88 |

## INDIVIDUAL HUNDREDS

**For England** (179)

| | | |
|---|---|---|
| 132*‡ | R. Abel, Sydney | 1891-92 |
| 120 | L. E. G. Ames, Lord's | 1934 |
| 185 | R. W. Barber, Sydney | 1965-66 |
| 134 | W. Barnes, Adelaide | 1884-85 |
| 129 | C. J. Barnett, Adelaide | 1936-37 |
| 126 | C. J. Barnett, Nottingham | 1938 |
| 132* | K. F. Barrington, Adelaide | 1962-63 |
| 101 | K. F. Barrington, Sydney | 1962-63 |
| 256 | K. F. Barrington, Manchester | 1964 |
| 102 | K. F. Barrington, Adelaide | 1965-66 |
| 115 | K. F. Barrington, Melbourne | 1965-66 |
| 119* | I. T. Botham, Melbourne | 1979-80 |
| 149* | I. T. Botham, Leeds | 1981 |
| 118 | I. T. Botham, Manchester | 1981 |
| 113 | G. Boycott, The Oval | 1964 |
| 142* | G. Boycott, Sydney | 1970-71 |
| 119* | G. Boycott, Adelaide | 1970-71 |
| 107 | G. Boycott, Nottingham | 1977 |
| 191 | G. Boycott, Leeds | 1977 |
| 128* | G. Boycott, Lord's | 1980 |
| 137 | G. Boycott, The Oval | 1981 |
| 103* | L. C. Braund, Adelaide | 1901-02 |
| 102 | L. C. Braund, Sydney | 1903-04 |
| 121 | J. Briggs, Melbourne | 1884-85 |
| 140 | J. T. Brown, Melbourne | 1894-95 |
| 121 | A. P. F. Chapman, Lord's | 1930 |
| 102† | D. C. S. Compton, Nottingham | 1938 |
| 147<br>103* | D. C. S. Compton, Adelaide | 1946-47 |
| 184 | D. C. S. Compton, Nottingham | 1948 |
| 145* | D. C. S. Compton, Manchester | 1948 |
| 102 | M. C. Cowdrey, Melbourne | 1954-55 |
| 100* | M. C. Cowdrey, Sydney | 1958-59 |
| 113 | M. C. Cowdrey, Melbourne | 1962-63 |
| 104 | M. C. Cowdrey, Melbourne | 1965-66 |

| | | |
|---|---|---|
| 104 | M. C. Cowdrey, Birmingham | 1968 |
| 188 | M. H. Denness, Melbourne | 1974-75 |
| 180 | E. R. Dexter, Birmingham | 1961 |
| 174 | E. R. Dexter, Manchester | 1964 |
| 158 | B. L. D'Oliveira, The Oval | 1968 |
| 117 | B. L. D'Oliveira, Melbourne | 1970-71 |
| 173† | K. S. Duleepsinhji, Lord's | 1930 |
| 120† | J. H. Edrich, Lord's | 1964 |
| 109 | J. H. Edrich, Melbourne | 1965-66 |
| 103 | J. H. Edrich, Sydney | 1965-66 |
| 164 | J. H. Edrich, The Oval | 1968 |
| 115* | J. H. Edrich, Perth | 1970-71 |
| 130 | J. H. Edrich, Adelaide | 1970-71 |
| 175 | J. H. Edrich, Lord's | 1975 |
| 119 | W. J. Edrich, Sydney | 1946-47 |
| 111 | W. J. Edrich, Leeds | 1948 |
| 146 | K. W. R. Fletcher, Melbourne | 1974-75 |
| 287† | R. E. Foster, Sydney | 1903-04 |
| 144 | C. B. Fry, The Oval | 1905 |
| 160 | M. W. Gatting, Manchester | 1985 |
| 100* | M. W. Gatting, Birmingham | 1985 |
| 196 | G. A. Gooch, The Oval | 1985 |
| 102 | D. I. Gower, Perth | 1978-79 |
| 114 | D. I. Gower, Adelaide | 1982-83 |
| 166 | D. I. Gower, Nottingham | 1985 |
| 215 | D. I. Gower, Birmingham | 1985 |
| 157 | D. I. Gower, The Oval | 1985 |
| 152† | W. G. Grace, The Oval | 1880 |
| 170 | W. G. Grace, The Oval | 1886 |
| 111 | T. W. Graveney, Sydney | 1954-55 |
| 110 | A. W. Greig, Brisbane | 1974-75 |
| 119† | G. Gunn, Sydney | 1907-08 |
| 122* | G. Gunn, Sydney | 1907-08 |
| 102* | W. Gunn, Manchester | 1893 |
| 251 | W. R. Hammond, Sydney | 1928-29 |
| 200 | W. R. Hammond, Melbourne | 1928-29 |
| 119* / 177 | W. R. Hammond, Adelaide | 1928-29 |
| 113 | W. R. Hammond, Leeds | 1930 |
| 112 | W. R. Hammond, Sydney | 1932-33 |
| 101 | W. R. Hammond, Sydney | 1932-33 |
| 231* | W. R. Hammond, Sydney | 1936-37 |
| 240 | W. R. Hammond, Lord's | 1938 |
| 169* | J. Hardstaff jun., The Oval | 1938 |
| 130 | T. W. Hayward, Manchester | 1899 |
| 137 | T. W. Hayward, The Oval | 1899 |
| 114 | J. W. Hearne, Melbourne | 1911-12 |
| 127* | E. H. Hendren, Lord's | 1926 |
| 169 | E. H. Hendren, Brisbane | 1928-29 |
| 132 | E. H. Hendren, Manchester | 1934 |
| 126* | J. B. Hobbs, Melbourne | 1911-12 |
| 187 | J. B. Hobbs, Adelaide | 1911-12 |
| 178 | J. B. Hobbs, Melbourne | 1911-12 |
| 107 | J. B. Hobbs, Lord's | 1912 |
| 122 | J. B. Hobbs, Melbourne | 1920-21 |
| 123 | J. B. Hobbs, Adelaide | 1920-21 |
| 115 | J. B. Hobbs, Sydney | 1924-25 |
| 154 | J. B. Hobbs, Melbourne | 1924-25 |
| 119 | J. B. Hobbs, Adelaide | 1924-25 |
| 119 | J. B. Hobbs, Lord's | 1926 |
| 100 | J. B. Hobbs, The Oval | 1926 |
| 142 | J. B. Hobbs, Melbourne | 1928-29 |
| 126 | K. L. Hutchings, Melbourne | 1907-08 |
| 100† | L. Hutton, Nottingham | 1938 |
| 364 | L. Hutton, The Oval | 1938 |
| 122* | L. Hutton, Sydney | 1946-47 |
| 156*‡ | L. Hutton, Adelaide | 1950-51 |
| 145 | L. Hutton, Lord's | 1953 |
| 103 | Hon. F. S. Jackson, The Oval | 1893 |
| 118 | Hon. F. S. Jackson, The Oval | 1899 |
| 128 | Hon. F. S. Jackson, Manchester | 1902 |
| 144* | Hon. F. S. Jackson, Leeds | 1905 |
| 113 | Hon. F. S. Jackson, Manchester | 1905 |
| 104 | G. L. Jessop, The Oval | 1902 |
| 106* | A. P. E. Knott, Adelaide | 1974-75 |
| 135 | A. P. E. Knott, Nottingham | 1977 |
| 137† | M. Leyland, Melbourne | 1928-29 |
| 109 | M. Leyland, Lord's | 1934 |
| 153 | M. Leyland, Manchester | 1934 |
| 110 | M. Leyland, The Oval | 1934 |
| 126 | M. Leyland, Brisbane | 1936-37 |
| 111* | M. Leyland, Melbourne | 1936-37 |
| 187 | M. Leyland, The Oval | 1938 |
| 131 | B. W. Luckhurst, Perth | 1970-71 |
| 109 | B. W. Luckhurst, Melbourne | 1970-71 |
| 120 | A. C. MacLaren, Melbourne | 1894-95 |
| 109 | A. C. MacLaren, Sydney | 1897-98 |
| 124 | A. C. MacLaren, Adelaide | 1897-98 |
| 116 | A. C. MacLaren, Sydney | 1901-02 |
| 140 | A. C. MacLaren, Nottingham | 1905 |
| 117 | H. Makepeace, Melbourne | 1920-21 |
| 104 | P. B. H. May, Sydney | 1954-55 |
| 101 | P. B. H. May, Leeds | 1956 |
| 113 | P. B. H. May, Melbourne | 1958-59 |
| 182* | C. P. Mead, The Oval | 1921 |
| 102† | Nawab of Pataudi, Sydney | 1932-33 |
| 216* | E. Paynter, Nottingham | 1938 |
| 174† | D. W. Randall, Melbourne | 1976-77 |
| 150 | D. W. Randall, Sydney | 1978-79 |
| 115 | D. W. Randall, Perth | 1982-83 |
| 154*† | K. S. Ranjitsinhji, Manchester | 1896 |
| 175 | K. S. Ranjitsinhji, Sydney | 1897-98 |
| 117 | W. W. Read, The Oval | 1884 |
| 179 | W. Rhodes, Melbourne | 1911-12 |
| 104 | P. E. Richardson, Manchester | 1956 |
| 175† | R. T. Robinson, Leeds | 1985 |
| 148 | R. T. Robinson, Birmingham | 1985 |
| 135* | A. C. Russell, Adelaide | 1920-21 |

| | | |
|---|---|---|
| 101 | A. C. Russell, Manchester | 1921 |
| 102* | A. C. Russell, The Oval | 1921 |
| 105 | J. Sharp, The Oval | 1909 |
| 113 | Rev. D. S. Sheppard, Manchester | 1956 |
| 113 | Rev. D. S. Sheppard, Melbourne | 1962-63 |
| 105* | A. Shrewsbury, Melbourne | 1884-85 |
| 164 | A. Shrewsbury, Lord's | 1886 |
| 106 | A. Shrewsbury, Lord's | 1893 |
| 156* | R. T. Simpson, Melbourne | 1950-51 |
| 135* | A. G. Steel, Sydney | 1882-83 |
| 148 | A. G. Steel, Lord's | 1884 |
| 134 | A. E. Stoddart, Adelaide | 1891-92 |
| 173 | A. E. Stoddart, Melbourne | 1894-95 |
| 112† | R. Subba Row, Birmingham | 1961 |
| 137 | R. Subba Row, The Oval | 1961 |
| 115† | H. Sutcliffe, Sydney | 1924-25 |
| 176<br>127 | H. Sutcliffe, Melbourne | 1924-25 |
| 143 | H. Sutcliffe, Melbourne | 1924-25 |
| 161 | H. Sutcliffe, The Oval | 1926 |
| 135 | H. Sutcliffe, Melbourne | 1928-29 |
| 161 | H. Sutcliffe, The Oval | 1930 |
| 194 | H. Sutcliffe, Sydney | 1932-33 |
| 138 | J. T. Tyldesley, Birmingham | 1902 |
| 100 | J. T. Tyldesley, Leeds | 1905 |
| 112* | J. T. Tyldesley, The Oval | 1905 |
| 149 | G. Ulyett, Melbourne | 1881-82 |
| 117 | A. Ward, Sydney | 1894-95 |
| 112 | C. Washbrook, Melbourne | 1946-47 |
| 143 | C. Washbrook, Leeds | 1948 |
| 109† | W. Watson, Lord's | 1953 |
| 133* | F. E. Woolley, Sydney | 1911-12 |
| 123 | F. E. Woolley, Sydney | 1924-25 |
| 149 | R. A. Woolmer, The Oval | 1975 |
| 120 | R. A. Woolmer, Lord's | 1977 |
| 137 | R. A. Woolmer, Manchester | 1977 |

† *Signifies hundred on first appearance in England–Australia Tests.*
‡ *Carried his bat.*

*Note:* In consecutive innings in 1928-29, W. R. Hammond scored 251 at Sydney, 200 and 32 at Melbourne, and 119* and 177 at Adelaide.

### **For Australia** (198)

| | | |
|---|---|---|
| 133* | W. W. Armstrong, Melbourne | 1907-08 |
| 158 | W. W. Armstrong, Sydney | 1920-21 |
| 121 | W. W. Armstrong, Adelaide | 1920-21 |
| 123* | W. W. Armstrong, Melbourne | 1920-21 |
| 118 | C. L. Badcock, Melbourne | 1936-37 |
| 165*† | C. Bannerman, Melbourne | 1876-77 |
| 136<br>130 | W. Bardsley, The Oval | 1909 |
| 193*‡ | W. Bardsley, Lord's | 1926 |
| 234 | S. G. Barnes, Sydney | 1946-47 |
| 141 | S. G. Barnes, Lord's | 1948 |
| 128 | G. J. Bonnor, Sydney | 1884-85 |
| 112 | B. C. Booth, Brisbane | 1962-63 |
| 103 | B. C. Booth, Melbourne | 1962-63 |
| 115 | A. R. Border, Perth | 1979-80 |
| 123* | A. R. Border, Manchester | 1981 |
| 106* | A. R. Border, The Oval | 1981 |
| 196 | A. R. Border, Lord's | 1985 |
| 146* | A. R. Border, Manchester | 1985 |
| 112 | D. G. Bradman, Melbourne | 1928-29 |
| 123 | D. G. Bradman, Melbourne | 1928-29 |
| 131 | D. G. Bradman, Nottingham | 1930 |
| 254 | D. G. Bradman, Lord's | 1930 |
| 334 | D. G. Bradman, Leeds | 1930 |
| 232 | D. G. Bradman, The Oval | 1930 |
| 103* | D. G. Bradman, Melbourne | 1932-33 |
| 304 | D. G. Bradman, Leeds | 1934 |
| 244 | D. G. Bradman, The Oval | 1934 |
| 270 | D. G. Bradman, Melbourne | 1936-37 |
| 212 | D. G. Bradman, Adelaide | 1936-37 |
| 169 | D. G. Bradman, Melbourne | 1936-37 |
| 144* | D. G. Bradman, Nottingham | 1938 |
| 102* | D. G. Bradman, Lord's | 1938 |
| 103 | D. G. Bradman, Leeds | 1938 |
| 187 | D. G. Bradman, Brisbane | 1946-47 |
| 234 | D. G. Bradman, Sydney | 1946-47 |
| 138 | D. G. Bradman, Nottingham | 1948 |
| 173* | D. G. Bradman, Leeds | 1948 |
| 105 | W. A. Brown, Lord's | 1934 |
| 133 | W. A. Brown, Nottingham | 1938 |
| 206*‡ | W. A. Brown, Lord's | 1938 |
| 181 | P. J. Burge, The Oval | 1961 |
| 103 | P. J. Burge, Sydney | 1962-63 |
| 160 | P. J. Burge, Leeds | 1964 |
| 120 | P. J. Burge, Melbourne | 1965-66 |
| 101*† | J. W. Burke, Adelaide | 1950-51 |
| 108† | G. S. Chappell, Perth | 1970-71 |
| 131 | G. S. Chappell, Lord's | 1972 |
| 113 | G. S. Chappell, The Oval | 1972 |
| 144 | G. S. Chappell, Sydney | 1974-75 |

| | | |
|---|---|---|
| 102 | G. S. Chappell, Melbourne | 1974-75 |
| 112 | G. S. Chappell, Manchester | 1977 |
| 114 | G. S. Chappell, Melbourne | 1979-80 |
| 117 | G. S. Chappell, Perth | 1982-83 |
| 115 | G. S. Chappell, Adelaide | 1982-83 |
| 111 | I. M. Chappell, Melbourne | 1970-71 |
| 104 | I. M. Chappell, Adelaide | 1970-71 |
| 118 | I. M. Chappell, The Oval | 1972 |
| 192 | I. M. Chappell, The Oval | 1975 |
| 104† | H. L. Collins, Sydney | 1920-21 |
| 162 | H. L. Collins, Adelaide | 1920-21 |
| 114 | H. L. Collins, Sydney | 1924-25 |
| 307 | R. M. Cowper, Melbourne | 1965-66 |
| 101 | J. Darling, Sydney | 1897-98 |
| 178 | J. Darling, Adelaide | 1897-98 |
| 160 | J. Darling, Sydney | 1897-98 |
| 104† | R. A. Duff, Melbourne | 1901-02 |
| 146 | R. A. Duff, The Oval | 1905 |
| 102 | J. Dyson, Leeds | 1981 |
| 170* | R. Edwards, Nottingham | 1972 |
| 115 | R. Edwards, Perth | 1974-75 |
| 100 | J. H. Fingleton, Brisbane | 1936-37 |
| 136 | J. H. Fingleton, Melbourne | 1936-37 |
| 161 | G. Giffen, Sydney | 1894-95 |
| 107† | H. Graham, Lord's | 1893 |
| 105 | H. Graham, Sydney | 1894-95 |
| 100 | J. M. Gregory, Melbourne | 1920-21 |
| 201 | S. E. Gregory, Sydney | 1894-95 |
| 103 | S. E. Gregory, Lord's | 1896 |
| 117 | S. E. Gregory, The Oval | 1899 |
| 112 | S. E. Gregory, Adelaide | 1903-04 |
| 116† | R. J. Hartigan, Adelaide | 1907-08 |
| 112† | R. N. Harvey, Leeds | 1948 |
| 122 | R. N. Harvey, Manchester | 1953 |
| 162 | R. N. Harvey, Brisbane | 1954-55 |
| 167 | R. N. Harvey, Melbourne | 1958-59 |
| 114 | R. N. Harvey, Birmingham | 1961 |
| 154 | R. N. Harvey, Adelaide | 1962-63 |
| 128 | A. L. Hassett, Brisbane | 1946-47 |
| 137 | A. L. Hassett, Nottingham | 1948 |
| 115 | A. L. Hassett, Nottingham | 1953 |
| 104 | A. L. Hassett, Lord's | 1953 |
| 112 | H. L. Hendry, Sydney | 1928-29 |
| 119 | A. M. J. Hilditch, Leeds | 1985 |
| 188 | C. Hill, Melbourne | 1897-98 |
| 135 | C. Hill, Lord's | 1899 |
| 119 | C. Hill, Sheffield | 1902 |
| 160 | C. Hill, Adelaide | 1907-08 |
| 124 | T. P. Horan, Melbourne | 1881-82 |
| 129 | K. J. Hughes, Brisbane | 1978-79 |
| 117 | K. J. Hughes, Lord's | 1980 |
| 137 | K. J. Hughes, Sydney | 1982-83 |
| 140 | F. A. Iredale, Adelaide | 1894-95 |
| 108 | F. A. Iredale, Manchester | 1896 |
| 164† | A. A. Jackson, Adelaide | 1928-29 |
| 147 | C. Kelleway, Adelaide | 1920-21 |
| 100 | A. F. Kippax, Melbourne | 1928-29 |
| 130 | W. M. Lawry, Lord's | 1961 |
| 102 | W. M. Lawry, Manchester | 1961 |
| 106 | W. M. Lawry, Manchester | 1964 |
| 166 | W. M. Lawry, Brisbane | 1965-66 |
| 119 | W. M. Lawry, Adelaide | 1965-66 |
| 108 | W. M. Lawry, Melbourne | 1965-66 |
| 135 | W. M. Lawry, The Oval | 1968 |
| 100 | R. R. Lindwall, Melbourne | 1946-47 |
| 134 | J. J. Lyons, Sydney | 1891-92 |
| 170 | C. G. Macartney, Sydney | 1920-21 |
| 115 | C. G. Macartney, Leeds | 1921 |
| 133* | C. G. Macartney, Lord's | 1926 |
| 151 | C. G. Macartney, Leeds | 1926 |
| 109 | C. G. Macartney, Manchester | 1926 |
| 187* | S. J. McCabe, Sydney | 1932-33 |
| 137 | S. J. McCabe, Manchester | 1934 |
| 112 | S. J. McCabe, Melbourne | 1936-37 |
| 232 | S. J. McCabe, Nottingham | 1938 |
| 104* | C. L. McCool, Melbourne | 1946-47 |
| 127 | R. B. McCosker, The Oval | 1975 |
| 107 | R. B. McCosker, Nottingham | 1977 |
| 170 | C. C. McDonald, Adelaide | 1958-59 |
| 133 | C. C. McDonald, Melbourne | 1958-59 |
| 147 | P. S. McDonnell, Sydney | 1881-82 |
| 103 | P. S. McDonnell, The Oval | 1884 |
| 124 | P. S. McDonnell, Adelaide | 1884-85 |
| 112 | C. E. McLeod, Melbourne | 1897-98 |
| 110* | R. W. Marsh, Melbourne | 1976-77 |
| 141* | K. R. Miller, Adelaide | 1946-47 |
| 145* | K. R. Miller, Sydney | 1950-51 |
| 109 | K. R. Miller, Lord's | 1953 |
| 155 | A. R. Morris, Melbourne | 1946-47 |
| 122 }<br>124* } | A. R. Morris, Adelaide | 1946-47 |
| 105 | A. R. Morris, Lord's | 1948 |
| 182 | A. R. Morris, Leeds | 1948 |
| 196 | A. R. Morris, The Oval | 1948 |
| 206 | A. R. Morris, Adelaide | 1950-51 |
| 153 | A. R. Morris, Brisbane | 1954-55 |
| 153* | W. L. Murdoch, The Oval | 1880 |
| 211 | W. L. Murdoch, The Oval | 1884 |
| 133 | M. A. Noble, Sydney | 1903-04 |
| 117 | N. C. O'Neill, The Oval | 1961 |
| 100 | N. C. O'Neill, Adelaide | 1962-63 |
| 116 | C. E. Pellew, Melbourne | 1920-21 |
| 104 | C. E. Pellew, Adelaide | 1920-21 |
| 110† | W. H. Ponsford, Sydney | 1924-25 |
| 128 | W. H. Ponsford, Melbourne | 1924-25 |
| 110 | W. H. Ponsford, The Oval | 1930 |
| 181 | W. H. Ponsford, Leeds | 1934 |
| 266 | W. H. Ponsford, The Oval | 1934 |
| 143* | V. S. Ransford, Lord's | 1909 |
| 171 | I. R. Redpath, Perth | 1970-71 |
| 105 | I. R. Redpath, Sydney | 1974-75 |
| 100 | A. J. Richardson, Leeds | 1926 |
| 138 | V. Y. Richardson, Melbourne | 1924-25 |

| | | |
|---|---|---|
| 146 | G. M. Ritchie, Nottingham | 1985 |
| 201* | J. Ryder, Adelaide | 1924-25 |
| 112 | J. Ryder, Melbourne | 1928-29 |
| 102 | H. J. H. Scott, The Oval | 1884 |
| 311 | R. B. Simpson, Manchester | 1964 |
| 225 | R. B. Simpson, Adelaide | 1965-66 |
| 207 | K. R. Stackpole, Brisbane | 1970-71 |
| 136 | K. R. Stackpole, Adelaide | 1970-71 |
| 114 | K. R. Stackpole, Nottingham | 1972 |
| 108 | J. M. Taylor, Sydney | 1924-25 |
| 143 | G. H. S. Trott, Lord's | 1896 |
| 135* | V. T. Trumper, Lord's | 1899 |
| 104 | V. T. Trumper, Manchester | 1902 |
| 185* | V. T. Trumper, Sydney | 1903-04 |
| 113 | V. T. Trumper, Adelaide | 1903-04 |
| 166 | V. T. Trumper, Sydney | 1907-08 |
| 113 | V. T. Trumper, Sydney | 1911-12 |
| 155† | K. D. Walters, Brisbane | 1965-66 |
| 115 | K. D. Walters, Melbourne | 1965-66 |
| 112 | K. D. Walters, Brisbane | 1970-71 |
| 103 | K. D. Walters, Perth | 1974-75 |
| 103† | D. M. Wellham, The Oval | 1981 |
| 162† | K. C. Wessels, Brisbane | 1982-83 |
| 100 | G. M. Wood, Melbourne | 1978-79 |
| 112 | G. M. Wood, Lord's | 1980 |
| 172 | G. M. Wood, Nottingham | 1985 |
| 141 | W. M. Woodfull, Leeds | 1926 |
| 117 | W. M. Woodfull, Manchester | 1926 |
| 111 | W. M. Woodfull, Sydney | 1928-29 |
| 107 | W. M. Woodfull, Melbourne | 1928-29 |
| 102 | W. M. Woodfull, Melbourne | 1928-29 |
| 155 | W. M. Woodfull, Lord's | 1930 |
| 102† | G. N. Yallop, Brisbane | 1978-79 |
| 121 | G. N. Yallop, Sydney | 1978-79 |
| 114 | G. N. Yallop, Manchester | 1981 |

† *Signifies hundred on first appearance in England–Australia Tests.*
‡ *Carried his bat.*

*Notes:* D. G. Bradman's scores in 1930 were 8 and 131 at Nottingham, 254 and 1 at Lord's, 334 at Leeds, 14 at Manchester, and 232 at The Oval.

D. G. Bradman scored a hundred in eight successive Tests against England in which he batted – three in 1936-37, three in 1938 and two in 1946-47. He was injured and unable to bat at The Oval in 1938.

W. H. Ponsford and K. D. Walters each hit hundreds in their first two Tests.

C. Bannerman and H. Graham each scored their maiden hundred in first-class cricket in their first Test.

No right-handed batsman has obtained two hundreds for Australia in a Test match against England, and no left-handed batsman for England against Australia.

H. Sutcliffe, in his first two games for England, scored 59 and 115 at Sydney and 176 and 127 at Melbourne in 1924-25. In the latter match, which lasted into the seventh day, he was on the field throughout except for 86 minutes, namely 27 hours and 52 minutes.

C. Hill made 98 and 97 at Adelaide in 1901-02, and F. E. Woolley 95 and 93 at Lord's in 1921.

H. Sutcliffe in 1924-25, C. G. Macartney in 1926 and A. R. Morris in 1946-47 made three hundreds in consecutive innings.

J. B. Hobbs and H. Sutcliffe shared eleven first-wicket three-figure partnerships.

L. Hutton and C. Washbrook twice made three-figure stands in each innings, at Adelaide in 1946-47 and at Leeds in 1948.

H. Sutcliffe, during his highest score of 194, v Australia in 1932-33, took part in three stands each exceeding 100, viz. 112 with R. E. S. Wyatt for the first wicket, 188 with W. R. Hammond for the second wicket, and 123 with the Nawab of Pataudi for the third wicket. In 1903-04 R. E. Foster, in his historic innings of 287, added 192 for the fifth wicket with L. C. Braund, 115 for the ninth with A. E. Relf, and 130 for the tenth with W. Rhodes.

When L. Hutton scored 364 at The Oval in 1938 he added 382 for the second wicket with M. Leyland, 135 for the third wicket with W. R. Hammond and 215 for the sixth wicket with J. Hardstaff jun.

D. C. S. Compton and A. R. Morris at Adelaide in 1946-47 provide the only instance of a player on each side hitting two separate hundreds in a Test match.

G. S. and I. M. Chappell at The Oval in 1972 provide the first instance in Test matches of brothers each scoring hundreds in the same innings.

## RECORD PARTNERSHIPS FOR EACH WICKET

### For England

| | | |
|---|---|---|
| 323 for 1st | J. B. Hobbs and W. Rhodes at Melbourne | 1911-12 |
| 382 for 2nd† | L. Hutton and M. Leyland at The Oval | 1938 |
| 262 for 3rd | W. R. Hammond and D. R. Jardine at Adelaide | 1928-29 |
| 222 for 4th | W. R. Hammond and E. Paynter at Lord's | 1938 |

| | | |
|---|---|---|
| 206 for 5th | E. Paynter and D. C. S. Compton at Nottingham | 1938 |
| 215 for 6th | L. Hutton and J. Hardstaff jun. at The Oval | 1938 |
| | G. Boycott and A. P. E. Knott at Nottingham | 1977 |
| 143 for 7th | F. E. Woolley and J. Vine at Sydney | 1911-12 |
| 124 for 8th | E. H. Hendren and H. Larwood at Brisbane | 1928-29 |
| 151 for 9th | W. H. Scotton and W. W. Read at The Oval | 1884 |
| 130 for 10th† | R. E. Foster and W. Rhodes at Sydney | 1903-04 |

**For Australia**

| | | |
|---|---|---|
| 244 for 1st | R. B. Simpson and W. M. Lawry at Adelaide | 1965-66 |
| 451 for 2nd† | W. H. Ponsford and D. G. Bradman at The Oval | 1934 |
| 276 for 3rd | D. G. Bradman and A. L. Hassett at Brisbane | 1946-47 |
| 388 for 4th† | W. H. Ponsford and D. G. Bradman at Leeds | 1934 |
| 405 for 5th† | S. G. Barnes and D. G. Bradman at Sydney | 1946-47 |
| 346 for 6th† | J. H. Fingleton and D. G. Bradman at Melbourne | 1936-37 |
| 165 for 7th | C. Hill and H. Trumble at Melbourne | 1897-98 |
| 243 for 8th† | R. J. Hartigan and C. Hill at Adelaide | 1907-08 |
| 154 for 9th† | S. E. Gregory and J. McC. Blackham at Sydney | 1894-95 |
| 127 for 10th† | J. M. Taylor and A. A. Mailey at Sydney | 1924-25 |

† *Denotes record partnership against all countries.*

## MOST RUNS IN A SERIES

| | | | |
|---|---|---|---|
| England in England | 732 (average 81.33) | D. I. Gower | 1985 |
| England in Australia | 905 (average 113.12) | W. R. Hammond | 1928-29 |
| Australia in England | 974 (average 139.14) | D. G. Bradman | 1930 |
| Australia in Australia | 810 (average 90.00) | D. G. Bradman | 1936-37 |

## TEN WICKETS OR MORE IN A MATCH

**For England** (37)

| | | |
|---|---|---|
| 13-163 (6-42, 7-121) | S. F. Barnes, Melbourne | 1901-02 |
| 14-102 (7-28, 7-74) | W. Bates, Melbourne | 1882-83 |
| 10-105 (5-46, 5-59) | A. V. Bedser, Melbourne | 1950-51 |
| 14-99 (7-55, 7-44) | A. V. Bedser, Nottingham | 1953 |
| 11-102 (6-44, 5-58) | C. Blythe, Birmingham | 1909 |
| 11-176 (6-78, 5-98) | I. T. Botham, Perth | 1979-80 |
| 10-253 (6-125, 4-128) | I. T. Botham, The Oval | 1981 |
| 11-74 (5-29, 6-45) | J. Briggs, Lord's | 1886 |
| 12-136 (6-49, 6-87) | J. Briggs, Adelaide | 1891-92 |
| 10-148 (5-34, 5-114) | J. Briggs, The Oval | 1893 |
| 10-104 (6-77, 4-27)† | R. M. Ellison, Birmingham | 1985 |
| 10-179 (5-102, 5-77)† | K. Farnes, Nottingham | 1934 |
| 10-60 (6-41, 4-19) | J. T. Hearne, The Oval | 1896 |
| 11-113 (5-58, 6-55) | J. C. Laker, Leeds | 1956 |
| 19-90 (9-37, 10-53) | J. C. Laker, Manchester | 1956 |
| 10-124 (5-96, 5-28) | H. Larwood, Sydney | 1932-33 |
| 11-76 (6-48, 5-28) | W. H. Lockwood, Manchester | 1902 |
| 12-104 (7-36, 5-68) | G. A. Lohmann, The Oval | 1886 |
| 10-87 (8-35, 2-52) | G. A. Lohmann, Sydney | 1886-87 |
| 10-142 (8-58, 2-84) | G. A. Lohmann, Sydney | 1891-92 |
| 12-102 (6-50, 6-52)† | F. Martin, The Oval | 1890 |
| 10-58 (5-18, 5-40) | R. Peel, Sydney | 1887-88 |
| 11-68 (7-31, 4-37) | R. Peel, Manchester | 1888 |
| 15-124 (7-56, 8-68) | W. Rhodes, Melbourne | 1903-04 |
| 10-156 (5-49, 5-107)† | T. Richardson, Manchester | 1893 |
| 11-173 (6-39, 5-134) | T. Richardson, Lord's | 1896 |

| | | |
|---|---|---|
| 13-244 (7-168, 6-76) | T. Richardson, Manchester | 1896 |
| 10-204 (8-94, 2-110) | T. Richardson, Sydney | 1897-98 |
| 11-228 (6-130, 5-98)† | M. W. Tate, Sydney | 1924-25 |
| 11-88 (5-58, 6-30) | F. S. Trueman, Leeds | 1961 |
| 10-130 (4-45, 6-85) | F. H. Tyson, Sydney | 1954-55 |
| 10-82 (4-37, 6-45) | D. L. Underwood, Leeds | 1972 |
| 11-215 (7-113, 4-102) | D. L. Underwood, Adelaide | 1974-75 |
| 15-104 (7-61, 8-43) | H. Verity, Lord's | 1934 |
| 10-57 (6-41, 4-16) | W. Voce, Brisbane | 1936-37 |
| 13-256 (5-130, 8-126) | J. C. White, Adelaide | 1928-29 |
| 10-49 (5-29, 5-20) | F. E. Woolley, The Oval | 1912 |

**For Australia** (35)

| | | |
|---|---|---|
| 10-239 (4-129, 6-110) | L. O'B. Fleetwood-Smith, Adelaide | 1936-37 |
| 10-160 (4-88, 6-72) | G. Giffen, Sydney | 1891-92 |
| 11-82 (5-45, 6-37)† | C. V. Grimmett, Sydney | 1924-25 |
| 10-201 (5-107, 5-94) | C. V. Grimmett, Nottingham | 1930 |
| 10-122 (5-65, 5-57) | R. M. Hogg, Perth | 1978-79 |
| 10-66 (5-30, 5-36) | R. M. Hogg, Melbourne | 1978-79 |
| 12-175 (5-85, 7-90)† | H. V. Hordern, Sydney | 1911-12 |
| 10-161 (5-95, 5-66) | H. V. Hordern, Sydney | 1911-12 |
| 10-164 (7-88, 3-76) | E. Jones, Lord's | 1899 |
| 11-134 (6-47, 5-87) | G. F. Lawson, Brisbane | 1982-83 |
| 10-181 (5-58, 5-123) | D. K. Lillee, The Oval | 1972 |
| 11-165 (6-26, 5-139) | D. K. Lillee, Melbourne | 1976-77 |
| 11-138 (6-60, 5-78) | D. K. Lillee, Melbourne | 1979-80 |
| 11-159 (7-89, 4-70) | D. K. Lillee, The Oval | 1981 |
| 11-85 (7-58, 4-27) | C. G. Macartney, Leeds | 1909 |
| 10-302 (5-160, 5-142) | A. A. Mailey, Adelaide | 1920-21 |
| 13-236 (4-115, 9-121) | A. A. Mailey, Melbourne | 1920-21 |
| 16-137 (8-84, 8-53)† | R. A. L. Massie, Lord's | 1972 |
| 10-152 (5-72, 5-80) | K. R. Miller, Lord's | 1956 |
| 13-77 (7-17, 6-60) | M. A. Noble, Melbourne | 1901-02 |
| 11-103 (5-51, 6-52) | M. A. Noble, Sheffield | 1902 |
| 10-129 (5-63, 5-66) | W. J. O'Reilly, Melbourne | 1932-33 |
| 11-129 (4-75, 7-54) | W. J. O'Reilly, Nottingham | 1934 |
| 10-122 (5-66, 5-56) | W. J. O'Reilly, Leeds | 1938 |
| 11-165 (7-68, 4-97) | G. E. Palmer, Sydney | 1881-82 |
| 10-126 (7-65, 3-61) | G. E. Palmer, Melbourne | 1882-83 |
| 13-110 (6-48, 7-62) | F. R. Spofforth, Melbourne | 1878-79 |
| 14-90 (7-46, 7-44) | F. R. Spofforth, The Oval | 1882 |
| 11-117 (4-73, 7-44) | F. R. Spofforth, Sydney | 1882-83 |
| 10-144 (4-54, 6-90) | F. R. Spofforth, Sydney | 1884-85 |
| 12-89 (6-59, 6-30) | H. Trumble, The Oval | 1896 |
| 10-128 (4-75, 6-53) | H. Trumble, Manchester | 1902 |
| 12-173 (8-65, 4-108) | H. Trumble, The Oval | 1902 |
| 12-87 (5-44, 7-43) | C. T. B. Turner, Sydney | 1887-88 |
| 10-63 (5-27, 5-36) | C. T. B. Turner, Lord's | 1888 |

† *Signifies ten wickets or more on first appearance in England–Australia Tests.*

*Note:* J. Briggs, J. C. Laker, T. Richardson in 1896, R. M. Hogg, A. A. Mailey, H. Trumble and C. T. B. Turner took ten wickets or more in successive Tests. J. Briggs was omitted, however, from the England team for the first Test match in 1893.

## MOST WICKETS IN A SERIES

| | | | |
|---|---|---|---|
| England in England | 46 (average 9.60) | J. C. Laker | 1956 |
| England in Australia | 38 (average 23.18) | M. W. Tate | 1924-25 |
| Australia in England | 42 (average 21.26) | T. M. Alderman (6 Tests) | 1981 |
| Australia in Australia | 41 (average 12.85) | R. M. Hogg (6 Tests) | 1978-79 |

## WICKET-KEEPING – MOST DISMISSALS

| | *M* | *Ct* | *St* | *Total* |
|---|---|---|---|---|
| †R. W. Marsh (Australia) | 42 | 141 | 7 | 148 |
| A. P. E. Knott (England) | 34 | 97 | 8 | 105 |
| †W. A. Oldfield (Australia) | 38 | 59 | 31 | 90 |
| A. A. Lilley (England) | 32 | 65 | 19 | 84 |
| A. T. W. Grout (Australia) | 22 | 69 | 7 | 76 |
| T. G. Evans (England) | 31 | 63 | 12 | 75 |

*† The number of catches by R. W. Marsh (141) and stumpings by W. A. Oldfield (31) are respective records in England–Australia Tests.*

## SCORERS OF OVER 2,000 RUNS

| | *T* | *I* | *NO* | *R* | *HI* | *Avge* |
|---|---|---|---|---|---|---|
| D. G. Bradman | 37 | 63 | 7 | 5,028 | 334 | 89.78 |
| J. B. Hobbs | 41 | 71 | 4 | 3,636 | 187 | 54.26 |
| G. Boycott | 38 | 71 | 9 | 2,945 | 191 | 47.50 |
| W. R. Hammond | 31 | 58 | 3 | 2,852 | 251 | 51.85 |
| H. Sutcliffe | 27 | 46 | 5 | 2,741 | 194 | 66.85 |
| C. Hill | 41 | 76 | 1 | 2,660 | 188 | 35.46 |
| J. H. Edrich | 32 | 57 | 3 | 2,644 | 175 | 48.96 |
| G. S. Chappell | 35 | 65 | 8 | 2,619 | 144 | 45.94 |
| M. C. Cowdrey | 43 | 75 | 4 | 2,433 | 113 | 34.26 |
| L. Hutton | 27 | 49 | 6 | 2,428 | 364 | 56.46 |
| R. N. Harvey | 37 | 68 | 5 | 2,416 | 167 | 38.34 |
| V. T. Trumper | 40 | 74 | 5 | 2,263 | 185* | 32.79 |
| W. M. Lawry | 29 | 51 | 5 | 2,233 | 166 | 48.54 |
| S. E. Gregory | 52 | 92 | 7 | 2,193 | 201 | 25.80 |
| W. W. Armstrong | 42 | 71 | 9 | 2,172 | 158 | 35.03 |
| I. M. Chappell | 30 | 56 | 4 | 2,138 | 192 | 41.11 |
| K. F. Barrington | 23 | 39 | 6 | 2,111 | 256 | 63.96 |
| A. R. Morris | 24 | 43 | 2 | 2,080 | 206 | 50.73 |
| D. I. Gower | 26 | 48 | 2 | 2,075 | 215 | 45.10 |

## BOWLERS WITH 100 WICKETS

| | *T* | *Balls* | *R* | *W* | *5 W/i* | *Avge* |
|---|---|---|---|---|---|---|
| D. K. Lillee | 29 | 8,516 | 3,507 | 167 | 11 | 21.00 |
| H. Trumble | 31 | 7,895 | 2,945 | 141 | 9 | 20.88 |
| I. T. Botham | 29 | 7,361 | 3,556 | 136 | 8 | 26.14 |
| R. G. D. Willis | 35 | 7,294 | 3,346 | 128 | 7 | 26.14 |
| M. A. Noble | 39 | 6,845 | 2,860 | 115 | 9 | 24.86 |
| R. R. Lindwall | 29 | 6,728 | 2,559 | 114 | 6 | 22.44 |
| W. Rhodes | 41 | 5,791 | 2,616 | 109 | 6 | 24.00 |
| S. F. Barnes | 20 | 5,749 | 2,288 | 106 | 12 | 21.58 |
| C. V. Grimmett | 22 | 9,224 | 3,439 | 106 | 11 | 32.44 |
| D. L. Underwood | 29 | 8,000 | 2,770 | 105 | 4 | 26.38 |
| A. V. Bedser | 21 | 7,065 | 2,859 | 104 | 7 | 27.49 |
| G. Giffen | 31 | 6,325 | 2,791 | 103 | 7 | 27.09 |
| W. J. O'Reilly | 19 | 7,864 | 2,587 | 102 | 8 | 25.36 |
| R. Peel | 20 | 5,216 | 1,715 | 102 | 6 | 16.81 |
| C. T. B. Turner | 17 | 5,195 | 1,670 | 101 | 11 | 16.53 |
| J. R. Thomson | 21 | 4,951 | 2,418 | 100 | 5 | 24.18 |

# ENGLAND v SOUTH AFRICA

| Season | Captains: England | Captains: South Africa | T | E | SA | D |
|---|---|---|---|---|---|---|
| 1888-89 | C. A. Smith[1] | O. R. Dunell[2] | 2 | 2 | 0 | 0 |
| 1891-92 | W. W. Read | W. H. Milton | 1 | 1 | 0 | 0 |
| 1895-96 | Lord Hawke[3] | E. A. Halliwell[4] | 3 | 3 | 0 | 0 |
| 1898-99 | Lord Hawke | M. Bisset | 2 | 2 | 0 | 0 |
| 1905-06 | P. F. Warner | P. W. Sherwell | 5 | 1 | 4 | 0 |
| 1907 | R. E. Foster | P. W. Sherwell | 3 | 1 | 0 | 2 |
| 1909-10 | H. D. G. Leveson Gower[5] | S. J. Snooke | 5 | 2 | 3 | 0 |
| 1912 | C. B. Fry | F. Mitchell[6] | 3 | 3 | 0 | 0 |
| 1913-14 | J. W. H. T. Douglas | H. W. Taylor | 5 | 4 | 0 | 1 |
| 1922-23 | F. T. Mann | H. W. Taylor | 5 | 2 | 1 | 2 |
| 1924 | A. E. R. Gilligan[7] | H. W. Taylor | 5 | 3 | 0 | 2 |
| 1927-28 | R. T. Stanyforth[8] | H. G. Deane | 5 | 2 | 2 | 1 |
| 1929 | J. C. White[9] | H. G. Deane | 5 | 2 | 0 | 3 |
| 1930-31 | A. P. F. Chapman | H. G. Deane[10] | 5 | 0 | 1 | 4 |
| 1935 | R. E. S. Wyatt | H. F. Wade | 5 | 0 | 1 | 4 |
| 1938-39 | W. R. Hammond | A. Melville | 5 | 1 | 0 | 4 |
| 1947 | N. W. D. Yardley | A. Melville | 5 | 3 | 0 | 2 |
| 1948-49 | F. G. Mann | A. D. Nourse | 5 | 2 | 0 | 3 |
| 1951 | F. R. Brown | A. D. Nourse | 5 | 3 | 1 | 1 |
| 1955 | P. B. H. May | J. E. Cheetham[11] | 5 | 3 | 2 | 0 |
| 1956-57 | P. B. H. May | C. B. van Ryneveld[12] | 5 | 2 | 2 | 1 |
| 1960 | M. C. Cowdrey | D. J. McGlew | 5 | 3 | 0 | 2 |
| 1964-65 | M. J. K. Smith | T. L. Goddard | 5 | 1 | 0 | 4 |
| 1965 | M. J. K. Smith | P. L. van der Merwe | 3 | 0 | 1 | 2 |
| | In South Africa | | 58 | 25 | 13 | 20 |
| | In England | | 44 | 21 | 5 | 18 |
| | Totals | | 102 | 46 | 18 | 38 |

*Notes:* The following deputised for the official touring captain or were appointed by the home authority for only a minor proportion of the series:

[1]M. P. Bowden (Second). [2]W. H. Milton (Second). [3]Sir T. C. O'Brien (First). [4]A. R. Richards (Third). [5]F. L. Fane (Fourth and Fifth). [6]L. J. Tancred (Second and Third). [7]J. W. H. T. Douglas (Fourth). [8]G. T. S. Stevens (Fifth). [9]A. W. Carr (Fourth and Fifth). [10]E. P. Nupen (First), H. B. Cameron (Fourth and Fifth). [11]D. J. McGlew (Third and Fourth). [12]D. J. McGlew (Second).

## HIGHEST INNINGS TOTALS

For England in England: 554-8 dec. at Lord's ........ 1947
in South Africa: 654-5 at Durban ........ 1938-39

For South Africa in England: 538 at Leeds ........ 1951
in South Africa: 530 at Durban ........ 1938-39

## LOWEST INNINGS TOTALS

For England in England: 76 at Leeds ........ 1907
in South Africa: 92 at Cape Town ........ 1898-99

For South Africa in England: 30 at Birmingham ........ 1924
in South Africa: 30 at Port Elizabeth ........ 1895-96

## INDIVIDUAL HUNDREDS

### For England (87)

| | | |
|---|---|---|
| 120 | R. Abel, Cape Town | 1888-89 |
| 148* | L. E. G. Ames, The Oval | 1935 |
| 115 | L. E. G. Ames, Cape Town | 1938-39 |
| 148* | K. F. Barrington, Durban | 1964-65 |
| 121 | K. F. Barrington, Johannesburg | 1964-65 |
| 117 | G. Boycott, Port Elizabeth | 1964-65 |
| 104† | L. C. Braund, Lord's | 1907 |
| 208 | D. C. S. Compton, Lord's | 1947 |
| 163† | D. C. S. Compton, Nottingham | 1947 |
| 115 | D. C. S. Compton, Manchester | 1947 |
| 113 | D. C. S. Compton, The Oval | 1947 |
| 114 | D. C. S. Compton, Johannesburg | 1948-49 |
| 112 | D. C. S. Compton, Nottingham | 1951 |
| 158 | D. C. S. Compton, Manchester | 1955 |
| 101 | M. C. Cowdrey, Cape Town | 1956-57 |
| 155 | M. C. Cowdrey, The Oval | 1960 |
| 105 | M. C. Cowdrey, Nottingham | 1965 |
| 104 | D. Denton, Johannesburg | 1909-10 |
| 172 | E. R. Dexter, Johannesburg | 1964-65 |
| 119† | J. W. H. T. Douglas, Durban | 1913-14 |
| 219 | W. J. Edrich, Durban | 1938-39 |
| 191 | W. J. Edrich, Manchester | 1947 |
| 189 | W. J. Edrich, Lord's | 1947 |
| 143 | F. L. Fane, Johannesburg | 1905-06 |
| 129 | C. B. Fry, The Oval | 1907 |
| 106† | P. A. Gibb, Johannesburg | 1938-39 |
| 120 | P. A. Gibb, Durban | 1938-39 |
| 138* | W. R. Hammond, Birmingham | 1929 |
| 101* | W. R. Hammond, The Oval | 1929 |
| 136* | W. R. Hammond, Durban | 1930-31 |
| 181 | W. R. Hammond, Cape Town | 1938-39 |
| 120 | W. R. Hammond, Durban | 1938-39 |
| 140 | W. R. Hammond, Durban | 1938-39 |
| 122 | T. W. Hayward, Johannesburg | 1895-96 |
| 132 | E. H. Hendren, Leeds | 1924 |
| 142 | E. H. Hendren, The Oval | 1924 |
| 124 | A. J. L. Hill, Cape Town | 1895-96 |
| 187 | J. B. Hobbs, Cape Town | 1909-10 |
| 211 | J. B. Hobbs, Lord's | 1924 |
| 100 | L. Hutton, Leeds | 1947 |
| 158 | L. Hutton, Johannesburg | 1948-49 |
| 123 | L. Hutton, Johannesburg | 1948-49 |
| 100 | L. Hutton, Leeds | 1951 |
| 110* | D. J. Insole, Durban | 1956-57 |
| 102 | M. Leyland, Lord's | 1929 |
| 161 | M. Leyland, The Oval | 1935 |
| 136* | F. G. Mann, Port Elizabeth | 1948-49 |
| 138† | P. B. H. May, Leeds | 1951 |
| 112 | P. B. H. May, Lord's | 1955 |
| 117 | P. B. H. May, Manchester | 1955 |
| 102 | C. P. Mead, Johannesburg | 1913-14 |
| 117 | C. P. Mead, Port Elizabeth | 1913-14 |
| 181 | C. P. Mead, Durban | 1922-23 |
| 122* | P. H. Parfitt, Johannesburg | 1964-65 |
| 108* | J. M. Parks, Durban | 1964-65 |
| 117†, 100 | E. Paynter, Johannesburg | 1938-39 |
| 243 | E. Paynter, Durban | 1938-39 |
| 175 | G. Pullar, The Oval | 1960 |
| 152 | W. Rhodes, Johannesburg | 1913-14 |
| 117† | P. E. Richardson, Johannesburg | 1956-57 |
| 108 | R. W. V. Robins, Manchester | 1935 |
| 140, 111 | A. C. Russell, Durban | 1922-23 |
| 137 | R. T. Simpson, Nottingham | 1951 |
| 121 | M. J. K. Smith, Cape Town | 1964-65 |
| 119† | R. H. Spooner, Lord's | 1912 |
| 122 | H. Sutcliffe, Lord's | 1924 |
| 102 | H. Sutcliffe, Johannesburg | 1927-28 |
| 114 | H. Sutcliffe, Birmingham | 1929 |
| 100 | H. Sutcliffe, Lord's | 1929 |
| 104, 109* | H. Sutcliffe, The Oval | 1929 |
| 100* | M. W. Tate, Lord's | 1929 |
| 122† | E. Tyldesley, Johannesburg | 1927-28 |
| 100 | E. Tyldesley, Durban | 1927-28 |
| 112 | J. T. Tyldesley, Cape Town | 1898-99 |
| 112 | B. H. Valentine, Cape Town | 1938-39 |
| 132*†‡ | P. F. Warner, Johannesburg | 1898-99 |
| 195 | C. Washbrook, Johannesburg | 1948-49 |
| 111 | A. J. Watkins, Johannesburg | 1948-49 |
| 134* | H. Wood, Cape Town | 1891-92 |
| 115* | F. E. Woolley, Johannesburg | 1922-23 |
| 134* | F. E. Woolley, Lord's | 1924 |
| 154 | F. E. Woolley, Manchester | 1929 |
| 113 | R. E. S. Wyatt, Manchester | 1929 |
| 149 | R. E. S. Wyatt, Nottingham | 1935 |

### For South Africa (58)

| | | |
|---|---|---|
| 138 | E. J. Barlow, Cape Town | 1964-65 |
| 144* | K. C. Bland, Johannesburg | 1964-65 |
| 127 | K. C. Bland, The Oval | 1965 |
| 120 | R. H. Catterall, Birmingham | 1924 |

| | | |
|---|---|---|
| 120 | R. H. Catterall, Lord's | 1924 |
| 119 | R. H. Catterall, Durban | 1927-28 |
| 117 | E. L. Dalton, The Oval | 1935 |
| 102 | E. L. Dalton, Johannesburg | 1938-39 |
| 116* | W. R. Endean, Leeds | 1955 |
| 123 | G. A. Faulkner, Johannesburg | 1909-10 |
| 112 | T. L. Goddard, Johannesburg | 1964-65 |
| 102 | C. M. H. Hathorn, Johannesburg | 1905-06 |
| 104* | D. J. McGlew, Manchester | 1955 |
| 133 | D. J. McGlew, Leeds | 1955 |
| 142 | R. A. McLean, Lord's | 1955 |
| 100 | R. A. McLean, Durban | 1956-57 |
| 109 | R. A. McLean, Manchester | 1960 |
| 103 | A. Melville, Durban | 1938-39 |
| 189<br>104* | A. Melville, Nottingham | 1947 |
| 117 | A. Melville, Lord's | 1947 |
| 123 | B. Mitchell, Cape Town | 1930-31 |
| 164* | B. Mitchell, Lord's | 1935 |
| 128 | B. Mitchell, The Oval | 1935 |
| 109 | B. Mitchell, Durban | 1938-39 |
| 120<br>189* | B. Mitchell, The Oval | 1947 |
| 120 | B. Mitchell, Cape Town | 1948-49 |
| 120 | A. D. Nourse, Cape Town | 1938-39 |
| 103 | A. D. Nourse, Durban | 1938-39 |
| 149 | A. D. Nourse, Nottingham | 1947 |
| 115 | A. D. Nourse, Manchester | 1947 |
| 129* | A. D. Nourse, Johannesburg | 1948-49 |
| 112 | A. D. Nourse, Cape Town | 1948-49 |
| 208 | A. D. Nourse, Nottingham | 1951 |
| 129 | H. G. Owen-Smith, Leeds | 1929 |
| 154 | A. J. Pithey, Cape Town | 1964-65 |
| 137 | R. G. Pollock, Port Elizabeth | 1964-65 |
| 125 | R. G. Pollock, Nottingham | 1965 |
| 156* | E. A. B. Rowan, Johannesburg | 1948-49 |
| 236 | E. A. B. Rowan, Leeds | 1951 |
| 115 | P. W. Sherwell, Lord's | 1907 |
| 141 | I. J. Siedle, Cape Town | 1930-31 |
| 106 | J. H. Sinclair, Cape Town | 1898-99 |
| 109 | H. W. Taylor, Durban | 1913-14 |
| 176 | H. W. Taylor, Johannesburg | 1922-23 |
| 101 | H. W. Taylor, Johannesburg | 1922-23 |
| 102 | H. W. Taylor, Durban | 1922-23 |
| 101 | H. W. Taylor, Johannesburg | 1927-28 |
| 121 | H. W. Taylor, The Oval | 1929 |
| 117 | H. W. Taylor, Cape Town | 1930-31 |
| 125 | P. G. V. van der Bijl, Durban | 1938-39 |
| 124 | K. G. Viljoen, Manchester | 1935 |
| 125 | W. W. Wade, Port Elizabeth | 1948-49 |
| 113 | J. H. B. Waite, Manchester | 1955 |
| 147 | G. C. White, Johannesburg | 1905-06 |
| 118 | G. C. White, Durban | 1909-10 |
| 108 | P. L. Winslow, Manchester | 1955 |

† *Signifies hundred on first appearance in England–South Africa Tests.*

‡ *P. F. Warner carried his bat through the second innings.*

*Notes:* The highest score by a South African batsman on début is 93* by A. W. Nourse at Johannesburg in 1905-06.

P. N. F. Mansell made 90 at Leeds in 1951, the best on début in England.

A. Melville's four hundreds were made in successive Test innings.

## RECORD PARTNERSHIP FOR EACH WICKET

### For England

| | | |
|---|---|---|
| 359 for 1st† | L. Hutton and C. Washbrook at Johannesburg | 1948-49 |
| 280 for 2nd | P. A. Gibb and W. J. Edrich at Durban | 1938-39 |
| 370 for 3rd† | W. J. Edrich and D. C. S. Compton at Lord's | 1947 |
| 197 for 4th | W. R. Hammond and L. E. G. Ames at Cape Town | 1938-39 |
| 237 for 5th | D. C. S. Compton and N. W. D. Yardley at Nottingham | 1947 |
| 206* for 6th | K. F. Barrington and J. M. Parks at Durban | 1964-65 |
| 115 for 7th | M. C. Bird and J. W. H. T. Douglas at Durban | 1913-14 |
| 154 for 8th | C. W. Wright and H. R. Bromley-Davenport at Johannesburg | 1895-96 |
| 71 for 9th | H. Wood and J. T. Hearne at Cape Town | 1891-92 |
| 92 for 10th | A. C. Russell and A. E. R. Gilligan at Durban | 1922-23 |

### For South Africa

| | | |
|---|---|---|
| 260 for 1st† | I. J. Siedle and B. Mitchell at Cape Town | 1930-31 |
| 198 for 2nd† | E. A. B. Rowan and C. B. van Ryneveld at Leeds | 1951 |
| 319 for 3rd | A. Melville and A. D. Nourse at Nottingham | 1947 |

| | | |
|---|---|---|
| 214 for 4th† | H. W. Taylor and H. G. Deane at The Oval | 1929 |
| 157 for 5th† | A. J. Pithey and J. H. B. Waite at Johannesburg | 1964-65 |
| 171 for 6th | J. H. B. Waite and P. L. Winslow at Manchester | 1955 |
| 123 for 7th | H. G. Deane and E. P. Nupen at Durban | 1927-28 |
| 109* for 8th | B. Mitchell and L. Tuckett at The Oval | 1947 |
| 137 for 9th† | E. L. Dalton and A. B. C. Langton at The Oval | 1935 |
| 103 for 10th† | H. G. Owen-Smith and A. J. Bell at Leeds | 1929 |

† *Denotes record partnership against all countries.*

## MOST RUNS IN A SERIES

| | | | |
|---|---|---|---|
| England in England | 753 (average 94.12) | D. C. S. Compton | 1947 |
| England in South Africa | 653 (average 81.62) | E. Paynter | 1938-39 |
| South Africa in England | 621 (average 69.00) | A. D. Nourse | 1947 |
| South Africa in South Africa | 582 (average 64.66) | H. W. Taylor | 1922-23 |

## TEN WICKETS OR MORE IN A MATCH

### For England (23)

| | | |
|---|---|---|
| 11-110 (5-25, 6-85)† | S. F. Barnes, Lord's | 1912 |
| 10-115 (6-52, 4-63) | S. F. Barnes, Leeds | 1912 |
| 13-57 (5-28, 8-29) | S. F. Barnes, The Oval | 1912 |
| 10-105 (5-57, 5-48) | S. F. Barnes, Durban | 1913-14 |
| 17-159 (8-56, 9-103) | S. F. Barnes, Johannesburg | 1913-14 |
| 14-144 (7-56, 7-88) | S. F. Barnes, Durban | 1913-14 |
| 12-112 (7-58, 5-54) | A. V. Bedser, Manchester | 1951 |
| 11-118 (6-68, 5-50) | C. Blythe, Cape Town | 1905-06 |
| 15-99 (8-59, 7-40) | C. Blythe, Leeds | 1907 |
| 10-104 (7-46, 3-58) | C. Blythe, Cape Town | 1909-10 |
| 15-28 (7-17, 8-11) | J. Briggs, Cape Town | 1888-89 |
| 13-91 (6-54, 7-37)† | J. J. Ferris, Cape Town | 1891-92 |
| 10-207 (7-115, 3-92) | A. P. Freeman, Leeds | 1929 |
| 12-171 (7-71, 5-100) | A. P. Freeman, Manchester | 1929 |
| 12-130 (7-70, 5-60) | G. Geary, Johannesburg | 1927-28 |
| 11-90 (6-7, 5-83) | A. E. R. Gilligan, Birmingham | 1924 |
| 10-119 (4-64, 6-55) | J. C. Laker, The Oval | 1951 |
| 15-45 (7-38, 8-7)† | G. A. Lohmann, Port Elizabeth | 1895-96 |
| 12-71 (9-28, 3-43) | G. A. Lohmann, Johannesburg | 1895-96 |
| 11-97 (6-63, 5-34) | J. B. Statham, Lord's | 1960 |
| 12-101 (7-52, 5-49) | R. Tattersall, Lord's | 1951 |
| 12-89 (5-53, 7-36) | J. H. Wardle, Cape Town | 1956-57 |
| 10-175 (5-95, 5-80) | D. V. P. Wright, Lord's | 1947 |

### For South Africa (6)

| | | |
|---|---|---|
| 11-112 (4-49, 7-63)† | A. E. Hall, Cape Town | 1922-23 |
| 11-150 (5-63, 6-87) | E. P. Nupen, Johannesburg | 1930-31 |
| 10-87 (5-53, 5-34) | P. M. Pollock, Nottingham | 1965 |
| 12-127 (4-57, 8-70) | S. J. Snooke, Johannesburg | 1905-06 |
| 13-192 (4-79, 9-113) | H. J. Tayfield, Johannesburg | 1956-57 |
| 12-181 (5-87, 7-94) | A. E. E. Vogler, Johannesburg | 1909-10 |

† *Signifies ten wickets or more on first appearance in England–South Africa Tests.*

*Note:* S. F. Barnes took ten wickets or more in his first five Tests v South Africa and in six of his seven Tests v South Africa. A. P. Freeman and G. A. Lohmann took ten wickets or more in successive matches.

## MOST WICKETS IN A SERIES

| | | | |
|---|---|---|---|
| England in England ......... | 34 (average 8.29) | S. F. Barnes ...... | 1912 |
| England in South Africa ..... | 49 (average 10.93) | S. F. Barnes ...... | 1913-14 |
| South Africa in England ..... | 26 (average 21.84) | H. J. Tayfield ..... | 1955 |
| South Africa in England ..... | 26 (average 22.57) | N. A. T. Adcock .. | 1960 |
| South Africa in South Africa . | 37 (average 17.18) | H. J. Tayfield ..... | 1956-57 |

## ENGLAND v WEST INDIES

| | *Captains* | | | | | |
|---|---|---|---|---|---|---|
| *Season* | *England* | *West Indies* | *T* | *E* | *WI* | *D* |
| 1928 | A. P. F. Chapman | R. K. Nunes | 3 | 3 | 0 | 0 |
| 1929-30 | Hon. F. S. G. Calthorpe | E. L. G. Hoad[1] | 4 | 1 | 1 | 2 |
| 1933 | D. R. Jardine[2] | G. C. Grant | 3 | 2 | 0 | 1 |
| 1934-35 | R. E. S. Wyatt | G. C. Grant | 4 | 1 | 2 | 1 |
| 1939 | W. R. Hammond | R. S. Grant | 3 | 1 | 0 | 2 |
| 1947-48 | G. O. Allen[3] | J. D. C. Goddard[4] | 4 | 0 | 2 | 2 |
| 1950 | N. W. D. Yardley[5] | J. D. C. Goddard | 4 | 1 | 3 | 0 |
| 1953-54 | L. Hutton | J. B. Stollmeyer | 5 | 2 | 2 | 1 |
| 1957 | P. B. H. May | J. D. C. Goddard | 5 | 3 | 0 | 2 |
| 1959-60 | P. B. H. May[6] | F. C. M. Alexander | 5 | 1 | 0 | 4 |

### THE WISDEN TROPHY

| | *Captains* | | | | | | |
|---|---|---|---|---|---|---|---|
| *Season* | *England* | *West Indies* | *T* | *E* | *WI* | *D* | *Held by* |
| 1963 | E. R. Dexter | F. M. M. Worrell | 5 | 1 | 3 | 1 | WI |
| 1966 | M. C. Cowdrey[7] | G. S. Sobers | 5 | 1 | 3 | 1 | WI |
| 1967-68 | M. C. Cowdrey | G. S. Sobers | 5 | 1 | 0 | 4 | E |
| 1969 | R. Illingworth | G. S. Sobers | 3 | 2 | 0 | 1 | E |
| 1973 | R. Illingworth | R. B. Kanhai | 3 | 0 | 2 | 1 | WI |
| 1973-74 | M. H. Denness | R. B. Kanhai | 5 | 1 | 1 | 3 | WI |
| 1976 | A. W. Greig | C. H. Lloyd | 5 | 0 | 3 | 2 | WI |
| 1980 | I. T. Botham | C. H. Lloyd[8] | 5 | 0 | 1 | 4 | WI |
| 1980-81† | I. T. Botham | C. H. Lloyd | 4 | 0 | 2 | 2 | WI |
| 1984 | D. I. Gower | C. H. Lloyd | 5 | 0 | 5 | 0 | WI |
| | In England .................... | | 49 | 14 | 20 | 15 | |
| | In West Indies ................ | | 36 | 7 | 10 | 19 | |
| | Totals ......................... | | 85 | 21 | 30 | 34 | |

† *The Test match at Georgetown, scheduled as the second of the series, was cancelled owing to political pressure.*

*Notes:* The following deputised for the official touring captain or were appointed by the home authority for only a minor proportion of the series:

[1]N. Betancourt (Second), M. P. Fernandes (Third), R. K. Nunes (Fourth). [2]R. E. S. Wyatt (Third). [3]K. Cranston (First). [4]G. A. Headley (First), G. E. Gomez (Second). [5]F. R. Brown (Fourth). [6]M. C. Cowdrey (Fourth and Fifth). [7]M. J. K. Smith (First), D. B. Close (Fifth). [8]I. V. A. Richards (Fifth).

## HIGHEST INNINGS TOTALS

For England in England: 619-6 dec. at Nottingham ........ 1957
in West Indies: 849 at Kingston ........ 1929-30

For West Indies in England: 687-8 dec. at The Oval ........ 1976
in West Indies: 681-8 dec. at Port-of-Spain ........ 1953-54

## LOWEST INNINGS TOTALS

For England in England: 71 at Manchester ........ 1976
in West Indies: 103 at Kingston ........ 1934-35

For West Indies in England: 86 at The Oval ........ 1957
in West Indies: 102 at Bridgetown ........ 1934-35

## INDIVIDUAL HUNDREDS

**For England** (81)

| | | |
|---|---|---|
| 105 | L. E. G. Ames, Port-of-Spain | 1929-30 |
| 149 | L. E. G. Ames, Kingston | 1929-30 |
| 126 | L. E. G. Ames, Kingston | 1934-35 |
| 174 | D. L. Amiss, Port-of-Spain | 1973-74 |
| 262* | D. L. Amiss, Kingston | 1973-74 |
| 118 | D. L. Amiss, Georgetown | 1973-74 |
| 203 | D. L. Amiss, The Oval | 1976 |
| 107† | A. H. Bakewell, The Oval | 1933 |
| 128† | K. F. Barrington, Bridgetown | 1959-60 |
| 121 | K. F. Barrington, Port-of-Spain | 1959-60 |
| 143 | K. F. Barrington, Port-of-Spain | 1967-68 |
| 116 | G. Boycott, Georgetown | 1967-68 |
| 128 | G. Boycott, Manchester | 1969 |
| 106 | G. Boycott, Lord's | 1969 |
| 112 | G. Boycott, Port-of-Spain | 1973-74 |
| 104* | G. Boycott, St John's, Antigua | 1980-81 |
| 120† | D. C. S. Compton, Lord's | 1939 |
| 133 | D. C. S. Compton, Port-of-Spain | 1953-54 |
| 154† | M. C. Cowdrey, Birmingham | 1957 |
| 152 | M. C. Cowdrey, Lord's | 1957 |
| 114 | M. C. Cowdrey, Kingston | 1959-60 |
| 119 | M. C. Cowdrey, Port-of-Spain | 1959-60 |
| 101 | M. C. Cowdrey, Kingston | 1967-68 |
| 148 | M. C. Cowdrey, Port-of-Spain | 1967-68 |
| 136*† | E. R. Dexter, Bridgetown | 1959-60 |
| 110 | E. R. Dexter, Georgetown | 1959-60 |
| 146 | J. H. Edrich, Bridgetown | 1967-68 |
| 104 | T. G. Evans, Manchester | 1950 |
| 129* | K. W. R. Fletcher, Bridgetown | 1973-74 |
| 106 | G. Fowler, Lord's | 1984 |
| 123 | G. A. Gooch, Lord's | 1980 |
| 116 | G. A. Gooch, Bridgetown | 1980-81 |
| 153 | G. A. Gooch, Kingston | 1980-81 |
| 154* | D. I. Gower, Kingston | 1980-81 |
| 258 | T. W. Graveney, Nottingham | 1957 |
| 164 | T. W. Graveney, The Oval | 1957 |
| 109 | T. W. Graveney, Nottingham | 1966 |
| 165 | T. W. Graveney, The Oval | 1966 |
| 118 | T. W. Graveney, Port-of-Spain | 1967-68 |
| 148 | A. W. Greig, Bridgetown | 1973-74 |
| 121 | A. W. Greig, Georgetown | 1973-74 |
| 116 | A. W. Greig, Leeds | 1976 |
| 140† | S. C. Griffith, Port-of-Spain | 1947-48 |
| 138 | W. R. Hammond, The Oval | 1939 |
| 107† | J. H. Hampshire, Lord's | 1969 |
| 106*† | F. C. Hayes, The Oval | 1973 |
| 205* | E. H. Hendren, Port-of-Spain | 1929-30 |
| 123 | E. H. Hendren, Georgetown | 1929-30 |
| 159 | J. B. Hobbs, The Oval | 1928 |
| 196† | L. Hutton, Lord's | 1939 |
| 165* | L. Hutton, The Oval | 1939 |
| 202*‡ | L. Hutton, The Oval | 1950 |
| 169 | L. Hutton, Georgetown | 1953-54 |
| 205 | L. Hutton, Kingston | 1953-54 |
| 113 | R. Illingworth, Lord's | 1969 |
| 127 | D. R. Jardine, Manchester | 1933 |
| 116 | A. P. E. Knott, Leeds | 1976 |
| 110 | A. J. Lamb, Lord's | 1984 |
| 100 | A. J. Lamb, Leeds | 1984 |
| 100* | A. J. Lamb, Manchester | 1984 |
| 135 | P. B. H. May, Port-of-Spain | 1953-54 |
| 285* | P. B. H. May, Birmingham | 1957 |
| 104 | P. B. H. May, Nottingham | 1957 |
| 126* | C. Milburn, Lord's | 1966 |
| 112† | J. T. Murray, The Oval | 1966 |
| 101*† | J. M. Parks, Port-of-Spain | 1959-60 |

| | | |
|---|---|---|
| 107 | W. Place, Kingston | 1947-48 |
| 126 | P. E. Richardson, Nottingham | 1957 |
| 107 | P. E. Richardson, The Oval | 1957 |
| 133 | J. D. Robertson, Port-of-Spain | 1947-48 |
| 152† | A. Sandham, Bridgetown | 1929-30 |
| 325 | A. Sandham, Kingston | 1929-30 |
| 108 | M. J. K. Smith, Port-of-Spain | 1959-60 |
| 106† | D. S. Steele, Nottingham | 1976 |
| 100† | R. Subba Row, Georgetown | 1959-60 |
| 122† | E. Tyldesley, Lord's | 1928 |
| 114† | C. Washbrook, Lord's | 1950 |
| 102 | C. Washbrook, Nottingham | 1950 |
| 116† | W. Watson, Kingston | 1953-54 |
| 100* | P. Willey, The Oval | 1980 |
| 102* | P. Willey, St John's, Antigua | 1980-81 |

**For West Indies** (87)

| | | |
|---|---|---|
| 105 | I. Barrow, Manchester | 1933 |
| 133 | B. F. Butcher, Lord's | 1963 |
| 209* | B. F. Butcher, Nottingham | 1966 |
| 107 | G. M. Carew, Port-of-Spain | 1947-48 |
| 103 | C. A. Davis, Lord's | 1969 |
| 101 | P. J. Dujon, Manchester | 1984 |
| 150 | R. C. Fredericks, Birmingham | 1973 |
| 138 | R. C. Fredericks, Lord's | 1976 |
| 109 | R. C. Fredericks, Leeds | 1976 |
| 112† | A. G. Ganteaume, Port-of-Spain | 1947-48 |
| 143 | H. A. Gomes, Birmingham | 1984 |
| 104* | H. A. Gomes, Leeds | 1984 |
| 134<br>101 | C. G. Greenidge, Manchester | 1976 |
| 115 | C. G. Greenidge, Leeds | 1976 |
| 214* | C. G. Greenidge, Lord's | 1984 |
| 223 | C. G. Greenidge, Manchester | 1984 |
| 184 | D. L. Haynes, Lord's | 1980 |
| 125 | D. L. Haynes, The Oval | 1984 |
| 176† | G. A. Headley, Bridgetown | 1929-30 |
| 114<br>112 | G. A. Headley, Georgetown | 1929-30 |
| 223 | G. A. Headley, Kingston | 1929-30 |
| 169* | G. A. Headley, Manchester | 1933 |
| 270* | G. A. Headley, Kingston | 1934-35 |
| 106<br>107 | G. A. Headley, Lord's | 1939 |
| 105* | D. A. J. Holford, Lord's | 1966 |
| 166 | J. K. Holt, Bridgetown | 1953-54 |
| 182 | C. C. Hunte, Manchester | 1963 |
| 108* | C. C. Hunte, The Oval | 1963 |
| 135 | C. C. Hunte, Manchester | 1966 |
| 121 | B. D. Julien, Lord's | 1973 |
| 158 | A. I. Kallicharran, Port-of-Spain | 1973-74 |
| 119 | A. I. Kallicharran, Bridgetown | 1973-74 |
| 110 | R. B. Kanhai, Port-of-Spain | 1959-60 |
| 104 | R. B. Kanhai, The Oval | 1966 |
| 153 | R. B. Kanhai, Port-of-Spain | 1967-68 |
| 150 | R. B. Kanhai, Georgetown | 1967-68 |
| 157 | R. B. Kanhai, Lord's | 1973 |
| 118† | C. H. Lloyd, Port-of-Spain | 1967-68 |
| 113* | C. H. Lloyd, Bridgetown | 1967-68 |
| 132 | C. H. Lloyd, The Oval | 1973 |
| 101 | C. H. Lloyd, Manchester | 1980 |
| 100 | C. H. Lloyd, Bridgetown | 1980-81 |
| 137 | S. M. Nurse, Leeds | 1966 |
| 136 | S. M. Nurse, Port-of-Spain | 1967-68 |
| 106 | A. F. Rae, Lord's | 1950 |
| 109 | A. F. Rae, The Oval | 1950 |
| 232† | I. V. A. Richards, Nottingham | 1976 |
| 135 | I. V. A. Richards, Manchester | 1976 |
| 291 | I. V. A. Richards, The Oval | 1976 |
| 145 | I. V. A. Richards, Lord's | 1980 |
| 182* | I. V. A. Richards, Bridgetown | 1980-81 |
| 114 | I. V. A. Richards, St John's, Antigua | 1980-81 |
| 117 | I. V. A. Richards, Birmingham | 1984 |
| 122 | C. A. Roach, Bridgetown | 1929-30 |
| 209 | C. A. Roach, Georgetown | 1929-30 |
| 120 | L. G. Rowe, Kingston | 1973-74 |
| 302 | L. G. Rowe, Bridgetown | 1973-74 |
| 123 | L. G. Rowe, Port-of-Spain | 1973-74 |
| 161† | O. G. Smith, Birmingham | 1957 |
| 168 | O. G. Smith, Nottingham | 1957 |
| 226 | G. S. Sobers, Bridgetown | 1959-60 |
| 147 | G. S. Sobers, Kingston | 1959-60 |
| 145 | G. S. Sobers, Georgetown | 1959-60 |
| 102 | G. S. Sobers, Leeds | 1963 |
| 161 | G. S. Sobers, Manchester | 1966 |
| 163* | G. S. Sobers, Lord's | 1966 |
| 174 | G. S. Sobers, Leeds | 1966 |
| 113* | G. S. Sobers, Kingston | 1967-68 |
| 152 | G. S. Sobers, Georgetown | 1967-68 |
| 150* | G. S. Sobers, Lord's | 1973 |
| 168* | C. L. Walcott, Lord's | 1950 |
| 220 | C. L. Walcott, Bridgetown | 1953-54 |
| 124 | C. L. Walcott, Port-of-Spain | 1953-54 |
| 116 | C. L. Walcott, Kingston | 1953-54 |
| 141 | E. D. Weekes, Kingston | 1947-48 |
| 129 | E. D. Weekes, Nottingham | 1950 |
| 206 | E. D. Weekes, Port-of-Spain | 1953-54 |
| 137 | K. H. Weekes, The Oval | 1939 |
| 131* | F. M. M. Worrell, Georgetown | 1947-48 |

| | | |
|---|---|---|
| 261 | F. M. M. Worrell, Nottingham | 1950 |
| 138 | F. M. M. Worrell, The Oval | 1950 |
| 167 | F. M. M. Worrell, Port-of-Spain | 1953-54 |
| 191*‡ | F. M. M. Worrell, Nottingham | 1957 |
| 197* | F. M. M. Worrell, Bridgetown | 1959-60 |

† *Signifies hundred on first appearance in England–West Indies Tests. S. C. Griffith provides the only instance for England of a player hitting his maiden century in first-class cricket in his first Test.*
‡ *Carried his bat.*

## RECORD PARTNERSHIPS FOR EACH WICKET

### For England

| | | |
|---|---|---|
| 212 for 1st | C. Washbrook and R. T. Simpson at Nottingham | 1950 |
| 266 for 2nd | P. E. Richardson and T. W. Graveney at Nottingham | 1957 |
| 264 for 3rd | L. Hutton and W. R. Hammond at The Oval | 1939 |
| 411 for 4th† | P. B. H. May and M. C. Cowdrey at Birmingham | 1957 |
| 130* for 5th | C. Milburn and T. W. Graveney at Lord's | 1966 |
| 163 for 6th | A. W. Greig and A. P. E. Knott at Bridgetown | 1973-74 |
| 197 for 7th† | M. J. K. Smith and J. M. Parks at Port-of-Spain | 1959-60 |
| 217 for 8th | T. W. Graveney and J. T. Murray at The Oval | 1966 |
| 109 for 9th | G. A. R. Lock and P. I. Pocock at Georgetown | 1967-68 |
| 128 for 10th | K. Higgs and J. A. Snow at The Oval | 1966 |

### For West Indies

| | | |
|---|---|---|
| 206 for 1st | R. C. Fredericks and L. G. Rowe at Kingston | 1973-74 |
| 287* for 2nd | C. G. Greenidge and H. A. Gomes at Lord's | 1984 |
| 338 for 3rd† | E. D. Weekes and F. M. M. Worrell at Port-of-Spain | 1953-54 |
| 399 for 4th† | G. S. Sobers and F. M. M. Worrell at Bridgetown | 1959-60 |
| 265 for 5th† | S. M. Nurse and G. S. Sobers at Leeds | 1966 |
| 274* for 6th† | G. S. Sobers and D. A. J. Holford at Lord's | 1966 |
| 155* for 7th‡ | G. S. Sobers and B. D. Julien at Lord's | 1973 |
| 99 for 8th | C. A. McWatt and J. K. Holt at Georgetown | 1953-54 |
| 150 for 9th | E. A. E. Baptiste and M. A. Holding at Birmingham | 1984 |
| 67* for 10th | M. A. Holding and C. E. H. Croft at St John's, Antigua | 1980-81 |

† *Denotes record partnership against all countries.*
‡ *231 runs were added for this wicket in two separate partnerships: G. S. Sobers retired ill and was replaced by K. D. Boyce when 155 had been added.*

## TEN WICKETS OR MORE IN A MATCH

### For England (10)

| | | |
|---|---|---|
| 11-98 (7-44, 4-54) | T. E. Bailey, Lord's | 1957 |
| 10-93 (5-54, 5-39) | A. P. Freeman, Manchester | 1928 |
| 13-156 (8-86, 5-70) | A. W. Greig, Port-of-Spain | 1973-74 |
| 11-48 (5-28, 6-20) | G. A. R. Lock, The Oval | 1957 |
| 11-96 (5-37, 6-59)† | C. S. Marriott, The Oval | 1933 |
| 10-142 (4-82, 6-60) | J. A. Snow, Georgetown | 1967-68 |
| 10-195 (5-105, 5-90)† | G. T. S. Stevens, Bridgetown | 1929-30 |
| 11-152 (6-100, 5-52) | F. S. Trueman, Lord's | 1963 |
| 12-119 (5-75, 7-44) | F. S. Trueman, Birmingham | 1963 |
| 11-149 (4-79, 7-70) | W. Voce, Port-of-Spain | 1929-30 |

### For West Indies (10)

| | | |
|---|---|---|
| 11-147 (5-70, 6-77)† | K. D. Boyce, The Oval | 1973 |
| 11-229 (5-137, 6-92) | W. Ferguson, Port-of-Spain | 1947-48 |
| 11-157 (5-59, 6-98)† | L. R. Gibbs, Manchester | 1963 |

| | | |
|---|---|---|
| 10-106 (5-37, 5-69) | L. R. Gibbs, Manchester | 1966 |
| 14-149 (8-92, 6-57) | M. A. Holding, The Oval | 1976 |
| 10-96 (5-41, 5-55)† | H. H. H. Johnson, Kingston | 1947-48 |
| 11-152 (5-66, 6-86) | S. Ramadhin, Lord's | 1950 |
| 10-123 (5-60, 5-63) | A. M. E. Roberts, Lord's | 1976 |
| 11-204 (8-104, 3-100)† | A. L. Valentine, Manchester | 1950 |
| 10-160 (4-121, 6-39) | A. L. Valentine, The Oval | 1950 |

† *Signifies ten wickets or more on first appearance in England–West Indies Tests.*

*Note:* F. S. Trueman took ten wickets or more in successive matches.

## ENGLAND v NEW ZEALAND

*Captains*

| *Season* | *England* | *New Zealand* | *T* | *E* | *NZ* | *D* |
|---|---|---|---|---|---|---|
| 1929-30 | A. H. H. Gilligan | T. C. Lowry | 4 | 1 | 0 | 3 |
| 1931 | D. R. Jardine | T. C. Lowry | 3 | 1 | 0 | 2 |
| 1932-33 | D. R. Jardine[1] | M. L. Page | 2 | 0 | 0 | 2 |
| 1937 | R. W. V. Robins | M. L. Page | 3 | 1 | 0 | 2 |
| 1946-47 | W. R. Hammond | W. A. Hadlee | 1 | 0 | 0 | 1 |
| 1949 | F. G. Mann[2] | W. A. Hadlee | 4 | 0 | 0 | 4 |
| 1950-51 | F. R. Brown | W. A. Hadlee | 2 | 1 | 0 | 1 |
| 1954-55 | L. Hutton | G. O. Rabone | 2 | 2 | 0 | 0 |
| 1958 | P. B. H. May | J. R. Reid | 5 | 4 | 0 | 1 |
| 1958-59 | P. B. H. May | J. R. Reid | 2 | 1 | 0 | 1 |
| 1962-63 | E. R. Dexter | J. R. Reid | 3 | 3 | 0 | 0 |
| 1965 | M. J. K. Smith | J. R. Reid | 3 | 3 | 0 | 0 |
| 1965-66 | M. J. K. Smith | B. W. Sinclair[3] | 3 | 0 | 0 | 3 |
| 1969 | R. Illingworth | G. T. Dowling | 3 | 2 | 0 | 1 |
| 1970-71 | R. Illingworth | G. T. Dowling | 2 | 1 | 0 | 1 |
| 1973 | R. Illingworth | B. E. Congdon | 3 | 2 | 0 | 1 |
| 1974-75 | M. H. Denness | B. E. Congdon | 2 | 1 | 0 | 1 |
| 1977-78 | G. Boycott | M. G. Burgess | 3 | 1 | 1 | 1 |
| 1978 | J. M. Brearley | M. G. Burgess | 3 | 3 | 0 | 0 |
| 1983 | R. G. D. Willis | G. P. Howarth | 4 | 3 | 1 | 0 |
| 1983-84 | R. G. D. Willis | G. P. Howarth | 3 | 0 | 1 | 2 |
| | In New Zealand | | 29 | 11 | 2 | 16 |
| | In England | | 31 | 19 | 1 | 11 |
| | Totals | | 60 | 30 | 3 | 27 |

*Notes:* The following deputised for the official touring captain or were appointed by the home authority for only a minor proportion of the series:

[1]R. E. S. Wyatt (Second). [2]F. R. Brown (Third and Fourth). [3]M. E. Chapple (First).

### HIGHEST INNINGS TOTALS

| | | |
|---|---|---|
| For England in England: | 546-4 dec. at Leeds | 1965 |
| in New Zealand: | 593-6 dec. at Auckland | 1974-75 |
| For New Zealand in England: | 551-9 dec. at Lord's | 1973 |
| in New Zealand: | 537 at Wellington | 1983-84 |

### LOWEST INNINGS TOTALS

| | | |
|---|---|---|
| For England in England: | 187 at Manchester | 1937 |
| in New Zealand: | 64 at Wellington | 1977-78 |
| For New Zealand in England: | 47 at Lord's | 1958 |
| in New Zealand: | 26 at Auckland | 1954-55 |

## INDIVIDUAL HUNDREDS

### For England (65)

122† G. O. Allen, Lord's ....... 1931
137† L. E. G. Ames, Lord's .... 1931
103 L. E. G. Ames, Christchurch ............... 1932-33
138*† D. L. Amiss, Nottingham . 1973
164* D. L. Amiss, Christchurch . 1974-75
134* T. E. Bailey, Christchurch . 1950-51
126† K. F. Barrington, Auckland 1962-63
163 K. F. Barrington, Leeds ... 1965
137 K. F. Barrington, Birmingham ................ 1965
103 I. T. Botham, Christchurch 1977-78
103 I. T. Botham, Nottingham . 1983
138 I. T. Botham, Wellington .. 1983-84
109 E. H. Bowley, Auckland .. 1929-30
115 G. Boycott, Leeds ........ 1973
131 G. Boycott, Nottingham ... 1978
114 D. C. S. Compton, Leeds .. 1949
116 D. C. S. Compton, Lord's . 1949
128* M. C. Cowdrey, Wellington 1962-63
119 M. C. Cowdrey, Lord's .... 1965
181 M. H. Denness, Auckland . 1974-75
141 E. R. Dexter, Christchurch 1958-59
100 B. L. D'Oliveira, Christchurch .............. 1970-71
117 K. S. Duleepsinhji, Auckland ................ 1929-30
109 K. S. Duleepsinhji, The Oval ................. 1931
310*† J. H. Edrich, Leeds ...... 1965
155 J. H. Edrich, Lord's ...... 1969
115 J. H. Edrich, Nottingham . 1969
100 W. J. Edrich, The Oval ... 1949
178 K. W. R. Fletcher, Lord's . 1973
216 K. W. R. Fletcher, Auckland ................ 1974-75
105† G. Fowler, The Oval ..... 1983
111† D. I. Gower, The Oval .... 1978
112* D. I. Gower, Leeds ....... 1983
108 D. I. Gower, Lord's ...... 1983
139† A. W. Greig, Nottingham . 1973
100* W. R. Hammond, The Oval 1931
227 W. R. Hammond, Christchurch .............. 1932-33
336* W. R. Hammond, Auckland ................ 1932-33
140 W. R. Hammond, Lord's .. 1937
114† J. Hardstaff jun., Lord's ... 1937
103 J. Hardstaff jun., The Oval ................ 1937
100 L. Hutton, Manchester .... 1937
101 L. Hutton, Leeds ......... 1949
206 L. Hutton, The Oval ...... 1949
125† B. R. Knight, Auckland ... 1962-63
101 A. P. E. Knott, Auckland . 1970-71
102*† A. J. Lamb, The Oval .... 1983
137* A. J. Lamb, Nottingham .. 1983
196 G. B. Legge, Auckland .... 1929-30
113* P. B. H. May, Leeds ...... 1958
101 P. B. H. May, Manchester . 1958
124* P. B. H. May, Auckland .. 1958-59
104*† C. A. Milton, Leeds ...... 1958
131*† P. H. Parfitt, Auckland ... 1962-63
158 C. T. Radley, Auckland ... 1977-78
164 D. W. Randall, Wellington 1983-84
104 D. W. Randall, Auckland . 1983-84
100† P. E. Richardson, Birmingham ................ 1958
121† J. D. Robertson, Lord's ... 1949
111 P. J. Sharpe, Nottingham . 1969
103† R. T. Simpson, Manchester 1949
117† H. Sutcliffe, The Oval .... 1931
109* H. Sutcliffe, Manchester ... 1931
109† C. J. Tavaré, The Oval ... 1983
103* C. Washbrook, Leeds ..... 1949

### For New Zealand (26)

104 M. G. Burgess, Auckland .. 1970-71
105 M. G. Burgess, Lord's .... 1973
174* J. V. Coney, Wellington ... 1983-84
104 B. E. Congdon, Christchurch .............. 1965-66
176 B. E. Congdon, Nottingham 1973
175 B. E. Congdon, Lord's .... 1973
128 J. J. Crowe, Auckland .... 1983-84
100 M. D. Crowe, Wellington . 1983-84
136 C. S. Dempster, Wellington 1929-30
120 C. S. Dempster, Lord's .... 1931
206 M. P. Donnelly, Lord's .... 1949
116 W. A. Hadlee, Christchurch .............. 1946-47
122 } 102 } G. P. Howarth, Auckland . 1977-78
123 G. P. Howarth, Lord's .... 1978
117† J. E. Mills, Wellington .... 1929-30
104 M. L. Page, Lord's ....... 1931
121 J. M. Parker, Auckland ... 1974-75
116 V. Pollard, Nottingham ... 1973
105* V. Pollard, Lord's ........ 1973
100 J. R. Reid, Christchurch .. 1962-63
114 B. W. Sinclair, Auckland .. 1965-66
113* I. D. S. Smith, Auckland .. 1983-84
101 B. Sutcliffe, Manchester ... 1949
116 B. Sutcliffe, Christchurch .. 1950-51
130 J. G. Wright, Auckland ... 1983-84

† *Signifies hundred on first appearance in England–New Zealand Tests.*

## RECORD PARTNERSHIPS FOR EACH WICKET

**For England**

| | | |
|---|---|---|
| 223 for 1st | G. Fowler and C. J. Tavaré at The Oval | 1983 |
| 369 for 2nd | J. H. Edrich and K. F. Barrington at Leeds | 1965 |
| 245 for 3rd | W. R. Hammond and J. Hardstaff jun. at Lord's | 1937 |
| 266 for 4th | M. H. Denness and K. W. R. Fletcher at Auckland | 1974-75 |
| 242 for 5th | W. R. Hammond and L. E. G. Ames at Christchurch | 1932-33 |
| 240 for 6th† | P. H. Parfitt and B. R. Knight at Auckland | 1962-63 |
| 149 for 7th | A. P. E. Knott and P. Lever at Auckland | 1970-71 |
| 246 for 8th† | L. E. G. Ames and G. O. Allen at Lord's | 1931 |
| 163* for 9th† | M. C. Cowdrey and A. C. Smith at Wellington | 1962-63 |
| 59 for 10th | A. P. E. Knott and N. Gifford at Nottingham | 1973 |

**For New Zealand**

| | | |
|---|---|---|
| 276 for 1st | C. S. Dempster and J. E. Mills at Wellington | 1929-30 |
| 131 for 2nd | B. Sutcliffe and J. R. Reid at Christchurch | 1950-51 |
| 190 for 3rd | B. E. Congdon and B. F. Hastings at Lord's | 1973 |
| 154 for 4th | J. G. Wright and J. J. Crowe at Auckland | 1983-84 |
| 177 for 5th | B. E. Congdon and V. Pollard at Nottingham | 1973 |
| 117 for 6th | M. G. Burgess and V. Pollard at Lord's | 1973 |
| 104 for 7th | B. Sutcliffe and V. Pollard at Birmingham | 1965 |
| 104 for 8th | A. W. Roberts and D. A. R. Moloney at Lord's | 1937 |
| 118 for 9th† | J. V. Coney and B. L. Cairns at Wellington | 1983-84 |
| 57 for 10th | F. L. H. Mooney and J. Cowie at Leeds | 1949 |

† *Denotes record partnership against all countries.*

## TEN WICKETS OR MORE IN A MATCH

**For England** (7)

| | | |
|---|---|---|
| 11-140 (6-101, 5-39) | I. T. Botham, Lord's | 1978 |
| 10-149 (5-98, 5-51) | A. W. Greig, Auckland | 1974-75 |
| 11-65 (4-14, 7-51) | G. A. R. Lock, Leeds | 1958 |
| 11-84 (5-31, 6-53) | G. A. R. Lock, Christchurch | 1958-59 |
| 11-70 (4-38, 7-32)† | D. L. Underwood, Lord's | 1969 |
| 12-101 (6-41, 6-60) | D. L. Underwood, The Oval | 1969 |
| 12-97 (6-12, 6-85) | D. L. Underwood, Christchurch | 1970-71 |

**For New Zealand** (3)

| | | |
|---|---|---|
| 10-144 (7-74, 3-70) | B. L. Cairns, Leeds | 1983 |
| 10-140 (4-73, 6-67) | J. Cowie, Manchester | 1937 |
| 10-100 (4-74, 6-26) | R. J. Hadlee, Wellington | 1977-78 |

† *Signifies ten wickets or more on first appearance in England–New Zealand Tests.*

*Note:* D. L. Underwood took twelve wickets in successive matches against New Zealand in 1969 and 1970-71.

## HAT-TRICK AND FOUR WICKETS IN FIVE BALLS

M. J. C. Allom, in his first Test match, v New Zealand at Christchurch in 1929-30, dismissed C. S. Dempster, T. C. Lowry, K. C. James, and F. T. Badcock to take four wickets in five balls (w-www).

## ENGLAND v INDIA

| Season | England (Captains) | India (Captains) | T | E | I | D |
|---|---|---|---|---|---|---|
| 1932 | D. R. Jardine | C. K. Nayudu | 1 | 1 | 0 | 0 |
| 1933-34 | D. R. Jardine | C. K. Nayudu | 3 | 2 | 0 | 1 |
| 1936 | G. O. Allen | Maharaj of Vizianagram | 3 | 2 | 0 | 1 |
| 1946 | W. R. Hammond | Nawab of Pataudi sen. | 3 | 1 | 0 | 2 |
| 1951-52 | N. D. Howard[1] | V. S. Hazare | 5 | 1 | 1 | 3 |
| 1952 | L. Hutton | V. S. Hazare | 4 | 3 | 0 | 1 |
| 1959 | P. B. H. May[2] | D. K. Gaekwad[3] | 5 | 5 | 0 | 0 |
| 1961-62 | E. R. Dexter | N. J. Contractor | 5 | 0 | 2 | 3 |
| 1963-64 | M. J. K. Smith | Nawab of Pataudi jun. | 5 | 0 | 0 | 5 |
| 1967 | D. B. Close | Nawab of Pataudi jun. | 3 | 3 | 0 | 0 |
| 1971 | R. Illingworth | A. L. Wadekar | 3 | 0 | 1 | 2 |
| 1972-73 | A. R. Lewis | A. L. Wadekar | 5 | 1 | 2 | 2 |
| 1974 | M. H. Denness | A. L. Wadekar | 3 | 3 | 0 | 0 |
| 1976-77 | A. W. Greig | B. S. Bedi | 5 | 3 | 1 | 1 |
| 1979 | J. M. Brearley | S. Venkataraghavan | 4 | 1 | 0 | 3 |
| 1979-80 | J. M. Brearley | G. R. Viswanath | 1 | 1 | 0 | 0 |
| 1981-82 | K. W. R. Fletcher | S. M. Gavaskar | 6 | 0 | 1 | 5 |
| 1982 | R. G. D. Willis | S. M. Gavaskar | 3 | 1 | 0 | 2 |
| 1984-85 | D. I. Gower | S. M. Gavaskar | 5 | 2 | 1 | 2 |
| | In England | | 32 | 20 | 1 | 11 |
| | In India | | 40 | 10 | 8 | 22 |
| | Totals | | 72 | 30 | 9 | 33 |

*Notes:* The 1932 Indian touring team was captained by the Maharaj of Porbandar but he did not play in the Test match.

The following deputised for the official touring captain or were appointed by the home authority for only a minor proportion of the series:

[1]D. B. Carr (Fifth). [2]M. C. Cowdrey (Fourth and Fifth). [3]P. Roy (Second).

### HIGHEST INNINGS TOTALS

For England in England: 633-5 dec. at Birmingham ........ 1979
in India: 652-7 dec. at Madras ........ 1984-85

For India in England: 510 at Leeds ........ 1967
in India: 553-8 dec. at Kanpur ........ 1984-85

### LOWEST INNINGS TOTALS

For England in England: 101 at The Oval ........ 1971
in India: 102 at Bombay ........ 1981-82

For India in England: 42 at Lord's ........ 1974
in India: 83 at Madras ........ 1976-77

## INDIVIDUAL HUNDREDS

### For England (59)

| | | |
|---|---|---|
| 188 | D. L. Amiss, Lord's | 1974 |
| 179 | D. L. Amiss, Delhi | 1976-77 |
| 151* | K. F. Barrington, Bombay | 1961-62 |
| 172 | K. F. Barrington, Kanpur | 1961-62 |
| 113* | K. F. Barrington, Delhi | 1961-62 |
| 137 | I. T. Botham, Leeds | 1979 |
| 114 | I. T. Botham, Bombay | 1979-80 |
| 142 | I. T. Botham, Kanpur | 1981-82 |
| 128 | I. T. Botham, Manchester | 1982 |
| 208 | I. T. Botham, The Oval | 1982 |
| 246*† | G. Boycott, Leeds | 1967 |
| 155 | G. Boycott, Birmingham | 1979 |
| 125 | G. Boycott, The Oval | 1979 |
| 105 | G. Boycott, Delhi | 1981-82 |
| 160 | M. C. Cowdrey, Leeds | 1959 |
| 107 | M. C. Cowdrey, Calcutta | 1963-64 |
| 151 | M. C. Cowdrey, Delhi | 1963-64 |
| 118 | M. H. Denness, Lord's | 1974 |
| 100 | M. H. Denness, Birmingham | 1974 |
| 126* | E. R. Dexter, Kanpur | 1961-62 |
| 109† | B. L. D'Oliveira, Leeds | 1967 |
| 100* | J. H. Edrich, Manchester | 1974 |
| 104 | T. G. Evans, Lord's | 1952 |
| 113 | K. W. R. Fletcher, Bombay | 1972-73 |
| 123* | K. W. R. Fletcher, Manchester | 1974 |
| 201 | G. Fowler, Madras | 1984-85 |
| 136 | M. W. Gatting, Bombay | 1984-85 |
| 207 | M. W. Gatting, Madras | 1984-85 |
| 129 | G. A. Gooch, Madras | 1981-82 |
| 200*† | D. I. Gower, Birmingham | 1979 |
| 175† | T. W. Graveney, Bombay | 1951-52 |
| 151 | T. W. Graveney, Lord's | 1967 |
| 148 | A. W. Greig, Bombay | 1972-73 |
| 106 | A. W. Greig, Lord's | 1974 |
| 103 | A. W. Greig, Calcutta | 1976-77 |
| 167 | W. R. Hammond, Manchester | 1936 |
| 217 | W. R. Hammond, The Oval | 1936 |
| 205* | J. Hardstaff jun., Lord's | 1946 |
| 150 | L. Hutton, Lord's | 1952 |
| 104 | L. Hutton, Manchester | 1952 |
| 107 | R. Illingworth, Manchester | 1971 |
| 127 | B. R. Knight, Kanpur | 1963-64 |
| 107 | A. J. Lamb, The Oval | 1982 |
| 125 | A. R. Lewis, Kanpur | 1972-73 |
| 214* | D. Lloyd, Birmingham | 1974 |
| 101 | B. W. Luckhurst, Manchester | 1971 |
| 106 | P. B. H. May, Nottingham | 1959 |
| 121 | P. H. Parfitt, Kanpur | 1963-64 |
| 131 | G. Pullar, Manchester | 1959 |
| 119 | G. Pullar, Kanpur | 1961-62 |
| 126 | D. W. Randall, Lord's | 1982 |
| 160 | R. T. Robinson, Delhi | 1984-85 |
| 119 | D. S. Sheppard, The Oval | 1952 |
| 100† | M. J. K. Smith, Manchester | 1959 |
| 149 | C. J. Tavaré, Delhi | 1981-82 |
| 136† | B. H. Valentine, Bombay | 1933-34 |
| 102 | C. F. Walters, Madras | 1933-34 |
| 137*† | A. J. Watkins, Delhi | 1951-52 |
| 128 | T. S. Worthington, The Oval | 1936 |

### For India (48)

| | | |
|---|---|---|
| 118† | L. Amarnath, Bombay | 1933-34 |
| 110† | M. Azharuddin, Calcutta | 1984-85 |
| 105 | M. Azharuddin, Madras | 1984-85 |
| 122 | M. Azharuddin, Kanpur | 1984-85 |
| 112† | A. A. Baig, Manchester | 1959 |
| 121 | F. M. Engineer, Bombay | 1972-73 |
| 101 | S. M. Gavaskar, Manchester | 1974 |
| 108 | S. M. Gavaskar, Bombay | 1976-77 |
| 221 | S. M. Gavaskar, The Oval | 1979 |
| 172 | S. M. Gavaskar, Bangalore | 1981-82 |
| 105† | Hanumant Singh, Delhi | 1963-64 |
| 164* | V. S. Hazare, Delhi | 1951-52 |
| 155 | V. S. Hazare, Bombay | 1951-52 |
| 127 | M. L. Jaisimha, Delhi | 1961-62 |
| 129 | M. L. Jaisimha, Calcutta | 1963-64 |
| 116 | Kapil Dev, Kanpur | 1981-82 |
| 102 | S. M. H. Kirmani, Bombay | 1984-85 |
| 192 | B. K. Kunderan, Madras | 1963-64 |
| 100 | B. K. Kunderan, Delhi | 1963-64 |
| 133 | V. L. Manjrekar, Leeds | 1952 |
| 189* | V. L. Manjrekar, Delhi | 1961-62 |
| 108 | V. L. Manjrekar, Madras | 1963-64 |
| 184 | V. Mankad, Lord's | 1952 |
| 114 | V. M. Merchant, Manchester | 1936 |
| 128 | V. M. Merchant, The Oval | 1946 |
| 154 | V. M. Merchant, Delhi | 1951-52 |
| 112 | Mushtaq Ali, Manchester | 1936 |
| 122* | R. G. Nadkarni, Kanpur | 1963-64 |
| 103 | Nawab of Pataudi jun., Madras | 1961-62 |
| 203* | Nawab of Pataudi jun., Delhi | 1963-64 |
| 148 | Nawab of Pataudi jun., Leeds | 1967 |
| 129* | S. M. Patil, Manchester | 1982 |
| 115 | D. G. Phadkar, Calcutta | 1951-52 |
| 140 | Pankaj Roy, Bombay | 1951-52 |
| 111 | Pankaj Roy, Madras | 1951-52 |
| 142 | R. J. Shastri, Bombay | 1984-85 |
| 111 | R. J. Shastri, Calcutta | 1984-85 |
| 130* | P. R. Umrigar, Madras | 1951-52 |
| 118 | P. R. Umrigar, Manchester | 1959 |

| | | | | | |
|---|---|---|---|---|---|
| 147* | P. R. Umrigar, Kanpur | 1961-62 | 113 | G. R. Viswanath, Lord's | 1979 |
| 103 | D. B. Vengsarkar, Lord's | 1979 | 107 | G. R. Viswanath, Delhi | 1981-82 |
| 157 | D. B. Vengsarkar, Lord's | 1982 | 222 | G. R. Viswanath, Madras | 1981-82 |
| 137 | D. B. Vengsarkar, Kanpur | 1984-85 | 140 | Yashpal Sharma, Madras | 1981-82 |
| 113 | G. R. Viswanath, Bombay | 1972-73 | | | |

† *Signifies hundred on first appearance in England–India Tests.*

*Note:* M. Azharuddin scored hundreds in each of his first three Tests.

## RECORD PARTNERSHIPS FOR EACH WICKET

**For England**

| | | |
|---|---|---|
| 178 for 1st | G. Fowler and R. T. Robinson at Madras | 1984-85 |
| 241 for 2nd | G. Fowler and M. W. Gatting at Madras | 1984-85 |
| 169 for 3rd | R. Subba Row and M. J. K. Smith at The Oval | 1959 |
| 266 for 4th | W. R. Hammond and T. S. Worthington at The Oval | 1936 |
| 254 for 5th† | K. W. R. Fletcher and A. W. Greig at Bombay | 1972-73 |
| 171 for 6th | I. T. Botham and R. W. Taylor at Bombay | 1979-80 |
| 125 for 7th | D. W. Randall and P. H. Edmonds at Lord's | 1982 |
| 168 for 8th | R. Illingworth and P. Lever at Manchester | 1971 |
| 83 for 9th | K. W. R. Fletcher and N. Gifford at Madras | 1972-73 |
| 70 for 10th | P. J. W. Allott and R. G. D. Willis at Lord's | 1982 |

**For India**

| | | |
|---|---|---|
| 213 for 1st | S. M. Gavaskar and C. P. S. Chauhan at The Oval | 1979 |
| 192 for 2nd | F. M. Engineer and A. L. Wadekar at Bombay | 1972-73 |
| 316 for 3rd†‡ | G. R. Viswanath and Yashpal Sharma at Madras | 1981-82 |
| 222 for 4th† | V. S. Hazare and V. L. Manjrekar at Leeds | 1952 |
| 214 for 5th† | M. Azharuddin and R. J. Shastri at Calcutta | 1984-85 |
| 130 for 6th | S. M. H. Kirmani and Kapil Dev at The Oval | 1982 |
| 235 for 7th† | R. J. Shastri and S. M. H. Kirmani at Bombay | 1984-85 |
| 128 for 8th | R. J. Shastri and S. M. H. Kirmani at Delhi | 1981-82 |
| 104 for 9th | R. J. Shastri and Madan Lal at Delhi | 1981-82 |
| 51 for 10th | R. G. Nadkarni and B. S. Chandrasekhar at Calcutta | 1963-64 |
| | S. M. H. Kirmani and C. Sharma at Madras | 1984-85 |

† *Denotes record partnership against all countries.*

‡ *415 runs were added between the fall of the 2nd and 3rd wickets: D. B. Vengsarkar retired hurt when he and Viswanath had added 99 runs.*

## TEN WICKETS OR MORE IN A MATCH

**For England** (7)

| | | |
|---|---|---|
| 10-78 (5-35, 5-43)† | G. O. Allen, Lord's | 1936 |
| 11-145 (7-49, 4-96)† | A. V. Bedser, Lord's | 1946 |
| 11-93 (4-41, 7-52) | A. V. Bedser, Manchester | 1946 |
| 13-106 (6-58, 7-48) | I. T. Botham, Bombay | 1979-80 |
| 11-163 (6-104, 5-59)† | N. A. Foster, Madras | 1984-85 |
| 10-70 (7-46, 3-24)† | J. K. Lever, Delhi | 1976-77 |
| 11-153 (7-49, 4-104) | H. Verity, Madras | 1933-34 |

**For India** (3)

| | | |
|---|---|---|
| 10-177 (6-105, 4-72) | S. A. Durani, Madras | 1961-62 |
| 12-108 (8-55, 4-53) | V. Mankad, Madras | 1951-52 |
| 12-181 (6-64, 6-117)† | L. Sivaramakrishnan, Bombay | 1984-85 |

† *Signifies ten wickets or more on first appearance in England–India Tests.*

*Note:* A. V. Bedser took eleven wickets in a match in the first two Tests of his career.

## ENGLAND v PAKISTAN

| Season | Captains: England | Captains: Pakistan | T | E | P | D |
|---|---|---|---|---|---|---|
| 1954 | L. Hutton[1] | A. H. Kardar | 4 | 1 | 1 | 2 |
| 1961-62 | E. R. Dexter | Imtiaz Ahmed | 3 | 1 | 0 | 2 |
| 1962 | E. R. Dexter[2] | Javed Burki | 5 | 4 | 0 | 1 |
| 1967 | D. B. Close | Hanif Mohammad | 3 | 2 | 0 | 1 |
| 1968-69 | M. C. Cowdrey | Saeed Ahmed | 3 | 0 | 0 | 3 |
| 1971 | R. Illingworth | Intikhab Alam | 3 | 1 | 0 | 2 |
| 1972-73 | A. R. Lewis | Majid J. Khan | 3 | 0 | 0 | 3 |
| 1974 | M. H. Denness | Intikhab Alam | 3 | 0 | 0 | 3 |
| 1977-78 | J. M. Brearley[3] | Wasim Bari | 3 | 0 | 0 | 3 |
| 1978 | J. M. Brearley | Wasim Bari | 3 | 2 | 0 | 1 |
| 1982 | R. G. D. Willis[4] | Imran Khan | 3 | 2 | 1 | 0 |
| 1983-84 | R. G. D. Willis[5] | Zaheer Abbas | 3 | 0 | 1 | 2 |
| | In England | | 24 | 12 | 2 | 10 |
| | In Pakistan | | 15 | 1 | 1 | 13 |
| | Totals | | 39 | 13 | 3 | 23 |

*Notes:* [1]D. S. Sheppard captained in Second and Third Tests. [2]M. C. Cowdrey captained in Third Test. [3]G. Boycott captained in Third Test. [4]D. I. Gower captained in Second Test. [5]D. I. Gower captained in Second and Third Tests.

### HIGHEST INNINGS TOTALS

For England in England: 558-6 dec. at Nottingham .......... 1954
in Pakistan: 546-8 dec. at Faisalabad .......... 1983-84

For Pakistan in England: 608-7 dec. at Birmingham .......... 1971
in Pakistan: 569-9 dec. at Hyderabad .......... 1972-73

### LOWEST INNINGS TOTALS

For England in England: 130 at The Oval .......... 1954
in Pakistan: 159 at Karachi .......... 1983-84

For Pakistan in England: 87 at Lord's .......... 1954
in Pakistan: 199 at Karachi .......... 1972-73

### INDIVIDUAL HUNDREDS

**For England** (36)

| | | |
|---|---|---|
| 112 | D. L. Amiss, Lahore | 1972-73 |
| 158 | D. L. Amiss, Hyderabad | 1972-73 |
| 183 | D. L. Amiss, The Oval | 1974 |
| 139† | K. F. Barrington, Lahore | 1961-62 |
| 148 | K. F. Barrington, Lord's | 1967 |
| 109* | K. F. Barrington, Nottingham | 1967 |
| 142 | K. F. Barrington, The Oval | 1967 |
| 100† | I. T. Botham, Birmingham | 1978 |
| 108 | I. T. Botham, Lord's | 1978 |
| 121* | G. Boycott, Lord's | 1971 |
| 112 | G. Boycott, Leeds | 1971 |
| 100* | G. Boycott, Hyderabad | 1977-78 |
| 278 | D. C. S. Compton, Nottingham | 1954 |
| 159† | M. C. Cowdrey, Birmingham | 1962 |
| 182 | M. C. Cowdrey, The Oval | 1962 |
| 100 | M. C. Cowdrey, Lahore | 1968-69 |
| 205 | E. R. Dexter, Karachi | 1961-62 |

| | | |
|---|---|---|
| 172 | E. R. Dexter, The Oval | 1962 |
| 114* | B. L. D'Oliveira, Dacca | 1968-69 |
| 122 | K. W. R. Fletcher, The Oval | 1974 |
| 152 | D. I. Gower, Faisalabad | 1983-84 |
| 173* | D. I. Gower, Lahore | 1983-84 |
| 153 | T. W. Graveney, Lord's | 1962 |
| 114 | T. W. Graveney, Nottingham | 1962 |
| 105 | T. W. Graveney, Karachi | 1968-69 |
| 116 | A. P. E. Knott, Birmingham | 1971 |
| 108*† | B. W. Luckhurst, Birmingham | 1971 |
| 139 | C. Milburn, Karachi | 1968-69 |
| 111 | P. H. Parfitt, Karachi | 1961-62 |
| 101* | P. H. Parfitt, Birmingham | 1962 |
| 119 | P. H. Parfitt, Leeds | 1962 |
| 101* | P. H. Parfitt, Nottingham | 1962 |
| 165 | G. Pullar, Dacca | 1961-62 |
| 106† | C. T. Radley, Birmingham | 1978 |
| 105 | D. W. Randall, Birmingham | 1982 |
| 101 | R. T. Simpson, Nottingham | 1954 |

**For Pakistan** (25)

| | | |
|---|---|---|
| 109 | Alim-ud-Din, Karachi | 1961-62 |
| 146 | Asif Iqbal, The Oval | 1967 |
| 104* | Asif Iqbal, Birmingham | 1971 |
| 102 | Asif Iqbal, Lahore | 1972-73 |
| 138† | Javed Burki, Lahore | 1961-62 |
| 140 | Javed Burki, Dacca | 1961-62 |
| 101 | Javed Burki, Lord's | 1962 |
| 111 / 104 | Hanif Mohammad, Dacca | 1961-62 |
| 187* | Hanif Mohammad, Lord's | 1967 |
| 122† | Haroon Rashid, Lahore | 1977-78 |
| 108 | Haroon Rashid, Hyderabad | 1977-78 |
| 138 | Intikhab Alam, Hyderabad | 1972-73 |
| 200 | Mohsin Khan, Lord's | 1982 |
| 104 | Mohsin Khan, Lahore | 1983-84 |
| 114† | Mudassar Nazar, Lahore | 1977-78 |
| 100* | Mushtaq Mohammad, Nottingham | 1962 |
| 100 | Mushtaq Mohammad, Birmingham | 1971 |
| 157 | Mushtaq Mohammad, Hyderabad | 1972-73 |
| 101 | Nasim-ul-Ghani, Lord's | 1962 |
| 119 | Sadiq Mohammad, Lahore | 1972-73 |
| 116 | Salim Malik, Faisalabad | 1983-84 |
| 112 | Wasim Raja, Faisalabad | 1983-84 |
| 274† | Zaheer Abbas, Birmingham | 1971 |
| 240 | Zaheer Abbas, The Oval | 1974 |

† *Signifies hundred on first appearance in England–Pakistan Tests.*

*Note:* Three batsmen – Majid J. Khan, Mushtaq Mohammad and D. L. Amiss – were dismissed for 99 at Karachi, 1972-73: the only instance in Test matches.

## RECORD PARTNERSHIPS FOR EACH WICKET

**For England**

| | | |
|---|---|---|
| 198 for 1st | G. Pullar and R. W. Barber at Dacca | 1961-62 |
| 248 for 2nd | M. C. Cowdrey and E. R. Dexter at The Oval | 1962 |
| 201 for 3rd | K. F. Barrington and T. W. Graveney at Lord's | 1967 |
| 188 for 4th | E. R. Dexter and P. H. Parfitt at Karachi | 1961-62 |
| 192 for 5th | D. C. S. Compton and T. E. Bailey at Nottingham | 1954 |
| 153* for 6th | P. H. Parfitt and D. A. Allen at Birmingham | 1962 |
| 167 for 7th | D. I. Gower and V. J. Marks at Faisalabad | 1983-84 |
| 99 for 8th | P. H. Parfitt and D. A. Allen at Leeds | 1962 |
| 76 for 9th | T. W. Graveney and F. S. Trueman at Lord's | 1962 |
| 79 for 10th | R. W. Taylor and R. G. D. Willis at Birmingham | 1982 |

**For Pakistan**

| | | |
|---|---|---|
| 173 for 1st | Mohsin Khan and Shoaib Mohammad at Lahore | 1983-84 |
| 291 for 2nd† | Zaheer Abbas and Mushtaq Mohammad at Birmingham | 1971 |
| 180 for 3rd | Mudassar Nazar and Haroon Rashid at Lahore | 1977-78 |
| 153 for 4th | Javed Burki and Mushtaq Mohammad at Lahore | 1961-62 |
| | Mohsin Khan and Zaheer Abbas at Lord's | 1982 |
| 197 for 5th | Javed Burki and Nasim-ul-Ghani at Lord's | 1962 |
| 145 for 6th | Mushtaq Mohammad and Intikhab Alam at Hyderabad | 1972-73 |
| 75 for 7th | Salim Malik and Abdul Qadir at Karachi | 1983-84 |
| 130 for 8th† | Hanif Mohammad and Asif Iqbal at Lord's | 1967 |
| 190 for 9th† | Asif Iqbal and Intikhab Alam at The Oval | 1967 |
| 62 for 10th | Sarfraz Nawaz and Asif Masood at Leeds | 1974 |

† *Denotes record partnership against all countries.*

## TEN WICKETS OR MORE IN A MATCH

**For England** (2)

| | | |
|---|---|---|
| 11-83 (6-65, 5-18)† | N. G. B. Cook, Karachi | 1983-84 |
| 13-71 (5-20, 8-51) | D. L. Underwood, Lord's | 1974 |

**For Pakistan** (2)

| | | |
|---|---|---|
| 10-194 (5-84, 5-110) | Abdul Qadir, Lahore | 1983-84 |
| 12-99 (6-53, 6-46) | Fazal Mahmood, The Oval | 1954 |

† *Signifies ten wickets or more on first appearance in England–Pakistan Tests.*

## FOUR WICKETS IN FIVE BALLS

C. M. Old, v Pakistan at Birmingham in 1978, dismissed Wasim Raja, Wasim Bari, Iqbal Qasim and Sikander Bakht to take four wickets in five balls (ww-ww).

# ENGLAND v SRI LANKA

| *Season* | *Captains* England | *Sri Lanka* | *T* | *E* | *SL* | *D* |
|---|---|---|---|---|---|---|
| 1981-82 | K. W. R. Fletcher | B. Warnapura | 1 | 1 | 0 | 0 |
| 1984 | D. I. Gower | L. R. D. Mendis | 1 | 0 | 0 | 1 |
| | Totals | | 2 | 1 | 0 | 1 |

Highest innings total for England: 370 at Lord's ... 1984
for Sri Lanka: 491-7 dec. at Lord's ... 1984
Lowest innings total for England: 223 at Colombo (PSO) ... 1981-82
for Sri Lanka: 175 at Colombo (PSO) ... 1981-82

## INDIVIDUAL HUNDREDS

**For England** (1)

| | | |
|---|---|---|
| 107† | A. J. Lamb, Lord's | 1984 |

**For Sri Lanka** (3)

| | | |
|---|---|---|
| 111 | L. R. D. Mendis, Lord's | 1984 |
| 102*† | S. A. R. Silva, Lord's | 1984 |
| 190 | S. Wettimuny, Lord's | 1984 |

† *Signifies hundred on first appearance in England–Sri Lanka Tests.*

Best bowling in an innings for England: 6-33 by J. E. Emburey at Colombo (PSO) 1981-82
for Sri Lanka: 4-70 by A. L. F. de Mel at Colombo (PSO) 1981-82
Best wicket partnerships for England: 87 for 6th by A. J. Lamb and R. M. Ellison at Lord's ... 1984
for Sri Lanka: 150 for 5th by S. Wettimuny and L. R. D. Mendis at Lord's ... 1984

## ENGLAND v REST OF THE WORLD

In 1970, owing to the cancellation of the South African tour to England, a series of matches was arranged, with the trappings of a full Test series, between England and the Rest of the World. It was played for the Guinness Trophy.

The following players represented the Rest of the World: E. J. Barlow (5), F. M. Engineer (2), L. R. Gibbs (4), Intikhab Alam (5), R. B. Kanhai (5), C. H. Lloyd (5), G. D. McKenzie (3), D. L. Murray (3), Mushtaq Mohammad (2), P. M. Pollock (1), R. G. Pollock (5), M. J. Procter (5), B. A. Richards (5), G. S. Sobers (5).

A list of players who appeared for England in these matches may be found on page 124.

## AUSTRALIA v SOUTH AFRICA

| | *Captains* | | | | | |
|---|---|---|---|---|---|---|
| *Season* | *Australia* | *South Africa* | *T* | *A* | *SA* | *D* |
| 1902-03*S* | J. Darling | H. M. Taberer[1] | 3 | 2 | 0 | 1 |
| 1910-11*A* | C. Hill | P. W. Sherwell | 5 | 4 | 1 | 0 |
| 1912*E* | S. E. Gregory | F. Mitchell[2] | 3 | 2 | 0 | 1 |
| 1921-22*S* | H. L. Collins | H. W. Taylor | 3 | 1 | 0 | 2 |
| 1931-32*A* | W. M. Woodfull | H. B. Cameron | 5 | 5 | 0 | 0 |
| 1935-36*S* | V. Y. Richardson | H. F. Wade | 5 | 4 | 0 | 1 |
| 1949-50*S* | A. L. Hassett | A. D. Nourse | 5 | 4 | 0 | 1 |
| 1952-53*A* | A. L. Hassett | J. E. Cheetham | 5 | 2 | 2 | 1 |
| 1957-58*S* | I. D. Craig | C. B. van Ryneveld[3] | 5 | 3 | 0 | 2 |
| 1963-64*A* | R. B. Simpson[4] | T. L. Goddard | 5 | 1 | 1 | 3 |
| 1966-67*S* | R. B. Simpson | P. L. van der Merwe | 5 | 1 | 3 | 1 |
| 1969-70*S* | W. M. Lawry | A. Bacher | 4 | 0 | 4 | 0 |
| | In South Africa | | 30 | 15 | 7 | 8 |
| | In Australia | | 20 | 12 | 4 | 4 |
| | In England | | 3 | 2 | 0 | 1 |
| | Totals | | 53 | 29 | 11 | 13 |

*S Played in South Africa. A Played in Australia. E Played in England.*

*Notes:* The following deputised for the official touring captain or were appointed by the home authority for only a minor proportion of the series:

[1]J. H. Anderson (Second), E. A. Halliwell (Third). [2]L. J. Tancred (Third). [3]D. J. McGlew (First). [4]R. Benaud (First).

### HIGHEST INNINGS TOTALS

For Australia in Australia: 578 at Melbourne ........ 1910-11
in South Africa: 549-7 dec. at Port Elizabeth ........ 1949-50
For South Africa in Australia: 595 at Adelaide ........ 1963-64
in South Africa: 622-9 dec. at Durban ........ 1969-70

### LOWEST INNINGS TOTALS

For Australia in Australia: 153 at Melbourne ........ 1931-32
in South Africa: 75 at Durban ........ 1949-50
For South Africa in Australia: 36† at Melbourne ........ 1931-32
in South Africa: 85 at Johannesburg ........ 1902-03

† *Scored 45 in the second innings giving the smallest aggregate of 81 (12 extras) in Test cricket.*

## INDIVIDUAL HUNDREDS

**For Australia** (55)

| | | |
|---|---|---|
| 159*‡ | W. W. Armstrong, Johannesburg | 1902-03 |
| 132 | W. W. Armstrong, Melbourne | 1910-11 |
| 132† | W. Bardsley, Sydney | 1910-11 |
| 121 | W. Bardsley, Manchester | 1912 |
| 164 | W. Bardsley, Lord's | 1912 |
| 122 | R. Benaud, Johannesburg | 1957-58 |
| 100 | R. Benaud, Johannesburg | 1957-58 |
| 169† | B. C. Booth, Brisbane | 1963-64 |
| 102* | B. C. Booth, Sydney | 1963-64 |
| 226† | D. G. Bradman, Brisbane | 1931-32 |
| 112 | D. G. Bradman, Sydney | 1931-32 |
| 167 | D. G. Bradman, Melbourne | 1931-32 |
| 299* | D. G. Bradman, Adelaide | 1931-32 |
| 121 | W. A. Brown, Cape Town | 1935-36 |
| 189 | J. W. Burke, Cape Town | 1957-58 |
| 109† | A. G. Chipperfield, Durban | 1935-36 |
| 203 | H. L. Collins, Johannesburg | 1921-22 |
| 112 | J. H. Fingleton, Cape Town | 1935-36 |
| 108 | J. H. Fingleton, Johannesburg | 1935-36 |
| 118 | J. H. Fingleton, Durban | 1935-36 |
| 119 | J. M. Gregory, Johannesburg | 1921-22 |
| 178 | R. N. Harvey, Cape Town | 1949-50 |
| 151* | R. N. Harvey, Durban | 1949-50 |
| 116 | R. N. Harvey, Port Elizabeth | 1949-50 |
| 100 | R. N. Harvey, Johannesburg | 1949-50 |
| 109 | R. N. Harvey, Brisbane | 1952-53 |
| 190 | R. N. Harvey, Sydney | 1952-53 |
| 116 | R. N. Harvey, Adelaide | 1952-53 |
| 205 | R. N. Harvey, Melbourne | 1952-53 |
| 112† | A. L. Hassett, Johannesburg | 1949-50 |
| 167 | A. L. Hassett, Port Elizabeth | 1949-50 |
| 163 | A. L. Hassett, Adelaide | 1952-53 |
| 142† | C. Hill, Johannesburg | 1902-03 |
| 191 | C. Hill, Sydney | 1910-11 |
| 100 | C. Hill, Melbourne | 1910-11 |
| 114 | C. Kelleway, Manchester | 1912 |
| 102 | C. Kelleway, Lord's | 1912 |
| 157 | W. M. Lawry, Melbourne | 1963-64 |
| 101† | S. J. E. Loxton, Johannesburg | 1949-50 |
| 137 | C. G. Macartney, Sydney | 1910-11 |
| 116 | C. G. Macartney, Durban | 1921-22 |
| 149 | S. J. McCabe, Durban | 1935-36 |
| 189* | S. J. McCabe, Johannesburg | 1935-36 |
| 154 | C. C. McDonald, Adelaide | 1952-53 |
| 118 } 101* } | J. Moroney, Johannesburg | 1949-50 |
| 111 | A. R. Morris, Johannesburg | 1949-50 |
| 157 | A. R. Morris, Port Elizabeth | 1949-50 |
| 127† | K. E. Rigg, Sydney | 1931-32 |
| 142 | J. Ryder, Cape Town | 1921-22 |
| 153 | R. B. Simpson, Cape Town | 1966-67 |
| 134 | K. R. Stackpole, Cape Town | 1966-67 |
| 159 | V. T. Trumper, Melbourne | 1910-11 |
| 214* | V. T. Trumper, Adelaide | 1910-11 |
| 161 | W. M. Woodfull, Melbourne | 1931-32 |

**For South Africa** (36)

| | | |
|---|---|---|
| 114† | E. J. Barlow, Brisbane | 1963-64 |
| 109 | E. J. Barlow, Melbourne | 1963-64 |
| 201 | E. J. Barlow, Adelaide | 1963-64 |
| 127 | E. J. Barlow, Cape Town | 1969-70 |
| 110 | E. J. Barlow, Johannesburg | 1969-70 |
| 126 | K. C. Bland, Sydney | 1963-64 |
| 162* | W. R. Endean, Melbourne | 1952-53 |
| 204 | G. A. Faulkner, Melbourne | 1910-11 |
| 115 | G. A. Faulkner, Adelaide | 1910-11 |
| 122* | G. A. Faulkner, Manchester | 1912 |
| 152 | C. N. Frank, Johannesburg | 1921-22 |
| 102 | B. L. Irvine, Port Elizabeth | 1969-70 |
| 182 | D. T. Lindsay, Johannesburg | 1966-67 |
| 137 | D. T. Lindsay, Durban | 1966-67 |
| 131 | D. T. Lindsay, Johannesburg | 1966-67 |
| 108 | D. J. McGlew, Johannesburg | 1957-58 |
| 105 | D. J. McGlew, Durban | 1957-58 |
| 231 | A. D. Nourse, Johannesburg | 1935-36 |
| 114 | A. D. Nourse, Cape Town | 1949-50 |
| 111 | A. W. Nourse, Johannesburg | 1921-22 |
| 122 | R. G. Pollock, Sydney | 1963-64 |
| 175 | R. G. Pollock, Adelaide | 1963-64 |
| 209 | R. G. Pollock, Cape Town | 1966-67 |
| 105 | R. G. Pollock, Port Elizabeth | 1966-67 |
| 274 | R. G. Pollock, Durban | 1969-70 |
| 140 | B. A. Richards, Durban | 1969-70 |
| 126 | B. A. Richards, Port Elizabeth | 1969-70 |
| 143 | E. A. B. Rowan, Durban | 1949-50 |

| | | | | | |
|---|---|---|---|---|---|
| 101 | J. H. Sinclair, Johannesburg | 1902-03 | 115 | J. H. B. Waite, Johannesburg | 1957-58 |
| 104 | J. H. Sinclair, Cape Town | 1902-03 | 134 | J. H. B. Waite, Durban | 1957-58 |
| 103 | S. J. Snooke, Adelaide | 1910-11 | 105 | J. W. Zulch, Adelaide | 1910-11 |
| 111 | K. G. Viljoen, Melbourne | 1931-32 | 150 | J. W. Zulch, Sydney | 1910-11 |

† *Signifies hundred on first appearance in Australia–South Africa Tests.*
‡ *Carried his bat.*

## RECORD PARTNERSHIPS FOR EACH WICKET

**For Australia**

| | | |
|---|---|---|
| 233 for 1st | J. H. Fingleton and W. A. Brown at Cape Town | 1935-36 |
| 275 for 2nd | C. C. McDonald and A. L. Hassett at Adelaide | 1952-53 |
| 242 for 3rd | C. Kelleway and W. Bardsley at Lord's | 1912 |
| 168 for 4th | R. N. Harvey and K. R. Miller at Sydney | 1952-53 |
| 143 for 5th | W. W. Armstrong and V. T. Trumper at Melbourne | 1910-11 |
| 107 for 6th | C. Kelleway and V. S. Ransford at Melbourne | 1910-11 |
| 160 for 7th | R. Benaud and G. D. McKenzie at Sydney | 1963-64 |
| 83 for 8th | A. G. Chipperfield and C. V. Grimmett at Durban | 1935-36 |
| 78 for 9th | D. G. Bradman and W. J. O'Reilly at Adelaide | 1931-32 |
| | K. D. Mackay and I. Meckiff at Johannesburg | 1957-58 |
| 82 for 10th | V. S. Ransford and W. J. Whitty at Melbourne | 1910-11 |

**For South Africa**

| | | |
|---|---|---|
| 176 for 1st | D. J. McGlew and T. L. Goddard at Johannesburg | 1957-58 |
| 173 for 2nd | L. J. Tancred and C. B. Llewellyn at Johannesburg | 1902-03 |
| 341 for 3rd† | E. J. Barlow and R. G. Pollock at Adelaide | 1963-64 |
| 206 for 4th | C. N. Frank and A. W. Nourse at Johannesburg | 1921-22 |
| 129 for 5th | J. H. B. Waite and W. R. Endean at Johannesburg | 1957-58 |
| 200 for 6th† | R. G. Pollock and H. R. Lance at Durban | 1969-70 |
| 221 for 7th | D. T. Lindsay and P. L. van der Merwe at Johannesburg | 1966-67 |
| 124 for 8th† | A. W. Nourse and E. A. Halliwell at Johannesburg | 1902-03 |
| 85 for 9th | R. G. Pollock and P. M. Pollock at Cape Town | 1966-67 |
| 53 for 10th | L. A. Stricker and S. J. Pegler at Adelaide | 1910-11 |

† *Denotes record partnership against all countries.*

## TEN WICKETS OR MORE IN A MATCH

**For Australia** (5)

| | | |
|---|---|---|
| 14-199 (7-116, 7-83) | C. V. Grimmett, Adelaide | 1931-32 |
| 10-88 (5-32, 5-56) | C. V. Grimmett, Cape Town | 1935-36 |
| 10-110 (3-70, 7-40) | C. V. Grimmett, Johannesburg | 1935-36 |
| 13-173 (7-100, 6-73) | C. V. Grimmett, Durban | 1935-36 |
| 11-24 (5-6, 6-18) | H. Ironmonger, Melbourne | 1931-32 |

**For South Africa** (2)

| | | |
|---|---|---|
| 10-116 (5-43, 5-73) | C. B. Llewellyn, Johannesburg | 1902-03 |
| 13-165 (6-84, 7-81) | H. J. Tayfield, Melbourne | 1952-53 |

*Note:* C. V. Grimmett took ten wickets or more in three consecutive matches in 1935-36.

## AUSTRALIA v WEST INDIES

| | Captains | | | | | | |
|---|---|---|---|---|---|---|---|
| *Season* | *Australia* | *West Indies* | *T* | *A* | *WI* | *T* | *D* |
| 1930-31*A* | W. M. Woodfull | G. C. Grant | 5 | 4 | 1 | 0 | 0 |
| 1951-52*A* | A. L. Hassett[1] | J. D. C. Goddard[2] | 5 | 4 | 1 | 0 | 0 |
| 1954-55*W* | I. W. Johnson | D. S. Atkinson[3] | 5 | 3 | 0 | 0 | 2 |
| 1960-61*A* | R. Benaud | F. M. M. Worrell | 5† | 2 | 1 | 1 | 1 |

### THE FRANK WORRELL TROPHY

| | Captains | | | | | | | |
|---|---|---|---|---|---|---|---|---|
| *Season* | *Australia* | *West Indies* | *T* | *A* | *WI* | *T* | *D* | *Held by* |
| 1964-65*W* | R. B. Simpson | G. S. Sobers | 5 | 1 | 2 | 0 | 2 | WI |
| 1968-69*A* | W. M. Lawry | G. S. Sobers | 5 | 3 | 1 | 0 | 1 | A |
| 1972-73*W* | I. M. Chappell | R. B. Kanhai | 5 | 2 | 0 | 0 | 3 | A |
| 1975-76*A* | G. S. Chappell | C. H. Lloyd | 6 | 5 | 1 | 0 | 0 | A |
| 1977-78*W* | R. B. Simpson | A. I. Kallicharran[4] | 5 | 1 | 3 | 0 | 1 | WI |
| 1979-80*A* | G. S. Chappell | C. H. Lloyd[5] | 3 | 0 | 2 | 0 | 1 | WI |
| 1981-82*A* | G. S. Chappell | C. H. Lloyd | 3 | 1 | 1 | 0 | 1 | WI |
| 1983-84*W* | K. J. Hughes | C. H. Lloyd[6] | 5 | 0 | 3 | 0 | 2 | WI |
| 1984-85*A* | A. R. Border[7] | C. H. Lloyd | 5 | 1 | 3 | 0 | 1 | WI |
| | In Australia | | 37 | 20 | 11 | 1 | 5 | |
| | In West Indies | | 25 | 7 | 8 | 0 | 10 | |
| | Totals | | 62 | 27 | 19 | 1 | 15 | |

† *The First Test at Brisbane resulted in a tie. This is the only instance of a Test match resulting in a tie.*

*A Played in Australia.* *W Played in West Indies.*

*Notes:* The following deputised for the official touring captain or were appointed by the home authority for only a minor proportion of the series:

[1]A. R. Morris (Third). [2]J. B. Stollmeyer (Fifth). [3]J. B. Stollmeyer (Second and Third). [4]C. H. Lloyd (First and Second). [5]D. L. Murray (First). [6]I. V. A. Richards (Second). [7]K. J. Hughes (First and Second).

### HIGHEST INNINGS TOTALS

| | | |
|---|---|---|
| For Australia in Australia: | 619 at Sydney | 1968-69 |
| in West Indies: | 758-8 dec. at Kingston | 1954-55 |
| For West Indies in Australia: | 616 at Adelaide | 1968-69 |
| in West Indies: | 573 at Bridgetown | 1964-65 |

### LOWEST INNINGS TOTALS

| | | |
|---|---|---|
| For Australia in Australia: | 76 at Perth | 1984-85 |
| in West Indies: | 90 at Port-of-Spain | 1977-78 |
| For West Indies in Australia: | 78 at Sydney | 1951-52 |
| in West Indies: | 109 at Georgetown | 1972-73 |

## INDIVIDUAL HUNDREDS

### For Australia (64)

| | | |
|---|---|---|
| 128 | R. G. Archer, Kingston | 1954-55 |
| 121 | R. Benaud, Kingston | 1954-55 |
| 117 | B. C. Booth, Port-of-Spain | 1964-65 |
| 126 | A. R. Border, Adelaide | 1981-82 |
| 100* | A. R. Border, Port-of-Spain | 1983-84 |
| 223 | D. G. Bradman, Brisbane | 1930-31 |
| 152 | D. G. Bradman, Melbourne | 1930-31 |
| 106 | G. S. Chappell, Bridgetown | 1972-73 |
| 123<br>109* | ‡G. S. Chappell, Brisbane | 1975-76 |
| 182* | G. S. Chappell, Sydney | 1975-76 |
| 124 | G. S. Chappell, Brisbane | 1979-80 |
| 117† | I. M. Chappell, Brisbane | 1968-69 |
| 165 | I. M. Chappell, Melbourne | 1968-69 |
| 106* | I. M. Chappell, Bridgetown | 1972-73 |
| 109 | I. M. Chappell, Georgetown | 1972-73 |
| 156 | I. M. Chappell, Perth | 1975-76 |
| 109† | G. J. Cosier, Melbourne | 1975-76 |
| 143 | R. M. Cowper, Port-of-Spain | 1964-65 |
| 102 | R. M. Cowper, Bridgetown | 1964-65 |
| 127*† | J. Dyson, Sydney | 1981-82 |
| 133 | R. N. Harvey, Kingston | 1954-55 |
| 133 | R. N. Harvey, Port-of-Spain | 1954-55 |
| 204 | R. N. Harvey, Kingston | 1954-55 |
| 132 | A. L. Hassett, Sydney | 1951-52 |
| 102 | A. L. Hassett, Melbourne | 1951-52 |
| 113† | A. M. J. Hilditch, Melbourne | 1984-85 |
| 130*† | K. J. Hughes, Brisbane | 1979-80 |
| 100* | K. J. Hughes, Melbourne | 1981-82 |
| 146† | A. F. Kippax, Adelaide | 1930-31 |
| 210 | W. M. Lawry, Bridgetown | 1964-65 |
| 105 | W. M. Lawry, Brisbane | 1968-69 |
| 205 | W. M. Lawry, Melbourne | 1968-69 |
| 151 | W. M. Lawry, Sydney | 1968-69 |
| 118 | R. R. Lindwall, Bridgetown | 1954-55 |
| 109* | R. B. McCosker, Melbourne | 1975-76 |
| 110 | C. C. McDonald, Port-of-Spain | 1954-55 |
| 127 | C. C. McDonald, Kingston | 1954-55 |
| 129 | K. R. Miller, Sydney | 1951-52 |
| 147 | K. R. Miller, Kingston | 1954-55 |
| 137 | K. R. Miller, Bridgetown | 1954-55 |
| 109 | K. R. Miller, Kingston | 1954-55 |
| 111 | A. R. Morris, Port-of-Spain | 1954-55 |
| 181† | N. C. O'Neill, Brisbane | 1960-61 |
| 120 | W. B. Phillips, Bridgetown | 1983-84 |
| 183 | W. H. Ponsford, Sydney | 1930-31 |
| 109 | W. H. Ponsford, Brisbane | 1930-31 |
| 132 | I. R. Redpath, Sydney | 1968-69 |
| 102 | I. R. Redpath, Melbourne | 1975-76 |
| 103 | I. R. Redpath, Adelaide | 1975-76 |
| 101 | I. R. Redpath, Melbourne | 1975-76 |
| 124 | C. S. Serjeant, Georgetown | 1977-78 |
| 201 | R. B. Simpson, Bridgetown | 1964-65 |
| 142 | K. R. Stackpole, Kingston | 1972-73 |
| 122 | P. M. Toohey, Kingston | 1977-78 |
| 136 | A. Turner, Adelaide | 1975-76 |
| 118 | K. D. Walters, Sydney | 1968-69 |
| 110 | K. D. Walters, Adelaide | 1968-69 |
| 242<br>103 | K. D. Walters, Sydney | 1968-69 |
| 102* | K. D. Walters, Bridgetown | 1972-73 |
| 112 | K. D. Walters, Port-of-Spain | 1972-73 |
| 173 | K. C. Wessels, Sydney | 1984-85 |
| 126 | G. M. Wood, Georgetown | 1977-78 |

‡ *G. S. Chappell is the only player to score hundreds in both innings of his first Test as captain.*

### For West Indies (63)

| | | |
|---|---|---|
| 108 | F. C. M. Alexander, Sydney | 1960-61 |
| 219 | D. S. Atkinson, Bridgetown | 1954-55 |
| 117 | B. F. Butcher, Port-of-Spain | 1964-65 |
| 101 | B. F. Butcher, Sydney | 1968-69 |
| 118 | B. F. Butcher, Adelaide | 1968-69 |
| 122 | C. C. Depeiza, Bridgetown | 1954-55 |
| 130 | P. J. L. Dujon, Port-of-Spain | 1983-84 |
| 139 | P. J. L. Dujon, Perth | 1984-85 |
| 125† | M. L. C. Foster, Kingston | 1972-73 |
| 169 | R. C. Fredericks, Perth | 1975-76 |
| 101† | H. A. Gomes, Georgetown | 1977-78 |
| 115 | H. A. Gomes, Kingston | 1977-78 |
| 126 | H. A. Gomes, Sydney | 1981-82 |
| 124* | H. A. Gomes, Adelaide | 1981-82 |
| 127 | H. A. Gomes, Perth | 1984-85 |
| 120* | H. A. Gomes, Adelaide | 1984-85 |
| 120* | C. G. Greenidge, Georgetown | 1983-84 |
| 127 | C. G. Greenidge, Kingston | 1983-84 |
| 103* | D. L. Haynes, Georgetown | 1983-84 |
| 145 | D. L. Haynes, Bridgetown | 1983-84 |
| 102* | G. A. Headley, Brisbane | 1930-31 |
| 105 | G. A. Headley, Sydney | 1930-31 |
| 110 | C. C. Hunte, Melbourne | 1960-61 |
| 101 | A. I. Kallicharran, Brisbane | 1975-76 |
| 127 | A. I. Kallicharran, Port-of-Spain | 1977-78 |
| 126 | A. I. Kallicharran, Kingston | 1977-78 |
| 106 | A. I. Kallicharran, Adelaide | 1979-80 |
| 117<br>115 | R. B. Kanhai, Adelaide | 1960-61 |

| | | |
|---|---|---|
| 129 | R. B. Kanhai, Bridgetown | 1964-65 |
| 121 | R. B. Kanhai, Port-of-Spain | 1964-65 |
| 105 | R. B. Kanhai, Bridgetown | 1972-73 |
| 129† | C. H. Lloyd, Brisbane | 1968-69 |
| 178 | C. H. Lloyd, Georgetown | 1972-73 |
| 149 | C. H. Lloyd, Perth | 1975-76 |
| 102 | C. H. Lloyd, Melbourne | 1975-76 |
| 121 | C. H. Lloyd, Adelaide | 1979-80 |
| 114 | C. H. Lloyd, Brisbane | 1984-85 |
| 123* | F. R. Martin, Sydney | 1930-31 |
| 201 | S. M. Nurse, Bridgetown | 1964-65 |
| 137 | S. M. Nurse, Sydney | 1968-69 |
| 101 | I. V. A. Richards, Adelaide | 1975-76 |
| 140 | I. V. A. Richards, Brisbane | 1979-80 |
| 178 | I. V. A. Richards, St John's, Antigua | 1983-84 |
| 208 | I. V. A. Richards, Melbourne | 1984-85 |
| 131* | R. B. Richardson, Bridgetown | 1983-84 |
| 154 | R. B. Richardson, St John's, Antigua | 1983-84 |
| 138 | R. B. Richardson, Brisbane | 1984-85 |
| 107 | L. G. Rowe, Brisbane | 1975-76 |
| 104† | O. G. Smith, Kingston | 1954-55 |
| 132 | G. S. Sobers, Brisbane | 1960-61 |
| 168 | G. S. Sobers, Sydney | 1960-61 |
| 110 | G. S. Sobers, Adelaide | 1968-69 |
| 113 | G. S. Sobers, Sydney | 1968-69 |
| 104 | J. B. Stollmeyer, Sydney | 1951-52 |
| 108 | C. L. Walcott, Kingston | 1954-55 |
| 126 } 110 } | C. L. Walcott, Port-of-Spain | 1954-55 |
| 155 } 110 } | C. L. Walcott, Kingston | 1954-55 |
| 139 | E. D. Weekes, Port-of-Spain | 1954-55 |
| 100† | A. B. Williams, Georgetown | 1977-78 |
| 108 | F. M. M. Worrell, Melbourne | 1951-52 |

† *Signifies hundred on first appearance in Australia–West Indies Tests.*

*Note:* F. C. M. Alexander hit the only hundred of his career in a Test match.

## RECORD PARTNERSHIPS FOR EACH WICKET

### For Australia

| | | |
|---|---|---|
| 382 for 1st† | W. M. Lawry and R. B. Simpson at Bridgetown | 1964-65 |
| 298 for 2nd | W. M. Lawry and I. M. Chappell at Melbourne | 1968-69 |
| 295 for 3rd† | C. C. McDonald and R. N. Harvey at Kingston | 1954-55 |
| 336 for 4th | W. M. Lawry and K. D. Walters at Sydney | 1968-69 |
| 220 for 5th | K. R. Miller and R. G. Archer at Kingston | 1954-55 |
| 206 for 6th | K. R. Miller and R. G. Archer at Bridgetown | 1954-55 |
| 134 for 7th | A. K. Davidson and R. Benaud at Brisbane | 1960-61 |
| 137 for 8th | R. Benaud and I. W. Johnson at Kingston | 1954-55 |
| 97 for 9th | K. D. Mackay and J. W. Martin at Melbourne | 1960-61 |
| 97 for 10th | T. G. Hogan and R. M. Hogg at Georgetown | 1983-84 |

### For West Indies

| | | |
|---|---|---|
| 250* for 1st | C. G. Greenidge and D. L. Haynes at Georgetown | 1983-84 |
| 165 for 2nd | M. C. Carew and R. B. Kanhai at Brisbane | 1968-69 |
| 308 for 3rd | R. B. Richardson and I. V. A. Richards at St John's, Antigua | 1983-84 |
| 198 for 4th | L. G. Rowe and A. I. Kallicharran at Brisbane | 1975-76 |
| 210 for 5th | R. B. Kanhai and M. L. C. Foster at Kingston | 1972-73 |
| 165 for 6th | R. B. Kanhai and D. L. Murray at Bridgetown | 1972-73 |
| 347 for 7th†‡ | D. St E. Atkinson and C. C. Depeiza at Bridgetown | 1954-55 |
| 82 for 8th | H. A. Gomes and A. M. E. Roberts at Adelaide | 1981-82 |
| 122 for 9th | D. A. J. Holford and J. L. Hendriks at Adelaide | 1968-69 |
| 56 for 10th | J. Garner and C. E. H. Croft at Brisbane | 1979-80 |

† *Denotes record partnership against all countries.*
‡ *The 347 partnership for the 7th wicket is the highest for this wicket in first-class cricket.*

## TEN WICKETS OR MORE IN A MATCH

**For Australia** (9)

| | | |
|---|---|---|
| 11-222 (5-135, 6-87)† | A. K. Davidson, Brisbane | 1960-61 |
| 11-183 (7-87, 4-96)† | C. V. Grimmett, Adelaide | 1930-31 |
| 10-115 (6-72, 4-43) | N. J. N. Hawke, Georgetown | 1964-65 |
| 10-144 (6-54, 4-90) | R. G. Holland, Sydney | 1984-85 |
| 11-79 (7-23, 4-56) | H. Ironmonger, Melbourne | 1930-31 |
| 11-181 (8-112, 3-69) | G. F. Lawson, Adelaide | 1984-85 |
| 10-127 (7-83, 3-44) | D. K. Lillee, Melbourne | 1981-82 |
| 10-159 (8-71, 2-88) | G. D. McKenzie, Melbourne | 1968-69 |
| 10-185 (3-87, 7-98) | B. Yardley, Sydney | 1981-82 |

**For West Indies** (3)

| | | |
|---|---|---|
| 10-113 (7-55, 3-58) | G. E. Gomez, Sydney | 1951-52 |
| 11-107 (5-45, 6-62) | M. A. Holding, Melbourne | 1981-82 |
| 10-107 (5-69, 5-38) | M. D. Marshall, Adelaide | 1984-85 |

† *Signifies ten wickets or more on first appearance in Australia–West Indies Tests.*

# AUSTRALIA v NEW ZEALAND

| | *Captains* | | | | | |
|---|---|---|---|---|---|---|
| *Season* | *Australia* | *New Zealand* | *T* | *A* | *NZ* | *D* |
| 1945-46*N* | W. A. Brown | W. A. Hadlee | 1 | 1 | 0 | 0 |
| 1973-74*A* | I. M. Chappell | B. E. Congdon | 3 | 2 | 0 | 1 |
| 1973-74*N* | I. M. Chappell | B. E. Congdon | 3 | 1 | 1 | 1 |
| 1976-77*N* | G. S. Chappell | G. M. Turner | 2 | 1 | 0 | 1 |
| 1980-81*A* | G. S. Chappell | G. P. Howarth[1] | 3 | 2 | 0 | 1 |
| 1981-82*N* | G. S. Chappell | G. P. Howarth | 3 | 1 | 1 | 1 |
| | In Australia | | 6 | 4 | 0 | 2 |
| | In New Zealand | | 9 | 4 | 2 | 3 |
| | Totals | | 15 | 8 | 2 | 5 |

*A Played in Australia. N Played in New Zealand.*

*Note:* The following deputised for the official touring captain: [1]M. G. Burgess (Second).

## HIGHEST INNINGS TOTALS

| | |
|---|---|
| For Australia in Australia: 477 at Adelaide | 1973-74 |
| in New Zealand: 552 at Christchurch | 1976-77 |
| For New Zealand in Australia: 317 at Melbourne | 1980-81 |
| in New Zealand: 484 at Wellington | 1973-74 |

## LOWEST INNINGS TOTALS

| | |
|---|---|
| For Australia in Australia: 162 at Sydney | 1973-74 |
| in New Zealand: 210 at Auckland | 1981-82 |
| For New Zealand in Australia: 121 at Perth | 1980-81 |
| in New Zealand: 42 at Wellington | 1945-46 |

## INDIVIDUAL HUNDREDS

**For Australia** (14)

| | | |
|---|---|---|
| 247* | G. S. Chappell, Wellington | 1973-74 |
| 133 | G. S. Chappell, Wellington | 1973-74 |
| 176 | G. S. Chappell, Christchurch | 1981-82 |
| 145 | I. M. Chappell, Wellington | 1973-74 |
| 121 | I. M. Chappell, Wellington | 1973-74 |
| 101 | G. J. Gilmour, Christchurch | 1976-77 |
| 132 | R. W. Marsh, Adelaide | 1973-74 |
| 159*‡ | I. R. Redpath, Auckland | 1973-74 |
| 122† | K. R. Stackpole, Melbourne | 1973-74 |
| 104* | K. D. Walters, Auckland | 1973-74 |
| 250 | K. D. Walters, Christchurch | 1976-77 |
| 107 | K. D. Walters, Melbourne | 1980-81 |
| 111† | G. M. Wood, Brisbane | 1980-81 |
| 100 | G. M. Wood, Auckland | 1981-82 |

**For New Zealand** (9)

| | | |
|---|---|---|
| 132 | B. E. Congdon, Wellington | 1973-74 |
| 107* | B. E. Congdon, Christchurch | 1976-77 |
| 161 | B. A. Edgar, Auckland | 1981-82 |
| 101 | B. F. Hastings, Wellington | 1973-74 |
| 117 | J. F. M. Morrison, Sydney | 1973-74 |
| 108 | J. M. Parker, Sydney | 1973-74 |
| 101 | G. M. Turner, Christchurch | 1973-74 |
| 110* | G. M. Turner, Christchurch | 1973-74 |
| 141 | J. G. Wright, Christchurch | 1981-82 |

† *Signifies hundred on first appearance in Australia–New Zealand Tests.*
‡ *Carried his bat.*

*Notes:* G. S. and I. M. Chappell at Wellington in 1973-74 provide the only instance in Test matches of brothers both scoring a hundred in each innings and in the same Test.

G. S. Chappell's match aggregate of 380 (247* and 133) for Australia at Wellington in 1973-74 is the record in Test matches.

## RECORD PARTNERSHIPS FOR EACH WICKET

**For Australia**

| | | |
|---|---|---|
| 106 for 1st | G. M. Wood and B. M. Laird at Auckland | 1981-82 |
| 141 for 2nd | I. R. Redpath and I. M. Chappell at Wellington | 1973-74 |
| 264 for 3rd | I. M. Chappell and G. S. Chappell at Wellington | 1973-74 |
| 106 for 4th | I. R. Redpath and I. C. Davis at Christchurch | 1973-74 |
| 93 for 5th | G. S. Chappell and K. D. Walters at Christchurch | 1976-77 |
| 92 for 6th | G. S. Chappell and R. W. Marsh at Christchurch | 1981-82 |
| 217 for 7th† | K. D. Walters and G. J. Gilmour at Christchurch | 1976-77 |
| 93 for 8th | G. J. Gilmour and K. J. O'Keeffe at Auckland | 1976-77 |
| 57 for 9th | R. W. Marsh and L. S. Pascoe at Perth | 1980-81 |
| 60 for 10th | K. D. Walters and J. D. Higgs at Melbourne | 1980-81 |

**For New Zealand**

| | | |
|---|---|---|
| 107 for 1st | G. M. Turner and J. M. Parker at Auckland | 1973-74 |
| 108 for 2nd | G. M. Turner and J. F. M. Morrison at Wellington | 1973-74 |
| 125 for 3rd | G. P. Howarth and J. M. Parker at Melbourne | 1980-81 |
| 229 for 4th† | B. E. Congdon and B. F. Hastings at Wellington | 1973-74 |
| 88 for 5th | J. V. Coney and M. G. Burgess at Perth | 1980-81 |
| 105 for 6th | M. G. Burgess and R. J. Hadlee at Auckland | 1976-77 |
| 66 for 7th | K. J. Wadsworth and D. R. Hadlee at Adelaide | 1973-74 |
| 53 for 8th | B. A. Edgar and R. J. Hadlee at Brisbane | 1980-81 |
| 73 for 9th | H. J. Howarth and D. R. Hadlee at Christchurch | 1976-77 |
| 47 for 10th | H. J. Howarth and M. G. Webb at Wellington | 1973-74 |

† *Denotes record partnership against all countries.*

## TEN WICKETS OR MORE IN A MATCH

**For Australia** (1)

11-123 (5-51, 6-72) D. K. Lillee, Auckland .............................. 1976-77

*Note:* The best match figures by a New Zealand bowler are 9-166 (5-82, 4-84), R. O. Collinge at Auckland, 1973-74, and 9-146 (3-89, 6-57), R. J. Hadlee at Melbourne, 1980-81.

# AUSTRALIA v INDIA

| *Season* | *Captains* *Australia* | *India* | *T* | *A* | *I* | *D* |
|---|---|---|---|---|---|---|
| 1947-48*A* | D. G. Bradman | L. Amarnath | 5 | 4 | 0 | 1 |
| 1956-57*I* | I. W. Johnson[1] | P. R. Umrigar | 3 | 2 | 0 | 1 |
| 1959-60*I* | R. Benaud | G. S. Ramchand | 5 | 2 | 1 | 2 |
| 1964-65*I* | R. B. Simpson | Nawab of Pataudi jun. | 3 | 1 | 1 | 1 |
| 1967-68*A* | R. B. Simpson[2] | Nawab of Pataudi jun.[3] | 4 | 4 | 0 | 0 |
| 1969-70*I* | W. M. Lawry | Nawab of Pataudi jun. | 5 | 3 | 1 | 1 |
| 1977-78*A* | R. B. Simpson | B. S. Bedi | 5 | 3 | 2 | 0 |
| 1979-80*I* | K. J. Hughes | S. M. Gavaskar | 6 | 0 | 2 | 4 |
| 1980-81*A* | G. S. Chappell | S. M. Gavaskar | 3 | 1 | 1 | 1 |
| | In Australia | | 17 | 12 | 3 | 2 |
| | In India | | 22 | 8 | 5 | 9 |
| | Totals | | 39 | 20 | 8 | 11 |

*A Played in Australia. I Played in India.*

*Notes:* The following deputised for the official touring captain or were appointed by the home authority for only a minor proportion of the series:

[1]R. R. Lindwall (Second). [2]W. M. Lawry (Third and Fourth). [3]C. G. Borde (First).

## HIGHEST INNINGS TOTALS

For Australia in Australia: 674 at Adelaide .............................. 1947-48
in India: 523-7 dec. at Bombay .............................. 1956-57

For India in Australia: 445 at Adelaide .............................. 1977-78
in India: 510-7 dec. at Delhi .............................. 1979-80

## LOWEST INNINGS TOTALS

For Australia in Australia: 83 at Melbourne .............................. 1980-81
in India: 105 at Kanpur .............................. 1959-60

For India in Australia: 58 at Brisbane .............................. 1947-48
in India: 135 at Delhi .............................. 1959-60

## INDIVIDUAL HUNDREDS

**For Australia** (36)

| | | | | | |
|---|---|---|---|---|---|
| 112 | S. G. Barnes, Adelaide | 1947-48 | 198* | A. L. Hassett, Adelaide | 1947-48 |
| 162† | A. R. Border, Madras | 1979-80 | 100 | K. J. Hughes, Madras | 1979-80 |
| 124 | A. R. Border, Melbourne | 1980-81 | 213 | K. J. Hughes, Adelaide | 1980-81 |
| 185† | D. G. Bradman, Brisbane | 1947-48 | 100 | W. M. Lawry, Melbourne | 1967-68 |
| 132 / 127* | D. G. Bradman, Melbourne | 1947-48 | 105 | A. L. Mann, Perth | 1977-78 |
| | | | 100* | A. R. Morris, Melbourne | 1947-48 |
| 201 | D. G. Bradman, Adelaide | 1947-48 | 163 | N. C. O'Neill, Bombay | 1959-60 |
| 161 | J. W. Burke, Bombay | 1956-57 | 113 | N. C. O'Neill, Calcutta | 1959-60 |
| 204† | G. S. Chappell, Sydney | 1980-81 | 114 | A. P. Sheahan, Kanpur | 1969-70 |
| 151 | I. M. Chappell, Melbourne | 1967-68 | 103 | R. B. Simpson, Adelaide | 1967-68 |
| 138 | I. M. Chappell, Delhi | 1969-70 | 109 | R. B. Simpson, Melbourne | 1967-68 |
| 108 | R. M. Cowper, Adelaide | 1967-68 | 176 | R. B. Simpson, Perth | 1977-78 |
| 165 | R. M. Cowper, Sydney | 1967-68 | 100 | R. B. Simpson, Adelaide | 1977-78 |
| 101 | L. E. Favell, Madras | 1959-60 | 103† | K. R. Stackpole, Bombay | 1969-70 |
| 153 | R. N. Harvey, Melbourne | 1947-48 | 102 | K. D. Walters, Madras | 1969-70 |
| 140 | R. N. Harvey, Bombay | 1956-57 | 125 | G. M. Wood, Adelaide | 1980-81 |
| 114 | R. N. Harvey, Delhi | 1959-60 | 121† | G. N. Yallop, Adelaide | 1977-78 |
| 102 | R. N. Harvey, Bombay | 1959-60 | 167 | G. N. Yallop, Calcutta | 1979-80 |

**For India** (23)

| | | | | | |
|---|---|---|---|---|---|
| 100 | M. Amarnath, Perth | 1977-78 | 128*† | Nawab of Pataudi, Madras | 1964-65 |
| 108 | N. J. Contractor, Bombay | 1959-60 | 174 | S. M. Patil, Adelaide | 1980-81 |
| 113† | S. M. Gavaskar, Brisbane | 1977-78 | 123 | D. G. Phadkar, Adelaide | 1947-48 |
| 127 | S. M. Gavaskar, Perth | 1977-78 | 109 | G. S. Ramchand, Bombay | 1956-57 |
| 118 | S. M. Gavaskar, Melbourne | 1977-78 | 112 | D. B. Vengsarkar, Bangalore | 1979-80 |
| 115 | S. M. Gavaskar, Delhi | 1979-80 | | | |
| 123 | S. M. Gavaskar, Bombay | 1979-80 | 137† | G. R. Viswanath, Kanpur | 1969-70 |
| 116 / 145 | V. S. Hazare, Adelaide | 1947-48 | 161* | G. R. Viswanath, Bangalore | 1979-80 |
| 101 | M. L. Jaisimha, Brisbane | 1967-68 | 131 | G. R. Viswanath, Delhi | 1979-80 |
| 101* | S. M. H. Kirmani, Bombay | 1979-80 | 114 | G. R. Viswanath, Melbourne | 1980-81 |
| 116 | V. Mankad, Melbourne | 1947-48 | | | |
| 111 | V. Mankad, Melbourne | 1947-48 | 100* | Yashpal Sharma, Delhi | 1979-80 |

† *Signifies hundred on first appearance in Australia–India Tests.*

## RECORD PARTNERSHIPS FOR EACH WICKET

**For Australia**

| | | |
|---|---|---|
| 191 for 1st | R. B. Simpson and W. M. Lawry at Melbourne | 1967-68 |
| 236 for 2nd | S. G. Barnes and D. G. Bradman at Adelaide | 1947-48 |
| 222 for 3rd | A. R. Border and K. J. Hughes at Madras | 1979-80 |
| 159 for 4th | R. N. Harvey and S. J. E. Loxton at Melbourne | 1947-48 |
| 223* for 5th | A. R. Morris and D. G. Bradman at Melbourne | 1947-48 |
| 151 for 6th | T. R. Veivers and B. N. Jarman at Bombay | 1964-65 |
| 64 for 7th | T. R. Veivers and J. W. Martin at Madras | 1964-65 |
| 73 for 8th | T. R. Veivers and G. D. McKenzie at Madras | 1964-65 |
| 87 for 9th | I. W. Johnson and W. P. A. Crawford at Madras | 1956-57 |
| 52 for 10th | K. J. Wright and J. D. Higgs at Delhi | 1979-80 |

**For India**

| | | |
|---|---|---|
| 192 for 1st | S. M. Gavaskar and C. P. S. Chauhan at Bombay | 1979-80 |
| 193 for 2nd | S. M. Gavaskar and M. Amarnath at Perth | 1977-78 |
| 159 for 3rd | S. M. Gavaskar and G. R. Viswanath at Delhi | 1979-80 |
| 159 for 4th | D. B. Vengsarkar and G. R. Viswanath at Bangalore | 1979-80 |
| 109 for 5th | A. A. Baig and R. B. Kenny at Bombay | 1959-60 |
| 188 for 6th | V. S. Hazare and D. G. Phadkar at Adelaide | 1947-48 |
| 132 for 7th | V. S. Hazare and H. R. Adhikari at Adelaide | 1947-48 |
| 127 for 8th | S. M. H. Kirmani and K. D. Ghavri at Bombay | 1979-80 |
| 57 for 9th | S. M. H. Kirmani and K. D. Ghavri at Sydney | 1980-81 |
| 39 for 10th | C. G. Borde and B. S. Chandrasekhar at Calcutta | 1964-65 |

## TEN WICKETS OR MORE IN A MATCH

**For Australia** (7)

| | | |
|---|---|---|
| 11-105 (6-52, 5-53) | R. Benaud, Calcutta | 1956-57 |
| 12-124 (5-31, 7-93) | A. K. Davidson, Kanpur | 1959-60 |
| 11-166 (5-99, 7-67) | G. Dymock, Kanpur | 1979-80 |
| 10-91 (6-58, 4-33)† | G. D. McKenzie, Madras | 1964-65 |
| 10-151 (7-66, 3-85) | G. D. McKenzie, Melbourne | 1967-68 |
| 10-144 (5-91, 5-53) | A. A. Mallett, Madras | 1969-70 |
| 11-31 (5-2, 6-29)† | E. R. H. Toshack, Brisbane | 1947-48 |

**For India** (6)

| | | |
|---|---|---|
| 10-194 (5-89, 5-105) | B. S. Bedi, Perth | 1977-78 |
| 12-104 (6-52, 6-52) | B. S. Chandrasekhar, Melbourne | 1977-78 |
| 10-130 (7-49, 3-81) | Ghulam Ahmed, Calcutta | 1956-57 |
| 11-122 (5-31, 6-91) | R. G. Nadkarni, Madras | 1964-65 |
| 14-124 (9-69, 5-55) | J. M. Patel, Kanpur | 1959-60 |
| 10-174 (4-100, 6-74) | E. A. S. Prasanna, Madras | 1969-70 |

† *Signifies ten wickets or more on first appearance in Australia–India Tests.*

# AUSTRALIA v PAKISTAN

| | *Captains* | | | | | |
|---|---|---|---|---|---|---|
| *Season* | *Australia* | *Pakistan* | *T* | *A* | *P* | *D* |
| 1956-57*P* | I. W. Johnson | A. H. Kardar | 1 | 0 | 1 | 0 |
| 1959-60*P* | R. Benaud | Fazal Mahmood[1] | 3 | 2 | 0 | 1 |
| 1964-65*P* | R. B. Simpson | Hanif Mohammad | 1 | 0 | 0 | 1 |
| 1964-65*A* | R. B. Simpson | Hanif Mohammad | 1 | 0 | 0 | 1 |
| 1972-73*A* | I. M. Chappell | Intikhab Alam | 3 | 3 | 0 | 0 |
| 1976-77*A* | G. S. Chappell | Mushtaq Mohammad | 3 | 1 | 1 | 1 |
| 1978-79*A* | G. N. Yallop[2] | Mushtaq Mohammad | 2 | 1 | 1 | 0 |
| 1979-80*P* | G. S. Chappell | Javed Miandad | 3 | 0 | 1 | 2 |
| 1981-82*A* | G. S. Chappell | Javed Miandad | 3 | 2 | 1 | 0 |
| 1982-83*P* | K. J. Hughes | Imran Khan | 3 | 0 | 3 | 0 |
| 1983-84*A* | K. J. Hughes | Imran Khan[3] | 5 | 2 | 0 | 3 |
| | In Pakistan | | 11 | 2 | 5 | 4 |
| | In Australia | | 17 | 9 | 3 | 5 |
| | Totals | | 28 | 11 | 8 | 9 |

*A Played in Australia. P Played in Pakistan.*

*Notes:* [1]Imtiaz Ahmed captained in Second Test. [2]K. J. Hughes captained in Second Test. [3]Zaheer Abbas captained in First, Second and Third Tests.

## HIGHEST INNINGS TOTALS

For Australia in Australia: 585 at Adelaide ............ 1972-73
in Pakistan: 617 at Faisalabad ............ 1979-80
For Pakistan in Australia: 624 at Adelaide ............ 1983-84
in Pakistan: 501-6 dec. at Faisalabad ............ 1982-83

## LOWEST INNINGS TOTALS

For Australia in Australia: 125 at Melbourne ............ 1981-82
in Pakistan: 80 at Karachi ............ 1956-57
For Pakistan in Australia: 62 at Perth ............ 1981-82
in Pakistan: 134 at Dacca ............ 1959-60

## INDIVIDUAL HUNDREDS

**For Australia** (32)

| | | |
|---|---|---|
| 142 | J. Benaud, Melbourne | 1972-73 |
| 105† | A. R. Border, Melbourne | 1978-79 |
| 150* / 153 | A. R. Border, Lahore | 1979-80 |
| 118 | A. R. Border, Brisbane | 1983-84 |
| 117* | A. R. Border, Adelaide | 1983-84 |
| 116* | G. S. Chappell, Melbourne | 1972-73 |
| 121 | G. S. Chappell, Melbourne | 1976-77 |
| 235 | G. S. Chappell, Faisalabad | 1979-80 |
| 201 | G. S. Chappell, Brisbane | 1981-82 |
| 150* | G. S. Chappell, Brisbane | 1983-84 |
| 182 | G. S. Chappell, Sydney | 1983-84 |
| 196 | I. M. Chappell, Adelaide | 1972-73 |
| 168 | G. J. Cosier, Melbourne | 1976-77 |
| 105† | I. C. Davis, Adelaide | 1976-77 |
| 106 | K. J. Hughes, Perth | 1981-82 |
| 106 | K. J. Hughes, Adelaide | 1983-84 |
| 105 | R. B. McCosker, Melbourne | 1976-77 |
| 118† | R. W. Marsh, Adelaide | 1972-73 |
| 134 | N. C. O'Neill, Lahore | 1959-60 |
| 159† | W. B. Phillips, Perth | 1983-84 |
| 135 | I. R. Redpath, Melbourne | 1972-73 |
| 106* | G. M. Ritchie, Faisalabad | 1982-83 |
| 127 | A. P. Sheahan, Melbourne | 1972-73 |
| 153† / 115 | R. B. Simpson, Karachi | 1964-65 |
| 107 | K. D. Walters, Adelaide | 1976-77 |
| 179 | K. C. Wessels, Adelaide | 1983-84 |
| 100 | G. M. Wood, Melbourne | 1981-82 |
| 172 | G. N. Yallop, Faisalabad | 1979-80 |
| 141 | G. N. Yallop, Perth | 1983-84 |
| 268 | G. N. Yallop, Melbourne | 1983-84 |

**For Pakistan** (25)

| | | |
|---|---|---|
| 152* | Asif Iqbal, Adelaide | 1976-77 |
| 120 | Asif Iqbal, Sydney | 1976-77 |
| 134* | Asif Iqbal, Perth | 1978-79 |
| 101* | Hanif Mohammad, Karachi | 1959-60 |
| 104 | Hanif Mohammad, Melbourne | 1964-65 |
| 129* | Javed Miandad, Perth | 1978-79 |
| 106* | Javed Miandad, Faisalabad | 1979-80 |
| 138 | Javed Miandad, Lahore | 1982-83 |
| 131 | Javed Miandad, Adelaide | 1983-84 |
| 166† | Khalid Ibadulla, Karachi | 1964-65 |
| 158 | Majid J. Khan, Melbourne | 1972-73 |
| 108 | Majid J. Khan, Melbourne | 1978-79 |
| 110* | Majid J. Khan, Lahore | 1979-80 |
| 111 | Mansoor Akhtar, Faisalabad | 1982-83 |
| 135 | Mohsin Khan, Lahore | 1982-83 |
| 149 | Mohsin Khan, Adelaide | 1983-84 |
| 152 | Mohsin Khan, Melbourne | 1983-84 |
| 121 | Mushtaq Mohammad, Sydney | 1972-73 |
| 113 | Qasim Omar, Adelaide | 1983-84 |
| 137 | Sadiq Mohammad, Melbourne | 1972-73 |
| 105 | Sadiq Mohammad, Melbourne | 1976-77 |
| 166 | Saeed Ahmed, Lahore | 1959-60 |
| 210* | Taslim Arif, Faisalabad | 1979-80 |
| 101 | Zaheer Abbas, Adelaide | 1976-77 |
| 126 | Zaheer Abbas, Faisalabad | 1982-83 |

† *Signifies hundred on first appearance in Australia–Pakistan Tests.*

## RECORD PARTNERSHIPS FOR EACH WICKET

**For Australia**

| | | |
|---|---|---|
| 134 for 1st | I. C. Davis and A. Turner at Melbourne | 1976-77 |
| 259 for 2nd | W. B. Phillips and G. N. Yallop at Perth | 1983-84 |
| 203 for 3rd | G. N. Yallop and K. J. Hughes at Melbourne | 1983-84 |
| 217 for 4th | G. S. Chappell and G. N. Yallop at Faisalabad | 1979-80 |
| 171 for 5th | G. S. Chappell and G. J. Cosier at Melbourne | 1976-77 |
| | A. R. Border and G. S. Chappell at Brisbane | 1983-84 |
| 139 for 6th | R. M. Cowper and T. R. Veivers at Melbourne | 1964-65 |
| 185 for 7th | G. N. Yallop and G. R. J. Matthews at Melbourne | 1983-84 |
| 117 for 8th | G. J. Cosier and K. J. O'Keeffe at Melbourne | 1976-77 |
| 83 for 9th | J. R. Watkins and R. A. L. Massie at Sydney | 1972-73 |
| 52 for 10th | D. K. Lillee and M. H. N. Walker at Sydney | 1976-77 |
| | G. F. Lawson and T. M. Alderman at Lahore | 1982-83 |

**For Pakistan**

| | | |
|---|---|---|
| 249 for 1st† | Khalid Ibadulla and Abdul Kadir at Karachi | 1964-65 |
| 233 for 2nd | Mohsin Khan and Qasim Omar at Adelaide | 1983-84 |
| 223* for 3rd | Taslim Arif and Javed Miandad at Faisalabad | 1979-80 |
| 155 for 4th | Mansoor Akhtar and Zaheer Abbas at Faisalabad | 1982-83 |
| 186 for 5th | Javed Miandad and Salim Malik at Adelaide | 1983-84 |
| 115 for 6th | Asif Iqbal and Javed Miandad at Sydney | 1976-77 |
| 104 for 7th | Intikhab Alam and Wasim Bari at Adelaide | 1972-73 |
| 111 for 8th | Majid J. Khan and Imran Khan at Lahore | 1979-80 |
| 56 for 9th | Intikhab Alam and Afaq Hussain at Melbourne | 1964-65 |
| 87 for 10th | Asif Iqbal and Iqbal Qasim at Adelaide | 1976-77 |

† *Denotes record partnership against all countries.*

## TEN WICKETS OR MORE IN A MATCH

**For Australia** (2)

| | | |
|---|---|---|
| 10-111 (7-87, 3-24)† | R. J. Bright, Karachi | 1979-80 |
| 10-135 (6-82, 4-53) | D. K. Lillee, Melbourne | 1976-77 |
| 11-118 (5-32, 6-86)† | C. G. Rackemann, Perth | 1983-84 |

**For Pakistan** (5)

| | | |
|---|---|---|
| 11-218 (4-76, 7-142) | Abdul Qadir, Faisalabad | 1982-83 |
| 13-114 (6-34, 7-80)† | Fazal Mahmood, Karachi | 1956-57 |
| 12-165 (6-102, 6-63) | Imran Khan, Sydney | 1976-77 |
| 11-118 (4-69, 7-49) | Iqbal Qasim, Karachi | 1979-80 |
| 11-125 (2-39, 9-86) | Sarfraz Nawaz, Melbourne | 1978-79 |

† *Signifies ten wickets or more on first appearance in Australia–Pakistan Tests.*

## AUSTRALIA v SRI LANKA

| | *Captains* | | | | | |
|---|---|---|---|---|---|---|
| *Season* | *Australia* | *Sri Lanka* | *T* | *A* | *SL* | *D* |
| 1982-83*SL* | G. S. Chappell | L. R. D. Mendis | 1 | 1 | 0 | 0 |

*SL Played in Sri Lanka.*

The only match played was at Kandy.

## INDIVIDUAL HUNDREDS

**For Australia** (2)

143* D. W. Hookes, Kandy ... 1982-83 | 141 K. C. Wessels, Kandy ... 1982-83

Highest score for Sri Lanka: 96 by S. Wettimuny.

Best bowling in an innings for Australia: 5-66 by T. G. Hogan.
for Sri Lanka: 2-113 by A. L. F. de Mel.

Best wicket partnerships for Australia: 170 for the 2nd by K. C. Wessels and G. N. Yallop.
155* for the 5th by D. W. Hookes and A. R. Border.
for Sri Lanka: 96 for the 5th by L. R. D. Mendis and A. Ranatunga.

Highest innings total for Australia: 514-4 dec.
for Sri Lanka: 271.

# SOUTH AFRICA v NEW ZEALAND

| *Season* | *South Africa* (Captains) | *New Zealand* (Captains) | *T* | *SA* | *NZ* | *D* |
|---|---|---|---|---|---|---|
| 1931-32*N* | H. B. Cameron | M. L. Page | 2 | 2 | 0 | 0 |
| 1952-53*N* | J. E. Cheetham | W. M. Wallace | 2 | 1 | 0 | 1 |
| 1953-54*S* | J. E. Cheetham | G. O. Rabone[1] | 5 | 4 | 0 | 1 |
| 1961-62*S* | D. J. McGlew | J. R. Reid | 5 | 2 | 2 | 1 |
| 1963-64*N* | T. L. Goddard | J. R. Reid | 3 | 0 | 0 | 3 |
| | In New Zealand | | 7 | 3 | 0 | 4 |
| | In South Africa | | 10 | 6 | 2 | 2 |
| | Totals | | 17 | 9 | 2 | 6 |

*N Played in New Zealand. S Played in South Africa.*

*Note:* [1]B. Sutcliffe captained in Fourth and Fifth Tests.

## HIGHEST INNINGS TOTALS

For South Africa in South Africa: 464 at Johannesburg ..................... 1961-62
in New Zealand: 524-8 at Wellington ..................... 1952-53

For New Zealand in South Africa: 505 at Cape Town ..................... 1953-54
in New Zealand: 364 at Wellington ..................... 1931-32

## LOWEST INNINGS TOTALS

For South Africa in South Africa: 148 at Johannesburg ..................... 1953-54
in New Zealand: 223 at Dunedin ..................... 1963-64

For New Zealand in South Africa: 79 at Johannesburg ..................... 1953-54
in New Zealand: 138 at Dunedin ..................... 1963-64

## INDIVIDUAL HUNDREDS

**For South Africa** (11)

| | | |
|---|---|---|
| 122* | X. C. Balaskas, Wellington | 1931-32 |
| 103† | J. A. J. Christy, Christchurch | 1931-32 |
| 116 | W. R. Endean, Auckland | 1952-53 |
| 255*† | D. J. McGlew, Wellington | 1952-53 |
| 127*‡ | D. J. McGlew, Durban | 1961-62 |
| 120 | D. J. McGlew, Johannesburg | 1961-62 |
| 101 | R. A. McLean, Durban | 1953-54 |
| 113 | R. A. McLean, Cape Town | 1961-62 |
| 113† | B. Mitchell, Christchurch | 1931-32 |
| 109† | A. R. A. Murray, Wellington | 1952-53 |
| 101 | J. H. B. Waite, Johannesburg | 1961-62 |

**For New Zealand** (7)

| | | |
|---|---|---|
| 109 | P. T. Barton, Port Elizabeth | 1961-62 |
| 101 | P. G. Z. Harris, Cape Town | 1961-62 |
| 107 | G. O. Rabone, Durban | 1953-54 |
| 135 | J. R. Reid, Cape Town | 1953-54 |
| 142 | J. R. Reid, Johannesburg | 1961-62 |
| 138 | B. W. Sinclair, Auckland | 1963-64 |
| 100† | H. G. Vivian, Wellington | 1931-32 |

† *Signifies hundred on first appearance in South Africa–New Zealand Tests.*
‡ *Carried his bat.*

## RECORD PARTNERSHIPS FOR EACH WICKET

**For South Africa**

| | | |
|---|---|---|
| 196 for 1st | J. A. J. Christy and B. Mitchell at Christchurch | 1931-32 |
| 76 for 2nd | J. A. J. Christy and H. B. Cameron at Wellington | 1931-32 |
| 112 for 3rd | D. J. McGlew and R. A. McLean at Johannesburg | 1961-62 |
| 135 for 4th | K. J. Funston and R. A. McLean at Durban | 1953-54 |
| 130 for 5th | W. R. Endean and J. E. Cheetham at Auckland | 1952-53 |
| 83 for 6th | K. C. Bland and D. T. Lindsay at Auckland | 1963-64 |
| 246 for 7th† | D. J. McGlew and A. R. A. Murray at Wellington | 1952-53 |
| 95 for 8th | J. E. Cheetham and H. J. Tayfield at Cape Town | 1953-54 |
| 60 for 9th | P. M. Pollock and N. A. T. Adcock at Port Elizabeth | 1961-62 |
| 47 for 10th | D. J. McGlew and H. D. Bromfield at Port Elizabeth | 1961-62 |

**For New Zealand**

| | | |
|---|---|---|
| 126 for 1st | G. O. Rabone and M. E. Chapple at Cape Town | 1953-54 |
| 51 for 2nd | W. P. Bradburn and B. W. Sinclair at Dunedin | 1963-64 |
| 94 for 3rd | M. B. Poore and B. Sutcliffe at Cape Town | 1953-54 |
| 171 for 4th | B. W. Sinclair and S. N. McGregor at Auckland | 1963-64 |
| 174 for 5th | J. R. Reid and J. E. F. Beck at Cape Town | 1953-54 |
| 100 for 6th | H. G. Vivian and F. T. Badcock at Wellington | 1931-32 |
| 84 for 7th | J. R. Reid and G. A. Bartlett at Johannesburg | 1961-62 |
| 73 for 8th | P. G. Z. Harris and G. A. Bartlett at Durban | 1961-62 |
| 69 for 9th | C. F. W. Allcott and I. B. Cromb at Wellington | 1931-32 |
| 49* for 10th | A. E. Dick and F. J. Cameron at Cape Town | 1961-62 |

† *Denotes record partnership against all countries.*

## TEN WICKETS OR MORE IN A MATCH

**For South Africa** (1)

| | | |
|---|---|---|
| 11-196 (6-128, 5-68)† | S. F. Burke, Cape Town | 1961-62 |

† *Signifies ten wickets or more on first appearance in South Africa–New Zealand Tests.*

*Note:* The best match figures by a New Zealand bowler are 8-180 (4-61, 4-119), J. C. Alabaster at Cape Town, 1961-62.

## WEST INDIES v NEW ZEALAND

| | *Captains* | | | | | |
|---|---|---|---|---|---|---|
| *Season* | *West Indies* | *New Zealand* | *T* | *WI* | *NZ* | *D* |
| 1951-52*N* | J. D. C. Goddard | B. Sutcliffe | 2 | 1 | 0 | 1 |
| 1955-56*N* | D. St E. Atkinson | J. R. Reid[1] | 4 | 3 | 1 | 0 |
| 1968-69*N* | G. S. Sobers | G. T. Dowling | 3 | 1 | 1 | 1 |
| 1971-72*W* | G. S. Sobers | G. T. Dowling[2] | 5 | 0 | 0 | 5 |
| 1979-80*N* | C. H. Lloyd | G. P. Howarth | 3 | 0 | 1 | 2 |
| 1984-85*W* | I. V. A. Richards | G. P. Howarth | 4 | 2 | 0 | 2 |
| | In New Zealand | | 12 | 5 | 3 | 4 |
| | In West Indies | | 9 | 2 | 0 | 7 |
| | Totals | | 21 | 7 | 3 | 11 |

*N Played in New Zealand.* *W Played in West Indies.*

*Notes:* The following deputised for the official touring captain or were appointed by the home authority for only a minor proportion of the series:

[1]H. B. Cave (First). [2]B. E. Congdon (Third, Fourth and Fifth).

### HIGHEST INNINGS TOTALS

For West Indies in West Indies: 564-8 at Bridgetown ........ 1971-72
in New Zealand: 546-6 dec. at Auckland ........ 1951-52

For New Zealand in West Indies: 543-3 dec. at Georgetown ........ 1971-72
in New Zealand: 460 at Christchurch ........ 1979-80

### LOWEST INNINGS TOTALS

For West Indies in West Indies: 133 at Bridgetown ........ 1971-72
in New Zealand: 77 at Auckland ........ 1955-56

For New Zealand in West Indies: 94 at Bridgetown ........ 1984-85
in New Zealand: 74 at Dunedin ........ 1955-56

### INDIVIDUAL HUNDREDS

**By West Indies** (23)

| | | |
|---|---|---|
| 109† | M. C. Carew, Auckland | 1968-69 |
| 183 | C. A. Davis, Bridgetown | 1971-72 |
| 163 | R. C. Fredericks, Kingston | 1971-72 |
| 100 | C. G. Greenidge, Port-of-Spain | 1984-85 |
| 105† | D. L. Haynes, Dunedin | 1979-80 |
| 122 | D. L. Haynes, Christchurch | 1979-80 |
| 100*† | A. I. Kallicharran, Georgetown | 1971-72 |
| 101 | A. I. Kallicharran, Port-of-Spain | 1971-72 |
| 100* | C. L. King, Christchurch | 1979-80 |
| 168† | S. M. Nurse, Auckland | 1968-69 |
| 258 | S. M. Nurse, Christchurch | 1968-69 |
| 105 | I. V. A. Richards, Bridgetown | 1984-85 |
| 185 | R. B. Richardson, Georgetown | 1984-85 |
| 214† 100* | L. G. Rowe, Kingston | 1971-72 |
| 100 | L. G. Rowe, Christchurch | 1979-80 |
| 142 | G. S. Sobers, Bridgetown | 1971-72 |
| 152 | J. B. Stollmeyer, Auckland | 1951-52 |
| 115 | C. L. Walcott, Auckland | 1951-52 |
| 123 | E. D. Weekes, Dunedin | 1955-56 |
| 103 | E. D. Weekes, Christchurch | 1955-56 |
| 156 | E. D. Weekes, Wellington | 1955-56 |
| 100 | F. M. M. Worrell, Auckland | 1951-52 |

**By New Zealand** (14)

| | | |
|---|---|---|
| 101 | M. G. Burgess, Kingston | 1971-72 |
| 166* | B. E. Congdon, Port-of-Spain | 1971-72 |
| 126 | B. E. Congdon, Bridgetown | 1971-72 |
| 112 | J. J. Crowe, Kingston | 1984-85 |
| 188 | M. D. Crowe, Georgetown | 1984-85 |
| 127 | B. A. Edgar, Auckland | 1979-80 |
| 103 | R. J. Hadlee, Christchurch | 1979-80 |
| 117* | B. F. Hastings, Christchurch | 1968-69 |
| 105 | B. F. Hastings, Bridgetown | 1971-72 |
| 147 | G. P. Howarth, Christchurch | 1979-80 |
| 182 | T. W. Jarvis, Georgetown | 1971-72 |
| 124† | B. R. Taylor, Auckland | 1968-69 |
| 223*‡ | G. M. Turner, Kingston | 1971-72 |
| 259 | G. M. Turner, Georgetown | 1971-72 |

† *Signifies hundred on first appearance in West Indies–New Zealand Tests.*
‡ *Carried his bat.*

*Notes:* E. D. Weekes in 1955-56 made three hundreds in consecutive innings.

L. G. Rowe and A. I. Kallicharran each scored hundreds in their first two innings in Test cricket, Rowe being the only batsman to do so in his first match.

## RECORD PARTNERSHIPS FOR EACH WICKET

**For West Indies**

| | | |
|---|---|---|
| 225 for 1st | C. G. Greenidge and D. L. Haynes at Christchurch | 1979-80 |
| 269 for 2nd | R. C. Fredericks and L. G. Rowe at Kingston | 1971-72 |
| 185 for 3rd | C. G. Greenidge and R. B. Richardson at Port-of-Spain | 1984-85 |
| 162 for 4th | E. D. Weekes and O. G. Smith at Dunedin | 1955-56 |
| | C. G. Greenidge and A. I. Kallicharran at Christchurch | 1979-80 |
| 189 for 5th | F. M. M. Worrell and C. L. Walcott at Auckland | 1951-52 |
| 254 for 6th | C. A. Davis and G. S. Sobers at Bridgetown | 1971-72 |
| 143 for 7th | D. St E. Atkinson and J. D. C. Goddard at Christchurch | 1955-56 |
| 83 for 8th | I. V. A. Richards and M. D. Marshall at Bridgetown | 1984-85 |
| 70 for 9th | M. D. Marshall and J. Garner at Bridgetown | 1984-85 |
| 31 for 10th | T. M. Findlay and G. C. Shillingford at Bridgetown | 1971-72 |

**For New Zealand**

| | | |
|---|---|---|
| 387 for 1st† | G. M. Turner and T. W. Jarvis at Georgetown | 1971-72 |
| 210 for 2nd† | G. P. Howarth and J. J. Crowe at Kingston | 1984-85 |
| 75 for 3rd | B. E. Congdon and B. F. Hastings at Christchurch | 1968-69 |
| 175 for 4th | B. E. Congdon and B. F. Hastings at Bridgetown | 1971-72 |
| 142 for 5th | M. D. Crowe and J. V. Coney at Georgetown | 1984-85 |
| 220 for 6th† | G. M. Turner and K. J. Wadsworth at Kingston | 1971-72 |
| 143 for 7th | M. D. Crowe and I. D. S. Smith at Georgetown | 1984-85 |
| 136 for 8th† | B. E. Congdon and R. S. Cunis at Port-of-Spain | 1971-72 |
| 62* for 9th | V. Pollard and R. S. Cunis at Auckland | 1968-69 |
| 41 for 10th | B. E. Congdon and J. C. Alabaster at Port-of-Spain | 1971-72 |

† *Denotes record partnership against all countries.*

## TEN WICKETS OR MORE IN A MATCH

**For West Indies** (1)

| | | |
|---|---|---|
| 11-120 (4-40, 7-80) | M. D. Marshall, Bridgetown | 1984-85 |

**For New Zealand** (3)

| | | |
|---|---|---|
| 10-124 (4-51, 6-73)† | E. J. Chatfield, Port-of-Spain | 1984-85 |
| 11-102 (5-34, 6-68)† | R. J. Hadlee, Dunedin | 1979-80 |
| 10-166 (4-71, 6-95) | G. B. Troup, Auckland | 1979-80 |

† *Signifies ten wickets or more on first appearance in West Indies–New Zealand Tests.*

## WEST INDIES v INDIA

| | Captains | | | | | |
|---|---|---|---|---|---|---|
| Season | West Indies | India | T | WI | I | D |
| 1948-49*I* | J. D. C. Goddard | L. Amarnath | 5 | 1 | 0 | 4 |
| 1952-53*W* | J. B. Stollmeyer | V. S. Hazare | 5 | 1 | 0 | 4 |
| 1958-59*I* | F. C. M. Alexander | Ghulam Ahmed[1] | 5 | 3 | 0 | 2 |
| 1961-62*W* | F. M. M. Worrell | N. J. Contractor[2] | 5 | 5 | 0 | 0 |
| 1966-67*I* | G. S. Sobers | Nawab of Pataudi jun. | 3 | 2 | 0 | 1 |
| 1970-71*W* | G. S. Sobers | A. L. Wadekar | 5 | 0 | 1 | 4 |
| 1974-75*I* | C. H. Lloyd | Nawab of Pataudi jun.[3] | 5 | 3 | 2 | 0 |
| 1975-76*W* | C. H. Lloyd | B. S. Bedi | 4 | 2 | 1 | 1 |
| 1978-79*I* | A. I. Kallicharran | S. M. Gavaskar | 6 | 0 | 1 | 5 |
| 1982-83*W* | C. H. Lloyd | Kapil Dev | 5 | 2 | 0 | 3 |
| 1983-84*I* | C. H. Lloyd | Kapil Dev | 6 | 3 | 0 | 3 |
| | In India | | 30 | 12 | 3 | 15 |
| | In West Indies | | 24 | 10 | 2 | 12 |
| | Totals | | 54 | 22 | 5 | 27 |

*I Played in India. W Played in West Indies.*

*Notes:* The following deputised for the official touring captain or were appointed by the home authority for only a minor proportion of the series:

[1]P. R. Umrigar (First), V. Mankad (Fourth), H. R. Adhikari (Fifth). [2]Nawab of Pataudi jun. (Third, Fourth and Fifth). [3]S. Venkataraghavan (Second).

## HIGHEST INNINGS TOTALS

For West Indies in West Indies: 631-8 dec. at Kingston ........ 1961-62
in India: 644-8 dec. at Delhi ........ 1958-59

For India in West Indies: 469-7 at Port-of-Spain ........ 1982-83
in India: 644-7 dec. at Kanpur ........ 1978-79

## LOWEST INNINGS TOTALS

For West Indies in West Indies: 214 at Port-of-Spain ........ 1970-71
in India: 151 at Madras ........ 1978-79

For India in West Indies: 97† at Kingston ........ 1975-76
in India: 90 at Calcutta ........ 1983-84

† *Five men absent hurt.*

## INDIVIDUAL HUNDREDS

### For West Indies (67)

250 S. F. A. F. Bacchus, Kanpur 1978-79
103 B. F. Butcher, Calcutta ... 1958-59
142 B. F. Butcher, Madras .... 1958-59
107† R. J. Christiani, Delhi .... 1948-49
125* C. A. Davis, Georgetown .. 1970-71
105 C. A. Davis, Port-of-Spain ........ 1970-71
110 P. J. L. Dujon, St John's, Antigua ........ 1982-83
100 R. C. Fredericks, Calcutta . 1974-75
104 R. C. Fredericks, Bombay . 1974-75
123 H. A. Gomes, Port-of-Spain 1982-83
101† G. E. Gomez, Delhi ...... 1948-49
107† C. G. Greenidge, Bangalore 1974-75
154* C. G. Greenidge, St John's, Antigua ........ 1982-83
194 C. G. Greenidge, Kanpur . 1983-84
136 D. L. Haynes, St John's, Antigua ........ 1982-83
123 J. K. Holt, Delhi ........ 1958-59
101 C. C. Hunte, Bombay ..... 1966-67
124† A. I. Kallicharran, Bangalore ........ 1974-75
103* A. I. Kallicharran, Port-of-Spain ........ 1975-76
187 A. I. Kallicharran, Bombay 1978-79

| | | |
|---|---|---|
| 256 | R. B. Kanhai, Calcutta ... | 1958-59 |
| 138 | R. B. Kanhai, Kingston ... | 1961-62 |
| 139 | R. B. Kanhai, Port-of-Spain | 1961-62 |
| 158* | R. B. Kanhai, Kingston ... | 1970-71 |
| 163 | C. H. Lloyd, Bangalore ... | 1974-75 |
| 242* | C. H. Lloyd, Bombay ..... | 1974-75 |
| 102 | C. H. Lloyd, Bridgetown .. | 1975-76 |
| 143 | C. H. Lloyd, Port-of-Spain . | 1982-83 |
| 106 | C. H. Lloyd, St John's, Antigua .............. | 1982-83 |
| 103 | C. H. Lloyd, Delhi ....... | 1983-84 |
| 161* | C. H. Lloyd, Calcutta ..... | 1983-84 |
| 130 | A. L. Logie, Bridgetown ... | 1982-83 |
| 125† | E. D. A. McMorris, Kingston ............. | 1961-62 |
| 115† | B. H. Pairaudeau, Port-of-Spain ................ | 1952-53 |
| 104 | A. F. Rae, Bombay ....... | 1948-49 |
| 109 | A. F. Rae, Madras ....... | 1948-49 |
| 192* | I. V. A. Richards, Delhi .. | 1974-75 |
| 142 | I. V. A. Richards, Bridgetown ................ | 1975-76 |
| 130 | I. V. A. Richards, Port-of-Spain ................ | 1975-76 |
| 177 | I. V. A. Richards, Port-of-Spain ................ | 1975-76 |
| 109 | I. V. A. Richards, Georgetown ................ | 1982-83 |
| 120 | I. V. A. Richards, Bombay | 1983-84 |
| 100 | O. G. Smith, Delhi ....... | 1958-59 |
| 142*† | G. S. Sobers, Bombay ..... | 1958-59 |
| 198 | G. S. Sobers, Kanpur ..... | 1958-59 |
| 106* | G. S. Sobers, Calcutta .... | 1958-59 |
| 153 | G. S. Sobers, Kingston .... | 1961-62 |
| 104 | G. S. Sobers, Kingston .... | 1961-62 |
| 108* | G. S. Sobers, Georgetown . | 1970-71 |
| 178* | G. S. Sobers, Bridgetown .. | 1970-71 |
| 132 | G. S. Sobers, Port-of-Spain | 1970-71 |
| 100* | J. S. Solomon, Delhi ...... | 1958-59 |
| 160 | J. B. Stollmeyer, Madras .. | 1948-49 |
| 104* | J. B. Stollmeyer, Port-of-Spain ................ | 1952-53 |
| 152† | C. L. Walcott, Delhi ...... | 1948-49 |
| 108 | C. L. Walcott, Calcutta ... | 1948-49 |
| 125 | C. L. Walcott, Georgetown | 1952-53 |
| 118 | C. L. Walcott, Kingston ... | 1952-53 |
| 128† | E. D. Weekes, Delhi ..... | 1948-49 |
| 194 | E. D. Weekes, Bombay ... | 1948-49 |
| 162<br>101 | E. D. Weekes, Calcutta ... | 1948-49 |
| 207 | E. D. Weekes, Port-of-Spain ................ | 1952-53 |
| 161 | E. D. Weekes, Port-of-Spain ................ | 1952-53 |
| 109 | E. D. Weekes, Kingston ... | 1952-53 |
| 111 | A. B. Williams, Calcutta .. | 1978-79 |
| 237 | F. M. M. Worrell, Kingston | 1952-53 |

**For India** (49)

| | | |
|---|---|---|
| 114*† | H. R. Adhikari, Delhi .... | 1948-49 |
| 101* | M. Amarnath, Kanpur .... | 1978-79 |
| 117 | M. Amarnath, Port-of-Spain ................ | 1982-83 |
| 116 | M. Amarnath, St John's, Antigua .............. | 1982-83 |
| 163* | M. L. Apte, Port-of-Spain . | 1952-53 |
| 109 | C. G. Borde, Delhi ....... | 1958-59 |
| 121 | C. G. Borde, Bombay ..... | 1966-67 |
| 125 | C. G. Borde, Madras ..... | 1966-67 |
| 104 | S. A. Durani, Port-of-Spain | 1961-62 |
| 109 | F. M. Engineer, Madras ... | 1966-67 |
| 102 | A. D. Gaekwad, Kanpur .. | 1978-79 |
| 116 | S. M. Gavaskar, Georgetown ................ | 1970-71 |
| 117* | S. M. Gavaskar, Bridgetown ................ | 1970-71 |
| 124<br>220 | S. M. Gavaskar, Port-of-Spain ................ | 1970-71 |
| 156 | S. M. Gavaskar, Port-of-Spain ................ | 1975-76 |
| 102 | S. M. Gavaskar, Port-of-Spain ................ | 1975-76 |
| 205 | S. M. Gavaskar, Bombay .. | 1978-79 |
| 107<br>182* | S. M. Gavaskar, Calcutta . | 1978-79 |
| 120 | S. M. Gavaskar, Delhi .... | 1978-79 |
| 147* | S. M. Gavaskar, Georgetown ................ | 1982-83 |
| 121 | S. M. Gavaskar, Delhi .... | 1983-84 |
| 236* | S. M. Gavaskar, Madras .. | 1983-84 |
| 134* | V. S. Hazare, Bombay .... | 1948-49 |
| 122 | V. S. Hazare, Bombay .... | 1948-49 |
| 126* | Kapil Dev, Delhi ........ | 1978-79 |
| 100* | Kapil Dev, Port-of-Spain .. | 1982-83 |
| 118 | V. L. Manjrekar, Kingston | 1952-53 |
| 112 | R. S. Modi, Bombay ...... | 1948-49 |
| 106† | Mushtaq Ali, Calcutta .... | 1948-49 |
| 115* | B. P. Patel, Port-of-Spain .. | 1975-76 |
| 150 | P. Roy, Kingston ........ | 1952-53 |
| 212 | D. N. Sardesai, Kingston .. | 1970-71 |
| 112 | D. N. Sardesai, Port-of-Spain ................ | 1970-71 |
| 150 | D. N. Sardesai, Bridgetown | 1970-71 |
| 102 | R. J. Shastri, St John's, Antigua .............. | 1982-83 |
| 102 | E. D. Solkar, Bombay .... | 1974-75 |
| 130 | P. R. Umrigar, Port-of-Spain ................ | 1952-53 |
| 117 | P. R. Umrigar, Kingston .. | 1952-53 |
| 172* | P. R. Umrigar, Port-of-Spain ................ | 1961-62 |
| 157* | D. B. Vengsarkar, Calcutta | 1978-79 |
| 109 | D. B. Vengsarkar, Delhi .. | 1978-79 |
| 159 | D. B. Vengsarkar, Delhi .. | 1983-84 |
| 100 | D. B. Vengsarkar, Bombay | 1983-84 |
| 139 | G. R. Viswanath, Calcutta . | 1974-75 |
| 112 | G. R. Viswanath, Port-of-Spain ................ | 1975-76 |
| 124 | G. R. Viswanath, Madras . | 1978-79 |
| 179 | G. R. Viswanath, Kanpur . | 1978-79 |

† *Signifies hundred on first appearance in West Indies–India Tests.*

## RECORD PARTNERSHIPS FOR EACH WICKET

**For West Indies**

| | | |
|---|---|---|
| 296 for 1st† | C. G. Greenidge and D. L. Haynes at St John's, Antigua | 1982-83 |
| 255 for 2nd | E. D. A. McMorris and R. B. Kanhai at Kingston | 1961-62 |
| 220 for 3rd | I. V. A. Richards and A. I. Kallicharran at Bridgetown | 1975-76 |
| 267 for 4th | C. L. Walcott and G. E. Gomez at Delhi | 1948-49 |
| 219 for 5th | E. D. Weekes and B. H. Pairaudeau at Port-of-Spain | 1952-53 |
| 250 for 6th | C. H. Lloyd and D. L. Murray at Bombay | 1974-75 |
| 130 for 7th | C. G. Greenidge and M. D. Marshall at Kanpur | 1983-84 |
| 124 for 8th† | I. V. A. Richards and K. D. Boyce at Delhi | 1974-75 |
| 161 for 9th† | C. H. Lloyd and A. M. E. Roberts at Calcutta | 1983-84 |
| 98* for 10th† | F. M. M. Worrell and W. W. Hall at Port-of-Spain | 1961-62 |

**For India**

| | | |
|---|---|---|
| 153 for 1st | S. M. Gavaskar and C. P. S. Chauhan at Bombay | 1978-79 |
| 344* for 2nd† | S. M. Gavaskar and D. B. Vengsarkar at Calcutta | 1978-79 |
| 159 for 3rd | M. Amarnath and G. R. Viswanath at Port-of-Spain | 1975-76 |
| 172 for 4th | G. R. Viswanath and A. D. Gaekwad at Kanpur | 1978-79 |
| 204 for 5th | S. M. Gavaskar and B. P. Patel at Port-of-Spain | 1975-76 |
| 170 for 6th | S. M. Gavaskar and R. J. Shastri at Madras | 1983-84 |
| 186 for 7th | D. N. Sardesai and E. D. Solkar at Bridgetown | 1970-71 |
| 107 for 8th | Yashpal Sharma and B. S. Sandhu at Kingston | 1982-83 |
| 143* for 9th | S. M. Gavaskar and S. M. H. Kirmani at Madras | 1983-84 |
| 62 for 10th | D. N. Sardesai and B. S. Bedi at Bridgetown | 1970-71 |

† *Denotes record partnership against all countries.*

## TEN WICKETS OR MORE IN A MATCH

**For West Indies** (2)

| | | |
|---|---|---|
| 11-126 (6-50, 5-76) | W. W. Hall, Kanpur | 1958-59 |
| 12-121 (7-64, 5-57) | A. M. E. Roberts, Madras | 1974-75 |

**For India** (3)

| | | |
|---|---|---|
| 11-235 (7-157, 4-78)† | B. S. Chandrasekhar, Bombay | 1966-67 |
| 10-223 (9-102, 1-121) | S. P. Gupte, Kanpur | 1958-59 |
| 10-135 (1-52, 9-83) | Kapil Dev, Ahmedabad | 1983-84 |

† *Signifies ten wickets or more on first appearance in West Indies–India Tests.*

## WEST INDIES v PAKISTAN

| | *Captains* | | | | | |
|---|---|---|---|---|---|---|
| *Season* | *West Indies* | *Pakistan* | *T* | *WI* | *P* | *D* |
| 1957-58*W* | F. C. M. Alexander | A. H. Kardar | 5 | 3 | 1 | 1 |
| 1958-59*P* | F. C. M. Alexander | Fazal Mahmood | 3 | 1 | 2 | 0 |
| 1974-75*P* | C. H. Lloyd | Intikhab Alam | 2 | 0 | 0 | 2 |
| 1976-77*W* | C. H. Lloyd | Mushtaq Mohammad | 5 | 2 | 1 | 2 |
| 1980-81*P* | C. H. Lloyd | Javed Miandad | 4 | 1 | 0 | 3 |
| | In West Indies | | 10 | 5 | 2 | 3 |
| | In Pakistan | | 9 | 2 | 2 | 5 |
| | Totals | | 19 | 7 | 4 | 8 |

*P Played in Pakistan. W Played in West Indies.*

## HIGHEST INNINGS TOTALS

For West Indies in West Indies: 790-3 dec. at Kingston .................... 1957-58
in Pakistan: 493 at Karachi .................... 1974-75

For Pakistan in West Indies: 657-8 dec. at Bridgetown .................... 1957-58
in Pakistan: 406-8 dec. at Karachi .................... 1974-75

## LOWEST INNINGS TOTALS

For West Indies in West Indies: 154 at Port-of-Spain .................... 1976-77
in Pakistan: 76 at Dacca .................... 1958-59

For Pakistan in West Indies: 106 at Bridgetown .................... 1957-58
in Pakistan: 104 at Lahore .................... 1958-59

## INDIVIDUAL HUNDREDS

**For West Indies** (17)

105*† L. Baichan, Lahore ....... 1974-75
120 R. C. Fredericks, Port-of-Spain .................. 1976-77
100 C. G. Greenidge, Kingston 1976-77
142† C. C. Hunte, Bridgetown .. 1957-58
260 C. C. Hunte, Kingston .... 1957-58
114 C. C. Hunte, Georgetown . 1957-58
101 B. D. Julien, Karachi ..... 1974-75
115 A. I. Kallicharran, Karachi 1974-75
217 R. B. Kanhai, Lahore ..... 1958-59
157 C. H. Lloyd, Bridgetown .. 1976-77
120* I. V. A. Richards, Multan . 1980-81
120 I. T. Shillingford, Georgetown .................. 1976-77
365* G. S. Sobers, Kingston .... 1957-58
125 } 109* } G. S. Sobers, Georgetown . 1957-58
145 C. L. Walcott, Georgetown 1957-58
197† E. D. Weekes, Bridgetown . 1957-58

**Pakistan** (14)

135 Asif Iqbal, Kingston ...... 1976-77
337† Hanif Mohammad, Bridgetown .................. 1957-58
103 Hanif Mohammad, Karachi 1958-59
122 Imtiaz Ahmed, Kingston .. 1957-58
123 Imran Khan, Lahore ..... 1980-81
100 Majid J. Khan, Karachi ... 1974-75
167 Majid J. Khan, Georgetown 1976-77
123 Mushtaq Mohammad, Lahore .......... 1974-75
121 Mushtaq Mohammad, Port-of-Spain .............. 1976-77
150 Saeed Ahmed, Georgetown 1957-58
107* Wasim Raja, Karachi ..... 1974-75
117* Wasim Raja, Bridgetown .. 1976-77
106 Wazir Mohammad, Kingston .................. 1957-58
189 Wazir Mohammad, Port-of-Spain ................ 1957-58

† *Signifies hundred on first appearance in West Indies–Pakistan Tests.*

## RECORD PARTNERSHIPS FOR EACH WICKET

**For West Indies**

| | | |
|---|---|---|
| 182 for 1st | R. C. Fredericks and C. G. Greenidge at Kingston ........... | 1976-77 |
| 446 for 2nd† | C. C. Hunte and G. S. Sobers at Kingston .................. | 1957-58 |
| 162 for 3rd | R. B. Kanhai and G. S. Sobers at Lahore .................. | 1958-59 |
| 188* for 4th | G. S. Sobers and C. L. Walcott at Kingston ................ | 1957-58 |
| 185 for 5th | E. D. Weekes and O. G. Smith at Bridgetown .............. | 1957-58 |
| 151 for 6th | C. H. Lloyd and D. L. Murray at Bridgetown .............. | 1976-77 |
| 70 for 7th | C. H. Lloyd and J. Garner at Bridgetown .................. | 1976-77 |
| 50 for 8th | B. D. Julien and V. A. Holder at Karachi .................. | 1974-75 |
| 46 for 9th | J. Garner and C. E. H. Croft at Port-of-Spain .............. | 1976-77 |
| 44 for 10th | R. Nanan and S. T. Clarke at Faisalabad .................. | 1980-81 |

**For Pakistan**

| | | |
|---|---|---|
| 159 for 1st‡ | Majid J. Khan and Zaheer Abbas at Georgetown | 1976-77 |
| 178 for 2nd | Hanif Mohammad and Saeed Ahmed at Karachi | 1958-59 |
| 169 for 3rd | Saeed Ahmed and Wazir Mohammad at Port-of-Spain | 1957-58 |
| 154 for 4th | Wazir Mohammad and Hanif Mohammad at Port-of-Spain | 1957-58 |
| 87 for 5th | Mushtaq Mohammad and Asif Iqbal at Kingston | 1976-77 |
| 166 for 6th | Wazir Mohammad and A. H. Kardar at Kingston | 1957-58 |
| 128 for 7th | Wasim Raja and Wasim Bari at Karachi | 1974-75 |
| 73 for 8th | Imran Khan and Sarfraz Nawaz at Port-of-Spain | 1976-77 |
| 73 for 9th | Wasim Raja and Sarfraz Nawaz at Bridgetown | 1976-77 |
| 133 for 10th† | Wasim Raja and Wasim Bari at Bridgetown | 1976-77 |

† *Denotes record partnership against all countries.*

‡ *219 runs were added for this wicket in two separate partnerships: Sadiq Mohammad retired hurt and was replaced by Zaheer Abbas when 60 had been added. The highest partnership by two opening batsmen is 152 by Hanif Mohammad and Imtiaz Ahmed at Bridgetown, 1957-58.*

## TEN WICKETS OR MORE IN A MATCH

**For Pakistan** (1)

12-100 (6-34, 6-66) Fazal Mahmood, Dacca ........ 1958-59

*Note:* The best match figures by a West Indian bowler are 9-187 (5-66, 4-121), A. M. E. Roberts at Lahore, 1974-75, and 9-95 (8-29, 1-66), C. E. H. Croft at Port-of-Spain, 1976-77.

# NEW ZEALAND v INDIA

| *Season* | *Captains* *New Zealand* | *India* | *T* | *NZ* | *I* | *D* |
|---|---|---|---|---|---|---|
| 1955-56*I* | H. B. Cave | P. R. Umrigar[1] | 5 | 0 | 2 | 3 |
| 1964-65*I* | J. R. Reid | Nawab of Pataudi jun. | 4 | 0 | 1 | 3 |
| 1967-68*N* | G. T. Dowling[2] | Nawab of Pataudi jun. | 4 | 1 | 3 | 0 |
| 1969-70*I* | G. T. Dowling | Nawab of Pataudi jun. | 3 | 1 | 1 | 1 |
| 1975-76*N* | G. M. Turner | B. S. Bedi[3] | 3 | 1 | 1 | 1 |
| 1976-77*I* | G. M. Turner | B. S. Bedi | 3 | 0 | 2 | 1 |
| 1980-81*N* | G. P. Howarth | S. M. Gavaskar | 3 | 1 | 0 | 2 |
| | In India | | 15 | 1 | 6 | 8 |
| | In New Zealand | | 10 | 3 | 4 | 3 |
| | Totals | | 25 | 4 | 10 | 11 |

*I Played in India. N Played in New Zealand.*

*Notes:* [1]Ghulam Ahmed captained in First Test. [2]B. W. Sinclair captained in First Test. [3]S. M. Gavaskar captained in First Test.

## HIGHEST INNINGS TOTALS

For New Zealand in New Zealand: 502 at Christchurch ........ 1967-68
in India: 462-9 dec. at Calcutta ........ 1964-65
450-2 dec. at Delhi ........ 1955-56

For India in New Zealand: 414 at Auckland ........ 1975-76
in India: 537-3 dec. at Madras ........ 1955-56

## LOWEST INNINGS TOTALS

| | | |
|---|---|---|
| For New Zealand in New Zealand: 100 at Wellington | | 1980-81 |
| in India: 127 at Bombay | | 1969-70 |
| For India in New Zealand: 81 at Wellington | | 1975-76 |
| in India: 88 at Bombay | | 1964-65 |

## INDIVIDUAL HUNDREDS

**For New Zealand** (16)

| | | | | | |
|---|---|---|---|---|---|
| 120 | G. T. Dowling, Bombay | 1964-65 | 120 | J. R. Reid, Calcutta | 1955-56 |
| 143 | G. T. Dowling, Dunedin | 1967-68 | 137*† | B. Sutcliffe, Hyderabad | 1955-56 |
| 239 | G. T. Dowling, Christchurch | 1967-68 | 230* | B. Sutcliffe, Delhi | 1955-56 |
| 102† | J. W. Guy, Hyderabad | 1955-56 | 151* | B. Sutcliffe, Calcutta | 1964-65 |
| 137* | G. P. Howarth, Wellington | 1980-81 | 105† | B. R. Taylor, Calcutta | 1964-65 |
| 104 | J. M. Parker, Bombay | 1976-77 | 117 | G. M. Turner, Christchurch | 1975-76 |
| 123* | J. F. Reid, Christchurch | 1980-81 | 113 | G. M. Turner, Kanpur | 1976-77 |
| 119* | J. R. Reid, Delhi | 1955-56 | 110 | J. G. Wright, Auckland | 1980-81 |

**For India** (20)

| | | | | | |
|---|---|---|---|---|---|
| 124† | S. Amarnath, Auckland | 1975-76 | 153 | Nawab of Pataudi jun., Calcutta | 1964-65 |
| 109 | C. G. Borde, Bombay | 1964-65 | 113 | Nawab of Pataudi jun., Delhi | 1964-65 |
| 116† | S. M. Gavaskar, Auckland | 1975-76 | 106* | G. S. Ramchand, Calcutta | 1955-56 |
| 119 | S. M. Gavaskar, Bombay | 1976-77 | 100 | Pankaj Roy, Calcutta | 1955-56 |
| 100*† | A. G. Kripal Singh, Hyderabad | 1955-56 | 173 | Pankaj Roy, Madras | 1955-56 |
| 118† | V. L. Manjrekar, Hyderabad | 1955-56 | 200* | D. N. Sardesai, Bombay | 1964-65 |
| 177 | V. L. Manjrekar, Delhi | 1955-56 | 106 | D. N. Sardesai, Delhi | 1964-65 |
| 102* | V. L. Manjrekar, Madras | 1964-65 | 223† | P. R. Umrigar, Hyderabad | 1955-56 |
| 223 | V. Mankad, Bombay | 1955-56 | 103* | G. R. Viswanath, Kanpur | 1976-77 |
| 231 | V. Mankad, Madras | 1955-56 | 143 | A. L. Wadekar, Wellington | 1967-68 |

† *Signifies hundred on first appearance in New Zealand–India Tests. B. R. Taylor provides the only instance for New Zealand of a player scoring his maiden hundred in first-class cricket in his first Test.*

## RECORD PARTNERSHIPS FOR EACH WICKET

**For New Zealand**

| | | |
|---|---|---|
| 126 for 1st | B. A. G. Murray and G. T. Dowling at Christchurch | 1967-68 |
| 155 for 2nd | G. T. Dowling and B. E. Congdon at Dunedin | 1967-68 |
| 222* for 3rd† | B. Sutcliffe and J. R. Reid at Delhi | 1955-56 |
| 103 for 4th | G. T. Dowling and M. G. Burgess at Christchurch | 1967-68 |
| 119 for 5th | G. T. Dowling and K. Thomson at Christchurch | 1967-68 |
| 87 for 6th | J. W. Guy and A. R. MacGibbon at Hyderabad | 1955-56 |
| 163 for 7th | B. Sutcliffe and B. R. Taylor at Calcutta | 1964-65 |
| 81 for 8th | V. Pollard and G. E. Vivian at Calcutta | 1964-65 |
| 69 for 9th | M. G. Burgess and J. C. Alabaster at Dunedin | 1967-68 |
| 61 for 10th | J. T. Ward and R. O. Collinge at Madras | 1964-65 |

**For India**

| | | |
|---|---|---|
| 413 for 1st† | V. Mankad and Pankaj Roy at Madras | 1955-56 |
| 204 for 2nd | S. M. Gavaskar and S. Amarnath at Auckland | 1975-76 |
| 238 for 3rd | P. R. Umrigar and V. L. Manjrekar at Hyderabad | 1955-56 |
| 171 for 4th | P. R. Umrigar and A. G. Kripal Singh at Hyderabad | 1955-56 |
| 127 for 5th | V. L. Manjrekar and G. S. Ramchand at Delhi | 1955-56 |
| 193* for 6th† | D. N. Sardesai and Hanumant Singh at Bombay | 1964-65 |
| 116 for 7th | B. P. Patel and S. M. H. Kirmani at Wellington | 1975-76 |
| 143 for 8th† | R. G. Nadkarni and F. M. Engineer at Madras | 1964-65 |
| 105 for 9th | S. M. H. Kirmani and B. S. Bedi at Bombay | 1976-77 |
| | S. M. H. Kirmani and N. S. Yadav at Auckland | 1980-81 |
| 57 for 10th | R. B. Desai and B. S. Bedi at Dunedin | 1967-68 |

† *Denotes record partnership against all countries.*

## TEN WICKETS OR MORE IN A MATCH

**For New Zealand** (1)

| | | |
|---|---|---|
| 11-58 (4-35, 7-23) | R. J. Hadlee, Wellington | 1975-76 |

**For India** (2)

| | | |
|---|---|---|
| 11-140 (3-64, 8-76) | E. A. S. Prasanna, Auckland | 1975-76 |
| 12-152 (8-72, 4-80) | S. Venkataraghavan, Delhi | 1964-65 |

## NEW ZEALAND v PAKISTAN

| | *Captains* | | | | | |
|---|---|---|---|---|---|---|
| *Season* | *New Zealand* | *Pakistan* | *T* | *NZ* | *P* | *D* |
| 1955-56*P* | H. B. Cave | A. H. Kardar | 3 | 0 | 2 | 1 |
| 1964-65*N* | J. R. Reid | Hanif Mohammad | 3 | 0 | 0 | 3 |
| 1964-65*P* | J. R. Reid | Hanif Mohammad | 3 | 0 | 2 | 1 |
| 1969-70*P* | G. T. Dowling | Intikhab Alam | 3 | 1 | 0 | 2 |
| 1972-73*N* | B. E. Congdon | Intikhab Alam | 3 | 0 | 1 | 2 |
| 1976-77*P* | G. M. Turner[1] | Mushtaq Mohammad | 3 | 0 | 2 | 1 |
| 1978-79*N* | M. G. Burgess | Mushtaq Mohammad | 3 | 0 | 1 | 2 |
| 1984-85*P* | J. V. Coney | Zaheer Abbas | 3 | 0 | 2 | 1 |
| 1984-85*N* | G. P. Howarth | Javed Miandad | 3 | 2 | 0 | 1 |
| | In Pakistan | | 15 | 1 | 8 | 6 |
| | In New Zealand | | 12 | 2 | 2 | 8 |
| | Totals | | 27 | 3 | 10 | 14 |

*N Played in New Zealand. P Played in Pakistan.*

*Note:* [1]J. M. Parker captained in Third Test.

## HIGHEST INNINGS TOTALS

| | |
|---|---|
| For New Zealand in New Zealand 492 at Wellington | 1984-85 |
| in Pakistan: 482-6 dec. at Lahore | 1964-65 |
| For Pakistan in New Zealand: 507-6 dec. at Dunedin | 1972-73 |
| in Pakistan: 565-9 dec. at Karachi | 1976-77 |
| 561 at Lahore | 1955-56 |

## LOWEST INNINGS TOTALS

| | |
|---|---|
| For New Zealand in New Zealand: 156 at Dunedin | 1972-73 |
| in Pakistan: 70 at Dacca | 1955-56 |
| For Pakistan in New Zealand: 169 at Auckland | 1984-85 |
| in Pakistan: 114 at Lahore | 1969-70 |

## INDIVIDUAL HUNDREDS

### For New Zealand (16)

| | | |
|---|---|---|
| 119* | M. G. Burgess, Dacca | 1969-70 |
| 111 | M. G. Burgess, Lahore | 1976-77 |
| 111* | J. V. Coney, Dunedin | 1984-85 |
| 129† | B. A. Edgar, Christchurch | 1978-79 |
| 110 | B. F. Hastings, Auckland | 1972-73 |
| 114 | G. P. Howarth, Napier | 1978-79 |
| 152 | W. K. Lees, Karachi | 1976-77 |
| 111 | S. N. McGregor, Lahore | 1955-56 |
| 107† | R. E. Redmond, Auckland | 1972-73 |
| 106 | J. F. Reid, Hyderabad | 1984-85 |
| 148 | J. F. Reid, Wellington | 1984-85 |
| 158* | J. F. Reid, Auckland | 1984-85 |
| 128 | J. R. Reid, Karachi | 1964-65 |
| 130 | B. W. Sinclair, Lahore | 1964-65 |
| 110† | G. M. Turner, Dacca | 1969-70 |
| 107 | J. G. Wright, Karachi | 1984-85 |

### For Pakistan (26)

| | | |
|---|---|---|
| 175 | Asif Iqbal, Dunedin | 1972-73 |
| 166 | Asif Iqbal, Lahore | 1976-77 |
| 104 | Asif Iqbal, Napier | 1978-79 |
| 103 | Hanif Mohammad, Dacca | 1955-56 |
| 100* | Hanif Mohammad, Christchurch | 1964-65 |
| 203* | Hanif Mohammad, Lahore | 1964-65 |
| 209 | Imtiaz Ahmed, Lahore | 1955-56 |
| 163† | Javed Miandad, Lahore | 1976-77 |
| 206 | Javed Miandad, Karachi | 1976-77 |
| 160* | Javed Miandad, Christchurch | 1978-79 |
| 104 } 103* | Javed Miandad, Hyderabad | 1984-85 |
| 110 | Majid J. Khan, Auckland | 1972-73 |
| 112 | Majid J. Khan, Karachi | 1976-77 |
| 119* | Majid J. Khan, Napier | 1978-79 |
| 126 | Mohammad Ilyas, Karachi | 1964-65 |
| 106 | Mudassar Nazar, Hyderabad | 1984-85 |
| 201 | Mushtaq Mohammad, Dunedin | 1972-73 |
| 101 | Mushtaq Mohammad, Hyderabad | 1976-77 |
| 107 | Mushtaq Mohammad, Karachi | 1976-77 |
| 166 | Sadiq Mohammad, Wellington | 1972-73 |
| 103* | Sadiq Mohammad, Hyderabad | 1976-77 |
| 172 | Saeed Ahmed, Karachi | 1964-65 |
| 119* | Salim Malik, Karachi | 1984-85 |
| 189 | Waqar Hassan, Lahore | 1955-56 |
| 135 | Zaheer Abbas, Auckland | 1978-79 |

† *Signifies hundred on first appearance in New Zealand–Pakistan Tests.*

*Note:* Mushtaq and Sadiq Mohammad, at Hyderabad in 1976-77, provide the fourth instance in Test matches, after the Chappells (thrice), of brothers each scoring hundreds in the same innings.

## RECORD PARTNERSHIPS FOR EACH WICKET

### For New Zealand

| | | |
|---|---|---|
| 159 for 1st | R. E. Redmond and G. M. Turner at Auckland | 1972-73 |
| 195 for 2nd | J. G. Wright and G. P. Howarth at Napier | 1978-79 |
| 178 for 3rd | B. W. Sinclair and J. R. Reid at Lahore | 1964-65 |
| 128 for 4th | B. F. Hastings and M. G. Burgess at Wellington | 1972-73 |
| 183 for 5th† | M. G. Burgess and R. W. Anderson at Lahore | 1976-77 |
| 145 for 6th | J. F. Reid and R. J. Hadlee at Wellington | 1984-85 |
| 186 for 7th† | W. K. Lees and R. J. Hadlee at Karachi | 1976-77 |
| 100 for 8th | B. W. Yuile and D. R. Hadlee at Karachi | 1969-70 |
| 96 for 9th | M. G. Burgess and R. S. Cunis at Dacca | 1969-70 |
| 151 for 10th† | B. F. Hastings and R. O. Collinge at Auckland | 1972-73 |

**For Pakistan**

| | | |
|---|---|---|
| 147 for 1st‡ | Sadiq Mohammad and Majid J. Khan at Karachi | 1976-77 |
| 114 for 2nd | Mohammad Ilyas and Saeed Ahmed at Rawalpindi | 1964-65 |
| 212 for 3rd | Mudassar Nazar and Javed Miandad at Hyderabad | 1984-85 |
| 350 for 4th† | Mushtaq Mohammad and Asif Iqbal at Dunedin | 1972-73 |
| 281 for 5th† | Javed Miandad and Asif Iqbal at Lahore | 1976-77 |
| 217 for 6th† | Hanif Mohammad and Majid J. Khan at Lahore | 1964-65 |
| 308 for 7th† | Waqar Hassan and Imtiaz Ahmed at Lahore | 1955-56 |
| 89 for 8th | Anil Dalpat and Iqbal Qasim at Karachi | 1984-85 |
| 52 for 9th | Intikhab Alam and Arif Butt at Auckland | 1964-65 |
| 65 for 10th | Salah-ud-Din and Mohammad Farooq at Rawalpindi | 1964-65 |

† *Denotes record partnership against all countries.*

‡ *In the preceding Test of this series, at Hyderabad, 164 runs were added for this wicket by Sadiq Mohammad, Majid J. Khan and Zaheer Abbas. Sadiq Mohammad retired hurt after 136 had been scored.*

## TEN WICKETS OR MORE IN A MATCH

**For Pakistan (4)**

| | | |
|---|---|---|
| 10-182 (5-91, 5-91) | Intikhab Alam, Dacca | 1969-70 |
| 11-130 (7-52, 4-78) | Intikhab Alam, Dunedin | 1972-73 |
| 10-128 (5-56, 5-72) | Wasim Akram, Dunedin | 1984-85 |
| 11-79 (5-37, 6-42)† | Zulfiqar Ahmed, Karachi | 1955-56 |

† *Signifies ten wickets or more on first appearance in New Zealand–Pakistan Tests.*

*Note:* The best match figures by a New Zealand bowler are 9-70 (4-36, 5-34), F. J. Cameron at Auckland, 1964-65.

# NEW ZEALAND v SRI LANKA

| | *Captains* | | | | | |
|---|---|---|---|---|---|---|
| *Season* | *New Zealand* | *Sri Lanka* | *T* | *NZ* | *SL* | *D* |
| 1982-83*N* | G. P. Howarth | D. S. de Silva | 2 | 2 | 0 | 0 |
| 1983-84*S* | G. P. Howarth | L. R. D. Mendis | 3 | 2 | 0 | 1 |
| | Totals | | 5 | 4 | 0 | 1 |

*N Played in New Zealand. S Played in Sri Lanka.*

## HIGHEST INNINGS TOTALS

For New Zealand in New Zealand: 344 at Christchurch ........ 1982-83
in Sri Lanka: 459 at Colombo (CCC) ........ 1983-84

For Sri Lanka in New Zealand: 240 at Wellington ........ 1982-83
in Sri Lanka: 289-9 dec. at Colombo (SSC) ........ 1983-84

## LOWEST INNINGS TOTALS

For New Zealand in New Zealand: 201 at Wellington ........ 1982-83
in Sri Lanka: 198 at Colombo (SSC) ........ 1983-84

For Sri Lanka in New Zealand: 93 at Wellington ........ 1982-83
in Sri Lanka: 97 at Kandy ........ 1983-84

## INDIVIDUAL HUNDREDS

| For New Zealand (1) | | | For Sri Lanka (1) | | |
|---|---|---|---|---|---|
| 180 | J. F. Reid, Colombo (CCC) | 1983-84 | 108† | R. L. Dias, Colombo (SSC) | 1983-84 |

† *Signifies hundred on first appearance in New Zealand–Sri Lanka Tests.*

Best wicket partnership for New Zealand: 133 for the 6th by J. F. Reid and J. V. Coney at Colombo (CCC) ........ 1983-84
for Sri Lanka: ‡159 for the 3rd by S. Wettimuny and R. L. Dias at Colombo (SSC) ........ 1983-84

‡ *163 runs were added for this wicket in two separate partnerships: S. Wettimuny retired hurt and was replaced by L. R. D. Mendis when 159 had been added.*

## TEN WICKETS OR MORE IN A MATCH

**For New Zealand** (1)

10-102 (5-73, 5-29) R. J. Hadlee, Colombo (CCC) ........ 1983-84

*Note:* The best match figures by a Sri Lankan bowler are 8-159 (5-86, 3-73), V. B. John at Colombo (SSC), 1983-84.

# INDIA v PAKISTAN

| | *Captains* | | | | | |
|---|---|---|---|---|---|---|
| *Season* | *India* | *Pakistan* | *T* | *I* | *P* | *D* |
| 1952-53*I* | L. Amarnath | A. H. Kardar | 5 | 2 | 1 | 2 |
| 1954-55*P* | V. Mankad | A. H. Kardar | 5 | 0 | 0 | 5 |
| 1960-61*I* | N. J. Contractor | Fazal Mahmood | 5 | 0 | 0 | 5 |
| 1978-79*P* | B. S. Bedi | Mushtaq Mohammad | 3 | 0 | 2 | 1 |
| 1979-80*I* | S. M. Gavaskar[1] | Asif Iqbal | 6 | 2 | 0 | 4 |
| 1982-83*P* | S. M. Gavaskar | Imran Khan | 6 | 0 | 3 | 3 |
| 1983-84*I* | Kapil Dev | Zaheer Abbas | 3 | 0 | 0 | 3 |
| 1984-85*P* | S. M. Gavaskar | Zaheer Abbas | 2 | 0 | 0 | 2 |
| | In India ........ | | 19 | 4 | 1 | 14 |
| | In Pakistan ........ | | 16 | 0 | 5 | 11 |
| | Totals ........ | | 35 | 4 | 6 | 25 |

*I Played in India. P Played in Pakistan.*

*Note:* [1]G. R. Viswanath captained in Sixth Test.

## HIGHEST INNINGS TOTALS

For India in India: 539-9 dec. at Madras ........ 1960-61
in Pakistan: 500 at Faisalabad ........ 1984-85

For Pakistan in India: 448-8 dec. at Madras ........ 1960-61
in Pakistan: 674-6 at Faisalabad ........ 1984-85

## LOWEST INNINGS TOTALS

For India in India: 106 at Lucknow ........ 1952-53
in Pakistan: 145 at Karachi ........ 1954-55

For Pakistan in India: 150 at Delhi ........ 1952-53
in Pakistan: 158 at Dacca ........ 1954-55

## INDIVIDUAL HUNDREDS

### For India (23)

| | | |
|---|---|---|
| 109* | M. Amarnath, Lahore | 1982-83 |
| 120 | M. Amarnath, Lahore | 1982-83 |
| 103* | M. Amarnath, Karachi | 1982-83 |
| 101* | M. Amarnath, Lahore | 1984-85 |
| 177* | C. G. Borde, Madras | 1960-61 |
| 201 | A. D. Gaekwad, Jullundur | 1983-84 |
| 111<br>137 | S. M. Gavaskar, Karachi | 1978-79 |
| 166 | S. M. Gavaskar, Madras | 1979-80 |
| 127*‡ | S. M. Gavaskar, Faisalabad | 1982-83 |
| 103* | S. M. Gavaskar, Bangalore | 1983-84 |
| 146* | V. S. Hazare, Bombay | 1952-53 |
| 127 | S. M. Patil, Faisalabad | 1984-85 |
| 128 | R. J. Shastri, Karachi | 1982-83 |
| 139 | R. J. Shastri, Faisalabad | 1984-85 |
| 110† | R. H. Shodhan, Calcutta | 1952-53 |
| 102 | P. R. Umrigar, Bombay | 1952-53 |
| 108 | P. R. Umrigar, Peshawar | 1954-55 |
| 115 | P. R. Umrigar, Kanpur | 1960-61 |
| 117 | P. R. Umrigar, Madras | 1960-61 |
| 112 | P. R. Umrigar, Delhi | 1960-61 |
| 146* | D. B. Vengsarkar, Delhi | 1979-80 |
| 145† | G. R. Viswanath, Faisalabad | 1978-79 |

### For Pakistan (31)

| | | |
|---|---|---|
| 103* | Alim-ud-Din, Karachi | 1954-55 |
| 104† | Asif Iqbal, Faisalabad | 1978-79 |
| 142 | Hanif Mohammad, Bahawalpur | 1954-55 |
| 160 | Hanif Mohammad, Bombay | 1960-61 |
| 135 | Imtiaz Ahmed, Madras | 1960-61 |
| 117 | Imran Khan, Faisalabad | 1982-83 |
| 154*† | Javed Miandad, Faisalabad | 1978-79 |
| 100 | Javed Miandad, Karachi | 1978-79 |
| 126 | Javed Miandad, Faisalabad | 1982-83 |
| 280* | Javed Miandad, Hyderabad | 1982-83 |
| 101*† | Mohsin Khan, Lahore | 1982-83 |
| 126 | Mudassar Nazar, Bangalore | 1979-80 |
| 119 | Mudassar Nazar, Karachi | 1982-83 |
| 231 | Mudassar Nazar, Hyderabad | 1982-83 |
| 152*† | Mudassar Nazar, Lahore | 1982-83 |
| 152 | Mudassar Nazar, Karachi | 1982-83 |
| 199 | Mudassar Nazar, Faisalabad | 1984-85 |
| 101 | Mushtaq Mohammad, Delhi | 1960-61 |
| 124*‡ | Nazar Mohammad, Lucknow | 1952-53 |
| 210 | Qasim Omar, Faisalabad | 1984-85 |
| 121† | Saeed Ahmed, Bombay | 1960-61 |
| 103 | Saeed Ahmed, Madras | 1960-61 |
| 107 | Salim Malik, Faisalabad | 1982-83 |
| 102* | Salim Malik, Faisalabad | 1984-85 |
| 125 | Wasim Raja, Jullundur | 1983-84 |
| 176† | Zaheer Abbas, Faisalabad | 1978-79 |
| 235* | Zaheer Abbas, Lahore | 1978-79 |
| 215 | Zaheer Abbas, Lahore | 1982-83 |
| 186 | Zaheer Abbas, Karachi | 1982-83 |
| 168 | Zaheer Abbas, Faisalabad | 1982-83 |
| 168* | Zaheer Abbas, Lahore | 1984-85 |

† *Signifies hundred on first appearance in India–Pakistan Tests.*
‡ *Carried his bat.*

## RECORD PARTNERSHIPS FOR EACH WICKET

### For India

| | | |
|---|---|---|
| 192 for 1st | S. M. Gavaskar and C. P. S. Chauhan at Lahore | 1978-79 |
| 125 for 2nd | S. M. Gavaskar and M. Amarnath at Hyderabad | 1982-83 |
| 190 for 3rd | M. Amarnath and Yashpal Sharma at Lahore | 1982-83 |
| 183 for 4th | V. S. Hazare and P. R. Umrigar at Bombay | 1952-53 |
| 200 for 5th | S. M. Patil and R. J. Shastri at Faisalabad | 1984-85 |
| 121 for 6th | A. D. Gaekwad and R. M. H. Binny at Jullundur | 1983-84 |
| 155 for 7th | R. M. H. Binny and Madan Lal at Bangalore | 1983-84 |
| 122 for 8th | S. M. H. Kirmani and Madan Lal at Faisalabad | 1982-83 |
| 149 for 9th† | P. G. Joshi and R. B. Desai at Bombay | 1960-61 |
| 109 for 10th† | H. R. Adhikari and Ghulam Ahmed at Delhi | 1952-53 |

**For Pakistan**

| | | |
|---|---|---|
| 162 for 1st | Hanif Mohammad and Imtiaz Ahmed at Madras | 1960-61 |
| 250 for 2nd | Mudassar Nazar and Qasim Omar at Faisalabad | 1984-85 |
| 451 for 3rd† | Mudassar Nazar and Javed Miandad at Hyderabad | 1982-83 |
| 287 for 4th | Javed Miandad and Zaheer Abbas at Faisalabad | 1982-83 |
| 213 for 5th | Zaheer Abbas and Mudassar Nazar at Karachi | 1982-83 |
| 207 for 6th | Salim Malik and Imran Khan at Faisalabad | 1982-83 |
| 142 for 7th | Zaheer Abbas and Ashraf Ali at Lahore | 1984-85 |
| 95 for 8th | Wasim Raja and Tahir Naqqash at Jullundur | 1983-84 |
| 60 for 9th | Wasim Bari and Iqbal Qasim at Bangalore | 1979-80 |
| 104 for 10th | Zulfiqar Ahmed and Amir Elahi at Madras | 1952-53 |

† *Denotes record partnership against all countries.*

## TEN WICKETS OR MORE IN A MATCH

**For India** (2)

| | | |
|---|---|---|
| 11-146 (4-90, 7-56) | Kapil Dev, Madras | 1979-80 |
| 13-131 (8-52, 5-79)† | V. Mankad, Delhi | 1952-53 |

**For Pakistan** (5)

| | | |
|---|---|---|
| 12-94 (5-52, 7-42) | Fazal Mahmood, Lucknow | 1952-53 |
| 11-79 (3-19, 8-60) | Imran Khan, Karachi | 1982-83 |
| 11-180 (6-98, 5-82) | Imran Khan, Faisalabad | 1982-83 |
| 10-175 (4-135, 6-40) | Iqbal Qasim, Bombay | 1979-80 |
| 11-190 (8-69, 3-121) | Sikander Bakht, Delhi | 1979-80 |

† *Signifies ten wickets or more on first appearance in India–Pakistan Tests.*

# INDIA v SRI LANKA

| | *Captains* | | | | | |
|---|---|---|---|---|---|---|
| *Season* | *India* | *Sri Lanka* | *T* | *I* | *SL* | *D* |
| 1982-83*I* | S. M. Gavaskar | B. Warnapura | 1 | 0 | 0 | 1 |

*I Played in India.*

The only match was played at Madras.

## INDIVIDUAL HUNDREDS

**For India** (2)

155† S. M. Gavaskar, Madras .. 1982-83 | 114*† S. M. Patil, Madras .... 1982-83

**For Sri Lanka** (2)

105, 105 †L. R. D. Mendis, Madras. 1982-83

† *Signifies hundred in first appearance in India–Sri Lanka Tests.*

Best bowling in an innings for India: 5-85 by D. R. Doshi.
for Sri Lanka: 5-68 by A. L. F. de Mel.

Best wicket partnership for India: 173 for the 2nd by S. M. Gavaskar and D. B. Vengsarkar.
for Sri Lanka: 153 for the 3rd by R. L. Dias and L. R. D. Mendis.

Highest innings total for India: 566-6 dec.
for Sri Lanka: 394.

## PAKISTAN v SRI LANKA

| | *Captains* | | | | | |
|---|---|---|---|---|---|---|
| *Season* | *Pakistan* | *Sri Lanka* | *T* | *P* | *SL* | *D* |
| 1981-82*P* | Javed Miandad | B. Warnapura[1] | 3 | 2 | 0 | 1 |

*P Played in Pakistan.*

*Note:* [1]L. R. D. Mendis captained in the Second Test.

### INDIVIDUAL HUNDREDS

**For Pakistan** (4)

| | | |
|---|---|---|
| 153† | Haroon Rashid, Karachi . | 1981-82 |
| 129 | Mohsin Khan, Lahore . . . | 1981-82 |
| 100*† | Salim Malik, Karachi . . . . | 1981-82 |
| 134† | Zaheer Abbas, Lahore . . . | 1981-82 |

**For Sri Lanka** (2)

| | | |
|---|---|---|
| 109 | R. L. Dias, Lahore . . . . . . | 1981-82 |
| 157 | S. Wettimuny, Faisalabad | 1981-82 |

† *Signifies hundred on first appearance in Pakistan–Sri Lanka Tests.*

### TEN WICKETS OR MORE IN A MATCH

**For Pakistan** (1)

14-116 (8-58, 6-58) Imran Khan, Lahore . . . . . . . . . . . . . . . . . . . . . . . . . . . . . . 1981-82

*Note:* The best match figures by a Sri Lankan bowler are 9-162 (4-103, 5-59), D. S. de Silva at Faisalabad, 1981-82.

Best wicket partnership for Pakistan: 161 for the 4th by Salim Malik and Javed Miandad at Karachi.
for Sri Lanka: 217 for the 2nd by S. Wettimuny and R. L. Dias at Faisalabad.

Highest innings total for Pakistan: 500-7 dec. at Lahore.
for Sri Lanka: 454 at Faisalabad.

Lowest innings total for Pakistan: 270 at Faisalabad.
for Sri Lanka: 149 at Karachi.

## SRI LANKAN RECORD PARTNERSHIPS FOR EACH WICKET

| | | |
|---|---|---|
| 77 for 1st | S. Wettimuny and H. M. Goonatillake v Pakistan at Faisalabad | 1981-82 |
| 217 for 2nd | S. Wettimuny and R. L. Dias v Pakistan at Faisalabad . . . . . . . | 1981-82 |
| 159* for 3rd‡ | S. Wettimuny and R. L. Dias v New Zealand at Colombo (SSC) | 1983-84 |
| 148 for 4th | S. Wettimuny and A. Ranatunga v England at Lord's . . . . . . . . . | 1984 |
| 150 for 5th | S. Wettimuny and L. R. D. Mendis v England at Lord's . . . . . . | 1984 |
| 138 for 6th | S. A. R. Silva and L. R. D. Mendis v England at Lord's . . . . . . | 1984 |
| 77 for 7th | A. N. Ranasinghe and D. S. de Silva v India at Madras . . . . . . | 1982-83 |
| 61 for 8th | R. S. Madugalle and D. S. de Silva v Pakistan at Faisalabad . . . | 1981-82 |
| 42 for 9th | J. R. Ratnayeke and A. L. F. de Mel v India at Madras . . . . . . | 1982-83 |
| 60 for 10th | V. B. John and A. M. J. G. Amerasinghe v New Zealand at Kandy | 1983-84 |

‡ *163 runs were added for this wicket in two separate partnerships: S. Wettimuny retired hurt and was replaced by L. R. D. Mendis when 159 had been added.*

# ONE-DAY INTERNATIONAL CRICKET

*Note:* One-day international matches do not have first-class status.

## 3,000 OR MORE RUNS

| | *M* | *I* | *NO* | *R* | *HI* | *100s* | *Avge* |
|---|---|---|---|---|---|---|---|
| I. V. A. Richards (*West Indies*) .... | 98 | 89 | 15 | 4,071 | 189* | 8 | 55.01 |
| D. L. Haynes (*West Indies*) ....... | 93 | 92 | 12 | 3,348 | 148 | 8 | 41.85 |

## HIGHEST INDIVIDUAL SCORE FOR EACH COUNTRY

| | | | |
|---|---|---|---|
| 189* | I. V. A. Richards | **West Indies** v England at Manchester ........... | 1984 |
| 175* | Kapil Dev | **India** v Zimbabwe at Tunbridge Wells ........... | 1983 |
| 171* | G. M. Turner | **New Zealand** v East Africa at Birmingham ....... | 1975 |
| 158 | D. I. Gower | **England** v New Zealand at Brisbane ............ | 1982-83 |
| 138* | G. S. Chappell | **Australia** v New Zealand at Sydney ............. | 1980-81 |
| 123 | Zaheer Abbas | **Pakistan** v Sri Lanka at Lahore ................ | 1981-82 |
| 121 | R. L. Dias | **Sri Lanka** v India at Bangalore ................ | 1982-83 |

## FIVE OR MORE HUNDREDS

| *Total* | | *E* | *A* | *WI* | *NZ* | *I* | *P* | *SL* | *Others* |
|---|---|---|---|---|---|---|---|---|---|
| 8 | D. L. Haynes (*West Indies*) ..... | 0 | 6 | – | 2 | 0 | 0 | 0 | 0 |
| 8 | I. V. A. Richards (*West Indies*) .. | 3 | 3 | – | 0 | 2 | 0 | 0 | 0 |
| 7 | D. I. Gower (*England*) ......... | – | 2 | 0 | 3 | 0 | 1 | 1 | 0 |
| 7 | Zaheer Abbas (*Pakistan*) ....... | 0 | 2 | 0 | 1 | 3 | – | 1 | 0 |
| 6 | C. G. Greenidge (*West Indies*) .. | 0 | 0 | – | 1 | 2 | 1 | 1 | 1 |

## HIGHEST PARTNERSHIP FOR EACH WICKET

| | | |
|---|---|---|
| 188 for 1st | K. Srikkanth (99) and R. J. Shastri (102), India v England at Cuttack | 1984-85 |
| 221 for 2nd | C. G. Greenidge (115) and I. V. A. Richards (149), West Indies v India at Jamshedpur ................................ | 1983-84 |
| 224* for 3rd | D. M. Jones (99*) and A. R. Border (118*), Australia v Sri Lanka at Adelaide ................................ | 1984-85 |
| 157* for 4th | R. B. Kerr (87*) and D. M. Jones (78*), Australia v England at Melbourne ................................ | 1984-85 |
| 152 for 5th | I. V. A. Richards (98) and C. H. Lloyd (89*), West Indies v Sri Lanka at Brisbane ................................ | 1984-85 |
| 144 for 6th | Imran Khan (102*) and Shahid Mahboob (77), Pakistan v Sri Lanka at Leeds ................................ | 1983 |
| 108 for 7th | Ramiz Raja (75) and Anil Dalpat (37), Pakistan v New Zealand at Christchurch ................................ | 1984-85 |
| 68 for 8th | B. E. Congdon (52*) and B. L. Cairns (23), New Zealand v England at Scarborough ................................ | 1978 |
| 126* for 9th | Kapil Dev (175*) and S. M. H. Kirmani (24*), India v Zimbabwe at Tunbridge Wells ................................ | 1983 |
| 106* for 10th | I. V. A. Richards (189*) and M. A. Holding (12*), West Indies v England at Manchester ................................ | 1984 |

## 100 OR MORE WICKETS

| | *M* | *Balls* | *R* | *W* | *BB* | *4Wi* | *Avge* |
|---|---|---|---|---|---|---|---|
| M. A. Holding (*West Indies*) ... | 87 | 4,734 | 2,613 | 122 | 5-26 | 5 | 21.41 |
| J. Garner (*West Indies*) ....... | 76 | 4,184 | 2,102 | 116 | 5-31 | 4 | 18.12 |
| D. K. Lillee (*Australia*) ....... | 63 | 3,593 | 2,145 | 103 | 5-34 | 6 | 20.82 |
| I. T. Botham (*England*) ....... | 75 | 3,936 | 2,639 | 100 | 4-56 | 1 | 26.39 |
| R. J. Hadlee (*New Zealand*) ... | 75 | 4,017 | 2,148 | 100 | 5-25 | 4 | 21.48 |

## BEST BOWLING FOR EACH COUNTRY

| | | | |
|---|---|---|---|
| 7-51 | W. W. Davis | **West Indies** v Australia at Leeds | 1983 |
| 6-14 | G. J. Gilmour | **Australia** v England at Leeds | 1975 |
| 6-14 | Imran Khan | **Pakistan** v India at Sharjah | 1984-85 |
| 5-20 | V. J. Marks | **England** v New Zealand at Wellington | 1983-84 |
| 5-23 | R. O. Collinge | **New Zealand** v India at Christchurch | 1975-76 |
| 5-26 | U. S. H. Karnain | **Sri Lanka** v New Zealand at Moratuwa | 1983-84 |
| 5-43 | Kapil Dev | **India** v Australia at Nottingham | 1983 |

## HAT-TRICK

Jalal-ud-Din — Pakistan v Australia at Hyderabad ... 1982-83

## CAREER DISMISSALS

| | *M* | *Ct* | *St* | *Total* |
|---|---|---|---|---|
| R. W. Marsh (*Australia*) | 91 | 119 | 4 | 123 |
| P. J. L. Dujon (*West Indies*) | 69 | 85 | 8 | 93 |
| Wasim Bari (*Pakistan*) | 51 | 52 | 10 | 62 |

## ALL-ROUND

### 1,000 Runs and 50 Wickets

| | *M* | *R* | *W* |
|---|---|---|---|
| I. T. Botham (*England*) | 75 | 1,248 | 100 |
| G. S. Chappell (*Australia*) | 73 | 2,329 | 71 |
| Imran Khan (*Pakistan*) | 55 | 1,023 | 56 |
| Kapil Dev (*India*) | 61 | 1,336 | 79 |
| Mudassar Nazar (*Pakistan*) | 71 | 1,497 | 73 |
| I. V. A. Richards (*West Indies*) | 98 | 4,071 | 62 |

### 1,000 Runs and 100 Dismissals

| | *M* | *R* | *D* |
|---|---|---|---|
| R. W. Marsh | 91 | 1,220 | 123 |

## HIGHEST INNINGS TOTALS

| | | | |
|---|---|---|---|
| 338-5 | (60 overs) | **Pakistan** v Sri Lanka at Swansea | 1983 |
| 334-4 | (60 overs) | **England** v India at Lord's | 1975 |
| 333-8 | (45 overs) | **West Indies** v India at Jamshedpur | 1983-84 |
| 333-9 | (60 overs) | England v Sri Lanka at Taunton | 1983 |
| 330-6 | (60 overs) | Pakistan v Sri Lanka at Nottingham | 1975 |
| 328-5 | (60 overs) | **Australia** v Sri Lanka at The Oval | 1975 |
| 323-2 | (50 overs) | Australia v Sri Lanka at Adelaide | 1984-85 |
| 322-6 | (60 overs) | England v New Zealand at The Oval | 1983 |
| 320-8 | (55 overs) | England v Australia at Birmingham | 1980 |
| 320-9 | (60 overs) | Australia v India at Nottingham | 1983 |
| 313-9 | (50 overs) | West Indies v Australia at St John's, Antigua | 1977-78 |
| 309-6 | (50 overs) | West Indies v Sri Lanka at Perth | 1984-85 |
| 309-5 | (60 overs) | **New Zealand** v East Africa at Birmingham | 1975 |
| 304-5 | (50 overs) | New Zealand v Sri Lanka at Auckland | 1982-83 |
| 302-8 | (50 overs) | Australia v New Zealand at Melbourne | 1982-83 |

*Note:* The highest score by **India** is 282-5 (47 overs) v West Indies at Berbice, Guyana, 1982-83, and the highest by **Sri Lanka** is 288-9 (60 overs) v Pakistan at Swansea, 1983.

## HIGHEST TOTAL BATTING SECOND

### Winning

| | | | |
|---|---|---|---|
| 297-6 | (48.5 overs) | New Zealand v England at Adelaide | 1982-83 |

### Losing

| | | | |
|---|---|---|---|
| 288-9 | (60 overs) | Sri Lanka v Pakistan at Swansea | 1983 |

## HIGHEST MATCH AGGREGATES

| | | | |
|---|---|---|---|
| 626-14 | (120 overs) | Pakistan v Sri Lanka at Swansea | 1983 |
| 619-19 | (118 overs) | England v Sri Lanka at Taunton | 1983 |
| 604-9 | (120 overs) | Australia v Sri Lanka at The Oval | 1975 |

## LOWEST INNINGS TOTALS

| | | | |
|---|---|---|---|
| 45 | (40.3 overs) | Canada v England at Manchester | 1979 |
| 63 | (25.5 overs) | **India** v Australia at Sydney | 1980-81 |
| 70 | (25.2 overs) | **Australia** v England at Birmingham | 1977 |
| 74 | (29 overs) | **New Zealand** v Australia at Wellington | 1981-82 |
| 79 | (34.2 overs) | India v Pakistan at Sialkot | 1978-79 |
| 85 | (47 overs) | **Pakistan** v England at Manchester | 1978 |
| 86 | (37.2 overs) | **Sri Lanka** v West Indies at Manchester | 1975 |
| 87 | (32.5 overs) | Pakistan v India at Sharjah | 1984-85 |
| 91 | (35.5 overs) | Sri Lanka v Australia at Adelaide | 1984-85 |
| 93 | (36.2 overs) | **England** v Australia at Leeds | 1975 |
| 94 | (31.7 overs) | England v Australia at Melbourne | 1978-79 |
| 94 | (52.3 overs) | East Africa v England at Birmingham | 1975 |
| 96 | (41 overs) | Sri Lanka v India at Sharjah | 1983-84 |

*Note:* This section does not take into account those matches in which the number of overs was reduced.

The lowest innings total by **West Indies** is 111 (41.4 overs) v Pakistan at Melbourne, 1983-84.

## TIED MATCH

West Indies 222-5 (50 overs), Australia 222-9 (50 overs) at Melbourne ......... 1983-84

## WORLD CUP FINALS

1975 West Indies (291-8) beat Australia (274) by 17 runs at Lord's.
1979 West Indies (286-9) beat England (194) by 92 runs at Lord's.
1983 India (183) beat West Indies (140) by 43 runs at Lord's.

# MISCELLANEOUS

## RELATIONS IN TEST CRICKET

### FATHERS AND SONS

*England*
M. C. Cowdrey (114 Tests, 1954-55–1974-75) and C. S. Cowdrey (5 Tests, 1984-85).
J. Hardstaff (5 Tests, 1907-08) and J. Hardstaff jun. (23 Tests, 1935–1948).
L. Hutton (79 Tests, 1937–1954-55) and R. A. Hutton (5 Tests, 1971).
F. T. Mann (5 Tests, 1922-23) and F. G. Mann (7 Tests, 1948-49–1949).
J. H. Parks (1 Test, 1937) and J. M. Parks (46 Tests, 1954–1967-68).
F. W. Tate (1 Test, 1902) and M. W. Tate (39 Tests, 1924–1935).
C. L. Townsend (2 Tests, 1899) and D. C. H. Townsend (3 Tests, 1934-35).

*Australia*
E. J. Gregory (1 Test, 1876-77) and S. E. Gregory (58 Tests, 1890–1912).

*South Africa*
F. Hearne (4 Tests, 1891-92–1895-96) and G. A. L. Hearne (3 Tests, 1922-23–1924).
*F. Hearne also played 2 Tests for England in 1888-89.*
J. D. Lindsay (3 Tests, 1947) and D. T. Lindsay (19 Tests, 1963-64–1969-70).
A. W. Nourse (45 Tests, 1902-03–1924) and A. D. Nourse (34 Tests, 1935–1951).
L. R. Tuckett (1 Test, 1913-14) and L. Tuckett (9 Tests, 1947–1948-49).

*West Indies*
G. A. Headley (22 Tests, 1929-30–1953-54) and R. G. A. Headley (2 Tests, 1973).
O. C. Scott (8 Tests, 1928–1930-31) and A. P. H. Scott (1 Test, 1952-53).

*New Zealand*
W. M. Anderson (1 Test, 1945-46) and R. W. Anderson (9 Tests, 1976-77–1978).
W. A. Hadlee (11 Tests, 1937–1950-51) and D. R. Hadlee (26 Tests, 1969–1977-78); R. J. Hadlee (57 Tests, 1972-73–1984-85).
H. G. Vivian (7 Tests, 1931–1937) and G. E. Vivian (5 Tests, 1964-65–1971-72).

*India*
L. Amarnath (24 Tests, 1933-34–1952-53) and M. Amarnath (49 Tests, 1969-70–1984-85); S. Amarnath (10 Tests, 1975-76–1978-79).
D. K. Gaekwad (11 Tests, 1952–1960-61) and A. D. Gaekwad (40 Tests, 1974-75–1984-85).
Nawab of Pataudi (Iftikhar Ali Khan) (3 Tests, 1946) and Nawab of Pataudi (Mansur Ali Khan) (46 Tests, 1961-62–1974-75).
*Nawab of Pataudi sen. also played 3 Tests for England, 1932-33–1934.*
V. Mankad (44 Tests, 1946–1958-59) and A. V. Mankad (22 Tests, 1969-70–1977-78).
Pankaj Roy (43 Tests, 1951-52–1960-61) and Pranab Roy (2 Tests, 1981-82).

*India and Pakistan*
M. Jahangir Khan (4 Tests, 1932–1936) and Majid J. Khan (63 Tests, 1964-65–1982-83).
S. Wazir Ali (7 Tests, 1932–1936) and Khalid Wazir (2 Tests, 1954).

*Pakistan*
Hanif Mohammad (55 Tests, 1954–1969-70) and Shoaib Mohammad (5 Tests, 1983-84–1984-85).
Nazar Mohammad (5 Tests, 1952-53) and Mudassar Nazar (52 Tests, 1976-77–1984-85).

### GRANDFATHERS AND GRANDSONS

*Australia*
V. Y. Richardson (19 Tests, 1924-25–1935-36) and G. S. Chappell (87 Tests, 1970-71–1983-84); I. M. Chappell (75 Tests, 1964-65–1979-80); T. M. Chappell (3 Tests, 1981).

## GREAT-GRANDFATHER AND GREAT-GRANDSON

*Australia*
W. H. Cooper (2 Tests, 1881-82 and 1884-85) and A. P. Sheahan (31 Tests, 1967-68–1973-74).

## BROTHERS IN SAME TEST TEAM

*England*
E. M., G. F. and W. G. Grace: 1 Test, 1880.
C. T. and G. B. Studd: 4 Tests, 1882-83.
A. and G. G. Hearne: 1 Test, 1891-92.
*F. Hearne, their brother, played in this match for South Africa.*
D. W. and P. E. Richardson: 1 Test, 1957.

*Australia*
E. J. and D. W. Gregory: 1 Test, 1876-77.
C. and A. C. Bannerman: 1 Test, 1878-79.
G. and W. F. Giffen: 2 Tests, 1891-92.
G. H. S. and A. E. Trott: 3 Tests, 1894-95.
I. M. and G. S. Chappell: 43 Tests, 1970-71–1979-80.

*South Africa*
S. J. and S. D. Snooke: 1 Test, 1907.
R. H. M. and P. A. M. Hands: 1 Test, 1913-14.
E. A. B. and A. M. B. Rowan: 9 Tests, 1948-49–1951.
P. M. and R. G. Pollock: 23 Tests, 1963-64–1969-70.
A. J. and D. B. Pithey: 5 Tests, 1963-64.

*West Indies*
G. C. and R. S. Grant: 4 Tests, 1934-35.
J. B. and V. H. Stollmeyer: 1 Test, 1939.
D. St E. and E. St E. Atkinson: 1 Test, 1957-58.

*New Zealand*
J. J. and M. D. Crowe: 18 Tests, 1983–1984-85.
D. R. and R. J. Hadlee: 10 Tests, 1973–1977-78.
H. J. and G. P. Howarth: 4 Tests, 1974-75–1976-77.
J. M. and N. M. Parker: 3 Tests, 1976-77.
B. P. and J. G. Bracewell: 1 Test, 1980-81.

*India*
S. Wazir Ali and S. Nazir Ali: 2 Tests, 1932–1933-34.
L. Ramji and Amar Singh: 1 Test, 1933-34.
C. K. and C. S. Nayudu: 4 Tests, 1933-34–1936.
A. G. Kripal Singh and A. G. Milkha Singh: 1 Test, 1961-62.
S. and M. Amarnath: 8 Tests, 1975-76–1978-79.

*Pakistan*
Wazir and Hanif Mohammad: 18 Tests, 1952-53–1959-60.
Wazir and Mushtaq Mohammad: 1 Test, 1958-59.
Hanif and Mushtaq Mohammad: 19 Tests, 1960-61–1969-70.
Hanif, Mushtaq and Sadiq Mohammad: 1 Test, 1969-70.
Mushtaq and Sadiq Mohammad: 26 Tests, 1969-70–1978-79.
Wasim and Ramiz Raja: 2 Tests, 1983-84.

*Sri Lanka*
M. D. and S. Wettimuny: 2 Tests, 1982-83.

# DOUBLE INTERNATIONALS

## CRICKET AND RUGBY UNION

| | Cricket | Rugby Union |
|---|---|---|
| Anderson, J. H. | South Africa (1) 1902-03 | South Africa (3) 1896 |
| Donnelly, M. P. | New Zealand (7) 1937-49 | England (1) 1947 |
| Elgie, M. K. | South Africa (3) 1961 | Scotland (8) 1954-55 |
| Harris, T. A. | South Africa (3) 1947-48 | South Africa (5) 1937-38 |
| Hands, R. H. M. | South Africa (1) 1913 | England (2) 1910 |
| Hornby, A. N. | England (3) 1878-84 | England (9) 1877-82 |
| Jones, P. S. T. | South Africa (1) 1902 | South Africa (3) 1896 |
| MacGregor, G. | England (8) 1890-93 | Scotland (13) 1890-96 |
| Milton, W. H. | South Africa (3) 1888-91 | England (2) 1874-75 |
| Mitchell, F. | England (2) 1898<br>South Africa (3) 1912 | England (6) 1895-96 |
| Owen-Smith, H. G. | South Africa (5) 1929 | England (9) 1934-37 |
| Powell, A. W. | South Africa (1) 1898 | South Africa (1) 1896 |
| Richards, A. R. | South Africa (1) 1895 | South Africa (3) 1891 |
| Stoddart, A. E. | England (16) 1887-97 | England (10) 1885-93 |
| Schwarz, R. O. | South Africa (20) 1905-12 | England (3) 1899-1901 |
| Sinclair, J. H. | South Africa (25) 1895-1910 | South Africa (1) 1903 |
| Smith, M. J. K. | England (50) 1958-72 | England (1) 1956 |
| Spooner, R. H. | England (10) 1905-12 | England (1) 1903 |
| Tindill, E. W. T. | New Zealand (5) 1937-46 | New Zealand (1) 1935 |
| Turnbull, M. J. | England (9) 1929-36 | Wales (2) 1933 |
| Van Ryneveld, C. B. | South Africa (19) 1951-57 | England (4) 1949 |
| Vernon, G. F. | England (1) 1882 | England (5) 1878-81 |
| Woods, S. M. J. | Australia (3) 1888<br>England (3) 1895 | England (13) 1890-95 |

## CRICKET AND ASSOCIATION FOOTBALL

| | Cricket | Association Football |
|---|---|---|
| Arnold, J. | England (1) 1931 | England (1) 1933 |
| Ducat, A. | England (1) 1921 | England (6) 1910-21 |
| Foster, R. E. | England (8) 1903-07 | England (6) 1900-02 |
| Fry, C. B. | England (26) 1895-1912 | England (2) 1891-1901 |
| Gay, L. H. | England (1) 1894 | England (4) 1891-94 |
| Gunn, W. | England (11) 1886-99 | England (2) 1884 |
| Hardinge, H. T. W. | England (1) 1921 | England (1) 1910 |
| Lyttelton, Hon. A. | England (4) 1880-84 | England (1) 1877 |
| Makepeace, H. | England (4) 1920 | England (4) 1906-12 |
| Milton, C. A. | England (6) 1958-59 | England (1) 1952 |
| Sharp, J. | England (3) 1909 | England (2) 1903-05 |
| Watson, W. | England (23) 1951-58 | England (4) 1950-51 |

# TEST MATCH GROUNDS

## In Chronological Sequence

| City and Ground | Date of First Test | Match |
|---|---|---|
| 1. Melbourne, Melbourne Cricket Ground | March 15, 1877 | Australia v England |
| 2. London, Kennington Oval | September 6, 1880 | England v Australia |
| 3. Sydney, Sydney Cricket Ground (No. 1) | February 17, 1882 | Australia v England |
| 4. Manchester, Old Trafford | July 11, 1884 | England v Australia |
| *This match was due to have started on July 10, but rain prevented any play.* | | |
| 5. London, Lord's | July 21, 1884 | England v Australia |

| | City and Ground | Date of First Test | Match |
|---|---|---|---|
| 6. | Adelaide, Adelaide Oval | December 12, 1884 | Australia v England |
| 7. | Port Elizabeth, St George's Park | March 12, 1889 | South Africa v England |
| 8. | Cape Town, Newlands | March 25, 1889 | South Africa v England |
| 9. | Johannesburg, Old Wanderers* | March 2, 1896 | South Africa v England |
| 10. | Nottingham, Trent Bridge | June 1, 1899 | England v Australia |
| 11. | Leeds, Headingley | June 29, 1899 | England v Australia |
| 12. | Birmingham, Edgbaston | May 29, 1902 | England v Australia |
| 13. | Sheffield, Bramall Lane* | July 3, 1902 | England v Australia |
| 14. | Durban, Lord's* | January 1, 1910 | South Africa v England |
| 15. | Durban, Kingsmead | January 18, 1923 | South Africa v England |
| 16. | Brisbane, Exhibition Ground* | November 30, 1928 | Australia v England |
| 17. | Christchurch, Lancaster Park | January 10, 1930 | New Zealand v England |
| 18. | Bridgetown, Kensington Oval | January 11, 1930 | West Indies v England |
| 19. | Wellington, Basin Reserve | January 24, 1930 | New Zealand v England |
| 20. | Port-of-Spain, Queen's Park Oval | February 1, 1930 | West Indies v England |
| 21. | Auckland, Eden Park | February 17, 1930 | New Zealand v England |

*This match was due to have started on February 14, but rain prevented any play on the first two days. February 16 was a Sunday.*

| | City and Ground | Date of First Test | Match |
|---|---|---|---|
| 22. | Georgetown, Bourda | February 21, 1930 | West Indies v England |
| 23. | Kingston, Sabina Park | April 3, 1930 | West Indies v England |
| 24. | Brisbane, Woolloongabba | November 27, 1931 | Australia v South Africa |
| 25. | Bombay, Gymkhana Ground* | December 15, 1933 | India v England |
| 26. | Calcutta, Eden Gardens | January 5, 1934 | India v England |
| 27. | Madras, Chepauk | February 10, 1934 | India v England |
| 28. | Delhi, Feroz Shah Kotla | November 10, 1948 | India v West Indies |
| 29. | Bombay, Brabourne Stadium* | December 9, 1948 | India v West Indies |
| 30. | Johannesburg, Ellis Park* | December 27, 1948 | South Africa v England |
| 31. | Kanpur, Green Park | January 12, 1952 | India v England |
| 32. | Lucknow, University Ground* | October 25, 1952 | India v Pakistan |
| 33. | Dacca, Dacca Stadium* | January 1, 1955 | Pakistan v India |
| 34. | Bahawalpur, Dring Stadium | January 15, 1955 | Pakistan v India |
| 35. | Lahore, Lawrence Gardens (Bagh-i-Jinnah)* | January 29, 1955 | Pakistan v India |
| 36. | Peshawar, Peshawar Club Ground | February 13, 1955 | Pakistan v India |
| 37. | Karachi, National Stadium | February 26, 1955 | Pakistan v India |
| 38. | Dunedin, Carisbrook | March 11, 1955 | New Zealand v England |
| 39. | Hyderabad, Fateh Maidan (Lal Bahadur Stadium) | November 19, 1955 | India v New Zealand |
| 40. | Madras Corporation Stadium* | January 6, 1956 | India v New Zealand |
| 41. | Johannesburg, New Wanderers | December 24, 1956 | South Africa v England |
| 42. | Lahore, Gaddafi Stadium | November 21, 1959 | Pakistan v Australia |
| 43. | Rawalpindi, Rawalpindi Club Ground | March 27, 1965 | Pakistan v New Zealand |
| 44. | Nagpur, Vidarbha Cricket Association Ground | October 3, 1969 | India v New Zealand |
| 45. | Perth, Western Australian Cricket Association Ground | December 11, 1970 | Australia v England |
| 46. | Hyderabad, Niaz Stadium | March 16, 1973 | Pakistan v England |
| 47. | Bangalore, Karnataka State Cricket Association Ground | November 22, 1974 | India v West Indies |
| 48. | Bombay, Wankhede Stadium | January 23, 1975 | India v West Indies |
| 49. | Faisalabad, Iqbal Park | October 16, 1978 | Pakistan v India |
| 50. | Napier, McLean Park | February 16, 1979 | New Zealand v Pakistan |
| 51. | Multan, Ibn-e-Qasim Bagh Stadium | December 30, 1980 | Pakistan v West Indies |
| 52. | St John's (Antigua), Recreation Ground | March 27, 1981 | West Indies v England |
| 53. | Colombo, P. Saravanamuttu Oval | February 17, 1982 | Sri Lanka v England |
| 54. | Kandy, Asgiriya Stadium | April 22, 1983 | Sri Lanka v Australia |
| 55. | Jullundur, Burlton Park | September 24, 1983 | India v Pakistan |
| 56. | Ahmedabad, Gujarat Stadium | November 12, 1983 | India v West Indies |
| 57. | Colombo, Sinhalese Sports Club Ground | March 16, 1984 | Sri Lanka v New Zealand |
| 58. | Colombo, Colombo Cricket Club Ground | March 24, 1984 | Sri Lanka v New Zealand |

* *Denotes no longer used for Test matches. In some instances the ground is no longer in existence.*

## LARGE ATTENDANCES

**Test Series**

| | | |
|---|---|---|
| 943,000 | Australia v England (5 Tests) | 1936-37 |
| *In England* | | |
| 549,650 | England v Australia (5 Tests) | 1953 |

**Test Match**

| | | |
|---|---|---|
| †350,534 | Australia v England, Melbourne (Third Test) | 1936-37 |
| 325,000+ | India v England, Calcutta (Second Test) | 1972-73 |
| *In England* | | |
| 158,000+ | England v Australia, Leeds (Fourth Test) | 1948 |
| 137,915 | England v Australia, Lord's (Second Test) | 1953 |

**Test Match Day**

| | | |
|---|---|---|
| 90,800 | Australia v West Indies, Melbourne (Fifth Test, 2nd day) | 1960-61 |

**Other First-Class Matches in England**

| | | |
|---|---|---|
| 80,000+ | Surrey v Yorkshire, The Oval (3 days) | 1906 |
| 78,792 | Yorkshire v Lancashire, Leeds (3 days) | 1904 |
| 76,617 | Lancashire v Yorkshire, Manchester (3 days) | 1926 |

**One-day International**

| | | |
|---|---|---|
| 86,133 | Australia v West Indies, Melbourne | 1983-84 |

† *Although no official figures are available, the attendance at the Fourth Test between India and England at Calcutta, 1981-82, was thought to have exceeded this figure.*

## LORD'S CRICKET GROUND

Lord's and the MCC were founded in 1787. The Club has enjoyed an uninterrupted career since that date, but there have been three grounds known as Lord's. The first (1787-1810) was situated where Dorset Square now is; the second (1809-13), at North Bank, had to be abandoned owing to the cutting of the Regent's Canal; and the third, opened in 1814, is the present one at St John's Wood. It was not until 1866 that the freehold of Lord's was secured by the MCC. The present pavilion was erected in 1890 at a cost of £21,000.

### HIGHEST INDIVIDUAL SCORES MADE AT LORD'S

| | | | |
|---|---|---|---|
| 316* | J. B. Hobbs | Surrey v Middlesex | 1926 |
| 315* | P. Holmes | Yorkshire v Middlesex | 1925 |
| 281* | W. H. Ponsford | Australians v MCC | 1934 |
| 278 | W. Ward | MCC v Norfolk (with E. H. Budd, T. Vigne and F. Ladbroke) | 1820 |
| 278 | D. G. Bradman | Australians v MCC | 1938 |
| 277* | E. H. Hendren | Middlesex v Kent | 1922 |

*Note:* The longest innings in a Test match at Lord's was played by S. Wettimuny (642 minutes, 190 runs) for Sri Lanka v England, 1984.

### HIGHEST TOTALS OBTAINED AT LORD'S

**First-Class Matches**

| | | |
|---|---|---|
| 729-6 | Australia v England | 1930 |
| 665 | West Indians v Middlesex | 1939 |
| 652-8 | West Indies v England | 1973 |

| | | |
|---|---|---|
| 629 | England v India | 1974 |
| 612-8 | Middlesex v Nottinghamshire | 1921 |
| 610-5 | Australians v Gentlemen | 1948 |
| 609-8 | Cambridge University v MCC and Ground | 1913 |
| 608-7 | Middlesex v Hampshire | 1919 |
| 607 | MCC and Ground v Cambridge University | 1902 |

**Minor Match**

| | | |
|---|---|---|
| 735-9 | MCC and Ground v Wiltshire | 1888 |

## BIGGEST HIT AT LORD'S

The only known instance of a batsman hitting a ball over the present pavilion at Lord's occurred when A. E. Trott, appearing for MCC against Australians on July 31, August 1, 2, 1899, drove M. A. Noble so far and high that the ball struck a chimney pot and fell behind the building.

## HIGHEST IN A MINOR COUNTY MATCH

| | | | |
|---|---|---|---|
| 323* | F. E. Lacey | Hampshire v Norfolk at Southampton | 1887 |

## HIGHEST IN MINOR COUNTIES CHAMPIONSHIP

| | | | |
|---|---|---|---|
| 282 | E. Garnett | Berkshire v Wiltshire at Reading | 1908 |
| 254 | H. E. Morgan | Glamorgan v Monmouthshire at Cardiff | 1901 |
| 253* | G. J. Whittaker | Surrey II v Gloucestershire II at The Oval | 1950 |
| 253 | A. Booth | Lancashire II v Lincolnshire at Grimsby | 1950 |
| 252 | J. A. Deed | Kent II v Surrey II at The Oval (on début) | 1924 |

## HIGHEST FOR ENGLISH PUBLIC SCHOOL

| | | | |
|---|---|---|---|
| 278 | J. L. Guise | Winchester v Eton at Eton | 1921 |

## HIGHEST IN OTHER MATCHES

| | | |
|---|---|---|
| 628* | A. E. J. Collins, Clark's House v North Town at Clifton College. (A Junior House match. His innings of 6 hours 50 minutes was spread over four afternoons.) | 1899 |
| 566 | C. J. Eady, Break-o'-Day v Wellington at Hobart | 1901-02 |
| 515 | D. R. Havewalla, B.B. and C.I. Rly v St Xavier's at Bombay | 1933-34 |
| 506* | J. C. Sharp, Melbourne GS v Geelong College at Melbourne | 1914-15 |
| 502* | Chaman Lal, Mehandra Coll., Patiala v Government Coll., Rupar at Patiala | 1956-57 |
| 485 | A. E. Stoddart, Hampstead v Stoics at Hampstead | 1886 |
| 475* | Mohammad Iqbal, Muslim Model HS v Islamia HS, Sialkot at Lahore | 1958-59 |
| 466* | G. T. S. Stevens, Beta v Lambda (University College School House match) at Neasden | 1919 |
| 459 | J. A. Prout, Wesley College v Geelong College at Geelong | 1908-09 |

## RECORD HIT

The Rev. W. Fellows, while at practice on the Christ Church ground at Oxford in 1856, drove a ball bowled by Charles Rogers 175 yards from hit to pitch.

## THROWING THE CRICKET BALL

140 yards 2 feet, Robert Percival, on the Durham Sands, Co. Durham Racecourse c1884
140 yards 9 inches, Ross Mackenzie, at Toronto .......................... 1872

*Notes:* W. F. Forbes, on March 16, 1876, threw 132 yards at the Eton College Sports. He was then 18 years of age.

William Yardley, while a boy at Rugby, threw 100 yards with his right hand and 78 yards with his left .

Charles Arnold, of Cambridge, once threw 112 yards with the wind and 108 against.

W. H. Game, at The Oval in 1875, threw the ball 111 yards and then back the same distance. W. G. Grace threw 109 yards one way and back 105, and George Millyard 108 with the wind and 103 against. At The Oval in 1868, W. G. Grace made three successive throws of 116, 117 and 118 yards, and then threw back over 100 yards. D. G. Foster (Warwickshire) threw 133 yards, and in 1930 he made a Danish record with 120.1 metres – about 130 yards.

## DATES OF FORMATION OF COUNTY CLUBS NOW FIRST-CLASS

| *County* | *First known county organisation* | *Present Club* | |
|---|---|---|---|
| | | *Original date* | *Reorganisation, if substantial* |
| Derbyshire | November 4, 1870 | November 4, 1870 | — |
| Essex | By May, 1790 | January 14, 1876 | — |
| Glamorgan | 1863 | July 6, 1888 | — |
| Gloucestershire | November 3, 1863 | 1871 | — |
| Hampshire | April 3, 1849 | August 12, 1863 | July, 1879 |
| Kent | August 6, 1842 | March 1, 1859 | December 6, 1870 |
| Lancashire | January 12, 1864 | January 12, 1864 | — |
| Leicestershire | By August, 1820 | March 25, 1879 | — |
| Middlesex | December 15, 1863 | February 2, 1864 | — |
| Northamptonshire | 1820 | 1820 | July 31, 1878 |
| Nottinghamshire | March/April, 1841 | March/April, 1841 | December 11, 1866 |
| Somerset | October 15, 1864 | August 18, 1875 | — |
| Surrey | August 22, 1845 | August 22, 1845 | — |
| Sussex | June 16, 1836 | March 1, 1839 | August, 1857 |
| Warwickshire | May, 1826 | 1882 | — |
| Worcestershire | 1844 | March 5, 1865 | — |
| Yorkshire | March 7, 1861 | January 8, 1863 | December 10, 1891 |

## DATES OF FORMATION OF CLUBS IN THE CURRENT MINOR COUNTIES CHAMPIONSHIP

| *County* | *First known county organisation* | *Present Club* |
|---|---|---|
| Bedfordshire | May, 1847 | November 3, 1899 |
| Berkshire | By May, 1841 | March 17, 1895 |
| Buckinghamshire | November, 1864 | January 15, 1891 |
| Cambridgeshire | March 13, 1844 | June 6, 1891 |
| Cheshire | 1819 | September 29, 1908 |
| Cornwall | 1813 | November 12, 1894 |

| *County* | *First known county organisation* | *Present Club* |
|---|---|---|
| Cumberland | January 2, 1884 | April 10, 1948 |
| Devon | 1824 | November 26, 1899 |
| Dorset | 1862 *or* 1871 | February 5, 1896 |
| Durham | January 24, 1874 | May 10, 1882 |
| Hertfordshire | 1838 | March 8, 1876 |
| Lincolnshire | 1853 | September 28, 1906 |
| Norfolk | January 11, 1827 | October 14, 1876 |
| Northumberland | 1834 | December, 1895 |
| Oxfordshire | 1787 | December 14, 1921 |
| Shropshire | 1819 or 1829 | June 28, 1956 |
| Staffordshire | November 24, 1871 | November 24, 1871 |
| Suffolk | July 27, 1864 | August, 1932 |
| Wiltshire | February 24, 1881 | January, 1893 |

## CONSTITUTION OF COUNTY CHAMPIONSHIP

There are references in the sporting press to a champion county as early as 1825, but the list is not continuous and in some years only two counties contested the title. The earliest reference in any cricket publication is from 1864, and at this time there were eight leading counties who have come to be regarded as first-class from that date – Cambridgeshire, Hampshire, Kent, Middlesex, Nottinghamshire, Surrey, Sussex and Yorkshire. The newly formed Lancashire club began playing inter-county matches in 1865, Gloucestershire in 1870 and Derbyshire in 1871, and they are therefore regarded as first-class from these respective dates. Cambridgeshire dropped out after 1871, Hampshire, who had not played inter-county matches in certain seasons, after 1885, and Derbyshire after 1887. Somerset, who had played matches against the first-class counties since 1879, were regarded as first-class from 1882 to 1885, and were admitted formally to the Championship in 1891. In 1894, Derbyshire, Essex, Leicestershire and Warwickshire were granted first-class status, but did not compete in the Championship until 1895 when Hampshire returned. Worcestershire, Northamptonshire and Glamorgan were admitted to the Championship in 1899, 1905 and 1921 respectively and are regarded as first-class from these dates. An invitation in 1921 to Buckinghamshire to enter the Championship was declined, owing to the lack of necessary playing facilities, and an application by Devon in 1948 was unsuccessful.

## MOST COUNTY CHAMPIONSHIP APPEARANCES

| | | | |
|---|---|---|---|
| 763 | W. Rhodes | Yorkshire | 1898-1930 |
| 707 | F. E. Woolley | Kent | 1906-38 |
| 665 | C. P. Mead | Hampshire | 1906-36 |

## MOST CONSECUTIVE COUNTY CHAMPIONSHIP APPEARANCES

| | | | |
|---|---|---|---|
| 423 | K. G. Suttle | Sussex | 1954-69 |
| 412 | J. G. Binks | Yorkshire | 1955-69 |
| 399 | J. Vine | Sussex | 1899-1914 |
| 344 | E. H. Killick | Sussex | 1898-1912 |
| 326 | C. N. Woolley | Northamptonshire | 1913-31 |
| 305 | A. H. Dyson | Glamorgan | 1930-47 |
| 301 | B. Taylor | Essex | 1961-72 |

*Notes:* J. Vine made 417 consecutive appearances for Sussex in all first-class matches between July 1900 and September 1914.

J. G. Binks did not miss a Championship match for Yorkshire between making his débût in June 1955 and retiring at the end of the 1969 season.

# FEATURES OF 1985

## Triple-Hundred and 300 Runs in a Day

I. V. A. Richards . . . 322 Somerset v Warwickshire at Taunton.

## Double-Hundreds

D. C. Boon . . . . . . . . 206* Australians v Northamptonshire at Northampton.
G. A. Gooch . . . . . . . 202 Essex v Nottinghamshire at Trent Bridge.
D. I. Gower . . . . . . . 215 England v Australia at Edgbaston.
C. G. Greenidge . . . . 204 Hampshire v Warwickshire at Edgbaston.
G. A. Hick . . . . . . . . 230 Zimbabweans v Oxford University at The Parks.
Javed Miandad . . . . . 200* Glamorgan v Australians at Neath.
C. T. Radley . . . . . . . 200 Middlesex v Northamptonshire at Uxbridge.
W. N. Slack . . . . . . . 201* Middlesex v Australians at Lord's.

## Hundred in Each Innings of a Match

G. D. Mendis . . . . . . 103 100* Sussex v Lancashire at Hastings.
R. T. Robinson . . . . . 103 130* Nottinghamshire v Glamorgan at Swansea.
C. L. Smith . . . . . . . . 110 100 Hampshire v Oxford University at The Parks.

## Fastest Hundred

(*For the Walter Lawrence Trophy*)

I. T. Botham . . . . . . . 50 balls Somerset v Warwickshire at Edgbaston.
In 49 minutes and from 26 scoring strokes – 94 in boundaries.

## Hundred Before Lunch

D. L. Bairstow . . . . . 100* Yorkshire v Leicestershire at Bradford (3rd day).
K. S. McEwan . . . . . 110 Essex v Cambridge University at Fenner's (3rd day).
A. Needham . . . . . . . 124 Surrey v Zimbabweans at The Oval (2nd day).

## Hundred on First-Class Début

A. C. Storie . . . . . . . 106 Northamptonshire v Hampshire at Northampton.
M. P. Maynard . . . . . 102 Glamorgan v Yorkshire at Swansea.

## First to 1,000 Runs

C. L. Smith (Hampshire) on June 13.

## First to 2,000 Runs

G. A. Gooch (Essex) on September 12.

## Carrying Bat Through Completed Innings

G. Boycott ........ 55* (131) Yorkshire v Surrey at Sheffield.
P. M. Roebuck† .... 33* (125) Somerset v Australians at Taunton.
W. N. Slack ....... 72* (195) Middlesex v Worcestershire at Lord's.

† *One man absent.* *Innings totals shown in brackets.*

## Most Runs off One Over

30 (662664) G. A. Gooch (off S. R. Gorman) Essex v Cambridge U. at Fenner's.

## Fifty Boundaries in an Innings

I. V. A. Richards (42 × 4, 8 × 6) Somerset v Warwickshire at Taunton.

## Twelve Sixes in an Innings

I. T. Botham Somerset v Warwickshire at Edgbaston.

## Three Sixes off Successive Balls

M. A. Lynch (off J. W. Lloyds) Surrey v Gloucestershire at The Oval.
M. P. Maynard (off P. Carrick) Glamorgan v Yorkshire at Swansea.

## Most Sixes in a Season

80 I. T. Botham (Somerset) – **world record**

## Notable Partnerships

**First Wicket**
351 G. Boycott/M. D. Moxon, Yorkshire v Worcs. at Worcester.
250* J. A. Hopkins/G. C. Holmes, Glamorgan v Worcs. at Abergavenny.

**Second Wicket**
351 G. A. Gooch/D. I. Gower, England v Australia at The Oval.
331 R. T. Robinson/D. I. Gower, England v Australia at Edgbaston.
263 N. R. Taylor/D. G. Aslett, Kent v Oxford U. at The Parks.
255 W. Larkins/R. J. Boyd-Moss, Northants v Worcs. at Worcester.
253 J. C. Balderstone/D. I. Gower, Leics. v Australians at Leicester.

**Third Wicket**
305 C. W. J. Athey/P. Bainbridge, Glos. v Derbyshire at Derby.

**Fourth Wicket**
306*† Javed Miandad/Younis Ahmed, Glam. v Australians at Neath.
277 G. A. Hick/D. L. Houghton, Zimbabweans v Oxford U. at The Parks.
259 M. C. J. Nicholas/R. A. Smith, Hampshire v Leics. at Bournemouth.

**Fifth Wicket**
289 C. T. Radley/P. R. Downton, Middlesex v Northants at Uxbridge.
252 A. J. Stewart/M. A. Lynch, Surrey v Kent at Canterbury.
227 T. S. Curtis/M. J. Weston, Worcs. v Surrey at Worcester.

**Eighth Wicket**
227† K. D. James/T. M. Tremlett, Hampshire v Somerset at Taunton.
186 K. W. R. Fletcher/D. E. East, Essex v Glos. at Southend.

**Tenth Wicket**
115 J. Stanworth/P. J. W. Allott, Lancashire v Glos. at Bristol.

† *County record.*

## Eight or More Wickets in an Innings

J. P. Agnew ....... 9-70 Leicestershire v Kent at Leicester.
A. H. Gray ........ 8-40 Surrey v Yorkshire at Sheffield.
R. J. Hadlee ....... 8-41 Nottinghamshire v Lancashire at Trent Bridge.
C. J. McDermott ... 8-141 Australia v England at Old Trafford.
V. J. Marks ....... 8-17 Somerset v Lancashire at Bath.
R. C. Ontong ...... 8-67 Glamorgan v Nottinghamshire at Trent Bridge.
G. J. Toogood ..... 8-52 Oxford University v Cambridge University at Lord's.

## Four Wickets in Five Balls

A. H. Gray........Surrey v Yorkshire at Sheffield.

## Hat-tricks

P. B. Clift ......... Leicestershire v Derbyshire at Chesterfield.
G. R. Dilley ....... Kent v Surrey at The Oval.
A. H. Gray ........ Surrey v Yorkshire at Sheffield.
P. W. Jarvis ....... Yorkshire v Derbyshire at Chesterfield.

## First to 100 Wickets

N. V. Radford (Worcestershire) on September 17.

## Match Doubles (100 Runs and 10 Wickets)

R. C. Ontong ...... 130 and 13-106 Glamorgan v Nottinghamshire at Trent Bridge.
G. J. Toogood ..... 149 and 10-93 Oxford U. v Cambridge U. at Lord's.

## 1,000 Runs and 50 Wickets

R. C. Ontong (Glamorgan).....1,121 runs and 64 wickets.

## Six or More Wicket-Keeping Dismissals in an Innings

8† D. E. East ..... (8 ct) Essex v Somerset at Taunton.
6 B. N. French ... (6 ct) Nottinghamshire v Derbyshire at Trent Bridge.

† **World record equalled** – the first eight wickets to fall.

## Highest Innings Totals

595-5 dec. ...... England v Australia at Edgbaston.
567-8 dec. ...... Middlesex v Northamptonshire at Uxbridge.
566-5 dec. ...... Somerset v Warwickshire at Taunton.
539 ............ Australia v England at Trent Bridge.
533 ............ England v Australia at Headingley.

## Lowest Innings Totals

24 .......... Oxford University v Leicestershire at The Parks.
47 .......... Oxford University v Lancashire at The Parks.
58 .......... Glamorgan v Sussex at Hove.
63 .......... Warwickshire v Surrey at The Oval.
76 .......... Australians v Hampshire at Southampton.
77 .......... Lancashire v Surrey at The Oval.

## Most Extras in an Innings

53 .......... Essex v Australians at Chelmsford.
52 .......... Leicestershire v Australians at Leicester.
52 .......... Derbyshire v Leicestershire at Chesterfield.
50 .......... England v Australia at The Oval.

## Career Aggregate Milestones†

40,000 runs ........ D. L. Amiss.
30,000 runs ........ C. H. Lloyd.
25,000 runs ........ C. T. Radley, I. V. A. Richards.
20,000 runs ........ G. A. Gooch, D. W. Randall, C. E. B. Rice.
15,000 runs ........ M. W. Gatting, D. I. Gower, W. Larkins, J. G. Wright.
10,000 runs ........ C. W. J. Athey, G. D. Mendis, G. Miller, P. M. Roebuck.
1,500 wickets ...... J. K. Lever.
1,000 wickets ...... R. J. Hadlee, Imran Khan.
500 wickets ........ A. M. Ferreira, M. A. Holding, Kapil Dev, V. J. Marks.
500 dismissals ...... B. N. French, G. W. Humpage.

† *Since September 1984.*

# FIRST-CLASS AVERAGES, 1985

## BATTING

(Qualification: 8 innings, average 10.00)

* *Signifies not out.* † *Denotes a left-handed batsman.*

| | *M* | *I* | *NO* | *R* | *HI* | *100s* | *Avge* |
|---|---|---|---|---|---|---|---|
| I. V. A. Richards (*Somerset*) | 19 | 24 | 0 | 1,836 | 322 | 9 | 76.50 |
| G. Boycott (*Yorkshire*) | 21 | 34 | 12 | 1,657 | 184 | 6 | 75.31 |
| G. A. Gooch (*Essex*) | 21 | 33 | 2 | 2,208 | 202 | 7 | 71.22 |
| I. T. Botham (*Somerset*) | 19 | 27 | 5 | 1,530 | 152 | 5 | 69.54 |
| Imran Khan (*Sussex*) | 14 | 21 | 8 | 890 | 117* | 1 | 68.46 |
| †Younis Ahmed (*Glamorgan*) | 22 | 30 | 8 | 1,421 | 177 | 5 | 64.59 |
| Javed Miandad (*Glamorgan*) | 20 | 29 | 6 | 1,441 | 200* | 4 | 62.65 |
| R. T. Robinson (*Nottinghamshire*) | 18 | 31 | 4 | 1,619 | 175 | 6 | 59.96 |
| C. L. Smith (*Hampshire*) | 23 | 39 | 4 | 2,000 | 143* | 7 | 57.14 |
| †J. G. Wright (*Derbyshire*) | 11 | 16 | 2 | 797 | 177* | 2 | 56.92 |
| M. W. Gatting (*Middlesex*) | 23 | 34 | 5 | 1,650 | 160 | 3 | 56.89 |
| P. Bainbridge (*Gloucestershire*) | 24 | 38 | 9 | 1,644 | 151* | 4 | 56.68 |
| C. E. B. Rice (*Nottinghamshire*) | 20 | 33 | 8 | 1,394 | 171* | 4 | 55.76 |
| †D. I. Gower (*Leicestershire*) | 21 | 29 | 2 | 1,477 | 215 | 6 | 54.70 |
| †W. N. Slack (*Middlesex*) | 26 | 43 | 8 | 1,900 | 201* | 4 | 54.28 |
| D. W. Randall (*Nottinghamshire*) | 25 | 47 | 7 | 2,151 | 117 | 5 | 53.77 |
| M. A. Lynch (*Surrey*) | 25 | 39 | 7 | 1,714 | 145 | 7 | 53.56 |
| C. T. Radley (*Middlesex*) | 27 | 38 | 12 | 1,375 | 200 | 3 | 52.88 |
| G. A. Hick (*Worcestershire and Zimbabweans*) | 17 | 25 | 1 | 1,265 | 230 | 4 | 52.70 |
| D. A. Thorne (*Warwickshire and Oxford U.*) | 12 | 20 | 3 | 849 | 124 | 1 | 49.94 |
| R. C. Ontong (*Glamorgan*) | 26 | 30 | 7 | 1,121 | 130 | 2 | 48.73 |
| †G. D. Barlow (*Middlesex*) | 20 | 32 | 4 | 1,343 | 141 | 6 | 47.96 |
| G. D. Mendis (*Sussex*) | 25 | 43 | 6 | 1,756 | 143* | 6 | 47.45 |
| D. L. Bairstow (*Yorkshire*) | 26 | 35 | 10 | 1,181 | 122* | 3 | 47.24 |
| †G. S. Clinton (*Surrey*) | 18 | 32 | 6 | 1,225 | 123 | 3 | 47.11 |
| N. R. Taylor (*Kent*) | 16 | 25 | 7 | 843 | 120* | 3 | 46.83 |
| C. W. J. Athey (*Gloucestershire*) | 24 | 38 | 7 | 1,442 | 170 | 5 | 46.51 |
| †D. M. Smith (*Worcestershire*) | 19 | 28 | 4 | 1,113 | 112 | 3 | 46.37 |
| P. Willey (*Leicestershire*) | 23 | 32 | 4 | 1,292 | 147 | 3 | 46.14 |
| P. M. Roebuck (*Somerset*) | 22 | 33 | 5 | 1,255 | 132* | 2 | 44.82 |
| C. J. Richards (*Surrey*) | 22 | 27 | 12 | 665 | 75* | 0 | 44.33 |
| P. A. Neale (*Worcestershire*) | 25 | 42 | 10 | 1,411 | 152* | 3 | 44.09 |
| T. E. Jesty (*Surrey*) | 24 | 36 | 8 | 1,216 | 141* | 4 | 43.42 |
| Kapil Dev (*Worcestershire*) | 12 | 21 | 2 | 816 | 100 | 1 | 42.94 |
| R. A. Smith (*Hampshire*) | 26 | 44 | 8 | 1,533 | 140* | 3 | 42.58 |
| A. M. Green (*Sussex*) | 25 | 43 | 4 | 1,646 | 133 | 3 | 42.20 |
| M. D. Moxon (*Yorkshire*) | 23 | 36 | 1 | 1,447 | 168 | 4 | 41.34 |
| C. G. Greenidge (*Hampshire*) | 19 | 32 | 2 | 1,236 | 204 | 2 | 41.20 |
| A. J. Lamb (*Northamptonshire*) | 19 | 26 | 4 | 903 | 122* | 2 | 41.04 |
| J. D. Love (*Yorkshire*) | 21 | 28 | 5 | 937 | 106 | 1 | 40.73 |
| A. C. Storie (*Northamptonshire*) | 7 | 12 | 2 | 407 | 106 | 1 | 40.70 |
| †B. C. Broad (*Nottinghamshire*) | 25 | 47 | 3 | 1,786 | 171 | 2 | 40.59 |
| K. J. Barnett (*Derbyshire*) | 25 | 41 | 2 | 1,568 | 134* | 4 | 40.20 |
| D. L. Amiss (*Warwickshire*) | 26 | 44 | 5 | 1,555 | 140 | 5 | 39.87 |
| †N. H. Fairbrother (*Lancashire*) | 25 | 39 | 4 | 1,395 | 164* | 3 | 39.85 |
| D. M. Ward (*Surrey*) | 6 | 10 | 3 | 279 | 143 | 1 | 39.85 |
| M. C. J. Nicholas (*Hampshire*) | 26 | 41 | 5 | 1,419 | 146 | 3 | 39.41 |
| P. R. Downton (*Middlesex*) | 22 | 29 | 7 | 856 | 104 | 1 | 38.90 |

| | M | I | NO | R | HI | 100s | Avge |
|---|---|---|---|---|---|---|---|
| R. J. Bailey (*Northamptonshire*) | 26 | 38 | 7 | 1,194 | 107* | 2 | 38.51 |
| †T. A. Lloyd (*Warwickshire*) | 18 | 34 | 2 | 1,230 | 160 | 2 | 38.43 |
| †K. D. James (*Hampshire*) | 8 | 11 | 4 | 268 | 124 | 1 | 38.28 |
| †S. P. Henderson (*Glamorgan*) | 7 | 12 | 4 | 306 | 111 | 1 | 38.25 |
| A. Needham (*Surrey*) | 25 | 37 | 5 | 1,223 | 138 | 3 | 38.21 |
| G. Cook (*Northamptonshire*) | 24 | 38 | 4 | 1,295 | 126 | 1 | 38.08 |
| N. F. M. Popplewell (*Somerset*) | 18 | 30 | 2 | 1,064 | 172 | 1 | 38.00 |
| R. O. Butcher (*Middlesex*) | 26 | 38 | 6 | 1,210 | 120 | 1 | 37.81 |
| G. W. Humpage (*Warwickshire*) | 25 | 42 | 6 | 1,360 | 159 | 2 | 37.77 |
| †M. R. Benson (*Kent*) | 24 | 43 | 3 | 1,501 | 162 | 3 | 37.52 |
| W. Larkins (*Northamptonshire*) | 26 | 42 | 0 | 1,549 | 163 | 3 | 36.88 |
| R. A. Harper (*Northamptonshire*) | 24 | 28 | 7 | 763 | 127 | 1 | 36.33 |
| J. C. Balderstone (*Leicestershire*) | 25 | 40 | 5 | 1,271 | 134 | 2 | 36.31 |
| †I. J. Gould (*Sussex*) | 24 | 25 | 8 | 616 | 101 | 1 | 36.23 |
| G. J. Toogood (*Oxford U.*) | 9 | 15 | 1 | 507 | 149 | 1 | 36.21 |
| B. R. Hardie (*Essex*) | 26 | 45 | 7 | 1,374 | 162 | 4 | 36.15 |
| T. A. Cotterell (*Cambridge U.*) | 9 | 12 | 4 | 289 | 69* | 0 | 36.12 |
| Asif Din (*Warwickshire*) | 6 | 11 | 2 | 325 | 89 | 0 | 36.11 |
| C. J. Tavaré (*Kent*) | 23 | 40 | 6 | 1,225 | 150* | 3 | 36.02 |
| J. J. Whitaker (*Leicestershire*) | 25 | 34 | 3 | 1,103 | 109 | 3 | 35.58 |
| †J. J. E. Hardy (*Hampshire*) | 16 | 25 | 4 | 742 | 107* | 1 | 35.33 |
| B. F. Davison (*Gloucestershire*) | 24 | 35 | 7 | 984 | 111 | 1 | 35.14 |
| G. S. le Roux (*Sussex*) | 18 | 16 | 4 | 421 | 61 | 0 | 35.08 |
| G. R. Cowdrey (*Kent*) | 6 | 9 | 2 | 242 | 53 | 0 | 34.57 |
| D. E. East (*Essex*) | 26 | 32 | 6 | 889 | 131 | 2 | 34.19 |
| †N. A. Felton (*Somerset*) | 18 | 27 | 0 | 922 | 112 | 1 | 34.14 |
| †S. G. Hinks (*Kent*) | 26 | 48 | 3 | 1,536 | 117 | 1 | 34.13 |
| P. W. G. Parker (*Sussex*) | 16 | 28 | 4 | 818 | 105 | 1 | 34.08 |
| K. S. McEwan (*Essex*) | 26 | 42 | 4 | 1,293 | 121 | 3 | 34.02 |
| G. Monkhouse (*Surrey*) | 16 | 14 | 8 | 203 | 47 | 0 | 33.83 |
| N. J. Lenham (*Sussex*) | 11 | 16 | 2 | 473 | 89 | 0 | 33.78 |
| D. G. Aslett (*Kent*) | 13 | 23 | 1 | 732 | 174 | 2 | 33.27 |
| I. P. Butcher (*Leicestershire*) | 25 | 39 | 3 | 1,192 | 120 | 1 | 33.11 |
| K. R. Brown (*Middlesex*) | 8 | 11 | 2 | 298 | 102 | 1 | 33.11 |
| V. P. Terry (*Hampshire*) | 25 | 41 | 2 | 1,284 | 148* | 2 | 32.92 |
| †R. J. Hadlee (*Nottinghamshire*) | 19 | 29 | 11 | 592 | 73* | 0 | 32.88 |
| K. W. R. Fletcher (*Essex*) | 23 | 28 | 7 | 688 | 78* | 0 | 32.76 |
| †A. R. Butcher (*Surrey*) | 26 | 46 | 3 | 1,407 | 126 | 2 | 32.72 |
| C. S. Cowdrey (*Kent*) | 20 | 36 | 3 | 1,079 | 159 | 2 | 32.69 |
| †A. I. Kallicharran (*Warwickshire*) | 21 | 35 | 2 | 1,052 | 152* | 2 | 31.87 |
| T. S. Curtis (*Worcestershire*) | 26 | 45 | 2 | 1,365 | 126* | 1 | 31.74 |
| R. A. Cobb (*Leicestershire*) | 16 | 23 | 4 | 601 | 78 | 0 | 31.63 |
| †A. J. T. Miller (*Middlesex and Oxford U.*) | 12 | 20 | 4 | 506 | 78 | 0 | 31.62 |
| J. D. Carr (*Middlesex and Oxford U.*) | 11 | 16 | 1 | 474 | 115 | 2 | 31.60 |
| A. J. Stewart (*Surrey*) | 23 | 36 | 4 | 1,009 | 158 | 1 | 31.53 |
| J. F. Steele (*Glamorgan*) | 11 | 12 | 3 | 283 | 100 | 1 | 31.44 |
| R. G. Williams (*Northamptonshire*) | 21 | 31 | 3 | 880 | 118 | 2 | 31.42 |
| J. G. Wyatt (*Somerset*) | 17 | 26 | 0 | 816 | 145 | 2 | 31.38 |
| E. A. E. Baptiste (*Kent*) | 23 | 36 | 5 | 972 | 82 | 0 | 31.35 |
| P. Johnson (*Nottinghamshire*) | 21 | 34 | 4 | 933 | 118 | 1 | 31.10 |
| D. J. Makinson (*Lancashire*) | 15 | 21 | 9 | 372 | 58* | 0 | 31.00 |
| D. W. Varey (*Lancashire*) | 22 | 34 | 3 | 960 | 112 | 1 | 30.96 |
| C. M. Wells (*Sussex*) | 26 | 37 | 6 | 960 | 100* | 1 | 30.96 |
| †R. E. Hayward (*Somerset*) | 9 | 12 | 3 | 278 | 100* | 1 | 30.88 |
| S. N. Hartley (*Yorkshire*) | 17 | 20 | 2 | 554 | 108* | 1 | 30.77 |
| G. C. Holmes (*Glamorgan*) | 27 | 40 | 3 | 1,129 | 112 | 2 | 30.51 |
| V. J. Marks (*Somerset*) | 26 | 34 | 5 | 885 | 82 | 0 | 30.51 |
| R. J. Harden (*Somerset*) | 12 | 17 | 5 | 366 | 107 | 1 | 30.50 |
| †J. W. Lloyds (*Gloucestershire*) | 25 | 33 | 6 | 818 | 101 | 1 | 30.29 |
| A. Hill (*Derbyshire*) | 10 | 14 | 3 | 333 | 120 | 1 | 30.27 |

| | *M* | *I* | *NO* | *R* | *HI* | *100s* | *Avge* |
|---|---|---|---|---|---|---|---|
| T. M. Tremlett (*Hampshire*) ....... | 24 | 29 | 14 | 450 | 102* | 1 | 30.00 |
| P. E. Robinson (*Yorkshire*) ........ | 13 | 16 | 1 | 450 | 79 | 0 | 30.00 |
| B. Roberts (*Derbyshire*) ........... | 25 | 42 | 4 | 1,128 | 100* | 2 | 29.68 |
| D. B. D'Oliveira (*Worcestershire*) ... | 26 | 44 | 2 | 1,244 | 139 | 2 | 29.61 |
| T. Davies (*Glamorgan*) ............ | 26 | 25 | 8 | 503 | 75 | 0 | 29.58 |
| D. P. Hughes (*Lancashire*) ......... | 10 | 16 | 2 | 411 | 75* | 0 | 29.35 |
| †D. J. Wild (*Northamptonshire*) ...... | 18 | 22 | 4 | 525 | 80 | 0 | 29.16 |
| M. J. Weston (*Worcestershire*) ...... | 19 | 30 | 1 | 845 | 132 | 1 | 29.13 |
| R. I. H. B. Dyer (*Warwickshire*) .... | 26 | 46 | 3 | 1,242 | 109* | 2 | 28.88 |
| †D. R. Turner (*Hampshire*) ......... | 7 | 9 | 2 | 202 | 49* | 0 | 28.85 |
| D. J. R. Martindale (*Nottinghamshire*) | 9 | 14 | 3 | 317 | 104* | 1 | 28.81 |
| A. M. Ferreira (*Warwickshire*) ..... | 25 | 38 | 10 | 805 | 101* | 1 | 28.75 |
| G. Miller (*Derbyshire*) ............ | 21 | 31 | 5 | 744 | 105 | 1 | 28.61 |
| †P. G. P. Roebuck (*Cambridge U.*) .. | 9 | 15 | 3 | 343 | 82 | 0 | 28.58 |
| J. E. Morris (*Derbyshire*) .......... | 18 | 27 | 1 | 722 | 109* | 1 | 27.76 |
| J. E. Emburey (*Middlesex*) ........ | 25 | 25 | 4 | 581 | 68 | 0 | 27.66 |
| J. F. Sykes (*Middlesex*) ........... | 11 | 13 | 3 | 275 | 126 | 1 | 27.50 |
| I. S. Anderson (*Derbyshire*) ........ | 19 | 35 | 3 | 876 | 95 | 0 | 27.37 |
| R. J. Boyd-Moss (*Northamptonshire*) . | 20 | 31 | 3 | 766 | 121 | 2 | 27.35 |
| †G. J. Lord (*Warwickshire*) ......... | 8 | 11 | 1 | 271 | 199 | 1 | 27.10 |
| †R. M. Ellison (*Kent*) ............. | 18 | 26 | 6 | 539 | 98 | 0 | 26.95 |
| †H. Morris (*Glamorgan*) ............ | 15 | 18 | 4 | 375 | 62 | 0 | 26.78 |
| D. N. Patel (*Worcestershire*) ....... | 26 | 42 | 3 | 1,042 | 88 | 0 | 26.71 |
| †J. Abrahams (*Lancashire*) ......... | 25 | 39 | 4 | 932 | 101* | 1 | 26.62 |
| P. J. Prichard (*Essex*) ............ | 21 | 34 | 4 | 779 | 95 | 0 | 25.96 |
| R. J. Blakey (*Yorkshire*) ........... | 14 | 22 | 2 | 518 | 90 | 0 | 25.90 |
| R. B. Phillips (*Australians and Rest of World XI*) .............. | 8 | 9 | 2 | 180 | 39 | 0 | 25.71 |
| M. R. Chadwick (*Lancashire*) ...... | 12 | 17 | 1 | 410 | 132 | 1 | 25.62 |
| S. J. Rhodes (*Worcestershire*) ....... | 26 | 34 | 13 | 538 | 58* | 0 | 25.61 |
| J. D. Birch (*Nottinghamshire*) ....... | 14 | 23 | 7 | 409 | 68* | 0 | 25.56 |
| †A. L. Jones (*Glamorgan*) .......... | 19 | 27 | 2 | 636 | 80 | 0 | 25.44 |
| K. P. Tomlins (*Middlesex*) ........ | 9 | 15 | 1 | 354 | 58 | 0 | 25.28 |
| R. J. Parks (*Hampshire*) ........... | 25 | 24 | 9 | 377 | 53* | 0 | 25.13 |
| †K. Sharp (*Yorkshire*) ............. | 20 | 34 | 4 | 750 | 96 | 0 | 25.00 |
| †C. Gladwin (*Essex*) ............... | 13 | 22 | 2 | 500 | 92* | 0 | 25.00 |
| †R. A. Pick (*Nottinghamshire*) ....... | 13 | 15 | 5 | 250 | 63 | 0 | 25.00 |
| D. J. Capel (*Northamptonshire*) ..... | 23 | 30 | 6 | 599 | 81 | 0 | 24.95 |
| J. A. Hopkins (*Glamorgan*) ........ | 23 | 34 | 2 | 794 | 114* | 1 | 24.81 |
| M. D. Marshall (*Hampshire*) ....... | 22 | 33 | 2 | 768 | 66* | 0 | 24.77 |
| M. Watkinson (*Lancashire*) ........ | 19 | 29 | 1 | 692 | 106 | 1 | 24.71 |
| M. A. Garnham (*Leicestershire*) .... | 23 | 26 | 4 | 542 | 100 | 1 | 24.63 |
| K. M. Curran (*Gloucestershire*) ..... | 26 | 34 | 3 | 762 | 83 | 0 | 24.58 |
| D. B. Pauline (*Surrey*) ............ | 13 | 18 | 2 | 392 | 77 | 0 | 24.50 |
| K. R. Pont (*Essex*) ............... | 10 | 15 | 3 | 294 | 62* | 0 | 24.50 |
| †B. C. Rose (*Somerset*) ............ | 5 | 9 | 1 | 196 | 81* | 0 | 24.50 |
| A. Sidebottom (*Yorkshire*) ......... | 11 | 11 | 3 | 196 | 55 | 0 | 24.50 |
| D. R. Pringle (*Essex*) ............. | 23 | 31 | 4 | 654 | 121* | 1 | 24.22 |
| P. A. Smith (*Warwickshire*) ........ | 24 | 37 | 3 | 815 | 93 | 0 | 23.97 |
| R. J. Doughty (*Surrey*) ........... | 11 | 12 | 2 | 239 | 65 | 0 | 23.90 |
| M. S. Turner (*Somerset*) .......... | 10 | 12 | 6 | 143 | 24* | 0 | 23.83 |
| M. Newell (*Nottinghamshire*) ....... | 7 | 13 | 0 | 309 | 74 | 0 | 23.76 |
| P. B. Clift (*Leicestershire*) ......... | 22 | 26 | 5 | 495 | 106 | 1 | 23.57 |
| P. Carrick (*Yorkshire*) ............ | 24 | 25 | 2 | 540 | 92 | 0 | 23.47 |
| J. R. T. Barclay (*Sussex*) .......... | 22 | 17 | 6 | 257 | 37* | 0 | 23.36 |
| P. G. Newman (*Derbyshire*) ....... | 20 | 29 | 3 | 604 | 115 | 1 | 23.23 |
| A. P. Wells (*Sussex*) .............. | 23 | 33 | 7 | 600 | 102 | 1 | 23.07 |
| N. E. Briers (*Leicestershire*) ........ | 23 | 29 | 4 | 576 | 129 | 1 | 23.04 |
| M. A. Holding (*Derbyshire*) ........ | 12 | 19 | 1 | 413 | 80 | 0 | 22.94 |
| A. E. Lea (*Cambridge U.*) ......... | 8 | 15 | 2 | 298 | 47* | 0 | 22.92 |
| R. J. Maru (*Hampshire*) ........... | 23 | 19 | 9 | 227 | 62 | 0 | 22.70 |

| | M | I | NO | R | HI | 100s | Avge |
|---|---|---|---|---|---|---|---|
| †M. R. Davis (*Somerset*) | 18 | 20 | 6 | 315 | 40* | 0 | 22.50 |
| W. R. Bristowe (*Oxford U.*) | 5 | 8 | 1 | 156 | 42* | 0 | 22.28 |
| P. W. Romaines (*Gloucestershire*) | 20 | 34 | 4 | 667 | 114* | 1 | 22.23 |
| N. F. Williams (*Middlesex*) | 22 | 21 | 4 | 378 | 67 | 0 | 22.23 |
| D. J. Fell (*Cambridge U.*) | 9 | 16 | 1 | 332 | 109* | 1 | 22.13 |
| I. A. Greig (*Sussex*) | 15 | 16 | 4 | 264 | 43 | 0 | 22.00 |
| A. W. Lilley (*Essex*) | 16 | 26 | 2 | 516 | 68* | 0 | 21.50 |
| A. A. Metcalfe (*Yorkshire*) | 6 | 12 | 0 | 257 | 109 | 1 | 21.41 |
| N. G. Cowley (*Hampshire*) | 13 | 14 | 4 | 213 | 51 | 0 | 21.30 |
| P. J. Newport (*Worcestershire*) | 18 | 26 | 10 | 338 | 36 | 0 | 21.12 |
| R. Sharma (*Derbyshire*) | 7 | 12 | 2 | 209 | 41* | 0 | 20.90 |
| †A. N. Jones (*Sussex*) | 12 | 9 | 5 | 83 | 26 | 0 | 20.75 |
| †C. H. Dredge (*Somerset*) | 15 | 13 | 7 | 124 | 31 | 0 | 20.66 |
| G. V. Palmer (*Somerset*) | 8 | 11 | 3 | 164 | 45* | 0 | 20.50 |
| W. P. Fowler (*Derbyshire*) | 10 | 14 | 1 | 266 | 79 | 0 | 20.46 |
| A. P. E. Knott (*Kent*) | 19 | 24 | 5 | 379 | 87* | 0 | 19.94 |
| P. J. Hartley (*Yorkshire*) | 12 | 11 | 3 | 159 | 35 | 0 | 19.87 |
| A. W. Stovold (*Gloucestershire*) | 22 | 37 | 2 | 694 | 112 | 2 | 19.82 |
| D. G. Moir (*Derbyshire*) | 8 | 9 | 0 | 178 | 46 | 0 | 19.77 |
| G. W. Johnson (*Kent*) | 11 | 16 | 4 | 237 | 30* | 0 | 19.75 |
| M. R. Price (*Glamorgan*) | 14 | 11 | 4 | 136 | 36 | 0 | 19.42 |
| A. J. Wright (*Gloucestershire*) | 9 | 16 | 3 | 249 | 47* | 0 | 19.15 |
| J. G. Thomas (*Glamorgan*) | 16 | 16 | 2 | 268 | 60* | 0 | 19.14 |
| D. A. Graveney (*Gloucestershire*) | 24 | 25 | 11 | 266 | 53* | 0 | 19.00 |
| R. S. Rutnagur (*Oxford U.*) | 11 | 15 | 2 | 246 | 66 | 0 | 18.92 |
| L. Potter (*Kent*) | 13 | 15 | 2 | 245 | 58 | 0 | 18.84 |
| S. P. Hughes (*Middlesex*) | 12 | 11 | 6 | 94 | 30* | 0 | 18.80 |
| P. C. MacLarnon (*Oxford U.*) | 7 | 10 | 1 | 168 | 56 | 0 | 18.66 |
| J. Simmons (*Lancashire*) | 21 | 30 | 4 | 485 | 101 | 1 | 18.65 |
| P. A. C. Bail (*Somerset*) | 5 | 9 | 2 | 127 | 78* | 0 | 18.14 |
| P. J. W. Allott (*Lancashire*) | 19 | 21 | 6 | 272 | 78 | 0 | 18.13 |
| †C. R. Andrew (*Cambridge U.*) | 8 | 15 | 1 | 253 | 66 | 0 | 18.07 |
| S. R. Gorman (*Cambridge U.*) | 9 | 15 | 5 | 177 | 43 | 0 | 17.70 |
| E. E. Hemmings (*Nottinghamshire*) | 21 | 22 | 5 | 297 | 56* | 0 | 17.47 |
| A. E. Warner (*Derbyshire*) | 15 | 20 | 2 | 314 | 60 | 0 | 17.44 |
| †G. Fowler (*Lancashire*) | 16 | 25 | 0 | 428 | 88 | 0 | 17.12 |
| †R. L. Ollis (*Somerset*) | 15 | 20 | 1 | 325 | 55 | 0 | 17.10 |
| N. V. Radford (*Worcestershire*) | 24 | 25 | 7 | 306 | 57* | 0 | 17.00 |
| D. A. Reeve (*Sussex*) | 17 | 15 | 5 | 170 | 56 | 0 | 17.00 |
| B. N. French (*Nottinghamshire*) | 25 | 34 | 8 | 439 | 52* | 0 | 16.88 |
| D. A. Hagan (*Oxford U.*) | 5 | 10 | 1 | 148 | 46 | 0 | 16.44 |
| N. A. Foster (*Essex*) | 15 | 14 | 2 | 196 | 63 | 0 | 16.33 |
| C. D. M. Tooley (*Oxford U.*) | 11 | 16 | 0 | 257 | 66 | 0 | 16.06 |
| C. A. Walsh (*Gloucestershire*) | 21 | 18 | 6 | 189 | 37 | 0 | 15.75 |
| N. A. Mallender (*Northamptonshire*) | 24 | 25 | 8 | 267 | 52* | 0 | 15.70 |
| S. C. Booth (*Somerset*) | 11 | 8 | 3 | 78 | 28 | 0 | 15.60 |
| P. I. Pocock (*Surrey*) | 24 | 18 | 6 | 183 | 41 | 0 | 15.25 |
| G. C. Small (*Warwickshire*) | 21 | 27 | 8 | 285 | 31* | 0 | 15.00 |
| K. D. Smith (*Warwickshire*) | 5 | 9 | 1 | 120 | 42 | 0 | 15.00 |
| J. D. Inchmore (*Worcestershire*) | 17 | 9 | 2 | 100 | 24 | 0 | 14.28 |
| †G. J. Parsons (*Leicestershire*) | 16 | 16 | 4 | 170 | 32 | 0 | 14.16 |
| R. J. Finney (*Derbyshire*) | 25 | 37 | 10 | 381 | 82 | 0 | 14.11 |
| †A. Walker (*Northamptonshire*) | 12 | 14 | 8 | 83 | 18* | 0 | 13.83 |
| I. Folley (*Lancashire*) | 21 | 27 | 8 | 262 | 69 | 0 | 13.78 |
| J. K. Lever (*Essex*) | 23 | 23 | 9 | 193 | 24* | 0 | 13.78 |
| R. K. Illingworth (*Worcestershire*) | 20 | 20 | 8 | 165 | 39* | 0 | 13.75 |
| T. Gard (*Somerset*) | 26 | 26 | 4 | 294 | 47 | 0 | 13.36 |
| †R. C. Russell (*Gloucestershire*) | 23 | 23 | 4 | 253 | 34 | 0 | 13.31 |
| S. J. O'Shaughnessy (*Lancashire*) | 13 | 23 | 2 | 275 | 63 | 0 | 13.09 |
| P. H. Edmonds (*Middlesex*) | 23 | 23 | 6 | 221 | 29* | 0 | 13.00 |
| P. A. J. De Freitas (*Leicestershire*) | 9 | 12 | 3 | 117 | 30* | 0 | 13.00 |

| | M | I | NO | R | HI | 100s | Avge |
|---|---|---|---|---|---|---|---|
| C. A. Connor (*Hampshire*) | 17 | 9 | 4 | 65 | 36 | 0 | 13.00 |
| †D. J. Thomas (*Surrey*) | 12 | 12 | 3 | 116 | 25* | 0 | 12.88 |
| A. R. K. Pierson (*Warwickshire*) | 12 | 14 | 7 | 90 | 17* | 0 | 12.85 |
| N. G. B. Cook (*Leicestershire*) | 18 | 16 | 4 | 152 | 45 | 0 | 12.66 |
| B. J. M. Maher (*Derbyshire*) | 14 | 18 | 6 | 150 | 46 | 0 | 12.50 |
| D. V. Lawrence (*Gloucestershire*) | 25 | 26 | 5 | 259 | 41 | 0 | 12.33 |
| J. Derrick (*Glamorgan*) | 14 | 15 | 2 | 160 | 52 | 0 | 12.30 |
| M. A. Fell (*Derbyshire*) | 5 | 8 | 0 | 98 | 27 | 0 | 12.25 |
| T. Patel (*Oxford U.*) | 9 | 17 | 4 | 159 | 47 | 0 | 12.23 |
| C. Maynard (*Lancashire*) | 19 | 27 | 5 | 266 | 43 | 0 | 12.09 |
| S. D. Fletcher (*Yorkshire*) | 14 | 10 | 7 | 36 | 15* | 0 | 12.00 |
| S. Wall (*Warwickshire*) | 12 | 16 | 5 | 128 | 28 | 0 | 11.63 |
| †K. E. Cooper (*Nottinghamshire*) | 22 | 16 | 4 | 139 | 46 | 0 | 11.58 |
| J. Garner (*Somerset*) | 15 | 11 | 3 | 92 | 22 | 0 | 11.50 |
| N. S. Taylor (*Surrey*) | 7 | 8 | 3 | 57 | 21* | 0 | 11.40 |
| C. Marples (*Derbyshire*) | 11 | 15 | 5 | 114 | 34 | 0 | 11.40 |
| Andrew G. Davies (*Cambridge U.*) | 9 | 13 | 2 | 124 | 43* | 0 | 11.27 |
| I. G. Swallow (*Yorkshire*) | 10 | 11 | 2 | 101 | 25* | 0 | 11.22 |
| †G. R. Dilley (*Kent*) | 17 | 19 | 5 | 153 | 31 | 0 | 10.92 |
| P. W. Jarvis (*Yorkshire*) | 14 | 16 | 2 | 151 | 28 | 0 | 10.78 |
| J. P. Agnew (*Leicestershire*) | 16 | 15 | 3 | 121 | 36 | 0 | 10.08 |
| N. G. Cowans (*Middlesex*) | 24 | 17 | 4 | 130 | 22* | 0 | 10.00 |

## BOWLING

(Qualification: 10 wickets in 10 innings)

† *Denotes left-arm bowler.*

| | O | M | R | W | BB | Avge |
|---|---|---|---|---|---|---|
| R. M. Ellison (*Kent*) | 432.1 | 113 | 1,118 | 65 | 7-87 | 17.20 |
| R. J. Hadlee (*Nottinghamshire*) | 473.5 | 136 | 1,026 | 59 | 8-41 | 17.38 |
| M. D. Marshall (*Hampshire*) | 688.1 | 193 | 1,680 | 95 | 7-59 | 17.68 |
| †G. E. Sainsbury (*Gloucestershire*) | 178 | 59 | 481 | 27 | 7-38 | 17.81 |
| C. A. Walsh (*Gloucestershire*) | 560.3 | 124 | 1,706 | 85 | 7-51 | 20.07 |
| Imran Khan (*Sussex*) | 422.1 | 114 | 1,040 | 51 | 5-49 | 20.39 |
| T. M. Tremlett (*Hampshire*) | 665.5 | 181 | 1,620 | 75 | 5-42 | 21.60 |
| Kapil Dev (*Worcestershire*) | 304.5 | 83 | 805 | 37 | 4-56 | 21.75 |
| M. A. Holding (*Derbyshire*) | 354.5 | 67 | 1,124 | 50 | 6-65 | 22.48 |
| P. J. W. Allott (*Lancashire*) | 560.2 | 167 | 1,328 | 58 | 6-71 | 22.89 |
| L. B. Taylor (*Leicestershire*) | 566.5 | 141 | 1,376 | 60 | 5-45 | 22.93 |
| N. G. Cowans (*Middlesex*) | 474.2 | 85 | 1,676 | 73 | 6-31 | 22.95 |
| A. H. Gray (*Surrey*) | 524 | 99 | 1,816 | 79 | 8-40 | 22.98 |
| K. M. Curran (*Gloucestershire*) | 469.5 | 104 | 1,419 | 61 | 5-35 | 23.26 |
| J. Garner (*Somerset*) | 295.4 | 75 | 739 | 31 | 5-46 | 23.83 |
| D. V. Lawrence (*Gloucestershire*) | 544.5 | 66 | 2,093 | 85 | 7-48 | 24.62 |
| N. V. Radford (*Worcestershire*) | 779.4 | 130 | 2,493 | 101 | 6-45 | 24.68 |
| †D. A. Graveney (*Gloucestershire*) | 410.1 | 133 | 1,013 | 41 | 4-91 | 24.70 |
| R. J. Doughty (*Surrey*) | 223.5 | 36 | 867 | 34 | 6-33 | 25.50 |
| †P. H. Edmonds (*Middlesex*) | 850.1 | 243 | 1,942 | 76 | 6-87 | 25.55 |
| J. D. Inchmore (*Worcestershire*) | 338.5 | 71 | 844 | 33 | 4-42 | 25.57 |
| K. E. Cooper (*Nottinghamshire*) | 604.3 | 187 | 1,566 | 61 | 7-10 | 25.67 |
| †J. K. Lever (*Essex*) | 720.3 | 188 | 1,995 | 77 | 6-47 | 25.90 |
| P. A. J. De Freitas (*Leicestershire*) | 234.2 | 43 | 703 | 27 | 5-39 | 26.03 |
| †R. J. Maru (*Hampshire*) | 704.5 | 197 | 1,923 | 73 | 5-16 | 26.34 |
| P. J. Newport (*Worcestershire*) | 362.2 | 57 | 1,214 | 46 | 5-18 | 26.39 |
| M. W. Gatting (*Middlesex*) | 92.5 | 17 | 293 | 11 | 3-55 | 26.63 |
| G. A. Gooch (*Essex*) | 284.2 | 66 | 773 | 29 | 5-46 | 26.65 |
| G. Monkhouse (*Surrey*) | 383.4 | 78 | 1,068 | 40 | 5-61 | 26.70 |

| | *O* | *M* | *R* | *W* | *BB* | *Avge* |
|---|---|---|---|---|---|---|
| W. W. Daniel (*Middlesex*) | 575.1 | 90 | 2,111 | 79 | 7-62 | 26.72 |
| G. C. Small (*Warwickshire*) | 592.3 | 114 | 1,850 | 69 | 5-24 | 26.81 |
| †D. L. Underwood (*Kent*) | 807 | 290 | 1,802 | 67 | 6-56 | 26.89 |
| J. W. Lloyds (*Gloucestershire*) | 180.1 | 42 | 575 | 21 | 5-37 | 27.38 |
| †R. J. Finney (*Derbyshire*) | 449.3 | 81 | 1,453 | 53 | 7-61 | 27.41 |
| J. P. Agnew (*Leicestershire*) | 445.4 | 89 | 1,512 | 55 | 9-70 | 27.49 |
| N. A. Foster (*Essex*) | 436.5 | 87 | 1,434 | 52 | 5-40 | 27.57 |
| R. C. Ontong (*Glamorgan*) | 586.5 | 145 | 1,777 | 64 | 8-67 | 27.76 |
| B. P. Patterson (*Lancashire*) | 364.3 | 59 | 1,144 | 41 | 7-49 | 27.90 |
| N. G. Cowley (*Hampshire*) | 247.5 | 60 | 699 | 25 | 3-17 | 27.96 |
| A. M. Ferreira (*Warwickshire*) | 673.3 | 129 | 2,167 | 77 | 5-41 | 28.14 |
| P. Willey (*Leicestershire*) | 399.3 | 117 | 1,017 | 36 | 6-43 | 28.25 |
| †R. K. Illingworth (*Worcestershire*) | 406.5 | 116 | 1,046 | 37 | 7-50 | 28.27 |
| G. S. le Roux (*Sussex*) | 402.2 | 72 | 1,132 | 40 | 6-46 | 28.30 |
| E. A. E. Baptiste (*Kent*) | 562 | 116 | 1,661 | 58 | 6-42 | 28.63 |
| B. J. Griffiths (*Northamptonshire*) | 313.4 | 76 | 918 | 32 | 6-76 | 28.68 |
| D. R. Pringle (*Essex*) | 604.1 | 146 | 1,556 | 53 | 6-42 | 29.35 |
| J. E. Emburey (*Middlesex*) | 797.1 | 230 | 1,737 | 59 | 6-35 | 29.44 |
| J. R. T. Barclay (*Sussex*) | 300.4 | 55 | 913 | 31 | 6-78 | 29.45 |
| †P. Carrick (*Yorkshire*) | 712.3 | 184 | 1,923 | 65 | 7-99 | 29.58 |
| D. A. Reeve (*Sussex*) | 475.5 | 107 | 1,424 | 48 | 5-24 | 29.66 |
| P. Bainbridge (*Gloucestershire*) | 200 | 46 | 570 | 19 | 5-60 | 30.00 |
| P. W. Jarvis (*Yorkshire*) | 371.5 | 53 | 1,330 | 44 | 7-105 | 30.22 |
| K. J. Barnett (*Derbyshire*) | 173.4 | 33 | 514 | 17 | 6-115 | 30.23 |
| N. F. Williams (*Middlesex*) | 490.2 | 69 | 1,784 | 58 | 5-15 | 30.75 |
| P. B. Clift (*Leicestershire*) | 593.3 | 169 | 1,446 | 47 | 5-38 | 30.76 |
| O. H. Mortensen (*Derbyshire*) | 340 | 75 | 1,026 | 33 | 5-87 | 31.09 |
| C. E. B. Rice (*Nottinghamshire*) | 284 | 82 | 779 | 25 | 4-24 | 31.16 |
| I. T. Botham (*Somerset*) | 406.2 | 67 | 1,376 | 44 | 5-109 | 31.27 |
| N. A. Mallender (*Northamptonshire*) | 521.4 | 98 | 1,533 | 49 | 5-83 | 31.28 |
| P. G. Newman (*Derbyshire*) | 400.5 | 76 | 1,315 | 42 | 4-29 | 31.30 |
| †I. Folley (*Lancashire*) | 453.3 | 113 | 1,286 | 41 | 6-8 | 31.36 |
| M. Watkinson (*Lancashire*) | 420.1 | 94 | 1,228 | 39 | 5-109 | 31.48 |
| J. G. Thomas (*Glamorgan*) | 340.3 | 51 | 1,232 | 39 | 4-47 | 31.58 |
| D. J. Capel (*Northamptonshire*) | 384.3 | 63 | 1,299 | 41 | 7-62 | 31.68 |
| P. A. Waterman (*Surrey*) | 115 | 25 | 382 | 12 | 3-22 | 31.83 |
| N. S. Taylor (*Surrey*) | 149 | 22 | 579 | 18 | 7-44 | 32.16 |
| K. B. S. Jarvis (*Kent*) | 530.4 | 115 | 1,674 | 51 | 5-43 | 32.82 |
| S. J. W. Andrew (*Hampshire*) | 284 | 53 | 992 | 30 | 6-43 | 33.06 |
| C. Penn (*Kent*) | 124.4 | 17 | 466 | 14 | 4-63 | 33.28 |
| A. C. S. Pigott (*Sussex*) | 184.4 | 39 | 633 | 19 | 3-22 | 33.31 |
| †N. Gifford (*Warwickshire*) | 611.5 | 188 | 1,541 | 46 | 5-128 | 33.50 |
| G. R. Dilley (*Kent*) | 350.2 | 71 | 1,075 | 32 | 5-53 | 33.59 |
| V. J. Marks (*Somerset*) | 812.4 | 197 | 2,421 | 72 | 8-17 | 33.62 |
| †D. J. Makinson (*Lancashire*) | 366 | 68 | 1,079 | 32 | 5-60 | 33.71 |
| P. I. Pocock (*Surrey*) | 576.2 | 131 | 1,632 | 48 | 7-42 | 34.00 |
| A. Walker (*Northamptonshire*) | 251.4 | 51 | 786 | 23 | 4-38 | 34.17 |
| S. J. O'Shaughnessy (*Lancashire*) | 142 | 21 | 521 | 15 | 4-68 | 34.73 |
| S. Wall (*Warwickshire*) | 301.1 | 44 | 973 | 28 | 4-59 | 34.75 |
| †A. M. G. Scott (*Cambridge U.*) | 243.3 | 34 | 879 | 25 | 5-68 | 35.16 |
| A. Sidebottom (*Yorkshire*) | 268.4 | 38 | 916 | 26 | 4-70 | 35.23 |
| D. B. Pauline (*Surrey*) | 161.4 | 32 | 567 | 16 | 5-52 | 35.43 |
| C. M. Old (*Warwickshire*) | 153.2 | 38 | 466 | 13 | 6-68 | 35.84 |
| P. M. Such (*Nottinghamshire*) | 405.1 | 105 | 1,152 | 32 | 5-73 | 36.00 |
| J. D. Carr (*Middlesex and Oxford U.*) | 249.1 | 65 | 616 | 17 | 6-61 | 36.23 |
| R. A. Harper (*Northamptonshire*) | 775.3 | 192 | 2,107 | 58 | 5-94 | 36.32 |
| D. N. Patel (*Worcestershire*) | 442 | 117 | 1,244 | 34 | 3-33 | 36.58 |
| †L. Potter (*Kent*) | 258.3 | 67 | 772 | 21 | 4-87 | 36.76 |
| T. E. Jesty (*Surrey*) | 144.2 | 28 | 517 | 14 | 2-32 | 36.92 |
| †D. J. Thomas (*Surrey*) | 361.4 | 62 | 1,186 | 32 | 5-51 | 37.06 |
| C. H. Dredge (*Somerset*) | 317.4 | 73 | 929 | 25 | 5-95 | 37.16 |

| | O | M | R | W | BB | Avge |
|---|---|---|---|---|---|---|
| I. A. Greig (*Sussex*) | 283 | 58 | 931 | 25 | 5-80 | 37.24 |
| P. J. Hartley (*Yorkshire*) | 315.5 | 40 | 1,175 | 31 | 5-75 | 37.90 |
| †R. J. Boyd-Moss (*Northamptonshire*) | 125.4 | 30 | 380 | 10 | 3-48 | 38.00 |
| S. R. Barwick (*Glamorgan*) | 473.4 | 96 | 1,376 | 36 | 7-43 | 38.22 |
| E. E. Hemmings (*Nottinghamshire*) | 716.3 | 171 | 2,103 | 55 | 6-51 | 38.23 |
| C. M. Wells (*Sussex*) | 537.4 | 144 | 1,457 | 38 | 4-76 | 38.34 |
| G. J. Toogood (*Oxford U.*) | 209.2 | 44 | 691 | 18 | 8-52 | 38.38 |
| K. Saxelby (*Nottinghamshire*) | 429 | 103 | 1,385 | 36 | 6-64 | 38.47 |
| G. C. Holmes (*Glamorgan*) | 347.3 | 86 | 1,041 | 27 | 4-49 | 38.55 |
| J. Simmons (*Lancashire*) | 543.1 | 155 | 1,427 | 37 | 4-55 | 38.56 |
| S. P. Hughes (*Middlesex*) | 266.2 | 43 | 932 | 24 | 5-64 | 38.83 |
| S. M. McEwan (*Worcestershire*) | 178 | 29 | 635 | 16 | 3-47 | 39.68 |
| D. S. Hoffman (*Warwickshire*) | 326.4 | 55 | 1,160 | 29 | 4-100 | 40.00 |
| C. Shaw (*Yorkshire*) | 417 | 95 | 1,286 | 32 | 5-76 | 40.18 |
| †S. C. Booth (*Somerset*) | 390.2 | 112 | 1,138 | 28 | 4-88 | 40.64 |
| R. G. Williams (*Northamptonshire*) | 312.2 | 75 | 979 | 24 | 5-34 | 40.79 |
| D. L. Acfield (*Essex*) | 588.4 | 130 | 1,674 | 41 | 6-81 | 40.82 |
| M. J. Weston (*Worcestershire*) | 273.5 | 72 | 777 | 19 | 3-37 | 40.89 |
| †M. R. Price (*Glamorgan*) | 258.4 | 63 | 697 | 17 | 4-97 | 41.00 |
| C. A. Connor (*Hampshire*) | 467.5 | 91 | 1,467 | 35 | 4-62 | 41.91 |
| R. A. Pick (*Nottinghamshire*) | 290 | 52 | 1,096 | 26 | 4-51 | 42.15 |
| A. E. Warner (*Derbyshire*) | 267.3 | 40 | 1,013 | 24 | 5-51 | 42.20 |
| †K. D. James (*Hampshire*) | 177.4 | 43 | 635 | 15 | 6-22 | 42.33 |
| A. N. Jones (*Sussex*) | 246 | 37 | 848 | 20 | 5-39 | 42.40 |
| G. Miller (*Derbyshire*) | 385.2 | 77 | 1,204 | 28 | 6-110 | 43.00 |
| G. J. Parsons (*Leicestershire*) | 356.2 | 75 | 1,010 | 23 | 6-11 | 43.91 |
| P. A. Smith (*Warwickshire*) | 237.2 | 24 | 1,143 | 26 | 4-25 | 43.96 |
| †C. E. Waller (*Sussex*) | 381.5 | 117 | 882 | 20 | 7-61 | 44.10 |
| A. Needham (*Surrey*) | 351.4 | 76 | 1,017 | 23 | 5-42 | 44.21 |
| J. F. Sykes (*Middlesex*) | 191.5 | 42 | 575 | 13 | 3-58 | 44.23 |
| †N. G. B. Cook (*Leicestershire*) | 558.1 | 186 | 1,332 | 30 | 4-59 | 44.40 |
| †A. R. Butcher (*Surrey*) | 158 | 35 | 449 | 10 | 3-43 | 44.90 |
| C. C. Ellison (*Cambridge U.*) | 223.5 | 58 | 591 | 13 | 3-76 | 45.46 |
| G. W. Johnson (*Kent*) | 156.3 | 24 | 501 | 11 | 5-78 | 45.54 |
| S. D. Fletcher (*Yorkshire*) | 345.5 | 48 | 1,253 | 26 | 4-91 | 48.19 |
| R. S. Rutnagur (*Oxford U.*) | 189 | 25 | 728 | 15 | 5-112 | 48.53 |
| M. S. Turner (*Somerset*) | 185.5 | 30 | 648 | 13 | 4-74 | 49.84 |
| S. J. Malone (*Glamorgan*) | 174.1 | 23 | 654 | 13 | 5-38 | 50.30 |
| C. S. Cowdrey (*Kent*) | 210.1 | 29 | 756 | 15 | 3-5 | 50.40 |
| J. Derrick (*Glamorgan*) | 226.1 | 39 | 706 | 14 | 4-60 | 50.42 |
| †D. A. Thorne (*Warwickshire and Oxford U.*) | 196.1 | 34 | 664 | 13 | 4-64 | 51.07 |
| †M. R. Davis (*Somerset*) | 366 | 60 | 1,249 | 24 | 4-83 | 52.04 |
| †J. F. Steele (*Glamorgan*) | 215.1 | 60 | 581 | 11 | 3-6 | 52.81 |
| G. J. F. Ferris (*Leicestershire*) | 231.3 | 32 | 826 | 15 | 3-84 | 55.06 |
| I. G. Swallow (*Yorkshire*) | 225 | 46 | 670 | 12 | 4-53 | 55.83 |
| †M. P. Lawrence (*Oxford U.*) | 341.5 | 65 | 1,154 | 20 | 3-99 | 57.70 |
| L. L. McFarlane (*Glamorgan*) | 259 | 42 | 1,008 | 16 | 4-100 | 63.00 |
| J. D. Quinlan (*Oxford U.*) | 189 | 37 | 635 | 10 | 4-76 | 63.50 |
| †T. A. Cotterell (*Cambridge U.*) | 232.4 | 54 | 742 | 11 | 3-53 | 67.45 |

The following bowlers took ten wickets but bowled in fewer than ten innings:

| | O | M | R | W | BB | Avge |
|---|---|---|---|---|---|---|
| †R. V. J. Coombs (*Somerset*) | 93 | 27 | 268 | 16 | 5-58 | 16.75 |
| I. L. Pont (*Essex*) | 115.5 | 15 | 485 | 19 | 5-103 | 25.52 |
| T. D. Topley (*Surrey and Essex*) | 161.1 | 37 | 464 | 17 | 4-57 | 27.29 |
| S. Turner (*Essex*) | 121.5 | 25 | 321 | 11 | 4-36 | 29.18 |
| †S. T. Jefferies (*Lancashire*) | 116.1 | 13 | 379 | 12 | 4-64 | 31.58 |
| †D. G. Moir (*Derbyshire*) | 186 | 48 | 517 | 12 | 3-102 | 43.08 |

# INDIVIDUAL SCORES OF 100 AND OVER

There were 309 three-figure innings in first-class cricket in 1985, nineteen fewer than in 1984. The list includes 227 hit in the County Championship, and 55 in other first-class games, but not the 23 hit by the Australian touring team, nor two of the four hit by the Zimbabwean touring team, which can be found in their respective sections.

* *Signifies not out.*

**I. V. A. Richards** (9)
322 Somerset v Warwicks, Taunton
186 Somerset v Hants, Taunton
135 Somerset v Middx, Lord's
125 Somerset v Worcs., Taunton
123 Somerset v Derbys., Derby
120 Somerset v Lancs., Old Trafford
112 Somerset v Sussex, Taunton
105 Somerset v Yorks., Headingley
100 Somerset v Glam., Cardiff

**G. A. Gooch** (7)
202 Essex v Notts., Trent Bridge
196 England v Australia, The Oval
173* Essex v Somerset, Taunton
145 Essex v Middx, Lord's
142 Essex v Yorks., Chelmsford
132* Essex v Surrey, Chelmsford
125 Essex v Kent, Dartford

**M. A. Lynch** (7)
145 Surrey v Warwicks., The Oval
144* Surrey v Middx, The Oval
133 Surrey v Yorks., Sheffield
121 Surrey v Yorks., The Oval
115 Surrey v Kent, Canterbury
110 Surrey v Glos., The Oval
108 Surrey v Middx, Lord's

**C. L. Smith** (7)
143* Hants v Yorks., Middlesbrough
121 Hants v Lancs., Liverpool
121 Hants v Kent, Folkestone
121 Hants v Somerset, Taunton
110 }
100 } Hants v Oxford U., The Parks
102 Hants v Somerset, Bournemouth

**G. D. Barlow** (6)
141 Middx v Northants, Northampton
132 Middx v Somerset, Lord's
115 Middx v Surrey, The Oval
112 Middx v Notts., Lord's
103* Middx v Worcs., Worcester
102 Middx v Leics., Lord's

**G. Boycott** (6)
184 Yorks. v Worcs., Worcester
125* Yorks. v Notts., Scarborough
115 Yorks. v Hants, Middlesbrough
114* Yorks. v Somerset, Headingley
105* Yorks. v Worcs., Harrogate
103* Yorks. v Warwicks., Edgbaston

**D. I. Gower** (6)
215 England v Australia, Edgbaston
166 England v Australia, Trent Bridge
157 England v Australia, The Oval
135 Leics. v Australians, Leicester
128 Leics. v Sussex, Hove
100* Leics. v Glam., Leicester

**G. D. Mendis** (6)
143* Sussex v Essex, Colchester
123 Sussex v Yorks., Hove
111* Sussex v Warwicks, Hove
109 Sussex v Hants, Portsmouth
103 }
100* } Sussex v Lancs, Hastings

**R. T. Robinson** (6)
175 England v Australia, Headingley
148 England v Australia, Edgbaston
103 }
130* } Notts. v Glam., Swansea
118 Notts. v Yorks., Scarborough
105 Notts. v Somerset, Taunton

**D. L. Amiss** (5)
140 Warwicks. v Northants, Northampton
125 Warwicks. v Oxford U., The Parks
117 Warwicks. v Notts., Nuneaton
103* Warwicks. v Yorks., Edgbaston
100* Warwicks. v Worcs., Worcester

**C. W. J. Athey** (5)
170 Glos. v Derbys., Derby
139* Glos. v Worcs., Gloucester
115 Glos. v Glam., Bristol
111* Glos. v Cambridge U., Cambridge
101 Glos. v Yorks., Gloucester

**I. T. Botham** (5)
152 Somerset v Essex, Taunton
149 Somerset v Hants, Taunton
138* Somerset v Warwicks., Edgbaston
134 Somerset v Northants, Weston-super-Mare
112 Somerset v Glam., Taunton

**D. W. Randall** (5)
117 Notts. v Essex, Trent Bridge
115 Notts. v Middx, Lord's
108* Notts. v Leics., Trent Bridge
106 Notts. v Surrey, The Oval
100* Notts. v Cambridge U., Fenner's

**Younis Ahmed** (5)
177 Glam. v Middx, Cardiff
143* Glam. v Hants, Cardiff
118* Glam. v Australians, Neath
113 Glam. v Oxford U., The Parks
100* Glam. v Worcs., Worcester

**P. Bainbridge** (4)
151* Glos. v Derbys., Derby
143* Glos. v Glam., Bristol
119 Glos. v Yorks., Gloucester
102 Glos. v Surrey, The Oval

**K. J. Barnett** (4)
134* Derbys. v Leics., Leicester
125 Derbys. v Yorks., Chesterfield
109 Derbys. v Sussex, Derby
103 Derbys. v Lancs., Chesterfield

**B. R. Hardie** (4)
162 Essex v Somerset, Southend
131 Essex v Northants, Ilford
113* Essex v Australians, Chelmsford
112* Essex v Cambridge U., Fenner's

**G. A. Hick** (4)
230 Zimbabweans v Oxford U., The Parks
192 Zimbabweans v Glam., Swansea
174* Worcs. v Somerset, Worcester
128 Worcs. v Northants, Worcester

**Javed Miandad** (4)
200* Glam. v Australians, Neath
164* Glam. v Lancs., Old Trafford
125 Glam. v Surrey, The Oval
107 Glam. v Somerset, Cardiff

**T. E. Jesty** (4)
141* Surrey v Yorks., The Oval
126 Surrey v Warwicks., Edgbaston
112* Surrey v Essex, The Oval
100* Surrey v Zimbabweans, The Oval

**M. D. Moxon** (4)
168 Yorks. v Worcs., Worcester
153 Yorks. v Somerset, Headingley
127 Yorks. v Lancs., Headingley
104 MCC v Essex, Lord's

**C. E. B. Rice** (4)
171* Notts. v Leics., Trent Bridge
156* Notts. v Warwicks., Nuneaton
108* Notts. v Essex, Trent Bridge
101 Notts. v Hants, Trent Bridge

**W. N. Slack** (4)
201* Middx v Australians, Lord's
112 Middx v Notts., Trent Bridge
109 Middx v Leics., Lord's
105 Middx v Kent, Lord's

**D. L. Bairstow** (3)
122* Yorks. v Derbys., Bradford
113* Yorks. v Derbys., Chesterfield
100* Yorks. v Leics., Bradford

**M. R. Benson** (3)
162 Kent v Hants, Southampton
107 Kent v Yorks., Maidstone
102 Kent v Lancs., Old Trafford

**G. S. Clinton** (3)
123 Surrey v Sussex, The Oval
117 Surrey v Worcs., Worcester
106 Surrey v Essex, The Oval

**N. H. Fairbrother** (3)
164* Lancs. v Hants, Liverpool
147 Lancs. v Yorks., Headingley
128 Lancs. v Yorks., Old Trafford

**M. W. Gatting** (3)
160 England v Australia, Old Trafford
114 Middx v Essex, Lord's
100* England v Australia, Edgbaston

**A. M. Green** (3)
133 Sussex v Surrey, The Oval
106 Sussex v Surrey, Horsham
100* Sussex v Glam., Hove

**W. Larkins** (3)
163 Northants v Worcs., Worcester
140 Northants v Notts., Northampton
117 Northants v Surrey, Northampton

**K. S. McEwan** (3)
121 Essex v Middx, Chelmsford
110 Essex v Cambridge U., Fenner's
106 Essex v Glos., Bristol

**P. A. Neale** (3)
152* Worcs. v Surrey, Worcester
108 Worcs. v Australians, Worcester
102 Worcs. v Derbys., Worcester

**A. Needham** (3)
138 Surrey v Warwicks., The Oval
132 Surrey v Notts., The Oval
124 Surrey v Zimbabweans, The Oval

**M. C. J. Nicholas** (3)
146 Hants v Leics., Bournemouth
121 MCC v Essex, Lord's
115* MCC v Australians, Lord's

**C. T. Radley** (3)
200 Middx v Northants, Uxbridge
127 Middx v Glam., Cardiff
105* Middx v Surrey, The Oval

**D. M. Smith** (3)
112 Worcs. v Hants, Portsmouth
104* Worcs. v Northants, Worcester
102 Worcs. v Glam., Worcester

**R. A. Smith** (3)
140* Hants v Derbys., Basingstoke
134* Hants v Leics., Bournemouth
120 Hants v Oxford U., The Parks

**C. J. Tavaré** (3)
150* Kent v Essex, Dartford
123 Kent v Yorks., Maidstone
102* Kent v Hants, Southampton

**N. R. Taylor** (3)
120* Kent v Oxford U., The Parks
102* Kent v Yorks., Scarborough
100 Kent v Worcs., Worcester

**J. J. Whitaker** (3)
109 Leics. v Surrey, Leicester
105 Leics. v Somerset, Taunton
103 Leics. v Glam., Swansea

**P. Willey** (3)
147 Leics. v Northants, Northampton
133 Leics. v Derbys., Leicester
101 Leics. v Derbys., Chesterfield

**D. G. Aslett** (2)
174 Kent v Oxford U., The Parks
111 Kent v Surrey, Canterbury

**R. J. Bailey** (2)
107* Northants v Australians, Northampton
101 Northants v Hants, Northampton

**J. C. Balderstone** (2)
134 Leics. v Australians, Leicester
101 Leics. v Glam., Swansea

**R. J. Boyd-Moss** (2)
121 Northants v Glam., Wellingborough
121 Northants v Worcs., Worcester

**B. C. Broad** (2)
171 Notts. v Derbys., Derby
131 Notts. v Yorks., Worksop

**A. R. Butcher** (2)
126 Surrey v Notts., The Oval
121 Surrey v Glam., The Oval

**J. D. Carr** (2)
115 Oxford U. v Somerset, The Parks
101 Oxford U. v Yorks., The Parks

**C. S. Cowdrey** (2)
159 Kent v Surrey, Canterbury
131 Kent v Hants, Folkestone

**D. B. D'Oliveira** (2)
139 Worcs. v Sussex, Eastbourne
113 Worcs. v Somerset, Taunton

**R. I. H. B. Dyer** (2)
109* Warwicks. v Zimbabweans, Edgbaston
106 Warwicks. v Somerset, Edgbaston

**D. E. East** (2)
131 Essex v Glos., Southend
100 Essex v Middx, Lord's

**C. G. Greenidge** (2)
204 Hants v Warwicks., Edgbaston
143 Hants v Northants, Southampton

**G. C. Holmes** (2)
112 Glam. v Leics., Leicester
106* Glam. v Worcs., Abergavenny

**G. W. Humpage** (2)
159 Warwicks. v Sussex, Hove
123* Warwicks. v Northants, Northampton

**A. I. Kallicharran** (2)
152* Warwicks. v Northants, Northampton
108 Warwicks. v Kent, Canterbury

**A. J. Lamb** (2)
122* MCC v Australians, Lord's
111 Northants v Essex, Northampton

**T. A. Lloyd** (2)
160 Warwicks. v Glam., Edgbaston
123 Warwicks. v Oxford U., The Parks

**R. C. Ontong** (2)
130 Glam. v Notts., Trent Bridge
122 Glam. v Sussex, Hove

**B. Roberts** (2)
100* Derbys. v Glos., Derby
100 Derbys. v Notts., Derby

**P. M. Roebuck** (2)
132* Somerset v Worcs., Taunton
123* Somerset v Oxford U., The Parks

**A. W. Stovold** (2)
112 Glos. v Derbys., Derby
104 Glos. v Sussex, Hove

**V. P. Terry** (2)
148* Hants v Somerset, Bournemouth
128* Hants v Notts., Trent Bridge

**R. G. Williams** (2)
118 Northants v Warwicks., Northampton
103 Northants v Derbys., Northampton

**J. G. Wright** (2)
177* Derbys. v Warwicks., Edgbaston
117 Derbys. v Worcs., Worcester

**J. G. Wyatt** (2)
145 Somerset v Oxford U., The Parks
100 Somerset v Hants, Bournemouth

The following each played one three-figure innings:

J. Abrahams, 101*, Lancs. v Oxford U., The Parks.

N. E. Briers, 129, Leics. v Essex, Chelmsford; K. R. Brown, 102, Middx v Australians, Lord's; I. P. Butcher, 120, Leics. v Notts., Trent Bridge; R. O. Butcher, 120, Middx v Worcs., Worcester.

M. R. Chadwick, 132, Lancs. v Somerset, Old Trafford; P. B. Clift, 106, Leics. v Essex, Chelmsford; G. Cook, 126, Northants v Warwicks., Northampton; T. S. Curtis, 126*, Worcs. v Surrey, Worcester.

B. F. Davison, 111, Glos. v Middx, Lord's; P. R. Downton, 104, Middx v Northants, Uxbridge.

D. J. Fell, 109*, Cambridge U., v Notts., Fenner's; N. A. Felton, 112, Somerset v Leics., Taunton; A. M. Ferreira, 101*, Warwicks. v Somerset, Taunton.

M. A. Garnham, 100, Leics. v Oxford U., The Parks; I. J. Gould, 101, Sussex v Leics., Hove.

R. J. Harden, 107*, Somerset v Cambridge U., Taunton; J. J. E. Hardy, 107*, Hants v Essex, Southampton; R. A. Harper, 127, Northants v Kent, Maidstone; S. N. Hartley, 108*, Yorks. v Oxford U., The Parks; K. A. Hayes, 117, Lancs. v Somerset, Old Trafford; R. E. Hayward, 100*, Somerset v Cambridge U., Taunton; S. P. Henderson, 111, Glam. v Sussex, Hove; A. Hill, 120, Derbys. v Hants, Basingstoke; S. G. Hinks, 117, Kent v Surrey, The Oval; J. A. Hopkins, 114*, Glam. v Worcs., Abergavenny.

Imran Khan, 117*, Sussex v Warwicks, Hove.

K. D. James, 124, Hants v Somerset, Taunton; P. Johnson, 118, Notts. v Leics., Trent Bridge.

Kapil Dev, 100, Worcs. v Middx, Lord's.

C. H. Lloyd, 131, Lancs. v Leics., Leicester; J. W. Lloyds, 101, Glos. v Essex, Southend; G. J. Lord, 199, Warwicks. v Yorks., Edgbaston; J. D. Love, 106, Yorks. v Oxford U., The Parks.

D. J. R. Martindale, 104*, Notts. v Lancs., Old Trafford; M. P. Maynard, 102, Glam. v Yorks., Swansea; A. A. Metcalfe, 109, Yorks. v Oxford U., The Parks; G. Miller, 105, Derbys. v Essex, Colchester; J. E. Morris, 109*, Derbys. v Warwicks., Chesterfield.

P. G. Newman, 115, Derbys. v Leics., Chesterfield.

P. W. G. Parker, 105, Sussex v Surrey, Horsham; N. F. M. Popplewell, 172, Somerset v Essex, Southend; D. R. Pringle, 121*, Essex v Surrey, The Oval.

P. W. Romaines, 114*, Glos. v Zimbabweans, Bristol.

J. Simmons, 101, Lancs. v Sussex, Hastings; J. F. Steele, 100, Glam. v Oxford U., The Parks; A. J. Stewart, 158, Surrey v Kent, Canterbury; A. C. Storie 106, Northants v Hants, Northampton; J. F. Sykes, 126, Middx v Cambridge U., Fenner's.

D. A. Thorne, 124, Oxford U. v Zimbabweans, The Parks; G. J. Toogood, 149, Oxford U. v Cambridge U., Lord's; T. M. Tremlett, 102*, Hants v Somerset, Taunton.

D. W. Varey, 112, Lancs. v Oxford U., The Parks.

D. M. Ward, 143, Surrey v Derbys., Derby; S. J. S. Warke, 144*, Ireland v Scotland, Dublin; M. Watkinson, 106, Lancs. v Surrey, Southport; A. P. Wells, 102, Sussex v Glam., Hove; C. M. Wells, 100*, Sussex v Warwicks., Hove; M. J. Weston, 132, Worcs. v Surrey, Worcester.

# TEN WICKETS IN A MATCH

There were sixteen instances of bowlers taking ten or more wickets in a match in first-class cricket in 1985, four fewer than in 1984. The list includes thirteen in the County Championship, and three in other first-class matches.

**R. M. Ellison** (2)
11-164 Kent v Northants, Maidstone
10-104 England v Australia, Edgbaston

**V. J. Marks** (2)
11-73 Somerset v Lancs., Bath
11-208 Somerset v Leics., Taunton

The following each took ten wickets in a match on one occasion:

J. P. Agnew, 11-118, Leics. v Kent, Leicester.
P. Carrick, 10-105, Yorks. v Derbys., Bradford.
A. M. Ferreira, 10-84, Warwicks. v Lancs., Old Trafford.
A. H. Gray, 10-119, Surrey v Yorks., Sheffield.
R. K. Illingworth, 13-59, Worcs. v Oxford U., The Parks.
M. A. Holding, 10-118, Derbys. v Warwicks., Chesterfield.
R. C. Ontong, 13-106, Glam. v Notts., Trent Bridge.
B. P. Patterson, 10-112, Lancs. v Essex, Ilford.
K. Saxelby, 10-113, Notts. v Kent, Tunbridge Wells.
G. J. Toogood, 10-93, Oxford U. v Cambridge U., Lord's.
D. L. Underwood, 10-36, Kent v Essex, Dartford.
C. A. Walsh, 13-128, Glos. v Warwicks., Cheltenham.

# SIX WICKETS IN AN INNINGS

There were 74 instances of bowlers taking six or more wickets in an innings in first-class cricket in 1985, four fewer than in 1984. The list includes 60 in the County Championship, three by the Australian touring side and eleven in other first-class matches.

**R. M. Ellison** (3)
7-87 Kent v Northants, Maidstone
6-61 Kent v Essex, Chelmsford
6-77 England v Australia, Edgbaston

**M. D. Marshall** (3)
7-59 Hants v Worcs., Portsmouth
6-42 Hants v Essex, Southampton
6-50 Hants v Warwicks., Edgbaston

**B. P. Patterson** (3)
7-49 Lancs. v Oxford U., The Parks
6-45 Lancs. v Essex, Ilford
6-77 Lancs. v Yorks., Old Trafford

**J. P. Agnew** (2)
9-70 Leics. v Kent, Leicester
6-86 Leics. v Surrey, Leicester

**E. A. E. Baptiste** (2)
6-42 Kent v Northants, Northampton
6-60 Kent v Leics., Leicester

**P. Carrick** (2)
7-99 Yorks. v Glam., Swansea
6-46 Yorks. v Derbys., Bradford

**K. E. Cooper** (2)
7-10 Notts. v Cambridge U., Fenner's
6-53 Notts. v Derbys., Derby

**N. G. Cowans** (2)
6-31 Middx v Leics., Leicester
6-68 MCC v Essex, Lord's

**R. J. Finney** (2)
7-61 Derbys. v Lancs., Old Trafford
6-62 Derbys. v Worcs., Worcester

**A. H. Gray** (2)
8-40 Surrey v Yorks., Sheffield
7-68 Surrey v Middx, Lord's

**R. J. Hadlee** (2)
8-41 Notts. v Lancs., Trent Bridge
7-34 Notts. v Middx, Lord's

**M. A. Holding** (2)
6-65 Derbys. v Notts., Derby
6-90 Derbys. v Warwicks., Chesterfield

**R. K. Illingworth** (2)
7-50 }
6-9 } Worcs. v Oxford U., The Parks

**J. K. Lever** (2)
6-47 Essex v Yorks., Chelmsford
6-49 Essex v Somerset, Southend

**C. J. McDermott** (2)
8-141 Australia v England, Old Trafford
6-70 Australia v England, Lord's

**V. J. Marks** (2)
8-17 Somerset v Lancs., Bath
7-143 Somerset v Leics., Taunton

**N. V. Radford** (2)
6-45 Worcs. v Warwicks., Edgbaston
6-76 Worcs. v Sussex, Eastbourne

**C. A. Walsh** (2)
7-51 }
6-77 } Glos. v Warwicks., Cheltenham

**P. Willey** (2)
6-43 Leics. v Hants, Leicester
6-73 Leics. v Surrey, Leicester

The following each took six wickets in an innings on one occasion:

D. L. Acfield, 6-81, Essex v Derbys., Colchester; S. J. W. Andrew, 6-43, Hants v Glos., Bournemouth; P. J. W. Allott, 6-71, Lancs. v Surrey, The Oval.
J. R. T. Barclay, 6-78, Sussex v Yorks., Hove; K. J. Barnett, 6-115, Derbys. v Yorks., Bradford; S. R. Barwick, 7-43, Glam. v Warwicks., Cardiff.
D. J. Capel, 7-62, Northants v Lancs., Lytham; J. D. Carr, 6-61, Middx v Glos., Lord's.
W. W. Daniel, 7-62, Middx v Leics., Leicester; R. J. Doughty, 6-33, Surrey v Warwicks., The Oval.
P. H. Edmonds, 6-87, Middx v Derbys., Lord's; J. E. Emburey, 6-35, Middx v Sussex, Hove.
I. Folley, 6-8, Lancs. v Oxford U., The Parks.
B. J. Griffiths, 6-76, Northants v Kent, Maidstone.
E. E. Hemmings, 6-51, Notts. v Lancs., Trent Bridge.
K. D. James, 6-22, Hants v Australians, Southampton; P. W. Jarvis, 7-105, Yorks. v Kent, Maidstone.
D. V. Lawrence, 7-48, Glos. v Sussex, Hove; G. S. le Roux, 6-46, Sussex v Essex, Colchester.
G. Miller, 6-110, Derbys. v Lancs., Old Trafford.
C. M. Old, 6-68, Warwicks. v Essex, Chelmsford; R. C. Ontong, 8-67, Glam. v Notts., Trent Bridge.
G. J. Parsons, 6-11, Leics. v Oxford U., The Parks; P. I. Pocock, 7-42, Surrey v Kent, The Oval; D. R. Pringle, 6-42, Essex v Glos., Bristol.
G. D. Rose, 6-41, Middx v Worcs., Worcester.
G. E. Sainsbury, 7-38, Glos. v Northants, Northampton; K. Saxelby, 6-64, Notts. v Kent, Tunbridge Wells.
N. S. Taylor, 7-44, Surrey v Cambridge U., Fenner's; J. R. Thomson, 6-44, Australians v Somerset, Taunton; G. J. Toogood, 8-52, Oxford U. v Cambridge U., Lord's.
D. L. Underwood, 6-56, Kent v Essex, Dartford.
C. E. Waller, 7-61, Sussex v Derbys., Derby.

# THE AUSTRALIANS IN ENGLAND, 1985

The 1985 Australian touring team, the 30th to play Test cricket in England, disappointed its supporters. After four matches in the Cornhill Test series, England and Australia had a victory apiece, and one further success by Australia in the remaining two Test matches would have ensured their retention of the Ashes. At this point, while England were felt to be the better side, it was beyond most objective pundits to foresee England's two crushing victories, each by an innings, that unveiled a conclusive superiority.

That so many of Australia's shortcomings remained only half-revealed for so long was attributable to the determined and often daring batsmanship of Allan Border, the captain, and the piecemeal support he received from Andrew Hilditch, Graeme Wood, Kepler Wessels, Greg Ritchie and the elegant batsman-wicketkeeper Wayne Phillips. Border created a new record by scoring hundreds in his first four first-class innings of the tour, and was always the batsman whose downfall meant most to both sides. The inconsistency of Australia's batting turned to downright fragility in the last two encounters as nerves snapped and technique was found wanting before the surging skill and confidence of a settled England team.

The bowling was even more disappointing. Geoff Lawson's bronchial problems reduced his effectiveness, and Bob Holland's leg-spin, hailed as an aesthetic asset and triumphant in the Lord's Test, was used unadventurously, proving of little value beyond containment as he operated from around the wicket for long spells, shunning use of the googly. The young all-rounder, Simon O'Donnell, after a handsome hundred in the match against MCC, seemed likely also to be as useful a bowler as Connolly had been a cricket generation ago, but he failed to hold his place for the final Test. Jeff Thomson, who turned 35 during the fifth Test, tried in vain to muster the speed and bite of bygone summers, while Dave Gilbert was plainly still learning his craft. The off-spin of the idiosyncratic Greg Matthews and slow left-arm of Murray Bennett, though tidy, posed little threat.

The outstanding success was Craig McDermott from Queensland, fiery, strong and seemingly more mature than his twenty years. Though, understandably, he could not always sustain the pace and accuracy that earned him eight wickets in England's only innings at Old Trafford, he was a perpetual menace, and returned a worthy 30 wickets in the Test series.

The selection of this touring party was hampered by the unavailability of those who chose to sign contracts for the disapproved tour of South Africa, though Kim Hughes and Graham Yallop signed only after their surprising omission from the team bound for England. They and bowlers Alderman, Hogg, Maguire and Rackemann would unquestionably have strengthened the side, almost to the same extent that the presence of Gooch, Emburey, Willey and Taylor – all newly liberated from the three-year TCCB ban for similar defections to South Africa – fortified England. Others overlooked included Hookes, Kerr and Jones. It was therefore essential that the team, from the day of its arrival in England, should put the complications and the persistent bouts of rumour aside and mould quickly into a unit. Externally, under the firm leadership of Border, the solicitous management of Robert Merriman, and the tactical control of his assistant, Geoff Dymock, this was achieved. But internally the lingering dissatisfaction caused by the inclusion of Dirk Wellham, Wood and Wayne Phillips, after they had changed their minds about touring South Africa, led to tensions in the camp. It was an echo of the

## THE AUSTRALIANS IN ENGLAND, 1985

[*Patrick Eagar*

The Australian party which toured England last year and lost the Ashes. *Back row:* G. R. Mackay (*physiotherapist*), R. B. Phillips, G. M. Ritchie, D. R. Gilbert, C. J. McDermott, S. P. O'Donnell, M. J. Bennett, R. G. Holland, G. R. J. Matthews, D. M. Wellham, M. P. Ringham (*scorer*). *Front row:* G. M. Wood, K. C. Wessels, J. R. Thomson, A. R. Border (*captain*), R. F. Merriman (*manager*), G. Dymock (*assistant manager*), A. M. J. Hilditch (*vice-captain*), G. F. Lawson, W. B. Phillips, D. C. Boon.

uneasiness felt within the 1977 Australian touring team, some of whom had not signed for the then forthcoming World Series breakaway movement.

By the end of the 1985 tour, the bowling figures told a significant tale. McDermott and Lawson finished with 52 of the 69 wickets taken by Australian bowlers in the six Tests, and the cost was extraordinarily high. Indeed, England's overall run-rate of 60.67 runs per 100 balls received (3.64 per over) was the fastest ever by either side in England-Australia Tests. The policy of going in with only four front-line bowlers was abandoned only in the fifth Test, at Edgbaston; and then England piled up 595 for five. The ability to bowl the testing length in the right direction was frequently lacking right through the ranks – a problem with England's bowlers too, until the latter stages of the series. This was a crucial differential.

Carrying on from where he left off on the 1981 tour, Border amassed runs this time at a faster rate, bristling with confidence until an excess at Old Trafford, when he was stumped. Thereafter, his wicket became even more difficult to capture. Hilditch surprised with his stroke-range in the opening Test, when he made 199 runs, but subsequently he failed to reach fifty and became notoriously susceptible to poorly played hook shots. Wood was in serious danger of losing his place before his marathon 172 at Trent Bridge, missed the next Test through injury, and failed in the important last two contests. Equally telling was Wessels's lack of success. So often effective in past Test matches, despite his ungainly method, he was kept well in check by sound England planning. David Boon, the powerful little Tasmanian, found Test cricket an agonising trial. His century against Essex saved his position for the third Test, and a double-century against Northamptonshire kept him in for the fourth, where he top-scored with 61 in Australia's wavering first innings. His slip catching, up till then a distinct asset, now let him down, and he disappeared for the rest of the series. Wellham, who scored consistently well outside the Tests, failed twice to Ellison when he came in for the Oval Test.

Ritchie was Australia's sole gain on the batting front. Elegant, though rounded of profile, the genial Queenslander followed a fine 94 in the Lord's Test, when he shared a double-century partnership with his captain, with an admirable six-hour 146 at Trent Bridge, and stood alone with an unbeaten 64 at The Oval as Australia crumpled for 241.

Only the reserve wicket-keeper, Ray Phillips, of the seventeen players was not called upon for Test duty on a tour blighted by rain which rendered the experiment of four-day matches against the counties inconclusive. It will remain a curiosity that such a damp summer could have housed so many Test match days of high scoring, admittedly on slow pitches. The Australians left these shores subdued but with hope for the next Ashes series. Border was still bewildered and unable to explain the disintegration, but deeper analysis in the months that followed, allowing that much Australian talent was otherwise occupied in South Africa, should guarantee a more closely fought series in 1986-87. – D.E.J.F.

## AUSTRALIAN TOUR RESULTS

*Test matches* – Played 6: Won 1, Lost 3, Drawn 2.

*First-class matches* – Played 20: Won 4, Lost 3, Drawn 13.

*Wins* – England, Somerset, Gloucestershire, Kent.

*Losses* – England (3).

*Draws* – England (2), Worcestershire, Sussex, MCC, Derbyshire, Yorkshire, Leicestershire, Hampshire, Essex, Glamorgan, Northamptonshire, Middlesex.

*Non first-class matches* – Played 9: Won 5, Lost 2, Drawn 2. Abandoned 1. *Wins* – England (2), Derbyshire, Oxford & Cambridge Universities, Minor Counties. *Losses* – England, Surrey. *Draws* – Lavinia, Duchess of Norfolk's XI, Ireland. *Abandoned* – Nottinghamshire.

## TEST MATCH AVERAGES

### ENGLAND – BATTING

| | *T* | *I* | *NO* | *R* | *HI* | *100s* | *Avge* |
|---|---|---|---|---|---|---|---|
| M. W. Gatting ...... | 6 | 9 | 3 | 527 | 160 | 2 | 87.83 |
| D. I. Gower .......... | 6 | 9 | 0 | 732 | 215 | 3 | 81.33 |
| R. T. Robinson ...... | 6 | 9 | 1 | 490 | 175 | 2 | 61.25 |
| G. A. Gooch ........ | 6 | 9 | 0 | 487 | 196 | 1 | 54.11 |
| A. J. Lamb ......... | 6 | 8 | 1 | 256 | 67 | 0 | 36.57 |
| J. E. Emburey ....... | 6 | 6 | 2 | 130 | 33 | 0 | 32.50 |
| I. T. Botham ......... | 6 | 8 | 0 | 250 | 85 | 0 | 31.25 |
| P. R. Downton ...... | 6 | 7 | 1 | 114 | 54 | 0 | 19.00 |
| P. H. Edmonds ...... | 5 | 5 | 0 | 47 | 21 | 0 | 9.40 |
| P. J. W. Allott ....... | 4 | 5 | 1 | 27 | 12 | 0 | 6.75 |

Played in two Tests: R. M. Ellison 3; L. B. Taylor 1*. Played in one Test: J. P. Agnew 2*; N. G. Cowans 22*; N. A. Foster 3, 0; A. Sidebottom 2; P. Willey 36, 3*.

**Signifies not out.*

### BOWLING

| | *O* | *M* | *R* | *W* | *BB* | *Avge* |
|---|---|---|---|---|---|---|
| R. M. Ellison ........ | 75.5 | 20 | 185 | 17 | 6-77 | 10.88 |
| I. T. Botham ......... | 251.4 | 36 | 855 | 31 | 5-109 | 27.58 |
| J. E. Emburey ....... | 248.4 | 75 | 544 | 19 | 5-82 | 28.63 |
| P. H. Edmonds ...... | 225.5 | 59 | 549 | 15 | 4-40 | 36.60 |
| P. J. W. Allott ....... | 113 | 22 | 297 | 5 | 2-74 | 59.40 |

Also bowled: J. P. Agnew 23–2–99–0; N. G. Cowans 33–6–128–2; N. A. Foster 23–1–83–1; M. W. Gatting 5–0–16–0; G. A. Gooch 41.2–10–102–2; A. J. Lamb 1–0–10–0; A. Sidebottom 18.4–3–65–1; L. B. Taylor 63.3–11–178–4.

### AUSTRALIA – BATTING

| | *T* | *I* | *NO* | *R* | *HI* | *100s* | *Avge* |
|---|---|---|---|---|---|---|---|
| A. R. Border ........ | 6 | 11 | 2 | 597 | 196 | 2 | 66.33 |
| G. M. Ritchie ....... | 6 | 11 | 1 | 422 | 146 | 1 | 42.20 |
| A. M. J. Hilditch .... | 6 | 11 | 0 | 424 | 119 | 1 | 38.54 |
| W. B. Phillips ....... | 6 | 11 | 1 | 350 | 91 | 0 | 35.00 |
| K. C. Wessels ....... | 6 | 11 | 0 | 368 | 83 | 0 | 33.45 |
| G. M. Wood ........ | 5 | 9 | 0 | 260 | 172 | 1 | 28.88 |
| S. P. O'Donnell ...... | 5 | 8 | 1 | 184 | 48 | 0 | 26.28 |
| D. C. Boon ......... | 4 | 7 | 0 | 124 | 61 | 0 | 17.71 |
| G. F. Lawson ....... | 6 | 9 | 1 | 119 | 53 | 0 | 14.87 |
| C. J. McDermott ..... | 6 | 9 | 1 | 103 | 35 | 0 | 12.87 |
| R. G. Holland ....... | 4 | 5 | 1 | 15 | 10 | 0 | 3.75 |

Played in two Tests: J. R. Thomson 4*, 2*, 28*, 4*. Played in one Test: M. J. Bennett 12, 11; D. R. Gilbert 1, 0*; G. R. J. Matthews 4, 17; D. M. Wellham 13, 5.

**Signifies not out.*

## BOWLING

| | *O* | *M* | *R* | *W* | *BB* | *Avge* |
|---|---|---|---|---|---|---|
| C. J. McDermott | 234.2 | 21 | 901 | 30 | 8-141 | 30.03 |
| G. F. Lawson | 246 | 38 | 830 | 22 | 5-103 | 37.72 |
| R. G. Holland | 172 | 41 | 465 | 6 | 5-68 | 77.50 |
| S. P. O'Donnell | 145.4 | 31 | 487 | 6 | 3-37 | 81.16 |

Also bowled: M. J. Bennett 32–8–111–1; A. R. Border 11–1–37–0; D. R. Gilbert 21–2–96–1; G. R. J. Matthews 9–2–21–0; G. M. Ritchie 1–0–10–0; J. R. Thomson 56–4–275–3; K. C. Wessels 6–2–18–0.

# AUSTRALIAN AVERAGES – FIRST-CLASS MATCHES

## BATTING

| | *M* | *I* | *NO* | *R* | *HI* | *100s* | *Avge* |
|---|---|---|---|---|---|---|---|
| A. R. Border | 14 | 21 | 2 | 1,355 | 196 | 8 | 71.31 |
| D. M. Wellham | 10 | 16 | 4 | 669 | 125* | 2 | 55.75 |
| D. C. Boon | 15 | 20 | 5 | 832 | 206* | 3 | 55.46 |
| G. M. Ritchie | 16 | 23 | 3 | 1,097 | 155 | 4 | 54.85 |
| W. B. Phillips | 14 | 22 | 3 | 899 | 128 | 1 | 47.31 |
| S. P. O'Donnell | 11 | 16 | 5 | 448 | 100* | 1 | 40.72 |
| K. C. Wessels | 16 | 26 | 1 | 905 | 156 | 1 | 36.20 |
| G. M. Wood | 16 | 25 | 3 | 691 | 172 | 2 | 31.40 |
| A. M. J. Hilditch | 17 | 27 | 0 | 829 | 119 | 1 | 30.70 |
| R. B. Phillips | 7 | 7 | 2 | 130 | 39 | 0 | 26.00 |
| G. R. J. Matthews | 10 | 12 | 3 | 216 | 51* | 0 | 24.00 |
| C. J. McDermott | 16 | 14 | 3 | 183 | 53* | 0 | 16.63 |
| J. R. Thomson | 11 | 11 | 6 | 82 | 28* | 0 | 16.40 |
| M. J. Bennett | 11 | 10 | 3 | 111 | 23 | 0 | 15.85 |
| G. F. Lawson | 13 | 13 | 2 | 154 | 53 | 0 | 14.00 |
| D. R. Gilbert | 10 | 8 | 3 | 39 | 12 | 0 | 7.80 |
| R. G. Holland | 13 | 10 | 1 | 59 | 35 | 0 | 6.55 |

**Signifies not out.*

## BOWLING

| | *O* | *M* | *R* | *W* | *BB* | *Avge* |
|---|---|---|---|---|---|---|
| C. J. McDermott | 421.5 | 49 | 1,609 | 51 | 8-141 | 31.54 |
| J. R. Thomson | 241.3 | 33 | 988 | 29 | 6-44 | 34.06 |
| R. G. Holland | 376 | 94 | 1,017 | 29 | 5-51 | 35.06 |
| G. F. Lawson | 347 | 61 | 1,165 | 31 | 5-103 | 37.58 |
| D. R. Gilbert | 253.2 | 42 | 885 | 21 | 4-41 | 42.14 |
| G. R. J. Matthews | 159.4 | 34 | 521 | 12 | 3-76 | 43.41 |
| M. J. Bennett | 266.4 | 62 | 766 | 16 | 4-39 | 47.87 |
| S. P. O'Donnell | 242.4 | 47 | 819 | 12 | 3-37 | 68.25 |

Also bowled: D. C. Boon 6–0–33–0; A. R. Border 13–2–38–0; A. M. J. Hilditch 7–2–29–0; G. M. Ritchie 6.3–0–33–1; K. C. Wessels 32–9–79–0.

## FIELDING

W. B. Phillips 21 (20 ct, 1st), R. B. Phillips 20 (17 ct, 3 st; 4 ct, 3 st as sub), A. R. Border 14 (1 as sub), D. C. Boon 13, K. C. Wessels 9, G. M. Ritchie 8 (1 as sub), A. M. J. Hilditch 7, M. J. Bennett 6, G. M. Wood 6, R. G. Holland 5, S. P. O'Donnell 5, D. R. Gilbert 3 (1 as sub), G. R. J. Matthews 3, C. J. McDermott 2, J. R. Thomson 2, G. F. Lawson 1, D. M. Wellham 1.

## HUNDREDS FOR AUSTRALIANS

The following 26 three-figure innings were played for the Australians, 23 in first-class matches and three in non first-class matches.

**A. R. Border** (8)
196 v England at Lord's (Second Test)
146* v England at Old Trafford (Fourth Test)
135 v Worcestershire at Worcester
130 v Gloucestershire at Bristol
125 v MCC at Lord's
106 v Somerset at Taunton
103 v Kent at Canterbury
100 v Derbyshire at Derby

**D. C. Boon** (4)
206* v Northamptonshire at Northampton
138 v Essex at Chelmsford
119 v Sussex at Hove
†108 v Oxford & Cambridge Universities at Fenner's

**G. M. Ritchie** (4)
155 v Kent at Canterbury
146 v England at Trent Bridge (Third Test)
115 v Leicestershire at Leicester
100* v Sussex at Hove

**D. M. Wellham** (3)
125* v Middlesex at Lord's
†107* v Minor Counties at Jesmond
105 v Gloucestershire at Bristol

**G. M. Wood** (3)
172 v England at Trent Bridge (Third Test)
†114* v England at Lord's (Third One-day International)
102* v Yorkshire at Headingley

**A. M. J. Hilditch** (1)
119 v England at Headingley (1st Test)

**S. P. O'Donnell** (1)
100* v MCC at Lord's

**W. B. Phillips** (1)
128 v Leicestershire at Leicester

**K. C. Wessels** (1)
156 v Somerset at Taunton

* *Signifies not out.* † *Not first-class.*

*Note:* Those matches which follow which were not first-class are signified by the use of a dagger.

## †LAVINIA, DUCHESS OF NORFOLK'S XI v AUSTRALIANS

At Arundel, May 5. Drawn. Toss won by Australians.

### Australians

| | |
|---|---|
| G. M. Wood run out | 28 |
| K. C. Wessels b Knight | 44 |
| D. M. Wellham b Sivaramakrishnan | 29 |
| G. M. Ritchie lbw b Knight | 72 |
| W. B. Phillips lbw b Knight | 5 |
| *A. R. Border c Willis b Ratnayake | 65 |
| G. R. J. Matthews not out | 4 |
| B 8, l-b 2, n-b 4 | 14 |
| 1/40 2/91 3/136 4/162 5/203 6/261 (6 wkts dec.) | 261 |

G. F. Lawson, M. J. Bennett, †R. B. Phillips and J. R. Thomson did not bat.

Bowling: Willis 14–2–28–0; Ratnayake 6.5–0–39–1; Sivaramakrishnan 11–1–86–1; Knight 14–3–47–3; Selvey 9–0–51–0.

### Lavinia, Duchess of Norfolk's XI

| | |
|---|---|
| D. C. Boon c Bennett b Lawson | 33 |
| N. J. Lenham b Thomson | 5 |
| B. Hassan c R. B. Phillips b Thomson | 4 |
| J. H. Hampshire c Wellham b Bennett | 8 |
| R. D. V. Knight not out | 63 |
| D. K. Standing b Bennett | 16 |
| R. J. Ratnayake not out | 1 |
| L-b 6, w 1, n-b 8 | 15 |
| 1/12 2/24 3/49 4/98 5/144 | (5 wkts) 145 |

†S. N. V. Waterton, L. Sivaramakrishnan, M. W. W. Selvey and *R. G. D. Willis did not bat.

Bowling: Lawson 11–4–20–1; Thomson 9–1–36–2; Matthews 16–5–31–0; Bennett 14–4–47–2; Wessels 2–1–5–0.

Umpires: W. L. Budd and J. G. Langridge.

## SOMERSET v AUSTRALIANS

At Taunton, May 8, 9, 10. Australians won by 233 runs with 170 minutes to spare. Toss won by Australians. Their first innings was dominated by a run-a-minute century from Border, who hit four 6s and ten 4s in an innings of 103 balls. Botham redressed Somerset's poor start by hitting one 6 and twelve 4s in 40 balls, reaching his fifty off 30 balls. He and Rose put on 105 in fifteen overs before Botham departed early on the second morning. Rose hit seventeen 4s in 40 overs before having his arm broken by McDermott, and then Marks and Gard proceeded briskly against the spinners, of whom Holland was the steadiest. Wessels, hitting 21 4s and two 6s in 217 minutes – his third 50 came off 30 balls – led the second innings, and some fine pace bowling by Thomson ruined Somerset's hopes of scoring 359 in five and a half hours. Only Roebuck, dropped three times before he was 12, Harden, in his first county match, and Marks offered any resistance, Roebuck becoming the first Somerset batsman to carry his bat against a touring side since F. S. Lee in 1934. On the second and third days, Ray Phillips deputised as wicket-keeper for Wayne Phillips, who was ill.

### Australians

| | | | |
|---|---|---|---|
| K. C. Wessels c Botham b Marks | 41 | – (2) c Botham b Booth | 156 |
| A. M. J. Hilditch c Davis b Botham | 20 | – (1) c Harden b Booth | 46 |
| D. M. Wellham c Davis b Botham | 64 | – (7) not out | 26 |
| *A. R. Border c Botham b Marks | 106 | | |
| D. C. Boon not out | 62 | – (8) not out | 21 |
| †W. B. Phillips not out | 56 | | |
| G. R. J. Matthews (did not bat) | | – (3) c Roebuck b Booth | 22 |
| C. J. McDermott (did not bat) | | – (4) c sub b Marks | 0 |
| J. R. Thomson (did not bat) | | – (5) lbw b Marks | 7 |
| R. G. Holland (did not bat) | | – (6) c Popplewell b Booth | 35 |
| L-b 7 | 7 | L-b 2, n-b 1 | 3 |
| 1/47 2/85 3/221 4/248 | (4 wkts dec.) 356 | 1/125 2/173 3/179 4/191 5/264 6/273 | (6 wkts dec.) 316 |

G. F. Lawson did not bat.

Bowling: *First Innings*—Davis 14–2–71–0; Turner 15–0–85–0; Botham 12–3–28–2; Marks 25–4–87–2; Popplewell 3–0–21–0; Booth 11–1–57–0. *Second Innings*—Botham 6–2–16–0; Davis 7–0–32–0; Turner 11–1–58–0; Marks 28–6–110–2; Booth 22–2–98–4.

## Somerset

| | | | |
|---|---|---|---|
| N. F. M. Popplewell c Boon b Thomson | 25 | – lbw b McDermott | 0 |
| P. M. Roebuck c Phillips b Lawson | 13 | – not out | 33 |
| R. L. Ollis run out | 11 | – lbw b Thomson | 4 |
| B. C. Rose retired hurt | 81 | – absent injured | |
| R. J. Harden c Phillips b McDermott | 0 | – (4) c sub (R. B. Phillips) b Thomson | 17 |
| *I. T. Botham st sub (R. B. Phillips) b Holland | 65 | – (5) c sub (R. B. Phillips) b Thomson | 4 |
| V. J. Marks c sub (R. B. Phillips) b Holland | 50 | – (6) c sub (R. B. Phillips) b Thomson | 48 |
| †T. Gard c Wessels b Holland | 30 | – (7) c sub (D. R. Gilbert) b Holland | 0 |
| M. S. Turner b Thomson | 9 | – (8) c sub (R. B. Phillips) b Thomson | 0 |
| M. R. Davis st sub (R. B. Phillips) b Holland | 11 | – (9) c Holland b Thomson | 4 |
| S. C. Booth not out | 4 | – (10) c Boon b Holland | 5 |
| B 4, l-b 4, n-b 7 | 15 | B 4, l-b 1, n-b 5 | 10 |
| 1/34 2/54 3/65 4/65 5/170 6/273 7/290 8/308 9/314 | 314 | 1/10 2/15 3/43 4/49 5/111 6/113 7/114 8/118 9/125 | 125 |

Bowling: *First Innings*—Thomson 17–3–75–2; Lawson 8–2–31–1; Holland 29.3–11–87–4; McDermott 11–1–71–1; Matthews 9–0–42–0. *Second Innings*—McDermott 12–2–46–1; Thomson 14–1–44–6; Holland 17.1–5–30–2.

Umpires: R. Julian and D. R. Shepherd.

## WORCESTERSHIRE v AUSTRALIANS

At Worcester, May 11, 12, 13. Drawn. Toss won by Worcestershire. The Australians looked well placed for victory at the end of the second day, only for rain to wash out the third. Neale, whose 145 not out in 1981 was the highest score made by a Worcestershire batsman against the Australians, scored the first hundred of the summer against the tourists, hitting one 6 and eighteen 4s in his 108 off 174 balls. Border, however, upstaged him with a second successive century, scoring exactly 100 of his 135 off 140 balls in boundaries – six 6s and sixteen 4s – and sharing hundred partnerships with Ritchie and Boon. Worcestershire were struggling at 93 for four in their second innings, a lead of only 32, after Lawson, who had been warned by umpire Palmer for intimidatory bowling at Neale the day before, had taken three for 11 in seven overs.

## Worcestershire

| | | | |
|---|---|---|---|
| M. J. Weston c Hilditch b McDermott | 11 | – c Phillips b Lawson | 31 |
| T. S. Curtis c and b Bennett | 76 | – c Wood b Lawson | 10 |
| D. M. Smith c Lawson b McDermott | 0 | | |
| D. N. Patel c Ritchie b Matthews | 30 | – lbw b Lawson | 4 |
| *P. A. Neale c Boon b Matthews | 108 | – not out | 13 |
| D. B. D'Oliveira c Ritchie b Bennett | 0 | – (3) b Gilbert | 11 |
| P. J. Newport not out | 29 | – (6) not out | 14 |
| †S. J. Rhodes not out | 20 | | |
| B 6, l-b 5, w 2, n-b 16 | 29 | L-b 1, w 4, n-b 5 | 10 |
| 1/18 2/19 3/81 4/193 5/213 6/273 (6 wkts dec.) | 303 | 1/40 2/50 3/58 4/71 (4 wkts) | 93 |

J. D. Inchmore, N. V. Radford and R. K. Illingworth did not bat.

Bowling: *First Innings*—Lawson 13–1–65–0; McDermott 13–3–39–2; Gilbert 19–1–90–0; Matthews 23.5–8–55–2; Bennett 19–8–43–2. *Second Innings*—McDermott 2–0–22–0; Gilbert 14.2–3–49–1; Lawson 7–4–11–3; Bennett 6–2–10–0.

### Australians

| | | | |
|---|---|---|---|
| A. M. J. Hilditch c Curtis b Inchmore | 7 | G. R. J. Matthews not out | 23 |
| G. M. Wood lbw b Inchmore | 34 | | |
| †R. B. Phillips c Radford b Patel | 39 | B 10, l-b 9, w 1, n-b 12 | 32 |
| G. M. Ritchie c Rhodes b Inchmore | 21 | | |
| *A. R. Border c Illingworth b Radford | 135 | 1/28 2/55 3/85 (5 wkts dec.) | 364 |
| D. C. Boon not out | 73 | 4/198 5/302 | |

M. J. Bennett, G. F. Lawson, C. J. McDermott and D. R. Gilbert did not bat.

Bowling: Radford 15–0–77–1; Inchmore 18–5–38–3; Weston 4–1–16–0; Patel 20–2–90–1; Newport 12–0–72–0; Illingworth 16–7–47–0; D'Oliveira 1–0–5–0.

Umpires: D. J. Constant and K. E. Palmer.

## †NOTTINGHAMSHIRE v AUSTRALIANS

At Trent Bridge, May 14. Abandoned without a ball bowled.

## †SURREY v AUSTRALIANS

At The Oval, May 16. Surrey won by six wickets. Toss won by Surrey.

### Australians

| | | | |
|---|---|---|---|
| G. M. Wood c Jesty b Butcher | 23 | M. J. Bennett c Jesty b Thomas | 46 |
| *A. M. J. Hilditch run out | 10 | | |
| K. C. Wessels c Needham b Pauline | 7 | B 4, l-b 2, w 9, n-b 9 | 24 |
| D. M. Wellham run out | 21 | | |
| G. M. Ritchie c Lynch b Butcher | 18 | 1/22 2/46 3/48 (7 wkts, 55 overs) | 216 |
| †W. B. Phillips not out | 66 | 4/85 5/100 6/108 | |
| S. P. O'Donnell b Needham | 1 | 7/216 | |

G. F. Lawson, J. R. Thomson and D. R. Gilbert did not bat.

Bowling: Thomas 9–1–35–1; Monkhouse 10–0–73–0; Butcher 11–3–24–2; Pauline 4–0–9–1; Needham 11–2–25–1; Pocock 10–1–44–0.

### Surrey

| | | | |
|---|---|---|---|
| A. R. Butcher c Gilbert b Bennett | 64 | D. B. Pauline not out | 7 |
| G. S. Clinton c Bennett b Thomson | 86 | B 6, l-b 7, w 6, n-b 5 | 24 |
| A. J. Stewart lbw b Gilbert | 14 | | |
| T. E. Jesty b Lawson | 8 | 1/140 2/185 3/187 (4 wkts, 54.1 overs) | 217 |
| M. A. Lynch not out | 14 | 4/201 | |

A. Needham, †C. J. Richards, D. J. Thomas, G. Monkhouse and *P. I. Pocock did not bat.

Bowling: Lawson 10.1–1–32–1; Gilbert 9–0–34–1; Thomson 10–0–39–1; O'Donnell 11–0–51–0; Wessels 3–0–16–0; Bennett 11–0–32–1.

Umpires: M. J. Kitchen and N. T. Plews.

## SUSSEX v AUSTRALIANS

At Hove, May 18, 19, 20, 21. Drawn. Toss won by Australians. This was the first of the four-day matches scheduled for the tourists against the counties, and apart from the gripping climax the cricket was generally disappointing, as was support for the fixture. Fewer than 3,000 paying spectators attended over the four days. Imran Khan and le Roux, the Sussex last-wicket pair, survived the final 28 balls from Holland and Matthews, and a missed catch. The tourists led on the first innings by 59, Boon scoring a splendid 119 off 224 balls, hitting twenty boundaries and displaying an impressive range of strokes and neat footwork. Mendis played a determined innings of 81 in the Sussex first innings, in which Barclay had to retire hurt after being struck in the face when he ducked into a sharply rising delivery from Thomson. Ritchie (one 6, eleven 4s) and Phillips (fourteen 4s) set up Australia's declaration with a partnership of 142 for the fifth wicket, whereupon Sussex, 17 for one overnight, struggled against the leg-spin of Holland and off-spin of Matthews in the three hours of play permitted on the last day by rain and bad light.

### Australians

| First innings | | Second innings | |
|---|---|---|---|
| *A. M. J. Hilditch c Gould b le Roux | 8 | (2) c Waller b C. M. Wells | 0 |
| G. M. Wood lbw b Imran | 8 | (1) c sub b Waller | 18 |
| K. C. Wessels c C. M. Wells b Waller | 56 | run out | 18 |
| G. M. Ritchie run out | 16 | (5) not out | 100 |
| D. C. Boon c A. P. Wells b C. M. Wells | 119 | (4) c sub b Greig | 21 |
| †W. B. Phillips c Parker b Barclay | 33 | c Greig b Green | 91 |
| G. R. J. Matthews lbw b Imran | 19 | c sub b Waller | 1 |
| S. P. O'Donnell not out | 37 | not out | 15 |
| R. G. Holland c Parker b Greig | 4 | | |
| D. R. Gilbert b Barclay | 7 | | |
| J. R. Thomson b Imran | 3 | | |
| B 1, l-b 4, n-b 6 | 11 | B 4, l-b 2, n-b 5 | 11 |
| 1/16 2/16 3/37 4/135 5/200 6/245 7/273 8/282 9/314 | 321 | 1/7 2/37 3/41 4/90 5/232 6/235 (6 wkts dec.) | 275 |

Bowling: *First Innings*—le Roux 10–2–19–1; Imran 21.2–10–55–3; C. M. Wells 20–5–73–1; Greig 12–2–43–1; Waller 33–9–61–1; Barclay 18–2–65–2. *Second Innings*—Imran 12–5–33–0; C. M. Wells 12–2–35–1; Waller 30–9–66–2; Greig 14–4–47–1; Green 21.3–4–76–1; Parker 1–0–12–0.

### Sussex

| First innings | | Second innings | |
|---|---|---|---|
| G. D. Mendis c and b Holland | 81 | c Gilbert b Thomson | 7 |
| A. M. Green b Gilbert | 27 | c Phillips b Holland | 29 |
| P. W. G. Parker b Matthews | 26 | (4) b O'Donnell | 12 |
| A. P. Wells c Hilditch b Matthews | 0 | (5) c Ritchie b Holland | 5 |
| C. M. Wells b Holland | 38 | (6) lbw b Holland | 0 |
| Imran Khan c Holland b O'Donnell | 0 | (7) not out | 44 |
| *J. R. T. Barclay retired hurt | 37 | (8) b Matthews | 19 |
| I. A. Greig lbw b Gilbert | 8 | (9) b Matthews | 15 |
| †I. J. Gould b Gilbert | 0 | (10) b Holland | 2 |
| G. S. le Roux c Phillips b Gilbert | 20 | (11) not out | 0 |
| C. E. Waller not out | 2 | (3) b Gilbert | 8 |
| L-b 3, w 1, n-b 19 | 23 | L-b 7, n-b 5 | 12 |
| 1/54 2/119 3/121 4/181 5/186 6/198 7/213 8/215 9/254 | 262 | 1/11 2/31 3/59 4/59 5/59 6/66 7/105 8/137 9/146 (9 wkts) | 153 |

Bowling: *First Innings*—Thomson 13.3–4–50–0; Gilbert 32–6–97–4; O'Donnell 14–4–25–1; Holland 23–5–49–2; Matthews 11–3–38–2. *Second Innings*—Thomson 7–1–31–1; Gilbert 7–2–15–1; O'Donnell 9–0–27–1; Holland 20–10–37–4; Matthews 11–2–36–2.

Umpires: D. G. L. Evans and J. H. Harris.

## MCC v AUSTRALIANS

At Lord's, May 22, 23, 24. Drawn. After two days on which the batsmen had very much the better of things, poor weather prevented a second Australian declaration and a chase for victory by MCC. Only 55 overs could be bowled on the last day. Put in by Nicholas, the Australians in their first innings scored at a gradually increasing tempo, Border making his third century in successive matches and the tall Victorian, O'Donnell, on his first appearance at headquarters and in only his twelfth first-class innings, racing to three figures in time to allow Border to declare with half an hour of the first day left. Of their 206 for the sixth wicket, the last hundred came in fifteen overs. Bad light, however, prevented any further play. On the second day MCC hit back through Nicholas and Lamb, who added an unbroken 239 in just over three hours. Both played very well, Nicholas after a shaky start reaching his hundred off 142 balls and Lamb needing 127 balls. Bad light again brought an early finish, following a declaration by Nicholas, and on the third day conditions were dismal. As a form of trial, the match pointed to the likelihood of a high-scoring Test series.

### Australians

| | | | |
|---|---|---|---|
| A. M. J. Hilditch b Sidebottom | 14 | – (2) c Sidebottom b Williams | 21 |
| G. M. Wood lbw b Willey | 33 | – (1) c French b Gooch | 48 |
| K. C. Wessels c Gooch b Sidebottom | 60 | | |
| *A. R. Border b Underwood | 125 | | |
| G. M. Ritchie c French b Williams | 22 | – (4) b Athey | 47 |
| D. M. Wellham c French b Williams | 0 | – (3) not out | 81 |
| S. P. O'Donnell not out | 100 | | |
| †R. B. Phillips not out | 0 | | |
| M. J. Bennett (did not bat) | | – (5) not out | 12 |
| L-b 8, n-b 15 | 23 | L-b 2, n-b 11 | 13 |
| 1/24 2/117 3/136 4/164 5/166 6/372 (6 wkts dec.) | 377 | 1/33 2/117 3/195 (3 wkts) | 222 |

G. F. Lawson and J. R. Thomson did not bat.

Bowling: *First Innings*—Williams 17–2–74–2; Sidebottom 20–3–73–2; Underwood 27–4–93–1; Thomas 15.2–2–76–0; Willey 16–4–53–1. *Second Innings*—Thomas 18–6–55–0; Williams 11–0–41–1; Underwood 4–3–3–0; Willey 4–2–14–0; Sidebottom 7–0–38–0; Gooch 16–2–46–1; Athey 9–0–23–1.

### MCC

| | |
|---|---|
| G. A. Gooch b Thomson | 15 |
| G. Fowler c O'Donnell b Lawson | 24 |
| *M. C. J. Nicholas not out | 115 |
| A. J. Lamb not out | 122 |
| B 4, l-b 7, w 3, n-b 1 | 15 |
| 1/28 2/52 (2 wkts dec.) | 291 |

C. W. J. Athey, P. Willey, A. Sidebottom, †B. N. French, D. J. Thomas, N. F. Williams and D. L. Underwood did not bat.

Bowling: Lawson 17–1–66–1; Thomson 14–1–65–1; O'Donnell 16–3–77–0; Bennett 15–1–53–0; Hilditch 3–0–19–0.

Umpires: J. Birkenshaw and A. G. T. Whitehead.

## DERBYSHIRE v AUSTRALIANS

At Derby, May 25, 26, 27. Drawn. Toss won by Australians. Border dominated the first day with a brilliant century, his fourth in successive first-class innings, to emulate C. G. Macartney who, on the 1921 tour, was the only previous Australian to score four consecutive hundreds in England. Derbyshire's weak attack was flayed by Border, who reached three figures in only 103 minutes from 112 balls. He hit five 6s and ten 4s, dominating a third-wicket stand of 148 with Wellham, before he gave away his wicket. Inadequate covering as well as rain ruled out play for the next two days and the match was abandoned so that a 55-over game could be staged on the scheduled fourth day of the match.

### Australians

| | |
|---|---|
| A. M. J. Hilditch c Maher b Miller | 60 |
| G. M. Wood c Roberts b Miller | 16 |
| D. M. Wellham c Maher b Moir | 77 |
| *A. R. Border c Wright b Moir | 100 |
| D. C. Boon not out | 10 |
| G. R. J. Matthews lbw b Miller | 1 |
| †W. B. Phillips not out | 0 |
| B 3, l-b 4, w 1, n-b 6 | 14 |
| 1/38 2/96 3/244 4/274 5/277 (5 wkts) | 278 |

M. J. Bennett, D. R. Gilbert, R. G. Holland and C. J. McDermott did not bat.

Bowling: Newman 7–2–27–0; Finney 14–1–52–0; Miller 39–5–125–3; Moir 27–7–67–2.

### Derbyshire

*K. J. Barnett, A. Hill, J. E. Morris, B. Roberts, J. G. Wright, W. P. Fowler, G. Miller, R. J. Finney, †B. J. M. Maher, D. G. Moir and P. G. Newman.

Umpires: H. D. Bird and B. J. Meyer.

## †DERBYSHIRE v AUSTRALIANS

At Derby, May 28. Australians won by six wickets. Toss won by Derbyshire.

### Derbyshire

| | | | |
|---|---|---|---|
| *K. J. Barnett b Lawson | 54 | †B. J. M. Maher not out | 18 |
| A. Hill c Phillips b McDermott | 2 | D. G. Moir c Wessels b Gilbert | 9 |
| J. E. Morris c Phillips b Gilbert | 6 | P. G. Newman not out | 1 |
| B. Roberts b Gilbert | 1 | L-b 4, w 1, n-b 12 | 17 |
| J. G. Wright lbw b Lawson | 42 | | |
| W. P. Fowler b Matthews | 0 | 1/9 2/31 3/33 (9 wkts, 55 overs) | 188 |
| G. Miller b Border | 23 | 4/105 5/110 6/119 | |
| R. J. Finney b Border | 15 | 7/149 8/176 9/186 | |

Bowling: McDermott 10–3–22–1; Gilbert 11–1–47–3; O'Donnell 11–1–34–0; Matthews 11–2–20–1; Lawson 7–0–34–2; Border 5–0–27–2.

### Australians

| | | | |
|---|---|---|---|
| †W. B. Phillips b Newman | 15 | S. P. O'Donnell not out | 0 |
| G. M. Wood c Morris b Moir | 41 | L-b 8, w 4, n-b 5 | 17 |
| K. C. Wessels c Fowler b Finney | 64 | | |
| D. C. Boon st Maher b Finney | 34 | 1/28 2/86 3/163 (4 wkts, 52.4 overs) | 192 |
| G. R. J. Matthews not out | 21 | 4/184 | |

A. M. J. Hilditch, G. F. Lawson, *A. R. Border, C. J. McDermott and D. R. Gilbert did not bat.

Bowling: Finney 11–2–39–2; Newman 11–2–38–1; Miller 11–4–12–0; Moir 11–1–40–1, Hill 3–0–17–0; Roberts 3–0–22–0; Fowler 2–0–10–0; Barnett 0.4–0–6–0.

Umpires: H. D. Bird and B. J. Meyer.

## †ENGLAND v AUSTRALIA

### First Texaco Trophy Match

At Old Trafford, May 30. Australia won by three wickets. After choosing to bat, England soon lost Fowler, Gower and Lamb, Lawson removing the last two with successive balls in the best spell of bowling in the match. But Gooch, back in the England side after serving a three-year ban for having played in South Africa, and Botham added 116 in 28 overs. The manner of Botham's dismissal, bowled while attempting a reverse sweep, marred an otherwise splendid innings. He was sixth out at 160 with a possible fifteen overs left, but Gatting ran out of partners and for England a final total of 219 was disappointing. For most of Australia's innings neither side could claim any advantage. If anything, England looked the likelier winners when Border was fifth out in the 44th over. But Phillips, until he fell to a spectacular catch by Gatting at short third man, Matthews and Lawson all found England's leg-stump attack to their liking, and Australia got home with five balls to spare. Brian Statham's choice of Botham as Man of the Match, at the end of a sunny day, caused some surprise, Botham having been seen to throw away his wicket at an important time.

*Man of the Match:* I. T. Botham. *Attendance:* 20,087; *receipts* £139,978.

## England

| | | | |
|---|---|---|---|
| G. A. Gooch c O'Donnell b Holland | 57 | P. H. Edmonds c Border b Lawson | 0 |
| G. Fowler c Phillips b McDermott | 10 | P. J. W. Allott b McDermott | 2 |
| *D. I. Gower b Lawson | 3 | N. G. Cowans c and b McDermott | 1 |
| A. J. Lamb c Phillips b Lawson | 0 | B 2, l-b 7, w 2, n-b 9 | 20 |
| I. T. Botham b Matthews | 72 | | — |
| M. W. Gatting not out | 31 | 1/21 2/27 3/27 4/143 (54 overs) | 219 |
| P. Willey b Holland | 12 | 5/160 6/181 7/203 | |
| †P. R. Downton c Matthews b Lawson | 11 | 8/203 9/213 | |

Bowling: Lawson 10–1–26–4; McDermott 11–0–46–3; O'Donnell 11–0–44–0; Matthews 11–1–45–1; Holland 11–2–49–2.

## Australia

| | | | |
|---|---|---|---|
| K. C. Wessels c Botham b Willey | 39 | G. R. J. Matthews not out | 29 |
| G. M. Wood c Downton b Cowans | 8 | G. F. Lawson not out | 14 |
| D. M. Wellham c and b Edmonds | 12 | B 2, l-b 12, w 4 | 18 |
| *A. R. Border c and b Allott | 59 | | — |
| D. C. Boon c Botham b Gooch | 12 | 1/15 2/52 3/74 (7 wkts, 54.1 overs) | 220 |
| †W. B. Phillips c Gatting b Cowans | 28 | 4/118 5/156 | |
| S. P. O'Donnell b Botham | 1 | 6/157 7/186 | |

C. J. McDermott and R. G. Holland did not bat.

Bowling: Cowans 10.1–1–44–2; Botham 11–2–41–1; Allott 11–0–47–1; Edmonds 11–2–33–1; Willey 9–1–31–1; Gooch 2–0–10–1.

Umpires: D. G. L. Evans and K. E. Palmer.

# †ENGLAND v AUSTRALIA

## Second Texaco Trophy Match

At Edgbaston, June 1. Australia won by four wickets. Both sides made one change for the second of their three one-day internationals, Robinson and Thomson replacing Fowler and Holland respectively, but the game followed a very similar course to the first, in equally fine weather. England, put in this time, were given a good start by Gooch and Robinson (63 in fourteen overs) but failed to make quite the most of it. Gooch scored a fine 115 (159 balls, nine 4s), but Lamb spent 21 overs over 25 and England were driven to desperate measures as their overs ran out. With the help of an early life – he was missed by Gower at short extra cover off Edmonds – Border continued his wonderful run of form, first steadying the innings with Wessels and then, in partnership with O'Donnell, putting Australia just ahead of the clock. England's defeat was their eighth in their last nine one-day internationals – in India, Australia, Sharjah and at home, and it left Australia with the Texaco Trophy.

*Man of the Match:* A. R. Border. *Attendance:* 17,000; *receipts* £111,650.

## England

| | | | |
|---|---|---|---|
| G. A. Gooch b McDermott | 115 | †P. R. Downton not out | 16 |
| R. T. Robinson c and b O'Donnell | 26 | P. H. Edmonds not out | 6 |
| *D. I. Gower c Phillips b O'Donnell | 0 | L-b 2, w 2, n-b 4 | 8 |
| A. J. Lamb b Thomson | 25 | | — |
| I. T. Botham c Wellham b Lawson | 29 | 1/63 2/69 3/134 (7 wkts, 55 overs) | 231 |
| M. W. Gatting c Lawson b McDermott | 6 | 4/193 5/206 6/208 | |
| P. Willey c Phillips b Lawson | 0 | 7/216 | |

P. J. W. Allott and N. G. Cowans did not bat.

Bowling: Lawson 11–0–53–2; McDermott 11–0–56–2; O'Donnell 11–2–32–2; Thomson 11–0–47–1; Matthews 10–0–38–0; Border 1–0–3–0.

TEXACO TROPHY
TEXACO

## Australia

| | | | |
|---|---|---|---|
| K. C. Wessels c and b Willey | 57 | S. P. O'Donnell b Botham | 28 |
| G. M. Wood lbw b Cowans | 5 | G. R. J. Matthews not out | 8 |
| D. M. Wellham lbw b Botham | 7 | L-b 13, w 2, n-b 1 | 16 |
| *A. R. Border not out | 85 | | |
| D. C. Boon b Allott | 13 | 1/10 2/19 3/116 (6 wkts, 54 overs) | 233 |
| †W. B. Phillips c Gatting b Cowans | 14 | 4/137 5/157 6/222 | |

G. F. Lawson, C. J. McDermott and J. R. Thomson did not bat.

Bowling: Botham 10–2–38–2; Cowans 11–2–42–2; Allott 10–1–40–1; Willey 11–1–38–1; Edmonds 10–0–48–0; Gooch 2–0–14–0.

Umpires: D. J. Constant and D. R. Shepherd.

# †ENGLAND v AUSTRALIA

## Third Texaco Trophy Match

At Lord's, June 3. England won by eight wickets. Having already won the one-day series, Australia gave Hilditch and Ritchie a game in place of Wessels and Wellham. England brought in Foster for Edmonds. Gower did his best day's work for a long time. It began with his winning the toss, and he made his first century for England, at home or abroad, since taking over as their official captain in June 1984. His second-wicket partnership of 202 in 37 overs with Gooch, when England went in needing 255 to win, gave his side a comfortable victory on another cloudless day before a capacity crowd. For the first time in eight innings on the Australian tour Border failed to reach 50, Gooch bowling him for 44. But Wood (165 balls, ten 4s, one 6) batted through the innings, and towards the end Boon made 45 in 47 balls. Once Gower had overcome an uncertain start, he and Gooch mastered the Australian bowling. Gooch batted 207 minutes, received 164 balls, and hit thirteen 4s and one 6. Gower was in for 159 minutes and 118 balls, hitting fourteen 4s and one 6.

*Man of the Match:* D. I. Gower. *Attendance:* 25,539; *receipts* £236,873.

*Men of the Series:* A. R. Border (Australia) and G. A. Gooch (England).

## Australia

| | | | |
|---|---|---|---|
| G. M. Wood not out | 114 | S. P. O'Donnell not out | 0 |
| A. M. J. Hilditch lbw b Foster | 4 | | |
| G. M. Ritchie c Gooch b Botham | 15 | B 2, l-b 13, w 6, n-b 1 | 22 |
| *A. R. Border b Gooch | 44 | | |
| D. C. Boon c Gower b Willey | 45 | 1/6 2/47 3/143 (5 wkts, 55 overs) | 254 |
| †W. B. Phillips run out | 10 | 4/228 5/252 | |

G. R. J. Matthews, G. F. Lawson, C. J. McDermott and J. R. Thomson did not bat.

Bowling: Cowans 8–2–22–0; Foster 11–0–55–1; Botham 8–1–27–1; Allott 7–1–45–0; Gooch 11–0–46–1; Willey 10–1–44–1.

## England

| | |
|---|---|
| G. A. Gooch not out | 117 |
| R. T. Robinson lbw b McDermott | 7 |
| *D. I. Gower c Border b McDermott | 102 |
| A. J. Lamb not out | 9 |
| B 2, l-b 9, w 2, n-b 9 | 22 |
| 1/25 2/227 (2 wkts, 49 overs) | 257 |

I. T. Botham, M. W. Gatting, P. Willey, †P. R. Downton, N. A. Foster, P. J. W. Allott and N. G. Cowans did not bat.

Bowling: Lawson 9–0–37–0; McDermott 10–0–51–2; Thomson 8–1–50–0; O'Donnell 11–0–54–0; Matthews 10–0–49–0; Border 1–0–5–0.

Umpires: H. D. Bird and B. J. Meyer.

## YORKSHIRE v AUSTRALIANS

At Headingley, June 5, 6, 7. Drawn. Toss won by Yorkshire. Bad weather ruined the contest, washing out the second day, interrupting the first and third, and denying the tourists much-needed match practice. Yorkshire fielded a weakened side, with three colts as seam bowlers. Wood made a solid century from 185 balls with seventeen boundaries, and in Yorkshire's reply Boycott took 130 deliveries for his unbeaten half-century.

### Australians

*A. M. J. Hilditch c Blakey b Fletcher . 18
G. M. Wood not out . . . . . . . . . . . . . . . .102
D. M. Wellham c Carrick b Pickles . . . 8
G. M. Ritchie not out . . . . . . . . . . . . . . . 58
L-b 4, w 3, n-b 2 . . . . . . . . . . . 9

1/33 2/53 (2 wkts dec.) 195

D. C. Boon, S. P. O'Donnell, †R. B. Phillips, M. J. Bennett, C. J. McDermott, R. G. Holland and D. R. Gilbert did not bat.

Bowling: Fletcher 13–2–48–1; Shaw 19–5–56–0; Pickles 14–6–40–1; Hartley 12.5–4–38–0; Carrick 3–1–9–0.

### Yorkshire

G. Boycott not out . . . . . . . . . . . . . . . . . 52
R. J. Blakey c Phillips b McDermott . . 31
K. Sharp c Hilditch b Bennett . . . . . . . . 24
J. D. Love not out . . . . . . . . . . . . . . . . . . 1
B 4, l-b 4, n-b 8 . . . . . . . . . . . . 16

1/70 2/122 (2 wkts) 124

*†D. L. Bairstow, S. N. Hartley, P. Carrick, P. A. Booth, C. S. Pickles, C. Shaw and S. D. Fletcher did not bat.

Bowling: McDermott 15–2–49–1; Gilbert 12–3–36–0; Bennett 8–3–14–1; O'Donnell 5–1–17–0.

Umpires: D. O. Oslear and B. Leadbeater.

## LEICESTERSHIRE v AUSTRALIANS

At Leicester, June 8, 9, 10, 11. Drawn. Toss won by Australians. Border, keen to give his fast bowlers a thorough workout before the first Test, put Leicestershire in on a bland pitch. Gower's innings of 214 minutes, including three 6s and twenty 4s, was the highlight of the opening day, overshadowing the four-hour hundred of Balderstone, the thirtieth of a long career. Together they put on 253 for the second wicket, a county record, although both survived chances, Balderstone in single figures and Gower, who reached his hundred with a 6 off Thomson, when he was 91. Thomson was the unlucky bowler in each instance. He and McDermott both bowled at a lively pace but Lawson, who developed a virus infection and took no further part after the first day, was well below par. Border, testing a groin injury, played a minor role when the Australians batted, but the left-handed wicket-keeper, Phillips, who hit two 6s and twenty 4s in 159 minutes, and Ritchie (two 6s, twelve 4s, 232 minutes) compiled untroubled hundreds against some ineffective bowling. McDermott struck a gigantic 6 and four 4s in his maiden first-class fifty. With the weather causing interruptions on the first three days and taking all but an hour from the fourth, the draw was the inevitable result.

### Leicestershire

| | | | |
|---|---|---|---|
| I. P. Butcher b McDermott | 35 | – not out | 19 |
| J. C. Balderstone c Ritchie b Thomson | 134 | – not out | 7 |
| *D. I. Gower c Boon b McDermott | 135 | | |
| P. Willey c Boon b McDermott | 2 | | |
| J. J. Whitaker c Phillips b Thomson | 18 | | |
| N. E. Briers lbw b Holland | 13 | | |
| †M. A. Garnham not out | 27 | | |
| G. J. Parsons b Thomson | 7 | | |
| N. G. B. Cook c Phillips b Thomson | 1 | | |
| J. P. Agnew c Boon b Thomson | 19 | | |
| L. B. Taylor c and b Matthews | 11 | | |
| B 2, l-b 12, w 2, n-b 36 | 52 | L-b 1, w 1 | 2 |
| 1/62 2/315 3/328 4/353 5/372 6/382 7/392 8/394 9/427 | 454 | | (no wkt) 28 |

Bowling: *First Innings*—Lawson 15–0–71–0; Thomson 24–6–103–5; McDermott 28–3–87–3; Holland 32–4–112–1; Matthews 16.5–3–67–1. *Second Innings*—Wessels 5–0–9–0; Boon 3–0–12–0; Holland 2–0–5–0; Ritchie 0.3–0–1–0.

### Australians

| | | | |
|---|---|---|---|
| K. C. Wessels lbw b Agnew | 2 | R. G. Holland b Agnew | 5 |
| A. M. J. Hilditch c Butcher b Willey | 56 | J. R. Thomson b Parsons | 2 |
| D. C. Boon b Agnew | 39 | G. F. Lawson absent ill | |
| †W. B. Phillips c Cook b Willey | 128 | | |
| G. M. Ritchie b Parsons | 115 | B 4, l-b 4, n-b 7 | 15 |
| *A. R. Border b Taylor | 25 | | |
| G. R. J. Matthews b Cook | 26 | 1/6 2/66 3/111 4/288 5/337 | 466 |
| C. J. McDermott not out | 53 | 6/388 7/437 8/453 9/466 | |

Bowling: Agnew 26–2–144–3; Taylor 16–3–72–1; Parsons 28–6–88–2; Cook 29–9–87–1; Willey 18–3–67–2.

Umpires: B. Dudleston and R. Palmer.

## ENGLAND v AUSTRALIA

### First Cornhill Test

At Headingley, June 13, 14, 15, 17, 18. England won by five wickets, Australia's third successive Test defeat at Leeds. The match had to withstand constant and inevitable comparisons with the epic Headingley Test of 1981, and to the end there was an outside chance that history would be reversed in an equally bizarre manner. Four years earlier, Australia, needing 130, had managed only 111. This time England, set 123, spluttered their way to victory with 13.2 overs left.

The game did not need the comparisons; it was a remarkable contest in its own right, effectively settled on a gloriously sunlit Saturday afternoon when the England batsmen seized the initiative spectacularly, led by Robinson, Man of the Match for scoring 175 in his first home Test, and Botham. The bat outshone the ball throughout, helped by a fast outfield. The pitch was less eccentric than many on this ground, but was uneven in bounce, and if either side had bowled more accurately, the scores would have been far lower.

Part of the bat's domination was dictated by conservative selection policies. Determined not to lose the first match in a six-Test series, both sets of selectors played an extra batsman. England brought back Gooch, Emburey, Willey, Botham and Allott, all of whom had, for different reasons, been unavailable for the previous Test in Kanpur. They replaced Fowler, Pocock, Cowdrey, Edmonds and Foster. Australia omitted Holland, who had engineered the triumph at Sydney in their previous Test, and were thus without a spinner at all. This looked a strange decision at the time, and stranger as the match wore on, when it seemed that Lawson, ill and in doubt in the days preceding the Test, was not wholly himself and that Thomson was off form.

None of this showed on the opening day when Australia, having won the toss, batted first and immediately took advantage of some short, wide bowling by England. Hilditch, after a wretched start to his tour, found form at the strategic moment (in contrast to his captain, Border, who went in the other direction), showing great skill, especially square of the wicket, and scoring 119 in 247 minutes, his second century in three Tests since being recalled against West Indies the previous December. At one stage Australia were 201 for two, but on a rain-affected second day England bounded back, taking the last four wickets in ten balls. Three of these fell in four balls to Botham, who narrowly missed a hat-trick when he whistled one past Lawson's defence.

On the Saturday, as the sun returned and all swing ceased, England took control. However defective the English bowling had appeared, the Australians were hopelessly exposed, and the youngsters McDermott (in his third Test) and O'Donnell (in his first) were forced to carry the attack. This proved impossible when Botham launched one of his most brilliant assaults: 60 off 51 balls in a golden hour of explosive batsmanship. While Botham was in, Robinson (firmly keeping his helmet on at the non-striker's end because Botham was a far greater danger than the bowling) was almost forgotten. But before and afterwards, he showed the technique and temperament that had made him a success in India. He surprised many people by the range and vigour of his strokeplay, especially off the back foot. His 175 took only 271 balls, good going for a supposed anchor-man.

The Australians reached exasperation on the Monday morning when Cowans and Downton put on 49 for the last wicket. Their old feeling that Headingley had something against Australians was heavily upon them, and they lost six wickets before wiping off the first-innings deficit of 202, despite another fine innings from Hilditch, well supported by Wessels. By now the bounce was becoming increasingly strange – Ritchie was bowled by a shooter – and England must have expected to wrap up the match early on the last day. The bookmakers stopped betting completely.

However, Phillips caused a delay with an innings too handsome and free to look like a serious match-saving effort but enough to keep England fielding until after lunch. They then had three hours twenty minutes to score the 123 runs they needed. But wickets kept falling, and England finally crawled over the finishing line like exhausted marathon runners. Even then, Willey, one of the not out batsmen, had given a simple chance off Thomson, which Border, at mid-wicket, put down. This would have been Thomson's 200th Test wicket and, as he had had a poor match, no-one was sure when his next chance might come.

However, this was quickly eclipsed as a talking point by the crowd's performance at the end. Less than three weeks after the deaths at the European Cup soccer final in Brussels, an invasion of the field in England's moment of triumph gave more than usual cause for concern. The mostly young spectators who rushed on prematurely – described by England's captain as "a pack of mad dogs" – almost certainly distracted Lawson as he tried to catch Lamb and prevent the winning runs. The attendance was 54,018 and the receipts £321,250, a record for a provincial Test. – M.E.

## Australia

| | First innings | | Second innings | |
|---|---|---|---|---|
| G. M. Wood | lbw b Allott | 14 | (2) c Lamb b Botham | 3 |
| A. M. J. Hilditch | c Downton b Gooch | 119 | (1) c Robinson b Emburey | 80 |
| K. C. Wessels | c Botham b Emburey | 36 | b Emburey | 64 |
| *A. R. Border | c Botham b Cowans | 32 | c Downton b Botham | 8 |
| D. C. Boon | lbw b Gooch | 14 | b Cowans | 22 |
| G. M. Ritchie | b Botham | 46 | b Emburey | 1 |
| †W. B. Phillips | c Gower b Emburey | 30 | c Lamb b Botham | 91 |
| C. J. McDermott | b Botham | 18 | (10) c Gooch b Emburey | 6 |
| S. P. O'Donnell | lbw b Botham | 0 | (8) c Downton b Botham | 24 |
| G. F. Lawson | c Downton b Allott | 0 | (9) c Downton b Emburey | 15 |
| J. R. Thomson | not out | 4 | not out | 2 |
| | L-b 13, w 4, n-b 1 | 18 | B 4, l-b 3, w 1 | 8 |
| | 1/23 2/155 3/201 4/229 5/229 6/284 7/326 8/326 9/327 | 331 | 1/5 2/144 3/151 4/159 5/160 6/192 7/272 8/307 9/318 | 324 |

Bowling: *First Innings*—Cowans 20–4–78–1; Allott 22–3–74–2; Botham 29.1–8–86–3; Gooch 21–4–57–2; Emburey 6–1–23–2. *Second Innings*—Botham 33–7–107–4; Allott 17–4–57–0; Emburey 43.4–14–82–5; Cowans 13–2–50–1; Gooch 9–3–21–0.

### England

| | | | |
|---|---|---|---|
| G. A. Gooch lbw b McDermott | 5 | lbw b O'Donnell | 28 |
| R. T. Robinson c Boon b Lawson | 175 | b Lawson | 21 |
| *D. I. Gower c Phillips b McDermott | 17 | c Border b O'Donnell | 5 |
| M. W. Gatting c Hilditch b McDermott | 53 | c Phillips b Lawson | 12 |
| A. J. Lamb b O'Donnell | 38 | not out | 31 |
| I. T. Botham b Thomson | 60 | b O'Donnell | 12 |
| P. Willey c Hilditch b Lawson | 36 | not out | 3 |
| †P. R. Downton c Border b McDermott | 54 | | |
| J. E. Emburey b Lawson | 21 | | |
| P. J. W. Allott c Boon b Thomson | 12 | | |
| N. G. Cowans not out | 22 | | |
| B 5, l-b 16, w 5, n-b 14 | 40 | L-b 7, w 1, n-b 3 | 11 |
| 1/14 2/50 3/186 4/264 5/344 6/417 7/422 8/462 9/484 | 533 | 1/44 2/59 3/71 4/83 5/110 | (5 wkts) 123 |

Bowling: *First Innings*—Lawson 26–4–117–3; McDermott 32–2–134–4; Thomson 34–3–166–2; O'Donnell 27–8–77–1; Border 3–0–16–0; Wessels 3–2–2–0. *Second Innings*—McDermott 4–0–20–0; Lawson 16–4–51–2; O'Donnell 15.4–5–37–3; Thomson 3–0–8–0.

Umpires: B. J. Meyer and K. E. Palmer.

## †OXFORD & CAMBRIDGE UNIVERSITIES v AUSTRALIANS

At Fenner's, Cambridge, June 20. Australians won by 79 runs. Toss won by Oxford & Cambridge Universities.

### Australians

| | |
|---|---|
| G. R. J. Matthews c Davies b Grimes | 15 |
| D. M. Wellham c Davies b Toogood | 11 |
| M. J. Bennett c Fell b Ellison | 14 |
| D. C. Boon c Thorne b Andrew | 108 |
| G. M. Ritchie c Davies b Toogood | 24 |
| *A. R. Border b Carr | 41 |
| †R. B. Phillips not out | 26 |
| G. F. Lawson st Davies b Andrew | 9 |
| R. G. Holland run out | 6 |
| B 2, l-b 4, w 5 | 11 |
| 1/17 2/37 3/56 4/110 5/188 6/233 7/252 8/265 | (8 wkts, 55 overs) 265 |

A. M. J. Hilditch and D. R. Gilbert did not bat.

Bowling: Grimes 7–0–43–1; Ellison 11–1–24–1; Toogood 11–1–57–2; Cotterell 9–0–47–0; Carr 7–1–33–1; Andrew 10–0–55–2.

### Oxford & Cambridge Universities

| | |
|---|---|
| *C. R. Andrew c Boon b Bennett | 40 |
| G. J. Toogood run out | 1 |
| P. G. P. Roebuck not out | 75 |
| J. D. Carr c and b Bennett | 6 |
| D. A. Thorne c Wellham b Bennett | 5 |
| D. J. Fell c Boon b Bennett | 0 |
| W. R. Bristowe lbw b Holland | 4 |
| †A. G. Davies not out | 51 |
| B 1, l-b 1, w 2 | 4 |
| 1/17 2/58 3/72 4/88 5/88 6/99 | (6 wkts, 55 overs) 186 |

T. A. Cotterell, C. C. Ellison and A. D. H. Grimes did not bat.

Bowling: Lawson 6–1–18–0; Gilbert 11–3–23–0; Matthews 11–2–41–0; Bennett 11–2–26–4; Holland 11–1–36–1; Border 4–0–35–0; Ritchie 1–0–5–0.

Umpires: K. J. Lyons and N. T. Plews.

## HAMPSHIRE v AUSTRALIANS

At Southampton, June 22, 23, 24, 25. Drawn. Toss won by Australians. Rain reduced the match to three days, all of which were affected by the weather. Holland, the leg-spinner, put in his claim for a Test place at Lord's with five for 51 as the county were dismissed for 221 on the second and third days, the opening day having been washed out. Then followed a most remarkable collapse by the Australians. James, a left-arm medium-pace bowler, playing in the match only because Hampshire were resting Marshall and Tremlett, returned a career-best six for 22 as the tourists were skittled out for 76 in 31.5 overs. It was their lowest total against Hampshire, the previous being 83 in 1909. After Connor had made the initial breakthrough, James's movement through the air saw him take six of the next seven wickets in nine overs at a personal cost of 16 runs. Only two 6s by Phillips, on his return from hospital for X-rays to his left hand, saved the Australians from the embarrassment of being asked to follow on. Hampshire's second-innings declaration at 64 for one set the tourists a target of 210 in 37 overs, and when seven wickets fell for 126 Hampshire had hopes of gaining their first win over the Australians since 1912. However, Bennett and McDermott remained together for the last thirteen overs.

### Hampshire

| | | | |
|---|---|---|---|
| V. P. Terry lbw b Holland | 60 | | |
| C. L. Smith c Phillips b McDermott | 29 | – not out | 41 |
| *M. C. J. Nicholas c Wood b Bennett | 17 | – (1) c Wood b Ritchie | 5 |
| R. A. Smith b Holland | 5 | – (3) not out | 17 |
| J. J. E. Hardy lbw b Holland | 27 | | |
| K. D. James c Phillips b Lawson | 8 | | |
| †R. J. Parks b Holland | 33 | | |
| N. G. Cowley lbw b Holland | 11 | | |
| R. J. Maru c Boon b McDermott | 4 | | |
| C. A. Connor not out | 4 | | |
| S. J. W. Andrew retired hurt | 1 | | |
| B 6, l-b 2, w 2, n-b 12 | 22 | B 1 | 1 |
| 1/62 2/98 3/120 4/121 5/150<br>6/174 7/200 8/215 9/215 | 221 | 1/22 (1 wkt dec.) | 64 |

Bowling: *First Innings*—Lawson 9–5–10–1; Gilbert 14–5–35–0; McDermott 12.2–1–39–2; Bennett 33–11–78–1; Holland 22–8–51–5. *Second Innings*—Lawson 2–2–0–0; Wessels 8–2–26–0; Ritchie 5–0–22–1; Boon 2–0–15–0.

### Australians

| | | | |
|---|---|---|---|
| G. M. Wood b Connor | 5 | – (2) c Parks b Connor | 0 |
| K. C. Wessels b James | 6 | – (1) c Parks b Connor | 6 |
| G. M. Ritchie lbw b James | 3 | – (4) c Connor b Maru | 62 |
| *A. R. Border c Parks b James | 8 | – (5) c Connor b Maru | 21 |
| D. C. Boon lbw b James | 0 | – (3) c Parks b Connor | 0 |
| M. J. Bennett c Nicholas b Maru | 13 | – (7) not out | 16 |
| G. F. Lawson c Cowley b James | 6 | – (8) lbw b Maru | 0 |
| C. J. McDermott b Connor | 5 | – (9) not out | 17 |
| R. G. Holland c R. A. Smith b James | 0 | | |
| D. R. Gilbert not out | 6 | | |
| †W. B. Phillips b Maru | 15 | – (6) c James b Cowley | 22 |
| L-b 1, w 2, n-b 6 | 9 | B 2, l-b 3, n-b 5 | 10 |
| 1/7 2/12 3/18 4/18 5/28<br>6/37 7/42 8/43 9/60 | 76 | 1/1 2/1 3/19 4/64<br>5/104 6/126 7/126 (7 wkts) | 154 |

Bowling: *First Innings*—Connor 16–2–46–2; James 11–2–22–6; Maru 4.5–3–7–2. *Second Innings*—Connor 4–0–27–3; James 5–1–26–0; Cowley 13–4–49–1; Maru 13–3–41–3; C. L. Smith 1–0–2–0; R. A. Smith 1–0–4–0.

Umpires: C. Cook and P. B. Wight.

## ENGLAND v AUSTRALIA

### Second Cornhill Test

At Lord's, June 27, 28, 29, July 1, 2. Australia won by four wickets. This was Border's match. The Australian captain scored 43 per cent of his side's runs, 237 out of 552, and led them superbly to maintain Australia's unbeaten run at cricket's headquarters since Verity bowled them to defeat in 1934. Border's 196 in Australia's first innings was his highest Test score, beating his 162 at Madras on his country's last tour of India, and he displayed a command and range of shot which few contemporary players could equal. The only time he seemed at all disconcerted in the match was when, with Australia needing 10 to win but batting anxiously, a statement was read out asking spectators not to run on to the pitch at the finish. However, the announcement had the desired effect and MCC were to be congratulated on their public relations over the question of crowd control.

A fine match was played in a good atmosphere with none of the "noises-off" that had marred the enjoyment of many people at the Test matches against West Indies the previous year. It was remarkable that play was able to start to time on the first day, for on the afternoon before, an MCC assistant secretary had worn wellington boots to inspect the sodden outfield. However, Mick Hunt, the groundsman, and some of his staff worked through the night to remove surface water and, although the pitch was soft and the square still wet, the umpires allowed the game to begin at the appointed time. Border won the toss and asked England to bat. The pitch being too slow at that stage for his leg-spinner, the 38-year-old Holland, Border was gambling on his three pace bowlers to bowl England out, and he was not disappointed. England brought in Edmonds and Foster for Cowans and Willey, and omitted Sidebottom from their original twelve players.

McDermott bowled magnificently for his six wickets. He had both England's openers, Gooch and Robinson, leg before, though Gooch's decision appeared a harsh one, the point of impact looking to be outside the line of the off stump as he played his shot. Gower dominated the England first innings with batting which persuaded the selectors to confirm him in the captaincy for the remaining four Tests. Lawson, still not bowling as fast or aggressively as he is able to, took the crucial wicket of Botham, having him caught on the cover boundary, driving at a slower delivery.

Play on the second day was interrupted five times and finally curtailed by bad light, to the annoyance of a capacity crowd. Loud disapproval was expressed when play was halted for the last time with England's spinners, Edmonds and Emburey, in action. Border, then 92 out of Australia's 183 for four, might have gone at 87 when his pull off Edmonds struck Gatting's wrist at short leg. As the fielder strove to control the ball, he seemed, prematurely, to try to throw it up in celebration of what would have been a remarkable catch. The ball escaped Gatting's despairing lunge, and in response to a somewhat half-hearted appeal umpire Bird ruled that it had not been retained in such a way as to satisfy Law 32.

Border's fifth-wicket stand of 216 with Ritchie ended soon after lunch on the third day when Botham, kept out of the attack in the morning to protect a slightly strained ankle, upset Ritchie's equanimity with a couple of bouncers and followed them with a straight delivery which had him leg before. Botham bowled as fast as for some time and his five wickets prevented the Australians from running away with the match. It was the 25th time he had claimed five wickets in an innings in a Test, a record for any country.

Trailing by 135, England needed a sound start to their second innings; but Gooch was caught behind, trying to leg glance McDermott, and Robinson's bat caught in his pad as he defended against Holland. Gower then took the controversial decision to send in not one, but two night-watchmen, Emburey and Allott. The promotion of two tailenders meant that a major batsman was likely to be left stranded later in the innings, and so it proved. On the Monday morning Lawson reduced England to 98 for six when he removed Emburey, Allott and Lamb, Gower having gone for a one-day-style 22. But Botham, suffering from a bruised toe sustained when he was hit by a golf ball at Wentworth the day before, added 131 with Gatting. They were on the way to turning likely defeat into possible victory when Holland went round the wicket at the Nursery End, aiming for the rough created by McDermott outside the right-hander's leg stump. McDermott had been officially warned by umpire Bird for running down the pitch. Botham's reply was to keep padding the ball away until, going for a big hit, he was caught just backward of point. Downton went next ball, caught at slip. Holland's five wickets on his first appearance in a Test in England were a splendid reward for accurate, intelligent bowling.

Australia faced 21 overs before the close, by when they were 46 for three, needing 127. Hilditch was caught hooking, Wood in the gully off a lifter, both off Botham, and Ritchie was bowled by the accurate Allott. Wood's wicket was Botham's 326th in Tests, making him England's most prolific wicket-taker. On the last morning Border's nerve held after Australia had declined to 65 to five, Wessels, the striker, being run out by a quick return from Gower at short leg and Boon bowled. Border was made Man of the Match and the game of cricket enhanced by a pleasurable Test. The overall attendance was 93,329 and receipts £668,312. – B.S.

## England

| | | | |
|---|---|---|---|
| G. A. Gooch lbw b McDermott | 30 | – c Phillips b McDermott | 17 |
| R. T. Robinson lbw b McDermott | 6 | – b Holland | 12 |
| *D. I. Gower c Border b McDermott | 86 | – (5) c Phillips b McDermott | 22 |
| M. W. Gatting lbw b Lawson | 14 | – (6) not out | 75 |
| A. J. Lamb c Phillips b Lawson | 47 | – (7) c Holland b Lawson | 9 |
| I. T. Botham c Ritchie b Lawson | 5 | – (8) c Border b Holland | 85 |
| †P. R. Downton c Wessels b McDermott | 21 | – (9) c Boon b Holland | 0 |
| J. E. Emburey lbw b O'Donnell | 33 | – (3) b Lawson | 20 |
| P. H. Edmonds c Border b McDermott | 21 | – (10) c Boon b Holland | 1 |
| N. A. Foster c Wessels b McDermott | 3 | – (11) c Border b Holland | 0 |
| P. J. W. Allott not out | 1 | – (4) b Lawson | 0 |
| B 1, l-b 4, w 1, n-b 17 | 23 | B 1, l-b 12, w 4, n-b 3 | 20 |
| 1/26 2/51 3/99 4/179 5/184 6/211 7/241 8/273 9/283 | 290 | 1/32 2/34 3/38 4/57 5/77 6/98 7/229 8/229 9/261 | 261 |

Bowling: *First Innings*—Lawson 25–2–91–3; McDermott 29.2–5–70–6; O'Donnell 22–3–82–1; Holland 23–6–42–0. *Second Innings*—McDermott 20–2–84–2; Lawson 23–0–86–3; Holland 32–12–68–5; O'Donnell 5–0–10–0.

## Australia

| | | | |
|---|---|---|---|
| G. M. Wood c Emburey b Allott | 8 | – (2) c Lamb b Botham | 6 |
| A. M. J. Hilditch b Foster | 14 | – (1) c Lamb b Botham | 0 |
| K. C. Wessels lbw b Botham | 11 | – run out | 28 |
| *A. R. Border c Gooch b Botham | 196 | – (5) not out | 41 |
| D. C. Boon c Downton b Botham | 4 | – (6) b Edmonds | 1 |
| G. M. Ritchie lbw b Botham | 94 | – (4) b Allott | 2 |
| †W. B. Phillips c Edmonds b Botham | 21 | – c Edmonds b Emburey | 29 |
| S. P. O'Donnell c Lamb b Edmonds | 48 | – not out | 9 |
| G. F. Lawson not out | 5 | | |
| C. J. McDermott run out | 9 | | |
| R. G. Holland b Edmonds | 0 | | |
| L-b 10, w 1, n-b 4 | 15 | L-b 11 | 11 |
| 1/11 2/24 3/80 4/101 5/317 6/347 7/398 8/414 9/425 | 425 | 1/0 2/9 3/22 4/63 5/65 6/116 (6 wkts) | 127 |

Bowling: *First Innings*—Foster 23–1–83–1; Allott 30–4–70–1; Botham 24–2–109–5; Edmonds 25.4–5–85–2; Gooch 3–1–11–0; Emburey 19–3–57–0. *Second Innings*—Botham 15–0–49–2; Allott 7–4–8–1; Edmonds 16–5–35–1; Emburey 8–4–24–1.

Umpires: H. D. Bird and D. G. L. Evans.

## ESSEX v AUSTRALIANS

At Chelmsford, July 6, 7, 8, 9. Drawn. Toss won by Australians. Foster, having pulled out of England's squad with a back strain four hours earlier, helped to stave off defeat by surviving the final seventeen overs of the match with East. The Essex quest to score a modest 204 for victory was cut short by Gilbert who, in a lively burst, claimed four of the first five wickets to fall. Although Hilditch performed well during the tourists' first innings, Essex gained a lead of 130, mainly through the efforts of Hardie, who resisted for more than four and a half hours for his century, and more robust contributions from Gooch, who hit thirteen 4s in his 68, and Phillip (65 balls). Thomson bowled 26 no-balls during the Essex innings. Boon, with his best score of the tour to date, and Wellham rescued the Australians from a poor start in their second innings before Gooch inspired a collapse with three wickets in eight deliveries. On the second day, play was interrupted for twenty minutes by a bomb scare, the crowd moving on to the playing area while the police searched the pavilion and stands.

## Australians

| First innings | | Second innings | |
|---|---|---|---|
| G. M. Wood c Lilley b Gooch | 33 | (2) c East b Pringle | 8 |
| *A. M. J. Hilditch c Pringle b Foster | 80 | (1) c Pringle b Foster | 35 |
| K. C. Wessels b Gooch | 23 | c Foster b Pringle | 0 |
| D. M. Wellham c Acfield b Phillip | 10 | b Foster | 63 |
| D. C. Boon c Gooch b Foster | 21 | b Gooch | 138 |
| S. P. O'Donnell c and b Gooch | 39 | b Pringle | 31 |
| G. R. J. Matthews b Acfield | 5 | c East b Gooch | 6 |
| †R. B. Phillips c and b Phillip | 28 | b Gooch | 9 |
| M. J. Bennett lbw b Phillip | 23 | c East b Gooch | 0 |
| D. R. Gilbert not out | 6 | b Pringle | 7 |
| J. R. Thomson b Phillip | 1 | not out | 21 |
| B 2, l-b 6, n-b 2 | 10 | B 5, l-b 4, w 1, n-b 5 | 15 |
| 1/105 2/125 3/142 4/155 5/182 6/217 7/217 8/261 9/277 | 279 | 1/41 2/45 3/49 4/211 5/273 6/291 7/296 8/296 9/303 | 333 |

Bowling: *First Innings*—Foster 27–6–96–2; Phillip 18.5–4–55–4; Acfield 18–5–36–1; Pringle 26–7–43–0; Gooch 21–7–41–3. *Second Innings*—Foster 20–3–92–2; Phillip 7–0–39–0; Pringle 27–5–69–4; Gooch 19.3–3–61–4; Acfield 22–6–58–0; Lilley 1–0–5–0.

## Essex

| First innings | | Second innings | |
|---|---|---|---|
| *G. A. Gooch c Hilditch b Matthews | 68 | c Boon b Gilbert | 27 |
| C. Gladwin c O'Donnell b Gilbert | 5 | lbw b Matthews | 27 |
| P. J. Prichard c Phillips b Gilbert | 7 | c Phillips b Gilbert | 4 |
| A. W. Lilley lbw b Gilbert | 15 | (7) c Wessels b Matthews | 11 |
| D. R. Pringle c Phillips b Thomson | 29 | c Phillips b Gilbert | 4 |
| B. R. Hardie not out | 113 | b Thomson | 17 |
| K. S. McEwan c and b Bennett | 18 | (4) lbw b Gilbert | 0 |
| N. Phillip c Matthews b Thomson | 50 | c Wood b Thomson | 22 |
| †D. E. East c Wessels b Thomson | 23 | not out | 30 |
| N. A. Foster c Phillips b Matthews | 14 | not out | 15 |
| D. L. Acfield c and b Matthews | 14 | | |
| B 12, l-b 8, w 5, n-b 28 | 53 | L-b 10, n-b 2 | 12 |
| 1/21 2/53 3/91 4/131 5/146 6/192 7/299 8/345 9/389 | 409 | 1/40 2/56 3/56 4/62 5/66 6/84 7/123 8/124 | (8 wkts) 169 |

Bowling: *First Innings*—Thomson 24–2–93–3; Gilbert 23–2–90–3; O'Donnell 15–1–58–0; Bennett 26–4–72–1; Matthews 15.4–1–76–3. *Second Innings*—Thomson 16–2–46–2; Gilbert 21–9–41–4; O'Donnell 4–0–22–0; Matthews 19–7–42–2; Bennett 4–2–8–0.

Umpires: J. H. Hampshire and M. J. Kitchen.

## ENGLAND v AUSTRALIA

### Third Cornhill Test

At Trent Bridge, July 11, 12, 13, 15, 16. Drawn. The match produced neither the excitement nor the outright result of the first two Tests, though it entertained with imposing individual performances, notably by Gower, Wood and Ritchie, all of whom made substantial centuries. Gower won the toss with a ten franc coin, thus breaking a losing sequence of six Tests, and decided to bat on a light-coloured pitch which promised and produced a feast of runs.

Robinson began at breakneck pace, England's first 50 coming in just twelve overs, but at 55 he edged a catch to Border off Lawson. This united Gower with the increasingly confident Gooch, and the partnership yielded 116 in 30 overs before Gooch lost concentration, guiding a cut to Wessels in the gully off Lawson. Gower's seemingly inevitable century, the tenth of his Test career, came with fifteen boundaries. Undefeated with 107 at the end of the first day, the England captain divulged his hopes of a total of about 600 to enable his bowlers to place strong pressure on the tourists, and there seemed no reason to dispute the prospect when England reached 358 for two just before lunch on the second day. Inexplicably they then lost eight wickets while scoring 98, a decline triggered by a cruel run-out for Gatting after he had contributed 74 to a 187-run partnership with his captain. Gower hit a straight drive off Holland's leg-spin, and the bowler's unintentional deflection found Gatting backing up too far. Just before tea Gower edged a delivery from O'Donnell to the wicket-keeper. His 166, off 283 balls, was an innings full of drives and cuts of quality, and he hit seventeen boundaries. Lawson, who captured five wickets in an innings for the tenth time in Tests, and McDermott shared six wickets in thirteen overs and England fell substantially short of Gower's target.

Australia began confidently enough with Hilditch and Wood, who had been on the verge of being omitted from the Test following a string of low scores, opening with an 87-run partnership. Hilditch then fell to Allott, but Wood and the night-watchman, Holland, carried Australia to 94 for one by stumps. Sidebottom, making his Test début following the withdrawal with a back injury of Foster, trapped Holland early next day. But Australia reached 205 before Wessels was caught at the wicket. Border, with a 6 and two 4s in his 23 off seventeen deliveries, was hinting at a repeat of his Lord's triumph when adjudged caught at slip off Edmonds, a controversial decision. When Boon then presented Emburey with a return catch for 15, Australia were vulnerable at 263 for five, no longer in danger of having to follow on but still 193 in arrears.

However, Wood, who reached his eighth Test century off 167 balls, found in Ritchie a partner prepared to attack the bowling, and a stand of 161 runs in 66 overs left Australia only 32 runs in arrears when Wood's marathon innings ended at 172, his highest in 51 Tests. After ten hours and 449 deliveries, Wood left the ground with his Test career revived and Australia's fighting qualities restored. Ritchie, who had missed a worthy century at Lord's by only 6 runs, confirmed his growing maturity with an innings of 146 (sixteen boundaries in six hours), and with O'Donnell making 46 Australia finished with a lead of 83. Botham, who was warned for running on the wicket and for intimidatory bowling by umpire Whitehead during an explosive over, in which he also had Ritchie caught off a no-ball, gave his all as usual, while Edmonds and Emburey bowled 121 overs between them for a return of five wickets. The unresponsive pitch, coupled with a toe injury to Sidebottom and Allott's stomach upset, eased the task for the Australians, but the batting of Wood and Ritchie was full of character.

England's second innings, held up by rain and bad light, was of little consequence, though Robinson boosted his average and standing with an unconquered 77. The overall winners were the slow and lifeless pitch, Gower for his captain's century (which won him the Man of the Match award), Wood for his spirited and courageous innings which rescued his international career, and Ritchie, a young batsman making an impact on Test cricket after some years of unfulfilled promise. The total attendance was 49,259 with takings of £305,000. – R.N.

## England

| | | | |
|---|---|---|---|
| G. A. Gooch c Wessels b Lawson | 70 | – c Ritchie b McDermott | 48 |
| R. T. Robinson c Border b Lawson | 38 | – not out | 77 |
| *D. I. Gower c Phillips b O'Donnell | 166 | – c Phillips b McDermott | 17 |
| M. W. Gatting run out | 74 | – not out | 35 |
| A. J. Lamb lbw b Lawson | 17 | | |
| I. T. Botham c O'Donnell b McDermott | 38 | | |
| †P. R. Downton c Ritchie b McDermott | 0 | | |
| A. Sidebottom c O'Donnell b Lawson | 2 | | |
| J. E. Emburey not out | 16 | | |
| P. H. Edmonds b Holland | 12 | | |
| P. J. W. Allott c Border b Lawson | 7 | | |
| L-b 12, w 1, n-b 3 | 16 | B 1, l-b 16, n-b 2 | 19 |
| 1/55 2/171 3/358 4/365 5/416 6/416 7/419 8/419 9/443 | 456 | 1/79 2/107 (2 wkts) | 196 |

Bowling: *First Innings*—Lawson 39.4–10–103–5; McDermott 35–3–147–2; O'Donnell 29–4–104–1; Holland 26–3–90–1. *Second Innings*—Lawson 13–4–32–0; McDermott 16–2–42–2; Holland 28–9–69–0; O'Donnell 10–2–26–0; Ritchie 1–0–10–0.

### Australia

G. M. Wood c Robinson b Botham . . .172
A. M. J. Hilditch lbw b Allott . . . . . . . . 47
R. G. Holland lbw b Sidebottom . . . . . . 10
K. C. Wessels c Downton b Emburey . . 33
*A. R. Border c Botham b Edmonds . . 23
D. C. Boon c and b Emburey . . . . . . . . 15
G. M. Ritchie b Edmonds . . . . . . . . . . .146
†W. B. Phillips b Emburey . . . . . . . . . . 2
S. P. O'Donnell c Downton b Botham . 46
G. F. Lawson c Gooch b Botham . . . . . 18
C. J. McDermott not out . . . . . . . . . . . . 0
B 6, l-b 7, w 2, n-b 12 . . . . . . . 27

1/87 2/128 3/205 4/234 5/263 6/424 7/437 8/491 9/539 — 539

Bowling: Botham 34.2–3–107–3; Sidebottom 18.4–3–65–1; Allott 18–4–55–1; Edmonds 66–18–155–2; Emburey 55–15–129–3; Gooch 8.2–2–13–0; Gatting 1–0–2–0.

Umpires: D. J. Constant and A. G. T. Whitehead.

## †MINOR COUNTIES v AUSTRALIANS

At Jesmond, July 18. Australians won by 125 runs. Toss won by Minor Counties.

### Australians

*A. M. J. Hilditch c Atkinson b Greensword. 41
G. M. Wood b O'Brien . . . . . . . . . . . . . 83
D. M. Wellham not out . . . . . . . . . . . . .107
D. C. Boon not out . . . . . . . . . . . . . . . . . 84
B 3, l-b 9, w 1, n-b 3 . . . . . . . . 16

1/112 2/169 (2 wkts, 55 overs) 331

S. P. O'Donnell, G. R. J. Matthews, M. J. Bennett, †R. B. Phillips, J. R. Thomson, D. R. Gilbert and R. G. Holland did not bat.

Bowling: Merry 11–2–56–0; Surridge 10–1–65–0; Barnard 11–0–59–0; Greensword 11–1–45–1; Plumb 4–0–29–0; O'Brien 4–0–28–1; Roope 4–0–37–0.

### Minor Counties

S. R. Atkinson c Matthews b Thomson. 0
R. J. Scott c Matthews b Thomson . . . . 4
S. Greensword c Wellham b Holland . . 38
G. R. J. Roope lbw b O'Donnell . . . . . . 76
S. G. Plumb c Phillips b Bennett . . . . . 17
*N. A. Riddell c O'Donnell b Bennett . 25
N. T. O'Brien b Gilbert . . . . . . . . . . . . . 6
†R. A. D. Mercer not out . . . . . . . . . . . . 17
W. G. Merry not out . . . . . . . . . . . . . . . 3
B 8, l-b 5, n-b 7 . . . . . . . . . . . . 20

1/4 2/9 3/57 4/103 5/152 6/171 7/186 (7 wkts, 55 overs) 206

A. S. Barnard and D. Surridge did not bat.

Bowling: Thomson 6–1–13–2; O'Donnell 11–3–23–1; Gilbert 10–1–32–1; Holland 10–3–39–1; Bennett 11–0–57–2; Matthews 6–2–20–0; Wood 1–0–9–0.

Umpires: D. B. Harrison and K. S. Shenton.

## GLAMORGAN v AUSTRALIANS

At Neath, July 20, 21, 22. Drawn. Toss won by Glamorgan. After a first day of record-breaking exploits by Glamorgan, there were only 95 minutes possible on the Sunday and the final day was washed out by heavy rain. However, the return of first-class cricket to the Gnoll after twelve years saw a multitude of records broken with brilliant strokeplay by Javed Miandad and Younis

Ahmed. Their unfinished partnership of 306 was a fourth-wicket record for the county and the best for any wicket against a touring team. The county's total of 409 for three declared was a record for a first-class match at Neath, and Javed's 200 (reached with a 6 over extra cover) the highest innings there. No player had scored more for Glamorgan against a touring team. Javed hit 30 4s and faced 225 deliveries in four and three-quarter hours in becoming the first to score four double-centuries for the county. The previous highest score on the ground had been W. J. Stewart's 155 for Warwickshire in 1959. Younis, with his attractive 118, made it the first occasion for two Glamorgan players to register centuries in a match against a touring team.

## Glamorgan

| | |
|---|---|
| J. A. Hopkins c and b Bennett | 30 |
| A. L. Jones b Bennett | 24 |
| G. C. Holmes c and b Bennett | 5 |
| Javed Miandad not out | 200 |
| Younis Ahmed not out | 118 |
| B 3, l-b 9, w 5, n-b 15 | 32 |
| 1/48 2/62 3/103 (3 wkts dec.) | 409 |

H. Morris, *R. C. Ontong, †T. Davies, M. R. Price, J. G. Thomas and S. R. Barwick did not bat.

Bowling: McDermott 14–4–55–0; Thomson 12–1–53–0; Bennett 25.4–5–101–3; Gilbert 18–0–99–0; Matthews 21–3–83–0; Boon 1–0–6–0.

## Australians

| | |
|---|---|
| G. M. Wood not out | 38 |
| *A. M. J. Hilditch lbw b Thomas | 15 |
| D. M. Wellham not out | 43 |
| B 5, w 2, n-b 2 | 9 |
| 1/42 (1 wkt) | 105 |

D. C. Boon, G. M. Ritchie, G. R. J. Matthews, M. J. Bennett, †R. B. Phillips, C. J. McDermott, J. R. Thomson and D. R. Gilbert did not bat.

Bowling: Thomas 10–1–49–1; Barwick 9.4–1–31–0; Younis 7–3–20–0.

Umpires: B. Dudleston and N. T. Plews.

## GLOUCESTERSHIRE v AUSTRALIANS

At Bristol, July 24, 25, 26. Australians won by 170 runs. Toss won by Australians. Their confrontation with Lawrence, under the glare of national publicity, roused such local interest that the gates were closed on the second day with well over 6,000 inside the ground. However, the day belonged to Border and Wellham, who temporarily removed the young fast bowler from the list of Test candidates with some punishing batting. Lawrence had taken three wickets in the first innings as Gloucestershire's three pacemen routed the touring side for 146 on a green pitch, only Matthews resisting for long. But Lawson hit back so effectively that Gloucestershire struggled in turn until, with the pitch easing on the second morning, a plucky effort by Lloyds secured them a narrow lead of 35. The Australian batsmen were then so dominant that only one maiden over was bowled in their second innings. Border's sixth century of the tour occupied only 108 balls, and although Wellham was sedate by comparison they averaged nearly 6 an over during their partnership of 236. Border hit four 6s and fourteen 4s in all; Wellham thirteen 4s. Gloucestershire, set 376 after Border's overnight declaration, quickly lost three wickets to Thomson, and although Athey batted impressively for 83 and was well supported by Curran, the tailenders fell cheaply. Russell was unable to bat in either innings because of a cracked thumb (Stovold kept wicket in the second innings) and Lawson did not bowl in Gloucestershire's second innings because of a neck injury.

### Australians

| | | | |
|---|---|---|---|
| K. C. Wessels b Lawrence | 0 | – not out | 61 |
| W. B. Phillips c Bainbridge b Curran | 22 | – b Walsh | 48 |
| D. M. Wellham c Russell b Lawrence | 10 | – b Graveney | 105 |
| *A. R. Border c Russell b Walsh | 5 | – c Stovold b Graveney | 130 |
| S. P. O'Donnell b Walsh | 3 | – not out | 31 |
| G. R. J. Matthews not out | 41 | | |
| †R. B. Phillips c Russell b Curran | 23 | | |
| G. F. Lawson b Lawrence | 0 | | |
| R. G. Holland b Curran | 0 | | |
| J. R. Thomson b Curran | 10 | | |
| D. R. Gilbert b Curran | 12 | | |
| B 4, l-b 5, n-b 11 | 20 | B 15, l-b 9, w 1, n-b 10 | 35 |
| 1/0 2/28 3/42 4/44 5/48 6/110 7/111 8/112 9/123 | 146 | 1/98 2/334 3/339 (3 wkts dec.) | 410 |

*In the second innings K. C. Wessels, when 21, retired hurt at 44 and resumed at 339.*

Bowling: *First Innings*—Lawrence 12–1–52–3; Walsh 11–2–33–2; Curran 12–4–35–5; Bainbridge 3–0–17–0. *Second Innings*—Lawrence 16–0–89–0; Walsh 9–0–37–1; Curran 12–0–43–0; Lloyds 13–0–83–0; Bainbridge 8–0–34–0; Graveney 20–1–100–2.

### Gloucestershire

| | | | |
|---|---|---|---|
| A. W. Stovold lbw b Lawson | 16 | – c Holland b Thomson | 8 |
| P. W. Romaines c R. B. Phillips b Thomson | 6 | – c R. B. Phillips b Thomson | 0 |
| A. J. Wright lbw b Lawson | 4 | – b Thomson | 9 |
| C. W. J. Athey lbw b Lawson | 0 | – b Holland | 83 |
| P. Bainbridge c Border b Gilbert | 23 | – b O'Donnell | 25 |
| K. M. Curran c Wessels b Thomson | 25 | – lbw b Gilbert | 58 |
| J. W. Lloyds c sub b Holland | 71 | – c Wessels b Holland | 0 |
| *D. A. Graveney lbw b O'Donnell | 23 | – not out | 4 |
| D. V. Lawrence b O'Donnell | 1 | – b Gilbert | 0 |
| C. A. Walsh not out | 2 | – b Holland | 4 |
| †R. C. Russell absent injured | | – absent injured | |
| L-b 2, n-b 8 | 10 | B 5, l-b 6, w 2, n-b 1 | 14 |
| 1/22 2/29 3/29 4/32 5/73 6/79 7/167 8/177 9/181 | 181 | 1/1 2/12 3/23 4/70 5/178 6/178 7/200 8/200 9/205 | 205 |

Bowling: *First Innings*—Lawson 10–0–42–3; Thomson 10–1–36–2; Gilbert 16–1–63–1; Holland 8–2–26–1; O'Donnell 8–1–12–2. *Second Innings*—Thomson 9–2–38–3; Gilbert 13–1–55–2; O'Donnell 10–5–13–1; Matthews 10–2–32–0; Holland 13.2–2–56–3.

Umpires: B. J. Meyer and D. R. Shepherd.

## NORTHAMPTONSHIRE v AUSTRALIANS

At Northampton, July 27, 28, 29, 30. Drawn. Toss won by Australians. The tourists recovered strongly after a poor start against a Northamptonshire attack missing Mallender and Walker, both injured. Wood was forced to retire with a broken nose with the score 35 after attempting to hook Griffiths, but then Boon, needing runs to preserve his Test place, responded with the highest score by an Australian against Northamptonshire. His unbeaten 206 contained a 6 and 28 4s, and with excellent support from Ritchie, Phillips and Matthews, the stocky Tasmanian completely dominated the bowling, particularly in the final session of the first day. The weather turned on Saturday night, severely restricting play on the second and third days, and preventing any cricket at all on the fourth. There was time, however, for Bailey (two 6s, twelve 4s, 173 minutes) to hit only the fourth century for the county against the Australians since 1905.

## Australians

| | | | |
|---|---|---|---|
| *A. M. J. Hilditch lbw b Griffiths | 0 | S. P. O'Donnell b Capel | 8 |
| G. M. Wood retired hurt | 20 | G. R. J. Matthews not out | 51 |
| K. C. Wessels c Lamb b Wheeler | 1 | B 2, l-b 10, w 2 | 14 |
| D. C. Boon not out | 206 | | |
| G. M. Ritchie run out | 49 | 1/4 2/13 3/109 (5 wkts dec.) | 404 |
| †W. B. Phillips b Williams | 55 | 4/215 5/254 | |

M. J. Bennett, C. J. McDermott and R. G. Holland did not bat.

Bowling: Griffiths 25–5–72–1; Wheeler 20–0–87–1; Capel 22–0–107–1; Larkins 6–0–26–0; Williams 21–5–66–1; Harper 11–3–27–0; Lamb 2–0–7–0.

## Northamptonshire

| | | | |
|---|---|---|---|
| *G. Cook lbw b McDermott | 24 | R. G. Williams not out | 35 |
| W. Larkins c sub b O'Donnell | 44 | B 12, l-b 11, n-b 7 | 30 |
| R. J. Boyd-Moss c Phillips b McDermott | 18 | | |
| R. J. Bailey not out | 107 | 1/55 2/82 3/149 (3 wkts) | 258 |

A. J. Lamb, D. J. Capel, †D. Ripley, R. A. Harper, M. B. H. Wheeler and B. J. Griffiths did not bat.

Bowling: McDermott 19–3–70–2; O'Donnell 16–1–81–1; Bennett 14–3–43–0; Holland 7–3–12–0; Matthews 13.2–3–29–0.

Umpires: J. W. Holder and A. A. Jones.

# ENGLAND v AUSTRALIA

## Fourth Cornhill Test

At Old Trafford, August 1, 2, 3, 5, 6. Drawn. After the first session and until the final hour England made all the running, but a prolonged defensive effort by Australia's middle order, organised by Border, enabled them to draw the game. They were helped in this by breaks for rain and an impossibly sluggish pitch, although the groundstaff worked diligently to keep the match going between frequent showers. It seemed a pity, none the less, that they were protecting a pitch that had been inexplicably wet at the start. It offered no pace and a low bounce. Batsmen who attacked with profit on it and wicket-taking bowlers, especially McDermott, could feel more satisfaction than usual.

England did not consider Sidebottom because of injury, Agnew being brought in. Australia replaced Wood, who was injured, by Matthews. Gower put Australia in, but his bowlers did not immediately vindicate the move. Wessels was the only Australian dismissed before lunch. Edmonds turned the game permanently England's way in the afternoon with three wickets. The most important of these was that of Border, who reacted to being tied down by going headlong down the pitch for a speculative drive and being stumped. Ritchie gave Edmonds a return catch in the same over and, at 122 for four, Australia's innings needed extensive repairs. Boon mustered all his skill and Phillips settled in with him, but England struck again at the start of the evening session through Botham. Like England's other faster bowlers, Botham had not been at his best in the morning. But now he had both Boon and Phillips caught cutting. Matthews and Lawson followed, but the new ball was propelled fruitlessly before Edmonds ended the day by finishing off the innings.

Robinson was slipped out early in England's reply by McDermott, but Australia enjoyed only isolated encouragement after this, largely because McDermott was the only bowler taking wickets. Lawson was accurate enough, but unrecognisable in terms of penetration. O'Donnell had Gooch dropped, but seldom menaced the batsmen's survival. Boon spilled that chance and also missed Gower off McDermott. The task of the Australian spinners looked forlorn.

Although 40 minutes were lost at the start of the second day, England had reached 233 for three by the close. Gooch and Gower, who went to a fine, tumbling catch on the square-leg boundary, made their exits within a few minutes of each other, but Gatting and Lamb became established in the final two hours. Play could not resume until two o'clock on Saturday, whereupon the cricket settled into a pattern, with Gatting driving and hooking while Lamb thrust fiercely through mid-wicket. They had added 156 when Lamb was run out by a beautiful piece of fielding from Matthews in the covers. Gatting was then 96, and after he reached his first home Test century his responsibilities increased when Botham was caught on the long-leg boundary. He had batted for nigh on six hours (266 balls) and nailed down his place as England's number four when he was caught behind. On Monday morning, as England went for further quick runs, McDermott hit the stumps three times and so marched off with eight for 141, the third youngest to take eight wickets in a Test. He had bowled 36 overs, defying the sponge-like pitch by obtaining occasional bounce, and was a deserving winner of the Man of the Match award.

Australia, 225 behind, were thus in by noon. Matthews had asked to open, to allow Wessels to drop back to number three, and he helped Australia past the first hurdle by remaining until lunch. Immediately afterwards he became the first of four batsmen to be prised out by the spinners before the close. Border conceded that evening that a last day of rain would not go amiss, and he was accommodated to the extent that only three overs could be bowled before lunch. England's dejection at not being able to get on to the pitch increased when play did start, Border soon surviving an awkward chance off the inside edge. Australia were 33 behind at the time, and they cleared the arrears after ten of the 50 overs to which the day was reduced had been bowled. Emburey had cheered England by bowling Ritchie, but Phillips was quite clear as to what his job was. He remained on nought for 50 balls. Border also gave England no more hope, seeing his side to safety in an innings of 334 balls and 346 minutes. A total of 62,127 spectators paid £368,968. – T.C.

## Australia

| | | | |
|---|---|---|---|
| K. C. Wessels c Botham b Emburey | 34 | – (3) c and b Emburey | 50 |
| A. M. J. Hilditch c Gower b Edmonds | 49 | – (1) b Emburey | 40 |
| D. C. Boon c Lamb b Botham | 61 | – (5) b Emburey | 7 |
| *A. R. Border st Downton b Edmonds | 8 | – not out | 146 |
| G. M. Ritchie c and b Edmonds | 4 | – (6) b Emburey | 31 |
| †W. B. Phillips c Downton b Botham | 36 | – (7) not out | 39 |
| G. R. J. Matthews b Botham | 4 | – (2) c and b Edmonds | 17 |
| S. P. O'Donnell b Edmonds | 45 | | |
| G. F. Lawson c Downton b Botham | 4 | | |
| C. J. McDermott lbw b Emburey | 0 | | |
| R. G. Holland not out | 5 | | |
| L-b 3, w 1, n-b 3 | 7 | B 1, l-b 6, n-b 3 | 10 |
| 1/71 2/97 3/118 4/122 5/193 6/198 7/211 8/223 9/224 | 257 | 1/38 2/85 3/126 4/138 5/213 (5 wkts) | 340 |

Bowling: *First Innings*—Botham 23–4–79–4; Agnew 14–0–65–0; Allott 13–1–29–0; Emburey 24–7–41–2; Edmonds 15.1–4–40–4. *Second Innings*—Botham 15–3–50–0; Allott 6–2–4–0; Edmonds 54–12–122–1; Emburey 51–17–99–4; Agnew 9–2–34–0; Gatting 4–0–14–0; Lamb 1–0–10–0.

## England

| | |
|---|---|
| G. A. Gooch lbw b McDermott | 74 |
| R. T. Robinson c Border b McDermott | 10 |
| *D. I. Gower c Hilditch b McDermott | 47 |
| M. W. Gatting c Phillips b McDermott | 160 |
| A. J. Lamb run out | 67 |
| I. T. Botham c O'Donnell b McDermott | 20 |
| †P. R. Downton b McDermott | 23 |
| J. E. Emburey not out | 31 |
| P. H. Edmonds b McDermott | 1 |
| P. J. W. Allott b McDermott | 7 |
| J. P. Agnew not out | 2 |
| B 7, l-b 16, n-b 17 | 40 |
| 1/21 2/142 3/148 4/304 5/339 6/430 7/448 8/450 9/470 (9 wkts dec.) | 482 |

Bowling: Lawson 37–7–114–0; McDermott 36–3–141–8; Holland 38–7–101–0; O'Donnell 21–6–82–0; Matthews 9–2–21–0.

Umpires: H. D. Bird and D. R. Shepherd.

## †IRELAND v AUSTRALIANS

At Downpatrick, August 8. Drawn. Toss won by Ireland. No play was possible after lunch because of rain.

### Australians

| | | | |
|---|---|---|---|
| A. M. J. Hilditch st Bailey b Halliday | 43 | W. B. Phillips not out | 0 |
| G. M. Wood run out | 2 | | |
| D. M. Wellham b Corlett | 6 | L-b 4 | 4 |
| *A. R. Border c Prior b McBrine | 91 | | |
| †R. B. Phillips not out | 5 | 1/25 2/37 3/87 4/151 (4 wkts) | 151 |

S. P. O'Donnell, G. R. J. Matthews, M. J. Bennett, D. R. Gilbert and R. G. Holland did not bat.

Bowling: Corlett 8–2–29–1; Elder 7–1–23–0; Halliday 9–3–37–1; McBrine 11–2–52–1; Anderson 3–1–6–0.

### Ireland

S. J. S. Warke, M. A. Masood, D. Dennison, I. J. Anderson, D. A. Lewis, J. A. Prior, S. C. Corlett, A. McBrine, †K. R. Bailey, *M. Halliday and J. W. G. Elder.

Umpires: M. A. C. Moore and P. F. G. Reith.

## MIDDLESEX v AUSTRALIANS

At Lord's, August 10, 11, 12, 13. Drawn. Toss won by Middlesex. Play was delayed until 4.30 on the first day and three o'clock on the second, and any remote chance of a finish even in four days was eliminated when, on the third morning, Lawson declined Gatting's offer of a declaration deal, arguing that the Australian batsmen needed practice. Middlesex scored 85 without loss on the opening day, the soggy outfield meaning that ten 3s were run. Brown introduced himself to Lord's – it was his fourth first-class match, but his first at home – by just beating Slack to his hundred. Although batting flawlessly for 295 minutes, he hit only five 4s. The county's opening stand of 213 was the highest against the tourists to date. Middlesex, 263 for three on Sunday evening, batted on until teatime on Monday. Slack, missed twice at the very start of his innings, finished with Middlesex's highest individual score against the Australians, beating E. H. Hendren's 138 in 1930; their total surpassed their best against an Australian side – 349 in 1926. Slack batted for 530 minutes, received 413 balls and hit 23 4s and one 6. Gatting rather upset the Australians' batting practice by taking three wickets in consecutive overs after Wood and Wessels had opened with a century stand, but Wellham batted throughout the last day.

### Middlesex

| | | | |
|---|---|---|---|
| W. N. Slack not out | 201 | †P. R. Downton not out | 24 |
| K. R. Brown st Phillips b Bennett | 102 | B 4, l-b 6, w 2, n-b 17 | 29 |
| *M. W. Gatting b McDermott | 7 | | |
| R. O. Butcher lbw b Holland | 0 | 1/213 2/251 3/252 (4 wkts dec.) | 397 |
| C. T. Radley c Boon b Bennett | 34 | 4/344 | |

J. E. Emburey, P. H. Edmonds, N. F. Williams, S. P. Hughes and N. G. Cowans did not bat.

Bowling: McDermott 25–3–108–1; Lawson 20–8–39–0; Thomson 18–4–54–0; Holland 30–3–87–1; Bennett 38–5–95–2; Wessels 3–1–4–0.

### Australians

| | | | |
|---|---|---|---|
| G. M. Wood c Edmonds b Gatting | 42 | M. J. Bennett c Emburey b Edmonds | 7 |
| K. C. Wessels c Radley b Gatting | 56 | *G. F. Lawson not out | 29 |
| D. C. Boon lbw b Gatting | 4 | B 10, l-b 5, w 5, n-b 13 | 33 |
| D. M. Wellham not out | 125 | | |
| G. M. Ritchie b Hughes | 27 | 1/107 2/111 3/116 (6 wkts dec.) | 396 |
| †W. B. Phillips c and b Edmonds | 73 | 4/168 5/319 6/329 | |

C. J. McDermott, J. R. Thomson and R. G. Holland did not bat.

Bowling: Williams 17–0–85–0; Cowans 17–3–72–0; Hughes 20–1–61–1; Gatting 13–1–55–3; Emburey 22–5–55–0; Edmonds 19–4–46–2; Brown 1–1–0–0; Butcher 1–0–7–0.

Umpires: D. O. Oslear and R. A. White.

## ENGLAND v AUSTRALIA

### Fifth Cornhill Test

At Edgbaston, August 15, 16, 17, 19, 20. England won by an innings and 118 runs to take a two-one lead in the series. Toss won by England. Rain, rivalling Australia as England's greatest adversary, rolled away on the final afternoon to allow just enough time for Gower's side to force a thoroughly warranted victory. There was, however, a dark cloud of controversy waiting to shed its gloom. Australia's captain asserted that the crucial, quite freak dismissal of Phillips should not have been allowed, claiming that enough doubt existed for the umpires to have judged in the batsman's favour. Border insisted that the incident cost Australia the match. Phillips hit a ball from Edmonds hard on to the instep of Lamb, who was taking swift evasive action at silly point. The rebound gently stood up for Gower, a couple of yards away, to catch, and 48 minutes later England won when it had seemed that the weather-induced frustrations which prevailed at Manchester would deny them again.

It was a pity Border blamed defeat on this one incident, especially as England had forged their supremacy with a succession of outstanding individual performances, none more so than Ellison's. The Kent swing bowler fought off the debilitating effects of a heavy cold to capture ten for 79 in the match, be named as Man of the Match, and announce his coming-of-age as a Test bowler. He and Taylor had replaced Agnew and Allott in the England side. Gower, in addition to savouring the fruits of victory and being appointed ahead of schedule for England's winter tour to the West Indies, exquisitely unveiled his strokemaking talents with a career-best 215 on the ground where he had scored his previous double-hundred for England, against India in 1979. Helped by some badly directed bowling, the England captain remorselessly punished Australia in a sumptuous, high-speed partnership of 331 with Robinson. Then Gatting, almost clinically, added a top-quality hundred – resourceful, chanceless and occupying only 125 balls.

England's domination was triggered off by Gower when he ran out Lawson for a fighting 53 off the first ball of the third day. The fifth delivery of the same over ended Australia's first innings for 335, the tourists being indebted to the obdurate Wessels for a dogged 83. With two days, both rain-interrupted, already gone, this was a position from which Australia should not have lost, but their wasteful bowling and an astonishing collapse early in their second innings cleared England's way.

By the third evening Gower and Robinson had already taken England into the lead with their respective centuries. Australia were rendered powerless as England amassed 355 for one, the only interruption being Thomson's dismissal of Gooch, his 200th Test wicket and 100th against England. England's huge second-wicket stand, when it concluded on Monday with Robinson playing on to Lawson, was the second highest for this wicket against Australia, short only of Hutton and Leyland's 382 at The Oval in 1938. It was the seventh alliance of over 300 by an England pair and the best in England since J. H. Edrich and Barrington added 369 against New Zealand at Headingley in 1965. Gower, by that time, had gone past Denis Compton's record aggregate of 562 in a home series against Australia.

England's declaration at 595 for five, a lead of 260, was sped by Lamb and briefly by Botham, who struck his first and fourth balls from McDermott for straight 6s and his second for 4. Ellison, bowling to a full length and achieving late swing, then ripped away the top layer of Australia's innings with a spell of four wickets for 1 run in fifteen balls, including Border's. Australia, going into a desperate final day at 37 for five, had their prayers for rain initially answered. Thick drizzle promised to save the match for them, but at 2.30 Phillips and Ritchie were finally summoned to fight it out. Phillips, in particular, displayed a strong nerve in making 59 before his controversial departure. Umpire Shepherd, not having a clear view of the incident, asked Constant, standing at square leg, for his version, and the latter unhesitatingly confirmed that the ball had at no time hit the ground. Australia's last four wickets offered little resistance.

A total of 51,550 spectators watched a match shortened by seven hours through bad weather and paid receipts of £318,500 – D.F.

## Australia

| | | | |
|---|---|---|---|
| G. M. Wood c Edmonds b Botham | 19 | – (2) c Robinson b Ellison | 10 |
| A. M. J. Hilditch c Downton b Edmonds | 39 | – (1) c Ellison b Botham | 10 |
| K. C. Wessels c Downton b Ellison | 83 | – c Downton b Ellison | 10 |
| *A. R. Border c Edmonds b Ellison | 45 | – (5) b Ellison | 2 |
| G. M. Ritchie c Botham b Ellison | 8 | – (6) c Lamb b Emburey | 20 |
| †W. B. Phillips c Robinson b Ellison | 15 | – (7) c Gower b Edmonds | 59 |
| S. P. O'Donnell c Downton b Taylor | 1 | – (8) b Botham | 11 |
| G. F. Lawson run out | 53 | – (9) c Gower b Edmonds | 3 |
| C. J. McDermott c Gower b Ellison | 35 | – (10) c Edmonds b Botham | 8 |
| J. R. Thomson not out | 28 | – (11) not out | 4 |
| R. G. Holland c Edmonds b Ellison | 0 | – (4) lbw b Ellison | 0 |
| L-b 4, w 1, n-b 4 | 9 | B 1, l-b 3, n-b 1 | 5 |
| 1/44 2/92 3/189 4/191 5/207 6/208 7/218 8/276 9/335 | 335 | 1/10 2/32 3/32 4/35 5/36 6/113 7/117 8/120 9/137 | 142 |

Bowling: *First Innings*—Botham 27–1–108–1; Taylor 26–5–78–1; Ellison 31.5–9–77–6; Edmonds 20–4–47–1; Emburey 9–2–21–0. *Second Innings*—Botham 14.1–2–52–3; Taylor 13–4–27–0; Ellison 9–3–27–4; Edmonds 15–9–13–2; Emburey 13–5–19–1.

## England

| | |
|---|---|
| G. A. Gooch c Phillips b Thomson | 19 |
| R. T. Robinson b Lawson | 148 |
| *D. I. Gower c Border b Lawson | 215 |
| M. W. Gatting not out | 100 |
| A. J. Lamb c Wood b McDermott | 46 |
| I. T. Botham c Thomson b McDermott | 18 |
| †P. R. Downton not out | 0 |
| B 7, l-b 20, n-b 22 | 49 |
| 1/38 2/369 3/463 4/572 5/592 (5 wkts dec.) | 595 |

J. E. Emburey, R. M. Ellison, P. H. Edmonds and L. B. Taylor did not bat.

Bowling: Lawson 37–1–135–2; McDermott 31–2–155–2; Thomson 19–1–101–1; Holland 25–4–95–0; O'Donnell 16–3–69–0; Border 6–1–13–0.

Umpires: D. J. Constant and D. R. Shepherd.

## KENT v AUSTRALIANS

At Canterbury, August 24, 25, 26, 27. Australians won by seven wickets. Toss won by Australians. Put in to bat when play started at 2.20, Kent were in early trouble until Baptiste and subsequently Potter and Graham Cowdrey batted well. Cowdrey achieved a maiden first-class half-century in 171 minutes before McDermott, with three for 16 in 6.1 overs, finished the innings. Wessels stood firm as Ellison troubled the tourists, and then Ritchie and Border engaged in an entertaining stand of 182 in 43 overs. Ritchie hit four 6s and eighteen 4s in a stay of 263 minutes; Border thirteen 4s in 202 minutes. Kent toiled in their second innings, with McDermott quickly polishing off the innings on the last morning. Luckhurst, Kent's 46-year-old manager, called out of retirement because of illness and injury to his team, remained unbeaten after 62 minutes. The tourists, needing 96 to win, achieved their target in the last over before lunch.

## Kent

| First innings | | Second innings | |
|---|---|---|---|
| N. R. Taylor lbw b Gilbert | 5 | c Phillips b Gilbert | 3 |
| S. G. Hinks c Phillips b Gilbert | 15 | c Wessels b McDermott | 0 |
| D. G. Aslett run out | 24 | c Phillips b Bennett | 13 |
| L. Potter lbw b Gilbert | 58 | b Bennett | 28 |
| E. A. E. Baptiste c Thomson b Bennett | 45 | (6) c Wood b McDermott | 11 |
| G. R. Cowdrey c Gilbert b Thomson | 51 | (5) b Bennett | 4 |
| R. M. Ellison run out | 29 | c Phillips b McDermott | 27 |
| *C. S. Cowdrey c Bennett b McDermott | 35 | (9) lbw b Bennett | 9 |
| †S. A. Marsh not out | 31 | (8) b McDermott | 0 |
| B. W. Luckhurst c Border b McDermott | 1 | not out | 9 |
| D. L. Underwood b McDermott | 3 | b McDermott | 0 |
| B 4, l-b 6, w 2, n-b 24 | 36 | B 4, l-b 8, w 1, n-b 9 | 22 |
| 1/9 2/34 3/57 4/137 5/194 6/232 7/271 8/301 9/326 | 333 | 1/3 2/3 3/42 4/56 5/68 6/79 7/81 8/90 9/124 | 126 |

Bowling: *First Innings*—McDermott 24.5–3–104–3; Gilbert 26–5–62–3; Wessels 10–4–22–0; Bennett 30–6–99–1; Hilditch 4–2–10–0; Border 2–1–1–0; Thomson 7–1–25–1. *Second Innings*—McDermott 11.2–3–18–5; Gilbert 17–2–57–1; Bennett 16–4–39–4.

## Australians

| First innings | | Second innings | |
|---|---|---|---|
| G. M. Wood c Marsh b Baptiste | 8 | (2) c Marsh b Baptiste | 18 |
| A. M. J. Hilditch c Marsh b Ellison | 16 | (1) c Potter b C. S. Cowdrey | 9 |
| K. C. Wessels c Marsh b Ellison | 51 | | |
| D. M. Wellham b Ellison | 1 | (3) c Hinks b Baptiste | 38 |
| G. M. Ritchie c Hinks b Potter | 155 | | |
| *A. R. Border c Marsh b Baptiste | 103 | | |
| †R. B. Phillips c Marsh b Baptiste | 8 | (4) not out | 23 |
| M. J. Bennett c Hinks b Underwood | 8 | (5) not out | 9 |
| C. J. McDermott b Baptiste | 5 | | |
| D. R. Gilbert c C. S. Cowdrey b Underwood | 0 | | |
| J. R. Thomson not out | 0 | | |
| B 1, l-b 3, w 1, n-b 4 | 9 | L-b 1, n-b 1 | 2 |
| 1/24 2/24 3/29 4/138 5/320 6/343 7/350 8/364 9/364 | 364 | 1/9 2/61 3/66 | (3 wkts) 99 |

Bowling: *First Innings*—Baptiste 27–7–89–4; Ellison 15–2–43–3; C. S. Cowdrey 4–1–19–0; Hinks 12–1–48–0; Underwood 31–6–71–2; Potter 19–3–90–1. *Second Innings*—Baptiste 10–0–36–2; C. S. Cowdrey 6–1–16–1; Potter 6–0–37–0; Aslett 2.1–0–9–0.

Umpires: J. A. Jameson and B. Leadbeater.

## ENGLAND v AUSTRALIA

### Sixth Cornhill Test

At The Oval, August 29, 30, 31, September 2. England won by an innings and 94 runs. Australia's modest chance of salvaging the Ashes effectively vanished on the opening morning when Gower won an exceptionally good toss and was then blessed by a good deal of luck in the first hour of what blossomed into a match-winning second-wicket stand of 351 with Gooch. The Essex opener, who had been rather overshadowed in the first five Tests by Robinson, his opening partner, made a chanceless 196 (27 4s, 423 minutes); but though Gower, too, went on to play brilliantly in scoring 157 (twenty 4s, 337 minutes), he had started loosely, lobbing the slips at 2 while attempting to kill a rising ball from McDermott, and surviving further narrow escapes at 31 and 35 during an over from Lawson. Given extra help by ill-directed bowling, much of it over-pitched and leg-side, England had sped to 100 for one off 25 overs by lunch, from which point Australia played like a losing side.

Several factors were involved in Australia's demoralisation, among them the cumulative effect of so little cricket between Tests because of rain, and the tour-long battle for full fitness of Lawson, their most experienced bowler. But ill-judged selection also played a part in it. At The Oval, where they had to win the match to save the series, a bowler was omitted in favour of a batsman. Holland was dropped in conditions better suited to a leg-spinner than in any previous Test. O'Donnell and Thomson were the others omitted, with the three places going to Bennett, Wellham and Gilbert, all of them playing their first Test of the series and Gilbert winning his first cap. England were unchanged, though Botham, who had twisted his left knee fielding for Somerset two days before, was declared fit only on the morning of the match. Agnew and Athey, Botham's stand-by, were left out of the thirteen.

Australia's one moment of supremacy came after 37 minutes when McDermott yorked Robinson with a late in-swinger. Had Gower's mis-hit gone to hand in the young Queenslander's next over, England would have been 29 for two. Instead, Australia were outplayed on a pitch of pace and generous, even bounce that shared its favours equally between bat and ball: a credit to Surrey's groundsman, Harry Brind. Because of their sluggish over-rate of thirteen an hour, Australia were already on "over-time", in the hottest weather for weeks, when Gower lashed a cut to deep gully after a partnership with Gooch in which the runs had come at 4.6 an over. Twenty-five minutes later Gatting was caught at the wicket off Bennett from a ball that turned – an ominous portent for Australia – but when England reached close of play on the first day at 376 for three, with Gooch 179, it seemed certain they were heading for a total of at least 600.

In the event, after Gooch and Emburey, the night-watchman, had added 27 in three overs off the new ball, Gooch mistimed a low full toss and McDermott checked in his follow-through to bring off a very good caught and bowled, wide to his right with his knuckle almost on the turf. Against long odds, the innings ended two hours later, improved fast bowling and over-confident batting accounting for most of the six wickets which fell for 61. But the early loss of Wood to a possibly unlucky decision, and the mortifying sight of vice-captain Hilditch falling into Botham's hooking trap for the third time in the series, combined with their drubbing on the first day, knocked the fight out of Australia. With the exception of Ritchie (195 minutes), they batted with little resolve or basic technique, even Border taking too little account of the extra pace in the pitch as he played on to Edmonds, attempting a forcing stroke against the spin. A brilliant overhead catch at second slip by Botham to remove Lawson hastened the end, and fifteen minutes after lunch on the third day, Australia followed on 223 behind.

After a lengthy stoppage through rain at 12 for no wicket, Hilditch and Wood picked up the second innings with an hour and three-quarters left before the revised time for drawing stumps, seven o'clock. But the faults of the first innings were soon in evidence. With only 1 run added, Botham bowled Wood, and three overs later Hilditch, having resisted several temptations to hook Botham, drove a widish ball from Taylor to cover point. When Wessels chased an even wider one from Botham, Australia were 37 for three, Downton taking a fine catch at full length to his left. Wellham, out of his depth against Ellison's out-swing, was lbw to a breakback, and at close of play Australia were 62 for four, still 161 behind, with Border 26.

As on the previous three, every seat had been sold in advance for the fourth day's play, a crowd of 15,000 assembling to see if Australia's captain had one more heroic saving innings in him. And as at Old Trafford in the fourth Test, the day began ominously for England when in overcast conditions Downton missed Border in the first over before he had added to his score, diving for a mistimed leg-glance off Ellison. However, the captain's resolution struck no chord among his team-mates. Ritchie, driving at a wide one, and Phillips, making room to cut, were swept aside in 50 minutes, and at eight minutes past noon Australia's last vestige of resistance disappeared when Border edged Ellison to second slip. There was time for Botham, leaping to his left to drag down a fast edge by McDermott, to add another to his galaxy of slip catches before Taylor caught and bowled Bennett to end the match and series. In 96 minutes Australia had lost six for 67, Ellison finishing with five for 46.

As in 1926 and 1953, when the Ashes were also regained at The Oval, several thousand spectators massed in front of the pavilion when the match was over, to hail the England captain and his team and to give Allan Border a heartfelt cheer. Gooch was named Man of the Match and Gower Player of the Series. The attendance was 60,000 and receipts £485,000. – J.D.T.

## England

| | | | |
|---|---|---|---|
| G. A. Gooch c and b McDermott | 196 | R. M. Ellison c Phillips b Gilbert | 3 |
| R. T. Robinson b McDermott | 3 | P. H. Edmonds lbw b Lawson | 12 |
| *D. I. Gower c Bennett b McDermott | 157 | L. B. Taylor not out | 1 |
| M. W. Gatting c Border b Bennett | 4 | | |
| J. E. Emburey c Wellham b Lawson | 9 | B 13, l-b 11, n-b 26 | 50 |
| A. J. Lamb c McDermott b Lawson | 1 | | |
| I. T. Botham c Phillips b Lawson | 12 | 1/20 2/371 3/376 4/403 5/405 | 464 |
| †P. R. Downton b McDermott | 16 | 6/418 7/425 8/447 9/452 | |

Bowling: Lawson 29.2–6–101–4; McDermott 31–2–108–4; Gilbert 21–2–96–1; Bennett 32–8–111–1; Border 2–0–8–0; Wessels 3–0–16–0.

## Australia

| | | | |
|---|---|---|---|
| G. M. Wood lbw b Botham | 22 | (2) b Botham | 6 |
| A. M. J. Hilditch c Gooch b Botham | 17 | (1) c Gower b Taylor | 9 |
| K. C. Wessels b Emburey | 12 | c Downton b Botham | 7 |
| *A. R. Border b Edmonds | 38 | c Botham b Ellison | 58 |
| D. M. Wellham c Downton b Ellison | 13 | lbw b Ellison | 5 |
| G. M. Ritchie not out | 64 | c Downton b Ellison | 6 |
| †W. B. Phillips b Edmonds | 18 | c Downton b Botham | 10 |
| M. J. Bennett c Robinson b Ellison | 12 | c and b Taylor | 11 |
| G. F. Lawson c Botham b Taylor | 14 | c Downton b Ellison | 7 |
| C. J. McDermott run out | 25 | c Botham b Ellison | 2 |
| D. R. Gilbert b Botham | 1 | not out | 0 |
| L-b 3, w 2 | 5 | B 4, n-b 4 | 8 |
| 1/35 2/52 3/56 4/101 5/109<br>6/144 7/171 8/192 9/235 | 241 | 1/13 2/16 3/37 4/51 5/71<br>6/96 7/114 8/127 9/129 | 129 |

Bowling: *First Innings*—Botham 20–3–64–3; Taylor 13–1–39–1; Ellison 18–5–35–2; Emburey 19–7–48–1; Edmonds 14–2–52–2. *Second Innings*—Botham 17–3–44–3; Taylor 11.3–1–34–2; Ellison 17–3–46–5; Emburey 1–0–1–0.

Umpires: H. D. Bird and K. E. Palmer.

---

## ESSO SCHOLARSHIPS

The four young Australian cricketers who received Esso Scholarships to play in England in 1985 were: G. A. Bishop (South Australia) for Leicestershire, B. A. Courtice (Queensland) for Nottinghamshire, A. I. C. Dodemaide (Victoria) for Sussex and S. R. Waugh (New South Wales) for Essex. Waugh was a replacement for D. R. Gilbert (New South Wales), who was a late selection for the Australian side to England.

THE ZIMBABWEANS IN ENGLAND, 1985

[*Ken Kelly*

Zimbabwe undertook a seven-weeks tour of England in 1985. Their team was: *Back row:* G. G. A. Saulez (*scorer*), D. L. Houghton, M. P. Jarvis, E. A. Brandes, A. C. Waller, A. H. Shah, K. G. Duers, L. L. de Grandhomme, K. G. Walton. *Front row:* D. H. Streak, G. A. Hick, I. P. Butchart, A. J. Pycroft (*captain*), D. A. Ellman-Brown (*manager*), A. J. Traicos (*vice-captain*), R. D. Brown, G. A. Paterson.

# THE ZIMBABWEANS IN ENGLAND, 1985

One of the purposes of Zimbabwe's seven-week tour, to give their players experience of English conditions in preparation for the 1986 ICC Trophy, was successfully accomplished, though in their six first-class matches five whole days' cricket were lost through rain and all but one of these matches finished as draws. The tourists won all their one-day games, however. Although the team missed the bowling of Peter Rawson, who was prevented from making the tour by business commitments, and Kevin Curran, who was under contract to Gloucestershire, the medium-paced contingent of Malcolm Jarvis, Kevin Duers and Eddo Brandes worked hard and quite effectively.

With 895 runs in all matches at an average of 52.65, Graeme Hick looked a world-class player in the making. His 230 against the University at Oxford was the third-highest score ever for Rhodesia, as it was, and Zimbabwe, behind only Ray Gripper's 279 against Orange Free State and Mike Procter's 254 against Western Province. Grant Paterson also had a good tour, narrowly missing centuries on three occasions, while David Houghton recorded his maiden first-class hundred against Oxford, sharing in the process a Zimbabwean record partnership of 277 for the fourth wicket. Andrew Pycroft played a captain's innings against Minor Counties, when his side were in trouble. He returned home early from the tour to be present at the birth of his first child.

Iain Butchart was the most successful all-rounder, his 40 wickets in all matches being twice as many as anyone else's. Ali Shah also made some useful contributions with bat and ball, and Lawrence de Grandhomme responded well to being given more than one long spell of bowling. After Pycroft's departure the captaincy was taken over by John Traicos, at 38 still Zimbabwe's most effective containing bowler and a major reason for their excellent record in one-day cricket. The side was quietly and efficiently managed by David Ellman-Brown.

## ZIMBABWEAN TOUR RESULTS

*First-class matches* – Played 6: Lost 1, Drawn 5.

*Loss* – Gloucestershire.

*Draws* – Oxford University, Glamorgan, Warwickshire, Minor Counties, Surrey.

*Non first-class matches* – Played 7: Won 5, Lost 2. *Wins* – Combined Services, Somerset, Scotland, Sussex, Lavinia, Duchess of Norfolk's XI. *Losses* – League Cricket Conference, Wales.

## ZIMBABWEAN TOUR AVERAGES – FIRST-CLASS MATCHES

### BATTING

| | *M* | *I* | *NO* | *R* | *HI* | *100s* | *Avge* |
|---|---|---|---|---|---|---|---|
| G. A. Hick | 6 | 9 | 0 | 598 | 230 | 2 | 66.44 |
| A. J. Pycroft | 4 | 6 | 2 | 245 | 110* | 1 | 61.25 |
| D. H. Streak | 3 | 3 | 1 | 72 | 29 | 0 | 36.00 |
| G. A. Paterson | 6 | 9 | 0 | 320 | 92 | 0 | 35.55 |
| A. C. Waller | 2 | 3 | 1 | 69 | 56* | 0 | 34.50 |
| D. L. Houghton | 6 | 8 | 1 | 231 | 104 | 1 | 33.00 |

| | *M* | *I* | *NO* | *R* | *HI* | *100s* | *Avge* |
|---|---|---|---|---|---|---|---|
| L. L. de Grandhomme .. | 5 | 6 | 1 | 157 | 59 | 0 | 31.40 |
| I. P. Butchart .......... | 6 | 8 | 1 | 134 | 82 | 0 | 19.14 |
| A. H. Shah ............ | 4 | 6 | 1 | 95 | 40 | 0 | 19.00 |
| A. J. Traicos .......... | 6 | 5 | 2 | 57 | 27* | 0 | 19.00 |
| K. G. Walton ......... | 3 | 5 | 1 | 57 | 20* | 0 | 14.25 |
| R. D. Brown .......... | 5 | 8 | 0 | 113 | 27 | 0 | 14.12 |
| E. A. Brandes ......... | 3 | 4 | 1 | 30 | 19 | 0 | 10.00 |
| M. P. Jarvis ........... | 4 | 3 | 1 | 10 | 6 | 0 | 5.00 |

Played in three matches: K. G. Duers 1, 0.

* *Signifies not out.*

## BOWLING

| | *O* | *M* | *R* | *W* | *BB* | *Avge* |
|---|---|---|---|---|---|---|
| I. P. Butchart .......... | 167 | 42 | 547 | 20 | 5-65 | 27.35 |
| L. L. de Grandhomme .. | 46 | 9 | 148 | 4 | 3-79 | 37.00 |
| M. P. Jarvis ........... | 110 | 13 | 392 | 10 | 3-37 | 39.20 |
| A. J. Traicos .......... | 167.1 | 48 | 439 | 8 | 2-33 | 54.87 |
| K. G. Duers ........... | 66 | 13 | 235 | 4 | 3-75 | 58.75 |

Also bowled: E. A. Brandes 47.4–3–190–3; G. A. Hick 71–9–236–3; A. H. Shah 28–7–106–0; D. H. Streak 20.3–4–69–3.

## FIELDING

A. J. Traicos 7, G. A. Hick 6, D. L. Houghton 3 (all ct), M. P. Jarvis 3 (2 as sub), L. L. de Grandhomme 2, A. J. Pycroft 2, A. C. Waller 2, K. G. Walton 2, R. D. Brown 1, I. P. Butchart 1, A. H. Shah 1, D. H. Streak 1.

*Note:* Those matches which follow which were not first-class are signified by the use of a dagger.

## OXFORD UNIVERSITY v ZIMBABWEANS

At The Parks, June 8, 10, 11. Drawn. Toss won by Zimbabweans. The opening match of Zimbabwe's seven-week tour ended in a draw when rain prevented any play after tea on the third day. Oxford, with five wickets standing, needed another 29 to avoid an innings defeat. Thorne underlined the tourists' bowling limitations with a maiden century (156 minutes, thirteen 4s), a feat recognised only on the second day when the match was confirmed as having first-class status. The Zimbabweans made a poor start in reply, losing their first three wickets for 64, but Hick and Houghton staged a remarkable recovery with a partnership of 277. Both completed maiden centuries and Hick, the Worcestershire all-rounder, went on to score 230, the fourth-highest individual score against Oxford in The Parks and the sixth-highest maiden first-class hundred in England. His innings lasted 4 hours, 42 minutes and included four 6s and 31 4s.

### Oxford University

| First innings | | Second innings | |
|---|---|---|---|
| *A. J. T. Miller not out | 36 | | |
| D. A. Hagan c Waller b Butchart | 13 | (1) c Hick b Duers | 4 |
| C. D. M. Tooley c Brown b Hick | 25 | b Butchart | 28 |
| R. S. Rutnagur lbw b Traicos | 17 | c Waller b Jarvis | 57 |
| D. A. Thorne lbw b Traicos | 124 | (6) not out | 5 |
| T. Patel c Traicos b Hick | 0 | (5) lbw b Jarvis | 3 |
| P. C. MacLarnon lbw b Butchart | 23 | (2) lbw b Jarvis | 44 |
| C. M. Denny b Butchart | 1 | (7) not out | 0 |
| †D. P. Taylor not out | 5 | | |
| B 6, l-b 11, n-b 1 | 18 | B 2, l-b 5, n-b 1 | 8 |
| 1/54 2/85 3/97 4/97 5/185 6/215 7/255 | (7 wkts dec.) 262 | 1/5 2/46 3/124 4/136 5/149 | (5 wkts) 149 |

M. P. Lawrence and J. G. Brettell did not bat.

*In the first innings, A. J. T. Miller, when 34, retired hurt at 50 and resumed at 215.*

Bowling: *First Innings*—Jarvis 12–2–23–0; Duers 20–7–63–0; Traicos 29–13–52–2; Butchart 16–6–51–3; Hick 21–7–55–2; de Grandhomme 1–0–1–0. *Second Innings*—Jarvis 14–3–37–3; Duers 7–3–16–1; Traicos 11–5–15–0; Butchart 12–1–51–1; Hick 8–0–23–0.

### Zimbabweans

| | |
|---|---|
| R. D. Brown c Denny b Rutnagur | 4 |
| G. A. Paterson lbw b Thorne | 5 |
| G. A. Hick b Thorne | 230 |
| *A. J. Pycroft c Hagan b Rutnagur | 24 |
| †D. L. Houghton c Hagan b Lawrence | 104 |
| A. C. Waller b Rutnagur | 12 |
| L. L. de Grandhomme not out | 32 |
| I. P. Butchart lbw b Thorne | 3 |
| A. J. Traicos lbw b Rutnagur | 0 |
| M. P. Jarvis lbw b Rutnagur | 6 |
| K. G. Duers run out | 1 |
| B 9, l-b 4, w 2, n-b 4 | 19 |
| 1/11 2/12 3/64 4/341 5/393 6/397 7/404 8/405 9/419 | 440 |

Bowling: Thorne 21.4–1–105–3; Rutnagur 29–4–112–5; Lawrence 28–3–111–1; MacLarnon 12–1–50–0; Brettell 6–0–49–0.

Umpires: J. W. Noble and A. R. Taylor.

†At Aldershot, June 14. Zimbabweans won by eight wickets. Combined Services 70 (A. J. Traicos four for 27); Zimbabweans 71 for two (G. A. Paterson 45 not out).

†At Bath, June 15. Zimbabweans won by four wickets. Somerset 191 for nine (55 overs) (R. J. Harden 56; K. G. Duers five for 26); Zimbabweans 195 for six (53.5 overs) (G. A. Hick 42).

## GLAMORGAN v ZIMBABWEANS

At Swansea, June 19, 20, 21. Drawn. Toss won by Glamorgan. The Zimbabweans were in a strong position to become the first team to win on a Glamorgan ground since the West Indians in May 1984, but heavy overnight rain washed out the final day. The tourists established a first-innings lead of 150 following a superb display by Hick, whose 192 in little more than four and a half hours featured three 6s and 22 4s. He and Paterson added 148 for the second wicket in 30 overs. Glamorgan lost four wickets before clearing the arrears and were only 37 runs in front at the end of the second day. Butchart bowled excellently on the first day to register his best figures of five for 65. Glamorgan rested seven of their leading players.

### Glamorgan

| | | | |
|---|---|---|---|
| J. A. Hopkins c Butchart b Streak | 13 | – c Houghton b Butchart | 44 |
| *A. L. Jones c Walton b Butchart | 80 | – c Traicos b Jarvis | 5 |
| G. C. Holmes c Pycroft b Streak | 9 | – c Pycroft b Traicos | 24 |
| H. Morris c Traicos b Jarvis | 34 | – c and b Hick | 36 |
| S. P. Henderson not out | 47 | – not out | 52 |
| M. R. Price c Houghton b Butchart | 18 | – not out | 20 |
| J. Derrick lbw b Butchart | 4 | | |
| I. Smith b Butchart | 0 | | |
| †M. L. Roberts lbw b Traicos | 0 | | |
| S. J. Malone c Shah b Butchart | 2 | | |
| L. L. McFarlane c Houghton b Traicos | 0 | | |
| B 4, l-b 1, n-b 2 | 7 | B 4, l-b 1, n-b 1 | 6 |
| 1/21 2/46 3/123 4/156 5/195 6/199 7/203 8/204 9/213 | 214 | 1/17 2/79 3/79 4/148 (4 wkts) | 187 |

Bowling: *First Innings*—Jarvis 18–3–58–1; Streak 9–3–27–2; Butchart 24–6–65–5; Traicos 20.4–6–45–2; Hick 4–0–14–0. *Second Innings*—Jarvis 13–0–52–1; Butchart 15–5–32–1; Traicos 16–5–39–1; de Grandhomme 9–4–26–0; Shah 6–2–13–0; Hick 6–1–20–1.

### Zimbabweans

| | |
|---|---|
| G. A. Paterson b Holmes | 69 |
| K. G. Walton run out | 1 |
| G. A. Hick c Holmes b Price | 192 |
| *A. J. Pycroft c Jones b Holmes | 0 |
| †D. L. Houghton lbw b McFarlane | 24 |
| A. H. Shah lbw b Holmes | 1 |
| L. L. de Grandhomme c Jones b McFarlane | 10 |
| I. P. Butchart lbw b Holmes | 4 |
| D. H. Streak not out | 26 |
| A. J. Traicos run out | 16 |
| M. P. Jarvis c Smith b Malone | 3 |
| B 5, l-b 6, n-b 7 | 18 |
| 1/3 2/151 3/151 4/251 5/256 6/283 7/288 8/333 9/360 | 364 |

Bowling: Malone 16.1–4–62–1; McFarlane 18–3–68–2; Derrick 15–2–56–0; Price 19–4–81–1; Holmes 17–4–49–4; Smith 6–1–37–0.

Umpires: J. Birkenshaw and R. Julian.

## WARWICKSHIRE v ZIMBABWEANS

At Edgbaston, June 22, 24, 25. Drawn. Toss won by Warwickshire. Three declarations, made because 385 minutes were lost to the weather, could not bring about a result in a game where batsmen were always on top. Dyer and Amiss added 152 for the second wicket in Warwickshire's first innings, with the opener scoring his first hundred of the season. In their second innings, Amiss when 7 became the fourteenth player to score 40,000 runs in first-class cricket, and Humpage, going in first, needed just 56 balls for his 76. Set a target of 289 in 51 overs, the Zimbabweans were always in the hunt while Hick was at the wicket. His 65 in 71 minutes was a powerful innings which underlined his immense potential.

### Warwickshire

| | | | |
|---|---|---|---|
| T. A. Lloyd lbw b Jarvis | 57 | – (5) b Jarvis | 3 |
| R. I. H. B. Dyer not out | 109 | – (3) c Traicos b Butchart | 7 |
| *D. L. Amiss b Butchart | 86 | – (6) not out | 18 |
| †G. W. Humpage not out | 45 | – (1) c Jarvis b Traicos | 76 |
| G. J. Lord (did not bat) | | – (2) c Hick b Butchart | 8 |
| A. M. Ferreira (did not bat) | | – (4) b Jarvis | 22 |
| A. R. K. Pierson (did not bat) | | – not out | 2 |
| B 2, l-b 9 | 11 | B 3 | 3 |
| 1/90 2/242 (2 wkts dec.) | 308 | 1/26 2/56 3/102 4/115 5/126 (5 wkts dec.) | 139 |

W. Morton, S. Wall, T. A. Munton and D. S. Hoffman did not bat.

Bowling: *First Innings*—Jarvis 21–4–80–1; Duers 19–2–62–0; Butchart 18–5–58–1; Traicos 18–3–44–0; Hick 9–0–30–0; Shah 6–1–23–0. *Second Innings*—Jarvis 7–0–35–2; Butchart 14–2–60–2; Traicos 7–0–41–1.

## Zimbabweans

| | | | |
|---|---|---|---|
| R. D. Brown c Ferreira b Pierson | 23 | – b Wall | 5 |
| G. A. Paterson c Morton b Wall | 10 | – c Humpage b Wall | 24 |
| G. A. Hick b Wall | 4 | – c Dyer b Pierson | 65 |
| *A. J. Pycroft c Humpage b Ferreira | 21 | – (7) not out | 46 |
| †D. L. Houghton run out | 35 | – (8) not out | 30 |
| A. C. Waller not out | 56 | – (4) lbw b Wall | 1 |
| A. H. Shah not out | 5 | – (6) c Pierson b Ferreira | 26 |
| I. P. Butchart (did not bat) | | – (5) b Ferreira | 18 |
| B 1, l-b 3, w 1 | 5 | B 9, l-b 6, n-b 1 | 16 |
| 1/13 2/19 3/55 4/68 5/146 | (5 wkts dec.) 159 | 1/30 2/39 3/47 4/91 5/130 6/152 | (6 wkts) 231 |

A. J. Traicos, M. P. Jarvis and K. G. Duers did not bat.

Bowling: *First Innings*—Wall 11–3–29–2; Hoffman 6–2–15–0; Munton 7–0–16–0; Ferreira 7–4–3–1; Morton 5–0–40–0; Pierson 11–2–33–1; Lord 5–0–19–0. *Second Innings*—Wall 14–2–42–3; Hoffman 6.3–1–18–0; Munton 2–0–19–0; Pierson 14–1–89–1; Ferreira 9–2–48–2.

Umpires: B. Leadbeater and H. J. Rhodes.

†At Coatbridge, June 28. Zimbabweans won by 70 runs in a one-day match which was arranged when the three-day fixture scheduled for June 26, 27, 28 was abandoned owing to rain. Zimbabweans 165 for eight (45 overs) (A. J. Pycroft 54); Scotland 95 (38.4 overs) (G. A. Hick four for 24).

## MINOR COUNTIES v ZIMBABWEANS

At Cleethorpes, June 29, 30, July 1. Drawn. Toss won by Zimbabweans. In reply to the tourists' modest total, in which only Pycroft and de Grandhomme passed 20, Minor Counties were able to declare their innings 79 ahead, thanks mainly to a second-wicket stand of 108 between Atkinson and Ottley. The Zimbabweans looked in danger of suffering their first defeat of the tour when they were reduced to 146 for six midway through the last afternoon. However, they were rescued by a patient century in four hours from Pycroft, an absentee the previous day with a stomach upset but now sharing a seventh-wicket stand of 123 with Butchart, whose 82 came off 94 balls with one 6 and twelve 4s.

## Zimbabweans

| | | | |
|---|---|---|---|
| G. A. Paterson b Arnold | 15 | – c Roope b Smith | 26 |
| K. G. Walton c Riddell b Smith | 15 | – c Mattocks b Merry | 1 |
| G. A. Hick c Mattocks b Arnold | 19 | – c Plumb b Smith | 38 |
| *A. J. Pycroft c Mattocks b Arnold | 44 | – (5) not out | **110** |
| †D. L. Houghton b Smith | 17 | – (6) c Smith b Herbert | 2 |
| R. D. Brown c Roope b Smith | 2 | – (4) c Roope b Herbert | 23 |
| L. L. de Grandhomme c Arnold b Smith | 59 | – c Riddell b Herbert | **0** |
| I. P. Butchart c Herbert b Arnold | 5 | – c Atkinson b Merry | **82** |
| E. A. Brandes lbw b Smith | 8 | – not out | **3** |
| D. H. Streak c Mattocks b Arnold | 17 | | |
| A. J. Traicos not out | 6 | | |
| B 2, l-b 3, n-b 2 | 7 | B 4, l-b 2, w 2 | **8** |
| 1/19 2/45 3/63 4/100 5/115 6/115 7/121 8/164 9/197 | 214 | 1/2 2/66 3/67 4/131 5/146 6/146 7/269 | **(7 wkts dec.) 293** |

Bowling: *First Innings*—Merry 19–2–59–0; Arnold 20–5–57–5; Smith 35–14–79–5; Herbert 8–1–14–0. *Second Innings*—Arnold 14–3–51–0; Merry 14–5–64–2; Smith 26–12–58–2; Plumb 10–1–31–0; Herbert 28–4–76–3; Ottley 2–1–1–0; Lanchbury 2–0–6–0.

## Minor Counties

| | |
|---|---|
| S. R. Atkinson c Hick b de Grandhomme | 63 |
| R. J. Lanchbury c Hick b Butchart | 0 |
| D. G. Ottley c sub b de Grandhomme | 47 |
| G. R. J. Roope b Butchart | 61 |
| S. G. Plumb c sub b de Grandhomme | 21 |
| *N. A. Riddell b Butchart | 23 |
| R. Herbert c Traicos b Brandes | 43 |
| T. S. Smith c Hick b Brandes | 9 |
| †D. E. Mattocks not out | 1 |
| B 5, l-b 16, w 3, n-b 1 | 25 |
| 1/2 2/110 3/128 4/175 5/209 6/269 7/292 8/293 (8 wkts dec.) | 293 |

W. G. Merry and K. A. Arnold did not bat.

Bowling: Brandes 12.4–0–46–2; Butchart 21–6–46–3; Traicos 23–8–39–0; Streak 3–0–13–0; de Grandhomme 27–5–79–3; Hick 10–1–49–0.

Umpires: S. Levison and T. G. Wilson.

†At Builth Wells, July 8, 9. Wales won by 67 runs. Wales 179 (I. P. Butchart five for 45) and 320 (G. Edwards 79, D. Harris 70; L. L. de Grandhomme five for 11); Zimbabweans 240 (D. L. Houghton 70, A. J. Pycroft 52, R. D. Brown 50; B. Lloyd four for 71) and 192 (I. P. Butchart 96; G. Edwards four for 72).

†At Middleton, Manchester, July 10, 11. League Cricket Conference won by seven wickets. League Cricket Conference 264 for seven dec. (D. Borthwick 65, R. J. Blakey 48, J. Foster 41) and 83 for three; Zimbabweans 163 (D. L. Houghton 52; A. Merrick six for 37) and 182 (D. L. Houghton 52).

†At Hove, July 13. Zimbabweans won by five wickets. Sussex 237 for six (55 overs) (A. P. Wells 80, N. J. Lenham 76); Zimbabweans 238 for five (54.4 overs) (G. A. Paterson 95, A. H. Shah 52, R. D. Brown 41).

†At Arundel, July 14. Zimbabweans won by seven wickets. Lavinia, Duchess of Norfolk's XI 217 for eight dec. (N. J. Lenham 74, J. M. Rice 49; A. H. Shah four for 43); Zimbabweans 220 for three (G. A. Paterson 88, K. G. Walton 78 not out).

## SURREY v ZIMBABWEANS

At The Oval, July 17, 18, 19. Drawn. Toss won by Zimbabweans. Rain prevented any play on the final day with Surrey, 337 ahead, well placed to force a win. Needham dominated the first morning with a hundred before lunch, reaching three figures in 109 minutes with sixteen 4s and scoring 124 of Surrey's 176 in the first session. In the afternoon it was the turn of Jesty, who shared an unbroken partnership of 116 with Davies, the wicket-keeper, making his first appearance for Surrey. The tourists then struggled against Surrey's seam bowlers, owing a great deal to de Grandhomme's determined batting in avoiding the follow-on. Stewart enlivened the final session of the second day with a dashing 88 not out as Surrey chased runs to set up a declaration, which the weather ensured did not eventuate.

### Surrey

| | | | |
|---|---|---|---|
| A. R. Butcher c de Grandhomme b Jarvis | 19 | – lbw b Jarvis | 14 |
| A. Needham c Traicos b Butchart | 124 | – b Streak | 38 |
| A. J. Stewart c and b de Grandhomme | 33 | – not out | 88 |
| T. E. Jesty not out | 100 | – b Traicos | 54 |
| M. A. Lynch b Butchart | 27 | – c Streak b Traicos | 15 |
| *G. P. Howarth lbw b Butchart | 0 | – not out | 3 |
| †Alec G. Davies not out | 26 | | |
| B 2, l-b 11, w 1 | 14 | B 2, l-b 5, w 1 | 8 |
| 1/51 2/180 3/182 4/227 5/227 | (5 wkts dec.) 343 | 1/31 2/77 3/179 4/205 | (4 wkts) 220 |

R. J. Doughty, G. Monkhouse, P. I. Pocock and P. A. Waterman did not bat.

Bowling: *First Innings*—Jarvis 16–0–71–1; Brandes 7–0–45–0; Butchart 17–5–58–3; Traicos 14–3–49–0; Shah 12–3–52–0; de Grandhomme 9–0–42–1; Streak 3.3–0–11–0; Hick 1–0–2–0. *Second Innings*—Jarvis 9–1–36–1; Brandes 13–1–53–0; Streak 5–1–18–1; Butchart 8–1–32–0; Hick 7–0–23–0; Shah 4–1–18–0; Traicos 9–1–33–2.

### Zimbabweans

| | |
|---|---|
| R. D. Brown c Davies b Needham | 27 |
| G. A. Paterson lbw b Waterman | 43 |
| D. H. Streak c Needham b Monkhouse | 29 |
| G. A. Hick lbw b Waterman | 10 |
| †D. L. Houghton lbw b Doughty | 19 |
| A. H. Shah c Davies b Doughty | 7 |
| I. P. Butchart c Stewart b Doughty | 4 |
| L. L. de Grandhomme lbw b Monkhouse | 48 |
| E. A. Brandes lbw b Pocock | 19 |
| *A. J. Traicos c Davies b Monkhouse | 8 |
| M. P. Jarvis not out | 1 |
| B 4, l-b 4, w 2, n-b 1 | 11 |
| 1/65 2/73 3/89 4/117 5/135 6/148 7/150 8/205 9/221 | 226 |

Bowling: Waterman 16–3–58–2; Doughty 16–1–61–3; Monkhouse 12.5–2–48–3; Pocock 12–4–24–1; Needham 13–5–27–1.

Umpires: J. Birkenshaw and D. O. Oslear.

## GLOUCESTERSHIRE v ZIMBABWEANS

At Bristol, July 20, 22, 23. Gloucestershire won by seven wickets. Toss won by Gloucestershire. The county side won a run-chase on the last day to inflict on the Zimbabweans their only defeat in a three-day match on the tour. Sainsbury and Curran, their countryman, proved too much for the visiting batsmen on the opening day, and when the second day was lost to rain Bainbridge conceded a lead of 91 to set up a day's cricket in which more than 500 runs were scored. Splendid hitting by Paterson (nineteen 4s) enabled Traicos to set Gloucestershire a target of 297 in 195 minutes. On a pitch playing perfectly, it was a fair challenge. Romaines "anchored" the chase while Bainbridge and Zaheer, who was making a guest appearance, fired off handsome strokes. By the time Davison arrived to confront his fellow countrymen, Romaines was ready to accelerate and the fourth-wicket pair knocked off the runs in an unbroken stand of 103, Gloucestershire having nine balls to spare.

## Zimbabweans

| | | | |
|---|---|---|---|
| R. D. Brown run out | 27 | – c Brassington b Twizell | 2 |
| G. A. Paterson b Sainsbury | 36 | – c Payne b Sainsbury | 92 |
| G. A. Hick c Brassington b Sainsbury | 1 | – (4) c Payne b Twizell | 39 |
| A. H. Shah b Sainsbury | 16 | – (3) c Curran b Bainbridge | 40 |
| †D. L. Houghton lbw b Sainsbury | 0 | | |
| K. G. Walton lbw b Payne | 20 | – (5) not out | 20 |
| I. P. Butchart c Davison b Curran | 18 | – (6) not out | 0 |
| L. L. de Grandhomme run out | 8 | | |
| E. A. Brandes c Zaheer b Curran | 0 | | |
| *A. J. Traicos not out | 27 | | |
| K. G. Duers b Curran | 0 | | |
| L-b 3 | 3 | B 1, l-b 11 | 12 |
| 1/60 2/62 3/68 4/70 5/83 6/107 7/121 8/121 9/145 | 156 | 1/8 2/126 3/146 4/203 (4 wkts dec.) | 205 |

Bowling: *First Innings*—Curran 18.3–7–37–3; Sainsbury 17–8–36–4; Twizell 13–4–33–0; Payne 17–4–43–1; Lloyds 2–1–4–0. *Second Innings*—Twizell 15–2–65–2; Sainsbury 13–2–42–1; Payne 8–0–59–0; Bainbridge 7–1–27–1.

## Gloucestershire

| | | | |
|---|---|---|---|
| P. W. Romaines b Brandes | 2 | – not out | 114 |
| A. J. Wright not out | 40 | – b Duers | 23 |
| *P. Bainbridge c Traicos b Butchart | 20 | – b Duers | 45 |
| †A. J. Brassington not out | 0 | | |
| Zaheer Abbas (did not bat) | | – (4) c Walton b Duers | 38 |
| B. F. Davison (did not bat) | | – (5) not out | 53 |
| L-b 3 | 3 | B 18, l-b 7, n-b 1 | 26 |
| 1/10 2/56 (2 wkts dec.) | 65 | 1/46 2/126 3/196 (3 wkts) | 299 |

K. M. Curran, J. W. Lloyds, I. R. Payne, G. E. Sainsbury and P. H. Twizell did not bat.

Bowling: *First Innings*—Brandes 7–1–16–1; Butchart 9–3–26–1; Duers 6–1–19–0; Traicos 4–3–1–0. *Second Innings*—Brandes 8–1–30–0; Butchart 13–2–68–0; Duers 14–0–75–3; Traicos 15.3–1–81–0; Hick 5–0–20–0.

*R. D. Brown kept wicket for part of the first innings and all of the second innings after D. L. Houghton had been injured.*

Umpires: H. J. Rhodes and D. S. Thompsett.

## LEICESTERSHIRE v ZIMBABWEANS

At Leicester, July 24, 25, 26. Cancelled owing to the non-availability of the ground at Grace Road.

# THE CRICKET COUNCIL

The Cricket Council, which was set up in 1968 and reconstituted in 1974 and 1983, acts as the governing body for cricket in the British Isles. It comprises the following, the officers listed being those for 1984-85.

*Chairman:* C. H. Palmer.
*Vice-Chairman:* J. D. Robson.
*8 Representatives of the Test and County Cricket Board:* C. H. Palmer, C. R. M. Atkinson, D. J. Insole, F. G. Mann, H. J. Pocock, A. C. Smith, A. D. Steven, F. M. Turner.
*5 Representatives of the National Cricket Association:* J. D. Robson, F. R. Brown, F. H. Elliott, J. Lane, J. G. Overy.
*3 Representatives of the Marylebone Cricket Club:* D. G. Clark, M. C. Cowdrey, G. H. G. Doggart.
*1 Representative (non-voting) of the Minor Counties Cricket Association:* G. L. B. August.
*1 Representative (non-voting) of the Irish Cricket Union:* D. Scott.
*1 Representative (non-voting) of the Scottish Cricket Union:* R. W. Barclay.

*Secretary:* D. B. Carr.

# THE TEST AND COUNTY CRICKET BOARD

The TCCB was set up in 1968 to be responsible for Test matches, official tours, and first-class and minor county competitions. It is composed of representatives of the seventeen first-class counties; Marylebone Cricket Club; Minor Counties Cricket Association; Oxford University Cricket Club, Cambridge University Cricket Club, the Irish Cricket Union and the Scottish Cricket Union.

## Officers 1984–85

*Chairman:* C. H. Palmer. (Chairman for 1985-86: R. Subba Row.)

*Chairmen of Committees:* C. H. Palmer (Executive); F. G. Mann (Adjudication); M. C. Cowdrey (County Pitches); D. J. Insole (Cricket, Overseas Tours); C. R. M. Atkinson (Discipline); A. D. Steven (Finance); B. Coleman (PR and Marketing); D. R. W. Silk (Registration); P. B. H. May (Selection); D. B. Carr (Umpires); M. D. Vockins (Under-25 and Second XI Competitions).

*Secretary:* D. B. Carr. *Assistant Secretary (Administration):* B. Langley. *Assistant Secretary (Cricket):* M. E. Gear. *PR and Marketing Manager:* P. M. Lush. *Sales and Promotion Manager:* K. Deshayes.

# THE NATIONAL CRICKET ASSOCIATION

With the setting up of the Cricket Council in 1968 it was necessary to form a separate organisation to represent the interests of all cricket below the first-class game, and it is the National Cricket Association that carries out this function. It comprises representatives from 51 county cricket associations and seventeen national cricketing organisations.

## Officers 1984-85

*President:* F. R. Brown.
*Chairman:* J. D. Robson.
*Vice-Chairman:* F. H. Elliott.
*Secretary:* B. J. Aspital.
*Director of Coaching:* K. V. Andrew.
*Hon. Treasurer:* D. A. Jackson.
*Assistant Secretary:* P. G. M. August.

# THE MARYLEBONE CRICKET CLUB, 1985

Patron – HER MAJESTY THE QUEEN

President – F. G. MANN

President Designate – J. G. W. DAVIES

Treasurer – D. G. CLARK

Chairman of Finance – SIR ANTHONY TUKE

Trustees – G. O. ALLEN, F. G. MANN, SIR OLIVER POPPLEWELL

Life Vice-Presidents – R. AIRD, G. O. ALLEN, F. R. BROWN, S. C. GRIFFITH

Secretary – J. A. BAILEY

(Lord's Cricket Ground, St John's Wood, NW8 8QN)

Assistant Secretaries – LT-COL. L. G. JAMES (Administration), LT-COL. J. R. STEPHENSON (Cricket), WG-CDR V. J. W. M. LAWRENCE (Chief Accountant)

Curator – S. E. A. GREEN

Ground Administrator – A. W. P. FLEMING

*MCC Committee for 1984-85:* F. G. Mann (President), G. O. Allen, A. N. S. Burnett, D. G. Clark, E. A. Clark, M. C. Cowdrey, A. H. A. Dibbs, G. H. G. Doggart, C. A. Fry, J. S. O. Haslewood, D. R. Male, M. E. L. Melluish, M. D. Mence, F. W. Millett, E. W. Phillips, Sir Oliver Popplewell, D. R. W. Silk, T. M. B. Sissons, Sir Anthony Tuke, J. A. F. Vallance, J. J. Warr.

At the 198th Annual Meeting of MCC, held at Lord's on May 1, 1985, at which the President took the chair, the retirement of G. O. Allen as a Trustee of the club from September 30, 1985, was announced. D. G. Clark was nominated to succeed him. Special mention was made that this brought to an end Mr Allen's 50 years on the Committee. His "unique services" to cricket, and to the MCC, were recorded.

The Income and Expenditure Account for 1984 showed a surplus of £169,270 after tax. This was considerably better than expected, owing to an excellent summer of both weather and cricket. Distribution from the TCCB was higher than anticipated and income from advertising was up by 21 per cent. There was also a reduction in exceptional expenditure, though urgent work arising in the Indoor School and from the refurbishment of the pavilion, following the move of the TCCB and the NCA to their new offices, was likely to result in exceptional expenditure in 1985 of over £300,000. The overall cost of the rebuilding of the Mound Stand referred to in the Annual Report would be in the region of £3m and a twenty-year bank loan of £1.5m on favourable terms had been provisionally arranged. The membership of the club on December 31, 1984, when there were 10,373 candidates on the waiting list, was 18,159, made up of 10,938 town members, 2,346 country members, 3,144 at the special over-65 rate, 374 at the under-25 rate, 265 at the special schoolmasters' rate, 767 on the abroad list, 77 life members, seventeen 60-year life members, 40 honorary cricket members and 191 honorary life members. In addition there were 36 out-match members. In 1984, 494 vacancies occurred, owing to 220 deaths, 126 resignations and 148 lapsed memberships.

The development programme in the Tennis and Squash Court area was completed in early 1985. Middlesex moved into their new offices in July 1984, and the TCCB and NCA into theirs in February 1985. Two new squash courts with viewing galleries were also opened. The final cost of the new building was £671,000, exclusive of VAT. Plans for the replacement of the Mound Stand, with a view to a new stand being in position by the Bicentenary of the club in 1987, were well advanced and would be considered at a Special General Meeting of the club on September 11, 1985. Members were also told that a new library would be built during the summer, incorporating part of the old and to be opened in September, with access from the main pavilion staircase across the bridge on the first floor.

J. G. W. Davies, OBE, was nominated by F. G. Mann to succeed him as President of MCC on October 1, 1985. Aged 73, Jack Davies, a past Treasurer of the club, was a vigorous all-rounder for Cambridge University and Kent. For many years he has been closely associated with Cambridge cricket. Those due for rotational retirement from the Committee of the club were A. N. S. Burnett, G. H. G. Doggart, J. S. O. Haslewood, M. E. L. Melluish and D. R. W. Silk. A. C. D. Ingleby-Mackenzie, D. J. Insole, M. M. Morton and P. B. H. May were elected to fill the vacancies, as from October 1, 1985.

At a Special General Meeting, which followed the Annual General Meeting on May 1, 1985, members gave approval to the Committee's request to be empowered to elect up to 2,000 Associate Members on such conditions and with such privileges as the Committee shall decide. The voting in favour, which included a postal ballot, was 1,740 to 544.

At a Special General Meeting, held in the Long Room at Lord's on September 11, 1985, plans for the redevelopment of the Mound Stand, to be completed by 1987, were approved. The design aims to retain the best features of the present stand, built in 1898 and 1899, and provides for new accommodation, including hospitality boxes, debenture seating, restaurants and bars. The voting, including a postal ballot, was 5,777 to 277.

## MCC v ESSEX

At Lord's, April 24, 25, 26. Drawn. Toss won by Essex. Runs came slowly in mostly very cold weather. On the first day only 260 were scored in six hours' cricket, Cowans having a lot to do with this by bowling a full length and a good line. On the second, Moxon, in his first innings at Lord's, made a painstaking 100 in 278 minutes. With one 6 and twenty 4s in his 121 Nicholas scored with greater freedom against an Essex attack without Lever and Foster. The 1984 county champions batted out the third day for a draw, although at 123 for four, with Fletcher absent with sinus trouble, there was some doubt whether they would.

## Essex

| | First innings | | Second innings | |
|---|---|---|---|---|
| G. A. Gooch | c Emburey b Allott | 15 | lbw b Allott | 41 |
| P. J. Prichard | c French b Cowans | 8 | c Bailey b Nicholas | 42 |
| B. R. Hardie | c Gower b Cowans | 31 | b Nicholas | 0 |
| K. S. McEwan | b Emburey | 41 | lbw b Emburey | 63 |
| D. R. Pringle | c Allott b Emburey | 47 | b Allott | 1 |
| *K. W. R. Fletcher | c Emburey b Cowans | 1 | | |
| K. R. Pont | b Cowans | 0 | (6) not out | 62 |
| †D. E. East | b Cowans | 7 | (7) not out | 39 |
| S. Turner | lbw b Cowans | 3 | | |
| J. H. Childs | b Allott | 6 | | |
| D. L. Acfield | not out | 1 | | |
| | B 1, l-b 1 | 2 | B 4, l-b 6 | 10 |
| | 1/23 2/23 3/97 4/97 5/102 6/102 7/110 8/118 9/141 | 162 | 1/86 2/86 3/99 4/123 5/178 | (5 wkts) 258 |

Bowling: *First Innings*—Cowans 21–8–68–6; Allott 22–6–63–2; Wells 7–1–22–0; Emburey 4.5–2–5–2; Edmonds 3–1–2–0. *Second Innings*—Cowans 18–1–85–0; Allott 22–11–41–2; Wells 10–1–19–0; Nicholas 10–4–28–2; Edmonds 16–7–32–0; Emburey 8–1–16–1; Moxon 5–0–19–0; Robinson 1–0–8–0.

## MCC

| | |
|---|---|
| M. D. Moxon c East b Acfield | 104 |
| R. T. Robinson c East b Pringle | 22 |
| *D. I. Gower c East b Pringle | 26 |
| M. C. J. Nicholas c Gooch b Pringle | 121 |
| R. J. Bailey b Turner | 33 |
| C. M. Wells c Pringle b Turner | 37 |
| J. E. Emburey c East b Pringle | 6 |
| †B. N. French c Prichard b Turner | 7 |
| P. H. Edmonds not out | 0 |
| P. J. W. Allott b Childs | 3 |
| N. G. Cowans not out | 3 |
| B 1, l-b 7, n-b 7 | 15 |
| 1/47 2/99 3/262 4/304 5/332 6/339 7/362 8/371 9/374 (9 wkts dec.) | 377 |

Bowling: Pringle 33–9–70–4; Turner 35–10–97–3; Pont 12–2–38–0; Acfield 22–2–65–1; Gooch 11–3–41–0; Childs 21–8–58–1.

Umpires: M. J. Kitchen and N. T. Plews.

†At Lord's, May 1. MCC won by 59 runs. MCC 264 for five dec. (G. Boycott 123; A. R. K. Pierson four for 88); MCC Young Cricketers 195 (G. P. Jenkins 92; D. A. Reeve six for 27).

At Lord's, May 22, 23, 24. MCC drew with AUSTRALIANS (See Australian tour section).

†At Fenner's, June 15, 16, 17. MCC drew with CAMBRIDGE UNIVERSITY (See Cambridge University section).

†At The Parks, June 22, 23, 24. MCC drew with OXFORD UNIVERSITY (See Oxford University section).

†At Swansea, July 24, 25, 26. MCC beat WALES by four wickets (See Other Matches, 1985).

†At Ayr, August 22, 23. MCC drew with SCOTLAND (See Other Matches, 1985).

†At Lord's, August 28, 29. Drawn, with the scores level. Ireland 310 for five dec. (M. A. Masood 138, D. G. Dennison 69, D. A. Lewis 40 not out; T. M. Lamb four for 63) and 153 (T. M. Lamb five for 52); MCC 218 for two dec. (Mansoor Akhtar 71 not out, R. W. Tolchard 64 not out) and 245 for eight (N. E. J. Pocock 65, J. Birkenshaw 61 not out, R. W. Tolchard 50; A. McBrine four for 72).

## MCC ENGLAND HONORARY CRICKET MEMBERS

C. J. Barnett
W. E. Bowes
H. Larwood
L. E. G. Ames, CBE
Sir Leonard Hutton
D. C. S. Compton, CBE
D. V. P. Wright
T. G. Evans, CBE
C. Washbrook
A. V. Bedser, CBE
W. J. Edrich, DFC
J. C. Laker
P. B. H. May, CBE
W. Watson
P. E. Richardson
T. E. Bailey
M. J. K. Smith, OBE
J. Hardstaff
J. B. Statham, CBE
F. S. Trueman
T. W. Graveney, OBE
G. A. R. Lock
C. Milburn
D. A. Allen
R. W. Barber
E. R. Dexter
P. H. Parfitt
F. H. Tyson
M. C. Cowdrey, CBE
J. T. Murray, MBE
J. M. Parks
D. B. Close, CBE
B. L. D'Oliveira, OBE
R. Illingworth, CBE
G. Pullar
F. J. Titmus, MBE
J. H. Wardle
D. J. Brown
M. H. Denness
J. M. Brearley, OBE
R. W. Taylor, MBE
R. G. D. Willis, MBE

## MCC HONORARY LIFE MEMBERS, 1985

*Australia:* G. S. Chappell.
*New Zealand:* G. M. Turner.
*Pakistan:* Asif Iqbal, Wasim Bari, Majid Jahangir Khan.
*South Africa:* M. J. Procter.
*West Indies:* R. C. Fredericks, A. M. E. Roberts.

---

## GETTY'S DONATION

J. Paul Getty II has donated £1.5 million towards the cost of the new Mound Stand at Lord's, due to be opened in 1987 and estimated to cost over £4 million.

# OTHER MATCHES AT LORD'S, 1985

June 3. Third Texaco Trophy match. ENGLAND beat AUSTRALIA by eight wickets (See Australian tour section).

June 27, 28, 29, July 1, 2. Second Cornhill Test. ENGLAND lost to AUSTRALIA by four wickets (See Australian tour section).

## OXFORD UNIVERSITY v CAMBRIDGE UNIVERSITY

July 3, 4, 5. Drawn. Toss won by Oxford University. Having outplayed Cambridge on the first two days, Oxford were denied the chance to finish them off when torrential rain ended the match soon after two o'clock on the last day. Proceedings were dominated to an extraordinary extent by Toogood, playing in the match for a fourth year. Intervening for the first time when Cambridge, who were put in, had been given a steady start, and bowling at medium pace, he bowled for most of the rest of Cambridge's first innings, finishing with eight for 52. Next day his 149 – he had scored his only other first-class hundred in the University Match of the year before – spanned most of the Oxford innings, and when Miller declared, in order to give Cambridge 50 minutes' batting before the close, Toogood took the two wickets to fall. In the whole history of the fixture, the only all-round feat superior to this was P. R. Le Couteur's in 1910 when he scored 160 in Oxford's only innings and took eleven Cambridge wickets in the match. Not until the last morning in the 1985 match did Cambridge play cricket at all worthy of the occasion.

### Cambridge University

| | | | |
|---|---|---|---|
| A. E. Lea (*High Arcal GS and Churchill*) c Carr b Toogood | 41 | – not out | 47 |
| *C. R. Andrew (*Barnard Castle and St John's*) b Toogood | 12 | – c Franks b Toogood | 12 |
| D. J. Fell (*John Lyon and Trinity*) b Lawrence | 8 | – lbw b Toogood | 0 |
| P. G. P. Roebuck (*Millfield and Emmanuel*) c Thorne b Toogood | 2 | – (5) not out | 34 |
| D. G. Price (*Haberdashers' Aske's and Homerton*) lbw b Toogood | 12 | | |
| †A. G. Davies (*Birkenhead and Robinson*) lbw b Toogood | 11 | | |
| T. A. Cotterell (*Downside and Peterhouse*) lbw b Toogood | 24 | | |
| S. R. Gorman (*St Peter's, York and Emmanuel*) b Toogood | 6 | – (4) c Toogood b Rutnagur | 43 |
| C. C. Ellison (*Tonbridge and Homerton*) c Franks b Toogood | 4 | | |
| A. M. G. Scott (*Seaford Head and Queen's*) c Franks b Thorne | 5 | | |
| J. E. Davidson (*Penglais and Trinity*) not out | 1 | | |
| B 3, l-b 1, w 3, n-b 1 | 8 | B 2, l-b 3 | 5 |
| 1/41 2/62 3/65 4/74 5/87 6/92 7/100 8/104 9/132 | 134 | 1/20 2/24 3/96 (3 wkts) | 141 |

Bowling: *First Innings*—Thorne 9.3–1–23–1; Quinlan 13–5–18–0; MacLarnon 4–1–13–0; Toogood 24–7–52–8; Lawrence 13–8–8–1; Carr 11–4–16–0. *Second Innings*—Thorne 9–3–14–0; Toogood 13–3–41–2; Quinlan 7–3–21–0; Rutnagur 13–2–35–1; Carr 11–5–25–0.

## Oxford University

| | |
|---|---|
| *A. J. T. Miller (*Haileybury and St Edmund Hall*) b Andrew | 78 |
| W. R. Bristowe (*Charterhouse and St Edmund Hall*) c Lea b Ellison | 16 |
| G. J. Toogood (*N. Bromsgrove HS and Lincoln*) c Andrew b Ellison | 149 |
| J. D. Carr (*Repton and Worcester*) not out | 84 |
| D. A. Thorne (*Bablake and Keble*) c Davies b Ellison | 17 |
| †J. G. Franks (*Stamford and St Edmund Hall*) c Gorman b Andrew | 0 |
| P. C. MacLarnon (*Loughborough GS and St Peter's*) b Andrew | 2 |
| B 3, l-b 8, w 5, n-b 2 | 18 |
| 1/22 2/172 3/318 4/351 5/352 6/364 (6 wkts dec.) | 364 |

C. D. M. Tooley (*St Dunstan's and Magdalen*), R. S. Rutnagur (*Westminster and New*), J. D. Quinlan (*Sherborne and St Peter's*) and M. P. Lawrence (*Manchester GS and Merton*) did not bat.

Bowling: Davidson 10–1–40–0; Ellison 27–6–76–3; Scott 11–1–43–0; Cotterell 25–8–78–0; Gorman 4–0–14–0; Lea 1–0–1–0; Andrew 25.4–5–101–3.

Umpires: B. Leadbeater and K. E. Palmer.

## OXFORD v CAMBRIDGE, RESULTS AND HUNDREDS

The University match dates back to 1827. Altogether there have been 141 official matches, Cambridge winning 53 and Oxford 46, with 42 drawn. Results since 1950:

1950 Drawn
1951 Oxford won by 21 runs
1952 Drawn
1953 Cambridge won by two wickets
1954 Drawn
1955 Drawn
1956 Drawn
1957 Cambridge won by an innings and 186 runs
1958 Cambridge won by 99 runs
1959 Oxford won by 85 runs
1960 Drawn
1961 Drawn
1962 Drawn
1963 Drawn
1964 Drawn
1965 Drawn
1966 Oxford won by an innings and 9 runs
1967 Drawn
1968 Drawn
1969 Drawn
1970 Drawn
1971 Drawn
1972 Cambridge won by an innings and 25 runs
1973 Drawn
1974 Drawn
1975 Drawn
1976 Oxford won by ten wickets
1977 Drawn
1978 Drawn
1979 Cambridge won by an innings and 52 runs
1980 Drawn
1981 Drawn
1982 Cambridge won by seven wickets
1983 Drawn
1984 Oxford won by five wickets
1985 Drawn

Seventy-eight three-figure innings have been played in the University matches. For those scored before 1919 see 1940 *Wisden*. Those subsequent to 1919 include the six highest, as shown here:

| | | |
|---|---|---|
| 238* | Nawab of Pataudi | 1931 Oxford |
| 211 | G. Goonesena | 1957 Cam. |
| 201* | M. J. K. Smith | 1954 Oxford |
| 201 | A. Ratcliffe | 1931 Cam. |
| 200 | Majid J. Khan | 1970 Cam. |
| 193 | D. C. H. Townsend | 1934 Oxford |
| 170 | M. Howell | 1919 Oxford |
| 167 | B. W. Hone | 1932 Oxford |
| 158 | P. M. Roebuck | 1975 Cam. |
| 157 | D. R. Wilcox | 1932 Cam. |
| 155 | F. S. Goldstein | 1968 Oxford |
| 149 | J. T. Morgan | 1929 Cam. |
| 149 | G. J. Toogood | 1985 Oxford |
| 146 | R. O'Brien | 1956 Cam. |
| 146 | D. R. Owen-Thomas | 1971 Cam. |
| 145* | H. E. Webb | 1948 Oxford |

| | | | | | |
|---|---|---|---|---|---|
| 145 | D. P. Toft | 1967 Oxford | 114 | J. F. Pretlove | 1955 Cam. |
| 142 | M. P. Donnelly | 1946 Oxford | 113* | J. M. Brearley | 1962 Cam. |
| 139 | R. J. Boyd-Moss | 1983 Cam. | 113 | E. R. T. Holmes | 1927 Oxford |
| 136 | E. T. Killick | 1930 Cam. | 112* | E. D. Fursdon | 1975 Oxford |
| 135 | H. A. Pawson | 1947 Oxford | 111* | G. W. Cook | 1957 Cam. |
| 131 | Nawab of Pataudi | 1960 Oxford | 109 | C. H. Taylor | 1923 Oxford |
| 129 | H. J. Enthoven | 1925 Cam. | 109 | G. J. Toogood | 1984 Oxford |
| 128* | A. J. T. Miller | 1984 Oxford | 108 | F. G. H. Chalk | 1934 Oxford |
| 127 | D. S. Sheppard | 1952 Cam. | 106 | Nawab of Pataudi | 1929 Oxford |
| 124 | A. K. Judd | 1927 Cam. | 105 | E. J. Craig | 1961 Cam. |
| 124 | A. Ratcliffe | 1932 Cam. | 104 | H. J. Enthoven | 1924 Cam. |
| 124 | R. J. Boyd-Moss | 1983 Cam. | 104 | M. J. K. Smith | 1955 Oxford |
| 122 | P. A. Gibb | 1938 Cam. | 103* | A. R. Lewis | 1962 Cam. |
| 121 | J. N. Grover | 1937 Oxford | 103* | D. R. Pringle | 1979 Cam. |
| 119 | J. M. Brearley | 1964 Cam. | 102* | A. P. F. Chapman | 1922 Cam. |
| 118 | H. Ashton | 1921 Cam. | 101* | R. W. V. Robins | 1928 Cam. |
| 118 | D. R. W. Silk | 1954 Cam. | 101 | N. W. D. Yardley | 1937 Cam. |
| 117 | M. J. K. Smith | 1956 Oxford | 100* | M. Manasseh | 1964 Oxford |
| 116* | D. R. W. Silk | 1953 Cam. | 100 | P. J. Dickinson | 1939 Cam. |
| 116 | M. C. Cowdrey | 1953 Oxford | 100 | N. J. Cosh | 1967 Cam. |
| 115 | A. W. Allen | 1934 Cam. | 100 | R. J. Boyd-Moss | 1982 Cam. |
| 114* | D. R. Owen-Thomas | 1972 Cam. | | | |

* *Signifies not out.*

## Highest Totals

| | | | | | |
|---|---|---|---|---|---|
| 503 | Oxford | 1900 | 432-9 | Cambridge | 1936 |
| 457 | Oxford | 1947 | 431 | Cambridge | 1932 |
| 453-8 | Oxford | 1931 | 425 | Cambridge | 1938 |

## Lowest Totals

| | | | | | |
|---|---|---|---|---|---|
| 32 | Oxford | 1878 | 42 | Oxford | 1890 |
| 39 | Cambridge | 1858 | 47 | Cambridge | 1838 |

*Notes:* A. P. F. Chapman and M. P. Donnelly enjoy the following distinction: Chapman scored a century at Lord's in the University match (102*, 1922); for Gentlemen v Players (160, 1922), (108, 1926); and for England v Australia (121, 1930). M. P. Donnelly scored a century at Lord's in the University match (142, 1946); for Gentlemen v Players (162*, 1947); and for New Zealand v England (206, 1949).

A. Ratcliffe's 201 for Cambridge remained a record for the match for only one day, being beaten by the Nawab of Pataudi's 238* for Oxford next day.

M. J. K. Smith (Oxford) and R. J. Boyd-Moss (Cambridge) are the only players who have scored three hundreds. Smith scored 201* in 1954, 104 in 1955, and 117 in 1956; Boyd-Moss scored 100 in 1982 and 139 and 124 in 1983. His aggregate of 489 surpassed Smith's previous record of 477.

The following players have scored two hundreds: W. Yardley (Cambridge) 100 in 1870 and 130 in 1872; H. J. Enthoven (Cambridge) 104 in 1924 and 129 in 1925; Nawab of Pataudi (Oxford) 106 in 1929 and 238* in 1931; A. Ratcliffe (Cambridge) 201 in 1931 and 124 in 1932; D. R. W. Silk (Cambridge) 116* in 1953 and 118 in 1954; J. M. Brearley (Cambridge) 113* in 1962 and 119 in 1964; D. R. Owen-Thomas (Cambridge) 146 in 1971 and 114* in 1972; G. J. Toogood (Oxford) 109 in 1984 and 149 in 1985.

F. C. Cobden, in the Oxford v Cambridge match in 1870, performed the hat-trick by taking the last three wickets and won an extraordinary game for Cambridge by 2 runs. The feat is without parallel in first-class cricket. Other hat-tricks, all for Cambridge, have been credited to A. G. Steel (1879), P. H. Morton (1880), J. F. Ireland (1911), and R. G. H. Lowe (1926).

S. E. Butler, in the 1871 match, took all the wickets in the Cambridge first innings. The feat is unique in University matches. He bowled 24.1 overs. In the follow-on he took five wickets for 57, making fifteen for 95 runs in the match.

The best all-round performances in the history of the match have come from P. R. Le Couteur, who scored 160 and took eleven Cambridge wickets for 66 runs in 1910, and G. J. Toogood, who in 1985 scored 149 and took ten Cambridge wickets for 93.

D. W. Jarrett (Oxford 1975, Cambridge 1976), S. M. Wookey (Cambridge 1975-76), Oxford 1978) and G. Pathmanathan (Oxford 1975-78, Cambridge 1983) are alone in gaining cricket Blues for both Universities.

## ETON v HARROW

July 6. Eton won by 3 runs, their 50th victory in the 150 years of the fixture achieved in a thrilling finish when Bowman-Shaw had Hills caught at deep square-leg. By taking six Eton wickets, Pethers established a new Harrow record of 59 wickets in a season and kept his side's target down to 142. But after Wiltshire and Wells had given Harrow a confident start they collapsed from 64 for two to 98 for nine. With Hills receiving brave and stubborn support from Middleton, 40 were then added for the last wicket before Bowman-Shaw crowned an outstanding all-round performance with 2.5 overs to spare. His sound defence had been a feature of the Eton innings.

### Eton

| | |
|---|---|
| J. A. D. Carr lbw b Fox | 13 |
| D. A. Clifton-Brown c Waud b Pethers | 4 |
| F. N. Bowman-Shaw b Raper | 42 |
| *S. R. Gardiner b Pethers | 2 |
| J. B. A. Jenkins c Middleton b Pethers | 1 |
| †A. D. A. Zagoritis lbw b Raper | 10 |
| W. A. C. Pym b Pethers | 42 |
| J. D. Norman b Pethers | 0 |
| C. R. Erith c Wiltshire b Pethers | 3 |
| N. J. Squire b Fox | 7 |
| T. R. Pearson not out | 2 |
| B 1, l-b 5, w 2, n-b 7 | 15 |
| 1/14 2/23 3/38 4/50 5/79 6/91 7/92 8/109 9/119 | 141 |

Bowling: Fox 16–5–24–2; Pethers 26.2–5–87–6; Raper 11–1–24–2.

### Harrow

| | |
|---|---|
| *R. C. Wiltshire lbw b Pearson | 23 |
| R. M. Wells c and b Bowman-Shaw | 18 |
| M. D. S. Raper b Norman | 14 |
| A. W. Sexton c Clifton-Brown b Bowman-Shaw | 9 |
| D. C. Manasseh c Gardiner b Bowman-Shaw | 4 |
| J. J. Pethers c Zagoritis b Norman | 5 |
| G. E. G. Waud c Zagoritis b Bowman-Shaw | 1 |
| R. A. Pyman lbw b Bowman-Shaw | 0 |
| †R. A. Hills c Squire b Bowman-Shaw | 46 |
| D. B. M. Fox c Zagoritis b Bowman-Shaw | 0 |
| M. R. Middleton not out | 1 |
| B 1, l-b 1, w 5, n-b 10 | 17 |
| 1/40 2/64 3/66 4/72 5/84 6/86 7/86 8/86 9/98 | 138 |

Bowling: Pearson 9–1–40–1; Erith 3–0–20–0; Pym 7–1–14–0; Bowman-Shaw 16.1–3–38–7; Norman 15–5–24–2.

Umpires: J. H. Budgen and D. J. Dennis.

## ETON v HARROW, RESULTS AND HUNDREDS

Of the 150 matches played Eton have won 50, Harrow 44 and 56 have been drawn. This is the generally published record, but Harrow men object strongly to the first game in 1805 being treated as a regular contest between the two schools, contending that it is no more correct to count that one than the fixture of 1857 which has been rejected.

The matches played during the war years 1915-18 and 1940-45 are not reckoned as belonging to the regular series.

Results since 1950:

1950 Drawn
1951 Drawn
1952 Harrow won by seven wickets
1953 Eton won by ten wickets
1954 Harrow won by nine wickets
1955 Eton won by 38 runs
1956 Drawn
1957 Drawn
1958 Drawn
1959 Drawn

| | | | |
|---|---|---|---|
| 1960 | Harrow won by 124 runs | 1973 | Drawn |
| 1961 | Harrow won by an innings and 12 runs | 1974 | Harrow won by eight wickets |
| 1962 | Drawn | 1975 | Harrow won by an innings and 151 runs |
| 1963 | Drawn | 1976 | Drawn |
| 1964 | Eton won by eight wickets | 1977 | Eton won by six wickets |
| 1965 | Harrow won by 48 runs | 1978 | Drawn |
| 1966 | Drawn | 1979 | Drawn |
| 1967 | Drawn | 1980 | Drawn |
| 1968 | Harrow won by seven wickets | 1981 | Drawn |
| 1969 | Drawn | 1982 | Drawn |
| 1970 | Eton won by 97 runs | 1983 | Drawn |
| 1971 | Drawn | 1984 | Drawn |
| 1972 | Drawn | 1985 | Eton won by 3 runs |

Forty-five three-figure innings have been played in matches between these two schools. Those since 1918:

| | | | | | |
|---|---|---|---|---|---|
| 161* | M. K. Fosh | 1975 Harrow | 106 | D. M. Smith | 1966 Eton |
| 159 | E. W. Dawson | 1923 Eton | 104 | R. Pulbrook | 1932 Harrow |
| 158 | I. S. Akers-Douglas | 1928 Eton | 103 | L. G. Crawley | 1921 Harrow |
| 153 | N. S. Hotchkin | 1931 Eton | 103 | T. Hare | 1947 Eton |
| 151 | R. M. Tindall | 1976 Harrow | 102* | P. H. Stewart-Brown | 1923 Harrow |
| 135 | J. C. Atkinson-Clark | 1930 Eton | 102 | R. V. C. Robins | 1953 Eton |
| 115 | E. Crutchley | 1939 Harrow | 100 | R. H. Cobbold | 1923 Eton |
| 112 | A. W. Allen | 1931 Eton | 100* | P. V. F. Cazalet | 1926 Eton |
| 112* | T. M. H. James | 1978 Harrow | 100 | A. N. A. Boyd | 1934 Eton |
| 111 | R. A. A. Holt | 1937 Harrow | 100* | P. M. Studd | 1935 Harrow |
| 109 | K. F. H. Hale | 1929 Eton | 100 | S. D. D. Sainsbury | 1947 Eton |
| 109 | N. S. Hotchkin | 1932 Eton | 100 | M. J. J. Faber | 1968 Eton |
| 107 | W. N. Coles | 1946 Eton | | | |

* *Signifies not out.*

In 1904, D. C. Boles of Eton, making 183, set up a new record for the match, beating the 152 obtained for Eton in 1841 by Emilius Bayley, afterwards the Rev. Sir John Robert Laurie Emilius Bayley Laurie. M. C. Bird, Harrow, in 1907, scored 100 not out and 131, the only batsman who has made two 100s in the match. N. S. Hotchkin, Eton, played the following innings: 1931, 153; 1932, 109 and 96; 1933, 88 and 12.

July 20. Benson and Hedges Cup final. LEICESTERSHIRE beat ESSEX by five wickets (See Benson and Hedges Cup section).

## MCC SCHOOLS v NATIONAL ASSOCIATION OF YOUNG CRICKETERS

July 24, 25. MCC Schools won by six wickets off the last ball, having bowled out NAYC twice while themselves losing only six wickets. Roseberry, who had by then joined Middlesex, thus led his side to victory for the second successive year – and again scored a hundred in the second innings. NAYC, sent in to bat, were in trouble against the accurate fast bowling of Fraser, Robinson and Atkinson, but their captain, Sabine, and Humphries, the wicket-keeper, brought about a recovery after lunch. At the close, however, MCC Schools were 158 for two, allowing Roseberry, who showed a high degree of considerate captaincy throughout the week, to declare before the start on Thursday. Fraser took another four wickets and Atherton, with leg-spin, four for 58 as NAYC were dismissed for 196. Chasing 263 at almost 5 an over, Roseberry and Bartlett opened with 160, the captain's 105 containing sixteen 4s. MCC then lost three more wickets before Atkinson of Millfield hit the winning single.

## National Association of Young Cricketers

| | | | |
|---|---|---|---|
| P. Vincent (*Gloucestershire*) b Robinson | 5 | – b Robinson | 17 |
| M. Holmes (*Cheshire*) c Atkins b Fraser | 1 | – c Atkins b Robinson | 8 |
| B. S. Percy (*Buckinghamshire*) b Robinson | 16 | – st Hegg b Atherton | 27 |
| I. Austin (*Lancashire*) c Hegg b Atkinson | 28 | – b Atherton | 45 |
| J. Mordrick (*Essex*) lbw b Fraser | 6 | – b Atherton | 14 |
| A. T. Morris (*Staffordshire*) c Hegg b Atkinson | 13 | – c Atkinson b Fraser | 43 |
| *D. Sabine (*Kent*) b Atherton | 58 | – c Hegg b Fraser | 14 |
| C. S. Mays (*Sussex*) b Fraser | 13 | – c Roseberry b Fraser | 3 |
| †M. Humphries (*Staffordshire*) st Hegg b Atherton | 43 | – not out | 7 |
| G. S. Garton (*Sussex*) b Atherton | 6 | – b Atherton | 1 |
| A. M. G. Scott (*Sussex*) not out | 4 | – b Fraser | 2 |
| B 6, l-b 10, w 9, n-b 6 | 31 | B 5, l-b 8, w 2 | 15 |
| 1/10 2/32 3/44 4/67 5/90 6/91 7/126 8/214 9/217 | 224 | 1/27 2/28 3/97 4/102 5/129 6/178 7/179 8/182 9/187 | 196 |

Bowling: *First Innings*—Fraser 14–3–60–3; Robinson 15–3–61–2; Atkinson 11–2–29–2; Atherton 11.5–3–27–3; Berry 10–0–31–0. *Second Innings*—Fraser 17–4–35–4; Robinson 7–1–29–2; Atkinson 6–1–28–0; Atherton 22–5–58–4; Berry 7–0–33–0.

## MCC Schools

| | | | |
|---|---|---|---|
| *M. A. Roseberry (*Durham*) lbw b Scott | 51 | – c Austin b Mays | 105 |
| P. D. Atkins (*Aylesbury GS*) not out | 53 | | |
| M. A. Atherton (*Manchester GS*) b Austin | 36 | – c Vincent b Austin | 47 |
| G. D. Hodgson (*Nelson Thomlinson*) not out | 12 | – not out | 15 |
| J. D. R. Benson (*Cambridge CAT*) (did not bat) | | – c Scott b Austin | 8 |
| J. C. M. Atkinson (*Millfield*) (did not bat) | | – not out | 1 |
| R. J. Bartlett (*Taunton*) (did not bat) | | – (2) b Scott | 73 |
| L-b 2, w 2, n-b 2 | 6 | B 5, l-b 9 | 14 |
| 1/62 2/142 (2 wkts dec.) | 158 | 1/160 2/217 3/245 4/262 (4 wkts) | 263 |

†W. K. Hegg (*Stand Coll.*), P. J. Berry (*Longlands Coll., Redcar*), A. G. J. Fraser (*Harrow Weald VIth Form*) and M. A. Robinson (*Hull GS*) did not bat.

Bowling: *First Innings*—Garton 5–0–39–0; Scott 12–1–42–1; Austin 13–4–35–1; Mays 16–7–40–0; Mordrick 2–2–0–0. *Second Innings*—Garton 8–1–32–0; Scott 20–2–86–1; Austin 10–1–54–2; Mays 11–1–52–1; Mordrick 5–1–25–0.

Umpires: D. F. Dean and F. S. Tillson.

The National Cricket Association after the match selected the following to play for NCA Young Cricketers against Combined Services. *M. A. Roseberry (Durham), R. J. Bartlett (Somerset), M. A. Atherton (Lancashire), G. D. Hodgson (Cumbria), I. Austin (Lancashire), J. D. R. Benson (Cambridgeshire), J. C. M. Atkinson (Somerset), C. S. Mays (Sussex), †W. K. Hegg (Lancashire), D. Sabine (Kent) and A. M. G. Scott (Sussex).

July 26. Drawn after rain interrupted play. NCA Young Cricketers 238 for three dec. (M. A. Roseberry 125, M. A. Atherton 70 not out); Combined Services 160 for four (Lt J. P. Barrett 74 not out, Lt C. W. P. Hobson 56 not out; J. C. M. Atkinson four for 27).

## WILLIAM YOUNGER CUP FINAL

August 31. Old Hill beat Reading by nine wickets. Old Hill of the Birmingham League gained their second successive William Younger Cup victory convincingly with seven and a half overs and nine wickets in hand, even though Reading had set a final record by making 227 for five after electing to bat first. For Old Hill, Oliver, formerly of Warwickshire, and wicket-keeper Watson shared an unbroken stand of 211 for the second wicket, Oliver's 137 not out, which included nine 6s, being a Younger Cup final record. Victory came in near darkness – some 90 minutes had been lost to the weather – with players of the calibre of Mushtaq Mohammad (Pakistan and Northamptonshire) and Boyns and Wilkinson (former Worcestershire all-rounders) not required to bat. Old Hill received £1,000, the losers £600.

### Reading

A. D. Walder c Boyns b Bagley ....... 75
A. Dindar b Bagley .................. 0
M. L. Simmons b Stockley ........... 32
D. B. Gorman not out ............... 74
M. A. Head lbw b Bagley ........... 14
S. Keen lbw b Boyns ................ 2
B. Jackson not out .................. 3
B 6, l-b 17, w 4 ............ 27

1/6 2/68 3/170 4/211 5/220 (5 wkts, 45 overs) 227

P. M. New, †G. E. J. Child, Mohammad Amjad and *J. H. Jones did not bat.

Bowling: Hackett 9–2–37–0; Bagley 9–0–49–3; Mushtaq 9–0–37–0; Stockley 9–1–33–1; Boyns 9–0–48–1.

### Old Hill

C. Hemsley lbw b Amjad ............. 15
†F. P. Watson not out ............... 65
P. R. Oliver not out .................137
L-b 8, w 1, n-b 2 ............ 11

1/17 (1 wkt, 37.3 overs) 228

Mushtaq Mohammad, C. N. Boyns, *K. W. Wilkinson, A. E. Brookes, S. Derham, G. Stockley, P. R. Bagley and N. Hackett did not bat.

Bowling: Jackson 6–0–43–0; Amjad 6–1–31–1; Jones 9–1–51–0; New 7–0–36–0; Simmons 3–0–23–0; Dindar 6.3–0–36–0.

Umpires: B. Knight and D. Wakefield.

## NATIONAL CLUB CRICKET CHAMPIONSHIP WINNERS 1969-85

### D. H. Robins Trophy

1969 HAMPSTEAD beat Pocklington Pixies by 14 runs.
1970 CHELTENHAM beat Stockport by three wickets.
1971 BLACKHEATH beat Ealing by eight wickets.
1972 SCARBOROUGH beat Brentham by six wickets.
1973 WOLVERHAMPTON beat The Mote by five wickets.
1974 SUNBURY beat Tunbridge Wells by seven wickets.
1975 YORK beat Blackpool by six wickets.

### John Haig Trophy

1976 SCARBOROUGH beat Dulwich by five wickets.
1977 SOUTHGATE beat Bowdon by six wickets.
1978 CHELTENHAM beat Bishop's Stortford by 15 runs.
1979 SCARBOROUGH beat Reading by two wickets.
1980 MOSELEY beat Gosport Borough by nine wickets.
1981 SCARBOROUGH beat Blackheath by 57 runs.
1982 SCARBOROUGH beat Finchley by 4 runs.

### William Younger Cup

1983 SHREWSBURY beat Hastings and St Leonards Priory by 2 runs.
1984 OLD HILL beat Bishop's Stortford by five wickets.
1985 OLD HILL beat Reading by nine wickets.

## NATIONAL VILLAGE CHAMPIONSHIP FINAL

September 1. Freuchie beat Rowledge by virtue of having lost fewer wickets with the scores level, so becoming, in the bicentenary year of Scottish cricket, the first Scottish village to win the final. Rowledge had won the toss and batted first, but against tigerish Scottish fielding the runs came slowly. Dunbar, whose 33 was top score of the match, and Offord were both run out by Andrew Crichton. Freuchie's captain and president, David Christie, saw the score to 134 for seven, when he was run out off the last ball of the 39th over, whereupon in great excitement in the gloaming of St John's Wood, the ninth-wicket pair played out a maiden 40th over to ensure victory. Freuchie, with kilts swirling and their piper skirling at their head, had marched into Lord's, where the national dress, including tie and jacket, was permitted wear in the Pavilion. Freuchie won £500 and Rowledge £250.

### Rowledge

| | |
|---|---|
| R. E. C. Simpson c A. N. Crichton b Cowan | 6 |
| A. P. Hook b McNaughton | 28 |
| N. S. Dunbar run out | 33 |
| C. Yates b D. Y. F. Christie | 10 |
| †P. Offord run out | 0 |
| R. J. Dunbar c Irvine b Trewartha | 12 |
| *A. J. Prior b Trewartha | 6 |
| P. R. Cooper b Cowan | 12 |
| B. A. Silver c Wilkie b Trewartha | 0 |
| A. B. Field not out | 10 |
| J. Reffold lbw b Trewartha | 0 |
| L-b 9, w 7, n-b 1 | 17 |
| 1/15 2/56 3/73 4/74 5/94 6/108 7/117 8/117 9/133 (39.3 overs) | 134 |

Bowling: Cowan 9–1–25–2; McNaughton 9–0–31–1; B. Christie 9–0–28–0; D. Y. F. Christie 5–0–17–1; Trewartha 7.3–0–24–4.

### Freuchie

| | |
|---|---|
| M. Wilkie b Field | 10 |
| †A. S. Duncan c Yates b Silver | 16 |
| A. N. Crichton lbw b Field | 0 |
| G. Wilson c Offord b Yates | 14 |
| D. Cowan b Silver | 16 |
| S. Irvine c and b Prior | 24 |
| G. Crichton not out | 24 |
| T. Trewartha b Reffold | 1 |
| *D. Y. F. Christie run out | 11 |
| B. Christie not out | 0 |
| B 6, l-b 8, w 2, n-b 2 | 18 |
| 1/23 2/25 3/42 4/52 5/85 6/91 7/101 8/134 (8 wkts, 40 overs) | 134 |

N. McNaughton did not bat.

Bowling: Field 9–1–15–2; Reffold 6–1–25–1; Prior 9–0–31–1; Yates 9–0–31–1; Silver 7–0–18–2.

Umpires: R. Axworthy and R. H. Duckett.

## VILLAGE CRICKET CHAMPIONSHIP WINNERS 1972-85

Sponsored by John Haig Ltd

1972 TROON (Cornwall) beat Astwood Bank (Worcestershire) by seven wickets.
1973 TROON (Cornwall) beat Gowerton (Glamorgan) by 12 runs.
1974 BOMARSUND (Northumberland) beat Collingham (Nottinghamshire) by three wickets.
(Played at Edgbaston after being rained off at Lord's).
1975 GOWERTON (Glamorgan) beat Isleham (Cambridgeshire) by six wickets.
1976 TROON (Cornwall) beat Sessay (Yorkshire) by 18 runs.
1977 COOKLEY (Worcestershire) beat Lindal Moor (Cumbria) by 28 runs.

Sponsored by *The Cricketer*

1978 LINTON PARK (Kent) beat Toft (Cheshire) by four wickets.

Sponsored by Samuel Whitbread and Co. Ltd

1979 EAST BIERLEY (Yorkshire) beat Ynysygerwyn (Glamorgan) by 92 runs.
1980 MARCHWIEL (Clwyd) beat Longparish (Hampshire) by 79 runs.
1981 ST FAGANS (Glamorgan) beat Broad Oak (Yorkshire) by 22 runs.
1982 ST FAGANS (Glamorgan) beat Collingham (Nottinghamshire) by six wickets.
1983 QUARNDON (Derbyshire) beat Troon (Cornwall) by eight wickets.
1984 MARCHWIEL (Clwyd) beat Hursley Park (Hampshire) by 8 runs.

No sponsor: organised by *The Cricketer*

1985 FREUCHIE (Fifeshire) beat Rowledge (Surrey) by virtue of fewer wickets lost with the scores level.

September 7. NatWest Bank Trophy final. ESSEX beat NOTTINGHAMSHIRE by 1 run (See NatWest Bank Trophy section).

# QUALIFICATION AND REGISTRATION

Regulations Governing the Qualification and Registration of Cricketers in Test and Competitive County Cricket

## 1. QUALIFICATIONS FOR ENGLAND

Subject to the overriding discretion of the Test and County Cricket Board, acting with the consent of the International Cricket Conference, the qualifications for playing for England shall be:

(a) That the cricketer was born in the British Isles; or

(b) That the cricketer's father or mother was born in the British Isles and that he himself is residing and has been resident therein during the preceding four consecutive years; or

(c) That the cricketer is residing and has been resident in the British Isles during the preceding ten consecutive years; or

(d) That the cricketer is residing and has been resident in the British Isles during the preceding four consecutive years and since the day before his fourteenth birthday.

All these qualifications apply only if the cricketer has not played for any other country in a Test match or (if the Board so decides) any other international match during the specified period of residence or in the case of (a) during the previous four years.

In the case of (b), if the cricketer has played first-class cricket in his country of origin before commencing his period of residence in the British Isles, the four-year period shall be increased to such number of years (not exceeding ten) as equals four years plus one year for each season of first-class cricket he played in his country of origin. In the case of (b) and (c), if, following the commencement of his period of residence in the British Isles, the cricketer plays first-class cricket in his country of origin (other than as an overseas cricketer in circumstances approved by the Board), then if previously qualified for England under (b) or (c) he shall cease to be so qualified. If he was in the course of acquiring residential qualification, his period of residence in the British Isles shall be treated as terminated, and a new period of residence will be required.

It is also required that the player shall have made a declaration in writing to the Board that it is his desire and intention to play for England and in (b), (c) and (d) that he shall be a British or Irish citizen.

## 2. QUALIFICATIONS FOR REGISTRATION FOR COMPETITIVE COUNTY CRICKET

(a) A cricketer qualified for England shall only be qualified for registration for:

(i) The county of his birth.
(ii) The county in which he is residing and has been resident for the previous twelve consecutive months.
(iii) The county for which his father regularly played.

(b) In addition, a cricketer qualified for England shall be qualified for registration for a county if:

(i) He has none of the above qualifications for any county and is not registered for one; or

(ii) Although qualified for and/or registered by one or more counties, the county or counties concerned have confirmed in writing that they do not wish to register him or retain his registration.

This paragraph (b), however, will not permit registration of a player who has been under contract to a county for the previous season and has failed to accept the offer of a new contract for the new season. It does not prevent his application for a Special Registration.

## 3. REGISTRATION

Normally new registrations take place during the close season, but in exceptional circumstances a county may apply to register a player in the course of a season.

No cricketer may be registered for more than one county at any one time or, subject to the overriding discretion of the Board, for more than one county during any one season. However, this shall not prevent a player qualified to play for England, and already registered for a minor county, from being registered for a first-class county with the consent of the minor county concerned, who will not lose his registration.

Except with the Board's approval no county may have registered for it more than 35 cricketers at any one time.

## 4. SPECIAL REGISTRATION

The qualification for county cricket may be wholly or partially waived by the Board and a cricketer qualified to play for England may be "specially registered" should the Board conclude that it would be in the best interest of competitive county cricket as a whole. For this purpose the Board shall have regard to the interests of the cricketer concerned and any other material considerations affecting the county concerned including, if applicable, the cricketer's age and the other Special Registrations of the county in previous years.

No application for Special Registration will be entertained in respect of a cricketer who has a contract of employment with another county in the absence of that county's consent, except during the period between January 1 and the start of the new season, if the cricketer's contract is due to expire in that period.

## 5. CRICKETERS NOT QUALIFIED TO PLAY FOR ENGLAND

No county shall be entitled to play more than one unqualified cricketer in any competitive match, except where two unqualified cricketers were registered for the county on November 28, 1978 or if *bona fide* negotiations had been begun before that date and were completed before the 1979 season.

The player must have remained registered without a break and had a contract of employment with the county since the start of the 1979 season, except in any season during which he was a member of an official touring team to the British Isles.

Although there is no restriction on the number of unqualified cricketers who may be registered by a county, it is the Board's policy that in normal circumstances *not more than two unqualified cricketers should be registered by any one county*.

If a registered overseas player is invited to play for his country for the whole or part of a tour of the British Isles, his county must release him and, except with the prior consent of the Board, may not play him during that tour.

*Note:* A citizen of a country within the European Economic Community, although he is not qualified to play for England, is not regarded as an unqualified cricketer for the purposes of registration, provided he satisfies the requirements as set out in Regulation 1 (except that for "British Isles" read "EEC").

## 6. NEGOTIATIONS BETWEEN COUNTIES AND CRICKETERS

No county may approach or be involved in discussions with any unregistered cricketer who is not qualified for that county with a view to offering him a trial or registering him:

(i) During the currency of a season without having given not less than fourteen days' previous notice in writing; or

(ii) During the close season without having given notice in writing

to any county for which he is qualified for registration by virtue of birth or residence before making any such approach or engaging in any such discussions.

No county may approach or be involved in discussions with any cricketer under the age of sixteen on April 15 in the current year, unless the cricketer is qualified for registration by that county or is not qualified for registration by any other first-class county.

## 7. RESIDENCE

A player does not interrupt his qualifying period of residence by undertaking government service or occasional winter work for business reasons outside the county in which his residence is situated.

The qualifying period cannot run while the cricketer has a contract with or is registered by another county.

# BRITANNIC ASSURANCE COUNTY CHAMPIONSHIP, 1985

For the third successive season the destination of the Championship remained in doubt until the last day, though in the end Middlesex's sweeping victory over Warwickshire, against the draws of their two nearest challengers, Hampshire and Gloucestershire, gave them a reasonably comfortable-looking cushion of eighteen points.

Glamorgan set the early pace and Surrey, having played more games, intruded briefly into third place in early August; but it was mostly Middlesex, Hampshire and Gloucestershire who exchanged the lead in the manner of long-distance runners. Middlesex led at the end of May, then Hampshire took over. Gloucestershire, buoyed up by effective team-building, established themselves in July and entered September with a narrow lead and a game in hand. But the west countrymen's late slump saw Middlesex sweep by for their ninth outright title win and their fourth in ten seasons. Hampshire overtook Gloucestershire, who were thus consigned to third place. Though a disappointment for Gloucestershire, after many weeks of the highest hopes, this still represented a huge advance for the wooden-spoonists of 1984.

Essex, champions for the previous two seasons, found their form only in August, when a late advance took them into fourth position. Four victories in the last six weeks also took the carefully built Worcestershire side to a satisfactory fifth position, marginally ahead of Surrey, who had gradually dropped out of contention. A good late run by Sussex, last at the end of May, enabled them to climb to seventh place, one lower than in 1984.

*Continued over.*

## BRITANNIC ASSURANCE CHAMPIONSHIP

| | | | | | *Bonus points* | | |
|---|---|---|---|---|---|---|---|
| *Win = 16 points* | *Played* | *Won* | *Lost* | *Drawn* | *Batting* | *Bowling* | *Points* |
| 1 – Middlesex (3) | 24 | 8 | 4 | 12 | 61 | 85 | 274 |
| 2 – Hampshire (15) | 24 | 7 | 2 | 15 | 66 | 78 | 256 |
| 3 – Gloucestershire (17) | 23 | 7 | 3 | 13 | 51 | 78 | 241 |
| 4 – Essex (1) | 23 | 7 | 2 | 14 | 42 | 70 | 224 |
| 5 – Worcestershire (10) | 24 | 5 | 6 | 13 | 65 | 68 | 221 |
| 6 – Surrey (8) | 24 | 5 | 5 | 14 | 62 | 76 | 218 |
| 7 – Sussex (6) | 23 | 6 | 1 | 16 | 52 | 57 | 205 |
| 8 – Nottinghamshire (2) | 24 | 4 | 2 | 18 | 66 | 69 | 199 |
| 9 – Kent (5) | 24 | 4 | 5 | 15 | 51 | 71 | 186 |
| 10 – Northamptonshire (11) | 24 | 5 | 4 | 15 | 52 | 51 | 183 |
| 11 – Yorkshire (14) | 23 | 3 | 4 | 16 | 58 | 59 | 165 |
| 12 – Glamorgan (13) | 24 | 4 | 4 | 16 | 41 | 50 | 163 |
| 13 – Derbyshire (12) | 24 | 3 | 9 | 12 | 46 | 69 | 163 |
| 14 – Lancashire (16) | 24 | 3 | 7 | 14 | 44 | 67 | 159 |
| 15 – Warwickshire (9) | 24 | 2 | 8 | 14 | 47 | 74 | 153 |
| 16 – Leicestershire (4) | 24 | 2 | 3 | 19 | 48 | 65 | 145 |
| 17 – Somerset (7) | 24 | 1 | 7 | 16 | 70 | 45 | 131 |

*1984 positions are shown in brackets.*

*The totals for Worcestershire and Glamorgan include 8 points for levelling the scores in drawn matches. Where sides are equal on points, the one with the most wins has priority.*

The following two matches were abandoned and are not included in the above table: May 22, 23, 24 – Yorkshire v Essex at Sheffield; June 22, 24, 25 – Gloucestershire v Sussex at Bristol.

Nottinghamshire, runners-up then, finished eighth and rarely looked likely to improve on this, while Kent followed an uninspired start with a mid-season surge before subsiding to ninth position. Northamptonshire, well placed in July, plunged down the table before two late wins gave them a respectable tenth place. Yorkshire's off-the-field activities were again more absorbing than their cricket: they made a useful start before sinking to the lower reaches. Glamorgan, front-runners in early May, spent the last two months avoiding one of the last places. They showed promise, however, as did Derbyshire, bottom without a victory in early July, who finished thirteenth. Fourteenth place represented a minor improvement for Lancashire, who had promised better early on. An early win for Warwickshire inspired optimism at Edgbaston, but their final position of fifteenth said little for their "patching-up" policy. Leicestershire maintained their depressing form of late 1984, finding positive results hard to come by, while last-placed Somerset, with two of the most exciting batsmen in the world, gained plenty of batting bonus points but little else. – R.W.B.

## REGULATIONS FOR BRITANNIC ASSURANCE CHAMPIONSHIP

(As applied in 1985)

**1. Prizemoney**

| | |
|---|---|
| First (Middlesex) | £20,000 |
| Second (Hampshire) | £10,000 |
| Third (Gloucestershire) | £5,000 |
| Fourth (Essex) | £2,500 |
| Fifth (Worcestershire) | £1,250 |
| Winner of each match | £250 |

**2. Scoring of Points**

(*a*) For a win, sixteen points, plus any points scored in the first innings.

(*b*) In a tie, each side to score eight points, plus any points scored in the first innings.

(*c*) If the scores are equal in a drawn match, the side batting in the fourth innings to score eight points, plus any points scored in the first innings.

(*d*) **First Innings Points** (awarded only for performances **in the first 100 overs** of each first innings and retained whatever the result of the match).

(i) A maximum of four batting points to be available as under:
150 to 199 runs – 1 point; 200 to 249 runs – 2 points; 250 to 299 runs – 3 points; 300 runs or over – 4 points.

(ii) A maximum of four bowling points to be available as under:
3 to 4 wickets taken – 1 point; 5 to 6 wickets taken – 2 points; 7 to 8 wickets taken – 3 points; 9 to 10 wickets taken – 4 points.

(*e*) If play starts when fewer than eight hours' playing time remains and a one innings match is played, no first innings points shall be scored. The side winning on the one innings to score twelve points.

(*f*) The side which has the highest aggregate of points gained at the end of the season shall be the Champion County. Should any sides in the Championship table be equal on points the side with most wins will have priority.

**3. Hours of Play**

1st and 2nd days ..... 11.00 a.m. to 6.30 p.m. (12 noon to 7.30 p.m. on Sundays) or after 117 overs, whichever is the later.

3rd day ............ 11.00 a.m. to 6.00 p.m. or after 110 overs, whichever is the later.

(*a*) If play is suspended (including any interval between innings) the minimum number of overs to be bowled in a day to be reduced by one over for each full $3\frac{1}{3}$ minutes of such suspension or suspensions in aggregate.

(*b*) If at 5.00 p.m. on the third day more than 90 overs have been bowled (or a proportionately reduced number in the event of any suspension), a minimum of 20 overs to be bowled in accordance with Law 17.6 and 17.7, except that all calculations in regard to suspensions or the start of a new innings to be based on $3\frac{1}{3}$ minutes per over. Play may cease on the third day at any time between 5.30 p.m. and 6.00 p.m. by mutual agreement of the captains.

(*c*) The captain's may agree or, in the event of disagreement, the umpires may decide to play 30 minutes (or minimum ten overs) extra time at the end of the first and/or second day's play if, in their opinion, it would bring about a definite result on that day. In the event of the possibility of a finish disappearing before the full period has expired, the whole period must be played out. Any time so claimed does not effect the timing for cessation of play on the third day.

(*d*) If an innings ends during the course of an over, that part shall count as a full over so far as the minimum number of overs per day is concerned.

*Intervals*

Lunch: 1.15 p.m. to 1.55 p.m. (1st and 2nd days), 2.15 p.m. to 2.55 p.m. on Sundays
1.00 p.m. to 1.40 p.m. (3rd day)

Tea: 4.10 p.m. to 4.30 p.m. (1st and 2nd days), 5.10 p.m. to 5.30 p.m. on Sundays, or when 40 overs remain to be bowled, whichever is the later.
3.40 p.m. to 4.00 p.m. (3rd day), or when 40 overs remain to be bowled, whichever is the later.

**4. Substitutes**

A substitute shall be allowed as of right in the event of a cricketer currently playing in a Championship match being required to join the England team for a Test match (or one-day international). Such substitutes may be permitted to bat or bowl in that match, subject to the approval of the TCCB. The player who is substituted may not take further part in the match, even though he might not be required by England. If batting at the time, the player substituted shall be retired "not out" and his substitute may be permitted to bat subject to the approval of the TCCB.

**5. New ball**

The captain of the fielding side shall have the choice of taking the new ball after 100 overs have been bowled with the old one.

**6. Covering of Pitches**

The whole pitch shall be covered:

(*a*) The night before a match and, if necessary, until the first ball is bowled.

(*b*) On each night of a match and, if necessary, throughout Sunday.

(*c*) In the event of play being suspended on account of bad light or rain during the specified hours of play.

**7. Declarations**

Law 14 will apply, but, in addition, a captain may also forfeit his first innings, subject to the provisions set out in Law 14.2. If, owing to weather conditions, the match has not started when fewer than eight hours of playing time remain, the first innings of each side shall automatically be forfeited and a one-innings match played.

## CHAMPION COUNTY SINCE 1864

*Note:* The earliest county champions were decided usually by the fewest matches lost, but in 1888 an unofficial points system was introduced. In 1890, the Championship was constituted officially. From 1977 to 1983 it was sponsored by Schweppes, and since 1984 by Britannic Assurance.

|  |  |
|---|---|
| 1864 | Surrey |
| 1865 | Nottinghamshire |
| 1866 | Middlesex |
| 1867 | Yorkshire |
| 1868 | Nottinghamshire |
| 1869 | Nottinghamshire |
| | Yorkshire |
| 1870 | Yorkshire |
| 1871 | Nottinghamshire |
| 1872 | Nottinghamshire |
| 1873 | Gloucestershire |
| | Nottinghamshire |
| 1874 | Gloucestershire |
| 1875 | Nottinghamshire |
| 1876 | Gloucestershire |
| 1877 | Gloucestershire |
| 1878 | Undecided |
| 1879 | Nottinghamshire |
| | Lancashire |
| 1880 | Nottinghamshire |
| 1881 | Lancashire |
| 1882 | Nottinghamshire |
| | Lancashire |
| 1883 | Nottinghamshire |
| 1884 | Nottinghamshire |
| 1885 | Nottinghamshire |
| 1886 | Nottinghamshire |
| 1887 | Surrey |
| 1888 | Surrey |
| 1889 | Surrey |
| | Lancashire |
| | Nottinghamshire |
| 1890 | Surrey |
| 1891 | Surrey |
| 1892 | Surrey |
| 1893 | Yorkshire |
| 1894 | Surrey |
| 1895 | Surrey |
| 1896 | Yorkshire |
| 1897 | Lancashire |
| 1898 | Yorkshire |
| 1899 | Surrey |
| 1900 | Yorkshire |
| 1901 | Yorkshire |
| 1902 | Yorkshire |
| 1903 | Middlesex |
| 1904 | Lancashire |
| 1905 | Yorkshire |
| 1906 | Kent |
| 1907 | Nottinghamshire |
| 1908 | Yorkshire |
| 1909 | Kent |
| 1910 | Kent |
| 1911 | Warwickshire |
| 1912 | Yorkshire |
| 1913 | Kent |
| 1914 | Surrey |
| 1919 | Yorkshire |
| 1920 | Middlesex |
| 1921 | Middlesex |
| 1922 | Yorkshire |
| 1923 | Yorkshire |
| 1924 | Yorkshire |
| 1925 | Yorkshire |
| 1926 | Lancashire |
| 1927 | Lancashire |
| 1928 | Lancashire |
| 1929 | Nottinghamshire |
| 1930 | Lancashire |
| 1931 | Yorkshire |
| 1932 | Yorkshire |
| 1933 | Yorkshire |
| 1934 | Lancashire |
| 1935 | Yorkshire |
| 1936 | Derbyshire |
| 1937 | Yorkshire |
| 1938 | Yorkshire |
| 1939 | Yorkshire |
| 1946 | Yorkshire |
| 1947 | Middlesex |
| 1948 | Glamorgan |
| 1949 | Middlesex |
| | Yorkshire |
| 1950 | Lancashire |
| | Surrey |
| 1951 | Warwickshire |
| 1952 | Surrey |
| 1953 | Surrey |
| 1954 | Surrey |
| 1955 | Surrey |
| 1956 | Surrey |
| 1957 | Surrey |
| 1958 | Surrey |
| 1959 | Yorkshire |
| 1960 | Yorkshire |
| 1961 | Hampshire |
| 1962 | Yorkshire |
| 1963 | Yorkshire |
| 1964 | Worcestershire |
| 1965 | Worcestershire |
| 1966 | Yorkshire |
| 1967 | Yorkshire |
| 1968 | Yorkshire |
| 1969 | Glamorgan |
| 1970 | Kent |
| 1971 | Surrey |
| 1972 | Warwickshire |
| 1973 | Hampshire |
| 1974 | Worcestershire |
| 1975 | Leicestershire |
| 1976 | Middlesex |
| 1977 | Middlesex |
| | Kent |
| 1978 | Kent |
| 1979 | Essex |
| 1980 | Middlesex |
| 1981 | Nottinghamshire |
| 1982 | Middlesex |
| 1983 | Essex |
| 1984 | Essex |
| 1985 | Middlesex |

*Notes:* The title has been won outright as follows: Yorkshire 31 times, Surrey 18, Nottinghamshire 13, Middlesex 9, Lancashire 8, Kent 6, Essex 3, Gloucestershire 3, Warwickshire 3, Worcestershire 3, Glamorgan 2, Hampshire 2, Derbyshire 1, Leicestershire 1.

Eight times the title has been shared as follows: Nottinghamshire 5, Lancashire 4, Middlesex 2, Surrey 2, Yorkshire 2, Gloucestershire 1, Kent 1.

The earliest date the Championship has been won in any season since it was expanded in 1895 was August 12, 1910, by Kent.

## BRITANNIC ASSURANCE CHAMPIONSHIP STATISTICS FOR 1985

| | | *For* | | | *Against* | |
|---|---|---|---|---|---|---|
| *County* | *Runs* | *Wickets* | *Avge* | *Runs* | *Wickets* | *Avge* |
| Derbyshire | 9,701 | 350 | 27.71 | 8,763 | 263 | 33.31 |
| Essex | 8,503 | 272 | 31.26 | 8,872 | 288 | 30.80 |
| Glamorgan | 8,180 | 245 | 33.38 | 9,128 | 233 | 39.17 |
| Gloucestershire | 7,772 | 272 | 28.57 | 7,697 | 328 | 23.46 |
| Hampshire | 10,284 | 281 | 36.59 | 9,649 | 348 | 27.72 |
| Kent | 9,626 | 320 | 30.08 | 9,535 | 308 | 30.95 |
| Lancashire | 8,221 | 340 | 24.17 | 8,729 | 274 | 31.85 |
| Leicestershire | 8,438 | 277 | 30.46 | 8,928 | 273 | 32.70 |
| Middlesex | 9,525 | 265 | 35.94 | 9,646 | 360 | 26.79 |
| Northamptonshire | 9,287 | 293 | 31.69 | 8,857 | 248 | 35.71 |
| Nottinghamshire | 10,563 | 297 | 35.56 | 9,872 | 307 | 32.15 |
| Somerset | 10,088 | 282 | 35.77 | 8,814 | 216 | 40.80 |
| Surrey | 9,994 | 272 | 36.74 | 10,395 | 309 | 33.64 |
| Sussex | 8,809 | 234 | 37.64 | 9,032 | 274 | 32.96 |
| Warwickshire | 9,277 | 329 | 28.19 | 10,159 | 289 | 35.15 |
| Worcestershire | 10,184 | 307 | 33.17 | 9,284 | 311 | 29.85 |
| Yorkshire | 8,874 | 262 | 33.87 | 9,966 | 269 | 37.04 |
| | 157,326 | 4,898 | 32.12 | 157,326 | 4,898 | 32.12 |

## COUNTY CHAMPIONSHIP – MATCH RESULTS, 1864-1985

| *County* | *Years of Play* | *Played* | *Won* | *Lost* | *Tied* | *Drawn* |
|---|---|---|---|---|---|---|
| Derbyshire | 1871-87; 1895-1985 | 1,998 | 490 | 743 | 0 | 765 |
| Essex | 1895-1985 | 1,961 | 543 | 577 | 5 | 836 |
| Glamorgan | 1921-1985 | 1,496 | 332 | 518 | 0 | 646 |
| Gloucestershire | 1870-1985 | 2,237 | 664 | 831 | 1 | 741 |
| Hampshire | 1864-85; 1895-1985 | 2,071 | 540 | 727 | 4 | 800 |
| Kent | 1864-1985 | 2,358 | 872 | 718 | 4 | 764 |
| Lancashire | 1865-1985 | 2,437 | 917 | 493 | 3 | 1,024 |
| Leicestershire | 1895-1985 | 1,928 | 412 | 733 | 1 | 782 |
| Middlesex | 1864-1985 | 2,139 | 810 | 547 | 5 | 777 |
| Northamptonshire | 1905-1985 | 1,695 | 401 | 612 | 3 | 679 |
| Nottinghamshire | 1864-1985 | 2,268 | 689 | 599 | 0 | 980 |
| Somerset | 1882-85, 1891-1985 | 1,969 | 468 | 825 | 3 | 673 |
| Surrey | 1864-1985 | 2,515 | 1,012 | 549 | 4 | 950 |
| Sussex | 1864-1985 | 2,409 | 687 | 831 | 5 | 886 |
| Warwickshire | 1895-1985 | 1,942 | 511 | 572 | 1 | 858 |
| Worcestershire | 1899-1985 | 1,883 | 452 | 687 | 1 | 743 |
| Yorkshire | 1864-1985 | 2,537 | 1,171 | 409 | 2 | 955 |
| Cambridgeshire | 1864-69; 1871 | 19 | 8 | 8 | 0 | 3 |
| | | 17,931 | 10,979 | 10,979 | 21 | 6,931 |

*Notes:* Matches abandoned without a ball bowled are wholly excluded.

Counties participated in the years shown, except that there were no matches in the years 1915-18 and 1940-45; Hampshire did not play inter-county matches in 1868-69, 1871-74 and 1879; Worcestershire did not take part in the Championship in 1919.

# COUNTY CHAMPIONSHIP – FINAL POSITIONS, 1890-1985

| | Derbyshire | Essex | Glamorgan | Gloucestershire | Hampshire | Kent | Lancashire | Leicestershire | Middlesex | Northamptonshire | Nottinghamshire | Somerset | Surrey | Sussex | Warwickshire | Worcestershire | Yorkshire |
|---|---|---|---|---|---|---|---|---|---|---|---|---|---|---|---|---|---|
| 1890 | — | — | — | 6 | — | 3 | 2 | — | 7 | — | 5 | — | 1 | 8 | — | — | 3 |
| 1891 | — | — | — | 9 | — | 5 | 2 | — | 3 | — | 4 | 5 | 1 | 7 | — | — | 8 |
| 1892 | — | — | — | 7 | — | 7 | 4 | — | 5 | — | 2 | 3 | 1 | 9 | — | — | 6 |
| 1893 | — | — | — | 9 | — | 4 | 2 | — | 3 | — | 6 | 8 | 5 | 7 | — | — | 1 |
| 1894 | — | — | — | 9 | — | 4 | 4 | — | 3 | — | 7 | 6 | 1 | 8 | — | — | 2 |
| 1895 | 5 | 9 | — | 4 | 10 | 14 | 2 | 12 | 6 | — | 12 | 8 | 1 | 11 | 6 | — | 3 |
| 1896 | 7 | 5 | — | 10 | 8 | 9 | 2 | 13 | 3 | — | 6 | 11 | 4 | 14 | 12 | — | 1 |
| 1897 | 14 | 3 | — | 5 | 9 | 12 | 1 | 13 | 8 | — | 10 | 11 | 2 | 6 | 7 | — | 4 |
| 1898 | 9 | 5 | — | 3 | 12 | 7 | 6 | 13 | 2 | — | 8 | 13 | 4 | 9 | 9 | — | 1 |
| 1899 | 15 | 6 | — | 9 | 10 | 8 | 4 | 13 | 2 | — | 10 | 13 | 1 | 5 | 7 | 12 | 3 |
| 1900 | 13 | 10 | — | 7 | 15 | 3 | 2 | 14 | 7 | — | 5 | 11 | 7 | 3 | 6 | 12 | 1 |
| 1901 | 15 | 10 | — | 14 | 7 | 7 | 3 | 12 | 2 | — | 9 | 12 | 6 | 4 | 5 | 11 | 1 |
| 1902 | 10 | 13 | — | 14 | 15 | 7 | 5 | 11 | 12 | — | 3 | 7 | 4 | 2 | 6 | 9 | 1 |
| 1903 | 12 | 8 | — | 13 | 14 | 8 | 4 | 14 | 1 | — | 5 | 10 | 11 | 2 | 7 | 6 | 3 |
| 1904 | 10 | 14 | — | 9 | 15 | 3 | 1 | 7 | 4 | — | 5 | 12 | 11 | 6 | 7 | 13 | 2 |
| 1905 | 14 | 12 | — | 8 | 16 | 6 | 2 | 5 | 11 | 13 | 10 | 15 | 4 | 3 | 7 | 8 | 1 |
| 1906 | 16 | 7 | — | 9 | 8 | 1 | 4 | 15 | 11 | 11 | 5 | 11 | 3 | 10 | 6 | 14 | 2 |
| 1907 | 16 | 7 | — | 10 | 12 | 8 | 6 | 11 | 5 | 15 | 1 | 14 | 4 | 13 | 9 | 2 | 2 |
| 1908 | 14 | 11 | — | 10 | 9 | 2 | 7 | 13 | 4 | 15 | 8 | 16 | 3 | 5 | 12 | 6 | 1 |
| 1909 | 15 | 14 | — | 16 | 8 | 1 | 2 | 13 | 6 | 7 | 10 | 11 | 5 | 4 | 12 | 8 | 3 |
| 1910 | 15 | 11 | — | 12 | 6 | 1 | 4 | 10 | 3 | 9 | 5 | 16 | 2 | 7 | 14 | 13 | 8 |
| 1911 | 14 | 6 | — | 12 | 11 | 2 | 4 | 15 | 3 | 10 | 8 | 16 | 5 | 13 | 1 | 9 | 7 |
| 1912 | 12 | 15 | — | 11 | 6 | 3 | 4 | 13 | 5 | 2 | 8 | 14 | 7 | 10 | 9 | 16 | 1 |
| 1913 | 13 | 15 | — | 9 | 10 | 1 | 8 | 14 | 6 | 4 | 5 | 16 | 3 | 7 | 11 | 12 | 2 |
| 1914 | 12 | 8 | — | 16 | 5 | 3 | 11 | 13 | 2 | 9 | 10 | 15 | 1 | 6 | 7 | 14 | 4 |
| 1919 | 9 | 14 | — | 8 | 7 | 2 | 5 | 9 | 13 | 12 | 3 | 5 | 4 | 11 | 15 | — | 1 |
| 1920 | 16 | 9 | — | 8 | 11 | 5 | 2 | 13 | 1 | 14 | 7 | 10 | 3 | 6 | 12 | 15 | 4 |
| 1921 | 12 | 15 | 17 | 7 | 6 | 4 | 5 | 11 | 1 | 13 | 8 | 10 | 2 | 9 | 16 | 14 | 3 |
| 1922 | 11 | 8 | 16 | 13 | 6 | 4 | 5 | 14 | 7 | 15 | 2 | 10 | 3 | 9 | 12 | 17 | 1 |
| 1923 | 10 | 13 | 16 | 11 | 7 | 5 | 3 | 14 | 8 | 17 | 2 | 9 | 4 | 6 | 12 | 15 | 1 |
| 1924 | 17 | 15 | 13 | 6 | 12 | 5 | 4 | 11 | 2 | 16 | 6 | 8 | 3 | 10 | 9 | 14 | 1 |
| 1925 | 14 | 7 | 17 | 10 | 9 | 5 | 3 | 12 | 6 | 11 | 4 | 15 | 2 | 13 | 8 | 16 | 1 |
| 1926 | 11 | 9 | 8 | 15 | 7 | 3 | 1 | 13 | 6 | 16 | 4 | 14 | 5 | 10 | 12 | 17 | 2 |
| 1927 | 5 | 8 | 15 | 12 | 13 | 4 | 1 | 7 | 9 | 16 | 2 | 14 | 6 | 10 | 11 | 17 | 3 |
| 1928 | 10 | 16 | 15 | 5 | 12 | 2 | 1 | 9 | 8 | 13 | 3 | 14 | 6 | 7 | 11 | 17 | 4 |
| 1929 | 7 | 12 | 17 | 4 | 11 | 8 | 2 | 9 | 6 | 13 | 1 | 15 | 10 | 4 | 14 | 16 | 2 |
| 1930 | 9 | 6 | 11 | 2 | 13 | 5 | 1 | 12 | 16 | 17 | 4 | 13 | 8 | 7 | 15 | 10 | 3 |
| 1931 | 7 | 10 | 15 | 2 | 12 | 3 | 6 | 16 | 11 | 17 | 5 | 13 | 8 | 4 | 9 | 14 | 1 |
| 1932 | 10 | 14 | 15 | 13 | 8 | 3 | 6 | 12 | 10 | 16 | 4 | 7 | 5 | 2 | 9 | 17 | 1 |
| 1933 | 6 | 4 | 16 | 10 | 14 | 3 | 5 | 17 | 12 | 13 | 8 | 11 | 9 | 2 | 7 | 15 | 1 |
| 1934 | 3 | 8 | 13 | 7 | 14 | 5 | 1 | 12 | 10 | 17 | 9 | 15 | 11 | 2 | 4 | 16 | 5 |
| 1935 | 2 | 9 | 13 | 15 | 16 | 10 | 4 | 6 | 3 | 17 | 5 | 14 | 11 | 7 | 8 | 12 | 1 |
| 1936 | 1 | 9 | 16 | 4 | 10 | 8 | 11 | 15 | 2 | 17 | 5 | 7 | 6 | 14 | 13 | 12 | 3 |
| 1937 | 3 | 6 | 7 | 4 | 14 | 12 | 9 | 16 | 2 | 17 | 10 | 13 | 8 | 5 | 11 | 15 | 1 |
| 1938 | 5 | 6 | 16 | 10 | 14 | 9 | 4 | 15 | 2 | 17 | 12 | 7 | 3 | 8 | 13 | 11 | 1 |
| 1939 | 9 | 4 | 13 | 3 | 15 | 5 | 6 | 17 | 2 | 16 | 12 | 14 | 8 | 10 | 11 | 7 | 1 |
| 1946 | 15 | 8 | 6 | 5 | 10 | 6 | 3 | 11 | 2 | 16 | 13 | 4 | 11 | 17 | 14 | 8 | 1 |
| 1947 | 5 | 11 | 9 | 2 | 16 | 4 | 3 | 14 | 1 | 17 | 11 | 11 | 6 | 9 | 15 | 7 | 7 |
| 1948 | 6 | 13 | 1 | 8 | 9 | 15 | 5 | 11 | 3 | 17 | 14 | 12 | 2 | 16 | 7 | 10 | 4 |
| 1949 | 15 | 9 | 8 | 7 | 16 | 13 | 11 | 17 | 1 | 6 | 11 | 9 | 5 | 13 | 4 | 3 | 1 |

| | Derbyshire | Essex | Glamorgan | Gloucestershire | Hampshire | Kent | Lancashire | Leicestershire | Middlesex | Northamptonshire | Nottinghamshire | Somerset | Surrey | Sussex | Warwickshire | Worcestershire | Yorkshire |
|---|---|---|---|---|---|---|---|---|---|---|---|---|---|---|---|---|---|
| 1950 | 5 | 17 | 11 | 7 | 12 | 9 | 1 | 16 | 14 | 10 | 15 | 7 | 1 | 13 | 4 | 6 | 3 |
| 1951 | 11 | 8 | 5 | 12 | 9 | 16 | 3 | 15 | 7 | 13 | 17 | 14 | 6 | 10 | 1 | 4 | 2 |
| 1952 | 4 | 10 | 7 | 9 | 12 | 15 | 3 | 6 | 5 | 8 | 16 | 17 | 1 | 13 | 10 | 14 | 2 |
| 1953 | 6 | 12 | 10 | 6 | 14 | 16 | 3 | 3 | 5 | 11 | 8 | 17 | 1 | 2 | 9 | 15 | 12 |
| 1954 | 3 | 15 | 4 | 13 | 14 | 11 | 10 | 16 | 7 | 7 | 5 | 17 | 1 | 9 | 6 | 11 | 2 |
| 1955 | 8 | 14 | 16 | 12 | 3 | 13 | 9 | 6 | 5 | 7 | 11 | 17 | 1 | 4 | 9 | 15 | 2 |
| 1956 | 12 | 11 | 13 | 3 | 6 | 16 | 2 | 17 | 5 | 4 | 8 | 15 | 1 | 9 | 14 | 9 | 7 |
| 1957 | 4 | 5 | 9 | 12 | 13 | 14 | 6 | 17 | 7 | 2 | 15 | 8 | 1 | 9 | 11 | 16 | 3 |
| 1958 | 5 | 6 | 15 | 14 | 2 | 8 | 7 | 12 | 10 | 4 | 17 | 3 | 1 | 13 | 16 | 9 | 11 |
| 1959 | 7 | 9 | 6 | 2 | 8 | 13 | 5 | 16 | 10 | 11 | 17 | 12 | 3 | 15 | 4 | 14 | 1 |
| 1960 | 5 | 6 | 11 | 8 | 12 | 10 | 2 | 17 | 3 | 9 | 16 | 14 | 7 | 4 | 15 | 13 | 1 |
| 1961 | 7 | 6 | 14 | 5 | 1 | 11 | 13 | 9 | 3 | 16 | 17 | 10 | 15 | 8 | 12 | 4 | 2 |
| 1962 | 7 | 9 | 14 | 4 | 10 | 11 | 16 | 17 | 13 | 8 | 15 | 6 | 5 | 12 | 3 | 2 | 1 |
| 1963 | 17 | 12 | 2 | 8 | 10 | 13 | 15 | 16 | 6 | 7 | 9 | 3 | 11 | 4 | 4 | 14 | 1 |
| 1964 | 12 | 10 | 11 | 17 | 12 | 7 | 14 | 16 | 6 | 3 | 15 | 8 | 4 | 9 | 2 | 1 | 5 |
| 1965 | 9 | 15 | 3 | 10 | 12 | 5 | 13 | 14 | 6 | 2 | 17 | 7 | 8 | 16 | 11 | 1 | 4 |
| 1966 | 9 | 16 | 14 | 15 | 11 | 4 | 12 | 8 | 12 | 5 | 17 | 3 | 7 | 10 | 6 | 2 | 1 |
| 1967 | 6 | 15 | 14 | 17 | 12 | 2 | 11 | 2 | 7 | 9 | 15 | 8 | 4 | 13 | 10 | 5 | 1 |
| 1968 | 8 | 14 | 3 | 16 | 5 | 2 | 6 | 9 | 10 | 13 | 4 | 12 | 15 | 17 | 11 | 7 | 1 |
| 1969 | 16 | 6 | 1 | 2 | 5 | 10 | 15 | 14 | 11 | 9 | 8 | 17 | 3 | 7 | 4 | 12 | 13 |
| 1970 | 7 | 12 | 2 | 17 | 10 | 1 | 3 | 15 | 16 | 14 | 11 | 13 | 5 | 9 | 7 | 6 | 4 |
| 1971 | 17 | 10 | 16 | 8 | 9 | 4 | 3 | 5 | 6 | 14 | 12 | 7 | 1 | 11 | 2 | 15 | 13 |
| 1972 | 17 | 5 | 13 | 3 | 9 | 2 | 15 | 6 | 8 | 4 | 14 | 11 | 12 | 16 | 1 | 7 | 10 |
| 1973 | 16 | 8 | 11 | 5 | 1 | 4 | 12 | 9 | 13 | 3 | 17 | 10 | 2 | 15 | 7 | 6 | 14 |
| 1974 | 17 | 12 | 16 | 14 | 2 | 10 | 8 | 4 | 6 | 3 | 15 | 5 | 7 | 13 | 9 | 1 | 11 |
| 1975 | 15 | 7 | 9 | 16 | 3 | 5 | 4 | 1 | 11 | 8 | 13 | 12 | 6 | 17 | 14 | 10 | 2 |
| 1976 | 15 | 6 | 17 | 3 | 12 | 14 | 16 | 4 | 1 | 2 | 13 | 7 | 9 | 10 | 5 | 11 | 8 |
| 1977 | 7 | 6 | 14 | 3 | 11 | 1 | 16 | 5 | 1 | 9 | 17 | 4 | 14 | 8 | 10 | 13 | 12 |
| 1978 | 14 | 2 | 13 | 10 | 8 | 1 | 12 | 6 | 3 | 17 | 7 | 5 | 16 | 9 | 11 | 15 | 4 |
| 1979 | 16 | 1 | 17 | 10 | 12 | 5 | 13 | 6 | 14 | 11 | 9 | 8 | 3 | 4 | 15 | 2 | 7 |
| 1980 | 9 | 8 | 13 | 7 | 17 | 16 | 15 | 10 | 1 | 12 | 3 | 5 | 2 | 4 | 14 | 11 | 6 |
| 1981 | 12 | 5 | 14 | 13 | 7 | 9 | 16 | 8 | 4 | 15 | 1 | 3 | 6 | 2 | 17 | 11 | 10 |
| 1982 | 11 | 7 | 16 | 15 | 3 | 13 | 12 | 2 | 1 | 9 | 4 | 6 | 5 | 8 | 17 | 14 | 10 |
| 1983 | 9 | 1 | 15 | 12 | 3 | 7 | 12 | 4 | 2 | 6 | 14 | 10 | 8 | 11 | 5 | 16 | 17 |
| 1984 | 12 | 1 | 13 | 17 | 15 | 5 | 16 | 4 | 3 | 11 | 2 | 7 | 8 | 6 | 9 | 10 | 14 |
| 1985 | 13 | 4 | 12 | 3 | 2 | 9 | 14 | 16 | 1 | 10 | 8 | 17 | 6 | 7 | 15 | 5 | 11 |

*Note:* From 1969 onwards, positions have been given in accordance with the Championship regulations which state that "Should *any* sides in the table be equal on points the side with most wins will have priority".

## DERBYSHIRE

*President:* The Duke of Devonshire
*Chairman:* C. N. Middleton
*Chairman, Cricket Committee:* G. L. Willatt
*Secretary/Chief Executive:* R. Pearman
County Ground, Nottingham Road, Derby DE2 6DA (Telephone: 0332-383211)
*Captain:* K. J. Barnett
*Coach:* P. E. Russell

Defeat by Durham in the NatWest Bank Trophy overshadowed what was at best a mixed season for Derbyshire. It was the first time they had been beaten by a minor county and the margin of defeat, seven wickets, was made even more embarrassing because it was at their own headquarters. Derbyshire were in the lower half of the Britannic Assurance Championship throughout the season but finished strongly in the John Player Sunday League to rise from bottom in 1984 to fourth. In a late flourish, they also won the Asda Trophy at Scarborough and beat Warwickshire in the Championship, but players and officials felt that they should have achieved more.

In no department did Derbyshire show the consistency required to maintain a realistic challenge for any of the four competitions. There were times when the attack relied too much on the West Indian fast bowler, Michael Holding, whose presence restricted the appearances of New Zealand's opening batsman, John Wright. Both overseas players have been retained for a further two seasons, despite the obvious disadvantage of only one being able to play at a time, and when Wright was absent, Kim Barnett had an uneasy feeling that the side could crumble if he himself failed with the bat. Happily, Barnett bowled his leg-spin more frequently than in previous seasons, although this was to some extent born out of frustration at inadequacies in this department. The left-arm spinner, Dallas Moir, was capped in the middle of the season but released, along with Bill Fowler and Ian Broome, at the end of it. He failed to take advantage of helpful conditions at Old Trafford and Bradford, as did Geoff Miller, who, beset by illness and worries about his benefit, had seldom been less effective with his off-spin.

Barnett remained a resilient and enterprising captain, despite the load on his shoulders, and again averaged over 40 with the bat. He fell away towards the end of the season when, planning to bowl more often, he dropped to number four and promoted Bruce Roberts to open. Roberts scored his maiden century against Gloucestershire and passed 1,000 runs for the first time, more than doubling his 1984 aggregate, but the change suited neither batsman. The advance of Roberts, who, like Miller, held some good slip catches, was cancelled out by the difficulties experienced by John Morris, the most naturally gifted of the county's younger players. Morris came through well with a century in the final Championship match after not always being sure of his place.

Alan Hill, the 1986 beneficiary, was unlucky with injuries. A ball from Malcolm Marshall at Basingstoke cracked a bone near his left knee (although he scored a century in the second innings) and after recovering from that he had a finger broken during practice. Hill's misfortune gave Iain Anderson a chance to revive his career. He was awarded a county cap after some solid Championship performances and showing a newly discovered freedom in Sunday games. When filling the overseas place, Wright confirmed his stature and played two magnificent innings, against Warwickshire at Edgbaston and in a victory at Worcester. Derbyshire were often rescued by their lower batsmen, especially Paul Newman and Holding who shared a Benson and Hedges Cup ninth-wicket record partnership of 83 against Nottinghamshire. Newman matured into a genuine all-rounder, with a maiden century against Leicestershire and 98 against Sussex. Of the new batsmen trying to force a way in, Andrew Brown made the best impression with a determined innings against Warwickshire at Chesterfield, where the pitches helped to produce good cricket.

Holding played a major part in two of the three Championship victories, over Glamorgan and Warwickshire, and was a calming influence in one-day games. He looked in the mood to shake Essex after Derbyshire, helped by some quick wickets in a rain-restricted match against Northamptonshire, had been fortunate to qualify for the quarter-finals of the Benson and Hedges Cup. Holding comprehensively bowled Graham Gooch before rain persisted long enough to force a new start on the third day, when Gooch had a more profitable second attempt. Roger Finney, capped during a snowstorm on the opening day of the season, was the leading wicket-taker but veered from highly effective to plain without much middle ground. He remains one of the more reliable players and his omission against Durham was one of several puzzling decisions by the county's selectors. Newman bowled steadily, but Ole Mortensen did not touch his best until the last six weeks of the season. When he did, Derbyshire were far more menacing. Alan Warner, engaged from Worcestershire, returned poor figures in the Championship but was more effective on Sundays. To his satisfaction, he took five wickets against his former county in a high-scoring match at Knypersley, where Derbyshire set a John Player League 6s record.

Neither wicket-keeper, attempting the unenviable task of succeeding Bob Taylor, quite established himself. Bernard Maher, Taylor's understudy for four seasons, never appeared sufficiently relaxed to produce his best and lost his place to Chris Marples, who also plays League football as Chesterfield's goalkeeper, a rare combination. Here, as in other positions, Derbyshire are feeling their way towards a successful blend, aware that they cannot think of themselves as a young side for ever. Barnett's promise was recognised by his selection as vice-captain of the England B team for the tour of Bangladesh, Sri Lanka and Zimbabwe. He was re-appointed as Derbyshire captain and benefited from a close relationship with Guy Willatt, who succeeded Charles Elliott as chairman of the cricket committee. – J.G.M.

# DERBYSHIRE 1985

[*Bill Smith*

*Back row:* I. Broome, J. P. Taylor, P. G. Newman, O. H. Mortensen, D. E. Malcolm, B. Roberts, W. P. Fowler, R. Sharma. *Middle row:* S. Tracey (*scorer*), A. M. Brown, R. J. Finney, B. J. M. Maher, J. E. Morris, A. E. Warner, R. Pearman (*chief executive*), J. Brown (*youth coach*). *Front row:* D. G. Moir, G. Miller, P. E. Russell (*coach*), K. J. Barnett (*captain*), R. W. Taylor, A. Hill, I. S. Anderson. *Inset:* M. A. Holding.

## DERBYSHIRE RESULTS

*All first-class matches – Played 25: Won 3, Lost 9, Drawn 13.*

*County Championship matches – Played 24: Won 3, Lost 9, Drawn 12.*

*Bonus points – Batting 46, Bowling 69.*

*Competition placings – Britannic Assurance County Championship, 13th; NatWest Bank Trophy, 1st round; Benson and Hedges Cup, q-f; John Player League, 4th.*

## BRITANNIC ASSURANCE CHAMPIONSHIP AVERAGES

### BATTING

| | *Birthplace* | *M* | *I* | *NO* | *R* | *HI* | *Avge* |
|---|---|---|---|---|---|---|---|
| ‡J. G. Wright ..... | *Darfield, NZ* | 10 | 16 | 2 | 797 | 177* | 56.92 |
| ‡K. J. Barnett ..... | *Stoke-on-Trent* | 24 | 41 | 1 | 1,568 | 134* | 40.20 |
| ‡A. Hill .......... | *Buxworth* | 9 | 14 | 3 | 333 | 120 | 30.27 |
| B. Roberts ....... | *Lusaka, N. Rhodesia* | 24 | 42 | 4 | 1,128 | 100* | 29.68 |
| ‡G. Miller ........ | *Chesterfield* | 20 | 31 | 5 | 744 | 105 | 28.61 |
| J. E. Morris ...... | *Crewe* | 17 | 27 | 1 | 722 | 109* | 27.76 |
| ‡I. S. Anderson .... | *Derby* | 19 | 35 | 3 | 876 | 95 | 27.37 |
| P. G. Newman ... | *Leicester* | 19 | 29 | 3 | 604 | 115 | 23.23 |
| M. A. Holding .... | *Kingston, Jamaica* | 12 | 19 | 1 | 413 | 80 | 22.94 |
| R. Sharma ....... | *Nairobi, Kenya* | 7 | 12 | 2 | 209 | 41* | 20.90 |
| W. P. Fowler ..... | *St Helens* | 9 | 14 | 1 | 266 | 79 | 20.46 |
| ‡D. G. Moir ...... | *Mtarfa, Malta* | 7 | 9 | 0 | 178 | 46 | 19.77 |
| A. E. Warner ..... | *Birmingham* | 15 | 20 | 2 | 314 | 60 | 17.44 |
| ‡R. J. Finney ...... | *Darley Dale* | 24 | 37 | 10 | 381 | 82 | 14.11 |
| B. J. M. Maher ... | *Hillingdon* | 13 | 18 | 6 | 150 | 46 | 12.50 |
| M. A. Fell ....... | *Newark* | 5 | 8 | 0 | 98 | 27 | 12.25 |
| C. Marples ....... | *Chesterfield* | 11 | 15 | 5 | 114 | 34 | 11.40 |
| O. H. Mortensen .. | *Vejle, Denmark* | 13 | 15 | 7 | 39 | 16* | 4.87 |

Also batted: A. M. Brown (*Heanor*) (2 matches) 3, 16, 74; D. E. Malcolm (*Kingston, Jamaica*) (1 match) 0; ‡P. E. Russell (*Ilkeston*) (3 matches) 3*, 2, 0*.

* *Signifies not out.* ‡ *Denotes county cap.*

The following played a total of twelve three-figure innings for Derbyshire in County Championship matches – K. J. Barnett 4, B. Roberts 2, J. G. Wright 2, A. Hill 1, G. Miller 1, J. E. Morris 1, P. G. Newman 1.

### BOWLING

| | *O* | *M* | *R* | *W* | *BB* | *Avge* |
|---|---|---|---|---|---|---|
| M. A. Holding ..... | 354.5 | 67 | 1,124 | 50 | 6-65 | 22.48 |
| R. J. Finney ....... | 435.3 | 80 | 1,401 | 53 | 7-61 | 26.43 |
| K. J. Barnett ...... | 173.4 | 33 | 514 | 17 | 6-115 | 30.23 |
| P. G. Newman .... | 393.5 | 74 | 1,288 | 42 | 4-29 | 30.66 |
| O. H. Mortensen ... | 340 | 75 | 1,026 | 33 | 5-87 | 31.09 |
| A. E. Warner ...... | 267.3 | 40 | 1,013 | 24 | 5-51 | 42.20 |
| G. Miller ......... | 346.2 | 72 | 1,079 | 25 | 6-110 | 43.16 |
| D. G. Moir ....... | 159 | 41 | 450 | 10 | 3-102 | 45.00 |

Also bowled: I. S. Anderson 3–1–9–0; D. E. Malcolm 17–2–82–3; J. E. Morris 5.1–0–55–0; B. Roberts 20–1–106–0; P. E. Russell 89.5–22–243–4; J. G. Wright 6–0–42–0.

## DERBYSHIRE v NORTHAMPTONSHIRE

At Derby, April 27, 29, 30. Northamptonshire won by 99 runs. Northamptonshire 18 pts, Derbyshire 3 pts. Toss won by Northamptonshire. Finney was awarded his county cap during an interruption because of snow on a bleak opening day after taking five of the first six Northamptonshire wickets to fall. Sleet and rain penetrated the covers, cutting out four hours of the second day, and Barnett forfeited Derbyshire's first innings in pursuit of a positive finish, enabling Cook to bat well twice before Derbyshire had buckled on a pad. Cook set a victory target of 381 in 105 overs, thus giving himself time to dismiss Derbyshire. Mallender made the early inroads and Williams bowled well.

### Northamptonshire

| | | | |
|---|---|---|---|
| *G. Cook c Moir b Mortensen | 87 | – not out | 69 |
| W. Larkins lbw b Finney | 46 | – lbw b Finney | 21 |
| R. G. Williams b Finney | 3 | – c Maher b Mortensen | 39 |
| A. J. Lamb lbw b Finney | 3 | – not out | 9 |
| R. J. Bailey lbw b Finney | 19 | | |
| D. J. Capel b Finney | 10 | | |
| D. J. Wild not out | 39 | | |
| †G. Sharp c and b Mortensen | 19 | | |
| N. A. Mallender not out | 3 | | |
| B 1, l-b 4, n-b 6 | 11 | N-b 2 | 2 |
| 1/106 2/112 3/116 4/142 5/171 6/180 7/227 | (7 wkts dec.) 240 | 1/24 2/130 | (2 wkts dec.) 140 |

A. Walker and R. F. Joseph did not bat.

Bonus points – Northamptonshire 2, Derbyshire 3.

Bowling: *First Innings*—Mortensen 18–5–60–2; Warner 16–3–74–0; Finney 21–4–68–5; Miller 16–4–33–0. *Second Innings*—Mortensen 14–2–38–1; Finney 6–0–25–1; Miller 13–2–50–0; Warner 11–2–27–0.

### Derbyshire

*Derbyshire forfeited their first innings.*

| | |
|---|---|
| *K. J. Barnett c Lamb b Mallender | 62 |
| A. Hill b Mallender | 4 |
| J. E. Morris c Sharp b Mallender | 4 |
| B. Roberts c Walker b Williams | 41 |
| W. P. Fowler b Williams | 79 |
| G. Miller c Cook b Williams | 19 |
| R. J. Finney c Cook b Williams | 5 |
| †B. J. M. Maher lbw b Joseph | 9 |
| D. G. Moir c Sharp b Walker | 20 |
| A. E. Warner run out | 16 |
| O. H. Mortensen c Cook b Williams | 3 |
| B 3, l-b 2, w 1, n-b 13 | 19 |
| 1/16 2/29 3/102 4/130 5/161 6/169 7/224 8/259 9/262 | 281 |

Bowling: Mallender 14–0–48–3; Joseph 16–2–70–1; Walker 13–5–29–1; Williams 32.1–8–91–4; Capel 9–2–22–0; Bailey 3–0–16–0.

Umpires: B. Leadbeater and B. J. Meyer.

At Leicester, May 8, 9, 10. DERBYSHIRE drew with LEICESTERSHIRE.

## DERBYSHIRE v LANCASHIRE

At Chesterfield, May 22, 23, 24. Drawn. Derbyshire 2 pts, Lancashire 4 pts. Toss won by Lancashire. Bad weather caused the loss of two-thirds of the first day. Barnett scored a determined century in 298 minutes, including a 6 and five 4s, his only significant support coming from Fowler in a fifth-wicket stand of 135. After a blank third morning, Lancashire declared at 20 for one, and when Derbyshire forfeited their second innings Lancashire had to score 224 in 55 overs. However, Holding took two wickets in his first three balls to persuade them that survival was the primary objective.

### Derbyshire

| | |
|---|---|
| *K. J. Barnett c Varey b Allott | 103 |
| A. Hill c Maynard b Allott | 6 |
| J. E. Morris c Hughes b Patterson | 1 |
| B. Roberts lbw b Simmons | 21 |
| †B. J. M. Maher c Ormrod b Patterson | 7 |
| W. P. Fowler c Ormrod b Patterson | 76 |
| G. Miller lbw b Allott | 3 |
| R. J. Finney c O'Shaughnessy b Simmons | 3 |
| A. E. Warner not out | 1 |
| M. A. Holding lbw b Allott | 1 |
| O. H. Mortensen lbw b Allott | 0 |
| L-b 10, w 3, n-b 8 | 21 |
| 1/10 2/12 3/65 4/94 5/229 6/238 7/241 8/241 9/243 | 243 |

Bonus points – Derbyshire 2, Lancashire 4.

Bowling: Allott 25.5–9–33–5; Patterson 22–2–77–3; Makinson 9–1–34–0; O'Shaughnessy 8–0–49–0; Simmons 23–8–40–2; Hughes 2–2–0–0.

*Derbyshire forfeited their second innings.*

### Lancashire

| | | | |
|---|---|---|---|
| J. A. Ormrod c Miller b Mortensen | 4 | – c Maher b Holding | 0 |
| D. W. Varey not out | 13 | – not out | 57 |
| S. J. O'Shaughnessy not out | 2 | – c Miller b Holding | 0 |
| N. H. Fairbrother (did not bat) | | – c Roberts b Finney | 27 |
| D. P. Hughes (did not bat) | | – c Miller b Holding | 13 |
| *J. Abrahams (did not bat) | | – not out | 18 |
| L-b 1 | 1 | L-b 2, w 3, n-b 6 | 11 |
| 1/15 (1 wkt dec.) | 20 | 1/0 2/0 3/46 4/80 (4 wkts) | 126 |

†C. Maynard, J. Simmons, B. P. Patterson, P. J. W. Allott and D. J. Makinson did not bat.

Bowling: *First Innings*—Holding 8–4–5–0; Mortensen 10–4–13–1; Warner 2–1–1–0. *Second Innings*—Holding 14–4–17–3; Mortensen 9–0–30–0; Warner 13–3–29–0; Finney 7–1–26–1; Roberts 6–1–20–0; Miller 5–4–2–0; Barnett 1–1–0–0.

Umpires: B. Dudleston and R. Julian.

At Derby, May 25, 26, 27. DERBYSHIRE drew with AUSTRALIANS (See Australian tour section).

At Derby, May 28. DERBYSHIRE lost to AUSTRALIANS by six wickets (See Australian tour section).

At Basingstoke, May 29, 30, 31. DERBYSHIRE lost to HAMPSHIRE by four wickets.

## DERBYSHIRE v GLOUCESTERSHIRE

At Derby, June 1, 3, 4. Gloucestershire won by 226 runs. Gloucestershire 22 pts, Derbyshire 5 pts. Toss won by Derbyshire. Lawrence (five for 38) and Walsh (five for 44) earned Gloucestershire victory when their hostile fast bowling hustled out Derbyshire for 82 in 24 overs. Until then, batsmen had dominated, 1,070 runs being scored for the loss of only twelve wickets. Athey (293 minutes, 25 4s) and Bainbridge (274 minutes, one 5, 21 4s) reached their highest scores and shared a partnership of 305, Gloucestershire's highest against Derbyshire and only 31 short of the county's third-wicket record. Roberts (120 minutes, two 6s, twelve 4s) achieved his maiden hundred in Derbyshire's reply and Stovold's composed 112 enabled Graveney to make the third declaration of the match, setting Derbyshire 309 in 125 minutes plus the final twenty overs. The target was soon forgotten as Derbyshire capitulated.

## Gloucestershire

| | | | |
|---|---|---|---|
| A. W. Stovold b Warner | 20 | – c Maher b Barnett | 112 |
| P. W. Romaines c Roberts b Finney | 32 | – c Mortensen b Holding | 5 |
| C. W. J. Athey c and b Barnett | 170 | – st Maher b Barnett | 58 |
| P. Bainbridge not out | 151 | – (5) not out | 36 |
| B. F. Davison not out | 15 | – (4) c Roberts b Barnett | 47 |
| K. M. Curran (did not bat) | | – not out | 14 |
| L-b 7, n-b 3 | 10 | B 3, l-b 10, w 1, n-b 5 | 19 |
| 1/30 2/65 3/370 (3 wkts dec.) | 398 | 1/10 2/157 3/235 4/236 (4 wkts dec.) | 291 |

J. W. Lloyds, *D. A. Graveney, †R. C. Russell, D. V. Lawrence and C. A. Walsh did not bat.

Bonus points – Gloucestershire 4, Derbyshire 1.

Bowling: *First Innings*—Holding 17–4–59–0; Mortensen 17–3–68–0; Warner 19–4–75–1; Finney 22–2–86–1; Miller 2–0–7–0; Roberts 4–0–27–0; Barnett 19–2–69–1. *Second Innings*—Holding 7–0–33–1; Mortensen 11–4–29–0; Finney 9–0–44–0; Warner 10–2–34–0; Barnett 28–4–84–3; Miller 21–4–54–0.

## Derbyshire

| | | | |
|---|---|---|---|
| †B. J. M. Maher c Stovold b Graveney | 46 | – (2) c Russell b Walsh | 1 |
| A. Hill retired hurt | 9 | – (10) not out | 10 |
| *K. J. Barnett b Lloyds | 83 | – (1) lbw b Walsh | 19 |
| J. E. Morris c Stovold b Lloyds | 22 | – (3) c Russell b Lawrence | 5 |
| B. Roberts not out | 100 | – (4) c Davison b Lawrence | 2 |
| W. P. Fowler lbw b Walsh | 13 | – (5) c Lloyds b Walsh | 0 |
| R. J. Finney c Romaines b Graveney | 82 | – b Lawrence | 1 |
| G. Miller not out | 1 | – (6) lbw b Lawrence | 11 |
| A. E. Warner (did not bat) | | – b Walsh | 12 |
| M. A. Holding (did not bat) | | – (8) c Bainbridge b Lawrence | 13 |
| O. H. Mortensen (did not bat) | | – lbw b Walsh | 0 |
| B 6, l-b 4, w 1, n-b 14 | 25 | W 2, n-b 6 | 8 |
| 1/135 2/177 3/178 4/206 5/375 (5 wkts dec.) | 381 | 1/7 2/22 3/28 4/28 5/28 6/34 7/53 8/59 9/82 | 82 |

Bonus points – Derbyshire 4, Gloucestershire 2.

Bowling: *First Innings*—Lawrence 13.2–1–70–0; Walsh 23–2–84–1; Graveney 34–8–94–2; Curran 7–0–42–0; Lloyds 15–2–75–2; Athey 1–0–6–0. *Second Innings*—Lawrence 12–1–38–5; Walsh 12–2–44–5.

Umpires: B. Leadbeater and R. A. White.

At Lord's, June 8, 10, 11. DERBYSHIRE drew with MIDDLESEX.

## DERBYSHIRE v SUSSEX

At Derby, June 12, 13, 14. Drawn. Derbyshire 5 pts, Sussex 4 pts. Toss won by Sussex. The first day was blank because of faulty covering, persuading Derbyshire to spend £7,000 on a new set. Barnett reached his third century of the season in 254 minutes, hitting ten 4s, and shared a partnership of 170 with Wright. However, Derbyshire's next eight wickets fell for the addition of 60 runs in a feeble collapse encouraged by Waller, who returned the best figures of his career, seven for 61. Sussex opted to bat for bonus points on the last day.

## Derbyshire

| | | | |
|---|---|---|---|
| *K. J. Barnett st Gould b Waller | 109 | P. G. Newman c Green b Waller | 0 |
| I. S. Anderson b C. M. Wells | 5 | †B. J. M. Maher not out | 0 |
| J. G. Wright c Waller b Pigott | 91 | O. H. Mortensen lbw b Waller | 0 |
| B. Roberts st Gould b Waller | 20 | | |
| J. E. Morris c Green b le Roux | 1 | B 4, l-b 1, w 3, n-b 2 | 10 |
| W. P. Fowler c Barclay b Waller | 16 | | |
| R. J. Finney c C. M. Wells b Waller | 1 | 1/26 2/196 3/219 4/223 5/241 | 256 |
| D. G. Moir c A. P. Wells b Waller | 3 | 6/253 7/253 8/255 9/256 | |

Bonus points – Derbyshire 2, Sussex 1 (Score at 100 overs: 237-4).

Bowling: le Roux 18–5–25–1; Pigott 16–3–56–1; C. M. Wells 16–7–36–1; Reeve 17–4–45–0; Barclay 11–4–24–0; Waller 34.3–15–61–7; Green 1–0–4–0.

## Sussex

| | | | |
|---|---|---|---|
| G. D. Mendis b Barnett | 41 | D. A. Reeve not out | 4 |
| A. M. Green c and b Moir | 68 | †I. J. Gould not out | 5 |
| P. W. G. Parker c and b Moir | 17 | | |
| A. P. Wells lbw b Barnett | 32 | L-b 1, n-b 6 | 7 |
| C. M. Wells c Morris b Moir | 18 | | |
| *J. R. T. Barclay c Barnett b Mortensen | 29 | 1/87 2/130 3/131 | (7 wkts dec.) 250 |
| G. S. le Roux c and b Mortensen | 29 | 4/179 5/183 6/233 7/244 | |

C. E. Waller and A. C. S. Pigott did not bat.

Bonus points – Sussex 3, Derbyshire 3.

Bowling: Mortensen 9–3–13–2; Newman 7.3–3–23–0; Finney 10–1–28–0; Moir 42–12–102–3; Barnett 31–7–83–2.

Umpires: A. A. Jones and N. T. Plews.

At Old Trafford, June 15, 17, 18. DERBYSHIRE lost to LANCASHIRE by three wickets.

## DERBYSHIRE v NOTTINGHAMSHIRE

At Derby, June 26, 27, 28. Drawn. Derbyshire 5 pts, Nottinghamshire 7 pts. Toss won by Derbyshire. Broad, who was dropped twice, retired briefly with a back injury when he was 45 and survived a confident appeal for a slip catch, battled through to 171, the highest of his career, in 366 minutes with 21 4s. Anderson's 95 earned him his county cap and Cooper bowled accurately before Holding tilted the game Derbyshire's way when Nottinghamshire batted a second time. Spirited defiance by Hadlee and Hemmings enabled Rice to set Derbyshire a target of 257 in 57 overs, a declaration which produced an excellent finish. Roberts, who hit a 6 and sixteen 4s, hit a hundred in 160 minutes, sharing a third-wicket stand of 154 with Anderson, but Hadlee put Derbyshire under pressure and they finished 23 runs short with two wickets remaining.

### Nottinghamshire

| First innings | | Second innings | |
|---|---|---|---|
| B. C. Broad c Miller b Newman | 171 | c Holding b Mortensen | 11 |
| M. Newell b Finney | 18 | c Miller b Holding | 1 |
| D. W. Randall c Maher b Finney | 5 | (4) b Holding | 23 |
| *C. E. B. Rice c sub b Miller | 51 | (5) b Holding | 13 |
| P. Johnson c Maher b Holding | 2 | (6) b Holding | 0 |
| J. D. Birch b Holding | 0 | (7) c Barnett b Holding | 23 |
| R. J. Hadlee c Miller b Newman | 8 | (8) c Roberts b Miller | 54 |
| †B. N. French run out | 44 | (3) b Holding | 11 |
| E. E. Hemmings b Newman | 17 | not out | 36 |
| K. E. Cooper c Miller b Newman | 0 | c Roberts b Finney | 6 |
| P. M. Such not out | 0 | not out | 0 |
| L-b 7, w 3, n-b 1 | 11 | B 5, l-b 3, w 5, n-b 2 | 15 |
| 1/71 2/74 3/79 4/79 5/169 6/184 7/277 8/321 9/325 | 327 | 1/11 2/15 3/51 4/65 5/65 6/76 7/112 8/174 9/188 | (9 wkts dec.) 193 |

*In the first innings B. C. Broad, when 45, retired hurt at 61 and resumed at 79.*

Bonus points – Nottinghamshire 3, Derbyshire 3 (Score at 100 overs: 296-7).

Bowling: *First Innings*—Holding 27–6–75–2; Mortensen 24–6–73–0; Finney 22–5–70–2; Newman 23.2–7–52–4; Miller 13–1–50–1. *Second Innings*—Holding 18–5–65–6; Mortensen 10–1–57–1; Miller 5–2–14–1; Finney 11–4–28–1; Newman 8–4–21–0.

### Derbyshire

| First innings | | Second innings | |
|---|---|---|---|
| *K. J. Barnett c Hadlee b Cooper | 32 | b Hadlee | 2 |
| I. S. Anderson c Randall b Rice | 95 | c Newell b Rice | 70 |
| W. P. Fowler c French b Cooper | 1 | c Rice b Hadlee | 4 |
| B. Roberts c Randall b Cooper | 49 | c French b Rice | 100 |
| R. Sharma c French b Cooper | 4 | (9) not out | 6 |
| G. Miller b Hemmings | 52 | c French b Rice | 19 |
| †B. J. M. Maher c French b Rice | 0 | (10) not out | 0 |
| R. J. Finney c Hadlee b Cooper | 0 | run out | 4 |
| P. G. Newman c Hadlee b Cooper | 4 | (7) b Hadlee | 2 |
| M. A. Holding c Such b Hemmings | 6 | (5) c Rice b Hadlee | 17 |
| O. H. Mortensen not out | 16 | | |
| B 1, l-b 2, n-b 2 | 5 | B 5, l-b 2, w 3 | 10 |
| 1/41 2/47 3/148 4/156 5/199 6/199 7/199 8/209 9/222 | 264 | 1/7 2/11 3/165 4/191 5/206 6/211 7/221 8/232 | (8 wkts) 234 |

Bonus points – Derbyshire 2, Nottinghamshire 4 (Score at 100 overs: 236-9).

Bowling: *First Innings*—Hadlee 13–5–28–0; Rice 12–4–38–2; Hemmings 41.2–10–110–2; Cooper 28–12–53–6; Such 15–5–32–0. *Second Innings*—Hadlee 17.5–5–44–4; Cooper 11–4–27–0; Hemmings 11–1–64–0; Such 6–1–32–0; Rice 11–1–60–3.

Umpires: J. H. Harris and D. O. Oslear.

## DERBYSHIRE v GLAMORGAN

At Derby, June 29, July 1, 2. Derbyshire won by ten wickets. Derbyshire 23 pts, Glamorgan 3 pts. Toss won by Derbyshire. Fine bowling by Holding and Newman gave Derbyshire an early advantage, and only a fifth-wicket stand of 101 between Javed Miandad and Ontong made Glamorgan's first innings respectable. An elegant 90 by Miller, coupled with a lively ninth-wicket stand between Newman and Warner, stretched Derbyshire's lead to 238 and Glamorgan were in trouble again at 25 for three. After two more wickets fell, Barnett claimed the extra half-hour on the second day but Younis Ahmed, Davies and Derrick battled splendidly. Holding and Newman again shared the wickets, leaving Derbyshire to score 79 for their first Championship victory of the season.

### Glamorgan

| First innings | | Second innings | |
|---|---|---|---|
| A. L. Jones c Maher b Holding | 10 | c Newman b Holding | 13 |
| H. Morris c Maher b Warner | 0 | c Holding b Warner | 2 |
| G. C. Holmes c Maher b Newman | 12 | c Miller b Newman | 52 |
| Javed Miandad c Anderson b Holding | 64 | b Holding | 2 |
| Younis Ahmed c Miller b Holding | 0 | b Newman | 96 |
| *R. C. Ontong c Morris b Holding | 29 | (7) c Maher b Newman | 27 |
| †T. Davies c Miller b Holding | 4 | (8) lbw b Barnett | 32 |
| J. Derrick c Roberts b Newman | 4 | (9) c Barnett b Holding | 52 |
| I. Smith c Sharma b Newman | 0 | (10) c Barnett b Newman | 12 |
| S. R. Barwick not out | 1 | (6) lbw b Miller | 1 |
| L. L. McFarlane b Newman | 3 | not out | 0 |
| B 2, l-b 16, w 5, n-b 10 | 33 | B 4, l-b 9, w 1, n-b 13 | 27 |
| 1/0 2/27 3/30 4/30 5/131 6/145 7/152 8/156 9/156 | 160 | 1/11 2/22 3/25 4/144 5/145 6/205 7/214 8/292 9/316 | 316 |

Bonus points – Glamorgan 1, Derbyshire 4.

Bowling: *First Innings*—Holding 21–7–33–5; Warner 11–1–45–1; Newman 13.1–2–29–4; Finney 10–1–35–0. *Second Innings*—Holding 18.3–3–62–3; Warner 15–3–67–1; Finney 9–3–28–0; Newman 26–2–94–4; Miller 11–2–44–1; Barnett 3–1–8–1.

### Derbyshire

| First innings | | Second innings | |
|---|---|---|---|
| *K. J. Barnett lbw b McFarlane | 67 | not out | 42 |
| I. S. Anderson c Davies b McFarlane | 7 | not out | 40 |
| J. E. Morris c Miandad b Derrick | 36 | | |
| B. Roberts lbw b McFarlane | 36 | | |
| R. Sharma c Ontong b Barwick | 26 | | |
| G. Miller c Davies b Holmes | 90 | | |
| †B. J. M. Maher b Holmes | 11 | | |
| R. J. Finney c Davies b McFarlane | 6 | | |
| P. G. Newman not out | 52 | | |
| A. E. Warner c Miandad b Barwick | 47 | | |
| M. A. Holding c Holmes b Ontong | 8 | | |
| L-b 2, w 3, n-b 7 | 12 | | |
| 1/21 2/81 3/150 4/155 5/243 6/275 7/288 8/291 9/377 | 398 | (no wkt) | 82 |

Bonus points – Derbyshire 3, Glamorgan 2 (Score at 100 overs: 280-6).

Bowling: *First Innings*—McFarlane 22–3–100–4; Barwick 28–3–91–2; Derrick 32–6–78–1; Holmes 26–5–89–2; Ontong 21.4–7–38–1. *Second Innings*—McFarlane 6–0–34–0; Barwick 8–2–23–0; Younis 4–2–8–0; Smith 1.4–0–17–0.

Umpires: J. H. Harris and D. O. Oslear.

At Worcester, July 6, 8, 9. DERBYSHIRE beat WORCESTERSHIRE by three wickets.

At Northampton, July 10, 11, 12. DERBYSHIRE drew with NORTHAMPTONSHIRE.

## DERBYSHIRE v LEICESTERSHIRE

At Chesterfield, July 13, 14, 15. Leicestershire won by seven wickets. Leicestershire 24 pts, Derbyshire 4 pts. Toss won by Leicestershire. The second hat-trick of Clift's career, coming with the first three balls of a new spell, reduced Derbyshire to 83 for seven early on the first afternoon. Willey consolidated the advantage by reaching his second century of the season against Derbyshire in 196 minutes, including nine 4s. Leicestershire, 223 ahead on first innings, captured six wickets quickly enough to claim the extra half-hour, so prolonging the second day to 7.55, but by then Newman, released by Leicestershire in 1979, was in and went on to complete a remarkable maiden century on the last day. He more than doubled his previous best score to reach 115 in 238 minutes, hitting seventeen 4s as the last four wickets added 201. Even then, however, time was on Leicestershire's side.

## Derbyshire

| | | | |
|---|---|---|---|
| *K. J. Barnett c Briers b Agnew | 20 | – lbw b Clift | 34 |
| I. S. Anderson c Whitticase b Agnew | 2 | – c Whitticase b Taylor | 5 |
| J. E. Morris c Whitticase b Clift | 53 | – b Taylor | 45 |
| B. Roberts lbw b Clift | 10 | – c Balderstone b Taylor | 13 |
| R. Sharma c Balderstone b Willey | 10 | – (6) c Whitticase b Taylor | 19 |
| G. Miller c Whitticase b Clift | 0 | – (7) c Whitticase b Taylor | 0 |
| P. G. Newman b Clift | 0 | – (8) c Briers b Agnew | 115 |
| R. J. Finney c Whitticase b Clift | 0 | – (9) c Briers b Willey | 26 |
| M. A. Holding c Butcher b Taylor | 37 | – (10) c Briers b Agnew | 12 |
| †B. J. M. Maher not out | 7 | – (5) lbw b Ferris | 0 |
| O. H. Mortensen b Ferris | 0 | – not out | 2 |
| B 2, n-b 12 | 14 | B 7, l-b 16, w 5, n-b 24 | 52 |
| 1/15 2/27 3/44 4/83 5/83 6/83 7/83 8/130 9/148 | 153 | 1/14 2/87 3/115 4/116 5/120 6/122 7/179 8/260 9/313 | 323 |

Bonus points – Derbyshire 1, Leicestershire 4.

Bowling: *First Innings*—Agnew 15–5–44–2; Taylor 13–3–33–1; Clift 16–5–38–5; Ferris 8.5–0–36–1; Willey 1–1–0–1. *Second Innings*—Agnew 26.1–7–79–2; Taylor 35–6–86–5; Ferris 19–2–76–1; Clift 22–10–40–1; Willey 11–7–19–1.

## Leicestershire

| | | | |
|---|---|---|---|
| I. P. Butcher c Roberts b Mortensen | 0 | – c Maher b Holding | 4 |
| J. C. Balderstone c Sharma b Holding | 49 | – c Morris b Holding | 20 |
| R. A. Cobb b Newman | 27 | – c Sharma b Holding | 8 |
| *P. Willey lbw b Finney | 101 | – not out | 48 |
| J. J. Whitaker lbw b Finney | 42 | – not out | 16 |
| N. E. Briers c Maher b Newman | 0 | | |
| P. B. Clift c Anderson b Finney | 31 | | |
| †P. Whitticase c Roberts b Holding | 47 | | |
| J. P. Agnew b Newman | 36 | | |
| L. B. Taylor c Miller b Newman | 0 | | |
| G. J. F. Ferris not out | 0 | | |
| B 8, l-b 7, w 7, n-b 21 | 43 | W 4, n-b 5 | 9 |
| 1/2 2/58 3/161 4/232 5/237 6/264 7/308 8/376 9/376 | 376 | 1/12 2/34 3/58 (3 wkts) | 105 |

Bonus points – Leicestershire 4, Derbyshire 3 (Score at 100 overs: 340-7).

Bowling: *First Innings*—Holding 30.3–3–95–2; Mortensen 21–1–95–1; Finney 23–5–77–3; Newman 31–8–89–4; Miller 4–3–5–0. *Second Innings*—Holding 12–2–38–3; Mortensen 4–0–28–0; Newman 10–0–35–0; Finney 2–0–4–0.

Umpires: J. Birkenshaw and A. A. Jones.

## DERBYSHIRE v YORKSHIRE

At Chesterfield, July 24, 25, 26. Drawn. Derbyshire 8 pts, Yorkshire 6 pts. Toss won by Yorkshire. Jarvis became the youngest bowler to perform a hat-trick for Yorkshire in first-class cricket, taking the record from F. S. Trueman, but Derbyshire built a strong position. Barnett scored his fourth century of the season, batting in all for 250 minutes with nine 4s, and Holding reached the highest score of his career. Yorkshire were always in danger of being made to follow on, but Bairstow reached 100 in 178 minutes and was unbeaten with a 6 and thirteen 4s as he saw them to safety. Yorkshire were set 366 to win in a minimum of 80 overs, but persistent bad light accounted for 59 of them and a resumption in the final hour was meaningless.

### Derbyshire

| | | | |
|---|---|---|---|
| *K. J. Barnett c Boycott b Jarvis | 125 | – c Shaw b Jarvis | 18 |
| I. S. Anderson c Bairstow b Sidebottom | 9 | – c Bairstow b Jarvis | 62 |
| J. E. Morris c Boycott b Shaw | 49 | – c Shaw b Hartley | 25 |
| B. Roberts c Pickles b Jarvis | 44 | – st Bairstow b Carrick | 24 |
| R. Sharma c Bairstow b Jarvis | 0 | – not out | 41 |
| G. Miller not out | 74 | – c sub b Carrick | 13 |
| P. G. Newman c Hartley b Jarvis | 0 | – c Bairstow b Jarvis | 0 |
| A. E. Warner c Bairstow b Shaw | 8 | – c Bairstow b Carrick | 16 |
| M. A. Holding c Shaw b Pickles | 80 | – c Sharp b Shaw | 12 |
| R. J. Finney c Sharp b Jarvis | 3 | – st Bairstow b Carrick | 1 |
| †C. Marples c Sharp b Pickles | 8 | | |
| B 1, l-b 10, w 6, n-b 3 | 20 | B 5, l-b 1 | 6 |
| 1/35 2/162 3/234 4/234 5/235 6/235 7/266 8/400 9/407 | 420 | 1/24 2/79 3/127 4/137 5/178 6/178 7/199 8/216 9/218 | (9 wkts dec.) 218 |

Bonus points – Derbyshire 4, Yorkshire 3 (Score at 100 overs: 379-7).

Bowling: *First Innings*—Jarvis 32–2–126–5; Sidebottom 22–1–94–1; Shaw 26–5–80–2; Pickles 22–2–91–2; Carrick 9–3–18–0. *Second Innings*—Jarvis 20–6–68–3; Shaw 7–2–22–1; Pickles 7–0–25–0; Hartley 10–1–35–1; Boycott 5–1–15–0; Carrick 12.4–4–47–4.

### Yorkshire

| | | | |
|---|---|---|---|
| G. Boycott c Sharma b Holding | 19 | – retired hurt | 4 |
| A. A. Metcalfe c Marples b Newman | 6 | – c Marples b Newman | 6 |
| K. Sharp c Anderson b Holding | 21 | – not out | 3 |
| S. N. Hartley c Holding b Newman | 0 | – not out | 4 |
| P. E. Robinson b Warner | 36 | | |
| *†D. L. Bairstow not out | 113 | | |
| P. Carrick c Morris b Holding | 21 | | |
| A. Sidebottom c Marples b Warner | 1 | | |
| P. W. Jarvis c Marples b Finney | 0 | | |
| C. S. Pickles c Miller b Warner | 12 | | |
| C. Shaw b Warner | 12 | | |
| B 13, l-b 9, w 1, n-b 9 | 32 | B 4 | 4 |
| 1/31 2/35 3/35 4/74 5/149 6/198 7/201 8/209 9/242 | 273 | 1/14 | (1 wkt) 21 |

Bonus points – Yorkshire 3, Derbyshire 4.

Bowling: *First Innings*—Holding 22–2–56–3; Finney 12–2–33–1; Newman 18–3–74–2; Warner 19.5–1–88–4. *Second Innings*—Holding 6.5–4–9–0; Warner 2–1–2–0; Newman 4–1–6–1.

Umpires: D. J. Constant and K. J. Lyons.

At Edgbaston, July 27, 29, 30. DERBYSHIRE drew with WARWICKSHIRE.

At Bradford, July 31, August 1, 2. DERBYSHIRE lost to YORKSHIRE by an innings and 24 runs.

## DERBYSHIRE v SURREY

At Derby, August 3, 5, 6. Surrey won by an innings and 80 runs. Surrey 24 pts, Derbyshire 5 pts. Toss won by Derbyshire. Jesty was taken ill before the start so Surrey summoned Ward, who had been due to play for his club, Banstead. Ward arrived at lunch when Surrey, who had been put in, were 115 for four but he, Richards and Doughty flayed some poor bowling. Ward, whose previous best was 35, hit a 6 and 21 4s in his 143, an exciting, unblemished maiden century, and added 130 in 29 overs with Doughty. Pauline produced the best bowling figures of his career and Derbyshire, following on 275 behind, collapsed to Monkhouse and Gray once the openers had been parted. Surrey were extremely efficient, Derbyshire less than adequate in any department.

## Surrey

| | |
|---|---|
| A. R. Butcher c Marples b Holding | 80 |
| A. Needham b Finney | 29 |
| A. J. Stewart c Roberts b Newman | 0 |
| M. A. Lynch lbw b Finney | 1 |
| D. B. Pauline b Finney | 6 |
| †C. J. Richards c Roberts b Miller | 70 |
| D. M. Ward b Miller | 143 |
| R. J. Doughty c Roberts b Barnett | 65 |
| G. Monkhouse lbw b Barnett | 29 |
| *P. I. Pocock not out | 10 |
| B 8, l-b 11, w 1, n-b 8 | 28 |
| 1/73 2/81 3/89 4/115 5/177 6/223 7/353 8/433 9/461 (9 wkts dec.) | 461 |

A. H. Gray did not bat.

Bonus points – Surrey 4, Derbyshire 4.

Bowling: Holding 16–2–70–1; Warner 13–3–49–0; Finney 22–5–90–3; Newman 17–1–80–1; Miller 14.3–1–79–2; Barnett 15–1–52–2; Roberts 2–0–22–0.

## Derbyshire

| | | | |
|---|---|---|---|
| *K. J. Barnett c Richards b Doughty | 27 | – c Monkhouse b Gray | 69 |
| I. S. Anderson c Stewart b Gray | 12 | – lbw b Gray | 32 |
| J. E. Morris lbw b Pauline | 2 | – (4) c Doughty b Monkhouse | 6 |
| B. Roberts lbw b Monkhouse | 10 | – (5) c Butcher b Doughty | 14 |
| A. Hill b Pauline | 0 | – (6) c Richards b Monkhouse | 10 |
| G. Miller c Butcher b Pauline | 13 | – (7) c Stewart b Monkhouse | 5 |
| P. G. Newman c Stewart b Gray | 35 | – (8) c Doughty b Monkhouse | 18 |
| A. E. Warner c Doughty b Gray | 60 | – (9) c Lynch b Monkhouse | 8 |
| M. A. Holding b Pauline | 0 | – (10) c Stewart b Gray | 1 |
| R. J. Finney not out | 1 | – (11) not out | 2 |
| †C. Marples c Doughty b Pauline | 4 | – (3) st Richards b Gray | 10 |
| B 8, l-b 5, w 9 | 22 | B 16, l-b 2, n-b 2 | 20 |
| 1/45 2/45 3/50 4/50 5/67 6/77 7/179 8/179 9/180 | 186 | 1/105 2/118 3/131 4/133 5/147 6/158 7/171 8/190 9/193 | 195 |

Bonus points – Derbyshire 1, Surrey 4.

Bowling: *First Innings*—Gray 20–5–68–3; Monkhouse 12–5–20–1; Pocock 2–1–3–0; Doughty 8–2–30–1; Pauline 19.4–7–52–5. *Second Innings*—Gray 21–6–44–4; Doughty 11–0–52–1; Monkhouse 30.5–9–61–5; Pauline 7–4–9–0; Pocock 7–2–6–0; Butcher 4–2–5–0; Needham 3–3–0–0.

Umpires: J. A. Jameson and K. E. Palmer.

At Colchester, August 10, 12, 13. DERBYSHIRE lost to ESSEX by 36 runs.

## DERBYSHIRE v WORCESTERSHIRE

At Buxton, August 14, 15, 16. Drawn. Worcestershire 1 pt. Toss won by Worcestershire. The Park was the only ground in the Championship at which play began promptly, but this rare distinction for Buxton lasted only an hour. Derbyshire, put in, struggled in damp conditions before rain returned to kill the match.

### Derbyshire

| | | | |
|---|---|---|---|
| I. S. Anderson lbw b Radford | 0 | J. G. Wright not out | 0 |
| B. Roberts lbw b Radford | 13 | L-b 2, w 1 | 3 |
| A. Hill not out | 7 | | |
| *K. J. Barnett c Rhodes b Newport | 2 | 1/0 2/17 3/25 | (3 wkts) 25 |

G. Miller, M. A. Fell, P. G. Newman, A. E. Warner, R. J. Finney and †C. Marples did not bat.

Bonus point – Worcestershire 1.

Bowling: Radford 8–5–4–2; Newport 8–2–19–1.

### Worcestershire

T. S. Curtis, D. B. D'Oliveira, D. M. Smith, D. N. Patel, *P. A. Neale, G. A. Hick, †S. J. Rhodes, P. J. Newport, N. V. Radford, R. K. Illingworth and J. D. Inchmore.

Umpires: B. Dudleston and M. J. Kitchen.

At Hove, August 17, 19, 20. DERBYSHIRE drew with SUSSEX.

At Trent Bridge, August 24, 26, 27. DERBYSHIRE lost to NOTTINGHAMSHIRE by ten wickets.

## DERBYSHIRE v SOMERSET

At Derby, August 28, 29, 30. Drawn. Derbyshire 7 pts, Somerset 8 pts. Toss won by Somerset. The first 49 overs were lost because of drizzle and a damp outfield. Derbyshire were again rescued by their lower order, the last four wickets adding 135, while Richards dominated Somerset's reply with a majestic century off 80 balls, his seventh of the season. His 123 was made in 131 minutes and, despite 90-yard boundaries on each side, contained two 6s and nineteen 4s. Wyatt batted solidly and Mortensen took five wickets for the first time in the season. Derbyshire, 64 behind, had little chance of making a challenging declaration, but the danger of defeat was averted by Morris, whose restrained innings was vividly supported by Holding after Marks had threatened to take control.

### Derbyshire

| | | | |
|---|---|---|---|
| I. S. Anderson lbw b Garner | 16 | – c Gard b Palmer | 26 |
| B. Roberts c Harden b Dredge | 1 | – c Gard b Dredge | 33 |
| A. M. Brown lbw b Garner | 3 | – b Marks | 16 |
| *K. J. Barnett c Harden b Palmer | 49 | – c Roebuck b Marks | 15 |
| J. E. Morris lbw b Dredge | 32 | – c Roebuck b Marks | 90 |
| M. A. Fell c Gard b Dredge | 19 | – c Garner b Marks | 6 |
| P. G. Newman c Garner b Palmer | 37 | – c sub b Marks | 9 |
| M. A. Holding c Wyatt b Garner | 27 | – c Gard b Atkinson | 34 |
| R. J. Finney c Palmer b Marks | 33 | – not out | 5 |
| †C. Marples b Marks | 34 | – not out | 8 |
| O. H. Mortensen not out | 0 | | |
| B 1, l-b 5, w 8, n-b 7 | 21 | B 4, l-b 6, w 1, n-b 8 | 19 |
| 1/4 2/15 3/28 4/95 5/134 6/137 7/179 8/206 9/270 | 272 | 1/49 2/70 3/102 4/107 5/129 6/157 7/236 8/248 | (8 wkts dec.) 261 |

Bonus points – Derbyshire 3, Somerset 4.

Bowling: *First Innings*—Garner 18–2–51–3; Dredge 29–10–63–3; Atkinson 11–2–54–0; Palmer 17–1–53–2; Richards 11–4–20–0; Marks 5–0–25–2. *Second Innings*—Garner 13–2–35–0; Dredge 14–5–42–1; Palmer 16–1–61–1; Marks 34–14–69–5; Atkinson 14–3–36–1; Harden 2–1–8–0.

## Somerset

J. G. Wyatt c Marples b Mortensen ... 90
P. M. Roebuck b Mortensen .......... 9
R. L. Ollis b Mortensen ............. 0
I. V. A. Richards c Marples b Mortensen . 123
R. J. Harden c Marples b Holding .... 3
*V. J. Marks c Holding b Mortensen .. 8
J. C. M. Atkinson c Brown b Barnett .. 40
G. V. Palmer c Marples b Newman ... 1
†T. Gard b Newman ................ 0
C. H. Dredge c Brown b Barnett ...... 31
J. Garner not out .................. 14
B 1, l-b 10, w 2, n-b 4 ....... 17

1/34 2/40 3/225 4/228 5/245 6/250 7/256 8/264 9/310 — 336

Bonus points – Somerset 4, Derbyshire 4.

Bowling: Holding 18–3–66–1; Mortensen 22–4–87–5; Finney 13–0–59–0; Newman 18–2–70–2; Barnett 10–0–43–2.

Umpires: J. A. Jameson and B. Leadbeater.

At Folkestone, August 31, September 2, 3. DERBYSHIRE drew with KENT.

## DERBYSHIRE v WARWICKSHIRE

At Chesterfield, September 11, 12, 13. Derbyshire won by ten wickets. Derbyshire 24 pts, Warwickshire 3 pts. Toss won by Warwickshire. After a bad start on a lively pitch, Derbyshire took complete control. Brown, in his third Championship innings, defended stubbornly and Morris, despite being forced to retire hurt when 92 because of a blow on the right arm from Small, reached his first century of the season in 145 minutes with a 6 and eight 4s. Holding flayed the Warwickshire bowling and then scattered their batsmen in a hostile opening spell. When the follow-on was enforced, he dismissed Lloyd and Kallicharran in his first four balls and went on to take ten for 118, his best match figures for the county. Asif Din batted well in both innings but Warwickshire were outplayed and beaten with two sessions to spare.

## Derbyshire

| | First innings | | Second innings |
|---|---|---|---|
| I. S. Anderson c Dyer b Smith | 3 | not out | 13 |
| B. Roberts b Smith | 4 | not out | 20 |
| A. M. Brown c Amiss b Wall | 74 | | |
| *K. J. Barnett c Dyer b Smith | 18 | | |
| J. E. Morris not out | 109 | | |
| R. Sharma c Humpage b Wall | 32 | | |
| P. G. Newman c Amiss b Smith | 5 | | |
| M. A. Holding b Wall | 62 | | |
| R. J. Finney c Asif Din b Gifford | 23 | | |
| †C. Marples c Amiss b Wall | 1 | | |
| O. H. Mortensen not out | 6 | | |
| L-b 10, w 1, n-b 6 | 17 | N-b 3 | 3 |
| 1/6 2/9 3/34 4/235 5/238 6/258 7/318 8/342 9/346 | (9 wkts dec.) 354 | | (no wkt) 36 |

Bonus points – Derbyshire 4, Warwickshire 3 (Score at 100 overs: 339-7).

*J. E. Morris, when 92, retired hurt at 168 and resumed at 342.*

Bowling: *First Innings*—Small 22–8–46–0; Smith 25–2–121–4; Wall 29–4–88–4; Ferreira 4–0–16–0; Gifford 27–2–73–1. *Second Innings*—Wall 4.5–0–23–0; Ferreira 4–3–13–0.

### Warwickshire

| | | |
|---|---|---|
| T. A. Lloyd c Barnett b Holding | 11 – c Marples b Holding | 0 |
| R. I. H. B. Dyer c Anderson b Mortensen | 6 – lbw b Finney | 27 |
| A. I. Kallicharran c Sharma b Holding | 6 – c Finney b Holding | 0 |
| D. L. Amiss c Sharma b Holding | 3 – lbw b Mortensen | 16 |
| †G. W. Humpage c Marples b Finney | 2 – c sub b Holding | 36 |
| Asif Din lbw b Holding | 44 – c Barnett b Holding | 89 |
| P. A. Smith c Brown b Finney | 2 – c sub b Holding | 31 |
| A. M. Ferreira lbw b Finney | 0 – c Finney b Holding | 17 |
| G. C. Small c Marples b Newman | 25 – b Mortensen | 15 |
| S. Wall not out | 9 – c Holding b Mortensen | 4 |
| *N. Gifford c Marples b Newman | 4 – not out | 11 |
| B 4, n-b 7 | 11 B 1, l-b 4, w 3, n-b 11 | 19 |
| 1/12 2/25 3/28 4/31 5/36 6/44 7/44 8/105 9/111 | 123 1/0 2/0 3/33 4/60 5/148 6/213 7/220 8/233 9/249 | 265 |

Bonus points – Derbyshire 4.

Bowling: *First Innings*—Holding 16–5–28–4; Mortensen 9–2–13–1; Newman 12.5–1–52–2; Finney 6–1–26–3. *Second Innings*—Holding 19–3–90–6; Mortensen 24.5–5–62–3; Finney 12–3–30–1; Newman 10–1–37–0; Roberts 4–0–17–0; Barnett 7–3–15–0; Anderson 3–1–9–0.

Umpires: J. Birkenshaw and R. Julian.

---

## FIELDING IN 1985

(Qualification: 20 dismissals)

80 G. W. Humpage (76 ct, 4 st)
76 D. E. East (72 ct, 4 st)
72 B. N. French (65 ct, 7 st)
65 R. C. Russell (59 ct, 6 st)
62 R. J. Parks (58 ct, 4 st)
62 P. R. Downton (57 ct, 5 st)
60 M. A. Garnham (53 ct, 7 st)
58 D. L. Bairstow (45 ct, 13 st)
57 S. J. Rhodes (54 ct, 3 st)
54 A. P. E. Knott (53 ct, 1 st)
50 C. Maynard (42 ct, 8 st)
49 T. Davies (44 ct, 5 st)
48 C. J. Richards (41 ct, 7 st)
39 I. J. Gould (35 ct, 4 st)
38 T. Gard (31 ct, 7 st)
36 M. A. Lynch
34 V. P. Terry
29 A. J. Stewart (28 ct, 1 st)
27 G. Miller
27 W. N. Slack
26 C. W. J. Athey
25 G. A. Gooch
25 J. W. Lloyds
25 D. Ripley (21 ct, 4 st)
24 D. L. Amiss
24 R. O. Butcher
24 C. Marples (23 ct, 1 st)
24 D. W. Randall
23 S. G. Hinks
22 P. H. Edmonds
22 J. E. Emburey
22 B. R. Hardie
22 R. A. Harper
22 B. Roberts
21 D. B. D'Oliveira
21 B. J. M. Maher (19 ct, 2 st)
21 C. E. B. Rice
20 I. P. Butcher
20 C. S. Cowdrey
20 M. W. Gatting
20 A. W. Stovold
20 C. J. Tavaré

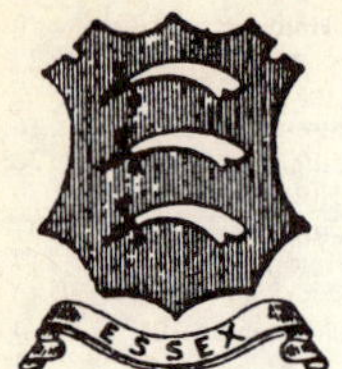


# ESSEX

*President:* T. N. Pearce
*Chairman:* D. J. Insole
*Chairman, Cricket Committee:* D. J. Insole
*Secretary/General Manager:* P. J. Edwards
County Ground, New Writtle Street,
Chelmsford CM2 0PG
(Telephone: 0245-354533)
*Captain:* 1985 – K. W. R. Fletcher
1986 – G. A. Gooch

The remarkable Essex success story continued in the rain-soaked summer of 1985 with two more titles to take the number in the last seven seasons to eight. In a dramatic end to the season, they not only retained the John Player Sunday League by defeating Yorkshire in the last match, but also emerged with the NatWest Bank Trophy for the first time in a thrilling clash at Lord's when they beat Nottinghamshire by just 1 run. Keith Fletcher thus became the first captain to have led a county to the game's four major honours.

For good measure, Essex also reached the final of the Benson and Hedges Cup, in which they were forced to admit second best against Leicestershire, and they finished fourth in the Britannic Assurance Championship. That may seem like failure, bearing in mind that they had carried off the title in the two previous years; but when one reflects that at the start of the second week of July they were at the foot of the table, with only one victory to their credit, to finish in so lofty a position was in fact a fine achievement.

Once again the county were left owing a great debt of gratitude to Graham Gooch, even though Test demands, following his three-year ban by the TCCB, limited his appearances. Statistics help convey the immense damage he inflicted upon opposing bowlers. In all competitions for club and country, he plundered ten centuries and in a total of 57 innings reached 50 on no fewer than 30 occasions. In first-class matches, he topped 2,000 for the second year running, this time for an average of over 70.

In 1986 Gooch will be skippering the side, following Fletcher's decision to step down after twelve years at the helm. In his own words, he has "a hard act to follow", but there is every reason to believe he will take the additional burden in his stride. Certainly, running his benefit last summer, coupled with the way he was singled out for attack by certain West Indian politicians, failed to affect his form.

Consistency was the main reason for Brian Hardie enjoying a highly rewarding season. The purists may sometimes frown at his ungainly style, but his was a major contribution to the county's success. His century in the NatWest Bank Trophy final enabled him to carry off the Man of the Match award. Ken McEwan, who by his own high standards failed to scale the heights of previous years, still topped 1,000 runs, and left everyone regretting his decision to retire, at the age of 33, and concentrate on the family's farming business in South Africa. McEwan gave splendid entertainment during his twelve years with Essex and provided the inspiration for many of their triumphs. However, his departure was tempered by the news that Australia's captain, Allan Border, would be taking his place.

Of the younger batsmen, Paul Prichard, once he had recovered from a hand injury, which kept him out of several matches early in the season, caught the eye with his easy, effortless style, though he failed to make a century. His fielding, in the covers or at mid-wicket, left an even bigger impression. His ability to cover so much ground so quickly, and turn and throw in one movement was a fine sight. Alan Lilley, too, excelled with his vulture-like exploits in the field; his catch to dismiss Gatting in the Benson and Hedges Cup at Chelmsford will long linger in the memory. But like Chris Gladwin, Lilley struggled to make any real impact with the bat, impetuosity rather than lack of talent bringing about the downfall of both of them more often than they can care to recollect.

It was perhaps ironic that Derek Pringle was seldom mentioned as an England candidate during the summer. Ironic because the all-rounder proved himself a better player than when thrust into the Test side two years earlier. He played most of his best innings when Essex were under pressure – a tribute to his application – and next to John Lever he was the most successful wicket-taker. As an additional bonus, if that is the correct word, he had rectified a no-balling problem which had caused so much frustration twelve months earlier. David East was also able to look back with satisfaction on the season. Not only did he equal the world wicket-keeping record of A. W. Grout by dismissing eight batsmen in an innings, he also had his best year with the bat, the highlight of which was a career-best 131 against Gloucestershire at Southend.

Lever was again the county's most successful bowler with 77 first-class wickets. The advancing years have not, so far, impaired his effectiveness or enthusiasm. He remains the perfect professional and a model for others to follow. That also applies to Stuart Turner, who, at the age of 42, continued to be a formidable opponent. A troublesome knee injury resulted in his being held back mainly for the one-day battles. Neil Foster usually shared the new ball with Lever and did enough to persuade the selectors to pick him for England's winter tour of the West Indies. But there is no doubting that niggling injuries prevented him from making the progress both he and his county would have liked.

Looking to the future, Essex, who decided not to offer their West Indian all-rounder, Norbert Phillip, another contract, will view it with continued optimism. They have a good blend of experience and youth, and Fletcher will still be around to exert his influence, for while he has decided to relinquish the full-time captaincy, he will lead the side when Gooch is unavailable. – N.F.

ESSEX 1985

[*Bill Smith*

*Back row:* K. S. McEwan, D. E. East, A. W. Lilley, D. R. Pringle, N. A. Foster, C. Gladwin, P. J. Prichard. *Front row:* B. R. Hardie, S. Turner, G. A. Gooch, K. W. R. Fletcher (*captain*), J. K. Lever, D. L. Acfield, K. R. Pont. *Insets:* I. L. Pont, N. Phillip.

## ESSEX RESULTS

*All first-class matches – Played 26: Won 7, Lost 2, Drawn 17. Abandoned 1.*

*County Championship matches – Played 23: Won 7, Lost 2, Drawn 14. Abandoned 1.*

*Bonus points – Batting 42, Bowling 70.*

*Competition placings – Britannic Assurance County Championship, 4th; NatWest Bank Trophy, winners; Benson and Hedges Cup, r/u; John Player League, winners.*

## BRITANNIC ASSURANCE CHAMPIONSHIP AVERAGES

### BATTING

| | Birthplace | M | I | NO | R | HI | Avge |
|---|---|---|---|---|---|---|---|
| ‡G. A. Gooch | *Leytonstone* | 11 | 17 | 2 | 1,368 | 202 | 91.20 |
| ‡D. E. East | *Clapton* | 23 | 26 | 3 | 754 | 131 | 32.78 |
| ‡K. S. McEwan | *Bedford, SA* | 23 | 36 | 4 | 1,035 | 121 | 32.34 |
| ‡B. R. Hardie | *Stenhousemuir* | 23 | 39 | 5 | 1,074 | 162 | 31.58 |
| ‡K. W. R. Fletcher | *Worcester* | 21 | 26 | 6 | 631 | 78* | 31.55 |
| P. J. Prichard | *Billericay* | 18 | 28 | 4 | 694 | 95 | 28.91 |
| ‡C. Gladwin | *East Ham* | 12 | 20 | 2 | 468 | 92* | 26.00 |
| ‡D. R. Pringle | *Nairobi, Kenya* | 21 | 27 | 4 | 573 | 121* | 24.91 |
| A. W. Lilley | *Ilford* | 14 | 23 | 2 | 474 | 68* | 22.57 |
| ‡N. A. Foster | *Colchester* | 13 | 10 | 1 | 164 | 63 | 18.22 |
| ‡K. R. Pont | *Wanstead* | 8 | 12 | 2 | 177 | 38 | 17.70 |
| I. L. Pont | *Brentwood* | 6 | 5 | 2 | 48 | 12 | 16.00 |
| ‡J. K. Lever | *Stepney* | 22 | 23 | 9 | 193 | 24* | 13.78 |
| ‡S. Turner | *Chester* | 4 | 6 | 0 | 75 | 35 | 12.50 |
| ‡N. Phillip | *Bioche, Dominica* | 3 | 5 | 0 | 57 | 21 | 11.40 |
| ‡D. L. Acfield | *Chelmsford* | 22 | 19 | 10 | 65 | 10* | 7.22 |

Also batted: J. H. Childs (*Plymouth*) (4 matches) 5, 3, 3*; J. P. Stephenson (*Stebbing*) (1 match) 10, 4; T. D. Topley (*Canterbury*) (4 matches) 0, 0, 9*.

** Signifies not out. ‡ Denotes county cap.*

The following played a total of thirteen three-figure innings for Essex in County Championship matches – G. A. Gooch 6, D. E. East 2, B. R. Hardie 2, K. S. McEwan 2, D. R. Pringle 1.

### BOWLING

| | O | M | R | W | BB | Avge |
|---|---|---|---|---|---|---|
| G. A. Gooch | 155.3 | 35 | 432 | 18 | 5-46 | 24.00 |
| N. A. Foster | 366.5 | 77 | 1,163 | 47 | 5-40 | 24.74 |
| I. L. Pont | 115.5 | 15 | 485 | 19 | 5-103 | 25.52 |
| J. K. Lever | 700.3 | 178 | 1,963 | 75 | 6-47 | 26.17 |
| T. D. Topley | 134.1 | 31 | 400 | 15 | 4-57 | 26.66 |
| D. R. Pringle | 518.1 | 125 | 1,374 | 45 | 6-42 | 30.53 |
| D. L. Acfield | 498.4 | 107 | 1,462 | 38 | 6-81 | 38.47 |

Also bowled: J. H. Childs 130–38–377–3; K. W. R. Fletcher 4–0–35–1; C. Gladwin 3–0–12–0; B. R. Hardie 6–1–35–1; A. W. Lilley 28.4–0–179–3; N. Phillip 50–10–148–2; K. R. Pont 76–10–305–7; S. Turner 86.5–15–224–8.

At Fenner's, April 20, 22, 23. ESSEX drew with CAMBRIDGE UNIVERSITY.

At Lord's, April 24, 25, 26. ESSEX drew with MCC.

## ESSEX v WARWICKSHIRE

At Chelmsford, April 27, 28, 29. Essex won by 89 runs. Essex 22 pts, Warwickshire 6 pts. Toss won by Warwickshire. An impressive display of seam bowling by Lever saw Essex begin their defence of the Championship title on a winning note, his second-innings wickets including those of Amiss, Humpage and Paul Smith in the same over. Old's ability to swing the ball justified Gifford's decision to put Essex in on the opening day, and Foster re-established the supremacy of ball over bat with four wickets in 21 balls to check Warwickshire after a century opening stand. Gooch, McEwan and Lilley all batted attractively to set up a declaration which left Warwickshire a target of 268 in 74 overs.

### Essex

| | | | |
|---|---|---|---|
| *G. A. Gooch c P. A. Smith b Small | 8 | – c Humpage b Old | 61 |
| P. J. Prichard lbw b Old | 6 | – c Small b Ferreira | 20 |
| B. R. Hardie b Old | 13 | – c Humpage b Small | 40 |
| K. S. McEwan b Old | 18 | – c P. A. Smith b Gifford | 69 |
| D. R. Pringle b Small | 10 | – c P. A. Smith b Small | 14 |
| A. W. Lilley c Humpage b Small | 30 | – c Humpage b P. A. Smith | 63 |
| K. R. Pont c Dyer b Old | 38 | – not out | 3 |
| †D. E. East c Lloyd b Ferreira | 36 | | |
| N. A. Foster b Old | 31 | | |
| J. K. Lever b Old | 0 | | |
| D. L. Acfield not out | 2 | | |
| B 2, l-b 10, w 4, n-b 4 | 20 | B 5, l-b 9, n-b 9 | 23 |
| 1/12 2/26 3/45 4/50 5/85 6/97 7/162 8/198 9/205 | 212 | 1/46 2/120 3/151 4/177 5/281 6/293 (6 wkts) | 293 |

Bonus points – Essex 2, Warwickshire 4.

Bowling: *First Innings*—Small 17–1–56–3; Old 19.2–6–68–6; Ferreira 18–3–76–1. *Second Innings*—Small 20–2–56–2; Old 21–5–78–1; Ferreira 17–0–80–1; P. A. Smith 7.5–0–60–1; Gifford 2–0–5–1.

### Warwickshire

| | | | |
|---|---|---|---|
| T. A. Lloyd c Pringle b Gooch | 68 | – c Hardie b Lever | 32 |
| R. I. H. B. Dyer c Pringle b Gooch | 53 | – lbw b Lever | 0 |
| K. D. Smith c Hardie b Pont | 4 | – c Gooch b Pringle | 9 |
| A. I. Kallicharran lbw b Foster | 12 | – c Pont b Foster | 32 |
| D. L. Amiss c Pringle b Foster | 10 | – b Lever | 5 |
| †G. W. Humpage lbw b Foster | 0 | – c Lilley b Lever | 0 |
| P. A. Smith c and b Lever | 37 | – c Prichard b Lever | 0 |
| A. M. Ferreira c East b Foster | 0 | – c Gooch b Pringle | 61 |
| C. M. Old c Lilley b Lever | 41 | – c Lilley b Pringle | 19 |
| G. C. Small lbw b Lever | 1 | – c Prichard b Pringle | 1 |
| *N. Gifford not out | 3 | – not out | 17 |
| L-b 8, n-b 1 | 9 | L-b 1, n-b 1 | 2 |
| 1/119 2/124 3/136 4/145 5/150 6/151 7/153 8/225 9/233 | 238 | 1/1 2/28 3/50 4/61 5/61 6/61 7/86 8/139 9/145 | 178 |

Bonus points – Warwickshire 2, Essex 4.

Bowling: *First Innings*—Lever 23.1–3–84–3; Foster 20–5–73–4; Pringle 16–7–34–0; Gooch 11–5–20–2; Pont 8–2–19–1. *Second Innings*—Lever 14–5–27–5; Foster 16–0–85–1; Pringle 17.5–3–65–4.

Umpires: D. O. Oslear and R. A. White.

At Trent Bridge, May 1, 2, 3. ESSEX drew with NOTTINGHAMSHIRE.

At Sheffield, May 22, 23, 24. YORKSHIRE v ESSEX. Abandoned.

At The Oval, May 25, 27, 28. ESSEX lost to SURREY by seven wickets.

## ESSEX v LEICESTERSHIRE

At Chelmsford, June 1, 3, 4. Drawn. Essex 4 pts, Leicestershire 6 pts. Toss won by Leicestershire. Agnew and Taylor, both returning after injury, made early inroads into the Essex innings before it was revived, first by Pringle and Fletcher and then by East. Centuries by Briers, in an innings of more than six hours, and Clift, his career best, helped provide the visitors with a healthy lead before the declaration, but on a pitch which became slower as the match progressed – plus a helping hand from the weather – a draw became more and more inevitable.

### Essex

| | | | |
|---|---|---|---|
| C. Gladwin c Butcher b Agnew | 17 | – (2) c Cook b Taylor | 37 |
| B. R. Hardie c Garnham b Agnew | 4 | – (1) b Agnew | 0 |
| A. W. Lilley b Clift | 11 | – (4) not out | 56 |
| K. S. McEwan c Garnham b Taylor | 1 | – (5) not out | 46 |
| D. R. Pringle c and b Taylor | 47 | | |
| *K. W. R. Fletcher c Cook b Parsons | 41 | | |
| †D. E. East c Briers b Agnew | 54 | | |
| S. Turner c and b Taylor | 1 | | |
| J. K. Lever b Agnew | 2 | – (3) lbw b Agnew | 6 |
| J. H. Childs c Garnham b Clift | 5 | | |
| D. L. Acfield not out | 4 | | |
| B 5, l-b 8, w 1, n-b 12 | 26 | B 1, l-b 1, w 1, n-b 14 | 17 |
| 1/18 2/23 3/24 4/48 5/131 6/148 7/160 8/200 9/202 | 213 | 1/9 2/34 3/66 | (3 wkts) 162 |

Bonus points – Essex 2, Leicestershire 4.

Bowling: *First Innings*—Agnew 18–4–59–4; Taylor 17–2–47–3; Parsons 14–1–49–1; Clift 17.4–6–36–2; Cook 5–3–9–0. *Second Innings*—Agnew 13–2–57–2; Taylor 11–3–26–1; Parsons 9–1–28–0; Clift 6–1–31–0; Cook 8–4–18–0.

## Leicestershire

I. P. Butcher c East b Pringle ........ 13
J. C. Balderstone c Hardie b Lever .... 10
R. A. Cobb c Gladwin b Pringle ...... 31
J. J. Whitaker b Pringle ............. 12
*N. E. Briers lbw b Acfield ..........129
†M. A. Garnham b Acfield .......... 51
P. B. Clift b Acfield ................106
G. J. Parsons not out ............... 6
N. G. B. Cook not out .............. 9
B 2, l-b 12, w 1, n-b 10 ...... 25

1/23 2/23 3/45 4/89 5/182 6/347 7/377 (7 wkts dec.) 392

J. P. Agnew and L. B. Taylor did not bat.

Bonus points – Leicestershire 2, Essex 2 (Score at 100 overs: 222-5).

Bowling: Lever 26–6–82–1; Pringle 31–6–71–3; Turner 19–4–54–0; Childs 48–16–96–0; Acfield 30–7–75–3.

Umpires: J. W. Holder and M. J. Kitchen.

# ESSEX v LANCASHIRE

At Ilford, June 8, 10, 11. Drawn. Essex 7 pts, Lancashire 5 pts. Toss won by Lancashire. The final hour was played in steady rain as both sides thought they had a chance of a victory. In the event, Essex were denied by Folley and Patterson, the last-wicket pair negotiating the final 29 deliveries of the match to frustrate the efforts of Gooch, who emerged with match figures of nine for 68. A career-best 63 by Foster highlighted the Essex first innings, but they collapsed sensationally on the third day in their second innings as Patterson bowled at a hostile pace. From an overnight 50 for one, they slumped to 75 for nine before Lever and Acfield paved the way for the declaration, which came during a lengthy hold-up because of rain.

## Essex

| | | | |
|---|---|---|---|
| G. A. Gooch b Patterson | 45 | – c Maynard b Allott | 19 |
| C. Gladwin lbw b Allott | 4 | – c Maynard b Patterson | 6 |
| A. W. Lilley c Fowler b Folley | 12 | – lbw b Allott | 10 |
| K. S. McEwan c Maynard b Patterson | 41 | – c Maynard b Patterson | 6 |
| D. R. Pringle c Varey b Simmons | 18 | – c Fowler b Patterson | 0 |
| *K. W. R. Fletcher b O'Shaughnessy | 50 | – (7) c Maynard b Patterson | 5 |
| B. R. Hardie c Abrahams b Simmons | 4 | – (6) c Maynard b Patterson | 4 |
| †D. E. East c Hughes b Patterson | 0 | – c Folley b Allott | 3 |
| N. A. Foster b Patterson | 63 | – b Patterson | 0 |
| J. K. Lever b O'Shaughnessy | 3 | – not out | 24 |
| D. L. Acfield not out | 10 | – not out | 8 |
| B 10, l-b 5, w 1, n-b 15 | 31 | B 9, l-b 8, w 1, n-b 5 | 23 |
| 1/5 2/38 3/102 4/111 5/149 6/156 7/165 8/209 9/235 | 281 | 1/26 2/51 3/59 4/59 5/59 6/65 7/72 8/72 9/75 (9 wkts dec.) | 108 |

Bonus points – Essex 3, Lancashire 4.

Bowling: *First Innings*—Allott 24–10–53–1; Patterson 23.5–4–67–4; O'Shaughnessy 13–2–49–2; Simmons 16–9–39–2; Folley 22–7–58–1. *Second Innings*—Allott 19–6–36–3; Patterson 18.3–1–45–6; O'Shaughnessy 2–0–5–0; Folley 2–0–5–0.

### Lancashire

| | | | |
|---|---|---|---|
| G. Fowler c Gooch b Lever | 24 | – c McEwan b Foster | 12 |
| D. W. Varey c McEwan b Lever | 26 | – b Lever | 48 |
| S. J. O'Shaughnessy c East b Lever | 5 | – c East b Gooch | 33 |
| N. H. Fairbrother c Lilley b Gooch | 41 | – c East b Foster | 0 |
| D. P. Hughes c Gooch b Foster | 17 | – c Pringle b Gooch | 39 |
| *J. Abrahams c East b Lever | 33 | – c East b Gooch | 1 |
| †C. Maynard c East b Gooch | 0 | – c Fletcher b Gooch | 3 |
| J. Simmons c East b Gooch | 10 | – c East b Gooch | 4 |
| I. Folley c Gooch b Lever | 9 | – (10) not out | 19 |
| P. J. W. Allott not out | 15 | – (9) b Lever | 3 |
| B. P. Patterson b Gooch | 2 | – not out | 5 |
| L-b 7, n-b 2 | 9 | L-b 7 | 7 |
| 1/34 2/50 3/74 4/115 5/127 6/127 7/149 8/167 9/178 | 191 | 1/31 2/77 3/78 4/115 5/127 6/133 7/137 8/150 9/150 | (9 wkts) 174 |

Bonus points – Lancashire 1, Essex 4.

Bowling: *First Innings*—Lever 24–10–66–5; Foster 18–6–46–1; Pringle 17–6–33–0; Acfield 4–1–17–0; Gooch 16.5–8–22–4. *Second Innings*—Lever 20–3–74–2; Foster 12–3–34–2; Gooch 14–0–46–5; Pringle 5–1–13–0.

Umpires: H. D. Bird and C. Cook.

## ESSEX v NORTHAMPTONSHIRE

At Ilford, June 12, 13, 14. Drawn. Essex 8 pts, Northamptonshire 6 pts. Toss won by Northamptonshire. A thrilling finish ended with Essex 7 runs short of victory with one wicket remaining after they had been set 192 in 70 minutes plus twenty overs. The match was a personal triumph for Hardie, who moved up the order to open in place of Gooch, playing in the Test match, and scored a total of 209 for once out. Northamptonshire batted consistently in their first innings after Cook had taken first use of a wicket still damp from the rain which fell at the end of the previous match. Storie confirmed his ability, getting quickly into line and playing straight. In Northamptonshire's second innings, which began with the night-watchman, Mallender, sharing a century opening stand with Cook, Lever bowled slow left-arm, his four wickets including his 1,500th in first-class matches.

### Northamptonshire

| | | | |
|---|---|---|---|
| *G. Cook c Hardie b Pont | 45 | – st East b Lever | 80 |
| W. Larkins c East b Turner | 11 | – (3) c Gladwin b Lever | 1 |
| R. G. Williams lbw b Turner | 11 | – (4) st East b Lever | 63 |
| A. C. Storie lbw b Lever | 81 | – (5) not out | 21 |
| R. J. Bailey c and b Pont | 13 | – (6) c Acfield b Lever | 38 |
| R. J. Boyd-Moss c East b Lever | 3 | | |
| D. J. Capel c Lever b Phillip | 52 | | |
| R. A. Harper lbw b Acfield | 12 | | |
| †G. Sharp c and b Lever | 13 | | |
| N. A. Mallender c Gladwin b Acfield | 10 | – (2) c East b Acfield | 40 |
| A. Walker not out | 15 | | |
| L-b 5, n-b 8 | 13 | B 12, l-b 7, n-b 4 | 23 |
| 1/41 2/68 3/75 4/99 5/114 6/214 7/234 8/250 9/257 | 279 | 1/110 2/117 3/156 4/206 5/266 | (5 wkts dec.) 266 |

Bonus points – Northamptonshire 3, Essex 4 (Score at 100 overs: 276-9).

Bowling: *First Innings*—Phillip 14–2–33–1; Lever 22–3–90–3; Turner 25–3–48–2; Pont 15–3–43–2; Acfield 25.1–4–60–2. *Second Innings*—Lever 34.4–6–84–4; Acfield 33–5–116–1; Phillip 7–1–29–0; Pont 5–1–18–0.

## Essex

| | | | |
|---|---|---|---|
| B. R. Hardie c Walker b Capel | 131 | – not out | 78 |
| C. Gladwin c Williams b Harper | 48 | – c Larkins b Harper | 12 |
| A. W. Lilley c Storie b Harper | 0 | – c Larkins b Harper | 4 |
| K. S. McEwan c Sharp b Mallender | 48 | – (5) b Mallender | 37 |
| *K. W. R. Fletcher c and b Mallender | 5 | – (6) c Cook b Mallender | 8 |
| K. R. Pont b Harper | 24 | – (7) b Mallender | 16 |
| N. Phillip c Cook b Harper | 19 | – (4) lbw b Walker | 6 |
| †D. E. East c Harper b Walker | 2 | – c Larkins b Harper | 1 |
| S. Turner c Walker b Mallender | 15 | – c Larkins b Mallender | 11 |
| J. K. Lever c Harper b Williams | 19 | – c and b Harper | 3 |
| D. L. Acfield not out | 10 | | |
| B 20, l-b 11, n-b 2 | 33 | B 4, l-b 5 | 9 |
| 1/125 2/125 3/228 4/240 5/261 6/297 7/307 8/315 9/325 | 354 | 1/15 2/31 3/44 4/124 5/144 6/166 7/169 8/181 9/185 | (9 wkts) 185 |

Bonus points – Essex 4, Northamptonshire 3 (Score at 100 overs: 321-8).

Bowling: *First Innings*—Mallender 26–6–46–3; Harper 37–6–118–4; Walker 21–5–72–1; Capel 17–1–58–1; Williams 9–1–29–1. *Second Innings*—Mallender 9–0–36–4; Walker 10–0–45–1; Harper 17–0–80–4; Williams 3–0–15–0.

Umpires: H. D. Bird and C. Cook.

At Swansea, June 15, 17, 18. ESSEX drew with GLAMORGAN.

At Northampton, June 22, 24, 25. ESSEX drew with NORTHAMPTONSHIRE.

## ESSEX v KENT

At Chelmsford, June 26, 27, 28. Drawn. Essex 6 pts, Kent 5 pts. Toss won by Essex. Following a highly productive century partnership for the third wicket between McEwan and Prichard on the second afternoon, Essex collapsed against a lively spell of seam and swing bowling by Ellison, who emphasised his recovery from an early-season injury with the best figures of his career. Even so, Essex were left with a first-innings lead of 69, an advantage which would have been greater had they not spilled several catches. When Kent batted again, Hinks, with a career-best 94 not out, batted soundly for two and a half hours to see Kent to an easy draw, a result which was always in the offing after the opening day had been lost to the weather.

## Kent

| | | | |
|---|---|---|---|
| M. R. Benson c Prichard b Pringle | 7 | – c and b Pringle | 7 |
| S. G. Hinks b Lever | 0 | – not out | 94 |
| C. J. Tavaré c East b Turner | 21 | – lbw b Turner | 10 |
| D. G. Aslett run out | 40 | – c East b Pont | 16 |
| *C. S. Cowdrey lbw b Pringle | 4 | – c East b Pont | 4 |
| E. A. E. Baptiste c Fletcher b Lever | 47 | – c East b Hardie | 42 |
| R. M. Ellison c East b Lever | 11 | – not out | 6 |
| G. W. Johnson c Hardie b Turner | 10 | | |
| †A. P. E. Knott b Turner | 0 | | |
| D. L. Underwood not out | 12 | | |
| K. B. S. Jarvis lbw b Turner | 6 | | |
| L-b 10, n-b 6 | 16 | B 1, l-b 2, w 1, n-b 1 | 5 |
| 1/7 2/11 3/43 4/52 5/107 6/141 7/142 8/143 9/156 | 174 | 1/7 2/49 3/81 4/85 5/166 | (5 wkts) 184 |

Bonus points – Kent 1, Essex 4.

Bowling: *First Innings*—Lever 26–9–68–3; Pringle 20–5–49–2; Turner 17.5–3–36–4; Acfield 2–0–11–0. *Second Innings*—Lever 8–2–25–0; Pringle 6–1–26–1; Turner 5–0–18–1; Pont 13–0–62–2; Acfield 9–2–28–0; Gladwin 3–0–12–0; Hardie 3–1–10–1.

## Essex

| | |
|---|---|
| B. R. Hardie c Tavaré b Jarvis | 18 |
| C. Gladwin c Knott b Ellison | 8 |
| P. J. Prichard c Knott b Ellison | 79 |
| K. S. McEwan c Knott b Jarvis | 82 |
| D. R. Pringle c Hinks b Ellison | 11 |
| *K. W. R. Fletcher c Knott b Ellison | 0 |
| K. R. Pont c Knott b Hinks | 17 |
| †D. E. East lbw b Jarvis | 7 |
| S. Turner lbw b Ellison | 2 |
| J. K. Lever b Ellison | 3 |
| D. L. Acfield not out | 1 |
| L-b 5, w 1, n-b 9 | 15 |
| 1/25 2/32 3/159 4/181 5/181 6/212 7/235 8/238 9/239 | 243 |

Bonus points – Essex 2, Kent 4.

Bowling: Jarvis 25–6–76–3; Baptiste 20–4–57–0; Ellison 31.2–8–61–6; Cowdrey 5–1–20–0; Underwood 3–1–6–0; Hinks 6–0–18–1.

Umpires: K. J. Lyons and A. G. T. Whitehead.

At Southampton, June 29, July 1, 2. ESSEX lost to HAMPSHIRE by an innings and 57 runs.

At Southend, July 6, 7, 8, 9. ESSEX drew with AUSTRALIANS (See Australian tour section).

## ESSEX v SOMERSET

At Southend, July 10, 11, 12. Essex won by 149 runs. Essex 20 pts, Somerset 5 pts. Toss won by Essex. Essex lifted themselves off the bottom of the Championship table with a victory inspired by Lever's best performance of the season. Set to score 248 in a minimum of 60 overs, Somerset capitulated in less than 40 after the first two days had favoured the batsmen. For Essex, Hardie, hitting 21 4s, equalled his previous highest score, batting through the opening day before falling early on the second, whereupon Popplewell so dominated Somerset's opening partnership that he scored all but 71 of the 243 it produced. His 172, his highest in first-class cricket, came from 231 deliveries and contained 27 4s. In contrast Roebuck's 69 was made off 240 balls.

## Essex

| | | | |
|---|---|---|---|
| B. R. Hardie c Gard b Dredge | 162 | – b Marks | 66 |
| C. Gladwin c Popplewell b Marks | 31 | – c and b Booth | 41 |
| P. J. Prichard b Marks | 41 | – c Marks b Booth | 7 |
| K. S. McEwan c Marks b Booth | 11 | – st Gard b Marks | 20 |
| D. R. Pringle c Hayward b Booth | 2 | – c Gard b Marks | 14 |
| *K. W. R. Fletcher c Hayward b Dredge | 71 | – not out | 11 |
| N. Phillip b Dredge | 21 | – c Popplewell b Booth | 7 |
| K. R. Pont c Roebuck b Dredge | 0 | – not out | 7 |
| †D. E. East c Hayward b Dredge | 25 | | |
| J. K. Lever c and b Booth | 7 | | |
| D. L. Acfield not out | 0 | | |
| L-b 6, w 4 | 10 | L-b 7, w 1 | 8 |
| 1/65 2/127 3/150 4/152 5/310 6/332 7/344 8/359 9/376 | 381 | 1/87 2/97 3/130 4/143 5/158 6/167 (6 wkts dec.) | 181 |

Bonus points – Essex 3, Somerset 1 (Score at 100 overs: 269-4).

Bowling: *First Innings*—Dredge 23–2–95–5; Davis 15–1–77–0; Marks 41–9–117–2; Booth 42.3–17–86–3. *Second Innings*—Dredge 3–0–21–0; Davis 3–0–14–0; Marks 18–0–69–3; Booth 18–1–70–3.

## Somerset

| First innings | | Second innings | |
|---|---|---|---|
| N. F. M. Popplewell lbw b Pringle | 172 | lbw b Lever | 6 |
| P. M. Roebuck c Pringle b Acfield | 69 | c Pont b Lever | 12 |
| N. A. Felton b Lever | 14 | c East b Pringle | 3 |
| J. G. Wyatt c Hardie b Acfield | 5 | c Hardie b Lever | 7 |
| R. E. Hayward not out | 13 | (6) c East b Lever | 0 |
| *V. J. Marks not out | 24 | (5) b Lever | 34 |
| R. L. Ollis (did not bat) | | c Fletcher b Lever | 0 |
| †T. Gard (did not bat) | | c Prichard b Acfield | 1 |
| M. R. Davis (did not bat) | | c Phillip b Acfield | 28 |
| S. C. Booth (did not bat) | | not out | 4 |
| C. H. Dredge (did not bat) | | b Acfield | 0 |
| B 4, l-b 11, w 1, n-b 2 | 18 | L-b 3 | 3 |
| 1/243 2/257 3/271 4/279 (4 wkts dec.) | 315 | 1/8 2/13 3/24 4/64 5/64 6/64 7/65 8/75 9/98 | 98 |

Bonus points – Somerset 4, Essex 1.

Bowling: *First Innings*—Lever 29–5–94–1; Phillip 10–4–17–0; Pringle 18–5–53–1; Acfield 35–4–109–2; Pont 8–1–27–0. *Second Innings*—Lever 20–7–49–6; Pringle 4–0–12–1; Acfield 15.4–9–34–3.

Umpires: K. J. Lyons and B. J. Meyer.

# ESSEX v GLOUCESTERSHIRE

At Southend, July 13, 15, 16. Drawn. Essex 8 pts, Gloucestershire 6 pts. Toss won by Gloucestershire. A maiden first-class century by East, in an innings of 160 minutes containing twenty 4s and two 6s, rescued Essex from a precarious 135 for seven and helped them establish a lead of 80. All his 131 runs came in an eighth-wicket stand of 186 with Fletcher. Athey provided the cornerstone of Gloucestershire's first innings before becoming a victim of Topley, a 21-year-old medium-pace bowler making his Championship début. The final morning was twice interrupted by rain, but there was time for Lloyds, opening because Stovold had a foot infection, to complete his first century for his new county.

## Gloucestershire

| First innings | | Second innings | |
|---|---|---|---|
| A. J. Wright c Hardie b Lever | 29 | c East b Phillip | 22 |
| A. W. Stovold c Pringle b Lever | 0 | | |
| C. W. J. Athey c Hardie b Topley | 76 | (4) c Hardie b Pringle | 41 |
| P. Bainbridge c East b Lever | 37 | (5) not out | 57 |
| B. F. Davison c Prichard b Pringle | 48 | (6) lbw b Topley | 12 |
| K. M. Curran c Hardie b Topley | 0 | (7) b Topley | 6 |
| J. W. Lloyds c East b Pringle | 6 | (2) c East b Topley | 101 |
| †R. C. Russell not out | 28 | (3) c McEwan b Pringle | 6 |
| *D. A. Graveney c Pringle b Lever | 1 | | |
| D. V. Lawrence c East b Lever | 24 | (8) not out | 1 |
| C. A. Walsh c Phillip b Acfield | 9 | | |
| B 3, l-b 3, w 3, n-b 3 | 12 | L-b 2, w 2 | 4 |
| 1/0 2/55 3/133 4/167 5/167 6/178 7/223 8/224 9/259 | 270 | 1/31 2/47 3/153 4/196 5/220 6/248 (6 wkts dec.) | 250 |

Bonus points – Gloucestershire 3, Essex 4.

Bowling: *First Innings*—Lever 28–9–82–5; Phillip 6–1–19–0; Pringle 24–4–58–2; Acfield 23.4–6–62–1; Topley 14–4–43–2. *Second Innings*—Lever 25–8–63–0; Phillip 13–2–50–1; Acfield 20–3–63–0; Pringle 16–7–38–2; Topley 15–5–34–3.

## Essex

| | | | |
|---|---|---|---|
| B. R. Hardie c Graveney b Walsh | 37 | †D. E. East lbw b Curran | 131 |
| C. Gladwin c Athey b Walsh | 12 | J. K. Lever b Curran | 8 |
| T. D. Topley lbw b Graveney | 0 | D. L. Acfield b Curran | 4 |
| P. J. Prichard c Russell b Lawrence | 17 | | |
| K. S. McEwan b Graveney | 14 | L-b 6, w 1, n-b 19 | 26 |
| D. R. Pringle c Russell b Graveney | 19 | | — |
| *K. W. R. Fletcher not out | 78 | 1/46 2/47 3/61 4/83 5/102 | 350 |
| N. Phillip lbw b Graveney | 4 | 6/129 7/135 8/321 9/346 | |

Bonus points – Essex 4, Gloucestershire 3 (Score at 100 overs: 305-7).

Bowling: Lawrence 17–2–79–1; Walsh 18–7–46–2; Graveney 43–14–131–4; Bainbridge 19–5–32–0; Curran 10–0–40–3; Lloyds 4–0–10–0; Athey 1–0–6–0.

Umpires: K. J. Lyons and B. J. Meyer.

At Dartford, July 24, 25, 26. ESSEX drew with Kent.

At Taunton, July 27, 29, 30. ESSEX beat SOMERSET by seven wickets.

## ESSEX v MIDDLESEX

At Chelmsford, August 3, 5, 6. Essex won by seven wickets. Essex 20 pts, Middlesex 2 pts. Toss won by Middlesex. McEwan, with his first Championship century of the summer, set up victory against opponents considerably weakened by Test calls. The South African struck sixteen 4s and was admirably supported by Pringle after two declarations had set the scene for a conclusive result following interference by the weather on the first two days. Slack and Butcher both batted attractively during Middlesex's first innings, when Lever again demonstrated the value of line and length while capturing five wickets, three of them coming in a 41-ball spell at a cost of just 2 runs.

## Middlesex

| | | | |
|---|---|---|---|
| G. D. Barlow c and b Pringle | 20 | | |
| W. N. Slack c Prichard b Lever | 72 | – run out | 22 |
| A. J. T. Miller c McEwan b Foster | 15 | – (1) not out | 13 |
| R. O. Butcher c Hardie b Foster | 61 | – (3) c East b Pont | 31 |
| *C. T. Radley b Pont | 17 | – (4) not out | 1 |
| J. D. Carr c sub b Pont | 1 | | |
| J. F. Sykes c East b Lever | 4 | | |
| †C. P. Metson b Lever | 12 | | |
| S. P. Hughes lbw b Lever | 16 | | |
| N. G. Cowans c Foster b Lever | 1 | | |
| W. W. Daniel not out | 1 | | |
| B 1, l-b 8, w 4, n-b 1 | 14 | L-b 3 | 3 |
| | — | | — |
| 1/43 2/84 3/127 4/189 5/196 6/197 7/200 8/230 9/233 | 234 | 1/26 2/65 (2 wkts dec.) | 70 |

Bonus points – Middlesex 2, Essex 4.

Bowling: *First Innings*—Lever 32.5–13–53–5; Foster 25–3–87–2; Pringle 17–7–26–1; Pont 15–3–58–2; Acfield 1–0–1–0. *Second Innings*—Foster 8–3–12–0; Pont 9–0–47–1; Pringle 2–0–8–0.

## Essex

| | | | |
|---|---|---|---|
| B. R. Hardie not out | 13 | – retired hurt | 12 |
| C. Gladwin not out | 19 | – c Metson b Daniel | 10 |
| P. J. Prichard (did not bat) | | – c Hughes b Cowans | 33 |
| K. S. McEwan (did not bat) | | – b Daniel | 121 |
| D. R. Pringle (did not bat) | | – not out | 69 |
| *K. W. R. Fletcher (did not bat) | | – not out | 8 |
| N-b 1 | 1 | L-b 3, n-b 19 | 22 |
| (no wkt dec.) | 33 | 1/35 2/103 3/234 (3 wkts) | 275 |

†D. E. East, N. A. Foster, I. L. Pont, J. K. Lever and D. L. Acfield did not bat.

Bowling: *First Innings*—Daniel 3–1–12–0; Cowans 5–3–12–0; Hughes 3–0–9–0. *Second Innings*—Daniel 20–0–87–2; Cowans 17–2–86–1; Hughes 14.4–1–58–0; Sykes 5–0–21–0; Carr 9–3–20–0.

Umpires: R. Julian and N. T. Plews.

# ESSEX v DERBYSHIRE

At Colchester, August 10, 12, 13. Essex won by 36 runs. Essex 17 pts, Derbyshire 4 pts. Toss won by Derbyshire. Essex squeezed to victory with fourteen balls to spare after Derbyshire had been invited to chase a target of 300. Miller, arriving with half the side out for 68, led a spirited bid for victory, scoring 105 off 124 balls in making only his second first-class century. Off-spinner Acfield, bowling unchanged, proved to be the Essex matchwinner with his best haul of the season. Following rain which washed out the opening day and interrupted play on the second, the third morning began with Essex scoring 101 in only 25 minutes as Wright and Morris tossed the ball up invitingly. Lilley smote four 6s and seven 4s while compiling 68 from 36 deliveries.

## Essex

| | | | |
|---|---|---|---|
| G. A. Gooch b Warner | 43 | | |
| B. R. Hardie c Marples b Newman | 17 | – (1) not out | 29 |
| P. J. Prichard c Roberts b Warner | 3 | | |
| K. S. McEwan c Hill b Newman | 26 | | |
| D. R. Pringle lbw b Warner | 0 | | |
| *K. W. R. Fletcher c Anderson b Miller | 52 | | |
| A. W. Lilley c Marples b Miller | 28 | – (2) not out | 68 |
| †D. E. East c Hill b Miller | 2 | | |
| N. A. Foster c Marples b Warner | 12 | | |
| J. K. Lever c Anderson b Warner | 4 | | |
| D. L. Acfield not out | 3 | | |
| L-b 4, n-b 5 | 9 | L-b 4 | 4 |
| 1/53 2/66 3/66 4/66 5/118 6/163 7/171 8/190 9/194 | 199 | (no wkt dec.) | 101 |

Bonus points – Essex 1, Derbyshire 4.

Bowling: *First Innings*—Warner 17.4–4–51–5; Newman 23–4–75–2; Miller 27–6–60–3; Finney 6.5–3–9–0; Barnett 0.1–0–0–0. *Second Innings*—Wright 6–0–42–0; Morris 5.1–0–55–0.

## Derbyshire

| | | | |
|---|---|---|---|
| I. S. Anderson not out | 1 | – run out | 39 |
| B. Roberts not out | 0 | – c Foster b Lever | 38 |
| A. Hill (did not bat) | | – c Pringle b Lever | 0 |
| J. E. Morris (did not bat) | | – b Foster | 4 |
| J. G. Wright (did not bat) | | – c Lever b Acfield | 10 |
| *K. J. Barnett (did not bat) | | – c Fletcher b Acfield | 0 |
| G. Miller (did not bat) | | – c Fletcher b Acfield | 105 |
| P. G. Newman (did not bat) | | – c Hardie b Acfield | 34 |
| A. E. Warner (did not bat) | | – c Prichard b Acfield | 8 |
| R. J. Finney (did not bat) | | – c Hardie b Acfield | 0 |
| †C. Marples (did not bat) | | – not out | 12 |
| | | B 7, l-b 5, n-b 1 | 13 |
| (no wkt dec.) | 1 | 1/47 2/47 3/53 4/68 5/68 6/141 7/222 8/246 9/249 | 263 |

Bowling: *First Innings*—Lever 2–1–1–0; Foster 1–1–0–0. *Second Innings*—Lever 23–7–53–2; Foster 19–5–81–1; Acfield 44.4–18–81–6; Pringle 9–0–36–0.

Umpires: D. S. Thompsett and A. G. T. Whitehead.

## ESSEX v SUSSEX

At Colchester, August 14, 15, 16. Drawn. Essex 3 pts, Sussex 7 pts. Toss won by Essex. The rain came to the rescue of Essex, still 80 in arrears with 35 overs remaining, to end a match in which Sussex always held the upper hand. Only Hardie and East came to terms with the hostility of le Roux in the home side's first innings, while Prichard returned to form in the second before the weather put paid to the visitors' hopes. The Sussex innings was built around the fifth Championship hundred of the season from Mendis, who remained unbeaten after six and a half hours of defiance, and the more robust efforts of Gould and le Roux.

## Essex

| | | | |
|---|---|---|---|
| B. R. Hardie c Reeve b Barclay | 74 | – b Barclay | 28 |
| C. Gladwin b Jones | 28 | – c Barclay b le Roux | 5 |
| P. J. Prichard c Barclay b Waller | 6 | – not out | 62 |
| †D. E. East c Green b le Roux | 42 | | |
| K. S. McEwan b Barclay | 0 | – (4) not out | 6 |
| D. R. Pringle c Gould b le Roux | 3 | | |
| *K. W. R. Fletcher b le Roux | 3 | | |
| A. W. Lilley b le Roux | 2 | | |
| N. A. Foster lbw b le Roux | 3 | | |
| J. K. Lever not out | 3 | | |
| D. L. Acfield c A. P. Wells b le Roux | 0 | | |
| B 6, l-b 7, n-b 7 | 20 | L-b 6, w 4, n-b 5 | 15 |
| 1/76 2/103 3/136 4/136 5/147 6/151 7/157 8/161 9/184 | 184 | 1/20 2/66 (2 wkts) | 116 |

Bonus points – Essex 1, Sussex 4.

Bowling: *First Innings*—le Roux 15.4–4–46–6; Jones 15–2–42–1; Reeve 6–1–25–0; Waller 9–2–22–1; Barclay 17–3–36–2. *Second Innings*—le Roux 9.2–1–34–1; Jones 5–0–29–0; Reeve 2–0–7–0; Barclay 8–0–30–1; Green 2–0–10–0.

## Sussex

| | |
|---|---|
| G. D. Mendis not out . . . . . . . . . . . . . . . . 143 | D. A. Reeve b Foster . . . . . . . . . . . . . . . . 7 |
| A. M. Green b Acfield . . . . . . . . . . . . . . 46 | A. N. Jones not out . . . . . . . . . . . . . . . . 5 |
| N. J. Lenham lbw b Acfield . . . . . . . . . 1 | |
| C. M. Wells c Gladwin b Acfield . . . . . 4 | B 3, l-b 7, w 1, n-b 2 . . . . . . . . 13 |
| A. P. Wells c and b Lever . . . . . . . . . . . 18 | |
| †I. J. Gould c Fletcher b Acfield . . . . . . 78 | 1/79 2/81 3/91 (8 wkts dec.) 380 |
| G. S. le Roux run out . . . . . . . . . . . . . . . . 60 | 4/124 5/257 6/342 |
| *J. R. T. Barclay b Foster . . . . . . . . . . . 5 | 7/350 8/374 |

C. E. Waller did not bat.

Bonus points – Sussex 3, Essex 2 (Score at 100 overs: 288-5).

Bowling: Lever 25–6–78–1; Foster 25–3–93–2; Acfield 42–6–125–4; Pringle 25–6–74–0.

Umpires: D. S. Thompsett and A. G. T. Whitehead.

At Worcester, August 17, 19, 20. ESSEX drew with WORCESTERSHIRE.

## ESSEX v SURREY

At Chelmsford, August 24, 26, 27. Drawn. Essex 7 pts, Surrey 5 pts. Toss won by Essex. Set to score 306 in 59 overs, Essex called off the chase once Gooch departed for 94 made from 115 deliveries. In the first innings he had amassed an unbeaten 132, containing eighteen 4s and one 6, from 144 balls, and received fine support in century stands from McEwan and Fletcher. Despite fine bowling from Foster, Surrey claimed maximum batting points, thanks chiefly to Clinton and Doughty, while in the second innings Needham gorged himself against Lilley, Hardie and Fletcher to strike an undefeated 92, including sixteen 4s, from 85 balls.

### Surrey

| | | |
|---|---|---|
| A. R. Butcher c Gooch b Foster . . . . . . . . . . . . . | 38 | – c East b Foster . . . . . . . . . . . . . . 39 |
| G. S. Clinton c Foster b Gooch . . . . . . . . . . . . . . | 81 | |
| †A. J. Stewart c East b Foster . . . . . . . . . . . . . . . | 5 | – (4) st East b Fletcher . . . . . . . . . 42 |
| M. A. Lynch c East b Gooch . . . . . . . . . . . . . . . . | 1 | – (3) c Acfield b Foster . . . . . . . . . 68 |
| *T. E. Jesty c Pringle b Foster . . . . . . . . . . . . . . | 17 | |
| A. Needham c Foster b Gooch . . . . . . . . . . . . . . | 19 | – (5) not out . . . . . . . . . . . . . . . . . . 92 |
| D. B. Pauline c East b Foster . . . . . . . . . . . . . . . | 21 | – (2) lbw b Foster . . . . . . . . . . . . . . 11 |
| M. A. Feltham lbw b Foster . . . . . . . . . . . . . . . . | 8 | – (6) b Pringle . . . . . . . . . . . . . . . . . . 27 |
| R. J. Doughty not out . . . . . . . . . . . . . . . . . . . . . | 61 | – (7) c and b Acfield . . . . . . . . . . . 2 |
| P. I. Pocock not out . . . . . . . . . . . . . . . . . . . . . . | 35 | |
| B 5, l-b 10, w 1 . . . . . . . . . . . . . . . . . . . . | 16 | B 9, l-b 9, w 4 . . . . . . . . . 22 |
| 1/91 2/103 3/104 (8 wkts dec.) | 302 | 1/17 2/122 3/127 (6 wkts dec.) 303 |
| 4/164 5/171 6/197 | | 4/239 5/290 6/303 |
| 7/198 8/210 | | |

A. H. Gray did not bat.

Bonus points – Surrey 4, Essex 3.

Bowling: *First Innings*—Lever 16.2–1–67–0; Foster 24–4–69–5; Pringle 19–4–42–0; Gooch 27–6–88–3; Acfield 4–1–21–0. *Second Innings*—Lever 11–3–37–0; Foster 16–1–59–3; Pringle 3–0–16–1; Gooch 2–0–19–0; Acfield 9.3–1–31–1; Lilley 11–0–63–0; Hardie 3–0–25–0; Fletcher 4–0–35–1.

**Essex**

| | | | |
|---|---|---|---|
| G. A. Gooch not out | 132 | – b Pocock | 94 |
| B. R. Hardie c Stewart b Doughty | 11 | – c sub b Gray | 13 |
| P. J. Prichard c Gray b Doughty | 9 | – lbw b Doughty | 1 |
| K. S. McEwan c sub b Pocock | 64 | – b Doughty | 0 |
| D. R. Pringle c Stewart b Pocock | 5 | – c Lynch b Butcher | 44 |
| *K. W. R. Fletcher not out | 56 | – (7) not out | 4 |
| A. W. Lilley (did not bat) | | – (6) b Gray | 6 |
| †D. E. East (did not bat) | | – not out | 9 |
| B 12, l-b 5, w 1, n-b 5 | 23 | B 9, l-b 6, w 2, n-b 12 | 29 |
| 1/23 2/46 3/154 4/180 | (4 wkts dec.) 300 | 1/30 2/31 3/31 4/176 5/176 6/188 | (6 wkts) 200 |

N. A. Foster, J. K. Lever and D. L. Acfield did not bat.

Bonus points – Essex 4, Surrey 1.

Bowling: *First Innings*—Gray 16–0–65–0; Doughty 11–0–73–2; Pauline 12–2–52–0; Feltham 9–1–56–0; Pocock 13–1–37–2. *Second Innings*—Gray 17–6–72–2; Doughty 8–1–30–2; Feltham 2–0–18–0; Pauline 3–0–18–0; Butcher 6–1–15–1; Pocock 16–6–24–1; Needham 3–1–8–0.

Umpires: J. H. Hampshire and A. A. Jones.

At Bristol, August 28, 29, 30. ESSEX beat GLOUCESTERSHIRE by 65 runs.

At Edgbaston, August 31, September 2, 3. ESSEX drew with WARWICKSHIRE.

At Lord's, September 11, 12, 13. ESSEX drew with MIDDLESEX.

## ESSEX v YORKSHIRE

At Chelmsford, September 14, 16, 17. Essex won by an innings and 4 runs. Essex 24 pts, Yorkshire 3 pts. Toss won by Essex. After Lever had produced his best figures of the season, six for 47, Yorkshire's wayward attack was subjected to a furious assault from Gooch as Essex built up a first-innings lead of 282. His 142 contained 25 4s and one 6 and took his aggregate from his last six first-class innings to 728. East scored 50 of his 62 in boundaries as he and Fletcher dealt out further punishment. Although there was a defiant 88 from Moxon and a resolute 52 from Neil Hartley, Yorkshire's resistance ended shortly after lunch on the final day. Boycott was unable to bat in the second innings, having fractured a thumb in the John Player League match two days earlier.

## Yorkshire

| | | | |
|---|---|---|---|
| G. Boycott c McEwan b Lever | 19 | – absent injured | |
| M. D. Moxon lbw b Lever | 2 | – (1) c Pringle b Lever | 88 |
| R. J. Blakey c East b Lever | 14 | – (2) c Gooch b Pringle | 31 |
| J. D. Love b Topley | 61 | – (3) lbw b Topley | 16 |
| S. N. Hartley b Gooch | 0 | – (4) c Hardie b Pont | 52 |
| P. E. Robinson b Lever | 0 | – (5) lbw b Pringle | 2 |
| *†D. L. Bairstow lbw b Lever | 8 | – (6) lbw b Lever | 46 |
| P. Carrick c McEwan b Topley | 6 | – (7) run out | 6 |
| P. J. Hartley c East b Lever | 5 | – (8) c McEwan b Topley | 12 |
| C. Shaw not out | 6 | – (9) not out | 2 |
| S. D. Fletcher c and b Topley | 0 | – (10) c Prichard b Lever | 13 |
| L-b 6, w 1, n-b 3 | 10 | L-b 5, w 1, n-b 4 | 10 |
| 1/7 2/42 3/43 4/44 5/49 6/79 7/100 8/107 9/127 | 131 | 1/76 2/109 3/164 4/171 5/236 6/248 7/262 8/263 9/278 | 278 |

Bonus points – Essex 4.

Bowling: *First Innings*—Lever 22–6–47–6; Pont 2–0–9–0; Topley 13–3–36–3; Gooch 9–0–33–1. *Second Innings*—Lever 21–5–69–3; Pont 11–0–69–1; Topley 33–7–107–2; Pringle 14–5–28–2.

## Essex

| | |
|---|---|
| G. A. Gooch c and b S. N. Hartley | 142 |
| B. R. Hardie c Bairstow b Shaw | 4 |
| P. J. Prichard lbw b P. J. Hartley | 6 |
| K. S. McEwan b Fletcher | 33 |
| D. R. Pringle b Shaw | 23 |
| A. W. Lilley c sub b Carrick | 38 |
| *K. W. R. Fletcher c sub b Shaw | 66 |
| †D. E. East c Love b P. J. Hartley | 62 |
| I. L. Pont not out | 9 |
| B 3, l-b 12, w 1, n-b 14 | 30 |
| 1/34 2/41 3/171 4/215 5/246 6/293 7/379 8/413 (8 wkts dec.) | 413 |

T. D. Topley and J. K. Lever did not bat.

Bonus points – Essex 4, Yorkshire 3.

Bowling: Fletcher 26–1–92–1; P. J. Hartley 24–0–145–2; Shaw 19.1–7–90–3; S. N. Hartley 6–0–25–1; Carrick 14–2–46–1.

Umpires: J. Birkenshaw and P. B. Wight.

## GLAMORGAN

*Patron:* HRH The Prince of Wales
*President:* His Honour Judge Rowe Harding
*Chairman:* G. Craven
*Chairman, Cricket Committee:* D. W. Lewis
*Secretary:* P. G. Carling
Sophia Gardens, Cardiff CF1 9XR
(Telephone: 0222-43478)
*Captain:* 1985 – R. C. Ontong
*Coach:* A. Jones

Assorted disappointments illuminated the fortunes – or, more appropriately, misfortunes – of Glamorgan throughout the 1985 season. The most optimistic recognised that top place in the Britannic Assurance Championship during the opening weeks hardly represented a realistic guide to the difficult days ahead. Yet even the eternal pessimist could not have envisaged the catalogue of injuries that was to cause so much disruption.

Basically the first team relied on a nucleus of battle-hardened players and the critical structure of this was delicately defined. So the loss of John Steele, the vastly experienced left-arm spinner, for the second half of the summer after shattering the bone of the little finger on his right hand while attempting to hold a return catch, proved a devastating setback. At a stroke, the balance of Rodney Ontong's bowling resources was badly upset.

Further misfortune followed as a variety of injuries reduced the efficiency of Gregory Thomas, considered by many to be the fastest white bowler in Britain. Ankle, hip and hamstring injuries hampered his progress, though he had his spirits uplifted immeasurably after the season had ended with the news that he had been selected to tour the West Indies with England. The England selectors admitted they were "playing a hunch", and Thomas saw the opportunity as a lifeline to haul himself back after so much frustration. He had taken 25 wickets during the first six games, yet finished with only 39, costing 31.58 runs each.

There was no such happy ending to the season for Alan Lewis Jones. The left-hander, who had established himself as a regular opening batsman the previous year with five centuries and 1,811 runs, dislocated his right shoulder while diving to make a stop in the covers in the opening John Player Sunday League match. He never regained convincing form following a month's absence at a vital time, and he suffered a further dislocation when throwing in during practice before the final fixture in September. This meant his undergoing an operation at the end of October and a long period of rehabilitation.

Javed Miandad suffered a recurrence of a "mystery" back strain that kept him out of the team for most of August. Nevertheless, he scored more runs than any other Glamorgan batsman, and only Younis Ahmed (and occasionally he also was absent for miscellaneous reasons) finished above him in the county's averages. Their exploits against the Australians virtually rewrote the record books, the most notable being Javed's 200 not out as the highest Glamorgan innings against a touring team and the highest in a first-class match at Neath. Younis scored 118 in their unbroken stand of 306, the record fourth-wicket partnership for the county. His 177 against Middlesex was the highest innings by a Glamorgan player at Sophia Gardens and the worth of these two Pakistani batsmen was immense.

John Hopkins lost form and disappointingly failed to reach 1,000 runs. Some compensation came for him with the award of a benefit in 1986. The development of Hugh Morris as a confident left-handed batsman continued, while Geoff Holmes was awarded his cap as he re-emphasised his value to the side, the scorer of 1,000 runs, reliable in times of crises, and extremely useful with his seam bowling.

Then came Matthew Maynard late in August, promoted from the second team to see what a nineteen-year-old could do against Yorkshire at Swansea. It was a memorable day for him. He went from 84 to 102 with three successive hits for 6 back over the head of the bowler, Carrick. There can have been few more remarkable maiden centuries in first-class cricket. Players such as Javed and Younis had scored hundreds in their first games for the Welsh county, but had made centuries previously with other counties. Frank Pinch scored a century in 1921, but had made similar scores at minor county level before Glamorgan's elevation to first-class status in that year. So Maynard's performance was of special significance, and he was the youngest Glamorgan century-maker on début at nineteen years and six days, compared with M. J. Turnbull's twenty years and five months when he made 106 against Worcestershire in 1926.

Another outstanding success was Ontong in his first full season as captain. He proved a tough, uncompromising leader, accepting that he would make mistakes but never allowing his team to be intimidated. "Often the difference between us winning and losing was very slender, and I don't think other counties underrate us any more", he said. He became the first Glamorgan player to achieve the Sunday League double of 100 wickets and 2,000 runs and was voted the county's Player of the Year for the Apex Award and the £1,000 prize. However, his most memorable feat was his innings of 130 and a match analysis of thirteen for 106 at Trent Bridge. This record individual feat by a Glamorgan player included career-best bowling figures of eight for 67 in Nottinghamshire's second innings and surpassed the previous match best of 107 and ten for 57 by Len Muncer against Derbyshire at Chesterfield in 1951.

Terry Davies, making further progress with his neat wicket-keeping, Younis and Holmes were awarded their county caps, but Stephen Henderson left after scoring a valedictory century at Hove, and others to go were Steve Malone, Les McFarlane and Mark Price. Steve Barwick at his best was a dangerous quick bowler, though he took only 36 wickets compared with 50 the previous summer.

Neath Borough Council, in conjunction with Neath Development Partnership, sponsored the Glamorgan fixture with the Australians at The Gnoll, and though this caused a measure of controversy because a section of the membership considered Swansea the traditional venue for the touring team's fixture, the package deal was too lucrative to be turned down. It brought Glamorgan around £20,000. – J.B.

GLAMORGAN 1985

[*Bill Smith*

*Back row:* T. Davies, G. C. Holmes, S. P. Henderson, S. R. Barwick, S. J. Malone, J. G. Thomas, J. Derrick, B. Denning (*scorer*). *Front row:* Younis Ahmed, Javed Miandad, R. C. Ontong (*captain*), J. F. Steele, J. A. Hopkins. *Insets:* A. L. Jones, H. Morris.

## GLAMORGAN RESULTS

*All first-class matches – Played 27: Won 4, Lost 4, Drawn 19.*

*County Championship matches – Played 24: Won 4, Lost 4, Drawn 16.*

*Bonus points – Batting 41, Bowling 50.*

*Competition placings – Britannic Assurance County Championship, 12th; NatWest Bank Trophy, q-f; Benson and Hedges Cup, 3rd in Group D; John Player League, 14th eq.*

## BRITANNIC ASSURANCE CHAMPIONSHIP AVERAGES

### BATTING

| | *Birthplace* | *M* | *I* | *NO* | *R* | *HI* | *Avge* |
|---|---|---|---|---|---|---|---|
| ‡Younis Ahmed | *Jullundur, Pakistan* | 20 | 28 | 7 | 1,190 | 177 | 56.66 |
| ‡Javed Miandad | *Karachi, Pakistan* | 18 | 27 | 5 | 1,194 | 164* | 54.27 |
| ‡R. C. Ontong | *Johannesburg, SA* | 24 | 29 | 7 | 1,105 | 130 | 50.22 |
| ‡G. C. Holmes | *Newcastle upon Tyne* | 24 | 36 | 3 | 1,062 | 112 | 32.18 |
| ‡T. Davies | *St Albans* | 24 | 24 | 7 | 457 | 75 | 26.88 |
| S. P. Henderson | *Oxford* | 6 | 10 | 2 | 207 | 111 | 25.87 |
| H. Morris | *Cardiff* | 13 | 16 | 4 | 305 | 62 | 25.41 |
| ‡A. L. Jones | *Alltwen* | 16 | 23 | 2 | 521 | 75 | 24.80 |
| ‡J. F. Steele | *Stafford* | 10 | 11 | 3 | 183 | 48 | 22.87 |
| ‡J. A. Hopkins | *Maesteg* | 20 | 30 | 2 | 626 | 114* | 22.35 |
| J. G. Thomas | *Trebanos* | 14 | 15 | 2 | 266 | 60* | 20.46 |
| M. R. Price | *Liverpool* | 12 | 9 | 3 | 98 | 36 | 16.33 |
| J. Derrick | *Cwmaman* | 13 | 14 | 2 | 156 | 52 | 13.00 |
| I. Smith | *Chopwell* | 5 | 4 | 0 | 27 | 12 | 6.75 |
| L. L. McFarlane | *Portland, Jamaica* | 11 | 4 | 2 | 12 | 8 | 6.00 |
| S. R. Barwick | *Neath* | 21 | 15 | 5 | 57 | 29 | 5.70 |
| S. J. Malone | *Chelmsford* | 7 | 4 | 1 | 0 | 0* | 0.00 |

Also batted: M. P. Maynard (*Oldham*) (4 matches) 102, 58, 38; P. D. North (*Newport*) (1 match) 0; S. P. James (*Lydney*) (1 match) did not bat.

* *Signifies not out.* ‡ *Denotes county cap.*

The following played a total of thirteen three-figure innings for Glamorgan in County Championship matches – Javed Miandad 3, Younis Ahmed 3, G. C. Holmes 2, R. C. Ontong 2, S. P. Henderson 1, J. A. Hopkins 1, M. P. Maynard 1.

### BOWLING

| | *O* | *M* | *R* | *W* | *BB* | *Avge* |
|---|---|---|---|---|---|---|
| R. C. Ontong | 563.5 | 137 | 1,726 | 62 | 8-67 | 27.83 |
| J. G. Thomas | 298.3 | 43 | 1,104 | 34 | 4-61 | 32.47 |
| S. R. Barwick | 464 | 95 | 1,345 | 36 | 7-43 | 37.36 |
| M. R. Price | 239.4 | 59 | 616 | 16 | 4-97 | 38.50 |
| J. Derrick | 211.1 | 37 | 650 | 14 | 4-60 | 46.42 |
| G. C. Holmes | 313.3 | 73 | 962 | 20 | 3-25 | 48.10 |
| J. F. Steele | 180.1 | 45 | 498 | 10 | 3-6 | 49.80 |
| L. L. McFarlane | 219 | 35 | 886 | 14 | 4-100 | 63.28 |

Also bowled: S. P. Henderson 8–2–31–0; J. A. Hopkins 6–1–22–0; Javed Miandad 27.3–2–120–3; A. L. Jones 1–0–24–0; S. J. Malone 129–12–517–9; M. P. Maynard 0.1–0–4–0; H. Morris 3–0–32–0; P. D. North 27–7–60–1; I. Smith 38.4–10–117–1; Younis Ahmed 67.4–19–158–2.

At The Parks, April 24, 25, 26. GLAMORGAN drew with OXFORD UNIVERSITY.

At The Oval, April 27, 28, 29. GLAMORGAN beat SURREY by seven wickets.

At Taunton, May 1, 2, 3. GLAMORGAN beat SOMERSET by nine wickets.

At Edgbaston, May 8, 9, 10. GLAMORGAN drew with WARWICKSHIRE.

## GLAMORGAN v MIDDLESEX

At Cardiff, May 22, 23, 24. Drawn. Glamorgan 2 pts, Middlesex 7 pts. Toss won by Glamorgan. Glamorgan having won two of their first three matches to head the Championship table, this was their first searching test. They made an immediate inroad, but Radley, as so often against Glamorgan, rallied the innings with 127 in 267 minutes, which not only enabled Gatting to declare but later to enforce the follow-on after the home side had collapsed against the pace of Cowans and Fraser. Glamorgan fought a dogged rearguard action, with rain to help them on the final morning, and went on to their highest total against Middlesex, their highest total at Sophia Gardens and their largest second innings in post-war cricket. Younis Ahmed's 177 in five and a quarter hours was the highest by a Glamorgan batsman at Sophia Gardens.

### Middlesex

| | |
|---|---|
| G. D. Barlow c Davies b Thomas | 4 |
| W. N. Slack run out | 19 |
| *M. W. Gatting b Thomas | 13 |
| R. O. Butcher c Miandad b Barwick | 23 |
| C. T. Radley b Thomas | 127 |
| †P. R. Downton c Henderson b Ontong | 67 |
| J. E. Emburey not out | 30 |
| P. H. Edmonds c Davies b Thomas | 0 |
| B 6, l-b 2, w 2, n-b 4 | 14 |
| 1/4 2/28 3/67 4/67 5/229 6/297 7/297 (7 wkts dec.) | 297 |

A. R. C. Fraser, N. G. Cowans and W. W. Daniel did not bat.

Bonus points – Middlesex 3, Glamorgan 2 (Score at 100 overs: 290-5).

Bowling: Thomas 18.3–2–61–4; Barwick 21–4–40–1; Holmes 9–4–29–0; Steele 24–4–67–0; Derrick 16–5–36–0; Ontong 16–5–56–1.

### Glamorgan

| | | | |
|---|---|---|---|
| J. A. Hopkins c Radley b Cowans | 9 | – lbw b Fraser | 3 |
| G. C. Holmes lbw b Cowans | 1 | – c Downton b Edmonds | 58 |
| Younis Ahmed c Downton b Daniel | 15 | – c Slack b Radley | 177 |
| J. Derrick b Daniel | 5 | | |
| Javed Miandad not out | 35 | – (4) b Edmonds | 95 |
| S. P. Henderson lbw b Cowans | 17 | – not out | 27 |
| *R. C. Ontong b Cowans | 3 | – not out | 22 |
| J. F. Steele c Gatting b Cowans | 3 | | |
| J. G. Thomas c Gatting b Fraser | 5 | | |
| †T. Davies c Downton b Fraser | 0 | – (5) c and b Radley | 75 |
| S. R. Barwick b Fraser | 4 | | |
| B 8, l-b 2, w 1, n-b 3 | 14 | B 4, l-b 8, w 2, n-b 7 | 21 |
| 1/6 2/34 3/34 4/58 5/79 6/85 7/96 8/107 9/107 | 111 | 1/29 2/121 3/299 4/399 5/445 (5 wkts dec.) | 478 |

Bonus points – Middlesex 4.

Bowling: *First Innings*—Daniel 10–1–38–2; Cowans 12–1–56–5; Fraser 2.5–0–7–3. *Second Innings*—Cowans 8–1–31–0; Daniel 21–6–57–0; Gatting 11–5–33–0; Fraser 17–3–64–1; Edmonds 41–11–106–2; Emburey 36–9–89–0; Radley 11–3–38–2; Slack 7–1–21–0; Downton 8–6–5–0; Butcher 7–3–8–0; Barlow 3–0–14–0.

Umpires: J. W. Holder and J. A. Jameson.

At Southampton, May 25, 27, 28. GLAMORGAN lost to HAMPSHIRE by three wickets.

At Hove, May 29, 30, 31. GLAMORGAN lost to SUSSEX by nine wickets.

## GLAMORGAN v WORCESTERSHIRE

At Abergavenny, June 8, 10, 11. Drawn. Glamorgan 7 pts, Worcestershire 3 pts. Toss won by Glamorgan. A stomach virus struck down six Worcestershire players, and with two others injured they finished with only three fully fit men and were unable to declare on the last day. The situation was explained over the public address system after a section of the small crowd had vented their disapproval of the visitors' batting on, and with their last two fit players at the wicket, rain at the tea interval put an end to Worcestershire's embarrassment. Hopkins (197 balls) and Holmes (189 balls) each scored a century before Glamorgan closed their first innings without losing a wicket. It was Holmes's first century for six years and his highest score. Kapil Dev, though handicapped by a swollen knee, struck six 6s and six 4s in making a colourful 92 off 108 deliveries against an assortment of bowlers.

### Worcestershire

| | | | |
|---|---|---|---|
| T. S. Curtis c Steele b Malone | 30 | – c Henderson b Miandad | 51 |
| D. B. D'Oliveira run out | 5 | – lbw b Barwick | 31 |
| D. M. Smith c Malone b Ontong | 55 | | |
| *P. A. Neale c McFarlane b Holmes | 77 | | |
| D. N. Patel c Davies b Barwick | 0 | – (3) b Miandad | 67 |
| M. J. Weston st Davies b Ontong | 16 | – (4) c Malone b Ontong | 36 |
| Kapil Dev lbw b McFarlane | 22 | – (5) b Steele | 92 |
| †S. J. Rhodes not out | 32 | – (6) c and b Steele | 7 |
| R. K. Illingworth c Hopkins b Holmes | 6 | – (7) not out | 15 |
| N. V. Radford lbw b Holmes | 16 | – (8) not out | 0 |
| J. D. Inchmore run out | 18 | | |
| B 8, l-b 5, n-b 4 | 17 | B 2, l-b 1, w 2, n-b 5 | 10 |
| 1/15 2/69 3/125 4/134 5/157 6/189 7/224 8/232 9/266 | 294 | 1/55 2/122 3/175 4/200 5/224 6/308 | (6 wkts) 309 |

Bonus points – Worcestershire 3, Glamorgan 4.

Bowling: *First Innings*—McFarlane 25–3–81–1; Barwick 26–4–78–1; Ontong 24–11–48–2; Malone 9–1–38–1; Holmes 12.1–3–36–3. *Second Innings*—McFarlane 10–5–18–0; Barwick 10–2–31–1; Ontong 17–5–66–1; Steele 25–9–44–2; Malone 3–0–5–0; Younis 12–2–35–0; Miandad 12–0–67–2; Hopkins 2–1–9–0; Henderson 8–2–31–0.

### Glamorgan

| | |
|---|---|
| J. A. Hopkins not out | 114 |
| G. C. Holmes not out | 106 |
| B 8, l-b 18, n-b 4 | 30 |
| (no wkt dec.) | 250 |

Younis Ahmed, Javed Miandad, S. P. Henderson, *R. C. Ontong, J. F. Steele, †T. Davies, L. L. McFarlane, S. R. Barwick and S. J. Malone did not bat.

Bonus points – Glamorgan 3.

Bowling: Kapil Dev 7–1–29–0; Radford 11–1–50–0; Illingworth 12–2–40–0; Inchmore 6–0–18–0; Weston 14.1–3–41–0; Patel 16–1–46–0.

Umpires: J. H. Harris and J. W. Holder.

## GLAMORGAN v ESSEX

At Swansea, June 15, 17, 18. Drawn. Glamorgan 2 pts, Essex 4 pts. Toss won by Glamorgan. Rain on the second day compelled declarations on the third if a result were to be achieved, but these led to the match finishing acrimoniously with disagreement between the captains. Essex made no attempt to attack the target of 309 off around 70 overs, claiming that an arrangement had been made for a figure of 280 from 63 overs and that Glamorgan had broken that agreement. Essex closed their first innings at their overnight score, 94 runs behind, and fed Glamorgan's batsmen with quick overs; too quick for Ontong's liking, and he considered that Essex were making more time for themselves by hastening the arrival of the agreed 280. Consequently he re-adjusted to balance the equation. Foster brought about the collapse of the home first innings, despite Steele's two hours of defiance; but thereafter runs often came easily off bowlers using up time.

### Glamorgan

| First innings | | Second innings | |
|---|---|---|---|
| J. A. Hopkins c East b Lever | 15 | c Acfield b Lilley | 60 |
| G. C. Holmes c Pringle b Foster | 34 | st East b Lilley | 92 |
| Younis Ahmed c East b Foster | 46 | c Childs b Lilley | 44 |
| Javed Miandad c Lilley b Acfield | 7 | | |
| S. P. Henderson c Hardie b Lever | 2 | not out | 0 |
| *R. C. Ontong b Pringle | 29 | (4) not out | 10 |
| J. F. Steele hit wkt b Foster | 20 | | |
| †T. Davies c Fletcher b Acfield | 4 | | |
| J. G. Thomas lbw b Foster | 7 | | |
| S. R. Barwick not out | 1 | | |
| S. J. Malone lbw b Foster | 0 | | |
| L-b 2, n-b 6 | 8 | B 6, l-b 2 | 8 |
| 1/44 2/50 3/80 4/106 5/114 6/145 7/159 8/172 9/173 | 173 | 1/108 2/191 3/214 (3 wkts dec.) | 214 |

Bonus points – Glamorgan 1, Essex 4.

Bowling: *First Innings*—Lever 16–2–51–2; Foster 22–8–40–5; Pringle 17–7–31–1; Acfield 15–6–34–2; Childs 12–5–15–0. *Second Innings*—Lever 4–0–15–0; Foster 4–1–6–0; Lilley 17.4–0–116–3; Childs 17–4–69–0.

### Essex

| First innings | | Second innings | |
|---|---|---|---|
| B. R. Hardie c Steele b Ontong | 25 | c Davies b Thomas | 3 |
| C. Gladwin c Davies b Thomas | 8 | not out | 92 |
| A. W. Lilley c Steele b Ontong | 9 | b Ontong | 16 |
| J. K. Lever not out | 16 | | |
| K. S. McEwan not out | 13 | (4) not out | 63 |
| B 1, l-b 1, w 5, n-b 1 | 8 | L-b 4, n-b 7 | 11 |
| 1/19 2/49 3/54 (3 wkts dec.) | 79 | 1/6 2/41 (2 wkts) | 185 |

*K. W. R. Fletcher, D. R. Pringle, †D. E. East, N. A. Foster, J. H. Childs and D. L. Acfield did not bat.

Bonus points – Glamorgan 1.

Bowling: *First Innings*—Thomas 14–3–45–1; Barwick 11.3–4–14–0; Steele 7–2–8–0; Ontong 3–0–10–2. *Second Innings*—Thomas 9–1–25–1; Barwick 4–2–4–0; Ontong 18–7–43–1; Malone 12–1–48–0; Steele 10–5–11–0; Miandad 12–2–37–0; Hopkins 4–0–13–0.

Umpires: R. Palmer and R. A. White.

At Swansea, June 19, 20, 21. GLAMORGAN drew with ZIMBABWEANS (See Zimbabwean tour section).

At Leicester, June 22, 24, 25. GLAMORGAN drew with LEICESTERSHIRE.

## GLAMORGAN v SOMERSET

At Cardiff, June 26, 27, 28. Drawn. Glamorgan 4 pts, Somerset 7 pts. Toss won by Somerset. After Somerset had recorded their highest total on a Welsh ground, passing the 408 at Swansea in 1921 (Glamorgan's inaugural year as a first-class county), this match became an absorbing contest as the home side fought to avoid the follow-on. Richards hit two 6s, one over the pavilion, and ten 4s in making 100 off 112 deliveries, and Popplewell, Felton and Roebuck also batted attractively. Glamorgan, held together by Javed (107 from 203 balls) and Younis, seemed to have no answer to Garner until Davies and Barwick put on 46 for the eighth wicket with a mixture of Davies's wristy strokes and Barwick's top-edges, so saving Steele, who had broken the small finger of his right hand attempting a return catch, from having to bat.

### Somerset

| | | | |
|---|---|---|---|
| N. F. M. Popplewell c sub b Ontong | 84 | – not out | 3 |
| P. M. Roebuck c Davies b Barwick | 59 | – not out | 2 |
| N. A. Felton b Ontong | 60 | | |
| I. V. A. Richards c Younis b McFarlane | 100 | | |
| R. E. Hayward not out | 57 | | |
| *V. J. Marks hit wkt b Ontong | 39 | | |
| J. Garner c sub b Ontong | 6 | | |
| M. S. Turner c Davies b Derrick | 6 | | |
| B 3, l-b 16, n-b 1 | 20 | N-b 2 | 2 |
| 1/142 2/156 3/311 4/323 5/403 6/413 7/431 | (7 wkts dec.) 431 | | (no wkt) 7 |

R. L. Ollis, †T. Gard and M. R. Davis did not bat.

Bonus points – Somerset 4, Glamorgan 1 (Score at 100 overs: 345-4).

Bowling: *First Innings*—McFarlane 20–3–78–1; Barwick 22–4–62–1; Holmes 14.1–4–42–0; Ontong 37–9–125–4; Derrick 20.3–1–81–1; Steele 2.5–0–24–0. *Second Innings*—McFarlane 2–0–5–0; Barwick 1–0–2–0.

### Glamorgan

| | |
|---|---|
| J. A. Hopkins lbw b Garner | 0 |
| A. L. Jones lbw b Davis | 15 |
| G. C. Holmes lbw b Garner | 17 |
| Javed Miandad b Garner | 107 |
| Younis Ahmed b Marks | 45 |
| *R. C. Ontong c Gard b Turner | 5 |
| †T. Davies not out | 50 |
| J. Derrick b Garner | 5 |
| S. R. Barwick b Richards | 29 |
| L. L. McFarlane b Garner | 8 |
| B 1, l-b 4, w 1, n-b 2 | 8 |
| 1/0 2/23 3/42 4/127 5/167 6/204 7/214 8/260 9/289 | (9 wkts dec.) 289 |

J. F. Steele did not bat.

Bonus points – Glamorgan 3, Somerset 3 (Score at 100 overs: 255-7).

Bowling: Garner 27.4–11–46–5; Davis 23–7–58–1; Turner 19–4–52–1; Richards 10–1–40–1; Marks 35–11–88–1.

Umpires: R. Julian and R. A. White.

At Derby, June 29, July 1, 2. GLAMORGAN lost to DERBYSHIRE by ten wickets.

## GLAMORGAN v NOTTINGHAMSHIRE

At Swansea, July 6, 8, 9. Drawn. Glamorgan 5 pts, Nottinghamshire 6 pts. Toss won by Nottinghamshire. A century in each innings by Robinson, the first time a visiting batsman had accomplished this feat at the St Helen's ground, enabled Nottinghamshire to declare twice. But Glamorgan saved the follow-on in their first innings with their bowlers, Thomas and Price, batting forcefully; and in the second innings they staged another recovery after being set to score 280 from a minimum of 58 overs. Robinson's 103 off 210 deliveries was followed by an unbeaten 130 from 153, the first time he had scored two hundreds in a match. Younis Ahmed and Davies prevented a threatened Glamorgan collapse.

### Nottinghamshire

| | | | |
|---|---|---|---|
| R. T. Robinson c Younis b McFarlane | 103 | not out | 130 |
| B. C. Broad c sub b Derrick | 37 | | |
| D. W. Randall b Thomas | 16 | (4) not out | 63 |
| *C. E. B. Rice c Davies b McFarlane | 27 | | |
| P. Johnson b Price | 1 | | |
| R. J. Hadlee not out | 53 | | |
| †B. N. French run out | 10 | (2) c Holmes b Thomas | 12 |
| E. E. Hemmings not out | 56 | (3) b Thomas | 12 |
| L-b 3, w 4, n-b 11 | 18 | L-b 3, w 1, n-b 9 | 13 |
| 1/109 2/140 3/187 4/196 5/196 6/207 | (6 wkts dec.) 321 | 1/24 2/42 | (2 wkts dec.) 230 |

P. M. Such, K. Saxelby and K. E. Cooper did not bat.

Bonus points – Nottinghamshire 3, Glamorgan 2 (Score at 100 overs: 290-6).

Bowling: *First Innings*—Thomas 20–2–76–1; McFarlane 16–5–42–2; Holmes 9–1–31–0; Derrick 21–2–69–1; Price 27–5–62–1; Ontong 15–4–38–0. *Second Innings*—Thomas 10–1–48–2; McFarlane 10–1–35–0; Derrick 6–0–33–0; Holmes 8–2–15–0; Ontong 14–4–49–0; Price 7–0–47–0.

### Glamorgan

| | | | |
|---|---|---|---|
| A. L. Jones b Hadlee | 17 | b Hadlee | 0 |
| †T. Davies c French b Cooper | 22 | (7) not out | 44 |
| G. C. Holmes c Johnson b Hadlee | 3 | c Hadlee b Saxelby | 12 |
| Javed Miandad c Hadlee b Saxelby | 1 | b Saxelby | 4 |
| Younis Ahmed c French b Saxelby | 39 | not out | 81 |
| H. Morris c French b Cooper | 39 | (2) c and b Such | 27 |
| *R. C. Ontong c Johnson b Such | 31 | (6) c French b Cooper | 1 |
| J. Derrick c Randall b Rice | 13 | | |
| J. G. Thomas not out | 60 | | |
| M. R. Price b Cooper | 36 | | |
| L. L. McFarlane not out | 1 | | |
| L-b 6, w 2, n-b 2 | 10 | L-b 2, w 2 | 4 |
| 1/25 2/29 3/36 4/56 5/110 6/133 7/166 8/171 9/263 | (9 wkts dec.) 272 | 1/0 2/19 3/23 4/62 5/63 | (5 wkts) 173 |

Bonus points – Glamorgan 3, Nottinghamshire 3 (Score at 100 overs: 259-8).

Bowling: *First Innings*—Hadlee 19–4–39–2; Saxelby 27–7–56–2; Hemmings 12–3–39–0; Such 13–5–40–1; Cooper 23–5–56–3; Rice 12–2–36–1. *Second Innings*—Hadlee 11–3–22–1; Saxelby 15–1–54–2; Cooper 11–4–28–1; Such 13–4–35–1; Hemmings 13–5–32–0.

Umpires: C. Cook and P. B. Wight.

## GLAMORGAN v LEICESTERSHIRE

At Swansea, July 10, 11, 12. Drawn. Glamorgan 4 pts, Leicestershire 5 pts. Toss won by Glamorgan. Javed and Younis rallied Glamorgan's cause in the second match of the Swansea Festival Week, but rain reduced the playing time on each of the last two days and consequently Leicestershire batted through because there was insufficient time to set a target. Balderstone and Whitaker scored centuries; Whitaker's 103 (fifteen 4s) being his third hundred in four Championship innings, while his partnership of 144 with Briers was a record for Leicestershire's fifth wicket against Glamorgan. Price, the Glamorgan left-arm spinner, recorded his best figures with four for 97 in the course of 52 overs.

### Glamorgan

A. L. Jones b Ferris . . . . . . . . . . . . . . . . 8
H. Morris c Balderstone b Clift . . . . . . . 12
G. C. Holmes run out . . . . . . . . . . . . . . . 23
Javed Miandad c Butcher b Clift . . . . . 89
Younis Ahmed st Garnham b Cook . . . 58
*R. C. Ontong not out . . . . . . . . . . . . . . . 56
†T. Davies b Ferris . . . . . . . . . . . . . . . . . . 10
J. Derrick not out . . . . . . . . . . . . . . . . . . . 22
L-b 3, w 1, n-b 7 . . . . . . . . . . . 11

1/15 2/25 3/97 4/162 5/211 6/228 (6 wkts dec.) 289

J. G. Thomas, M. R. Price and L. L. McFarlane did not bat.

Bonus points – Glamorgan 3, Leicestershire 2 (Score at 100 overs: 279-6).

Bowling: Taylor 17–3–22–0; Ferris 21.3–3–76–2; Clift 18–3–51–2; Willey 17–3–58–0; Cook 28–10–79–1.

### Leicestershire

I. P. Butcher c Ontong b Price . . . . . . . 72
J. C. Balderstone c Davies b Price . . . .101
R. A. Cobb c Miandad b Ontong . . . . . 4
*P. Willey c and b Ontong . . . . . . . . . . . 20
J. J. Whitaker b McFarlane . . . . . . . . . .103
N. E. Briers c Miandad b Price . . . . . . . 36
†M. A. Garnham not out . . . . . . . . . . . . . 18
N. G. B. Cook b Price . . . . . . . . . . . . . . 5
P. B. Clift not out . . . . . . . . . . . . . . . . . . . 4
B 8, l-b 7, w 2, n-b 13 . . . . . . . 30

1/168 2/177 3/211 4/211 5/355 6/361 7/382 (7 wkts) 393

L. B. Taylor and G. J. F. Ferris did not bat.

Bonus points – Leicestershire 3, Glamorgan 1 (Score at 100 overs: 285-4).

Bowling: Thomas 20.2–6–57–0; McFarlane 20–2–95–1; Holmes 9–2–27–0; Derrick 9–1–27–0; Price 52–20–97–4; Ontong 31–8–66–2; Younis 12–8–9–0.

Umpires: C. Cook and P. B. Wight.

At Old Trafford, July 13, 15, 16. GLAMORGAN drew with LANCASHIRE.

At Neath, July 20, 21, 22. GLAMORGAN drew with AUSTRALIANS (See Australian tour section).

At Worcester, July 24, 25, 26. GLAMORGAN drew with WORCESTERSHIRE.

At Bristol, July 27, 29. 30. GLAMORGAN drew with GLOUCESTERSHIRE.

## GLAMORGAN v KENT

At Swansea, August 3, 4, 5. Drawn. Glamorgan 3 pts, Kent 3 pts. Toss won by Kent. The captains took positive action to create an interesting finish after rain had washed out the second day, Glamorgan's first innings and Kent's second being forfeited so that Glamorgan were set to score 252 from 56 overs. Thomas, their fast bowler, had broken down with a torn hamstring, and when Javed Miandad retired hurt with a serious muscle spasm in his back at 97 for four, Glamorgan effectively had only four wickets left; but Ontong and Morris added 85 in fifteen colourful overs before heavy rain intervened yet again.

### Kent

| | |
|---|---|
| *M. R. Benson c Davies b Holmes | 35 |
| S. G. Hinks c Morris b Holmes | 36 |
| C. J. Tavaré c Jones b Ontong | 9 |
| N. R. Taylor c Miandad b Barwick | 33 |
| L. Potter b Holmes | 11 |
| E. A. E. Baptiste c Davies b Younis | 52 |
| R. M. Ellison c and b Miandad | 33 |
| G. R. Cowdrey not out | 29 |
| C. Penn not out | 4 |
| B 3, l-b 1, n-b 5 | 9 |
| 1/57 2/82 3/86 4/117 5/172 6/180 7/247 (7 wkts dec.) | 251 |

†S. N. V. Waterton and D. L. Underwood did not bat.

Bonus points – Kent 3, Glamorgan 3.

Bowling: Thomas 8–2–28–0; Barwick 17–4–45–1; Ontong 20–6–39–1; Holmes 25–11–49–3; Younis 15–4–38–1; Miandad 3.3–0–16–1; Morris 3–0–32–0.

*Kent forfeited their second innings.*

### Glamorgan

*Glamorgan forfeited their first innings.*

| | |
|---|---|
| J. A. Hopkins c Waterton b Baptiste | 15 |
| A. L. Jones c Waterton b Ellison | 19 |
| G. C. Holmes c Waterton b Baptiste | 10 |
| Javed Miandad retired hurt | 22 |
| Younis Ahmed b Baptiste | 18 |
| H. Morris lbw b Potter | 38 |
| *R. C. Ontong c Tavaré b Potter | 57 |
| M. R. Price not out | 14 |
| †T. Davies not out | 9 |
| L-b 1, n-b 7 | 8 |
| 1/31 2/48 3/53 4/77 5/182 6/191 (6 wkts) | 210 |

J. G. Thomas and S. R. Barwick did not bat.

Bowling: Ellison 7–0–27–1; Baptiste 15–2–47–3; Underwood 18–3 80 0; Penn 5–0–26–0; Potter 4.5–0–29–2.

Umpires: J. H. Hampshire and R. Palmer.

## GLAMORGAN v WARWICKSHIRE

At Cardiff, August 10, 12, 13. Drawn. Glamorgan 4 pts, Warwickshire 2 pts. Toss won by Warwickshire. Amiss prevented a threatened rout after the first three wickets had fallen for 4 runs, batting with admirable temperament and technique on the opening day of the Cardiff Cricket Festival, which sadly was to be victim to the wet weather. Barwick found movement in the air and off the seam to return the best figures of the season by a Glamorgan bowler, but only seven balls were bowled on the second day and the last day was lost completely.

### Warwickshire

R. I. H. B. Dyer c Davies b Barwick .. 0
G. J. Lord c Ontong b McFarlane .... 4
A. I. Kallicharran lbw b Barwick ..... 0
D. L. Amiss c Jones b Ontong ........ 77
†G. W. Humpage c Davies b Derrick .. 36
P. A. Smith lbw b Barwick .......... 34
A. M. Ferreira c and b Barwick ...... 3
C. M. Old c and b Barwick .......... 33
G. C. Small c Davies b Barwick ...... 6
A. R. K. Pierson c McFarlane b Barwick 4
*N. Gifford not out ................. 1
B 9, l-b 5, n-b 8 ............ 22

1/0 2/4 3/4 4/74 5/168 6/176 7/180 8/214 9/217 — 220

Bonus points – Warwickshire 2, Glamorgan 4.

Bowling: Barwick 20.5–6–43–7; McFarlane 9–1–42–1; Derrick 15–1–47–1; Holmes 11–2–32–0; Ontong 13–3–42–1.

### Glamorgan

J. A. Hopkins c Humpage b Small .... 13
A. L. Jones not out ................. 38
G. C. Holmes lbw b Ferreira ......... 13
Younis Ahmed not out ............... 28
B 1, l-b 4 ..................... 5

1/30 2/54 (2 wkts) 97

H. Morris, *R. C. Ontong, M. R. Price, †T. Davies, J. Derrick, L. L. McFarlane and S. R. Barwick did not bat.

Bowling: Small 11.1–3–19–1; Old 13–3–30–0; Ferreira 9–2–27–1; Gifford 9–4–14–0; Pierson 2–1–2–0.

Umpires: J. Birkenshaw and B. J. Meyer.

## GLAMORGAN v HAMPSHIRE

At Cardiff, August 14, 15, 16. Glamorgan won by five wickets. Glamorgan 17 pts, Hampshire 3 pts. Toss won by Glamorgan. After no play on the first day and only 67 overs on the second, the captains brought the game back to life by each forfeiting an innings on the final day. So Glamorgan set off in pursuit of a target of 271 runs from 89 overs, which proved no difficult task once Younis Ahmed and Ontong had countered the opposition's early command. They added a decisive 172, Younis reaching his fifth century of the season off 128 deliveries and finishing unbeaten with 143 (one 6, fourteen 4s). He was awarded his county cap, having previously been capped by Surrey and Worcestershire.

### Hampshire

C. G. Greenidge lbw b McFarlane .... 77
*V. P. Terry b Derrick .............. 28
R. A. Smith lbw b Price ............. 68
J. J. E. Hardy not out ............... 64
D. R. Turner not out ............... 22
B 4, l-b 3, n-b 4 ............ 11

1/90 2/123 3/223 (3 wkts dec.) 270

M. D. Marshall, N. G. Cowley, T. M. Tremlett, †R. J. Parks, R. J. Maru and C. A. Connor did not bat.

Bonus points – Hampshire 3, Glamorgan 1.

Bowling: Barwick 10–1–36–0; McFarlane 14–5–49–1; Derrick 15–3–37–1; Holmes 9–2–20–0; Price 19–2–82–1; Ontong 13–5–39–0.

*Hampshire forfeited their second innings.*

## Glamorgan

*Glamorgan forfeited their first innings.*

A. L. Jones lbw b Marshall .......... 0
J. A. Hopkins c Turner b Maru ...... 13
G. C. Holmes b Cowley ............. 18
Younis Ahmed not out ..............143
H. Morris c Maru b Cowley .......... 0
*R. C. Ontong c Connor b Cowley .... 69
J. Derrick not out ................... 13
B 2, l-b 8, n-b 5 ............ 15

1/1 2/24 3/69 4/75 5/247 (5 wkts) 271

M. R. Price, †T. Davies, L. L. McFarlane and S. R. Barwick did not bat.

Bowling: Marshall 20–6–36–1; Connor 8–1–25–0; Maru 30–2–112–1; Tremlett 10–3–33–0; Cowley 15–1–53–3; Smith 0.4–0–2–0.

Umpires: J. Birkenshaw and B. J. Meyer.

At Wellingborough, August 17, 19, 20. GLAMORGAN drew with NORTHAMPTONSHIRE.

## GLAMORGAN v YORKSHIRE

At Swansea, August 24, 26, 27. Yorkshire won by 34 runs. Yorkshire 18 pts, Glamorgan 3 pts. Toss won by Yorkshire. Yet another instance of manipulation on the final day to overcome the weather saw Yorkshire win in an eventful climax after forfeiting their second innings. Carrick made 92 in 133 minutes with adventurous hitting (three 6s, eleven 4s) low in the order and then took seven for 99 to win the match on an old-fashioned St Helen's slow turner. Glamorgan, set to score 272 at a tempting 2.59 runs per over, initially appeared capable of succeeding as Morris and Holmes put on 92 for the second wicket. But then Carrick instituted the collapse, although Maynard played an historic innings. At nineteen years, six days, he became the youngest batsman to score a Glamorgan century on début, taking the record from M. J. Turnbull, who had been twenty years, five months and five days when he scored an unbeaten 106 against Worcestershire at Cardiff Arms Park in 1926. Maynard struck his century in 87 minutes off 98 balls with five 6s and thirteen 4s, racing from 84 to 102 by hitting three consecutive deliveries from Carrick straight back into the terraces. Frank Pinch registered a century on his first-class début in 1921, but had played for Glamorgan in the Minor Counties competition. Javed Miandad and Younis Ahmed also scored début centuries, but both had obtained hundreds previously in first-class cricket.

## Yorkshire

G. Boycott c Holmes b Ontong ....... 64
M. D. Moxon c Holmes b Ontong ..... 31
R. J. Blakey b Ontong .............. 7
S. N. Hartley lbw b Ontong .......... 4
J. D. Love lbw b Ontong ............ 14
P. E. Robinson c and b Price ........ 54
*†D. L. Bairstow c Davies b North ... 9
P. Carrick c Younis b Price .......... 92
I. G. Swallow lbw b Price ........... 10
P. J. Hartley not out ................. 3
B 4, l-b 2, w 4 ............. 10

1/81 2/101 3/110 (9 wkts dec.) 298
4/123 5/136 6/163 7/220
8/291 9/298

C. Shaw did not bat.

Bonus points – Yorkshire 2, Glamorgan 3 (Score at 100 overs: 230-7).

Bowling: Barwick 11–3–25–0; Smith 13–4–33–0; Price 35.3–11–61–3; North 27–7–60–1; Ontong 29–5–91–5; Holmes 3–0–22–0.

*Yorkshire forfeited their second innings.*

### Glamorgan

| | | | |
|---|---|---|---|
| H. Morris not out | 8 | – c Blakey b Carrick | 62 |
| J. Derrick lbw b P. J. Hartley | 0 | – lbw b Shaw | 0 |
| G. C. Holmes not out | 14 | – lbw b Carrick | 42 |
| Younis Ahmed (did not bat) | | – st Bairstow b Carrick | 8 |
| *R. C. Ontong (did not bat) | | – lbw b Swallow | 1 |
| M. P. Maynard (did not bat) | | – c P. J. Hartley b Carrick | 102 |
| †T. Davies (did not bat) | | – c S. N. Hartley b Carrick | 0 |
| M. R. Price (did not bat) | | – c S. N. Hartley b Carrick | 0 |
| I. Smith (did not bat) | | – b Carrick | 11 |
| S. R. Barwick (did not bat) | | – b Swallow | 0 |
| P. D. North (did not bat) | | – not out | 0 |
| B 4, l-b 1 | 5 | L-b 4, w 1, n-b 6 | 11 |
| 1/0 | (1 wkt dec.) 27 | 1/6 2/98 3/119 4/120 5/127 6/132 7/136 8/166 9/185 | 237 |

Bowling: *First Innings*—Shaw 2–1–3–0; P. J. Hartley 1–1–0–1; Swallow 7–1–16–0; Carrick 6–3–4–0. *Second Innings*—P. J. Hartley 7–2–11–0; Shaw 9–3–19–1; Carrick 34–8–99–7; Swallow 29–4–104–2.

Umpires: B. Dudleston and D. S. Thompsett.

At Trent Bridge, August 28, 29, 30. GLAMORGAN beat NOTTINGHAMSHIRE by an innings and 11 runs.

## GLAMORGAN v GLOUCESTERSHIRE

At Cardiff, August 31, September 2, 3. Drawn. Glamorgan 9 pts, Gloucestershire 1 pt. Toss won by Glamorgan. The home county took eight points as the side batting in the fourth innings with the scores tied. To reach this exciting stage after rain had washed out most of the first day, all the second day and everything before tea on the final day, there were two forfeitures of innings. This set Glamorgan to score 152 from what turned out to be 37 overs after Athey had hit an unbeaten 71, including 24 off one over by Jones in the Gloucestershire innings. Glamorgan recovered from 33 for four as Javed Miandad and Maynard unleashed some big hitting; but the home side narrowly failed to score the 7 runs needed off the final over. From the last delivery, Ontong was run out looking for the second run which would have won the match.

### Gloucestershire

| | |
|---|---|
| P. W. Romaines lbw b Holmes | 3 |
| J. W. Lloyds c and b Holmes | 39 |
| C. W. J. Athey not out | 71 |
| P. Bainbridge st Davies b Price | 20 |
| B. F. Davison c Hopkins b Ontong | 0 |
| D. V. Lawrence not out | 4 |
| B 3, l-b 8, w 3 | 14 |
| 1/15 2/65 3/115 4/122 (4 wkts dec.) | 151 |

K. M. Curran, I. R. Payne, †R. C. Russell, *D. A. Graveney and C. A. Walsh did not bat.

Bonus points – Gloucestershire 1, Glamorgan 1.

Bowling: Barwick 9–0–31–0; Holmes 11–3–29–2; Smith 8–3–18–0; Price 11–1–28–1; Ontong 5–1–6–1; Jones 1–0–24–0; Maynard 0.1–0–4–0.

*Gloucestershire forfeited their second innings.*

## Glamorgan

*Glamorgan forfeited their first innings.*

| | | | |
|---|---|---|---|
| J. A. Hopkins b Walsh | 12 | M. R. Price b Walsh | 1 |
| A. L. Jones st Russell b Lloyds | 7 | †T. Davies not out | 1 |
| G. C. Holmes c Russell b Curran | 1 | | |
| H. Morris c Russell b Lloyds | 8 | B 3, l-b 4, n-b 2 | 9 |
| Javed Miandad st Russell b Graveney | 60 | | |
| M. P. Maynard c Graveney b Walsh | 38 | 1/13 2/19 3/26 4/33 5/100 (8 wkts) | 151 |
| *R. C. Ontong run out | 14 | 6/144 7/145 8/151 | |

I. Smith and S. R. Barwick did not bat.

Bowling: Walsh 11–3–40–3; Curran 10–3–30–1; Graveney 10–0–45–1; Lloyds 6–1–29–2.

Umpires: R. A. White and A. G. T. Whitehead.

## GLAMORGAN v SUSSEX

At Cardiff, September 14, 16, 17. Drawn. Toss won by Glamorgan. There was little more than 60 minutes of play, and that late on the first day, because of rain.

## Glamorgan

| | |
|---|---|
| J. A. Hopkins not out | 16 |
| H. Morris not out | 14 |
| L-b 1, n-b 1 | 2 |
| (no wkt) | 32 |

S. P. James, G. C. Holmes, I. Smith, *R. C. Ontong, M. P. Maynard, †T. Davies, M. R. Price, J. G. Thomas and S. R. Barwick did not bat.

Bowling: Imran 7–3–10–0; Jones 6–2–10–0; Reeve 5–0–11–0.

## Sussex

G. D. Mendis, A. M. Green, N. J. Lenham, C. M. Wells, Imran Khan, A. P. Wells, †I. J. Gould, *J. R. T. Barclay, A. N. Jones, I. C. Waring and D. A. Reeve.

Umpires: D. J. Constant and D. R. Shepherd.

## GLOUCESTERSHIRE

*Patron:* HRH The Princess of Wales
*President:* J. K. Graveney
*Chairman:* D. N. Perry
*Chairman, Cricket Committee:* D. G. Stone
*Secretary/Manager:* D. G. Collier
Phoenix County Ground, Nevil Road, Bristol BS7 9EJ (Telephone: 0272-45216)
*Captain:* D. A. Graveney
*Senior Coach:* J. N. Shepherd
*Youth Coach:* G. G. Wiltshire

Gloucestershire's rise from last to third place in the Britannic Assurance Championship was one of the features of the season, and for much of it the team seemed well capable of winning the title for the first time since 1877. However, a combination of bad luck with the weather and loss of form by some of the batsmen saw the prize slip away. Although Gloucestershire were mathematically in contention until the last day of the last match, only one of the final eleven games was won.

Having played themselves into a position to gain a draw at Bournemouth, which would have seriously damaged Hampshire's chances, Gloucestershire lost their last seven wickets while 30 runs were scored, undermined less by Marshall than Maru's left-arm spin. The following match, against Essex at Bristol, saw Gloucestershire dominant until McEwan's fine century in the second innings. Even so, 223 to win was not a particularly testing target for Championship contenders. The score passed 90 with eight wickets still in hand, but then Pringle caused a collapse from which there was no recovery. Then, when Northamptonshire opened up a rain-ruined match at Bristol to give Gloucestershire a chance of sixteen points, the visitors' tenth-wicket pair survived the final nine overs to force a draw.

The county's successful season, with a much-strengthened team, was a heartening one for supporters who had suffered, not always in silence, the setbacks of 1984. Gloucestershire became one of the most feared bowling sides in the competition, three powerful and fit young men – David Lawrence, Courtney Walsh and Kevin Curran – forming perhaps the most formidable pace attack the county had ever fielded.

Lawrence, patiently nursed along, returned from a winter in Australia still raw but decidedly fast. He soon became the talk of the county circuit, although he was unable to convince the England selectors to give him a Test match. Walsh started quietly but settled down to bowl very well, showing exceptional variety for a bowler who was still only 22. Curran, from Zimbabwe and qualified by virtue of holding an Irish passport, swung and seamed the ball at a lively pace. All three were always available and keen to bowl, encouraged no doubt by the amount of grass left on home pitches. Even Bristol suddenly became a paradise for fast bowlers, although, strangely, Gloucestershire were still unable to win a Championship match there.

Ironically, the helpful conditions which assisted their fast-bowling trio to claim 213 Championship wickets between them also served to undermine the form and confidence of some of their batsmen. Paul Romaines was the first to suffer. Although continuing to do well in limited-overs cricket, he passed 50 only twice in Championship games and was twice dropped for lengthy periods. Andrew Stovold hit two early centuries, but then he had a bad time at Cheltenham, followed by a pair against Essex, and was left out for the last three games of the season. Bill Athey, immune from uncertainty until early August, was called to The Oval as reserve batsman for the sixth Test match; but his season, too, tailed away. He was responsible for four of the county's twelve Championship hundreds. Tony Wright was tried as an opening batsman, but he was unable to hold a regular place.

Gloucestershire's batsman of the year was their new vice-captain, Phil Bainbridge. He often had to pull the team out of difficult situations and always did so in an attractive way. Nor was he ever found wanting for courage. When he had a finger broken against Leicestershire, he stayed in to make top score. It was sad that his season should end with his being carried on a stretcher from the pitch at The Oval after being knocked out by a ball from Monkhouse. The consolation of a place on the England B tour was then denied him, although he had done enough to earn one.

Brian Davison, although not a heavy scorer in his first season with Gloucestershire, was a valuable aid to David Graveney and brought a robustness to the middle order which was good for morale. Curran was also a violent stroke-maker. Not yet a Procter or a Botham, he tended to give his wicket away when well set, but he has it in him to become a formidable all-rounder. Jeremy Lloyds, the other new signing, began as number seven but made his lone century as an emergency opening batsman late in the season. With the pacemen doing most of the work his off-spin was not often in demand.

When spin was required, Graveney did a good job. As captain, his handling of a young and relatively inexperienced attack was good, things being very different from the previous year when Gloucestershire only once managed to bowl a team out twice. All the bowlers owed a debt to Jack Russell, a splendid wicket-keeper, neat and tidy even when the ball was coming through at difficult heights. Andy Brassington, a faithful deputy but rarely called upon, has been rewarded with a benefit in 1988. The forgotten man of the staff was Gary Sainsbury. Before Walsh's arrival he took eleven wickets in two games, yet he made only two further appearances, both of them successful, and had to be content with Sunday cricket and a high place in the averages.

Over 160 hours were lost to weather in the Championship alone, and the rain also played a part in Gloucestershire's failure to qualify for the knockout stages of the Benson and Hedges Cup. Nottinghamshire won a high-scoring third-round match in the NatWest Bank Trophy. In the John Player Sunday League, Gloucestershire equalled their previous best final position of sixth.

In the end the £5,000 prizemoney from Britannic, for finishing third, did little more than help pay the fine imposed for a miserably slow over-rate. But this apart, Gloucestershire's cricket was refreshingly challenging. Some opponents found it hard to believe that a team could have undergone such a remarkable change between one year and the next. Curran, Davison, Lawrence, Lloyds and Walsh were all awarded county caps in a happy ceremony during the final match at Bristol. – G.J.W.

GLOUCESTERSHIRE 1985

[*Bill Smith*

*Back row:* R. C. Russell, C. W. J. Athey, A. J. Wright, P. W. Romaines, J. W. Lloyds, I. R. Payne. *Middle row:* G. G. Wiltshire (*coach*), P. H. Twizell, D. V. Lawrence, E. J. Cunningham, G. E. Sainsbury, D. A. Burrows, K. M. Curran, A. G. Avery (*scorer*). *Front row:* A. J. Brassington, J. N. Shepherd, D. A. Graveney (*captain*), D. G. Collier (*secretary/manager*), P. Bainbridge, A. W. Stovold. *Insets:* C. A. Walsh, B. F. Davison.

## GLOUCESTERSHIRE RESULTS

*All first-class matches – Played 26: Won 8, Lost 4, Drawn 14. Abandoned 1.*

*County Championship matches – Played 23: Won 7, Lost 3, Drawn 13. Abandoned 1.*

*Bonus points – Batting 51, Bowling 78.*

*Competition placings – Britannic Assurance County Championship, 3rd; NatWest Bank Trophy, q-f; Benson and Hedges Cup, 4th in Group A; John Player League, 6th eq.*

## BRITANNIC ASSURANCE CHAMPIONSHIP AVERAGES

### BATTING

| | *Birthplace* | *M* | *I* | *NO* | *R* | *HI* | *Avge* |
|---|---|---|---|---|---|---|---|
| ‡P. Bainbridge | *Stoke-on-Trent* | 21 | 33 | 8 | 1,456 | 151* | 58.24 |
| ‡C. W. J. Athey | *Middlesbrough* | 21 | 35 | 6 | 1,247 | 170 | 43.00 |
| ‡B. F. Davison | *Bulawayo, S. Rhodesia* | 22 | 33 | 6 | 902 | 111 | 33.40 |
| ‡J. W. Lloyds | *Penang, Malaya* | 22 | 30 | 5 | 734 | 101 | 29.36 |
| ‡K. M. Curran | *Rusape, S. Rhodesia* | 23 | 31 | 3 | 677 | 83 | 24.17 |
| I. R. Payne | *Kennington* | 6 | 6 | 1 | 106 | 37 | 21.20 |
| ‡A. W. Stovold | *Bristol* | 20 | 33 | 2 | 656 | 112 | 21.16 |
| ‡D. A. Graveney | *Bristol* | 22 | 23 | 10 | 239 | 53* | 18.38 |
| A. J. Wright | *Stevenage* | 7 | 12 | 2 | 173 | 47* | 17.30 |
| ‡C. A. Walsh | *Kingston, Jamaica* | 20 | 16 | 5 | 183 | 37 | 16.63 |
| ‡P. W. Romaines | *Bishop Auckland* | 17 | 28 | 2 | 423 | 64 | 16.26 |
| ‡D. V. Lawrence | *Gloucester* | 23 | 24 | 5 | 258 | 41 | 13.57 |
| ‡R. C. Russell | *Stroud* | 21 | 23 | 4 | 253 | 34 | 13.31 |
| G. E. Sainsbury | *Wanstead* | 4 | 5 | 3 | 11 | 8* | 5.50 |

Also batted: ‡A. J. Brassington (*Bagnall*) (2 matches) 3*; R. G. P. Ellis (*Paddington*) (1 match) 3, 20. ‡J. N. Shepherd (*St Andrew, Barbados*) played in one match but did not bat.

* *Signifies not out.* ‡ *Denotes county cap.*

The following played a total of twelve three-figure innings for Gloucestershire in County Championship matches – C. W. J. Athey 4, P. Bainbridge 4, A. W. Stovold 2, B. F. Davison 1, J. W. Lloyds 1.

### BOWLING

| | *O* | *M* | *R* | *W* | *BB* | *Avge* |
|---|---|---|---|---|---|---|
| G. E. Sainsbury | 138 | 45 | 380 | 21 | 7-38 | 18.09 |
| C. A. Walsh | 540.3 | 122 | 1,636 | 82 | 7-51 | 19.95 |
| D. A. Graveney | 360.5 | 116 | 887 | 38 | 4-91 | 23.34 |
| D. V. Lawrence | 500.5 | 59 | 1,923 | 79 | 7-48 | 24.34 |
| K. M. Curran | 414.2 | 87 | 1,288 | 52 | 5-42 | 24.76 |
| P. Bainbridge | 182 | 45 | 492 | 18 | 5-60 | 27.33 |
| J. W. Lloyds | 131.1 | 25 | 450 | 15 | 5-37 | 30.00 |

Also bowled: C. W. J. Athey 41.1–6–189–8; R. G. P. Ellis 3–1–7–1; I. R. Payne 39–9–112–3; P. W. Romaines 10–0–42–3; J. N. Shepherd 14–3–41–0.

At Fenner's, April 27, 29, 30. GLOUCESTERSHIRE drew with CAMBRIDGE UNIVERSITY.

## GLOUCESTERSHIRE v LANCASHIRE

At Bristol, May 1, 2, 3. Lancashire won by 74 runs. Lancashire 24 pts, Gloucestershire 5 pts. Toss won by Gloucestershire. Lancashire took maximum points for the first time in a sequence of 40 matches in this meeting between the Championship tailenders of 1984. Their success was due largely to a last-wicket partnership of 115 between Allott and Stanworth, which completed a first-innings recovery from 94 for six. Allott, who had a fine all-round match, hit his career-best 78 from only 72 balls during the one period of the game when bowlers of pace lost control of events on a well-grassed pitch. Lawrence's nine wickets in the match provided Gloucestershire with some consolation, and Bainbridge batted bravely with a fractured cheekbone as they sought an improbable target of 295 in 95 overs.

### Lancashire

| | | | |
|---|---|---|---|
| G. Fowler b Lawrence | 30 | – c Russell b Lawrence | 0 |
| J. A. Ormrod lbw b Lawrence | 4 | – c and b Sainsbury | 2 |
| S. J. O'Shaughnessy lbw b Curran | 2 | – not out | 40 |
| N. H. Fairbrother c Russell b Lawrence | 0 | – c Russell b Sainsbury | 24 |
| *J. Abrahams c Russell b Lawrence | 29 | – c Russell b Curran | 26 |
| M. Watkinson c Stovold b Curran | 57 | – c Athey b Lawrence | 14 |
| J. Simmons c Athey b Lawrence | 2 | – c Davison b Sainsbury | 8 |
| S. T. Jefferies b Curran | 57 | – c Curran b Sainsbury | 24 |
| †J. Stanworth not out | 50 | – c Russell b Lawrence | 0 |
| I. Folley c Stovold b Graveney | 0 | – c Lloyds b Sainsbury | 0 |
| P. J. W. Allott b Sainsbury | 78 | – c Davison b Lawrence | 15 |
| B 3, l-b 6 | 9 | L-b 4, w 6, n-b 2 | 12 |
| 1/13 2/22 3/23 4/51 5/88 6/94 7/163 8/196 9/203 | 318 | 1/0 2/26 3/41 4/68 5/77 6/89 7/89 8/121 9/126 | 165 |

Bonus points – Lancashire 4, Gloucestershire 4.

Bowling: *First Innings*—Lawrence 28–6–79–5; Curran 26–10–82–3; Sainsbury 21.4–6–79–1; Graveney 18–5–50–1; Lloyds 4–1–19–0. *Second Innings*—Lawrence 22.5–6–70–4; Curran 16–4–47–1; Sainsbury 20–7–44–5.

### Gloucestershire

| | | | |
|---|---|---|---|
| A. W. Stovold c Ormrod b Allott | 2 | – c Allott b Jefferies | 7 |
| P. W. Romaines c Stanworth b Allott | 18 | – c Simmons b Allott | 7 |
| †R. C. Russell b Jefferies | 1 | – (9) c O'Shaughnessy b Simmons | 0 |
| C. W. J. Athey lbw b Allott | 24 | – (3) lbw b O'Shaughnessy | 15 |
| J. W. Lloyds b Allott | 33 | – (7) b Jefferies | 35 |
| B. F. Davison c and b Watkinson | 40 | – (5) run out | 11 |
| P. Bainbridge c Fairbrother b Watkinson | 3 | – (4) c Stanworth b Jefferies | 67 |
| K. M. Curran b Jefferies | 46 | – (6) lbw b Allott | 39 |
| *D. A. Graveney c Simmons b O'Shaughnessy | 6 | – (8) st Stanworth b Simmons | 27 |
| D. V. Lawrence b Jefferies | 7 | – not out | 6 |
| G. E. Sainsbury not out | 1 | – lbw b Jefferies | 1 |
| B 2, l-b 4, n-b 2 | 8 | L-b 2, n-b 3 | 5 |
| 1/2 2/41 3/46 4/103 5/115 6/139 7/176 8/178 9/178 | 189 | 1/11 2/19 3/34 4/50 5/134 6/163 7/207 8/210 9/213 | 220 |

Bonus points – Gloucestershire 1, Lancashire 4.

Bowling: *First Innings*—Allott 19–5–44–4; Jefferies 13.1–0–45–3; Watkinson 16–5–60–2; O'Shaughnessy 11–3–34–1. *Second Innings*—Allott 19–10–25–2; Jefferies 19–2–64–4; Watkinson 8–0–34–0; O'Shaughnessy 8–1–27–1; Simmons 21–6–53–2; Folley 5–2–15–0.

Umpires: J. H. Harris and D. R. Shepherd.

At Worcester, May 8, 9, 10. GLOUCESTERSHIRE beat WORCESTERSHIRE by 40 runs.

At Hove, May 22, 23, 24. GLOUCESTERSHIRE drew with SUSSEX.

## GLOUCESTERSHIRE v SOMERSET

At Bristol, May 25, 27, 28. Drawn. Gloucestershire 4 pts, Somerset 2 pts. Toss won by Gloucestershire. A local businessman put up £1,000 as a sidestake to encourage positive play in this West Country derby, but the game was ruined by the weather. Play was not possible on the second and third days and was restricted on the Saturday when, after a good opening partnership, Somerset were forced on to the defensive by the Gloucestershire quick bowlers. Lawrence claimed three wickets in thirteen balls and then Graveney found some turn to work his way through the tail.

### Somerset

| | |
|---|---|
| J. G. Wyatt c Russell b Curran | 46 |
| N. F. M. Popplewell c Russell b Curran | 31 |
| N. A. Felton c Russell b Lawrence | 29 |
| I. V. A. Richards c Lloyds b Bainbridge | 26 |
| R. L. Ollis c and b Graveney | 8 |
| *I. T. Botham c Stovold b Lawrence | 5 |
| V. J. Marks c Athey b Lawrence | 0 |
| †T. Gard c Stovold b Graveney | 30 |
| M. R. Davis c Lloyds b Graveney | 7 |
| J. Garner not out | 8 |
| M. S. Turner not out | 13 |
| L-b 5, w 1, n-b 2 | 8 |
| 1/66 2/91 3/126 4/136 5/141 6/141 7/166 8/183 9/194 | (9 wkts) 211 |

Bonus points – Somerset 2, Gloucestershire 4.

Bowling: Lawrence 22–3–76–3; Walsh 15–3–38–0; Curran 10–1–36–2; Bainbridge 9–2–30–1; Graveney 11–3–22–3; Lloyds 3–1–4–0.

### Gloucestershire

A. W. Stovold, P. W. Romaines, C. W. J. Athey, P. Bainbridge, B. F. Davison, J. W. Lloyds, K. M. Curran, *D. A. Graveney, †R. C. Russell, D. V. Lawrence and C. A. Walsh.

Umpires: D. G. L. Evans and K. J. Lyons.

At Derby, June 1, 3, 4. GLOUCESTERSHIRE beat DERBYSHIRE by 226 runs.

At Bath, June 8, 10, 11. GLOUCESTERSHIRE drew with SOMERSET.

At Tunbridge Wells, June 12, 13, 14. GLOUCESTERSHIRE beat Kent by 59 runs.

At Northampton, June 15, 17, 18. GLOUCESTERSHIRE beat NORTHAMPTONSHIRE by eight wickets.

## GLOUCESTERSHIRE v SUSSEX

At Bristol, June 22, 24, 25. Abandoned.

## GLOUCESTERSHIRE v HAMPSHIRE

At Bristol, June 26, 27, 28. Drawn. Gloucestershire 5 pts, Hampshire 4 pts. Toss won by Gloucestershire. So well did Hampshire recover in this battle of Championship contenders that when rain ended play with 28 overs remaining they were dictating events. A start was not possible until four o'clock on the first day, but Gloucestershire's three-pronged pace attack made up for lost time in helpful conditions. Only Greenidge looked comfortable. However, Hampshire's pacemen routed the top of the Gloucestershire order just as effectively, and it needed a spirited revival, led by Curran's 50 off 48 balls, to effect a lead of 81. With conditions easing, Greenidge again batted well and Robin Smith hurried Hampshire to a declaration which left Gloucestershire to make 232 in a minimum of 50 overs. Tremlett and Maru were causing problems when a downpour brought Gloucestershire relief.

### Hampshire

| First innings | | Second innings | |
|---|---|---|---|
| C. G. Greenidge lbw b Curran | 43 | c Athey b Lawrence | 68 |
| V. P. Terry c Russell b Lawrence | 1 | b Walsh | 34 |
| *M. C. J. Nicholas c Lloyds b Lawrence | 0 | c Curran b Bainbridge | 32 |
| R. A. Smith c Athey b Walsh | 19 | (5) c Walsh b Athey | 79 |
| C. L. Smith lbw b Curran | 1 | (4) c Lloyds b Walsh | 24 |
| J. J. E. Hardy c Graveney b Lawrence | 4 | c Lloyds b Athey | 42 |
| M. D. Marshall c Russell b Walsh | 18 | c Lawrence b Athey | 8 |
| T. M. Tremlett not out | 14 | not out | 2 |
| †R. J. Parks c Lloyds b Curran | 1 | | |
| R. J. Maru c Athey b Curran | 2 | | |
| C. A. Connor b Lawrence | 0 | | |
| L-b 2, w 1, n-b 4 | 7 | B 2, l-b 14, n-b 7 | 23 |
| 1/9 2/22 3/48 4/54 5/63 6/78 7/95 8/102 9/106 | 110 | 1/80 2/145 3/147 4/184 5/290 6/303 7/312 (7 wkts dec.) | 312 |

Bonus points – Gloucestershire 4.

Bowling: *First Innings*—Lawrence 13–3–41–4; Walsh 15–3–44–2; Curran 18–9–23–4. *Second Innings*—Lawrence 15–2–51–1; Walsh 23–6–62–2; Curran 13–3–56–0; Bainbridge 21–3–72–1; Lloyds 8–1–52–0; Athey 2.1–0–3–3.

### Gloucestershire

| First innings | | Second innings | |
|---|---|---|---|
| A. W. Stovold lbw b Marshall | 14 | c Parks b Maru | 17 |
| P. W. Romaines c Terry b Connor | 2 | c R. A. Smith b Tremlett | 7 |
| C. W. J. Athey c Terry b Tremlett | 8 | c Terry b Tremlett | 13 |
| P. Bainbridge c Parks b Marshall | 2 | (6) not out | 3 |
| B. F. Davison c C. L. Smith b Marshall | 0 | (4) not out | 9 |
| K. M. Curran c Parks b Marshall | 50 | (5) b Maru | 2 |
| J. W. Lloyds c Greenidge b Tremlett | 23 | | |
| *D. A. Graveney not out | 3 | | |
| †R. C. Russell c Terry b Tremlett | 34 | | |
| D. V. Lawrence c C. L. Smith b Tremlett | 2 | | |
| C. A. Walsh c Marshall b Maru | 37 | | |
| B 6, l-b 3, n-b 7 | 16 | N-b 2 | 2 |
| 1/16 2/16 3/20 4/20 5/69 6/90 7/114 8/122 9/181 | 191 | 1/21 2/35 3/47 4/49 (4 wkts) | 53 |

*In the first innings D. A. Graveney, when 0, retired hurt at 90 and resumed at 181.*

Bonus points – Gloucestershire 1, Hampshire 4.

Bowling: *First Innings*—Marshall 20–3–57–4; Connor 19–3–63–1; Tremlett 16.4–4–43–4; Maru 6–1–19–1. *Second Innings*—Marshall 5–1–8–0; Connor 3–0–12–0; Maru 8–3–19–2; Tremlett 6–3–14–2.

Umpires: A. A. Jones and K. E. Palmer.

At Trent Bridge, June 29, 30, July 1. GLOUCESTERSHIRE drew with NOTTINGHAMSHIRE.

## GLOUCESTERSHIRE v YORKSHIRE

At Gloucester, July 6, 8, 9. Gloucestershire won by eight wickets. Gloucestershire 24 pts, Yorkshire 6 pts. Toss won by Gloucestershire. Yorkshire's second-innings collapse – all out for 83 in less than 23 overs, or two hours – owed little to the state of the pitch. Rather, top-class fast bowling by Lawrence, Walsh and Curran proved too much for a side down on its luck and lacking the services of Moxon because of a finger injury. Yet in their first innings, Bairstow's spirited 80 and Carrick's highest score for two years had earned maximum batting points. Gloucestershire's reply was built around a third-wicket stand of 213 between Athey and Bainbridge. Athey's second hundred in successive innings against his former county took 263 minutes while Bainbridge, in 171 minutes, provided more sparkle but was dropped three times. Graveney's decision to declare when still behind was quickly justified and Gloucestershire just failed to finish the match in two days.

### Yorkshire

| | | | |
|---|---|---|---|
| G. Boycott c Russell b Lawrence | 24 | – c Graveney b Walsh | 10 |
| M. D. Moxon c Russell b Curran | 31 | – absent injured | |
| A. A. Metcalfe b Lawrence | 14 | – c Athey b Lawrence | 3 |
| K. Sharp b Walsh | 23 | – b Curran | 9 |
| J. D. Love b Athey | 1 | – b Lawrence | 18 |
| *†D. L. Bairstow c Lawrence b Graveney | 80 | – c Walsh b Lawrence | 11 |
| P. Carrick c Athey b Graveney | 73 | – (2) c Lloyds b Walsh | 2 |
| A. Sidebottom b Walsh | 24 | – (7) b Curran | 12 |
| P. W. Jarvis b Graveney | 0 | – (8) b Lawrence | 0 |
| G. B. Stevenson c Russell b Walsh | 21 | – (9) b Lawrence | 8 |
| S. D. Fletcher not out | 1 | – (10) not out | 2 |
| L-b 10, w 1, n-b 4 | 15 | N-b 8 | 8 |
| 1/45 2/68 3/72 4/106 5/175 6/257 7/263 8/263 9/286 | 307 | 1/2 2/17 3/18 4/45 5/54 6/62 7/64 8/81 9/83 | 83 |

Bonus points – Yorkshire 4, Gloucestershire 4.

Bowling: *First Innings*—Lawrence 13–1–60–2; Walsh 21–4–78–3; Curran 17–1–48–1; Bainbridge 14–5–36–0; Athey 8–1–34–1; Graveney 20–6–41–3. *Second Innings*—Lawrence 11.3–1–50–5; Walsh 5–1–15–2; Curran 6–0–18–2.

### Gloucestershire

| | | | |
|---|---|---|---|
| A. W. Stovold lbw b Sidebottom | 39 | – not out | 56 |
| P. W. Romaines b Jarvis | 11 | – lbw b Stevenson | 9 |
| C. W. J. Athey c and b Carrick | 101 | – retired hurt | 13 |
| P. Bainbridge c Bairstow b Carrick | 119 | – (5) not out | 4 |
| B. F. Davison not out | 12 | | |
| K. M. Curran b Carrick | 0 | | |
| J. W. Lloyds b Stevenson | 1 | | |
| *D. A. Graveney not out | 0 | | |
| C. A. Walsh (did not bat) | | (4) c Sidebottom b Love | 5 |
| L-b 6, n-b 12 | 18 | L-b 3, n-b 1 | 4 |
| 1/25 2/68 3/281 4/294 5/294 6/295 | (6 wkts dec.) 301 | 1/34 2/83 | (2 wkts) 91 |

†R. C. Russell and D. V. Lawrence did not bat.

Bonus points – Gloucestershire 4, Yorkshire 2.

Bowling: *First Innings*—Jarvis 21–3–67–1; Sidebottom 18–1–57–1; Fletcher 8–1–26–0; Stevenson 16.4–2–74–1; Carrick 27–9–67–3; Sharp 1–0–4–0. *Second Innings*—Jarvis 10–1–47–0; Stevenson 6–1–13–1; Sidebottom 4–1–14–0; Sharp 2–0–6–0; Love 1–0–8–1.

Umpires: R. Julian and R. Palmer.

## GLOUCESTERSHIRE v WORCESTERSHIRE

At Gloucester, July 10, 11, 12. Gloucestershire won by 110 runs. Gloucestershire 23 pts, Worcestershire 4 pts. Toss won by Worcestershire. Gloucestershire returned to the head of the Championship table with their second win of the week at the Winget Ground. This time Walsh took the fast-bowling honours, effecting two Worcestershire collapses, but Gloucestershire had equal reason to be grateful to the patient Athey, who batted almost all of the opening day for his second hundred of the week on a slow, uncertain pitch. Worcestershire made a spirited reply, reaching 240 before their last five wickets fell in fifteen balls, and Gloucestershire in their second innings struggled as Newport enjoyed a career-best return. They might have been in difficulty but for Bainbridge's timely 81. Lawrence began Worcestershire's second-innings decline and Kapil Dev's half-century off 55 balls, an innings of high class featuring nine 4s, was only a temporary check.

### Gloucestershire

| | | | |
|---|---|---|---|
| A. W. Stovold b Radford | 6 | lbw b Radford | 7 |
| A. J. Wright lbw b Illingworth | 20 | c and b Illingworth | 33 |
| C. W. J. Athey not out | 139 | (5) lbw b Kapil Dev | 6 |
| P. Bainbridge c and b Illingworth | 58 | lbw b Newport | 81 |
| B. F. Davison b Newport | 29 | (6) b Newport | 13 |
| K. M. Curran c Weston b McEwan | 0 | (7) not out | 15 |
| J. W. Lloyds c Patel b Newport | 0 | (3) b Kapil Dev | 0 |
| †R. C. Russell run out | 22 | (9) c Rhodes b Newport | 3 |
| D. V. Lawrence not out | 12 | (8) b Newport | 0 |
| *D. A. Graveney (did not bat) | | b Newport | 1 |
| B 7, l-b 12, n-b 2 | 21 | L-b 9, n-b 2 | 11 |
| 1/11 2/52 3/148 4/221 5/222 6/223 7/295 (7 wkts dec.) | 307 | 1/13 2/14 3/82 4/103 5/145 6/156 7/156 8/164 9/170 (9 wkts dec.) | 170 |

C. A. Walsh did not bat.

Bonus points – Gloucestershire 3, Worcestershire 2 (Score at 100 overs: 252-6).

Bowling: *First Innings*—Kapil Dev 8–1–18–0; Radford 16–4–40–1; Newport 20–3–47–2; Illingworth 26–8–55–2; McEwan 16–3–51–1; Patel 29–9–77–0. *Second Innings*—Kapil Dev 15–3–36–2; Radford 7–1–22–1; Illingworth 27–12–48–1; Patel 8–1–37–0; Newport 9.1–2–18–5.

### Worcestershire

| | | | |
|---|---|---|---|
| T. S. Curtis b Graveney | 62 | c Lloyds b Lawrence | 6 |
| D. B. D'Oliveira lbw b Lawrence | 5 | b Lawrence | 15 |
| *P. A. Neale b Graveney | 46 | c Russell b Curran | 4 |
| D. N. Patel c Graveney b Lloyds | 9 | b Graveney | 4 |
| M. J. Weston c Russell b Bainbridge | 17 | b Curran | 4 |
| Kapil Dev c Lloyds b Walsh | 72 | c Lloyds b Walsh | 57 |
| †S. J. Rhodes not out | 19 | lbw b Walsh | 8 |
| P. J. Newport lbw b Graveney | 0 | b Graveney | 5 |
| R. K. Illingworth run out | 0 | b Walsh | 6 |
| N. V. Radford b Walsh | 0 | lbw b Walsh | 10 |
| S. M. McEwan b Walsh | 0 | not out | 0 |
| B 2, l-b 9, n-b 1 | 12 | W 4, n-b 2 | 6 |
| 1/19 2/111 3/122 4/126 5/183 6/240 7/242 8/242 9/242 | 242 | 1/19 2/25 3/31 4/31 5/36 6/88 7/107 8/115 9/117 | 125 |

Bonus points – Worcestershire 2, Gloucestershire 4.

Bowling: *First Innings*—Lawrence 6–2–28–1; Walsh 16–4–52–3; Curran 3–0–14–0; Graveney 40–16–62–3; Lloyds 21–3–62–1; Bainbridge 10–4–13–1. *Second Innings*—Lawrence 8–1–11–2; Walsh 12.4–2–39–4; Curran 8–1–42–2; Graveney 9–5–17–2; Lloyds 4–1–16–0.

Umpires: R. Julian and R. Palmer.

At Southend, July 13, 15, 16. GLOUCESTERSHIRE drew with ESSEX.

At Bristol, July 20, 22, 23. GLOUCESTERSHIRE beat ZIMBABWEANS by seven wickets (See Zimbabwean tour section).

At Bristol, July 24, 25, 26. GLOUCESTERSHIRE lost to AUSTRALIANS by 170 runs (See Australian tour section).

## GLOUCESTERSHIRE v GLAMORGAN

At Bristol, July 27, 29, 30. Drawn. Gloucestershire 6 pts, Glamorgan 5 pts. Toss won by Glamorgan, who must have wondered at the wisdom of putting Gloucestershire in to bat as they amassed 400 runs in the first 100 overs. But the rain, which washed out the second day and did not permit a start until after lunch on the third, allowed Gloucestershire little profit from the match. Athey, watched by the chairman of selectors, needed only 153 minutes for his fifth hundred of the season, in which he hit sixteen 4s, and Bainbridge again benefited from dropped catches – two in the slips – to play a big innings. Davison and Curran took advantage of the tiring and lack-lustre bowling as they thumped the ball to all parts of the ground. Glamorgan adopted an aggressive approach when play finally resumed, Holmes in particular batting well, and Gloucestershire could manage only two bowling points on a well-grassed but slow pitch.

### Gloucestershire

A. W. Stovold c Davies b Barwick .... 10
P. W. Romaines run out ............. 12
C. W. J. Athey c Davies b Barwick ...115
P. Bainbridge not out ...............143
B. F. Davison b Holmes ............. 65
K. M. Curran c and b Ontong ........ 54
J. W. Lloyds c Davies b Malone ...... 1
*D. A. Graveney not out ............ 3
B 4, l-b 1, w 6, n-b 2 ........ 13

1/15 2/60 3/191 4/276 5/389 6/394 (6 wkts dec.) 416

†A. J. Brassington, D. V. Lawrence and C. A. Walsh did not bat.

Bonus points – Gloucestershire 4, Glamorgan 2 (Score at 100 overs: 400-6).

Bowling: McFarlane 20–0–115–0; Barwick 17–5–41–2; Holmes 23–3–96–1; Malone 21.3–0–106–1; Younis 12–3–27–0; Ontong 10–2–26–1.

### Glamorgan

J. A. Hopkins c Curran b Athey ...... 70
A. L. Jones c Davison b Walsh ....... 0
G. C. Holmes c Brassington b Bainbridge 53
Javed Miandad b Walsh ............. 13
Younis Ahmed retired hurt .......... 12
H. Morris not out .................. 30
*R. C. Ontong c Athey b Bainbridge .. 24
†T. Davies not out .................. 24
B 4, l-b 7, w 3, n-b 13 ....... 27

1/2 2/97 3/149 4/154 5/220 (5 wkts) 253

S. J. Malone, L. L. McFarlane and S. R. Barwick did not bat.

Bonus points – Glamorgan 3, Gloucestershire 2.

Bowling: Lawrence 13–1–42–0; Walsh 19–1–72–2; Curran 11–2–43–0; Bainbridge 11–2–28–2; Graveney 6–3–21–0; Athey 8–1–36–1.

Umpires: N. T. Plews and A. G. T. Whitehead.

At Lord's, July 31, August 1, 2. GLOUCESTERSHIRE drew with MIDDLESEX.

## GLOUCESTERSHIRE v LEICESTERSHIRE

At Cheltenham, August 10, 12, 13. Drawn. Gloucestershire 4 pts, Leicestershire 6 pts. Toss won by Leicestershire. Taylor, who learned of his selection for England during this match, gave a splendid exhibition of fast-medium bowling after Gloucestershire had been put in on a seamer's pitch. Only a stout effort by Bainbridge, batting with a broken index finger after being struck by Agnew, enabled his side to reach 134. Leicestershire struggled in turn and were only 9 ahead when the sixth wicket fell. However, Willey defied the fast bowlers for nearly three hours to earn a lead of 115. With the third day, like the second, interrupted by rain, Gloucestershire had only the draw to aim for, and but for Wright's stubborness in difficult conditions, they might not have achieved that.

### Gloucestershire

| | | | |
|---|---|---|---|
| A. W. Stovold b Taylor | 20 | – c Garnham b Taylor | 2 |
| A. J. Wright c Butcher b Taylor | 0 | – not out | 47 |
| C. W. J. Athey b Taylor | 8 | – (4) c Garnham b Agnew | 6 |
| P. Bainbridge c Garnham b Clift | 33 | | |
| J. W. Lloyds c Balderstone b Agnew | 1 | – c Clift b Agnew | 6 |
| K. M. Curran b Taylor | 23 | – c Garnham b Taylor | 36 |
| I. R. Payne c Garnham b De Freitas | 27 | – not out | 10 |
| †R. C. Russell c Willey b Agnew | 1 | | |
| *D. A. Graveney c Garnham b Clift | 0 | | |
| D. V. Lawrence c Clift b Taylor | 14 | – (3) c De Freitas b Agnew | 8 |
| C. A. Walsh not out | 0 | | |
| L-b 1, n-b 6 | 7 | L-b 2, n-b 4 | 6 |
| 1/13 2/29 3/30 4/31 5/75 6/111 7/114 8/115 9/124 | 134 | 1/5 2/14 3/28 4/38 5/85 | (5 wkts) 121 |

Bonus points – Leicestershire 4.

Bowling: *First Innings*—Agnew 15–4–35–2; Taylor 17.4–3–45–5; De Freitas 14–4–20–1; Clift 14–3–33–2. *Second Innings*—Agnew 15–3–40–3; Taylor 16–5–34–2; De Freitas 12–2–36–0; Willey 2–1–9–0.

### Leicestershire

| | |
|---|---|
| I. P. Butcher c Russell b Walsh | 21 |
| J. C. Balderstone c Russell b Curran | 34 |
| R. A. Cobb lbw b Payne | 24 |
| *D. I. Gower c Lloyds b Curran | 4 |
| P. Willey c Wright b Lawrence | 52 |
| J. J. Whitaker c Russell b Payne | 17 |
| †M. A. Garnham c Payne b Walsh | 6 |
| P. B. Clift b Payne | 29 |
| P. A. J. De Freitas not out | 29 |
| J. P. Agnew b Walsh | 5 |
| L. B. Taylor b Lawrence | 4 |
| B 1, l-b 5, w 4, n-b 14 | 24 |
| 1/48 2/86 3/94 4/98 5/128 6/143 7/188 8/234 9/242 | 249 |

Bonus points – Leicestershire 2, Gloucestershire 4.

Bowling: Lawrence 9.3–0–38–2; Walsh 26–6–82–3; Curran 19–2–55–2; Payne 24–7–68–3.

Umpires: M. J. Kitchen and R. Palmer.

## GLOUCESTERSHIRE v NOTTINGHAMSHIRE

At Cheltenham, August 14, 15, 16. Drawn. Gloucestershire 4 pts, Nottinghamshire 2 pts. Toss won by Gloucestershire. Another rain-ruined game, with no play possible on the third day, began with Nottinghamshire reaching 98 for one in the 34 overs allowed by the weather on the first day. Randall, opening in the absence of Robinson, and Broad both played well, but on the second day, also truncated, Lloyds seized his chance to show his abilities as an off-spinner by taking five wickets in an innings for the first time for his new county. Nottinghamshire took encouragement from a mature, attacking innings from the 21-year-old Martindale, whose efforts ensured the second batting point.

## Nottinghamshire

| | |
|---|---|
| D. W. Randall c Russell b Walsh | 41 |
| B. C. Broad c Payne b Lloyds | 48 |
| *C. E. B. Rice c Davison b Lloyds | 6 |
| P. Johnson c Stovold b Lloyds | 12 |
| D. J. R. Martindale c Lawrence b Curran | 42 |
| K. P. Evans c Russell b Walsh | 11 |
| †B. N. French lbw b Curran | 7 |
| R. A. Pick c Stovold b Lloyds | 18 |
| K. Saxelby lbw b Lawrence | 7 |
| K. E. Cooper not out | 10 |
| P. M. Such st Russell b Lloyds | 0 |
| B 5, l-b 5, n-b 4 | 14 |
| 1/98 2/98 3/117 4/118 5/153 6/172 7/179 8/203 9/215 | 216 |

Bonus points – Nottinghamshire 2, Gloucestershire 4.

Bowling: Lawrence 10–1–45–1; Walsh 18–8–42–2; Graveney 20–4–46–0; Curran 12–4–29–2; Payne 3–1–7–0; Lloyds 12.1–3–37–5.

## Gloucestershire

| | |
|---|---|
| A. W. Stovold retired hurt | 10 |
| A. J. Wright not out | 5 |
| C. W. J. Athey not out | 0 |
| (no wkt) | 15 |

B. F. Davison, J. W. Lloyds, K. M. Curran, I. R. Payne, †R. C. Russell, *D. A. Graveney, D. V. Lawrence and C. A. Walsh did not bat.

Bowling: Saxelby 4–2–9–0; Pick 4–0–6–0.

Umpires: J. A. Jameson and R. Palmer.

## GLOUCESTERSHIRE v WARWICKSHIRE

At Cheltenham, August 17, 19, 20. Gloucestershire won by seven wickets. Gloucestershire 23 pts, Warwickshire 4 pts. Toss won by Warwickshire. Gloucestershire went back to the top of the Championship table by forcing victory on the third day, when play was impossible in most other parts of the country. On one of the fastest pitches ever prepared at the College ground, the first day saw some stirring cricket with over 400 runs scored and twenty wickets taken. Warwickshire, swept aside by Walsh and Lawrence in under two and a half hours as the ball flew, hit back so well that Gloucestershire would have been 50 for six had not two easy catches been put down. In contrast, Gloucestershire held sixteen catches at or close to the wicket in the match. Curran and Lloyds, the players reprieved, turned the game as Small tired and Smith lost control, one of his overs containing six no-balls and costing 22 runs. Gloucestershire's first-innings lead of 126 looked certain to be decisive, weather permitting. Only eight overs were possible on the Monday, but in bleak conditions the following day Walsh bowled superbly to overcome resistance from Amiss, Humpage and Ferreira. The West Indian's match return of thirteen for 128 was the best of his career, as were his first-innings figures of seven for 51.

## Warwickshire

| | | | |
|---|---|---|---|
| R. I. H. B. Dyer c Russell b Walsh | 9 | – c Lloyds b Walsh | 10 |
| G. J. Lord c Athey b Lawrence | 0 | – c Lloyds b Walsh | 18 |
| A. I. Kallicharran c Lawrence b Walsh | 34 | – c Russell b Curran | 20 |
| D. L. Amiss c Athey b Lawrence | 14 | – c Stovold b Lawrence | 45 |
| †G. W. Humpage c Russell b Lawrence | 0 | – c Russell b Walsh | 45 |
| P. A. Smith c Russell b Walsh | 38 | – c Russell b Walsh | 8 |
| A. M. Ferreira c Russell b Walsh | 4 | – not out | 34 |
| D. A. Thorne c Graveney b Walsh | 0 | – c Russell b Walsh | 0 |
| G. C. Small not out | 7 | – c Athey b Walsh | 10 |
| A. R. K. Pierson b Walsh | 2 | – b Lawrence | 3 |
| *N. Gifford b Walsh | 4 | – c Athey b Lawrence | 0 |
| B 4, l-b 10, n-b 1 | 15 | L-b 2, w 7, n-b 9 | 18 |
| 1/9 2/15 3/42 4/46 5/99 6/104 7/104 8/121 9/123 | 127 | 1/29 2/32 3/80 4/151 5/155 6/166 7/166 8/186 9/201 | 211 |

Bonus points – Gloucestershire 4.

Bowling: *First Innings*—Lawrence 11–2–34–3; Walsh 15.5–3–51–7; Curran 5–0–28–0. *Second Innings*—Lawrence 24.2–2–95–3; Walsh 24–6–77–6; Curran 5–2–30–1; Payne 2–0–7–0.

## Gloucestershire

| | | | |
|---|---|---|---|
| A. W. Stovold c Pierson b Smith | 6 | – b Ferreira | 10 |
| A. J. Wright b Small | 7 | – c Gifford b Small | 7 |
| C. W. J. Athey c Humpage b Smith | 0 | – not out | 18 |
| B. F. Davison c Ferreira b Small | 0 | | |
| J. W. Lloyds c Humpage b Ferreira | 54 | – not out | 23 |
| K. M. Curran b Small | 63 | – (4) lbw b Ferreira | 10 |
| I. R. Payne c Humpage b Ferreira | 11 | | |
| †R. C. Russell c Humpage b Small | 17 | | |
| *D. A. Graveney not out | 29 | | |
| D. V. Lawrence b Small | 9 | | |
| C. A. Walsh b Ferreira | 31 | | |
| B 1, l-b 7, w 1, n-b 17 | 26 | B 5, l-b 8, w 5 | 18 |
| 1/17 2/17 3/17 4/19 5/152 6/152 7/169 8/192 9/206 | 253 | 1/18 2/19 3/48 | (3 wkts) 86 |

Bonus points – Gloucestershire 3, Warwickshire 4.

Bowling: *First Innings*—Small 21–3–80–5; Smith 11–1–80–2; Ferreira 22–1–85–3. *Second Innings*—Small 9–4–20–1; Smith 1–0–12–0; Ferreira 9–0–27–2; Gifford 1–0–14–0.

Umpires: C. Cook and J. H. Harris.

At Bournemouth, August 24, 26, 27. GLOUCESTERSHIRE lost to HAMPSHIRE by seven wickets.

## GLOUCESTERSHIRE v ESSEX

At Bristol, August 28, 29, 30. Essex won by 65 runs. Essex 20 pts, Gloucestershire 5 pts. Toss won by Gloucestershire. At one stage pressing for victory in two days, Gloucestershire finished a badly beaten team, their batting lacking the poise expected from Championship contenders. For a long time all had gone well. The reigning champions had been put in on another Bristol "green top", the fast bowlers had done their stuff and Gloucestershire had gone ahead with six wickets in hand. The lead was restricted to 88 by a good spell from Foster, but when the first three Essex second-innings wickets went for 70, all was still according to plan. However, McEwan, on his farewell appearance at Bristol, then took control with a splendidly composed century. Batting was on a different plane to what had gone before. With most of the later Essex batsmen also contributing, Gloucestershire found themselves requiring 223 to win. A poor start, with Stovold completing a pair, was efficiently repaired by Romaines and Bainbridge so that at tea 128 were needed from 40 overs with seven wickets in hand. The ensuing collapse against Pringle, who took six for 42, was as complete as it was unexpected.

## Essex

| | | |
|---|---|---|
| B. R. Hardie c Stovold b Lawrence | 19 – lbw b Curran | 35 |
| J. P. Stephenson b Walsh | 10 – c and b Lawrence | 4 |
| P. J. Prichard lbw b Walsh | 19 – c Lloyds b Graveney | 24 |
| K. S. McEwan b Curran | 16 – c and b Graveney | 106 |
| D. R. Pringle lbw b Walsh | 0 – lbw b Walsh | 25 |
| *K. W. R. Fletcher lbw b Curran | 16 – c Lloyds b Graveney | 30 |
| A. W. Lilley lbw b Curran | 10 – c Stovold b Lawrence | 29 |
| †D. E. East c Romaines b Walsh | 1 – c Curran b Lawrence | 12 |
| N. A. Foster b Walsh | 11 – c Romaines b Graveney | 10 |
| J. K. Lever b Curran | 4 – not out | 18 |
| D. L. Acfield not out | 0 – b Walsh | 4 |
| L-b 1, n-b 4 | 5 B 1, l-b 6, w 2, n-b 4 | 13 |
| 1/34 2/38 3/59 4/61 5/83 6/86 7/87 8/107 9/107 | 111 1/10 2/68 3/70 4/159 5/231 6/238 7/262 8/288 9/288 | 310 |

Bonus points – Gloucestershire 4.

Bowling: *First Innings*—Lawrence 6–1–24–1; Walsh 20–9–51–5; Payne 6–1–22–0; Curran 8.1–0–13–4. *Second Innings*—Lawrence 27–2–93–3; Walsh 17–6–37–2; Curran 14–1–49–1; Payne 4–0–8–0; Graveney 32–6–91–4; Lloyds 8–1–25–0.

## Gloucestershire

| | | |
|---|---|---|
| P. W. Romaines c East b Lever | 16 – lbw b Pringle | 35 |
| J. W. Lloyds c Fletcher b Pringle | 34 – b Foster | 1 |
| A. W. Stovold c East b Foster | 0 – c Pringle b Lever | 0 |
| P. Bainbridge lbw b Foster | 0 – c Foster b Acfield | 69 |
| B. F. Davison c Stephenson b Pringle | 42 – c Lever b Acfield | 10 |
| K. M. Curran c Fletcher b Foster | 42 – lbw b Pringle | 1 |
| I. R. Payne lbw b Lever | 19 – lbw b Pringle | 2 |
| †R. C. Russell c East b Foster | 0 – c East b Pringle | 7 |
| *D. A. Graveney c Prichard b Foster | 12 – not out | 12 |
| D. V. Lawrence not out | 22 – b Pringle | 0 |
| C. A. Walsh c East b Pringle | 7 – c Foster b Pringle | 16 |
| L-b 5 | 5 B 1, l-b 3 | 4 |
| 1/30 2/51 3/51 4/57 5/124 6/146 7/147 8/169 9/174 | 199 1/4 2/5 3/91 4/104 5/118 6/120 7/124 8/135 9/139 | 157 |

Bonus points – Gloucestershire 1, Essex 4.

Bowling: *First Innings*—Lever 16–4–59–2; Foster 32–7–79–5; Pringle 19.2–3–56–3. *Second Innings*—Lever 12–1–27–1; Foster 8–0–20–1; Pringle 20.2–6–42–6; Acfield 20–4–64–2.

Umpires: J. H. Hampshire and R. Julian.

At Cardiff, August 31, September 2, 3. GLOUCESTERSHIRE drew with GLAMORGAN.

## GLOUCESTERSHIRE v NORTHAMPTONSHIRE

At Bristol, September 4, 5, 6. Drawn. Gloucestershire 2 pts, Northamptonshire 4 pts. Toss won by Northamptonshire. Gloucestershire's last realistic hopes of winning the Championship disappeared with this result. Play did not start until four o'clock on the second day, when Griffiths proved a handful and only Graveney's best score of the season, after taking eleven overs to get off the mark, enabled his side to gain two batting points. Northamptonshire, sportingly, gave their opponents the chance of sixteen points by forfeiting their first innings, and after Graveney's declaration they set off willingly in pursuit of 245 in 66 overs. Walsh brought about a collapse, and with Graveney an effective foil there were still nine overs remaining when the last pair came together. However, Mallender played well and Griffiths clung on to leave Gloucestershire disappointed and frustrated.

## Gloucestershire

| | | | |
|---|---|---|---|
| P. W. Romaines b Griffiths | 8 | – (2) not out | 2 |
| J. W. Lloyds c Boyd-Moss b Griffiths | 30 | | |
| C. W. J. Athey c Ripley b Griffiths | 8 | | |
| P. Bainbridge b Harper | 7 | | |
| B. F. Davison c Harper b Capel | 5 | | |
| K. M. Curran lbw b Capel | 14 | | |
| I. R. Payne b Mallender | 37 | | |
| *D. A. Graveney not out | 53 | – (1) not out | 14 |
| †R. C. Russell c Capel b Harper | 20 | | |
| D. V. Lawrence b Boyd-Moss | 26 | | |
| C. A. Walsh c Williams b Boyd-Moss | 9 | | |
| B 3, l-b 3, n-b 5 | 11 | | |
| 1/21 2/37 3/51 4/60 5/78 6/84 7/122 8/165 9/210 | 228 | (no wkt dec.) | 16 |

Bonus points – Gloucestershire 2, Northamptonshire 4.

Bowling: *First Innings*—Mallender 14–1–48–1; Griffiths 14–4–36–3; Capel 10–4–21–2; Harper 23–7–75–2; Williams 9–2–21–0; Boyd-Moss 4.1–0–21–2. *Second Innings*—Harper 2–0–4–0; Boyd-Moss 2–0–12–0.

## Northamptonshire

*Northamptonshire forfeited their first innings.*

| | |
|---|---|
| *G. Cook c Romaines b Lawrence | 0 |
| W. Larkins run out | 39 |
| R. J. Boyd-Moss b Walsh | 14 |
| R. J. Bailey lbw b Walsh | 8 |
| R. G. Williams c Davison b Walsh | 1 |
| D. J. Wild c Athey b Graveney | 49 |
| D. J. Capel b Walsh | 15 |
| R. A. Harper lbw b Graveney | 9 |
| †D. Ripley c Romaines b Graveney | 0 |
| N. A. Mallender not out | 43 |
| B. J. Griffiths not out | 1 |
| L-b 3, n-b 6 | 9 |
| 1/0 2/50 3/67 4/68 5/71 6/100 7/129 8/129 9/164 (9 wkts) | 188 |

Bowling: Lawrence 8–2–30–1; Walsh 27–6–72–4; Curran 16–5–37–0; Graveney 15–6–46–3.

Umpires: K. J. Lyons and N. T. Plews.

At The Oval, September 14, 16, 17. GLOUCESTERSHIRE drew with SURREY.

## HAMPSHIRE

*President:* C. G. A. Paris
*Chairman:* 1985 – G. Ford
*Chairman, Cricket Committee:* C. J. Knott
*Secretary.* 1985 – A. K. James
*Chief Executive:* 1986 – A. F. Baker
Northlands Road, Southampton SO9 2TY
(Telephone: 0703-333788)
*Captain:* M. C. J. Nicholas
*Coach:* P. J. Sainsbury

The 1985 season brought such a resurgence to Hampshire cricket that success should not be far away. Their contribution to the summer was both positive and attractive, as the results show: runners-up in the Britannic Assurance Championship, third in the John Player Sunday League, a place in the semi-finals of the NatWest Bank Trophy and the quarter-finals of the Benson and Hedges Cup. It was a dramatic and major improvement on the previous year.

Much of the credit for this must go to Mark Nicholas, who was in his first full season as captain. He had taken over in August, 1984, when Nick Pocock announced his retirement and all was not smooth. Trevor Jesty, feeling he should have been offered the job, left to join Surrey; but Nicholas proved Hampshire right in their decision. He led the team with a refreshing keenness and a quickly found maturity, and support for his captaincy came from outside the county. He led MCC against both the champion county and the Australians at Lord's, and was later appointed captain for the England B tour to Bangladesh, Sri Lanka and Zimbabwe.

Hampshire clearly enjoyed their cricket, but the season brought its disappointments. Defeat in the semi-final of the NatWest Bank Trophy, which Essex won by virtue of having lost fewer wickets when the scores finished level, was high among them. In the captain's words, it left Hampshire with the stigma of being the only county not to have appeared in a Lord's final. Yet this should not be allowed to cloud a season of achievement and promise.

But for the weather Hampshire could well have amassed an almost unassailable lead in the Championship by mid-June. After successive wins over Somerset and Derbyshire, they would have made it four in a row but for rain robbing them of victory at both Middlesbrough and Edgbaston. However, the weather could not be held totally to blame, for their own lapses in the field cost Hampshire dearly. Middlesex should have been beaten at Bournemouth, where the eventual champions, having been set 265 in 63 overs, stared defeat in the face at 82 for eight, before being helped in saving the match by at least two dropped catches. A further setback was their failure to beat a weakened Somerset at Bournemouth early in August; and in their penultimate Championship fixture of the season they let slip a total of nine chances in Northamptonshire's two innings.

In the John Player League, Hampshire finished third behind Essex and Sussex, their biggest misfortune here being that they suffered more "no result" matches than the two sides above them. They then lost their penultimate game against Derbyshire at Southampton, which they should never have done.

Hampshire possessed perhaps the most formidable batting line-up in the county game. They were never bowled out twice in a first-class match. This considerable potential was given consistency by Chris Smith, who was the third-highest run-getter in the country and the first Hampshire batsman to score 2,000 first-class runs in a season since Barry Richards in 1968. Smith's younger brother, Robin, who qualified as English at the start of the season, confirmed his talent by scoring over 1,500 runs and could well become an international cricketer of some repute.

Gordon Greenidge had a disappointing season, judged by his own high standards, not reaching 1,000 runs until the last seven days of the season. He scored very freely in the John Player League, in which he finished with an average of 81.66. Nicholas and Paul Terry both topped 1,000 runs, while Tim Tremlett, Jon Hardy and Kevan James all scored centuries.

Such was Hampshire's batting strength that the highly promising Hardy was unable to claim a regular place and at the end of the season was given permission to seek another county. By the same token, the dependable David Turner was given only seven first-class games, though he was a vital member of the one-day side.

The return of Malcolm Marshall, who had been, like Greenidge, on tour with the West Indians in 1984, was vital to Hampshire's bowling. He overcame a succession of slow pitches to take 95 wickets, a performance which his captain described as remarkable. There were notable contributions, too, from the ever-willing Tremlett, who was the first bowler in the country to reach the 50 mark and went on to record his best haul of wickets in a first-class season, and from Rajesh Maru, the slow left-arm spinner. Tremlett gained recognition with his selection for the England B tour, and at a time of scarcity of top-class spinners, there were those who felt Maru would have been an asset in the same side. He made a significant advance by taking 73 first-class wickets at an average of 26.34.

Stephen Andrew, at nineteen a fine fast bowling prospect, had moments of high promise, while James, like Maru a recruit from Middlesex, looked a useful acquisition. He hit a maiden first-class hundred against Somerset at Taunton and achieved remarkable success with his left-arm medium pace against the Australians, taking six for 22 as the tourists were dismissed for 76 at Southampton.

Thus Hampshire enjoyed a season in which only the icing on the cake was missing. There was a quiet efficiency about their cricket, as typified by the dependable wicket-keeper, Bobby Parks. – B.H.

HAMPSHIRE 1985

[*Bill Smith*

*Back row:* M. E. O'Connor, C. A. Connor, R. A. Smith, T. M. Tremlett, K. D. James, R. J. Parks, R. J. Maru. *Front row:* M. D. Marshall, V. P. Terry, M. C. J. Nicholas (*captain*), C. G. Greenidge, C. L. Smith. *Insets:* N. G. Cowley, S. J. W. Andrew, J. J. E. Hardy, D. R. Turner.

## HAMPSHIRE RESULTS

*All first-class matches – Played 26: Won 7, Lost 2, Drawn 17.*

*County Championship matches – Played 24: Won 7, Lost 2, Drawn 15.*

*Bonus points – Batting 66, Bowling 78.*

*Competition placings – Britannic Assurance County Championship, r/u; NatWest Bank Trophy, s-f; Benson and Hedges Cup, q-f; John Player League, 3rd.*

## BRITANNIC ASSURANCE CHAMPIONSHIP AVERAGES

### BATTING

| | *Birthplace* | *M* | *I* | *NO* | *R* | *HI* | *Avge* |
|---|---|---|---|---|---|---|---|
| ‡C. L. Smith | *Durban, SA* | 21 | 35 | 3 | 1,720 | 143* | 53.75 |
| ‡C. G. Greenidge | *St Peter, Barbados* | 19 | 32 | 2 | 1,236 | 204 | 41.20 |
| ‡R. A. Smith | *Durban, SA* | 24 | 40 | 6 | 1,351 | 140* | 39.73 |
| K. D. James | *Lambeth* | 6 | 9 | 3 | 217 | 124 | 36.16 |
| J. J. E. Hardy | *Nakaru, Kenya* | 14 | 22 | 4 | 624 | 107* | 34.66 |
| ‡M. C. J. Nicholas | *London* | 22 | 35 | 3 | 1,109 | 146 | 34.65 |
| ‡V. P. Terry | *Osnabruck, WG* | 24 | 40 | 2 | 1,224 | 148* | 32.21 |
| ‡T. M. Tremlett | *Wellington, Somerset* | 24 | 29 | 15 | 450 | 102* | 32.14 |
| ‡M. D. Marshall | *St Michael, Barbados* | 22 | 33 | 2 | 768 | 66* | 24.77 |
| ‡R. J. Parks | *Cuckfield* | 24 | 23 | 9 | 344 | 53* | 24.57 |
| ‡N. G. Cowley | *Shaftesbury* | 12 | 13 | 4 | 202 | 51 | 22.44 |
| R. J. Maru | *Nairobi, Kenya* | 21 | 18 | 8 | 223 | 62 | 22.30 |
| ‡D. R. Turner | *Chippenham* | 6 | 8 | 1 | 153 | 44 | 21.85 |
| C. A. Connor | *The Valley, Anguilla* | 15 | 8 | 3 | 61 | 36 | 12.20 |
| S. J. W. Andrew | *London* | 10 | 4 | 3 | 8 | 6* | 8.00 |

* *Signifies not out.* ‡ *Denotes county cap.*

The following played a total of fifteen three-figure innings for Hampshire in County Championship matches – C. L. Smith 5, C. G. Greenidge 2, R. A. Smith 2, V. P. Terry 2, J. J. E. Hardy 1, K. D. James 1, M. C. J. Nicholas 1, T. M. Tremlett 1.

### BOWLING

| | *O* | *M* | *R* | *W* | *BB* | *Avge* |
|---|---|---|---|---|---|---|
| M. D. Marshall | 688.1 | 193 | 1,680 | 95 | 7-59 | 17.68 |
| T. M. Tremlett | 665.5 | 181 | 1,620 | 75 | 5-42 | 21.60 |
| N. G. Cowley | 234.5 | 56 | 650 | 24 | 3-17 | 27.08 |
| R. J. Maru | 652 | 178 | 1,809 | 64 | 5-16 | 28.26 |
| S. J. W. Andrew | 258 | 46 | 915 | 28 | 6-43 | 32.67 |
| C. A. Connor | 417.5 | 83 | 1,310 | 29 | 4-62 | 45.17 |

Also bowled: C. G. Greenidge 4–1–16–0; K. D. James 126–17–549–7; M. C. J. Nicholas 119–21–436–6; C. L. Smith 61–6–269–4; R. A. Smith 26.4–8–72–4.

## HAMPSHIRE v KENT

At Southampton, April 27, 28, 29. Drawn. Hampshire 7 pts, Kent 5 pts. Toss won by Kent. Hampshire's first match of the season produced 1,151 runs and a thrilling finish which saw them fall just 2 runs short of victory. Kent were given a good start by Benson and Hinks, but Cowley broke the stand with his first ball to trigger a collapse which saw seven wickets fall for 70 runs before Knott and Dilley staged a recovery. In Hampshire's first innings Robin Smith batted brilliantly for his 85, hitting one 6 and fifteen 4s in 165 minutes. When Kent batted again, Benson hit a career-best 162 (one 6, nineteen 4s) in 249 minutes and Tavaré an undefeated 102 (four 6s, twelve 4s) in 117 minutes to enable Cowdrey to set Hampshire a target of 269 in 51 overs. Terry and Chris Smith put them on course, but 14 off the final over, bowled by Dilley, proved just too demanding.

### Kent

| | | | |
|---|---|---|---|
| M. R. Benson c Nicholas b Connor | 61 | – c James b Cowley | 162 |
| S. G. Hinks b Cowley | 39 | – lbw b C. L. Smith | 65 |
| C. J. Tavaré c Parks b Tremlett | 7 | – not out | 102 |
| D. G. Aslett c R. A. Smith b Tremlett | 0 | | |
| *C. S. Cowdrey b James | 25 | | |
| G. W. Johnson c Terry b Tremlett | 8 | | |
| †A. P. E. Knott b Cowley | 55 | | |
| C. Penn c Parks b Tremlett | 1 | | |
| G. R. Dilley b Cowley | 24 | – (4) not out | 0 |
| D. L. Underwood c James b Tremlett | 5 | | |
| K. B. S. Jarvis not out | 0 | | |
| L-b 4, w 1, n-b 2 | 7 | B 1, l-b 4, n-b 10 | 15 |
| 1/85 2/106 3/106 4/112 5/123 6/151 7/155 8/207 9/213 | 232 | 1/142 2/319 (2 wkts dec.) | 344 |

Bonus points – Kent 2, Hampshire 4.

Bowling: *First Innings*—Connor 26–6–83–1; James 14–1–62–1; Tremlett 24–5–66–5; Cowley 7.4–1–17–3. *Second Innings*—Connor 16–1–64–0; James 19–2–77–0; Nicholas 8–1–28–0; Tremlett 13–5–24–0; Cowley 22–1–96–1; C. L. Smith 9–0–50–1.

### Hampshire

| | | | |
|---|---|---|---|
| V. P. Terry c Penn b Jarvis | 69 | – lbw b Cowdrey | 88 |
| C. L. Smith b Jarvis | 18 | – lbw b Jarvis | 84 |
| *M. C. J. Nicholas c Knott b Cowdrey | 12 | – (4) not out | 33 |
| J. J. E. Hardy b Jarvis | 0 | – (5) not out | 21 |
| R. A. Smith run out | 85 | – (3) b Dilley | 23 |
| D. R. Turner c Cowdrey b Underwood | 44 | | |
| N. G. Cowley c Johnson b Underwood | 8 | | |
| K. D. James not out | 33 | | |
| T. M. Tremlett c Cowdrey b Penn | 23 | | |
| †R. J. Parks not out | 3 | | |
| L-b 6, n-b 7 | 13 | B 2, l-b 8, w 1, n-b 7 | 18 |
| 1/30 2/68 3/68 4/172 5/195 6/216 7/249 8/303 (8 wkts dec.) | 308 | 1/167 2/207 3/209 (3 wkts) | 267 |

C. A. Connor did not bat.

Bonus points – Hampshire 3, Kent 3 (Score at 100 overs: 264-7).

Bowling: *First Innings*—Dilley 21–3–71–0; Jarvis 29–6–99–3; Penn 15.3–5–44–1; Cowdrey 9.3–4–24–1; Underwood 31–15–41–2; Johnson 8–1–23–0. *Second Innings*—Dilley 12–0–53–1; Jarvis 10–0–48–1; Johnson 5–2–17–0; Underwood 6–1–28–0; Cowdrey 14–0–84–1; Penn 4–0–27–0.

Umpires: C. Cook and R. Palmer.

At Northampton, May 4, 6, 7. HAMPSHIRE drew with NORTHAMPTONSHIRE.

At The Parks, May 8, 9, 10. HAMPSHIRE drew with OXFORD UNIVERSITY.

At Taunton, May 22, 23, 24. HAMPSHIRE beat SOMERSET by five wickets.

## HAMPSHIRE v GLAMORGAN

At Southampton, May 25, 27, 28. Hampshire won by three wickets. Hampshire 20 pts, Glamorgan 5 pts. Toss won by Hampshire. Bowlers dominated the first day when 21 wickets fell. Glamorgan, sent in to bat, lost seven wickets for 88 before they were rallied by Ontong, who was 10 short of his century when the innings ended. Hampshire were then dismissed for 115 with Malone, the seam bowler they released in 1984, returning Championship-best figures of five for 38. Rain precluded play on the second day, but the third produced an exciting finish after Glamorgan's declaration asked Hampshire to score 259 in 44 overs. The win was set up by a third-wicket partnership of 166 in 27 overs between Greenidge and Chris Smith, who batted quite superbly in making 96 off 95 balls. With Hampshire needing 8 runs off the last two balls, Tremlett hit Thomas for 6 over mid-wicket and then ran 2 with the help of a mis-field.

### Glamorgan

| | | | |
|---|---|---|---|
| J. A. Hopkins c Cowley b Connor | 3 | (5) lbw b Tremlett | 10 |
| G. C. Holmes c and b Connor | 11 | (1) c R. A. Smith b Tremlett | 34 |
| S. P. Henderson c Terry b Connor | 3 | (6) c Parks b James | 9 |
| Javed Miandad c Parks b Marshall | 1 | c Parks b Tremlett | 42 |
| *R. C. Ontong not out | 90 | (8) not out | 15 |
| J. F. Steele c Parks b Tremlett | 9 | (9) run out | 1 |
| J. Derrick c Nicholas b Marshall | 17 | (2) lbw b Marshall | 0 |
| †T. Davies c Terry b Marshall | 0 | (3) b James | 31 |
| J. G. Thomas c Greenidge b Nicholas | 42 | (7) c Greenidge b R. A. Smith | 17 |
| S. J. Malone b Marshall | 0 | | |
| S. R. Barwick run out | 5 | (10) not out | 1 |
| L-b 5, n-b 11 | 16 | B 6, l-b 3, n-b 7 | 16 |
| 1/14 2/19 3/20 4/24 5/53 6/88 7/88 8/168 9/186 | 197 | 1/1 2/59 3/120 4/120 5/135 6/139 7/168 8/170 (8 wkts dec.) | 176 |

Bonus points – Glamorgan 1, Hampshire 4.

Bowling: *First Innings*—Marshall 21.2–4–57–4; Connor 19–2–70–3; Tremlett 12–3–21–1; James 4–1–26–0; Cowley 4–0–7–0; Nicholas 4–0–11–1. *Second Innings*—Marshall 12–3–33–1; Connor 12–4–18–0; Tremlett 18–2–53–3; James 11–2–45–2; Cowley 2–2–0–0; C. L. Smith 5–1–6–0; R. A. Smith 4–0–12–1.

### Hampshire

| | First innings | | Second innings | |
|---|---|---|---|---|
| C. G. Greenidge c Barwick b Thomas | 0 | – | run out | 65 |
| V. P. Terry c Davies b Malone | 4 | – | lbw b Thomas | 0 |
| *M. C. J. Nicholas c Steele b Thomas | 6 | – | c Henderson b Thomas | 4 |
| C. L. Smith not out | 29 | – | b Thomas | 96 |
| R. A. Smith c Davies b Thomas | 2 | – | c Steele b Ontong | 35 |
| M. D. Marshall c Miandad b Malone | 12 | – | st Davies b Ontong | 18 |
| K. D. James c Miandad b Barwick | 2 | – | run out | 4 |
| T. M. Tremlett lbw b Malone | 1 | – | (9) not out | 10 |
| N. G. Cowley hit wkt b Malone | 14 | – | (8) not out | 9 |
| †R. J. Parks c Davies b Malone | 18 | | | |
| C. A. Connor c Davies b Barwick | 9 | | | |
| L-b 3, w 1, n-b 14 | 18 | | B 5, l-b 6, n-b 7 | 18 |
| 1/3 2/14 3/24 4/31 5/53 6/57 7/57 8/85 9/91 | 115 | | 1/1 2/13 3/179 4/182 5/223 6/236 7/241 (7 wkts) | 259 |

Bonus points – Glamorgan 4.

*In the first innings C. L. Smith, when 14, retired hurt at 37 and resumed at 91.*

Bowling: *First Innings*—Thomas 11–1–41–3; Malone 16–5–38–5; Barwick 13.5–4–33–2. *Second Innings*—Thomas 17–0–96–3; Malone 5–0–26–0; Barwick 7–2–26–0; Derrick 3–0–20–0; Holmes 2–1–5–0; Steele 2–0–24–0; Ontong 7–0–51–2.

Umpires: R. Palmer and A. G. T. Whitehead.

## HAMPSHIRE v DERBYSHIRE

At Basingstoke, May 29, 30, 31. Hampshire won by four wickets. Hampshire 22 pts, Derbyshire 6 pts. Toss won by Hampshire. Derbyshire were in trouble at 118 for seven, but Moir, Newman and Warner staged a tail-end recovery. Hampshire also made a poor start to their first innings, and Derbyshire, with a lead of 28, built steadily through Hill, who batted for 5 hours, 45 minutes for his 120. Hampshire, set to score 379 in 79 overs, got home with an over to spare thanks to a career-best 140 not out (four 6s, thirteen 4s, 165 balls) from Robin Smith, who finished the match by straight-driving Miller for two successive 6s. The Smith brothers laid the platform for the victory by putting on 161 in 38 overs for the fourth wicket.

### Derbyshire

| | First innings | | Second innings | |
|---|---|---|---|---|
| *K. J. Barnett lbw b Marshall | 6 | – | c Tremlett b Marshall | 17 |
| A. Hill run out | 20 | – | c C. L. Smith b James | 120 |
| J. G. Wright c Parks b Connor | 29 | – | c James b Maru | 44 |
| B. Roberts lbw b Tremlett | 0 | – | lbw b Marshall | 66 |
| W. P. Fowler b James | 12 | – | c Parks b Marshall | 0 |
| G. Miller c Parks b Connor | 15 | – | c Marshall b Connor | 46 |
| R. J. Finney c Connor b Tremlett | 16 | – | not out | 27 |
| †B. J. M. Maher c Marshall b Tremlett | 8 | – | not out | 18 |
| D. G. Moir lbw b Marshall | 40 | | | |
| P. G. Newman not out | 56 | | | |
| A. E. Warner b Connor | 24 | | | |
| L-b 9, w 1, n-b 10 | 20 | | L-b 3, w 1, n-b 8 | 12 |
| 1/6 2/58 3/59 4/65 5/76 6/99 7/118 8/128 9/176 | 246 | | 1/26 2/100 3/190 4/190 5/302 6/304 (6 wkts dec.) | 350 |

Bonus points – Derbyshire 2, Hampshire 4.

Bowling: *First Innings*—Marshall 19–5–57–2; James 19–5–67–1; Connor 15.4–5–40–3; Tremlett 18–6–30–3; Maru 6–0–43–0. *Second Innings*—Marshall 16–5–39–3; James 18–2–63–1; Connor 22–3–98–1; Tremlett 19–7–43–0; Maru 33–13–81–1; Nicholas 4–0–23–0.

### Hampshire

| | | |
|---|---|---|
| C. G. Greenidge c Miller b Finney | 17 – lbw b Newman | 42 |
| V. P. Terry lbw b Warner | 6 – b Miller | 61 |
| *M. C. J. Nicholas c Moir b Finney | 0 – c Roberts b Newman | 4 |
| C. L. Smith b Miller | 45 – lbw b Moir | 83 |
| R. A. Smith c and b Moir | 12 – not out | 140 |
| M. D. Marshall c Roberts b Warner | 64 – c Roberts b Miller | 8 |
| K. D. James c and b Miller | 0 – c Barnett b Moir | 3 |
| R. J. Maru c Miller b Newman | 32 | |
| T. M. Tremlett c Maher b Warner | 15 – (8) not out | 13 |
| †R. J. Parks not out | 10 | |
| C. A. Connor lbw b Newman | 0 | |
| B 1, l-b 5, n-b 11 | 17 L-b 16, w 2, n-b 8 | 26 |
| 1/27 2/27 3/31 4/83 5/93 6/125 7/158 8/203 9/214 | 218 1/80 2/84 3/137 4/298 5/309 6/326 | (6 wkts) 380 |

Bonus points – Hampshire 2, Derbyshire 4.

Bowling: *First Innings*—Warner 16–2–67–3; Finney 14–1–56–2; Newman 6.3–1–30–2; Moir 14–5–51–1; Miller 6–4–8–2. *Second Innings*—Warner 11–1–63–0; Finney 11–0–62–0; Miller 29–3–132–2; Newman 8–1–39–2; Moir 20–3–68–2.

Umpires: A. A. Jones and A. G. T. Whitehead.

At Middlesbrough, June 1, 3, 4. HAMPSHIRE drew with YORKSHIRE.

At Edgbaston, June 8, 10, 11. HAMPSHIRE drew with WARWICKSHIRE.

## HAMPSHIRE v MIDDLESEX

At Bournemouth, June 12, 13, 14. Drawn. Hampshire 5 pts, Middlesex 5 pts. Toss won by Hampshire. Leading the Championship at this point, Hampshire were denied victory after setting Middlesex a target of 265 in 63 overs and dismissing eight of their batsmen for just 82 runs. However, Sykes, in only his fourth first-class match, and Hughes thwarted Hampshire with an unbeaten ninth-wicket partnership of 84 in 29 overs. In a bid to break through, Nicholas switched his bowlers ten times during the final twenty overs. Batting was never easy on a slow wicket, but during Hampshire's second innings Chris Smith became the first player to reach 1,000 runs in the season.

## Hampshire

| First Innings | | Second Innings | |
|---|---|---|---|
| C. G. Greenidge b Williams | 21 | lbw b Williams | 1 |
| V. P. Terry c Butcher b Hughes | 25 | c and b Edmonds | 57 |
| *M. C. J. Nicholas c Brown b Hughes | 54 | c Tomlins b Hughes | 10 |
| C. L. Smith c Edmonds b Hughes | 4 | run out | 40 |
| R. A. Smith c Hughes b Edmonds | 8 | run out | 45 |
| M. D. Marshall c Tomlins b Edmonds | 15 | c Williams b Sykes | 55 |
| T. M. Tremlett lbw b Daniel | 6 | (8) c Butcher b Edmonds | 12 |
| †R. J. Parks b Edmonds | 17 | (7) lbw b Daniel | 4 |
| N. G. Cowley c and b Edmonds | 19 | not out | 21 |
| R. J. Maru b Daniel | 5 | | |
| C. A. Connor not out | 2 | | |
| B 1, l-b 1, n-b 6 | 8 | B 7, l-b 2, n-b 9 | 18 |
| 1/24 2/59 3/63 4/74 5/121 6/135 7/157 8/163 9/182 | 184 | 1/8 2/52 3/93 4/158 5/192 6/198 7/229 8/263 | (8 wkts dec.) 263 |

Bonus points – Hampshire 1, Middlesex 4.

Bowling: *First Innings*—Williams 12–0–51–1; Daniel 15–5–52–2; Edmonds 31–13–44–4; Hughes 16–6–35–3. *Second Innings*—Williams 15–1–59–1; Daniel 15–2–49–1; Hughes 11–4–24–1; Edmonds 41–13–66–2; Sykes 22.1–6–56–1.

## Middlesex

| First Innings | | Second Innings | |
|---|---|---|---|
| G. D. Barlow lbw b Tremlett | 11 | lbw b Tremlett | 5 |
| W. N. Slack lbw b Tremlett | 24 | c Parks b Connor | 1 |
| K. P. Tomlins c Parks b Marshall | 42 | b Maru | 36 |
| R. O. Butcher c Connor b Marshall | 4 | lbw b Marshall | 23 |
| *C. T. Radley lbw b Marshall | 7 | c Connor b Marshall | 5 |
| †K. R. Brown lbw b Marshall | 11 | c sub b Maru | 2 |
| P. H. Edmonds lbw b Marshall | 0 | lbw b Marshall | 3 |
| N. F. Williams b Tremlett | 34 | c Greenidge b Maru | 3 |
| J. F. Sykes c Terry b Maru | 24 | not out | 52 |
| S. P. Hughes not out | 12 | not out | 30 |
| W. W. Daniel b Tremlett | 1 | | |
| L-b 11, n-b 2 | 13 | W 4, n-b 2 | 6 |
| 1/34 2/54 3/69 4/86 5/106 6/106 7/125 8/168 9/174 | 183 | 1/5 2/9 3/38 4/50 5/61 6/76 7/80 8/82 | (8 wkts) 166 |

Bonus points – Middlesex 1, Hampshire 4.

Bowling: *First Innings*—Marshall 26–9–68–5; Connor 12–2–36–0; Tremlett 19.3–8–30–4; Maru 13–8–10–1; Cowley 9–3–28–0. *Second Innings*—Connor 7–3–17–1; Marshall 24–7–59–3; Tremlett 7–3–15–1; Maru 23–7–63–3; Cowley 6–3–12–0.

Umpires: J. H. Harris and R. A. White.

At Hove, June 15, 17, 18. HAMPSHIRE drew with SUSSEX.

At Southampton, June 22, 23, 24, 25. HAMPSHIRE drew with AUSTRALIANS (See Australian tour section).

At Bristol, June 26, 27, 28. HAMPSHIRE drew with GLOUCESTERSHIRE.

## HAMPSHIRE v ESSEX

At Southampton, June 29, July 1, 2. Hampshire won by an innings and 57 runs. Hampshire 23 pts, Essex 3 pts. Toss won by Hampshire. They were in command from the moment they put Essex in on a green wicket and Marshall and Tremlett dismissed them for less than 100. Hampshire went ahead before losing their first wicket and built a commanding lead as Hardy, sharing stands of 68 and 115 with Tremlett and Parks respectively, reached a maiden first-class century. His unbeaten 107 was made in 265 minutes and included two 6s and fourteen 4s. Essex were soon in trouble again and only a brave innings from McEwan saved them from defeat in two days. They ended the second day at 172 for seven and Hampshire needed just six overs to clinch victory the following morning.

### Essex

| First innings | | Second innings | |
|---|---|---|---|
| B. R. Hardie b Marshall | 4 | c Nicholas b Tremlett | 28 |
| C. Gladwin c C. L. Smith b Marshall | 25 | c Parks b Andrew | 4 |
| P. J. Prichard b Marshall | 0 | lbw b Marshall | 1 |
| K. S. McEwan c Parks b Tremlett | 2 | c Parks b Maru | 56 |
| D. R. Pringle c Terry b Marshall | 5 | b Marshall | 3 |
| *K. W. R. Fletcher c Parks b Tremlett | 2 | c Parks b Tremlett | 8 |
| K. R. Pont c Turner b Tremlett | 5 | hit wkt b Marshall | 34 |
| †D. E. East c Andrew b Marshall | 0 | lbw b Maru | 11 |
| S. Turner c Nicholas b Tremlett | 35 | st Parks b Tremlett | 11 |
| J. K. Lever not out | 14 | not out | 2 |
| D. L. Acfield b Marshall | 1 | b Tremlett | 4 |
| L-b 2, n-b 1 | 3 | B 5, l-b 5, w 2, n-b 9 | 21 |
| 1/18 2/18 3/34 4/34 5/41 6/41 7/42 8/54 9/93 | 96 | 1/4 2/19 3/57 4/90 5/106 6/132 7/152 8/172 9/176 | 183 |

Bonus points – Hampshire 4.

Bowling: *First Innings*—Marshall 16.5–5–42–6; Andrew 8–0–33–0; Tremlett 10–2–19–4. *Second Innings*—Marshall 21–7–54–3; Andrew 13–1–49–1; Tremlett 21–6–45–4; Maru 12–7–15–2; Nicholas 1–0–10–0.

### Hampshire

| | |
|---|---|
| V. P. Terry c McEwan b Lever | 51 |
| C. L. Smith c East b Lever | 59 |
| *M. C. J. Nicholas lbw b Turner | 13 |
| R. A. Smith lbw b Pringle | 11 |
| J. J. E. Hardy not out | 107 |
| D. R. Turner c Prichard b Pringle | 0 |
| M. D. Marshall c Hardie b Pringle | 8 |
| T. M. Tremlett lbw b Acfield | 26 |
| †R. J. Parks not out | 53 |
| L-b 3, n-b 5 | 8 |
| 1/97 2/125 3/125 4/145 5/145 6/153 7/221 | (7 wkts dec.) 336 |

R. J. Maru and S. J. W. Andrew did not bat.

Bonus points – Hampshire 3, Essex 3 (Score at 100 overs: 251-7).

Bowling: Lever 39–9–109–2; Pringle 32–6–75–3; Turner 20–5–68–1; Pont 7–2–27–0; Acfield 22–7–54–1.

Umpires: J. A. Jameson and P. B. Wight.

At Liverpool, July 6, 8, 9. HAMPSHIRE beat LANCASHIRE by four wickets.

## HAMPSHIRE v SUSSEX

At Portsmouth, July 10, 11, 12. Drawn. Hampshire 5 pts, Sussex 8 pts. Toss won by Sussex. They lost their first two wickets quickly before Mendis, with his fourth century in four days, led a recovery which eventually saw them obtain maximum batting points. Mendis, given good support by the Wells brothers in stands of 81 and 83, was seventh out for 109, made off 263 balls and containing one 6 and fourteen 4s. Hampshire's reply fell away, the last eight wickets going for 67 runs after Chris Smith and Maru, sent in as night-watchman, had put on 115 in 34 overs for the second wicket. Sussex built a formidable lead before Barclay's declaration left Hampshire a target of 327 in 83 overs. At this point Mendis was just 4 runs short of becoming only the twelfth player to score five centuries in six consecutive innings, having received only four balls in the preceding five overs. Hampshire were in with a chance of victory until the Smith brothers fell within 8 runs of each other. Hardy then checked Sussex's progress and Tremlett and Maru finally thwarted them by safely negotiating the last seven overs.

## Sussex

| First innings | | Second innings | |
|---|---|---|---|
| G. D. Mendis st Parks b Maru | 109 | – not out | 96 |
| A. M. Green run out | 0 | – c Maru b Andrew | 44 |
| P. W. G. Parker c Terry b Marshall | 0 | – c Nicholas b Andrew | 7 |
| C. M. Wells b Tremlett | 49 | – lbw b Andrew | 24 |
| A. P. Wells b Marshall | 33 | – run out | 3 |
| *J. R. T. Barclay run out | 0 | | |
| I. A. Greig c Parks b Andrew | 22 | – not out | 8 |
| †I. J. Gould c Parks b Marshall | 51 | – (6) run out | 11 |
| G. S. le Roux not out | 33 | | |
| A. N. Jones not out | 21 | | |
| B 4, l-b 1, w 2, n-b 2 | 9 | B 4, l-b 7, w 2, n-b 3 | 16 |
| 1/4 2/4 3/85 4/168 5/168 6/208 7/272 8/274 | (8 wkts dec.) 327 | 1/89 2/99 3/165 4/168 5/185 | (5 wkts dec.) 209 |

C. E. Waller did not bat.

Bonus points – Sussex 4, Hampshire 3.

Bowling: *First Innings*—Marshall 25–5–70–3; Andrew 20–6–63–1; Nicholas 3–0–18–0; Tremlett 22–4–58–1; Maru 30–6–113–1. *Second Innings*—Marshall 2–1–10–0; Andrew 26–3–94–3; Tremlett 19–4–43–0; Nicholas 9–2–31–0; Maru 10–2–20–0.

## Hampshire

| First innings | | Second innings | |
|---|---|---|---|
| V. P. Terry lbw b le Roux | 12 | – lbw b le Roux | 1 |
| C. L. Smith c Gould b Jones | 60 | – c and b le Roux | 68 |
| R. J. Maru b Jones | 62 | – (10) not out | 6 |
| *M. C. J. Nicholas c A. P. Wells b le Roux | 5 | – (3) c Gould b Jones | 19 |
| J. J. E. Hardy lbw b le Roux | 0 | – c Gould b C. M. Wells | 54 |
| R. A. Smith run out | 19 | – (4) c C. M. Wells b Greig | 15 |
| D. R. Turner lbw b C. M. Wells | 20 | – (6) lbw b le Roux | 11 |
| M. D. Marshall c Gould b Jones | 4 | – (9) c C. M. Wells b Greig | 9 |
| T. M. Tremlett c Parker b Greig | 11 | – (8) not out | 2 |
| †R. J. Parks not out | 3 | – (7) lbw b Greig | 11 |
| S. J. W. Andrew c and b C. M. Wells | 0 | | |
| L-b 8, w 1, n-b 5 | 14 | L-b 7, w 1, n-b 9 | 17 |
| 1/28 2/143 3/148 4/148 5/148 6/173 7/187 8/206 9/208 | 210 | 1/2 2/61 3/104 4/112 5/161 6/187 7/195 8/204 | (8 wkts) 213 |

Bonus points – Hampshire 2, Sussex 4.

Bowling: *First Innings*—le Roux 18–5–52–3; Jones 21–4–63–3; C. M. Wells 9.5–5–16–2; Greig 16–5–44–1; Waller 8–3–27–0. *Second Innings*—le Roux 21.5–5–51–3; Jones 17–3–50–1; Greig 15–4–43–3; C. M. Wells 16–7–31–1; Waller 12–5–27–0; Barclay 1–0–4–0.

Umpires: H. D. Bird and D. R. Shepherd.

## HAMPSHIRE v WORCESTERSHIRE

At Portsmouth, July 13, 15, 16. Drawn. Hampshire 7 pts, Worcestershire 6 pts. Toss won by Worcestershire. The consistent Chris Smith saved Hampshire from collapse after the top half of their batting was unhinged by Newport, and James supported him courageously, for it was later discovered that he had broken a bone in his right wrist from the first ball he received. David Smith, whose century included one 6 and eleven 4s, provided the Worcestershire innings with backbone as Marshall took seven for 59 to gain for his county a slender lead. Terry and Nicholas were the main contributors to Hampshire's second innings before Worcestershire were set to score 218 in 56 overs. Smith gave them impetus, but ultimately Worcestershire were keeping Hampshire at bay as Rhodes and Newport saw out the last seven overs.

## Hampshire

| | | | |
|---|---|---|---|
| V. P. Terry b Newport | 13 | – b Newport | 76 |
| C. L. Smith b Illingworth | 89 | – c Newport b Radford | 10 |
| *M. C. J. Nicholas c Rhodes b Newport | 16 | – (6) not out | 73 |
| R. A. Smith b Newport | 2 | – (5) b Newport | 28 |
| J. J. E. Hardy c D'Oliveira b Weston | 10 | – (4) c Illingworth b Radford | 0 |
| M. D. Marshall c Patel b Radford | 14 | – (7) c Rhodes b Newport | 0 |
| K. D. James st Rhodes b Patel | 42 | | |
| T. M. Tremlett c Rhodes b Newport | 29 | – not out | 4 |
| †R. J. Parks c Illingworth b Newport | 20 | | |
| R. J. Maru c D'Oliveira b Radford | 1 | – (3) b Radford | 0 |
| C. A. Connor not out | 0 | | |
| L-b 11, w 2, n-b 6 | 19 | B 5, l-b 1, n-b 14 | 20 |
| 1/47 2/70 3/81 4/97 5/120 6/183 7/217 8/239 9/247 | 255 | 1/31 2/32 3/33 4/83 5/206 6/206 (6 wkts dec.) | 211 |

Bonus points – Hampshire 3, Worcestershire 4.

Bowling: *First Innings*—Ellcock 14–0–34–0; Radford 26–5–59–2; Newport 22–0–89–5; Weston 8–2–33–1; Illingworth 10–5–23–1; Patel 6–3–6–1. *Second Innings*—Ellcock 14–0–57–0; Radford 18–1–67–3; Newport 14–2–54–3; Illingworth 10–3–27–0.

## Worcestershire

| | | | |
|---|---|---|---|
| T. S. Curtis b Marshall | 6 | – c and b Maru | 8 |
| D. B. D'Oliveira c Nicholas b Marshall | 10 | – (5) c R. A. Smith b Maru | 31 |
| D. M. Smith b Maru | 112 | – c Parks b Marshall | 87 |
| D. N. Patel lbw b Marshall | 38 | – (2) c Parks b James | 0 |
| *P. A. Neale lbw b Nicholas | 12 | – (4) b Marshall | 20 |
| M. J. Weston b Maru | 26 | – c Parks b Maru | 10 |
| †S. J. Rhodes c Nicholas b Marshall | 3 | – not out | 6 |
| P. J. Newport lbw b Marshall | 3 | – (9) not out | 0 |
| N. V. Radford b Marshall | 8 | – (8) c Terry b Maru | 0 |
| R. M. Ellcock lbw b Marshall | 3 | | |
| R. K. Illingworth not out | 0 | | |
| B 2, l-b 21, w 1, n-b 4 | 28 | L-b 4 | 4 |
| 1/15 2/34 3/145 4/191 5/219 6/224 7/234 8/236 9/244 | 249 | 1/0 2/32 3/109 4/124 5/138 6/161 7/161 (7 wkts) | 166 |

Bonus points – Worcestershire 2, Hampshire 4 (Score at 100 overs: 248-9).

Bowling: *First Innings*—Connor 21–5–49–0; Marshall 30.3–12–59–7; Tremlett 18–7–47–0; Maru 21–9–33–2; C. L. Smith 2–0–3–0; Nicholas 9–1–35–1. *Second Innings*—Marshall 14–7–29–2; James 5–1–15–1; Connor 3–1–5–0; Maru 18.5–7–52–4; Tremlett 9–2–27–0; C. L. Smith 6–0–34–0.

Umpires: H. D. Bird and D. R. Shepherd.

At Guildford, July 27, 29, 30. HAMPSHIRE drew with SURREY.

## HAMPSHIRE v SOMERSET

At Bournemouth, August 3, 5, 6. Drawn. Hampshire 8 pts, Somerset 2 pts. Toss won by Hampshire. Somerset, without Botham, Richards and Garner, were reduced to 76 for five before Wyatt, Harden and Palmer, three of their young players, staged a rally. Centuries by Terry, his first in the Championship for a year, and Chris Smith enabled Hampshire to declare with a first-innings lead of 114. Terry's unbeaten 148 included three 6s and fourteen 4s, while Smith's sixth first-class hundred of the season contained five 6s and eleven 4s. Although the wicket remained docile, Hampshire had hopes of victory when Roebuck was out with the scores level and, later, when Marshall removed Marks and Palmer with successive balls. However, they were frustrated by a first Championship century from Wyatt, whose innings spanned 6 hours, 22 minutes and included eleven 4s.

### Somerset

| | | | |
|---|---|---|---|
| N. F. M. Popplewell c C. L. Smith b Connor | 15 | – c Parks b Marshall | 10 |
| P. M. Roebuck c Maru b Tremlett | 6 | – lbw b Marshall | 46 |
| N. A. Felton b Marshall | 2 | – c Parks b Connor | 8 |
| J. G. Wyatt b Connor | 29 | – b Nicholas | 100 |
| R. E. Hayward lbw b Tremlett | 4 | – c Terry b Tremlett | 7 |
| R. J. Harden c and b Tremlett | 46 | – lbw b Tremlett | 11 |
| *V. J. Marks c Nicholas b Connor | 13 | – c Parks b Marshall | 9 |
| G. V. Palmer c Parks b Maru | 38 | – c Maru b Marshall | 0 |
| †T. Gard c Nicholas b Maru | 26 | – not out | 11 |
| M. R. Davis not out | 33 | – not out | 3 |
| C. H. Dredge c Parks b Cowley | 9 | | |
| L-b 4, w 2, n-b 5 | 11 | B 6, l-b 8, w 4, n-b 13 | 31 |
| 1/20 2/25 3/25 4/38 5/76 6/99 7/145 8/163 9/219 | 232 | 1/31 2/54 3/114 4/133 5/164 6/177 7/177 8/231 | (8 wkts) 236 |

Bonus points – Somerset 2, Hampshire 4.

Bowling: *First Innings*—Marshall 24–6–51–1; Connor 23–3–61–3; Tremlett 26–9–60–3; Maru 12–2–39–2; Cowley 6.1–1–13–1; C. L. Smith 2–0–4–0. *Second Innings*—Marshall 33–10–70–4; Connor 22–6–49–1; Tremlett 23–7–42–2; Maru 24–10–31–0; Cowley 7–0–14–0; R. A. Smith 1–0–3–0; Nicholas 7–3–13–1.

### Hampshire

| | |
|---|---|
| C. G. Greenidge c Harden b Marks | 70 |
| V. P. Terry not out | 148 |
| C. L. Smith c Harden b Davis | 102 |
| R. A. Smith not out | 6 |
| L-b 10, w 2, n-b 8 | 20 |
| 1/132 2/317 (2 wkts dec.) | 346 |

*M. C. J. Nicholas, M. D. Marshall, N. G. Cowley, T. M. Tremlett, R. J. Maru, †R. J. Parks and C. A. Connor did not bat.

Bonus points – Hampshire 4.

Bowling: Dredge 27–13–44–0; Davis 20–3–67–1; Palmer 19–3–74–0; Marks 25–5–100–1; Harden 2–0–17–0; Popplewell 6–1–34–0.

Umpires: M. J. Kitchen and D. O. Oslear.

## HAMPSHIRE v SURREY

At Southampton, August 10, 12, 13. Drawn. Hampshire 5 pts, Surrey 6 pts. Toss won by Surrey. The loss of the morning session because of rain on the first two days effectively prevented a result. After being put in, Hampshire lost two wickets for 57, but Chris Smith and Nicholas rebuilt the innings before the declaration in the 100th over after maximum batting points had been obtained. Surrey's response was to declare 103 behind and then, using only occasional bowlers, they reduced Hampshire to 9 for two. However, Robin Smith batted brightly and Surrey were set a target of 278 in 44 overs. But with Butcher and Needham soon out, they declined to chase for victory. It was Hampshire's nineteenth successive match without defeat, their previous best having been eighteen in 1958.

## Hampshire

| | | | |
|---|---|---|---|
| C. G. Greenidge c Richards b Doughty | 2 | – c Monkhouse b Richards | 6 |
| V. P. Terry st Richards b Monkhouse | 24 | – c Stewart b Butcher | 1 |
| C. L. Smith b Jesty | 77 | | |
| *M. C. J. Nicholas lbw b Monkhouse | 94 | | |
| R. A. Smith c Lynch b Monkhouse | 2 | – (3) b Butcher | 50 |
| J. J. E. Hardy lbw b Monkhouse | 40 | – (4) c Ward b Richards | 38 |
| M. D. Marshall c Stewart b Gray | 8 | – (5) c Stewart b Butcher | 17 |
| T. M. Tremlett c Jesty b Gray | 5 | – (7) not out | 18 |
| †R. J. Parks c Doughty b Gray | 11 | – (6) not out | 40 |
| R. J. Maru not out | 11 | | |
| C. A. Connor not out | 2 | | |
| L-b 9, w 5, n-b 13 | 27 | L-b 2, w 1, n-b 1 | 4 |
| 1/3 2/57 3/161 4/164 5/251 6/260 7/270 8/284 9/293 (9 wkts dec.) | 303 | 1/5 2/9 3/91 4/105 5/124 (5 wkts dec.) | 174 |

Bonus points – Hampshire 4, Surrey 4.

Bowling: *First Innings*—Gray 29.4–4–83–3; Doughty 18–2–75–1; Monkhouse 33–5–82–4; Pocock 8–0–20–0; Jesty 11–2–34–1. *Second Innings*—Butcher 12–2–43–3; Richards 19–1–78–2; Lynch 3–0–27–0; Stewart 4–0–24–0.

## Surrey

| | | | |
|---|---|---|---|
| A. R. Butcher c Nicholas b Connor | 40 | – c Terry b Connor | 1 |
| A. Needham c C. L. Smith b Marshall | 2 | – lbw b Marshall | 13 |
| A. J. Stewart c Parks b Connor | 71 | – b R. A. Smith | 44 |
| *T. E. Jesty c Parks b Connor | 1 | – not out | 23 |
| M. A. Lynch not out | 47 | – c Greenidge b R. A. Smith | 19 |
| D. M. Ward not out | 23 | – not out | 2 |
| B 1, l-b 6, w 1, n-b 8 | 16 | B 2, l-b 1, w 1, n-b 1 | 5 |
| 1/20 2/101 3/107 4/147 (4 wkts dec.) | 200 | 1/2 2/17 3/78 4/104 (4 wkts) | 107 |

†C. J. Richards, R. J. Doughty, G. Monkhouse, A. H. Gray and P. I. Pocock did not bat.

Bonus points – Surrey 2, Hampshire 1.

Bowling: *First Innings*—Marshall 7–1–20–1; Connor 22–5–79–3; Tremlett 8–2–28–0; Nicholas 5–0–13–0; Maru 18.4–2–49–0; R. A. Smith 1–0–4–0. *Second Innings*—Marshall 7–0–23–1; Connor 4–0–8–1; Maru 15–2–58–0; Tremlett 3–1–4–0; R. A. Smith 12–7–11–2.

Umpires: A. A. Jones and P. B. Wight.

At Cardiff, August 14, 15, 16. HAMPSHIRE lost to GLAMORGAN by five wickets.

At Leicester, August 17, 19, 20. HAMPSHIRE drew with LEICESTERSHIRE.

## HAMPSHIRE v GLOUCESTERSHIRE

At Bournemouth, August 24, 26, 27. Hampshire won by seven wickets. Hampshire 21 pts, Gloucestershire 4 pts. Toss won by Hampshire. Their decision to put their opponents in soon paid dividends in this important match. After a start delayed until three o'clock, only Bainbridge and Lloyds batted with any confidence as Andrew, the young fast-medium bowler, well supported by Marshall and Tremlett, produced career-best figures of six for 43. Hampshire's batsmen did not fare much better against Gloucestershire's seam bowlers, but Chris Smith's patience and the adventure of Marshall and Parks saw them establish a first-innings lead of 57. A fourth-wicket partnership of 121 between Bainbridge and Davison saved Gloucestershire from complete disaster in their second innings when their first three wickets fell for 6 runs and their last seven for 30 in sixteen overs as Maru, with some turn and confident flight, set up a victory target of 101. Nicholas, in sparkling form, saw Hampshire home with an unbeaten 71 off 68 balls.

### Gloucestershire

| | | | |
|---|---|---|---|
| A. W. Stovold lbw b Marshall | 2 | b Marshall | 2 |
| A. J. Wright b Andrew | 0 | c R. A. Smith b Andrew | 0 |
| C. W. J. Athey c Terry b Tremlett | 18 | lbw b Marshall | 3 |
| P. Bainbridge c Nicholas b Andrew | 43 | c Parks b Maru | 46 |
| B. F. Davison c Parks b Andrew | 15 | c Nicholas b Maru | 77 |
| K. M. Curran b Andrew | 0 | lbw b Marshall | 3 |
| J. W. Lloyds not out | 34 | c Hardy b Maru | 0 |
| †R. C. Russell b Marshall | 5 | c C. L. Smith b Marshall | 5 |
| *D. A. Graveney b Tremlett | 3 | not out | 2 |
| D. V. Lawrence c Nicholas b Andrew | 1 | b Maru | 0 |
| C. A. Walsh b Andrew | 8 | c Andrew b Maru | 4 |
| L-b 3, w 3, n-b 5 | 11 | B 4, l-b 4, w 1, n-b 6 | 15 |
| 1/2 2/6 3/37 4/64 5/64 6/93 7/98 8/124 9/127 | 140 | 1/2 2/2 3/6 4/127 5/130 6/131 7/151 8/151 9/153 | 157 |

Bonus points – Hampshire 4.

Bowling: *First Innings*—Marshall 23–10–31–2; Andrew 20–8–43–6; Tremlett 19–3–47–2; Nicholas 7–3–13–0; Maru 2–0–3–0. *Second Innings*—Marshall 20–6–38–4; Andrew 7–1–31–1; Tremlett 11–1–42–0; Nicholas 4–0–22–0; Maru 12–4–16–5.

### Hampshire

| | | | |
|---|---|---|---|
| C. G. Greenidge run out | 18 | lbw b Walsh | 7 |
| V. P. Terry b Lawrence | 17 | b Walsh | 13 |
| C. L. Smith c Graveney b Curran | 41 | c Stovold b Walsh | 4 |
| *M. C. J. Nicholas lbw b Lawrence | 4 | not out | 71 |
| R. A. Smith c Russell b Curran | 6 | not out | 0 |
| J. J. E. Hardy c Lloyds b Walsh | 10 | | |
| M. D. Marshall b Lawrence | 41 | | |
| T. M. Tremlett b Bainbridge | 6 | | |
| †R. J. Parks c Walsh b Lawrence | 33 | | |
| R. J. Maru lbw b Lawrence | 0 | | |
| S. J. W. Andrew not out | 6 | | |
| L-b 8, n-b 7 | 15 | L-b 4, n-b 3 | 7 |
| 1/35 2/45 3/56 4/69 5/103 6/107 7/123 8/175 9/175 | 197 | 1/15 2/19 3/79 | (3 wkts) 102 |

Bonus points – Hampshire 1, Gloucestershire 4.

Bowling: *First Innings*—Lawrence 19.2–2–78–5; Walsh 22–9–44–1; Curran 17–3–44–2; Bainbridge 4–1–23–1. *Second Innings*—Lawrence 7–0–32–0; Walsh 10.2–2–37–3; Curran 6–1–22–0; Graveney 2–0–7–0.

Umpires: N. T. Plews and R. A. White.

## HAMPSHIRE v LEICESTERSHIRE

At Bournemouth, August 28, 29, 30. Hampshire won by an innings and 56 runs. Hampshire 24 pts, Leicestershire 1 pt. Toss won by Hampshire. Only three batsmen reached double figures as Leicestershire were shot out for 100 by Tremlett and Marshall, the former enjoying a spell of four for 4 in 26 balls. Hampshire themselves suffered three quick setbacks before Nicholas and Robin Smith came together in a prosperous fourth-wicket partnership of 259, made off 82 overs. It fell just 4 runs short of the Hampshire record. Nicholas's 146, his first Championship hundred of the season, spanned 291 minutes and included 21 4s, while Smith hit one 6 and seventeen 4s in his unbeaten 134 in 322 minutes. Leicestershire finished the second day at 180 for five, still needing another 92 to avoid an innings defeat, a fate which came quickly on the final morning. Cobb did not resume his innings after being hit on the foot by a ball from Marshall the previous evening.

### Leicestershire

| | | | |
|---|---|---|---|
| I. P. Butcher c Maru b Tremlett | 38 | – b Andrew | 29 |
| J. C. Balderstone c Terry b Andrew | 2 | – lbw b Marshall | 20 |
| R. A. Cobb lbw b James | 3 | – retired hurt | 33 |
| *P. Willey c Terry b Tremlett | 5 | – lbw b Andrew | 20 |
| J. J. Whitaker lbw b Tremlett | 0 | – c Parks b Maru | 65 |
| N. E. Briers b Marshall | 5 | – c Nicholas b Maru | 3 |
| †M. A. Garnham c James b Tremlett | 3 | – c R. A. Smith b Maru | 10 |
| P. B. Clift c Nicholas b Marshall | 7 | – (9) c Parks b Andrew | 0 |
| G. J. Parsons not out | 11 | – (10) c and b Maru | 5 |
| P. A. J. De Freitas c Marshall b Tremlett | 17 | – (11) not out | 2 |
| N. G. B. Cook c Tremlett b Marshall | 0 | – (8) c C. L. Smith b Andrew | 7 |
| L-b 4, w 2, n-b 3 | 9 | B 1, l-b 5, w 1, n-b 14 | 21 |
| 1/13 2/35 3/50 4/50 5/54 6/62 7/66 8/73 9/100 | 100 | 1/46 2/60 3/111 4/143 5/166 6/200 7/200 8/208 9/215 | 215 |

Bonus points – Hampshire 4.

Bowling: *First Innings*—James 8–2–31–1; Andrew 5–2–11–1; Marshall 15.2–8–12–3; Tremlett 13–5–42–5. *Second Innings*—Andrew 23–5–58–4; James 4–0–18–0; Tremlett 21–8–35–0; Marshall 23–11–53–1; Maru 23.4–12–45–4.

### Hampshire

| | |
|---|---|
| C. G. Greenidge lbw b De Freitas | 6 |
| V. P. Terry c Butcher b De Freitas | 3 |
| C. L. Smith c Butcher b De Freitas | 18 |
| *M. C. J. Nicholas c Balderstone b Cook | 146 |
| R. A. Smith not out | 134 |
| M. D. Marshall b De Freitas | 43 |
| K. D. James not out | 2 |
| B 6, l-b 4, w 9 | 19 |
| 1/8 2/15 3/32 4/291 5/362 (5 wkts dec.) | 371 |

T. M. Tremlett, †R. J. Parks, R. J. Maru and S. J. W. Andrew did not bat.

Bonus points – Hampshire 4, Leicestershire 1 (Score at 100 overs: 333-4).

Bowling: De Freitas 27–3–80–4; Parsons 20–2–78–0; Clift 24–10–52–0; Cook 19–3–86–1; Briers 4–1–17–0; Willey 12–2–48–0.

Umpires: N. T. Plews and R. A. White.

At Folkestone, September 4, 5, 6. HAMPSHIRE drew with KENT.

## HAMPSHIRE v NORTHAMPTONSHIRE

At Southampton, September 11, 12, 13. Northamptonshire won by one wicket. Northamptonshire 23 pts, Hampshire 8 pts. Toss won by Northamptonshire. This was a vital game in Hampshire's bid for the Championship, and although it went to the last ball, their failure to win could be attributed to poor catching. With Greenidge in fine form, passing 1,000 runs for the fifteenth time in his career as he scored 143 (one 6, 23 4s) in 308 minutes, Hampshire were able to gain maximum batting points before making early inroads into the Northamptonshire batting. Marshall took three wickets in five balls to reduce Northamptonshire to 30 for four, and half the side were out for 61. But Hampshire put down five catches, and Cook, Capel and Harper changed the complexion of the game. Hampshire's second-innings declaration set a target of 241 in 55 overs and in a tense finish Harper hit the last ball, bowled by Maru, for 6. His unbeaten 27 was made off only fifteen balls and contained four 6s. Earlier Lamb's 60 had kept Northamptonshire in the hunt, although at 9 and at 38 he survived chances.

## Hampshire

| First innings | | Second innings | |
|---|---|---|---|
| C. G. Greenidge c Boyd-Moss b Capel | 143 | – b Harper | 68 |
| V. P. Terry c Harper b Griffiths | 7 | – b Capel | 25 |
| C. L. Smith c Ripley b Griffiths | 19 | – c Wild b Capel | 2 |
| *M. C. J. Nicholas c Boyd-Moss b Griffiths | 33 | – c Larkins b Harper | 13 |
| R. A. Smith c Ripley b Griffiths | 10 | – not out | 55 |
| J. J. E. Hardy c Lamb b Harper | 8 | | |
| M. D. Marshall c Ripley b Harper | 14 | – (6) not out | 66 |
| T. M. Tremlett b Capel | 13 | | |
| †R. J. Parks not out | 17 | | |
| R. J. Maru not out | 24 | | |
| B 1, l-b 9, n-b 2 | 12 | B 7, l-b 6, n-b 2 | 15 |
| 1/34 2/68 3/146 4/173 5/198 6/216 7/258 8/264 | (8 wkts dec.) 300 | 1/96 2/98 3/98 4/122 | (4 wkts dec.) 244 |

S. J. W. Andrew did not bat.

Bonus points – Hampshire 4, Northamptonshire 3.

Bowling: *First Innings*—Mallender 10–0–45–0; Griffiths 27–11–64–4; Capel 21–3–72–2; Harper 29–9–78–2; Boyd-Moss 3–2–3–0; Wild 8–1–28–0. *Second Innings*—Mallender 5–2–29–0; Griffiths 12–3–44–0; Harper 24–3–76–2; Boyd-Moss 1–0–2–0; Capel 14–4–34–2; Wild 10–0–46–0.

## Northamptonshire

| First innings | | Second innings | |
|---|---|---|---|
| *G. Cook b Maru | 73 | – lbw b Nicholas | 36 |
| W. Larkins c sub b Andrew | 0 | – c Maru b Nicholas | 48 |
| R. J. Boyd-Moss c Terry b Marshall | 10 | – c Terry b Maru | 6 |
| A. J. Lamb c Parks b Marshall | 0 | – c C. L. Smith b Marshall | 60 |
| R. J. Bailey c Terry b Marshall | 0 | – lbw b Maru | 23 |
| D. J. Wild b Marshall | 17 | – c Parks b Maru | 25 |
| D. J. Capel c Greenidge b Tremlett | 81 | – st Parks b Maru | 0 |
| R. A. Harper c Terry b Tremlett | 76 | – not out | 27 |
| †D. Ripley not out | 13 | – run out | 1 |
| N. A. Mallender c Terry b Tremlett | 4 | – c Tremlett b Maru | 4 |
| B. J. Griffiths c R. A. Smith b Tremlett | 12 | – not out | 1 |
| B 2, l-b 4, w 7, n-b 5 | 18 | L-b 8, n-b 2 | 10 |
| 1/4 2/30 3/30 4/30 5/61 6/147 7/268 8/275 9/280 | 304 | 1/76 2/93 3/98 4/148 5/196 6/196 7/214 8/228 9/234 | (9 wkts) 241 |

Bonus points – Northamptonshire 4, Hampshire 4 (Score at 100 overs: 300-9).

Bowling: *First Innings*—Marshall 23–6–75–4; Andrew 18–5–73–1; Tremlett 24.4–11–53–4; Maru 32–11–88–1; Nicholas 3–0–9–0. *Second Innings*—Marshall 11–2–31–1; Andrew 7–1–19–0; Tremlett 6–2–13–0; Maru 21–1–114–5; Nicholas 10–2–22–2; C. L. Smith 5–0–34–0.

Umpires: K. J. Lyons and D. O. Oslear.

At Trent Bridge, September 14, 16, 17. HAMPSHIRE drew with NOTTINGHAMSHIRE.

# KENT

*Patron:* HRH The Duke of Kent
*President:* J. A. Porter
*Chairman:* H. J. Pocock
*Chairman, Cricket Committee:* A. H. Phebey
*Secretary:* D. B. Dalby
St Lawrence Ground, Old Dover Road,
Canterbury CT1 3NZ
(Telephone: 0227-456886)
*Cricket Manager:* B. W. Luckhurst
*Captain:* C. S. Cowdrey
*Director of Coaching:* J. C. T. Page

With, on paper, one of the strongest squads in the country, Kent seemed set to return to their winning ways of the 1970s in the year chosen by the club to launch its Project Appeal. Designed to raise money for the building of a new multi-purpose stand at Canterbury, the Appeal depended to some extent on a good summer, both from the weather and playing viewpoints.

Neither was forthcoming, for in a season when the weather was a continual frustration, the county side again suffered from a lack of consistency. It was a testing summer for the new captain, Christopher Cowdrey, the fifth different incumbent since his father, Colin, was succeeded by Denness in 1972. Injuries to key players, including Cowdrey himself, did not help to maintain a settled situation, and just when it seemed that Kent were on the threshold of better things they were eclipsed by Leicestershire in a Benson and Hedges Cup semi-final through a batting failure such as had been the hallmark of their early-season form in the Britannic Assurance Championship.

Three successive home defeats – one at Canterbury and two in the festival at Tunbridge Wells – were a nasty setback, but Cowdrey always believed that the side was good enough to start winning. "Win one and we'll win four", he predicted, and he was nearly right. They won three of the next four after beating Lancashire at Old Trafford towards the end of June. But the Championship improvement was not maintained, and by the beginning of August the wind of change was blowing.

It was announced then that Graham Johnson, in his 21st season with the county, would not be offered a new contract for 1986. Two Second XI players, Lindsay Wood and Kevin Masters, received similar news. By the end of the month Johnson's contract had been cancelled forthwith, disciplinary action taken on account of his refusal to play against the Australians at Canterbury. Whatever the rights and wrongs of this affair, the decision inevitably had an unsettling effect in the dressing-room, and this was to spill over until well into the close season.

The atmosphere was difficult enough anyway, particularly for the batsmen, because Kent's large staff included a rich array of young talent waiting in the wings. The pressure on individuals seemingly made itself felt on the side as a whole, reflected most noticeably in a dramatic decline in the John Player Sunday League. Halfway through the summer Kent led that table, having lost only one of their first eight games. There followed a crushing defeat by Northamptonshire at Maidstone and not another Sunday game was won.

The side's batting strength was boosted by the success as an opener of the left-handed Simon Hinks, who scored over 1,400 runs with some powerful strokeplay in his first full Championship season. His partner, Mark Benson, was equally successful, and Chris Tavaré, besides scoring 1,225 Championship runs, was much the most successful Sunday batsman.

Cowdrey struggled after a brilliant start, but, like Tavaré during the previous summer, he would be reluctant to admit that this had anything to do with the cares of captaincy. Derek Aslett lost his place midway through the season to Neil Taylor, who took his chance eagerly and successfully, and by the end of the season Graham Cowdrey, the captain's younger brother, had forced his way into the first team on the strength of his high scoring for the Second XI.

Injuries mainly troubled the bowlers, which meant that the attack was often unsettled. Kevin Jarvis bowled consistently until a knee injury troubled him during the closing weeks, and Graham Dilley, having done very well to return to the game after a serious neck operation, bowled fast and well at times but without a lot of luck. He also had some early minor injury problems that were not connected with his neck condition. Richard Ellison, after missing the start of the summer with a badly damaged ankle, found his form with a vengeance as a bowler during the Tunbridge Wells week and was rewarded with a return to the England side.

Eldine Baptiste, back after a season on tour with the West Indians, passed 50 wickets and scored 899 Championship runs. Derek Underwood was again the leading wicket-taker, although pitches restricted the amount of bowling he was given during the first half of the season. By the end of the summer he had a new spin partner, another left-arm bowler, in Laurie Potter, who had switched from medium pace. But no sooner had Potter been cast in the mould of Johnson's successor as the permanent all-rounder than he decided to go in search of another county.

Alan Knott, with little chance to reveal his batting talents, still kept wicket so consistently and well that he was very close to an England recall. Towards the end of the summer, however, his ankle injury manifested itself again, and it was a sad day when, on the penultimate afternoon of the season, he announced his retirement. The club duly acknowledged his "outstanding services to the county and to English cricket", adding that "his ability and professionalism have ranked him among the truly great players in the history of the game".

But Knott's retirement, Johnson's departure, Potter's release and the non-re-engagement of Wood and Masters were not the end of the upheavals. Dilley, who is Johnson's brother-in-law, asked unsuccessfully to have his own contract terminated; Stuart Waterton, one of Knott's understudies, left for Northamptonshire, and Graham Cowdrey was widely, if not accurately, quoted as looking for a move. The revival that had been hoped for when the season began still seemed a long way off. – D.M.

KENT 1985

[*Bill Smith*

*Back row:* S. C. Goldsmith, R. P. Davis, A. P. Igglesden, D. J. M. Kelleher. *Middle row:* C. Lewis (*scorer*), B. W. Luckhurst (*cricket manager*), K. D. Masters, L. Potter, C. Penn, S. G. Hinks, L. J. Wood, G. R. Cowdrey, S. A. Marsh, S. N. V. Waterton, R. Chappell (*physiotherapist*), J. C. T. Page (*director of coaching*). *Front row:* N. R. Taylor, G. R. Dilley, G. W. Johnson, D. G. Aslett, M. R. Benson, C. S. Cowdrey (*captain*), D. L. Underwood, A. P. E. Knott, C. J. Tavaré, K. B. S. Jarvis, R. M. Ellison. *Inset:* E. A. E. Baptiste.

## KENT RESULTS

*All first-class matches – Played 26: Won 4, Lost 6, Drawn 16.*

*County Championship matches – Played 24: Won 4, Lost 5, Drawn 15.*

*Bonus points – Batting 51, Bowling 71.*

*Competition placings Britannic Assurance County Championship, 9th; NatWest Bank Trophy, q-f; Benson and Hedges Cup, s-f; John Player League, 10th eq.*

## BRITANNIC ASSURANCE CHAMPIONSHIP AVERAGES

### BATTING

| | *Birthplace* | *M* | *I* | *NO* | *R* | *HI* | *Avge* |
|---|---|---|---|---|---|---|---|
| ‡N. R. Taylor | *Orpington* | 14 | 22 | 6 | 715 | 102* | 44.68 |
| G. R. Cowdrey | *Farnborough, Kent* | 5 | 7 | 2 | 187 | 53 | 37.40 |
| ‡M. R. Benson | *Shoreham* | 23 | 42 | 3 | 1,446 | 162 | 37.07 |
| ‡C. J. Tavaré | *Orpington* | 23 | 40 | 6 | 1,225 | 150* | 36.02 |
| ‡S. G. Hinks | *Northfleet* | 24 | 44 | 3 | 1,423 | 117 | 34.70 |
| ‡C. S. Cowdrey | *Farnborough, Kent* | 19 | 34 | 3 | 1,035 | 159 | 33.38 |
| ‡E. A. E. Baptiste | *St John's, Antigua* | 21 | 33 | 4 | 897 | 82 | 30.93 |
| ‡D. G. Aslett | *Dover* | 11 | 20 | 1 | 521 | 111 | 27.42 |
| ‡R. M. Ellison | *Ashford* | 14 | 22 | 5 | 457 | 98 | 26.88 |
| C. Penn | *Dover* | 8 | 7 | 2 | 102 | 50 | 20.40 |
| ‡A. P. E. Knott | *Belvedere* | 19 | 24 | 5 | 379 | 87* | 19.94 |
| ‡G. W. Johnson | *Beckenham* | 10 | 14 | 3 | 198 | 30* | 18.00 |
| L. Potter | *Bexleyheath* | 11 | 13 | 2 | 159 | 55 | 14.45 |
| ‡G. R. Dilley | *Dartford* | 16 | 19 | 5 | 153 | 31 | 10.92 |
| ‡D. L. Underwood | *Bromley* | 23 | 23 | 9 | 121 | 16* | 8.64 |
| ‡K. B. S. Jarvis | *Dartford* | 18 | 18 | 5 | 41 | 7 | 3.15 |

Also batted: S. A. Marsh (*Westminster*) (2 matches) 25, 3; S. N. V. Waterton (*Dartford*) (2 matches) 16*, 6*.

* *Signifies not out.* ‡ *Denotes county cap.*

The following played a total of twelve three-figure innings for Kent in County Championship matches – M. R. Benson 3, C. J. Tavaré 3, C. S. Cowdrey 2, N. R. Taylor 2, D. G. Aslett 1, S. G. Hinks 1.

### BOWLING

| | *O* | *M* | *R* | *W* | *BB* | *Avge* |
|---|---|---|---|---|---|---|
| R. M. Ellison | 318.2 | 78 | 863 | 44 | 7-87 | 19.61 |
| D. L. Underwood | 745 | 277 | 1,635 | 64 | 6-56 | 25.54 |
| E. A. E. Baptiste | 518 | 106 | 1,521 | 52 | 6-42 | 29.25 |
| L. Potter | 203.3 | 57 | 554 | 18 | 4-87 | 30.77 |
| K. B. S. Jarvis | 513.4 | 111 | 1,636 | 51 | 5-43 | 32.07 |
| C. Penn | 124.4 | 17 | 466 | 14 | 4-63 | 33.28 |
| G. R. Dilley | 323.1 | 62 | 1,031 | 27 | 5-53 | 38.18 |
| C. S. Cowdrey | 200.1 | 27 | 721 | 14 | 3-5 | 51.50 |

Also bowled: D. G. Aslett 6–0–25–0; M. R. Benson 20.2–0–138–1; S. G. Hinks 21–0–72–1; G. W. Johnson 115.3–16–409–9; N. R. Taylor 52–8–168–5.

At Southampton, April 27, 28, 29. KENT drew with HAMPSHIRE.

## KENT v SURREY

At Canterbury, May 1, 2, 3. Drawn. Kent 7 pts, Surrey 8 pts. Toss won by Kent, who lost Benson to the first ball of the day and were rescued from a position of 16 for three after eleven overs by Hinks, who hit fifteen 4s in his stay of 217 minutes, and Cowdrey in a stand of 173 in 52 overs. Cowdrey's career-best score came in 286 minutes and contained two 6s and seventeen 4s. Surrey made an equally poor start as Dilley's pace brought three wickets for 6 runs in 24 balls before Stewart and Lynch put on 252 off 56 overs for the fifth wicket. Lynch reached his century in 185 minutes, with one 6 and eighteen 4s, and Stewart batted 268 minutes, hitting three 6s and 24 4s in his highest score. Kent, 109 behind, were in serious trouble until Aslett and Cowdrey saved them with a sixth-wicket stand of 217 off 59 overs. Aslett hit fourteen 4s in his century, in 187 minutes, while Cowdrey, who batted for 190 minutes, struck one 6 and thirteen 4s, failing by 5 runs to score his second century of the match.

### Kent

| | | | |
|---|---|---|---|
| M. R. Benson lbw b Thomas | 0 | – lbw b Thomas | 11 |
| S. G. Hinks c Pocock b Jesty | 92 | – lbw b Pauline | 6 |
| C. J. Tavaré b Taylor | 1 | – (5) b Pocock | 13 |
| D. G. Aslett lbw b Thomas | 2 | – (6) c Clinton b Jesty | 111 |
| *C. S. Cowdrey b Needham | 159 | – (7) lbw b Butcher | 95 |
| N. R. Taylor c Stewart b Needham | 2 | – (4) b Pauline | 13 |
| G. W. Johnson c Lynch b Thomas | 6 | – (8) not out | 7 |
| †A. P. E. Knott c Jesty b Thomas | 2 | – (9) c Richards b Jesty | 0 |
| G. R. Dilley b Needham | 31 | – (3) c Pauline b Thomas | 0 |
| D. L. Underwood not out | 16 | – not out | 4 |
| K. B. S. Jarvis c and b Thomas | 6 | | |
| B 4, l-b 7, w 1, n-b 7 | 19 | B 9, l-b 6, w 1, n-b 6 | 22 |
| 1/0 2/11 3/16 4/189 5/203 6/220 7/227 8/298 9/317 | 336 | 1/14 2/14 3/18 4/46 5/46 6/263 7/271 8/271 | (8 wkts dec.) 282 |

Bonus points – Kent 4, Surrey 4 (Score at 100 overs: 329-9).

Bowling: *First Innings*—Thomas 25.2–7–51–5; Taylor 19–6–69–1; Pocock 26–2–89–0; Pauline 4–0–18–0; Needham 17–1–67–3; Jesty 11–2–31–1. *Second Innings*—Thomas 16–3–40–2; Taylor 2.2–0–6–0; Pocock 20–4–59–1; Pauline 13.4–1–50–2; Jesty 12–3–32–2; Needham 13–0–40–0; Butcher 14–3–40–1; Lynch 1–1–0–0.

### Surrey

| | |
|---|---|
| A. R. Butcher c Benson b Dilley | 16 |
| G. S. Clinton lbw b Jarvis | 3 |
| *P. I. Pocock c Taylor b Dilley | 6 |
| A. J. Stewart c Aslett b Dilley | 158 |
| T. E. Jesty c Knott b Dilley | 3 |
| M. A. Lynch b Dilley | 115 |
| D. B. Pauline not out | 56 |
| †C. J. Richards c Cowdrey b Johnson | 38 |
| A. Needham c Hinks b Johnson | 3 |
| D. J. Thomas b Johnson | 2 |
| N. S. Taylor not out | 21 |
| B 3, l-b 8, n-b 13 | 24 |
| 1/3 2/11 3/34 4/41 5/293 6/328 7/390 8/412 9/417 | (9 wkts dec.) 445 |

Bonus points – Surrey 4, Kent 3 (Score at 100 overs: 397-7).

Bowling: Jarvis 22–7–62–1; Underwood 16–3–57–0; Dilley 24–4–97–5; Johnson 30–2–142–3; Cowdrey 13–0–58–0; Hinks 5–0–18–0.

Umpires: J. A. Jameson and M. J. Kitchen.

At Lord's, May 8, 9, 10. KENT drew with MIDDLESEX.

At Northampton, May 22, 23, 24. KENT drew with NORTHAMPTONSHIRE.

At The Parks, May 29, 30, 31. KENT drew with OXFORD UNIVERSITY.

## KENT v WORCESTERSHIRE

At Canterbury, June 1, 3, 4. Worcestershire won by seven wickets. Worcestershire 22 pts, Kent 5 pts. Toss won by Kent. The bowlers held the upper hand, until the final morning, in a game of fluctuating fortunes. Kent struggled in their first innings, mainly against the spin of Patel and Illingworth, with Kapil Dev catching superbly in the slips. Worcestershire's recovery was centred around the left-handed Smith, who reached 50 in 88 minutes with one 6 and six 4s, and although their lead was slight, Kent lost four wickets before clearing the arrears of 15. Indeed, only a resolute seventh-wicket stand between Tavaré and Knott prevented a finish in two days. Worcestershire, left 132 to win, faltered on the last morning before the night-watchman, Illingworth, was joined by Smith, and with application and resolution they steered their side home by adding 86 in 85 minutes. Smith reached his 50 with the winning hit.

### Kent

| | | | |
|---|---|---|---|
| M. R. Benson c Rhodes b Kapil Dev | 6 | – (7) b Patel | 1 |
| N. R. Taylor c Kapil Dev b Inchmore | 16 | – (1) lbw b Kapil Dev | 2 |
| C. J. Tavaré c Rhodes b Radford | 8 | – c Kapil Dev b Illingworth | 60 |
| S. G. Hinks c Kapil Dev b Patel | 21 | – (2) lbw b Radford | 2 |
| *C. S. Cowdrey c Kapil Dev b Patel | 38 | – (4) lbw b Kapil Dev | 1 |
| E. A. E. Baptiste c Neale b Illingworth | 41 | – (5) c Smith b Radford | 3 |
| †A. P. E. Knott c Rhodes b Patel | 0 | – (8) b Illingworth | 35 |
| G. W. Johnson not out | 30 | – (6) c Inchmore b Patel | 20 |
| G. R. Dilley c Kapil Dev b Illingworth | 7 | – lbw b Patel | 1 |
| D. L. Underwood c Smith b Illingworth | 7 | – not out | 13 |
| K. B. S. Jarvis b Kapil Dev | 2 | – b Radford | 0 |
| B 3, l-b 8, n-b 2 | 13 | B 3, l-b 1, n-b 4 | 8 |
| 1/16 2/27 3/54 4/56 5/122 6/136 7/144 8/160 9/170 | 189 | 1/2 2/6 3/7 4/13 5/46 6/47 7/104 8/125 9/139 | 146 |

Bonus points – Kent 1, Worcestershire 4.

Bowling: *First Innings*—Kapil Dev 9.5–3–22–2; Radford 10–4–28–1; Patel 18–4–49–3; Inchmore 9–3–29–1; Illingworth 16–5–50–3. *Second Innings*—Kapil Dev 15–4–30–2; Radford 8.4–1–26–3; Patel 15–2–45–3; Inchmore 2–1–2–0; Illingworth 20–5–39–2.

### Worcestershire

| | | | |
|---|---|---|---|
| M. J. Weston c Johnson b Dilley | 0 | – c and b Baptiste | 7 |
| T. S. Curtis c Knott b Jarvis | 0 | – c Knott b Underwood | 15 |
| D. M. Smith c Knott b Jarvis | 64 | – (5) not out | 50 |
| *P. A. Neale c Cowdrey b Underwood | 42 | | |
| R. K. Illingworth c Tavaré b Jarvis | 2 | – (4) not out | 39 |
| †S. J. Rhodes not out | 37 | – (3) lbw b Jarvis | 9 |
| D. N. Patel b Jarvis | 4 | | |
| D. B. D'Oliveira c Knott b Jarvis | 0 | | |
| Kapil Dev c Taylor b Underwood | 17 | | |
| N. V. Radford c and b Cowdrey | 2 | | |
| J. D. Inchmore c Johnson b Cowdrey | 23 | | |
| B 4, l-b 5, n-b 4 | 13 | B 7, l-b 2, w 1, n-b 2 | 12 |
| 1/4 2/8 3/105 4/112 5/119 6/125 7/125 8/149 9/156 | 204 | 1/7 2/25 3/46 | (3 wkts) 132 |

Bonus points – Worcestershire 2, Kent 4.

Bowling: *First Innings*—Dilley 3–1–6–1; Jarvis 22–5–53–5; Underwood 34–12–75–2; Cowdrey 10.4–0–41–2; Johnson 8–4–16–0; Baptiste 2–0–4–0. *Second Innings*—Jarvis 13–1–35–1; Baptiste 5–1–17–1; Underwood 19–8–29–1; Cowdrey 4–0–17–0; Johnson 8–0–25–0.

Umpires: B. Dudleston and R. Palmer.

## KENT v NOTTINGHAMSHIRE

At Tunbridge Wells, June 8, 10, 11. Nottinghamshire won by four wickets. Nottinghamshire 21 pts, Kent 5 pts. Toss won by Kent. Pace and seam bowlers held sway throughout. Benson batted with assurance, but when he was fourth out at 123 the remaining Kent wickets crashed for 40 runs in 22 overs. Robinson held Nottinghamshire's innings together for 211 minutes, but their collapse was even worse than Kent's – the last seven wickets fell for 23 runs in twelve overs. Aslett and Ellison raised Kent's hopes with a stand of 49 off twelve overs for the sixth wicket before Saxelby, with three for 0 in seven balls, wrapped up the innings. Nottinghamshire, needing 157 to win, lost two wickets in Jarvis's first over, but on the last morning Randall played very well on a difficult wicket to lay the foundations of the victory.

### Kent

| | | | |
|---|---|---|---|
| M. R. Benson lbw b Saxelby | 71 | – c Rice b Saxelby | 4 |
| S. G. Hinks b Hadlee | 15 | – b Hemmings | 42 |
| C. J. Tavaré c Broad b Rice | 17 | – c French b Cooper | 14 |
| D. G. Aslett lbw b Saxelby | 2 | – c Rice b Cooper | 49 |
| *C. S. Cowdrey c French b Cooper | 31 | – b Hadlee | 21 |
| E. A. E. Baptiste c Robinson b Saxelby | 5 | – b Hadlee | 0 |
| R. M. Ellison c Hadlee b Saxelby | 6 | – c Robinson b Saxelby | 41 |
| †A. P. E. Knott b Saxelby | 2 | – b Saxelby | 15 |
| G. R. Dilley retired hurt | 0 | – (11) not out | 0 |
| D. L. Underwood not out | 3 | – (9) lbw b Saxelby | 0 |
| K. B. S. Jarvis lbw b Saxelby | 0 | – (10) run out | 0 |
| L-b 9, w 1, n-b 1 | 11 | B 1, n-b 4 | 5 |
| 1/31 2/80 3/85 4/123 5/133 6/149 7/157 8/163 9/163 | 163 | 1/12 2/44 3/80 4/105 5/108 6/157 7/185 8/185 9/186 | 191 |

Bonus points – Kent 1, Nottinghamshire 4.

Bowling: *First Innings*—Hadlee 15–3–23–1; Saxelby 23–6–64–6; Hemmings 12–2–22–0; Cooper 15–4–42–1; Rice 5–3–3–1. *Second Innings*—Hadlee 17–2–45–2; Saxelby 19.1–5–49–4; Hemmings 10–2–20–1; Cooper 14–1–44–2; Rice 10–2–32–0.

### Nottinghamshire

| | | | |
|---|---|---|---|
| R. T. Robinson run out | 90 | – lbw b Jarvis | 0 |
| B. C. Broad lbw b Jarvis | 0 | – c Tavaré b Ellison | 11 |
| D. W. Randall c Aslett b Baptiste | 26 | – (4) c Knott b Dilley | 40 |
| *C. E. B. Rice c Hinks b Jarvis | 28 | – (5) c Hinks b Ellison | 5 |
| †B. N. French not out | 1 | | |
| P. Johnson b Jarvis | 23 | – c Jarvis b Ellison | 40 |
| J. D. Birch b Jarvis | 4 | – not out | 25 |
| R. J. Hadlee c Tavaré b Baptiste | 3 | – not out | 18 |
| E. E. Hemmings c Cowdrey b Jarvis | 0 | | |
| K. Saxelby run out | 10 | | |
| K. E. Cooper b Baptiste | 3 | – (3) lbw b Jarvis | 0 |
| L-b 5, w 4, n-b 1 | 10 | L-b 13, w 1, n-b 4 | 18 |
| 1/5 2/67 3/133 4/175 5/177 6/184 7/184 8/184 9/197 | 198 | 1/0 2/2 3/47 4/55 5/93 6/124 | (6 wkts) 157 |

*In the first innings B. N. French, when 0, retired hurt at 135 and resumed at 197.*

Bonus points – Nottinghamshire 1, Kent 4.

Bowling: *First Innings*—Jarvis 22.1–8–43–5; Dilley 9–0–31–0; Ellison 10–0–28–0; Baptiste 14–4–44–3; Cowdrey 6–1–24–0; Underwood 7–0–23–0. *Second Innings*—Jarvis 16–3–42–2; Dilley 14–3–32–1; Baptiste 12–1–37–0; Ellison 12.5–4–33–3; Underwood 2–2–0–0.

Umpires: J. Birkenshaw and P. B. Wight.

## KENT v GLOUCESTERSHIRE

At Tunbridge Wells, June 12, 13, 14. Gloucestershire won by 59 runs. Gloucestershire 22 pts, Kent 4 pts. Toss won by Kent. A sound innings by Bainbridge and a belligerent assault by Curran revived Gloucestershire's fortunes. Then Russell and Lawrence batted enterprisingly before Kent encountered batting problems of their own. By lunch on the second day Gloucestershire were batting again and had extended their lead to 91. Davison, racing to 50 in 70 minutes, and Lloyds, with an invaluable half-century in 130 minutes, halted a collapse and ensured that Kent would have to make the highest score of the match to win – 260 off 100 overs. They started badly but recovered well, Benson and Aslett adding 78 off seventeen overs; but when Benson was fourth out, having batted for 146 minutes, Kent's resistance was virtually ended. Walsh bowled a marathon spell of two hours, twenty minutes on a pitch so receptive to pace and seam that Underwood bowled only fourteen overs of spin all week.

### Gloucestershire

| | | | |
|---|---|---|---|
| A. W. Stovold c Cowdrey b Baptiste | 20 | – c Benson b Baptiste | 1 |
| P. W. Romaines c Knott b Jarvis | 5 | – c Knott b Ellison | 6 |
| C. W. J. Athey b Ellison | 6 | – c Knott b Baptiste | 26 |
| P. Bainbridge c Underwood b Jarvis | 52 | – b Baptiste | 5 |
| B. F. Davison c Tavaré b Jarvis | 15 | – lbw b Jarvis | 53 |
| K. M. Curran b Cowdrey | 43 | – c Baptiste b Cowdrey | 10 |
| J. W. Lloyds b Cowdrey | 0 | – c Knott b Ellison | 50 |
| †R. C. Russell c Benson b Ellison | 28 | – c Knott b Ellison | 19 |
| *D. A. Graveney lbw b Ellison | 2 | – c Hinks b Ellison | 8 |
| D. V. Lawrence c Baptiste b Ellison | 27 | – lbw b Ellison | 4 |
| C. A. Walsh not out | 1 | – not out | 11 |
| L-b 3, n-b 2 | 5 | L-b 2, w 3, n-b 1 | 6 |
| 1/22 2/26 3/32 4/65 5/129 6/129 7/157 8/168 9/193 | 204 | 1/2 2/8 3/32 4/45 5/66 6/105 7/175 8/178 9/184 | 199 |

Bonus points – Gloucestershire 2, Kent 4.

Bowling: *First Innings*—Jarvis 17–6–46–3; Baptiste 12–0–38–1; Ellison 19.4–6–46–4; Underwood 4–1–18–0; Cowdrey 14–3–53–2. *Second Innings*—Baptiste 21–5–57–3; Ellison 21.2–7–46–5; Cowdrey 19–3–52–1; Underwood 1–0–1–0; Jarvis 11–1–41–1.

### Kent

| | | | |
|---|---|---|---|
| M. R. Benson lbw b Lawrence | 0 | – (5) c Graveney b Bainbridge | 80 |
| S. G. Hinks c Russell b Curran | 12 | – (1) c Lloyds b Lawrence | 1 |
| C. J. Tavaré lbw b Curran | 34 | – (2) c Russell b Walsh | 4 |
| D. G. Aslett lbw b Curran | 0 | – c Russell b Walsh | 30 |
| *C. S. Cowdrey c Stovold b Bainbridge | 29 | – (3) run out | 13 |
| E. A. E. Baptiste c Russell b Walsh | 3 | – c Russell b Walsh | 0 |
| R. M. Ellison c Lloyds b Walsh | 24 | – c Romaines b Lawrence | 18 |
| D. L. Underwood c Athey b Curran | 2 | – (10) c Bainbridge b Lawrence | 11 |
| G. W. Johnson c Russell b Walsh | 18 | – (8) lbw b Walsh | 16 |
| †A. P. E. Knott c Lloyds b Curran | 11 | – (9) not out | 10 |
| K. B. S. Jarvis not out | 0 | – run out | 0 |
| L-b 4, w 3, n-b 4 | 11 | B 1, l-b 5, n-b 11 | 17 |
| 1/0 2/49 3/49 4/50 5/58 6/111 7/114 8/119 9/144 | 144 | 1/5 2/22 3/100 4/138 5/142 6/146 7/174 8/176 9/195 | 200 |

Bonus points – Gloucestershire 4.

Bowling: *First Innings*—Lawrence 13–1–48–1; Walsh 19–5–43–3; Curran 18.2–3–42–5; Bainbridge 5–2–7–1. *Second Innings*—Lawrence 13.5–2–51–3; Walsh 24–1–59–4; Curran 8–0–52–0; Bainbridge 8–2–32–1.

Umpires: J. Birkenshaw and P. B. Wight.

At Trent Bridge, June 15, 17, 18. KENT drew with NOTTINGHAMSHIRE.

At Old Trafford, June 22, 24, 25. KENT beat LANCASHIRE by 25 runs.

At Chelmsford, June 26, 27, 28. KENT drew with ESSEX.

At The Oval, July 6, 8, 9. KENT beat SURREY by 176 runs.

## KENT v YORKSHIRE

At Maidstone, July 10, 11, 12. Kent won by 100 runs. Kent 23 pts, Yorkshire 8 pts. Toss won by Yorkshire. Kent recovered from a dubious start through a fifth-wicket stand of 127 off 31 overs between Cowdrey and Baptiste, the latter hitting fourteen 4s in his 113-minute innings. Ellison then cracked a 74-minute half-century (six 4s, two 6s) before Jarvis, with four for 3 in 26 balls, finished off the innings to return his best-ever figures. Yorkshire batted soundly and declared at their fourth bonus point, whereupon Benson and Tavaré set up Kent's declaration by putting on 232 in 60 overs. Benson's century, coming in 195 minutes, contained one 6 and seven 4s, while Tavaré hit four 6s and fourteen 4s in his stay of 179 minutes. Needing 299 to win in 66 overs, Yorkshire made a dreadful start and would have suffered a much heavier defeat but for Love, who batted for 203 minutes, hitting seventeen 4s, as Underwood produced a remarkable spell of bowling.

### Kent

| | | | |
|---|---|---|---|
| M. R. Benson c Bairstow b Jarvis | 12 | – c sub b Carrick | 107 |
| G. W. Johnson c Sharp b Shaw | 29 | | |
| C. J. Tavaré c Carrick b Jarvis | 28 | – c Jarvis b Carrick | 123 |
| S. G. Hinks b Carrick | 18 | – (2) b Jarvis | 11 |
| *C. S. Cowdrey b Jarvis | 48 | – (4) not out | 14 |
| E. A. E. Baptiste c Bairstow b Carrick | 82 | – (5) not out | 3 |
| R. M. Ellison not out | 64 | | |
| †S. A. Marsh c Boycott b Jarvis | 25 | | |
| G. R. Dilley b Jarvis | 1 | | |
| D. L. Underwood b Jarvis | 1 | | |
| K. B. S. Jarvis b Jarvis | 4 | | |
| B 5, l-b 4, w 3, n-b 4 | 16 | L-b 9, w 1, n-b 2 | 12 |
| 1/24 2/63 3/87 4/99 5/226 6/228 7/314 8/316 9/322 | 328 | 1/14 2/246 3/255 (3 wkts dec.) | 270 |

Bonus points – Kent 4, Yorkshire 4.

Bowling: *First Innings*—Jarvis 26.4–3–105–7; Stevenson 15–4–49–0; Fletcher 17–4–45–0; Shaw 17–2–53–1; Carrick 23–7–67–2. *Second Innings*—Jarvis 16–0–60–1; Fletcher 17–2–70–0; Shaw 11–1–52–0; Carrick 24–2–79–2.

### Yorkshire

| | First innings | | Second innings | |
|---|---|---|---|---|
| G. Boycott c Marsh b Baptiste | 25 | – run out | 9 |
| A. A. Metcalfe c Tavaré b Jarvis | 3 | – run out | 0 |
| K. Sharp c Tavaré b Ellison | 36 | – b Jarvis | 10 |
| J. D. Love c Marsh b Dilley | 19 | – c Johnson b Underwood | 93 |
| S. N. Hartley c Cowdrey b Underwood | 60 | – lbw b Ellison | 9 |
| *†D. L. Bairstow b Jarvis | 29 | – c Hinks b Underwood | 42 |
| P. Carrick lbw b Dilley | 45 | – c Cowdrey b Underwood | 0 |
| P. W. Jarvis not out | 25 | – (9) c Cowdrey b Underwood | 9 |
| G. B. Stevenson not out | 35 | – (8) c Hinks b Jarvis | 15 |
| C. Shaw (did not bat) | | – c Baptiste b Ellison | 0 |
| S. D. Fletcher (did not bat) | | – not out | 0 |
| B 10, l-b 10, n-b 3 | 23 | B 1, l-b 6, w 1, n-b 3 | 11 |
| 1/8 2/71 3/71 4/121 5/153 6/217 7/244 | (7 wkts dec.) 300 | 1/1 2/21 3/25 4/57 5/122 6/124 7/139 8/195 9/198 | 198 |

Bonus points – Yorkshire 4, Kent 3.

Bowling: *First Innings*—Dilley 17–4–47–2; Jarvis 23–4–72–2; Underwood 13–8–17–1; Baptiste 24–3–101–1; Ellison 13–2–43–1. *Second Innings*—Dilley 10–2–41–0; Jarvis 11–2–49–2; Ellison 13.3–5–43–2; Baptiste 7–0–33–0; Underwood 18–14–8–4; Johnson 2–0–17–0.

Umpires: J. H. Harris and K. E. Palmer.

## KENT v NORTHAMPTONSHIRE

At Maidstone, July 13, 15, 16. Kent won by four wickets. Kent 22 pts, Northamptonshire 7 pts. Toss won by Northamptonshire. A magnificent maiden first-class century by the West Indian all-rounder, Harper, rescued his side. They were 59 for six, a collapse spearheaded by splendid seam and swing bowling from Ellison, before Harper scored 127 out of 182 in 176 minutes, his innings featuring two 6s and twenty 4s. Kent's bad start was retrieved by Benson and the recovery continued by Cowdrey and Penn, the night-watchman, who struck three 4s and three 6s in reaching 50 out of 78 in 53 minutes. But Kent then lost their last six wickets for 30 in fourteen overs, Griffiths taking four for 7 in 38 balls. Batting again, Northamptonshire had a second-wicket stand of 97 between Larkins and Boyd-Moss, but Cowdrey gave his side the edge with three wickets in an over. Ellison, with career-best figures in the first innings, finished with ten wickets in a match for the first time. Chasing 280 to win in a minimum of 90 overs, Kent were given a great start by Benson, and then Baptiste, with a rapid fifty in 48 minutes, steered them home with 2.3 overs to spare.

### Northamptonshire

| | First innings | Second innings | |
|---|---|---|---|
| *G. Cook c Knott b Ellison | 1 | – c Baptiste b Ellison | 16 |
| W. Larkins c and b Cowdrey | 8 | – b Underwood | 67 |
| R. J. Boyd-Moss c Cowdrey b Ellison | 0 | – c Benson b Baptiste | 63 |
| R. G. Williams c Knott b Ellison | 24 | – c Taylor b Ellison | 6 |
| R. J. Bailey c Knott b Baptiste | 16 | – c Knott b Cowdrey | 44 |
| D. J. Capel c Knott b Ellison | 5 | – c Underwood b Penn | 10 |
| D. J. Wild c Taylor b Ellison | 26 | – c Benson b Cowdrey | 7 |
| R. A. Harper c Johnson b Ellison | 127 | – c Taylor b Ellison | 18 |
| †D. Ripley c Penn b Baptiste | 13 | – lbw b Cowdrey | 0 |
| N. A. Mallender not out | 21 | – not out | 2 |
| B. J. Griffiths b Ellison | 0 | – c Penn b Ellison | 0 |
| B 1, l-b 8, w 3, n-b 2 | 14 | B 1, l-b 6, w 2, n-b 5 | 14 |
| 1/1 2/1 3/21 4/41 5/57 6/59 7/130 8/189 9/241 | 255 | 1/33 2/130 3/147 4/186 5/216 6/223 7/224 8/224 9/247 | 247 |

Bonus points – Northamptonshire 3, Kent 4.

Bowling: *First Innings*—Baptiste 18–2–58–2; Ellison 27.3–6–87–7; Cowdrey 11–0–56–1; Underwood 9–2–22–0; Penn 5–0–23–0. *Second Innings*—Ellison 24.4–6–77–4; Baptiste 21–6–68–1; Underwood 24–11–48–1; Penn 12–2–42–1; Cowdrey 4–0–5–3.

## Kent

| First innings | | Second innings | |
|---|---|---|---|
| M. R. Benson c Ripley b Mallender | 53 | b Williams | 97 |
| S. G. Hinks b Griffiths | 16 | b Griffiths | 14 |
| N. R. Taylor c Ripley b Griffiths | 5 | lbw b Harper | 43 |
| D. G. Aslett b Capel | 5 | run out | 41 |
| *C. S. Cowdrey c Harper b Griffiths | 67 | c Larkins b Williams | 7 |
| C. Penn c Ripley b Griffiths | 50 | | |
| E. A. E. Baptiste c Larkins b Griffiths | 0 | (6) not out | 58 |
| R. M. Ellison c Larkins b Harper | 1 | (7) run out | 2 |
| G. W. Johnson c Boyd-Moss b Harper | 12 | (8) not out | 3 |
| †A. P. E. Knott not out | 7 | | |
| D. L. Underwood lbw b Griffiths | 1 | | |
| L-b 3, n-b 3 | 6 | B 6, l-b 5, n-b 5 | 16 |
| 1/39 2/47 3/58 4/110 5/193 6/197 7/202 8/208 9/222 | 223 | 1/34 2/150 3/170 4/194 5/256 6/258 | (6 wkts) 281 |

Bonus points – Kent 2, Northamptonshire 4.

Bowling: *First Innings*—Mallender 11–1–54–1; Griffiths 30.1–2–76–6; Harper 15–0–64–2; Capel 10–1–26–1. *Second Innings*—Griffiths 14–4–52–1; Capel 13–3–38–0; Harper 38.3–6–108–1; Larkins 2–0–4–0; Wild 4–1–7–0; Williams 19–3–61–2.

Umpires: J. H. Harris and K. E. Palmer.

# KENT v ESSEX

At Dartford, July 24, 25, 26. Drawn. Kent 8 pts, Essex 3 pts. Toss won by Essex. Four brilliant catches by wicket-keeper Knott and Underwood's best return of the season conspired to dismiss Essex relatively cheaply. Kent were soon building a big lead. Benson and Hinks with an opening stand of 134 off 31 overs paved the way, and Tavaré and Taylor hit 131 off 39 overs. Tavaré, batting for 289 minutes, hit five 6s and twenty 4s in recording the highest score by a Kent batsman on this ground. The previous highest was M. C. Cowdrey's 145 in 1965. Essex always struggled, apart from Gooch who looked in tremendous form during his 362 minutes at the crease, hitting twenty 4s. His innings was the inspiration for survival to the tailenders, who held on gamely to deny Kent. Underwood, whose first-innings analysis included a spell of four for 11, took ten or more wickets in a match for the 47th time in his career.

## Essex

| First innings | | Second innings | |
|---|---|---|---|
| *G. A. Gooch c Knott b Jarvis | 17 | c Benson b Potter | 125 |
| C. Gladwin b Underwood | 53 | c Knott b Dilley | 8 |
| P. J. Prichard b Jarvis | 9 | c Knott b Underwood | 9 |
| K. S. McEwan lbw b Underwood | 46 | b Ellison | 14 |
| B. R. Hardie b Underwood | 2 | c Knott b Dilley | 24 |
| D. R. Pringle c Knott b Baptiste | 19 | b Underwood | 15 |
| K. R. Pont c Tavaré b Underwood | 8 | b Underwood | 15 |
| †D. E. East c Knott b Jarvis | 30 | not out | 26 |
| J. K. Lever not out | 10 | lbw b Underwood | 0 |
| J. H. Childs c Knott b Underwood | 3 | not out | 3 |
| D. L. Acfield c Tavaré b Underwood | 0 | | |
| L-b 10, n-b 6 | 16 | L-b 7, w 1, n-b 13 | 21 |
| 1/33 2/49 3/130 4/135 5/140 6/156 7/186 8/200 9/209 | 213 | 1/20 2/54 3/80 4/146 5/206 6/220 7/245 8/245 | (8 wkts) 260 |

Bonus points – Essex 2, Kent 4.

Bowling: *First Innings*—Jarvis 18–2–59–3; Dilley 16–5–41–0; Baptiste 13–3–32–1; Ellison 5–1–15–0; Underwood 22.1–6–56–6. *Second Innings*—Jarvis 11–3–36–0; Dilley 23–6–58–2; Underwood 48–18–80–4; Potter 15–5–29–1; Ellison 13.5–3–29–1; Baptiste 10–4–21–0.

## Kent

| | | | |
|---|---|---|---|
| *M. R. Benson c McEwan b Acfield | 64 | †A. P. E. Knott c Gooch b Pringle | 1 |
| S. G. Hinks c Gooch b Acfield | 74 | G. R. Dilley c Prichard b Pringle | 5 |
| D. L. Underwood c East b Childs | 6 | | |
| C. J. Tavaré not out | 150 | B 1, l-b 7 | 8 |
| N. R. Taylor c East b Pont | 79 | | |
| L. Potter c Hardie b Acfield | 29 | 1/134 2/146 3/152 | (9 wkts dec.) 476 |
| E. A. E. Baptiste b Acfield | 47 | 4/283 5/346 6/422 | |
| R. M. Ellison b Childs | 13 | 7/458 8/459 9/476 | |

K. B. S. Jarvis did not bat.

Bonus points – Kent 4, Essex 1 (Score at 100 overs: 308-4).

Bowling: Lever 14–6–28–0; Pringle 30.2–8–83–2; Acfield 42–8–164–4; Childs 36–12–129–2; Pont 9–1–64–1.

Umpires: R. Julian and R. A. White.

At Leicester, July 27, 29, 30. KENT drew with LEICESTERSHIRE.

At Eastbourne, July 31, August 1, 2. KENT drew with SUSSEX.

At Swansea, August 3, 4, 5. KENT drew with GLAMORGAN.

# KENT v SUSSEX

At Canterbury, August 10, 12, 13. Sussex won by 54 runs. Sussex 20 pts, Kent 3 pts. Toss won by Sussex. Rain prevented any play on the first day of the Festival Week, and when the match did get under way, Sussex were indebted to splendid batting by Lenham, who hit nine 4s in a career-best innings. Kent forfeited their first innings, and Sussex soon declared to set a target of 345 in 96 overs. Tavaré and Taylor added 93 off 29 overs as Kent made a bold bid, and Potter hit 55 in 110 minutes. However, le Roux arrested the advance and then Reeve bowled Sussex to victory with twenty balls to spare as Kent maintained their challenge to the last.

## Sussex

| | | | |
|---|---|---|---|
| G. D. Mendis c Knott b Jarvis | 27 | – not out | 22 |
| A. M. Green b Baptiste | 21 | – not out | 4 |
| N. J. Lenham c Knott b Potter | 89 | | |
| C. M. Wells b Underwood | 61 | | |
| A. P. Wells c Penn b Underwood | 36 | | |
| †I. J. Gould c Jarvis b Underwood | 20 | | |
| G. S. le Roux c Jarvis b Potter | 22 | | |
| *J. R. T. Barclay c sub b Potter | 9 | | |
| D. A. Reeve c Penn b Benson | 14 | | |
| A. C. S. Pigott c Tavaré b Underwood | 0 | | |
| C. E. Waller not out | 6 | | |
| B 1, l-b 4, n-b 7 | 12 | L-b 1 | 1 |
| 1/50 2/50 3/174 4/232 5/253 6/266 7/294 8/296 9/300 | 317 | (no wkt dec.) | 27 |

Bonus points – Sussex 4, Kent 3 (Score at 100 overs: 300-8).

Bowling: *First Innings*—Jarvis 27–5–71–1; Dilley 12–1–42–0; Baptiste 5–1–11–1; Penn 13–2–44–0; Underwood 35–6–87–4; Potter 13–1–46–3; Taylor 3–0–7–0; Benson 0.3–0–4–1. *Second Innings*—Taylor 3–0–9–0; Benson 2.5–0–17–0.

## Kent

*Kent forfeited their first innings.*

| | |
|---|---|
| *M. R. Benson c Reeve b Waller | 26 |
| S. G. Hinks b le Roux | 15 |
| C. J. Tavaré c Barclay b Reeve | 64 |
| N. R. Taylor lbw b le Roux | 41 |
| L. Potter b le Roux | 55 |
| E. A. E. Baptiste c sub b Reeve | 5 |
| †A. P. E. Knott b Reeve | 29 |
| C. Penn b Reeve | 27 |
| G. R. Dilley b Reeve | 0 |
| D. L. Underwood not out | 4 |
| K. B. S. Jarvis c Barclay b le Roux | 4 |
| L-b 9, w 4, n-b 7 | 20 |
| 1/33 2/62 3/155 4/159 5/177 6/217 7/280 8/281 9/282 | 290 |

Bowling: le Roux 17.4–1–72–4; Pigott 4.3–1–12–0; Reeve 32–11–70–5; Waller 19.3–4–64–1; C. M. Wells 11–4–34–0; Barclay 8–2–29–0.

Umpires: J. W. Holder and K. J. Lyons.

## KENT v WARWICKSHIRE

At Canterbury, August 14, 15, 16. Drawn. Kent 4 pts, Warwickshire 8 pts. Toss won by Warwickshire. Rain prevented a start until 2.30 on the first day, whereupon Kallicharran batted beautifully, reaching his hundred out of 166 in 260 minutes with one 6 and eleven 4s. Enterprising batting by Humpage and Ferreira then enabled Warwickshire to declare at their fourth batting point. Kent struggled and finally collapsed, losing their last six wickets for 30 runs in twelve overs as Ferreira took three for 1 in nine balls and Gifford three for 22 in six overs. Warwickshire themselves collapsed against the pace of Jarvis and Dilley before Ferreira rescued them and Kent were set 275 to win in 63 overs. Rain intervened after nine balls of their innings to wash out what could have been an intriguing finish.

## Warwickshire

| First innings | | Second innings | |
|---|---|---|---|
| G. J. Lord c Hinks b Dilley | 7 | (2) b Jarvis | 0 |
| R. I. H. B. Dyer lbw b Penn | 59 | (1) lbw b Jarvis | 8 |
| A. I. Kallicharran c Penn b Dilley | 108 | b Dilley | 1 |
| D. L. Amiss c Hinks b Penn | 2 | c Benson b Jarvis | 3 |
| A. R. K. Pierson b Penn | 9 | (7) not out | 17 |
| †G. W. Humpage b Penn | 52 | (5) c Penn b Dilley | 34 |
| P. A. Smith c Knott b Underwood | 1 | (6) c and b Penn | 22 |
| A. M. Ferreira not out | 34 | not out | 41 |
| C. M. Old not out | 12 | | |
| B 1, l-b 5, n-b 10 | 16 | B 4, l-b 2, n-b 6 | 12 |
| 1/17 2/160 3/167 4/192 5/230 6/233 7/271 (7 wkts dec.) | 300 | 1/5 2/10 3/12 4/27 5/57 6/79 (6 wkts dec.) | 138 |

G. C. Small and *N. Gifford did not bat.

Bonus points – Warwickshire 4, Kent 3.

Bowling: *First Innings*—Jarvis 23–6–66–0; Dilley 16–3–64–2; Baptiste 14–2–47–0; Underwood 22–9–46–1; Penn 14–2–71–4. *Second Innings*—Jarvis 21–6–66–3; Dilley 20–6–52–2; Penn 5–1–10–1; Underwood 4–2–4–0.

## Kent

| | | |
|---|---|---|
| *M. R. Benson c Humpage b Small | 13 – not out | 4 |
| S. G. Hinks c Smith b Small | 5 – not out | 0 |
| C. J. Tavaré c Humpage b Smith | 21 | |
| N. R. Taylor b Gifford | 39 | |
| L. Potter run out | 3 | |
| E. A. E. Baptiste c Humpage b Ferreira | 40 | |
| †A. P. E. Knott c Humpage b Gifford | 10 | |
| C. Penn lbw b Ferreira | 0 | |
| G. R. Dilley c Pearson b Gifford | 15 | |
| D. L. Underwood c Humpage b Ferreira | 0 | |
| K. B. S. Jarvis not out | 0 | |
| B 4, n-b 14 | 18 | |
| 1/11 2/33 3/48 4/61 5/134 6/148 7/149 8/154 9/154 | 164 | (no wkt) 4 |

Bonus points – Kent 1, Warwickshire 4.

Bowling: *First Innings*—Small 8–0–20–2; Old 5–1–18–0; Ferreira 19–3–56–3; Smith 6–1–27–1; Pearson 3–0–13–0; Gifford 10.4–3–26–3. *Second Innings*—Small 1–0–1–0; Smith 0.3–0–3–0.

Umpires: J. W. Holder and K. J. Lyons.

At Scarborough, August 17, 19, 20. KENT drew with YORKSHIRE.

At Canterbury, August 24, 25, 26, 27. KENT lost to AUSTRALIANS by seven wickets (See Australian tour section).

At Worcester, August 28, 29, 30. KENT lost to WORCESTERSHIRE by five wickets.

## KENT v DERBYSHIRE

At Folkestone, August 31, September 2, 3. Drawn. Kent 8 pts, Derbyshire 3 pts. Toss won by Derbyshire. Rain curtailed play on the first day when Derbyshire struggled on a wicket seemingly helping spin bowlers. Kent were boosted by their captain, Cowdrey, who reached 50 in 99 minutes, and on the final morning Baptiste hit eleven 4s as he featured in a lively stand of 61 off ten overs with Graham Cowdrey. Kent, declaring 153 ahead, pinned their victory hopes on the left-arm spin of Underwood and Potter but Derbyshire now batted in a resolute mood. Barnett set the pattern, batting through 50 overs: Roberts resisted for 33 overs and Newman took twenty overs for his single. It was enough to foil Kent.

## Derbyshire

| | | | |
|---|---|---|---|
| I. S. Anderson c Waterton b Baptiste | 2 | – c Waterton b Baptiste | 2 |
| B. Roberts b Baptiste | 33 | – b Underwood | 17 |
| J. E. Morris b Underwood | 38 | – lbw b Underwood | 1 |
| *K. J. Barnett c Benson b Baptiste | 0 | – c Hinks b Potter | 14 |
| M. A. Fell b Underwood | 12 | – c G. R. Cowdrey b Underwood | 7 |
| P. G. Newman c C. S. Cowdrey b Potter | 29 | – lbw b Potter | 1 |
| M. A. Holding c and b Underwood | 0 | – st Waterton b Potter | 12 |
| R. J. Finney c Benson b Baptiste | 11 | – not out | 3 |
| †C. Marples c Potter b Underwood | 3 | – not out | 0 |
| P. E. Russell not out | 0 | | |
| O. H. Mortensen c Tavaré b Potter | 4 | | |
| B 2, l-b 3, w 2, n-b 8 | 15 | B 6, l-b 3, n-b 4 | 13 |
| 1/2 2/52 3/55 4/91 5/99 6/99 7/135 8/143 9/143 | 147 | 1/9 2/24 3/31 4/45 5/50 6/54 7/70 | (7 wkts) 70 |

Bonus points – Kent 4.

Bowling: *First Innings*—Dilley 12–4–19–0; Baptiste 16–3–48–4; Underwood 33–17–34–4; C. S. Cowdrey 4–1–19–0; Potter 14–7–22–2. *Second Innings*—Dilley 5–0–15–0; Baptiste 10–6–10–1; Underwood 37–28–23–3; Potter 30.4–22–13–3; Taylor 1–1–0–0.

## Kent

| | |
|---|---|
| M. R. Benson c Marples b Holding | 4 |
| S. G. Hinks b Russell | 24 |
| C. J. Tavaré c Marples b Mortensen | 33 |
| N. R. Taylor b Newman | 25 |
| *C. S. Cowdrey lbw b Holding | 62 |
| E. A. E. Baptiste c Anderson b Russell | 71 |
| L. Potter c Marples b Mortensen | 4 |
| G. R. Cowdrey c Newman b Holding | 33 |
| †S. N. V. Waterton not out | 16 |
| G. R. Dilley not out | 18 |
| B 2, l-b 7, n-b 1 | 10 |
| 1/14 2/31 3/72 4/131 5/169 6/188 7/249 8/265 | (8 wkts dec.) 300 |

D. L. Underwood did not bat.

Bonus points – Kent 4, Derbyshire 3.

Bowling: Holding 31–4–114–3; Mortensen 18–6–54–2; Russell 25.1–5–67–2; Newman 11–4–20–1; Barnett 7–2–24–0; Finney 3–0–12–0.

Umpires: D. J. Constant and K. J. Lyons.

## KENT v HAMPSHIRE

At Folkestone, September 4, 5, 6. Drawn. Kent 5 pts, Hampshire 8 pts. Toss won by Hampshire. Greenidge gave Hampshire a splendid start and Chris Smith, having taken 188 minutes for his first fifty, raced to his seventh hundred of the season in another 31 minutes. He hit three 6s and eleven 4s in his stay of 247 minutes. Kent began badly but were rescued by Chris Cowdrey, who batted for 243 minutes, hitting two 6s and ten 4s and figuring in a last-wicket stand of 62 with Underwood. The innings featured a controversial run-out when Benson, going for a single, was well down the wicket only to see his partner, Taylor, on the ground after colliding with the bowler, Maru. Benson, trying to get back, was run out by Marshall's throw from deep mid-off. The umpires decided that it was a legitimate dismissal although Cowdrey, while agreeing that the obstruction was not deliberate, felt that as it was accidental obstruction, Benson should have been called back. Hampshire set Kent 231 to win in 62 overs and seemed well on the way to victory as Kent slumped to 47 for four. However, Chris Cowdrey and Baptiste put on 110 in 31 overs and Kent held on for the draw.

## Hampshire

| | | |
|---|---|---|
| C. G. Greenidge c Marsh b Baptiste | 84 | – c Potter b Baptiste 50 |
| V. P. Terry c Tavaré b Underwood | 5 | – b Underwood 67 |
| C. L. Smith c G. R. Cowdrey b Potter | 121 | – not out 9 |
| *M. C. J. Nicholas st Marsh b Potter | 36 | – c C. S. Cowdrey b Underwood 2 |
| R. A. Smith st Marsh b Underwood | 48 | – b Baptiste 1 |
| M. D. Marshall c C. S. Cowdrey b Potter | 5 | – c Tavaré b Baptiste 15 |
| N. G. Cowley c Benson b Underwood | 0 | |
| T. M. Tremlett not out | 15 | |
| †R. J. Parks st Marsh b Potter | 2 | |
| R. J. Maru run out | 2 | |
| B 1, l-b 8, n-b 6 | 15 | B 1, l-b 6, n-b 5 12 |
| 1/31 2/115 3/176 4/284 5/295 6/296 7/315 8/328 9/333 | (9 wkts dec.) 333 | 1/117 2/129 3/135 4/137 5/156 (5 wkts dec.) 156 |

S. J. W. Andrew did not bat.

Bonus points – Hampshire 4, Kent 2 (Score at 100 overs: 301-6).

Bowling: *First Innings*—Baptiste 17–4–44–1; Ellison 14–6–35–0; Underwood 34–11–76–3; C. S. Cowdrey 15–3–66–0; Potter 25–5–87–4; Taylor 5–1–16–0. *Second Innings*—Baptiste 19.1–7–40–3; Ellison 4–1–12–0; Potter 7–2–21–0; Underwood 18–3–76–2.

## Kent

| | | |
|---|---|---|
| M. R. Benson run out | 27 | – lbw b Tremlett 10 |
| S. G. Hinks b Marshall | 16 | – b Andrew 14 |
| C. J. Tavaré c Marshall b Maru | 8 | – b Cowley 3 |
| N. R. Taylor lbw b Cowley | 7 | – b Maru 18 |
| *C. S. Cowdrey c Terry b Marshall | 131 | – lbw b Maru 39 |
| E. A. E. Baptiste c Greenidge b Marshall | 19 | – c Marshall b Cowley 68 |
| G. R. Cowdrey c Terry b Cowley | 10 | – (8) c Parks b Marshall 1 |
| L. Potter c Nicholas b Tremlett | 11 | – (9) not out 6 |
| R. M. Ellison c Parks b Andrew | 10 | – (7) not out 0 |
| †S. A. Marsh lbw b Cowley | 3 | |
| D. L. Underwood not out | 4 | |
| B 2, l-b 5, n-b 6 | 13 | B 11, l-b 1, w 1 13 |
| 1/38 2/53 3/53 4/64 5/106 6/136 7/173 8/193 9/197 | 259 | 1/22 2/24 3/33 4/47 5/157 6/157 7/162 (7 wkts) 172 |

Bonus points – Kent 3, Hampshire 4 (Score at 100 overs: 259-9).

Bowling: *First Innings*—Marshall 24.3–5–46–3; Andrew 9–1–35–1; Tremlett 15–6–19–1; Cowley 25–6–51–3; Maru 27–2–101–1. *Second Innings*—Marshall 14.4–3–31–1; Andrew 6–1–15–1; Tremlett 11–2–24–1; Maru 17–4–66–2; Cowley 13–5–24–2.

Umpires: B. Dudleston and D. J. Constant.

## KENT v SOMERSET

At Canterbury, September 14, 16, 17. Drawn. Kent 4 pts, Somerset 5 pts. Toss won by Somerset. There was a disappointing end to the season, with the weather again influencing the match. Only 40 overs were possible on the first day, with Somerset struggling to 78 for four, but on the second day Felton, batting in all for 278 minutes, steered them to two bonus points. Kent declared in arrears at their overnight score, and with Somerset hurried along by Bail, who batted for 167 minutes and hit eleven 4s, Kent were set 270 to win in a minimum of 58 overs. The target never looked like being achieved as they collapsed to 44 for four. Taylor, who reached 50 in 97 minutes, and Graham Cowdrey rescued the innings, and Tavaré, batting at No. 7 because he had been off the field with a leg injury, dropped anchor for 70 minutes to deny Somerset's victory bid.

## Somerset

| | | | |
|---|---|---|---|
| J. G. Wyatt c Potter b Ellison | 4 | – st Waterton b Underwood | 39 |
| P. M. Roebuck c G. R. Cowdrey b Underwood | 17 | | |
| N. A. Felton c C. S. Cowdrey b Baptiste | 84 | – b Underwood | 24 |
| P. A. C. Bail c G. R. Cowdrey b Underwood | 2 | – (2) not out | 78 |
| B. C. Rose c Tavaré b Baptiste | 12 | – (4) c G. R. Cowdrey b Underwood | 15 |
| *V. J. Marks c Potter b Ellison | 46 | – (5) b Underwood | 23 |
| †T. Gard c Hinks b Taylor | 3 | | |
| M. R. Davis c Ellison b Underwood | 9 | | |
| J. Garner c Jarvis b Taylor | 13 | | |
| C. H. Dredge not out | 8 | | |
| R. V. J. Coombs b Underwood | 1 | | |
| L-b 11, n-b 1 | 12 | B 8, l-b 1, n-b 1 | 10 |
| 1/15 2/42 3/49 4/62 5/125 6/152 7/175 8/189 9/210 | 211 | 1/76 2/106 3/137 4/189 (4 wkts dec.) | 189 |

Bonus points – Somerset 2, Kent 4.

Bowling: *First Innings*—Jarvis 12–3–40–0; Ellison 22–8–41–2; Baptiste 24–6–54–2; Underwood 27.2–10–44–4; Taylor 12–4–20–2; Potter 2–1–1–0. *Second Innings*—Jarvis 5–2–16–0; Baptiste 7–1–25–0; Underwood 25.5–8–69–4; Potter 15–1–36–0; Taylor 8–1–34–0.

## Kent

| | | | |
|---|---|---|---|
| L. Potter c Gard b Garner | 4 | – lbw b Davis | 0 |
| S. G. Hinks c Dredge b Davis | 5 | – c Dredge b Garner | 5 |
| C. J. Tavaré b Coombs | 14 | – (7) not out | 10 |
| N. R. Taylor b Garner | 24 | – (3) st Gard b Coombs | 54 |
| *C. S. Cowdrey lbw b Coombs | 12 | – (4) c sub b Coombs | 9 |
| E. A. E. Baptiste lbw b Garner | 45 | – (5) c sub b Coombs | 10 |
| G. R. Cowdrey not out | 20 | – (6) c Gard b Coombs | 41 |
| R. M. Ellison c Wyatt b Coombs | 0 | – not out | 1 |
| †S. N. V. Waterton not out | 6 | | |
| N-b 1 | 1 | L-b 1, n-b 1 | 2 |
| 1/4 2/14 3/34 4/50 5/88 6/108 7/113 (7 wkts dec.) | 131 | 1/2 2/7 3/25 4/44 5/97 6/124 (6 wkts) | 132 |

D. L. Underwood and K. B. S. Jarvis did not bat.

Bonus points – Somerset 3.

Bowling: *First Innings*—Garner 12–1–34–3; Davis 8–2–21–1; Coombs 18–3–57–3; Dredge 6–1–13–0; Marks 4–1–6–0. *Second Innings*—Garner 9–4–10–1; Davis 6–3–13–1; Coombs 23–11–54–4; Marks 19–4–54–0; Bail 2–2–0–0.

Umpires: R. Julian and B. J. Meyer.

# LANCASHIRE

*Patron:* HM The Queen
*President:* C. D. Peaker
*Chairman:* C. S. Rhoades
*Secretary:* C. D. Hassell
County Cricket Ground, Old Trafford,
Manchester M16 0PX
(Telephone: 061-848 7021)
*Cricket Manager:* J. D. Bond
*Captain:* 1985 – J. Abrahams
1986 – C. H. Lloyd
*Coaches:* J. S. Savage and P. Lever

In a season of four competitions a team can confidently be expected to show improvement on the previous year in at least one of them. Lancashire's solitary progression came in the Britannic Assurance Championship with three wins to the one of 1984 and a rise of two places in the table. They still finished in the bottom half, completing a decade of relegation-type cricket burdened with uncertain batting and unimpressive bowling. Unfortunately, their performances in the limited-overs tournaments were just as depressing and they won only five matches all summer, one of them against Suffolk in the NatWest Bank Trophy.

Another miserable Championship season was reflected in only one batsman, Neil Fairbrother, scoring 1,000 runs and none of the bowlers taking 50 wickets. Yet two wins in the first seven games helped Lancashire to stay away from the bottom half of the table until August. The season started in a blaze of glory with a 74-run win over Gloucestershire at Bristol in the second game. That was to prove the only match in which the opposition were bowled out twice; and just to round it off nicely as a bowlers' match, they got most of the runs as well, with four of them hitting half-centuries. Paul Allott, in fact, was the game's top scorer with 78, the highest ever by a Lancashire number eleven. The brittleness of the batting was evident then and was emphasised in the following match at The Oval when Lancashire lost to Surrey by 233 runs, with Fairbrother the top scorer in either innings with 48.

Fairbrother played several fine innings, including two centuries against Yorkshire, as he continued his impressive form of 1984 and reached nearly 1,400 runs. His fielding, too, was in a high class and he was by far the most heartening part of Lancashire's season. The former Cambridge University batsman, David Varey, was given an unexpectedly early opportunity in the team and outlasted both original opening batsmen, Alan Ormrod and Graeme Fowler. He was second behind Fairbrother in his total of runs in a season in which he played in 22 matches, rarely failed to get into double figures, yet scored only one century – against Oxford University – and two fifties.

The first three batsmen at the start of the season, Ormrod, Fowler and Steve O'Shaughnessy, all lost their places in a dismal summer in which runs dried up. Each scored 1,000 runs in 1984; between them they could not total 800 in 1985. Ormrod played in the first four Championship matches, dropped into the second team, where he broke a cheekbone, and was not retained at the end of the season. O'Shaughnessy hit one half-century in thirteen games and not even the award of his county cap could inspire him to recapture his form of the previous year. Yet the saddest and most bewildering change in fortune came to Fowler, who had returned to Lancashire after playing a significant part in England's success in India, where his peak had come with a double-century in the Madras Test. His confidence could not have been higher, yet it quickly drained with a succession of low scores, culminating in his being dropped from England's Texaco Trophy team after failing in the first of the three matches. He went into the Championship match with Hampshire at Liverpool at the beginning of July with just one first-class half-century behind him. But worse was to come as he injured his neck during catching practice and had to be taken by ambulance to hospital after lying prostrate on the ground for nearly half an hour. Torn neck muscles were diagnosed and he did not play again for three weeks. The break from cricket did not help him and more low scores saw him slip into the second team and out of consideration for either of the England teams chosen for the winter tours.

The captain, John Abrahams, also had a miserable season and missed 1,000 runs for the first time since being capped in 1982. He was relieved of the captaincy at the end of the season, Clive Lloyd being restored as captain for his second benefit season in 1986 after playing in only four Championship matches in 1985, when he became virtually just a one-day player. This was Lancashire's answer to their problem of having engaged three overseas players, with Steve Jefferies and Patrick Patterson, both opening bowlers, being used mainly in the Championship games. Jefferies again made little impression and was released, but Patterson showed flashes of genuine pace, especially in the early stages of the season when he took six for 77 against Yorkshire, seven for 49 against Oxford University and had a career-best match return of ten for 113 against Essex in successive matches. There was to be no repeat but Lancashire were sufficiently encouraged to keep him.

Allott was again the outstanding bowler, the leading wicket-taker with 49 despite missing several matches through England calls. He lacked real support, except during Patterson's burst, and a few sheepish glances must have been cast towards Worcestershire where Neal Radford, released by Lancashire at the end of 1984 after five mediocre seasons, was becoming the only bowler in the country to take 100 wickets.

Two of Lancashire's wins came in run-chases, one against Derbyshire, who set a target of 213 in 37 overs, the other over Somerset in a match in which both teams forfeited an innings and Mark Chadwick, 21, and Kevin Hayes, 22, the former Oxford University captain, scored maiden Championship centuries. Seven matches were ruined by rain, including the first-ever Championship match at Lytham, and in a season in which Lancashire batted second in two-thirds of the games, they finished up six times hanging on with tailenders together.

Not even the limited-overs game enabled Lancashire to snatch glory as they did in 1984, when they won the Benson and Hedges Cup. Along with Leicestershire, they had five abandoned games in the John Player League and fell from fourth place the previous year to fourteenth. After beating Suffolk in the first round of the NatWest Bank Trophy they were beaten by Worcestershire, and they failed to reach the knockout stages of the Benson and Hedges Cup after winning only one zonal game. – B.B.

LANCASHIRE 1985

[*Bill Smith*

*Back row:* N. H. Fairbrother, D. W. Varey, B. P. Patterson, M. Watkinson, D. J. Makinson, M. R. Chadwick. *Front row:* P. J. W. Allott, J. Simmons, J. Abrahams (*captain*), G. Fowler, C. Maynard. *Insets:* I. Folley, C. H. Lloyd, S. J. O'Shaughnessy, D. P. Hughes.

## LANCASHIRE RESULTS

*All first-class matches – Played 25: Won 4, Lost 7, Drawn 14.*

*County Championship matches – Played 24: Won 3, Lost 7, Drawn 14.*

*Bonus points – Batting 44, Bowling 67.*

*Competition placings – Britannic Assurance County Championship, 14th; NatWest Bank Trophy, 2nd round; Benson and Hedges Cup, 5th in Group B; John Player League, 14th eq.*

## BRITANNIC ASSURANCE CHAMPIONSHIP AVERAGES

### BATTING

| | *Birthplace* | *M* | *I* | *NO* | *R* | *HI* | *Avge* |
|---|---|---|---|---|---|---|---|
| ‡C. H. Lloyd | *Georgetown, BG* | 4 | 7 | 1 | 288 | 131 | 48.00 |
| K. A. Hayes | *Thurnscoe* | 5 | 7 | 0 | 310 | 117 | 44.28 |
| S. T. Jefferies | *Cape Town, SA* | 4 | 7 | 0 | 274 | 93 | 39.14 |
| ‡N. H. Fairbrother | *Warrington* | 24 | 38 | 3 | 1,327 | 164* | 37.91 |
| D. J. Makinson | *Eccleston* | 14 | 21 | 9 | 372 | 58* | 31.00 |
| D. W. Varey | *Darlington* | 21 | 33 | 3 | 848 | 87 | 28.26 |
| ‡P. J. W. Allott | *Altrincham* | 14 | 15 | 5 | 242 | 78 | 24.20 |
| ‡D. P. Hughes | *Newton-le-Willows* | 9 | 15 | 1 | 336 | 68 | 24.00 |
| ‡J. Abrahams | *Cape Town, SA* | 24 | 38 | 3 | 831 | 77* | 23.74 |
| M. Watkinson | *Westhoughton* | 18 | 28 | 1 | 633 | 106 | 23.44 |
| M. R. Chadwick | *Rochdale* | 11 | 16 | 1 | 347 | 132 | 23.13 |
| ‡J. Simmons | *Clayton-le-Moors* | 21 | 30 | 4 | 485 | 101 | 18.65 |
| ‡G. Fowler | *Accrington* | 15 | 24 | 0 | 404 | 88 | 16.83 |
| I. Folley | *Burnley* | 20 | 27 | 8 | 262 | 69 | 13.78 |
| ‡S. J. O'Shaughnessy | *Bury* | 13 | 23 | 2 | 275 | 63 | 13.09 |
| C. Maynard | *Haslemere* | 18 | 26 | 4 | 240 | 43 | 10.90 |
| J. Stanworth | *Oldham* | 6 | 10 | 2 | 70 | 50* | 8.75 |
| ‡J. A. Ormrod | *Ramsbottom* | 4 | 7 | 0 | 54 | 23 | 7.71 |
| B. P. Patterson | *Portland, Jamaica* | 15 | 15 | 5 | 38 | 22 | 3.80 |

Also batted: I. C. Davidson (*Worsley*) (1 match) 13, 0; A. N. Hayhurst (*Manchester*) (1 match) 17; S. Henriksen (*Copenhagen, Denmark*) (1 match) 10*, 0*; A. J. Murphy (*Manchester*) (2 matches) 2*, 1, 0.

* *Signifies not out.* ‡ *Denotes county cap.*

The following played a total of eight three-figure innings for Lancashire in County Championship matches – N. H. Fairbrother 3, M. R. Chadwick 1, K. A. Hayes 1, C. H. Lloyd 1, J. Simmons 1, M. Watkinson 1.

### BOWLING

| | *O* | *M* | *R* | *W* | *BB* | *Avge* |
|---|---|---|---|---|---|---|
| P. J. W. Allott | 403.2 | 128 | 927 | 49 | 6-71 | 18.91 |
| S. T. Jefferies | 116.1 | 13 | 379 | 12 | 4-64 | 31.58 |
| B. P. Patterson | 341.5 | 54 | 1,085 | 34 | 6-45 | 31.91 |
| D. J. Makinson | 346 | 62 | 1,029 | 31 | 5-60 | 33.19 |
| S. J. O'Shaughnessy | 142 | 21 | 521 | 15 | 4-68 | 34.73 |
| M. Watkinson | 391.5 | 83 | 1,182 | 34 | 5-109 | 34.76 |
| I. Folley | 436.3 | 100 | 1,271 | 35 | 4-39 | 36.31 |
| J. Simmons | 543.1 | 155 | 1,427 | 37 | 4-55 | 38.56 |

Also bowled: J. Abrahams 25.2–7–93–3; M. R. Chadwick 5–0–20–0; I. C. Davidson 10–3–24–2; N. H. Fairbrother 26–7–75–1; A. N. Hayhurst 13–4–37–3; S. Henriksen 12–1–44–1; D. P. Hughes 21–12–26–1; A. J. Murphy 56.2–15–207–6.

## LANCASHIRE v SUSSEX

At Old Trafford, April 27, 28, 29. Drawn. Lancashire 3 pts, Sussex 4 pts. Toss won by Lancashire. The highlight of a match in which the first two days were affected by rain and the third washed out was a career-best innings of 93 by Jefferies after Lancashire had lost six wickets for 99 runs. Colin Wells had taken four of these and later his brother Alan scored an adventurous fifty after Sussex had slipped to 23 for four.

### Lancashire

| | |
|---|---|
| G. Fowler lbw b C. M. Wells | 10 |
| J. A. Ormrod c Gould b le Roux | 5 |
| S. J. O'Shaughnessy lbw b Greig | 1 |
| N. H. Fairbrother b C. M. Wells | 8 |
| *J. Abrahams b Greig | 67 |
| M. Watkinson b C. M. Wells | 5 |
| J. Simmons c Parker b C. M. Wells | 28 |
| S. T. Jefferies c Gould b Greig | 93 |
| †J. Stanworth c Gould b Greig | 1 |
| I. Folley lbw b Greig | 0 |
| P. J. W. Allott not out | 8 |
| L-b 4, n-b 7 | 11 |
| 1/10 2/17 3/21 4/42 5/60 6/99 7/178 8/197 9/204 | 237 |

Bonus points – Lancashire 2, Sussex 4.

Bowling: Imran 22–7–49–0; le Roux 19–6–28–1; C. M. Wells 32–11–76–4; Greig 25–3–80–5.

### Sussex

| | |
|---|---|
| G. D. Mendis lbw b Allott | 0 |
| A. M. Green lbw b Jefferies | 11 |
| P. W. G. Parker b Allott | 0 |
| Imran Khan not out | 36 |
| C. M. Wells c Fairbrother b Allott | 4 |
| A. P. Wells not out | 55 |
| L-b 6, n-b 1 | 7 |
| 1/0 2/10 3/12 4/23 | (4 wkts) 113 |

*J. R. T. Barclay, I. A. Greig, †I. J. Gould, G. S. le Roux and C. E. Waller did not bat.

Bonus point – Lancashire 1.

Bowling: Allott 13–5–22–3; Jefferies 11–4–36–1; Watkinson 6–3–10–0; O'Shaughnessy 11–1–31–0; Simmons 5–3–8–0.

Umpires: J. Birkenshaw and J. W. Holder.

At Bristol, May 1, 2, 3. LANCASHIRE beat GLOUCESTERSHIRE by 74 runs.

At The Oval, May 8, 9, 10. LANCASHIRE lost to SURREY by 233 runs.

At Chesterfield, May 22, 23, 24. LANCASHIRE drew with DERBYSHIRE.

## LANCASHIRE v YORKSHIRE

At Old Trafford, May 25, 26, 27. Drawn. Lancashire 7 pts, Yorkshire 6 pts. Toss won by Lancashire. For the second successive Whitsuntide, rain denied Lancashire the chance to press home a strong advantage in the Roses match, which ended with Yorkshire 6 runs behind with four second-innings wickets down. Patterson, playing his third Championship match, took three wickets in his first six overs to force Yorkshire to struggle for the rest of their first innings. Lancashire themselves were in trouble at 16 for two at the end of the first day, but the night-watchman, Folley, resisted for 53 overs, and Fairbrother hit his first Roses century, and his highest score, as together they put on 142. Allott took three wickets for 4 runs in his first five overs in the second innings, but only 24 overs were possible on the last day.

## Yorkshire

| | | | |
|---|---|---|---|
| M. D. Moxon b Patterson | 7 | – b Allott | 4 |
| R. J. Blakey b Patterson | 1 | – c Maynard b O'Shaughnessy | 35 |
| K. Sharp c Allott b O'Shaughnessy | 8 | – (4) c Maynard b Allott | 0 |
| J. D. Love lbw b Patterson | 3 | – (5) not out | 16 |
| S. N. Hartley c Simmons b Folley | 52 | | |
| *†D. L. Bairstow b Allott | 27 | – not out | 0 |
| A. Sidebottom b Patterson | 35 | | |
| P. Carrick b Patterson | 7 | | |
| I. G. Swallow c Maynard b Patterson | 1 | | |
| P. W. Jarvis c O'Shaughnessy b Folley | 28 | – (3) c Maynard b Allott | 1 |
| S. D. Fletcher not out | 15 | | |
| B 2, l-b 6, w 4, n-b 9 | 21 | B 1, n-b 1 | 2 |
| 1/3 2/13 3/19 4/26 5/87 6/138 7/154 8/156 9/163 | 205 | 1/10 2/16 3/16 4/58 | (4 wkts) 58 |

Bonus points – Yorkshire 2, Lancashire 4.

Bowling: *First Innings*—Patterson 25–5–77–6; Allott 27–10–49–1; O'Shaughnessy 13–2–38–1; Simmons 9–2–21–0; Folley 11.2–5–12–2. *Second Innings*—Patterson 11–4–21–0; Allott 13–8–18–3; O'Shaughnessy 6–3–13–1; Folley 3–1–5–0.

## Lancashire

| | |
|---|---|
| G. Fowler c Bairstow b Sidebottom | 4 |
| D. W. Varey lbw b Jarvis | 6 |
| I. Folley c and b Carrick | 69 |
| S. J. O'Shaughnessy c Love b Sidebottom | 4 |
| N. H. Fairbrother c Sharp b Fletcher | 128 |
| D. P. Hughes b Carrick | 0 |
| *J. Abrahams c Bairstow b Fletcher | 21 |
| †C. Maynard b Jarvis | 7 |
| J. Simmons lbw b Jarvis | 4 |
| P. J. W. Allott not out | 6 |
| B. P. Patterson c Sharp b Jarvis | 3 |
| B 1, l-b 6, n-b 10 | 17 |
| 1/9 2/13 3/25 4/167 5/167 6/238 7/253 8/258 9/261 | 269 |

Bonus points – Lancashire 3, Yorkshire 4.

Bowling: Sidebottom 10–1–34–2; Jarvis 26.1–5–57–4; Fletcher 17–2–50–2; Carrick 22–5–55–2; Swallow 17–4–50–0; Moxon 2–0–16–0.

Umpires: B. Dudleston and D. R. Shepherd.

At The Parks, June 1, 3, 4. LANCASHIRE beat OXFORD UNIVERSITY by 370 runs.

At Ilford, June 8, 10, 11. LANCASHIRE drew with ESSEX.

At Bath, June 12, 13, 14. LANCASHIRE lost to SOMERSET by an innings and 62 runs.

## LANCASHIRE v DERBYSHIRE

At Old Trafford, June 15, 17, 18. Lancashire won by three wickets. Lancashire 22 pts, Derbyshire 5 pts. Toss won by Derbyshire. Lancashire's first Championship win at Old Trafford since August 1983 was excitingly achieved with one ball to spare after they had been generously set a target of 213 in 37 overs. Off the last over 10 runs were required, and Makinson hit the penultimate ball for 6. Lancashire's hopes of a substantial first-innings lead evaporated when their last seven wickets fell for 41 runs, five of them to Finney who, like Makinson earlier, had career-best figures. Derbyshire persisted with the spinners on the final day and Miller was hit for six 6s as Lancashire forged ahead to their second win of the season.

## Derbyshire

| | First innings | | Second innings | |
|---|---|---|---|---|
| *K. J. Barnett lbw b Makinson | 9 | – c Abrahams b Simmons | 43 |
| I. S. Anderson c Maynard b Patterson | 5 | – b Makinson | 12 |
| J. G. Wright c and b Simmons | 75 | – c Hughes b Folley | 95 |
| B. Roberts b Makinson | 8 | – st Maynard b Folley | 15 |
| J. E. Morris c Abrahams b Makinson | 2 | – c Abrahams b Simmons | 19 |
| W. P. Fowler c Hughes b Simmons | 6 | – b Folley | 7 |
| D. G. Moir c Simmons b Makinson | 14 | – st Maynard b Simmons | 10 |
| G. Miller b Makinson | 45 | – not out | 18 |
| R. J. Finney c Hughes b Simmons | 0 | – c Patterson b Simmons | 3 |
| †B. J. M. Maher not out | 2 | – not out | 5 |
| O. H. Mortensen c sub b Simmons | 3 | | |
| B 4, l-b 12, w 8, n-b 8 | 32 | B 4, l-b 16, w 1, n-b 3 | 24 |
| 1/18 2/21 3/48 4/52 5/66 6/107 7/175 8/179 9/198 | 201 | 1/57 2/91 3/130 4/194 5/207 6/213 7/223 8/233 | (8 wkts dec.) 251 |

Bonus points – Derbyshire 2, Lancashire 4.

Bowling: *First Innings*—Patterson 15–2–32–1; Makinson 29–7–60–5; O'Shaughnessy 7–1–21–0; Simmons 33.2–16–55–4; Folley 5–2–17–0. *Second Innings*—Patterson 7–1–23–0; Makinson 10–2–14–1; O'Shaughnessy 3–0–14–0; Folley 30–12–83–3; Simmons 30–13–89–4; Abrahams 1–0–8–0.

## Lancashire

| | First innings | | Second innings | |
|---|---|---|---|---|
| G. Fowler c Roberts b Miller | 21 | – c and b Miller | 34 |
| D. W. Varey c Moir b Finney | 39 | – c Mortensen b Miller | 14 |
| S. J. O'Shaughnessy c and b Miller | 24 | – run out | 4 |
| N. H. Fairbrother lbw b Finney | 51 | – (5) c and b Miller | 44 |
| D. P. Hughes c Maher b Finney | 68 | – (4) c and b Miller | 20 |
| *J. Abrahams c Wright b Finney | 8 | – c Morris b Miller | 41 |
| †C. Maynard c Anderson b Finney | 0 | – c Fowler b Miller | 16 |
| J. Simmons b Miller | 4 | – not out | 21 |
| I. Folley not out | 8 | | |
| D. J. Makinson lbw b Finney | 5 | – (9) not out | 11 |
| B. P. Patterson c Moir b Finney | 0 | | |
| B 1, l-b 9, w 1, n-b 1 | 12 | L-b 6, w 4 | 10 |
| 1/43 2/81 3/93 4/199 5/210 6/218 7/219 8/223 9/236 | 240 | 1/43 2/53 3/54 4/112 5/121 6/155 7/199 | (7 wkts) 215 |

Bonus points – Lancashire 2, Derbyshire 3 (Score at 100 overs: 232-8).

Bowling: *First Innings*—Mortensen 21–7–32–0; Finney 27.2–4–61–7; Miller 43–11–93–3; Moir 13–1–44–0. *Second Innings*—Mortensen 3.5–0–24–0; Miller 18–3–110–6; Finney 5–0–16–0, Moir 10–0–59–0

Umpires: J. W. Holder and D. O. Oslear.

## LANCASHIRE v KENT

At Old Trafford, June 22, 24, 25. Kent won by 25 runs. Kent 22 pts, Lancashire 4 pts. Toss won by Kent. Benson scored a punishing 102 out of the opening stand of 152 before Simmons took four wickets in an innings for the fourth successive time. Simmons also scored a half-century in each innings but could not stop Kent, who set a target of 260 in 59 overs, pulling off their first Championship win of the season with nine balls to spare.

## Kent

| | | | |
|---|---|---|---|
| M. R. Benson b Simmons | 102 | – c Maynard b Allott | 4 |
| S. G. Hinks c Makinson b Simmons | 44 | – c Maynard b Makinson | 18 |
| C. J. Tavaré c Maynard b Allott | 49 | – lbw b Makinson | 21 |
| D. G. Aslett c Hughes b Simmons | 11 | – (5) st Maynard b Simmons | 38 |
| *C. S. Cowdrey c Abrahams b Folley | 6 | – (6) c Fairbrother b Allott | 39 |
| E. A. E. Baptiste b Simmons | 43 | – (4) not out | 81 |
| R. M. Ellison lbw b Allott | 12 | – not out | 8 |
| †A. P. E. Knott lbw b Allott | 5 | | |
| G. W. Johnson b Patterson | 6 | | |
| D. L. Underwood run out | 6 | | |
| K. B. S. Jarvis not out | 0 | | |
| B 4, l-b 12, n-b 3 | 19 | B 1, l-b 3, w 1, n-b 3 | 8 |
| 1/152 2/159 3/173 4/184 5/235 6/283 7/289 8/292 9/299 | 303 | 1/6 2/40 3/69 4/139 5/189 (5 wkts dec.) | 217 |

Bonus points – Kent 3, Lancashire 2 (Score at 100 overs: 276-5).

Bowling: *First Innings*—Patterson 19–5–33–1; Allott 19.5–5–58–3; Makinson 11–2–44–0; Simmons 39–15–85–4; Folley 25–8–67–1. *Second Innings*—Simmons 7–0–59–1; Makinson 10–2–41–2; Allott 14–3–54–2; Patterson 6–1–16–0; Folley 6–0–43–0.

## Lancashire

| | | | |
|---|---|---|---|
| G. Fowler lbw b Jarvis | 0 | – c Benson b Jarvis | 18 |
| D. W. Varey c Hinks b Underwood | 41 | – b Jarvis | 12 |
| *J. Abrahams c Tavaré b Baptiste | 37 | – b Underwood | 44 |
| N. H. Fairbrother b Johnson | 28 | – c Cowdrey b Jarvis | 45 |
| D. P. Hughes st Knott b Underwood | 27 | – b Johnson | 3 |
| †C. Maynard c Knott b Underwood | 3 | – c Baptiste b Johnson | 18 |
| J. Simmons c Knott b Jarvis | 51 | – not out | 62 |
| I. Folley b Underwood | 2 | – (11) b Johnson | 0 |
| D. J. Makinson not out | 32 | – (8) c Tavaré b Johnson | 6 |
| P. J. W. Allott not out | 8 | – (9) c Cowdrey b Underwood | 20 |
| B. P. Patterson (did not bat) | | – (10) b Johnson | 0 |
| B 3, l-b 16, n-b 13 | 32 | B 1, l-b 2, n-b 3 | 6 |
| 1/0 2/75 3/109 4/146 5/150 6/172 7/179 8/252 (8 wkts dec.) | 261 | 1/26 2/30 3/112 4/123 5/129 6/180 7/199 8/231 9/234 | 234 |

Bonus points – Lancashire 2, Kent 3 (Score at 100 overs: 248-7).

Bowling: *First Innings*—Jarvis 16–3–52–2; Ellison 9–1–26–0; Underwood 35–15–55–4; Baptiste 20–7–42–1; Johnson 24–3–67–1. *Second Innings*—Jarvis 9–2–29–3; Ellison 5–1–17–0; Baptiste 4–1–14–0; Underwood 20–2–93–2; Johnson 19.3–3–78–5.

Umpires: D. J. Constant and M. J. Kitchen.

## LANCASHIRE v WARWICKSHIRE

At Old Trafford, June 26, 27, 28. Drawn. Lancashire 6 pts, Warwickshire 6 pts. Toss won by Warwickshire. Fowler's first Championship half-century of the season, in his sixteenth first-class innings, helped Lancashire, in the first innings, to get within 32 of Warwickshire, for whom Dyer and Humpage shared a partnership of 112. Lancashire were set to score 259 to win in 60 overs, but with Ferreira reducing them to 93 for six with a spell of five for 16, and taking ten wickets in a Championship match for the first time, the home county could do nothing more than hold on for a draw.

### Warwickshire

| First innings | | Second innings | |
|---|---|---|---|
| T. A. Lloyd c Maynard b Makinson | 6 | c Fairbrother b Watkinson | 62 |
| R. I. H. B. Dyer c Abrahams b Makinson | 68 | c Patterson b O'Shaughnessy | 55 |
| K. D. Smith c Abrahams b Patterson | 0 | b O'Shaughnessy | 1 |
| D. L. Amiss lbw b Makinson | 12 | c Patterson b O'Shaughnessy | 0 |
| †G. W. Humpage c O'Shaughnessy b Folley | 75 | c Watkinson b Folley | 31 |
| A. M. Ferreira c O'Shaughnessy b Patterson | 4 | b O'Shaughnessy | 10 |
| Asif Din c Maynard b Makinson | 15 | not out | 43 |
| G. C. Small c Fairbrother b Watkinson | 6 | run out | 0 |
| A. R. K. Pierson c Maynard b Watkinson | 2 | | |
| S. Wall c Maynard b Watkinson | 28 | (9) not out | 1 |
| *N. Gifford not out | 1 | | |
| B 4, l-b 7, w 1, n-b 10 | 22 | B 1, l-b 14, w 2, n-b 6 | 23 |
| 1/7 2/9 3/41 4/153 5/165 6/198 7/205 8/205 9/218 | 239 | 1/135 2/136 3/136 4/147 5/163 6/197 7/199 (7 wkts dec.) | 226 |

Bonus points – Warwickshire 2, Lancashire 4.

Bowling: *First Innings*—Patterson 18–5–60–2; Makinson 25–10–48–4; Watkinson 22.1–6–62–3; O'Shaughnessy 3–0–13–0; Folley 17–3–42–1; Abrahams 2–0–3–0. *Second Innings*—Patterson 10–0–49–0; Makinson 9–1–24–0; Watkinson 15–1–54–1; O'Shaughnessy 13–0–68–4; Folley 4–0–16–1.

### Lancashire

| First innings | | Second innings | |
|---|---|---|---|
| G. Fowler c Dyer b Gifford | 88 | c Amiss b Ferreira | 36 |
| D. W. Varey c Humpage b Ferreira | 16 | st Humpage b Gifford | 14 |
| S. J. O'Shaughnessy b Ferreira | 2 | b Ferreira | 11 |
| N. H. Fairbrother c Humpage b Ferreira | 1 | lbw b Ferreira | 14 |
| D. P. Hughes c Humpage b Small | 8 | not out | 43 |
| *J. Abrahams c Amiss b Small | 36 | c Wall b Ferreira | 0 |
| †C. Maynard b Ferreira | 12 | c Asif Din b Ferreira | 0 |
| M. Watkinson b Small | 4 | b Gifford | 11 |
| I. Folley lbw b Small | 0 | b Gifford | 18 |
| D. J. Makinson not out | 24 | not out | 4 |
| B. P. Patterson c Humpage b Ferreira | 1 | | |
| L-b 6, w 3, n-b 6 | 15 | B 4, l-b 6, n-b 4 | 14 |
| 1/38 2/51 3/59 4/74 5/145 6/176 7/182 8/182 9/197 | 207 | 1/53 2/70 3/74 4/92 5/92 6/93 7/118 8/152 (8 wkts) | 165 |

Bonus points – Lancashire 2, Warwickshire 4.

Bowling: *First Innings*—Small 23–6–71–4; Wall 21–1–44–0; Ferreira 29.4–10–43–5; Pierson 6–2–15–0; Gifford 15–5–28–1. *Second Innings*—Small 12–2–49–0; Wall 7–1–34–0; Ferreira 17–6–41–5; Gifford 19–11–23–3; Pierson 3–1–4–0; Asif Din 2–1–4–0.

Umpires: D. J. Constant and M. J. Kitchen.

At Hastings, June 29, July 1, 2. LANCASHIRE lost to SUSSEX by 73 runs.

## LANCASHIRE v HAMPSHIRE

At Liverpool, July 6, 8, 9. Hampshire won by four wickets. Hampshire 22 pts, Lancashire 5 pts. Toss won by Lancashire. Fairbrother's second century of the season, and the best of his career, was followed by Chris Smith scoring his fifth century of the summer on an easy-paced pitch. Nicholas's declaration, 70 runs in arrears, was rewarded when, in the final 90 minutes of the second day, Lancashire crashed to 63 for five, and were bowled out the following morning, leaving Hampshire to score 186 for their fifth victory. It was not achieved without alarm and needed Greenidge, who sprained his ankle during the Sunday game at Old Trafford, to bat with a runner at the fall of the fifth wicket. Fowler had to be taken by ambulance to hospital on the second morning after collapsing with a neck injury during catching practice before the game. Torn neck muscles were diagnosed.

### Lancashire

| | | | |
|---|---|---|---|
| G. Fowler lbw b Marshall | 0 | – absent injured | |
| D. W. Varey b Tremlett | 33 | – (8) lbw b Marshall | 0 |
| *J. Abrahams b Marshall | 42 | – (1) run out | 7 |
| N. H. Fairbrother not out | 164 | – (3) c Parks b Marshall | 0 |
| C. H. Lloyd c Parks b Andrew | 44 | – (4) b Maru | 24 |
| M. Watkinson c Marshall b C. L. Smith | 35 | – (5) lbw b Marshall | 11 |
| J. Simmons b Andrew | 49 | – (6) c Terry b Marshall | 2 |
| †C. Maynard not out | 7 | – (7) b Maru | 20 |
| D. J. Makinson (did not bat) | | – not out | 12 |
| P. J. W. Allott (did not bat) | | – c R. A. Smith b Maru | 15 |
| I. Folley (did not bat) | | – (2) b Andrew | 6 |
| B 2, l-b 12, n-b 13 | 27 | B 1, l-b 5, w 2, n-b 7 | 15 |
| 1/0 2/57 3/92 4/161 5/256 6/387 (6 wkts dec.) | 401 | 1/10 2/12 3/35 4/58 5/62 6/72 7/72 8/86 9/115 | 115 |

Bonus points – Lancashire 4, Hampshire 2.

Bowling: *First Innings*—Marshall 17–1–48–2; Andrew 15–0–79–2; Tremlett 21–4–77–1; Nicholas 16–4–50–0; Maru 25–2–117–0; Smith 5–1–16–1. *Second Innings*—Marshall 15–4–45–4; Andrew 6–1–15–1; Maru 9.2–2–38–3; Tremlett 3–0–11–0.

### Hampshire

| | | | |
|---|---|---|---|
| C. G. Greenidge retired hurt | 13 | – (7) not out | 22 |
| V. P. Terry c Abrahams b Folley | 54 | – (1) lbw b Allott | 19 |
| C. L. Smith c Folley b Simmons | 121 | – (2) b Makinson | 4 |
| *M. C. J. Nicholas c Makinson b Folley | 61 | – (3) c Abrahams b Folley | 41 |
| R. A. Smith not out | 44 | – (4) b Allott | 9 |
| J. J. E. Hardy c and b Folley | 12 | – (5) b Makinson | 54 |
| M. D. Marshall c and b Folley | 15 | – (6) c and b Folley | 24 |
| †R. J. Parks not out | 3 | | |
| T. M. Tremlett (did not bat) | | – (8) not out | 7 |
| L-b 7, n-b 1 | 8 | B 2, l-b 6, n-b 1 | 9 |
| 1/100 2/253 3/258 4/283 5/307 (5 wkts dec.) | 331 | 1/16 2/32 3/42 4/102 5/145 6/169 (6 wkts) | 189 |

R. J. Maru and S. J. W. Andrew did not bat.

Bonus points – Hampshire 4, Lancashire 1 (Score at 100 overs: 301-4).

Bowling: *First Innings*—Allott 16–3–37–0; Makinson 17–4–52–0; Simmons 34–5–82–1; Watkinson 14–1–57–0; Folley 30–5–96–4. *Second Innings*—Allott 12–2–48–2; Makinson 8–1–27–2; Simmons 9–1–23–0; Folley 20–4–58–2; Watkinson 11–2–25–0.

Umpires: N. T. Plews and R. A. White.

At Edgbaston, July 10, 11, 12. LANCASHIRE lost to WARWICKSHIRE by one wicket.

## LANCASHIRE v GLAMORGAN

At Old Trafford, July 13, 15, 16. Drawn. Lancashire 6 pts, Glamorgan 6 pts. Toss won by Lancashire. Javed Miandad, reaching 1,000 runs for the season during the course of his third century, lost three partners to run-outs, two of them to brilliant fielding by Fairbrother. Davies's 29 included a 6 when the ball hit a fieldsman's helmet. Varey withdrew from the match after the first day because of the death of his father and permission was given for Hayes to come into the match and bat in both innings. Sixteen wickets fell on the final day, when Lancashire were set to score 240 in 45 overs.

## Glamorgan

| | | | |
|---|---|---|---|
| J. A. Hopkins c Simmons b Watkinson | 12 | lbw b Jefferies | 7 |
| A. L. Jones c Watkinson b O'Shaughnessy | 34 | c Hayes b Abrahams | 75 |
| G. C. Holmes lbw b O'Shaughnessy | 30 | lbw b Jefferies | 0 |
| Javed Miandad not out | 164 | lbw b Watkinson | 1 |
| Younis Ahmed run out | 47 | c Maynard b Jefferies | 2 |
| *R. C. Ontong run out | 38 | not out | 65 |
| †T. Davies run out | 29 | | |
| M. R. Price c Abrahams b Folley | 0 | (7) b Abrahams | 6 |
| J. G. Thomas c and b Simmons | 4 | (8) c Watkinson b Abrahams | 5 |
| B 4, l-b 14, w 3, n-b 4 | 25 | B 4, l-b 1, n-b 5 | 10 |
| 1/27 2/77 3/96 4/211 5/299 6/373 7/378 8/383 (8 wkts dec.) | 383 | 1/28 2/28 3/29 4/32 5/135 6/157 7/171 (7 wkts dec.) | 171 |

L. L. McFarlane and S. R. Barwick did not bat.

Bonus points – Glamorgan 4, Lancashire 2 (Score at 100 overs: 310-5).

Bowling: *First Innings*—Makinson 25–3–75–0; Jefferies 25–2–79–0; Watkinson 22–5–55–1; O'Shaughnessy 10–1–38–2; Simmons 18.1–4–49–1; Folley 22–2–69–1. *Second Innings*—Jefferies 12–1–30–3; Watkinson 8–1–21–1; Simmons 8–4–9–0; Makinson 3–0–16–0; O'Shaughnessy 3–1–13–0; Folley 2–1–8–0; Fairbrother 2–1–3–0; Abrahams 6.2–0–46–3; Chadwick 5–0–20–0.

## Lancashire

| | | | |
|---|---|---|---|
| K. A. Hayes c Davies b Thomas | 5 | c Miandad b Barwick | 39 |
| M. R. Chadwick c Davies b Thomas | 9 | b Ontong | 22 |
| S. J. O'Shaughnessy c Hopkins b Ontong | 34 | b Thomas | 63 |
| N. H. Fairbrother b McFarlane | 57 | b Barwick | 11 |
| *J. Abrahams not out | 77 | (7) c Thomas b Ontong | 29 |
| M. Watkinson c Hopkins b Thomas | 65 | (5) c Thomas b Ontong | 9 |
| S. T. Jefferies c Holmes b Ontong | 57 | (6) c McFarlane b Ontong | 6 |
| J. Simmons (did not bat) | | st Davies b Ontong | 11 |
| †C. Maynard (did not bat) | | not out | 12 |
| D. J. Makinson (did not bat) | | not out | 0 |
| B 5, l-b 1, w 2, n-b 3 | 11 | B 8, l-b 4, n-b 1 | 13 |
| 1/14 2/17 3/85 4/106 5/192 6/315 (6 wkts dec.) | 315 | 1/38 2/70 3/88 4/107 5/117 6/186 7/186 8/215 (8 wkts) | 215 |

I. Folley did not bat.

Bonus points – Lancashire 4, Glamorgan 2.

Bowling: *First Innings*—Thomas 16–3–39–3; Barwick 18–2–61–0; McFarlane 11–1–61–1; Ontong 36.5–9–116–2; Price 12–3–32–0. *Second Innings*—Thomas 13.5–1–58–1; Barwick 13–3–63–2; Ontong 18–1–82–5.

Umpires: B. Leadbeater and R. Palmer.

## LANCASHIRE v SURREY

At Southport, July 24, 25, 26. Drawn. Lancashire 7 pts, Surrey 6 pts. Toss won by Lancashire. Three early wickets from Doughty made Lancashire struggle, but Watkinson hit a maiden century in a 200-minute innings in which he shared a ninth-wicket stand of 76 with Folley. Allott bowled 26 overs in unbroken sunshine to prove his fitness for the fourth Test but was upstaged on the second day by Gray, who took three wickets in an over, including that of Fairbrother, out first ball in each innings. Gray's effort was in vain, however, for only 45 minutes of play were possible on the final day.

## Lancashire

| | | | |
|---|---|---|---|
| M. R. Chadwick c Richards b Gray | 32 | – lbw b Doughty | 14 |
| D. W. Varey c Richards b Doughty | 1 | – not out | 47 |
| S. J. O'Shaughnessy b Doughty | 1 | – c Lynch b Gray | 1 |
| N. H. Fairbrother c Lynch b Doughty | 0 | – b Gray | 0 |
| *J. Abrahams c Lynch b Monkhouse | 51 | – c Monkhouse b Gray | 1 |
| M. Watkinson c Lynch b Doughty | 106 | – c Lynch b Gray | 32 |
| J. Simmons c Butcher b Pocock | 4 | – b Doughty | 39 |
| †C. Maynard c Gray b Monkhouse | 3 | – c Richards b Gray | 0 |
| D. J. Makinson c Stewart b Gray | 12 | – not out | 2 |
| I. Folley b Needham | 28 | | |
| P. J. W. Allott not out | 15 | | |
| B 4, l-b 16, w 1, n-b 4 | 25 | L-b 4, n-b 5 | 9 |
| 1/11 2/18 3/18 4/67 5/131 6/152 7/159 8/186 9/262 | 278 | 1/30 2/31 3/31 4/33 5/97 6/140 7/142 | (7 wkts) 145 |

Bonus points – Lancashire 3, Surrey 4.

Bowling: *First Innings*—Gray 22–4–64–2; Doughty 17–4–56–4; Monkhouse 22–3–61–2; Pocock 21–6–53–1; Needham 11.2–1–24–1. *Second Innings*—Gray 14–2–51–5; Doughty 13–1–49–2; Needham 13–6–13–0; Monkhouse 6–3–12–0; Pocock 4–1–15–0; Butcher 1–0–1–0.

## Surrey

| | |
|---|---|
| A. R. Butcher c Maynard b Allott | 17 |
| G. S. Clinton c Simmons b Allott | 21 |
| P. I. Pocock b Makinson | 6 |
| A. J. Stewart c Varey b Allott | 61 |
| *T. E. Jesty c Maynard b Allott | 2 |
| M. A. Lynch b O'Shaughnessy | 31 |
| A. Needham b Folley | 31 |
| †C. J. Richards c Allott b Watkinson | 37 |
| R. J. Doughty c Maynard b Watkinson | 22 |
| G. Monkhouse c Chadwick b Simmons | 1 |
| A. H. Gray not out | 0 |
| L-b 1, w 1 | 2 |
| 1/30 2/43 3/47 4/55 5/98 6/159 7/179 8/224 9/231 | 231 |

Bonus points – Surrey 2, Lancashire 4.

Bowling: Allott 26–7–62–4; Makinson 16–1–61–1; Simmons 7.1–4–11–1; Watkinson 10–2–21–2; O'Shaughnessy 5–1–28–1; Folley 17–2–47–1.

Umpires: H. D. Bird and J. Birkenshaw.

At Uxbridge, July 27, 29, 30. LANCASHIRE drew with MIDDLESEX.

At Leicester, July 31, August 1, 2. LANCASHIRE drew with LEICESTERSHIRE.

At Worcester, August 3, 5, 6. LANCASHIRE lost to WORCESTERSHIRE by seven wickets.

At Headingley, August 10, 12, 13. LANCASHIRE drew with YORKSHIRE.

## LANCASHIRE v NORTHAMPTONSHIRE

At Lytham, August 14, 15, 16. Drawn. Lancashire 2 pts, Northamptonshire 4 pts. Toss won by Northamptonshire. The first Championship match at Lytham, which replaced Blackpool in the fixture list, was so affected by rain that only 72.1 overs were possible. Sixty of those were bowled on the final day when Capel and Makinson, who hit seven 6s off Williams, had career-best performances.

### Lancashire

| | | | |
|---|---|---|---|
| M. R. Chadwick lbw b Mallender | 8 | I. Folley lbw b Capel | 0 |
| D. W. Varey b Capel | 36 | D. J. Makinson not out | 58 |
| K. A. Hayes c Cook b Griffiths | 22 | B. P. Patterson b Capel | 22 |
| N. H. Fairbrother c Griffiths b Capel | 19 | | |
| *J. Abrahams c Ripley b Capel | 4 | B 7, l-b 6, n-b 1 | 14 |
| M. Watkinson lbw b Capel | 12 | | |
| J. Simmons b Capel | 20 | 1/8 2/60 3/87 4/95 5/111 | 225 |
| †J. Stanworth c Capel b Williams | 10 | 6/116 7/133 8/133 9/153 | |

Bonus points – Lancashire 2, Northamptonshire 4.

Bowling: Mallender 16–4–28–1; Griffiths 20–8–35–1; Capel 20–5–62–7; Harper 3–2–1–0; Williams 12–2–80–1; Cook 1–0–6–0.

### Northamptonshire

| | |
|---|---|
| B. J. Griffiths not out | 2 |
| †D. Ripley not out | 0 |
| (no wkt) | 2 |

*G. Cook, W. Larkins, R. J. Boyd-Moss, R. G. Williams, R. J. Bailey, D. J. Wild, D. J. Capel, R. A. Harper and N. A. Mallender did not bat.

Bowling: Watkinson 0.1–0–2–0.

Umpires: J. H. Hampshire and R. A. White.

## LANCASHIRE v NOTTINGHAMSHIRE

At Old Trafford, August 17, 19, 20. Drawn. Lancashire 5 pts, Nottinghamshire 6 pts. Toss won by Nottinghamshire. Varey, formerly of Cambridge University, and Hayes, formerly of Oxford, both had Championship-best scores on the opening day. Martindale, aged 21, playing in only his fourth Championship match, scored his maiden century and shared in a partnership of 143 with Broad before Nottinghamshire declared 81 behind. Rain washed out the final day.

### Lancashire

| | | | |
|---|---|---|---|
| M. R. Chadwick b Pick | 14 | – not out | 2 |
| D. W. Varey st French b Hemmings | 87 | – b Pick | 3 |
| K. A. Hayes lbw b Hemmings | 71 | | |
| N. H. Fairbrother b Cooper | 66 | | |
| *J. Abrahams c Rice b Hemmings | 34 | | |
| M. Watkinson lbw b Cooper | 0 | | |
| J. Simmons b Cooper | 4 | | |
| D. J. Makinson run out | 32 | | |
| †J. Stanworth c and b Pick | 2 | – (3) not out | 0 |
| I. Folley not out | 8 | | |
| B. P. Patterson b Pick | 1 | | |
| B 1, l-b 10, n-b 4 | 15 | | |
| 1/17 2/172 3/185 4/279 5/279 6/283 7/289 8/308 9/326 | 334 | 1/5 (1 wkt) | 5 |

Bonus points – Lancashire 3, Nottinghamshire 3 (Score at 100 overs: 289-7).

Bowling: *First Innings*—Saxelby 12–3–40–0; Pick 25.4–8–64–3; Cooper 20–7–50–3; Rice 17–3–60–0; Evans 9–1–38–0; Hemmings 27–9–71–3. *Second Innings*—Pick 6–2–5–1; Rice 5–5–0–0.

### Nottinghamshire

| | | | |
|---|---|---|---|
| D. W. Randall b Patterson | 2 | †B. N. French not out | 19 |
| B. C. Broad b Patterson | 84 | | |
| *C. E. B. Rice b Patterson | 5 | B 4, l-b 8, n-b 9 | 21 |
| P. Johnson b Watkinson | 18 | | |
| D. J. R. Martindale not out | 104 | 1/16 2/27 3/51 | (5 wkts dec.) 253 |
| K. P. Evans lbw b Simmons | 0 | 4/194 5/207 | |

E. E. Hemmings, K. Saxelby, R. A. Pick and K. E. Cooper did not bat.

Bonus points – Nottinghamshire 3, Lancashire 2.

Bowling: Patterson 21–5–43–3; Makinson 6.3–1–16–0; Simmons 26.3–5–76–1; Watkinson 20–5–50–1; Folley 18.2–4–56–0.

Umpires: J. Birkenshaw and A. A. Jones.

## LANCASHIRE v SOMERSET

At Old Trafford, August 24, 26, 27. Lancashire won by six wickets. Lancashire 17 pts, Somerset 4 pts. Toss won by Somerset. Lancashire's third win came after the opening day was lost to rain and both teams had forfeited an innings. For Somerset, Richards hit his sixth century of the season with eleven 4s and five 6s, sharing in a stand of 206 in 46 overs with Roebuck, while Botham batted for just 47 balls, striking seven 4s and four 6s. Lancashire were left with the final day – a minimum of 105 overs – in which to secure victory, which was achieved mainly through a partnership of 176 between Hayes and Chadwick, both uncapped and aged 22. Each scored his maiden Championship century.

### Somerset

| | | | |
|---|---|---|---|
| P. M. Roebuck lbw b Patterson | 88 | R. J. Harden not out | 19 |
| J. G. Wyatt lbw b Allott | 5 | *I. T. Botham not out | 76 |
| R. L. Ollis c Simmons b Watkinson | 4 | B 2, l-b 6, w 1, n-b 8 | 17 |
| I. V. A. Richards c Fairbrother b Simmons | 120 | 1/8 2/23 3/229 4/230 | (4 wkts dec.) 329 |

J. C. M. Atkinson, V. J. Marks, †T. Gard, J. Garner and C. H. Dredge did not bat.

Bonus points – Somerset 4, Lancashire 1.

Bowling: Patterson 15–3–61–1; Allott 16–4–58–1; Watkinson 21–3–52–1; Simmons 18–3–95–1; Fairbrother 11–0–55–0.

*Somerset forfeited their second innings.*

### Lancashire

*Lancashire forfeited their first innings.*

| | | | |
|---|---|---|---|
| M. R. Chadwick c Dredge b Marks | 132 | *J. Abrahams not out | 2 |
| D. W. Varey b Atkinson | 22 | | |
| K. A. Hayes c Roebuck b Garner | 117 | B 1, l-b 3, w 1, n-b 6 | 11 |
| N. H. Fairbrother not out | 31 | | |
| G. Fowler c Harden b Marks | 15 | 1/73 2/249 3/302 4/324 | (4 wkts) 330 |

M. Watkinson, †C. Maynard, J. Simmons, P. J. W. Allott and B. P. Patterson did not bat.

Bowling: Garner 15–4–24–1; Dredge 18–2–79–0; Botham 5–1–14–0; Marks 43–10–125–2; Atkinson 15.5–2–54–1; Richards 8–0–30–0.

Umpires: J. W. Holder and P. B. Wight.

At Trent Bridge, August 31, September 2, 3. LANCASHIRE drew with NOTTINGHAMSHIRE.

## LANCASHIRE v LEICESTERSHIRE

At Old Trafford, September 14, 16, 17. Drawn. Lancashire 3 pts, Leicestershire 3 pts. Toss won by Leicestershire. A first-wicket stand of 108 and a last-wicket stand of 73 enabled Leicestershire to set the pace on the opening day. The second day was lost to rain, and after another double forfeiture of innings, Lancashire were left to score 337 to win in a minimum of 92 overs. Fairbrother and Abrahams put on 130 but it was Leicestershire who almost forced victory before Maynard and Folley, the last pair, held out at the end.

### Leicestershire

| | |
|---|---|
| J. C. Balderstone c Chadwick b Folley | 45 |
| I. P. Butcher b Folley | 78 |
| R. A. Cobb lbw b Simmons | 35 |
| J. J. Whitaker st Maynard b Folley | 18 |
| *D. I. Gower c and b Folley | 18 |
| P. Willey b Hayhurst | 38 |
| †M. A. Garnham b Allott | 24 |
| G. J. Parsons c Maynard b Hayhurst | 0 |
| P. A. J. De Freitas c Simmons b Hayhurst | 1 |
| P. B. Clift st Maynard b Simmons | 50 |
| G. J. F. Ferris not out | 22 |
| L-b 7 | 7 |
| 1/108 2/131 3/163 4/189 5/203 6/245 7/245 8/247 9/263 | 336 |

Bonus points – Leicestershire 3, Lancashire 3 (Score at 100 overs: 262-8).

Bowling: Allott 21–4–65–1; Watkinson 17–4–52–0; Hayhurst 13–4–37–3; Folley 41–10–120–4; Simmons 27–12–55–2.

*Leicestershire forfeited their second innings.*

### Lancashire

*Lancashire forfeited their first innings.*

| | |
|---|---|
| D. W. Varey b Clift | 31 |
| M. R. Chadwick b Parsons | 11 |
| A. N. Hayhurst lbw b De Freitas | 17 |
| N. H. Fairbrother c Garnham b Parsons | 91 |
| C. H. Lloyd c Balderstone b Clift | 9 |
| *J. Abrahams b Parsons | 65 |
| M. Watkinson c Garnham b Ferris | 16 |
| J. Simmons c Butcher b De Freitas | 0 |
| †C. Maynard not out | 21 |
| P. J. W. Allott b Ferris | 2 |
| I. Folley not out | 1 |
| B 6, l-b 8, w 12, n-b 3 | 29 |
| 1/11 2/61 3/76 4/113 5/243 6/250 7/255 8/279 9/287 | (9 wkts) 293 |

Bowling: Ferris 15–4–24–2; Parsons 15–3–31–3; Willey 31–8–69–0; De Freitas 27–2–80–2; Clift 30–11–66–2; Balderstone 1–0–9–0.

Umpires: A. A. Jones and K. E. Palmer.

# LEICESTERSHIRE

*President:* W. Bentley
*Chairman:* C. H. Palmer
*Chairman, Cricket Committee:* J. J. Palmer
*Secretary/Cricket Manager:* F. M. Turner
County Cricket Ground, Grace Road,
Leicester LE2 8AD
(Telephone: 0533-831880/832128)
*Captain:* D. I. Gower
*Coach:* K. Higgs

Leicestershire's pleasure at winning the Benson and Hedges Cup, their first major trophy since the John Player League title in 1977, was tempered by their lowest Championship placing since 1964 and a spate of late-season departures from discontented players.

They were, in fairness, one of the hardest-hit of all the counties by the weather, creating a John Player Sunday League record of five "no result" wash-outs, and losing no fewer than 116 playing hours in first-class matches, most of them at home. In the Britannic Assurance Championship alone, the time lost added up to one quarter of their total fixtures. The absence of key players for lengthy periods also had a significant effect. Les Taylor and Jonathan Agnew did not appear together until June because of injury, and Test calls further restricted their Championship appearances. Taylor missed three games, Agnew four, with the captain, David Gower, absent in twelve and the vice-captain, Peter Willey, in four.

However, the county's inability to win more than two games was more broadly based on a disturbing lack of penetration in attack, a problem not solely confined to the low, slow pitches at Grace Road. Much had been expected of the young Antiguan, George Ferris, fit again after missing almost the whole of 1984 with a knee injury; but he struggled all season, capturing only fifteen wickets, and in September the club announced the signing of another Antiguan pace bowler, 21-year old Winston Benjamin.

Gordon Parsons also disappointed. After taking 67 first-class wickets and scoring 853 runs the previous summer, he now finished with only 23 wickets and 170 runs. He was no longer an automatic choice by mid-July and successfully applied to be released from his contract late in the season. Leicestershire, however, looked to have unearthed a very useful replacement in the nineteen-year-old Phillip De Freitas, Dominican-born but English-qualified, who was signed from the Lord's groundstaff. He impressed many observers with his high, whippy action and ability to extract bounce and movement from the pitch.

Nick Cook, the England left-arm spinner, had another disappointing season, taking only 30 first-class wickets at an average of well over 40. He, too, applied successfully to be released from his contract, announcing that he was disillusioned with life at Grace Road and felt "unwanted". This the club denied, pointing out that he had bowled more overs in the season than anyone except Paddy Clift. Cook's claim that he was normally asked to operate on pitches prepared primarily for a seam attack had some merit. In addition, he had never been more than an occasional choice for one-day matches. At 29, he felt he would be better moving from his native county to one that could offer him better prospects of regular cricket, and when the club acceded "with reluctance", he joined Northamptonshire.

The third senior player to leave was the first-team wicket-keeper, Mike Garnham, who had still to win his county cap and felt disillusioned with Leicestershire and the game in general. Despite an invaluable contribution in the Benson and Hedges final, his form was not good for much of the summer, which undoubtedly had to do with a conscious decision made before the season began, and implemented in September, to retire from the game and pursue a career in business. He did, however, make himself available for 1986 "in emergencies". While there was no obvious replacement for Cook, Leicestershire appeared to have a natural replacement for Garnham in Phil Whitticase, who also showed encouraging signs of becoming a more than useful batsman.

The final chapter in Leicestershire's end-of-season disturbances, which may well have had a bearing on their form from late August being so abysmal, involved the veteran opener, Chris Balderstone. At the age of 44, he was the first Leicestershire player to 1,000 runs and had a decisive influence on their Benson and Hedges success with two Gold Awards and a vital half-century in the quarter-final at Southampton. Despite this, the committee voted not to offer him another contract, without, to the amazement of all concerned, consulting their captain. Once Gower learned of the decision, he, Willey and the club's secretary/manager made successful representations on Balderstone's behalf.

The other batting successes were Ian Butcher, though he suffered a late slump in form, James Whitaker, who overcame an early-season "drought", Gower, despite his limited appearances, Russell Cobb, when he came in for Gower, and, above all, Willey.

Willey topped the averages, and played a succession of crucial innings in the Benson and Hedges Cup. He also bowled with great economy in the one-day games, besides taking 35 first-class wickets. For the second year running, he won the Leicestershire Player of the Year award.

Leicestershire were still in contention for the John Player League title until they lost their last three matches, their 87 for nine in the final game at Chesterfield being their lowest total in an unreduced contest since 1973. There was further disappointment, too, in the NatWest Bank Trophy when Hampshire gained revenge for their earlier Benson and Hedges defeat by winning a second-round clash on the same ground at Southampton. This preserved Leicestershire's record of only once having advanced as far as the semi-final stage of the premier knockout competition – M.J.

LEICESTERSHIRE 1985

[*Bill Smith*

*Back row:* M. A. Garnham, I. P. Butcher, J. J. Whitaker, J. P. Agnew, N. E. Briers, N. G. B. Cook, R. A. Cobb. *Front row:* J. C. Balderstone, L. B. Taylor, D. I. Gower (*captain*), P. Willey, P. B. Clift. *Insets:* G. J. Parsons, P. A. J. De Freitas, P. Whitticase.

## LEICESTERSHIRE RESULTS

*All first-class matches – Played 26: Won 3, Lost 3, Drawn 20.*

*County Championship matches – Played 24: Won 2, Lost 3, Drawn 19.*

*Bonus points – Batting 48, Bowling 65.*

*Competition placings – Britannic Assurance County Championship, 16th; NatWest Bank Trophy, 2nd round; Benson and Hedges Cup, winners; John Player League, 6th eq.*

## BRITANNIC ASSURANCE CHAMPIONSHIP AVERAGES

### BATTING

| | *Birthplace* | *M* | *I* | *NO* | *R* | *HI* | *Avge* |
|---|---|---|---|---|---|---|---|
| ‡P. Willey | *Sedgefield* | 19 | 28 | 3 | 1,194 | 147 | 47.76 |
| ‡D. I. Gower | *Tunbridge Wells* | 12 | 17 | 2 | 575 | 128 | 38.33 |
| J. J. Whitaker | *Skipton* | 23 | 32 | 3 | 1,085 | 109 | 37.41 |
| P. Whitticase | *Solihull* | 3 | 5 | 1 | 149 | 55* | 37.25 |
| ‡J. C. Balderstone | *Huddersfield* | 23 | 37 | 4 | 1,130 | 101 | 34.24 |
| R. A. Cobb | *Leicester* | 16 | 23 | 4 | 601 | 78 | 31.63 |
| ‡I. P. Butcher | *Farnborough, Kent* | 23 | 36 | 2 | 1,043 | 120 | 30.67 |
| ‡N. E. Briers | *Leicester* | 21 | 27 | 4 | 561 | 129 | 24.39 |
| ‡P. B. Clift | *Salisbury, S. Rhodesia* | 21 | 25 | 5 | 472 | 106 | 23.60 |
| M. Blackett | *Edmonton* | 2 | 4 | 2 | 41 | 28* | 20.50 |
| M. A. Garnham | *Johannesburg, SA* | 21 | 24 | 3 | 415 | 51 | 19.76 |
| P. A. J. De Freitas | *Scotts Head, Dominica* | 8 | 11 | 3 | 117 | 30* | 14.62 |
| ‡G. J. Parsons | *Slough* | 14 | 14 | 4 | 139 | 32 | 13.90 |
| ‡N. G. B. Cook | *Leicester* | 17 | 15 | 4 | 151 | 45 | 13.72 |
| G. J. F. Ferris | *Urlings Village, Antigua* | 10 | 9 | 6 | 29 | 22* | 9.66 |
| ‡L. B. Taylor | *Earl Shilton* | 16 | 15 | 7 | 77 | 20* | 9.62 |
| ‡J. P. Agnew | *Macclesfield* | 14 | 13 | 2 | 100 | 36 | 9.09 |

Also batted: D. J. Billington (*Leyland*) (1 match) 19.

* *Signifies not out.* ‡ *Denotes county cap.*

The following played a total of twelve three-figure innings for Leicestershire in County Championship matches – J. J. Whitaker 3, P. Willey 3, D. I. Gower 2, J. C. Balderstone 1, N. E. Briers 1, I. P. Butcher 1, P. B. Clift 1.

### BOWLING

| | *O* | *M* | *R* | *W* | *BB* | *Avge* |
|---|---|---|---|---|---|---|
| L. B. Taylor | 472.2 | 120 | 1,102 | 52 | 5-45 | 21.19 |
| J. P. Agnew | 396.4 | 85 | 1,269 | 52 | 9-70 | 24.40 |
| P. Willey | 343.5 | 102 | 834 | 31 | 6-43 | 26.90 |
| P. A. J. De Freitas | 208.4 | 34 | 619 | 21 | 5-39 | 29.47 |
| P. B. Clift | 577.3 | 165 | 1,407 | 45 | 5-38 | 31.26 |
| N. G. B. Cook | 529.1 | 177 | 1,245 | 29 | 4-59 | 42.93 |
| G. J. F. Ferris | 231.3 | 32 | 826 | 15 | 3-84 | 55.06 |
| G. J. Parsons | 306.2 | 61 | 869 | 14 | 3-31 | 62.07 |

Also bowled: J. C. Balderstone 15–3–68–1; N. E. Briers 88–18–303–8; I. P. Butcher 2–1–5–0; D. I. Gower 2.1–0–16–0.

## LEICESTERSHIRE v YORKSHIRE

At Leicester, April 27, 28, 29. Drawn. Leicestershire 3 pts, Yorkshire 8 pts. Toss won by Yorkshire, who had by far the better of a draw which was almost inevitable with more than half the match lost to a combination of rain, bad light and, on the opening day, a snowstorm. Yorkshire's four-pronged pace attack reaped the rewards for accurate bowling on a pitch of occasional low bounce and offering movement off the seam, but the Leicestershire bowlers could not match them.

### Leicestershire

| | | | |
|---|---|---|---|
| I. P. Butcher c Moxon b Stevenson | 33 | – not out | 23 |
| J. C. Balderstone b Jarvis | 37 | – not out | 13 |
| *D. I. Gower c Bairstow b Dennis | 28 | | |
| P. Willey lbw b Stevenson | 19 | | |
| N. E. Briers c Sharp b Stevenson | 4 | | |
| †M. A. Garnham c and b Dennis | 8 | | |
| G. J. Parsons lbw b Sidebottom | 8 | | |
| P. B. Clift not out | 7 | | |
| N. G. B. Cook c Carrick b Sidebottom | 0 | | |
| G. J. F. Ferris c Bairstow b Jarvis | 4 | | |
| L. B. Taylor b Jarvis | 5 | | |
| L-b 6, w 1, n-b 10 | 17 | B 4, l-b 2, w 1, n-b 3 | 10 |
| 1/73 2/73 3/120 4/129 5/141 6/144 7/159 8/159 9/164 | 170 | (no wkt) | 46 |

Bonus points – Leicestershire 1, Yorkshire 4.

Bowling: *First Innings*—Sidebottom 16–3–52–2; Dennis 16–2–37–2; Jarvis 13–4–36–3; Stevenson 13–2–39–3. *Second Innings*—Sidebottom 4.4–3–5–0; Dennis 4.2–0–13–0; Jarvis 4–1–9–0; Stevenson 3–0–13–0.

### Yorkshire

| | |
|---|---|
| G. Boycott c Garnham b Ferris | 4 |
| M. D. Moxon c Willey b Ferris | 60 |
| K. Sharp b Parsons | 96 |
| J. D. Love c and b Clift | 44 |
| P. E. Robinson c Willey b Clift | 42 |
| *†D. L. Bairstow not out | 24 |
| A. Sidebottom not out | 15 |
| B 4, l-b 4, w 2, n-b 11 | 21 |
| 1/13 2/96 3/202 4/258 5/289 (5 wkts dec.) | 306 |

P. Carrick, G. B. Stevenson, P. W. Jarvis and S. J. Dennis did not bat.

Bonus points – Yorkshire 4, Leicestershire 2.

Bowling: Ferris 28–6–95–2; Taylor 14–3–45–0; Parsons 21–4–60–1; Clift 18–3–52–2; Cook 12–3–27–0; Briers 4–0–19–0.

Umpires: H. D. Bird and J. A. Jameson.

At The Parks, May 1, 2. LEICESTERSHIRE beat OXFORD UNIVERSITY by an innings and 75 runs.

## LEICESTERSHIRE v DERBYSHIRE

At Leicester, May, 8, 9, 10. Drawn. Leicestershire 8 pts, Derbyshire 6 pts. Toss won by Leicestershire. On a green pitch, Derbyshire subsided from 152 for two to 226 all out, Briers returning a career-best four for 29. Willey, eligible for England once more after the three-year ban, scored his seventh century for Leicestershire since arriving from Northamptonshire in 1984, his second fifty coming in only 36 minutes with ten 4s after the first had taken 204 minutes. Bad weather on the second day ruined the match as a contest, and with a draw the only possible result Barnett completed a routine century, sharing a third-wicket partnership of 191 in 204 minutes with Roberts, who narrowly missed a maiden Championship hundred.

## Derbyshire

| | | |
|---|---|---|
| *K. J. Barnett c Garnham b Clift | 49 – not out | 134 |
| A. Hill lbw b Clift | 89 – run out | 33 |
| J. E. Morris c Butcher b Clift | 20 – b Clift | 0 |
| B. Roberts c Cook b Briers | 14 – b Briers | 96 |
| W. P. Fowler c Garnham b Briers | 6 | |
| G. Miller lbw b Briers | 0 | |
| R. J. Finney b Parsons | 0 | |
| †B. J. M. Maher b Ferris | 8 | |
| A. E. Warner not out | 8 | |
| P. G. Newman c Clift b Briers | 10 | |
| D. E. Malcolm b Ferris | 0 | |
| B 9, l-b 4, n-b 9 | 22 | B 4, l-b 6, n-b 6 16 |
| 1/82 2/109 3/152 4/170 5/172 6/173 7/199 8/206 9/226 | 226 | 1/88 2/88 3/279 (3 wkts dec.) 279 |

Bonus points – Derbyshire 2, Leicestershire 4.

Bowling: *First Innings*—Ferris 20.1–5–59–2; Parsons 24–5–72–1; Clift 26–9–53–3; Briers 12–1–29–4. *Second Innings*—Ferris 20–4–52–0; Clift 33–12–69–1; Cook 29–12–50–0; Briers 16.5–3–56–1; Willey 21–9–33–0; Balderstone 1–0–9–0.

## Leicestershire

| | |
|---|---|
| I. P. Butcher c Roberts b Malcolm | 6 |
| J. C. Balderstone b Newman | 14 |
| *D. I. Gower lbw b Malcolm | 57 |
| P. Willey c Maher b Newman | 133 |
| J. J. Whitaker b Newman | 8 |
| N. E. Briers c Maher b Warner | 2 |
| P. B. Clift b Warner | 8 |
| †M. A. Garnham c Roberts b Malcolm | 4 |
| G. J. Parsons b Newman | 32 |
| N. G. B. Cook c Hill b Warner | 5 |
| G. J. F. Ferris not out | 2 |
| B 1, l-b 6, w 1, n-b 22 | 30 |
| 1/9 2/51 3/122 4/132 5/136 6/151 7/175 8/273 9/291 | 301 |

Bonus points – Leicestershire 4, Derbyshire 4.

Bowling: Newman 29.3–7–92–4; Malcolm 17–2–82–3; Warner 25–3–79–3; Finney 8–5–13–0; Roberts 4–0–20–0; Miller 4–2–8–0.

Umpires: C. Cook and A. G. T. Whitehead.

# LEICESTERSHIRE v NOTTINGHAMSHIRE

At Leicester, May 22, 23, 24. Drawn. Leicestershire 2 pts, Nottinghamshire 4 pts. Toss won by Leicestershire. Rain washed out all but 38 overs of the opening day, and all but eighteen on the third. When play was possible, the batsmen prospered on a lifeless pitch, Randall especially batting enterprisingly for Nottinghamshire after Robinson and Broad had established the innings in a three-hour partnership.

## Nottinghamshire

| | | |
|---|---|---|
| R. T. Robinson c Garnham b Briers | 94 – not out | 25 |
| B. C. Broad c Butcher b Parsons | 70 – c Cobb b Briers | 8 |
| D. W. Randall not out | 89 – not out | 10 |
| P. Johnson lbw b Cook | 1 | |
| *C. E. B. Rice not out | 34 | |
| B 6, l-b 5, w 1, n-b 1 | 13 | L-b 3 3 |
| 1/152 2/210 3/217 | (3 wkts dec.) 301 | 1/28 (1 wkt) 46 |

J. D. Birch, R. J. Hadlee, †C. W. Scott, E. E. Hemmings, K. Saxelby and K. E. Cooper did not bat.

Bonus points – Nottinghamshire 4, Leicestershire 1.

Bowling: *First Innings*—Ferris 24–1–108–0; Parsons 26–5–76–1; Clift 17–8–25–0; Cook 13–5–33–1; Briers 11–2–48–1. *Second Innings*—Ferris 5–1–17–0; Clift 7.1–1–14–0; Briers 6–2–12–1.

## Leicestershire

| | |
|---|---|
| I. P. Butcher c Hadlee b Hemmings | 52 |
| J. C. Balderstone not out | 72 |
| *D. I. Gower not out | 30 |
| B 5, l-b 6 | 11 |
| 1/107 (1 wkt dec.) | 165 |

J. J. Whitaker, N. E. Briers, R. A. Cobb, P. B. Clift, †M. A. Garnham, G. J. Parsons, N. G. B. Cook and G. J. F. Ferris did not bat.

Bonus points – Leicestershire 1.

Bowling: Hadlee 5–1–9–0; Saxelby 15–3–45–0; Cooper 13–4–36–0; Hemmings 20–5–64–1.

Umpires: B. Leadbeater and K. J. Lyons.

# LEICESTERSHIRE v NORTHAMPTONSHIRE

At Leicester, May 25, 27, 28. Drawn. Leicestershire 3 pts, Northamptonshire 1 pt. Toss won by Leicestershire. Balderstone, Gower and Whitaker all completed half-centuries, but Leicestershire's failure to achieve maximum batting points had much to do with the high-class off-spin bowling of Harper, who on his first appearance for Northamptonshire took four of the five wickets to fall. Rain washed out play on the final two days.

## Leicestershire

| | |
|---|---|
| I. P. Butcher c and b Harper | 13 |
| J. C. Balderstone c Sharp b Harper | 83 |
| *D. I. Gower c Larkins b Harper | 52 |
| P. Willey c Sharp b Mallender | 6 |
| J. J. Whitaker c and b Harper | 79 |
| N. E. Briers not out | 47 |
| P. B. Clift not out | 1 |
| B 9, l-b 5, w 1, n-b 8 | 23 |
| 1/34 2/158 3/165 4/172 5/300 (5 wkts) | 304 |

†M. A. Garnham, G. J. Parsons, N. G. B. Cook and G. J. F. Ferris did not bat.

Bonus points – Leicestershire 3, Northamptonshire 1 (Score at 100 overs: 260-4).

Bowling: Mallender 17–2–45–1; Capel 20–3–67–0; Harper 44–13–103–4; Wheeler 14–3–30–0; Larkins 9–6–11–0; Williams 16–5–34–0.

## Northamptonshire

*G. Cook, W. Larkins, R. G. Williams, A. J. Lamb, R. J. Bailey, D. J. Capel, D. J. Wild, R. A. Harper, †G. Sharp, N. A. Mallender and M. B. H. Wheeler.

Umpires: B. Leadbeater and R. A. White.

At Trent Bridge, May 29, 30, 31. LEICESTERSHIRE drew with NOTTINGHAMSHIRE.

At Chelmsford, June 1, 3, 4. LEICESTERSHIRE drew with ESSEX.

At Leicester, June 8, 9, 10, 11. LEICESTERSHIRE drew with AUSTRALIANS (see Australian tour section).

## LEICESTERSHIRE v WARWICKSHIRE

At Hinckley, June 12, 13, 14. Leicestershire won by four wickets. Leicestershire 16 pts. Toss won by Leicestershire. The two captains, Briers and Gifford, agreed to early first-innings declarations in a bid to make up for lost time after rain had prevented any play until three o'clock on the second day. Both declarations came before the tea interval. Warwickshire struggled against Agnew and Clift on a slow pitch with uneven bounce, Kallicharran taking eighteen overs to reach double figures, and Cobb's career-best 65 saw Leicestershire to their first win of the season with four overs to spare.

### Warwickshire

| First innings | | Second innings | |
|---|---|---|---|
| T. A. Lloyd not out | 8 | – c Balderstone b Agnew | 6 |
| R. I. H. B. Dyer not out | 1 | – b Taylor | 9 |
| A. I. Kallicharran (did not bat) | | – lbw b Clift | 36 |
| D. L. Amiss (did not bat) | | – c Cobb b Clift | 14 |
| †G. W. Humpage (did not bat) | | – c and b Agnew | 3 |
| S. Wall (did not bat) | | – c Garnham b Agnew | 7 |
| P. A. Smith (did not bat) | | – lbw b Taylor | 16 |
| A. M. Ferreira (did not bat) | | – c Billington b Agnew | 17 |
| G. C. Small (did not bat) | | – c and b Clift | 25 |
| *N. Gifford (did not bat) | | – not out | 6 |
| D. S. Hoffman (did not bat) | | – b Agnew | 0 |
| L-b 1, w 5, n-b 1 | 7 | B 5, l-b 7, n-b 9 | 21 |
| (no wkt dec.) | 16 | 1/18 2/18 3/42 4/54 5/77 6/98 7/109 8/154 9/154 | 160 |

Bowling: *First Innings*—Agnew 3–1–11–0; Taylor 3–3–0–0; Clift 2–0–2–0; Parsons 1–0–2–0. *Second Innings*—Agnew 25–7–46–5; Taylor 18–3–51–2; Clift 19–12–25–3; Parsons 9–2–25–0; Cook 2–1–1–0.

### Leicestershire

| First innings | | Second innings | |
|---|---|---|---|
| J. C. Balderstone b Hoffman | 5 | – c Humpage b Hoffman | 7 |
| R. A. Cobb not out | 8 | – c Ferreira b Small | 65 |
| D. J. Billington (did not bat) | | – b Ferreira | 19 |
| J. J. Whitaker (did not bat) | | – b Ferreira | 37 |
| *N. E. Briers (did not bat) | | – b Gifford | 16 |
| G. J. Parsons (did not bat) | | – not out | 10 |
| †M. A. Garnham (did not bat) | | – c Amiss b Ferreira | 0 |
| P. B. Clift (did not bat) | | – not out | 1 |
| L-b 1, n-b 1 | 2 | B 2, l-b 5 | 7 |
| 1/15 (1 wkt dec.) | 15 | 1/15 2/64 3/117 4/144 5/154 6/159 (6 wkts) | 162 |

N. G. B. Cook, J. P. Agnew and L. B. Taylor did not bat.

Bowling: *First Innings*—Hoffman 5.1–2–3–1; Wall 5–2–11–0. *Second Innings*—Small 15–3–56–1; Hoffman 4–0–15–1; Ferreira 16.4–0–54–3; Gifford 21–7–30–1.

Umpires: M. J. Kitchen and D. R. Shepherd.

At Lord's, June 15, 17, 18. LEICESTERSHIRE drew with MIDDLESEX.

## LEICESTERSHIRE v GLAMORGAN

At Leicester, June 22, 24, 25. Drawn. Leicestershire 3 pts, Glamorgan 1 pt. Toss won by Glamorgan. A typically slow Grace Road pitch was no excuse for Glamorgan's unenterprising batting as they occupied the first four sessions in reaching 197. On the first day 33 overs were lost to the weather. Steele, on his first return to Leicestershire since leaving the club in 1983, batted four hours, two minutes (76 overs) for his 48. However, Gower put the pitch into perspective with a brilliant century off 112 balls, with nineteen 4s, his first in the Championship at Grace Road since 1981. Holmes made his third first-class century before Glamorgan's second declaration set Leicestershire to make 306 in 270 minutes. Although wickets fell steadily, they abandoned the chase only after the loss of their eighth wicket. With the last pair together, Cook, who had to survive the last six deliveries of the game from Thomas, was dropped off the second of them by Steele at silly-point.

## Glamorgan

| | | | |
|---|---|---|---|
| A. L. Jones st Garnham b Cook | 18 | – (2) b Balderstone | 60 |
| J. A. Hopkins run out | 15 | – (1) b Agnew | 0 |
| G. C. Holmes c Willey b Briers | 55 | – c Whitaker b Cook | 112 |
| Javed Miandad b Taylor | 1 | – not out | 61 |
| Younis Ahmed c Garnham b Taylor | 0 | | |
| *R. C. Ontong lbw b Agnew | 5 | | |
| J. F. Steele b Taylor | 48 | | |
| †T. Davies lbw b Agnew | 38 | | |
| J. G. Thomas b Agnew | 0 | | |
| S. R. Barwick not out | 0 | | |
| B 1, l-b 14, n-b 2 | 17 | B 14, l-b 7, w 1, n-b 4 | 26 |
| 1/31 2/47 3/50 4/52 5/66 6/124 7/197 8/197 9/197 (9 wkts dec.) | 197 | 1/0 2/134 3/259 (3 wkts dec.) | 259 |

S. J. Malone did not bat.

Bonus points – Glamorgan 1, Leicestershire 2 (Score at 100 overs: 158-6).

Bowling: *First Innings*—Agnew 22–7–43–3; Taylor 31.4–11–33–3; Parsons 23–4–50–0; Cook 35–15–46–1; Briers 7–3–10–1. *Second Innings*—Agnew 11.5–3–32–1; Taylor 18–5–57–0; Cook 23.2–7–67–1; Briers 7.1–1–29–0; Parsons 9–3–21–0; Balderstone 1–0–1–1; Willey 8–1–31–0.

## Leicestershire

| | | | |
|---|---|---|---|
| I. P. Butcher lbw b Thomas | 0 | – lbw b Barwick | 26 |
| J. C. Balderstone not out | 51 | – b Thomas | 65 |
| *D. I. Gower not out | 100 | – c Davies b Ontong | 27 |
| P. Willey (did not bat) | | – c Davies b Ontong | 41 |
| J. J. Whitaker (did not bat) | | – b Thomas | 4 |
| N. E. Briers (did not bat) | | – run out | 2 |
| †M. A. Garnham (did not bat) | | – b Ontong | 42 |
| G. J. Parsons (did not bat) | | – c Thomas b Steele | 13 |
| N. G. B. Cook (did not bat) | | – not out | 34 |
| J. P. Agnew (did not bat) | | – lbw b Ontong | 0 |
| L. B. Taylor (did not bat) | | – not out | 0 |
| | | B 6, l-b 5 | 11 |
| 1/6 (1 wkt dec.) | 151 | 1/62 2/117 3/135 4/149 5/157 6/196 7/223 8/243 9/265 (9 wkts) | 265 |

Bonus point – Leicestershire 1.

Bowling: *First Innings*—Thomas 9–3–31–1; Barwick 8–1–39–0; Holmes 7–1–27–0; Malone 3–0–20–0; Steele 5.1–1–29–0; Ontong 2–1–5–0. *Second Innings*—Thomas 18–3–72–2; Malone 6–0–25–0; Barwick 12–2–30–1; Holmes 5–1–24–0; Ontong 24–5–66–4; Steele 6–0–37–1.

Umpires: R. Julian and J. A. Jameson.

At Bradford, June 26, 27, 28. LEICESTERSHIRE drew with YORKSHIRE.

## LEICESTERSHIRE v SURREY

At Leicester, June 29, July 1, 2. Drawn. Leicestershire 8 pts, Surrey 6 pts. Toss won by Leicestershire. Their tenth draw from eleven games kept Leicestershire at the foot of the Championship table, Surrey having little trouble batting through most of the final day to avoid defeat. Play did not begin until 3.10 on the Saturday, by the close of which Surrey were struggling at 148 for six. Richards, in a ninth-wicket stand of 55 with Taylor, saw them past 200 on the Monday, whereupon Leicestershire strengthened their position. Cobb hit his highest score and Whitaker his first century of the season, which came on the final morning after he was 95 not out and Leicestershire 302 for six overnight. Willey whittled away at Surrey's second-innings resistance but time was never on Leicestershire's side.

### Surrey

| | | |
|---|---|---|
| A. R. Butcher lbw b Agnew | 33 – c Cobb b Willey | 41 |
| G. S. Clinton lbw b Agnew | 49 – lbw b Agnew | 11 |
| A. J. Stewart c Garnham b Parsons | 1 – b Willey | 42 |
| *T. E. Jesty b Agnew | 0 – b Willey | 14 |
| M. A. Lynch c Garnham b Agnew | 0 – b Willey | 21 |
| A. Needham c Garnham b Taylor | 18 – lbw b Agnew | 56 |
| D. B. Pauline c Garnham b Taylor | 8 – c Cobb b Willey | 3 |
| †C. J. Richards not out | 75 – c and b Willey | 11 |
| A. H. Gray lbw b Agnew | 1 – b Agnew | 10 |
| N. S. Taylor c Garnham b Parsons | 6 – not out | 5 |
| P. I. Pocock b Agnew | 1 – not out | 2 |
| L-b 10, n-b 8 | 18 B 2, l-b 6 | 8 |
| 1/60 2/75 3/76 4/80 5/93 6/107 7/149 8/150 9/205 | 210 1/23 2/93 3/100 4/133 5/138 6/144 7/193 8/212 9/217 | (9 wkts) 224 |

Bonus points – Surrey 2, Leicestershire 4.

Bowling: *First Innings*—Agnew 28.1–6–86–6; Taylor 24–7–49–2; Parsons 13–1–56–2; Willey 2–2–0–0; Cook 4–2–9–0. *Second Innings*—Agnew 17–5–49–3; Taylor 7–3–13–0; Cook 33–16–64–0; Willey 41–14–73–6; Balderstone 7–2–17–0.

### Leicestershire

| | |
|---|---|
| I. P. Butcher lbw b Gray | 6 |
| J. C. Balderstone c Jesty b Gray | 7 |
| R. A. Cobb lbw b Gray | 78 |
| *P. Willey b Jesty | 43 |
| J. J. Whitaker b Pocock | 109 |
| N. E. Briers lbw b Gray | 0 |
| †M. A. Garnham run out | 32 |
| G. J. Parsons b Needham | 15 |
| N. G. B. Cook b Needham | 4 |
| J. P. Agnew st Richards b Pocock | 8 |
| L. B. Taylor not out | 2 |
| B 6, l-b 15, n-b 16 | 37 |
| 1/16 2/27 3/130 4/201 5/203 6/278 7/323 8/327 9/331 | 341 |

Bonus points – Leicestershire 4, Surrey 4 (Score at 100 overs: 331-9).

Bowling: Gray 21–5–56–4; Taylor 17–0–78–0; Pauline 10–2–40–0; Jesty 4–0–23–1; Butcher 8–4–16–0; Needham 31–8–69–2; Pocock 11.4–2–38–2.

Umpires: D. J. Constant and K. E. Palmer.

At Taunton, July 6, 8, 9. LEICESTERSHIRE drew with SOMERSET.

At Swansea, July 10, 11, 12. LEICESTERSHIRE drew with GLAMORGAN.

At Chesterfield, July 13, 14, 15. LEICESTERSHIRE beat DERBYSHIRE by seven wickets.

At Leicester, July 24, 25, 26. LEICESTERSHIRE v ZIMBABWEANS. Cancelled.

## LEICESTERSHIRE v KENT

At Leicester, July 27, 29, 30. Drawn. Leicestershire 7 pts, Kent 5 pts. Toss won by Kent. After Baptiste had taken six consecutive wickets in a two-hour spell to restrict Leicestershire to 251 on a green but slow pitch, Agnew took the first nine Kent wickets. With Jarvis facing, the England fast bowler had the chance to record his first-ever hat-trick, and also become the first since N. I. Thomson of Sussex, in 1964, to take all ten wickets in a first-class innings in England. Agnew, however, bowled a no-ball, and Jarvis subsequently fell to Clift. Agnew's nine for 70 was a career best. Rain prevented any play before lunch on the second and third days, and when Kent were set 243 to win in 40 overs, a draw seemed the likeliest result. Opinions changed as they subsided to 73 for six in twenty overs against Agnew and Taylor, but Knott and Taylor hung on.

### Leicestershire

| | | | |
|---|---|---|---|
| I. P. Butcher c Benson b Dilley | 17 | c sub b Jarvis | 8 |
| J. C. Balderstone c Knott b Ellison | 34 | not out | 82 |
| *D. I. Gower lbw b Ellison | 27 | c Baptiste b Taylor | 24 |
| P. Willey c Knott b Baptiste | 47 | (5) not out | 18 |
| J. J. Whitaker b Baptiste | 73 | | |
| N. E. Briers c Ellison b Baptiste | 6 | | |
| †M. A. Garnham c and b Baptiste | 0 | | |
| P. B. Clift c Knott b Baptiste | 21 | | |
| N. G. B. Cook c Knott b Baptiste | 3 | | |
| J. P. Agnew not out | 8 | (4) c Dilley b Taylor | 6 |
| L. B. Taylor b Ellison | 6 | | |
| L-b 4, w 2, n-b 3 | 9 | L-b 1, w 1, n-b 1 | 3 |
| 1/44 2/55 3/98 4/184 5/209 6/211 7/212 8/224 9/239 | 251 | 1/10 2/79 3/97 (3 wkts dec.) | 141 |

Bonus points – Leicestershire 3, Kent 4.

Bowling: *First Innings*—Dilley 10–0–47–1; Jarvis 18–2–71–0; Ellison 18.4–4–58–3; Baptiste 22–6–60–6; Underwood 4–1–11–0. *Second Innings*—Dilley 3–0–4–0; Jarvis 2–0–17–1; Taylor 11–0–50–2; Benson 10–0–69–0.

### Kent

| | | | |
|---|---|---|---|
| M. R. Benson lbw b Agnew | 5 | c Briers b Taylor | 12 |
| S. G. Hinks b Agnew | 54 | b Agnew | 41 |
| C. J. Tavaré c Garnham b Agnew | 1 | b Taylor | 8 |
| N. R. Taylor not out | 59 | not out | 20 |
| *C. S. Cowdrey b Agnew | 0 | (6) c Garnham b Taylor | 0 |
| E. A. E. Baptiste c Garnham b Agnew | 5 | (5) c Garnham b Agnew | 0 |
| †A. P. E. Knott lbw b Agnew | 15 | (8) not out | 36 |
| G. R. Dilley lbw b Agnew | 0 | | |
| R. M. Ellison c Garnham b Agnew | 0 | (7) b Taylor | 4 |
| D. L. Underwood b Agnew | 0 | | |
| K. B. S. Jarvis c Butcher b Clift | 7 | | |
| L-b 4, w 2, n-b 11 | 17 | B 5, l-b 1, w 1 | 7 |
| 1/13 2/17 3/116 4/117 5/123 6/143 7/145 8/145 9/145 | 163 | 1/38 2/58 3/64 4/66 5/67 6/73 (6 wkts) | 128 |

Bonus points – Kent 1, Leicestershire 4.

Bowling: *First Innings*—Agnew 19–2–70–9; Taylor 12–4–27–0; Clift 21.4–7–61–1; Willey 1–0–1–0. *Second Innings*—Agnew 11–1–48–2; Taylor 15–6–42–4; Clift 7–1–25–0; Cook 5–2–6–0; Willey 2–1–1–0.

Umpires: B. J. Meyer and J. Birkenshaw.

## LEICESTERSHIRE v LANCASHIRE

At Leicester, July 31, August 1, 2. Drawn. Leicestershire 8 pts, Lancashire 7 pts. Toss won by Lancashire. On a pitch of uncertain bounce, Lancashire's weakened seam attack allowed Leicestershire to recover from 190 for six. Lancashire, in turn, were rescued by Clive Lloyd's first century in the Championship for three years. With his side at one stage five wickets down and needing another 63 to avoid the follow-on, Lloyd struck nineteen 4s and one 6 in his 131. Willey's defensive declaration left Lancashire to make 257 in one hour plus twenty overs, and although De Freitas, Leicestershire's nineteen-year-old Dominican-born, English-qualified seamer, returned five for 39 on his Championship début, the home team ran out of time with victory beckoning.

### Leicestershire

| | | | |
|---|---|---|---|
| I. P. Butcher c Maynard b Watkinson | 33 | – b Makinson | 1 |
| J. C. Balderstone b Murphy | 20 | – lbw b Murphy | 26 |
| R. A. Cobb lbw b Watkinson | 59 | – not out | 66 |
| *P. Willey c Maynard b Makinson | 11 | – c Fairbrother b Makinson | 37 |
| J. J. Whitaker c Lloyd b Watkinson | 7 | – not out | 66 |
| N. E. Briers lbw b Makinson | 61 | | |
| †M. A. Garnham c Simmons b Makinson | 9 | | |
| P. B. Clift c Maynard b Watkinson | 23 | | |
| G. J. Parsons lbw b Watkinson | 29 | | |
| P. A. J. De Freitas not out | 30 | | |
| L. B. Taylor b Makinson | 20 | | |
| B 1, l-b 8, w 11, n-b 5 | 25 | B 4, l-b 3, n-b 4 | 11 |
| 1/54 2/62 3/85 4/98 5/175 6/190 7/226 8/262 9/285 | 327 | 1/12 2/33 3/100 | (3 wkts dec.) 207 |

Bonus points – Leicestershire 4, Lancashire 4 (Score at 100 overs: 322-9).

Bowling: *First Innings*—Makinson 25.3–1–110–4; Watkinson 40–10–109–5; Murphy 20–4–71–1; Fairbrother 4–2–5–0; Simmons 11–4–23–0. *Second Innings*—Watkinson 17–4–47–0; Makinson 22–7–53–2; Murphy 8–4–18–1; Simmons 22–1–68–0; Abrahams 7–2–14–0.

### Lancashire

| | | | |
|---|---|---|---|
| M. R. Chadwick c Garnham b Taylor | 13 | – c Garnham b Taylor | 8 |
| D. W. Varey b Willey | 41 | – c Garnham b Taylor | 20 |
| G. Fowler c Cobb b De Freitas | 10 | – c Butcher b De Freitas | 13 |
| N. H. Fairbrother c Garnham b Parsons | 13 | – c Cobb b De Freitas | 1 |
| C. H. Lloyd c Clift b Taylor | 131 | – (7) lbw b Taylor | 16 |
| *J. Abrahams c and b Taylor | 9 | – (5) c Garnham b De Freitas | 4 |
| M. Watkinson lbw b Clift | 14 | – (6) b De Freitas | 9 |
| J. Simmons c Garnham b Clift | 0 | – (9) not out | 4 |
| †C. Maynard c Garnham b Taylor | 7 | – (10) not out | 0 |
| D. J. Makinson c Willey b Parsons | 15 | – (8) c Taylor b De Freitas | 1 |
| A. J. Murphy not out | 2 | | |
| B 10, w 2, n-b 11 | 23 | B 1, l-b 1, n-b 3 | 5 |
| 1/32 2/50 3/83 4/95 5/115 6/183 7/183 8/203 9/231 | 278 | 1/27 2/32 3/40 4/49 5/56 6/65 7/77 8/77 | (8 wkts) 81 |

Bonus points – Lancashire 3, Leicestershire 4 (Score at 100 overs: 253-9).

Bowling: *First Innings*—Taylor 27.3–5–52–4; Clift 29–10–64–2; De Freitas 23–5–71–1; Parsons 20–5–58–2; Willey 6–2–23–1. *Second Innings*—Taylor 10.5–3–12–3; De Freitas 13–3–39–5; Briers 12–5–28–0.

Umpires: B. J. Meyer and J. Birkenshaw.

At Cheltenham, August 10, 12, 13. LEICESTERSHIRE drew with GLOUCESTERSHIRE.

## LEICESTERSHIRE v HAMPSHIRE

At Leicester, August 17, 19, 20. Drawn. Leicestershire 4 pts, Hampshire 3 pts. Toss won by Hampshire. A potentially exciting contest was ruined when rain prevented any play after an opening day on which fifteen wickets fell, all but two of them to the spin bowlers. Willey returned his best figures for Leicestershire, including four wickets for 16 in 21 balls, as Hampshire tumbled to 162 all out on a wicket that accommodated turn from the outset. Then it was Leicestershire's turn as they subsided from 72 for one to 99 for five against the off-spin of Cowley and the slow left-arm spin of Maru.

### Hampshire

| | |
|---|---|
| C. G. Greenidge c Garnham b De Freitas | 10 |
| V. P. Terry b Agnew | 10 |
| R. A. Smith lbw b Willey | 40 |
| J. J. E. Hardy c Willey b Cook | 15 |
| D. R. Turner b Willey | 10 |
| *M. C. J. Nicholas st Garnham b Cook | 1 |
| M. D. Marshall b Willey | 36 |
| N. G. Cowley c Briers b Willey | 20 |
| T. M. Tremlett c Garnham b Willey | 0 |
| †R. J. Parks b Willey | 3 |
| R. J. Maru not out | 0 |
| B 4, l-b 9, n-b 4 | 17 |
| 1/19 2/27 3/60 4/97 5/98 6/104 7/139 8/145 9/161 | 162 |

Bonus points – Hampshire 1, Leicestershire 4.

Bowling: Agnew 12–3–32–1; De Freitas 9–5–12–1; Clift 7–3–17–0; Cook 23–7–45–2; Willey 19.1–4–43–6.

### Leicestershire

| | |
|---|---|
| I. P. Butcher c Greenidge b Maru | 41 |
| J. C. Balderstone c Maru b Cowley | 10 |
| R. A. Cobb c Terry b Cowley | 26 |
| *P. Willey c Greenidge b Maru | 7 |
| J. J. Whitaker b Maru | 0 |
| N. E. Briers not out | 8 |
| N. G. B. Cook not out | 5 |
| B 6, l-b 3 | 9 |
| 1/23 2/72 3/90 4/90 5/99 | (5 wkts) 106 |

†M. A. Garnham, P. B. Clift, P. A. J. De Freitas and J. P. Agnew did not bat.

Bonus points – Hampshire 2.

Bowling: Marshall 4–1–11–0; Tremlett 6–2–11–0; Maru 22–8–41–3; Cowley 20–6–34–2.

Umpires: P. B. Wight and K. J. Lyons.

At Northampton, August 24, 26, 27. LEICESTERSHIRE drew with NORTHAMPTONSHIRE.

At Bournemouth, August 28, 29, 30. LEICESTERSHIRE lost to HAMPSHIRE by an innings and 56 runs.

## LEICESTERSHIRE v WORCESTERSHIRE

At Leicester, August 31, September 2, 3. Drawn. Leicestershire 4 pts, Worcestershire 8 pts. Toss won by Worcestershire. A total of 353 minutes lost to the weather ultimately denied Worcestershire, who dictated the game from the moment Butcher fell to the first ball of the match. Accurate seam bowling hustled Leicestershire out for 153, and an injury to Agnew while fielding, coupled with the absence of Taylor on Test duty, left Leicestershire short of firepower.

Radford took nine wickets in the game, and Worcestershire might well have overcome the loss of time but for the resistance of Garnham, who announced his retirement during the match, and Blackett, who held the visitors at bay for 166 minutes on his first home Championship appearance.

### Leicestershire

| | | | |
|---|---|---|---|
| I. P. Butcher lbw b Radford | 0 | – lbw b Radford | 6 |
| J. C. Balderstone b McEwan | 7 | – c Hick b Radford | 28 |
| N. E. Briers c Rhodes b Weston | 45 | – c Inchmore b Radford | 0 |
| *P. Willey c and b Weston | 56 | – c Rhodes b McEwan | 35 |
| J. J. Whitaker c Curtis b Inchmore | 15 | – lbw b Radford | 4 |
| M. Blackett c Patel b Radford | 10 | – not out | 28 |
| †M. A. Garnham b McEwan | 3 | – lbw b Radford | 41 |
| P. B. Clift lbw b McEwan | 13 | – lbw b Hick | 7 |
| P. A. J. De Freitas b Radford | 0 | – b Patel | 9 |
| J. P. Agnew b Radford | 1 | – lbw b Patel | 1 |
| G. J. F. Ferris not out | 0 | – not out | 0 |
| L-b 2, n-b 1 | 3 | L-b 1, n-b 7 | 8 |
| 1/0 2/27 3/84 4/123 5/123 6/139 7/143 8/143 9/153 | 153 | 1/22 2/22 3/52 4/56 5/82 6/130 7/137 8/156 9/166 (9 wkts) | 167 |

Bonus points – Leicestershire 1, Worcestershire 4.

Bowling: *First Innings*—Radford 14.1–3–55–4; Inchmore 13–4–26–1; McEwan 18–5–47–3; Weston 19–7–23–2. *Second Innings*—Radford 23–4–64–5; Inchmore 12–3–34–0; Weston 3–0–14–0; Patel 20–14–16–2; McEwan 10–2–27–1; Hick 4–2–11–1.

### Worcestershire

| | | | |
|---|---|---|---|
| T. S. Curtis lbw b De Freitas | 65 | †S. J. Rhodes not out | 13 |
| D. B. D'Oliveira c Garnham b Ferris | 9 | N. V. Radford not out | 6 |
| G. A. Hick b Willey | 21 | | |
| D. M. Smith lbw b Willey | 48 | B 5, l-b 6, n-b 22 | 33 |
| *P. A. Neale lbw b De Freitas | 0 | | |
| D. N. Patel run out | 69 | 1/16 2/80 3/160 4/160 (7 wkts dec.) | 343 |
| M. J. Weston c Butcher b De Freitas | 79 | 5/160 6/319 7/324 | |

J. D. Inchmore and S. M. McEwan did not bat.

Bonus points – Worcestershire 4, Leicestershire 3.

Bowling: Agnew 6–1–17–0; Ferris 21–1–91–1; De Freitas 22–0–93–3; Willey 28–8–56–2; Clift 20–1–75–0.

Umpires: J. A. Jameson and J. Birkenshaw.

## LEICESTERSHIRE v MIDDLESEX

At Leicester, September 4, 5, 6. Middlesex won by ten wickets. Middlesex 23 pts, Leicestershire 5 pts. Toss won by Middlesex. Cowans, returning a career-best six for 31, helped Middlesex make up for a loss of over three hours to the weather on the opening day, and only Gower, who hit eleven 4s in a 47-ball 49, offered any resistance. On a far from straightforward pitch, Middlesex were indebted to Radley's four-hour 87 for their decisive first-innings advantage. Leicestershire collapsed for a second time, this time to Daniel's best return of the season. The West Indian dismissed Butcher first ball, then removed Gower and Willey as the home side slumped to 24 for three. Whitaker, despatching anything short with authority, played a mature innings until ninth out, hitting one 6 and thirteen 4s in 125 balls before being caught at mid-wicket. This victory, their seventh of the season, took Middlesex to the top of the Championship table.

## Leicestershire

| | First innings | | Second innings | |
|---|---|---|---|---|
| I. P. Butcher | b Daniel | 11 | b Daniel | 0 |
| J. C. Balderstone | c Butcher b Cowans | 19 | c Brown b Cowans | 14 |
| *D. I. Gower | c Slack b Cowans | 49 | b Daniel | 18 |
| P. Willey | c Brown b Cowans | 9 | b Daniel | 0 |
| J. J. Whitaker | c Downton b Daniel | 7 | c Hughes b Daniel | 89 |
| N. E. Briers | lbw b Cowans | 0 | b Williams | 8 |
| P. B. Clift | lbw b Cowans | 30 | lbw b Cowans | 34 |
| P. A. J. De Freitas | c Radley b Hughes | 11 | b Daniel | 11 |
| †P. Whitticase | c Downton b Williams | 15 | lbw b Daniel | 0 |
| L. B. Taylor | not out | 1 | not out | 5 |
| G. J. F. Ferris | lbw b Cowans | 1 | lbw b Daniel | 0 |
| | L-b 5 | 5 | L-b 3, n-b 3 | 6 |
| | 1/16 2/57 3/86 4/97 5/97 6/97 7/120 8/155 9/155 | 158 | 1/0 2/24 3/24 4/47 5/94 6/139 7/177 8/179 9/183 | 185 |

Bonus points – Leicestershire 1, Middlesex 4.

Bowling: *First Innings*—Daniel 17–3–52–2; Williams 15–2–39–1; Cowans 9.3–1–31–6; Hughes 6–1–27–1; Embury 3–1–4–0. *Second Innings*—Daniel 14.1–1–62–7; Williams 11–1–51–1; Hughes 8–3–23–0; Cowans 8–1–32–2; Emburey 11–3–14–0.

## Middlesex

| | First innings | | Second innings | |
|---|---|---|---|---|
| W. N. Slack | lbw b Taylor | 38 | not out | 13 |
| K. R. Brown | c De Freitas b Taylor | 5 | not out | 25 |
| *M. W. Gatting | b Ferris | 39 | | |
| R. O. Butcher | run out | 1 | | |
| C. T. Radley | b Clift | 87 | | |
| †P. R. Downton | c Whitticase b Ferris | 32 | | |
| J. E. Emburey | c Whitticase b Clift | 1 | | |
| N. F. Williams | lbw b Taylor | 30 | | |
| S. P. Hughes | not out | 18 | | |
| N. G. Cowans | b Ferris | 12 | | |
| W. W. Daniel | c Willey b De Freitas | 2 | | |
| | B 18, n-b 15 | 33 | B 4, l-b 5, w 1, n-b 1 | 11 |
| | 1/47 2/47 3/50 4/118 5/210 6/215 7/226 8/271 9/288 | 298 | (no wkt) | 49 |

Bonus points – Middlesex 3, Leicestershire 4 (Score at 100 overs: 298-9).

Bowling: *First Innings*—Ferris 25–1–84–3; Taylor 30–4–68–3; De Freitas 18.1–3–54–1; Clift 21–7–50–2; Willey 6–0–24–0. *Second Innings*—De Freitas 6–1–12–0; Clift 5–1–12–0; Balderstone 2–1–3–0; Gower 1.1–0–13–0.

Umpires: J. H. Hampshire and R. Julian.

At Hove, September 7, 9, 10. LEICESTERSHIRE lost to SUSSEX by two wickets.

At Old Trafford, September 14, 16, 17. LEICESTERSHIRE drew with LANCASHIRE.

# MIDDLESEX

*Patron:* HRH The Duke of Edinburgh
*President:* F. G. Mann
*Chairman:* M. P. Murray
*Chairman, Cricket Committee:* R. V. C. Robins
*Secretary:* T. M. Lamb
Lord's Cricket Ground, St John's Wood, London NW8 8QN (Telephone: 01-289 1300)
*Captain:* M. W. Gatting
*Coach:* D. Bennett

For the fifth time in ten seasons Middlesex won the County Championship, probably the most satisfying of their successes since the first title of this modern era back in 1976. Before the start of the 1985 season it was considered that the Britannic Assurance Championship might be beyond a county squad certain to be weakened by Test calls. Mike Gatting and Phil Edmonds had spent the winter establishing themselves in the England side and John Emburey was again available for Tests. Paul Downton and Norman Cowans were also almost sure to be required. Indeed, in these notes last year I presumed to wonder – "Are the reserves adequate?" The answer came that they were, and the "regulars" surpassed themselves in camouflaging the inevitable shortfall in runs, wickets and experience when Tests were being played.

In one sense – because they played throughout the campaign – the title belonged more to men like Graham Barlow, Wilf Slack, Clive Radley, Roland Butcher and Wayne Daniel than to the county's current England players. The captain, Gatting, and Downton each missed ten matches, and Edmonds and Emburey nine. As he luxuriated in achieving another ambition, to win the Championship, Gatting was swift to compliment his colleagues. His words about success arising from an all-round team effort were heartfelt. Middlesex were the best team and had proved it.

By the time Gatting, Downton, Edmonds and Cowans went off to play in the one-day internationals, Middlesex had recorded two wins in five games – both at Lord's, the only victories they had there. When Emburey joined the others for the Tests, Radley took charge for nine of the next thirteen games. Only one of these was won, a remarkable two-day effort at Worcester where Butcher played his best innings of the season and Graham Rose marked his Championship début with some decisive bowling. But all the time that Radley was captain the bonus points ticked up, in fives and sixes, and two important, possibly Championship-deciding, draws were earned against Hampshire and Gloucestershire. Because of the grim weather such handfuls of points assumed disproportionate importance. Wins and points were rarer than in the previous two sunlit summers. In 1984 Middlesex were third with a very similar record to 1985 (eight wins, 269 points); in 1983 they were second with three more wins and over 300 points.

Radley's thinking was: "We didn't expect that the makeshift side could win much, but we looked for every bonus point and tried to make sure that no challenger took advantage of us being under strength." Between Tests Gatting returned to supervise victory over Nottinghamshire at Trent

Bridge and a double over Northamptonshire. The Uxbridge win against Northamptonshire on July 26 was the last for six weeks, but Middlesex fell no lower after that than second. When they beat Leicestershire on September 6 they went top, and they wrapped up the title on the season's last day at Edgbaston.

Gatting again scored substantially, though his major innings were for England. The huge quantities of runs that he produced for Middlesex from 1981 to 1984, making him the highest Test-qualified Englishman for four consecutive seasons, were not there. He batted entertainingly and forcefully, but more briefly, failing to reach a century until September. In contrast to 1984, however, the batting coped effectively without Gatting's constant big scores.

Those principally responsible for this more even state of affairs were Barlow, Slack and Radley. The openers' reliable form was the real bonus, for Barlow had struggled to complete his benefit season the previous year because of a hip injury and had become pessimistic about his playing future. Happily, a faith healer restored him and he employed his regained physical freedom to join with Slack in a string of substantial starts. They recorded two double-century stands, four century partnerships and thirteen more of over 40, which meant that Gatting, or whoever was at number three, came in with the ball no longer new. Keith Brown, calm and with a secure defence, was a genuine find. Down the order Radley, Downton and Emburey enjoyed more profitable seasons with the bat, Radley enhancing his already high reputation for excavating runs from the deepest pit.

Daniel and Neil Williams provided the extra wickets that were needed with the spinners so often absent. Daniel, fully earning his benefit, was as dedicated as ever. He shortened his run, but there was no noticeable reduction in speed, or, certainly, in hostility.

The team's view was that the longer limited-overs competitions provided them with their best opportunities of continuing their winning sequence. This reckoned without Essex, who established themselves alongside Lancashire and Surrey in Middlesex's one-day cricket "black museum". Two trips to Chelmsford – in the Benson and Hedges Cup semi-finals and the second round of the NatWest Bank Trophy – resulted in similar defeats by 62 and 84 runs. In the John Player Sunday League it was a return to the dark days. Middlesex were equal first on June 16, but their solitary victory after that came in a ten-over thrash and they finished equal twelfth.

Gatting optimistically asserted at the end of the season that he will be aiming for the Sunday title in 1986 to complete a unique collection of four different trophies in four years. He was to the point in analysing his successful start as captain: "I inherited Mike Brearley's side and tried to keep them playing the same purposeful cricket. They can be a hard team to lead because many have developed their own views through having played for so long at a high level. There were some slightly unprofessional moments, but we managed to show the younger players that Middlesex expect the highest playing standards."

Though his team found the sort of resilience that Surrey needed in the 1950s in overcoming Test calls, it may be even harder in 1986, when Middlesex's England regulars could miss as many as thirteen Championship matches. – T.C.

## MIDDLESEX 1985

[*Bill Smith*

*Back row:* P. C. R. Tufnell, K. R. Brown, N. R. C. MacLaurin, A. R. Harwood, G. K. Brown, S. P. Hughes, C. P. Metson. *Middle row:* J. E. Miller (*physiotherapist*), D. Bennett (*coach*), N. G. Cowans, J. F. Sykes, A. R. C. Fraser, G. D. Rose, W. N. Slack, N. F. Williams, K. P. Tomlins, H. P. Sharp (*scorer*). *Front row:* P. R. Downton, W. W. Daniel, G. D. Barlow, J. E. Emburey, M. W. Gatting (*captain*), C. T. Radley, P. H. Edmonds, R. O. Butcher.

## MIDDLESEX RESULTS

*All first-class matches – Played 26: Won 8, Lost 4, Drawn 14.*

*County Championship matches – Played 24: Won 8, Lost 4, Drawn 12.*

*Bonus points – Batting 61, Bowling 85.*

*Competition placings – Britannic Assurance County Championship, winners; NatWest Bank Trophy, 2nd round; Benson and Hedges Cup, s-f; John Player League, 12th eq.*

## BRITANNIC ASSURANCE CHAMPIONSHIP AVERAGES

### BATTING

| | *Birthplace* | *M* | *I* | *NO* | *R* | *HI* | *Avge* |
|---|---|---|---|---|---|---|---|
| ‡C. T. Radley ..... | *Hertford* | 24 | 33 | 9 | 1,260 | 200 | 52.50 |
| ‡M. W. Gatting .... | *Kingsbury* | 14 | 21 | 2 | 929 | 114 | 48.89 |
| ‡G. D. Barlow ..... | *Folkestone* | 20 | 32 | 4 | 1,343 | 141 | 47.96 |
| ‡W. N. Slack ...... | *Troumaca, St Vincent* | 24 | 41 | 7 | 1,618 | 112 | 47.58 |
| ‡P. R. Downton ... | *Farnborough, Kent* | 14 | 20 | 5 | 663 | 104 | 44.20 |
| ‡R. O. Butcher .... | *St Philip, Barbados* | 24 | 36 | 6 | 1,154 | 120 | 38.46 |
| ‡J. E. Emburey .... | *Peckham* | 15 | 16 | 2 | 432 | 68 | 30.85 |
| K. R. Brown ..... | *Edmonton* | 7 | 10 | 2 | 196 | 67 | 24.50 |
| ‡K. P. Tomlins .... | *Kingston-upon-Thames* | 8 | 13 | 0 | 306 | 58 | 23.53 |
| ‡N. F. Williams ... | *Hope Well, St Vincent* | 19 | 20 | 4 | 311 | 46 | 19.43 |
| ‡S. P. Hughes ..... | *Kingston-upon-Thames* | 11 | 11 | 6 | 94 | 30* | 18.80 |
| J. F. Sykes ....... | *Shoreditch* | 10 | 12 | 3 | 149 | 52* | 16.55 |
| ‡P. H. Edmonds ... | *Lusaka, N. Rhodesia* | 15 | 16 | 5 | 155 | 29* | 14.09 |
| C. P. Metson ..... | *Cuffley* | 8 | 9 | 3 | 59 | 14* | 9.83 |
| J. D. Carr ....... | *St John's Wood* | 5 | 7 | 0 | 59 | 29 | 8.42 |
| ‡N. G. Cowans .... | *Enfield St Mary, Jamaica* | 19 | 14 | 2 | 99 | 15* | 8.25 |
| ‡W. W. Daniel .... | *St Philip, Barbados* | 22 | 15 | 5 | 48 | 19* | 4.80 |

Also batted: A. J. T. Miller (*Chesham*) (2 matches) 16, 15, 13*; G. D. Rose (*Tottenham*) (2 matches) 4, 15; A. R. C. Fraser (*Billinge*) (1 match) did not bat.

* *Signifies not out.* ‡ *Denotes county cap.*

The following played a total of fifteen three-figure innings for Middlesex in County Championship matches – G. D. Barlow 6, C. T. Radley 3, W. N. Slack 3, R. O. Butcher 1, P. R. Downton 1, M. W. Gatting 1.

### BOWLING

| | *O* | *M* | *R* | *W* | *BB* | *Avge* |
|---|---|---|---|---|---|---|
| N. G. Cowans ..... | 362.4 | 65 | 1,268 | 60 | 6-31 | 21.13 |
| P. H. Edmonds .... | 542 | 158 | 1,206 | 51 | 6-87 | 23.64 |
| W. W. Daniel ..... | 575.1 | 89 | 2,111 | 79 | 7-62 | 26.72 |
| N. F. Williams .... | 434.2 | 65 | 1,542 | 54 | 5-15 | 28.55 |
| J. E. Emburey ..... | 451 | 124 | 976 | 30 | 6-35 | 32.53 |
| S. P. Hughes ...... | 246.2 | 42 | 871 | 23 | 5-64 | 37.86 |
| J. F. Sykes ........ | 175.5 | 41 | 540 | 13 | 3-58 | 41.53 |

Also bowled: G. D. Barlow 3–0–14–0; R. O. Butcher 18–5–39–2; J. D. Carr 65.1–17–154–9; P. R. Downton 8–6–5–0; A. R. C. Fraser 19.5–3–71–4; M. W. Gatting 73.5–15–222–8; C. T. Radley 13–3–43–2; G. D. Rose 45.1–8–142–9; W. N. Slack 9–1–29–0; K. P. Tomlins 2–0–9–0.

## MIDDLESEX v WORCESTERSHIRE

At Lord's, April 27, 29, 30. Middlesex won by eight wickets. Middlesex 19 pts, Worcestershire 8 pts. Toss won by Middlesex, whose decision to insert Worcestershire was justified when Williams and Daniel accounted for the top half of the order. But then Kapil Dev warmed a freezing day – it snowed later – with a dashing innings, his first eight scoring shots all being 4s. He hit eight more and also two 6s, including a straight blow off Cowans to bring up his century in 75 minutes off 78 balls. D'Oliveira and Newport were unbeaten on the second morning, and Newport continued his good day with five wickets, the highlight of which was extracting Gatting's middle stump. Slack carried his bat through the innings. Middlesex came through strongly on the last day, their catching especially being of a high class, and despite losing Gatting cheaply, they strolled home with nineteen overs in hand.

### Worcestershire

| | | | |
|---|---|---|---|
| M. J. Weston lbw b Williams | 44 | – b Williams | 0 |
| T. S. Curtis c Tomlins b Daniel | 8 | – c Tomlins b Daniel | 5 |
| D. M. Smith lbw b Williams | 9 | – c Downton b Cowans | 28 |
| D. N. Patel c Slack b Daniel | 19 | – c Downton b Cowans | 24 |
| *P. A. Neale c Emburey b Williams | 8 | – c and b Cowans | 2 |
| D. B. D'Oliveira not out | 73 | – b Emburey | 0 |
| Kapil Dev lbw b Daniel | 100 | – (8) c Daniel b Williams | 33 |
| P. J. Newport not out | 28 | – (7) c Gatting b Emburey | 1 |
| †S. J. Rhodes (did not bat) | | – (10) c Downton b Williams | 0 |
| R. K. Illingworth (did not bat) | | – (11) not out | 0 |
| N. V. Radford (did not bat) | | – (9) lbw b Emburey | 0 |
| B 1, l-b 4, w 3, n-b 4 | 12 | B 2, l-b 1, n-b 7 | 10 |
| 1/34 2/60 3/73 4/94 5/96 6/223 (6 wkts dec.) | 301 | 1/0 2/18 3/53 4/61 5/64 6/64 7/68 8/68 9/98 | 103 |

Bonus points – Worcestershire 4, Middlesex 2.

Bowling: *First Innings*—Daniel 23–2–90–3; Cowans 15.4–4–74–0; Williams 26–8–68–3; Emburey 9–2–30–0; Gatting 3–0–17–0; Edmonds 8–2–17–0. *Second Innings*—Williams 10.3–4–28–3; Daniel 10–1–43–1; Cowans 7–3–15–3; Emburey 7–1–14–3.

### Middlesex

| | | | |
|---|---|---|---|
| W. N. Slack not out | 72 | – c Rhodes b Newport | 40 |
| †P. R. Downton lbw b Newport | 16 | – not out | 69 |
| *M. W. Gatting b Newport | 12 | – lbw b Radford | 12 |
| R. O. Butcher c Patel b Kapil Dev | 4 | – not out | 80 |
| C. T. Radley c Rhodes b Radford | 6 | | |
| K. P. Tomlins c D'Oliveira b Kapil Dev | 6 | | |
| J. E. Emburey c Rhodes b Newport | 56 | | |
| P. H. Edmonds c Patel b Newport | 0 | | |
| N. F. Williams c Rhodes b Radford | 8 | | |
| N. G. Cowans lbw b Radford | 0 | | |
| W. W. Daniel b Newport | 1 | | |
| L-b 2, w 4, n-b 8 | 14 | L-b 3, w 1, n-b 6 | 10 |
| 1/30 2/43 3/48 4/61 5/70 6/161 7/162 8/190 9/190 | 195 | 1/81 2/96 (2 wkts) | 211 |

Bonus points – Middlesex 1, Worcestershire 4.

Bowling: *First Innings*—Kapil Dev 13–4–35–2; Radford 17–3–43–3; Newport 19.4–5–57–5; Weston 6–2–19–0; Illingworth 12–4–31–0; Patel 3–0–8–0. *Second Innings*—Radford 15–2–65–1; Newport 12–2–48–1; Weston 7–2–20–0; Illingworth 7.4–1–42–0; Patel 4–0–33–0.

Umpires: M. J. Kitchen and N. T. Plews.

At Fenner's, May 1, 2, 3. MIDDLESEX drew with CAMBRIDGE UNIVERSITY.

At Headingley, May 4, 6, 7. MIDDLESEX lost to YORKSHIRE by 2 runs.

## MIDDLESEX v KENT

At Lord's, May 8, 9, 10. Drawn. Middlesex 8 pts, Kent 4 pts. Toss won by Kent. Slack, having made 99 the previous day, went one better as he underpinned the Middlesex innings for 285 minutes. Batting was not easy, and after the seam bowlers had done their work Underwood caused problems before Radley and Emburey saw Middlesex towards four points. For Kent, Cowdrey batted more determinedly than many of his colleagues, most of whom fell to pace after exploratory work. At 151 for three, with Gatting playing soundly, Middlesex were handsomely placed on the second evening, but Kent's approach was defensive next morning and they did not respond when set 324 to win in a minimum of 77 overs.

### Middlesex

| | | | |
|---|---|---|---|
| G. D. Barlow c Aslett b Cowdrey | 32 | – c Tavaré b Penn | 20 |
| W. N. Slack b Cowdrey | 105 | – c Knott b Penn | 14 |
| *M. W. Gatting c Knott b Jarvis | 11 | – c Knott b Jarvis | 90 |
| R. O. Butcher c Hinks b Underwood | 35 | – lbw b Jarvis | 1 |
| C. T. Radley c and b Underwood | 50 | – not out | 85 |
| †P. R. Downton c Penn b Underwood | 23 | – c Knott b Penn | 15 |
| J. E. Emburey not out | 22 | – c Knott b Penn | 0 |
| P. H. Edmonds not out | 6 | – not out | 21 |
| L-b 6, w 3, n-b 10 | 19 | B 1, l-b 5, w 1, n-b 4 | 11 |
| 1/69 2/110 3/178 4/206 5/262 6/282 (6 wkts dec.) | 303 | 1/33 2/38 3/49 4/178 5/209 6/209 (6 wkts dec.) | 257 |

N. F. Williams, N. G. Cowans and W. W. Daniel did not bat.

Bonus points – Middlesex 4, Kent 2.

Bowling: *First Innings*—Jarvis 21–2–73–1; Baptiste 23–5–55–0; Penn 17–3–57–0; Cowdrey 25–4–69–2; Underwood 14–7–43–3. *Second Innings*—Jarvis 23–5–83–2; Baptiste 19–5–41–0; Penn 16.1–1–63–4; Cowdrey 5–1–21–0; Underwood 7–0–35–0; Johnson 4–0–8–0.

### Kent

| | | | |
|---|---|---|---|
| M. R. Benson c Downton b Cowans | 10 | – not out | 62 |
| S. G. Hinks c Butcher b Daniel | 13 | – b Emburey | 35 |
| C. J. Tavaré c Downton b Cowans | 13 | – not out | 18 |
| D. G. Aslett c Gatting b Daniel | 12 | | |
| *C. S. Cowdrey b Edmonds | 95 | | |
| E. A. E. Baptiste c Daniel b Williams | 15 | | |
| G. W. Johnson b Daniel | 28 | | |
| †A. P. E. Knott c Slack b Edmonds | 18 | | |
| C. Penn not out | 20 | | |
| D. L. Underwood c Slack b Edmonds | 0 | | |
| K. B. S. Jarvis b Daniel | 5 | | |
| B 4, w 1, n-b 3 | 8 | B 6, w 2, n-b 1 | 9 |
| 1/16 2/26 3/42 4/64 5/88 6/167 7/209 8/220 9/224 | 237 | 1/78 (1 wkt) | 124 |

Bonus points – Kent 2, Middlesex 4.

Bowling: *First Innings*—Williams 14–2–72–1; Cowans 20–1–81–2; Daniel 18–3–32–4; Emburey 7–2–15–0; Gatting 3–0–14–0; Edmonds 7–3–19–3. *Second Innings*—Daniel 7–2–25–0; Cowans 5–2–4–0; Williams 4–1–5–0; Emburey 26–9–55–1; Edmonds 24–10–28–0; Gatting 1–0–1–0.

Umpires: H. D. Bird and D. O. Oslear.

At Cardiff, May 22, 23, 24. MIDDLESEX drew with GLAMORGAN.

## MIDDLESEX v SUSSEX

At Lord's, May 25, 27, 28. Middlesex won by an innings and 27 runs. Middlesex 24 pts, Sussex 2 pts. Toss won by Sussex. A one-sided match, on the same pitch on which MCC had just played the Australians, was always going Middlesex's way from the time Williams justified his being given the new ball. Gould, Sussex's acting-captain, initiated a minor revival against his former colleagues, but Middlesex were 87 ahead at the end of the first day after vigorous batting by Gatting and Butcher. Although only 30 overs were possible on the second day, Middlesex made them count, Downton playing stylishly and Emburey unconventionally. Sussex set themselves to bat all the last day, but were beaten soon after tea. Edmonds made the breakthrough and Cowans went through the middle order after lunch.

### Sussex

| | | | |
|---|---|---|---|
| G. D. Mendis b Williams | 5 | – c Slack b Edmonds | 33 |
| A. M. Green c Downton b Cowans | 2 | – run out | 38 |
| P. W. G. Parker c Downton b Williams | 9 | – b Daniel | 1 |
| A. P. Wells c Emburey b Cowans | 1 | – lbw b Cowans | 16 |
| C. M. Wells c Gatting b Cowans | 2 | – b Daniel | 42 |
| Imran Khan c Slack b Daniel | 11 | – lbw b Cowans | 1 |
| I. A. Greig c Edmonds b Daniel | 12 | – c Daniel b Cowans | 11 |
| *†I. J. Gould not out | 46 | – b Emburey | 17 |
| D. A. Reeve b Daniel | 23 | – b Emburey | 0 |
| C. E. Waller c Downton b Cowans | 4 | – b Cowans | 0 |
| A. N. Jones c Downton b Cowans | 8 | – not out | 3 |
| L-b 3, n-b 6 | 9 | L-b 6, w 1, n-b 11 | 18 |
| 1/2 2/12 3/17 4/17 5/23 6/33 7/51 8/108 9/124 | 132 | 1/54 2/55 3/83 4/107 5/110 6/126 7/168 8/168 9/171 | 180 |

Bonus points – Middlesex 4.

Bowling: *First Innings*—Williams 9–2–35–2; Cowans 13–2–44–5; Daniel 10–1–25–3; Gatting 6–1–14–0; Emburey 4–0–11–0. *Second Innings*—Daniel 18–5–72–2; Cowans 10–4–18–4; Williams 11–0–38–0; Edmonds 15–3–28–1; Emburey 15–9–18–2.

### Middlesex

| | |
|---|---|
| G. D. Barlow c Gould b Jones | 31 |
| W. N. Slack lbw b Reeve | 23 |
| *M. W. Gatting b C. M. Wells | 40 |
| R. O. Butcher lbw b C. M. Wells | 70 |
| C. T. Radley c Gould b Imran | 25 |
| †P. R. Downton not out | 85 |
| J. E. Emburey c Green b C. M. Wells | 39 |
| N. F. Williams not out | 6 |
| B 4, l-b 11, w 5 | 20 |
| 1/48 2/77 3/136 4/183 5/233 6/329 (6 wkts dec.) | 339 |

P. H. Edmonds, N. G. Cowans and W. W. Daniel did not bat.

Bonus points – Middlesex 4, Sussex 2.

Bowling: Imran 19–3–67–1; Jones 11–1–55–1; Greig 18–2–60–0; Reeve 17–5–64–1; Waller 8–1–24–0; C. M. Wells 24–5–54–3.

Umpires: J. Birkenshaw and K. E. Palmer.

At The Oval, May 29, 30, 31. MIDDLESEX drew with SURREY.

## MIDDLESEX v DERBYSHIRE

At Lord's, June 8, 10, 11. Drawn. Middlesex 5 pts, Derbyshire 6 pts. Toss won by Derbyshire. Morris, batting after only three balls, sustained Derbyshire well, playing all the bowlers with great assurance until, seeking his century, he was caught at extra cover. Mortensen had

Middlesex in trouble towards the end of the first day, and Gatting was unable to dig them out of it on the second, being last out as the innings folded about him. However, Derbyshire lacked the nerve or skill to turn the screw with quick scoring, taking 89 overs to make 196. Play was interrupted 50 minutes into the third day, and when the weather cleared Middlesex were set 280 at approximately 6 runs an over. They had barely begun when the gloom descended again.

## Derbyshire

| | | | |
|---|---|---|---|
| *K. J. Barnett c Downton b Daniel | 0 | – c Downton b Williams | 72 |
| I. S. Anderson c Gatting b Edmonds | 27 | – c Slack b Daniel | 55 |
| J. E. Morris c Emburey b Edmonds | 99 | – lbw b Cowans | 10 |
| B. Roberts c Downton b Edmonds | 17 | – not out | 39 |
| W. P. Fowler c Downton b Edmonds | 16 | – not out | 30 |
| G. Miller b Edmonds | 7 | | |
| R. J. Finney c Butcher b Williams | 10 | | |
| D. G. Moir c Slack b Williams | 46 | | |
| †B. J. M. Maher c Gatting b Williams | 0 | | |
| M. A. Holding st Downton b Edmonds | 6 | | |
| O. H. Mortensen not out | 2 | | |
| B 1, l-b 3, n-b 2 | 6 | B 4, l-b 5, w 1, n-b 5 | 15 |
| 1/0 2/76 3/106 4/160 5/169 6/170 7/190 8/190 9/199 | 236 | 1/132 2/139 3/160 (3 wkts dec.) | 221 |

Bonus points – Derbyshire 2, Middlesex 4.

Bowling: *First Innings*—Daniel 12–5–33–1; Cowans 7–3–19–0; Williams 13.4–4–43–3; Emburey 26–7–50–0; Edmonds 32–11–87–6. *Second Innings*—Daniel 14–3–27–1; Cowans 10–1–31–1; Williams 11–2–27–1; Emburey 34–14–59–0; Edmonds 37–10–67–0; Butcher 1–0–1–0.

## Middlesex

| | | | |
|---|---|---|---|
| G. D. Barlow b Holding | 18 | – c Maher b Mortensen | 12 |
| W. N. Slack b Mortensen | 0 | – not out | 4 |
| *M. W. Gatting c Fowler b Moir | 77 | – not out | 1 |
| R. O. Butcher c Miller b Mortensen | 11 | | |
| C. T. Radley lbw b Mortensen | 7 | | |
| †P. R. Downton c Anderson b Finney | 0 | | |
| J. E. Emburey c Barnett b Holding | 9 | | |
| P. H. Edmonds c Maher b Mortensen | 27 | | |
| N. F. Williams c Roberts b Finney | 0 | | |
| N. G. Cowans c Fowler b Finney | 13 | | |
| W. W. Daniel not out | 8 | | |
| B 6, l-b 2 | 8 | | |
| 1/0 2/25 3/36 4/60 5/67 6/87 7/128 8/131 9/163 | 178 | 1/15 (1 wkt) | 17 |

Bonus points – Middlesex 1, Derbyshire 4.

Bowling: *First Innings*—Holding 17–3–66–2; Mortensen 20–5–47–4; Finney 12–2–45–3; Miller 1–0–1–0; Moir 2–0–11–1. *Second Innings*—Holding 2–0–6–0; Mortensen 1.5–0–11–1.

Umpires: K. J. Lyons and D. O. Oslear.

At Bournemouth, June 12, 13, 14. MIDDLESEX drew with HAMPSHIRE.

## MIDDLESEX v LEICESTERSHIRE

At Lord's, June 15, 17, 18. Drawn. Middlesex 6 pts, Leicestershire 4 pts. Toss won by Middlesex. Barlow hit six boundaries in the first seven overs of the match, thereby giving a false impression of how Middlesex would play it. For after Barlow's dismissal the batsmen toiled.

Slack faced 147 balls for his 53 and Tomlins 149 for his 43. On the second day Leicestershire were progressing nicely at 172 for four when Daniel, who had been bowling very short, began pitching the ball up and claimed a wicket in each of five successive overs. When Middlesex batted a second time Barlow again played beautifully as he and Slack put on 146 on the second evening. They went on to compile their second double-century stand of the season, and Leicestershire were set 296 to win in a minimum of 73 overs. They lost all interest when bad light caused the first of many stoppages, and although Middlesex kept trying between breaks, Williams, who was warned for excessive bouncers, and Daniel pounded the ball in too short to be effective. Their methods encouraged the umpires to suspend play for a total of 23 overs.

## Middlesex

| | | | |
|---|---|---|---|
| G. D. Barlow c Garnham b Agnew | 31 | – c sub b Parsons | 102 |
| W. N. Slack c Agnew b Cook | 53 | – b Cook | 109 |
| K. P. Tomlins lbw b Cook | 43 | – c Whitaker b Clift | 1 |
| R. O. Butcher lbw b Taylor | 24 | – not out | 11 |
| *C. T. Radley b Clift | 41 | – not out | 3 |
| J. F. Sykes b Cook | 4 | | |
| P. H. Edmonds b Cook | 13 | | |
| N. F. Williams not out | 16 | | |
| †C. P. Metson c Garnham b Taylor | 6 | | |
| S. P. Hughes c Garnham b Taylor | 0 | | |
| W. W. Daniel c Cobb b Agnew | 8 | | |
| L-b 13, n-b 5 | 18 | B 2, l-b 2, n-b 5 | 9 |
| 1/51 2/120 3/141 4/165 5/177 6/223 7/223 8/243 9/247 | 257 | 1/203 2/210 3/227 (3 wkts dec.) | 235 |

Bonus points – Middlesex 2, Leicestershire 3 (Score at 100 overs: 232-7).

Bowling: *First Innings*—Agnew 18.3–2–78–2; Taylor 17–3–45–3; Parsons 16–7–22–0; Clift 19–5–31–1; Cook 35–13–59–4; Briers 2–0–9–0. *Second Innings*—Agnew 11–0–53–0; Taylor 8–3–12–0; Clift 16–3–45–1; Parsons 17–3–55–1; Cook 23–5–66–1.

## Leicestershire

| | | | |
|---|---|---|---|
| I. P. Butcher c Metson b Edmonds | 29 | – not out | 71 |
| J. C. Balderstone c Metson b Williams | 7 | – b Daniel | 0 |
| R. A. Cobb c Metson b Hughes | 48 | – c Metson b Daniel | 13 |
| J. J. Whitaker b Edmonds | 7 | – retired hurt | 30 |
| *N. E. Briers b Daniel | 45 | – c Barlow b Hughes | 10 |
| †M. A. Garnham b Daniel | 27 | – not out | 6 |
| P. B. Clift b Daniel | 0 | | |
| G. J. Parsons b Daniel | 5 | | |
| N. G. B. Cook lbw b Daniel | 0 | | |
| J. P. Agnew c Williams b Edmonds | 6 | | |
| L. B. Taylor not out | 0 | | |
| B 1, l-b 13, n-b 9 | 23 | B 2, l-b 4, nb 13 | 19 |
| 1/9 2/56 3/70 4/134 5/172 6/172 7/187 8/189 9/197 | 197 | 1/16 2/47 3/130 (3 wkts) | 149 |

Bonus points – Leicestershire 1, Middlesex 4.

Bowling: *First Innings*—Daniel 16.3–3–48–5; Williams 11–1–30–1; Edmonds 17–5–38–3; Hughes 16–1–67–1. *Second Innings*—Daniel 13–2–61–2; Williams 10–1–50–0; Edmonds 10–3–25–0; Hughes 5–3–5–1; Sykes 2–1–2–0.

Umpires: J. Birkenshaw and D. G. L. Evans.

At Trent Bridge, June 22, 24, 25. MIDDLESEX beat NOTTINGHAMSHIRE by ten wickets.

At Worcester, June 26, 27, 28. MIDDLESEX beat WORCESTERSHIRE by three wickets.

At Northampton, July 6, 8, 9. MIDDLESEX beat NORTHAMPTONSHIRE by 141 runs.

## MIDDLESEX v NOTTINGHAMSHIRE

At Lord's, July 10, 11, 12. Nottinghamshire won by five wickets. Nottinghamshire 22 pts, Middlesex 6 pts. Toss won by Nottinghamshire. A level match finally tilted Nottinghamshire's way, though Middlesex took a firm early grip with another productive stand between Barlow and Slack, their seventh century partnership in eleven games. Rice dismissed Barlow and controlled events during the afternoon as Tomlins tried to sustain the Middlesex innings. Randall "walked" when the umpire had not given him out in Nottinghamshire's first innings, which Williams ended with three wickets in a span of ten balls. Middlesex were comfortably increasing their lead on the second evening when Hadlee made a decisive intervention with three late wickets and a slip catch. Early next morning he removed Barlow, 94 overnight, with a diving return catch. Needing 246 in 92 overs, Nottinghamshire won on the foundation of Broad and Randall's alliance of 173 in 44 overs. Randall played with increasing joy, reaching his century only four minutes after Broad passed 50 and hitting eighteen 4s.

### Middlesex

| | | | |
|---|---|---|---|
| G. D. Barlow c Randall b Rice | 97 | – c and b Hadlee | 112 |
| W. N. Slack run out | 35 | – c Johnson b Hadlee | 8 |
| K. P. Tomlins c French b Rice | 46 | – run out | 15 |
| R. O. Butcher lbw b Cooper | 5 | – c and b Hadlee | 34 |
| *C. T. Radley c French b Cooper | 22 | – c Hadlee b Cooper | 0 |
| J. D. Carr c French b Hemmings | 1 | – c Broad b Hadlee | 1 |
| J. F. Sykes lbw b Hemmings | 4 | – c Johnson b Hadlee | 3 |
| N. F. Williams c Birch b Rice | 9 | – c Rice b Cooper | 11 |
| †C. P. Metson c Randall b Rice | 5 | – b Hadlee | 2 |
| S. P. Hughes not out | 8 | – not out | 1 |
| W. W. Daniel st French b Hemmings | 0 | – c French b Hadlee | 0 |
| B 5, l-b 4, w 4, n-b 1 | 14 | B 8, l-b 2, w 1, n-b 3 | 14 |
| 1/137 2/137 3/145 4/206 5/213 6/217 7/227 8/234 9/239 | 246 | 1/25 2/50 3/137 4/138 5/141 6/155 7/190 8/198 9/201 | 201 |

Bonus points – Middlesex 2, Nottinghamshire 4.

Bowling: *First Innings*—Hadlee 15–6–31–0; Saxelby 16–6–41–0; Cooper 22–9–67–2; Hemmings 18.2–3–41–3; Rice 21–4–57–4. *Second Innings*—Hadlee 21.3–8–34–7; Cooper 23–3–88–2; Hemmings 12–4–15–0; Rice 9–3–16–0; Saxelby 7–0–30–0; Such 4–1–8–0.

### Nottinghamshire

| | | | |
|---|---|---|---|
| B. C. Broad b Hughes | 53 | – c Metson b Sykes | 56 |
| †B. N. French b Williams | 16 | – c Carr b Daniel | 9 |
| D. W. Randall c Metson b Williams | 45 | – c Carr b Sykes | 115 |
| *C. E. B. Rice c Metson b Daniel | 0 | – (5) not out | 22 |
| P. Johnson c Tomlins b Sykes | 32 | – (4) b Carr | 12 |
| J. D. Birch b Sykes | 1 | – c and b Sykes | 5 |
| R. J. Hadlee not out | 21 | – not out | 9 |
| E. E. Hemmings c Butcher b Williams | 10 | | |
| K. Saxelby lbw b Williams | 1 | | |
| K. E. Cooper b Williams | 0 | | |
| P. M. Such lbw b Daniel | 0 | | |
| B 1, l-b 5, n-b 17 | 23 | B 8, l-b 4, n-b 9 | 21 |
| 1/47 2/106 3/107 4/155 5/156 6/172 7/191 8/193 9/193 | 202 | 1/18 2/191 3/208 4/208 5/230 | (5 wkts) 249 |

Bonus points – Nottinghamshire 2, Middlesex 4.

Bowling: *First Innings*—Daniel 14.5–2–63–2; Williams 18–1–71–5; Hughes 12–1–44–1; Sykes 6–1–18–2. *Second Innings*—Daniel 11–2–49–1; Williams 10–2–44–0; Hughes 11–1–41–0; Sykes 21–7–58–3; Carr 15.1–5–45–1; Butcher 1–1–0–0.

Umpires: M. J. Kitchen and B. Leadbeater.

## MIDDLESEX v SOMERSET

At Lord's, July 13, 15, 16. Drawn. Middlesex 7 pts, Somerset 7 pts. Toss won by Middlesex. Barlow, maintaining his heavy-scoring mid-season form, had to work diligently to overcome an unusually slow pitch, though either side of reaching his century he played some muscular shots. Somerset's spinners, Booth, Marks and Richards, achieved some turn and just had the better of the middle order. Richards followed up many glorious innings on the ground with another. Despite reintroducing himself to the Lord's crowd spectacularly, hitting Sykes for three 6s, it was one of his less flamboyant efforts. He used the short Tavern boundary cleverly for the majority of his sixteen 4s. Somerset attempted in vain to establish the big lead that Richards's batting had promised, and the match was already looking like stalemate before rain removed 22 overs from the final day.

### Middlesex

| | | | |
|---|---|---|---|
| G. D. Barlow c and b Booth | 132 | – c Booth b Richards | 38 |
| W. N. Slack c Gard b Davis | 26 | – c Gard b Dredge | 20 |
| K. P. Tomlins c Marks b Richards | 9 | – st Gard b Booth | 58 |
| R. O. Butcher lbw b Dredge | 20 | – b Marks | 28 |
| *C. T. Radley c Harden b Booth | 22 | – not out | 52 |
| J. D. Carr c Gard b Booth | 13 | – c Popplewell b Harden | 8 |
| J. F. Sykes c Richards b Davis | 14 | – not out | 0 |
| G. D. Rose c Richards b Booth | 15 | | |
| N. F. Williams c Felton b Marks | 39 | | |
| S. P. Hughes b Marks | 0 | | |
| †C. P. Metson not out | 4 | | |
| L-b 8, n-b 7 | 15 | B 6, l-b 10, w 1, n-b 4 | 21 |
| 1/49 2/79 3/151 4/211 5/233 6/234 7/252 8/275 9/286 | 309 | 1/49 2/89 3/134 4/179 5/223 (5 wkts dec.) | 225 |

Bonus points – Middlesex 3, Somerset 3 (Score at 100 overs: 276-8).

Bowling: *First Innings*—Dredge 25–4–72–1; Davis 23–2–65–2; Richards 15–4–32–1; Marks 17.3–5–44–2; Booth 29–8–88–4. *Second Innings*—Dredge 12–4–40–1; Davis 9–0–44–0; Richards 14–3–34–1; Marks 28–9–49–1; Booth 22–8–38–1; Harden 4.3–1–4–1.

### Somerset

| | |
|---|---|
| N. F. M. Popplewell b Hughes | 25 |
| P. M. Roebuck c Tomlins b Williams | 11 |
| N. A. Felton lbw b Rose | 16 |
| I. V. A. Richards c Butcher b Sykes | 135 |
| R. E. Hayward b Williams | 38 |
| R. J. Harden c Butcher b Sykes | 29 |
| *V. J. Marks b Williams | 0 |
| †T. Gard c Metson b Rose | 9 |
| M. R. Davis b Carr | 35 |
| S. C. Booth c Butcher b Sykes | 9 |
| C. H. Dredge not out | 9 |
| L-b 17, w 1, n-b 11 | 29 |
| 1/27 2/46 3/82 4/226 5/248 6/249 7/272 8/316 9/330 | 345 |

Bonus points – Somerset 4, Middlesex 4.

Bowling: Williams 26–2–86–3; Hughes 23–2–99–1; Rose 21–6–44–2; Sykes 24.4–5–97–3; Carr 3–1–2–1.

Umpires: B. Dudleston and M. J. Kitchen.

## MIDDLESEX v NORTHAMPTONSHIRE

At Uxbridge, July 24, 25, 26. Middlesex won by an innings and 161 runs. Middlesex 23 pts, Northamptonshire 2 pts. Toss won by Northamptonshire. Middlesex were eager to take maximum advantage of a week with their Test players available for two successive matches on what has been a lucky ground for them. They began it almost perfectly. Daniel and Cowans, aided by some excellent slip-catching, brought Harper in at 73 for six, but the West Indian hit out in the most extravagant Caribbean style, striking eight 6s and seven 4s off 85 balls, scoring all but 21 of the last 118 runs. Nevertheless Northamptonshire were all out in 39.1 overs, and

Middlesex had no trouble taking the lead before the end of the first day. On the second they sacrificed a batting point in their strategy of building a big lead. Radley (one 6, one 5, 26 4s) hit his first-ever double-hundred, and his partnership with Downton, who reached three figures for the first time in a first-class match, put on 289 in 107 overs. In all Radley batted for 382 minutes. To win, Middlesex needed nine wickets on the last day and were troubled only by bad light and Lamb, who held them up after Edmonds had taken three wickets in two overs at the start. However, a diving catch by Barlow straight after tea, followed by the immediate dismissal of Harper, brought Middlesex a win that took them back to the top of the table.

## Northamptonshire

| | | | |
|---|---|---|---|
| *G. Cook c Emburey b Daniel | 4 | – b Daniel | 16 |
| W. Larkins c Emburey b Cowans | 4 | – c and b Edmonds | 34 |
| R. J. Boyd-Moss run out | 11 | – (4) b Edmonds | 4 |
| A. J. Lamb lbw b Cowans | 5 | – (5) c Barlow b Gatting | 61 |
| R. J. Bailey c Radley b Williams | 36 | – (6) c Gatting b Edmonds | 6 |
| R. G. Williams c Gatting b Daniel | 7 | – (7) lbw b Cowans | 29 |
| D. J. Wild c Emburey b Williams | 10 | – (8) not out | 23 |
| R. A. Harper not out | 97 | – (9) c Slack b Daniel | 0 |
| †D. Ripley b Cowans | 4 | – (10) b Daniel | 5 |
| N. A. Mallender b Cowans | 0 | – (3) c Slack b Edmonds | 10 |
| B. J. Griffiths run out | 1 | – b Daniel | 0 |
| B 4, l-b 2, n-b 6 | 12 | B 12, l-b 4, n-b 11 | 27 |
| 1/8 2/13 3/30 4/33 5/45 6/73 7/93 8/162 9/162 | 191 | 1/35 2/64 3/68 4/69 5/87 6/149 7/197 8/202 9/215 | 215 |

Bonus points – Northamptonshire 1, Middlesex 4.

Bowling: *First Innings*—Daniel 12–0–83–2; Cowans 11.1–0–30–4; Williams 8–2–35–2; Edmonds 8–1–37–0. *Second Innings*—Daniel 18.1–2–73–4; Cowans 8–3–12–1; Edmonds 23–8–54–4; Gatting 3–1–6–1; Emburey 27–13–41–0; Williams 5–0–13–0.

## Middlesex

| | |
|---|---|
| G. D. Barlow c and b Griffiths | 32 |
| W. N. Slack lbw b Griffiths | 16 |
| *M. W. Gatting c Ripley b Harper | 51 |
| R. O. Butcher c Harper b Williams | 39 |
| C. T. Radley c Bailey b Williams | 200 |
| †P. R. Downton b Williams | 104 |
| J. E. Emburey c Boyd-Moss b Wild | 68 |
| N. F. Williams not out | 19 |
| P. H. Edmonds b Williams | 1 |
| N. G. Cowans not out | 15 |
| B 11, l-b 5, n-b 6 | 22 |
| 1/42 2/59 3/127 4/147 5/436 6/491 7/547 8/552 (8 wkts dec.) | 567 |

W. W. Daniel did not bat.

Bonus points – Middlesex 3, Northamptonshire 1 (Score at 100 overs: 288-4).

Bowling: Mallender 27–5–90–0; Griffiths 26–5–95–2; Harper 38–14–87–1; Larkins 14–1–47–0; Williams 42–10–131–4; Boyd-Moss 8–1–39–0; Wild 11.5–1–62–1.

Umpires: J. H. Harris and J. A. Jameson.

## MIDDLESEX v LANCASHIRE

At Uxbridge, July 27, 29, 30. Drawn. Middlesex 4 pts, Lancashire 1 pt. Toss won by Middlesex. Middlesex's hopes of another rich haul of points were ruined when rain washed out the last two days. On the first day they had built a commanding platform. Barlow and Slack provided a sound start before falling in the same over to Watkinson. Butcher then played even more destructively than Gatting in a stand of 158 in 39 overs, his half-century containing ten 4s and one 6. Rain ended the game for good at 5.23, though there was sufficient hope of play for Middlesex to declare on the Monday.

## Middlesex

| | | | |
|---|---|---|---|
| G. D. Barlow c Maynard b Watkinson | 28 | C. T. Radley not out | 64 |
| W. N. Slack b Watkinson | 32 | †P. R. Downton not out | 19 |
| *M. W. Gatting c Maynard b Watkinson | 74 | B 7, n-b 8 | 15 |
| R. O. Butcher c Simmons b Watkinson | 86 | 1/62 2/63 3/221 4/250 (4 wkts dec.) | 318 |

J. E. Emburey, N. F. Williams, P. H. Edmonds, N. G. Cowans and W. W. Daniel did not bat.

Bonus points – Middlesex 4, Lancashire 1.

Bowling: Allott 22–11–30–0; Patterson 12–0–69–0; Watkinson 22.2–5–71–4; Simmons 19–2–62–0; Folley 16–0–79–0.

## Lancashire

G. Fowler, D. W. Varey, M. R. Chadwick, *J. Abrahams, N. H. Fairbrother, M. Watkinson, †C. Maynard, J. Simmons, I. Folley, P. J. W. Allott and B. P. Patterson.

Umpires: J. H. Harris and J. A. Jameson.

# MIDDLESEX v GLOUCESTERSHIRE

At Lord's, July 31, August 1, 2. Drawn. Middlesex 6 pts, Gloucestershire 7 pts. Toss won by Middlesex. Lacking their Test players, Middlesex were reasonably content to keep Gloucestershire to bonus points in a contest between the first and second teams in the Championship table. Rain allowed only ten overs on the last day, preventing Gloucestershire from pushing for victory. After making little attempt on the first day to break the hold achieved by Walsh and Graveney, Middlesex batted on into the second. Gloucestershire were much more positive, Bainbridge hitting eleven 4s in his first 50 off 56 balls and Davison playing in his usual dominant way for 204 minutes. But at 268 for three Carr, the Oxford Blue, began working his way through the middle order, taking six consecutive wickets with his off-breaks as only 83 were added.

## Middlesex

| | | | |
|---|---|---|---|
| G. D. Barlow c Brassington b Walsh | 10 | – not out | 16 |
| W. N. Slack c Curran b Graveney | 44 | – not out | 25 |
| A. J. T. Miller b Lloyds | 16 | | |
| R. O. Butcher b Graveney | 37 | | |
| *C. T. Radley c Brassington b Lloyds | 57 | | |
| J. D. Carr c and b Lawrence | 29 | | |
| J. F. Sykes c Bainbridge b Graveney | 16 | | |
| N. F. Williams c Stovold b Walsh | 18 | | |
| †C. P. Metson not out | 14 | | |
| N. G. Cowans b Walsh | 15 | | |
| W. W. Daniel c Brassington b Walsh | 4 | | |
| B 5, l-b 7, w 5, n-b 12 | 29 | B 4, l-b 2 | 6 |
| 1/19 2/81 3/95 4/150 5/201 6/219 7/244 8/260 9/280 | 289 | | (no wkt) 47 |

Bonus points – Middlesex 3, Gloucestershire 3 (Score at 100 overs: 250-7).

Bowling: *First Innings*—Lawrence 17–2–50–1; Walsh 28.3–5–86–4; Curran 6–1–16–0; Bainbridge 5–1–13–0; Lloyds 19–3–41–2; Graveney 40–16–71–3. *Second Innings*—Lawrence 5.2–0–24–0; Walsh 4–2–9–0; Lloyds 1–0–8–0.

### Gloucestershire

| | | | |
|---|---|---|---|
| A. W. Stovold c Metson b Carr | 92 | C. A. Walsh b Carr | 0 |
| P. W. Romaines c Metson b Cowans | 12 | D. V. Lawrence c and b Carr | 13 |
| C. W. J. Athey c Cowans b Daniel | 16 | †A. J. Brassington not out | 3 |
| P. Bainbridge c Butcher b Williams | 60 | B 13, l-b 7, n-b 7 | 27 |
| B. F. Davison c Sykes b Carr | 111 | | |
| K. M. Curran c Butcher b Carr | 6 | 1/21 2/56 3/144 (9 wkts dec.) | 351 |
| J. W. Lloyds c Barlow b Carr | 5 | 4/268 5/299 6/322 | |
| *D. A. Graveney not out | 6 | 7/325 8/325 9/346 | |

Bonus points – Gloucestershire 4, Middlesex 3 (Score at 100 overs: 326-8).

Bowling: Daniel 18–2–67–1; Cowans 13–0–64–1; Williams 13–0–53–1; Sykes 32–5–86–0; Carr 29–6–61–6.

Umpires: B. Leadbeater and R. A. White.

At Chelmsford, August 3, 5, 6. MIDDLESEX lost to ESSEX by seven wickets.

At Lord's, August 10, 11, 12, 13. MIDDLESEX drew with AUSTRALIANS (See Australian tour section).

At Weston-super-Mare, August 14, 15, 16. MIDDLESEX drew with SOMERSET.

## MIDDLESEX v SURREY

At Lord's, August 17, 19, 20. Drawn. Middlesex 5 pts, Surrey 5 pts. Toss won by Surrey. Cowans bowled with great fire in overcoming a pitch that played with reasonable blandness. After taking Surrey's first three wickets cheaply, he returned after lunch to remove Stewart and Jesty. Daniel's supporting contribution were the wickets of Lynch and of Monkhouse, who had helped in a slight recovery. Middlesex were making fair progress at 115 for three when Gray took two late wickets on the first evening. On the second day Radley made a dogged, unbeaten 47 while Gray removed his partners, and a fine match was building up. However, a storm during lunch prevented Surrey from resuming until 5.15. They then made 112 for two before the close with Lynch, in partnership with Clinton for 38 overs, playing at his most destructive for 125 minutes and hitting his sixth hundred of the summer. Middlesex, eventually set to make 283 in 67 overs, were going quite well when rain ended the chase.

### Surrey

| | | | |
|---|---|---|---|
| A. R. Butcher lbw b Cowans | 13 | – c Sykes b Cowans | 12 |
| G. S. Clinton c Barlow b Cowans | 0 | – c and b Hughes | 63 |
| A. Needham c and b Cowans | 6 | – (6) c and b Sykes | 10 |
| A. J. Stewart lbw b Cowans | 44 | – (3) lbw b Cowans | 6 |
| M. A. Lynch c and b Daniel | 26 | – (4) b Hughes | 108 |
| *T. E. Jesty c Sykes b Cowans | 7 | – (5) lbw b Carr | 27 |
| †C. J. Richards b Hughes | 0 | – not out | 9 |
| R. J. Doughty b Hughes | 22 | – c Butcher b Sykes | 5 |
| G. Monkhouse c Metson b Daniel | 47 | | |
| P. I. Pocock not out | 8 | – (9) not out | 3 |
| A. H. Gray run out | 3 | | |
| B 2, l-b 9, n-b 7 | 18 | B 4, l-b 16, w 2, n-b 6 | 28 |
| 1/4 2/12 3/40 4/83 5/100 6/109 7/109 8/165 9/185 | 194 | 1/20 2/28 3/205 4/212 5/249 6/261 7/266 (7 wkts dec.) | 271 |

Bonus points – Surrey 1, Middlesex 4.

Bowling: *First Innings*—Daniel 16.2–2–47–2; Cowans 15–3–61–5; Hughes 20–5–56–2; Sykes 6–1–13–0; Carr 3–1–6–0. *Second Innings*—Daniel 16–2–61–0; Cowans 16–0–70–2; Hughes 15–1–71–2; Sykes 9–1–29–2; Carr 6–1–20–1.

## Middlesex

| | | | |
|---|---|---|---|
| G. D. Barlow c Richards b Doughty | 9 | – not out | 28 |
| W. N. Slack lbw b Gray | 36 | – not out | 23 |
| K. R. Brown c Stewart b Butcher | 20 | | |
| R. O. Butcher c Stewart b Gray | 26 | | |
| *C. T. Radley not out | 47 | | |
| S. P. Hughes lbw b Gray | 0 | | |
| J. D. Carr c Stewart b Gray | 6 | | |
| J. F. Sykes c Richards b Gray | 4 | | |
| †C. P. Metson c Lynch b Gray | 0 | | |
| N. G. Cowans b Monkhouse | 13 | | |
| W. W. Daniel b Gray | 0 | | |
| B 2, l-b 8, w 3, n-b 9 | 22 | W 1, n-b 4 | 5 |
| 1/15 2/74 3/78 4/115 5/115 6/130 7/144 8/150 9/175 | 183 | (no wkt) | 56 |

Bonus points – Middlesex 1, Surrey 4.

Bowling: *First Innings*—Gray 26–7–68–7; Doughty 7–2–21–1; Monkhouse 18–1–46–1; Butcher 12–3–26–1; Pocock 3–0–12–0. *Second Innings*—Gray 5–0–29–0; Doughty 4.4–0–27–0.

Umpires: B. Dudleston and A. G. T. Whitehead.

At Hove, August 24, 26, 27. MIDDLESEX lost to SUSSEX by 103 runs.

At Leicester, September 4, 5, 6. MIDDLESEX beat LEICESTERSHIRE by ten wickets.

## MIDDLESEX v ESSEX

At Lord's, September 11, 12, 13. Drawn. Middlesex 7 pts, Essex 4 pts. Toss won by Essex. Williams and Gatting were outstanding on the first day, when Middlesex were fully in control. Yet the next two days brought them just one more point. Williams, cutting the ball away from the bat at high pace, took three wickets in his first eleven balls and collected two more by the end of his eighth over for figures of five for 11. Gooch, batting down the order following a meeting with the secretary of the TCCB, could not repair the damage. Slack went first ball, but thereafter Middlesex made excellent progress throughout the afternoon as Gatting and Butcher took advantage of a weakened Essex attack, adding 158 in 47 overs. They ended the day at 236 for three, but the next morning Topley and Pont swept aside the remaining seven wickets for 43 runs in nineteen overs, whereupon Gooch and Hardie continued their prolific September form. As Middlesex's catching deteriorated, Essex added 179 on the last day. Middlesex needed 275 in 51 overs, and although there was a possibility while Gatting and Butcher were together, Gatting was soon organising a holding operation.

## Essex

| First Innings | | Second Innings | |
|---|---|---|---|
| P. J. Prichard c Downton b Williams | 0 | (3) b Edmonds | 6 |
| B. R. Hardie c Butcher b Williams | 5 | c Downton b Edmonds | 48 |
| A. W. Lilley c Emburey b Williams | 4 | (5) c Brown b Cowans | 60 |
| K. S. McEwan b Williams | 0 | b Edmonds | 4 |
| *K. W. R. Fletcher c Downton b Williams | 13 | (6) b Edmonds | 39 |
| G. A. Gooch c Downton b Cowans | 19 | (1) lbw b Gatting | 145 |
| †D. E. East b Gatting | 18 | b Daniel | 100 |
| I. L. Pont c Emburey b Gatting | 11 | c and b Daniel | 12 |
| J. K. Lever not out | 10 | b Cowans | 7 |
| T. D. Topley b Daniel | 0 | not out | 9 |
| D. L. Acfield run out | 2 | b Williams | 1 |
| L-b 1, n-b 9 | 10 | B 7, l-b 9, n-b 14 | 30 |
| 1/2 2/5 3/5 4/14 5/28 6/61 7/69 8/81 9/86 | 92 | 1/111 2/130 3/146 4/274 5/274 6/378 7/433 8/443 9/460 | 461 |

Bonus points – Middlesex 4.

Bowling: *First Innings*—Daniel 9.4–0–51–1; Williams 9–4–15–5; Gatting 6–0–20–2; Cowans 6–2–5–1. *Second Innings*—Daniel 20–2–91–2; Williams 20.3–2–73–1; Cowans 18–3–62–2; Edmonds 40–7–101–4; Emburey 27–2–78–0; Gatting 14–2–40–1.

## Middlesex

| First Innings | | Second Innings | |
|---|---|---|---|
| W. N. Slack c Gooch b Lever | 0 | c Gooch b Pont | 20 |
| K. R. Brown c Gooch b Topley | 25 | c Gooch b Pont | 20 |
| *M. W. Gatting c McEwan b Topley | 114 | not out | 83 |
| R. O. Butcher c Lever b Acfield | 77 | (5) c Lever b Gooch | 20 |
| C. T. Radley lbw b Pont | 21 | (6) lbw b Gooch | 0 |
| †P. R. Downton c Gooch b Topley | 1 | (7) b Topley | 12 |
| J. E. Emburey c Prichard b Pont | 10 | (8) c and b Gooch | 16 |
| N. F. Williams run out | 2 | (9) not out | 4 |
| P. H. Edmonds c McEwan b Topley | 7 | (4) b Pont | 10 |
| N. G. Cowans c Lilley b Pont | 4 | | |
| W. W. Daniel not out | 0 | | |
| B 2, l-b 12, w 1, n-b 3 | 18 | B 4, l-b 5, w 1, n-b 1 | 11 |
| 1/0 2/47 3/205 4/242 5/243 6/264 7/267 8/275 9/279 | 279 | 1/33 2/48 3/66 4/117 5/118 6/133 7/169 | (7 wkts) 196 |

Bonus points – Middlesex 3, Essex 4.

Bowling: *First Innings*—Lever 12–3–22–1; Pont 23–4–81–3; Topley 27.1–8–57–4; Acfield 21–4–74–1; Gooch 14–3–31–0. *Second Innings*—Lever 10–1–30–0; Pont 17–5–74–3; Gooch 15.4–1–46–3; Topley 8–1–37–1.

Umpires: C. Cook and J. H. Hampshire.

At Edgbaston, September 14, 16, 17. MIDDLESEX beat WARWICKSHIRE by an innings and 74 runs.

# NORTHAMPTONSHIRE

*President:* 1985 – D. C. Lucas
*Chairman, Cricket Committee:* A. P. Arnold
*Secretary/Manager:* S. P. Coverdale
County Ground, Wantage Road,
Northampton NN1 4TJ
(Telephone: 0604-32917)
*Captain:* G. Cook
*Coach:* B. L. Reynolds

The start of the 1985 season coincided with the end of an era for Northamptonshire, with the retirement of the county's tireless secretary, Ken Turner, along with the club's President and former opening batsman, Dennis Brookes, after a combined total of nearly 90 years' service. The veteran all-rounder, David Steele, had also decided to call it a day during the winter. The new order began to establish itself with the appointment of Stephen Coverdale, a 30-year-old Yorkshireman, as secretary-manager, the election of a streamlined general committee and the arrival in May of the West Indian off-spinner, Roger Harper.

With the biggest problem always likely to be that of bowling teams out twice to win Britannic Assurance Championship games, Geoff Cook, looking ahead to his fifth season in charge, felt his side's best chance of a trophy would be in one of the limited-overs competitions.

In the event, Northamptonshire challenged keenly until the final week for the John Player Sunday League, when defeat at Worcester and victory for leading rivals pushed them down into fifth place. They made an unlucky exit from the Benson and Hedges Cup, losing to Kent on bowlers' striking-rate in their group matches after rain had nullified an excellent start by Northamptonshire's opening batsmen in the quarter-final at Northampton. There could be no blame attached to the elements, though, for the defeat by Gloucestershire in the second round of the NatWest Bank Trophy.

Northamptonshire's Championship campaign progressed in fits and starts, and tenth position, one higher than in 1984, was a good deal better than looked likely when, owing to the never-distant rain and some inconsistent performances, they occupied fifteenth place at the end of August. However, victories in the last two games – against Hampshire and Worcestershire – ensured a respectable finish to a season which began with hopes high after a win in the opening game at Derby. Surrey and Warwickshire were beaten in successive matches at the end of June, but four games were lost, two of them heavily to the eventual champions, Middlesex.

Full credit was due to Cook, in his benefit year and weakened by a serious winter operation, for the enterprising and imaginative way he again led the side. One of the county game's most respected figures, he also remained one of its most consistent batsmen, passing 1,000 first-class runs for the tenth time in eleven seasons. His regular opening partner, Wayne Larkins, was the leading scorer for the fourth year running with 1,549 runs, and, despite failing on numerous occasions to turn a dazzling start into a century, his magnificent 117 against Surrey proved again his match-winning capabilities.

The best of Allan Lamb was seen in the one-day games, his Championship appearances being limited to only eleven through England calls, so that apart from Cook and Larkins only Robert Bailey reached 1,000 runs. With the committee aware of the difficulties he was likely to face in his second full season, the 21-year-old Bailey was given his county cap after a century against Hampshire in the first home Championship match. Later he battled through a lean spell to return with an unbeaten 107 against the Australians. Robin Boyd-Moss, out of action until early June with a back injury, and Richard Williams showed their best form only in patches, but a bonus was the emergence of Alastair Storie, born in Glasgow and brought up in South Africa. His technique and determination produced 407 runs in his first seven county games, including a century on his début, against Hampshire. Still only twenty, he would appear to have a bright future.

The all-round contribution of Harper was considerable, and could well be even greater in a summer of harder pitches. A popular and committed addition to the team, he got through more Championship overs than any Northamptonshire bowler since Brian Crump in 1968. With the arrival of Nick Cook from Leicestershire, the county should have one of the best spin attacks in the country in 1986. In addition, Harper played a number of spectacular innings and his fielding was sometimes an inspiration. Only his performances in one-day cricket fell short of expectations. The two local all-rounders, David Capel and Duncan Wild, both had their moments, Capel's notably with the ball towards the end of the season. In few other sides would the elegant Wild have received such limited batting opportunities after scoring impressively at numbers three and four in 1984.

Northamptonshire's most pressing need is still of a fast bowling partner for Neil Mallender, who started the season looking sharper and stronger following a successful winter in New Zealand, but he suffered later through lack of genuine support. Alan Walker bowled economically in the limited-overs competitions, but he was dogged by an injury and had to give way to Jim Griffiths, who, once given his chance, bowled well and topped the averages.

Two young fast bowlers with first-team experience, Ray Joseph from Guyana and Matthew Wheeler, were released at the end of the season, and Northamptonshire will now be looking for progress from the nineteen-year-old Gareth Smith, a left-arm fast bowler from the Durham Senior League.

In August the vice-captain, George Sharp, who broke a finger at Edgbaston late in June, retired to concentrate on a business career after fifteen years as the county's first-choice wicket-keeper. His departure should open up a regular place for David Ripley, Sharp's deputy for the past two seasons, though soon after the end of the season Stuart Waterton, another promising young wicket-keeper, was signed from Kent. – A.R.

NORTHAMPTONSHIRE 1985

[*Bill Smith*

*Back row*: A. C. Storie, A. Walker, D. J. Capel, R. A. Harper, B. J. Griffiths, R. A. Bailey, D. J. Wild. *Front row*: W. Larkins, A. J. Lamb, G. Cook (*captain*), G. Sharp, N. A. Mallender. *Insets*: R. J. Boyd-Moss, R. G. Williams, D. Ripley.

## NORTHAMPTONSHIRE RESULTS

*All first-class matches – Played 25: Won 5, Lost 4, Drawn 16.*

*County Championship matches – Played 24: Won 5, Lost 4, Drawn 15.*

*Bonus points – Batting 52, Bowling 51.*

*Competition placings – Britannic Assurance County Championship, 10th; NatWest Bank Trophy, 2nd round; Benson and Hedges Cup, q-f; John Player League, 5th.*

## BRITANNIC ASSURANCE CHAMPIONSHIP AVERAGES

### BATTING

| | *Birthplace* | *M* | *I* | *NO* | *R* | *HI* | *Avge* |
|---|---|---|---|---|---|---|---|
| A. C. Storie ...... | *Bishopbriggs, Glasgow* | 7 | 12 | 2 | 407 | 106 | 40.70 |
| R. A. Harper ..... | *Georgetown, BG* | 22 | 26 | 7 | 734 | 127 | 38.63 |
| ‡G. Cook ......... | *Middlesbrough* | 23 | 37 | 4 | 1,271 | 126 | 38.51 |
| ‡W. Larkins ....... | *Roxton* | 24 | 39 | 0 | 1,490 | 163 | 38.20 |
| ‡R. J. Bailey ...... | *Stoke-on-Trent* | 24 | 36 | 6 | 1,054 | 101 | 35.13 |
| ‡A. J. Lamb ....... | *Langebaanweg, SA* | 11 | 17 | 2 | 525 | 111 | 35.00 |
| ‡R. G. Williams ... | *Bangor* | 20 | 30 | 2 | 845 | 118 | 30.17 |
| D. J. Wild ....... | *Northampton* | 18 | 22 | 4 | 525 | 80 | 29.16 |
| ‡R. J. Boyd-Moss .. | *Hatton, Ceylon* | 19 | 30 | 3 | 748 | 121 | 27.70 |
| D. J. Capel ...... | *Northampton* | 22 | 30 | 6 | 599 | 81 | 24.95 |
| ‡N. A. Mallender .. | *Kirksandall* | 23 | 25 | 8 | 267 | 52* | 15.70 |
| A. Walker ....... | *Emley* | 12 | 14 | 8 | 83 | 18* | 13.83 |
| ‡G. Sharp ......... | *West Hartlepool* | 11 | 13 | 1 | 111 | 25 | 9.25 |
| D. Ripley ........ | *Leeds* | 13 | 14 | 4 | 83 | 27 | 8.30 |
| ‡B. J. Griffiths ..... | *Wellingborough* | 12 | 9 | 4 | 17 | 12 | 3.40 |

Also batted: R. F. Joseph (*Belladrum, BG*) (2 matches) 26*. M. B. H. Wheeler (*Windlesham*) played in one match but did not bat.

* *Signifies not out.* ‡ *Denotes county cap.*

The following played a total of twelve three-figure innings for Northamptonshire in County Championship matches – W. Larkins 3, R. J. Boyd-Moss 2, R. G. Williams 2, R. J. Bailey 1, G. Cook 1, R. A. Harper 1, A. J. Lamb 1, A. C. Storie 1.

### BOWLING

| | *O* | *M* | *R* | *W* | *BB* | *Avge* |
|---|---|---|---|---|---|---|
| B. J. Griffiths ...... | 288.4 | 71 | 846 | 31 | 6-76 | 27.29 |
| D. J. Capel ....... | 362.3 | 63 | 1,192 | 40 | 7-62 | 29.80 |
| N. A. Mallender ... | 506.4 | 97 | 1,479 | 48 | 5-83 | 30.81 |
| A. Walker ........ | 251.4 | 51 | 786 | 23 | 4-38 | 34.17 |
| R. A. Harper ...... | 737.4 | 185 | 1,996 | 56 | 5-94 | 35.64 |
| R. J. Boyd-Moss ... | 125.4 | 30 | 380 | 10 | 3-48 | 38.00 |
| R. G. Williams .... | 291.2 | 70 | 913 | 23 | 5-34 | 39.69 |

Also bowled: R. J. Bailey 3–0–16–0; G. Cook 1–0–6–0; R. F. Joseph 38–5–143–4; A. J. Lamb 1–1–0–0; W. Larkins 77–16–258–1; G. Sharp 1–0–2–0; A. C. Storie 18–6–51–0; M. B. H. Wheeler 14–3–30–0; D. J. Wild 82.5–7–368–2.

At Derby, April 27, 29, 30. NORTHAMPTONSHIRE beat DERBYSHIRE by 99 runs.

## NORTHAMPTONSHIRE v HAMPSHIRE

At Northampton, May 4, 6, 7. Drawn. Northamptonshire 7 pts, Hampshire 6 pts. Toss won by Northamptonshire. They were rescued on the last day by their nineteen-year-old newcomer, Storie, Glasgow-born but brought up in South Africa, who hit a resolute century on his Championship début. From 60 without loss overnight, they had lost nine wickets in adding 123 against a hostile pace attack, but Storie, who opened, batted patiently for six hours, ten minutes until last out, valiantly supported at the end by the West Indian, Joseph. Both sides had scored freely in the first innings. For Northamptonshire, Bailey hit a fine century and was immediately capped, and Nicholas, who led some spirited Hampshire batting, narrowly missed one.

### Northamptonshire

| | | | |
|---|---|---|---|
| W. Larkins b Tremlett | 83 | – c Terry b Andrew | 41 |
| A. C. Storie c Nicholas b Connor | 10 | – c Hardy b Maru | 106 |
| R. G. Williams c Terry b Tremlett | 50 | – c Parks b Connor | 6 |
| A. J. Lamb c and b Maru | 43 | – c Parks b Connor | 8 |
| R. J. Bailey st Parks b Cowley | 101 | – c Cowley b Connor | 0 |
| D. J. Capel lbw b Cowley | 26 | – c Parks b Cowley | 16 |
| D. J. Wild not out | 34 | – c Terry b Connor | 2 |
| *†G. Sharp b Maru | 2 | – c R. A. Smith b Tremlett | 9 |
| N. A. Mallender b Maru | 0 | – c Parks b Andrew | 13 |
| A. Walker not out | 18 | – c Parks b Maru | 11 |
| R. F. Joseph (did not bat) | | – not out | 26 |
| L-b 2, n-b 4 | 6 | L-b 4, n-b 2 | 6 |
| 1/18 2/121 3/155 4/258 5/310 6/325 7/328 8/328 (8 wkts dec.) | 373 | 1/63 2/72 3/84 4/88 5/125 6/131 7/145 8/161 9/183 | 244 |

Bonus points – Northamptonshire 4, Hampshire 2 (Score at 100 overs: 328-6).

Bowling: *First Innings*—Andrew 11–1–61–0; Connor 25–3–97–1; Tremlett 24–5–74–2; Nicholas 6–3–13–0; Maru 29–6–94–3; Cowley 16–3–32–2. *Second Innings*—Connor 24–7–62–4; Andrew 24–4–67–2; Maru 27.3–9–43–2; Tremlett 16–7–30–1; Cowley 23–10–33–1; C. L. Smith 4–3–5–0; R. A. Smith 1–1–0–0.

### Hampshire

| | | | |
|---|---|---|---|
| V. P. Terry b Joseph | 0 | | |
| C. L. Smith c Sharp b Joseph | 6 | | |
| R. J. Maru c Larkins b Mallender | 32 | – (2) not out | 0 |
| C. A. Connor b Capel | 36 | | |
| *M. C. J. Nicholas lbw b Mallender | 94 | | |
| R. A. Smith b Joseph | 14 | | |
| J. J. E. Hardy c Capel b Walker | 45 | | |
| N. G. Cowley c Sharp b Walker | 8 | | |
| T. M. Tremlett not out | 33 | | |
| †R. J. Parks not out | 52 | | |
| S. J. W. Andrew (did not bat) | | – (1) not out | 2 |
| B 5, l-b 12, n-b 7 | 24 | | |
| 1/13 2/14 3/70 4/115 5/153 6/232 7/254 8/261 (8 wkts dec.) | 352 | (no wkt) | 2 |

Bonus points – Hampshire 4, Northamptonshire 3.

Bowling: *First Innings*—Mallender 20–3–69–2; Joseph 22–3–73–3; Walker 16–0–53–2; Capel 21–6–76–1; Williams 19.4–5–64–0. *Second Innings*—Sharp 1–0–2–0; Lamb 1–1–0–0.

Umpires: R. Julian and D. O. Oslear.

## NORTHAMPTONSHIRE v KENT

At Northampton, May 22, 23, 24. Drawn. Northamptonshire 4 pts, Kent 6 pts. Toss won by Kent. A record ninth-wicket stand of 136 for any county against Northamptonshire by Ellison and Knott put Kent in control after they had lost eight wickets for 56 against the lively pace of Griffiths and Walker. When this pair suffered injuries, however, Ellison and Knott grimly mastered the depleted home attack. After a good opening by Cook and Larkins, Northamptonshire collapsed to 162 during a devastating spell by Baptiste, his best-ever bowling. Kent increased their advantage to set a target of 231 in 44 overs, but after the early loss of the home openers, Williams and Bailey opted to play out time.

### Kent

| | | | |
|---|---|---|---|
| M. R. Benson lbw b Walker | 24 | – b Harper | 30 |
| S. G. Hinks c Wild b Walker | 35 | – c Bailey b Capel | 1 |
| C. J. Tavaré b Walker | 0 | – c Harper b Capel | 32 |
| D. G. Aslett lbw b Walker | 4 | – c sub b Capel | 40 |
| *C. S. Cowdrey b Griffiths | 5 | – lbw b Capel | 1 |
| E. A. E. Baptiste c Larkins b Griffiths | 18 | – not out | 1 |
| L. Potter c Wild b Griffiths | 3 | | |
| R. M. Ellison b Mallender | 71 | | |
| G. W. Johnson c Sharp b Mallender | 5 | | |
| †A. P. E. Knott not out | 87 | | |
| G. R. Dilley not out | 5 | | |
| B 2, l-b 8, n-b 3 | 13 | L-b 7, w 9, n-b 1 | 17 |
| 1/56 2/60 3/63 4/68 5/72 6/92 7/93 8/112 9/248 | (9 wkts dec.) 270 | 1/10 2/65 3/99 4/121 5/122 | (5 wkts dec.) 122 |

Bonus points – Kent 2, Northamptonshire 3 (Score at 100 overs 209-8).

Bowling: *First Innings*—Mallender 32–4–91–2; Griffiths 28–9–45–3; Walker 20–5–38–4; Harper 17–4–44–0; Capel 13–2–35–0; Williams 2–0–7–0. *Second Innings*—Mallender 8–1–24–0; Capel 10.3–1–47–4; Harper 10–0–44–1.

### Northamptonshire

| | | | |
|---|---|---|---|
| *G. Cook b Potter | 39 | – c Aslett b Ellison | 12 |
| W. Larkins c Hinks b Baptiste | 52 | – c Potter b Baptiste | 13 |
| R. G. Williams lbw b Cowdrey | 1 | – not out | 37 |
| R. J. Bailey c Knott b Ellison | 38 | – not out | 50 |
| D. J. Capel c Benson b Baptiste | 6 | | |
| D. J. Wild c Knott b Baptiste | 10 | | |
| R. A. Harper lbw b Baptiste | 0 | | |
| †G. Sharp c and b Baptiste | 9 | | |
| N. A. Mallender lbw b Baptiste | 2 | | |
| A. Walker not out | 0 | | |
| L-b 3, w 1, n-b 1 | 5 | L-b 5, n-b 3 | 8 |
| 1/71 2/78 3/132 4/134 5/144 6/147 7/155 8/157 9/162 | (9 wkts dec.) 162 | 1/21 2/27 | (2 wkts) 120 |

B. J. Griffiths did not bat.

Bonus points – Northamptonshire 1, Kent 4.

Bowling: *First Innings*—Dilley 11–4–27–0; Ellison 15–4–37–1; Baptiste 19.3–5–42–6; Cowdrey 12–2–36–1; Potter 8–2–17–1. *Second Innings*—Dilley 5–1–13–0; Ellison 6–1–17–1; Baptiste 5–0–26–1; Cowdrey 5–1–12–0; Potter 8–0–31–0; Johnson 7–1–16–0.

Umpires: K. E. Palmer and R. A. White.

At Leicester, May 25, 27, 28. NORTHAMPTONSHIRE drew with LEICESTERSHIRE.

## NORTHAMPTONSHIRE v WARWICKSHIRE

At Northampton, May 29, 30, 31. Drawn. Northamptonshire 5 pts, Warwickshire 8 pts. Toss won by Northamptonshire. In a game of 1,264 runs and five centuries, Warwickshire finally fell 21 runs short of a target of 342 in 74 overs. Their challenge revolved around a magnificent fourth-wicket stand of 232 between Amiss and Humpage in 155 minutes, but Harper's skilful off-spin bowling ultimately checked them. Northamptonshire's first innings was dominated by a fighting century from Cook and hectic hitting by Harper after a collapse which saw six wickets fall for 29, while Williams, Capel and Storie led the bid for a worthwhile declaration in the second. Warwickshire's first innings featured a superb, unbeaten 152 by Kallicharran, who hit three 6s and 21 4s, while Amiss provided excellent support in a third-wicket stand of 197.

### Northamptonshire

| | | | |
|---|---|---|---|
| *G. Cook c Ferreira b Hoffman | 126 | – run out | 5 |
| W. Larkins lbw b Small | 45 | – c Amiss b Gifford | 36 |
| R. G. Williams run out | 0 | – c Lloyd b Hoffman | 118 |
| R. J. Bailey c Smith b Gifford | 14 | – lbw b Gifford | 6 |
| D. J. Capel c Humpage b Ferreira | 1 | – c Amiss b Small | 63 |
| A. C. Storie lbw b Ferreira | 0 | – not out | 50 |
| D. J. Wild c Humpage b Ferreira | 0 | – c Humpage b Smith | 17 |
| R. A. Harper c Hoffman b Wall | 76 | – lbw b Smith | 18 |
| †G. Sharp b Wall | 9 | – c Small b Gifford | 0 |
| N. A. Mallender c Lloyd b Ferreira | 13 | – c Humpage b Smith | 4 |
| A. Walker not out | 7 | – not out | 10 |
| B 1, l-b 7, w 2, n-b 2 | 12 | L-b 9, w 1, n-b 2 | 12 |
| 1/68 2/68 3/85 4/97 5/97 6/97 7/204 8/244 9/291 | 303 | 1/18 2/68 3/78 4/176 5/265 6/289 7/312 8/317 9/322 (9 wkts dec.) | 339 |

Bonus points – Northamptonshire 4, Warwickshire 4.

Bowling: *First Innings*—Small 18–4–68–1; Wall 14–0–67–2; Gifford 33–16–68–1; Ferreira 20.5–2–81–4; Hoffman 6–1–11–1. *Second Innings*—Small 11–2–39–1; Wall 15–0–71–0; Gifford 32–5–99–3; Hoffman 15–1–68–1; Ferreira 8–4–18–0; Lloyd 1–0–1–0; Smith 6–0–34–3.

### Warwickshire

| | | | |
|---|---|---|---|
| T. A. Lloyd c Sharp b Capel | 28 | – b Mallender | 0 |
| R. I. H. B. Dyer b Harper | 10 | – c Larkins b Capel | 4 |
| A. I. Kallicharran not out | 152 | – c Sharp b Harper | 11 |
| D. L. Amiss c Cook b Wild | 83 | – c Sharp b Harper | 140 |
| †G. W. Humpage not out | 18 | – not out | 123 |
| P. A. Smith (did not bat) | | – st Sharp b Harper | 24 |
| A. M. Ferreira (did not bat) | | – st Sharp b Harper | 1 |
| G. C. Small (did not bat) | | – not out | 2 |
| B 2, l-b 7, n-b 1 | 10 | B 10, l-b 6 | 16 |
| 1/27 2/47 3/244 (3 wkts dec.) | 301 | 1/0 2/6 3/30 4/262 5/307 6/315 (6 wkts) | 321 |

*N. Gifford, S. Wall and D. S. Hoffman did not bat.

Bonus points – Warwickshire 4, Northamptonshire 1.

Bowling: *First Innings*—Mallender 15–4–33–0; Walker 13–2–28–0; Capel 13–2–51–1; Harper 29.2–10–74–1; Williams 13–4–48–0; Wild 15–1–58–1. *Second Innings*—Mallender 12–2–51–1; Capel 8–2–24–1; Williams 13–3–42–0; Harper 29–3–116–4; Walker 11.3–0–54–0; Wild 3–0–18–0.

Umpires: D. J. Constant and J. W. Holder.

## NORTHAMPTONSHIRE v SUSSEX

At Northampton, June 8, 10, 11. Drawn. Northamptonshire 7 pts, Sussex 6 pts. Toss won by Northamptonshire. After three declarations in a rain-affected match, Sussex were set to score 247 in 48 overs and had lost four wickets for 47 when more rain ended the game. Keen Sussex bowling had Northamptonshire struggling at the start before half-centuries by Lamb, Boyd-Moss and Capel ensured maximum bonus points. Sussex also began badly against the fast bowlers but Colin Wells, Imran and Barclay secured a second batting point before Barclay declared 101 behind. Williams led Northamptonshire's chase for quick runs to set a target, but the weather had the final say.

### Northamptonshire

| | | | |
|---|---|---|---|
| *G. Cook c Green b Pigott | 2 | b Reeve | 13 |
| W. Larkins lbw b C. M. Wells | 41 | c Parker b Waller | 23 |
| R. G. Williams b Reeve | 2 | c Gould b C. M. Wells | 41 |
| A. J. Lamb b Reeve | 65 | b Waller | 11 |
| R. J. Bailey b C. M. Wells | 7 | lbw b C. M. Wells | 18 |
| R. J. Boyd-Moss lbw b Imran | 67 | not out | 22 |
| D. J. Capel c C. M. Wells b Imran | 58 | not out | 14 |
| R. A. Harper not out | 38 | | |
| †G. Sharp b Imran | 2 | | |
| N. A. Mallender c Pigott b Imran | 6 | | |
| A. Walker not out | 0 | | |
| B 2, l-b 9, w 1, n-b 2 | 14 | L-b 2, w 1 | 3 |
| 1/3 2/22 3/91 4/99 5/129 6/234 7/277 8/285 9/293 (9 wkts dec.) | 302 | 1/25 2/75 3/79 4/101 5/113 (5 wkts dec.) | 145 |

Bonus points – Northamptonshire 4, Sussex 4.

Bowling: *First Innings*—Imran 30–2–116–4; Pigott 7–1–25–1; Reeve 19–6–57–2; Waller 20.2–4–57–0; C. M. Wells 22–10–36–2. *Second Innings*—Pigott 6–1–26–0; Reeve 8–1–37–1; C. M. Wells 14.5–3–56–2; Waller 12–4–24–2.

### Sussex

| | | | |
|---|---|---|---|
| G. D. Mendis b Walker | 13 | c Lamb b Walker | 1 |
| A. M. Green b Mallender | 8 | b Mallender | 2 |
| P. W. G. Parker c Sharp b Walker | 5 | not out | 13 |
| A. P. Wells c Harper b Mallender | 5 | run out | 12 |
| C. M. Wells lbw b Mallender | 48 | (6) not out | 0 |
| Imran Khan c Sharp b Mallender | 38 | (5) c Harper b Williams | 18 |
| *J. R. T. Barclay not out | 37 | | |
| †I. J. Gould c Lamb b Harper | 26 | | |
| D. A. Reeve c Lamb b Walker | 2 | | |
| A. C. S. Pigott not out | 10 | | |
| L-b 7, n-b 2 | 9 | L-b 1 | 1 |
| 1/11 2/16 3/34 4/42 5/120 6/129 7/175 8/178 (8 wkts dec.) | 201 | 1/3 2/3 3/18 4/47 (4 wkts) | 47 |

C. E. Waller did not bat.

Bonus points – Sussex 2, Northamptonshire 3.

Bowling: *First Innings*—Mallender 22–3–57–4; Walker 21–6–42–3; Capel 9–4–19–0; Harper 17.2–5–39–1; Larkins 13–4–34–0; Williams 2–0–3–0. *Second Innings*—Mallender 6–1–10–1; Walker 4–4–0–1; Harper 6–1–32–0; Capel 2–1–4–0; Williams 3–3–0–1.

Umpires: D. R. Shepherd and A. G. T. Whitehead.

At Ilford, June 12, 13, 14. NORTHAMPTONSHIRE drew with ESSEX.

## NORTHAMPTONSHIRE v GLOUCESTERSHIRE

At Northampton, June 15, 17, 18. Gloucestershire won by eight wickets. Gloucestershire 23 pts, Northamptonshire 2 pts. Toss won by Gloucestershire. Although rain threatened Gloucestershire's victory, it was achieved when they hit the 71 needed from eleven overs with nine balls remaining. They had grafted to a useful first-innings total, and then the left-arm seam bowler, Sainsbury, a late replacement for the injured Walsh, exploited the conditions for a career-best performance that forced Northamptonshire to follow on. The home county were then helped by 257 minutes of resistance from Storie, some lusty hitting from Harper and the intervention of the weather. There was no play before lunch on the last day, and when it rained again after half an hour's play a draw seemed the likeliest result. However, conditions improved to allow 21 overs – sufficient for Gloucestershire to capture the last three Northamptonshire wickets and purposefully press home their advantage to go to the top of the Championship table. It was Northamptonshire's first Championship defeat of the season.

### Gloucestershire

| | | | |
|---|---|---|---|
| A. W. Stovold b Mallender | 31 | – c Storie b Walker | 8 |
| P. W. Romaines lbw b Larkins | 55 | – c Sharp b Mallender | 30 |
| C. W. J. Athey c Cook b Boyd-Moss | 82 | – not out | 12 |
| P. Bainbridge b Harper | 67 | | |
| B. F. Davison b Boyd-Moss | 2 | – (4) not out | 22 |
| K. M. Curran c Walker b Mallender | 28 | | |
| J. W. Lloyds c Bailey b Boyd-Moss | 20 | | |
| †R. C. Russell not out | 0 | | |
| B 1, l-b 8, n-b 1 | 10 | L-b 1 | 1 |
| 1/79 2/103 3/238 4/243 5/250 6/293 7/295 | (7 wkts dec.) 295 | 1/31 2/40 | (2 wkts) 73 |

*D. A. Graveney, D. V. Lawrence and G. E. Sainsbury did not bat.

Bonus points – Gloucestershire 3, Northamptonshire 2 (Score at 100 overs: 278-5).

Bowling: *First Innings*—Mallender 13.1–7–19–2; Walker 16–4–47–0; Capel 9–2–16–0; Storie 18–6–51–0; Harper 26–5–71–1; Larkins 13–4–34–1; Boyd-Moss 13–2–48–3. *Second Innings*—Mallender 5–0–45–1; Walker 4.3–0–27–1.

### Northamptonshire

| | | | |
|---|---|---|---|
| *G. Cook lbw b Sainsbury | 6 | – c Russell b Lawrence | 36 |
| W. Larkins b Sainsbury | 6 | – lbw b Curran | 15 |
| R. G. Williams c Russell b Sainsbury | 24 | – c Athey b Curran | 1 |
| N. A. Mallender c Bainbridge b Graveney | 0 | – (10) not out | 14 |
| A. C. Storie c Graveney b Sainsbury | 4 | – (4) lbw b Curran | 71 |
| R. J. Bailey lbw b Sainsbury | 1 | – (5) st Russell b Graveney | 16 |
| R. J. Boyd-Moss c Russell b Sainsbury | 2 | – (6) lbw b Graveney | 19 |
| D. J. Capel c and b Graveney | 0 | – (7) b Lloyds | 22 |
| R. A. Harper b Sainsbury | 39 | – (8) c Stovold b Lawrence | 40 |
| †G. Sharp c Davison b Graveney | 25 | – (9) lbw b Lawrence | 2 |
| A. Walker not out | 2 | – b Graveney | 4 |
| B 1, l-b 7, w 1, n-b 1 | 10 | B 1, l-b 3, w 1, n-b 1 | 6 |
| 1/9 2/26 3/27 4/34 5/40 6/47 7/48 8/52 9/93 | 119 | 1/30 2/36 3/65 4/82 5/106 6/156 7/205 8/208 9/233 | 246 |

Bonus points – Gloucestershire 4.

Bowling: *First Innings*—Lawrence 5–0–16–0; Sainsbury 17.2–8–38–7; Graveney 17–4–35–3; Bainbridge 4–0–22–0. *Second Innings*—Curran 23–5–60–3; Sainsbury 24–5–69–0; Lawrence 14–2–61–3; Athey 2–2–0–0; Graveney 21.4–13–27–3; Lloyds 9–4–18–1; Bainbridge 5–2–7–0.

Umpires: K. J. Lyons and P. B. Wight.

## NORTHAMPTONSHIRE v ESSEX

At Northampton, June 22, 24, 25. Drawn. Northamptonshire 3 pts, Essex 2 pts. Toss won by Northamptonshire. Only ten balls were bowled on the first day, and none on the second, but that was enough to prevent there being a one-innings match. With the captains unable to agree on declarations and forfeitures, the two sides spent the final day playing for bonus points. Lamb hit his 25th hundred for Northamptonshire off 184 balls with fourteen boundaries.

### Northamptonshire

| | | | |
|---|---|---|---|
| *G. Cook c Foster b Lever | 8 | D. J. Capel not out | 5 |
| W. Larkins c East b Lever | 31 | | |
| A. C. Storie c Pringle b Foster | 45 | B 2, l-b 8, n-b 2 | 12 |
| A. J. Lamb b Acfield | 111 | | |
| R. J. Bailey not out | 47 | 1/28 2/53 3/152 4/232 5/257 | (5 wkts dec.) 269 |
| R. J. Boyd-Moss lbw b Foster | 10 | | |

R. A. Harper, †G. Sharp, N. A. Mallender and A. Walker did not bat.

Bonus points – Northamptonshire 3, Essex 2.

Bowling: Lever 13–5–36–2; Foster 22–9–53–2; Gooch 22–6–61–0; Pringle 18–4–52–0; Acfield 25–5–57–1.

### Essex

G. A. Gooch, C. Gladwin, P. J. Prichard, K. S. McEwan, D. R. Pringle, *K. W. R. Fletcher, B. R. Hardie, †D. E. East, N. A. Foster, J. K. Lever and D. L. Acfield.

Umpires: B. Dudleston and N. T. Plews.

## NORTHAMPTONSHIRE v SURREY

At Northampton, June 26, 27, 28. Northamptonshire won by five wickets. Northamptonshire 20 pts, Surrey 6 pts. Toss won by Surrey. Larkins batted splendidly to carry Northamptonshire to a target of 255 in 45 overs with fourteen balls to spare. His 117, his first hundred of the season, came off 111 balls (three 6s, thirteen 4s), and he was joined in a vital, match-winning stand of 135 by Bailey. After this pair had gone, Boyd-Moss kept up the momentum with 42 off 23 balls, and Harper clinched the issue with the eighth 6 of Northamptonshire's innings. Until this fourth innings, bowlers had controlled the game, although Clinton and Pauline batted with much-needed discipline to restore Surrey's first innings, which did not commence until late on the first day because of rain. For the home side, only Cook resisted a Surrey attack in which Gray and Pocock were always menacing on a pitch offering movement off the seam, bounce and spin. Clinton again batted well as Surrey consolidated but their efforts were soon to be undone by Larkins's brilliance.

## Surrey

| | | | |
|---|---|---|---|
| A. R. Butcher lbw b Mallender | 0 | – lbw b Capel | 27 |
| G. S. Clinton c Cook b Harper | 80 | – lbw b Walker | 49 |
| A. J. Stewart lbw b Mallender | 3 | – b Harper | 12 |
| *T. E. Jesty c Harper b Walker | 5 | – not out | 36 |
| M. A. Lynch b Harper | 34 | – c Sharp b Harper | 0 |
| P. I. Pocock c Harper b Mallender | 9 | | |
| A. Needham lbw b Mallender | 0 | – (6) st Sharp b Harper | 31 |
| D. B. Pauline c Walker b Boyd-Moss | 50 | – not out | 10 |
| †C. J. Richards not out | 26 | | |
| D. J. Thomas not out | 25 | – (7) c Larkins b Harper | 4 |
| B 10, l-b 8 | 18 | B 3, l-b 9, w 4 | 16 |
| 1/2 2/8 3/19 4/66 5/86 6/86 7/185 8/203 (8 wkts dec.) | 250 | 1/43 2/60 3/90 4/136 5/138 6/152 (6 wkts dec.) | 185 |

A. H. Gray did not bat.

Bonus points – Surrey 2, Northamptonshire 3 (Score at 100 overs: 240-8).

Bowling: *First Innings*—Mallender 21.3–7–43–4; Walker 15–5–36–1; Harper 35–9–63–2; Capel 8–2–30–0; Williams 12–4–22–0; Boyd-Moss 11–3–38–1. *Second Innings*—Mallender 8–1–31–0; Walker 11–1–43–1; Capel 9–1–44–1; Harper 14–4–55–4; Boyd-Moss 1–1–0–0.

## Northamptonshire

| | | | |
|---|---|---|---|
| *G. Cook lbw b Pocock | 70 | – c Lynch b Thomas | 17 |
| W. Larkins c Clinton b Thomas | 31 | – c Clinton b Gray | 117 |
| R. G. Williams b Gray | 29 | – c Clinton b Gray | 10 |
| A. C. Storie lbw b Gray | 6 | | |
| R. J. Bailey c Stewart b Pocock | 16 | – (4) st Richards b Pocock | 39 |
| R. J. Boyd-Moss c Clinton b Pocock | 0 | – (5) b Gray | 42 |
| D. J. Capel c Stewart b Gray | 11 | – (6) not out | 5 |
| R. A. Harper c Butcher b Gray | 4 | – (7) not out | 8 |
| †G. Sharp b Pocock | 10 | | |
| N. A. Mallender c Lynch b Gray | 1 | | |
| A. Walker not out | 0 | | |
| B 1, l-b 1, n-b 1 | 3 | B 7, l-b 7, n-b 5 | 19 |
| 1/70 2/119 3/134 4/149 5/150 6/161 7/166 8/179 9/181 | 181 | 1/36 2/62 3/197 4/200 5/248 (5 wkts) | 257 |

Bonus points – Northamptonshire 1, Surrey 4.

Bowling: *First Innings*—Thomas 10–0–42–1; Gray 15–3–44–5; Butcher 1–0–18–0; Needham 11–1–44–0; Pocock 16.4–6–31–4. *Second Innings*—Thomas 8–0–46–2; Gray 11–1–74–2; Pocock 17.4–1–78–1; Needham 6–0–45–0.

Umpires: B. Dudleston and N. T. Plews.

At Edgbaston, June 29, July 1, 2. NORTHAMPTONSHIRE beat WARWICKSHIRE by 31 runs.

## NORTHAMPTONSHIRE v MIDDLESEX

At Northampton, July 6, 8, 9. Middlesex won by 141 runs. Middlesex 24 pts, Northamptonshire 4 pts. Toss won by Middlesex. Middlesex dominated the game throughout, putting together a solid first-day total thanks to Barlow's fourth Championship century of the season. He batted for four and a half hours and shared an opening stand of 134 in 39 overs with Slack. Despite a brave innings from Cook, who was troubled by a badly bruised hand which forced him to retire early on, Northamptonshire trailed by 142. Brisk scoring by Radley and Downton allowed Gatting to give his bowlers four hours to dismiss Northamptonshire on a wearing pitch. The damage was done by the spin of Edmonds, for the second time, and Emburey after Daniel had made the initial breakthrough. Boyd-Moss resisted stubbornly and Mallender hit freely for a maiden Championship fifty but Middlesex won comfortably with sixteen overs in hand.

### Middlesex

| | | | |
|---|---|---|---|
| G. D. Barlow c Capel b Williams | 141 | – lbw b Mallender | 17 |
| W. N. Slack c Ripley b Mallender | 70 | – lbw b Mallender | 12 |
| *M. W. Gatting run out | 19 | – c Ripley b Capel | 24 |
| R. O. Butcher b Capel | 4 | – c Larkins b Capel | 35 |
| C. T. Radley hit wkt b Mallender | 26 | – not out | 63 |
| †P. R. Downton c Harper b Capel | 27 | – not out | 57 |
| J. E. Emburey c Harper b Capel | 51 | | |
| N. F. Williams lbw b Mallender | 2 | | |
| P. H. Edmonds not out | 4 | | |
| N. G. Cowans c sub b Capel | 0 | | |
| W. W. Daniel not out | 19 | | |
| B 6, l-b 13, n-b 4 | 23 | B 8, l-b 2, w 3, n-b 2 | 15 |
| 1/134 2/186 3/190 4/273 5/277 6/344 7/362 8/362 9/364 (9 wkts dec.) | 386 | 1/22 2/37 3/84 4/97 (4 wkts dec.) | 223 |

Bonus points – Middlesex 4, Northamptonshire 2 (Score at 100 overs: 329-5).

Bowling: *First Innings*—Mallender 26–7–79–3; Walker 9–0–50–0; Harper 37–12–77–0; Capel 23–2–84–4; Larkins 5–0–31–0; Williams 8–2–30–1; Boyd-Moss 4–1–16–0. *Second Innings*—Mallender 15–3–43–2; Capel 23–4–71–2; Harper 12–3–38–0; Boyd-Moss 7–0–33–0; Williams 5–0–28–0.

### Northamptonshire

| | | | |
|---|---|---|---|
| *G. Cook not out | 72 | – c Gatting b Daniel | 16 |
| W. Larkins b Daniel | 42 | – c Emburey b Daniel | 31 |
| R. J. Boyd-Moss b Daniel | 4 | – c Radley b Edmonds | 32 |
| A. J. Lamb b Edmonds | 60 | – b Edmonds | 25 |
| R. J. Bailey b Daniel | 0 | – c Slack b Emburey | 4 |
| R. G. Williams b Edmonds | 24 | – c and b Edmonds | 0 |
| D. J. Capel c Cowans b Edmonds | 6 | – b Emburey | 1 |
| R. A. Harper c Gatting b Edmonds | 4 | – c Butcher b Daniel | 6 |
| †D. Ripley b Edmonds | 1 | – c Emburey b Edmonds | 27 |
| N. A. Mallender run out | 11 | – not out | 52 |
| A. Walker lbw b Gatting | 0 | – c Downton b Emburey | 4 |
| L-b 11, n-b 9 | 20 | B 12, l-b 9, n-b 5 | 26 |
| 1/32 2/69 3/69 4/108 5/124 6/183 7/189 8/195 9/244 | 244 | 1/44 2/55 3/82 4/89 5/94 6/95 7/119 8/137 9/178 | 224 |

Bonus points – Northamptonshire 2, Middlesex 4.

Bowling: *First Innings*—Daniel 17–3–89–3; Cowans 11–0–51–0; Williams 7–1–18–0; Edmonds 26–10–49–5; Emburey 17–7–24–0; Gatting 2–1–2–1. *Second Innings*—Daniel 18–4–83–3; Cowans 2–0–9–0; Williams 3–0–7–0; Edmonds 25–5–81–4; Emburey 12.5–3–23–3.

Umpires: J. W. Holder and J. A. Jameson.

## NORTHAMPTONSHIRE v DERBYSHIRE

At Northampton, July 10, 11, 12. Drawn. Northamptonshire 7 pts, Derbyshire 4 pts. Toss won by Northamptonshire. Derbyshire, after a generally lack-lustre display, had a struggle to save the game with their seventh-wicket pair seeing out the final eighteen overs. Set 290 to win in 60 overs they flourished briefly through Anderson and Roberts, but the challenge faltered against the off-spin of Williams, who had featured on the first day with a 275-minute hundred to rescue Northamptonshire from a shaky start. Williams shared a stand of 132 with the commanding Bailey, whose strokeplay (fourteen 4s) and that of Wild contrasted with the grim, unenterprising Derbyshire reply. Only Miller was able to provide any sparkle. Bailey, again, and Capel were impressive as Northamptonshire forged on towards a declaration on the last day.

### Northamptonshire

| First innings | | Second innings | |
|---|---|---|---|
| *G. Cook lbw b Finney | 3 | c Miller b Finney | 12 |
| W. Larkins c Miller b Mortensen | 0 | lbw b Mortensen | 5 |
| R. J. Boyd-Moss c Wright b Mortensen | 5 | lbw b Mortensen | 16 |
| R. G. Williams lbw b Newman | 103 | c Barnett b Newman | 9 |
| R. J. Bailey c Miller b Newman | 81 | lbw b Finney | 52 |
| D. J. Capel lbw b Finney | 5 | c Finney b Mortensen | 71 |
| D. J. Wild c Roberts b Finney | 80 | not out | 32 |
| R. A. Harper not out | 34 | not out | 7 |
| †D. Ripley not out | 3 | | |
| B 1, l-b 14, w 1, n-b 4 | 20 | B 8, l-b 6, n-b 1 | 15 |
| 1/1 2/6 3/30 4/162 5/183 6/261 7/330 (7 wkts dec.) | 334 | 1/23 2/25 3/46 4/52 5/180 6/180 (6 wkts dec.) | 219 |

N. A. Mallender and B. J. Griffiths did not bat.

Bonus points – Northamptonshire 4, Derbyshire 2 (Score at 100 overs: 317-6).

Bowling: *First Innings*—Mortensen 23–2–62–2; Finney 22–2–75–3; Newman 14–1–52–2; Miller 19–2–70–0; Russell 27–9–60–0. *Second Innings*—Mortensen 18–4–70–3; Finney 15.4–2–57–2; Newman 6–0–27–1; Russell 5–0–21–0; Barnett 3–0–15–0; Miller 2–0–15–0.

### Derbyshire

| First innings | | Second innings | |
|---|---|---|---|
| †B. J. M. Maher b Harper | 19 | | |
| I. S. Anderson b Griffiths | 0 | b Williams | 51 |
| R. J. Finney b Griffiths | 12 | (8) not out | 0 |
| *K. J. Barnett c Cook b Williams | 44 | (1) c Mallender b Williams | 27 |
| J. G. Wright st Ripley b Harper | 47 | (3) c Wild b Williams | 5 |
| B. Roberts b Boyd-Moss | 41 | (4) c Ripley b Williams | 44 |
| R. Sharma c Cook b Harper | 15 | (6) c Larkins b Williams | 13 |
| G. Miller not out | 60 | (5) c Larkins b Boyd-Moss | 4 |
| P. G. Newman lbw b Griffiths | 6 | (7) not out | 8 |
| P. E. Russell c Ripley b Griffiths | 2 | | |
| O. H. Mortensen c Ripley b Mallender | 1 | | |
| B 5, l-b 8, n-b 4 | 17 | B 7, l-b 3 | 10 |
| 1/5 2/29 3/58 4/84 5/167 6/181 7/219 8/237 9/243 | 264 | 1/50 2/60 3/132 4/137 5/137 6/154 (6 wkts) | 162 |

Bonus points – Derbyshire 2, Northamptonshire 3 (Score at 100 overs: 226-7).

Bowling: *First Innings*—Mallender 24.4–6–62–1; Griffiths 17–7–37–4; Capel 8–2–23–0; Harper 39–12–76–3; Williams 14–4–32–1; Boyd-Moss 10–4–21–1. *Second Innings*—Mallender 10–2–30–0; Griffiths 4–1–15–0; Harper 20–5–65–0; Williams 20–6–34–5; Boyd-Moss 2–0–8–1.

Umpires: J. W. Holder and J. A. Jameson.

At Maidstone, July 13, 15, 16. NORTHAMPTONSHIRE lost to KENT by four wickets.

At Uxbridge, July 24, 25, 26. NORTHAMPTONSHIRE lost to MIDDLESEX by an innings and 161 runs.

At Northampton, July 27, 28, 29, 30. NORTHAMPTONSHIRE drew with AUSTRALIANS (See Australian tour section).

## NORTHAMPTONSHIRE v NOTTINGHAMSHIRE

At Northampton, August 3, 5, 6. Drawn. Northamptonshire 4 pts, Nottinghamshire 2 pts. Toss won by Nottinghamshire. Rain brought a halt with fourteen overs remaining and the match still in the balance. Nottinghamshire, set 329 to win in 71 overs, were put on course by Randall and Johnson with an exciting third-wicket partnership of 131 in twenty overs, but with half the side out they still required 83 runs. Earlier the two captains had attempted to counteract the effect of several stoppages with three declarations. Cook and Larkins launched Northamptonshire's first innings with 174 for the first wicket in between the showers, Larkins dominating with a 6 and nineteen 4s in his 140. Hadlee declared 149 behind on gaining a batting point, whereupon Larkins launched an even more furious assault, his 62 coming from only 21 scoring strokes.

### Northamptonshire

| | | | |
|---|---|---|---|
| *G. Cook b Cooper | 79 | – not out | 77 |
| W. Larkins c Hassan b Hemmings | 140 | – c Cooper b Saxelby | 62 |
| R. J. Boyd-Moss c Hemmings b Saxelby | 35 | – not out | 36 |
| R. J. Bailey not out | 30 | | |
| R. G. Williams not out | 10 | | |
| B 1, l-b 4, n-b 2 | 7 | W 1, n-b 3 | 4 |
| 1/174 2/250 3/265 (3 wkts dec.) | 301 | 1/81 (1 wkt dec.) | 179 |

D. J. Wild, D. J. Capel, R. A. Harper, †D. Ripley, N. A. Mallender and B. J. Griffiths did not bat.

Bonus points – Northamptonshire 4, Nottinghamshire 1.

Bowling: *First Innings*—Hadlee 9–0–23–0; Cooper 24.5–7–78–1; Saxelby 16–4–66–1; Pick 15–3–58–0; Hemmings 30–11–71–1. *Second Innings*—Cooper 11–5–22–0; Pick 8–0–62–0; Saxelby 10–0–67–1; Hemmings 8–0–28–0.

### Nottinghamshire

| | | | |
|---|---|---|---|
| B. C. Broad c Ripley b Williams | 57 | – c Bailey b Mallender | 77 |
| D. W. Randall c Ripley b Griffiths | 45 | – (3) c Mallender b Williams | 84 |
| B. Hassan not out | 17 | – (2) run out | 6 |
| P. Johnson not out | 23 | – c Mallender b Williams | 61 |
| *R. J. Hadlee (did not bat) | | – c Mallender b Harper | 4 |
| D. J. R. Martindale (did not bat) | | – not out | 3 |
| L-b 7, w 3 | 10 | B 4, l-b 7, n-b 1 | 12 |
| 1/95 2/112 (2 wkts dec.) | 152 | 1/33 2/105 3/236 4/242 5/247 (5 wkts) | 247 |

†B. N. French, E. E. Hemmings, K. Saxelby, K. E. Cooper and R. A. Pick did not bat.

Bonus point – Nottinghamshire 1.

Bowling: *First Innings*—Mallender 9–2–29–0; Griffiths 17–5–33–1; Wild 10–2–38–0; Harper 6–0–21–0; Williams 5.3–1–24–1. *Second Innings*—Mallender 12–0–47–1; Griffiths 8–0–49–0; Harper 21.1–4–89–1; Williams 8–0–51–2.

Umpires: A. A. Jones and A. G. T. Whitehead.

At Weston-super-Mare, August 10, 12, 13. NORTHAMPTONSHIRE drew with SOMERSET.

At Lytham, August 14, 15, 16. NORTHAMPTONSHIRE drew with LANCASHIRE.

## NORTHAMPTONSHIRE v GLAMORGAN

At Wellingborough, August 17, 19, 20. Drawn. Northamptonshire 5 pts, Glamorgan 2 pts. Toss won by Glamorgan. The 100th Championship meeting between the two counties was abandoned at lunch on the third day, less than two hours' play having been possible over the last two days of the match. Put in to bat on a soft pitch, Northamptonshire slowly took control as Boyd-Moss scored his first hundred of the season in 225 minutes with fourteen boundaries. Williams looked set to follow him to three figures but fell 6 runs short, having secured his side's fourth batting point with one ball to spare. Wild and Harper both played lively innings, and after Cook's overnight declaration Glamorgan quickly ran into trouble, losing three wickets in nine balls. Younis and Morris started a recovery but yet again the weather had the final say.

### Northamptonshire

| | |
|---|---|
| *G. Cook lbw b Derrick | 18 |
| W. Larkins c Price b Barwick | 11 |
| R. J. Boyd-Moss b McFarlane | 121 |
| R. J. Bailey c Davies b Derrick | 13 |
| R. G. Williams c Ontong b Price | 94 |
| D. J. Wild b Derrick | 41 |
| D. J. Capel not out | 25 |
| R. A. Harper c Davies b Ontong | 30 |
| †D. Ripley c Davies b Derrick | 0 |
| N. A. Mallender c sub b Ontong | 0 |
| B. J. Griffiths not out | 0 |
| B 4, l-b 12, n-b 3 | 19 |
| 1/21 2/43 3/81 4/215 5/301 6/317 7/360 8/367 9/372 (9 wkts dec.) | 372 |

Bonus points – Northamptonshire 4, Glamorgan 2 (Score at 100 overs: 301-5).

Bowling: Barwick 15–6–32–1; McFarlane 16–2–69–1; Derrick 21–7–60–4; Ontong 25–7–68–2; Holmes 14–3–47–0; Price 24–4–80–1.

### Glamorgan

| | |
|---|---|
| J. A. Hopkins c Cook b Griffiths | 6 |
| A. L. Jones c Ripley b Mallender | 3 |
| G. C. Holmes c Ripley b Griffiths | 1 |
| Younis Ahmed not out | 35 |
| H. Morris not out | 28 |
| N-b 2 | 2 |
| 1/9 2/10 3/11 (3 wkts) | 75 |

*R. C. Ontong, M. R. Price, †T. Davies, J. Derrick, L. L. McFarlane and S. R. Barwick did not bat.

Bonus point – Northamptonshire 1.

Bowling: Mallender 6–0–17–1; Griffiths 13.3–5–43–2; Harper 8–2–15–0.

Umpires: B. Leadbeater and J. H. Hampshire.

## NORTHAMPTONSHIRE v LEICESTERSHIRE

At Northampton, August 24, 26, 27. Drawn. Northamptonshire 4 pts, Leicestershire 5 pts. Toss won by Northamptonshire. The game ended in disappointment for Bailey, who missed out on a century when stumps were drawn at 5.30, having previously played out a maiden from Butcher. The 21-year-old produced a responsible innings of just over three hours to steer his side to safety, helped principally by Harper, who came to the wicket with Northamptonshire 169 for seven and only 36 runs ahead. Leicestershire's victory effort was led by Clift, bowling off-spin instead of his usual medium pace, a move made necessary by an injury to Willey, who had dominated the first two days of the match. The former Northamptonshire all-rounder bowled with excellent control on a helpful pitch in the first innings, claiming four for 9 in his first 61 balls, and then slowly built Leicestershire's lead in a stay of five and a half hours in which he hit twenty boundaries. Apart from Bailey, Williams also narrowly missed a century for the second game running.

## Northamptonshire

| | | | |
|---|---|---|---|
| *G. Cook b Willey | 35 | – c Willey b Cook | 4 |
| W. Larkins c Whitaker b Willey | 31 | – b Cook | 48 |
| R. J. Boyd-Moss lbw b Willey | 1 | – c Garnham b Clift | 13 |
| A. J. Lamb lbw b Clift | 4 | – c Cobb b Clift | 32 |
| R. J. Bailey lbw b Willey | 6 | – not out | 99 |
| R. G. Williams c and b Cook | 96 | – c Gower b Clift | 7 |
| D. J. Wild c Garnham b Cook | 8 | – c Garnham b Clift | 1 |
| D. J. Capel c and b Agnew | 2 | – lbw b Willey | 3 |
| R. A. Harper b Cook | 8 | – not out | 15 |
| †D. Ripley c Cobb b Willey | 10 | | |
| N. A. Mallender not out | 2 | | |
| L-b 3, n-b 4 | 7 | B 10, l-b 5, n-b 6 | 21 |
| 1/67 2/68 3/76 4/80 5/92 6/119 7/144 8/176 9/204 | 210 | 1/37 2/64 3/86 4/118 5/136 6/148 7/169 | (7 wkts) 243 |

Bonus points – Northamptonshire 2, Leicestershire 3 (Score at 100 overs: 200-8).

Bowling: *First Innings*—Agnew 16–5–38–1; Taylor 7–2–30–0; Clift 16–4–28–1; Willey 34–15–64–5; Cook 31–9–47–3. *Second Innings*—Agnew 9–0–46–0; Taylor 4–2–9–0; Cook 47–25–67–2; Willey 19–4–44–1; Clift 30–7–54–4; Gower 1–0–3–0; Butcher 2–1–5–0.

## Leicestershire

| | |
|---|---|
| I. P. Butcher c Ripley b Mallender | 9 |
| R. A. Cobb lbw b Capel | 18 |
| *D. I. Gower lbw b Capel | 4 |
| P. Willey lbw b Boyd-Moss | 147 |
| J. J. Whitaker c Cook b Harper | 43 |
| N. E. Briers c and b Harper | 7 |
| †M. A. Garnham c Cook b Harper | 40 |
| P. B. Clift c Ripley b Harper | 0 |
| N. G. B. Cook b Harper | 45 |
| J. P. Agnew st Ripley b Boyd-Moss | 2 |
| L. B. Taylor not out | 1 |
| B 6, l-b 17, n-b 4 | 27 |
| 1/15 2/30 3/35 4/100 5/117 6/237 7/237 8/333 9/339 | 343 |

Bonus points – Leicestershire 2, Northamptonshire 2 (Score at 100 overs: 231-5).

Bowling: Mallender 22–5–56–1; Harper 45–13–94–5; Boyd-Moss 30.3–10–44–2; Capel 15–1–67–2; Williams 23–7–59–0.

Umpires: R. Julian and D. O. Oslear.

At Headingley, August 31, September 2, 3. NORTHAMPTONSHIRE drew with YORKSHIRE.

At Bristol, September 4, 5, 6. NORTHAMPTONSHIRE drew with GLOUCESTERSHIRE.

At Southampton, September 11, 12, 13. NORTHAMPTONSHIRE beat HAMPSHIRE by one wicket.

At Worcester, September 14, 16, 17. NORTHAMPTONSHIRE beat WORCESTERSHIRE by three wickets.

# NOTTINGHAMSHIRE

*President:* J. W. Baddiley
*Chairman:* C. F. Ward
*Chairman, Cricket Committee:* R. T. Simpson
*Secretary:* B. Robson
County Cricket Ground, Trent Bridge,
Nottingham NG2 6AG
(Telephone: 0602-821525)
*Cricket Manager:* K. A. Taylor
*Captain:* C. E. B. Rice

At the outset of the 1985 summer, Nottinghamshire's hopes of taking a major prize were directed towards a one-day trophy, and their ambitions came very near to being fulfilled in a memorable NatWest Bank Trophy final against Essex. Who that saw it will forget Derek Randall's courageous bid to provide the county with their first-ever limited-overs trophy? In the end, though, Nottinghamshire succumbed again to the side that had pipped them for both the Britannic Assurance Championship and John Player Sunday League twelve months earlier.

Victory in the Lord's showpiece would have given Clive Rice and his men all the satisfaction they could have hoped for in a summer that had more than its fair share of frustrations, and, even as it was, there were a number of heartening pointers from their performance. When they won the Championship in 1981 and finished second in 1984, there were questions asked about the character and responsibility of their batting line-up. Apart from the occasional lapse, that area of doubt was all but removed in 1985.

In Tim Robinson and Chris Broad they possess an opening partnership that has emerged as one of the country's best – if not the best. It was a source of some surprise that Broad, who scored 1,786 first-class runs, lost his identity as a Test player. His disappointment, however, has coincided with Robinson's remarkable adaptation to Test cricket. It is a long time since an English batsman made such an accomplished job of the international opportunity put before him, and Robinson has continued to give the county great service. In 1985 he topped Nottinghamshire's batting averages despite his frequent departures to do battle with Australia.

Rice, in his benefit season, also had a healthy average, but the most pleasing aspect of Nottinghamshire's batting were the displays of Randall, who had his most successful season on the county circuit. Considering that at the end of 1984 he had been considering retirement, Randall's consistency, which brought him 2,151 first-class runs, was all the more remarkable, and for the most part he made his runs in relaxed, uninhibited fashion.

Paul Johnson, a prodigious stroke-maker, was on course to become the youngest player in Nottinghamshire's history to score 1,000 runs when an appendix operation curtailed his season and excluded him from the NatWest final. But he looks to have a flourishing future, and there was more than an indication that Duncan Martindale will follow suit. Yorkshire-born but a product of Cheshire Schools, Martindale showed in his first season on the staff that he has talent, technique and temperament, well illustrated at the climax of the NatWest final.

If Nottinghamshire are to continue to compete at the highest level, there is, however, a clear need to improve the bowling department, which still leans too heavily on Richard Hadlee. Following his rigorous tour of the West Indies, the brilliant New Zealander was in no state to get near his great double achievement of 1984, but he remained the only Nottinghamshire bowler to command total respect. After a quiet start to the season he emerged as clear leader of the county's bowling averages, and for a player who always sets himself targets a career-best eight for 41 against Lancashire will have given him satisfaction.

Kevin Cooper had an excellent start to the summer and looked to be heading for a bigger haul than the 61 wickets he eventually picked up, but after him and Hadlee the bowling left something to be desired. The two off-spinners, Eddie Hemmings and Peter Such, suffered, like all slow bowlers, from the number of dead pitches they went to work on, and Kevin Saxelby and Andrew Pick, who improved after a poor start, will both be hoping for better results in 1986. Then, the almost certain loss of Hadlee for part of the season, with the New Zealand tourists, will cast further doubts over Nottinghamshire's ability to bowl opponents out twice. Ken Taylor and his staff must unearth, or recruit, a pace bowler from some quarter if Nottinghamshire are to remain a force, and their interest in the South African, Hugh Page, is understandable.

One area where there are no such deficiencies is wicket-keeping. Bruce French, a patient Test deputy, proved once more that he is among the most gifted around.

Reflections on Nottinghamshire's 1985 season would not be complete without recognition of the Second XI's championship success under the astute leadership of Mike Bore. The Under-25 side also reached the semi-final of their competition, a hopeful sign. – J.L.

NOTTINGHAMSHIRE 1985

[*Bill Smith*

*Back row:* P. M. Such, K. Saxelby, B. C. Broad, K. E. Cooper, B. N. French, P. Johnson. *Front row:* D. W. Randall, R. J. Hadlee, C E. B. Rice (*captain*), J. D. Birch, E. E. Hemmings. *Insets:* R. T. Robinson, D. J. R. Martindale, R. A. Pick.

## NOTTINGHAMSHIRE RESULTS

*All first-class matches – Played 25: Won 4, Lost 2, Drawn 19.*

*County Championship matches – Played 24: Won 4, Lost 2, Drawn 18.*

*Bonus points – Batting 66, Bowling 69.*

*Competition placings – Britannic Assurance County Championship, 8th; NatWest Bank Trophy, r/u; Benson and Hedges Cup, 3rd in Group A; John Player League, 12th eq.*

## BRITANNIC ASSURANCE CHAMPIONSHIP AVERAGES

### BATTING

| | *Birthplace* | *M* | *I* | *NO* | *R* | *HI* | *Avge* |
|---|---|---|---|---|---|---|---|
| ‡R. T. Robinson | *Sutton-in-Ashfield* | 11 | 21 | 3 | 1,107 | 130* | 61.50 |
| ‡C. E. B. Rice | *Johannesburg, SA* | 20 | 33 | 8 | 1,394 | 171* | 55.76 |
| ‡D. W. Randall | *Retford* | 24 | 45 | 6 | 1,977 | 117 | 50.69 |
| ‡B. C. Broad | *Bristol* | 24 | 45 | 3 | 1,706 | 171 | 40.61 |
| ‡R. J. Hadlee | *Christchurch, NZ* | 19 | 29 | 11 | 592 | 73* | 32.88 |
| P. Johnson | *Newark* | 20 | 32 | 4 | 890 | 118 | 31.78 |
| D. J. R. Martindale | *Harrogate* | 9 | 14 | 3 | 317 | 104* | 28.81 |
| ‡B. Hassan | *Nairobi, Kenya* | 3 | 5 | 1 | 109 | 34 | 27.25 |
| ‡J. D. Birch | *Nottingham* | 13 | 21 | 6 | 392 | 68* | 26.13 |
| R. A. Pick | *Nottingham* | 12 | 14 | 4 | 240 | 63 | 24.00 |
| ‡E. E. Hemmings | *Leamington Spa* | 21 | 22 | 5 | 297 | 56* | 17.47 |
| ‡B. N. French | *Warsop* | 23 | 33 | 8 | 432 | 52* | 17.28 |
| M. Newell | *Blackburn* | 6 | 11 | 0 | 177 | 59 | 16.09 |
| ‡K. E. Cooper | *Hucknall* | 21 | 16 | 4 | 139 | 46 | 11.58 |
| C. D. Fraser-Darling | *Sheffield* | 2 | 4 | 1 | 33 | 23* | 11.00 |
| ‡K. Saxelby | *Worksop* | 17 | 13 | 4 | 78 | 29* | 8.66 |
| P. M. Such | *Helensburgh* | 14 | 12 | 5 | 18 | 8 | 2.57 |

Also batted: J. A. Afford (*Crowland*) (2 matches) 2; K. P. Evans (*Calverton*) (2 matches) 11, 0; C. W. Scott (*Thorpe-on-the-Hill*) played in one match but did not bat.

* *Signifies not out.* ‡ *Denotes county cap.*

The following played a total of sixteen three-figure innings for Nottinghamshire in County Championship matches – D. W. Randall 4, C. E. B. Rice 4, R. T. Robinson 4, B. C. Broad 2, P. Johnson 1, D. J. R. Martindale 1.

### BOWLING

| | *O* | *M* | *R* | *W* | *BB* | *Avge* |
|---|---|---|---|---|---|---|
| R. J. Hadlee | 473.5 | 136 | 1,026 | 59 | 8-41 | 17.38 |
| K. E. Cooper | 576.3 | 168 | 1,552 | 53 | 6-53 | 29.28 |
| C. E. B. Rice | 284 | 82 | 779 | 25 | 4-24 | 31.16 |
| P. M. Such | 405.1 | 105 | 1,152 | 32 | 5-73 | 36.00 |
| K. Saxelby | 404 | 95 | 1,333 | 35 | 6-64 | 38.08 |
| E. E. Hemmings | 716.3 | 171 | 2,103 | 55 | 6-51 | 38.23 |
| R. A. Pick | 267 | 44 | 1,021 | 25 | 4-51 | 40.84 |

Also bowled: J. A. Afford 22–3–76–2; J. D. Birch 5–0–14–0; B. C. Broad 9.3–2–40–2; K. P. Evans 9–1–38–0; C. D. Fraser-Darling 19–3–88–0; P. Johnson 23–3–129–1; D. J. R. Martindale 2–0–8–0; M. Newell 9–2–38–1; D. W. Randall 28–2–174–5.

At Fenner's, April 24, 25, 26. NOTTINGHAMSHIRE drew with CAMBRIDGE UNIVERSITY.

At Taunton, April 27, 28, 29. NOTTINGHAMSHIRE beat SOMERSET by nine wickets.

## NOTTINGHAMSHIRE v ESSEX

At Trent Bridge, May 1, 2, 3. Drawn. Nottinghamshire 6 pts, Essex 7 pts. Toss won by Essex. Splendid batting, particularly by Gooch, highlighted a match which could have gone either way in the final session. Although Gooch and Prichard put on 121 for the first wicket in Essex's first innings, the visitors fell away somewhat after Rice had broken the back of their batting with a spell of three for 4 in seven overs. The Nottinghamshire captain then took on the Essex bowlers with an unbeaten 108 in four and a half hours to restrict Essex's first-innings lead to 46 after Foster had threatened to give them control. A marvellous 202, which included two 6s and 32 4s, in 199 minutes by Gooch enabled Essex to set Nottinghamshire a target of 326. Randall's 117 gave them hope, but when he and Johnson were out, Birch was content to steer them to a draw.

### Essex

| | | | |
|---|---|---|---|
| G. A. Gooch b Pick | 67 | – c Rice b Pick | 202 |
| P. J. Prichard c French b Pick | 70 | – c French b Saxelby | 5 |
| B. R. Hardie c French b Rice | 5 | – c French b Rice | 9 |
| K. S. McEwan b Rice | 9 | – c Rice b Such | 28 |
| D. R. Pringle b Rice | 29 | – (6) not out | 27 |
| *K. W. R. Fletcher c French b Rice | 8 | – (7) not out | 5 |
| K. R. Pont c Pick b Cooper | 10 | | |
| †D. E. East c Broad b Such | 20 | – (5) c sub b Such | 17 |
| N. A. Foster st French b Such | 17 | | |
| J. K. Lever not out | 19 | | |
| D. L. Acfield b Such | 8 | | |
| L-b 7, w 2, n-b 2 | 11 | B 2, w 1, n-b 1 | 4 |
| 1/121 2/136 3/156 4/156 5/167 6/186 7/215 8/229 9/253 | 273 | 1/13 2/71 3/171 4/219 5/291 (5 wkts dec.) | 297 |

Bonus points – Essex 3, Nottinghamshire 4.

Bowling: *First Innings*—Saxelby 15–4–67–0; Pick 19–4–72–2; Cooper 23–13–21–1; Such 18.5–3–82–3; Rice 16–7–24–4. *Second Innings*—Saxelby 11–1–62–1; Pick 17–2–103–1; Rice 6–3–18–1; Such 20–1–79–2; Cooper 5–0–33–0.

### Nottinghamshire

| | | | |
|---|---|---|---|
| B. C. Broad c Hardie b Foster | 18 | – c Gooch b Foster | 7 |
| R. T. Robinson c McEwan b Foster | 5 | – lbw b Foster | 1 |
| D. W. Randall c East b Foster | 0 | – c Fletcher b Acfield | 117 |
| R. A. Pick c East b Foster | 16 | – (8) c McEwan b Pringle | 13 |
| *C. E. B. Rice not out | 108 | – (4) c East b Lever | 0 |
| P. Johnson c Foster b Pringle | 31 | – (5) c McEwan b Lever | 84 |
| J. D. Birch lbw b Foster | 31 | – (6) not out | 68 |
| †B. N. French c Gooch b Lever | 4 | – (7) b Acfield | 1 |
| K. Saxelby c East b Pringle | 2 | – not out | 0 |
| K. E. Cooper b Lever | 1 | | |
| P. M. Such c East b Lever | 4 | | |
| L-b 5, w 1, n-b 1 | 7 | B 3, l-b 5, w 2, n-b 1 | 11 |
| 1/18 2/18 3/35 4/62 5/96 6/154 7/167 8/178 9/181 | 227 | 1/8 2/11 3/12 4/142 5/269 6/279 7/302 (7 wkts) | 302 |

Bonus points – Nottinghamshire 2, Essex 4.

Bowling: *First Innings*—Lever 27.3–9–63–3; Foster 27–6–83–5; Pringle 23–9–58–2; Acfield 2–1–5–0; Gooch 9–3–13–0. *Second Innings*—Lever 20–4–67–2; Foster 16–5–64–2; Gooch 10–1–36–0; Pringle 15.4–2–57–1; Acfield 22–1–70–2.

Umpires: J. Birkenshaw and K. E. Palmer.

At Trent Bridge, May 14. NOTTINGHAMSHIRE v AUSTRALIANS. Abandoned.

At Leicester, May 22, 23, 24. NOTTINGHAMSHIRE drew with LEICESTERSHIRE.

## NOTTINGHAMSHIRE v LEICESTERSHIRE

At Trent Bridge, May 29, 30, 31. Drawn. Nottinghamshire 7 pts, Leicestershire 4 pts. Toss won by Nottinghamshire. On an easy-paced pitch, Nottinghamshire dominated much of the game but were unable to force a positive result. Rice scored 171 (two 6s, 22 4s) in 301 minutes, while Johnson hit his first century on his home ground, his 118 (22 4s) coming in 155 minutes as he shared with Rice a stand worth 208. But for Butcher, Leicestershire might have perished in reply, but his 288-minute innings of 120, which included one 6 and ten 4s, took Leicestershire past the follow-on figure. Randall hit 108 in 176 minutes to set up Rice's second declaration, but Leicestershire, thanks largely to another excellent contribution from Butcher, held out for a draw.

### Nottinghamshire

| | | | |
|---|---|---|---|
| B. C. Broad c Cook b Ferris | 10 | – c and b Clift | 11 |
| M. Newell c Cobb b Cook | 4 | – c Garnham b Parsons | 0 |
| D. W. Randall lbw b Clift | 48 | – not out | 108 |
| *C. E. B. Rice not out | 171 | | |
| P. Johnson lbw b Cook | 118 | – (6) not out | 9 |
| J. D. Birch b Cook | 2 | – (5) b Cook | 18 |
| R. J. Hadlee not out | 9 | | |
| †B. N. French (did not bat) | | – (4) c and b Cook | 4 |
| B 4, l-b 4, w 3, n-b 9 | 20 | B 4, l-b 2, w 3, n-b 3 | 12 |
| 1/21 2/24 3/125 4/333 5/345 (5 wkts dec.) | 382 | 1/4 2/43 3/83 4/138 (4 wkts dec.) | 162 |

E. E. Hemmings, K. E. Cooper and P. M. Such did not bat.

Bonus points – Nottinghamshire 4, Leicestershire 2 (Score at 100 overs: 354-5).

Bowling: *First Innings*—Ferris 15–4–64–1; Parsons 24–7–68–0; Clift 29–8–100–1; Cook 37–5–120–3; Briers 3–0–22–0. *Second Innings*—Ferris 9–0–44–0; Parsons 13–0–40–1; Clift 13–2–29–1; Cook 20–8–43–2.

### Leicestershire

| First innings | | Second innings | |
|---|---|---|---|
| I. P. Butcher c Birch b Such | 120 | – b Hemmings | 74 |
| J. C. Balderstone lbw b Cooper | 18 | – b Hemmings | 28 |
| R. A. Cobb c Randall b Such | 3 | – lbw b Hemmings | 14 |
| J. J. Whitaker c Rice b Such | 22 | – c French b Hadlee | 8 |
| *N. E. Briers b Hemmings | 0 | – not out | 44 |
| M. Blackett c French b Hemmings | 0 | – (8) not out | 3 |
| P. B. Clift c Rice b Hadlee | 22 | – c Such b Hemmings | 24 |
| G. J. Parsons c Rice b Cooper | 0 | | |
| †M. A. Garnham c Rice b Cooper | 32 | – (6) b Such | 11 |
| N. G. B. Cook b Rice | 18 | | |
| G. J. F. Ferris not out | 0 | | |
| B 5, l-b 4, w 1, n-b 2 | 12 | B 1, l-b 3 | 4 |
| 1/59 2/69 3/125 4/126 5/126 6/159 7/175 8/213 9/247 | 247 | 1/50 2/104 3/125 4/125 5/149 6/191 | (6 wkts) 210 |

Bonus points – Leicestershire 2, Nottinghamshire 3 (Score at 100 overs: 226-8).

Bowling: *First Innings*—Hadlee 19–5–37–1; Cooper 19.3–7–39–3; Hemmings 36–15–76–2; Such 27–8–74–3; Rice 5–1–12–1. *Second Innings*—Hadlee 11–3–32–1; Cooper 7–1–20–0; Such 24–8–64–1; Hemmings 32–8–89–4; Rice 2–1–1–0.

Umpires: B. J. Meyer and D. R. Shepherd.

At Tunbridge Wells, June 8, 10, 11. NOTTINGHAMSHIRE beat KENT by four wickets.

At The Oval, June 12, 13, 14. NOTTINGHAMSHIRE drew with SURREY.

## NOTTINGHAMSHIRE v KENT

At Trent Bridge, June 15, 17, 18. Drawn. Nottinghamshire 6 pts, Kent 4 pts. Toss won by Nottinghamshire. Troubled Kent, with a succession of defeats behind them, were content to make sure of not losing the game. Put in, they recovered from 130 for seven to 258 all out with Ellison falling just 2 runs short of a first Championship hundred. Nottinghamshire scored briskly in reply and declared 6 runs behind, but on a slow pitch Kent piled on the runs against some generous bowling before setting a target of 329 in only 70 minutes plus twenty overs. Initially, Broad and Rice took up the challenge, but it was never possible once Kent went on the defensive and the game drifted aimlessly to a draw.

### Kent

| First innings | | Second innings | |
|---|---|---|---|
| M. R. Benson c Rice b Cooper | 55 | – c French b Broad | 50 |
| S. G. Hinks b Hadlee | 7 | – c Rice b Randall | 67 |
| C. J. Tavaré run out | 11 | – not out | 94 |
| D. G. Aslett b Cooper | 26 | – c Johnson b Randall | 53 |
| *C. S. Cowdrey b Hadlee | 10 | – c Randall b Johnson | 5 |
| E. A. E. Baptiste c French b Saxelby | 11 | – b Newell | 24 |
| R. M. Ellison lbw b Cooper | 98 | | |
| †A. P. E. Knott c French b Cooper | 0 | – (7) not out | 20 |
| G. R. Dilley c Johnson b Hemmings | 13 | | |
| D. L. Underwood lbw b Hadlee | 13 | | |
| K. B. S. Jarvis not out | 0 | | |
| B 4, l-b 4, w 1, n-b 5 | 14 | B 3, l-b 5, w 1 | 9 |
| 1/31 2/76 3/76 4/88 5/109 6/126 7/130 8/171 9/245 | 258 | 1/91 2/129 3/222 4/235 5/271 | (5 wkts dec.) 322 |

Bonus points – Kent 2, Nottinghamshire 3 (Score at 100 overs: 214-8).

Bowling: *First Innings*—Hadlee 24–8–36–3; Saxelby 26–5–91–1; Cooper 30.3–14–43–4; Rice 24–8–57–0; Hemmings 14–3–23–1. *Second Innings*—Hadlee 5–1–9–0; Saxelby 7–0–39–0; Cooper 6–1–13–0; Hemmings 4–0–12–0; Birch 5–0–14–0; Broad 4–1–16–1; Randall 12–2–60–2; Johnson 20–2–112–1; Newell 9–2–38–1; Rice 2–1–1–0.

## Nottinghamshire

| | | | |
|---|---|---|---|
| B. C. Broad c Knott b Ellison | 43 | – not out | 71 |
| M. Newell c Hinks b Dilley | 0 | | |
| D. W. Randall c Knott b Ellison | 37 | – not out | 13 |
| *C. E. B. Rice lbw b Baptiste | 37 | – (2) c Baptiste b Underwood | 71 |
| P. Johnson c Benson b Baptiste | 11 | | |
| J. D. Birch not out | 60 | | |
| R. J. Hadlee not out | 52 | | |
| B 5, l-b 4, w 1, n-b 2 | 12 | B 1, l-b 1, w 2 | 4 |
| 1/1 2/77 3/90 4/113 5/143 (5 wkts dec.) | 252 | 1/128 (1 wkt) | 159 |

†B. N. French, E. E. Hemmings, K. Saxelby and K. E. Cooper did not bat.

Bonus points – Nottinghamshire 3, Kent 2.

Bowling: *First Innings*—Dilley 18–5–60–1; Jarvis 15–0–66–0; Baptiste 19–2–48–2; Ellison 14–3–36–2; Underwood 7.4–1–33–0. *Second Innings*—Aslett 6–0–25–0; Benson 4–0–31–0; Jarvis 5–0–27–0; Baptiste 4–0–23–0; Hinks 5–0–26–0; Underwood 5–0–25–1.

Umpires: H. D. Bird and B. Dudleston.

# NOTTINGHAMSHIRE v MIDDLESEX

At Trent Bridge, June 22, 24, 25. Middlesex won by ten wickets. Middlesex 24 pts, Nottinghamshire 4 pts. Toss won by Middlesex. Despite the threat of rain, Middlesex coasted to a thoroughly deserved victory with 5.5 overs to spare. They restricted Nottinghamshire to 202 with some fine seam bowling in the first innings and then Slack's four and a half hour 112 plus significant contributions from Barlow, Gatting and Butcher gave them a lead of 235. Nottinghamshire, although beginning promisingly, faired little better a second time and slid from 108 without loss to 249 against the pace of Williams and Cowans. Certainly Middlesex did not suffer unduly from the absence of the incapacitated Daniel on the last day.

## Nottinghamshire

| | | | |
|---|---|---|---|
| R. T. Robinson b Daniel | 18 | – b Edmonds | 73 |
| B. C. Broad c Downton b Daniel | 27 | – c Slack b Edmonds | 40 |
| D. W. Randall run out | 50 | – b Williams | 3 |
| *C. E. B. Rice c Edmonds b Williams | 12 | – c Downton b Williams | 14 |
| P. Johnson c Slack b Cowans | 1 | – b Williams | 1 |
| J. D. Birch c Gatting b Cowans | 0 | – c Slack b Cowans | 4 |
| R. J. Hadlee c Downton b Gatting | 27 | – not out | 28 |
| †B. N. French not out | 28 | – c Butcher b Cowans | 0 |
| E. E. Hemmings c Butcher b Daniel | 11 | – c Downton b Cowans | 7 |
| K. Saxelby c Downton b Daniel | 1 | – b Williams | 10 |
| K. E. Cooper c Slack b Williams | 12 | – b Cowans | 46 |
| L-b 14, w 1 | 15 | B 1, l-b 12, n-b 10 | 23 |
| 1/25 2/60 3/85 4/86 5/92 6/138 7/154 8/183 9/185 | 202 | 1/108 2/115 3/131 4/135 5/147 6/147 7/147 8/155 9/167 | 249 |

Bonus points – Nottinghamshire 2, Middlesex 4.

Bowling: *First Innings*—Daniel 21–5–64–4; Cowans 16–4–47–2; Williams 17.4–2–57–2; Gatting 5–1–20–1. *Second Innings*—Williams 21–2–92–4; Cowans 14.2–2–47–4; Edmonds 30–8–55–2; Gatting 5–2–5–0; Emburey 12–3–37–0.

## Middlesex

G. D. Barlow c sub b Hemmings ............ 81 – not out ..................... 6
W. N. Slack c Robinson b Hemmings ........112 – not out ..................... 9
*M. W. Gatting c Rice b Cooper ............ 76
R. O. Butcher c Hemmings b Rice ........... 71
†P. R. Downton c Cooper b Hadlee .......... 0
C. T. Radley c Hadlee b Cooper ............ 0
J. E. Emburey c Hadlee b Hemmings ......... 44
N. F. Williams st French b Hemmings ........ 21
P. H. Edmonds not out ..................... 1
N. G. Cowans not out ...................... 4
B 5, l-b 19, w 1, n-b 2 ............. 27

1/171 2/242 3/301 (8 wkts dec.) 437 (no wkt) 15
4/306 5/307 6/397
7/420 8/432

W. W. Daniel did not bat.

Bonus points – Middlesex 4, Nottinghamshire 2 (Score at 100 overs: 308-5).

Bowling: *First Innings*—Hadlee 26–5–78–1; Saxelby 3–0–13–0; Cooper 31–3–105–2; Rice 28–9–92–1; Hemmings 34–6–125–4. *Second Innings*—Cooper 1–0–5–0; Broad 1.1–0–3–0; Randall 1–0–7–0.

Umpires: J. H. Hampshire and R. Palmer.

At Derby, June 26, 27, 28. NOTTINGHAMSHIRE drew with DERBYSHIRE.

## NOTTINGHAMSHIRE v GLOUCESTERSHIRE

At Trent Bridge, June 29, 30, July 1. Drawn. Nottinghamshire 7 pts, Gloucestershire 6 pts. Toss won by Gloucestershire. Solid, rather than spectacular, batting gave Nottinghamshire a useful platform which began to look formidable when Gloucestershire lost their first six wickets for 58. However, Lloyds fashioned a recovery with an invaluable 88 not out in 165 minutes, and Gloucestershire were able to declare only 59 runs behind. Rice and Johnson put on 124 for the fourth wicket in 23 overs to set up a promising finish with 50 overs remaining. Hadlee again dismissed both Gloucestershire openers cheaply, but Athey and Bainbridge made sure there were no further worries for the visitors, even though victory was well beyond them.

## Nottinghamshire

B. C. Broad c Athey b Bainbridge .......... 35 – c Russell b Sainsbury ......... 7
M. Newell c Russell b Curran .............. 9 – c Russell b Sainsbury ......... 15
D. W. Randall c Curran b Lawrence ......... 65 – b Sainsbury ................. 9
*C. E. B. Rice c Athey b Walsh ............ 46 – c Walsh b Lawrence ........... 68
P. Johnson c Russell b Lawrence ........... 16 – b Athey ..................... 60
J. D. Birch b Lawrence .................... 23 – not out ..................... 16
R. J. Hadlee c Athey b Walsh .............. 0 – not out ..................... 26
†B. N. French c Bainbridge b Curran ........ 28
E. E. Hemmings c Lawrence b Walsh ......... 11
K. Saxelby b Lawrence ..................... 10
K. E. Cooper not out ...................... 5
B 4, l-b 8, w 4, n-b 8 .............. 24 B 1, l-b 3, w 2, n-b 6 .... 12

1/36 2/73 3/146 4/178 5/192 272 1/14 2/35 3/40 (5 wkts dec.) 213
6/193 7/230 8/251 9/266 4/164 5/170

Bonus points – Nottinghamshire 3, Gloucestershire 4.

Bowling: *First Innings*—Lawrence 17–0–73–4; Walsh 22–4–62–3; Curran 17–4–54–2; Sainsbury 8–0–36–0; Bainbridge 14–2–34–1; Lloyds 1–0–1–0. *Second Innings*—Lawrence 16–1–68–1; Sainsbury 14–5–30–3; Walsh 8–1–47–0; Curran 2–1–4–0; Bainbridge 7–1–33–0; Athey 5–0–27–1.

## Gloucestershire

| | | | |
|---|---|---|---|
| A. W. Stovold c Johnson b Hadlee | 7 | – c Randall b Hadlee | 2 |
| P. W. Romaines b Hadlee | 8 | – c Rice b Hadlee | 1 |
| C. W. J. Athey b Cooper | 9 | – c Cooper b Hemmings | 54 |
| *P. Bainbridge c French b Rice | 4 | – not out | 56 |
| B. F. Davison c French b Saxelby | 32 | – not out | 1 |
| K. M. Curran c Saxelby b Rice | 10 | | |
| G. E. Sainsbury c Hadlee b Saxelby | 1 | | |
| J. W. Lloyds not out | 88 | | |
| †R. C. Russell b Rice | 7 | | |
| D. V. Lawrence c Randall b Cooper | 41 | | |
| C. A. Walsh not out | 0 | | |
| B 2, l-b 3, n-b 1 | 6 | L-b 4 | 4 |
| 1/12 2/17 3/30 4/30 5/48 6/58 7/103 8/133 9/213 (9 wkts dec.) | 213 | 1/2 2/7 3/111 (3 wkts) | 118 |

Bonus points – Gloucestershire 2, Nottinghamshire 4.

Bowling: *First Innings*—Hadlee 19–7–59–2; Saxelby 17–7–45–2; Cooper 14–4–37–2; Rice 11–2–40–3; Hemmings 14–5–27–0. *Second Innings*—Hadlee 8–3–16–2; Saxelby 9–3–21–0; Cooper 8–3–16–0; Hemmings 11–1–61–1.

Umpires: M. J. Kitchen and N. T. Plews.

At Swansea, July 6, 8, 9. NOTTINGHAMSHIRE drew with GLAMORGAN.

At Lord's, July 10, 11, 12. NOTTINGHAMSHIRE beat MIDDLESEX by five wickets.

At Nuneaton, July 13, 15, 16. NOTTINGHAMSHIRE drew with WARWICKSHIRE.

## NOTTINGHAMSHIRE v SUSSEX

At Trent Bridge, July 24, 25, 26. Drawn. Nottinghamshire 7 pts, Sussex 3 pts. Toss won by Sussex. Nottinghamshire made an excellent start with Broad and Robinson sharing a stand of 139 in 57 overs, but in spite of 64 from Randall, the expected acceleration never materialised. In the end they batted throughout the day for maximum batting points. A first-class spell of four for 12 by Hadlee inspired a Sussex collapse in which their last eight wickets fell for 62 runs and Nottinghamshire were 250 runs ahead with seven wickets intact at the close of the second day. Sussex were set 329 to win from 87 overs, and on a pitch which had eased considerably they accepted the challenge. A fourth-wicket partnership of 123 in 29 overs between Imran and Colin Wells put them on course, but with eighteen overs being lost because of stoppages for rain and bad light, a draw became inevitable.

### Nottinghamshire

| | First Innings | | Second Innings | |
|---|---|---|---|---|
| R. T. Robinson b Imran | 73 | | | |
| B. C. Broad lbw b Imran | 63 | – (1) lbw b Waller | 14 |
| D. W. Randall c Gould b Imran | 64 | – c Gould b Reeve | 18 |
| P. Johnson c Gould b le Roux | 23 | – c Green b Imran | 54 |
| B. Hassan c Parker b Imran | 22 | – (2) b Reeve | 34 |
| *R. J. Hadlee c Barclay b Imran | 4 | – not out | 12 |
| †B. N. French not out | 7 | – (5) b Imran | 40 |
| E. E. Hemmings not out | 27 | – (7) c and b C. M. Wells | 0 |
| R. A. Pick (did not bat) | | – (8) b Imran | 4 |
| K. Saxelby (did not bat) | | – (9) not out | 5 |
| B 1, l-b 8, w 4, n-b 4 | 17 | B 4, l-b 5, n-b 6 | 15 |
| 1/139 2/152 3/208 4/260 5/263 6/266 | (6 wkts dec.) 300 | 1/39 2/73 3/76 4/164 5/183 6/184 7/189 | (7 wkts dec.) 196 |

J. A. Afford did not bat.

Bonus points – Nottinghamshire 3, Sussex 2 (Score at 100 overs: 266-6).

Bowling: *First Innings*—Imran 26–5–59–5; le Roux 17–0–58–1; Reeve 22–2–64–0; C. M. Wells 11–1–41–0; Waller 31–12–61–0; Barclay 5–3–8–0. *Second Innings*—Imran 19–1–50–3; le Roux 10–3–12–0; Waller 14–3–56–1; Reeve 9–0–45–2; C. M. Wells 5–0–24–1.

### Sussex

| | First Innings | | Second Innings | |
|---|---|---|---|---|
| G. D. Mendis c Hassan b Pick | 42 | – b Hemmings | 41 |
| A. M. Green c Randall b Saxelby | 3 | – c Randall b Hadlee | 4 |
| P. W. G. Parker c Hassan b Hemmings | 40 | – c sub b Afford | 33 |
| Imran Khan b Afford | 22 | – not out | 56 |
| C. M. Wells c French b Hadlee | 15 | – c French b Hadlee | 71 |
| A. P. Wells c Johnson b Hemmings | 6 | – not out | 7 |
| *J. R. T. Barclay c French b Hadlee | 1 | | |
| †I. J. Gould c French b Hadlee | 5 | | |
| G. S. le Roux c Afford b Hadlee | 8 | | |
| D. A. Reeve not out | 12 | | |
| C. E. Waller lbw b Saxelby | 8 | | |
| L-b 5, w 1 | 6 | B 6 | 6 |
| 1/16 2/66 3/106 4/116 5/128 6/134 7/134 8/143 9/150 | 168 | 1/13 2/70 3/84 4/207 | (4 wkts) 218 |

Bonus points – Sussex 1, Nottinghamshire 4.

Bowling: *First Innings*—Hadlee 18–3–39–4; Saxelby 10.5–3–27–2; Pick 7–2–21–1; Hemmings 25–4–51–2; Afford 6–1–25–1. *Second Innings*—Hadlee 15–3–36–2; Saxelby 11–2–36–0; Hemmings 21–3–80–1; Afford 10–2–37–1; Pick 6–1–23–0.

Umpires: J. W. Holder and D. O. Oslear.

## NOTTINGHAMSHIRE v YORKSHIRE

At Worksop, July 27, 29, 30. Drawn. Nottinghamshire 7 pts, Yorkshire 5 pts. Toss won by Nottinghamshire. In contrast to many matches at Worksop, this game petered out into a disappointing draw. Nottinghamshire made a positive start with an innings of 131 from Broad, his second century of the season, but Yorkshire laboured before declaring 63 runs behind. A brisk 64 by Broad and 47 not out in 53 minutes from Randall took Nottinghamshire to a second declaration, but Yorkshire, needing 263 at just over 5 an over, settled for a comfortable draw once Hadlee had removed Moxon and Sharp in his first two overs.

**Nottinghamshire**

| | | | |
|---|---|---|---|
| B. C. Broad c S. N. Hartley b Shaw | 131 | – c Boycott b Moxon | 64 |
| D. W. Randall c Bairstow b Jarvis | 38 | – c Bairstow b S. N. Hartley | 48 |
| B. Hassan c Sharp b Jarvis | 30 | | |
| P. Johnson lbw b Jarvis | 13 | – not out | 47 |
| D. J. R. Martindale c Bairstow b P. J. Hartley | 18 | – (3) not out | 27 |
| *R. J. Hadlee c Moxon b Shaw | 47 | | |
| †B. N. French c Carrick b Shaw | 19 | | |
| E. E. Hemmings not out | 6 | | |
| B 8, l-b 14, w 2, n-b 4 | 28 | L-b 11, n-b 2 | 13 |
| 1/84 2/161 3/184 4/252 5/274 6/315 7/330 (7 wkts dec.) | 330 | 1/111 2/124 (2 wkts dec.) | 199 |

K. Saxelby, K. E. Cooper and P. M. Such did not bat.

Bonus points – Nottinghamshire 4, Yorkshire 2 (Score at 100 overs: 321-6).

Bowling: *First Innings*—Jarvis 24–2–89–3; P. J. Hartley 22–2–71–1; Shaw 24.2–3–77–3; Carrick 16–4–33–0; Swallow 15–3–38–0. *Second Innings*—Jarvis 4–1–10–0; Shaw 8–0–48–0; S. N. Hartley 16.4–5–63–1; Moxon 5–0–35–1; P. J. Hartley 7–0–32–0.

**Yorkshire**

| | | | |
|---|---|---|---|
| G. Boycott c French b Hadlee | 0 | – not out | 55 |
| M. D. Moxon c Broad b Hadlee | 70 | – c Randall b Hadlee | 0 |
| K. Sharp b Saxelby | 48 | – c Such b Hadlee | 0 |
| S. N. Hartley c Broad b Saxelby | 10 | | |
| P. E. Robinson c Hassan b Saxelby | 46 | – (4) not out | 18 |
| *†D. L. Bairstow c Cooper b Such | 35 | | |
| P. Carrick c and b Such | 4 | | |
| I. G. Swallow not out | 25 | | |
| P. W. Jarvis not out | 8 | | |
| B 13, l-b 5, n-b 3 | 21 | B 4, l-b 2, n-b 3 | 9 |
| 1/8 2/128 3/148 4/148 5/198 6/223 7/245 (7 wkts dec.) | 267 | 1/1 2/1 (2 wkts) | 82 |

C. Shaw and P. J. Hartley did not bat.

Bonus points – Yorkshire 3, Nottinghamshire 3.

Bowling: *First Innings*—Hadlee 25–8–60–2; Cooper 19–6–59–0; Hemmings 19–7–38–0; Saxelby 23–4–68–3; Such 14–5–24–2. *Second Innings*—Hadlee 9–2–9–2; Cooper 7–3–8–0; Such 12–2–25–0; Hemmings 8–1–19–0; Johnson 2–1–5–0; Martindale 2–0–8–0; Randall 1–0–2–0.

Umpires: D. J. Constant and D. O. Oslear.

At Northampton, August 3, 5, 6. NOTTINGHAMSHIRE drew with NORTHAMPTONSHIRE.

## NOTTINGHAMSHIRE v WORCESTERSHIRE

At Trent Bridge, August 10, 12, 13. Drawn. Nottinghamshire 8 pts, Worcestershire 6 pts. Toss won by Worcestershire. Worcestershire, on the receiving end for most of the game, almost produced an improbable victory in the final session. Penetrative bowling by Saxelby restricted them to 202 in their first innings, and Robinson and Hemmings, the night-watchman, gave Nottinghamshire a good start with a century partnership which Rice and Johnson built on. A gritty 69 by Neale in 212 minutes held up Nottinghamshire, and they were further inconvenienced by Radford's 41 from 68 deliveries, but maximum points still looked within their grasp when they needed 106 in 21 overs. However, wickets fell at an alarming rate, and but for Randall's 53, Nottinghamshire would have suffered defeat instead of finishing at 98 for seven.

**Worcestershire**

| | | | |
|---|---|---|---|
| T. S. Curtis c French b Hadlee | 43 | – c Hadlee b Such | 20 |
| D. B. D'Oliveira retired hurt | 8 | – (7) b Hemmings | 4 |
| D. M. Smith b Saxelby | 15 | – c Randall b Hemmings | 2 |
| D. N. Patel c Rice b Saxelby | 5 | – c Randall b Cooper | 39 |
| *P. A. Neale c Robinson b Cooper | 37 | – c and b Such | 69 |
| G. A. Hick c Johnson b Hadlee | 20 | – c Broad b Such | 10 |
| †S. J. Rhodes c French b Saxelby | 10 | – (2) c Hadlee b Hemmings | 6 |
| P. J. Newport c French b Saxelby | 24 | – c sub b Such | 14 |
| N. V. Radford c Johnson b Such | 10 | – b Cooper | 41 |
| R. K. Illingworth not out | 17 | – not out | 6 |
| S. M. McEwan run out | 5 | – b Cooper | 0 |
| L-b 6, w 1, n-b 1 | 8 | B 9, l-b 4, n-b 1 | 14 |
| 1/34 2/40 3/110 4/130 5/135 6/160 7/179 8/179 9/202 | 202 | 1/29 2/29 3/41 4/111 5/128 6/148 7/178 8/179 9/225 | 225 |

Bonus points – Worcestershire 2, Nottinghamshire 4.

Bowling: *First Innings*—Hadlee 16–4–45–2; Saxelby 22–8–47–4; Cooper 12–2–29–1; Hemmings 5–0–12–0; Rice 7–1–19–0; Such 24–6–44–1. *Second Innings*—Hadlee 4–2–3–0; Saxelby 6–2–16–0; Cooper 17–7–26–3; Such 38–12–74–4; Hemmings 39–12–93–3.

**Nottinghamshire**

| | | | |
|---|---|---|---|
| R. T. Robinson c Smith b Radford | 82 | – c D'Oliveira b Radford | 2 |
| B. C. Broad b Newport | 3 | – c Curtis b Newport | 0 |
| E. E. Hemmings b Illingworth | 30 | – (8) not out | 13 |
| D. W. Randall c Patel b Illingworth | 0 | – (3) b Newport | 53 |
| *C. E. B. Rice b Patel | 85 | – (4) b Radford | 0 |
| P. Johnson c Rhodes b McEwan | 48 | – (5) c Rhodes b Newport | 5 |
| R. J. Hadlee c Rhodes b Patel | 2 | – run out | 4 |
| †B. N. French c Rhodes b McEwan | 3 | – (6) b Newport | 11 |
| K. Saxelby not out | 29 | – not out | 3 |
| K. E. Cooper c Radford b Newport | 7 | | |
| P. M. Such b Patel | 0 | | |
| B 4, l-b 18, w 2, n-b 9 | 33 | B 1, l-b 6 | 7 |
| 1/17 2/117 3/117 4/136 5/213 6/221 7/237 8/297 9/310 | 322 | 1/2 2/2 3/6 4/23 5/49 6/59 7/93 | (7 wkts) 98 |

Bonus points – Nottinghamshire 4, Worcestershire 4.

Bowling: *First Innings*—Radford 23–1–78–1; Newport 21–1–93–2; McEwan 12–2–38–2; Illingworth 12–0–37–2; Patel 17.1–4–54–3. *Second Innings*—Radford 9.5–1–33–2; Newport 10–0–47–4; Illingworth 1–0–11–0.

Umpires: J. H. Harris and K. E. Palmer.

At Cheltenham, August 14, 15, 16. NOTTINGHAMSHIRE drew with GLOUCESTERSHIRE.

At Old Trafford, August 17, 19, 20. NOTTINGHAMSHIRE drew with LANCASHIRE.

## NOTTINGHAMSHIRE v DERBYSHIRE

At Trent Bridge, August 24, 26, 27. Nottinghamshire won by ten wickets. Nottinghamshire 23 pts, Derbyshire 2 pts. Toss won by Derbyshire. Nottinghamshire ended a sequence of seven successive draws with an emphatic victory over their neighbours. A splendid 94 in 162 minutes by Randall helped Nottinghamshire build a useful platform, and when Pick's best bowling of the season and six catches by French left Derbyshire facing the follow-on, there was no escape for them. Wright and Barnett put on 120 for the third wicket, but once they were separated, Hemmings, Such and Hadlee brought the innings to a swift conclusion. Nottinghamshire were left with the simplest of tasks in their second innings, but satisfaction was tempered by the news that Johnson, taken ill overnight with appendicitis, would miss the rest of the season.

## Nottinghamshire

| | | | |
|---|---|---|---|
| R. T. Robinson c Marples b Mortensen | 52 | – not out | 11 |
| B. C. Broad c Anderson b Mortensen | 13 | – not out | 17 |
| D. W. Randall c Anderson b Miller | 94 | | |
| P. Johnson c Wright b Finney | 3 | | |
| D. J. R. Martindale lbw b Finney | 52 | | |
| *R. J. Hadlee c Marples b Warner | 15 | | |
| †B. N. French not out | 32 | | |
| E. E. Hemmings c Barnett b Warner | 7 | | |
| R. A. Pick c Wright b Warner | 9 | | |
| K. E. Cooper lbw b Mortensen | 4 | | |
| P. M. Such b Mortensen | 5 | | |
| B 4, l-b 6, w 3, n-b 14 | 27 | L-b 2 | 2 |
| 1/60 2/73 3/81 4/206 5/249 6/255 7/277 8/289 9/297 | 313 | | (no wkt) 30 |

Bonus points – Nottinghamshire 3, Derbyshire 2 (Score at 100 overs: 274-6).

Bowling: *First Innings*—Warner 23–1–87–3; Finney 18–5–55–2; Newman 24–4–70–0; Mortensen 27.3–10–49–4; Miller 18–5–42–1. *Second Innings*—Mortensen 4–1–11–0; Newman 3.3–1–17–0.

## Derbyshire

| | | | |
|---|---|---|---|
| I. S. Anderson c French b Hadlee | 0 | – c Randall b Such | 3 |
| B. Roberts c French b Pick | 1 | – lbw b Hemmings | 33 |
| J. G. Wright b Pick | 6 | – c French b Pick | 76 |
| *K. J. Barnett run out | 23 | – c Johnson b Such | 51 |
| M. A. Fell c Randall b Pick | 0 | – (7) b Hemmings | 6 |
| G. Miller c French b Cooper | 34 | – (8) c Randall b Hemmings | 9 |
| P. G. Newman c French b Cooper | 20 | – (9) c and b Hemmings | 11 |
| A. E. Warner c Such b Hemmings | 6 | – (10) lbw b Hadlee | 1 |
| R. J. Finney c French b Pick | 4 | – (6) b Hadlee | 17 |
| †C. Marples not out | 21 | – (5) b Such | 0 |
| O. H. Mortensen c French b Hemmings | 1 | – not out | 1 |
| L-b 4, n-b 5 | 9 | L-b 5, w 1, n-b 3 | 9 |
| 1/2 2/6 3/19 4/20 5/57 6/72 7/79 8/84 9/124 | 125 | 1/39 2/39 3/159 4/159 5/179 6/194 7/204 8/204 9/205 | 217 |

Bonus points – Nottinghamshire 4.

Bowling: *First Innings*—Hadlee 2.2–2–2–1; Pick 12–3–51–4; Cooper 16.4–4–36–2; Such 5–0–22–0; Hemmings 7.2–2–10–2. *Second Innings*—Cooper 10–4–16–0; Pick 12–1–46–1; Broad 4–1–20–0; Hemmings 37.3–15–79–4; Such 24–11–45–3; Hadlee 7–4–6–2.

Umpires: J. Birkenshaw and M. J. Kitchen.

## NOTTINGHAMSHIRE v GLAMORGAN

At Trent Bridge, August 28, 29, 30. Glamorgan won by an innings and 11 runs. Glamorgan 24 pts, Nottinghamshire 4 pts. Toss won by Nottinghamshire. The match was a remarkable personal success for the Glamorgan captain, Ontong, who scored a brilliant hundred and had match figures of thirteen for 106. Nottinghamshire prospered at first but from 150 for two collapsed against Ontong's off-spin as he took four wickets in five overs without conceding a run. Next Ontong, helped by the nineteen-year-old Maynard, rescued Glamorgan after the loss of four wickets, and his 130, occupying 247 minutes and including one 6 and fourteen 4s, earned a lead of 131 which was to prove decisive. Nottinghamshire began their second innings comfortably, but from 59 they lost all ten wickets for the addition of 61 runs as Ontong enjoyed his best-ever return.

## Nottinghamshire

| First innings | | Second innings | |
|---|---|---|---|
| B. C. Broad c Jones b Barwick | 5 | b Ontong | 32 |
| M. Newell c Ontong b Holmes | 44 | b Price | 24 |
| D. W. Randall b Smith | 32 | c sub b Ontong | 0 |
| *C. E. B. Rice c Morris b Ontong | 63 | c Jones b Ontong | 9 |
| D. J. R. Martindale lbw b Ontong | 4 | b Ontong | 1 |
| J. D. Birch b Barwick | 22 | lbw b Ontong | 3 |
| †B. N. French c Morris b Ontong | 0 | c Hopkins b Ontong | 12 |
| C. D. Fraser-Darling c Holmes b Ontong | 0 | (9) c Hopkins b Price | 8 |
| R. A. Pick c Davies b Barwick | 8 | (10) not out | 17 |
| E. E. Hemmings c Maynard b Ontong | 9 | (8) c sub b Ontong | 4 |
| P. M. Such not out | 0 | c sub b Ontong | 0 |
| B 4, l-b 5, n-b 2 | 11 | L-b 5, w 5 | 10 |
| 1/10 2/62 3/150 4/158 5/159 6/159 7/163 8/176 9/195 | 198 | 1/59 2/61 3/63 4/76 5/77 6/88 7/97 8/99 9/118 | 120 |

Bonus points – Nottinghamshire 1, Glamorgan 4.

Bowling: *First Innings*—Barwick 17.1–3–44–3; Smith 12–3–39–1; Derrick 12–2–31–0; Holmes 14–5–32–1; Ontong 15–6–39–5; Price 1–0–4–0. *Second Innings*—Barwick 6–2–11–0; Smith 4–0–10–0; Price 20–6–27–2; Ontong 18.3–3–67–8.

## Glamorgan

| | |
|---|---|
| A. L. Jones c Birch b Hemmings | 35 |
| J. A. Hopkins c Newell b Such | 25 |
| G. C. Holmes c Fraser-Darling b Hemmings | 11 |
| H. Morris c Fraser-Darling b Such | 0 |
| *R. C. Ontong c Martindale b Hemmings | 130 |
| M. P. Maynard b Pick | 58 |
| †T. Davies c Martindale b Hemmings | 21 |
| M. R. Price not out | 28 |
| J. Derrick st French b Hemmings | 4 |
| I. Smith b Rice | 4 |
| S. R. Barwick c French b Pick | 1 |
| L-b 9, n-b 3 | 12 |
| 1/59 2/65 3/65 4/81 5/203 6/260 7/302 8/309 9/328 | 329 |

Bonus points – Glamorgan 4, Nottinghamshire 3 (Score at 100 overs: 311-8).

Bowling: Pick 17.2–5–54–2; Rice 15–3–28–1; Such 31–4–99–2; Hemmings 35–7–115–5; Fraser-Darling 4–0–24–0.

Umpires: M. J. Kitchen and P. B. Wight.

## NOTTINGHAMSHIRE v LANCASHIRE

At Trent Bridge, August 31, September 2, 3. Drawn. Nottinghamshire 4 pts, Lancashire 4 pts. Toss won by Lancashire. Bowlers dominated a rain-affected match but a sporting declaration by Rice just failed to produce a winner. Put in to bat, Nottinghamshire were bowled out without gaining a batting point. Allott impressed with five wickets, but he was eclipsed by Hadlee's career-best figures of eight for 41 as Lancashire were hustled out for 126. Rain resulted in the loss of 90 overs before Nottinghamshire were in a position to declare, offering a target of 199 in 39 overs. Hayes accepted the challenge with 55 in 75 minutes, but the off-spinners, Such and Hemmings, swung the initiative Nottinghamshire's way so that Lancashire were content to settle for a draw.

## Nottinghamshire

| | | | |
|---|---|---|---|
| D. W. Randall c Maynard b Watkinson | 21 | – (2) c Varey b Folley | 50 |
| B. C. Broad lbw b Watkinson | 15 | – (1) c Hayes b Patterson | 32 |
| *C. E. B. Rice st Maynard b Simmons | 70 | – retired hurt | 41 |
| D. J. R. Martindale c Maynard b Allott | 13 | – lbw b Simmons | 11 |
| J. D. Birch c Maynard b Allott | 0 | – not out | 13 |
| R. J. Hadlee c Maynard b Allott | 4 | – c Hayes b Folley | 22 |
| †B. N. French c Fairbrother b Simmons | 3 | – not out | 2 |
| R. A. Pick c and b Simmons | 1 | | |
| E. E. Hemmings b Allott | 2 | | |
| J. A. Afford c Patterson b Allott | 2 | | |
| P. M. Such not out | 0 | | |
| L-b 7, w 1, n-b 1 | 9 | B 1, l-b 7, w 1, n-b 4 | 13 |
| 1/32 2/49 3/90 4/94 5/104 6/123 7/127 8/138 9/138 | 140 | 1/44 2/132 3/152 4/178 (4 wkts dec.) | 184 |

Bonus points – Lancashire 4.

Bowling: *First Innings*—Patterson 10–2–29–0; Allott 19.5–3–47–5; Watkinson 14–1–52–2; Simmons 5–2–5–3. *Second Innings*—Allott 12–3–29–0; Patterson 10–1–40–1; Watkinson 7-1–18–0; Simmons 17–2–46–1; Folley 10–0–43–2.

## Lancashire

| | | | |
|---|---|---|---|
| M. R. Chadwick c Randall b Such | 18 | – c Hemmings b Hadlee | 10 |
| D. W. Varey lbw b Hadlee | 24 | – st French b Hemmings | 26 |
| K. A. Hayes c French b Hadlee | 1 | – lbw b Hemmings | 55 |
| N. H. Fairbrother b Hadlee | 8 | – c Rice b Hemmings | 5 |
| *J. Abrahams c French b Hadlee | 35 | – c Broad b Hemmings | 11 |
| I. Folley c Birch b Hadlee | 0 | – (9) not out | 0 |
| M. Watkinson not out | 22 | – (6) c Afford b Hemmings | 14 |
| J. Simmons c French b Hadlee | 8 | – (7) not out | 14 |
| †C. Maynard c French b Hadlee | 0 | – (8) c Broad b Hemmings | 10 |
| P. J. W. Allott c Hemmings b Such | 6 | | |
| B. P. Patterson c French b Hadlee | 0 | | |
| L-b 3, n-b 1 | 4 | B 4, l-b 8, n-b 1 | 13 |
| 1/35 2/38 3/46 4/79 5/86 6/93 7/113 8/115 9/126 | 126 | 1/14 2/71 3/99 4/109 5/120 6/134 7/150 (7 wkts) | 158 |

Bonus points – Nottinghamshire 4.

Bowling: *First Innings*—Hadlee 29.3–16–41–8; Pick 7–0–15–0; Rice 7–4–8–0; Such 24–11–32–2; Hemmings 4–0–17–0; Afford 3–0–10–0. *Second Innings*—Hadlee 10–0–34–1; Pick 8–1–31–0; Such 6–1–23–0; Hemmings 12–0–51–6; Rice 1–0–3–0; Afford 3–0–4–0.

Umpires: R. Julian and N. T. Plews.

At Scarborough, September 11, 12, 13. NOTTINGHAMSHIRE drew with YORKSHIRE.

## NOTTINGHAMSHIRE v HAMPSHIRE

At Trent Bridge, September 14, 16, 17. Drawn. Nottinghamshire 4 pts, Hampshire 7 pts. Toss won by Nottinghamshire. Hampshire needed to win this match to stand any chance of the Championship, but on the final day that issue became academic. Rice's fourth hundred of the season – his 101 came in 207 minutes, with fourteen 4s – frustrated Hampshire on the opening day, and then stoppages took a toll on their victory chances. Terry hit his second hundred of the season and went on to an unbeaten 128 in 263 minutes (eighteen 4s) before Hampshire's declaration, but bad light prevented the commencement of Nottinghamshire's second innings that evening. On the third day Nicholas invited Nottinghamshire to score runs quickly, and eventually Hampshire were set to chase 280 in 149 minutes plus twenty overs. Nicholas kept them in the hunt after an initial setback, but the innings lost momentum with the news that Middlesex had won the title at Edgbaston. In the end it was Nottinghamshire who were scenting victory as the last Hampshire pair played out Cooper's final four balls.

## Nottinghamshire

| | | | |
|---|---|---|---|
| R. T. Robinson b Maru | 51 | – b Tremlett | 1 |
| B. C. Broad c Hardy b Tremlett | 25 | – c R. A. Smith b Andrew | 5 |
| D. W. Randall b Marshall | 48 | – c Terry b R. A. Smith | 58 |
| *C. E. B. Rice c sub b Tremlett | 101 | – c Terry b Nicholas | 20 |
| D. J. R. Martindale c Andrew b Maru | 24 | – b Maru | 14 |
| R. J. Hadlee c and b Maru | 0 | – not out | 71 |
| †B. N. French c R. A. Smith b Maru | 2 | – c Greenidge b C. L. Smith | 11 |
| E. E. Hemmings c Andrew b Tremlett | 19 | | |
| R. A. Pick c Maru b Tremlett | 10 | – (8) not out | 45 |
| K. E. Cooper b Maru | 1 | | |
| P. M. Such not out | 1 | | |
| B 5, l-b 7, n-b 3 | 15 | B 5, l-b 1, w 2, n-b 1 | 9 |
| 1/66 2/99 3/164 4/223 5/225 6/235 7/281 8/289 9/295 | 297 | 1/1 2/18 3/52 4/75 5/126 6/150 (6 wkts dec.) | 234 |

Bonus points – Nottinghamshire 3, Hampshire 4.

Bowling: *First Innings*—Marshall 24–4–62–1; Andrew 14–0–73–0; Tremlett 25–5–53–4; Nicholas 9–2–31–0; Maru 27.3–4–66–5. *Second Innings*—Andrew 3–0–18–1; Tremlett 2–1–1–1; Nicholas 10–0–80–1; C. L. Smith 18–0–85–1; Maru 1–0–4–1; R. A. Smith 7–0–40–1.

## Hampshire

| | | | |
|---|---|---|---|
| C. G. Greenidge c Martindale b Pick | 3 | – lbw b Such | 40 |
| V. P. Terry not out | 128 | – c Broad b Hadlee | 2 |
| C. L. Smith c Randall b Hadlee | 22 | – c Hadlee b Pick | 6 |
| *M. C. J. Nicholas c Martindale b Pick | 40 | – run out | 84 |
| R. A. Smith c Martindale b Hemmings | 7 | – c Robinson b Cooper | 39 |
| J. J. E. Hardy not out | 45 | – b Cooper | 8 |
| M. D. Marshall (did not bat) | | – b Pick | 23 |
| T. M. Tremlett (did not bat) | | – c Pick b Cooper | 26 |
| †R. J. Parks (did not bat) | | – b Hadlee | 12 |
| R. J. Maru (did not bat) | | – not out | 17 |
| S. J. W. Andrew (did not bat) | | – not out | 0 |
| L-b 4, w 1, n-b 2 | 7 | L-b 7, w 1, n-b 3 | 11 |
| 1/9 2/62 3/152 4/167 (4 wkts dec.) | 252 | 1/13 2/22 3/83 4/160 5/186 6/217 7/239 8/243 9/266 (9 wkts) | 268 |

Bonus points – Hampshire 3, Nottinghamshire 1.

Bowling: *First Innings*—Hadlee 15–5–36–1; Pick 15–1–67–2; Cooper 11–3–16–0; Rice 8–0–43–0; Such 10–1–47–0; Hemmings 12–3–39–1. *Second Innings*—Hadlee 12–3–20–2; Pick 12–1–44–2; Hemmings 15–1–69–0; Cooper 14–1–78–3; Such 11–0–50–1.

Umpires: J. H. Hampshire and A. G. T. Whitehead.

## SOMERSET

*President:* C. R. M. Atkinson
*Chairman:* M. F. Hill
*Chairman, Cricket Committee:*
1985 – C. R. M. Atkinson
1986 – B. A. Langford
*Secretary:* A. S. Brown
The County Ground, St James's Street,
Taunton TA1 1JT (Telephone: 0823-72946)
*Captain:* 1985 – I. T. Botham
1986 – P. M. Roebuck
*Coach:* P. J. Robinson

Expected by many to be a challenging force, Somerset suffered one of their worst seasons since the 1970s' resurgence, despite the return of Vivian Richards and Joel Garner and the astonishing batting exploits of the captain, Ian Botham, and Richards. One of the outcomes of a somewhat bizarre season came in early October. Citing his many interests outside Somerset cricket as the reason, Botham resigned the captaincy, Peter Roebuck being appointed, and accepted a one-year contract instead of the two years he was offered.

While achieving the highest number of batting points in the Britannic Assurance Championship table, Somerset were bottom for the first time since 1969, with only one victory. Two late successes took them to tenth in the John Player Sunday League, fourteen points behind the winners in a very close competition. Three heavy defeats in the Benson and Hedges Cup zonal matches came with sides depleted by the late arrival of Garner and Richards from Test duties for West Indies. A controversial NatWest Bank Trophy quarter-final ended with a crushing Hampshire victory. Only three home successes were registered over first-class opposition, just one of them at Taunton.

Besides some superb one-day batting, Botham made the first three of his five centuries from 76, 76 and 50 balls respectively, created a new record of 6s in a first-class season, and averaged 100 in the Championship. His friend Richards, with nine centuries, including a memorable 322, averaged 76. Together they scored 3,047 Championship runs.

In this context the season's final results were remarkably disappointing, but the reasons are fairly clear. Principally, a savage spate of injuries completely upset team plans; also, the bowlers, with the exception of the vice-captain, Vic Marks, could not match expectations. Botham, missing half the season on England duty and the last few games with injury, took only eleven Championship wickets; Garner, now 32 and considerably hampered by knee troubles, took 31 in fifteen matches. Mark Davis failed to sustain his advance of 1984, while Gary Palmer, Andrew Jones and a newcomer, Murray Turner, could not provide the necessary seam support. Stephen Booth's gentle left-arm spin was not assertive enough for important results, and by the end of May a sombre pattern had been set.

Before the season started, injuries to Colin Dredge, which kept him out for half the season, and Nigel Felton had added to the effect of losing three experienced batsmen – Peter Denning, Philip Slocombe and Jeremy

Lloyds – at the end of 1984. The experienced Brian Rose suffered a broken arm on May 9, which ruined his season. Two of the opening batsmen, Roebuck and Julian Wyatt, sustained severe hand injuries, which cost long absences, while the reliable wicket-keeper, Trevor Gard, missed two weeks with concussion suffered in a mid-pitch collision.

Early in the season, second-innings batting collapses brought heavy defeats against Nottinghamshire, Glamorgan and the Australians, while, despite the dazzling efforts of Botham and Richards, Hampshire won at Taunton by five wickets with three balls to spare. Three conclusive Benson and Hedges Cup defeats added to the gloom. Young players necessarily were being rushed in, and the former Hampshire batsman, Richard Hayward, was brought in to try to plug the gaps. But victories remained very scarce.

However, Nigel Popplewell, making a fine effort as an opener, came in with some grand attacking efforts, including a splendid 172 against Essex, to provide some stability. Then, regrettably, he decided to leave county cricket at the age of 28 to concentrate on his law studies. His cheerful optimism and overall contribution will be sorely missed. Roebuck returned from injury and with his usual gritty tenacity reached 1,000 runs; Wyatt's season reached its high point with his first Championship century, a fine, fighting effort which saved the return match against Hampshire, and Felton, considering his injuries in April and August, also produced some spirited innings.

With so many matches being upset or ruined by the weather, Somerset's declarations contained several which looked generous at the time, and proved so. Curiously, however, they only once lost twenty wickets in a match, and only once took twenty, this when Marks had a golden morning at Bath against some feeble Lancashire batting in Somerset's only Championship victory.

Turner, an all-rounder, and Richard Ollis had a few good days, but not enough to attract another contract, and gradually the season came to its nadir in early August. A match containing several sharp controversies ended in devastating victory by Hampshire in the NatWest quarter-final at Taunton, following a promising Somerset bowling start, a long delay for rain and then the dismemberment of the Somerset attack by Paul Terry and Robin Smith.

Richard Harden, aged nineteen, had shown considerable batting ability by now, and some promising experiments were to come in the final month. Jonathan Atkinson, the seventeen-year-old son of C.R.M., former Somerset captain and now President of the club, began with a superb innings of 79 and suggested an interesting future. Robert Coombs, a 26-year-old former Dorset player, currently at Exeter University, made a splendid start with a good bowling action and attacking bent as he took sixteen wickets in three matches at 16.75 apiece with his left-arm spinners. Paul Bail, another nineteen-year-old, made a maiden Championship fifty in the final match.

At the end of an acutely disappointing season for supporters who had been expecting a continuation of recent successes, there were other signs of comfort and hope. Apart from at the rain-ruined Weston Festival, support remained remarkably high – a tribute to the astonishing batting feats of Botham and Richards. Home pitches generally struck a good balance, Gordon Prosser's efforts at Bath being especially important. – E.H.

SOMERSET 1985

[*Bill Smith*

*Back row:* R. V. J. Coombs, J. G. Wyatt, M. R. Davis, T. Gard, G. V. Palmer, R. J. Harden, P. A. C. Bail, N. A. Felton, D. A. Oldam (*scorer*). *Front row:* C. H. Dredge, P. M. Roebuck, V. J. Marks, B. C. Rose, J. Garner. *Insets:* I. V. A. Richards, I. T. Botham (*captain*), N. F. M. Popplewell.

## SOMERSET RESULTS

*All first-class matches – Played 26: Won 1, Lost 8, Drawn 17.*

*County Championship matches – Played 24: Won 1, Lost 7, Drawn 16.*

*Bonus points – Batting 70, Bowling 45.*

*Competition placings – Britannic Assurance County Championship, 17th; NatWest Bank Trophy, q-f; Benson and Hedges Cup, 4th in Group D; John Player League, 10th eq.*

## BRITANNIC ASSURANCE CHAMPIONSHIP AVERAGES

### BATTING

| | *Birthplace* | *M* | *I* | *NO* | *R* | *HI* | *Avge* |
|---|---|---|---|---|---|---|---|
| ‡I. T. Botham | *Heswall* | 11 | 17 | 5 | 1,211 | 152 | 100.91 |
| ‡I. V. A. Richards | *St John's, Antigua* | 19 | 24 | 0 | 1,836 | 322 | 76.50 |
| J. C. M. Atkinson | *Butleigh* | 6 | 5 | 1 | 167 | 79 | 41.75 |
| ‡P. M. Roebuck | *Oxford* | 19 | 29 | 3 | 1,058 | 132* | 40.69 |
| ‡N. F. M. Popplewell | *Chislehurst* | 16 | 27 | 1 | 972 | 172 | 37.38 |
| M. S. Turner | *Shaftesbury* | 7 | 10 | 6 | 134 | 24* | 33.50 |
| N. A. Felton | *Guildford* | 17 | 25 | 0 | 794 | 112 | 31.76 |
| ‡V. J. Marks | *Middle Chinnock* | 24 | 32 | 5 | 787 | 82 | 29.14 |
| J. G. Wyatt | *Paulton* | 15 | 23 | 0 | 620 | 100 | 26.95 |
| R. J. Harden | *Bridgwater* | 10 | 13 | 4 | 240 | 52* | 26.66 |
| M. R. Davis | *Kilve* | 15 | 17 | 6 | 274 | 40* | 24.90 |
| G. V. Palmer | *Taunton* | 7 | 11 | 3 | 164 | 45* | 20.50 |
| ‡C. H. Dredge | *Frome* | 14 | 12 | 6 | 119 | 31 | 19.83 |
| R. E. Hayward | *Hillingdon* | 8 | 11 | 2 | 178 | 57* | 19.77 |
| P. A. C. Bail | *Burnham-on-Sea* | 5 | 9 | 2 | 127 | 78* | 18.14 |
| R. L. Ollis | *Clifton* | 12 | 16 | 1 | 271 | 55 | 18.06 |
| S. C. Booth | *Leeds* | 8 | 6 | 2 | 69 | 28 | 17.25 |
| ‡B. C. Rose | *Dartford* | 4 | 8 | 0 | 115 | 43 | 14.37 |
| ‡J. Garner | *Barbados* | 15 | 11 | 3 | 92 | 22 | 11.50 |
| ‡T. Gard | *South Petherton* | 23 | 23 | 3 | 230 | 47 | 11.50 |
| A. P. Jones | *Southampton* | 3 | 4 | 2 | 3 | 1* | 1.50 |

Also batted: R. V. J. Coombs (*Barnet*) (4 matches) 0, 0, 1; S. A. R. Ferguson (*Lagos, Nigeria*) (1 match) 8; S. J. Turner (*Cuckfield*) (1 match) 9*.

* *Signifies not out.* ‡ *Denotes county cap.*

The following played a total of eighteen three-figure innings for Somerset in County Championship matches – I. V. A. Richards 9, I. T. Botham 5, N. A. Felton 1, N. F. M. Popplewell 1, P. M. Roebuck 1, J. G. Wyatt 1.

### BOWLING

| | *O* | *M* | *R* | *W* | *BB* | *Avge* |
|---|---|---|---|---|---|---|
| R. V. J. Coombs | 93 | 27 | 268 | 16 | 5-58 | 16.75 |
| J. Garner | 295.4 | 75 | 739 | 31 | 5-46 | 23.83 |
| V. J. Marks | 745.4 | 180 | 2,208 | 67 | 8-17 | 32.95 |
| C. H. Dredge | 286 | 61 | 863 | 21 | 5-95 | 41.09 |
| I. T. Botham | 130.4 | 25 | 464 | 11 | 4-63 | 42.18 |
| S. C. Booth | 275.2 | 73 | 819 | 19 | 4-88 | 43.10 |
| M. R. Davis | 298 | 45 | 1,029 | 19 | 4-83 | 54.15 |

Also bowled: J. C. M. Atkinson 65–9–250–2; P. A. C. Bail 4–2–4–0; R. J. Harden 8.3–2–29–1; A. P. Jones 37–4–142–3; G. V. Palmer 147–13–627–7; N. F. M. Popplewell 18–1–95–0; I. V. A. Richards 183–48–494–7; P. M. Roebuck 7–0–28–0; B. C. Rose 1–0–8–0; M. S. Turner 121.4–22–403–8; J. G. Wyatt 9–0–58–1.

At The Parks, April 20, 22, 23. SOMERSET drew with OXFORD UNIVERSITY.

## SOMERSET v NOTTINGHAMSHIRE

At Taunton, April 27, 28, 29. Nottinghamshire won by nine wickets. Nottinghamshire 22 pts, Somerset 8 pts. Toss won by Somerset. In cold, windy weather the visitors ran away with the game on the last day after two even days. Ollis and Rose rescued a poor start by Somerset then Botham, batting for 77 balls and hitting five 6s and eleven 4s, completed things. Marks and Davis caused a slump after Robinson, hitting fifteen 4s in 57 overs, had taken Nottinghamshire to 185 for two. Somerset, 61 for one overnight, collapsed before Such and Cooper on the third day, but Botham, batting low in the order because of a leg injury, struck five 6s from 32 balls. Half-centuries from Broad and Robinson ended the match just after tea.

### Somerset

| | | | |
|---|---|---|---|
| J. G. Wyatt c Rice b Cooper | 28 | – c French b Cooper | 18 |
| P. M. Roebuck c Johnson b Saxelby | 12 | – c French b Cooper | 36 |
| N. F. M. Popplewell c French b Rice | 2 | – run out | 13 |
| R. L. Ollis c French b Rice | 44 | – c Broad b Such | 0 |
| B. C. Rose c Robinson b Pick | 43 | – c French b Such | 7 |
| *I. T. Botham c French b Pick | 90 | – (8) c Robinson b Such | 50 |
| V. J. Marks b Rice | 10 | – (6) b Such | 3 |
| †T. Gard c French b Pick | 1 | – (9) c Rice b Cooper | 1 |
| G. V. Palmer not out | 45 | – (7) c Randall b Such | 0 |
| M. R. Davis not out | 21 | – run out | 1 |
| A. P. Jones (did not bat) | | – not out | 1 |
| L-b 17, n-b 1 | 18 | L-b 2, w 1 | 3 |
| 1/27 2/44 3/44 4/121 5/201 6/239 7/243 8/246 | (8 wkts dec.) 314 | 1/47 2/70 3/70 4/70 5/77 6/77 7/96 8/119 9/131 | 133 |

Bonus points – Somerset 4, Nottinghamshire 3 (Score at 100 overs: 308-8).

Bowling: *First Innings*—Saxelby 23–7–49–1; Pick 25–5–79–3; Cooper 25–5–119–1; Rice 18–6–38–3; Such 10–5–12–0. *Second Innings*—Saxelby 6–0–25–0; Pick 5–0–16–0; Such 18.2–5–73–5; Cooper 18–10–17–3.

### Nottinghamshire

| | | | |
|---|---|---|---|
| B. C. Broad c Gard b Jones | 27 | – not out | 56 |
| R. T. Robinson c Gard b Davis | 105 | – c Ollis b Jones | 54 |
| D. W. Randall c Gard b Davis | 18 | – not out | 32 |
| *C. E. B. Rice c Wyatt b Marks | 27 | | |
| P. Johnson b Davis | 0 | | |
| J. D. Birch c Popplewell b Marks | 38 | | |
| †B. N. French c Gard b Marks | 18 | | |
| R. A. Pick c Roebuck b Marks | 15 | | |
| K. Saxelby c Gard b Marks | 0 | | |
| K. E. Cooper not out | 17 | | |
| P. M. Such c sub b Davis | 8 | | |
| B 1, l-b 8, w 2, n-b 4 | 15 | B 7, l-b 4, w 1, n-b 6 | 18 |
| 1/86 2/119 3/185 4/187 5/188 6/235 7/244 8/244 9/275 | 288 | 1/98 | (1 wkt) 160 |

Bonus points – Nottinghamshire 3, Somerset 4.

Bowling: *First Innings*—Davis 24.5–3–83–4; Palmer 10–0–46–0; Marks 23–5–66–5; Botham 7–1–22–0; Jones 14–2–62–1. *Second Innings*—Davis 9–1–30–0; Palmer 7–1–28–0; Marks 18–4–52–0; Jones 12–2–39–1.

Umpires: B. Dudleston and A. G. T. Whitehead.

## SOMERSET v GLAMORGAN

At Taunton, May 1, 2, 3. Glamorgan won by nine wickets. Glamorgan 24 pts, Somerset 5 pts. Toss won by Glamorgan. A poor start was handsomely relieved by the brilliance of Miandad and Holmes, who added 183 in 44 overs to establish a solid Glamorgan innings. Somerset slipped to 89 for five before Botham, with a remarkable 100 from 76 balls, and Ollis put on 133, Botham ending with 112 out of 139 with eight 6s and seven 4s. Steele's spell of three for 6 forced the follow-on from an unlikely position, and then only Popplewell, hitting nine 4s in a bold rescue bid over 48 overs, made progress. Steele's two wickets and Holmes's very lively spell on the second evening, which accounted for Botham and Popplewell, enabled Glamorgan to win their first victory in Somerset since 1970 before lunch on the final day.

### Glamorgan

| First innings | | Second innings | |
|---|---|---|---|
| J. A. Hopkins lbw b Davis | 8 | – c Gard b Jones | 12 |
| A. L. Jones c Rose b Palmer | 11 | – not out | 18 |
| G. C. Holmes st Gard b Marks | 88 | – not out | 9 |
| Javed Miandad c Gard b Davis | 86 | | |
| Younis Ahmed c Wyatt b Palmer | 59 | | |
| *R. C. Ontong b Davis | 64 | | |
| J. G. Thomas c Jones b Botham | 37 | | |
| J. F. Steele not out | 11 | | |
| B 5, l-b 4, w 8, n-b 6 | 23 | L-b 1, w 2, n-b 1 | 4 |
| 1/11 2/26 3/209 4/209 5/301 6/367 7/387 (7 wkts dec.) | 387 | 1/24 (1 wkt) | 43 |

J. Derrick, †T. Davies and S. R. Barwick did not bat.

Bonus points – Glamorgan 4, Somerset 3.

Bowling: *First Innings*—Botham 18–4–45–1; Davis 20.3–2–61–3; Palmer 20–2–97–2; Marks 26–6–109–1; Jones 5–0–20–0; Popplewell 9–0–46–0. *Second Innings*—Davis 5–0–14–0; Botham 2–1–4–0; Marks 4–2–7–0; Jones 2–0–9–1; Rose 1–0–8–0.

### Somerset

| First innings | | Second innings | |
|---|---|---|---|
| J. G. Wyatt lbw b Derrick | 45 | – c Jones b Barwick | 19 |
| P. M. Roebuck b Thomas | 2 | – b Barwick | 26 |
| †T. Gard c Davies b Thomas | 1 | – (6) lbw b Holmes | 0 |
| N. F. M. Popplewell c Thomas b Derrick | 5 | – (3) b Holmes | 81 |
| R. L. Ollis lbw b Barwick | 38 | – (4) c Barwick b Steele | 14 |
| B. C. Rose b Derrick | 8 | – (5) c sub b Steele | 0 |
| *I. T. Botham c Derrick b Steele | 112 | – lbw b Holmes | 3 |
| V. J. Marks not out | 9 | – (9) c Davies b Ontong | 18 |
| G. V. Palmer c Jones b Steele | 0 | – (10) c Miandad b Ontong | 0 |
| M. R. Davis run out | 0 | – (8) lbw b Thomas | 21 |
| A. P. Jones c Holmes b Steele | 0 | – not out | 1 |
| B 5, l-b 7, w 2, n-b 3 | 17 | B 1, l-b 6, n-b 1 | 8 |
| 1/6 2/12 3/47 4/79 5/89 6/222 7/228 8/228 9/233 | 237 | 1/30 2/53 3/111 4/119 5/120 6/134 7/153 8/190 9/190 | 191 |

Bonus points – Somerset 2, Glamorgan 4.

Bowling: *First Innings*—Thomas 22–7–43–2; Barwick 21–6–54–1; Ontong 14–1–69–0; Derrick 12–0–53–3; Steele 2.1–1–6–3. *Second Innings*—Thomas 12–0–50–1; Barwick 12–3–33–2; Derrick 10–2–23–0; Ontong 11.5–2–36–2; Holmes 12–3–25–3; Steele 10–5–17–2.

Umpires: D. J. Constant and P. B. Wight.

At Taunton, May 8, 9, 10. SOMERSET lost to AUSTRALIANS by 233 runs (See Australian tour section).

## SOMERSET v HAMPSHIRE

At Taunton, May 22, 23, 24. Hampshire won by five wickets with three balls to spare. Hampshire 24 pts, Somerset 6 pts. Toss won by Hampshire. Two remarkable recoveries set the scene for a very exciting finish. In the first, Botham saved Somerset with an astonishing 149 out of 193 in 106 balls, hitting six 6s and twenty 4s. His hundred came off 76 balls, equalling his performance against Glamorgan. Then defiant and well-composed maiden hundreds by Tremlett and James, who established a new eighth-wicket record for Hampshire of 227 in 72 overs, not only banished any possibility of the follow-on but also put Hampshire ahead on first innings. Richards, hitting ten 6s and nineteen 4s in 176 balls, set the declaration target at 323 in 72 overs. Chris Smith and Terry, attacking the spin of Marks, added 180 in 41 overs before Garner and Botham effected a change. However, Marshall, boldly flinging the bat and hitting two 6s and five 4s, solved the problem of getting 40 off the last 32 balls, finishing with 2, 4, 6 off the first three balls of Garner's final over.

### Somerset

| First innings | | Second innings | |
|---|---|---|---|
| J. G. Wyatt c R. A. Smith b Marshall | 7 | b Connor | 13 |
| P. M. Roebuck b Tremlett | 18 | | |
| N. F. M. Popplewell c James b Marshall | 28 | (2) c Greenidge b Tremlett | 68 |
| I. V. A. Richards c Greenidge b Tremlett | 0 | (3) c Greenidge b Tremlett | 186 |
| R. L. Ollis lbw b Tremlett | 4 | (4) c Terry b Marshall | 34 |
| *I. T. Botham b Marshall | 149 | (5) c Connor b C. L. Smith | 19 |
| V. J. Marks c Cowley b Connor | 17 | (6) not out | 1 |
| †T. Gard run out | 9 | | |
| M. R. Davis not out | 18 | | |
| J. Garner lbw b Cowley | 14 | | |
| M. S. Turner lbw b Cowley | 17 | (7) not out | 19 |
| B 4, l-b 6, w 2, n-b 5 | 17 | L-b 9, w 1, n-b 8 | 18 |
| 1/12 2/51 3/51 4/58 5/70 6/108 7/166 8/251 9/272 | 298 | 1/34 2/146 3/298 4/328 5/338 (5 wkts dec.) | 358 |

Bonus points – Somerset 3, Hampshire 4.

Bowling: *First Innings*—Marshall 22–4–81–3; Connor 18–5–68–1; James 13–1–64–0; Tremlett 15–5–36–3; Cowley 5.4–1–39–2. *Second Innings*—Marshall 13–0–50–1; Connor 14–2–67–1; James 11–0–81–0; Cowley 15–2–80–0; Tremlett 14–4–43–2; C. L. Smith 4–1–28–1.

### Hampshire

| First innings | | Second innings | |
|---|---|---|---|
| C. G. Greenidge lbw b Botham | 12 | c Botham b Garner | 2 |
| *V. P. Terry lbw b Garner | 3 | c Popplewell b Marks | 83 |
| C. L. Smith st Gard b Richards | 16 | b Botham | 121 |
| D. R. Turner c Gard b Turner | 38 | (5) c Davis b Botham | 8 |
| R. A. Smith c Marks b Richards | 5 | (4) c Popplewell b Garner | 33 |
| M. D. Marshall c sub b Garner | 24 | not out | 49 |
| N. G. Cowley c Gard b Garner | 0 | | |
| K. D. James c Davis b Marks | 124 | (7) not out | 7 |
| T. M. Tremlett not out | 102 | | |
| B 1, l-b 7, w 2 | 10 | B 12, l-b 10 | 22 |
| 1/11 2/21 3/68 4/76 5/87 6/94 7/107 8/334 (8 wkts dec.) | 334 | 1/4 2/184 3/251 4/257 5/283 (5 wkts) | 325 |

†R. J. Parks and C. A. Connor did not bat.

Bonus points – Hampshire 4, Somerset 3 (Score at 100 overs: 301-7).

Bowling: *First Innings*—Garner 22–7–39–3; Botham 15–2–69–1; Turner 21–4–46–1; Richards 20–8–55–2; Davis 15–3–53–0; Marks 17.3–3–64–1. *Second Innings*—Garner 12.3–2–45–2; Botham 13–0–60–2; Davis 11–1–37–0; Turner 4–0–22–0; Marks 17–1–105–1; Richards 8–1–34–0.

Umpires: C. Cook and R. Palmer.

At Bristol, May 25, 27, 28. SOMERSET drew with GLOUCESTERSHIRE.

At Headingley, May 29, 30, 31. SOMERSET drew with YORKSHIRE.

## SOMERSET v WARWICKSHIRE

At Taunton, June 1, 3, 4. Drawn. Somerset 6 pts, Warwickshire 6 pts. Toss won by Somerset. Everything was dwarfed by a magnificent 322 out of 479 by Richards, who came in when Bail had retired after a blow on the helmet and Felton was out next ball. His first 100 came from 105 balls, his second from 76, and his third in 63. In all he faced 258 deliveries in 294 minutes, and his 133 scoring strokes included eight 6s and 42 4s. Championship-best batting performances by Ferreira and Smith featured in a solid reply, but after the change bowlers had fed Somerset runs to provoke an acceptable challenge, Warwickshire displayed no interest in the final requirement of 351 in 205 minutes or a minimum of 53 overs.

### Somerset

| First innings | | Second innings | |
|---|---|---|---|
| N. F. M. Popplewell c Tedstone b Hoffman | 55 | c Hoffman b Small | 27 |
| P. A. C. Bail retired hurt | 8 | c Kallicharran b Small | 0 |
| N. A. Felton c Kallicharran b Small | 0 | (4) c Small b Lloyd | 45 |
| I. V. A. Richards b Ferreira | 322 | | |
| R. L. Ollis c Hoffman b Ferreira | 55 | lbw b Wall | 0 |
| *V. J. Marks c Tedstone b Gifford | 65 | not out | 66 |
| M. R. Davis not out | 25 | | |
| M. S. Turner not out | 17 | (7) not out | 24 |
| †T. Gard (did not bat) | | (3) run out | 47 |
| B 1, l-b 9, w 1, n-b 8 | 19 | L-b 13, n-b 4 | 17 |
| 1/28 2/150 3/324 4/507 5/533 (5 wkts dec.) | 566 | 1/1 2/62 3/103 4/105 5/175 (5 wkts dec.) | 226 |

J. Garner and S. C. Booth did not bat.

*P. A. C. Bail retired hurt at 28-0.*

Bonus points – Somerset 4, Warwickshire 2.

Bowling: *First Innings*—Small 16–3–70–1; Wall 18–3–72–0; Smith 11–0–73–0; Ferreira 23–0–121–2; Hoffman 14–0–85–1; Gifford 18–1–135–1. *Second Innings*—Small 8–0–31–2; Smith 9–1–43–0; Hoffman 2–0–12–0; Wall 5–2–7–1; Lloyd 16–0–64–1; Kallicharran 11.4–0–56–0.

### Warwickshire

| First innings | | Second innings | |
|---|---|---|---|
| T. A. Lloyd lbw b Richards | 61 | c Gard b Garner | 7 |
| R. I. H. B. Dyer lbw b Turner | 33 | not out | 63 |
| A. I. Kallicharran c Garner b Davis | 36 | c Gard b Marks | 89 |
| D. L. Amiss c Davis b Marks | 81 | not out | 14 |
| P. A. Smith c Turner b Marks | 93 | | |
| A. M. Ferreira not out | 101 | | |
| †G. A. Tedstone b Turner | 22 | | |
| G. C. Small c Davis b Turner | 3 | | |
| S. Wall lbw b Turner | 1 | | |
| D. S. Hoffman run out | 0 | | |
| *N. Gifford not out | 0 | | |
| B 1, l-b 6, w 1, n-b 3 | 11 | L-b 5, w 1, n-b 2 | 8 |
| 1/84 2/108 3/151 4/312 5/312 6/399 7/419 8/431 9/431 (9 wkts dec.) | 442 | 1/18 2/158 (2 wkts) | 181 |

Bonus points – Warwickshire 4, Somerset 2 (Score at 100 overs: 372-5).

Bowling: *First Innings*—Garner 20–3–59–0; Davis 23.4–1–115–1; Turner 22.4–2–74–4; Richards 12–4–31–1; Marks 25–3–97–2; Booth 13–3–59–0. *Second Innings*—Garner 6–2–16–1; Davis 9–2–19–0; Marks 16–1–56–1; Turner 1–0–9–0; Booth 21–4–72–0; Bail 2–0–4–0.

Umpires: A. A. Jones and P. B. Wight.

## SOMERSET v GLOUCESTERSHIRE

At Bath, June 8, 10, 11. Drawn. Somerset 6 pts, Gloucestershire 8 pts. Toss won by Somerset. After Gloucestershire's early collapse, Athey and Davison began the recovery, which was ably continued by Curran and Lloyds, both of whom were missed early but went on to make their highest scores for the county. Despite a brisk start by Popplewell, Somerset were in danger of following on at 159 for six with a player injured, but Botham, hitting five 6s and seven 4s from 47 balls, reduced the deficit to 89 on the third day, a wet in-field having limited the second day to only 35 overs. Another early collapse prompted Gloucestershire caution, but the danger was sealed off before more rain brought the match to a close.

### Gloucestershire

| | | | |
|---|---|---|---|
| A. W. Stovold b Garner | 0 | – c Botham b Garner | 2 |
| P. W. Romaines c Felton b Botham | 2 | – not out | 22 |
| C. W. J. Athey lbw b Garner | 52 | – (4) c sub b Davis | 2 |
| P. Bainbridge lbw b Garner | 0 | – (3) c sub b Davis | 17 |
| B. F. Davison c Gard b Davis | 43 | – b Marks | 26 |
| K. M. Curran c Botham b Marks | 83 | | |
| J. W. Lloyds not out | 95 | – (6) not out | 6 |
| *D. A. Graveney b Marks | 0 | | |
| †R. C. Russell lbw b Marks | 0 | | |
| D. V. Lawrence c Ollis b Marks | 8 | | |
| C. A. Walsh not out | 33 | | |
| B 11, l-b 5 | 16 | B 9 | 9 |
| 1/0 2/8 3/15 4/80 5/139 6/262 7/262 8/264 9/294 (9 wkts dec.) | 332 | 1/2 2/27 3/31 4/68 (4 wkts) | 84 |

Bonus points – Gloucestershire 4, Somerset 4 (Score at 100 overs: 305-9).

Bowling: *First Innings*—Garner 28–7–68–3; Botham 16–2–54–1; Richards 27–7–62–0; Davis 11–1–57–1; Marks 17–5–65–4; Booth 4–0–10–0. *Second Innings*—Garner 7–2–21–1; Davis 8–3–17–2; Marks 12–5–24–1; Booth 10–5–13–0.

### Somerset

| | |
|---|---|
| N. F. M. Popplewell c Lawrence b Curran | 44 |
| N. A. Felton lbw b Curran | 15 |
| R. E. Hayward b Lloyds | 12 |
| R. L. Ollis b Graveney | 19 |
| S. C. Booth b Curran | 10 |
| I. V. A. Richards c Stovold b Walsh | 27 |
| *I. T. Botham not out | 76 |
| V. J. Marks c Graveney b Walsh | 1 |
| M. R. Davis c Athey b Graveney | 14 |
| J. Garner b Graveney | 1 |
| †T. Gard absent injured | |
| B 8, l-b 2, w 6, n-b 8 | 24 |
| 1/63 2/72 3/107 4/107 5/147 6/159 7/184 8/229 9/243 | 243 |

Bonus points – Somerset 2, Gloucestershire 4.

Bowling: Lawrence 10–1–79–0; Walsh 19–3–65–2; Curran 15–5–52–3; Lloyds 5–2–12–1; Graveney 8.1–3–25–3.

Umpires: D. J. Constant and J. H. Hampshire.

## SOMERSET v LANCASHIRE

At Bath, June 12, 13, 14. Somerset won by an innings and 62 runs. Somerset 22 pts, Lancashire 3 pts. Toss won by Somerset. As it was the only dry part of the square, the same pitch was used as for the Gloucestershire game, and Somerset won for the first time in 1985, out-playing their opponents. Missed chances off Richards and Felton, who added 103 in 35 overs, enabled a solid innings to be established, whereupon some undisciplined batting by Lancashire – Folley,

Hughes (twice), Varey and Maynard excepted – brought about their downfall. Garner was chiefly responsible for their narrow failure to avoid the follow-on, but career-best figures by Marks, eight for 17, in their second innings considerably exaggerated the difficulties of a slow, turning pitch.

### Somerset

| | | | |
|---|---|---|---|
| N. F. M. Popplewell b Folley | 39 | M. R. Davis not out | 40 |
| N. A. Felton c Hughes b Folley | 76 | †S. J. Turner not out | 9 |
| R. E. Hayward lbw b Simmons | 9 | | |
| I. V. A. Richards st Maynard b Folley | 65 | L-b 18, w 1, n-b 1 | 20 |
| R. L. Ollis b Simmons | 9 | | |
| *V. J. Marks c Hughes b Simmons | 27 | 1/68 2/95 3/198 (7 wkts dec.) | 304 |
| R. J. Harden c O'Shaughnessy b Simmons | 10 | 4/201 5/238 6/241 7/262 | |

S. C. Booth and J. Garner did not bat.

Bonus points – Somerset 2, Lancashire 2 (Score at 100 overs: 241-5).

Bowling: Patterson 22–6–75–0; O'Shaughnessy 6–1–18–0; Watkinson 8–2–26–0; Simmons 45–15–78–4; Folley 44–16–89–3.

### Lancashire

| | | | |
|---|---|---|---|
| D. W. Varey c Turner b Garner | 1 | – b Booth | 33 |
| I. Folley c Marks b Booth | 38 | – c Popplewell b Marks | 5 |
| S. J. O'Shaughnessy b Booth | 9 | – (4) b Marks | 0 |
| N. H. Fairbrother lbw b Marks | 5 | – (5) b Marks | 3 |
| D. P. Hughes c Booth b Garner | 57 | – (6) c Booth b Marks | 23 |
| *J. Abrahams b Marks | 14 | – (7) c Ollis b Marks | 0 |
| G. Fowler b Richards | 14 | – (3) b Marks | 4 |
| M. Watkinson c Turner b Garner | 7 | – c Ollis b Marks | 0 |
| †C. Maynard b Garner | 0 | – st Turner b Marks | 15 |
| J. Simmons st Turner b Marks | 6 | – c Marks b Booth | 0 |
| B. P. Patterson not out | 0 | – not out | 0 |
| B 2 | 2 | B 4, w 1, n-b 1 | 6 |
| 1/6 2/45 3/54 4/54 5/85<br>6/128 7/142 8/142 9/153 | 153 | 1/19 2/40 3/40 4/48 5/58<br>6/58 7/64 8/88 9/89 | 89 |

Bonus points – Lancashire 1, Somerset 4.

Bowling: *First Innings*—Garner 14.4–8–18–4; Davis 6–3–19–0; Booth 15–4–44–2; Marks 30–11–56–3; Richards 10–4–14–1. *Second Innings*—Garner 8–3–16–0; Davis 6–1–16–0; Marks 22–15–17–8; Booth 10.5–1–36–2.

Umpires: D. J. Constant and J. H. Hampshire.

At Bath, June 15. SOMERSET lost to ZIMBABWEANS by four wickets (See Zimbabwean tour section).

At The Oval, June 22, 24, 25. SOMERSET drew with SURREY.

At Cardiff, June 26, 27, 28. SOMERSET drew with GLAMORGAN.

## SOMERSET v CAMBRIDGE UNIVERSITY

At Taunton, June 29, July 1, 2. Drawn. Maiden first-class centuries by Harden, batting for 41 overs, and Hayward, in 61 overs, followed Cambridge's winning the toss. But on a slow pitch the University faltered against a varied attack, only Roebuck, in an accomplished innings of 56 overs, and Price enabling the follow-on to be avoided. Felton's brisk batting set up a requirement of 344 in 295 minutes, and if achieving it was ever considered an early collapse quickly put it out of reach. Andrew, surviving two chances, patiently saved his side by batting for 79 overs, Roebuck again giving good support, before Davies and Cotterell saw them through.

## Somerset

| First innings | | Second innings | |
|---|---|---|---|
| J. G. Wyatt c Davies b Ellison | 25 | – lbw b Scott | 26 |
| *P. M. Roebuck c and b Scott | 28 | | |
| N. A. Felton c Price b Scott | 54 | – (4) c Andrew b Gorman | 74 |
| R. E. Hayward not out | 100 | | |
| R. L. Ollis lbw b Scott | 0 | – (3) c Lea b Scott | 39 |
| R. J. Harden run out | 107 | – not out | 2 |
| C. H. Dredge not out | 5 | | |
| †T. Gard (did not bat) | | – (2) retired hurt | 34 |
| M. R. Davis (did not bat) | | – (5) c Fell b Scott | 26 |
| B 1, l-b 7, w 2, n-b 2 | 12 | B 4, l-b 4, n-b 2 | 10 |
| 1/34 2/85 3/144 4/144 5/321 (5 wkts dec.) | 331 | 1/42 2/94 3/207 4/211 (4 wkts dec.) | 211 |

M. S. Turner and S. C. Booth did not bat.

Bowling: *First Innings*—Davidson 16–0–61–0; Ellison 30.5–9–89–1; Scott 19–3–67–3; Gorman 12–2–37–0; Cotterell 15–2–69–0. *Second Innings*—Davidson 8–1–35–0; Ellison 10–0–39–0; Scott 14–2–45–3; Cotterell 12–1–52–0; Gorman 3.5–0–32–1.

## Cambridge University

| First innings | | Second innings | |
|---|---|---|---|
| A. E. Lea c Booth b Dredge | 6 | – c Booth b Davis | 0 |
| *C. R. Andrew c Dredge b Davis | 0 | – c Harden b Dredge | 62 |
| S. R. Gorman hit wkt b Davis | 8 | – (8) not out | 9 |
| D. J. Fell b Booth | 13 | – (3) b Davis | 0 |
| P. G. P. Roebuck c Davis b Booth | 82 | – (4) c Davis b Turner | 43 |
| D. G. Price c Ollis b Booth | 29 | – (5) c Ollis b Booth | 1 |
| †A. G. Davies b Turner | 9 | – (6) lbw b Harden | 32 |
| T. A. Cotterell b Turner | 9 | – (7) not out | 28 |
| C. C. Ellison c Turner b Dredge | 4 | | |
| J. E. Davidson c Booth b Dredge | 22 | | |
| A. M. G. Scott not out | 1 | | |
| B 11, l-b 2, w 2, n-b 1 | 16 | B 2, l-b 6, w 2, n-b 1 | 11 |
| 1/9 2/19 3/30 4/47 5/103 6/128 7/143 8/174 9/182 | 199 | 1/6 2/6 3/81 4/85 5/132 6/158 (6 wkts) | 186 |

Bowling: *First Innings*—Davis 17–4–50–2; Dredge 18.4–8–36–3; Booth 27–11–50–3; Turner 16–2–49–2; Wyatt 1–0–1–0. *Second Innings*—Davis 9–2–32–2; Dredge 13–4–30–1; Booth 36–18–52–1; Turner 14–3–33–1; Roebuck 9–3–19–0; Ollis 4–1–8–0; Harden 4–3–4–1.

Umpires: B. Dudleston and D. R. Shepherd.

## SOMERSET v LEICESTERSHIRE

At Taunton, July 6, 8, 9. Drawn. Somerset 7 pts, Leicestershire 7 pts. Toss won by Somerset. Felton, in 79 overs, provided a solid platform for a sound Somerset performance, lifted by entertaining interludes from Richards and Botham. Whitaker, over 68 overs, did a similar job for the visitors, aided by Willey and Clift. Botham, rounding off a steady Somerset second innings with five 6s in 30 balls, mainly against the spinners, set a target of 273 in three hours. But Somerset's spin bowlers – Marks, who finished with match figures of eleven for 208, and Booth – soon removed this as a realistic ambition. Indeed, after Willey had played well for 38 overs, wickets fell to suggest a Somerset success, but Taylor, for eleven overs, and Garnham, for the final fourteen, held firm.

### Somerset

| First Innings | | Second Innings | |
|---|---|---|---|
| N. F. M. Popplewell lbw b Clift | 24 | c Taylor b Cook | 53 |
| P. M. Roebuck c Butcher b Taylor | 21 | b Clift | 49 |
| N. A. Felton c Balderstone b Taylor | 112 | c Garnham b Clift | 58 |
| I. V. A. Richards c Garnham b Taylor | 47 | | |
| R. E. Hayward lbw b Cook | 28 | (4) lbw b Willey | 8 |
| *I. T. Botham st Garnham b Cook | 48 | (5) not out | 50 |
| V. J. Marks b Taylor | 20 | (6) c Cook b Clift | 8 |
| †T. Gard c Garnham b Agnew | 15 | | |
| C. H. Dredge c Balderstone b Taylor | 0 | | |
| S. C. Booth not out | 17 | | |
| M. S. Turner st Garnham b Cook | 18 | (7) not out | 15 |
| B 5, l-b 5, n-b 7 | 17 | L-b 6, n-b 1 | 7 |
| 1/33 2/61 3/134 4/193 5/261 6/311 7/318 8/318 9/339 | 367 | 1/74 2/152 3/175 4/175 5/209 (5 wkts dec.) | 248 |

Bonus points – Somerset 4, Leicestershire 4.

Bowling: *First Innings*—Agnew 19–3–85–1; Taylor 28–4–77–5; Clift 23–3–86–1; Willey 10–1–32–0; Cook 19.5–4–77–3. *Second Innings*—Taylor 7–2–13–0; Agnew 13–3–49–0; Cook 23–7–73–1; Willey 23–6–60–1; Clift 10–1–47–3.

### Leicestershire

| First Innings | | Second Innings | |
|---|---|---|---|
| I. P. Butcher lbw b Dredge | 38 | lbw b Booth | 3 |
| J. C. Balderstone c Popplewell b Marks | 27 | b Marks | 36 |
| *D. I. Gower c and b Marks | 4 | c Felton b Marks | 3 |
| P. Willey c Gard b Marks | 43 | c Gard b Booth | 80 |
| J. J. Whitaker c Popplewell b Marks | 105 | c Dredge b Botham | 19 |
| N. E. Briers c Richards b Booth | 34 | run out | 17 |
| †M. A. Garnham lbw b Marks | 1 | (9) not out | 8 |
| P. B. Clift not out | 40 | c Booth b Marks | 0 |
| N. G. B. Cook lbw b Marks | 8 | (10) not out | 8 |
| J. P. Agnew c and b Marks | 17 | | |
| L. B. Taylor not out | 20 | (7) b Marks | 8 |
| B 1, l-b 4, n-b 1 | 6 | B 3, l-b 5, n-b 2 | 10 |
| 1/66 2/66 3/76 4/152 5/241 6/242 7/269 8/283 9/321 (9 wkts dec.) | 343 | 1/26 2/29 3/88 4/127 5/167 6/175 7/176 8/178 (8 wkts) | 192 |

Bonus points – Leicestershire 3, Somerset 3 (Score at 100 overs: 285-8).

Bowling: *First Innings*—Botham 3–1–2–0; Turner 10–2–37–0; Marks 49–11–143–7; Booth 27–9–89–1; Dredge 15–1–50–1; Richards 6–0–17–0. *Second Innings*—Dredge 3–0–12–0; Turner 3–1–8–0; Booth 17–3–63–2; Marks 27–8–65–4; Botham 12–5–32–1; Roebuck 1–0–4–0.

Umpires: A. A. Jones and B. Leadbeater.

At Southend, July 10, 11, 12. SOMERSET lost to ESSEX by 149 runs.

At Lord's, July 13, 15, 16. SOMERSET drew with MIDDLESEX.

At Edgbaston, July 24, 25, 26. SOMERSET drew with WARWICKSHIRE.

## SOMERSET v ESSEX

At Taunton, July 27, 29, 30. Essex won by seven wickets. Essex 20 pts, Somerset 4 pts. Toss won by Essex. Following an early slump by Somerset on a green pitch against Ian Pont on his Essex début, Felton and Wyatt added 92 in 30 overs. Botham, hitting four 6s and sixteen 4s, then made a remarkable 152 out of 195 in 121 balls to complete the recovery. Bad light stopped play after an over of Essex's reply and no play was possible on the Monday. Essex declared on the final morning, and after Somerset's forfeiture, Essex easily achieved the target of 296 in 90 overs, having 21 overs to spare. Garner was unable to bowl because of a knee injury. Usefully supported, Gooch carried the innings with superb batting in easy conditions, his unbeaten 173 coming off 190 balls and containing two 6s and 21 4s. East's eight catches in the Somerset innings gave him an Essex record and equalled the world record of A. W. T. Grout of Queensland in 1959-60.

## Somerset

| | |
|---|---|
| N. F. M. Popplewell c East b I. L. Pont | 27 |
| P. M. Roebuck c East b I. L. Pont | 17 |
| N. A. Felton c East b K. R. Pont | 49 |
| I. V. A. Richards c East b I. L. Pont | 5 |
| J. G. Wyatt c East b Pringle | 50 |
| *I. T. Botham c East b I. L. Pont | 152 |
| V. J. Marks c East b Pringle | 17 |
| †T. Gard not out | 27 |
| M. R. Davis c East b Pringle | 7 |
| C. H. Dredge b I. L. Pont | 1 |
| J. Garner not out | 4 |
| L-b 4, w 1, n-b 2 | 7 |
| 1/36 2/45 3/56 4/148 5/162 6/246 7/343 8/352 9/353 | (9 wkts dec.) 363 |

Bonus points – Somerset 4, Essex 4.

Bowling: Pringle 30–2–90–3; I. L. Pont 24–2–103–5; Topley 24–3–86–0; K. R. Pont 11–0–45–1; Acfield 11–1–35–0.

*Somerset forfeited their second innings.*

## Essex

| | | | |
|---|---|---|---|
| G. A. Gooch c Gard b Wyatt | 19 | – not out | 173 |
| B. R. Hardie not out | 25 | – b Dredge | 20 |
| P. J. Prichard not out | 18 | – b Dredge | 44 |
| K. S. McEwan (did not bat) | | – lbw b Dredge | 0 |
| D. R. Pringle (did not bat) | | – not out | 45 |
| L-b 4, w 2 | 6 | L-b 11, n-b 3 | 14 |
| 1/25 | (1 wkt dec.) 68 | 1/84 2/165 3/165 | (3 wkts) 296 |

*K. W. R. Fletcher, K. R. Pont, †D. E. East, T. D. Topley, D. L. Acfield and I. L. Pont did not bat.

Bowling: *First Innings*—Garner 1–1–0–0; Wyatt 6–0–40–1; Roebuck 6–0–24–0. *Second Innings*—Botham 8–0–61–0; Davis 16–2–65–0; Dredge 22–0–82–3; Marks 18–2–48–0; Wyatt 3–0–18–0; Popplewell 2–0–11–0.

Umpires: K. J. Lyons and R. Palmer.

At Bournemouth, August 3, 5, 6. SOMERSET drew with HAMPSHIRE.

## SOMERSET v NORTHAMPTONSHIRE

At Weston-super-Mare, August 10, 12, 13. Drawn. Somerset 4 pts, Northamptonshire 3 pts. Toss won by Somerset. Somerset's poor start was redressed by Richards and Roebuck's adding 103 in 32 overs, and then, following a slump to 194 for six, Botham and the seventeen-year-old Atkinson, on his county début, put on a remarkable 177 in 31 overs. Botham struck ten 6s, establishing a new record of 74 6s in a season, and eight 4s as he made 134 in 147 balls, while Atkinson's refreshing composure and willingness to attack brought him three 6s and eleven 4s in 91 balls. Rain reduced Northamptonshire's reply to 1.2 overs on the Saturday evening, another 27.4 overs were possible in four periods on Monday, and rain washed out the final day.

## Somerset

| | | | |
|---|---|---|---|
| J. G. Wyatt run out | 16 | †T. Gard c Lamb b Griffiths | 11 |
| P. M. Roebuck c Ripley b Griffiths | 53 | C. H. Dredge not out | 25 |
| N. A. Felton c Ripley b Mallender | 9 | A. P. Jones b Mallender | 1 |
| I. V. A. Richards lbw b Griffiths | 58 | B 3, l-b 8, n-b 2 | 13 |
| R. J. Harden b Mallender | 10 | | |
| *I. T. Botham c Cook b Mallender | 134 | 1/23 2/40 3/143 4/144 | 409 |
| V. J. Marks st Ripley b Harper | 0 | 5/193 6/194 7/371 | |
| J. C. M. Atkinson c Larkins b Mallender | 79 | 8/371 9/393 | |

Bonus points – Somerset 4, Northamptonshire 3 (Score at 100 overs: 383-8).

Bowling: Mallender 26.2–5–83–5; Griffiths 29–4–127–3; Harper 24–4–52–1; Larkins 17–1–82–0; Williams 1–0–7–0; Wild 7–0–47–0.

## Northamptonshire

| | |
|---|---|
| *G. Cook not out | 39 |
| W. Larkins lbw b Dredge | 29 |
| R. J. Boyd-Moss not out | 19 |
| 1/57 (1 wkt) | 87 |

A. J. Lamb, R. J. Bailey, R. G. Williams, D. J. Wild, B. J. Griffiths, R. A. Harper, †D. Ripley and N. A. Mallender did not bat.

Bowling: Botham 1–0–4–0; Atkinson 5–1–22–0; Dredge 14–1–41–1; Jones 4–0–12–0; Richards 5–1–8–0.

Umpires: C. Cook and B. Leadbeater.

# SOMERSET v MIDDLESEX

At Weston-super-Mare, August 14, 15, 16. Drawn. Somerset 5 pts, Middlesex 5 pts. Toss won by Somerset. A courageous 60-over innings by Felton, after an early blow had broken a finger, saw Somerset through a mid-innings slump, after which Marks, with ten 4s in 32 overs, and Atkinson put on 56 in eleven overs. The innings ended just after tea on the third day following a blank first day, only 68 overs on Thursday, and a delay until 3.30 on the final day. Seeking one batting point from their 36 overs, Middlesex began slowly, then accelerated. Slack and Barlow put on 65 in 22 overs, Radley kept the innings together as attacking strokes cost wickets against Coombs, a 26-year-old left-arm spinner on his county début, and Hughes completed Middlesex's mission with four balls to spare.

## Somerset

| | | | |
|---|---|---|---|
| J. G. Wyatt lbw b Sykes | 42 | †T. Gard c Brown b Hughes | 0 |
| P. M. Roebuck lbw b Daniel | 0 | C. H. Dredge not out | 2 |
| N. A. Felton b Cowans | 63 | R. V. J. Coombs lbw b Hughes | 0 |
| I. V. A. Richards c Metson b Hughes | 8 | B 9, l-b 6, w 1, n-b 12 | 28 |
| R. J. Harden c Sykes b Hughes | 0 | | |
| S. A. R. Ferguson c Butcher b Daniel | 8 | 1/5 2/75 3/86 4/90 | 245 |
| *V. J. Marks c and b Daniel | 69 | 5/119 6/185 7/241 | |
| J. C. M. Atkinson c Metson b Hughes | 25 | 8/243 9/245 | |

Bonus points – Somerset 2, Middlesex 4.

Bowling: Daniel 19–2–81–3; Cowans 13–1–36–1; Hughes 18.4–2–64–5; Sykes 23–10–49–1.

### Middlesex

G. D. Barlow st Gard b Coombs ...... 32
W. N. Slack c Roebuck b Coombs .... 52
K. R. Brown b Coombs ............. 1
R. O. Butcher c Gard b Coombs ...... 2
*C. T. Radley not out ............... 24
K. P. Tomlins st Gard b Coombs ..... 14
N. G. Cowans b Marks ............. 10
J. F. Sykes b Marks ............... 0
†C. P. Metson lbw b Marks .......... 2
S. P. Hughes not out ............... 5
B 1, l-b 7 ................. 8

1/65 2/75 3/89 4/96 5/118 6/135 7/135 8/141 (8 wkts) 150

W. W. Daniel did not bat.

Bonus points – Middlesex 1, Somerset 3.

Bowling: Dredge 7–2–12–0; Atkinson 9–0–36–0; Coombs 14–1–58–5; Marks 6–0–36–3.

Umpires: C. Cook and B. Leadbeater.

At Old Trafford, August 24, 26, 27. SOMERSET lost to LANCASHIRE by six wickets.

At Derby, August 28, 29, 30. SOMERSET drew with DERBYSHIRE.

## SOMERSET v SUSSEX

At Taunton, August 31, September 2, 3. Drawn. Somerset 3 pts, Sussex 1 pt. Toss won by Somerset. The only play possible was 87 overs on the first day. Roebuck, in 60 overs, and Wyatt both survived chances and fought well on a seaming pitch to establish the innings. Richards, missed when 36, went on to score his eighth hundred of the season, finishing with 112 out of 146, his 115-ball innings containing one 6 and sixteen 4s.

### Somerset

J. G. Wyatt lbw b Greig ............ 35
P. M. Roebuck lbw b Jones ........... 60
P. A. C. Bail run out ............... 21
I. V. A. Richards c Lenham b Greig ..112
R. J. Harden not out ................ 20
J. C. M. Atkinson not out ........... 19
L-b 4, w 1, n-b 3 ........... 8

1/61 2/101 3/187 4/247 (4 wkts) 275

*V. J. Marks, †T. Gard, C. H. Dredge, J. Garner and R. V. J. Coombs did not bat.

Bonus points – Somerset 3, Sussex 1.

Bowling: le Roux 12–2–36–0; Jones 17–2–57–1; C. M. Wells 18–4–58–0; Greig 25–5–70–2; Waller 9–3–30–0; Barclay 6–1–20–0.

### Sussex

G. D. Mendis, A. M. Green, N. J. Lenham, C. M. Wells, A. P. Wells, I. A. Greig, †I. J. Gould, *J. R. T. Barclay, C. E. Waller, A. N. Jones and G. S. le Roux.

Umpires: D. O. Oslear and J. H. Hampshire.

At Worcester, September 4, 5, 6. SOMERSET lost to WORCESTERSHIRE by 124 runs.

## SOMERSET v WORCESTERSHIRE

At Taunton, September 11, 12, 13. Drawn. Somerset 4 pts, Worcestershire 8 pts. Toss won by Somerset. On a pitch receptive to seam, Somerset recovered through Roebuck (a tenacious 78 overs), Richards and particularly Marks, who hit fourteen 4s in a stay of 38 overs. D'Oliveira, hitting two 6s and fourteen 4s, and Curtis, after sharp early chances, put on a splendid 197 for the first wicket in 61 overs. Coombs, especially, slowed the scoring for a time but Smith, Patel and Weston added 182 in the final 33 overs to see Worcestershire to their highest total of the season. Another sturdy effort from Roebuck, this time off 112 overs, was augmented by Richards after Somerset had entered the last day 186 behind. Richards, reaching 100 in 96 balls, eventually hit four 6s and seventeen 4s as he led their stand of 195 in 42 overs.

## Somerset

| Batsman | First innings | | Second innings | |
|---|---|---|---|---|
| J. G. Wyatt | lbw b Radford | 2 | lbw b Radford | 19 |
| P. M. Roebuck | b Hick | 85 | not out | 132 |
| N. A. Felton | c Rhodes b Inchmore | 4 | c Hick b Patel | 25 |
| I. V. A. Richards | c Hick b Inchmore | 52 | c McEwan b Weston | 125 |
| R. J. Harden | c Rhodes b McEwan | 4 | not out | 33 |
| *V. J. Marks | c Curtis b Hick | 82 | | |
| G. V. Palmer | not out | 23 | | |
| †T. Gard | lbw b Radford | 0 | | |
| C. H. Dredge | c D'Oliveira b Radford | 3 | | |
| J. Garner | c Neale b McEwan | 1 | | |
| R. V. J. Coombs | b Radford | 0 | | |
| | B 6, l-b 16, w 1, n-b 1 | 24 | B 9, l-b 2, n-b 7 | 18 |
| | 1/2 2/13 3/95 4/110 5/244 6/260 7/261 8/267 9/280 | 280 | 1/32 2/94 3/289 (3 wkts dec.) | 352 |

Bonus points – Somerset 3, Worcestershire 4.

Bowling: *First Innings*—Radford 22.5–5–59–4; Inchmore 20–3–48–2; McEwan 16–3–54–2; Patel 7–0–35–0; Weston 14–4–28–0; Hick 10–2–34–2. *Second Innings*—Radford 27–3–68–1; McEwan 14–1–77–0; Weston 23–6–67–1; Inchmore 11–5–21–0; Patel 6–2–27–1; Hick 21–3–81–0.

## Worcestershire

|  |  |  |
|---|---|---|
| T. S. Curtis | c Roebuck b Coombs | 83 |
| D. B. D'Oliveira | c Gard b Coombs | 113 |
| G. A. Hick | c Dredge b Coombs | 38 |
| D. M. Smith | c Harden b Garner | 61 |
| *P. A. Neale | b Coombs | 9 |
| D. N. Patel | c Richards b Dredge | 41 |
| M. J. Weston | c Wyatt b Marks | 40 |
| †S. J. Rhodes | not out | 33 |
| N. V. Radford | not out | 10 |
| | B 13, l-b 11, w 1, n-b 13 | 38 |
| | 1/197 2/233 3/271 4/284 5/380 6/383 7/446 (7 wkts dec.) | 466 |

J. D. Inchmore and S. M. McEwan did not bat.

Bonus points – Worcestershire 4, Somerset 1 (Score at 100 overs 311-4).

Bowling: Garner 18–2–76–1; Dredge 22–3–88–1; Richards 12–5–56–0; Palmer 10–1–36–0; Coombs 38–12–99–4; Marks 28–6–87–1.

Umpires: J. A Jameson and N. T. Plews.

At Canterbury, September 14, 16, 17. SOMERSET drew with KENT.

# SURREY

*Patron:* HM The Queen
*President:* 1985-86 – Lord Carr of Hadley
1986-87 – M. F. Turner
*Chairman:* D. H. Newton
*Chairman, Cricket Committee:* J. C. Laker
*Secretary:* I. F. B. Scott-Browne
Kennington Oval, London SE11 5SS
(Telephone: 01-582 6660)
*Cricket Manager:* M. J. Stewart
*Captain:* 1985 – G. P. Howarth
*Coach:* G. G. Arnold

Nobody would have blamed Surrey's manager, Micky Stewart, for welcoming the end of the 1985 season. By his own admission, it was the most difficult summer since he returned to The Oval in 1979 to try to regenerate team performances. It was riddled by injury, depressed by a feeble effort in the one-day competitions, and disappointing even in the last hour of the season when Surrey were inched out of the Britannic Assurance Championship prizemoney.

Stewart's strategy was badly disrupted in early May when disc trouble ruled out his bowling spearhead, Sylvester Clarke, for the entire season, although, paradoxically, Surrey were to benefit from his absence by the discovery of a new West Indian fast bowling talent in the 6ft 8in Tony Gray. Gray's arrival on a chilly May morning, as a replacement for Clarke, caused problems over the captaincy. The overseas qualification regulations precluded Surrey's New Zealand-born captain, Geoff Howarth, from playing in the same side as Gray. It was an embarrassing problem for the committee, whose response was to appoint their new acquisition from Hampshire, Trevor Jesty, to skipper the team for the remainder of the season. In the event Gray supported their difficult decision by taking 79 first-class wickets, the fifth-best bag in the country.

If sixth in the Championship could be viewed as a worthwhile challenge, a deeper analysis shows that Surrey should have fared better. They held a place in the top four during the first two months of the season, were third in the middle of August, and mathematically could still have struck for the title in the final week had Sussex not eliminated them with a successful run-chase in the penultimate match. Because of their crippling log of injuries, the bowling was not strong enough to force crucial victories in any of the last six matches.

Yet with 76, Surrey finished with the third best total of bowling points, although their wickets were taken at a high cost and too low a striking-rate. This, in fact, was the prime reason why they gave a poor account of themselves in one-day cricket. They languished in the John Player Sunday League, going three months without a victory, though that was due partly to the weather.

Surrey failed to qualify for the knockout stages in the strongest group of the Benson and Hedges Cup. Essex, in fact, demonstrated their considerable one-day prowess by overwhelming Surrey by nine wickets.

In the NatWest Bank Trophy, they went out in the first round to Kent at Canterbury, where, as the cliché puts it, they snatched defeat from the jaws of victory by failing to defend such a substantial score as 293 for eight.

Stewart's intended faster attack before the season started was Clarke, David Thomas, Graham Monkhouse, Mark Feltham and Kevin Mackintosh, and one by one they went down. Mackintosh was always out of the running with a prolonged back injury, Feltham took most of the summer recovering from a car accident in South Africa, Monkhouse had a wrist broken while batting against Middlesex, and Thomas, incapacitated by a damaged groin, was rarely seen after the beginning of July.

It was fortunate that the batting maintained a high level of consistency, especially that of Monte Lynch, who showed an increased maturity and, at times, touched brilliance with seven Championship hundreds, two of them against the 1985 champions, Middlesex. He also took two off Middlesex in 1984 and seems to be fostering a vendetta against them since he suffered the ignominy of collecting a "pair" before lunch on the same day of a rain-hit match at Lord's in 1977, his first season. Lynch's close-to-the-wicket catching was also a sight to behold. He collected 36 victims, the most by any fielder in the country. In this respect Jack Richards also excelled behind the stumps.

Grahame Clinton came of age as a consistent run-scorer. The slightly built left-hander topped 1,200 runs with three centuries; but he was also a regular visitor to hospital and treatment room. He broke a hand, an injury which he aggravated later, and in September he sustained a fractured cheekbone when hit by a ball from Lancashire's Paul Allott in a Sunday League match. Even so, Clinton's opening alliance with Alan Butcher, who was steady rather than spectacular, was one of the most successful in the country.

Andrew Needham, pressed into service to open when Clinton was indisposed, scored 1,000 runs for the first time, while Alec Stewart achieved the same distinction in his first full season. Both received their county caps, along with Gray, on the final day of the Championship campaign. Jesty began with a blaze of runs, but the big scores began to dry up with the extra responsibilities of captaincy, thrust on him when his unbeaten hundred set up the victory over Essex at the end of May. Surrey's first Championship win under him was then seven weeks and nine matches away, Yorkshire being overcome by nine wickets at Sheffield on July 16, a victory which highlighted an eight-wicket return by Gray, including a hat-trick. Gray's willingness to listen, absorb and learn from the advice of older, wiser cricketers paid off, though a double-edged consequence was the ominous preparation of a class bowler to face England on their winter tour to the Caribbean.

The summer ended on both a happy and sad note. No sooner had The Oval housed England's Ashes-regaining Test against Australia than Surrey said their goodbyes to Howarth, who left the county after fifteen seasons with the determined intention of re-establishing himself in New Zealand cricket. – D.F.

SURREY 1985

[*Bill Smith*

*Back row:* A. J. Stewart, Zahid Sadiq, D. M. Ward, P. A. Waterman, K. T. Medlycott, N. J. Falkner. *Middle row:* G. G. Arnold (*coach*), T. E. Jesty, G. Monkhouse, C. K. Bullen, N. S. Taylor, M. A. Feltham, D. B. Pauline, J. Deary (*physiotherapist*), T. Billson (*scorer*). *Front row:* M. A. Lynch, S. T. Clarke, A. R. Butcher, M. J. Stewart (*manager*), P. I. Pocock, C. J. Richards, G. S. Clinton, D. J. Thomas. *Insets:* A. H. Gray, G. P. Howarth (*captain*), A. Needham.

# SURREY RESULTS

*All first-class matches – Played 27: Won 6, Lost 5, Drawn 16.*

*County Championship matches – Played 24: Won 5, Lost 5, Drawn 14.*

*Bonus points – Batting 62, Bowling 76.*

*Competition placings – Britannic Assurance County Championship, 6th; NatWest Bank Trophy, 1st round; Benson and Hedges Cup, 3rd in Group C; John Player League, 17th.*

## BRITANNIC ASSURANCE CHAMPIONSHIP AVERAGES

### BATTING

| | *Birthplace* | *M* | *I* | *NO* | *R* | *HI* | *Avge* |
|---|---|---|---|---|---|---|---|
| ‡M. A. Lynch | *Georgetown, BG* | 24 | 37 | 7 | 1,672 | 145 | 55.73 |
| D. M. Ward | *Croydon* | 5 | 8 | 3 | 256 | 143 | 51.20 |
| ‡G. S. Clinton | *Sidcup* | 18 | 32 | 6 | 1,225 | 123 | 47.11 |
| ‡C. J. Richards | *Penzance* | 22 | 27 | 12 | 665 | 75* | 44.33 |
| ‡T. E. Jesty | *Gosport* | 23 | 34 | 7 | 1,062 | 141* | 39.33 |
| ‡A. Needham | *Calow* | 23 | 33 | 4 | 1,032 | 138 | 35.58 |
| ‡A. R. Butcher | *Croydon* | 24 | 42 | 3 | 1,335 | 126 | 34.23 |
| ‡G. Monkhouse | *Carlisle* | 15 | 14 | 8 | 203 | 47 | 33.83 |
| ‡A. J. Stewart | *Merton* | 21 | 32 | 3 | 886 | 158 | 30.55 |
| D. B. Pauline | *Aberdeen* | 12 | 16 | 2 | 374 | 77 | 26.71 |
| R. J. Doughty | *Bridlington* | 10 | 12 | 2 | 239 | 65 | 23.90 |
| ‡P. I. Pocock | *Bangor* | 23 | 18 | 6 | 183 | 41 | 15.25 |
| C. K. Bullen | *Clapham* | 2 | 4 | 0 | 53 | 19 | 13.25 |
| ‡D. J. Thomas | *Solihull* | 11 | 12 | 3 | 116 | 25* | 12.88 |
| N. S. Taylor | *Holmfirth* | 6 | 7 | 3 | 51 | 21* | 12.75 |
| ‡A. H. Gray | *Port-of-Spain, Trinidad* | 19 | 10 | 1 | 48 | 20 | 5.33 |

Also batted: M. A. Feltham (*Wandsworth*) (1 match) 8, 27; K. T. Medlycott (*Whitechapel*) (1 match) 5; P. A. Waterman (*Hendon*) (4 matches) 0, 1*.

* *Signifies not out.* ‡ *Denotes county cap.*

The following played a total of nineteen three-figure innings for Surrey in County Championship matches – M. A. Lynch 7, G. S. Clinton 3, T. E. Jesty 3, A. R. Butcher 2, A. Needham 2, A. J. Stewart 1, D. M. Ward 1.

### BOWLING

| | *O* | *M* | *R* | *W* | *BB* | *Avge* |
|---|---|---|---|---|---|---|
| A. H. Gray | 524 | 99 | 1,816 | 79 | 8-40 | 22.98 |
| R. J. Doughty | 207.5 | 35 | 806 | 31 | 6-33 | 26.00 |
| G. Monkhouse | 370.5 | 76 | 1,020 | 37 | 5-61 | 27.56 |
| D. J. Thomas | 328.2 | 54 | 1,055 | 32 | 5-51 | 32.96 |
| P. I. Pocock | 564.2 | 127 | 1,608 | 47 | 7-42 | 34.21 |
| T. E. Jesty | 144.2 | 28 | 517 | 14 | 2-32 | 36.92 |
| D. B. Pauline | 158.4 | 31 | 560 | 15 | 5-52 | 37.33 |
| A. R. Butcher | 150 | 32 | 439 | 10 | 3-43 | 43.90 |
| A. Needham | 326.4 | 67 | 978 | 22 | 5-42 | 44.45 |

Also bowled: C. K. Bullen 7–1–39–0; G. S. Clinton 6–0–46–0; M. A. Feltham 11–1–74–0; M. A. Lynch 6–1–46–0; C. J. Richards 27–2–120–4; A. J. Stewart 6–0–43–0; N. S. Taylor 120.2–16–516–9; P. A. Waterman 69–11–284–5.

## SURREY v GLAMORGAN

At The Oval, April 27, 28, 29. Glamorgan won by seven wickets. Glamorgan 21 pts, Surrey 6 pts. Toss won by Surrey. Butcher unveiled Surrey's season with a splendidly aggressive 121 in less than three hours, but Glamorgan refused to be overrun, responding positively to Pocock's declaration to begin their Championship campaign with a win. A ferocious 85 not out by Lynch lifted Surrey to 300 and a declaration, and Glamorgan had to be salvaged by a fifth-wicket partnership of 167 between Miandad and Ontong. Pocock's second closure of the match left Glamorgan a target of 218 in 145 minutes, Surrey's acting-captain basing his strategy on a pitch which was beginning to take spin. However, Hopkins upset his calculations with some robust blows in his 90 and Glamorgan got home with twelve balls remaining.

### Surrey

| First innings | | Second innings | |
|---|---|---|---|
| A. R. Butcher b Ontong | 121 | c Thomas b McFarlane | 35 |
| G. S. Clinton b Holmes | 39 | b Malone | 26 |
| A. J. Stewart b Thomas | 10 | c Jones b Ontong | 12 |
| T. E. Jesty c Steele b Holmes | 1 | b Ontong | 40 |
| M. A. Lynch not out | 85 | c and b Steele | 10 |
| D. B. Pauline lbw b Thomas | 20 | c McFarlane b Steele | 20 |
| †C. J. Richards b Thomas | 0 | not out | 11 |
| D. J. Thomas not out | 17 | c Steele b Thomas | 20 |
| L-b 5, w 1, n-b 1 | 7 | B 4, l-b 2, w 1 | 7 |
| 1/102 2/125 3/138 4/219 5/266 6/266 | (6 wkts dec.) 300 | 1/65 2/71 3/88 4/99 5/143 6/150 7/181 | (7 wkts dec.) 181 |

G. Monkhouse, N. S. Taylor and *P. I. Pocock did not bat.

Bonus points – Surrey 4, Glamorgan 2.

Bowling: *First Innings*—Thomas 19–1–72–3; Malone 20.3–4–70–0; McFarlane 9–0–43–0; Holmes 13–2–39–2; Steele 11–3–22–0; Ontong 11–0–49–1. *Second Innings*—Thomas 7.3–2–24–1; Malone 9–0–34–1; McFarlane 9–4–19–1; Ontong 21–6–47–2; Steele 19–5–51–2.

### Glamorgan

| First innings | | Second innings | |
|---|---|---|---|
| J. A. Hopkins lbw b Monkhouse | 9 | c Jesty b Thomas | 90 |
| A. L. Jones c Lynch b Taylor | 21 | c sub b Pocock | 47 |
| G. C. Holmes lbw b Taylor | 5 | c Pauline b Thomas | 42 |
| Javed Miandad b Pocock | 125 | not out | 23 |
| Younis Ahmed c Richards b Taylor | 4 | not out | 8 |
| *R. C. Ontong lbw b Thomas | 61 | | |
| J. F. Steele not out | 15 | | |
| J. G. Thomas not out | 14 | | |
| L-b 3, w 1, n-b 6 | 10 | B 3, l-b 5 | 8 |
| 1/31 2/37 3/49 4/53 5/220 6/240 | (6 wkts dec.) 264 | 1/96 2/180 3/201 | (3 wkts) 218 |

†T. Davies, S. J. Malone and L. L. McFarlane did not bat.

Bonus points – Glamorgan 3, Surrey 2.

Bowling: *First Innings*—Thomas 20–6–53–1; Taylor 20–4–57–3; Monkhouse 25–5–75–1; Jesty 5–1–27–0; Pocock 14–4–32–1; Pauline 2.1–0–17–0. *Second Innings*—Thomas 18–1–104–2; Taylor 6–1–25–0; Pocock 14–0–61–1; Jesty 2–0–20–0.

Umpires: R. Julian and P. B. Wight.

At Canterbury, May 1, 2, 3. SURREY drew with KENT.

## SURREY v LANCASHIRE

At The Oval, May 8, 9, 10. Surrey won by 233 runs. Surrey 24 pts, Lancashire 5 pts. Toss won by Surrey, who acquired a substantial initiative when Butcher and Clinton put together an opening partnership of 167. That the innings progressed fitfully thereafter was due mainly to the persistence of Allott, who was rewarded with the splendid figures of six for 71. Jesty's 75 sustained the middle of the innings, which gave Needham a platform to take five wickets with his off-breaks and earn Surrey a lead of 119. Allott again served his side handsomely, adding 39 with the Dane, Henriksen (who thwarted Needham's hat-trick attempt), to edge Lancashire past the follow-on mark. Jesty launched Surrey towards a declaration with a richly entertaining 96, and Lancashire were set a target of 311 in 79 overs. When Thomas took four of the first five wickets to fall, they were never remotely in with a chance and succumbed for a meagre 77.

### Surrey

| First innings | | Second innings | |
|---|---|---|---|
| A. R. Butcher c Simmons b O'Shaughnessy | 81 | – c Stanworth b Jefferies | 21 |
| G. S. Clinton b Allott | 87 | – (6) c O'Shaughnessy b Simmons | 3 |
| A. J. Stewart c Abrahams b O'Shaughnessy | 14 | – lbw b Simmons | 14 |
| T. E. Jesty c and b Henriksen | 75 | – b Watkinson | 96 |
| M. A. Lynch run out | 0 | – st Stanworth b Simmons | 11 |
| A. Needham c Stanworth b Allott | 43 | | |
| †C. J. Richards c Stanworth b Allott | 3 | – (2) c Simmons b Allott | 32 |
| D. J. Thomas c Stanworth b Allott | 15 | – (7) not out | 2 |
| G. Monkhouse not out | 10 | – (8) lbw b Watkinson | 0 |
| *P. I. Pocock c and b Allott | 0 | | |
| N. S. Taylor b Allott | 0 | | |
| B 4, l-b 8, n-b 1 | 13 | B 2, l-b 6, n-b 4 | 12 |
| 1/167 2/189 3/194 4/194 5/287 6/293 7/316 8/341 9/341 | 341 | 1/29 2/52 3/127 4/180 5/188 6/191 7/191 (7 wkts dec.) | 191 |

Bonus points – Surrey 4, Lancashire 3 (Score at 100 overs: 339-7).

Bowling: *First Innings*—Allott 24.5–7–71–6; Jefferies 23–2–72–0; Henriksen 12–1–44–1; Simmons 25–7–71–0; Watkinson 10–2–46–0; Abrahams 2–0–16–0; O'Shaughnessy 6–2–9–2. *Second Innings*—Allott 17–4–50–1; Jefferies 13–2–53–1; Watkinson 11.5–5–23–2; Simmons 15–2–57–3.

### Lancashire

| First innings | | Second innings | |
|---|---|---|---|
| G. Fowler c Lynch b Taylor | 19 | – b Thomas | 5 |
| J. A. Ormrod c Lynch b Monkhouse | 23 | – c Lynch b Pocock | 16 |
| S. J. O'Shaughnessy c Lynch b Monkhouse | 16 | – lbw b Thomas | 0 |
| N. H. Fairbrother b Needham | 48 | – c Needham b Monkhouse | 3 |
| M. Watkinson b Taylor | 15 | – (7) b Pocock | 9 |
| *J. Abrahams c Lynch b Thomas | 8 | – (5) c Monkhouse b Thomas | 5 |
| S. T. Jefferies c Jesty b Needham | 29 | – (6) c Richards b Thomas | 8 |
| J. Simmons c Jesty b Needham | 6 | – c Stewart b Pocock | 4 |
| †J. Stanworth b Needham | 0 | – c and b Needham | 0 |
| P. J. W. Allott c Jesty b Needham | 29 | – st Richards b Needham | 19 |
| S. Henriksen not out | 10 | – not out | 0 |
| B 5, l-b 4, n-b 10 | 19 | L-b 1, w 5, n-b 2 | 8 |
| 1/32 2/63 3/66 4/92 5/125 6/168 7/174 8/183 9/183 | 222 | 1/6 2/6 3/18 4/25 5/36 6/51 7/55 8/58 9/62 | 77 |

Bonus points – Lancashire 2, Surrey 4.

Bowling: *First Innings*—Thomas 19–3–44–1; Taylor 15–2–57–2; Pocock 22–8–46–0; Monkhouse 9–1–24–2; Needham 17–6–42–5. *Second Innings*—Thomas 9–1–20–4; Monkhouse 8–0–22–1; Needham 6.2–1–15–2; Taylor 1–0–2–0; Pocock 5–1–17–3.

Umpires: B. Dudleston and J. W. Holder.

At The Oval, May 16. SURREY beat AUSTRALIANS by six wickets (See Australian tour section).

At Edgbaston, May 22, 23, 24. SURREY lost to WARWICKSHIRE by four wickets.

## SURREY v ESSEX

At The Oval, May 25, 27, 28. Surrey won by seven wickets. Surrey 18 pts, Essex 4 pts. Toss won by Surrey. Jesty made this rain-affected match a personal triumph by scoring his second hundred inside a week for his new county and easing the way to victory over the county champions with 21.3 overs to spare. He was awarded his county cap by the club captain, Howarth, and then told that he would lead the county for the rest of the season in Howarth's absence. Essex, put in, reached 114 without loss, then slumped to 150 for five before Pringle's first Championship hundred for two years revived the innings. He added 173 with East for the sixth wicket. A weekend storm prevented any play on the second day, but lost time was made up by Surrey's declaration and Essex's forfeiture of their second innings. This left Surrey with a target of 327 in 105 overs which, with Jesty's contribution and a sound century from Clinton, they did not find a serious challenge.

### Essex

| | | | |
|---|---|---|---|
| G. A. Gooch c Monkhouse b Gray | 57 | †D. E. East c sub b Pocock | 69 |
| B. R. Hardie lbw b Monkhouse | 54 | N. A. Foster not out | 2 |
| A. W. Lilley lbw b Monkhouse | 0 | B 3, l-b 6, w 1, n-b 5 | 15 |
| K. S. McEwan c Richards b Gray | 2 | | |
| D. R. Pringle not out | 121 | 1/114 2/114 3/119 (6 wkts dec.) | 336 |
| *K. W. R. Fletcher lbw b Jesty | 16 | 4/124 5/150 6/323 | |

J. H. Childs, J. K. Lever and D. L. Acfield did not bat.

Bonus points – Essex 4, Surrey 2 (Score at 100 overs: 323-6).

Bowling: Thomas 19–3–51–0; Gray 16–1–72–2; Monkhouse 24–3–90–2; Pocock 16–4–32–1; Butcher 4–1–16–0; Jesty 12–3–37–1; Needham 10–3–29–0.

*Essex forfeited their second innings.*

### Surrey

| | | | |
|---|---|---|---|
| †C. J. Richards not out | 5 | | |
| G. S. Clinton not out | 4 | – c Hardie b Childs | 106 |
| A. R. Butcher (did not bat) | | – (1) c Fletcher b Lever | 25 |
| A. J. Stewart (did not bat) | | – (3) c East b Pringle | 43 |
| T. E. Jesty (did not bat) | | – (4) not out | 112 |
| M. A. Lynch (did not bat) | | – (5) not out | 31 |
| L-b 1 | 1 | B 1, l-b 6, w 2, n-b 1 | 10 |
| (no wkt dec.) | 10 | 1/58 2/131 3/264 (3 wkts) | 327 |

A. Needham, D. J. Thomas, G. Monkhouse, *P. I. Pocock and A. H. Gray did not bat.

Bowling: *First Innings*—Lever 4–2–3–0; Foster 4–1–6–0. *Second Innings*—Lever 16–1–60–1; Foster 16–1–74–0; Pringle 21.4–4–70–1; Gooch 5–2–17–0; Acfield 8–2–31–0; Childs 17–1–68–1.

Umpires: M. J. Kitchen and P. B. Wight.

## SURREY v MIDDLESEX

At The Oval, May 29, 30, 31. Drawn. Surrey 4 pts, Middlesex 7 pts. Toss won by Surrey. Lynch's second century of the season, equalling his highest score for Surrey, helped by 141 minutes of support from Richards, transformed a precarious position into a creditable draw. Just over three and a half hours remained when Lynch went in, with Surrey still 20 runs behind and four second-innings wickets down. In addition, Monkhouse had suffered a broken left arm when he was hit by a ball from Williams on the second evening. Emburey had inspired the collapse with three wickets in twenty deliveries. Middlesex, who led the Championship table by a point from Surrey before the match, owed their control to centuries from Barlow and Radley and to some effective seam bowling on the opening day, when Surrey's first innings was held together by Stewart.

## Surrey

| | | | |
|---|---|---|---|
| A. R. Butcher run out | 1 | – c Slack b Williams | 3 |
| G. S. Clinton c Emburey b Williams | 0 | – c Radley b Butcher | 80 |
| A. J. Stewart run out | 77 | – (5) c Slack b Emburey | 2 |
| *T. E. Jesty c Brown b Williams | 0 | – (6) c Butcher b Emburey | 4 |
| M. A. Lynch c Hughes b Daniel | 31 | – (7) not out | 144 |
| A. Needham run out | 12 | – (4) c Butcher b Emburey | 73 |
| †C. J. Richards c Brown b Hughes | 38 | – (9) not out | 44 |
| D. J. Thomas c Sykes b Daniel | 12 | – c Butcher b Sykes | 9 |
| G. Monkhouse not out | 8 | – (3) retired hurt | 6 |
| P. I. Pocock c Daniel b Emburey | 41 | | |
| A. H. Gray run out | 1 | | |
| B 3, l-b 16, w 4, n-b 11 | 34 | B 10, l-b 9, w 2, n-b 16 | 37 |
| 1/4 2/11 3/11 4/57 5/110 6/171 7/199 8/202 9/251 | 255 | 1/6 2/168 3/172 4/177 5/188 6/222 (6 wkts dec.) | 402 |

Bonus points – Surrey 3, Middlesex 4.

Bowling: *First Innings*—Daniel 13–4–33–2; Williams 16–3–82–2; Hughes 13–3–58–1; Emburey 11–2–44–1; Sykes 4–1–19–0. *Second Innings*—Williams 16–4–70–1; Daniel 11–0–25–0; Emburey 41–7–103–3; Sykes 16–3–71–1; Hughes 14–0–79–0; Butcher 5–1–13–1; Slack 2–0–8–0; Tomlins 2–0–9–0; Radley 2–0–5–0.

## Middlesex

| | |
|---|---|
| G. D. Barlow c Clinton b Monkhouse | 115 |
| W. N. Slack b Monkhouse | 96 |
| K. P. Tomlins c Needham b Pocock | 14 |
| R. O. Butcher c Butcher b Jesty | 29 |
| C. T. Radley not out | 105 |
| *J. E. Emburey c Stewart b Thomas | 10 |
| N. F. Williams c Lynch b Pocock | 32 |
| †K. R. Brown not out | 20 |
| B 12, l-b 11, n-b 8 | 31 |
| 1/225 2/244 3/264 4/291 5/306 6/388 (6 wkts dec.) | 452 |

J. F. Sykes, S. P. Hughes and W. W. Daniel did not bat.

Bonus points – Middlesex 3, Surrey 1 (Score at 100 overs: 283-3).

Bowling: Thomas 31–4–106–1; Gray 9–1–40–0; Needham 38–2–110–0; Monkhouse 26–6–43–2; Pocock 41–13–110–2; Butcher 4–1–14–0; Jesty 3–0–6–1.

Umpires: M. J. Kitchen and P. B. Wight.

At Horsham, June 1, 3, 4. SURREY drew with SUSSEX.

At Fenner's, June 8, 10, 11. SURREY drew with CAMBRIDGE UNIVERSITY.

## SURREY v NOTTINGHAMSHIRE

At The Oval, June 12, 13, 14. Drawn. Surrey 5 pts, Nottinghamshire 5 pts. Toss won by Surrey. Randall and Butcher both scored hundreds and narrowly missed making a second each, with Randall playing delightfully in reaching his fourth century of the season off 127 balls on a first day reduced by 33 overs through rain. Nottinghamshire's declaration was followed by Butcher and Needham enjoying a partnership of 232 – Surrey's highest for the first wicket against Nottinghamshire, surpassing Hobbs and Sandham's 203 in 1927 – after Clinton had retired hurt in the first over with 1 run on the board. Surrey declared as soon as the scores were level, whereupon Randall struck 97 before Rice set a target of 266 in 130 minutes. Butcher, timing the ball splendidly, thrashed a 75-ball 97 with one 6 and eleven 4s, but the task proved too great and Surrey finished well adrift.

## Nottinghamshire

| First Innings | | Second Innings | |
|---|---|---|---|
| B. C. Broad c Waterman b Butcher | 30 | c Clinton b Needham | 62 |
| M. Newell b Pocock | 59 | c Richards b Gray | 3 |
| D. W. Randall c Stewart b Pocock | 106 | b Needham | 97 |
| *C. E. B. Rice not out | 41 | | |
| P. Johnson not out | 51 | | |
| J. D. Birch (did not bat) | – | (5) not out | 36 |
| R. J. Hadlee (did not bat) | – | (4) c Pocock b Butcher | 8 |
| †B. N. French (did not bat) | – | (6) not out | 52 |
| B 2, l-b 4, w 3, n-b 5 | 14 | L-b 3, n-b 4 | 7 |
| 1/65 2/169 3/226 (3 wkts dec.) | 301 | 1/11 2/151 3/166 4/177 (4 wkts dec.) | 265 |

E. E. Hemmings, K. Saxelby and K. E. Cooper did not bat.

Bonus points – Nottinghamshire 4, Surrey 1.

Bowling: *First Innings*—Thomas 20–3–54–0; Gray 12–0–50–0; Butcher 15–3–35–1; Waterman 11–0–50–0; Pocock 17–2–54–2; Jesty 3–0–21–0; Needham 9–1–31–0. *Second Innings*—Thomas 13–2–49–0; Gray 12–4–29–1; Pocock 12–5–15–0; Butcher 31–4–93–1; Waterman 3–1–8–0; Needham 30–11–49–2; Lynch 2–0–19–0.

## Surrey

| First Innings | | Second Innings | |
|---|---|---|---|
| A. R. Butcher b Hemmings | 126 | c Johnson b Cooper | 97 |
| G. S. Clinton not out | 1 | c French b Cooper | 22 |
| A. Needham st French b Hemmings | 132 | (4) not out | 33 |
| †C. J. Richards not out | 15 | (6) not out | 0 |
| M. A. Lynch run out | 13 | (3) b Cooper | 10 |
| D. J. Thomas (did not bat) | – | (5) c Broad b Cooper | 4 |
| B 2, l-b 10, n-b 2 | 14 | | |
| 1/233 2/273 3/297 (3 wkts dec.) | 301 | 1/83 2/115 3/148 4/163 (4 wkts) | 166 |

A. J. Stewart, *T. E. Jesty, P. I. Pocock, A. H. Gray and P. A. Waterman did not bat.

Bonus points – Surrey 4, Nottinghamshire 1.

*In the first innings G. S. Clinton, when 0, retired hurt at 1 and resumed at 297.*

Bowling: *First Innings*—Hadlee 11–4–19–0; Saxelby 13–4–50–0; Cooper 17–2–65–0; Hemmings 29–5–119–2; Rice 13–4–36–0. *Second Innings*—Hadlee 5–0–26–0; Hemmings 3–0–30–0; Saxelby 10–0–72–0; Cooper 9–1–38–4.

Umpires: D. G. L. Evans and K. J. Lyons.

At Worcester, June 15, 17, 18. SURREY drew with WORCESTERSHIRE.

## SURREY v SOMERSET

At The Oval, June 22, 24, 25. Drawn. Surrey 4 pts, Somerset 1 pt. Toss won by Somerset. A Somerset collapse was hastened by Pauline's gentle seam bowling on a rain-disrupted first day. Pauline, who had taken only six previous first-class wickets, included Richards among his trio of victims as Somerset slipped from 85 for one to 122 for six. The giant West Indian, Gray, claimed his best figures for Surrey by winding up the Somerset innings on the second day, when drizzle and a heavier downpour restricted play to just an hour. Every effort was made to wring a positive conclusion out of the match on the final day. Surrey declared immediately, and then

Botham thrashed 72 not out in 50 balls from an irregular seam attack of Clinton, wicket-keeper Richards and Stewart, who had never previously bowled a first-class delivery. Surrey's target was 293 in 73 overs, but heavy rain had the final say.

## Somerset

| | | | |
|---|---|---|---|
| N. F. M. Popplewell c Richards b Gray | 30 | – c Lynch b Richards | 35 |
| P. M. Roebuck c Butcher b Gray | 34 | – c Needham b Richards | 0 |
| N. A. Felton c Lynch b Pauline | 21 | | |
| I. V. A. Richards b Pauline | 5 | | |
| R. E. Hayward c Richards b Pauline | 2 | | |
| *I. T. Botham c Richards b Gray | 32 | – (3) not out | 72 |
| V. J. Marks c Needham b Gray | 2 | | |
| †T. Gard c Jesty b Thomas | 15 | | |
| M. R. Davis b Gray | 11 | | |
| J. Garner c Lynch b Thomas | 7 | | |
| M. S. Turner not out | 0 | | |
| B 5, l-b 10, w 1, n-b 13 | 29 | B 4, l-b 3 | 7 |
| 1/44 2/85 3/100 4/117 5/118 6/122 7/168 8/170 9/184 | 188 | 1/4 2/114 (2 wkts dec.) | 114 |

Bonus points – Somerset 1, Surrey 4.

Bowling: *First Innings*—Thomas 20–4–55–2; Gray 20.2–4–69–5; Pauline 16–3–42–3; Butcher 7–4–7–0. *Second Innings*—Clinton 6–0–46–0; Richards 8–1–42–2; Stewart 2–0–19–0.

## Surrey

| | | | |
|---|---|---|---|
| A. R. Butcher not out | 6 | – (2) c Richards b Botham | 37 |
| G. S. Clinton not out | 4 | – (1) not out | 16 |
| A. J. Stewart (did not bat) | | – not out | 0 |
| | | L-b 5 | 5 |
| (no wkt dec.) | 10 | 1/54 (1 wkt) | 58 |

*T. E. Jesty, M. A. Lynch, A. Needham, †C. J. Richards, D. J. Thomas, P. I. Pocock, A. H. Gray and D. B. Pauline did not bat.

Bowling: *First Innings*—Garner 2–1–6–0; Davis 2–1–4–0. *Second Innings*—Garner 7–1–30–0; Davis 7–0–21–0; Botham 0.4–0–2–1.

Umpires: J. Birkenshaw and R. A. White.

At Northampton, June 26, 27, 28. SURREY lost to NORTHAMPTONSHIRE by five wickets.

At Leicester, June 29, July 1, 2. SURREY drew with LEICESTERSHIRE.

## SURREY v KENT

At The Oval, July 6, 8, 9. Kent won by 176 runs. Kent 24 pts, Surrey 5 pts. Toss won by Kent. Surrey, without a Championship victory in the seven matches since Jesty's appointment as acting-captain, had their ambitions torpedoed by outstanding individual performances from Hinks and Dilley. Hinks stabilised Kent's first innings with 81, then hit his maiden first-class century in the second against an injury-weakened attack. In between, Dilley performed the hat-trick on the first evening, and on the last day bowled Kent to their third Championship win in five matches with a burst of five wickets. Lynch, Surrey's mainstay, kept the deficit down to 120 with the first of two half-centuries, reaching 50 out of 80 in 67 balls. Kent, aggressively sustained by a stand of 173 in two hours between Hinks and Tavaré, set Surrey to score 370 in 97 overs, and in spite of Lynch's 66 they were outplayed.

## Kent

| | | | |
|---|---|---|---|
| M. R. Benson lbw b Gray | 4 | – c Richards b Gray | 18 |
| S. G. Hinks b Pocock | 81 | – b Taylor | 117 |
| C. J. Tavaré c Bullen b Jesty | 43 | – c Richards b Gray | 65 |
| D. G. Aslett b Pocock | 13 | – not out | 28 |
| *C. S. Cowdrey c Bullen b Pocock | 19 | – not out | 6 |
| E. A. E. Baptiste b Pocock | 41 | | |
| R. M. Ellison c Jesty b Taylor | 34 | | |
| †A. P. E. Knott c Gray b Pocock | 2 | | |
| G. R. Dilley lbw b Pocock | 14 | | |
| D. L. Underwood not out | 12 | | |
| K. B. S. Jarvis c Needham b Pocock | 0 | | |
| B 4, l-b 17, w 5, n-b 12 | 38 | B 8, l-b 4, n-b 3 | 15 |
| 1/22 2/132 3/164 4/171 5/207 6/257 7/272 8/282 9/287 | 301 | 1/40 2/213 3/231 (3 wkts dec.) | 249 |

Bonus points – Kent 4, Surrey 4.

Bowling: *First Innings*—Gray 23–4–51–1; Taylor 16–1–89–1; Pauline 19–1–66–0; Jesty 6–2–19–1; Needham 1–1–0–0; Butcher 6–0–13–0; Pocock 24.5–9–42–7. *Second Innings*—Gray 17–4–34–2; Taylor 6–0–35–1; Pocock 14–3–50–0; Needham 10–1–47–0; Pauline 3.1–2–2–0; Jesty 7.5–0–30–0; Bullen 7–1–39–0.

## Surrey

| | | | |
|---|---|---|---|
| A. R. Butcher c Cowdrey b Jarvis | 39 | – c Knott b Dilley | 4 |
| D. B. Pauline c Hinks b Dilley | 20 | – c Knott b Underwood | 30 |
| N. S. Taylor b Dilley | 0 | – (10) not out | 1 |
| A. Needham c Hinks b Dilley | 0 | – (3) c Hinks b Dilley | 1 |
| *T. E. Jesty c Tavaré b Ellison | 9 | – (4) b Dilley | 9 |
| M. A. Lynch c Jarvis b Baptiste | 55 | – (5) c Knott b Baptiste | 66 |
| D. M. Ward not out | 23 | – (6) c Knott b Dilley | 18 |
| †C. J. Richards lbw b Jarvis | 15 | – (7) c Baptiste b Jarvis | 26 |
| C. K. Bullen run out | 12 | – (8) c Ellison b Dilley | 16 |
| A. H. Gray run out | 0 | – (9) b Jarvis | 0 |
| P. I. Pocock c Hinks b Baptiste | 0 | – c Hinks b Jarvis | 12 |
| B 3, w 1, n-b 4 | 8 | L-b 9, w 1 | 10 |
| 1/32 2/32 3/32 4/46 5/126 6/130 7/156 8/180 9/181 | 181 | 1/10 2/23 3/33 4/110 5/114 6/150 7/168 8/170 9/180 | 193 |

Bonus points – Surrey 1, Kent 4.

Bowling: *First Innings*—Dilley 19–5–49–3; Jarvis 18–5–53–2; Ellison 5–0–20–1; Baptiste 11.2–0–42–2; Underwood 1–1–0–0; Cowdrey 7–1–14–0. *Second Innings*—Dilley 13–2–53–5; Jarvis 12.3–5–54–3; Ellison 6–1–29–0; Baptiste 9–3–26–1; Underwood 15–8–22–1.

Umpires: B. J. Meyer and D. R. Shepherd.

At Sheffield, July 13, 15, 16. SURREY beat YORKSHIRE by nine wickets.

At The Oval, July 17, 18, 19. SURREY drew with ZIMBABWEANS (See Zimbabwean tour section).

At Southport, July 24, 25, 26. SURREY drew with LANCASHIRE.

## SURREY v HAMPSHIRE

At Guildford, July 27, 29, 30. Drawn. Surrey 4 pts, Hampshire 3 pts. Toss won by Hampshire. Rain allowed only five hours' play in a match which promised to have a bearing on the outcome of the Championship prizemoney, if not the Championship itself. Hampshire, third in the table, began with great urgency on the first day with Chris and Robin Smith exploiting the short boundaries and fast outfield. However, astute bowling, especially from Pocock, slowed the rate dramatically, wickets fell, and Hampshire were 247 for six when rain accounted for the final two hours. Only fourteen overs were possible on the second day, and none at all on the third.

### Hampshire

| | |
|---|---|
| C. G. Greenidge c Richards b Gray | 29 |
| V. P. Terry b Doughty | 13 |
| C. L. Smith c Richards b Gray | 58 |
| R. A. Smith c Needham b Pocock | 57 |
| *M. C. J. Nicholas c Doughty b Pocock | 5 |
| M. D. Marshall c Needham b Pocock | 22 |
| N. G. Cowley c Richards b Doughty | 51 |
| T. M. Tremlett c Lynch b Gray | 10 |
| †R. J. Parks c Richards b Gray | 0 |
| R. J. Maru not out | 15 |
| C. A. Connor c Clinton b Gray | 12 |
| L-b 9, w 1, n-b 9 | 19 |
| 1/50 2/50 3/144 4/171 5/179 6/212 7/254 8/254 9/264 | 291 |

Bonus points – Hampshire 3, Surrey 4.

Bowling: Gray 24.1–5–83–5; Monkhouse 18–3–51–0; Doughty 15–2–69–2; Jesty 8–3–18–0; Pocock 22–3–61–3.

### Surrey

| | |
|---|---|
| A. R. Butcher not out | 4 |
| G. S. Clinton not out | 0 |
| (no wkt) | 4 |

A. Needham, *T. E. Jesty, M. A. Lynch, A. J. Stewart, †C. J. Richards, G. Monkhouse, R. J. Doughty, A. H. Gray and P. I. Pocock did not bat.

Bowling: Connor 1–0–4–0.

Umpires: C. Cook and M. J. Kitchen.

## SURREY v WARWICKSHIRE

At The Oval, July 31, August 1. Surrey won by an innings and 203 runs. Surrey 24 pts, Warwickshire 3 pts. Toss won by Surrey. The winning of the toss was of crucial importance as Surrey chose to have first use of a pitch which disintegrated alarmingly. Having amassed a formidable score on the first day, they then bowled out Warwickshire twice on the second. Needham and Lynch collected career-best hundreds, and a brisk 33 from Doughty set up the declaration which left Surrey time to take two wickets before the close. Lynch's bristling innings included two 6s into the pavilion while Needham's effort came as emergency opening batsman after a net injury had ruled out Clinton. The wet weather had interfered with the preparation of the pitch, as Warwickshire discovered to their cost on the second day. Surrey's spearhead of Gray and Monkhouse forced the follow-on soon after lunch, and then it was Doughty's turn to provide the penetration with six wickets, his best return for his new county, and hurry along the two-day victory.

### Surrey

| | |
|---|---|
| A. R. Butcher c Humpage b Ferreira | 27 |
| A. Needham c Kallicharran b Gifford | 138 |
| A. J. Stewart lbw b Monkhouse | 1 |
| *T. E. Jesty c and b Smith | 26 |
| M. A. Lynch c and b Ferreira | 145 |
| D. B. Pauline b Hoffman | 10 |
| †C. J. Richards c Amiss b Hoffman | 7 |
| R. J. Doughty not out | 33 |
| K. T. Medlycott lbw b Ferreira | 5 |
| A. H. Gray c Humpage b Ferreira | 5 |
| L-b 2, w 1, n-b 13 | 16 |
| 1/73 2/75 3/118 4/282 5/312 6/340 7/392 8/402 9/413 | (9 wkts dec.) 413 |

G. Monkhouse did not bat.

Bonus points – Surrey 4, Warwickshire 3 (Score at 100 overs: 408-8).

Bowling: Hoffman 19–1–77–2; Smith 13–1–69–1; Monkhouse 17–2–61–1; Ferreira 18–1–85–4; Gifford 25–6–74–1; Pierson 9–0–45–0.

### Warwickshire

| | | | |
|---|---|---|---|
| R. I. H. B. Dyer lbw b Monkhouse | 2 | – c Stewart b Doughty | 2 |
| G. J. Lord lbw b Gray | 2 | – c Richards b Doughty | 7 |
| A. R. K. Pierson c Richards b Monkhouse | 3 | – (8) not out | 9 |
| A. I. Kallicharran b Monkhouse | 23 | – (3) c Richards b Gray | 7 |
| D. L. Amiss c Pauline b Gray | 4 | – (4) c Jesty b Doughty | 3 |
| †G. W. Humpage lbw b Monkhouse | 27 | – (5) b Gray | 7 |
| P. A. Smith c Richards b Doughty | 50 | – (6) c Jesty b Doughty | 4 |
| A. M. Ferreira b Doughty | 0 | – (7) c Richards b Gray | 0 |
| *N. Gifford b Gray | 26 | – run out | 4 |
| S. Monkhouse not out | 2 | – b Doughty | 5 |
| D. S. Hoffman c Richards b Jesty | 0 | – b Doughty | 12 |
| L-b 5, n-b 3 | 8 | W 3 | 3 |
| 1/5 2/6 3/25 4/37 5/39 6/73 7/82 8/145 9/145 | 147 | 1/9 2/11 3/19 4/23 5/28 6/28 7/32 8/39 9/51 | 63 |

Bonus points – Surrey 4.

Bowling: *First Innings*—Gray 14–4–43–3; Monkhouse 16–3–46–4; Doughty 7–1–32–2; Pauline 2–0–21–0; Jesty 0.3–0–0–1. *Second Innings*—Gray 8–1–24–3; Doughty 9.4–4–33–6; Monkhouse 2–1–6–0.

Umpires: C. Cook and B. Dudleston.

At Derby, August 3, 5, 6. SURREY beat DERBYSHIRE by an innings and 80 runs.

At Southampton, August 10, 12, 13. SURREY drew with HAMPSHIRE.

## SURREY v YORKSHIRE

At The Oval, August 14, 15, 16. Drawn. Surrey 4 pts, Yorkshire 7 pts. Toss won by Yorkshire. Surrey's wicket-keeper, Richards, broke his nose in the pre-match practice, their captain, Jesty, was asked to bat first, and a general malaise set in as Yorkshire's quick bowlers, Shaw and Peter Hartley, wrecked the first innings on a blameless pitch. Surrey, still mathematically capable of winning the Championship, were bustled out in 53 overs, but hundreds from Lynch and Jesty, plus rain either side of lunch and at tea, on the final day precluded Yorkshire's hopes of victory. Yorkshire, sustained by 81 from the eighteen-year-old opener, Blakey, and 69 by Love, who was dropped when 35, consolidated on the second day, establishing a useful lead of 157. Lynch and Jesty, however, gave Yorkshire little scope to capitalise, and although the weather was to be the decisive influence, they must doubtless have reflected on a simple chance missed when Jesty was 98.

### Surrey

| | | | |
|---|---|---|---|
| A. R. Butcher c Sharp b Shaw | 12 | – lbw b P. J. Hartley | 0 |
| A. Needham c Blakey b Shaw | 15 | – b P. J. Hartley | 16 |
| †A. J. Stewart lbw b Oldham | 7 | – (4) lbw b Oldham | 20 |
| *T. E. Jesty c Carrick b P. J. Hartley | 3 | – (6) not out | 141 |
| M. A. Lynch b P. J. Hartley | 4 | – b S. N. Hartley | 121 |
| D. M Ward b Oldham | 7 | – (7) b S. N. Hartley | 5 |
| D. B. Pauline c Carrick b Shaw | 15 | – (3) b Oldham | 17 |
| R. J. Doughty c Blakey b Shaw | 2 | – b S. N. Hartley | 0 |
| P. I. Pocock c Oldham b P. J. Hartley | 13 | – (10) not out | 0 |
| A. H. Gray b P. J. Hartley | 20 | | |
| G. Monkhouse not out | 15 | – (9) b S. N. Hartley | 7 |
| B 5, l-b 1, n-b 1 | 7 | B 5, l-b 6, n-b 3 | 14 |
| 1/23 2/28 3/31 4/41 5/41 6/60 7/65 8/81 9/85 | 120 | 1/0 2/33 3/37 4/76 5/267 6/289 7/308 8/334 | (8 wkts dec.) 341 |

Bonus points – Yorkshire 4.

Bowling: *First Innings*—P. J. Hartley 16.5–4–43–4; Shaw 19–6–53–4; Oldham 12–4–13–2; S. N. Hartley 5–2–5–0. *Second Innings*—P. J. Hartley 21–4–85–2; Shaw 7–0–38–0; Oldham 19–5–56–2; Carrick 15–3–76–0; S. N. Hartley 12–0–51–4; Sharp 1–0–4–0; Moxon 4–0–20–0.

### Yorkshire

| | | | |
|---|---|---|---|
| M. D. Moxon lbw b Doughty | 10 | – not out | 10 |
| R. J. Blakey st Stewart b Pauline | 81 | – not out | 0 |
| S. N. Hartley c Stewart b Monkhouse | 22 | | |
| J. D. Love c Stewart b Monkhouse | 69 | | |
| P. E. Robinson c Lynch b Monkhouse | 18 | | |
| K. Sharp b Monkhouse | 1 | | |
| *†D. L. Bairstow lbw b Gray | 13 | | |
| P. Carrick c Monkhouse b Gray | 36 | | |
| P. J. Hartley c Stewart b Gray | 8 | | |
| C. Shaw c Ward b Pocock | 1 | | |
| S. Oldham not out | 2 | | |
| B 5, l-b 9, n-b 2 | 16 | L-b 1 | 1 |
| 1/17 2/88 3/173 4/207 5/211 6/212 7/233 8/253 9/262 | 277 | | (no wkt) 11 |

Bonus points – Yorkshire 3, Surrey 4 (Score at 100 overs: 273-9).

Bowling: *First Innings*—Gray 23.3–5–68–3; Doughty 16–2–58–1; Monkhouse 24–8–46–4; Pocock 23–8–45–1; Needham 7–1–22–0; Pauline 8–2–24–1. *Second Innings*—Monkhouse 3–1–2–0; Doughty 2–0–8–0.

Umpires: J. H. Harris and R. Julian.

At Lord's, August 17, 19, 20. SURREY drew with MIDDLESEX.

At Chelmsford, August 24, 26, 27. SURREY drew with ESSEX.

## SURREY v SUSSEX

At The Oval, September 4, 5, 6. Sussex won by three wickets. Sussex 22 pts, Surrey 5 pts. Toss won by Sussex. Surrey's minimal but lingering interest in the Championship title was swept away by a successful Sussex run-chase which reached its climax in a spurt of 41 from 31 deliveries by Gould and Greig in the gathering autumnal gloom. Rain on the first evening had obliged Jesty to prolong Surrey's first innings for nearly two hours on the second day. Clinton, who passed 50 for the tenth time in the season, progressed to his third hundred, featuring in century stands with Lynch and Jesty. Surrey's declaration was answered by a vigorous Sussex reply, runs coming at the rate of 4 an over on a pitch containing less pace than some prepared at The Oval during the summer. Green, enjoying an outstanding season, struck a career-best 133 from just 135 balls to push his aggregate past 1,600 runs, while brisk contributions from Mendis and Imran enabled Barclay to declare only 49 behind. Stewart's return to form set up a target of 248 in 48 overs. Imran and le Roux thrashed 72 in eleven overs and the victory, Sussex's third in five matches, was boldly achieved by Gould and Greig.

## Surrey

| Batsman | First innings | Runs | Second innings | Runs |
|---|---|---|---|---|
| A. R. Butcher | c Mendis b C. M. Wells | 28 | b Jones | 5 |
| G. S. Clinton | c Greig b Imran | 123 | c Greig b Jones | 11 |
| M. A. Lynch | b Jones | 59 | lbw b le Roux | 1 |
| A. J. Stewart | b Jones | 0 | not out | 81 |
| *T. E. Jesty | c Gould b Imran | 82 | lbw b Jones | 5 |
| A. Needham | not out | 25 | lbw b Jones | 1 |
| †C. J. Richards | not out | 12 | c A. P. Wells b Jones | 42 |
| D. J. Thomas | (did not bat) | | b le Roux | 5 |
| G. Monkhouse | (did not bat) | | not out | 35 |
| | B 1, l-b 10, w 2, n-b 7 | 20 | B 3, l-b 4, w 1, n-b 4 | 12 |
| | 1/66 2/169 3/169 4/305 5/322 (5 wkts dec.) | 349 | 1/17 2/19 3/23 4/34 5/37 6/108 7/127 (7 wkts dec.) | 198 |

A. H. Gray and P. I. Pocock did not bat.

Bonus points – Surrey 4, Sussex 2.

Bowling: *First Innings*—Imran 28–5–98–2; le Roux 13–2–34–0; C. M. Wells 14–5–33–1; Jones 15–0–60–2; Greig 23–1–99–0; Barclay 5–2–14–0. *Second Innings*—le Roux 17–3–41–2; Jones 16–4–39–5; Imran 12–1–34–0; C. M. Wells 7–2–32–0; Greig 3–1–19–0; Barclay 4–0–17–0; Green 4–0–9–0.

## Sussex

| Batsman | First innings | Runs | Second innings | Runs |
|---|---|---|---|---|
| G. D. Mendis | c Jesty b Monkhouse | 50 | c Clinton b Pocock | 46 |
| A. M. Green | st Richards b Needham | 133 | c Lynch b Gray | 16 |
| N. J. Lenham | c Lynch b Thomas | 5 | c Richards b Thomas | 2 |
| Imran Khan | not out | 84 | st Richards b Monkhouse | 59 |
| C. M. Wells | c Richards b Monkhouse | 6 | c Stewart b Pocock | 0 |
| A. P. Wells | not out | 9 | (8) c Monkhouse b Pocock | 14 |
| G. S. le Roux | (did not bat) | | (6) c Jesty b Monkhouse | 40 |
| †I. J. Gould | (did not bat) | | (7) not out | 30 |
| I. A. Greig | (did not bat) | | not out | 28 |
| | B 4, l-b 6, w 1, n-b 2 | 13 | B 1, l-b 12, n-b 1 | 14 |
| | 1/95 2/108 3/236 4/255 (4 wkts dec.) | 300 | 1/33 2/40 3/92 4/94 5/166 6/185 7/208 (7 wkts) | 249 |

*J. R. T. Barclay and A. N. Jones did not bat.

Bonus points – Sussex 4, Surrey 1.

Bowling: *First Innings*—Gray 13–0–74–0; Thomas 12–1–47–1; Monkhouse 19–5–51–2; Butcher 5–1–11–0; Pocock 6.4–0–34–0; Needham 12–3–44–1; Jesty 8–0–29–0. *Second Innings*—Gray 11.4–0–76–1; Thomas 8–0–38–1; Monkhouse 12–2–47–2; Pocock 15–1–75–3.

Umpires: J. A. Jameson and R. Palmer.

## SURREY v GLOUCESTERSHIRE

At The Oval, September 14, 16, 17. Drawn. Surrey 6 pts, Gloucestershire 7 pts. Toss won by Gloucestershire. Gloucestershire entered their last match with a slight chance of overhauling Middlesex and Hampshire to win the Championship for the first time since 1877, while Surrey had prizemoney to play for. Ultimately, both sides failed to achieve their objectives, with

Gloucestershire finishing third and Surrey sixth after spending much of the summer in the top four. The weather was again a decisive factor, bad light and rain ending the first day's play as Surrey were struggling against the visitors' pace attack at 41 for four. On Monday, their innings was shored up by Richards and the tailenders. Gloucestershire began badly, but from 8 for three the dependable Bainbridge led the recovery with his fourth Championship century and a useful lead of 72 was achieved. Surrey's Lynch set about the bowling with gusto, at one stage taking 20 off an over from Lloyds, to rush to his seventh hundred of a summer splendid with runs and close catches. His stand with Needham produced 147 and Gloucestershire were set 187 at 7 an over. They knew by then that Middlesex were racing towards the title at Edgbaston, but victory could still have earned them second place and an extra £5,000 in prizemoney. However, after a fine start by Romaines and Ellis – 48 in seven overs – the effort began to tail away. Bainbridge was carried off on a stretcher with suspected concussion after being hit on the forehead by Monkhouse.

## Surrey

| | | | |
|---|---|---|---|
| A. R. Butcher c Russell b Walsh | 46 | – c Russell b Lawrence | 7 |
| A. Needham c Ellis b Lawrence | 0 | – c Graveney b Athey | 63 |
| M. A. Lynch c Romaines b Walsh | 4 | – c Lawrence b Ellis | 110 |
| A. J. Stewart c Athey b Walsh | 1 | – b Romaines | 6 |
| *T. E. Jesty c Curran b Walsh | 7 | – b Athey | 12 |
| C. K. Bullen lbw b Curran | 19 | – c Lawrence b Romaines | 6 |
| †C. J. Richards b Lloyds | 56 | – not out | 39 |
| R. J. Doughty lbw b Curran | 4 | – c Athey b Romaines | 4 |
| G. Monkhouse c Russell b Curran | 30 | – not out | 3 |
| P. I. Pocock c Ellis b Curran | 27 | | |
| P. A. Waterman not out | 1 | | |
| L-b 1, w 1, n-b 8 | 10 | L-b 4, w 2, n-b 2 | 8 |
| 1/5 2/12 3/14 4/32 5/68 6/96 7/101 8/164 9/204 | 205 | 1/19 2/166 3/182 4/199 5/207 6/217 7/228 (7 wkts dec.) | 258 |

Bonus points – Surrey 2, Gloucestershire 4.

Bowling: *First Innings*—Lawrence 14–3–29–1; Walsh 23–3–79–4; Curran 17–3–51–4; Graveney 9–3–28–0; Lloyds 8–1–17–1. *Second Innings*—Lawrence 7–1–37–1; Walsh 7–1–31–0; Graveney 5–1–28–0; Curran 1–0–8–0; Lloyds 3–1–24–0; Athey 14–2–77–2; Romaines 10–0–42–3; Ellis 3–1–7–1.

## Gloucestershire

| | | | |
|---|---|---|---|
| P. W. Romaines c Lynch b Doughty | 0 | – st Richards b Monkhouse | 35 |
| R. G. P. Ellis b Waterman | 3 | – c Lynch b Doughty | 20 |
| C. W. J. Athey run out | 4 | – lbw b Monkhouse | 16 |
| P. Bainbridge c Butcher b Pocock | 102 | – (7) retired hurt | 4 |
| B. F. Davison c Butcher b Waterman | 59 | – b Pocock | 1 |
| K. M. Curran c Stewart b Pocock | 26 | – (4) c Jesty b Monkhouse | 9 |
| J. W. Lloyds c Butcher b Pocock | 21 | (6) lbw b Pocock | 3 |
| *D. A. Graveney c Lynch b Needham | 19 | – not out | 3 |
| †R. C. Russell not out | 17 | – not out | 0 |
| D. V. Lawrence b Needham | 0 | | |
| C. A. Walsh c Jesty b Pocock | 12 | | |
| B 2, l-b 2, w 2, n-b 8 | 14 | B 1, l-b 5, w 1, n-b 3 | 10 |
| 1/4 2/4 3/8 4/156 5/195 6/228 7/231 8/261 9/264 | 277 | 1/48 2/65 3/83 4/89 5/89 6/101 (6 wkts) | 101 |

Bonus points – Gloucestershire 3, Surrey 4.

Bowling: *First Innings*—Doughty 14–3–52–1; Waterman 13–2–47–2; Jesty 2–1–1–0; Monkhouse 12–1–61–0; Pocock 23–5–57–4; Needham 15–2–55–2. *Second Innings*—Doughty 5–0–26–1; Waterman 2–0–17–0; Monkhouse 8–1–43–3; Pocock 7.4–3–9–2; Butcher 1–1–0–0; Needham 2–2–0–0.

Umpires: B. Leadbeater and D. O. Oslear.

# SUSSEX

*President:* A. M. Caffyn
*Chairman:* Dr D. Rice
*Chairman, Cricket & Ground Sub-Committee:* D. J. Church
*Secretary:* R. H. Renold
County Ground, Eaton Road,
Hove BN3 3AN
(Telephone: 0273-732161)
*Captain:* J. R. T. Barclay
*Coach:* S. J. Storey

This was a disappointing season for Sussex, following high hopes of winning at least one competition and making a really determined bid to become county champions for the first time. When battle was done, they had to settle for seventh place in the Britannic Assurance Championship, one lower than the previous season, and as runners-up in the John Player Sunday League.

Optimism had appeared fully justified with a side strong in batting and an attack spearheaded by Imran Khan and Garth le Roux; but there was a lack of consistency right from the start. Sussex were in Jekyll and Hyde form in their first weekend of one-day matches against Essex and Surrey, losing one day and winning the next; and in Championship fixtures a sound start from the opening pair of Gehan Mendis and Allan Green would frequently be wasted.

Green, opening the season in fine form, was awarded his county cap, batting stylishly and scoring briskly. His maiden century was quickly followed by another, while Mendis, later in the summer, came very close to joining the small band of batsmen who have scored five first-class centuries in six successive innings, being foiled, when only 4 runs short, by a declaration. Mendis had hit a century in both innings against Lancashire at Hastings, a third in the second innings against Warwickshire and a fourth in the first innings against Hampshire at Portsmouth. He was 96 not out in the second innings against Hampshire when John Barclay declared. The Sussex captain explained that he was scheming to beat Hampshire and that a declaration was due, but Mendis was upset at missing such a rare opportunity.

Another upset in the camp came when Ian Greig, a popular member of the staff, was told he would not be retained on grounds of economy. By then Sussex were out of the Benson and Hedges Cup and the NatWest Bank Trophy and occupying a lowly Championship position. The season of rich promise was becoming a little sour. But at least a string of Sunday victories raised spirits. Sussex were, in fact, foiled only by Essex in the John Player League.

It was a season of good individual performances, notably by Imran, who had agreed to play in a selected number of Championship matches and all the one-day games. He headed both batting and bowling averages, scoring nearly 1,000 runs in only fourteen matches and saying that it was his most enjoyable season in England. Sussex's other overseas player, the giant le Roux, also had a successful season, being second in the bowling averages and fifth in the batting. Dermot Reeve was a valuable and hard-working member of the fast attack, and, following another injury to Tony Pigott, Adrian Jones came in and bowled some hostile deliveries down the Hove slope. Jones was also a tailender of belligerent intent who had some rousing knocks with the bat.

Paul Parker's season was not a particularly happy one. He scored 680 Championship runs, less than half his tally in 1984, and injury caused him to play a dozen fewer matches. Having come back late in the season, he broke down and was forced to bat with a runner. The wicket-keeper, Ian Gould, could not complain of an uneventful season. He hit a fighting century, his first for the club, to set up a fine victory over Leicestershire at Hove, and residents of the quiet borough of Hove always knew when Sussex were fielding, Gould's appeals echoing round the neighbouring avenues.

The Wells brothers, who had both hit over 1,000 runs in the previous season, were less successful, although Colin, the elder, was only 40 runs short. However, he sent down more overs than any other Sussex bowler. Alan, who still has to win his county cap, had a few vigorous knocks. He also fielded well in the deep, where he held a number of exciting high hits.

Barclay led the side confidently and with his usual zest, striving always to keep a game moving in the hope of getting a result. As he batted well down the order, his contribution in this aspect was disappointing, but he bowled his off-spinners thoughtfully and set a keen lead in the field with his obvious enthusiasm. Like all connected with the club, he was delighted to see Neil Lenham, only nineteen, bat with commendable coolness and skill, indicating that his rich promise would be fulfilled. Watching the widely experienced Imran displaying his rich talents, and the up-and-coming Lenham blossoming into a player of county class, proved one of the interesting features of the season.

Cricket on the rural Horsham ground was again watched by good crowds; the Central Ground at Hastings staged two victories for Sussex over Lancashire, in the Championship and the John Player League; but the Eastbourne Week was unusually wet and dismal, attendances and receipts being well down on 1984. Sussex are trying to urge local councils, away from their Hove headquarters, to provide greater financial support towards the staging of first-class cricket. "Showing the flag" round the county has proved popular but expensive.

During the season three old Sussex stalwarts died: George Cox, Jim Hammond and Jim Cornford. Watching the match at Hove against the Australians was Hugh Bartlett who, in 1938, hammered them for a century in only 57 minutes. – J.A.

SUSSEX 1985

[Bill Smith

*Back row:* D. K. Standing, N. J. Lenham, A. M. Bredin, D. A. Reeve, M. S. Scott, A. M. Green. *Middle row:* C. P. Cale (*assistant coach*), A. C. S. Pigott, C. P. Phillipson, C. M. Wells, I. C. Waring, G. S. le Roux, A. N. Jones, A. P. Wells, S. J. Storey (*coach*). *Front row:* I. J. Gould, I. A. Greig, J. R. T. Barclay (*captain*), C. E. Waller, G. D. Mendis, P. W. G. Parker. *Inset:* Imran Khan.

## SUSSEX RESULTS

*All first-class matches – Played 25: Won 7, Lost 1, Drawn 17. Abandoned 1.*

*County Championship matches – Played 23: Won 6, Lost 1, Drawn 16. Abandoned 1.*

*Bonus points – Batting 52, Bowling 57.*

*Competition placings – Britannic Assurance County Championship, 7th; NatWest Bank Trophy, 2nd round; Benson and Hedges Cup, 4th in Group C; John Player League, 2nd.*

## BRITANNIC ASSURANCE CHAMPIONSHIP AVERAGES

### BATTING

| | *Birthplace* | *M* | *I* | *NO* | *R* | *HI* | *Avge* |
|---|---|---|---|---|---|---|---|
| ‡Imran Khan | *Lahore, Pakistan* | 13 | 19 | 7 | 846 | 117* | 70.50 |
| ‡G. D. Mendis | *Colombo, Ceylon* | 23 | 39 | 5 | 1,604 | 143* | 47.17 |
| ‡A. M. Green | *Pulborough* | 23 | 39 | 4 | 1,547 | 133 | 44.20 |
| ‡I. J. Gould | *Slough* | 22 | 23 | 8 | 614 | 101 | 40.93 |
| ‡G. S. le Roux | *Cape Town, SA* | 17 | 14 | 3 | 401 | 61 | 36.45 |
| ‡P. W. G. Parker | *Bulawayo, S. Rhodesia* | 14 | 24 | 4 | 680 | 105 | 34.00 |
| N. J. Lenham | *Worthing* | 11 | 16 | 2 | 473 | 89 | 33.78 |
| ‡C. M. Wells | *Newhaven* | 23 | 33 | 5 | 840 | 100* | 30.00 |
| ‡I. A. Greig | *Queenstown, SA* | 13 | 14 | 4 | 241 | 43 | 24.10 |
| A. P. Wells | *Newhaven* | 21 | 29 | 6 | 532 | 102 | 23.13 |
| A. N. Jones | *Woking* | 11 | 9 | 5 | 83 | 26 | 20.75 |
| ‡J. R. T. Barclay | *Bonn, WG* | 20 | 14 | 4 | 192 | 37* | 19.20 |
| D. A. Reeve | *Hong Kong* | 16 | 15 | 5 | 170 | 56 | 17.00 |
| ‡C. E. Waller | *Guildford* | 15 | 7 | 2 | 27 | 8 | 5.40 |

Also batted: ‡A. C. S. Pigott (*London*) (8 matches) 10*, 0*, 0; D. K. Standing (*Brighton*) (1 match) 7, 3. P. Moores (*Macclesfield*) and I. C. Waring (*Chesterfield*) each played in one match but did not bat.

* *Signifies not out.* ‡ *Denotes county cap.*

The following played a total of fourteen three-figure innings for Sussex in County Championship matches – G. D. Mendis 6, A. M. Green 3, I. J. Gould 1, Imran Khan 1, P. W. G. Parker 1, A. P. Wells 1, C. M. Wells 1.

### BOWLING

| | *O* | *M* | *R* | *W* | *BB* | *Avge* |
|---|---|---|---|---|---|---|
| Imran Khan | 388.5 | 99 | 952 | 48 | 5-49 | 19.83 |
| G. S. le Roux | 392.2 | 70 | 1,113 | 39 | 6-46 | 28.53 |
| D. A. Reeve | 451.1 | 101 | 1,377 | 45 | 5-24 | 30.60 |
| J. R. T. Barclay | 252.4 | 39 | 804 | 24 | 6-78 | 33.50 |
| A. C. S. Pigott | 166.4 | 31 | 612 | 17 | 3-22 | 36.00 |
| C. M. Wells | 470.4 | 126 | 1,275 | 34 | 4-76 | 37.50 |
| I. A. Greig | 233 | 44 | 794 | 20 | 5-80 | 39.70 |
| A. N. Jones | 231 | 33 | 814 | 20 | 5-39 | 40.70 |
| C. E. Waller | 318.5 | 99 | 755 | 17 | 7-61 | 44.41 |

Also bowled: I. J. Gould 4–0–75–0; A. M. Green 32–6–77–2; G. D. Mendis 4–0–65–1.

At Old Trafford, April 27, 28, 29. SUSSEX drew with LANCASHIRE.

At Fenner's, May 8, 9, 10. SUSSEX beat CAMBRIDGE UNIVERSITY by 83 runs.

At Hove, May 18, 19, 20, 21. SUSSEX drew with AUSTRALIANS (See Australian tour section).

## SUSSEX v GLOUCESTERSHIRE

At Hove, May 22, 23, 24. Drawn. Sussex 1 pt, Gloucestershire 7 pts. Toss won by Gloucestershire. There were ten stoppages during a match ruined by rain, bad light and sea fret drifting across the ground. Sussex were sent in on a lively pitch which Lawrence exploited with enthusiasm, returning a career-best seven for 48 from hostile bowling down the slope. Bainbridge chipped in as Sussex lost their last five wickets for 9 runs in seven overs. Gloucestershire took a first-innings lead of 53 by the close of the second day, with a sound 104 from Stovold, and would have been more strongly placed except for Reeve's three wickets towards the close. After a day of stops and starts on the Friday, the game was called off at a quarter to five.

### Sussex

| | | | |
|---|---|---|---|
| G. D. Mendis c Russell b Lawrence | 45 | – (3) c Wright b Curran | 16 |
| A. M. Green run out | 1 | – (1) c Davison b Curran | 17 |
| P. W. G. Parker b Lawrence | 6 | – (2) not out | 36 |
| A. P. Wells lbw b Lawrence | 0 | – not out | 7 |
| C. M. Wells lbw b Lawrence | 7 | | |
| *J. R. T. Barclay c Bainbridge b Lawrence | 27 | | |
| I. A. Greig c Stovold b Lawrence | 8 | | |
| †I. J. Gould c Bainbridge b Lawrence | 0 | | |
| D. A. Reeve b Bainbridge | 1 | | |
| C. E. Waller not out | 1 | | |
| A. N. Jones b Bainbridge | 5 | | |
| B 9, l-b 9, w 1, n-b 21 | 40 | B 7, l-b 1, n-b 5 | 13 |
| 1/5 2/36 3/36 4/47 5/117 6/132 7/132 8/133 9/134 | 141 | 1/37 2/81 (2 wkts) | 89 |

Bonus points – Gloucestershire 4.

Bowling: *First Innings*—Lawrence 17–2–48–7; Walsh 5.1–0–22–0; Shepherd 12–3–31–0; Curran 6.5–2–13–0; Bainbridge 9–4–9–2. *Second Innings*—Lawrence 6.4–0–19–0; Walsh 10–4–26–0; Bainbridge 4–2–7–0; Shepherd 2–0–10–0; Curran 9–3–19–2.

### Gloucestershire

| | |
|---|---|
| A. W. Stovold lbw b Reeve | 104 |
| P. W. Romaines c Gould b Reeve | 64 |
| A. J. Wright lbw b Reeve | 3 |
| P. Bainbridge c Gould b Reeve | 27 |
| B. F. Davison not out | 29 |
| K. M. Curran not out | 11 |
| L-b 7, n-b 6 | 13 |
| 1/165 2/169 3/193 4/235 (4 wkts dec.) | 251 |

*D. A. Graveney, J. N. Shepherd, †R. C. Russell, D. V. Lawrence and C. A. Walsh did not bat.

Bonus points – Gloucestershire 3, Sussex 1.

Bowling: Jones 20–2–75–0; Reeve 29.2–6–86–4; C. M. Wells 18–6–27–0; Greig 12–2–44–0; Waller 5–2–12–0.

Umpires: J. H. Harris and D. G. L. Evans.

At Lord's, May 25, 27, 28. SUSSEX lost to MIDDLESEX by an innings and 27 runs.

## SUSSEX v GLAMORGAN

At Hove, May 29, 30, 31. Sussex won by nine wickets. Sussex 24 pts, Glamorgan 2 pts. Toss won by Sussex. Although Glamorgan rallied from a first-innings dismissal of only 58, 245 runs in arrears, to score 447 in some eight and a half hours when they followed on, Sussex raced to their victory target of 203 with eleven balls remaining for the loss of only Mendis. Green hit his maiden century off just 106 deliveries with one 6 and twelve 4s. For Glamorgan, Ontong's 122 (eighteen 4s, 185 balls) and 111 by Henderson (seventeen 4s, 184 balls) looked to be changing the course of the game, and Steele was obdurate to the last. Sussex had begun the game in handsome fashion through Green and Parker, and Alan Wells hit two 6s and thirteen 4s in his 102 off 200 balls. By the close of the first day Imran and Reeve had reduced Glamorgan to 29 for five, Reeve claiming three wickets in four balls and going on to achieve his best return in the Championship.

### Sussex

| First innings | | Second innings | |
|---|---|---|---|
| G. D. Mendis b Malone | 17 | b Ontong | 70 |
| A. M. Green c Davies b Barwick | 45 | not out | 100 |
| P. W. G. Parker lbw b Holmes | 60 | not out | 30 |
| A. P. Wells c Hopkins b Ontong | 102 | | |
| C. M. Wells c Hopkins b Ontong | 11 | | |
| Imran Khan not out | 44 | | |
| I. A. Greig not out | 17 | | |
| B 1, l-b 1, w 1, n-b 4 | 7 | B 1, l-b 4, w 1 | 6 |
| 1/55 2/66 3/184 4/214 5/259 (5 wkts dec.) | 303 | 1/136 (1 wkt) | 206 |

*†I. J. Gould, D. A. Reeve, A. C. S. Pigott and C. E. Waller did not bat.

Bonus points – Sussex 4, Glamorgan 2.

Bowling: *First Innings*—Thomas 4–0–13–0; Barwick 19.4–5–61–1; Malone 18–1–68–1; Steele 24–8–48–0; Holmes 22–8–54–1; Ontong 12–1–57–2. *Second Innings*—Malone 6–0–39–0; Barwick 13–0–52–0; Ontong 10–1–52–1; Holmes 6.1–1–31–0; Steele 4–0–27–0.

### Glamorgan

| First innings | | Second innings | |
|---|---|---|---|
| J. A. Hopkins b Imran | 13 | b Reeve | 35 |
| G. C. Holmes c Gould b Imran | 1 | run out | 25 |
| Younis Ahmed c Gould b Reeve | 6 | c Parker b Imran | 35 |
| †T. Davies b Imran | 4 | (8) b Pigott | 4 |
| Javed Miandad c Gould b Reeve | 0 | (4) b Reeve | 9 |
| S. P. Henderson c Green b Reeve | 2 | (5) c Mendis b Reeve | 111 |
| *R. C. Ontong c Mendis b Reeve | 19 | (6) c A. P. Wells b Pigott | 122 |
| J. F. Steele not out | 7 | (7) b Imran | 42 |
| J. G. Thomas c Green b Imran | 0 | c Parker b Green | 29 |
| S. J. Malone b Reeve | 0 | (11) not out | 0 |
| S. R. Barwick b Pigott | 4 | (10) c Greig b Green | 6 |
| L-b 1, n-b 1 | 2 | B 3, l-b 19, w 4, n-b 3 | 29 |
| 1/1 2/20 3/20 4/20 5/22 6/31 7/51 8/52 9/53 | 58 | 1/56 2/93 3/112 4/117 5/338 6/367 7/377 8/424 9/440 | 447 |

Bonus points – Sussex 4.

Bowling: *First Innings*—Imran 12–5–16–4; Pigott 6–1–17–1; Reeve 9–4–24–5. *Second Innings*—Imran 31.5–10–75–2; Reeve 29–6–107–3; Pigott 26–6–65–2; Greig 26–7–65–0; C. M. Wells 14–4–50–0; Waller 18–3–43–0; Green 13–5–20–2.

Umpires: C. Cook and N. T. Plews.

## SUSSEX v SURREY

At Horsham, June 1, 3, 4. Drawn. Sussex 8 pts, Surrey 6 pts. Toss won by Surrey. There had seemed the prospect of an exciting finish until rain, which had been threatening all morning, put an end to Surrey's attempt to make 402 for victory off 85 overs. For Sussex, Green had batted in a most confident manner in two splendid innings of 90 and 106, hitting eleven 4s in his first fifty in the second innings and another six as he reached treble figures in 157 minutes. Parker's first-innings hundred contained two 6s and fourteen 4s. Jesty, however, kept Surrey in contention, hitting a 6 and seventeen 4s before Parker, at square leg, took a magnificent diving catch off a firmly hit pull, and Richards ensured that the follow-on was avoided.

### Sussex

| | | | |
|---|---|---|---|
| G. D. Mendis c Needham b Thomas | 0 | – c Clinton b Thomas | 46 |
| A. M. Green b Waterman | 90 | – c Richards b Thomas | 106 |
| P. W. G. Parker c Lynch b Taylor | 105 | – c Richards b Waterman | 14 |
| A. P. Wells c and b Needham | 11 | – b Thomas | 43 |
| C. M. Wells c and b Jesty | 56 | – c Lynch b Thomas | 4 |
| D. K. Standing b Pocock | 7 | – c Lynch b Pocock | 3 |
| I. A. Greig c Stewart b Waterman | 43 | – not out | 34 |
| *†I. J. Gould not out | 58 | – not out | 15 |
| D. A. Reeve not out | 11 | | |
| B 3, l-b 4, n-b 3 | 10 | B 4, l-b 7, w 1, n-b 4 | 16 |
| 1/0 2/187 3/212 4/218 5/252 6/293 7/351 (7 wkts dec.) | 391 | 1/84 2/124 3/202 4/220 5/225 6/249 (6 wkts dec.) | 281 |

A. C. S. Pigott and C. E. Waller did not bat.

Bonus points – Sussex 4, Surrey 3.

Bowling: *First Innings*—Thomas 19–5–53–1; Waterman 14–2–69–2; Jesty 17–6–60–1; Taylor 12–2–64–1; Butcher 4–0–18–0; Pocock 18–2–73–1; Needham 10–4–47–1. *Second Innings*—Thomas 19–2–88–4; Waterman 9–2–47–1; Taylor 6–0–34–0; Jesty 8–1–22–0; Pocock 19–2–74–1; Needham 3–1–5–0.

### Surrey

| | | | |
|---|---|---|---|
| A. R. Butcher lbw b Reeve | 8 | – c Green b Reeve | 28 |
| G. S. Clinton lbw b Reeve | 17 | – c Parker b Pigott | 0 |
| A. J. Stewart c Gould b Reeve | 39 | – c Greig b Pigott | 28 |
| P. I. Pocock run out | 0 | | |
| D. J. Thomas lbw b Pigott | 1 | | |
| *T. E. Jesty c Parker b C. M. Wells | 99 | – (4) not out | 28 |
| M. A. Lynch lbw b Greig | 27 | – (5) not out | 61 |
| A. Needham lbw b C. M. Wells | 35 | | |
| †C. J. Richards not out | 20 | | |
| N. S. Taylor b Pigott | 18 | | |
| P. A. Waterman b Pigott | 0 | | |
| L-b 6, n-b 1 | 7 | B 4, l-b 2, n-b 2 | 8 |
| 1/9 2/30 3/33 4/40 5/86 6/139 7/226 8/239 9/271 | 271 | 1/1 2/55 3/59 (3 wkts) | 153 |

Bonus points – Surrey 3, Sussex 4.

Bowling: *First Innings*—Pigott 17.5–3–94–3; Reeve 24–8–49–3; C. M. Wells 12–1–33–2; Greig 9–3–41–1; Waller 14–3–48–0. *Second Innings*—Pigott 9–0–43–2; Reeve 10–4–34–1; C. M. Wells 7–1–19–0; Greig 3–0–26–0; Waller 5–1–17–0; Green 2–0–8–0.

Umpires: K. J. Lyons and N. T. Plews.

At Northampton, June 8, 10, 11. SUSSEX drew with NORTHAMPTONSHIRE.

At Derby, June 12, 13, 14. SUSSEX drew with DERBYSHIRE.

## SUSSEX v HAMPSHIRE

At Hove, June 15, 17, 18. Drawn. Sussex 5 pts, Hampshire 6 pts. Toss won by Hampshire. They arrived as Championship leaders, with 50 more points than Sussex, but by the end were struggling to avoid their first defeat of the season in the competition. Nicholas had declared the visitors' first innings 36 runs behind the Sussex total, and following another stylish innings by Green, the only batsman to master a slow pitch of uneven bounce, in a first-wicket stand of 166 with Mendis, Sussex set a target of 275 in 58 overs. Imran sent back both openers with only 24 on the board, but the decisive bowling was Greig's four for 9 in a six-over spell which saw Hampshire 86 for six with twenty overs remaining. However, Hardy and Tremlett held out until the last 21 balls, whereupon Tremlett and Maru defied in deteriorating light the bombardment of Imran and le Roux, who posted ten fieldsmen around the batsmen but without success.

### Sussex

| | First Innings | | Second Innings | |
|---|---|---|---|---|
| G. D. Mendis | c Parks b Tremlett | 11 | c sub b Tremlett | 62 |
| A. M. Green | c Parks b Maru | 54 | c Marshall b Maru | 93 |
| P. W. G. Parker | c Parks b Connor | 80 | not out | 53 |
| A. P. Wells | lbw b Tremlett | 14 | c Hardy b Maru | 15 |
| C. M. Wells | c Parks b Andrew | 1 | not out | 1 |
| Imran Khan | c Maru b Andrew | 7 | | |
| *J. R. T. Barclay | b Connor | 14 | | |
| I. A. Greig | c Terry b Maru | 13 | | |
| †I. J. Gould | c Andrew b Maru | 10 | | |
| G. S. le Roux | not out | 32 | | |
| C. E. Waller | lbw b Connor | 8 | | |
| | B 5, l-b 4, n-b 4 | 13 | B 9, w 1, n-b 4 | 14 |
| 1/37 2/96 3/128 4/147 5/155 6/178 7/205 8/209 9/234 | | 257 | 1/166 2/169 3/226 (3 wkts dec.) | 238 |

Bonus points – Sussex 3, Hampshire 4 (Score at 100 overs: 252-9).

Bowling: *First Innings*—Marshall 15–7–28–0; Connor 24.1–4–79–3; Tremlett 25–5–70–2; Andrew 14–4–39–2; Maru 24–11–32–3. *Second Innings*—Marshall 10–0–22–0; Andrew 9–2–39–0; Connor 15–2–47–0; Tremlett 10–2–23–1; Maru 23–4–68–2; Greenidge 4–1–16–0; Nicholas 4–0–14–0.

### Hampshire

| | First Innings | | Second Innings | |
|---|---|---|---|---|
| C. G. Greenidge | c A. P. Wells b C. M. Wells | 56 | lbw b Imran | 9 |
| V. P. Terry | c Parker b Waller | 36 | lbw b Imran | 4 |
| *M. C. J. Nicholas | c Greig b Imran | 23 | c and b Greig | 29 |
| R. A. Smith | b Greig | 47 | c sub b Greig | 24 |
| J. J. E. Hardy | c Green b Greig | 27 | b Imran | 20 |
| M. D. Marshall | lbw b Imran | 13 | c and b Greig | 0 |
| †R. J. Parks | not out | 0 | b Greig | 5 |
| T. M. Tremlett | (did not bat) | | not out | 21 |
| R. J. Maru | (did not bat) | | not out | 1 |
| | B 4, l-b 7, w 2, n-b 6 | 19 | B 1, l-b 5, w 2, n-b 2 | 10 |
| 1/77 2/122 3/122 4/191 5/217 6/221 | (6 wkts dec.) | 221 | 1/13 2/24 3/71 4/74 5/74 6/86 7/119 (7 wkts) | 123 |

C. A. Connor and S. J. W. Andrew did not bat.

Bonus points – Hampshire 2, Sussex 2.

Bowling: *First Innings*—Imran 16–8–28–2; le Roux 16–1–64–0; C. M. Wells 16–4–46–1; Greig 14–3–46–2; Waller 22–10–26–1. *Second Innings*—Imran 16.4–7–25–3; le Roux 11–3–19–0; C. M. Wells 5–1–12–0; Waller 13–5–24–0; Greig 14–4–37–4.

Umpires: D. J. Constant and J. H. Harris.

At Bristol, June 22, 24, 25. GLOUCESTERSHIRE v SUSSEX. Abandoned.

## SUSSEX v LANCASHIRE

At Hastings, June 29, July 1, 2. Sussex won by 73 runs. Sussex 23 pts, Lancashire 3 pts. Toss won by Sussex. A career-first second hundred in the same match by Mendis, completed off the last ball of the second day, and Green's seventh fifty in his last ten Championship innings, opened the way for Barclay to set Lancashire a challenging target of 331 off 105 overs. Their slump to 60 for five presaged an early start for Liverpool, but then Simmons, batting for 168 minutes and hitting fourteen 4s, arrested the decline and rallied the innings. Barclay, having bowled only eleven overs in the Championship to date, bowled with skill and variation through a marathon spell for his five wickets and had the final say with a dazzling slip catch to dismiss Simmons. Lancashire's first innings had ended spectacularly with five wickets tumbling for 13, three of those clean-bowled in a fourteen-ball spell by Imran, who had earlier been warned by umpire Whitehead for persistent short-pitched bowling at Abrahams.

### Sussex

| | | | |
|---|---|---|---|
| G. D. Mendis run out | 103 | – not out | 100 |
| A. M. Green c Simmons b Makinson | 8 | – not out | 78 |
| P. W. G. Parker c Abrahams b Makinson | 1 | | |
| A. P. Wells c Abrahams b Makinson | 0 | | |
| Imran Khan c Fairbrother b Folley | 70 | | |
| C. M. Wells not out | 69 | | |
| I. A. Greig c Fowler b Watkinson | 40 | | |
| G. S. le Roux not out | 1 | | |
| L-b 6, w 3, n-b 9 | 18 | B 4, l-b 6, n-b 5 | 15 |
| 1/16 2/20 3/20 4/131 5/244 6/307 (6 wkts dec.) | 310 | (no wkt dec.) | 193 |

*J. R. T. Barclay, A. C. S. Pigott and †P. Moores did not bat.

Bonus points – Sussex 3, Lancashire 2 (Score at 100 overs: 250-5).

Bowling: *First Innings*—Patterson 10.3–0–51–0; Makinson 20–3–61–3; Watkinson 17–6–51–1; Simmons 34–9–91–0; Folley 29–9–50–1. *Second Innings*—Patterson 7–1–18–0; Makinson 12–3–24–0; Watkinson 7–0–34–0; Simmons 15–0–64–0; Folley 11–0–43–0.

### Lancashire

| | | | |
|---|---|---|---|
| G. Fowler lbw b C. M. Wells | 23 | – c Mendis b Pigott | 20 |
| D. W. Varey b Imran | 5 | – c Greig b Barclay | 10 |
| I. Folley c Moores b le Roux | 6 | – (9) b Imran | 0 |
| *J. Abrahams b le Roux | 29 | – (3) c A. P. Wells b Pigott | 0 |
| N. H. Fairbrother not out | 59 | – (4) b Barclay | 23 |
| D. P. Hughes c Parker b Barclay | 13 | – (5) c A. P. Wells b Barclay | 3 |
| M. Watkinson lbw b Barclay | 13 | – (6) c Greig b Barclay | 31 |
| †C. Maynard b Imran | 0 | – c Pigott b Barclay | 34 |
| J. Simmons b Imran | 0 | – (7) c Barclay b Pigott | 101 |
| D. J. Makinson run out | 0 | – c A. P. Wells b Imran | 11 |
| B. P. Patterson b Imran | 0 | – not out | 1 |
| B 5, l-b 10, w 3, n-b 7 | 25 | B 10, l-b 7, w 5, n-b 1 | 23 |
| 1/8 2/19 3/67 4/90 5/123 6/160 7/162 8/162 9/165 | 173 | 1/28 2/32 3/41 4/57 5/60 6/118 7/207 8/211 9/241 | 257 |

Bonus points – Lancashire 1, Sussex 4.

Bowling: *First Innings*—Imran 19.4–7–28–4; le Roux 17–3–42–2; C. M. Wells 7–2–19–1; Pigott 12–4–39–0; Barclay 12–4–30–2. *Second Innings*—le Roux 10–2–34–0; Imran 17–3–49–2; Barclay 30–3–99–5; Pigott 9.3–5–22–3; Greig 5–0–23–0; Green 3–0–13–0.

Umpires: A. A. Jones and A. G. T. Whitehead.

## SUSSEX v WARWICKSHIRE

At Hove, July 6, 8, 9. Drawn. Sussex 7 pts, Warwickshire 5 pts. Toss won by Warwickshire. The visiting bowlers toiled as the Sussex batsmen delighted a Saturday crowd basking in the hot sunshine. Imran and Colin Wells in particular savaged the weakened attack in a stand of 197, the last hundred coming off sixteen overs. Green, capped earlier in the week, continued his rich vein of form. Imran, bowling down the hill at a scorching pace, had Warwickshire on the run on the second morning before Humpage, assisted by Amiss, Smith and Asif Din, showed there were no hidden evils in the easy-paced pitch. Humpage's hundred came in just over three hours, with fifteen boundaries. Sussex put on 73 without loss in the last 65 minutes, and with Mendis completing his third century in four Championship innings on the last morning, Barclay was able to set a target of 291 in 70 overs. A cover of afternoon cloud encouraged the Sussex swing bowlers, but Smith and Lethbridge held out for the final fourteen overs after Imran's three for 4 in eighteen balls had threatened to brush Warwickshire aside.

### Sussex

| | | | |
|---|---|---|---|
| G. D. Mendis c Humpage b Smith | 21 | not out | 111 |
| A. M. Green b Smith | 96 | b Hoffman | 72 |
| P. W. G. Parker c Dyer b Lethbridge | 44 | c Dyer b Gifford | 33 |
| Imran Khan not out | 117 | | |
| C. M. Wells not out | 100 | | |
| B 1, l-b 9, w 2, n-b 15 | 27 | L-b 7, w 2, n-b 3 | 12 |
| 1/62 2/128 3/208 (3 wkts dec.) | 405 | 1/180 2/228 (2 wkts dec.) | 228 |

A. P. Wells, I. A. Greig, †I. J. Gould, *J. R. T. Barclay, G. S. le Roux and A. C. S. Pigott did not bat.

Bonus points – Sussex 4, Warwickshire 1 (Score at 100 overs: 400-3).

Bowling: *First Innings*—Small 16–3–68–0; Hoffman 17–5–74–0; Smith 17–2–68–2; Lethbridge 19–2–94–1; Gifford 30–9–90–0; Asif Din 2–1–1–0. *Second Innings*—Small 12–3–47–0; Hoffman 14–1–69–1; Lethbridge 11–0–47–0; Gifford 11–3–33–1; Smith 5–1–25–0.

### Warwickshire

| | | | |
|---|---|---|---|
| T. A. Lloyd c Pigott b Imran | 15 | c Green b C. M. Wells | 63 |
| R. I. H. B. Dyer c Gould b Imran | 8 | b C. M. Wells | 38 |
| A. I. Kallicharran c Pigott b Imran | 2 | c Gould b le Roux | 6 |
| D. L. Amiss c Mendis b Greig | 31 | c A. P. Wells b Imran | 22 |
| †G. W. Humpage b Imran | 159 | b Imran | 10 |
| P. A. Smith c Parker b Pigott | 61 | not out | 14 |
| Asif Din not out | 38 | b Imran | 0 |
| C. Lethbridge b Imran | 15 | not out | 22 |
| B 1, l-b 11, n-b 2 | 14 | B 4, l-b 6, w 1 | 11 |
| 1/14 2/18 3/36 4/90 5/216 6/326 7/343 (7 wkts dec.) | 343 | 1/99 2/108 3/116 4/134 5/149 6/159 (6 wkts) | 186 |

G. C. Small, D. S. Hoffman and *N. Gifford did not bat.

Bonus points – Warwickshire 4, Sussex 3.

Bowling: *First Innings*—le Roux 14–3–41–0; Pigott 15–1–60–1; Imran 19.1–2–49–5; C. M. Wells 19–5–68–0; Greig 16–4–49–1; Barclay 16–1–64–0. *Second Innings*—Imran 21–8–42–3; le Roux 14–4–23–1; Pigott 12–2–37–0; C. M. Wells 13–4–30–2; Barclay 5–0–33–0; Greig 2–0–11–0.

Umpires: H. D. Bird and K. J. Lyons.

At Portsmouth, July 10, 11, 12. SUSSEX drew with HAMPSHIRE.

At Hove, July 13. SUSSEX lost to ZIMBABWEANS by five wickets (See Zimbabwean tour section).

At Trent Bridge, July 24, 25, 26. SUSSEX drew with NOTTINGHAMSHIRE.

## SUSSEX v WORCESTERSHIRE

At Eastbourne, July 27, 29, 30. Drawn. Sussex 3 pts, Worcestershire 8 pts. Toss won by Sussex. Barclay's decision to insert Worcestershire on a slow pitch of low bounce was not backed up by his fielders, D'Oliveira being one of those to benefit from missed chances as he moved solidly and patiently to a career-best 139 in almost six hours. Sussex found batting a different proposition on Monday morning as Radford, keeping a full length and moving the ball, bowled the top four in his first six overs. Only Gould, with his highest score for Sussex, prevented the follow-on. Worcestershire finished a satisfactory day 93 without loss and added a further 102 in 70 minutes on the final morning before Neale gave his bowlers at least 80 overs to force a win. Radford found the edge of Mendis's bat with his first delivery but rain prevented a resumption of play after lunch.

### Worcestershire

| First innings | | Second innings | |
|---|---|---|---|
| T. S. Curtis lbw b le Roux | 4 | c Green b Waller | 54 |
| D. B. D'Oliveira c Pigott b Wells | 139 | lbw b Waller | 49 |
| D. M. Smith b le Roux | 62 | c Pigott b Barclay | 34 |
| G. A. Hick b Pigott | 22 | b Reeve | 35 |
| D. N. Patel c Green b Pigott | 29 | (6) not out | 0 |
| *P. A. Neale not out | 25 | (7) not out | 7 |
| †S. J. Rhodes c Gould b Pigott | 4 | | |
| P. J. Newport not out | 4 | | |
| J. D. Inchmore (did not bat) | | (5) st Gould b Barclay | 10 |
| B 4, l-b 6, n-b 7 | 17 | L-b 5, n-b 1 | 6 |
| 1/6 2/122 3/181 4/230 5/287 6/301 (6 wkts dec.) | 306 | 1/101 2/110 3/169 4/188 5/188 (5 wkts dec.) | 195 |

N. V. Radford and R. K. Illingworth did not bat.

Bonus points – Worcestershire 4, Sussex 2.

Bowling: *First Innings*—le Roux 17–3–53–2; Pigott 20.5–3–102–3; Wells 18–3–63–1; Reeve 22–8–66–0; Waller 18–9–12–0; Barclay 1–1–0–0. *Second Innings*—le Roux 8–2–21–0; Pigott 5–0–14–0; Wells 12–7–14–0; Reeve 23–2–83–1; Waller 14.3–2–56–2; Barclay 1–0–2–2.

### Sussex

| First innings | | Second innings | |
|---|---|---|---|
| G. D. Mendis b Radford | 13 | c Rhodes b Radford | 0 |
| A. M. Green b Radford | 1 | not out | 10 |
| N. J. Lenham b Radford | 6 | not out | 7 |
| C. M. Wells b Radford | 3 | | |
| *J. R. T. Barclay lbw b Radford | 14 | | |
| †I. J. Gould c Inchmore b Illingworth | 95 | | |
| G. S. le Roux b Newport | 20 | | |
| P. W. G. Parker b Illingworth | 7 | | |
| D. A. Reeve b Radford | 4 | | |
| A. C. S. Pigott not out | 0 | | |
| C. E. Waller b Illingworth | 0 | | |
| B 1, l-b 12, n-b 1 | 14 | B 2, l-b 3 | 5 |
| 1/3 2/24 3/27 4/28 5/91 6/145 7/164 8/174 9/176 | 177 | 1/0 (1 wkt) | 22 |

Bonus points – Sussex 1, Worcestershire 4.

Bowling: *First Innings*—Radford 21–4–76–6; Inchmore 14–4–23–0; Newport 14–2–46–1; Illingworth 8.3–3–19–3. *Second Innings*—Radford 5–2–10–1; Inchmore 4–1–7–0.

Umpires: R. Julian and J. H. Hampshire.

## SUSSEX v KENT

At Eastbourne, July 31, August 1, 2. Drawn. Sussex 3 pts, Kent 4 pts. Toss won by Sussex. Chasing a target of 271, Kent were in a strong position at 162 for one with 23 overs remaining when a gale-force wind finally gave way to persistent rain, leaving Hinks 1 run short of his second first-class hundred. The tall left-handed opening batsman had already played a major role in setting up an exciting finish by allowing Benson, with whom he shared a century opening stand, to declare Kent's first innings 27 in arrears and so challenge Barclay to make a match of it after the home team had moved aimlessly through a shortened first day at two and a half runs an over. The fact that Underwood took the new ball for Kent underlined the prospect of a slow pitch which encouraged neither batsman nor bowler, and only the brilliance of Imran's mid-afternoon strokeplay, which brought seventeen boundaries, raised the spirit and the innings.

### Sussex

| | | | |
|---|---|---|---|
| G. D. Mendis b Baptiste | 29 | – b Baptiste | 11 |
| A. M. Green b Jarvis | 24 | – b Penn | 78 |
| N. J. Lenham c Knott b Penn | 18 | – c Tavaré b Penn | 36 |
| Imran Khan c and b Underwood | 89 | – b Potter | 30 |
| C. M. Wells b Baptiste | 39 | – c Underwood b Taylor | 42 |
| A. P. Wells c and b Baptiste | 1 | – not out | 19 |
| †I. J. Gould not out | 10 | – not out | 19 |
| *J. R. T. Barclay not out | 8 | | |
| B 1, l-b 4, w 1, n-b 3 | 9 | B 1, l-b 3, n-b 4 | 8 |
| 1/51 2/66 3/98 4/173 5/199 6/209 | (6 wkts dec.) 227 | 1/13 2/81 3/153 4/183 5/221 | (5 wkts dec.) 243 |

G. S. le Roux, D. A. Reeve and C. E. Waller did not bat.

Bonus points – Sussex 2, Kent 2.

Bowling: *First Innings*—Dilley 8–1–31–0; Underwood 28–11–45–1; Baptiste 26–0–86–3; Jarvis 18–7–42–1; Penn 6–0–18–1. *Second Innings*—Jarvis 10–1–31–0; Baptiste 8–3–21–1; Underwood 22–7–43–0; Penn 12–1–41–2; Potter 18–2–70–1; Taylor 5–0–16–1; Benson 3–0–17–0.

### Kent

| | | | |
|---|---|---|---|
| *M. R. Benson c sub b Barclay | 80 | – b Waller | 22 |
| S. G. Hinks st Gould b Waller | 85 | – not out | 99 |
| C. J. Tavaré run out | 8 | – not out | 38 |
| N. R. Taylor not out | 17 | | |
| L. Potter not out | 3 | | |
| B 4, l-b 2, n-b 1 | 7 | L-b 2, n-b 1 | 3 |
| 1/132 2/161 3/185 | (3 wkts dec.) 200 | 1/47 | (1 wkt) 162 |

E. A. E. Baptiste, C. Penn, †A. P. E. Knott, G. R. Dilley, D. L. Underwood and K. B. S. Jarvis did not bat.

Bonus points – Kent 2, Sussex 1.

Bowling: *First Innings*—le Roux 8–1–32–0; Imran 7–3–8–0; C. M. Wells 6–1–22–0; Reeve 8–0–37–0; Waller 23–6–31–1; Barclay 21–5–57–1; Green 3–0–7–0. *Second Innings*—Imran 11–3–17–0; le Roux 4–0–16–0; Reeve 11–2–41–0; Waller 9–2–33–1; Barclay 7–0–40–0; C. M. Wells 3–2–13–0.

Umpires: J. H. Hampshire and R. Julian.

At Canterbury, August 10, 12, 13. SUSSEX beat KENT by 54 runs.

At Colchester, August 14, 15, 16. SUSSEX drew with ESSEX.

## SUSSEX v DERBYSHIRE

At Hove, August 17, 19, 20. Drawn. Sussex 5 pts, Derbyshire 8 pts. Toss won by Derbyshire. Cricket's ancient enemy won the day when Sussex, chasing a target of 388 in a minimum of 97 overs, were halted in mid-stride at 228 for three with 34 overs remaining. That a match dominated for the first two days by Derbyshire should have finished with Sussex challenging for victory owed everything to a neat innings from their young batsman, Lenham, some rumbustious batting by Imran in a partnership of 98 with Colin Wells, and nineteen no-balls in their first innings, without which Sussex might well have had to follow on. Holding (8) and Finney (6) were the chief culprits. On the other hand, it was due mostly to their bowlers, Newman and Holding, that Derbyshire's innings had recovered so well from the attentions of the Sussex seam attack on the opening day.

### Derbyshire

| | | | |
|---|---|---|---|
| I. S. Anderson lbw b Imran | 68 | – c Gould b Imran | 7 |
| B. Roberts lbw b Imran | 7 | – lbw b Imran | 14 |
| A. Hill c Gould b Imran | 2 | – lbw b Reeve | 23 |
| *K. J. Barnett b le Roux | 1 | – c Reeve b C. M. Wells | 80 |
| M. A. Fell lbw b Reeve | 21 | – c Reeve b C. M. Wells | 27 |
| G. Miller lbw b Reeve | 4 | – c and b Barclay | 18 |
| P. G. Newman lbw b le Roux | 98 | – c sub b C. M. Wells | 6 |
| A. E. Warner c Gould b le Roux | 5 | – b Reeve | 23 |
| M. A. Holding not out | 67 | – c Gould b Imran | 18 |
| R. J. Finney c Lenham b C. M. Wells | 13 | – not out | 9 |
| †C. Marples b Reeve | 1 | – c sub b Reeve | 4 |
| B 3, l-b 7, w 1, n-b 14 | 25 | B 5, l-b 4, n-b 6 | 15 |
| 1/7 2/9 3/14 4/40 5/50 6/188 7/194 8/273 9/305 | 312 | 1/10 2/21 3/69 4/156 5/165 6/178 7/209 8/225 9/231 | 244 |

Bonus points – Derbyshire 4, Sussex 4.

Bowling: *First Innings*—Imran 22–3–61–3; le Roux 15–2–50–3; Reeve 29–7–87–3; Jones 8–0–45–0; C. M. Wells 16–3–43–1; Barclay 3–0–16–0. *Second Innings*—Imran 14–6–38–3; Jones 10–1–32–0; Reeve 17.5–5–51–3; C. M. Wells 21–3–74–3; Barclay 15–2–40–1.

### Sussex

| | | | |
|---|---|---|---|
| G. D. Mendis lbw b Finney | 7 | – c Marples b Holding | 16 |
| A. M. Green b Finney | 4 | – c Anderson b Miller | 37 |
| N. J. Lenham c Anderson b Finney | 11 | – b Holding | 49 |
| C. M. Wells c Holding b Finney | 11 | – (5) not out | 33 |
| D. A. Reeve lbw b Holding | 13 | | |
| Imran Khan lbw b Holding | 9 | – (4) not out | 77 |
| A. P. Wells b Finney | 24 | | |
| †I. J. Gould c Warner b Holding | 0 | | |
| *J. R. T. Barclay c Marples b Newman | 23 | | |
| G. S. le Roux c Barnett b Newman | 20 | | |
| A. N. Jones not out | 9 | | |
| B 9, l-b 10, n-b 19 | 38 | B 5, n-b 11 | 16 |
| 1/11 2/17 3/42 4/55 5/68 6/78 7/78 8/104 9/147 | 169 | 1/41 2/72 3/134 | (3 wkts) 228 |

Bonus points – Sussex 1, Derbyshire 4.

Bowling: *First Innings*—Holding 21–3–78–3; Finney 20–6–41–5; Warner 5–0–10–0; Newman 5.3–0–21–2. *Second Innings*—Holding 13–0–59–2; Newman 15–3–52–0; Finney 12.4–2–38–0; Miller 17–2–49–1; Barnett 3–2–6–0; Warner 3–0–19–0.

Umpires: B. J. Meyer and J. W. Holder.

## SUSSEX v MIDDLESEX

At Hove, August 24, 26, 27. Sussex won by 103 runs. Sussex 20 pts, Middlesex 6 pts. Toss won by Sussex. Barclay elected to bat first on the easy-paced pitch to which this match was transferred when the intended pitch – well grassed and rolled hard – was soaked by overnight rain. Play began at 2.30, whereupon Sussex found further favour from the weather when, after three overs into a stiff gale, Cowans relinquished the new ball. Emburey, taking five for 10 off 38 balls, set Sussex back on the second day, and Butcher's 60 off 90 balls allowed Gatting to declare in arrears in the hope of being set a target. When it came – 292 off 58 overs – Middlesex, with the exception of Butcher and Gatting, disintegrated just when a win would have taken them to the top of the Championship table. Reeve, who began the day with a half-century as night-watchman, ended it, and the Middlesex innings, with three wickets in a six-ball spell.

### Sussex

| | | | |
|---|---|---|---|
| G. D. Mendis c Downton b Daniel | 72 | – c Emburey b Edmonds | 19 |
| A. M. Green c Edmonds b Emburey | 89 | – c Slack b Emburey | 38 |
| N. J. Lenham run out | 32 | – (4) st Downton b Emburey | 39 |
| C. M. Wells c Gatting b Emburey | 32 | – (5) c Butcher b Gatting | 35 |
| A. P. Wells c Downton b Edmonds | 13 | – (6) not out | 9 |
| †I. J. Gould c and b Emburey | 5 | – (7) not out | 4 |
| I. A. Greig c Barlow b Emburey | 3 | | |
| G. S. le Roux c Radley b Edmonds | 14 | | |
| *J. R. T. Barclay c Edmonds b Emburey | 5 | | |
| D. A. Reeve not out | 8 | – (3) c Gatting b Butcher | 56 |
| A. N. Jones st Downton b Emburey | 0 | | |
| L-b 6, n-b 8 | 14 | L-b 5, n-b 2 | 7 |
| 1/138 2/183 3/228 4/252 5/256 6/258 7/265 8/278 9/286 | 287 | 1/32 2/67 3/133 4/186 5/195 (5 wkts dec.) | 207 |

Bonus points – Sussex 3, Middlesex 4.

Bowling: *First Innings*—Daniel 21–2–84–1; Cowans 11–2–37–0; Hughes 11–0–28–0; Edmonds 37–7–97–2; Emburey 18.2–3–35–6. *Second Innings*—Daniel 8–1–22–0; Cowans 2–0–12–0; Edmonds 29–6–74–1; Emburey 22–4–46–2; Gatting 5.5–0–31–1; Butcher 4–0–17–1.

### Middlesex

| | | | |
|---|---|---|---|
| G. D. Barlow c Jones b Barclay | 38 | – c Gould b Jones | 13 |
| W. N. Slack c A. P. Wells b Reeve | 50 | – c Gould b C. M. Wells | 29 |
| *M. W. Gatting b Reeve | 3 | – b Reeve | 51 |
| R. O. Butcher not out | 60 | – not out | 58 |
| C. T. Radley c Barclay b Greig | 35 | – lbw b le Roux | 8 |
| †P. R. Downton not out | 4 | – c Greig b le Roux | 9 |
| J. E. Emburey (did not bat) | | – b C. M. Wells | 0 |
| P. H. Edmonds (did not bat) | | – b Reeve | 11 |
| S. P. Hughes (did not bat) | | – lbw b Reeve | 4 |
| N. G. Cowans (did not bat) | | – lbw b Reeve | 0 |
| W. W. Daniel (did not bat) | | – run out | 0 |
| B 4, l-b 5, n-b 4 | 13 | L-b 5 | 5 |
| 1/77 2/91 3/107 4/199 (4 wkts dec.) | 203 | 1/21 2/57 3/115 4/138 5/162 6/163 7/179 8/183 9/183 | 188 |

Bonus points – Middlesex 2, Sussex 1.

Bowling: *First Innings*—le Roux 5–2–16–0; Jones 7–3–33–0; Barclay 11–1–35–1; Reeve 15–6–30–2; C. M. Wells 13–0–43–0; Greig 7–0–37–1. *Second Innings*—le Roux 10–0–39–2; Jones 5–0–29–1; Reeve 15–1–64–4; C. M. Wells 10–2–27–2; Barclay 4–0–24–0.

Umpires: R. Palmer and H. J. Rhodes.

## SUSSEX v YORKSHIRE

At Hove, August 28, 29, 30. Drawn. Sussex 7 pts, Yorkshire 4 pts. Toss won by Sussex. Chasing 278 runs in 44 overs, Sussex came to the final over, bowled by Peter Hartley, needing 21 for victory: too much even for Imran, who with Jones took 11 from it. Both sides having occupied the crease for the best part of a day apiece over their first innings, the third day became something of a run-feast with 552 runs taken from a mixed bag of bowlers. Love and Robinson were both on course for the fastest hundred of the season in a partnership of 152 off ten overs, and in keeping with the somewhat bizarre nature of the day, both Imran and Parker employed runners in their seventh-wicket partnership, while S. J. Storey, the Sussex coach, stood at square-leg because umpire Cook was ill.

### Yorkshire

| | | | |
|---|---|---|---|
| G. Boycott lbw b Imran | 43 | – retired hurt | 11 |
| M. D. Moxon b Barclay | 70 | – c Gould b le Roux | 20 |
| R. J. Blakey lbw b Wells | 3 | – hit wkt b Mendis | 48 |
| S. N. Hartley c Green b Barclay | 49 | – c Mendis b Wells | 47 |
| J. D. Love c Lenham b Barclay | 46 | – not out | 78 |
| P. E. Robinson b Barclay | 15 | – c sub b Barclay | 79 |
| *†D. L. Bairstow c Parker b Barclay | 29 | | |
| P. Carrick c Lenham b Barclay | 2 | | |
| C. S. Pickles c Wells b le Roux | 9 | | |
| P. J. Hartley not out | 5 | | |
| C. Shaw b Imran | 0 | | |
| B 5, l-b 15, w 1, n-b 15 | 36 | B 2, l-b 1, n-b 7 | 10 |
| 1/91 2/104 3/176 4/211 5/245 6/288 7/290 8/296 9/307 | 307 | 1/42 2/131 3/141 4/293 (4 wkts dec.) | 293 |

Bonus points – Yorkshire 3, Sussex 3 (Score at 100 overs: 297-8).

Bowling: *First Innings*—le Roux 17–3–47–1; Imran 18.3–7–33–2; Wells 15–2–29–1; Reeve 22–6–54–0; Jones 14–3–46–0; Barclay 19–1–78–6. *Second Innings*—le Roux 11–1–38–1; Jones 11–2–31–0; Reeve 4–1–3–0; Wells 14–3–30–1; Barclay 14.4–1–42–1; Green 4–1–6–0; Mendis 4–0–65–1; Gould 4–0–75–0.

### Sussex

| | | | |
|---|---|---|---|
| G. D. Mendis c Love b P. J. Hartley | 123 | – c Bairstow b P. J. Hartley | 6 |
| A. M. Green c Bairstow b Shaw | 54 | – b Carrick | 39 |
| P. W. G. Parker b S. N. Hartley | 76 | – (8) c Blakey b Carrick | 10 |
| Imran Khan not out | 39 | – (7) c Robinson b P. J. Hartley | 39 |
| C. M. Wells lbw b P. J. Hartley | 4 | – (4) c sub b P. J. Hartley | 46 |
| N. J. Lenham not out | 10 | – (3) c sub b P. J. Hartley | 41 |
| †I. J. Gould (did not bat) | | – (6) st Bairstow b Carrick | 8 |
| G. S. le Roux (did not bat) | | – (5) st Bairstow b Carrick | 61 |
| A. N. Jones (did not bat) | | – not out | 6 |
| B 1, l-b 5, w 2, n-b 9 | 17 | B 4, l-b 8 | 12 |
| 1/104 2/239 3/270 4/297 (4 wkts dec.) | 323 | 1/6 2/92 3/92 4/185 5/203 6/215 7/243 8/268 (8 wkts) | 268 |

*J. R. T. Barclay and D. A. Reeve did not bat.

Bonus points – Sussex 4, Yorkshire 1 (Score at 100 overs: 305-4).

Bowling: *First Innings*—Shaw 22–7–43–1; P. J. Hartley 24–1–100–2; Carrick 30–7–77–0; Pickles 19.3–1–69–0; Boycott 4–1–11–0; S. N. Hartley 4–0–17–1. *Second Innings*—P. J. Hartley 19–1–97–4; Shaw 12–0–60–0; Carrick 22–0–99–4.

Umpires: C. Cook and A. A. Jones.

At Taunton, August 31, September 2, 3. SUSSEX drew with SOMERSET.

At The Oval, September 4, 5, 6. SUSSEX beat SURREY by three wickets.

## SUSSEX v LEICESTERSHIRE

At Hove, September 7, 9, 10. Sussex won by two wickets. Sussex 22 pts, Leicestershire 5 pts. Toss won by Leicestershire. Real cricket weather favoured the last match at Hove, and Gower set the seal on it with a most cultured innings, his second-innings 128 containing sixteen 4s and a seemingly effortless 6 off Jones. The Sussex fast bowler, working up a good pace down the hill, had had the better of Gower on the first day, however, when only Willey, for 176 minutes, and Whitticase remained for long. By dint of Gower's brilliance, Sussex were asked to score 289 to win off at least 67 overs and looked out of the hunt at 65 for four. Gould, despite an injured finger, turned their fortunes with his first-ever hundred for the county, and there were only three balls left when Barclay and Reeve raced through for a leg-bye to end Sussex's home season on a winning note.

### Leicestershire

| Batsman | First innings | | Second innings | |
|---|---|---|---|---|
| I. P. Butcher | b Jones | 6 | b Jones | 4 |
| J. C. Balderstone | b le Roux | 28 | b Reeve | 31 |
| R. A. Cobb | lbw b le Roux | 3 | c sub b C. M. Wells | 23 |
| *D. I. Gower | b Jones | 2 | c Reeve b Barclay | 128 |
| P. Willey | not out | 74 | c Barclay b Reeve | 34 |
| J. J. Whitaker | c Mendis b Reeve | 18 | c Reeve b Barclay | 0 |
| P. B. Clift | lbw b C. M. Wells | 0 | c Greig b Jones | 14 |
| P. A. J. De Freitas | lbw b Reeve | 0 | b Jones | 7 |
| †P. Whitticase | c Gould b le Roux | 32 | not out | 55 |
| J. P. Agnew | c Gould b le Roux | 0 | (11) not out | 10 |
| L. B. Taylor | b le Roux | 0 | (10) c Mendis b Reeve | 5 |
| | L-b 2, n-b 6 | 8 | L-b 4, w 1, n-b 10 | 15 |
| | 1/12 2/27 3/32 4/43 5/80 6/81 7/86 8/159 9/159 | 171 | 1/5 2/61 3/69 4/169 5/170 6/193 7/210 8/276 9/295 (9 wkts dec.) | 326 |

Bonus points – Leicestershire 1, Sussex 4.

Bowling: *First Innings*—le Roux 14.5–2–41–5; Jones 10–0–41–2; Reeve 20–2–53–2; C. M. Wells 11–3–30–1; Barclay 1–0–4–0. *Second Innings*—le Roux 12–1–48–0; Jones 23–4–77–3; Reeve 26–3–83–3; C. M. Wells 20–5–56–1; Barclay 27–5–58–2.

### Sussex

| Batsman | First innings | | Second innings | |
|---|---|---|---|---|
| G. D. Mendis | b Willey | 33 | c sub b Taylor | 4 |
| A. M. Green | lbw b Taylor | 4 | b De Freitas | 9 |
| N. J. Lenham | b Willey | 50 | c Clift b Willey | 77 |
| C. M. Wells | lbw b Willey | 1 | b Clift | 1 |
| A. P. Wells | b De Freitas | 6 | lbw b Willey | 21 |
| D. A. Reeve | c sub b Taylor | 10 | (10) not out | 5 |
| †I. J. Gould | c Butcher b Taylor | 0 | (6) c Whitaker b Clift | 101 |
| G. S. le Roux | b De Freitas | 27 | (7) c and b Clift | 34 |
| *J. R. T. Barclay | not out | 12 | not out | 8 |
| I. A. Greig | lbw b Taylor | 0 | (8) c sub b Clift | 2 |
| A. N. Jones | b Willey | 26 | | |
| | B 7, l-b 6, w 2, n-b 25 | 40 | B 1, l-b 20, w 2, n-b 4 | 27 |
| | 1/8 2/100 3/108 4/114 5/122 6/123 7/164 8/176 9/176 | 209 | 1/6 2/31 3/36 4/65 5/162 6/268 7/271 8/273 (8 wkts) | 289 |

Bonus points – Sussex 2, Leicestershire 4.

Bowling: *First Innings*—Agnew 12–1–43–0; Taylor 17–4–50–4; De Freitas 23–5–59–2; Clift 19–5–36–0; Willey 12.4–7–8–4. *Second Innings*—Taylor 13–2–51–1; De Freitas 14.3–1–63–1; Clift 22–3–60–4; Willey 15–4–65–2; Balderstone 3–0–29–0.

Umpires: M. J. Kitchen and R. Palmer.

At Cardiff, September 14, 16, 17. SUSSEX drew with GLAMORGAN.

# WARWICKSHIRE

*President:* The Earl of Aylesford
*Chairman:* 1985 – A. D. Steven
*Chairman, Cricket Committee:* J. I. McDowall
*Secretary:* A. C. Smith
County Ground, Edgbaston,
Birmingham B5 7QU
(Telephone: 021-440 4292)
*Cricket Manager:* D. J. Brown
*Captain:* N. Gifford
*Coach:* A. S. M. Oakman

A finish of fifteenth in the Britannic Assurance Championship, sixth in the John Player Sunday League, and, after not qualifying for the knockout stages of the Benson and Hedges Cup, elimination from the NatWest Bank Trophy in the second round, fairly reflects the poorest playing record by Warwickshire for many years.

After a promising start, their season disintegrated so comprehensively that on the way down the Championship table they gathered only one batting point in their last five matches. Four of these games were lost – to Gloucestershire, Worcestershire, Derbyshire and Middlesex – because of bowling problems which had begun earlier in the season with injuries to Chris Old and Stephen Wall. This was particularly disappointing, because at Cheltenham, Edgbaston (twice) and Chesterfield the pitches could hardly have been more helpful to the faster bowlers, while the spinners were also on top in the final Championship-settling game against Middlesex.

Yet an anomaly in the bonus points system resulted in almost as many being won compared with the previous year (121 in 1985, 131 in 1984), despite only two victories in 1985 compared with the eight of 1984. So many times was the painfully weak Warwickshire attack hit for big totals quickly that they picked up more bowling points than twelve other sides, some of them as their opponents raced towards totals of 400 or more in 100 overs. Perhaps consideration should be given to the idea of allowing bowling points to be won only up to and including 300, the total at which batting points cease. Only Glamorgan, Derbyshire and Lancashire secured fewer batting points than the powerful-looking Edgbaston line-up.

The two knockout competitions were a disaster, with Warwickshire failing to progress past the zonal stage of the Benson and Hedges Cup owing to some unintelligent cricket at the end of their match against Worcestershire. In the NatWest, they lost at Trent Bridge to the eventual losing finalists because their seam attack bowled poorly on a pitch that was not far short of dangerous.

From that mid-season moment Warwickshire fell apart. In the most open John Player League for years, because of the havoc created by rain, the side was well in the running for honours until the match against Derbyshire at Edgbaston. Then, after scoring what at that time was their second-highest total of the season, even in a match reduced because of weather, they never looked like defending an asking-rate of over seven and a half runs per over. They eventually finished equal sixth, a marginal improvement on their 1984 position.

Gladstone Small had a satisfactory season with 69 wickets in the first-class game, but the burden of carrying the new-ball attack almost single-handed took its toll. Anton Ferreira's bag of 77 wickets was more impressive than his control; an apparent decline in his general fitness was reflected in the cost of his wickets.

Among the younger fast bowlers, Paul Smith was the biggest disappointment with 26 wickets at 43.96. Far from showing signs of the undoubted talent he possesses, his bowling regressed to a point where line and length were hopelessly neglected. Wall looked the best of the other seamers, although Dean Hoffman showed promise when a spate of injuries forced his selection for a number of games. Norman Gifford carried the spin bowling department – and most of the attack as well – but understandably his penetrative powers are not as sharp as they were.

Among the batsmen, only Andy Lloyd, Dennis Amiss and Geoff Humpage had satisfactory seasons, and it was small wonder that the general decline in the team's performance finally afflicted them as well. Particularly disappointing was the comparatively poor season of Alvin Kallicharran, who was regularly troubled by shoulder injuries. Lloyd broke a thumb in mid-July, but completed a successful season of rehabilitation after his eye injury sustained the previous year on his Test début.

Amiss scored five first-class hundreds after a tantalising series of near-misses early in the season to take his tally to 96, and in passing 40,000 runs he moved past R. E. S. Wyatt, J. H. Edrich, W. Rhodes, M. J. K. Smith and L. Hutton into thirteenth position in the list of leading career aggregates. Humpage scored 1,360 runs. This allied to his club record of 80 wicket-keeping victims, which also put him top of the country's wicket-keeping table, meant that again he was easily the country's leading wicket-keeper–batsman. Robin Dyer was adequate but no more. He needs to develop the art of raising the tempo of his batting as an innings grows. Of the younger batsmen, Gordon Lord did well with limited opportunities, and he hit a magnificent 199 against Yorkshire.

Off the field, Warwickshire's administrative links with Lord's were strengthened by the appointments of past and present club captains, Bob Willis and Gifford, as assistant-managers on England's two winter tours. But a dismal season ended with rumblings of a specially convened meeting of members, and if new bowling talent is not quickly found and developed by the Edgbaston cricket management, then the poor playing record of 1985 could be the beginning of a depressing era. – J.D.B.

WARWICKSHIRE 1985

[*Bill Smith*

*Back row:* A. S. M. Oakman (*coach*), S. Wall, G. C. Small, P. A. Smith, W. Hogg, C. M. Old, T. A. Munton, R. I. H. B. Dyer, D. S. Hoffman, W. Morton, R. N. Abberley (*head coach indoor cricket school*). *Middle row:* T. A. Lloyd, G. W. Humpage, D. L. Amiss, D. J. Brown (*cricket manager*), N. Gifford (*captain*), A. I. Kallicharran, K. D. Smith. *Front row:* P. W. Threlfall, W. J. P. Matthews, G. J. Lord, C. Lethbridge, Asif Din, G. A. Tedstone.

## WARWICKSHIRE RESULTS

*All first-class matches – Played 26: Won 3, Lost 8, Drawn 15.*

*County Championship matches – Played 24: Won 2, Lost 8, Drawn 14.*

*Bonus points – Batting 47, Bowling 74.*

*Competition placings – Britannic Assurance County Championship, 15th; NatWest Bank Trophy, 2nd round; Benson and Hedges Cup, 4th in Group B; John Player League, 6th eq.*

## BRITANNIC ASSURANCE CHAMPIONSHIP AVERAGES

### BATTING

| | *Birthplace* | *M* | *I* | *NO* | *R* | *HI* | *Avge* |
|---|---|---|---|---|---|---|---|
| ‡D. L. Amiss | *Birmingham* | 24 | 40 | 4 | 1,326 | 140 | 36.83 |
| ‡G. W. Humpage | *Birmingham* | 23 | 38 | 5 | 1,197 | 159 | 36.27 |
| Asif Din | *Kampala, Uganda* | 6 | 11 | 2 | 325 | 89 | 36.11 |
| ‡T. A. Lloyd | *Oswestry* | 16 | 30 | 2 | 989 | 160 | 35.32 |
| ‡A. I. Kallicharran | *Berbice, BG* | 21 | 35 | 2 | 1,052 | 152* | 31.87 |
| G. J. Lord | *Birmingham* | 7 | 10 | 1 | 263 | 199 | 29.22 |
| R. I. H. B. Dyer | *Hertford* | 24 | 42 | 2 | 1,112 | 106 | 27.80 |
| ‡A. M. Ferreira | *Pretoria, SA* | 23 | 35 | 8 | 693 | 101* | 25.66 |
| P. A. Smith | *Jesmond* | 23 | 35 | 3 | 783 | 93 | 24.46 |
| ‡C. M. Old | *Middlesbrough* | 7 | 7 | 2 | 122 | 41 | 24.40 |
| ‡G. C. Small | *St George, Barbados* | 21 | 27 | 8 | 285 | 31* | 15.00 |
| ‡K. D. Smith | *Jesmond* | 4 | 7 | 0 | 99 | 42 | 14.14 |
| S. Wall | *Ulverston* | 10 | 15 | 5 | 125 | 28 | 12.50 |
| A. R. K. Pierson | *Enfield* | 10 | 12 | 5 | 85 | 17* | 12.14 |
| ‡N. Gifford | *Ulverston* | 24 | 25 | 8 | 132 | 26 | 7.76 |
| D. S. Hoffman | *Birmingham* | 15 | 15 | 4 | 39 | 13* | 3.54 |

Also batted: C. Lethbridge (*Castleford*) (3 matches) 15, 22*, 47; S. Monkhouse (*Bury*) (1 match) 2*, 5; G. A. Tedstone (*Southport*) (1 match) 22; D. A. Thorne (*Coventry*) (1 match) 0, 0.

** Signifies not out.* ‡ *Denotes county cap.*

The following played a total of twelve three-figure innings for Warwickshire in County Championship matches – D. L. Amiss 4, G. W. Humpage 2, A. I. Kallicharran 2, R. I. H. B. Dyer 1, A. M. Ferreira 1, T. A. Lloyd 1, G. J. Lord 1.

### BOWLING

| | *O* | *M* | *R* | *W* | *BB* | *Avge* |
|---|---|---|---|---|---|---|
| G. C. Small | 592.3 | 114 | 1,850 | 69 | 5-24 | 26.81 |
| A. M. Ferreira | 624.3 | 118 | 2,039 | 71 | 5-41 | 28.71 |
| N. Gifford | 611.5 | 188 | 1,541 | 46 | 5-128 | 33.50 |
| C. M. Old | 153.2 | 38 | 466 | 13 | 6-68 | 35.84 |
| D. S. Hoffman | 287.1 | 41 | 1,081 | 26 | 4-100 | 41.57 |
| P. A. Smith | 234.2 | 24 | 1,130 | 26 | 4-25 | 43.46 |
| S. Wall | 243.1 | 36 | 790 | 18 | 4-59 | 43.88 |

Also bowled: Asif Din 5.2–2–7–1; A. I. Kallicharran 11.4–0–56–0; C. Lethbridge 65–7–263–5; T. A. Lloyd 31–1–127–4; S. Monkhouse 17–2–61–1; A. R. K. Pierson 89–19–340–1.

At Chelmsford, April 27, 28, 29. WARWICKSHIRE lost to ESSEX by 89 runs.

## WARWICKSHIRE v GLAMORGAN

At Edgbaston, May 8, 9, 10. Drawn. Warwickshire 8 pts, Glamorgan 4 pts. Toss won by Glamorgan. Warwickshire just failed to clinch a win when, after dropping a vital catch towards the end of the Glamorgan second innings, they were left to score 37 off only two overs. The home side were always on top after Lloyd hit 160 in 311 minutes in his first innings on the ground since he was injured playing for England against West Indies eleven months previously. Javed Miandad, with 98, took his Championship record on the ground to 659 in six innings, and his second-innings 52 prevented some hostile bowling by Small from achieving a home win.

### Glamorgan

| | | | |
|---|---|---|---|
| J. A. Hopkins c Ferreira b Old | 0 | lbw b Ferreira | 32 |
| G. C. Holmes c Wall b Small | 0 | lbw b Small | 8 |
| S. P. Henderson c Humpage b Ferreira | 26 | c Humpage b Ferreira | 10 |
| Javed Miandad lbw b Wall | 98 | b Small | 52 |
| Younis Ahmed b Smith | 18 | lbw b Wall | 32 |
| *R. C. Ontong c Amiss b Ferreira | 55 | c Humpage b Wall | 16 |
| J. F. Steele c Humpage b Wall | 1 | b Small | 26 |
| J. Derrick lbw b Wall | 1 | c Humpage b Small | 20 |
| J. G. Thomas c Humpage b Small | 27 | c Dyer b Small | 19 |
| †T. Davies not out | 12 | not out | 13 |
| S. R. Barwick c Humpage b Wall | 0 | c Dyer b Ferreira | 4 |
| B 2, l-b 8, w 1, n-b 4 | 15 | B 4, l-b 12, w 1, n-b 6 | 23 |
| 1/1 2/1 3/55 4/82 5/172 6/179 7/187 8/228 9/252 | 253 | 1/11 2/41 3/88 4/108 5/148 6/167 7/216 8/237 9/238 | 255 |

Bonus points – Glamorgan 3, Warwickshire 4.

Bowling: *First Innings*—Small 15–4–44–2; Old 7–4–15–1; Wall 20.2–5–59–4; Ferreira 19–3–66–2; Smith 8–0–47–1; Gifford 6–2–12–0. *Second Innings*—Small 31–8–84–5; Wall 20–4–42–2; Smith 10–3–31–0; Ferreira 26.1–5–77–3; Gifford 8–5–5–0.

### Warwickshire

| | | | |
|---|---|---|---|
| T. A. Lloyd b Ontong | 160 | | |
| R. I. H. B. Dyer b Derrick | 80 | | |
| K. D. Smith c Davies b Thomas | 42 | | |
| D. L. Amiss c Ontong b Derrick | 86 | (3) not out | 2 |
| †G. W. Humpage c Miandad b Barwick | 40 | (2) b Thomas | 0 |
| P. A. Smith lbw b Barwick | 3 | | |
| A. M. Ferreira c Steele b Thomas | 4 | (1) not out | 18 |
| G. C. Small c and b Thomas | 26 | | |
| S. Wall not out | 20 | | |
| L-b 6, w 1, n-b 4 | 11 | W 2 | 2 |
| 1/186 2/270 3/310 4/379 5/386 6/391 7/433 8/472 | (8 wkts dec.) 472 | 1/11 | (1 wkt) 22 |

*N. Gifford and C. M. Old did not bat.

Bonus points – Warwickshire 4, Glamorgan 1 (Score at 100 overs: 318-3).

Bowling: *First Innings*—Thomas 31–2–142–3; Barwick 29–6–100–2; Derrick 18.4–7–55–2; Holmes 11–2–36–0; Steele 28–2–83–0; Ontong 18–3–50–1. *Second Innings*—Thomas 1–0–13–1; Barwick 1–0–9–0.

Umpires: J. H. Harris and B. J. Meyer.

## WARWICKSHIRE v SURREY

At Edgbaston, May 22, 23, 24. Warwickshire won by four wickets. Warwickshire 23 pts, Surrey 7 pts. Toss won by Warwickshire. A typically docile batting pitch allowed a result only because of three declarations and a fourteen-over spell from occasional bowler Lloyd which enabled Pocock to set the home side to make 283 in 50 overs. Thanks to a brilliant 76 off 51 deliveries by Kallicharran, and Humpage's second quick-fire half-century of the match, the home side won with five balls to spare. Small again bowled with fire and penetration, and but for Jesty's first century since leaving Hampshire, which included two 6s and fifteen 4s, Surrey would not have enjoyed a first-innings lead. Surrey's new fast bowler, Gray, from Trinidad, had a promising first match with six for 122.

### Surrey

| | | | |
|---|---|---|---|
| A. R. Butcher c Humpage b Small | 10 | – b Lloyd | 86 |
| G. S. Clinton c Humpage b Old | 21 | – c Humpage b Lloyd | 72 |
| A. J. Stewart b Small | 0 | – not out | 42 |
| T. E. Jesty c Humpage b Ferreira | 126 | – c Kallicharran b Lloyd | 4 |
| M. A. Lynch c Ferreira b Small | 45 | – not out | 24 |
| D. B. Pauline b Small | 77 | | |
| A. Needham c and b Small | 25 | | |
| †C. J. Richards not out | 15 | | |
| G. Monkhouse not out | 12 | | |
| L-b 13, w 1, n-b 2 | 16 | B 6, n-b 1 | 7 |
| 1/14 2/22 3/44 4/107 5/284 6/312 7/321 (7 wkts dec.) | 347 | 1/165 2/168 3/172 (3 wkts dec.) | 235 |

*P. I. Pocock and A. H. Gray did not bat.

Bonus points – Surrey 4, Warwickshire 3.

Bowling: *First Innings*—Small 22–1–66–5; Old 23–4–81–1; Hoffman 14–0–65–0; Ferreira 22–2–89–1; Gifford 19–10–33–0. *Second Innings*—Small 5–0–17–0; Old 7–0–32–0; Gifford 10–2–28–0; Lloyd 14–1–62–3; Hoffman 6–1–25–0; Ferreira 14–3–57–0.

### Warwickshire

| | | | |
|---|---|---|---|
| T. A. Lloyd run out | 34 | – c Monkhouse b Pocock | 46 |
| R. I. H. B. Dyer c Clinton b Gray | 48 | – b Gray | 64 |
| A. I. Kallicharran c Richards b Gray | 6 | – c Jesty b Gray | 76 |
| D. L. Amiss c Butcher b Needham | 57 | – c Jesty b Gray | 0 |
| †G. W. Humpage c Stewart b Jesty | 70 | – not out | 55 |
| P. A. Smith c Pauline b Needham | 31 | – c Richards b Gray | 5 |
| A. M. Ferreira not out | 36 | – c Lynch b Pocock | 19 |
| C. M. Old c Clinton b Needham | 0 | – not out | 10 |
| G. C. Small not out | 2 | | |
| B 10, l-b 2, w 2, n-b 2 | 16 | L b 9, w 1 | 10 |
| 1/81 2/97 3/103 4/209 5/249 6/269 7/273 (7 wkts dec.) | 300 | 1/77 2/188 3/188 4/193 5/207 6/256 (6 wkts) | 285 |

*N. Gifford and D. S. Hoffman did not bat.

Bonus points – Warwickshire 4, Surrey 3.

Bowling: *First Innings*—Gray 16–4–54–2; Pauline 7–3–14–0; Butcher 7–1–20–0; Monkhouse 11–2–47–0; Pocock 26–6–65–0; Needham 19–3–52–3; Jesty 7–0–36–1. *Second Innings*—Gray 12–0–68–4; Pauline 4–0–18–0; Pocock 19.1–2–108–2; Monkhouse 5–0–24–0; Needham 8–1–48–0; Butcher 1–0–10–0.

Umpires: J. H. Hampshire and D. R. Shepherd.

At Worcester, May 25, 26, 27. WARWICKSHIRE drew with WORCESTERSHIRE.

At Northampton, May 29, 30, 31. WARWICKSHIRE drew with NORTHAMPTONSHIRE.

At Taunton, June 1, 3, 4. WARWICKSHIRE drew with SOMERSET.

## WARWICKSHIRE v HAMPSHIRE

At Edgbaston, June 8, 10, 11. Drawn. Warwickshire 3 pts, Hampshire 8 pts. Toss won by Warwickshire. A total of 245 minutes lost to bad light and rain on the last day prevented Hampshire from winning a match which they had controlled from the start. With victory in sight, rain washed out the last three hours' play. Their two West Indian Test players, Greenidge and Marshall, dominated throughout, with the opening batsman hitting his fifth double-century for the county, and the opening bowler having a match analysis of nine for 118, despite being sparingly used on the last day because of the poor light. Greenidge's innings of five hours included two 6s and 26 4s, and only Gifford of the home bowlers avoided heavy punishment. Similarly, only Amiss and Humpage, with a second-innings fourth-wicket stand of 77, coped with Marshall's extra pace.

### Warwickshire

| | | | |
|---|---|---|---|
| R. I. H. B. Dyer lbw b Marshall | 0 | – lbw b Marshall | 4 |
| K. D. Smith lbw b Marshall | 16 | – run out | 27 |
| A. I. Kallicharran lbw b Marshall | 0 | – c Terry b Marshall | 5 |
| D. L. Amiss lbw b Marshall | 15 | – lbw b Tremlett | 57 |
| †G. W. Humpage lbw b Tremlett | 14 | – c Parks b Connor | 45 |
| P. A. Smith lbw b Tremlett | 24 | – c Terry b Marshall | 11 |
| A. M. Ferreira c Marshall b Tremlett | 36 | – c Greenidge b Tremlett | 22 |
| G. C. Small not out | 9 | – not out | 13 |
| S. Wall b Tremlett | 0 | – not out | 3 |
| D. S. Hoffman b Marshall | 2 | | |
| *N. Gifford c C. L. Smith b Marshall | 0 | | |
| L-b 7, w 1, n-b 3 | 11 | B 1, l-b 4, n-b 6 | 11 |
| 1/2 2/2 3/24 4/38 5/75 6/99 7/124 8/124 9/127 | 127 | 1/9 2/37 3/37 4/114 5/149 6/163 7/182 | (7 wkts) 198 |

Bonus points – Hampshire 4.

Bowling: *First Innings*—Connor 13–6–28–0; Marshall 20–6–50–6; Tremlett 15–1–42–4. *Second Innings*—Connor 17–3–44–1; Marshall 24–7–68–3; Tremlett 23–5–69–2; Maru 7–3–6–0; Cowley 4.2–2–6–0.

### Hampshire

| | |
|---|---|
| V. P. Terry c Humpage b Wall | 5 |
| C. G. Greenidge c K. D. Smith b Gifford | 204 |
| *M. C. J. Nicholas c Amiss b Ferreira | 28 |
| C. L. Smith lbw b Hoffman | 52 |
| R. A. Smith b Gifford | 36 |
| M. D. Marshall c Humpage b Gifford | 10 |
| T. M. Tremlett b P. A. Smith | 4 |
| †R. J. Parks lbw b Gifford | 26 |
| N. G. Cowley not out | 29 |
| R. J. Maru not out | 13 |
| B 1, l-b 14, w 2, n-b 9 | 26 |
| 1/6 2/93 3/225 4/325 5/347 6/352 7/364 8/392 | (8 wkts dec.) 433 |

C. A. Connor did not bat.

Bonus points – Hampshire 4, Warwickshire 3 (Score at 100 overs: 386-7).

Bowling: Small 18–3–84–0; Wall 9–1–37–1; Hoffman 25–3–85–1; Ferreira 11–2–68–1; Gifford 34–9–89–4; P. A. Smith 13–1–55–1.

Umpires: D. G. L. Evans and B. Leadbeater.

At Hinckley, June 12, 13, 14. WARWICKSHIRE lost to LEICESTERSHIRE by four wickets.

At The Parks, June 15, 17, 18. WARWICKSHIRE beat OXFORD UNIVERSITY by 21 runs.

At Edgbaston, June 22, 24, 25. WARWICKSHIRE drew with ZIMBABWEANS (See Zimbabwean tour section).

At Old Trafford, June 26, 27, 28. WARWICKSHIRE drew with LANCASHIRE.

## WARWICKSHIRE v NORTHAMPTONSHIRE

At Edgbaston, June 29, July 1, 2. Northamptonshire won by 31 runs. Northamptonshire 20 pts, Warwickshire 6 pts. Toss won by Warwickshire. Northamptonshire fought back well after hostile bowling from Small dismissed them for 142 in their first innings. Despite Asif Din's first half-century for two years, Warwickshire could not establish a big lead, but after Ferreira and Gifford had bowled well to dismiss the visitors for 282, a target of 213 in 72 overs was not an over-taxing one. However, a mid-innings collapse of five wickets for 5 runs, brought about by Mallender and Harper, swung the game Northamptonshire's way and they eventually won with 22 balls to spare. Sharp suffered a fractured finger on the first day and Ripley appeared as substitute wicket-keeper for Northamptonshire.

### Northamptonshire

| | | | |
|---|---|---|---|
| *G. Cook c Humpage b Small | 0 | c Amiss b Gifford | 19 |
| W. Larkins c Humpage b Ferreira | 42 | c Dyer b Ferreira | 33 |
| R. J. Boyd-Moss c Humpage b Small | 17 | c Gifford b Ferreira | 17 |
| A. C. Storie c Humpage b Wall | 2 | c Amiss b Ferreira | 11 |
| R. J. Bailey c and b Wall | 20 | b Hoffman | 67 |
| D. J. Capel c Dyer b Ferreira | 22 | c Humpage b Gifford | 0 |
| D. J. Wild lbw b Ferreira | 9 | c Amiss b Hoffman | 55 |
| R. A. Harper lbw b Small | 5 | lbw b Small | 34 |
| †G. Sharp c Amiss b Small | 2 | (10) not out | 9 |
| N. A. Mallender not out | 2 | (9) c Humpage b Gifford | 10 |
| A. Walker c Ferreira b Small | 9 | c Wall b Asif Din | 3 |
| B 1, l-b 6, w 2, n-b 3 | 12 | B 3, l-b 16, w 3, n-b 2 | 24 |
| 1/0 2/45 3/51 4/84 5/88 6/123 7/124 8/127 9/132 | 142 | 1/59 2/70 3/95 4/106 5/113 6/222 7/229 8/261 9/271 | 282 |

Bonus points – Warwickshire 4.

Bowling: *First Innings*—Small 15.3–2–45–5; Wall 11–3–36–2; Ferreira 17–3–53–3; Gifford 1–0–1–0. *Second Innings*—Small 23–3–65–1; Smith 8–0–48–0; Wall 5–0–21–0; Hoffman 14–1–38–2; Gifford 34–7–69–3; Ferreira 12–4–20–3; Asif Din 1.2–0–2–1.

### Warwickshire

| | | | |
|---|---|---|---|
| T. A. Lloyd c Bailey b Capel | 14 | c sub b Walker | 0 |
| R. I. H. B. Dyer run out | 44 | lbw b Mallender | 44 |
| D. L. Amiss c Cook b Capel | 28 | c Harper b Walker | 36 |
| †G. W. Humpage lbw b Capel | 15 | c sub b Mallender | 23 |
| P. A. Smith c Sharp b Walker | 4 | c Storie b Harper | 3 |
| A. M. Ferreira b Capel | 1 | (7) b Harper | 0 |
| Asif Din c Harper b Walker | 60 | (6) lbw b Mallender | 0 |
| G. C. Small b Walker | 27 | not out | 31 |
| S. Wall c Cook b Harper | 0 | b Harper | 28 |
| *N. Gifford c Walker b Harper | 1 | run out | 11 |
| D. S. Hoffman not out | 0 | c Cook b Harper | 1 |
| B 5, l-b 10, w 1, n-b 2 | 18 | B 2, l-b 2 | 4 |
| 1/22 2/62 3/82 4/98 5/101 6/141 7/193 8/194 9/208 | 212 | 1/1 2/71 3/105 4/110 5/110 6/110 7/110 8/155 9/176 | 181 |

Bonus points – Warwickshire 2, Northamptonshire 4.

Bowling: *First Innings*—Walker 23.3–9–59–3; Mallender 24–7–55–0; Capel 24–4–58–4; Larkins 1–0–4–0; Harper 17–10–21–2. *Second Innings*—Mallender 20–6–36–3; Walker 14–2–55–2; Capel 4–1–21–0; Harper 26.2–9–47–4; Larkins 3–0–11–0; Boyd-Moss 1–0–7–0.

Umpires: J. H. Hampshire and K. E. Palmer.

At Hove, July 6, 8, 9. WARWICKSHIRE drew with SUSSEX.

## WARWICKSHIRE v LANCASHIRE

At Edgbaston, July 10, 11, 12. Warwickshire won by one wicket. Warwickshire 20 pts, Lancashire 4 pts. Toss won by Lancashire. Twenty wickets fell on the first day on a helpful but never dangerous pitch, and on the final evening Warwickshire won a thrilling victory with one over to spare, thanks to a splendid all-round performance by Ferreira. Batsmen on both sides showed more application in their respective second innings. Fairbrother's 85 and Watkinson's career-best 87 enabled Lancashire to set a target of 348, 14 of which were on the board when bad light ended play 25 minutes early. Lloyd and Kallicharran both played well for 91 and 56 respectively, but from 191 for one the home side lost six wickets while adding 80, and only an unbeaten 42 by Ferreira denied Lancashire the win that the bowling of Watkinson in particular had seemed to earn them.

### Lancashire

| | | | |
|---|---|---|---|
| M. R. Chadwick c and b Small | 4 | – b Small | 13 |
| D. W. Varey b Ferreira | 34 | – c Humpage b Ferreira | 32 |
| S. J. O'Shaughnessy c Humpage b Ferreira | 7 | – c Ferreira b Small | 12 |
| N. H. Fairbrother c Humpage b Smith | 5 | – (5) c Small b Ferreira | 85 |
| *J. Abrahams c Gifford b Smith | 1 | – (4) c Ferreira b Hoffman | 16 |
| M. Watkinson lbw b Ferreira | 16 | – c Amiss b Gifford | 87 |
| †C. Maynard c Ferreira b Small | 6 | – c Gifford b Ferreira | 3 |
| D. J. Makinson lbw b Smith | 36 | – b Small | 27 |
| I. Folley c Kallicharran b Hoffman | 1 | – not out | 26 |
| I. C. Davidson b Smith | 13 | – c Dyer b Ferreira | 0 |
| B. P. Patterson not out | 3 | – c and b Gifford | 0 |
| B 6, l-b 10, n-b 6 | 22 | B 4, l-b 13, w 1, n-b 2 | 20 |
| 1/28 2/50 3/51 4/52 5/59 6/76 7/85 8/86 9/139 | 148 | 1/21 2/53 3/74 4/105 5/205 6/216 7/276 8/320 9/320 | 321 |

Bonus points – Warwickshire 4.

Bowling: *First Innings*—Small 17–6–38–2; Hoffman 10–1–30–1; Ferreira 21–3–35–3; Smith 11–2–25–4; Gifford 6–2–4–0. *Second Innings*—Small 30–6–82–3; Hoffman 22–7–52–1; Ferreira 24–7–64–4; Smith 5–1–24–0; Gifford 29–14–52–2; Pierson 6–0–30–0.

### Warwickshire

| | | |
|---|---|---|
| T. A. Lloyd b Patterson | 10 – c Chadwick b Davidson | 91 |
| R. I. H. B. Dyer c Varey b Makinson | 1 – c O'Shaughnessy b Watkinson | 28 |
| A. I. Kallicharran lbw b Makinson | 3 – c and b Davidson | 56 |
| D. L. Amiss c Maynard b Patterson | 1 – lbw b Watkinson | 31 |
| †G. W. Humpage c Maynard b Makinson | 0 – c Abrahams b Watkinson | 25 |
| P. A. Smith c Watkinson b Patterson | 48 – c Davidson b Folley | 15 |
| A. M. Ferreira b Watkinson | 14 – not out | 42 |
| G. C. Small c and b Watkinson | 15 b Watkinson | 7 |
| A. R. K. Pierson not out | 9 – (10) c Chadwick b Makinson | 11 |
| *N. Gifford run out | 4 – (9) c and b Folley | 3 |
| D. S. Hoffman c Folley b Watkinson | 0 – not out | 5 |
| B 4, l-b 7, w 3, n-b 3 | 17 B 8, l-b 18, w 3, n-b 8 | 37 |
| 1/7 2/10 3/15 4/17 5/19 6/44 7/60 8/105 9/121 | 122 1/104 2/191 3/204 4/247 5/269 6/271 7/293 8/308 9/326 | (9 wkts) 351 |

Bonus points – Lancashire 4.

Bowling: *First Innings*—Patterson 10–3–23–3; Makinson 10–1–44–3; Watkinson 8.2–1–25–3; O'Shaughnessy 2–0–19–0. *Second Innings*—Patterson 20–1–81–0; Makinson 25–4–59–1; Watkinson 28–6–96–4; O'Shaughnessy 5–1–11–0; Folley 21–1–54–2; Davidson 10–3–24–2.

Umpires: J. H. Hampshire and D. O. Oslear.

## WARWICKSHIRE v NOTTINGHAMSHIRE

At Nuneaton, July 13, 15, 16. Drawn. Warwickshire 8 pts, Nottinghamshire 7 pts. Toss won by Nottinghamshire. With Amiss scoring his 95th first-class hundred, and Lloyd reaching the 90s for the second successive innings, Warwickshire were always in charge of a game in which the good pitch, and the loss of 192 minutes overall, ensured a draw. For the visitors, Rice hit an unbeaten 156 – his third hundred of the season. Well supported by night-watchman Pick and then by Cooper, he hit 25 boundaries in a stay of 250 minutes, but then unluckily broke a finger in the second innings when his side had been set to score 310 off 52 overs. The lively Hoffman confirmed his promise with six wickets in the match.

### Warwickshire

| | | |
|---|---|---|
| T. A. Lloyd c Rice b Saxelby | 94 – c Randall b Pick | 17 |
| R. I. H. B. Dyer c French b Saxelby | 2 – c Hadlee b Hemmings | 49 |
| A. I. Kallicharran c French b Pick | 8 – c Broad b Randall | 38 |
| D. L. Amiss c French b Cooper | 117 – c Broad b Randall | 25 |
| †G. W. Humpage c Broad b Hemmings | 29 – not out | 56 |
| P. A. Smith c Fraser-Darling b Saxelby | 51 – b Randall | 9 |
| A. M. Ferreira c Fraser-Darling b Saxelby | 32 – not out | 26 |
| G. C. Small b Saxelby | 5 | |
| A. R. K. Pierson not out | 14 | |
| *N. Gifford not out | 17 | |
| B 2, l-b 10, w 1, n-b 2 | 15 B 5, l-b 7, w 2, n-b 4 | 18 |
| 1/16 2/25 3/164 4/239 5/260 6/323 7/337 8/354 | (8 wkts dec.) 384 1/28 2/104 3/113 4/153 5/165 | (5 wkts dec.) 238 |

D. S. Hoffman did not bat.

Bonus points – Warwickshire 4, Nottinghamshire 3.

Bowling: *First Innings*—Hadlee 7–3–14–0; Saxelby 24–8–73–5; Pick 16–2–82–1; Cooper 13–1–60–1; Fraser-Darling 11–3–51–0; Rice 8–0–36–0; Hemmings 21–5–56–1. *Second Innings*—Hadlee 4–1–5–0; Saxelby 3–0–11–0; Fraser-Darling 4–0–13–0; Pick 3–0–11–1; Hemmings 14–0–71–1; Randall 13–0–103–3; Johnson 1–0–12–0.

### Nottinghamshire

| First innings | | Second innings | |
|---|---|---|---|
| B. C. Broad c Ferreira b Small | 25 | – c Lloyd b Small | 13 |
| †B. N. French c Humpage b Small | 6 | – (7) c Humpage b Gifford | 0 |
| R. A. Pick b Ferreira | 63 | – (9) not out | 4 |
| D. W. Randall c Humpage b Hoffman | 6 | – (2) c Humpage b Hoffman | 67 |
| *C. E. B. Rice not out | 156 | – (3) retired hurt | 0 |
| P. Johnson c Smith b Gifford | 2 | – (4) b Gifford | 88 |
| R. J. Hadlee c Humpage b Small | 14 | – (6) c Dyer b Hoffman | 1 |
| C. D. Fraser-Darling lbw b Hoffman | 2 | – (5) not out | 23 |
| E. E. Hemmings c Humpage b Hoffman | 6 | – (8) b Gifford | 4 |
| K. Saxelby b Hoffman | 0 | | |
| K. E. Cooper lbw b Gifford | 23 | | |
| B 2, l-b 5, w 1, n-b 2 | 10 | L-b 2, w 3, n-b 1 | 6 |
| 1/31 2/46 3/53 4/159 5/179 6/224 7/237 8/253 9/253 | 313 | 1/26 2/160 3/180 4/181 5/187 6/193 (6 wkts) | 206 |

Bonus points – Nottinghamshire 4, Warwickshire 4.

Bowling: *First Innings*—Small 24–0–78–3; Hoffman 20–2–100–4; Smith 2–0–10–0; Gifford 19.2–4–38–2; Ferreira 20–1–80–1. *Second Innings*—Small 9–3–24–1; Hoffman 11–3–53–2; Gifford 20–4–67–3; Ferreira 8–1–50–0; Pierson 2–0–10–0.

Umpires: R. Julian and D. O. Oslear.

## WARWICKSHIRE v SOMERSET

At Edgbaston, July 24, 25, 26. Drawn. Warwickshire 7 pts, Somerset 4 pts. Toss won by Somerset. Despite two quick-fire innings from Richards, the match was dominated by a performance from Botham which ranks alongside any ever seen on the ground. In 67 minutes he faced 65 deliveries and hit an unbeaten 138 out of 169 scored while he was batting. He hit twelve 6s and thirteen 4s in a whirlwind demonstration of his correct technique, which is backed by a phenomenal strength. Botham's hundred, the fastest of the season, took just 26 scoring strokes – one more than the record – and when he reached three figures off 50 deliveries, 94 runs had come in boundaries. For the home side, Dyer scored his first Championship hundred of the season on a dry pitch. That it was low of bounce and gave generous turn to the slow bowlers made the display by Botham even more remarkable.

### Somerset

| First innings | | Second innings | |
|---|---|---|---|
| N. F. M. Popplewell c Gifford b Hoffman | 4 | – c Amiss b Gifford | 70 |
| P. M. Roebuck c Humpage b Ferreira | 40 | – c Amiss b Gifford | 81 |
| N. A. Felton c Humpage b Hoffman | 10 | – b Gifford | 8 |
| I. V. A. Richards c Smith b Lethbridge | 65 | – (5) c Humpage b Pierson | 53 |
| B. C. Rose c Humpage b Ferreira | 16 | – (6) run out | 14 |
| *I. T. Botham c Humpage b Lethbridge | 5 | – (7) not out | 138 |
| V. J. Marks c Gifford b Ferreira | 6 | – (8) not out | 8 |
| †T. Gard c Amiss b Ferreira | 7 | – (4) c Dyer b Gifford | 16 |
| M. R. Davis c Humpage b Hoffman | 1 | | |
| S. C. Booth c Dyer b Gifford | 28 | | |
| C. H. Dredge not out | 10 | | |
| B 4, l-b 3, w 7, n-b 1 | 15 | B 10, l-b 18, w 2 | 30 |
| 1/4 2/30 3/120 4/121 5/126 6/133 7/155 8/164 9/168 | 207 | 1/112 2/132 3/188 4/213 5/249 6/345 (6 wkts dec.) | 418 |

Bonus points – Somerset 2, Warwickshire 4.

Bowling: *First Innings*—Hoffman 16–2–53–3; Smith 9–2–19–0; Ferreira 24–10–61–4; Lethbridge 19–4–62–2; Gifford 1.5–0–5–1. *Second Innings*—Hoffman 5–0–33–0; Smith 7–2–33–0; Lethbridge 4–0–17–0; Ferreira 9–4–15–0; Pierson 34–8–164–1; Gifford 42–20–128–4.

## Warwickshire

| | | | |
|---|---|---|---|
| R. I. H. B. Dyer c Booth b Marks | 106 | – c Botham b Davis | 4 |
| G. J. Lord b Davis | 9 | – not out | 17 |
| A. I. Kallicharran c Rose b Dredge | 48 | – not out | 51 |
| D. L. Amiss c Booth b Marks | 14 | | |
| C. Lethbridge c Richards b Booth | 47 | | |
| †G. W. Humpage c and b Botham | 33 | | |
| P. A. Smith lbw b Botham | 62 | | |
| A. M. Ferreira b Botham | 4 | | |
| A. R. K. Pierson not out | 2 | | |
| *N. Gifford run out | 0 | | |
| D. S. Hoffman b Botham | 0 | | |
| B 5, l-b 4, w 4 | 13 | B 2 | 2 |
| 1/14 2/86 3/113 4/181 5/230 6/332 7/336 8/338 9/338 | 338 | 1/4 | (1 wkt) 74 |

Bonus points – Warwickshire 3, Somerset 2 (Score at 100 overs: 286-5).

Bowling: *First Innings*—Botham 22–7–63–4; Davis 14–2–56–1; Dredge 11–4–21–1; Richards 8–2–26–0; Marks 40–13–91–2; Booth 23–3–72–1. *Second Innings*—Davis 3–1–3–1; Marks 12.4–5–22–0; Booth 2–0–15–0; Botham 8–1–32–0.

Umpires: J. H. Hampshire and H. J. Rhodes.

# WARWICKSHIRE v DERBYSHIRE

At Edgbaston, July 27, 29, 30. Drawn. Warwickshire 3 pts, Derbyshire 3 pts. Toss won by Derbyshire. Play was possible only on the first day, when the New Zealand Test player, Wright, dominated Derbyshire's innings. He completed the 40th first-class hundred of his career off 205 deliveries and hit 25 boundaries to avert a threatened crisis at 144 for six. His unbeaten 177 was the highest innings for Derbyshire at Edgbaston.

## Derbyshire

| | |
|---|---|
| *K. J. Barnett lbw b Hoffman | 12 |
| I. S. Anderson c Humpage b Ferreira | 24 |
| J. E. Morris c Amiss b Smith | 18 |
| B. Roberts st Humpage b Gifford | 13 |
| J. G. Wright not out | 177 |
| G. Miller b Lethbridge | 15 |
| P. G. Newman c Kallicharran b Gifford | 4 |
| A. E. Warner lbw b Lethbridge | 8 |
| D. G. Moir lbw b Hoffman | 3 |
| R. J. Finney not out | 44 |
| B 3, l-b 10, w 3, n-b 10 | 26 |
| 1/24 2/58 3/62 4/93 5/139 6/144 7/169 8/209 | (8 wkts) 344 |

†C. Marples did not bat.

Bonus points – Derbyshire 3, Warwickshire 3 (Score at 100 overs: 250-8).

Bowling: Hoffman 16–4–30–2; Smith 14–1–66–1; Ferreira 18–3–54–1; Gifford 36–11–81–2; Pierson 24–7–57–0; Lethbridge 12–1–43–2.

## Warwickshire

G. J. Lord, R. I. H. B. Dyer, A. I. Kallicharran, D. L. Amiss, †G. W. Humpage, P. A. Smith, A. M. Ferreira, C. Lethbridge, A. R. K. Pierson, *N. Gifford and D. S. Hoffman.

Umpires: K. E. Palmer and P. B. Wight.

At The Oval, July 31, August 1, 2. WARWICKSHIRE lost to SURREY by an innings and 203 runs.

## WARWICKSHIRE v YORKSHIRE

At Edgbaston, August 3, 5, 6. Drawn. Warwickshire 8 pts, Yorkshire 3 pts. Toss won by Warwickshire. Despite a mammoth first innings in which Lord scored a magnificent maiden century and Amiss registered his 96th hundred, Warwickshire were unable to fashion a win. Lord's 199 took only 223 minutes (252 balls, four 6s, 29 4s), and he shared a third-wicket partnership of 206 with Kallicharran, a record for Warwickshire against Yorkshire. Amiss's unbeaten 103 equalled the 72 hundreds hit for the county by William Quaife. Yorkshire, from 125 for eight, recovered through a stand of 74 between Peter Hartley and Carrick, whose 68 not out almost avoided the follow-on. In their second innings, Yorkshire were indebted to Boycott, who became the seventh player in history, and the first since the war, to score 100 hundreds for his county. He batted for five hours and faced 257 deliveries, from which he hit ten 4s.

### Warwickshire

R. I. H. B. Dyer c Sharp b Jarvis ..... 10
G. J. Lord run out ..................199
A. I. Kallicharran c Bairstow b P. J. Hartley . 81
D. L. Amiss not out ................103
†G. W. Humpage c Bairstow b Jarvis . 31
P. A. Smith not out ................ 9
B 1, l-b 14, w 1, n-b 7 ....... 23

1/39 2/245 3/345 4/428 (4 wkts dec.) 456

A. M. Ferreira, C. M. Old, G. C. Small, A. R. K. Pierson and *N. Gifford did not bat.

Bonus points – Warwickshire 4, Yorkshire 1.

Bowling: Jarvis 23–2–119–2; P. J. Hartley 27–1–122–1; Shaw 20–4–61–0; Swallow 18–4–71–0; Carrick 11–0–68–0.

### Yorkshire

| | First innings | | Second innings | |
|---|---|---|---|---|
| G. Boycott | c Humpage b Smith | 38 | not out | 103 |
| M. D. Moxon | lbw b Old | 5 | c Amiss b Old | 26 |
| K. Sharp | b Smith | 21 | b Smith | 3 |
| P. E. Robinson | b Ferreira | 0 | c Dyer b Smith | 0 |
| S. N. Hartley | lbw b Small | 8 | lbw b Gifford | 34 |
| *†D. L. Bairstow | lbw b Small | 21 | not out | 49 |
| P. Carrick | not out | 68 | | |
| I. G. Swallow | lbw b Ferreira | 2 | | |
| P. W. Jarvis | b Small | 5 | | |
| P. J. Hartley | b Smith | 35 | | |
| C. Shaw | b Small | 1 | | |
| | L-b 6, n-b 18 | 24 | B 4, l-b 6, n-b 12 | 22 |
| | 1/17 2/69 3/70 4/76 5/100 6/110 7/115 8/125 9/199 | 228 | 1/60 2/93 3/93 4/156 (4 wkts) | 237 |

Bonus points – Yorkshire 2, Warwickshire 4.

Bowling: *First Innings*—Small 17.5–2–42–4; Old 12–2–40–1; Smith 15–1–77–3; Ferreira 18–3–54–2; Gifford 2–1–9–0. *Second Innings*—Small 19–2–47–0; Old 29–7–69–1; Ferreira 19–3–58–0; Smith 10–2–30–2; Gifford 9–2–23–1.

Umpires: B. Dudleston and B. Leadbeater.

At Cardiff, August 10, 12, 13. WARWICKSHIRE drew with GLAMORGAN.

At Canterbury, August 14, 15, 16. WARWICKSHIRE drew with KENT.

At Cheltenham, August 17, 19, 20. WARWICKSHIRE lost to GLOUCESTERSHIRE by seven wickets.

## WARWICKSHIRE v WORCESTERSHIRE

At Edgbaston, August 24, 26, 27. Worcestershire won by 185 runs. Worcestershire 20 pts, Warwickshire 4 pts. Toss won by Warwickshire. After enjoying first use of a seaming pitch, Warwickshire eventually capitulated, giving their worst performance of the season on the second and third days. For Worcestershire, Radford and Inchmore bowled much better than their counterparts, who after the first day never came to grips with a pitch which called for accuracy to exploit the generous movement available. On the second morning Warwickshire lost nine wickets for 61, and then Worcestershire were allowed to reach 50 in eight overs, which gave Neale and his side an advantage they never let slip. Hick gave his captain good support in a stand of 108 for the fourth wicket which set up the declaration. Thereafter the home side subsided for the second time in the match.

### Worcestershire

| First innings | | Second innings | |
|---|---|---|---|
| T. S. Curtis b Wall | 7 | b Small | 5 |
| D. B. D'Oliveira c Humpage b Small | 4 | c and b Ferreira | 38 |
| D. M. Smith c Humpage b Small | 2 | retired hurt | 42 |
| D. N. Patel lbw b Small | 4 | b Small | 27 |
| *P. A. Neale c Amiss b Ferreira | 5 | not out | 92 |
| G. A. Hick b Small | 2 | c Dyer b Hoffman | 62 |
| †S. J. Rhodes c Dyer b Ferreira | 15 | not out | 30 |
| P. J. Newport hit wkt b Small | 28 | | |
| N. V. Radford b Ferreira | 34 | | |
| J. D. Inchmore c Humpage b Wall | 0 | | |
| S. M. McEwan not out | 7 | | |
| L-b 6, n-b 1 | 7 | L-b 19, w 1, n-b 2 | 22 |
| 1/7 2/13 3/17 4/17 5/19 6/41 7/52 8/90 9/90 | 115 | 1/8 2/103 3/140 4/248 (4 wkts dec.) | 318 |

Bonus points – Warwickshire 4.

Bowling: *First Innings*—Small 15–7–24–5; Wall 15–5–34–2; Hoffman 5–2–11–0; Ferreira 14.2–4–40–3. *Second Innings*—Small 25–4–97–2; Wall 19–2–57–0; Ferreira 29–6–83–1; Hoffman 10–2–34–1; Gifford 15–5–28–0.

### Warwickshire

| First innings | | Second innings | |
|---|---|---|---|
| T. A. Lloyd b Inchmore | 22 | c D'Oliveira b Inchmore | 44 |
| R. I. H. B. Dyer c D'Oliveira b Radford | 2 | c Rhodes b McEwan | 10 |
| A. I. Kallicharran c Rhodes b Radford | 7 | c Curtis b Inchmore | 12 |
| D. L. Amiss c Rhodes b Inchmore | 2 | b Patel | 27 |
| †G. W. Humpage not out | 44 | b Newport | 1 |
| P. A. Smith c Rhodes b Radford | 3 | run out | 12 |
| A. M. Ferreira b Inchmore | 1 | lbw b Patel | 22 |
| G. C. Small c Patel b Radford | 0 | not out | 21 |
| S. Wall lbw b Radford | 0 | c sub b Hick | 3 |
| *N. Gifford b Inchmore | 7 | b Inchmore | 0 |
| D. S. Hoffman c Hick b Radford | 0 | c and b Patel | 2 |
| L-b 3, w 1, n-b 2 | 6 | | |
| 1/3 2/34 3/34 4/45 5/48 6/53 7/54 8/56 9/88 | 94 | 1/37 2/65 3/70 4/73 5/106 6/106 7/142 8/151 9/151 | 154 |

Bonus points – Worcestershire 4.

Bowling: *First Innings*—Radford 16.5–3–45–6; Inchmore 17–3–42–4; Newport 2–1–1–0; Patel 1–0–3–0. *Second Innings*—Radford 12–3–34–0; Inchmore 20–5–35–3; Newport 9–4–29–1; McEwan 7–0–22–1; Patel 18–7–33–3; Hick 5–4–1–1.

Umpires: K. J. Lyons and D. R. Shepherd.

## WARWICKSHIRE v ESSEX

At Edgbaston, August 31, September 2, 3. Drawn. Warwickshire 2 pts, Essex 5pts. Toss won by Warwickshire. In a rain-ruined match, Warwickshire's batting problems continued with their third consecutive failure to obtain a batting point. They were bowled out in 48.5 overs, with Humpage yet again offering the sternest resistance. Small took three early wickets when Essex batted, but Prichard and East pulled the innings round with an unbroken sixth-wicket stand of 128. Rain, having allowed only an hour's play on the second day, washed out the final day.

### Warwickshire

| | | | |
|---|---|---|---|
| T. A. Lloyd c Prichard b Foster | 9 | G. C. Small lbw b Acfield | 2 |
| R. I. H. B. Dyer c East b Foster | 26 | *N. Gifford b Pont | 0 |
| A. I. Kallicharran lbw b Lever | 5 | D. S. Hoffman c East b Pont | 0 |
| D. L. Amiss c East b Foster | 1 | | |
| †G. W. Humpage b Pont | 49 | L-b 6, w 2 | 8 |
| Asif Din lbw b Pringle | 4 | | — |
| P. A. Smith not out | 28 | 1/23 2/33 3/38 4/75 5/82 | 142 |
| A. M. Ferreira c Acfield b Pont | 10 | 6/122 7/138 8/141 9/142 | |

Bonus points – Essex 4.

Bowling: Lever 14–4–33–1; Foster 15–3–40–3; Pringle 9–3–36–1; Pont 5.5–0–15–4; Acfield 5–1–12–1.

### Essex

| | | | |
|---|---|---|---|
| B. R. Hardie b Small | 0 | *K. W. R. Fletcher run out | 2 |
| A. W. Lilley c Gifford b Small | 0 | †D. E. East not out | 69 |
| P. J. Prichard not out | 69 | L-b 6, w 3, n-b 6 | 15 |
| K. S. McEwan c Amiss b Small | 11 | | — |
| D. R. Pringle lbw b Hoffman | 4 | 1/0 2/2 3/24 4/39 5/42 | (5 wkts) 170 |

I. L. Pont, N. A. Foster, J. K. Lever and D. L. Acfield did not bat.

Bonus points – Essex 1, Warwickshire 2.

Bowling: Small 18–5–67–3; Smith 5–0–23–0; Hoffman 7–0–21–1; Ferreira 14–4–43–0; Gifford 7–4–10–0.

Umpires: A. A. Jones and B. Leadbeater.

At Chesterfield, September 11, 12, 13. WARWICKSHIRE lost to DERBYSHIRE by ten wickets.

## WARWICKSHIRE v MIDDLESEX

At Edgbaston, September 14, 16, 17. Middlesex won by an innings and 74 runs. Middlesex 24 pts, Warwickshire 3 pts. Toss won by Warwickshire. Middlesex clinched the Championship title with an emphatic win in a match which they dominated from the start. After bowling out Warwickshire with a mixture of seam and spin in just 63 overs, they reinforced their early advantage by taking a lead of 258 through forceful contributions from Slack, Brown, Gatting and Emburey. With the pitch taking spin on the final day, only Amiss looked likely to deny Edmonds and Emburey. The result was a fitting one for both sides, Middlesex deservedly taking the title and Warwickshire slumping to fifteenth place from ninth in 1984.

## Warwickshire

| | | | |
|---|---|---|---|
| T. A. Lloyd c Slack b Williams | 32 | – c Radley b Edmonds | 28 |
| R. I. H. B. Dyer c Radley b Williams | 52 | – b Edmonds | 28 |
| A. I. Kallicharran lbw b Emburey | 18 | – st Downton b Emburey | 0 |
| D. L. Amiss c Downton b Daniel | 6 | – c Brown b Emburey | 39 |
| †G. W. Humpage c Cowans b Emburey | 1 | – c Radley b Edmonds | 8 |
| Asif Din c Edmonds b Emburey | 3 | – c Slack b Edmonds | 29 |
| P. A. Smith b Daniel | 1 | – b Daniel | 20 |
| A. M. Ferreira c Slack b Williams | 34 | – c Slack b Emburey | 2 |
| G. C. Small not out | 26 | – c Gatting b Emburey | 0 |
| S. Wall b Emburey | 4 | – not out | 17 |
| *N. Gifford c Slack b Daniel | 0 | – b Daniel | 4 |
| L-b 4, n-b 6 | 10 | L-b 4, n-b 5 | 9 |
| 1/40 2/72 3/89 4/97 5/102 6/109 7/151 8/155 9/178 | 187 | 1/56 2/57 3/75 4/91 5/137 6/141 7/146 8/146 9/176 | 184 |

Bonus points – Warwickshire 1, Middlesex 4.

Bowling: *First Innings*—Daniel 14–3–51–3; Williams 13–2–43–3; Cowans 10–2–26–0; Gatting 2–0–6–0; Emburey 21–8–47–4; Edmonds 3–1–10–0. *Second Innings*—Daniel 9.3–1–37–2; Williams 3–0–16–0; Emburey 33–9–64–4; Edmonds 27–9–63–4.

## Middlesex

| | |
|---|---|
| W. N. Slack b Gifford | 74 |
| K. R. Brown b Gifford | 67 |
| *M. W. Gatting lbw b Small | 76 |
| R. O. Butcher b Ferreira | 1 |
| C. T. Radley c and b Gifford | 12 |
| †P. R. Downton c sub b Ferreira | 40 |
| J. E. Emburey c Humpage b Gifford | 68 |
| N. F. Williams c Small b Ferreira | 46 |
| P. H. Edmonds not out | 29 |
| N. G. Cowans st Humpage b Gifford | 0 |
| W. W. Daniel run out | 3 |
| L-b 21, n-b 8 | 29 |
| 1/129 2/164 3/180 4/209 5/268 6/318 7/392 8/433 9/438 | 445 |

Bonus points – Middlesex 4, Warwickshire 2 (Score at 100 overs: 300-5).

Bowling: Small 28–5–96–1; Smith 4–0–19–0; Wall 25–3–87–0; Ferreira 29–7–94–3; Gifford 48–8–128–5.

Umpires: H. D. Bird and C. Cook.

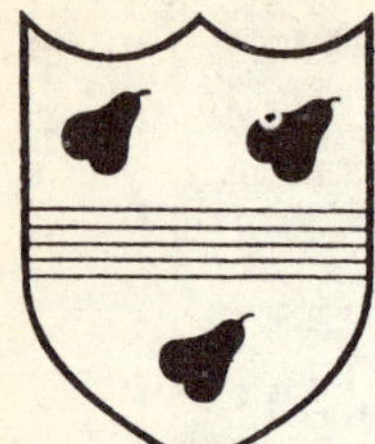

# WORCESTERSHIRE

*President:* The Duke of Westminster
*Chairman:* Dr J. A. Burnett
*Chairman, Cricket Committee:* M. G. Jones
*Secretary:* M. D. Vockins
County Ground, New Road, Worcester
WR2 4QQ (Telephone: 0905-422694)
*Captain:* P. A. Neale
*Coach:* B. L. D'Oliveira

If there were an award for talent-spotting it would surely have gone to Worcestershire in 1985. The signing of Neal Radford was one of the more inspired transactions of recent times, the former Lancashire paceman becoming the only bowler in the country to finish the season with more than 100 first-class wickets. No-one had achieved that feat at New Road since Norman Gifford in 1970. Equally successful in his début season with the county was the 21-year-old wicket-keeper, Steven Rhodes, whose 57 dismissals and 538 runs were rewarded with selection for the England B tour during the winter of 1985-86. Where else on the county circuit did two newcomers so distinguish themselves last season?

But the success story did not end there. David Smith, despite a succession of injury problems, ended only his second season at Worcester with a place in the England party for the West Indies. With his reputation for being difficult behind him, the elegant left-hander topped the batting averages with 1,113 runs from 28 first-class innings, including Championship centuries against Hampshire, Glamorgan and Northamptonshire. He also made career-best scores in the two limited-overs knockout competitions, hitting 126 against Warwickshire in the Benson and Hedges Cup and 109 against Lancashire in the NatWest Bank Trophy.

Then there was Graeme Hick, the prolific young Zimbabwean who looks set to follow in Glenn Turner's footsteps and become Worcestershire's leading overseas batsman. He started the summer with seven centuries outside the first-class game before joining up with the Zimbabweans. For them he scored 230 in the opening game against Oxford University, one of the highest maiden first-class centuries ever made, and followed this with 192 against Glamorgan. On returning to Worcestershire he hit his first Championship century, an innings of 174 not out against Somerset, to which he added 128 against Northamptonshire. Four other batsmen – making six in all – topped 1,000 runs for the season, the captain, Phil Neale, achieving the target for the seventh time. Damian D'Oliveira, awarded his county cap in July, made a career-best 139 against Sussex at Eastbourne and registered a maiden one-day hundred in the John Player Sunday League. This provided the first instance of a father (Basil) and son scoring centuries in the competition.

Dipak Patel, who with Radford was put on stand-by for England's two winter tours, had an indifferent season by his own standards, scoring 1,042 runs and taking 34 wickets. Kapil Dev might also have reached the 1,000 mark but for having to cut short the season to captain India in Sri Lanka.

He topped the bowling averages with 37 wickets at 21.75, though there was never any doubt that Radford would carry off the Worcestershire Supporters' Association Player of the Year award.

The veteran John Inchmore, in his benefit year, was a popular winner of the Dick Lygon award for the clubman of the year. Philip Newport, despite missing the end of the season with a pelvic injury, was the second-highest wicket-taker, his 46 victims in the Championship representing his best season to date.

Yet, for all these individual successes, it was only in the final few weeks of the summer that Worcestershire underlined their collective talents by climbing into an elevated position in the Championship table. They started August in sixteenth place. But three wins in four matches over Lancashire, Warwickshire and Kent hoisted them up into fourth position, with Leicestershire denying them another success by narrowly avoiding an innings defeat at Grace Road. Another win over Somerset consolidated Worcestershire's standing, though defeat in the final game against Northamptonshire saw them slip to finish fifth, a rise of five places on the previous season.

Strangely, Worcestershire were found wanting in the John Player Sunday League, slipping from fifth in 1984 to sixteenth. However, they did qualify for the quarter-finals of the Benson and Hedges Cup for the first time for five years, after winning their qualifying group, and they reached the semi-finals of the NatWest Bank Trophy, their best in the 60-overs competition since 1974. Unfortunately, the weather ruined their hopes of further progress in both competitions. Worcestershire "lost" to Middlesex in the Benson and Hedges because their opponents had a better striking-rate in the zonal games. Ironically Worcestershire had won their qualifying group, and Middlesex had finished second in theirs. Then, after scoring 232 for eight against Nottinghamshire in the NatWest semi-final, they had the visitors struggling when rain and bad light curtailed play for the day. Replanning their strategy overnight, Nottinghamshire got home next morning with four balls to spare.

Two operations on a shoulder injury restricted Paul Pridgeon, the previous season's top wicket-taker, to only one first-class outing, against Cambridge. He hopes to be fully recovered for 1986. David Humphries, having lost the wicket-keeping role to Rhodes, was released at the end of the season, together with David Banks, Simon Kimber and Harshad Patel. Kapil Dev's registration has been retained, but with the Indians touring England in 1986, and his original contract now expired, it is open to question whether he will play a full season at New Road again. With or without him, however, Worcestershire have the talent and potential to emerge as genuine challengers for honours in 1986. – C.M.

## WORCESTERSHIRE 1985

[*Bill Smith*

*Back row:* N. V. Radford, D. B. D'Oliveira, T. S. Curtis, M. J. Weston, P. J. Newport, S. M. McEwan, R. M. Ellcock, R. K. Illingworth, S. J. Rhodes. *Front row:* Kapil Dev, J. D. Inchmore, P. A. Neale (*captain*), D. N. Patel, D. M. Smith. *Insets:* D. A. Banks, G. A. Hick, A. P. Pridgeon.

## WORCESTERSHIRE RESULTS

*All first-class matches – Played 27: Won 6, Lost 6, Drawn 15.*

*County Championship matches – Played 24: Won 5, Lost 6, Drawn 13.*

*Bonus points – Batting 65, Bowling 68.*

*Competition placings – Britannic Assurance County Championship, 5th; NatWest Bank Trophy, s-f; Benson and Hedges Cup, q-f; John Player League, 16th.*

## BRITANNIC ASSURANCE CHAMPIONSHIP AVERAGES

### BATTING

| | *Birthplace* | *M* | *I* | *NO* | *R* | *HI* | *Avge* |
|---|---|---|---|---|---|---|---|
| ‡D. M. Smith ..... | *Balham* | 18 | 27 | 4 | 1,113 | 112 | 48.39 |
| G. A. Hick ....... | *Salisbury, Rhodesia* | 10 | 15 | 1 | 664 | 174* | 47.42 |
| Kapil Dev ....... | *Chandigarh, India* | 12 | 21 | 2 | 816 | 100 | 42.94 |
| ‡P. A. Neale ...... | *Scunthorpe* | 24 | 40 | 9 | 1,290 | 152* | 41.61 |
| ‡T. S. Curtis ...... | *Chislehurst* | 24 | 42 | 2 | 1,279 | 126* | 31.97 |
| ‡D. B. D'Oliveira .. | *Cape Town, SA* | 24 | 41 | 2 | 1,200 | 139 | 30.76 |
| ‡D. N. Patel ...... | *Nairobi, Kenya* | 24 | 39 | 3 | 1,006 | 88 | 27.94 |
| M. J. Weston ..... | *Worcester* | 17 | 27 | 1 | 706 | 132 | 27.15 |
| S. J. Rhodes ...... | *Bradford* | 24 | 32 | 12 | 518 | 58* | 25.90 |
| P. J. Newport .... | *High Wycombe* | 16 | 23 | 8 | 277 | 36 | 18.46 |
| D. A. Banks ...... | *Penselt* | 4 | 5 | 1 | 70 | 30 | 17.50 |
| ‡N. V. Radford .... | *Luanshya, N. Rhodesia* | 23 | 25 | 7 | 306 | 57* | 17.00 |
| ‡J. D. Inchmore ... | *Ashington* | 16 | 9 | 2 | 100 | 24 | 14.28 |
| R. K. Illingworth .. | *Bradford* | 18 | 19 | 8 | 129 | 39* | 11.72 |
| S. M. McEwan ... | *Worcester* | 9 | 7 | 4 | 12 | 7* | 4.00 |

Also batted: R. M. Ellcock (*Bridgetown, Barbados*) (1 match) 3.

* *Signifies not out.* ‡ *Denotes county cap.*

The following played a total of twelve three-figure innings for Worcestershire in County Championship matches – D. M. Smith 3, D. B. D'Oliveira 2, G. A. Hick 2, P. A. Neale 2, T. S. Curtis 1, Kapil Dev 1, M. J. Weston 1.

### BOWLING

| | *O* | *M* | *R* | *W* | *BB* | *Avge* |
|---|---|---|---|---|---|---|
| Kapil Dev ........ | 304.5 | 83 | 805 | 37 | 4-56 | 21.75 |
| P. J. Newport ..... | 334.2 | 57 | 1,089 | 46 | 5-18 | 23.67 |
| N. V. Radford ..... | 764.4 | 130 | 2,416 | 100 | 6-45 | 24.16 |
| J. D. Inchmore .... | 320.5 | 66 | 806 | 30 | 4-42 | 26.86 |
| S. M. McEwan .... | 169 | 28 | 611 | 16 | 3-47 | 38.18 |
| D. N. Patel ....... | 381 | 101 | 1,084 | 28 | 3-33 | 38.71 |
| R. K. Illingworth ... | 344.4 | 92 | 940 | 24 | 4-76 | 39.16 |
| M. J. Weston ...... | 259.5 | 66 | 746 | 17 | 3-37 | 43.88 |

Also bowled: D. B. D'Oliveira 9–0–30–1; R. M. Ellcock 28–0–91–0; G. A. Hick 74–17–265–5.

At Lord's, April 27, 29, 30. WORCESTERSHIRE lost to MIDDLESEX by eight wickets.

## WORCESTERSHIRE v GLOUCESTERSHIRE

At Worcester, May 8, 9, 10. Gloucestershire won by 40 runs. Gloucestershire 23 pts, Worcestershire 5 pts. Toss won by Worcestershire. The home side, needing 307 to win with all second-innings wickets standing on the final day, slumped to 79 for five before D'Oliveira fashioned a splendid fightback with 99 off only 81 deliveries. In 101 minutes, he hammered three 6s and thirteen 4s, dominating a seventh-wicket stand of 70 in eight overs with Kapil Dev. But Bainbridge, who had steadied Gloucestershire's first innings, removed both batsmen in quick succession, trapping D'Oliveira lbw with a delivery which kept low. Worcestershire still required 79 off the final twenty overs, but their last two wickets could add only 39.

### Gloucestershire

| | | | |
|---|---|---|---|
| A. W. Stovold b Newport | 28 | – lbw b Kapil Dev | 19 |
| P. W. Romaines c Patel b Radford | 4 | – c Kapil Dev b Radford | 12 |
| C. W. J. Athey c Rhodes b Radford | 30 | – c Rhodes b Kapil Dev | 27 |
| P. Bainbridge lbw b Radford | 83 | – lbw b Kapil Dev | 0 |
| B. F. Davison lbw b Kapil Dev | 35 | – b Weston | 23 |
| K. M. Curran c Kapil Dev b Weston | 0 | – b Radford | 33 |
| J. W. Lloyds b Kapil Dev | 9 | – c D'Oliveira b Weston | 15 |
| *D. A. Graveney c Rhodes b Newport | 35 | – lbw b Kapil Dev | 0 |
| †R. C. Russell c Kapil Dev b Newport | 9 | – st Rhodes b Patel | 24 |
| D. V. Lawrence b Newport | 15 | – lbw b Radford | 14 |
| G. E. Sainsbury not out | 0 | – not out | 8 |
| B 4, l-b 11, w 2, n-b 5 | 22 | B 7, l-b 10, w 5, n-b 3 | 25 |
| 1/14 2/44 3/81 4/147 5/158 6/187 7/218 8/252 9/257 | 270 | 1/26 2/48 3/48 4/63 5/115 6/119 7/123 8/143 9/162 | 200 |

Bonus points – Gloucestershire 3, Worcestershire 4.

Bowling: *First Innings*—Kapil Dev 20–6–74–2; Radford 25–6–68–3; Newport 11.4–2–48–4; Weston 19–7–49–1; Illingworth 4–1–16–0. *Second Innings*—Kapil Dev 25–7–63–4; Radford 24–5–57–3; Weston 26–12–58–2; Patel 3.4–1–5–1.

### Worcestershire

| | | | |
|---|---|---|---|
| M. J. Weston c Russell b Bainbridge | 47 | – (3) c Graveney b Sainsbury | 10 |
| T. S. Curtis b Lawrence | 3 | – c and b Bainbridge | 24 |
| D. M. Smith c Sainsbury b Lawrence | 15 | – (4) c Stovold b Sainsbury | 11 |
| D. N. Patel c Romaines b Curran | 15 | – (5) c Russell b Bainbridge | 2 |
| *P. A. Neale run out | 19 | – (6) c Russell b Lawrence | 21 |
| D. B. D'Oliveira c Graveney b Sainsbury | 14 | – (7) lbw b Bainbridge | 99 |
| Kapil Dev c and b Bainbridge | 9 | – (8) c Graveney b Bainbridge | 23 |
| P. J. Newport c Lloyds b Curran | 18 | – (9) c Romaines b Lawrence | 23 |
| N. V. Radford c Lloyds b Sainsbury | 0 | – (10) b Bainbridge | 10 |
| †S. J. Rhodes not out | 9 | – (1) lbw b Sainsbury | 18 |
| R. K. Illingworth c Athey b Lawrence | 3 | – not out | 6 |
| L-b 2, w 1, n-b 9 | 12 | L-b 5, n-b 14 | 19 |
| 1/21 2/56 3/86 4/88 5/120 6/122 7/131 8/132 9/157 | 164 | 1/41 2/59 3/63 4/65 5/79 6/138 7/208 8/227 9/247 | 266 |

Bonus points – Worcestershire 1, Gloucestershire 4.

Bowling: *First Innings*—Lawrence 12.4–1–64–3; Curran 12–4–27–2; Sainsbury 16–7–37–2; Bainbridge 16–3–34–2. *Second Innings*—Lawrence 15.3–1–92–2; Curran 22–4–62–0; Sainsbury 17–7–47–3; Bainbridge 17–4–60–5.

Umpires: K. E. Palmer and R. A. White.

At Worcester, May 11, 12, 13. WORCESTERSHIRE drew with AUSTRALIANS (See Australian tour section).

At The Parks, May 22, 23. WORCESTERSHIRE beat OXFORD UNIVERSITY by an innings and 22 runs.

## WORCESTERSHIRE v WARWICKSHIRE

At Worcester, May 25, 26, 27. Drawn. Worcestershire 5 pts, Warwickshire 7 pts. Toss won by Worcestershire. Rain shortened the second day by 23 overs, and washed out the final day altogether after Warwickshire had established a first-innings lead of 101. Amiss, with his 92nd first-class century, enabled the visitors to recover after they had lost their first four wickets to Radford. Gifford declared at their overnight score. In turn Kapil Dev, with 56 off 62 balls, and Curtis, in the anchor role, pulled Worcestershire round from 97 for five.

### Warwickshire

| | | | |
|---|---|---|---|
| T. A. Lloyd c Smith b Radford | 13 | – not out | 8 |
| R. I. H. B. Dyer b Radford | 45 | – lbw b Radford | 0 |
| A. I. Kallicharran c Rhodes b Radford | 63 | | |
| D. L. Amiss not out | 100 | | |
| †G. W. Humpage c Rhodes b Radford | 0 | | |
| P. A. Smith lbw b Weston | 9 | | |
| A. M. Ferreira b Weston | 43 | | |
| C. M. Old b Patel | 7 | | |
| G. C. Small lbw b Patel | 0 | | |
| *N. Gifford b Kapil Dev | 8 | | |
| D. S. Hoffman not out | 13 | – (3) not out | 4 |
| L-b 5, w 2, n-b 7 | 14 | L-b 2, w 1, n-b 1 | 4 |
| 1/25 2/110 3/150 4/150 5/167 6/246 7/253 8/257 9/294 (9 wkts dec.) | 315 | 1/8 (1 wkt) | 16 |

Bonus points – Warwickshire 3, Worcestershire 3 (Score at 100 overs: 253-7).

Bowling: *First Innings*—Kapil Dev 23–5–50–1; Radford 28–3–110–4; Patel 18–8–35–2; Inchmore 17–3–51–0; Illingworth 13–4–28–0; Weston 14–1–36–2. *Second Innings*—Kapil Dev 4–1–6–0; Radford 3–0–8–1.

### Worcestershire

| | |
|---|---|
| M. J. Weston c and b Old | 10 |
| T. S. Curtis c Smith b Small | 66 |
| D. M. Smith lbw b Hoffman | 10 |
| *P. A. Neale c Humpage b Small | 5 |
| D. N. Patel b Small | 3 |
| D. B. D'Oliveira c Humpage b Old | 5 |
| Kapil Dev b Gifford | 56 |
| †S. J. Rhodes lbw b Ferreira | 7 |
| R. K. Illingworth c Humpage b Gifford | 5 |
| N. V. Radford b Ferreira | 9 |
| J. D. Inchmore not out | 15 |
| B 3, l-b 12, w 6, n-b 2 | 23 |
| 1/37 2/60 3/72 4/82 5/97 6/170 7/178 8/186 9/190 | 214 |

Bonus points – Worcestershire 2, Warwickshire 4.

Bowling: Small 20–6–53–3; Old 17–6–35–2; Hoffman 10–2–37–1; Ferreira 20.5–5–55–2; Gifford 11–6–19–2.

Umpires: A. A. Jones and D. O. Oslear.

At Canterbury, June 1, 3, 4. WORCESTERSHIRE beat KENT by seven wickets.

At Abergavenny, June 8, 10, 11. WORCESTERSHIRE drew with GLAMORGAN.

At Fenner's, June 12, 13, 14. WORCESTERSHIRE drew with CAMBRIDGE UNIVERSITY.

## WORCESTERSHIRE v SURREY

At Worcester, June 15, 17, 18. Drawn. Worcestershire 5 pts, Surrey 6 pts. Toss won by Worcestershire. Only fifteen wickets fell for 993 runs, with four batsmen scoring centuries. Curtis (126 not out) and Weston (132) broke Worcestershire's 84-year-old record fifth-wicket partnership against Surrey with a stand of 227 on the opening day, Curtis batting in all for a marathon six hours, five minutes. Clinton replied with 117 in 248 minutes before Surrey declared their first innings 50 runs behind. Neale then weighed in with an undefeated 152, including 24 4s and the 6 off Needham with which he reached three figures, to set the visitors 304 to win off 58 overs. Surrey had reached 82 for two off 28 before bad light forced an early finish.

### Worcestershire

| | | | |
|---|---|---|---|
| T. S. Curtis not out | 126 | – lbw b Thomas | 13 |
| D. B. D'Oliveira lbw b Thomas | 0 | – lbw b Thomas | 1 |
| D. M. Smith lbw b Pauline | 49 | | |
| *P. A. Neale lbw b Pauline | 0 | – (3) not out | 152 |
| D. N. Patel c Jesty b Butcher | 25 | – (4) b Thomas | 29 |
| M. J. Weston b Butcher | 132 | – (5) c Thomas b Pauline | 33 |
| P. J. Newport not out | 3 | – not out | 2 |
| †S. J. Rhodes (did not bat) | | – (6) c Waterman b Pauline | 0 |
| B 4, l-b 7, w 1, n-b 7 | 19 | B 4, l-b 12, w 5, n-b 2 | 23 |
| 1/7 2/65 3/65 4/117 5/344 (5 wkts dec.) | 354 | 1/1 2/42 3/129 4/217 5/217 (5 wkts dec.) | 253 |

R. K. Illingworth, N. V. Radford and J. D. Inchmore did not bat.

Bonus points – Worcestershire 4, Surrey 2 (Score at 100 overs: 348-5).

Bowling: *First Innings*—Thomas 21–4–55–1; Gray 19–3–77–0; Pauline 18–2–71–2; Butcher 7–1–38–2; Waterman 9–2–24–0; Needham 11–2–22–0; Pocock 18–4–56–0. *Second Innings*—Thomas 21–5–59–3; Gray 19–5–67–0; Pocock 1–0–5–0; Waterman 8–2–22–0; Pauline 10–1–46–2; Needham 8–1–38–0.

### Surrey

| | | | |
|---|---|---|---|
| A. R. Butcher b Patel | 66 | – lbw b Radford | 10 |
| G. S. Clinton b Illingworth | 117 | – not out | 46 |
| A. Needham lbw b Radford | 63 | – run out | 1 |
| *T. E. Jesty not out | 28 | – not out | 17 |
| M. A. Lynch not out | 11 | | |
| B 1, l-b 13, n-b 5 | 19 | L-b 5, w 1, n-b 2 | 8 |
| 1/121 2/227 3/288 (3 wkts dec.) | 304 | 1/26 2/54 (2 wkts) | 82 |

D. B. Pauline, †C. J. Richards, D. J. Thomas, P. I. Pocock, A. H. Gray and P. A. Waterman did not bat.

Bonus points – Surrey 4, Worcestershire 1.

Bowling: *First Innings*—Radford 19–3–63–1; Inchmore 13–2–31–0; Newport 9–1–42–0; Weston 2–1–13–0; Illingworth 17–4–67–1; Patel 18–2–74–1. *Second Innings*—Radford 7–0–30–1; Inchmore 5–0–21–0; Weston 9–3–18–0; Newport 7–3–8–0.

Umpires: J. H. Hampshire and D. R. Shepherd.

At Harrogate, June 22, 23, 24. WORCESTERSHIRE drew with YORKSHIRE.

## WORCESTERSHIRE v MIDDLESEX

At Worcester, June 26, 27, 28. Middlesex won by three wickets. Middlesex 21 pts, Worcestershire 2 pts. Toss won by Middlesex. Worcestershire were bowled out twice in the span of 111 overs after the entire first day had been lost to the weather. Middlesex declared 88 runs behind on the first innings as soon as Barlow (103 not out) had completed his third century of the season, whereupon they then dismissed the home side for 137 with Rose, making his Championship début in place of Daniel, who was suffering from a stomach upset, taking six for 41 in ten overs. He captured his first three wickets in seventeen deliveries as Worcestershire slumped to 55 for six. Needing 226 to win in 55 overs, Middlesex lost both openers with only 11 on the board. But a swashbuckling 120 off 111 balls from Butcher, who hit fifteen 4s and two 6s in 142 minutes, saw them home with 25 balls to spare for a victory that put them top of the Championship table.

### Worcestershire

| | | | |
|---|---|---|---|
| T. S. Curtis b Williams | 1 | – b Cowans | 7 |
| D. B. D'Oliveira c Metson b Williams | 28 | – c Sykes b Williams | 1 |
| *P. A. Neale c Sykes b Hughes | 18 | – c Butcher b Rose | 12 |
| D. N. Patel lbw b Hughes | 48 | – b Hughes | 6 |
| Kapil Dev lbw b Cowans | 49 | – c Hughes b Rose | 38 |
| M. J. Weston c Metson b Hughes | 5 | – b Rose | 0 |
| D. A. Banks lbw b Cowans | 6 | – lbw b Rose | 1 |
| P. J. Newport c Barlow b Cowans | 6 | – c Slack b Rose | 18 |
| †S. J. Rhodes not out | 46 | – c Metson b Rose | 28 |
| R. K. Illingworth run out | 13 | – c Metson b Williams | 1 |
| N. V. Radford c sub b Rose | 7 | – not out | 16 |
| L-b 9, w 4, n-b 6 | 19 | B 5, l-b 1, n-b 3 | 9 |
| 1/17 2/55 3/55 4/129 5/146 6/174 7/180 8/185 9/229 | 246 | 1/13 2/13 3/32 4/36 5/45 6/55 7/78 8/91 9/100 | 137 |

Bonus points – Worcestershire 2, Middlesex 4.

Bowling: *First Innings*—Cowans 19–4–71–3; Williams 15–1–50–2; Hughes 17–5–38–3; Rose 13.2–0–57–1; Sykes 5–0–21–0. *Second Innings*—Cowans 6–1–11–1; Williams 12–4–34–2; Hughes 12–3–45–1; Rose 10.5–2–41–6.

### Middlesex

| | | | |
|---|---|---|---|
| G. D. Barlow not out | 103 | – c Rhodes b Radford | 9 |
| W. N. Slack b Patel | 35 | – b Kapil Dev | 0 |
| K. P. Tomlins c Rhodes b Illingworth | 7 | – c Illingworth b Radford | 15 |
| R. O. Butcher not out | 7 | – c Rhodes b Kapil Dev | 120 |
| *C. T. Radley (did not bat) | | – b Kapil Dev | 37 |
| N. F. Williams (did not bat) | | – lbw b Illingworth | 1 |
| J. F. Sykes (did not bat) | | – not out | 24 |
| G. D. Rose (did not bat) | | – b Kapil Dev | 4 |
| †C. P. Metson (did not bat) | | – not out | 14 |
| B 2, l-b 4 | 6 | L-b 2 | 2 |
| 1/100 2/133 (2 wkts dec.) | 158 | 1/1 2/11 3/46 4/182 5/183 6/191 7/195 (7 wkts) | 226 |

S. P. Hughes and N. G. Cowans did not bat.

Bonus point – Middlesex 1.

Bowling: *First Innings*—Kapil Dev 6–0–30–0; Radford 11–0–39–0; Newport 9–2–32–0; Weston 2–0–10–0; Patel 10–5–10–1; Illingworth 7–2–31–1. *Second Innings*—Kapil Dev 16–0–74–4; Radford 11–0–50–2; Newport 4–2–20–0; Illingworth 15.5–1–54–1; Weston 4–1–26–0.

Umpires: C. Cook and B. J. Meyer.

## WORCESTERSHIRE v YORKSHIRE

At Worcester, June 29, July 1, 2. Drawn. Worcestershire 11 pts, Yorkshire 7 pts. Toss won by Worcestershire, who failed by only 1 run to reach a victory target of 292 in 55 overs but were rewarded with an extra eight points for being the side batting second in a match in which the scores finished level. They needed 11 runs off the last over, and when Newport hit Fletcher's fourth delivery for 6, the requirement was down to 2. However, only another single came from the last two balls. Patel and Neale had set up the thrilling finish with a stand of 117 in 23 overs, Neale falling to a brilliant catch by Bairstow before Kapil Dev provided Pickles with his first Championship wicket. The Saturday had produced Yorkshire's highest opening partnership for 53 years – since Holmes and Sutcliffe's 555 against Essex – with a stand of 351 between Boycott, who was out off the last ball of the day for 184, his 147th first-class century, and Moxon, who made a career-best 168. Moxon's six-hour innings included one 6 and twenty 4s, while Boycott hit 21 boundaries. It was the latter's first partnership of 300 for his county.

### Yorkshire

| | | | |
|---|---|---|---|
| G. Boycott c Newport b Radford | 184 | – c Patel b Kapil Dev | 50 |
| M. D. Moxon c and b Weston | 168 | | |
| A. A. Metcalfe c Rhodes b Kapil Dev | 5 | – (2) c Patel b Kapil Dev | 4 |
| K. Sharp not out | 9 | – (3) c D'Oliveira b Radford | 4 |
| J. D. Love (did not bat) | | – (4) b Newport | 48 |
| *†D. L. Bairstow (did not bat) | | – (5) not out | 49 |
| A. Sidebottom (did not bat) | | – not out | 0 |
| P. Carrick (did not bat) | | – (6) c Rhodes b Kapil Dev | 21 |
| L-b 21, n-b 2 | 23 | B 1, l-b 15, n-b 2 | 18 |
| 1/351 2/363 3/389 (3 wkts dec.) | 389 | 1/7 2/12 3/109 4/124 5/189 (5 wkts dec.) | 194 |

C. S. Pickles, S. D. Fletcher and C. Shaw did not bat.

Bonus points – Yorkshire 4 (Score at 100 overs: 307-0).

Bowling: *First Innings*—Kapil Dev 22–5–54–1; Radford 24.5–5–84–1; Newport 23–3–73–0; Illingworth 23–2–84–0; Weston 20–2–67–1; D'Oliveira 1–0–6–0. *Second Innings*—Kapil Dev 14–3–58–3; Radford 18–1–74–1; Newport 9–3–23–1; Weston 6–0–23–0.

### Worcestershire

| | | | |
|---|---|---|---|
| T. S. Curtis c Boycott b Sidebottom | 51 | – (2) c Bairstow b Sidebottom | 17 |
| D. B. D'Oliveira c sub b Fletcher | 0 | – (6) st Bairstow b Carrick | 37 |
| *P. A. Neale lbw b Sidebottom | 4 | – c Bairstow b Fletcher | 58 |
| D. N. Patel c Love b Shaw | 32 | – lbw b Sidebottom | 78 |
| Kapil Dev b Fletcher | 44 | – lbw b Pickles | 9 |
| M. J. Weston lbw b Sidebottom | 12 | – (7) b Fletcher | 26 |
| D. A. Banks c Bairstow b Fletcher | 30 | – (8) b Fletcher | 12 |
| †S. J. Rhodes not out | 58 | – (1) lbw b Fletcher | 20 |
| P. J. Newport not out | 23 | – (10) not out | 7 |
| N. V. Radford (did not bat) | | – (9) not out | 10 |
| B 1, l-b 14, w 1, n-b 22 | 38 | L-b 9, n-b 8 | 17 |
| 1/1 2/9 3/60 4/126 5/167 6/172 7/233 (7 wkts dec.) | 292 | 1/35 2/47 3/164 4/191 5/215 6/258 7/266 8/284 (8 wkts) | 291 |

R. K. Illingworth did not bat.

Bonus points – Worcestershire 3, Yorkshire 3 (Score at 100 overs: 268-7).

Bowling: *First Innings*—Sidebottom 20–2–76–3; Fletcher 19–8–39–3; Shaw 27–8–70–1; Pickles 27–6–70–0; Carrick 19–9–22–0. *Second Innings*—Sidebottom 17–1–88–2; Fletcher 19–1–91–4; Shaw 10–3–54–0; Pickles 4–0–27–1; Carrick 5–0–22–1.

Umpires: C. Cook and B. J. Meyer.

## WORCESTERSHIRE v DERBYSHIRE

At Worcester, July 6, 8, 9. Derbyshire won by three wickets. Derbyshire 22 pts, Worcestershire 7 pts. Toss won by Worcestershire. A second-wicket stand of 193 in 55 overs between Wright and Anderson paved the way for an improbable Derbyshire victory after Worcestershire had looked to be in control throughout the first two days. Although Finney enjoyed a ten-ball spell of four for 0 in Worcestershire's first innings, Kapil Dev and Radford took four wickets each in the visitors' reply to secure a lead of 81; and then Neale completed his third century of the season on the final morning prior to setting Derbyshire a target of 335 off 85 overs. Wright's 23rd century for Derbyshire, off 170 balls, included seventeen 4s. But from 244 for two, when they needed 91 to win off nineteen overs, Derbyshire slipped to 326 for seven before clinching an exciting win with eight balls to spare.

### Worcestershire

| | | | |
|---|---|---|---|
| T. S. Curtis lbw b Finney | 22 | – b Finney | 10 |
| D. B. D'Oliveira lbw b Finney | 63 | – lbw b Newman | 34 |
| *P. A. Neale c Maher b Warner | 46 | – c Warner b Russell | 102 |
| D. N. Patel c Anderson b Miller | 88 | – b Miller | 43 |
| Kapil Dev b Finney | 16 | – (6) not out | 3 |
| M. J. Weston lbw b Finney | 0 | – (5) c Barnett b Russell | 47 |
| †S. J. Rhodes c Miller b Finney | 0 | | |
| P. J. Newport lbw b Finney | 0 | | |
| N. V. Radford c Roberts b Warner | 38 | | |
| R. K. Illingworth c Miller b Warner | 1 | | |
| S. M. McEwan not out | 0 | | |
| B 4, l-b 10, w 7 | 21 | B 1, l-b 9, w 2, n-b 2 | 14 |
| 1/38 2/142 3/149 4/179 5/179 6/179 7/179 8/271 9/285 | 295 | 1/28 2/65 3/147 4/247 5/253 (5 wkts dec.) | 253 |

Bonus points – Worcestershire 3, Derbyshire 4.

Bowling: *First Innings*—Warner 19–3–88–3; Finney 22–4–62–6; Newman 15–5–37–0; Russell 16–4–61–0; Miller 14.5–1–33–1. *Second Innings*—Warner 16–2–58–0; Finney 15–4–38–1; Russell 16.4–4–34–2; Newman 19–3–72–1; Miller 10–1–41–1.

### Derbyshire

| | | | |
|---|---|---|---|
| *K. J. Barnett b McEwan | 27 | – c Radford b McEwan | 29 |
| I. S. Anderson c Rhodes b Kapil Dev | 36 | – c Rhodes b Illingworth | 94 |
| †B. J. M. Maher c Patel b Kapil Dev | 9 | | |
| J. G. Wright lbw b Kapil Dev | 7 | – (3) c and b Illingworth | 117 |
| B. Roberts c Curtis b Radford | 0 | – (4) b Illingworth | 30 |
| R. Sharma lbw b Radford | 35 | – (5) b Illingworth | 8 |
| G. Miller c Rhodes b Radford | 6 | – (6) not out | 24 |
| P. G. Newman c Patel b McEwan | 21 | – (7) lbw b Kapil Dev | 10 |
| A. E. Warner lbw b Kapil Dev | 50 | – (8) c Radford b Kapil Dev | 0 |
| R. J. Finney b Radford | 4 | – (9) not out | 6 |
| P. E. Russell not out | 3 | | |
| L-b 9, n-b 7 | 16 | L-b 9, w 1, n-b 8 | 18 |
| 1/48 2/60 3/76 4/81 5/81 6/92 7/121 8/202 9/203 | 214 | 1/51 2/244 3/259 4/273 5/304 6/326 7/326 (7 wkts) | 336 |

Bonus points – Derbyshire 2, Worcestershire 4.

Bowling: *First Innings*—Kapil Dev 26–9–56–4; Radford 24–3–78–4; McEwan 10–3–29–2; Newport 6–0–33–0; Illingworth 3–1–5–0; Patel 2–1–4–0. *Second Innings*—Kapil Dev 13–3–51–2; Radford 17–3–73–0; McEwan 7–2–26–1; Newport 7–3–16–0; Patel 23–3–85–0; Illingworth 17.4–2–76–4.

Umpires: B. Dudleston and D. O. Oslear.

At Gloucester, July 10, 11, 12. WORCESTERSHIRE lost to GLOUCESTERSHIRE by 110 runs.

At Portsmouth, July 13, 15, 16. WORCESTERSHIRE drew with HAMPSHIRE.

## WORCESTERSHIRE v GLAMORGAN

At Worcester, July 24, 25, 26. Drawn. Worcestershire 8 pts, Glamorgan 6 pts. Toss won by Glamorgan. Worcestershire looked poised for their first home Championship win of the season when they had 28 overs in which to capture the visitors' last four wickets. But they were thwarted, in the main, by Ontong, who held the Glamorgan tail together until the close. On the opening day, Smith completed his third century in ten days, hitting thirteen 4s in his 102, to which Younis responded with a typically fluent 100 not out, hitting two 6s and twelve 4s. Glamorgan enterprisingly declared 40 runs behind, and on the last day were eventually left with 55 overs to score 266 for victory. They were in trouble against the home seam attack, even though Kapil Dev was unable to bowl because of a calf strain, before Ontong came to the rescue, playing out nineteen overs with Davies and the last nine with Price.

### Worcestershire

| | | | |
|---|---|---|---|
| T. S. Curtis c Davies b Younis | 41 | – c Davies b Thomas | 3 |
| D. B. D'Oliveira c Holmes b Barwick | 51 | – b Holmes | 7 |
| D. M. Smith run out | 102 | – c Miandad b Barwick | 32 |
| D. N. Patel c Davies b Barwick | 45 | – run out | 24 |
| *P. A. Neale c Ontong b Holmes | 10 | – (6) c Ontong b Barwick | 6 |
| Kapil Dev b Price | 24 | – (7) c Morris b Ontong | 60 |
| †S. J. Rhodes not out | 41 | – (8) c Davies b Price | 39 |
| P. J. Newport not out | 12 | – (5) c Davies b Barwick | 36 |
| N. V. Radford (did not bat) | | – st Davies b Ontong | 8 |
| J. D. Inchmore (did not bat) | | – c Jones b Price | 5 |
| R. K. Illingworth (did not bat) | | – not out | 0 |
| B 12, l-b 6, w 1, n-b 4 | 23 | B 1, l-b 2, w 1, n-b 1 | 5 |
| 1/85 2/111 3/195 4/240 5/280 6/308 (6 wkts dec.) | 349 | 1/5 2/15 3/53 4/82 5/98 6/121 7/199 8/216 9/225 | 225 |

Bonus points – Worcestershire 4, Glamorgan 2 (Score at 100 overs: 338-6).

Bowling: *First Innings*—Thomas 15–3–66–0; Barwick 15–2–52–2; Holmes 19–2–62–1; Price 21–6–57–1; Younis 12–0–39–1; Ontong 20–6–55–0. *Second Innings*—Thomas 2.2–0–4–1; Barwick 27–4–79–3; Younis 0.4–0–2–0; Holmes 19–2–63–1; Ontong 12–3–35–2; Price 10.1–1–39–2.

## Glamorgan

| | | | |
|---|---|---|---|
| J. A. Hopkins c Smith b Radford | 3 | – lbw b Radford | 6 |
| A. L. Jones b Patel | 69 | – c Rhodes b Inchmore | 3 |
| G. C. Holmes c Smith b Newport | 67 | – (6) c Curtis b Newport | 2 |
| Javed Miandad c Curtis b Radford | 27 | – c D'Oliveira b Newport | 5 |
| Younis Ahmed not out | 100 | – b Inchmore | 34 |
| H. Morris c Rhodes b Inchmore | 2 | – (3) run out | 35 |
| *R. C. Ontong c D'Oliveira b Patel | 7 | – not out | 40 |
| †T. Davies c Smith b Radford | 18 | – c Neale b Radford | 12 |
| J. G. Thomas run out | 0 | | |
| M. R. Price c Rhodes b Radford | 5 | – (9) not out | 8 |
| S. R. Barwick not out | 0 | | |
| L-b 3, n-b 8 | 11 | B 1, l-b 5, w 1, n-b 4 | 11 |
| 1/3 2/115 3/156 4/179 5/204 6/226 7/291 8/292 9/305 | (9 wkts dec.) 309 | 1/12 2/18 3/39 4/87 5/89 6/99 7/130 | (7 wkts) 156 |

Bonus points – Glamorgan 4, Worcestershire 4.

Bowling: *First Innings*—Kapil Dev 4–0–18–0; Radford 24.5–3–94–4; Newport 15–2–57–1; Patel 22–7–57–2; Inchmore 15–2–39–1; Illingworth 15–4–41–0. *Second Innings*—Radford 18.4–5–53–2; Inchmore 11–3–33–2; Newport 12–0–44–2; Patel 7–3–10–0; Illingworth 6–1–10–0.

Umpires: K. E. Palmer and A. G. T. Whitehead.

At Eastbourne, July 27, 29, 30. WORCESTERSHIRE drew with SUSSEX.

## WORCESTERSHIRE v LANCASHIRE

At Worcester, August 3, 5, 6. Worcestershire won by seven wickets. Worcestershire 23 pts, Lancashire 5 pts. Toss won by Lancashire. Lancashire had good reason to rue their decision to dispense with the services of their former fast bowler, Radford, after providing Worcestershire with their first home Championship win of the season. Radford, clearly with a point to prove, dismissed Fowler and Abrahams without scoring in his first eight balls; followed up with 57 not out in 69 minutes to engineer a first-innings lead of 96; and would have had a hat-trick in Lancashire's second innings had not Inchmore dropped Makinson at third slip. On a pitch which assisted the quick bowlers, Worcestershire's four seamers shared all Lancashire's wickets. Only Lloyd, with an undefeated 50, stood firm as Lancashire's batting disintegrated for the second time in the match, leaving the home side a target of 70 which they reached with more than three hours to spare.

## Lancashire

| | | | |
|---|---|---|---|
| G. Fowler lbw b Radford | 0 | – c Rhodes b Radford | 4 |
| D. W. Varey c Rhodes b Newport | 29 | – c Rhodes b Newport | 34 |
| *J. Abrahams lbw b Radford | 0 | – c Smith b Radford | 0 |
| N. H. Fairbrother b Inchmore | 42 | – b Newport | 30 |
| C. H. Lloyd lbw b Newport | 14 | – not out | 50 |
| M. Watkinson b Kapil Dev | 19 | – (7) lbw b Radford | 0 |
| J. Simmons c Rhodes b Kapil Dev | 19 | – (6) c Kapil Dev b Radford | 0 |
| D. J. Makinson c Smith b Newport | 24 | – lbw b Kapil Dev | 20 |
| †J. Stanworth lbw b Kapil Dev | 0 | – c D'Oliveira b Inchmore | 7 |
| I. Folley not out | 14 | – b Newport | 4 |
| A. J. Murphy c Rhodes b Newport | 1 | – b Inchmore | 0 |
| L-b 5, n-b 1 | 6 | B 6, l-b 6, w 2, n-b 2 | 16 |
| 1/1 2/1 3/47 4/67 5/104 6/112 7/133 8/133 9/157 | 168 | 1/8 2/16 3/71 4/88 5/91 6/91 7/139 8/159 9/164 | 165 |

Bonus points – Lancashire 1, Worcestershire 4.

Bowling: *First Innings*—Kapil Dev 19–7–42–3; Radford 21–3–63–2; Inchmore 11–5–9–1; Patel 5–2–9–0; Newport 17.5–2–35–4; Illingworth 3–2–5–0. *Second Innings*—Radford 23–6–70–4; Kapil Dev 18–6–30–1; Inchmore 17–3–28–2; Newport 16–4–25–3.

## Worcestershire

| | | | |
|---|---|---|---|
| T. S. Curtis c Lloyd b Watkinson | 0 | – st Stanworth b Fairbrother | 33 |
| D. B. D'Oliveira lbw b Murphy | 30 | – c Lloyd b Murphy | 14 |
| D. M. Smith b Folley | 67 | – not out | 15 |
| †S. J. Rhodes c Fowler b Murphy | 8 | | |
| D. N. Patel c Simmons b Murphy | 8 | – (4) run out | 0 |
| *P. A. Neale c sub b Makinson | 3 | – (5) not out | 3 |
| Kapil Dev c Simmons b Folley | 28 | | |
| P. J. Newport lbw b Folley | 5 | | |
| N. V. Radford not out | 57 | | |
| R. K. Illingworth b Makinson | 9 | | |
| J. D. Inchmore b Folley | 24 | | |
| B 3, l-b 15, w 2, n-b 5 | 25 | L-b 4, w 1 | 5 |
| 1/0 2/44 3/58 4/95 5/107 6/147 7/160 8/175 9/209 | 264 | 1/51 2/61 3/61 | (3 wkts) 70 |

Bonus points – Worcestershire 3, Lancashire 4.

Bowling: *First Innings*—Watkinson 11–2–29–1; Makinson 24–2–81–2; Murphy 20–5–84–3; Folley 9.5–3–39–4; Simmons 4–1–13–0. *Second Innings*—Makinson 7–2–29–0; Murphy 8.2–2–34–1; Fairbrother 2–0–3–1.

Umpires: J. Birkenshaw and D. J. Constant.

At Trent Bridge, August 10, 12, 13. WORCESTERSHIRE drew with NOTTINGHAMSHIRE.

At Buxton, August 14, 15, 16. WORCESTERSHIRE drew with DERBYSHIRE.

## WORCESTERSHIRE v ESSEX

At Worcester, August 17, 19, 20. Drawn. Worcestershire 6 pts, Essex 6 pts. Toss won by Essex. Worcestershire were in the driving seat at the end of the rain-curtailed second day, but no play at all was possible on the final day. Radford took his season's haul of first-class victims to 71 with five for 79 as Essex recovered from 39 for four to reach 217 in the first innings, and claimed another three on the second evening. Prichard batted four hours for his 95, adding 95 with Fletcher for the fifth wicket. D'Oliveira, with 50 in 81 minutes before the close on the first day, Neale and Hick helped Worcestershire to a lead of 14, though Illingworth was unable to bat because of illness.

### Essex

| | | | |
|---|---|---|---|
| B. R. Hardie b Newport | 4 | – b Radford | 6 |
| A. W. Lilley lbw b Radford | 7 | – c Curtis b Radford | 11 |
| P. J. Prichard b Patel | 95 | – not out | 35 |
| K. S. McEwan b Radford | 11 | – lbw b Radford | 11 |
| D. R. Pringle b Inchmore | 1 | | |
| *K. W. R. Fletcher b Radford | 34 | | |
| †D. E. East c Rhodes b Radford | 7 | | |
| N. A. Foster lbw b Patel | 15 | | |
| I. L. Pont b Radford | 11 | – (5) not out | 5 |
| J. K. Lever b Patel | 11 | | |
| D.L. Acfield not out | 3 | | |
| B 1, l-b 5, w 6, n-b 6 | 18 | L-b 1, w 1, n-b 2 | 4 |
| 1/12 2/12 3/38 4/39 5/134 6/142 7/184 8/197 9/211 | 217 | 1/17 2/31 3/50 | (3 wkts) 72 |

Bonus points – Essex 2, Worcestershire 4.

Bowling: *First Innings*—Radford 26–1–79–5; Newport 15–4–48–1; Inchmore 15–5–18–1; Illingworth 9–2–23–0; Patel 18.1–5–38–3; Hick 2–0–5–0. *Second Innings*—Radford 14–4–37–3; Newport 5–1–18–0; Inchmore 5–1–11–0; Patel 3–1–5–0.

### Worcestershire

| | |
|---|---|
| T. S. Curtis lbw b Pringle | 15 |
| D. B. D'Oliveira lbw b Lever | 50 |
| P. J. Newport c Hardie b Pringle | 17 |
| D. M. Smith c East b Lever | 8 |
| D. N. Patel c East b Lever | 11 |
| *P. A. Neale c Hardie b Acfield | 62 |
| G. A. Hick b Foster | 56 |
| †S. J. Rhodes lbw b Foster | 1 |
| N. V. Radford b Foster | 0 |
| J. D. Inchmore not out | 5 |
| R. K. Illingworth absent ill | |
| N-b 6 | 6 |
| 1/55 2/67 3/77 4/99 5/109 6/210 7/222 8/222 9/231 | 231 |

Bonus points – Worcestershire 2, Essex 4.

Bowling: Lever 30–9–67–3; Foster 16.5–2–59–3; Pringle 18–4–42–2; Pont 9–1–29–0; Acfield 7–0–28–1.

Umpires: H. D. Bird and R. Palmer.

At Edgbaston, August 24, 26, 27. WORCESTERSHIRE beat WARWICKSHIRE by 185 runs.

## WORCESTERSHIRE v KENT

At Worcester, August 28, 29, 30. Worcestershire won by five wickets. Worcestershire 22 pts, Kent 4 pts. Toss won by Kent. Injury-hit Worcestershire, who had started August in sixteenth place in the Championship, conjured an unexpected victory with five balls to spare to finish the month in seventh spot. Without Kapil Dev, Smith, Radford, Illingworth, Ellcock and Pridgeon, they were further handicapped at lunch on the first day when Newport was rushed to hospital for a minor pelvic operation. Two declarations on the final day left the home side a victory target of 270 off a minimum of 62 overs, which was extended by seven overs owing to

Cowdrey's persistance with spin. The match was finely balanced until Curtis and Weston, 76 off 66 balls, came together to put on 123 in twenty overs for the fifth wicket. Curtis fittingly struck the winning runs in the final over with his fourteenth boundary, having received 201 balls. Taylor's third century of the season in Kent's first innings included thirteen 4s and one 6, while during the game D'Oliveira passed 1,000 runs for the first time.

## Kent

| | | |
|---|---|---|
| M. R. Benson c D'Oliveira b Weston | 39 | – b Patel 44 |
| S. G. Hinks c D'Oliveira b Weston | 31 | – c D'Oliveira b Hick 44 |
| C. J. Tavaré c Rhodes b Inchmore | 27 | – b Patel 21 |
| N. R. Taylor b Inchmore | 100 | – (6) not out 11 |
| *C. S. Cowdrey b Inchmore | 12 | – not out 28 |
| E. A. E. Baptiste c Weston b McEwan | 6 | – (4) lbw b Inchmore 11 |
| L. Potter c Curtis b Weston | 15 | |
| G. R. Cowdrey c Neale b D'Oliveira | 53 | |
| †A. P. E. Knott run out | 1 | |
| G. R. Dilley c Banks b Inchmore | 4 | |
| D. L. Underwood not out | 0 | |
| L-b 9, w 1, n-b 1 | 11 | L-b 10, n-b 1 11 |
| 1/67 2/80 3/142 4/160 5/167 6/198 7/294 8/294 9/299 | 299 | 1/83 2/89 3/120 4/132 (4 wkts dec.) 170 |

Bonus points – Kent 3, Worcestershire 4.

Bowling: *First Innings*—Newport 7–1–19–0; Inchmore 20–3–50–4; McEwan 17–1–63–1; Patel 14–2–58–0; Hick 19–6–62–0; Weston 22–7–37–3; D'Oliveira 1–0–1–1. *Second Innings*—McEwan 7–1–27–0; Inchmore 11–2–35–1; Weston 7–0–32–0; Patel 11–1–38–2; Hick 4–0–28–1.

## Worcestershire

| | | |
|---|---|---|
| T. S. Curtis c Potter b Underwood | 12 | – not out 97 |
| D. B. D'Oliveira c Taylor b Underwood | 48 | – c Knott b Baptiste 0 |
| G. A. Hick b Underwood | 35 | – b Potter 47 |
| D. N. Patel not out | 62 | – c and b Underwood 4 |
| *P. A. Neale not out | 35 | – b Underwood 36 |
| M. J. Weston (did not bat) | | – b Dilley 76 |
| †S. J. Rhodes (did not bat) | | – not out 4 |
| B 1, l-b 2, n-b 5 | 8 | L-b 6, w 1, n-b 2 9 |
| 1/54 2/77 3/108 | (3 wkts dec.) 200 | 1/5 2/81 3/86 4/137 5/260 (5 wkts) 273 |

D. A. Banks, P. J. Newport, J. D. Inchmore and S. M. McEwan did not bat.

Bonus points – Worcestershire 2, Kent 1.

Bowling: *First Innings*—Dilley 9–2–19–0; Baptiste 13–2–53–0; Underwood 29–10–66–3; C. S. Cowdrey 10–0–36–0; Potter 8–2–23–0. *Second Innings*—Dilley 10.1–0–50–1; Baptiste 9–2–49–1; Underwood 23–7–75–2; C. S. Cowdrey 7–2–14–0; Potter 15–2–63–1; Taylor 4–1–16–0.

Umpires: J. W. Holder and K. J. Lyons.

At Leicester, August 31, September 2, 3. WORCESTERSHIRE drew with LEICESTERSHIRE.

## WORCESTERSHIRE v SOMERSET

At Worcester, September 4, 5, 6. Worcestershire won by 124 runs. Worcestershire 21 pts, Somerset 2 pts. Toss won by Somerset. Hick's first Championship hundred, which took him past 1,000 runs in his 21st innings of the season, set up Worcestershire's third Championship victory in four matches. Producing a string of handsome off-side strokes, particularly on the front foot, the young Zimbabwean struck two 6s and 24 4s in his unbeaten 174 off 243 balls. He dominated partnerships of 135 with Curtis and 146 unbroken with his captain, Neale. Rain having cut the match by allowing only 27 overs on the first day (Worcestershire 73 for one), Marks declared before the start of the final day, when Richards kept wicket in place of the injured Gard and Somerset were set a target of 295 in 66 overs. Radford, increasing his haul for the season to 90, and Inchmore quickly effected a collapse on a pitch of easy pace, after which Somerset subsided gradually.

## Worcestershire

| | | | |
|---|---|---|---|
| T. S. Curtis c Roebuck b Marks | 58 | – c Richards b Garner | 0 |
| D. B. D'Oliveira c Roebuck b Dredge | 5 | – c Dredge b Marks | 64 |
| G. A. Hick not out | 174 | – b Dredge | 2 |
| D. M. Smith c Wyatt b Dredge | 0 | | |
| *P. A. Neale not out | 37 | – not out | 55 |
| D. N. Patel (did not bat) | | – (4) c Richards b Garner | 1 |
| M. J. Weston (did not bat) | | – (6) not out | 14 |
| L-b 11, w 1, n-b 14 | 26 | B 6, l-b 1, n-b 8 | 15 |
| 1/12 2/147 3/154 (3 wkts dec.) | 300 | 1/0 2/7 3/10 4/87 (4 wkts dec.) | 151 |

†S. J. Rhodes, N. V. Radford, J. D. Inchmore and S. M. McEwan did not bat.

Bonus points – Worcestershire 4, Somerset 1.

Bowling: *First Innings*—Garner 19–3–56–0; Dredge 25–7–65–2; Atkinson 9–0–44–0; Palmer 11–0–61–0; Marks 20–3–63–1. *Second Innings*—Garner 8–2–23–2; Dredge 10–2–23–1; Palmer 8–0–48–0; Marks 8–0–46–1; Atkinson 1.1–1–4–0.

## Somerset

| | | | |
|---|---|---|---|
| J. G. Wyatt b Inchmore | 1 | – lbw b Radford | 0 |
| P. M. Roebuck not out | 45 | – c Rhodes b Inchmore | 28 |
| P. A. C. Bail lbw b Inchmore | 4 | – lbw b Radford | 1 |
| I. V. A. Richards c Inchmore b McEwan | 44 | – (5) c Rhodes b Inchmore | 0 |
| R. J. Harden not out | 52 | – (4) b Inchmore | 3 |
| J. C. M. Atkinson (did not bat) | | – c Patel b Radford | 4 |
| *V. J. Marks (did not bat) | | – c Hick b Weston | 49 |
| G. V. Palmer (did not bat) | | – b Radford | 29 |
| C. H. Dredge (did not bat) | | – not out | 21 |
| J. Garner (did not bat) | | – c Neale b Weston | 22 |
| †T. Gard (did not bat) | | – absent injured | |
| L-b 4, n-b 7 | 11 | L-b 8, n-b 5 | 13 |
| 1/5 2/11 3/77 (3 wkts dec.) | 157 | 1/0 2/2 3/11 4/11 5/26 6/73 7/124 8/132 9/170 | 170 |

Bonus points – Somerset 1, Worcestershire 1.

Bowling: *First Innings*—Radford 11–2–43–0, Inchmore 11–3–40–2; McEwan 7–2–23–1; Patel 8–3–19–0; Hick 6–0–28–0. *Second Innings*—Radford 17–6–45–4; Inchmore 12–1–41–3; McEwan 8–1–33–0; Patel 5–2–9–0; Weston 5.4–1–34–2.

Umpires: J. W. Holder and R. A. White.

At Taunton, September 11, 12, 13. WORCESTERSHIRE drew with SOMERSET.

## WORCESTERSHIRE v NORTHAMPTONSHIRE

At Worcester, September 14, 16, 17. Northamptonshire won by three wickets. Northamptonshire 21 pts, Worcestershire 5 pts. Toss won by Northamptonshire. Defeat for Worcestershire on the final day of the season was softened on two counts. Radford finished his first season with the county by becoming the only bowler in the country to take 100 first-class wickets. And, although slipping from fourth to fifth place in the table, Worcestershire could still celebrate an improvement of five places over their 1984 Championship position. Centuries from Hick and Smith provided the backbone of Worcestershire's first innings, but they were upstaged when Larkins and Boyd-Moss put on 255 off 56 overs before Northamptonshire declared 43 runs behind. Inexplicably, the home side collapsed to 184 all out on the final morning, Capel and Harper doing the damage with four wickets apiece. Northamptonshire's requirement of 228 from 74 overs began to look less comfortable when Radford quickly accounted for Larkins and Boyd-Moss, but he had to wait for another 30 overs before Bailey became his 100th victim following a stand of 107 with Cook. The visitors eventually edged home with just seven balls to spare.

## Worcestershire

| | | | |
|---|---|---|---|
| T. S. Curtis lbw b Griffiths | 55 | – lbw b Capel | 46 |
| D. B. D'Oliveira c Harper b Walker | 5 | – c Larkins b Capel | 16 |
| G. A. Hick c Cook b Capel | 128 | – b Capel | 12 |
| D. M. Smith not out | 104 | – c and b Capel | 29 |
| *P. A. Neale not out | 72 | – (7) c Cook b Harper | 5 |
| D. N. Patel (did not bat) | | – b Harper | 28 |
| M. J. Weston (did not bat) | | – (5) c Boyd-Moss b Harper | 7 |
| †S. J. Rhodes (did not bat) | | – run out | 4 |
| N. V. Radford (did not bat) | | – b Walker | 10 |
| J. D. Inchmore (did not bat) | | – b Harper | 0 |
| S. M. McEwan (did not bat) | | – not out | 0 |
| B 5, l-b 13, n-b 10 | 28 | B 8, l-b 4, w 5, n-b 10 | 27 |
| 1/17 2/134 3/228 (3 wkts dec.) | 392 | 1/41 2/64 3/115 4/126 5/129 6/143 7/169 8/170 9/184 | 184 |

Bonus points – Worcestershire 4, Northamptonshire 1.

Bowling: *First Innings*—Walker 19–1–70–1; Griffiths 19–1–73–1; Capel 10–0–63–1; Harper 12–2–44–0; Boyd-Moss 28–6–88–0; Wild 11–1–36–0. *Second Innings*—Walker 10.1–2–38–1; Griffiths 10–2–22–0; Capel 19–0–59–4; Wild 3–0–28–0; Harper 16–8–25–4.

## Northamptonshire

| | | | |
|---|---|---|---|
| *G. Cook b Radford | 23 | – c Smith b Radford | 72 |
| W. Larkins b Radford | 163 | – c D'Oliveira b Radford | 15 |
| R. J. Boyd-Moss c Smith b Weston | 121 | – lbw b Radford | 7 |
| A. J. Lamb not out | 22 | – lbw b McEwan | 6 |
| R. J. Bailey not out | 1 | – c Rhodes b Radford | 52 |
| D. J. Wild (did not bat) | | – b Inchmore | 30 |
| D. J. Capel (did not bat) | | – not out | 29 |
| R. A. Harper (did not bat) | | – lbw b Inchmore | 2 |
| †D. Ripley (did not bat) | | – not out | 6 |
| B 3, l-b 4, w 1, n-b 11 | 19 | L-b 5, n-b 7 | 12 |
| 1/49 2/304 3/338 (3 wkts dec.) | 349 | 1/27 2/37 3/44 4/151 5/164 6/208 7/212 (7 wkts) | 231 |

A. Walker and B. J. Griffiths did not bat.

Bonus points – Northamptonshire 4, Worcestershire 1.

Bowling: *First Innings*—Radford 30–3–125–2; Inchmore 11–1–49–0; Weston 19–0–68–1; McEwan 9–1–59–0; Patel 11–1–41–0. *Second Innings*—Radford 24.5–5–68–4; Inchmore 17–0–59–2; McEwan 11–1–35–1; Hick 3–0–15–0; Patel 17–5–49–0.

Umpires: B. Dudleston and M. J. Kitchen.

# YORKSHIRE

*Patron:* HRH The Duchess of Kent
*President:* Viscount Mountgarret
*Chairman:* H. R. Kirk
*Chairman, Cricket Committee:*
1985 – A. L. Vann
*Secretary:* J. Lister
Headingley Cricket Ground, Leeds LS6 3BU
(Telephone: 0532-787394)
*Captain:* D. L. Bairstow

Yorkshire, by accident rather than design, found themselves in a transitional period during 1985, when the level of performance proved as disappointing as the results. They struggled in the lower reaches of the Britannic Assurance Championship for much of the summer and faded badly in the John Player Sunday League after developing a promising challenge for the title. The picture was equally gloomy in the two knockout competitions, for Yorkshire failed to qualify from their zonal group in the Benson and Hedges Cup and fell at the second hurdle in the NatWest Bank Trophy.

Significantly, their three capped seam bowlers, Arnie Sidebottom, Graham Stevenson and Simon Dennis, plagued by all manner of strains and illness, made very little contribution, while the highly regarded Paul Jarvis, whose brighter moments included a hat-trick against Derbyshire at Chesterfield, and Stuart Fletcher also suffered frustrating injuries. Sidebottom, although gaining a Test place, managed only 203 overs in the Championship and rarely hit his most effective rhythm, while Stevenson and Dennis hardly featured at all because of long-standing fitness problems.

In the circumstances, an unexpectedly heavy burden fell on the inexperienced shoulders of Chris Shaw, Peter Hartley and Chris Pickles, a trio of medium-paced bowlers who all did better than might have been reasonably expected. Inevitably, these three have been added to the contracted staff for 1986, when Yorkshire will have eight seam bowlers pressing for selection. Clearly this is an expensive situation and one that cannot continue for long. It will put a lot of pressure on the bowlers, particularly as Sidebottom, Stevenson and Dennis have been so injury-prone in recent years.

The left-arm spinner, Phil Carrick, comfortably the leading wicket-taker, emerged from his benefit season as the side's most prominent all-rounder, but even he had some barren spells and did not impress when forced into a defensive role on good pitches. Matters were further complicated by the failure of the young spinners, Ian Swallow and Paul Booth, to make any real progress. Booth appeared to lose confidence and did not achieve much turn, while on the few occasions he received a chance in the first team Swallow could not command the essential accuracy. Bearing this in mind, more scope might have been given to Kevin Sharp, who showed some promise as an off-spinner.

As captain, David Bairstow operated in difficult circumstances in his second season in charge. Against a troubled "political" background, his leadership continued to lack real authority. Too often an air of confusion hung over the proceedings, with Yorkshire sitting back to see what happened instead of making positive moves to influence the course of events.

Although the bowling limitations – and at times very poor fielding – handicapped Yorkshire's prospects, the batting was also to blame for much of the rather dreary cricket played by the county side. The Cricket Committee chairman, Tony Vann, urged in his pre-season message that defeat should be risked in pursuit of victory, but his words fell on deaf ears. Yorkshire never really chased a target; nor did they score their runs sufficiently quickly to create scope for meaningful declarations, without which the majority of matches were destined for stalemate on a succession of low, slow pitches.

Geoff Boycott, who recorded his 100th century for the county at Edgbaston on August 6, inevitably found himself at the centre of some heated argument about his rate of scoring. He was dreadfully slow at the end of the season when completing the 149th century of his career, which came against Nottinghamshire at Scarborough and bracketed him with Herbert Sutcliffe as the county's leading centurion. But others fell short of requirements to a greater extent. Neither Jim Love, despite a healthy average, nor Sharp had a particularly happy time. They did not manage a century between them in the Championship. Indeed, only some marvellous innings from Bairstow and one or two timely contributions from the robust Phil Robinson prevented shortcomings in this direction being more clearly exposed. The four Championship defeats all stemmed from sorry collapses which reflected a shortage of determination as well as faulty technique.

Boycott again headed the averages by a substantial margin, with his partner, Martyn Moxon, also operating reliably and with rather more urgency for much of the time. Young Richard Blakey advanced from the second team to replace the unhappy Ashley Metcalfe as the most reliable number three and the likely successor to Boycott in due course.

Yorkshire's work was also very patchy in the Sunday League. Although some splendid victories were achieved, other games were lost through a lack of basic professionalism. If this was understandable in the case of the younger players, some of the more senior members of the team should have shown a greater sense of purpose.

There were indications that the dressing-room would accept an outsider – even an overseas player – if he happened to be the type of experienced campaigner to raise the overall standards. The committee, however, while not unanimous on the matter, presented a united face against such a move. All the same, a crop of eager, willing and talented juniors do need guidance if they are to revive Yorkshire's fortunes. They would also benefit from a more settled situation within the committee, and these two aspects are to an important extent related. – J.C.

YORKSHIRE 1985

[*Bill Smith*

*Back row:* A. A. Metcalfe, P. A. Booth, S. N. Hartley, S. J. Dennis, S. D. Fletcher, K. Sharp. *Front row:* M. D. Moxon, G. Boycott, D. L. Bairstow (*captain*), A. Sidebottom, J. D. Love. *Insets:* P. Carrick, P. W. Jarvis, S. Oldham, I. G. Swallow, C. Shaw, P. E. Robinson.

## YORKSHIRE RESULTS

*All first-class matches – Played 25: Won 3, Lost 4, Drawn 18. Abandoned 1.*

*County Championship matches – Played 23: Won 3, Lost 4, Drawn 16. Abandoned 1.*

*Bonus points – Batting 58, Bowling 59.*

*Competition placings – Britannic Assurance County Championship, 11th; NatWest Bank Trophy, 2nd round; Benson and Hedges Cup, 3rd in Group B; John Player League, 6th eq.*

## BRITANNIC ASSURANCE CHAMPIONSHIP AVERAGES

### BATTING

| | *Birthplace* | *M* | *I* | *NO* | *R* | *HI* | *Avge* |
|---|---|---|---|---|---|---|---|
| ‡G. Boycott | *Fitzwilliam* | 19 | 31 | 11 | 1,545 | 184 | 77.25 |
| ‡D. L. Bairstow | *Bradford* | 23 | 31 | 9 | 1,148 | 122* | 52.18 |
| ‡M. D. Moxon | *Barnsley* | 20 | 31 | 1 | 1,224 | 168 | 40.80 |
| ‡J. D. Love | *Leeds* | 19 | 26 | 4 | 830 | 93 | 37.72 |
| P. E. Robinson | *Keighley* | 13 | 16 | 1 | 450 | 79 | 30.00 |
| ‡A. Sidebottom | *Barnsley* | 8 | 9 | 2 | 191 | 55 | 27.28 |
| R. J. Blakey | *Huddersfield* | 13 | 21 | 2 | 487 | 90 | 25.63 |
| ‡S. N. Hartley | *Shipley* | 15 | 19 | 1 | 446 | 60 | 24.77 |
| ‡G. B. Stevenson | *Ackworth* | 4 | 6 | 2 | 99 | 35* | 24.75 |
| ‡K. Sharp | *Leeds* | 17 | 29 | 3 | 613 | 96 | 23.57 |
| ‡P. Carrick | *Leeds* | 23 | 25 | 2 | 540 | 92 | 23.47 |
| P. J. Hartley | *Keighley* | 12 | 11 | 3 | 159 | 35 | 19.87 |
| A. A. Metcalfe | *Horsforth* | 5 | 10 | 0 | 125 | 77 | 12.50 |
| S. D. Fletcher | *Keighley* | 12 | 10 | 7 | 36 | 15* | 12.00 |
| I. G. Swallow | *Barnsley* | 10 | 11 | 2 | 101 | 25* | 11.22 |
| P. W. Jarvis | *Redcar* | 14 | 16 | 2 | 151 | 28 | 10.78 |
| C. Shaw | *Hemsworth* | 16 | 13 | 5 | 57 | 12 | 7.12 |

Also batted: P. A. Booth (*Huddersfield*) (2 matches) 0; S. Oldham (*Sheffield*) (2 matches) 6, 2*; C. S. Pickles (*Mirfield*) (5 matches) 31*, 12, 9. ‡S. J. Dennis (*Scarborough*) (1 match) did not bat

* *Signifies not out.* ‡ *Denotes county cap.*

The following played a total of twelve three-figure innings for Yorkshire in County Championship matches – G. Boycott 6, D. L. Bairstow 3, M. D. Moxon 3.

### BOWLING

| | *O* | *M* | *R* | *W* | *BB* | *Avge* |
|---|---|---|---|---|---|---|
| P. Carrick | 709.3 | 183 | 1,914 | 65 | 7-99 | 29.44 |
| P. W. Jarvis | 371.5 | 53 | 1,330 | 44 | 7-105 | 30.22 |
| A. Sidebottom | 203.2 | 28 | 667 | 22 | 4-70 | 30.31 |
| P. J. Hartley | 315.5 | 40 | 1,175 | 31 | 5-75 | 37.90 |
| C. Shaw | 398 | 90 | 1,230 | 32 | 5-76 | 38.43 |
| S. D. Fletcher | 323.5 | 45 | 1,185 | 24 | 4-91 | 49.37 |
| I. G. Swallow | 225 | 46 | 670 | 12 | 4-53 | 55.83 |

Also bowled: P. A. Booth 80.1–29–189–3; G. Boycott 10–2–29–0; S. J. Dennis 20.2–2–50–2; S. N. Hartley 74.4–10–272–9; J. D. Love 1–0–8–1; M. D. Moxon 27–1–131–4; S. Oldham 39–10–102–4; C. S. Pickles 112.3–24–345–5; K. Sharp 26–8–60–1; G. B. Stevenson 72.4–10–252–6.

At Leicester, April 27, 28, 29. YORKSHIRE drew with LEICESTERSHIRE.

## YORKSHIRE v MIDDLESEX

At Headingley, May 4, 6, 7. Yorkshire won by 2 runs. Yorkshire 20 pts, Middlesex 6 pts. Toss won by Yorkshire. Batting first, Yorkshire scored steadily but needed a brave contribution from their captain, Bairstow, who defied a painful leg strain to hurry them to maximum batting points. Middlesex, scoring freely, declared behind and appeared poised for due reward when Daniel, achieving extra pace, started a collapse. Again Bairstow fought valiantly, but Middlesex were set to make only 215 in 60 overs. They had reached 109 for one in 32 overs when Sharp, from mid-wicket, ran out Gatting. The aggressive Sidebottom then took three wickets in seventeen balls as Middlesex stumbled, and in a tense finish Jarvis also claimed three wickets to bring Yorkshire victory with four balls to spare. Blakey, eighteen and making his début, kept wicket in Bairstow's absence and held four catches, two of which were far from straightforward.

### Yorkshire

| | | | |
|---|---|---|---|
| A. Sidebottom c Butcher b Daniel | 55 | (8) c Gatting b Cowans | 23 |
| M. D. Moxon c Slack b Daniel | 10 | (1) c Downton b Daniel | 2 |
| K. Sharp b Cowans | 15 | (4) c Emburey b Daniel | 20 |
| J. D. Love b Emburey | 33 | (5) b Daniel | 4 |
| P. E. Robinson b Gatting | 62 | (6) c Gatting b Williams | 19 |
| R. J. Blakey c Downton b Edmonds | 32 | (2) c sub b Edmonds | 4 |
| P. W. Jarvis c Gatting b Williams | 13 | (3) c Downton b Williams | 10 |
| P. Carrick c and b Edmonds | 14 | (9) run out | 1 |
| *†D. L. Bairstow c Butcher b Edmonds | 26 | (7) not out | 33 |
| G. B. Stevenson not out | 14 | c Williams b Cowans | 6 |
| S. D. Fletcher not out | 2 | c Slack b Cowans | 0 |
| B 5, l-b 17, w 2, n-b 4 | 28 | L-b 7, w 6 | 13 |
| 1/38 2/74 3/98 4/135 5/203 6/235 7/243 8/279 9/294 (9 wkts dec.) | 304 | 1/6 2/6 3/32 4/38 5/61 6/69 7/108 8/121 9/135 | 135 |

Bonus points – Yorkshire 4, Middlesex 4.

Bowling: *First Innings*—Daniel 18–1–73–2; Cowans 15–3–53–1; Williams 22–4–56–1; Edmonds 26–10–44–3; Emburey 13.5–3–47–1; Gatting 5–1–9–1. *Second Innings*—Daniel 13–4–19–3; Gatting 2–1–4–0; Edmonds 5–2–16–1; Emburey 17–3–28–0; Cowans 9–3–30–3; Williams 6–0–31–2.

### Middlesex

| | | | |
|---|---|---|---|
| W. N. Slack not out | 86 | c Carrick b Stevenson | 99 |
| †P. R. Downton c and b Carrick | 70 | c Blakey b Carrick | 13 |
| *M. W. Gatting c Stevenson b Carrick | 40 | run out | 23 |
| R. O. Butcher not out | 14 | lbw b Sidebottom | 2 |
| C. T. Radley (did not bat) | | c Blakey b Sidebottom | 4 |
| G. D. Barlow (did not bat) | | c Blakey b Sidebottom | 0 |
| J. E. Emburey (did not bat) | | c Blakey b Fletcher | 8 |
| P. H. Edmonds (did not bat) | | b Jarvis | 22 |
| N. G. Cowans (did not bat) | | b Jarvis | 12 |
| N. F. Williams (did not bat) | | lbw b Jarvis | 10 |
| W. W. Daniel (did not bat) | | not out | 1 |
| B 1, l-b 4, w 5, n-b 5 | 15 | L-b 11, n-b 7 | 18 |
| 1/116 2/188 (2 wkts dec.) | 225 | 1/62 2/109 3/113 4/123 5/123 6/149 7/178 8/184 9/205 | 212 |

Bonus points – Middlesex 2.

Bowling: *First Innings*—Sidebottom 15–4–34–0; Stevenson 7–0–24–0; Jarvis 11–1–45–0; Fletcher 10–1–42–0; Carrick 26 8 55 2; Sharp 5–0–20–0. *Second Innings*—Sidebottom 21–3–47–3; Jarvis 11.2–1–51–3; Fletcher 7–0–30–1; Carrick 8–1–33–1; Stevenson 12–1–40–1.

Umpires: H. D. Bird and K. E. Palmer.

## YORKSHIRE v ESSEX

At Sheffield, May 22, 23, 24. Abandoned.

At Old Trafford, May 25, 26, 27. YORKSHIRE drew with LANCASHIRE.

## YORKSHIRE v SOMERSET

At Headingley, May 29, 30, 31. Drawn. Yorkshire 8 pts, Somerset 4 pts. Toss won by Yorkshire. Somerset, lacking seven senior players, were unable to contain Yorkshire on an easy-paced pitch. Moxon equalled his highest score in first-class cricket, sharing a stand of 223 in 69 overs with Blakey, who hit a career-best 90. This was a record for Yorkshire's second wicket against Somerset. Richards was equally commanding after recovering from a minor illness. His fifth century for Somerset against Yorkshire included eleven 4s and one 6 and also left Sidebottom with a split hand, the result of a fierce straight-drive. Boycott, returning after a long lay-off because of injury, also reached three figures before Somerset were given a target of 350 in what amounted to 85 overs. Once Richards departed, however, Marks, who was dropped before he had scored by Bairstow, organised a successful defensive operation.

### Yorkshire

| | | | |
|---|---|---|---|
| G. Boycott c Gard b Palmer | 20 | – not out | 114 |
| M. D. Moxon c Palmer b Turner | 153 | – c Garner b Palmer | 16 |
| R. J. Blakey b Marks | 90 | – c Richards b Turner | 7 |
| K. Sharp c Booth b Garner | 42 | – b Marks | 44 |
| J. D. Love not out | 62 | – not out | 30 |
| B 4, l-b 5, w 3, n-b 4 | 15 | L-b 7, w 2, n-b 3 | 12 |
| 1/51 2/274 3/280 4/383 (4 wkts dec.) | 383 | 1/34 2/49 3/138 (3 wkts dec.) | 223 |

*†D. L. Bairstow, A. Sidebottom, P. Carrick, P. W. Jarvis, S. D. Fletcher and P. A. Booth did not bat.

Bonus points – Yorkshire 4, Somerset 1 (Score at 100 overs: 336-3).

Bowling: *First Innings*—Garner 16.5–5–39–1; Turner 19–5–83–1; Richards 7–1–21–0; Palmer 13–3–58–1; Marks 28–1–105–1; Booth 21–7–64–0; Popplewell 1–0–4–0. *Second Innings*—Garner 11–2–27–0; Turner 22–4–72–1; Palmer 16–1–65–1; Richards 10–3–14–0; Marks 12–2–38–1.

## Somerset

| First innings | | Second innings | |
|---|---|---|---|
| N. F. M. Popplewell lbw b Jarvis | 10 | c Bairstow b Jarvis | 11 |
| P. A. C. Bail b Sidebottom | 4 | lbw b Jarvis | 9 |
| †T. Gard c Bairstow b Sidebottom | 0 | (8) not out | 0 |
| N. A. Felton b Sidebottom | 28 | (3) b Jarvis | 31 |
| R. L. Ollis not out | 5 | hit wkt b Jarvis | 37 |
| I. V. A. Richards c sub b Fletcher | 105 | (4) lbw b Fletcher | 53 |
| *V. J. Marks run out | 62 | (6) c Bairstow b Fletcher | 51 |
| G. V. Palmer c Jarvis b Carrick | 11 | (7) not out | 17 |
| M. S. Turner lbw b Jarvis | 5 | | |
| J. Garner c Bairstow b Carrick | 2 | | |
| S. C. Booth lbw b Booth | 1 | | |
| B 5, l-b 10, n-b 9 | 24 | B 4, l-b 8, w 3, n-b 6 | 21 |
| 1/11 2/12 3/22 4/98 5/196 6/235 7/246 8/250 9/256 | 257 | 1/19 2/30 3/118 4/126 5/209 6/216 (6 wkts) | 230 |

Bonus points – Somerset 3, Yorkshire 4.

*In the first innings R. L. Ollis, when 0, retired ill at 25 and resumed at 246.*

Bowling: *First Innings*—Sidebottom 18.1–2–48–3; Jarvis 18–3–65–2; Fletcher 11.5–0–62–1; Carrick 22–7–36–2; Booth 11.1–4–31–1. *Second Innings*—Fletcher 16–3–53–2; Jarvis 20–7–59–4; Booth 18–8–21–0; Carrick 22–1–74–0; Sharp 9–4–11–0.

Umpires: J. Birkenshaw and J. A. Jameson.

## YORKSHIRE v HAMPSHIRE

At Middlesbrough, June 1, 3, 4. Drawn. Yorkshire 4 pts, Hampshire 7 pts. Toss won by Hampshire. They scored too slowly on the first day, when, on a pitch of easy pace, Yorkshire were reduced to three specialist bowlers following the retirement through injury of Jarvis and Oldham. Chris Smith used up 105 overs to make his unbeaten 143, he and Robin sharing the highest partnership by brothers against Yorkshire – 146 for the fourth wicket. Yorkshire, under the influence of Boycott, made a solid reply to which Bairstow contributed a robust 47 from 33 balls, but Marshall's burst of four for 7 in 31 deliveries kept Yorkshire in arrears. Hampshire allowed their second innings also to drift along until Marshall and Chris Smith hit out, and Yorkshire's final target became 282 in 215 minutes. This was an impossible task on a pitch increasingly allowing turn, and the advantage lay with Hampshire when rain stopped play an hour early.

## Hampshire

| First innings | | Second innings | |
|---|---|---|---|
| C. G. Greenidge st Bairstow b Carrick | 26 | c Moxon b Carrick | 22 |
| V. P. Terry lbw b Fletcher | 9 | c Bairstow b Fletcher | 14 |
| *M. C. J. Nicholas c Blakey b Carrick | 12 | c Moxon b Carrick | 11 |
| C. L. Smith not out | 143 | (5) c sub b Carrick | 68 |
| R. A. Smith c Jarvis b Moxon | 63 | (4) c Bairstow b Booth | 30 |
| M. D. Marshall c Bairstow b Booth | 50 | c Fletcher b Sharp | 60 |
| N. G. Cowley c Booth b Carrick | 19 | (8) not out | 4 |
| T. M. Tremlett not out | 12 | (7) not out | 10 |
| L-b 1, n-b 6 | 7 | L-b 4 | 4 |
| 1/24 2/51 3/51 4/197 5/269 6/322 (6 wkts dec.) | 341 | 1/33 2/41 3/78 4/78 5/165 6/219 (6 wkts dec.) | 223 |

R. J. Maru, †R. J. Parks and C. A. Connor did not bat.

Bonus points – Hampshire 3, Yorkshire 1 (Score at 100 overs: 259-4).

Bowling: *First Innings*—Fletcher 25–4–100–1; Jarvis 3–0–13–0; Oldham 8–2–33–0; Carrick 43–12–102–3; Booth 32–9–76–1; Moxon 6–0–16–1. *Second Innings*—Fletcher 11–3–44–1; Carrick 36–8–99–3; Booth 19–8–61–1; Sharp 8–4–15–1.

## Yorkshire

| | | | |
|---|---|---|---|
| G. Boycott lbw b Marshall | 115 | – c Greenidge b Tremlett | 25 |
| M. D. Moxon c Maru b Tremlett | 25 | – c Parks b Cowley | 31 |
| R. J. Blakey c Parks b Marshall | 43 | – c Nicholas b Cowley | 18 |
| K. Sharp c Greenidge b Cowley | 19 | – c R. A. Smith b Maru | 2 |
| J. D. Love c Parks b Maru | 1 | – lbw b Cowley | 5 |
| *†D. L. Bairstow lbw b Marshall | 47 | – not out | 16 |
| P. Carrick c Maru b Marshall | 0 | – not out | 13 |
| P. W. Jarvis b Marshall | 0 | | |
| S. Oldham c Tremlett b Maru | 6 | | |
| P. A. Booth c Marshall b Maru | 0 | | |
| S. D. Fletcher not out | 0 | | |
| B 8, l-b 8, n-b 11 | 27 | L-b 3, w 1 | 4 |
| 1/48 2/136 3/182 4/203 5/255 6/262 7/262 8/274 9/276 | 283 | 1/33 2/77 3/78 4/82 5/90 | (5 wkts) 114 |

Bonus points – Yorkshire 3, Hampshire 4.

Bowling: *First Innings*—Marshall 20–8–48–5; Connor 9–2–29–0; Maru 22.2–6–65–3; Tremlett 17–4–35–1; Cowley 21–3–90–1. *Second Innings*—Marshall 6–3–8–0; Connor 3–0–8–0; Maru 19.1–8–45–1; Tremlett 7–0–25–1; Cowley 13–6–21–3; C. L. Smith 1–0–4–0.

Umpires: J. Birkenshaw and J. A. Jameson.

At Headingley, June 5, 6, 7. YORKSHIRE drew with AUSTRALIANS (See Australian tour section).

At The Parks, June 12, 13, 14. YORKSHIRE drew with OXFORD UNIVERSITY.

## YORKSHIRE v WORCESTERSHIRE

At Harrogate, June 22, 23, 24. Drawn. Yorkshire 5 pts, Worcestershire 7 pts. Toss won by Yorkshire. Worcestershire, put in, scored briskly against steady bowling, although they were helped by some poor Yorkshire ground-fielding and several dropped catches. Yorkshire batted badly in reply and would have been in serious danger of following on had not Boycott stood firm. He was well supported by Sidebottom and Swallow. Sidebottom, having been called up by England, conceded a flurry of no-balls in Worcestershire's second innings, during which Yorkshire sat back and waited for the declaration. When it came they had to score 271 in a minimum of 53 overs for victory. Kapil Dev bowled much too well, however, and they made no attempt to win a game in which Worcestershire played the more enterprising cricket.

## Worcestershire

| | First innings | | Second innings | |
|---|---|---|---|---|
| T. S. Curtis b Carrick | | 72 | c Carrick b Fletcher | 35 |
| D. B. D'Oliveira lbw b Fletcher | | 60 | c Jarvis b Moxon | 34 |
| *P. A. Neale c Boycott b Swallow | | 38 | c Boycott b Sidebottom | 36 |
| D. N. Patel c Moxon b Sidebottom | | 45 | not out | 30 |
| †S. J. Rhodes b Sidebottom | | 3 | | |
| Kapil Dev c Bairstow b Sidebottom | | 24 | (5) not out | 40 |
| M. J. Weston c Bairstow b Sidebottom | | 8 | | |
| D. A. Banks not out | | 21 | | |
| R. K. Illingworth c Boycott b Moxon | | 0 | | |
| N. V. Radford not out | | 4 | | |
| L-b 5, w 2, n-b 18 | | 25 | B 1, l-b 1, w 1, n-b 7 | 10 |
| 1/111 2/183 3/198 4/232 5/256 6/269 7/294 8/295 | (8 wkts dec.) | 300 | 1/71 2/85 3/124 (3 wkts dec.) | 185 |

J. D. Inchmore did not bat.

Bonus points – Worcestershire 4, Yorkshire 3.

Bowling: *First Innings*—Sidebottom 26.3–6–70–4; Jarvis 10–0–39–0; Fletcher 23–1–90–1; Carrick 12–5–23–1; Swallow 15–4–56–1; Moxon 3–0–17–1. *Second Innings*—Sidebottom 11–0–48–1; Fletcher 11–0–62–1; Moxon 7–1–27–1; Carrick 9–5–14–0; Swallow 11–1–32–0.

## Yorkshire

| | First innings | | Second innings | |
|---|---|---|---|---|
| G. Boycott not out | | 105 | not out | 64 |
| M. D. Moxon c Rhodes b Kapil Dev | | 11 | lbw b Kapil Dev | 3 |
| R. J. Blakey lbw b Kapil Dev | | 0 | c Patel b Illingworth | 17 |
| K. Sharp c D'Oliveira b Radford | | 4 | (5) not out | 27 |
| J. D. Love c Rhodes b Kapil Dev | | 4 | | |
| *†D. L. Bairstow b Weston | | 13 | (4) b Illingworth | 5 |
| P. Carrick c Kapil Dev b Radford | | 11 | | |
| A. Sidebottom c Kapil Dev b Illingworth | | 26 | | |
| I. G. Swallow not out | | 20 | | |
| B 7, l-b 10, w 1, n-b 3 | | 21 | B 1, l-b 7 | 8 |
| 1/13 2/19 3/29 4/36 5/62 6/93 7/162 | (7 wkts dec.) | 215 | 1/3 2/49 3/65 (3 wkts) | 124 |

P. W. Jarvis and S. D. Fletcher did not bat.

Bonus points – Yorkshire 2, Worcestershire 3.

Bowling: *First Innings*—Kapil Dev 19–12–15–3; Radford 23.1–4–59–2; Inchmore 1.5–0–6–0; Weston 10–5–30–1; Illingworth 30–9–49–1; Patel 9–1–39–0. *Second Innings*—Kapil Dev 8–3–14–1; Radford 8–3–20–0; Illingworth 19–9–29–2; D'Oliveira 7–0–23–0; Patel 8–1–30–0.

Umpires: J. W. Holder and D. O. Oslear.

## YORKSHIRE v LEICESTERSHIRE

At Bradford, June 26, 27, 28. Drawn. Yorkshire 5 pts, Leicestershire 4 pts. Toss won by Yorkshire who, pinned down by some accurate Leicestershire bowling, ground along at around 2 runs an over and batted on into the second day in the hope that a slow pitch might take spin. Leicestershire were much more attacking with Willey giving a positive lead while adding 115 in 33 overs with Butcher. The acting-captain declared 70 behind to put pressure on Bairstow, who hammered his way into the record books with a century before lunch, making his runs from 119 balls in 94 minutes. He then set a target of 312 in four hours, during which Yorkshire eventually bowled 73 overs. Balderstone and Butcher put on 145 in 43 overs, but Yorkshire went on the defensive with as many as five men on the boundary. As wickets fell, Leicestershire settled for a draw.

### Yorkshire

| | First innings | | Second innings | |
|---|---|---|---|---|
| G. Boycott c Butcher b Agnew | 4 | – | not out | 82 |
| M. D. Moxon c Willey b Taylor | 33 | – | st Garnham b Cook | 45 |
| R. J. Blakey c Butcher b Agnew | 5 | | | |
| K. Sharp lbw b Cook | 81 | | | |
| J. D. Love c Butcher b Willey | 23 | | | |
| *†D. L. Bairstow c Butcher b Cook | 77 | – | (3) not out | 100 |
| P. Carrick lbw b Parsons | 17 | | | |
| I. G. Swallow c Cobb b Agnew | 7 | | | |
| C. S. Pickles not out | 31 | | | |
| C. Shaw not out | 11 | | | |
| L-b 2, w 5, n-b 4 | 11 | | B 1, l-b 8, w 3, n-b 2 | 14 |
| 1/10 2/26 3/87 4/153 5/153 6/203 7/230 8/266 (8 wkts dec.) | 300 | | 1/73 (1 wkt dec.) | 241 |

S. D. Fletcher did not bat.

Bonus points – Yorkshire 2, Leicestershire 2 (Score at 100 overs: 208-6).

Bowling: *First Innings*—Agnew 30–9–73–3; Taylor 25.4–12–59–1; Parsons 30–8–61–1; Cook 35–9–82–2; Willey 10–2–23–1. *Second Innings*—Agnew 11–1–56–0; Taylor 8–4–14–0; Cook 19–2–71–1; Willey 12–0–50–0; Briers 3–0–24–0; Parsons 2.2–0–17–0.

### Leicestershire

| | First innings | | Second innings | |
|---|---|---|---|---|
| J. C. Balderstone c Moxon b Shaw | 1 | – | run out | 79 |
| I. P. Butcher b Swallow | 82 | – | c Blakey b Swallow | 76 |
| R. A. Cobb b Fletcher | 0 | – | (8) not out | 12 |
| *P. Willey c Moxon b Carrick | 60 | – | (3) c Swallow b Carrick | 10 |
| J. J. Whitaker c Pickles b Carrick | 43 | – | (4) c Love b Carrick | 19 |
| N. E. Briers c Love b Carrick | 0 | – | (5) not out | 32 |
| †M. A. Garnham c Boycott b Carrick | 33 | – | c Bairstow b Carrick | 6 |
| G. J. Parsons not out | 1 | – | (6) st Bairstow b Carrick | 4 |
| B 4, l-b 3, n-b 3 | 10 | | L-b 8, n-b 3 | 11 |
| 1/4 2/7 3/122 4/152 5/161 6/172 7/230 (7 wkts dec.) | 230 | | 1/145 2/169 3/179 4/204 5/216 6/226 (6 wkts) | 249 |

N. G. B. Cook, J. P. Agnew and L. B. Taylor did not bat.

Bonus points – Leicestershire 2, Yorkshire 3.

Bowling: *First Innings*—Fletcher 14–1–56–1; Shaw 10–1–30–1; Pickles 6–3–16–0; Carrick 26–5–73–4; Swallow 15–1–48–1. *Second Innings*—Fletcher 20–5–72–0; Shaw 7–0–26–0; Carrick 26–3–76–4; Pickles 5–1–16–0; Swallow 15–1–51–1.

Umpires: J. W. Holder and B. Leadbeater.

At Worcester, June 29, July 1, 2. YORKSHIRE drew with WORCESTERSHIRE.

At Gloucester, July 6, 8, 9. YORKSHIRE lost to GLOUCESTERSHIRE by eight wickets.

At Maidstone, July 10, 11, 12. YORKSHIRE lost to KENT by 100 runs.

## YORKSHIRE v SURREY

At Sheffield, July 13, 15, 16. Surrey won by nine wickets. Surrey 24 pts, Yorkshire 3 pts. Toss won by Surrey, who had early problems on a pitch which did offer slight help to the seamers. However, Yorkshire had no-one to exploit the conditions and their catching again let them down. Lynch, producing some well-timed drives, dominated the first day before Gray took over. Achieving lift and varying his pace, Gray cut through some faint-hearted batting with a burst of four wickets in five balls, including the hat-trick. Boycott, solid and well organised, completed 1,000 runs in an English season for the 23rd time and carried his bat through a completed Yorkshire innings for the eighth time. Metcalfe did better against a tired attack when Yorkshire followed on, but the Bridlington-born Doughty bowled with commendable persistence and only Bairstow, reaching 50 from 31 balls, really challenged Surrey's grip on the match.

## Surrey

| | | | |
|---|---|---|---|
| A. R. Butcher c and b Jarvis | 21 | – not out | 24 |
| G. S. Clinton lbw b Jarvis | 67 | – lbw b Shaw | 6 |
| A. Needham c Sharp b Carrick | 27 | – not out | 19 |
| *T. E. Jesty c S. N. Hartley b Carrick | 3 | | |
| M. A. Lynch c Love b Jarvis | 133 | | |
| D. M. Ward c Sharp b Swallow | 35 | | |
| †C. J. Richards c and b Carrick | 19 | | |
| R. J. Doughty c Bairstow b Jarvis | 19 | | |
| P. I. Pocock c Sharp b Carrick | 10 | | |
| A. H. Gray lbw b Jarvis | 8 | | |
| G. Monkhouse not out | 0 | | |
| B 4, l-b 9, n-b 9 | 22 | L-b 2 | 2 |
| 1/35 2/94 3/104 4/151 5/253 6/306 7/345 8/346 9/364 | 364 | 1/14 | (1 wkt) 51 |

Bonus points – Surrey 4, Yorkshire 3 (Score at 100 overs: 357-8).

Bowling: *First Innings*—Jarvis 26.4–4–107–5; P. J. Hartley 18–2–62–0; Shaw 13–4–34–0; Carrick 31–5–98–4; Swallow 14–2–50–1. *Second Innings*—Jarvis 7–2–15–0; Shaw 5–2–11–1; S. N. Hartley 3–0–14–0; P. J. Hartley 2–0–9–0.

## Yorkshire

| | | | |
|---|---|---|---|
| G. Boycott not out | 55 | – c Richards b Jesty | 29 |
| A. A. Metcalfe c Richards b Gray | 7 | – c Lynch b Gray | 77 |
| K. Sharp b Gray | 0 | – lbw b Doughty | 30 |
| S. N. Hartley c Doughty b Jesty | 27 | – c Lynch b Gray | 5 |
| P. Carrick b Gray | 20 | – c Richards b Doughty | 7 |
| *†D. L. Bairstow c Lynch b Gray | 0 | – lbw b Monkhouse | 65 |
| P. W. Jarvis c Richards b Gray | 1 | – c Richards b Jesty | 11 |
| I. G. Swallow c Doughty b Gray | 0 | – lbw b Pocock | 3 |
| P. J. Hartley b Gray | 13 | – c Clinton b Doughty | 33 |
| C. Shaw b Doughty | 1 | – not out | 9 |
| J. D. Love c Richards b Gray | 0 | – absent injured | |
| B 2, l-b 2, w 2, n-b 1 | 7 | B 1, l-b 7, w 2, n-b 1 | 11 |
| 1/18 2/18 3/68 4/105 5/105 6/107 7/107 8/125 9/130 | 131 | 1/53 2/143 3/147 4/155 5/155 6/230 7/236 8/236 9/280 | 280 |

Bonus points – Surrey 4.

Bowling: *First Innings*—Gray 17.4–6–40–8; Doughty 17–4–40–1; Jesty 9–3–21–1; Monkhouse 7–2–14–0; Needham 2–0–12–0. *Second Innings*—Gray 19–5–79–2; Doughty 24.3–7–75–3; Monkhouse 20–6–46–1; Jesty 8–1–50–2; Pocock 20–10–22–1.

Umpires: J. W. Holder and R. A. White.

At Headingley, July 19. YORKSHIRE lost to AN INTERNATIONAL XI by 33 runs (See Other Matches, 1985).

At Chesterfield, July 24, 25, 26. YORKSHIRE drew with DERBYSHIRE.

At Worksop, July 27, 29, 30. YORKSHIRE drew with NOTTINGHAMSHIRE.

## YORKSHIRE v DERBYSHIRE

At Bradford, July 31, August 1, 2. Yorkshire won by an innings and 24 runs. Yorkshire 22 pts, Derbyshire 3 pts. Toss won by Derbyshire. On a slow pitch which gave generous help to the spinners from the start, Carrick bowled for more than four hours to destroy Derbyshire's first innings, during which Roberts resisted for 50 overs. Moir, however, was not sufficiently accurate when Yorkshire batted, and Barnett, with leg-spin, proved Derbyshire's most effective bowler, returning career-best figures. Bairstow, despite a painful back, applied himself carefully for more than three and a half hours to ensure that Yorkshire gained a healthy lead. In their second innings, Derbyshire surrendered without much fight, throwing away wickets with some careless strokes as the ball turned. Yorkshire's catching, which had been patchy for much of the season, proved far more reliable and this was a decisive factor as they achieved their first Championship win since May.

### Derbyshire

| First innings | | Second innings | |
|---|---|---|---|
| *K. J. Barnett c Bairstow b Shaw | 34 | (6) c Bairstow b Carrick | 0 |
| I. S. Anderson c and b Carrick | 39 | (1) st Bairstow b Swallow | 14 |
| J. E. Morris c Sharp b Shaw | 9 | lbw b Carrick | 22 |
| B. Roberts c Bairstow b P. J. Hartley | 41 | (2) c Swallow b Carrick | 6 |
| J. G. Wright c and b Swallow | 12 | lbw b Carrick | 6 |
| G. Miller b Carrick | 23 | (4) c and b Swallow | 11 |
| P. G. Newman lbw b Jarvis | 11 | b Swallow | 2 |
| A. E. Warner st Bairstow b Carrick | 7 | (10) b Carrick | 6 |
| D. G. Moir b Swallow | 4 | (8) lbw b Carrick | 38 |
| R. J. Finney not out | 6 | (9) c Shaw b Swallow | 0 |
| †C. Marples c S. N. Hartley b Carrick | 1 | not out | 7 |
| L-b 10, w 2 | 12 | B 2, l-b 11, n-b 4 | 17 |
| 1/64 2/82 3/94 4/111 5/144 6/167 7/183 8/189 9/198 | 199 | 1/13 2/32 3/59 4/65 5/68 6/71 7/73 8/81 9/110 | 129 |

Bonus points – Derbyshire 1, Yorkshire 4.

Bowling: *First Innings*—Jarvis 16–2–40–1; P. J. Hartley 11–2–23–1; Carrick 39.4–16–59–4; Shaw 10–2–27–2; Swallow 14–4–40–2. *Second Innings*—Jarvis 6–1–9–0; P. J. Hartley 2–0–5–0; Carrick 35.1–17–46–6; Swallow 32–13–53–4; Boycott 1–0–3–0.

### Yorkshire

| | |
|---|---|
| G. Boycott c Anderson b Moir | 7 |
| M. D. Moxon lbw b Barnett | 43 |
| K. Sharp c Anderson b Barnett | 37 |
| P. E. Robinson b Moir | 39 |
| S. N. Hartley lbw b Barnett | 7 |
| *†D. L. Bairstow not out | 122 |
| P. Carrick c Miller b Barnett | 33 |
| I. G. Swallow c Miller b Moir | 17 |
| P. W. Jarvis c Wright b Barnett | 18 |
| P. J. Hartley b Newman | 1 |
| C. Shaw st Marples b Barnett | 0 |
| B 6, l-b 11, w 2, n-b 9 | 28 |
| 1/25 2/81 3/110 4/138 5/142 6/220 7/260 8/321 9/341 | 352 |

Bonus points – Yorkshire 2, Derbyshire 2 (Score at 100 overs: 206-5).

Bowling: Finney 6–3–4–0; Newman 15–5–22–1; Miller 33–9–79–0; Moir 58–20–115–3; Barnett 46.3–10–115–6.

Umpires: N. T. Plews and A. A. Jones.

At Edgbaston, August 3, 5, 6. YORKSHIRE drew with WARWICKSHIRE.

## YORKSHIRE v LANCASHIRE

At Headingley, August 10, 12 13. Drawn. Yorkshire 5 pts, Lancashire 7 pts. Toss won by Lancashire. Electing to bat first, Lancashire recovered from a hesitant start to build a useful first innings on a pitch of unreliable bounce and just a hint of pace. Fairbrother, missed in the slips when 82, completed his second Roses century of the summer in four hours with nineteen 4s and one 6. Peter Hartley had his best bowling return for Yorkshire. Rain cut into Yorkshire's reply, and although this destroyed the competitive element, both sides were nevertheless guilty of negative cricket. Moxon occupied the crease for six and a half hours in making 127 and he, like Bairstow, had the satisfaction of passing 1,000 runs for the season. Lancashire bowled their overs very slowly and set defensive fields, while Yorkshire made no apparent attempt to score quickly.

### Lancashire

M. R. Chadwick c Jarvis b Shaw ..... 37
D. W. Varey b Shaw ............... 13
S. J. O'Shaughnessy c Carrick b P. J. Hartley . 4
N. H. Fairbrother b P. J. Hartley .....147
D. P. Hughes lbw b Shaw ........... 2
*J. Abrahams c Bairstow b P. J. Hartley 23
†C. Maynard c Carrick b P. J. Hartley . 43
D. J. Makinson not out ............. 40
P. J. W. Allott c Bairstow b P. J. Hartley 3
I. Folley not out .................. 0
B 1, l-b 5, w 2, n-b 7 ........ 15

1/35 2/53 3/57 4/67 5/147 6/222 7/318 8/326 (8 wkts dec.) 327

B. P. Patterson did not bat.

Bonus points – Lancashire 4, Yorkshire 2 (Score at 100 overs: 318-6).

Bowling: Jarvis 23–2–94–0; P. J. Hartley 30–6–91–5; Shaw 29–8–77–3; Swallow 8–1–21–0; Carrick 14–4–38–0.

### Yorkshire

M. D. Moxon c Maynard b Folley ....127
P. Carrick c Fairbrother b Patterson ... 0
I. G. Swallow b Patterson ........... 9
K. Sharp c Hughes b Allott .......... 0
P. E. Robinson b Allott ............. 20
S. N. Hartley lbw b Makinson ........ 19
J. D. Love c Chadwick b Patterson ... 27
*†D. L. Bairstow c O'Shaughnessy b Folley . 28
P. W. Jarvis c O'Shaughnessy b Hughes 22
P. J. Hartley not out ................ 21
C. Shaw not out ................... 9
B 6, l-b 12, w 3, n-b 25 ...... 46

1/2 2/37 3/42 4/95 5/159 6/213 7/260 8/281 9/308 (9 wkts dec.) 328

Bonus points – Yorkshire 3, Lancashire 3 (Score at 100 overs: 281-8).

Bowling: Allott 23–9–38–2; Patterson 29–2–95–3; Makinson 22–4–56–1; O'Shaughnessy 7–1–23–0; Folley 15–3–57–2; Fairbrother 7–4–9–0; Hughes 19–10–26–1; Abrahams 7–5–6–0.

Umpires: H. D. Bird and B. Dudleston.

At The Oval, August 14, 15, 16. YORKSHIRE drew with SURREY.

## YORKSHIRE v KENT

At Scarborough, August 17, 19, 20. Drawn. Yorkshire 5 pts, Kent 2 pts. Toss won by Kent. Batting first, Kent collapsed against some accurate seam bowling by Yorkshire's young attack on an easy-paced pitch after the start was delayed by overnight rain. The Kent innings stretched well into the second day, with Taylor needing 276 balls for his century. Shaw had a career-best return of five for 76, and although he bowled accurately throughout, his form did not explain Kent's subdued approach. Yorkshire in contrast scored slowly only against the spinners, who found little assistance but gave nothing away. Bairstow declared 67 behind to open up the game, but the possibility of an interesting finish disappeared when torrential rain washed out the last day.

## Kent

| | | | |
|---|---|---|---|
| M. R. Benson c Bairstow b Shaw | 17 | not out | 6 |
| S. G. Hinks lbw b P. J. Hartley | 9 | b Shaw | 0 |
| C. J. Tavaré c Pickles b Shaw | 22 | | |
| N. R. Taylor not out | 102 | (3) not out | 5 |
| *C. S. Cowdrey lbw b Shaw | 0 | | |
| L. Potter lbw b Pickles | 15 | | |
| C. Penn c Bairstow b Shaw | 0 | | |
| †A. P. E. Knott b P. J. Hartley | 18 | | |
| G. R. Dilley c Moxon b Pickles | 15 | | |
| D. L. Underwood lbw b P. J. Hartley | 1 | | |
| K. B. S. Jarvis lbw b Shaw | 7 | | |
| L-b 5, w 2, n-b 4 | 11 | B 6, l-b 1 | 7 |
| 1/14 2/29 3/78 4/81 5/101 6/102 7/129 8/182 9/183 | 217 | 1/2 | (1 wkt) 18 |

Bonus points – Kent 2, Yorkshire 4 (Score at 100 overs: 200-9).

Bowling: *First Innings*—P. J. Hartley 30–6–78–3; Shaw 40.3–13–76–5; Pickles 22–11–31–2; S. N. Hartley 6–2–12–0; Carrick 9–5–15–0. *Second Innings*—P. J. Hartley 5–1–6–0; Shaw 4–1–4–1; Carrick 1–0–1–0.

## Yorkshire

| | |
|---|---|
| G. Boycott not out | 62 |
| M. D. Moxon lbw b Underwood | 43 |
| R. J. Blakey not out | 35 |
| B 4, l-b 2, n-b 4 | 10 |
| 1/79 (1 wkt dec.) | 150 |

J. D. Love, P. E. Robinson, S. N. Hartley, *†D. L. Bairstow, P. Carrick, C. Shaw, P. J. Hartley and C. S. Pickles did not bat.

Bonus point – Yorkshire 1.

Bowling: Dilley 3–0–9–0; Jarvis 8–3–18–0; Underwood 23–8–41–1; Potter 20–4–66–0; Hinks 5–0–10–0.

Umpires: D. O. Oslear and R. A. White.

At Swansea, August 24, 26, 27. YORKSHIRE beat GLAMORGAN by 34 runs.

At Hove, August 28, 29, 30. YORKSHIRE drew with SUSSEX.

## YORKSHIRE v NORTHAMPTONSHIRE

At Headingley, August 31, September 2, 3. Drawn. Yorkshire 2 pts, Northamptonshire 2 pts. Toss won by Yorkshire. Rain, which allowed only 73 overs, ruined the match. Northamptonshire made steady progress on an easy-paced pitch, despite losing three wickets for 14 runs in 25 balls to Fletcher's medium-pace. Bailey and Capel were engaged in an enterprising stand which had added 90 in 27 overs when the weather closed in at lunch on the second day.

### Northamptonshire

| | | | |
|---|---|---|---|
| *G. Cook c Bairstow b Shaw | 41 | D. J. Capel not out | 35 |
| W. Larkins lbw b S. N. Hartley | 25 | | |
| R. J. Boyd-Moss c Robinson b Fletcher | 31 | B 4, l-b 14, n-b 9 | 27 |
| R. J. Bailey not out | 73 | | — |
| R. G. Williams b Fletcher | 0 | 1/61 2/82 3/126 4/128 (5 wkts) | 242 |
| D. J. Wild b Fletcher | 10 | 5/152 | |

R. A. Harper, †D. Ripley, N. A. Mallender and B. J. Griffiths did not bat.

Bonus points – Northamptonshire 2, Yorkshire 2.

Bowling: P. J. Hartley 18–4–60–0; Fletcher 24–4–62–3; Shaw 19–3–52–1; S. N. Hartley 12–0–50–1.

### Yorkshire

G. Boycott, M. D. Moxon, R. J. Blakey, J. D. Love, P. E. Robinson, S. N. Hartley, *†D. L. Bairstow, P. Carrick, C. Shaw, P. J. Hartley and S. D. Fletcher.

Umpires: B. J. Meyer and P. B. Wight.

## YORKSHIRE v NOTTINGHAMSHIRE

At Scarborough, September 11, 12, 13. Drawn. Yorkshire 5 pts, Nottinghamshire 8 pts. Toss won by Yorkshire. Batting first, Yorkshire struggled on a slow pitch and lost wickets to careless strokes against accurate bowling by Hadlee and Hemmings in particular. Robinson, hitting seventeen boundaries, dominated the Nottinghamshire reply, but used up more than five hours in making his century. Rice surprisingly declared with a lead of only 39 which left the contest in "no man's land". Bairstow had hardly sufficient time in which to build a position from which he might pursue victory and Boycott held up the progress of the game by scoring a very cautious hundred, his 149th, which put him level with Herbert Sutcliffe as the leading Yorkshireman in the all-time list of century-makers. Boycott used up 261 deliveries and Bairstow finally set a target of 268 in 54 overs. Nottinghamshire were very much on top as they passed 200 for the loss of only two wickets in 45 overs. Randall completed 2,000 runs in the course of an imaginative effort, but Peter Hartley achieved a career-best bowling return, and a spell in which four wickets fell for 4 runs in three overs ensured a draw.

### Yorkshire

| | | | |
|---|---|---|---|
| G. Boycott c Randall b Hemmings | 76 | – not out | 125 |
| M. D. Moxon c French b Hadlee | 15 | – c Randall b Hadlee | 65 |
| R. J. Blakey c Robinson b Such | 12 | – lbw b Cooper | 4 |
| J. D. Love b Hadlee | 36 | – c Randall b Pick | 79 |
| S. N. Hartley c Broad b Cooper | 37 | | |
| *†D. L. Bairstow b Hemmings | 6 | – (5) c Hemmings b Broad | 25 |
| P. Carrick c Martindale b Hemmings | 41 | | |
| I. G. Swallow c and b Hemmings | 7 | | |
| P. J. Hartley c French b Hadlee | 23 | | |
| C. Shaw b Hadlee | 5 | | |
| S. D. Fletcher not out | 3 | | |
| L-b 1 | 1 | B 1, l-b 3, n-b 4 | 8 |
| | — | | — |
| 1/21 2/45 3/106 4/160 5/178 | 262 | 1/129 2/143 3/262 (4 wkts dec.) | 306 |
| 6/184 7/199 8/248 9/254 | | 4/306 | |

Bonus points – Yorkshire 3, Nottinghamshire 4.

Bowling: *First Innings*—Hadlee 17.4–3–52–4; Pick 9–1–29–0; Cooper 12–4–22–1; Such 22–5–53–1; Rice 5–3–10–0; Hemmings 28–6–95–4. *Second Innings*—Hadlee 11–4–14–1; Pick 18–2–82–1; Rice 6–2–11–0; Cooper 15–4–40–1; Such 15–1–83–0; Hemmings 22–7–69–0; Randall 1–0–2–0; Broad 0.2–0–1–1.

## Nottinghamshire

| | First innings | | Second innings | |
|---|---|---|---|---|
| R. T. Robinson | st Bairstow b Carrick | 118 | lbw b P. J. Hartley | 19 |
| B. C. Broad | c and b Fletcher | 50 | st Bairstow b Carrick | 72 |
| D. W. Randall | b Fletcher | 0 | c Blakey b Carrick | 73 |
| *C. E. B. Rice | c Carrick b Shaw | 39 | c Bairstow b P. J. Hartley | 24 |
| D. J. R. Martindale | lbw b Carrick | 4 | (6) lbw b P. J. Hartley | 0 |
| R. J. Hadlee | not out | 73 | (5) b P. J. Hartley | 3 |
| †B. N. French | not out | 5 | c Shaw b Carrick | 15 |
| E. E. Hemmings | (did not bat) | | lbw b P. J. Hartley | 10 |
| R. A. Pick | (did not bat) | | not out | 17 |
| K. E. Cooper | (did not bat) | | not out | 4 |
| | B 1, l-b 6, w 1, n-b 4 | 12 | B 7, l-b 6, w 1, n-b 5 | 19 |
| | 1/93 2/93 3/168 4/175 5/286 | (5 wkts dec.) 301 | 1/47 2/163 3/204 4/206 5/207 6/208 7/222 8/245 | (8 wkts) 256 |

P. M. Such did not bat.

Bonus points – Nottinghamshire 4, Yorkshire 2.

Bowling: *First Innings*—Fletcher 18–4–50–2; P. J. Hartley 16–2–60–0; Carrick 40–14–106–2; Swallow 15–3–40–0; Shaw 11–2–38–1. *Second Innings*—Fletcher 10–0–49–0; P. J. Hartley 15–1–75–5; Shaw 9–2–32–0; Carrick 20–2–87–3.

Umpires: J. W. Holder and A. A. Jones.

At Chelmsford, September 14, 16, 17. YORKSHIRE lost to ESSEX by an innings and 4 runs.

---

## RECORD TESTIMONIAL

The Yorkshire batsman, G. Boycott's testimonial in 1984 realised £147,954. The previou record of £128,000 had been raised by J. Simmons (Lancashire) in 1980.

# THE UNIVERSITIES IN 1985

## OXFORD

President – M. J. K. SMITH (St Edmund Hall)

Hon. Treasurer – Dr S. R. PORTER (St Cross)

Captain – A. J. T. MILLER (Haileybury and St Edmund Hall)

Secretary – D. A. THORNE (Bablake School, Coventry and Keble)

Captain for 1986 – D. A. THORNE

Secretary – M. P. LAWRENCE (Manchester Grammar School and Merton)

Not even the wet season could prevent The Parks from again becoming a batsman's paradise, at any rate for visiting batsmen. Twenty-two centuries were scored in the ten first-class matches played there, all but three against the University.

When Andrew Miller had all the old Blues at his disposal, at the start and end of the season, Oxford performed quite well. But the absence, while preparing for finals, of John Carr, who opened with 115 against Somerset and marked his return with a century off Yorkshire, Willie Bristowe and the wicket-keeper, Jonathan Franks, left gaps which were never adequately filled. It was hardly surprising, therefore, that the side suffered some heavy defeats.

There were mitigating circumstances for the first-innings score of 24 all out against Leicestershire, the University's lowest since the war: the pitch was difficult enough to be reported later to Lord's. However, the 47 in the second innings against Lancashire did reveal a sad lack of technique against good spin bowling. It underlined the need for a coach to be available throughout the term, and not just in the weeks leading up to the start of the season.

Generally the batting fared quite well, enabling Miller more than once to declare with scores in excess of 250. This was due mainly to the excellent form of David Thorne, who had a splendid season. In ten of his seventeen innings in The Parks he exceeded 50, and if a troublesome back affected his bowling, it did nothing to inhibit his efforts with the bat, his average of not much under 60 being the best by an Oxford player for many years. Thorne scored Oxford's other century in The Parks, 124 against the Zimbabweans, having earlier been denied a maiden century against Glamorgan when the last six batsmen accumulated only 8 runs between them and he finished with 98 not out. Miller and Giles Toogood, who had a remarkable match at Lord's, batted well at times, though neither achieved the consistency of the previous year. On occasions Patrick MacLarnon, Richard Rutnagur and Christopher

OXFORD UNIVERSITY 1985

[*Bill Smith*

*Back row:* R. S. Rutnagur, M. P. Lawrence, P. C. MacLarnon, C. D. M. Tooley, J. D. Quinlan, W. R. Bristowe, T. Patel. *Front row:* J. D. Carr, D. A. Thorne, A. J. T. Miller (*captain*), G. J. Toogood, J. G. Franks.

Tooley also made valuable contributions. The disappointment was Tikendra Patel, a prolific scorer in club cricket.

The bowling was weak in all aspects, the problems being compounded by poor catching. The opening attack of Jeremy Quinlan and Thorne, when he was fit enough to bowl, was of gentle medium pace and posed few threats to county batsmen, while Carr's absence deprived the side of their only off-spinner. The bulk of the slow bowling was undertaken by Mark Lawrence, slow left-arm, who took most wickets but was expensive. He suffered from an over-ambitious policy of close fielders when the situation demanded more defensive placings.

Heavy rain after lunch on the third day at Lord's denied Oxford a possible win over Cambridge in what will always be recalled as Toogood's match. His eight for 52 in Cambridge's first innings and 149 in Oxford's first amounted to an all-round performance that has seldom been equalled in the long history of the fixture. – P.F.

## OXFORD UNIVERSITY RESULTS

*First-class matches* – Played 11: Lost 4, Drawn 7.

## FIRST-CLASS AVERAGES – BATTING

| | *M* | *I* | *NO* | *R* | *HI* | *Avge* |
|---|---|---|---|---|---|---|
| D. A. Thorne ......... | 11 | 18 | 3 | 849 | 124 | 56.60 |
| J. D. Carr ............ | 6 | 9 | 1 | 415 | 115 | 51.87 |
| G. J. Toogood ........ | 9 | 15 | 1 | 507 | 149 | 36.21 |
| A. J. T. Miller ........ | 10 | 17 | 3 | 462 | 78 | 33.00 |
| J. G. Franks .......... | 3 | 4 | 1 | 71 | 35 | 23.66 |
| W. R. Bristowe ........ | 5 | 8 | 1 | 156 | 42* | 22.28 |
| R. S. Rutnagur ........ | 11 | 15 | 2 | 246 | 66 | 18.92 |
| P. C. MacLarnon ...... | 7 | 10 | 1 | 168 | 56 | 18.66 |
| D. A. Hagan .......... | 5 | 10 | 1 | 148 | 46 | 16.44 |
| C. D. M. Tooley ....... | 11 | 16 | 0 | 257 | 66 | 16.06 |
| T. Patel ............... | 9 | 17 | 4 | 159 | 47 | 12.23 |
| J. D. Quinlan ......... | 7 | 6 | 2 | 34 | 22* | 8.50 |
| C. M. Denny .......... | 4 | 6 | 1 | 28 | 19 | 5.60 |
| D. S. Harrison ........ | 4 | 5 | 2 | 12 | 6 | 4.00 |
| M. P. Lawrence ....... | 11 | 9 | 3 | 20 | 9* | 3.33 |
| D. P. Taylor .......... | 4 | 6 | 2 | 5 | 5* | 1.25 |

Played in four matches: J. G. Brettell 0, 0*.

* *Signifies not out.*

The following played a total of four three-figure innings for Oxford University – J. D. Carr 2, D. A. Thorne 1, G. J. Toogood 1.

## BOWLING

| | *O* | *M* | *R* | *W* | *BB* | *Avge* |
|---|---|---|---|---|---|---|
| G. J. Toogood ........ | 209.2 | 44 | 691 | 18 | 8-52 | 38.38 |
| R. S. Rutnagur ........ | 189 | 25 | 728 | 15 | 5-112 | 48.53 |
| D. A. Thorne ......... | 196.1 | 34 | 664 | 13 | 4-64 | 51.07 |
| M. P. Lawrence ....... | 341.5 | 65 | 1,154 | 20 | 3-99 | 57.70 |
| J. D. Carr ............ | 184 | 48 | 462 | 8 | 4-65 | 57.75 |
| J. D. Quinlan ......... | 189 | 37 | 635 | 10 | 4-76 | 63.50 |

Also bowled: J. G. Brettell 62.4–14–266–4; W. R. Bristowe 1–0–5–0; D. A. Hagan 1–0–6–0; P. C. MacLarnon 60.3–10–229–1.

## OXFORD UNIVERSITY v SOMERSET

At The Parks, April 20, 22, 23. Drawn. Toss won by Somerset. Rain prevented any play on the first day of a match which bore several similarities to the fixture the previous season. As they did in 1984, Roebuck and Wyatt opened with centuries in a first-wicket partnership of 245, and after Wyatt's dismissal for 145 (280 minutes, fifteen 4s), Popplewell joined Roebuck in an unbroken stand of 106. Oxford's reply on the third morning began badly when Miller and Bristowe went cheaply. However, Carr, who scored 100 in 1984, and Toogood responded with a splendid third-wicket partnership of 154, Carr hitting twenty 4s in an innings of 153 minutes and 115 balls.

### Somerset

| | |
|---|---|
| J. G. Wyatt c Tooley b Quinlan | 145 |
| P. M. Roebuck not out | 123 |
| N. F. M. Popplewell not out | 67 |
| L-b 5, n-b 11 | 16 |
| 1/245 (1 wkt dec.) | 351 |

R. L. Ollis, V. J. Marks, *I. T. Botham, M. S. Turner, †T. Gard, G. V. Palmer, M. R. Davis and S. C. Booth did not bat.

Bowling: Thorne 16–3–49–0; Quinlan 21–6–62–1; Toogood 21–3–70–0; Lawrence 25–3–87–0; Carr 38–8–78–0.

### Oxford University

| | |
|---|---|
| *A. J. T. Miller c Botham b Turner | 6 |
| W. R. Bristowe b Turner | 4 |
| G. J. Toogood c Gard b Davis | 59 |
| J. D. Carr b Marks | 115 |
| D. A. Thorne c Wyatt b Booth | 31 |
| †J. G. Franks not out | 10 |
| T. Patel not out | 12 |
| B 4, n-b 6 | 10 |
| 1/8 2/11 3/165 4/223 5/227 (5 wkts dec.) | 247 |

R. S. Rutnagur, C. D. M. Tooley, M. P. Lawrence and J. D. Quinlan did not bat.

Bowling: Davis 21–7–35–1; Turner 8.1–2–20–2; Palmer 20–6–56–0; Booth 19–7–62–1; Popplewell 6.5–1–41–0; Marks 14–7–16–1; Botham 6–1–13–0.

Umpires: H. D. Bird and D. S. Thompsett.

## OXFORD UNIVERSITY v GLAMORGAN

At The Parks, April 24, 25, 26. Drawn. Toss won by Oxford University. Glamorgan were made to pay for two errors by their wicket-keeper, Davies. Thorne, dropped before he had scored, finished with an unbeaten 98 and only a startling collapse denied the all-rounder his maiden century. Carr survived a stumping chance when 20 and went on to score 81, so that despite the last six batsmen managing only 8 runs between them, the University scored 282. Carr's first 44 runs were all from boundaries and in all he hit sixteen 4s. Glamorgan's reply was a massive 456. Younis, with one 6 and 21 4s in his 113, and Steele, hitting his first century for the county, led the run-spree. Oxford, facing a deficit of 174 with three hours remaining, lost Bristowe for 7, but Miller and Franks steadied the innings with a partnership of 55.

## Oxford University

| | | | |
|---|---|---|---|
| *A. J. T. Miller c Steele b Ontong | 18 | not out | 61 |
| W. R. Bristowe b Thomas | 25 | lbw b Malone | 7 |
| †J. G. Franks c Davies b Malone | 35 | b Holmes | 26 |
| J. D. Carr c Davies b Holmes | 81 | c Ontong b Malone | 0 |
| D. A. Thorne not out | 98 | lbw b Ontong | 7 |
| T. Patel c Steele b Holmes | 0 | not out | 0 |
| C. D. M. Tooley run out | 4 | | |
| R. S. Rutnagur c Jones b Steele | 0 | | |
| C. M. Denny lbw b Thomas | 0 | | |
| J. D. Quinlan c Ontong b Thomas | 4 | | |
| M. P. Lawrence b Thomas | 0 | | |
| B 8, l-b 4, n-b 5 | 17 | B 4, l-b 3, n-b 1 | 8 |
| 1/47 2/55 3/132 4/193 5/201 6/249 7/253 8/254 9/278 | 282 | 1/22 2/77 3/82 4/105 | (4 wkts) 109 |

Bowling: *First Innings*—Thomas 22–7–47–4; McFarlane 14–3–28–0; Malone 20–5–55–1; Ontong 19–7–38–1; Steele 30–12–75–1; Holmes 12–6–27–2. *Second Innings*—Thomas 10–0–32–0; Malone 9–2–20–2; McFarlane 8–1–26–0; Holmes 5–3–3–1; Steele 5–3–8–0; Ontong 4–1–13–1.

## Glamorgan

| | |
|---|---|
| A. L. Jones c and b Thorne | 6 |
| J. A. Hopkins c Carr b Quinlan | 81 |
| G. C. Holmes lbw b Rutnagur | 29 |
| Javed Miandad c Franks b Quinlan | 47 |
| Younis Ahmed st Franks b Quinlan | 113 |
| *R. C. Ontong c Tooley b Lawrence | 16 |
| J. F. Steele b Lawrence | 100 |
| †T. Davies not out | 46 |
| J. G. Thomas c Denny b Rutnagur | 2 |
| L. L. McFarlane c Miller b Rutnagur | 0 |
| S. J. Malone c Thorne b Lawrence | 2 |
| B 4, l-b 10 | 14 |
| 1/7 2/82 3/148 4/178 5/222 6/333 7/440 8/451 9/453 | 456 |

Bowling: Thorne 26–6–75–1; Quinlan 30–4–117–3; Lawrence 30.5–6–99–3; Rutnagur 22–1–76–3; Carr 27–8–75–0.

Umpires: H. D. Bird and D. S. Thompsett.

## OXFORD UNIVERSITY v LEICESTERSHIRE

At The Parks, May 1, 2. Leicestershire won by an innings and 75 runs. Toss won by Leicestershire. On a virtually unplayable pitch, which was later reported to Lord's, Oxford University were bowled out twice on the second day. The batsmen were unable to cope with deliveries that lifted sharply off a length and were dismissed for 24 in 90 minutes, their second-ever lowest score, as Parsons returned career-best figures of six for 11. Eight batsmen failed to score. Oxford did better in the second innings, Miller and Toogood opening with 52 and Thorne and Patel making useful contributions, but it was a losing struggle on the still unpredictable pitch. The match ended in the first over of the extra half-hour claimed by Gower. Gower's decision to bat looked to have backfired when Leicestershire lost three wickets for 21; but Butcher, run out 5 short of his century, and Parsons steadied the innings, and Garnham completed the recovery with a maiden hundred (eleven 4s) off 226 balls.

## Leicestershire

| | |
|---|---|
| J. C. Balderstone c Denny b Quinlan | 0 |
| I. P. Butcher run out | 95 |
| J. J. Whitaker c Harrison b Quinlan | 0 |
| N. E. Briers c Patel b Quinlan | 2 |
| G. J. Parsons c Toogood b Carr | 24 |
| †M. A. Garnham st Harrison b Carr | 100 |
| *D. I. Gower b Quinlan | 9 |
| P. Willey b Carr | 57 |
| P. A. J. De Freitas b Carr | 0 |
| P. B. Clift c Patel b Toogood | 23 |
| L. B. Taylor not out | 0 |
| B 12, l-b 1, w 3, n-b 4 | 20 |
| 1/11 2/15 3/21 4/95 5/135 6/172 7/268 8/268 9/326 | 330 |

Bowling: Thorne 23–5–68–0; Quinlan 21–3–76–4; Lawrence 5–1–23–0; Toogood 11.4–1–48–1; Carr 36–14–65–4; Rutnagur 8–0–37–0.

## Oxford University

| | | | |
|---|---|---|---|
| *A. J. T. Miller c Gower b Taylor | 0 | c Butcher b Clift | 28 |
| G. J. Toogood c Garnham b Parsons | 0 | c Whitaker b Parsons | 39 |
| C. D. M. Tooley b De Freitas | 13 | b Taylor | 17 |
| J. D. Carr c Garnham b Parsons | 0 | c Whitaker b Taylor | 2 |
| D. A. Thorne c Balderstone b Parsons | 0 | b Willey | 47 |
| T. Patel lbw b Parsons | 2 | c Garnham b De Freitas | 35 |
| R. S. Rutnagur c Garnham b Parsons | 0 | b Clift | 17 |
| C. M. Denny c Garnham b Parsons | 5 | c Garnham b De Freitas | 3 |
| †D. S. Harrison c Clift b De Freitas | 0 | c Garnham b De Freitas | 6 |
| J. D. Quinlan not out | 0 | not out | 22 |
| M. P. Lawrence b De Freitas | 0 | c Gower b Willey | 0 |
| N-b 4 | 4 | B 4, l-b 2, w 1, n-b 8 | 15 |
| 1/0 2/0 3/3 4/3 5/11 6/11 7/24 8/24 9/24 | 24 | 1/52 2/84 3/86 4/90 5/152 6/193 7/201 8/201 9/230 | 231 |

Bowling: *First Innings*—Taylor 8–5–10–1; Parsons 11–5–11–6; De Freitas 3.4–2–3–3. *Second Innings*—De Freitas 22–7–81–3; Parsons 11–3–42–1; Clift 18–4–39–2; Taylor 7–2–14–2; Willey 17.4–6–49–2.

Umpires: K. J. Lyons and N. T. Plews.

# OXFORD UNIVERSITY v HAMPSHIRE

At The Parks, May 8, 9, 10. Drawn. Toss won by Hampshire. Oxford University comfortably drew a high-scoring match which saw Hampshire's Chris Smith score a hundred in each innings. In the first innings he figured in a second-wicket stand of 151 – 80 with Turner, who retired with a heavy cold, and 71 with his brother, Robin, who later added 151 with James. Oxford made a positive reply, with Miller and Tooley putting on 100 for the second wicket and Thorne and Patel joining in a fourth-wicket partnership of 133. Following Miller's declaration, 70 runs in arrears, Chris Smith scored 100 out of an opening partnership of 133 with Hardy and the county declared at 252 for two, setting Oxford to score 323 in 150 minutes. The target was purely academic.

## Hampshire

| | | | |
|---|---|---|---|
| J. J. E. Hardy c and b Toogood | 43 | c Thorne b Lawrence | 48 |
| C. L. Smith c Patel b Brettell | 110 | c Rutnagur b Lawrence | 100 |
| D. R. Turner retired ill | 49 | | |
| R. A. Smith st Harrison b Toogood | 120 | not out | 40 |
| *M. C. J. Nicholas c Lawrence b Rutnagur | 0 | (3) not out | 52 |
| K. D. James not out | 43 | | |
| B 2, l-b 5, n-b 1 | 8 | B 9, l-b 3 | 12 |
| 1/71 2/222 3/222 4/373 (4 wkts dec.) | 373 | 1/133 2/186 (2 wkts dec.) | 252 |

R. J. Maru, †C. F. E. Goldie, C. A. Connor, S. J. W. Andrew and I. J. Chivers did not bat.

Bowling: *First Innings*—Thorne 10-0-42-0; Quinlan 10-1-62-0; Toogood 31.4-11-106-2; Lawrence 19-1-98-0; Rutnagur 6-1-26-1; Brettell 5-1-32-1. *Second Innings*—Thorne 6-1-24-0; Quinlan 16-3-43-0; Toogood 10-3-35-0; Brettell 10.4-3-43-0; Lawrence 12-1-75-2; Rutnagur 3-0-20-0.

## Oxford University

| | | | |
|---|---|---|---|
| *A. J. T. Miller c Goldie b Andrew | 44 | c C. L. Smith b Chivers | 36 |
| G. J. Toogood b Connor | 0 | not out | 26 |
| C. D. M. Tooley b Andrew | 66 | c C. L. Smith b Maru | 3 |
| T. Patel c Connor b Maru | 47 | not out | 0 |
| D. A. Thorne b Maru | 85 | | |
| R. S. Rutnagur st Goldie b Maru | 15 | | |
| C. M. Denny b James | 19 | | |
| †D. S. Harrison not out | 5 | | |
| J. D. Quinlan lbw b James | 0 | | |
| M. P. Lawrence not out | 9 | | |
| B 1, l-b 4, n-b 8 | 13 | L-b 4 | 4 |
| 1/6 2/106 3/119 4/252 5/253 6/286 7/292 8/292 | (8 wkts dec.) 303 | 1/59 2/69 | (2 wkts) 69 |

J. G. Brettell did not bat.

Bowling: *First Innings*—Andrew 19-4-56-2; Connor 23-3-63-1; James 23.4-15-24-2; Chivers 15-2-67-0; Maru 29-10-62-3; C. L. Smith 4-0-26-0. *Second Innings*—Andrew 7-3-21-0; James 12-8-14-0; Connor 7-2-21-0; Chivers 7-3-5-1; Maru 6-3-4-1.

Umpires: A. A. Jones and R. Palmer.

# OXFORD UNIVERSITY v WORCESTERSHIRE

At The Parks, May 22, 23. Worcestershire won by an innings and 22 runs. Toss won by Worcestershire. Oxford were routed by the slow left-arm spin of Illingworth after being put in on a rain-affected pitch. Miller and Hagan, who was making his first-class début, gave the innings a sound start, but after lunch the last seven wickets fell for 23 in 65 minutes. Illingworth's haul was a career-best six for 9. Worcestershire made a poor start, but Weston and Banks saw them establish a commanding lead by the second day. Following Worcestershire's declaration, Oxford's openers gave their side an even better start, but after both had fallen to Patel, Illingworth struck again with an improved career-best of seven for 50, and when Patel claimed the extra half-hour, the University were condemned to their second innings defeat in two days.

## Oxford University

| | | | |
|---|---|---|---|
| *A. J. T. Miller lbw b Weston | 22 | – b Patel | 72 |
| D. A. Hagan c Patel b Weston | 33 | – c Weston b Patel | 46 |
| G. J. Toogood c and b Illingworth | 16 | – c Hick b Illingworth | 1 |
| C. D. M. Tooley c Kimber b Illingworth | 26 | – lbw b Illingworth | 4 |
| D. A. Thorne b Patel | 2 | – c D'Oliveira b Patel | 16 |
| T. Patel c Curtis b Illingworth | 0 | – c D'Oliveira b Illingworth | 0 |
| R. S. Rutnagur c Patel b Illingworth | 2 | – c D'Oliveira b Illingworth | 0 |
| P. C. MacLarnon b Illingworth | 0 | – (9) st Rhodes b Illingworth | 22 |
| †D. P. Taylor c Banks b Patel | 0 | – (8) b Illingworth | 0 |
| M. P. Lawrence not out | 0 | – b Illingworth | 4 |
| J. G. Brettell c D'Oliveira b Illingworth | 0 | – not out | 0 |
| L-b 2, w 1, n-b 1 | 4 | B 6, l-b 7, w 1, n-b 4 | 18 |
| 1/56 2/67 3/82 4/89 5/92 6/102 7/105 8/105 9/105 | 105 | 1/106 2/117 3/129 4/146 5/151 6/153 7/153 8/162 9/168 | 183 |

Bowling: *First Innings*—Newport 9–0–29–0; McEwan 4–0–14–0; Weston 10–5–15–2; Kimber 7–1–18–0; Illingworth 13.4–7–9–6; Patel 12–5–18–2. *Second Innings*—Newport 7–0–24–0; McEwan 5–1–10–0; Illingworth 32.3–10–50–7; Kimber 2–0–14–0; Patel 29–9–52–3; D'Oliveira 6–1–20–0; Hick 1–1–0–0.

## Worcestershire

M. J. Weston st Taylor b Brettell ..... 97
T. S. Curtis c Patel b Thorne ......... 0
*D. N. Patel b Thorne .............. 2
D. B. D'Oliveira st Taylor b Brettell ... 33
G. A. Hick c MacLarnon b Lawrence . 3
D. A. Banks c Brettell b Lawrence .... 76
P. J. Newport lbw b Thorne ......... 18
†S. J. Rhodes lbw b Thorne .......... 0
R. K. Illingworth c MacLarnon b Lawrence . 36
S. J. S. Kimber not out .............. 14
S. M. McEwan not out .............. 13
B 7, l-b 11 .................. 18

1/1 2/13 3/100 4/115 5/146 6/182 7/186 8/265 9/286 (9 wkts dec.) 310

Bowling: Thorne 22–4–64–4; Toogood 5–0–14–0; Brettell 26–6–87–2; Lawrence 38–8–127–3.

Umpires: H. J. Rhodes and P. B. Wight.

## OXFORD UNIVERSITY v KENT

At The Parks, May 29, 30, 31. Drawn. Toss won by Kent. Aslett and Taylor thrashed Oxford's weak attack for 263 off 59 overs for the second wicket, the partnership being dominated by Aslett, who hit five 6s and 22 4s in 140 minutes compared to Taylor's 250-minute century (fourteen 4s). At 103 for five Oxford were in danger of following on until Thorne and Rutnagur added 93 for the sixth wicket, and when Miller declared in arrears, Kent's lead of 97 was quickly extended by Benson and Hinks, who put on 132 for the first wicket. The third declaration of the match left Oxford to score 300 in 203 minutes, but they were never in a position to make a serious challenge. Thorne and Toogood checked a partial collapse with a fourth-wicket partnership of 73 and the University held on comfortably for a draw.

## Kent

S. G. Hinks c Taylor b Thorne ............... 10 – (2) b Brettell ................. 88
N. R. Taylor not out .......................120
D. G. Aslett c Thorne b Rutnagur ...........174
G. W. Johnson c Patel b MacLarnon ......... 12 – (3) not out ................. 27
E. A. E. Baptiste not out ................... 19
*M. R. Benson (did not bat) ................ – (1) c Rutnagur b Lawrence ..... 55
R. M. Ellison (did not bat) .................. – (4) not out ................. 23
B 8, l-b 6 ......................... 14 B 5, l-b 4 .............. 9

1/24 2/287 3/324 (3 wkts dec.) 349 1/132 2/158 (2 wkts dec.) 202

L. Potter, †S. N. V. Waterton, G. R. Dilley and K. B. S. Jarvis did not bat.

Bowling: *First Innings*—Thorne 13–3–44–1; Toogood 19–4–71–0; Lawrence 23–4–89–0; Rutnagur 24–3–82–1; Brettell 6–2–31–0; MacLarnon 4.3–2–18–1. *Second Innings*—Thorne 6–1–29–0; Toogood 9–2–33–0; MacLarnon 10–3–29–0; Rutnagur 10–3–45–0; Lawrence 13–2–33–1; Brettell 9–2–24–1.

## Oxford University

| | | | |
|---|---|---|---|
| *A. J. T. Miller c Potter b Dilley | 0 | c Benson b Johnson | 32 |
| D. A. Hagan run out | 0 | lbw b Dilley | 5 |
| G. J. Toogood c Waterton b Ellison | 34 | b Aslett | 38 |
| C. D. M. Tooley c Aslett b Dilley | 12 | b Johnson | 0 |
| D. A. Thorne c and b Potter | 89 | c Potter b Taylor | 66 |
| T. Patel b Potter | 16 | not out | 28 |
| R. S. Rutnagur c Waterton b Dilley | 66 | not out | 0 |
| P. C. MacLarnon not out | 10 | | |
| †D. P. Taylor b Dilley | 0 | | |
| L-b 18, w 4, n-b 3 | 25 | L-b 4 | 4 |
| 1/2 2/15 3/41 4/68 5/103 6/196 7/246 8/252 | (8 wkts dec.) 252 | 1/7 2/51 3/51 4/124 5/164 | (5 wkts) 173 |

M. P. Lawrence and J. G. Brettell did not bat.

Bowling: *First Innings*—Dilley 22.1–8–40–4; Jarvis 17–4–38–0; Baptiste 7–3–15–0; Johnson 24–4–58–0; Ellison 20–11–26–1; Potter 15–3–57–2; Aslett 1–1–0–0. *Second Innings*—Dilley 5–1–4–1; Ellison 3–2–1–0; Johnson 17–4–34–2; Potter 15–4–34–0; Taylor 12–1–52–1; Aslett 8–0–44–1.

Umpires: J. H. Harris and H. J. Rhodes.

## OXFORD UNIVERSITY v LANCASHIRE

At The Parks, June 1, 3, 4. Lancashire won by 370 runs. Toss won by Lancashire. With the exception of Thorne in the first innings, Oxford were completely outplayed by Lancashire, who preferred batting practice rather than enforcing the follow-on and winning in two days. With Thorne troubled by a back injury, Toogood shared the new ball with Quinlan and they were meat and drink to Varey and Chadwick, who opened with a partnership of 157. Nor was there any respite for the bowlers as Hughes and Fairbrother put on an unbeaten 135 before the declaration. Hagan was the only batsman other than Thorne to reach double figures in Oxford's first innings, and they fared even worse when set a final target of 418 on the last day. Half the side was out for 44, and the last five wickets fell for the addition of just 3 runs in 30 minutes after tea. The main destroyer was Folley, who enjoyed career-best figures of six for 8 in sixteen overs. Patterson's return in Oxford's first innings was also a career best.

## Lancashire

| | | | |
|---|---|---|---|
| M. R. Chadwick c Quinlan b Lawrence | 63 | | |
| D. W. Varey c Thorne b Rutnagur | 112 | | |
| N. H. Fairbrother not out | 68 | | |
| D. P. Hughes not out | 75 | | |
| R. G. Watson (did not bat) | – | (1) lbw b Rutnagur | 18 |
| *J. Abrahams (did not bat) | – | (2) not out | 101 |
| M. Watkinson (did not bat) | – | (3) c Hagan b Lawrence | 59 |
| †C. Maynard (did not bat) | – | (4) not out | 26 |
| B 10, l-b 9, w 1 | 20 | B 7, l-b 4, w 8 | 19 |
| 1/157 2/203 | (2 wkts dec.) 338 | 1/53 2/158 | (2 wkts dec.) 223 |

D. J. Makinson, I. Folley and B. P. Patterson did not bat.

Bowling: *First Innings*—Quinlan 21–3–90–0; Toogood 16–3–57–0; Lawrence 40–8–95–1; Rutnagur 15–1–72–1; MacLarnon 1–0–5–0. *Second Innings*—Quinlan 12–3–37–0; Toogood 11–2–38–0; Rutnagur 13–1–53–1; MacLarnon 12–1–39–0; Lawrence 8–0–45–1.

## Oxford University

| Batsman | First innings | | Second innings | |
|---|---|---|---|---|
| *A. J. T. Miller | c Maynard b Patterson | 2 | c Fairbrother b Folley | 10 |
| D. A. Hagan | lbw b Patterson | 20 | lbw b Makinson | 1 |
| G. J. Toogood | c Maynard b Patterson | 0 | c Fairbrother b Watkinson | 11 |
| P. C. MacLarnon | c Maynard b Patterson | 6 | (8) b Folley | 0 |
| C. D. M. Tooley | c Chadwick b Patterson | 0 | (4) c Maynard b Abrahams | 6 |
| D. A. Thorne | b Watkinson | 76 | (5) c Maynard b Folley | 7 |
| T. Patel | b Patterson | 0 | (6) c Abrahams b Folley | 4 |
| R. S. Rutnagur | b Watkinson | 3 | (7) b Folley | 1 |
| †D. P. Taylor | b Watkinson | 0 | not out | 0 |
| J. D. Quinlan | c Maynard b Patterson | 8 | st Maynard b Folley | 0 |
| M. P. Lawrence | not out | 6 | c Folley b Watkinson | 1 |
| | B 1, l-b 10, n-b 12 | 23 | B 1, l-b 3, n-b 2 | 6 |
| | 1/10 2/20 3/38 4/38 5/68 6/74 7/83 8/91 9/132 | 144 | 1/2 2/25 3/25 4/40 5/44 6/45 7/45 8/46 9/46 | 47 |

Bowling: *First Innings*—Patterson 17.4–3–49–7; Makinson 13–2–45–0; Watkinson 15–5–32–3; Folley 1–0–7–0. *Second Innings*—Patterson 5–2–10–0; Makinson 7–4–5–1; Watkinson 13.2–6–14–2; Folley 16–13–8–6; Abrahams 6–3–6–1.

Umpires: J. H. Harris and H. J. Rhodes.

At The Parks, June 8, 10, 11. OXFORD UNIVERSITY drew with ZIMBABWEANS (See Zimbabwean tour section).

## OXFORD UNIVERSITY v YORKSHIRE

At The Parks, June 12, 13, 14. Drawn. Toss won by Oxford University. Oxford's hopes of being set a realistic target were killed off by Bairstow, who delayed his declaration until tea. This left the University the impossible target of 314 in two hours. Miller had kept the game alive by declaring 54 behind, and at lunch on the third day Yorkshire led by 175. A declaration was expected once Metcalfe had completed his century, when the county were 270 ahead and two and a half hours remained. Instead Yorkshire batted on, making a nonsense of Bairstow's pre-match pledge of playing to win. The match began with Yorkshire losing four wickets for 88 after being put in, but Love (one 6, seventeen 4s) and Hartley (sixteen 4s) put the bowling into perspective with a fourth-wicket partnership of 193. Carr marked his return for Oxford with a sparkling hundred (seventeen 4s) and Thorne and Toogood gave him good support.

## Yorkshire

| Batsman | First innings | | Second innings | |
|---|---|---|---|---|
| G. Boycott | c Thorne b Quinlan | 15 | c Bristowe b Lawrence | 45 |
| M. D. Moxon | b Lawrence | 25 | b Quinlan | 7 |
| A. A. Metcalfe | c Bristowe b Lawrence | 23 | c Hagan b Carr | 109 |
| K. Sharp | b Rutnagur | 17 | not out | 69 |
| J. D. Love | c Lawrence b Toogood | 106 | | |
| S. N. Hartley | not out | 108 | | |
| P. A. Booth | c and b Toogood | 4 | | |
| *†D. L. Bairstow | not out | 8 | (5) c Harrison b Carr | D 7 |
| A. Sidebottom | (did not bat) | | (6) not out | 3 |
| | B 4, l-b 6, w 2, n-b 4 | 16 | B 6, l-b 7, w 3, n-b 3 | 19 |
| | 1/38 2/49 3/78 4/88 5/281 6/298 (6 wkts dec.) | 322 | 1/10 2/109 3/225 4/235 (4 wkts dec.) | 259 |

S. D. Fletcher and S. J. Dennis did not bat.

Bowling: *First Innings*—Thorne 8–0–43–0; Quinlan 24–5–57–1; Rutnagur 23–7–73–1; Lawrence 20–6–46–2; Carr 18–5–44–0; Toogood 13–1–49–2. *Second Innings*—Quinlan 14–1–52–1; Rutnagur 4–1–17–0; Lawrence 24–5–77–1; Carr 19–4–45–2; Toogood 13–2–34–0; MacLarnon 2–0–10–0; Bristowe 1–0–5–0; Hagan 1–0–6–0.

### Oxford University

| Batsman | First innings | | Second innings | |
|---|---|---|---|---|
| D. A. Hagan c and b Booth | 14 | not out | 12 |
| W. R. Bristowe c Fletcher b Dennis | 9 | not out | 42 |
| G. J. Toogood c Boycott b Booth | 43 | | |
| J. D. Carr c Love b Booth | 101 | | |
| *D. A. Thorne c Moxon b Fletcher | 56 | | |
| C. D. M. Tooley c Metcalfe b Sidebottom | 12 | | |
| R. S. Rutnagur not out | 25 | | |
| B 1, l-b 3, n-b 4 | 8 | L-b 4, w 1, n-b 3 | 8 |
| 1/12 2/33 3/121 4/198 5/232 6/268 (6 wkts dec.) | 268 | (no wkt) | 62 |

P. C. MacLarnon, †D. S. Harrison, M. P. Lawrence and J. D. Quinlan did not bat.

Bowling: *First Innings*—Sidebottom 13.4–3–59–1; Dennis 13–2–36–1; Booth 29–7–86–3; Fletcher 9–1–20–1; Sharp 5–1–14–0; Hartley 9–2–39–0; Moxon 2–0–10–0. *Second Innings*—Sidebottom 6–1–14–0; Moxon 7–3–12–0; Booth 8–4–13–0; Sharp 4–2–15–0; Metcalfe 3–0–4–0.

Umpires: D. Lloyd and A. G. T. Whitehead.

## OXFORD UNIVERSITY v WARWICKSHIRE

At The Parks, June 15, 17, 18. Warwickshire won by 21 runs. Toss won by Warwickshire. Oxford's last first-class match of the season in The Parks ended in a narrow defeat. Set a target of 272 in four hours, they were in contention until the last 30 minutes, whereupon the last five wickets fell for 22 runs. Toogood put on 84 with Bristowe for the third wicket, 61 with Thorne for the next, and the momentum was maintained by Thorne and Tooley, who figured in another partnership of 61 for the sixth wicket. However, Tooley's dismissal signalled the collapse and Thorne ran out of partners. Warwickshire staged a spectacular recovery on the opening day after losing Dyer and David Smith for 2, Lloyd and Amiss completing hundreds during a third-wicket partnership of 228, and Ferreira hitting a punishing unbeaten half-century. MacLarnon, opening because of a thumb injury to Miller, and Thorne also scored half-centuries as the University made steady progress towards a declaration shortly before the close on the second day. Amiss's generous response led to the exciting finish.

### Warwickshire

| Batsman | First innings | Second innings | |
|---|---|---|---|
| T. A. Lloyd b Lawrence | 123 | b Carr | 58 |
| R. I. H. B. Dyer c Rutnagur b Toogood | 2 | c MacLarnon b Thorne | 12 |
| K. D. Smith c Carr b Toogood | 0 | not out | 21 |
| *D. L. Amiss c Miller b Toogood | 125 | (6) c Harrison b Lawrence | 0 |
| †G. W. Humpage b Rutnagur | 13 | (4) b Carr | 29 |
| P. A. Smith c Bristowe b Lawrence | 29 | (5) c Harrison b Lawrence | 3 |
| A. M. Ferreira not out | 58 | not out | 32 |
| W. Morton c and b Thorne | 3 | | |
| S. Wall c Miller b Thorne | 3 | | |
| A. R. K. Pierson not out | 3 | | |
| L-b 1, w 1, n-b 10 | 12 | B 5, l-b 4, n-b 2 | 11 |
| 1/2 2/2 3/230 4/256 5/297 6/306 7/340 8/364 (8 wkts dec.) | 371 | 1/54 2/84 3/120 4/123 5/123 (5 wkts dec.) | 166 |

D. S. Hoffman did not bat.

Bowling: *First Innings*—Thorne 18–3–63–2; Toogood 11–1–43–3; Rutnagur 15–1–60–1; Carr 16–0–65–0; Lawrence 33–7–98–2; MacLarnon 11–2–41–0. *Second Innings*—Thorne 8–3–21–1; Toogood 1–1–0–0; MacLarnon 4–0–24–0; Rutnagur 4–0–20–0; Lawrence 10–2–43–2; Carr 8–0–49–2.

### Oxford University

| | | | |
|---|---|---|---|
| P. C. MacLarnon c Morton b Pierson | 56 | – c Dyer b Ferreira | 5 |
| W. R. Bristowe c and b Morton | 14 | – c Humpage b Pierson | 39 |
| G. J. Toogood st Humpage b Pierson | 14 | – (4) c Humpage b Pierson | 77 |
| J. D. Carr c Lloyd b Ferreira | 32 | – (3) b Hoffman | 0 |
| D. A. Thorne b Hoffman | 55 | – not out | 68 |
| R. S. Rutnagur b Wall | 43 | – lbw b Pierson | 0 |
| C. D. M. Tooley c Amiss b Morton | 15 | – c Humpage b Wall | 26 |
| T. Patel c Ferreira b Wall | 7 | – c Wall b Ferreira | 5 |
| *A. J. T. Miller not out | 8 | – run out | 9 |
| †D. S. Harrison not out | 1 | – b Wall | 0 |
| M. P. Lawrence (did not bat) | | – c Humpage b Wall | 0 |
| B 3, l-b 6, n-b 12 | 21 | B 9, l-b 6, w 2, n-b 4 | 21 |
| 1/40 2/88 3/111 4/146 5/221 6/239 7/250 8/258 (8 wkts dec.) | 266 | 1/21 2/22 3/106 4/167 5/167 6/228 7/239 8/249 9/250 | 250 |

Bowling: *First Innings*—Wall 18–2–49–2; Hoffman 11–5–24–1; Morton 36–7–98–2; Ferreira 19–2–40–1; Pierson 20–7–33–2; P. A. Smith 3–0–13–0. *Second Innings*—Hoffman 16–6–22–1; Wall 15–1–63–3; Ferreira 14–3–37–2; Pierson 21–1–92–3; Morton 5–0–21–0.

Umpires: D. Lloyd and A. G. T. Whitehead.

†At The Parks, June 22, 24, 25. Drawn. MCC 52 for one; Oxford University did not bat.

At Lord's, July 3, 4, 5. OXFORD UNIVERSITY drew with CAMBRIDGE UNIVERSITY (See Other Matches at Lord's).

## CAMBRIDGE

President – SIR JOHN BUTTERFIELD (Downing)

Captain – C. R. ANDREW (Barnard Castle and St John's)

Secretary – A. G. DAVIES (Birkenhead and Robinson)

Captain for 1986 – D. G. PRICE (Haberdashers' Aske's and Homerton)

Secretary – S. R. GORMAN (St Peter's, York and Emmanuel)

Run-scoring continued to be a problem for Cambridge on the generally slow, and disappointingly low, wickets at Fenner's. For inexperienced batsmen needing all the help they could get from the elements, the wet University season offered no encouragement, every game proving to be a battle for survival.

But, with one or two timely interventions by the rain, disasters against the counties were avoided, and it was not until the team reached Lord's that their batting shortcomings were fully exposed. Initially there had been some encouragement in the form of David Fell, a freshman with Middlesex connections. In his maiden first-class innings he scored 85 against Essex; in his fourth came an unbeaten century against Nottinghamshire, the only three-figure score by a Cambridge player during the University season. His first four innings produced 235 runs, but his form and confidence declined, so that his remaining twelve first-class innings realised only another 97 runs.

The seniors never made runs consistently and it was left to Archie Cotterell, who, though failing to realise his potential as a left-arm spinner, became the most reliable runmaker in the side. Rob Andrew, the captain, found it difficult to maintain his promise of the previous season. He missed the first game through playing rugby for England against Wales, and although he led the side with some skill afterwards, he could not score the runs that were so badly needed. Paul Roebuck was another who failed to maintain the progress of the previous year, and Andrew Davies, while again keeping wicket tidily, found runs in short supply. Not until he had completed his final examinations did he get into double figures.

What encouraging signs there were had to do with the bowling, which stood up well in the face of assaults by some of the country's premier batsmen. Alastair Scott, a left-arm, medium-paced freshman, bowled with some skill but little luck on generally unresponsive pitches. In his first season he took 25 wickets to top the averages, while Charles Ellison, brother of the England bowler, was second with thirteen victims. There was variety in the bowling with the captain's off-spin accompanying the similar style of the promising Shaun Gorman and Cotterell's left-arm spin. Disappointingly, Alexander Grimes failed to maintain the progress he had shown as a freshman the previous year, a failure that led to his being left out at Lord's.

The meeting with Oxford turned out to be a great disappointment from the Cambridge point of view. More cheerful was the news that J. G. W. Davies, the club's fixture secretary and longest-serving senior member, was to become President of MCC. – D.G.H.

## CAMBRIDGE UNIVERSITY RESULTS

*First-class matches* – Played 9: Lost 1, Drawn 8.

## FIRST-CLASS AVERAGES – BATTING

| | *M* | *I* | *NO* | *R* | *HI* | *Avge* |
|---|---|---|---|---|---|---|
| T. A. Cotterell ........ | 9 | 12 | 4 | 289 | 69* | 36.12 |
| P. G. P. Roebuck ...... | 9 | 15 | 3 | 343 | 82 | 28.58 |
| A. E. Lea ............ | 8 | 15 | 2 | 298 | 47* | 22.92 |
| D. J. Fell ............. | 9 | 16 | 1 | 332 | 109* | 22.13 |
| A. D. H. Grimes ...... | 6 | 3 | 1 | 43 | 22* | 21.50 |
| C. C. Ellison .......... | 7 | 6 | 0 | 109 | 51 | 18.16 |
| C. R. Andrew ......... | 8 | 15 | 1 | 253 | 66 | 18.07 |
| S. R. Gorman ......... | 9 | 15 | 5 | 177 | 43 | 17.70 |
| J. E. Davidson ........ | 4 | 4 | 2 | 25 | 22 | 12.50 |
| A. G. Davies .......... | 9 | 13 | 2 | 124 | 43* | 11.27 |
| M. S. Ahluwalia ....... | 4 | 7 | 1 | 55 | 31 | 9.16 |
| D. G. Price ........... | 6 | 9 | 1 | 60 | 29 | 7.50 |
| A. M. G. Scott ........ | 9 | 7 | 4 | 12 | 5* | 4.00 |

Played in one match: D. W. Browne 10; S. N. Siddiqi 0.

* *Signifies not out.*

D. J. Fell played the only three-figure innings for Cambridge University.

CAMBRIDGE UNIVERSITY 1985

[*Bill Smith*

*Back row:* M. S. Ahluwalia, D. J. Fell, S. R. Gorman, C. C. Ellison, J. E. Davidson, D. G. Price, A. M. G. Scott. *Front row:* T. A. Cotterell, A. G. Davies, C. R. Andrew (*captain*), A. E. Lea, P. G. P. Roebuck.

## BOWLING

| | O | M | R | W | BB | Avge |
|---|---|---|---|---|---|---|
| A. M. G. Scott | 243.3 | 34 | 879 | 25 | 5-68 | 35.16 |
| C. C. Ellison | 223.5 | 58 | 591 | 13 | 3-76 | 45.46 |
| C. R. Andrew | 80.2 | 10 | 279 | 6 | 3-101 | 46.50 |
| A. D. H. Grimes | 130 | 28 | 480 | 9 | 3-99 | 53.33 |
| T. A. Cotterell | 232.4 | 54 | 742 | 11 | 3-53 | 67.45 |

Also bowled: J. E. Davidson 80–12–254–4; S. R. Gorman 117.4–17–465–3; A. E. Lea 2–0–9–0; D. G. Price 1–0–7–0; S. N. Siddiqi 2–0–12–0.

†At Fenner's, April 19. Loughborough Students won by 24 runs. Loughborough Students 192 (N. Folland 78); Cambridge University 168.

## CAMBRIDGE UNIVERSITY v ESSEX

At Fenner's, April 20, 22, 23. Drawn. Toss won by Essex. The county champions devoted much of the game to batting practice, with the result that the University were able to secure a draw. On the first day Gooch was in prime form, hitting four 6s and eight 4s in 154 minutes before being bowled 1 short of his hundred. Pont, playing for a place, and Fletcher later batted well in a century partnership. The early stages of the University's reply were dominated by Fell, a freshman making his first-class début. He reached 50 in 79 balls and hit nine 4s in his 85. Cotterell, captaining the side in the absence of Andrew, who was playing rugby for England, scored an unbeaten 69 before declaring. In the second innings Hardie scored a century in three and a half hours, but McEwan took only 110 minutes to reach three figures. Gooch hit out, taking 30, including four 6s, off one over from Gorman, the off-spinner, who was another making his first first-class appearance. Cambridge, left with three hours' batting, played safely through for a draw.

### Essex

| | | | |
|---|---|---|---|
| G. A. Gooch b Ellison | 99 | – (5) c Ahluwalia b Scott | 88 |
| P. J. Prichard c Ellison b Grimes | 14 | – (1) b Ellison | 10 |
| K. S. McEwan b Grimes | 26 | – (4) c Fell b Gorman | 110 |
| B. R. Hardie c Davies b Grimes | 27 | – (2) not out | 112 |
| A. W. Lilley c Davies b Ellison | 16 | | |
| K. R. Pont c Ahluwalia b Cotterell | 55 | | |
| *K. W. R. Fletcher not out | 56 | | |
| †D. E. East not out | 34 | – (3) c Cotterell b Grimes | 2 |
| L-b 8, w 4 | 12 | B 1, l-b 3, w 1 | 5 |
| 1/31 2/66 3/106 4/184 5/185 6/289 (6 wkts dec.) | 339 | 1/19 2/28 3/186 4/327 (4 wkts dec.) | 327 |

J. K. Lever, J. H. Childs and D. L. Acfield did not bat.

Bowling: *First Innings*—Grimes 20–2–99–3; Ellison 26–8–75–2; Scott 18–3–63–0; Cotterell 18–3–59–1; Gorman 9–0–28–0; Price 1–0–7–0. *Second Innings*—Grimes 15–2–94–1; Ellison 18–3–60–1; Scott 11.3–1–63–1; Cotterell 4–1–19–0; Gorman 13–3–79–1; Lea 1–0–8–0.

### Cambridge University

| | | |
|---|---|---|
| A. E. Lea c McEwan b Pont | 9 – not out | 31 |
| M. S. Ahluwalia lbw b Gooch | 0 – run out | 1 |
| D. J. Fell c McEwan b Lever | 85 – c Pont b Acfield | 37 |
| D. G. Price c East b Pont | 5 – not out | 0 |
| P. G. P. Roebuck c McEwan b Lever | 14 | |
| †A. G. Davies c East b Childs | 5 | |
| *T. A. Cotterell not out | 69 | |
| S. R. Gorman not out | 27 | |
| B 1, l-b 7 | 8 | |
| 1/9 2/9 3/16 4/60 5/65 6/157 (6 wkts dec.) | 222 – 1/5 2/66 (2 wkts) | 69 |

C. C. Ellison, A. D. H. Grimes and A. M. G. Scott did not bat.

Bowling: *First Innings*—Lever 15–6–28–2; Pont 19–9–43–2; Gooch 20–6–50–1; Childs 30–10–70–1; Acfield 16–6–23–0. *Second Innings*—Lever 5–4–4–0; Pont 8–3–12–0; Childs 16–8–23–0; Acfield 12–4–30–1.

Umpires: D. J. Constant and D. Lloyd.

## CAMBRIDGE UNIVERSITY v NOTTINGHAMSHIRE

At Fenner's, April 24, 25, 26. Drawn. Toss won by Nottinghamshire. Cambridge were heartened by the bowling of Scott, the freshman left-arm seamer, whose five wickets included a spell of four wickets in nine overs. Cooper, taking seven for 10 from nineteen overs, dismissed the students for 115 but the county did not enforce the follow-on and Randall scored a century in 98 minutes from 87 balls with a 6 and fourteen 4s. Cambridge, left with four hours' batting, saved the match comfortably as Fell followed his 87 against Essex in the previous match with an unbeaten 109. He hit a 6 and seventeen 4s, reaching three figures in 171 minutes and sharing a century partnership with Lea.

### Nottinghamshire

| | | |
|---|---|---|
| B. C. Broad c Roebuck b Scott | 29 – lbw b Scott | 51 |
| M. Newell lbw b Grimes | 74 – run out | 58 |
| D. W. Randall lbw b Scott | 74 – (4) not out | 100 |
| P. Johnson c Fell b Scott | 20 – (3) c Lea b Ellison | 23 |
| *J. D. Birch b Scott | 5 – not out | 12 |
| K. P. Evans lbw b Scott | 13 | |
| †C. W. Scott not out | 39 | |
| R. A. Pick not out | 10 | |
| B 1, l-b 3, n-b 1 | 5 L-b 7 | 7 |
| 1/52 2/164 3/196 4/204 5/209 6/226 (6 wkts dec.) | 269 – 1/76 2/113 3/171 (3 wkts dec.) | 251 |

K. Saxelby, K. E. Cooper and J. A. Afford did not bat.

Bowling: *First Innings*—Grimes 17–6–39–1; Ellison 23–3–57–0; Scott 19–3–68–5; Cotterell 36–11–86–0; Gorman 5–1–15–0. *Second Innings*—Grimes 17–3–69–0; Ellison 16–4–54–1; Scott 18–1–72–1; Cotterell 3–2–2–0; Andrew 2–0–16–0; Gorman 7–2–31–0.

## Cambridge University

| | | |
|---|---|---|
| A. E. Lea c Scott b Pick | 27 | – b Broad 46 |
| *C. R. Andrew c Newell b Cooper | 5 | – c Newell b Cooper 2 |
| D. J. Fell c Scott b Cooper | 4 | – not out 109 |
| P. G. P. Roebuck lbw b Evans | 0 | – not out 14 |
| D. G. Price c Birch b Cooper | 1 | |
| †A. G. Davies c Evans b Cooper | 0 | |
| T. A. Cotterell c Scott b Saxelby | 20 | |
| S. R. Gorman c Scott b Cooper | 24 | |
| A. D. H. Grimes c Scott b Cooper | 18 | |
| A. M. G. Scott not out | 0 | |
| C. C. Ellison b Cooper | 0 | |
| B 2, l-b 13, w 1 | 16 | B 1, l-b 20 21 |
| 1/15 2/23 3/28 4/29 5/31 6/72 7/76 8/114 9/115 | 115 | 1/9 2/119 (2 wkts) 192 |

Bowling: *First Innings*—Cooper 19–14–10–7; Saxelby 15–5–26–1; Pick 13–6–37–1; Evans 13–3–26–1; Afford 3–2–1–0. *Second Innings*—Cooper 9–5–4–1; Saxelby 10–3–26–0; Pick 10–2–38–0; Evans 8–4–5–0; Birch 12–3–33–0; Broad 6–1–18–1; Newell 3–0–24–0; Johnson 3–1–23–0.

Umpires: D. J. Constant and D. Lloyd.

## CAMBRIDGE UNIVERSITY v GLOUCESTERSHIRE

At Fenner's, April 27, 29, 30. Drawn. Toss won by Gloucestershire. Rain and bad light seriously affected the game, enabling the University to bat out for another draw. Only 147 minutes' play was possible on the first day before a heavy snowstorm ruled out further action. This meant the county having to bat into the second day, Athey reaching his hundred after 239 minutes. The off-spin of Lloyds, making his first appearance for the county, had Cambridge in trouble before play was halted by bad light. Cambridge declared before the start of the third day's play and Gloucestershire batted for 98 minutes before setting the University a target of 292 in three hours. Two further stoppages ensured that they were able to survive.

## Gloucestershire

| | | |
|---|---|---|
| A. W. Stovold c Roebuck b Grimes | 9 | – c Davies b Scott 5 |
| P. W. Romaines c Grimes b Ellison | 62 | – not out 60 |
| C. W. J. Athey not out | 112 | |
| P. Bainbridge not out | 75 | |
| B. F. Davison (did not bat) | | – (3) c Davies b Scott 29 |
| K. M. Curran (did not bat) | | – (4) c Davies b Scott 2 |
| J. W. Lloyds (did not bat) | | – (5) not out 13 |
| B 3, l-b 1, w 1, n-b 2 | 7 | L-b 5 5 |
| 1/11 2/124 | (2 wkts dec.) 265 | 1/10 2/58 3/82 (3 wkts dec.) 114 |

*D. A. Graveney, †R. C. Russell, D. V. Lawrence and G. E. Sainsbury did not bat.

Bowling: *First Innings*—Grimes 11–2–33–1; Scott 23–1–72–0; Ellison 10–0–34–1; Cotterell 15–1–57–0; Gorman 21–5–49–0; Andrew 3–0–16–0. *Second Innings*—Scott 15–4–48–3; Andrew 15–0–53–0; Cotterell 1–0–8–0.

### Cambridge University

| | | | |
|---|---|---|---|
| A. E. Lea c Stovold b Lloyds | 21 | – c Lloyds b Curran | 3 |
| *C. R. Andrew c and b Lawrence | 5 | – b Lawrence | 5 |
| D. J. Fell b Sainsbury | 12 | – (4) c Lloyds b Lawrence | 4 |
| P. G. P. Roebuck not out | 35 | – (5) c Athey b Lloyds | 28 |
| D. G. Price c Athey b Lloyds | 1 | – (3) st Russell b Graveney | 6 |
| †A. G. Davies c Romaines b Lloyds | 3 | – b Lloyds | 1 |
| T. A. Cotterell c Russell b Lloyds | 7 | – not out | 1 |
| S. R. Gorman not out | 0 | – not out | 0 |
| B 3, l-b 1 | 4 | L-b 3 | 3 |
| 1/7 2/38 3/54 4/60 5/70 6/88 (6 wkts dec.) | 88 | 1/9 2/9 3/13 4/32 5/39 6/50 (6 wkts) | 51 |

C. C. Ellison, A. D. H. Grimes and A. M. G. Scott did not bat.

Bowling: *First Innings*—Lawrence 8–3–18–1; Curran 8–4–11–0; Sainsbury 7–3–17–1; Lloyds 19–8–24–4; Graveney 13.2–6–14–0. *Second Innings*—Lawrence 8–3–11–2; Curran 5–2–5–1; Sainsbury 3–1–6–0; Graveney 16–10–12–1; Lloyds 15–8–14–2.

Umpires: D. G. L. Evans and J. H. Hampshire.

†At Fenner's, April 28. Cambridge University won by six wickets. Oxford University 162 for nine (55 overs); Cambridge University 166 for four (D. J. Fell 84 not out).

## CAMBRIDGE UNIVERSITY v MIDDLESEX

At Fenner's, May 1, 2, 3. Drawn. Toss won by Cambridge University. Rain again prevented a finish when Cambridge were batting to save the match. The first five in the county batting order made full use of the opportunity to score half-centuries before Gatting, having played the best innings, declared. Andrew maintained the sequence with a half-century in an opening partnership, but after he and Gorman had put on 84, seven wickets went down for 50 before Cotterell organised another 97 runs from the tail to avoid the follow-on. In their second innings Middlesex continued from where they had left off. Williams, opening, scored a careful 67 and Sykes, the reserve off-spinner, struck a splendid maiden century in three hours, profiting from dropped catches as he hit twenty 4s from 184 balls. The University faced one over before lunch, after which bad light and drizzle prevented any further play.

### Middlesex

| | | | |
|---|---|---|---|
| W. N. Slack c Andrew b Scott | 81 | | |
| †P. R. Downton c Davies b Cotterell | 55 | | |
| *M. W. Gatting b Cotterell | 80 | | |
| R. O. Butcher c Gorman b Andrew | 56 | | |
| C. T. Radley not out | 54 | – (7) not out | 0 |
| K. P. Tomlins not out | 34 | – (4) c Browne b Cotterell | 14 |
| J. E. Emburey (did not bat) | | – (1) b Grimes | 7 |
| N. F. Williams (did not bat) | | – (2) b Andrew | 67 |
| J. F. Sykes (did not bat) | | – (3) st Davies b Cotterell | 126 |
| N. G. Cowans (did not bat) | | – (5) c Fell b Cotterell | 6 |
| A. R. C. Fraser (did not bat) | | – (6) c Roebuck b Andrew | 1 |
| B 3, l-b 4, n-b 2 | 9 | L-b 5 | 5 |
| 1/88 2/206 3/226 4/287 (4 wkts dec.) | 369 | 1/12 2/161 3/188 4/222 5/226 6/226 (6 wkts dec.) | 226 |

Bowling: *First Innings*—Grimes 9–3–11–0; Scott 17–1–75–1; Siddiqi 2–0–12–0; Gorman 19–2–79–0; Cotterell 37–3–153–2; Andrew 12–1–32–1. *Second Innings*—Grimes 8–0–41–1; Scott 12–1–55–0; Andrew 16.4–3–45–2; Cotterell 19–5–53–3; Gorman 7–0–27–0.

## Cambridge University

| | | | |
|---|---|---|---|
| *C. R. Andrew lbw b Cowans | 66 | – not out | 0 |
| S. R. Gorman c Downton b Fraser | 28 | – not out | 0 |
| D. J. Fell lbw b Fraser | 2 | | |
| S. N. Siddiqi b Fraser | 0 | | |
| D. G. Price c Downton b Fraser | 5 | | |
| D. W. Browne c Downton b Cowans | 10 | | |
| †A. G. Davies c Sykes b Williams | 0 | | |
| T. A. Cotterell c Emburey b Cowans | 40 | | |
| P. G. P. Roebuck c Gatting b Cowans | 37 | | |
| A. D. H. Grimes not out | 22 | | |
| A. M. G. Scott c Downton b Cowans | 0 | | |
| B 10, l-b 4, n-b 7 | 21 | | |
| 1/84 2/88 3/92 4/112 5/114 6/123 7/134 8/185 9/225 | 231 | (no wkt) | 0 |

Bowling: *First Innings*—Fraser 24–7–48–4; Williams 11–2–42–1; Emburey 28–12–55–0; Sykes 16–1–35–0; Cowans 12.4–2–37–5. *Second Innings*—Gatting 1–1–0–0.

Umpires: D. G. L. Evans and J. H. Hampshire.

# CAMBRIDGE UNIVERSITY v SUSSEX

At Fenner's, May 8, 9, 10. Sussex won by 83 runs. Toss won by Sussex. Having lost half the first day to the weather, Barclay, the first county captain to shun practice at the expense of a result, contrived to force victory. The Sussex first innings lasted until lunch on the second day, and then Cambridge, having batted slowly, declared 104 behind at the close. Sussex pushed on, and Barclay's lunch-time declaration set the University to score 211 in four hours. This was beyond them, and even survival proved too much. They were bowled out with twelve of the final twenty overs remaining.

## Sussex

| | | | |
|---|---|---|---|
| G. D. Mendis lbw b Scott | 23 | – not out | 41 |
| A. M. Green b Cotterell | 42 | – c Davies b Ellison | 1 |
| P. W. G. Parker c Ahluwalia b Grimes | 61 | – c Andrew b Scott | 39 |
| A. P. Wells c Davies b Cotterell | 45 | – not out | 18 |
| C. M. Wells not out | 45 | | |
| *J. R. T. Barclay not out | 9 | | |
| B 6, l-b 5 | 11 | B 4, l-b 3 | 7 |
| 1/35 2/102 3/156 4/198 | (4 wkts dec.) 236 | 1/6 2/76 | (2 wkts dec.) 106 |

I. A. Greig, †I. J. Gould, A. C. S. Pigott, D. A. Reeve and A. N. Jones did not bat.

Bowling: *First Innings*—Grimes 9–2–24–1; Ellison 37–12–76–0; Andrew 3–1–5–0; Scott 12–1–34–1; Cotterell 32–12–81–2; Gorman 2–1–5–0. *Second Innings*—Grimes 9–3–16–0; Ellison 8–3–10–1; Scott 7–1–41–1; Gorman 3–0–21–0; Andrew 3–0–11–0.

## Cambridge University

| | | | |
|---|---|---|---|
| A. E. Lea c Barclay b Reeve | 36 | (2) c Green b Barclay | 18 |
| S. R. Gorman c Green b Barclay | 31 | (8) lbw b Greig | 0 |
| *C. R. Andrew b Pigott | 35 | (1) c Gould b Pigott | 9 |
| P. G. P. Roebuck lbw b Reeve | 1 | c and b Barclay | 5 |
| D. J. Fell lbw b Barclay | 9 | (3) c Greig b Barclay | 27 |
| M. S. Ahluwalia not out | 4 | (5) c Pigott b C. M. Wells | 15 |
| †A. G. Davies not out | 0 | (6) lbw b Greig | 7 |
| T. A. Cotterell (did not bat) | | (7) b Greig | 0 |
| A. D. H. Grimes (did not bat) | | lbw b C. M. Wells | 3 |
| C. C. Ellison (did not bat) | | b Reeve | 21 |
| A. M. G. Scott (did not bat) | | not out | 5 |
| B 7, l-b 9 | 16 | B 9, l-b 8 | 17 |
| 1/66 2/78 3/82 4/91 5/131 (5 wkts dec.) | 132 | 1/18 2/53 3/69 4/74 5/87 6/87 7/87 8/100 9/107 | 127 |

Bowling: *First Innings*—Pigott 9–4–10–1; Jones 8–3–12–0; Greig 11–4–21–0; C. M. Wells 8–4–17–0; Barclay 20–9–25–2; Reeve 16–4–31–2. *Second Innings*—Pigott 9–4–11–1; Jones 7–1–22–0; Reeve 8.4–2–16–1; Barclay 10–5–19–3; Greig 13–4–26–3; C. M. Wells 10–5–16–2.

Umpires: B. Leadbeater and H. J. Rhodes.

†At Fenner's, May 12. Cambridge University won by 71 runs. Cambridge University 183 for nine dec. (I. R. Redmayne five for 45); Cryptics 112 (J. E. Davidson eight for 58).

†At Fenner's, June 4. Cambridgeshire won by eight wickets. Cambridge University 149; Cambridgeshire 150 for two (J. D. R. Benson 47 not out, R. Milne 43 not out).

## CAMBRIDGE UNIVERSITY v SURREY

At Fenner's, June 8, 10, 11. Drawn. Toss won by Surrey. Fielding an inexperienced team, Surrey were never in charge, and, with ten overs still to be bowled, were possibly saved by rain after losing five wickets for 43 in the fourth innings. The University reached 142 in their first innings, being rescued from 58 for seven by Ellison, who hit a robust 51 in a partnership of 60 for the eighth wicket with Fell. A careful half-century by Howarth, in his first senior game of the season, enabled Surrey to declare with a slight advantage. The Cambridge top half again failed to impress, but more runs from their lower order ensured that their opponents, batting a man short after an injury to Bullen, would need 148 to win. That was never likely once Davidson had taken three quick wickets.

## Cambridge University

| | | | |
|---|---|---|---|
| A. E. Lea lbw b Waterman | 0 | lbw b Taylor | 3 |
| S. R. Gorman b Waterman | 0 | b Waterman | 1 |
| *C. R. Andrew lbw b Topley | 24 | (4) b Taylor | 14 |
| P. G. P. Roebuck c and b Taylor | 9 | (5) c Needham b Taylor | 2 |
| D. J. Fell lbw b Waterman | 4 | (3) lbw b Taylor | 14 |
| M. S. Ahluwalia c Topley b Bullen | 31 | c Butcher b Taylor | 4 |
| †A. G. Davies b Medlycott | 0 | lbw b Waterman | 13 |
| T. A. Cotterell b Topley | 8 | b Taylor | 43 |
| C. C. Ellison c Butcher b Taylor | 51 | b Pauline | 29 |
| A. M. G. Scott b Bullen | 1 | not out | 0 |
| J. E. Davidson not out | 2 | b Taylor | 0 |
| L-b 6, w 2, n-b 4 | 12 | B 16, l-b 10, w 1, n-b 11 | 38 |
| 1/0 2/5 3/18 4/23 5/43 6/44 7/58 8/118 9/125 | 142 | 1/11 2/13 3/43 4/50 5/53 6/64 7/97 8/147 9/160 | 161 |

Bowling: *First Innings*—Waterman 14–6–22–3; Taylor 9.3–2–19–2; Topley 13–3–42–2; Medlycott 10–5–17–1; Bullen 21–10–36–2. *Second Innings*—Waterman 16–5–18–2; Taylor 19.1–4–44–7; Needham 12–4–12–0; Medlycott 14–7–22–0; Topley 14–3–22–0; Butcher 8–3–10–0; Pauline 3–2–7–1.

## Surrey

| | | | |
|---|---|---|---|
| A. R. Butcher c Gorman b Davidson | 39 | – b Davidson | 0 |
| D. B. Pauline b Ellison | 5 | – b Davidson | 13 |
| A. J. Stewart c Scott b Ellison | 0 | – c Davidson b Ellison | 2 |
| †D. M. Ward c Davies b Scott | 17 | – st Davies b Cotterell | 6 |
| *G. P. Howarth c Davidson b Gorman | 53 | – c Roebuck b Davidson | 2 |
| A. Needham lbw b Scott | 15 | – not out | 14 |
| K. T. Medlycott lbw b Scott | 3 | – not out | 3 |
| N. S. Taylor lbw b Scott | 6 | | |
| T. D. Topley not out | 6 | | |
| B 4, l-b 2, w 3, n-b 3 | 12 | L-b 2, n-b 1 | 3 |
| 1/16 2/18 3/66 4/66 5/109 6/113 7/138 8/156 (8 wkts dec.) | 156 | 1/6 2/15 3/16 4/18 5/40 (5 wkts) | 43 |

P. A. Waterman and C. K. Bullen did not bat.

Bowling: *First Innings*—Davidson 22–5–47–1; Ellison 11–6–16–2; Scott 20–4–60–4; Gorman 9.5–1–27–1. *Second Innings*—Davidson 9–3–22–3; Ellison 7–4–5–1; Scott 3–0–13–0; Cotterell 1.4–0–1–1.

Umpires: J. A. Jameson and D. S. Thompsett.

# CAMBRIDGE UNIVERSITY v WORCESTERSHIRE

At Fenner's, June 12, 13, 14. Drawn. Toss won by Cambridge University. The worst weather of the term restricted play to 130 minutes on the first day and prevented any on the third. Banks, taking three hours to score 50, led a virtual Worcestershire Second Eleven to 216 for five before the declaration at lunch on the second day. The University were in some trouble before Davies and Cotterell, both playing their last first-class innings for Cambridge at Fenner's, shared an unbroken partnership of 84.

## Worcestershire

| | |
|---|---|
| H. V. Patel b Cotterell | 39 |
| L. K. Smith b Cotterell | 28 |
| D. A. Banks not out | 50 |
| M. Hussain b Grimes | 4 |
| P. Bent lbw b Scott | 14 |
| S. R. Lampitt lbw b Scott | 0 |
| *†D. J. Humphries not out | 62 |
| B 4, l-b 4, w 4, n-b 7 | 19 |
| 1/63 2/78 3/92 4/124 5/124 (5 wkts dec.) | 216 |

S. J. S. Kimber, M. Scothern, A. P. Pridgeon and B. J. Barrett did not bat.

Bowling: Grimes 15–5–54–1; Davidson 15–2–49–0; Scott 24–7–60–2; Cotterell 14–5–24–2; Gorman 2–0–21–0.

## Cambridge University

| | |
|---|---|
| A. E. Lea lbw b Kimber | 10 |
| S. R. Gorman c Humphries b Barrett | 0 |
| *C. R. Andrew lbw b Scothern | 2 |
| P. G. P. Roebuck lbw b Kimber | 37 |
| D. J. Fell lbw b Pridgeon | 4 |
| M. S. Ahluwalia c Humphries b Kimber | 0 |
| †A. G. Davies not out | 43 |
| T. A. Cotterell not out | 40 |
| B 4, l-b 2, n-b 1 | 7 |
| 1/1 2/6 3/39 4/46 5/47 6/59 (6 wkts) | 143 |

A. D. H. Grimes, A. M. G. Scott and J. E. Davidson did not bat.

Bowling: Barrett 18–7–40–1; Scothern 16–6–42–1; Pridgeon 9–2–14–1; Kimber 11–1–40–3; Lampitt 1–0–1–0.

Umpires: J. A. Jameson and D. S. Thompsett.

†At Fenner's, June 15, 16, 17. Drawn. Cambridge University 246 for six dec. (C. R. Andrew 71, M. S. Ahluwalia 68) and 202 for three dec. (C. R. Andrew 62, P. G. P. Roebuck 54 not out); MCC 286 (N. J. Kemp 87, G. Boycott 68, R. A. Hutton 45 not out; J. E. Davidson seven for 57) and 90 for four.

†At Fenner's, June 22, 23, 24. Drawn. Combined Services 256 for five dec. (B. W. P. Bennett 120, J. Barratt 62) and 64 for two; Cambridge University 249 for three (A. E. Lea 130, C. R. Andrew 65).

†At Brecon, June 26, 27, 28. Wales won by an innings and 15 runs. Wales 278 for eight dec. (G. P. Ellis 117, D. A. Francis 97; J. E. Davidson six for 84); Cambridge University 71 (S. Carey seven for 26) and 192 (C. R. Andrew 75).

At Taunton, June 29, July 1, 2. CAMBRIDGE UNIVERSITY drew with SOMERSET.

At Lord's, July 3, 4, 5. CAMBRIDGE UNIVERSITY drew with OXFORD UNIVERSITY (See Other Matches at Lord's).

---

## YOUNG CRICKETER OF THE YEAR

(*Elected by the Cricket Writers Club*)

1950 R. Tattersall
1951 P. B. H. May
1952 F. S. Trueman
1953 M. C. Cowdrey
1954 P. J. Loader
1955 K. F. Barrington
1956 B. Taylor
1957 M. J. Stewart
1958 A. C. D. Ingleby-Mackenzie
1959 G. Pullar
1960 D. A. Allen
1961 P. H. Parfitt
1962 P. J. Sharpe
1963 G. Boycott
1964 J. M. Brearley
1965 A. P. E. Knott
1966 D. L. Underwood
1967 A. W. Greig
1968 R. M. H. Cottam
1969 A. Ward
1970 C. M. Old
1971 J. Whitehouse
1972 D. R. Owen-Thomas
1973 M. Hendrick
1974 P. H. Edmonds
1975 A. Kennedy
1976 G. Miller
1977 I. T. Botham
1978 D. I. Gower
1979 P. W. G. Parker
1980 G. R. Dilley
1981 M. W. Gatting
1982 N. G. Cowans
1983 N. A. Foster
1984 R. J. Bailey
1985 D. V. Lawrence

An additional award, in memory of Norman Preston, Editor of *Wisden* from 1952 to 1980, was made to C. W. J. Athey in 1980.

# OXFORD AND CAMBRIDGE BLUES

From 1946 to 1985, and some others

A full list of Blues from 1837 may be found in all Wisdens published between 1923 and 1939. Between 1948 and 1972 the list was confined to all those who had won Blues after 1880, plus some of "special interest for personal or family reasons". Between 1972 and 1982 the list was restricted to those who had won Blues since 1919. Such adjustments have been necessary owing to the exigencies of space.

## OXFORD

Aamer Hameed (Central Model HS and Punjab U.) 1979
Abell, G. E. B. (Marlborough) 1924, 1926-27
Allan, J. M. (Edinburgh Academy) 1953-56
Allerton, J. W. O. (Stowe) 1969
Allison, D. F. (Greenmore Coll.) 1970
Altham, H. S. (Repton) 1911-12
Arenhold, J. A. (Diocesan Coll., SA) 1954

Baig, A. A. (Aliya and Osmania U., India) 1959-62
Baig, M. A. (Osmania U., India) 1962-64
Bailey, J. A. (Christ's Hospital) (Capt. in 1958) 1956-58
Barber, A. T. (Shrewsbury) (Capt. in 1929) 1927-29
Barker, A. H. (Charterhouse) 1964-65, 1967
Bartlett, J. H. (Chichester) 1946, 1951
Bettington, R. H. B. (The King's School, Parramatta) (Capt. in 1923) 1920-23
Bird, W. S. (Malvern) (Capt. in 1906) 1904-06
Birrell, H. B. (St Andrews, SA) 1953-54
Blake, P. D. S. (Eton) (Capt. in 1952) 1950-52
Bloy, N. C. F. (Dover) 1946-47
Boobbyer, B. (Uppingham) 1949-52
Bosanquet, B. J. T. (Eton) 1898-1900
Botton, N. D. (King Edward's, Bath) 1974
Bowman, R. C. (Fettes) 1957
Brettell, D. N. (Cheltenham) 1977
Bristowe, W. R. (Charterhouse) 1984-85
Brooks, R. A. (Quintin and Bristol U.) 1967
Burchnall, R. L. (Winchester) 1970-71
Burki, J. (St Mary's, Rawalpindi and Punjab U.) 1958-60
Burton, M. St J. W. (Umtali HS, Rhodesia and Rhodes U.) (Capt. in 1970) 1969-71
Bury, T. E. O. (Charterhouse) 1980
Bush, J. E. (Magdalen Coll. Sch.) 1952

Campbell, A. N. (Berkhamsted) 1970
Campbell, I. P. (Canford) 1949-50
Campbell, I. P. F. (Repton) (Capt. in 1913) 1911-13
Cantlay, C. P. T. (Radley) 1975
Carr, D. B. (Repton) (Capt. in 1950) 1949-51
Carr, J. D. (Repton) 1983-85
Carroll, P. R. (Newington Coll. and Sydney U.) 1971
Chalk, F. G. H. (Uppingham) (Capt. in 1934) 1931-34
Chesterton, G. H. (Malvern) 1949
Claughton, J. A. (King Edward's, Birmingham) (Capt. in 1978) 1976-79
Clements, S. M. (Ipswich) (Capt. in 1979) 1976, 1979
Clube, S. V. M. (St John's, Leatherhead) 1956
Corlett, S. C. (Worksop) 1971-72
Corran, A. J. (Gresham's) 1958-60
Coutts, I. D. F. (Dulwich) 1952
Cowan, R. S. (Lewes Priory CS) 1980-82
Cowdrey, M. C. (Tonbridge) (Capt. in 1954) 1952-54
Coxon, A. J. (Harrow CS) 1952
Crawley, A. M. (Harrow) 1927-30
Crutchley, G. E. V. (Harrow) 1912
Cullinan, M. R. (Hilton Coll., SA) 1983-84
Curtis, I. J. (Whitgift) 1980, 1982
Cushing, V. G. B. (KCS Wimbledon) 1973
Cuthbertson, J. L. (Rugby) 1962-63

Davidson, W. W. (Brighton) 1947-48
Davis, F. J. (Blundell's) 1963
Delisle, G. P. S. (Stonyhurst) 1955-56
de Saram, F. C. (Royal Coll., Colombo) 1934-35
Divecha, R. V. (Podar HS and Bombay U.) 1950-51
Dixon, E. J. H. (St Edward's, Oxford) (Capt. in 1939) 1937-39
Donnelly, M. P. (New Plymouth BHS and Canterbury U., NZ) (Capt. in 1947) 1946-47
Dowding, A. L. (St Peter's, Adelaide) (Capt. in 1953) 1952-53
Drybrough, C. D. (Highgate) (Capt. in 1961-62) 1960-62
Duff, A. R. (Radley) 1960-61
Dyer, A. W. (Mill Hill) 1965-66
Dyson, E. M. (QEGS, Wakefield) 1958

Eagar, M. A. (Rugby) 1956-59
Easter, J. N. C. (St Edward's, Oxford) 1967-68
Edbrooke, R. M. (Queen Elizabeth's Hospital) 1984
Ellis, R. G. P. (Haileybury) (Capt. in 1982) 1981-83

Elviss, R. W. (Leeds GS) 1966-67
Ezekowitz, R. A. B. (Westville BHS, Durban and Cape Town U., SA) 1980-81

Faber, M. J. J. (Eton) 1972
Fane, F. L. (Charterhouse) 1897-98
Fasken, D. K. (Wellington) 1953-55
Fellows-Smith, J. P. (Durban HS, SA) 1953-55
Fillary, E. W. J. (St Lawrence) 1963-65
Findlay, W. (Eton) (Capt. in 1903) 1901-03
Fisher, P. B. (St Ignatius, Enfield) 1975-78
Foster, G. N. (Malvern) 1905-08
Foster, H. K. (Malvern) 1894-96
Foster, R. E. (Malvern) (Capt. in 1900) 1897-1900
Franks, J. G. (Stamford) 1984-85
Fry, C. A. (Repton) 1959-61
Fry, C. B. (Repton) (Capt. in 1894) 1892-95
Fursdon, E. D. (Sherborne) 1974-75

Gamble, N. W. (Stockport GS) 1967
Garofall, A. R. (Latymer Upper) 1967-68
Gibbs, P. J. K. (Hanley GS) 1964-66
Gibson, I. (Manchester GS) 1955-58
Gilliat, R. M. C. (Charterhouse) (Capt. in 1966) 1964-67
Gilligan, F. W. (Dulwich) (Capt. in 1920) 1919-20
Glover, T. R. (Lancaster RGS) (Capt. in 1975) 1973-75
Goldstein, F. S. (Falcon Coll., Bulawayo) (Capt. in 1968-69) 1966-69
Green, D. M. (Manchester GS) 1959-61
Grover, J. N. (Winchester) (Capt. in 1938) 1936-38
Groves, M. G. M. (Diocesan Coll., SA) 1964-66
Guest, M. R. J. (Rugby) 1964-66
Guise, J. L. (Winchester) (Capt. in 1925) 1924-25
Gurr, D. R. (Aylesbury GS) 1976-77

Halliday, S. J. (Downside) 1980
Hamblin, C. B. (King's, Canterbury) 1971-73
Hamilton, A. C. (Charterhouse) 1975
Harris, C. R. (Buckingham RLS) 1964
Harris, Hon. G. R. C. (Lord Harris) (Eton) 1871-72, 1874
Hayes, K. A. (QEGS, Blackburn) (Capt. in 1984) 1981-84
Heal, M. G. (St Brendan's, Bristol) 1970, 1972
Heard, H. (QE Hosp. Sch.) 1969-70
Henderson, D. (St Edward's, Oxford) 1950
Henley, D. F. (Harrow) 1947
Heseltine, P. G. (Holgate GS) 1983
Hiller, R. B. (Bec) 1966
Hobbs, J. A. D. (Liverpool Coll.) 1957
Hofmeyr, M. B. (Pretoria, SA) (Capt. in 1951) 1949-51
Holmes, E. R. T. (Malvern) (Capt. in 1927) 1925-27
Hone, B. W. (Adelaide U.) (Capt. in 1933) 1931-33
Howell, M. (Repton) (Capt. in 1919) 1914, 1919
Huxford, P. N. (Richard Hale) 1981

Imran Khan (Aitchison Coll., Lahore and Worcester RGS) (Capt. in 1974) 1973-75

Jakobson, T. R. (Charterhouse) 1961
Jardine, D. R. (Winchester) 1920-21, 1923
Jardine, M. R. (Fettes) (Capt. in 1891) 1889-92
Jarrett, D. W. (Wellington) 1975
Johns, R. L. (St Albans and Keele U.) 1970
Jones, A. K. C. (Solihull) (Capt. in 1973) 1971-73
Jones, P. C. H. (Milton HS, Rhodesia and Rhodes U.) (Capt. in 1972) 1971-72
Jose, A. D. (Adelaide U.) 1950-51
Jowett, D. C. P. R. (Sherborne) 1952-55
Jowett, R. L. (Bradford GS) 1957-59

Kamm, A. (Charterhouse) 1954
Kardar, A. H. (Islamia Coll. and Punjab U.) 1947-49
Kayum, D. A. (Selhurst GS and Chatham House GS) 1977-78
Keighley, W. G. (Eton) 1947-48
Kentish, E. S. M. (Cornwall Coll., Jamaica) 1956
Khan, A. J. (Aitchison Coll., Lahore and Punjab U.) 1968-69
Kingsley, P. G. T. (Winchester) (Capt. in 1930) 1928-30
Kinkead-Weekes, R. C. (Eton) 1972
Knight, D. J. (Malvern) 1914, 1919
Knight, J. M. (Oundle) 1979
Knott, C. H. (Tonbridge) (Capt. in 1924) 1922-24
Knott, F. H. (Tonbridge) (Capt. in 1914) 1912-14
Knox, F. P. (Dulwich) (Capt. in 1901) 1899-1901

Lamb, Hon. T. M. (Shrewsbury) 1973-74
Lawrence, M. P. (Manchester GS) 1984-85
Lee, R. J. (Church of England GS and Sydney U.) 1972-74
Legge, G. B. (Malvern) (Capt. in 1926) 1925-26
L'Estrange, M. G. (St Aloysius Coll. and Sydney U.) 1977, 1979
Leveson Gower, H. D. G. (Winchester) (Capt. in 1896) 1893-96
Lewis, D. J. (Cape Town U.) 1951
Lloyd, M. F. D. (Magdalen Coll. Sch.) 1974
Luddington, R. S. (KCS, Wimbledon) 1982

McCanlis, M. A. (Cranleigh) (Capt. in 1928) 1926-28

Macindoe, D. H. (Eton) (Capt. in 1946) 1937-39, 1946
McKinna, G. H. (Manchester GS) 1953
MacLarnon, P. C. (Loughborough GS) 1985
Majendie, N. L. (Winchester) 1962-63
Mallett, A. W. H. (Dulwich) 1947-48
Mallett, N. V. H. (St Andrew's Coll. and Cape Town U.) 1981
Manasseh, M. (Epsom) 1964
Marie, G. V. (Western Australia U. and Reading U.) (Capt. in 1979, but injury prevented him playing v Cambridge) 1978
Marks, V. J. (Blundell's) (Capt. in 1976-77) 1975-78
Marsden, R. (Merchant Taylors', Northwood) 1982
Marshall, J. C. (Rugby) 1953
Marsham, C. D. B. (Private) (Capt. in 1857-58) 1854-58
Marsham, C. H. B. (Eton) (Capt. in 1902) 1900-02
Marsham, C. J. B. (Private) 1851
Marsham, R. H. B. (Private) 1856
Marsland, G. P. (Rossall) 1954
Martin, J. D. (Magdalen Coll. Sch.) (Capt. in 1965) 1962-63, 1965
Maudsley, R. H. (Malvern) 1946-47
May, B. (Prince Edward's, Salisbury and Cape Town U.) (Capt. in 1971) 1970-72
Melville, A. (Michaelhouse, SA) (Capt. in 1931-32) 1930-33
Melville, C. D. M. (Michaelhouse, SA) 1957
Metcalfe, S. G. (Leeds GS) 1956
Millener, D. J. (Auckland GS and Auckland U.) 1969-70
Miller, A. J. T. (Haileybury) (Capt. in 1985) 1983-85
Minns, R. E. F. (King's, Canterbury) 1962-63
Mitchell, W. M. (Dulwich) 1951-52
Mitchell-Innes, N. S. (Sedbergh) (Capt. in 1936) 1934-37
Moore, D. N. (Shrewsbury) (Capt. in 1931, when he did not play v Cambridge owing to illness) 1930
Morgan, A. H. (Hastings GS) 1969
Morrill, N. D. (Sandown GS and Millfield) 1979
Moulding, R. P. (Haberdashers' Aske's) (Capt. in 1981) 1978-83
Mountford, P. N. G. (Bromsgrove) 1963

Neate, F. W. (St Paul's) 1961-62
Newton-Thompson, J. O. (Diocesan Coll., SA) 1946
Niven, R. A. (Berkhamsted) 1968-69, 1973

O'Brien, T. C. (St Charles' College, Notting-Hill) 1884-85
Orders, J. O. D. (Winchester) 1978-81
Owen-Smith, H. G. (Diocesan College, SA) 1931-33

Palairet, L. C. H. (Repton) (Capt. in 1892-93) 1890-93
Pataudi, Nawab of (Chief's College, Lahore) 1929-31
Pataudi, Nawab of (Winchester) (Capt. in 1961, when he did not play v Cambridge owing to a car accident and 1963) 1960, 1963
Pathmanathan, G. (Royal Coll., Colombo and Sri Lanka U.) 1975-78
Paver, R. G. L. (Fort Victoria HS and Rhodes U.) 1973-74
Pawson, A. C. (Winchester) 1903
Pawson, A. G. (Winchester) (Capt. in 1910) 1908-11
Pawson, H. A. (Winchester) (Capt. in 1948) 1947-48
Pearce, J. P. (Ampleforth) 1979
Peebles, I. A. R. (Glasgow Academy) 1930
Petchey, M. D. (Latymer Upper) 1983
Phillips, J. B. M. (King's, Canterbury) 1955
Piachaud, J. D. (St Thomas's, Colombo) 1958-61
Pithey, D. B. (Plumtree HS and Cape Town U.) 1961-62
Porter, S. R. (Peers School) 1973
Potter, I. C. (King's, Canterbury) 1961-62
Potts, H. J. (Stand GS) 1950
Price, V. R. (Bishop's Stortford) (Capt. in 1921) 1919-22
Pycroft, J. (Bath) 1836

Quinlan, J. D. (Sherborne) 1985

Rawlinson, H. T. (Eton) 1983-84
Raybould, J. G. (Leeds GS) 1959
Ridge, S. P. (Dr Challenor's GS) 1982
Ridley, G. N. S. (Milton HS, Rhodesia) (Capt. in 1967) 1965-68
Ridley, R. M. (Clifton) 1968-70
Robertson-Glasgow, R. C. (Charterhouse) 1920-23
Robinson, G. A. (Preston Cath. Coll.) 1971
Robinson, H. B. O. (North Shore Coll., Vancouver) 1947-48
Rogers, J. J. (Sedbergh) 1979-81
Ross, C. J. (Wanganui CS and Wellington U., NZ) (Capt. in 1980) 1978-80
Rudd, C. R. D. (Eton) 1949
Rumbold, J. S. (St Andrew's Coll., NZ) 1946
Rutnagur, R. S. (Westminster) 1985

Sabine, P. N. B. (Marlborough) 1963
Sale, R. (Repton) 1910
Sale, R. (Repton) 1939, 1946
Sanderson, J. F. W. (Westminster) 1980
Saunders, C. J. (Lancing) 1964
Savage, R. Le Q. (Marlborough) 1976-78
Sayer, D. M. (Maidstone GS) 1958-60
Scott, M. D. (Winchester) 1957
Singleton, A. P. (Shrewsbury) (Capt. in 1937) 1934-37
Siviter, K. (Liverpool) 1976

Smith, A. C. (King Edward's, Birmingham) (Capt. in 1959-60) 1958-60
Smith, G. O. (Charterhouse) 1895-96
Smith, M. J. K. (Stamford) (Capt. in 1956) 1954-56
Stallibrass, M. J. D. (Lancing) 1974
Stevens, G. T. S. (UCS) (Capt. in 1922) 1920-23
Sutcliffe, S. P. (King George V GS, Southport) 1980-81
Sutton, M. A. (Ampleforth) 1946

Tavaré, C. J. (Sevenoaks) 1975-77
Taylor, C. H. (Westminster) 1923-26
Taylor, T. J. (Stockport GS) 1981-82
Thackeray, P. R. (St Edward's, Oxford and Exeter U.) 1974
Thomas, R. J. A. (Radley) 1965
Thorne, D. A. (Bablake) 1984-85
Toft, D. P. (Tonbridge) 1966-67
Toogood, G. J. (N. Bromsgrove HS) (Capt. in 1983) 1982-85
Tooley, C. D. M. (St Dunstan's) 1985
Topham, R. D. N. (Shrewsbury and Australian National U., Canberra) 1976
Travers, B. H. (Sydney U.) 1946, 1948
Twining, R. H. (Eton) (Capt. in 1912) 1910-13

van der Bijl, P. G. (Diocesan Coll., SA) 1932
Van Ryneveld, C. B. (Diocesan Coll., SA) (Capt. in 1949) 1948-50
Varey, J. G. (Birkenhead) 1982-83

Wagstaffe, M. C. (Rossall and Exeter U.) 1972
Walford, M. M. (Rugby) 1936, 1938
Walker, D. F. (Uppingham) (Capt. in 1935) 1933-35
Waller, G. de W. (Hurstpierpoint) 1974
Walsh, D. R. (Marlborough) 1967-69
Walshe, A. P. (Milton HS, Rhodesia) 1953, 1955-56
Walton, A. C. (Radley) (Capt. in 1957) 1955-57
Ward, J. M. (Newcastle-u-Lyme HS) 1971-73
Warner, P. F. (Rugby) 1895-96
Watson, A. G. M. (St Lawrence) 1965-66, 1968
Webb, H. E. (Winchester) 1948
Webbe, A. J. (Harrow) (Capt. in 1877-78) 1875-78
Wellings, E. M. (Cheltenham) 1929, 1931
Westley, S. A. (Lancaster RGS) 1968-69
Wheatley, G. A. (Uppingham) 1946
Whitcombe, P. A. (Winchester) 1947-49
Whitcombe, P. J. (Worcester RGS) 1951-52
Wiley, W. G. A. (Diocesan Coll., SA) 1952
Williams, C. C. P. (Westminster) (Capt. in 1955) 1953-55
Wilson, P. R. B. (Milton HS, Rhodesia and Cape Town U.) 1968, 1970
Wilson, R. W. (Warwick) 1957
Wingfield Digby, A. R. (Sherborne) 1971, 1975-77
Winn, C. E. (KCS, Wimbledon) 1948-51
Woodcock, R. G. (Worcester RGS) 1957-58
Wookey, S. M. (Malvern and Cambridge U.) 1978
Wordsworth, Chas. (Harrow) (Capt. both years, first Oxford Capt.) 1827, 1829
Worsley, D. R. (Bolton) (Capt. in 1964) 1961-64
Wrigley, M. H. (Harrow) 1949

## CAMBRIDGE

Acfield, D. L. (Brentwood) 1967-68
Aers, D. R. (Tonbridge) 1967
Aird, R. (Eton) 1923
Alexander, F. C. M. (Wolmer's Coll., Jamaica) 1952-53
Allbrook, M. E. (Tonbridge) 1975-78
Allen, G. O. (Eton) 1922-23
Allom, M. J. C. (Wellington) 1927-28
Andrew, C. R. (Barnard Castle) (Capt. in 1985) 1984-85
Ashton, C. T. (Winchester) (Capt. in 1923) 1921-23
Ashton, G. (Winchester) (Capt. in 1921) 1919-21
Ashton, H. (Winchester) (Capt. in 1922) 1920-22
Atkins, G. (Dr Challenor's GS) 1960
Aworth, C. J. (Tiffin) (Capt. in 1975) 1973-75

Bailey, T. E. (Dulwich) 1947-48
Baker, R. K. (Brentwood) 1973-74
Bannister, C. S. (Caterham) 1976
Barber, R. W. (Ruthin) 1956-57
Barford, M. T. (Eastbourne) 1970-71
Barrington, W. E. J. (Lancing) 1982
Bartlett, H. T. (Dulwich) (Capt. in 1936) 1934-36
Beaumont, D. J. (West Bridgford GS and Bramshill Coll.) 1978
Benke, A. F. (Cheltenham) 1962
Bennett, B. W. P. (Welbeck and RMA Sandhurst) 1979
Bennett, C. T. (Harrow) (Capt. in 1925) 1923, 1925
Bernard, J. R. (Clifton) 1958-60
Bhatia, A. N. (Doon School, India) 1969
Bligh, Hon. Ivo F. W. (Lord Darnley) (Eton) (Capt. in 1881) 1878-81
Blofeld, H. C. (Eton) 1959
Bodkin, P. E. (Bradfield) (Capt. in 1946) 1946
Boyd-Moss, R. J. (Bedford) 1980-83
Brearley, J. M. (City of London) (Capt. in 1963-64) 1961-64
Breddy, M. N. (Cheltenham GS) 1984

Brodie, J. B. (Union HS, SA) 1960
Brodrick, P. D. (Royal GS, Newcastle) 1961
Bromley, R. C. (Christ's Coll. and Canterbury U., NZ) 1970
Brooker, M. E. W. (Lancaster RGS and Burnley GS) 1976
Brown, F. R. (The Leys) 1930-31
Burnett, A. C. (Lancing) 1949
Burnley, I. D. (Queen Elizabeth, Darlington) 1984
Bushby, M. H. (Dulwich) (Capt. in 1954) 1952-54

Calthorpe, Hon. F. S. G. (Repton) 1912-14, 1919
Cameron, J. H. (Taunton) 1935-37
Cangley, B. G. M. (Felsted) 1947
Carling, P. G. (Kingston GS) 1968, 1970
Chambers, R. E. J. (Forest) 1966
Chapman, A. P. F. (Oakham and Uppingham) 1920-22
Close, P. A. (Haileybury) 1965
Cobden, F. C. (Harrow) 1870-72
Cockett, J. A. (Aldenham) 1951
Coghlan, T. B. L. (Rugby) 1960
Conradi, E. R. (Oundle) 1946
Cook, G. W. (Dulwich) 1957-58
Cooper, N. H. C. (St Brendan's, Bristol and East Anglia U.) 1979
Cosh, N. J. (Dulwich) 1966-68
Cotterell, T. A. (Downside) 1983-85
Cottrell, G. A. (Kingston GS) (Capt. in 1968) 1966-68
Cottrell, P. R. (Chislehurst and Sidcup GS) 1979
Coverdale, S. P. (St Peter's, York) 1974-77
Craig, E. J. (Charterhouse) 1961-63
Crawford, N. C. (Shrewsbury) 1979-80
Crawley, E. (Harrow) 1887-89
Crawley, L. G. (Harrow) 1923-25
Croft, P. D. (Gresham's) 1955
Crookes, D. V. (Michaelhouse, SA) 1953
Curtis, T. S. (Worcester RGS) 1983

Daniell, J. (Clifton) 1899-1901
Daniels, D. M. (Rutlish) 1964-65
Datta, P. B. (Asutosh Coll., Calcutta) 1947
Davies, A. G. (Birkenhead) 1984-85
Davies, J. G. W. (Tonbridge) 1933-34
Davidson, J. E. (Penglais) 1985
Dawson, E. W. (Eton) (Capt. in 1927) 1924-27
Day, S. H. (Malvern) (Capt. in 1901) 1899-1902
Dewes, A. R. (Dulwich) 1978
Dewes, J. G. (Aldenham) 1948-50
Dexter, E. R. (Radley) (Capt. in 1958) 1956-58
Dickinson, D. C. (Clifton) 1953
Doggart, A. G. (Bishop's Stortford) 1921-22
Doggart, G. H. G. (Winchester) (Capt. in 1950) 1948-50
Doggart, S. J. G. (Winchester) 1980-83
Douglas-Pennant, S. (Eton) 1959
Duleepsinhji, K. S. (Cheltenham) 1925-26, 1928

Edmonds, P. H. (Gilbert Rennie HS, Lusaka, Skinner's and Cranbrook) (Capt. in 1973) 1971-73
Edwards, T. D. W. (Sherborne) 1981
Elgood, B. C. (Bradfield) 1948
Ellison, C. C. (Tonbridge) 1982-83, 1985
Enthoven, H. J. (Harrow) (Capt. in 1926) 1923-26
Estcourt, N. S. D. (Plumtree, Southern Rhodesia) 1954

Falcon, M. (Harrow) (Capt. in 1910) 1908-11
Farnes, K. (Royal Liberty School, Romford) 1931-33
Fell, D. J. (John Lyon) 1985
Field, M. N. (Bablake) 1974
Fitzgerald, J. F. (St Brendan's, Bristol) 1968
Ford, A. F. J. (Repton) 1878-81
Ford, F. G. J. (Repton) (Capt. in 1889) 1887-90
Ford, W. J. (Repton) 1873
Fosh, M. K. (Harrow) 1977-78

Gardiner, S. J. (St Andrew's, Bloemfontein) 1978
Garlick, P. L. (Sherborne) 1984
Gibb, P. A. (St Edward's, Oxford) 1935-38
Gibson, C. H. (Eton) 1920-21
Gilligan, A. E. R. (Dulwich) 1919-20
Goldie, C. F. E. (St Paul's) 1981-82
Goodfellow, A. (Marlborough) 1961-62
Goonesena, G. (Royal Coll., Colombo) (Capt. in 1957) 1954-57
Gorman, S. R. (St Peter's, York) 1985
Grace, W. G., jun. (Clifton) 1895-96
Grant, G. C. (Trinidad) 1929-30
Grant, R. S. (Trinidad) 1933
Green, D. J. (Burton GS) (Capt. in 1959) 1957-59
Greig, I. A. (Queen's Coll., SA) (Capt. in 1979) 1977-79
Grierson, H. (Bedford GS) 1911
Grimes, A. D. H. (Tonbridge) 1984
Griffith, M. G. (Marlborough) 1963-65
Griffith, S. C. (Dulwich) 1935
Griffiths, W. H. (Charterhouse) 1946-48

Hadley, R. J. (Sanfields CS) 1971-73
Hall, J. E. (Ardingly) 1969
Hall, P. J. (Geelong) 1949
Harvey, J. R. W. (Marlborough) 1965
Hawke, Hon. M. B. (Eton) (Capt. in 1885) 1882-83, 1885
Hayes, P. J. (Brighton) 1974-75, 1977
Hays, D. L. (Highgate) 1966, 1968
Hayward, W. I. D. (St Peter's Coll., Adelaide) 1950-51, 1953
Haywood, D. C. (Nottingham HS) 1968

Hazelrigg, A. G. (Eton) (Capt. in 1932) 1930-32
Henderson, S. P. (Downside and Durham U.) (Capt. in 1983) 1982-83
Hewitt, S. G. P. (Bradford GS) 1983
Hignell, A. J. (Denstone) (Capt. in 1977-78) 1975-78
Hobson, B. S. (Taunton) 1946
Hodgson, K. I. (Oundle) 1981-83
Hodson, R. P. (QEGS, Wakefield) 1972-73
Holliday, D. C. (Oundle) 1979-81
Howat, M. G. (Abingdon) 1977, 1980
Howland, C. B. (Dulwich) (Capt. in 1960) 1958-60
Hughes, G. (Cardiff HS) 1965
Human, J. H. (Repton) (Capt. in 1934) 1932-34
Hurd, A. (Chigwell) 1958-60
Hutton, R. A. (Repton) 1962-64
Huxter, R. J. A. (Magdalen Coll. Sch.) 1981

Insole, D. J. (Monoux, Walthamstow) (Capt. in 1949) 1947-49

Jackson, E. J. W. (Winchester) 1974-76
Jackson, F. S. (Harrow) (Capt. in 1892-93) 1890-93
Jahangir Khan (Lahore), 1933-36
James, R. M. (St John's, Leatherhead) 1956-58
Jameson, T. E. N. (Taunton and Durham U.) 1970
Jarrett, D. W. (Wellington and Oxford U.) 1976
Jefferson, R. I. (Winchester) 1961
Jenner, Herbert (Eton) (Capt. in 1827, First Cambridge Capt.) 1827
Jessop, G. L. (Cheltenham GS) (Capt. in 1899) 1896-99
Johnson, P. D. (Nottingham HS) 1970-72
Jones, A. O. (Bedford Modern) 1893
Jorden, A. M. (Monmouth) (Capt. in 1969-70) 1968-70

Kelland, P. A. (Repton) 1950
Kemp-Welch, G. D. (Charterhouse) (Capt. in 1931) 1929-31
Kendall, M. P. (Gillingham GS) 1972
Kenny, C. J. M. (Ampleforth) 1952
Kerslake, R. C. (Kingswood) 1963-64
Killick, E. T. (St Paul's) 1928-30
Kirby, D. (St Peter's, York) (Capt. in 1961) 1959-61
Kirkman, M. C. (Dulwich) 1963
Knight, R. D. V. (Dulwich) 1967-70
Knightley-Smith, W. (Highgate) 1953

Lacey, F. E. (Sherborne) 1882
Lacy-Scott, D. G. (Marlborough) 1946
Lea, A. E. (High Arcal GS) 1984-85
Lewis, A. R. (Neath GS) (Capt. in 1962) 1960-62
Lewis, L. K. (Taunton) 1953
Littlewood, D. J. (Enfield GS) 1978
Lowry, T. C. (Christ's College, NZ) (Capt. in 1924) 1923-24
Lumsden, V. R. (Munro College, Jamaica) 1953-55
Lyttelton, 4th Lord (Eton) 1838
Lyttelton, Hon. Alfred (Eton) (Capt. in 1879) 1876-79
Lyttelton, Hon. C. F. (Eton) 1908-09
Lyttelton, Hon. C. G. (Lord Cobham) (Eton) 1861-64
Lyttelton, Hon. Edward (Eton) (Capt. in 1878) 1875-78
Lyttelton, Hon. G. W. S. (Eton) 1866-67

McAdam, K. P. W. J. (Prince of Wales, Nairobi and Millfield) 1965-66
MacBryan, J. C. W. (Exeter) 1920
McCarthy, C. N. (Maritzburg Coll., SA) 1952
McDowall, J. I. (Rugby) 1969
MacGregor, G. (Uppingham) (Capt. in 1891) 1888-91
McLachlan, A. A. (St Peter's, Adelaide) 1964-65
McLachlan, I. M. (St Peter's, Adelaide) 1957-58
Majid J. Khan (Aitchison Coll., Lahore and Punjab U.) (Capt. in 1971-72) 1970-72
Malalasekera, V. P. (Royal Coll., Colombo) 1966-67
Mann, E. W. (Harrow) (Capt. in 1905) 1903-05
Mann, F. G. (Eton) 1938-39
Mann, F. T. (Malvern) 1909-11
Marlar, R. G. (Harrow) (Capt. in 1953) 1951-53
Marriott, C. S. (St Columba's) 1920-21
Mathews, K. P. A. (Felsted) 1951
May, P. B. H. (Charterhouse) 1950-52
Melluish, M. E. L. (Rossall) (Capt. in 1956) 1954-56
Meyer, R. J. O. (Haileybury) 1924-26
Miller, M. E. (Prince Henry GS, Hohne, WG) 1963
Mills, J. M. (Oundle) (Capt. in 1948) 1946-48
Mills, J. P. C. (Oundle) (Capt. in 1982) 1979-82
Mischler, N. M. (St Paul's) 1946-47
Mitchell, F. (St Peter's, York) (Capt. in 1896) 1894-97
Morgan, J. T. (Charterhouse) (Capt. in 1930) 1928-30
Morgan, M. N. (Marlborough) 1954
Morris, R. J. (Blundell's) 1949
Morrison, J. S. F. (Charterhouse) (Capt. in 1919) 1912, 1914, 1919
Moses, G. H. (Ystalyfera GS) 1974
Moylan, A. C. D. (Clifton) 1977

Mubarak, A. M. (Royal Coll., Colombo and Sri Lanka U.) 1978-80
Murray, D. L. (Queen's RC, Trinidad) (Capt. in 1966) 1965-66
Murrills, T. J. (The Leys) (Capt. in 1976) 1973-74, 1976

Nevin, M. R. S. (Winchester) 1969
Norris, D. W. W. (Harrow) 1967 68

O'Brien, R. P. (Wellington) 1955-56
Odendaal, A. (Queen's Coll. and Stellenbosch U., SA) 1980
Owen-Thomas, D. R. (KCS, Wimbledon) 1969-72

Palfreman, A. B. (Nottingham HS) 1966
Palmer, R. W. M. (Bedford) 1982
Parker, G. W. (Crypt, Gloucester) (Capt. in 1935) 1934-35
Parker, P. W. G. (Collyer's GS) 1976-78
Parsons, A. B. D. (Brighton) 1954-55
Pathmanathan, G. (Royal Coll., Colombo, Sri Lanka U. and Oxford U.) 1983
Paull, R. K. (Millfield) 1967
Payne, M. W. (Wellington) (Capt. in 1907) 1904-07
Pearman, H. (King Alfred's and St Andrew's U.) 1969
Pearson, A. J. G. (Downside) 1961-63
Peck, I. G. (Bedford) (Capt. in 1980-81) 1980-81
Pepper, J. (The Leys) 1946-48
Pieris, P. I. (St Thomas's, Colombo) 1957-58
Pollock, A. J. (Shrewsbury) (Capt. in 1984) 1982-84
Ponniah, C. E. M. (St Thomas's, Colombo) 1967-69
Ponsonby, Hon. F. G. B. (Lord Bessborough) (Harrow) 1836
Popplewell, N. F. M. (Radley) 1977-79
Popplewell, O. B. (Charterhouse) 1949-51
Pretlove, J. F. (Alleyn's) 1954-56
Price, D. G. (Haberdashers' Aske's) 1984-85
Prideaux, R. M. (Tonbridge) 1958-60
Pringle, D. R. (Felsted) (Capt. in 1982, when he did not play v Oxford owing to Test selection) 1979-81
Pritchard, G. C. (King's, Canterbury) 1964
Pryer, B. J. K. (City of London) 1948
Pyemont, C. P. (Marlborough) 1967

Ranjitsinhji, K. S. (Rajkumar Coll., India) 1893
Ratcliffe, A. (Rydal) 1930-32
Reddy, N. S. K. (Doon School, India) 1959-61
Rimell, A. G. J. (Charterhouse) 1949-50
Robins, R. W. V. (Highgate) 1926-28
Roebuck, P. G. P. (Millfield) 1984-85
Roebuck, P. M. (Millfield) 1975-77
Roopnaraine, R. (Queen's RC, BG) 1965-66
Rose, M. H. (Pocklington) 1963-64
Ross, N. P. G. (Marlborough) 1969
Roundell, J. (Winchester) 1973
Russell, D. P. (West Park GS, St Helens) 1974-75
Russell, S. G. (Tiffin) (Capt. in 1967) 1965-67
Russom, N. (Huish's GS) 1980-81

Scott, A. M. G. (Seaford Head) 1985
Seabrook, F. J. (Haileybury) (Capt. in 1928) 1926-28
Seager, C. P. (Peterhouse, Rhodesia) 1971
Selvey, M. W. W. (Battersea GS and Manchester U.) 1971
Sheppard, D. S. (Sherborne) (Capt. in 1952) 1950-52
Short, R. L. (Denstone) 1969
Shuttleworth, G. M. (Blackburn GS) 1946-48
Silk, D. R. W. (Christ's Hospital) (Capt. in 1955) 1953-55
Singh, S. (Khalsa Coll. and Punjab U.) 1955-56
Sinker, N. D. (Winchester) 1966
Slack, J. K. E. (UCS) 1954
Smith, C. S. (William Hulme's GS) 1954-57
Smith, D. J. (Stockport GS) 1955-56
Smyth, R. I. (Sedbergh) 1973-75
Snowden, W. (Merchant Taylors', Crosby) (Capt. in 1974) 1972-75
Spencer, J. (Brighton and Hove GS) 1970-72
Steele, H. K. (King's Coll., NZ) 1971-72
Stevenson, M. H. (Rydal) 1949-52
Studd, C. T. (Eton) (Capt. in 1883) 1880-83
Studd, G. B. (Eton) (Capt. in 1882) 1879-82
Studd, J. E. K. (Eton) (Capt. in 1884) 1881-84
Studd, P. M. (Harrow) (Capt. in 1939) 1937-39
Studd, R. A. (Eton) 1895
Subba Row, R. (Whitgift) 1951-53
Surridge, D. (Richard Hale and Southampton U.) 1979
Swift, B. T. (St Peter's, Adelaide) 1957

Taylor, C. R. V. (Birkenhead) 1971-73
Thomson, R. H. (Bexhill) 1961-62
Thwaites, I. G. (Eastbourne) 1964
Tindall, M. (Harrow) (Capt. in 1937) 1935-37
Tordoff, G. G. (Normanton GS) 1952
Trapnell, B. M. W. (UCS) 1946
Turnbull, M. J. (Downside) (Capt. in 1929) 1926, 1928-29

Urquhart, J. R. (King Edward VI School, Chelmsford) 1948

Valentine, B. H. (Repton) 1929
Varey, D. W. (Birkenhead) 1982-83

Wait, O. J. (Dulwich) 1949, 1951
Warr, J. J. (Ealing County GS) (Capt. in 1951) 1949-52
Watts, H. E. (Downside) 1947

Webster, W. H. (Highgate) 1932
Weedon, M. J. H. (Harrow) 1962
Wells, T. U. (King's Coll., NZ) 1950
Wheatley, O. S. (King Edward's, Birmingham) 1957-58
Wheelhouse, A. (Nottingham HS) 1959
White, R. C. (Hilton Coll., SA) (Capt. in 1965) 1962-65
Wilcox, D. R. (Dulwich) (Capt. in 1933) 1931-33
Wilenkin, B. C. G. (Harrow) 1956
Wilkin, C. L. A. (St Kitts GS) 1970
Willard, M. J. L. (Judd) 1959-61
Willatt, G. L. (Repton) (Capt. in 1947) 1946-47
Windows, A. R. (Clifton) 1962-64
Wood, G. E. C. (Cheltenham) (Capt. in 1920) 1914, 1919-20
Wookey, S. M. (Malvern) 1975-76
Wooller, W. (Rydal) 1935-36
Wright, S. (Mill Hill) 1973

Yardley, N. W. D. (St Peter's, York) (Capt. in 1938) 1935-38
Young, R. A. (Repton) (Capt. in 1908) 1905-08

## STATUS OF MATCHES IN THE UK

**(*a*) Automatic First-Class Matches**

The following matches of three or more days' duration should automatically be considered first-class:

(i) County Championship matches.

(ii) Official representative tourist matches from Full Member Countries, unless specifically excluded.

(iii) MCC v any First-Class County.

(iv) Oxford v Cambridge and either University against First-Class Counties.

(v) Scotland v Ireland.

**(*b*) Excluded from First-Class Status**

The following matches of three or more days' duration should not normally be accorded first-class status:

(i) County "friendly" matches.

(ii) Matches played by Scotland or Ireland, other than their annual match against each other.

(iii) Unofficial tourist matches, unless circumstances are exceptional.

(iv) MCC v Oxford/Cambridge.

(v) Matches involving privately raised teams, unless included officially in a touring team's itinerary.

**(*c*) Consideration of Doubtful Status**

Matches played by unofficial touring teams of exceptional ability can be considered in advance and decisions taken accordingly.

Certain other matches comprising 22 recognised first-class cricketers might also be considered in advance.

# OTHER MATCHES, 1985

†At Cambusdoon, Ayr, August 22, 23. Drawn. Scotland 138 for six dec.; MCC 101 for two (D. Lloyd 51).

## IRELAND v SCOTLAND

At Dublin, June 15, 16, 17. Drawn. Toss won by Scotland. Ireland gained the upper hand midway through the first afternoon and remained in the ascendant thereafter. When rain ruined the final stages, allowing only a token amount of play late on the third day, Scotland were 275 runs behind with all their second wickets in hand. Despite Warke's 65, Ireland, having been put in on a slow, damp pitch, were 137 for seven and in some difficulty before the last three wickets added 112, Halliday and Elder sharing a partnership of 45 at the end. Stevenson, a new cap and a last-minute replacement in the Scotland side, took four for 66 with his slow left-arm spin. Having dismissed Scotland 75 runs in arrears, Ireland moved further ahead, finishing the second day at 222 for two. Stephen Warke emulated his father, Larry, by making a hundred against Scotland, his unbeaten 144, the highest score against Scotland in Ireland, occupying four hours, with seventeen 4s. He gave no chance until he was 102.

### Ireland

| | | | |
|---|---|---|---|
| S. J. S. Warke st Brown b Stevenson | 65 | – not out | 144 |
| M. F. Cohen b Ker | 9 | – lbw b Duthie | 22 |
| M. P. Rea c Duthie b Thomson | 5 | – c Snodgrass b Donald | 39 |
| R. T. Wills c Donald b Stevenson | 9 | | |
| J. A. Prior c Donald b Thomson | 19 | – (4) not out | 11 |
| G. D. Harrison c Snodgrass b Stevenson | 10 | | |
| S. C. Corlett st Brown b Stevenson | 12 | | |
| A. McBrine c Brown b Duthie | 24 | | |
| †P. B. Jackson c Simpson b Thomson | 28 | | |
| *M. Halliday run out | 47 | | |
| J. W. G. Elder not out | 11 | | |
| B 5, l-b 3, w 2 | 10 | L-b 3 | 3 |
| 1/28 2/49 3/73 4/94 5/122 6/124 7/137 8/180 9/204 | 249 | 1/65 2/174 (2 wkts dec.) | 222 |

Bowling: *First Innings*—Duthie 14–4–25–1; McPate 8–1–24–0; Ker 15–7–21–1; Thomson 33–6–89–3; Donald 10–3–16–0; Stevenson 30–10–66–4. *Second Innings*—Duthie 18–7–47–1; McPate 6–3–14–0; Ker 5–1–14–0; Thomson 23–6–54–0; Donald 8–0–47–1; Stevenson 16–2–43–0.

### Scotland

| | | | |
|---|---|---|---|
| W. A. Donald b Corlett | 16 | – not out | 19 |
| D. J. Simpson b Elder | 6 | – not out | 1 |
| *R. G. Swan c Prior b Elder | 2 | | |
| A. B. Russell c and b Halliday | 51 | | |
| †A. Brown lbw b Corlett | 57 | | |
| D. L. Snodgrass c Elder b Halliday | 12 | | |
| P. G. Duthie b Corlett | 1 | | |
| J. E. Ker b Halliday | 4 | | |
| W. A. McPate c Prior b Halliday | 14 | | |
| A. Stevenson b Corlett | 9 | | |
| J. Thomson not out | 0 | | |
| L-b 2 | 2 | W 2 | 2 |
| 1/8 2/14 3/30 4/118 5/144 6/146 7/151 8/151 9/168 | 174 | (no wkt) | 22 |

Bowling: *First Innings*—Corlett 24.2–7–56–4; Elder 15–5–27–2; Halliday 27–10–64–4; McBrine 12–6–25–0. *Second Innings*—McBrine 4–2–3–0; Harrison 6–3–11–0; Prior 6–4–8–0.

Umpires: E. Harkness and S. Moore.

## THE TILCON TROPHY

When the rain-soaked outfield and drizzle prevented any orthodox play on the final day, the Tilcon Trophy at the Harrogate Festival was decided by all 22 players from the finalists, Warwickshire and Nottinghamshire, bowling two balls each at a single stump. The contest, devised by the two umpires, D. O. Oslear and J. W. Holder, in preference to tossing a coin for the prizemoney, was the first such bowling contest to decide a competition involving first-class teams in England. Warwickshire, with hits from Dyer, Lord, Pierson, Asif Din and Gifford, won £1,550; the runners-up, Nottinghamshire, whose only success came from Saxelby, took £500.

On the first day Nottinghamshire, put in by Yorkshire on a placid pitch, began slowly, Broad taking 30 overs to compile 30 runs. Play was held up for ten minutes while the footholds were cut by hand mower. Acceleration came from French, who made his best one-day score and whose eighth-wicket stand of 58 in eight overs with Hemmings was a record for the competition. Restricted by Cooper, Yorkshire, in reply, were always behind the required run-rate, and a mid-innings collapse sealed their fate. On the second day a devastating spell of four for 6 in 23 balls, including three wickets in four balls (the third delivery was a no-ball), from Wall of Warwickshire reduced Gloucestershire to 49 for five after they had elected to bat. Although a sixth-wicket partnership of 92 between Payne and Bainbridge brought respectability, Warwickshire had no trouble in passing their total with 8.3 overs to spare, thanks mainly to a second-wicket stand of 126 between Lloyd and Lord, as well as 26 extras, 21 of them wides and no-balls.

†June 19. Nottinghamshire won by 98 runs. Nottinghamshire 267 for seven (55 overs) (B. C. Broad 60, B. N. French 58 not out); Yorkshire 169 (49.5 overs) (G. Boycott 46). *Man of the Match*: B. N. French.

†June 20. Warwickshire won by seven wickets. Gloucestershire 198 (55 overs) (I. R. Payne 58, P. Bainbridge 55; S. Wall five for 21); Warwickshire 202 for three (46.3 overs) (T. A. Lloyd 70, G. J. Lord 64). *Man of the Match*: S. Wall.

†At Headingley, July 19. International XI won by 33 runs. International XI 233 for six (40 overs) (Mohsin Khan 73); Yorkshire 200 (39.3 overs) (D. L. Bairstow 110).

†At Swansea, July 24, 25, 26. MCC won by four wickets. Wales 298 for eight dec. (G. Edwards 81, H. Williams 56, R. Williams 40 not out) and 221 for seven dec. (G. Ellis 62); MCC 260 for four dec. (N. E. Briers 139) and 262 for six (N. E. Briers 83, B. Dudleston 75).

## THE ASDA CHALLENGE

The Asda Challenge at Scarborough opened with a last-over win by Derbyshire over Yorkshire, whose total of 206 owed much to Hartley's efforts after they had been put in on a damp pitch. Derbyshire, reduced by Pickles to 86 for four from 79 for one, were rescued by a fierce half-century off 50 balls from Morris. Against Nottinghamshire on the second day, Lancashire, who won the toss, were taken towards a comfortable victory by a fourth-wicket partnership of 116 between Lloyd and Fairbrother, after economical bowling by Simmons had restricted their opponents to 146. It was a bowler who took the honours in the final, in which Finney's five for 22 hampered Lancashire before Anderson and Roberts, in reply, put on 132 for Derbyshire's first wicket as they cruised to victory.

†September 4. Derbyshire won by three wickets. Yorkshire 206 for nine (50 overs) (S. N. Hartley 72, K. Sharp 55); Derbyshire 209 for seven (49.1 overs) (J. E. Morris 56, I. S. Anderson 42, P. G. Newman 40). *Man of the Match*: J. E. Morris.

†September 5. Lancashire won by six wickets. Nottinghamshire 146 for nine (50 overs); Lancashire 147 for four (47.1 overs) (C. H. Lloyd 73 not out, N. H. Fairbrother 51). *Man of the Match*: C. H. Lloyd.

†September 6. Derbyshire won by eight wickets. Lancashire 175 for seven (50 overs) (C. H. Lloyd 50; R. J. Finney five for 32); Derbyshire 177 for two (45.2 overs) (I. S. Anderson 75 not out, B. Roberts 70). *Man of the Match*: R. J. Finney.

## D. B. CLOSE'S XI v REST OF THE WORLD XI

At Scarborough, September 8, 9, 10. D. B. Close's XI won by 30 runs. Toss won by D. B. Close's XI.

### D. B. Close's XI

| | | | |
|---|---|---|---|
| W. Larkins c Harper b Benjamin | 6 | – c Phillips b Stephenson | 9 |
| M. D. Moxon c Harper b Stirling | 51 | – c Mushtaq b Doshi | 36 |
| M. W. Gatting c Stephenson b Doshi | 88 | – (5) b Stirling | 19 |
| K. Sharp st Phillips b Harper | 14 | – (3) b Benjamin | 13 |
| C. T. Radley not out | 27 | – (4) b Benjamin | 0 |
| †D. L. Bairstow st Phillips b Doshi | 12 | – lbw b Stirling | 6 |
| *D. B. Close not out | 20 | – not out | 22 |
| P. H. Edmonds (did not bat) | | – run out | 19 |
| J. E. Emburey (did not bat) | | – b Harper | 6 |
| B 4, l-b 4 | 8 | L-b 3, w 4 | 7 |
| 1/8 2/98 3/163 4/167 5/195 | (5 wkts dec.) 226 | 1/35 2/36 3/39 4/83 5/85 6/90 7/127 8/137 | (8 wkts dec.) 137 |

N. A. Mallender and N. G. Cowans did not bat.

Bowling: *First Innings*—Benjamin 12–3–30–1; Stirling 8–3–21–1; Doshi 20–4–75–2; Harper 23–4–73–1; Mushtaq 2–0–5–0; Stephenson 6–1–14–0. *Second Innings*—Stirling 11–2–39–2; Benjamin 9–2–31–2; Stephenson 8–3–24–1; Doshi 12–2–29–1; Harper 3.5–0–11–1.

### Rest of the World

| | | | |
|---|---|---|---|
| Sadiq Mohammad c Larkins b Emburey | 24 | – c Moxon b Close | 65 |
| B. A. Young c Bairstow b Mallender | 0 | – b Edmonds | 14 |
| M. D. Crowe lbw b Moxon | 7 | – c Mallender b Edmonds | 6 |
| †R. B. Phillips c Emburey b Edmonds | 35 | – b Emburey | 15 |
| G. R. Viswanath c Moxon b Edmonds | 7 | – c Close b Emburey | 0 |
| *Mushtaq Mohammad c Close b Emburey | 16 | – b Emburey | 9 |
| R. A. Harper c Sharp b Edmonds | 15 | – c and b Edmonds | 14 |
| F. D. Stephenson c Gatting b Emburey | 40 | – run out | 0 |
| W. Benjamin not out | 0 | – b Close | 15 |
| D. A. Stirling st Bairstow b Edmonds | 3 | – b Edmonds | 20 |
| D. R. Doshi c Radley b Emburey | 0 | – not out | 0 |
| B 5, l-b 5, w 1, n-b 4 | 15 | B 2, l-b 10, w 1 | 13 |
| 1/1 2/25 3/38 4/57 5/95 6/98 7/151 8/158 9/161 | 162 | 1/29 2/43 3/70 4/76 5/90 6/105 7/109 8/130 9/170 | 171 |

Bowling: *First Innings*—Cowans 6–2–9–0; Mallender 12–1–35–1; Moxon 3–1–13–1; Emburey 22.4–6–47–4; Edmonds 22–8–48–4. *Second Innings*—Cowans 4–1–9–0; Mallender 3–0–19–0; Emburey 12–5–39–3; Edmonds 22.2–6–59–4; Close 6–1–33–2.

Umpires: J. Birkenshaw and B. Leadbeater.

# NATWEST BANK TROPHY, 1985

Essex, who won the 60-overs competition for the first time when they beat Nottinghamshire by 1 run in a gripping finish at Lord's, became the fifth holders of the NatWest Bank Trophy. In addition to the trophy, they received a cheque for £17,000, while Nottinghamshire, finalists for the first time, received £8,500. The losing semi-finalists, Hampshire and Worcestershire, each received £4,250, and Glamorgan, Gloucestershire, Kent and Somerset, the losing quarter-finalists, each received £2,125. Brian Hardie, of Essex, received £550 as Man of the Match in the final. The Man of the Match in each semi-final received £275; in each quarter-final £200; in each second-round match £125 and in each first-round match £100. Total prizemoney for the competition was £47,000, £6,400 more than in 1984.

## FIRST ROUND

### BEDFORDSHIRE v GLOUCESTERSHIRE

At Luton, July 3. Gloucestershire won by 141 runs. Toss won by Bedfordshire.
*Man of the Match:* C. W. J. Athey.

#### Gloucestershire

A. W. Stovold b Wake . . . . . . . . . . . . . . 71
P. W. Romaines lbw b Hoare . . . . . . . . 26
C. W. J. Athey c Lines b Marvin . . . . . 72
B. F. Davison c and b Hoare . . . . . . . . . 28
P. Bainbridge c Pearson b Marvin . . . . 11
K. M. Curran c Steele b Lines . . . . . . . . 9
I. R. Payne not out . . . . . . . . . . . . . . . . . 18
D. V. Lawrence not out . . . . . . . . . . . . . 1
B 5, l-b 14, w 7, n-b 6 . . . . . . . 32

1/101 2/132 3/184 4/208 5/224 6/263 (6 wkts, 60 overs) 268

*D. A. Graveney, †R. C. Russell and C. A. Walsh did not bat.

Bowling: Marvin 11–0–56–2; Proudman 12–2–40–0; Hoare 12–0–64–2; Steele 12–1–29–0; Wake 12–1–47–1; Lines 1–0–13–1.

#### Bedfordshire

K. Gentle st Russell b Payne . . . . . . . . . 13
D. S. Steele b Walsh . . . . . . . . . . . . . . . . 0
A. S. Pearson c Stovold b Lawrence . . . 4
M. Morgan b Lawrence . . . . . . . . . . . . . 7
S. J. Lines b Graveney . . . . . . . . . . . . . . 2
*I. G. Peck c Russell b Curran . . . . . . . 1
P. D. B. Hoare c Romaines b Bainbridge 12
B. L. Marvin lbw b Graveney . . . . . . . . 0
J. R. Wake c Russell b Curran . . . . . . . 37
†P. G. M. August lbw b Walsh . . . . . . . 16
C. J. Proudman not out . . . . . . . . . . . . . 14
B 2, l-b 17, w 2 . . . . . . . . . . . . 21

1/1 2/12 3/31 4/34 5/37 6/41 7/41 8/79 9/96 (54 overs) 127

Bowling: Lawrence 5–0–20–2; Walsh 7–3–7–2; Payne 12–4–11–1; Curran 12–7–9–2; Graveney 10–3–41–2; Bainbridge 8–0–20–1.

Umpires: K. J. Lyons and P. J. Eele.

### CHESHIRE v YORKSHIRE

At Birkenhead, July 3. Yorkshire won by ten wickets. Toss won by Yorkshire.
*Man of the Match:* M. D. Moxon.

### Cheshire

Mudassar Nazar c Bairstow b Sidebottom 1
I. Tansley run out 18
I. Cockbain lbw b Jarvis 17
N. T. O'Brien c and b Stevenson 13
S. C. Yates b Stevenson 6
J. J. Hitchmough b Jarvis 22
K. Teasdale b Sidebottom 46
*J. A. Sutton not out 15
B 2, l-b 8, w 5, n-b 6 21

1/3 2/38 3/45 4/60 5/66 6/108 7/159 (7 wkts, 60 overs) 159

D. J. Parry, †J. K. Pickup and P. J. Hacker did not bat.

Bowling: Sidebottom 12–0–42–2; Fletcher 12–3–35–0; Stevenson 12–4–17–2; Jarvis 12–1–36–2; Carrick 12–5–19–0.

### Yorkshire

G. Boycott not out 70
M. D. Moxon not out 82
B 1, l-b 1, w 5, n-b 1 8

(no wkt, 44.1 overs) 160

S. N. Hartley, K. Sharp, J. D. Love, *†D. L. Bairstow, A. Sidebottom, P. Carrick, G. B. Stevenson, P. W. Jarvis and S. D. Fletcher did not bat.

Bowling: Hacker 8–0–32–0; Mudassar 9–0–34–0; Sutton 11–1–43–0; O'Brien 7–3–17–0; Parry 9.1–0–32–0.

Umpires: J. Birkenshaw and C. Smith.

## DERBYSHIRE v DURHAM

At Derby, July 3. Durham won by seven wickets to become the first minor county to beat first-class opposition on two occasions. Toss won by Durham.
*Man of the Match:* S. Greensword.

### Derbyshire

*K. J. Barnett b Patel 53
I. S. Anderson c Fothergill b Johnson 4
J. E. Morris b Johnson 12
B. Roberts c Fothergill b Patel 13
R. Sharma c Johnson b Patel 11
G. Miller c Hurst b Greensword 0
M. A. Holding lbw b Greensword 27
P. G. Newman c Riddell b Johnston 19
†B. J. M. Maher c Johnson b Greensword 0
A. E. Warner b Johnston 17
O. H. Mortensen not out 4
L-b 5, w 6 11

1/14 2/40 3/83 4/94 5/99 6/99 7/142 8/144 9/158 (58.4 overs) 171

Bowling: Scott 8–1–29–0; Johnston 11.4–0–31–2; Johnson 12–0–35–2; Burn 3–0–17–0; Patel 12–3–34–3; Greensword 12–4–20–3.

### Durham

J. W. Lister c Roberts b Mortensen 42
D. C. Jackson lbw b Warner 0
S. Greensword c Roberts b Holding 40
*N. A. Riddell not out 49
A. S. Patel not out 21
B 1, l-b 12, w 5, n-b 2 20

1/62 2/63 3/114 (3 wkts, 55.4 overs) 172

P. Burn, G. Hurst, †A. R. Fothergill, G. Johnson, A. W. Scott and J. Johnston did not bat.

Bowling: Holding 12–2–36–1; Warner 12–1–46–1; Newman 12–1–25–0; Mortensen 10.4–2–37–1; Miller 9–4–15–0.

Umpires: J. H. Harris and D. O. Oslear.

## ESSEX v OXFORDSHIRE

At Chelmsford, July 3. Essex won by 226 runs. Toss won by Oxfordshire.
*Man of the Match:* D. R. Pringle.

### Essex

| | | | |
|---|---|---|---|
| G. A. Gooch b Busby | 5 | A. W. Lilley not out | 4 |
| B. R. Hardie c and b Evans | 51 | | |
| P. J. Prichard run out | 94 | B 2, l-b 12, w 3 | 17 |
| K. S. McEwan b Porter | 66 | | |
| D. R. Pringle b Arnold | 55 | 1/16 2/91 3/210 (6 wkts, 60 overs) | 307 |
| *K. W. R. Fletcher run out | 15 | 4/247 5/303 6/307 | |

†D. E. East, N. A. Foster, J. K. Lever and D. L. Acfield did not bat.

Bowling: Busby 12–1–66–1; Arnold 12–0–64–1; Ricks 9–0–49–0; Evans 12–1–41–1; Porter 12–1–52–1; Garner 3–0–21–0.

### Oxfordshire

| | | | |
|---|---|---|---|
| M. D. Nurton b Lever | 6 | R. N. Busby c East b Acfield | 8 |
| G. C. Ford b Pringle | 18 | K. A. Arnold lbw b Acfield | 0 |
| D. A. J. Wise c East b Gooch | 3 | †A. Crossley not out | 0 |
| *P. J. Garner b Pringle | 2 | L-b 8, w 6 | 14 |
| C. J. Clements lbw b Pringle | 1 | | |
| S. R. Porter c Gooch b Pringle | 3 | 1/20 2/36 3/36 4/37 (43.2 overs) | 81 |
| R. A. Evans lbw b Pringle | 9 | 5/41 6/43 7/63 | |
| C. D. Ricks b Foster | 17 | 8/81 9/81 | |

Bowling: Lever 8–4–7–1; Foster 9.2–0–29–1; Gooch 12–3–22–1; Pringle 12–5–12–5; Acfield 2–0–3–2.

Umpires: A. Jepson and H. J. Rhodes.

## HAMPSHIRE v BERKSHIRE

At Southampton, July 3. Hampshire won by 187 runs. Toss won by Berkshire.
*Man of the Match:* V. P. Terry.

### Hampshire

| | | | |
|---|---|---|---|
| C. G. Greenidge st Child b Roope | 89 | J. J. E. Hardy not out | 1 |
| V. P. Terry not out | 165 | B 5, l-b 7, w 13, n-b 2 | 27 |
| R. A. Smith c Child b Sluman | 37 | | |
| *M. C. J. Nicholas c Harvey b Jones | 8 | 1/52 2/247 3/271 (4 wkts, 60 overs) | 339 |
| C. L. Smith run out | 12 | 4/319 | |

M. D. Marshall, K. D. James, T. M. Tremlett, †R. J. Parks and S. J. W. Andrew did not bat.

Bowling: Roberts 11–1–70–0; Jones 12–1–82–1; New 12–0–41–0; Roope 12–0–77–1; Sluman 12–1–53–1; Lickley 1–0–4–0.

### Berkshire

| | | | |
|---|---|---|---|
| M. G. Lickley c R. A. Smith b Tremlett | 20 | T. E. Roberts c C. L. Smith b Andrew | 7 |
| J. A. Claughton st Parks b C. L. Smith | 19 | L. P. Sluman not out | 12 |
| M. L. Simmons lbw b Tremlett | 3 | J. H. Jones c Tremlett b R. A. Smith | 0 |
| G. R. J. Roope c Greenidge b Nicholas | 26 | L-b 6, w 4, n-b 3 | 13 |
| D. B. Gorman c Tremlett b C. L. Smith | 28 | | |
| *J. F. Harvey c R. A. Smith b C. L. Smith | 1 | 1/31 2/36 3/70 4/78 (58.5 overs) | 152 |
| †G. E. J. Child c Parks b Nicholas | 10 | 5/80 6/103 7/122 | |
| P. M. New b R. A. Smith | 13 | 8/139 9/141 | |

Bowling: James 12–0–31–0; Marshall 3–2–1–0; Andrew 10–1–28–1; Tremlett 7–5–2–2; Nicholas 12–1–39–2; C. L. Smith 12–3–32–3; R. A. Smith 2.5–0–13–2.

Umpires: J. A. Jameson and D. S. Thompsett.

## HERTFORDSHIRE v WORCESTERSHIRE

At Hitchin, July 3. Worcestershire won by 58 runs. Toss won by Worcestershire.
*Man of the Match*: E. P. Neal.

### Worcestershire

| | |
|---|---|
| T. S. Curtis run out . . . . . . . . . . . . . . . . . 63 | D. A. Banks not out . . . . . . . . . . . . . . . . 11 |
| †S. J. Rhodes c Smith b Merry . . . . . . . 6 | N. V. Radford not out . . . . . . . . . . . . . . . 0 |
| *P. A. Neale lbw b Merry . . . . . . . . . . . 73 | B 2, l-b 5, w 3 . . . . . . . . . . . . . 10 |
| D. N. Patel lbw b Garofall . . . . . . . . . . 4 | —— |
| Kapil Dev c Ottley b Garofall . . . . . . . . 8 | 1/10 2/127 3/140 (7 wkts, 60 overs) 241 |
| D. B. D'Oliveira c Hailey b Surridge . . 31 | 4/154 5/162 |
| M. J. Weston c Hailey b Surridge . . . . . 35 | 6/207 7/241 |

P. J. Newport and R. K. Illingworth did not bat.

Bowling: Surridge 11–2–39–2; Merry 12–3–25–2; Smith 11–1–49–0; Garofall 12–1–56–2; Hailey 6–0–31–0; Neal 8–0–34–0.

### Hertfordshire

| | |
|---|---|
| *F. E. Collyer c and b Radford . . . . . . . 14 | W. G. Merry not out . . . . . . . . . . . . . . . 5 |
| W. M. Osman lbw b Radford . . . . . . . . 15 | D. Surridge run out . . . . . . . . . . . . . . . . . 0 |
| D. G. Ottley b Patel . . . . . . . . . . . . . . . . 9 | R. J. Hailey b Weston . . . . . . . . . . . . . . 2 |
| N. Gilbert st Rhodes b Patel . . . . . . . . . 33 | B 6, w 4, n-b 5 . . . . . . . . . . . . . 15 |
| E. P. Neal c Banks b D'Oliveira . . . . . . 52 | —— |
| T. S. Smith run out . . . . . . . . . . . . . . . . . 31 | 1/31 2/33 3/59 4/90 (57.5 overs) 183 |
| A. R. Garofall c Radford b D'Oliveira . 2 | 5/167 6/168 7/170 |
| †M. W. C. Olley run out . . . . . . . . . . . . 5 | 8/177 9/179 |

Bowling: Kapil Dev 9–0–28–0; Radford 8–2–24–2; Newport 2–0–11–0; Illingworth 12–2–21–0; Patel 12–2–22–2; D'Oliveira 8–0–37–2; Weston 6.5–0–34–1.

Umpires: D. J. Constant and C. T. Spencer.

## KENT v SURREY

At Canterbury, July 3. Kent won by six wickets. Toss won by Kent.
*Man of the Match*: S. G. Hinks.

### Surrey

| | |
|---|---|
| A. R. Butcher c Johnson b Cowdrey . . . 18 | †C. J. Richards not out . . . . . . . . . . . . . 9 |
| G. S. Clinton c Johnson b Cowdrey . . .146 | D. B. Pauline run out . . . . . . . . . . . . . . . 5 |
| A. J. Stewart b Baptiste . . . . . . . . . . . . . 37 | L-b 8, w 6, n-b 1 . . . . . . . . . . . 15 |
| *T. E. Jesty c Knott b Underwood . . . . 1 | —— |
| M. A. Lynch c Knott b Ellison . . . . . . . 31 | 1/28 2/93 3/169 (8 wkts, 60 overs) 293 |
| A. Needham run out . . . . . . . . . . . . . . . . 26 | 4/176 5/235 6/248 |
| D. J. Thomas c Baptiste b Cowdrey . . . 5 | 7/286 8/293 |

A. H. Gray and P. I. Pocock did not bat.

Bowling: Jarvis 9–1–35–0; Baptiste 12–0–59–1; Ellison 11–0–58–1; Cowdrey 12–1–74–3; Johnson 6–1–23–0; Underwood 10–2–36–1.

### Kent

| | |
|---|---|
| M. R. Benson c Jesty b Needham . . . . . 78 | E. A. E. Baptiste not out . . . . . . . . . . . . 0 |
| S. G. Hinks c Thomas b Needham . . . . 95 | B 4, l-b 8, w 8, n-b 5 . . . . . . . . 25 |
| C. J. Tavaré not out . . . . . . . . . . . . . . . . 62 | —— |
| D. G. Aslett c Richards b Gray . . . . . . 24 | 1/88 2/201 3/250 (4 wkts, 58 overs) 296 |
| *C. S. Cowdrey c Pauline b Gray . . . . . 12 | 4/282 |

R. M. Ellison, G. W. Johnson, †A. P. E. Knott, D. L. Underwood and K. B. S. Jarvis did not bat.

Bowling: Thomas 10–0–56–0; Gray 11–0–66–2; Pocock 8–0–35–0; Pauline 7–0–29–0; Butcher 4–0–26–0; Jesty 7–2–17–0; Needham 11–0–55–2.

Umpires: W. L. Budd and A. G. T. Whitehead.

## MIDDLESEX v CUMBERLAND

At Uxbridge, July 3. Middlesex won by 131 runs. Toss won by Cumberland.
*Man of the Match:* W. N. Slack.

### Middlesex

| | |
|---|---|
| G. D. Barlow c Drury b Sample | 35 |
| W. N. Slack b Sample | 98 |
| *M. W. Gatting c Boustead b Reidy | 16 |
| R. O. Butcher c Reidy b Halliwell | 59 |
| C. T. Radley b Halliwell | 18 |
| †P. R. Downton b Halliwell | 9 |
| J. E. Emburey b Sample | 2 |
| N. F. Williams lbw b Halliwell | 5 |
| N. G. Cowans c Boustead b Sample | 4 |
| P. H. Edmonds not out | 1 |
| W. W. Daniel not out | 7 |
| B 1, l-b 18, w 10 | 29 |
| 1/61 2/94 3/194 4/237 5/253 6/264 7/269 8/275 9/275 (9 wkts, 60 overs) | 283 |

Bowling: Sample 12–1–58–4; Halliwell 12–0–57–4; Reidy 12–4–40–1; Elleray 9–2–37–0; Woods 8–1–33–0; Lloyd 7–0–39–0.

### Cumberland

| | |
|---|---|
| M. D. Woods c Slack b Edmonds | 18 |
| D. Lloyd c Downton b Daniel | 12 |
| *J. R. Moyes c Edmonds b Emburey | 37 |
| B. W. Reidy c Daniel b Edmonds | 9 |
| G. J. Clarke b Edmonds | 23 |
| D. B. Drury b Edmonds | 4 |
| D. Halliwell b Emburey | 3 |
| E. K. Sample lbw b Gatting | 4 |
| †W. N. Boustead not out | 17 |
| J. B. Elleray run out | 8 |
| Qasim Omar absent injured | |
| B 6, l-b 4, w 4, n-b 3 | 17 |
| 1/24 2/52 3/72 4/105 5/115 6/118 7/123 8/125 9/152 (53.3 overs) | 152 |

Bowling: Daniel 9–1–31–1; Cowans 7–1–13–0; Williams 6–0–24–0; Edmonds 12–2–39–4; Emburey 12–2–28–2; Gatting 7.3–3–7–1.

Umpires: C. Cook and M. J. Kitchen.

## NORFOLK v LEICESTERSHIRE

At Norwich, July 3. Leicestershire won by 140 runs. Toss won by Leicestershire.
*Man of the Match:* L. B. Taylor.

### Leicestershire

| | |
|---|---|
| J. C. Balderstone b Topley | 35 |
| I. P. Butcher c Mattocks b Parvez Mir | 12 |
| *D. I. Gower run out | 41 |
| P. Willey c Whittaker b Topley | 17 |
| J. J. Whitaker c Carter b Bunting | 26 |
| N. E. Briers c Handley b Thomas | 27 |
| †M. A. Garnham not out | 29 |
| P. B. Clift c Mattocks b Thomas | 3 |
| J. P. Agnew b Thomas | 5 |
| L. B. Taylor not out | 0 |
| L-b 8, w 7, n-b 3 | 18 |
| 1/23 2/95 3/97 4/121 5/160 6/176 7/182 8/194 (8 wkts, 60 overs) | 213 |

G. J. F. Ferris did not bat.

Bowling: Whittaker 10–1–25–0; Parvez Mir 12–2–44–1; Thomas 9–0–50–3; Topley 12–1–37–2; Plumb 12–4–19–0; Bunting 5–0–30–1.

### Norfolk

| | | | |
|---|---|---|---|
| *F. L. Q. Handley lbw b Agnew | 1 | P. K. Whittaker c Garnham b Taylor | 1 |
| J. R. Carter c Gower b Clift | 8 | T. D. Topley lbw b Willey | 1 |
| R. D. Huggins c Garnham b Taylor | 29 | R. A. Bunting c Ferris b Butcher | 6 |
| Parvez Mir c Willey b Taylor | 1 | B 1, l-b 2, w 1, n-b 2 | 6 |
| S. G. Plumb c and b Willey | 9 | | — |
| N. D. Cook lbw b Clift | 0 | 1/3 2/21 3/22 4/45 (46.3 overs) | 73 |
| †D. E. Mattocks b Taylor | 0 | 5/46 6/48 7/53 | |
| D. R. Thomas not out | 11 | 8/55 9/58 | |

Bowling: Agnew 7–2–11–1; Ferris 6–1–9–0; Clift 9–2–18–2; Taylor 11–4–14–4; Willey 12–8–4–2; Gower 1–0–8–0; Butcher 0.3–0–6–1.

Umpires: R. A. White and D. J. Dennis.

## NOTTINGHAMSHIRE v STAFFORDSHIRE

At Trent Bridge, July 3. Nottinghamshire won by 96 runs. Toss won by Nottinghamshire. *Man of the Match:* P. Johnson.

### Nottinghamshire

| | | | |
|---|---|---|---|
| R. T. Robinson b Maguire | 10 | †B. N. French b Maguire | 49 |
| B. C. Broad b Webster | 2 | E. E. Hemmings not out | 31 |
| D. W. Randall c Marshall b Webster | 2 | L-b 15, w 7, n-b 2 | 24 |
| *C. E. B. Rice c Griffiths b Maguire | 0 | | — |
| P. Johnson not out | 101 | 1/13 2/21 3/21 (7 wkts, 60 overs) | 243 |
| R. J. Hadlee c Archer b Webster | 16 | 4/31 5/53 6/71 | |
| K. P. Evans c Archer b Webster | 8 | 7/190 | |

K. Saxelby and K. E. Cooper did not bat.

Bowling: Maguire 12–0–64–3; Webster 12–1–38–4; Blank 12–2–36–0; Wenlock 12–1–45–0; Flower 12–3–45–0.

### Staffordshire

| | | | |
|---|---|---|---|
| D. Cartledge c Randall b Hadlee | 6 | D. C. Blank not out | 20 |
| P. A. Marshall c French b Saxelby | 1 | R. W. Flower not out | 9 |
| D. B. Vengsarkar b Saxelby | 4 | | |
| G. S. Warner c Broad b Hemmings | 51 | L-b 4, w 3, n-b 3 | 10 |
| D. A. Wenlock lbw b Saxelby | 0 | | — |
| *N. J. Archer c Hadlee b Cooper | 10 | 1/6 2/12 3/13 (8 wkts, 60 overs) | 147 |
| †A. Griffiths c Johnson b Evans | 6 | 4/17 5/31 6/45 | |
| A. J. Webster b Hemmings | 30 | 7/103 8/124 | |

K. R. Maguire did not bat.

Bowling: Hadlee 5–3–9–1; Saxelby 12–2–19–3; Rice 6–0–22–0; Cooper 11–3–24–1; Evans 12–4–24–1; Hemmings 12–4–37–2; Johnson 1–0–5–0; Randall 1–0–3–0.

Umpires: D. Harrison and N. T. Plews.

## SCOTLAND v GLAMORGAN

At Edinburgh, July 3. Glamorgan won by eight wickets. Toss won by Glamorgan. *Man of the Match:* G. C. Holmes.

### Scotland

| | | | |
|---|---|---|---|
| *R. G. Swan c Morris b Holmes | 27 | J. E. Ker not out | 19 |
| S. M. C. Alleyne c Davis b Barwick | 4 | W. A. McPate b Derrick | 1 |
| †A. Brown lbw b Holmes | 4 | A. W. J. Stevenson c Davies b Holmes | 1 |
| I. G. Kennedy c Davies b Holmes | 15 | B 1, l-b 5, w 14, n-b 1 | 21 |
| O. Henry c Davies b Derrick | 20 | | |
| A. B. Russell lbw b Derrick | 1 | 1/22 2/35 3/49 4/63 (60 overs) | 137 |
| D. L. Snodgrass c Morris b Holmes | 24 | 5/80 6/86 7/86 | |
| P. G. Duthie c Ontong b Derrick | 0 | 8/132 9/133 | |

Bowling: McFarlane 12–2–34–0; Barwick 7–1–12–1; Younis 12–2–24–0; Holmes 12–4–24–5; Derrick 11–3–14–4; Ontong 6–0–23–0.

### Glamorgan

| | |
|---|---|
| A. L. Jones not out | 60 |
| H. Morris c Brown b McPate | 23 |
| G. C. Holmes lbw b Ker | 20 |
| Javed Miandad not out | 21 |
| B 2, l-b 7, w 7, n-b 1 | 17 |
| 1/76 2/112 (2 wkts, 39.4 overs) | 141 |

Younis Ahmed, *R. C. Ontong, †T. Davies, J. Derrick, M. R. Price, S. R. Barwick and L. L. McFarlane did not bat.

Bowling: Ker 10–2–31–1; Duthie 12–2–29–0; McPate 11–2–43–1; Stevenson 2–0–11–0; Henry 3–0–7–0; Snodgrass 1.4–0–11–0.

Umpires: S. Levison and J. W. Holder.

## SHROPSHIRE v NORTHAMPTONSHIRE

At Telford, July 3. Northamptonshire won by 100 runs. Toss won by Northamptonshire. *Man of the Match:* G. Cook.

### Northamptonshire

| | | | |
|---|---|---|---|
| *G. Cook c Ashley b Barnard | 130 | R. A. Harper c Jones b Barnard | 0 |
| W. Larkins c Ashley b Barnard | 34 | D. J. Capel not out | 1 |
| R. J. Boyd-Moss run out | 51 | B 4, l-b 5, w 11, n-b 1 | 21 |
| A. J. Lamb c Foster b Smith | 7 | | |
| R. J. Bailey not out | 18 | 1/81 2/231 3/235 (6 wkts, 60 overs) | 270 |
| R. G. Williams c Mushtaq b Barnard | 8 | 4/243 5/262 6/269 | |

†D. Ripley, N. A. Mallender and D. J. Wild did not bat.

Bowling: Smith 12–2–48–1; Nash 12–1–55–0; Mushtaq 12–2–42–0; Barnard 12–0–47–4; Ranells 12–0–69–0.

### Shropshire

| | | | |
|---|---|---|---|
| M. Davies st Ripley b Wild | 6 | M. A. Nash c Ripley b Bailey | 11 |
| J. B. R. Jones lbw b Mallender | 0 | †D. J. Ashley c and b Lamb | 5 |
| J. Foster c Harper b Williams | 63 | A. S. Barnard not out | 2 |
| Mushtaq Mohammad c Larkins b Williams | 21 | B 10, l-b 3, w 16, n-b 1 | 30 |
| I. Hutchinson c Cook b Boyd-Moss | 8 | | |
| *S. C. Gale b Boyd-Moss | 1 | 1/2 2/46 3/78 4/100 (54.2 overs) | 170 |
| P. L. Ranells b Boyd-Moss | 13 | 5/127 6/127 7/139 | |
| J. A. Smith c Larkins b Williams | 10 | 8/159 9/164 | |

Bowling: Mallender 5–2–4–1; Capel 7–1–19–0; Wild 8–1–33–1; Boyd-Moss 12–1–47–3; Williams 12–3–35–3; Harper 9–4–13–0; Bailey 1–0–2–1; Lamb 0.2–0–4–1.

Umpires: R. Palmer and T. G. Wilson.

## SOMERSET v BUCKINGHAMSHIRE

At Taunton, July 3. Somerset won by seven wickets. Toss won by Somerset.
*Man of the Match:* J. Garner.

### Buckinghamshire

M. E. Milton c Gard b Davis ........ 33
T. P. Russell c Garner b Dredge ...... 23
K. I. Hodgson c Garner b Dredge ..... 7
N. G. Hames c and b Marks .......... 12
S. Burrow c Gard b Garner .......... 27
*D. E. Smith b Garner .............. 9
G. R. Black lbw b Garner ........... 2
†R. G. Humphrey b Garner .......... 3
H. L. Alleyne c Felton b Richards .... 0
M. Jean-Jacques not out ............. 0
A. W. Lyon b Garner ................ 0
B 3, l-b 6, w 7, n-b 6 ........ 22

1/58 2/71 3/82 4/88 5/117 6/130 7/133 8/134 9/138 (47.4 overs) 138

Bowling: Garner 8.4–2–18–5; Botham 8–0–21–0; Dredge 8–2–20–2; Davis 9–1–31–1; Marks 12–2–32–1; Richards 2–0–7–1.

### Somerset

P. M. Roebuck b Milton ............ 39
N. F. M. Popplewell c Humphrey b Alleyne. 9
N. A. Felton not out ................ 72
I. V. A. Richards c Russell b Black ... 4
R. E. Hayward not out .............. 8
L-b 1, w 6 ................. 7

1/19 2/106 3/111 (3 wkts, 41.3 overs) 139

*I. T. Botham, V. J. Marks, †T. Gard, M. R. Davis, C. H. Dredge and J. Garner did not bat.

Bowling: Alleyne 8–1–26–1; Jean-Jacques 5–0–11–0; Lyon 7–1–28–0; Burrow 8–2–27–0; Milton 6–1–13–1; Black 7–1–32–1; Smith 0.3–0–1–0.

Umpires: B. Dudleston and D. R. Shepherd.

## SUFFOLK v LANCASHIRE

At Bury St Edmunds, July 3. Lancashire won by 100 runs. Toss won by Lancashire.
*Man of the Match:* N. H. Fairbrother.

### Lancashire

G. Fowler b Graham ................ 41
*J. A. Abrahams c Wright b Hayes ... 15
C. H. Lloyd st Brown b Herbert ...... 30
S. J. O'Shaughnessy st Brown b Hayes . 14
D. P. Hughes c and b Wright ........ 31
N. H. Fairbrother not out ........... 52
M. Watkinson c Graham b Green .... 31
†C. Maynard not out ............... 0
B 4, l-b 4, w 11 ............ 19

1/50 2/74 3/106 4/116 5/174 6/225 (6 wkts, 60 overs) 233

J. Simmons, D. J. Makinson and P. J. W. Allott did not bat.

Bowling: Green 12–1–71–1; Wright 12–0–48–1; Graham 12–0–49–1; Hayes 12–1–20–2; Herbert 12–2–37–1.

### Suffolk

P. D. Barker b Allott ............... 7
G. Morgan b Allott ................. 3
M. S. A. McEvoy c Maynard b Simmons 21
*S. M. Clements c O'Shaughnessy b Abrahams. 21
R. Herbert c Fairbrother b O'Shaughnessy. 17
P. J. Caley c Simmons b O'Shaughnessy 15
†A. D. Brown b O'Shaughnessy ....... 1
P. J. Hayes not out ................ 12
H. J. W. Wright c Watkinson b Abrahams. 14
R. C. Green not out ................ 7
B 8, l-b 6, w 1 ............ 15

1/7 2/24 3/49 4/68 5/92 6/94 7/97 8/124 (8 wkts, 60 overs) 133

C. C. Graham did not bat.

Bowling: Allott 7–3–8–2; Makinson 5–0–17–0; Simmons 12–9–3–1; O'Shaughnessy 12–2–28–3; Abrahams 11–2–36–2; Watkinson 12–5–22–0; Hughes 1–0–5–0.

Umpires: R. H. Duckett and R. Julian.

## SUSSEX v IRELAND

At Hove, July 3. Sussex won by 244 runs, a record margin for the competition. Le Roux took a hat-trick as Ireland were reduced to a new lowest innings total for the 60-overs competition. Toss won by Ireland.

*Man of the Match:* P. W. G. Parker.

### Sussex

| | |
|---|---|
| G. D. Mendis c Bailey b Corlett | 3 |
| A. M. Green b Lewis | 6 |
| *P. W. G. Parker b Elder | 109 |
| Imran Khan b McBrine | 38 |
| C. M. Wells c Wake b Elder | 76 |
| A. P. Wells not out | 4 |
| I. A. Greig c Patterson b Corlett | 8 |
| G. S. le Roux not out | 0 |
| B 5, l-b 8, w 16, n-b 10 | 39 |
| 1/8 2/23 3/105 4/259 5/271 6/282 (6 wkts, 60 overs) | 283 |

C. E. Waller, A. C. S. Pigott and †P. Moores did not bat.

Bowling: Corlett 12–0–72–2; Patterson 9–0–39–0; Lewis 5–0–28–1; Halliday 12–0–40–0; McBrine 12–3–22–1; Elder 10–0–69–2.

### Ireland

| | |
|---|---|
| S. J. S. Warke b le Roux | 6 |
| D. Dennison lbw b le Roux | 4 |
| R. T. Wills lbw b le Roux | 0 |
| D. A. Lewis b Imran | 4 |
| J. A. Prior b le Roux | 0 |
| T. J. T. Patterson c Greig b le Roux | 0 |
| S. C. Corlett c Moores b Pigott | 11 |
| J. McBrine c Parker b Pigott | 7 |
| *M. Halliday c C. M. Wells b Waller | 3 |
| †K. R. Bailey not out | 0 |
| J. W. G. Elder b Pigott | 0 |
| L-b 2, w 2 | 4 |
| 1/10 2/10 3/15 4/15 5/15 6/15 7/28 8/39 9/39 (26.4 overs) | 39 |

Bowling: Imran 8–3–13–1; le Roux 7–4–7–5; Greig 5–1–13–0; Pigott 5.4–2–4–3; Waller 1–1–0–1.

Umpires: A. A. Jones and P. B. Wight.

## WARWICKSHIRE v DEVON

At Edgbaston, July 3. Warwickshire won by three wickets. Toss won by Warwickshire.

*Man of the Match:* K. G. Rice.

### Devon

| | |
|---|---|
| Agha Zahid c Hoffman b Gifford | 31 |
| K. G. Rice c Dyer b Kallicharran | 107 |
| N. A. Folland c Humpage b Gifford | 12 |
| C. F. Rudd run out | 11 |
| N. R. Gaywood b Kallicharran | 5 |
| *J. H. Edwards not out | 22 |
| C. J. Edwards b Lloyd | 5 |
| J. K. Tierney c Lloyd b Kallicharran | 5 |
| †R. M. Oliver not out | 7 |
| B 1, l-b 4, w 11 | 16 |
| 1/79 2/125 3/159 4/173 5/173 6/188 7/205 (7 wkts, 60 overs) | 221 |

M. J. Goulding and J. Davey did not bat.

Bowling: Small 8–0–26–0; Smith 3–0–20–0; Hoffman 10–0–44–0; Pierson 12–2–32–0; Gifford 12–1–49–2; Kallicharran 12–0–41–3; Lloyd 3–1–4–1.

### Warwickshire

| | |
|---|---|
| T. A. Lloyd c Folland b Davey | 9 |
| R. I. H. B. Dyer b Tierney | 18 |
| A. I. Kallicharran run out | 66 |
| D. L. Amiss c Oliver b Tierney | 5 |
| †G. W. Humpage c Folland b Agha Zahid | 14 |
| P. A. Smith not out | 51 |
| Asif Din lbw b Tierney | 25 |
| G. C. Small b Goulding | 18 |
| A. R. K. Pierson not out | 1 |
| B 2, l-b 7, w 6 | 15 |
| 1/13 2/37 3/53 4/87 5/130 6/173 7/219 (7 wkts, 53.2 overs) | 222 |

*N. Gifford and D. S. Hoffman did not bat.

Bowling: Davey 8–0–43–1; Goulding 9–3–33–1; Tierney 12–2–47–3; Agha Zahid 12–1–43–1; Rudd 12–0–44–0; Folland 0.2–0–3–0.

Umpires: J. H. Hampshire and B. J. Meyer.

## SECOND ROUND

## ESSEX v MIDDLESEX

At Chelmsford, July 17. Essex won by 84 runs. Toss won by Essex.
*Man of the Match:* G. A. Gooch.

### Essex

| | |
|---|---|
| *G. A. Gooch b Edmonds | 66 |
| B. R. Hardie c Butcher b Emburey | 68 |
| P. J. Prichard c Emburey b Cowans | 11 |
| K. S. McEwan b Williams | 1 |
| D. R. Pringle b Cowans | 5 |
| C. Gladwin c Downton b Edmonds | 15 |
| A. W. Lilley b Daniel | 17 |
| †D. E. East c Gatting b Emburey | 8 |
| S. Turner c Cowans b Emburey | 3 |
| N. A. Foster run out | 0 |
| J. K. Lever not out | 1 |
| L-b 12, w 5, n-b 2 | 19 |
| 1/118 2/135 3/141 4/156 5/168 6/196 7/208 8/213 9/213 (60 overs) | 214 |

Bowling: Daniel 12–1–40–1; Williams 12–1–33–1; Cowans 12–0–39–2; Edmonds 12–0–49–2; Emburey 12–1–41–3.

### Middlesex

| | |
|---|---|
| G. D. Barlow lbw b Lever | 8 |
| W. N. Slack b Gooch | 32 |
| *M. W. Gatting c Prichard b Foster | 17 |
| C. T. Radley c and b Pringle | 27 |
| R. O. Butcher b Pringle | 2 |
| †P. R. Downton run out | 15 |
| J. E. Emburey c sub b Turner | 10 |
| N. F. Williams not out | 7 |
| P. H. Edmonds lbw b Pringle | 0 |
| W. W. Daniel c East b Pringle | 2 |
| N. G. Cowans b Pringle | 0 |
| B 1, l-b 1, w 6, n-b 2 | 10 |
| 1/19 2/59 3/65 4/68 5/93 6/109 7/124 8/124 9/129 (50 overs) | 130 |

Bowling: Lever 9–1–17–1; Foster 12–4–31–1; Turner 10–0–34–1; Pringle 9–1–23–5; Gooch 10–3–23–1.

Umpires: B. Dudleston and P. B. Wight.

## GLAMORGAN v SUSSEX

At Cardiff, July 17. Glamorgan won by four wickets. Toss won by Glamorgan.
*Man of the Match:* J. G. Thomas.

### Sussex

G. D. Mendis lbw b Barwick .......... 28
A. M. Green lbw b Thomas .......... 1
P. W. G. Parker b Thomas .......... 7
Imran Khan c Davies b Barwick ...... 28
C. M. Wells b Thomas .............. 35
A. P. Wells run out ................ 6
I. A. Greig b McFarlane ............ 1
†I. J. Gould not out ............... 23
G. S. le Roux lbw b Thomas ......... 0
*J. R. T. Barclay c Davies b Thomas .. 0
A. C. S. Pigott lbw b Holmes ........ 0
L-b 2, w 1, n-b 4 ........... 7

1/19 2/28 3/67 4/68 (51.3 overs) 136
5/85 6/86 7/135
8/135 9/135

Bowling: Thomas 7–2–17–5; McFarlane 12–1–54–1; Barwick 8–4–8–2; Holmes 11.3–2–19–1; Ontong 5–1–15–0; Price 8–1–21–0.

### Glamorgan

A. L. Jones c A. P. Wells b C. M. Wells 21
J. A. Hopkins b Pigott .............. 15
G. C. Holmes lbw b Pigott ........... 3
Javed Miandad c Barclay b Imran .... 29
H. Morris b le Roux ................ 19
*R. C. Ontong not out .............. 30
†T. Davies run out .................. 12
J. G. Thomas not out ................ 2
B 1, l-b 5, w 1, n-b 2 ........ 9

1/36 2/36 3/41 (6 wkts, 48.5 overs) 140
4/85 5/105 6/133

M. R. Price, L. L. McFarlane and S. R. Barwick did not bat.

Bowling: Imran 12–2–21–1; le Roux 10.5–0–38–1; C. M. Wells 10–2–21–1; Pigott 12–1–37–2; Greig 4–0–17–0.

Umpires: B. Leadbeater and R. Palmer.

## GLOUCESTERSHIRE v NORTHAMPTONSHIRE

At Bristol, July 17. Gloucestershire won by 37 runs. Toss won by Northamptonshire.
*Man of the Match:* K. M. Curran.

### Gloucestershire

P. W. Romaines c Ripley b Mallender . 5
J. W. Lloyds lbw b Larkins .......... 40
C. W. J. Athey lbw b Wild .......... 44
P. Bainbridge c Ripley b Larkins ..... 7
B. F. Davison run out ............... 81
K. M. Curran c Ripley b Capel ....... 36
I. R. Payne not out ................. 32
C. A. Walsh c Mallender b Williams .. 2
*D. A. Graveney c Bailey b Capel .... 12
D. V. Lawrence not out .............. 0
B 4, l-b 10, w 1, n-b 3 ....... 18

1/6 2/77 3/95 4/109 (8 wkts, 60 overs) 277
5/222 6/229
7/232 8/269

†R. C. Russell did not bat.

Bowling: Mallender 6–0–19–1; Joseph 8–0–47–0; Wild 12–2–38–1; Larkins 12–3–38–2; Capel 12–0–74–2; Williams 10–0–47–1.

### Northamptonshire

*G. Cook c Athey b Bainbridge ...... 54
W. Larkins run out ................. 75
R. J. Boyd-Moss run out ............. 11
A. J. Lamb c Lloyds b Curran ........ 42
R. J. Bailey c Russell b Bainbridge .... 8
R. G. Williams c Romaines b Curran .. 8
D. J. Capel c Russell b Curran ....... 3
D. J. Wild b Lawrence ............... 1
†D. Ripley b Curran ................. 5
N. A. Mallender not out ............. 8
R. F. Joseph b Lawrence ............ 6
L-b 6, w 5, n-b 8 ........... 19

1/129 2/136 3/160 4/195 (56.3 overs) 240
5/210 6/210 7/216
8/218 9/226

Bowling: Lawrence 9.3–1–53–2; Walsh 11–1–39–0; Curran 10–0–34–4; Payne 9–0–52–0; Bainbridge 12–2–35–2; Graveney 5–0–21–0.

Umpires: J. H. Harris and A. A. Jones.

## HAMPSHIRE v LEICESTERSHIRE

At Southampton, July 17. Hampshire won by four wickets. Toss won by Hampshire.
*Man of the Match:* V. P. Terry.

### Leicestershire

| | |
|---|---|
| I. P. Butcher c Terry b Nicholas | 31 |
| J. C. Balderstone c Terry b Tremlett | 15 |
| *D. I. Gower c Connor b Nicholas | 12 |
| P. Willey st Parks b Cowley | 52 |
| J. J. Whitaker b Tremlett | 46 |
| N. E. Briers not out | 31 |
| P. B. Clift b Marshall | 7 |
| †M. A. Garnham not out | 7 |
| B 1, l-b 5, w 4, n-b 1 | 11 |
| 1/25 2/55 3/74 4/143 5/179 6/201 (6 wkts, 60 overs) | 212 |

G. J. Parsons, J. P. Agnew and L. B. Taylor did not bat.

Bowling: Marshall 12–0–45–1; Connor 12–1–49–0; Tremlett 12–3–44–2; Nicholas 12–1–40–2; Cowley 12–1–28–1.

### Hampshire

| | |
|---|---|
| C. G. Greenidge b Briers | 67 |
| V. P. Terry c Gower b Clift | 63 |
| C. L. Smith c Garnham b Agnew | 10 |
| *M. C. J. Nicholas c and b Taylor | 16 |
| R. A. Smith not out | 24 |
| J. J. E. Hardy c Balderstone b Willey | 1 |
| M. D. Marshall b Parsons | 1 |
| N. G. Cowley not out | 20 |
| L-b 9, w 1, n-b 1 | 11 |
| 1/22 2/143 3/158 4/169 5/171 6/172 (6 wkts, 59.1 overs) | 213 |

T. M. Tremlett, †R. J. Parks and C. A. Connor did not bat.

Bowling: Agnew 12–0–44–1; Taylor 11–0–52–1; Parsons 11.1–3–31–1; Willey 11–0–36–1; Clift 12–2–33–1; Briers 2–0–8–1.

Umpires: B. J. Meyer and D. R. Shepherd.

## KENT v DURHAM

At Canterbury, July 17. Kent won by 79 runs. Toss won by Durham.
*Man of the Match:* M. R. Benson.

### Kent

| | |
|---|---|
| M. R. Benson b Scott | 78 |
| S. G. Hinks b Johnson | 47 |
| C. J. Tavaré c Riddell b Kippax | 6 |
| D. G. Aslett run out | 25 |
| *C. S. Cowdrey c Greensword b Kippax | 19 |
| E. A. E. Baptiste b Kippax | 3 |
| R. M. Ellison not out | 39 |
| †A. P. E. Knott b Scott | 16 |
| G. R. Dilley not out | 1 |
| B 4, l-b 6, w 4 | 14 |
| 1/71 2/88 3/139 4/183 5/187 6/193 7/240 (7 wkts, 60 overs) | 248 |

D. L. Underwood and K. B. S. Jarvis did not bat.

Bowling: Scott 10–2–45–2; Wilkinson 11–0–61–0; Johnson 11–2–39–1; Kippax 12–1–32–3; Greensword 12–0–38–0; Patel 4–0–23–0.

### Durham

J. W. Lister c Knott b Jarvis .......... 0
S. R. Atkinson c Benson b Ellison .... 18
D. C. Jackson c Knott b Ellison ...... 24
S. Greensword c Baptiste b Cowdrey .. 34
*N. A. Riddell c and b Baptiste ...... 11
A. S. Patel b Underwood ............ 2
P. J. Kippax c Knott b Jarvis ........ 30
†R. A. D. Mercer c Baptiste b Underwood 0
A. W. Scott b Underwood ............ 7
G. Johnson not out .................. 20
J. S. Wilkinson lbw b Dilley .......... 3
L-b 11, w 8, n-b 1 .......... 20

1/0 2/43 3/53 4/82 5/94 6/100 7/102 8/118 9/166 (59.1 overs) 169

Bowling: Jarvis 11–0–56–2; Dilley 10.1–1–25–1; Baptiste 12–3–22–1; Ellison 7–2–13–2; Underwood 12–5–26–3; Cowdrey 7–0–16–1.

Umpires: S. Cook and K. J. Lyons.

## LANCASHIRE v WORCESTERSHIRE

At Old Trafford, July 17, 18. Worcestershire won by 14 runs, having compiled their highest total in the competition. It was also the highest conceded by Lancashire. Toss won by Lancashire.
*Man of the Match:* C. H. Lloyd.

### Worcestershire

T. S. Curtis run out .................. 32
D. N. Patel lbw b Henriksen .......... 19
D. M. Smith run out .................109
*P. A. Neale c Simmons b Henriksen .. 81
Kapil Dev not out .................. 38
D. B. D'Oliveira c Hayhurst b Makinson 12
M. J. Weston not out ................ 7
L-b 7, w 5, n-b 2 ............ 14

1/30 2/86 3/239 4/267 5/289 (5 wkts, 60 overs) 312

†S. J. Rhodes, J. D. Inchmore, N. V. Radford and R. K. Illingworth did not bat.

Bowling: Makinson 12–3–69–1; Henriksen 10–1–51–2; Watkinson 12–1–67–0; O'Shaughnessy 9–1–40–0; Simmons 12–0–48–0; Hayhurst 5–0–30–0.

### Lancashire

M. R. Chadwick lbw b Inchmore ..... 43
A. N. Hayhurst lbw b Kapil Dev ..... 7
S. J. O'Shaughnessy c Smith b Inchmore 22
N. H. Fairbrother c Rhodes b Radford . 15
*J. Abrahams c Rhodes b Radford .... 15
C. H. Lloyd c Neale b Kapil Dev ..... 91
M. Watkinson b Radford ............ 56
J. Simmons lbw b Kapil Dev ......... 13
†C. Maynard b Kapil Dev ........... 0
D. J. Makinson b Kapil Dev .......... 17
S. Henriksen not out ................ 1
B 1, l-b 9, w 5, n-b 3 ........ 18

1/9 2/72 3/87 4/109 5/114 6/218 7/270 8/270 9/283 (59 overs) 298

Bowling: Kapil Dev 12–0–52–5; Radford 12–0–50–3; Inchmore 12–0–51–2; Weston 2–0–19–0; Illingworth 10–0–55–0; Patel 11–0–61–0.

Umpires: R. Julian and R. A. White.

## NOTTINGHAMSHIRE v WARWICKSHIRE

At Trent Bridge, July 17. Nottinghamshire won by 86 runs. Toss won by Warwickshire.
*Man of the Match:* R. T. Robinson.

### Nottinghamshire

R. T. Robinson not out . . . . . . . . . . . . . 98
B. C. Broad c Humpage b Smith . . . . . . 14
D. W. Randall b Hoffman . . . . . . . . . . . 19
P. Johnson c Humpage b Lethbridge . . 20
B. Hassan c Dyer b Hoffman . . . . . . . . . 17
*R. J. Hadlee b Small . . . . . . . . . . . . . . . 56
†B. N. French not out . . . . . . . . . . . . . . 7
L-b 16, w 4 . . . . . . . . . . . . . . . . 20

1/32 2/43 3/81 4/119 5/211 (5 wkts, 60 overs) 251

R. A. Pick, E. E. Hemmings, K. Saxelby and K. E. Cooper did not bat.

Bowling: Small 12–3–38–1; Hoffman 12–1–56–2; Smith 7–0–40–1; Ferreira 12–2–55–0; Lethbridge 12–2–39–1; Gifford 5–1–7–0.

### Warwickshire

T. A. Lloyd retired hurt . . . . . . . . . . . . . 0
R. I. H. B. Dyer c Broad b Hemmings . 15
A. I. Kallicharran c French b Cooper . . 27
D. L. Amiss c sub b Hemmings . . . . . . 64
†G. W. Humpage c Randall b Saxelby . 11
P. A. Smith c Randall b Cooper . . . . . . 2
A. M. Ferreira st French b Hemmings . 18
C. Lethbridge c French b Cooper . . . . . 4
G. C. Small not out . . . . . . . . . . . . . . . . 6
*N. Gifford c Hassan b Pick . . . . . . . . . 2
D. S. Hoffman b Cooper . . . . . . . . . . . . 3
L-b 8, w 3, n-b 2 . . . . . . . . . . . 13

1/37 2/67 3/86 4/100 5/147 6/151 7/155 8/158 9/165 (51.2 overs) 165

Bowling: Hadlee 8–1–26–0; Saxelby 8–3–14–1; Cooper 11.2–1–49–4; Pick 12–3–41–1; Hemmings 12–2–27–3.

Umpires: N. T. Plews and J. H. Hampshire.

## YORKSHIRE v SOMERSET

At Headingley, July 17, 18. Somerset won by four wickets. Toss won by Somerset.
*Man of the Match:* I. V. A. Richards.

### Yorkshire

G. Boycott lbw b Dredge . . . . . . . . . . . . 24
A. A. Metcalfe lbw b Richards . . . . . . . 33
K. Sharp c Botham b Marks . . . . . . . . . 5
S. N. Hartley c Richards b Dredge . . . . 69
P. E. Robinson b Marks . . . . . . . . . . . . . 0
*†D. L. Bairstow c Popplewell b Marks 13
P. Carrick c and b Botham . . . . . . . . . . 16
P. W. Jarvis c Davis b Dredge . . . . . . . 16
C. Shaw not out . . . . . . . . . . . . . . . . . . . 6
S. Oldham not out . . . . . . . . . . . . . . . . . 0
B 5, l-b 9, w 5, n-b 7 . . . . . . . . 26

1/69 2/69 3/81 4/83 5/124 6/173 7/194 8/207 (8 wkts, 60 overs) 208

S. D. Fletcher did not bat.

Bowling: Garner 12–2–34–0; Davis 5–0–24–0; Botham 11–0–42–1; Dredge 8–0–28–3; Richards 12–0–36–1; Marks 12–3–30–3.

### Somerset

P. M. Roebuck lbw b Oldham . . . . . . . . 16
N. F. M. Popplewell c Carrick b Shaw . 18
N. A. Felton lbw b Fletcher . . . . . . . . . 25
I. V. A. Richards not out . . . . . . . . . . . . 87
B. C. Rose b Fletcher . . . . . . . . . . . . . . . 1
*I. T. Botham b Fletcher . . . . . . . . . . . . 37
V. J. Marks b Jarvis . . . . . . . . . . . . . . . . 4
†T. Gard not out . . . . . . . . . . . . . . . . . . . 0
B 4, l-b 13, w 2, n-b 2 . . . . . . . 21

1/27 2/55 3/76 4/81 5/185 6/206 (6 wkts, 48.1 overs) 209

J. Garner, M. R. Davis and C. H. Dredge did not bat.

Bowling: Jarvis 10–1–61–1; Shaw 10.1–3–14–1; Oldham 10–0–45–1; Carrick 4–0–17–0; Fletcher 12–2–34–3; Hartley 2–0–21–0.

Umpires: J. A. Jameson and J. W. Holder.

## QUARTER-FINALS

### ESSEX v KENT

At Chelmsford, August 7, 8. Essex won by six wickets. Toss won by Kent. Kent soon regretted their decision to bat first as the clouds rolled in and the Essex seamers took full advantage of the conditions. Only Taylor batted with authority, and he was needlessly run out. Bad weather took the tie into a second day, when conditions were much more favourable for batting. Essex seemed to be coasting to victory as Gooch and Prichard sent up the hundred, but Ellison removed both, plus McEwan, in an eventful 32nd over. Fletcher and Pringle, however, steadied the innings and steered Essex into the semi-finals.

*Man of the Match:* R. M. Ellison.

**Kent**

| | |
|---|---|
| M. R. Benson b Gooch | 22 |
| S. G. Hinks b Lever | 2 |
| C. J. Tavaré c Pringle b Turner | 12 |
| N. R. Taylor run out | 51 |
| *C. S. Cowdrey c East b Gooch | 7 |
| E. A. E. Baptiste c East b Foster | 0 |
| R. M. Ellison b Turner | 8 |
| †A. P. E. Knott c East b Foster | 24 |
| G. R. Dilley c Prichard b Lever | 19 |
| D. L. Underwood not out | 19 |
| K. B. S. Jarvis not out | 2 |
| L-b 2, w 4 | 6 |
| 1/5 2/31 3/47 4/87 5/88 6/102 7/121 8/137 9/151 (9 wkts, 60 overs) | 172 |

Bowling: Lever 12–5–25–2; Foster 12–2–32–2; Pringle 12–3–37–0; Gooch 12–1–37–2; Turner 12–0–39–2.

**Essex**

| | |
|---|---|
| G. A. Gooch c Knott b Ellison | 43 |
| B. R. Hardie c Knott b Ellison | 5 |
| P. J. Prichard c Knott b Ellison | 42 |
| K. S. McEwan c Cowdrey b Ellison | 0 |
| D. R. Pringle not out | 32 |
| *K. W. R. Fletcher not out | 39 |
| L-b 11, w 2 | 13 |
| 1/14 2/101 3/101 4/102 (4 wkts, 56.4 overs) | 174 |

A. W. Lilley, S. Turner, †D. E. East, N. A. Foster and J. K. Lever did not bat.

Bowling: Dilley 11.4–3–28–0; Ellison 12–3–22–4; Jarvis 10–1–60–0; Baptiste 12–0–33–0; Underwood 11–5–20–0.

Umpires: R. Julian and A. G. T. Whitehead.

### GLAMORGAN v WORCESTERSHIRE

At Swansea, August 7, 8. Worcestershire won by four wickets. Toss won by Worcestershire. Glamorgan, already weakened by the absence through injury of Thomas, their fast bowler, and Javed Miandad, faced an uncomfortable 24 overs late on the first day, play not starting until just before six o'clock. Put in, they lost four wickets for 51 runs. Next morning there was a recovery as Ontong and Morris batted defiantly to add 102, but the damage had been done. Inchmore took three of the last four wickets for 11 runs to finish with five for 25, his best figures in a 60-overs match. Smith and Patel continued Worcestershire's hold on the game, Smith hitting one 6 and thirteen 4s in an excellent 97 off 158 deliveries.

*Man of the Match:* J. D. Inchmore.

## Glamorgan

A. L. Jones c Patel b Kapil Dev . . . . . . 6
J. A. Hopkins b Inchmore . . . . . . . . . . . 12
G. C. Holmes c Smith b Newport . . . . . 1
H. Morris c Rhodes b Kapil Dev . . . . . 75
M. R. Price c Kapil Dev b Illingworth . 6
Younis Ahmed b Inchmore . . . . . . . . . . 3
*R. C. Ontong run out . . . . . . . . . . . . . . 55
†T. Davies b Inchmore . . . . . . . . . . . . . . 7
J. Derrick b Inchmore . . . . . . . . . . . . . . 4
S. R. Barwick c Rhodes b Inchmore . . . 4
L. L. McFarlane not out . . . . . . . . . . . . . 1
L-b 10, w 4 . . . . . . . . . . . . . . . . 14

1/15 2/18 3/31 4/49 (59.5 overs) 188
5/55 6/157 7/176
8/182 9/186

Bowling: Kapil Dev 12–1–36–2; Radford 12–4–30–0; Newport 10–1–32–1; Inchmore 11.5–4–25–5; Patel 4–0–14–0; Illingworth 10–0–41–1.

## Worcestershire

T. S. Curtis b Barwick . . . . . . . . . . . . . . 0
D. B. D'Oliveira c Hopkins b McFarlane 7
D. M. Smith c Jones b Price . . . . . . . . . 97
D. N. Patel c Younis b Barwick . . . . . . 54
*P. A. Neale c Barwick b Price . . . . . . . 15
Kapil Dev b Price . . . . . . . . . . . . . . . . . . 0
†S. J. Rhodes not out . . . . . . . . . . . . . . . 6
P. J. Newport not out . . . . . . . . . . . . . . . 4
L-b 6, w 1, n-b 2 . . . . . . . . . . . 9

1/0 2/38 3/145 (6 wkts, 54.3 overs) 192
4/177 5/182 6/187

J. D. Inchmore, N. V. Radford and R. K. Illingworth did not bat.

Bowling: Barwick 8–0–49–2; McFarlane 9–2–32–1; Ontong 12–2–36–0; Derrick 12–3–27–0; Price 7–1–22–3; Holmes 6.3–0–20–0.

Umpires: J. H. Hampshire and R. Palmer.

## GLOUCESTERSHIRE v NOTTINGHAMSHIRE

At Bristol, August 7, 8, 9. Nottinghamshire won by 10 runs. Toss won by Nottinghamshire. An opening partnership of 146 in 37 overs between Robinson and Broad was the foundation of Nottinghamshire's success. After a blank Wednesday the Nottinghamshire pair made splendid progress, despite a slow outfield, as the Gloucestershire bowlers fell short of their usual high standard. Conceding 33 extras did not help Gloucestershire's cause either. Gloucestershire did not lose a wicket in scoring 42 before the match went into a third day, but Nottinghamshire bowled eighteen overs in this period to strengthen their grip. Bainbridge initiated a rally with a rapid 55, and with Curran and Payne adding 91 Gloucestershire reached 251 for five with five overs remaining. Wickets then tumbled, and 15 runs off the final over, bowled by Saxelby, proved too great a task for Russell and Walsh.

*Man of the Match:* R. T. Robinson.

## Nottinghamshire

R. T. Robinson run out . . . . . . . . . . . . . 90
B. C. Broad c Bainbridge b Graveney . 58
D. W. Randall c Athey b Graveney . . . 12
P. Johnson b Bainbridge . . . . . . . . . . . . 24
*C. E. B. Rice c Graveney b Bainbridge 35
R. J. Hadlee c Russell b Bainbridge . . . 6
†B. N. French run out . . . . . . . . . . . . . . 14
E. E. Hemmings b Walsh . . . . . . . . . . . . 3
R. A. Pick not out . . . . . . . . . . . . . . . . . 6
K. E. Saxelby not out . . . . . . . . . . . . . . . 6

B 2, l-b 19, w 10, n-b 2 . . . . . . 33

1/146 2/166 3/195 (8 wkts, 60 overs) 287
4/243 5/255 6/256
7/273 8/277

K. E. Cooper did not bat.

Bowling: Lawrence 7–0–39–0; Walsh 10–0–61–1; Curran 12–3–34–0; Payne 10–0–36–0; Graveney 9–0–42–2; Bainbridge 12–0–54–3.

### Gloucestershire

A. W. Stovold c Hadlee b Pick ....... 21
J. W. Lloyds b Cooper ............... 20
C. W. J. Athey c Randall b Cooper ... 12
B. F. Davison run out ................ 27
P. Bainbridge c Hadlee b Saxelby ..... 55
K. M. Curran c French b Hadlee ...... 36
I. R. Payne run out .................. 53
*D. A. Graveney b Hadlee ........... 4
†R. C. Russell not out ............... 14
D. V. Lawrence c and b Saxelby ...... 1
C. A. Walsh not out .................. 6
B 2, l-b 20, w 4, n-b 2 ....... 28

1/43 2/64 3/70 4/147 5/160 6/251 7/253 8/263 9/264 (9 wkts, 60 overs) 277

Bowling: Hadlee 12–1–42–2; Saxelby 12–2–34–2; Cooper 12–2–40–2; Pick 12–0–49–1; Rice 6–0–49–0; Hemmings 6–0–41–0.

Umpires: M. J. Kitchen and D. O. Oslear.

## SOMERSET v HAMPSHIRE

At Taunton, August 7, 8. Hampshire won by 149 runs. Toss won by Somerset. Put in, Hampshire recovered from 51 for three through a fine stand of 144 in 25 overs between Terry, missed off Botham when 9 then moving to a splendid 105 in 169 balls, and Robin Smith, whose determined start and clean striking produced 110 in 97 balls with one 6 and eleven 4s. Rain and bad light seriously interrupted play, and after Somerset had collapsed to 43 for five, a low sun reflecting off an adjacent building at 7.45 pm ended play to considerable agitation from a capacity crowd of 8,500. A spirited stand of 91 in nineteen overs between Marks and Botham, who hit two 6s and seven 4s in 55 balls, offered Somerset a faint hope next morning, but this was swiftly extinguished when Marshall and Cowley took the vital wickets.

*Man of the Match*: R. A. Smith.

### Hampshire

C. G. Greenidge run out ............. 10
V. P. Terry c and b Dredge ..........105
C. L. Smith c Richards b Davis ...... 3
*M. C. J. Nicholas c Gard b Richards . 2
R. A. Smith b Dredge ...............110
D. R. Turner not out ................ 38
M. D. Marshall not out ............. 2
B 3, l-b 9, w 7, n-b 10 ....... 29

1/24 2/39 3/51 4/195 5/290 (5 wkts, 60 overs) 299

N. G. Cowley, T. M. Tremlett, †R. J. Parks and C. A. Connor did not bat.

Bowling: Garner 12–1–50–0; Botham 12–2–57–0; Dredge 12–2–54–2; Davis 12–2–57–1; Richards 9–0–49–1; Marks 3–0–20–0.

### Somerset

N. F. M. Popplewell b Marshall ...... 2
P. M. Roebuck lbw b Tremlett ....... 6
N. A. Felton c Connor b Nicholas .... 9
I. V. A. Richards c C. L. Smith b Tremlett 16
J. G. Wyatt run out ................ 3
*I. T. Botham c Parks b Marshall ..... 64
V. J. Marks b Cowley ............... 26
J. Garner b Cowley ................. 0
M. R. Davis c R. A. Smith b Cowley .. 6
†T. Gard run out ................... 7
C. H. Dredge not out ............... 0
B 5, w 2, n-b 4 ............. 11

1/2 2/24 3/24 4/37 5/43 6/134 7/136 8/136 9/149 (39.2 overs) 150

Bowling: Marshall 9–2–17–2; Connor 6.2–1–14–0; Nicholas 9–0–40–1; Tremlett 9–0–33–2; Cowley 6–0–41–3.

Umpires: C. Cook and B. Leadbeater.

## SEMI-FINALS

## HAMPSHIRE v ESSEX

At Southampton, August 21, 22. Essex won by virtue of losing fewer wickets. Toss won by Essex. Hampshire could be forgiven for thinking all the luck went against them in a match which left them still the only county not to have reached a Lord's final. Fletcher did not hesitate in putting them in on a damp wicket, and the Essex bowling was tight and accurate. By the 21st over Greenidge and Terry were out for 36, with the game swinging further to Essex at 54 when Chris Smith ran himself out. After the departure of Nicholas, Turner led a Hampshire recovery and a total of 224 was more than had looked likely. The Essex reply was built around Gooch, who was most fortunate not to be adjudged run out just after completing his fifty. Bad light forced the game into a second day, when Essex entered the final over 1 run behind and one fewer wicket down. Greenidge bowled a wide with his first delivery to put the scores level and Turner blocked out the rest of the over.

*Man of the Match:* G. A. Gooch.

### Hampshire

C. G. Greenidge c Pringle b Foster . . . 10
V. P. Terry lbw b Turner . . . . . . . . . . . . 7
C. L. Smith run out . . . . . . . . . . . . . . . . 26
*M. C. J. Nicholas lbw b Turner . . . . . 39
R. A. Smith b Turner . . . . . . . . . . . . . . . 24
D. R. Turner c McEwan b Foster . . . . . 36
M. D. Marshall b Lever . . . . . . . . . . . . . 29
N. G. Cowley c East b Foster . . . . . . . . 20
T. M. Tremlett not out . . . . . . . . . . . . . . 8
†R. J. Parks not out . . . . . . . . . . . . . . . . 6
L-b 10, w 6, n-b 3 . . . . . . . . . . 19

1/18 2/36 3/54 4/112 5/117 6/169 7/208 8/208 (8 wkts, 60 overs) 224

C. A. Connor did not bat.

Bowling: Lever 12–4–35–1; Foster 12–2–58–3; Pringle 12–2–58–0; Turner 12–2–38–3; Gooch 12–1–25–0.

### Essex

G. A. Gooch not out . . . . . . . . . . . . . . . . 93
B. R. Hardie lbw b Nicholas . . . . . . . . . 5
P. J. Prichard c Turner b Nicholas . . . . 14
K. S. McEwan c Parks b Connor . . . . . 35
D. R. Pringle run out . . . . . . . . . . . . . . . 8
*K. W. R. Fletcher lbw b Connor . . . . . 19
A. W. Lilley c Cowley b Connor . . . . . . 26
†D. E. East c R. A. Smith b Cowley . . 1
S. Turner not out . . . . . . . . . . . . . . . . . . . 7
L-b 6, w 6, n-b 4 . . . . . . . . . . . 16

1/32 2/48 3/111 4/161 5/167 6/208 7/212 (7 wkts, 60 overs) 224

N. A. Foster and J. K. Lever did not bat.

Bowling: Marshall 12–1–41–0; Connor 12–0–52–3; Tremlett 12–1–38–0; Nicholas 12–0–41–2; Cowley 11–0–45–1; Greenidge 1–0–1–0.

Umpires: B. J. Meyer and N. T. Plews.

## WORCESTERSHIRE v NOTTINGHAMSHIRE

At Worcester, August 21, 22. Nottinghamshire won by four wickets with four balls to spare. Toss won by Worcestershire. Robinson won his third successive Man of the Match award for a magnificent match-winning 139. When bad light ended play early on Wednesday evening, Nottinghamshire with six wickets in hand needed 96 to win off the last fourteen overs, and after a delayed start the following morning Robinson added another 64 off 45 balls to his overnight 75. Before being run out in the penultimate over, he faced 173 deliveries, hit thirteen 4s, and had put his side within 6 runs of the final at Lord's. On a sluggish pitch which yielded little bounce, the backbone of Worcestershire's innings was a second-wicket stand of 112 between Curtis, whose 92 was his highest one-day score, and Smith. The absence of Kapil Dev, recalled to lead India in Sri Lanka, left an obvious void in the home side, and the gamble of recalling King, making his first appearance for fifteen months, failed to pay off.

### Worcestershire

T. S. Curtis c and b Pick . . . . . . . . . . . . 92
D. B. D'Oliveira lbw b Hadlee . . . . . . . 0
D. M. Smith b Rice . . . . . . . . . . . . . . . . 57
C. L. King run out . . . . . . . . . . . . . . . . 11
D. N. Patel b Hadlee . . . . . . . . . . . . . . . 20
*P. A. Neale c Johnson b Pick . . . . . . . 9
M. J. Weston run out . . . . . . . . . . . . . . . 7
†S. J. Rhodes not out . . . . . . . . . . . . . . . 9
N. V. Radford run out . . . . . . . . . . . . . . 16
J. D. Inchmore not out . . . . . . . . . . . . . . 0
L-b 4, w 5, n-b 2 . . . . . . . . . . . 11

1/4 2/116 3/168 4/170 5/185 6/206 7/207 8/227 (8 wkts, 60 overs) 232

P. J. Newport did not bat.

Bowling: Hadlee 12–2–35–2; Rice 11–0–61–1; Cooper 12–2–43–0; Hemmings 12–2–37–0; Pick 12–2–46–2; Evans 1–0–6–0.

### Nottinghamshire

R. T. Robinson run out . . . . . . . . . . . . .139
B. C. Broad lbw b Radford . . . . . . . . . . 4
D. W. Randall lbw b King . . . . . . . . . . 9
*C. E. B. Rice c Rhodes b Inchmore . . 25
P. Johnson b Patel . . . . . . . . . . . . . . . . . 1
R. J. Hadlee c and b Patel . . . . . . . . . . . 18
†B. N. French not out . . . . . . . . . . . . . . 11
E. E. Hemmings not out . . . . . . . . . . . . . 4
L-b 14, w 4, n-b 4 . . . . . . . . . . 22

1/25 2/47 3/106 4/114 5/175 6/227 (6 wkts, 59.2 overs) 233

R. A. Pick, K. P. Evans and K. E. Cooper did not bat.

Bowling: Radford 12–2–36–1; Inchmore 12–1–40–1; Newport 9.2–1–43–0; King 8–0–36–1; Weston 6–0–21–0; Patel 12–0–43–2.

Umpires: D. O. Oslear and J. Birkenshaw.

## FINAL

## ESSEX v NOTTINGHAMSHIRE

At Lord's, September 7. Essex won by 1 run, their first success in the knockout competition and their seventh title in as many years. It was a marvellous match, in which Randall all but conjured up an improbable victory for Nottinghamshire who had seen Gooch and Hardie put on 202, the highest partnership in any Lord's final, after Essex had been put in. Hardie's innings of 110, made from 149 balls, outshone Gooch's in its vigorous strokeplay, though he needed some luck when the ball moved about early on. When both were dismissed in quick succession, Nottinghamshire might have contained Essex for the rest of their innings, but McEwan was dropped by Broad off Saxelby at 16 and made 30 out of the 56 added with Pringle from the last four overs.

Robinson and Broad then, in turn, encountered few problems in putting on 143 for Nottinghamshire's first wicket, but the innings faltered from the moment Broad was run out, underestimating the power of Pont's throw from the mid-wicket boundary. When Robinson, Rice and Hadlee all went trying to force the pace, Randall was joined by Martindale, appearing in his first one-day match. With 37 still required and only three overs left Essex seemed clear-cut winners. Randall, however, at last began to negotiate most of the strike, improvising to find the gaps, and Pringle bowled the last over to him with 18 needed. To defeat Pringle's leg-stump attack, Randall made room to play on the off side, taking 16 from the first five deliveries so that, remarkably, Nottinghamshire were now only one stroke away from winning. With the last ball, however, Pringle succeeded in tucking Randall up as he again tried to move inside the line, and Prichard plucked down the resulting catch at short-midwicket. Hardie took the Man of the Match award from Peter May, and the match was watched by 21,500 (excluding members). – M.J.C.

### Essex

G. A. Gooch b Pick ................ 91
B. R. Hardie run out ................ 110
K. S. McEwan not out ............... 46
D. R. Pringle not out ............... 29
B 1, l-b 3 .................. 4

1/202 2/203 (2 wkts, 60 overs) 280

P. J. Prichard, *K. W. R. Fletcher, A. W. Lilley, †D. E. East, S. Turner, I. L. Pont and J. K. Lever did not bat.

Bowling: Hadlee 12–4–48–0; Cooper 9–3–27–0; Saxelby 12–0–73–0; Rice 7–0–38–0; Pick 8–0–36–1; Hemmings 12–1–54–0.

### Nottinghamshire

R. T. Robinson c Hardie b Turner .... 80
B. C. Broad run out ................ 64
*C. E. B. Rice c Hardie b Turner ..... 12
D. W. Randall c Prichard b Pringle ... 66
R. J. Hadlee b Pont ................ 22
D. J. R. Martindale not out .......... 20
L-b 14, n-b 1 ............... 15

1/143 2/153 3/173 4/214 5/279 (5 wkts, 60 overs) 279

†B. N. French, E. E. Hemmings, R. A. Pick, K. Saxelby and K. E. Cooper did not bat.

Bowling: Lever 12–2–53–0; Pont 12–0–54–1; Turner 12–1–43–2; Gooch 12–0–47–0; Pringle 12–1–68–1.

Umpires: D. J. Constant and B. J. Meyer.

## NATWEST BANK TROPHY RECORDS

(Including Gillette Cup, 1963-80)

### Batting

**Highest individual scores:** 206, A. I. Kallicharran, Warwickshire v Oxfordshire, Edgbaston, 1984; 177, C. G. Greenidge, Hampshire v Glamorgan, Southampton, 1975; 165 not out, V. P. Terry, Hampshire v Berkshire, Southampton, 1985; 158, G. D. Barlow, Middlesex v Lancashire, Lord's, 1984; 158, Zaheer Abbas, Gloucestershire v Leicestershire, Leicester, 1983; 156, D. I. Gower, Leicestershire v Derbyshire, Leicester, 1984; 155, J. J. Whitaker, Leicestershire v Wiltshire, Swindon, 1984. (93 hundreds were scored in the Gillette Cup; 44 hundreds have been scored in the NatWest Bank Trophy.)

**Fastest hundred:** R. E. Marshall in 77 minutes, Hampshire v Bedfordshire at Goldington, 1968.

**Highest innings total:** 392 for five off 60 overs, Warwickshire v Oxfordshire, Edgbaston, 1984; 371 for four off 60 overs, Hampshire v Glamorgan, Southampton, 1975; 354 for seven off 60 overs, Leicestershire v Wiltshire, Swindon, 1984; 349 for six off 60 overs, Lancashire v Gloucestershire, Bristol, 1984; 339 for four off 60 overs, Hampshire v Berkshire, Southampton, 1985; 330 for four off 60 overs, Somerset v Glamorgan, Cardiff, 1978; 327 for seven off 60 overs, Gloucestershire v Berkshire, Reading, 1966; 327 for six off 60 overs, Essex v Scotland, Chelmsford, 1984; 326 for six off 60 overs, Leicestershire v Worcestershire, Leicester, 1979; 321 for four off 60 overs, Hampshire v Bedfordshire, Goldington, 1968; 317 for four off 60 overs, Yorkshire v Surrey (in the final), Lord's, 1965; 312 for five off 60 overs, Worcestershire v Lancashire, Old Trafford, 1985.

**Highest innings total by a minor county:** 256 off 58 overs, Oxfordshire v Warwickshire, Edgbaston, 1983.

**Highest totals by a side batting second:** 306 for six off 59.3 overs, Gloucestershire v Leicestershire, Leicester, 1983; 298 off 59 overs, Lancashire v Worcestershire, Old Trafford, 1985; 297 for four off 57.1 overs, Somerset v Warwickshire, Taunton, 1978; 296 for four off 58 overs, Kent v Surrey, Canterbury, 1985; 290 for seven off 59.3 overs, Yorkshire v Worcestershire, Headingley, 1982; 287 for six off 59 overs, Warwickshire v Glamorgan, Edgbaston, 1976; 287 off 60 overs, Essex v Somerset, Taunton, 1978; 282 for nine off 60 overs, Leicestershire v Gloucestershire, Leicester, 1975. Gloucestershire's 306 for six v Leicestershire, Leicester, 1983 was the highest by a side batting second and winning the match.

**Highest innings by a side batting first and losing:** 302 for five off 60 overs, Leicestershire v Gloucestershire, Leicester, 1983.

**Lowest innings in the final at Lord's:** 118 off 60 overs, Lancashire v Kent, 1974.

**Lowest completed innings totals:** 39 off 26.4 overs, Ireland v Sussex, Hove, 1985; 41 off 20 overs, Cambridgeshire v Buckinghamshire, Cambridge, 1972; 41 off 19.4 overs, Middlesex v Essex, Westcliff, 1972; 41 off 36.1 overs, Shropshire v Essex, Wellington, 1974.

**Lowest total by a side batting first and winning:** 98 off 56.2 overs, Worcestershire v Durham, Chester-le-Street, 1968.

**Shortest innings:** 10.1 overs (60 for one), Worcestershire v Lancashire, Worcester, 1963.

*Matches re-arranged on a reduced number of overs are excluded from the above.*

**Record partnerships for each wicket**

| | | |
|---|---|---|
| 227 for 1st | R. E. Marshall and B. L. Reed, Hampshire v Bedfordshire at Goldington | 1968 |
| 223 for 2nd | M. J. Smith and C. T. Radley, Middlesex v Hampshire at Lord's | 1977 |
| 179 for 3rd | G. A. Gooch and K. S. McEwan, Essex v Scotland at Chelmsford | 1984 |
| 234* for 4th | D. Lloyd and C. H. Lloyd, Lancashire v Gloucestershire at Old Trafford | 1978 |
| 166 for 5th | M. A. Lynch and G. R. J. Roope, Surrey v Durham at The Oval | 1982 |
| 105 for 6th | G. S. Sobers and R. A. White, Nottinghamshire v Worcestershire at Worcester | 1974 |
| 160* for 7th | C. J. Richards and I. R. Payne, Surrey v Lincolnshire at Sleaford | 1983 |
| 69 for 8th | S. J. Rouse and D. J. Brown, Warwickshire v Middlesex at Lord's | 1977 |
| 87 for 9th | M. A. Nash and A. E. Cordle, Glamorgan v Lincolnshire at Swansea | 1974 |
| 81 for 10th | S. Turner and R. E. East, Essex v Yorkshire at Headingley | 1982 |

The record partnership for any wicket in the NatWest Bank Trophy is:

| | | |
|---|---|---|
| 202 for 1st | G. A. Gooch and B. R. Hardie, Essex v Nottinghamshire (in the final), Lord's | 1985 |

## Bowling

**Hat-tricks:** J. D. F. Larter, Northamptonshire v Sussex, Northampton, 1963; D. A. D. Sydenham, Surrey v Cheshire, Hoylake, 1964; R. N. S. Hobbs, Essex v Middlesex, Lord's, 1968; N. M. McVicker, Warwickshire v Lincolnshire, Edgbaston, 1971; G. S. le Roux, Sussex v Ireland, Hove, 1985.

**Four wickets in five balls:** D. A. D. Sydenham, Surrey v Cheshire, Hoylake, 1964.

**Best analyses:** seven for 15, A. L. Dixon, Kent v Surrey, The Oval, 1967; seven for 30, P. J. Sainsbury, Hampshire v Norfolk, Southampton, 1965; seven for 32, S. P. Davis, Durham v Lancashire, Chester-le-Street, 1983; seven for 33, R. D. Jackman, Surrey v Yorkshire, Harrogate, 1970; seven for 37, N. A. Mallender, Northamptonshire v Worcestershire, Northampton, 1984.

## Results

**Largest victories in runs:** Sussex by 244 runs v Ireland, Hove, 1985; Warwickshire by 227 runs v Oxfordshire, Edgbaston, 1984; Essex by 226 runs v Oxfordshire, Chelmsford, 1985; Leicestershire by 214 runs v Staffordshire, Longton, 1975; Sussex by 200 runs v Durham, Hove, 1964; and in the final by 175 runs, Yorkshire v Surrey, Lord's 1965.

**Quickest finishes:** both at 2.20 p.m. Worcestershire beat Lancashire by nine wickets at Worcester, 1963; Essex beat Middlesex by eight wickets at Westcliff, 1972.

**Scores level:** Nottinghamshire 215, Somerset 215 for nine at Taunton, 1964; Surrey 196, Sussex 196 for eight at The Oval, 1970; Somerset 287 for six, Essex 287 at Taunton, 1978; Surrey 195 for seven, Essex 195 at Chelmsford, 1980; Essex 149, Derbyshire 149 for eight at Derby, 1981; Northamptonshire 235 for nine, Derbyshire 235 for six in the final at Lord's, 1981; Middlesex 222 for nine, Somerset 222 for eight at Lord's, 1983; Hampshire 224 for eight, Essex 224 for seven at Southampton, 1985. Under the rules the side which lost fewer wickets won.

**Minor Counties:** Durham became the first minor county to defeat a first-class county when they beat Yorkshire at Harrogate by five wickets in 1973, Lincolnshire became the second when they beat Glamorgan at Swansea by six wickets in 1974 and Shropshire the first in the NatWest Bank Trophy when they beat Yorkshire at Telford by 37 runs in 1984. Hertfordshire were the first minor county to reach the third round when they beat Essex at Hitchin by 33 runs in 1976. Durham became the first minor county to defeat first-class opposition on two occasions when they beat Derbyshire at Derby in 1985.

## WINNERS

### Gillette Cup

1963 SUSSEX beat Worcestershire by 14 runs.
1964 SUSSEX beat Warwickshire by eight wickets.
1965 YORKSHIRE beat Surrey by 175 runs.
1966 WARWICKSHIRE beat Worcestershire by five wickets.
1967 KENT beat Somerset by 32 runs.
1968 WARWICKSHIRE beat Sussex by four wickets.
1969 YORKSHIRE beat Derbyshire by 69 runs.
1970 LANCASHIRE beat Sussex by six wickets.
1971 LANCASHIRE beat Kent by 24 runs.
1972 LANCASHIRE beat Warwickshire by four wickets.
1973 GLOUCESTERSHIRE beat Sussex by 40 runs.
1974 KENT beat Lancashire by four wickets.
1975 LANCASHIRE beat Middlesex by seven wickets.
1976 NORTHAMPTONSHIRE beat Lancashire by four wickets.
1977 MIDDLESEX beat Glamorgan by five wickets.
1978 SUSSEX beat Somerset by five wickets.
1979 SOMERSET beat Northamptonshire by 45 runs.
1980 MIDDLESEX beat Surrey by seven wickets.

### NatWest Bank Trophy

1981 DERBYSHIRE beat Northamptonshire by losing fewer wickets with the scores level.
1982 SURREY beat Warwickshire by nine wickets.
1983 SOMERSET beat Kent by 24 runs.
1984 MIDDLESEX beat Kent by four wickets.
1985 ESSEX beat Nottinghamshire by 1 run.

# BENSON AND HEDGES CUP, 1985

Leicestershire, who had previously won the competition in 1974 and 1977, won the Benson and Hedges Cup when they beat Essex by five wickets at Lord's. In addition to the trophy, which they hold for a year, Leicestershire received £17,000 in prizemoney. Essex, as runners-up, took £8,500.

The losing semi-finalists, Kent and Middlesex, received £4,250 each, while Derbyshire, Hampshire, Northamptonshire and Worcestershire, the losing quarter-finalists, each received £2,125. The winners of the group matches received £725 each.

Peter Willey, nominated by Denis Compton for the Gold Award in the final in recognition of his fine all-round performance, received £550, while the Gold Award winners in the semi-finals each received £275, in the quarter-finals £200, and in the group matches £125 each.

Total prizemoney for the competition was £78,400, an increase of £14,200 over the previous year. Benson and Hedges increased their total sponsorship to the TCCB for 1985 to £400,000, linked to inflation for 1986 and 1987.

## FINAL GROUP TABLE

| | Played | Won | Lost | No Result | Points |
|---|---|---|---|---|---|
| *Group A* | | | | | |
| NORTHAMPTONSHIRE | 4 | 2 | 0 | 2 | 6 |
| DERBYSHIRE | 4 | 2 | 1 | 1 | 5 |
| Nottinghamshire | 4 | 2 | 1 | 1 | 5 |
| Gloucestershire | 4 | 2 | 2 | 0 | 4 |
| Scotland | 4 | 0 | 4 | 0 | 0 |
| *Group B* | | | | | |
| WORCESTERSHIRE | 4 | 3 | 1 | 0 | 6 |
| LEICESTERSHIRE | 4 | 3 | 1 | 0 | 6 |
| Yorkshire | 4 | 2 | 2 | 0 | 4 |
| Warwickshire | 4 | 1 | 3 | 0 | 2 |
| Lancashire | 4 | 1 | 3 | 0 | 2 |
| *Group C* | | | | | |
| ESSEX | 4 | 4 | 0 | 0 | 8 |
| MIDDLESEX | 4 | 2 | 2 | 0 | 4 |
| Surrey | 4 | 2 | 2 | 0 | 4 |
| Sussex | 4 | 2 | 2 | 0 | 4 |
| Oxford & Cambridge Univs | 4 | 0 | 4 | 0 | 0 |
| *Group D* | | | | | |
| HAMPSHIRE | 4 | 4 | 0 | 0 | 8 |
| KENT | 4 | 3 | 1 | 0 | 6 |
| Glamorgan | 4 | 2 | 2 | 0 | 4 |
| Somerset | 4 | 1 | 3 | 0 | 2 |
| Minor Counties | 4 | 0 | 4 | 0 | 0 |

*The top two teams in each section qualified for the quarter-finals.*

*Where two or more teams finished with the same number of points, the position in the group was determined by their bowlers' striking-rates.*

## BOWLERS' STRIKING-RATES

| | Balls | Wickets | Striking-Rate |
|---|---|---|---|
| *Group A* | | | |
| NORTHAMPTONSHIRE | 983 | 24 | 40.95 |
| DERBYSHIRE | 853 | 24 | 35.54 |
| Nottinghamshire | 994 | 25 | 39.76 |
| Gloucestershire | 1,310 | 32 | 40.93 |
| Scotland | 1,235 | 29 | 42.58 |
| *Group B* | | | |
| WORCESTERSHIRE | 1,186 | 29 | 40.89 |
| LEICESTERSHIRE | 1,212 | 25 | 48.48 |
| Yorkshire | 1,170 | 38 | 30.78 |
| Warwickshire | 1,271 | 24 | 52.95 |
| Lancashire | 1,161 | 24 | 48.37 |
| *Group C* | | | |
| ESSEX | 1,094 | 36 | 30.38 |
| MIDDLESEX | 1,120 | 29 | 38.62 |
| Surrey | 1,182 | 27 | 43.77 |
| Sussex | 1,211 | 26 | 46.57 |
| Oxford & Cambridge Univs | 1,149 | 15 | 76.60 |
| *Group D* | | | |
| HAMPSHIRE | 1,087 | 38 | 28.60 |
| KENT | 1,195 | 36 | 33.19 |
| Glamorgan | 1,131 | 36 | 31.41 |
| Somerset | 1,144 | 29 | 39.44 |
| Minor Counties | 914 | 17 | 53.76 |

## GROUP A

## GLOUCESTERSHIRE v NOTTINGHAMSHIRE

At Bristol, May 4. Gloucestershire won by 33 runs. Toss won by Nottinghamshire.
*Gold Award:* P. W. Romaines.

### Gloucestershire

A. W. Stovold c Robinson b Evans .... 60
P. W. Romaines c Evans b Saxelby ...125
C. W. J. Athey c French b Saxelby .... 8
B. F. Davison c Randall b Rice ...... 38
P. Bainbridge run out ............... 20
K. M. Curran not out ............... 15
B 4, l-b 16, w 1, n-b 1 ....... 22

1/153 2/170 3/239 4/265 5/288 (5 wkts, 55 overs) 288

J. W. Lloyds, *D. A. Graveney, †R. C. Russell, D. V. Lawrence and J. N. Shepherd did not bat.

Bowling: Saxelby 11–0–62–2; Pick 11–0–54–0; Evans 11–0–47–1; Rice 11–1–50–1; Hemmings 11–0–55–0.

### Nottinghamshire

| | |
|---|---|
| B. C. Broad run out | 17 |
| R. T. Robinson c sub b Graveney | 56 |
| D. W. Randall c Davison b Shepherd | 62 |
| *C. E. B. Rice c sub b Shepherd | 11 |
| P. Johnson lbw b Bainbridge | 16 |
| J. D. Birch b Curran | 37 |
| K. P. Evans lbw b Curran | 20 |
| †B. N. French c Shepherd b Curran | 4 |
| E. E. Hemmings c Russell b Lawrence | 2 |
| K. Saxelby not out | 2 |
| R. A. Pick not out | 3 |
| L-b 15, w 9, n-b 1 | 25 |
| 1/44 2/126 3/154 4/164 5/187 6/231 7/241 8/249 9/253 (9 wkts, 55 overs) | 255 |

Bowling: Lawrence 11–0–54–1; Curran 11–1–45–3; Shepherd 11–1–42–2; Graveney 11–0–48–1; Bainbridge 11–0–51–1.

Umpires: J. H. Harris and D. R. Shepherd.

## SCOTLAND v DERBYSHIRE

At Aberdeen, May 4. Derbyshire won by 93 runs. Toss won by Scotland.
*Gold Award:* A. Hill.

### Derbyshire

| | |
|---|---|
| *K. J. Barnett lbw b Duthie | 3 |
| A. Hill not out | 107 |
| J. E. Morris c Brown b Duthie | 2 |
| B. Roberts c Duthie b Donald | 56 |
| W. P. Fowler b Ker | 4 |
| G. Miller c Ker b McPate | 26 |
| R. J. Finney b McPate | 9 |
| D. G. Moir lbw b Duthie | 2 |
| A. E. Warner c Ker b McPate | 2 |
| P. G. Newman b McPate | 7 |
| †B. J. M. Maher not out | 2 |
| B 2, l-b 6 | 8 |
| 1/3 2/9 3/132 4/141 5/187 6/206 7/209 8/212 9/225 (9 wkts, 55 overs) | 228 |

Bowling: McPate 11–2–42–4; Duthie 11–4–39–3; Thomson 5–0–17–0; Ker 8–1–40–1; Donald 11–1–36–1; Henry 9–0–46–0.

### Scotland

| | |
|---|---|
| W. A. Donald lbw b Finney | 10 |
| P. G. Duthie b Warner | 7 |
| *R. G. Swan lbw b Miller | 7 |
| O. Henry c Finney b Moir | 59 |
| D. J. Simpson b Finney | 7 |
| A. B. Russell b Miller | 22 |
| T. M. Black st Maher b Moir | 1 |
| †A. Brown not out | 9 |
| J. E. Ker lbw b Finney | 0 |
| W. A. McPate lbw b Finney | 0 |
| J. Thomson b Finney | 0 |
| L-b 5, w 2, n-b 6 | 13 |
| 1/11 2/29 3/33 4/46 5/98 6/109 7/135 8/135 9/135 (43.5 overs) | 135 |

Bowling: Warner 5–0–13–1; Newman 6–2–10–0; Finney 10.5–1–40–5; Miller 11–2–24–2; Moir 11–3–43–2.

Umpires: B. J. Meyer and R. A. White.

## NORTHAMPTONSHIRE v GLOUCESTERSHIRE

At Northampton, May 11. Northamptonshire won by four wickets. Toss won by Northamptonshire.
*Gold Award:* R. G. Williams.

### Gloucestershire

| | | | |
|---|---|---|---|
| A. W. Stovold b Walker | 11 | I. R. Payne run out | 2 |
| P. W. Romaines c Sharp b Walker | 19 | †R. C. Russell b Walker | 0 |
| C. W. J. Athey b Walker | 77 | D. V. Lawrence not out | 0 |
| P. Bainbridge c Larkins b Williams | 27 | B 3, l-b 9, w 1, n-b 2 | 15 |
| B. F. Davison c Larkins b Bailey | 41 | | |
| K. M. Curran c Sharp b Mallender | 16 | 1/31 2/33 3/95 (53.5 overs) | 217 |
| *D. A. Graveney c Cook b Mallender | 0 | 4/161 5/205 6/205 7/211 | |
| J. N. Shepherd run out | 9 | 8/217 9/217 | |

Bowling: Mallender 10–0–38–2; Walker 9.5–0–46–4; Joseph 11–2–32–0; Capel 8–1–35–0; Williams 11–2–32–1; Bailey 4–0–22–1.

### Northamptonshire

| | | | |
|---|---|---|---|
| *G. Cook lbw b Lawrence | 11 | D. J. Wild not out | 15 |
| W. Larkins lbw b Payne | 48 | †G. Sharp not out | 6 |
| R. G. Williams c Payne b Lawrence | 58 | B 3, l-b 9, w 1, n-b 6 | 19 |
| A. J. Lamb lbw b Payne | 0 | | |
| R. J. Bailey c Russell b Curran | 52 | 1/30 2/98 3/100 (6 wkts, 54.5 overs) | 220 |
| D. J. Capel c Athey b Shepherd | 11 | 4/164 5/194 6/210 | |

N. A. Mallender, A. Walker and R. F. Joseph did not bat.

Bowling: Lawrence 11–1–41–2; Curran 10.5–1–46–1; Shepherd 11–0–49–1; Bainbridge 6–0–20–0; Graveney 11–1–27–0; Payne 5–0–25–2.

Umpires: J. H. Hampshire and J. W. Holder.

## SCOTLAND v NOTTINGHAMSHIRE

At Glasgow, May 11. Nottinghamshire won by 28 runs. Toss won by Nottinghamshire. *Gold Award:* R. T. Robinson.

### Nottinghamshire

| | | | |
|---|---|---|---|
| B. C. Broad c Russell b Duthie | 0 | K. Saxelby not out | 12 |
| R. T. Robinson c Swan b McPate | 120 | K. E. Cooper not out | 0 |
| D. W. Randall b De Neef | 7 | | |
| *C. E. B. Rice c Brown b Thomson | 25 | L-b 9 | 9 |
| P. Johnson c Thomson b Henry | 0 | | |
| J. D. Birch c and b Henry | 4 | 1/4 2/19 3/67 (8 wkts, 55 overs) | 216 |
| †B. N. French c Brown b Donald | 8 | 4/74 5/88 6/111 | |
| E. E. Hemmings lbw b McPate | 31 | 7/196 8/215 | |

P. M. Such did not bat.

Bowling: Duthie 11–2–43–1; De Neef 6–0–22–1; McPate 11–1–56–2; Thomson 11–2–30–1; Henry 11–1–29–2; Donald 5–0–27–1.

### Scotland

| | | | |
|---|---|---|---|
| W. A. Donald c Randall b Cooper | 44 | P. G. Duthie b Such | 4 |
| K. Scott c Randall b Cooper | 2 | W. A. McPate b Such | 1 |
| *R. G. Swan c Birch b Such | 27 | J. Thomson not out | 2 |
| O. Henry c Johnson b Hemmings | 1 | L-b 4, w 1 | 5 |
| D. J. Simpson c Saxelby b Hemmings | 5 | | |
| †A. Brown run out | 21 | 1/3 2/66 3/71 (9 wkts, 55 overs) | 188 |
| D. De Neef c French b Rice | 3 | 4/79 5/83 6/88 7/153 | |
| A. B. Russell not out | 73 | 8/166 9/168 | |

Bowling: Saxelby 11–1–51–0; Cooper 11–3–31–2; Rice 11–2–30–1; Hemmings 11–3–22–2; Such 11–1–50–3.

Umpires: D. G. L. Evans and J. A. Jameson.

## DERBYSHIRE v NORTHAMPTONSHIRE

At Derby, May 14, 15. No result. Toss won by Derbyshire. No play was possible until 3.20 on the second day, when the match was reduced to 25 overs a side. However, bad light and rain had the last word after only 22 overs of Northamptonshire's innings.

### Northamptonshire

| | | | |
|---|---|---|---|
| W. Larkins b Miller | 10 | D. J. Wild not out | 2 |
| R. J. Bailey c Maher b Mortensen | 25 | †G. Sharp not out | 1 |
| A. J. Lamb lbw b Finney | 2 | B 2, l-b 9, n-b 1 | 12 |
| R. G. Williams b Warner | 24 | | |
| D. J. Capel c Barnett b Miller | 7 | 1/31 2/37 3/60 (6 wkts, 22 overs) | 88 |
| *G. Cook lbw b Holding | 5 | 4/67 5/78 6/86 | |

R. F. Joseph, N. A. Mallender and A. Walker did not bat.

Bowling: Mortensen 5–0–19–1; Finney 5–0–25–1; Miller 5–1–16–2; Warner 4–0–9–1; Holding 3–0–8–1.

### Derbyshire

*K. J. Barnett, A. Hill, J. E. Morris, B. Roberts, W. P. Fowler, G. Miller, R. J. Finney, †B. J. M. Maher, A. E. Warner, M. A. Holding and O. H. Mortensen.

Umpires: J. W. Holder and N. T. Plews.

## GLOUCESTERSHIRE v SCOTLAND

At Bristol, May 14, 15. Gloucestershire won by 53 runs after the match had been interrupted by rain on the first day when Scotland were 38 for three off 13.3 overs. Toss won by Scotland.
*Gold Award:* K. M. Curran.

### Gloucestershire

| | | | |
|---|---|---|---|
| A. W. Stovold c Black b Duthie | 9 | †R. C. Russell c Russell b McPate | 0 |
| P. W. Romaines c Donald b Duthie | 5 | D. V. Lawrence not out | 22 |
| C. W. J. Athey c Donald b Ker | 22 | | |
| P. Bainbridge b McPate | 53 | L-b 6, w 4 | 10 |
| B. F. Davison c Brown b Ker | 6 | | |
| K. M. Curran not out | 53 | 1/10 2/15 3/63 (8 wkts, 55 overs) | 184 |
| J. N. Shepherd c Henry b Ker | 1 | 4/71 5/122 6/129 | |
| *D. A. Graveney run out | 3 | 7/138 8/139 | |

C. A. Walsh did not bat.

Bowling: De Neef 11–0–37–0; Duthie 11–2–35–2; McPate 11–1–38–2; Henry 11–2–39–0; Ker 11–1–29–3.

### Scotland

| | | | |
|---|---|---|---|
| W. A. Donald c Russell b Lawrence | 7 | J. E. Ker c Stovold b Graveney | 16 |
| D. J. Simpson run out | 2 | D. De Neef c Athey b Walsh | 2 |
| *R. J. Swan c Russell b Curran | 14 | W. A. McPate not out | 4 |
| O. Henry c Athey b Walsh | 1 | L-b 6, w 6, n-b 10 | 22 |
| †A. Brown c Stovold b Curran | 12 | | |
| A. B. Russell run out | 29 | 1/18 2/23 3/31 (53.3 overs) | 131 |
| T. M. Black c Bainbridge b Graveney | 22 | 4/46 5/65 6/89 7/91 | |
| P. G. Duthie c Russell b Shepherd | 0 | 8/122 9/126 | |

Bowling: Lawrence 6–0–13–1; Walsh 10.3–3–19–2; Shepherd 11–3–15–1; Curran 11–1–26–2; Bainbridge 8–0–33–0; Graveney 7–1–19–2.

Umpires: A. G. T. Whitehead and P. B. Wight.

## NORTHAMPTONSHIRE v SCOTLAND

At Northampton, May 16. Northamptonshire won by six wickets. Toss won by Northamptonshire. Donald and Swan established a Scottish second-wicket record of 96 for the competition.

*Gold Award:* W. Larkins.

### Scotland

W. A. Donald c Harper b Mallender .. 59
D. J. Simpson c Sharp b Griffiths ..... 0
*R. G. Swan b Capel ............... 37
O. Henry b Walker .................. 54
A. B. Russell c Sharp b Mallender .... 12
†A. Brown run out .................. 0
T. M. Black b Mallender ............ 0
P. G. Duthie run out ............... 4
D. De Neef c Lamb b Walker ........ 1
J. E. Ker not out .................. 0
B 1, l-b 7, w 6, n-b 4 ........ 18

1/0 2/96 3/129 4/161 5/162 6/163 7/183 8/183 9/185 (9 wkts, 55 overs) 185

W. A. McPate did not bat.

Bowling: Mallender 11–1–46–3; Griffiths 7–2–13–1; Walker 11–0–41–2; Harper 11–1–37–0; Williams 11–3–25–0; Capel 4–0–15–1.

### Northamptonshire

*G. Cook c Russell b De Neef ....... 6
W. Larkins c Swan b Black ..........105
R. G. Williams c Henry b Black ...... 27
A. J. Lamb c Brown b De Neef ...... 20
R. J. Bailey not out ................ 20
D. J. Capel not out ................ 11
B 1, w 1 .................. 2

1/16 2/140 3/143 4/165 (4 wkts, 40.5 overs) 191

†G. Sharp, R. A. Harper, N. A. Mallender, A. Walker and B. J. Griffiths did not bat.

Bowling: De Neef 7–2–32–2; Duthie 10–1–46–0; McPate 4–2–22–0; Ker 3.5–0–20–0; Henry 11–3–36–0; Black 5–0–34–2.

Umpires: J. H. Hampshire and B. J. Meyer.

## NOTTINGHAMSHIRE v DERBYSHIRE

At Trent Bridge, May 16. Nottinghamshire won by 53 runs, a margin which would have been much bigger but for a Benson and Hedges Cup record ninth-wicket stand of 83 between Newman and Holding. Toss won by Derbyshire.

*Gold Award:* C. E. B. Rice.

### Nottinghamshire

B. C. Broad c Holding b Mortensen ... 1
R. T. Robinson lbw b Newman ....... 32
D. W. Randall c Maher b Miller ...... 29
*C. E. B. Rice not out .............. 73
P. Johnson c Roberts b Mortensen .... 4
J. D. Birch c Maher b Mortensen ..... 2
R. J. Hadlee c Hill b Warner ........ 39
†B. N. French not out .............. 3
B 1, l-b 10, w 2 ........... 13

1/3 2/51 3/83 4/94 5/98 6/178 (6 wkts, 55 overs) 196

E. E. Hemmings, K. E. Cooper and K. Saxelby did not bat.

Bowling: Holding 11–1–47–0; Mortensen 11–0–30–3; Warner 11–0–52–1; Newman 11–2–42–1; Miller 11–2–14–1.

### Derbyshire

| | | | |
|---|---|---|---|
| *K. J. Barnett lbw b Saxelby | 2 | P. G. Newman not out | 56 |
| A. Hill c Johnson b Hadlee | 0 | M. A. Holding c Rice b Hemmings | 38 |
| J. E. Morris lbw b Saxelby | 9 | O. H. Mortensen c Randall b Hemmings | 2 |
| B. Roberts c Rice b Cooper | 0 | B 3, l-b 3, w 10 | 16 |
| W. P. Fowler lbw b Rice | 11 | | |
| G. Miller c Rice b Cooper | 7 | 1/3 2/15 3/16 (47.4 overs) | 143 |
| †B. J. M. Maher c Rice b Cooper | 0 | 4/16 5/30 6/34 7/36 | |
| A. E. Warner c Hadlee b Cooper | 2 | 8/38 9/121 | |

Bowling: Hadlee 8–1–15–1; Saxelby 8–5–6–2; Cooper 11–3–30–4; Rice 5–0–19–1; Hemmings 10.4–1–31–2; Birch 5–0–36–0.

Umpires: J. W. Holder and B. Leadbeater.

## DERBYSHIRE v GLOUCESTERSHIRE

At Chesterfield, May 18, 20. Derbyshire won on faster scoring-rate after rain ended play on the first day and prevented any play on the second.

*Gold Award:* K. J. Barnett.

### Derbyshire

| | | | |
|---|---|---|---|
| *K. J. Barnett c Stovold b Curran | 86 | A. E. Warner c Graveney b Shepherd | 0 |
| A. Hill c Athey b Graveney | 31 | G. Miller not out | 1 |
| J. E. Morris b Curran | 2 | | |
| B. Roberts c Stovold b Walsh | 48 | B 1, l-b 3, w 10, n-b 6 | 20 |
| W. P. Fowler not out | 7 | | |
| P. G. Newman b Walsh | 4 | 1/75 2/78 3/178 (7 wkts, 55 overs) | 202 |
| M. A. Holding b Shepherd | 3 | 4/185 5/191 6/194 7/194 | |

†B. J. M. Maher and O. H. Mortensen did not bat.

Bowling: Lawrence 11–1–31–0; Walsh 11–0–43–2; Shepherd 11–0–49–2; Graveney 11–2–23–1; Curran 11–1–52–2.

### Gloucestershire

| | |
|---|---|
| A. W. Stovold c Warner b Mortensen | 28 |
| P. W Romaines c Roberts b Warner | 21 |
| C. W. J. Athey not out | 2 |
| P. Bainbridge not out | 0 |
| W 3, n-b 1 | 4 |
| 1/43 2/55 (2 wkts, 21 overs) | 55 |

B. F. Davison, K. M. Curran, J. N. Shepherd, D. V. Lawrence, *D. A. Graveney, †R. C. Russell and C. A. Walsh did not bat.

Bowling: Holding 5–1–10–0; Mortensen 10.2–1–35–1; Warner 6–3–10–1.

Umpires: H. D. Bird and J. A. Jameson.

## NOTTINGHAMSHIRE v NORTHAMPTONSHIRE

At Trent Bridge, May 18, 20. No result. Toss won by Northamptonshire. No play was possible on the second day.

### Nottinghamshire

B. C. Broad c Mallender b Harper .... 70
R. T. Robinson c Mallender b Harper . 39
D. W. Randall c and b Harper ....... 54
*C. E. B. Rice c Cook b Mallender ... 36
R. J. Hadlee not out ................ 29
J. D. Birch c Harper b Walker ....... 3
K. P. Evans not out ................. 2
B 1, l-b 5, w 1, n-b 2 ........ 9

1/82 2/156 3/173 4/217 5/227 (5 wkts, 55 overs) 242

†B. N. French, E. E. Hemmings, K. E. Cooper and K. Saxelby did not bat.

Bowling: Mallender 11–0–71–1; Griffiths 11–2–24–0; Walker 11–1–62–1; Williams 11–1–31–0; Harper 11–0–48–3.

### Northamptonshire

*G. Cook not out .................. 7
W. Larkins c Birch b Hadlee ......... 0
R. G. Williams not out .............. 20
W 1, n-b 1 ................ 2

1/1 (1 wkt, 8 overs) 29

A. J. Lamb, R. J. Bailey, D. J. Capel, R. A. Harper, †G. Sharp, N. A. Mallender, A. Walker and B. J. Griffiths did not bat.

Bowling: Hadlee 4–0–14–1; Saxelby 3–0–15–0; Cooper 1–1–0–0.

Umpires: A. A. Jones and R. Julian.

## GROUP B

## LANCASHIRE v LEICESTERSHIRE

At Old Trafford, May 4, 6. Leicestershire won by three wickets. Toss won by Leicestershire. *Gold Award:* J. C. Balderstone.

### Lancashire

G. Fowler c Garnham b Ferris ....... 12
J. A. Ormrod run out ............... 0
S. J. O'Shaughnessy b Parsons ........ 11
K. A. Hayes b Ferris ............... 0
*J. Abrahams run out ............... 34
N. H. Fairbrother c Garnham b Parsons 4
M. Watkinson c Garnham b Parsons .. 34
J. Simmons c Garnham b Ferris ...... 0
†J. Stanworth not out ............... 8
P. J. W. Allott b Ferris ............. 1
B. P. Patterson not out .............. 15
B 6, l-b 14, w 2, n-b 4 ....... 26

1/2 2/22 3/22 4/26 5/35 6/111 7/111 8/120 9/121 (9 wkts, 55 overs) 145

Bowling: Ferris 11–1–31–4; Parsons 11–2–32–3; Clift 11–4–19–0; De Freitas 11–3–25–0; Willey 11–4–18–0.

### Leicestershire

I. P. Butcher c Ormrod b Watkinson .. 14
J. C. Balderstone not out ............ 58
*D. I. Gower c Ormrod b O'Shaughnessy 24
P. Willey c Abrahams b Simmons ..... 1
J. J. Whitaker b O'Shaughnessy ...... 0
N. E. Briers b O'Shaughnessy ........ 19
†M. A. Garnham b O'Shaughnessy .... 2
G. J. Parsons b Patterson ........... 0
P. B. Clift not out .................. 11
L-b 13, n-b 5 .............. 18

1/32 2/73 3/74 4/77 5/113 6/117 7/118 (7 wkts, 53.2 overs) 147

G. J. F. Ferris and P. A. J. De Freitas did not bat.

Bowling: Allott 9.2–1–35–0; Patterson 11–1–34–1; Watkinson 9–1–32–1; Simmons 11–8–5–1; O'Shaughnessy 11–5–17–4; Abrahams 2–0–11–0.

Umpires: K. J. Lyons and N. T. Plews.

## WORCESTERSHIRE v WARWICKSHIRE

At Worcester, May 4. Worcestershire won by 4 runs. Toss won by Warwickshire.
*Gold Award:* D. M. Smith.

### Worcestershire

M. J. Weston lbw b Small ........... 0
T. S. Curtis b Small ................. 75
D. M. Smith c Amiss b Ferreira ......126
Kapil Dev c Kallicharran b Wall ..... 32
D. N. Patel b Ferreira ............... 3
*P. A. Neale run out ............... 0
D. B. D'Oliveira run out ............ 9
J. D. Inchmore run out .............. 0
N. V. Radford not out ............... 13
†S. J. Rhodes not out ................ 3
B 4, l-b 5, w 6, n-b 1 ........ 16

1/1 2/175 3/236 4/251 5/251 6/251 7/252 8/269 (8 wkts, 55 overs) 277

R. K. Illingworth did not bat.

Bowling: Small 11–1–47–2; Old 10–1–41–0; Gifford 11–0–31–0; Ferreira 10–0–72–2; Wall 8–0–45–1; Kallicharran 5–0–32–0.

### Warwickshire

T. A. Lloyd run out .................. 22
R. I. H. B. Dyer run out ............ 9
A. I. Kallicharran st Rhodes b Illingworth.104
D. L. Amiss c Rhodes b Weston ...... 12
†G. W. Humpage run out ............ 62
P. A. Smith c Patel b Kapil Dev ...... 18
A. M. Ferreira b Radford ........... 5
C. M. Old not out ................... 17
B 1, l-b 19, w 4 ............ 24

1/22 2/40 3/61 4/217 5/234 6/241 7/272 (7 wkts, 55 overs) 273

G. C. Small, S. Wall and *N. Gifford did not bat.

Bowling: Kapil Dev 11–2–44–1; Radford 11–1–50–1; Inchmore 11–2–44–0; Weston 11–0–55–1; Illingworth 5–0–23–1; Patel 6–0–37–0.

Umpires: P. B. Wight and B. Dudleston.

## LEICESTERSHIRE v YORKSHIRE

At Leicester, May 11. Yorkshire won by 1 run. Toss won by Leicestershire.
*Gold Award:* D. L. Bairstow.

### Yorkshire

A. Sidebottom b Ferris ............... 21
M. D. Moxon run out ................ 37
K. Sharp c Balderstone b Agnew ...... 3
J. D. Love not out .................. 90
P. E. Robinson c Gower b Clift ...... 42
*†D. L. Bairstow not out ............ 31
B 2, l-b 11, w 2, n-b 5 ....... 20

1/31 2/36 3/90 4/176 (4 wkts, 55 overs) 244

D. Byas, P. Carrick, G. B. Stevenson, P. W. Jarvis and S. D. Fletcher did not bat.

Bowling: Ferris 11–2–63–1; Agnew 11–3–34–1; Parsons 11–0–44–0; Clift 11–0–55–1; Willey 11–0–35–0.

### Leicestershire

| | | | |
|---|---|---|---|
| I. P. Butcher run out | 101 | G. J. Parsons not out | 25 |
| J. C. Balderstone c Bairstow b Sidebottom | 26 | J. P. Agnew run out | 1 |
| *D. I. Gower c Stevenson b Sidebottom | 0 | G. J. F. Ferris not out | 0 |
| P. Willey c Bairstow b Jarvis | 60 | L-b 4, w 2, n-b 5 | 11 |
| J. J. Whitaker c Bairstow b Jarvis | 0 | | —— |
| N. E. Briers c Bairstow b Jarvis | 2 | 1/38 2/38 3/150 (9 wkts, 55 overs) | 243 |
| P. B. Clift run out | 9 | 4/150 5/157 6/175 7/201 | |
| †M. A. Garnham c Bairstow b Stevenson | 8 | 8/237 9/241 | |

Bowling: Sidebottom 11–0–41–2; Jarvis 11–1–39–3; Stevenson 11–0–64–1; Carrick 11–0–34–0; Fletcher 11–0–61–0.

Umpires: A. G. T. Whitehead and C. Cook.

## WARWICKSHIRE v LANCASHIRE

At Edgbaston, May 11. Warwickshire won by 63 runs. Toss won by Lancashire.
*Gold Award:* T. A. Lloyd.

### Warwickshire

| | | | |
|---|---|---|---|
| T. A. Lloyd not out | 137 | †G. W. Humpage c Fowler b Makinson | 8 |
| R. I. H. B. Dyer b Simmons | 40 | P. A. Smith not out | 14 |
| D. L. Amiss c Watkinson b O'Shaughnessy | 16 | B 1, l-b 8, n-b 1 | 10 |
| | | | —— |
| A. I. Kallicharran c Fairbrother b Jefferies | 57 | 1/119 2/140 (4 wkts, 55 overs) | 282 |
| | | 3/235 4/259 | |

A. M. Ferreira, C. Lethbridge, G. C. Small, S. Wall and *N. Gifford did not bat.

Bowling: Allott 11–3–33–0; Jefferies 7–0–45–1; Makinson 10–0–60–1; Simmons 11–2–33–1; Watkinson 6–0–42–0; O'Shaughnessy 10–0–60–1.

### Lancashire

| | | | |
|---|---|---|---|
| G. Fowler c and b Wall | 9 | †C. Maynard c Kallicharran b Ferreira | 41 |
| D. W. Varey c Humpage b Small | 8 | P. J. W. Allott c Lethbridge b Ferreira | 2 |
| S. J. O'Shaughnessy c Wall b Gifford | 66 | D. J. Makinson not out | 0 |
| N. H. Fairbrother b Smith | 6 | L-b 7, w 7, n-b 3 | 17 |
| *J. Abrahams c Smith b Ferreira | 5 | | —— |
| M. Watkinson b Smith | 0 | 1/13 2/17 3/37 (52 overs) | 219 |
| S. T. Jefferies c Small b Gifford | 32 | 4/52 5/53 6/121 7/149 | |
| J. Simmons c and b Small | 33 | 8/210 9/219 | |

Bowling: Small 8–2–18–2; Wall 11–1–31–1; Smith 7–0–30–2; Ferreira 10–0–48–3; Lethbridge 5–0–37–0; Gifford 11–0–48–2.

Umpires: J. H. Harris and B. J. Meyer.

## LANCASHIRE v YORKSHIRE

At Old Trafford, May 14, 15. Lancashire won by 2 runs in a match reduced by rain to 32 overs a side, no play being possible until 2.40 on the second day. Toss won by Yorkshire.
*Gold Award:* S. J. O'Shaughnessy.

### Lancashire

| | | | |
|---|---|---|---|
| G. Fowler st Bairstow b Carrick | 29 | J. Simmons not out | 3 |
| D. W. Varey c Bairstow b Sidebottom | 5 | P. J. W. Allott c Moxon b Stevenson | 4 |
| S. J. O'Shaughnessy c Bairstow b Fletcher | 48 | D. J. Makinson b Jarvis | 5 |
| C. H. Lloyd c Moxon b Stevenson | 8 | L-b 7, w 2 | 9 |
| N. H. Fairbrother b Stevenson | 16 | | |
| *J. Abrahams c Bairstow b Jarvis | 18 | 1/15 2/52 3/84 (31.5 overs) | 146 |
| M. Watkinson b Stevenson | 0 | 4/101 5/125 6/131 7/133 | |
| †C. Maynard c Fletcher b Jarvis | 1 | 8/133 9/138 | |

Bowling: Sidebottom 7–0–21–1; Jarvis 6.5–0–34–3; Carrick 6–0–35–1; Fletcher 6–0–23–1; Stevenson 6–0–26–4.

### Yorkshire

| | | | |
|---|---|---|---|
| D. Byas lbw b Makinson | 2 | A. Sidebottom b Watkinson | 7 |
| M. D. Moxon c Maynard b O'Shaughnessy | 24 | P. Carrick not out | 16 |
| K. Sharp run out | 45 | P. W. Jarvis c Varey b Allott | 3 |
| G. B. Stevenson b O'Shaughnessy | 3 | S. D. Fletcher not out | 0 |
| J. D. Love b O'Shaughnessy | 12 | L-b 7, n-b 2 | 9 |
| P. E. Robinson run out | 13 | 1/7 2/48 3/56 (9 wkts, 32 overs) | 144 |
| *†D. L. Bairstow c Fairbrother b Watkinson | 10 | 4/78 5/106 6/109 7/120 | |
| | | 8/132 9/140 | |

Bowling: Makinson 6–0–23–1; Allott 7–0–23–1; O'Shaughnessy 7–0–20–3; Simmons 6–0–27–0; Watkinson 6–0–44–2.

Umpires: B. Leadbeater and D. O. Oslear.

## LEICESTERSHIRE v WORCESTERSHIRE

At Leicester, May 14, 15. Leicestershire won by 17 runs in a match reduced by rain to 37 overs a side, no play being possible until 2.00 on the second day. Toss won by Worcestershire.
*Gold Award:* J. C. Balderstone.

### Leicestershire

| | | | |
|---|---|---|---|
| I. P. Butcher c Kapil Dev b Weston | 25 | P. B. Clift b Illingworth | 4 |
| J. C. Balderstone run out | 77 | †M. A. Garnham not out | 0 |
| *D. I. Gower c Radford b Patel | 37 | | |
| P. Willey c Smith b Kapil Dev | 15 | B 2, l-b 9, w 7 | 18 |
| J. J. Whitaker c and b Inchmore | 15 | | |
| G. J. Parsons not out | 16 | 1/52 2/126 3/148 (7 wkts, 37 overs) | 212 |
| N. E. Briers run out | 5 | 4/170 5/199 6/205 7/212 | |

J. P. Agnew and G. J. F. Ferris did not bat.

Bowling: Kapil Dev 6–1–25–1; Radford 7–0–36–0; Inchmore 6–0–39–1; Weston 3–0–22–1; Patel 8–0–34–1; Illingworth 7–0–45–1.

### Worcestershire

| | | | |
|---|---|---|---|
| M. J. Weston c Garnham b Parsons | 46 | J. D. Inchmore b Clift | 1 |
| T. S. Curtis b Willey | 21 | †S. J. Rhodes not out | 27 |
| D. M. Smith lbw b Ferris | 24 | | |
| Kapil Dev c Briers b Parsons | 0 | B 4, l-b 11, w 2 | 17 |
| D. N. Patel run out | 3 | | |
| *P. A. Neale not out | 43 | 1/48 2/88 3/88 (7 wkts, 37 overs) | 195 |
| D. B. D'Oliveira c Briers b Clift | 13 | 4/94 5/111 6/150 7/151 | |

N. V. Radford and R. K. Illingworth did not bat.

Bowling: Agnew 7–0–27–0; Clift 8–0–39–2; Parsons 7–1–53–2; Willey 8–0–20–1; Ferris 7–0–41–1.

Umpires: R. Palmer and J. H. Hampshire.

## WORCESTERSHIRE v LANCASHIRE

At Worcester, May 16. Worcestershire won by six wickets. Toss won by Worcestershire. *Gold Award:* P. A. Neale.

### Lancashire

G. Fowler c Rhodes b Radford ....... 8
D. W. Varey b Patel ................. 16
S. J. O'Shaughnessy run out ........... 90
*J. Abrahams c Rhodes b Patel ....... 57
C. H. Lloyd not out ................. 43
M. Watkinson lbw b Patel ........... 3
†C. Maynard not out ............... 22
B 2, l-b 9, w 6, n-b 2 ........ 19

1/13 2/57 3/185 4/188 5/193 (5 wkts, 55 overs) 258

P. J. W. Allott, D. J. Makinson, J. Simmons and S. Henriksen did not bat.

Bowling: Kapil Dev 11–0–51–0; Radford 9–3–34–1; Illingworth 11–1–42–0; Inchmore 11–1–48–0; Patel 11–0–50–3; D'Oliveira 2–0–22–0.

### Worcestershire

M. J. Weston b Makinson ........... 14
T. S. Curtis c and b O'Shaughnessy ... 19
D. M. Smith c Maynard b Watkinson . 41
*P. A. Neale not out ............... 94
D. N. Patel c Maynard b Makinson ... 16
D. B. D'Oliveira not out ............. 47
L-b 15, w 7, n-b 8 .......... 30

1/29 2/69 3/140 4/161 (4 wkts, 53.1 overs) 261

Kapil Dev, †S. J. Rhodes, J. D. Inchmore, N. V. Radford and R. K. Illingworth did not bat.

Bowling: Allott 11–1–41–0; Makinson 11–0–45–2; Henriksen 7–0–32–0; O'Shaughnessy 6–0–38–1; Simmons 10–1–42–0; Watkinson 8.1–0–48–1.

Umpires: A. A. Jones and D. O. Oslear.

## YORKSHIRE v WARWICKSHIRE

At Headingley, May 16. Yorkshire won by seven wickets. Toss won by Yorkshire. *Gold Award:* P. Carrick.

### Warwickshire

T. A. Lloyd c Hartley b Jarvis ........ 1
R. I. H. B. Dyer c Robinson b Jarvis .. 4
A. I. Kallicharran c Stevenson b Carrick 33
D. L. Amiss c Sharp b Stevenson ..... 35
†G. W. Humpage c Bairstow b Carrick 10
P. A. Smith c Bairstow b Stevenson ... 25
A. M. Ferreira b Sidebottom ......... 27
C. Lethbridge c Bairstow b Stevenson . 0
G. C. Small lbw b Stevenson ......... 4
S. Wall lbw b Jarvis ................. 6
*N. Gifford not out .................. 0
L-b 7, w 6, n-b 1 ........... 14

1/1 2/9 3/70 4/90 5/98 6/143 7/144 8/146 9/157 (53.1 overs) 159

Bowling: Sidebottom 11–2–21–1; Jarvis 10.1–2–31–3; Stevenson 10–1–34–4; Fletcher 11–0–32–0; Carrick 11–1–34–2.

### Yorkshire

| | | | |
|---|---|---|---|
| M. D. Moxon b Wall | 43 | S. N. Hartley not out | 4 |
| P. Carrick lbw b Small | 53 | L-b 11, w 8, n-b 9 | 28 |
| K. Sharp b Ferreira | 24 | | — |
| J. D. Love not out | 13 | 1/111 2/129 3/150 (3 wkts, 53 overs) | 165 |

A. Sidebottom, P. E. Robinson, *†D. L. Bairstow, G. B. Stevenson, P. W. Jarvis and S. D. Fletcher did not bat.

Bowling: Small 11–5–22–1; Wall 11–2–30–1; Ferreira 8–1–25–1; Smith 3–0–16–0; Lethbridge 9–1–38–0; Gifford 11–3–23–0.

Umpires: J. Birkenshaw and R. A. White.

## WARWICKSHIRE v LEICESTERSHIRE

At Edgbaston, May 18, 20. Leicestershire won by seven wickets. Toss won by Warwickshire. *Gold Award:* J. J. Whitaker.

### Warwickshire

| | | | |
|---|---|---|---|
| T. A. Lloyd lbw b Parsons | 21 | A. M. Ferreira not out | 42 |
| R. I. H. B. Dyer c Garnham b Agnew | 10 | | |
| A. I. Kallicharran c Garnham b Parsons | 55 | L-b 5, w 1, n-b 7 | 13 |
| D. L. Amiss c Garnham b Clift | 53 | | — |
| †G. W. Humpage not out | 51 | 1/33 2/33 3/147 (5 wkts, 55 overs) | 246 |
| P. A. Smith c Willey b Parsons | 1 | 4/151 5/153 | |

C. Lethbridge, G. C. Small, S. Wall and *N. Gifford did not bat.

Bowling: Agnew 11–1–68–1; Parsons 11–1–44–3; Clift 11–4–16–1; Ferris 11–0–74–0; Willey 11–0–39–0.

### Leicestershire

| | | | |
|---|---|---|---|
| I. P. Butcher c Humpage b Ferreira | 44 | J. J. Whitaker not out | 73 |
| J. C. Balderstone c Wall b Ferreira | 27 | L-b 11, w 3, n-b 2 | 16 |
| *D. I. Gower c Humpage b Small | 19 | | — |
| P. Willey not out | 68 | 1/41 2/96 3/101 (3 wkts, 51.5 overs) | 247 |

N. E. Briers, P. B. Clift, †M. A. Garnham, G. J. Parsons, J. P. Agnew and G. J. F. Ferris did not bat.

Bowling: Small 11–2–35–1; Wall 9–3–35–0; Ferreira 10.5–1–56–2; Smith 4–0–29–0; Gifford 11–0–36–0; Lethbridge 5–0–33–0; Kallicharran 1–0–12–0.

Umpires: K. E. Palmer and P. B. Wight.

## YORKSHIRE v WORCESTERSHIRE

At Bradford, May 18. Worcestershire won by 84 runs. Toss won by Yorkshire. *Gold Award:* A. Sidebottom.

### Worcestershire

M. J. Weston lbw b Sidebottom ...... 0
T. S. Curtis b Jarvis ............... 50
D. M. Smith c Bairstow b Sidebottom . 77
*P. A. Neale c Swallow b Booth ...... 35
D. N. Patel c Moxon b Booth ........ 1
D. B. D'Oliveira c Bairstow b Sidebottom 7
Kapil Dev b Sidebottom ............. 1
†S. J. Rhodes lbw b Sidebottom ...... 3
N. V. Radford c Swallow b Jarvis ..... [illegible]
J. D. Inchmore not out .............. 1[illegible]
R. K. Illingworth not out ............ [illegible]
B 1, l-b 7, w 2, n-b 1 ........ 1[illegible]

1/2 2/111 3/164 4/167 5/173 6/180 7/181 8/184 9/198 (9 wkts, 55 overs) 21[illegible]

Bowling: Sidebottom 11–4–27–5; Jarvis 9–1–46–2; Swallow 11–1–42–0; Carrick 11–0–27–0 Stevenson 5–0–36–0; Booth 8–0–28–2.

### Yorkshire

M. D. Moxon c Kapil Dev b Radford . 6
P. Carrick c Rhodes b Kapil Dev ..... 5
K. Sharp c and b Weston ............ 10
J. D. Love b Inchmore .............. 11
S. N. Hartley c Patel b Weston ....... 16
*†D. L. Bairstow c Rhodes b Illingworth. 15
G. B. Stevenson c Rhodes b Illingworth 2
A. Sidebottom c Kapil Dev b Illingworth 21
I. G. Swallow not out ............... 1[illegible]
P. W. Jarvis b Illingworth ........... 2[illegible]
P. A. Booth c Rhodes b Patel ........ [illegible]
B 1, l-b 8, w 2, n-b 2 ........ 1[illegible]

1/9 2/11 3/27 4/45 5/66 6/69 7/86 8/103 9/128 (50.4 overs) 13[illegible]

Bowling: Kapil Dev 7–4–6–1; Radford 6–1–11–1; Inchmore 8–1–20–1; Weston 11–2–27–2 Illingworth 11–2–36–4; Patel 7.4–0–21–1.

Umpires: R. Palmer and R. A. White.

## GROUP C

## ESSEX v SUSSEX

At Chelmsford, May 4, 6. Essex won by five wickets. Toss won by Essex.
*Gold Award:* G. A. Gooch.

### Sussex

G. D. Mendis b Foster .............. 14
A. M. Green run out ................ 38
P. W. G. Parker c East b Lever ...... 4
A. P. Wells b Gooch ................ 21
C. M. Wells lbw b Turner ........... 1
*J. R. T. Barclay not out ........... 29
I. A. Greig c Hardie b Gooch ........ 0
†I. J. Gould c East b Foster .......... 13
G. S. le Roux lbw b Foster .......... [illegible]
D. A. Reeve b Foster ............... [illegible]
A. N. Jones b Pringle ............... [illegible]
B 12, w 4, n-b 3 ........... 1[illegible]

1/21 2/40 3/72 4/77 5/89 6/89 7/123 8/123 9/130 (51.2 overs) 14[illegible]

Bowling: Lever 9–1–28–1; Foster 11–1–39–4; Pringle 9.2–1–21–1; Gooch 11–3–23–2 Turner 11–2–20–1.

### Essex

G. A. Gooch b Greig ............... 46
P. J. Prichard b Greig .............. 32
B. R. Hardie b le Roux ............. 27
K. S. McEwan c Gould b le Roux .... 9
D. R. Pringle c Greig b le Roux ...... 0
*K. W. R. Fletcher not out .......... 12
A. W. Lilley not out ............... [illegible]
L-b 1, w 1, n-b 7 .......... [illegible]

1/77 2/84 3/108 4/108 5/130 (5 wkts, 39.2 overs) 14[illegible]

S. Turner, †D. E. East, N. A. Foster and J. K. Lever did not bat.

Bowling: le Roux 11–2–39–3; Reeve 6–2–22–0; Greig 11–3–29–2; C. M. Wells 2–0–16–0 Barclay 6–1–15–0; Jones 3.2–0–22–0.

Umpires: J. A. Jameson and B. Leadbeater.

## SURREY v OXFORD & CAMBRIDGE UNIVS

At The Oval, May 4. Surrey won by seven wickets. Toss won by Oxford & Cambridge Univs.
*Gold Award:* T. E. Jesty.

### Oxford & Cambridge Univs

C. R. Andrew c Richards b Pauline . . . 24
*A. J. T. Miller c Butcher b Jesty . . . . . 57
G. J. Toogood b Pauline . . . . . . . . . . . . 2
D. J. Carr c Richards b Jesty . . . . . . . . 0
P. G. P. Roebuck lbw b Jesty . . . . . . . . 15
D. J. Fell c Clinton b Monkhouse . . . . . 31
D. A. Thorne c Lynch b Jesty . . . . . . . . 1
J. G. Franks b Monkhouse . . . . . . . . . . 0
†A. G. Davies c Richards b Monkhouse 13
A. D. H. Grimes not out . . . . . . . . . . . . 0
A. M. G. Scott not out . . . . . . . . . . . . . . 2
B 6, l-b 9, w 4, n-b 2 . . . . . . . . 21

1/59 2/80 3/87 (9 wkts, 55 overs) 166
4/109 5/109 6/113 7/119
8/162 9/162

Bowling: Thomas 8–2–14–0; Taylor 5–2–16–0; Monkhouse 11–0–47–3; Pauline 10–2–28–2; Jesty 11–0–23–4; Pocock 10–3–23–0.

### Surrey

A. R. Butcher b Grimes . . . . . . . . . . . . . 1
G. S. Clinton c Franks b Andrew . . . . . 63
D. B. Pauline not out . . . . . . . . . . . . . . . 69
M. A. Lynch c Davies b Carr . . . . . . . . 11
A. Needham not out . . . . . . . . . . . . . . . . 8
L-b 11, w 3, n-b 1 . . . . . . . . . . . 15

1/8 2/131 3/147 (3 wkts, 42.2 overs) 167

T. E. Jesty, †C. J. Richards, D. J. Thomas, G. Monkhouse, N. S. Taylor and *P. I. Pocock did not bat.

Bowling: Grimes 9–2–23–1; Thorne 11–2–29–0; Scott 8–2–32–0; Toogood 2–0–13–0; Andrew 4–0–15–1; Carr 6–1–30–1; Fell 1.2–0–7–0; Miller 1–0–7–0.

Umpires: D. J. Constant and R. Palmer.

## OXFORD & CAMBRIDGE UNIVS v MIDDLESEX

At Fenner's, Cambridge, May 11. Middlesex won by nine wickets. Toss won by Oxford & Cambridge Univs.
*Gold Award:* P. H. Edmonds.

### Oxford & Cambridge Univs

C. R. Andrew b Edmonds . . . . . . . . . . . 38
*A. J. T. Miller b Daniel . . . . . . . . . . . . 3
G. J. Toogood b Edmonds . . . . . . . . . . . 15
J. D. Carr st Downton b Emburey . . . . 8
P. G. P. Roebuck b Edmonds . . . . . . . . 33
D. A. Thorne c Radley b Williams . . . . 7
D. J. Fell st Downton b Edmonds . . . . . 10
†A. G. Davies b Daniel . . . . . . . . . . . . . 5
T. A. Cotterell st Downton b Edmonds 6
C. C. Ellison not out . . . . . . . . . . . . . . . 1
A. M. G. Scott not out . . . . . . . . . . . . . . 0
L-b 7, w 2, n-b 3 . . . . . . . . . . . 12

1/15 2/50 3/63 (9 wkts, 55 overs) 138
4/82 5/93 6/109 7/130
8/137 9/138

Bowling: Daniel 11–3–22–2; Williams 11–2–23–1; Fraser 11–1–24–0; Emburey 11–4–19–1; Edmonds 11–2–43–5.

### Middlesex

G. D. Barlow st Davies b Cotterell . . . . 34
W. N. Slack not out . . . . . . . . . . . . . . . 58
*M. W. Gatting not out . . . . . . . . . . . . . 39
B 3, l-b 5 . . . . . . . . . . . . . . . . . . . . 8

1/86 (1 wkt, 39.1 overs) 139

K. P. Tomlins, C. T. Radley, †P. R. Downton, J. E. Emburey, P. H. Edmonds, N. F. Williams, A. R. C. Fraser and W. W. Daniel did not bat.

Bowling: Thorne 5–0–16–0; Ellison 4.1–0–12–0; Scott 4–0–16–0; Carr 11–2–23–0; Cotterell 11–2–38–1; Andrew 4–1–26–0.

Umpires: J. Birkenshaw and R. A. White.

## SUSSEX v SURREY

At Hove, May 11. Sussex won by three wickets. Toss won by Sussex.
*Gold Award:* G. S. le Roux.

### Surrey

| | |
|---|---|
| A. R. Butcher c Gould b le Roux | 24 |
| G. S. Clinton c C. M. Wells b Imran | 5 |
| A. J. Stewart c Gould b Imran | 1 |
| T. E. Jesty c A. P. Wells b C. M. Wells | 61 |
| M. A. Lynch lbw b le Roux | 9 |
| D. B. Pauline lbw b le Roux | 1 |
| †C. J. Richards c and b C. M. Wells | 1 |
| D. J. Thomas c Gould b Imran | 7 |
| G. Monkhouse not out | 24 |
| *P. I. Pocock c Reeve b le Roux | 14 |
| N. S. Taylor b Greig | 2 |
| L-b 18, w 2, n-b 1 | 21 |
| 1/20 2/30 3/65 4/89 5/94 6/103 7/127 8/128 9/160 (52.3 overs) | 170 |

Bowling: Imran 11–2–24–3; le Roux 11–0–40–4; Reeve 10–3–44–0; Greig 9.3–1–31–1; C. M. Wells 11–5–13–2.

### Sussex

| | |
|---|---|
| G. D. Mendis b Thomas | 42 |
| A. M. Green c and b Taylor | 2 |
| P. W. G. Parker lbw b Thomas | 0 |
| A. P. Wells c Richards b Jesty | 62 |
| C. M. Wells c and b Pauline | 19 |
| Imran Khan c Richards b Monkhouse | 14 |
| *J. R. T. Barclay not out | 20 |
| I. A. Greig c Richards b Monkhouse | 1 |
| †I. J. Gould not out | 2 |
| B 2, l-b 4, w 4, n-b 2 | 12 |
| 1/2 2/3 3/106 4/123 5/149 6/151 7/163 (7 wkts, 54 overs) | 174 |

D. A. Reeve and G. S. le Roux did not bat.

Bowling: Thomas 10–2–34–2; Taylor 8–1–30–1; Monkhouse 10–1–30–2; Jesty 10–1–30–1; Pocock 11–2–31–0; Pauline 5–2–13–1.

Umpires: B. Dudleston and R. Julian.

## SURREY v ESSEX

At The Oval, May 14, 15. Essex won by nine wickets. Toss won by Essex.
*Gold Award:* N. A. Foster.

### Surrey

| | |
|---|---|
| A. R. Butcher c East b Foster | 13 |
| G. S. Clinton lbw b Foster | 4 |
| A. J. Stewart c Gooch b Turner | 16 |
| T. E. Jesty not out | 69 |
| M. A. Lynch c Gooch b Turner | 7 |
| D. B. Pauline c Prichard b Gooch | 8 |
| †C. J. Richards c East b Pringle | 3 |
| D. J. Thomas lbw b Foster | 4 |
| G. Monkhouse c McEwan b Foster | 5 |
| *P. I. Pocock c East b Foster | 0 |
| N. S. Taylor b Lever | 0 |
| L-b 4, w 6 | 10 |
| 1/7 2/19 3/55 4/75 5/116 6/124 7/128 8/138 9/138 (46.5 overs) | 139 |

Bowling: Lever 7.5–1–29–1; Foster 8–0–32–5; Pringle 9–2–18–1; Turner 11–2–23–2; Gooch 11–1–33–1.

### Essex

G. A. Gooch lbw b Pocock .......... 81
P. J. Prichard retired hurt .......... 4
B. R. Hardie not out .......... 43
K. S. McEwan not out .......... 7
L-b 1, w 3, n-b 1 .......... 5

1/126 (1 wkt, 34.4 overs) 140

D. R. Pringle, *K. W. R. Fletcher, A. W. Lilley, S. Turner, †D. E. East, N. A. Foster and J. K. Lever did not bat.

Bowling: Thomas 11–3–28–0; Taylor 5.4–0–38–0; Pauline 6–0–40–0; Monkhouse 4–0–19–0; Pocock 6–1–12–1; Butcher 2–1–2–0.

Umpires: A. A. Jones and R. Julian.

## SUSSEX v MIDDLESEX

At Hove, May 14, 15. Middlesex won by 31 runs. Toss won by Sussex.
*Gold Award:* M. W. Gatting.

### Middlesex

G. D. Barlow lbw b Greig .......... 19
W. N. Slack lbw b le Roux .......... 1
*M. W. Gatting not out .......... 143
R. O. Butcher c Parker b le Roux .......... 29
C. T. Radley c Imran b C. M. Wells .......... 40
†P. R. Downton run out .......... 1
J. E. Emburey not out .......... 18
L-b 20, w 4, n-b 5 .......... 29

1/8 2/46 3/108 4/216 5/219 (5 wkts, 55 overs) 280

P. H. Edmonds, N. F. Williams, A. R. C. Fraser and W. W. Daniel did not bat.

Bowling: le Roux 11–1–49–2; Reeve 11–0–56–0; Greig 11–0–58–1; Imran 11–3–48–0; C. M. Wells 11–0–49–1.

### Sussex

G. D. Mendis b Emburey .......... 15
A. M. Green b Daniel .......... 9
P. W. G. Parker c Radley b Edmonds .......... 48
A. P. Wells b Fraser .......... 38
Imran Khan c Slack b Edmonds .......... 10
C. M. Wells c Fraser b Daniel .......... 55
I. A. Greig c Radley b Daniel .......... 31
G. S. le Roux run out .......... 21
†I. J. Gould not out .......... 3
*J. R. T. Barclay b Williams .......... 0
D. A. Reeve b Daniel .......... 3
B 2, l-b 6, w 1, n-b 7 .......... 16

1/13 2/43 3/119 4/119 5/153 6/204 7/237 8/243 9/244 (53.4 overs) 249

Bowling: Daniel 10.4–1–58–4; Williams 11–0–47–1; Fraser 11–1–48–1; Emburey 10–3–40–1; Edmonds 11–0–48–2.

Umpires: K. J. Lyons and K. E. Palmer.

## MIDDLESEX v ESSEX

At Lord's, May 16. Essex won by four wickets, after dismissing Middlesex for 73, their lowest Benson and Hedges Cup innings total. Toss won by Essex.
*Gold Award:* J. K. Lever.

### Middlesex

| | | | |
|---|---|---|---|
| G. D. Barlow c Hardie b Lever | 0 | N. F. Williams lbw b Pringle | 3 |
| W. N. Slack b Turner | 11 | A. R. C. Fraser c Gooch b Foster | 0 |
| *M. W. Gatting b Lever | 1 | W. W. Daniel c East b Foster | 2 |
| R. O. Butcher c Pringle b Lever | 2 | W 1 | 1 |
| C. T. Radley lbw b Lever | 6 | | — |
| †P. R. Downton c Hardie b Lever | 7 | 1/0 2/6 3/12 (29.1 overs) | 73 |
| J. E. Emburey not out | 38 | 4/14 5/24 6/27 7/49 | |
| P. H. Edmonds b Foster | 2 | 8/64 9/65 | |

Bowling: Lever 11–4–13–5; Pringle 7–0–19–1; Turner 5–1–13–1; Foster 6.1–0–28–3.

### Essex

| | | | |
|---|---|---|---|
| G. A. Gooch c Slack b Fraser | 27 | †D. E. East not out | 0 |
| B. R. Hardie retired hurt | 4 | S. Turner not out | 1 |
| A. W. Lilley c Emburey b Williams | 1 | | |
| K. S. McEwan c Emburey b Williams | 4 | L-b 2, w 2, n-b 4 | 8 |
| D. R. Pringle c Downton b Daniel | 8 | | — |
| *K. W. R. Fletcher c Downton b Williams | 18 | 1/12 2/17 3/49 (6 wkts, 23 overs) | 74 |
| N. Phillip run out | 3 | 4/70 5/70 6/73 | |

N. A. Foster and J. K. Lever did not bat.

Bowling: Williams 11–5–20–3; Daniel 7–4–21–1; Fraser 5–0–31–1.

Umpires: R. Palmer and P. B. Wight.

## OXFORD & CAMBRIDGE UNIVS v SUSSEX

At The Parks, Oxford, May 16. Sussex won by 108 runs. Toss won by Oxford & Cambridge Univs.

*Gold Award:* Imran Khan.

### Sussex

| | | | |
|---|---|---|---|
| G. D. Mendis c Davies b Grimes | 0 | G. S. le Roux c Davies b Grimes | 5 |
| A. M. Green c Carr b Grimes | 10 | †I. J. Gould not out | 18 |
| P. W. G. Parker c Carr b Scott | 48 | | |
| A. P. Wells c Davies b Carr | 49 | L-b 6, w 7, n-b 6 | 19 |
| Imran Khan not out | 82 | | — |
| C. M. Wells c and b Grimes | 10 | 1/0 2/26 3/98 (7 wkts, 55 overs) | 241 |
| I. A. Greig lbw b Grimes | 0 | 4/152 5/177 6/177 7/201 | |

*J. R. T. Barclay and C. E. Waller did not bat.

Bowling: Grimes 11–1–36–5; Thorne 11–1–45–0; Cotterell 11–2–47–0; Carr 11–0–66–1; Scott 11–0–41–1.

### Oxford & Cambridge Univs

| | | | |
|---|---|---|---|
| *A. J. T. Miller b Waller | 41 | D. J. Fell c Parker b Greig | 6 |
| C. R. Andrew c Gould b Imran | 2 | †A. G. Davies not out | 4 |
| G. J. Toogood st Gould b Barclay | 2 | W 1 | 1 |
| J. D. Carr run out | 18 | | — |
| P. G. P. Roebuck not out | 31 | 1/4 2/11 3/62 (6 wkts, 55 overs) | 133 |
| D. A. Thorne b Greig | 28 | 4/68 5/120 6/126 | |

T. A. Cotterell, A. M. G. Scott and A. D. H. Grimes did not bat.

Bowling: le Roux 8–2–12–0; Imran 11–3–16–1; Barclay 10–0–31–1; Waller 11–4–21–1; C. M. Wells 9–2–20–0; Green 3–1–22–0; Greig 3–0–11–2.

Umpires: B. Dudleston and J. H. Harris.

## ESSEX v OXFORD & CAMBRIDGE UNIVS

At Chelmsford, May 18. Essex won by 130 runs. Toss won by Essex. Off the last ball of the Essex innings, Fletcher was run out going for the run which brought up McEwan's hundred, but in the absence of an appeal he was not given out by umpire Oslear and McEwan's score of 100 not out was allowed to stand.
*Gold Award:* G. A. Gooch.

### Essex

| | |
|---|---|
| G. A. Gooch b Cotterell . . . . . . . . . . . . . 89 | *K. W. R. Fletcher not out . . . . . . . . . . 0 |
| B. R. Hardie c Davies b Thorne . . . . . .113 | L-b 3, w 12, n-b 3 . . . . . . . . . . 18 |
| A. W. Lilley c Thorne b Scott . . . . . . . . 8 | —— |
| K. S. McEwan not out . . . . . . . . . . . . . .100 | 1/126 2/149 3/318 (4 wkts, 55 overs) 333 |
| D. R. Pringle c Thorne b Grimes . . . . . 5 | 4/326 |

S. Turner, †D. E. East, N. A. Foster, N. Phillip and D. L. Acfield did not bat.

Bowling: Grimes 6–0–59–1; Thorne 9–0–67–1; Scott 11–1–48–1; Cotterell 11–1–60–1; Carr 11–1–54–0; Andrew 7–0–42–0.

### Oxford & Cambridge Univs

| | |
|---|---|
| *C. R. Andrew not out . . . . . . . . . . . . . . 82 | W. R. Bristowe b Pringle . . . . . . . . . . . . 0 |
| A. J. T. Miller c Gooch b Foster . . . . . . 1 | |
| D. J. Fell c East b Phillip . . . . . . . . . . . 4 | L-b 5, w 8, n-b 6 . . . . . . . . . . . 19 |
| J. D. Carr b Foster . . . . . . . . . . . . . . . . . 67 | —— |
| D. A. Thorne b Lilley . . . . . . . . . . . . . . . 28 | 1/11 2/17 3/143 (6 wkts, 55 overs) 203 |
| G. J. Toogood c and b Pringle . . . . . . . 2 | 4/200 5/203 6/203 |

†A. G. Davies, T. A. Cotterell, A. D. H. Grimes and A. M. G. Scott did not bat.

Bowling: Foster 11–1–39–2; Phillip 11–2–51–1; Acfield 11–2–33–0; Pringle 10–0–38–2; Turner 11–1–33–0; Lilley 1–0–4–1.

Umpires: D. O. Oslear and N. T. Plews.

## MIDDLESEX v SURREY

At Lord's, May 18. Surrey won by 8 runs. Toss won by Surrey.
*Gold Award:* A. R. Butcher.

### Surrey

| | |
|---|---|
| A. R. Butcher c and b Emburey . . . . . . 56 | D. J. Thomas not out . . . . . . . . . . . . . . 6 |
| G. S. Clinton not out . . . . . . . . . . . . . . .106 | L-b 9, w 1, n-b 4 . . . . . . . . . . . 14 |
| A. J. Stewart c Emburey b Daniel . . . . 12 | —— |
| T. E. Jesty c and b Emburey . . . . . . . . . 27 | 1/101 2/131 3/194 (4 wkts, 55 overs) 227 |
| M. A. Lynch run out . . . . . . . . . . . . . . . 6 | 4/208 |

A. Needham, †C. J. Richards, G. Monkhouse, P. A. Waterman and *P. I. Pocock did not bat.

Bowling: Daniel 11–1–53–1; Williams 11–1–62–0; Fraser 11–1–30–0; Edmonds 11–0–40 0; Emburey 11–1–33–2.

### Middlesex

| | |
|---|---|
| G. D. Barlow c Lynch b Butcher . . . . . . 44 | N. F. Williams not out . . . . . . . . . . . . . . 29 |
| W. N. Slack lbw b Butcher . . . . . . . . . . 20 | W. W. Daniel run out . . . . . . . . . . . . . . . 8 |
| *M. W. Gatting c Clinton b Pocock . . . 51 | A. R. C. Fraser c Richards b Monkhouse 2 |
| R. O. Butcher c Butcher b Pocock . . . . 18 | B 4, l-b 1, w 6, n-b 1 . . . . . . . . 12 |
| C. T. Radley b Pocock . . . . . . . . . . . . . . 11 | —— |
| †P. R. Downton c Waterman b Jesty . . 24 | 1/60 2/81 3/121 (53.2 overs) 219 |
| J. E. Emburey c Richards b Butcher . . . 0 | 4/135 5/174 6/174 7/174 |
| P. H. Edmonds lbw b Butcher . . . . . . . . 0 | 8/183 9/206 |

Bowling: Thomas 10–1–37–0; Waterman 6–0–27–0; Butcher 11–1–36–4; Monkhouse 10.2–0–54–1; Pocock 10–0–36–3; Jesty 6–0–24–1.

Umpires: C. Cook and J. H. Hampshire.

## GROUP D

## GLAMORGAN v KENT

At Cardiff, May 4. Kent won by 20 runs, despite a partnership of 102 between Ontong and Derrick, which was a Glamorgan record for the eighth wicket in all limited-overs competitions. Toss won by Kent.

*Gold Award:* E. A. E. Baptiste.

### Kent

M. R. Benson st Davies b Ontong ..... 25
S. G. Hinks c Ontong b Steele ........ 49
C. J. Tavaré c and b Steele .......... 8
†A. P. E. Knott c Hopkins b Holmes .. 23
D. G. Aslett c Steele b Ontong ....... 7
*C. S. Cowdrey c Barwick b Thomas .. 54
E. A. E. Baptiste run out ............ 4
G. W. Johnson not out .............. 14
G. R. Dilley not out ................ 10
B 1, l-b 4, w 2 ............ 7

1/76 2/84 3/90 4/101 5/152 6/163 7/184 (7 wkts, 55 overs) 201

D. L. Underwood and K. B. S. Jarvis did not bat.

Bowling: Thomas 9–1–38–1; Barwick 7–3–24–0; Ontong 11–2–20–2; Steele 11–1–44–2; Holmes 11–2–43–1; Derrick 6–0–27–0.

### Glamorgan

J. A. Hopkins b Jarvis .............. 8
A. L. Jones c and b Jarvis ........... 4
G. C. Holmes c Tavaré b Baptiste .... 4
Javed Miandad lbw b Baptiste ....... 14
Younis Ahmed c Aslett b Baptiste .... 5
J. F. Steele lbw b Baptiste ........... 0
*R. C. Ontong run out .............. 58
J. G. Thomas c Johnson b Cowdrey ... 5
J. Derrick c and b Baptiste .......... 42
†T. Davies c Tavaré b Jarvis ......... 7
S. R. Barwick not out ............... 6
B 6, l-b 12, n-b 10 .......... 28

1/7 2/21 3/22 4/41 5/42 6/43 7/58 8/160 9/169 (52.3 overs) 181

Bowling: Jarvis 9.3–3–38–3; Baptiste 10–0–30–5; Johnson 11–1–24–0; Cowdrey 11–0–35–1; Underwood 11–2–36–0.

Umpires: C. Cook and M. J. Kitchen.

## MINOR COUNTIES v SOMERSET

At Shrewsbury, May 4. Somerset won by seven wickets. Toss won by Somerset.

*Gold Award:* M. R. Davis.

### Minor Counties

F. L. Q. Handley c Gard b Davis ..... 5
W. M. Osman lbw b Botham ......... 1
P. J. Garner b Turner ............... 17
N. T. O'Brien c Rose b Davis ........ 2
S. G. Plumb b Botham ............... 0
*N. A. Riddell c Davis b Turner ...... 10
J. S. Hitchmough b Palmer .......... 4
†A. Griffiths not out ................ 11
W. G. Merry c Gard b Davis ........ 8
A. S. Barnard b Turner ............. 5
D. Surridge c Gard b Botham ........ 3
B 1, l-b 16, w 8, n-b 2 ....... 27

1/10 2/10 3/12 4/17 5/38 6/42 7/53 8/70 9/85 (34.5 overs) 93

Bowling: Davis 11–3–21–3; Botham 8.5–4–15–3; Palmer 4–0–18–1; Turner 10–2–22–3; Marks 1–1–0–0.

### Somerset

P. M. Roebuck b Plumb .............. 36
J. G. Wyatt lbw b Merry ............ 2
N. F. M. Popplewell b Hitchmough ... 20
B. C. Rose not out ................. 18
R. L. Ollis not out ................ 13
B 3, w 2 ........................... 5

1/3 2/44 3/74 (3 wkts, 39.2 overs) 94

*I. T. Botham, V. J. Marks, †T. Gard, G. V. Palmer, M. R. Davis and M. S. Turner did not bat.

Bowling: Merry 11–4–17–1; Barnard 7–4–7–0; Surridge 9–3–24–0; Hitchmough 9–0–33–1; Plumb 3.2–1–10–1.

Umpires: J. Birkenshaw and J. W. Holder.

## GLAMORGAN v MINOR COUNTIES

At Swansea, May 11. Glamorgan won by nine wickets. Toss won by Glamorgan.
*Gold Award:* S. R. Barwick.

### Minor Counties

F. L. Q. Handley c Hopkins b Thomas 0
W. M. Osman lbw b Barwick ......... 1
P. J. Garner c Steele b Thomas ....... 5
N. T. O'Brien c Steele b Barwick ..... 6
S. G. Plumb c Derrick b Barwick ..... 13
*N. A. Riddell b Holmes ............ 9
J. S. Hitchmough c Steele b Holmes ... 9
†A. Griffiths c Miandad b Holmes .... 17
W. G. Merry b Thomas ............. 7
D. Surridge c Younis b Barwick ...... 1
A. S. Barnard not out ............... 0
B 4, l-b 1, w 1, n-b 2 ........ 8

1/0 2/2 3/8 4/26 5/31 6/44 7/57 8/75 9/76 (32.1 overs) 76

Bowling: Thomas 8–2–26–3; Barwick 7.1–2–11–4; Holmes 11–4–26–3; Derrick 6–2–8–0.

### Glamorgan

J. A. Hopkins c Riddell b Surridge .... 18
G. C. Holmes not out ................ 53
S. P. Henderson not out ............. 1
L-b 1, w 1, n-b 3 ........... 5

1/64 (1 wkt, 20.2 overs) 77

Younis Ahmed, Javed Miandad, *R. C. Ontong, J. G. Thomas, J. Derrick, J. F. Steele, †T. Davies and S. R. Barwick did not bat.

Bowling: Merry 2–2–0–0; Barnard 7–2–15–0; Surridge 7–0–31–1; Hitchmough 3–0–19–0; Plumb 1.2–0–11–0.

Umpires: D. O. Oslear and D. R. Shepherd.

## KENT v HAMPSHIRE

At Canterbury, May 11, 13. Hampshire won by 90 runs. Toss won by Kent. A match begun on 11 May was declared void when rain and bad light ended play after only three overs. For the second match, R. M. Ellison replaced G. W. Johnson for Kent.
*Gold Award:* M. C. J. Nicholas.

### Hampshire

V. P. Terry b Dilley .................. 8
C. L. Smith c Ellison b Cowdrey ...... 25
*M. C. J. Nicholas b Underwood ..... 45
D. R. Turner b Ellison ............... 31
R. A. Smith c Hinks b Cowdrey ...... 30
J. J. E. Hardy c Benson b Cowdrey ... 4
N. G. Cowley b Baptiste ............. 11
K. D. James run out ................. 0
†R. J. Parks not out .................. 11
T. M. Tremlett not out ............... 17
L-b 19, w 10, n-b 4 .......... 33

1/20 2/90 3/97 4/152 5/161 6/180 7/180 8/189 (8 wkts, 43 overs) 215

C. A. Connor did not bat.

Bowling: Jarvis 4–0–27–0; Dilley 5–0–23–1; Baptiste 8–0–38–1; Ellison 9–0–41–1; Underwood 8–2–29–1; Cowdrey 9–0–38–3.

### Kent

M. R. Benson c Parks b Connor ...... 0
S. G. Hinks c C. L. Smith b Cowley .. 21
C. J. Tavaré c Parks b James ........ 12
D. G. Aslett c Turner b Tremlett ..... 49
*C. S. Cowdrey c James b Cowley .... 2
E. A. E. Baptiste c Parks b Nicholas .. 3
†A. P. E. Knott b Connor ........... 19
R. M. Ellison b Connor .............. 0
G. R. Dilley c Nicholas b Connor ..... 0
D. L. Underwood run out ............ 3
K. B. S. Jarvis not out ............... 0
B 4, l-b 5, w 4, n-b 3 ........ 16

1/1 2/33 3/39 4/44 5/50 6/103 7/103 8/104 9/123 (33.4 overs) 125

Bowling: Connor 7–1–27–4; James 6–0–16–1; Cowley 8–0–22–2; Nicholas 8–1–27–1; Tremlett 4.4–0–24–1.

Umpires: N. T. Plews and A. A. Jones.

## HAMPSHIRE v GLAMORGAN

At Southampton, May 14, 15. Hampshire won by 116 runs. Toss won by Glamorgan. *Gold Award:* C. G. Greenidge.

### Hampshire

C. G. Greenidge c and b Holmes ..... 99
V. P. Terry c Holmes b Thomas ...... 2
*M. C. J. Nicholas c Davies b Derrick . 74
R. A. Smith c Holmes b Thomas ..... 47
D. R. Turner b Barwick ............. 18
M. D. Marshall c Davies b Thomas ... 10
N. G. Cowley b Thomas ............ 6
K. D. James run out ................ 14
T. M. Tremlett c Davies b Barwick ... 1
†R. J. Parks not out ................ 0
B 1, l-b 19, w 2, n-b 1 ....... 23

1/9 2/157 3/211 4/253 5/270 6/272 7/283 8/284 9/294 (9 wkts, 55 overs) 294

C. A. Connor did not bat.

Bowling: Thomas 10–1–38–4; Barwick 10–0–43–2; Steele 4–0–36–0; Derrick 9–2–47–1; Ontong 11–0–55–0; Holmes 11–0–55–1.

### Glamorgan

J. A. Hopkins lbw b Connor ......... 5
G. C. Holmes c Turner b Marshall .... 36
S. P. Henderson c Nicholas b James ... 16
Javed Miandad st Parks b Cowley .... 57
Younis Ahmed c and b Marshall ...... 1
*R. C. Ontong c Parks b Tremlett .... 19
J. G. Thomas c Connor b Tremlett .... 9
J. Derrick c R. A. Smith b Cowley .... 6
J. F. Steele c Parks b Tremlett ....... 8
†T. Davies not out .................. 6
S. R. Barwick c and b Tremlett ....... 3
B 1, l-b 4, w 3, n-b 4 ........ 12

1/19 2/52 3/106 4/112 5/140 6/147 7/154 8/168 9/174 (46.1 overs) 178

Bowling: Marshall 8–2–18–2; James 11–0–41–1; Connor 9–0–34–1; Cowley 9–1–26–2; Tremlett 9.1–0–54–4.

Umpires: J. H. Harris and M. J. Kitchen.

## SOMERSET v KENT

At Taunton, May 14. Kent won by 102 runs. Toss won by Somerset.
*Gold Award:* C. J. Tavaré.

### Kent

M. R. Benson run out .............. 34
S. G. Hinks b Davis .............. 9
C. J. Tavaré b Davis ..............143
D. G. Aslett lbw b Palmer .............. 3
*C. S. Cowdrey c Botham b Palmer ... 41
E. A. E. Baptiste not out .............. 43
†A. P. E. Knott run out .............. 5
G. W. Johnson not out .............. 2
L-b 3, w 3, n-b 7 .............. 13

1/20 2/58 3/73 4/172 5/286 6/291 (6 wkts, 55 overs) 293

G. R. Dilley, D. L. Underwood and K. B. S. Jarvis did not bat.

Bowling: Botham 11–1–62–0; Davis 11–0–84–2; Turner 11–2–42–0; Palmer 11–1–56–2; Marks 11–1–46–0.

### Somerset

P. M. Roebuck b Dilley .............. 0
J. G. Wyatt b Cowdrey .............. 22
N. F. M. Popplewell b Underwood .... 37
R. L. Ollis c Tavaré b Baptiste ....... 2
*I. T. Botham c Knott b Cowdrey .... 45
V. J. Marks c Tavaré b Johnson ...... 29
R. J. Harden c Baptiste b Johnson .... 7
G. V. Palmer c Knott b Johnson ...... 2
M. R. Davis c Tavaré b Jarvis ....... 16
M. S. Turner c Baptiste b Jarvis ...... 19
†T. Gard not out .............. 1
L-b 5, w 3, n-b 3 .............. 11

1/2 2/37 3/40 4/101 5/135 6/148 7/152 8/152 9/180 (48.4 overs) 191

Bowling: Dilley 8–0–18–1; Jarvis 7.4–2–33–2; Baptiste 6–1–20–1; Cowdrey 7–0–51–2; Underwood 11–1–23–1; Johnson 9–0–41–3.

Umpires: B. Dudleston and D. G. L. Evans.

## HAMPSHIRE v SOMERSET

At Southampton, May 16. Hampshire won by seven wickets. Toss won by Somerset.
*Gold Award:* R. J. Parks.

### Somerset

J. G. Wyatt c Parks b Tremlett ....... 8
P. M. Roebuck c Parks b Tremlett .... 3
N. F. M. Popplewell c and b Nicholas 7
R. L. Ollis c Parks b James .............. 24
*I. T. Botham b Marshall .............. 48
V. J. Marks c Parks b Tremlett ....... 7
R. J. Harden c Parks b Marshall ...... 13
G. V. Palmer not out .............. 15
M. R. Davis b Connor .............. 4
M. S. Turner not out .............. 8
B 1, l-b 15, w 13, n-b 1 ...... 30

1/16 2/17 3/39 4/48 5/118 6/125 7/150 8/159 (8 wkts, 55 overs) 167

†T. Gard did not bat.

Bowling: Marshall 11–1–32–2; Connor 11–1–42–1; Tremlett 11–3–24–3; James 11–4–18–1; Nicholas 5–0–17–1; Cowley 6–2–18–0.

### Hampshire

| | | | |
|---|---|---|---|
| C. G. Greenidge c Ollis b Davis | 13 | D. R. Turner not out | 52 |
| V. P. Terry c Botham b Davis | 12 | L-b 5, w 6 | 11 |
| *M. C. J. Nicholas lbw b Palmer | 18 | | — |
| R. A. Smith not out | 63 | 1/23 2/25 3/62 (3 wkts, 46.5 overs) | 169 |

N. G. Cowley, M. D. Marshall, K. D. James, T. M. Tremlett, †R. J. Parks and C. A. Connor did not bat.

Bowling: Botham 11–3–27–0; Davis 10–2–35–2; Palmer 7–0–29–1; Turner 9.5–0–53–0; Marks 9–2–20–0.

Umpires: R. Julian and K. J. Lyons.

## KENT v MINOR COUNTIES

At Canterbury, May 16. Kent won by five wickets. Toss won by Kent.
*Gold Award:* D. L. Underwood.

### Minor Counties

| | | | |
|---|---|---|---|
| Mudassar Nazar b Underwood | 9 | D. Surridge lbw b Dilley | 0 |
| W. M. Osman c Hinks b Underwood | 5 | K. Arnold not out | 3 |
| R. J. Lanchbury c Hinks b Baptiste | 10 | | |
| S. Greensword c Baptiste b Jarvis | 28 | B 1, l-b 6, w 3, n-b 4 | 14 |
| *N. A. Riddell b Jarvis | 0 | | — |
| G. R. J. Roope c Tavaré b Jarvis | 11 | 1/17 2/28 3/35 (8 wkts, 55 overs) | 132 |
| S. G. Plumb not out | 37 | 4/73 5/73 6/76 | |
| †A. Griffiths b Dilley | 15 | 7/120 8/122 | |

P. C. Graham did not bat.

Bowling: Jarvis 10–1–42–3; Dilley 10–2–24–2; Underwood 11–7–6–2; Baptiste 11–4–23–1; Johnson 11–6–22–0; Cowdrey 2–0–8–0.

### Kent

| | | | |
|---|---|---|---|
| M. R. Benson c Roope b Surridge | 21 | †A. P. E. Knott not out | 0 |
| S. G. Hinks c Riddell b Surridge | 4 | | |
| C. J. Tavaré c Riddell b Plumb | 13 | B 1, l-b 4, w 11, n-b 1 | 17 |
| D. G. Aslett not out | 21 | | — |
| *C. S. Cowdrey run out | 49 | 1/17 2/42 3/50 (5 wkts, 37.4 overs) | 133 |
| E. A. E. Baptiste c Roope b Graham | 8 | 4/118 5/130 | |

G. W. Johnson, G. R. Dilley, D. L. Underwood and K. B. S. Jarvis did not bat.

Bowling: Surridge 11–3–27–2; Arnold 5–1–24–0; Plumb 9–1–36–1; Graham 8–2–35–1; Mudassar 4.4–2–6–0.

Umpires: C. Cook and J. A. Jameson.

## MINOR COUNTIES v HAMPSHIRE

At Reading, May 18. Hampshire won by 135 runs. Toss won by Hampshire.
*Gold Award:* C. G. Greenidge.

### Hampshire

C. G. Greenidge c Arnold b Greensword . 123
V. P. Terry c Griffiths b Barnard . . . . . 7
*M. C. J. Nicholas b Mudassar . . . . . . . 6
R. A. Smith run out . . . . . . . . . . . . . . . . 29
D. R. Turner not out . . . . . . . . . . . . . . . 63
M. D. Marshall c Barnard b Plumb . . . 2
N. G. Cowley run out . . . . . . . . . . . . . . 0
K. D. James run out . . . . . . . . . . . . . . . . 8
†R. J. Parks run out . . . . . . . . . . . . . . . . 6
T. M. Tremlett not out . . . . . . . . . . . . . . 0
B 2, l-b 14, w 4 . . . . . . . . . . . . 20

1/26 2/66 3/160 4/194 5/204 6/210 7/240 8/262 (8 wkts, 55 overs) 264

C. A. Connor did not bat.

Bowling: Surridge 10–2–30–0; Barnard 10–2–38–1; Mudassar 11–1–56–1; Arnold 8–0–55–0; Plumb 9–1–38–1; Greensword 7–0–31–1.

### Minor Counties

Mudassar Nazar lbw b James . . . . . . . . 13
W. M. Osman run out . . . . . . . . . . . . . . 2
R. J. Lanchbury b Connor . . . . . . . . . . . 0
S. Greensword b Nicholas . . . . . . . . . . . 30
G. R. J. Roope lbw b Marshall . . . . . . . 14
S. G. Plumb b Cowley . . . . . . . . . . . . . . 17
*N. A. Riddell c Parks b Nicholas . . . . 14
†A. Griffiths c and b Nicholas . . . . . . . . 11
K. Arnold b Nicholas . . . . . . . . . . . . . . . 2
D. Surridge not out . . . . . . . . . . . . . . . . . 3
A. S. Barnard b Connor . . . . . . . . . . . . . 10
B 2, l-b 7, w 3, n-b 1 . . . . . . . . 13

1/19 2/19 3/19 4/41 5/68 6/98 7/109 8/113 9/116 (46.2 overs) 129

Bowling: Connor 8.2–4–16–2; James 6–3–12–1; Tremlett 7–3–16–0; Marshall 4–1–10–1; Cowley 11–1–32–1; Nicholas 10–2–34–4.

Umpires: D. J. Constant and K. J. Lyons.

## SOMERSET v GLAMORGAN

At Taunton, May 18. Glamorgan won by 93 runs. Toss won by Glamorgan.
*Gold Award:* R. C. Ontong.

### Glamorgan

J. A. Hopkins c Ollis b Botham . . . . . . 4
G. C. Holmes c Popplewell b Turner . . 70
Younis Ahmed c Wyatt b Marks . . . . . . 55
Javed Miandad run out . . . . . . . . . . . . . 57
S. P. Henderson run out . . . . . . . . . . . . . 2
*R. C. Ontong c Gard b Davis . . . . . . . 15
J. G. Thomas c Davis b Botham . . . . . . 0
J. Derrick not out . . . . . . . . . . . . . . . . . . 12
J. F. Steele run out . . . . . . . . . . . . . . . . . 0
†T. Davies run out . . . . . . . . . . . . . . . . . . 3
S. R. Barwick run out . . . . . . . . . . . . . . . 1
L-b 7, w 10, n-b 1 . . . . . . . . . . 18

1/5 2/102 3/187 4/192 5/214 6/218 7/222 8/223 9/235 (54 overs) 237

Bowling: Botham 11–1–43–2, Davis 10–0–43–1; Palmer 11–0–58–0; Turner 11–0–39–1; Marks 11–1–47–1.

### Somerset

P. M. Roebuck lbw b Thomas . . . . . . . . 0
J. G. Wyatt lbw b Thomas . . . . . . . . . . 7
N. F. M. Popplewell c Barwick b Ontong 39
R. L. Ollis b Ontong . . . . . . . . . . . . . . . . 0
*I. T. Botham c Miandad b Ontong . . . 23
V. J. Marks lbw b Ontong . . . . . . . . . . . 0
R. J. Harden c Holmes b Derrick . . . . . 11
G. V. Palmer b Ontong . . . . . . . . . . . . . 3
M. R. Davis c Hopkins b Holmes . . . . . 28
M. S. Turner b Holmes . . . . . . . . . . . . . 15
†T. Gard not out . . . . . . . . . . . . . . . . . . . 0
L-b 10, w 6, n-b 2 . . . . . . . . . . 18

1/2 2/10 3/20 4/49 5/49 6/80 7/87 8/110 9/131 (46.2 overs) 144

Bowling: Thomas 5–1–6–2; Barwick 7–1–22–0; Steele 11–2–26–0; Ontong 11–2–30–5; Holmes 5.2–0–24–2; Derrick 7–0–26–1.

Umpires: J. Birkenshaw and M. J. Kitchen.

## QUARTER-FINALS

## ESSEX v DERBYSHIRE

At Chelmsford, June 5, 6, 7. Essex won by 18 runs. Toss won by Derbyshire. An innings of controlled aggression by Gooch, who struck nine 4s, paved the way for this Essex triumph in a match of twenty overs per side on the third day set aside for the tie after the game which commenced on the first day was abandoned. Gladwin and McEwan also batted well. Derbyshire never posed a serious threat despite the brave efforts of Fowler and Roberts. In the abandoned match, Derbyshire, put in, had scored 167 in 55 overs and Essex in reply were 4 for the loss of Gooch off 1.4 overs.

*Gold Award:* G. A. Gooch.

### Essex

| | |
|---|---|
| G. A. Gooch not out | 72 |
| C. Gladwin b Finney | 29 |
| K. S. McEwan b Warner | 24 |
| D. R. Pringle c Miller b Warner | 5 |
| *K. W. R. Fletcher run out | 6 |
| B 1, l-b 9, w 1, n-b 3 | 14 |
| 1/85 2/127 3/138 4/150 (4 wkts, 20 overs) | 150 |

B. R. Hardie, A. W. Lilley, N. Phillip, †D. E. East, N. A. Foster and J. K. Lever did not bat.

Bowling: Holding 4–0–20–0; Mortensen 4–0–15–0; Newman 4–0–30–0; Finney 4–0–34–1; Warner 4–0–41–2.

### Derbyshire

| | |
|---|---|
| *K. J. Barnett c Hardie b Phillip | 5 |
| W. P. Fowler run out | 28 |
| J. E. Morris c Phillip b Gooch | 5 |
| B. Roberts c Lilley b Lever | 26 |
| R. J. Finney c Lever b Gooch | 14 |
| P. G. Newman b Lever | 9 |
| M. A. Holding not out | 19 |
| A. E. Warner not out | 13 |
| B 1, l-b 8, w 3, n-b 1 | 13 |
| 1/15 2/30 3/45 4/81 5/100 6/100 (6 wkts, 20 overs) | 132 |

G. Miller, †B. J. M. Maher and O. H. Mortensen did not bat.

Bowling: Lever 4–0–23–2; Foster 4–0–14–0; Gooch 4–0–28–2; Phillip 4–0–18–1; Pringle 4–0–40–0.

Umpires: B. J. Meyer and A. G. T. Whitehead.

## HAMPSHIRE v LEICESTERSHIRE

At Southampton, June 5. Leicestershire won by 4 runs. Toss won by Hampshire. This splendid match was settled with just one ball remaining, and defeat left Hampshire still with the unenviable record of being the only first-class county not to have reached a Lord's final. The Leicestershire innings was founded on a century opening partnership between Butcher and Balderstone, both of whom were missed early on, and there was a fine contribution from Willey. Yet their total seemed well within the grasp of Hampshire, a side adept at chasing runs. After losing three wickets for 54 in 22 overs, Hampshire then looked to Robin Smith, who responded so well that 36 runs were needed from the final six overs. However, his dismissal settled the outcome.

*Gold Award:* P. Willey.

### Leicestershire

I. P. Butcher c Parks b Connor . . . . . . . 55
J. C. Balderstone lbw b Marshall . . . . . 60
*D. I. Gower c Marshall b Tremlett . . . 17
P. Willey c R. A. Smith b James . . . . . 56
J. J. Whitaker not out . . . . . . . . . . . . . . 24
P. B. Clift not out . . . . . . . . . . . . . . . . . . 11
L-b 10, w 3, n-b 7 . . . . . . . . . . 20

1/104 2/128 3/176 4/211 (4 wkts, 55 overs) 243

N. E. Briers, †M. A. Garnham, G. J. Parsons, L. B. Taylor and J. P. Agnew did not bat.

Bowling: Connor 11–0–40–1; Marshall 11–1–38–1; James 11–1–61–1; Tremlett 11–0–48–1; Cowley 11–0–46–0.

### Hampshire

C. G. Greenidge c Whitaker b Clift . . . 10
V. P. Terry lbw b Taylor . . . . . . . . . . . . 14
*M. C. J. Nicholas b Willey . . . . . . . . . 41
C. L. Smith run out . . . . . . . . . . . . . . . . 8
R. A. Smith b Clift . . . . . . . . . . . . . . . . . 81
M. D. Marshall lbw b Taylor . . . . . . . . . 25
K. D. James c Gower b Agnew . . . . . . . 27
N. G. Cowley c Whitaker b Agnew . . . 8
T. M. Tremlett run out . . . . . . . . . . . . . . 1
†R. J. Parks not out . . . . . . . . . . . . . . . . 8
C. A. Connor c Willey b Agnew . . . . . . 0
B 1, l-b 6, w 4, n-b 5 . . . . . . . . 16

1/25 2/36 3/54 4/118 5/177 6/210 7/225 8/229 9/234 (54.5 overs) 239

Bowling: Agnew 10.5–0–38–3; Taylor 11–0–43–2; Clift 11–2–43–2; Parsons 11–1–59–0; Willey 11–0–49–1.

Umpires: D. J. Constant and D. G. L. Evans.

## NORTHAMPTONSHIRE v KENT

At Northampton, June 5, 6, 7. No result. Kent qualified for the semi-finals on their superior striking-rate in the zonal matches. Toss won by Kent. Only 34 overs were bowled on the first afternoon and rain prevented further play on the second and third days. Northamptonshire had made rapid progress, with Larkins hitting ten 4s in an innings of 70 balls and Cook scoring an excellent 78 before Hinks hit his stumps when he was attempting a quick single.

### Northamptonshire

*G. Cook run out . . . . . . . . . . . . . . . . . . 78
W. Larkins c Underwood b Dilley . . . . 52
R. G. Williams not out . . . . . . . . . . . . . . 11
A. J. Lamb not out . . . . . . . . . . . . . . . . . 8
L-b 3, w 6 . . . . . . . . . . . . . . . . . 9

1/131 2/147 (2 wkts, 34 overs) 158

R. J. Bailey, D. J. Capel, R. A. Harper, †G. Sharp, A. Walker, N. A. Mallender and B. J. Griffiths did not bat.

Bowling: Dilley 8–2–21–1; Jarvis 6–1–23–0; Baptiste 8–1–37–0; Ellison 5–0–30–0; Cowdrey 5–1–30–0; Underwood 2–0–14–0.

### Kent

N. R. Taylor, S. G. Hinks, C. J. Tavaré, D. G. Aslett, *C. S. Cowdrey, E. A. E. Baptiste, R. M. Ellison, †A. P. E. Knott, G. R. Dilley, D. L. Underwood and K. B. S. Jarvis.

Umpires: H. D. Bird and J. A. Jameson.

## WORCESTERSHIRE v MIDDLESEX

At Worcester, June 5, 6, 7. No result. Middlesex qualified for the semi-finals on their superior striking-rate in the zonal matches. Toss won by Middlesex. Worcestershire, having finished top of their qualifying group, had their hopes of a semi-final place wrecked by the weather after scoring 220 on the opening day. Rain restricted Middlesex's reply to only thirteen overs.

### Worcestershire

| | |
|---|---|
| M. J. Weston lbw b Daniel | 0 |
| T. S. Curtis c Edmonds b Emburey | 39 |
| D. M. Smith c Emburey b Edmonds | 57 |
| *P. A. Neale c Downton b Cowans | 33 |
| Kapil Dev st Downton b Edmonds | 21 |
| D. N. Patel st Downton b Edmonds | 13 |
| D. B. D'Oliveira c Downton b Daniel | 6 |
| †S. J. Rhodes run out | 24 |
| R. K. Illingworth run out | 0 |
| N. V. Radford lbw b Daniel | 0 |
| J. D. Inchmore not out | 5 |
| B 6, l-b 9, w 4, n-b 3 | 22 |
| 1/0 2/106 3/124 4/168 5/168 6/179 7/204 8/205 9/207 (54 overs) | 220 |

Bowling: Daniel 10–1–26–3; Cowans 11–1–60–1; Williams 11–0–45–0; Emburey 11–1–37–1; Edmonds 11–1–37–3.

### Middlesex

| | |
|---|---|
| G. D. Barlow run out | 6 |
| W. N. Slack not out | 20 |
| *M. W. Gatting not out | 7 |
| B 5, l-b 1, w 2, n-b 4 | 12 |
| 1/21 (1 wkt, 13 overs) | 45 |

R. O. Butcher, C. T. Radley, †P. R. Downton, J. E. Emburey, P. H. Edmonds, N. F. Williams, N. G. Cowans and W. W. Daniel did not bat.

Bowling: Kapil Dev 5–2–13–0; Radford 5–0–16–0; Inchmore 2–0–7–0; Weston 1–0–3–0.

Umpires: K. E. Palmer and D. R. Shepherd.

## SEMI-FINALS

## ESSEX v MIDDLESEX

At Chelmsford, June 19, 20. Essex won by 62 runs. Toss won by Middlesex, who looked well in control until Lilley pulled off a breathtaking catch at point to dismiss Gatting. Thereafter, Essex made rapid inroads, capturing the last five wickets in four overs to ensure a place in the final. Apart from Gatting, only Slack faced the home attack with any authority. Gooch laid the foundation of Essex's total after they had been put in.

*Gold Award:* J. E. Emburey.

### Essex

| | |
|---|---|
| G. A. Gooch b Emburey | 58 |
| B. R. Hardie b Williams | 14 |
| P. J. Prichard c Emburey b Cowans | 31 |
| K. S. McEwan c Downton b Cowans | 3 |
| D. R. Pringle b Edmonds | 2 |
| *K. W. R. Fletcher lbw b Emburey | 24 |
| A. W. Lilley lbw b Emburey | 11 |
| S. Turner c Butcher b Emburey | 7 |
| †D. E. East not out | 12 |
| N. A. Foster not out | 23 |
| L-b 5, w 1, n-b 11 | 17 |
| 1/34 2/87 3/97 4/108 5/141 6/151 7/166 8/167 (8 wkts, 55 overs) | 202 |

J. K. Lever did not bat.

Bowling: Daniel 11–0–56–0; Williams 11–1–39–1; Cowans 11–0–35–2; Edmonds 11–0–31–1; Emburey 11–2–36–4.

### Middlesex

G. D. Barlow run out . . . . . . . . . . . . . . . 7
W. N. Slack b Turner . . . . . . . . . . . . . . . 60
*M. W. Gatting c Lilley b Turner . . . . . 28
C. T. Radley b Pringle . . . . . . . . . . . . . . 7
R. O. Butcher lbw b Pringle . . . . . . . . . 11
†P. R. Downton c Hardie b Turner . . . 0
J. E. Emburey not out . . . . . . . . . . . . . . 8
P. H. Edmonds run out . . . . . . . . . . . . . 0
N. F. Williams run out . . . . . . . . . . . . . . 4
N. G. Cowans lbw b Foster . . . . . . . . . . 0
W. W. Daniel b Foster . . . . . . . . . . . . . . 0
L-b 2, w 10, n-b 3 . . . . . . . . . . 15

1/9 2/63 3/87 4/113 5/123 6/132 7/134 8/140 9/140 (46 overs) 140

Bowling: Lever 8–1–21–0; Foster 9–1–31–2; Pringle 7–1–25–2; Turner 11–3–27–3; Gooch 11–2–34–0.

Umpires: M. J. Kitchen and A. G. T. Whitehead.

## LEICESTERSHIRE v KENT

At Leicester, June 19. Leicestershire won by eight wickets. Toss won by Leicestershire. It was somewhat ironic that on the first full day of sunshine at Grace Road all season, there was no cricket left by 4.18. For by then, Leicestershire were back in the pavilion, winners with more than 33 overs to spare. There was some evidence of moisture early on, and Gower's bowlers used the pitch so well that the match, with Kent 76 for seven, was virtually decided by lunch. Butcher batted attractively when Leicestershire chased their modest target, but the Gold Award went, for the first time, to Clift, who bowled right through his eleven overs because of a leg strain, conceded only 20 runs, and took two important wickets just when Kent were hinting that they might recover from their wretched start.

### Kent

M. R. Benson c Garnham b Agnew . . . 14
S. G. Hinks c Butcher b Agnew . . . . . . 11
C. J. Tavaré b Parsons . . . . . . . . . . . . . . 4
D. G. Aslett lbw b Clift . . . . . . . . . . . . . 11
*C. S. Cowdrey b Clift . . . . . . . . . . . . . . 12
E. A. E. Baptiste lbw b Willey . . . . . . . 15
R. M. Ellison c Gower b Taylor . . . . . . 15
†A. P. E. Knott b Willey . . . . . . . . . . . . 0
G. W. Johnson not out . . . . . . . . . . . . . . 13
D. L. Underwood c Gower b Taylor . . . 2
K. B. S. Jarvis lbw b Taylor . . . . . . . . . 0
L-b 3, w 1 . . . . . . . . . . . . . . . . . 4

1/24 2/27 3/35 4/47 5/70 6/70 7/72 8/99 9/101 (45.5 overs) 101

Bowling: Agnew 9–1–24–2; Taylor 8.5–2–16–3; Parsons 9–1–14–1; Clift 11–3–20–2; Willey 8–1–24–2.

### Leicestershire

I. P. Butcher c Knott b Jarvis . . . . . . . . 55
J. C. Balderstone c Knott b Ellison . . . . 12
*D. I. Gower not out . . . . . . . . . . . . . . . 26
P. Willey not out . . . . . . . . . . . . . . . . . . . 5
L-b 1, w 1, n-b 2 . . . . . . . . . . . 4

1/14 2/91 (2 wkts, 21.5 overs) 102

J. J. Whitaker, N. E. Briers, P. B. Clift, †M. A. Garnham, G. J. Parsons, J. P. Agnew and L. B. Taylor did not bat.

Bowling: Jarvis 6–0–34–1; Ellison 10.5–2–43–1; Baptiste 5–1–24–0.

Umpires: D. R. Shepherd and B. Leadbeater.

## FINAL

## ESSEX v LEICESTERSHIRE

At Lord's, July 20. Leicestershire won by five wickets. Beating Gooch in the toss (Fletcher was absent with strained side muscles), Gower put Essex in on an overcast morning and a slow pitch still damp from its preparation. An early shower held up play briefly, but that was all the rain there was. Runs were hard to come by, especially in the morning. In the 219 balls they received between them, Gooch, Hardie and McEwan, all good strikers of the ball, managed only six boundaries, Willey's wily off-spin and Taylor's accurate medium-pace pinning them down when they were looking to raise the run-rate.

Needing to score at just under 4 runs an over to win, which should not have been especially demanding, Leicestershire lost their openers for 33, Butcher to a brilliant catch at mid-wicket by Prichard. Gower and Willey then added 83 in seventeen overs before Gower went to another fine catch, this time by Lilley at cover point. When Whitaker and Briers fell cheaply, Leicestershire still had 81 to make in fifteen overs, which was no easy matter. Willey, however, was finding gaps on the leg side by now, and Garnham made him a confidently dashing partner. With all manner of strokes they won the match for Leicestershire with three overs to spare, making Denis Compton's choice of Willey for the Gold Award a mere formality.

Attendance: 21,448 (excluding members); takings: £261,936.

### Essex

| | |
|---|---|
| *G. A. Gooch b Willey | 57 |
| B. R. Hardie c and b Clift | 25 |
| P. J. Prichard b Taylor | 32 |
| K. S. McEwan c Garnham b Taylor | 29 |
| D. R. Pringle c Agnew b Taylor | 10 |
| C. Gladwin b Clift | 14 |
| A. W. Lilley b Agnew | 12 |
| †D. E. East not out | 7 |
| S. Turner run out | 3 |
| N. A. Foster not out | 6 |
| B 1, l-b 15, w 1, n-b 1 | 18 |
| 1/71 2/101 3/147 4/163 5/164 6/191 7/195 8/198 (8 wkts, 55 overs) | 213 |

J. K. Lever did not bat.

Bowling: Willey 11–0–41–1; Clift 11–1–40–2; Agnew 11–1–51–1; Taylor 11–3–26–3; Parsons 11–0–39–0.

### Leicestershire

| | |
|---|---|
| J. C. Balderstone c Prichard b Pringle | 12 |
| I. P. Butcher c Prichard b Turner | 19 |
| *D. I. Gower c Lilley b Foster | 43 |
| P. Willey not out | 86 |
| J. J. Whitaker b Gooch | 1 |
| N. E. Briers lbw b Gooch | 6 |
| †M. A. Garnham not out | 34 |
| B 2, l-b 9, w 2, n-b 1 | 14 |
| 1/33 2/37 3/120 4/123 5/135 (5 wkts, 52 overs) | 215 |

P. B. Clift, G. J. Parsons, J. P. Agnew and L. B. Taylor did not bat.

Bowling: Lever 11–0–50–0; Foster 11–2–32–1; Pringle 10–0–42–1; Turner 10–1–40–1; Gooch 10–1–40–2.

Umpires: H. D. Bird and K. E. Palmer.

## BENSON AND HEDGES CUP RECORDS

**Highest individual scores:** 198 not out, G. A. Gooch, Essex v Sussex, Hove 1982; 173 not out, C. G. Greenidge, Hampshire v Minor Counties (South), Amersham, 1973; 158 not out, B. F. Davison, Leicestershire v Warwickshire, Coventry, 1972. (118 hundreds have been scored in the competition.)

**Highest totals in 55 overs:** 350 for three, Essex v Oxford & Cambridge Univs, Chelmsford, 1979; 327 for four, Leicestershire v Warwickshire, Coventry, 1972; 327 for two, Essex v Sussex, Hove, 1982; 321 for one, Hampshire v Minor Counties (South), Amersham, 1973.

**Highest total by a side batting second:** 291 for five (53.5 overs), Warwickshire v Lancashire, Old Trafford, 1981.

**Highest match aggregate:** 593 for fourteen wickets, Gloucestershire (282) v Hampshire (311-4), Bristol, 1974.

**Lowest totals:** 56 in 26.2 overs, Leicestershire v Minor Counties, Wellington, 1982; 59 in 34 overs, Oxford & Cambridge Univs v Glamorgan, Fenner's, 1983; 60 in 26 overs, Sussex v Middlesex, Hove, 1978; 62 in 26.5 overs, Gloucestershire v Hampshire, Bristol, 1975.

**Best bowling:** Seven for 12, W. W. Daniel, Middlesex v Minor Counties (East), Ipswich, 1978; seven for 22, J. R. Thomson, Middlesex v Hampshire, Lord's, 1981; seven for 32, R. G. D. Willis, Warwickshire v Yorkshire, Edgbaston, 1981.

**Hat-tricks:** G. D. McKenzie, Leicestershire v Worcestershire, Worcester, 1972; K. Higgs, Leicestershire v Surrey in the final, Lord's, 1974; A. A. Jones, Middlesex v Essex, Lord's 1977; M. J. Procter, Gloucestershire v Hampshire, Southampton, 1977; W. Larkins, Northamptonshire v Oxford & Cambrige Univs, Northampton, 1980; E. A. Moseley, Glamorgan v Kent, Cardiff, 1981; G. C. Small, Warwickshire v Leicestershire, Leicester, 1984.

**Record partnership for each wicket**

| | | |
|---|---|---|
| 241 for 1st | S. M. Gavaskar and B. C. Rose, Somerset v Kent at Canterbury . . . | 1980 |
| 285* for 2nd | C. G. Greenidge and D. R. Turner, Hampshire v Minor Counties (South) at Amersham . . . | 1973 |
| 268* for 3rd | G. A. Gooch and K. W. R. Fletcher, Essex v Sussex at Hove . . . | 1982 |
| 184* for 4th | D. Lloyd and B. W. Reidy, Lancashire v Derby at Chesterfield . . . | 1980 |
| 134 for 5th | M. Maslin and D. N. F. Slade, Minor Counties (East) v Nottinghamshire at Trent Bridge . . . | 1976 |
| 114 for 6th | Majid J. Khan and G. P. Ellis, Glamorgan v Gloucestershire at Bristol | 1975 |
| 149* for 7th | J. D. Love and C. M. Old, Yorkshire v Scotland at Bradford . . . | 1981 |
| 109 for 8th | R. E. East and N. Smith, Essex v Northamptonshire at Chelmsford | 1977 |
| 83 for 9th | P. G. Newman and M. A. Holding, Derbyshire v Nottinghamshire at Trent Bridge . . . | 1985 |
| 80* for 10th | D. L. Bairstow and M. Johnson, Yorkshire v Derbyshire at Derby . . | 1981 |

## WINNERS 1972-85

1972 LEICESTERSHIRE beat Yorkshire by five wickets.
1973 KENT beat Worcestershire by 39 runs.
1974 SURREY beat Leicestershire by 27 runs.
1975 LEICESTERSHIRE beat Middlesex by five wickets.
1976 KENT beat Worcestershire by 43 runs.
1977 GLOUCESTERSHIRE beat Kent by 64 runs.
1978 KENT beat Derbyshire by six wickets.
1979 ESSEX beat Surrey by 35 runs.
1980 NORTHAMPTONSHIRE beat Essex by 6 runs.
1981 SOMERSET beat Surrey by seven wickets.
1982 SOMERSET beat Nottinghamshire by nine wickets.
1983 MIDDLESEX beat Essex by 4 runs.
1984 LANCASHIRE beat Warwickshire by six wickets.
1985 LEICESTERSHIRE beat Essex by five wickets.

## WINS BY OXFORD AND CAMBRIDGE UNIVERSITIES

1973 OXFORD beat Northamptonshire at Northampton by two wickets.
1975 OXFORD & CAMBRIDGE beat Worcestershire at Fenner's by 66 runs.
1975 OXFORD & CAMBRIDGE beat Northamptonshire at The Parks by three wickets.
1976 OXFORD & CAMBRIDGE beat Yorkshire at Barnsley by seven wickets.
1984 OXFORD & CAMBRIDGE beat Gloucestershire at Bristol by 27 runs.

## WINS BY MINOR COUNTIES

1980 MINOR COUNTIES beat Gloucestershire at Chippenham by 3 runs.
1981 MINOR COUNTIES beat Hampshire at Southampton by 3 runs.
1982 MINOR COUNTIES beat Leicestershire at Wellington by 131 runs.

# JOHN PLAYER LEAGUE, 1985

When Essex, the eventual winners and the first side since Kent in the early 1970s to retain the title, started their eighth match in the John Player League on July 14, they were fifteenth in the table, having won only one of their first seven games. Of their remaining nine they won eight and the other was washed out. Owing to the weather an unprecedented number of 27 matches ended with no result, and nine victories was the lowest number recorded by a side finishing first.

In theory, Sussex, Northamptonshire and Hampshire could all have won the title when the last round of matches began. But Essex kept their lead by beating Yorkshire by two wickets with one ball to spare at Chelmsford, an exciting climax to the Sunday season. Sussex, who had already won at Cardiff, were able to watch on television as the first prize was denied them. Derbyshire achieved fourth place, their highest since they finished third in 1970, by beating Leicestershire at Chesterfield in their final game. The table was led by Kent from May 26 until the end of July; but having had six victories in their first eight matches, they never won again and dropped down to tenth place.

Despite the appalling weather, Essex's receipts were well up on 1984, though that was due not least to the admission price having risen from £2.50 to £3.50. Their final match drew a crowd of 8,500 and accounted for record takings of £16,000. For finishing first Essex won £17,000, an increase of £3,000 on the previous year. Sussex, winners in 1982, fourth in 1983 and third in 1984, received £8,500 as runners-up in 1985. Hampshire's third place was worth £3,750, and Derbyshire's fourth place £2,250.

C. W. J. Athey (Gloucestershire) was the season's top scorer with 663 runs at an average of 60.27, the highest individual score being G. A. Gooch's 171 for Essex against Nottinghamshire at Trent Bridge. By taking his total aggregate for the competition to 6,486 runs at an average of 32.75, D. L. Amiss (Warwickshire) passed the previous record of 6,144 set by G. M. Turner (Worcestershire). In his last season with Essex, K. S. McEwan scored his ninth Sunday League hundred, the same number as C. G. Greenidge (Hampshire)

*Continued over.*

## JOHN PLAYER LEAGUE TABLE

| | | *M* | *W* | *L* | *T* | *NR* | *Pts* | *6s* | *4w* |
|---|---|---|---|---|---|---|---|---|---|
| 1 | Essex (1) | 16 | 9 | 3 | 1 | 3 | 44 | 21 | 4 |
| 2 | Sussex (3) | 16 | 10 | 5 | 0 | 1 | 42 | 41 | 6 |
| 3 | Hampshire (9) | 16 | 8 | 4 | 0 | 4 | 40 | 27 | 2 |
| 4 | Derbyshire (17) | 16 | 8 | 5 | 0 | 3 | 38 | 39 | 3 |
| 5 | Northamptonshire (12) | 16 | 7 | 4 | 1 | 4 | 38 | 33 | 2 |
| 6 | Gloucestershire (13) | 16 | 8 | 8 | 0 | 0 | 32 | 39 | 3 |
| | Warwickshire (7) | 16 | 7 | 7 | 0 | 2 | 32 | 30 | 2 |
| | Yorkshire (13) | 16 | 6 | 6 | 0 | 4 | 32 | 26 | 0 |
| | Leicestershire (13) | 16 | 5 | 5 | 1 | 5 | 32 | 11 | 0 |
| 10 | Kent (9) | 16 | 6 | 7 | 0 | 3 | 30 | 16 | 2 |
| | Somerset (13) | 16 | 5 | 6 | 0 | 5 | 30 | 32 | 3 |
| 12 | Nottinghamshire (2) | 16 | 6 | 8 | 0 | 2 | 28 | 24 | 0 |
| | Middlesex (5) | 16 | 5 | 7 | 0 | 4 | 28 | 20 | 0 |
| 14 | Glamorgan (9) | 16 | 4 | 7 | 1 | 4 | 26 | 14 | 2 |
| | Lancashire (4) | 16 | 3 | 6 | 2 | 5 | 26 | 22 | 2 |
| 16 | Worcestershire (5) | 16 | 5 | 9 | 0 | 2 | 24 | 28 | 1 |
| 17 | Surrey (8) | 16 | 4 | 9 | 0 | 3 | 22 | 37 | 1 |

*1984 positions in brackets.*

and I. V. A. Richards (Somerset), and passed 5,000 runs in the competition. The highest total of the season was Northamptonshire's 306 for two against Surrey at Guildford. Against Worcestershire at Knypersley, Derbyshire's batsmen hit a record eighteen 6s in an innings.

K. M. Curran (Gloucestershire) and N. Gifford (Warwickshire) both took 26 wickets, which was the most for the season, Gifford's six for 20 against Northamptonshire at Edgbaston being the best analysis. S. Turner (Essex) joined J. K. Lever (Essex) and D. L. Underwood (Kent) as the only bowlers to have taken 300 wickets in the competition. Turner has also scored more than 3,000 runs. Lever, with 329 wickets (average 21.31), is the leading bowler.

T. Davies (Glamorgan) with 17 victims (11ct, 6st) led the wicket-keeping table. D. L. Bairstow (Yorkshire) and G. Sharp (Northamptonshire) both claimed their 200th victim in the competition, a number passed previously only by R. W. Taylor (Derbyshire), A. P. E. Knott (Kent) and E. W. Jones (Glamorgan).

## CHAMPIONS: 1969-85

| | | | |
|---|---|---|---|
| 1969 | Lancashire | 1978 | Hampshire |
| 1970 | Lancashire | 1979 | Somerset |
| 1971 | Worcestershire | 1980 | Warwickshire |
| 1972 | Kent | 1981 | Essex |
| 1973 | Kent | 1982 | Sussex |
| 1974 | Leicestershire | 1983 | Yorkshire |
| 1975 | Hampshire | 1984 | Essex |
| 1976 | Kent | 1985 | Essex |
| 1977 | Leicestershire | | |

## DISTRIBUTION OF PRIZEMONEY

**The total prizemoney was £69,700.**

£17,000 and John Player Trophy: ESSEX.
£8,500 to runners-up: SUSSEX.
£3,750 for third place: HAMPSHIRE.
£2,250 for fourth place: DERBYSHIRE.
£275 each match to the winners – shared if tied or no result.

**Batting award:** £400 to M. A. Lynch (Surrey) who hit sixteen 6s in the season.

*Other leading 6-hitters:*

15 – I. V. A. Richards (Somerset), P. W. Romaines (Gloucestershire).
13 – I. T. Botham (Somerset), M. A. Holding (Derbyshire), Imran Khan (Sussex).
12 – B. Roberts (Derbyshire).
11 – B. F. Davison (Gloucestershire), A. J. Lamb (Northamptonshire), W. Larkins (Northamptonshire).
9 – G. A. Gooch (Essex).
8 – C. W. J. Athey (Gloucestershire), C. G. Greenidge (Hampshire), C. M. Wells (Sussex).

In all 460 6s were hit in the League in 1985.

**Fastest televised match fifty:**
23 balls – G. S. le Roux, Sussex v Glamorgan, Cardiff, September 15.

**Bowling award:** £400 to J. K. Lever (Essex) who took four wickets or more in an innings on three occasions.

K. M. Curran (Gloucestershire), Imran Khan (Sussex) and A. E. Warner (Derbyshire) each took four wickets in an innings twice; 24 players each took four wickets in an innings once.

# DERBYSHIRE

## DERBYSHIRE v NORTHAMPTONSHIRE

At Derby, May 12. Northamptonshire won by nine wickets. Toss won by Northamptonshire.

### Derbyshire

| | |
|---|---|
| B. Roberts b Mallender | 8 |
| *K. J. Barnett b Capel | 17 |
| J. E. Morris c Sharp b Walker | 2 |
| W. P. Fowler c Larkins b Capel | 4 |
| A. Hill c Harper b Walker | 25 |
| G. Miller c Harper b Williams | 8 |
| †B. J. M. Maher run out | 2 |
| D. G. Moir c Bailey b Capel | 9 |
| A. E. Warner not out | 15 |
| P. G. Newman not out | 12 |
| L-b 11, w 5, n-b 1 | 17 |
| 1/13 2/24 3/35 4/43 5/61 6/65 7/86 8/93 (8 wkts, 40 overs) | 119 |

O. H. Mortensen did not bat.

Bowling: Mallender 8–1–25–1; Walker 8–1–28–2; Harper 8–1–19–0; Capel 8–1–21–3; Williams 8–1–15–1.

### Northamptonshire

| | |
|---|---|
| *G. Cook b Mortensen | 0 |
| W. Larkins not out | 45 |
| A. J. Lamb not out | 69 |
| L-b 4, n-b 3 | 7 |
| 1/0 (1 wkt, 24.2 overs) | 121 |

R. J. Bailey, D. J. Capel, R. G. Williams, †G. Sharp, D. J. Wild, R. A. Harper, N. A. Mallender and A. Walker did not bat.

Bowling: Mortensen 8–3–14–1; Newman 5.2–1–34–0; Moir 6–0–29–0; Miller 3–0–28–0; Warner 2–0–12–0.

Umpires: J. Birkenshaw and R. A. White.

At Scarborough, May 19. YORKSHIRE v DERBYSHIRE. No result.

## DERBYSHIRE v GLOUCESTERSHIRE

At Derby, June 2. Derbyshire won by 16 runs. Toss won by Derbyshire.

### Derbyshire

| | |
|---|---|
| *K. J. Barnett c Athey b Bainbridge | 69 |
| A. Hill b Graveney | 26 |
| J. E. Morris c Athey b Payne | 44 |
| B. Roberts c Romaines b Walsh | 10 |
| W. P. Fowler c Romaines b Curran | 20 |
| D. G. Moir run out | 4 |
| R. J. Finney c Russell b Walsh | 1 |
| †B. J. M. Maher run out | 1 |
| M. A. Holding not out | 20 |
| A. E. Warner run out | 17 |
| L-b 10, n-b 1 | 11 |
| 1/62 2/143 3/147 4/164 5/176 6/183 7/184 8/184 9/223 (9 wkts, 40 overs) | 223 |

O. H. Mortensen did not bat.

Bowling: Walsh 8–0–35–2; Curran 8–1–44–1; Payne 6–0–35–1; Graveney 8–0–34–1; Shepherd 6–0–43–0; Bainbridge 4–0–22–1.

### Gloucestershire

P. W. Romaines c Barnett b Finney . . . 73
J. W. Lloyds b Holding . . . . . . . . . . . . . 9
C. W. J. Athey c Barnett b Finney . . . . 44
B. F. Davison c Mortensen b Warner . . 28
P. Bainbridge c Barnett b Warner . . . . . 7
K. M. Curran b Holding . . . . . . . . . . . . 2
J. N. Shepherd not out . . . . . . . . . . . . . . 11
*D. A. Graveney c Mortensen b Holding 6
I. R. Payne not out . . . . . . . . . . . . . . . . . 13
B 3, l-b 5, w 5, n-b 1 . . . . . . . . 14

1/26 2/114 3/145 (7 wkts, 40 overs) 207
4/165 5/169 6/177 7/180

†R. C. Russell and C. A. Walsh did not bat.

Bowling: Warner 8–0–44–2; Holding 8–0–36–3; Mortensen 8–0–44–0; Moir 8–0–34–0; Finney 8–0–41–2.

Umpires: B. Leadbeater and R. A. White.

At Lord's, June 9. DERBYSHIRE beat MIDDLESEX on faster scoring-rate.

At Old Trafford, June 16. DERBYSHIRE lost to LANCASHIRE by seven wickets.

## DERBYSHIRE v GLAMORGAN

At Derby, June 30. No result. Toss won by Glamorgan.

### Glamorgan

H. Morris b Holding . . . . . . . . . . . . . . . . 53
A. L. Jones c Morris b Newman . . . . . . 53
Javed Miandad not out . . . . . . . . . . . . . . 8
Younis Ahmed not out . . . . . . . . . . . . . . 5
L-b 8, w 5 . . . . . . . . . . . . . . . . . 13

1/109 2/124 (2 wkts, 29 overs) 132

G. C. Holmes, *R. C. Ontong, J. Derrick, M. R. Price, †T. Davies, S. R. Barwick and L. L. McFarlane did not bat.

Bowling: Warner 5–0–16–0; Holding 5–3–6–1; Finney 8–0–40–0; Miller 6–0–33–0; Newman 5–0–29–1.

### Derbyshire

*K. J. Barnett, I. S. Anderson, J. E. Morris, B. Roberts, R. Sharma, G. Miller, R. J. Finney, †B. J. M. Maher, M. A. Holding, P. G. Newman and A. E. Warner.

Umpires: J. H. Harris and D. O. Oslear.

## DERBYSHIRE v WORCESTERSHIRE

At Knypersley, July 7. Derbyshire won by 33 runs, having hit a John Player League record eighteen 6s in a new county record total for the competition. Toss won by Worcestershire.

## Derbyshire

*K. J. Barnett c Rhodes b Kapil Dev . . 9
I. S. Anderson b Weston . . . . . . . . . . . . 52
J. E. Morris c Rhodes b Radford . . . . . 9
B. Roberts st Rhodes b Illingworth . . . . 70
G. Miller b Illingworth . . . . . . . . . . . . . . 17
M. A. Holding b Radford . . . . . . . . . . . 37
P. G. Newman run out . . . . . . . . . . . . . . 46
A. E. Warner c Illingworth b Kapil Dev 10
R. J. Finney c McEwan b Weston . . . . 4
†B. J. M. Maher not out . . . . . . . . . . . . 14
O. H. Mortensen not out . . . . . . . . . . . . 0
L-b 19, w 2, n-b 3 . . . . . . . . . . 24

1/19 2/32 3/126 (9 wkts, 40 overs) 292
4/162 5/185 6/231 7/274
8/274 9/278

Bowling: Kapil Dev 8–0–48–2; Radford 7–0–47–2; Newport 7–0–38–0; McEwan 7–0–41–0; Weston 6–0–53–2; Illingworth 4–0–32–2; Patel 1–0–14–0.

## Worcestershire

T. S. Curtis run out . . . . . . . . . . . . . . . . . 76
D. N. Patel c Miller b Warner . . . . . . . 4
*P. A. Neale b Newman . . . . . . . . . . . . 54
Kapil Dev b Warner . . . . . . . . . . . . . . . . 36
D. B. D'Oliveira c Roberts b Warner . . 19
M. J. Weston c Barnett b Warner . . . . . 19
†S. J. Rhodes c Barnett b Warner . . . . . 4
N. V. Radford b Holding . . . . . . . . . . . . 16
P. J. Newport not out . . . . . . . . . . . . . . . 10
R. K. Illingworth not out . . . . . . . . . . . . 3
B 4, l-b 8, w 6 . . . . . . . . . . . . . . 18

1/6 2/130 3/167 (8 wkts, 40 overs) 259
4/203 5/203 6/216
7/238 8/249

S. M. McEwan did not bat.

Bowling: Finney 8–1–50–0; Warner 8–0–39–5; Mortensen 8–0–49–0; Newman 8–0–50–1; Holding 8–0–59–1.

Umpires: B. Dudleston and D. O. Oslear.

# DERBYSHIRE v SOMERSET

At Derby, July 21. Derbyshire won by four wickets in a match reduced by rain to 33 overs a side. Toss won by Derbyshire.

## Somerset

P. M. Roebuck lbw b Newman . . . . . . . 18
N. F. M. Popplewell c Marples b Holding 5
I. V. A. Richards c and b Newman . . . 51
*I. T. Botham c Holding b Mortensen . 34
B. C. Rose b Warner . . . . . . . . . . . . . . . 24
V. J. Marks not out . . . . . . . . . . . . . . . . 20
N. A. Felton run out . . . . . . . . . . . . . . . . 15
J. Garner run out . . . . . . . . . . . . . . . . . . 1
B 2, l-b 5, w 1 . . . . . . . . . . . . . 8

1/6 2/56 3/89 (7 wkts, 33 overs) 176
4/128 5/143 6/174 7/176

†T. Gard, M. R. Davis and C. H. Dredge did not bat.

Bowling: Holding 7–0–36–1; Warner 6–0–27–1; Mortensen 7–0–45–1; Miller 6–0–33–0, Newman 7–1–28–2.

## Derbyshire

*K. J. Barnett c Davis b Marks . . . . . . 44
I. S. Anderson c Davis b Garner . . . . . . 64
J. E. Morris run out . . . . . . . . . . . . . . . . 10
B. Roberts c and b Botham . . . . . . . . . . 19
G. Miller c Garner b Botham . . . . . . . . 14
R. Sharma b Botham . . . . . . . . . . . . . . . 8
M. A. Holding not out . . . . . . . . . . . . . . 2
P. G. Newman not out . . . . . . . . . . . . . . 4
B 2, l-b 6, w 3, n-b 1 . . . . . . . . 12

1/59 2/79 3/137 (6 wkts, 32.5 overs) 177
4/145 5/163 6/172

A. E. Warner, †C. Marples and O. H. Mortensen did not bat.

Bowling: Garner 7–2–26–1; Davis 6–0–29–0; Marks 7–1–41–1; Richards 5–0–20–0; Botham 5.5–0–31–3; Dredge 2–0–22–0.

Umpires: J. A. Jameson and B. J. Meyer.

At Edgbaston, July 28. DERBYSHIRE beat WARWICKSHIRE by five wickets.

## DERBYSHIRE v SURREY

At Derby, August 4. No result. Toss won by Surrey.

### Derbyshire

*K. J. Barnett b Monkhouse .......... 10
I. S. Anderson not out ............... 14
J. E. Morris not out .................. 0
L-b 1 ....................... 1

1/25 (1 wkt, 3.2 overs) 25

B. Roberts, G. Miller, P. G. Newman, M. A. Holding, A. E. Warner, R. J. Finney, †C. Marples and O. H. Mortensen did not bat.

Bowling: Waterman 2–0–17–0; Monkhouse 1.2–0–7–1.

### Surrey

*A. R. Butcher, D. B. Pauline, †A. J. Stewart, D. M. Ward, M. A. Lynch, A. Needham, K. T. Medlycott, R. J. Doughty, G. Monkhouse, A. H. Gray and P. A. Waterman.

Umpires: K. E. Palmer and J. A. Jameson.

At Colchester, August 11. DERBYSHIRE lost to ESSEX by nine wickets.

At Hove, August 18. DERBYSHIRE lost to SUSSEX by 20 runs.

## DERBYSHIRE v NOTTINGHAMSHIRE

At Heanor, August 25. Derbyshire won by seven wickets in a match reduced by rain to 37 overs a side. Toss won by Derbyshire.

### Nottinghamshire

R. T. Robinson run out ............. 38
B. C. Broad b Holding ............... 14
D. W. Randall lbw b Mortensen ...... 11
*C. E. B. Rice c Morris b Roberts .... 15
P. Johnson c Newman b Finney ...... 37
R. J. Hadlee c Fell b Finney ......... 17
†B. N. French lbw b Mortensen ...... 4
C. D. Fraser-Darling b Newman ...... 7
E. E. Hemmings not out ............. 16
R. A. Pick not out ................. 7
L-b 5, w 4, n-b 4 ........... 13

1/27 2/46 3/82 4/89 5/139 6/144 7/148 8/167 (8 wkts, 37 overs) 179

K. E. Cooper did not bat.

Bowling: Holding 7–0–33–1; Finney 8–0–35–2; Mortensen 8–0–36–2; Newman 6–0–20–1; Roberts 4–0–28–1; Barnett 4–0–22–0.

### Derbyshire

I. S. Anderson c French b Pick ....... 6
B. Roberts not out ................... 77
*K. J. Barnett c Randall b Fraser-Darling 34
M. A. Fell c Johnson b Cooper ....... 10
J. E. Morris not out ................. 38
L-b 9, w 5, n-b 1 ........... 15

1/12 2/72 3/113 (3 wkts, 31.2 overs) 180

M. A. Holding, P. G. Newman, A. M. Brown, R. J. Finney, †C. Marples and O. H. Mortensen did not bat.

Bowling: Hadlee 7–1–30–0; Cooper 8–0–38–1; Pick 7–1–34–1; Fraser-Darling 2–0–24–1; Rice 6–0–30–0; Hemmings 1–0–12–0; Randall 2–0–3–0.

Umpires: J. Birkenshaw and M. J. Kitchen.

At Folkestone, September 1. DERBYSHIRE beat KENT by 9 runs.

At Southampton, September 8. DERBYSHIRE beat HAMPSHIRE by 7 runs.

## DERBYSHIRE v LEICESTERSHIRE

At Chesterfield, September 15. Derbyshire won by nine wickets. Toss won by Derbyshire.

### Leicestershire

*D. I. Gower c Barnett b Mortensen .. 6
N. E. Briers c Marples b Mortensen ... 4
J. J. Whitaker b Mortensen .......... 0
P. Willey c Roberts b Mortensen ...... 8
†M. A. Garnham not out ............ 28
I. P. Butcher c Marples b Newman ... 6
P. B. Clift c Finney b Russell ........ 12
G. J. Parsons c and b Russell ........ 3
P. A. J. De Freitas c Brown b Finney . 1
G. J. F. Ferris b Holding ............ 4
L. B. Taylor not out ................ 1
B 1, l-b 7, w 5, n-b 1 ........ 14

1/8 2/11 3/20 4/23 5/37 6/59 7/63 8/64 9/84 (9 wkts, 40 overs) 87

Bowling: Mortensen 8–4–10–4; Holding 8–1–17–1; Finney 8–1–18–1; Russell 8–3–18–2; Newman 8–0–16–1.

### Derbyshire

I. S. Anderson not out .............. 37
B. Roberts c Briers b Parsons ........ 0
*K. J. Barnett not out ............... 41
L-b 3, w 5, n-b 4 .......... 12

1/0 (1 wkt, 23.2 overs) 90

J. E. Morris, A. M. Brown, P. G. Newman, M. A. Holding, P. E. Russell, †C. Marples, R. J. Finney and O. H. Mortensen did not bat.

Bowling: Taylor 4–1–13–0; Parsons 5–1–15–1; Ferris 3–0–21–0; Clift 5–2–11–0; Willey 2–0–9–0; De Freitas 2–0–4–0; Briers 1–0–6–0; Butcher 1–0–4–0; Whitaker 0.2–0–4–0.

Umpires: A. A. Jones and K. E. Palmer.

# ESSEX

## ESSEX v SUSSEX

At Chelmsford, May 5. Sussex won by nine wickets. Toss won by Sussex.

### Essex

G. A. Gooch b le Roux ............... 7
P. J. Prichard c Barclay b C. M. Wells. 8
K. S. McEwan b Reeve .............. 36
D. R. Pringle c Mendis b Greig ...... 6
*K. W. R. Fletcher c A. P. Wells b Jones 34
N. Phillip c Gould b Greig .......... 19
A. W. Lilley lbw b Greig ............ 4
B. R. Hardie b le Roux .............. 2
†D. E. East lbw b Greig ........... 0
S. Turner not out ................... 10
J. K. Lever run out ................. 14
B 1, l-b 6, w 1 ............ 8

1/13 2/15 3/40 4/75 5/113 6/119 7/124 8/124 9/124 (38.4 overs) 148

Bowling: C. M. Wells 8–0–24–1; le Roux 8–3–16–2; Greig 8–1–26–4; Reeve 7.4–0–35–1; Jones 7–0–40–1.

### Sussex

| | |
|---|---|
| G. D. Mendis not out | 78 |
| A. M. Green c Fletcher b Lever | 45 |
| P. W. G. Parker not out | 12 |
| L-b 12, n-b 3 | 15 |
| 1/91 (1 wkt, 37.4 overs) | 150 |

A. N. Jones, C. M. Wells, A. P. Wells, †I. J. Gould, I. A. Greig, *J. R. T. Barclay, D. A. Reeve and G. S. le Roux did not bat.

Bowling: Phillip 8–0–27–0; Lever 8–2–15–1; Gooch 6.4–0–37–0; Turner 7–1–27–0; Pringle 8–1–32–0.

Umpires: J. A. Jameson and B. Leadbeater.

At The Oval, May 26. SURREY v ESSEX. No result.

## ESSEX v LEICESTERSHIRE

At Chelmsford, June 2. Tied. Toss won by Leicestershire.

### Essex

| | |
|---|---|
| B. R. Hardie c Garnham b Clift | 15 |
| A. W. Lilley lbw b De Freitas | 49 |
| K. S. McEwan b Clift | 2 |
| D. R. Pringle c Garnham b Clift | 3 |
| *K. W. R. Fletcher c Clift b De Freitas | 17 |
| N. Phillip c Briers b Taylor | 20 |
| †D. E. East c Taylor b De Freitas | 2 |
| K. R. Pont c Balderstone b Agnew | 4 |
| S. Turner b Agnew | 8 |
| J. K. Lever run out | 1 |
| D. L. Acfield not out | 0 |
| L-b 7, w 8, n-b 3 | 18 |
| 1/40 2/50 3/66 4/100 5/102 6/114 7/125 8/136 9/139 (39.2 overs) | 139 |

Bowling: Agnew 8–1–21–2; Taylor 7.2–0–28–1; Parsons 8–0–31–0; Clift 8–1–25–3; De Freitas 8–0–27–3.

### Leicestershire

| | |
|---|---|
| I. P. Butcher run out | 41 |
| J. C. Balderstone c McEwan b Acfield | 19 |
| *N. E. Briers lbw b Acfield | 14 |
| J. J. Whitaker b Acfield | 1 |
| †M. A. Garnham run out | 22 |
| P. B. Clift run out | 10 |
| G. J. Parsons run out | 0 |
| P. A. J. De Freitas lbw b Lever | 1 |
| N. G. B. Cook run out | 1 |
| J. P. Agnew not out | 4 |
| L-b 13, w 6, n-b 7 | 26 |
| 1/63 2/80 3/83 4/108 5/131 6/132 7/133 8/134 9/139 (9 wkts, 40 overs) | 139 |

L. B. Taylor did not bat.

Bowling: Lever 8–1–22–1; Phillip 6–0–39–0; Pringle 8–2–16–0; Turner 8–3–23–0; Pont 2–0–7–0; Acfield 8–3–19–3.

Umpires: J. W. Holder and M. J. Kitchen.

## ESSEX v LANCASHIRE

At Ilford, June 9. No result after rain ended play. Toss won by Essex.

### Lancashire

| | |
|---|---|
| G. Fowler lbw b Pringle | 30 |
| S. J. O'Shaughnessy c Fletcher b Lever | 60 |
| C. H. Lloyd not out | 64 |
| D. P. Hughes not out | 14 |
| B 1, l-b 9, w 3, n-b 2 | 15 |
| 1/66 2/118 (2 wkts, 28 overs) | 183 |

*J. Abrahams, †C. Maynard, M. Watkinson, J. Simmons, P. J. W. Allott, S. Henriksen and D. J. Makinson did not bat.

Bowling: Lever 8–1–47–1; Phillip 7–0–34–0; Turner 6–0–40–0; Pringle 7–0–52–1.

### Essex

| | |
|---|---|
| G. A. Gooch b Henriksen | 0 |
| A. W. Lilley run out | 24 |
| K. S. McEwan not out | 38 |
| D. R. Pringle b Simmons | 18 |
| N. Phillip not out | 4 |
| B 1, l-b 4, w 2 | 7 |
| 1/0 2/39 3/78 (3 wkts, 15 overs) | 91 |

*K. W. R. Fletcher, B. R. Hardie, S. Turner, †D. E. East, J. K. Lever and D. L. Acfield did not bat.

Bowling: Henriksen 5–0–35–1; Allott 4–0–19–0; Makinson 3–0–12–0; Simmons 3–0–20–1.

Umpires: H. D. Bird and C. Cook.

At Swansea, June 16. ESSEX beat GLAMORGAN by 14 runs.

At Luton, June 23. ESSEX lost to NORTHAMPTONSHIRE by six wickets.

At Bournemouth, June 30. ESSEX lost to HAMPSHIRE by eight wickets.

## ESSEX v GLOUCESTERSHIRE

At Southend, July 14. Essex won by seven wickets. Toss won by Gloucestershire.

### Gloucestershire

| | |
|---|---|
| P. W. Romaines b Pringle | 60 |
| P. Bainbridge c East b Phillip | 0 |
| C. W. J. Athey c Fletcher b Pringle | 37 |
| B. F. Davison c East b Pringle | 22 |
| K. M. Curran c Fletcher b Pringle | 40 |
| A. J. Wright c Hardie b Pringle | 9 |
| I. R. Payne c Fletcher b Lever | 4 |
| †R. C. Russell not out | 3 |
| C. A. Walsh not out | 1 |
| B 1, l-b 4, w 2, n-b 1 | 8 |
| 1/6 2/86 3/100 4/141 5/175 6/175 7/180 (7 wkts, 40 overs) | 184 |

*D. A. Graveney and G. E. Sainsbury did not bat.

Bowling: Lever 8–0–31–1; Phillip 8–0–22–1; Turner 6–0–22–0; Pringle 8–0–41–5; Acfield 8–0–43–0; Pont 2–0–20–0.

### Essex

| | | | |
|---|---|---|---|
| B. R. Hardie c Davison b Curran | 73 | *K. W. R. Fletcher not out | 5 |
| P. J. Prichard b Payne | 33 | B 5, l-b 7, w 3 | 15 |
| K. S. McEwan not out | 58 | | |
| D. R. Pringle c Russell b Curran | 2 | 1/63 2/171 3/180 (3 wkts, 36.3 overs) | 186 |

K. R. Pont, N. Phillip, S. Turner, †D. E. East, J. K. Lever and D. L. Acfield did not bat.

Bowling: Sainsbury 6.3–0–27–0; Curran 7–0–37–2; Payne 6–0–30–1; Walsh 8–0–34–0; Graveney 7–0–31–0; Bainbridge 2–0–15–0.

Umpires: K. J. Lyons and B. J. Meyer.

## ESSEX v KENT

At Chelmsford, July 21. Essex won by 13 runs. Toss won by Kent.

### Essex

| | | | |
|---|---|---|---|
| *G. A. Gooch c Potter b Ellison | 86 | C. Gladwin not out | 21 |
| B. R. Hardie b Jarvis | 5 | | |
| K. S. McEwan c Knott b Jarvis | 3 | L-b 12, w 2 | 14 |
| D. R. Pringle c Jarvis b Underwood | 45 | | |
| N. Phillip b Jarvis | 3 | 1/25 2/31 3/148 (5 wkts, 40 overs) | 193 |
| A. W. Lilley not out | 16 | 4/151 5/154 | |

P. J. Prichard, S. Turner, †D. E. East and J. K. Lever did not bat.

Bowling: Jarvis 8–0–30–3; Ellison 8–0–56–1; Cowdrey 8–0–21–0; Baptiste 8–1–29–0; Underwood 8–0–45–1.

### Kent

| | | | |
|---|---|---|---|
| M. R. Benson lbw b Turner | 9 | †A. P. E. Knott c East b Pringle | 3 |
| S. G. Hinks b Phillip | 11 | D. L. Underwood b Phillip | 1 |
| C. J. Tavaré c Lever b Turner | 45 | K. B. S. Jarvis lbw b Phillip | 0 |
| D. G. Aslett b Turner | 8 | B 1, l-b 11, w 6, n-b 5 | 23 |
| L. Potter run out | 52 | | |
| E. A. E. Baptiste c McEwan b Lever | 23 | 1/16 2/34 3/53 (37.3 overs) | 180 |
| R. M. Ellison not out | 5 | 4/90 5/168 6/169 7/171 | |
| *C. S. Cowdrey c East b Pringle | 0 | 8/175 9/179 | |

Bowling: Lever 7–0–30–1; Phillip 7.3–0–35–3; Turner 8–1–23–3; Gooch 7–0–52–0; Pringle 8–0–28–2.

Umpires: A. A. Jones and M. J. Kitchen.

At Taunton, July 28. ESSEX beat SOMERSET by five wickets.

## ESSEX v MIDDLESEX

At Chelmsford, August 4. No result.

## ESSEX v DERBYSHIRE

At Colchester, August 11. Essex won by nine wickets in a match reduced by rain to 28 overs a side. Toss won by Essex.

## Derbyshire

*K. J. Barnett c East b Turner ........ 18
I. S. Anderson c East b Gooch ....... 16
J. E. Morris c Gooch b Lever ........ 44
B. Roberts b Foster .................. 8
G. Miller b Pringle .................. 0
M. A. Holding c Foster b Pringle ..... 10
P. G. Newman run out ................. 1
A. E. Warner c Lever b Foster ........ 0
R. J. Finney c East b Lever .......... 14
†C. Marples not out .................. 4
O. H. Mortensen run out .............. 0
B 1, l-b 2, w 5 ...................... 8

1/37 2/39 3/71 4/72 5/84 6/87 7/89 8/118 9/120 (26.1 overs) 123

Bowling: Lever 6.1–0–22–2; Foster 7–0–35–2; Turner 3–0–15–1; Gooch 4–0–19–1; Pringle 6–0–29–2.

## Essex

G. A. Gooch not out .................. 51
B. R. Hardie b Miller ................ 45
K. S. McEwan not out ................. 23
L-b 2, w 3 ........................... 5

1/77 (1 wkt, 27.2 overs) 124

P. J. Prichard, D. R. Pringle, *K. W. R. Fletcher, N. A. Foster, †D. E. East, S. Turner, J. K. Lever and A. W. Lilley did not bat.

Bowling: Holding 7–1–21–0; Mortensen 4–0–21–0; Newman 7–1–33–0; Miller 7–0–37–1; Warner 2.2–0–10–0.

Umpires: A. G. T. Whitehead and D. S. Thompsett.

At Worcester, August 18. ESSEX beat WORCESTERSHIRE by seven wickets.

At Edgbaston, September 1. ESSEX beat WARWICKSHIRE by 21 runs.

At Trent Bridge, September 8. ESSEX beat NOTTINGHAMSHIRE by 44 runs.

# ESSEX v YORKSHIRE

At Chelmsford, September 15. Essex won by two wickets, with one ball to spare, to become John Player League champions for the second consecutive year. Toss won by Essex.

## Yorkshire

G. Boycott run out ................... 7
M. D. Moxon b Gooch .................. 28
K. Sharp run out ..................... 114
J. D. Love b Gooch ................... 3
S. N. Hartley c Pringle b Gooch ...... 5
*†D. L. Bairstow run out ............. 28
P. Carrick c East b Pringle .......... 15
C. S. Pickles not out ................ 6
S. Oldham not out .................... 1
L-b 17, w 5, n-b 2 ................... 24

1/14 2/58 3/62 4/80 5/194 6/206 7/225 (7 wkts, 40 overs) 231

C. Shaw and S. D. Fletcher did not bat.

Bowling: Lever 8–0–37–0; Foster 8–1–38–0; Turner 8–0–59–0; Gooch 8–0–26–3; Pringle 8–0–54–1.

### Essex

| | | | |
|---|---|---|---|
| G. A. Gooch c Fletcher b Shaw | 12 | S. Turner not out | 7 |
| B. R. Hardie c Bairstow b Fletcher | 21 | N. A. Foster not out | 2 |
| K. S. McEwan c Shaw b Hartley | 62 | | |
| D. R. Pringle c Carrick b Oldham | 60 | L-b 13, w 7, n-b 1 | 21 |
| *K. W. R. Fletcher c Carrick b Pickles | 7 | | |
| A. W. Lilley b Fletcher | 8 | 1/27 2/53 3/137 (8 wkts, 39.5 overs) | 232 |
| †D. E. East b Oldham | 7 | 4/151 5/170 6/183 | |
| P. J. Prichard c Pickles b Oldham | 25 | 7/194 8/230 | |

J. K. Lever did not bat.

Bowling: Pickles 8–0–38–1; Shaw 8–0–46–1; Fletcher 8–0–45–2; Hartley 8–0–47–1; Oldham 7.5–0–43–3.

Umpires: P. B. Wight and J. Birkenshaw.

# GLAMORGAN

## GLAMORGAN v KENT

At Cardiff, May 5. Kent won on faster scoring-rate, having been set a revised target of 135 off 30 overs after rain had caused a brief interruption. Toss won by Kent.

### Glamorgan

| | | | |
|---|---|---|---|
| J. A. Hopkins b Jarvis | 16 | J. Derrick run out | 5 |
| A. L. Jones c Cowdrey b Johnson | 28 | J. F. Steele not out | 0 |
| G. C. Holmes b Johnson | 33 | B 4, l-b 14, w 7 | 25 |
| Javed Miandad lbw b Jarvis | 29 | | |
| Younis Ahmed c Knott b Cowdrey | 18 | 1/24 2/73 3/93 (8 wkts, 39 overs) | 175 |
| *R. C. Ontong b Jarvis | 12 | 4/119 5/145 6/160 | |
| J. G. Thomas b Baptiste | 9 | 7/168 8/175 | |

†T. Davies and S. R. Barwick did not bat.

Bowling: Jarvis 8–1–24–3; Baptiste 8–0–32–1; Potter 8–0–36–0; Cowdrey 7–1–32–1; Johnson 8–1–33–2.

### Kent

| | | | |
|---|---|---|---|
| M. R. Benson lbw b Barwick | 4 | †A. P. E. Knott lbw b Ontong | 3 |
| S. G. Hinks b Barwick | 26 | G. W. Johnson not out | 10 |
| C. J. Tavaré not out | 67 | B 1, l-b 5 | 6 |
| D. G. Aslett st Davies b Holmes | 14 | | |
| *C. S. Cowdrey st Davies b Holmes | 1 | 1/5 2/40 3/85 (6 wkts, 29.2 overs) | 138 |
| E. A. E. Baptiste c Thomas b Holmes | 7 | 4/87 5/97 6/103 | |

N. R. Taylor, L. Potter and K. B. S. Jarvis did not bat.

Bowling: Thomas 6–0–41–0; Barwick 6–2–8–2; Holmes 8–0–36–3; Ontong 6.2–0–33–1; Steele 3–0–14–0.

Umpires: C. Cook and M. J. Kitchen.

At Taunton, May 12. GLAMORGAN beat SOMERSET by two wickets.

At Lord's, May 19. GLAMORGAN beat MIDDLESEX by seven wickets.

At Basingstoke, May 26. HAMPSHIRE v GLAMORGAN. No result.

## GLAMORGAN v WORCESTERSHIRE

At Ebbw Vale, June 9. Glamorgan won by 22 runs in a match reduced by rain first to 23 and later to 21 overs a side. Toss won by Worcestershire.

### Glamorgan

J. A. Hopkins c Weston b Inchmore . . . 25
Javed Miandad not out . . . . . . . . . . . . . . . 95
Younis Ahmed c Weston b Inchmore . . 6
S. P. Henderson run out . . . . . . . . . . . . . 12
G. C. Holmes not out . . . . . . . . . . . . . . . 0
L-b 8, w 1 . . . . . . . . . . . . . . . . . . 9

1/46 2/67 3/141 (3 wkts, 21 overs) 147

*R. C. Ontong, J. F. Steele, J. Derrick, †T. Davies, L. L. McFarlane and S. R. Barwick did not bat.

Bowling: Kapil Dev 4–0–28–0; Radford 5–0–31–0; Inchmore 5–0–34–2; Newport 5–0–30–0; Weston 2–0–16–0.

### Worcestershire

D. N. Patel c Steele b Barwick . . . . . . . 22
D. B. D'Oliveira c Ontong b McFarlane 8
Kapil Dev run out . . . . . . . . . . . . . . . . . . 5
*P. A. Neale c Davies b Holmes . . . . . . 0
J. D. Inchmore c Ontong b Holmes . . . 8
M. J. Weston run out . . . . . . . . . . . . . . . 18
T. S. Curtis b McFarlane . . . . . . . . . . . . 30
†S. J. Rhodes b Holmes . . . . . . . . . . . . . 3
N. V. Radford run out . . . . . . . . . . . . . . 13
P. J. Newport not out . . . . . . . . . . . . . . . 2
R. K. Illingworth not out . . . . . . . . . . . 0
B 1, l-b 13, w 2 . . . . . . . . . . . . 16

1/27 2/37 3/41 4/49 5/50 6/81 7/93 8/113 9/123 (9 wkts, 21 overs) 125

Bowling: McFarlane 4–0–17–2; Barwick 5–0–25–1; Derrick 5–0–33–0; Holmes 5–0–19–3; Steele 2–0–17–0.

Umpires: J. H. Harris and J. W. Holder.

## GLAMORGAN v ESSEX

At Swansea, June 16. Essex won by 14 runs. Toss won by Glamorgan.

### Essex

B. R. Hardie lbw b Holmes . . . . . . . . . . 14
A. W. Lilley b Holmes . . . . . . . . . . . . . . 28
K. S. McEwan c Barwick b Ontong . . . 43
D. R. Pringle run out . . . . . . . . . . . . . . . 39
*K. W. R. Fletcher not out . . . . . . . . . . 37
N. Phillip b Thomas . . . . . . . . . . . . . . . . 23
†D. E. East lbw b Thomas . . . . . . . . . . . 1
N. A. Foster c Steele b Ontong . . . . . . . 1
K. R. Pont not out . . . . . . . . . . . . . . . . . 6
L-b 12, w 1 . . . . . . . . . . . . . . . . 13

1/45 2/50 3/131 4/131 5/177 6/181 7/182 (7 wkts, 40 overs) 205

J. K. Lever and D. L. Acfield did not bat.

Bowling: Thomas 8–0–41–2; Barwick 4–0–17–0; Derrick 8–0–36–0; Holmes 8–1–42–2; Steele 4–0–23–0; Ontong 8–0–34–2.

### Glamorgan

J. A. Hopkins c McEwan b Phillip .... 7
G. C. Holmes b Lever .............. 15
Younis Ahmed c Pringle b Foster ..... 10
Javed Miandad b Lever ............. 86
S. P. Henderson c East b Pont ....... 23
*R. C. Ontong c Acfield b Lever ...... 17
J. G. Thomas c Foster b Pringle ...... 5
J. Derrick b Pringle ................ 8
J. F. Steele b Lever ................. 0
†T. Davies run out .................. 2
S. R. Barwick not out ................ 0
B 4, l-b 8, w 4, n-b 2 ........ 18

1/23 2/30 3/51 4/104 5/127 6/149 7/172 8/175 9/189 (39.3 overs) 191

Bowling: Phillip 5–0–21–1; Lever 7.3–0–40–4; Foster 8–0–35–1; Acfield 6–0–32–0; Pringle 8–0–33–2; Pont 5–1–18–1.

Umpires: R. Palmer and R. A. White.

At Leicester, June 23. GLAMORGAN lost to LEICESTERSHIRE by 11 runs.

At Derby, June 30. DERBYSHIRE v GLAMORGAN. No result.

## GLAMORGAN v NOTTINGHAMSHIRE

At Swansea, July 7. Nottinghamshire won by three wickets. Toss won by Nottinghamshire.

### Glamorgan

J. A. Hopkins c and b Hadlee ........ 0
A. L. Jones b Saxelby ............... 0
Younis Ahmed c French b Hadlee .... 5
Javed Miandad b Saxelby ........... 89
G. C. Holmes run out .............. 45
*R. C. Ontong not out ............. 34
J. G. Thomas c Robinson b Saxelby ... 12
M. R. Price run out ................ 3
B 1, l-b 2, w 7, n-b 1 ........ 11

1/1 2/6 3/16 4/120 5/178 6/184 7/197 (7 wkts, 40 overs) 199

†T. Davies, J. Derrick and L. L. McFarlane did not bat.

Bowling: Hadlee 8–1–27–2; Saxelby 8–0–40–3; Cooper 8–0–41–0; Rice 8–0–48–0; Hemmings 8–0–40–0.

### Nottinghamshire

B. C. Broad c Davies b Ontong ....... 40
R. T. Robinson b Price ............. 77
*C. E. B. Rice run out .............. 18
R. J. Hadlee run out ................ 0
P. Johnson c Younis b Thomas ....... 7
D. W. Randall run out ............... 9
J. D. Birch not out ................. 39
†B. N. French c Ontong b Thomas .... 0
E. E. Hemmings not out ............. 1
B 2, l-b 5, w 1, n-b 3 ........ 11

1/85 2/130 3/136 4/147 5/150 6/165 7/179 (7 wkts, 40 overs) 202

K. Saxelby and K. E. Cooper did not bat.

Bowling: Thomas 8–0–53–2; McFarlane 5–0–34–0; Derrick 8–0–31–0; Ontong 8–1–31–1; Price 7–0–22–1; Holmes 4–0–24–0.

Umpires: C. Cook and P. B. Wight.

At Old Trafford, July 14. GLAMORGAN tied with LANCASHIRE.

At Bristol, July 28. GLAMORGAN lost to GLOUCESTERSHIRE by six wickets.

## GLAMORGAN v WARWICKSHIRE

At Cardiff, August 11. No result.

At Wellingborough, August 18. NORTHAMPTONSHIRE v GLAMORGAN. No result.

## GLAMORGAN v YORKSHIRE

At Swansea, August 25. Glamorgan won on faster scoring-rate after Yorkshire had failed to reach a target reduced by rain to 96 off twenty overs, the match already having been reduced to 28 overs a side. Toss won by Yorkshire.

### Glamorgan

| | | | |
|---|---|---|---|
| H. Morris c Robinson b Oldham | 7 | I. Smith run out | 3 |
| G. C. Holmes st Bairstow b Carrick | 27 | S. R. Barwick b Oldham | 1 |
| Younis Ahmed c Bairstow b Carrick | 28 | L. L. McFarlane not out | 0 |
| *R. C. Ontong st Bairstow b Carrick | 35 | L-b 6, w 2, n-b 2 | 10 |
| M. P. Maynard c S. N. Hartley b Shaw | 18 | | |
| M. R. Price c Moxon b Shaw | 7 | 1/24 2/69 3/78 (28 overs) | 138 |
| †T. Davies run out | 1 | 4/123 5/125 6/129 7/133 | |
| J. Derrick b Shaw | 1 | 8/134 9/137 | |

Bowling: P. J. Hartley 3-0-16-0; Pickles 6-2-26-0; Oldham 6-0-27-2; Carrick 6-0-36-3; Boycott 3-0-12-0; Shaw 4-0-15-3.

### Yorkshire

| | | | |
|---|---|---|---|
| G. Boycott run out | 38 | P. J. Hartley b Holmes | 0 |
| M. D. Moxon c Younis b Barwick | 6 | S. Oldham not out | 0 |
| S. N. Hartley b Ontong | 29 | | |
| J. D. Love c and b Holmes | 1 | B 1, l-b 6, w 1, n-b 2 | 10 |
| P. E. Robinson b Holmes | 2 | | |
| *†D. L. Bairstow b Holmes | 3 | 1/11 2/64 3/67 (8 wkts, 20 overs) | 93 |
| P. Carrick not out | 3 | 4/79 5/83 6/88 | |
| C. S. Pickles b Holmes | 1 | 7/90 8/90 | |

C. Shaw did not bat.

Bowling: Barwick 4-0-18-1; McFarlane 1-0-7-0; Derrick 5-0-31-0; Ontong 6-1-14-1; Holmes 4-0-16-5.

Umpires: B. Dudleston and D. S. Thompsett.

## GLAMORGAN v SURREY

At Cardiff, September 1. Surrey won on faster scoring-rate when rain ended play after an earlier shower had reduced their target to 138 in 34 overs. Toss won by Surrey.

### Glamorgan

| | | | |
|---|---|---|---|
| A. L. Jones b Pocock | 10 | I. Smith b Butcher | 2 |
| H. Morris lbw b Pocock | 18 | S. R. Barwick not out | 1 |
| Javed Miandad b Jesty | 33 | L. L. McFarlane not out | 0 |
| G. C. Holmes c Jesty b Pauline | 5 | L-b 8, w 15 | 23 |
| *R. C. Ontong c Clinton b Pauline | 0 | | |
| M. P. Maynard st Richards b Butcher | 12 | 1/31 2/39 3/56 (9 wkts, 36 overs) | 146 |
| M. R. Price b Gray | 22 | 4/56 5/91 6/93 7/123 | |
| †T. Davies c Lynch b Gray | 20 | 8/144 9/146 | |

Bowling: Thomas 3–1–14–0; Gray 7–0–34–2; Pocock 8–1–24–2; Pauline 7–0–24–2; Butcher 7–1–26–2; Jesty 4–0–16–1.

### Surrey

| | |
|---|---|
| A. R. Butcher not out | 81 |
| G. S. Clinton not out | 25 |
| W 1, n-b 1 | 2 |
| (no wkt, 21.4 overs) | 108 |

A. J. Stewart, *T. E. Jesty, M. A. Lynch, D. J. Thomas, †C. J. Richards, R. J. Doughty, A. H. Gray, P. I. Pocock and D. B. Pauline did not bat.

Bowling: Barwick 4–1–8–0; McFarlane 2–0–12–0; Ontong 8–0–42–0; Holmes 2–0–16–0; Price 5.4–0–30–0.

Umpires: R. A. White and A. G. T. Whitehead.

## GLAMORGAN v SUSSEX

At Cardiff, September 15. Sussex won by 93 runs. Toss won by Glamorgan.

### Sussex

| | | | |
|---|---|---|---|
| G. D. Mendis st Davies b Ontong | 21 | C. M. Wells not out | 0 |
| A. M. Green b Barwick | 22 | | |
| Imran Khan not out | 66 | B 5, l-b 7, w 2 | 14 |
| †I. J. Gould b Holmes | 34 | | |
| G . S. le Roux b Thomas | 54 | 1/31 2/66 3/120 (5 wkts, 40 overs) | 214 |
| I. A. Greig run out | 3 | 4/206 5/210 | |

A. P. Wells, *J. R. T. Barclay, D. A. Reeve and A. N. Jones did not bat.

Bowling: Thomas 8–1–47–1; Barwick 6–0–48–1; Ontong 8–3–13–1; Holmes 8–0–43–1; Price 5–0–21–0; Derrick 5–0–30–0.

### Glamorgan

| | | | |
|---|---|---|---|
| J. A. Hopkins lbw b C. M. Wells | 10 | †T. Davies c C. M. Wells b Jones | 6 |
| H. Morris c Gould b Jones | 45 | J. Derrick c C. M. Wells b Jones | 10 |
| Younis Ahmed lbw b C. M. Wells | 0 | S. R. Barwick not out | 1 |
| G. C. Holmes c A. P. Wells b Jones | 21 | B 3 | 3 |
| M. P. Maynard c C. M. Wells b Reeve | 1 | | |
| *R. C. Ontong b Reeve | 13 | 1/18 2/26 3/75 (37 overs) | 121 |
| J. G. Thomas c C. M. Wells b Jones | 1 | 4/83 5/83 6/85 7/103 | |
| M. R. Price b Reeve | 10 | 8/104 9/115 | |

Bowling: C. M. Wells 8–3–18–2; Imran 7–2–18–0; Barclay 6–1–24–0; Reeve 8–0–26–3; Jones 8–1–32–5.

Umpires: D. J. Constant and D. R. Shepherd.

# GLOUCESTERSHIRE

## GLOUCESTERSHIRE v NOTTINGHAMSHIRE

At Bristol, May 5. Gloucestershire won by 11 runs. Toss won by Nottinghamshire.

### Gloucestershire

| | | | |
|---|---|---|---|
| A. W. Stovold b Rice | 1 | J. N. Shepherd b Evans | 2 |
| P. W. Romaines c Saxelby b Hemmings | 58 | *D. A. Graveney not out | 56 |
| C. W. J. Athey c Robinson b Such | 40 | B 1, l-b 5, w 1, n-b 2 | 9 |
| B. F. Davison c Birch b Such | 34 | | — |
| P. Bainbridge b Hemmings | 3 | 1/1 2/78 3/122 (6 wkts, 40 overs) | 249 |
| K. M. Curran not out | 46 | 4/130 5/150 6/164 | |

I. R. Payne, †R. C. Russell and D. V. Lawrence did not bat.

Bowling: Saxelby 8–0–35–0; Rice 8–0–49–1; Such 8–0–50–2; Evans 8–0–68–1; Hemmings 8–1–41–2.

### Nottinghamshire

| | | | |
|---|---|---|---|
| B. C. Broad c Russell b Shepherd | 28 | E. E. Hemmings not out | 7 |
| R. T. Robinson b Lawrence | 2 | K. Saxelby not out | 12 |
| *C. E. B. Rice b Curran | 7 | | |
| P. Johnson b Shepherd | 31 | B 1, l-b 11, w 3, n-b 1 | 16 |
| D. W. Randall run out | 7 | | — |
| J. D. Birch c Athey b Lawrence | 63 | 1/4 2/13 3/71 (8 wkts, 40 overs) | 238 |
| K. P. Evans c Davison b Bainbridge | 28 | 4/73 5/86 6/142 | |
| †B. N. French c and b Lawrence | 37 | 7/218 8/218 | |

P. M. Such did not bat.

Bowling: Lawrence 8–0–47–3; Curran 8–0–56–1; Shepherd 8–0–43–2; Graveney 8–0–37–0; Bainbridge 4–1–19–1; Payne 4–0–24–0.

Umpires: J. H. Harris and D. R. Shepherd.

At Lord's, May 12. GLOUCESTERSHIRE lost to MIDDLESEX by eight wickets.

At Old Trafford, May 19. GLOUCESTERSHIRE beat LANCASHIRE by six wickets.

## GLOUCESTERSHIRE v KENT

At Bristol, May 26. Kent won by seven wickets in a match reduced by rain to ten overs a side after a first match had been abandoned after one over, during which Kent scored 1 run for no wicket. Toss won by Kent.

### Gloucestershire

| | | | |
|---|---|---|---|
| B. F. Davison c Underwood b Dilley | 6 | *D. A. Graveney not out | 13 |
| C. W. J. Athey not out | 31 | B 4, l-b 3, w 4 | 11 |
| K. M. Curran b Cowdrey | 17 | | — |
| J. W. Lloyds run out | 4 | 1/7 2/46 3/50 (4 wkts, 10 overs) | 87 |
| P. Bainbridge c Cowdrey b Baptiste | 5 | 4/62 | |

P. W. Romaines, J. N. Shepherd, †R. C. Russell, D. V. Lawrence and C. A. Walsh did not bat.

Bowling: Dilley 2–0–21–1; Cowdrey 2–0–15–1; Baptiste 2–0–14–1; Underwood 2–0–12–0; Ellison 2–0–18–0.

### Kent

| | | | |
|---|---|---|---|
| S. G. Hinks b Lawrence | 6 | M. R. Benson not out | 6 |
| C. J. Tavaré b Shepherd | 32 | L-b 4, w 3 | 7 |
| E. A. E. Baptiste b Walsh | 13 | | |
| *C. S. Cowdrey not out | 24 | 1/9 2/49 3/74 (3 wkts, 9.3 overs) | 88 |

D. G. Aslett, R. M. Ellison, †A. P. E. Knott, G. W. Johnson, G. R. Dilley and D. L. Underwood did not bat.

Bowling: Lawrence 2–0–20–1; Shepherd 2–0–22–1; Walsh 2–0–16–1; Curran 1.3–0–11–0; Bainbridge 2–0–15–0.

Umpires: D. G. L. Evans and K. J. Lyons.

At Derby, June 2. GLOUCESTERSHIRE lost to DERBYSHIRE by 16 runs.

At Bath, June 9. GLOUCESTERSHIRE lost to SOMERSET by 83 runs.

At Northampton, June 16. GLOUCESTERSHIRE beat NORTHAMPTONSHIRE by 15 runs.

## GLOUCESTERSHIRE v SUSSEX

At Swindon, June 23. Sussex won by nine wickets in a match reduced to 37 overs a side by rain, which interrupted the game during the eighth over of Gloucestershire's innings. Toss won by Sussex.

### Gloucestershire

| | | | |
|---|---|---|---|
| P. W. Romaines b le Roux | 23 | K. M. Curran b le Roux | 50 |
| P. Bainbridge b Imran | 0 | B 2, l-b 5, w 2, n-b 2 | 11 |
| C. W. J. Athey c Moores b Imran | 1 | | |
| B. F. Davison c Mendis b Imran | 8 | 1/7 2/9 3/17 (5 wkts, 37 overs) | 126 |
| A. W. Stovold not out | 33 | 4/39 5/126 | |

I. R. Payne, *D. A. Graveney, †R. C. Russell, D. V. Lawrence and C. A. Walsh did not bat.

Bowling: Imran 8–2–11–3; C. M. Wells 8–0–21–0; le Roux 8–0–39–2; Greig 8–1–18–0; Pigott 5–0–30–0.

### Sussex

| | |
|---|---|
| G. D. Mendis not out | 60 |
| A. M. Green b Curran | 5 |
| P. W. G. Parker not out | 55 |
| L-b 5, w 3 | 8 |
| 1/7 (1 wkt, 32.4 overs) | 128 |

Imran Khan, C. M. Wells, A. P. Wells, *J. R. T. Barclay, I. A. Greig, †P. Moores, G. S. le Roux and A. C. S. Pigott did not bat.

Bowling: Lawrence 8–0–40–0; Curran 8–3–16–1; Payne 8–2–28–0; Walsh 5.4–0–25–0; Bainbridge 3–0–14–0.

Umpires: A. A. Jones and K. E. Palmer.

## GLOUCESTERSHIRE v YORKSHIRE

At Gloucester, July 7. Gloucestershire won by 13 runs. Toss won by Gloucestershire.

### Gloucestershire

| | |
|---|---|
| P. W. Romaines c Jarvis b Carrick .... 30 | I. R. Payne not out .................. 10 |
| P. Bainbridge b Fletcher ............ 20 | *D. A. Graveney not out ............ 1 |
| C. W. J. Athey b Stevenson .......... 21 | L-b 12, w 1, n-b 1 .......... 14 |
| B. F. Davison b Stevenson ..........103 | |
| A. W. Stovold run out .............. 17 | 1/56 2/56 3/116 (6 wkts, 40 overs) 216 |
| K. M. Curran b Fletcher ............ 0 | 4/179 5/180 6/211 |

†R. C. Russell, G. E. Sainsbury and C. A. Walsh did not bat.

Bowling: Sidebottom 8–0–34–0; Jarvis 8–0–31–0; Carrick 8–1–45–1; Fletcher 8–0–49–2; Stevenson 8–0–45–2.

### Yorkshire

| | |
|---|---|
| K. Sharp b Payne .................... 26 | P. Carrick c Walsh b Bainbridge ...... 1 |
| A. A. Metcalfe c Bainbridge b Curran 5 | A. Sidebottom not out .............. 14 |
| J. D. Love not out ..................100 | B 1, l-b 14, w 7 ............ 22 |
| *†D. L. Bairstow b Graveney ........ 11 | |
| G. B. Stevenson lbw b Graveney ...... 1 | 1/22 2/65 3/82 (6 wkts, 40 overs) 203 |
| S. N. Hartley c Athey b Bainbridge ... 23 | 4/86 5/142 6/149 |

M. D. Moxon, P. W. Jarvis and S. D. Fletcher did not bat.

Bowling: Curran 4–0–22–1; Sainsbury 8–0–31–0; Payne 8–1–27–1; Graveney 7–0–28–2; Walsh 8–2–38–0; Bainbridge 5–0–42–2.

Umpires: R. Julian and R. Palmer.

At Southend, July 14. GLOUCESTERSHIRE lost to ESSEX by seven wickets.

## GLOUCESTERSHIRE v GLAMORGAN

At Bristol, July 28. Gloucestershire won by six wickets. Toss won by Glamorgan.

### Glamorgan

| | |
|---|---|
| H. Morris c Athey b Curran ......... 5 | M. R. Price b Curran ................ 11 |
| A. L. Jones b Sainsbury ............ 17 | S. R. Barwick b Curran ............. 0 |
| Younis Ahmed st Brassington b Graveney 20 | L. L. McFarlane not out ............. 1 |
| Javed Miandad b Curran ............ 57 | B 4, l-b 6, w 1 .......... 11 |
| G. C. Holmes c Curran b Bainbridge .. 25 | |
| J. A. Hopkins c Bainbridge b Payne ... 0 | 1/18 2/38 3/59 (9 wkts, 40 overs) 166 |
| *R. C. Ontong run out .............. 12 | 4/124 5/124 6/146 7/147 |
| †T. Davies not out ................. 7 | 8/165 9/165 |

Bowling: Sainsbury 8–0–26–1; Curran 8–2–25–4; Payne 8–0–31–1; Graveney 6–0–27–1; Walsh 8–0–33–0; Bainbridge 2–0–14–1.

### Gloucestershire

| | |
|---|---|
| P. W. Romaines b Holmes ........... 23 | P. Bainbridge not out ............... 2 |
| J. W. Lloyds c and b McFarlane ...... 7 | L-b 7, w 2, n-b 2 ........... 11 |
| C. W. J. Athey lbw b McFarlane ..... 3 | |
| B. F. Davison not out ............... 85 | 1/21 2/30 3/65 (4 wkts, 33.3 overs) 168 |
| K. M. Curran c Holmes b Barwick .... 37 | 4/162 |

I. R. Payne, *D. A. Graveney, †A. J. Brassington, C. A. Walsh and G. E. Sainsbury did not bat.

Bowling: Barwick 7–0–18–1; McFarlane 6.3–1–35–2; Younis 2–0–7–0; Price 2–0–17–0; Ontong 8–1–25–0; Holmes 8–0–59–1.

Umpires: N. T. Plews and A. G. T. Whitehead.

## GLOUCESTERSHIRE v LEICESTERSHIRE

At Cheltenham, August 11. Leicestershire won by 7 runs in a match reduced by rain to ten overs a side. Toss won by Gloucestershire.

### Leicestershire

| | |
|---|---|
| P. Willey c Payne b Sainsbury | 11 |
| N. E. Briers b Graveney | 21 |
| *D. I. Gower c Payne b Curran | 11 |
| J. J. Whitaker c Payne b Curran | 13 |
| †M. A. Garnham b Curran | 8 |
| G. J. Parsons c Wright b Curran | 4 |
| P. A. J. De Freitas b Walsh | 2 |
| P. B. Clift run out | 1 |
| R. A. Cobb not out | 0 |
| J. P. Agnew not out | 4 |
| B 2 | 2 |
| 1/22 2/39 3/56 4/56 5/63 6/69 7/73 8/73 (8 wkts, 10 overs) | 77 |

L. B. Taylor did not bat.

Bowling: Sainsbury 2–0–17–1; Payne 2–0–23–0; Graveney 2–0–12–1; Curran 2–0–11–4; Walsh 2–0–12–1.

### Gloucestershire

| | |
|---|---|
| A. W. Stovold not out | 47 |
| R. G. P. Ellis run out | 21 |
| K. M. Curran c De Freitas b Clift | 0 |
| I. R. Payne not out | 0 |
| B 2 | 2 |
| 1/62 2/62 (2 wkts, 10 overs) | 70 |

C. W. J. Athey, A. J. Wright, J. W. Lloyds, †R. C. Russell, *D. A. Graveney, C. A. Walsh and G. E. Sainsbury did not bat.

Bowling: Willey 1–0–6–0; De Freitas 2–0–10–0; Clift 2–0–10–1; Agnew 2–0–16–0; Parsons 1–0–14–0; Taylor 2–0–12–0.

Umpires: M. J. Kitchen and R. Palmer.

## GLOUCESTERSHIRE v WARWICKSHIRE

At Cheltenham, August 18. Gloucestershire won by 13 runs in a match reduced by rain to ten overs a side. Toss won by Warwickshire.

### Gloucestershire

| | |
|---|---|
| R. G. P. Ellis run out | 7 |
| K. M. Curran not out | 48 |
| C. W. J. Athey b Small | 21 |
| *B. F. Davison c Thorne b Small | 6 |
| A. J. Wright not out | 0 |
| L-b 2, w 1 | 3 |
| 1/27 2/75 3/81 (3 wkts, 10 overs) | 85 |

P. W. Romaines, I. R. Payne, †R. C. Russell, P. H. Twizell, C. A. Walsh and G. E. Sainsbury did not bat.

Bowling: Hoffman 2–0–9–0; Smith 2–0–21–0; Gifford 2–0–9–0; Ferreira 2–0–25–0; Small 2–0–19–2.

### Warwickshire

†G. W. Humpage c Sainsbury b Curran 29
G. J. Lord c Athey b Sainsbury ....... 0
A. I. Kallicharran c and b Twizell .... 11
D. L. Amiss c Davison b Payne ...... 1
P. A. Smith run out ................ 0
A. M. Ferreira c Walsh b Curran ..... 15
Asif Din b Curran ................. 8
D. A. Thorne c Russell b Walsh ...... 2
G. C. Small not out ................ 2
*N. Gifford not out ................. 1
L-b 3 ..................... 3

1/5 2/37 3/39 4/39 5/53 6/67 7/61 8/71 (8 wkts, 10 overs) 72

D. S. Hoffman did not bat.

Bowling: Sainsbury 2-0-15-1; Payne 2-0-11-1; Twizell 2-0-23-1; Curran 2-0-9-3; Walsh 2-0-11-1.

Umpires: C. Cook and J. H. Harris.

At Bournemouth, August 25. GLOUCESTERSHIRE lost to HAMPSHIRE on scoring rate.

## GLOUCESTERSHIRE v WORCESTERSHIRE

At Moreton-in-Marsh, September 8. Gloucestershire won by nine wickets. Toss won by Gloucestershire.

### Worcestershire

T. S. Curtis c Bainbridge b Sainsbury .. 1
D. B. D'Oliveira b Sainsbury ......... 17
G. A. Hick c and b Bainbridge ....... 90
D. N. Patel run out ................. 63
*P. A. Neale c Athey b Bainbridge .... 16
M. J. Weston run out ............... 2
L. K. Smith c and b Curran ......... 3
†S. J. Rhodes c Russell b Curran ..... 0
J. D. Inchmore not out .............. 10
S. M. McEwan b Curran ............ 0
B. J. Barrett not out ................ 5
B 1, l-b 3, w 2 ............. 6

1/3 2/42 3/174 4/176 5/182 6/196 7/196 8/196 9/199 (9 wkts, 40 overs) 213

Bowling: Lawrence 5-0-28-0; Sainsbury 8-0-28-2; Payne 8-0-43-0; Graveney 6-0-35-0; Bainbridge 5-1-34-2; Curran 8-0-41-3.

### Gloucestershire

P. W. Romaines b Inchmore .......... 65
C. W. J. Athey not out ...............121
K. M. Curran not out ................ 14
L-b 10, w 4, n-b 3 .......... 17

1/186 (1 wkt, 38 overs) 217

P. Bainbridge, B. F. Davison, J. W. Lloyds, †R. C. Russell, I. R. Payne, *D. A. Graveney, D. V. Lawrence and G. E. Sainsbury did not bat.

Bowling: Weston 8-0-28-0; Inchmore 7-0-33-1; McEwan 8-0-37-0; Barrett 8-0-43-0; Patel 6-0-51-0; Hick 1-0-15-0.

Umpires: K. E. Palmer and A. G. T. Whitehead.

At The Oval, September 15. GLOUCESTERSHIRE beat SURREY by 86 runs.

# HAMPSHIRE

At Northampton, May 5. HAMPSHIRE lost to NORTHAMPTONSHIRE by eight wickets.

At Canterbury, May 12. KENT v HAMPSHIRE. No result.

## HAMPSHIRE v SURREY

At Southampton, May 19. Hampshire won by 48 runs. Toss won by Surrey.

### Hampshire

C. G. Greenidge c Butcher b Thomas . . 5
V. P. Terry c Richards b Butcher . . . . . 17
*M. C. J. Nicholas b Monkhouse . . . . . 7
R. A. Smith c Lynch b Pocock . . . . . . .104
D. R. Turner b Monkhouse . . . . . . . . . . 39
M. D. Marshall c Clinton b Monkhouse 14
N. G. Cowley c Jesty b Pocock . . . . . . . 6
K. D. James not out . . . . . . . . . . . . . . . . 1
L-b 5, w 10 . . . . . . . . . . . . . . . . 15

1/14 2/27 3/59 (7 wkts, 38 overs) 208
4/142 5/186 6/206 7/208

T. M. Tremlett, †R. J. Parks and C. A. Connor did not bat.

Bowling: Thomas 7–0–49–1; Monkhouse 8–0–44–3; Butcher 8–0–35–1; Pauline 8–0–33–0; Pocock 7–0–42–2.

### Surrey

A. R. Butcher c Parks b Connor . . . . . . 8
G. S. Clinton b Connor . . . . . . . . . . . . . 4
A. J. Stewart b Tremlett . . . . . . . . . . . . . 17
T. E. Jesty b Tremlett . . . . . . . . . . . . . . . 16
M. A. Lynch b Marshall . . . . . . . . . . . . . 15
D. J. Thomas c Terry b Cowley . . . . . . 30
D. B. Pauline lbw b Cowley . . . . . . . . . . 14
A. Needham c Nicholas b James . . . . . 21
†C. J. Richards not out . . . . . . . . . . . . . 19
G. Monkhouse c Greenidge b James . . 5
*P. I. Pocock not out . . . . . . . . . . . . . . . 1
L-b 8, w 2 . . . . . . . . . . . . . . . . . 10

1/14 2/15 3/47 (9 wkts, 38 overs) 160
4/52 5/86 6/102 7/116
8/147 9/157

Bowling: Connor 7–1–13–2; Marshall 8–1–32–1; James 8–2–30–2; Tremlett 7–0–40–2; Cowley 8–0–37–2.

Umpires: D. J. Constant and K. J. Lyons.

## HAMPSHIRE v GLAMORGAN

At Basingstoke, May 26. No result.

At Middlesbrough, June 2. HAMPSHIRE lost to YORKSHIRE by six wickets.

At Edgbaston, June 9. HAMPSHIRE lost to WARWICKSHIRE by five wickets.

At Hove, June 16. HAMPSHIRE beat SUSSEX by nine wickets.

## HAMPSHIRE v ESSEX

At Bournemouth, June 30. Hampshire won by eight wickets. Toss won by Essex.

**Essex**

B. R. Hardie b Marshall ... 0
P. J. Prichard c Terry b Nicholas ... 14
K. S. McEwan c James b Nicholas ... 24
D. R. Pringle c Parks b Marshall ... 40
*K. W. R. Fletcher c R. A. Smith b Tremlett. 30
N. Phillip b Connor ... 4
K. R. Pont b Marshall ... 19
†D. E. East c Turner b Nicholas ... 4
S. Turner not out ... 15
J. K. Lever c and b Connor ... 0
D. L. Acfield not out ... 1
L-b 6, w 4 ... 10

1/0 2/38 3/45 4/100 5/107 6/139 7/141 8/150 9/160 (9 wkts, 40 overs) 161

Bowling: Marshall 8–1–24–3; James 8–0–20–0; Tremlett 8–1–36–1; Nicholas 8–0–39–3; Connor 8–0–36–2.

**Hampshire**

V. P. Terry c Fletcher b Pont ... 23
D. R. Turner b Phillip ... 7
*M. C. J. Nicholas not out ... 61
R. A. Smith not out ... 61
L-b 8, w 1, n-b 1 ... 10

1/20 2/62 (2 wkts, 36.4 overs) 162

C. L. Smith, M. D. Marshall, J. J. E. Hardy, K. D. James, T. M. Tremlett, †R. J. Parks and C. A. Connor did not bat.

Bowling: Lever 6.4–1–32–0; Phillip 8–0–34–1; Turner 8–1–41–0; Pringle 6–2–13–0; Pont 8–0–34–1.

Umpires: J. A. Jameson and P. B. Wight.

At Old Trafford, July 7. HAMPSHIRE beat LANCASHIRE by 3 runs.

## HAMPSHIRE v WORCESTERSHIRE

At Portsmouth, July 14. Hampshire won by 10 runs. Toss won by Worcestershire.

**Hampshire**

V. P. Terry c D'Oliveira b Weston ... 35
D. R. Turner b Radford ... 4
*M. C. J. Nicholas c Neale b Inchmore 18
R. A. Smith c Inchmore b Radford ... 62
C. L. Smith not out ... 63
J. J. E. Hardy not out ... 0
L-b 20, w 4 ... 24

1/9 2/71 3/71 4/205 (4 wkts, 40 overs) 206

†R. J. Parks, N. G. Cowley, K. D. James, T. M. Tremlett and C. A. Connor did not bat.

Bowling: Kapil Dev 8–0–43–0; Radford 8–1–53–2; Newport 8–0–41–0; Inchmore 8–1–25–1; Weston 8–0–24–1.

**Worcestershire**

T. S. Curtis c Hardy b Tremlett ... 71
D. N. Patel c Parks b James ... 13
*P. A. Neale c Nicholas b Cowley ... 4
Kapil Dev c R. A. Smith b Cowley ... 22
D. B. D'Oliveira c Terry b Connor ... 6
M. J. Weston c Terry b Tremlett ... 7
†S. J. Rhodes not out ... 41
J. D. Inchmore not out ... 20
B 2, l-b 6, w 3, n-b 1 ... 12

1/39 2/48 3/84 4/105 5/132 6/139 (6 wkts, 40 overs) 196

P. J. Newport, N. V. Radford and R. K. Illingworth did not bat.

Bowling: James 8–1–20–1; Connor 8–0–37–1; Nicholas 8–0–47–0; Cowley 8–0–26–2; Tremlett 8–0–58–2.

Umpires: H. D. Bird and D. R. Shepherd.

## HAMPSHIRE v SOMERSET

At Southampton, August 4. No result.

At Leicester, August 18. LEICESTERSHIRE v HAMPSHIRE. No result.

## HAMPSHIRE v GLOUCESTERSHIRE

At Bournemouth, August 25. Hampshire won on faster scoring-rate after rain ended play. Toss won by Hampshire.

### Gloucestershire

| | | | |
|---|---|---|---|
| P. W. Romaines b Cowley | 17 | *D. A. Graveney not out | 4 |
| J. W. Lloyds c Parks b Marshall | 3 | †R. C. Russell not out | 1 |
| C. W. J. Athey c Tremlett b Marshall | 69 | | |
| K. M. Curran lbw b Cowley | 0 | B 2, l-b 4, w 2, n-b 1 | 9 |
| P. Bainbridge lbw b Nicholas | 1 | | |
| A. J. Wright c R. A. Smith b Tremlett | 8 | 1/7 2/43 3/43 (8 wkts, 40 overs) | 152 |
| I. R. Payne b Connor | 37 | 4/48 5/63 6/136 | |
| C. A. Walsh b Connor | 3 | 7/145 8/150 | |

G. E. Sainsbury did not bat.

Bowling: Marshall 8–2–18–2; Connor 8–0–32–2; Nicholas 8–1–27–1; Tremlett 8–0–43–1; Cowley 8–1–26–2.

### Hampshire

| | |
|---|---|
| C. G. Greenidge not out | 57 |
| V. P. Terry lbw b Walsh | 5 |
| C. L. Smith lbw b Sainsbury | 1 |
| D. R. Turner not out | 20 |
| L-b 2, w 2, n-b 1 | 5 |
| 1/9 2/14 (2 wkts, 20.2 overs) | 88 |

*M. C. J. Nicholas, R. A. Smith, M. D. Marshall, N. G. Cowley, T. M. Tremlett, †R. J. Parks and C. A. Connor did not bat.

Bowling: Sainsbury 7–1–30–1; Walsh 4–0–13–1; Payne 6–0–20–0; Curran 3.2–0–23–0.

Umpires: N. T. Plews and R. A. White.

## HAMPSHIRE v MIDDLESEX

At Southampton, September 1. Hampshire won by six wickets. Toss won by Hampshire.

### Middlesex

| | | | |
|---|---|---|---|
| G. D. Barlow b Nicholas | 4 | N. F. Williams not out | 5 |
| W. N. Slack c R. A. Smith b Tremlett | 27 | S. P. Hughes b Connor | 9 |
| *C. T. Radley c and b Tremlett | 1 | A. R. C. Fraser run out | 1 |
| R. O. Butcher st Parks b Nicholas | 36 | B 3, l-b 5, w 6 | 14 |
| K. R. Brown c Terry b Cowley | 14 | | — |
| G. D. Rose b Marshall | 30 | 1/19 2/32 3/43 (37.5 overs) | 146 |
| J. F. Sykes b Connor | 3 | 4/87 5/97 6/112 7/126 | |
| †C. P. Metson b Connor | 2 | 8/130 9/141 | |

Bowling: Connor 8–0–25–3; Marshall 7.5–0–35–1; Nicholas 8–0–22–2; Tremlett 6–0–32–2; Cowley 8–2–24–1.

### Hampshire

| | | | |
|---|---|---|---|
| C. G. Greenidge c Butcher b Fraser | 2 | C. L. Smith not out | 9 |
| V. P. Terry lbw b Fraser | 55 | B 1, l-b 4, w 5, n-b 1 | 11 |
| D. R. Turner b Sykes | 30 | | — |
| R. A. Smith not out | 25 | 1/4 2/87 3/109 (4 wkts, 37.3 overs) | 149 |
| *M. C. J. Nicholas c Metson b Hughes | 17 | 4/133 | |

M. D. Marshall, N. G. Cowley, T. M. Tremlett, †R. J. Parks and C. A. Connor did not bat.

Bowling: Fraser 8–1–13–2; Williams 7.3–0–34–0; Rose 7–0–47–0; Hughes 7–0–28–1; Sykes 8–0–22–1.

Umpires: D. G. L. Evans and D. R. Shepherd.

## HAMPSHIRE v DERBYSHIRE

At Southampton, September 8. Derbyshire won by 7 runs. Toss won by Hampshire.

### Derbyshire

| | | | |
|---|---|---|---|
| I. S. Anderson run out | 31 | A. M. Brown not out | 2 |
| B. Roberts lbw b Marshall | 3 | P. E. Russell not out | 0 |
| *K. J. Barnett c C. L. Smith b Tremlett | 37 | | |
| J. E. Morris run out | 7 | L-b 8, w 3, n-b 4 | 15 |
| M. A. Holding c Terry b Connor | 57 | | — |
| P. G. Newman b Connor | 12 | 1/7 2/71 3/83 (8 wkts, 40 overs) | 186 |
| R. J. Finney b Connor | 14 | 4/87 5/160 6/162 | |
| †C. Marples c Terry b Tremlett | 8 | 7/179 8/185 | |

O. H. Mortensen did not bat.

Bowling: Marshall 8–1–29–1; Connor 8–1–21–3; Cowley 8–2–24–0; Nicholas 8–0–54–0; Tremlett 8–0–50–2.

### Hampshire

| | | | |
|---|---|---|---|
| C. G. Greenidge c Marples b Finney | 20 | T. M. Tremlett b Mortensen | 17 |
| V. P. Terry c Marples b Mortensen | 3 | †R. J. Parks b Holding | 5 |
| D. R. Turner b Newman | 34 | C. A. Connor not out | 2 |
| R. A. Smith run out | 26 | B 1, l-b 14, w 6, n-b 3 | 24 |
| *M. C. J. Nicholas c Marples b Holding | 3 | | — |
| C. L. Smith b Mortensen | 34 | 1/32 2/34 3/95 (39.5 overs) | 179 |
| M. D. Marshall b Finney | 4 | 4/99 5/112 6/129 7/144 | |
| N. G. Cowley c Newman b Finney | 7 | 8/158 9/169 | |

Bowling: Finney 8–0–42–3; Holding 8–0–34–2; Mortensen 7.5–0–34–3; Newman 8–1–28–1; Russell 8–0–26–0.

Umpires: B. Dudleston and D. O. Oslear.

At Trent Bridge, September 15. HAMPSHIRE beat NOTTINGHAMSHIRE by 36 runs.

# KENT

At Cardiff, May 5. KENT beat GLAMORGAN on faster scoring-rate.

## KENT v HAMPSHIRE

At Canterbury, May 12. No result, rain and bad light having ended play. Toss won by Hampshire.

### Kent

M. R. Benson c Nicholas b Tremlett .. 21
S. G. Hinks run out .......... 0
C. J. Tavaré c R. A. Smith b Cowley ..101
D. G. Aslett st Parks b Cowley ....... 8
*C. S. Cowdrey c R. A. Smith b Tremlett 5
E. A. E. Baptiste b Tremlett ......... 50
R. M. Ellison b Connor ........... 5
†A. P. E. Knott c Nicholas b Tremlett . 7
G. W. Johnson not out ........... 5
D. L. Underwood b Tremlett ......... 2
B 4, l-b 5, w 4, n-b 1 ........ 14

1/0 2/46 3/89 (9 wkts, 40 overs) 218
4/116 5/175 6/204 7/210
8/214 9/218

K. B. S. Jarvis did not bat.

Bowling: James 8–0–31–0; Connor 8–2–42–1; Cowley 7–0–40–2; Tremlett 8–1–28–5; Maru 7–0–45–0; Nicholas 2–0–23–0.

### Hampshire

V. P. Terry not out .............. 16
D. R. Turner b Ellison ........... 3
R. A. Smith not out ............. 4
L-b 7 ................... 7

1/8 (1 wkt, 11.1 overs) 30

C. L. Smith, *M. C. J. Nicholas, R. J. Maru, N. G. Cowley, T. M. Tremlett, †R. J. Parks, K. D. James and C. A. Connor did not bat.

Bowling: Jarvis 5–0–11–0; Ellison 5.1–2–11–1; Baptiste 1–0–1–0.

Umpires: A. A. Jones and N. T. Plews.

At Bristol, May 26. KENT beat GLOUCESTERSHIRE by seven wickets.

## KENT v WORCESTERSHIRE

At Canterbury, June 2. Kent won by 35 runs. Toss won by Kent.

### Kent

M. R. Benson c Weston b Inchmore ... 93
N. R. Taylor run out ............ 12
C. J. Tavaré c Smith b Weston ....... 4
S. G. Hinks c D'Oliveira b Illingworth . 21
*C. S. Cowdrey c Weston b Patel ..... 3
E. A. E. Baptiste not out ............ 54
R. M. Ellison run out ............ 19
†A. P. E. Knott not out ........... 5
B 2, l-b 8, w 3, n-b 2 ........ 15

1/41 2/59 3/106 (6 wkts, 40 overs) 226
4/118 5/157 6/211

G. W. Johnson, G. R. Dilley and D. L. Underwood did not bat.

Bowling: Kapil Dev 8–0–55–0; Radford 7–0–41–0; Weston 8–0–29–1; Inchmore 8–0–37–1; Patel 5–0–28–1; Illingworth 4–0–26–1.

### Worcestershire

| | | | |
|---|---|---|---|
| M. J. Weston c Hinks b Ellison | 13 | N. V. Radford b Ellison | 8 |
| T. S. Curtis c Taylor b Cowdrey | 23 | J. D. Inchmore not out | 6 |
| D. M. Smith c Knott b Baptiste | 7 | R. K. Illingworth not out | 8 |
| *P. A. Neale c Taylor b Cowdrey | 10 | L-b 12, w 2 | 14 |
| D. N. Patel b Underwood | 27 | | |
| D. B. D'Oliveira c Taylor b Baptiste | 18 | 1/28 2/37 3/54 (9 wkts, 40 overs) | 191 |
| Kapil Dev b Dilley | 16 | 4/60 5/102 6/109 7/149 | |
| †S. J. Rhodes c Knott b Hinks | 41 | 8/176 9/180 | |

Bowling: Dilley 7–0–36–1; Ellison 8–1–30–2; Baptiste 8–0–35–2; Cowdrey 8–0–25–2; Underwood 8–0–50–1; Hinks 1–0–3–1.

Umpires: B. Dudleston and R. Palmer.

At Trent Bridge, June 16. KENT beat NOTTINGHAMSHIRE by 42 runs.

At Old Trafford, June 23. KENT lost to LANCASHIRE by four wickets.

## KENT v MIDDLESEX

At Canterbury, June 30. Kent won by five wickets. Toss won by Middlesex.

### Middlesex

| | | | |
|---|---|---|---|
| G. D. Barlow c Aslett b Baptiste | 72 | J. F. Sykes run out | 25 |
| W. N. Slack c Benson b Underwood | 25 | †C. P. Metson not out | 8 |
| R. O. Butcher c Cowdrey b Jarvis | 15 | L-b 14, n-b 1 | 15 |
| *C. T. Radley c Hinks b Jarvis | 3 | | |
| K. P. Tomlins c and b Underwood | 1 | 1/87 2/119 3/124 (7 wkts, 40 overs) | 169 |
| N. F. Williams lbw b Ellison | 5 | 4/125 5/129 6/150 7/169 | |

S. P. Hughes, W. W. Daniel and N. G. Cowans did not bat.

Bowling: Jarvis 8–0–40–2; Ellison 7–0–30–1; Johnson 8–0–21–0; Baptiste 8–1–27–1; Underwood 8–1–30–2; Cowdrey 1–0–7–0.

### Kent

| | | | |
|---|---|---|---|
| M. R. Benson b Hughes | 34 | R. M. Ellison not out | 13 |
| S. G. Hinks c Metson b Daniel | 15 | | |
| C. J. Tavaré b Hughes | 44 | L-b 3, w 3, n-b 4 | 10 |
| D. G. Aslett b Daniel | 39 | | |
| *C. S. Cowdrey not out | 15 | 1/30 2/72 3/140 (5 wkts, 37.5 overs) | 173 |
| E. A. E. Baptiste lbw b Hughes | 3 | 4/140 5/148 | |

G. W. Johnson, †A. P. E. Knott, D. L. Underwood and K. B. S. Jarvis did not bat.

Bowling: Cowans 7–0–34–0; Daniel 8–0–26–2; Williams 6.5–0–47–0; Sykes 8–0–32–0; Hughes 8–0–31–3.

Umpires: R. Julian and R. A. White.

At The Oval, July 7. KENT beat SURREY by 37 runs.

## KENT v NORTHAMPTONSHIRE

At Maidstone, July 14. Northamptonshire won by ten wickets. Toss won by Northamptonshire.

### Kent

M. R. Benson b Mallender . . . . . . . . . . . 8
S. G. Hinks c Capel b Walker . . . . . . . . 13
C. J. Tavaré not out . . . . . . . . . . . . . . . . 65
D. G. Aslett b Mallender . . . . . . . . . . . . 0
*C. S. Cowdrey c Ripley b Mallender . . 4
E. A. E. Baptiste c Larkins b Capel . . . 1
R. M. Ellison run out . . . . . . . . . . . . . . . 5
G. W. Johnson not out . . . . . . . . . . . . . . 36
L-b 3, w 3 . . . . . . . . . . . . . . . . 6

1/16 2/32 3/32 4/36 5/40 6/54 (6 wkts, 40 overs) 138

†A. P. E. Knott, D. L. Underwood and K. B. S. Jarvis did not bat.

Bowling: Walker 6.1–1–16–1; Mallender 8–2–37–3; Larkins 8–1–24–0; Capel 8–1–18–1; Harper 8–2–27–0; Williams 1.5–0–13–0.

### Northamptonshire

W. Larkins not out . . . . . . . . . . . . . . . . . 75
R. J. Bailey not out . . . . . . . . . . . . . . . . . 59
L-b 3, w 2 . . . . . . . . . . . . . . . . . 5

(no wkt, 28.4 overs) 139

*G. Cook, R. J. Boyd-Moss, R. G. Williams, D. J. Capel, D. J. Wild, R. A. Harper, †D. Ripley, N. A. Mallender and A. Walker did not bat.

Bowling: Jarvis 5–0–18–0; Ellison 5–0–25–0; Cowdrey 4–0–25–0; Baptiste 6–0–26–0; Underwood 6–0–25–0; Johnson 2.4–0–17–0.

Umpires: J. H. Harris and K. E. Palmer.

At Chelmsford, July 21. KENT lost to ESSEX by 13 runs.

At Leicester, July 28. LEICESTERSHIRE v KENT. No result.

## KENT v SUSSEX

At Canterbury, August 11. No result.

At Scarborough, August 18. KENT lost to YORKSHIRE on scoring-rate.

## KENT v DERBYSHIRE

At Folkestone, September 1. Derbyshire won by 9 runs. Toss won by Kent.

### Derbyshire

I. S. Anderson c Hinks b Baptiste . . . . . 34
B. Roberts b Potter . . . . . . . . . . . . . . . . . 48
J. E. Morris c Tavaré b C. S. Cowdrey . 1
*K. J. Barnett c Taylor b Underwood . 13
M. A. Fell b Potter . . . . . . . . . . . . . . . . 21
M. A. Holding b Jarvis . . . . . . . . . . . . . 10
P. G. Newman c G. R. Cowdrey b Potter 1
R. J. Finney c and b Potter . . . . . . . . . . 0
†C. Marples not out . . . . . . . . . . . . . . . . 20
P. E. Russell not out . . . . . . . . . . . . . . . . 3
B 2, l-b 13, w 4 . . . . . . . . . . . . 19

1/74 2/80 3/94 4/127 5/140 6/142 7/143 8/143 (8 wkts, 40 overs) 170

O. H. Mortensen did not bat.

Bowling: Dilley 7–0–19–0; Jarvis 8–0–41–1; Baptiste 5–0–27–1; C. S. Cowdrey 6–0–39–1; Underwood 8–2–20–1; Potter 6–1–9–4.

## Kent

| | | | |
|---|---|---|---|
| L. Potter c Anderson b Newman | 20 | G. R. Dilley c Finney b Holding | 10 |
| S. G. Hinks b Mortensen | 32 | D. L. Underwood not out | 3 |
| C. J. Tavaré c Holding b Finney | 18 | K. B. S. Jarvis not out | 1 |
| N. R. Taylor b Russell | 13 | B 3, l-b 10, w 1 | 14 |
| *C. S. Cowdrey c Finney b Russell | 20 | | |
| E. A. E. Baptiste c Morris b Russell | 9 | 1/44 2/61 3/81 (9 wkts, 40 overs) | 161 |
| G. R. Cowdrey c Barnett b Holding | 21 | 4/97 5/121 6/123 7/133 | |
| †A. P. E. Knott run out | 0 | 8/150 9/160 | |

Bowling: Mortensen 8–0–28–1; Holding 8–3–18–2; Russell 8–1–32–3; Newman 8–0–41–1; Finney 8–0–29–1.

Umpires: D. J. Constant and K. J. Lyons.

# KENT v WARWICKSHIRE

At Canterbury, September 8. Warwickshire won by 31 runs. Toss won by Kent. Warwickshire's total was the highest by any county against Kent in the competition.

## Warwickshire

| | | | |
|---|---|---|---|
| T. A. Lloyd lbw b Underwood | 69 | A. M. Ferreira not out | 20 |
| †G. W. Humpage c Marsh b Ellison | 27 | D. A. Thorne not out | 3 |
| A. I. Kallicharran c Marsh b Ellison | 97 | L-b 13, w 7, n-b 4 | 24 |
| D. L. Amiss c Taylor b Cowdrey | 9 | | |
| Asif Din c Hinks b Ellison | 23 | 1/50 2/170 3/188 (6 wkts, 40 overs) | 284 |
| P. A. Smith c Tavaré b Baptiste | 12 | 4/233 5/256 6/257 | |

G. C. Small, A. R. K. Pierson and *N. Gifford did not bat.

Bowling: Dilley 6–0–32–0; Ellison 8–0–61–3; Potter 4–0–21–0; Baptiste 6–0–53–1; Cowdrey 8–0–60–1; Underwood 8–0–44–1.

## Kent

| | | | |
|---|---|---|---|
| M. R. Benson c Amiss b Small | 12 | †S. A. Marsh c Pierson b Ferreira | 2 |
| S. G. Hinks st Humpage b Pierson | 28 | G. R. Dilley not out | 10 |
| C. J. Tavaré c Kallicharran b Gifford | 59 | | |
| E. A. E. Baptiste b Thorne | 60 | L-b 4, w 2, n-b 2 | 8 |
| *C. S. Cowdrey c Pierson b Gifford | 8 | | |
| R. M. Ellison c Pierson b Ferreira | 30 | 1/18 2/60 3/148 (9 wkts, 40 overs) | 253 |
| N. R. Taylor lbw b Thorne | 11 | 4/160 5/181 6/203 7/235 | |
| L. Potter b Small | 25 | 8/242 9/253 | |

D. L. Underwood did not bat.

Bowling: Small 8–0–43–2; Smith 6–0–23–0; Ferreira 8–0–48–2; Pierson 4–0–29–1; Gifford 8–0–58–1; Thorne 6–0–48–2.

Umpires: A. A. Jones and N. T. Plews.

# KENT v SOMERSET

At Canterbury, September 15. Somerset won by three wickets. Toss won by Kent.

### Kent

L. Potter c Harden b Dredge ......... 11
S. G. Hinks c Felton b Palmer ....... 32
C. J. Tavaré c Garner b Palmer ...... 27
N. R. Taylor c Garner b Palmer ...... 21
E. A. E. Baptiste lbw b Palmer ....... 0
*C. S. Cowdrey c Dredge b Palmer .... 4
G. R. Cowdrey b Garner ............. 20
R. M. Ellison run out ............... 6
†S. N. V. Waterton not out .......... 10
D. L. Underwood not out ............ 2
B 1, l-b 7, w 1, n-b 1 ........ 10

1/36 2/57 3/94 4/94 5/97 6/107 7/126 8/129 (8 wkts, 40 overs) 143

K. B. S. Jarvis did not bat.

Bowling: Garner 8–2–20–1; Davis 8–0–24–0; Dredge 8–0–30–1; Marks 8–0–27–0; Palmer 8–0–34–5.

### Somerset

J. G. Wyatt lbw b Jarvis ............ 2
P. M. Roebuck lbw b C. S. Cowdrey .. 16
N. A. Felton c Waterton b Baptiste ... 47
B. C. Rose c Waterton b C. S. Cowdrey 1
*V. J. Marks c Waterton b Baptiste ... 39
R. J. Harden run out ............... 20
J. Garner b Ellison ................. 3
G. V. Palmer not out ................ 8
C. H. Dredge not out ............... 1
L-b 6, w 1 .................. 7

1/2 2/44 3/48 4/97 5/116 6/135 7/136 (7 wkts, 39.5 overs) 144

M. R. Davis and †T. Gard did not bat.

Bowling: Jarvis 8–1–27–1; Ellison 7.5–0–23–1; C. S. Cowdrey 8–0–23–2; Baptiste 8–0–36–2; Underwood 8–0–29–0.

Umpires: R. Julian and B. J. Meyer.

# LANCASHIRE

## LANCASHIRE v LEICESTERSHIRE

At Old Trafford, May 5. No result. Toss won by Leicestershire.

### Lancashire

G. Fowler b Clift ................... 11
S. J. O'Shaughnessy c Ferris b Willey .. 23
K. A. Hayes b Willey ............... 3
N. H. Fairbrother b Ferris .......... 35
*J. Abrahams b De Freitas .......... 2
M. Watkinson c Butcher b Parsons .... 8
J. Simmons c Willey b De Freitas ..... 16
P. J. W. Allott c Briers b Ferris ...... 3
†J. Stanworth c Garnham b De Freitas 2
D. J. Makinson not out ............. 3
B. P. Patterson not out .............. 3
B 6, l-b 8, w 1, n-b 3 ........ 18

1/29 2/38 3/40 4/68 5/85 6/100 7/108 8/113 9/121 (9 wkts, 40 overs) 127

Bowling: Ferris 8–3–14–2; Parsons 8–0–33–1; Clift 8–1–28–1; Willey 8–3–11–2; De Freitas 8–1–27–3.

### Leicestershire

*D. I. Gower lbw b Allott ........... 6
N. E. Briers not out ................ 0
P. Willey not out ................... 2

1/6 (1 wkt, 3.2 overs) 8

I. P. Butcher, J. J. Whitaker, †M. A. Garnham, P. B. Clift, G. J. Parsons, G. J. F. Ferris, P. A. J. De Freitas and J. P. Addison did not bat.

Bowling: Allott 2–0–2–1; Patterson 1.2–0–6–0.

Umpires: K. J. Lyons and N. T. Plews.

At Edgbaston, May 12. LANCASHIRE lost to WARWICKSHIRE by 23 runs.

## LANCASHIRE v GLOUCESTERSHIRE

At Old Trafford, May 19. Gloucestershire won by six wickets. Toss won by Gloucestershire.

### Lancashire

| | | | |
|---|---|---|---|
| G. Fowler b Bainbridge | 35 | †C. Maynard c Athey b Bainbridge | 15 |
| S. J. O'Shaughnessy c Graveney b Curran | 20 | J. Simmons not out | 5 |
| *J. Abrahams b Curran | 3 | L-b 14, w 12, n-b 4 | 30 |
| D. P. Hughes c Lawrence b Bainbridge | 28 | | |
| N. H. Fairbrother not out | 49 | 1/38 2/47 3/90 (6 wkts, 40 overs) | 220 |
| S. T. Jefferies run out | 35 | 4/97 5/168 6/192 | |

S. Henriksen, P. J. W. Allott and D. J. Makinson did not bat.

Bowling: Lawrence 8–0–59–0; Walsh 8–1–35–0; Shepherd 8–0–37–0; Curran 8–0–31–2; Bainbridge 8–1–44–3.

### Gloucestershire

| | | | |
|---|---|---|---|
| J. W. Lloyds c and b Jefferies | 1 | P. Bainbridge not out | 10 |
| P. W. Romaines c Maynard b Henriksen | 65 | L-b 8, w 3, n-b 3 | 14 |
| C. W. J. Athey c Abrahams b Makinson | 44 | | |
| B. F. Davison c Fowler b Makinson | 57 | 1/17 2/97 3/122 (4 wkts, 38.1 overs) | 223 |
| K. M. Curran not out | 32 | 4/209 | |

J. N. Shepherd, *D. A. Graveney, †R. C. Russell, C. A. Walsh and D. V. Lawrence did not bat.

Bowling: Makinson 8–1–44–2; Allott 7–0–36–0; Jefferies 6–0–45–1; O'Shaughnessy 5.1–0–25–0; Simmons 5–0–19–0; Henriksen 7–0–46–1.

Umpires: H. D. Bird and J. A. Jameson.

At Northampton, June 2. LANCASHIRE tied with NORTHAMPTONSHIRE.

At Ilford, June 9. ESSEX v LANCASHIRE. No result.

## LANCASHIRE v DERBYSHIRE

At Old Trafford, June 16. Lancashire won by seven wickets. Toss won by Lancashire.

### Derbyshire

| | | | |
|---|---|---|---|
| *K. J. Barnett b O'Shaughnessy | 21 | R. J. Finney not out | 0 |
| †B. J. M. Maher c Fowler b Makinson | 7 | M. A. Holding b Makinson | 0 |
| J. E. Morris c Abrahams b Watkinson | 52 | O. H. Mortensen not out | 0 |
| B. Roberts c Makinson b Simmons | 42 | L-b 6, w 1 | 7 |
| W. P. Fowler c Fairbrother b Watkinson | 14 | | |
| D. G. Moir c Fairbrother b Makinson | 13 | 1/16 2/56 3/99 (9 wkts, 40 overs) | 182 |
| G. Miller c Maynard b Makinson | 20 | 4/115 5/148 6/158 7/178 | |
| P. G. Newman c Abrahams b Watkinson | 6 | 8/181 9/181 | |

Bowling: Henriksen 8–0–18–0; Makinson 8–0–28–4; O'Shaughnessy 8–0–55–1; Simmons 8–0–37–1; Watkinson 8–1–38–3.

### Lancashire

| | | | |
|---|---|---|---|
| G. Fowler not out | 98 | *J. Abrahams not out | 38 |
| S. J. O'Shaughnessy b Mortensen | 13 | B 1, l-b 3, w 7 | 11 |
| C. H. Lloyd c Newman b Miller | 16 | | —— |
| D. P. Hughes c Moir b Finney | 10 | 1/22 2/58 3/94 (3 wkts, 39 overs) | 186 |

N. H. Fairbrother, M. Watkinson, †C. Maynard, J. Simmons, D. J. Makinson and S. Henriksen did not bat.

Bowling: Holding 8–1–37–0; Mortensen 7–0–29–1; Moir 8–0–25–0; Miller 6–0–25–1; Finney 5–0–30–1; Newman 5–0–36–0.

Umpires: J. W. Holder and D. O. Oslear.

## LANCASHIRE v KENT

At Old Trafford, June 23. Lancashire won by four wickets. Toss won by Lancashire.

### Kent

| | | | |
|---|---|---|---|
| M. R. Benson c Maynard b Allott | 8 | G. W. Johnson not out | 11 |
| S. G. Hinks c O'Shaughnessy b Allott | 0 | D. L. Underwood not out | 5 |
| C. J. Tavaré b Simmons | 27 | | |
| D. G. Aslett lbw b Allott | 0 | B 5, l-b 8, w 5 | 18 |
| *C. S. Cowdrey c Fairbrother b Simmons | 37 | | —— |
| E. A. E. Baptiste b Watkinson | 18 | 1/0 2/17 3/17 (8 wkts, 40 overs) | 142 |
| R. M. Ellison c and b Makinson | 4 | 4/72 5/98 6/105 | |
| †A. P. E. Knott c Fowler b Allott | 14 | 7/110 8/128 | |

K. B. S. Jarvis did not bat.

Bowling: Makinson 8–1–20–1; Allott 8–2–28–4; Watkinson 8–2–25–1; O'Shaughnessy 8–0–29–0; Simmons 8–2–27–2.

### Lancashire

| | | | |
|---|---|---|---|
| G. Fowler c Johnson b Underwood | 33 | M. Watkinson not out | 34 |
| S. J. O'Shaughnessy c Knott b Ellison | 13 | J. Simmons not out | 4 |
| *J. Abrahams b Cowdrey | 1 | L-b 16, w 4 | 20 |
| C. H. Lloyd c Johnson b Baptiste | 17 | | —— |
| D. P. Hughes b Ellison | 19 | 1/23 2/32 3/65 (6 wkts, 38.2 overs) | 143 |
| N. H. Fairbrother b Underwood | 2 | 4/79 5/81 6/123 | |

†C. Maynard, P. J. W. Allott and D. J. Makinson did not bat.

Bowling: Jarvis 7.2–0–32–0; Ellison 7–3–16–2; Cowdrey 8–0–34–1; Baptiste 8–2–17–1; Underwood 8–1–28–2.

Umpires: D. J. Constant and M. J. Kitchen.

At Hastings, June 30. LANCASHIRE lost to SUSSEX by 69 runs.

## LANCASHIRE v HAMPSHIRE

At Old Trafford, July 7. Hampshire won by 3 runs. Toss won by Lancashire.

**Hampshire**

C. G. Greenidge retired hurt ......... 59
V. P. Terry c Abrahams b Watkinson . 45
*M. C. J. Nicholas c Fowler b Henriksen 26
R. A. Smith lbw b Simmons ......... 12
C. L. Smith not out ................. 47
J. J. E. Hardy b Allott ............... 36
M. D. Marshall b Allott ............. 0
L-b 8, w 2 ................. 10

1/99 2/145 3/151 4/235 5/235 (5 wkts, 40 overs) 235

K. D. James, T. M. Tremlett, †R. J. Parks and C. A. Connor did not bat.

Bowling: Makinson 7–1–31–0; Allott 8–0–55–2; Simmons 8–0–39–1; Watkinson 7–0–35–1, O'Shaughnessy 3–0–24–0; Henriksen 7–0–43–1.

**Lancashire**

G. Fowler b James ................. 5
S. J. O'Shaughnessy c Parks b Connor . 7
C. H. Lloyd b Tremlett .............. 22
*J. Abrahams b Tremlett ............ 66
N. H. Fairbrother b Nicholas ........ 44
M. Watkinson b Marshall ............ 5
J. Simmons b Nicholas ............... 39
†C. Maynard run out ............... 1
D. J. Makinson b Connor ............ 13
P. J. W. Allott not out .............. 7
S. Henriksen b Nicholas .............. 1
B 1, l-b 12, w 7, n-b 2 ....... 22

1/17 2/23 3/75 4/132 5/157 6/171 7/173 8/224 9/228 (40 overs) 232

Bowling: James 8–0–41–1; Connor 8–0–37–2; Nicholas 8–0–53–3; Tremlett 8–0–51–2; Marshall 8–0–37–1.

Umpires: N. T. Plews and R. A. White.

## LANCASHIRE v GLAMORGAN

At Old Trafford, July 14. Tied. Toss won by Glamorgan.

**Lancashire**

M. R. Chadwick lbw b Thomas ...... 0
S. J. O'Shaughnessy c Younis b Ontong 42
*J. Abrahams c Davies b Ontong ..... 11
C. H. Lloyd c Davies b Barwick ......108
N. H. Fairbrother c Jones b Barwick .. 39
M. Watkinson not out .............. 11
J. Simmons c Holmes b Barwick ...... 1
L-b 6, n-b 1 ............... 7

1/1 2/30 3/69 4/166 5/213 6/219 (6 wkts, 40 overs) 219

I. Folley, †C. Maynard, D. J. Makinson and S. Henriksen did not bat.

Bowling: Thomas 8–0–43–1; Barwick 8–1–35–3; Ontong 8–0–33–2; Price 8–0–40–0; Malone 4–0–32–0; Holmes 4–0–30–0.

**Glamorgan**

H. Morris run out ................... 91
A. L. Jones c Abrahams b Makinson .. 6
Younis Ahmed lbw b Simmons ....... 22
Javed Miandad st Maynard b Simmons 51
G. C. Holmes not out ............... 26
*R. C. Ontong c and b Makinson ..... 4
J. G. Thomas not out ............... 4
B 4, l-b 9, w 2 ............ 15

1/9 2/59 3/164 4/192 5/208 (5 wkts, 40 overs) 219

M. R. Price, †T. Davies, S. R. Barwick and S. J. Malone did not bat.

Bowling: Makinson 7–1–38–2; Henriksen 7–0–35–0; Simmons 8–1–34–2; O'Shaughnessy 3–0–24–0; Folley 8–0–41–0; Watkinson 7–0–34–0.

Umpires: B. Leadbeater and R. Palmer.

At Lord's, July 28. LANCASHIRE lost to MIDDLESEX by six wickets.

At Worcester, August 4. WORCESTERSHIRE v LANCASHIRE. No result.

At Headingley, August 11. YORKSHIRE v LANCASHIRE. No result.

### LANCASHIRE v NOTTINGHAMSHIRE

At Old Trafford, August 18. Lancashire won by five wickets in a match reduced by rain to 20 overs a side. Toss won by Lancashire.

#### Nottinghamshire

| | | | |
|---|---|---|---|
| B. C. Broad c Maynard b Makinson | 1 | †B. N. French not out | 27 |
| D. W. Randall run out | 2 | | |
| *C. E. B. Rice run out | 13 | L-b 12 | 12 |
| P. Johnson b Makinson | 4 | | |
| J. D. Birch b Watkinson | 17 | 1/3 2/3 3/11 (5 wkts, 20 overs) | 115 |
| R. J. Hadlee not out | 39 | 4/35 5/48 | |

E. E. Hemmings, R. A. Pick, K. Saxelby and K. E. Cooper did not bat.

Bowling: Allott 6–0–28–0; Makinson 5–0–27–2; Simmons 4–0–13–0; Watkinson 5–0–35–1.

#### Lancashire

| | | | |
|---|---|---|---|
| G. Fowler c Cooper b Saxelby | 6 | D. J. Makinson not out | 12 |
| S. J. O'Shaughnessy b Hadlee | 8 | | |
| C. H. Lloyd c Hemmings b Hadlee | 46 | L-b 6, w 2, n-b 1 | 9 |
| D. P. Hughes c Hadlee b Cooper | 14 | | |
| N. H. Fairbrother not out | 26 | 1/13 2/16 3/62 (5 wkts, 19.4 overs) | 121 |
| J. Simmons b Hadlee | 0 | 4/87 5/88 | |

*J. Abrahams, M. Watkinson, †C. Maynard and P. J. W. Allott did not bat.

Bowling: Hadlee 6–1–28–3; Saxelby 3–0–10–1; Pick 3.4–0–26–0; Cooper 4–0–25–1; Rice 3–0–26–0.

Umpires: A. A. Jones and J. Birkenshaw.

### LANCASHIRE v SOMERSET

At Old Trafford, August 25. No result.

At The Oval, September 8. LANCASHIRE lost to SURREY by eight wickets.

## LEICESTERSHIRE

At Old Trafford, May 5. LANCASHIRE v LEICESTERSHIRE. No result.

### LEICESTERSHIRE v YORKSHIRE

At Leicester, May 12. Yorkshire won by seven wickets. Toss won by Yorkshire.

### Leicestershire

J. C. Balderstone c Bairstow b Sidebottom 0
N. E. Briers b Fletcher 77
*D. I. Gower c Fletcher b Jarvis 27
P. Willey lbw b Jarvis 2
J. J. Whitaker not out 86
P. B. Clift b Fletcher 16
G. J. Parsons not out 3
B 2, l-b 5, w 4, n-b 1 12

1/6 2/59 3/63 4/165 5/211 (5 wkts, 40 overs) 223

†M. A. Garnham, P. A. J. De Freitas, J. P. Agnew and G. J. F. Ferris did not bat.

Bowling: Stevenson 8–0–56–0; Sidebottom 8–0–43–1; Jarvis 8–1–37–2; Carrick 8–1–22–0; Fletcher 8–0–58–2.

### Yorkshire

M. D. Moxon b Parsons 28
D. Byas st Garnham b Willey 15
K. Sharp not out 73
J. D. Love c Garnham b Clift 13
P. E. Robinson not out 78
L-b 8, w 5, n-b 4 17

1/34 2/57 3/86 (3 wkts, 36.5 overs) 224

*†D. L. Bairstow, A. Sidebottom, G. B. Stevenson, P. Carrick, P. W. Jarvis and S. D. Fletcher did not bat.

Bowling: Agnew 7–0–41–0; Ferris 6.5–0–33–0; Willey 8–0–24–1; Parsons 8–0–42–1; Clift 5–0–51–1; De Freitas 2–0–25–0.

Umpires: C. Cook and A. G. T. Whitehead.

At Trent Bridge, May 19. NOTTINGHAMSHIRE v LEICESTERSHIRE. No result.

## LEICESTERSHIRE v NORTHAMPTONSHIRE

At Leicester, May 26. No result, rain having ended play after 32 minutes. Toss won by Northamptonshire.

### Leicestershire

I. P. Butcher c Capel b Mallender 8
N. E. Briers not out 6
*D. I. Gower not out 17
L-b 3, w 1 4

1/9 (1 wkt, 10 overs) 35

P. Willey, J. J. Whitaker, P. B. Clift, †M. A. Garnham, G. J. Parsons, R. A. Cobb, N. G. B. Cook and G. J. F. Ferris did not bat.

Bowling: Walker 4–0–20–0; Mallender 5–2–4–1; Larkins 1–0–8–0.

### Northamptonshire

*G. Cook, W. Larkins, R. J. Bailey, A. J. Lamb, †G. Sharp, D. J. Wild, R. A. Harper, D. J. Capel, R. G. Williams, N. A. Mallender and A. Walker.

Umpires: B. Leadbeater and R. A. White.

At Chelmsford, June 2. LEICESTERSHIRE tied with ESSEX.

At Lord's, June 16. LEICESTERSHIRE lost to MIDDLESEX by 5 runs.

## LEICESTERSHIRE v GLAMORGAN

At Leicester, June 23. Leicestershire won by 11 runs. Toss won by Glamorgan.

### Leicestershire

I. P. Butcher c Hopkins b Barwick .... 2
N. E. Briers c Thomas b Derrick ..... 60
*D. I. Gower c Davies b Thomas ..... 2
P. Willey c Davies b Ontong ......... 40
J. J. Whitaker not out .............. 40
M. Blackett c Davies b Thomas ...... 8
†M. A. Garnham not out ............ 10
L-b 11, w 4 ................. 15

1/13 2/24 3/101 4/126 5/157 (5 wkts, 40 overs) 177

G. J. Parsons, P. A. J. De Freitas, J. P. Agnew and L. B. Taylor did not bat.

Bowling: Barwick 8–1–10–1; Thomas 8–1–32–2; Steele 8–0–30–0; Ontong 8–1–38–1; Holmes 7–0–44–0; Derrick 1–0–12–1.

### Glamorgan

J. A. Hopkins c Garnham b Parsons .. 14
A. L. Jones c Garnham b Agnew ..... 3
S. P. Henderson b Taylor ............ 11
Javed Miandad run out .............. 62
G. C. Holmes c Garnham b Parsons ... 0
*R. C. Ontong c Garnham b Parsons .. 40
J. G. Thomas b De Freitas .......... 3
†T. Davies c Briers b Agnew ......... 12
J. F. Steele b Agnew ................ 9
J. Derrick not out .................. 7
S. R. Barwick b Taylor .............. 0
L-b 5 ...................... 5

1/7 2/28 3/30 4/30 5/126 6/129 7/140 8/159 9/164 (39.3 overs) 166

Bowling: Agnew 8–0–36–3; Taylor 5.3–0–12–2; Parsons 8–1–30–3; Willey 8–1–18–0; De Freitas 8–0–51–1; Briers 2–0–14–0.

Umpires: J. A. Jameson and R. Julian.

## LEICESTERSHIRE v SURREY

At Leicester, June 30. Leicestershire won on faster scoring-rate after Surrey failed to achieve their revised target of 109 off twenty overs, 75 minutes of their innings having been lost to rain. Toss won by Surrey.

### Leicestershire

I. P. Butcher c Stewart b Taylor ...... 48
N. E. Briers b Jesty ................ 54
J. J. Whitaker b Pauline ............ 0
*P. Willey c and b Pauline ........... 39
†M. A. Garnham run out ............. 36
G. J. Parsons c Pauline b Gray ....... 17
M. Blackett not out .................. 4
P. A. J. De Freitas not out .......... 1
B 2, l-b 6, w 7, n-b 2 ........ 17

1/81 2/81 3/137 4/155 5/191 6/213 (6 wkts, 40 overs) 216

R. A. Cobb, J. P. Agnew and L. B. Taylor did not bat.

Bowling: Gray 8–0–36–1; Taylor 8–0–47–1; Jesty 8–1–38–1; Pauline 8–0–43–2; Pocock 8–0–44–0.

### Surrey

A. R. Butcher lbw b Agnew .......... 1
G. S. Clinton b Parsons ............. 28
M. A. Lynch c Blackett b De Freitas .. 14
*T. E. Jesty c Garnham b Agnew ..... 12
A. J. Stewart c Whitaker b Taylor .... 25
A. Needham lbw b Taylor ........... 0
†C. J. Richards run out ............. 4
D. B. Pauline not out ............... 10
A. H. Gray not out .................. 2
B 1, l-b 3, w 1 ............ 5

1/4 2/32 3/58 4/66 5/69 6/73 7/88 (7 wkts, 20 overs) 101

N. S. Taylor and P. I. Pocock did not bat.

Bowling: Taylor 7–1–21–2; Agnew 7–2–36–2; De Freitas 3–0–16–1; Parsons 3–0–24–1.

Umpires: D. J. Constant and R. Palmer.

At Taunton, July 7. LEICESTERSHIRE beat SOMERSET by 43 runs.

## LEICESTERSHIRE v WARWICKSHIRE

At Leicester, July 21. Leicestershire won by nine wickets, having been set a revised target of 173 in 37 overs after the loss of fifteen minutes to rain. Toss won by Leicestershire.

### Warwickshire

| | |
|---|---|
| G. J. Lord c Taylor b Parsons | 53 |
| †G. W. Humpage b Willey | 28 |
| A. I. Kallicharran c Briers b Clift | 19 |
| D. L. Amiss b Taylor | 16 |
| P. A. Smith not out | 28 |
| A. M. Ferreira c Whitaker b Clift | 11 |
| Asif Din b Clift | 25 |
| L-b 5, n-b 2 | 7 |
| 1/44 2/105 3/105 4/137 5/151 6/187 (6 wkts, 40 overs) | 187 |

G. C. Small, *N. Gifford, D. S. Hoffman and D. A. Thorne did not bat.

Bowling: Agnew 8–0–43–0; Taylor 8–1–27–1; Parsons 8–0–50–1; Willey 8–2–27–1; Clift 8–1–35–3.

### Leicestershire

| | |
|---|---|
| I. P. Butcher lbw b Small | 0 |
| N. E. Briers not out | 51 |
| *D. I. Gower not out | 114 |
| B 3, l-b 4, w 2, n-b 1 | 10 |
| 1/0 (1 wkt, 29.3 overs) | 175 |

P. Willey, J. J. Whitaker, P. B. Clift, P. A. J. De Freitas, †M. A. Garnham, G. J. Parsons, J. P. Agnew and L. B. Taylor did not bat.

Bowling: Small 5–1–24–1; Hoffman 4–0–17–0; Thorne 6–0–33–0; Ferreira 6–0–39–0; Gifford 4–0–21–0; Smith 4.3–0–34–0.

Umpires: J. Birkenshaw and B. Leadbeater.

## LEICESTERSHIRE v KENT

At Leicester, July 28. No result.

At Cheltenham, August 11. LEICESTERSHIRE beat GLOUCESTERSHIRE by 7 runs.

## LEICESTERSHIRE v HAMPSHIRE

At Leicester, August 18. No result after rain ended play. Toss won by Hampshire.

### Leicestershire

| | |
|---|---|
| I. P. Butcher b Marshall | 3 |
| N. E. Briers not out | 13 |
| *P. Willey not out | 1 |
| W 1 | 1 |
| 1/14 (1 wkt, 8 overs) | 18 |

J. J. Whitaker, R. A. Cobb, M. Blackett, †M. A. Garnham, P. B. Clift, P. A. J. De Freitas, G. J. Parsons and J. P. Agnew did not bat.

Bowling: Connor 4–0–11–0; Marshall 4–0–7–1.

### Hampshire

C. G. Greenidge, V. P. Terry, *M. C. J. Nicholas, R. A. Smith, D. R. Turner, J. J. E. Hardy, M. D. Marshall, N. G. Cowley, T. M. Tremlett, †R. J. Parks and C. A. Connor.

Umpires: K. J. Lyons and P. B. Wight.

## LEICESTERSHIRE v WORCESTERSHIRE

At Leicester, September 1. Worcestershire won by 8 runs. Toss won by Leicestershire.

### Worcestershire

| | |
|---|---|
| T. S. Curtis c Balderstone b Ferris | 1 |
| D. B. D'Oliveira lbw b Willey | 18 |
| G. A. Hick c Clift b Willey | 21 |
| D. N. Patel b Ferris | 76 |
| *P. A. Neale lbw b De Freitas | 28 |
| M. J. Weston lbw b De Freitas | 32 |
| D. A. Banks c Garnham b Ferris | 0 |
| †S. J. Rhodes c Willey b De Freitas | 6 |
| N. V. Radford not out | 6 |
| J. D. Inchmore not out | 1 |
| L-b 3, w 1, n-b 2 | 6 |
| 1/2 2/40 3/47 4/100 5/139 6/161 7/182 8/194 (8 wkts, 40 overs) | 195 |

S. M. McEwan did not bat.

Bowling: Parsons 8–0–34–0; Ferris 8–0–40–3; Willey 8–0–21–2; Clift 8–0–42–0; De Freitas 8–0–55–3.

### Leicestershire

| | |
|---|---|
| N. E. Briers b Inchmore | 24 |
| I. P. Butcher c Banks b Weston | 7 |
| *P. Willey c Patel b McEwan | 21 |
| J. J. Whitaker c Rhodes b Patel | 46 |
| †M. A. Garnham c Patel b McEwan | 0 |
| P. B. Clift c Patel b McEwan | 9 |
| G. J. Parsons lbw b Patel | 8 |
| J. C. Balderstone c Neale b Patel | 5 |
| P. A. J. De Freitas run out | 27 |
| M. Blackett not out | 21 |
| G. J. F. Ferris not out | 9 |
| L-b 6, w 3, n-b 1 | 10 |
| 1/19 2/39 3/66 4/66 5/82 6/120 7/125 8/130 9/177 (9 wkts, 40 overs) | 187 |

Bowling: Weston 8–0–18–1; Radford 8–0–53–0; Inchmore 8–0–41–1; McEwan 8–0–36–3; Patel 8–0–33–3.

Umpires: J. Birkenshaw and J. A. Jameson.

At Hove, September 8. LEICESTERSHIRE lost to SUSSEX by 7 runs.

At Chesterfield, September 15. LEICESTERSHIRE lost to DERBYSHIRE by nine wickets.

# MIDDLESEX

At Bradford, May 5. YORKSHIRE v MIDDLESEX. No result.

## MIDDLESEX v GLOUCESTERSHIRE

At Lord's, May 12. Middlesex won by eight wickets in a match reduced by rain to 28 overs a side. Toss won by Middlesex.

### Gloucestershire

| | |
|---|---|
| A. W. Stovold c Downton b Daniel | 0 |
| P. W. Romaines lbw b Daniel | 3 |
| C. W. J. Athey not out | 67 |
| B. F. Davison b Daniel | 5 |
| P. Bainbridge c Barlow b Fraser | 12 |
| K. M. Curran c and b Emburey | 47 |
| J. N. Shepherd not out | 1 |
| L-b 7, w 5, n-b 2 | 14 |
| 1/0 2/5 3/11 4/29 5/134 (5 wkts, 28 overs) | 149 |

*D. A. Graveney, I. R. Payne, †R. C. Russell and D. V. Lawrence did not bat.

Bowling: Daniel 8 2 40 3; Williams 8-0-18-0; Fraser 8-1-45-1; Emburey 4-0-39-1.

### Middlesex

| | |
|---|---|
| G. D. Barlow c Curran b Payne | 40 |
| W. N. Slack lbw b Shepherd | 3 |
| *M. W. Gatting not out | 69 |
| R. O. Butcher not out | 29 |
| L-b 8, w 1 | 9 |
| 1/7 2/99 (2 wkts, 26.2 overs) | 150 |

C. T. Radley, †P. R. Downton, J. E. Emburey, P. H. Edmonds, N. F. Williams, A. R. C. Fraser and W. W. Daniel did not bat.

Bowling: Lawrence 5.2-0-34-0; Shepherd 6-0-33-1; Curran 4-0-22-0; Bainbridge 7-0-35-0; Payne 4-1-18-1.

Umpires: J. H. Hampshire and J. W. Holder.

## MIDDLESEX v GLAMORGAN

At Lord's, May 19. Glamorgan won by seven wickets. Toss won by Glamorgan.

### Middlesex

| | |
|---|---|
| G. D. Barlow st Davies b Holmes | 59 |
| W. N. Slack run out | 35 |
| *M. W. Gatting c Henderson b Steele | 16 |
| R. O. Butcher c Derrick b Steele | 7 |
| C. T. Radley not out | 23 |
| †P. R. Downton c Hopkins b Steele | 2 |
| J. E. Emburey c Davies b Steele | 1 |
| P. H. Edmonds c Derrick b Steele | 7 |
| N. F. Williams c and b Thomas | 1 |
| W. W. Daniel not out | 7 |
| L-b 5, w 3 | 8 |
| 1/101 2/104 3/124 4/128 5/135 6/137 7/145 8/151 (8 wkts, 40 overs) | 166 |

A. R. C. Fraser did not bat.

Bowling: Barwick 5-0-19-0; Thomas 6-0-27-1; Derrick 6-1-28-0; Holmes 8-0-40-1; Ontong 8-0-17-0; Steele 7-0-30-5.

### Glamorgan

J. A. Hopkins not out ................ 72
G. C. Holmes c and b Williams ...... 8
Younis Ahmed c Radley b Emburey ... 37
Javed Miandad c Downton b Williams 32
S. P. Henderson not out ............. 11
L-b 5, w 2 .................. 7

1/19 2/89 3/138 (3 wkts, 38.2 overs) 167

*R. C. Ontong, J. F. Steele, J. Derrick, J. G. Thomas, †T. Davies and S. R. Barwick did not bat.

Bowling: Williams 8–1–29–2; Daniel 8–1–22–0; Fraser 8–0–31–0; Emburey 8–0–48–1; Edmonds 5.2–0–26–0; Gatting 1–0–6–0.

Umpires: C. Cook and J. H. Hampshire.

## MIDDLESEX v SUSSEX

At Lord's, May 26. Middlesex won by seven wickets in a match reduced by rain to ten overs a side. Toss won by Middlesex.

### Sussex

P. W. G. Parker c Emburey b Williams 23
A. P. Wells b Edmonds ............ 42
Imran Khan not out ................ 17
*I. J. Gould not out ................ 1
B 1, l-b 1, n-b 2 ............ 4

1/44 2/84 (2 wkts, 10 overs) 87

G. D. Mendis, C. M. Wells, I. A. Greig, C. P. Phillipson, A. C. S. Pigott, D. A. Reeve and A. N. Jones did not bat.

Bowling: Daniel 2–0–15–0; Cowans 2–0–15–0; Edmonds 2–0–19–1; Williams 2–0–25–1; Emburey 2–0–11–0.

### Middlesex

G. D. Barlow c Phillipson b Pigott .... 2
*M. W. Gatting b Pigott ............ 15
R. O. Butcher c A. P. Wells b Imran .. 49
C. T. Radley not out ................ 9
†P. R. Downton not out .............. 5
L-b 5, w 3 .................. 8

1/6 2/68 3/77 (3 wkts, 9.4 overs) 88

W. N. Slack, J. E. Emburey, P. H. Edmonds, N. F. Williams, N. G. Cowans and W. W. Daniel did not bat.

Bowling: Pigott 2–0–17–2; Imran 2–0–10–1; Reeve 2–0–19–0; Greig 2–0–20–0; C. M. Wells 1.4–0–17–0.

Umpires: J. Birkenshaw and K. E. Palmer.

## MIDDLESEX v DERBYSHIRE

At Lord's, June 9. Derbyshire won on faster-scoring rate after rain ended play. Toss won by Middlesex.

### Derbyshire

*K. J. Barnett c Barlow b Emburey ... 14
†B. J. M. Maher lbw b Emburey ...... 13
J. E. Morris c Radley b Cowans ...... 2
B. Roberts c Downton b Daniel ...... 56
W. P. Fowler c Barlow b Williams .... 22
D. G. Moir run out .................. 0
R. J. Finney b Williams ............. 1
P. G. Newman c Cowans b Daniel .... 17
M. A. Holding c Emburey b Edmonds . 12
A. E. Warner not out ............... 5
O. H. Mortensen not out ............ 0
B 1, l-b 8, w 8, n-b 2 ........ 19

1/29 2/32 3/38 (9 wkts, 40 overs) 161
4/94 5/95 6/108 7/137
8/153 9/155

Bowling: Cowans 8-1-11-1; Daniel 6-0-25-2; Emburey 8-1-25-2; Williams 8-0-38-2; Gatting 2-0-16-0; Edmonds 8-1-37-1.

### Middlesex

G. D. Barlow not out . . . . . . . . . . . . . . . . 66
W. N. Slack not out . . . . . . . . . . . . . . . . . 42
B 1, l-b 8, w 3, n-b 1 . . . . . . . . 13

(no wkt, 25.2 overs) 121

*M. W. Gatting, R. O. Butcher, C. T. Radley, †P. R. Downton, J. E. Emburey, P. H. Edmonds, N. F. Williams, N. G. Cowans and W. W. Daniel did not bat.

Bowling: Holding 8-1-23-0; Mortensen 8-1-25-0; Warner 5-0-41-0; Newman 4.2-0-23-0.

Umpires: K. J. Lyons and D. O. Oslear.

## MIDDLESEX v LEICESTERSHIRE

At Lord's, June 16. Middlesex won by 5 runs. Toss won by Leicestershire.

### Middlesex

G. D. Barlow lbw b Parsons . . . . . . . . . 15
W. N. Slack b Parsons . . . . . . . . . . . . . . 33
*C. T. Radley c and b Cook . . . . . . . . . 16
R. O. Butcher c and b Cook . . . . . . . . . 0
K. P. Tomlins c Whitaker b Clift . . . . . 36
J. F. Sykes c Garnham b De Freitas . . . 3
N. F. Williams c Taylor b Agnew . . . . . 15
P. H. Edmonds c Agnew b Cook . . . . . 0
†C. P. Metson not out . . . . . . . . . . . . . . . 14
S. P. Hughes not out . . . . . . . . . . . . . . . . . 18
B 1, l-b 10, w 2 . . . . . . . . . . . . 13

1/42 2/65 3/70 4/79 5/92 6/95 7/130 8/130 (8 wkts, 40 overs) 163

W. W. Daniel did not bat.

Bowling: Agnew 8-0-50-1; Taylor 4-1-12-0; Clift 8-1-20-1; Parsons 8-0-27-2; Cook 8-0-26-3; De Freitas 4-0-17-1.

### Leicestershire

I. P. Butcher c Edmonds b Hughes . . . . 25
J. C. Balderstone b Daniel . . . . . . . . . . . 3
*N. E. Briers c Metson b Daniel . . . . . . 1
J. J. Whitaker c and b Williams . . . . . . 53
P. B. Clift c Edmonds b Slack . . . . . . . . 1
G. J. Parsons c Williams b Edmonds . . 15
†M. A. Garnham run out . . . . . . . . . . . . 41
P. A. J. De Freitas not out . . . . . . . . . . 8
N. G. B. Cook b Daniel . . . . . . . . . . . . . 0
L-b 6, w 2, n-b 3 . . . . . . . . . . . 11

1/17 2/31 3/39 4/42 5/88 6/145 7/158 8/158 (8 wkts, 40 overs) 158

J. P. Agnew and L. B. Taylor did not bat.

Bowling: Williams 8-0-34-1; Daniel 8-2-23-3; Hughes 8-0-28-1; Slack 8-0-43-1; Edmonds 8-1-24-1.

Umpires: J. Birkenshaw and D. G. L. Evans.

At Trent Bridge, June 23. MIDDLESEX lost to NOTTINGHAMSHIRE by 7 runs.

At Canterbury, June 30. MIDDLESEX lost to KENT by five wickets.

At Tring, July 7. MIDDLESEX lost to NORTHAMPTONSHIRE by five wickets.

## MIDDLESEX v SOMERSET

At Lord's, July 14. No result. Toss won by Middlesex.

### Somerset

N. F. M. Popplewell c Hughes b Williams 5
P. M. Roebuck run out 15
N. A. Felton run out 22
I. V. A. Richards c Williams b Sykes 16
B. C. Rose c Radley b Rose 53
*V. J. Marks run out 35
R. J. Harden b Hughes 0
R. E. Hayward not out 5
L-b 4, w 4, n-b 4 12

1/7 2/44 3/48 4/80 5/140 6/155 7/163 (7 wkts, 37 overs) 163

†T. Gard, C. H. Dredge and M. S. Turner did not bat.

Bowling: Williams 8–0–34–1; Fraser 6–1–21–0; Sykes 8–0–20–1; Rose 8–0–46–1; Hughes 7–0–38–1.

### Middlesex

G. D. Barlow, W. N. Slack, K. P. Tomlins, R. O. Butcher, *C. T. Radley, G. D. Rose, J. F. Sykes, N. F. Williams, †C. P. Metson, S. P. Hughes and A. R. C. Fraser.

Umpires: B. Dudleston and M. J. Kitchen.

At Worcester, July 21. MIDDLESEX lost to WORCESTERSHIRE by 22 runs.

## MIDDLESEX v LANCASHIRE

At Lord's, July 28. Middlesex won by six wickets in a match reduced by rain to ten overs a side. Toss won by Middlesex.

### Lancashire

G. Fowler b Edmonds 21
C. H. Lloyd b Hughes 13
S. J. O'Shaughnessy c Butcher b Emburey 13
M. Watkinson run out 3
D. P. Hughes b Daniel 5
J. Simmons b Daniel 0
N. H. Fairbrother not out 1
L-b 2, w 4 6

1/23 2/48 3/54 4/60 5/60 6/62 (6 wkts, 10 overs) 62

*J. Abrahams, †C. Maynard, D. J. Makinson and P. J. W. Allott did not bat.

Bowling: Daniel 2–0–10–2; Hughes 2–0–9–1; Fraser 2–0–15–0; Edmonds 2–0–15–1; Emburey 2–0–11–1.

### Middlesex

G. D. Barlow run out 14
*M. W. Gatting lbw b Allott 22
R. O. Butcher c Fairbrother b Allott 9
C. T. Radley c Fowler b O'Shaughnessy 1
J. E. Emburey not out 8
†P. R. Downton not out 9
L-b 2 2

1/26 2/46 3/46 4/48 (4 wkts, 9.5 overs) 65

J. D. Carr, S. P. Hughes, P. H. Edmonds, A. R. C. Fraser and W. W. Daniel did not bat.

Bowling: Allott 2–0–4–2; Makinson 1.5–0–16–0; Watkinson 2–0–17–0; Simmons 2–0–16–0; O'Shaughnessy 2–0–10–1.

Umpires: J. H. Harris and J. A. Jameson.

At Chelmsford, August 4. ESSEX v MIDDLESEX. No result.

## MIDDLESEX v SURREY

At Lord's, August 18. No result after rain ended play. Toss won by Surrey.

### Middlesex

| | |
|---|---|
| G. D. Barlow c Stewart b Gray | 16 |
| W. N. Slack b Gray | 18 |
| *C. T. Radley c Jesty b Gray | 9 |
| R. O. Butcher b Butcher | 43 |
| K. R. Brown c Lynch b Feltham | 11 |
| J. D. Carr lbw b Butcher | 4 |
| J. F. Sykes b Butcher | 10 |
| N. F. Williams st Stewart b Butcher | 8 |
| †C. P. Metson run out | 3 |
| S. P. Hughes not out | 22 |
| A. R. C. Fraser lbw b Jesty | 7 |
| B 2, l-b 13, w 12, n-b 1 | 28 |
| 1/35 2/45 3/51 4/86 5/111 6/130 7/138 8/145 9/146 (37.2 overs) | 179 |

Bowling: Gray 8–1–22–3; Doughty 5–0–39–0; Feltham 8–0–45–1; Pauline 8–0–36–0; Butcher 8–0–22–4; Jesty 0.2–0–0–1.

### Surrey

| | |
|---|---|
| A. R. Butcher not out | 20 |
| G. S. Clinton not out | 12 |
| W 1, n-b 1 | 2 |
| (no wkt, 7.5 overs) | 34 |

†A. J. Stewart, *T. E. Jesty, M. A. Lynch, A. Needham, D. B. Pauline, D. M. Ward, R. J. Doughty, M. A. Feltham and A. H. Gray did not bat.

Bowling: Fraser 4–0–14–0; Williams 3.5–0–20–0.

Umpires: B. Dudleston and A. G. T. Whitehead.

At Southampton, September 1. MIDDLESEX lost to HAMPSHIRE by six wickets.

At Edgbaston, September 15. MIDDLESEX lost to WARWICKSHIRE by 6 runs.

# NORTHAMPTONSHIRE

## NORTHAMPTONSHIRE v HAMPSHIRE

At Northampton, May 5. Northamptonshire won by eight wickets. Toss won by Hampshire. The unbroken stand of 207 between Lamb and Bailey was a John Player League record for the third wicket.

### Hampshire

| | |
|---|---|
| V. P. Terry c Sharp b Walker | 24 |
| D. R. Turner c Lamb b Capel | 65 |
| *M. C. J. Nicholas c Bailey b Larkins | 38 |
| R. A. Smith c Cook b Larkins | 26 |
| C. L. Smith c Larkins b Capel | 1 |
| J. J. E. Hardy run out | 10 |
| N. G. Cowley lbw b Mallender | 24 |
| K. D. James not out | 20 |
| T. M. Tremlett not out | 5 |
| L-b 10, w 1 | 11 |
| 1/81 2/118 3/148 4/153 5/172 6/176 7/218 (7 wkts, 40 overs) | 224 |

†R. J. Parks and C. A. Connor did not bat.

Bowling: Mallender 5–1–31–1; Joseph 4–0–21–0; Walker 8–0–50–1; Williams 8–0–35–0; Capel 8–0–35–2; Larkins 7–0–42–2.

### Northamptonshire

| | |
|---|---|
| *G. Cook c Parks b Connor | 1 |
| W. Larkins b Connor | 5 |
| A. J. Lamb not out | 125 |
| R. J. Bailey not out | 79 |
| L-b 12, w 4, n-b 1 | 17 |
| 1/1 2/20 (2 wkts, 39.1 overs) | 227 |

D. J. Capel, R. G. Williams, †G. Sharp, D. J. Wild, R. F. Joseph, N. A. Mallender and A. Walker did not bat.

Bowling: James 8–0–25–0; Connor 7.1–0–36–2; Nicholas 8–0–43–0; Tremlett 8–0–53–0; Cowley 8–0–58–0.

Umpires: R. Julian and D. O. Oslear.

At Derby, May 12. NORTHAMPTONSHIRE beat DERBYSHIRE by nine wickets.

At Leicester, May 26. LEICESTERSHIRE v NORTHAMPTONSHIRE. No result.

## NORTHAMPTONSHIRE v LANCASHIRE

At Northampton, June 2. Tied. Toss won by Northamptonshire.

### Lancashire

| | |
|---|---|
| M. R. Chadwick c Wild b Griffiths | 6 |
| S. J. O'Shaughnessy c Cook b Walker | 19 |
| *J. Abrahams c Harper b Capel | 59 |
| D. P. Hughes c Bailey b Williams | 20 |
| C. H. Lloyd b Mallender | 46 |
| N. H. Fairbrother c Walker b Harper | 10 |
| †C. Maynard b Mallender | 11 |
| M. Watkinson not out | 22 |
| J. Simmons not out | 0 |
| B 1, l-b 10, w 1 | 12 |
| 1/16 2/42 3/91 4/148 5/171 6/172 7/199 (7 wkts, 40 overs) | 205 |

D. J. Makinson and S. Henriksen did not bat.

Bowling: Griffiths 6–1–22–1; Mallender 8–1–32–2; Walker 8–0–39–1; Williams 8–1–33–1; Harper 7–0–46–1; Capel 3–0–22–1.

### Northamptonshire

| | |
|---|---|
| *G. Cook run out | 98 |
| W. Larkins b Watkinson | 48 |
| R. G. Williams st Maynard b Simmons | 5 |
| R. J. Bailey b O'Shaughnessy | 26 |
| R. A. Harper b Watkinson | 9 |
| D. J. Capel not out | 3 |
| B 1, l-b 12, w 3 | 16 |
| 1/88 2/97 3/154 4/191 5/205 (5 wkts, 40 overs) | 205 |

D. J. Wild, †G. Sharp, N. A. Mallender, A. Walker and B. J. Griffiths did not bat.

Bowling: Henriksen 8–0–22–0; Makinson 8–0–28–0; O'Shaughnessy 8–0–56–1; Watkinson 8–0–41–2; Simmons 8–0–45–1.

Umpires: J. H. Harris and R. Julian.

## NORTHAMPTONSHIRE v GLOUCESTERSHIRE

At Northampton, June 16. Gloucestershire won by 15 runs in a match reduced by rain to 38 overs a side. Toss won by Northamptonshire.

### Gloucestershire

P. W. Romaines st Sharp b Harper . . . .105
P. Bainbridge run out . . . . . . . . . . . . . . . . 41
C. W. J. Athey st Sharp b Harper . . . . 8
B. F. Davison run out . . . . . . . . . . . . . . . 18
K. M. Curran c Mallender b Walker . . 9
J. W. Lloyds run out . . . . . . . . . . . . . . . . 4
C. A. Walsh b Walker . . . . . . . . . . . . . . 0
I. R. Payne not out . . . . . . . . . . . . . . . . . 9
*D. A. Graveney not out . . . . . . . . . . . . 5
B 2, l-b 1, w 8, n-b 1 . . . . . . . . 12

1/108 2/149 3/176 (7 wkts, 38 overs) 211
4/183 5/196 6/197 7/197

†A. W. Stovold and D. V. Lawrence did not bat.

Bowling: Mallender 8–0–36–0; Griffiths 8–0–32–0; Walker 7–0–36–2; Harper 8–0–41–2; Capel 5–0–46–0; Larkins 2–0–17–0.

### Northamptonshire

*G. Cook lbw b Walsh . . . . . . . . . . . . . . . 51
W. Larkins c Stovold b Curran . . . . . . . 2
R. J. Boyd-Moss c Graveney b Lawrence 1
R. J. Bailey c Walsh b Payne . . . . . . . . 9
D. J. Capel run out . . . . . . . . . . . . . . . . . 44
D. J. Wild not out . . . . . . . . . . . . . . . . . 63
R. A. Harper run out . . . . . . . . . . . . . . . 9
†G. Sharp b Curran . . . . . . . . . . . . . . . . 4
N. A. Mallender b Walsh . . . . . . . . . . . . 3
A. Walker run out . . . . . . . . . . . . . . . . . . 0
B. J. Griffiths lbw b Walsh . . . . . . . . . . 1
L-b 5, w 3, n-b 1 . . . . . . . . . . . 9

1/13 2/16 3/55 (37 overs) 196
4/82 5/166 6/180 7/191
8/194 9/194

Bowling: Curran 7–0–28–2; Lawrence 8–0–44–1; Payne 6–0–39–1; Graveney 6–0–34–0; Walsh 8–0–28–3; Bainbridge 2–0–18–0.

Umpires: K. J. Lyons and P. B. Wight.

## NORTHAMPTONSHIRE v ESSEX

At Luton, June 23. Northamptonshire won by six wickets. Toss won by Northamptonshire.

### Essex

G. A. Gooch b Walker . . . . . . . . . . . . . . 50
A. W. Lilley b Capel . . . . . . . . . . . . . . . 17
K. S. McEwan c Lamb b Capel . . . . . . 70
D. R. Pringle c Griffiths b Mallender . . 51
N. Phillip c Harper b Walker . . . . . . . . 16
*K. W. R. Fletcher not out . . . . . . . . . . 7
S. Turner not out . . . . . . . . . . . . . . . . . . 2
L-b 2, w 1 . . . . . . . . . . . . . . . . . 3

1/41 2/108 3/170 (5 wkts, 40 overs) 216
4/204 5/207

B. R. Hardie, †D. E. East, J. K. Lever and D. L. Acfield did not bat.

Bowling: Griffiths 8–1–45–0; Mallender 8–0–41–1; Capel 8–0–50–2; Harper 8–2–29–0; Walker 8–0–49–2.

### Northamptonshire

*G. Cook c Turner b Gooch . . . . . . . . . 57
W. Larkins c Hardie b Turner . . . . . . . . 38
A. J. Lamb not out . . . . . . . . . . . . . . . . . 82
R. J. Bailey c Gooch b Turner . . . . . . . 9
D. J. Capel c Phillip b Gooch . . . . . . . . 13
D. J. Wild not out . . . . . . . . . . . . . . . . . . 5
L-b 10, w 1, n-b 2 . . . . . . . . . . 13

1/76 2/112 3/141 (4 wkts, 39.2 overs) 217
4/188

R. A. Harper, †G. Sharp, N. A. Mallender, A. Walker and B. J. Griffiths did not bat.

Bowling: Lever 8–0–29–0; Phillip 5–0–40–0; Acfield 3–0–22–0; Pringle 7.2–0–47–0; Turner 8–0–35–2; Gooch 8–0–34–2.

Umpires: B. Dudleston and N. T. Plews.

At Edgbaston, June 30. NORTHAMPTONSHIRE lost to WARWICKSHIRE by 9 runs.

## NORTHAMPTONSHIRE v MIDDLESEX

At Tring, July 7. Northamptonshire won by five wickets. Toss won by Middlesex.

### Middlesex

| | | | |
|---|---|---|---|
| G. D. Barlow c Ripley b Mallender | 1 | J. E. Emburey not out | 11 |
| W. N. Slack st Ripley b Williams | 74 | S. P. Hughes not out | 10 |
| *M. W. Gatting lbw b Larkins | 54 | L-b 17, w 2, n-b 1 | 20 |
| C. T. Radley st Ripley b Williams | 37 | | |
| R. O. Butcher c Capel b Wild | 0 | 1/3 2/105 3/160 (6 wkts, 40 overs) | 230 |
| †P. R. Downton c Wild b Mallender | 23 | 4/165 5/198 6/213 | |

N. F. Williams, P. H. Edmonds and W. W. Daniel did not bat.

Bowling: Capel 4–0–12–0; Mallender 7–0–21–2; Wild 7–0–47–1; Larkins 8–0–46–1; Harper 8–0–52–0; Williams 6–0–35–2.

### Northamptonshire

| | | | |
|---|---|---|---|
| W. Larkins b Williams | 25 | R. G. Williams not out | 9 |
| R. J. Bailey not out | 103 | | |
| A. J. Lamb c Radley b Edmonds | 33 | B 1, l-b 3, w 1 | 5 |
| R. A. Harper b Edmonds | 1 | | |
| R. J. Boyd-Moss st Downton b Edmonds | 9 | 1/33 2/91 3/93 (5 wkts, 39.5 overs) | 231 |
| *G. Cook st Downton b Emburey | 46 | 4/114 5/206 | |

D. J. Capel, D. J. Wild, †D. Ripley and N. A. Mallender did not bat.

Bowling: Daniel 8–0–38–0; Williams 5.5–0–47–1; Edmonds 8–0–33–3; Emburey 8–0–38–1; Hughes 8–0–49–0; Slack 2–0–22–0.

Umpires: J. W. Holder and J. A. Jameson.

At Maidstone, July 14. NORTHAMPTONSHIRE beat KENT by ten wickets.

## NORTHAMPTONSHIRE v SUSSEX

At Northampton, July 21. Sussex won by 2 runs. Toss won by Northamptonshire.

### Sussex

| | | | |
|---|---|---|---|
| G. D. Mendis c Larkins b Harper | 32 | †I. J. Gould not out | 17 |
| A. M. Green b Mallender | 3 | G. S. le Roux not out | 1 |
| P. W. G. Parker run out | 85 | L-b 7, w 10 | 17 |
| Imran Khan c Larkins b Harper | 0 | | |
| C. M. Wells c Larkins b Wild | 8 | 1/18 2/67 3/67 (6 wkts, 40 overs) | 210 |
| A. P. Wells c Ripley b Wild | 47 | 4/83 5/182 6/207 | |

D. A. Reeve, *J. R. T. Barclay and A. C. S. Pigott did not bat.

Bowling: Mallender 8–1–35–1; Capel 6–0–43–0; Larkins 8–1–25–0; Harper 7–0–32–2; Wild 8–0–49–2; Williams 3–0–19–0.

### Northamptonshire

| | | | |
|---|---|---|---|
| W. Larkins c Gould b le Roux | 43 | D. J. Wild not out | 32 |
| R. J. Bailey b C. M. Wells | 0 | †D. Ripley b Barclay | 11 |
| A. J. Lamb c C. M. Wells b le Roux | 22 | | |
| R. J. Boyd-Moss c Green b Pigott | 21 | L-b 17, w 4 | 21 |
| *G. Cook lbw b C. M. Wells | 37 | | |
| R. G. Williams c le Roux b Pigott | 10 | 1/7 2/74 3/75 (9 wkts, 40 overs) | 208 |
| D. J. Capel b C. M. Wells | 0 | 4/118 5/141 6/141 7/158 | |
| R. A. Harper run out | 11 | 8/162 9/208 | |

N. A. Mallender did not bat.

Bowling: Imran 8–0–44–0; C. M. Wells 8–0–31–3; le Roux 8–0–25–2; Reeve 8–0–24–0; Pigott 7–0–58–2; Barclay 1–0–9–1.

Umpires: D. G. L. Evans and J. H. Hampshire.

## NORTHAMPTONSHIRE v NOTTINGHAMSHIRE

At Northampton, August 4. No result.

At Weston-super-Mare, August 11. SOMERSET v NORTHAMPTONSHIRE. No result.

## NORTHAMPTONSHIRE v GLAMORGAN

At Wellingborough, August 18. No result after rain ended play. Toss won by Glamorgan.

### Northamptonshire

| | |
|---|---|
| W. Larkins lbw b Holmes | 37 |
| R. J. Bailey c Davies b Ontong | 7 |
| R. J. Boyd-Moss st Davies b Holmes | 6 |
| R. G. Williams c Younis b Holmes | 3 |
| *G. Cook c Davies b Price | 11 |
| D. J. Wild run out | 1 |
| D. J. Capel c Price b Younis | 24 |
| R. A. Harper c Price b Younis | 11 |
| †D. Ripley c Ontong b Barwick | 7 |
| N. A. Mallender not out | 1 |
| A. Walker st Davies b Younis | 4 |
| B 1, l-b 4, n-b 4 | 9 |
| 1/22 2/42 3/48 4/57 5/65 6/91 7/108 8/116 9/116 (39.3 overs) | 121 |

Bowling: Barwick 8–0–32–1; McFarlane 5–1–6–0; Ontong 8–0–18–1; Holmes 8–0–23–3; Price 4–0–17–1; Younis 6.3–0–20–3.

### Glamorgan

| | |
|---|---|
| J. A. Hopkins not out | 21 |
| H. Morris not out | 5 |
| L-b 10 | 10 |
| (no wkt, 12 overs) | 36 |

Javed Miandad, G. C. Holmes, Younis Ahmed, *R. C. Ontong, M. R. Price, †T. Davies, S. J. Malone, L. L. McFarlane and S. R. Barwick did not bat.

Bowling: Mallender 5–0–13–0; Walker 6–4–11–0; Larkins 1–0–2–0.

Umpires: J. H. Hampshire and B. Leadbeater.

At Guildford, August 25. NORTHAMPTONSHIRE beat SURREY by 93 runs.

At Headingley, September 1. NORTHAMPTONSHIRE beat YORKSHIRE by three wickets.

At Worcester, September 15. NORTHAMPTONSHIRE lost to WORCESTERSHIRE on scoring-rate.

# NOTTINGHAMSHIRE

At Bristol, May 5. NOTTINGHAMSHIRE lost to GLOUCESTERSHIRE by 11 runs.

## NOTTINGHAMSHIRE v LEICESTERSHIRE

At Trent Bridge, May 19. No result. Toss won by Leicestershire.

### Nottinghamshire

B. C. Broad b Willey ................ 54
R. T. Robinson c Gower b Ferris ..... 7
*C. E. B. Rice c De Freitas b Willey .. 36
J. D. Birch not out ................. 55
R. J. Hadlee not out .................. 25
L-b 7, w 1, n-b 1 ........... 9

1/18 2/84 3/116 (3 wkts, 35 overs) 186

P. Johnson, D. W. Randall, †B. N. French, E. E. Hemmings, K. E. Cooper and K. Saxelby did not bat.

Bowling: Parsons 8–0–32–0; Ferris 5–0–25–1; Willey 8–0–40–2; De Freitas 8–0–39–0; Clift 6–0–43–0.

### Leicestershire

*D. I. Gower, N. E. Briers, P. Willey, J. J. Whitaker, I. P. Butcher, R. A. Cobb, P. B. Clift, †M. A. Garnham, G. J. Parsons, P. A. J. De Freitas and G. J. F. Ferris.

Umpires: A. A. Jones and R. Julian.

## NOTTINGHAMSHIRE v SOMERSET

At Trent Bridge, May 26. Somerset won by seven wickets in a match reduced by rain to 26 overs a side. Toss won by Somerset.

### Nottinghamshire

B. C. Broad c Gard b Garner ........ 1
R. T. Robinson not out ............. 44
*C. E. B. Rice lbw b Garner ......... 4
P. Johnson c Wyatt b Richards ....... 30
J. D. Birch c sub b Richards ........ 5
D. W. Randall not out .............. 9
B 1, l-b 4, w 1, n-b 1 ........ 7

1/9 2/17 3/64 4/74 (4 wkts, 26 overs) 100

R. J. Hadlee, †B. N. French, E. E. Hemmings, K. E. Cooper and K. Saxelby did not bat.

Bowling: Garner 7–0–33–2; Botham 6–0–21–0; Turner 4–1–11–0; Davis 3–0–19–0; Richards 3–0–6–2; Marks 3–0–5–0.

### Somerset

N. F. M. Popplewell c Rice b Saxelby . 29
N. A. Felton c Robinson b Saxelby ... 12
I. V. A. Richards c Broad b Hadlee ... 9
*I. T. Botham not out ............... 40
V. J. Marks not out ................ 9
L-b 5, w 2 ................. 7

1/30 2/41 3/56 (3 wkts, 20.5 overs) 106

J. G. Wyatt, R. L. Ollis, M. R. Davis, J. Garner, M. S. Turner and †T. Gard did not bat.

Bowling: Saxelby 8–2–28–2; Hadlee 8–1–28–1; Cooper 2.5–0–31–0; Rice 2–0–14–0.

Umpires: J. H. Hampshire and J. W. Holder.

At Horsham, June 2. NOTTINGHAMSHIRE beat SUSSEX by two wickets.

## NOTTINGHAMSHIRE v KENT

At Trent Bridge, June 16. Kent won by 42 runs. Toss won by Nottinghamshire.

### Kent

M. R. Benson b Saxelby . . . . . . . . . . . . . 90
S. G. Hinks c Rice b Hemmings . . . . . . 14
C. J. Tavaré c and b Cooper . . . . . . . . . 3
D. G. Aslett c Saxelby b Evans . . . . . . . 44
*C. S. Cowdrey c Johnson b Hemmings 27
E. A. E. Baptiste run out . . . . . . . . . . . . 1
R. M. Ellison not out . . . . . . . . . . . . . . . 20
†A. P. E. Knott c Saxelby b Hadlee . . . 1
G. W. Johnson b Hadlee . . . . . . . . . . . . 2
G. R. Dilley run out . . . . . . . . . . . . . . . . 12
K. B. S. Jarvis not out . . . . . . . . . . . . . . 0
L-b 8, w 2 . . . . . . . . . . . . . . . . . 10

1/37 2/40 3/126 4/184 5/185 6/189 7/192 8/196 9/223 (9 wkts, 40 overs) 224

Bowling: Hadlee 8–0–31–2; Saxelby 8–1–44–1; Hemmings 6–0–30–2; Cooper 8–1–41–1; Rice 7–0–37–0; Evans 3–0–33–1.

### Nottinghamshire

B. C. Broad c Knott b Jarvis . . . . . . . . . 12
*C. E. B. Rice b Baptiste . . . . . . . . . . . . 31
P. Johnson b Jarvis . . . . . . . . . . . . . . . . . 4
J. D. Birch b Jarvis . . . . . . . . . . . . . . . . 0
D. W. Randall st Knott b Johnson . . . . 15
R. J. Hadlee c Baptiste b Cowdrey . . . . 42
K. P. Evans c Benson b Baptiste . . . . . . 28
†B. N. French b Jarvis . . . . . . . . . . . . . . 25
E. E. Hemmings c Dilley b Ellison . . . . 6
K. Saxelby not out . . . . . . . . . . . . . . . . . 0
K. E. Cooper b Jarvis . . . . . . . . . . . . . . . . 0
L-b 13, w 5, n-b 1 . . . . . . . . . . 19

1/22 2/29 3/31 4/64 5/82 6/141 7/159 8/181 9/182 (37.4 overs) 182

Bowling: Dilley 7–0–34–0; Jarvis 6.4–1–24–5; Ellison 6–0–21–1; Cowdrey 5–0–21–1; Johnson 6–2–24–1; Baptiste 7–0–45–2.

Umpires: H. D. Bird and B. Dudleston.

## NOTTINGHAMSHIRE v MIDDLESEX

At Trent Bridge, June 23. Nottinghamshire won by 7 runs. Toss won by Middlesex.

### Nottinghamshire

R. T. Robinson c and b Emburey . . . . . 15
B. C. Broad b Williams . . . . . . . . . . . . . 69
*C. E. B. Rice c Downton b Edmonds 3
P. Johnson c Gatting b Edmonds . . . . . 28
R. J. Hadlee not out . . . . . . . . . . . . . . . . 37
D. W. Randall c Slack b Williams . . . . 8
J. D. Birch run out . . . . . . . . . . . . . . . . . 2
K. P. Evans not out . . . . . . . . . . . . . . . . . 0
B 1, l-b 8, w 7 . . . . . . . . . . . . . 16

1/41 2/47 3/119 4/148 5/168 6/173 (6 wkts, 40 overs) 178

†B. N. French, C. D. Fraser-Darling and K. E. Cooper did not bat.

Bowling: Daniel 8–0–33–0; Cowans 8–2–31–0; Edmonds 8–1–21–2; Emburey 8–1–28–1; Williams 7–0–47–2; Gatting 1–0–9–0.

### Middlesex

G. D. Barlow c French b Hadlee . . . . . 0
W. N. Slack b Evans . . . . . . . . . . . . . . . . 40
*M. W. Gatting b Hadlee . . . . . . . . . . . 7
R. O. Butcher c and b Hadlee . . . . . . . . 4
C. T. Radley c and b Evans . . . . . . . . . . 8
†P. R. Downton run out . . . . . . . . . . . . . 70
J. E. Emburey c Randall b Cooper . . . . 1
N. F. Williams c Johnson b Fraser-Darling. 3
P. H. Edmonds c Broad b Evans . . . . . . 2
N. G. Cowans b Rice . . . . . . . . . . . . . . . 20
W. W. Daniel not out . . . . . . . . . . . . . . . 2
L-b 8, w 5, n-b 1 . . . . . . . . . . . 14

1/0 2/15 3/24 4/53 5/85 6/88 7/109 8/126 9/165 (39.4 overs) 171

Bowling: Hadlee 8–0–23–3; Cooper 8–0–24–1; Fraser-Darling 8–0–45–1; Rice 7.4–1–35–1; Evans 8–1–36–3.

Umpires: J. H. Hampshire and R. Palmer.

At Swansea, July 7. NOTTINGHAMSHIRE beat GLAMORGAN by three wickets.

At Edgbaston, July 14. NOTTINGHAMSHIRE lost to WARWICKSHIRE by 9 runs.

At Guildford, July 21. NOTTINGHAMSHIRE beat SURREY by 12 runs.

## NOTTINGHAMSHIRE v YORKSHIRE

At Trent Bridge, July 28. Nottinghamshire won by six wickets in a match restricted by rain to ten overs a side. Toss won by Nottinghamshire.

### Yorkshire

| | | | |
|---|---|---|---|
| *†D. L. Bairstow c Hadlee b Pick | 9 | P. W. Jarvis run out | 2 |
| K. Sharp run out | 16 | C. S. Pickles not out | 1 |
| S. N. Hartley c French b Saxelby | 15 | | |
| P. E. Robinson c French b Saxelby | 1 | B 1, l-b 1, w 1 | 3 |
| A. A. Metcalfe b Hadlee | 10 | | |
| M. D. Moxon not out | 12 | 1/19 2/31 3/42 (7 wkts, 10 overs) | 70 |
| P. Carrick b Saxelby | 1 | 4/43 5/57 6/60 7/63 | |

S. Oldham and C. Shaw did not bat.

Bowling: Hemmings 2-0-11-0; Cooper 2-0-15-0; Pick 2-0-15-1; Saxelby 2-0-6-3; Hadlee 2-0-21-1.

### Nottinghamshire

| | | | |
|---|---|---|---|
| D. W. Randall c Hartley b Jarvis | 15 | †B. N. French not out | 19 |
| B. Hassan c Bairstow b Oldham | 4 | L-b 3, w 1 | 4 |
| P. Johnson c Bairstow b Shaw | 12 | | |
| R. J. Hadlee c and b Jarvis | 7 | 1/15 2/28 3/40 (4 wkts, 9.2 overs) | 73 |
| B. C. Broad not out | 12 | 4/51 | |

K. P. Evans, E. E. Hemmings, R. A. Pick, K. Saxelby and K. E. Cooper did not bat.

Bowling: Carrick 1-0-6-0; Shaw 2-0-18-1; Oldham 2-0-16-1; Pickles 2-0-17-0; Jarvis 2-0-7-2; Hartley 0.2-0-6-0.

Umpires: D. J. Constant and D. O. Oslear.

At Northampton, August 4. NORTHAMPTONSHIRE v NOTTINGHAMSHIRE. No result.

## NOTTINGHAMSHIRE v WORCESTERSHIRE

At Trent Bridge, August 11. Nottinghamshire won by 24 runs in a match reduced by rain to 21 overs a side. Toss won by Worcestershire.

### Nottinghamshire

| | | | |
|---|---|---|---|
| P. Johnson b Inchmore | 0 | E. E. Hemmings lbw b Inchmore | 5 |
| D. W. Randall run out | 22 | R. A. Pick not out | 4 |
| *C. E. B. Rice b Newport | 24 | | |
| B. C. Broad c Rhodes b McEwan | 28 | L-b 6, w 2 | 8 |
| R. J. Hadlee c Radford b Newport | 25 | | |
| R. T. Robinson c Newport b Weston | 5 | 1/0 2/49 3/49 (7 wkts, 21 overs) | 139 |
| †B. N. French not out | 18 | 4/89 5/106 6/110 7/117 | |

K. Saxelby and K. E. Cooper did not bat.

Bowling: Inchmore 4-0-15-2; Radford 3-0-14-0; Newport 4-0-29-2; McEwan 4-0-35-1; Patel 1-0-9-0; Weston 5-0-31-1.

## Worcestershire

T. S. Curtis c Rice b Cooper ........ 7
D. N. Patel c Pick b Saxelby ........ 12
D. M. Smith c French b Pick ........ 36
G. A. Hick run out ........ 0
*P. A. Neale c Robinson b Pick ........ 23
M. J. Weston not out ........ 16
†S. J. Rhodes run out ........ 10
N. V. Radford not out ........ 4
L-b 6, n-b 1 ........ 7

1/19 2/22 3/22 4/83 5/84 6/98 (6 wkts, 21 overs) 115

P. J. Newport, J. D. Inchmore and S. M. McEwan did not bat.

Bowling: Hadlee 5-0-25-0; Cooper 4-0-14-1; Saxelby 4-0-15-1; Rice 4-0-32-0; Pick 4-0-23-2.

Umpires: J. H. Harris and K. E. Palmer

At Old Trafford, August 18. NOTTINGHAMSHIRE lost to LANCASHIRE by five wickets.

At Heanor, August 25. NOTTINGHAMSHIRE lost to DERBYSHIRE by seven wickets.

# NOTTINGHAMSHIRE v ESSEX

At Trent Bridge, September 8. Essex won by 44 runs after Gooch, with 171 off 135 balls including three 6s and eighteen 4s and Hardie had compiled a John Player League record first-wicket stand of 239. Gooch reached his hundred off 85 balls. Toss won by Nottinghamshire.

## Essex

G. A. Gooch c Rice b Pick ........ 171
B. R. Hardie b Rice ........ 60
K. S. McEwan c Robinson b Rice ........ 1
*K. W. R. Fletcher not out ........ 0
A. W. Lilley not out ........ 9
B 2, l-b 7, w 2 ........ 11

1/239 2/242 3/242 (3 wkts, 40 overs) 252

P. J. Prichard, D. R. Pringle, †D. E. East, S. Turner, I. L. Pont and J. K. Lever did not bat.

Bowling: Hadlee 8-0-35-0; Cooper 8-0-38-0; Rice 8-0-51-2; Pick 8-0-62-1; Hemmings 6-0-32-0; Evans 2-0-25-0.

## Nottinghamshire

R. T. Robinson b Turner ........ 43
B. C. Broad b Pont ........ 14
*C. E. B. Rice c Pringle b Gooch ........ 37
D. W. Randall c Lever b Pringle ........ 22
R. J. Hadlee b Gooch ........ 2
D. J. R. Martindale c Fletcher b Pringle ........ 33
K. P. Evans c Lilley b Lever ........ 12
†B. N. French not out ........ 19
E. E. Hemmings c East b Lever ........ 1
R. A. Pick c Turner b Lever ........ 11
K. E. Cooper c Hardie b Lever ........ 0
B 4, l-b 6, w 2 ........ 12

1/44 2/72 3/117 4/120 5/129 6/175 7/176 8/179 9/199 (37 overs) 208

Bowling: Lever 7-0-35-4; Pont 8-0-39-1; Turner 8-0-45-1; Pringle 8-0-50-2; Gooch 6-0-29-2.

Umpires: H. D. Bird and J. W. Holder.

# NOTTINGHAMSHIRE v HAMPSHIRE

At Trent Bridge, September 15. Hampshire won by 36 runs. Toss won by Nottinghamshire.

### Hampshire

C. G. Greenidge b Rice .............. 122
V. P. Terry b Cooper .............. 19
D. R. Turner c Rice b Hemmings ..... 20
R. A. Smith c and b Hadlee .......... 30
M. D. Marshall b Rice .............. 33
N. G. Cowley not out .............. 1
B 3, l-b 14, n-b 1 .......... 18

1/63 2/114 3/192 4/242 5/243 (5 wkts, 40 overs) 243

C. L. Smith, T. M. Tremlett, †R. J. Parks, C. A. Connor and *M. C. J. Nicholas did not bat.

Bowling: Hadlee 8–0–46–1; Pick 8–2–43–0; Cooper 8–0–49–1; Rice 8–0–43–2; Hemmings 8–0–48–1.

### Nottinghamshire

R. T. Robinson c Parks b Connor ..... 18
B. C. Broad c Parks b Cowley ........ 28
*C. E. B. Rice b Nicholas ........... 29
D. W. Randall c Greenidge b Tremlett . 4
D. J. R. Martindale c Parks b Marshall 7
R. Evans c C. L. Smith b Nicholas .... 20
R. J. Hadlee c Nicholas b Tremlett ... 18
†B. N. French b Marshall ........... 18
E. E. Hemmings c Parks b Nicholas ... 35
R. A. Pick not out .............. 8
K. E. Cooper b Nicholas ............ 8
B 4, l-b 7, w 2, n-b 1 ........ 14

1/31 2/59 3/69 4/89 5/91 6/122 7/138 8/189 9/189 (39.3 overs) 207

Bowling: Connor 8–0–45–1; Marshall 8–0–39–2; Cowley 8–0–33–1; Tremlett 8–1–29–2; Nicholas 7.3–0–50–4.

Umpires: J. H. Hampshire and A. G. T. Whitehead.

# SOMERSET

At Worcester, May 5. WORCESTERSHIRE v SOMERSET. No result.

## SOMERSET v GLAMORGAN

At Taunton, May 12. Glamorgan won by two wickets. Toss won by Glamorgan.

### Somerset

P. M. Roebuck not out .............. 74
J. G. Wyatt lbw b Barwick .......... 13
N. F. M. Popplewell c Holmes b Ontong 8
*I. T. Botham c Thomas b Steele ..... 36
V. J. Marks c Thomas b Steele ....... 7
R. L. Ollis lbw b Ontong ............ 2
G. V. Palmer b Derrick .............. 3
R. C. J. Sully b Barwick ............ 2
M. R. Davis c Davies b Thomas ...... 11
M. S. Turner not out ................ 8
L-b 6, w 4 ................ 10

1/21 2/49 3/95 4/103 5/114 6/119 7/128 8/153 (8 wkts, 40 overs) 174

†T. Gard did not bat.

Bowling: Thomas 8–0–42–1; Barwick 8–0–35–2; Steele 8–0–34–2; Ontong 8–1–37–2; Derrick 8–1–20–1.

### Glamorgan

J. A. Hopkins c Ollis b Palmer ....... 64
G. C. Holmes c Davis b Turner ...... 21
S. P. Henderson c Popplewell b Marks . 0
Javed Miandad b Palmer ............ 31
Younis Ahmed b Botham ............ 4
*R. C. Ontong run out .............. 4
J. G. Thomas c sub b Davis ......... 12
J. Derrick b Botham ................ 8
J. F. Steele not out ................ 9
†T. Davies not out ................ 6
B 4, l-b 7, w 5 ............ 16

1/55 2/58 3/122 4/129 5/133 6/139 7/155 8/160 (8 wkts, 40 overs) 175

S. R. Barwick did not bat.

Bowling: Botham 8–1–19–2; Davis 8–0–47–1; Marks 8–0–16–1; Sully 2–0–15–0; Turner 8–0–34–1; Palmer 6–0–33–2.

Umpires: D. O. Oslear and D. R. Shepherd.

At Trent Bridge, May 26. SOMERSET beat NOTTINGHAMSHIRE by seven wickets.

## SOMERSET v WARWICKSHIRE

At Taunton, June 2. Warwickshire won by seven wickets. Toss won by Warwickshire.

### Somerset

N. F. M. Popplewell lbw b Smith ..... 21
N. A. Felton c Humpage b Smith ..... 2
R. E. Hayward b Hoffman ........... 6
I. V. A. Richards b Gifford .......... 62
R. L. Ollis lbw b Hoffman ........... 19
*V. J. Marks b Gifford .............. 1
G. V. Palmer run out ............... 21
M. R. Davis lbw b Gifford .......... 5
M. S. Turner b Small ............... 4
J. Garner not out .................. 21
†T. Gard not out ................... 2
L-b 16, w 3 .................. 19

1/4 2/22 3/58 (9 wkts, 40 overs) 183
4/116 5/118 6/128 7/135
8/148 9/174

Bowling: Small 8–0–26–1; Smith 8–0–33–2; Hoffman 8–2–18–2; Ferreira 8–0–50–0; Gifford 8–0–40–3.

### Warwickshire

T. A. Lloyd c Popplewell b Garner .... 0
R. I. H. B. Dyer run out ............ 50
A. I. Kallicharran run out ........... 33
D. L. Amiss not out ................ 78
†G. W. Humpage not out ............ 20
L-b 4, w 1, n-b 1 ........... 6

1/6 2/51 3/118 (3 wkts, 37.5 overs) 187

P. A. Smith, A. M. Ferreira, D. S. Hoffman, G. C. Small, *N. Gifford and Asif Din did not bat.

Bowling: Garner 8–1–22–1; Davis 8–0–41–0; Marks 8–0–36–0; Turner 6–0–39–0; Richards 5–0–26–0; Palmer 2.5–0–19–0.

Umpires: A. A. Jones and P. B. Wight.

## SOMERSET v GLOUCESTERSHIRE

At Bath, June 9. Somerset won by 83 runs. Toss won by Gloucestershire. Popplewell kept wicket when Gard suffered from concussion.

### Somerset

N. F. M. Popplewell c Athey b Walsh . 58
N. A. Felton c Graveney b Bainbridge . 52
I. V. A. Richards c Lawrence b Curran 56
*I. T. Botham c Athey b Lawrence .... 7
V. J. Marks lbw b Bainbridge ........ 0
R. E. Hayward not out .............. 38
M. S. Turner c Russell b Walsh ...... 7
J. Garner not out .................. 16
L-b 8, w 3, n-b 2 ........... 13

1/107 2/146 3/161 (6 wkts, 40 overs) 247
4/163 5/200 6/228

R. L. Ollis, †T. Gard and M. R. Davis did not bat.

Bowling: Lawrence 8–0–39–1; Curran 8–0–56–1; Shepherd 8–0–58–0; Graveney 3–0–20–0; Walsh 8–0–38–2; Bainbridge 5–0–28–2.

### Gloucestershire

| | | | |
|---|---|---|---|
| P. W. Romaines run out | 11 | *D. A. Graveney c Davis b Botham | 18 |
| P. Bainbridge b Davis | 14 | †R. C. Russell st Popplewell b Botham | 14 |
| C. W. J. Athey c sub b Marks | 41 | D. V. Lawrence not out | 3 |
| B. F. Davison b Turner | 28 | B 3, l-b 6, w 2 | 11 |
| C. A. Walsh c Popplewell b Turner | 1 | | |
| K. M. Curran c Botham b Turner | 13 | 1/28 2/31 3/80 (37 overs) | 164 |
| A. W. Stovold b Botham | 6 | 4/82 5/106 6/114 7/121 | |
| J. N. Shepherd st Popplewell b Marks | 4 | 8/135 9/150 | |

Bowling: Garner 5–0–21–0; Davis 8–0–32–1; Turner 8–1–36–3; Marks 8–0–28–2; Botham 6–0–28–3; Richards 2–0–10–0.

Umpires: D. J. Constant and J. H. Hampshire.

## SOMERSET v YORKSHIRE

At Bath, June 16. Yorkshire won by 51 runs. Toss won by Somerset.

### Yorkshire

| | | | |
|---|---|---|---|
| M. D. Moxon b Garner | 86 | P. Carrick not out | 12 |
| A. A. Metcalfe b Garner | 13 | A. Sidebottom run out | 1 |
| K. Sharp c Felton b Marks | 22 | L-b 11, w 1, n-b 1 | 13 |
| J. D. Love b Garner | 37 | | |
| *†D. L. Bairstow b Garner | 31 | 1/26 2/84 3/161 (7 wkts, 40 overs) | 215 |
| S. N. Hartley lbw b Garner | 0 | 4/201 5/202 6/203 7/215 | |

S. J. Dennis, P. W. Jarvis and C. S. Pickles did not bat.

Bowling: Garner 8–1–27–5; Davis 8–0–52–0; M. S. Turner 8–0–46–0; Marks 8–1–44–1; Richards 8–0–35–0.

### Somerset

| | | | |
|---|---|---|---|
| N. A. Felton run out | 16 | J. Garner c Sharp b Sidebottom | 8 |
| N. F. M. Popplewell b Pickles | 25 | M. S. Turner b Jarvis | 5 |
| I. V. A. Richards c Hartley b Pickles | 1 | †S. J. Turner not out | 8 |
| R. E. Hayward b Jarvis | 8 | B 1, l-b 8, w 2, n-b 2 | 13 |
| *V. J. Marks c Bairstow b Dennis | 25 | | |
| R. L. Ollis c Moxon b Sidebottom | 46 | 1/34 2/40 3/56 (38.3 overs) | 164 |
| R. J. Harden run out | 1 | 4/63 5/103 6/118 7/134 | |
| M. R. Davis lbw b Jarvis | 8 | 8/144 9/150 | |

Bowling: Sidebottom 7.3–2–29–2; Pickles 8–0–28–2; Jarvis 7–0–26–3; Dennis 8–0–32–1; Carrick 8–0–40–0.

Umpires: C. Cook and A. A. Jones.

At The Oval, June 23. SOMERSET beat SURREY by 61 runs.

## SOMERSET v LEICESTERSHIRE

At Taunton, July 7. Leicestershire won by 43 runs. Toss won by Leicestershire.

### Leicestershire

I. P. Butcher c Hayward b Dredge .... 9
N. E. Briers lbw b Botham .......... 9
*D. I. Gower c Dredge b Turner ...... 45
P. Willey c Felton b Marks .......... 21
J. J. Whitaker c Roebuck b Marks .... 16
†M. A. Garnham c and b Marks ..... 6
P. B. Clift not out .................. 27
G. J. Parsons not out ............... 24
L-b 9, w 8, n-b 2 ........... 19

1/24 2/30 3/68 4/112 5/121 6/121 (6 wkts, 40 overs) 176

R. A. Cobb, J. P. Agnew and L. B. Taylor did not bat.

Bowling: Davis 8–1–28–0; Botham 8–0–37–1; Dredge 7–1–28–1; Marks 8–1–21–3; Turner 5–0–34–1; Richards 4–0–19–0.

### Somerset

P. M. Roebuck c Briers b Parsons .... 19
N. F. M. Popplewell c Cobb b Clift ... 25
N. A. Felton c and b Willey ......... 4
I. V. A. Richards c Garnham b Taylor . 32
*I. T. Botham c Garnham b Parsons .. 6
V. J. Marks c sub b Taylor .......... 7
R. E. Hayward lbw b Taylor .......... 2
M. R. Davis c Taylor b Clift ......... 7
M. S. Turner b Willey ............... 2
C. H. Dredge not out ................ 13
†T. Gard c and b Clift ............... 4
B 2, l-b 5, w 5 ............. 12

1/47 2/53 3/57 4/86 5/93 6/100 7/114 8/114 9/118 (34 overs) 133

Bowling: Agnew 5–0–22–0; Taylor 8–1–22–3; Parsons 8–0–31–2; Clift 6–1–17–3; Willey 7–0–34–2.

Umpires: A. A. Jones and B. Leadbeater.

At Lord's, July 14. MIDDLESEX v SOMERSET. No result.

At Derby, July 21. SOMERSET lost to DERBYSHIRE by four wickets.

## SOMERSET v ESSEX

At Taunton, July 28. Essex won by five wickets. Toss won by Essex.

### Somerset

P. M. Roebuck b Pont ............... 0
N. F. M. Popplewell c McEwan b Turner 33
N. A. Felton lbw b Pont ............ 3
I. V. A. Richards b Topley .......... 5
J. G. Wyatt c East b Topley ......... 4
*I. T. Botham c Prichard b Gooch .... 58
V. J. Marks c Gooch b Acfield ....... 19
J. Garner c Gooch b Pringle ......... 26
M. R. Davis run out ................ 1
†T. Gard not out .................... 11
C. H. Dredge not out ................ 3
L-b 5, w 4, n-b 1 ........... 10

1/8 2/14 3/29 4/48 5/50 6/116 7/144 8/146 9/161 (9 wkts, 40 overs) 173

Bowling: Pringle 7–0–36–1; Pont 5–0–18–2; Topley 8–1–26–2; Turner 8–0–37–1; Gooch 8–0–33–1; Acfield 4–0–18–1.

### Essex

G. A. Gooch c Garner b Botham ..... 37
P. J. Prichard st Gard b Marks ....... 15
K. S. McEwan not out ............... 54
D. R. Pringle c Gard b Davis ........ 14
B. R. Hardie c Botham b Richards .... 9
A. W. Lilley b Botham ............... 12
†D. E. East not out .................. 14
L-b 13, w 4, n-b 2 .......... 19

1/39 2/57 3/105 4/126 5/157 (5 wkts, 38.5 overs) 174

I. L. Pont, S. Turner, T. D. Topley and D. L. Acfield did not bat.

Bowling: Garner 8–1–26–0; Botham 7–0–35–2; Marks 7–0–34–1; Dredge 5–0–17–0; Davis 5–0–19–1; Richards 6.5–2–30–1.

Umpires: R. Palmer and K. J. Lyons.

At Southampton, August 4. HAMPSHIRE v SOMERSET. No result.

## SOMERSET v NORTHAMPTONSHIRE

At Weston-super-Mare, August 11. No result.

At Old Trafford, August 25. LANCASHIRE v SOMERSET. No result.

## SOMERSET v SUSSEX

At Taunton, September 1. Somerset won by eight wickets. Toss won by Somerset. Richards hit 26 off one over from Barclay, and won the match with four consecutive 4s off le Roux.

### Sussex

| | |
|---|---|
| G. D. Mendis c Gard b Palmer | 3 |
| †I. J. Gould c Dredge b Garner | 9 |
| Imran Khan c Roebuck b Dredge | 67 |
| C. M. Wells b Marks | 46 |
| G. S. le Roux b Richards | 30 |
| A. P. Wells c Roebuck b Dredge | 1 |
| I. A. Greig c Richards b Garner | 6 |
| C. P. Phillipson not out | 5 |
| N. J. Lenham not out | 1 |
| B 3, l-b 5, w 5, n-b 3 | 16 |
| 1/12 2/17 3/115 4/167 5/170 6/170 7/178 (7 wkts, 40 overs) | 184 |

*J. R. T. Barclay and A. N. Jones did not bat.

Bowling: Garner 8–2–28–2; Palmer 8–0–22–1; Dredge 8–0–39–2; Marks 8–1–41–1; Richards 8–0–46–1.

### Somerset

| | |
|---|---|
| P. M. Roebuck run out | 34 |
| J. G. Wyatt b Imran | 0 |
| N. F. M. Popplewell not out | 74 |
| I. V. A. Richards not out | 66 |
| L-b 10, w 4 | 14 |
| 1/1 2/88 (2 wkts, 32.4 overs) | 188 |

R. J. Harden, *V. J. Marks, J. C. M. Atkinson, G. V. Palmer, †T. Gard, C. H. Dredge and J. Garner did not bat.

Bowling: Imran 7–0–37–1; C. M. Wells 8–2–21–0; Jones 8–1–25–0; Greig 2–0–10–0; le Roux 6.4–0–59–0; Barclay 1–0–26–0.

Umpires: D. O. Oslear and J. H. Hampshire.

At Canterbury, September 15. SOMERSET beat KENT by three wickets.

# SURREY

## SURREY v WARWICKSHIRE

At The Oval, May 5. Surrey won by 4 runs. Toss won by Warwickshire. Surrey's total of 304 was a county record for the competition, and the match aggregate of 604 was a new John Player League record.

### Surrey

| | | | |
|---|---|---|---|
| A. R. Butcher hit wkt b Smith | 72 | †C. J. Richards not out | 14 |
| G. S. Clinton c Amiss b Gifford | 34 | D. B. Pauline not out | 1 |
| A. J. Stewart c Small b Gifford | 86 | B 7, l-b 12, w 11 | 30 |
| T. E. Jesty b Smith | 2 | | |
| M. A. Lynch b Smith | 43 | 1/80 2/170 3/182 (6 wkts, 40 overs) | 304 |
| D. J. Thomas b Gifford | 22 | 4/256 5/258 6/296 | |

A. Needham, G. Monkhouse and *P. I. Pocock did not bat.

Bowling: Small 8–0–48–0; Old 5–0–30–0; Ferreira 8–0–56–0; Wall 6–0–40–0; Gifford 7–0–55–3; Smith 6–0–56–3.

### Warwickshire

| | | | |
|---|---|---|---|
| T. A. Lloyd b Pauline | 24 | G. C. Small run out | 1 |
| R. I. H. B. Dyer c and b Thomas | 0 | S. Wall not out | 6 |
| A. I. Kallicharran c Clinton b Jesty | 70 | *N. Gifford not out | 2 |
| D. L. Amiss c Lynch b Jesty | 23 | B 3, l-b 15, w 5, n-b 1 | 24 |
| †G. W. Humpage lbw b Pocock | 47 | | |
| C. M. Old c Butcher b Pauline | 31 | 1/5 2/96 3/121 (9 wkts, 40 overs) | 300 |
| P. A. Smith c Stewart b Monkhouse | 34 | 4/144 5/212 6/217 7/289 | |
| A. M. Ferreira c and b Monkhouse | 38 | 8/291 9/293 | |

Bowling: Monkhouse 8–0–53–2; Thomas 8–0–54–1; Jesty 8–0–50–2; Pauline 8–0–71–2; Pocock 8–0–54–1.

Umpires: D. J. Constant and R. Palmer.

At Hove, May 12. SURREY beat SUSSEX by eight wickets.

At Southampton, May 19. SURREY lost to HAMPSHIRE by 48 runs.

## SURREY v ESSEX

At The Oval, May 26. No result. Toss won by Surrey.

### Essex

| | | | |
|---|---|---|---|
| G. A. Gooch c Richards b Gray | 1 | *K. W. R. Fletcher not out | 0 |
| B. R. Hardie b Gray | 20 | W 2, n-b 2 | 4 |
| K. S. McEwan b Pocock | 29 | | |
| D. R. Pringle not out | 9 | 1/2 2/47 3/63 (3 wkts, 17.2 overs) | 63 |

A. W. Lilley, S. Turner N. Phillip, †D. E. East, J. K. Lever and D. L. Acfield did not bat.

Bowling: Gray 8–0–26–2; Monkhouse 4–0–18–0; Thomas 4–0–14–0; Pauline 1–0–5–0; Pocock 0.2–0–0–1.

### Surrey

D. M. Ward, G. S. Clinton, A. J. Stewart, T. E. Jesty, M. A. Lynch, D. J. Thomas, D. B. Pauline, A. H. Gray, †C. J. Richards, G. Monkhouse and *P. I. Pocock.

Umpires: M. J. Kitchen and P. B. Wight.

At Worcester, June 16. SURREY lost to WORCESTERSHIRE by eight wickets.

## SURREY v SOMERSET

At The Oval, June 23. Somerset won by 61 runs. Toss won by Surrey.

### Somerset

P. M. Roebuck c Lynch b Pauline .... 43
N. F. M. Popplewell run out ......... 4
N. A. Felton c Lynch b Pauline ...... 7
I. V. A. Richards c Lynch b Gray .... 86
*I. T. Botham c Clinton b Needham .. 29
V. J. Marks c Needham b Gray ...... 26
J. Garner c and b Thomas ........... 30
R. E. Hayward not out .............. 10
B 1, l-b 10, w 5, n-b 3 ....... 19

1/9 2/35 3/129 4/157 5/189 6/228 7/254 (7 wkts, 40 overs) 254

†T. Gard, M. S. Turner and M. R. Davis did not bat.

Bowling: Thomas 8–0–34–1; Gray 8–0–30–2; Pauline 8–0–36–2; Butcher 5–0–39–0; Jesty 8–0–51–0; Needham 3–0–53–1.

### Surrey

A. R. Butcher c sub b Garner ........ 12
G. S. Clinton b Davis ............... 29
A. J. Stewart b Davis ................ 2
*T. E. Jesty run out ................. 8
M. A. Lynch st Garner b Richards .... 58
D. M. Ward st Gard b Richards ...... 8
D. J. Thomas b Richards ............ 34
A. Needham c Botham b Richards .... 15
†C. J. Richards not out ............. 10
D. B. Pauline not out ................ 5
L-b 9, w 3 ................. 12

1/23 2/37 3/52 4/56 5/117 6/154 7/178 8/178 (8 wkts, 40 overs) 193

A. H. Gray did not bat.

Bowling: Garner 8–0–26–1; Davis 8–0–26–2; Marks 8–1–22–0; Turner 4–0–25–0; Botham 4–0–39–0; Richards 7–0–39–4; Felton 1–0–7–0.

Umpires: J. Birkenshaw and R. A. White.

At Leicester, June 30. SURREY lost to LEICESTERSHIRE on scoring-rate.

## SURREY v KENT

At The Oval, July 7. Kent won by 37 runs. Toss won by Kent.

### Kent

M. R. Benson b Gray ................ 5
S. G. Hinks b Gray .................. 2
C. J. Tavaré not out ................ 84
D. G. Aslett c Pauline b Jesty ........ 31
*C. S. Cowdrey c and b Jesty ........ 38
E. A. E. Baptiste st Richards b Pocock 25
R. M. Ellison c Richards b Gray ..... 2
†A. P. E. Knott b Pocock ........... 10
G. W. Johnson not out ............... 1
L-b 13, w 10, n-b 1 ......... 24

1/13 2/15 3/85 4/155 5/201 6/204 7/217 (7 wkts, 40 overs) 222

D. L. Underwood and K. B. S. Jarvis did not bat.

Bowling: Pauline 8–1–34–0; Gray 8–0–31–3; Waterman 8–0–35–0; Pocock 8–0–52–2; Jesty 8–0–57–2.

**Surrey**

| | |
|---|---|
| A. R. Butcher c Baptiste b Cowdrey | 52 |
| D. B. Pauline run out | 19 |
| M. A. Lynch c Hinks b Cowdrey | 12 |
| *T. E. Jesty c and b Underwood | 2 |
| †C. J. Richards b Cowdrey | 3 |
| A. Needham not out | 43 |
| D. M. Ward c Johnson b Underwood | 16 |
| C. K. Bullen b Jarvis | 10 |
| A. H. Gray b Ellison | 1 |
| P. A. Waterman b Ellison | 8 |
| P. I. Pocock not out | 6 |
| L-b 6, w 7 | 13 |
| 1/47 2/68 3/74 4/83 5/104 6/131 7/156 8/159 9/175 (9 wkts, 40 overs) | 185 |

Bowling: Jarvis 8–0–35–1; Ellison 8–0–33–2; Cowdrey 8–0–35–3; Baptiste 8–0–42–0; Underwood 8–1–34–2.

Umpires: B. J. Meyer and D. R. Shepherd.

At Bradford, July 14. SURREY lost to YORKSHIRE by two wickets.

## SURREY v NOTTINGHAMSHIRE

At Guildford, July 21. Nottinghamshire won by 12 runs. Toss won by Surrey.

**Nottinghamshire**

| | |
|---|---|
| R. T. Robinson c Stewart b Monkhouse | 22 |
| B. C. Broad c Stewart b Jesty | 69 |
| D. W. Randall c Monkhouse b Gray | 65 |
| *R. J. Hadlee c Waterman b Gray | 18 |
| P. Johnson c Jesty b Waterman | 6 |
| †B. N. French not out | 3 |
| B. Hassan run out | 15 |
| E. E. Hemmings run out | 3 |
| L-b 16, w 3, n-b 3 | 22 |
| 1/56 2/158 3/182 4/199 5/200 6/220 7/223 (7 wkts, 40 overs) | 223 |

R. A. Pick, K. Saxelby and K. E. Cooper did not bat.

Bowling: Waterman 8–0–44–1; Monkhouse 8–0–25–1; Gray 8–0–50–2; Jesty 8–0–46–1; Pocock 8–0–42–0.

**Surrey**

| | |
|---|---|
| A. R. Butcher b Hemmings | 46 |
| G. S. Clinton c Randall b Cooper | 72 |
| M. A. Lynch c French b Hemmings | 9 |
| *T. E. Jesty b Pick | 0 |
| A. J. Stewart c French b Pick | 0 |
| A. Needham not out | 52 |
| †C. J. Richards c Hadlee b Saxelby | 18 |
| G. Monkhouse b Hadlee | 5 |
| P. I. Pocock b Hadlee | 2 |
| A. H. Gray not out | 1 |
| L-b 3, w 2, n-b 1 | 6 |
| 1/90 2/112 3/115 4/115 5/153 6/187 7/208 8/210 (8 wkts, 40 overs) | 211 |

P. A. Waterman did not bat.

Bowling: Hadlee 8–2–33–2; Saxelby 8–0–46–1; Cooper 8–0–58–1; Hemmings 8–1–29–2; Pick 8–0–42–2.

Umpires: C. Cook and K. E. Palmer.

At Derby, August 4. DERBYSHIRE v SURREY. No result.

At Lord's, August 18. MIDDLESEX v SURREY. No result.

## SURREY v NORTHAMPTONSHIRE

At Guildford, August 25. Northamptonshire won by 93 runs, after scoring their highest total in the competition and the third-highest ever. It was discovered later that two five-ball overs were bowled in their innings. Toss won by Surrey.

### Northamptonshire

W. Larkins c Ward b Felton .........126
R. J. Bailey lbw b Pauline ........... 21
A. J. Lamb not out ...................132
R. A. Harper not out ............... 13
B 4, l-b 7, w 3 ............. 14

1/56 2/232 (2 wkts, 40 overs) 306

R. J. Boyd-Moss, R. G. Williams, D. J. Wild, D. J. Walker, *G. Cook, †D. Ripley and N. A. Mallender did not bat.

Bowling: Waterman 8–1–46–0; Doughty 8–0–46–0; Felton 8–0–72–1; Pauline 8–0–53–1; Needham 4–0–33–0; Butcher 4–0–45–0.

### Surrey

*A. R. Butcher c Ripley b Walker .... 9
G. S. Clinton b Mallender ............ 13
M. A. Lynch c Harper b Wild ......... 55
†A. J. Stewart b Harper .............. 11
A. Needham run out ................. 51
D. M. Ward c Cook b Harper ......... 9
R. J. Doughty c Walker b Wild ...... 10
M. A. Feltham b Walker ............. 31
D. B. Pauline c Wild b Williams ...... 3
C. K. Bullen c Wild b Williams ...... 9
P. A. Waterman not out .............. 0
L-b 9, w 2, n-b 1 ........... 12

1/21 2/29 3/96 4/104 5/132 6/155 7/183 8/197 9/212 (35.1 overs) 213

Bowling: Mallender 5–0–19–1; Walker 6.1–0–26–2; Harper 8–0–40–2; Larkins 3–0–39–0; Wild 8–0–44–2; Williams 5–0–36–2.

Umpires: J. H. Hampshire and A. A. Jones.

At Cardiff, September 1. SURREY beat GLAMORGAN on faster scoring-rate.

## SURREY v LANCASHIRE

At The Oval, September 8. Surrey won by eight wickets. Toss won by Surrey.

### Lancashire

G. Fowler c Needham b Pauline ...... 23
S. J. O'Shaughnessy b Feltham ....... 29
C. H. Lloyd b Pauline ............... 4
N. H. Fairbrother lbw b Pauline ...... 3
D. P. Hughes c Stewart b Pocock ..... 23
*J. Abrahams c Richards b Doughty .. 25
M. Watkinson c Lynch b Pocock ..... 12
J. Simmons run out .................. 11
A. N. Hayhurst not out ............. 12
†C. Maynard not out ................ 3
B 1, l-b 7, w 6, n-b 1 ........ 15

1/46 2/63 3/65 4/67 5/119 6/123 7/136 8/146 (8 wkts, 40 overs) 160

P. J. W. Allott did not bat.

Bowling: Jesty 8–0–30–0; Monkhouse 5–0–12–0; Pauline 8–0–34–3; Feltham 8–2–23–1; Doughty 6–0–30–1; Pocock 5–0–23–2.

### Surrey

A. Needham c Hayhurst b Watkinson . 9
G. S. Clinton retired hurt ............ 40
M. A. Lynch c Simmons b O'Shaughnessy 24
A. J. Stewart not out ............... 71
*T. E. Jesty not out ................ 14
L-b 3, w 3 ................. 6

1/9 2/42 (2 wkts, 37 overs) 164

D. B. Pauline, †C. J. Richards, M. A. Feltham, G. Monkhouse, P. I. Pocock and R. J. Doughty did not bat.

Bowling: Allott 8–0–33–0; Watkinson 6–2–19–1; Simmons 8–0–41–0; O'Shaughnessy 8–0–22–1; Fairbrother 2–0–15–0; Hayhurst 5–0–31–0.

Umpires: B. J. Meyer and P. B. Wight.

## SURREY v GLOUCESTERSHIRE

At The Oval, September 15. Gloucestershire won by 86 runs. Toss won by Surrey.

### Gloucestershire

P. W. Romaines c Jesty b Pocock . . . . . 78
C. W. J. Athey not out . . . . . . . . . . . . . .115
K. M. Curran c Doughty b Feltham . . . 14
B. F. Davison not out . . . . . . . . . . . . . . . 10
B 1, l-b 6, w 2, n-b 1 . . . . . . . . 10

1/164 2/198 (2 wkts, 40 overs) 227

R. G. P. Ellis, P. Bainbridge, J. W. Lloyds, *D. A. Graveney, C. A. Walsh, †R. C. Russell and G. E. Sainsbury did not bat.

Bowling: Jesty 6–0–32–0; Monkhouse 5–1–18–0; Feltham 6–0–30–1; Waterman 8–0–54–0; Pocock 8–0–44–1; Doughty 7–0–42–0.

### Surrey

N. J. Falkner c Graveney b Athey . . . . 44
†C. J. Richards c Athey b Curran . . . . . 21
M. A. Lynch b Sainsbury . . . . . . . . . . . . 2
A. J. Stewart lbw b Sainsbury . . . . . . . . 0
*T. E. Jesty b Athey . . . . . . . . . . . . . . . . 32
D. M. Ward c and b Graveney . . . . . . . 5
R. J. Doughty run out . . . . . . . . . . . . . . . 0
M. A. Feltham c Sainsbury b Graveney 23
G. Monkhouse st Russell b Graveney . . 0
P. I. Pocock c Davison b Graveney . . . 3
P. A. Waterman not out . . . . . . . . . . . . . 0
L-b 5, w 6 . . . . . . . . . . . . . . . . . . 11

1/27 2/34 3/34 (29.3 overs) 141
4/102 5/115 6/115 7/115
8/121 9/141

Bowling: Sainsbury 8–1–26–2; Curran 4–0–23–1; Bainbridge 5–1–30–0; Athey 6–0–21–2; Graveney 6.3–1–36–4.

Umpires: B. Leadbeater and D. O. Oslear.

# SUSSEX

At Chelmsford, May 5. SUSSEX beat ESSEX by nine wickets.

## SUSSEX v SURREY

At Hove, May 12. Surrey won by eight wickets after rain had reduced their target to 170 off 35 overs. Toss won by Surrey. Barclay took his 100th wicket in John Player League matches.

### Sussex

G. D. Mendis c Clinton b Thomas . . . . 70
A. M. Green b Pauline . . . . . . . . . . . . . . 36
P. W. G. Parker b Pocock . . . . . . . . . . . 20
A. P. Wells c Stewart b Thomas . . . . . . 20
C. M. Wells run out . . . . . . . . . . . . . . . . 11
I. A. Greig c Bullen b Monkhouse . . . . 1
†I. J. Gould not out . . . . . . . . . . . . . . . . 9
G. S. le Roux not out . . . . . . . . . . . . . . . 18
B 2, l-b 2, w 4, n-b 1 . . . . . . . . 9

1/92 2/123 3/140 (6 wkts, 40 overs) 194
4/166 5/166 6/169

A. N. Jones, *J. R. T. Barclay and I. C. Waring did not bat.

Bowling: Thomas 8–0–22–2; Monkhouse 8–0–58–1; Pocock 8–0–25–1; Bullen 6–0–35–0; Pauline 8–0–40–1; Jesty 2–0–10–0.

### Surrey

| | |
|---|---|
| A. R. Butcher st Gould b Barclay | 67 |
| G. S. Clinton c Parker b Jones | 67 |
| A. J. Stewart not out | 22 |
| T. E. Jesty not out | 4 |
| L-b 7, w 1, n-b 5 | 13 |
| 1/132 2/165 (2 wkts, 31.2 overs) | 173 |

M. A. Lynch, D. B. Pauline, D. J. Thomas, C. K. Bullen, †C. J. Richards, G. Monkhouse and *P. I. Pocock did not bat.

Bowling: C. M. Wells 6–0–21–0; le Roux 6–0–30–0; Waring 4–0–21–0; Barclay 4–0–24–1; Greig 7–0–45–0; Jones 4.2–0–25–1.

Umpires: B. Dudleston and R. Julian.

At Lord's, May 26. SUSSEX lost to MIDDLESEX by seven wickets.

## SUSSEX v NOTTINGHAMSHIRE

At Horsham, June 2. Nottinghamshire won by two wickets. Toss won by Sussex.

### Sussex

| | |
|---|---|
| G. D. Mendis b Hadlee | 2 |
| A. M. Green b Hadlee | 11 |
| P. W. G. Parker c Birch b Cooper | 8 |
| Imran Khan c French b Evans | 72 |
| A. P. Wells c Randall b Rice | 27 |
| C. M. Wells not out | 47 |
| I. A. Greig c Rice b Saxelby | 12 |
| *†I. J. Gould run out | 1 |
| D. A. Reeve not out | 0 |
| L-b 8, w 4, n-b 4 | 16 |
| 1/15 2/16 3/53 4/100 5/155 6/189 7/195 (7 wkts, 40 overs) | 196 |

I. C. Waring and A. C. S. Pigott did not bat.

Bowling: Hadlee 8–2–36–2; Saxelby 8–1–32–1; Cooper 8–1–34–1; Rice 8–0–40–1; Evans 8–0–46–1.

### Nottinghamshire

| | |
|---|---|
| B. C. Broad lbw b C. M. Wells | 24 |
| *C. E. B. Rice c Parker b Reeve | 67 |
| P. Johnson c Imran b Reeve | 7 |
| J. D. Birch b Pigott | 49 |
| D. W. Randall b Reeve | 9 |
| R. J. Hadlee b Reeve | 4 |
| K. P. Evans c Mendis b Pigott | 18 |
| †B. N. French run out | 2 |
| E. E. Hemmings not out | 2 |
| K. Saxelby not out | 3 |
| B 1, l-b 9, w 2 | 12 |
| 1/43 2/72 3/111 4/147 5/161 6/187 7/192 8/193 (8 wkts, 40 overs) | 197 |

K. E. Cooper did not bat.

Bowling: C. M. Wells 8–0–32–1; Imran 8–1–28–0; Pigott 7–0–45–2; Reeve 8–0–32–4; Waring 7–0–37–0; Greig 2–0–13–0.

Umpires: K. J. Lyons and N. T. Plews.

At Sheffield, June 9. SUSSEX beat YORKSHIRE by 36 runs.

## SUSSEX v HAMPSHIRE

At Hove, June 16. Hampshire won by nine wickets. Toss won by Hampshire.

### Sussex

G. D. Mendis lbw b Tremlett ........ 11
A. M. Green c and b Cowley ....... 43
P. W. G. Parker c Parks b Connor .... 4
Imran Khan not out .................104
A. P. Wells run out .................. 25
C. M. Wells not out ................ 42
L-b 7, w 1, n-b 1 ........... 9

1/36 2/55 3/69 4/116 (4 wkts, 40 overs) 238

I. A. Greig, G. S. le Roux, †I. J. Gould, *J. R. T. Barclay and A. C. S. Pigott did not bat.

Bowling: James 8–0–56–0; Marshall 8–0–46–0; Tremlett 8–0–37–1; Connor 8–0–41–1; Cowley 8–0–51–1.

### Hampshire

C. G. Greenidge not out .............124
V. P. Terry c and b Pigott ............ 82
*M. C. J. Nicholas not out ........... 8
B 4, l-b 17, n-b 4 ............ 25

1/221 (1 wkt, 38.5 overs) 239

R. A. Smith, J. J. E. Hardy, N. G. Cowley, M. D. Marshall, K. D. James, T. M. Tremlett, †R. J. Parks and C. A. Connor did not bat.

Bowling: le Roux 8–1–41–0; C. M. Wells 8–0–41–0; Pigott 8–0–46–1; Imran 8–0–34–0; Barclay 3–0–27–0; Greig 3.5–0–29–0.

Umpires: D. J. Constant and J. H. Harris.

At Swindon, June 23. SUSSEX beat GLOUCESTERSHIRE by nine wickets.

## SUSSEX v LANCASHIRE

At Hastings, June 30. Sussex won by 69 runs. Toss won by Lancashire.

### Sussex

G. D. Mendis run out ................ 19
A. M. Green b Henriksen ............ 70
P. W. G. Parker b O'Shaughnessy ..... 22
Imran Khan run out ................. 80
C. M. Wells not out ................. 35
A. P. Wells not out ................. 0
L-b 5, n-b 3 ............... 8

1/30 2/94 3/136 4/221 (4 wkts, 40 overs) 234

I. A. Greig, G. S. le Roux, *J. R. T. Barclay, A. C. S. Pigott and †P. Moores did not bat.

Bowling: Makinson 8–0–46–0; Henriksen 8–0–40–1; Watkinson 8–0–42–0; O'Shaughnessy 8–0–43–1; Simmons 8–0–58–0.

### Lancashire

G. Fowler c Moores b le Roux ....... 20
S. J. O'Shaughnessy c Mendis b le Roux 19
*J. Abrahams c Moores b Greig ...... 6
C. H. Lloyd c Parker b Pigott ........ 26
D. P. Hughes b Imran ............... 21
N. H. Fairbrother c and b Pigott ..... 3
M. Watkinson b Imran ............... 2
J. Simmons not out ................. 32
†C. Maynard not out ............... 19
L-b 10, w 7 ................ 17

1/44 2/54 3/56 4/103 5/104 6/110 7/110 (7 wkts, 40 overs) 165

S. Henriksen and D. J. Makinson did not bat.

Bowling: C. M. Wells 8–0–47–0; Imran 8–2–14–2; Greig 8–0–29–1; le Roux 5–1–9–2; Pigott 8–0–31–2; Barclay 2–0–20–0; A. P. Wells 1–0–5–0.

Umpires: A. G. T. Whitehead and A. A. Jones.

## SUSSEX v WARWICKSHIRE

At Hove, July 7. Sussex won by 20 runs. Toss won by Sussex.

### Sussex

| | |
|---|---|
| G. D. Mendis b Smith ........ 11 | I. A. Greig not out ........ 7 |
| A. M. Green c Amiss b Gifford ........ 29 | A. P. Wells not out ........ 2 |
| P. W. G. Parker c and b Smith ........ 1 | L-b 9, n-b 3 ........ 12 |
| Imran Khan c Amiss b Small ........ 83 | |
| C. M. Wells b Small ........ 53 | 1/30 2/36 3/50 (6 wkts, 40 overs) 209 |
| †I. J. Gould c Humpage b Small ........ 11 | 4/171 5/187 6/200 |

G. S. le Roux, *J. R. T. Barclay and A. C. S. Pigott did not bat.

Bowling: Small 8–0–38–3; Smith 7–0–25–2; Hoffman 8–0–51–0; Pierson 8–1–28–0; Gifford 8–0–47–1; Kallicharran 1–0–11–0.

### Warwickshire

| | |
|---|---|
| T. A. Lloyd b Pigott ........ 21 | A. R. K. Pierson lbw b Imran ........ 4 |
| R. I. H. B. Dyer c Gould b le Roux ........ 15 | *N. Gifford b Barclay ........ 12 |
| A. I. Kallicharran b Pigott ........ 0 | D. S. Hoffman run out ........ 2 |
| D. L. Amiss c A. P. Wells b Greig ........ 25 | B 3, l-b 14, w 7, n-b 2 ........ 26 |
| †G. W. Humpage c Pigott b C. M. Wells 23 | |
| P. A. Smith not out ........ 50 | 1/48 2/48 3/49 (38.5 overs) 189 |
| Asif Din b Greig ........ 5 | 4/90 5/109 6/117 7/130 |
| G. C. Small c C. M. Wells b Imran ........ 6 | 8/158 9/184 |

Bowling: Imran 8–1–29–2; C. M. Wells 8–1–16–1; Pigott 8–1–38–2; le Roux 6.5–0–39–1; Greig 7–0–48–2; Barclay 1–0–2–1.

Umpires: H. D. Bird and K. J. Lyons.

At Northampton, July 21. SUSSEX beat NORTHAMPTONSHIRE by 2 runs.

## SUSSEX v WORCESTERSHIRE

At Eastbourne, July 28. Sussex won by 45 runs in a match reduced by rain to 23 overs a side. Toss won by Worcestershire.

### Sussex

| | |
|---|---|
| G. D. Mendis c Weston b Newport ........ 18 | I. A. Greig not out ........ 0 |
| P. W. G. Parker c Hick b Newport ........ 53 | B 1, l-b 3, w 2, n-b 1 ........ 7 |
| Imran Khan c Hick b Radford ........ 71 | |
| C. M. Wells c D'Oliveira b Hick ........ 13 | 1/37 2/85 3/114 (4 wkts, 23 overs) 169 |
| A. P. Wells not out ........ 7 | 4/168 |

*J. R. T. Barclay, †I. J. Gould, G. S. le Roux, D. A. Reeve and A. C. S. Pigott did not bat.

Bowling: Radford 5–0–35–1; Inchmore 5–0–27–0; Weston 2–0–15–0; Newport 5–0–32–2; Patel 4–0–41–0; Hick 2–0–15–1.

### Worcestershire

| | | | |
|---|---|---|---|
| T. S. Curtis b C. M. Wells | 7 | †S. J. Rhodes c Reeve b Barclay | 11 |
| D. N. Patel c A. P. Wells b C. M. Wells | 10 | M. J. Weston not out | 1 |
| D. M. Smith c Mendis b Reeve | 27 | L-b 8, w 7, n-b 1 | 16 |
| G. A. Hick c C. M. Wells b Reeve | 21 | | |
| D. B. D'Oliveira c Barclay b Reeve | 16 | 1/19 2/23 3/70 (6 wkts, 23 overs) | 124 |
| *P. A. Neale not out | 15 | 4/85 5/97 6/122 | |

P. J. Newport, N. V. Radford and J. D. Inchmore did not bat.

Bowling: le Roux 4–0–17–0; C. M. Wells 5–0–16–2; Imran 5–0–15–0; Reeve 5–0–26–3; Pigott 2–0–25–0; Barclay 1–0–15–1; Greig 1–0–2–0.

Umpires: J. H. Hampshire and R. Julian.

At Canterbury, August 11. KENT v SUSSEX. No result.

## SUSSEX v DERBYSHIRE

At Hove, August 18. Sussex won by 20 runs. Toss won by Derbyshire.

### Sussex

| | | | |
|---|---|---|---|
| G. D. Mendis c Marples b Holding | 15 | C. P. Phillipson not out | 15 |
| †I. J. Gould b Mortensen | 11 | *J. R. T. Barclay not out | 7 |
| Imran Khan c and b Miller | 31 | | |
| C. M. Wells c Fell b Miller | 16 | B 1, l-b 13, w 7, n-b 1 | 22 |
| A. P. Wells c Anderson b Warner | 18 | | |
| G. S. le Roux c and b Holding | 8 | 1/25 2/44 3/82 (7 wkts, 40 overs) | 156 |
| I. A. Greig run out | 13 | 4/90 5/115 6/121 7/132 | |

D. A. Reeve and A. C. S. Pigott did not bat.

Bowling: Holding 8–1–37–2; Finney 8–0–27–0; Mortensen 8–2–13–1; Newman 7–1–26–0; Miller 4–0–8–2; Warner 5–0–31–1.

### Derbyshire

| | | | |
|---|---|---|---|
| I. S. Anderson c Gould b Reeve | 22 | R. J. Finney c Gould b Imran | 0 |
| B. Roberts lbw b le Roux | 17 | †C. Marples run out | 10 |
| *K. J. Barnett c Imran b C. M. Wells | 10 | O. H. Mortensen not out | 0 |
| M. A. Fell c Mendis b le Roux | 0 | L-b 6, w 1, n-b 3 | 10 |
| G. Miller c Gould b Reeve | 2 | | |
| M. A. Holding b Imran | 58 | 1/44 2/46 3/50 (33.2 overs) | 136 |
| P. G. Newman c Barclay b le Roux | 7 | 4/55 5/89 6/124 7/125 | |
| A. E. Warner c Gould b Imran | 0 | 8/125 9/126 | |

Bowling: C. M. Wells 7–0–24–1; Imran 7.2–2–28–3; Reeve 8–1–28–2; le Roux 8–0–27–3; Pigott 1–0–13–0; Greig 2–0–10–0.

Umpires: J. W. Holder and B. J. Meyer.

At Taunton, September 1. SUSSEX lost to SOMERSET by eight wickets.

## SUSSEX v LEICESTERSHIRE

At Hove, September 8. Sussex won by 7 runs. Toss won by Sussex.

### Sussex

G. D. Mendis c Willey b Taylor ...... 19
A. M. Green c and b Agnew .......... 7
Imran Khan c Butcher b Clift ........ 11
C. M. Wells lbw b Taylor ........... 0
G. S. le Roux c Agnew b Parsons ..... 31
†I. J. Gould b De Freitas ............ 28
I. A. Greig c De Freitas b Parsons .... 39
A. P. Wells b Willey ................ 16
D. A. Reeve c Gower b Taylor ....... 19
*J. R. T. Barclay not out ............ 4
A. N. Jones not out ................ 1
L-b 6, w 1, n-b 4 ............ 11

1/18 2/23 3/35 4/52 5/89 6/128 7/155 8/175 9/182 (9 wkts, 40 overs) 186

Bowling: Agnew 8–0–25–1; Taylor 8–1–26–3; Clift 8–2–17–1; Parsons 8–0–44–2; De Freitas 4–0–44–1; Willey 4–0–24–1.

### Leicestershire

*D. I. Gower c A. P. Wells b Jones ... 46
N. E. Briers c Jones b C. M. Wells ... 25
J. J. Whitaker b Reeve ............... 5
P. Willey c Mendis b Jones .......... 20
†M. A. Garnham b Jones ............ 28
I. P. Butcher c Barclay b Imran ...... 3
P. B. Clift lbw b Imran ............. 4
G. J. Parsons b Imran .............. 11
P. A. J. De Freitas b Imran .......... 3
J. P. Agnew not out ................ 13
L. B. Taylor not out ................ 6
B 1, l-b 10, w 3, n-b 1 ....... 15

1/76 2/81 3/83 4/126 5/137 6/141 7/148 8/157 9/158 (9 wkts, 40 overs) 179

Bowling: Imran 8–0–37–4; C. M. Wells 8–0–29–1; le Roux 8–0–38–0; Reeve 8–0–31–1; Jones 8–0–33–3.

Umpires: M. J. Kitchen and R. Palmer.

At Cardiff, September 15. SUSSEX beat GLAMORGAN by 93 runs.

# WARWICKSHIRE

At The Oval, May 5. WARWICKSHIRE lost to SURREY by 4 runs.

## WARWICKSHIRE v LANCASHIRE

At Edgbaston, May 12. Warwickshire won by 23 runs. Toss won by Lancashire. Amiss achieved a new John Player League record of 6,174 runs, passing by 30 G. M. Turner's previous record.

### Warwickshire

T. A. Lloyd b Simmons ............. 44
R. I. H. B. Dyer b Allott ............ 0
A. I. Kallicharran c Abrahams b Watkinson. 43
D. L. Amiss c O'Shaughnessy b Watkinson. 53
†G. W. Humpage b Makinson ........ 53
P. A. Smith not out ................. 5
Asif Din not out .................. 1
B 11, w 3 ................. 14

1/5 2/71 3/104 4/204 5/212 (5 wkts, 40 overs) 213

A. M. Ferreira, G. C. Small, S. Wall and *N. Gifford did not bat.

Bowling: Allott 8–0–38–1; Makinson 8–1–25–1; Simmons 8–0–43–1; O'Shaughnessy 8–0–44–0; Watkinson 8–0–52–2.

### Lancashire

| | |
|---|---|
| G. Fowler c Small b Kallicharran | 46 |
| S. J. O'Shaughnessy c Gifford b Smith | 39 |
| C. H. Lloyd c Ferreira b Kallicharran | 25 |
| *J. Abrahams st Humpage b Gifford | 23 |
| N. H. Fairbrother b Ferreira | 28 |
| M. Watkinson st Humpage b Kallicharran | 0 |
| †C. Maynard b Small | 4 |
| J. Simmons run out | 14 |
| P. J. W. Allott b Ferreira | 1 |
| K. A. Hayes not out | 2 |
| D. J. Makinson c Kallicharran b Small | 1 |
| L-b 6, n-b 1 | 7 |
| 1/76 2/104 3/131 4/157 5/158 6/165 7/177 8/185 9/189 (39.1 overs) | 190 |

Bowling: Small 7.1–0–30–2; Wall 4–0–26–0; Gifford 8–0–41–1; Smith 6–0–26–1; Kallicharran 8–0–32–3; Ferreira 6–0–29–2.

Umpires: J. H. Harris and B. J. Meyer.

At Taunton, June 2. WARWICKSHIRE beat SOMERSET by seven wickets.

## WARWICKSHIRE v HAMPSHIRE

At Edgbaston, June 9. Warwickshire won by five wickets in a match reduced by rain to 36 overs a side. Toss won by Warwickshire.

### Hampshire

| | |
|---|---|
| C. G. Greenidge c Humpage b Small | 23 |
| V. P. Terry lbw b Hoffman | 18 |
| *M. C. J. Nicholas b Gifford | 10 |
| R. A. Smith b Gifford | 2 |
| C. L. Smith c Kallicharran b Ferreira | 39 |
| M. D. Marshall c Small b Gifford | 11 |
| K. D. James c Gifford b Small | 34 |
| N. G. Cowley b Ferreira | 25 |
| T. M. Tremlett not out | 3 |
| †R. J. Parks not out | 3 |
| L-b 6, w 1 | 7 |
| 1/34 2/50 3/54 4/55 5/79 6/124 7/168 8/170 (8 wkts, 36 overs) | 175 |

C. A. Connor did not bat.

Bowling: Small 8–0–41–2; Smith 4–0–22–0; Gifford 8–2–19–3; Hoffman 8–0–41–1; Ferreira 8–0–46–2.

### Warwickshire

| | |
|---|---|
| R. I. H. B. Dyer c James b Cowley | 16 |
| G. J. Lord c Terry b James | 1 |
| A. I. Kallicharran c R. A. Smith b Tremlett | 69 |
| D. L. Amiss c Parks b Marshall | 12 |
| †G. W. Humpage b Marshall | 4 |
| P. A. Smith not out | 27 |
| A. M. Ferreira not out | 34 |
| L-b 11, w 2 | 13 |
| 1/4 2/56 3/80 4/89 5/120 (5 wkts, 34.2 overs) | 176 |

Asif Din, G. C. Small, *N. Gifford and D. S. Hoffman did not bat.

Bowling: James 7.2–0–29–1; Connor 6–0–33–0; Tremlett 6–1–22–1; Cowley 7–0–44–1; Marshall 8–0–37–2.

Umpires: D. G. L. Evans and B. Leadbeater.

## WARWICKSHIRE v NORTHAMPTONSHIRE

At Edgbaston, June 30. Warwickshire won by 9 runs after the loss of 33 minutes to rain caused a reduction to 35 overs a side. Toss won by Northamptonshire.

### Warwickshire

| | |
|---|---|
| T. A. Lloyd c Ripley b Wild | 12 |
| R. I. H. B. Dyer b Walker | 5 |
| A. I. Kallicharran c Williams b Wild | 44 |
| D. L. Amiss c Boyd-Moss b Larkins | 7 |
| †G. W. Humpage c Boyd-Moss b Larkins | 23 |
| P. A. Smith b Harper | 3 |
| Asif Din run out | 18 |
| A. M. Ferreira b Harper | 2 |
| G. C. Small b Walker | 3 |
| N. Gifford not out | 12 |
| D. S. Hoffman not out | 0 |
| B 1, l-b 10, w 2 | 13 |
| 1/10 2/28 3/57 4/97 5/103 6/108 7/109 8/115 9/141 (9 wkts, 35 overs) | 142 |

Bowling: Mallender 6–0–25–0; Walker 6–0–30–2; Wild 7–1–20–2; Larkins 8–0–27–2; Harper 8–0–29–2.

### Northamptonshire

| | |
|---|---|
| *G. Cook c Humpage b Small | 0 |
| W. Larkins c and b Gifford | 26 |
| R. J. Boyd-Moss c Ferreira b Gifford | 51 |
| R. J. Bailey lbw b Hoffman | 2 |
| R. G. Williams b Gifford | 4 |
| D. J. Capel run out | 15 |
| D. J. Wild st Humpage b Gifford | 0 |
| R. A. Harper st Humpage b Gifford | 0 |
| †D. Ripley b Gifford | 1 |
| N. A. Mallender not out | 4 |
| A. Walker not out | 6 |
| B 1, l-b 9, w 14 | 24 |
| 1/0 2/80 3/83 4/90 5/105 6/106 7/107 8/111 9/125 (9 wkts, 35 overs) | 133 |

Bowling: Small 8–0–30–1; Smith 3–0–14–0; Ferreira 8–1–29–0; Hoffman 7–0–23–1; Gifford 8–0–20–6; Kallicharran 1–0–7–0.

Umpires: J. H. Hampshire and K. E. Palmer.

At Hove, July 7. WARWICKSHIRE lost to SUSSEX by 20 runs.

## WARWICKSHIRE v NOTTINGHAMSHIRE

At Edgbaston, July 14. Warwickshire won by 9 runs. Toss won by Nottinghamshire.

### Warwickshire

| | |
|---|---|
| T. A. Lloyd b Hadlee | 4 |
| R. I. H. B. Dyer c Hemmings b Hadlee | 1 |
| A. I. Kallicharran b Hemmings | 28 |
| D. L. Amiss c Randall b Evans | 55 |
| †G. W. Humpage not out | 51 |
| P. A. Smith lbw b Evans | 3 |
| A. M. Ferreira c Evans b Saxelby | 9 |
| G. C. Small b Saxelby | 17 |
| B 1, l-b 12, w 3 | 16 |
| 1/4 2/11 3/75 4/126 5/131 6/133 7/184 (7 wkts, 40 overs) | 184 |

A. R. K. Pierson, *N. Gifford and D. S. Hoffman did not bat.

Bowling: Hadlee 8–1–30–2; Saxelby 8–0–27–2; Cooper 4–0–26–0; Rice 8–1–33–0; Hemmings 8–2–25–1; Evans 4–0–30–2.

### Nottinghamshire

B. C. Broad c and b Gifford ......... 23
†B. N. French lbw b Hoffman ........ 6
*C. E. B. Rice c Humpage b Ferreira .. 12
P. Johnson b Ferreira ............... 63
D. W. Randall lbw b Gifford ......... 16
R. J. Hadlee b Small ................ 36
J. D. Birch lbw b Ferreira ......... 0
K. P. Evans c Pierson b Small ....... 5
E. E. Hemmings c Dyer b Ferreira .... 0
K. Saxelby not out .................. 5
K. E. Cooper not out ................ 4
L-b 4, n-b 1 ................ 5

1/14 2/35 3/67 (9 wkts, 40 overs) 175
4/116 5/126 6/126 7/158
8/159 9/171

Bowling: Small 8–1–16–2; Hoffman 8–0–35–1; Ferreira 7–0–42–4; Gifford 8–1–26–2; Pierson 7–0–42–0; Smith 2–0–10–0.

Umpires: D. O. Oslear and R. Julian.

At Leicester, July 21. WARWICKSHIRE lost to LEICESTERSHIRE by nine wickets.

## WARWICKSHIRE v DERBYSHIRE

At Edgbaston, July 28. Derbyshire won by five wickets in a match reduced by rain to 30 overs a side. Toss won by Derbyshire.

### Warwickshire

†G. W. Humpage b Warner .......... 4
G. J. Lord c Anderson b Warner .....103
A. I. Kallicharran run out .......... 9
D. L. Amiss b Newman ............. 21
P. A. Smith b Holding .............. 21
A. M. Ferreira c Mortensen b Warner . 38
Asif Din b Warner ................. 6
C. Lethbridge not out ............... 2
G. C. Small not out ................ 3
L-b 7, w 7, n-b 3 ........... 17

1/9 2/37 3/95 (7 wkts, 30 overs) 224
4/166 5/179 6/218 7/218

*N. Gifford and D. S. Hoffman did not bat.

Bowling: Warner 6–0–44–4; Holding 6–0–37–1; Finney 6–0–58–0; Mortensen 6–0–39–0; Newman 6–0–39–1.

### Derbyshire

*K. J. Barnett not out ............... 82
I. S. Anderson c Amiss b Small ....... 11
J. E. Morris c Humpage b Small ...... 5
B. Roberts lbw b Smith .............. 42
G. Miller c Smith b Lethbridge ....... 38
M. A. Holding c Smith b Small ....... 13
P. G. Newman not out .............. 8
B 5, l-b 16, w 4, n-b 1 ....... 26

1/33 2/45 3/106 (5 wkts, 29.2 overs) 225
4/165 5/199

A. E. Warner, R. J. Finney, †C. Marples and O. H. Mortensen did not bat.

Bowling: Small 6–0–36–3; Hoffman 4–0–26–0; Ferreira 5.2–0–47–0; Lethbridge 6–0–43–1; Smith 3–0–25–1; Gifford 5–0–27–0.

Umpires: K. E. Palmer and P. B. Wight.

## WARWICKSHIRE v YORKSHIRE

At Edgbaston, August 4. No result.

At Cardiff, August 11. GLAMORGAN v WARWICKSHIRE. No result.

At Cheltenham, August 18. WARWICKSHIRE lost to GLOUCESTERSHIRE by 13 runs.

At Worcester, August 25. WARWICKSHIRE lost to WORCESTERSHIRE on scoring-rate.

## WARWICKSHIRE v ESSEX

At Edgbaston, September 1. Essex won by 21 runs. Toss won by Warwickshire.

### Essex

B. R. Hardie run out ................ 21
P. J. Prichard lbw b Smith ........... 6
K. S. McEwan b Ferreira ............118
D. R. Pringle not out ............... 81
*K. W. R. Fletcher not out .......... 2
B 5, l-b 13, w 3, n-b 2 ....... 23

1/18 2/59 3/249 (3 wkts, 40 overs) 251

A. W. Lilley, I. L. Pont, †D. E. East, S. Turner, N. A. Foster and J. K. Lever did not bat.

Bowling: Small 8-0-36-0; Smith 6-0-25-1; Thorne 2-0-13-0; Pierson 8-0-30-0; Gifford 8-0-57-0; Ferreira 8-0-72-1.

### Warwickshire

T. A. Lloyd c East b Pont ........... 18
†G. W. Humpage c Foster b Pringle ... 62
A. I. Kallicharran c Lilley b Turner ... 5
D. L. Amiss c East b Pringle ......... 45
Asif Din c Lilley b Foster ........... 44
P. A. Smith b Lever .................. 4
A. M. Ferreira b Lever .............. 19
D. A. Thorne not out ................ 5
G. C. Small b Lever .................. 4
*N. Gifford b Lever .................. 0
A. R. K. Pierson b Pringle ........... 0
L-b 15, w 5, n-b 4 .......... 24

1/48 2/61 3/106 (39.1 overs) 230
4/166 5/173 6/215 7/217
8/226 9/229

Bowling: Lever 8-0-44-4; Foster 8-0-43-1; Pont 8-0-39-1; Turner 8-0-50-1; Pringle 7.1-0-39-3.

Umpires: A. A. Jones and B. Leadbeater.

At Canterbury, September 8. WARWICKSHIRE beat KENT by 31 runs.

## WARWICKSHIRE v MIDDLESEX

At Edgbaston, September 15. Warwickshire won by 6 runs. Toss won by Warwickshire.

### Warwickshire

T. A. Lloyd c Downton b Hughes ..... 33
†G. W. Humpage c Slack b Rose ..... 17
A. I. Kallicharran b Emburey ........ 16
D. L. Amiss run out ................. 16
Asif Din c Downton b Fraser ........ 20
P. A. Smith st Downton b Emburey ... 20
A. M. Ferreira b Williams ........... 14
D. A. Thorne st Downton b Emburey . 5
G. C. Small run out .................. 1
A. R. K. Pierson b Williams ......... 3
*N. Gifford not out .................. 1
B 1, l-b 14, w 4, n-b 1 ....... 20

1/34 2/65 3/84 (39 overs) 166
4/113 5/138 6/138 7/155
8/157 9/165

Bowling: Williams 8-0-38-2; Fraser 8-0-28-1; Rose 8-0-38-1; Emburey 8-1-25-3; Hughes 7-0-22-1.

### Middlesex

| | | | |
|---|---|---|---|
| W. N. Slack lbw b Gifford | 33 | N. F. Williams not out | 10 |
| K. R. Brown lbw b Asif Din | 33 | S. P. Hughes b Ferreira | 2 |
| R. O. Butcher st Humpage b Gifford | 8 | A. R. C. Fraser run out | 0 |
| C. T. Radley st Humpage b Gifford | 1 | B 4, l-b 13, w 5 | 22 |
| M. A. Roseberry b Small | 15 | | |
| †P. R. Downton b Ferreira | 23 | 1/69 2/86 3/87 (39.5 overs) | 160 |
| *J. E. Emburey b Small | 8 | 4/92 5/127 6/139 7/139 | |
| G. D. Rose c Asif Din b Ferreira | 5 | 8/147 9/160 | |

Bowling: Small 8–0–43–2; Smith 3–0–7–0; Pierson 8–1–25–0; Ferreira 7.5–0–29–3; Gifford 8–1–16–3; Asif Din 5–0–23–1.

Umpires: H. D. Bird and C. Cook.

# WORCESTERSHIRE

## WORCESTERSHIRE v SOMERSET

At Worcester, May 5. No result when rain, which had already reduced the match to ten overs a side, ended play. Toss won by Somerset.

### Worcestershire

| | | | |
|---|---|---|---|
| M. J. Weston run out | 8 | N. V. Radford not out | 12 |
| D. B. D'Oliveira c Palmer b Davis | 7 | T. S. Curtis not out | 5 |
| Kapil Dev b Davis | 10 | | |
| J. D. Inchmore run out | 3 | L-b 3 | 3 |
| D. M. Smith c Davis b Palmer | 25 | | |
| D. N. Patel lbw b Botham | 0 | 1/8 2/23 3/26 (7 wkts, 10 overs) | 75 |
| *P. A. Neale c Botham b Turner | 2 | 4/41 5/41 6/50 7/58 | |

†S. J. Rhodes and P. J. Newport did not bat.

Bowling: Marks 2–0–15–0; Davis 2–0–12–2; Turner 2–0–20–1; Botham 2–0–5–1; Palmer 2–0–20–1.

### Somerset

| | |
|---|---|
| *I. T. Botham not out | 28 |
| B. C. Rose not out | 15 |
| L-b 1, w 1 | 2 |
| (no wkt, 5.1 overs) | 45 |

P. M. Roebuck, J. G. Wyatt, N. F. M. Popplewell, R. L. Ollis, V. J. Marks, †T. Gard, G. V. Palmer, M. S. Turner and M. R. Davis did not bat.

Bowling: Inchmore 2–0–15–0; Newport 1–0–6–0; Kapil Dev 1.1–0–11–0; Radford 1–0–12–0.

Umpires: B. Dudleston and P. B. Wight.

At Canterbury, June 2. WORCESTERSHIRE lost to KENT by 35 runs.

At Ebbw Vale, June 9. WORCESTERSHIRE lost to GLAMORGAN by 22 runs.

## WORCESTERSHIRE v SURREY

At Worcester, June 16. Worcestershire won by eight wickets. Toss won by Worcestershire.

### Surrey

A. R. Butcher lbw b Radford ........ 4
G. S. Clinton c Rhodes b Radford .... 6
A. Needham c Neale b Inchmore ..... 2
M. A. Lynch c Newport b Weston .... 52
*T. E. Jesty c D'Oliveira b Illingworth . 21
D. M. Ward not out ................ 42
D. B. Pauline c Smith b Patel ........ 5
D. J. Thomas c Smith b Radford ..... 26
†C. J. Richards b Inchmore .......... 10
B 2, l-b 14, w 9 ............ 25

1/2 2/21 3/21 (8 wkts, 40 overs) 193
4/102 5/106 6/118
7/180 8/193

A. H. Gray and P. I. Pocock did not bat.

Bowling: Radford 8–0–23–3; Inchmore 8–2–36–2; Newport 5–0–33–0; Weston 8–0–32–1; Illingworth 7–1–23–1; Patel 4–1–30–1.

### Worcestershire

D. N. Patel st Richards b Needham ... 47
D. B. D'Oliveira b Thomas ..........103
D. M. Smith not out ................ 18
G. A. Hick not out ................. 11
B 8, l-b 5, w 5 ............ 18

1/39 2/178 (2 wkts, 38.1 overs) 197

*P. A. Neale, M. J. Weston, †S. J. Rhodes, P. J. Newport, R. K. Illingworth, N. V. Radford and J. D. Inchmore did not bat.

Bowling: Gray 7.1–0–34–0; Thomas 7–0–25–1; Pauline 4–0–24–0; Butcher 5–0–14–0; Jesty 4–0–26–0; Pocock 7–0–43–0; Needham 4–0–18–1.

Umpires: J. H. Hampshire and D. R. Shepherd.

## WORCESTERSHIRE v YORKSHIRE

At Worcester, June 30. Yorkshire won by 14 runs. Toss won by Yorkshire.

### Yorkshire

A. A. Metcalfe c Rhodes b Weston .... 12
K. Sharp not out ...................112
J. D. Love c Kapil Dev b Patel ....... 7
*†D. L. Bairstow b Illingworth ....... 25
S. N. Hartley b Radford ............. 19
G. B. Stevenson b Radford .......... 10
P. Carrick not out .................. 4
L-b 19, w 7 ................ 26

1/39 2/63 3/136 (5 wkts, 40 overs) 215
4/192 5/208

A. Sidebottom, C. S. Pickles, P. W. Jarvis and S. D. Fletcher did not bat.

Bowling: Kapil Dev 8–0–43–0; Radford 7–0–38–2; Weston 3–0–15–1; Patel 8–0–26–1; Newport 8–0–36–0; Illingworth 6–0–38–1.

### Worcestershire

D. N. Patel run out ................. 54
D. B. D'Oliveira b Pickles ........... 12
D. M. Smith c Bairstow b Pickles ..... 3
Kapil Dev run out ................... 0
*P. A. Neale b Stevenson ............ 18
M. J. Weston b Stevenson ........... 15
D. A. Banks b Jarvis ................ 13
S. J. Rhodes lbw b Sidebottom ....... 13
P. J. Newport not out ............... 18
N. V. Radford not out .............. 30
B 2, l-b 16, w 3, n-b 4 ....... 25

1/25 2/42 3/42 (8 wkts, 40 overs) 201
4/75 5/109 6/127
7/142 8/157

R. K. Illingworth did not bat.

Bowling: Sidebottom 8–0–50–1; Pickles 8–0–32–2; Fletcher 8–0–39–0; Stevenson 8–0–39–2; Jarvis 8–1–23–1.

Umpires: C. Cook and B. J. Meyer.

At Knypersley, July 7. WORCESTERSHIRE lost to DERBYSHIRE by 33 runs.

At Portsmouth, July 14. WORCESTERSHIRE lost to HAMPSHIRE by 10 runs.

## WORCESTERSHIRE v MIDDLESEX

At Worcester, July 21. Worcestershire won by 22 runs. Toss won by Middlesex.

### Worcestershire

| | | | |
|---|---|---|---|
| T. S. Curtis lbw b Daniel | 16 | J. D. Inchmore run out | 5 |
| D. N. Patel c Radley b Williams | 15 | N. V. Radford b Hughes | 14 |
| D. M. Smith b Emburey | 3 | R. K. Illingworth not out | 1 |
| *P. A. Neale c Downton b Hughes | 5 | L-b 7, w 6, n-b 2 | 15 |
| D. B. D'Oliveira c Radley b Gatting | 45 | | |
| Kapil Dev c Slack b Gatting | 22 | 1/26 2/36 3/38 (9 wkts, 40 overs) | 197 |
| M. J. Weston b Gatting | 11 | 4/41 5/85 6/120 7/137 | |
| †S. J. Rhodes not out | 45 | 8/159 9/196 | |

Bowling: Daniel 7–0–39–1; Williams 6–0–28–1; Emburey 8–0–23–1; Hughes 7–0–40–2; Edmonds 4–0–23–0; Gatting 8–1–37–3.

### Middlesex

| | | | |
|---|---|---|---|
| G. D. Barlow lbw b Radford | 14 | P. H. Edmonds b Kapil Dev | 4 |
| W. N. Slack b Radford | 20 | S. P. Hughes not out | 5 |
| *M. W. Gatting not out | 62 | | |
| C. T. Radley c Rhodes b Radford | 0 | L-b 12, w 5 | 17 |
| R. O. Butcher c Radford b Patel | 13 | | |
| †P. R. Downton c Smith b Illingworth | 31 | 1/33 2/38 3/44 (8 wkts, 40 overs) | 175 |
| J. E. Emburey b Illingworth | 9 | 4/74 5/138 6/156 | |
| N. F. Williams b Illingworth | 0 | 7/156 8/170 | |

W. W. Daniel did not bat.

Bowling: Kapil Dev 8–0–44–1; Radford 8–2–19–3; Inchmore 8–0–42–0; Patel 8–2–28–1; Illingworth 8–1–30–3.

Umpires: D. J. Constant and J. W. Holder.

At Eastbourne, July 28. WORCESTERSHIRE lost to SUSSEX by 45 runs.

## WORCESTERSHIRE v LANCASHIRE

At Worcester, August 4. No result.

At Trent Bridge, August 11. WORCESTERSHIRE lost to NOTTINGHAMSHIRE by 24 runs.

## WORCESTERSHIRE v ESSEX

At Worcester, August 18. Essex won by seven wickets in a match reduced by rain to ten overs a side. Toss won by Essex.

### Worcestershire

| | |
|---|---|
| D. N. Patel run out | 2 |
| D. B. D'Oliveira b Pont | 15 |
| D. M. Smith not out | 34 |
| G. A. Hick c Fletcher b Turner | 8 |
| *P. A. Neale b Turner | 17 |
| T. S. Curtis not out | 6 |
| L-b 5, w 1 | 6 |
| 1/8 2/26 3/35 4/62 (4 wkts, 10 overs) | 88 |

M. J. Weston, †S. J. Rhodes, P. J. Newport, N. V. Radford and J. D. Inchmore did not bat.

Bowling: Foster 2–0–14–0; Pont 2–0–15–1; Turner 2–0–16–2; Lever 2–0–24–0; Pringle 2–0–14–0.

### Essex

| | |
|---|---|
| B. R. Hardie run out | 27 |
| A. W. Lilley b Newport | 26 |
| K. S. McEwan c Radford b Weston | 22 |
| D. R. Pringle not out | 4 |
| *K. W. R. Fletcher not out | 7 |
| L-b 3 | 3 |
| 1/44 2/71 3/82 (3 wkts, 9.2 overs) | 89 |

P. J. Prichard, †D. E. East, S. Turner, N. A. Foster, J. K. Lever and I. L. Pont did not bat.

Bowling: Radford 2–0–13–0; Inchmore 2–0–13–0; Weston 2–0–20–1; Newport 2–0–23–1; Patel 1.2–0–17–0.

Umpires: H. D. Bird and R. Palmer.

## WORCESTERSHIRE v WARWICKSHIRE

At Worcester, August 25. Worcestershire won on faster scoring-rate. Toss won by Warwickshire.

### Worcestershire

| | |
|---|---|
| T. S. Curtis b Smith | 57 |
| D. B. D'Oliveira lbw b Wall | 3 |
| D. M. Smith b Gifford | 35 |
| G. A. Hick lbw b Gifford | 2 |
| *D. N. Patel c Hoffman b Gifford | 45 |
| M. J. Weston c Ferreira b Wall | 4 |
| †S. J. Rhodes not out | 32 |
| N. V. Radford not out | 18 |
| B 1, l-b 11, w 3, n-b 1 | 16 |
| 1/5 2/94 3/102 4/108 5/128 6/189 (6 wkts, 40 overs) | 212 |

P. J. Newport, J. D. Inchmore and S. M. McEwan did not bat.

Bowling: Wall 8–1–31–2; Hoffman 8–0–32–0; Smith 8–0–39–1; Ferreira 8–0–59–0; Gifford 8–0–39–3.

### Warwickshire

| | |
|---|---|
| T. A. Lloyd run out | 5 |
| G. J. Lord lbw b Inchmore | 13 |
| A. I. Kallicharran c and b Radford | 1 |
| D. L. Amiss lbw b Radford | 27 |
| †G. W. Humpage c Smith b Hick | 24 |
| P. A. Smith c Smith b Inchmore | 17 |
| A. M. Ferreira b Radford | 0 |
| D. A. Thorne c Hick b Radford | 7 |
| S. Wall b Inchmore | 2 |
| *N. Gifford b Hick | 16 |
| D. S. Hoffman not out | 1 |
| L-b 5, w 6, n-b 1 | 12 |
| 1/21 2/21 3/25 4/54 5/86 6/86 7/100 8/102 9/122 (26.3 overs) | 125 |

Bowling: Radford 6.3–0–24–4; Inchmore 6–0–21–3; Newport 5–0–27–0; Hick 7–0–36–2; Patel 2–0–12–0.

Umpires: R. Julian and D. O. Oslear.

At Leicester, September 1. WORCESTERSHIRE beat LEICESTERSHIRE by 8 runs.

At Moreton-in-Marsh, September 8. WORCESTERSHIRE lost to GLOUCESTERSHIRE by nine wickets.

## WORCESTERSHIRE v NORTHAMPTONSHIRE

At Worcester, September 15. Worcestershire won on faster scoring-rate after rain ended play. Toss won by Northamptonshire.

### Worcestershire

T. S. Curtis lbw b Mallender ......... 4
D. B. D'Oliveira c and b Walker ..... 3
G. A. Hick c Harper b Williams ...... 52
D. N. Patel c Ripley b Mallender ..... 0
*P. A. Neale run out ............... 83
D. M. Smith not out ................ 34
M. J. Weston b Walker ............. 1
†S. J. Rhodes c Cook b Walker ....... 2
N. V. Radford c Mallender b Walker .. 4
L-b 4, w 7, n-b 1 ........... 12

1/4 2/13 3/13 4/131 5/181 6/183 7/191 8/195 (8 wkts, 40 overs) 195

J. D. Inchmore and S. M. McEwan did not bat.

Bowling: Mallender 7–0–32–2; Walker 8–0–21–4; Larkins 6–0–22–0; Wild 6–0–37–0; Harper 6–0–40–0; Williams 7–0–39–1.

### Northamptonshire

W. Larkins lbw b Radford ........... 6
R. J. Bailey c Rhodes b Weston ...... 1
A. J. Lamb c Rhodes b Weston ....... 0
*G. Cook lbw b Patel ............... 54
R. G. Williams c Rhodes b McEwan .. 15
D. J. Capel c McEwan b Radford ..... 26
R. A. Harper c Patel b Inchmore ..... 18
D. J. Wild b Inchmore .............. 1
†D. Ripley run out ................. 16
N. A. Mallender not out ............ 12
A. Walker not out .................. 2
L-b 8, w 6, n-b 2 ........... 16

1/9 2/9 3/13 4/50 5/99 6/131 7/136 8/138 9/165 (9 wkts, 37 overs) 167

Bowling: Radford 8–0–31–2; Weston 8–2–14–2; Inchmore 8–0–39–2; McEwan 5–0–27–1; Patel 8–0–48–1.

Umpires: M. J. Kitchen and B. Dudleston.

# YORKSHIRE

## YORKSHIRE v MIDDLESEX

At Bradford, May 5. No result. Toss won by Middlesex.

### Yorkshire

A. Sidebottom c Butcher b Williams ... 0
M. D. Moxon b Williams ............ 1
K. Sharp c Butcher b Emburey ....... 29
J. D. Love c Gatting b Daniel ........ 0
P. E. Robinson b Emburey .......... 25
S. N. Hartley c Emburey b Fraser ..... 17
*†D. L. Bairstow c Gatting b Fraser ... 19
G. B. Stevenson c Williams b Fraser .. 13
P. W. Jarvis c Barlow b Daniel ....... 0
S. Oldham not out .................. 14
S. D. Fletcher not out .............. 0
B 1, l-b 6, w 6, n-b 1 ........ 14

1/0 2/12 3/14 4/60 5/65 6/95 7/114 8/117 9/118 (9 wkts, 37 overs) 132

Bowling: Williams 6–0–23–2; Daniel 8–1–25–2; Edmonds 8–1–22–0; Fraser 7–0–46–3; Emburey 8–7–9–2.

### Middlesex

W. N. Slack, G. D. Barlow, *M. W. Gatting, R. O. Butcher, C. T. Radley, †P. R. Downton, J. E. Emburey, P. H. Edmonds, N. F. Williams, A. R. C. Fraser and W. W. Daniel.

Umpires: H. D. Bird and K. E. Palmer.

At Leicester, May 12. YORKSHIRE beat LEICESTERSHIRE by seven wickets.

## YORKSHIRE v DERBYSHIRE

At Scarborough, May 19. No result.

## YORKSHIRE v HAMPSHIRE

At Middlesbrough, June 2. Yorkshire won by six wickets after compiling their highest total in the competition. Toss won by Hampshire.

### Hampshire

| | | | |
|---|---|---|---|
| C. G. Greenidge c Shaw b Booth | 78 | N. G. Cowley not out | 8 |
| V. P. Terry c Hartley b Shaw | 70 | | |
| R. A. Smith c Booth b Carrick | 44 | L-b 3 | 3 |
| *M. C. J. Nicholas b Fletcher | 26 | | |
| C. L. Smith c Love b Fletcher | 27 | 1/108 2/177 3/215 (6 wkts, 40 overs) | 257 |
| M. D. Marshall c Fletcher b Shaw | 1 | 4/222 5/225 6/257 | |

K. D. James, T. M. Tremlett, †R. J. Parks and C. A. Connor did not bat.

Bowling: Fletcher 8–0–68–2; Shaw 8–0–46–2; Carrick 8–0–38–1; Booth 8–0–57–1; Pickles 8–0–45–0.

### Yorkshire

| | | | |
|---|---|---|---|
| M. D. Moxon c R. A. Smith b Cowley | 47 | S. N. Hartley not out | 13 |
| A. A. Metcalfe c Marshall b Tremlett | 18 | L-b 12, n-b 2 | 14 |
| K. Sharp not out | 81 | | |
| J. D. Love st Parks b Tremlett | 46 | 1/43 2/83 3/166 (4 wkts, 39.3 overs) | 259 |
| *†D. L. Bairstow run out | 40 | 4/234 | |

P. Carrick, P. A. Booth, S. D. Fletcher, C. S. Pickles and C. Shaw did not bat.

Bowling: Connor 8–0–55–0; Marshall 8–1–39–0; Tremlett 8–0–55–2; James 7.3–1–44–0; Cowley 8–0–54–1.

Umpires: J. Birkenshaw and J. A. Jameson.

## YORKSHIRE v SUSSEX

At Sheffield, June 9. Sussex won by 36 runs. Toss won by Yorkshire.

### Sussex

| | | | |
|---|---|---|---|
| G. D. Mendis c Hartley b Shaw | 1 | I. A. Greig c Pickles b Fletcher | 7 |
| A. M. Green c Sharp b Pickles | 51 | †I. J. Gould not out | 10 |
| P. W. G. Parker lbw b Pickles | 25 | L-b 2, w 1, n-b 3 | 6 |
| Imran Khan c and b Fletcher | 13 | | |
| A. P. Wells not out | 57 | 1/6 2/48 3/85 (6 wkts, 40 overs) | 197 |
| C. M. Wells c Pickles b Carrick | 27 | 4/101 5/149 6/169 | |

*J. R. T. Barclay, D. A. Reeve and A. C. S. Pigott did not bat.

Bowling: Sidebottom 8–2–29–0; Shaw 8–1–47–1; Carrick 8–0–39–1; Pickles 8–1–37–2; Fletcher 8–0–43–2.

### Yorkshire

M. D. Moxon c Gould b Barclay ...... 67
A. A. Metcalfe c Barclay b Imran ..... 0
K. Sharp c Gould b Imran ........... 0
J. D. Love b Pigott ................. 13
*†D. L. Bairstow c Pigott b Imran .... 38
S. N. Hartley b Imran ............... 7
A. Sidebottom c Gould b Pigott ...... 1
P. Carrick c Parker b Pigott ......... 6
C. S. Pickles b Barclay ............... 3
C. Shaw c C. M. Wells b Pigott ...... 7
S. D. Fletcher not out ................ 0
L-b 15, w 3, n-b 1 .......... 19

1/0 2/4 3/40 4/125 5/141 6/142 7/145 8/149 9/157 (36.5 overs) 161

Bowling: C. M. Wells 8–2–17–0; Imran 8–1–15–4; Pigott 6.5–0–28–4; Reeve 8–0–41–0; Greig 4–0–30–0; Barclay 2–0–15–2.

Umpires: D. R. Shepherd and A. G. T. Whitehead.

At Bath, June 16. YORKSHIRE beat SOMERSET by 51 runs.

At Worcester, June 30. YORKSHIRE beat WORCESTERSHIRE by 14 runs.

At Gloucester, July 7. YORKSHIRE lost to GLOUCESTERSHIRE by 13 runs.

## YORKSHIRE v SURREY

At Bradford, July 14. Yorkshire won by two wickets, having reached a new county record for the competition for the second time in the season. Lynch had earlier achieved a new John Player League record score for Surrey. Toss won by Surrey.

### Surrey

A. R. Butcher c and b Jarvis ......... 11
G. S. Clinton c Sharp b Oldham ...... 12
M. A. Lynch b Jarvis ...............136
*T. E. Jesty c Hartley b Carrick ...... 18
A. Needham c Shaw b Fletcher ....... 23
D. M. Thomas c Shaw b Hartley ..... 20
D. M. Ward not out ................ 19
†C. J. Richards not out ............. 14
B 1, l-b 4, w 3, n-b 1 ........ 9

1/20 2/28 3/91 4/201 5/213 6/239 (6 wkts, 36 overs) 262

A. H. Gray, G. Monkhouse and P. I. Pocock did not bat.

Bowling: Jarvis 7–1–27–2; Oldham 8–0–16–1; Shaw 7–0–66–0; Fletcher 7–0–79–1; Carrick 4–0–41–1; Hartley 3–0–28–1.

### Yorkshire

S. N. Hartley c Clinton b Jesty ....... 72
A. A. Metcalfe c Jesty b Monkhouse .. 28
K. Sharp b Thomas ................. 61
P. E. Robinson run out .............. 60
*†D. L. Bairstow run out ............ 5
J. D. Love c Jesty b Thomas ......... 1
P. Carrick c Clinton b Thomas ....... 18
P. W. Jarvis not out ................ 6
C. Shaw run out .................... 1
S. Oldham not out .................. 0
B 1, l-b 7, w 3 ............. 11

1/69 2/141 3/214 4/226 5/233 6/241 7/257 8/262 (8 wkts, 35.5 overs) 263

S. D. Fletcher did not bat.

Bowling: Thomas 7–0–47–3; Gray 7.5–0–39–0; Monkhouse 7–0–52–1; Pocock 7–0–73–0; Jesty 7–0–44–1.

Umpires: J. W. Holder and R. A. White.

At Trent Bridge, July 28. YORKSHIRE lost to NOTTINGHAMSHIRE by six wickets.

At Edgbaston, August 4. WARWICKSHIRE v YORKSHIRE. No result.

## YORKSHIRE v LANCASHIRE

At Headingley, August 11. No result.

## YORKSHIRE v KENT

At Scarborough, August 18. Yorkshire won on faster scoring-rate, by 0.025 of a run, after Kent had failed by 1 run to reach a revised target of 134 off 35 overs following an interruption by rain. Toss won by Kent.

### Yorkshire

| | |
|---|---|
| M. D. Moxon c Jarvis b Underwood | 41 |
| A. A. Metcalfe c Knott b Jarvis | 5 |
| J. D. Love b Dilley | 10 |
| P. E. Robinson b Dilley | 2 |
| S. N. Hartley c Dilley b Potter | 20 |
| *†D. L. Bairstow c Dilley b Penn | 35 |
| P. Carrick c Knott b Potter | 2 |
| C. S. Pickles not out | 13 |
| P. J. Hartley c Underwood b Jarvis | 2 |
| C. Shaw run out | 5 |
| S. Oldham not out | 2 |
| B 8, w 3, n-b 5 | 16 |
| 1/22 2/36 3/47 4/74 5/99 6/102 7/137 8/145 9/151 (9 wkts, 40 overs) | 153 |

Bowling: Jarvis 8–0–37–2; Dilley 8–0–24–2; Penn 8–0–41–1; Potter 8–0–30–2; Underwood 8–2–13–1.

### Kent

| | |
|---|---|
| M. R. Benson c Bairstow b Shaw | 26 |
| N. R. Taylor b P. J. Hartley | 2 |
| C. J. Tavaré c S. N. Hartley b Shaw | 7 |
| S. G. Hinks c Love b Oldham | 14 |
| *C. S. Cowdrey c Robinson b Oldham | 16 |
| L. Potter c Pickles b Oldham | 8 |
| C. Penn b Carrick | 20 |
| †A. P. E. Knott run out | 18 |
| G. R. Dilley run out | 3 |
| D. L. Underwood not out | 0 |
| B 1, l-b 6, w 11, n-b 1 | 19 |
| 1/13 2/37 3/52 4/64 5/79 6/81 7/127 8/128 9/133 (9 wkts, 35 overs) | 133 |

K. B. S. Jarvis did not bat.

Bowling: P. J. Hartley 8–1–20–1; Pickles 8–1–21–0; Shaw 8–0–40–2; Oldham 8–0–35–3; Carrick 3–0–10–1.

Umpires: D. O. Oslear and R. A. White.

At Swansea, August 25. YORKSHIRE lost to GLAMORGAN on scoring-rate.

## YORKSHIRE v NORTHAMPTONSHIRE

At Headingley, September 1. Northamptonshire won by three wickets. Toss won by Northamptonshire.

### Yorkshire

| | |
|---|---|
| M. D. Moxon lbw b Mallender | 6 |
| S. N. Hartley c Wild b Larkins | 56 |
| K. Sharp run out | 12 |
| J. D. Love lbw b Larkins | 0 |
| P. E. Robinson c Larkins b Wild | 23 |
| *†D. L. Bairstow b Wild | 11 |
| P. Carrick b Wild | 2 |
| C. S. Pickles b Wild | 8 |
| S. Oldham not out | 28 |
| C. Shaw not out | 10 |
| B 1, l-b 17, w 6, n-b 1 | 25 |
| 1/7 2/42 3/42 4/91 5/123 6/130 7/140 8/141 (8 wkts, 40 overs) | 181 |

S. D. Fletcher did not bat.

Bowling: Walker 7–0–19–0; Mallender 7–0–40–1; Harper 8–0–20–0; Larkins 8–0–32–2; Wild 8–1–33–4; Williams 2–0–19–0.

## Northamptonshire

| | |
|---|---|
| W. Larkins c Bairstow b Shaw | 59 |
| R. J. Bailey b Oldham | 32 |
| R. J. Boyd-Moss c and b Carrick | 10 |
| R. G. Williams c Pickles b Fletcher | 17 |
| *G. Cook c Hartley b Shaw | 31 |
| R. A. Harper b Shaw | 0 |
| D. J. Capel not out | 16 |
| D. J. Wild run out | 7 |
| †D. Ripley not out | 0 |
| B 4, l-b 2, w 3, n-b 4 | 13 |
| 1/74 2/108 3/110 4/159 5/162 6/163 7/181 (7 wkts, 40 overs) | 185 |

N. A. Mallender and A. Walker did not bat.

Bowling: Pickles 8–0–44–0; Fletcher 8–0–38–1; Oldham 8–0–26–1; Shaw 8–0–36–3; Carrick 8–0–35–1.

Umpires: B. J. Meyer and P. B. Wight.

At Chelmsford, September 15. YORKSHIRE lost to ESSEX by two wickets.

# JOHN PLAYER LEAGUE RECORDS

## Batting

**Highest score:** 176 – G. A. Gooch, Essex v Glamorgan (Southend), 1983. (251 hundreds have been scored in the League.)

**Most runs in a season:** 814 – C. E. B. Rice (Nottinghamshire), 1977.

**Most sixes in an innings:** 10 – C. G. Greenidge, Hampshire v Warwickshire (Edgbaston), 1979; G. B. Stevenson, Yorkshire v Somerset (Middlesbrough), 1984.

**Most sixes by a team in an innings:** 18 – Derbyshire v Worcestershire (Knypersley), 1985.

**Most sixes in a season:** 26 – I. V. A. Richards (Somerset), 1977.

**Highest total:** 310 for five – Essex v Glamorgan (Southend), 1983.

**Highest total – batting second:** 301 for six – Warwickshire v Essex (Colchester), 1982.

**Highest match aggregate:** 604 – Surrey (304) v Warwickshire (300 for nine) (The Oval), 1985.

**Lowest total:** 23: – Middlesex v Yorkshire (Headingley), 1974.

**Shortest completed innings:** 16 overs – Northamptonshire 59 v Middlesex (Tring), 1974.

**Shortest match:** 2 hr 13 min (40.3 overs) – Essex v Northamptonshire (Ilford), 1971.

**Biggest victories:** 190 runs, Kent beat Northamptonshire (Brackley), 1973.

There have been twenty instances of victory by ten wickets – by Derbyshire, Essex, Glamorgan, Hampshire, Kent, Leicestershire (twice), Middlesex (twice), Northamptonshire, Somerset (twice), Surrey (twice), Warwickshire (twice), Worcestershire and Yorkshire (three times).

**Ties:** Nottinghamshire v Kent (Trent Bridge), 1969, in a match reduced to twenty overs.
Gloucestershire v Hampshire (Bristol), 1972.
Gloucestershire v Northamptonshire (Bristol), 1972.
Surrey v Worcestershire (Byfleet), 1973.
Middlesex v Lancashire (Lord's), 1974.
Sussex v Leicestershire (Hove), 1974.
Lancashire v Worcestershire (Old Trafford), 1975.
Somerset v Glamorgan (Taunton), 1975.
Warwickshire v Kent (Edgbaston), 1980.
Kent v Lancashire (Maidstone), 1981.
Yorkshire v Nottinghamshire (Hull), 1982.
Hampshire v Lancashire (Southampton), 1982.

Surrey v Hampshire (The Oval), 1982.
Worcestershire v Nottinghamshire (Hereford), 1983.
Lancashire v Worcestershire (Old Trafford), 1983, in a match reduced to nineteen overs.
Warwickshire v Worcestershire (Edgbaston), 1983, Warwickshire's innings having been reduced to ten overs.
Middlesex v Essex (Lord's), 1984.
Essex v Leicestershire (Chelmsford), 1985.
Northamptonshire v Lancashire (Northampton), 1985.
Lancashire v Glamorgan (Old Trafford), 1985.

**Record partnerships for each wicket**

| | | |
|---|---|---|
| 239 for 1st | G. A. Gooch and B. R. Hardie, Essex v Nottinghamshire at Trent Bridge | 1985 |
| 273 for 2nd | G. A. Gooch and K. S. McEwan, Essex v Nottinghamshire at Trent Bridge | 1983 |
| 215 for 3rd | W. Larkins and R. G. Williams, Northamptonshire v Worcestershire at Luton | 1982 |
| 178 for 4th | J. J. Whitaker and P. Willey, Leicestershire v Glamorgan at Swansea | 1984 |
| 179 for 5th | I. T. Botham and I. V. A. Richards, Somerset v Hampshire at Taunton | 1981 |
| 121 for 6th | C. P. Wilkins and A. J. Borrington, Derbyshire v Warwickshire at Chesterfield | 1972 |
| 101 for 7th | S. J. Windaybank and D. A. Graveney, Gloucestershire v Nottinghamshire at Trent Bridge | 1981 |
| 95* for 8th | D. Breakwell and K. F. Jennings, Somerset v Nottinghamshire at Trent Bridge | 1976 |
| 105 for 9th | D. G. Moir and R. W. Taylor, Derbyshire v Kent at Derby | 1984 |
| 57 for 10th | D. A. Graveney and J. B. Mortimore, Gloucestershire v Lancashire at Tewkesbury | 1973 |

## Bowling

**Best analyses:** eight for 26, K. D. Boyce, Essex v Lancashire at Old Trafford, 1971; seven for 15, R. A. Hutton, Yorkshire v Worcestershire at Headingley, 1969; seven for 39, A. Hodgson, Northamptonshire v Somerset at Northampton, 1976; six for 6, R. W. Hooker, Middlesex v Surrey at Lord's, 1969; six for 7, M. Hendrick, Derbyshire v Nottinghamshire at Trent Bridge, 1972.

**Four wickets in four balls:** A. Ward, Derbyshire v Sussex at Derby, 1970.

**Hat-tricks:** A. Ward, Derbyshire v Sussex at Derby, 1970; R. Palmer, Somerset v Gloucestershire at Bristol, 1970; K. D. Boyce, Essex v Somerset at Westcliff, 1971; G. D. McKenzie, Leicestershire v Essex at Leicester, 1972; R. G. D. Willis, Warwickshire v Yorkshire at Edgbaston, 1973; W. Blenkiron, Warwickshire v Derbyshire at Buxton, 1974; A. Buss, Sussex v Worcestershire at Hastings, 1974; J. M. Rice, Hampshire v Northamptonshire at Southampton, 1975; M. A. Nash, Glamorgan v Worcestershire at Worcester, 1975; A. Hodgson, Northamptonshire v Somerset at Northampton, 1976; A. E. Cordle, Glamorgan v Hampshire at Portsmouth, 1979; C. J. Tunnicliffe, Derbyshire v Worcestershire at Derby, 1979; M. D. Marshall, Hampshire v Surrey at Southampton, 1981; I. V. A. Richards, Somerset v Essex at Chelmsford, 1982; P. W. Jarvis, Yorkshire v Derbyshire at Derby, 1982; R. M. Ellison, Kent v Hampshire at Canterbury, 1983.

**Most economical analysis:** 8–8–0–0, B. A. Langford, Somerset v Essex at Yeovil, 1969.

**Most expensive analyses:** 8–0–88–1, E. E. Hemmings, Nottinghamshire v Somerset at Trent Bridge, 1983; 7.5–0–89–3, G. Miller Derbyshire v Gloucestershire at Gloucester, 1984.

**Most wickets in a season:** 34 – R. J. Clapp (Somerset) 1974.

# MINOR COUNTIES' CHAMPIONSHIP, 1985

By MICHAEL BERRY and ROBERT BROOKE

Cheshire, the losing finalists twelve months earlier, made a triumphant return to Worcester to lift the third and last Minor Counties' Championship to be sponsored by the United Friendly Insurance Company. After three years of support, neither United Friendly nor English Estates, the sponsors of the one-day knockout competition, won by Durham in 1985, has renewed its backing.

**Cheshire** were clear winners of the Western Division for the second successive season, and owed a great deal to the leadership and bowling of their captain, Arthur Sutton, at 46 in his 27th season with the county and a survivor of the only other Cheshire side to win the Championship – in 1967. In spite of the loss of Tony Murphy, to Lancashire, and John S. Hitchmough, to a club v county disagreement, Cheshire showed great versatility in winning five Championship games. Major contributions came from Neil O'Brien, who had figures of eight for 56 against Buckinghamshire, Ian Tansley, who made 541 runs, and Mudassar Nazar (488 runs and 20 wickets). This was Mudassar's final season with the county, because from 1986 a new ruling comes into force excluding all non-England qualified players from the competition.

As in 1984, there was no obvious challenge to Cheshire in the Western Division. The inclement weather caused a major disruption of the season, and the other counties soon had their sights on qualifying for the NatWest Bank Trophy rather than disturbing Cheshire at the top. So close was the competition to finish in the top six that only nine points finally separated Devon, the runners-up, and Wiltshire, in bottom place.

On the bowling front **Devon** again relied on Tony Allin and the veteran left-arm seamer, Doug Yeabsley, the latter taking 28 wickets to improve his career total to 683. Nick Gaywood and Kevin Rice emerged as proficient run-scorers, and Richard Twose and Richard Turpin, a wicket-keeper, were impressive newcomers.

**Berkshire** and **Cornwall**, with one win each, finished one point behind Devon. Cornwall's victory came early in the season when they beat Shropshire off the last ball with Julian Charles, from the Windward Islands, playing a leading all-round role. Their major success was Alan Buzza, slow left-arm, who took 29 wickets, including the best return of the summer, nine for 69 against Buckinghamshire at Truro. Berkshire suffered from the rain at the start, but their win against Buckinghamshire in their last match saw them move into third place. Graham Roope scored 483 runs and the consistent Peter Lewington took 25 wickets. Because of Reading's progress to the final of the William Younger Cup, Berkshire were able to introduce several youngsters who showed great potential.

**Dorset** failed to win a match in the Championship but had some memorable moments. They were finalists in the English Estates Trophy, after beating Cornwall, Buckinghamshire and Shropshire, but lost in the final by 100 runs to Durham. In the Championship Andrew Kennedy, formerly of Lancashire, made the highest individual score in the competition since 1979 – 171 not out to prevent defeat by Shropshire. Dorset were in the news again when Ian Sanders was "timed out" when caught in the lavatory as three wickets fell in four balls against Oxfordshire at Bournemouth. Kennedy and Simon Halliday, an Oxford Blue and England rugby international, each scored more than twice as many runs as the other batsmen, and the Reverend Andrew Wingfield Digby had one of his best seasons, his 33 wickets including a best of eight for 50 against Oxfordshire.

Mike Nurton was again **Oxfordshire's** leading run-maker with 390, while Simon Porter, an off-spinner, finished with 26 wickets. In a season which had few highlights, Oxfordshire's fast bowler, Keith Arnold, made a promising representative début in the first-class fixture against Zimbabwe at Cleethorpes.

**Somerset II** failed to reproduce their 1984 form – despite good performances from Gary Palmer, Paul Bail, Mark Harman and Richard Ollis, who scored 170 against Berkshire – and both Shropshire and Buckinghamshire dropped dramatically, failing to qualify for the NatWest Bank Trophy. **Buckinghamshire's** best display was in their opening match when they established a new record total in the English Estates knockout competition of 306 for two off 55 overs against Staffordshire. Andrew Harwood, a 21-year-old opening batsman on Middlesex's books, hit 111 not out and Stephen Burrow 111 in a second-wicket stand of 187. In reply Staffordshire were dismissed for 190. Gary Black, who returned eight for 47 against Wiltshire, was another major contributor to a side that suffered the loss of its captain, Richard Hayward, to Somerset for most of the season.

**Shropshire**, who re-introduced Phil Oliver, the former Warwickshire player, in their final match against Devon, had a frustrating season. They lost more than most to the weather, and their disappointment at not winning a Championship game for the first time in fifteen years was followed by Steve Gale being relieved of the captaincy after only one season. The captaincy issue was also under discussion at **Wiltshire**, where Richard Cooper took over from Philip Thorn amid much pre-season controversy. However, Cooper had little to celebrate apart from the individual success of Mark Watts, a fast bowler, who took 31 wickets including eight for 59 against Oxfordshire.

In the Eastern Division, another close finish saw the final placings decided on the penultimate day of the programme, when **Suffolk** took first-innings points from Durham to overhaul Staffordshire at the top. A side of few stars, Suffolk were missing Colin Rutterford, their captain, owing to injury, but they were ably led by Simon Clements, a former captain of Oxford University. However, Clements missed the final because of a holiday commitment, and Mike McEvoy, who had returned to Minor Counties cricket after trying to establish himself in the first-class game at Worcestershire, took over the captaincy. McEvoy made 403 runs in the season and was backed up by Phil Caley and Clements. Russ Green, their opening bowler, marked his return from Glamorgan with 31 wickets.

**Staffordshire** were runners-up for the second successive season. They displayed plenty of enterprise under Nick Archer to win three and lose three of their nine Championship games. Five of their batsmen figured in the leading 30 in the Championship, David Cartledge (445) and Paul Marshall (438) scoring the most runs. They had a fast bowler of genuine quality in Hugh Page, the Transvaal all-rounder, who replaced Dilip Vengsarkar as their overseas player midway through the season.

David Lloyd, the former England and Lancashire player, scored 382 runs for **Cumberland** and Graham Clarke, a new recruit who is a fine prospect for the future, totalled 306. Malcolm Woods and David Halliwell led the bowling, with Woods achieving the hat-trick in his seven for 12 in the victory over Durham at Carlisle. **Durham**, the 1984 champions, won the English Estates one-day trophy and also claimed a celebrated win against Derbyshire in the NatWest Bank Trophy, becoming the only minor county with two wins against first-class opposition in the 60 overs competition. Neil Riddell captained by example in aggregating 594 runs and Ashok Patel backed him up with 480. Peter Kippax, Durham's 45-year-old leg-spinner, returned from injury to capture 26 wickets and Andy Scott, an Australian fast bowler, had 27.

**Hertfordshire** and **Northumberland** had what might have been labelled ordinary seasons until they met at Balls Park, Hertford in August. In a remarkable match, played on a hastily prepared, rain-affected wicket, Hertfordshire made 51 for six declared and 47 and Northumberland 51 for five declared and 22, the lowest Championship total in their history. Peter Graham took seven for 18 in the Hertfordshire second innings while Northumberland's collapse was effected by Brian Collins who, recalled at the age of 43, returned eight for 7. The only batsman from either county to find any sort of form over the season was Northumberland's Ken Pearson with 392 runs.

**Cambridgeshire** squeezed into the NatWest Bank Trophy draw by beating Lincolnshire in their last game. Derrick Parry, the former West Indian Test off-spinner, came within 14 runs of the double of 500 runs and 50 wickets. A popular player in his seven years with the county, Parry will be badly missed now that he is banned by the new ruling on overseas players. Nigel Gadsby hit 357 runs to give Parry good support.

**Norfolk** were plagued by rain during the Lakenham fortnight, when they hosted all five of their home games. It was the worst-affected Lakenham festival for twenty years and resulted in Norfolk's failure to qualify for the NatWest Bank Trophy for the first time in five years. Parvez Mir received the Wilfred Rhodes Trophy for the leading batsman to add to the Frank Edwards Trophy he was awarded in 1984 as the top bowler.

**Lincolnshire** and **Bedfordshire** filled the two bottom places but collective indifference was tempered by individual triumphs. Neil Priestley, a talented wicket-keeper, made 551 runs for Lincolnshire, and their long-serving opening batsman, Geoff Robinson, joined Sutton of

Cheshire and Nurton of Oxfordshire in becoming the third current player to reach 10,000 runs in the Championship. Bedfordshire, meanwhile, had the leading run-maker of the season in Kevin Gentle, who finished with 627 at 39.18, while Alan Fordham combined his Second XI duties with Northamptonshire to crack 454 runs in eight innings. David Steele collected 25 wickets on his return to the Minor County circuit, but Bedfordshire's bowling was weakened by an injury to Keith Jones, who had begun the season with his 100th consecutive appearance for the county.

## UNITED FRIENDLY INSURANCE MINOR COUNTIES' CHAMPIONSHIP, 1985

| | *Played* | *Won* | *Lost* | *Won 1st Inns* | *Drawn Tied 1st Inns* | *Lost 1st Inns* | *No Result* | *Points* |
|---|---|---|---|---|---|---|---|---|
| **Eastern Division** | | | | | | | | |
| Suffolk[NW] | 9 | 3 | 1* | 1 | 1 | 3 | 0 | 41 |
| Staffordshire[NW] | 9 | 3 | 3* | 1 | 0 | 1 | 1 | 39 |
| Cumberland[NW] | 9 | 2 | 1* | 1 | 0 | 3 | 2 | 33 |
| Durham[NW] | 9 | 2 | 1 | 3 | 1 | 2 | 0 | 33 |
| Hertfordshire[NW] | 9 | 2 | 0 | 1 | 0 | 4 | 2 | 31 |
| Northumberland[NW] | 9 | 1 | 1† | 4 | 2 | 0 | 1 | 30 |
| Cambridgeshire[NW] | 9 | 2 | 2 | 2 | 0 | 3 | 0 | 29 |
| Norfolk | 9 | 1 | 1* | 2 | 2 | 1 | 2 | 28 |
| Lincolnshire | 9 | 0 | 3* | 3 | 0 | 1 | 2 | 17 |
| Bedfordshire | 9 | 0 | 3 | 2 | 2 | 2 | 0 | 12 |
| **Western Division** | | | | | | | | |
| Cheshire[NW] | 9 | 5 | 0 | 2 | 0 | 2 | 0 | 58 |
| Devon[NW] | 9 | 1 | 0 | 3 | 1 | 4 | 0 | 25 |
| Berkshire[NW] | 9 | 1 | 2* | 1 | 1 | 2 | 2 | 24 |
| Cornwall[NW] | 9 | 1 | 1 | 2 | 1 | 2 | 2 | 24 |
| Dorset[NW] | 9 | 0 | 1* | 5 | 0 | 3 | 0 | 21 |
| Oxfordshire[NW] | 9 | 0 | 0 | 4 | 2 | 2 | 1 | 20 |
| Somerset II | 9 | 0 | 0 | 3 | 1 | 3 | 2 | 18 |
| Buckinghamshire | 9 | 0 | 2* | 3 | 1 | 3 | 0 | 17 |
| Shropshire | 9 | 0 | 2* | 2 | 0 | 2 | 3 | 17 |
| Wiltshire | 9 | 0 | 0 | 2 | 1 | 4 | 2 | 16 |

* *Denotes first-innings points in one match lost outright.*

† *Denotes tie on first innings in one match lost outright.*

[NW] *Denotes qualified for NatWest Bank Trophy in 1986.*

*Win = 10 pts, first-innings win = 3 pts, first-innings tie = 2 pts, first-innings loss = 1 pt, No result = 2 pts.*

## CHAMPIONSHIP PLAY-OFF

### CHESHIRE v SUFFOLK

At Worcester, September 7. Cheshire won by 58 runs. Toss won by Suffolk. A second-wicket stand of 84 between Cockbain, the former Lancashire player, and Hitchmough, followed by some brisk batting from Teasdale and Sutton, laid the platform for Cheshire's victory. Suffolk, in reply, lost McEvoy early, and their challenge fell away after Morgan and Caley had briefly threatened a recovery.

*Man of the Match:* J. A. Sutton (Cheshire).

### Cheshire

| | | | |
|---|---|---|---|
| I. Tansley c McEvoy b Wright | 0 | K. B. K. Ibadulla b Green | 2 |
| J. J. Hitchmough c Brown b Hayes | 32 | †J. K. Pickup lbw b Green | 0 |
| I. Cockbain b Hayes | 45 | A. J. Murphy run out | 1 |
| N. T. O'Brien c McEvoy b Bailey | 21 | Extras | 30 |
| S. C. Yates c Green b Wright | 21 | | |
| S. T. Crawley lbw b Herbert | 1 | 1/1 2/85 3/94 4/131 (53.2 overs) | 194 |
| *J. A. Sutton run out | 24 | 5/140 6/145 7/183 | |
| K. Teasdale not out | 17 | 8/189 9/189 | |

Bowling: Green 10–1–43–2; Wright 10.2–2–44–2; Hayes 11–3–16–2; Bailey 11–3–35–1; Herbert 11–0–33–1.

### Suffolk

| | | | |
|---|---|---|---|
| P. D. Barker c Teasdale b Murphy | 1 | R. C. Green b Murphy | 9 |
| *M. S. A. McEvoy run out | 5 | M. D. Bailey not out | 8 |
| R. Herbert c Teasdale b Murphy | 16 | †A. D. Brown not out | 4 |
| G. Morgan b Sutton | 31 | Extras | 17 |
| P. J. Caley b O'Brien | 27 | | |
| R. Bond lbw b Sutton | 14 | 1/3 2/26 3/28 4/79 (9 wkts, 55 overs) | 136 |
| P. J. Hayes c Yates b Sutton | 2 | 5/102 6/107 7/110 | |
| H. J. W. Wright b O'Brien | 2 | 8/110 9/122 | |

Bowling: Murphy 11–1–29–3; Crawley 11–2–22–0; Sutton 11–1–27–3; Teasdale 11–1–33–0; O'Brien 11–4–15–2.

Umpires: K. S. Shenton and T. G. Wilson.

## ENGLISH ESTATES TROPHY FINAL

## DORSET v DURHAM

At Fenner's, July 14. Durham won by 100 runs. Toss won by Dorset. Atkinson's fluent 85 found support from Greensword, Riddell and Patel as Durham set Dorset a difficult target. Rash strokes and the tight Durham bowling ended Dorset's hopes as they lost half their side for 57 before Sanders, who had earlier finished with four wickets, hit out at the end for 31 to take them into three figures.

*Man of the Match:* S. R. Atkinson (Durham).

Durham 229 (55 overs) (S. R. Atkinson 85; I. E. W. Sanders four for 47); Dorset 129 (47.2 overs).

*In the averages that follow, * against a score signifies not out, * against a name signifies the captain and † signifies a wicket-keeper.*

## BEDFORDSHIRE

Secretary – A. J. PEARCE, 15 Dene Way, Upper Caldecote, Biggleswade SG18 9DL

*Matches 9: Lost – Cumberland, Cambridgeshire, Suffolk. Won on first innings – Hertfordshire, Lincolnshire. Tied on first innings – Durham, Norfolk. Lost on first innings – Northumberland, Staffordshire.*

## Batting Averages

| | M | I | NO | R | HI | 100s | Avge |
|---|---|---|---|---|---|---|---|
| A. Fordham | 4 | 8 | 0 | 454 | 123 | 1 | 56.75 |
| K. Gentle | 9 | 18 | 2 | 627 | 104* | 1 | 39.18 |
| D. S. Steele | 6 | 10 | 3 | 239 | 39 | 0 | 34.14 |
| S. J. Lines | 8 | 15 | 2 | 368 | 65 | 0 | 28.30 |
| K. V. Jones | 5 | 8 | 3 | 112 | 34* | 0 | 22.40 |
| *I. G. Peck | 8 | 11 | 2 | 197 | 51* | 0 | 21.88 |
| A. S. Pearson | 8 | 15 | 1 | 270 | 51 | 0 | 19.28 |
| M. Morgan | 7 | 13 | 3 | 191 | 34 | 0 | 19.10 |
| B. L. Marvin | 6 | 7 | 1 | 90 | 27 | 0 | 15.00 |
| †N. S. Randall | 6 | 7 | 2 | 61 | 33* | 0 | 12.20 |
| S. J. Renshaw | 5 | 6 | 2 | 17 | 8 | 0 | 4.25 |
| J. R. Wake | 8 | 9 | 0 | 26 | 7 | 0 | 2.88 |

Played in seven matches: C. J. Proudman 0*, 0, 1*, 9*, 2*. Played in four matches: P. D. B. Hoare 2, 0, 1, 13*, 0. Played in three matches: †P. G. M. August 0*, 0, 9. Played in two matches: S. E. Blott 3*; T. Patel 1, 3, 3*, 4. Played in one match: T. Thomas 16.

## Bowling Averages

| | O | M | R | W | BB | Avge |
|---|---|---|---|---|---|---|
| K. V. Jones | 125.4 | 39 | 323 | 17 | 4-60 | 19.00 |
| D. S. Steele | 160.4 | 43 | 490 | 25 | 5-39 | 19.60 |
| S. J. Renshaw | 82 | 13 | 328 | 13 | 4-55 | 25.23 |
| J. R. Wake | 140.3 | 31 | 478 | 17 | 5-71 | 28.11 |

Also bowled: S. E. Blott 56–14–172–8; B. L. Marvin 54.3–8–210–7; C. J. Proudman 78–11–241–7; A. S. Pearson 30–4–81–5; P. D. B. Hoare 26–4–100–4; S. J. Lines 3–0–17–1; M. Morgan 8–0–21–0; I. G. Peck 5–0–53–0; T. Patel 2.5–0–15–0; A. Fordham 1.5–0–36–0.

# BERKSHIRE

Secretary – C. F. V. MARTIN, Paradise Cottage, Paradise Road, Henley-on-Thames, Oxon RG9 1UB

*Matches 9: Won – Buckinghamshire. Lost – Cheshire, Devon. Won on first innings – Somerset. Tied on first innings – Wiltshire. Lost on first innings – Dorset, Oxfordshire. No result – Cornwall, Shropshire.*

## Batting Averages

| | M | I | NO | R | HI | 100s | Avge |
|---|---|---|---|---|---|---|---|
| G. R. J. Roope | 9 | 15 | 4 | 483 | 76* | 0 | 43.90 |
| M. L. Simmons | 5 | 6 | 2 | 173 | 64 | 0 | 43.25 |
| *J. F. Harvey | 9 | 12 | 5 | 226 | 43* | 0 | 32.28 |
| M. G. Lickley | 9 | 15 | 2 | 381 | 78* | 0 | 29.30 |
| G. E. Loveday | 4 | 7 | 0 | 156 | 46 | 0 | 22.28 |
| T. M. H. James | 4 | 6 | 2 | 88 | 21* | 0 | 22.00 |
| D. B. Gorman | 6 | 8 | 1 | 152 | 45* | 0 | 21.71 |
| K. S. Murray | 6 | 8 | 0 | 159 | 44 | 0 | 19.87 |
| †M. E. Stevens | 4 | 7 | 4 | 41 | 16 | 0 | 13.66 |

Played in nine matches: P. J. Lewington 7*, 0*, 0*. Played in seven matches: J. H. Jones 3*, 3, 0; L. P. Sluman 0, 23*. Played in six matches: T. E. Roberts 13, 1*. Played in five matches: †G. E. J. Child 8, 19*. Played in three matches: J. A. Claughton 7, 0, 11, 12, 35; P. M. New 15. Played in two matches: G. Scott 15, 2*, 0, 57*. Played in one match: J. A. Woollhead 0.

## Bowling Averages

| | O | M | R | W | BB | Avge |
|---|---|---|---|---|---|---|
| J. H. Jones ......... | 108.5 | 20 | 308 | 15 | 4-44 | 20.53 |
| P. J. Lewington ...... | 199.3 | 61 | 525 | 25 | 5-63 | 21.00 |
| T. E. Roberts ....... | 75.4 | 19 | 236 | 10 | 4-22 | 23.60 |

Also bowled: L. P. Sluman 98–20–264–9; P. M. New 38–11–116–6; T. M. H. James 44.5–7–183–5; G. R. J. Roope 42–9–126–5; M. G. Lickley 17–4–66–1; J. F. Harvey 5.4–2–46–1; J. R. Woollhead 7.5–5–11–0; D. B. Gorman 3–0–30–0.

# BUCKINGHAMSHIRE

Secretary – S. J. TOMLIN, Orchard Leigh Cottage, Bigfrith Lane, Cookham Dean SL6 9PH

*Matches 9: Lost – Berkshire, Cheshire. Won on first innings – Shropshire, Somerset II, Wiltshire. Tied on first innings – Cornwall. Lost on first innings – Devon, Dorset, Oxfordshire.*

## Batting Averages

| | M | I | NO | R | HI | 100s | Avge |
|---|---|---|---|---|---|---|---|
| P. Dolphin .......... | 3 | 6 | 1 | 155 | 92* | 0 | 31.00 |
| G. R. Black .......... | 8 | 15 | 3 | 319 | 68 | 0 | 26.58 |
| P. D. Atkins ......... | 4 | 7 | 1 | 133 | 54 | 0 | 22.16 |
| *R. E. Hayward ..... | 4 | 8 | 0 | 169 | 53 | 0 | 21.12 |
| N. G. Hames ......... | 6 | 12 | 1 | 205 | 88 | 0 | 18.63 |
| *D. E. Smith ........ | 7 | 13 | 3 | 183 | 56 | 0 | 18.30 |
| †T. P. Russell ....... | 9 | 16 | 0 | 291 | 77 | 0 | 18.18 |
| S. Burrow ........... | 5 | 10 | 1 | 123 | 26* | 0 | 13.66 |
| S. G. Lynch .......... | 6 | 10 | 6 | 54 | 24* | 0 | 13.50 |
| K. J. Graham ....... | 3 | 6 | 2 | 54 | 32 | 0 | 13.50 |
| †R. G. Humphrey .... | 5 | 7 | 1 | 62 | 21* | 0 | 10.33 |
| A. W. Lyon ......... | 9 | 7 | 1 | 27 | 10 | 0 | 4.50 |

Played in five matches: C. D. Booden 0*, 0*, 0*, 2*, 1, 0*. Played in four matches: H. L. Alleyne 1, 0, 9; S. J. Edwards 4, 2*, 8, 68*, 50. Played in three matches: J. K. Edwards 33, 12, 29, 36, 59; A. R. Harwood 4, 27, 35, 4; M. Jean-Jacques 39*, 0, 1. Played in two matches: J. D. Atkins 9, 1, 8; T. J. Barry 15*, 1, 0; M. E. Milton 3, 16, 5, 2. Played in one match: P. D. M. Ashton 2*, 2; P. A. Cooper 26, 15.

## Bowling Averages

| | O | M | R | W | BB | Avge |
|---|---|---|---|---|---|---|
| G. R. Black ......... | 105.4 | 26 | 252 | 22 | 8-47 | 11.45 |
| H. L. Alleyne ....... | 109 | 29 | 238 | 18 | 7-61 | 13.22 |
| S. Burrow ........... | 142.2 | 56 | 284 | 21 | 4-24 | 13.52 |
| S. G. Lynch ......... | 86 | 18 | 261 | 13 | 3-21 | 20.07 |
| A. W. Lyon ......... | 268.5 | 71 | 608 | 24 | 4-13 | 25.33 |

Also bowled; C. D. Booden 86–18–272–9; M. Jean-Jacques 50.4–16–130–6; S. J. Edwards 41–19–54–3; T. J. Barry 17–3–49–2; M. E. Milton 13–0–58–2; D. E. Smith 3.1–0–30–1; A. R. Harwood 2–1–1–0; R. E. Hayward 2–0–25–0.

# CAMBRIDGESHIRE

Secretary – P. W. GOODEN, The Redlands, Oakington Road, Cottenham, Cambridge CB4 4TW

*Matches 9: Won – Bedfordshire, Lincolnshire. Lost – Norfolk, Staffordshire. Won on first innings – Hertfordshire, Suffolk. Lost on first innings – Cumberland, Durham, Northumberland.*

## Batting Averages

| | M | I | NO | R | HI | 100s | Avge |
|---|---|---|---|---|---|---|---|
| D. R. Parry ......... | 8 | 14 | 3 | 486 | 108 | 1 | 44.18 |
| N. T. Gadsby ....... | 8 | 14 | 1 | 357 | 83* | 0 | 27.46 |
| J. D. R. Benson ..... | 9 | 16 | 2 | 266 | 40 | 0 | 19.00 |
| P. C. M. Osborn ..... | 5 | 8 | 0 | 140 | 32 | 0 | 17.50 |
| D. C. Collard ....... | 8 | 11 | 3 | 134 | 44* | 0 | 16.75 |
| G. W. Presland ...... | 6 | 8 | 0 | 126 | 45 | 0 | 15.75 |
| D. R. Vincent ....... | 6 | 11 | 0 | 163 | 41 | 0 | 14.81 |
| *G. V. Miller ........ | 9 | 16 | 0 | 214 | 52 | 0 | 13.37 |
| M. G. Stephenson .... | 8 | 12 | 5 | 84 | 18* | 0 | 12.00 |
| A. D. Cuthill ........ | 5 | 8 | 1 | 56 | 16 | 0 | 8.00 |
| †P. C. Brooker ...... | 6 | 8 | 6 | 11 | 4* | 0 | 5.50 |
| M. Brown .......... | 5 | 8 | 1 | 30 | 9 | 0 | 4.28 |

Played in two matches: D. H. Baker 0, 34, 0, 10; D. C. Holliday 15, 10, 33, 3; R. A. Milne 1, 0, 1; Mohammad Afzal 10, 11, 7*; P. A. Redfarn 10, 32, 16. Played in one match: N. J. Adams 7, 1; I. Lawrence 0, 5; J. Mawhinney 22, 60*; G. S. Rice 6; †G. G. Whitbread 0, 29*; D. C. Wing 0.

## Bowling Averages

| | O | M | R | W | BB | Avge |
|---|---|---|---|---|---|---|
| D. R. Parry ......... | 329 | 84 | 753 | 53 | 6-59 | 14.20 |
| M. G. Stephenson .... | 152.5 | 36 | 414 | 19 | 4-37 | 21.78 |
| D. C. Collard ....... | 105.1 | 20 | 316 | 12 | 6-53 | 26.33 |

Also bowled: M. Brown 68–13–237–7; P. C. M. Osborn 56–4–219–5; G. W. Presland 75.1–8–254–3; J. D. R. Benson 35.1–5–137–3; J. Mawhinney 19–2–107–2; G. S. Rice 17–2–53–0; D. C. Wing 14–0–43–0; D. C. Holliday 2–0–16–0.

# CHESHIRE

Secretary – J. B. PICKUP, 2 Castle Street, Northwich CW8 1AB

*Matches 9: Won – Berkshire, Buckinghamshire, Cornwall, Dorset, Shropshire. Won on first innings – Devon, Wiltshire. Lost on first innings – Oxfordshire, Somerset II.*

## Batting Averages

| | M | I | NO | R | HI | 100s | Avge |
|---|---|---|---|---|---|---|---|
| Mudassar Nazar ..... | 7 | 12 | 3 | 488 | 112* | 1 | 54.22 |
| I. Tansley ........... | 9 | 16 | 2 | 541 | 118* | 1 | 38.64 |
| S. C. Yates ......... | 8 | 11 | 2 | 284 | 83 | 0 | 31.55 |
| N. T. O'Brien ........ | 9 | 14 | 1 | 353 | 64 | 0 | 27.15 |
| J. J. Hitchmough .... | 9 | 15 | 1 | 360 | 74 | 0 | 25.71 |
| K. Teasdale ......... | 8 | 11 | 2 | 190 | 51 | 0 | 21.11 |
| *J. A. Sutton ........ | 9 | 13 | 4 | 184 | 46* | 0 | 20.44 |
| I. Cockbain ......... | 8 | 13 | 1 | 243 | 48 | 0 | 20.25 |
| K. B. K. Ibadulla .... | 7 | 9 | 5 | 60 | 24* | 0 | 15.00 |

Played in seven matches: †J. K. Pickup 1*, 1, 9*, 3*. Played in three matches: S. T. Crawley 16*, 35, 2, 4, 1. Played in two matches: W. K. R. Benjamin 3*, 7, 3; †P. N. Hughes 9*; S. J. Monks 11, 11; P. G. Wakefield 11*, 1*; P. J. Hacker and A. J. Murphy did not bat. Played in one match: J. S. Hitchmough 6; D. J. Parry 1, 2; A. Greenwood did not bat.

## Bowling Averages

| | O | M | R | W | BB | Avge |
|---|---|---|---|---|---|---|
| A. J. Murphy | 73.2 | 19 | 162 | 17 | 6-48 | 9.52 |
| J. A. Sutton | 203 | 70 | 555 | 38 | 7-47 | 14.60 |
| Mudassar Nazar | 129 | 32 | 305 | 20 | 4-36 | 15.25 |
| W. K. R. Benjamin | 76 | 15 | 264 | 13 | 4-56 | 20.30 |
| N. T. O'Brien | 137.2 | 37 | 388 | 19 | 8-56 | 20.42 |

Also bowled: J. S. Hitchmough 31–8–70–7; S. T. Crawley 66.4–10–203–6; K. B. K. Ibadulla 65–15–220–5; P. J. Hacker 40–3–138–4; K. Teasdale 31–10–71–2; P. G. Wakefield 24–6–72–1; S. C. Yates 4–1–17–1; I. Cockbain 11–5–24–0; A. Greenwood 8–1–29–0; D. J. Parry 5–2–14–0; I. Tansley 4–0–14–0; J. J. Hitchmough 4–0–27–0.

# CORNWALL

Secretary – T. D. MENEER, c/o L. P. DAWE, 22 Berkeley Vale, Falmouth

*Matches 9: Won – Shropshire. Lost – Cheshire. Won on first innings – Oxfordshire, Somerset II. Tied on first innings – Buckinghamshire. Lost on first innings – Devon, Dorset. No result – Berkshire, Wiltshire.*

## Batting Averages

| | M | I | NO | R | HI | 100s | Avge |
|---|---|---|---|---|---|---|---|
| G. Furze | 8 | 7 | 5 | 88 | 52* | 0 | 44.00 |
| M. S. T. Dunstan | 6 | 8 | 2 | 218 | 72 | 0 | 36.33 |
| P. J. Stephens | 4 | 7 | 1 | 123 | 39 | 0 | 20.50 |
| *E. G. Willcock | 9 | 14 | 1 | 252 | 66 | 0 | 19.38 |
| J. D. Charles | 8 | 13 | 1 | 231 | 67 | 0 | 19.25 |
| A. Snowdon | 9 | 13 | 5 | 135 | 38* | 0 | 16.87 |
| C. J. Trudgeon | 7 | 11 | 0 | 184 | 55 | 0 | 16.72 |
| T. J. Angove | 5 | 7 | 0 | 94 | 29 | 0 | 13.42 |
| J. M. Cradick | 9 | 14 | 2 | 145 | 31 | 0 | 12.08 |
| A. J. Buzza | 9 | 7 | 3 | 32 | 19 | 0 | 8.00 |
| A. Machin | 4 | 8 | 1 | 55 | 17 | 0 | 7.85 |
| †T. L. Gall | 9 | 11 | 1 | 71 | 43* | 0 | 7.10 |

Played in seven matches: D. A. Toseland 2, 7, 3*, 4, 0. Played in two matches: A. J. Dengler 5*. Played in one match: A. P. Hancock 1, 14; S. Hooper 42; A. Lawry did not bat.

## Bowling Averages

| | O | M | R | W | BB | Avge |
|---|---|---|---|---|---|---|
| A. J. Buzza | 167 | 43 | 522 | 29 | 9-69 | 18.00 |
| D. A. Toseland | 201.3 | 83 | 390 | 21 | 4-41 | 18.57 |
| A. Snowdon | 93.3 | 23 | 287 | 14 | 3-43 | 20.50 |
| J. D. Charles | 121.1 | 19 | 396 | 10 | 5-78 | 39.60 |

Also bowled: G. Furze 98–16–294–7; A. J. Dengler 12–3–28–2; A. Machin 16–6–27–0; E. G. Willcock 4–0–37–0; A. Lawry 2–1–3–0; A. P. Hancock 2–0–14–0.

# CUMBERLAND

Secretary – M. BEATY, 9 Abbey Drive, Natland, Kendal, Cumbria LA9 7QN

*Matches 9: Won – Bedfordshire, Durham. Lost – Staffordshire. Won on first innings – Cambridgeshire. Lost on first innings – Lincolnshire, Northumberland, Suffolk. No result – Hertfordshire, Norfolk.*

## Batting Averages

| | M | I | NO | R | HI | 100s | Avge |
|---|---|---|---|---|---|---|---|
| *J. R. Moyes | 8 | 12 | 4 | 356 | 129 | 1 | 44.50 |
| D. Lloyd | 7 | 11 | 1 | 382 | 93 | 0 | 38.20 |
| B. W. Reidy | 5 | 8 | 0 | 216 | 70 | 0 | 27.00 |
| D. Halliwell | 7 | 8 | 5 | 80 | 42* | 0 | 26.66 |
| G. J. Clarke | 8 | 13 | 1 | 306 | 91 | 0 | 25.50 |
| M. D. Woods | 8 | 15 | 1 | 351 | 64 | 0 | 25.07 |
| C. J. Stockdale | 8 | 12 | 3 | 199 | 54 | 0 | 22.11 |
| Qasim Omar | 3 | 6 | 0 | 116 | 57 | 0 | 19.33 |
| †D. B. Drury | 7 | 7 | 2 | 96 | 27 | 0 | 19.20 |

Played in eight matches: †W. N. Boustead 13*, 10, 12, 5*. Played in six matches: E. K. Sample 6, 0, 0*, 7, 11*. Played in four matches; Iqbal Sikandar 23*, 11, 4*, 7, 74. Played in three matches: G. D. Hodgson 65, 13, 4, 0*, 2. Played in two matches: M. G. Scothern did not bat. Played in one match: D.J. Lupton 1*, 6*; G. H. McMeekin 18; J. J. Ashurst, J. B. Elleray and M. G. Nicholson did not bat.

## Bowling Averages

| | O | M | R | W | BB | Avge |
|---|---|---|---|---|---|---|
| M. D. Woods | 85.4 | 28 | 236 | 20 | 7-12 | 11.80 |
| D. Halliwell | 180.2 | 46 | 476 | 26 | 4-46 | 18.30 |

Also bowled: B. W. Reidy 93.2–34–225–9; E. K. Sample 92–13–342–7; D. Lloyd 71.5–21–177–7; Iqbal Sikandar 68–25–183–6; M. G. Scothern 22–3–73–4; D. J. Lupton 26–11–44–2; J. B. Elleray 22–7–83–2; J. J. Ashurst 5–0–26–0; W. N. Boustead 0.1–0–0–0.

# DEVON

Secretary – Rev. K. J. WARREN, The Rectory, Lapford, Crediton EX17 6PX

*Matches 9: Won – Berkshire. Won on first innings – Buckinghamshire, Cornwall, Wiltshire. Tied on first innings – Oxfordshire. Lost on first innings – Cheshire, Dorset, Shropshire, Somerset II.*

## Batting Averages

| | M | I | NO | R | HI | 100s | Avge |
|---|---|---|---|---|---|---|---|
| R. P. Twose | 4 | 8 | 0 | 272 | 91 | 0 | 34.00 |
| C. J. Edwards | 9 | 16 | 7 | 283 | 53* | 0 | 31.44 |
| K. G. Rice | 6 | 12 | 0 | 313 | 82 | 0 | 26.08 |
| Agha Zahid | 6 | 11 | 0 | 278 | 83 | 0 | 25.27 |
| C. F. Rudd | 3 | 6 | 1 | 125 | 40 | 0 | 25.00 |
| N. A. Folland | 9 | 18 | 2 | 395 | 95 | 0 | 24.68 |
| N. R. Gaywood | 9 | 18 | 2 | 379 | 61 | 0 | 23.68 |
| A. W. Allin | 8 | 10 | 5 | 118 | 40 | 0 | 23.60 |
| N. G. Folland | 6 | 12 | 1 | 229 | 41 | 0 | 20.81 |
| *J. H. Edwards | 9 | 12 | 6 | 105 | 36 | 0 | 17.50 |
| M. Taylor | 5 | 6 | 1 | 25 | 10* | 0 | 5.00 |

Played in eight matches: D. I. Yeabsley 1*. Played in five matches: †R. C. Turpin 0*, 0, 34*, 48*. Played in four matches: †R. M. Oliver 6*, 0*. Played in three matches: K. Donohoe 1*; J. K. Tierney 2, 16*, 4, 16. Played in one match: N. G. Wonnacott 1*; M. J. Goulding did not bat.

## Bowling Averages

| | O | M | R | W | BB | Avge |
|---|---|---|---|---|---|---|
| D. I. Yeabsley | 245 | 72 | 593 | 28 | 6-36 | 21.17 |
| A. W. Allin | 233.1 | 75 | 608 | 25 | 6-47 | 24.32 |

Also bowled: Agha Zahid 72–16–225–9; C. F. Rudd 50.5–17–111–9; M. Taylor 126.4–25–416–8; K. Donohoe 61–7–244–6; N. G. Wonnacott 8–3–55–2; C. J. Edwards 5.2–1–23–2; M. J. Goulding 17.3–2–97–1; J. H. Edwards 12–2–38–1; J. K. Tierney 21–0–103–0; N. R. Gaywood 5–0–37–0; N. A. Folland 4–0–13–0.

## DORSET

Secretary – D. J. W. BRIDGE, Long Acre, Tinney's Lane, Sherborne DT9 3DY

*Matches 9: Lost – Cheshire. Won on first innings – Berkshire, Buckinghamshire, Cornwall, Devon, Wiltshire. Lost on first innings – Oxfordshire, Shropshire, Somerset II.*

### Batting Averages

| | *M* | *I* | *NO* | *R* | *HI* | *100s* | *Avge* |
|---|---|---|---|---|---|---|---|
| S. J. Halliday ........ | 7 | 13 | 3 | 526 | 96* | 0 | 52.60 |
| *A. Kennedy ........ | 9 | 16 | 2 | 589 | 171* | 1 | 42.07 |
| V. B. Lewis ......... | 9 | 15 | 4 | 257 | 59 | 0 | 23.36 |
| C. Stone ............ | 8 | 12 | 0 | 266 | 59 | 0 | 22.16 |
| R. V. Lewis ......... | 7 | 12 | 2 | 189 | 53* | 0 | 18.90 |
| S. Sawney .......... | 4 | 6 | 0 | 88 | 42 | 0 | 14.66 |
| A. R. Wingfield Digby | 7 | 9 | 1 | 111 | 35 | 0 | 13.87 |
| I. E. W. Sanders ..... | 8 | 10 | 2 | 88 | 28* | 0 | 11.00 |
| T. J. Kent .......... | 5 | 8 | 0 | 87 | 24 | 0 | 10.87 |

Played in six matches: R. V. J. Coombs 4, 13*; B. K. Shantry 4*, 16*, 3. Played in five matches: †A. R. Richardson 1*, 1*, 2, 0, 20. Played in four matches: †D. A. Ridley 8, 9, 4. Played in three matches: I. C. D. Stuart 11, 8*, 9, 10*, 0. Played in two matches: N. A. W. Ackland 24, 0, 13; C. A. Graham 13, 6*, 14, 13; A. B. O'Sullivan 1, 1*, 0*; R. J. Scott 37, 19, 6, 39. Played in one match: A. S. Drummond 11, 12; St J. M. N. Farley, 0, 0; P. L. Garlick did not bat.

### Bowling Averages

| | *O* | *M* | *R* | *W* | *BB* | *Avge* |
|---|---|---|---|---|---|---|
| A. R. Wingfield Digby | 166.4 | 49 | 518 | 33 | 8-50 | 15.69 |
| I. E. W. Sanders ..... | 135.1 | 41 | 385 | 21 | 6-46 | 18.33 |
| C. Stone ............ | 117 | 37 | 345 | 15 | 4-53 | 23.00 |
| B. K. Shantry ....... | 129 | 23 | 371 | 18 | 4-27 | 20.61 |

Also bowled: R. V. J. Coombs 84–23–226–6; A. Kennedy 38.2–9–136–5; P. L. Garlick 16–2–59–4; A. B. O'Sullivan 22–5–88–3; S. Sawney 15–3–38–0; I. C. D. Stuart 7–2–17–0; A. S. Drummond 2–1–5–0.

## DURHAM

Secretary – J. ILEY, Roselea, Springwell Avenue, Durham DH1 4LY

*Matches 9: Won – Norfolk, Suffolk. Lost – Cumberland. Won on first innings – Cambridgeshire, Hertfordshire, Staffordshire. Tied on first innings – Bedfordshire. Lost on first innings – Lincolnshire, Northumberland.*

## Batting Averages

| | M | I | NO | R | HI | 100s | Avge |
|---|---|---|---|---|---|---|---|
| *N. A. Riddell | 9 | 17 | 3 | 594 | 91 | 0 | 42.42 |
| S. R. Atkinson | 6 | 11 | 0 | 380 | 94 | 0 | 34.54 |
| A. S. Patel | 9 | 17 | 3 | 480 | 106 | 1 | 34.28 |
| S. Greensword | 9 | 15 | 3 | 346 | 69 | 0 | 28.83 |
| †R. A. D. Mercer | 8 | 12 | 5 | 160 | 61 | 0 | 22.85 |
| G. Hurst | 9 | 17 | 4 | 294 | 61 | 0 | 22.61 |
| P. J. Kippax | 9 | 10 | 4 | 116 | 36* | 0 | 19.33 |
| P. Burn | 4 | 6 | 2 | 73 | 20* | 0 | 18.25 |
| J. W. Lister | 5 | 10 | 0 | 147 | 80 | 0 | 14.70 |
| D. C. Jackson | 5 | 8 | 0 | 117 | 46 | 0 | 14.62 |

Played in six matches: G. Johnson 2, 7; A.W. Scott 72*, 24*, 9*, 5*. Played in four matches: P. Beaney 5, 4, 0*. J. Johnston 5, 0*, 0*. Played in two matches: J. N. Whitehouse 21, 0. Played in one match: I. E. Conn 0, 0*; †A. R. Fothergill 15; B. R. Lander 4, 2*; M. A. Roseberry 6, 27.

## Bowling Averages

| | O | M | R | W | BB | Avge |
|---|---|---|---|---|---|---|
| P. J. Kippax | 207.3 | 58 | 496 | 26 | 5-34 | 19.07 |
| A. W. Scott | 160.5 | 23 | 543 | 27 | 4-52 | 20.11 |
| S. Greensword | 203.1 | 63 | 511 | 18 | 3-42 | 28.38 |
| G. Johnson | 139 | 25 | 429 | 15 | 3-33 | 28.60 |

Also bowled: A. S. Patel 89–21–302–9; J. Johnston 105–18–356–6; P. Beaney 54–14–179–6; I. E. Conn 16–3–40–4; B. R. Lander 27–7–62–2; J. N. Whitehouse 22–6–48–1; N. A. Riddell 7.5–0–77–0; S. R. Atkinson 1–0–9–0.

# HERTFORDSHIRE

Secretary – D. DREDGE, 38 Santers Lane, Potters Bar, EN6 2BX

*Matches 9: Won – Northumberland, Staffordshire. Won on first innings – Suffolk. Lost on first innings – Bedfordshire, Cambridgeshire, Durham, Norfolk. No result – Cumberland, Lincolnshire.*

## Batting Averages

| | M | I | NO | R | HI | 100s | Avge |
|---|---|---|---|---|---|---|---|
| W. M. Osman | 4 | 8 | 0 | 271 | 88 | 0 | 33.87 |
| C. S. Bannister | 4 | 8 | 0 | 221 | 58 | 0 | 27.62 |
| E. P. Neal | 5 | 10 | 1 | 227 | 54 | 0 | 25.22 |
| T. S. Smith | 7 | 13 | 3 | 213 | 40* | 0 | 21.30 |
| †M. W. C. Olley | 8 | 13 | 4 | 190 | 67 | 0 | 21.11 |
| N. Gilbert | 5 | 9 | 1 | 165 | 61* | 0 | 20.62 |
| *F. E. Collyer | 5 | 9 | 1 | 159 | 54 | 0 | 19.87 |
| S. A. Dean | 5 | 10 | 0 | 196 | 52 | 0 | 19.60 |
| A. R. Garofall | 6 | 9 | 2 | 130 | 24* | 0 | 18.57 |
| D. G. Ottley | 6 | 11 | 0 | 176 | 29 | 0 | 16.00 |
| P. A. Driver | 6 | 11 | 1 | 132 | 44 | 0 | 13.20 |
| R. J. Hailey | 6 | 6 | 2 | 2 | 1* | 0 | 0.50 |

Played in five matches: W. G. Merry 6, 2, 4, 2, 16*; A. P. Wright 12, 0, 10, 8*, 1. Played in four matches: D. Surridge 4*, 19*, 0*, 0. Played in three matches: T. C. E. Stancombe 5*, 21*, 0, 18. Played in two matches: B. G. Collins 5*, 0, 0. Played in one match: R. H. Pomphrey 0; C. Thomas 11, 19.

## Bowling Averages

| | *O* | *M* | *R* | *W* | *BB* | *Avge* |
|---|---|---|---|---|---|---|
| B. G. Collins | 50 | 15 | 115 | 12 | 8-7 | 9.58 |
| D. Surridge | 88.1 | 18 | 222 | 10 | 4-48 | 22.20 |
| W. G. Merry | 104 | 31 | 272 | 10 | 3-22 | 27.20 |
| R. J. Hailey | 96.2 | 25 | 284 | 10 | 4-26 | 28.40 |
| T. S. Smith | 172 | 45 | 465 | 13 | 3-46 | 35.76 |

Also bowled: E. P. Neal 49.4–9–181–9; A. R. Garofall 78–15–231–8; A. P. Wright 51–14–145–6; T. C. E. Stancombe 35–5–114–3; D. G. Ottley 1–0–5–1; C. Thomas 7–0–32–0; C. S. Bannister 2–0–9–0.

# LINCOLNSHIRE

Secretary – D. H. Wright, 18 Spencer Road, Ketton, Stamford

*Matches 9: Lost – Cambridgeshire, Staffordshire, Suffolk. Won on first innings – Cumberland, Durham, Norfolk. Lost on first innings – Bedfordshire. No result – Hertfordshire, Northumberland.*

## Batting Averages

| | *M* | *I* | *NO* | *R* | *HI* | *100s* | *Avge* |
|---|---|---|---|---|---|---|---|
| †N. Priestley | 8 | 15 | 4 | 551 | 126* | 1 | 50.09 |
| M. A. Fell | 6 | 11 | 0 | 297 | 67 | 0 | 27.00 |
| J. R. Ratnayeke | 4 | 6 | 1 | 101 | 37* | 0 | 20.20 |
| P. R. Butler | 7 | 12 | 4 | 138 | 25* | 0 | 17.25 |
| G. Robinson | 8 | 15 | 0 | 250 | 51 | 0 | 16.66 |
| S. A. Bradford | 6 | 9 | 4 | 73 | 26* | 0 | 14.60 |
| D. Marshall | 8 | 8 | 3 | 55 | 25* | 0 | 11.00 |
| R. L. Burton | 6 | 6 | 1 | 51 | 30* | 0 | 10.20 |
| *H. Pougher | 8 | 9 | 0 | 67 | 24 | 0 | 7.44 |

Played in seven matches: J. P. Quincey 20, 7, 2, 0, 26. Played in four matches: C. Beckett 2, 7, 4*. Played in three matches: P. D. Johnson 15*, 35, 32*, 83, 56. Played in two matches: J. G. Franks 5, 2, 10, 57; P. L. Tillison 5, 0; P. A. Todd 1, 5, 17, 48; C. Wicks 47, 4, 25, 13. Played in one match: S. W. Bartlett 0, 0; C. S. Knapton 0*, 7; A. R. Turpin 11, 10*; L. A. Ward 27, 0; P. Wood 0, 5*.

## Bowling Averages

| | *O* | *M* | *R* | *W* | *BB* | *Avge* |
|---|---|---|---|---|---|---|
| J. R. Ratnayeke | 85.2 | 14 | 314 | 18 | 6-30 | 17.44 |
| D. Marshall | 204 | 44 | 575 | 22 | 4-41 | 26.13 |

Also bowled: J. P. Quincey 87–14–275–6; P. Wood 41–8–114–6; S. A. Bradford 63–14–208–5; R. L. Burton 109–21–313–5; C. Beckett 43–10–160–5; P. L. Tillison 40–7–115–4; P. R. Butler 4–0–18–3; P. A. Todd 16.2–4–37–2; M. A. Fell 14–1–70–2; C. S. Knapton 12–3–27–0; S. W. Bartlett 7–1–20–0; G. Robinson 3–1–8–0; A. R. Turpin 1.3–0–5–0; H. Pougher 1.1–0–9–0.

# NORFOLK

Secretary – D. K. WILD, Charnwood, Hall Farm Place,
New Road, Bawburgh, Norwich NR9 3LW

*Matches 9: Won – Cambridgeshire. Lost – Durham. Won on first innings – Hertfordshire, Suffolk. Tied on first innings – Bedfordshire, Northumberland. Lost on first innings – Lincolnshire. No result – Cumberland, Staffordshire.*

### Batting Averages

| | M | I | NO | R | HI | 100s | Avge |
|---|---|---|---|---|---|---|---|
| Parvez Mir | 6 | 9 | 4 | 332 | 126* | 1 | 66.40 |
| S. G. Plumb | 9 | 12 | 4 | 286 | 58* | 0 | 35.75 |
| J. R. Carter | 6 | 10 | 2 | 224 | 81 | 0 | 28.00 |
| R. D. Huggins | 9 | 14 | 6 | 209 | 45 | 0 | 26.12 |
| *F. L. Q. Handley | 4 | 6 | 0 | 150 | 63 | 0 | 25.00 |
| N. D. Cook | 5 | 6 | 1 | 89 | 46 | 0 | 17.80 |
| P. C. Rice | 5 | 8 | 2 | 88 | 25 | 0 | 14.66 |
| Nasir Zaidi | 9 | 8 | 2 | 55 | 11 | 0 | 9.16 |

Played in nine matches: D. R. Thomas 0*, 19*, 0, 3, 19. Played in eight matches: R. A. Bunting 0*, 2, 0*; P. K. Whittaker 0, 22, 3, 0*, 8*. Played in six matches: †D. E. Mattocks 0, 6, 8. Played in four matches: J. Whitehead 3, 23*. Played in three matches: R. L. Bradford 9, 19, 8, 26. Played in two matches: †F. P. Bailey 0; E. R. Hodson 5. Played in one match: P. A. Motum 20; T. L. Powell 7; †M. M. Jervis and J. S. Tate did not bat.

### Bowling Averages

| | O | M | R | W | BB | Avge |
|---|---|---|---|---|---|---|
| D. R. Thomas | 118.3 | 30 | 300 | 18 | 4-16 | 16.66 |
| R. A. Bunting | 143.1 | 36 | 358 | 18 | 4-27 | 19.88 |
| Nasir Zaidi | 93.4 | 27 | 262 | 13 | 6-46 | 20.15 |
| Parvez Mir | 196 | 65 | 447 | 20 | 4-39 | 22.35 |
| S. G. Plumb | 170.2 | 49 | 426 | 18 | 4-59 | 23.66 |

Also bowled: P. K. Whittaker 99–20–325–6; J. S. Tate 10–6–8–1; R. D. Huggins 1–1–0–0.

## NORTHUMBERLAND

Secretary – R. E. WOOD, Northumberland County Cricket Ground, Osborne Avenue, Jesmond, Newcastle upon Tyne NE2 1JS

*Matches 9: Won – Staffordshire. Lost – Hertfordshire. Won on first innings – Bedfordshire, Cambridgeshire, Cumberland, Durham. Tied on first innings – Norfolk, Suffolk. No result – Lincolnshire.*

### Batting Averages

| | M | I | NO | R | HI | 100s | Avge |
|---|---|---|---|---|---|---|---|
| K. Pearson | 8 | 15 | 3 | 392 | 115* | 1 | 32.66 |
| P. G. Ingham | 5 | 9 | 3 | 190 | 63 | 0 | 31.66 |
| K. C. Williams | 6 | 9 | 2 | 204 | 57* | 0 | 29.14 |
| G. R. Morris | 7 | 9 | 2 | 195 | 75* | 0 | 27.85 |
| *M. E. Younger | 8 | 11 | 3 | 216 | 59* | 0 | 27.00 |
| G. D. Halliday | 7 | 13 | 3 | 238 | 54 | 0 | 23.80 |
| D. Smart | 5 | 6 | 2 | 82 | 27 | 0 | 20.50 |

Played in seven matches: P. C. Graham 0, 4. Played in six matches: P. G. Cormack, 2, 27, 0, 2. Played in five matches: †K. Corby 0*, 15, 2*, 9*; R. Arrowsmith 2*, 0. Played in four matches: B. C. Keenleyside 22*, 0. Played in three matches: I. W. Darling 9; †B. Storey 10*, 1. Played in two matches: B. S. Brar 0*; R. Dreyer 22, 7, 54*. Played in one match: M. B. Anderson 16, 6; A. S. Thompson 1; B. R. Evans, A. Hardy and C. J. Harker did not bat.

### Bowling Averages

| | O | M | R | W | BB | Avge |
|---|---|---|---|---|---|---|
| P. C. Graham | 152.1 | 42 | 402 | 25 | 7-18 | 16.08 |
| G. D. Halliday | 50.1 | 12 | 185 | 11 | 3-3 | 16.81 |
| R. Arrowsmith | 108.2 | 30 | 314 | 12 | 3-20 | 26.16 |

Also bowled: K. C. Williams 106.1–37–214–7; B. C. Keenleyside 34–7–98–7; M. E. Younger 41–7–185–5; B. S. Brar 26–4–109–4; I. W. Darling 49–15–131–3; B. R. Evans 23–2–70–1; P. G. Cormack 7–0–54–1; M. B. Anderson 4–1–19–1; A. Hardy 13–2–52–0; C. J. Harker 10–2–43–0; K. Pearson 7.2–1–32–0; P. G. Ingham 4–0–30–0.

## OXFORDSHIRE

Secretary – J. E. O. SMITH, 2 The Green, Horton-cum-Studley OX9 1AE

*Matches 9: Won on first innings – Berkshire, Buckinghamshire, Cheshire, Dorset. Tied on first innings – Devon, Somerset II. Lost on first innings – Cornwall, Wiltshire. No result – Shropshire.*

### Batting Averages

| | *M* | *I* | *NO* | *R* | *HI* | *100s* | *Avge* |
|---|---|---|---|---|---|---|---|
| C. J. Clements | 3 | 6 | 1 | 186 | 89 | 0 | 37.20 |
| M. D. Nurton | 9 | 17 | 5 | 390 | 72* | 0 | 32.50 |
| *P. J. Garner | 9 | 15 | 0 | 306 | 59 | 0 | 20.40 |
| D. A. J. Wise | 7 | 13 | 1 | 231 | 48 | 0 | 19.25 |
| K. A. Arnold | 8 | 7 | 1 | 101 | 27* | 0 | 16.83 |
| G. C. Ford | 4 | 7 | 0 | 111 | 46 | 0 | 15.85 |
| T. A. Lester | 6 | 9 | 3 | 91 | 30 | 0 | 15.16 |
| G. R. Hobbins | 5 | 9 | 2 | 105 | 41* | 0 | 15.00 |
| †A. Crossley | 9 | 12 | 2 | 147 | 25 | 0 | 14.70 |
| C. D. Ricks | 6 | 10 | 3 | 99 | 37* | 0 | 14.14 |
| S. R. Porter | 9 | 10 | 1 | 90 | 43 | 0 | 10.00 |
| R. N. Busby | 8 | 6 | 3 | 23 | 14* | 0 | 7.66 |
| R. A. Evans | 7 | 9 | 2 | 19 | 5* | 0 | 2.71 |

Played in four matches: I. J. Curtis 0*, 0*, 6*, 9*. Played in three matches: M. L. Beaumont 9, 0, 0, 7, 7. Played in one match: M. J. Thomas 1*, 11; D. C. Woods 0*, 0.

### Bowling Averages

| | *O* | *M* | *R* | *W* | *BB* | *Avge* |
|---|---|---|---|---|---|---|
| S. R. Porter | 110 | 13 | 436 | 26 | 6-60 | 16.76 |
| I. J. Curtis | 69.1 | 22 | 186 | 11 | 5-39 | 16.90 |
| R. N. Busby | 147.5 | 37 | 429 | 17 | 5-67 | 35.23 |
| R. A. Evans | 153 | 35 | 503 | 12 | 2-48 | 41.91 |
| K. A. Arnold | 181.3 | 51 | 533 | 11 | 2-38 | 48.45 |

Also bowled: C. D. Ricks 46–7–188–4; G. R. Hobbins 18–4–66–2; P. J. Garner 1–1–0–0.

## SHROPSHIRE

Secretary – N. H. BIRCH, 8 Port Hill Close, Copthorne, Shrewsbury

*Matches 9: Lost – Cheshire, Cornwall. Won on first innings – Devon, Dorset. Lost on first innings – Buckinghamshire, Wiltshire. No result – Berkshire, Oxfordshire, Somerset II.*

### Batting Averages

| | *M* | *I* | *NO* | *R* | *HI* | *100s* | *Avge* |
|---|---|---|---|---|---|---|---|
| K. Humphreys | 6 | 7 | 1 | 224 | 84* | 0 | 37.33 |
| J. Foster | 9 | 11 | 1 | 356 | 65 | 0 | 35.60 |
| Mushtaq Mohammad | 7 | 7 | 1 | 192 | 80* | 0 | 32.00 |
| J. A. Smith | 9 | 8 | 2 | 141 | 54* | 0 | 23.50 |
| *S. C. Gale | 9 | 11 | 3 | 160 | 56 | 0 | 20.00 |
| P. L. Ranells | 9 | 9 | 1 | 154 | 42 | 0 | 19.25 |
| J. C. C. Pettegree | 6 | 6 | 1 | 91 | 29 | 0 | 18.20 |
| †D. J. Ashley | 9 | 7 | 1 | 82 | 38* | 0 | 13.66 |

Played in nine matches: J. S. Roberts 2, 0*, 0*. Played in six matches: J. P. Dawson 17, 6*, 3*, 6. Played in four matches: M. A. Nash 1*, 0, 0. Played in three matches: W. Bott 2, 2*, 0, 0; M. Davies 0, 39, 2; J. B. R. Jones 12, 59, 2, 41. Played in two matches: A. S. Barnard 3, 0; C. N. Boyns 32. Played in one match; M. I. Chaudry 3; P. R. Oliver 16*; S. Ogrizovic did not bat.

## Bowling Averages

| | O | M | R | W | BB | Avge |
|---|---|---|---|---|---|---|
| J. P. Dawson | 154 | 41 | 394 | 21 | 4-51 | 18.76 |
| Mushtaq Mohammad | 148 | 45 | 378 | 20 | 6-68 | 18.90 |
| J. A. Smith | 136 | 31 | 373 | 17 | 2-16 | 21.94 |
| J. S. Roberts | 168.1 | 39 | 440 | 15 | 5-33 | 29.33 |

Also bowled: M. A. Nash 60–19–156–5; P. L. Ranells 59–14–152–5; C. N. Boyns 49.5–11–141–3; W. Bott 20–0–86–1; S. Ogrizovic 7–1–33–1; P. R. Oliver 10.5–2–54–1; A. S. Barnard 29–3–100–0; S. C. Gale 1–0–2–0.

# SOMERSET SECOND ELEVEN

Secretary – A. S. BROWN, County Cricket Ground, Taunton TA1 1JT

*Matches 9: Won on first innings – Cheshire, Devon, Dorset. Tied on first innings – Oxfordshire. Lost on first innings – Berkshire, Buckinghamshire, Cornwall. No result – Shropshire, Wiltshire.*

## Batting Averages

| | M | I | NO | R | HI | 100s | Avge |
|---|---|---|---|---|---|---|---|
| R. J. Harden | 6 | 8 | 4 | 190 | 51* | 0 | 47.50 |
| R. L. Ollis | 6 | 9 | 2 | 330 | 170* | 1 | 47.14 |
| †S. J. Turner | 7 | 7 | 3 | 134 | 49 | 0 | 33.50 |
| M. S. Turner | 6 | 7 | 3 | 104 | 37 | 0 | 26.00 |
| G. V. Palmer | 8 | 9 | 1 | 183 | 47 | 0 | 22.87 |
| P. A. C. Bail | 9 | 15 | 1 | 238 | 57 | 0 | 17.00 |
| S. A. R. Ferguson | 6 | 10 | 0 | 170 | 63 | 0 | 17.00 |
| J. G. Wyatt | 5 | 8 | 2 | 90 | 32* | 0 | 15.00 |
| A. P. Jones | 8 | 6 | 2 | 26 | 8* | 0 | 6.50 |

Played in nine matches: M. D. Harman 2*, 8, 4, 3, 0. Played in six matches: S. C. Booth 0, 7*, 0, 1. Played in four matches: †A. J. H. Dunning 47*, 22, 17*, 0, 5; *P. J. Robinson 12*, 0*. Played in three matches: M. R. Davis 22, 0*; C. H. Dredge 17, 3. Played in two matches: J. C. M. Atkinson 1; R. G. Twose 2*, 22, 1, 40. Played in one match: R. J. Bartlett 25, 1; M. D. Crowe 30; B. C. Rose 48*; N. R. Williams 18; D. Beal did not bat.

## Bowling Averages

| | O | M | R | W | BB | Avge |
|---|---|---|---|---|---|---|
| S. C. Booth | 118.1 | 29 | 273 | 14 | 5-47 | 19.50 |
| G. V. Palmer | 107 | 21 | 403 | 20 | 4-47 | 20.15 |
| M. S. Turner | 86 | 24 | 251 | 12 | 4-58 | 20.91 |
| M. D. Harman | 171.4 | 33 | 459 | 21 | 5-21 | 21.85 |
| A. P. Jones | 105 | 23 | 250 | 11 | 3-38 | 22.72 |

Also bowled: M. R. Davis 46–7–142–8; C. H. Dredge 60–22–105–7; P. J. Robinson 19.5–4–38–4; D. Beal 5–1–8–1; J. C. M. Atkinson 12–1–38–0; P. A. C. Bail 1–1–0–0; M. D. Crowe 0.1–0–3–0.

# STAFFORDSHIRE

Secretary – L. W. HANCOCK, 4 Kingsland Avenue, Oakhill, Stoke-on-Trent ST4 5LA

*Matches 9: Won – Cambridgeshire, Cumberland, Lincolnshire. Lost – Hertfordshire, Northumberland, Suffolk. Won on first innings – Bedfordshire. Lost on first innings – Durham. No result – Norfolk.*

## Batting Averages

| | M | I | NO | R | HI | 100s | Avge |
|---|---|---|---|---|---|---|---|
| G. S. Warner | 5 | 9 | 4 | 272 | 82* | 0 | 54.40 |
| *N. J. Archer | 9 | 12 | 7 | 260 | 63* | 0 | 52.00 |
| J. A. Waterhouse | 5 | 9 | 4 | 187 | 50* | 0 | 37.40 |
| D. Cartledge | 8 | 14 | 1 | 445 | 78 | 0 | 34.23 |
| P. A. Marshall | 9 | 17 | 4 | 438 | 133* | 1 | 33.69 |
| H. A. Page | 5 | 7 | 3 | 123 | 35 | 0 | 30.75 |
| S. J. Dean | 7 | 11 | 0 | 236 | 68 | 0 | 21.45 |
| †A. Griffiths | 9 | 7 | 2 | 61 | 24 | 0 | 12.20 |

Played in nine matches: R. W. Flower 0, 14*, 3. Played in eight matches: D. C. Blank 1, 17*, 10, 21*. Played in seven matches: A. J. Webster 20, 44, 38*, 2, 22. Played in three matches: S. J. Bailey 3, 42, 6*, 16, 1; M. E. W. Brooker 2; K. R. Maguire 4*; D. B. Vengsarkar 31, 3, 30. Played in two matches: P. N. Gill 52, 42, 5, 4; M. J. Ikin 0, 4; D. A. Wenlock 0.

## Bowling Averages

| | O | M | R | W | BB | Avge |
|---|---|---|---|---|---|---|
| D. Cartledge | 43.5 | 16 | 135 | 11 | 4-5 | 12.27 |
| H. A. Page | 144 | 36 | 369 | 25 | 7-50 | 14.76 |
| D. C. Blank | 163.3 | 38 | 425 | 25 | 7-25 | 17.00 |
| K. R. Maguire | 72.3 | 10 | 244 | 11 | 4-46 | 22.18 |
| R. W. Flower | 186.3 | 58 | 532 | 22 | 6-36 | 24.18 |
| A. J. Webster | 162 | 33 | 511 | 21 | 6-53 | 24.33 |

Also bowled: M. E. W. Brooker 50–12–138–3; M. J. Ikin 19–4–74–3; D. A. Wenlock 42–8–139–1; D. B. Vengsarkar 4–1–14–1; P. N. Gill 2–0–18–0; P. A. Marshall 1–0–9–0; N. J. Archer 0.4–0–4–0.

# SUFFOLK

Secretary – R. S. BARKER, 301 Henley Road, Ipswich IP1 6TB

*Matches 9: Won – Bedfordshire, Lincolnshire, Staffordshire. Lost – Durham. Won on first innings – Cumberland. Tied on first innings – Northumberland. Lost on first innings – Cambridgeshire, Hertfordshire, Norfolk.*

## Batting Averages

| | M | I | NO | R | HI | 100s | Avge |
|---|---|---|---|---|---|---|---|
| M. S. A. McEvoy | 8 | 14 | 1 | 403 | 70 | 0 | 31.00 |
| P. J. Caley | 9 | 13 | 3 | 307 | 67 | 0 | 30.70 |
| P. J. Hayes | 9 | 12 | 6 | 161 | 43* | 0 | 26.83 |
| *S. M. Clements | 9 | 14 | 1 | 307 | 72 | 0 | 23.61 |
| G. Morgan | 9 | 14 | 1 | 273 | 97* | 0 | 21.00 |
| P. D. Barker | 9 | 15 | 1 | 252 | 58 | 0 | 18.00 |
| R. Herbert | 9 | 14 | 1 | 222 | 45* | 0 | 17.07 |
| R. C. Green | 9 | 9 | 3 | 78 | 19 | 0 | 13.00 |
| †A. D. Brown | 9 | 6 | 3 | 30 | 9* | 0 | 10.00 |

Played in seven matches: M. D. Bailey 4,17, 0*, 4*, 10. Played in four matches: H. J. W. Wright 30*, 16, 0, 15, 11. Played in two matches: P. W. Harvey 12, 0*; S. J. Priscott 0. Played in one match: C. C. Graham 1; R. J. Robinson 1, 4; *C. Rutterford 8; A. Squire 0.

### Bowling Averages

| | *O* | *M* | *R* | *W* | *BB* | *Avge* |
|---|---|---|---|---|---|---|
| H. J. W. Wright . . . . . | 79 | 28 | 183 | 11 | 7-30 | 16.63 |
| M. D. Bailey . . . . . . . . | 92 | 19 | 246 | 14 | 5-48 | 17.57 |
| R. C. Green . . . . . . . . . . | 199.3 | 41 | 578 | 31 | 6-49 | 18.64 |
| R. Herbert . . . . . . . . . . | 182.4 | 38 | 512 | 22 | 5-37 | 23.27 |
| P. J. Hayes . . . . . . . . . | 110.1 | 23 | 338 | 12 | 4-21 | 28.16 |

Also bowled: P. J. Caley 38–6–121–4, P. W. Harvey 20–1–73–3; C. Rutterford 8–1–33–2; R. J. Robinson 16–1–53–1; C. C. Graham 6–0–17–1; S. J. Priscott 25–5–102–0; S. M Clements 2–2–0–0; G. Morgan 1–1–0–0; P. D. Barker 7–3–11–0.

## WILTSHIRE

*Matches 9: Won on first innings – Oxfordshire, Shropshire. Tied on first innings – Berkshire. Lost on first innings – Buckinghamshire, Cheshire, Devon, Dorset. No result – Cornwall, Somerset II.*

### Batting Averages

| | *M* | *I* | *NO* | *R* | *HI* | *100s* | *Avge* |
|---|---|---|---|---|---|---|---|
| R. J. Lanchbury . . . . . | 8 | 11 | 1 | 274 | 72 | 0 | 27.40 |
| B. H. White . . . . . . . . . | 6 | 9 | 0 | 246 | 67 | 0 | 27.33 |
| D. J. M. Mercer . . . . . | 9 | 11 | 1 | 217 | 77 | 0 | 21.70 |
| C. C. Ellison . . . . . . . . | 5 | 6 | 3 | 63 | 27* | 0 | 21.00 |
| J. E. Skinner . . . . . . . . | 8 | 11 | 0 | 225 | 64 | 0 | 20.45 |
| P. Meehan . . . . . . . . . . | 7 | 7 | 3 | 80 | 32 | 0 | 20.00 |
| M. A. Watts . . . . . . . . | 9 | 9 | 3 | 104 | 34* | 0 | 17.33 |
| M. C. Seaman . . . . . . . | 9 | 13 | 0 | 207 | 38 | 0 | 15.92 |
| †J. Cullip . . . . . . . . . . . | 6 | 7 | 3 | 60 | 21 | 0 | 15.00 |
| *R. C. Cooper . . . . . . . | 9 | 13 | 2 | 161 | 32 | 0 | 14.63 |
| K. St J. D. Emery . . . . | 5 | 6 | 3 | 40 | 16* | 0 | 13.33 |

Played in four matches: †W. R. Johnson 8, 0*; J. J. Newman 33, 0, 51, 0. Played in three matches: J. M. Rice 38*, 12, 12*, 4, 39. Played in two matches: R. J. Merryweather 1*, 0; J. D. Quinlan 0. Played in one match: J. C. Barrett 7, 5; R. J. Greatorex 0, 11; D. R. Pike 1, 14; R. Wilson 0.

### Bowling Averages

| | *O* | *M* | *R* | *W* | *BB* | *Avge* |
|---|---|---|---|---|---|---|
| M. A. Watts . . . . . . . . | 187.1 | 47 | 489 | 31 | 8-59 | 15.77 |
| K. St J. D. Emery . . . . | 87.2 | 10 | 274 | 14 | 3-31 | 19.57 |

Also bowled: P. Meehan 92–26–282–6; C. C. Ellison 78–11–237–6; J. M. Rice 53–14–144–6; R. C. Cooper 57–22–122–5; J. C. Barrett 31–6–101–4; J. E. Skinner 15–0–47–3; R. Wilson 14–0–77–1; R. J. Merryweather 12–2–35–1; J. D. Quinlan 32.4–6–115–0, D. H. White 2–1–3–0; D. R. Pike 2–0–3–0.

## TOP TEN MINOR COUNTIES AVERAGES, 1985

### BATTING

(Qualification: 8 innings)

| | *M* | *I* | *NO* | *R* | *HI* | *100s* | *Avge* |
|---|---|---|---|---|---|---|---|
| Parvez Mir (*Norfolk*) . . . . . . . . . | 6 | 9 | 4 | 332 | 126* | 1 | 66.40 |
| A. Fordham (*Bedfordshire*) . . . . . | 4 | 8 | 0 | 454 | 123 | 1 | 56.75 |
| G. S. Warner (*Staffordshire*) . . . . | 5 | 9 | 4 | 272 | 82* | 0 | 54.40 |

| | *M* | *I* | *NO* | *R* | *HI* | *100s* | *Avge* |
|---|---|---|---|---|---|---|---|
| Mudassar Nazar (*Cheshire*) | 7 | 12 | 3 | 488 | 112* | 1 | 54.22 |
| S. J. Halliday (*Dorset*) | 7 | 13 | 3 | 526 | 96* | 0 | 52.60 |
| N. J. Archer (*Staffordshire*) | 9 | 12 | 7 | 260 | 63* | 0 | 52.00 |
| N. Priestley (*Lincolnshire*) | 8 | 15 | 4 | 551 | 126* | 1 | 50.09 |
| R. J. Harden (*Somerset II*) | 6 | 8 | 4 | 190 | 51* | 0 | 47.50 |
| R. L. Ollis (*Somerset II*) | 6 | 9 | 2 | 330 | 170* | 1 | 47.14 |
| J. R. Moyes (*Cumberland*) | 8 | 12 | 4 | 356 | 129 | 1 | 44.50 |

## BOWLING

(Qualification: 20 wickets)

| | *O* | *M* | *R* | *W* | *BB* | *Avge* |
|---|---|---|---|---|---|---|
| G. R. Black (*Buckinghamshire*) | 105.4 | 26 | 252 | 22 | 8-47 | 11.45 |
| M. D. Woods (*Cumberland*) | 85.4 | 28 | 236 | 20 | 7-12 | 11.80 |
| S. Burrow (*Buckinghamshire*) | 142.2 | 56 | 284 | 21 | 4-24 | 13.52 |
| D. R. Parry (*Cambridgeshire*) | 329 | 84 | 753 | 53 | 6-59 | 14.20 |
| J. A. Sutton (*Cheshire*) | 203 | 70 | 555 | 38 | 7-47 | 14.60 |
| H. A. Page (*Staffordshire*) | 144 | 36 | 369 | 25 | 7-50 | 14.76 |
| Mudassar Nazar (*Cheshire*) | 129 | 32 | 305 | 20 | 4-36 | 15.25 |
| A. R. Wingfield Digby (*Dorset*) | 166.4 | 49 | 518 | 33 | 8-50 | 15.69 |
| M. A. Watts (*Wiltshire*) | 187.1 | 47 | 489 | 31 | 8-59 | 15.77 |
| P. C. Graham (*Northumberland*) | 152.1 | 42 | 402 | 25 | 7-18 | 16.08 |

## THE MINOR COUNTIES CHAMPIONS

| | | | | | |
|---|---|---|---|---|---|
| 1895 | Norfolk / Durham / Worcestershire | 1924 | Berkshire | 1958 | Yorkshire II |
| 1896 | Worcestershire | 1925 | Buckinghamshire | 1959 | Warwickshire II |
| 1897 | Worcestershire | 1926 | Durham | 1960 | Lancashire II |
| 1898 | Worcestershire | 1927 | Staffordshire | 1961 | Somerset II |
| 1899 | Northamptonshire / Buckinghamshire | 1928 | Berkshire | 1962 | Warwickshire II |
| 1900 | Glamorgan / Durham / Northamptonshire | 1929 | Oxfordshire | 1963 | Cambridgeshire |
| 1901 | Durham | 1930 | Durham | 1964 | Lancashire II |
| 1902 | Wiltshire | 1931 | Leicestershire II | 1965 | Somerset II |
| 1903 | Northamptonshire | 1932 | Buckinghamshire | 1966 | Lincolnshire |
| 1904 | Northamptonshire | 1933 | Undecided | 1967 | Cheshire |
| 1905 | Norfolk | 1934 | Lancashire II | 1968 | Yorkshire II |
| 1906 | Staffordshire | 1935 | Middlesex II | 1969 | Buckinghamshire |
| 1907 | Lancashire II | 1936 | Hertfordshire | 1970 | Bedfordshire |
| 1908 | Staffordshire | 1937 | Lancashire II | 1971 | Yorkshire II |
| 1909 | Wiltshire | 1938 | Buckinghamshire | 1972 | Bedfordshire |
| 1910 | Norfolk | 1939 | Surrey II | 1973 | Shropshire |
| 1911 | Staffordshire | 1946 | Suffolk | 1974 | Oxfordshire |
| 1912 | In abeyance | 1947 | Yorkshire II | 1975 | Hertfordshire |
| 1913 | Norfolk | 1948 | Lancashire II | 1976 | Durham |
| 1920 | Staffordshire | 1949 | Lancashire II | 1977 | Suffolk |
| 1921 | Staffordshire | 1950 | Surrey II | 1978 | Devon |
| 1922 | Buckinghamshire | 1951 | Kent II | 1979 | Suffolk |
| 1923 | Buckinghamshire | 1952 | Buckinghamshire | 1980 | Durham |
| | | 1953 | Berkshire | 1981 | Durham |
| | | 1954 | Surrey II | 1982 | Oxfordshire |
| | | 1955 | Surrey II | 1983 | Hertfordshire |
| | | 1956 | Kent II | 1984 | Durham |
| | | 1957 | Yorkshire II | 1985 | Cheshire |

# SECOND ELEVEN CHAMPIONSHIP, 1985

Although injuries to first-team players often depleted **Derbyshire's** side, five batsmen made seven centuries. Their failure to progress beyond fifteenth place was attributed to a weak attack, in which Paul Taylor's performance deteriorated. Devon Malcolm continued to progress, as did Chris Rudd with his off-breaks, but Dallas Moir, who took six for 9 against Leicestershire at Derby, was not retained at the end of the season.

The batting for **Essex** was headed by Alan Lilley, whose two hundreds included 224 not out against Kent at Eton Manor, and John Stephenson, who scored the most runs despite being available only after the end of his university term. The attack suffered from first-team calls, but Stephen Waugh, on an Esso Scholarship from New South Wales, was an asset with both bat and ball, taking six for 116 against Surrey at Chelmsford and six for 81 in the second innings against Gloucestershire at the same ground. Ian Pont took six for 15, including a hat-trick, in Gloucestershire's first innings. Neil Burns kept wicket efficiently as well as being a useful batsman.

**Glamorgan's** young side owed much to the consistent batting of Matthew Maynard, who, despite playing no three-figure innings for the Second Eleven, made a hundred on his first-class début. Philip North and Michael Cann both impressed as young slow bowlers, each taking 32 wickets and North collecting five in an innings four times.

**Gloucestershire**, for whom Tony Wright scored the side's only century, earned a mere six batting points and subsided to the bottom of the table. Gary Sainsbury took the most wickets, including a return of seven for 51 against Warwickshire at Old Edwardians CC in the last match of the season.

**Hampshire's** batting was strengthened by David Turner, Nigel Cowley and Jon Hardy, when they were not playing for the first team. The stand of 284 against Somerset at Southampton between Turner (175) and Tony Middleton (125) was a second-wicket record for the county Second Eleven. With the exception of Stephen Andrew, the attack lacked penetration.

Outstanding for **Kent** was Graham Cowdrey, who passed 1,000 runs for the second successive season and was the only player from any county to reach four figures in the Championship in 1985. His innings of 255 against Glamorgan at Sittingbourne was a spectacular performance. Neil Taylor, having lost his place in the first team at the beginning of the season, applied himself admirably to head the batting averages, while Laurie Potter, consistent with the bat, improved greatly with the ball. Alan Igglesden returned seven for 60 against Middlesex at Canterbury, but Kevin Masters was disappointing and was not retained, along with the left-arm spinner, Lindsay Wood, who took the most wickets but seemed unlikely to command a first-team place as long as Derek Underwood remains in the side.

In their third game **Lancashire** dismissed Warwickshire for 36 in their nine-wicket win at Knowle & Dorridge, Steve Jefferies collecting seven for 21. He also took six for 67 against Yorkshire at Headingley, where Tony Murphy returned six for 54. Only three centuries were hit, Mark Chadwick's unbeaten 173 against Derbyshire at Blackburn being a career best, and Andy Hayhurst's 120 against the same county at Derby being his first.

For **Leicestershire**, Glenn Bishop, an Esso Scholar from South Australia, had a superb season, always going for his shots in an attractive manner. Tim Boon, striving for fitness after breaking a thigh in a car accident in South Africa, also batted well, while Russell Cobb was a dependable opener, and promise was shown by David Billington and Mark Blackett. Phil Whitticase had an excellent season behind the stumps. Despite a surfeit of no-balls, Phillip De Freitas was an exciting addition to the side, his 44 wickets including returns of six for 30 against Worcestershire at Market Harborough, six for 56 against Northamptonshire at Leicester and six for 88 against the same county at Woughton. George Ferris also bowled too many no-balls, but Winston Benjamin, on a Caribbean Connection Scholarship, and Lloyd Tennant both showed promise.

The outstanding batsman for **Middlesex** was Keith Brown, whose 828 runs included 193 against Northamptonshire at Harefield, where he shared with the Oxford Blue, Andrew Miller

(115), a first-wicket stand of 274. Philip Tufnell and Angus Fraser took 47 and 44 wickets respectively and John Grimble achieved the side's best return of seven for 64 against Hampshire at South Hampstead. Graham Rose was the leading all-rounder.

Without a win, **Northamptonshire's** inexperienced side slipped to sixteenth place, frustrated by the weather on at least four occasions when victory seemed within their grasp. Alan Fordham scored hundreds against Derbyshire at Shipley and against Middlesex at Harefield, one each also coming from Mark Gouldstone and Rob Carter, back on the playing staff after two years as assistant coach. Matthew Wheeler took the most wickets, six of them for 84 against Leicestershire at Woughton.

**Nottinghamshire**, benefiting from Surrey's punishment for fielding an ineligible player, won the Championship for only the second time, their previous success having been in 1972. Their team was built around a regular nucleus of nine players, of whom Mike Newell was the leading batsman, well supported by Duncan Martindale and Andy Courtice, on an Esso Scholarship from Queensland. Andy Afford had a useful season, claiming 45 wickets, although the best return was seven for 48 by Eddie Hemmings against Derbyshire at Caythorpe. Peter Such (six for 12) combined with Mike Bore (four for 8) to dismiss Glamorgan for 71 at Ebbw Vale.

Injuries hampered **Somerset**, who slipped back to fourteenth position. Yet seven batsmen each scored a century, Simon Ferguson and Richard Harden batting especially well. Martin Crowe made 326 runs in his three innings, his 150 against Glamorgan at Taunton being especially noteworthy. Andrew Jones showed much improvement with the ball, Mark Harman suffered more missed chances than most, and the promise shown by Robert Coombs, on his return from Exeter University, brought his promotion to the first team.

**Surrey**, the runners-up for the second successive season, would have taken first place but for the deduction of 24 points for including an ineligible player, Zorol Barthey, in their win over Sussex at Hove. Chris Bullen and Nick Falkner were the most prolific batsmen, while Nick Taylor's 45 wickets included eleven for 148 against Essex at Chelmsford.

**Sussex**, bottom in 1984, shot up to fourth place, contending strongly for the title until the end of the season. Some big totals were compiled by a strong batting side which featured Neil Lenham, David Standing, Ian Greig and Tony Dodemaide, an Esso Scholar from Victoria. Adrian Jones and Ian Waring shared the new ball, Jones taking six for 46 against Middlesex at the Lensbury Club. Two newcomers prospered, Andrew Bredin collecting 25 wickets with his left-arm spin and Peter Moores, formerly at Worcestershire, impressing behind the stumps.

Asif Din batted for **Warwickshire** with increasing assurance to hit four centuries, and was well supported by the promising Wayne Matthews, Gordon Lord and David Smith, who hit 207 not out against Somerset at Edgbaston. Willie Morton bowled his left-arm spinners with less confidence than in 1984, but was none the less the leading wicket-taker. Brian McMillan was the side's fastest bowler, while progress was made by the medium-pacer, Timothy Munton, and the off-spinner, Adrian Pierson.

**Worcestershire**, who slid down to tenth place, suffered on slow pitches from an inadequate attack, which was dominated by pace and lacked a class spin bowler. Ricardo Ellcock, their fastest, and Paul Pridgeon were both restricted by injury, although Pridgeon took the most wickets, including a return of seven for 80 against Gloucestershire at Worcester. Graeme Hick was again outstanding, totalling the second-highest aggregate in only six innings, including 187 against Glamorgan at Worcester and 100 not out against Warwickshire at Old Hill. Lawrence Smith and Paul Bent also performed well.

First-team injuries seriously depleted **Yorkshire**, winners in 1984, who plummeted to twelfth place. In all, 32 players were called upon, twelve making their débuts. The fielding in particular reflected their inexperience, Rob Andrew excepted, and the batting was inconsistent. Ashley Metcalfe and Phil Robinson were hampered by ankle injuries, but David Byas batted encouragingly, beginning his first season with a maiden century against Kent at Canterbury. Paul Booth took by far the most wickets with his slow left-arm spin and there was good support from the off-break bowling of Ian Swallow. The seam bowlers, Chris Shaw, Chris Pickles and Peter Hartley, all performed well at times, Hartley excelling with a return of seven for 58 against Lancashire at Headingley and an exhilarating innings of 100 not out against Kent at York.

## SECOND ELEVEN CHAMPIONSHIP FINAL TABLE

| | Played | Won | Lost | Drawn | Bonus Points Batting | Bonus Points Bowling | Total Points | Average |
|---|---|---|---|---|---|---|---|---|
| 1–Nottinghamshire (9) | 15 | 7 | 2 | 6 | 21 | 46 | 171‡ | 11.40 |
| 2–Surrey (2) | 13 | 6 | 2 | 5 | 29 | 38 | 147* | 11.30 |
| 3–Middlesex (5) | 14 | 5 | 2 | 7 | 33 | 44 | 157 | 11.21 |
| 4–Sussex (17) | 12 | 4 | 4 | 4 | 22 | 39 | 125 | 10.41 |
| 5–Lancashire (8) | 16 | 4 | 3 | 9 | 35 | 50 | 149 | 9.31 |
| 6–Essex (7) | 13 | 3 | 5 | 5 | 23 | 43 | 114 | 8.76 |
| 7–Warwickshire (4) | 18 | 4 | 3 | 11 | 39 | 46 | 149 | 8.27 |
| 8–Kent (6) | 15 | 2 | 3 | 10 | 38 | 44 | 114 | 7.60 |
| 9–Glamorgan (13) | 14 | 3 | 2 | 9 | 22 | 35 | 105 | 7.50 |
| 10–Worcestershire (3) | 11 | 2 | 1 | 8 | 20 | 29 | 81 | 7.36 |
| 11–Leicestershire (14) | 14 | 2 | 2 | 10 | 29 | 40 | 101 | 7.21 |
| 12–Yorkshire (1) | 14 | 3 | 3 | 8 | 25 | 26 | 95† | 6.87 |
| 13–Hampshire (11) | 12 | 1 | 4 | 7 | 24 | 41 | 81 | 6.75 |
| 14–Somerset (10) | 11 | 1 | 2 | 8 | 27 | 24 | 63† | 5.72 |
| 15–Derbyshire (16) | 12 | 1 | 3 | 8 | 24 | 25 | 61† | 5.08 |
| 16–Northamptonshire (12) | 13 | 0 | 3 | 10 | 23 | 35 | 58 | 4.46 |
| 17–Gloucestershire (15) | 9 | 0 | 4 | 5 | 6 | 23 | 29 | 3.22 |

*1984 positions in brackets.*

† *Includes 12 points for one win in a one-innings match.*

‡ *Includes 24 points for two wins in one-innings matches.*

* *24 points deducted for playing an ineligible cricketer in the match v Sussex at Hove.*

*Note:* The averages to determine the positions in the Championship are worked to two, uncorrected decimal places.

The following matches were abandoned without a ball being bowled: Nottinghamshire v Northamptonshire, May 22, 23, 24; Surrey v Yorkshire, June 5, 6, 7; Surrey v Lancashire, August 14, 15, 16.

*In the averages that follow, * against a score signifies not out, * against a name signifies the captain and † signifies a wicket-keeper.*

## DERBYSHIRE SECOND ELEVEN

*Matches 12: Won – Worcestershire. Lost – Nottinghamshire (twice), Yorkshire. Drawn – Glamorgan, Lancashire (twice), Leicestershire (twice), Northamptonshire (twice), Yorkshire.*

### Batting Averages

| | I | NO | R | HI | Avge |
|---|---|---|---|---|---|
| W. P. Fowler | 10 | 3 | 498 | 131 | 71.14 |
| M. A. Fell | 9 | 2 | 447 | 118* | 63.85 |
| †B. J. M. Maher | 8 | 2 | 376 | 105 | 62.66 |
| R. Sharma | 14 | 2 | 460 | 107 | 38.33 |
| A. M. Brown | 18 | 2 | 602 | 105 | 37.62 |
| J. E. Morris | 6 | 0 | 190 | 72 | 31.66 |
| I. S. Anderson | 6 | 0 | 122 | 37 | 20.33 |
| †C. Marples | 11 | 3 | 158 | 28 | 19.75 |
| C. F. B. P. Rudd | 10 | 5 | 89 | 29 | 17.80 |
| *R. W. Taylor | 6 | 3 | 51 | 20 | 17.00 |
| J. P. Taylor | 8 | 3 | 64 | 22* | 12.80 |
| S. D. Myles | 9 | 0 | 103 | 34 | 11.44 |
| I. Broome | 10 | 1 | 56 | 17 | 6.22 |

Also batted: C. S. Dale 3, 17*; †A. Fothergill 18; R. Gaunt 21, 1, 3, 8; D. Hallack 34, 12, 13, 8; P. J. Heseltine 0; A. Hill 49, 20*; T. J. Hopper 7; J. B. McGregor 18, 10; D. E. Malcolm 6, 11, 22, 19, 0; S. N. C. Massey 27*; D. G. Moir 10*, 9, 14, 1, 39; O. H. Mortensen 1*; A. G. Pierrepont 5*, 2; S. K. Sharma 6*; J. Tindale 0, 7, 1, 25, 15; N. A. Willetts 15. P. G. Newman, K. J. Shine and M. Wakefield did not bat.

## Bowling Averages

| | *O* | *M* | *R* | *W* | *Avge* |
|---|---|---|---|---|---|
| O. H. Mortensen | 36.4 | 13 | 62 | 6 | 10.33 |
| D. G. Moir | 232.5 | 56 | 629 | 27 | 23.29 |
| D. E. Malcolm | 196 | 45 | 559 | 22 | 25.40 |
| W. P. Fowler | 103.4 | 30 | 303 | 10 | 30.30 |
| C. F. B. P. Rudd | 164.5 | 46 | 420 | 12 | 35.00 |
| I. Broome | 199.3 | 50 | 602 | 16 | 37.62 |
| J. P. Taylor | 172 | 30 | 605 | 11 | 55.00 |

Also bowled: I. S. Anderson 31–8–118–3; C. S. Dale 10–4–15–0; D. Hallack 28–4–87–3; T. J. Hopper 31–9–89–3; J. B. McGregor 3–0–26–0; S. N. C. Massey 17–4–53–2; S. D. Myles 13–5–27–1; P. G. Newman 14–2–42–1; A. G. Pierrepont 12–1–44–0; R. Sharma 59–9–172–3; K. J. Shine 13–4–32–0; J. Tindale 5–1–35–0; M. Wakefield 11–4–31–0.

# ESSEX SECOND ELEVEN

*Matches 13: Won – Gloucestershire, Northamptonshire, Sussex. Lost – Middlesex (twice), Nottinghamshire, Surrey, Sussex. Drawn – Hampshire, Kent (twice), Northamptonshire, Surrey.*

## Batting Averages

| | *M* | *I* | *NO* | *R* | *HI* | *Avge* |
|---|---|---|---|---|---|---|
| A. W. Lilley | 5 | 8 | 1 | 520 | 224* | 74.28 |
| J. P. Stephenson | 6 | 11 | 2 | 576 | 117 | 64.00 |
| S. R. Waugh | 7 | 11 | 2 | 404 | 74 | 44.88 |
| †N. D. Burns | 13 | 20 | 5 | 466 | 99* | 31.06 |
| K. R. Pont | 6 | 9 | 0 | 256 | 74 | 28.44 |
| N. Phillip | 4 | 6 | 1 | 129 | 47 | 25.80 |
| C. Gladwin | 7 | 14 | 1 | 311 | 52 | 23.92 |
| I. Redpath | 12 | 20 | 1 | 392 | 118* | 20.63 |
| M. G. Field-Buss | 13 | 25 | 2 | 426 | 60 | 18.52 |
| *R. E. East | 10 | 12 | 3 | 128 | 26 | 14.22 |
| T. D. Topley | 7 | 10 | 1 | 114 | 33 | 12.66 |
| N. Hussain | 2 | 4 | 0 | 49 | 25 | 12.25 |
| I. L. Pont | 9 | 10 | 2 | 88 | 36 | 11.00 |
| A. K. Golding | 8 | 12 | 2 | 103 | 23 | 10.30 |
| K. D. Moye | 11 | 13 | 2 | 98 | 25* | 8.90 |
| A. Seymour | 5 | 6 | 1 | 17 | 10 | 3.40 |

Played in five matches: J. H. Childs 0, 18*, 6*, 5*, 13*. Played in two matches: A. G. J. Fraser 13*, 1*, 5*, 0; S. Turner 12*, 0, 37*. Played in one match: R. Blitz 37; M. Boden 0; P. Jobson 20; A. Mordrick 0, 2; M. Offiah 0; R. Pook 0, 9; S. J. Poulter 17, 4; W. Sexton 11, 6.

## Bowling Averages

| | *O* | *M* | *R* | *W* | *Avge* |
|---|---|---|---|---|---|
| S. Turner | 60.5 | 22 | 109 | 11 | 9.90 |
| A. G. J. Fraser | 37.3 | 6 | 104 | 8 | 13.00 |
| J. H. Childs | 71.4 | 21 | 213 | 13 | 16.38 |
| S. R. Waugh | 118.3 | 16 | 390 | 20 | 19.50 |
| N. Phillip | 49 | 11 | 129 | 6 | 21.50 |
| I. L. Pont | 201.2 | 32 | 621 | 24 | 25.87 |
| A. K. Golding | 198.5 | 47 | 600 | 23 | 26.08 |
| T. D. Topley | 193 | 42 | 560 | 20 | 28.00 |
| M. G. Field-Buss | 240.4 | 55 | 719 | 21 | 34.23 |
| K. D. Moye | 211.5 | 44 | 747 | 20 | 37.35 |

Also bowled: M. Boden 8–3–8–0; R. E. East 0.4–0–1–0; C. Gladwin 8–1–17–0; A. W. Lilley 34–8–97–1; R. Mordrick 6–1–30–0; M. Offiah 12–1–66–0; K. R. Pont 61.3–19–127–3; S. J. Poulter 22.1–6–87–2; I. Redpath 9.4–0–86–1; A. Seymour 1–0–8–0; J. P. Stephenson 1–0–4–1.

## GLAMORGAN SECOND ELEVEN

*Matches 14: Won – Lancashire, Nottinghamshire, Warwickshire. Lost – Kent, Worcestershire. Drawn – Derbyshire, Gloucestershire (twice), Somerset (twice), Warwickshire, Worcestershire (twice), Yorkshire.*

### Batting Averages

| | *I* | *NO* | *R* | *HI* | *Avge* |
|---|---|---|---|---|---|
| J. A. Hopkins | 5 | 0 | 345 | 140 | 86.25 |
| J. Derrick | 5 | 1 | 207 | 95 | 51.75 |
| A. L. Jones | 4 | 0 | 178 | 80 | 44.50 |
| M. P. Maynard | 20 | 2 | 756 | 83 | 42.00 |
| S. P. James | 10 | 3 | 246 | 70 | 35.14 |
| A. Jones | 7 | 2 | 175 | 48 | 35.00 |
| P. A. Cottey | 21 | 7 | 469 | 81 | 33.50 |
| C. M. Elward | 12 | 2 | 317 | 76 | 31.70 |
| S. W. Maddock | 5 | 2 | 90 | 42 | 30.00 |
| H. Morris | 4 | 0 | 117 | 70 | 29.25 |
| I. Smith | 18 | 2 | 409 | 59 | 25.56 |
| M. J. Cann | 18 | 2 | 350 | 56 | 21.87 |
| M. R. Price | 9 | 3 | 118 | 38 | 19.66 |
| †M. L. Roberts | 15 | 5 | 187 | 50 | 18.70 |
| S. P. Henderson | 6 | 0 | 52 | 20 | 8.66 |
| S. R. James | 5 | 0 | 40 | 19 | 8.00 |
| P. D. North | 7 | 2 | 54 | 22 | 7.71 |

Also batted: S. Dean 40, 0.

### Bowling Averages

| | *O* | *M* | *R* | *W* | *Avge* |
|---|---|---|---|---|---|
| P. D. North | 267.1 | 79 | 753 | 32 | 23.53 |
| S. J. Malone | 166 | 42 | 434 | 16 | 27.12 |
| M. J. Cann | 304 | 82 | 883 | 32 | 27.59 |
| S. L. Watkin | 213.5 | 49 | 582 | 16 | 36.37 |
| M. P. Maynard | 43 | 5 | 160 | 4 | 40.00 |
| I. Smith | 182 | 38 | 634 | 14 | 45.28 |
| L. L. McFarlane | 109 | 27 | 390 | 8 | 48.75 |
| M. R. Price | 130 | 33 | 399 | 5 | 79.80 |

Also bowled: J. Davidson 17–4–34–3; J. Derrick 37–13–86–3; S. Merricks 19–6–36–3; H. Rogers 39–9–131–1; D. R. Williams 37–3–169–2.

## GLOUCESTERSHIRE SECOND ELEVEN

*Matches 9: Lost – Essex, Somerset, Warwickshire, Worcestershire. Drawn – Glamorgan (twice), Hampshire, Somerset, Worcestershire.*

### Batting Averages

| | *M* | *I* | *NO* | *R* | *HI* | *Avge* |
|---|---|---|---|---|---|---|
| I. R. Payne | 5 | 8 | 1 | 270 | 70 | 38.47 |
| R. T. Evans | 5 | 9 | 1 | 263 | 85* | 32.87 |
| A. J. Wright | 5 | 10 | 0 | 321 | 108 | 32.10 |
| R. G. P. Ellis | 7 | 12 | 0 | 283 | 87 | 23.58 |

| | M | I | NO | R | HI | Avge |
|---|---|---|---|---|---|---|
| P. G. P. Roebuck | 3 | 6 | 1 | 104 | 43 | 20.80 |
| E. J. Cunningham | 6 | 11 | 0 | 215 | 95 | 19.54 |
| R. Edwards | 2 | 3 | 0 | 57 | 35 | 19.00 |
| L. K. Smith | 3 | 5 | 0 | 79 | 30 | 15.80 |
| J. N. Shepherd | 7 | 10 | 1 | 136 | 52 | 15.11 |
| I. P. C. Blakemore | 2 | 3 | 0 | 41 | 22 | 13.66 |
| P. M. Vincent | 2 | 3 | 0 | 40 | 30 | 13.33 |
| G. E. Sainsbury | 7 | 11 | 4 | 89 | 19* | 12.71 |
| W. M. Smith | 5 | 9 | 0 | 92 | 28 | 10.22 |
| P. H. Twizell | 9 | 13 | 2 | 102 | 39* | 9.27 |
| A. J. Brassington | 6 | 8 | 1 | 55 | 14* | 7.85 |
| D. A. Burrows | 9 | 10 | 3 | 36 | 8* | 5.14 |
| D. J. Taylor | 2 | 4 | 0 | 15 | 8 | 3.75 |

Played in two matches: L. M. Roll 7, 0; J. A. Smith 0*, 16*, 6*, 9*. Played in one match: B. J. Bridle 18; M. Frost 0, 0*; R. C. Gloster 11; W. Johnson 9, 0; J. W. Lloyds 4; J. R. Lumley 8; S. Murphy 7; P. W. Romaines 16; D. J. Russell 6, 0*; N. Trestrail 17.

## Bowling Averages

| | O | M | R | W | Avge |
|---|---|---|---|---|---|
| G. E. Sainsbury | 144.5 | 43 | 344 | 23 | 14.95 |
| I. R. Payne | 72 | 20 | 180 | 11 | 16.36 |
| J. W. Lloyds | 26.2 | 8 | 81 | 4 | 20.25 |
| J. N. Shepherd | 66 | 18 | 151 | 7 | 21.57 |
| P. H. Twizell | 128 | 29 | 344 | 12 | 28.66 |
| W. M. Smith | 62 | 18 | 140 | 4 | 35.00 |
| I. P. C. Blakemore | 38.1 | 2 | 144 | 4 | 36.00 |
| D. A. Burrows | 118.4 | 10 | 435 | 11 | 39.54 |
| E. J. Cunningham | 99 | 24 | 245 | 6 | 40.83 |

Also bowled: M. Frost 18–2–75–3; S. Murphy 23–9–54–3; L. M. Roll 15–6–26–0; J. A. Smith 14–4–51–1; D. J. Taylor 53–20–133–1.

# HAMPSHIRE SECOND ELEVEN

*Matches 12: Won – Somerset. Lost – Middlesex, Surrey (twice), Sussex. Drawn – Essex, Gloucestershire, Kent (twice), Middlesex, Somerset, Sussex.*

## Batting Averages

| | M | I | NO | R | HI | Avge |
|---|---|---|---|---|---|---|
| D. R. Turner | 6 | 11 | 0 | 591 | 173 | 53.72 |
| *J. J. E. Hardy | 5 | 9 | 0 | 461 | 102 | 51.22 |
| N. G. Cowley | 4 | 7 | 1 | 235 | 73* | 39.16 |
| M. E. O'Connor | 9 | 12 | 5 | 235 | 92* | 33.57 |
| K. D. James | 6 | 9 | 3 | 189 | 88 | 31.50 |
| T. C. Middleton | 12 | 21 | 2 | 588 | 125 | 30.94 |
| R. J. Maru | 4 | 5 | 1 | 109 | 97* | 27.25 |
| R. J. Scott | 9 | 15 | 1 | 333 | 92 | 23.78 |
| R. C. W. Mason | 8 | 12 | 3 | 211 | 83* | 23.44 |
| †C. F. E. Goldie | 12 | 14 | 3 | 233 | 43 | 21.18 |
| C. A. Connor | 4 | 5 | 3 | 42 | 17* | 21.00 |
| P. J. Bakker | 12 | 8 | 5 | 53 | 31 | 17.66 |
| I. J. Chivers | 11 | 12 | 1 | 152 | 39 | 13.81 |
| G. N. Harrison | 4 | 4 | 1 | 33 | 16 | 11.00 |
| D. J. Hacker | 11 | 18 | 0 | 189 | 35 | 10.50 |
| S. J. W. Andrew | 8 | 7 | 1 | 62 | 23 | 10.33 |
| L. K. Hayes-Rosario | 2 | 3 | 0 | 23 | 13 | 7.66 |

Played in one match: A. N. Aymes 53*, 18; J. R. Ayling 10*, 7; J. K. Barrow 17; R. R. Savage 6; R. K. McGlashan did not bat.

## Bowling Averages

| | *O* | *M* | *R* | *W* | *Avge* |
|---|---|---|---|---|---|
| S. J. W. Andrew | 249.4 | 46 | 790 | 35 | 22.57 |
| K. D. James | 150.3 | 45 | 382 | 15 | 25.46 |
| R. J. Maru | 107.1 | 22 | 318 | 11 | 28.90 |
| G. N. Harrison | 45 | 13 | 126 | 4 | 31.50 |
| I. J. Chivers | 220.4 | 48 | 755 | 23 | 32.82 |
| P. J. Bakker | 336.1 | 75 | 1,080 | 27 | 40.00 |
| N. G. Cowley | 137.4 | 56 | 282 | 7 | 40.28 |
| C. A. Connor | 136 | 28 | 408 | 9 | 45.33 |

Also bowled: R. K. McGlashan 8–5–8–3; R. J. Scott 23–5–70–2; D. R. Turner 1–0–4–0; T. C. Middleton 7.2–4–30–0; J. R. Ayling 6–1–17–0; J. K. Barrow 4–0–19–0; R. C. W. Mason 9–2–29–0.

# KENT SECOND ELEVEN

*Matches 15: Won – Glamorgan, Middlesex. Lost – Lancashire, Surrey, Sussex. Drawn – Essex (twice), Hampshire (twice), Lancashire, Middlesex, Surrey, Sussex, Yorkshire (twice).*

## Batting Averages

| | *M* | *I* | *NO* | *R* | *HI* | *Avge* |
|---|---|---|---|---|---|---|
| N. R. Taylor | 8 | 14 | 2 | 755 | 139* | 62.91 |
| †S. N. V. Waterton | 14 | 23 | 8 | 898 | 143* | 59.86 |
| *G. R. Cowdrey | 15 | 26 | 2 | 1,300 | 255 | 54.16 |
| C. Penn | 7 | 9 | 2 | 212 | 54 | 30.28 |
| L. Potter | 9 | 15 | 1 | 410 | 103* | 29.28 |
| S. C. Goldsmith | 14 | 22 | 2 | 525 | 92 | 26.25 |
| †S. A. Marsh | 14 | 22 | 1 | 399 | 52 | 19.00 |
| K. D. Masters | 13 | 9 | 5 | 74 | 23 | 18.50 |
| R. P. Davis | 11 | 11 | 4 | 125 | 30* | 17.85 |
| D. J. M. Kelleher | 14 | 19 | 7 | 195 | 54* | 16.25 |
| T. Ward | 5 | 9 | 2 | 113 | 36 | 16.14 |
| D. G. Aslett | 4 | 6 | 0 | 82 | 19 | 13.66 |
| L. J. Wood | 15 | 15 | 5 | 93 | 24* | 9.30 |

Also batted: G. R. Dilley 12; A. Duncan 4; R. M. Ellison 70, 2; J. Hinks 46, 0; A. P. Igglesden 1, 1, 1*, 0, 0, 0; G. W. Johnson 98, 50, 40; R. Pepper 27, 12, 4, 4; S. Porteous 6; D. Sabine 6, 0, 28; R. Short 21, 90; P. Steinhobel 26.

## Bowling Averages

| | *O* | *M* | *R* | *W* | *Avge* |
|---|---|---|---|---|---|
| R. P. Davis | 216.5 | 65 | 616 | 27 | 22.81 |
| C. Penn | 182.5 | 40 | 490 | 21 | 23.33 |
| A. P. Igglesden | 176.3 | 35 | 575 | 21 | 27.38 |
| L. Potter | 135.5 | 27 | 423 | 15 | 28.20 |
| L. J. Wood | 439.1 | 125 | 1,266 | 42 | 30.14 |
| K. D. Masters | 333 | 63 | 1,152 | 33 | 34.90 |
| D. J. M. Kelleher | 319.5 | 63 | 1,166 | 26 | 44.84 |

Also bowled: D. G. Aslett 1–0–5–0; G. R. Cowdrey 19.4–3–73–3; G. R. Dilley 20–6–34–2; A. Duncan 10–3–19–0; R. M. Ellison 27–9–72–2; S. C. Goldsmith 2–0–15–0; G. W. Johnson 24–5–83–1; D. Sabine 5–0–19–0; R. Short 10–1–36–0; N. R. Taylor 31–7–89–3.

## LANCASHIRE SECOND ELEVEN

*Matches 16: Won – Kent, Northamptonshire, Warwickshire, Yorkshire. Lost – Glamorgan, Leicestershire, Nottinghamshire. Drawn – Derbyshire (twice), Kent, Leicestershire, Northamptonshire, Nottinghamshire, Somerset, Warwickshire, Yorkshire. Abandoned – Surrey.*

### Batting Averages

| | *M* | *I* | *NO* | *R* | *HI* | *Avge* |
|---|---|---|---|---|---|---|
| B. P. Patterson | 4 | 4 | 3 | 50 | 37* | 50.00 |
| N. A. Bradshaw | 2 | 3 | 1 | 85 | 60* | 42.50 |
| M. R. Chadwick | 13 | 22 | 2 | 839 | 173* | 41.95 |
| S. T. Jefferies | 12 | 17 | 4 | 504 | 127 | 38.76 |
| G. Fowler | 3 | 4 | 0 | 125 | 71 | 31.25 |
| R. G. Watson | 12 | 18 | 3 | 464 | 89 | 30.93 |
| D. W. Varey | 3 | 4 | 0 | 119 | 58 | 29.75 |
| D. J. Makinson | 3 | 5 | 0 | 136 | 85 | 27.20 |
| A. N. Hayhurst | 15 | 22 | 1 | 549 | 120 | 26.14 |
| K. A. Hayes | 13 | 21 | 0 | 531 | 78 | 25.28 |
| †C. Maynard | 2 | 3 | 0 | 71 | 39 | 23.66 |
| *H. Pilling | 10 | 10 | 3 | 165 | 46 | 23.57 |
| M. Watkinson | 3 | 4 | 0 | 91 | 35 | 22.75 |
| †J. Stanworth | 14 | 18 | 3 | 340 | 80 | 22.66 |
| S. P. Titchard | 2 | 3 | 1 | 44 | 31 | 22.00 |
| J. A. Ormrod | 7 | 13 | 2 | 237 | 45* | 21.54 |
| M. A. Atherton | 2 | 3 | 0 | 58 | 47 | 19.33 |
| I. Folley | 5 | 8 | 1 | 126 | 39 | 18.00 |
| S. J. O'Shaughnessy | 7 | 10 | 0 | 172 | 58 | 17.20 |
| S. Henriksen | 11 | 13 | 6 | 118 | 47 | 16.85 |
| D. P. Hughes | 8 | 13 | 0 | 192 | 62 | 14.76 |
| I. C. Davidson | 12 | 13 | 4 | 86 | 26 | 9.55 |
| A. J. Murphy | 11 | 10 | 5 | 11 | 9* | 2.20 |

Played in four matches: G. J. Speak 0. Played in one match: J. Abrahams 4, 86; G. N. Hodgson 22, 13; G. Lloyd 3, 0; C. Smith 26; M. Wakefield 1*; T. Foley, †J. Macaulay, S. J. L. Merricks and D. Page did not bat.

### Bowling Averages

| | *O* | *M* | *R* | *W* | *Avge* |
|---|---|---|---|---|---|
| J. Abrahams | 6 | 4 | 9 | 4 | 2.25 |
| I. Folley | 158 | 63 | 296 | 15 | 19.73 |
| D. J. Makinson | 102.4 | 34 | 221 | 11 | 20.09 |
| M. Watkinson | 78 | 18 | 201 | 10 | 20.10 |
| D. P. Hughes | 140.4 | 50 | 328 | 16 | 20.50 |
| A. J. Murphy | 303.2 | 67 | 869 | 38 | 22.86 |
| S. T. Jefferies | 308.3 | 62 | 929 | 39 | 23.82 |
| B. P. Patterson | 113 | 25 | 324 | 13 | 24.92 |
| A. N. Hayhurst | 150 | 28 | 424 | 17 | 24.94 |
| S. Henriksen | 230.5 | 54 | 672 | 25 | 26.88 |
| G. J. Speak | 32 | 5 | 137 | 4 | 34.25 |
| I. C. Davidson | 246.3 | 62 | 686 | 20 | 34.30 |
| S. J. O'Shaughnessy | 75.2 | 9 | 247 | 7 | 35.28 |

Also bowled: M. A. Atherton 8–3–16–2; M. R. Chadwick 4–1–18–0; K. A. Hayes 12–4–27–1; S. J. L. Merricks 4–0–20–1; D. Page 9–1–24–1; S. P. Titchard 2–0–16–0; M. Wakefield 23–7–64–2.

## LEICESTERSHIRE SECOND ELEVEN

*Matches 14: Won – Lancashire, Northamptonshire. Lost – Nottinghamshire, Worcestershire. Drawn – Derbyshire (twice), Lancashire, Middlesex, Northamptonshire, Nottinghamshire, Surrey, Warwickshire, Worcestershire (twice).*

### Batting Averages

| | *M* | *I* | *NO* | *R* | *HI* | *Avge* |
|---|---|---|---|---|---|---|
| T. J. Boon | 5 | 7 | 1 | 363 | 125 | 60.50 |
| P. D. Bowler | 5 | 4 | 1 | 161 | 60 | 53.66 |
| G. A. Bishop | 11 | 17 | 0 | 909 | 109 | 53.47 |
| R. A. Cobb | 6 | 9 | 0 | 417 | 112 | 46.33 |
| M. Blackett | 9 | 17 | 1 | 427 | 92 | 26.68 |
| D. J. Billington | 12 | 13 | 1 | 319 | 92 | 26.58 |
| N. G. B. Cook | 4 | 5 | 1 | 100 | 27 | 25.00 |
| J. P. Addison | 13 | 19 | 1 | 339 | 64 | 18.83 |
| †P. Whitticase | 14 | 19 | 6 | 190 | 35* | 14.61 |
| P. A. J. De Freitas | 12 | 16 | 1 | 185 | 52 | 12.33 |
| A. J. Dutton | 5 | 7 | 0 | 75 | 34 | 10.71 |
| J. P. Wright | 8 | 11 | 0 | 109 | 26 | 9.90 |
| K. Higgs | 10 | 10 | 3 | 61 | 16 | 8.71 |
| L. Tennant | 13 | 13 | 5 | 56 | 23 | 7.00 |
| G. J. F. Ferris | 7 | 10 | 3 | 40 | 17 | 5.71 |

Also batted: J. P. Agnew 6, 0*; W. K. Benjamin 3, 4*, 21; N. E. Briers 48, 5; S. T. Crawley 45, 9; K. N. Foyle 11, 9; G. A. R. Harris 0, 0; P. Murphy 0; G. J. Parsons 5, 1, 70; R. V. Patel 24, M. J. Robinson 13, 31; O. P. J. Stephenson 0*; L. B. Taylor 1*, 23*, 17; M. Turner 1; M. Whitmore 7, 5.

### Bowling Averages

| | *O* | *M* | *R* | *W* | *Avge* |
|---|---|---|---|---|---|
| L. B. Taylor | 107 | 28 | 261 | 14 | 18.64 |
| G. J. F. Ferris | 148.5 | 29 | 430 | 22 | 19.54 |
| P. A. J. De Freitas | 392.4 | 101 | 957 | 44 | 21.75 |
| J. P. Agnew | 37 | 8 | 89 | 4 | 22.25 |
| W. K. Benjamin | 74.3 | 20 | 160 | 7 | 22.85 |
| K. Higgs | 130.3 | 27 | 262 | 11 | 23.81 |
| N. G. B. Cook | 138.4 | 56 | 286 | 9 | 31.77 |
| G. A. R. Harris | 55.4 | 10 | 170 | 5 | 34.00 |
| A. J. Dutton | 81 | 20 | 205 | 6 | 34.16 |
| J. P. Addison | 145 | 38 | 437 | 11 | 39.72 |
| L. Tennant | 203.2 | 31 | 734 | 14 | 52.42 |

Also bowled: M. Blackett 2–0–6–0; P. D. Bowler 68–13–208–1; N. E. Briers 2–0–16–0; S. T. Crawley 21.3–5–70–2; K. P. Higgs 20–6–49–1; P. Murphy 4–0–16–0; G. J. Parsons 58–13–193–3; R. V. Patel 2–0–18–0; P. J. Stephenson 21–4–51–1; P. Whitticase 2–2–0–0; J. P. Wright 15–5–32–2.

## MIDDLESEX SECOND ELEVEN

*Matches 14: Won – Essex (twice), Hampshire, Surrey, Sussex. Lost – Kent, Warwickshire. Drawn – Hampshire, Kent, Leicestershire, Northamptonshire, Surrey, Sussex, Warwickshire.*

## Batting Averages

| | *M* | *I* | *NO* | *R* | *HI* | *Avge* |
|---|---|---|---|---|---|---|
| *†K. R. Brown | 10 | 16 | 1 | 828 | 193 | 55.20 |
| J. D. Cullinan | 3 | 4 | 0 | 208 | 123 | 52.00 |
| J. A. Grimble | 2 | 3 | 2 | 49 | 30* | 49.00 |
| K. P. Tomlins | 5 | 8 | 1 | 284 | 112 | 40.57 |
| A. J. T. Miller | 7 | 11 | 2 | 365 | 115 | 40.55 |
| A. J. Moulding | 2 | 3 | 0 | 108 | 55 | 36.00 |
| S. P. Hughes | 6 | 7 | 3 | 133 | 58* | 33.25 |
| A. R. Harwood | 9 | 17 | 2 | 488 | 104 | 32.53 |
| G. D. Rose | 14 | 21 | 5 | 518 | 81 | 32.37 |
| J. F. Sykes | 10 | 16 | 2 | 344 | 67 | 24.57 |
| †C. P. Metson | 5 | 7 | 2 | 120 | 32 | 24.00 |
| N. R. C. McLaurin | 12 | 18 | 0 | 420 | 67 | 23.33 |
| C. K. Brown | 13 | 21 | 1 | 446 | 81 | 22.30 |
| G. W. Bean | 3 | 4 | 1 | 65 | 46* | 21.66 |
| P. C. R. Tufnell | 13 | 11 | 8 | 64 | 19* | 21.33 |
| D. J. Fell | 2 | 3 | 0 | 53 | 36 | 17.66 |
| D. G. Cummins | 3 | 4 | 0 | 70 | 38 | 17.50 |
| J. D. Carr | 5 | 6 | 0 | 102 | 54 | 17.00 |
| N. F. Williams | 2 | 4 | 1 | 50 | 35 | 16.66 |
| A. R. C. Fraser | 12 | 13 | 4 | 120 | 36 | 13.33 |
| M. A. Roseberry | 6 | 10 | 0 | 130 | 24 | 13.00 |

Played in two matches: N. F. Sargent 2. Played in one match: F. F. De Freitas 5, 0*; D. J. Foster 14; A. G. J. Fraser 2; S. J. Priscott 1*; G. C. Rolfe 9, 0; A. J. Smales 0, 0; C. J. Stockdale 25, 0; T. Rajapaksa did not bat.

## Bowling Averages

| | *O* | *M* | *R* | *W* | *Avge* |
|---|---|---|---|---|---|
| J. A. Grimble | 46.1 | 12 | 131 | 9 | 14.55 |
| N. F. Williams | 79.1 | 16 | 197 | 12 | 16.41 |
| S. P. Hughes | 127.1 | 30 | 319 | 16 | 19.93 |
| J. D. Carr | 84.3 | 32 | 248 | 12 | 20.66 |
| A. R. C. Fraser | 383.5 | 96 | 940 | 44 | 21.36 |
| G. D. Rose | 285.3 | 65 | 785 | 30 | 26.16 |
| P. C. R. Tufnell | 473 | 138 | 1,244 | 47 | 26.46 |
| J. F. Sykes | 230 | 63 | 587 | 20 | 29.35 |

Also bowled: G. K. Brown 14–2–35–1; K. R. Brown 2–0–11–0; A. G. J. Fraser 17–4–63–1; F. F. De Freitas 9–1–26–1; A. R. Harwood 37–9–84–2; N. R. C. McLaurin 3–0–20–0; S. J. Priscott 3–1–6–1; T. Rajapaksa 6–2–15–0; M. A. Roseberry 3–0–19–0; A. J. Smales 2–1–2–1.

# NORTHAMPTONSHIRE SECOND ELEVEN

*Matches 13: Lost – Essex, Lancashire, Leicestershire. Drawn – Derbyshire (twice), Essex, Lancashire, Leicestershire, Middlesex, Nottinghamshire, Surrey, Yorkshire (twice). Abandoned – Nottinghamshire.*

## Batting Averages

| | *M* | *I* | *NO* | *R* | *HI* | *Avge* |
|---|---|---|---|---|---|---|
| R. M. Carter | 11 | 17 | 7 | 489 | 101* | 48.90 |
| †A. Fordham | 8 | 14 | 0 | 582 | 118 | 41.57 |
| D. J. Wild | 6 | 9 | 0 | 368 | 83 | 40.88 |
| M. Gouldstone | 13 | 23 | 1 | 791 | 132 | 35.95 |
| R. J. Boyd-Moss | 4 | 7 | 1 | 198 | 48 | 33.00 |
| T. Ritchie | 5 | 7 | 1 | 183 | 56 | 30.50 |
| A. Ramage | 8 | 14 | 3 | 249 | 46 | 22.63 |

| | *M* | *I* | *NO* | *R* | *HI* | *Avge* |
|---|---|---|---|---|---|---|
| †D. Ripley | 5 | 8 | 1 | 146 | 46 | 20.85 |
| K. St J. D. Emery | 3 | 5 | 0 | 98 | 59 | 19.60 |
| A. C. Storie | 10 | 17 | 1 | 270 | 51 | 16.87 |
| R. F. Joseph | 5 | 6 | 0 | 83 | 21 | 13.83 |
| T. Scriven | 11 | 18 | 2 | 210 | 34 | 13.12 |
| M. B. H. Wheeler | 8 | 12 | 4 | 67 | 20 | 8.37 |
| †S. Inwood | 3 | 6 | 0 | 49 | 31 | 8.16 |
| G. Smith | 4 | 5 | 2 | 22 | 9* | 7.33 |
| M. Baker | 4 | 6 | 2 | 26 | 8 | 6.50 |
| J. Griffiths | 5 | 6 | 1 | 23 | 12 | 4.60 |
| M. G. Beeby | 6 | 6 | 2 | 16 | 11 | 4.00 |
| R. Tredwell | 6 | 8 | 2 | 13 | 10* | 2.16 |

Also batted: R. J. Bailey 21; †D. Borthwick 6, 7, 0, 20; A. Buzza 0, 0; D. J. Capel 39, 42, 30, 38; †M. Humphries 10, 4; I. Hutchinson 22, 54*; W. Law 7, 0; N. Lindsay 0, 1, 0, 2; A. Penberthy 11, 12; I. Reynolds 34, 2; †G. Sharp 1, 24; A. Walker 0, 17, 7, 2.

## Bowling Averages

| | *O* | *M* | *R* | *W* | *Avge* |
|---|---|---|---|---|---|
| R. M. Carter | 67 | 18 | 166 | 9 | 18.44 |
| G. Smith | 51.5 | 13 | 119 | 6 | 19.83 |
| R. F. Joseph | 113 | 27 | 383 | 19 | 20.15 |
| M. Baker | 41.3 | 7 | 114 | 5 | 22.80 |
| R. Tredwell | 92.4 | 25 | 246 | 10 | 24.60 |
| D. J. Wild | 73 | 17 | 203 | 8 | 25.37 |
| M. B. H. Wheeler | 203.3 | 46 | 637 | 24 | 26.54 |
| A. Walker | 72.2 | 28 | 137 | 5 | 27.40 |
| J. Griffiths | 131.1 | 40 | 304 | 11 | 27.63 |
| N. Lindsay | 51.2 | 12 | 142 | 5 | 28.40 |
| A. Ramage | 132.3 | 21 | 459 | 16 | 28.68 |
| T. Scriven | 116.4 | 33 | 323 | 7 | 46.14 |
| M. G. Beeby | 80 | 11 | 289 | 3 | 96.33 |

Also bowled: R. J. Bailey 4–1–20–0; R. J. Boyd-Moss 37–8–113–2; A. Buzza 8–3–17–0; D. J. Capel 15–3–68–0; K. St J. D. Emery 26–0–157–1; A. C. Storie 13–3–47–0.

# NOTTINGHAMSHIRE SECOND ELEVEN

*Matches 15: Won – Derbyshire* (*twice*), *Essex, Lancashire, Leicestershire, Yorkshire* (*twice*). *Lost – Glamorgan, Sussex. Drawn – Glamorgan, Lancashire, Leicestershire, Northamptonshire, Warwickshire* (*twice*). *Abandoned – Northamptonshire.*

## Batting Averages

| | *M* | *I* | *NO* | *R* | *HI* | *Avge* |
|---|---|---|---|---|---|---|
| M. Newell | 13 | 21 | 1 | 879 | 111 | 43.95 |
| D. J. R. Martindale | 12 | 19 | 2 | 703 | 108 | 41.35 |
| B. A. Courtice | 11 | 19 | 1 | 724 | 138 | 40.22 |
| C. D. Fraser-Darling | 13 | 20 | 5 | 399 | 70 | 26.60 |
| R. J. Evans | 16 | 27 | 2 | 647 | 111 | 25.88 |
| B. Hassan | 4 | 6 | 0 | 145 | 58 | 24.16 |
| †C. W. Scott | 14 | 20 | 2 | 400 | 57 | 22.22 |
| R. A. Pick | 8 | 12 | 3 | 196 | 44* | 21.77 |
| H. A. Page | 2 | 3 | 0 | 53 | 39 | 17.66 |
| D. J. Halliday | 3 | 2 | 0 | 35 | 34 | 17.50 |
| K. P. Evans | 12 | 18 | 1 | 271 | 54 | 15.94 |
| M. K. Bore | 14 | 20 | 6 | 214 | 30 | 15.28 |
| J. A. Afford | 14 | 16 | 8 | 97 | 27 | 12.12 |
| J. C. Bacon | 3 | 3 | 0 | 28 | 21 | 9.33 |

| | M | I | NO | R | HI | Avge |
|---|---|---|---|---|---|---|
| J. D. Birch | 3 | 6 | 0 | 44 | 24 | 7.33 |
| B. Pollard | 2 | 4 | 0 | 28 | 12 | 7.00 |
| D. Storer | 2 | 4 | 2 | 13 | 7* | 6.50 |
| D. J. Millns | 14 | 17 | 3 | 85 | 22* | 6.07 |
| P. M. Such | 6 | 6 | 2 | 16 | 7 | 4.00 |

Played in two matches: P. B. Wormald 12, 6. Played in one match: M. R. Dickinson 16, 11; A. D. H. Grimes 5, 0; D. G. Harding 7, 2; E. E. Hemmings 11*, 0; S. Khan 3; S. A. J. Kippax 4; R. S. M. Morris 6, 7; K. Saxelby 35, 22.

## Bowling Averages

| | O | M | R | W | Avge |
|---|---|---|---|---|---|
| E. E. Hemmings | 57.1 | 28 | 71 | 10 | 7.10 |
| P. M. Such | 216.3 | 88 | 417 | 26 | 16.03 |
| M. K. Bore | 291.3 | 118 | 589 | 35 | 16.82 |
| H. A. Page | 64.2 | 12 | 198 | 11 | 18.00 |
| J. A. Afford | 388.1 | 118 | 976 | 45 | 21.68 |
| C. D. Fraser-Darling | 223.2 | 57 | 562 | 25 | 22.48 |
| K. P. Evans | 135 | 38 | 341 | 12 | 28.41 |
| R. A. Pick | 126 | 30 | 314 | 11 | 28.54 |
| P. B. Wormald | 42.3 | 6 | 149 | 5 | 29.80 |
| D. J. Millns | 179 | 30 | 656 | 17 | 38.58 |

Also bowled: J. C. Bacon 18–8–37–3; R. J. Evans 9–4–20–0; A. D. H. Grimes 4–0–11–0; D. J. Halliday 10–2–26–0; D. G. Harding 10–4–25–1; S. Khan 2–0–14–0; S. A. J. Kippax 2–0–23–0; K. Saxelby 17.2–7–27–3; D. Storer 16–3–55–1.

# SOMERSET SECOND ELEVEN

*Matches 11: Won – Gloucestershire. Lost – Hampshire, Warwickshire. Drawn – Glamorgan (twice), Gloucestershire, Hampshire, Lancashire, Warwickshire, Worcestershire (twice).*

## Batting Averages

| | M | I | NO | R | HI | Avge |
|---|---|---|---|---|---|---|
| M. D. Crowe | 2 | 3 | 0 | 326 | 150 | 108.66 |
| J. G. Wyatt | 3 | 5 | 0 | 364 | 141 | 72.80 |
| S. A. R. Ferguson | 7 | 11 | 5 | 436 | 153* | 72.66 |
| R. E. Hayward | 4 | 6 | 1 | 259 | 107 | 51.80 |
| †A. J. H. Dunning | 3 | 4 | 0 | 207 | 134 | 51.75 |
| R. J. Harden | 8 | 12 | 2 | 449 | 133* | 44.90 |
| G. V. Palmer | 6 | 7 | 3 | 177 | 75* | 44.25 |
| P. A. C. Bail | 9 | 14 | 0 | 513 | 119 | 36.64 |
| A. P. Jones | 8 | 8 | 2 | 173 | 74 | 28.83 |
| S. Larder | 3 | 5 | 0 | 140 | 92 | 28.00 |
| S. J. Fitchett | 5 | 7 | 0 | 169 | 55 | 24.14 |
| †R. L. Ollis | 5 | 7 | 0 | 169 | 92 | 24.14 |
| M. D. Harman | 5 | 7 | 4 | 57 | 28* | 19.00 |
| K. S. Murray | 4 | 7 | 0 | 116 | 37 | 16.57 |
| †J. M. Robinson | 3 | 5 | 2 | 47 | 24 | 15.66 |
| †S. J. Turner | 7 | 5 | 0 | 77 | 16 | 15.40 |
| R. A. Bunting | 2 | 3 | 0 | 24 | 14 | 8.00 |
| R. V. J. Coombs | 3 | 4 | 2 | 9 | 3* | 4.50 |

Played in five matches: S. C. Booth 15, 0. Played in two matches: D. Beal 1*, 2; N. Cowans 17; M. R. Davis 1; N. A. Felton 32, 0; *P. J. Robinson 16, 1. Played in one match: J. C. M. Atkinson 9*; M. Allingham 12*; A. M. Babington 1*, 18; R. J. Bartlett 44, 20; M. A. Cottam 0, 4*; G. H. Dean 11; T. J. Hopper 8, 0; S. Larder 4; S. Massey 8, 38; D. Neville 2, 9*; P. Oldham 18; M. J. Robinson 9, 45; P. M. Roebuck 55; M. S. Turner 4, 61*; N. Waters 14, 13; D. Wood 19, 68; H. Trump did not bat.

## Bowling Averages

| | *O* | *M* | *R* | *W* | *Avge* |
|---|---|---|---|---|---|
| M. R. Davis | 49 | 5 | 133 | 9 | 14.77 |
| S. C. Booth | 193.5 | 79 | 400 | 18 | 22.22 |
| G. V. Palmer | 107 | 29 | 276 | 12 | 23.00 |
| N. Cowans | 59.5 | 6 | 217 | 8 | 27.12 |
| A. P. Jones | 206.5 | 33 | 837 | 24 | 34.87 |
| M. D. Harman | 236 | 69 | 598 | 17 | 35.17 |
| R. V. J. Coombs | 127.3 | 42 | 324 | 9 | 36.00 |
| M. S. Turner | 54.5 | 10 | 163 | 4 | 40.75 |
| G. H. Dean | 23.3 | 3 | 87 | 2 | 43.50 |

Also bowled: M. Allingham 3–0–12–0; J. C. M. Atkinson 16–3–44–0; A. M. Babington 28–3–108–1; P. A. C. Bail 10.1–5–26–0; D. Beal 48–8–191–0; R. A. Bunting 37–4–154–2; M. A. Cottam 18–2–71–1; G. H. Dean 23.3–3–87–2; S. A. R. Ferguson 5–0–18–1; R. J. Harden 23–1–62–3; R. E. Hayward 1–0–1–0; T. J. Hopper 18–4–74–1; S. Massey 10–3–31–0; D. Neville 13–1–50–1; M. J. Robinson 30–4–138–3; P. J. Robinson 27–5–87–0; P. M. Roebuck 8–4–9–0.

# SURREY SECOND ELEVEN

*Matches 13: Won – Essex, Hampshire (twice), Kent, Sussex (twice; points deducted after the win at Hove, Surrey having played an ineligible cricketer). Lost – Middlesex, Yorkshire. Drawn – Essex, Kent, Leicestershire, Middlesex, Northamptonshire. Abandoned – Lancashire, Yorkshire.*

## Batting Averages

| | *M* | *I* | *NO* | *R* | *HI* | *Avge* |
|---|---|---|---|---|---|---|
| C. K. Bullen | 12 | 16 | 3 | 650 | 116 | 50.00 |
| R. J. Doughty | 7 | 11 | 3 | 331 | 56 | 41.37 |
| A. J. Stewart | 3 | 5 | 0 | 187 | 62 | 37.40 |
| N. J. Falkner | 13 | 22 | 4 | 669 | 132 | 37.16 |
| †Alec G. Davies | 7 | 8 | 0 | 273 | 125 | 34.12 |
| Zahid Sadiq | 11 | 17 | 2 | 477 | 108 | 31.80 |
| R. I. Ali Khan | 4 | 6 | 0 | 183 | 60 | 30.50 |
| D. M. Ward | 13 | 22 | 2 | 570 | 114* | 28.50 |
| N. S. Taylor | 11 | 9 | 3 | 143 | 45 | 23.83 |
| M. A. Feltham | 7 | 9 | 2 | 160 | 32 | 22.85 |
| K. T. Medlycott | 12 | 14 | 2 | 252 | 95 | 21.00 |
| T. D. Topley | 5 | 5 | 2 | 62 | 27* | 20.66 |
| D. B. Pauline | 6 | 11 | 0 | 221 | 61 | 20.09 |
| G. P. Howarth | 6 | 9 | 1 | 150 | 32 | 18.75 |
| P. A. Waterman | 9 | 7 | 4 | 45 | 25 | 15.00 |

Played in two matches: †B. G. Parkinson 11*, 4; N. M. Kendrick did not bat. Played in one match: F. S. Ahangama 11*; †A. N. Aymes 24*, 6; D. Z. Barthley 5; M. P. Bicknell 5; L. K. Hayes-Rosario 18; M. Jean-Jacques 0; M. Malik 3*; G. Monkhouse 3*; †M. R. C. Olley 24*, 1*; D. J. Thomas 21*, 16; P. H. L. Wilson 4, 1*; G. G. Arnold did not bat.

## Bowling Averages

| | *O* | *M* | *R* | *W* | *Avge* |
|---|---|---|---|---|---|
| M. P. Bicknell | 41 | 11 | 98 | 7 | 14.00 |
| R. J. Doughty | 170 | 41 | 501 | 28 | 17.89 |
| M. A. Feltham | 141.2 | 29 | 386 | 18 | 21.44 |
| N. S. Taylor | 297.1 | 48 | 966 | 45 | 21.46 |
| T. D. Topley | 183.3 | 56 | 421 | 18 | 23.38 |
| P. H. L. Wilson | 45.5 | 13 | 145 | 5 | 29.00 |
| P. A. Waterman | 231.5 | 53 | 670 | 22 | 30.45 |
| C. K. Bullen | 181.1 | 56 | 471 | 14 | 33.64 |
| D. B. Pauline | 87 | 20 | 254 | 5 | 50.80 |

Also bowled: F. S. Ahangama 18–3–88–1; G. G. Arnold 17–3–41–3; L. K. Hayes-Rosario 3–1–11–0; G. P. Howarth 2–1–1–0; M. Jean-Jacques 16–2–64–2; N. M. Kendrick 10–1–42–1; M. Malik 4–0–20–0; G. Monkhouse 30–5–76–3; D. J. Thomas 10–3–30–3.

## SUSSEX SECOND ELEVEN

*Matches 12: Won – Essex, Hampshire, Kent, Nottinghamshire. Lost – Essex, Middlesex, Surrey (twice). Drawn – Hampshire, Kent, Middlesex, Warwickshire.*

### Batting Averages

| | *I* | *NO* | *R* | *HI* | *Avge* |
|---|---|---|---|---|---|
| A. P. Wells | 3 | 0 | 211 | 109 | 70.33 |
| N. J. Lenham | 14 | 0 | 566 | 123 | 40.42 |
| D. K. Standing | 21 | 6 | 534 | 75 | 35.60 |
| A. I. C. Dodemaide | 15 | 3 | 406 | 125 | 33.83 |
| I. A. Greig | 9 | 0 | 265 | 48 | 29.44 |
| *C. P. Phillipson | 20 | 4 | 457 | 71* | 28.56 |
| A. C. S. Pigott | 5 | 1 | 110 | 34* | 27.50 |
| M. S. Scott | 22 | 2 | 413 | 55 | 20.65 |
| A. N. Jones | 12 | 2 | 197 | 41* | 19.70 |
| I. Wadey | 4 | 1 | 57 | 31 | 19.00 |
| K. Bauermeister | 5 | 1 | 63 | 31 | 15.75 |
| J. Prentis | 4 | 0 | 59 | 55 | 14.75 |
| †P. Moores | 17 | 2 | 205 | 49 | 13.66 |
| I. C. Waring | 12 | 5 | 93 | 26* | 13.28 |
| J. Roycroft | 4 | 0 | 52 | 44 | 13.00 |
| A. M. Bredin | 12 | 1 | 86 | 28 | 7.81 |
| C. S. Mays | 4 | 0 | 27 | 12 | 6.75 |
| A. M. G. Scott | 3 | 2 | 3 | 3 | 3.00 |

Also batted: P. Boarer 21, D. Briance 11, G. Garton 4, 2; †I. J. Gould 98, 86; J. Hall 0*; S. Leach 0; D. A. Reeve 27*, 11; M. Speight 56, 19*.

### Bowling Averages

| | *O* | *M* | *R* | *W* | *Avge* |
|---|---|---|---|---|---|
| K. Bauermeister | 31.5 | 4 | 115 | 7 | 16.42 |
| A. N. Jones | 181 | 44 | 494 | 27 | 18.29 |
| G. Garton | 23 | 3 | 76 | 4 | 19.00 |
| I. A. Greig | 151 | 44 | 392 | 20 | 19.60 |
| A. C. S. Pigott | 69 | 16 | 207 | 8 | 25.87 |
| I. C. S. Waring | 242 | 34 | 797 | 29 | 27.48 |
| A. M. Bredin | 251.2 | 80 | 701 | 25 | 28.04 |
| A. I. C. Dodemaide | 158 | 23 | 495 | 14 | 35.35 |
| D. K. Standing | 116.1 | 32 | 246 | 6 | 41.00 |

Also bowled: P. Boarer 18.4–4–64–3; C. S. Mays 21–5–76–1; C. P. Phillipson 20–6–62–2; D. A. Reeve 29–12–61–2; A. M. G. Scott 23–7–67–2; A. P. Wells 6–1–68–1.

## WARWICKSHIRE SECOND ELEVEN

*Matches 18: Won – Gloucestershire, Leicestershire, Middlesex, Somerset. Lost – Glamorgan, Lancashire, Yorkshire. Drawn – Glamorgan, Lancashire, Leicestershire, Middlesex, Nottinghamshire (twice), Somerset, Sussex, Worcestershire (twice), Yorkshire.*

### Batting Averages

| | *M* | *I* | *NO* | *R* | *HI* | *Avge* |
|---|---|---|---|---|---|---|
| Asif Din | 13 | 18 | 5 | 904 | 191 | 69.53 |
| A. Moles | 3 | 5 | 2 | 191 | 83 | 63.66 |
| K. D. Smith | 14 | 18 | 2 | 842 | 207* | 52.62 |
| B. M. McMillan | 12 | 14 | 5 | 367 | 79 | 40.77 |
| G. J. Lord | 13 | 19 | 1 | 715 | 163* | 39.72 |
| R. T. Evans | 2 | 4 | 1 | 116 | 74 | 38.66 |
| W. J. P. Matthews | 18 | 27 | 2 | 938 | 115* | 37.52 |
| D. A. Thorne | 7 | 11 | 4 | 257 | 73 | 36.71 |
| C. Lethbridge | 8 | 8 | 3 | 162 | 84* | 32.40 |
| †G. A. Tedstone | 18 | 25 | 5 | 618 | 107 | 30.90 |
| W. Morton | 17 | 14 | 3 | 275 | 59 | 25.00 |
| M. Hussain | 2 | 4 | 0 | 98 | 84 | 24.50 |
| S. Wall | 6 | 5 | 2 | 72 | 33 | 24.00 |
| I. W. E. Stokes | 2 | 4 | 0 | 86 | 29 | 21.50 |
| *R. N. Abberley | 10 | 5 | 1 | 77 | 56 | 19.25 |
| T. Stancombe | 5 | 3 | 1 | 38 | 34 | 19.00 |
| P. Threlfall | 10 | 5 | 2 | 27 | 21 | 9.00 |
| D. S. Hoffman | 9 | 5 | 1 | 19 | 13 | 4.75 |
| A. R. K. Pierson | 4 | 3 | 1 | 8 | 8 | 4.00 |
| T. A. Munton | 15 | 9 | 2 | 17 | 7* | 2.42 |

Played in two matches: W. Hogg 2*, 0*, 0, 0*. Played in one match: G. M. Charlesworth 9, 101*; G. W. Humpage 11; D. K. Page 5; C. Rudd 1; P. A. Smith 83; N. Ashton, D. T. Dismore and S. Monkhouse did not bat.

### Bowling Averages

| | *O* | *M* | *R* | *W* | *Avge* |
|---|---|---|---|---|---|
| A. Moles | 23 | 5 | 69 | 5 | 13.80 |
| A. R. K. Pierson | 132.5 | 45 | 300 | 13 | 23.07 |
| B. M. McMillan | 196.5 | 35 | 583 | 25 | 23.32 |
| G. J. Lord | 86.5 | 23 | 236 | 10 | 23.60 |
| W. Morton | 432.4 | 93 | 1,259 | 52 | 24.21 |
| S. Wall | 114 | 30 | 242 | 9 | 26.88 |
| T. A. Munton | 297.3 | 47 | 904 | 32 | 28.25 |
| Asif Din | 141.4 | 37 | 445 | 11 | 40.45 |
| P. Threlfall | 139.2 | 18 | 531 | 13 | 40.84 |
| C. Lethbridge | 163 | 42 | 430 | 10 | 43.00 |
| D. S. Hoffman | 176 | 41 | 515 | 11 | 46.81 |
| T. Stancombe | 89 | 9 | 353 | 5 | 70.60 |

Also bowled: D. P. Dismore 11–2–28–1; W. Hogg 30–6–68–2; G. W. Humpage 3–0–18–0; W. J. P. Matthews 4.4–0–32–2; S. Monkhouse 8–2–23–0; D. K. Page 22–2–57–3; C. Rudd 12.4–2–53–1; P. A. Smith 26–5–96–1; G. A. Tedstone 1–0–4–0; D. A. Thorne 36–3–106–3.

## WORCESTERSHIRE SECOND ELEVEN

*Matches 11: Won – Glamorgan, Gloucestershire. Lost – Derbyshire. Drawn – Glamorgan, Gloucestershire, Leicestershire (twice), Somerset (twice), Warwickshire (twice).*

### Batting Averages

| | *I* | *NO* | *R* | *HI* | *Avge* |
|---|---|---|---|---|---|
| G. A. Hick | 6 | 2 | 407 | 187 | 101.75 |
| P. Bent | 7 | 3 | 306 | 88 | 76.50 |
| †L. K. Smith | 12 | 0 | 506 | 96 | 42.16 |
| *†D. J. Humphries | 12 | 2 | 359 | 106 | 35.90 |
| D. A. Banks | 10 | 1 | 281 | 83 | 31.22 |
| S. J. S. Kimber | 11 | 3 | 224 | 62 | 28.00 |
| H. V. Patel | 16 | 1 | 368 | 101 | 24.53 |

| | I | NO | R | HI | Avge |
|---|---|---|---|---|---|
| S. M. McEwan | 5 | 2 | 66 | 44 | 22.00 |
| M. Hussain | 5 | 0 | 106 | 42 | 21.20 |
| S. Lampitt | 8 | 2 | 120 | 25 | 20.00 |

Also batted: B. J. Barrett, A. Brewer, R. M. Ellcock, D. Goodall, P. Humphries, J. D. Inchmore, D. Leatherdale, S. Lloyd, I. McLaren, P. J. Newport, E. Nicholson, P. North, J. Pickles, A. P. Pridgeon, D. Richmond, M. G. Scothern, M. Sedgley, J. S. Smith, M. J. Weston, D. Wise, J. Wright.

## Bowling Averages

| | O | M | R | W | Avge |
|---|---|---|---|---|---|
| J. D. Inchmore | 28 | 6 | 59 | 5 | 11.80 |
| M. G. Scothern | 28 | 6 | 78 | 6 | 13.00 |
| M. Boocock | 39 | 12 | 104 | 5 | 20.80 |
| M. J. Weston | 47 | 13 | 146 | 7 | 20.85 |
| S. Lampitt | 74.2 | 17 | 221 | 10 | 22.10 |
| A. P. Pridgeon | 145.3 | 29 | 448 | 20 | 22.40 |
| B. J. Barrett | 53 | 13 | 147 | 6 | 24.50 |
| S. M. McEwan | 116.2 | 22 | 405 | 15 | 27.00 |
| R. M. Ellcock | 143 | 32 | 497 | 17 | 29.23 |
| S. J. S. Kimber | 156.3 | 30 | 527 | 17 | 31.00 |
| G. A. Hick | 64 | 18 | 157 | 5 | 31.40 |

Also bowled: D. A. Banks, P. Bent, A. Brewer, D. Goodall, D. J. Humphries, M. Hussain, I. McLaren, P. J. Newport, P. North, H. V. Patel, D. Richmond, L. K. Smith, J. Wright.

# YORKSHIRE SECOND ELEVEN

*Matches 14: Won – Derbyshire, Surrey, Warwickshire. Lost – Lancashire, Nottinghamshire (twice). Drawn – Derbyshire, Glamorgan, Kent (twice), Lancashire, Northamptonshire (twice), Warwickshire. Abandoned – Surrey.*

## Batting Averages

| | M | I | NO | R | HI | Avge |
|---|---|---|---|---|---|---|
| C. Shaw | 6 | 7 | 3 | 213 | 86 | 53.25 |
| *C. Johnson | 13 | 17 | 6 | 551 | 126* | 50.09 |
| I. G. Swallow | 7 | 9 | 4 | 250 | 62 | 50.00 |
| P. E. Robinson | 7 | 11 | 1 | 445 | 125 | 44.50 |
| A. A. Metcalfe | 9 | 14 | 1 | 526 | 110 | 40.46 |
| D. Byas | 13 | 20 | 1 | 606 | 111 | 31.89 |
| R. J. Blakey | 9 | 14 | 0 | 380 | 93 | 27.14 |
| C. R. Andrew | 7 | 12 | 2 | 269 | 71 | 26.90 |
| †J. Goldthorp | 6 | 8 | 2 | 154 | 60 | 25.66 |
| †D. N. Pike | 8 | 8 | 3 | 127 | 46 | 25.40 |
| N. G. Nicholson | 5 | 8 | 1 | 174 | 77 | 24.85 |
| A. Bethel | 3 | 4 | 0 | 84 | 68 | 21.00 |
| C. S. Pickles | 7 | 10 | 2 | 142 | 41 | 17.75 |
| P. A. Booth | 12 | 15 | 3 | 203 | 50 | 16.91 |
| J. D. Love | 2 | 4 | 0 | 64 | 35 | 16.00 |
| J. Glendenen | 4 | 8 | 0 | 63 | 23 | 7.87 |
| G. Liley | 3 | 6 | 2 | 17 | 9 | 4.25 |
| S. Oldham | 5 | 4 | 0 | 12 | 9 | 3.00 |

Played in four matches: P. J. Hartley 100*, 0, 13; M. A. Robinson 0, 1, 0*. Played in three matches: P. Adamson 16*. Played in two matches: S. Atkinson 0, 0; S. D. Fletcher 6; G. B. Stevenson 58, 29, 24; A. Sidebottom 17, 43; M. Varley 4; P. Berry did not bat. Played in one match: M. Beardshall 16, 12; S. N. Hartley 13, 68; K. Sharp 53, 39*; R. Thorpe 3, 14; S. Parkinson 3*, 0.

## Bowling Averages

| | *O* | *M* | *R* | *W* | *Avge* |
|---|---|---|---|---|---|
| C. Shaw | 169.3 | 40 | 480 | 20 | 24.00 |
| P. A. Booth | 431.2 | 121 | 1,180 | 43 | 27.44 |
| P. J. Hartley | 115.4 | 22 | 347 | 12 | 28.91 |
| C. S. Pickles | 145.3 | 43 | 429 | 14 | 30.64 |
| S. D. Fletcher | 63 | 11 | 204 | 6 | 34.00 |
| S. Oldham | 114.5 | 37 | 273 | 8 | 34.12 |
| C. R. Andrew | 69 | 15 | 217 | 6 | 36.16 |
| I. G. Swallow | 191.5 | 49 | 568 | 15 | 37.85 |
| M. A. Robinson | 105.4 | 22 | 350 | 7 | 50.00 |

Also bowled: P. Adamson 31–6–107–3; M. Beardshall 22–4–103–1; P. Berry 36–8–140–1; A. Bethel 13–3–39–0; D. Byas 4–1–15–1; G. Liley 89–11–314–3; N. G. Nicholson 3–1–5–0; S. Parkinson 34.2–6–142–1; A. Sidebottom 25.5–3–66–3; G. B. Stevenson 40–13–98–2; R. Thorpe 30–4–125–3.

## SECOND ELEVEN CHAMPIONS

| | | | | | |
|---|---|---|---|---|---|
| 1959 | Gloucestershire | 1968 | Surrey | 1977 | Yorkshire |
| 1960 | Northamptonshire | 1969 | Kent | 1978 | Sussex |
| 1961 | Kent | 1970 | Kent | 1979 | Warwickshire |
| 1962 | Worcestershire | 1971 | Hampshire | 1980 | Glamorgan |
| 1963 | Worcestershire | 1972 | Nottinghamshire | 1981 | Hampshire |
| 1964 | Lancashire | 1973 | Essex | 1982 | Worcestershire |
| 1965 | Glamorgan | 1974 | Middlesex | 1983 | Leicestershire |
| 1966 | Surrey | 1975 | Surrey | 1984 | Yorkshire |
| 1967 | Hampshire | 1976 | Kent | 1985 | Nottinghamshire |

---

## COUNTY CAPS AWARDED IN 1985

| | |
|---|---|
| Derbyshire | I. S. Anderson, R. J. Finney, D. G. Moir. |
| Glamorgan | T. Davies, G. C. Holmes, Younis Ahmed. |
| Gloucestershire | C. W. J. Athey, K. M. Curran, B. F. Davison, D. V. Lawrence, J. W. Lloyds, R. C. Russell, C. A. Walsh. |
| Hampshire | R. A. Smith. |
| Kent | S. G. Hinks. |
| Lancashire | N. H. Fairbrother, S. J. O'Shaughnessy. |
| Northamptonshire | R. J. Bailey. |
| Surrey | A. H. Gray, A. Needham, A. J. Stewart. |
| Sussex | A. M. Green. |
| Worcestershire | D. B. D'Oliveira, N. V. Radford. |

*No caps were awarded by Essex, Leicestershire, Middlesex, Nottinghamshire, Somerset, Warwickshire or Yorkshire.*

# WARWICK UNDER-25 COMPETITION, 1985

**Zone A:** Nottinghamshire again finished top of Zone A by winning four of their six matches. They began in convincing style by defeating Yorkshire by 45 runs and then Derbyshire on faster scoring-rate in a rain-affected match. Their second encounter with Derbyshire was delayed by rain: after Nottinghamshire had batted, Derbyshire were set only 68 to win off 26 overs, which they managed for the loss of three wickets. In their remaining matches Nottinghamshire lost only to Lancashire. Yorkshire and Lancashire were joint runners-up, both winning three and losing three of their matches. Derbyshire won only two. This northern group was the only one that had none of its matches completely abandoned.

**Zone B:** This was the group worst hit by the weather, with one-third of the matches ending without a result. The final placings were not decided until the last match when Middlesex, in second place, needed to beat Leicestershire to finish top. Middlesex were bowled out for 166 in 39.3 overs, and when rain came Leicestershire had been reduced to 81 for nine. Middlesex therefore won on faster scoring-rate. Northamptonshire were the early leaders in the group after beating Leicestershire twice and Essex once. M. Field-Buss (75 and five for 32) steered Essex to victory in their other match against Northamptonshire. Unfortunately, the two matches involving the strongest teams in Zone B, Middlesex and Northamptonshire, were both abandoned. Essex and Leicestershire managed only one win each.

**Zone C:** Kent and Surrey were the front-runners in this group, each occupying first position at various times. Surrey started well by beating Hampshire and Kent convincingly before falling foul of the weather and then losing their return match with Kent. They recovered from this setback to beat Sussex and Hampshire again and to finish their programme with eighteen points out of a possible 24. Kent's only defeat was against Surrey, when they were contained to 205 for seven in their 40 overs, L. Potter making 61. Surrey passed this in the last over for the loss of four wickets (A. J. Stewart 85). Kent never slipped again. They defeated Surrey the next week by nine wickets, then Sussex by seven wickets, Hampshire by four wickets and Sussex again, by 50 runs, in their final match. They thus dropped only four points all season and so won the group. Sussex managed two victories. A poor Hampshire team were the only county in all zones not to gain a single point.

**Zone D:** Warwickshire, winners of Zone D, had their first two matches, against Somerset, abandoned. They then beat Gloucestershire in a high-scoring game. Set to score 223 in their 40 overs, they passed the total for the loss of two wickets in the 36th over with Asif Din 83 not out. In the return match Gloucestershire were dismissed for 83 and comfortably beaten. Perhaps the most exciting match of the whole competition was that between Warwickshire and Worcestershire at Edgbaston. The visitors scored 222 for six in their 40 overs, mainly through a brilliant innings of 142 not out by Graeme Hick. In response the all-round strength of Warwickshire's batting was almost decisive, with the reliable Asif Din making 64 and P. A. Smith 55. At the conclusion of Warwickshire's 40 overs the scores were level and the match tied. Worcestershire and Somerset were joint second with two wins each. Gloucestershire suffered four defeats and won only once.

**Semi-final:** *Warwickshire v Middlesex at Edgbaston, August 11.* Abandoned. Although Middlesex were drawn at home, Lord's was not available for the match. The venues were therefore reversed and the match fell foul of the weather. Since only one day was allocated to the semi-finals, and not a ball could be bowled, the team qualifying for the final had to be decided by the statisticians. The rules stated that the winners should be the team with the higher percentage of wins in the zonal matches, or, if that failed, the higher percentage of away wins. Both teams had won three of their group matches, but Warwickshire, having won more away matches than Middlesex, qualified for the final.

**Semi-final:** *Kent v Nottinghamshire at Maidstone, August 18.* Kent won by 63 runs. Having won the toss and elected to field, Nottinghamshire found some degree of assistance in the Mote pitch. Page ripped through the early Kent batting before Graham Cowdrey played a fine innings of 56. This proved crucial, for Nottinghamshire found runs equally difficult to score. When Masters took three quick wickets in his opening spell, Kent gained the initiative which they never allowed to slip.

## FINAL

## WARWICKSHIRE v KENT

At Edgbaston, August 25. Warwickshire won by 45 runs. Kent won the toss and, with a side weakened by first team calls for the county's match against the Australians, elected to field. Warwickshire's openers, Matthews and Moles, were put under no great pressure by the Kent bowlers on a typical Edgbaston pitch. When Moles fell to Sabine at 34, Asif Din played an innings of high class. Set to score more than five and a half runs an over to win, Kent made a steady start through Pepper and Ward, who put on 86 for the first wicket. When Pepper was out and Waterton settled in, the match was delicately poised. But accurate Warwickshire bowling proved too much for Kent's batsmen and scoring fell below the required rate. When Ward was caught for 68 no other Kent batsman reached double figures.

### Warwickshire

W. J. P. Matthews c Steinhober b Wood 39
A. J. Moles b Sabine . . . . . . . . . . . . . . . . 19
*Asif Din c Pepper b Davis . . . . . . . . . . 75
G. M. Charlesworth c Pepper b Kelleher 16
†G. A. Tedstone c Masters b Sabine . . . 38
B. M. McMillan run out . . . . . . . . . . . . . . 11
W. Morton c Goldsmith b Masters . . . . 2
E. T. Milburn not out . . . . . . . . . . . . . . . 7
A. R. K. Pierson b Masters . . . . . . . . . . 4
T. A. Munton not out . . . . . . . . . . . . . . . 4
B 4, l-b 12, n-b 2 . . . . . . . . . . . 18

1/34 2/118 3/168 (8 wkts, 40 overs) 233
4/194 5/206 6/213
7/219 8/228

T. Stancombe did not bat.

Bowling: Masters 8-0-37-2; Kelleher 8-0-38-1; Sabine 8-0-51-2; Wood 8-0-37-1; Davis 8-0-54-1.

### Kent

R. Pepper c Matthews b Morton . . . . . . 34
T. Ward c Tedstone b Stancombe . . . . . 68
*†S. N. V. Waterton not out . . . . . . . . . 58
P. Steinhober b Morton . . . . . . . . . . . . . 8
S. C. Goldsmith run out . . . . . . . . . . . . . 1
D. Sabine run out . . . . . . . . . . . . . . . . . . 1
V. Wells b McMillan . . . . . . . . . . . . . . . . 4
D. J. M. Kelleher c Tedstone b McMillan 5
R. P. Davis c Asif Din b McMillan . . . 1
L. J. Wood not out . . . . . . . . . . . . . . . . . 2
L-b 5, n-b 1 . . . . . . . . . . . . . . . 6

1/86 2/118 3/135 (8 wkts, 40 overs) 188
4/138 5/141 6/157
7/171 8/173

K. D. Masters did not bat.

Bowling: Munton 8-1-35-0; McMillan 7-2-25-3; Stancombe 8-0-45-1; Pierson 8-1-34-0; Morton 8-0-35-2; Asif Din 1-0-9-0.

Umpires: D. R. Shepherd and K. J. Lyons.

# UAU CHAMPIONSHIP, 1985

For the past twenty years the UAU Championship has been dominated by five universities – Durham, Exeter, Loughborough, Manchester and Southampton. Between them they have taken or shared the title on eighteen separate occasions. In 1985 three of the semi-finalists again came from this élite circle, but it was the outsiders, Birmingham, who went on to win the UAU title for the first time since 1955.

A feature of the 1980s has been the cold and intemperate early-season weather and 1985 was no exception; but by the beginning of June eight universities had reached the knockout stages of the competition. Birmingham began their passage to the final by defeating Aston at West Hills in a game restricted by the weather to 50 overs. Within that allocation Aston managed only 148 for eight, a target passed by Birmingham in the 33rd over for the loss of five wickets. Dave Orr, with an undefeated 54, led the way for Birmingham.

Kent visited Southampton and batted first. Throughout they struggled to make runs and, after 58 overs, were finally dismissed for 114, Gary Pilcher taking four for 35 in eighteen overs. Southampton's early reply was positive, led by Andy Barnes (49), but a mid-order collapse, engineered by Chris Lane (18.5–3–50–5), caused anxiety before Southampton reached 115 in the 52nd over with two wickets remaining.

The semi-final between Birmingham and Southampton was played at Liverpool University on June 18. It was a one-sided and short-lived affair. Losing their first three wickets for 8 runs, Southampton made a poor start and were dismissed shortly after lunch for 119. For Birmingham, Sean Travers took five for 34 in thirteen overs. Southampton's moderate total was passed for the loss of only two wickets, John Burrell (71 not out) and Orr putting on 87 in an unbeaten third-wicket stand.

In the opposite half of the draw Durham met their neighbours, Newcastle, in the quarter-finals. Newcastle chose to bat on a firm, easy-paced pitch, but their final score of 153 for six off 60 overs (Ted Sly 64) was quite inadequate against a batting line-up which earlier in the season had put on more than 400 against them. For Durham, the gentle medium-pace of Graham Charlesworth claimed four for 24 off 23 overs. Led by John Stephenson, whose 84 not out contained eleven 4s, Durham cruised to victory for the loss of two wickets.

Exeter visited Swansea, who had already defeated the 1984 champions, Bristol. But Swansea's challenge was now dashed on a pitch described as "bad" in the captains' report. Batting first Exeter struggled to 148 for nine in their 60 overs, only their captain, Alistair Dunning (64), coping with the conditions. Faced with the spin of Rob Coombs (19.2–14–27–5) and Bill Tebbit (14–2–50–4), Swansea crumbled to 108 all out.

Each year the championship seems to produce one game of outstanding quality. In 1985 it was the semi-final between Durham and Exeter, played at the Firs, Manchester. Overnight rain on an uncovered pitch produced awkward conditions for batting, and the game was dominated by the bowlers as Exeter's spin met Durham's seam attack. Durham, put in to bat, made cautious progress until Philip Fitzherbert's 63 took the score to 121 in the over before lunch. After the interval Durham were pinned down by the flighted left-arm spin of Coombs, but Julian Pettegree (41) and Charlesworth made valuable contributions before Durham's innings closed at 203 in the 59th over.

Exeter's early reply cost them the game. They lost their first three batsmen without a run between them and were always under pressure from an exclusively seam attack well supported by tight fielding. The damage was done by Durham's opening bowlers, John Whitehouse and Andy Forman (28.3–6–73–5). It was an impressive début by Forman, who used his height and strength to extract bounce and movement from the pitch and bowled unchanged throughout the innings. Exeter were dismissed for 162 in the 58th over.

## FINAL

### DURHAM v BIRMINGHAM

At Northern CC, Crosby, June 19. Birmingham won by two wickets. Choosing to bat on an amiable pitch, Durham were 59 after ten overs, Travers having conceded 39 of these in five overs. Ashton checked the flow of runs and gained the valuable wicket of Stephenson, caught sweeping. Fordham continued his onslaught until, at 94, he was caught at deep square leg off Roll's only over of the match. After such a promising start Durham's middle-order batting was undistinguished, and by lunch they had slumped to 131 for six off 38 overs. Pettegree and Charlesworth brought greater respectability to Durham's final total of 216. In reply Birmingham made an uneasy start, losing two early wickets and falling behind the clock. However, Burrell and Orr pushed the score to 89 before, in the final session of the day, Layton, going round the wicket, claimed the wickets of Orr and Crawley in quick succession. Two more wickets then fell to Charlesworth, leaving Birmingham 150 for six with time running out. Parsons then hammered a quick 40 and took the score to 197, only 20 short of victory. Whitehouse now returned to the attack and immediately removed Ashton, but Burrell steered Birmingham to victory with three balls remaining.

## Durham

A. Fordham c Travers b Roll ........ 52
J. P. Stephenson c Parsons b Ashton .. 27
*B. G. Evans c Waterfield b Travers .. 21
P. B. Fitzherbert b Ashton ........... 0
R. C. W. Mason b Travers .......... 13
J. C. C. Pettegree b Travers .......... 43
†C. P. Metson c Salmon b Travers .... 4
G. M. Charlesworth st Waterfield b Ashton. 40
J. N. Whitehouse st Waterfield b Ashton. 3
R. Layton run out .................. 6
A. Forman not out .................. 0
B 1, l-b 2, w 2, n-b 2 ........ 7

1/59 2/94 3/98 4/104 5/123 6/131 7/196 8/207 9/216 (58.2 overs) 216

Bowling: Travers 18–3–85–4; Parsons 11–1–35–0; Ashton 24.2–5–61–4; Roll 1–0–8–1; Crawley 4–0–24–0.

## Birmingham

A. J. Salmon b Whitehouse .......... 2
J. T. Burrell not out ................ 97
L. M. Roll c Charlesworth b Whitehouse 3
D. J. M. Orr c Fordham b Layton .... 28
*S. T. Crawley hit wkt b Layton ...... 1
J. C. America c Fordham b Charlesworth 9
S. F. Travers c Pettegree b Charlesworth. 13
M. J. Parsons b Charlesworth ........ 40
N. K. Ashton b Whitehouse .......... 4
N. W. Leigh not out ................ 1
B 8, l-b 8, w 2, n-b 1 ........ 19

1/4 2/20 3/89 4/91 5/128 6/150 7/197 8/206 (8 wkts, 59.3 overs) 217

†D. C. R. Waterfield did not bat.

Bowling: Whitehouse 11–2–23–3; Forman 9–2–27–0; Layton 17–2–56–2; Mason 3–0–8–0; Charlesworth 17.3–0–69–3; Stephenson 2–0–19–0.

Umpires: Mr Brise and M. A. Maysbury.

## WINNERS

*Since 1960. A full list of previous winners from 1927 onwards may be found on page 819 of* Wisden *1984.*

1960 Loughborough Colleges
1961 Loughborough Colleges
1962 Manchester
1963 Loughborough Colleges
1964 Loughborough Colleges
1965 Hull
1966 Southampton and Newcastle
1967 Manchester
1968 Southampton
1969 Southampton
1970 Southampton
1971 Loughborough Colleges
1972 Durham
1973 Loughborough Colleges and Leicester
1974 Durham
1975 Loughborough Colleges
1976 Loughborough
1977 Durham
1978 Manchester
1979 Manchester
1980 Exeter
1981 Durham
1982 Exeter
1983 Exeter
1984 Bristol
1985 Birmingham

# THE LANCASHIRE LEAGUES, 1985

By CHRIS ASPIN

The high standard of cricket in the Lancashire leagues makes the county side's lack of success in recent years all the more disappointing. It would be possible to list eleven players who would grace the first-class game, but who have been overlooked by Lancashire. There are signs, however, that attitudes are changing.

Haslingden won the Lancashire League for the second time in three years, finishing ten points ahead of the 1984 wooden spoonists, Todmorden, whose greatly improved form also took them to the final of the *Lancashire Evening Telegraph* Cup. (Rawtenstall 187 for eight; Todmorden 153.) Haslingden, who have lost only eight league games in the past three seasons, again owed their superiority to the hostile bowling of Hartley Alleyne and the great strength of their amateur batting. Two of their young players, Ian Austin and John Entwistle, set up a number of records on June 8 when they shared an unbroken stand of 268 for the third wicket against Church. It was the highest partnership for any wicket since the League was formed, the previous best (248) having been jointly held by Eddie Paynter and Des Fothergill (Enfield v Colne, 1949) and Everton Weekes and Stanley Entwistle (Bacup v Colne, 1954). Austin, a nineteen-year-old left-hander, who hopes to make cricket his career, hit seven 6s and seventeen 4s in his 149 not out. Entwistle made 106 not out. The partnership lasted 163 minutes and the last six overs yielded 80 runs. Austin's score and Haslingden's total of 280 for two were both records for the League in limited-overs cricket.

Mudassar Nazar (Burnley) headed the batting averages with 874 runs at 51.41, but the highest aggregate was the 918 accumulated by the Todmorden professional, Darryl Scott from South Australia. He also took 64 wickets at 15.25. Other professionals to impress were another South Australian, David Hookes (Ramsbottom), with 877 runs at 35.08 and the former England opening batsman, David Lloyd (Accrington), with 725 at 32.95. The leading amateurs were Peter Wood (Rawtenstall) with 710 at 39.44, Philip Pickles (Rawtenstall) with 641 at 33.74 and Brian Knowles (Haslingden) with 632 at 35.11. Rawtenstall's West Indian fast bowler, Anthony Merrick, topped the bowling averages with 86 wickets at 11.29, but Alleyne took the most wickets – 95 at 11.84. Burnley's spin bowler, Trevor Jones, took 64 wickets at 12.83 and John Seedle, of East Lancashire, 50 at 12.68.

Officials were happy to see the end of a season which was not only one of the coldest on record – gate receipts were down from £19,750 to £13,417 – but which was also a source of considerable embarrassment when the new rules covering rain-affected matches were first applied. So unclear were the instructions that widely differing interpretations were put on them, giving the League committee no alternative but to order one entire day's programme to be replayed.

Littleborough became champions of the Central Lancashire League for the thirteenth time, thanks largely to their West Indian professional, Ezra Moseley, who worked up great pace and wrecked the opposition batting match after match. In one weekend, he took fourteen wickets for 24 and finished the season with 121 league and cup victims at only 7.85 apiece. Royton were runners-up and the beaten finalists in the Lees Wood Cup. (Royton 77; Oldham 81 for one.)

Two professionals, Robert Haynes (Radcliffe) and Steve Wundke

(Heywood), both scored four centuries and topped 1,000 runs. The only other player to reach 1,000 was the nineteen-year-old Dexter Fitton in his first season as professional for Stockport. Mohsin Khan (Walsden) scored 986 at 49.95 and Basil Abrahams (Castleton Moor) 930 at 40.43. Oldham's Australian amateur, Harvey Jolly, hit 871 runs at 39.59 and Richard Eastwood (Walsden) 729 at 31.69. The highest individual innings of the season was the 156 by the Werneth amateur, Andy Wild, against Castleton Moor.

Moseley and Vanburn Holder were the only players to take more than 100 wickets, Holder finishing with 101 at 12.46. Carl Rackemann (Oldham) took 89 wickets, including six for 48 in the Cup final, at 13.11. There were also outstanding performances by two amateur bowlers: Craig Hopkinson (Royton) with 77 at 8.71, and Mel Whittle (Oldham) with 87 at 12.73.

## MATTHEW BROWN LANCASHIRE LEAGUE

| | *P* | *W* | *L* | *D* | *Pts* | *Professional* | *Runs* | *Avge* | *Wkts* | *Avge* |
|---|---|---|---|---|---|---|---|---|---|---|
| Haslingden | 26 | 19 | 3 | 4 | 86 | H. L. Alleyne | 199 | 14.88 | 95 | 11.84 |
| Todmorden | 26 | 17 | 5 | 4 | 78 | D. B. Scott | 918 | 45.90 | 64 | 15.25 |
| East Lancashire | 26 | 15 | 6 | 5 | 75 | C. D. Mitchley | 427 | 30.50 | 62 | 13.74 |
| Burnley | 26 | 14 | 8 | 4 | 65 | Mudassar Nazar | 874 | 51.41 | 31 | 27.45 |
| Accrington | 26 | 12 | 10 | 4 | 64 | D. Lloyd | 725 | 32.95 | 48 | 13.83 |
| Rawtenstall | 26 | 11 | 9 | 6* | 58 | T. A. Merrick | 153 | 10.85 | 86 | 11.29 |
| Ramsbottom | 26 | 11 | 12 | 3* | 56 | D. W. Hookes | 877 | 35.08 | 47 | 19.32 |
| Rishton | 26 | 9 | 13 | 4 | 45 | M. K. van Vuuren | 535 | 24.32 | 68 | 20.46 |
| Church | 26 | 9 | 14 | 3 | 44 | I. W. Callen | 375 | 22.06 | 51 | 21.70 |
| Nelson | 26 | 9 | 13 | 4 | 44 | T. A. Hunte | 374 | 20.78 | 44 | 18.02 |
| Lowerhouse | 26 | 9 | 14 | 3 | 43 | K. Azad | 537 | 26.85 | 54 | 33.25 |
| Enfield | 26 | 8 | 14 | 4 | 41 | H. A. Page | 344 | 18.11 | 64 | 14.42 |
| Bacup | 26 | 7 | 15 | 4 | 36 | A. L. F. de Mel | 573 | 35.81 | 62 | 14.14 |
| Colne | 26 | 4 | 18 | 4 | 24 | C. R. Norris | 578 | 27.52 | 39 | 21.62 |

* *Includes 2 points for a tie.*

*Note:* One bonus point awarded for bowling out the opposition.

## TSB CENTRAL LANCASHIRE LEAGUE

| | *P* | *W* | *L* | *D* | *Pts* | *Professional* | *Runs* | *Avge* | *Wkts* | *Avge* |
|---|---|---|---|---|---|---|---|---|---|---|
| Littleborough | 30 | 18 | 3 | 9 | 89 | E. A. Moseley | 506 | 33.73 | 121 | 7.85 |
| Royton | 30 | 16 | 8 | 6 | 78 | V. A. Holder | 348 | 14.50 | 101 | 12.46 |
| Oldham | 30 | 16 | 4 | 10 | 75 | C. G. Rackemann | 58 | 9.67 | 89 | 13.11 |
| Heywood | 30 | 15 | 4 | 11 | 70 | S. C. Wundke | 1,039 | 54.68 | 77 | 12.82 |
| Werneth | 30 | 12 | 9 | 9 | 61 | E. L. Reifer | 480 | 20.87 | 72 | 17.08 |
| Rochdale | 30 | 11 | 7 | 12 | 57 | N. A. Phillips | 670 | 27.92 | 85 | 15.58 |
| Walsden | 30 | 12 | 7 | 11 | 57 | Mohsin Khan | 986 | 49.95 | 28 | 24.89 |
| Ashton | 30 | 10 | 11 | 9 | 51 | Madan Lal | 698 | 30.35 | 68 | 14.85 |
| Middleton | 30 | 8 | 12 | 10* | 49 | K. Boden | 728 | 31.65 | 77 | 16.48 |
| Norden | 30 | 9 | 11 | 10 | 48 | Anwar Khan | 342 | 24.43 | 63 | 14.67 |
| Castleton Moor | 30 | 8 | 15 | 7 | 45 | B. Abrahams | 930 | 40.43 | 26 | 20.73 |
| Radcliffe | 30 | 7 | 12 | 11 | 40 | R. C. Haynes | 1,117 | 46.54 | 82 | 17.22 |
| Crompton | 30 | 8 | 14 | 8* | 39 | Shahid Aziz | 144 | 16.00 | 75 | 15.71 |
| Stockport | 30 | 6 | 15 | 9 | 37 | D. Fitton | 1,040 | 47.27 | 41 | 24.44 |
| Milnrow | 30 | 6 | 16 | 8 | 30 | P. Sutcliffe | 353 | 14.71 | 30 | 25.17 |
| †Hyde | 30 | 4 | 17 | 9 | 25 | — | — | — | — | — |

* *Includes 2 points for a tie.*

† *Hyde called on four professionals during the season.*

*Note:* Five points awarded for an outright win; three for a limited win.

# IRISH CRICKET IN 1985

By DEREK SCOTT

Most of the Irish tend to get upset if referred to as bogmen. In 1985 they could hardly justify any undue indignation. The rain, which mostly came at the weekends, turned many grounds into marshes and at least two could not be played upon from early July onwards.

In Munster only one of three competitions could be completed, Limerick being the league winners. In Leinster (Dublin) the three strongest teams won a trophy each: Phoenix won the league (a twelve-match competition) without being beaten, Leinster took the knockout cup, and the 50-overs-each league, run in August, was won by Malahide. Donemana did the league/cup double in the north-west and provided the Irish team with a new slow left-arm bowler in A. McBrine.

The Northern Cricket Union League was retained by Waringstown, Lisburn being the somewhat unexpected cup winners. Lisburn and Ireland lost the services of Dermott Monteith, who was badly injured in a hit-and-run road accident in February 1985. Woodvale, a team with five international players, wereBddemoted for the first time ever.

Downpatrick maintained the northern dominance of the Schweppes All-Ireland Cup. In the four years of this popular national competition, a Northern Cricket Union team has always won. In 1985 North Down, near neighbours of the winners, were the beaten finalists in a low-scoring and somewhat damp and sodden match.

The Interprovincial Competition (Guinness Cup) should consist of fifteen matches played by six teams. But seven matches could not be played owing to rain and the winner was decided on a percentage system, North Leinster and North-West both finishing with 100 per cent. North Leinster won all three matches they succeeded in playing but North-West could finish only one match. North-West beat the weakest team, Munster, but the rules ordained that they shared the cup with North Leinster.

The abandonment of half this competition created a difficult task for the Irish selectors, a problem that was added to by the unavailability of the long-standing captain, Monteith, and also Jack Short, the opening bat, whose Civil Service job took him to Paris, and Simon Corlett, who could not make the August tour to Britain. Not since 1972, when only two matches were played, have Ireland failed to win at least one match per season. Seven matches, of various lengths, were scheduled, of which one never started, that against Wales at Menai Bridge on the British tour.

Scotland were the first opponents, at Castle Avenue, Dublin. For the third successive year Ireland held the upper hand, but there is still only one victory in the record books. The Irish lead at close of the second day was 297, but then the rains came. For Ireland, the feature was Stephen Warke's scores of 65 and 144 not out. Stephen's father, Larry, had also made a century against Scotland, a record shared with the Pollocks, father William and his son, Stuart.

In early July the team emerged from the rain and the mud to find glorious sunshine and a fast pitch at Hove for the NatWest Bank Trophy. They also met one of the best opening attacks in England, and 39 was all they could muster after a reasonable bowling and fielding display. It was not much consolation for the Irish to see Sussex hustled out by Glamorgan in the next round. Next, Australia came to Downpatrick in August for a one-day match. There was a huge crowd, and despite dreadful conditions Allan Border insisted on playing.

There was only two hours' play but the crowd went home happy after watching the Australian captain himself score a scintillating 91 in 77 minutes.

The British tour opened with a defeat by the Club Cricket Conference in a two-day match at Norbury. Ireland began well but lost their grip and were beaten by 67 runs after the last pair had made 21 to avoid a follow-on. Next stop was a one-day match at Arundel, sponsored by Allied Irish Banks Limited. This resulted in an honourable draw. Lavinia, Duchess of Norfolk's team made 223 for five (K. R. Brown 77, K. P. Tomlins 41 not out, P. Willey 40). M. A. Masood, returning to the Irish team after a year's absence, then scored 111 in 148 minutes. J. Spencer, with four for 25, put a stop to Ireland's winning aspirations, 181 for six being the final score.

The Welsh monsoon followed, after which it was back to Lord's for two days of warm sunshine, a hard, flat pitch and a 50-yard boundary on the Grand Stand side. The scores finished level. Having been put in, Ireland declared at 310 for five, their highest score at Lord's. Masood made 138 in 140 minutes. MCC then declared their own first innings overnight, 92 behind, and bowled Ireland out in their second innings for 153. Needing 246 in 115 minutes plus twenty overs, MCC reached 245 for eight, including 32 off the last three overs. J. Birkenshaw needed 6 off the last ball, but a waist-high full toss went only for 4. Five new caps were awarded in 1985 – to M. P. Rea (batsman), H. Milling and J. McDevitt (opening bowlers), K. R. Bailey (wicket-keeper) and A. McBrine (slow left-arm).

The controversy of the year was the banning of professional players from the Dublin competitions (they were allowed to be employed solely as coaches), and any player not qualified to play for Ireland was ineligible for the Schweppes Cup.

After a gap of twelve years the Irish team were scheduled to make a major overseas tour – to Zimbabwe in January 1986. The selected party was M. Halliday (*captain*), S. J. S. Warke (*vice-captain*), M. F. Cohen, D. G. Dennison, J. W. G. Elder, R. Haire, P. B. Jackson, D. A. Lewis, A. McBrine, J. J. McDevitt, M. A. Masood, H. Milling, T. J. T. Patterson, J. A. Prior, D. Vincent. Haire and Vincent were uncapped players. The manager was A. Linehan, a former Irish captain. Corlett and Rea were not available.

The schools international against Wales at Neath was a high-scoring draw with Wales holding the upper hand. The Under-nineteen party at the international tournament in Bermuda was captained by Paul O'Riordan, son of A. J. The record of three wins and three defeats was considered reasonably satisfactory.

## SCOTTISH CRICKET IN 1985

By WATSON BLAIR

The Bi-Centenary year of cricket in Scotland will be remembered for the success of Freuchie in the National Village Championship at Lord's and the excessive rain which ruined the heavy international and domestic programme. Freuchie's triumph was further rewarded by their being unanimously elected Team of the Month for August, and in October they received the Team of the Year award, both sponsored by Famous Grouse. Other winners of the monthly award were Uddingston, Irvine, St Michael's and Stewarts/Melville.

League and cup abandonments and postponements, especially from early June onwards, created problems. For example, in the D. M. Hall and Son Western Union Championship, Poloc, winners in 1981 and 1983, again annexed the trophy but set up a new record of a kind. The champions achieved their success from only half of the scheduled eighteen-match programme. The margin between Poloc and Clydesdale, the runners-up, was a mere four points. Clydesdale, however, obtained some compensation by defeating Poloc in the final of the Knight, Frank and Rutley Scottish Cup on September 8 at Hamilton Crescent, Glasgow. The final had been postponed on three occasions, and when it was finally staged the playing area was covered in sawdust. Although without Afzal Butt, their Pakistani professional who had returned home, Clydesdale won by 2 runs, Poloc's last wicket falling to the last ball of the match. In addition to the Scottish Cup, Clydesdale won the West League and Rowan Charity Cups.

Ferguslie, Kelburne and Drumpellier finished third, fourth and fifth respectively behind Poloc and Clydesdale in the Western Union, and all, as a result, have qualified for inclusion in the 1986 Scottish Cup. This will be the last time that any league will have five qualifiers: the rules for 1987 are to be amended. With the Scottish Counties Championship now comprising ten clubs, the top four will qualify for the 1987 competition. To make room for the extra qualifier the cup winners will count as one of the qualifiers from its league, which is not the case at present.

The Edinburgh Woollen Mill Border League was again won by Kelso. In retaining the title they lost only one match and that was against Berwick, who were making their first appearance in the competition. Berwick created a very favourable impression and thoroughly merited their final position as runners-up. With nine wins and one draw, Peebles County finished top of the Reserve League. Stenhousemuir, strengthened by the Pakistani leg-spinner, Abdul Qadir, emerged as narrow winners over Heriot's FP in the Ryden and Partners East League. Despite the dismal weather conditions, Qadir took the league bowling prize with 54 wickets at 8.28 apiece and also topped the batting averages with 333 runs at 66.20. Carlton and Kirkcaldy finished third and fourth respectively. In Division Two, Cupar topped the final table, closely followed by Stewarts/Melville. Freuchie, incidentally, were third. The Masterton Trophy, sponsored by Radio Forth in 1985, gave Kirkcaldy a comfortable win over Stenhousemuir and the trophy for the first time. India's Sandeep Patil played a major part in Kirkcaldy's success.

For the first time since 1952 Stirling County won the Beneagles Scottish Counties Championship, with Ayrshire again in second place. Aberdeenshire were third. An Australian, Brett McKirdy, played a leading role in Stirling's win. Aberdeenshire defeated Perthshire in the final of the Beneagles Quaich.

Division One of the Abbey Life Glasgow and District League was won by North Kelvide/Old Aloysians. Helensburgh were second. Divisions Two, Three and Four were won by Woodhall, Hyndland and St Michael's respectively. NKOA won the Reserve Division and also the knockout cup, beating Glasgow Academicals in the final. St Michael's from Dumfries, newcomers to the league, had a 100 per cent record. Foster Lewis, a 22-year-old Antiguan, had an amazing season. In 27 innings for St Michael's he scored 1,625 runs (average 65), including six centuries and nine half-centuries. No fewer than 67 6s and 141 4s flowed from his bat. His fast bowling produced a final analysis of 175–55–312–56 (average 5.4).

Luncarty became the first club to retain the championship of the Perthshire League. Arbroath United and Meigle were first and second in the Strathmore Union, while Ross County and Northern Counties occupied similar positions in the MacAllan North of Scotland League. George Mundell of Ross County took all ten wickets against Highland. The new Mann Investments SCU Small Clubs Cup proved successful. The final at Cupar saw Dundee University Staff defeat Stoneywood by four wickets. On the national scene Greenock won the Scottish section of the William Younger Cup but fell to Leyland in the quarter-finals.

The West District, for the second time in three years, reached the final of the NCA County Championship after beating Yorkshire CA and Middlesex CA. Following three cancellations the final was eventually staged at Cambusdoon, Ayr, where the West, forced to make numerous changes to a successful line-up, lost to Worcestershire CA by nine wickets.

Scotland had to combat both weather and stiff opposition in the international arena, with disappointing and frustrating results. All four Benson and Hedges Cup matches, against Derbyshire, Nottinghamshire, Gloucestershire and Northamptonshire, were lost, and the NatWest Trophy match against Glamorgan brought another defeat. The three-day games against Ireland, Zimbabwe and MCC were all ruined by rain, while Scotland B's encounters with Durham University, Nottinghamshire Second XI and Leicestershire Second XI produced a defeat, a draw and a wash-out respectively. All these were two-day matches.

A. B. Russell (Stirling County), A. W. J. Stevenson (Drumpellier), S. M. C. Alleyne (Carlton), N. W. Burnett (Aberdeenshire), D. Fleming (West Lothian County) and G. R. Kirkwood (Poloc) were all capped for Scotland for the first time. The wet summer also adversely affected Scotland's Young Cricketers. After losing to Staffordshire CA, the Under-nineteen side drew with the Welsh Schools and lost to the English Schools.

The year in review also saw the introduction of *Scottish Cricket*, a publication issued by the Scottish Cricket Union. The three issues in April, July and October were well received. Indeed, with increased sponsorship and the advent of new clubs in the Shetlands and the south-west of Scotland, the future of cricket in the country, under the auspices of a revamped SCU, appears secure.

---

## CRICKET IN ANTARCTICA

What was almost certainly the most southerly game of cricket ever played, and the coldest, took place in Antarctica, 700 kilometres from the South Pole, on January 11, 1985, between two teams drawn from the 60 scientists, lawyers, environmentalists and administrators engaged in an international workshop being held at the Beardmore South Camp and concerned with the Antarctic Treaty. New Zealand's representative on the Treaty, Christopher Beeby, captained the Gondwanaland Occasionals with players from Australia, New Zealand and South Africa. A British delegate to the Conference, Arthur Watts, captained the Beardmore Casuals, a basically British team. The stumps were improvised, the pitch, such as it was, had been rolled by a Hercules transport aircraft, and the "midnight sun" allowed play to continue until 11.00 p.m. The Occasionals (129) beat the Casuals (102) by 27 runs.

# SCHOOLS CRICKET IN 1985

After the Oxford Festival and the match at Lord's against NAYC, the representative English Schools programme was limited to one game, the fixture v Wales at Headingley being abandoned without a ball bowled. M. A. Roseberry captained the side at Lord's, where he scored two centuries for the second successive year, before moving on to join Middlesex. The captaincy was taken over by M. A. Atherton, whose quietly astute leadership was as significant as were his sound batting and well-controlled leg-spin. Other batsmen to attract notice were D. G. Hodgson, J. D. R. Benson, P. D. Atkins and R. J. Bartlett, who won the Len Newbery Gray-Nicolls Award for the most improved schoolboy cricketer. The leading fast bowler was M. A. Robinson – who was outstanding against Scotland – while A. G. J. Fraser and J. C. M. Atkinson provided sound support. Atherton's spin was supplemented by the off-breaks of P. J. Berry. Supported by an excellent wicket-keeper in W. K. Hegg, the fielding was good, Benson receiving the A. A. Thomson fielding prize of the Cricket Society.

Asked to bat first in the game against Scottish CU Colts at West of Scotland Ground, English Schools began well through Bartlett (67) and Atkins (34), who put on an opening partnership of 110, which was followed by another century stand in 55 minutes from Hodgson (47) and Benson (56). In reply to English Schools' total of 255 for nine in 60 overs, Scotland were then dismissed for 73, thanks to some hostile bowling from Robinson, who took eight for 35 in sixteen overs. Following on, the home side lost two more wickets to Robinson as they collapsed to 38 for five. A spirited stand of 57 between J. Williams (30) and M. Smith (32), before Atherton polished off the tail, brought some respectability and a total of 120, which left English Schools the winners by an innings and 62 runs.

The first MCC Schools Festival at Oxford was an undoubted success; for four days, positive cricket of a high standard was played in an excellent spirit. On the first two days, HMC Southern Schools played The Rest while ESCA North played ESCA South. On the third day all 44 players were rearranged into two further trial games, and on the fourth day a final trial – MCC Schools East v West – was played with the best 22, after which the MCC Schools XI for Lord's was chosen.

## HMC SOUTHERN SCHOOLS v THE REST

At New College, Oxford, July 20, 21. Drawn. Rain, which interrupted the first day, left a damp pitch, on which the bowlers dominated throughout, only Bartlett and, briefly, Hussain of the Southern Schools batsmen looking at all comfortable in their first innings. The Rest found the going even harder against first Robinson then the spinners, Harding and Heath. After Atherton's declaration 53 behind, the medium pace of Pethers and the spin of Cox and Atherton reduced Southern Schools to 77 for six before a fine partnership between Speight and Bartlett – the latter played better than anyone – enabled O'Gorman to set a target of 252 in 190 minutes. Although the wicket had eased, only Foster and Atherton could master the spin attack, and once they had gone, off successive balls from Harding (the pick of the bowlers), no-one else lasted long until Pethers and Bashford survived the last six overs.

## HMC Southern Schools

| Batsman | First innings | | Second innings | |
|---|---|---|---|---|
| J. R. Ayling (*Portsmouth GS*) | lbw b Makin | 15 | (3) b Pethers | 8 |
| R. J. Bartlett (*Taunton*) | st Bashford b Cox | 57 | (8) c Atherton b Makin | 69 |
| *T. J. G. O'Gorman (*St George's, Weybridge*) | b Pringle | 10 | (4) c Makin b Atherton | 3 |
| R. Owen-Browne (*Tonbridge*) | b Atherton | 7 | (6) st Bashford b Atherton | 2 |
| N. Hussain (*Forest*) | c Foster b Cox | 29 | (1) st Bashford b Cox | 27 |
| I. L. M. Henry (*Winchester*) | c Bashford b Cox | 7 | (2) b Pethers | 2 |
| †M. P. Speight (*Hurstpierpoint*) | not out | 11 | c Foster b Cox | 39 |
| J. D. Robinson (*Lancing*) | not out | 16 | (5) c Pringle b Atherton | 21 |
| S. D. Heath (*KES Birmingham*) | (did not bat) | | b Pringle | 14 |
| R. P. Haywood (*Felsted*) | (did not bat) | | not out | 2 |
| | Extras | 13 | Extras | 11 |
| | 1/38 2/93 3/95 4/110 5/137 6/138 | (6 wkts dec.) 165 | 1/18 2/37 3/43 4/48 5/69 6/77 7/145 8/179 9/198 | (9 wkts dec.) 198 |

G. D. Harding (*Nottingham HS*) (did not bat).

Bowling: *First Innings*—Makin 10–3–17–1; Pethers 6–0–13–0; Pringle 12–2–40–1; Cox 17–1–55–3; Atherton 8–1–27–1. *Second Innings*—Makin 11–0–39–1; Pethers 9–3–16–2; Cox 18–6–70–2; Atherton 15–5–36–3; Pringle 10–2–26–1.

## The Rest

| Batsman | First innings | | Second innings | |
|---|---|---|---|---|
| S. G. Foster (*Barnard Castle*) | b Robinson | 1 | (3) c and b Harding | 58 |
| *M. A. Atherton (*Manchester GS*) | c Speight b Robinson | 2 | (4) c Henry b Harding | 19 |
| M. D. I. Sheppard (*Forest*) | c O'Gorman b Harding | 19 | (1) c Hussain b Ayling | 4 |
| N. A. Willetts (*KES Birmingham*) | c and b Ayling | 22 | (2) b Robinson | 13 |
| N. R. Venning (*Haileybury*) | c Harding b Heath | 11 | b Heath | 6 |
| G. D. Reynolds (*Wellington C*) | c Speight b Heath | 4 | b Harding | 12 |
| N. J. Pringle (*Taunton*) | c Owen-Browne b Heath | 22 | b Heath | 4 |
| J. J. Pethers (*Harrow*) | not out | 15 | not out | 14 |
| M. C. Cox (*Abingdon*) | not out | 9 | (10) c Robinson b Harding | 9 |
| J. C. Makin (*Marlborough*) | (did not bat) | | (9) b Harding | 0 |
| †P. Bashford (*Bishop's Stortford*) | (did not bat) | | not out | 0 |
| | Extras | 7 | Extras | 14 |
| | 1/1 2/18 3/47 4/47 5/51 6/80 7/96 | (7 wkts dec.) 112 | 1/8 2/21 3/104 4/104 5/116 6/120 7/131 8/131 9/147 | (9 wkts) 153 |

Bowling: *First Innings*—Haywood 11–3–22–0; Robinson 16–3–35–2; Ayling 4–3–4–1; Harding 12–8–14–1; Heath 13–5–30–3. *Second Innings*—Robinson 7–2–9–1; Ayling 7–1–12–1; Heath 21–7–69–2; Harding 27–11–49–5.

## ESCA NORTH v ESCA SOUTH

At Keble College, Oxford, July 21, 22. Drawn. Struggling at 99 for seven in reply to South's 178 for five declared at the end of a rain-affected first day, North were rescued on the second morning by an unbroken partnership of 128 between Hegg and Berry. After a sound start to South's second innings by Atkins and Earl, Roseberry introduced occasional bowlers in the hope of encouraging the declaration, which eventually set a target of 191 in 130 minutes. North made a valiant but unavailing effort to score the runs, Hodgson heading the chase.

## ESCA South

| | | | |
|---|---|---|---|
| P. D. Atkins (*Bucks.*) c Philbrook b Lerigo | 15 | – not out | 139 |
| R. Earl (*Suffolk*) b Fisher | 8 | – b Smith | 60 |
| J. D. R. Benson (*Cambs.*) c Roseberry b Smith | 65 | – c Lerigo b Smith | 19 |
| C. Hutchings (*Warwicks.*) not out | 48 | | |
| R. Thomas (*London*) c Fisher b Smith | 3 | | |
| *J. C. M. Atkinson (*Somerset*) c Philbrook b Berry | 26 | | |
| †S. Inwood (*Northants*) not out | 4 | – (4) b Philbrook | 5 |
| Extras | 9 | Extras | 14 |
| 1/15 2/42 3/122 4/140 5/170 (5 wkts dec.) | 178 | 1/121 2/137 (2 wkts dec.) | 237 |

M. Taylor (*Middx*), A. G. J. Fraser (*Middx*), J. Boiling (*Surrey*) and C. Beagles (*Essex*) did not bat.

Bowling: *First Innings*—Robinson 16–3–47–0; Fisher 9–1–32–1; Lerigo 13–3–28–1; Berry 12–3–45–1; Smith 6–1–17–2. *Second Innings*—Robinson 10–3–23–0; Fisher 4–0–27–0; Lerigo 5–1–11–0; Berry 17–5–40–0; Smith 12.3–0–38–2; Roseberry 5–1–7–0; Philbrook 10–3–27–1; Crawley 3–1–4–0; Hodgson 6–0–46–0.

## ESCA North

| | | | |
|---|---|---|---|
| *M. A. Roseberry (*Durham*) b Atkinson | 14 | – b Fraser | 12 |
| S. D. Philbrook (*Lancs.*) b Atkinson | 2 | – c Benson b Fraser | 9 |
| N. J. Speak (*Lancs.*) lbw b Atkinson | 18 | – lbw b Fraser | 7 |
| D. G. Hodgson (*Cumbria*) c Benson b Boiling | 9 | – st Inwood b Boiling | 65 |
| M. A. Crawley (*Lancs.*) c Inwood b Taylor | 11 | – c Atkins b Fraser | 0 |
| O. Smith (*Avon*) b Beagles | 35 | – c Taylor b Boiling | 34 |
| S. D. Lerigo (*Yorks.*) b Beagles | 6 | – c Atkins b Boiling | 3 |
| †W. K. Hegg (*Lancs.*) not out | 55 | – not out | 1 |
| P. J. Berry (*Cleveland*) not out | 63 | – not out | 1 |
| Extras | 12 | Extras | 7 |
| 1/14 2/23 3/35 4/54 5/86 6/94 7/97 (7 wkts dec.) | 225 | 1/20 2/30 3/33 4/45 5/133 6/133 7/136 (7 wkts) | 139 |

M. A. Robinson (*Humberside*) and J. Fisher (*Leics.*) did not bat.

Bowling: *First Innings*—Fraser 12–3–35–0; Atkinson 18–8–38–3; Boiling 15–7–42–1; Taylor 12–3–40–1; Beagles 8–1–40–2; Earl 5–1–18–0. *Second Innings*—Fraser 21–6–60–4; Atkinson 9–1–16–0; Boiling 6–0–32–3; Taylor 6–0–24–0.

At Oxford, July 22. J. C. M. Atkinson's XI won by five wickets. M. A. Atherton's XI 165 for eight dec. (S. D. Philbrook 48); J. C. M. Atkinson's XI 166 for five (R. J. Bartlett 51).

At Oxford, July 22. Drawn. M. A. Roseberry's XI 192 for four dec. (M. A. Roseberry 97); T. J. G. O'Gorman's XI 136 for six (C. Hutchings 43).

At Oxford, July 23. Drawn. MCC Schools East 243 for five dec. (J. D. R. Benson 106, M. A. Roseberry 51); MCC Schools West 225 for nine (P. D. Atkins 58, R. J. Bartlett 49, N. A. Willetts 43; P. J. Berry seven for 67).

Details of the match between MCC Schools and the National Association of Young Cricketers may be found in Other Matches at Lord's, 1985.

*Reports from the Schools:*

The dismal weather in 1985 caused a number of schools matches to be abandoned and curtailed many more. The batsmen generally struggled, only N. A. Stanley of Bedford Modern passing 1,000 runs (1,042 at 65.12) from among the schools reviewed here. The bowlers, however, prospered, eight taking 60 wickets and Matthew Taylor, of Enfield GS, collecting 73 at 10.61. The leading all-rounders were N. Hussain of Forest School, with 978 runs and 48 wickets, and C. M. Graham of Victoria College, Jersey, with 758 runs and 60 wickets. A Combined Public Schools of Western Australia party toured here during the summer and provided strong opposition wherever they played.

**Abingdon** attributed their unbeaten record to a strong team spirit, inspired by the sound captaincy of M. A. Marsden, and an outstanding attack, led by J. S. Hutchison (medium right-arm in-swing) – whose 46 wickets included a return of eight for 25 v Radley – and the slow left-arm spin of M. C. Cox, who took 53 wickets. J. C. P. Haynes established a reliable opening partnership with M. T. Boobbyer, whose 965 runs were more than twice the next highest. Boobbyer's four centuries included three in five days. **Aldenham's** best players were N. A. Fenn, who made two hundreds, and left-arm spinner D. J. Stenning, who took 48 wickets. Both are expected to return in 1986, as are ten of the **Alleyn's** side, who were perhaps too reliant on their captain, J. Bridgeman. C. O'Gorman showed promise as a fast bowler and A. Stevens and S. Naish played some responsible innings. **Allhallows** ended the season in style, winning three out of four matches on a Kent tour, after earlier disappointments. Unreliable middle-order batting failed to capitalise on the efforts of W. R. Frost, and the bowlers generally lacked form, the exception being the captain, E. R. M. Gard, whose 45 wickets took his tally over the past two seasons to more than 100.

After losing six matches, **Ampleforth** dropped two senior members, whereupon their fortunes changed. The spinners, B. R. Simonds-Gooding and J. G. Cummings, began taking wickets, and the fourteen-year-old R. Booth showed promise as a wicket-keeper as well as sharing in a ninth-wicket partnership of 80 with Simonds-Gooding v Blundell's. In a moderate season a young **Ardingly** side lacked consistency with the bat, although seventeen fifties were shared by six batsmen, and support for the right-arm medium pace of J. E. K. Henderson. Twelve players with first-team experience should be available in 1986. For **Arnold**, another with a young side, highlights were centuries by A. D. Lyon and a fourteen-year-old, A. D. Jones. Lyon's 124 not out v King William's College, Isle of Man, was the highest for the school for many years.

Injuries to key players hampered **Bablake**, whose attack often lacked penetration. Their leading bowler was the off-spinner, D. J. Barr. D. C. Percival, often unavailable owing to injury, played for Warwickshire Under-19, together with the wicket-keeper, N. A. Matkin, and A. M. J. Kearns. The latter, whose three centuries were a school record, shared in an unbroken partnership of 222 with Percival against King Henry VIII, Coventry. In a season of rebuilding, **Bancroft's** owed much to their captain and opening bat, J. P. Thomas, and the all-rounder, K. R. Gold, who bowled his off-breaks to good effect and was an excellent fielder. R. W. Hubbard, a medium-pace bowler and opening batsman, took eight for 15 v Enfield GS, and promise was shown by V. D. Masani with the bat and N. K. Patel with the new ball. A successful season for **Bangor GS** culminated in a tour which featured a win v Stockport GS and exciting draws v Arnold and King's, Macclesfield. The captain, C. M. McCall, an astute tactician, represented Irish Schools, as did R. B. Millar, who also kept wicket for the Irish Under-19 side in Bermuda.

Unbeaten with sixteen wins in 21 matches, **Barnard Castle School** batted well down the order and possessed an attack capable of bowling out most sides. D. W. T. McGarr and R. J. Irving both took 50 wickets, while the captain, S. G. Foster, enjoyed a good all-round season. For **Bedford School** there were convincing and satisfying wins v St Edward's, Felsted and Wellington. At other times, though, the fielding was unreliable and the batting prone to collapse. J. E. Crooker was the outstanding bowler with 45 wickets, while C. J. Honan scored 966 runs. **Bedford Modern School** recorded victories v Kimbolton, Wellingborough, Ardingly, Stowe, Bedford School (by ten wickets) and Royal GS, Colchester. The match v Oundle was drawn with the scores level. The captain, N. A. Stanley, dominated the batting with 1,042 runs and was well supported by T. J. F. Hill and A. J. Trott, while P. A. Owen took 69 wickets at an average of 10.14 with slow left-arm spin, collecting five in an innings on six occasions, including seven for 67 v Oundle.

In a somewhat undistinguished season, **Berkhamsted** beat Magdalen College School, Framlingham and St Lawrence. P. A. Brown, the captain, was the leading batsman, with two centuries, and the attack relied heavily on S. P. Hunt (slow left-arm) and M. A. Hodges (right-arm medium). **Birkenhead** had one of their least distinguished seasons for many years. The batting, apart from the left-handed opener, A. R. Wilby, was sadly lacking in sound technique and application, and the bowling, without variety from an experienced spin bowler, was too predictable. In a memorable season, the young side at **Bishop's Stortford** – runners-up to Millfield in the Barclays Bank Under-17 competition – lost only to Ipswich, defeating The Perse, Brentwood, Monkton Combe, Dean Close and Ardingly, as well as tying with King Edward's, Bath, both sides being bowled out for 59. This was the school's first tie as far as can be remembered. L. S. P. Fishpool, an outstanding off-spinner, took seven for 16 against King Edward's and thoughout the season, during which he also scored the most runs, he was ably supported by the fifteen-year-old P. E. B. Armitage (leg-spin), S. R. Hartnell (slow left-arm) and A. M. Reynolds (medium). The excellent wicket-keeping of P. Bashford set the standard for a first-class fielding side. A tour of Sri Lanka was planned for the Christmas holiday.

Outstanding for **Blundell's** was the slow left-arm bowler, R. K. Giles, who, with 55 wickets, took more than twice as many as anyone else. B. A. Barwell scored 148 v King's, Taunton, and wins were recorded v Downside, Oundle, Plymouth and Uppingham. For **Bradfield College**, who had convincing wins v Westminster, Canford and Charterhouse, a highlight was A. J. Goodsir's return of six for 32 v Wellington College. Positive and entertaining cricket brought **Bradford GS** a record thirteen wins, including those v St Peter's York, Bristol GS, Hymer's College, Bolton School and Woodhouse Grove. With more than 4,000 runs scored, their strength lay in the batting, P. A. Greenwood, C. E. Nichols and R. M. Nichols setting the platform for the fast-scoring A. A. D. Gillgrass and G. M. Bentley. The attack, headed by M. E. Joy (medium), was accurate but less effective than had been hoped, the left-arm spinner, I. J. McClay, failing to find the consistency of the previous two seasons. **Brentwood**, whose bowlers had difficulty taking wickets on slow pitches and whose batting generally struggled, were nevertheless encouraged by centuries from R. S. Newman in the win v Framlingham and from the promoted J. G. Northwood in the final match v the Old Boys. Pre-eminent for **Brighton College** was D. J. Panto, whose 62 wickets included nine for 17 v Christ's Hospital, eight for 44 v Worth and seven for 68 v Epsom. **Bromsgrove**, unbeaten by schools but with ten drawn games, were especially satisfied to beat King Edward's School, Birmingham, for the first time since 1969. In their most successful season for 30 years, **Bryanston** owed much to consistency in batting, led by the left-handed G. Ecclestone, who headed both batting and bowling averages. With N. Goodenough-Bayly and J. Beale, he formed a penetrative attack which claimed 121 wickets between them.

A young **Canford** side were encouraged by wins v King's Taunton and Combined Public Schools of Western Australia who, needing 3 to win with three wickets in hand, were beaten by 1 run. R. J. Stearn (medium) took six wickets for 55 against the Western Australians and eight for 71 against Blundell's. Much promise was shown by the young left-hander, C. H. Forward, who topped 500 runs in his first season. Well led by S. R. A. Miles, **Caterham** recorded notable victories v Kingston GS, Trinity, Sevenoaks, St Dunstan's and Reigate GS. The side's highest score of 116 not out came from the left-hander P. J. Sidall, while the fourteen-year-old A. D. Brown made two centuries and was the leading bowler, five times taking five wickets in an innings, including seven for 24 v Trinity. Another fine return was the left-arm opener, S. G. Randall's seven for 55 v Rutlish. It was a disappointing season in terms of results for a young **Charterhouse** side. B. T. A. Holdsworth collected the most runs in his first year and fourteen-year-old A. T. Grundy scored the side's only other hundred. **Cheltenham College** reported their best results for more than ten years, with wins v Marlborough, Malvern (bowled out for 55), Shrewsbury, against whom J. T. Morgan made an unbeaten century, and Clifton, who were bowled out for 116, thanks to a return of six for 18 by O. G. Davies. P. D. Richardson, with his attacking fast bowling and powerful batting, led the side by example.

In a mixed season for **Chigwell School**, highlights were a 162-run victory v Buckhurst Hill County HS, the defeat of The Perse, who were bowled out for 59 by the fast bowling of D. J. Clark and P. W. Hutchings, and a second-wicket partnership of 125 in the win over Brentwood between A. J. Lee and J. R. Maskey, who captained the side well. A young **Christ College, Brecon**, side exceeded all expectations, and were beaten only by a strong Old Boys' side. The captain, J. W. Lewis, set an aggressive example in the field and batted powerfully and purposefully, his two unbeaten hundreds including 107 out of 140 in the nine-wicket defeat of Monmouth. Sound performances also came from the opening batsman, S. J. Harrett, and from S. J. Thomas, while with the ball D. O. Lloyd-Jones took seven wickets in a match three times. A young **Clifton College** side, whose batting tended to be brittle, fared better than their record might suggest, playing many close matches. A highlight was W. M. I. Bailey's unbeaten 107 against Felsted; batting at No. 7, he rescued the side from 48 for seven, enabling them to declare at 214 for nine. The attack was sound, excellent performances by M. C. H. Jones and A. A. R. Niven almost bringing about remarkable victories v Marlborough – who, needing 113, were reduced to 74 for eight – and Cheltenham, who recovered from 98 for nine to achieve a target of 117.

Losing only one schools match and reaching the final of the Kent Under-19 Cup, **Colfe's** owed their success to the free scoring of the openers, C. A. Spencer and J. Waddell, ably supported by the forceful strokeplay of the captain, M. A. Saleemi. An inexperienced attack depended too much on K. J. Boxall who, with Spencer and Saleemi, played for Kent Under-19. Another side short of bowling were **Colston's**, who beat Monkton Combe and Prior Park, but often failed to capitalise on good positions won by their batsmen. J. N. Stutt scored three centuries, bringing his total for the First XI to eight. **Cranleigh** enjoyed an encouraging season, during which they established a schools' cricket festival, inviting Merchant Taylors', Northwood, Bryanston, Rossall and St Peter's, York. S. J. Watkinson (medium) took 54 wickets, surpassing the previous best since the last war (49), achieved by N. A. Paul in 1953, and including eight for 21 v St John's, Leatherhead, seven for 49 v King's, Canterbury, and six for 39 v Rossall, all of whom were beaten. He was well supported by I. Z. Khan and the colt, R. G. Gutteridge.

In a season of mixed fortunes, in which only one match of seventeen was drawn, **Dame Allan's School** bowled out Ponteland HS for 55 (A. J. Silversides 5–1–9–4), having earlier in the season themselves been dismissed for 29 by St Cuthbert's. The playing record of **Dauntsey's**, for whom a colt, J. Porter, emerged as a promising opening batsman, and whose attack was spearheaded by I. M. Alexander (fast-medium), shows a preponderance of draws, a number of which were the product of conservative declarations. **Dean Close**, fielding an inexperienced side, were pleasantly surprised by their results. The team was built around K. B. Hemshall (in-swing), who led the attack with M. H. Paget-Wilkes, as well as captaining the side and batting at No. 3. T. A. Edginton showed promise both as a batsman and slow left-arm bowler, while P. J. Kirby emerged to play some useful innings. The fortunes of **Denstone** faded somewhat after a promising start, but they did enjoy a close win v the Western Australian Public Schools side.

**Downside** beat Royal GS, Lancaster, and Strathallan at the latter's festival, and compiled 286 for four in beating Taunton by six wickets. In a disappointing season for **Dulwich**, whose young side struggled, only R. F. Parker batted consistently, while the bowling rested heavily on the shoulders of the left-arm spinner, I. C. Tredgett, whose 48 wickets included eight for 43 v Mill Hill. For **Durham**, unbeaten by schools for the third successive year, their outstanding captain, M. A. Roseberry, was available only rarely, yet he scored more runs than anyone else, at an average of 65.50, and fittingly made 104 in his last innings for the school. He captained MCC Schools and NCA Young Cricketers at Lord's, ending his career as a schoolboy with a century there to take his total at headquarters to four. He also played for Durham and in the John Player League for Middlesex. His brother, the fourteen-year-old A. Roseberry, followed him in the school's batting averages.

Rain and the inability of the bowling to dismiss opposing sides brought an exceptional number of drawn games for **Eastbourne College**. The wicket-keeper, F. J. Westlake, was the outstanding batsman, his 120 v St John's, Leatherhead, being a solid, impressive innings. Also notable was the performance of J. J. R. A. Harley, the side's leading bowler (medium), who made 111 and took five for 10 v Ardingly. For two of their four wins, **The Edinburgh Academy** were indebted to M. B. Holmes (fast-medium away-swing), who took nine for 33 v Merchiston Castle and seven for 19 v Abbot Beyne. **Elizabeth College, Guernsey**, played some exciting drawn games, notably that v St George's, Weybridge. Promising young players were P. J. Woods with the bat and R. P. C. Cox (fast-medium) with the ball, while M. J. Bacon (leg-spin) and A. B. Howe (off-spin) had their moments. F. N. Stratford, able to play for only half the season, none the less topped both batting and bowling averages. **Ellesmere**, without a win, looked too often to their captain, J. Holmes, whose aggregate of 723 runs was a school record and more than twice as many as the next highest. A. R. L. Stubbs bowled his off-spinners to good effect, and with more support the results might have been more favourable. Outstanding for **Eltham College** was the captain and left-arm spin bowler, R. J. Hart, who scored 707 runs and took 61 wickets, including seven for 30 v Claysmore. L. A. O'Leary was a consistent opener, and other centuries were scored by A. J. Prifti and N. D. A. Baxter, while the fifteen-year-old J. A. Chase showed considerable all-round promise.

Less successful were **Emanuel**, with only one win – v Latymer Upper. Their side was built around C. Noble, who totalled 64 wickets at 9.78 and scored 600 runs, including 78 and seven for 21 v Trinity. The **Enfield GS** XI was dominated by the Taylor brothers, Matthew (fast-medium) establishing a record for the school with 73 wickets, including eight for 27 v Latymer Upper and seven for 39 v Bancroft's, while Malcolm was the leading batsman with 679 runs. The captain of **Epsom College**, G. J. R. Corcoran, totalled 910 runs, including an unbeaten 139 out of 170 v Brighton College. Other highlights were J. B. Appleton's return of seven for 55 v the Grasshoppers and A. C. R. Davidson's 167 not out v The Hague CC on a tour to the Netherlands. A well-balanced **Eton** side, unbeaten by schools, relied successfully on a medium-pace seam attack to dismiss opposing sides and victories were recorded v St Edward's Oxford, Wellington College, Marlborough and Harrow, against whom F. N. Bowman-Shaw returned seven for 38 at Lord's. In a season of rebuilding, **Exeter's** young side provided much encouragement for the future, the only defeat by a school being at the hands of Queen's, Taunton. The 659 runs amassed by F. O. S. MacDonald were thought to be a school record, and the continually improving fast bowling of M. C. Jacquiss brought him 40 wickets.

For **Fettes** J. Ellworthy performed a hat-trick and M. Adam twice took three wickets in four balls, but the brittleness of the batting meant that a competent attack rarely had a substantial total to defend and the final record was the worst for many years. A wealth of outstanding performances was recorded by **Forest School**, for whom the captain, M. D. I. Sheppard, and N. Hussain were by far the most prolific batsmen. Sheppard hit three hundreds and averaged 76.00; Hussain made two, falling only 22 short of 1,000 runs for the second successive season; and together they put on an opening stand of 237 v St Edmunds, Canterbury. Hussain's leg-spin brought him 41 wickets, including seven for 27 v Brentwood and seven for 86 v Combined Public Schools of Western Australia.

The captain of **Giggleswick**, M. T. Howard, was a dependable opening batsman, and their leading bowler, A. J. Fowler, went on to open the bowling for Yorkshire Schools Senior XI. An unbeaten **Glasgow Academy** XI batted in depth, the openers, M. S. Robertson and G. G. H. Gemmell, laying a solid foundation on which A. G. M. Baird and wicket-keeper-batsman G. B. A. Dyer could build. E. J. Miller and D. H. K. Robbins laboured hard for little reward at medium pace, while G. G. R. Gemmell bowled economically to top the averages. Three from **Glenalmond** – G. M. Sommerville, L. M. Porter and A. E. Kennedy – played for Scotland Under-19, which was captained by the school's captain of 1983, J. Sutton. Wins came v Fettes, Merchiston Castle and Strathallan, with J. A. Higgins the pick of the emerging young batsmen. A young **Gresham's** side was built around the all-round skills of their captain, J. Lewis, who was well supported with the ball by R. Jackson and T. Berwick. The batting was again brittle.

Dominant at **Haberdashers' Aske's, Elstree**, was their captain, R. Bate, who had a fine season with the bat. A tour to Devon was undertaken in the summer, with a tour to the Far East planned for Christmas. Superb ground fielding and excellent catches lifted the performance of an experienced **Haileybury** XI, whose captain, N. R. Venning, led a solid batting line-up. J. T. Lumley (in-swing) spearheaded the attack, with good support from R. R. W. Bonallack (leg-spin). Batting in depth, with four centuries scored, **Hampton School** were defeated only once. The bowling acquired greater edge as the season progressed, the left-arm spin of J. P. Shepherd again proving effective. The fielding was keen, notably that of S. J. Eggleton and A. P. Hood, while S. J. Young was tidy and agile in his first season behind the stumps. Also good in the field, **Harrow** achieved some of their eight victories by wide margins, notably those v Haileybury (by eight wickets), Winchester (seven wickets) and Charterhouse (an innings and 108 runs). Their strength lay in the seam bowling of D. B. M. Fox and J. J. Pethers, who returned eight for 33 v Charterhouse and six for 87 in the thrilling match v Eton at Lord's.

A young **Hereford Cathedral School** side was well led by P. J. Butler, who batted consistently if less prolifically than anticipated, while promise was shown by N. R. Denny with the bat and A. M. Herbert (fast-medium) with the ball. **Highgate** struggled to achieve their three wins, their progress being limited by the batsmen's inability to dominate, especially on the lifeless home pitches. Although the attack was steady, the only noteworthy return was six for 20 v Old Cholmelians by the young D. N. Amato, who emerged as a fine all-round prospect. For a young **Hipperholme GS** side, carefully captained by D. Smith, W. Clarke and M. Kirkbride confirmed with the bat the promise they had shown as colts, and I. Crabtree became the first player in at least 25 years to carry his bat for the school. With contributions from all their players, **Hurstpierpoint** beat Ardingly, Seaford, Cranleigh, Bloxham, Sussex Clergy, Sussex Martlets and MCC. The captain, M. P. Speight, who made the major contribution with the bat, played for NCA England South in Bermuda. A tour to India was planned for Christmas.

Highlights for **Ipswich School** were wins v Bishop's Stortford, Framlingham and Brighton College. J. J. Zagni (slow left-arm) topped both averages, followed by N. J. Gregory and R. J. Beales with the bat and S. Young (off-spin) with the ball. N. Barrett kept well to the spin bowlers and nine catches were held at short leg by P. Finch. **Kelly College's** fragile middle- and lower-order batting too often failed to capitalise on useful individual performances, the best of which was P. G. Shering's 107 v Plymouth College, and their attack, though accurate, rarely troubled good batsmen. The absence of a safe catcher in the slips proved a handicap. None the less, seven victories were recorded. **Kimbolton School**, who won the Berkhamsted festival, were ably led by A. N. Caswell, whose bowling, decidedly quick, proved too much for schoolboy batsmen once pitches became harder. The left-handed opening batsman, G. J. Kerr, established a school record with his aggregate of 712 runs at 47.46. An enthusiastic but inexperienced **King Edward VI College, Stourbridge**, XI was carried by C. M. Tolley, although there was potential in the bowling of B. Darby (medium) and G. D. Tomkins (slow left-arm). In a successful season for **King Edward VI School, Southampton**, the batting of the captain, G. J. M. Cottrell, and the opener, R. S. Mayhew, was supplemented by accurate bowling. J. E. Shepherd collected a school record of 56 wickets with his off-breaks.

Victory at the excellently organised UCS festival rounded off a rewarding season for **King Edward VII School, Lytham**, in which they defeated Burnley GS, Cowley, Batley GS, Stockport GS, Sir John Deannes College, UCS London and Solihull. Prominent for **King Edward's School, Birmingham**, were the captain, N. A. Willetts (slow left-arm), who headed both averages, S. D. Heath (opening bat and leg-breaks) and the No. 3 batsman, N. Martin, who between them scored 2,378 runs and took 100 wickets. Big wins were recorded v Wrekin (by 218 runs) and Solihull (eight wickets), although some of the best games resulted in draws. For **King Henry VIII School, Coventry**, in a moderate season, the major contribution with the bat came from A. G. Dow, in his first year in the XI. The attack often had trouble achieving a breakthrough, although N. A. Ansari (seven for 43 v RGS Worcester), and the captain, D. C. Bridges, enjoyed some good returns.

Inconsistent batting restricted the wins of **King William's College, Isle of Man**, to those v Stockport, King's School Chester – against whom S. W. Ellis (medium) took seven for 33 and scored 71 – and Liverpool College, who were dismissed for 38, seven of the wickets falling for 25 runs to A. J. Corlett (left-arm medium-fast). A similar problem handicapped **King's College, Taunton**, who had wins v Queen's Taunton, Sherborne, Downside and the XL Club. H. D. W. Wordsworth (medium) was the best bowler and achieved a record for the school of 52 wickets, including nine for 64 v Taunton School. N. P. Barnett was the leading batsman for **King's College School, Wimbledon**, hitting a fine century v Epsom College, while the captain, J. P. Feltham, bowled with fire and received good support from his fellow opening bowler, S. P. Gibson, and the off-spinner, R. M. Wight. Beaten only by MCC – by 7 runs – **King's School, Bruton**, attributed their success to the hostile seam attack of the left-armer, S. J. Griffin, who took eight for 25 v Canford, and M. A. Walton, effectively backed up by the left-arm spin of C. G. Cowell. The tactical appreciation of the captain, J. Cassell, was good, and his three centuries provided a solid foundation for rather suspect batting. The ground fielding was keen, although the catching did not reach the same standard.

With eight wins, and defeats only by Cranleigh and MCC, **The King's School, Canterbury**, founded their XI on the skills of three young players – J. P. Taylor, opening batsman and swing bowler; the No. 3 batsman, M. B. Ryeland, whose medium-fast bowling brought him the most wickets; and the opening batsman, P. P. Lacamp, who made 574 runs in his first season. Fine team performances under the all-round example of S. A. Tonks characterised the season for **King's School, Chester**, for whom A. J. Martin reached three figures twice and a newcomer, D. B. Claringbold, took the most wickets. Never bowled out, yet dismissing the opposition seven times, **The King's School, Ely**, were unbeaten in a record season, their eleven wins including those v Gresham's, Kimbolton and The Leys, the last coming in the final of the County Schools Under-19 competition. The attack was spearheaded by two hostile opening bowlers, J. R. G. Bouverie and M. E. V. Gallop, while the leading run-scorers were the captain, M. G. D. Chamberlain, and the hard-hitting K. Worrall.

Excellent fielding and several all-round contributions brought success for **The King's School, Macclesfield**, who recorded victories v Arnold, Blackpool (twice), Bolton, Stockport GS, Birkenhead, Bury GS and Ipswich and were well led by C. J. Belfield, a forcing batsman. Batting in depth, and with sound leadership from M. P. Mernagh, the young side of **King's School, Rochester**, overcame the handicap of limited bowling resources to record seven wins. **King's School, Worcester**, were hampered by a wayward attack and batting that was inconsistent when in pursuit of large totals. N. A. Marsh began with 272 runs in his first four innings but then his rich form deserted him. Despite frequently bowling themselves into a promising position, **Kingston GS** were frustrated by their fragile batting, which was carried almost entirely by the captain, S. C. R. Cox. Dismissed only once in single figures, he made 114 v Reed's as well as 103 not out v MCC. The left-arm opening bowler, R. A. White, led the attack accurately and played for Surrey Under-16 and Under-19 sides.

**Lancing College**, unbeaten by schools, equalled the school record for games won, with fewer lost, and took the Langdale Cup in their fourth successive final. Both averages were topped by the captain, J. D. Robinson, whose batting average of 78.18 was the highest since G.H. Heslop's 89.18 in 1914, and whose aggregate of 860 was the highest since E. Cawston made 966 in 1929. His career total for the school exceeded 3,000. A. P. Miller and one of the openers, R. M. Osborn, were the other batsmen of note, while S. F. Cloke developed considerably as an opening bowling partner for Robinson, his 53 wickets being the most for Lancing by a fast bowler, and only five short of the school's record. **Leeds GS**, whose best result was a four-wicket win v Queen Elizabeth GS, Wakefield, owed much to the prolific batting of J. R. Goldthorp, an England Under-15 player who hit hundreds v Pocklington and Bradford GS. The leg-spin and googlies of the injured G. R. Tyler were often missed. A highlight for **Leighton Park** was their progress to the regional final of the Barclays Bank Cup, where they yielded to St John's, Leatherhead. J. R. Wood, who played for English Schools, scored more than three times more runs than the next highest, at an average of 75.09, and took the most wickets with his fast, straight bowling, despite breaking down with a back injury at the beginning of the Barclays Bank final and not bowling again. Under the conscientious captaincy of D. Doraisamy team spirit was strong, J. Berridge and J. Shingles maturing considerably. P. Newell-Price bowled a nagging length at medium pace and J. Thomas was an effective strike bowler.

**The Leys**, who achieved victories v St Paul's and Greshams, often struggled to score enough runs to set a target. They were encouraged by the progress of C. K. Butler (left-arm medium), who took seven for 18 v St Paul's. The attack of **Lord Wandsworth College** lacked penetration and, apart from left-hander A. J. Phillips, their batsmen failed to score quickly enough to secure victories. Beating Royal GS High Wycombe, Wellingborough and Oxford School, **Lord Williams's School, Thame**, lost only to Old Thamensians and Wesley College, Western Australia. A strong attack was led by R. J. Carr (fast-medium), and the captain, G. A. Westlake, gave a confident start to the batting, supported by P. M. Jobson, who played for Essex Second XI. A young **Loretto** side did well to lose only once, recording good victories v Kelvinside Academy and Fettes. Two Under-16 players excelled, the left-handed opening batsman, T. R. McCreath, playing for Scotland Under-16, and I. S. Pattullo (left-arm medium) troubling opposing batsmen.

**Magdalen College School** were frustrated by their inability to bowl sides out, achieving this only twice and winning both times – v The Oratory and Bloxham. However, their strong batting prevented defeat against schools except on two occasions, T. M. Morgan-Wynne and M. E. Mackinlay both passing 500 runs. **Malvern College** won the Lord's Taverners' Colts Trophy, in the final of which a promising thirteen-year-old, J. R. Wileman, put on 152 for the second wicket with G. N. Lunt. The XI, however, was fragile in its batting and had a mixed season. For **Manchester GS**, who were undefeated, the captain, M. A. Atherton, was outstanding, scoring four successive unbeaten centuries in June v Hulme GS Oldham, Royal GS Lancaster, Arnold and William Hulme's GS. He played for MCC Schools and captained English Schools as well as travelling with North of England Under-19 to Bermuda. M. A. Crawley, who also went to Bermuda, reached three figures v Stockport, as did G. Yates v Birkenhead. Although Atherton bowled some accurate leg-spin, leading wicket-takers were the opening bowler, E. J. Bryant, and Yates, whose off-spin could be difficult to play. Excellent team spirit and sound fielding were also significant, N. Davenport excelling in the deep. Highlights for **Marlborough** were N. E. Sykes's 100 not out off 56 balls v Rugby and a return of seven for 41 v Haileybury by J. C. Makin.

**Merchant Taylors', Crosby**, who had several exciting finishes, were heartened by their improved batting, dominated by the captain, M. J. Cooke, with A. Walmsley and S. A. Jones. The attack was again spearheaded by the faster bowlers, T. J. Judge and the left-armer, S. R. Edgington, who were well supported by P. E. Church (off-spin) and N. A. Harley (left-arm medium). The fielding was of a high standard, the example being set, in his first full season behind the stumps, by R. W. Glynne-Jones, who was also a notable batting prospect. Losing only to Stowe, **Merchant Taylors', Northwood**, equalled the school record of eleven wins, which included those v St Albans, St Paul's, Watford GS, Aldenham, City of London, Highgate,

Westminster, Dulwich and St Peter's, York. Attractive and aggressive batting was led by G. Cornelius and M. A. St C. Stewart, who featured in nine half-century opening stands, while the guileful leg-spin of Cornelius and the accurate pace attack restricted opposing batsmen. **Millfield** boasted a well-balanced XI, who recorded convincing wins over Sherborne, King's Taunton, Downside and Blundell's. They batted in depth, the captain, J. C. M. Atkinson, scoring three centuries, including 192 v Bristol University, and being soundly supported by I. J. M. Smith, R. J. Turner and R. W. Hill. H. R. J. Trump (off-spin) and P. J. Stephenson (slow left-arm) were the top wicket-takers, although the fast bowlers, Atkinson and M. T. Parkinson, were close behind them. Atkinson represented MCC Schools and English Schools, and went on to play first-class cricket for Somerset. The school won the Barclays Bank Under-17 competition for the second year running.

For their victories v Aldenham, UCS, Highgate and Dulwich, **Mill Hill** owed much to the match-winning bowling of O. I. Akpofure, who against Highgate hit the stumps seven times for 22 runs. R. S. W. Roberts and later S. R. Premadasa stood in as captain when J. M. Cicale was unable to play. Good wins v Allhallows and Eltham College were highlights for **Milton Abbey School**, for whom C. D. Lindsay proved a valuable all-rounder. **Monkton Combe**, who finished their season with a successful tour of the south-west, had two accurate fast bowlers in J. W. L. Sinfield and J. A. Jenkins, but the batting lacked a consistent high scorer. Outstanding in a wet and depressing season for **Monmouth** were B. T. B. Katolina, who was by far the most effective bowler, and S. P. James, who scored the most runs, including 102 v Cheltenham College, and played for Glamorgan in the County Championship.

**Norwich School**, who enjoyed a successful end-of-term tour of the Netherlands, owed much to the positive captaincy as well as the all-round skills of N. J. E. Foster. The ability of R. J. Wilson (fast-medium) to take wickets on any surface was important, and the potential shown by the young batsmen, Crane and Heath, was encouraging. The batting of an inexperienced **Nottingham HS** side was dominated by the captain, J. G. Morris, and a left-hander, M. Saxelby. N. Hunt, in his first season, promised much for the future. The leading bowlers were T. Deas (leg-spin) and G. Harding (off-spin), the latter playing for HMC Schools. Another young side, **Oakham**, lost only to Wellingborough in schools matches. The batting was pleasingly strong, and R. Wightman, bowling left-arm seam, was particularly effective with the ball. Although **Oundle's** attack lacked penetration, the team fielded well and batted competently to bring off wins v The Leys, Mill Hill, Bedford School, St Edward's and Uppingham. For runs, **The Perse** relied to a great extent on their captain, C. P. Wass, and S. C. Riley, but the attack, led by Wass (fast-medium) and S. T. Whiteside (left-arm medium), was better balanced. Ipswich School, Royal GS Newcastle and Wrekin were the schools defeated. **Plymouth College** began the season with a flourish, but struggled when key players were lost to examinations. S. Crawford often scored freely, but the attack relied too much on B. Johns, Crawford and S. Woodward.

Under the lively captaincy of J. J. Mansfield, **Pocklington** won eleven matches, eight of them against schools. For the first time three boys passed 600 runs – M. J. Baker (746), Mansfield (628) and M. J. Taylor (621) – while 60 wickets were taken by T. P. D. Balderson (66) and J. D. Nuttall (60). J. R. Ayling, the captain of **Portsmouth GS**, was another who led by example, his 775 runs at 70.45 and 50 wickets at 7.74 both being more than three times as many as the next highest. He captained Hampshire Schools and played for Hampshire Second XI. After an early defeat by Winchester, there were wins v Charterhouse, Lord Wandsworth, Bournemouth, Churcher's College and Milton Abbey. A rather defensive outlook hampered **Prior Park College**, although a fast bowler, A. A. D'Souza, performed admirably, moving the ball both ways and sometimes reverting to off-spin. The batting, headed by B. V. Kebbie, the captain, was adequate, sound contributions coming from the wicket-keeper and left-hand bat, M. I. Woodhouse, and A. D. Hadley. For **Queen Elizabeth GS, Wakefield**, S. Das showed much potential as a batsman, and M. Smith developed into a useful all-rounder. **Queen's College, Taunton**, fielded a hostile opening attack in the Essien brothers, C. A. E. and D., and their 82 wickets, at an average of 8.54, proved a decisive factor in most of the eight victories. Inconsistent batting, especially on wet wickets, was responsible for their four defeats.

Similar problems faced **Radley**, who played better than their results might suggest. The leg-spin of J. C. Smellie was usually good to watch, and R. D. Stormonth-Darling's medium-pace leg-cutters brought him 43 wickets in his first season. Wet wickets also hampered the batsmen of **Ratcliffe College**, where P. Mestecky showed great promise as a fast-medium bowler and D. H. Cole performed admirably behind the stumps. Three of the XI played for county Under-19 sides – Cole and Mestecky for Leicestershire and P. H. E. Morel for Sussex. **Reading School** failed to fulfil early expectations, their one win coming v Reading Blue Coat School, against whom the captain, A. N. S. Hampton, hit the side's only hundred. In a strong batting side, J. R. Jamieson established a **Reed's School** record with 877 runs. Although their attack lacked penetration, they won five matches and were defeated only by **Reigate GS**, who were none the less disappointed by their overall performance after anticipating a good season. Heartening victories were also achieved v RGS Colchester, Trinity and Emanuel. M. T. Holman bowled well in his first season.

An experienced **Repton** XI were unable to maintain their early promise on the slow June pitches. The batting was built around N. P. Stocks, who scored two unbeaten centuries, and the captain, B. P. H. Richardson, who also kept wicket to a good standard. The consistent R. W. A. Pyne and P. J. A. Heathcote bore the brunt of the attack. **Rossall** did better then expected with six wins, including those v Giggleswick, Stonyhurst and Bolton School. The left-handed C. J. D. Lees was the most prolific batsman, although some of the younger players showed promise, especially C. D. Foster, the wicket-keeper. A. G. Smith, the leading wicket-taker, bowled with great fire on occasions. **Royal GS, Guildford**, lacked the experience to turn a number of winning positions into victories, although they beat Reigate GS, Emanuel and Rutlish. Slow scoring and dropped catches, from which the left-arm opening bowler, G. Harmer, suffered most, hampered **Royal GS, Newcastle**. Only the captain, J. Harrison, accumulated runs briskly, and the side could have produced better cricket with more application. A young but enthusiastic **Rugby** side was led by T. P. Skipper, who kept wicket well and headed the batting averages, reaching three figures v Marlborough and Clifton, against whom G. Blissett returned six for 38. H. Bhatia, a leg-spinner, again enjoyed rich pickings. After losing to Birkenhead School and Liverpool College, **Rydal School** improved significantly to beat King's Chester, Cowley and Northern CC. With nine of the side returning in 1986, they have good reason for optimism.

Vulnerable in a crisis, the batsmen of **St Dunstan's College** often failed to capitalise on the advantage gained by their bowlers – of whom G. Pointer was decidedly fast for a schoolboy – and at least five matches were drawn that could have been won. **St Edmund's, Canterbury**, had a disappointing season, owing to the fact that their batting and bowling, potentially strong, rarely excelled on the same day. Showing a willingness to graft which was at times lacking in others, K. J. Hopper, a left-hander, twice carried his bat. Only four opposing sides were dismissed, the seam attack rather lacking line and length, and it was the leg-spinner, P. J. Bryant, who collected most wickets, including six for 4 v Duke of York's RMS. Unbeaten by schools since 1982, **St George's, Weybridge**, fielded a mature, well-balanced side, which compiled a record total of 304 for four v St Benedict's. T. J. G. O'Gorman was pre-eminent with 910 runs – making a total for the first XI of 3,373, including eleven hundreds – and 37 wickets, which took his total to 117. A. J. Woodhead, with 52 wickets in 1985, took his haul to 151 in three seasons. **St John's, Leatherhead**, failed to maintain their unbeaten record of the two previous seasons, but, with most of the side returning in 1986, have high hopes for the future. Although their captain, G. G. Philpott, enjoyed some success, **St Lawrence, Ramsgate**, encountered difficulty in bowling sides out. On the other hand, there was some good batting, with A. O. Uzor scoring two hundreds.

Frequently failing to realise their potential, **St Peter's, York**, reported a frustrating season. However, the left-handed J. E. B. Burdass excelled with the bat and a colt, N. D. Muirhead (left-hand bat, right-arm medium-fast), had a promising first season. Positive attacking cricket brought **Sedbergh** wins v Pocklington, Ampleforth, William Hulme's GS, Royal GS Lancaster and Stonyhurst, although they were less successful v club sides, being especially vulnerable against spin bowling. A. R. Wright and R. E. F. Stephenson, in particular, batted aggressively, and a well-balanced attack was supported by fielding which reached a high standard as the season progressed. An enjoyable ten-day tour of the Netherlands was undertaken. A young **Sevenoaks** side developed in confidence to record four victories. The captain and wicket-keeper, J. D. Mitchell, batted reliably, as did C. J. Crang, but the bowling depended too much on A. B. Hood (fast-medium) and A. Griffiths (slow left-arm). Another inexperienced side to mature during the season were **Shrewsbury**, well captained by E. L. Home, who scored the most runs, with J. A. Skelton proving a consistent all-rounder.

The season for **Simon Langton GS** being severely curtailed by the weather and teachers' industrial action, the highlight was a tour of Devon, in which they won all five matches. Particularly impressive were the left-handed A. J. Falconer and M. C. Dobson (right-hand bat, slow left-arm bowler), who, with the wicket-keeper, R. J. Davies, played for Kent Under-19. Unbeaten by schools, but with only two wins, **Sir Roger Manwood's** owed much to R. D. Spence and S. A. Smith, who shared an unbroken stand of 155 v St Edmund's, Canterbury, Spence also compiling an unbeaten 121 v Duke of York's RMS. J. A. T. Ingram (medium) carried the bowling, taking six wickets in an innings on three occasions. In a poor season for **Solihull**, worthy of note were the increasingly successful leg-spin bowling of W. Mohammed and the batting of R. J. Lucas and S. J. Townley, the latter playing the side's only three-figure innings – 109 v UCS London.

A young and enthusiastic **Stonyhurst** XI were well led by S. J. Bishop. C. H. Guyer headed the batting and M. Docherty took most wickets. They defeated Wrekin, the XL Club and Ampleforth, against whom R. J. Fee took seven for 41. **Stowe**, who beat Free Foresters, Repton and Merchant Taylors', Northwood, had a strong attack, in which C. Whitmore (fast-medium) took his school tally to 126 wickets and R. B. K. Giles (right-arm swing) showed considerable promise. R. S. M. Morris, with hundreds v St Edward's and Merchant Taylors', frequently held together a tentative batting line-up. Despite a good win v Edinburgh Academy, **Strathallan** were disappointed with their overall performance on wet pitches which suited neither the pace of T. J. Pawson nor the strokeplay of R. S. Hamilton and G. S. R. Robertson. However, the development of Robertson as an all-rounder and the perseverance with which A. W. Tench bowled were encouraging. Pre-eminent for **Sutton Valence** was the captain, J. P. Sunnucks, a forcing right-hand bat and fast bowler, who scored 150 not out and took six for 49 in the defeat of Caterham School.

An outstanding **Taunton School** side enjoyed their most successful season for 80 years, with convincing victories v Clifton, Bradford GS, Queen's Taunton, Blundell's, King's Taunton, Monmouth, Fettes, Sherborne, Millfield and the XL Club. High-scoring batsmen were N. J. Waters and R. J. Bartlett, the latter playing for MCC Schools and English Schools. Six schools were decisively beaten by **Tiffin**, whose batting was again headed by the captain and opening bat, A. M. Morley-Brown, whose 838 runs included three centuries. Two more centuries were scored by R. L. Hunt, including one before lunch in 85 minutes v Emanuel. With the ball, the left-arm orthodox spinner, M. R. Coote, claimed 46 wickets, twice as many as the next bowler. **Tonbridge School** were unbeaten, with wins v Sevenoaks, Charterhouse, Dulwich, Bedford, Wellington College, Winchester, Felsted, Kent Schools, Tonbridge CC and MCC, the last mentioned for the first time in ten years. The left-handed R. Owen-Browne was a distinguished all-rounder, hitting three hundreds, and one each came from J. I. Longley, who scored the most runs, S. T. Pollington and K. B. Saro-Wiwa. **Trinity, Croydon**, were encouraged to record more wins than losses, the most pleasing being those v KCS Wimbledon and St Dunstan's. Two matches were won on a tour of Guernsey, the other two being drawn. Noteworthy in a satisfactory season for **Truro School** were the fast-medium bowling of R. M. H. Bell and two centuries from the all-rounder, P. S. Holmes.

In a period of rebuilding, **Uppingham** depended very much on A. G. W. Lewin, the captain, for runs, although the bowling possessed both variety and depth. D. B. J. Cooke, with off-spinners, was the most successful bowler. Unbeaten by schools and with sixteen wins, **Victoria College, Jersey**, owed much to their captain, C. M. Graham, and A. J. Wright, who each collected more than 700 runs and more than 50 wickets. They were well supported by the spin of A. D. Brown, D. V. Carnegie and R. V. Melwani. Enjoying a third successive unbeaten season, **Warwick School** defeated Bablake, King's Worcester, MCC, Old Warwickians and the XL Club. Their strength lay in the batting, led by J. D. Stanton, whose 715 runs included two hundreds. The bowling depended mainly on the leg-spin of A. J. Moffatt and off-spin of P. J. Squires. **Watford GS**, whose eight wins included those v Alleyn's, Hitchin School, Tiffin, Royal GS High Wycombe, St Albans School and Enfield GS, were unfortunate to lose the services of their captain, C. S. Dyce, who was injured after making two centuries in four matches. A. G. Thomas, an agile wicket-keeper, took over the captaincy, and the depth in the batting compensated for Dyce's absence. Two left-arm spinners, S. J. Mann and S. J. Easterbrook, bowled with guile and penetration – Mann took his school haul to 118 wickets – and were well supported in the field.

In a pleasing season, **Wellingborough** beat Bloxham, Oakham, Alleyn's and MCC (off the last ball). Two fifteen-year-olds, M. I. Ingram (opening bat) and T. K. Marriott (slow left-arm) performed consistently throughout. Head and shoulders above the rest of the **Wellington College** side was the captain, G. D. Reynolds, who virtually carried the batting on his own, as well as being an excellent fielder and useful medium-pace bowler. The middle-order batting was fragile and the attack not particularly strong, yet wins came v Bradfield, Charterhouse, Haileybury, Repton, Free Foresters, against whom J. S. Hodgson returned seven for 63, and the Royal Corps of Transport. The season for **Wellington School**, Somerset, began with a flourish, but a later lack of confidence resulted in too many drawn matches. Particular features were the spirited batting of J. Clist and the seam bowling of M. Coleman. Uncertain batting undermined a young

**Westminster** XI, who managed no wins in a poor season. **Whitgift** reported happier times with victories v Kingston GS, Christ's Hospital (bowled out for 36), and Reigate GS, against whom M. P. J. Ellingham scored 100. Keen fielding assisted A. J. Bowers (medium) and H. Gallagher (slow left-arm), who led the attack.

Positive cricket brought an exciting and satisfying season for **William Hulme's GS**. M. J. Cross and A. G. Hinchcliffe worked up a good pace on occasions, and P. D. Fearnley and K. G. Rushton led successful run-chases v Stockport GS and Ellesmere College. A first-wicket stand of 128 between G. P. Benson and the captain, the left-handed A. G. Cleary, ensured the downfall of Denstone, and Cross took Birkenhead's last wicket with the last ball to snatch another victory. **Winchester** were less successful than had been hoped, too often failing to force a win in drawn games. Highlights were B. C. Winzer's return of seven for 55 v Marlborough and a second-wicket partnership of 170 v Wellington College between A. N. Patterson-Moutray and the captain, I. L. M. Henry, who took his First XI record to 2,300 runs, 103 wickets and 48 catches. **Woodbridge School** struggled for runs, but the bowling was sound, N. D. J. Henchie (slow-medium) collecting five wickets or more on five occasions and A. A. C. Donnison (medium-fast) taking three wickets in four balls v the Old Boys.

**Woodhouse Grove School** beat Batley GS, Silcoates, Hawkes CC, Leeds GS, Hipperholme GS and Giggleswick. B. S. Percy was outstanding, his 687 runs breaking the school record, set in 1962 by J. N. Spence, and including 150 not out v Leeds GS, 110 v Queen Elizabeth GS, Wakefield, and 126 not out v Ashville, against whom he put on an unbroken 248 for the second wicket with the captain, N. A. Ledgard, who made 112 not out. Percy, who captained Yorkshire Senior Schools, also took 34 wickets with his seamers and off-breaks, although the most successful bowler was L. Savill (fast-medium), whose 40 wickets included a return of eight for 32 v Silcoates and a hat-trick v Leeds GS. Triumphant in the Woodard Festival, where they beat Hurstpierpoint, Ellesmere and Bloxham, **Worksop** attributed their success to their depth in batting and the splendid off-spin bowling of the captain, E. R. Hughes, often in combination with the slow-medium deliveries of J. P. Wilkins. These two played a leading role in the defeat of Repton. Inaccurate bowling and batting collapses were overcome by **Wrekin** after half-term, bringing wins v Ellesmere, Liverpool College and Worksop. C. Fenton was the most consistent batsman, while the fast bowlers, P. Richardson and P. Hawkins, became a hostile opening pair who were given accurate support from O. Davies (medium) and J. Whitfield (left-arm orthodox spin). P. Needes kept wicket well. In a mediocre season for **Wycliffe College**, several notable bowling returns were recorded: A. S. Dickenson (off-breaks) took five for 8 and R. A. Boulton (fast-medium) five for 11 in the match v Marling, while G. S. Campbell (medium) returned seven for 21 v a Malvern XI, as well as scoring the side's only century – v Ratcliffe College.

## THE SCHOOLS

(Qualification: Batting 100 runs; Bowling: 10 wickets)

* *On name indicates captain.* * *On figure indicates not out.*

*Note:* The line for batting reads Innings–Not Outs–Runs–Highest Innings–Average; that for bowling reads Overs–Maidens–Runs–Wickets–Average.

## ABINGDON SCHOOL

*Played 19: Won 8, Lost 0, Drawn 11. Abandoned 2*

Master i/c: N. H. Payne

*Batting*—M. T. Boobbyer 18–3–965–136*–64.33; *M. A. Marsden 16–8–231–43–28.87; J. C. P. Haynes 19–1–482–74–26.77; J. N. Bouch 14–5–212–61–23.55; S. G. Sutcliffe 17–1–372–59*–23.25; M. C. Cox 16–2–264–66*–18.85.

*Bowling*—M. C. Cox 150–40–483–53–9.11; M. A. Marsden 188–57–390–36–10.83; J. S. Hutchinson 215–75–523–46–11.36.

## ALDENHAM SCHOOL

*Played 15: Won 5, Lost 5, Drawn 5. Abandoned 3*

Master i/c: P. K. Smith

*Batting*—N. A. Fenn 15–2–512–124–39.38; *N. J. Davies 15–2–374–64–28.76; M. L. Vickers 15–2–352–68–27.07; D. J. Stenning 14–4–140–45–14.00; A. G. Fraser 13–0–127–33–9.76; M. H. Moledina 12–1–100–37–9.09.

*Bowling*—D. J. Stenning 215.1–65–618–48–12.87; M. L. Vickers 133.3–30–330–24–13.75; R. E. Sugarman 119–26–404–16–25.25.

## ALLEYN'S SCHOOL

*Played 15: Won 3, Lost 5, Drawn 7. Abandoned 2*

Master i/c: J. F. C. Nash

*Batting*—O. Lucking 12–6–189–34–31.50; *J. Bridgeman 14–0–357–80–25.50; A. Stevens 13–1–247–81*–20.58; C. O'Gorman 14–0–281–65–20.07; S. Naish 14–3–199–39–18.09; O. Butler 12–1–125–20–11.36; B. Bennett 14–1–141–29–10.84.

*Bowling*—C. O'Gorman 80–16–259–19–13.63; G. Edwards 142.5–34–357–24–14.87; B. Bennett 88.5–20–247–14–17.64; O. Lucking 89.5–20–240–13–18.46; T. Wareham 95–16–330–15–22.00.

## ALLHALLOWS SCHOOL

*Played 16: Won 5, Lost 7, Drawn 4. Abandoned 2*

Master i/c: P. L. Petherbridge

*Batting*—*E. R. M. Gard 13–8–150–31–30.00; W. R. Frost 16–1–380–79–25.33; R. W. Metcalfe 15–0–273–62–18.20; S. B. Claro 15–3–176–47–14.66; D. K. M. Shaw 16–1–190–45–12.66; J. P. Enticott 12–0–100–24–8.33.

*Bowling*—S. B. Claro 95.4–24–243–19–12.78; S. P. White 64–10–237–14–16.92; E. R. M. Gard 232.5–35–774–45–17.20; P. J. P. Turner 69–12–233–11–21.18.

## AMPLEFORTH COLLEGE

*Played 17: Won 2, Lost 7, Drawn 8*

Masters i/c: J. G. Willcox and Rev. J. F. Stephens

*Batting*—R. E. O'Kelly 18–2–395–64*–24.68; S. J. Kennedy 18–1–413–75–24.29; T. M. Bingham 18–0–436–80–24.22; D. S. Bennett 18–0–414–91–23.00; M. X. Butler 16–5–235–53*–21.36; B. R. Simonds-Gooding 13–2–175–38*–15.90; P. E. Hartigan 16–2–189–41–13.50; M. P. Swainston 10–0–115–43–11.50; J. G. Cummings 12–2–107–20–10.70.

*Bowling*—P. A. Cox 122–31–356–22–16.18; B. R. Simonds-Gooding 269–78–724–41–17.65; J. G. Cummings 199–48–689–36–19.13; M. X. Butler 160–37–461–15–30.73.

## ARDINGLY COLLEGE

*Played 21: Won 6, Lost 9, Drawn 6*

Master i/c: T. J. Brooker — Cricket professional: G. R. J. Roope

*Batting*—G. Fagarazzi 13–8–149–28*–29.80; C. M. Thorne 20–0–560–83–28.00; A. J. Dixon 11–1–247–62*–24.70; J. J. Anderson 20–0–449–81–22.45; *R. A. R. Smith 20–0–440–68–22.00; M. N. S. Dembrey 16–1–270–68–18.00; A. M. E. Gould 19–2–303–74–17.82; N. J. Clark 9–2–111–24–15.85; T. P. R. Goodwin 15–1–204–49–14.57.

*Bowling*—J. J. Anderson 62.2–17–219–12–18.25; J. E. K. Henderson 215.1–53–692–29–23.86; J. F. W. Pollitt 111.1–14–402–15–26.80; T. J. Card 158.2–17–651–22–29.59; A. M. E. Gould 228–35–832–27–30.81; G. Fagarazzi 94–9–408–11–37.09.

## ARNOLD SCHOOL

*Played 19: Won 4, Lost 4, Drawn 11*

Master i/c: S. T. Godfrey

*Batting*—A. D. Lyon 8–1–353–124*–50.42; A. D. Jones 17–4–499–101*–38.38; K. I. Harrison 8–2–197–46*–32.83; S. E. Davies 17–0–496–86–29.17; S. B. Guy 13–2–212–57–19.27; A. J. Parker 15–5–183–36*–18.30; J. M. Muir 18–0–324–72–18.00; R. G. Halsall 17–1–279–60–17.43.

*Bowling*—A. J. MacGregor 174–43–485–30–16.16; P. D. Knapman 60–7–228–12–19.00; J. A. N. McFarlane 150–29–495–23–21.52; A. J. Parker 175–39–485–22–22.04; R. G. Halsall 162–30–566–21–26.95.

## ASHVILLE COLLEGE

*Played 21: Won 5, Lost 6, Drawn 10*

Master i/c: J. M. Bromley Cricket professional: P. Carrick

*Batting*—S. R. Holgate 15–3–463–103*–38.58; R. C. Garner 11–7–107–28*–26.75; T. L. Holgate 21–1–498–76–24.90; M. J. Smart 8–3–121–42*–24.20; N. M. Rogers 19–1–397–90–22.05; S. J. Ashman 19–1–382–78*–21.22; J. S. Crabtree 20–1–310–50–16.31; J. E. Hill 20–4–204–41*–12.75.

*Bowling*—M. W. Yates 132–41–330–27–12.22; J. A. Gunning 65–8–254–14–18.14; J. S. Crabtree 263–68–808–38–21.26; A. J. D. Pickup 125–7–538–18–29.88.

## BABLAKE SCHOOL

*Played 20: Won 4, Lost 8, Drawn 8. Abandoned 2*

Master i/c: B. J. Sutton

*Batting*—A. M. J. Kearns 20–8–731–112*–60.91; D. C. Percival 8–1–248–104*–35.42; M. R. Edwards 17–1–454–91*–28.37; N. A. Matkin 16–1–269–50*–17.93; S. Wain 10–1–110–56–12.22; P. A. Hill 18–1–198–56–11.64; *M. D. Foxton 17–1–129–25–8.06.

*Bowling*—D. J. Barr 148.2–28–395–28–14.10; R. T. Cassidy 71–18–201–12–16.75; A. M. J. Kearns 175–36–559–27–20.70; P. A. Hill 69.5–11–337–11–30.63.

## BANCROFT'S SCHOOL

*Played 16: Won 4, Lost 6, Drawn 6. Abandoned 2*

Master i/c: J. G. Bromfield

*Batting*—*J. P. Thomas 16–1–455–84–30.33; V. D. Masani 16–1–326–77–21.73; K. R. Gold 12–4–151–31–18.87; R. W. Hubbard 17–0–305–61–17.94; A. Phillips 14–0–156–36–11.14; A. Knight 16–0–162–71–10.12.

*Bowling*—N. K. Patel 154–32–424–27–15.70; K. R. Gold 164.5–29–492–30–16.40; R. W. Hubbard 154.4–32–458–26–17.61; M. Goff 71.2–7–286–12–23.83.

## BANGOR GRAMMAR SCHOOL

*Played 22: Won 13, Lost 3, Drawn 6. Abandoned 1*

Master i/c: C. C. J. Harte

*Batting*—*C. M. McCall 21–3–668–100*–37.11; R. B. Millar 15–2–368–57–28.30; I. J. Boal 19–3–332–48–20.75; S. McGookin 21–3–298–73*–16.55; S. R. N. McClatchey 12–4–125–37–15.62; J. Taylor 21–6–230–41*–15.33; D. P. Monteith 17–3–207–36*–14.78; N. J. E. Johnston 14–6–112–32*–14.00.

*Bowling*—N. Sinclair 118.3–37–266–26–10.23; S. R. N. McClatchey 128.1–30–348–34–10.23; N. J. E. Johnston 118–27–318–26–12.23; C. Mawhinney 153–26–447–33–13.54; S. Skelly 83.3–11–281–18–15.61.

## BARNARD CASTLE SCHOOL

*Played 21: Won 16, Lost 0, Drawn 5. Abandoned 1*

Master i/c: C. P. Johnson

*Batting*—*S. G. Foster 21–4–737–165*–43.35; J. Ashman 20–2–537–132–29.83; R. L. Pettit 21–2–525–91–27.63; N. J. Foster 17–2–405–70–27.00; R. D. Whittaker 8–1–180–62–25.71; R. J. Lawrence 16–2–245–47–17.50; M. E. Jobling 16–3–219–33–16.84; K. Bowyer-Sidwell 16–3–120–23–9.23.

*Bowling*—D. W. T. McGarr 206.3–70–472–50–9.44; S. G. Foster 196.5–70–401–42–9.54; R. J. Irving 253.5–83–526–50–10.52; N. J. Foster 207–62–549–36–15.25.

## BEDFORD SCHOOL

*Played 21: Won 7, Lost 5, Drawn 9. Abandoned 1*

Master i/c: P. D. Briggs Cricket professional: R. G. Caple

*Batting*—C. J. Honan 22–2–966–102*–48.30; D. W. M. Mitchell 14–5–369–64*–41.00; N. J. Young 21–3–606–105*–33.66; *E. H. Castenskiold 21–3–563–130*–31.27; A. P. N. Walton 16–3–294–53*–22.61; J. F. Hopkisson 19–3–345–50*–21.56; J. J. Doubleday 14–3–157–33*–14.27.

*Bowling*—E. H. Castenskiold 63–17–170–11–15.45; A. R. Murphy 100–27–256–14–18.28; J. E. Crooker 347–98–836–45–18.57; J. C. White 170–27–502–23–21.82; C. J. Honan 178–35–697–26–26.80; C. D. L. Hoppe 209–43–676–22–30.72.

## BEDFORD MODERN SCHOOL

*Played 22: Won 6, Lost 6, Drawn 10*

Master i/c: A. D. Curtis

*Batting*—*N. A. Stanley 21–5–1,042–119*–65.12; T. J. F. Hill 17–1–488–77–30.50; A. J. Trott 19–1–517–82–28.72; D. C. Garratt 7–0–129–50–18.42; C. N. Wright 13–3–139–32–13.90.

*Bowling*—P. A. Owen 368.1–102–700–69–10.14; A. D. McCartney 236.5–53–676–35–19.31; N. A. Stanley 129.1–26–359–18–19.94; M. R. White 196.2–52–523–21–24.90; J. D. Webb 187.3–43–462–15–30.80.

## BERKHAMSTED SCHOOL

*Played 13: Won 3, Lost 2, Drawn 8. Abandoned 3*

Master i/c: F. J. Davis Cricket professional: M. Herring

*Batting*—*P. A. Brown 10–1–510–156*–56.66; S. T. Fox 12–1–206–58*–18.72; D. C. Salter 11–0–183–35–16.63; M. A. Hodges 13–0–200–40–15.38; S. P. Hunt 13–0–176–42–13.53.

*Bowling*—S. P. Hunt 266–57–732–44–16.63; M. A. Hodges 192–39–549–28–19.60.

## BIRKENHEAD SCHOOL

*Played 16: Won 6, Lost 3, Drawn 7*

Master i/c: M. H. Bowyer

*Batting*—A. R. Wilby 12-3-448-80*-49.77; *D. R. K. Windler 14-5-246-64*-27.33; M. J. Wilkie 9-2-130-35-18.57; N. V. Jeffreys 10-2-138-46-17.25; P. Rennie 12-3-125-49*-13.88; B. C. Jackson 12-2-127-36-12.70.

*Bowling*—E. N. Kitchen 140.9-41-354-30-11.80; S. N. Davies 121.4-28-300-20-15.00; D. R. K. Windler 123.5-29-324-21-15.42; N. V. Jeffreys 88.4-18-276-17-16.23; P. Rennie 115.4-26-357-12-29.75.

## BISHOP'S STORTFORD COLLEGE

*Played 17: Won 6, Lost 1, Drawn 9, Tied 1. Abandoned 4*

Master i/c: D. A. Hopper Cricket professional: E. G. Witherden

*Batting*—L. S. P. Fishpool 16-2-594-80-42.42; P. Bashford 11-6-130-36*-26.00; T. A. G. Lucas 16-1-297-44-19.80; *D. E. O. Barber 15-1-259-52-18.50; G. M. E. Hackwell 11-2-153-48-17.00; P. D. K. Brooker 13-1-180-35-15.00; S. R. Hartnell 13-1-179-51*-14.91.

*Bowling*—L. S. P. Fishpool 216.4-85-408-54-7.55; S. R. Hartnell 97.3-18-297-16-18.56; A. M. Reynolds 142.4-21-415-22-18.86; P. E. B. Armitage 84.4-18-287-15-19.13.

## BLOXHAM SCHOOL

*Played 16: Won 5, Lost 6, Drawn 5. Abandoned 1*

Master i/c: I. K. George

*Batting*—R. T. C. Shouler 14-2-330-67-27.50; *P. J. Rice 15-0-322-65-21.46; M. J. Eden 15-2-276-39-21.23; E. J. Davies 15-4-226-64-20.54; J. M. Tarrant 12-0-230-38-19.16; M. W. Nash 14-1-223-54*-17.15.

*Bowling*—C. J. Jory 46-10-137-11-12.45; P. M. G. Rozee 206-49-643-36-17.86; J. J. Davidson 71-7-261-14-18.64; J. R. Hartwell 163-43-480-24-20.00; R. T. C. Shouler 76-16-256-12-21.33.

## BLUNDELL'S SCHOOL

*Played 15: Won 4, Lost 2, Drawn 9. Abandoned 1*

Master i/c: E. R. Crowe Cricket professional: E. Steele

*Batting*—J. C. Hunt 15-0-595-130-39.66; B. A. Barwell 15-2-470-148-36.15; A. R. Giles 15-0-465-79-31.00; S. B. North 15-4-227-57*-20.63; R. M. Bayly 15-1-281-71-20.07; R. K. Giles 10-1-121-33-13.44.

*Bowling*—R. K. Giles 298.1-88-832-55-15.12; M. A. Scott 130.5-30-399-19-21.00; B. A. Barwell 183-52-487-21-23.19; R. W. Sockett 117-31-309-12-25.75; D. H. Merton 137.3-39-345-11-31.36.

## BRADFIELD COLLEGE

*Played 14: Won 5, Lost 1, Drawn 8. Abandoned 1*

Master i/c: R. A. Brooks Cricket professional: J. F. Harvey

*Batting*—R. M. F. Cox 13-1-421-85-35.08; J. B. McC. Grant 13-5-218-50*-27.25; *A. R. Gent 9-3-153-52-25.50; D. R. H. Spencer 13-1-295-57-24.58; D. W. Reed 13-1-251-66-20.91.

*Bowling*—R. M. F. Cox 57–12–170–15–11.33; A. J. Goodsir 172–60–362–30–12.06; A. R. Gent 104–30–212–15–14.13; M. E. Morris 123–36–335–16–20.93.

## BRADFORD GRAMMAR SCHOOL

*Played 26: Won 13, Lost 4, Drawn 9*

Master i/c: A. G. Smith

*Batting*—C. E. Nichols 21–5–796–130*–49.75; *A. A. D. Gillgrass 19–4–652–97*–43.46; G. M. Bentley 23–8–619–92*–41.26; P. A. Greenwood 26–3–714–86*–31.04; R. M. Nichols 23–2–470–93–22.38; R. A. Leach 16–7–110–22*–12.22.

*Bowling*—P. A. Wallace 98.5–22–345–21–16.42; R. K. Fisher 175.4–48–536–31–17.29; M. E. Joy 234.4–43–751–43–17.46; T. R. Emmott 146.2–40–444–18–24.66; C. E. Nichols 119.4–24–382–15–25.46; I. J. McClay 237.3–55–811–27–30.03.

## BRENTWOOD SCHOOL

*Played 11: Won 2, Lost 4, Drawn 5. Abandoned 4*

Master i/c: P. J. Whitcombe Cricket professional: K. C. Preston

*Batting*—A. J. Davis 5–1–187–79*–46.75; J. G. Northwood 7–1–197–102*–32.83; R. S. Newman 9–1–260–108*–32.50; *A. P. Connelly 11–0–255–62–23.18; I. P. Walker 9–2–137–57*–19.57; D. J. Martin 10–1–166–41–18.44.

*Bowling*—R. S. Newman 125.1–31–304–12–25.33; Q. Ashby 137–25–461–10–46.10.

## BRIGHTON COLLEGE

*Played 20: Won 9, Lost 2, Drawn 9*

Master i/c: J. Spencer

*Batting*—M. J. Edmunds 18–3–582–115–38.80; *A. J. Herbert 19–2–589–95–34.64; G. Forster 17–4–365–75*–28.07; M. W. Greenwood 19–1–470–74–26.11; C. P. Sweet 16–5–251–50–22.81; S. Elcock 13–2–204–47–18.54; D. J. Panto 13–3–179–29*–17.90.

*Bowling*—D. J. Panto 287.5–59–802–62–12.93; A. J. Herbert 196.2–37–541–17–31.82; R. Bourne 207–45–540–16–33.75; C. P. Sweet 90–12–269–12–22.41.

## BROMSGROVE SCHOOL

*Played 14: Won 3, Lost 1, Drawn 10*

Master i/c: P. R. Sawtell

*Batting*—P. C. Duffy 4–1–134–83*–44.66; A. J. Hudson 12–1–264–65–24.00; *K. B. Eyre 10–0–223–68–22.30; C. B. Lunt 13–3–186–55*–18.60; D. S. Bridge 10–4–110–41–18.33; A. H. Ross 12–1–177–75–16.09; I. F. Barwick 9–0–107–30–11.88.

*Bowling*—K. B. Eyre 85–17–254–21–12.09; D. S. Bridge 149.4–46–375–22–17.04; D. J. Winteridge 110.3–29–312–18–17.33; A. H. Ross 67–11–220–10–22.00.

## BRYANSTON SCHOOL

*Played 18: Won 10, Lost 1, Drawn 7. Abandoned 1*

Master i/c: M. C. Wagstaffe

*Batting*—G. Ecclestone 16–4–700–100*–58.33; J. Potts 15–1–398–47–28.42; J. De Bagota 16–5–302–80*–27.45; *G. Binns 18–1–391–60–23.00; M. Greenwood 11–2–162–61*–18.00; P. De Glanville 14–2–211–60–17.58; A. Davison 13–1–201–37–16.75.

*Bowling*—G. Ecclestone 182.2–37–433–39–11.10; N. Goodenough-Bayly 227.4–64–597–43–13.88; J. Beale 192.3–36–565–39–14.48; J. De Bagota 117–30–434–16–27.12.

## CANFORD SCHOOL

*Played 15: Won 2, Lost 7, Drawn 6*

Master i/c: H. A. Jarvis Cricket professional: D. Shackleton

*Batting*—C. H. Forward 15–1–568–70–40.57; G. G. Yates 13–1–233–57–19.41; P. A. Hendy 11–1–148–52*–14.80; S. R. Knight 14–0–205–41–14.64; M. P. Heasman 10–0–138–34–13.80; R. E. Johnson 14–1–178–37–13.69; J. H. G. Layard 13–2–100–45*–9.09; *J. M. Seward 15–1–110–16–7.85.

*Bowling*—R. J. Stearn 182.3–45–592–42–14.09; T. C. Legallais 118.2–23–371–23–16.13; J. M. Seward 100.4–22–362–17–21.29; S. J. Hipwell 143.1–32–510–17–30.00.

## CATERHAM SCHOOL

*Played 15: Won 8, Lost 3, Drawn 4*

Masters i/c: A. G. Simon and D. J. Tooze Cricket professional: J. Wilson

*Batting*—A. D. Brown 15–3–633–102*–52.75; *S. R. A. Miles 15–2–498–97–38.30; N. D. Thomas 15–2–285–70*–21.92; M. G. Cole 6–1–102–71–20.40; P. J. Siddall 12–1–223–116*–20.27; S. R. W. Evered 13–1–174–40–14.50; S. G. Randall 9–1–100–39*–12.50.

*Bowling*—A. D. Brown 224–56–599–48–12.47; J. N. Holder 199.2–54–496–28–17.71; S. G. Randall 120–27–399–19–21.00; N. D. Thomas 129.4–35–331–12–27.58.

## CHARTERHOUSE

*Played 20: Won 3, Lost 8, Drawn 9. Abandoned 1*

Master i/c: M. F. D. Lloyd Cricket professional: R. V. Lewis

*Batting*—B. T. A. Holdsworth 20–3–515–112*–30.29; C. A. Coe 18–4–390–87–27.85; *E. J. M. Baker 16–2–375–91–26.78; A. T. Grundy 17–3–337–108–24.07; R. V. Fyson 8–1–128–33–18.28; D. R. S. Neill 19–1–280–64–15.55; J. C. Golder 20–0–300–45–15.00; T. L. Beaumont 12–2–141–62–14.10.

*Bowling*—W. D. Blacklidge 225.2–63–605–30–20.16; C. A. Coe 274.3–58–770–31–24.83; E. J. M. Baker 99.3–16–350–12–29.16; A. E. Ivermee 214.5–46–693–23–30.13; B. T. A. Holdsworth 105–24–339–11–30.81; T. L. Beaumont 142.3–22–513–12–42.75.

## CHELTENHAM COLLEGE

*Played 15: Won 8, Lost 3, Drawn 4. Abandoned 3*

Master i/c: J. P. Watson Cricket professional: J. E. Skinner

*Batting*—J. W. Tucker 13–4–422–64–46.88; W. J. Davies 11–4–238–57–34.00; O. G. Davies 12–3–266–66*–29.55; J. T. Morgan 12–1–283–100*–25.72; P. R. Kenyon 15–1–320–65–22.85; *P. D. Richardson 13–3–194–88*–19.40; C. M. Harris 15–0–270–55–18.00; L. C. Barnes 15–0–233–40–15.53.

*Bowling*—O. G. Davies 98–20–290–29–10.00; T. G. D. Sykes 187–31–391–30–13.03; W. J. Davies 127–27–451–34–13.26; P. D. Richardson 144.5–30–366–23–15.91; C. M. Harris 100.3–17–315–13–24.23.

## CHIGWELL SCHOOL

*Played 14: Won 3, Lost 4, Drawn 7*

Master i/c: D. N. Morrison

*Batting*—A. J. Lee 13–3–449–80*–44.90; *J. R. Maskey 14–4–282–60*–28.20; A. J. Beasant 8–3–104–81–20.80; R. D. Mullett 13–0–198–89–15.23; J. N. Haigh 13–3–137–35*–13.70.

*Bowling*—D. J. Clark 101.4–16–350–20–17.50; P. W. Hutchings 89–20–267–13–20.53; M. G. Chalkley 107.5–17–328–15–21.86; J. R. Maskey 110.1–18–394–17–23.17.

## CHRIST COLLEGE, BRECON

*Played 14: Won 8, Lost 1, Drawn 5. Abandoned 2*

Master i/c: C. W. Kleiser

*Batting*—*J. W. Lewis 14–5–680–107*–75.55; S. J. Thomas 13–5–274–55*–34.25; S. J. Harrett 12–2–252–43–25.20; D. A. Luxton 10–4–101–35*–16.83; N. S. Johnson 13–0–153–42–11.76.

*Bowling*—D. O. Lloyd-Jones 171–64–320–40–8.00; J. W. Lewis 127.4–27–340–26–13.07; I. R. Bolger 105.1–36–261–14–18.64; R. P. Sykes 108–28–280–11–25.45.

## CHRIST'S HOSPITAL

*Played 12: Won 2, Lost 7, Drawn 3*

Master i/c: R. H. Sutcliffe Cricket professional: A. Karim

*Batting*—N. R. Godfrey 12–0–252–73–21.00; G. R. Houghton 9–0–140–45–15.55.

*Bowling*—P. T. V. Jenkins 100–13–306–18–17.00; P. J. English 92–20–258–13–19.84; J. O. J. Bennett 91–14–367–17–21.58.

## CITY OF LONDON SCHOOL

*Played 16: Won 6, Lost 1, Drawn 9*

Master i/c: R. D. A. Woodberry Cricket professional: L. M. Smith

*Batting*—W. A. M. Solomon 8–3–242–93*–48.40; D. M. Kutner 15–4–509–80*–46.27; O. J. Gibbs 13–1–327–114*–27.25; W. A. Saunders 10–1–225–54–25.00; P. A. Rayman 7–1–111–42–18.50.

*Bowling*—R. I. Millett 102–16–382–24–15.91; H. B. Moffatt 102–23–294–11–26.72; D. M. Kutner 85.4–10–312–10–31.20; S. S. Shergill 73–5–359–10–35.90.

## CLIFTON COLLEGE

*Played 17: Won 1, Lost 8, Drawn 8. Abandoned 1*

Master i/c: D. C. Henderson Cricket professional: F. J. Andrew

*Batting*—B. C. Lawry 16–0–365–92–22.81; W. M. Lawry 18–0–363–59–20.16; *M. C. H. Jones 18–1–334–53–19.64; W. M. I. Bailey 16–1–278–107*–18.53; S. J. Platts 15–5–171–33–17.10; A. J. A. Cole 16–1–221–48–14.73; A. G. Y. Scott 10–1–122–29–13.55; M. T. Hembrow 17–0–224–35–13.17; D. J. Cottrell 17–2–167–48–11.13.

*Bowling*—B. C. Lawry 49–7–188–10–18.80; S. J. Midgley 153–36–446–23–19.39; M. T. Hembrow 136–35–395–19–20.78; M. C. H. Jones 281–60–941–43–21.88; A. A. R. Niven 162–32–545–24–22.70.

## COLFE'S SCHOOL

*Played 20: Won 9, Lost 3, Drawn 8*

Master i/c: M. L. Taylor

*Batting*—C. A. Spencer 20-4-832-118*-52.00; *M. A. Saleemi 17-4-564-86-43.38; J. Waddell 20-3-737-89*-43.35; J. P. Young 9-4-117-60*-23.40; P. R. Whiteland 14-3-253-62*-23.00; G. D. H. Rameaux 15-1-170-40-12.14.

*Bowling*—K. J. Boxall 212.3-42-620-36-17.22; J. E. M. Streeter 73.3-7-250-14-17.85; M. J. Pires 96-14-424-18-23.55; M. A. Saleemi 125.4-22-426-16-26.62; E. R. J. Churchill 110.4-13-440-15-29.33.

## COLSTON'S SCHOOL

*Played 18: Won 3, Lost 5, Drawn 10. Abandoned 2*

Master i/c: M. P. B. Tayler Cricket professional: R. A. Sinfield

*Batting*—J. N. Stutt 18-0-855-111-47.50; *D. A. Blake 16-4-465-57*-38.75; S. R. Curtis 6-2-141-40*-35.25; J. M. Ward 15-5-291-61*-29.10; A. R. Davey 15-0-329-70-21.93; P. T. Ward 13-5-117-21*-14.62; C. E. J. Tenbroeke 12-3-119-26*-13.22; J. Louch 11-3-101-37-12.62.

*Bowling*—J. Louch 150-24-426-30-14.20; I. Coles 198-47-480-32-15.00; I. D. Stephens 118.4-25-407-16-25.43; J. M. Ward 110-14-419-16-26.18.

## CRANLEIGH SCHOOL

*Played 15: Won 4, Lost 5, Drawn 6. Abandoned 1*

Master i/c: C. J. Lush

*Batting*—R. Radbourne 14-0-326-64-23.28; S. W. Clements 15-1-309-56-22.07; R. G. Gutteridge 15-1-300-61-21.42; *G. C. Clack 15-0-265-37-17.66; S. J. Watkinson 15-0-182-61-12.13.

*Bowling*—S. J. Watkinson 245-58-651-54-12.05; R. G. Gutteridge 159-38-506-26-19.46; I. Z. Khan 168-43-494-20-24.70.

## DAME ALLAN'S SCHOOL

*Played 17: Won 8, Lost 8, Drawn 1. Abandoned 1*

Master i/c: J. P. E. Proctor

*Batting*—J. F. Davidson 17-3-341-57*-24.35; *D. J. Parker 15-0-185-43-12.33; B. J. F. Hopper 17-1-195-47*-12.18; M. J. Little 15-1-155-37-11.07; O. C. Roberts 16-0-147-26-9.18.

*Bowling*—I. R. Leedham 41.1-7-133-13-10.23; A. J. Silversides 72-13-278-25-11.12; D. J. Parker 173.4-38-500-37-13.51; S. Hargraves 154.2-42-439-31-14.16.

## DAUNTSEY'S SCHOOL

*Played 15: Won 2, Lost 4, Drawn 9. Abandoned 2*

Master i/c: M. K. F. Johnson Cricket professional: A. Willows

*Batting*—A. Brooks 16-1-461-76*-30.73; J. Porter 13-1-340-65-28.33; S. J. Brazier 14-2-253-84*-21.08; P. S. Fennell 13-5-152-30*-19.00; I. M. Alexander 12-3-151-64*-16.77; A. Lamont 13-0-119-25-9.15.

*Bowling*—A. Brooks 109.5–13–389–26–14.96; I. M. Alexander 161–36–361–15–24.06; P. S. Fennell 128.2–26–388–15–25.86; C. R. B. Page 121–19–414–15–27.60.

## DEAN CLOSE SCHOOL

*Played 16: Won 2, Lost 6, Drawn 8. Abandoned 3*

Master i/c. C. M. Kenyon Cricket professional: D. Walker

*Batting*—P. D. Moon 13–4–256–58*–28.44; *K. B. Hemshall 16–2–355–62*–25.35; D. E. Davies-Thomas 16–2–323–87*–23.07; P. J. Kirby 16–0–362–72–22.62; M. H. Paget-Wilkes 16–2–208–62*–14.85; T. J. Harmer 11–2–132–23–14.66; T. A. Edginton 12–2–144–29–14.40.

*Bowling*—M. H. Paget-Wilkes 150.5–29–415–25–16.60; T. A. Edginton 242.4–46–768–38–20.21; K. B. Hemshall 112.3–27–331–14–23.64; S. P. Connelly 146.1–27–521–20–26.05.

## DENSTONE COLLEGE

*Played 17: Won 5, Lost 4, Drawn 8*

Masters i/c: D. Dexter and A. N. James

*Batting*—*J. Davison 15–2–338–77*–26.00; S. J. Martin 14–1–323–75*–24.84; D. P. Bickley 13–4–183–36–20.33; J. H. A. Hughes 13–4–144–21–16.00; D. J. North 16–3–202–42–15.53; N. D. Baker 10–0–148–39–14.80; A. T. Swales 11–1–143–37*–14.30; S. R. C. Ellis 14–0–190–57–13.57.

*Bowling*—D. P. Bickley 147.4–39–364–26–14.00; A. J. Sloan 112.1–22–297–20–14.85; A. G. R. Collier 130–22–437–27–16.18; A. T. Swales 98–13–350–13–26.92.

## DOUAI SCHOOL

*Played 13: Won 2, Lost 5, Drawn 6*

Master i/c: J. Shaw

*Batting*—N. A. Peters 11–1–327–51–32.70; *R. J. Weston 13–1–282–52*–23.50; M. I. D. Strong 12–2–205–43*–20.50; C. J. Flanagan 13–1–140–50*–11.66; K. H. Blackwell 13–1–120–26–10.00.

*Bowling*—G. F. Chesterman 140–28–353–33–10.69; R. J. Weston 114–14–487–13–37.46.

## DOVER COLLEGE

*Played 14: Won 3, Lost 7, Drawn 4*

Master i/c: R. Quinton-Jones

*Batting*—*M. F. Elks 13–4–328–80*–36.44; S. R. Howkins 11–1–323–63–32.30; J. Huxtable 11–0–241–46–21.90; S. Sukum 13–0–276–53–21.23.

*Bowling*—A. Brai 95.2–20–285–19–15.00; S. R. Carrion 139.5–22–477–19–25.10; M. F. Elks 62.3–4–323–12–26.91.

## DOWNSIDE SCHOOL

*Played 13: Won 5, Lost 7, Drawn 1. Abandoned 1*

Master i/c: D. Baty

*Batting*—*E. O. Thesiger 13–3–314–73–31.40; J. P. Garton 13–0–313–87–24.07; A. J. Morley-Hall 12–2–226–67*–22.60; N. B. Morgan 12–1–184–46–16.72; S. B. O'Gorman 11–0–182–32–16.54; P. J. A. Baldwin 13–0–213–45–16.38.

*Bowling*—B. J. Toomey 74–13–215–16–13.43; G. D. Brent 140.2–26–502–27–18.59; E. O. Thesiger 126.2–32–387–18–21.50; A. J. Morley-Hall 88.4–17–337–14–24.07; A. J. Chisholm 121–18–351–12–29.25.

## DULWICH COLLEGE

*Played 18: Won 1, Lost 11, Drawn 6*

Master i/c: N. D. Cousins    Cricket professionals: W. A. Smith and A. R. Ranson

*Batting*—R. F. Parker 18–0–552–66–30.66; *J. S. H. Lennox 18–0–454–61–25.22; J. P. S. Jones 18–3–361–51–24.06; C. J. A. McLelland 10–1–189–82–21.00; T. D. J. Ufton 13–0–100–31–7.69.

*Bowling*—I. C. Tredgett 317.1–60–963–48–20.06; P. M. King 48.4–10–287–12–23.91; R. F. Hollis 84.5–15–263–11–23.90; S. A. Patel 194.4–32–567–15–37.80.

## DURHAM SCHOOL

*Played 15: Won 6, Lost 0, Drawn 9. Abandoned 2*

Master i/c: N. J. Willings    Cricket professional: M. Hirsch

*Batting*—*M. A. Roseberry 8–0–524–104–65.50; A. Roseberry 13–3–341–74–34.10; R. J. Stewart 12–4–241–70–30.12; S. H. Whitfield 7–2–117–52–23.40; A. R. Gibson 13–3–228–53–22.80; S. C. Hussain 15–2–277–63*–21.30; J. S. Salway 9–1–121–53–15.12.

*Bowling*—M. A. Roseberry 88.2–29–158–18–8.77; S. H. Whitfield 132.5–42–291–20–14.55; R. A. Sowerby 163.4–38–510–28–18.21; R. J. Stewart 130–36–417–22–18.95; P. D. Marshall 154.3–36–448–21–21.33.

## EASTBOURNE COLLEGE

*Played 21: Won 5, Lost 3, Drawn 13*

Master i/c: N. L. Wheeler    Cricket professional: A. E. James

*Batting*—F. J. Westlake 20–2–720–120–40.00; J. J. R. A. Harley 18–2–460–111–28.75; *G. C. Richards 20–2–496–74–27.55; R. M. Day 18–0–490–67–27.22; A. M. Thorpe-Beeston 18–6–250–76*–20.83; B. D. Richardson 17–1–301–42–18.81; R. C. A. Clarke 14–2–203–50–16.91.

*Bowling*—L. M. Valmas 181–41–469–30–15.63; M. A. Chapple 186–40–485–28–17.32; J. J. R. A. Harley 239–47–731–39–18.74; A. D. Ferrier 103–18–397–11–36.09.

## THE EDINBURGH ACADEMY

*Played 16: Won 4, Lost 5, Drawn 7*

Masters i/c: A. R. Dyer and D. M. Standley

*Batting*—*J. D. Kudianavala 15–2–465–65–35.76; D. I. Sutherland 17–0–416–71–24.47; R. N. Barber 15–4–227–52–20.63; A. J. Swarbrick 15–6–178–42–19.77; C. C. R. Robertson 12–1–201–49–18.27; T. M. Harston 8–0–115–73–14.37.

*Bowling*—M. B. Holmes 116.2–41–295–25–11.80; J. D. Kudianavala 221–59–607–38–15.97; C. C. R. Robertson 193–58–448–26–17.23; I. D. Lamond 88.4–19–260–13–20.00.

## ELIZABETH COLLEGE, GUERNSEY

*Played 17: Won 2, Lost 4, Drawn 11. Abandoned 4*

Master i/c: M. E. Kinder

*Batting*—F. N. Stratford 11–1–230–47*–23.00; T. N. Hemery 8–0–162–67–20.25; T. Winstowe 11–1–186–52–18.60; M. J. Bacon 17–2–239–54–15.93; P. J. Woods 15–2–188–35–14.46; J. Paul 17–2–210–41–14.00; *J. Crocker 13–0–177–64–13.61; J. Ovenden 14–2–149–38–12.41.

*Bowling*—F. N. Stratford 92.3–20–248–12–20.66; R. P. C. Cox 122.4–24–436–21–20.76; M. J. Bacon 64–11–249–10–24.90; J. Crocker 98–22–299–11–27.18; A. B. Howe 115–21–383–14–27.35; T. Winstowe 110–23–365–10–36.50.

## ELLESMERE COLLEGE

*Played 18: Won 0, Lost 8, Drawn 10. Abandoned 1*

Master i/c and cricket professional: R. K. Sethi

*Batting*—*J. Holmes 18–3–723–101*–48.20; A. R. L. Stubbs 18–0–356–66–19.77; G. H. Burton 18–0–305–38–16.94; N. Owen 16–3–220–41–16.92; P. D. Parton 14–0–128–38–9.14; J. J. Birchall 15–0–127–31–8.46.

*Bowling*—C. M. Reed 47–16–119–10–11.90; A. R. L. Stubbs 242.4–58–717–34–21.08; J. J. Birchall 178–36–521–22–23.68; J. Holmes 119–33–332–14–23.71; N. Owen 141–28–442–14–31.57.

## ELTHAM COLLEGE

*Played 24: Won 9, Lost 2, Drawn 13*

Masters i/c: B. M. Withecombe and P. C. McCartney

*Batting*—L. A. O'Leary 19–6–686–100*–52.76; *R. J. Hart 24–7–707–82*–41.58; A. J. Prifti 16–8–241–116*–30.12; J. A. Chase 16–1–320–76–21.33; N. D. A. Baxter 20–2–376–113–20.88; J. Peek 14–3–197–55–17.90; T. J. Prifti 20–2–321–50–17.83; M. A. Barker 16–3–161–58–12.38.

*Bowling*—T. J. Prifti 27.3–8–77–14–5.50; R. J. Hart 341.5–92–899–61–14.73; I. W. Marsh 275.3–73–783–41–19.09; R. J. Churchill 92.4–16–253–13–19.46; J. A. Chase 166.5–33–454–23–19.73; A. J. Prifti 138.4–33–457–23–19.86; N. D. A. Baxter 74.5–16–247–10–24.70.

## EMANUEL SCHOOL

*Played 16: Won 1, Lost 8, Drawn 7. Abandoned 4*

Master i/c: P. M. Bermingham (1985), R. M. Woodall (1986)

*Batting*—H. Jones 17–4–485–56*–37.30; *C. Noble 17–0–600–78–35.29; J. Masters 16–3–447–100*–34.38; B. Hall 16–0–444–57–27.75; J. Saeed 16–0–394–47–24.62; R. Vivekananden 14–1–261–77*–20.07; N. Razzell 7–0–138–56–19.71.

*Bowling*—C. Noble 204–22–626–64–9.78; E. Cook 67–10–356–13–27.38; P. Brown 156–18–627–22–28.50; R. Vivekananden 115–13–556–16–34.75; G. Sizeland 86–8–472–13–36.30.

## ENFIELD GRAMMAR SCHOOL

*Played 22: Won 8, Lost 6, Drawn 8*

Master i/c: J. J. Conroy

*Batting*—Malcolm Taylor 22–3–679–75*–35.73; G. Casey 6–2–130–53–32.50; C. Berry 20–6–420–57–30.00; *Matthew Taylor 20–2–495–71*–27.50; S. Horne 19–0–461–91–24.26; P. Beadle 15–1–224–53–16.00; P. Dunwell 13–4–103–35–11.44; S. Chandler 17–1–178–45–11.12; M. Hunnisett 13–1–129–32–10.75; N. Watson 14–2–127–26–10.58.

*Bowling*—Matthew Taylor 334–87–775–73–10.61; M. Hunnisett 182.1–38–605–28–21.60; M. Davies 126–28–376–11–34.18; P. Dunwell 163.2–23–576–15–38.40.

## EPSOM COLLEGE

*Played 18: Won 6, Lost 7, Drawn 5*

Master i/c: J. T. J. Houlson

*Batting*—*G. J. R. Corcoran 18–2–910–139*–56.87; A. C. R. Davidson 15–2–471–167*–36.23; J. A. Baldwin 14–1–336–71–25.84; N. P. Beale 15–5–198–55–19.80; J. S. Jessop 11–0–214–47–19.45; P. J. Williams 16–4–210–52*–17.50; A. D. Woods 14–1–209–35–16.07; M. L. Davies 9–1–109–41–13.62.

*Bowling*—J. B. Appleton 164–26–596–28–21.28; N. P. Beale 162.3–35–536–25–21.44; G. J. R. Corcoran 139–24–472–21–22.47; P. J. Williams 71.2–6–287–12–23.91; J. A. Baldwin 138.3–28–445–17–26.17; M. F. De Jongh 96.1–16–381–12–31.75.

## ETON COLLEGE

*Played 10: Won 4, Lost 1, Drawn 5. Abandoned 2*

Master i/c: P. R. Thackeray Cricket professional: J. M. Rice

*Batting*—W. A. C. Pym 6–2–122–42–30.50; F. N. Bowman-Shaw 11–0–318–70–28.90; J. A. D. Carr 11–2–250–69–27.77; *S. R. Gardiner 11–3–209–101*–26.12; J. B. A. Jenkins 11–0–208–102–18.90.

*Bowling*—F. N. Bowman-Shaw 80.1–15–244–17–14.35; T. R. Pearson 114.5–25–293–19–15.42; C. R. Erith 141.1–28–442–28–15.78.

## EXETER SCHOOL

*Played 15: Won 1, Lost 2, Drawn 12*

Master i/c: D. Beckett

*Batting*—F. O. S. MacDonald 15–3–659–106*–54.91; M. P. Turner 12–0–273–47–22.75; A. W. Pinn 13–1–254–81–21.16; N. J. Taverner 15–3–236–36–19.66; *B. J. A. Nealon 8–1–122–35*–17.42; D. M. Richards 10–2–102–27–12.75; K. D. Lines 12–0–110–28–9.16.

*Bowling*—B. J. A. Nealon 89.2–25–235–16–14.68; M. C. Jaquiss 182–36–669–40–16.72; K. D. Lines 70–11–315–10–31.50.

## FELSTED SCHOOL

*Played 18: Won 4, Lost 4, Drawn 10*

Master i/c: M. Surridge Cricket professional: G. O. Barker

*Batting*—N. V. Knight 7–2–205–73*–41.00; D. H. J. Griggs 18–2–623–108*–38.93; T. I. Haynes 17–2–429–98–28.60; B. J. S. Cooper 12–5–199–44–28.42; J. E. Bathgate 16–5–284–61–25.81; A. V. Knight 17–3–356–76*–25.42; *P. A. Nicholls 18–1–413–101–24.29; R. P. Haywood 12–4–114–25*–14.25.

*Bowling*—R. P. Haywood 248.3–63–630–45–14.00; D. H. J. Griggs 162.5–35–515–26–19.80; B. J. S. Cooper 214–44–686–33–20.78.

## FETTES COLLEGE

*Played 16: Won 1, Lost 6, Drawn 9*

Master i/c: V. G. B. Cushing

*Batting*—G. Lawrie 15–0–375–87–25.00; T. Salvesen 15–1–292–37–20.85; *T. Usher 15–6–158–26*–17.55; M. Ramcharan 15–2–201–32–15.46; A. Peacock 15–1–195–63–13.92; R. Baillie 17–2–169–44*–11.26.

*Bowling*—M. Adam 154–33–407–27–15.07; A. Peacock 118–30–280–16–17.50; J. Elworthy 120–33–390–20–19.50; T. Salvesen 145–43–401–18–22.27; T. Usher 88–12–372–14–26.57.

## FOREST SCHOOL

*Played 18: Won 8, Lost 3, Drawn 6, Tied 1*

Master i/c: K. A. Paisley Cricket professional: H. A. Faragher

*Batting*—*M. D. I. Sheppard 15–4–836–134*–76.00; N. Hussain 17–0–978–141–57.52; A. J. Hamlin 15–5–301–66–30.10; A. Sharma 7–2–108–28*–21.60; D. J. Richards 15–5–182–42–18.20.

*Bowling*—D. J. Richards 117–30–340–26–13.07; N. Hussain 252.3–65–731–41–17.82; M. D. I. Sheppard 110.4–23–325–17–19.11; R. J. Davis 124–34–288–12–24.00; A. Sharma 180.4–48–466–19–24.52.

## FRAMLINGHAM COLLEGE

*Played 14: Won 5, Lost 5, Drawn 4. Abandoned 1*

Master i/c: S. M. Bloomfield Cricket professional: C. Rutterford

*Batting*—C. E. Wright 8–1–239–74–34.14; M. Pegg 13–2–373–103*–33.90; S. Newbery 13–1–400–111*–33.33; *R. D. O. Earl 13–1–397–74–33.08; H. D. Corrie 12–1–318–85–28.90; A. J. Pattinson 7–1–108–36–18.00.

*Bowling*—C. E. Wright 85.3–13–324–20–16.20; R. D. O. Earl 187.1–38–588–29–20.27; D. Latimer-Jones 91.5–11–333–13–25.61; N. J. Williams 136–23–450–17–26.47.

## GIGGLESWICK SCHOOL

*Played 16: Won 2, Lost 6, Drawn 8. Abandoned 1*

Master i/c: J. Mayall Cricket professional: C. Mitchley

*Batting*—*M. T. Haward 16–0–492–70–30.75; S. N. Youdale 15–5–302–59–30.20; C. C. Haward 13–3–187–50–18.70; D. S. Stoten 14–2–179–50–14.91; A. J. Fowler 13–1–144–25–12.00.

*Bowling*—J. M. Flint 34–6–111–10–11.10; A. J. Fowler 188–43–551–36–15.30; C. C. Haward 120–23–472–21–22.47; S. J. Pighills 85–13–341–11–31.00.

## THE GLASGOW ACADEMY

*Played 11. Won 2, Lost 0, Drawn 9, Abandoned 1*

Master i/c: R. M. I. Williams Cricket professional: P. C. Cooper

*Batting*—G. B. A. Dyer 10–2–258–41*–32.25; *A. G. M. Baird 10–1–253–43–28.11; G. G. H. Gemmell 11–2–198–46–22.00; M. S. Robertson 11–0–124–35–11.27.

*Bowling*—G. G. R. Gemmell 68–11–183–15–12.20; D. H. K. Robbins 109–25–342–21–16.28; E. J. Miller 109–28–261–15–17.40.

## GLENALMOND

*Played 15: Won 4, Lost 4, Drawn 7. Abandoned 1*

Master i/c: A. James Cricket professional: W. J. Dennis

*Batting*—J. A. Higgins 12–2–214–51–21.40; A. M. Stevenson 15–2–267–58–20.53; A. E. Kennedy 15–2–253–69–19.46; G. M. Sommerville 15–0–287–59–19.13; A. B. P. Sanderson 13–4–155–31*–17.22; A. R. Linklater 11–1–117–48–11.70.

*Bowling*—R. S. Worsnop 130.2–43–299–22–13.59; L. M. Porter 189–48–527–32–16.46; E. L. Calder 92–23–255–13–19.61; A. E. Kennedy 107–19–372–11–33.81.

## GRESHAM'S SCHOOL

*Played 14: Won 3, Lost 3, Drawn 8. Abandoned 2*

Master i/c: A. M. Ponder

*Batting*—G. Webster 14–0–280–65–20.00; R. Dean 8–0–154–47–19.25; J. Allen 14–1–243–72–18.69; G. Roper 10–2–127–35*–15.87; *J. Lewis 14–0–211–53–15.07.

*Bowling*—T. Berwick 63–9–232–17–13.64; J. Lewis 194–39–476–32–14.87; R. Jackson 143–38–396–23–17.21; G. Roper 134–21–417–11–37.90

## HABERDASHERS' ASKE'S SCHOOL, ELSTREE

*Played 20: Won 4, Lost 2, Drawn 14*

Master i/c: D. I. Yeabsley

*Batting*—*R. Bate 20–2–871–117*–48.38; J. D. Wellard 16–2–404–92*–28.85; J. C. Burrows 19–1–443–77–24.61; A. J. Griffiths 17–3–286–45–20.42; S. C. Seimon 15–4–207–77*–18.81; J. N. S. Crawford 13–4–162–47*–18.00; G. Atkins 11–2–111–25–12.33; S. G. Lloyd 14–0–159–34–11.35.

*Bowling*—A. J. Griffiths 250.5–41–733–31–23.64; R. C. Downes 278.4–50–977–41–23.82; M. Griffiths 111.3–13–507–10–50.70.

## HAILEYBURY

*Played 18: Won 6, Lost 3, Drawn 9. Abandoned 1*

Master i/c: M. S. Seymour Cricket professional: P. M. Ellis

*Batting*—*N. R. Venning 18–1–659–91–38.76; R. L. Croft 17–3–403–105*–28.78; M. G. Smith 18–2–420–67–26.25; J. T. Lumley 15–2–283–45–21.76; J. P. B. Hall 15–6–173–35–19.22; R. R. W. Bonallack 19–2–310–80*–18.23; N. D. Matthews 14–1–193–56*–14.84; S. J. Clarke 15–2–148–39*–11.38.

*Bowling*—J. T. Lumley 244.4–67–566–41–13.80; R. R. W. Bonallack 185.2–38–533–35–15.22; M. G. Smith 138.1–41–345–22–15.68; R. L. Gerrard-Wright 189–41–498–31–16.06.

## HAMPTON SCHOOL

*Played 16: Won 8, Lost 1, Drawn 7. Abandoned 2*

Master i/c: G. R. Cocksworth

*Batting*—M. G. Williams 5–2–151–57*–50.33; A. R. Collins 14–4–499–144–49.90; *J. P. Shepherd 11–2–448–115–49.77; A. P. Hood 12–2–375–119–37.50; S. J. Eggleton 8–4–143–46*–35.75; S. J. Young 9–1–162–38–20.25; A. N. Westaway 11–2–153–58–17.00; R. M. Holloway 10–2–120–33–15.00.

*Bowling*—A. R. Collins 43.5–13–83–11–7.54; T. S. J. Drake 52–18–108–13–8.30; J. P. Shepherd 157–47–424–34–12.47; M. G. Williams 77–28–175–14–12.50; S. J. Kale 162.1–46–405–25–16.20; P. Laver 138.2–36–478–17–28.11.

## HARROW SCHOOL

*Played 14: Won 8, Lost 3, Drawn 2, Tied 1*

Master i/c: W. Snowden Cricket professional: P. Davies

*Batting*—A. W. Sexton 12–5–304–53*–43.42; *R. C. Wiltshire 14–1–439–74–33.76; M. D. S. Raper 13–3–288–80*–28.80; R. M. Wells 14–2–342–70*–28.50; J. J. Pethers 13–1–275–60–22.91; G. E. G. Waud 10–2–133–32–16.62.

*Bowling*—J. J. Pethers 240.1–51–600–59–10.16; M. D. S. Raper 66.2–9–188–14–13.42; D. B. M. Fox 159–34–391–27–14.48; D. C. Manasseh 125–24–354–17–20.82.

## HEREFORD CATHEDRAL SCHOOL

*Played 11: Won 4, Lost 2, Drawn 5*

Master i/c: A. H. Connop

*Batting*—*P. J. Butler 9–1–271–56–33.87; N. R. Denny 8–1–206–89–29.42; A. M. Herbert 8–2–152–55*–25.33; I. J. Bowler 11–1–225–55–22.50; R. J. Binnersley 8–2–124–32–20.66; R. C. Wood 10–2–138–61–17.25; A. S. MacDonald 10–4–101–24–16.83.

*Bowling*—D. Boucher 75–16–206–18–11.44; A. M. Herbert 116–33–279–22–12.68; A. S. MacDonald 90.1–15–331–18–18.38.

## HIGHGATE SCHOOL

*Played 12: Won 3, Lost 5, Drawn 4. Abandoned 3*

Master i/c: R. W. Halstead Cricket professional: R. E. Jones

*Batting*—N. Cowasjee 11–0–218–45–19.81; D. N. Amato 12–3–164–37–18.22; T. de R. Sheppard 9–0–144–45–16.00; J. H. Winn 12–1–156–38–14.18; *C. W. J. Wawn 12–0–120–46–10.00.

*Bowling*—D. N. Amato 63.5–13–177–10–17.70; M. G. Griffiths 120.3–25–379–18–21.05; A. Margai 106–26–293–12–24.41; D. Stead 99.1–18–326–13–25.07.

## HIPPERHOLME GRAMMAR SCHOOL

*Played 14: Won 4, Lost 9, Drawn 1*

Master i/c: W. S. Gardner

*Batting*—M. Kirkbride 11–1–230–39–23.00; W. Clarke 9–0–178–55–19.77; *D. Smith 10–0–112–29–11.20; I. Crabtree 13–3–112–48*–11.20

*Bowling*—C. Senior 30–7–115–11–10.45; G. Broadbent 53–9–178–17–10.47; W. Clarke 134.3–38–306–25–12.24; M. Kirkbride 89–13–318–14–22.71.

## HURSTPIERPOINT COLLEGE

*Played 20: Won 7, Lost 3, Drawn 10. Abandoned 1*

Master i/c: M. E. Allbrook Cricket professional: D. J. Semmence

*Batting*—*M. P. Speight 11–4–556–122*–79.42; M. J. Hastwell 5–3–139–51*–69.50; M. D. Rose 14–7–190–44*–27.14; C. J. Davey 19–1–461–79–25.61; A. J. Inman 17–2–366–72–24.40; M. R. Cass 9–3–132–32*–22.00; S. A. Kerr 15–2–219–53*–16.84; M. J. K. Brown 17–1–210–59–13.12; A. G. Dexter 11–2–102–19–11.33.

*Bowling*—M. J. Hastwell 48–16–105–10–10.50; M. S. Drake 175.2–26–556–30–18.53; J. A. Rose 150–12–233–10–23.30; A. G. Dexter 143–26–545–22–24.77; M. J. Lowndes 107–29–370–14–26.42; M. R. Cass 169–24–596–22–27.09; A. J. Inman 152.3–35–513–17–30.17.

## IPSWICH SCHOOL

*Played 14: Won 3, Lost 3, Drawn 8*

Master i/c: P. Rees Cricket professional: K. Winder

*Batting*—J. J. Zagni 14–3–563–104–51.18; N. J. Gregory 4–0–120–54–30.00; R. J. Beales 11–2–267–47*–29.66; *J. Bryden 14–0–359–87–25.64; P. Finch 14–0–277–82–19.78; A. M. Paul 13–1–218–65*–18.16; S. Young 10–1–111–26–12.33; A. Walker 11–1–102–33–10.20.

*Bowling*—J. J. Zagni 244.4–68–617–32–19.28; S. Young 186.2–55–539–25–21.56; B. J. Gibbons 116.5–34–345–12–28.75; N. E. Horne 112.4–31–307–10–30.70.

## KELLY COLLEGE

*Played 16: Won 7, Lost 4, Drawn 5*

Master i/c: T. Ryder

*Batting*—*R. M. Summerell 16–5–452–78*–41.09; D. R. Williams 12–3–300–53*–33.33; P. G. Shering 13–1–274–107–22.83; M. B. Druce 15–4–219–53*–19.90; M. Jenkins 10–1–178–51*–19.77; A. J. Gateley 14–1–242–61–18.61.

*Bowling*—S. G. Smith 108.3–42–231–29–7.96; M. B. Druce 68–6–197–21–9.38; R. M. Summerell 69–15–215–19–11.31; M. G. B. Kirwin 93–29–250–19–13.15; P. G. Shering 103.5–32–236–17–13.88.

**KENT COLLEGE** – See page 876.

## KIMBOLTON SCHOOL

*Played 17: Won 7, Lost 3, Drawn 7. Abandoned 2*

Master i/c: T. J. Williams

*Batting*—G. J. Kerr 17–2–712–113*–47.46; R. Hall 16–0–354–83–22.12; *A. N. Caswell 16–3–277–46–21.30; S. G. Moffat 15–1–296–52*–21.14; R. M. Godden 13–0–261–69–20.07; D. J. Peacock 14–3–149–24–13.54.

*Bowling*—J. P. Hurley 39–8–96–10–9.60; A. W. Caswell 275–81–654–37–17.67; P. D. Hammond 190–44–520–26–20.00; A. W. T. Ramply 96–14–333–16–20.81; P. D. Atkinson 92–22–283–12–23.58.

## KING EDWARD VI COLLEGE, STOURBRIDGE

*Played 10: Won 3, Lost 4, Drawn 3. Abandoned 2*

Master i/c: M. L. Ryan

*Batting*—C. M. Tolley 10–0–477–111–47.70; A. W. Harris 12–3–378–88–42.00; R. J. George 12–0–242–50–20.16; P. J. Gwilliam 9–0–155–38–17.22.

*Bowling*—C. M. Tolley 126.1–48–193–25–7.72; B. Darby 97.4–24–263–18–14.61; G. D. Tomkins 54.2–13–151–11–13.72; P. J. Gwilliam 105–29–243–14–17.35.

## KING EDWARD VI SCHOOL, SOUTHAMPTON

*Played 23: Won 8, Lost 2, Drawn 13. Abandoned 1*

Master i/c: R. J. Putt

*Batting*—*G. J. M. Cottrell 23–4–702–84–36.94; R. S. Mayhew 22–3–658–114*–34.63; J. E. Shepherd 17–4–255–80–19.61; J. L. Gillespie 10–1–168–65–18.66; M. A. Noyce 22–0–407–92–18.50; P. A. Arnold 19–1–300–36*–16.66; A. J. Donaldson 15–4–103–24*–9.36.

*Bowling*—J. E. Shepherd 222.1–45–757–56–13.51; J. A. Donaldson 242.4–42–719–44–16.34; A. J. Donaldson 132.5–23–473–27–17.51; B. D. Godber 105–16–353–15–23.53.

## KING EDWARD VII SCHOOL, LYTHAM

*Played 20: Won 7, Lost 8, Drawn 5. Abandoned 2*

Master i/c: A. Jones

*Batting*—M. Mullarkey 18–5–392–75–30.15; M. Cope 11–2–238–49–26.44; M. Hawthornthwaite 20–3–401–100–23.58; A. Cooper 17–5–194–39–16.16; D. Chrispin 20–0–276–54–13.80.

*Bowling*—M. McMinn 89–23–235–23–10.21; A. Stammers 153.2–57–308–29–10.62; I. Ball 130.2–40–278–21–13.23; M. Mullarkey 135.2–35–376–24–15.66; M. Hawthornthwaite 51.4–14–160–10–16.00; *C. Lodge 130.5–35–412–18–22.88.

## KING EDWARD'S SCHOOL, BIRMINGHAM

*Played 19: Won 10, Lost 2, Drawn 7. Abandoned 4*

Master i/c: D. H. Benson Cricket professional: P. J. Knowles

*Batting*—*N. A. Willetts 18–2–889–146–55.56; N. Martin 20–3–772–118–45.41; S. D. Heath 18–1–717–106*–42.17; A. C. D. Crossley 20–4–303–55–18.93; J. Sharratt 8–2–113–32–18.83; M. J. Hills 16–2–131–39–9.35.

*Bowling*—N. A. Willetts 214.1–66–502–45–11.15; S. D. Heath 274.4–53–718–63–11.39; I. P. Crawford 186–45–509–24–21.20; E. J. Shedd 111.3–37–287–12–23.91.

## KING HENRY VIII SCHOOL, COVENTRY

*Played 20: Won 5, Lost 5, Drawn 10. Abandoned 1*

Master i/c: G. P. C. Courtois

*Batting*—A. G. Dow 16–1–470–85–31.33; C. P. D. Reynolds 12–2–227–38–22.70; S. J. Miles 13–4–197–61*–21.88; N. A. Ansari 16–2–298–84–21.28; *D. C. Bridges 14–5–165–47–18.33; P. S. J. Bond 16–1–238–42–15.86; P. M. D. Cunnington 15–1–219–64*–15.64; P. G. J. Cunnington 19–2–252–55–14.82; C. A. Wynn-Evans 18–6–153–29–12.75.

*Bowling*—C. A. Wynn-Evans 39–5–177–10–17.70; N. A. Ansari 151.4–24–609–27–22.55; D. C. Bridges 178.3–31–672–19–35.36; I. D. Harris 114.2–10–548–14–39.14.

## KING WILLIAM'S COLLEGE, ISLE OF MAN

*Played 16: Won 3, Lost 7, Drawn 6*

Master i/c: T. M. Manning Cricket professional: D. Mark

*Batting*—*R. F. M. Cook 16–1–324–58–21.60; J. C. Radford 16–1–257–71–17.13; G. R. Murray 14–1–202–51*–15.53; S. W. Ellis 15–1–204–71*–14.57; A. P. Woodward 14–4–136–38–13.60; P. W. Townsend 15–1–163–43–11.64; R. Bell 15–0–123–25–8.20.

*Bowling*—A. P. Woodward 96.1–14–255–13–19.61; S. W. Ellis 252.3–58–743–33–22.51; A. J. Corlett 200.4–32–591–26–22.73.

## KING'S COLLEGE, TAUNTON

*Played 13: Won 4, Lost 4, Drawn 5. Abandoned 2*

Master i/c: P. A. Dossett Cricket professional: R. E. Marshall

*Batting*—R. G. Twose 13–3–478–116*–47.80; *J. T. S. Chippendale 14–2–295–82–24.58; S. D. Painter 11–2–221–50–24.55; J. P. Brunt 14–1–278–55*–21.38; H. D. W. Wordsworth 12–0–202–84–16.83; R. S. Hereward 9–1–102–47–12.75; S. A. R. Drayton 11–1–127–27–12.70.

*Bowling*—H. D. W. Wordsworth 241.3–62–708–52–13.61; R. G. Twose 174–36–559–27–20.70; G. K. Barber 178–34–553–21–26.33.

## KING'S COLLEGE SCHOOL, WIMBLEDON

*Played 16: Won 6, Lost 4, Drawn 6. Abandoned 1*

Master i/c: A. G. P. Lang Cricket professional: R. A. Dare

*Batting*—N. P. Barnett 15–2–439–133–33.76; *J. P. Feltham 14–2–304–92–25.33; R. M. Wight 12–1–205–49–18.63; A. D. Mallinson 11–0–202–51–18.36; R. M. Hussey 12–3–162–41–18.00; J. M. Moritz 15–1–224–53–16.00; P. R. Endean 9–1–107–30–13.37.

*Bowling*—J. P. Feltham 187.4–65–390–25–15.60; R. M. Wight 150.1–32–548–32–17.12; S. P. Gibson 196.5–45–598–27–22.14.

## KING'S SCHOOL, BRUTON

*Played 14: Won 6, Lost 1, Drawn 7. Abandoned 1*

Master i/c: A. S. Linney

*Batting*—*J. Cassell 14–1–598–132–46.00; M. A. Walton 14–0–361–64–25.78; S. J. Griffin 9–5–101–28*–25.25; S. G. F. Canning 9–4–113–29*–22.60; C. G. Cowell 14–1–258–64–19.84; A. R. Mayson 14–3–216–34*–19.63; A. J. Duguid 12–4–157–40–19.62; P. D. B. Lee 13–0–169–36–13.00.

*Bowling*—S. J. Griffin 148–40–336–28–12.00; M. A. Walton 179–20–438–34–12.88; C. G. Cowell 147.1–26–520–33–15.75.

## THE KING'S SCHOOL, CANTERBURY

*Played 16: Won 8, Lost 2, Drawn 6*

Master i/c: A. W. Dyer Cricket professional: D. V. P. Wright

*Batting*—P. P. Lacamp 16–1–574–80–38.26; M. B. Ryeland 16–2–415–68–29.64; O. B. Morgan 8–2–176–66*–29.33; J. P. Taylor 17–1–468–87–29.25; *J. R. Seagrave 11–1–254–78–25.40; R. E. Patterson 9–4–104–34*–20.80; I. D. S. Linney 17–5–220–34*–18.33; D. M. Ives 12–4–103–30–12.87.

*Bowling*—M. B. Ryeland 226–65–519–40–12.97; M. Durham 41.1–9–157–12–13.08; J. P. Taylor 244.4–88–521–35–14.88; E. J. T. Brett 94.3–9–345–18–19.16; A. J. Puleston 189.4–58–504–22–22.90.

## THE KING'S SCHOOL, CHESTER

*Played 15: Won 2, Lost 4, Drawn 9. Abandoned 2*

Master i/c: A. R. Neeves

*Batting*—A. J. Martin 14–1–426–107*–32.76; C. A. Lewis 12–0–263–86–21.91; T. R. M. Jones 13–2–207–63–18.81; T. R. Blackmore 11–0–162–33–14.72; P. J. McLoughlin 13–1–163–37–13.58; *S. A. Tonks 12–3–106–27*–11.77.

*Bowling*—J. S. W. Hawkins 67.1–14–197–16–12.31; D. B. Claringbold 152–50–372–26–14.30; S. A. Tonks 120–26–329–22–14.95; P. J. McLoughlin 93.3–12–350–19–18.42; G. S. Powell 73–17–191–10–19.10.

## THE KING'S SCHOOL, ELY

*Played 14: Won 11, Lost 0, Drawn 3*

Master i/c: C. R. Gordon Jones Cricket professional: T. J. Morley

*Batting*—*M. G. D. Chamberlain 11–2–422–100*–46.88; K. Worrall 10–2–319–103*–39.87; R. A. Hall 10–3–233–78–33.28; J. K. Morse 11–2–291–64–32.33; M. E. V. Gallop 10–4–158–83*–26.33; A. H. Ditta 9–2–162–49–23.14.

*Bowling*—R. G. Bickell 38.5–14–95–13–7.30; M. G. D. Chamberlain 29.1–7–81–11–7.36; M. E. V. Gallop 150.2–40–352–37–9.51; J. R. G. Bouverie 124.5–28–282–28–10.07; A. H. Ditta 83–12–261–20–13.05.

## THE KING'S SCHOOL, MACCLESFIELD

*Played 23: Won 8, Lost 3, Drawn 12. Abandoned 1*

Master i/c: D. M. Harbord

*Batting*—*C. J. Belfield 23–4–815–82*–42.89; R. D. Diggle 21–3–554–92*–30.77; N. E. J. Hampson 18–5–341–57–26.23; T. P. Melvin 17–2–304–63–20.26; C. R. Fisher 17–3–223–33*–15.92; R. B. Stott 22–0–350–56–15.90; J. F. D. Harcombe 13–5–126–29–15.75; J. G. R. Burdekin 19–6–163–37*–12.53.

*Bowling*—J. G. R. Burdekin 207–57–506–34–14.88; C. W. Fitches 261–64–714–43–16.60; R. D. Diggle 199–47–569–33–17.24; T. P. Melvin 189–39–630–36–17.50; A. J. Palin 74–20–216–11–19.63; J. F. D. Harcombe 114–17–407–12–33.91.

## THE KING'S SCHOOL, ROCHESTER

*Played 16: Won 7, Lost 1, Drawn 8*

Master i/c: J. Irvine

*Batting*—R. N. Eastburn 13–3–340–54*–34.00; S. R. C. Smith 12–1–367–94–33.36; S. I. Andrews 14–3–332–80–30.18; A. J. Anthony 11–4–169–36–24.14; S. J. Chambers 12–3–185–54–20.55; D. C. Walsh 14–3–205–52*–18.63; *M. P. Mernagh 14–0–239–66–17.07.

*Bowling*—M. P. Mernagh 301.2–86–682–42–16.23; J. A. Fife 212.2–57–583–31–18.80; S. R. C. Smith 92.5–17–284–15–18.93.

## KING'S SCHOOL, WORCESTER

*Played 17: Won 2, Lost 5, Drawn 10. Abandoned 1*

Master i/c: D. P. Iddon

*Batting*—S. J. Jevons 7–2–181–52*–36.20; N. A. Marsh 16–2–468–120*–33.42; N. H. Sanders 12–2–285–66–28.50; D. L. Evans 4–0–103–70–25.75; J. A. Cooper 8–1–167–49–23.85; *J. E. Mackie 17–0–337–66–19.82; S. Mees 14–0–262–61–18.71; D. J. C. Cameron-Mitchell 15–3–181–43*–15.08; T. A. Preston 10–0–114–39–11.40.

*Bowling*—C. P. Burnham 73–10–306–12–25.50; R. J. Brown 98–17–320–12–26.66; A. P. Blackmore 161–31–562–20–28.10; D. J. C. Cameron-Mitchell 117.2–27–391–12–32.58

## KINGSTON GRAMMAR SCHOOL

*Played 17: Won 2, Lost 9, Drawn 6. Abandoned 3*

Master i/c: R. J. Sturgeon

*Batting*—*S. C. R. Cox 17–2–811–114–54.06; R. J. Pollitt 16–2–339–71–24.21; D. J. Railton 15–0–219–36–14.60; S. J. Dixon 13–5–102–38*–12.75; R. W. Mort 15–3–114–47*–9.50; P. Vamadevan 14–1–104–29–8.00; S. Kumar 16–2–100–24–7.14.

*Bowling*—S. P. Bull 101.2–20–428–20–21.40; R. A. White 179.5–57–434–20–21.70; S. Kumar 100–18–366–14–26.14; N. J. Stafford 100.1–13–366–13–28.15; F. C. Williams 67.2–7–342–11–31.09.

## KINGSWOOD SCHOOL, BATH

*Played 11: Won 1, Lost 3, Drawn 7*

Master i/c: R. J. Lewis

*Batting*—T. Gleghorn 9–3–123–43–20.50; A. D. Ducker 11–0–222–76–20.18; R. A. P. Kent 11–1–187–71–18.70; *R. J. Lloyd-Williams 11–0–180–45–16.36; C. N. J. Law 11–0–127–29–11.54.

*Bowling*—W. P. B. Wright 113–31–374–18–20.77; G. R. Walker 118–18–381–15–25.40.

## LANCING COLLEGE

*Played 19: Won 12, Lost 2, Drawn 5. Abandoned 1*

Master i/c: E. A. Evans-Jones Cricket professional: D. V. Smith

*Batting*—*J. D. Robinson 17–6–860–102–78.18; A. P. Miller 19–2–591–67–34.76; R. M. Osborn 19–3–348–50–21.75; P. A. Parvin 15–4–198–51*–18.00.

*Bowling*—J. D. Robinson 157.1–49–374–36–10.38; S. F. Cloke 247.5–56–654–53–12.33; T. W. Poerscourt-Edgerton 161.3–46–353–27–13.07; T. P. Mackenzie 178–38–508–29–17.51.

## LEEDS GRAMMAR SCHOOL

*Played 16: Won 7, Lost 4, Drawn 5*

Master i/c: I. R. Briars

*Batting*—J. R. Goldthorp 12–4–626–139*–78.25; J. F. Harrison 10–0–248–85–24.80; T. C. D. Hollis 12–2–201–46–20.10; R. S. J. Tovey 11–1–142–50*–14.20; C. M. Siddle 12–0–168–28–14.00; I. A. Davison 10–1–122–27–13.55; A. J. McFarlane 14–2–104–47–8.66.

*Bowling*—A. J. Metcalfe 64.4–8–245–17–14.41; G. R. Tyler 68.3–19–206–13–15.84; R. S. J. Tovey 167–31–604–29–20.82; A. P. Joyce 124.3–20–508–18–28.22.

## LEIGHTON PARK SCHOOL

*Played 18: Won 9, Lost 4, Drawn 5. Abandoned 1*

Master i/c: S. C. Shaw

*Batting*—J. R. Wood 15–4–826–155–75.09; J. Berridge 12–3–260–71*–28.88; *D. Doraisamy 11–1–196–43–19.60; J. Shingles 15–1–203–31–14.50; J. Evans 13–4–128–38–14.22; M. Harris 15–0–182–40–12.13.

*Bowling*—J. R. Wood 81–23–220–28–7.85; J. Thomas 67–27–183–16–11.43; D. Doraisamy 103–29–288–20–14.40; P. Newell-Price 147–28–393–27–14.55; J. Berridge 90–22–308–15–20.53.

## THE LEYS SCHOOL

*Played 22: Won 5, Lost 4, Drawn 13*

Master i/c: P. R. Chamberlain Cricket professional: D. Gibson

*Batting*—*S. D. Bailey 21–4–482–62–28.35; S. P. Barker 22–2–457–73–22.85; R. E. Symes 18–1–264–66–15.52; M. J. Biddle 20–1–292–42–15.36; A. D. Smart 16–4–176–36–14.66; T. C. Bent 20–4–216–55–13.50; D. R. K. Nesbitt 20–0–255–52–12.75.

*Bowling*—C. K. Butler 73–17–226–22–10.27; S. D. Bailey 102–21–267–22–12.13; C. R. D. Bullen 50–8–160–11–14.54; A. D. Smart 144.2–29–406–20–20.30; J. A. S. Webb 105.3–15–337–14–24.07; S. P. Barker 105–27–315–13–24.23; T. C. Bent 156–27–460–12–38.33.

## LIVERPOOL COLLEGE

*Played 14: Won 2, Lost 3, Drawn 9. Abandoned 1*

Master i/c: J. R. H. Robertson Cricket professional: W. J. Clutterbuck

*Batting*—*A. N. Hughes 15–0–522–89–34.80; S. R. Downes 12–3–271–54*–30.11; I. D. Williams 11–3–174–53–21.75; A. W. B. Smith 11–1–205–72–20.50; R. J. Fletcher 11–1–173–53–17.30; C. St H. Bishop 12–2–108–26–10.80.

*Bowling*—W. E. Bickerstaffe 162–34–469–35–13.40; N. R. J. Lawson 91–17–285–15–19.00; J. J. Ashcroft 83–8–364–12–30.33; I. D. Williams 90.2–17–332–10–33.20.

## LLANDOVERY COLLEGE

*Played 13: Won 1, Lost 7, Drawn 5. Abandoned 2*

Master i/c: T. G. Marks

*Batting*—*S. Meredith 10–0–322–73–32.20; N. J. Evans 6–1–114–63*–22.80; T. A. S. Williams 8–1–126–51*–18.00; J. Fitzsimmons 12–1–145–39–13.18; C. Hughes 12–1–142–40–12.90; D. J. R. Evans 12–0–147–37–12.25.

*Bowling*—D. J. R. Evans 51–13–170–17–10.00; J. Fitzsimmons 84–10–315–15–21.00; R. Pickering 70–10–248–11–22.54.

## LORD WANDSWORTH COLLEGE

*Played 9: Won 1, Lost 2, Drawn 6. Abandoned 2*

Master i/c: A. G. Whibley

*Batting*—A. J. Phillips 9–1–311–70–38.87; J. W. Goulden 8–2–165–51–27.50; *S. I. R. Alcoran 9–0–201–42–22.33; S. H. Blows 8–0–161–61–20.12.

*Bowling*—J. W. Goulden 61–7–231–16–14.43; C. R. W. Gould 85.4–22–291–11–26.45.

## LORD WILLIAMS'S SCHOOL, THAME

*Played 12: Won 5, Lost 2, Drawn 5*

Masters i/c: A. M. Brannan and G. M. D. Howat

*Batting*—*G. A. Westlake 11–1–453–82–45.30; P. M. Jobson 9–1–301–89–37.62; R. J. Gregory 11–3–198–47–24.75; R. J. Carr 10–1–172–35–19.11; S. Fairn 7–1–110–25–18.33.

*Bowling*—I. D. McStay 41.4–11–85–10–8.50; S. Fairn 57–18–92–10–9.20; R. J. Carr 143–35–388–27–14.37; P. M. Jobson 75.3–14–348–16–21.75.

## LORETTO SCHOOL

*Played 14: Won 4, Lost 1, Drawn 9. Abandoned 1*

Master i/c: R. G. Selley

*Batting*—T. R. McCreath 12–1–303–59–27.54; M. D. Hinton 13–3–242–68*–24.20; E. K. R. Foy 13–3–209–36*–20.90; R. C. Fraser 12–1–171–54*–15.54; A. Shepherd-Cross 11–1–151–40*–15.10.

*Bowling*—I. J. Pattullo 166–51–452–25–18.08; C. T. G. Craig 87–17–249–13–19.15; J. A. N. Macaulay 109–26–284–13–21.84; E. K. R. Foy 174–64–409–18–22.72.

## MAGDALEN COLLEGE SCHOOL

*Played 17: Won 2, Lost 5, Drawn 10. Abandoned 2*

Master i/c: N. A. Rollings

*Batting*—T. M. Morgan-Wynne 15–0–540–91–36.00; M. E. Mackinlay 17–1–566–102–35.37; *J. F. Atkins 16–2–332–115*–23.71; C. R. Hutton 16–2–282–64*–20.14; J. C. Vaughan 15–1–208–57*–14.85; A. P. Goringe 11–2–118–31*–13.11.

*Bowling*—A. L. C. Winchester 110.5–17–390–17–22.94; N. G. Hollis 133–21–498–20–24.90; J. C. K. Lewis 88.4–18–304–11–27.63; M. E. Mackinlay 71.5–15–281–10–28.10; R. J. Suckling 112.4–13–404–14–28.85.

## MALVERN COLLEGE

*Played 18: Won 4, Lost 4, Drawn 10. Abandoned 1*

Master i/c: A. J. Murtagh Cricket professionals: R. W. Tolchard and G. D. Morton

*Batting*—J. R. Wileman 9–2–272–70*–38.85; S. J. E. Hemsworth 13–3–357–66–35.70; *A. D. Cambell-Ferguson 17–4–378–60–29.07; K. Ramanathan 17–1–374–105*–23.37; A. M. Searle 14–3–238–56–21.63; G. N. Lunt 11–1–119–32*–11.90; R. J. Kidd 12–0–138–53–11.50; A. J. Davies 11–0–126–54–11.45.

*Bowling*—B. A. W. Bellamy 184.3–37–517–27–19.14; J. Green 85–12–275–13–21.15; G. N. Lunt 87–9–361–14–25.78; K. Ramanathan 156.1–30–509–18–28.27; S. J. E. Hemsworth 105.5–21–399–12–33.25.

## MANCHESTER GRAMMAR SCHOOL

*Played 15: Won 8, Lost 0, Drawn 7. Abandoned 2*

Master i/c: D. Moss

*Batting*—*M. A. Atherton 10–6–748–123*–187.00; G. Yates 12–3–458–101–50.88; M. A. Crawley 12–5–350–100*–50.00; M. H. Taylor 8–3–103–28–20.60; P. M. Crawley 12–2–177–45*–17.70; M. A. McGrath 9–1–138–40–17.25.

*Bowling*—E. J. Bryant 149–31–337–28–12.03; M. A. Crawley 115.4–34–213–15–14.20; M. A. Atherton 168–69–331–21–15.76; G. Yates 237.4–83–523–29–18.03.

## MARLBOROUGH COLLEGE

*Played 16: Won 7, Lost 3, Drawn 6*

Master i/c: P. J. Lough Cricket professional: R. R. Savage

*Batting*—*N. E. Sykes 18–3–492–100*–32.80; N. J. Fallowfield 17–4–398–68*–30.61; P. R. A. Shone 19–0–575–96–30.26; J. C. Makin 14–4–283–84*–28.30; C. A. Hicks 19–3–417–86*–26.06; A. J. Fane 12–0–299–92–24.91; O. J. M. Tress 19–1–386–73–21.44; R. N. A. Graham 13–2–141–34–12.81.

*Bowling*—J. C. Makin 246.1–57–647–46–14.06; N. J. Fallowfield 114.1–31–354–21–16.85; D. S. B. Moorhead 151.3–42–590–27–21.85; R. N. A. Graham 213.1–43–757–23–32.91.

## MERCHANT TAYLORS' SCHOOL, CROSBY

*Played 16: Won 4, Lost 3, Drawn 9. Abandoned 1*

Master i/c: Rev. D. A. Smith

*Batting*—*M. J. Cooke 14–4–520–105*–52.00; A. Walmsley 13–2–422–104*–38.36; A. G. Forshaw 14–4–236–69*–23.60; D. G. Jones 14–3–219–41*–19.90; S. A. Jones 14–0–277–41–19.78; N. A. Hanley 12–1–176–29–16.00.

*Bowling*—N. A. Hanley 67.3–14–229–21–10.90; P. E. Church 120.3–22–348–23–15.13; T. J. Judge 185.2–46–554–32–17.31; S. R. Edgington 126.5–37–356–17–20.94.

## MERCHANT TAYLORS' SCHOOL, NORTHWOOD

*Played 18: Won 11, Lost 1, Drawn 6. Abandoned 3*

Master i/c: W. M. B. Ritchie

*Batting*—G. Cornelius 17–4–550–88–42.30; *S. R. C. Mee 14–4–363–64–36.30; M. A. St C. Stewart 17–2–535–60–35.66; M. J. P. Collins 11–3–254–86–31.75; R. S. H. Jones 13–3–214–42*–21.40; J. D. Northcott 11–2–100–33*–11.11.

*Bowling*—P. C. Perrotta 193–71–358–31–11.54; I. Young 61.4–18–129–11–11.72; G. Cornelius 209.5–73–493–42–11.73; D. W. R. Wiles 215–55–503–32–15.71; A. R. Thompson 143.3–45–336–20–16.80.

## MILLFIELD SCHOOL

*Played 16: Won 7, Lost 1, Drawn 8. Abandoned 3*

Master i/c: F. N. Fenner Cricket professional: G. W. Wilson

*Batting*—*J. C. M. Atkinson 15–0–685–192–45.66; I. J. M. Smith 17–5–486–131–40.50; J. L. Fuller 10–2–323–86–40.37; R. J. Turner 15–1–483–125–34.50; P. A. Baverstock 8–2–206–61–34.33; R. W. Hill 15–2–417–108*–32.07; L. J. Ford 16–0–373–73–23.31; H. R. J. Trump 9–2–142–52*–20.28.

*Bowling*—J. C. M. Atkinson 115.1–36–276–25–11.04; O. J. Strachan 86–14–308–17–18.11; H. R. J. Trump 220.1–49–654–29–22.55; P. J. Stephenson 192.5–45–654–26–25.15; M. T. Parkinson 156–29–612–24–25.50.

## MILL HILL SCHOOL

*Played 19: Won 5, Lost 5, Drawn 9. Abandoned 1*

Masters i/c: C. Dean and R. J. Denning Cricket professional: J. A. Howarth

*Batting*—R. S. W. Roberts 17–4–652–117*–50.15; *J. M. Cicale 8–2–219–57–36.50; P. B. Mensah 7–3–130–50*–32.50; B. Hartman 8–1–185–45–26.42; S. R. Premadasa 17–1–401–60–25.06; C. R. Younger 13–5–164–48–20.50; M. E. K. Matthews 13–0–201–52–15.46; J. B. Campbell 17–0–250–36–14.70; B. Chandaria 11–0–112–50–10.18.

*Bowling*—O. I. Akpofure 258.1–63–747–43–17.37; J. M. Bourn 132.4–38–379–20–18.95; R. S. W. Roberts 277.3–46–842–31–27.16.

## MILTON ABBEY SCHOOL

*Played 13: Won 3, Lost 7, Drawn 3. Abandoned 1*

Master i/c: S. T. Smail

*Batting*—C. D. Lindsay 12–1–230–55–20.90; R. C. Hunnisett 13–0–231–80–17.76; E. S. H. Spicer 13–0–201–49–15.46; M. H. K. Bulmer 12–0–167–37–13.91; R. J. Pownall 11–2–115–34–12.77; *R. B. Burchnall 12–2–125–24–12.50; C. F. Meyrick 13–0–157–51–12.07; J. M. A. Boscawen 13–1–138–38–11.50.

*Bowling*—G. Cameron-Clarke 102.1–28–288–22–13.09; C. F. Meyrick 134.1–25–409–25–16.36; C. D. Lindsay 140–31–380–21–18.09; M. J. Harper 100–26–306–12–25.50.

## MONKTON COMBE SCHOOL

*Played 18: Won 7, Lost 4, Drawn 7*

Master i/c: P. C. Sibley Cricket professional: N. D. Botton

*Batting*—J. F. Perry 12-2-297-84-29.70; A. W. Veitch 18-5-370-70-28.46; *R. M. B. Salmon 16-0-361-57-22.56; D. R. S. Gurney-Champion 16-2-288-58-20.57; J. D. L. Pearce 16-0-245-53-15.31; J. W. L. Sinfield 10-1-137-43-15.22; O. Q. J. Wyncoll 14-6-103-29-12.87; T. W. Fussell 17-1-185-33-11.56.

*Bowling*—A. D. W. Kenworthy 81-21-206-17-12.11; R. M. B. Salmon 57-14-204-15-13.60; J. A. Jenkins 178-35-483-35-13.80; J. W. L. Sinfield 261-61-639-39-16.38; O. Q. J. Wyncoll 102-18-376-20-18.80.

## MONMOUTH SCHOOL

*Played 11: Won 3, Lost 2, Drawn 6. Abandoned 1*

Master i/c: G. F. Edmunds Cricket professional: G. I. Burgess

*Batting*—S. P. James 12-2-581-102-58.10; B. T. B. Kantolinna 9-2-164-72*-23.42; M. F. Kear 11-1-223-69-22.30; C. N. Button 11-1-166-46*-16.60; R. D. Bryant 9-1-132-38-16.50; R. I. Clitheroe 11-0-151-26-13.72.

*Bowling*—B. T. B. Kantolinna 155.5-47-412-32-12.87; A. J. Kear 85-18-282-10-28.20; M. F. Kear 104.5-32-369-10-36.90.

## NORWICH SCHOOL

*Played 16: Won 7, Lost 2, Drawn 7. Abandoned 4*

Master i/c: P. J. Henderson

*Batting*—*N. J. E. Foster 15-4-348-62*-31.63; J. G. Crane 15-4-276-92*-25.09; R. M. S. Scott 11-5-135-35*-22.50; G. J. Morgan-Hughes 8-0-167-53-20.87; T. D. Hanson 13-3-188-41-18.80; J. R. Marsh 14-0-148-36-10.57; J. D. O. Spear 13-2-116-34-10.54.

*Bowling*—N. J. E. Foster 108.4-24-230-24-9.58; R. M. S. Scott 74-20-219-20-10.95; R. J. Wilson 146.5-34-405-32-12.65; J. G. Crane 64-9-216-13-16.61.

## NOTTINGHAM HIGH SCHOOL

*Played 22: Won 7, Lost 2, Drawn 13. Abandoned 2*

Master i/c: D. A. Slack Cricket professional: H. Latchman

*Batting*—M. Saxelby 17-2-688-111-45.86; *J. G. Morris 20-4-640-88*-40.00; A. Floyd 16-3-265-39-20.38; N. Hunt 14-2-243-51-20.25; G. Heathcote 18-2-320-56*-20.00; T. Deas 17-1-287-66-17.93; P. Briggs 13-1-202-55*-16.83; G. Harding 17-6-130-23-11.81.

*Bowling*—T. Deas 251-54-868-45-19.29; G. Harding 315-89-779-36-21.63; M. Saxelby 137.5-42-369-14-26.35; J. Hampson 143-41-363-13-27.92; J. W. A. Morris 160-30-506-18-28.11.

## OAKHAM SCHOOL

*Played 19: Won 4, Lost 3, Drawn 12. Abandoned 1*

Master i/c: J. Wills Cricket professional: I. H. S. Balfour

*Batting*—D. M. Robjohns 15-1-502-72-35.85; A. S. England 12-6-215-63-35.83; D. J. K. Webb 15-2-404-73-31.07; T. R. Shaw 16-1-436-102*-29.06; C. M. E. Calvert 13-1-302-51-25.16; *A. C. Welch 17-4-231-54-17.76; M. J. H. Linney 11-3-137-39-17.12; B. M. James 15-1-126-40-9.00.

*Bowling*—R. D. Wightman 233.2–68–564–44–12.81; D. H. Batty 105–15–345–19–18.15; S. V. Aldis 175–37–514–27–19.03; A. C. Welch 165.4–35–400–14–28.57.

## THE ORATORY SCHOOL

*Played 18: Won 6, Lost 6, Drawn 6*

Master i/c: P. L. Tomlinson

*Batting*—M. D. Boyne 18–2–637–76*–39.81; G. D. Stevens 14–5–280–51*–31.11; M. T. S. Barnes 17–1–471–76*–29.43; A. L. Sims 18–3–438–75*–29.20; *S. G. Olszowski 17–2–433–81–28.86; P. A. Akwei 17–2–330–78–22.00; A. J. C. Rispoli 17–2–305–57*–20.33; D. N. C. Cocking 12–1–155–37–14.09.

*Bowling*—T. R. Seys 285–56–646–41–15.75; G. D. Stevens 176–30–486–27–18.00; A. J. C. Rispoli 86–16–290–16–18.12; D. N. C. Cocking 90–16–328–15–21.86.

## OUNDLE SCHOOL

*Played 19: Won 5, Lost 6, Drawn 8. Abandoned 1*

Master i/c: M. J. Goatly Cricket professional: A. J. Watkins

*Batting*—P. W. O. Massey 17–2–470–100*–31.33; R. B. Waters 17–3–341–53–24.35; C. P. Hanson 16–0–383–106–23.93; A. R. Pinnington 12–6–131–41–21.83; C. G. Saul 15–2–264–42–20.30; C. A. Barraclough 14–1–262–55*–20.15; G. M. Jones 13–1–230–45–19.16; *M. J. Sewell 18–1–300–45–17.64; C. D. Squire 16–1–230–52*–15.33.

*Bowling*—A. R. Pinnington 171.2–33–518–29–17.86; M. J. Sewell 219.3–56–612–23–26.60; T. H. Palmer 95–21–325–12–27.08; R. B. Waters 183.5–44–593–21–28.23; P. W. O. Massey 67.1–7–301–11–27.36; G. M. M. Bisdee 141–26–464–16–29.00.

## THE PERSE SCHOOL

*Played 16: Won 3, Lost 4, Drawn 9. Abandoned 1*

Master i/c: A. W. Billinghurst

*Batting*—*C. P. Wass 16–2–495–123*–35.35; S. C. Riley 16–0–359–53–22.43; D. R. S. Woodhouse 12–2–182–42*–18.20; T. A. G. Miller 12–3–135–30–15.00; O. Graham 12–1–141–23–12.81; N. M. Law 16–4–137–21*–11.41.

*Bowling*—C. P. Wass 202.1–59–421–25–16.84; S. T. Whiteside 188.5–58–475–22–21.59; S. C. Riley 123–21–351–12–29.25; N. M. Law 85.5–14–321–10–32.10.

## PLYMOUTH COLLEGE

*Played 17: Won 7, Lost 5, Drawn 5. Abandoned 1*

Master i/c: T. J. Stevens

*Batting*—*S. Crawford 13–3–704–131–70.40; J. Hatch 10–3–329–64–47.00; S. Wright 14–5–384–100*–42.66; S. Stevenson 14–2–424–70–35.33; G. Waldock 15–3–378–58*–31.50; S. Woodward 9–2–131–33–18.71; A. Widdecombe 9–1–121–59*–15.12.

*Bowling*—B. Johns 129–29–439–24–18.29; S. Crawford 136–40–428–23–18.60; S. Woodward 132.5–22–593–28–21.17; A. Hackett 76.4–12–286–10–28.60; J. Potts 57.5–8–287–10–28.70; J. Hatch 78–9–359–11–32.63.

## POCKLINGTON SCHOOL

*Played 22: Won 11, Lost 5, Drawn 6. Abandoned 2*

Master i/c: D. Nuttall

*Batting*—M. J. Baker 22-4-746-78*-41.44; *J. J. Mansfield 22-3-628-103-33.05; M. J. Taylor 23-1-621-67-28.22; T. P. D. Balderson 20-5-315-42*-21.00; C. Talago 10-3-134-44-19.14; S. J. Clarke 18-0-272-52-15.11; J. E. Haynes 11-0-149-44-13.54; A. Pettinger 16-4-150-30*-12.50; P. J. Kemp 14-5-101-25*-11.22.

*Bowling*—T. P. D. Balderson 364.3-60-1,101-66-16.68; C. Talago 86.5-18-275-16-17.18; J. D. Nuttall 381.2-87-1,062-60-17.70; J. Mears 44-6-215-12-17.91; A. R. Dale 130-16-428-15-28.53.

## PORTSMOUTH GRAMMAR SCHOOL

*Played 16: Won 7, Lost 2, Drawn 7*

Master i/c: R. H. G. Wilkins Cricket professional: J. W. Southern

*Batting*—J. R. Ayling 14-3-775-127-70.45; P. Hayward-Surry 12-1-189-54-17.18; P. J. Russell 14-1-206-105-15.84; G. E. Burnett 12-3-135-37-15.00; A. E. Peel 13-0-173-37-13.30.

*Bowling*—J. R. Ayling 193-54-387-50-7.74; P. Hayward-Surry 87-22-238-12-19.83; P. E. O. Webb 54-6-204-10-20.40; G. E. Burnett 127-27-344-16-21.50; M. E. W. Rice-Oxley 49-5-178-7-25.42.

## PRIOR PARK COLLEGE

*Played 14: Won 5, Lost 3, Drawn 6. Abandoned 1*

Master i/c: J. J. Gibney Cricket professional: P. B. Fisher

*Batting*—*B. V. Kebbie 11-1-318-100*-31.80; M. I. Woodhouse 13-3-271-63*-27.10; S. M. Brady 8-1-175-104*-25.00; I. P. Fox 9-4-107-41*-21.40; A. D. Hadley 13-0-221-34-17.00; B. R. Woodford 11-2-141-33-15.66; B. D. Moorhouse 11-1-147-31-14.70.

*Bowling*—A. A. D'Souza 152.3-35-381-34-11.20; B. D. Moorhouse 58-12-170-10-17.00; B. V. Kebbie 112.3-15-329-12-27.41.

## QUEEN ELIZABETH GRAMMAR SCHOOL, WAKEFIELD

*Played 12: Won 4, Lost 3, Drawn 5*

Master i/c: T. Barker

*Batting*—S. Das 8-1-214-78*-30.57; M. Smith 10-0-212-58-21.20; M. Whitmore 9-0-152-45-16.88; J. Wild 7-0-116-42-16.57; *J. Berry 8-0-100-33-12.50.

*Bowling*—M. Smith 119-37-235-28-8.39; J. Berry 104-17-334-19-17.57.

## QUEEN'S COLLEGE, TAUNTON

*Played 16: Won 8, Lost 4, Drawn 4*

Master i/c: J. W. Davies

*Batting*—*R. J. Veillard 15-5-292-66*-29.20; M. K. Jones 16-0-429-77-26.81; A. M. Tanner 16-3-327-70-25.15; J. J. Wilson 16-1-333-57-22.20; M. R. E. Scholfield 11-1-218-106-21.80; C. A. E. Essien 10-4-114-36*-19.00; A. J. Turner 16-1-275-88-18.33.

*Bowling*—C. A. E. Essien 187-74-383-47-8.14; D. Essien 149-55-318-35-9.08; D. Knight 62-15-176-12-14.66; R. J. Veillard 47-7-154-10-15.40; A. M. Tanner 79-20-248-16-15.50; G. Hawkins 57-19-166-10-16.60.

## RADLEY COLLEGE

*Played 16: Won 3, Lost 5, Drawn 8*

Master i/c: G. de W. Waller — Cricket professional: A. G. Robinson

*Batting*—J. S. Myers 5–2–164–78*–54.66; N. F. Craven 13–3–271–46–27.10; *N. E. Marsh 14–0–377–107–26.92; R. J. Flury 13–1–287–60–23.91; C. H. H. Pegg 7–1–134–79–22.33; J. R. G. Stephenson 13–0–220–53–16.92; J. C. Smellie 11–1–169–44–16.90; A. R. Eliot 12–3–117–31–13.00; M. J. Marvin 10–1–117–53–13.00.

*Bowling*—J. C. Smellie 123–35–269–23–11.69; R. D. Stormonth-Darling 254–84–546–43–12.69; J. R. G. Stephenson 166–38–428–20–21.40; N. E. Marsh 166–50–376–17–22.11.

## RATCLIFFE COLLEGE

*Played 14: Won 2, Lost 4, Drawn 8. Abandoned 5*

Master i/c: C. W. Swan

*Batting*—P. H. E. Morel 13–6–215–55–30.71; R. J. d'Mello 14–0–333–75–23.78; J. Farnell 14–1–217–40–16.69; D. H. Cole 13–1–157–52*–13.08.

*Bowling*—P. A. Mestecky 155–47–388–24–16.16; D. J. Herrington 82–16–280–15–18.66; P. H. E. Morel 87–14–289–10–28.90.

## READING SCHOOL

*Played 15: Won 1, Lost 8, Drawn 6. Abandoned 1*

Master i/c: R. G. Owen — Cricket professional: A. Dindar

*Batting*—J. E. Grimsdale 14–0–395–66–28.21; A. T. G. Johnstone 13–1–313–69–26.08; *A. N. S. Hampton 15–0–376–100–25.06; J. N. S. Hampton 14–1–312–75*–24.00; J. S. Pritchard 14–3–227–37*–20.63; N. Heppel 9–0–137–31–15.22; M. W. Palmer 14–1–190–31–14.61; A. J. Hathaway 11–3–105–22*–13.12; A. Wrenn 13–1–110–21–9.16.

*Bowling*—J. S. Pritchard 220.2–59–562–42–13.38; M. W. Palmer 70.2–10–228–13–17.53; P. D. Bunch 71–10–254–11–23.09; A. J. Hathaway 98–17–343–13–26.38; A. N. S. Hampton 114–22–377–14–26.92.

## REED'S SCHOOL

*Played 16: Won 6, Lost 1, Drawn 9*

Master i/c: G. R. Martin

*Batting*—J. R. Jamieson 16–3–877–153*–67.46; D. Jaksic 11–4–228–71–32.57; J. D. F. Paris 16–2–454–60–32.42; B. Eyre-Varnier 13–1–276–59–23.00; *S. H. K. Maddock 14–3–226–41–20.54; L. E. Jones 11–5–109–28*–18.16; D. M. Keyes 11–0–187–83–17.00.

*Bowling*—J. D. F. Paris 102.5–16–351–22–15.95; D. M. Paterson 174.1–47–564–26–21.69; T. T. Oliver 146–28–600–23–26.08; A. D. I. Darroch-Warren 85–16–337–10–33.70; D. Jaksic 185–42–522–15–34.80.

## REIGATE GRAMMAR SCHOOL

*Played 16: Won 5, Lost 6, Drawn 5. Abandoned 3*

Master i/c: D. C. R. Jones — Cricket professional: H. Newton

*Batting*—T. S. M. Linnington 13–1–380–73–31.66; P. A. Rowlinson 10–1–266–49–29.55; T. J. Lander 16–1–349–71–23.26; S. J. Chenery 8–1–160–55–22.85; *A. S. Clayton 16–0–360–54–22.50.

*Bowling*—M. T. Holman 159.4–32–468–33–14.18; T. S. M. Linnington 119.2–25–481–26–18.50; P. A. Rowlinson 189.1–63–448–24–18.66.

## REPTON SCHOOL

*Played 20: Won 5, Lost 7, Drawn 8. Abandoned 2*

Master i/c: M. Stones Cricket professional: M. K. Kettle

*Batting*—N. P. Stocks 17–6–589–100*–53.54; *B. P. H. Richardson 18–4–557–81*–39.78; G. M. Cook 19–0–414–68–21.78; A. A. Bradwell 18–2–315–55*–19.68; C. E. Wall 13–1–208–38–17.33.

*Bowling*—R. W. A. Pyne 231–52–654–41–15.95; P. J. Brownhill 150–33–460–28–16.42; P. J. A. Heathcote 203–38–640–33–19.39; D. J. Anderson 115–33–278–13–21.38; C. E. Wall 74–14–275–10–27.50.

## ROSSALL SCHOOL

*Played 17: Won 6, Lost 4, Drawn 7. Abandoned 2*

Master i/c: R. J. Clapp

*Batting*—*C. J. D. Lees 18–3–386–79*–25.73; S. M. Chalmers 17–2–353–58*–23.53; P. L. Smith 15–5–212–41–21.20; C. D. Foster 16–0–298–61–18.62; P. Cartwright 17–0–272–67–16.00; A. G. Bowman 11–4–105–39*–15.00; M. P. D. Greenwood 18–1–242–48–14.23; P. A. Clayton 12–2–113–40–11.30.

*Bowling*—P. M. Hudson 37–10–89–10–8.90; A. G. Smith 263–59–719–41–17.53; C. J. D. Lees 181–27–646–29–22.27; J. A. Bailey 136–31–417–17–24.52.

## THE ROYAL GRAMMAR SCHOOL, GUILDFORD

*Played 13: Won 3, Lost 3, Drawn 7*

Master i/c: S. B. R. Shore

*Batting*—S. Forber 12–3–231–69–25.66; C. Livingston 12–0–266–97–22.16; N. Bowman 7–1–129–66*–21.50; *P. Gullick 13–1–248–100*–20.66; N. Canning 13–0–213–45–16.38; M. Cain 13–0–189–51–14.53.

*Bowling*—C. Livingston 122.5–24–367–27–13.59; A. Oldroyd 44–13–136–10–13.60; N. Canning 107–16–306–22–13.90; T. Jeveons 96.5–20–248–15–16.53; W. Haynes 48.4–8–190–10–19.00; P. Gullick 62–12–214–10–21.40.

## ROYAL GRAMMAR SCHOOL, NEWCASTLE

*Played 15: Won 3, Lost 5, Drawn 7. Abandoned 3*

Master i/c: D. W. Smith

*Batting*—P. Hollis 14–3–289–58*–26.27; T. Meears-White 8–2–136–39*–22.66; C. J. Hall 10–0–219–82–21.90; *J. Harrison 15–2–242–54–18.61; M. Scott 15–1–254–53–18.14.

*Bowling*—P. Hollis 83–23–209–12–17.41; G. Harmer 177.4–45–496–26–19.07; S. Johnson 112–24–297–15–19.80; A. Atkinson 83.3–13–282–14–20.14; M. Preston 164.4–30–595–29–20.51; S. Curtis 90.1–13–291–12–24.25.

## RUGBY SCHOOL

*Played 15: Won 4, Lost 4, Drawn 7. Abandoned 1*

Master i/c: K. Siviter Cricket professional: W. J. Stewart

*Batting*—*T. P. Skipper 17-1-665-112-41.56; Y. J. Khan 17-2-338-64*-22.53; A. G. H. Lamberty 9-2-139-38-19.85; J. O. Onile-Ere 16-3-234-55*-18.00; R. A. Sutton 15-3-190-39*-15.83; T. H. A. Arulampalam 17-1-247-45-15.43; A. J. Holmes 16-2-186-37-13.28.

*Bowling*—G. Blissitt 212-67-484-33-14.66; H. Bhatia 281.4-84-762-43-17.72; J. O. Onile-Ere 112-32-317-13-24.38; J. J. Bourne 153-46-487-15-32.46.

## RYDAL SCHOOL

*Played 10: Won 4, Lost 3, Drawn 3*

Master i/c: M. H. Stevenson Cricket professional: R. W. C. Pitman

*Batting*—C. Robinson 9-1-238-75-29.75; M. Sherrington 10-1-196-46-21.77; M. Morrison 10-1-176-37-19.55; E. Jones 9-2-119-48-17.00.

*Bowling*—I. Lloyd 129.3-36-300-19-15.78; M. Sherrington 136-43-287-16-17.93; C. Robinson 95.1-25-260-14-18.57.

## ST DUNSTAN'S COLLEGE

*Played 17: Won 4, Lost 3, Drawn 10. Abandoned 1*

Master i/c: C. Matten

*Batting*—G. Pointer 12-3-292-69-32.44; S. Tyler 17-1-423-80-26.43; K. Norman 14-1-255-78*-19.61; A. Dowler 10-0-195-42-19.50; M. Slade 12-1-189-51-17.18; R. Moyse 11-3-121-32-15.12; C. Steer 9-2-102-34-14.57; R. Cosgrove 13-1-173-47-14.41; A. Colley 11-0-141-47-12.81; E. Moseley 12-1-128-21-11.63.

*Bowling*—N. Cross 53-9-177-14-12.64; G. Pointer 146-45-375-29-12.93; M. Slade 128-27-346-22-15.72; K. Norman 190-44-583-29-20.10; A. Dowler 129-34-342-14-24.42.

## ST EDMUND'S SCHOOL, CANTERBURY

*Played 14: Won 3, Lost 6, Drawn 5*

Master i/c: H. W. Scott Cricket professional: D. V. P. Wright

*Batting*—K. J. Hopper 12-3-346-75*-38.44; M. L. Lunn 12-3-251-47-27.88; S. D. Beckett 10-0-277-86-27.70; P. A. H. Maffett 13-4-227-56-25.22; D. H. Hopkins 14-0-296-58-21.14; A. J. C. Eagar 14-5-173-57*-19.22.

*Bowling*—P. J. Bryant 70.4-11-270-15-18.00; D. M. Fenton 43-1-200-11-18.18; M. L. Lunn 96-16-368-14-26.28; *S. M. Tarrant 120-20-428-14-30.57.

## ST EDWARD'S SCHOOL, OXFORD

*Played 15: Won 1, Lost 7, Drawn 7*

Master i/c: P. G. Badger Cricket professional: B. R. Edrich

*Batting*—A. G. C. Brown 15-1-421-70-30.07; P. G. St J. Daniel 14-1-220-64-16.92; *R. W. Sadler 13-0-205-70-15.76; G. J. Young 13-1-188-50-15.66; J. D. Ball 15-0-230-50-15.33; S. K. Gray 11-2-137-47*-15.22; D. N. Webster 13-2-111-34*-10.09.

*Bowling*—R. A. Spalding 154.3-37-440-28-15.71; R. W. Sadler 110.7-20-360-19-18.94; J. M. Kelly 198-53-522-21-24.85.

## ST GEORGE'S COLLEGE, WEYBRIDGE

*Played 20: Won 12, Lost 2, Drawn 6. Abandoned 2*

Master i/c: B. V. O'Gorman

*Batting*—*T. J. G. O'Gorman 20-5-910-116*-60.66; P. Segal 12-6-285-67-47.50; C. Crossley 20-2-681-145-37.83; P. E. R. Jansen 16-3-389-113-29.92; I. Marsh 15-1-358-62-25.57; A. J. Woodhead 13-1-201-75-16.75; N. Henderson 13-4-125-36*-13.88; A. J. Smith 17-0-208-32-12.23.

*Bowling*—A. J. Woodhead 313.4-103-635-52-12.21; T. J. G. O'Gorman 185-36-526-37-14.21; G. Parmenter 176-37-430-26-16.53; P. Segal 178.3-56-375-22-17.04; H. J. S. Harper 126.2-24-319-15-21.26.

## ST JOHN'S SCHOOL, LEATHERHEAD

*Played 16: Won 2, Lost 4, Drawn 10*

Master i/c: A. B. Gale Cricket professional: E. Shepperd

*Batting*—S. G. Foster 12-1-266-51-24.18; A. C. Martin 16-1-362-72-24.13; S. J. Walster 16-1-314-58-20.93; S. E. Penfold 15-2-234-76*-18.00; J. P. Harwood 16-1-260-50-17.33; *H. R. A. F. Davies 14-5-127-26*-14.11; A. S. Campbell 16-0-190-46-11.87.

*Bowling*—A. C. Martin 98.5-28-272-13-20.92; S. J. Walster 212-54-524-24-21.83; D. S. McDaniel 120-25-384-14-27.42; J. R. Meier 146.4-33-504-18-28.00.

## ST LAWRENCE COLLEGE

*Played 17: Won 5, Lost 4, Drawn 8. Abandoned 2*

Master i/c: N. O. S. Jones Cricket professional: L. D'Arcy

*Batting*—A. O. Uzor 17-1-578-113*-36.12; E. V. Phillips 16-4-391-77*-32.58; J. W. D. Stevens 16-7-257-31-28.55; *G. G. Philpott 17-2-392-97*-26.13; M. J. Stevens 10-3-165-44-23.57; J. P. D. Yonge 9-2-142-68-20.28; M. Carrington 11-1-196-47-19.60.

*Bowling*—G. G. Philpott 216.4-35-806-30-26.86; M. J. Stevens 200-38-727-24-30.29; A. O. Uzor 164.4-18-617-17-36.29; M. Carrington 108.2-12-421-10-42.10.

## ST PAUL'S SCHOOL

*Played 18: Won 2, Lost 6, Drawn 10*

Master i/c: G. Hughes Cricket professional: E. W. Whitfield

*Batting*—P. E. Hoult 10-2-285-86*-35.62; *M. G. Boulton 19-2-558-88*-32.82; J. P. Partridge 19-0-601-118-31.63; P. J. Littler 19-3-400-80-25.00; R. W. Bool 15-4-258-43-23.45; R. Frost 14-0-287-62-20.50; P. L. Graham 15-4-225-65-20.45; E. M. Clayman 12-3-140-51-15.55.

*Bowling*—R. Frost 162.3-26-483-22-21.95; C. R. S. Dare 81-19-268-11-24.36; J. J. Farrell 227.1-61-706-23-30.69; R. J. Smith 109.2-17-425-11-38.63; A. P. F. Simpson 150.4-32-453-10-45.30.

## ST PETER'S SCHOOL, YORK

*Played 19: Won 3, Lost 6, Drawn 10. Abandoned 2*

Master i/c: D. Kirby Cricket professional: K. Mohan

*Batting*—J. E. B. Burdass 19-2-623-97-36.64; D. M. D. White 5-1-112-55*-28.00; P. J. E. Brierley 16-6-250-47-25.00; N. D. Muirhead 18-1-364-64-21.41; *G. Y. Taylor 10-0-199-45-19.90; C. E. Gilman 16-0-210-51-13.12; J. Brewster 14-2-154-51*-12.83.

*Bowling*—G. Y. Taylor 111-26-332-16-20.75; I. J. Barker 140.5-39-441-21-21.00; N. D. Muirhead 158.5-26-545-21-25.95; J. Brewster 112.4-17-526-18-29.22; S. Forman 160-21-483-13-37.15.

## SEDBERGH SCHOOL

*Played 15: Won 6, Lost 3, Drawn 6*

Master i/c: M. J. Morris

*Batting*—R. E. F. Stephenson 15-2-610-105-46.92; *A. R. Wright 15-4-460-96*-41.81; J. I. Foggitt 12-3-252-62-28.00; G. J. Porritt 12-2-161-52-16.10; N. D. D. Roberts 12-3-143-52*-15.88; A. J. D. Wheatley 13-2-170-52-15.45; M. W. Mewburn 14-0-193-38-13.78.

*Bowling*—A. Farrington 141.1-52-335-22-15.22; M. W. Mewburn 171-33-461-30-15.36; J. I. Foggitt 119.4-30-343-22-15.59; N. D. D. Roberts 177.2-41-419-24-17.45; S. M. Short 139-25-414-18-23.00.

## SEVENOAKS SCHOOL

*Played 15: Won 4, Lost 7, Drawn 4. Abandoned 2*

Master i/c: I. J. B. Walker

*Batting*—*J. D. Mitchell 15-2-390-67*-30.00; C. J. Crang 12-2-245-45-24.50; M. J. Hodgson 15-2-289-88-22.23; N. C. Baker 11-0-210-69-19.09; S. C. West 15-0-263-67-17.53.

*Bowling*—A. Griffiths 167-33-542-36-15.05; A. B. Hood 140.3-29-388-23-16.86; M. J. Hodgson 111-12-396-14-28.28.

## SHERBORNE SCHOOL

*Played 16: Won 1, Lost 4, Drawn 11. Abandoned 2*

Master i/c: A. J. Hignell Cricket professional: C. Stone

*Batting*—S. W. D. Rintoul 16-0-681-134-42.56; P. M. S. Slade 14-3-267-67*-24.27; *D. M. G. Wright 16-3-293-82*-22.53; A. Kardooni 16-0-342-71-21.37; N. H. Peters 15-2-270-53-20.76; A. J. Romer-Lee 9-0-181-67-20.11; J. D. Milne 15-0-231-43-15.40.

*Bowling*—N. H. Peters 209-56-488-37-13.18; D. J. Stober 76.2-12-275-13-21.15; P. M. S. Slade 103.3-17-430-20-21.50; A. C. James 191-58-596-22-27.09.

## SHREWSBURY SCHOOL

*Played 23: Won 3, Lost 2, Drawn 18*

Master i/c: C. M. B. Williams Cricket professional: P. H. Bromley

*Batting*—*E. L. Home 21-1-649-87-32.45; J. R. Prichard 19-2-516-93-30.35; J. A. Skelton 19-3-462-70-28.87; R. W. H. Lanyon 11-3-230-67*-28.75; D. J. Burrows 21-6-422-66-28.13; C. M. Bullock 8-3-136-52-27.20; C. R. Haines 16-4-275-62-22.91; E. J. Everall 15-1-264-55-18.85; N. J. Miller 15-4-184-32-16.72; J. E. Lush 11-1-108-33-10.80.

*Bowling*—J. A. Skelton 277.1-74-669-43-15.55; D. J. Burrows 225.3-53-642-34-18.88; E. L. Home 178.3-40-558-19-29.36; D. J. Magennis 178.4-32-542-18-30.11; M. J. Lascelles 226.5-51-776-23-33.73.

## SIMON LANGTON GRAMMAR SCHOOL

*Played 7: Won 5, Lost 0, Drawn 2. Abandoned 1*

Master i/c: R. F. Harriott Cricket professional: I. M. Gillespie

*Batting*—A. J. Falconer 5–0–286–101–57.20; M. C. Dobson 4–0–201–74–50.25; *I. M. Scoones 7–1–157–58*–26.16; R. J. Davies 6–1–109–65–21.80; I. F. Hadfield 6–0–128–64–21.33.

*Bowling*—M. C. Dobson 58.3–17–152–17–8.94; A. Carruthers 25–3–116–10–11.60.

## SIR ROGER MANWOOD'S SCHOOL

*Played 10: Won 2, Lost 1, Drawn 7*

Master i/c: P. W. Kullman

*Batting*—R. D. Spence 10–2–426–121*–53.25; S. A. Smith 10–3–329–64–47.00.

*Bowling*—J. A. T. Ingram 121.3–35–314–32–9.81; J. A. N. Goold 58–9–170–10–17.00.

## SOLIHULL SCHOOL

*Played 17: Won 1, Lost 8, Drawn 8. Abandoned 1*

Master i/c: M. R. Brough Cricket professional: A. Moles

*Batting*—R. J. Lucas 17–0–633–91–37.23; S. J. Townsley 16–0–394–109–24.62; M. A. Fitzpatrick 16–3–298–74–22.92; A. J. P. Morton 12–4–136–18–17.00; W. Mohammed 11–2–144–56–16.00; M. Crockart 10–2–112–42*–14.00; N. J. Spall 10–0–102–44–10.20; *L. Myers 15–2–124–29*–9.53.

*Bowling*—P. St J. Heath 44.5–3–232–10–23.20; M. J. Sawle 138.4–22–428–15–28.53; L. Myers 120.3–20–405–14–28.92; W. Mohammed 169–23–730–22–33.18.

## STAMFORD SCHOOL

*Played 15: Won 1, Lost 4, Drawn 10. Abandoned 1*

Master i/c: I. Poyser

*Batting*—C. P. Grindal 14–2–361–58–30.08; *R. C. Hibbitt 16–2–377–103–26.92; R. P. C. Plant 5–1–104–39–26.00; P. N. Bell 16–1–344–54–22.93; D. F. Clowarch 13–1–230–59–19.16; J. R. Cobb 14–0–204–57–14.57; C. K. Tebb 12–2–123–35–12.30.

*Bowling*—R. C. Hibbitt 41–11–149–11–13.54; S. Atkinson 50.4–4–311–13–23.92; J. R. S. Allin 83–19–282–11–25.63; J. P. W. Taylor 104.2–17–402–10–40.20.

## STOCKPORT GRAMMAR SCHOOL

*Played 14: Won 0, Lost 8, Drawn 6. Abandoned 2*

Master i/c: C. Dunkerley

*Batting*—N. J. Vernon 8–2–159–43–26.50; N. E. Samarji 8–1–177–90–25.28; P. H. Duff 9–0–153–53–17.00; *B. N. Kabbani 10–0–127–30–12.70; M. K. Duckworth 14–0–173–54–12.35.

*Bowling*—R. H. Coathup 79–18–214–14–15.28; A. J. Tipping 92–19–275–16–17.18; M. J. Seed 171.1–36–552–24–23.00.

## STONYHURST COLLEGE

*Played 12: Won 4, Lost 2, Drawn 6*

Master i/c: J. M. Fairburn

*Batting*—C. H. Guyer 11–2–235–62*–26.11; *S. J. Bishop 12–6–141–42–23.50; M. L. D. Cash 11–0–231–52–21.00; S. C. Blake 10–0–157–32–15.70.

*Bowling*—M. Docherty 228–97–362–36–10.05; M. A. Porter 79–22–184–13–14.15; R. J. Fee 194–53–463–28–16.53.

## STOWE SCHOOL

*Played 18: Won 4, Lost 1, Drawn 13. Abandoned 3*

Master i/c: R. Marsden Cricket professional: M. J. Harris

*Batting*—R. S. M. Morris 18–6–628–110*–52.33; *M. S. Riley 18–1–386–100*–22.70; T. E. Perei 15–0–310–48–20.66; C. J. Rotheroe 17–1–319–61–19.93; A. J. Philips 15–2–192–54*–14.76; N. J. Hughes 15–2–173–51–13.30; J. M. J. Philips 13–2–136–30–12.36.

*Bowling*—J. P. Rigg 197–79–351–26–13.50; C. Whitmore 203–47–639–44–14.52; R. B. K. Giles 169–38–467–25–18.68; L. B. Turner 158–30–411–19–21.63; R. S. M. Morris 103–16–334–10–33.40.

## STRATHALLAN SCHOOL

*Played 16: Won 5, Lost 5, Drawn 6. Abandoned 4*

Master i/c: R. J. W. Proctor

*Batting*—R. E. M. Reah 14–5–240–54*–26.66; *R. S. Hamilton 15–0–388–61–25.86; G. S. R. Robertson 16–1–327–75*–21.80; R. S. B. McCulloch 14–3–196–62–17.81; M. L. Heggie 14–2–175–43–14.58.

*Bowling*—G. S. R. Robertson 58.3–11–136–15–9.06; T. J. Pawson 176.5–40–480–33–14.54; A. W. Tench 151.1–37–423–28–15.10; R. D. Baird 70.4–15–220–14–15.71; K. D. Smith 93.3–19–321–11–29.18

## SUTTON VALENCE SCHOOL

*Played 14: Won 4, Lost 4, Drawn 6. Abandoned 2*

Master i/c: D. Rickard

*Batting*—*J. P. Sunnucks 14–4–689–150*–68.90; S. N. Walton 12–3–257–86*–28.55; D. Paine 13–1–243–73–20.25; G. N. Lister 12–1–201–52–18.27; S. R. Sunnucks 10–2–141–53–17.62; D. G. Plommer 11–1–104–18–10.40.

*Bowling*—J. P. Sunnucks 162–36–426–31–13.74; D. Paine 94–16–315–17–18.52; S. R. Sunnucks 106–15–414–20–20.70; A. M. Pound 96–19–327–15–21.80; R. J. Ashton 101–24–308–10–30.80.

## TAUNTON SCHOOL

*Played 18: Won 11, Lost 1, Drawn 6. Abandoned 1*

Master i/c: R. P. Smith Cricket professional: A. Kennedy

*Batting*—R. J. Bartlett 12–2–686–134–68.60; N. J. Waters 18–5–891–125*–68.53; M. N. Adam 9–5–175–60*–43.75; *J. C. Pike 14–3–447–70–40.63; C. A. Wilson 16–0–409–80–25.56; C. J. Walker 15–3–305–76*–25.41; D. A. Penny 10–1–145–68–16.11.

*Bowling*—N. J. Pringle 165.2–48–379–30–12.63; N. J. Waters 103.3–20–314–24–13.08; C. J. Walker 65–15–158–11–14.36; V. J. Pike 113.3–33–376–26–14.46; J. C. Pike 64–14–180–11–16.36; M. N. Adam 97.4–24–281–16–17.56; D. A. Penny 126–30–366–13–28.15.

## TIFFIN SCHOOL

*Played 19: Won 6, Lost 5, Drawn 8. Abandoned 2*

Master i/c: M. J. Williams

*Batting*—*A. M. Morley-Brown 19–2–838–131–49.29; R. L. Hunt 19–3–594–111–37.12; G. J. Affleck 16–2–356–80*–25.42; M. R. Coote 16–5–214–48–19.45; N. P. Warren 11–0–212–61–19.27; S. P. Randall 16–0–299–71–18.68; D. W. Harry 10–4–103–37*–17.16; N. D. Cecil 11–3–106–24–13.25; A. R. Green 14–3–107–57–9.72.

*Bowling*—N. P. Warren 71.2–21–183–15–12.20; P. K. Somers 51.4–12–143–10–14.30; M. R. Coote 255–83–677–46–14.71; K. C. P. Pamphilon 134.3–35–424–23–18.43; A. M. Morley-Brown 114.4–22–367–18–20.38; S. P. Randall 100.1–19–349–14–24.92.

## TONBRIDGE SCHOOL

*Played 17: Won 10, Lost 0, Drawn 7*

Master i/c: D. R. Walsh Cricket professional: H. J. C. Mutton

*Batting*—*R. Owen-Browne 18–6–670–111*–55.83; J. I. Longley 18–3–687–100*–45.80; J. A. G. Waters 8–4–128–33–32.00; K. B. Saro-Wiwa 14–4–311–102*–31.10; J. J. Mantovani 7–2–139–41–27.80; S. T. Pollington 18–0–437–103–24.27; H. M. Tebay 12–1–226–78–20.54; J. S. Lazell 13–2–197–36–17.90.

*Bowling*—J. P. Nolan 191–43–501–32–15.65; R. Owen-Browne 203–63–393–23–17.08; W. L. C. Sackville-West 160–34–476–26–18.30; W. J. Chaloner 155–46–428–23–18.60; J. Owen-Browne 163–38–428–21–20.38.

## TRINITY SCHOOL

*Played 27: Won 7, Lost 5, Drawn 15*

Masters i/c: B. Widger and A. Gist

*Batting*—K. P. Morley 24–2–564–64*–25.63; G. M. Vigor 27–5–561–59*–25.50; D. J. Trafford 22–6–377–72–23.56; *J. B. Gamage 26–1–567–86*–22.68; A. S. Warner 25–3–496–68–22.54; N. A. Zain 18–3–169–35–11.26; J. Allen 25–3–234–35–10.63; M. R. D. Hollands 16–1–154–33–10.26.

*Bowling*—P. A. Gardner 90–19–238–18–13.22; D. M. P. Turner 69.5–9–221–15–14.73; D. J. Trafford 281.2–65–831–40–20.77; A. S. Warner 203.4–37–699–32–21.84; J. W. Harlow 354.1–81–1,017–45–22.60; P. J. Mander 128.4–19–466–15–31.06.

## TRURO SCHOOL

*Played 14: Won 4, Lost 5, Drawn 4, Tied 1*

Master i/c: A. J. D. Aldwinckle

*Batting*—P. S. Holmes 13–4–468–151*–52.00; S. J. Richards 14–0–405–80–28.92; P. G. Phillips 8–2–105–35*–17.50; *M. W. Yates 12–1–169–65–15.36; R. J. Daniel 9–1–113–66*–14.12; R. J. Heath 13–0–110–23–8.46.

*Bowling*—R. M. H. Bell 118–26–325–27–12.03; S. J. Richards 77–13–259–17–15.23; R. J. Heath 78.2–7–234–12–19.50; P. C. Nance 76.1–9–260–13–20.00; P. S. Holmes 138.2–24–454–22–20.63.

## UPPINGHAM SCHOOL

*Played 13: Won 3, Lost 3, Drawn 7. Abandoned 2*

Master i/c: P. L. Bodily Cricket professional: M. R. Hallam

*Batting*—*A. G. W. Lewin 14–4–511–92*–51.10; R. W. K. Brown 13–1–389–91–32.41; J. H. S. Phillips 9–0–168–46–18.66; C. M. Frost 12–0–220–57–18.33; D. B. J. Cooke 10–4–104–42*–17.33; P. D. Bennett 13–2–181–51*–16.45.

*Bowling*—D. B. J. Cooke 177.4–39–637–25–25.48; B. O. H. Robson 109.5–17–398–15–26.53; T. Dickens 90.4–13–276–10–27.60; A. S. Waters 120.3–27–401–12–33.41; S. R. Mason 109.5–13–347–10–34.70.

## VICTORIA COLLEGE, JERSEY

*Played 28: Won 16, Lost 3, Drawn 9*

Master i/c: D. A. R. Ferguson Cricket professional: R. A. Pearce

*Batting*—*C. M. Graham 22–4–758–118*–42.11; A. J. Wright 24–6–733–92–40.72; I. G. Le Couteur 15–7–290–52*–36.25; J. R. H. Dodd 15–2–308–59–23.69; P. J. Le Cornu 25–5–427–61–21.35; J. W. Kellett 21–2–396–121–20.84; A. J. Clarke 8–3–100–47–20.00; A. E. Sadarangani 12–2–129–43–12.90; G. E. Mauger 25–1–299–35–12.45; A. D. Brown 20–5–167–28*–11.13.

*Bowling*—A. J. Wright 223–61–599–56–10.69; C. M. Graham 295.4–85–806–60–13.43; R. V. Melwani 75–13–274–20–13.70; A. D. Brown 208–37–689–43–16.02; D. V. Carnegie 141–26–527–27–19.51; N. T. Greenwood 117.2–23–402–18–22.33.

## WARWICK SCHOOL

*Played 14: Won 5, Lost 0, Drawn 9. Abandoned 1*

Master i/c: I. B. Moffatt Cricket professional: N. Horner

*Batting*—J. D. Stanton 14–3–715–117–65.00; I. D. Bolton 13–1–440–100*–36.66; A. J. Moffatt 14–1–426–84–32.76; J. D. Morris 9–5–111–35*–27.75; D. J. Stanley 12–4–194–27*–24.25; S. A. Bolt 10–3–157–36*–22.42; *G. M. Robinson 11–0–178–36–16.18; T. R. Luckman 13–1–135–38*–11.25.

*Bowling*—A. J. Moffatt 83.5–17–331–19–17.42; P. J. Squires 86–18–263–13–20.23; J. D. Stanton 72.2–17–301–14–21.50; J. D. Morris 74–20–245–10–24.50; S. J. Holdsworth 157.3–44–448–14–32.00.

## WATFORD GRAMMAR SCHOOL

*Played 16: Won 8, Lost 3, Drawn 5. Abandoned 3*

Master i/c: D. Green

*Batting*—*C. S. Dyce 4–2–312–101–156.00; C. E. Ahye 9–6–133–37*–44.33; P. D. Ahye 14–1–470–78–36.15; M. J. H. Hanson 7–2–154–64*–30.80; R. M. Nicholls 14–2–306–74–25.50; A. A. Chaudry 11–1–246–61–24.60; G. D. Gregory 14–1–288–95*–22.15; M. J. Roberts 8–0–116–63–14.50.

*Bowling*—S. J. Mann 270.4–70–767–45–17.04; A. A. Chaudry 128–31–326–17–19.17; S. J. Easterbrook 207–68–590–26–22.69.

## WELLINGBOROUGH SCHOOL

*Played 15: Won 7, Lost 1, Drawn 7*

Master i/c: C. J. Ford Cricket professional: J. C. J. Dye

*Batting*—R. G. Smith 11–7–207–55*–51.75; M. I. Ingram 14–3–437–61*–39.72; A. Mabbutt 15–0–562–77–37.46; *P. S. H. Wilson 14–3–398–106–36.18; T. K. Marriott 12–4–142–37*–17.75; M. H. Griffiths 13–2–174–49–15.81; S. P. H. Gane 12–2–135–47*–13.50.

*Bowling*—M. D. Dutoy 181–34–533–36–14.80; T. K. Marriott 180–50–554–31–17.87; S. P. H. Gane 125–20–446–24–18.58; R. J. Brawn 110–20–347–11–31.54.

## WELLINGTON COLLEGE, BERKSHIRE

*Played 17: Won 7, Lost 3, Drawn 7. Abandoned 1*

Master i/c: D. J. Mordaunt Cricket professional: P. J. Lewington

*Batting*—*G. D. Reynolds 18–4–730–106–52.14; T. B. Cockroft 14–1–280–77–21.53; P. A. Huxtable 18–1–334–61–19.64; J. S. Hodgson 18–1–306–72–18.00; A. J. Braithwaite 14–1–210–51–16.15; P. J. Istead 13–0–210–45–16.15; J. M. Benkert 10–1–107–39–11.88; J. P. Bishop 14–3–121–27–11.00.

*Bowling*—J. S. Hodgson 234.4–57–655–39–16.79; G. D. Reynolds 111.4–37–258–15–17.20; A. J. L. Hunter 177–52–427–23–18.56; T. B. Cockroft 224–65–610–27–22.59.

## WELLINGTON SCHOOL, SOMERSET

*Played 10: Won 2, Lost 2, Drawn 6*

Master i/c: I. F. Loudon

*Batting*—J. Clist 10–0–277–88–27.70; T. D. Over 10–2–198–65–24.75; M. Salter 10–0–152–48–15.20; J. W. Hine 10–1–130–36–14.44.

*Bowling*—M. Colman 116–32–431–30–14.36; B. W. Loudon 96.4–36–401–15–26.73; G. C. Cloud 94.3–26–388–13–29.84.

## WESTMINSTER SCHOOL

*Played 11: Won 0, Lost 8, Drawn 3*

Master i/c: J. A. Cogan Cricket professional: R. Gilson

*Batting*—J. D. Kershen 11–0–203–56–18.45; *A. C. King 11–0–173–30–15.72; J. G. R. Griffiths 11–0–161–49–14.63; D. J. Cogan 11–0–105–38–9.54.

*Bowling*—M. D. F. Pennington 102–16–287–12–23.91.

## WHITGIFT SCHOOL

*Played 18: Won 4, Lost 4, Drawn 10*

Master i/c: P. C. Fladgate Cricket professional: A. Long

*Batting*—M. P. J. Ellingham 17–3–483–100–34.50; N. J. Taylor 18–1–402–79*–23.64; I. L. H. Scarisbrick 19–4–337–77*–22.46; T. P. Bureau 17–2–301–58–20.06; G. J. Thompson 14–2–223–39–18.58; *K. S. R. Ebenezer 15–2–231–37–17.76.

*Bowling*—A. J. Bowers 206–53–567–35–16.20; H. Gallagher 160.3–29–560–33–16.96; P. J. Wallis 107–27–296–15–19.73; R. Slatford 155.2–37–410–19–21.57; M. H. P. Raeburn 140.5–42–392–16–24.50.

## WILLIAM HULME'S GRAMMAR SCHOOL

*Played 24: Won 8, Lost 5, Drawn 11*

Master i/c: I. J. Shaw

*Batting*—G. J. O'Driscoll 4–1–131–65–43.66; G. P. Benson 17–1–410–62–25.62; *A. G. Cleary 21–3–454–77*–25.22; K. G. Rushton 21–4–428–75–25.17; P. D. Fearnley 21–2–469–70–24.68; M. J. Cross 16–8–187–74*–23.37; C. W. Timm 15–1–270–70–19.28; S. M. Kennedy 17–3–250–49–17.85; D. M. J. Timm 16–1–242–55–16.13; M. L. Jackson 17–1–187–35–11.68.

*Bowling*—D. M. J. Timm 95.5–15–286–18–15.88; A. G. Hinchcliffe 155.1–50–454–28–16.21; A. N. Jameson 93–9–341–17–20.05; M. J. Cross 231.2–33–766–36–21.27; G. P. Benson 168.5–43–454–16–28.37; K. G. Rushton 145.3–23–541–13–41.61.

## WINCHESTER COLLEGE

*Played 19: Won 5, Lost 3, Drawn 11*

Master i/c: J. F. X. Miller Cricket professional: V. Broderick

*Batting*—*I. L. M. Henry 17–4–696–99*–53.53; M. I. Riaz 7–2–133–80*–26.60; A. N. Patterson-Moutray 14–2–308–101*–25.66; A. W. Ellis 12–0–218–56–18.16; J. G. B. Warren 16–0–277–65–17.31; C. H. M. Ridley 15–2–200–29–15.38; B. D. Thornycroft 16–1–195–44–13.00; R. C. Waddington 12–0–107–25–8.91.

*Bowling*—J. P. K. Bygrave 171.3–51–423–30–14.10; I. L. M. Henry 220–44–643–45–14.28; B. C. Winzer 243.2–53–698–32–21.81; C. H. M. Ridley 178.3–39–615–27–22.77.

## WOODBRIDGE SCHOOL

*Played 11: Won 3, Lost 2, Drawn 6. Abandoned 2*

Master i/c: I. Gwyther Cricket professional: J. A. Pugh

*Batting*—S. I. Bacon 10–3–203–94*–29.00; M. G. C. Harvey 11–3–204–47*–25.50; J. R. Harper 9–1–121–33*–15.12; S. G. Kingston 11–0–131–44–11.90.

*Bowling*—N. D. J. Henchie 164–42–403–41–9.82; J. R. Harper 93.2–26–204–18–11.33; A. A. C. Donnison 112.1–27–307–21–14.61; T. R. C. Watts 70–20–200–12–16.66.

## WOODHOUSE GROVE SCHOOL

*Played 13: Won 6, Lost 4, Drawn 3. Abandoned 1*

Master i/c: E. R. Howard Cricket professional: P. J. Kippax

*Batting*—B. S. Percy 12–4–687–150*–85.87; *N. A. Ledgard 12–2–366–112*–36.60; J. E. J. Fidler 4–1–107–87–35.66; M. E. Fox 11–3–105–17–13.12; C. R. Kippax 11–2–118–40*–13.11; T. G. Wood 13–0–132–23–10.15.

*Bowling*—B. S. Percy 195–60–381–34–11.20; L. Savill 188.4–45–485–40–12.12.

## WORKSOP COLLEGE

*Played 15: Won 5, Lost 2, Drawn 8. Abandoned 1*

Master i/c: N. S. Broadbent Cricket professional: R. G. Davies

*Batting*—D. B. Storer 15–6–466–103–51.77; R. J. Darwin 15–0–312–73–20.80; *E. R. Hughes 14–2–233–46–19.41; B. D. Hackett 10–2–151–50*–18.87; N. E. Green 14–1–235–57–18.07; M. J. W. Hallam 15–0–263–69–17.53; J. P. Wilkins 14–3–153–49–13.90.

*Bowling*—E. R. Hughes 190–54–471–37–12.72; S. Leggate 51–17–208–12–17.33; B. D. Hackett 124–39–310–17–18.23; D. B. Storer 91.2–22–208–11–18.90; J. P. Wilkins 174–62–457–20–22.85.

## WREKIN COLLEGE

*Played 19: Won 6, Lost 6, Drawn 7. Abandoned 1*

Master i/c: T. J. Murphy Cricket professional: T. Harrison

*Batting*—C. Fenton 18–2–539–77*–33.68; G. Berry 18–5–243–67*–18.69; G. Lynch 16–0–285–53–17.81; *O. Davies 18–1–302–75*–17.76; P. Richardson 17–1–225–51–14.06; J. Rimmer 18–0–252–52–14.00; D. Horton 16–3–110–36*–8.46; C. Rogers 16–0–118–17–7.37.

*Bowling*—P. Richardson 292–64–839–51–16.45; P. Hawkins 256–58–637–35–18.20; J. Whitfield 98–25–301–15–20.06; O. Davies 188–26–707–33–21.42.

## WYCLIFFE COLLEGE

*Played 14: Won 4, Lost 4, Drawn 6. Abandoned 1*

Master i/c: M. Eagers Cricket professional: K. Biddulph

*Batting*—G. S. Campbell 11–2–315–102–35.00; *A. S. Dickenson 13–3–254–69*–25.40; S. J. Reed 13–2–229–41*–20.81; J. A. H. Tovey 6–1–100–31*–20.00; R. A. Boulton 9–3–104–29–17.33; R. Green 10–2–110–36–13.75; P. R. Pitman 12–1–117–29–10.63.

*Bowling*—G. S. Campbell 79.1–16–308–22–14.00; A. S. Dickenson 148–30–426–25–17.04; R. A. Boulton 178.1–46–477–27–17.66.

## KENT COLLEGE

*Played 11: Won 2, Lost 2, Drawn 7*

Master i/c: C. S. Day

The season did not quite live up to expectations. A. J. MacGregor batted with authority, his 126 v St Edmund's being an especially fine innings, but the bowling lacked sufficient penetration. T. Dudgeon (slow left-arm) bowled with control and confidence, and there was promise in the seam bowling of A. R. Rajan.

*Batting*—A. J. MacGregor 11–0–398–126–36.18; P. A. Miles 6–2–110–48*–27.50; J. D. Scotchbrook 11–0–271–87–24.63; N. M. L. Barker 11–1–236–69*–23.60; R. J. R. Woodward 11–0–209–70–19.00; *P. C. Goodban 8–1–106–34–15.14.

*Bowling*—T. Dudgeon 161.1–27–540–37–14.59; A. R. Rajan 94–8–317–21–15.09.

---

# CRICKET ASSOCIATIONS AND SOCIETIES

AUCKLAND CRICKET SOCIETY: *Secretary* Tom Lindsay, PO Box 56059, Auckland, New Zealand.

AUSTRALIAN CRICKET SOCIETY: *Secretary* Christopher Harte, GPO Box 696, Adelaide, 5001, South Australia.

ADELAIDE BRANCH: *Secretary* Gerald Fishpool, 49 Johnstone Street, Glengowrie, 5044, South Australia.

BRISBANE BRANCH: *Secretary* Robert Spence, GPO Box 1498, Brisbane, 4001, Queensland.

CANBERRA BRANCH: *Secretary* Julian Oakley, GPO Box 650, Canberra, 2600, ACT.

MELBOURNE BRANCH: *Secretary* Colin Barnes, 4 Hornby Street, Beaumaris, 3193, Victoria.

PERTH BRANCH: *Secretary* Athol Barrett, 15a Barsden Street, Cottesloe, 6011, Western Australia.

SYDNEY BRANCH: *Secretary* Ronald Cardwell, 24 New Street, Balgowlah Heights, 2093, New South Wales.

BLACKLEY CRICKET SOCIETY: *Secretary* D. Butterfield, 7 Bayswater Terrace, West Yorkshire, HX3 0NB.

CAMBRIDGE UNIVERSITY CRICKET SOCIETY: *Secretary* Leo McKinstry, Sidney Sussex College, Cambridge, CB2 3HU.

CHESTERFIELD CRICKET LOVERS' SOCIETY: *Secretary* B. Hollings, 24 Woodland Way, Old Tupton, Chesterfield, Derbyshire.

COUNCIL OF CRICKET SOCIETIES, THE: *Secretary* B. L. Mellis, The Old Vicarage, Church Hill, Bramhope, West Yorkshire LS16 9BA.

CRICKET SOCIETY, THE: *Secretary* J. M. Bridgeman, 42 Woodlands Park Road, King's Norton, Birmingham, B30 1HA.

CRICKET SOCIETY, THE (Midland Branch): *Secretary* Dr A. A. Walker, "Sarnia", Hernes Nest, Bewdley, DX12 2N.

CRICKET STATISTICIANS, ASSOCIATION OF: *Secretary* P. Wynne-Thomas, The Bungalow, Haughton Mill, Retford, Nottinghamshire.

EAST RIDING CRICKET SOCIETY: *Secretary* H. K. Cooke, 104 Well Lane, Willerby, Kingston upon Hull, East Yorkshire.

ESSEX CRICKET SOCIETY: *Secretary* P. T. Roberts, 21 Hadrian Close, Lodge Park, Witham, Essex, CM8 1XA.

FYLDE COAST CRICKET SOCIETY: *Secretary* S. Kennedy, 36 Torquay Avenue, Marton, Blackpool, Lancashire.

HAMPSHIRE CRICKET SOCIETY: *Secretary* F. Bailey, 7 Lightfoot Grove, Basingstoke, Hampshire.

HEAVY WOOLLEN CRICKET SOCIETY: *Secretary* G. S. Cooper, 27 Milford Grove, Gomersal, Cleckheaton, West Yorkshire.

INDIA, THE CRICKET SOCIETY OF: *Secretary* Sandeep Singh Nakai, House No. 122, Sector 8-A, Chandigarh, India.

LANCASHIRE AND CHESHIRE CRICKET SOCIETY: *Secretary* H. W. Pardoe, Crantock, 117a Barlow Moor Road, Didsbury, Manchester, M20 8TS.

LINCOLNSHIRE CRICKET LOVERS' SOCIETY: *Secretary* C. Kennedy, 26 Eastwood Avenue, Grimsby, South Humberside, DN34 5BE.

MERSEYSIDE CRICKET SOCIETY: *Secretary* W. T. Robins, 11 Yew Tree Road, Hunts Cross, Liverpool, L25 9QN.

NATAL CRICKET SOCIETY: *Secretary* Haydn Bradfield, PO Box 3046, Durban 4000, South Africa.

NORTHERN CRICKET SOCIETY: *Secretary* Eric Haywood, 11 Sandringham Drive, Leeds 17.

NOTTINGHAM CRICKET SOCIETY: *Secretary* G. Blagdurn, 2 Inham Circus, Chilwell Beeston, Nottinghamshire, NG9 4FN.

NUNTHORPE GRAMMAR SCHOOL CRICKET SOCIETY: *Secretary* H. J. George, 2 Braeside Gardens, Acomb, Yorkshire YO2 4EZ.

OXFORD UNIVERSITY CRICKET SOCIETY: *Secretary* Andrew Glover, University College, Oxford.

PAKISTAN ASSOCIATION OF CRICKET STATISTICIANS: *Secretary* Abid Ali Kazi, 5-A, 11/1 Sunset Lane, Phase 11, Defence Housing Society, Karachi, Pakistan.

ROTHERHAM CRICKET SOCIETY: *Secretary* J. A. R. Atkin, 15 Gallow Tree Road, Rotherham, South Yorkshire, S65 3EE.

SCOTLAND, CRICKET SOCIETY OF: *Secretary* A. J. Robertson, 5 Riverside Road, Eaglesham, Glasgow, G76 0DA.

SOMERSET WYVERNS: *Secretary* M. Richards, "Wyvern", 3 Ash Road, Tring, Hertfordshire.

SOPHIANS, THE: *Secretary* A. K. Hignell, 79 Coed Glas Road, Llanishen, Cardiff.

SOUTH AFRICAN CRICKET SOCIETY: *Secretary* Anthony D. Collis, PO Box 78040, Sandton, Transvaal, 2146, South Africa.

STOURBRIDGE AND DISTRICT CRICKET SOCIETY: *Secretary* R. Barber, 6 Carlton Avenue, Stourbridge, DY9 9ED.

SUSSEX CRICKET SOCIETY: *Secretary* A. A. Dumbrell, 6 Southdown Avenue, Brighton, East Sussex, BN1 6EG.

UPPINGHAM SCHOOL CRICKET SOCIETY: *Secretary* Dr E. J. R. Boston, The Common Room, Uppingham School, Rutland.

WALES, CRICKET SOCIETY OF: *Secretary* C. N. Fookes, 5 Melrose Close, St Mellons, Cardiff, CF3 9SW.

WEST LANCASHIRE CRICKET SOCIETY: *Secretary* D. H. Stringfellow, 36 Cardigan Road, Southport, Merseyside, PR8 4SF.

WOMBWELL CRICKET LOVERS' SOCIETY: *Secretary* J. Sokell, 42 Woodstock Road, Barnsley, South Yorkshire, S75 1DX.

ZIMBABWE, CRICKET SOCIETY OF: *Secretary* L. G. Morgenrood, 10 Elsworth Avenue, Balgravia, Harare, Zimbabwe.

# OVERSEAS CRICKET, 1984-85

*Note:* Throughout this section, matches not first-class are denoted by the use of a dagger.

## ENGLAND IN INDIA (AND SRI LANKA), 1984-85

By JOHN THICKNESSE

England got more than they bargained for on their tour of India, and it was much to their credit that they became the first team from any country to win a series there coming from behind. Within a few hours of their arrival in New Delhi, in the early morning of Wednesday, October 31, they were awoken with the news of the assassination of Mrs Gandhi, the Indian Prime Minister. The memory of this was still fresh when, on the eve of the first Test, less than four weeks later, the British Deputy High Commissioner, Mr Percy Norris, a cricket-lover who had entertained the touring party at a reception in his home the previous evening, was shot dead as he was being driven to his Bombay office. Both outrages took place within a mile or two of where the team were staying.

In political and world terms, Mrs Gandhi's assassination of course had the greater impact, and for 72 hours India's capital city, while "safe" for those content to obey High Commission advice to stay close to their hotel, was an uneasy place to be. Happily, thanks to a generous gesture from the Sri Lankan Cricket Board, and the sympathetic co-operation of that country's President, who had flown to New Delhi for the funeral and invited the team to share his plane on the return journey, they found sanctuary in Colombo. There, for the next nine days, they found opportunities for play and practice which would have been impossible in India during the period of official mourning.

Mr Norris's murder affected them more personally, and with a Test due to start next day they felt under threat themselves. Had the decision been left to the team, or more particularly to a majority of the representatives of the British press, there is little doubt they would have taken the first available flight home. But as in Delhi, Tony Brown, the England manager, retained his sense of perspective, took advice from all relevant bodies, including the Foreign Office, and after consultation with the Test and County Cricket Board at Lord's, decided the best course was to stay and play. The decision had its dangers, based as it was on an educated guess that there was no connection between the timing of the murder and the team's presence in Bombay, but in the event there were no alarms during the Test; nor indeed any further political troubles on the tour.

Nevertheless, to safeguard the team, the itinerary was revised to postpone until near the end their appearance in the north of India, where because of the large Sikh population there was continuing unrest. Armed guards and escorts also became such a feature of the tour that before long they were hardly noticed. The fixture against North Zone, which was due to have been played at Jammu, was switched to the Wankhede Stadium, Bombay, between the first and second Tests. With Kapil Dev resting from the North Zone team, it was predictable that spectators for that game would be numbered in hundreds; but the smallness of the crowds was generally a disappointing feature of the tour. Only for the one-day internationals, and an abortive Test in Calcutta, were "Ground Full" signs in use.

England had already been badly beaten by India's Under-25 XI – their first sight of Laxman Sivaramakrishnan and Mohammad Azharuddin – when they started the series disastrously, losing the first Test by eight wickets despite Mike Gatting's long-awaited maiden Test hundred. Siva, still eighteen at that stage and playing his first home Test, took twelve for 181 with leg-breaks and googlies and, in what was to prove his last Test, Swaroop Kishen had an unsatisfactory match as umpire. It all looked depressingly familiar to those who had been on Fletcher's tour three years before, and it was tempting to write off England's chances there and then. However, the expected sequence of dull draws on soul-destroying pitches did not follow. The second Test, in Delhi, where Tim Robinson scored 160 impressively in eight and three-quarter hours, was snatched by England's spinners, Phil Edmonds and Pat Pocock, when India succumbed to the pressure of relentless accuracy on the final afternoon; and a month later the series was decided by an exceptional display in the fourth Test in Madras.

England, losing the toss, were in charge within an hour of the start of the Madras match when Neil Foster and Norman Cowans shared three wickets. Foster, playing his first Test of the series, took six for 104 (his match figures were eleven for 163) to bowl India out for 272, and then Graeme Fowler and Gatting thrust home the advantage by becoming the first pair of England batsmen to score 200 in the same Test. It was necessary to go back to the sixth Test at Sydney in 1978-79 to find the last occasion when England controlled a Test abroad so surely. They won by nine wickets in the final session, a splendid and uplifting match for Peter May to watch on his first overseas trip as the chairman of selectors.

When the Kanpur Test was drawn, England had won a winter series for the first time for six years, and also, by four-one, the one-day internationals. Creditably as they performed, however, they owed a lot to India's shortcomings. Sunil Gavaskar's lack of form – 140 runs compared to 500 against Fletcher's team – was probably the biggest factor in the turnabout: having got his 30th Test hundred behind him, against West Indies twelve months before, and so passed Sir Donald Bradman's record, he seemed short of motivation. Following a quarrel about division of prizemoney, there were signs, too, of disharmony within his team, of which a foolhardy stroke by Kapil Dev, helping England win the Delhi Test, and his subsequent dropping were symptomatic. The minimum 80-overs-a-day playing condition cut out the petty time-wasting that had marred Fletcher's tour, while the emergence of a top-class umpire in V. K. Ramaswamy in the last two Tests was a relief to all concerned.

Leadership did not seem to come naturally to David Gower. However, he developed a good team spirit and it was an advantage for him that Gatting, his vice-captain, and Edmonds, another forceful character, had the self-confidence and drive to influence matters on the field, their stature bolstered by personal success. Gatting, coming into his own at last, fell only 19 runs short of K. F. Barrington's record Test aggregate for England in India, while Edmonds bowled well throughout the tour, despite being at sixes and sevens with his run-up. (His Test average of 41.71 was a travesty of justice.) Robinson, Fowler and Foster were the other main successes, and it was not until the team reached Australia and went badly off the boil, losing all three matches in the so-called "World Championship of Cricket", that Ian Botham's absence was an obvious disadvantage.

## ENGLAND TOUR RESULTS

### In Sri Lanka

*First-class match* – Played 1: Drawn 1. *Draw* – Sri Lanka Cricket Board President's XI.
*Non first-class match* – Played 1: No result 1. No result – Sri Lankan XI.

### In India

*Test matches* – Played 5: Won 2, Lost 1, Drawn 2.
*First-class matches* – Played 11: Won 3, Lost 2, Drawn 6.
*Wins* – India (2), East Zone.
*Losses* – India, Indian Under-25 XI.
*Draws* – India (2), Indian Cricket Board President's XI, West Zone, North Zone, South Zone.
*Non first-class matches* – Played 5: Won 4, Lost 1. *Wins* – India (4). *Loss* – India.

## TEST MATCH AVERAGES

### INDIA – BATTING

| | *T* | *I* | *NO* | *R* | *HI* | *100s* | *Avge* |
|---|---|---|---|---|---|---|---|
| M. Azharuddin | 3 | 5 | 1 | 439 | 122 | 3 | 109.75 |
| S. M. H. Kirmani | 5 | 7 | 2 | 291 | 102 | 1 | 58.20 |
| M. Amarnath | 5 | 8 | 1 | 407 | 95 | 0 | 58.14 |
| R. J. Shastri | 5 | 9 | 2 | 383 | 142 | 2 | 54.71 |
| K. Srikkanth | 2 | 4 | 1 | 141 | 84 | 0 | 47.00 |
| Kapil Dev | 4 | 6 | 0 | 253 | 60 | 0 | 42.16 |
| D. B. Vengsarkar | 5 | 8 | 1 | 284 | 137 | 1 | 40.57 |
| Chetan Sharma | 3 | 4 | 3 | 40 | 17* | 0 | 40.00 |
| S. M. Patil | 2 | 3 | 0 | 91 | 41 | 0 | 30.33 |
| M. Prabhakar | 2 | 4 | 1 | 86 | 35* | 0 | 28.66 |
| S. M. Gavaskar | 5 | 8 | 0 | 140 | 65 | 0 | 17.50 |
| L. Sivaramakrishnan | 5 | 5 | 1 | 59 | 25 | 0 | 14.75 |
| N. S. Yadav | 4 | 6 | 3 | 43 | 28* | 0 | 14.33 |
| A. D. Gaekwad | 3 | 5 | 0 | 71 | 28 | 0 | 14.20 |

Played in one Test: A. Malhotra 27, G. Sharma did not bat.

**Signifies not out.*

### BOWLING

| | *O* | *M* | *R* | *W* | *BB* | *Avge* |
|---|---|---|---|---|---|---|
| L. Sivaramakrishnan | 274.3 | 63 | 723 | 23 | 6-64 | 31.43 |
| N. S. Yadav | 134 | 31 | 362 | 9 | 4-86 | 40.22 |
| Kapil Dev | 161.5 | 33 | 436 | 10 | 4-81 | 43.60 |
| G. Sharma | 71 | 20 | 132 | 3 | 3-115 | 44.00 |
| Chetan Sharma | 50.3 | 6 | 200 | 4 | 4-38 | 50.00 |
| R. J. Shastri | 184 | 48 | 390 | 7 | 3-52 | 55.71 |

Also bowled: M. Amarnath 21–4–49–2; M. Azharuddin 1–0–8–0; A. D. Gaekwad 1–0–1–0; S. M. Gavaskar 0.4–0–10–0; A. Malhotra 2–0–3–0; M. Prabhakar 29–4–102–1; K. Srikkanth 2–0–11–0.

### ENGLAND – BATTING

| | *T* | *I* | *NO* | *R* | *HI* | *100s* | *Avge* |
|---|---|---|---|---|---|---|---|
| M. W. Gatting | 5 | 9 | 3 | 575 | 207 | 2 | 95.83 |
| R. T. Robinson | 5 | 9 | 2 | 444 | 160 | 1 | 63.42 |
| P. R. Downton | 5 | 6 | 3 | 183 | 74 | 0 | 61.00 |
| G. Fowler | 5 | 8 | 0 | 438 | 201 | 1 | 54.75 |

| | *T* | *I* | *NO* | *R* | *HI* | *100s* | *Avge* |
|---|---|---|---|---|---|---|---|
| A. J. Lamb | 5 | 7 | 1 | 241 | 67 | 0 | 40.16 |
| P. H. Edmonds | 5 | 6 | 0 | 175 | 49 | 0 | 29.16 |
| D. I. Gower | 5 | 7 | 1 | 167 | 78 | 0 | 27.83 |
| C. S. Cowdrey | 5 | 6 | 1 | 96 | 38 | 0 | 19.20 |
| P. I. Pocock | 5 | 5 | 2 | 39 | 22* | 0 | 13.00 |
| N. A. Foster | 2 | 2 | 0 | 13 | 8 | 0 | 6.50 |
| R. M. Ellison | 3 | 4 | 0 | 12 | 10 | 0 | 3.00 |
| N. G. Cowans | 5 | 5 | 1 | 10 | 9 | 0 | 2.50 |

* *Signifies not out.*

## BOWLING

| | *O* | *M* | *R* | *W* | *BB* | *Avge* |
|---|---|---|---|---|---|---|
| N. A. Foster | 87 | 18 | 286 | 14 | 6-104 | 20.42 |
| P. H. Edmonds | 276.1 | 104 | 584 | 14 | 4-60 | 41.71 |
| N. G. Cowans | 181.5 | 41 | 627 | 14 | 3-103 | 44.78 |
| P. I. Pocock | 237.5 | 53 | 655 | 13 | 4-93 | 50.38 |
| C. S. Cowdrey | 61 | 2 | 288 | 4 | 2-65 | 72.00 |
| R. M. Ellison | 105 | 24 | 289 | 4 | 4-66 | 72.25 |

Also bowled: G. Fowler 1-1-0-0; M. W. Gatting 13-1-36-0; D. I. Gower 3-0-13-0; A. J. Lamb 1-0-6-1; R. T. Robinson 1-1-0-0.

# ENGLAND AVERAGES – FIRST-CLASS MATCHES IN INDIA AND SRI LANKA

## BATTING

| | *M* | *I* | *NO* | *R* | *HI* | *100s* | *Avge* |
|---|---|---|---|---|---|---|---|
| M. W. Gatting | 11 | 17 | 5 | 1,029 | 207 | 3 | 85.75 |
| M. D. Moxon | 3 | 4 | 0 | 231 | 153 | 1 | 57.75 |
| R. T. Robinson | 11 | 18 | 3 | 861 | 160 | 3 | 57.40 |
| G. Fowler | 10 | 15 | 0 | 727 | 201 | 3 | 48.46 |
| A. J. Lamb | 10 | 14 | 2 | 441 | 67 | 0 | 36.75 |
| D. I. Gower | 11 | 15 | 1 | 482 | 86 | 0 | 34.42 |
| N. A. Foster | 7 | 8 | 4 | 128 | 29 | 0 | 32.00 |
| P. R. Downton | 9 | 11 | 3 | 238 | 74 | 0 | 29.75 |
| C. S. Cowdrey | 9 | 11 | 1 | 211 | 70 | 0 | 21.10 |
| V. J. Marks | 6 | 8 | 1 | 142 | 66 | 0 | 20.28 |
| P. H. Edmonds | 11 | 12 | 0 | 241 | 49 | 0 | 20.08 |
| R. M. Ellison | 8 | 10 | 1 | 152 | 83* | 0 | 16.88 |
| P. J. W. Allott | 3 | 3 | 1 | 29 | 14 | 0 | 14.50 |
| B. N. French | 4 | 5 | 0 | 63 | 19 | 0 | 12.60 |
| P. I. Pocock | 8 | 9 | 3 | 48 | 22* | 0 | 8.00 |
| N. G. Cowans | 10 | 8 | 1 | 21 | 10 | 0 | 3.00 |

Played in one match: J. P. Agnew 12*.

* *Signifies not out.*

## BOWLING

| | *O* | *M* | *R* | *W* | *BB* | *Avge* |
|---|---|---|---|---|---|---|
| N. A. Foster | 230.1 | 58 | 655 | 29 | 6-104 | 22.58 |
| J. P. Agnew | 45 | 4 | 205 | 7 | 5-102 | 29.28 |
| P. H. Edmonds | 498.1 | 184 | 1,019 | 32 | 4-13 | 31.84 |
| N. G. Cowans | 267.5 | 60 | 916 | 25 | 3-59 | 36.64 |
| P. I. Pocock | 321.1 | 73 | 932 | 23 | 4-57 | 40.52 |
| V. J. Marks | 121 | 28 | 321 | 7 | 4-48 | 45.85 |
| C. S. Cowdrey | 114 | 12 | 442 | 9 | 3-61 | 49.11 |
| R. M. Ellison | 210.1 | 57 | 550 | 11 | 4-66 | 50.00 |

Also bowled: P. J. W. Allott 62.1-11-209-2; G. Fowler 1-1-0-0; M. W. Gatting 34-2-90-1; D. I. Gower 3-0-13-0; A. J. Lamb 2-1-6-1, R. T. Robinson 1-1-0-0.

## FIELDING

P. R. Downton 23 (20 ct, 3 st), B. N. French 14 (12 ct, 2 st), A. J. Lamb 13, C. Cowdrey 10 (1 as sub), M. W. Gatting 10, D. I. Gower 10, P. H. Edmonds 5, G. Fowler 4 (1 as sub), N. G. Cowans 3, R. M. Ellison 3 (1 as sub), N. A. Foster 2, M. D. Moxon 2, P. I. Pocock 2, V. J. Marks 1, R. T. Robinson 1.

## SRI LANKA CRICKET BOARD PRESIDENT'S XI v AN ENGLAND XI

At Cricket Club of Ceylon, Colombo, November 7, 8, 9. Drawn. The opening match of England's rearranged itinerary was notable for the maiden first-class hundred of nineteen-year-old P. A. de Silva, who had played for Sri Lanka in their Test at Lord's the previous August. Struck on the head by his second ball from Foster, he none the less showed composure, technique, a wide range of strokes and admirable enterprise in an innings lasting 186 minutes and containing eighteen 4s. Slightly built and quick-footed, he drove and hooked powerfully, refusing to let the spinners tie him down on a pitch that helped them. Gatting and Gower shared 30 4s while adding 166 in 140 minutes against a young attack in which E. A. R. de Silva (unrelated to P. A.) showed promise as a leg-spinner. A delay of 75 minutes on the final day destroyed any chance of a result.

### Sri Lanka Cricket Board President's XI

| | | | |
|---|---|---|---|
| D. M. Vonhagt c Downton b Cowans | 6 | c Fowler b Edmonds | 53 |
| C. P. Amerasinghe c Robinson b Foster | 7 | c Gower b Pocock | 27 |
| S. Warnakulasuriya c Downton b Ellison | 5 | c Edmonds b Pocock | 0 |
| P. A. de Silva c Cowans b Pocock | 105 | c Lamb b Ellison | 13 |
| *R. S. Madugalle st Downton b Edmonds | 46 | (7) c sub b Edmonds | 12 |
| A. Ranatunga c Lamb b Pocock | 42 | (6) not out | 10 |
| R. S. Mahanama not out | 37 | (5) b Pocock | 8 |
| †R. G. de Alwis c Foster b Cowans | 42 | (6) c Ellison b Pocock | 1 |
| R. J. Ratnayake c Gatting b Cowans | 4 | not out | 10 |
| E. A. R. de Silva c Downton b Foster | 2 | | |
| L-b 2 | 2 | | |
| 1/14 2/14 3/33 4/132 5/191 6/221 7/285 8/291 9/298 (9 wkts dec.) | 298 | 1/49 2/49 3/70 4/85 5/99 6/114 7/119 (7 wkts) | 134 |

G. N. de Silva did not bat.

Bowling: *First Innings*—Cowans 15-3-59-3; Foster 15.3-6-37-2; Ellison 11-1-45-1; Edmonds 33-10-93-1; Pocock 19-6-62-2. *Second Innings*—Cowans 9-0-31-0; Foster 7-1-25-0; Pocock 19-5-57-4; Ellison 7-2-12-1; Edmonds 6-3-9-2.

### An England XI

| | |
|---|---|
| G. Fowler c Madugalle b G. N. de Silva | 1 |
| R. T. Robinson lbw b Ratnayake | 2 |
| M. W. Gatting c Vonhagt b E. A. R. de Silva | 97 |
| *D. I. Gower c Ranatunga b G. N. de Silva | 86 |
| A. J. Lamb c Warnakulasuriya b Ratnayake | 53 |
| R. M. Ellison run out | 14 |
| P. H. Edmonds c Amerasinghe b E. A. R. de Silva | 2 |
| †P. R. Downton b E. A. R. de Silva | 0 |
| N. A. Foster not out | 7 |
| P. I. Pocock c de Alwis b G. N. de Silva | 5 |
| L-b 3, n-b 3 | 6 |
| 1/2 2/17 3/183 4/192 5/230 6/255 7/257 8/261 9/273 (9 wkts dec.) | 273 |

N. G. Cowans did not bat.

Bowling: G. N. de Silva 22.3-5-77-3; Ratnayake 22-5-78-2; Ranatunga 10-0-45-0; E. A. R. de Silva 29-9-60-3; Warnakulasuriya 2-0-10-0.

Umpires: E. C. Seneviratne and H. C. Felsinger.

†At Saravanamuttu Stadium, Colombo, November 10. No result – rain. Sri Lankan XI 178 (38 overs) (S. Wettimuny 43, R. L. Dias 45) v An England XI.

## INDIAN CRICKET BOARD PRESIDENT'S XI v AN ENGLAND XI

At Jaipur, November 13, 14, 15. Drawn. Gower was encouraged by a sprinkling of grass into choosing to field. However, though the President's XI lost three cheap wickets and were over-cautious in recovering, the pitch played flawlessly. Edmonds bowled accurately, despite experimenting with a two-strides run-up after front-foot problems in Colombo, but he was flattered by his figures as Malhotra consumed 280 minutes for his hundred, completed on the second morning. Gaekwad thereupon declared, but there was no energetic response from England. Robinson, Gower, Ellison and Marks took their chance of practice, and the innings ran eight hours before Gower called a halt.

### Indian Cricket Board President's XI

| Batsman | First innings | Runs | Second innings | Runs |
|---|---|---|---|---|
| *A. D. Gaekwad | c Gower b Ellison | 23 | | |
| P. Shastri | c Gatting b Cowans | 6 | (1) c Edmonds b Cowdrey | 30 |
| M. Azharuddin | b Cowans | 2 | not out | 52 |
| A. Malhotra | not out | 102 | | |
| Gursharan Singh | b Edmonds | 41 | (4) st French b Edmonds | 0 |
| S. Mudkavi | c Cowdrey b Edmonds | 15 | (5) not out | 21 |
| †K. S. More | not out | 4 | (2) c French b Cowans | 12 |
| | W 5 | 5 | B 1, l-b 1 | 2 |
| | 1/18 2/20 3/44 4/127 5/165 (5 wkts dec.) | 198 | 1/24 2/69 3/70 (3 wkts) | 117 |

A. Patel, A. Raghuram Bhat, R. R. Kulkarni and Randhir Singh did not bat.

Bowling: *First Innings*—Cowans 13-4-29-2; Allott 12.1-4-33-0; Ellison 14-3-42-1; Edmonds 30-9-48-2; Marks 15-3-41-0; Gatting 1-0-5-0. *Second Innings*—Cowans 6-1-35-1; Allott 9-1-29-0; Edmonds 11-5-15-1; Marks 9-1-30-0; Cowdrey 4-1-6-1.

### An England XI

|  |  |  |
|---|---|---|
| G. Fowler | c More b Bhat | 28 |
| R. T. Robinson | c and b Mudkavi | 81 |
| M. W. Gatting | c Mudkavi b Bhat | 36 |
| *D. I. Gower | c Shastri b Kulkarni | 82 |
| C. S. Cowdrey | b Kulkarni | 8 |
| R. M. Ellison | not out | 83 |
| V. J. Marks | c Azharuddin b Mudkavi | 66 |
| P. H. Edmonds | c Kulkarni b Patel | 6 |
| †B. N. French | b Mudkavi | 19 |
| P. J. W. Allott | not out | 5 |
| | B 5, l-b 15, w 4, n-b 6 | 30 |
| | 1/56 2/142 3/221 4/244 5/279 6/394 7/404 8/436 (8 wkts dec.) | 444 |

N. G. Cowans did not bat.

Bowling: Kulkarni 22-2-78-2; Randhir 18-2-72-0; Bhat 31-4-97-2; Patel 30-3-112-1; Mudkavi 18-2-65-3.

Umpires: Swaroop Kishen and P. D. Reporter.

## INDIAN UNDER-25 XI v AN ENGLAND XI

At Gujarat Stadium, Ahmedabad, November 17, 18, 19. Indian Under-25 XI won by an innings and 59 runs. England's first defeat by an innings outside a Test match since 1962-63 when, as MCC, they lost to New South Wales at Sydney, came with nine of the final twenty overs unbowled as they collapsed against the spinners. Sivaramakrishnan, a slightly built eighteen-year-old leg-spinner, who had played one Test against West Indies, made good use of the rough outside the leg stump, bowling round the wicket, and Shastri handled his attack adroitly. There was help for seam bowling on the first morning, but after winning the toss England were let down by undisciplined batting, from which point they were never in the match. Srikkanth and Viswanath got the colts off to a good start, and Azharuddin and Madhavan, a left-hander, sealed their advantage by adding 240 in 270 minutes. England were outplayed in all departments, missing three catches and bowling with little penetration.

## An England XI

| | | | |
|---|---|---|---|
| G. Fowler c and b Prabhakar | 19 | lbw b Ghai | 9 |
| R. T. Robinson c Sivaramakrishnan b Ghai | 11 | c Viswanath b Sharma | 3 |
| M. W. Gatting run out | 52 | b Prabhakar | 16 |
| A. J. Lamb c Shastri b Prabhakar | 18 | c Sivaramakrishnan b Sharma | 34 |
| *D. I. Gower c and b Shastri | 21 | c sub b Sivaramakrishnan | 8 |
| R. M. Ellison c Shastri b Sivaramakrishnan | 5 | b Sivaramakrishnan | 3 |
| V. J. Marks b Ghai | 37 | st Viswanath b Sivaramakrishnan | 2 |
| †P. R. Downton b Sharma | 11 | st Viswanath b Sivaramakrishnan | 6 |
| N. A. Foster b Ghai | 11 | not out | 20 |
| P. J. W. Allott c Madhavan b Ghai | 14 | c Viswanath b Sharma | 10 |
| P. I. Pocock not out | 2 | c Ghai b Sharma | 0 |
| B 4, l-b 4, w 1, n-b 6 | 15 | B 1, l-b 2, n-b 3 | 6 |
| 1/36 2/40 3/62 4/105 5/117 6/145 7/183 8/198 9/209 | 216 | 1/12 2/17 3/65 4/71 5/75 6/79 7/85 8/86 9/115 | 117 |

Bowling: *First Innings*—Ghai 12.5–2–42–4; Prabhakar 10–2–43–2; Sharma 12–2–41–1; Khanvilkar 3–0–15–0; Sivaramakrishnan 10–1–38–1; Shastri 11–1–29–1. *Second Innings*—Ghai 10–1–36–1; Prabhakar 9–3–21–1; Sivaramakrishnan 20–11–27–4; Sharma 12–6–22–4; Shastri 8–3–8–0.

## Indian Under-25 XI

| | | | |
|---|---|---|---|
| †S. Viswanath c Downton b Allott | 31 | M. Prabhakar run out | 0 |
| K. Srikkanth b Pocock | 92 | R. S. Ghai not out | 0 |
| M. Azharuddin c Lamb b Marks | 151 | B 1, l-b 9, w 2, n-b 2 | 14 |
| Gursharan Singh lbw b Allott | 0 | | |
| R. Madhavan not out | 103 | 1/65 2/141 3/145 (6 wkts dec.) | 392 |
| R. Khanvilkar c Ellison b Pocock | 1 | 4/385 5/388 6/388 | |

*R. J. Shastri, G. Sharma and L. Sivaramakrishnan did not bat.

Bowling: Allott 27–4–99–2; Foster 22–5–59–0; Ellison 34–10–86–0; Pocock 22.2–2–94–2; Marks 10–3–34–1; Gatting 5–0–10–0.

Umpires: S. K. Bose and D. N. Dotiwala.

## WEST ZONE v AN ENGLAND XI

At Rajkot, November 21, 22, 23, 24. Drawn. That only seven wickets fell in the opening three days paints the picture of this match. On a pitch too heavily loaded in their favour, batsmen who concentrated, and who had the patience or footwork to overcome its lack of bounce, were likely to succeed. Four made hundreds, Vengsarkar an undefeated 200 in eight hours. Edmonds's four for 99 off 49 overs was a fine exhibition of variation and control. After the defeat at Ahmedabad, it was an important toss for Gower to win because the alternative could have been five or six sessions in the field in temperatures of 90 degrees. Fowler (255 minutes), Robinson (356 minutes) and Gatting (171 minutes with fifteen 4s and six 6s) made the most of it.

### An England XI

| | | | |
|---|---|---|---|
| G. Fowler c Jadeja b Patel | 116 | (5) b Patel | 2 |
| R. T. Robinson b Sandhu | 103 | (6) not out | 34 |
| *D. I. Gower st Pandit b Gudge | 57 | | |
| M. W. Gatting not out | 136 | | |
| A. J. Lamb not out | 30 | (8) st Pandit b Patel | 22 |
| P. H. Edmonds (did not bat) | | (1) c Sandhu b Keshwala | 8 |
| R. M. Ellison (did not bat) | | (2) c Sandhu b Patel | 25 |
| V. J. Marks (did not bat) | | (3) b Keshwala | 0 |
| †P. R. Downton (did not bat) | | (4) c and b Patel | 35 |
| N. G. Cowans (did not bat) | | (7) c Gudge b Patel | 10 |
| B 2, l-b 8, w 1, n-b 5 | 16 | B 1, l-b 1 | 2 |
| 1/190 2/246 3/317 (3 wkts dec.) | 458 | 1/33 2/33 3/46 4/48 5/99 6/111 7/138 (7 wkts dec.) | 138 |

P. J. W. Allott did not bat.

Bowling: *First Innings*—Kulkarni 22–5–58–0; Sandhu 31–7–99–1; Keshwala 5–0–12–0; Patel 39–7–102–1; Gudge 26–6–114–1; Rajput 4–1–10–0; Patil 6–0–35–0; Vengsarkar 1–0–7–0; Jadeja 1–0–11–0. *Second Innings*—Kulkarni 8–1–25–0; Sandhu 6.2–1–25–0; Keshwala 8.4–5–11–2; Patel 19.5–8–42–5; Gudge 10–0–33–0.

### West Zone

| | |
|---|---|
| L. S. Rajput b Edmonds | 79 |
| S. Kalyani lbw b Cowans | 9 |
| *D. B. Vengsarkar not out | 200 |
| S. M. Patil c Gower b Edmonds | 4 |
| B. Jadeja c Downton b Ellison | 48 |
| †C. S. Pandit run out | 22 |
| S. Keshwala c Gower b Edmonds | 19 |
| B. S. Sandhu c Downton b Edmonds | 0 |
| A. Patel not out | 9 |
| L-b 3 | 3 |
| 1/20 2/155 3/159 4/266 5/340 6/374 7/374 (7 wkts dec.) | 393 |

S. Gudge and R. R. Kulkarni did not bat.

Bowling: Allott 14–2–48–0; Cowans 19–4–76–1; Ellison 12–5–28–1; Edmonds 49–18–99–4; Marks 39.2–5–120–0; Gatting 5–0–19–0.

Umpires: B. Ganguli and M. G. Subramaniam.

## INDIA v ENGLAND

### First Test Match

At Bombay, November 28, 29, December 1, 2, 3. India won by eight wickets. A combination of bad batting in England's first innings and erratic umpiring by Swaroop Kishen in their second helped India end a sequence of 31 Tests without a win in a fast-moving and entertaining match. Their previous victory had also been at the Wankhede Stadium and at England's expense, just over three years earlier when Fletcher's team lost by 128 runs and protested about the umpiring.

In that respect the games were not dissimilar. Where they differed was that on this occasion England won the toss and through Fowler and Robinson – the latter, with Cowdrey, was one of two new caps – were building a satisfactory opening when Fowler was caught and bowled off a full toss. This was Sivaramakrishnan's first wicket in Test cricket and started a collapse from which England never recovered, seven wickets falling for 68 on a slow pitch of even bounce. India were in danger of losing their advantage when, through batting more in keeping with one-day cricket, they became 156 for five in the 34th over. But Shastri survived a straightforward stumping chance at 38 off Edmonds, and with Kirmani turned the game with an Indian seventh-wicket record stand of 235.

When they were out to successive balls, caught by Lamb at deep mid-wicket, both had made maiden hundreds against England without offering a further chance. Kirmani, first out, hit ten 4s in 319 minutes, Shastri seventeen 4s and a 6 in 390 minutes, a composed innings that confirmed he could hold his Test place on his batting skill alone. Cowans bowled some fast overs, surprising Gavaskar with his bounce. But England's attack in general was short of penetration, Ellison suffering from his inexperience in using the new ball. In the light of

Ellison's selection ahead of Allott (who was in the twelve), Gower's failure to give him a new ball in any of the four previous games was strange. On the credit side was England's fielding, especially Robinson's, in an Indian innings spanning nine hours, twenty minutes.

England, needing 270 to make India bat again, lost Robinson to a highly questionable lbw decision in the final 50 minutes of the third day's play. India were kept waiting till 45 minutes after lunch on the fourth day for their next success, Fowler and Gatting adding 135 in 199 minutes on a slow, turning pitch. Then Fowler was lbw to Sivaramakrishnan before umpire Kishen gave Gower out, caught at silly-point from what the batsman believed was a rebound off his pad. Next over, when Lamb, groping for a leg-break, was brilliantly stumped off Sivaramakrishnan, bowling round the wicket, England had slumped from 138 for one to 152 for four in 27 minutes. Cowdrey saw Gatting past his first Test hundred (in his 54th innings, two more than R. B. Simpson needed for Australia), but at 199 fell to another controversial catch at silly-point.

Gatting, sensing an assault was needed for England to escape, scored 40 of his final 46 in 4s. Then Sivaramakrishnan deceived him in the air, causing him to sky a catch to long-off, making England 222 for six. The ease with which Pocock batted for 78 minutes on the last day, adding 62 for the ninth wicket with Downton, showed that Gatting may have miscalculated. But the stroke, far less the intention, took little credit from his 309 minutes of mixed aggression and solidity which brought him 21 4s. The tiny Sivaramakrishnan, if somewhat flattered by match figures of twelve for 181, looked a fine prospect and an engaging natural cricketer.

## England

| | | | |
|---|---|---|---|
| G. Fowler c and b Sivaramakrishnan | 28 | – lbw b Sivaramakrishnan | 55 |
| R. T. Robinson c Kirmani b Sivaramakrishnan | 22 | – lbw b Kapil Dev | 1 |
| M. W. Gatting c and b Sivaramakrishnan | 15 | – c Patil b Sivaramakrishnan | 136 |
| *D. I. Gower b Kapil Dev | 13 | – c Vengsarkar b Shastri | 2 |
| A. J. Lamb c Shastri b Kapil Dev | 9 | – st Kirmani b Sivaramakrishnan | 1 |
| C. S. Cowdrey c Kirmani b Yadav | 13 | – c Vengsarkar b Yadav | 14 |
| R. M. Ellison b Sivaramakrishnan | 1 | – (8) c Vengsarkar b Yadav | 0 |
| †P. R. Downton not out | 37 | – (7) lbw b Sivaramakrishnan | 62 |
| P. H. Edmonds c Gaekwad b Shastri | 48 | – c Kapil Dev b Sivaramakrishnan | 8 |
| P. I. Pocock c Kirmani b Sivaramakrishnan | 8 | – not out | 22 |
| N. G. Cowans c Shastri b Sivaramakrishnan | 0 | – c Vengsarkar b Sivaramakrishnan | 0 |
| B 1 | 1 | B 4, l-b 8, n-b 4 | 16 |
| 1/46 2/51 3/78 4/78 5/93 6/94 7/114 8/175 9/193 | 195 | 1/3 2/138 3/145 4/152 5/199 6/222 7/228 8/255 9/317 | 317 |

Bowling: *First Innings*—Kapil Dev 22–8–44–2; Chetan 11–4–28–0; Shastri 17–8–23–1; Amarnath 3–2–1–0; Sivaramakrishnan 31.2–10–64–6; Yadav 12–2–34–1. *Second Innings*—Kapil Dev 21–8–34–1; Chetan 9–2–39–0; Sivaramakrishnan 46–10–117–6; Yadav 29–9–64–2; Shastri 29–8–50–1; Gaekwad 1–0–1–0.

## India

| | | | |
|---|---|---|---|
| *S. M. Gavaskar c Downton b Cowans | 27 | – c Gower b Cowans | 5 |
| A. D. Gaekwad run out | 24 | – st Downton b Edmonds | 1 |
| D. B. Vengsarkar c Lamb b Cowans | 34 | – not out | 21 |
| M. Amarnath c Cowdrey b Pocock | 49 | – not out | 22 |
| S. M. Patil c Gower b Edmonds | 20 | | |
| R. J. Shastri c Lamb b Pocock | 142 | | |
| Kapil Dev b Cowdrey | 42 | | |
| †S. M. H. Kirmani c Lamb b Pocock | 102 | | |
| Chetan Sharma not out | 5 | | |
| N. S. Yadav not out | 7 | | |
| B 4, l-b 2, n-b 7 | 13 | B 2 | 2 |
| 1/47 2/59 3/116 4/156 5/156 6/218 7/453 8/453 | (8 wkts dec.) 465 | 1/5 2/7 | (2 wkts) 51 |

L. Sivaramakrishnan did not bat.

Bowling: *First Innings*—Ellison 18–3–85–0; Cowans 28–6–109–2; Edmonds 33–6–82–1; Pocock 46–10–133–3; Cowdrey 5–0–30–1; Gatting 7–0–20–0. *Second Innings*—Edmonds 8–3–21–1; Cowans 5–2–18–1; Pocock 2.1–0–10–0.

Umpires: Swaroop Kishen and B. Ganguli.

## †INDIA v ENGLAND

### First One-day International

At Pune, December 5. England won by four wickets. For a change in one-day matches in India, with their 9.30 start, the toss played no significant role. Though Gower chose to field, the sun soon dried the dew and India should have made at least 40 more than their 214 for six after a second-wicket stand of 118 in 24 overs. Vengsarkar, missed three times between 77 and 83, failed to push the score along, taking 40 overs for his 105 in perfect batting conditions. England in turn nearly threw the match away, losing six for 129 through poor cricket. But Gatting was undismayed and, with sensible support from Downton, won it impressively with his first hundred in a one-day international. Their unbroken stand of 86 was scored off 14 overs.

*Man of the Match:* D. B. Vengsarkar and M. W. Gatting (shared).

### India

K. Srikkanth b Edmonds ............ 50
*S. M. Gavaskar b Foster ........... 0
D. B. Vengsarkar b Ellison ..........105
S. M. Patil run out ................ 2
Yashpal Sharma c Ellison b Foster .... 37
R. J. Shastri c Ellison b Foster ....... 11
R. M. H. Binny not out ............ 0
L-b 2, w 7 ................ 9

1/1 2/119 3/126 4/189 5/212 6/214 (6 wkts, 45 overs) 214

†K. S. More, M. Prabhakar, R. S. Ghai and Chetan Sharma did not bat.

Bowling: Cowans 8–0–32–0; Foster 10–0–44–3; Ellison 7–0–45–1; Marks 10–0–48–0; Edmonds 10–0–43–1.

### England

G. Fowler c Yashpal b Chetan ....... 5
R. T. Robinson lbw b Ghai .......... 15
M. W. Gatting not out ..............115
A. J. Lamb c and b Prabhakar ....... 3
V. J. Marks run out ................ 31
*D. I. Gower c Shastri b Binny ....... 3
R. M. Ellison run out ............... 4
†P. R. Downton not out ............ 27
L-b 8, n-b 4 ............... 12

1/14 2/43 3/47 4/114 5/117 6/129 (6 wkts, 43.2 overs) 215

P. H. Edmonds, N. A. Foster and N. G. Cowans did not bat.

Bowling: Chetan 8.2–0–50–1; Prabhakar 10–1–27–1; Ghai 9–0–38–1; Shastri 8–0–49–0; Binny 8–0–43–1.

Umpires: Mohammad Ghouse and S. Banerjee.

## NORTH ZONE v AN ENGLAND XI

At Bombay, December 7, 8, 9. Drawn. This match was switched from Jammu, when the tour itinerary was rearranged, as a precaution against reaction from Mrs Gandhi's assassination in the northern state of Jammu and Kashmir. Played at the Wankhede Stadium, it was watched by no more than a few hundred on each day and as a consequence lacked atmosphere. England, winning the toss, bowled a side out for the first time in more than five weeks, though eight of North Zone's wickets fell when a damp pitch had turned in favour of the ball. Robinson, sharing stands of 101 with Moxon, who was playing his first innings on tour, and 124 with Cowdrey, batted 309 minutes for his second hundred in five innings. England, leading by 191, left themselves four hours to bowl North Zone out a second time but never looked like doing so.

## North Zone

| | | | |
|---|---|---|---|
| C. P. S. Chauhan lbw b Ellison | 24 | – c French b Foster | 8 |
| †S. C. Khanna c and b Foster | 12 | | |
| Navjot Singh c French b Foster | 0 | | |
| A. Malhotra run out | 47 | – not out | 50 |
| Yashpal Sharma c French b Pocock | 22 | – not out | 26 |
| K. Azad c Moxon b Pocock | 0 | | |
| Gursharan Singh c and b Edmonds | 0 | – (3) lbw b Marks | 53 |
| *Madan Lal run out | 42 | | |
| M. Prabhakar c Lamb b Ellison | 30 | – (2) b Foster | 31 |
| R. S. Ghai lbw b Ellison | 0 | | |
| Maninder Singh not out | 4 | | |
| B 3, l-b 2 | 5 | B 1, l-b 6, n-b 1 | 8 |
| 1/15 2/15 3/51 4/99 5/99 6/106 7/107 8/175 9/175 | 186 | 1/40 2/51 3/118 (3 wkts) | 176 |

Bowling: *First Innings*—Foster 22–4–58–2; Ellison 19.1–9–29–3; Cowdrey 9–3–24–0; Edmonds 15–4–36–1; Pocock 14–4–34–2. *Second Innings*—Foster 8–0–50–2; Ellison 8–3–19–0; Cowdrey 7–0–19–0; Marks 10–3–14–1; Edmonds 13–2–37–0; Pocock 9–3–30–0; Lamb 1–1–0–0.

## An England XI

| | |
|---|---|
| P. I. Pocock c Navjot b Ghai | 2 |
| R. T. Robinson c Malhotra b Maninder | 138 |
| M. D. Moxon lbw b Ghai | 42 |
| *D. I. Gower lbw b Ghai | 7 |
| A. J. Lamb c Prabhakar b Maninder | 20 |
| C. S. Cowdrey lbw b Prabhakar | 70 |
| V. J. Marks c Madan Lal b Ghai | 19 |
| R. M. Ellison b Ghai | 10 |
| P. H. Edmonds b Ghai | 15 |
| †B. N. French lbw b Ghai | 19 |
| N. A. Foster not out | 22 |
| B 3, l-b 6, n-b 4 | 13 |
| 1/3 2/104 3/123 4/158 5/282 6/292 7/305 8/331 9/342 | 377 |

Bowling: Prabhakar 17–5–49–1; Ghai 27–4–110–7; Madan Lal 11–1–30–0; Maninder 31–4–107–2; Azad 14–1–48–0; Chauhan 2–0–24–0.

Umpires: R. Mehra and V. Vikramraju.

# INDIA v ENGLAND

## Second Test Match

At Delhi, December 12, 13, 15, 16, 17. England won by eight wickets. An excellent all-round performance was unexpectedly rewarded after lunch on the final day when, by taking India's last six wickets for 28, England were left with a simple task to square the series. A target of 125 in 59 minutes and twenty overs proved no problem on a small ground running fast and Lamb made the winning hit with 8.2 overs in hand. Though a draw should have been within India's grasp on a slow, turning pitch, Edmonds and Pocock bowled superbly, promoting and sustaining the collapse by relentless accuracy to precisely set attacking fields. The crucial wicket was that of Patil, fifth out at 207. Pegged down by the spinners for 40 overs, he revealed a note of desperation in his final stroke, an attempted pull off Edmonds, which resulted in a mis-hit to mid-wicket.

The result ended England's longest-ever spell without a victory and was especially well deserved as Gower lost what seemed a crucial toss and, as at Bombay, the umpiring left something to be desired. Of several questionable decisions, seemingly the only one that favoured England came at the end of India's first innings when Sivaramakrishnan was adjudged run out by Robinson's direct hit on the non-striker's stumps from cover point.

England, fielding the team beaten in the first Test, were given a flying start by Ellison, who had Gavaskar caught at the wicket in the second over with an out-swinger. Edmonds and Pocock then took control so that at tea, when India were 144 for six, the advantage of batting first on a suspect pitch had almost disappeared. Soon afterwards, however, Kirmani was missed at slip by Lamb off Edmonds, and with Kapil Dev surviving a hard-hit caught and bowled to Pocock's left, the last four wickets held out till after lunch on the second day, adding 167.

England soon lost Fowler. But first with Gatting, then Lamb, and later Cowdrey and Downton, Robinson made certain of a lengthy lead on first innings with a determined maiden Test hundred. In eight and three-quarter hours at the crease, with seventeen 4s, he gave his only chance when he was 54, Kirmani missing stumping him off Sivaramakrishnan's googly, which almost hit the off stump. Eliminating the threat of the occasional low bounce by wary play against short balls on the stumps, Robinson shared three-figure stands with Lamb and Downton before, early on the fourth day, he was caught at the wicket off his gloves from a ball from Kapil Dev that lifted unexpectedly off a length.

Most of Robinson's runs came off his legs and behind square on the off side, where by opening the blade he repeatedly found gaps; but when the spinners over-pitched, he off-drove with certainty and power. Downton, with his highest Test score, and Edmonds consolidated by adding 55 for the seventh wicket. But when Edmonds was out to a mis-hit in the over after lunch, Sivaramakrishnan polished off the innings in 40 minutes, restricting England's lead to 111, and completing his third successive bag of six wickets in the series.

Cowans increased England's advantage by dismissing Prabhakar, who was opening in place of Gaekwad (ankle injury), and Vengsarkar in four overs. But Gavaskar and Amarnath, punishing the spinners, took India to 128 for two at close of play, 17 ahead. On a pitch lasting much better than expected, a draw now seemed much the likeliest result. But when Edmonds hit Amarnath's off stump with a ball that curled in and spun away in the second over of the final day, and an hour later Gavaskar, making room to force Pocock through his three-man off-side field, was bowled by one that turned sharply and kept low, the scene was set for the afternoon collapse. Patil and Kapil, who mis-hit Pocock to long-off the ball after driving him for 6, were wickets India threw away.

## India

| | | | |
|---|---|---|---|
| *S. M. Gavaskar c Downton b Ellison | 1 | – b Pocock | 65 |
| A. D. Gaekwad b Pocock | 28 | – (8) c Downton b Edmonds | 0 |
| D. B. Vengsarkar st Downton b Edmonds | 24 | – b Cowans | 1 |
| M. Amarnath c Gower b Pocock | 42 | – b Edmonds | 64 |
| S. M. Patil c Pocock b Edmonds | 30 | – c Lamb b Edmonds | 41 |
| R. J. Shastri c Fowler b Pocock | 2 | – not out | 25 |
| Kapil Dev c Downton b Ellison | 60 | – c Lamb b Pocock | 7 |
| †S. M. H. Kirmani c Gatting b Ellison | 27 | – (9) b Pocock | 6 |
| M. Prabhakar c Downton b Ellison | 25 | – (2) c Downton b Cowans | 5 |
| N. S. Yadav not out | 28 | – c Lamb b Edmonds | 1 |
| L. Sivaramakrishnan run out | 25 | – c and b Pocock | 0 |
| B 1, l-b 12, n-b 2 | 15 | B 6, l-b 10, w 1, n-b 3 | 20 |
| 1/3 2/56 3/68 4/129 5/131 6/140 7/208 8/235 9/258 | 307 | 1/12 2/15 3/136 4/172 5/207 6/214 7/216 8/225 9/234 | 235 |

Bowling: *First Innings*—Cowans 20–5–70–0; Ellison 26–6–66–4; Edmonds 44.2–16–83–2; Pocock 33–8–70–3; Gatting 2–0–5–0. *Second Innings*—Cowans 13–2–43–2; Ellison 7–1–20–0; Edmonds 44–24–60–4; Pocock 38.4–9–93–4; Gatting 1–0–3–0.

## England

| | | | |
|---|---|---|---|
| G. Fowler c Gaekwad b Prabhakar | 5 | – c Vengsarkar b Sivaramakrishnan | 29 |
| R. T. Robinson c Gavaskar b Kapil Dev | 160 | – run out | 18 |
| M. W. Gatting b Yadav | 26 | – not out | 30 |
| A. J. Lamb c Vengsarkar b Yadav | 52 | – not out | 37 |
| *D. I. Gower lbw b Sivaramakrishnan | 5 | | |
| C. S. Cowdrey c Gavaskar b Sivaramakrishnan | 38 | | |
| †P. R. Downton c Kapil Dev b Sivaramakrishnan | 74 | | |
| P. H. Edmonds c Shastri b Sivaramakrishnan | 26 | | |
| R. M. Ellison b Sivaramakrishnan | 10 | | |
| P. I. Pocock b Sivaramakrishnan | 0 | | |
| N. G. Cowans not out | 0 | | |
| B 6, l-b 13, n-b 3 | 22 | B 4, l-b 7, n-b 2 | 13 |
| 1/15 2/60 3/170 4/181 5/237 6/343 7/398 8/411 9/415 | 418 | 1/41 2/68 | (2 wkts) 127 |

Bowling: *First Innings*—Kapil Dev 32-5-87-1; Prabhakar 21-3-68-1; Sivaramakrishnan 49.1-17-99-6; Yadav 36-6-95-2; Shastri 29-4-44-0; Amarnath 2-0-6-0. *Second Innings*—Kapil Dev 6-0-20-0; Prabhakar 3-0-18-0; Sivaramakrishnan 8-0-41-1; Yadav 2-0-7-0; Shastri 4-0-20-0; Gavaskar 0.4-0-10-0.

Umpires: D. N. Dotiwala and P. D. Reporter.

## EAST ZONE v AN ENGLAND XI

At Gauhati, December 19, 20, 21. England won by an innings and 121 runs with a day to spare. Fowler's watchful 114 in four and a half hours on a slow, turning pitch was the basis of England's victory, which was achieved just before lunch on the third day of a scheduled four-day match. East Zone, propped up by Arun Lal, the one Test batsman in an inexperienced team, seemingly had prospects of scoring 141 to avoid the follow-on when they passed 60 with only two men out. But Marks dismissed Arun Lal and Bharadwaj with successive balls, whereupon resistance crumbled, Marks and Edmonds at one point bowling 44 overs while four wickets fell for 45. Foster's out-swing did the early damage in the follow-on, despite two straightforward slip catches being missed off him, and Edmonds's control and spin overwhelmed the tail.

### An England XI

| | |
|---|---|
| G. Fowler c sub b Kumar | 114 |
| M. D. Moxon c Jayaprakash b Doshi | 36 |
| A. J. Lamb b Jayaprakash | 23 |
| *M. W. Gatting c Arun Lal b Kumar | 37 |
| C. S. Cowdrey st Deora b Jayaprakash | 9 |
| V. J. Marks b Kumar | 7 |
| P. H. Edmonds run out | 6 |
| P. R. Downton c Dubey b Kumar | 3 |
| †B. N. French c Deora b Doshi | 13 |
| N. A. Foster not out | 26 |
| N. G. Cowans c Bharadwaj b Kumar | 1 |
| B 5, l-b 5, w 3, n-b 2 | 15 |
| 1/86 2/119 3/180 4/193 5/220 6/243 7/248 8/251 9/277 | 290 |

Bowling: Randhir 8-1-19-0; Sinha 5-1-37-0; Doshi 37-6-90-2; Kumar 38.3-14-81-5; Jayaprakash 11-0-53-2.

### East Zone

| First innings | | Second innings | |
|---|---|---|---|
| K. Dubey lbw b Foster | 0 | c Gatting b Foster | 8 |
| Arun Lal b Marks | 42 | c Cowdrey b Foster | 2 |
| A. Mitra lbw b Edmonds | 7 | c Cowdrey b Foster | 0 |
| A. Jayaprakash b Marks | 16 | lbw b Cowans | 2 |
| A. Bharadwaj c and b Marks | 0 | b Marks | 30 |
| A. Das c French b Marks | 7 | b Edmonds | 3 |
| †R. Deora c French b Gatting | 12 | c Gatting b Edmonds | 0 |
| Randhir Singh not out | 9 | run out | 0 |
| A. Sinha c Gatting b Cowans | 9 | st French b Edmonds | 0 |
| *D. R. Doshi c French b Cowans | 4 | b Edmonds | 0 |
| A. Kumar b Edmonds | 2 | not out | 6 |
| B 4, l-b 4, w 1 | 9 | B 1 | 1 |
| 1/0 2/26 3/69 4/69 5/70 6/83 7/95 8/106 9/112 | 117 | 1/3 2/3 3/12 4/14 5/17 6/27 7/37 8/38 9/38 | 52 |

Bowling: *First Innings*—Foster 10-4-14-1; Cowans 9-2-18-2; Edmonds 33-16-25-2; Marks 29-11-48-4; Gatting 4-1-4-1. *Second Innings*—Foster 15-6-32-3; Cowans 6-3-4-1; Edmonds 9-3-13-4; Marks 0.4-0-2-1.

Umpires: M. Y. Gupte and V. K. Ramaswamy.

## †INDIA v ENGLAND

### Second One-day International

At Cuttack, December 27. England won on faster scoring-rate. Lynx-eyed batting by Marks, Downton and Ellison in light which was theoretically "unplayable" for most of the last hour enabled England to snatch a win. Helped by six missed chances, Srikkanth and Shastri shared an opening stand of 188 – India's highest for any wicket in one-day internationals – after Gower had chosen to field. But a poor attempt was made to capitalise on this following Srikkanth's dismissal in the 37th over, only 64 being added in 12.2 overs as Shastri moved too slowly to his hundred. The pitch was easy-paced. England's hopes faded, however, when Lamb was run out in the 33rd over at 145. Then Marks and Downton added 58 in nine overs and India lost control. Downton and Ellison had just completed the win (by 0.08 of a run) when the game was abandoned, after 46 overs, in the gloaming.

*Man of the Match:* R. J. Shastri.

### India

| | | | |
|---|---|---|---|
| K. Srikkanth lbw b Gatting | 99 | *S. M. Gavaskar not out | 6 |
| R. J. Shastri b Gatting | 102 | | |
| D. B. Vengsarkar c Gower b Marks | 23 | B 5, l-b 5, w 3, n-b 2 | 15 |
| Yashpal Sharma lbw b Marks | 4 | | |
| M. Amarnath not out | 1 | 1/188 2/235 (5 wkts, 49 overs) | 252 |
| R. M. H. Binny b Marks | 2 | 3/243 4/243 5/246 | |

†K. S. More, M. Prabhakar, R. S. Ghai and A. Patel did not bat.

Bowling: Foster 5–0–26–0; Cowans 10–0–39–0; Ellison 6–0–31–0; Edmonds 10–0–47–0; Marks 8–0–50–3; Gatting 10–0–49–2.

### England

| | | | |
|---|---|---|---|
| G. Fowler c Shastri b Binny | 15 | †P. R. Downton not out | 44 |
| R. T. Robinson b Prabhakar | 1 | R. M. Ellison not out | 14 |
| M. W. Gatting b Patel | 59 | L-b 9, w 1, n-b 5 | 15 |
| *D. I. Gower c Prabhakar b Binny | 21 | | |
| A. J. Lamb run out | 28 | 1/3 2/50 3/93 (6 wkts, 46 overs) | 241 |
| V. J. Marks run out | 44 | 4/128 5/145 6/203 | |

P. H. Edmonds, N. A. Foster and N. G. Cowans did not bat.

Bowling: Ghai 8–0–40–0; Prabhakar 10–1–34–1; Binny 7–0–48–2; Patel 10–0–53–1; Shastri 10–0–48–0; Amarnath 1–0–9–0.

Umpires: J. D. Ghosh and P. G. Pandit.

## INDIA v ENGLAND

### Third Test Match

At Calcutta, December 31, January 1, 3, 4, 5. Drawn. Smog and rain, which restricted play to twenty minutes on the second day, followed by Gavaskar's perverse decision to continue India's innings from 417 for seven at lunch time on the fourth, made certain of a pointless and tedious draw. Gavaskar's lack of ambition, or evident direction, while Azharuddin and Shastri were adding 214 for the fifth wicket at under 2 runs an over, so incensed the crowd that there were fears a riot might develop. That section of the crowd nearest the pavilion hooted and booed, shouting "Gavaskar down, Gavaskar out" when the Indian captain made a brief appearance outside the dressing-room while Prabhakar and Chetan Sharma were batting at a snail's pace, and he was pelted with fruit when eventually he led India out to field, the game being held up for eight minutes while groundstaff cleared the outfield. Gower helped prompt his declaration even then reluctant – twenty minutes after lunch with three overs of derisive off-breaks, while Edmonds took a leaf out of Warwick Armstrong's book at The Oval in 1921 by reading a newspaper as the captain waited at his mark to bowl. Gavaskar subsequently denied that police had warned him there was a threat to law and order should he delay the declaration any longer, though it was broadcast as a fact by an Indian commentator on BBC radio.

All this, combined with the distraction of a protracted meeting between India's selectors three days before the match to review Kapil Dev's omission, ensured a Test that had less to do with cricket than machinations off the field. The five selectors, who had been requested to reconsider Kapil's case by N. K. P. Salve, the BCCI chairman, unanimously decided against his reinstatement, although Gavaskar, who had no vote, was said to be in favour of it following the all-rounder's "repentance" for the stroke that helped England win the second Test in Delhi. The selectors, under the chairmanship of C. G. Borde, further established their authority over Gavaskar by insisting that the 21-year-old Azharuddin took the batting place vacated by Patil. The captain's preference was for Srikkanth, who as an opener would have given Gavaskar the chance he was seeking to bat at number five.

In the event Azharuddin vindicated the selectors' judgement by becoming the eighth Indian (ninth with the elder Nawab of Pataudi for England) to make a hundred in his maiden Test. A willowy 5ft 11in, he confirmed the impression made at Jaipur and Ahmedabad of placid temperament, sound technique and flawless application, batting 443 minutes before being caught in the gully from a ball that lifted off a length. After a well-contested first day, however, the tempo of Azharuddin's stand with Shastri, which was India's record in all Tests for the fifth wicket, killed the match.

Though the pitch was slow, England's outcricket was mostly of exceptional standard throughout India's innings of thirteen and three-quarter hours. There was, however, no justification for India's failure to try to accelerate. Shastri, who batted on all five days of the match, was the worst offender, taking an hour longer for his second fifty than his first, seven hours in all, and spending an hour in the 90s. Only eight hours remained when England's first innings started and the batsmen seemed for the most part unable to apply themselves to what had long since been a fruitless exercise. On the final day the crowd dropped to 60,000, a phenomenon for a Test at Eden Gardens.

## India

| First innings | | Second innings | |
|---|---|---|---|
| *S. M. Gavaskar c Gatting b Edmonds | 13 | | |
| A. D. Gaekwad c Downton b Cowans | 18 | | |
| D. B. Vengsarkar b Edmonds | 48 | | |
| M. Amarnath c Cowdrey b Edmonds | 42 | | |
| M. Azharuddin c Gower b Cowans | 110 | | |
| R. J. Shastri b Cowans | 111 | (1) not out | 7 |
| †S. M. H. Kirmani c Fowler b Pocock | 35 | | |
| M. Prabhakar not out | 35 | (2) lbw b Lamb | 21 |
| Chetan Sharma not out | 13 | | |
| N. S. Yadav (did not bat) | – | (3) not out | 0 |
| L-b 8, w 1, n-b 3 | 12 | N-b 1 | 1 |
| 1/28 2/35 3/126 4/127 5/341 6/356 7/407 | (7 wkts dec.) 437 | 1/29 | (1 wkt) 29 |

L. Sivaramakrishnan did not bat.

Bowling: *First Innings*—Cowans 41–12–103–3; Ellison 53–14–117–0; Edmonds 47–22–72–3; Pocock 52–14–108–1; Gatting 2–1–1–0; Cowdrey 2–0–15–0; Gower 3–0–13–0. *Second Innings*—Cowans 4–1–6–0; Cowdrey 4–0–10–0; Edmonds 4–3–2–0; Ellison 1–0–1–0; Pocock 2–1–4–0; Lamb 1–0–6–1; Robinson 1–1–0–0; Fowler 1–1–0–0.

## England

| | |
|---|---|
| G. Fowler c Vengsarkar b Sivaramakrishnan | 49 |
| R. T. Robinson b Yadav | 36 |
| *D. I. Gower c Shastri b Yadav | 19 |
| P. I. Pocock c Azharuddin b Sivaramakrishnan | 5 |
| M. W. Gatting b Yadav | 48 |
| A. J. Lamb c Kirmani b Chetan | 67 |
| C. S. Cowdrey lbw b Yadav | 27 |
| †P. R. Downton not out | 6 |
| P. H. Edmonds c Gavaskar b Chetan | 8 |
| R. M. Ellison c and b Chetan | 1 |
| N. G. Cowans b Chetan | 1 |
| L-b 2, n-b 7 | 9 |
| 1/71 2/98 3/110 4/152 5/163 6/229 7/261 8/270 9/273 | 276 |

Bowling: Chetan 12.3–0–38–4; Prabhakar 5–1–16–0; Sivaramakrishnan 28–7–90–2; Yadav 32–10–86–4; Shastri 23–6–44–0.

Umpires: B. Ganguli and V. Vikramraju.

## SOUTH ZONE v AN ENGLAND XI

At Secunderabad, January 7, 8, 9, 10. Drawn. The return of first-class cricket to the Gymkhana Ground after an interval of 33 years provided a new experience for a recent England touring team in India – a pitch with a thick mat of grass which gave lift and bounce on all four days.

England, winning the toss, should have gone on to win the match. But inaccurate seam bowling, compounded by bad catching, enabled South Zone to reach 306, Srikkanth being let off in the slips at 14, 24 and 32. Moxon, overcoming cramp in his hands to bat for seven and a quarter hours, helped to earn a lead of 28, and victory looked probable when South Zone slipped to 210 for eight with three and a half hours still to play. But Ayub and Raman shared a second valuable ninth-wicket stand and England's attempt to score 232 at six an over foundered before the final twenty overs.

## South Zone

| First Innings | | Second Innings | |
|---|---|---|---|
| *K. Srikkanth c Moxon b Agnew | 90 | (3) lbw b Cowdrey | 18 |
| M. R. Srinivasaprasad c French b Agnew | 0 | (1) lbw b Foster | 18 |
| †S. Viswanath c Gatting b Foster | 34 | (2) c sub b Agnew | 12 |
| R. Madhavan c Edmonds b Foster | 0 | c French b Cowdrey | 13 |
| M. Azharuddin b Agnew | 18 | (7) c French b Edmonds | 52 |
| R. M. H. Binny b Agnew | 19 | b Cowdrey | 14 |
| R. Kanvilkar c French b Cowdrey | 21 | (8) c Cowdrey b Agnew | 9 |
| K. A. Qayyum c Edmonds b Cowans | 18 | (5) b Foster | 39 |
| A. Ayub c French b Foster | 58 | not out | 35 |
| W. V. Raman lbw b Agnew | 26 | not out | 24 |
| T. A. P. Sekar not out | 0 | | |
| B 10, n-b 12 | 22 | B 4, l-b 2, n-b 19 | 25 |
| 1/7 2/62 3/62 4/131 5/157 6/174 7/200 8/234 9/306 | 306 | 1/29 2/40 3/52 4/67 5/100 6/143 7/168 8/210 (8 wkts dec.) | 259 |

Bowling: *First Innings*—Cowans 9–2–37–1; Agnew 19–1–102–5; Foster 19.4–6–45–3; Edmonds 13–7–28–0; Marks 7–2–27–0; Cowdrey 11–1–44–1; Gatting 3–0–13–0. *Second Innings*—Agnew 26–3–103–2; Foster 24–8–49–2; Cowdrey 22–5–61–3; Gatting 3–0–3–0; Edmonds 10–3–32–1; Marks 1–0–5–0.

## An England XI

| First Innings | | Second Innings | |
|---|---|---|---|
| M. D. Moxon b Raman | 153 | c Viswanath b Kanvilkar | 0 |
| R. T. Robinson c Raman b Sekar | 13 | run out | 32 |
| *D. I. Gower c Srinivasaprasad b Sekar | 13 | c Kanvilkar b Raman | 41 |
| C. S. Cowdrey c Srikkanth b Ayub | 22 | b Raman | 6 |
| M. W. Gatting c Kanvilkar b Raman | 50 | not out | 30 |
| V. J. Marks c Srinivasaprasad b Raman | 0 | (7) not out | 11 |
| †B. N. French c Kanvilkar b Ayub | 1 | (6) c Viswanath b Ayub | 11 |
| P. H. Edmonds c Srinivasaprasad b Raman | 29 | | |
| N. A. Foster c Viswanath b Sekar | 29 | | |
| J. P. Agnew not out | 12 | | |
| N. G. Cowans c Azharuddin b Raman | 0 | | |
| L-b 5, n-b 7 | 12 | N-b 1 | 1 |
| 1/18 2/45 3/88 4/176 5/176 6/179 7/226 8/297 9/332 | 334 | 1/1 2/12 3/80 4/80 5/102 (5 wkts) | 132 |

Bowling: *First Innings*—Sekar 24–4–74–3; Binny 11–1–41–0; Kanvilkar 12–3–28–0; Ayub 34–4–116–2; Raman 28.4–11–59–5; Srinivasaprasad 1–0–8–0; Srikkanth 1–0–3–0. *Second Innings*—Sekar 7–2–17–0; Kanvilkar 4–0–20–1; Ayub 10–0–48–1; Raman 8–0–39–2; Srikkanth 1–0–8–0.

Umpires: S. K. Ghosh and S. R. Ramachandra Rao.

## INDIA v ENGLAND

### Fourth Test Match

At Madras, January 13, 14, 15, 17, 18. England won by nine wickets. Well-sustained swing bowling by Foster, playing his first match of the series, gave England a grip they were never to lose when India, winning the toss, were dismissed in five hours twelve minutes. After bowling

Gavaskar as he made to drive and having Vengsarkar caught at second slip, forcing off the back foot, in his opening spell, Foster returned after lunch to break the one stand of substance, 110 for the fourth wicket between Amarnath and Azharuddin, before adding two tailenders to his bag to finish with six for 104, his best in Test cricket.

Helped by faulty Indian catching, England took full advantage of conditions which by the second day had become ideal for batting. The outfield guaranteed full value for every well-placed stroke. India's attack was strengthened by the return of Kapil Dev: but he could make no impact as Fowler, partnered by Robinson and Gatting, shared two successive wicket records for England against India and joined Hutton (The Oval, 1938) as the only English batsman to establish in one innings such records that still stand.

Fowler, at 36 and 75, and Robinson, at 44, survived chances close to the bat in their stand of 178. India paid dearly for the lapses. Gatting, given the freedom to play his natural forcing game, helped Fowler take the score to 293 by close of play, and on the third day to complete a second-wicket stand of 241. Fowler, missed again at 160, had batted 565 minutes (three 6s, one 5, 21 4s and 409 balls) when Kapil had him caught behind. Two and a half hours later, when Gatting was caught at long-on after batting 506 minutes (three 6s, twenty 4s and 308 balls) they had the distinction of becoming the first Englishmen ever to have scored double-hundreds in the same Test innings.

Despite defensive field-placing, the second-wicket stand was made at more than 3 runs an over, a rate which increased to nearly 5 while Gatting and Lamb were adding 144 for the third wicket. Another 41 were scored off eight overs on the fourth morning before, after thirteen hours in the field, India were spared further punishment by Gower's declaration at 652 for seven – England's highest total against India. Facing a deficit of 380 with ten and a half hours left for play, India briefly seemed in danger of annihilation when Foster shot out Gavaskar, Vengsarkar and Srikkanth in his first four overs – Gavaskar for the second time in the match in seventeen deliveries. But with the pitch still doing little for the spinners, Amarnath and Azharuddin counter-attacked superbly, adding 190 in three and a half hours, with Pocock the main sufferer, before Foster returned to have Amarnath well caught at long-leg off a hook.

Azharuddin revealed a brilliant range of off-side strokes square with the wicket in becoming only the fourth player to score a hundred in his first two Tests before falling to Pocock, caught at silly point, early on the final day. Kapil Dev and Kirmani went on to score 82 off nineteen overs for the seventh wicket, but when Kapil Dev fell to the new ball there could be only one result. Had Fowler, at deep backward point, caught Kirmani with India 362 for nine, England would have been celebrating their first innings victory since 1979, when India themselves lost at Edgbaston 61 Tests earlier. The match was well umpired by two officials standing for the first time in a Test.

## India

| | | | |
|---|---|---|---|
| *S. M. Gavaskar b Foster | 17 | – c Gatting b Foster | 3 |
| K. Srikkanth c Downton b Cowans | 0 | – c Cowdrey b Foster | 16 |
| D. B. Vengsarkar c Lamb b Foster | 17 | – c Downton b Foster | 2 |
| M. Amarnath c Downton b Foster | 78 | – c Cowans b Foster | 95 |
| M. Azharuddin b Cowdrey | 48 | – c Gower b Pocock | 105 |
| R. J. Shastri c Downton b Foster | 2 | – c Cowdrey b Edmonds | 33 |
| Kapil Dev c Cowans b Cowdrey | 53 | – c Gatting b Cowans | 49 |
| †S. M. H. Kirmani not out | 30 | – c Lamb b Edmonds | 75 |
| N. S. Yadav b Foster | 2 | – (10) c Downton b Cowans | 5 |
| L. Sivaramakrishnan c Cowdrey b Foster | 13 | – (9) lbw b Foster | 5 |
| Chetan Sharma c Lamb b Cowans | 5 | – not out | 17 |
| L-b 3, n-b 4 | 7 | B 1, l-b 4, n-b 2 | 7 |
| 1/17 2/17 3/45 4/155 5/167 6/167 7/241 8/243 9/263 | 272 | 1/7 2/19 3/22 4/212 5/259 6/259 7/341 8/350 9/361 | 412 |

Bowling: *First Innings*—Cowans 12.5–3–39–2; Foster 23–2–104–6; Edmonds 6–1–33–0; Cowdrey 19–1–65–2; Pocock 7–1–28–0. *Second Innings*—Cowans 15–1–73–2; Foster 28–8–59–5; Cowdrey 5–0–26–0; Edmonds 41.5–13–119–2; Pocock 33–8–130–1.

## England

| | | | |
|---|---|---|---|
| G. Fowler c Kirmani b Kapil Dev | 201 | – c Kirmani b Sivaramakrishnan | 2 |
| R. T. Robinson c Kirmani b Sivaramakrishnan | 74 | – not out | 21 |
| M. W. Gatting c sub (G. Sharma) b Shastri | 207 | – not out | 10 |
| A. J. Lamb b Amarnath | 62 | | |
| P. H. Edmonds lbw b Shastri | 36 | | |
| N. A. Foster b Amarnath | 5 | | |
| *D. I. Gower b Kapil Dev | 18 | | |
| C. S. Cowdrey not out | 3 | | |
| †P. R. Downton not out | 3 | | |
| B 7, l-b 19, n-b 17 | 43 | L-b 1, w 1 | 2 |
| 1/178 2/419 3/563 4/599 5/604 6/640 7/646 | (7 wkts dec.) 652 | 1/7 | (1 wkt) 35 |

P. I. Pocock and N. G. Cowans did not bat.

Bowling: *First Innings*—Kapil Dev 36–5–131–2; Chetan 18–0–95–0; Sivaramakrishnan 44–6–145–1; Yadav 23–4–76–0; Shastri 42–7–143–2; Amarnath 12–1–36–2. *Second Innings*—Kapil Dev 3–0–20–0; Sivaramakrishnan 4–0–12–1; Shastri 1–0–2–0.

Umpires: M. Y. Gupte and V. K. Ramaswamy.

## †INDIA v ENGLAND

### Third One-day International

At Bangalore, January 20. England won by three wickets. India ran into one of England's best displays of fielding and did well to reach 205 for six off 46 overs after losing the toss. Gavaskar and Srikkanth overcame early problems on a slightly damp pitch to score 70 in nineteen overs, but Marks set India back and only the wristy power of Azharuddin saw them past 200. England made trouble for themselves when Gatting was run out, but Fowler and Gower, in a stand of 70 (thirteen overs), and then Lamb, who made the winning hit with an over in hand, swung the game round. Bottles thrown on to the ground by sections of a capacity crowd caused a delay of twenty minutes five overs from the end, Gavaskar leading India off the field in protest.

*Man of the Match:* A. J. Lamb.

## India

| | |
|---|---|
| *S. M. Gavaskar c Gatting b Marks | 40 |
| K. Srikkanth b Cowans | 29 |
| D. B. Vengsarkar st Downton b Marks | 23 |
| Kapil Dev c Gower b Marks | 8 |
| Yashpal Sharma run out | 8 |
| R. J. Shastri b Edmonds | 33 |
| M. Azharuddin not out | 47 |
| †S. Viswanath not out | 6 |
| B 4, l-b 6, w 1 | 11 |
| 1/70 2/70 3/90 4/108 5/119 6/185 | (6 wkts, 46 overs) 205 |

T. A. P. Sekar, R. S. Ghai and A. Patel did not bat.

Bowling: Cowans 10–1–31–1; Foster 6–0–33–0; Ellison 6–0–25–0; Marks 10–1–35–3; Edmonds 10–0–44–1; Gatting 4–0–27–0.

## England

| | |
|---|---|
| G. Fowler run out | 45 |
| R. T. Robinson c Viswanath b Kapil Dev | 2 |
| M. W. Gatting run out | 3 |
| *D. I. Gower b Shastri | 38 |
| A. J. Lamb not out | 59 |
| V. J. Marks c Gavaskar b Patel | 17 |
| †P. R. Downton c Shastri b Kapil Dev | 12 |
| P. H. Edmonds c Viswanath b Kapil Dev | 7 |
| R. M. Ellison not out | 1 |
| L-b 10, w 7, n-b 5 | 22 |
| 1/15 2/21 3/91 4/103 5/144 6/186 7/204 | (7 wkts, 45 overs) 206 |

N. A. Foster and N. G. Cowans did not bat.

Bowling: Kapil Dev 10–0–38–3; Sekar 9–0–36–0; Patel 10–1–42–1; Ghai 4–0–37–0; Shastri 10–2–29–1; Yashpal 2–0–14–0.

Umpires: S. K. Das and S. V. Ramani.

## †INDIA v ENGLAND

### Fourth One-day International

At Nagpur, January 23. India won by three wickets. The advantage of winning the toss in matches starting at 9.30 was again illustrated when England needed Cowdrey's powerful 46 off 42 balls to reach 240 for seven, despite an opening stand of 70 between Fowler and Moxon (21 overs). Rain the day before was a factor in England's requiring 34 overs to reach a rate of 4 runs an over. Moxon, who with Cowdrey and Agnew was playing his first international, was missed at 45 and 59 in an innings lasting 42 overs. India faced problems at 31 for three. But Azharuddin, who showed that straight 6s were also in his repertoire, added 59 with Gavaskar, whereupon Kapil Dev, dropped at long-off at 16, scored 54 off 41 balls to swing the game. England's fielding generally was as untidy as, in Bangalore, it had been brilliant.

*Man of the Match:* Kapil Dev.

### England

| | |
|---|---|
| G. Fowler b Shastri | 37 |
| M. D. Moxon c Srikkanth b Kapil Dev | 70 |
| M. W. Gatting b Shastri | 1 |
| *D. I. Gower c and b Shastri | 11 |
| A. J. Lamb st Viswanath b Shastri | 30 |
| C. S. Cowdrey not out | 46 |
| V. J. Marks b Sekar | 4 |
| †P. R. Downton c Rajput b Sekar | 13 |
| P. H. Edmonds not out | 8 |
| B 3, l-b 15, w 1, n-b 1 | 20 |
| 1/70 2/78 3/100 4/156 5/176 6/199 7/221 (7 wkts, 50 overs) | 240 |

N. G. Cowans and J. P. Agnew did not bat.

Bowling: Kapil Dev 10–1–42–1; Prabhakar 10–1–36–0; Sekar 10–0–50–2; Patel 10–1–54–0; Shastri 10–1–40–4.

### India

| | |
|---|---|
| K. Srikkanth b Cowans | 6 |
| L. S. Rajput c Downton b Cowans | 0 |
| D. B. Vengsarkar c Downton b Agnew | 11 |
| M. Azharuddin b Cowdrey | 47 |
| *S. M. Gavaskar b Agnew | 52 |
| Kapil Dev c Gatting b Cowans | 54 |
| R. J. Shastri not out | 24 |
| M. Prabhakar b Agnew | 4 |
| †S. Viswanath not out | 23 |
| B 3, l-b 14, w 1, n-b 2 | 20 |
| 1/5 2/11 3/31 4/90 5/166 6/197 7/204 (7 wkts, 47.4 overs) | 241 |

T. A. P. Sekar and A. Patel did not bat.

Bowling: Cowans 10–0–44–3; Agnew 10–0–38–3; Marks 6–0–32–0; Edmonds 10–0–44–0; Cowdrey 7.4–0–52–1; Gatting 4–0–14–0.

Umpires: R. Mrutyunjan and A. L. Narasimhan.

## †INDIA v ENGLAND

### Fifth One-day International

At Chandigarh, January 27. England won by 7 runs. England broke the sequence of victories by the team winning the toss in a match reduced by overnight rain to fifteen overs each, which by the conditions of the tour was the minimum that qualified for one-day international status. A crowd of 25,000, by far the biggest assembly to have been allowed in Punjab since the storming of the Golden Temple in Amritsar seven months earlier, were rewarded for a delay of more than five hours by a spirited game in which there was never much between the scoring-rates. India were looking as likely to win as England until Shastri ran himself out with six balls remaining.

Cowdrey, who hit the stumps from mid-wicket, bowled the final over and conceded only 3 of the 11 runs India then needed.

*Man of the Match:* R. J. Shastri. *Man of the Series:* R. J. Shastri.

## England

| | | | |
|---|---|---|---|
| G. Fowler run out | 17 | V. J. Marks run out | 2 |
| M. W. Gatting c Azharuddin b Sekar | 31 | R. M. Ellison not out | 4 |
| *D. I. Gower b Sekar | 19 | L-b 5 | 5 |
| A. J. Lamb not out | 33 | | — |
| C. S. Cowdrey c Rajput b Shastri | 5 | 1/31 2/71 3/74 (6 wkts, 15 overs) | 121 |
| P. H. Edmonds c Azharuddin b Sekar | 5 | 4/86 5/93 6/104 | |

†B. N. French, N. A. Foster and J. P. Agnew did not bat.

Bowling: Kapil Dev 3–0–17–0; Prabhakar 3–0–26–0; Chetan 3–0–20–0; Sekar 3–0–23–3; Shastri 3–0–30–1.

## India

| | | | |
|---|---|---|---|
| R. J. Shastri run out | 53 | L. S. Rajput not out | 1 |
| K. Srikkanth run out | 9 | | |
| Kapil Dev c Agnew b Edmonds | 17 | L-b 4, w 12 | 16 |
| M. Azharuddin c Gatting b Edmonds | 10 | | — |
| Yashpal Sharma b Cowdrey | 6 | 1/22 2/49 3/83 (5 wkts, 15 overs) | 114 |
| *S. M. Gavaskar not out | 2 | 4/111 5/112 | |

M. Prabhakar, †S. Viswanath, Chetan Sharma and T. A. P. Sekar did not bat.

Bowling: Agnew 3–0–23–0; Foster 3–0–17–0; Ellison 3–0–20–0; Edmonds 3–0–20–2; Gatting 2–0–27–0; Cowdrey 1–0–3–1.

Umpires: Nagaraja Rao and R. B. Gupta.

## INDIA v ENGLAND

### Fifth Test Match

At Kanpur, January 31, February 1, 3, 4, 5. Drawn. Only when England lost three quick wickets to Gopal Sharma midway through the fourth day did India look capable of bringing off a win to square the series. Facing India's 553 for eight declared, their highest total against England, to which Azharuddin contributed his third hundred in as many Tests, England were still 68 short of saving the follow-on with four wickets standing. But, with valuable and positive help from Edmonds, Gower produced a captain's innings of 78 that made certain of a draw, though on the final day India made an heroic effort not to let it die a peaceful death.

India made two changes from the team beaten in Madras, Gopal Sharma, a 24-year-old off-spinner, making his Test début as replacement for Yadav, and Malhotra, a middle-order batsman, coming in for Chetan Sharma. The latter seemed a strange decision in view of the fact that India had to win to save the rubber, but it was justified by the deadness of the pitch: had he played, Chetan Sharma would have been unlikely to do more than take the shine off the new ball, a role performed by Amarnath. England were unchanged, which meant they called on only twelve players in the series – the teams at Madras and Kanpur plus Ellison.

India, winning the toss for the fourth time in succession, soon lost Gavaskar to a Cowans breakback. Though there was no pace in the pitch, the ball swung early on, but neither Cowans nor Foster bowled accurately enough to make full use of it and Srikkanth and Azharuddin built India's foundations by adding 150 for the second wicket off only 37 overs. Srikkanth, missed at 16 and 59, had reached his highest score in Tests when Foster had him caught behind, while Azharuddin played some glorious wristy strokes against the spinners. On Srikkanth's dismissal, however, India, cramped by Edmonds in a long containing spell, lost impetus. Amarnath's 15 lasted twenty overs and when Azharuddin scored only 8 runs in the final hour, they reached close of play at 228 for three. Azharuddin, passing the night on 98, turned Foster off his legs in the fourth over of the second day to carve his niche in history. He batted 374 minutes before pulling a short ball to mid-wicket. Vengsarkar, missed at 65, gave no further chance in a six-hour 137. Only while Shastri and Kapil were together did India make much attempt to increase the tempo before declaring after five overs on the third day.

It was a help to England that the rest day had come after two days, sparing Fowler and Robinson the extra burden of beginning the reply after eleven and a half hours in the field. England's main misgivings at that stage centred on a worn spot on a spinners' length in line with the middle stump, seemingly caused by Kapil running on the pitch late in India's innings. But in the event it hardly increased in size during the remainder of the match, making the odd ball which kept low the only real hazard. Fowler and Robinson went a long way towards ensuring England's safety by staying together for 73 overs; and when on the fourth day the score grew to 276 for four an hour after lunch, a draw seemed the only possible result.

Then Gopal Sharma, small and bouncy, had his say with a spell of three for 4 in 29 balls, and it was left to Gower and Edmonds to repair the damage with a stand of 100 for the seventh wicket. Only four and a quarter hours remained when Kapil brought England's first innings to an end with three for 19 on the final day. But India made a last attempt to snatch a win through Srikkanth and Azharuddin, who despite five men on the boundary scored 95 for the second wicket off 12.1 overs. Gavaskar's declaration left his bowlers 46 overs to bowl England out a second time, but against batsmen looking no further than a draw, they made no progress. Gatting, replacing Robinson when he got dust behind a contact lens with the score at 36, finished 19 runs short of K. F. Barrington's 594, the England record for a series against India.

## India

| | | | |
|---|---|---|---|
| *S. M. Gavaskar b Cowans | 9 | | |
| K. Srikkanth c Downton b Foster | 84 | – not out | 41 |
| M. Azharuddin c sub (R. M. Ellison) b Cowdrey | 122 | – not out | 54 |
| M. Amarnath b Cowans | 15 | | |
| D. B. Vengsarkar c Downton b Foster | 137 | | |
| A. Malhotra lbw b Pocock | 27 | | |
| R. J. Shastri b Edmonds | 59 | – (1) run out | 2 |
| Kapil Dev c Gower b Foster | 42 | | |
| †S. M. H. Kirmani not out | 16 | | |
| L. Sivaramakrishnan not out | 16 | | |
| B 9, l-b 12, w 5 | 26 | | |
| 1/19 2/169 3/209 4/277 5/362 6/457 7/511 8/533 (8 wkts dec.) | 553 | 1/2 (1 wkt dec.) | 97 |

G. Sharma did not bat.

Bowling: *First Innings*—Cowans 36–9–115–2; Foster 36–8–123–3; Pocock 24–2–79–1; Edmonds 48–16–112–1; Cowdrey 21–1–103–1. *Second Innings*—Cowans 7–0–51–0; Cowdrey 5–0–39–0; Gatting 1–0–7–0.

## England

| | | | |
|---|---|---|---|
| G. Fowler c Kirmani b Shastri | 69 | | |
| R. T. Robinson lbw b Kapil Dev | 96 | – retired hurt | 16 |
| M. W. Gatting c and b Sharma | 62 | – not out | 41 |
| A. J. Lamb c Srikkanth b Shastri | 13 | | |
| *D. I. Gower lbw b Shastri | 78 | – (1) not out | 32 |
| C. S. Cowdrey c Kirmani b Sharma | 1 | | |
| †P. R. Downton b Sharma | 1 | | |
| P. H. Edmonds lbw b Kapil Dev | 49 | | |
| N. A. Foster c Kirmani b Kapil Dev | 8 | | |
| P. I. Pocock not out | 4 | | |
| N. G. Cowans b Kapil Dev | 9 | | |
| B 10, l-b 17 | 27 | L-b 2 | 2 |
| 1/156 2/196 3/222 4/276 5/278 6/286 7/386 8/402 9/404 | 417 | (no wkt) | 91 |

Bowling: *First Innings*—Kapil Dev 36.5–7–81–4; Amarnath 4–1–6–0; Sharma 60–16–115–3; Sivaramakrishnan 54–11–133–0; Shastri 32–13–52–3; Malhotra 2–0–3–0. *Second Innings*—Kapil Dev 5–0–19–0; Shastri 7–2–12–0; Sharma 11–4–17–0; Sivaramakrishnan 10–2–22–0; Srikkanth 2–0–11–0; Azharuddin 1–0–8–0.

Umpires: P. D. Reporter and V. K. Ramaswamy.

# CAREER FIGURES OF PLAYERS RETIRING OR NOT RETAINED

## BATTING

| | *M* | *I* | *NO* | *R* | *HI* | *100s* | *Avge* | *1,000r in season* |
|---|---|---|---|---|---|---|---|---|
| B. Hassan | 332 | 549 | 54 | 14,394 | 182* | 15 | 29.07 | 5 |
| S. P. Henderson | 70 | 116 | 17 | 2,416 | 209* | 4 | 24.40 | 0 |
| D. J. Humphries | 175 | 252 | 46 | 5,116 | 133* | 4 | 24.83 | 0 |
| G. W. Johnson | 390 | 605 | 78 | 12,922 | 168 | 11 | 24.51 | 3 |
| C. Lethbridge | 50 | 58 | 13 | 1,033 | 87* | 0 | 22.95 | 0 |
| K. S. McEwan | 382 | 631 | 56 | 23,135 | 218 | 61 | 40.23 | 12 |
| L. L. McFarlane | 56 | 41 | 20 | 127 | 15* | 0 | 6.04 | 0 |
| S. J. Malone | 57 | 45 | 15 | 180 | 23 | 0 | 6.00 | 0 |
| C. M. Old | 378 | 462 | 91 | 7,756 | 116* | 6 | 20.90 | 0 |
| R. L. Ollis | 37 | 60 | 4 | 1,017 | 99* | 0 | 18.16 | 0 |
| J. A. Ormrod | 500 | 846 | 95 | 23,205 | 204* | 32 | 30.89 | 13 |
| N. Phillip | 230 | 244 | 37 | 7,013 | 134 | 1 | 33.87 | 0 |
| H. Pilling | 333 | 542 | 68 | 15,279 | 149* | 25 | 32.23 | 8 |
| N. F. M. Popplewell | 143 | 214 | 27 | 5,070 | 143 | 4 | 27.11 | 2 |
| M. S. Scott | 32 | 60 | 3 | 1,383 | 109 | 1 | 24.26 | 0 |
| G. Sharp | 306 | 396 | 81 | 6,254 | 98 | 0 | 19.85 | 0 |
| K. D. Smith | 197 | 346 | 29 | 8,734 | 140 | 9 | 27.55 | 4 |

## BOWLING AND FIELDING

| | *R* | *W* | *BB* | *Avge* | *5 W/i* | *10 W/m* | *Ct* | *St* |
|---|---|---|---|---|---|---|---|---|
| B. Hassan | 407 | 6 | 3-33 | 67.83 | 0 | 0 | 308 | 1 |
| S. P. Henderson | 216 | 3 | 2-48 | 72.00 | 0 | 0 | 46 | 0 |
| D. J. Humphries | – | – | – | – | – | – | 294 | 60 |
| G. W. Johnson | 17,559 | 566 | 7-76 | 31.02 | 22 | 3 | 316 | 0 |
| C. Lethbridge | 2,996 | 77 | 5-68 | 38.90 | 1 | 0 | 16 | 0 |
| K. S. McEwan | 309 | 4 | 1-0 | 77.25 | 0 | 0 | 335 | 7 |
| L. L. McFarlane | 4,140 | 102 | 6-59 | 40.58 | 1 | 0 | 11 | 0 |
| S. J. Malone | 4,236 | 118 | 7-55 | 35.85 | 3 | 1 | 13 | 0 |
| C. M. Old | 25,081 | 1,070 | 7-22 | 23.44 | 39 | 2 | 214 | 0 |
| R. L. Ollis | 2 | 0 | – | – | 0 | 0 | 19 | 0 |
| J. A. Ormrod | 1,094 | 25 | 5-27 | 43.76 | 1 | 0 | 399 | 0 |
| N. Phillip | 17,032 | 688 | 7-33 | 24.75 | 30 | 2 | 75 | 0 |
| H. Pilling | 195 | 1 | 1-42 | 195.00 | 0 | 0 | 89 | 0 |
| N. F. M. Popplewell | 4,441 | 103 | 5-33 | 43.11 | 1 | 0 | 110 | 0 |
| M. S. Scott | 37 | 0 | – | – | 0 | 0 | 9 | 0 |
| G. Sharp | – | – | – | – | – | – | 564 | 90 |
| K. D. Smith | – | – | – | – | – | – | 70 | 0 |

---

# INTERNATIONAL AMBASSADORS

An "International Ambassadors XI", assembled by the Rev. A. R. Wingfield Digby, the Director of the Christians in Sport Organisation and a former Oxford cricket Blue, made a three-weeks tour of southern India in October and November 1985. The fifteen-strong party contained several past and present county players and was captained by V. J. Marks. The aims of the tour were to raise money for the Spastics Society of India and act as an encouragement to churches in that part of the country, as well as to play nine one-day matches. Four of these were against opposition that contained Indian Test cricketers, one of them, at Coimbatore, being played under lights and attracting a crowd of 35,000.

# THE AUSTRALIANS IN INDIA, 1984-85

By MIKE COWARD

It took some time for the full relevance of Australia's brief goodwill tour of India, to play a series of one-day internationals, to become apparent. In the end, what started as a public relations exercise to help the Indian authorities celebrate the Golden Jubilee of the Ranji Trophy had a considerable impact on Australian cricket. Indeed, the shock waves are still being felt.

From a cricketing standpoint, it was a most successful undertaking. Australia won the five-match series three-nil – the matches at Trivandrum and Jamshedpur were abandoned after rain – which was a considerable achievement after India's success in the World Cup the previous year. However, with the benefit of hindsight, Australia's first success in such a series on the sub-continent can be seen to have been the least significant happening. While he had personal success, Kim Hughes lost support within his team and within a few weeks had resigned the Australian captaincy. The Indian excursion culminated with a gala dinner in Bombay, a priceless moment in the history of Indian cricket, and on their way home several of the Australian players had their first significant contact with representatives of the South African Cricket Union. Clandestine discussions with organisers of "rebel" teams took place in Singapore, leading in April 1985 to another major crisis for Australia's cricketing authorities.

The visit to India will also be remembered for the farce of Jamshedpur, where a one-day international could not be started as scheduled because the players' gear had been misplaced by officials. This was an incident which caused great embarrassment to the Board of Control for Cricket in India, who have been charged with the responsibility of organising, jointly with Pakistan, the 1987 World Cup.

India, who had reinstated Sunil Gavaskar as captain following Kapil Dev's sequence of failures after their 1983 World Cup triumph, did not seem as intensely committed to the one-day series as the Australians and were comprehensively beaten. Kepler Wessels was named Man of the Series. The Australians, who proved very popular, won prizemoney of 25,000 rupees (£2,000), most of which they donated to a home for crippled children in Ahmedabad.

## †INDIA v AUSTRALIA

### First One-day International

At New Delhi, September 28. Australia won by 48 runs. Four outstanding individual performances enabled Australia to open their campaign with a convincing victory at the floodlit Jawaharlal Nehru Stadium. Accustomed to making the adjustments required to compete successfully under lights, they controlled the match from the time Wessels and Hughes added 128 for the second wicket. Wessels, returning after knee surgery, played splendidly for his first century in 30 limited-overs internationals, while Hughes was in characteristically flamboyant mood. Rackemann (four for 41 in ten overs) and Phillips (three catches and one stumping) provided admirable support.

*Man of the Match:* K. C. Wessels.

### Australia

K. C. Wessels c Parkar b Madan Lal . . 107
G. M. Wood c Khanna b Chetan . . . . . 0
*K. J. Hughes c Parkar b Patel . . . . . . . 72
G. N. Yallop st Khanna b Azad . . . . . . 22
A. R. Border st Khanna b Azad . . . . . . 0
†W. B. Phillips run out . . . . . . . . . . . . . . 1
T. G. Hogan lbw b Madan Lal . . . . . . . 6
G. F. Lawson c Vengsarkar b Kapil Dev 2
R. M. Hogg not out . . . . . . . . . . . . . . . . 0
C. G. Rackemann run out . . . . . . . . . . . 2
B 3, l-b 4, n-b 1 . . . . . . . . . . . . 8

1/14 2/142 3/200 4/200 5/204 6/213 7/216 8/220 9/220 (9 wkts, 48 overs) 220

J. N. Maguire did not bat.

Bowling: Kapil Dev 9–1–43–1; Chetan 9–0–49–1; Madan Lal 7–2–23–2; Patel 10–2–27–1; Shastri 3–0–23–0; Azad 10–1–48–2.

### India

†S. C. Khanna c Phillips b Rackemann 13
G. A. Parkar c Lawson b Rackemann . 16
D. B. Vengsarkar c Yallop b Maguire . 33
S. M. Patil lbw b Hogg . . . . . . . . . . . . . 22
*S. M. Gavaskar c Wood b Rackemann 25
K. Azad c Phillips b Maguire . . . . . . . . 0
Kapil Dev b Hogan . . . . . . . . . . . . . . . . 39
R. J. Shastri st Phillips b Hogan . . . . . . 5
Madan Lal c Lawson b Rackemann . . . 1
Chetan Sharma not out . . . . . . . . . . . . . . 9
A. Patel c Phillips b Hogan . . . . . . . . . . 0
L-b 2, n-b 7 . . . . . . . . . . . . . . . 9

1/17 2/44 3/76 4/96 5/97 6/148 7/160 8/161 9/172 (40.5 overs) 172

Bowling: Lawson 5–0–23–0; Rackemann 10–1–41–4; Hogg 6–1–21–1; Maguire 10–1–41–2; Hogan 9.5–1–44–3.

Umpires: B. Ganguli and P. D. Reporter.

## †INDIA v AUSTRALIA

## Second One-day International

At Trivandrum, October 1. No result. Heavy rain frustrated the Australians after they had been given the responsibility of taking the "gospel" of cricket to Kerala, the most Christianised part of India. Historically more interested in snake-boat races, soccer, volleyball and athletics, the Keralans saw Vengsarkar reach his 1,000 runs in limited-over internationals. Rackemann was again Australia's most successful bowler on a pitch barely adequate for cricket at this level.

### India

†S. C. Khanna c Phillips b Rackemann. 4
G. A. Parkar c Phillips b Rackemann . 3
D. B. Vengsarkar b Hogan . . . . . . . . . . . 77
S. M. Patil c Yallop b Rackemann . . . . 16
Kapil Dev b Wessels . . . . . . . . . . . . . . . 12
K. Azad c and b Hogan . . . . . . . . . . . . . 6
*S. M. Gavaskar c Wood b Hogan . . . . 14
R. J. Shastri c Rackemann b Hogan . . . 2
Madan Lal b Border . . . . . . . . . . . . . . . . 9
Chetan Sharma not out . . . . . . . . . . . . . . 13
A. Patel c Hughes b Border . . . . . . . . . . 6
B 5, l-b 6, n-b 2 . . . . . . . . . . . . 13

1/7 2/10 3/53 4/80 5/103 6/136 7/146 8/146 9/166 (37 overs) 175

Bowling: Lawson 7–0–29–0; Rackemann 8–4–7–3; Maguire 5–0–38–0; Wessels 7–0–44–1; Hogan 8–0–33–4; Border 2–0–13–2.

### Australia

G. M. Wood not out . . . . . . . . . . . . . . . . 7
K. C. Wessels lbw b Kapil Dev . . . . . . 12
A. R. Border not out . . . . . . . . . . . . . . . . 4
B 1, l-b 4, w 1 . . . . . . . . . . . . . 6

1/24 (1 wkt, 7.4 overs) 29

*K. J. Hughes, G. N. Yallop, S. B. Smith, †W. B. Phillips, T. G. Hogan, G. F. Lawson, C. G. Rackemann and J. N. Maguire did not bat.

Bowling: Kapil Dev 4-1-14-1; Chetan 3.4-1-10-0.

Umpires: V. K. Ramaswamy and Swaroop Kishen.

## †INDIA v AUSTRALIA

### Third One-day International

At Jamshedpur, October 3. No result. The match, the "portmanteau affair", was halted by rain after just five overs at the beautifully turfed Kennan Stadium. Rain swept in from the valleys of the Dalma Mountains only 25 minutes after proceedings had started three hours late because the truck carrying the Indian and Australian players' clothes and equipment had gone missing.

### India

| | |
|---|---|
| †S. C. Khanna c Border b Rackemann | 3 |
| G. A. Parkar b Rackemann | 12 |
| D. B. Vengsarkar not out | 1 |
| Kapil Dev not out | 0 |
| L-b 4, n-b 1 | 5 |
| 1/6 2/21 (2 wkts, 5.1 overs) | 21 |

*S. M. Gavaskar, R. J. Shastri, A. Patel, R. M. H. Binny, Madan Lal, K. Azad and Chetan Sharma did not bat.

Bowling: Lawson 3-0-14-0; Rackemann 2.1-0-3-2.

### Australia

G. M. Wood, K. C. Wessels, A. R. Border, *K. J. Hughes, G. N. Yallop, S. B. Smith, †W. B. Phillips, R. M. Hogg, G. F. Lawson, J. N. Maguire and C. G. Rackemann.

## †INDIA v AUSTRALIA

### Fourth One-day International

At Ahmedabad, October 5. Australia won by seven wickets to clinch the series. Despite a sound opening partnership of 104 between Shastri and Binny, and some bold late hitting by Azad, India could manage only 206 from their 46 overs. Their bowling, too reliant on Kapil Dev, could not contain the Australians, for whom Wessels, Wood, Border and Hughes batted with the minimum of fuss.

*Man of the Match:* G. F. Lawson.

### India

| | |
|---|---|
| R. J. Shastri st Phillips b Hogan | 45 |
| R. M. H. Binny st Phillips b Hogan | 57 |
| D. B. Vengsarkar b Lawson | 14 |
| S. M. Patil c Hughes b Wessels | 3 |
| Kapil Dev b Lawson | 28 |
| *S. M. Gavaskar b Lawson | 4 |
| K. Azad not out | 39 |
| Madan Lal not out | 6 |
| B 1, l-b 5, n-b 4 | 10 |
| 1/104 2/111 3/122 4/133 5/145 6/161 (6 wkts, 46 overs) | 206 |

†S. M. H. Kirmani, Chetan Sharma and A. Patel did not bat.

Bowling: Lawson 10–2–25–3; Rackemann 8–0–50–0; Maguire 8–0–56–0; Wessels 10–0–29–1; Hogan 10–2–40–2.

### Australia

| | | | |
|---|---|---|---|
| K. C. Wessels c Kirmani b Patel | 42 | G. N. Yallop not out | 32 |
| G. M. Wood run out | 32 | B 1, l-b 10, n-b 2 | 13 |
| A. R. Border not out | 62 | | |
| *K. J. Hughes lbw b Kapil Dev | 29 | 1/67 2/89 3/162 (3 wkts, 43.5 overs) | 210 |

S. B. Smith, †W. B. Phillips, T. G. Hogan, J. N. Maguire, G. F. Lawson and C. G. Rackemann did not bat.

Bowling: Kapil Dev 8–1–27–1; Chetan 7–1–21–0; Binny 2–0–21–0; Madan Lal 7.5–0–35–0; Patel 10–0–44–1; Azad 9–0–51–0.

Umpires: D. N. Dotiwala and V. Vikramraju.

## †INDIA v AUSTRALIA

### Fifth One-day International

At Indore, October 6. Australia won by six wickets. A capacity crowd at the Nehru Stadium watched India, thanks chiefly to an immaculate 102 by Shastri, reach their highest total of the series. But Phillips, Smith, Yallop, Ritchie and Wessels were in such command that they made light of the required scoring-rate of 6 runs an over and Australia won with 3.5 overs to spare.

*Man of the Match:* R. J. Shastri.

### India

| | | | |
|---|---|---|---|
| G. A. Parkar b Rackemann | 6 | †S. C. Khanna not out | 1 |
| R. J. Shastri b Maguire | 102 | | |
| R. M. H. Binny c Ritchie b Maguire | 37 | B 5, l-b 3, w 4, n-b 4 | 16 |
| *S. M. Gavaskar b Maguire | 40 | | |
| K. Azad c Smith b Rackemann | 11 | 1/23 2/83 3/198 (5 wkts, 44 overs) | 235 |
| Kapil Dev not out | 22 | 4/207 5/217 | |

Madal Lal, M. Prabhakar, B. S. Sandhu and A. Patel did not bat.

Bowling: Lawson 10–2–48–0; Rackemann 8–1–37–2; Maguire 10–0–61–3; Bennett 10–0–37–0; Wessels 6–0–44–0.

### Australia

| | | | |
|---|---|---|---|
| S. B. Smith c Kapil Dev b Patel | 56 | K. C. Wessels not out | 35 |
| †W. B. Phillips c Patel b Kapil Dev | 33 | L-b 4, n-b 1 | 5 |
| G. N. Yallop b Patel | 42 | | |
| G. M. Ritchie not out | 59 | 1/53 2/122 3/153 (4 wkts, 40.1 overs) | 236 |
| *K. J. Hughes c Prabhakar b Patel | 6 | 4/163 | |

G. F. Lawson, M. J. Bennett, C. G. Rackemann, J. N. Maguire and G. M. Wood did not bat.

Bowling: Kapil Dev 8–0–62–1; Prabhakar 2–0–15–0; Sandhu 6–0–38–0; Madan Lal 6–0–19–0; Patel 10–0–43–3; Azad 2–0–16–0; Shastri 6–0–35–0; Gavaskar 0.1–0–4–0.

Umpires: S. R. Bose and P. G. Pandit.

†At Bombay, October 8. Australians won by five wickets. Bombay 190 for six (47 overs) (L. S. Rajput 66); Australians 191 for five (S. B. Smith 81 retired hurt, A. R. Border 70).

# THE INDIANS IN PAKISTAN, 1984-85

By QAMAR AHMED

The last of the annual three-match Test series between Pakistan and India ended in tragic circumstances when, midway through the tour, the news came of the assassination of India's Prime Minister, Mrs Indira Gandhi. It was a shock to all concerned, and the tour was called off with the third Test at Karachi and the last one-day international still to be played. At the time the second one-day international was in progress and immediately abandoned. The first one-day international, at Quetta at the start of the tour, had been won by Pakistan by 46 runs, while the first two Test matches had been drawn.

Once again umpires came under heavy criticism from a visiting captain, this time Sunil Gavaskar. He said after the first Test at Lahore that "despite the best efforts of the Pakistan umpires to favour the home team we have managed to draw the Test and that is a miracle. Before embarking on the tour of Pakistan we expected close decisions but what happened in the Lahore Test was pre-planned and pre-determined". The Indian captain's statement created a furore in the Pakistani camp and the Pakistan captain, Zaheer Abbas, retaliated by saying that Gavaskar was applying "pressure tactics". Nevertheless, some of the decisions given during the Test matches were certainly unsatisfactory.

The pitches remained as docile as ever, providing hardly any assistance to the bowlers. The second Test at Faisalabad produced 1,174 runs for the loss of only sixteen wickets. Even the mayor of that city condemned the ground authorities for producing "heartbreaking strips", blaming them for keeping spectators away.

Statistical highlights of the tour were the 100th Test appearance of Gavaskar, at Lahore, Abdul Qadir's 100th Test wicket, at Faisalabad, and Zaheer Abbas's twelfth Test century, which equalled Hanif Mohammad's record for Pakistan. In the absence of Imran Khan and Sarfraz Nawaz, Pakistan's opening attack lacked penetration, except in the first Test when India were dismissed for 156 in reply to Pakistan's total of 428. Following on, they were saved by some fine batting by Mohinder Amarnath and Ravi Shastri.

## INDIAN TOUR RESULTS

*Test matches* – Played 2: Drawn 2.
*Non first-class matches* – Played 3: Won 1, Lost 1, No result 1. *Win* – Pakistan XI. *Loss* – Pakistan. *No result* – Pakistan.

## TEST MATCH AVERAGES

### PAKISTAN – BATTING

| | *T* | *I* | *NO* | *R* | *HI* | *100s* | *Avge* |
|---|---|---|---|---|---|---|---|
| Zaheer Abbas ....... | 2 | 2 | 1 | 194 | 168* | 1 | 194.00 |
| Salim Malik .......... | 2 | 2 | 1 | 147 | 102* | 1 | 147.00 |
| Qasim Omar ........ | 2 | 2 | 0 | 256 | 210 | 1 | 128.00 |
| Mudassar Nazar ..... | 2 | 2 | 0 | 214 | 199 | 1 | 107.00 |

| | *T* | *I* | *NO* | *R* | *HI* | *100s* | *Avge* |
|---|---|---|---|---|---|---|---|
| Ashraf Ali .......... | 2 | 2 | 1 | 74 | 65 | 0 | 74.00 |
| Mohsin Khan ....... | 2 | 2 | 0 | 63 | 59 | 0 | 31.50 |
| Javed Miandad ...... | 2 | 2 | 0 | 50 | 34 | 0 | 25.00 |
| Jalal-ud-Din ......... | 2 | 1 | 0 | 2 | 2 | 0 | 2.00 |

Played in two Tests: Azeem Hafeez 17*. Played in one Test: Abdul Qadir did not bat; Manzoor Elahi 26; Tauseef Ahmed 10; Wasim Raja 3.

**Signifies not out.*

## BOWLING

| | *O* | *M* | *R* | *W* | *BB* | *Avge* |
|---|---|---|---|---|---|---|
| Adbul Qadir ........ | 38 | 8 | 104 | 4 | 4-104 | 26.00 |
| Azeem Hafeez ....... | 110 | 28 | 297 | 11 | 6-46 | 27.00 |
| Mudassar Nazar ..... | 51 | 8 | 140 | 3 | 2-32 | 46.66 |
| Jalal-ud-Din ......... | 75 | 13 | 204 | 3 | 2-61 | 68.00 |

Also bowled: Javed Miandad 1–0–4–0; Manzoor Elahi 25–5–74–1; Tauseef Ahmed 63–22–112–1; Wasim Raja 24.3–4–56–2.

## INDIA – BATTING

| | *T* | *I* | *NO* | *R* | *HI* | *100s* | *Avge* |
|---|---|---|---|---|---|---|---|
| M. Amarnath ....... | 2 | 3 | 1 | 174 | 101* | 1 | 87.00 |
| R. J. Shastri ........ | 2 | 3 | 0 | 210 | 139 | 1 | 70.00 |
| A. D. Gaekwad ...... | 2 | 3 | 0 | 138 | 74 | 0 | 46.00 |
| S. M. Patil .......... | 2 | 3 | 0 | 134 | 127 | 1 | 44.66 |
| S. M. Gavaskar ...... | 2 | 3 | 0 | 120 | 48 | 0 | 40.00 |
| Kapil Dev .......... | 2 | 3 | 1 | 52 | 33* | 0 | 26.00 |
| D. B. Vengsarkar .... | 2 | 3 | 0 | 74 | 41 | 0 | 24.66 |
| Chetan Sharma ...... | 2 | 2 | 1 | 22 | 18* | 0 | 22.00 |
| S. M. H. Kirmani .... | 2 | 2 | 0 | 8 | 6 | 0 | 4.00 |

Played in one Test: R. M. H. Binny 0, 13; Madan Lal 0; Maninder Singh 4*; N. S. Yadav 29.

**Signifies not out.*

## BOWLING

| | *O* | *M* | *R* | *W* | *BB* | *Avge* |
|---|---|---|---|---|---|---|
| R. J. Shastri ........ | 96 | 30 | 189 | 4 | 3-90 | 47.25 |
| Chetan Sharma ...... | 61 | 2 | 233 | 4 | 3-94 | 58.25 |

Also bowled: M. Amarnath 12.5–0–55–0; R. M. H. Binny 8–1–20–0; A. D. Gaekwad 28–5–79–2; Kapil Dev 35–4–126–1; Madan Lal 27–3–94–1; Maninder Singh 40–10–90–1; N. S. Yadav 75–18–196–1.

## †PAKISTAN v INDIA

### First One-day International

At Quetta, October 12. Pakistan won by 46 runs. India, having put Pakistan in, bowled below their best and two newcomers, Naved Anjum and Manzoor Elahi, batted quite maturely for Pakistan. India were then all out in the 38th over, mainly owing to some good bowling by Manzoor, Naved and Tahir Naqqash.

*Man of the Match:* Manzoor Elahi.

### Pakistan

| | | | |
|---|---|---|---|
| Mohsin Khan lbw b Chetan | 13 | Mudassar Nazar not out | 7 |
| Saadat Ali c Khanna b Sandhu | 12 | Tahir Naqqash not out | 0 |
| *Zaheer Abbas c and b Maninder | 55 | | |
| Javed Miandad run out | 25 | L-b 12, w 3 | 15 |
| Naved Anjum c Amarnath b Kapil Dev | 30 | | |
| Manzoor Elahi b Kapil Dev | 36 | 1/27 2/39 3/113 (7 wkts, 40 overs) | 199 |
| †Ashraf Ali c Maninder b Kapil Dev | 6 | 4/122 5/165 6/174 7/199 | |

Rashid Khan and Tauseef Ahmed did not bat.

Bowling: Kapil Dev 8–0–36–3; Chetan 7–0–42–1; Sandhu 7–0–35–1; Madan Lal 5–1–20–0; Maninder 5–0–24–1; Shastri 8–0–30–0.

### India

| | | | |
|---|---|---|---|
| R. J. Shastri lbw b Tahir | 6 | Chetan Sharma not out | 20 |
| †S. C. Khanna lbw b Tahir | 31 | B. S. Sandhu b Naved | 7 |
| R. M. H. Binny c Miandad b Mudassar | 19 | Maninder Singh b Rashid | 4 |
| *S. M. Gavaskar st Ashraf b Tauseef | 25 | | |
| S. M. Patil c Ashraf b Naved | 11 | B 2, l-b 10, w 5, n-b 2 | 19 |
| Kapil Dev b Manzoor | 0 | | |
| M. Amarnath b Manzoor | 5 | 1/33 2/42 3/83 4/91 5/92 (37.1 overs) | 153 |
| Madan Lal run out | 6 | 6/110 7/114 8/123 9/136 | |

Bowling: Tahir 6–0–35–2; Rashid 6.1–1–20–1; Mudassar 8–2–14–1; Tauseef 8–0–27–1; Manzoor 4–0–18–2; Naved 5–0–27–2.

Umpires: Javed Akhtar and Khizer Hayat.

†At Rawalpindi, October 14 (Charity Match). India XI won by 57 runs. India XI 260 for two (39 overs) (D. B. Vengsarkar 88 not out, S. M. Patil 72 not out, A. D. Gaekwad 63); Pakistan XI 203 for eight (39 overs) (Maninder Singh four for 41).

## PAKISTAN v INDIA

### First Test Match

At Lahore, October 17, 18, 19, 21, 22. Drawn. After winning the toss Pakistan compiled a massive 428 for nine declared, which incorporated an innings of 168 not out by Zaheer, his twelfth Test century. Against some fine medium-pace bowling by Azeem, India then collapsed to 156 and had to follow on, 272 behind. However, they were saved by a fine century from Amarnath and a patient 71 from Shastri after Gaekwad had established India's second innings with a stay of 207 minutes. Gaekwad's bat and pad decision, given by umpire Shakoor Rana, resulted in an exchange of words between the batsman and the Pakistani players which forced both umpires to intervene. India were 180 for four when the last day's play began, still requiring 92 to wipe off the deficit, but Amarnath and Shastri took the score to 290 before the fifth wicket fell. Kapil Dev joined Amarnath to see India to a draw, passing 2,500 Test runs during the course of his innings. Gavaskar made his 100th Test appearance.

### Pakistan

| | | | |
|---|---|---|---|
| Mohsin Khan b Chetan | 4 | Tauseef Ahmed c Gavaskar b Maninder | 10 |
| Mudassar Nazar c Gavaskar b Chetan | 15 | Jalal-ud-Din lbw b Shastri | 2 |
| Qasim Omar c Amarnath b Shastri | 46 | Azeem Hafeez not out | 17 |
| Javed Miandad c Amarnath b Chetan | 34 | L-b 7, w 1, n-b 11 | 19 |
| *Zaheer Abbas not out | 168 | | |
| Salim Malik c and b Shastri | 45 | 1/6 2/54 3/100 (9 wkts dec.) | 428 |
| Wasim Raja c Amarnath b Kapil Dev | 3 | 4/110 5/195 6/212 7/354 | |
| †Ashraf Ali c Gavaskar b Gaekwad | 65 | 8/394 9/397 | |

Bowling: Kapil Dev 30–4–104–1; Chetan 29–2–94–3; Binny 8–1–20–0; Maninder 40–10–90–1; Shastri 46–13–90–3; Amarnath 4–0–19–0; Gaekwad 1–0–4–1.

## India

| | | | |
|---|---|---|---|
| *S. M. Gavaskar c Salim b Azeem | 48 | – lbw b Jalal | 37 |
| A. D. Gaekwad b Jalal | 4 | – c Salim b Tauseef | 60 |
| D. B. Vengsarkar c Ashraf b Azeem | 41 | – c Mudassar b Azeem | 28 |
| M. Amarnath b Wasim Raja | 36 | – not out | 101 |
| S. M. Patil c Salim b Azeem | 0 | – b Jalal | 7 |
| R. J. Shastri lbw b Azeem | 0 | – lbw b Salim | 71 |
| Kapil Dev lbw b Azeem | 3 | – (8) not out | 33 |
| R. M. H. Binny lbw b Mudassar | 0 | – (7) lbw b Wasim Raja | 13 |
| †S. M. H. Kirmani c sub (Ramiz Raja) b Mudassar | 2 | | |
| Chetan Sharma b Azeem | 4 | | |
| Maninder Singh not out | 4 | | |
| B 2, l-b 7, w 1, n-b 4 | 14 | B 6, l-b 7, w 4, n-b 4 | 21 |
| 1/7 2/94 3/112 4/114 5/114 6/119 7/120 8/130 9/135 | 156 | 1/85 2/114 3/148 4/164 5/290 6/315 | (6 wkts) 371 |

Bowling: *First Innings*—Jalal 17–5–40–1; Azeem 23–7–46–6; Mudassar 16–2–32–2; Tauseef 13–3–19–0; Wasim Raja 5.3–0–10–1. *Second Innings*—Jalal 24–3–61–2; Azeem 43–12–114–1; Mudassar 14–3–34–0; Tauseef 50–19–93–1; Wasim Raja 19–4–46–1; Salim 5–2–6–1; Miandad 1–0–4–0.

Umpires: Shakoor Rana and Khizar Hayat.

# PAKISTAN v INDIA

## Second Test Match

At Faisalabad, October 24, 25, 26, 28, 29. Drawn. In five days of slow, predictable cricket 1,174 runs were scored for the loss of only sixteen wickets, and when stumps were drawn on the final day, Pakistan had yet to finish their first innings. Five batsmen scored centuries. For India, whose total of 500 was their highest in Pakistan, Shastri made his highest Test score and Gavaskar passed 8,500 Test runs. For Pakistan Abdul Qadir reached 100 Test wickets when he had Yadav caught. Pakistan's 674 for six was their highest-ever Test score, beating their 657 for eight against West Indies at Bridgetown in 1957-58. Mudassar and Qasim Omar shared a record second-wicket stand of 250, Mudassar batting nine hours, twenty minutes for his 199. Qasim Omar's 210, his second Test hundred, took 11 hours, 25 minutes.

## India

| | |
|---|---|
| *S. M. Gavaskar c Omar b Qadir | 35 |
| A. D. Gaekwad c and b Manzoor | 74 |
| D. B. Vengsarkar c Mohsin b Qadir | 5 |
| M. Amarnath hit wkt b Azeem | 37 |
| S. M. Patil c Zaheer b Mudassar | 127 |
| R. J. Shastri c Ashraf b Qadir | 139 |
| Kapil Dev c Manzoor b Azeem | 16 |
| Madan Lal c Ashraf b Azeem | 0 |
| †S. M. H. Kirmani c sub (Shoaib Mohammad) b Azeem | 6 |
| N. S. Yadav c Salim b Qadir | 29 |
| Chetan Sharma not out | 18 |
| B 1, l-b 6, n-b 7 | 14 |
| 1/88 2/100 3/148 4/170 5/370 6/412 7/420 8/441 9/461 | 500 |

Bowling: Jalal 34–5–103–0; Azeem 44–9–137–4; Mudassar 21–3–74–1; Manzoor 25–5–74–1; Qadir 38–8–104–4; Salim 1–0–1–0.

## Pakistan

| | |
|---|---|
| Mohsin Khan c Gavaskar b Chetan | 59 |
| Mudassar Nazar c Kirmani b Yadav | 199 |
| Qasim Omar c Yadav b Gaekwad | 210 |
| Javed Miandad st Kirmani b Shastri | 16 |
| *Zaheer Abbas c Kirmani b Madan Lal | 26 |
| Salim Malik not out | 102 |
| Manzoor Elahi run out | 26 |
| †Ashraf Ali not out | 9 |
| B 7, l-b 6, w 1, n-b 13 | 27 |
| 1/141 2/391 3/430 4/494 5/608 6/650 | (6 wkts) 674 |

Abdul Qadir, Jalal-ud-Din and Azeem Hafeez did not bat.

Bowling: Kapil Dev 5-0-22-0; Chetan Sharma 32-0-139-1; Madan Lal 27-3-94-1; Yadav 75-18-196-1; Shastri 50-17-99-1; Gaekwad 27-5-75-1; Amarnath 8.5-0-36-0.

Umpires: Mahboob Shah and Amanullah Khan.

## †PAKISTAN v INDIA

### Second One-day International

At Sialkot, October 31. No result. The match was abandoned following news of the assassination of India's Prime Minister. Pakistan, after winning the toss, had put India in.

### India

| | | | |
|---|---|---|---|
| A. D. Gaekwad b Mudassar | 12 | R. J. Shastri not out | 6 |
| G. A. Parkar b Mudassar | 20 | L-b 9, w 6, n-b 4 | 19 |
| D. B. Vengsarkar not out | 94 | | |
| S. M. Patil b Tauseef | 59 | 1/35 2/53 3/196 (3 wkts, 40 overs) | 210 |

*M. Amarnath, R. M. H. Binny, †S. M. H. Kirmani, Madan Lal, B. S. Sandhu and Maninder Singh did not bat.

Bowling: Rashid 8-0-43-0; Tahir 8-0-55-0; Mudassar 8-1-27-2; Manzoor 8-3-24-0; Naved 1-0-10-0; Tauseef 7-0-42-1.

### Pakistan

Sajid Ali, Saadat Ali, *Zaheer Abbas, Javed Miandad, Naved Anjum, Manzoor Elahi, Mudassar Nazar, †Ashraf Ali, Tahir Naqqash, Tauseef Ahmed and Rashid Khan.

Umpires: Mian Mohammad Aslam and Shakoor Rana.

## †PAKISTAN v INDIA

### Third One-day International

At Peshawar, November 2. Cancelled.

## PAKISTAN v INDIA

### Third Test Match

At Karachi, November 4, 5, 6, 8, 9. Cancelled.

# THE WEST INDIANS IN AUSTRALIA, 1984-85

By TONY COZIER

Although this was the fourth time that the West Indians had toured Australia in six seasons since the disbanding of World Series Cricket, it was the first full Test series between the teams in Australia since 1975-76 when West Indies, then, as now, under the captaincy of Clive Lloyd, suffered a crushing five-one defeat.

It was, therefore, cause for considerable satisfaction for Lloyd and those players who had survived the débâcle nine seasons earlier – his vice-captain, Vivian Richards, Gordon Greenidge and Michael Holding – that the roles were reversed this time. Lloyd, in the farewell series of an illustrious career, could enjoy fully the sweeping triumph of his powerful team which won the first three Tests by wide margins, would almost certainly have won the fourth but for a delayed declaration, and had its record tarnished only by defeat in the last. It was Australia who now endured the traumatic effects of a heavy defeat, their captain, Kim Hughes, resigning after two Tests under the pressure of "constant criticism", and their selectors using no fewer than nineteen players in the series.

The result was not entirely unexpected. West Indies arrived in Australia with an imposing record – comfortable victors over India in India, a similarly emphatic record over much the same Australian team in the Caribbean and a clean sweep over England in England, all accomplished in the preceding year. In Greenidge and Desmond Haynes they possessed the most consistent pair of opening batsmen in the game; in Richards and Lloyd the two most experienced and commanding middle-order batsmen. Even with such credentials, though, the batting was no more formidable than the fast bowling, spearheaded by Holding, Joel Garner and Malcolm Marshall. It is not often the case that a touring team can be said to have had no single individual failure, but it was so with this West Indian team. There may have been disappointments, notably Greenidge and Haynes, but every member could claim to have played some part in the triumph, which extended to the limited-overs World Series Cup tournament, also involving Sri Lanka, that followed the Tests.

As he had been in the series of three Tests three seasons earlier, the steady and effective Larry Gomes was the leading batsman, but Lloyd himself, Richie Richardson, Jeffrey Dujon and Marshall all played important innings. In each of the first four Tests, West Indies lost their first five wickets for under 200 and yet totalled over 400 three times and over 350 once. It was only in their matches on the Sydney Cricket Ground, where the pitch provided considerable assistance to the spinners, that they twice faltered and lost, to New South Wales and by an innings in the final Test.

If the batting provided West Indies with worthwhile totals, it was the fast bowling which converted these into victory. Marshall and Garner, who put pressure on the batsmen from the start, had 47 wickets between them. In four consecutive innings Marshall took five wickets; he was clearly the Man of the Series with 28 wickets and some important contributions with the bat as well. Injury kept Holding out of the third and fourth Tests, but his influence on the third morning of the first, when eight Australian wickets fell for 45, emphasised his continuing quality. His young Jamaican protégé, Courtney Walsh, in his début series, did a good job as a support bowler, often into the wind.

To complete their all-round excellence, West Indies caught and fielded with spectacular efficiency, particularly close to the wicket. Richardson, in the slips, and Roger Harper, anywhere, set especially high standards.

Against such formidable opposition, and with controversy over their captaincy and team selection, it was little wonder that so few Australians did themselves justice. The left-handed Kepler Wessels overcame a horrid start to the series to top 500 runs, but although in the fourth Test Andrew Hilditch enjoyed a happy return to Test cricket after an absence of five years, no-one else batted consistently. The experienced Geoff Lawson was the only Australian bowler to take more than fifteen wickets, and even he was only occasionally at his best. The clear potential of the nineteen-year-old Craig McDermott, strong and decidedly fast, was one bonus in an otherwise gloomy season for Australia.

Nowhere was the gap between the teams more pronounced than in the field. The West Indians held their catches with as much frequency as the Australians dropped theirs, many of them at critical periods. In the Tests alone Australia let no fewer than 30 slip through their uncertain grasp.

Unfortunately, the series was marred by strained relations between the teams, involving verbal altercations on the field and causing an official protest from the West Indians against one Australian player, Lawson.

For all that, West Indies, managed again by their former fast bowler, the affable Wesley Hall, retained their popularity with Australian crowds and their captain received fond farewells wherever he went. He was awarded the Order of Australia by the Australian government for his services to the game.

## WEST INDIAN TOUR RESULTS

*Test matches* – Played 5: Won 3, Lost 1, Drawn 1.
*First-class matches* – Played 11: Won 4, Lost 2, Drawn 5.
*Wins* – Australia (3), Western Australia.
*Losses* – Australia, New South Wales.
*Draws* – Australia, Queensland, South Australia, Victoria, Tasmania.
*Non first-class matches* – Played 19: Won 18, Lost 1.
*Wins* – Australia (7), Sri Lanka (5), South Australian Country XI, Western Australia Country XI (2), Victorian Country XI, Prime Minister's XI, Australian Capital Territory. *Loss* – Australia.

## TEST MATCH AVERAGES

### AUSTRALIA – BATTING

| | *T* | *I* | *NO* | *R* | *HI* | *100s* | *Avge* |
|---|---|---|---|---|---|---|---|
| A. M. J. Hilditch . . . . | 2 | 3 | 0 | 185 | 113 | 1 | 61.66 |
| K. C. Wessels . . . . . . . | 5 | 9 | 0 | 505 | 173 | 1 | 56.11 |
| W. B. Phillips . . . . . . . | 2 | 4 | 0 | 136 | 54 | 0 | 34.00 |
| A. R. Border . . . . . . . . | 5 | 9 | 0 | 246 | 69 | 0 | 27.33 |
| D. C. Boon . . . . . . . . . | 3 | 5 | 0 | 132 | 51 | 0 | 26.40 |
| G. M. Wood . . . . . . . . | 5 | 9 | 0 | 207 | 56 | 0 | 23.00 |
| G. F. Lawson . . . . . . . | 5 | 9 | 2 | 131 | 49 | 0 | 18.71 |
| R. M. Hogg . . . . . . . . . | 4 | 7 | 3 | 54 | 21* | 0 | 13.50 |
| J. Dyson . . . . . . . . . . . | 3 | 6 | 0 | 77 | 30 | 0 | 12.83 |
| S. J. Rixon . . . . . . . . . | 3 | 5 | 0 | 53 | 20 | 0 | 10.60 |
| K. J. Hughes . . . . . . . . | 4 | 8 | 0 | 81 | 37 | 0 | 10.12 |
| T. M. Alderman . . . . | 3 | 6 | 1 | 34 | 23 | 0 | 6.80 |
| R. G. Holland . . . . . . . | 3 | 4 | 1 | 15 | 7* | 0 | 5.00 |

Played in two Tests: M. J. Bennett 22*, 3*, 23; C. J. McDermott 0, 4. Played in one Test: G. R. J. Matthews 5, 2; C. G. Rackemann 0, 0; G. M. Ritchie 37; G. N. Yallop 2, 1.

*Signifies not out.

## BOWLING

| | O | M | R | W | BB | Avge |
|---|---|---|---|---|---|---|
| G. F. Lawson ....... | 194.4 | 39 | 589 | 23 | 8-112 | 25.60 |
| C. J. McDermott ..... | 69 | 8 | 273 | 10 | 3-65 | 27.30 |
| R. G. Holland ....... | 130.3 | 26 | 404 | 14 | 6-54 | 28.85 |
| T. M. Alderman ..... | 99 | 31 | 339 | 9 | 6-128 | 37.66 |
| M. J. Bennett ....... | 78.5 | 16 | 214 | 5 | 3-79 | 42.80 |
| R. M. Hogg ......... | 147.1 | 23 | 474 | 11 | 4-101 | 43.09 |

Also bowled: A. R. Border 9–0–49–0; G. R. J. Matthews 14.3–2–67–2; C. G. Rackemann 28–3–106–0; K. C. Wessels 6–0–15–0.

## WEST INDIES – BATTING

| | T | I | NO | R | HI | 100s | Avge |
|---|---|---|---|---|---|---|---|
| H. A. Gomes ........ | 5 | 9 | 2 | 451 | 127 | 2 | 64.42 |
| C. H. Lloyd ......... | 5 | 8 | 1 | 356 | 114 | 1 | 50.85 |
| P. J. L. Dujon ....... | 5 | 8 | 1 | 341 | 139 | 1 | 48.71 |
| I. V. A. Richards .... | 5 | 9 | 1 | 342 | 208 | 1 | 42.75 |
| M. D. Marshall ...... | 5 | 6 | 1 | 174 | 57 | 0 | 34.80 |
| D. L. Haynes ........ | 5 | 9 | 0 | 247 | 63 | 0 | 27.44 |
| C. G. Greenidge ..... | 5 | 8 | 0 | 214 | 95 | 0 | 26.75 |
| R. B. Richardson .... | 5 | 9 | 0 | 236 | 138 | 1 | 26.22 |
| R. A. Harper ........ | 2 | 3 | 0 | 40 | 26 | 0 | 13.33 |
| C. A. Walsh ........ | 5 | 6 | 3 | 32 | 18* | 0 | 10.66 |
| J. Garner ........... | 5 | 6 | 2 | 41 | 17 | 0 | 10.25 |

Played in three Tests: M. A. Holding 1, 1, 0, 0.

*Signifies not out.

## BOWLING

| | O | M | R | W | BB | Avge |
|---|---|---|---|---|---|---|
| M. A. Holding ....... | 88.1 | 20 | 249 | 15 | 6-21 | 16.60 |
| M. D. Marshall ...... | 215.2 | 45 | 554 | 28 | 5-38 | 19.78 |
| R. A. Harper ........ | 72 | 15 | 211 | 8 | 4-43 | 26.37 |
| J. Garner ........... | 177.4 | 33 | 566 | 19 | 4-67 | 29.78 |
| C. A. Walsh ........ | 146.2 | 29 | 432 | 13 | 3-55 | 33.23 |

Also bowled: H. A. Gomes 15–4–30–2; I. V. A. Richards 16–4–32–1.

## WEST INDIAN AVERAGES – FIRST-CLASS MATCHES

### BATTING

| | *M* | *I* | *NO* | *R* | *HI* | *100s* | *Avge* |
|---|---|---|---|---|---|---|---|
| C. H. Lloyd | 10 | 16 | 2 | 732 | 114 | 1 | 52.28 |
| H. A. Gomes | 10 | 15 | 3 | 621 | 127 | 2 | 51.75 |
| P. J. L. Dujon | 9 | 13 | 2 | 536 | 151* | 2 | 48.72 |
| D. L. Haynes | 10 | 17 | 1 | 635 | 155 | 1 | 39.68 |
| I. V. A. Richards | 10 | 17 | 1 | 606 | 208 | 2 | 37.87 |
| A. L. Logie | 5 | 7 | 0 | 250 | 134 | 1 | 35.71 |
| R. B. Richardson | 10 | 17 | 1 | 557 | 145 | 2 | 34.81 |
| C. G. Greenidge | 9 | 15 | 0 | 469 | 95 | 0 | 31.26 |
| M. D. Marshall | 7 | 9 | 2 | 212 | 57 | 0 | 30.28 |
| W. W. Davis | 5 | 7 | 2 | 110 | 50 | 0 | 22.00 |
| T. R. O. Payne | 3 | 5 | 0 | 93 | 55 | 0 | 18.60 |
| E. A. E. Baptiste | 4 | 6 | 0 | 107 | 54 | 0 | 17.83 |
| C. A. Walsh | 9 | 10 | 6 | 55 | 18* | 0 | 13.75 |
| R. A. Harper | 6 | 9 | 1 | 104 | 38* | 0 | 13.00 |
| J. Garner | 8 | 9 | 4 | 58 | 17 | 0 | 11.60 |
| M. A. Holding | 6 | 7 | 0 | 49 | 21 | 0 | 7.00 |

* *Signifies not out.*

### BOWLING

| | *O* | *M* | *R* | *W* | *BB* | *Avge* |
|---|---|---|---|---|---|---|
| M. D. Marshall | 267.3 | 59 | 699 | 36 | 5-38 | 19.41 |
| M. A. Holding | 161.3 | 40 | 410 | 20 | 6-21 | 20.50 |
| I. V. A. Richards | 94 | 26 | 175 | 7 | 4-18 | 25.00 |
| C. A. Walsh | 311.1 | 58 | 946 | 37 | 6-119 | 25.56 |
| J. Garner | 237.4 | 58 | 668 | 25 | 4-19 | 26.72 |
| E. A. E. Baptiste | 121.2 | 28 | 350 | 11 | 4-67 | 31.81 |
| R. A. Harper | 253.5 | 56 | 658 | 17 | 5-72 | 38.70 |
| H. A. Gomes | 68 | 17 | 137 | 3 | 1-0 | 45.66 |
| W. W. Davis | 117.4 | 24 | 421 | 8 | 3-58 | 52.62 |

Also bowled: P. J. L. Dujon 7–3–43–1; C. G. Greenidge 3–0–7–0; D. L. Haynes 6–0–27–0; A. L. Logie 10–1–29–1; R. B. Richardson 10–1–40–0.

### FIELDING

P. J. L. Dujon 28 (all ct, 1 as sub), R. B. Richardson 16 (2 as sub), T. R. O. Payne 10 (all ct, 1 as sub), C. G. Greenidge 9, I. V. A. Richards 9, R. A. Harper 8 (2 as sub), C. H. Lloyd 7, M. A. Holding 6, D. L. Haynes 5, J. Garner 4 (1 as sub), M. D. Marshall 4, H. A. Gomes 3 (1 as sub), C. A. Walsh 2, E. A. E. Baptiste 1, W. W. Davis 1.

## QUEENSLAND v WEST INDIANS

At Brisbane, October 19, 20, 21, 22. Drawn. Although rain interfered too frequently for the possibility of a result, the opening match carried some significant indicators for the Test series. Garner dismissed Wessels in his first over, the first in a sequence of similar successes, and also removed another Test candidate, Ritchie, as Queensland were dismissed cheaply. When the West Indians batted, Richardson attacked Thomson to such effect that the fast bowler conceded 44 from five overs, diminishing his chances of a return to the Test team. On a pitch freshened by rain, the West Indians lost their last eight wickets for 60 to the steady Maguire and the lively McDermott.

### Queensland

| | | | |
|---|---|---|---|
| K. C. Wessels c Richards b Garner | 0 | – c Dujon b Marshall | 7 |
| R. B. Kerr c Richards b Marshall | 24 | – not out | 0 |
| *A. R. Border c Dujon b Davis | 23 | – not out | 0 |
| G. M. Ritchie c and b Garner | 4 | | |
| G. S. Trimble c and b Davis | 42 | | |
| T. V. Hohns c Dujon b Garner | 6 | | |
| †R. B. Phillips not out | 38 | | |
| C. J. McDermott b Davis | 7 | | |
| J. N. Maguire c Dujon b Garner | 1 | | |
| C. G. Rackemann c Richards b Marshall | 0 | | |
| J. R. Thomson c Lloyd b Marshall | 2 | | |
| B 1, l-b 7, n-b 25 | 33 | N-b 3 | 3 |
| 1/0 2/54 3/68 4/70 5/84 6/138 7/166 8/173 9/176 | 180 | 1/8 | (1 wkt) 10 |

Bowling: *First Innings*—Garner 14–8–19–4; Marshall 17.1–5–37–3; Davis 23–8–58–3; Baptiste 12–2–39–0; Gomes 10–4–16–0; Richards 1–0–3–0. *Second Innings*—Marshall 3–2–7–1; Davis 2.4–1–3–0.

### West Indians

| | |
|---|---|
| D. L. Haynes c Phillips b Rackemann | 10 |
| R. B. Richardson c Border b Maguire | 65 |
| H. A. Gomes b Maguire | 18 |
| I. V. A. Richards c Ritchie b Maguire | 23 |
| A. L. Logie c Phillips b Maguire | 8 |
| *C. H. Lloyd c Hohns b Thomson | 21 |
| †P. J. L. Dujon c Phillips b McDermott | 5 |
| M. D. Marshall c Thomson b Maguire | 1 |
| E. A. E. Baptiste c Wessels b McDermott | 4 |
| W. W. Davis c Phillips b Maguire | 1 |
| J. Garner not out | 6 |
| L-b 5, w 2, n-b 8 | 15 |
| 1/29 2/91 3/117 4/127 5/136 6/141 7/150 8/156 9/160 | 177 |

Bowling: Rackemann 8–1–38–1; Thomson 5.1–0–48–1; Maguire 15–1–48–6; McDermott 14.1–3–38–2.

Umpires: M. W. Johnson and C. D. Timmins.

†At Loxton, October 24. West Indians won by seven wickets and batted on. South Australian Country XI 165 for eight (50 overs) (G. McCallum 45); West Indians 230 for five (40.5 overs) (R. B. Richardson 87 not out, A. L. Logie 44, H. A. Gomes 42).

## SOUTH AUSTRALIA v WEST INDIANS

At Adelaide, October 26, 27, 28, 29. Drawn. The West Indians' batting in their first innings reflected a lack of practice, only Richards of the main batsmen, with nine 4s in a dominant 80, coping confidently with varied bowling. A century partnership for the fifth wicket between O'Connor and Haysman was the foundation of a useful lead for the state team, but Greenidge and Haynes emphatically erased this in less than two hours. Greenidge's first nine scoring strokes were 4s and his example was followed by Richards (one 6, ten 4s) and Dujon (one 6, nineteen 4s in his highest first-class score). South Australia, handicapped by injuries to four players, had to recruit Davis and Payne from the ranks of the West Indians' reserves as substitutes, Davis catching Richards. There were times on the last day when the West Indians appeared likely to clinch victory, but the veteran Inverarity batted solidly to ensure they were denied it.

### West Indians

| | | | |
|---|---|---|---|
| C. G. Greenidge c Benton b Carmichael | 26 | – run out | 79 |
| D. L. Haynes c Hilditch b McCurdy | 7 | – c Phillips b McCurdy | 94 |
| H. A. Gomes b Carmichael | 16 | – c sub b Benton | 9 |
| I. V. A. Richards c McCurdy b May | 80 | – c sub b O'Connor | 102 |
| *C. H. Lloyd c Phillips b Carmichael | 7 | – (6) b Benton | 63 |
| †P. J. L. Dujon run out | 10 | – (5) not out | 151 |
| M. D. Marshall c Hilditch b May | 35 | – not out | 2 |
| E. A. E. Baptiste c O'Connor b Inverarity | 30 | | |
| R. A. Harper c Bishop b Inverarity | 1 | | |
| M. A. Holding st Phillips b May | 21 | | |
| C. A. Walsh not out | 0 | | |
| L-b 8, n-b 1 | 9 | B 6, l-b 7, n-b 1 | 14 |
| 1/22 2/49 3/56 4/86 5/107 6/187 7/190 8/202 9/228 | 242 | 1/135 2/156 3/217 4/346 5/486 (5 wkts dec.) | 514 |

Bowling: *First Innings*—McCurdy 14–6–39–1; Carmichael 15–2–72–3; Benton 4–1–18–0; May 20–1–87–3; Inverarity 5–0–18–2. *Second Innings*—McCurdy 13.2–2–75–1; Benton 32–2–144–2; Carmichael 23–4–85–0; May 5–1–21–0; Hookes 12.4–0–43–0; Inverarity 24–0–105–0; Haysman 2.4–0–5–0; O'Connor 5–0–22–1; Hilditch 0.2–0–1–0.

### South Australia

| | | | |
|---|---|---|---|
| A. M. J. Hilditch c Dujon b Marshall | 2 | – lbw b Baptiste | 49 |
| G. A. Bishop c Greenidge b Walsh | 29 | – c Holding b Walsh | 18 |
| *D. W. Hookes c Gomes b Walsh | 27 | – (8) c Greenidge b Gomes | 24 |
| †W. B. Phillips b Marshall | 0 | – (3) retired hurt | 2 |
| D. F. O'Connor lbw b Walsh | 51 | – (4) c sub b Baptiste | 33 |
| M. D. Haysman lbw b Holding | 91 | – (5) lbw b Richards | 3 |
| J. J. Benton c sub b Harper | 9 | – run out | 6 |
| R. J. Inverarity b Marshall | 17 | – (6) not out | 40 |
| T. B. A. May lbw b Marshall | 4 | – not out | 14 |
| R. J. McCurdy not out | 18 | | |
| I. R. Carmichael c Baptiste b Holding | 22 | | |
| L-b 7, w 1, n-b 17 | 25 | L-b 4, n-b 7 | 11 |
| 1/2 2/46 3/51 4/64 5/167 6/192 7/249 8/249 9/256 | 295 | 1/22 2/107 3/111 4/118 5/125 6/173 (6 wkts) | 200 |

Bowling: *First Innings*—Marshall 21–5–75–4; Walsh 18–5–53–3; Holding 21.2–4–54–2; Baptiste 8–3–11–0; Harper 24–8–72–1; Richards 5–1–23–0. *Second Innings*—Marshall 11–2–26–0; Walsh 16–4–49–1; Holding 8–2–19–0; Baptiste 18–7–44–2; Harper 2–0–6–0; Richards 17–7–20–1; Gomes 14–3–25–1; Greenidge 3–0–7–0.

Umpires: A. R. Crafter and B. E. Martin.

†At Corrigin, October 31. West Indians won by 81 runs. West Indians 235 for eight (40 overs) (A. L. Logie 85); Western Australia Country XI 154 for nine (40 overs).

## WESTERN AUSTRALIA v WEST INDIANS

At Perth, November 2, 3, 4. West Indians won by nine wickets. Sent in, Western Australia punished much wayward bowling, particularly by Davis, to end the first day 317 for three. Wood, who hit seventeen 4s, and Shipperd, who was denied a century by a leg injury that forced him to retire hurt, added 199 in 3 hours, 35 minutes to form the basis of the state's total. Hughes declared overnight, whereupon the swing of Alderman and MacLeay reduced the West Indians to 204 for seven before Lloyd, with three 6s and eleven 4s in two hours' batting, and Davis added 90 in 77 minutes and reduced the deficit to 15. Holding, resorting to his full run with the breeze at his back, and Walsh then swept through Western Australia's second innings in 37.5 overs. Haynes and Richardson completed the victory with a flourish.

### Western Australia

| | | | |
|---|---|---|---|
| G. M. Wood c Dujon b Walsh | 141 | – (5) c Richardson b Holding | 13 |
| M. R. J. Veletta c Holding b Walsh | 6 | – c Dujon b Walsh | 3 |
| G. Shipperd retired hurt | 97 | – (7) not out | 27 |
| *K. J. Hughes c Holding b Walsh | 12 | – c and b Walsh | 13 |
| G. R. Marsh not out | 26 | – (3) b Walsh | 1 |
| S. C. Clements not out | 9 | – (1) c sub b Holding | 9 |
| K. H. MacLeay (did not bat) | | – (6) c Richardson b Holding | 1 |
| †W. D. Hill (did not bat) | | – c Dujon b Walsh | 7 |
| T. G. Hogan (did not bat) | | – c Richards b Davis | 19 |
| W. M. Clark (did not bat) | | – c Haynes b Davis | 7 |
| T. M. Alderman (did not bat) | | – b Walsh | 4 |
| B 5, l-b 3, n-b 18 | 26 | B 1, l-b 1, n-b 5 | 7 |
| 1/40 2/239 3/255 | (3 wkts dec.) 317 | 1/14 2/14 3/18 4/31 5/43 6/43 7/70 8/95 9/106 | 111 |

Bowling: *First Innings*—Holding 26–7–57–0; Davis 23–0–128–0; Walsh 20–4–54–3; Gomes 19–3–44–0; Richards 12–2–26–0. *Second Innings*—Holding 12–4–26–3; Walsh 18.5–4–60–5; Davis 7–2–23–2.

### West Indians

| | | | |
|---|---|---|---|
| C. G. Greenidge c Hughes b Alderman | 42 | – c Alderman b MacLeay | 12 |
| D. L. Haynes lbw b Alderman | 15 | – not out | 60 |
| R. B. Richardson c Wood b MacLeay | 42 | – not out | 50 |
| I. V. A. Richards c Hogan b MacLeay | 1 | | |
| A. L. Logie c Wood b Alderman | 18 | | |
| †P. J. L. Dujon c Hill b MacLeay | 12 | | |
| *C. H. Lloyd c Hill b MacLeay | 95 | | |
| M. A. Holding c Clark b Alderman | 10 | | |
| W. W. Davis b MacLeay | 50 | | |
| C. A. Walsh not out | 5 | | |
| H. A. Gomes absent ill | | | |
| L-b 3, n-b 9 | 12 | B 4, l-b 2, n-b 1 | 7 |
| 1/38 2/82 3/100 4/113 5/127 6/153 7/204 8/294 9/302 | 302 | 1/28 | (1 wkt) 129 |

Bowling: *First Innings*—Alderman 19–7–52–4; MacLeay 22–2–115–5; Clark 18–4–80–0; Hogan 12–2–52–0. *Second Innings*—Alderman 8–1–32–0; MacLeay 10–2–42–1; Clark 5–1–21–0; Hogan 3–0–20–0; Clements 0.2–0–8–0.

Umpires: P. J. McConnell and R. J. Evans.

## AUSTRALIA v WEST INDIES

### First Test Match

At Perth, November 9, 10, 11, 12. West Indies won by an innings and 112 runs with some magnificent fast bowling on a bouncy pitch supported by spectacular catching. Yet, midway through the opening day, Australia had established an early advantage after Hughes had decided to bowl first. Two days of rain preceding the match had left the pitch under-prepared and unpredictable and Alderman, on his return to Test cricket on the ground where he had been injured two seasons earlier in a clash with an intruding spectator, took four wickets for 5 runs from 26 balls to leave West Indies 104 for five.

Gomes and Dujon halted the decline, in spite of blows to the head. Neither was wearing a helmet at the time. Dujon, who was hit by a ball from Alderman before he had scored, called for one but then temporarily retired, complaining of blurred vision. By the end of the first day, at 211 for six, West Indies could not be entirely satisfied. However, Dyson missed a straightforward chance at second slip off Alderman early next day when Gomes was 45, and it was not until an hour after lunch that the partnership was eventually broken, Dujon then being caught behind after hitting 21 4s in four hours' batting. Gomes was last out after a determined innings lasting seven and three-quarter hours.

Australia lost three wickets for 36 in just over the hour available to them on the second afternoon and the result was virtually settled in the first session of the third day when Australia lost eight wickets for 45. All out for their lowest total ever against West Indies, they immediately lost Wessels in the first over when they followed on. West Indies were irresistible, Holding taking six for 20 from 8.2 overs, Garner and Marshall offering no respite at the other end, and the fielders supporting the effort with several brilliant catches. If their cricket became somewhat ragged as Dyson and Wood added 91 in Australia's second innings, with Garner being no-balled six times in an over for overstepping, in the final session Marshall and Walsh claimed two wickets each and only a pugnacious last-wicket partnership of 59 between Lawson and Alderman delayed Australia's inevitable defeat early on the fourth day.

### West Indies

| | |
|---|---|
| C. G. Greenidge c Rackemann b Alderman | 30 |
| D. L. Haynes c Yallop b Hogg | 56 |
| R. B. Richardson b Alderman | 0 |
| H. A. Gomes b Hogg | 127 |
| I. V. A. Richards c Phillips b Alderman | 10 |
| *C. H. Lloyd c Phillips b Alderman | 0 |
| †P. J. L. Dujon c Phillips b Alderman | 139 |
| M. D. Marshall c Hughes b Hogg | 21 |
| M. A. Holding c Wood b Alderman | 1 |
| J. Garner c Phillips b Hogg | 17 |
| C. A. Walsh not out | 9 |
| B 1, l-b 1, n-b 4 | 6 |
| 1/83 2/83 3/89 4/104 5/104 6/186 7/335 8/337 9/387 | 416 |

Bowling: Alderman 39–12–128–6; Hogg 32–6–101–4; Lawson 24–3–79–0; Rackemann 28–3–106–0.

### Australia

| First innings | | Second innings | |
|---|---|---|---|
| K. C. Wessels c Holding b Garner | 13 | (2) c Lloyd b Garner | 0 |
| J. Dyson c Lloyd b Marshall | 0 | (1) b Marshall | 30 |
| G. M. Wood c Lloyd b Garner | 6 | c Richardson b Walsh | 56 |
| A. R. Border c Dujon b Holding | 15 | c Haynes b Marshall | 6 |
| *K. J. Hughes c Marshall b Holding | 4 | lbw b Marshall | 37 |
| G. N. Yallop c Greenidge b Holding | 2 | c Haynes b Walsh | 1 |
| †W. B. Phillips c Marshall b Holding | 22 | c Dujon b Garner | 16 |
| G. F. Lawson c Dujon b Marshall | 1 | not out | 38 |
| R. M. Hogg b Holding | 0 | b Marshall | 0 |
| C. G. Rackemann c Richardson b Holding | 0 | b Garner | 0 |
| T. M. Alderman not out | 0 | c Richardson b Holding | 23 |
| B 4, l-b 2, n-b 7 | 13 | L-b 7, n-b 14 | 21 |
| 1/1 2/18 3/28 4/40 5/46 6/55 7/58 8/63 9/63 | 76 | 1/4 2/94 3/107 4/107 5/124 6/166 7/168 8/168 9/169 | 228 |

Bowling: *First Innings*—Marshall 15–5–25–2; Garner 7–0–24–2; Holding 9.2–3–21–6. *Second Innings*—Garner 16–5–52–3; Marshall 21–4–68–4; Holding 11.3–1–53–1; Walsh 20–4–43–2; Gomes 1–0–1–0; Richards 1–0–4–0.

Umpires: A. R. Crafter and P. J. McConnell.

## NEW SOUTH WALES v WEST INDIANS

At Sydney, November 16, 17, 18, 19. New South Wales won by 71 runs, inflicting on the West Indians their first defeat in a first-class match, outside Tests, since 1980. The pitch responded to spin throughout and New South Wales won because they were better served in that department by Holland (leg-spin) and Bennett (orthodox left-arm). Dyson's dogged 98, spanning four hours, ten minutes, was the backbone of the state's first innings. However, the West Indian batsmen did not apply themselves with the care and attention demanded by the situation until Lloyd, who handed the captaincy over to Richards for the match, came in at No. 7; and when he ran out of partners it was likely that a deficit of 75 would be crucial. Harper and Richards ran through the New South Wales second innings with their off-spin, and again Lloyd was the only batsman to cope capably with Holland and Bennett in the West Indians' second innings. The tourists were convincingly beaten early on the last day, a week after their huge victory in the first Test.

### New South Wales

| | | | |
|---|---|---|---|
| J. Dyson run out | 98 | – c sub b Harper | 16 |
| S. B. Smith b Davis | 33 | – lbw b Garner | 8 |
| *D. M. Wellham c Greenidge b Harper | 36 | – c Richardson b Harper | 29 |
| P. S. Clifford c Greenidge b Baptiste | 24 | – b Richards | 6 |
| G. R. J. Matthews c Payne b Davis | 2 | – b Harper | 1 |
| Imran Khan c Payne b Garner | 30 | – b Richards | 9 |
| †S. J. Rixon c Richardson b Baptiste | 0 | – b Harper | 15 |
| P. H. Marks run out | 4 | – c and b Richards | 7 |
| M. J. Bennett not out | 16 | – c Harper b Richards | 6 |
| D. R. Gilbert c Harper b Davis | 6 | – not out | 10 |
| R. G. Holland lbw b Baptiste | 20 | – b Harper | 8 |
| B 3, l-b 5, n-b 10 | 18 | B 8, l-b 4, n-b 2 | 14 |
| 1/65 2/160 3/184 4/188 5/216 6/217 7/224 8/241 9/252 | 287 | 1/9 2/35 3/55 4/62 5/77 6/81 7/98 8/106 9/116 | 129 |

Bowling: *First Innings*—Garner 19–8–38–1; Davis 26–6–72–3; Baptiste 22.1–5–65–3; Harper 37–11–84–1; Richards 5–0–20–0. *Second Innings*—Davis 9–3–21–0; Garner 8–6–2–1; Baptiste 7–5–4–0; Harper 27.5–5–72–5; Richards 21–10–18–4.

### West Indians

| | | | |
|---|---|---|---|
| C. G. Greenidge c Rixon b Imran | 9 | – lbw b Imran | 9 |
| D. L. Haynes b Imran | 26 | – c Marks b Bennett | 21 |
| R. B. Richardson c sub b Gilbert | 8 | – c Dyson b Holland | 1 |
| A. L. Logie b Bennett | 37 | – c Matthews b Holland | 6 |
| *I. V. A. Richards c and b Bennett | 27 | – (6) c and b Bennett | 4 |
| †T. R. O. Payne b Holland | 4 | – (5) c and b Bennett | 14 |
| C. H. Lloyd not out | 64 | – c Gilbert b Bennett | 47 |
| E. A. E. Baptiste c Rixon b Holland | 19 | – c Dyson b Bennett | 0 |
| R. A. Harper st Rixon b Holland | 4 | – b Bennett | 8 |
| W. W. Davis b Holland | 1 | – c Dyson b Holland | 11 |
| J. Garner lbw b Gilbert | 2 | – not out | 9 |
| B 3, l-b 8 | 11 | L-b 3 | 3 |
| 1/16 2/35 3/62 4/97 5/112 6/132 7/171 8/175 9/177 | 212 | 1/17 2/31 3/31 4/45 5/49 6/68 7/74 8/88 9/113 | 133 |

Bowling: *First Innings*—Imran 14–2–42–2; Gilbert 9.3–2–25–2; Holland 30–6–81–4; Bennett 14–1–53–2. *Second Innings*—Imran 5–1–6–1; Gilbert 12–0–45–0; Holland 18–3–38–3; Bennett 15.3–6–32–6; Matthews 4–1–9–0.

Umpires: R. A. French and A. G. Marshall.

## AUSTRALIA v WEST INDIES

### Second Test Match

At Brisbane, November 23, 24, 25, 26. West Indies won by eight wickets. Another shattering defeat in four days for Australia led immediately to the resignation of their captain, Hughes, emotionally announced at a post-match press conference. Trying unsuccessfully to hold back his tears, Hughes, in a prepared statement, said: "The constant criticism, speculation and innuendo by former players and a section of the media over the past four or five years have finally taken their toll."

Australia were again betrayed by their batting, in spite of an excellent pitch and the injuries which restricted Holding to 6.2 overs in their first innings and Walsh to five in their second. Garner bowled Wessels with the last ball of the first over after Lloyd had chosen to field, and Australia never recovered from this psychological setback. For the second time in successive Tests Hughes was caught at long-leg hooking, and it needed Phillips's aggression to carry Australia past 150. Garner became the fifth West Indies bowler to take 200 Test wickets when he bowled Lawson. Australia's bowlers, not least the leg-spinner Holland, in his début Test, kept West Indies in check until Lloyd joined Richardson at 184 for five midway through the second day. From the time he hooked Alderman for 6 twenty minutes after coming in, the West Indian captain was at his commanding best, dominating a sixth-wicket partnership of 152 in 122 minutes with Richardson that committed Australia to a forlorn second-innings struggle.

Richardson, badly dropped off Hogg by Hughes at mid-off when 40, had 24 4s from the 232 balls he faced. Lloyd was 109 at the close, his nineteenth Test century, but was soon out next morning, having hit three 6s and fourteen 4s from 154 balls in 208 minutes. Marshall contributed an attractive half-century before Lawson ended the innings by dismissing Walsh for his 100th Test wicket.

Wessels, attacking boldly, and Dyson lifted Australian hopes of a second-innings revival with an opening stand of 88, but they were out at the same score in successive overs and only contrasting half-centuries from the solid Boon, in his début Test, and the powerful Phillips put any spirit into the Australian effort after that.

A verbal clash on the field during the brief West Indies second innings when Haynes was bowled by Lawson brought the former a reprimand and a fine from the management, who also complained about Lawson's part in the incident.

### Australia

| First innings | | Second innings | |
|---|---|---|---|
| J. Dyson c Dujon b Holding | 13 | (2) c Dujon b Marshall | 21 |
| K. C. Wessels b Garner | 0 | (1) c Gomes b Walsh | 61 |
| G. M. Wood c Marshall b Walsh | 20 | c Richardson b Holding | 3 |
| A. R. Border c Lloyd b Marshall | 17 | c sub (R. A. Harper) b Holding | 24 |
| *K. J. Hughes c Marshall b Garner | 34 | lbw b Holding | 4 |
| D. C. Boon c Richardson b Marshall | 11 | c Holding b Marshall | 51 |
| †W. B. Phillips c Dujon b Walsh | 44 | (8) c sub (R. A. Harper) b Holding | 54 |
| G. F. Lawson b Garner | 14 | (9) c Richards b Marshall | 14 |
| T. M. Alderman c Lloyd b Walsh | 0 | (7) c Richardson b Marshall | 1 |
| R. G. Holland c Dujon b Garner | 6 | b Marshall | 0 |
| R. M. Hogg not out | 0 | not out | 21 |
| B 4, l-b 1, n-b 11 | 16 | B 4, l-b 5, n-b 8 | 17 |
| 1/1 2/33 3/33 4/81 5/97 6/102 7/122 8/136 9/173 | 175 | 1/88 2/88 3/99 4/106 5/131 6/212 7/236 8/236 9/271 | 271 |

Bowling: *First Innings*—Garner 18.4–5–67–4; Marshall 14.4–5–39–2; Holding 6.2–2–9–1; Walsh 16–5–55–3. *Second Innings*—Marshall 34–7–82–5; Garner 20–4–80–0; Holding 30–7–92–4; Walsh 5–2–7–1; Richards 1–0–1–0.

### West Indies

| | | | |
|---|---|---|---|
| C. G. Greenidge c Border b Lawson | 44 | | |
| D. L. Haynes b Alderman | 21 | (1) b Lawson | 7 |
| R. B. Richardson c Phillips b Alderman | 138 | (2) c Alderman b Hogg | 5 |
| H. A. Gomes b Holland | 13 | (3) not out | 9 |
| I. V. A. Richards c Boon b Lawson | 6 | (4) not out | 3 |
| †P. J. L. Dujon c Phillips b Holland | 14 | | |
| *C. H. Lloyd c Hughes b Alderman | 114 | | |
| M. D. Marshall b Lawson | 57 | | |
| M. A. Holding b Lawson | 1 | | |
| J. Garner not out | 0 | | |
| C. A. Walsh c Phillips b Lawson | 0 | | |
| B 2, l-b 6, n-b 8 | 16 | L-b 2 | 2 |
| 1/36 2/99 3/129 4/142 5/184 6/336 7/414 8/423 9/424 | 424 | 1/6 2/18 | (2 wkts) 26 |

Bowling: *First Innings*—Lawson 30.4–8–116–5; Alderman 29–10–107–3; Hogg 21–3–71–0; Holland 27–5–97–2; Border 5–0–25–0. *Second Innings*—Lawson 5–0–10–1; Hogg 4.1–0–14–1.

Umpires: R. A. French and M. W. Johnson.

## VICTORIA v WEST INDIANS

At Melbourne, November 30, December 1, 2, 3. Drawn. A lifeless pitch, the loss of important time to the weather, and the reluctance of the captains to make early declarations rendered the match meaningless to all except the statisticians. Haynes, in spite of the after-effects of influenza, batted five hours, ten minutes and hit 24 4s in his highest score in Australia, while Richardson's second century in successive matches lasted just under five hours and included twenty 4s, four in one over from Dodemaide. The West Indians' stand-in captain, Gomes, closed at tea on the second day, and between interruptions for rain Victoria batted through the rest of the match, the West Indians using novice bowlers in the closing stages while their players made no effort to conceal their disinterest. Taylor's mammoth effort of eight and a half hours included sixteen 4s.

### West Indians

| | |
|---|---|
| C. G. Greenidge b Bright | 78 |
| D. L. Haynes b O'Donnell | 155 |
| R. B. Richardson b Bright | 145 |
| A. L. Logie c Siddons b Hughes | 40 |
| *H. A. Gomes c Jones b O'Donnell | 28 |
| P. J. L. Dujon b Robinson | 17 |
| †T. R. O. Payne run out | 18 |
| R. A. Harper not out | 38 |
| W. W. Davis not out | 24 |
| L-b 8, n-b 7 | 15 |
| 1/187 2/263 3/380 4/426 5/457 6/484 7/503 | (7 wkts dec.) 558 |

J. Garner and C. A. Walsh did not bat.

Bowling: Hughes 25–4–88–1; Dodemaide 30–4–137–0; O'Donnell 22–1–112–2; Bright 40–11–98–2; Robinson 23–2–99–1; Whiteside 5–0–16–0.

### Victoria

| | |
|---|---|
| G. F. Richardson c Harper b Walsh | 12 |
| D. Robinson c Harper b Walsh | 52 |
| D. M. Jones c Payne b Harper | 71 |
| W. G. Whiteside lbw b Walsh | 57 |
| M. D. Taylor not out | 234 |
| J. Siddons c Payne b Walsh | 35 |
| S. P. O'Donnell b Logie | 78 |
| A. I. C. Dodemaide c Payne b Dujon | 3 |
| †M. G. Dimattina not out | 1 |
| B 6, l-b 22, n-b 30 | 58 |
| 1/37 2/151 3/166 4/327 5/433 6/572 7/599 | (7 wkts) 601 |

*R. J. Bright and M. G. Hughes did not bat.

Bowling: Davis 25–3–110–0; Walsh 36–6–141–4; Garner 19–3–43–0; Harper 51–12–118–1; Gomes 10–3–22–0; Haynes 6–0–27–0; Richardson 10–1–40–0; Logie 10–1–29–1; Dujon 7–3–43–1.

Umpires: R. C. Bailhache and R. C. Isherwood.

## AUSTRALIA v WEST INDIES

### Third Test Match

At Adelaide, December 7, 8, 9, 10, 11. West Indies won by 191 runs, extending their sequence of consecutive Test victories to eleven. The match marked the centenary of Test cricket at the Adelaide Oval and was watched by 22 captains who had led their countries in Tests there. Unfortunately, the cricket did not measure up to the occasion, the tempo always being slow and the over-rate seldom rising above thirteen an hour in often oppressive heat; this in spite of the presence of spinners in both teams, Harper replacing the injured Holding for West Indies.

West Indies' first innings followed a familiar pattern after Lloyd had opted to bat. When Greenidge's hook was caught on the boundary by Hogg soon after tea on the opening day, denying him his first Test century in Australia, the total was an unconvincing 172 for five. Australia's catching lapses had already cost them dearly, Greenidge having been dropped at 16 and 36, and Dujon now escaped, first ball, to Wessels at second slip of Lawson. Next morning, Holland at long-leg missed Lloyd's mistimed hook off Lawson. Lloyd, then 44, added another 34 and the partnership was worth 150 before Lawson dismissed both in a final spell of four for 27 from eight overs.

Australia responded strongly to 91 for one at the end of the second day, but the loss of Wessels, who was forced to retire hurt just before stumps after being struck on the forearm by Walsh, upset the order, and next day wickets fell steadily, including Hughes's first ball to Garner. Only when Wessels returned and found an able partner in Lawson was there sufficient purpose in the batting, the pair adding 87. Two away from his century, Wessels (sixteen 4s, 164 balls, 248 minutes) dragged Marshall's third delivery with the second new ball back into his stumps.

Ahead by 72, West Indies lost three second-innings wickets for 45 before Gomes, in successive partnerships with Haynes, Richards and Dujon, placed them in a winning position. Gomes's ninth Test century, and sixth against Australia, was filled with fluent strokes and included ten 4s.

Australia's theoretical target was 365 on the last day, but the limit of their expectations was to hold out for a draw. They fell well short of even that objective, bowled out five minutes before tea. Wessels, who passed his 1,000 runs in Tests, was the only batsman to last for any significant time, batting two and a half hours with fourteen 4s before becoming one of off-spinner Harper's four wickets to a ball that turned and lifted.

### West Indies

| | | | |
|---|---|---|---|
| C. G. Greenidge c Hogg b Lawson | 95 | – lbw b Lawson | 4 |
| D. L. Haynes c Hughes b Hogg | 0 | – c Wood b Lawson | 50 |
| R. B. Richardson c Border b Lawson | 8 | – (4) lbw b Hogg | 3 |
| H. A. Gomes c Rixon b Lawson | 60 | – (5) not out | 120 |
| I. V. A. Richards c Rixon b Lawson | 0 | – (6) c Rixon b Hogg | 42 |
| *C. H. Lloyd b Lawson | 78 | – (7) c Rixon b Lawson | 6 |
| †P. J. L. Dujon lbw b Lawson | 77 | – (8) c Boon b Holland | 32 |
| M. D. Marshall c Rixon b Lawson | 9 | | |
| R. A. Harper c Rixon b Lawson | 9 | – (3) c Rixon b Hogg | 26 |
| J. Garner not out | 8 | | |
| C. A. Walsh b Holland | 0 | | |
| B 5, l-b 4, n-b 3 | 12 | L-b 2, n-b 7 | 9 |
| 1/4 2/25 3/157 4/157 5/172 6/322 7/331 8/348 9/355 | 356 | 1/4 2/39 3/45 4/121 5/218 6/225 7/292 (7 wkts dec.) | 292 |

Bowling: *First Innings*—Lawson 40–7–112–8; Hogg 28–7–75–1; Alderman 19–8–38–0; Holland 30.2–5–109–1; Wessels 5–0–13–0. *Second Innings*—Lawson 24–6–69–3; Hogg 21–2–77–3; Holland 18.1–1–54–1; Alderman 12–1–66–0; Border 4–0–24–0.

## Australia

| | | | |
|---|---|---|---|
| G. M. Wood c Greenidge b Harper | 41 | – (7) c Dujon b Harper | 19 |
| J. Dyson c Dujon b Walsh | 8 | – lbw b Marshall | 5 |
| K. C. Wessels b Marshall | 98 | – (1) c Dujon b Harper | 70 |
| †S. J. Rixon c Richards b Marshall | 0 | – (6) lbw b Harper | 16 |
| K. J. Hughes c Dujon b Garner | 0 | – (4) b Marshall | 2 |
| *A. R. Border c Garner b Marshall | 21 | – (3) b Marshall | 18 |
| D. C. Boon c Dujon b Marshall | 12 | – (5) c Harper b Garner | 9 |
| G. F. Lawson c Dujon b Garner | 49 | – c Dujon b Marshall | 2 |
| R. G. Holland c Haynes b Walsh | 2 | – not out | 7 |
| R. M. Hogg not out | 7 | – b Harper | 7 |
| T. M. Alderman c Richardson b Marshall | 10 | – b Marshall | 0 |
| B 2, l-b 8, n-b 26 | 36 | B 7, l-b 7, n-b 4 | 18 |
| 1/28 2/91 3/91 4/122 5/138 6/145 7/232 8/241 9/265 | 284 | 1/22 2/70 3/78 4/97 5/126 6/150 7/153 8/153 9/170 | 173 |

Bowling: *First Innings*—Marshall 26–8–69–5; Garner 26–5–61–2; Walsh 24–8–88–2; Harper 21–4–56–1. *Second Innings*—Marshall 15.5–4–38–5; Garner 16–2–58–1; Walsh 4–0–20–0; Harper 15–6–43–4.

Umpires: A. R. Crafter and M. W. Johnson.

## TASMANIA v WEST INDIANS

At Devonport, December 14, 15, 16, 17. Drawn. After being sent in, the West Indians batted in such carefree fashion that they were all out before tea, having hit one 6 and 23 4s in their 184. In contrast, Tasmania spent ten hours, twelve minutes building a lead of 203 at marginally over 2 runs an over. Goodman, who added 150 with Ray for the first wicket, needed six and a half hours for his 123. The West Indians again batted enterprisingly in their second innings in spite of their deficit, Logie leading the way with his first century in Australia. He added 126 with Payne and 115 with Gomes, who had been forced to retire in the first innings after being struck by a ball from Tasmania's West Indian professional, Patterson. The match was played throughout in bitingly cold weather, and Walsh and Baptiste gave Tasmania a fright in their second innings before it finished.

## West Indians

| | | | |
|---|---|---|---|
| R. B. Richardson c Woolley b Brown | 8 | – c Hyatt b Patterson | 2 |
| †T. R. O. Payne c Ray b Brown | 2 | – b Ray | 55 |
| A. L. Logie lbw b Brown | 7 | – c Woolley b Saunders | 134 |
| I. V. A. Richards b Patterson | 16 | – c Bennett b Ray | 11 |
| H. A. Gomes retired hurt | 14 | – c Boon b Brown | 85 |
| *C. H. Lloyd c Hyatt b Patterson | 30 | – c Ray b Patterson | 49 |
| E. A. E. Baptiste c Buckingham b Faulkner | 54 | – c sub b Brown | 0 |
| R. A. Harper c Goodman b Faulkner | 2 | – c Goodman b Patterson | 11 |
| M. A. Holding c Hyatt b Brown | 16 | – absent injured | |
| C. A. Walsh b Faulkner | 16 | – not out | 2 |
| W. W. Davis not out | 17 | – (9) b Brown | 6 |
| L-b 1, n-b 1 | 2 | B 2, l-b 4, n-b 3 | 9 |
| 1/4 2/16 3/17 4/34 5/114 6/121 7/134 8/154 9/184 | 184 | 1/2 2/128 3/148 4/263 5/345 6/345 7/345 8/352 9/364 | 364 |

Bowling: *First Innings*—Patterson 17–2–67–2; Brown 13–3–72–4; Faulkner 17–5–42–3; Saunders 1–0–2–0. *Second Innings*—Patterson 21.2–3–74–3; Brown 10–3–29–3; Saunders 20–2–104–1; Hyatt 20–2–77–0; Ray 21–2–74–2.

### Tasmania

| | | | |
|---|---|---|---|
| M. Ray c Harper b Richards | 59 | – c Richardson b Baptiste | 11 |
| G. W. Goodman b Walsh | 123 | – lbw b Baptiste | 22 |
| D. C. Boon c Holding b Walsh | 32 | – retired hurt | 1 |
| R. J. Bennett c Payne b Walsh | 0 | – c Richards b Walsh | 4 |
| D. J. Buckingham c Payne b Walsh | 25 | – b Baptiste | 24 |
| *†R. D. Woolley c Lloyd b Baptiste | 35 | – not out | 22 |
| S. L. Saunders c sub b Walsh | 0 | – c Payne b Walsh | 13 |
| P. I. Faulkner c Payne b Walsh | 23 | – (9) not out | 0 |
| R. S. Hyatt b Harper | 29 | – (8) c sub b Baptiste | 6 |
| R. L. Brown not out | 21 | | |
| B. P. Patterson b Baptiste | 4 | | |
| B 4, l-b 5, n-b 27 | 36 | B 1, l-b 4, n-b 2 | 7 |
| 1/150 2/239 3/241 4/243 5/305 6/305 7/309 8/356 9/362 | 387 | 1/32 2/41 3/53 4/74 5/95 6/110 | (6 wkts) 110 |

Bowling: *First Innings*—Holding 6–3–5–0; Davis 2–1–6–0; Walsh 40–5–119–6; Baptiste 38.2–6–120–2; Harper 38–5–95–1; Richards 17–2–33–1. *Second Innings*—Walsh 16–1–38–2; Baptiste 15.5–0–67–4.

Umpires: S. G. Randell and W. Elliott.

†At Echuca, December 19. West Indians won by 64 runs. West Indians 279 for nine (50 overs) (E. A. E. Baptiste 75, D. L. Haynes 48); Victorian Country XI 215 for four (50 overs) (S. Bray 96 not out).

## AUSTRALIA v WEST INDIES

### Fourth Test Match

At Melbourne, December 22, 23, 24, 26, 27. Drawn. West Indies just failed to complete their twelfth consecutive Test victory because of Lloyd's surprising caution in delaying his second-innings declaration until quarter of an hour into the final day. This cost precious time that West Indies could have used as Australia desperately held out at the end of the match.

As was the case in each of the previous Tests, West Indies lost their first five wickets for under 200 but then rallied to a sizeable total after Border had put them in. McDermott, in his début Test, dismissed Richardson, Gomes and Dujon in the space of seven balls in his second spell, but after ten consecutive Test innings without a half-century Richards returned to form with a vengeance. Understandably careful on the opening day, at the end of which he was 82, he accelerated on the second to reach his third double-century in Tests before he was last out, caught at long-on. His main scoring strokes in six and a quarter hours were three 6s and 22 4s, and his partnership of 139 with Marshall pushed West Indies to a virtually invincible total.

Hilditch, returning to Test cricket after a break of five years, and Wessels launched a strong Australian reply with a second-wicket partnership of 123, but once Harper bowled Hilditch and Hughes failed again, the innings went into a disappointing though not unusual decline. Only a last-wicket stand of 43 between Bennett and Hogg prevented the follow-on. Once again Wessels fell in the 90s to Marshall, who took five wickets for the fourth consecutive innings.

Poor light ended play an hour early on the third day, and incisive bowling by Lawson and McDermott restrained West Indies' second innings until Dujon and Lloyd put on 86 prior to Lloyd's declaration, the former benefiting from two chances. Lawson was the subject of an official protest from the West Indians after an incident involving Greenidge and was fined $500 and bonded for $1,500 for his overall behaviour on the field.

When Garner dismissed Wood, Wessels and Hughes (first ball) with the total at 17 well before lunch, West Indies appeared certain to win, but Hilditch, appreciating a slow, featureless pitch, dug in for a determined century (seven 4s, 339 minutes, 273 balls) and received crucial assistance from Border, Rixon and, finally, Bennett.

## West Indies

| | | | |
|---|---|---|---|
| C. G. Greenidge c Bennett b Lawson | 10 | lbw b Lawson | 1 |
| D. L. Haynes c Border b Lawson | 13 | b McDermott | 63 |
| R. B. Richardson b McDermott | 51 | b Lawson | 3 |
| H. A. Gomes c Matthews b McDermott | 68 | c Bennett b McDermott | 18 |
| I. V. A. Richards c Hughes b Matthews | 208 | lbw b McDermott | 0 |
| †P. J. L. Dujon b McDermott | 0 | not out | 49 |
| *C. H. Lloyd c Lawson b Matthews | 19 | not out | 34 |
| M. D. Marshall c Rixon b Hogg | 55 | | |
| R. A. Harper c and b Hogg | 5 | | |
| J. Garner lbw b Lawson | 8 | | |
| C. A. Walsh not out | 18 | | |
| B 1, l-b 11, n-b 12 | 24 | B 4, l-b 9, n-b 5 | 18 |
| 1/27 2/30 3/153 4/154 5/154 6/223 7/362 8/376 9/426 | 479 | 1/2 2/12 3/63 4/63 5/100 (5 wkts dec.) | 186 |

Bowling: *First Innings*—Lawson 37-9-108-3; Hogg 27-2-96-2; McDermott 27-2-118-3; Bennett 20-0-78-0; Matthews 14.3-2-67-2. *Second Innings*—Lawson 19-4-54-2; Hogg 14-3-40-0; McDermott 21-6-65-3; Bennett 3-0-12-0; Wessels 1-0-2-0.

## Australia

| | | | |
|---|---|---|---|
| A. M. J. Hilditch b Harper | 70 | b Gomes | 113 |
| G. M. Wood lbw b Garner | 12 | c Dujon b Garner | 5 |
| K. C. Wessels c Dujon b Marshall | 90 | b Garner | 0 |
| K. J. Hughes c Dujon b Walsh | 0 | lbw b Garner | 0 |
| *A. R. Border c Richards b Walsh | 35 | c Dujon b Richards | 41 |
| G. R. J. Matthews b Marshall | 5 | b Harper | 2 |
| †S. J. Rixon c Richardson b Marshall | 0 | c Richardson b Harper | 17 |
| M. J. Bennett not out | 22 | not out | 3 |
| G. F. Lawson c Walsh b Garner | 8 | b Walsh | 0 |
| C. J. McDermott b Marshall | 0 | | |
| R. M. Hogg lbw b Marshall | 19 | | |
| B 5, l-b 7, w 1, n-b 22 | 35 | B 6, l-b 2, n-b 9 | 17 |
| 1/38 2/161 3/163 4/220 5/238 6/238 7/240 8/253 9/253 | 296 | 1/17 2/17 3/17 4/128 5/131 6/162 7/198 8/198 (8 wkts) | 198 |

Bowling: *First Innings*—Marshall 31.5-6-86-5; Garner 24-6-74-2; Walsh 21-5-57-2; Harper 14-1-58-1; Richards 1-0-9-0. *Second Innings*—Marshall 20-4-36-0; Garner 19-1-49-3; Walsh 18-4-44-1; Harper 22-4-54-2; Richards 6-2-7-1; Gomes 2-2-0-1.

Umpires: P. J. McConnell and S. G. Randell.

## AUSTRALIA v WEST INDIES

### Fifth Test Match

At Sydney, December 30, 31, January 1, 2. Australia won by an innings and 55 runs with more than a day to spare. This was West Indies' first defeat since they lost, also to Australia, at Melbourne 27 Tests earlier in the 1981-82 series. It was their first by an innings since 1968-69, also at Melbourne. The architects of such a complete reversal were the Australian spinners, Holland and Bennett, who had bowled New South Wales to victory over the West Indians earlier in the season. They again fully exploited a turning pitch and the uncertainty of the West Indian batting in such conditions.

West Indies contributed to their own demise by omitting their one specialist spinner, Harper, from their side, in spite of the overwhelming evidence all season that the Sydney pitch encouraged spin. Afterwards Lloyd admitted the selection was a mistake, although he himself, in his 110th and final Test, fought bravely in both innings to save his team.

Following two days of persistent rain that left the pitch damp, Australia chose to bat first, but soon lost Hilditch to Holding, who, recovered from the muscle strain that kept him out of the previous two Tests, had returned as Harper's replacement. But gully escapes for Wood when 6 and Wessels when 13, and a missed opportunity to run out Wessels as soon as he came in, were early indications that the luck had swung Australia's way. There was some life in the pitch throughout the first day when Wood was hit on the helmet by Marshall and Ritchie, after taking a nasty crack on the cheek from Walsh, was forced to retire. But it was never fast and Australia steadily built their highest total of the series. Wessels led the way with his fourth Test century, batting just over eight hours before he chopped Holding into his stumps soon after tea on the second day. He would have hit more than fourteen 4s but for a sluggish outfield. Rain reduced the second day by an hour and a quarter and delayed the end of Australia's innings until an hour into the third day.

West Indies struggled throughout their first innings and were following on before the end of the day. McDermott dismissed Greenidge and Richardson, but Holland was the chief destroyer. Among his six victims were Richards, who edged a sharp leg-break to slip, and Lloyd, who was caught off bat and pad just when he and Dujon were threatening a counter-attack.

Richards and Lloyd both batted with skill and determination in the difficult conditions in the second innings, Richards for a little over two hours before Bennett deceived him with a superb faster ball, Lloyd for two and a quarter hours before he punched a hard, low catch to extra-cover off McDermott. As Lloyd left a Test ground for the last time, he received a standing ovation from the crowd of almost 25,000.

Relations between the teams, already strained following incidents earlier in the series, were further affected by a verbal clash between Richards on the one hand and Rixon and Border on the other, following an unsuccessful appeal against Richards in the first innings. The umpires reported the matter to the Australian Cricket Board, but no action was taken against the players involved.

Marshall, with 28 wickets in spite of his lack of success in this match, was voted Man of the Series.

## Australia

| | |
|---|---|
| A. M. J. Hilditch c Dujon b Holding | 2 |
| G. M. Wood c Haynes b Gomes | 45 |
| K. C. Wessels b Holding | 173 |
| G. M. Ritchie run out | 37 |
| *A. R. Border c Greenidge b Walsh | 69 |
| D. C. Boon b Garner | 49 |
| †S. J. Rixon c Garner b Holding | 20 |
| M. J. Bennett c Greenidge b Garner | 23 |
| G. F. Lawson not out | 5 |
| C. J. McDermott c Greenidge b Walsh | 4 |
| B 7, l-b 20, n-b 17 | 44 |
| 1/12 2/126 3/338 4/342 5/350 6/392 7/450 8/463 9/471 (9 wkts dec.) | 471 |

R. G. Holland did not bat.

Bowling: Marshall 37–2–111–0; Garner 31–5–101–2; Holding 31–7–74–3; Walsh 38.2–1–118–2; Gomes 12–2–29–1; Richards 7–2–11–0.

## West Indies

| | | | |
|---|---|---|---|
| C. G. Greenidge c Rixon b McDermott | 18 | – b Holland | 12 |
| D. L. Haynes c Wessels b Holland | 34 | – lbw b McDermott | 3 |
| R. B. Richardson b McDermott | 2 | – c Wood b Bennett | 26 |
| H. A. Gomes c Bennett b Holland | 28 | – c Wood b Lawson | 8 |
| I. V. A. Richards c Wessels b Holland | 15 | – b Bennett | 58 |
| *C. H. Lloyd c Wood b Holland | 33 | – c Border b McDermott | 72 |
| †P. J. L. Dujon c Hilditch b Bennett | 22 | – c and b Holland | 8 |
| M. D. Marshall st Rixon b Holland | 0 | – not out | 32 |
| M. A. Holding c McDermott b Bennett | 0 | – c Wessels b Holland | 0 |
| J. Garner c Rixon b Holland | 0 | – c Rixon b Bennett | 8 |
| C. A. Walsh not out | 1 | – c Bennett b Holland | 4 |
| L-b 3, n-b 7 | 10 | B 2, l-b 12, n-b 8 | 22 |
| 1/26 2/34 3/72 4/103 5/106 6/160 7/160 8/160 9/160 | 163 | 1/7 2/31 3/46 4/93 5/153 6/180 7/231 8/231 9/244 | 253 |

Bowling: *First Innings*—Lawson 9–1–27–0; McDermott 9–0–34–2; Bennett 22.4–7–45–2; Holland 22–7–54–6. *Second Innings*—Lawson 6–1–14–1; McDermott 12–0–56–2; Bennett 33–9–79–3; Holland 33–8–90–4.

Umpires: R. C. Isherwood and M. W. Johnson.

†At Canberra, January 22. West Indians won by 15 runs. West Indians 284 for eight (50 overs) (H. A. Gomes 91 not out, C. H. Lloyd 50, C. G. Greenidge 44); Prime Minister's XI 269 for seven (50 overs) (A. R. Border 114, P. I. Faulkner 59 not out).

†At Canberra, January 23. West Indians won by eight wickets. Australian Capital Territory 212 for two (50 overs) (P. Woods 58, K. Norris 49 not out); West Indians 213 for two (36.4 overs) (D. L. Haynes 86, T. R. O. Payne 67).

†At Albany, January 29. West Indians won by 11 runs. West Indians 237 for nine dec. (39.4 overs) (R. B. Richardson 75, D. L. Haynes 41); Western Australia Country XI 226 for seven (42 overs) (T. Waldron 72).

*West Indies' matches v Australia and Sri Lanka in the Benson and Hedges World Series Cup may be found in that section.*

# THE NEW ZEALANDERS IN SRI LANKA AND PAKISTAN, 1984-85

By QAMAR AHMED

On their fifth tour of Pakistan the New Zealanders arrived with high hopes of giving Pakistan a hard fight in the three-match Test series. Instead they lost the first two Tests by wide margins. The final Test at Karachi was drawn, though New Zealand came near to winning it through some fine bowling by their orthodox left-arm spinner Stephen Boock, who took seventeen wickets in the three Test matches. The tourists also lost the one-day international series one-three, having shared their two-match series in Sri Lanka *en route* to Pakistan. Their two first-class games, against the BCCP Patron's XI and the Punjab Governor's XI, ended in draws.

New Zealand were weakened by the absence of Richard Hadlee and Geoff Howarth, who were unavailable for the tour. Without Hadlee their opening attack appeared unimpressive, though the newcomer, Derek Stirling, was the find of the tour. He improved fast and at times seemed very lively even on docile wickets. John Reid was the most difficult batsman for the Pakistani bowlers to dislodge, and the experienced John Wright played a fine innings of 107 in Karachi, which nearly won the Test there for New Zealand. Martin Crowe suffered through lack of concentration and doubtful umpiring decisions.

The tour, which had begun on a cordial note, started, in fact, to turn sour when the New Zealanders were angered by the attitude of the umpires and some of their decisions. Soon after the second Test, at Hyderabad, their captain and manager issued an official and critical statement, and the controversy escalated when the tourists started to walk off the field in the final Test when umpire Shakoor Rana denied them an appeal for a catch at the wicket against Javed Miandad, a century-maker in each innings of the second Test. The game was held up as the fielders gathered near the pavilion and refused to go back to resume play. It required persuasion from other senior members of the touring team to persuade the captain, Jeremy Coney, to let the game continue. An enquiry committee, set up to look into the complaints made by the tourists, found that four decisions against them and two against the home team were questionable. The committee was headed by Pakistan's former captain, Hanif Mohammad.

The star of the Test series was the left-arm spinner, Iqbal Qasim, who had missed Pakistan's previous thirteen Test matches and now finished with eighteen wickets in the series at an average of 22.11.

## NEW ZEALAND TOUR RESULTS

*Test matches* – Played 3: Lost 2, Drawn 1.
*First-class matches* – Played 5: Lost 2, Drawn 3.
*Losses* – Pakistan (2).
*Draws* – Pakistan, BCCP Patron's XI, Punjab Governor's XI.
*Non first-class matches* – Played 7: Won 2, Lost 5.
*Wins* – Sri Lanka, Pakistan. *Losses* – Sri Lanka, Pakistan (3), Pakistan XI.

# TEST MATCH AVERAGES

## PAKISTAN – BATTING

| | *T* | *I* | *NO* | *R* | *HI* | *100s* | *Avge* |
|---|---|---|---|---|---|---|---|
| Javed Miandad | 3 | 6 | 2 | 337 | 104 | 2 | 84.25 |
| Salim Malik | 3 | 5 | 2 | 204 | 119* | 1 | 68.00 |
| Iqbal Qasim | 3 | 3 | 1 | 75 | 45* | 0 | 37.50 |
| Mudassar Nazar | 3 | 6 | 0 | 181 | 106 | 1 | 30.16 |
| Mohsin Khan | 2 | 4 | 0 | 107 | 58 | 0 | 26.75 |
| Qasim Omar | 3 | 6 | 0 | 140 | 45 | 0 | 23.33 |
| Anil Dalpat | 3 | 3 | 0 | 64 | 52 | 0 | 21.33 |
| Zaheer Abbas | 3 | 5 | 0 | 93 | 43 | 0 | 18.60 |
| Abdul Qadir | 3 | 3 | 0 | 32 | 14 | 0 | 10.66 |
| Azeem Hafeez | 3 | 3 | 1 | 11 | 11 | 0 | 5.50 |

Played in one Test: Manzoor Elahi 19, 4*; Shoaib Mohammad 31, 34; Tauseef Ahmed 0*; Wasim Raja 51, 60*.

* *Signifies not out.*

## BOWLING

| | *O* | *M* | *R* | *W* | *BB* | *Avge* |
|---|---|---|---|---|---|---|
| Mudassar Nazar | 48.4 | 14 | 105 | 5 | 3-8 | 21.00 |
| Iqbal Qasim | 166.5 | 46 | 398 | 18 | 5-79 | 22.11 |
| Abdul Qadir | 105.3 | 24 | 307 | 12 | 5-108 | 25.58 |
| Azeem Hafeez | 103.4 | 30 | 271 | 10 | 4-132 | 27.10 |

Also bowled: Manzoor Elahi 2–1–2–0; Tauseef Ahmed 6–0–26–0; Wasim Raja 33–8–97–1; Zaheer Abbas 14.2–2–39–2.

## NEW ZEALAND – BATTING

| | *T* | *I* | *NO* | *R* | *HI* | *100s* | *Avge* |
|---|---|---|---|---|---|---|---|
| J. F. Reid | 3 | 5 | 0 | 232 | 106 | 1 | 46.40 |
| J. G. Wright | 3 | 5 | 0 | 213 | 107 | 1 | 42.60 |
| J. J. Crowe | 3 | 5 | 0 | 201 | 62 | 0 | 40.20 |
| M. D. Crowe | 3 | 5 | 0 | 173 | 55 | 0 | 34.60 |
| I. D. S. Smith | 3 | 5 | 1 | 92 | 41 | 0 | 23.00 |
| D. A. Stirling | 3 | 5 | 1 | 55 | 16 | 0 | 13.75 |
| J. V. Coney | 3 | 5 | 0 | 60 | 26 | 0 | 12.00 |
| E. J. Gray | 2 | 4 | 0 | 48 | 25 | 0 | 12.00 |
| B. A. Edgar | 3 | 5 | 0 | 56 | 26 | 0 | 11.20 |
| J. G. Bracewell | 2 | 3 | 0 | 30 | 30 | 0 | 10.00 |
| S. L. Boock | 3 | 5 | 1 | 29 | 13 | 0 | 7.25 |

Played in one Test: E. J. Chatfield 6*, 0; P. E. McEwan 40*.

* *Signifies not out.*

## BOWLING

| | O | M | R | W | BB | Avge |
|---|---|---|---|---|---|---|
| S. L. Boock | 172.4 | 54 | 431 | 17 | 7-87 | 25.35 |
| M. D. Crowe | 49 | 9 | 165 | 6 | 2-29 | 27.50 |
| D. A. Stirling | 92.1 | 16 | 338 | 8 | 4-88 | 42.25 |
| E. J. Gray | 59 | 5 | 183 | 4 | 2-19 | 45.75 |
| J. G. Bracewell | 82.1 | 21 | 217 | 4 | 3-44 | 54.25 |

Also bowled: E. J. Chatfield 41.2–14–69–3; J. V. Coney 21–9–26–0; J. J. Crowe 2–0–9–0; P. E. McEwan 6–1–13–0; J. F. Reid 2–0–7–0; J. G. Wright 1–0–1–0.

# NEW ZEALAND AVERAGES – FIRST-CLASS MATCHES

## BATTING

| | M | I | NO | R | HI | 100s | Avge |
|---|---|---|---|---|---|---|---|
| M. D. Crowe | 4 | 7 | 1 | 294 | 71 | 0 | 49.00 |
| J. G. Wright | 4 | 7 | 0 | 309 | 107 | 1 | 44.14 |
| J. F. Reid | 5 | 9 | 2 | 301 | 106 | 1 | 43.00 |
| J. J. Crowe | 5 | 8 | 0 | 298 | 62 | 0 | 37.25 |
| B. A. Edgar | 5 | 9 | 0 | 224 | 75 | 0 | 24.88 |
| J. V. Coney | 4 | 6 | 0 | 139 | 79 | 0 | 23.16 |
| I. D. S. Smith | 4 | 7 | 1 | 133 | 41 | 0 | 22.16 |
| E. J. Gray | 4 | 7 | 0 | 133 | 56 | 0 | 19.00 |
| J. G. Bracewell | 4 | 5 | 1 | 55 | 30 | 0 | 13.75 |
| D. A. Stirling | 4 | 6 | 1 | 55 | 16 | 0 | 11.00 |
| S. L. Boock | 5 | 6 | 1 | 30 | 13 | 0 | 6.00 |

Played in two matches: B. L. Cairns 7, 10*; E. J. Chatfield 6*, 0; P. E. McEwan 40*, 33*, 44. M. C. Snedden played in one match but did not bat.

**Signifies not out.*

## BOWLING

| | O | M | R | W | BB | Avge |
|---|---|---|---|---|---|---|
| E. J. Chatfield | 51.2 | 17 | 93 | 4 | 3-57 | 23.25 |
| S. L. Boock | 221.4 | 75 | 501 | 21 | 7-87 | 23.85 |
| E. J. Gray | 90 | 12 | 253 | 10 | 3-24 | 25.30 |
| M. D. Crowe | 55 | 11 | 181 | 6 | 2-29 | 30.16 |
| D. A. Stirling | 111.5 | 19 | 392 | 9 | 4-88 | 43.55 |
| J. G. Bracewell | 117.1 | 31 | 294 | 6 | 3-44 | 49.55 |

Also bowled: B. L. Cairns 23–5–75–2; J. V. Coney 21–9–26–0; J. J. Crowe 2–0–9–0; P. E. McEwan 6–1–13–0; J. F. Reid 2–0–7–0; M. C. Snedden 11–1–52–2; J. G. Wright 1–0–1–0.

## FIELDING

I. D. S. Smith 10 (8 ct, 2 st), J. J. Crowe 7, M. D. Crowe 6, J. V. Coney 4, J. F. Reid 4, B. L. Cairns 3, E. J. Gray 3, P. E. McEwan 2, M. C. Snedden 2, S. L. Boock 1, J. G. Wright 1.

## †SRI LANKA v NEW ZEALAND

At Saravanamuttu Stadium, Colombo, November 3. Sri Lanka won by four wickets. New Zealand, captained by Coney, were restricted on an easy-paced pitch by tight out-cricket. Sri Lanka were in turn reduced to 79 for five before the nineteen-year-old Aravinda de Silva came to the rescue with an unbeaten half-century.

*Man of the Match:* P. A. de Silva.

### New Zealand

J. G. Wright c Silva b John . . . . . . . . . . 11
B. A. Edgar c Silva b Ratnayeke . . . . . . 6
M. D. Crowe b Ranatunga . . . . . . . . . . . . 23
J. F. Reid c Ratnayeke b de Mel . . . . . 21
J. J. Crowe not out . . . . . . . . . . . . . . . . . 57
*J. V. Coney c P. A. de Silva b John . . 24
B. L. Cairns c P. A. de Silva b John . . 4
†I. D. S. Smith not out . . . . . . . . . . . . . . 5
B 1, l-b 14, w 3, n-b 2 . . . . . . . 20

1/20 2/36 3/58 4/84 5/124 6/133 (6 wkts, 45 overs) 171

S. L. Boock, M. C. Snedden and E. J. Chatfield did not bat.

Bowling: de Mel 9–3–26–1; John 9–2–37–3; Ratnayeke 9–0–40–1; Ranatunga 9–0–23–1; D. S. de Silva 9–1–25–0.

### Sri Lanka

S. Wettimuny c Edgar b Cairns . . . . . . . 1
†S. A. R. Silva c Boock b Chatfield . . . 21
R. S. Madugalle c Wright b Chatfield . . 31
A. Ranatunga c Reid b Coney . . . . . . . . 9
R. L. Dias c Wright b Boock . . . . . . . . . 34
*L. R. D. Mendis c J. J. Crowe b Coney 3
P. A. de Silva not out . . . . . . . . . . . . . . . 50
A. L. F. de Mel not out . . . . . . . . . . . . . 15
B 3, l-b 5, n-b 2 . . . . . . . . . . . . 10

1/13 2/43 3/62 4/75 5/79 6/144 (6 wkts, 39.4 overs) 174

D. S. de Silva, J. R. Ratnayeke and V. B. John did not bat.

Bowling: Snedden 6–1–30–0; Cairns 6.4–2–37–1; Chatfield 9–0–34–2; Boock 9–0–29–1; Coney 4–0–16–2; M. D. Crowe 5–0–18–0.

Umpires: D. P. Buultjens and H. C. Felsinger.

*Wides and no-balls not debited to bowlers' analyses.*

## †SRI LANKA v NEW ZEALAND

At Moratuwa, November 4. New Zealand won by seven wickets. Put in, Sri Lanka quickly lost their openers to Martin Crowe and lunched at 58 for five on their way to a modest total, to which no batsman contributed more than 15. New Zealand also made a poor start, but Martin Crowe, with 52 off 57 balls, including one 6 and eight 4s, saw them to a comfortable victory.

*Man of the Match:* M. D. Crowe.

### Sri Lanka

S. Wettimuny b M. D. Crowe . . . . . . . . 3
†S. A. R. Silva c Smith b M. D. Crowe 9
R. S. Madugalle run out . . . . . . . . . . . . . 0
R. L. Dias st Smith b Coney . . . . . . . . . 10
*L. R. D. Mendis c Snedden b Stirling . 13
A. Ranatunga run out . . . . . . . . . . . . . . . 15
P. A. de Silva run out . . . . . . . . . . . . . . . 15
A. L. F. de Mel c Reid b Stirling . . . . . 15
D. S. de Silva b Chatfield . . . . . . . . . . . . 13
J. R. Ratnayeke not out . . . . . . . . . . . . . 8
V. B. John not out . . . . . . . . . . . . . . . . . . 0
B 3, l-b 6, w 1, n-b 3 . . . . . . . . 13

1/12 2/12 3/22 4/35 5/47 6/66 7/91 8/91 9/114 (9 wkts, 41 overs) 114

Bowling: Chatfield 9–2–17–1; Snedden 7–2–14–0; M. D. Crowe 9–3–17–2; Stirling 9–1–28–2; Coney 4–0–7–1; McEwan 3–0–18–0.

## New Zealand

| | | | |
|---|---|---|---|
| J. G. Wright b de Mel | 6 | J. J. Crowe not out | 7 |
| P. E. McEwan c P. A. de Silva b de Mel | 9 | L-b 3, w 5, n-b 2 | 10 |
| J. F. Reid c Dias b Ranatunga | 34 | | |
| M. D. Crowe not out | 52 | 1/15 2/19 3/98 (3 wkts, 31.4 overs) | 118 |

*J. V. Coney, E. J. Gray, †I. D. S. Smith, D. A. Stirling, M. C. Snedden and E. J. Chatfield did not bat.

Bowling: de Mel 7–3–23–2; John 9–2–37–0; Ratnayeke 6–1–9–0; D. S. de Silva 4–1–14–0; Ranatunga 5.4–1–25–1.

Umpires: K. T. Francis and P. W. Vidanagamage.

*Wides and no-balls not debited to bowlers' analyses.*

# BCCP PATRON'S XI v NEW ZEALANDERS

At Rawalpindi, November 8, 9, 10. Drawn. After winning the toss the New Zealanders were all out for 234 in their first innings, Edgar making 60 and Martin Crowe 71. The young left-arm medium-pacer, Wasim Akram, finished with seven for 50. But it would have needed a fourth day to have got anywhere near a result.

## New Zealanders

| | | | |
|---|---|---|---|
| *J. G. Wright c Salim b Akram | 3 | lbw b Akram | 93 |
| B. A. Edgar c Anil b Akram | 60 | c and b Hafeez | 71 |
| M. D. Crowe c Anil b Ghaffar | 71 | (4) not out | 50 |
| J. J. Crowe c Ramiz b Hafeez | 45 | (5) b Hafeez | 3 |
| J. F. Reid lbw b Akram | 1 | (3) lbw b Akram | 0 |
| E. J. Gray c Miandad b Ghaffar | 25 | b Hafeez | 4 |
| †I. D. S. Smith lbw b Akram | 11 | c Miandad b Ghaffar | 30 |
| J. G. Bracewell not out | 5 | | |
| B. L. Cairns b Akram | 7 | | |
| D. A. Stirling c Anil b Akram | 0 | | |
| S. L. Boock b Akram | 1 | | |
| L-b 3, n-b 2 | 5 | L-b 5, n-b 5 | 10 |
| 1/8 2/108 3/161 4/165 5/199 6/220 7/220 8/228 9/232 | 234 | 1/166 2/167 3/181 4/184 5/190 6/261 (6 wkts dec.) | 261 |

Bowling: *First Innings*—Asif 16–3–50–0; Akram 20.5–6–50–7; Hafeez 21–3–73–1; Ghaffar 13–3–58–2. *Second Innings*—Akram 19–4–54–2; Asif 10–2–50–0; Ghaffar 8.3–1–50–1; Hafeez 21–4–63–3; Salim 4–0–15–0; Miandad 6–1–24–0.

## BCCP Patron's XI

| | | | |
|---|---|---|---|
| Masood Anwar lbw b Cairns | 26 | c M. D. Crowe b Bracewell | 9 |
| Shoaib Mohammad not out | 108 | not out | 5 |
| Ramiz Raja st Smith b Boock | 18 | not out | 11 |
| *Javed Miandad c Reid b Gray | 23 | | |
| Salim Malik c and b Gray | 10 | | |
| Sagheer Abbas c Smith b Boock | 0 | | |
| †Anil Dalpat c J. J. Crowe b Gray | 12 | | |
| Ghaffar Kazmi c Smith b Stirling | 8 | | |
| Hafeez-ur-Rehman not out | 1 | | |
| L-b 6, n-b 17 | 23 | B 1, l-b 1, n-b 3 | 5 |
| 1/54 2/96 3/163 4/182 5/183 6/200 7/219 (7 wkts dec.) | 229 | 1/14 (1 wkt) | 30 |

Asif Afridi and Wasim Akram did not bat.

Bowling: *First Innings*—Stirling 15.4–2–44–1; Cairns 13–2–45–1; Bracewell 12–3–34–0; Boock 21–5–46–2; M. D. Crowe 6–2–16–0; Gray 17–3–38–3. *Second Innings*—Stirling 4–1–10–0; Cairns 4–2–6–0; Bracewell 5–3–4–1; Gray 3–1–8–0.

Umpires: Javed Akhtar and Mian Mohammad Aslam.

## †PAKISTAN v NEW ZEALAND

### First One-day International

At Peshawar, November 12. Pakistan won by 46 runs. After winning the toss New Zealand put Pakistan in and claimed their first three wickets for only 38 runs. But Miandad, along with the newcomer, Naved Anjum, and Mudassar took Pakistan to a respectable 191 for five. New Zealand in turn lost half their side for 44 to the medium pace of Zakir Khan.

*Man of the Match:* Zakir Khan.

### Pakistan

| | |
|---|---|
| Saadat Ali c Cairns b Chatfield | 1 |
| Sajid Ali c J. J. Crowe b Cairns | 16 |
| *Zaheer Abbas lbw b Cairns | 13 |
| Javed Miandad not out | 80 |
| Naved Anjum c M. D. Crowe b Stirling | 29 |
| Manzoor Elahi c Stirling b Snedden | 15 |
| Mudassar Nazar not out | 17 |
| B 2, l-b 8, w 8, n-b 2 | 20 |
| 1/14 2/27 3/38 4/87 5/123 (5 wkts, 39 overs) | 191 |

Sarfraz Nawaz, †Anil Dalpat, Tauseef Ahmed and Zakir Khan did not bat.

Bowling: Stirling 8–0–32–1; Cairns 8–0–38–2; Chatfield 7–0–38–1; M. D. Crowe 8–0–37–0; Snedden 8–0–36–1.

### New Zealand

| | |
|---|---|
| J. G. Wright lbw b Manzoor | 8 |
| J. J. Crowe c Anil b Zakir | 8 |
| M. D. Crowe c Anil b Zakir | 8 |
| P. E. McEwan lbw b Zakir | 3 |
| J. F. Reid c Miandad b Zakir | 14 |
| *J. V. Coney c and b Mudassar | 23 |
| †I. D. S. Smith c Sajid b Mudassar | 59 |
| M. C. Snedden c Anil b Mudassar | 1 |
| B. L. Cairns c Zaheer b Tauseef | 7 |
| D. A. Stirling run out | 2 |
| E. J. Chatfield not out | 1 |
| L-b 4, w 7 | 11 |
| 1/19 2/19 3/22 4/39 5/44 6/99 7/103 8/113 9/142 (36.2 overs) | 145 |

Bowling: Manzoor 8–1–27–1; Zakir 8–2–19–4; Sarfraz 4–1–18–0; Naved 3–0–13–0; Tauseef 7–0–30–1; Mudassar 6.2–0–34–3.

Umpires: Adheer Zaadi and Javed Akhtar.

## PAKISTAN v NEW ZEALAND

### First Test Match

At Lahore, November 16, 17, 18, 19, 20. Pakistan won by six wickets, twenty minutes into the final morning. With Sarfraz Nawaz having announced his retirement soon after the first one-day international, Pakistan went into the first Test with only one opening bowler, Azeem Hafeez: Mudassar used the new ball from the other end. But it was the spinners who stole the limelight. Iqbal Qasim, who was not in the original side and was flown overnight to join the team, finished with match figures of eight for 106. However, New Zealand batted poorly after winning the toss, only Martin Crowe and the wicket-keeper, Smith, putting up much resistance against Iqbal Qasim and Mudassar. In the second innings, after conceding a lead of 64, New Zealand's batsmen displayed much better technique against the spinners. Wright, after a blow on his head from a bouncer by Azeem, recovered to make 65 before being run out. Zaheer Abbas completed his 5,000 runs in Test cricket.

### New Zealand

| | | | |
|---|---|---|---|
| J. J. Crowe c Anil b Mudassar | 0 | (5) b Iqbal | 43 |
| B. A. Edgar b Mudassar | 3 | lbw b Azeem | 26 |
| M. D. Crowe c Omar b Qadir | 55 | c sub (Ramiz Raja) b Iqbal | 33 |
| J. G. Wright c Anil b Azeem | 1 | (1) run out | 65 |
| J. F. Reid lbw b Mudassar | 2 | (4) b Qadir | 6 |
| *J. V. Coney c Mohsin b Iqbal | 7 | c Anil b Azeem | 26 |
| E. J. Gray c sub (Ramiz Raja) b Iqbal | 12 | (8) c Mudassar b Qadir | 6 |
| †I. D. S. Smith c Iqbal b Azeem | 41 | (9) not out | 11 |
| D. A. Stirling b Iqbal | 16 | (10) c Anil b Iqbal | 10 |
| S. L. Boock c Miandad b Iqbal | 13 | (7) c Miandad b Qadir | 0 |
| E. J. Chatfield not out | 6 | c Omar b Iqbal | 0 |
| B 1 | 1 | B 8, l-b 2, w 1, n-b 4 | 15 |
| 1/0 2/11 3/28 4/31 5/50 6/76 7/120 8/124 9/146 | 157 | 1/66 2/123 3/138 4/140 5/208 6/209 7/220 8/220 9/235 | 241 |

Bowling: *First Innings*—Mudassar 11–5–8–3; Azeem 18–9–40–2; Qadir 21–6–58–1; Iqbal 22.4–10–41–4; Tauseef 2–0–9–0. *Second Innings*—Mudassar 10–1–30–0; Azeem 13–5–37–2; Tauseef 4–0–17–0; Iqbal 30–10–65–4; Qadir 26–4–82–3.

### Pakistan

| | | | |
|---|---|---|---|
| Mudassar Nazar c Reid b Stirling | 26 | b Boock | 16 |
| Mohsin Khan c Reid b Gray | 58 | c and b Gray | 38 |
| Qasim Omar c J. J. Crowe b Boock | 13 | lbw b Stirling | 20 |
| Javed Miandad c Reid b Gray | 11 | not out | 48 |
| *Zaheer Abbas c M. D. Crowe b Boock | 43 | c Smith b Gray | 31 |
| Salim Malik lbw b Stirling | 10 | not out | 24 |
| Abdul Qadir c Coney b Chatfield | 14 | | |
| †Anil Dalpat b M. D. Crowe | 11 | | |
| Iqbal Qasim c Coney b Chatfield | 22 | | |
| Azeem Hafeez c Boock b Chatfield | 11 | | |
| Tauseef Ahmed not out | 0 | | |
| N-b 2 | 2 | L-b 4 | 4 |
| 1/54 2/84 3/103 4/114 5/144 6/165 7/188 8/189 9/212 | 221 | 1/33 2/77 3/77 4/138 (4 wkts) | 181 |

Bowling: *First Innings*—Stirling 27–7–71–2; M. D. Crowe 7–1–21–1; Gray 8–1–19–2; Chatfield 28.2–7–57–3; Boock 24–7–53–2. *Second Innings*—Stirling 15.1–2–60–1; Chatfield 13–7–12–0; Boock 17–2–56–1; Gray 18–0–45–2; Coney 2–1–4–0.

Umpires: Mahboob Shah and Shakeel Khan.

## †PAKISTAN v NEW ZEALAND

### Second One-day International

At Faisalabad, November 23. Pakistan won by 5 runs. In a rain-ruined game, reduced to twenty overs to each side, Pakistan were again asked to bat. Thanks to Salim Malik's 41 and a belligerent 39 not out from Manzoor Elahi they managed to set New Zealand a target of more than 7 runs an over. But Smith and Stirling were run out at vital stages and they fell 5 runs short.

*Man of the Match:* Salim Malik.

## Pakistan

| | | | |
|---|---|---|---|
| Salim Malik b Snedden | 41 | Shoaib Mohammad not out | 10 |
| Mohsin Khan b M. D. Crowe | 0 | | |
| *Zaheer Abbas c Stirling b Snedden | 25 | L-b 7, w 4, n-b 1 | 12 |
| Javed Miandad run out | 20 | | |
| Manzoor Elahi not out | 39 | 1/3 2/67 3/81 (5 wkts, 20 overs) | 157 |
| Mudassar Nazar lbw b M. D. Crowe | 10 | 4/105 5/128 | |

†Anil Dalpat, Zakir Khan, Wasim Akram and Tauseef Ahmed did not bat.

Bowling: M. D. Crowe 4–0–17–2; Coney 2–0–10–0; Cairns 4–0–25–0; Chatfield 2–0–25–0; Snedden 4–0–41–2; Stirling 4–0–32–0.

## New Zealand

| | | | |
|---|---|---|---|
| J. G. Wright b Mudassar | 55 | D. A. Stirling run out | 1 |
| J. J. Crowe lbw b Zakir | 7 | *J. V. Coney not out | 17 |
| M. D. Crowe c Zaheer b Mudassar | 19 | | |
| P. E. McEwan lbw b Mudassar | 7 | B 2, l-b 7, w 7 | 16 |
| B. L. Cairns c Salim b Mudassar | 10 | | |
| J. G. Bracewell not out | 16 | 1/20 2/61 3/78 (7 wkts, 20 overs) | 152 |
| †I. D. S. Smith run out | 4 | 4/106 5/112 6/127 7/132 | |

M. C. Snedden and E. J. Chatfield did not bat.

Bowling: Akram 4–0–31–0; Zakir 4–0–28–1; Manzoor 4–0–31–0; Mudassar 4–0–27–4; Tauseef 4–0–26–0.

Umpires: Ikram Rabbani and Amanullah Khan.

## PAKISTAN v NEW ZEALAND

### Second Test Match

At Hyderabad, November 25, 26, 27, 29. Pakistan won by seven wickets with a day to spare. New Zealand succumbed again to Pakistan's spinners, Iqbal Qasim and Qadir, who between them captured fourteen wickets in the match. There was also a fine display of spin bowling by Boock, who finished with seven for 87 in Pakistan's first innings. Eventually, needing 227 to win, Pakistan lost two wickets for only 14 in their second innings, but Mudassar and Miandad added 212 for the third wicket – a record for Pakistan against New Zealand – before Mudassar was out for 106, minutes away from victory. Miandad became the second Pakistani after Hanif Mohammad to score two centuries in a Test match, his 103 not out in the second innings making him his country's leading century-maker with thirteen. Following severe criticism by the New Zealand captain and manager of the umpiring the BCCP set up an enquiry to look into the complaints. This was the 1,000th Test match since the first one was played between Australia and England in March 1877.

## New Zealand

| | | | |
|---|---|---|---|
| J. G. Wright c Anil b Iqbal | 18 | – c Anil b Iqbal | 22 |
| B. A. Edgar c Salim b Qadir | 11 | – lbw b Mudassar | 1 |
| M. D. Crowe b Qadir | 19 | – (4) st Anil b Iqbal | 21 |
| J. F. Reid lbw b Azeem | 106 | – (3) lbw b Qadir | 21 |
| *J. V. Coney c Manzoor b Qadir | 6 | – b Iqbal | 5 |
| J. J. Crowe c Salim b Zaheer | 39 | – lbw b Iqbal | 57 |
| †I. D. S. Smith c Iqbal b Zaheer | 6 | – c Mudassar b Azeem | 34 |
| E. J. Gray lbw b Mudassar | 25 | – c Omar b Iqbal | 5 |
| J. G. Bracewell c Mudassar b Qadir | 0 | – c and b Qadir | 0 |
| D. A. Stirling not out | 11 | – b Qadir | 11 |
| S. L. Boock lbw b Qadir | 12 | – not out | 4 |
| B 13, n-b 1 | 14 | B 1, l-b 4, n-b 3 | 8 |
| 1/30 2/30 3/74 4/88 5/150 6/164 7/237 8/239 9/243 | 267 | 1/2 2/34 3/58 4/71 5/80 6/125 7/149 8/149 9/167 | 189 |

Bowling: *First Innings*—Mudassar 7–4–14–1; Azeem 18–4–29–1; Iqbal 33–6–80–1; Qadir 40.3–11–108–5; Manzoor 2–1–2–0; Zaheer 8–1–21–2. *Second Innings*—Mudassar 5–2–8–1; Azeem 8–3–33–1; Iqbal 24.1–7–79–5; Qadir 18–3–59–3; Zaheer 1–0–5–0.

## Pakistan

| | | | |
|---|---|---|---|
| Mudassar Nazar c M. D. Crowe b Bracewell | 28 | – c Coney b Boock | 106 |
| Mohsin Khan c Gray b Boock | 9 | – b M. D. Crowe | 2 |
| Qasim Omar c Coney b Boock | 45 | – lbw b M. D. Crowe | 0 |
| Javed Miandad c J. J. Crowe b Boock | 104 | – not out | 103 |
| †Anil Dalpat b Bracewell | 1 | | |
| *Zaheer Abbas st Smith b Boock | 2 | | |
| Salim Malik b Boock | 1 | | |
| Manzoor Elahi c J. J. Crowe b Boock | 19 | – (5) not out | 4 |
| Abdul Qadir lbw b Boock | 11 | | |
| Iqbal Qasim c J. J. Crowe b Bracewell | 8 | | |
| Azeem Hafeez not out | 0 | | |
| L-b 2 | 2 | B 5, l-b 7, n-b 3 | 15 |
| 1/26 2/50 3/153 4/154 5/159 6/169 7/191 8/215 9/230 | 230 | 1/14 2/14 3/226 | (3 wkts) 230 |

Bowling: *First Innings*—Stirling 3–1–11–0; M. D. Crowe 3–0–8–0; Coney 10–4–8–0; Boock 37–12–87–7; Bracewell 16.1–3–44–3; Gray 22–4–70–0. *Second Innings*—Stirling 4–0–26–0; M. D. Crowe 8–1–29–2; Boock 23.4–4–69–1; Gray 11–0–49–0; Bracewell 13–2–36–0; Coney 4–1–9–0.

Umpires: Mian Mohammad Aslam and Khizar Hayat.

## †PAKISTAN v NEW ZEALAND

### Third One-day International

At Sialkot, December 2. New Zealand won by 34 runs. Pakistan, after winning the toss, put the visitors in and Mohsin Kamal with medium pace and the off-spinner Tauseef Ahmed bowled well to restrict them to 187 in 36 overs. Martin Crowe batted superbly. Wickets fell at regular intervals when Pakistan batted for the New Zealanders to record their first win of the tour in Pakistan.

*Man of the Match:* M. D. Crowe.

## New Zealand

| | |
|---|---|
| J. G. Wright c Salim Malik b Kamal . . 24 | †I. D. S. Smith c Salim Malik b Tauseef 9 |
| J. G. Bracewell c Salim Malik b Kamal 1 | D. A. Stirling c Salim Malik b Tauseef . 4 |
| J. F. Reid run out . . . . . . . . . . . . . . . . . . 34 | M. C. Snedden not out . . . . . . . . . . . . . 0 |
| M. D. Crowe b Kamal . . . . . . . . . . . . . . 67 | L-b 6, w 21, n-b 1 . . . . . . . . . . 28 |
| J. J. Crowe not out . . . . . . . . . . . . . . . . 15 | — |
| P. E. McEwan st Salim Yousuf b Tauseef 4 | 1/14 2/47 3/128 (9 wkts, 36 overs) 187 |
| B. L. Cairns b Tauseef . . . . . . . . . . . . . . 0 | 4/156 5/162 6/166 |
| *J. V. Coney run out . . . . . . . . . . . . . . . 1 | 7/168 8/178 9/187 |

Bowling: Kamal 8–0–46–3; Zakir 8–0–22–0; Mudassar 8–0–58–0; Manzoor 6–0–17–0; Tauseef 6–0–38–4.

## Pakistan

| | |
|---|---|
| Mohsin Khan lbw b Stirling . . . . . . . . . 2 | †Salim Yousuf lbw b Bracewell . . . . . . . 1 |
| Shoaib Mohammad lbw b M. D. Crowe 22 | Tauseef Ahmed not out . . . . . . . . . . . . . 27 |
| Salim Malik b M. D. Crowe . . . . . . . . . 6 | Zakir Khan not out . . . . . . . . . . . . . . . . . 8 |
| Javed Miandad c Wright b Cairns . . . . 14 | L-b 6, w 3, n-b 3 . . . . . . . . . . . 12 |
| *Zaheer Abbas c J. J. Crowe b Bracewell 42 | — |
| Manzoor Elahi b Cairns . . . . . . . . . . . . . 16 | 1/2 2/14 3/42 4/52 (8 wkts, 36 overs) 153 |
| Mudassar Nazar c Stirling b Snedden . . 3 | 5/90 6/97 7/100 8/133 |

Mohsin Kamal did not bat.

Bowling: Stirling 8–0–36–1; M. D. Crowe 5–0–21–2; Cairns 6–0–30–2; Snedden 8–0–29–1; Bracewell 8–0–23–2; Coney 1–0–8–0.

Umpires: Shakoor Rana and Rab Nawaz.

# PUNJAB GOVERNOR'S XI v NEW ZEALANDERS

At Bahawalpur, December 4, 5, 6. Drawn. The New Zealanders made good use of a perfect batting strip, Gray, Coney and Jeff Crowe being the main scorers. In reply the Governor's XI struggled against some good spin bowling by Gray, who finished with three for 24 in eleven overs, but the result was the predictable draw.

## New Zealanders

| First innings | | Second innings | |
|---|---|---|---|
| B. A. Edgar b Tahir . . . . . . . . . . . . . . . . . . . . . . | 23 | c Masood b Tahir . . . . . . . . . . . . | 14 |
| E. J. Gray b Tahir . . . . . . . . . . . . . . . . . . . . . . | 56 | | |
| *J. V. Coney lbw b Mohsin Kamal . . . . . . . . . . | 79 | | |
| J. J. Crowe c Shaukat b Mohsin Kamal . . . . . . . | 49 | | |
| P. E. McEwan not out . . . . . . . . . . . . . . . . . . . . | 33 | (2) b Anwar . . . . . . . . . . . . . . . . . | 44 |
| †J. F. Reid not out . . . . . . . . . . . . . . . . . . . . . . | 13 | (3) not out . . . . . . . . . . . . . . . . . . | 55 |
| J. G. Bracewell (did not bat) . . . . . . . . . . . . . . | | (4) c Atiqur b Anwar . . . . . . . . . | 20 |
| B. L. Cairns (did not bat) . . . . . . . . . . . . . . . . . | | (5) not out . . . . . . . . . . . . . . . . . . | 10 |
| B 8, l-b 9, w 10, n-b 11 . . . . . . . . . . . . | 38 | B 4, l-b 2, n-b 3 . . . . . . . . | 9 |
| | — | | — |
| 1/52 2/129 3/203 4/258 (4 wkts dec.) | 291 | 1/52 2/90 3/122 (3 wkts) | 152 |

M. C. Snedden, S. L. Boock and E. J. Chatfield did not bat.

Bowling: *First Innings*—Mohsin Kamal 24–2–75–2; Atiqur 10–1–39–0; Tahir 22–5–64–2; Altaf 19–6–56–0; Anwar 18–6–29–0; Mohsin Khan 1–0–6–0; Sajid 1–0–5–0. *Second Innings*—Mohsin Kamal 5–1–24–0; Atiqur 4–0–16–0; Altaf 9–1–29–0; Tahir 6–0–27–1; Anwar 7–1–19–2; Mohsin Khan 3–0–18–0; Sajid 1–0–13–0.

### Punjab Governor's XI

| | | | |
|---|---|---|---|
| *Mohsin Khan c Snedden b Chatfield | 36 | Tahir Naqqash c Cairns b Gray | 34 |
| Sajid Ali lbw b Snedden | 4 | Mohsin Kamal c Cairns b Gray | 9 |
| Sultan Rana c J. J. Crowe b Cairns | 6 | Atiqur Rehman not out | 1 |
| Shaukat Mirza c Cairns b Boock | 51 | | |
| Mansoor Rana lbw b Bracewell | 1 | B 1, l-b 1, w 4, n-b 8 | 14 |
| †Masood Iqbal c Snedden b Gray | 4 | | — |
| Anwar Miandad lbw b Snedden | 28 | 1/20 2/48 3/75 4/86 5/134 | 189 |
| Mohammad Altaf b Boock | 1 | 6/143 7/144 8/144 9/188 | |

Bowling: Snedden 11–1–52–2; Cairns 6–1–24–1; Chatfield 10–3–24–1; Bracewell 18–4–39–1; Boock 28–16–24–2; Gray 11–3–24–3.

Umpires: Masroor Ali and Amanullah Khan.

## †PAKISTAN v NEW ZEALAND

### Fourth One-day International

At Multan, December 7. Pakistan won by one wicket. The match was delayed for half an hour because of an overcrowded stadium and a minor clash between spectators and groundstaff. Consequently the overs were reduced to 35 per side, and New Zealand came near to levelling the one-day series. Chasing a target of 214, Pakistan needed 8 to win in the last over with their last pair at the wicket, and had the match ended with the scores level victory would have gone to New Zealand for having lost fewer wickets. However, off the last ball Mohsin Kamal and Tauseef snatched a single as the visitors appealed for a run-out.

*Man of the Match*: Zaheer Abbas.

### New Zealand

| | | | |
|---|---|---|---|
| J. G. Wright b Tauseef | 11 | J. G. Bracewell not out | 14 |
| P. E. McEwan c Saadat b Kamal | 22 | D. A. Stirling not out | 1 |
| J. F. Reid run out | 10 | | |
| M. D. Crowe run out | 28 | B 18, l-b 8, w 10, n-b 1 | 37 |
| J. J. Crowe run out | 13 | | — |
| *J. V. Coney c Salim b Zaheer | 34 | 1/40 2/47 3/64 (8 wkts, 35 overs) | 213 |
| †I. D. S. Smith c Miandad b Saadat | 41 | 4/110 5/114 6/179 | |
| B. L. Cairns c Salim b Saadat | 2 | 7/183 8/211 | |

M. C. Snedden did not bat.

Bowling: Kamal 5–0–21–1; Shahid 4–0–18–0; Tauseef 7–0–30–1; Mudassar 7–0–40–0; Zaheer 6–0–35–1; Manzoor 2–0–19–0; Saadat 4–0–24–2.

### Pakistan

| | | | |
|---|---|---|---|
| Saadat Ali c Bracewell b Stirling | 6 | Shahid Mahboob lbw b M. D. Crowe | 1 |
| Shoaib Mohammad c Bracewell b Coney | 35 | †Masood Iqbal run out | 2 |
| *Zaheer Abbas b Bracewell | 73 | Mohsin Kamal not out | 5 |
| Javed Miandad c Smith b Snedden | 32 | L-b 5, w 1, n-b 2 | 8 |
| Salim Malik c Cairns b Snedden | 28 | | — |
| Manzoor Elahi c Bracewell b Snedden | 8 | 1/8 2/80 3/148 (9 wkts, 35 overs) | 214 |
| Mudassar Nazar run out | 1 | 4/154 5/164 6/169 7/199 | |
| Tauseef Ahmed not out | 15 | 8/203 9/206 | |

Bowling: M. D. Crowe 5–0–22–1; Stirling 7–0–44–1; Snedden 7–0–38–3; Cairns 5–0–42–0; Coney 4–0–27–1; Bracewell 7–0–36–1.

Umpires: Said Shah and B. K. Tahir.

## PAKISTAN v NEW ZEALAND

### Third Test Match

At Karachi, December 10, 11, 12, 14, 15. Drawn. New Zealand batted well to make 426 in reply to Pakistan's 328 runs in the first innings, though the home side were handicapped by injuries to Abdul Qadir, struck on the foot while batting, and Mudassar, who was troubled by a sore neck. The New Zealanders then had Pakistan in their clutches with five second-innings wickets gone for only 130 before a match-saving stand of 178 for the sixth wicket between Wasim Raja and Salim Malik, the latter making his fifth Test century. New Zealand threatened to walk off the field after an appeal for caught behind against Miandad was denied, play being held up for several minutes.

### Pakistan

| First innings | | Second innings | |
|---|---|---|---|
| Mudassar Nazar c Smith b Stirling | 5 | c McEwan b Stirling | 0 |
| Shoaib Mohammad c Smith b Stirling | 31 | c McEwan b Boock | 34 |
| Qasim Omar lbw b Boock | 45 | c and b M. D. Crowe | 17 |
| Javed Miandad c Smith b M. D. Crowe | 13 | c J. J. Crowe b Boock | 58 |
| *Zaheer Abbas c Smith b Stirling | 14 | c Smith b Bracewell | 3 |
| Salim Malik c and b M. D. Crowe | 50 | not out | 119 |
| Wasim Raja lbw b Stirling | 51 | not out | 60 |
| Abdul Qadir c Wright b Boock | 7 | | |
| †Anil Dalpat b Boock | 52 | | |
| Iqbal Qasim not out | 45 | | |
| Azeem Hafeez lbw b Boock | 0 | | |
| B 5, l-b 6, w 1, n-b 3 | 15 | B 2, l-b 8, n-b 7 | 17 |
| 1/14 2/80 3/92 4/102 5/124 6/204 7/226 8/315 9/319 | 328 | 1/5 2/37 3/119 4/126 5/130 | (5 wkts) 308 |

Bowling: *First Innings*—Stirling 29–5–88–4; M. D. Crowe 21–4–81–2; McEwan 4–1–6–0; Boock 41–19–83–4; Coney 5–3–5–0; Bracewell 20–5–54–0. *Second Innings*—Stirling 14–1–82–1; M. D. Crowe 10–3–26–1; Boock 30–10–83–2; Bracewell 33–11–83–1; McEwan 2–0–7–0; J. J. Crowe 2–0–9–0; Wright 1–0–1–0; Reid 2–0–7–0.

### New Zealand

| | |
|---|---|
| J. G. Wright c Anil b Iqbal | 107 |
| B. A. Edgar run out | 15 |
| J. F. Reid c Iqbal b Azeem | 97 |
| M. D. Crowe lbw b Wasim Raja | 45 |
| J. J. Crowe c Miandad b Azeem | 62 |
| *J. V. Coney c and b Iqbal | 16 |
| P. E. McEwan not out | 40 |
| †I. D. S. Smith c Salim b Iqbal | 0 |
| D. A. Stirling c Omar b Iqbal | 7 |
| J. G. Bracewell c Anil b Azeem | 30 |
| S. L. Boock c Anil b Azeem | 0 |
| B 1, l-b 5, n-b 1 | 7 |
| 1/83 2/163 3/258 4/292 5/338 6/352 7/353 8/361 9/426 | 426 |

Bowling: Mudassar 15.4–2–45–0; Azeem 46.4–9–132–4; Iqbal 57–13–133–4; Wasim Raja 33–8–97–1; Zaheer 5.2–1–13–0.

Umpires: Javed Akhtar and Shakoor Rana.

†At Karachi, December 16 (Hanif Mohammad's Benefit Match). Pakistan XI won by 23 runs. Pakistan XI 257 for five (35 overs) (Manzoor Elahi 68 not out, Javed Miandad 58, Shoaib Mohammad 44); New Zealanders 234 for five (35 overs).

# THE PAKISTANIS IN NEW ZEALAND, 1984-85

By R. T. BRITTENDEN

Pakistan's fourth visit to New Zealand was not without incident. The successes of the home side were almost outnumbered by the comings and goings of the Pakistan players. Pakistan lost a Test in New Zealand for the first time and went down two-nil in the three-match series, a result which reversed that in Pakistan a few weeks earlier. New Zealand also took the four-match one-day international series three-nil. Though lacking in lustre in most respects, Pakistan still made a good effort to square the Test series in the final match at Dunedin.

The touring team were without the talented Imran Khan, reports that he would join them from Australia proving unfounded. After joining the party just before the opening Test, and playing in the first two without success, the leg-spinner, Abdul Qadir, was sent home for disciplinary reasons. The only visible expression of discontent was his half-hearted effort to field a ball on the last afternoon of the drawn match against Wellington, whereupon he was ordered from the field by the acting-captain, Zaheer Abbas, who had arrived in time only for the last two Tests. Rashid Khan, a medium-paced bowler, was flown in to take a place in the team for the third Test.

Pakistan must have been disappointed by their performance. The captain, Javed Miandad, hardly surprisingly, failed to maintain the dizzy heights of his previous successes against New Zealand. The batsmen generally tended to go for their runs, more in one-day fashion, rather than grafting for them on slow pitches with variable bounce. The batting success – and a favourite with spectators – was the diminutive Qasim Omar. Despite a limited back-lift, he was extremely strong off the back foot. After making an unbeaten century in the first match of the tour, he went on to a notable double in the low-scoring final Test and finished by topping both Test and tour aggregates and averages.

Other encouraging features for Pakistan were the progress of Azeem Hafeez and the emergence of Wasim Akram, both left-arm seamers. Akram, in only his second Test, took ten wickets, at eighteen the youngest Test player to have achieved this feat. It was a measure of Pakistan's recognition of New Zealand conditions that they went into the last Test without a spinner. But so slowly did Pakistan bowl their overs that they often struggled to reach the modest fourteen an hour required by the playing conditions for the Test matches.

At his best against bowling up to fast-medium in pace, the New Zealand left-hander, John Reid, enjoyed particular success. He scored two centuries and during the series reached 1,000 Test runs in a shorter time than any New Zealander before him – twelve matches and twenty innings. Jeremy Coney and Martin Crowe were both impressive, and Richard Hadlee again stood out with the sustained hostility and accuracy of his bowling.

In what must have been a very trying tour for him, the Pakistan manager, Mr Yawar Saeed, remained calm and courteous.

## PAKISTANI TOUR RESULTS

*Test matches* – Played 3: Lost 2, Drawn 1.
*First-class matches* – Played 5: Won 1, Lost 2, Drawn 2.
*Win* – Canterbury.
*Losses* – New Zealand (2).
*Draws* – New Zealand, Wellington.

*Non first-class matches* – Played 4: Lost 3, No result 1. *Losses* – New Zealand (3). *No result* – New Zealand.

## TEST MATCH AVERAGES

### NEW ZEALAND – BATTING

| | *T* | *I* | *NO* | *R* | *HI* | *100s* | *Avge* |
|---|---|---|---|---|---|---|---|
| J. F. Reid | 3 | 5 | 1 | 333 | 158* | 2 | 83.25 |
| J. V. Coney | 3 | 5 | 2 | 226 | 111* | 1 | 75.33 |
| M. D. Crowe | 3 | 5 | 0 | 295 | 84 | 0 | 59.00 |
| R. J. Hadlee | 3 | 4 | 0 | 131 | 89 | 0 | 32.75 |
| J. G. Wright | 3 | 5 | 0 | 121 | 66 | 0 | 24.20 |
| I. D. S. Smith | 3 | 4 | 0 | 90 | 65 | 0 | 22.50 |
| B. L. Cairns | 3 | 4 | 1 | 65 | 36 | 0 | 21.66 |
| G. P. Howarth | 3 | 5 | 0 | 103 | 33 | 0 | 20.60 |
| J. J. Crowe | 3 | 5 | 1 | 59 | 30 | 0 | 14.75 |
| E. J. Chatfield | 3 | 4 | 4 | 27 | 21* | 0 | – |

Played in two Tests: S. L. Boock 0, 10. Played in one Test: B. P. Bracewell 3, 4.

* *Signifies not out.*

### BOWLING

| | *O* | *M* | *R* | *W* | *BB* | *Avge* |
|---|---|---|---|---|---|---|
| R. J. Hadlee | 118.5 | 29 | 306 | 16 | 6-51 | 19.12 |
| S. L. Boock | 49 | 20 | 127 | 6 | 5-117 | 21.16 |
| E. J. Chatfield | 108 | 31 | 234 | 9 | 3-47 | 26.00 |
| B. L. Cairns | 120.2 | 28 | 305 | 10 | 4-49 | 30.50 |
| B. P. Bracewell | 33 | 3 | 129 | 4 | 2-48 | 32.25 |

Also bowled: J. V. Coney 10–2–23–1.

### PAKISTAN – BATTING

| | *T* | *I* | *NO* | *R* | *HI* | *100s* | *Avge* |
|---|---|---|---|---|---|---|---|
| Qasim Omar | 3 | 5 | 0 | 248 | 96 | 0 | 49.60 |
| Mudassar Nazar | 3 | 5 | 0 | 162 | 89 | 0 | 32.40 |
| Salim Malik | 3 | 5 | 1 | 116 | 66 | 0 | 29.00 |
| Javed Miandad | 3 | 5 | 0 | 138 | 79 | 0 | 27.60 |
| Mohsin Khan | 3 | 5 | 0 | 133 | 40 | 0 | 26.60 |
| Abdul Qadir | 2 | 3 | 0 | 64 | 54 | 0 | 21.33 |
| Anil Dalpat | 3 | 5 | 0 | 65 | 21 | 0 | 13.00 |
| Wasim Raja | 2 | 3 | 0 | 29 | 14 | 0 | 9.66 |
| Wasim Akram | 2 | 4 | 3 | 9 | 8* | 0 | 9.00 |
| Azeem Hafeez | 3 | 5 | 0 | 37 | 17 | 0 | 7.40 |
| Zaheer Abbas | 2 | 4 | 0 | 24 | 12 | 0 | 6.00 |

Played in one Test: Iqbal Qasim 27*; Rashid Khan 0, 37; Shoaib Mohammad 7; Tahir Naqqash 0, 1.

* *Signifies not out.*

## BOWLING

| | *O* | *M* | *R* | *W* | *BB* | *Avge* |
|---|---|---|---|---|---|---|
| Wasim Akram ....... | 93.4 | 21 | 233 | 12 | 5-56 | 19.41 |
| Tahir Naqqash ...... | 33.2 | 5 | 81 | 3 | 2-23 | 27.00 |
| Iqbal Qasim ......... | 57 | 13 | 124 | 4 | 2-19 | 31.00 |
| Azeem Hafeez ....... | 162 | 40 | 484 | 12 | 5-127 | 40.33 |
| Mudassar Nazar ..... | 78 | 15 | 198 | 4 | 2-85 | 49.50 |

Also bowled: Abdul Qadir 81–19–212–2; Javed Miandad 3–1–7–0; Rashid Khan 32–9–97–2; Salim Malik 8.2–2–34–0; Shoaib Mohammad 1–0–4–0; Wasim Raja 3–0–13–0.

## PAKISTANI AVERAGES – FIRST-CLASS MATCHES

## PAKISTAN – BATTING

| | *M* | *I* | *NO* | *R* | *HI* | *100s* | *Avge* |
|---|---|---|---|---|---|---|---|
| Qasim Omar ........ | 5 | 9 | 1 | 464 | 114* | 1 | 51.55 |
| Ramiz Raja ......... | 2 | 3 | 1 | 81 | 70* | 0 | 40.50 |
| Mudassar Nazar ..... | 4 | 6 | 0 | 237 | 89 | 0 | 39.50 |
| Javed Miandad ...... | 4 | 7 | 0 | 267 | 112 | 1 | 38.14 |
| Salim Malik .......... | 5 | 9 | 2 | 229 | 66 | 0 | 32.71 |
| Mohsin Khan ....... | 5 | 9 | 0 | 244 | 71 | 0 | 27.11 |
| Zaheer Abbas ....... | 3 | 5 | 0 | 116 | 92 | 0 | 23.20 |
| Abdul Qadir ........ | 3 | 4 | 0 | 70 | 54 | 0 | 17.50 |
| Wasim Akram ....... | 3 | 5 | 4 | 15 | 8* | 0 | 15.00 |
| Wasim Raja ......... | 4 | 6 | 1 | 56 | 19 | 0 | 11.20 |
| Anil Dalpat ......... | 5 | 7 | 0 | 77 | 21 | 0 | 11.00 |
| Tahir Naqqash ...... | 3 | 4 | 0 | 35 | 20 | 0 | 8.75 |
| Azeem Hafeez ....... | 3 | 5 | 0 | 37 | 17 | 0 | 7.40 |

Played in two matches: Iqbal Qasim 27*, 16*; Mohsin Kamal 0, 8*. Played in one match: Rashid Khan 0, 37; Shoaib Mohammad 7.

* *Signifies not out.*

## BOWLING

| | *O* | *M* | *R* | *W* | *BB* | *Avge* |
|---|---|---|---|---|---|---|
| Wasim Raja ......... | 24.3 | 3 | 92 | 6 | 3-27 | 15.33 |
| Wasim Akram ....... | 122.4 | 30 | 302 | 12 | 5-56 | 25.16 |
| Tahir Naqqash ...... | 83.2 | 16 | 217 | 6 | 2-11 | 36.16 |
| Mohsin Kamal ...... | 40.4 | 4 | 192 | 5 | 2-28 | 38.40 |
| Azeem Hafeez ....... | 162 | 40 | 484 | 12 | 5-127 | 40.33 |
| Iqbal Qasim ......... | 90 | 23 | 191 | 4 | 2-19 | 47.75 |
| Mudassar Nazar ..... | 106 | 16 | 275 | 5 | 2-85 | 55.00 |
| Abdul Qadir ........ | 112 | 28 | 285 | 5 | 3-71 | 57.00 |

Also bowled: Javed Miandad 7–1–23–1; Qasim Omar 4–1–8–0; Ramiz Raja 2–1–4–0; Rashid Khan 32–9–97–2; Salim Malik 16.4–4–65–0; Shoaib Mohammad 1–0–4–0.

## FIELDING

Anil Dalpat 11 (10 ct, 1 st), Javed Miandad 5, Qasim Omar 4, Abdul Qadir 3, Mohsin Khan 3, Shoaib Mohammad 3, Mudassar Nazar 2, Ramiz Raja 2, Tahir Naqqash 2, Iqbal Qasim 1, Mohsin Kamal 1, Rashid Khan 1, Salim Malik 1, Wasim Akram 1, Wasim Raja 1.

## CANTERBURY v PAKISTANIS

At Christchurch, January 8, 9, 10. Pakistanis won by eight wickets. A bland pitch produced some attractive batting from both sides. There was an assertive century by Wright and brisk innings from McEwan, Latham and Hadlee before Canterbury declared. Although nearly 200 for two at one stage, the tourists collapsed and were all out for 289. One of the few Maoris to play first-class cricket, Garry MacDonald took four catches from his left-arm slow bowling, a New Zealand record. Canterbury declared again after Wright, Latham and Fulton had contributed generously to a spectacular display. The Pakistanis needed 230 in 110 minutes and twenty overs but with Hadlee suffering from a muscle strain this was a generous closure, and the visitors duly won with 26 deliveries to spare.

### Canterbury

| | | | |
|---|---|---|---|
| J. G. Wright b Miandad | 106 | – lbw b Mudassar | 57 |
| A. P. Nathu c Akram b Tahir | 21 | – c Omar b Kamal | 17 |
| P. E. McEwan c Kamal b Wasim Raja | 73 | – retired hurt | 13 |
| R. T. Latham c Ramiz b Kamal | 62 | – (5) c Tahir b Wasim Raja | 75 |
| R. J. Hadlee not out | 30 | – (7) c Omar b Kamal | 0 |
| *R. W. Fulton not out | 7 | – not out | 34 |
| V. R. Brown (did not bat) | | – (4) c Omar b Wasim Raja | 2 |
| G. K. MacDonald (did not bat) | | – st Anil b Wasim Raja | 2 |
| B 1, l-b 2, w 3, n-b 4 | 10 | L-b 5, n-b 4 | 9 |
| 1/66 2/189 3/260 4/281 (4 wkts dec.) | 309 | 1/47 2/121 3/130 4/200 5/200 6/209 (6 wkts dec.) | 209 |

S. R. McNally, C. H. Thiele and †A. W. Hart did not bat.

Bowling: *First Innings*—Akram 14–3–39–0; Kamal 12–1–78–1; Tahir 16–1–65–1; Mudassar 8–1–32–0; Wasim Raja 11–1–50–1; Salim 5–0–26–0; Miandad 4–0–16–1. *Second Innings*—Akram 15–6–30–0; Kamal 13.4–1–66–2; Tahir 13–3–36–0; Mudassar 20–0–45–1; Wasim Raja 7.3–0–27–3; Salim 0.2–0–0–0.

### Pakistanis

| | | | |
|---|---|---|---|
| Mudassar Nazar c Wright b MacDonald | 75 | | |
| Mohsin Khan c Fulton b Hadlee | 1 | – (1) c MacDonald b Thiele | 71 |
| Qasim Omar c MacDonald b Hadlee | 27 | – (2) not out | 114 |
| *Javed Miandad c McEwan b MacDonald | 112 | – (3) c Fulton b Brown | 17 |
| Salim Malik c Hart b Brown | 22 | – (4) not out | 23 |
| Ramiz Raja c and b MacDonald | 4 | | |
| Wasim Raja c and b MacDonald | 8 | | |
| †Anil Dalpat c and b MacDonald | 8 | | |
| Tahir Naqqash c Fulton b Brown | 14 | | |
| Wasim Akram not out | 6 | | |
| Mohsin Kamal c and b MacDonald | 0 | | |
| B 3, l-b 3, n-b 6 | 12 | B 4, l-b 1, n-b 3 | 8 |
| 1/5 2/55 3/194 4/234 5/239 6/253 7/262 8/279 9/288 | 289 | 1/131 2/178 (2 wkts) | 233 |

Bowling: *First Innings*—Hadlee 17–2–63–2; McNally 9–0–35–0; Thiele 10–1–46–0; Brown 22–4–77–2; MacDonald 20.4–4–62–6. *Second Innings*—Hadlee 3–0–15–0; McNally 11.4–2–54–0; Thiele 15–0–92–1; Brown 11–0–48–1; MacDonald 4–1–19–0.

Umpires: F. R. Goodall and G. C. Morris.

## †NEW ZEALAND v PAKISTAN

### First One-day International

At Napier, January 12. New Zealand won by 110 runs. Restored to the New Zealand captaincy after not being available for the Pakistan tour, Howarth was dropped off the first ball of the match and went on to make 68. New Zealand scored swiftly against sluggish fielding. Pakistan began miserably and Howarth kept a tight grip on the game. Only Miandad really battled it out.

*Man of the Match:* R. J. Hadlee.

## New Zealand

| | | | |
|---|---|---|---|
| *G. P. Howarth st Anil b Iqbal | 68 | J. V. Coney not out | 24 |
| J. G. Wright c Kamal b Tahir | 24 | R. J. Hadlee not out | 34 |
| J. F. Reid b Mudassar | 11 | B 4, l-b 17, w 14 | 35 |
| M. D. Crowe c Omar b Tahir | 32 | | |
| †I. D. S. Smith run out | 14 | 1/62 2/103 3/157 (6 wkts, 50 overs) | 277 |
| J. J. Crowe run out | 35 | 4/160 5/189 6/225 | |

B. L. Cairns, E. J. Chatfield and J. G. Bracewell did not bat.

Bowling: Azeem 10–0–47–0; Kamal 10–0–61–0; Tahir 10–0–60–2; Mudassar 10–0–51–1; Iqbal 10–1–37–1.

## Pakistan

| | | | |
|---|---|---|---|
| Mohsin Khan b Cairns | 4 | †Anil Dalpat not out | 21 |
| Mudassar Nazar c Smith b Hadlee | 17 | Azeem Hafeez c Hadlee b Howarth | 15 |
| Qasim Omar c Smith b Hadlee | 0 | Mohsin Kamal not out | 0 |
| *Javed Miandad run out | 38 | B 4, l-b 3, w 4 | 11 |
| Salim Malik run out | 11 | | |
| Wasim Raja c Smith b Chatfield | 30 | 1/24 2/24 3/26 (9 wkts, 50 overs) | 167 |
| Tahir Naqqash lbw b Cairns | 11 | 4/46 5/91 6/106 7/125 | |
| Iqbal Qasim b Chatfield | 9 | 8/132 9/161 | |

Bowling: Hadlee 8–0–30–2; Cairns 10–0–27–2; Chatfield 10–2–20–2; Coney 10–0–45–0; Bracewell 10–1–28–0; Howarth 1–0–4–1; Wright 1–0–6–0.

Umpires: D. A. Kinsella and S. J. Woodward.

# †NEW ZEALAND v PAKISTAN

## Second One-day International

At Hamilton, January 15. New Zealand won by four wickets with seven balls to spare. Pakistan gave a much better performance, despite starting diffidently, only 28 runs coming from their first fifteen overs. Then Miandad batted brilliantly on a slow pitch, taking runs readily from each bowler in turn. With slow-medium swing, and with the ball coming on to the bat very reluctantly, Coney took two for 16 from his ten overs. Wasim Raja kept Pakistan in the game with some economical medium-paced bowling, but the Crowes and Coney eventually took control.

*Man of the Match:* Javed Miandad.

## Pakistan

| | | | |
|---|---|---|---|
| Mohsin Khan c Smith b Chatfield | 49 | Mudassar Nazar not out | 22 |
| Wasim Raja c Reid b Coney | 15 | B 1, l-b 10, w 3, n-b 2 | 16 |
| Qasim Omar b Coney | 15 | | |
| *Javed Miandad not out | 90 | 1/32 2/62 3/131 (4 wkts, 50 overs) | 221 |
| Salim Malik run out | 14 | 4/160 | |

Shoaib Mohammad, †Anil Dalpat, Iqbal Qasim, Tahir Naqqash and Azeem Hafeez did not bat.

Bowling: Cairns 10–2–58–0; Hadlee 10–3–46–0; Coney 10–1–16–2; Bracewell 10–0–51–0; Chatfield 10–0–39–1.

### New Zealand

| | |
|---|---|
| *G. P. Howarth c Anil b Wasim Raja | 5 |
| J. G. Wright c Miandad b Salim | 39 |
| J. F. Reid b Wasim Raja | 17 |
| M. D. Crowe c Tahir b Iqbal | 59 |
| J. J. Crowe b Iqbal | 35 |
| J. V. Coney not out | 31 |
| †I. D. S. Smith c Azeem b Tahir | 13 |
| R. J. Hadlee not out | 13 |
| L-b 5, w 5 | 10 |
| 1/9 2/36 3/90 4/154 5/164 6/191 (6 wkts, 48.5 overs) | 222 |

B. L. Cairns, J. G. Bracewell and E. J. Chatfield did not bat.

Bowling: Wasim Raja 10–0–29–2; Salim 10–1–34–1; Iqbal 10–0–58–2; Azeem 7.5–0–36–0; Mudassar 7–0–41–0; Tahir 4–0–19–1.

Umpires: D. A. Kinsella and T. A. McCall.

## NEW ZEALAND v PAKISTAN

### First Test Match

At Wellington, January 18, 19, 20, 21, 22. Drawn. Suggestions that the Basin Reserve pitch would play into the hands of the Pakistan spinners proved unfounded. There was plenty of turn, but it was very slow.

New Zealand, who won the toss, were vulnerable at 138 for four, but Reid, showing good footwork, held firm control, and his later partners made comparative merry. Elegant on the drive and safe in defence, Reid batted 572 minutes for his 148, facing 427 balls and hitting fifteen 4s. With Hadlee he set a New Zealand sixth-wicket record against Pakistan of 145. New Zealand batted briefly into the third morning, reaching their highest total against Pakistan. Azeem Hafeez, who took half the wickets, showed commendable resolution and control.

Mohsin Khan, strong off his pads, had the lion's share of an opening stand of 62 for Pakistan before Boock initiated a minor collapse. Although Miandad then helped the assertive Salim Malik add 59, by the end of the day Pakistan were reeling at 236 for seven, still needing 56 to avoid the follow-on. It was not a happy day for the tourists. Shoaib Mohammad, playing his only innings on a nine-match tour, was unluckily run out, and Mudassar crashed a ball into the shins of Cairns at silly-point, from where it rebounded to be caught by the bowler.

But on the fourth morning it was all Pakistan. Adbul Qadir, 23 on the previous evening, reached his highest Test score, and obstinate stands with Anil Dalpat and Iqbal Qasim were stretched by rain stoppages so that New Zealand, with a lead of 170, were not batting again until an hour after lunch on the fourth day. Then, having taken 19 from the first two overs, they managed only 31 from the next nineteen, because of some very accurate left-arm slow bowling by Iqbal Qasim. Heavy rain overnight and more next morning caused the match to be abandoned at 11.45am on the last day.

### New Zealand

| | | | |
|---|---|---|---|
| *G. P. Howarth run out | 33 | – c Anil b Azeem | 17 |
| J. G. Wright c Shoaib b Azeem | 11 | – lbw b Mudassar | 11 |
| J. F. Reid b Azeem | 148 | – c Qadir b Iqbal | 3 |
| M. D. Crowe c Anil b Iqbal | 37 | – c Qadir b Iqbal | 33 |
| J. J. Crowe c Shoaib b Iqbal | 4 | – not out | 19 |
| J. V. Coney b Qadir | 48 | – not out | 18 |
| R. J. Hadlee c Miandad b Azeem | 89 | | |
| †I. D. S. Smith c and b Mudassar | 65 | | |
| B. L. Cairns b Azeem | 36 | | |
| S. L. Boock c Anil b Azeem | 0 | | |
| E. J. Chatfield not out | 3 | | |
| B 5, l-b 12, n-b 1 | 18 | L-b 2 | 2 |
| 1/24 2/61 3/126 4/138 5/230 6/375 7/414 8/488 9/488 | 492 | 1/24 2/30 3/42 4/73 (4 wkts) | 103 |

Bowling: *First Innings*—Mudassar 29-5-80-1; Azeem 48-12-127-5; Qadir 51-13-142-1; Iqbal 41-5-105-2; Wasim Raja 2-0-10-0; Shoaib 1-0-4-0; Miandad 3-1-7-0. *Second Innings*—Azeem 15-3-51-1; Mudassar 6-3-13-1; Iqbal 16-8-19-2; Qadir 8-1-18-0.

## Pakistan

| | |
|---|---|
| Mudassar Nazar c and b Boock | 38 |
| Mohsin Khan c Wright b Boock | 40 |
| Shoaib Mohammad run out | 7 |
| Qasim Omar b Boock | 8 |
| *Javed Miandad c Smith b Boock | 30 |
| Salim Malik c Cairns b Hadlee | 66 |
| Wasim Raja c M. D. Crowe b Boock | 14 |
| Abdul Qadir c Smith b Hadlee | 54 |
| †Anil Dalpat c Smith b Chatfield | 15 |
| Iqbal Qasim not out | 27 |
| Azeem Hafeez c Boock b Cairns | 3 |
| B 9, l-b 9, n-b 2 | 20 |
| 1/62 2/85 3/95 4/102 5/161 6/187 7/223 8/288 9/309 | 322 |

Bowling: Hadlee 32-11-70-2; Cairns 27.4-5-65-1; Chatfield 25-10-52-1; Boock 45-18-117-5.

Umpires: G. C. Morris and S. J. Woodward.

## NEW ZEALAND v PAKISTAN

### Second Test Match

At Auckland, January 25, 26, 27, 28. New Zealand won by an innings and 99 runs, with 130 minutes and a full day to spare. Sent in on a pitch which was not nearly as lively as its green tinge suggested it might be, Pakistan reached 58 for two at lunch and proceeded quite cheerfully to 93 before Omar was caught at slip off the persistent Chatfield. Zaheer, seldom successful against New Zealand bowling, was well caught, also at slip, and Miandad was the victim of a ball from Chatfield which got up very quickly. Pakistan finished a day shortened by rain and bad light by 135 minutes in desperate trouble at 147 for eight.

On the second day New Zealand, after winding up the Pakistan innings in 23 minutes, scored 248 for three wickets, and on the third they reached 451 for nine. Wright, full of aggression, shared an opening stand of 60 with Howarth and one of 48 with Reid, but it was the partnership between Reid and Martin Crowe – 137 in 143 minutes – which put New Zealand on the road to victory. Reid blended his commendable powers of concentration with forcing strokes in an innings lasting just over eight hours. Crowe reached a fine 84 before he was out in unusual circumstances. Because of the slow over-rate play went on, in order to fulfil the requirement of fourteen overs an hour, after six o'clock and in the last over he was superbly caught at short leg by a substitute fieldsman, Shoaib Mohammad, when the ball ran up his pad and took the edge of his bat.

Reid reached his fifth Test century early on a rain-affected third day. At 123 he had to retire after being hit in the mouth, but later returned. New Zealand's lead of 282, only 16 short of its record margin, set at Lord's in 1973, was more than enough to account for Pakistan, whose batsmen, Mudassar excepted, seemed to decide their chances of long batting life were slim on a pitch of variable bounce. They chased runs with a vigour undiminished by their rapid comings and goings, and the match was over before tea on the fourth day. Having gone in first, Mudassar was last out after 231 minutes of good, watchful batting.

## Pakistan

| | | | |
|---|---|---|---|
| Mudassar Nazar lbw b Hadlee | 12 | – b Cairns | 89 |
| Mohsin Khan c Coney b Cairns | 26 | – c Coney b Hadlee | 1 |
| Qasim Omar c M. D. Crowe b Cairns | 33 | – c Cairns b Chatfield | 22 |
| *Javed Miandad c Smith b Chatfield | 26 | – (5) c Smith b Chatfield | 1 |
| Zaheer Abbas c J. J. Crowe b Cairns | 6 | – (6) c sub (J. G. Bracewell) b Hadlee | 12 |
| Salim Malik not out | 41 | – (4) c Cairns b Chatfield | 0 |
| Wasim Raja c Smith b Chatfield | 4 | – c Wright b Boock | 11 |
| Abdul Qadir run out | 0 | – lbw b Cairns | 10 |
| †Anil Dalpat c J. J. Crowe b Hadlee | 7 | – lbw b Cairns | 6 |
| Wasim Akram c M. D. Crowe b Hadlee | 0 | – (11) not out | 0 |
| Azeem Hafeez c Boock b Hadlee | 6 | – (10) lbw b Cairns | 17 |
| L-b 5, n-b 3 | 8 | L-b 11, n-b 3 | 14 |
| 1/33 2/58 3/93 4/105 5/111 6/115 7/123 8/147 9/151 | 169 | 1/13 2/54 3/54 4/57 5/79 6/122 7/140 8/152 9/178 | 183 |

Bowling: *First Innings*—Hadlee 19.5–3–60–4; Cairns 29–10–73–3; Chatfield 14–5–24–2; Coney 4–1–7–0. *Second Innings*—Hadlee 17–1–66–2; Chatfield 19–5–47–3; Cairns 19.4–8–49–4; Boock 4–2–10–1.

## New Zealand

| | |
|---|---|
| *G. P. Howarth c Miandad b Mudassar | 13 |
| J. G. Wright c Salim b Akram | 66 |
| J. F. Reid not out | 158 |
| M. D. Crowe c sub (Shoaib Mohammad) b Qadir | 84 |
| S. L. Boock c Wasim Raja b Azeem | 10 |
| J. J. Crowe run out | 30 |
| J. V. Coney c Anil b Mudassar | 25 |
| R. J. Hadlee c Mohsin b Azeem | 13 |
| †I. D. S. Smith c Miandad b Akram | 7 |
| B. L. Cairns b Azeem | 23 |
| E. J. Chatfield not out | 1 |
| B 6, l-b 9, n-b 6 | 21 |
| 1/60 2/108 3/245 4/278 5/359 6/366 7/387 8/411 9/447 (9 wkts dec.) | 451 |

Bowling: Azeem 47–10–157–3; Akram 34.4–4–105–2; Mudassar 34–5–85–2; Qadir 22–5–52–1; Wasim Raja 1–0–3–0; Salim 8.2–2–34–0.

Umpires: F. R. Goodall and S. J. Woodward.

## WELLINGTON v PAKISTANIS

At Wellington, February 1, 2, 3. Drawn. This was not a very satisfactory match. Zaheer's 92 lifted the batting level, but it took the Pakistanis 320 minutes to make 217 for nine declared. The left-arm spinner, Gray, bowling into a stiff breeze, caused most trouble after Chatfield had taken three early wickets, the first of them giving him the Wellington record of 331, one more than R. W. Blair. After Wellington had declared in arrears, Pakistan batted quietly on the third morning before the use of part-time bowlers encouraged a more vigorous approach. Salim Malik scored 61 from 67 deliveries and Wellington were eventually left with 83 minutes and twenty overs to score 235. Early losses precluded a chase and the match was called off with eleven overs unbowled.

### Pakistanis

| | | | |
|---|---|---|---|
| Mohsin Khan c Maguiness b Cederwall | 12 | lbw b Chatfield | 27 |
| Qasim Omar c McSweeney b Chatfield | 20 | c and b Chatfield | 55 |
| Ramiz Raja c McSweeney b Chatfield | 7 | not out | 70 |
| Salim Malik b Chatfield | 7 | b Larsen | 61 |
| *Zaheer Abbas c Vance b Gray | 92 | | |
| Wasim Raja st McSweeney b Gray | 19 | (5) not out | 0 |
| Adbul Qadir st McSweeney b Gray | 6 | | |
| †Anil Dalpat c and b Gray | 4 | | |
| Tahir Naqqash c Maguiness b Gray | 20 | | |
| Iqbal Qasim not out | 16 | | |
| Mohsin Kamal not out | 8 | | |
| B 2, l-b 2, n-b 2 | 6 | L-b 3, n-b 6 | 9 |
| 1/35 2/35 3/44 4/57 5/98 6/116 7/128 8/179 9/198 (9 wkts dec.) | 217 | 1/51 2/120 3/221 (3 wkts dec.) | 222 |

Bowling: *First Innings*—Chatfield 27–5–60–3; Cederwall 9–0–42–1; Maguiness 16–4–42–0; Gray 29–8–68–5; Larsen 2–1–1–0. *Second Innings*—Chatfield 18–5–17–2; Cederwall 16–3–56–0; Maguiness 19–3–68–0; Gray 4–1–12–0; Larsen 6–2–7–1; Ormiston 6–0–37–0; Ritchie 3–0–22–0.

### Wellington

| | | | |
|---|---|---|---|
| J. G. Boyle b Kamal | 16 | c Iqbal b Tahir | 15 |
| E. J. Gray c Anil b Kamal | 11 | lbw b Tahir | 1 |
| *R. H. Vance b Qadir | 66 | not out | 23 |
| R. W. Ormiston c Anil b Qadir | 67 | not out | 10 |
| D. F. Oakley c and b Qadir | 2 | | |
| †E. B. McSweeney c Ramiz b Wasim Raja | 26 | | |
| T. D. Ritchie b Wasim Raja | 1 | | |
| G. R. Larsen not out | 0 | | |
| G. N. Cederwall not out | 1 | | |
| B 3, l-b 11, w 1 | 15 | L-b 2, n-b 2 | 4 |
| 1/25 2/41 3/157 4/159 5/198 6/199 7/204 (7 wkts dec.) | 205 | 1/2 2/27 (2 wkts) | 53 |

S. J. Maguiness and E. J. Chatfield did not bat.

Bowling: *First Innings*—Tahir 13–4–24–0; Kamal 9–1–28–2; Iqbal 28–6–66–0; Qadir 28–7–71–3; Wasim Raja 3–2–2–2. *Second Innings*—Tahir 8–3–11–2; Kamal 6–1–20–0; Iqbal 5–4–1–0; Qadir 3–2–2–0; Omar 4–1–8–0; Salim 3–2–5–0; Ramiz Raja 2–1–4–0.

Umpires: R. L. McHarg and S. J. Woodward.

## †NEW ZEALAND v PAKISTAN

### Third One-day International

At Christchurch, February 6. New Zealand won by 13 runs. On a splendid batting pitch, Wright and Reid scored 92 in 67 minutes, but the promise of a really substantial score was not fulfilled as Pakistan's bowling and fielding became much more determined. Pakistan lost three wickets quickly before Miandad and Zaheer added 83 in an hour. Although their sixth wicket fell at 129, Ramiz then drove strongly and sprinted furiously, an enthusiastic approach which brought about a sharp decline in New Zealand's performance. He scored 75 from as many deliveries and added 108 with Dalpat. But his spirited effort did not last quite long enough: 26 were needed from the last three overs and 15 from the last, in which Hadlee took three wickets with his first four balls.

*Man of the Match*: J. F. Reid.

## New Zealand

| | | | |
|---|---|---|---|
| *G. P. Howarth c Anil b Azeem | 12 | †I. D. S. Smith not out | 5 |
| J. G. Wright c Salim b Tahir | 65 | J. G. Bracewell not out | 20 |
| J. F. Reid c Salim b Azeem | 88 | | |
| M. D. Crowe run out | 20 | B 3, l-b 5, w 4 | 12 |
| B. L. Cairns c and b Mudassar | 8 | | |
| R. J. Hadlee c Anil b Tahir | 9 | 1/29 2/121 3/166 (8 wkts, 50 overs) | 264 |
| J. V. Coney c Iqbal b Azeem | 12 | 4/177 5/192 6/216 | |
| J. J. Crowe c Wasim Raja b Tahir | 13 | 7/237 8/241 | |

E. J. Chatfield did not bat.

Bowling: Wasim Raja 10–1–34–0; Azeem 10–0–56–3; Iqbal 5–0–33–0; Mudassar 10–0–56–1; Tahir 8–0–40–3; Salim 3–0–16–0; Zaheer 4–0–21–0.

## Pakistan

| | | | |
|---|---|---|---|
| Mudassar Nazar c J. J. Crowe b Cairns | 8 | Tahir Naqqash c Howarth b Hadlee | 11 |
| Qasim Omar run out | 1 | Azeem Hafeez not out | 1 |
| Salim Malik b Cairns | 0 | Iqbal Qasim b Hadlee | 0 |
| Zaheer Abbas st Smith b Bracewell | 58 | B 4, l-b 6, w 4, n-b 4 | 18 |
| *Javed Miandad c M. D. Crowe b Cairns | 30 | | |
| Ramiz Raja run out | 75 | 1/1 2/1 3/22 4/105 (49.4 overs) | 251 |
| Wasim Raja c Howarth b Chatfield | 12 | 5/105 6/129 7/237 | |
| †Anil Dalpat c M. D. Crowe b Hadlee | 37 | 8/250 9/250 | |

Bowling: Cairns 10–4–39–3; Hadlee 9.4–1–32–3; Chatfield 10–0–75–1; Coney 10–0–44–0; Bracewell 10–1–51–1.

Umpires: F. R. Goodall and G. C. Morris.

# NEW ZEALAND v PAKISTAN

## Third Test Match

At Dunedin, February 9, 10, 11, 13, 14. New Zealand won by two wickets. Expectations of a seamers' pitch persuaded both sides to go into the match without a spin bowler. Brendon Bracewell was recalled by New Zealand after five years without a Test. Pakistan struggled to 76 for one at lunch – Howarth won the toss for the third successive time – and lost Mohsin only through bad calling. Miandad and Omar batted beautifully while adding 141, with Miandad, at 27 years of age, becoming the youngest player ever to reach 5,000 Test runs, and Pakistan seemed on course for a big total; but for no good reason they lost five wickets for 10 runs in the last half-hour of the opening day.

New Zealand in turn suffered a collapse in the awkward conditions, only Martin Crowe looking capable of significant progress. His attacking strokes were strong and sweetly timed, and he waited for his opportunities with a welcome maturity. Of the Pakistan bowlers, Wasim Akram made a very good impression. His line was good, his energy unbounded, and he moved the ball readily off the seam.

In Pakistan's second innings Omar again played with distinction, and when the last pair, Rashid Khan and Akram, scored 42 together New Zealand were left to make 278 to win. The bounce was unreliable, there was considerable sideways movement from the seamers, and when Akram wrecked the top of the order New Zealand were a sorry 23 for four wickets. Martin Crowe and Coney – so often at his best in a crisis – fought through to 114 by the close of play, then batted patiently and proficiently on the last morning. Crowe was out shortly before lunch, his stand with Coney having realised 157 in 229 minutes.

Pakistan prospered again in the early afternoon, taking New Zealand's seventh wicket at 216. Cairns, not wearing a helmet, was then hit on the head by Akram and at 228 Bracewell went, whereupon Chatfield joined Coney. Cairns had declared a willingness to bat again if necessary but he was badly concussed and could barely have walked to the wicket without assistance. In fact he spent three days in hospital. By tea Chatfield, no batsman but with a mixture of determination and good fortune, had helped Coney to take the score to 235. Coney, on 97, was dropped behind off Rashid from the first ball of the final session. He had already been missed by Akram at 37, an easy caught and bowled.

In the last over before tea Akram had received an official warning for over-use of short-pitched balls. Now Pakistan's deep-set fields gave Coney plenty of singles – he had 21 on end at one stage – but Chatfield showed such willingness to take the strike that in their unbroken, match-winning stand of 50 he had 84 balls to Coney's 48. Coney reached his second Test century and Chatfield made his best Test score, his runs being almost outnumbered by his bruises. The excitement was intense as the two Wellington players inched their side to victory.

## Pakistan

| First innings | | Second innings | |
|---|---|---|---|
| Mudassar Nazar c J. J. Crowe b Hadlee | 18 | c Coney b Bracewell | 5 |
| Mohsin Khan run out | 39 | c M. D. Crowe b Hadlee | 27 |
| Qasim Omar c J. J. Crowe b Coney | 96 | c Smith b Chatfield | 89 |
| *Javed Miandad c Smith b Hadlee | 79 | c Reid b Hadlee | 2 |
| Zaheer Abbas c Reid b Hadlee | 6 | lbw b Cairns | 0 |
| Rashid Khan c M. D. Crowe b Hadlee | 0 | (9) b Bracewell | 37 |
| †Anil Dalpat b Bracewell | 16 | b Chatfield | 21 |
| Salim Malik lbw b Hadlee | 0 | (6) b Cairns | 9 |
| Tahir Naqqash c Wright b Hadlee | 0 | (8) run out | 1 |
| Azeem Hafeez c Smith b Bracewell | 4 | b Chatfield | 7 |
| Wasim Akram not out | 1 | not out | 8 |
| B 1, l-b 2, n-b 12 | 15 | B 1, l-b 9, n-b 7 | 17 |
| 1/25 2/100 3/241 4/245 5/245 6/251 7/251 8/255 9/273 | 274 | 1/5 2/72 3/75 4/76 5/103 6/157 7/166 8/169 9/181 | 223 |

Bowling: *First Innings*—Hadlee 24–5–51–6; Bracewell 18.2–1–81–2; Cairns 22–0–77–0; Chatfield 24–6–46–0; Coney 6–1–16–1. *Second Innings*—Hadlee 26–9–59–2; Bracewell 14.4–2–48–2; Cairns 22–5–41–2; Chatfield 26–5–65–3.

## New Zealand

| First innings | | Second innings | |
|---|---|---|---|
| *G. P. Howarth b Akram | 23 | c Mohsin b Akram | 17 |
| J. G. Wright c Omar b Azeem | 32 | c Mohsin b Azeem | 1 |
| J. F. Reid b Akram | 24 | c Anil b Akram | 0 |
| M. D. Crowe c Miandad b Akram | 57 | c Mudassar b Tahir | 84 |
| J. J. Crowe lbw b Akram | 6 | lbw b Akram | 0 |
| J. V. Coney c Anil b Rashid | 24 | not out | 111 |
| R. J. Hadlee c Anil b Rashid | 18 | b Azeem | 11 |
| †I. D. S. Smith lbw b Tahir | 12 | c Miandad b Akram | 6 |
| B. L. Cairns c Anil b Akram | 6 | retired hurt | 0 |
| B. P. Bracewell c Rashid b Tahir | 3 | c Tahir b Akram | 4 |
| E. J. Chatfield not out | 2 | not out | 21 |
| B 7, l-b 5, n-b 1 | 13 | B 5, l-b 6, w 1, n-b 11 | 23 |
| 1/41 2/81 3/84 4/92 5/149 6/185 7/203 8/205 9/216 | 220 | 1/4 2/5 3/23 4/23 5/180 6/208 7/216 8/228 | (8 wkts) 278 |

Bowling: *First Innings*—Rashid 23–7–64–2; Azeem 20–6–65–1; Akram 26–7–56–5; Tahir 16.4–4–23–2. *Second Innings*—Azeem 32–9–84–2; Akram 33–10–72–5; Rashid 9–2–33–0; Tahir 16.4–1–58–1; Mudassar 9–2–20–0.

Umpires: F. R. Goodall and G. C. Morris.

## †NEW ZEALAND v PAKISTAN

### Fourth One-day International

At Auckland, February 16, 17. No result. Pakistan were facing another defeat when rain ended the match. Their main batsmen could make nothing of some accurate bowling, the seventh wicket falling at 92. But Ramiz Raja repeated his cheerful Christchurch display and received splendid assistance from Tahir Naqqash. These two scored 64 together in seven overs.

## Pakistan

| | |
|---|---|
| Mudassar Nazar c M. D. Crowe b Chatfield | 10 |
| Qasim Omar c Smith b Snedden | 6 |
| Zaheer Abbas c Smith b Chatfield | 4 |
| *Javed Miandad run out | 9 |
| Ramiz Raja st Smith b Bracewell | 59 |
| Salim Malik lbw b Chatfield | 7 |
| Wasim Raja c Howarth b Bracewell | 0 |
| †Anil Dalpat c Bracewell b McEwan | 3 |
| Tahir Naqqash c Wright b Snedden | 61 |
| Rashid Khan not out | 8 |
| Wasim Akram b Hadlee | 2 |
| B 3, l-b 9, w 8 | 20 |
| 1/17 2/25 3/25 4/61 5/70 6/73 7/92 8/156 9/182 (49.1 overs) | 189 |

Bowling: Chatfield 10–2–20–3; Hadlee 9.1–3–24–1; Snedden 10–3–36–2; McEwan 10–0–54–1; Bracewell 10–1–43–2.

## New Zealand

*G. P. Howarth, J. G. Wright, J. F. Reid, M. D. Crowe, J. V. Coney, R. J. Hadlee, †I. D. S. Smith, P. E. McEwan, J. G. Bracewell, M. C. Snedden and E. J. Chatfield.

Umpires: T. A. McCall and S. J. Woodward.

# THE SRI LANKANS IN AUSTRALIA, 1984-85

Sri Lanka undertook a programme of 22 matches between December 1984 and March 1985. Their one first-class fixture, against an under-strength Western Australia side, was won, but the main purpose of the tour was to take part, with Australia and West Indies, in the triangular World Series Cup, followed by participation in the Benson and Hedges "World Championship of Cricket", and in most of the twelve one-day internationals which this involved their bowling gave the Sri Lankans scant chance of success. Their one victory came at Melbourne in the second of their five WSC matches against Australia. The West Indians overwhelmed them.

The batting leant too heavily on the captain, Duleep Mendis, and Roy Dias, though Amal Silva, Aravinda de Silva and Arjuna Ranatunga had their moments. In the last match of the tour something of a sensation was caused when the West Indian batsmen, Richardson and Gomes, had to retire through injury after being struck in the face on an unpredictable Melbourne pitch. Richardson was hit by Ashantha de Mel and Gomes, whose nose was broken, by Rumesh Ratnayake. Allegations calling Ratnayake's action into question brought a strong denial from Neil Chanmugam, the Sri Lankan manager, and were not substantiated by the evidence of television.

## WESTERN AUSTRALIA v SRI LANKANS

At Perth, December 31, January 1, 2. Sri Lankans won by seven wickets. Western Australia fielded five players new to first-class cricket, and after a first-innings declaration their performance declined. In Sri Lanka's first innings Mendis and de Silva enjoyed a partnership of 98 in 50 minutes which wrested the initiative. John, de Mel and Ratnayeke then ran through the Western Australian second innings, enabling the tourists to win with over a day to spare.

### Western Australia

| | | | |
|---|---|---|---|
| G. R. Marsh c Silva b de Mel | 8 | b John | 13 |
| S. C. Clements c Dias b Ratnayeke | 60 | c John b Ratnayeke | 19 |
| M. W. McPhee c de Mel b Ranatunga | 19 | b John | 6 |
| R. W. Gartrell c Wettimuny b de Mel | 21 | c Kuruppu b John | 3 |
| P. Gonnella c Dias b de Mel | 22 | c sub b John | 10 |
| D. D. Smith c Kuruppu b Ratnayeke | 0 | c Kuruppu b John | 2 |
| †T. J. Zoehrer not out | 69 | lbw b Ratnayeke | 0 |
| *W. M. Clark run out | 25 | b Ratnayeke | 1 |
| G. E. Bush not out | 1 | c sub b de Mel | 21 |
| B. A. Reid (did not bat) | – | not out | 0 |
| E. G. Spalding (did not bat) | – | lbw b de Mel | 0 |
| B 4, l-b 7, n-b 9 | 20 | L-b 2, n-b 2 | 4 |
| 1/17 2/80 3/109 4/135 5/141 6/143 7/206 (7 wkts dec.) | 245 | 1/15 2/25 3/41 4/42 5/53 6/55 7/55 8/59 9/79 | 79 |

Bowling: *First Innings*—John 19–2–60–0; de Mel 19–3–66–3; Ratnayeke 15–1–66–2; Ratnayake 1–0–9–0; Ranatunga 8.3–2–20–1; Wettimuny 3.3–0–13–0. *Second Innings*—John 11–2–28–5; de Mel 6.3–0–24–2; Ratnayeke 12–4–25–3.

### Sri Lankans

| | | | |
|---|---|---|---|
| S. Wettimuny c Zoehrer b Spalding | 6 | c Zoehrer b Spalding | 13 |
| S. A. R. Silva c Zoehrer b Clark | 41 | c Zoehrer b Spalding | 11 |
| †D. S. B. P. Kuruppu c Zoehrer b Smith | 21 | not out | 1 |
| R. L. Dias b Smith | 3 | c Zoehrer b Reid | 54 |

| | | |
|---|---|---|
| *L. R. D. Mendis run out | 67 | |
| P. A. de Silva c Smith b Spalding | 40 | |
| J. R. Ratnayeke run out | 4 | – not out 18 |
| A. L. F. de Mel c Gonnella b Bush | 0 | |
| R. J. Ratnayake not out | 18 | |
| V. B. John not out | 10 | |
| L-b 4, n-b 3 | 7 | B 4, l-b 3, w 1, n-b 3 11 |
| 1/21 2/71 3/77 4/87 5/185 6/189 7/191 | (8 wkts dec.) 217 | 1/17 2/35 3/98 (3 wkts) 108 |

A. Ranatunga did not bat.

Bowling: *First Innings*—Spalding 15–3–59–2; Reid 10–1–40–0; Bush 11–1–43–1; Clark 11–5–34–1; Smith 6–1–29–2; Gonnella 1–0–8–0. *Second Innings*—Spalding 5–0–42–2; Reid 12.1–3–33–1; Bush 9–3–26–0.

Umpires: W. M. Powell and D. G. Weser.

†At Brisbane, January 5. Sri Lankans won by five wickets. Queensland 212 for five (50 overs) (G. S. Trimble 100 not out, B. A. Courtice 44); Sri Lankans 213 for five (47.3 overs) (L. R. D. Mendis 72 not out, R. S. Madugalle 45).

†At Brisbane, January 6. Sri Lankans won on faster scoring-rate after rain ended play. Sri Lankans 240 for six (50 overs) (R. L. Dias 110 not out, P. A. de Silva 45); Queensland 153 for no wkt (30.1 overs) (R. B. Kerr 87 not out, B. A. Courtice 55 not out).

†At Fremantle, January 30, 31. Sri Lankans won by two wickets. Western Australian Colts 225 for four dec. (P. Gonnella 100 not out, G. Ireland 55) and 166 for five dec. (R. Gartsell 52); Sri Lankans 190 for seven dec. and 192 for eight (L. R. D. Mendis 50; B. Mulder four for 74).

†At Maryborough, February 6. Sri Lankans won by 108 runs. Sri Lankans 313 for eight (50 overs) (D. S. B. P. Kuruppu 72, R. S. Madugalle 71, L. R. D. Mendis 71); Central Highlands 205 (47.3 overs) P. Brady 79; U. S. H. Karnain five for 23).

†At Shepparton, February 8. Sri Lankans won by 100 runs. Sri Lankans 279 for eight (50 overs) (S. A. R. Silva 105, R. S. Madugalle 80); Goulburn-Murray 179 (49 overs) (J. Hill 50).

†At Yea, February 10. Sri Lankans won by 78 runs. Sri Lankans 253 (48.4 overs) (S. Wettimuny 70; T. Selby five for 42); Upper Goulburn 175 (50 overs).

†At Leongatha, February 12. Sri Lankans won by four wickets. South Gippsland 203 (50 overs) (I. Eddy 51); Sri Lankans 204 for six (45 overs) (L. R. D. Mendis 62 not out).

†At Morwell, February 14. Sri Lankans won by seven wickets and batted on. Gippsland 100 (35.1 overs); Sri Lankans 238 for seven (50 overs) (A. Ranatunga 89, R. S. Madugalle 62).

†At Hastings, February 16. Sri Lankans won by 150 runs. Sri Lankans 327 for nine (49 overs) (J. R. Ratnayeke 100, S. A. R. Silva 61, D. S. B. P. Kuruppu 59, A. Ranatunga 56; L. Slocombe four for 66); Mornington Peninsula 177 (43.2 overs) (D. M. Vonhagt four for 45).

*Sri Lanka's matches v Australia and West Indies in the Benson and Hedges World Series Cup may be found in that section.*

## AUSTRALIA v NEW ZEALAND, 1985-86

New Zealand beat Australia in a Test series for the first time, when they toured that country in November and December, 1985. R. J. Hadlee's haul of 33 wickets was the third-highest in a three-match series, and the highest by a New Zealand bowler. He took fifteen wickets in the first Test, a feat surpassed only by J. C. Laker, S. F. Barnes and R. A. L. Massie, while his return of nine for 52 in the first innings was the fourth-best in all Tests and the best for New Zealand. He was also involved in the dismissal of the tenth batsman, catching G. F. Lawson off the bowling of V. R. Brown.

*First Test:* At Brisbane, November 8, 9, 10, 11, 12. New Zealand won by an innings and 41 runs. Australia 179 (K. C. Wessels 70; R. J. Hadlee nine for 52) and 333 (A. R. Border 152 not out, G. R. J. Matthews 115; R. J. Hadlee six for 71); New Zealand 553 for seven dec. (M. D. Crowe 188, J. F. Reid 108, R. J. Hadlee 54, J. G. Wright 46, Extras 45).

*Second Test:* At Sydney, November 22, 23, 24, 25, 26. Australia won by four wickets. New Zealand 293 (J. G. Bracewell 83 not out, B. A. Edgar 50; R. G. Holland six for 106) and 193 (B. A. Edgar 52, J. G. Wright 43; R. G. Holland four for 68); Australia 227 (G. M. Ritchie 89, G. R. J. Matthews 50; R. J. Hadlee five for 65) and 260 for six (D. C. Boon 81, W. B. Phillips 63).

*Third Test:* At Perth, November 30, December 1, 2, 3, 4. New Zealand won by six wickets. Australia 203 (R. J. Hadlee five for 65) and 259 (A. R. Border 83, D. C. Boon 50, G. M. Ritchie 44; R. J. Hadlee six for 90); New Zealand 299 (B. A. Edgar 74, M. D. Crowe 71; G. F. Lawson four for 79) and 164 for four (M. D. Crowe 42 not out).

*Full details of the New Zealanders' tour of Australia will appear in the 1987 edition of* Wisden.

---

## SRI LANKA v INDIA, 1985-86

India, led by Kapil Dev, toured Sri Lanka in August and September, 1985. The first and third Tests were drawn but Sri Lanka achieved their first-ever Test victory when they took the second Test at Colombo by 149 runs. India's only success came in the first one-day international, Sri Lanka winning the second and the third being drawn after rain ended play.

*First Test:* Sinhalese Sports Club Ground, Colombo, August 30, 31, September 1, 3, 4. Drawn. India 218 (S. M. Gavaskar 51; A. L. F. de Mel five for 64) and 251 (D. B. Vengsarkar 98 not out, L. S. Rajput 61, R. J. Shastri 40; R. J. Ratnayake six for 85); Sri Lanka 347 (A. Ranatunga 111, R. S. Madugalle 103, L. R. D. Mendis 51) and 61 for four.

*Second Test:* P. Saravanamuttu Stadium, Colombo, September 6, 7, 8, 10, 11. Sri Lanka won by 149 runs. Sri Lanka 385 (S. A. R. Silva 111, R. L. Dias 95, R. S. Madugalle 54, L. R. D. Mendis 51; Chetan Sharma five for 118) and 206 for three dec. (P. A. de Silva 75, R. L. Dias 60 not out); India 244 (K. Srikkanth 64, M. Amarnath 60, S. M. Gavaskar 52; R. J. Ratnayake four for 76) and 198 (Kapil Dev 78; R. J. Ratnayake five for 49).

*Third Test:* Kandy, September 14, 15, 16, 18, 19. Drawn. India 249 (D. B. Vengsarkar 62, S. M. Gavaskar 49, K. Srikkanth 40; F. S. Ahangama five for 52) and 325 for five dec. (M. Amarnath 116 not out, R. J. Shastri 81, K. Srikkanth 47, M. Azharuddin 43); Sri Lanka 198 (L. R. D. Mendis 53; Maninder Singh four for 31) and 307 for seven (L. R. D. Mendis 124, R. L. Dias 106).

*Full details of the Indians' tour of Sri Lanka will appear in the 1987 edition of* Wisden.

# THE NEW ZEALANDERS IN WEST INDIES, 1984-85

By TONY COZIER

New Zealand's second tour of West Indies, condensed into seven weeks with four Tests, three three-day first-class matches and five one-day internationals, was a struggle from start to finish. The assessment of their own captain, Geoff Howarth, was that his team were two years past their peak; and the absence of their most reliable batsman of recent series, the left-handed John Reid, who declined to tour because of teaching commitments, was a telling setback. They confronted a strong, confident West Indies team, to whom the main threat was the amount of cricket they had played internationally in the previous eighteen months.

In the circumstances, the New Zealanders were outclassed. They managed to draw the first two Tests, the first with the help of the weather, before losing the third and fourth by wide margins. They also lost all five one-day internationals, in which they showed little interest, and were under pressure to draw the three matches against combined teams. As was the case on their previous tour in 1972, they did not win a single match, but on that occasion they lost none either.

Their batsmen foundered against the West Indian fast bowlers, of whom Malcolm Marshall, with 27 wickets at 18 apiece, was the fastest, most aggressive and most feared. Only New Zealand's tall, upright vice-captain, Jeremy Coney, batted with any consistency, and he, ironically, had his left forearm fractured in the final Test during a particularly torrid spell from Marshall and Joel Garner which brought justified complaints from the New Zealand manager and captain about intimidatory bowling.

The Crowe brothers, Martin and Jeff, were always positive in their attitude and were the only New Zealand century-makers of the series; Martin in the second Test, Jeff in the fourth. Yet in six other innings in the series Martin managed only 28 runs and Jeff only one other score above 50. The disappointing form of the experienced John Wright and Howarth himself, and the failure of the nineteen-year-old opening batsman, Ken Rutherford, exposed the middle order to constant pressure.

Richard Hadlee confirmed his standing as a fast bowler of genuine class, but, unlike Marshall, he lacked support of similar quality. Ewen Chatfield did his job honestly and as well as his limitations would allow, but neither the left-arm Gary Troup nor the lively but erratic Derek Stirling matched expectations. When Hadlee was resting, New Zealand had little alternative but to bowl defensively.

It was the first series for the West Indians since the retirement of their long-serving captain, Clive Lloyd, following their tour of Australia. Vivian Richards was appointed to replace him, but the time was too brief and the play too one-sided to determine whether he would have a different style of leadership. Certainly, the new responsibility had no adverse effect on Richards's batting. The opposite was probably the case, as he scored consistently with important innings in the first and third Tests. Except for the second Test, when they made full use of the perfect batting conditions of the Bourda ground, West Indies scored steadily rather than spectacularly, but at no time was their superiority threatened.

It was the first time the two teams had met since the troubled short series in New Zealand five years earlier, but any fears that there might have been disagreeable repercussions proved groundless. The New Zealanders were popular tourists and the matches were played in an excellent spirit.

## NEW ZEALAND TOUR RESULTS

*Test matches* – Played 4: Drawn 2, Lost 2.
*First-class matches* – Played 7: Drawn 5, Lost 2.
*Draws* – West Indies (2), Shell Shield XI, West Indies Under-23 XI, President's XI.
*Losses* – West Indies (2).
*Non first-class matches* – Played 5: Lost 5. *Losses* – West Indies (5).

## TEST MATCH AVERAGES

### WEST INDIES – BATTING

| | *T* | *I* | *NO* | *R* | *HI* | *100s* | *Avge* |
|---|---|---|---|---|---|---|---|
| R. B. Richardson .... | 4 | 6 | 0 | 378 | 185 | 1 | 63.00 |
| I. V. A. Richards .... | 4 | 6 | 1 | 310 | 105 | 1 | 62.00 |
| D. L. Haynes ........ | 4 | 8 | 2 | 344 | 90 | 0 | 57.33 |
| C. G. Greenidge ..... | 4 | 7 | 2 | 264 | 100 | 1 | 52.80 |
| J. Garner ........... | 4 | 3 | 2 | 49 | 37* | 0 | 49.00 |
| A. L. Logie ......... | 4 | 6 | 1 | 166 | 52 | 0 | 33.20 |
| P. J. L. Dujon ....... | 4 | 6 | 1 | 156 | 70 | 0 | 31.20 |
| H. A. Gomes ........ | 4 | 6 | 0 | 158 | 53 | 0 | 26.33 |
| M. D. Marshall ...... | 4 | 4 | 0 | 90 | 63 | 0 | 22.50 |
| M. A. Holding ....... | 3 | 3 | 0 | 21 | 12 | 0 | 7.00 |

Played in two Tests: W. W. Davis 16, 0. Played in one Test: C. G. Butts 9, R. A. Harper 0, 11*; C. A. Walsh 12*.

*Signifies not out.

### BOWLING

| | *O* | *M* | *R* | *W* | *BB* | *Avge* |
|---|---|---|---|---|---|---|
| M. D. Marshall ...... | 170.1 | 30 | 486 | 27 | 7-80 | 18.00 |
| W. W. Davis ........ | 63.3 | 11 | 188 | 10 | 4-19 | 18.80 |
| M. A. Holding ....... | 82 | 24 | 218 | 9 | 4-79 | 24.22 |
| J. Garner ........... | 136.2 | 37 | 302 | 10 | 2-14 | 30.20 |

Also bowled: C. G. Butts 47–12–113–0; H. A. Gomes 18–3–44–0; R. A. Harper 36–18–52–2; A. L. Logie 1–1–0–0; I. V. A. Richards 39–7–89–1; R. B. Richardson 2–2–0–0; C. A. Walsh 25–5–75–3.

### NEW ZEALAND – BATTING

| | *T* | *I* | *NO* | *R* | *HI* | *100s* | *Avge* |
|---|---|---|---|---|---|---|---|
| J. V. Coney ......... | 4 | 6 | 1 | 241 | 83 | 0 | 48.20 |
| J. J. Crowe ......... | 4 | 7 | 0 | 252 | 112 | 1 | 36.00 |
| M. D. Crowe ........ | 4 | 7 | 0 | 216 | 188 | 1 | 30.85 |
| J. G. Wright ........ | 4 | 7 | 0 | 213 | 64 | 0 | 30.42 |
| R. J. Hadlee ........ | 4 | 7 | 1 | 137 | 39* | 0 | 22.83 |
| G. P. Howarth ....... | 4 | 7 | 0 | 158 | 84 | 0 | 22.57 |
| I. D. S. Smith ....... | 4 | 7 | 1 | 111 | 53 | 0 | 18.50 |
| E. J. Chatfield ....... | 4 | 6 | 5 | 13 | 4* | 0 | 13.00 |
| S. L. Boock ......... | 3 | 4 | 0 | 26 | 22 | 0 | 6.50 |
| K. R. Rutherford .... | 4 | 7 | 0 | 12 | 5 | 0 | 1.71 |

Played in two Tests: B. L. Cairns 8, 3. Played in one Test: J. G. Bracewell 25*, 27; D. A. Stirling 6, 3; G. B. Troup 0, 2.

**Signifies not out.*

## BOWLING

| | O | M | R | W | BB | Avge |
|---|---|---|---|---|---|---|
| R. J. Hadlee ........ | 143 | 33 | 409 | 15 | 4-53 | 27.26 |
| J. V. Coney .......... | 51 | 11 | 137 | 5 | 2-38 | 27.40 |
| E. J. Chatfield ....... | 152 | 36 | 441 | 13 | 6-73 | 33.92 |
| B. L. Cairns ......... | 95 | 14 | 315 | 5 | 2-47 | 63.00 |

Also bowled: S. L. Boock 110–25–339–2; J. G. Bracewell 25–5–68–1; M. D. Crowe 20–4–55–3; G. P. Howarth 9–5–17–0; K. R. Rutherford 9.4–1–48–1; I. D. S. Smith 3–1–5–0; D. A. Stirling 14.1–0–82–2; G. B. Troup 20–1–100–2; J. G. Wright 3–1–2–0.

# NEW ZEALAND AVERAGES – FIRST-CLASS MATCHES

## BATTING

| | M | I | NO | R | HI | 100s | Avge |
|---|---|---|---|---|---|---|---|
| J. V. Coney ......... | 6 | 10 | 2 | 447 | 99 | 0 | 55.87 |
| M. D. Crowe ........ | 5 | 9 | 0 | 396 | 188 | 2 | 44.00 |
| J. G. Wright ........ | 7 | 13 | 0 | 458 | 101 | 1 | 35.23 |
| J. J. Crowe ......... | 7 | 13 | 0 | 354 | 112 | 1 | 27.23 |
| R. J. Hadlee ........ | 4 | 7 | 1 | 137 | 39* | 0 | 22.83 |
| K. R. Rutherford .... | 7 | 13 | 1 | 256 | 109* | 1 | 21.33 |
| J. G. Bracewell ...... | 4 | 7 | 1 | 113 | 50 | 0 | 18.83 |
| B. L. Cairns ......... | 5 | 7 | 1 | 111 | 52* | 0 | 18.50 |
| I. D. S. Smith ....... | 4 | 7 | 1 | 111 | 53 | 0 | 18.50 |
| G. P. Howarth ...... | 7 | 13 | 0 | 186 | 84 | 0 | 14.30 |
| E. J. Chatfield ....... | 5 | 7 | 5 | 17 | 4* | 0 | 8.50 |
| D. A. Stirling ....... | 4 | 7 | 2 | 42 | 17 | 0 | 8.40 |
| R. T. Hart .......... | 3 | 6 | 0 | 34 | 8 | 0 | 5.66 |
| G. B. Troup ......... | 3 | 5 | 3 | 11 | 8* | 0 | 5.50 |
| S. L. Boock ......... | 6 | 8 | 0 | 42 | 22 | 0 | 5.25 |

**Signifies not out.*

## BOWLING

| | O | M | R | W | BB | Avge |
|---|---|---|---|---|---|---|
| D. A. Stirling ....... | 60.1 | 7 | 308 | 13 | 4-66 | 23.69 |
| R. J. Hadlee ........ | 143 | 33 | 409 | 15 | 4-53 | 27.26 |
| J. V. Coney .......... | 52 | 11 | 143 | 5 | 2-38 | 28.60 |
| J. G. Bracewell ...... | 88 | 19 | 223 | 7 | 3-58 | 31.85 |
| E. J. Chatfield ....... | 179 | 45 | 493 | 14 | 6-73 | 35.21 |
| B. L. Cairns ......... | 156.5 | 22 | 495 | 14 | 3-45 | 35.35 |
| G. B. Troup ......... | 56 | 8 | 250 | 5 | 2-41 | 50.00 |
| S. L. Boock ......... | 177.1 | 42 | 493 | 6 | 2-63 | 82.16 |

Also bowled: M. D. Crowe 20–4–55–3; G. P. Howarth 9–5–17–0; K. R. Rutherford 9.4–1–48–1; I. D. S. Smith 3–1–5–0; J. G. Wright 3–1–2–0.

## FIELDING

J. J. Crowe 11, I. D. S. Smith 9 (8 ct [1 as sub], 1 st), M. D. Crowe 7, J. G. Bracewell 5 (2 as sub), G. P. Howarth 4, J. V. Coney 3, K. R. Rutherford 3, E. J. Chatfield 2, R. T. Hart 2, S. L. Boock 1, R. J. Hadlee 1, D. A. Stirling 1, G. B. Troup 1, J. G. Wright 1.

## SHELL SHIELD XI v NEW ZEALANDERS

At Kingston, March 15, 16, 17. Drawn. The highlight of the New Zealanders' first innings was an enterprising third-wicket partnership of 102 in an hour and a half between the Crowe brothers, who were both among off-spinner Butts's seven victims. Kelly's maiden first-class century after eight seasons included fifteen 4s, mostly powerful off-side strokes, and his third-wicket stand with the left-handed Mohamed carried the Shield XI past 200. However, the New Zealanders bowled steadily to restrict their lead. The tourists were in trouble against Mahabir's leg-spin at 72 for four just after lunch on the last day, but Wright and Martin Crowe steered them out of it by adding 74.

### New Zealanders

| First innings | | Second innings | |
|---|---|---|---|
| K. R. Rutherford b Gray | 12 | (5) lbw b Mahabir | 0 |
| †R. T. Hart b Butts | 8 | hit wkt b Gray | 8 |
| J. J. Crowe c D. Williams b Butts | 67 | c Gray b Mahabir | 14 |
| M. D. Crowe c A. B. Williams b Butts | 118 | (6) run out | 62 |
| J. G. Wright c D. Williams b Butts | 9 | (1) c Hooper b Gray | 69 |
| *G. P. Howarth lbw b Butts | 0 | (4) c Best b Mahabir | 4 |
| J. G. Bracewell c A. B. Williams b Butts | 0 | lbw b Gray | 10 |
| B. L. Cairns lbw b Mahabir | 21 | c Best b Mahabir | 10 |
| D. A. Stirling c Gray b Mahabir | 6 | c D. Williams b Gray | 0 |
| G. B. Troup not out | 1 | not out | 8 |
| S. L. Boock b Butts | 6 | lbw b Gray | 3 |
| B 1, l-b 12, n-b 6 | 19 | B 3, l-b 3, n-b 5 | 11 |
| 1/19 2/43 3/145 4/179 5/179 6/179 7/216 8/242 9/257 | 267 | 1/19 2/59 3/72 4/74 5/146 6/170 7/173 8/176 9/188 | 199 |

Bowling: *First Innings*—Gray 14-4-33-1; Daley 18-6-42-0; Butts 38.3-6-90-7; Mahabir 23-4-65-2; Hooper 4-0-24-0. *Second Innings*—Gray 19.2-2-55-5; Daley 9-2-30-0; Butts 23-7-36-0; Mahabir 26-7-72-4.

### Shell Shield XI

| First innings | | Second innings | |
|---|---|---|---|
| C. A. Best c Hart b Troup | 28 | not out | 9 |
| A. L. Kelly c Troup b Bracewell | 132 | b Cairns | 0 |
| E. E. Lewis lbw b Boock | 5 | not out | 3 |
| T. Mohamed c Bracewell b Stirling | 60 | | |
| *A. B. Williams c Rutherford b Stirling | 4 | | |
| C. L. Hooper c Bracewell b Stirling | 36 | | |
| A. G. Daley b Bracewell | 0 | | |
| †D. Williams lbw b Bracewell | 9 | | |
| C. G. Butts c M. D. Crowe b Boock | 7 | | |
| A. H. Gray lbw b Troup | 9 | | |
| G. Mahabir not out | 0 | | |
| B 8, l-b 6, w 7, n-b 5 | 26 | L-b 3, n-b 1 | 4 |
| 1/85 2/107 3/230 4/234 5/255 6/255 7/279 8/292 9/314 | 316 | 1/10 | (1 wkt) 16 |

Bowling: *First Innings*—Stirling 17-2-92-3; Troup 15-3-41-2; Cairns 16-1-48-0; Boock 26-6-63-2; Bracewell 27-8-58-3. *Second Innings*—Troup 2-0-12-0; Cairns 1-0-1-1.

Umpires: J. Gayle and A. Gaynor.

## WEST INDIES UNDER-23 XI v NEW ZEALANDERS

At Basseterre, St Kitts, March 22, 23, 24. Drawn. After conceding a first-innings lead of 114, the New Zealanders had to battle hard on the final day to avoid defeat, a solid, unbeaten century from their young opener, Rutherford, who batted for just under five hours, and his fifth-wicket partnership of 119 with Coney carrying them to eventual safety. Their first innings was dominated by Wright, whose opening partner scored just four singles in a little over two hours at the wicket. After Wright was out, the off-spinner, Hooper, swept through the lower order. Stirling, lively but erratic, removed the first three home wickets for 26 late on the first day, but Lawrence and Hunte led a recovery by adding 144 and the New Zealanders were under pressure for most of their second innings.

### New Zealanders

| | | | |
|---|---|---|---|
| J. G. Wright c Richardson b Merrick | 101 | b Merrick | 40 |
| †R. T. Hart c Hooper b Gray | 4 | (4) b Merrick | 7 |
| J. J. Crowe lbw b Gray | 4 | lbw b Merrick | 0 |
| K. R. Rutherford lbw b Merrick | 19 | (2) not out | 109 |
| *G. P. Howarth c Williams b Hooper | 8 | c Simmons b Gray | 6 |
| J. V. Coney c Merrick b Hooper | 1 | not out | 58 |
| J. G. Bracewell b Hooper | 1 | | |
| B. L. Cairns c Simmons b Hooper | 11 | | |
| D. A. Stirling not out | 8 | | |
| E. J. Chatfield lbw b Hooper | 4 | | |
| S. L. Boock lbw b Merrick | 0 | | |
| L-b 3, n-b 7 | 10 | B 10, l-b 6, n-b 2 | 18 |
| 1/64 2/89 3/127 4/142 5/142 6/144 7/153 8/158 9/162 | 171 | 1/79 2/79 3/110 4/119 | (4 wkts) 238 |

Bowling: *First Innings*—Walsh 10–4–27–0; Gray 14–4–36–2; Merrick 18.5–7–33–3; Harper 13–4–37–0; Hooper 14–3–35–5. *Second Innings*—Walsh 17–3–67–0; Gray 15–6–29–1; Merrick 19–3–40–3; Harper 10–3–27–0; Hooper 17–1–59–0.

### West Indies Under-23 XI

| | |
|---|---|
| P. V. Simmons lbw b Stirling | 1 |
| L. L. Lawrence c Crowe b Bracewell | 79 |
| R. B. Richardson c Coney b Stirling | 1 |
| A. F. D. Jackman c Crowe b Stirling | 6 |
| T. A. Hunte c Crowe b Bracewell | 69 |
| C. L. Hooper c Howarth b Cairns | 37 |
| *R. A. Harper c Stirling b Cairns | 20 |
| †D. Williams lbw b Boock | 13 |
| A. H. Gray c and b Chatfield | 7 |
| T. A. Merrick c Rutherford b Stirling | 8 |
| C. A. Walsh not out | 10 |
| B 14, l-b 12, w 5, n-b 3 | 34 |
| 1/3 2/9 3/26 4/170 5/181 6/245 7/246 8/255 9/270 | 285 |

Bowling: Stirling 16–4–68–4; Chatfield 27–9–52–1; Cairns 18–4–39–2; Bracewell 25–5–59–2; Boock 23.1–8–35–1; Coney 1–0–6–0.

Umpires: A. Weekes and P. White.

## †WEST INDIES v NEW ZEALAND

### First One-day International

At St John's, Antigua, March 20. West Indies won by 23 runs. West Indies overcame an uncertain start on a lively pitch as Richards, with a 6 and seven 4s off 85 balls, and Haynes added 127 for the third wicket. But the most telling innings was Harper's unbeaten 45 at the end from 29 balls with three 6s and three 4s. New Zealand never appeared likely to present a challenge, although the Crowe brothers batted well in adding 91 before Harper dismissed them both in successive overs. The ground was packed for the Antiguan Richards's first match as West Indies' official captain.

*Man of the Match:* R. A. Harper.

### West Indies

| | | | |
|---|---|---|---|
| C. G. Greenidge c Smith b Troup | 3 | M. A. Holding b Hadlee | 9 |
| D. L. Haynes b Troup | 54 | J. Garner not out | 1 |
| R. B. Richardson b Hadlee | 3 | | |
| *I. V. A. Richards b Coney | 70 | B 1, l-b 6, w 3, n-b 3 | 13 |
| A. L. Logie c Cairns b Coney | 11 | | |
| †P. J. L. Dujon st Smith b Coney | 14 | 1/4 2/7 3/134 (8 wkts, 46 overs) | 231 |
| R. A. Harper not out | 45 | 4/141 5/160 6/191 | |
| E. A. E. Baptiste b Cairns | 8 | 7/208 8/226 | |

W. W. Davis did not bat.

Bowling: Troup 10-0-52-2; Hadlee 10-0-29-2; Chatfield 8-0-38-0; Cairns 8-0-42-1; Coney 10-0-63-3.

### New Zealand

| | | | |
|---|---|---|---|
| J. G. Wright b Holding | 0 | *G. P. Howarth not out | 12 |
| R. T. Hart c Dujon b Garner | 3 | G. B. Troup not out | 16 |
| J. J. Crowe b Harper | 53 | | |
| M. D. Crowe lbw b Harper | 41 | B 2, l-b 18, w 5, n-b 6 | 31 |
| B. L. Cairns c Richards b Holding | 20 | | |
| J. V. Coney run out | 18 | 1/5 2/20 3/111 (8 wkts, 46 overs) | 208 |
| R. J. Hadlee c Harper b Holding | 2 | 4/124 5/151 6/158 | |
| †I. D. S. Smith c Holding b Garner | 12 | 7/173 8/180 | |

E. J. Chatfield did not bat.

Bowling: Garner 10-4-26-2; Holding 10-2-33-3; Baptiste 10-1-49-0; Davis 8-0-46-0; Harper 8-0-34-2.

Umpires: A. Weekes and P. White.

## †WEST INDIES v NEW ZEALAND

### Second One-day International

At Port-of-Spain, March 27. West Indies won by six wickets after rain had reduced the match to 22 overs an innings. Sent in on a pitch that rendered Garner and Davis almost unplayable, New Zealand were 9 for three in the sixth over and were struggling to recover when the weather intervened. West Indies then had a straightforward task, even though New Zealand had the consolation of taking four wickets. The match was a disappointment to a crowd of over 25,000.

*Man of the Match:* W. W. Davis.

### New Zealand

| | | | |
|---|---|---|---|
| J. G. Wright c Dujon b Davis | 5 | J. V. Coney not out | 19 |
| K. R. Rutherford c Dujon b Davis | 2 | L-b 1, w 1, n-b 3 | 5 |
| J. J. Crowe c Richards b Davis | 0 | | |
| M. D. Crowe not out | 20 | 1/6 2/9 3/9 (3 wkts, 22 overs) | 51 |

*G. P. Howarth, †I. D. S. Smith, R. J. Hadlee, B. L. Cairns, G. B. Troup and E. J. Chatfield did not bat.

Bowling: Garner 6-2-6-0; Davis 6-2-7-3; Holding 5-0-16-0; Baptiste 5-0-21-0.

## West Indies

| | | | |
|---|---|---|---|
| D. L. Haynes b Chatfield | 4 | †P. J. L. Dujon not out | 4 |
| R. B. Richardson c Smith b Troup | 3 | L-b 2, w 1, n-b 2 | 5 |
| H. A. Gomes c Smith b Troup | 4 | | —— |
| *I. V. A. Richards c Cairns b Rutherford | 27 | 1/4 2/11 3/21 (4 wkts, 17 overs) | 55 |
| A. L. Logie not out | 8 | 4/51 | |

R. A. Harper, E. A. E. Baptiste, M. A. Holding, J. Garner and W. W. Davis did not bat.

Bowling: Chatfield 6–0–15–1; Troup 5–1–22–2, Coney 3–1–4–0; Rutherford 3–0–12–1.

Umpires: C. E. Cumberbatch and S. Mohammed.

## WEST INDIES v NEW ZEALAND

### First Test Match

At Port-of-Spain, March 29, 30, 31, April 2, 3. Drawn. New Zealand's sixth-wicket pair, Coney and Hadlee, resisting doggedly for just over two hours on the final afternoon, frustrated West Indies much as Australia had done in the corresponding Test at Queen's Park Oval the previous season. Richards surprisingly batted on winning the toss in his first Test as appointed captain and his batsmen were at full stretch surviving the early stages on a pitch that encouraged the fast bowlers. Hadlee dismissed Haynes and Gomes in his third over, and Greenidge and Richardson did well to get through this period and build their partnership of 185. Greenidge, dropped at third slip by Howarth off Hadlee when 40, had twelve 4s in his twelfth Test century, but he and Richardson were out in consecutive overs and the innings faltered on the second morning as six wickets fell for 76 – four of them for 16, from eight overs, to the steady Chatfield.

Wright and Jeff Crowe mounted a strong New Zealand response with 109 for the second wicket, but the rest of the batting lacked purpose and West Indies gained a lead of 45, in spite of two chances each to Hadlee and Smith. Rain, which limited play on the third day to two hours, meant West Indies needed to make up time to force a result and Richards led the effort with 78 off 88 balls. Haynes, however, could not emulate him and Richards was obliged to continue his second innings 45 minutes into the final day before declaring. Chatfield's innings and match figures were his best in Tests, just reward for his consistency.

From the time the unfortunate Rutherford was run out without facing a ball, thus completing a pair in his first Test, New Zealand were struggling; and when Marshall dismissed the Crowes and Howarth in a spell of eleven overs after lunch, a West Indian victory appeared likely. But Marshall had exhausted himself by then and none of the other bowlers could make the same impression on a slow pitch. By the time Coney was out, only fourteen of the last twenty overs remained. Hadlee, who joined the élite group of those who have scored over 2,000 runs and taken over 200 wickets in Tests when he had scored 31, and Smith held out.

## West Indies

| | | | |
|---|---|---|---|
| C. G. Greenidge b Boock | 100 | | |
| D. L. Haynes c Rutherford b Hadlee | 0 | – (1) c M. D. Crowe b Chatfield | 78 |
| H. A. Gomes c Smith b Hadlee | 0 | – c and b Chatfield | 25 |
| R. B. Richardson c Hadlee b Coney | 78 | – (2) c Smith b Chatfield | 3 |
| *I. V. A. Richards b Hadlee | 57 | – (4) b Cairns | 78 |
| A. L. Logie b Chatfield | 24 | – (5) b Cairns | 42 |
| †P. J. L. Dujon b Chatfield | 15 | – (6) b Chatfield | 5 |
| M. D. Marshall c sub (J. G. Bracewell) b Chatfield | 0 | – (7) c Coney b Chatfield | 1 |
| R. A. Harper c Howarth b Chatfield | 0 | – (8) not out | 11 |
| M. A. Holding lbw b Hadlee | 12 | – (9) c J. J. Crowe b Chatfield | 8 |
| J. Garner not out | 0 | | |
| B 1, l-b 16, n-b 4 | 21 | L-b 3, n-b 7 | 10 |
| | —— | | —— |
| 1/5 2/9 3/194 4/196 5/236 6/267 7/267 8/269 9/302 | 307 | 1/10 2/58 3/172 4/226 5/239 6/240 7/241 8/261 (8 wkts dec.) | 261 |

Bowling: *First Innings*—Hadlee 24.3–6–82–4; Chatfield 28–11–51–4; Cairns 26–3–93–0; Boock 19–5–47–1; Coney 9–3–17–1. *Second Innings*—Hadlee 17–2–58–0; Chatfield 22–4–73–6; Cairns 19–2–70–2; Boock 14–4–57–0.

## New Zealand

| | | | |
|---|---|---|---|
| J. G. Wright c Richardson b Harper | 40 | lbw b Holding | 19 |
| K. R. Rutherford c Haynes b Marshall | 0 | run out | 0 |
| J. J. Crowe c and b Harper | 64 | c Garner b Marshall | 27 |
| M. D. Crowe lbw b Holding | 3 | c Haynes b Marshall | 2 |
| *G. P. Howarth c sub (P. V. Simmons) b Holding | 45 | b Marshall | 14 |
| J. V. Coney lbw b Marshall | 25 | c Dujon b Marshall | 44 |
| R. J. Hadlee c Garner b Holding | 18 | not out | 39 |
| †I. D. S. Smith c Logie b Holding | 10 | not out | 11 |
| B. L. Cairns c Harper b Garner | 8 | | |
| S. L. Boock c sub (P. V. Simmons) b Garner | 3 | | |
| E. J. Chatfield not out | 4 | | |
| B 12, l-b 11, n-b 19 | 42 | B 17, l-b 6, n-b 8 | 31 |
| 1/1 2/110 3/113 4/132 5/182 6/223 7/225 8/248 9/250 | 262 | 1/0 2/40 3/59 4/76 5/83 6/158 | (6 wkts) 187 |

Bowling: *First Innings*—Marshall 25–3–78–2; Garner 21.3–8–41–2; Holding 29–8–79–4; Harper 22–11–33–2; Richards 2–0–7–0; Gomes 1–0–1–0. *Second Innings*—Marshall 26–4–65–4; Garner 18–2–41–0; Holding 17–6–36–1; Harper 14–7–19–0; Richards 2–1–1–0; Gomes 2–1–2–0; Richardson 1–1–0–0; Logie 1–1–0–0.

Umpires: D. M. Archer and C. E. Cumberbatch.

## WEST INDIES v NEW ZEALAND

### Second Test Match

At Georgetown, April 6, 7, 8, 10, 11. Drawn. Batsmen took advantage of a lifeless pitch and a fast outfield to score 1,219 runs for the loss of 22 wickets. Richardson gave a delightful exhibition of off-side strokes, of which the square-drive was the most frequent, on the opening day when he struck 21 4s in an unbeaten 140. He and Haynes added 191 in 3 hours, 35 minutes as West Indies, 271 for two at the close, established the basis of their huge total. Next day, Richardson could not refind his touch, taking another three hours, twenty minutes to add 45 before being run out. His fourth Test century lasted seven and three-quarter hours. It was left to the other West Indian batsmen to accelerate the scoring, Logie and Dujon adding 104 in better than even time.

New Zealand had no alternative but to bat for a draw, and at 98 for four midway through the third afternoon they faced a familiar crisis. But by then Martin Crowe had overcome an uncertain start, and Coney played confidently from the time he came in. The pair carried the total to 230 for four when rain ended play 55 minutes early.

The early dismissal of Coney on the fourth morning, to a slip catch off Holding, ended the fifth-wicket stand at 142, a New Zealand record against West Indies, and it was not until Martin Crowe raised his century and erased the follow-on requirement with the same stroke that New Zealand could breathe more easily. No West Indies bowler, least of all the new off-spinner, Butts, could get any response from the pitch, and Crowe and Smith attacked so effectively that they added 143 in less than three hours for the seventh wicket, another New Zealand record against West Indies. Crowe was last man out, batting for longer than he had ever done before in a first-class match (nine and a half hours), one 6 and 22 4s being his main strokes. The final day amounted to no more than batting practice for West Indies on a pitch that remained ideal for batting to the end.

### West Indies

| | First innings | | Second innings | |
|---|---|---|---|---|
| C. G. Greenidge b Chatfield | 10 | – c and b Coney | 69 |
| D. L. Haynes b Hadlee | 90 | – c Smith b Hadlee | 9 |
| R. B. Richardson run out | 185 | – (4) c J. J. Crowe b Cairns | 60 |
| H. A. Gomes lbw b Cairns | 53 | – (5) c sub (J. G. Bracewell) b Rutherford | 35 |
| *I. V. A. Richards st Smith b Coney | 40 | – (8) not out | 7 |
| A. L. Logie c Howarth b Hadlee | 52 | – (7) not out | 41 |
| †P. J. L. Dujon not out | 60 | – (6) b Cairns | 3 |
| C. G. Butts (did not bat) | | – (3) c Smith b Hadlee | 9 |
| B 1, l-b 16, w 1, n-b 3 | 21 | B 7, l-b 25, w 1, n-b 2 | 35 |
| 1/30 2/221 3/327 4/394 5/407 6/511 (6 wkts dec.) | 511 | 1/22 2/46 3/150 4/191 5/207 6/225 (6 wkts) | 268 |

M. D. Marshall, M. A. Holding and J. Garner did not bat.

Bowling: *First Innings*—Hadlee 25.5–5–83–2; Chatfield 30–3–122–1; Cairns 32–5–105–1; Boock 43–11–107–0; Coney 18–2–62–1; Howarth 4–1–15–0. *Second Innings*—Hadlee 16–3–32–2; Chatfield 16–3–43–0; Boock 18–3–52–0; Cairns 18–4–47–2; Coney 10–3–20–1; Rutherford 9–1–38–1; Howarth 5–4–2–0; Wright 3–1–2–0.

### New Zealand

| | |
|---|---|
| J. G. Wright run out | 27 |
| K. R. Rutherford c Dujon b Garner | 4 |
| J. J. Crowe b Marshall | 22 |
| M. D. Crowe lbw b Garner | 188 |
| *G. P. Howarth c Haynes b Marshall | 4 |
| J. V. Coney c Richards b Holding | 73 |
| R. J. Hadlee c Dujon b Marshall | 16 |
| †I. D. S. Smith lbw b Marshall | 53 |
| B. L. Cairns b Holding | 3 |
| S. L. Boock b Holding | 0 |
| E. J. Chatfield not out | 3 |
| B 12, l-b 2, w 6, n-b 27 | 47 |
| 1/8 2/45 3/81 4/98 5/240 6/261 7/404 8/415 9/415 | 440 |

Bowling: Marshall 33–3–110–4; Garner 27.5–5–72–2; Holding 28–6–89–3; Butts 47–12–113–0; Richards 8–1–22–0; Gomes 8–2–20–0.

Umpires: L. H. Barker and D. J. Narine.

## †WEST INDIES v NEW ZEALAND

### Third One-day International

At Berbice, Guyana, April 14. West Indies won by 130 runs. Haynes led West Indies to a commanding total with his seventh century in one-day internationals, hitting sixteen 4s and sharing partnerships of 125 for the third wicket with Richards and 80 from ten overs in 36 minutes with Logie. The accuracy of West Indies' bowling was evidenced by the fact that the first seven New Zealand batsmen were bowled, leaving the total 75 for seven, only Cairns with 33 from 27 deliveries, including three huge 6s off Harper, avoiding a complete anticlimax.

*Man of the Match:* D. L. Haynes.

### West Indies

| | |
|---|---|
| D. L. Haynes not out | 146 |
| R. B. Richardson c Smith b Hadlee | 7 |
| H. A. Gomes c Smith b Chatfield | 13 |
| *I. V. A. Richards c Wright b Bracewell | 51 |
| A. L. Logie c Troup b Cairns | 26 |
| R. A. Harper c Smith b Troup | 1 |
| †P. J. L. Dujon not out | 4 |
| L-b 5, w 1, n-b 5 | 11 |
| 1/18 2/47 3/172 4/252 5/253 (5 wkts, 50 overs) | 259 |

E. A. E. Baptiste, M. A. Holding, J. Garner and W. W. Davis did not bat.

Bowling: Troup 7–0–28–1; Hadlee 10–1–47–1; Chatfield 10–1–36–1; Bracewell 9–0–50–1; Cairns 10–0–68–1; Coney 4–0–25–0.

### New Zealand

*G. P. Howarth b Garner . . . . . . . . . . . 3
J. G. Wright b Garner . . . . . . . . . . . . . . 0
J. J. Crowe b Davis . . . . . . . . . . . . . . . . 9
M. D. Crowe b Holding . . . . . . . . . . . . . 20
J. V. Coney b Baptiste . . . . . . . . . . . . . . 11
†I. D. S. Smith b Baptiste . . . . . . . . . . . 1
R. J. Hadlee b Harper . . . . . . . . . . . . . . 16
J. G. Bracewell c Richards b Gomes . . 15
B. L. Cairns c Davis b Harper . . . . . . . 33
G. B. Troup not out . . . . . . . . . . . . . . . . 6
E. J. Chatfield b Gomes . . . . . . . . . . . . . 6
B 2, l-b 4, w 1, n-b 2 . . . . . . . . 9

1/4 2/8 3/24 4/41 (48.1 overs) 129
5/48 6/55 7/75 8/115 9/121

Bowling: Garner 6–1–16–2; Davis 6–3–7–1; Holding 6–0–12–1; Baptiste 7–2–18–2; Harper 10–1–35–2; Richards 10–4–23–0; Gomes 2.1–0–6–2; Logie 1–0–6–0.

Umpires: L. H. Barker and D. J. Narine.

## †WEST INDIES v NEW ZEALAND

### Fourth One-day International

At Port-of-Spain, April 17. West Indies won by ten wickets, a result that was settled as soon as New Zealand lost the toss and had to bat first on a green and difficult pitch. Garner made the most of it with four for 10 from his opening six overs, and although Coney and Hadlee took advantage of his absence to add 58 the eventual total left West Indies with no problems.

*Man of the Match:* J. Garner.

### New Zealand

*G. P. Howarth c Dujon b Garner . . . . 6
J. G. Wright c Dujon b Garner . . . . . . . 1
J. J. Crowe c Richardson b Garner . . . . 4
M. D. Crowe b Garner . . . . . . . . . . . . . . 1
J. V. Coney c Dujon b Richards . . . . . . 33
†I. D. S. Smith c and b Holding . . . . . . 3
R. J. Hadlee c Richards b Davis . . . . . . 41
B. L. Cairns b Harper . . . . . . . . . . . . . . 12
J. G. Bracewell run out . . . . . . . . . . . . . 1
G. B. Troup run out . . . . . . . . . . . . . . . . 4
E. J. Chatfield not out . . . . . . . . . . . . . . 1
L-b 3, w 2, n-b 4 . . . . . . . . . . . 9

1/6 2/10 3/14 4/18 (42.2 overs) 116
5/25 6/83 7/100
8/104 9/114

Bowling: Garner 6–1–10–4; Davis 6.2–1–10–1; Baptiste 5–0–31–0; Holding 7–1–24–1; Harper 10–2–18–1; Richards 8–1–20–1.

### West Indies

D. L. Haynes not out . . . . . . . . . . . . . . . 85
R. B. Richardson not out . . . . . . . . . . . . 28
L-b 2, n-b 2 . . . . . . . . . . . . . . . 4

(no wkt, 25.2 overs) 117

H. A. Gomes, *I. V. A. Richards, A. L. Logie, †P. J. L. Dujon, E. A. E. Baptiste, R. A. Harper, M. A. Holding, W. W. Davis and J. Garner did not bat.

Bowling: Hadlee 6–1–18–0; Troup 8–2–30–0; Cairns 7–0–50–0; Chatfield 4–0–14–0; Bracewell 0.2–0–3–0.

Umpires: C. E. Cumberbatch and S. Mohammed.

## PRESIDENT'S XI v NEW ZEALANDERS

At Castries, April 19, 20, 21. Drawn. As in their previous two first-class matches, the New Zealanders found themselves under pressure on the final day as a result of unconvincing batting. They recovered well on the opening day from 68 for four to be able to declare at stumps, Coney falling 1 run short of his century when out hooking. Cairns's unbeaten 52 off 36 balls included three 6s. The President's XI, batting inconsistently, conceded a lead of 43, but their fast bowlers, Walsh and Merrick, committed the New Zealanders to a stern last day by removing the first four wickets for 40 on the third afternoon. That became 129 for eight the next morning, but Rutherford, despite a wrist injury, held firm with the tail and there was not enough time for the President's XI to make a serious attempt at a winning target of 225.

## New Zealanders

| First innings | | Second innings | |
|---|---|---|---|
| K. R. Rutherford b Hooper | 51 | (7) c Jackman b Hooper | 53 |
| †R. T. Hart c Payne b Merrick | 4 | (1) c Gray b Walsh | 3 |
| J. J. Crowe hit wkt b Walsh | 3 | b Walsh | 14 |
| G. P. Howarth run out | 0 | b Merrick | 10 |
| J. G. Wright c Payne b Merrick | 25 | (2) c Payne b Walsh | 1 |
| *J. V. Coney c sub b Walsh | 99 | (5) c Seeram b Gray | 48 |
| J. G. Bracewell run out | 50 | (8) lbw b Gray | 0 |
| B. L. Cairns not out | 52 | (9) b Merrick | 6 |
| D. A. Stirling not out | 2 | (10) b Merrick | 17 |
| S. L. Boock (did not bat) | | (6) b Walsh | 7 |
| G. B. Troup (did not bat) | | not out | 0 |
| B 1, l-b 1, w 1, n-b 18 | 21 | B 8, l-b 7, n-b 7 | 22 |
| 1/17 2/31 3/31 4/68 5/204 6/236 7/288 (7 wkts dec.) | 307 | 1/4 2/15 3/28 4/40 5/55 6/119 7/119 8/129 9/154 | 181 |

Bowling: *First Innings*—Walsh 16–1–80–2; Gray 13–0–44–0; Merrick 17–2–61–2; Mahabir 23–2–69–0; Hooper 15–2–51–1. *Second Innings*—Walsh 17–0–61–4; Merrick 19–5–45–3; Gray 12–1–51–2; Mahabir 2–1–1–0; Hooper 2.5–0–8–1.

## President's XI

| First innings | | Second innings | |
|---|---|---|---|
| *C. A. Best c sub b Troup | 16 | not out | 53 |
| P. V. Simmons b Stirling | 5 | lbw b Cairns | 7 |
| A. F. D. Jackman lbw b Cairns | 29 | b Cairns | 22 |
| R. M. Otto b Stirling | 4 | b Cairns | 12 |
| †T. R. O. Payne c Boock b Stirling | 56 | lbw b Boock | 9 |
| R. N. Seeram not out | 75 | not out | 2 |
| C. L. Hooper c Hart b Stirling | 0 | | |
| A. H. Gray run out | 1 | | |
| T. A. Merrick c Howarth b Bracewell | 31 | | |
| C. A. Walsh b Cairns | 13 | | |
| G. Mahabir lbw b Cairns | 3 | | |
| B 14, l-b 9, w 3, n-b 5 | 31 | L-b 6, w 2, n-b 1 | 9 |
| 1/21 2/28 3/40 4/64 5/145 6/149 7/169 8/221 9/260 | 264 | 1/24 2/63 3/81 4/106 (4 wkts) | 114 |

Bowling: *First Innings*—Stirling 13–1–66–4; Troup 14–4–58–1; Cairns 15.5–3–45–3; Boock 12–3–34–0; Bracewell 11–1–38–1. *Second Innings*—Troup 5–0–39–0; Cairns 11–0–47–3; Boock 6–0–22–1.

Umpires: J. Simon and A. Weekes.

## †WEST INDIES v NEW ZEALAND

### Fifth One-day International

At Bridgetown, April 23. West Indies won by 112 runs, completing a clean sweep in the series with the same one-sidedness of the four previous matches. Haynes continued his remarkable sequence of heavy scoring with another century, his eighth, surviving a return chance to Chatfield when 13 and hitting two 6s and eight 4s in 151 balls to equal Richards's record number of hundreds in one-day internationals. With Gomes he added 184 from 33 overs. New Zealand's batting had little to recommend it to a crowd of 10,000, Rutherford taking 69 balls to make 18.

*Man of the Match:* D. L. Haynes.

## West Indies

| | |
|---|---|
| D. L. Haynes c Coney b Chatfield | 116 |
| R. B. Richardson c Coney b Chatfield | 21 |
| H. A. Gomes c J. J. Crowe b Cairns | 78 |
| *I. V. A. Richards not out | 33 |
| A. L. Logie not out | 11 |
| L-b 5, w 1 | 6 |
| 1/31 2/215 3/223 (3 wkts, 49 overs) | 265 |

†P. J. L. Dujon, R. A. Harper, E. A. E. Baptiste, M. A. Holding, J. Garner and W. W. Davis did not bat.

Bowling: Troup 10-0-57-0; Hadlee 9-1-26-0; Chatfield 10-1-61-2; Cairns 10-1-63-1; Coney 10-0-53-0.

## New Zealand

| | |
|---|---|
| *G. P. Howarth c Dujon b Davis | 6 |
| J. G. Wright c Richards b Garner | 22 |
| K. R. Rutherford c Holding b Harper | 18 |
| M. D. Crowe c Logie b Davis | 6 |
| J. V. Coney b Baptiste | 5 |
| J. J. Crowe c Logie b Harper | 30 |
| B. L. Cairns c Logie b Harper | 5 |
| †I. D. S. Smith c Garner b Davis | 37 |
| R. J. Hadlee not out | 16 |
| G. B. Troup not out | 0 |
| B 2, l-b 2, w 1, n-b 3 | 8 |
| 1/30 2/30 3/36 4/47 5/83 6/91 7/103 8/152 (8 wkts, 49 overs) | 153 |

E. J. Chatfield did not bat.

Bowling: Garner 6-2-10-1; Davis 8-0-32-3; Baptiste 7-1-11-1; Holding 6-1-10-0; Harper 10-3-38-3; Richards 8-0-31-0; Gomes 3-1-16-0; Logie 1-0-1-0.

Umpires: D. M. Archer and L. H. Barker.

# WEST INDIES v NEW ZEALAND

## Third Test Match

At Bridgetown, April 26, 27, 28, 30, May 1. West Indies won by ten wickets, their fifth consecutive victory at Kensington Oval being completed early on the final day in spite of the accumulated loss of seven and three-quarter hours of play to the sudden and definite end of Barbados's dry season. West Indies' record on the ground, and uncertainty over how the pitch would play after persistent overnight and morning rain had delayed the start until midway through the first day, appeared uppermost in the New Zealanders' minds when they had to bat first on losing the toss. As it turned out, the pitch lacked any real devil, but by the time more rain halted play soon after tea New Zealand were 18 for four. They fell next day for the lowest Test total ever recorded on the ground, 3 fewer than Australia's the previous season, and in the final half-hour West Indies were already within 3 runs of the lead when Martin Crowe, in his first bowl of the tour, dismissed Richardson, going on to remove Gomes in the same over. Haynes quickly followed and West Indies did not take command until Marshall joined Richards at 174 for seven. The pair added 83 as Richards, with three 6s and twelve 4s, completed his nineteenth Test century in just under three and a quarter hours.

Poor light halted play an hour early on the third day and a sodden outfield delayed play for another hour on the fourth, a welcome respite for New Zealand. However, Marshall, delivering from round the wicket with speed and hostility, proved irresistible. The main defiance came from Wright, who batted for two and three-quarter hours before he was caught at slip. Coney and Boock carried the match into the final day by adding 77 for the eighth wicket; but Marshall dismissed Boock just before stumps and then returned next morning to finish things off. His match return of eleven for 120 was his best in Tests, ten of his wickets coming from deliveries bowled from round the wicket.

### New Zealand

| | First innings | | Second innings | |
|---|---|---|---|---|
| *G. P. Howarth c Greenidge b Garner | 1 | – | c Haynes b Marshall | 5 |
| J. G. Wright c Dujon b Marshall | 0 | – | c Richardson b Davis | 64 |
| K. R. Rutherford c Richards b Marshall | 0 | – | c Holding b Marshall | 2 |
| M. D. Crowe hit wkt b Holding | 14 | – | c Dujon b Marshall | 2 |
| J. J. Crowe c Dujon b Davis | 21 | – | b Davis | 4 |
| J. V. Coney c Richardson b Marshall | 12 | – | c Logie b Marshall | 83 |
| †I. D. S. Smith c Greenidge b Marshall | 2 | – | c and b Marshall | 26 |
| R. J. Hadlee c Logie b Davis | 29 | – | c Greenidge b Davis | 3 |
| D. A. Stirling c Logie b Davis | 6 | – | b Marshall | 3 |
| S. L. Boock c Dujon b Garner | 1 | – | c Haynes b Marshall | 22 |
| E. J. Chatfield not out | 0 | – | not out | 4 |
| N-b 8 | 8 | | B 8, l-b 1, w 2, n-b 19 | 30 |
| 1/1 2/1 3/1 4/18 5/37 6/44 7/80 8/87 9/90 | 94 | | 1/26 2/35 3/45 4/60 5/108 6/141 7/149 8/226 9/235 | 248 |

Bowling: *First Innings*—Marshall 15–3–40–4; Garner 15–9–14–2; Holding 7–4–12–1; Davis 10.4–5–28–3. *Second Innings*—Marshall 25.3–6–80–7; Garner 19–5–56–0; Davis 18–0–66–3; Holding 1–0–2–0; Richards 13–3–25–0; Gomes 4–0–10–0.

### West Indies

| | First innings | | Second innings | |
|---|---|---|---|---|
| C. G. Greenidge c J. J. Crowe b Hadlee | 2 | – | not out | 4 |
| D. L. Haynes c Smith b Hadlee | 62 | – | not out | 5 |
| R. B. Richardson lbw b M. D. Crowe | 22 | | | |
| H. A. Gomes c J. J. Crowe b M. D. Crowe | 0 | | | |
| W. W. Davis c Smith b Stirling | 16 | | | |
| *I. V. A. Richards c M. D. Crowe b Boock | 105 | | | |
| A. L. Logie c J. J. Crowe b Chatfield | 7 | | | |
| †P. J. L. Dujon b Hadlee | 3 | | | |
| M. D. Marshall c J. J. Crowe b Chatfield | 63 | | | |
| J. Garner not out | 37 | | | |
| M. A. Holding c Smith b Stirling | 1 | | | |
| B 2, l-b 8, w 6, n-b 2 | 18 | | W 1 | 1 |
| 1/12 2/91 3/91 4/95 5/142 6/161 7/174 8/257 9/327 | 336 | | | (no wkt) 10 |

Bowling: *First Innings*—Hadlee 26–5–86–3; Chatfield 28–10–57–2; Stirling 14.1–0–82–2; M. D. Crowe 10–2–25–2; Boock 15–1–76–1. *Second Innings*—Boock 1–1–0–0; Rutherford 0.4–0–10–0.

Umpires: D. M. Archer and L. H. Barker.

## WEST INDIES v NEW ZEALAND

### Fourth Test Match

At Kingston, May 4, 5, 6, 8. West Indies won by ten wickets. Another weak first-innings batting performance by New Zealand committed them to the follow-on, and, even though Howarth and Jeff Crowe put new life into their effort on the third day with a New Zealand Test record second-wicket partnership of 210, their second innings folded once these two were separated, West Indies winning with more than a day to spare.

West Indies appeared to be building a substantial first-innings total after being sent in until Hadlee intervened with the wickets of Richards and Logie, with successive balls, and then Gomes, and the West Indian total was hardly a daunting one. However, New Zealand again started badly and their confidence and courage were put to a severe test over the final 55 minutes of the second day, after an interruption for rain, when Marshall and Garner unsettled the batsmen with a profusion of short-pitched deliveries. One ball from Garner fractured Coney's forearm, a crucial loss for New Zealand, and Rutherford ducked into Garner's first ball to him, which hit him on the helmet. Earlier in the day Hadlee had delivered five bouncers in an over to Garner, but at no stage did the umpires intervene under Law 42.8 as they would have had justifiable cause for doing. Wright batted through the ordeal for a gritty half-century, but he was soon out hooking in the second innings when Howarth, in his one major innings of the series, and the adventurous Jeff Crowe raised New Zealand spirits by taking the total to 211 for one by the end of the third day. Crowe was already past his second Test century.

However, New Zealand's recovery was halted on the fourth day by the naggingly accurate bowling of Marshall and Garner, who conceded only 6 runs from their first nine overs. Richards then offered the batsmen the temptation to break free by coming on himself, and Crowe quickly on-drove a catch to mid-wicket, having batted for four and three-quarter hours in all. Howarth was brilliantly caught at gully in the next over to his first attacking stroke of the day, whereupon the innings collapsed, the last eight wickets falling for 60. West Indies were left with the formality of scoring 59 to win.

## West Indies

| First innings | | Second innings | |
|---|---|---|---|
| C. G. Greenidge c J. J. Crowe b M. D. Crowe | 46 | not out | 33 |
| D. L. Haynes c J. J. Crowe b Coney | 76 | not out | 24 |
| R. B. Richardson c M. D. Crowe b Coney | 30 | | |
| H. A. Gomes c Wright b Hadlee | 45 | | |
| *I. V. A. Richards lbw b Hadlee | 23 | | |
| A. L. Logie c M. D. Crowe b Hadlee | 0 | | |
| †P. J. L. Dujon c Bracewell b Troup | 70 | | |
| M. D. Marshall lbw b Bracewell | 26 | | |
| W. W. Davis c M. D. Crowe b Troup | 0 | | |
| J. Garner c M. D. Crowe b Hadlee | 12 | | |
| C. A. Walsh not out | 12 | | |
| B 7, l-b 9, w 1, n-b 6 | 23 | B 1, l-b 1 | 2 |
| 1/82 2/144 3/164 4/207 5/207 6/273 7/311 8/311 9/339 | 363 | (no wkt) | 59 |

Bowling: *First Innings*—Hadlee 28.4–11–53–4; Troup 17–1–87–2; Chatfield 26–5–85–0; M. D. Crowe 10–2–30–1; Bracewell 21–5–54–1; Coney 14–3–38–2. *Second Innings*—Hadlee 5–1–15–0; Troup 3–0–13–0; Chatfield 2–0–10–0; Bracewell 4–0–14–0; Smith 3–1–5–0.

## New Zealand

| First innings | | Second innings | |
|---|---|---|---|
| *G. P. Howarth c Gomes b Marshall | 5 | c Garner b Walsh | 84 |
| J. G. Wright b Davis | 53 | c Dujon b Garner | 10 |
| J. J. Crowe c Richardson b Garner | 2 | c Marshall b Richards | 112 |
| M. D. Crowe c Davis b Walsh | 6 | c Dujon b Walsh | 1 |
| J. V. Coney retired hurt | 4 | absent injured | |
| K. R. Rutherford c Dujon b Marshall | 1 | (5) lbw b Marshall | 5 |
| †I. D. S. Smith b Garner | 0 | (6) b Marshall | 9 |
| R. J. Hadlee c Dujon b Davis | 18 | (7) c Walsh b Marshall | 14 |
| J. G. Bracewell not out | 25 | (8) c Gomes b Marshall | 27 |
| G. B. Troup c Marshall b Davis | 0 | (9) c Richardson b Garner | 2 |
| E. J. Chatfield b Davis | 2 | (10) not out | 0 |
| B 4, l-b 1, w 2, n-b 15 | 22 | B 4, l-b 7, n-b 8 | 19 |
| 1/11 2/15 3/37 4/65 5/68 6/106 7/113 8/122 9/138 | 138 | 1/13 2/223 3/223 4/228 5/238 6/242 7/259 8/281 9/283 | 283 |

Bowling: *First Innings*—Marshall 17–3–47–2; Garner 16–0–37–2; Davis 13.5–5–19–4; Walsh 9–1–30–1. *Second Innings*—Marshall 28.4–8–66–4; Garner 19–8–41–2; Davis 21–1–75–0; Walsh 16–4–45–2; Richards 14–2–34–1; Gomes 3–0–11–0; Richardson 1–1–0–0.

Umpires: D. M. Archer and J. R. Gayle.

# BENSON AND HEDGES WORLD SERIES CUP, 1984-85

## †AUSTRALIA v WEST INDIES

At Melbourne, January 6. West Indies won by seven wickets. Australia lost a wicket to the first ball of the match and were 68 for two after twenty overs, but Border and Boon, both missed in the 30s, led their revival by adding 115 from 127 balls. Haynes's unbeaten 123 from 131 balls, with fifteen 4s, and his stands of 71 with Richardson and 94 in fourteen overs with Richards swept West Indies to a comfortable victory.

*Man of the Match:* D. L. Haynes. *Attendance:* 58,929.

### Australia

G. M. Wood c Holding b Garner ..... 0
A. M. J. Hilditch c Holding b Baptiste 27
K. C. Wessels run out ..... 33
*A. R. Border c Baptiste b Garner ..... 73
D. C. Boon b Marshall ..... 55
†W. B. Phillips c Greenidge b Garner . 23
S. P. O'Donnell not out ..... 7
G. F. Lawson not out ..... 8
L-b 7, w 4, n-b 3 ..... 14

1/0 2/48 3/78 4/193 5/220 6/224 (6 wkts, 50 overs) 240

M. J. Bennett, C. J. McDermott and R. M. Hogg did not bat.

Bowling: Garner 10–2–41–3; Marshall 10–0–32–1; Baptiste 9–0–73–1; Holding 10–1–41–0; Richards 10–1–37–0; Gomes 1–0–9–0.

### West Indies

C. G. Greenidge b Bennett ..... 12
D. L. Haynes not out ..... 123
R. B. Richardson c Boon b Lawson ... 34
I. V. A. Richards c Phillips b McDermott 47
H. A. Gomes not out ..... 2
B 1, l-b 17, w 5 ..... 23

1/69 2/140 3/234 (3 wkts, 44.5 overs) 241

*C. H. Lloyd, †P. J. L. Dujon, M. D. Marshall, E. A. E. Baptiste, M. A. Holding and J. Garner did not bat.

Bowling: Lawson 10–0–45–1; McDermott 9.5–0–52–1; Hogg 8–0–43–0; O'Donnell 3–0–24–0; Bennett 10–2–23–1; Wessels 2–0–18–0; Border 2–0–18–0.

Umpires: A. R. Crafter and P. J. McConnell.

## †AUSTRALIA v SRI LANKA

At Sydney, January 8 (day/night). Australia won by six wickets after a hard struggle in which the fifteen no-balls and wides bowled by Sri Lanka's medium-pacers were crucial. Playing their first day-night match, the Sri Lankans chose to bat first and used the afternoon to compile a very useful total. However, Wood was in dashing form for Australia, and when he retired with cramp Border guided his side to victory.

*Man of the Match:* A. R. Border. *Attendance:* 26,000 (estimated).

### Sri Lanka

S. Wettimuny c Phillips b Rackemann 20
†S. A. R. Silva c Bennett b Hogg ..... 68
D. S. B. P. Kuruppu c Wood b Bennett 22
R. L. Dias c Border b O'Donnell ..... 60
*L. R. D. Mendis b Hogg ..... 16
P. A. de Silva b Hogg ..... 17
A. L. F. de Mel b Hogg ..... 0
J. R. Ratnayeke not out ..... 8
R. J. Ratnayake not out ..... 4
B 5, l-b 5, w 13, n-b 1 ..... 24

1/66 2/104 3/160 4/181 5/214 6/214 7/229 (7 wkts, 49 overs) 239

D. S. de Silva and V. B. John did not bat.

Bowling: Hogg 10–0–47–4; O'Donnell 9–2–39–1; McDermott 10–1–49–0; Bennett 10–1–44–1; Rackemann 10–0–50–1.

### Australia

| | |
|---|---|
| A. M. J. Hilditch run out . . . . . . . . . . . . 23 | S. P. O'Donnell not out . . . . . . . . . . . . . 20 |
| G. M. Wood retired hurt . . . . . . . . . . . . 52 | |
| K. C. Wessels c Silva b Ratnayeke . . . . 1 | B 4, l-b 4, w 4, n-b 6 . . . . . . . . 18 |
| *A. R. Border not out . . . . . . . . . . . . . . . 79 | |
| D. C. Boon c sub b de Mel . . . . . . . . . . 44 | 1/68 2/70 3/171 (4 wkts, 46.2 overs) 240 |
| †W. B. Phillips c Silva b de Mel . . . . . . 3 | 4/176 |

M. J. Bennett, C. J. McDermott, R. M. Hogg and C. G. Rackemann did not bat.

Bowling: de Mel 9.3–9–59–2; John 9–1–40–0; Ratnayake 8.5–0–32–0; Ratnayeke 9–0–69–1; D. S. de Silva 10–1–32–0.

Umpires: R. A. French and P. J. McConnell.

## †SRI LANKA v WEST INDIES

At Hobart, January 10. West Indies won by eight wickets. Sri Lanka never had a chance after they had lost the toss and been put in on a lively pitch. Garner was particularly awkward in his opening spell, but Mendis's swashbuckling 56, which included 29 off nine balls from Richards, and an unbroken stand of 52 from eleven overs between Karnain and Ratnayake, represented a spirited recovery. West Indies, however, were never in any danger and won with 9.2 overs to spare.

*Man of the Match:* L. R. D. Mendis. *Attendance:* 6,000 (estimated).

### Sri Lanka

| | |
|---|---|
| S. Wettimuny c Richards b Garner . . . . 8 | J. R. Ratnayeke b Richards . . . . . . . . . . 8 |
| †S. A. R. Silva c Dujon b Garner . . . . . 4 | U. S. H. Karnain not out . . . . . . . . . . . . 20 |
| D. S. B. P. Kuruppu c Richardson b Holding. 8 | R. J. Ratnayake not out . . . . . . . . . . . . . 23 |
| R. L. Dias c Dujon b Walsh . . . . . . . . . 27 | B 12, l-b 10, w 12, n-b 1 . . . . . 35 |
| *L. R. D. Mendis run out . . . . . . . . . . . 56 | 1/19 2/24 3/39 (7 wkts, 50 overs) 197 |
| P. A. de Silva c sub b Richards . . . . . . . 8 | 4/115 5/127 6/142 7/145 |

D. S. de Silva and V. B. John did not bat.

Bowling: Marshall 10–3–37–0; Garner 10–1–19–2; Holding 10–1–25–1; Walsh 10–1–47–1; Richards 10–2–47–2.

### West Indies

| | |
|---|---|
| C. G. Greenidge c Kuruppu b D. S. de Silva. 61 | A. L. Logie not out . . . . . . . . . . . . . . . . . 34 |
| D. L. Haynes c Silva b Ratnayake . . . . 32 | L-b 11, w 5, n-b 3 . . . . . . . . . . 19 |
| R. B. Richardson not out . . . . . . . . . . . . 52 | 1/50 2/144 (2 wkts, 40.4 overs) 198 |

*I. V. A. Richards, H. A. Gomes, †P. J. L. Dujon, M. D. Marshall, M. A. Holding, J. Garner and C. A. Walsh did not bat.

Bowling: John 6.4–2–30–0; Ratnayeke 7–0–41–0; Ratnayake 7–0–31–1; D. S. de Silva 10–3–29–1; Karnain 8–0–41–0; P. A. de Silva 2–0–15–0.

Umpires: R. C. Isherwood and S. G. Randell.

## †SRI LANKA v WEST INDIES

At Brisbane, January 12. West Indies won by 90 runs. West Indies, without Greenidge and Haynes, both injured, started uncertainly after being put in but finally reached the highest total in a WSC match at Brisbane through a one-day international fifth-wicket record stand of 152 between Richards (three 6s and six 4s) and Lloyd (three 6s and seven 4s). Dias's stylish 80 was an innings of genuine quality, but Sri Lanka were always losing.

*Man of the Match:* I. V. A. Richards. *Attendance:* 9,626.

### West Indies

R. B. Richardson c Silva b John ...... 1
T. R. O. Payne c John b Karnain ..... 20
H. A. Gomes c Silva b Karnain ..... 28
*I. V. A. Richards c Silva b John ..... 98
A. L. Logie c P. A. de Silva b D. S. de Silva. 10
C. H. Lloyd not out ................ 89
†P. J. L. Dujon c Mendis b Ratnayake 11
M. D. Marshall not out ............. 1
B 1, l-b 5, w 4, n-b 2 ........ 12

1/7 2/45 3/73 4/92 5/244 6/269 (6 wkts, 50 overs) 270

M. A. Holding, W. W. Davis and J. Garner did not bat.

Bowling: G. N. de Silva 10–0–42–0; John 10–2–52–2; Ratnayake 10–0–39–1; Karnain 10–0–55–2; D. S. de Silva 8–0–57–1; Dias 2–0–19–0.

### Sri Lanka

S. Wettimuny c Dujon b Garner ...... 2
†S. A. R. Silva b Davis .............. 20
D. S. B. P. Kuruppu c Payne b Holding 4
R. L. Dias c Dujon b Holding ........ 80
*L. R. D. Mendis b Holding ......... 14
P. A. de Silva c Richards b Davis ..... 13
U. S. H. Karnain st Dujon b Richards . 9
R. J. Ratnayake st Dujon b Richards .. 19
D. S. de Silva b Lloyd .............. 9
V. B. John c Logie b Gomes ......... 0
G. N. de Silva not out .............. 2
L-b 3, w 3, n-b 2 ........... 8

1/4 2/29 3/35 4/59 5/88 6/114 7/144 8/176 9/177 (48.1 overs) 180

Bowling: Marshall 5–2–9–0; Garner 5–2–14–1; Holding 10–0–38–3; Davis 10–0–29–2; Richards 10–0–45–2; Gomes 8–0–42–1; Lloyd 0.1–0–0–1.

Umpires: R. A. French and M. W. Johnson.

## †AUSTRALIA v WEST INDIES

At Brisbane, January 13. West Indies won by five wickets. Put in, Australia batted so slowly early in their innings that the later batsmen were under considerable pressure to accelerate the run-rate. Wessels spent 25 overs making 47 and the consequence was four run-outs later, three by Lloyd, who hit the stumps to remove Border and O'Donnell and returned to the bowler to dismiss Rixon. As they had the day before, Richards and Lloyd shared a robust and decisive partnership for West Indies.

*Man of the Match:* C. H. Lloyd. *Attendance:* 22,012.

### Australia

G. M. Wood c Dujon b Richards ..... 38
A. M. J. Hilditch c Garner b Davis ... 19
K. C. Wessels c Logie b Richards ..... 47
*A. R. Border run out .............. 7
D. C. Boon lbw b Richards .......... 4
S. P. O'Donnell run out ............ 25
†S. J. Rixon run out ................ 3
M. J. Bennett c Logie b Marshall ..... 3
G. F. Lawson c Dujon b Garner ...... 7
C. J. McDermott run out ............ 13
R. M. Hogg not out ................ 6
L-b 10, w 4, n-b 5 .......... 19

1/49 2/77 3/97 4/107 5/153 6/160 7/162 8/171 9/173 (50 overs) 191

Bowling: Marshall 10–2–42–1; Garner 10–1–33–1; Holding 10–0–31–0; Davis 10–0–37–1; Richards 10–0–38–3.

### West Indies

| | |
|---|---|
| D. L. Haynes c Hogg b O'Donnell | 46 |
| R. B. Richardson b McDermott | 16 |
| H. A. Gomes b McDermott | 0 |
| I. V. A. Richards c Border b Hogg | 49 |
| *C. H. Lloyd not out | 52 |
| A. L. Logie c Rixon b O'Donnell | 7 |
| †P. J. L. Dujon not out | 6 |
| B 5, l-b 8, w 5, n-b 1 | 19 |
| 1/50 2/50 3/74 4/172 5/188 (5 wkts, 37.4 overs) | 195 |

M. D. Marshall, M. A. Holding, W. W. Davis and J. Garner did not bat.

Bowling: Lawson 10–1–35–0; Hogg 8–1–41–1; O'Donnell 9–0–47–2; McDermott 7–1–33–2; Bennett 3–0–21–0; Boon 0.4–0–5–0.

Umpires: M. W. Johnson and S. G. Randell.

## †AUSTRALIA v WEST INDIES

At Sydney, January 15 (day/night). West Indies won by five wickets. After Border had elected to bat, Wessels's slowness (out for 63 in the 39th over) and crucial run-outs again hampered Australia's effort. McDermott, generating great speed, dismissed Haynes and Gomes in the same over and Lawson then had Richardson lbw, but Border took McDermott off after six overs, Richards plundered O'Donnell, and the result was never in doubt after that. Richards's hundred, from 122 balls, included one 6 and eight 4s and was his eighth in one-day internationals.

*Man of the Match:* I. V. A. Richards. *Attendance:* 45,779.

### Australia

| | |
|---|---|
| G. M. Wood c Holding b Davis | 21 |
| K. C. Wessels st Dujon b Richards | 63 |
| D. C. Boon run out | 20 |
| *A. R. Border run out | 24 |
| G. M. Ritchie not out | 30 |
| S. P. O'Donnell b Marshall | 17 |
| †S. J. Rixon not out | 2 |
| L-b 10, w 3, n-b 10 | 23 |
| 1/42 2/103 3/137 4/161 5/197 (5 wkts, 50 overs) | 200 |

G. F. Lawson, M. J. Bennett, C. J. McDermott and R. G. Holland did not bat.

Bowling: Marshall 10–0–38–1; Garner 10–1–44–0; Holding 10–1–36–0; Davis 10–2–31–1; Richards 10–0–41–1.

### West Indies

| | |
|---|---|
| D. L. Haynes c O'Donnell b McDermott | 13 |
| R. B. Richardson lbw b Lawson | 9 |
| H. A. Gomes c Wessels b McDermott | 0 |
| I. V. A. Richards not out | 103 |
| *C. H. Lloyd c Rixon b McDermott | 38 |
| A. L. Logie c Rixon b Lawson | 12 |
| †P. J. L. Dujon not out | 15 |
| B 1, l-b 5, w 2, n-b 3 | 11 |
| 1/23 2/23 3/25 4/115 5/138 (5 wkts, 43.3 overs) | 201 |

M. D. Marshall, M. A. Holding, W. W. Davis and J. Garner did not bat.

Bowling: Lawson 10–1–32–2; McDermott 10–0–30–3; Bennett 6–0–40–0; O'Donnell 7.3–0–43–0; Holland 10–0–50–0.

Umpires: R. C. Isherwood and S. G. Randell.

## †SRI LANKA v WEST INDIES

At Sydney, January 17 (day/night). West Indies won by 65 runs. Sri Lanka's inexperience was exposed in every department. Lloyd having won the toss, Greenidge and Haynes took advantage of loose bowling and fielding to put on 128 from 28 overs, and Richardson, Richards and Logie also enjoyed themselves. Once Sri Lanka had lost four wickets for 64 the match was as good as over, although Dias again demonstrated his class and Karnain hit effectively at the end.

*Man of the Match:* C. G. Greenidge. *Attendance:* 9,179.

### West Indies

C. G. Greenidge b D. S. de Silva ..... 67
D. L. Haynes run out ................ 54
R. B. Richardson not out ............. 57
*I. V. A. Richards b de Mel .......... 30
A. L. Logie not out ................. 47
L-b 5, w 5, n-b 2 ........... 12

1/128 2/128 3/186 (3 wkts, 50 overs) 267

†P. J. L. Dujon, M. D. Marshall, R. A. Harper, M. A. Holding, W. W. Davis and C. A. Walsh did not bat.

Bowling: de Mel 10-1-50-1; John 10-0-53-0; Ratnayeke 3-0-19-0; Ratnayake 10-0-58-0; D. S. de Silva 10-1-48-1; Karnain 7-1-34-0.

### Sri Lanka

†S. A. R. Silva c Greenidge b Marshall 5
J. R. Ratnayeke c Dujon b Davis ..... 17
P. A. de Silva c Dujon b Holding ..... 21
*L. R. D. Mendis c Dujon b Holding .. 2
R. L. Dias not out .................. 65
R. S. Madugalle b Harper ........... 25
U. S. H. Karnain not out ............ 41
B 2, l-b 7, w 4, n-b 13 ....... 26

1/12 2/54 3/54 4/64 5/124 (5 wkts, 50 overs) 202

R. J. Ratnayake, A. L. F. de Mel, D. S. de Silva and V. B. John did not bat.

Bowling: Marshall 10-1-33-1; Walsh 10-1-45-0; Davis 10-0-52-1; Holding 10-2-32-2; Harper 10-0-31-1.

Umpires: M. W. Johnson and B. E. Martin.

## †AUSTRALIA v SRI LANKA

At Melbourne, January 19. Sri Lanka won by four wickets. Having chosen to field first, Sri Lanka excelled themselves after a discouraging start wherein Wessels and Wood raced away to score 68 in Australia's first seventeen overs. Ratnayake dismissed them both and, together with the veteran leg-spinner, D. S. de Silva, bowled well enough to restrict Australia to a reachable total. For Sri Lanka Dias and Mendis put on an invaluable 64 in eleven overs and P. A. de Silva played a responsible innings, crowned when he hit the winning runs with a 6 off the second ball of the final over.

*Man of the Match:* R. J. Ratnayake. *Attendance:* 16,635.

### Australia

G. M. Wood b Ratnayake ........... 42
K. C. Wessels b Ratnayake .......... 28
G. M. Ritchie c Madugalle b Karnain . 13
*A. R. Border st Silva b D. S. de Silva . 1
D. C. Boon c Wettimuny b Dias ...... 34
†W. B. Phillips c de Mel b Dias ...... 67
S. P. O'Donnell b Ratnayake ......... 7
G. F. Lawson c Madugalle b Dias .... 11
M. J. Bennett not out ............... 6
C. J. McDermott b Ratnayake ....... 0
R. M. Hogg not out ................ 5
L-b 9, w 3 ................. 12

1/68 2/73 3/74 4/88 5/160 6/191 7/204 8/220 9/220 (9 wkts, 50 overs) 226

Bowling: de Mel 7-1-45-0; John 10-1-32-0; Ratnayake 10-3-37-4; D. S. de Silva 10-0-33-1; Karnain 9-0-45-1; Dias 4-0-25-3.

### Sri Lanka

S. Wettimuny lbw b Hogg ........... 17
†S. A. R. Silva c Hogg b O'Donnell ... 23
R. S. Madugalle c Border b O'Donnell . 24
R. L. Dias run out .................. 48
*L. R. D. Mendis c Wessels b Hogg ... 35
P. A. de Silva not out ............... 46
U. S. H. Karnain b Lawson .......... 16
R. J. Ratnayake not out ............. 5
B 1, l-b 14, n-b 1 ........... 16

1/38 2/52 3/86 4/150 5/161 6/196 (6 wkts, 49.2 overs) 230

A. L. F. de Mel, D. S. de Silva and V. B. John did not bat.

Bowling: Lawson 10–0–51–1; McDermott 9.2–1–36–0; Hogg 10–1–31–2; O'Donnell 10–1–43–2; Bennett 9–1–48–0; Wessels 1–0–6–0.

Umpires: R. A. French and M. W. Johnson.

## †AUSTRALIA v WEST INDIES

At Melbourne, January 20. West Indies won by 65 runs. Nothing went right for Australia after they had won the toss. They dropped Richards at 5, 6, and 62 and fielded poorly as West Indies equalled their previous highest WSC total. The decision to omit Bennett meant Wessels and Border sharing ten overs that cost them 74. A wholesale shuffling of their batting order reflected Australian panic and, after losing their first four wickets for 34, they could not make any sort of show.

*Man of the Match:* I. V. A. Richards. *Attendance:* 53,367.

### West Indies

C. G. Greenidge c Phillips b Hogg .... 33
D. L. Haynes c and b O'Donnell ...... 23
R. B. Richardson c Phillips b O'Donnell 21
I. V. A. Richards c Boon b McDermott 74
*C. H. Lloyd run out ............... 16
A. L. Logie c Border b Wessels ....... 72
†P. J. L. Dujon c Phillips b Hogg ..... 23
M. A. Holding not out ............... 2
M. D. Marshall not out .............. 2
B 1, l-b 3, w 1 .............. 5

1/56 2/58 3/103 (7 wkts, 50 overs) 271
4/138 5/201 6/252 7/268

J. Garner and W. W. Davis did not bat.

Bowling: Lawson 10–0–47–0; McDermott 10–0–50–1; Hogg 10–1–56–2; O'Donnell 10–0–40–2; Wessels 8–0–58–1; Border 2–0–16–0.

### Australia

G. M. Wood c Dujon b Marshall ..... 9
†W. B. Phillips c Greenidge b Garner . 4
D. M. Jones c Haynes b Marshall ..... 0
S. P. O'Donnell run out ............. 11
*A. R. Border c Richards b Holding ... 61
D. C. Boon b Richards ............... 34
G. M. Ritchie b Davis ............... 6
K. C. Wessels b Richards ........... 21
G. F. Lawson not out ................ 18
C. J. McDermott run out ............. 19
B 6, l-b 12, w 1, n-b 4 ....... 23

1/14 2/15 3/21 (9 wkts, 50 overs) 206
4/34 5/115 6/126 7/163
8/169 9/206

R. M. Hogg did not bat.

Bowling: Marshall 9–1–29–2; Garner 9–2–17–1; Holding 10–1–36–1; Davis 10–1–52–1; Richards 10–0–43–2; Logie 1–0–10–0; Richardson 1–0–1–0.

Umpires: R. C. Isherwood and P. G. McConnell.

## †AUSTRALIA v SRI LANKA

At Sydney, January 23. Australia won by three wickets. With Sri Lanka still in contention to reach the final, Australia were keen to avoid another embarrassment, and they started well enough after inserting Sri Lanka with Wessels taking two quick wickets. From 55 for four, however, Mendis and Aravinda de Silva added a splendid 139, leaving their side with what looked a useful score, especially when Wood and Smith were out early. But Sri Lanka's bowling fell away rather badly and in the end Wessels, Border and Jones comfortably achieved the required run-rate.

*Man of the Match:* K. C. Wessels. *Attendance:* 22,152.

### Sri Lanka

| | | | |
|---|---|---|---|
| †S. A. R. Silva run out | 2 | R. J. Ratnayake b McDermott | 7 |
| S. Wettimuny b Wessels | 21 | U. S. H. Karnain not out | 10 |
| R. S. Madugalle c Phillips b Hogg | 7 | L-b 9, w 1, n-b 3 | 13 |
| R. L. Dias c Phillips b Wessels | 19 | | |
| *L. R. D. Mendis c Phillips b Lawson | 80 | 1/3 2/23 3/54 (6 wkts, 50 overs) | 240 |
| P. A. de Silva not out | 81 | 4/55 5/194 6/204 | |

A. L. F. de Mel, D. S. de Silva and V. B. John did not bat.

Bowling: Lawson 10–2–32–1; McDermott 10–1–59–1; Hogg 10–2–33–1; O'Donnell 10–0–46–0; Wessels 10–0–61–2.

### Australia

| | | | |
|---|---|---|---|
| G. M. Wood c Ratnayake b de Mel | 0 | S. P. O'Donnell c Karnain b de Mel | 2 |
| S. B. Smith c Silva b John | 4 | G. F. Lawson not out | 0 |
| K. C. Wessels c Mendis b Karnain | 82 | | |
| *A. R. Border st Silva b D. S. de Silva | 57 | L-b 10, w 3 | 13 |
| D. M. Jones not out | 62 | | |
| D. C. Boon lbw b John | 3 | 1/0 2/29 3/119 (7 wkts, 47.1 overs) | 242 |
| †W. B. Phillips b Ratnayake | 19 | 4/187 5/195 6/231 7/238 | |

C. J. McDermott and R. M. Hogg did not bat.

Bowling: de Mel 8–0–53–2; John 10–1–35–2; D. S. de Silva 10–0–62–1; Karnain 10–0–38–1; Ratnayake 8.1–0–37–1; Dias 1–0–7–0.

Umpires: A. R. Crafter and S. G. Randell.

## †SRI LANKA v WEST INDIES

At Adelaide, January 26. West Indies won by eight wickets. Sri Lanka, put in, were outplayed from start to finish. They were unable to score a run from Davis's first five overs; slumped to 22 for three in the thirteenth over, and were given only slim hope by Dias and Mendis who added 93 from eighteen overs. Greenidge, whose sixth century in one-day internationals included ten 4s (and two chances before he was 40), and Haynes emphasised the insignificance of the Sri Lankan total by scoring 133 from 22 overs.

*Man of the Match:* C. G. Greenidge. *Attendance:* 7,402.

### Sri Lanka

| | | | |
|---|---|---|---|
| †S. A. R. Silva c Garner b Davis | 5 | U. S. H. Karnain not out | 20 |
| D. S. B. P. Kuruppu c Dujon b Walsh | 7 | R. J. Ratnayake not out | 12 |
| R. S. Madugalle b Davis | 1 | B 2, l-b 9, w 2, n-b 4 | 17 |
| R. L. Dias b Holding | 66 | | |
| *L. R. D. Mendis c Richards b Davis | 45 | 1/5 2/13 3/22 (6 wkts, 50 overs) | 204 |
| A. Ranatunga c sub b Holding | 31 | 4/115 5/164 6/181 | |

A. L. F. de Mel, D. S. de Silva and G. N. de Silva did not bat.

Bowling: Garner 10–2–27–0; Davis 10–5–21–3; Walsh 10–0–54–1; Holding 10–0–46–2; Richards 10–0–45–0.

### West Indies

| | |
|---|---|
| C. G. Greenidge not out | 110 |
| D. L. Haynes b D. S. de Silva | 51 |
| H. A. Gomes c and b Ranatunga | 24 |
| A. L. Logie not out | 7 |
| L-b 4, w 1, n-b 8 | 13 |
| 1/133 2/178 (2 wkts, 37.2 overs) | 205 |

*I. V. A. Richards, C. H. Lloyd, †P. J. L. Dujon, M. A. Holding, J. Garner, W. W. Davis and C. A. Walsh did not bat.

Bowling: de Mel 4–0–34–0; G. N. de Silva 8.2–1–56–0; Ratnayake 10–0–41–0; D. S. de Silva 7–0–36–1; Ranatunga 8–1–34–1.

Umpires: R. A. French and B. E. Martin.

## †AUSTRALIA v WEST INDIES

At Adelaide, January 27. West Indies won by six wickets. Wood was both the hero and the villain of Australia's inadequate total. Carrying his bat for 104 from 142 deliveries, Australia having been asked to bat, he was involved in all three run-outs and was clearly at fault in that of Phillips, who was hitting the ball well when their stand of 82 was ended. West Indies, aided once more by poor catching which gave chances to Greenidge at 9 and 31, Richards at 17 and 19, and Lloyd at 1, won with 6.2 overs to spare.

*Man of the Match:* J. Garner. *Attendance:* 30,728.

### Australia

K. C. Wessels run out . . . . . . . . . . . . . . . 1
G. M. Wood not out . . . . . . . . . . . . . . . . 104
*A. R. Border lbw b Marshall . . . . . . . . 0
D. M. Jones b Garner . . . . . . . . . . . . . . 11
S. B. Smith c Dujon b Davis . . . . . . . . . 21
†W. B. Phillips run out . . . . . . . . . . . . . . 36
S. P. O'Donnell c Dujon b Garner . . . . 9
G. F. Lawson hit wkt b Marshall . . . . . 4
C. J. McDermott c Logie b Garner . . . . 2
R. J. McCurdy run out . . . . . . . . . . . . . . . 1
R. M. Hogg not out . . . . . . . . . . . . . . . . 3
L-b 5, n-b 3 . . . . . . . . . . . . . . 8

1/4 2/4 3/19 4/72 5/154 6/167 7/178 8/181 9/184 (9 wkts, 50 overs) 200

Bowling: Garner 10–3–17–3; Marshall 10–1–35–2; Davis 10–0–53–1; Holding 10–0–51–0; Richards 10–0–39–0.

### West Indies

C. G. Greenidge lbw b McDermott . . . 39
D. L. Haynes b McCurdy . . . . . . . . . . . . 14
R. B. Richardson c Smith b McDermott 34
I. V. A. Richards c Border b McCurdy . 51
*C. H. Lloyd not out . . . . . . . . . . . . . . . 47
A. L. Logie not out . . . . . . . . . . . . . . . . 2
B 2, l-b 8, w 1, n-b 3 . . . . . . . . 14

1/31 2/93 3/103 4/199 (4 wkts, 43.4 overs) 201

†P. J. L. Dujon, M. D. Marshall, W. W. Davis, M. A. Holding and J. Garner did not bat.

Bowling: Lawson 9–0–32–0; McCurdy 9.4–2–38–2; McDermott 7–0–37–2; Hogg 8–0–46–0; O'Donnell 10–1–38–0.

Umpires: A. R. Crafter and M. W. Johnson.

## †AUSTRALIA v SRI LANKA

At Adelaide, January 28. Australia won by 232 runs. Australia's total was the highest ever made in a 50-over international match, Border and Jones running riot in an unbeaten stand of 224, the highest for any wicket in limited-overs internationals. Sri Lanka, who had chosen to bowl first, were demoralised and their batsmen had no answer to the pace of Lawson and McCurdy.

*Man of the Match:* A. R. Border. *Attendance:* 19,637.

### Australia

G. M. Wood c D. S. de Silva b Karnain 30
S. B. Smith c Silva b Karnain ........ 55
D. M. Jones not out ................ 99
*A. R. Border not out ...............118
B 6, l-b 8, w 4, n-b 3 ........ 21

1/94 2/99 (2 wkts, 50 overs) 323

D. C. Boon, K. C. Wessels, †W. B. Phillips, G. F. Lawson, S. P. O'Donnell, R. J. McCurdy and R. M. Hogg did not bat.

Bowling: Ratnayake 10–1–51–0; John 10–1–64–0; G. N. de Silva 10–0–50–0; D. S. de Silva 5–0–42–0; Karnain 8–0–56–2; Ranatunga 6–0–36–0; Dias 1–0–10–0.

### Sri Lanka

†S. A. R. Silva lbw b McCurdy ....... 0
A. Ranatunga c Phillips b McCurdy ... 5
P. A. de Silva lbw b Lawson ......... 6
R. L. Dias c Smith b Lawson ........ 3
*L. R. D. Mendis c Boon b McCurdy . 7
R. S. Madugalle lbw b O'Donnell ..... 8
U. S. H. Karnain c Wessels b O'Donnell 21
R. J. Ratnayake c Jones b Hogg ...... 2
D. S. de Silva not out ............... 15
V. B. John c Hogg b Wessels ......... 8
G. N. de Silva st Phillips b Wessels ... 7
B 1, l-b 5, w 3 ............ 9

1/3 2/12 3/14 4/23 5/25 6/45 7/52 8/66 9/75 (35.5 overs) 91

Bowling: Lawson 7–5–5–2; McCurdy 5–1–19–3; Hogg 8–1–18–1; O'Donnell 9–1–19–2; Wessels 4.5–0–16–2; Boon 2–0–8–0.

Umpires: B. E. Martin and R. C. Isherwood.

## †SRI LANKA v WEST INDIES

At Perth, February 2. West Indies won by 82 runs, so becoming the first team to win all its matches in the preliminary round of a WSC tournament. Put in by Mendis, they started with the stated intention of attempting to beat Australia's record total of 323 for two set the previous weekend against Sri Lanka but fell just short. Gomes's first hundred in a one-day international included his first 6 hit for West Indies in an international match and he had three in all, along with six 4s, as Sri Lanka went to pieces in the field. The left-handed Silva's 85 from 96 balls was the feature of Sri Lanka's innings.

*Man of the Match:* H. A. Gomes. *Attendance:* 11,154.

### West Indies

C. G. Greenidge b Ratnayake ........ 42
D. L. Haynes c Silva b John ......... 27
H. A. Gomes c Dias b de Mel ........101
*I. V. A. Richards b John ........... 46
A. L. Logie run out ................. 6
C. H. Lloyd not out ................ 54
†P. J. L. Dujon c de Silva b de Mel ... 13
M. D. Marshall not out ............. 2
L-b 10, w 6, n-b 2 .......... 18

1/47 2/99 3/216 4/223 5/241 6/280 (6 wkts, 50 overs) 309

W. W. Davis, J. Garner and C. A. Walsh did not bat.

Bowling: de Mel 10–0–67–2; John 10–0–44–2; Ratnayake 10–0–58–1; Ratnayeke 10–0–48–0; Karnain 6–0–35–0; Ranatunga 3–0–39–0; Dias 1–0–8–0.

### Sri Lanka

S. Wettimuny run out ............... 0
†S. A. R. Silva c Dujon b Walsh ...... 85
J. R. Ratnayeke b Richards .......... 24
R. L. Dias run out ................. 1
*L. R. D. Mendis c Dujon b Walsh ... 8
P. A. de Silva c Dujon b Richards .... 5
A. Ranatunga not out ............... 63
U. S. H. Karnain not out ............ 28
L-b 6, w 5, n-b 2 .......... 13

1/0 2/100 3/102 4/120 5/133 6/137 (6 wkts, 50 overs) 227

R. J. Ratnayake, A. L. F. de Mel and V. B. John did not bat.

Bowling: Garner 6–3–6–0; Davis 6–1–34–0; Marshall 6–0–17–0; Walsh 10–0–52–2; Richards 10–0–47–2; Gomes 7–0–41–0; Haynes 5–0–24–0.

Umpires: A. R. Crafter and S. G. Randell.

## †AUSTRALIA v SRI LANKA

At Perth, February 3. Australia won by nine wickets. With no chance of making the final Sri Lanka, electing to bat first this time, proved easy victims for Australia, who won with 26 overs to spare.

*Man of the Match:* S. B. Smith.

### Sri Lanka

| | |
|---|---|
| †S. A. R. Silva c Phillips b O'Donnell | 51 |
| D. M. Vonhagt c Wessels b Alderman | 8 |
| *L. R. D. Mendis c Wood b Lawson | 2 |
| R. L. Dias c Alderman b Lawson | 4 |
| P. A. de Silva st Phillips b Wessels | 52 |
| A. Ranatunga c Phillips b Hogg | 10 |
| U. S. H. Karnain c Border b Hogg | 8 |
| J. R. Ratnayeke run out | 1 |
| R. J. Ratnayake c Phillips b O'Donnell | 16 |
| A. L. F. de Mel not out | 11 |
| V. B. John b McCurdy | 0 |
| L-b 2, w 5, n-b 1 | 8 |
| 1/16 2/19 3/26 4/94 5/110 6/123 7/126 8/147 9/166 (44.3 overs) | 171 |

Bowling: Lawson 7–1–24–2; Alderman 10–0–41–1; McCurdy 5.3–0–15–1; O'Donnell 10–0–42–2; Hogg 10–1–40–2; Wessels 2–0–7–1.

### Australia

| | |
|---|---|
| K. C. Wessels c Silva b John | 8 |
| S. B. Smith not out | 73 |
| †W. B. Phillips not out | 75 |
| L-b 8, w 6, n-b 2 | 16 |
| 1/15 (1 wkt, 23.5 overs) | 172 |

S. P. O'Donnell, *A. R. Border, G. M. Wood, D. M. Jones, G. F. Lawson, R. J. McCurdy, R. M. Hogg and T. M. Alderman did not bat.

Bowling: de Mel 8–0–45–0; John 6.5–0–43–1; Ratnayake 5–0–40–0; Ratnayeke 4–0–36–0.

Umpires: B. E. Martin and P. J. McConnell.

## QUALIFYING TABLE

| | *P* | *W* | *L* | *Pts* |
|---|---|---|---|---|
| West Indies | 10 | 10 | 0 | 20 |
| Australia | 10 | 4 | 6 | 8 |
| Sri Lanka | 10 | 1 | 9 | 2 |

## †AUSTRALIA v WEST INDIES

### First Final Match

At Sydney, February 6 (day/night). Australia won by 26 runs. A magnificent, unbeaten 127 by Border, rated one of the best one-day innings he had seen by Border's opposite number, Lloyd – and the best of all by the former England captain, Tony Greig – gave Australia the total and inspiration they needed. Border came in after both openers had been dismissed by lifting balls from Garner, took a painful blow on the chest from Garner early on, and saw the total slump to 64 for four in the eighteenth over before Phillips helped him add 105 in 20.4 overs. As Border hit thirteen 4s from the 140 deliveries he faced, West Indies' outcricket became unusually ragged. They delivered twenty no-balls and fielded poorly. They also batted unconvincingly, Richards offering three chances in 68, although Marshall and Garner raised their hopes temporarily by adding 63 for the ninth wicket.

*Attendance:* 29,588.

## Australia

| | | | |
|---|---|---|---|
| S. B. Smith c Richardson b Garner | 6 | S. P. O'Donnell lbw b Garner | 17 |
| G. M. Wood c Richards b Garner | 0 | G. F. Lawson not out | 14 |
| K. C. Wessels c Dujon b Marshall | 11 | B 2, l-b 6, n-b 11 | 19 |
| *A. R. Border not out | 127 | | |
| D. M. Jones b Davis | 3 | 1/3 2/7 3/58 (6 wkts, 50 overs) | 247 |
| †W. B. Phillips c Garner b Holding | 50 | 4/64 5/169 6/205 | |

C. J. McDermott, R. J. McCurdy and R. M. Hogg did not bat.

Bowling: Garner 10–3–29–3; Holding 10–0–40–1; Marshall 10–0–55–1; Davis 10–0–57–1; Richards 10–0–58–0.

## West Indies

| | | | |
|---|---|---|---|
| D. L. Haynes b Lawson | 11 | M. A. Holding b O'Donnell | 1 |
| R. B. Richardson lbw b McCurdy | 0 | J. Garner run out | 27 |
| H. A. Gomes lbw b McCurdy | 9 | W. W. Davis not out | 8 |
| I. V. A. Richards b McDermott | 68 | L-b 7, n-b 1 | 8 |
| *C. H. Lloyd c Wessels b McDermott | 20 | | |
| A. L. Logie c Wood b Hogg | 12 | 1/10 2/20 3/20 (47.3 overs) | 221 |
| †P. J. L. Dujon b McDermott | 14 | 4/82 5/107 6/137 7/140 | |
| M. D. Marshall b McCurdy | 43 | 8/147 9/210 | |

Bowling: Lawson 9–1–41–1; McCurdy 9.3–1–40–3; Hogg 10–0–35–1; McDermott 10–0–44–3; O'Donnell 9–0–54–1.

Umpires: A. R. Crafter and M. W. Johnson.

## †AUSTRALIA v WEST INDIES

### Second Final Match

At Melbourne, February 10. West Indies won by four wickets when Dujon hit successive off-side boundaries off the first two balls of the final over from Hogg. It was a magnificent match, and until Logie and Dujon came together Australia held the upper hand. Their highest total in the tournament against West Indies, coming after Lloyd had put them in, was based on an opening partnership of 135 in 30 overs between Smith and Wood and a boisterous 56 from 37 balls by Phillips. Garner and Marshall both conceded 60 runs for the first time in a one-day international. Haynes and Richardson, who had replaced the injured Greenidge in the finals, gave West Indies the ideal start with 78 in sixteen overs, and Gomes consolidated with a confident 47. However, O'Donnell dismissed both Richardson and Gomes, and Lawson, returning early for his final spell, removed Richards and Lloyd cheaply. When Lloyd went in the 37th over, West Indies were 92 behind. But Lawson exhausted his allotted overs in the 39th. Logie (60 off 56 balls with five 4s) and Dujon then unleashed strokes in all directions and ran skilfully to make victory possible. Luck was on their side as Logie was dropped at 28 and 32, and there were several close shaves between the wickets.

*Attendance:* 39,746.

### Australia

| | | | |
|---|---|---|---|
| S. B. Smith b Davis | 54 | D. M. Jones not out | 13 |
| G. M. Wood c Richards b Holding | 81 | B 2, l-b 10, w 7, n-b 9 | 28 |
| *A. R. Border c Dujon b Marshall | 39 | | —— |
| †W. B. Phillips not out | 56 | 1/135 2/186 3/203 (3 wkts, 50 overs) | 271 |

K. C. Wessels, S. P. O'Donnell, G. F. Lawson, C. J. McDermott, R. J. McCurdy and R. M. Hogg did not bat.

Bowling: Garner 10–0–60–0; Marshall 10–0–64–1; Holding 10–1–41–1; Davis 10–0–43–1; Richards 10–0–51–0.

### West Indies

| | | | |
|---|---|---|---|
| D. L. Haynes c Wessels b Hogg | 44 | †P. J. L. Dujon not out | 39 |
| R. B. Richardson c Wessels b O'Donnell | 50 | M. D. Marshall not out | 0 |
| H. A. Gomes b O'Donnell | 47 | B 2, l-b 8, n-b 1 | 11 |
| I. V. A. Richards lbw b Lawson | 9 | | —— |
| *C. H. Lloyd c O'Donnell b Lawson | 13 | 1/78 2/137 3/154 (6 wkts, 49.2 overs) | 273 |
| A. L. Logie hit wkt b McCurdy | 60 | 4/158 5/179 6/265 | |

M. A. Holding, W. W. Davis and J. Garner did not bat.

Bowling: Lawson 10–0–34–2; McCurdy 10–0–69–1; McDermott 10–0–56–0; Hogg 9.2–0–58–1; O'Donnell 10–0–46–2.

Umpires: R. C. Isherwood and P. J. McConnell.

## †AUSTRALIA v WEST INDIES

### Third Final Match

At Sydney, February 12 (day/night). West Indies won by seven wickets, securing the World Series Cup for the fourth time in a match that proved an anti-climax. Australia, put in, laboured against West Indies' bowling and fielding, which reverted to its highest standards, and could manage only 67 for four by the halfway stage of their innings. Wood had also retired hurt with a cracked finger. O'Donnell hit two 6s and three 4s in his highest score of the tournament, but West Indies made light work of their target as Haynes and Richards added 128 from 29 overs.

*Man of the Finals:* A. R. Border and M. A. Holding (shared). *Attendance:* 31,399.

### Australia

| | | | |
|---|---|---|---|
| G. M. Wood not out | 36 | C. J. McDermott c Dujon b Holding | 0 |
| K. C. Wessels c Richards b Holding | 17 | R. J. McCurdy run out | 12 |
| R. B. Kerr c Logie b Davis | 4 | R. M. Hogg c Richards b Garner | 1 |
| *A. R. Border c Garner b Holding | 4 | B 2, l-b 4, w 4, n-b 2 | 12 |
| D. M. Jones b Richards | 16 | | —— |
| †W. B. Phillips c Dujon b Holding | 3 | 1/47 2/51 3/57 (50 overs) | 178 |
| S. P. O'Donnell c and b Garner | 69 | 4/64 5/80 6/89 7/89 | |
| G. F. Lawson c Richards b Holding | 4 | 8/124 9/176 | |

Bowling: Garner 10–4–34–2; Marshall 10–0–37–0; Davis 10–1–23–1; Holding 10–1–26–5; Richards 10–0–52–1.

### West Indies

| | | | |
|---|---|---|---|
| D. L. Haynes not out | 76 | A. L. Logie not out | 11 |
| R. B. Richardson run out | 3 | B 4, l-b 2, n-b 4 | 10 |
| H. A. Gomes c Border b McDermott | 3 | | —— |
| I. V. A. Richards c sub b McDermott | 76 | 1/14 2/34 3/162 (3 wkts, 47 overs) | 179 |

*C. H. Lloyd, †P. J. L. Dujon, M. D. Marshall, M. A. Holding, W. W. Davis and J. Garner did not bat.

Bowling: Lawson 10–1–22–0; McCurdy 10–2–31–0; McDermott 10–2–36–2; Hogg 9–0–42–0; O'Donnell 8–0–42–0.

Umpires: R. A. French and P. J. McConnell.

# BENSON AND HEDGES WORLD CHAMPIONSHIP OF CRICKET, 1984-85

To mark the 150th anniversary of the founding of the state of Victoria, the Victorian Cricket Association promoted what they called a "World Championship of Cricket". The seven Test-playing countries entered representative sides, England and India arriving straight from their meeting in India, New Zealand and Pakistan from theirs in New Zealand, and Sri Lanka and West Indies already being in Australia. At a cost of over £3 million, lights were installed on the Melbourne Cricket Ground: to see them switched on for the first time, during the opening match between England and Australia, there was a crowd of 82,494. Of the thirteen matches, nine were in Melbourne and four in Sydney.

The tournament was won by India, who played excellent cricket throughout, winning all their five matches comfortably. This was in sharp contrast to their poor showing against England in their recent one-day series in India. Gavaskar, who led them astutely, attributed his side's remarkable improvement to their being removed from the keen, at times impatient expectations of the Indian public. Gavaskar stood by his previously declared intention to give up the captaincy of India at the end of the tournament.

Shastri and Srikkanth made an outstanding pair of opening batsmen for India, whose bowling was accurate and well balanced and fielding reliable. As India were the current holders of the World Cup, which they had won in England in 1983, their victory completed a notable double. They were well suited by the Melbourne and Sydney pitches, which were both slow and took turn, and also by the slow outfields, which called for no great turn of foot. Azharuddin and Sivaramakrishnan, their young newcomers, also created a fine impression, Siva's leg-breaks providing a welcome change at the end of an Australian season that had been monopolised by the West Indian fast bowlers.

Though losing twice to India, Pakistan had the satisfaction of beating West Indies in the second of the semi-finals. This was Clive Lloyd's last match as captain of West Indies. Although the tournament was inevitably denuded by England's failure to make an impact and Australia's early elimination, the VCA had the satisfaction of knowing that, but for their efforts and the sponsorship which these attracted, they would have had a longer wait for a set of lights to match Sydney's. By the time of the final, the programme of one-day international matches in Australia had lasted, with scarcely a lull, for no less than ten weeks. This was another factor in keeping down the overall attendance for the tournament to 245,302, which was some way below the anticipated figure. – J.W.

## †AUSTRALIA v ENGLAND

At Melbourne, February 17 (day/night). Australia won by seven wickets. The opening match produced a close struggle until Kerr and Jones, both 23, swept Australia to victory with an unbroken fourth-wicket partnership of 157. The new floodlights and England's first appearance in the country for two years proved the main attraction of the tournament. Putting Downton in first so as to fit another batsman, Cowdrey, into the middle order, England, after winning the toss, reached 150 for three in 35 overs. Lamb was in particularly good form. But they lost their way when he, Cowdrey and Gatting were out in quick succession. Australia were then given a good start by Wessels, who was soon into his stride under the powerful new lights. The loss of Wessels, Hughes and Border in the fourteenth and sixteenth overs had brought England back into the game when Jones joined Kerr. Gaining in confidence with every over these two went on to win the match with 22 balls to spare. Australia were fined £440 for bowling only 49 of the 50 overs expected of them before six o'clock. The match started at 2.30 and finished at 9.58, Australia's victory being greeted by a firework display.

*Man of the Match:* R. B. Kerr. *Attendance:* 82,494.

### England

G. Fowler c and b McDermott ....... 26
†P. R. Downton c McCurdy b McDermott. 27
*D. I. Gower c Alderman b McCurdy . 6
A. J. Lamb c Kerr b Lawson ......... 53
M. W. Gatting c Alderman b O'Donnell 34
C. S. Cowdrey lbw b McDermott ..... 0
V. J. Marks b Lawson .............. 24
P. H. Edmonds b Lawson ........... 20
R. M. Ellison not out ............... 2
J. P. Agnew not out ................ 2
B 3, l-b 12, n-b 5 ........... 20

1/61 2/66 3/76 4/159 5/159 6/166 7/200 8/211 (8 wkts, 49 overs) 214

N. G. Cowans did not bat.

Bowling: Lawson 10–3–31–3; Alderman 10–0–48–0; McDermott 10–0–39–3; McCurdy 10–1–42–1; O'Donnell 9–0–39–1.

### Australia

K. C. Wessels c Gatting b Ellison ..... 39
R. B. Kerr not out ................. 87
K. J. Hughes run out .............. 0
*A. R. Border c Cowans b Marks ..... 1
D. M. Jones not out ................ 78
B 1, l-b 3, n-b 6 ............ 10

1/57 2/57 3/58 (3 wkts, 45.2 overs) 215

†W. B. Phillips, S. P. O'Donnell, G. F. Lawson, C. J. McDermott, R. J. McCurdy and T. M. Alderman did not bat.

Bowling: Cowans 10–0–52–0; Ellison 10–4–34–1; Agnew 8–0–59–0; Marks 7.2–0–33–1; Edmonds 10–0–33–0.

Umpires: A. R. Crafter and R. C. Isherwood.

## †NEW ZEALAND v WEST INDIES

At Sydney, February 19, 21 (day/night). No result. No play was possible owing to rain on February 19, the day originally scheduled for the match, and only 18.4 overs on the reserve day, two days later. Having won the toss and chosen to bat, New Zealand made a slow start against Garner and Marshall, losing Howarth in the ninth over. They were lengthening their stride when the rain returned. Each side took one point.

*Attendance:* 7,499.

### New Zealand

*G. P. Howarth c Dujon b Garner .... 8
J. G. Wright c Logie b Davis ........ 22
J. F. Reid not out .................. 22
L-b 1, n-b 4 ............... 5

1/21 2/57 (2 wkts, 18.4 overs) 57

M. D. Crowe, P. E. McEwan, J. V. Coney, R. J. Hadlee, †I. D. S. Smith, B. L. Cairns, M. C. Snedden and E. J. Chatfield did not bat.

Bowling: Garner 6–3–11–1; Marshall 6–1–13–0; Davis 3.4–0–23–1; Holding 3–0–9–0.

### West Indies

D. L. Haynes, R. B. Richardson, H. A. Gomes, I. V. A. Richards, *C. H. Lloyd, A. L. Logie, †P. J. L. Dujon, M. D. Marshall, M. A. Holding, J. Garner and W. W. Davis.

Umpires: M. W. Johnson and S. G. Randell.

## †INDIA v PAKISTAN

At Melbourne, February 20 (day/night). India won by six wickets. Except when Imran Khan was taking three wickets in six overs for 13 runs at the start of India's innings, Pakistan had a very disappointing match. Having won the toss and chosen to bat, they soon fell badly behind the clock as India's medium-paced bowlers moved the ball around. When Gavaskar introduced spin, Shastri was more economical than anyone and Siva took two useful wickets. India fielded excellently. Playing his first match for Pakistan for over a year, Imran threatened to turn the tables on India when they went in needing 184 to win; but Azharuddin and Gavaskar, coming together at 27 for three, added 132 in 31 overs so that in the end India won easing up. Fresh from his triumphs against England in India, Azharuddin created a brilliant impression on his first appearance in Australia. He survived one chance – to the wicket-keeper off Tahir Naqqash when he was 37 – and his 93 not out came off 135 balls.

*Man of the Match:* M. Azharuddin. *Attendance:* 6,956.

### Pakistan

Mohsin Khan c Viswanath b Binny ... 3
Qasim Omar c and b Sivaramakrishnan 57
Zaheer Abbas c and b Sivaramakrishnan 25
*Javed Miandad c Sivaramakrishnan b Binny. 17
Ramiz Raja c Shastri b Kapil Dev .... 29
Imran Khan c Madan Lal b Kapil Dev 14
Mudassar Nazar run out ............. 6
Tahir Naqqash c Amarnath b Madan Lal 0
Rashid Khan c Shastri b Binny ....... 17
†Anil Dalpat c Kapil Dev b Binny .... 9
Wasim Akram not out .............. 0
L-b 3, w 2, n-b 1 ........... 6

1/8 2/73 3/98 4/119 5/144 (49.2 overs) 183
6/151 7/155 8/156 9/183

Bowling: Kapil Dev 9–1–31–2; Binny 8.2–3–35–4; Madan Lal 9–2–27–1; Amarnath 3–0–11–0; Sivaramakrishnan 10–0–49–2; Shastri 10–1–27–0.

### India

R. J. Shastri c Miandad b Imran ..... 2
K. Srikkanth c Mohsin b Imran ...... 12
M. Azharuddin not out .............. 93
D. B. Vengsarkar c Mudassar b Imran . 0
*S. M. Gavaskar lbw b Mudassar ..... 54
M. Amarnath not out ............... 11
L-b 9, w 3 ................. 12

1/2 2/27 3/27 (4 wkts, 45.5 overs) 184
4/159

Kapil Dev, R. M. H. Binny, Madan Lal, †S. Viswanath and L. Sivaramakrishnan did not bat.

Bowling: Imran 10–1–27–3; Akram 8.5–0–38–0; Rashid 7–0–38–0; Tahir 10–0–34–0; Mudassar 10–0–38–1.

Umpires: R. A. French and P. J. McConnell.

## †NEW ZEALAND v SRI LANKA

At Melbourne, February 23 (day/night). New Zealand won by 51 runs, their victory assuring them of a place in the semi-finals. Winning the toss and batting they had an anxious struggle for runs, being 100 for four after 27 overs and 170 for seven after 38, with only the last four in the order left. Reid, the backbone of the innings, took 38 overs to make 62. An eighth-wicket partnership of 43 between Smith and Cairns gave New Zealand's bowlers some runs to play with, but Sri Lanka started their innings well enough to suggest a close finish. Coney, however, and Hadlee, returning after being given only two overs at the start, reduced them from 60 for two to 75 for six, and although some spirited resistance remained it was not enough to threaten the winners.

*Man of the Match:* J. F. Reid. *Attendance:* 8,759.

### New Zealand

| | | | |
|---|---|---|---|
| *G. P. Howarth c Madugalle b John | 11 | B. L. Cairns c de Mel b Ratnayake | 25 |
| J. G. Wright b John | 4 | M. C. Snedden b Ratnayake | 7 |
| J. F. Reid c Dias b Karnain | 62 | E. J. Chatfield not out | 2 |
| M. D. Crowe run out | 22 | L-b 6, w 5 | 11 |
| P. E. McEwan b John | 27 | | |
| J. V. Coney c de Silva b Karnain | 21 | 1/11 2/21 3/64 4/100 (49.4 overs) | 223 |
| R. J. Hadlee c de Mel b Ranatunga | 9 | 5/145 6/161 7/170 | |
| †I. D. S. Smith b Ratnayake | 22 | 8/213 9/216 | |

Bowling: John 10–1–29–3; de Mel 10–0–48–0; Ratnayake 8.5–1–40–3; de Silva 5–0–25–0; Karnain 9.5–0–50–2; Ranatunga 6–0–25–1.

### Sri Lanka

| | | | |
|---|---|---|---|
| †S. A. R. Silva c Crowe b Chatfield | 33 | R. J. Ratnayake c Hadlee b Coney | 1 |
| J. R. Ratnayeke run out | 8 | D. S. de Silva not out | 24 |
| R. S. Madugalle lbw b Coney | 8 | V. B. John c Chatfield b Cairns | 11 |
| R. L. Dias c Smith b Coney | 9 | L-b 9, n-b 1 | 10 |
| *L. R. D. Mendis c and b Hadlee | 7 | | |
| A. Ranatunga c Wright b Coney | 34 | 1/26 2/48 3/60 4/67 (42.4 overs) | 172 |
| U. S. H. Karnain lbw b Hadlee | 0 | 5/75 6/75 7/118 | |
| A. L. F. de Mel run out | 27 | 8/125 9/143 | |

Bowling: Cairns 8.4–1–25–1; Hadlee 6–1–23–2; Chatfield 10–3–25–1; Snedden 8–0–44–0; Coney 10–0–46–4.

Umpires: B. E. Martin and P. J. McConnell.

## †AUSTRALIA v PAKISTAN

At Melbourne, February 24. Pakistan won by 62 runs. An excellent opening partnership of 141 in 29 overs between Mohsin and Mudassar, marked by fine strokeplay and well-judged running between the wickets, gave Pakistan an advantage which they never lost. McDermott, bowling under handicap, conceded 11 runs in his first over and 36 in his first five, and when Wasim Akram produced the outstanding opening spell of the tournament, to reduce Australia to 42 for five, the match was as good as over. Bowling left-arm over the wicket at a lively medium pace, the eighteen-year-old Akram removed Wessels, Kerr, Jones, Border and Hughes in his first six overs. For a seventh successive time for Australia in Melbourne, Hughes was out for fewer than 5.

*Man of the Match:* Wasim Akram. *Attendance:* 19,224.

### Pakistan

| | | | |
|---|---|---|---|
| Mudassar Nazar c McDermott b O'Donnell | 69 | Ramiz Raja c Alderman b Lawson | 3 |
| Mohsin Khan b Alderman | 81 | Tahir Naqqash not out | 5 |
| Qasim Omar b O'Donnell | 31 | L-b 8, w 9, n-b 2 | 19 |
| *Javed Miandad b McCurdy | 19 | | |
| Zaheer Abbas b Lawson | 3 | 1/141 2/190 3/190 (6 wkts, 50 overs) | 262 |
| Imran Khan not out | 32 | 4/196 5/224 6/229 | |

Rashid Khan, †Anil Dalpat and Wasim Akram did not bat.

Bowling: Lawson 10–2–45–2; Alderman 10–0–42–1; McDermott 8–0–51–0; McCurdy 10–0–58–1; O'Donnell 10–1–42–2; Wessels 2–0–16–0.

### Australia

| | | | |
|---|---|---|---|
| K. C. Wessels b Akram | 10 | C. J. McDermott run out | 4 |
| R. B. Kerr b Akram | 2 | R. J. McCurdy run out | 1 |
| D. M. Jones b Akram | 11 | T. M. Alderman b Imran | 2 |
| *A. R. Border hit wkt b Akram | 11 | B 2, l-b 9, w 2 | 13 |
| K. J. Hughes c Tahir b Akram | 1 | | |
| †W. B. Phillips c Miandad b Tahir | 44 | 1/4 2/15 3/30 4/37 (42.3 overs) | 200 |
| S. P. O'Donnell not out | 74 | 5/42 6/121 7/178 | |
| G. F. Lawson c Ramiz b Mudassar | 27 | 8/184 9/187 | |

Bowling: Imran 6.3–0–24–1; Akram 8–1–21–5; Rashid 10–0–51–0; Zaheer 3–0–16–0; Tahir 7–0–37–1; Mudassar 8–0–40–1.

Umpires: R. C. Isherwood and M. W. Johnson.

## †ENGLAND v INDIA

At Sydney, February 26 (day/night). India won by 86 runs. Put in by Gower, India were given a great start by Srikkanth, who made 42 of the first 52 runs in ten overs. Of only sixteen boundaries hit in the match, Srikkanth scored ten. Once he had been brilliantly thrown out from long leg by Cowans, England bowled and fielded much better. Then, needing 236 to win, they looked to be on the way to getting them until Gower hit a full toss straight to deep mid-wicket. Their last eight wickets after that realised just 55 runs, Siva and Shastri both turning the ball on a much-used pitch.

*Man of the Match:* K. Srikkanth. *Attendance:* 9,609.

### India

| | | | |
|---|---|---|---|
| R. J. Shastri c Fowler b Ellison | 13 | Madan Lal c Downton b Foster | 0 |
| K. Srikkanth run out | 57 | †S. Viswanath run out | 8 |
| M. Azharuddin c and b Cowans | 45 | | |
| D. B. Vengsarkar run out | 43 | L-b 2 | 2 |
| Kapil Dev c Downton b Cowans | 29 | | |
| *S. M. Gavaskar not out | 30 | 1/67 2/74 3/147 (9 wkts, 50 overs) | 235 |
| M. Amarnath c Lamb b Cowans | 6 | 4/183 5/197 6/216 | |
| R. M. H. Binny c Marks b Foster | 2 | 7/220 8/220 9/235 | |

L. Sivaramakrishnan did not bat.

Bowling: Cowans 10–0–59–3; Ellison 10–1–46–1; Foster 10–0–33–2; Edmonds 10–1–38–0; Marks 10–0–57–0.

### England

| | | | |
|---|---|---|---|
| G. Fowler c Viswanath b Binny | 26 | R. M. Ellison c Viswanath b Madan Lal | 1 |
| M. D. Moxon c and b Sivaramakrishnan | 48 | N. A. Foster c Srikkanth b Madan Lal | 1 |
| *D. I. Gower c Vengsarkar b Sivaramakrishnan | 25 | N. G. Cowans not out | 3 |
| A. J. Lamb b Sivaramakrishnan | 13 | B 3, l-b 4, w 1, n-b 1 | 9 |
| M. W. Gatting c Viswanath b Shastri | 7 | | |
| †P. R. Downton c Shastri b Kapil Dev | 9 | 1/41 2/94 3/113 4/126 (41.4 overs) | 149 |
| V. J. Marks st Viswanath b Shastri | 2 | 5/126 6/130 7/142 | |
| P. H. Edmonds st Viswanath b Shastri | 5 | 8/144 9/146 | |

Bowling: Kapil Dev 7–0–21–1; Binny 8–0–33–1; Madan Lal 6.4–0–19–2; Sivaramakrishnan 10–0–39–3; Shastri 10–2–30–3.

Umpires: R. A. French and B. E. Martin.

## †SRI LANKA v WEST INDIES

At Melbourne, February 27 (day/night). West Indies won by eight wickets. By scoring the 136 they needed for victory in only 23.1 overs, West Indies made sure of finishing first in their group by virtue of a faster run-rate than New Zealand. The significance of this for them was that their semi-final would be played in Melbourne rather than on a turning pitch in Sydney, possibly against the Indian spinners. Not that the Melbourne pitch for this match was entirely kind to the West Indians. After Sri Lanka had had a hard struggle to make 135 for seven, West Indies lost Richardson and Gomes, hit in the face by rising balls from de Mel and Rumesh Ratnayake respectively. Gomes lost two teeth and suffered a broken nose. Morning rain (the start was delayed by half an hour and the match reduced from 50 to 47 overs a side) and evening dew may have accounted for the uneven bounce, though after the match aspersions were cast on Ratnayake's action.

*Man of the Match:* J. R. Ratnayeke. *Attendance:* 4,508.

### Sri Lanka

| | |
|---|---|
| †S. A. R. Silva c Haynes b Garner | 4 |
| J. R. Ratnayeke c Haynes b Holding | 50 |
| R. L. Dias c Dujon b Davis | 16 |
| A. Ranatunga b Richards | 1 |
| *L. R. D. Mendis run out | 1 |
| R. S. Madugalle not out | 36 |
| D. S. de Silva c and b Richards | 5 |
| U. S. H. Karnain c and b Richards | 1 |
| A. L. F. de Mel not out | 15 |
| B 1, l-b 4, w 1 | 6 |
| 1/7 2/52 3/53 4/57 5/86 6/102 7/106 (7 wkts, 47 overs) | 135 |

R. J. Ratnayake and V. B. John did not bat.

Bowling: Marshall 10–1–26–0; Garner 10–3–16–1; Davis 9–0–35–1; Holding 9–1–26–1; Richards 9–0–27–3.

### West Indies

| | |
|---|---|
| D. L. Haynes b de Mel | 36 |
| R. B. Richardson retired hurt | 11 |
| H. A. Gomes retired hurt | 20 |
| I. V. A. Richards c de Mel b Ratnayake | 12 |
| *C. H. Lloyd not out | 14 |
| A. L. Logie not out | 29 |
| B 1, l-b 7, w 2, n-b 4 | 14 |
| 1/86 2/90 (2 wkts, 23.1 overs) | 136 |

†P. J. L. Dujon, M. D. Marshall, M. A. Holding, J. Garner and W. W. Davis did not bat.

Bowling: de Mel 8–0–47–1; John 7–0–39–0; Ratnayake 7–0–29–1; Ranatunga 1.1–0–13–0.

Umpires: A. R. Crafter and S. G. Randell.

## †ENGLAND v PAKISTAN

At Melbourne, March 2 (day/night). Pakistan won by 67 runs. With no points and the lowest run-rate in their group, England needed not only to beat Pakistan but to score very fast in doing so. In the event they did well to restrict them, after Miandad had won the toss, to 213 for eight in 50 overs, fewer than had seemed probable when, with Mudassar again in good form, Pakistan reached 77 for one in twenty overs. Edmonds and Marks were mainly responsible for keeping Pakistan in check. Batting under the lights, England knew that if they passed Pakistan's total in 33 overs or less they would lead them in the competition and still have a chance of a place in the semi-finals. While Lamb, going in in the first over, was making a brilliant 81 in 69 balls it was a possibility, but when he was fifth out in the 22nd over, well caught at long leg, no-one managed to keep up the chase.

*Man of the Match:* A. J. Lamb. *Attendance:* 7,139.

### Pakistan

| | |
|---|---|
| Mudassar Nazar c Foster b Edmonds | 77 |
| Mohsin Khan c Moxon b Ellison | 9 |
| Ramiz Raja c Moxon b Marks | 21 |
| *Javed Miandad c Downton b Foster | 11 |
| Imran Khan b Ellison | 35 |
| Salim Malik c Gatting b Foster | 8 |
| Qasim Omar b Cowans | 12 |
| Tahir Naqqash not out | 21 |
| †Anil Dalpat b Ellison | 8 |
| Azeem Hafeez not out | 0 |
| B 5, l-b 4, n-b 2 | 11 |
| 1/37 2/93 3/114 4/126 5/144 6/181 7/183 8/212 (8 wkts, 50 overs) | 213 |

Wasim Akram did not bat.

Bowling: Cowans 10–0–52–1; Ellison 10–0–42–3; Foster 10–0–56–2; Marks 10–2–25–1; Edmonds 10–1–29–1.

### England

| | |
|---|---|
| G. Fowler c Anil b Imran | 0 |
| *D. I. Gower c Tahir b Imran | 27 |
| A. J. Lamb c Akram b Azeem | 81 |
| M. W. Gatting c Mudassar b Tahir | 11 |
| †P. R. Downton run out | 6 |
| R. M. Ellison c Anil b Tahir | 6 |
| V. J. Marks run out | 1 |
| M. D. Moxon c Imran b Azeem | 3 |
| P. H. Edmonds not out | 0 |
| N. A. Foster run out | 1 |
| N. G. Cowans b Tahir | 0 |
| B 1, l-b 7, w 1, n-b 1 | 10 |
| 1/0 2/56 3/102 4/125 5/138 6/139 7/141 8/145 9/146 (24.2 overs) | 146 |

Bowling: Imran 7–0–33–2; Akram 10–0–59–0; Azeem 3–0–22–2; Tahir 4.2–0–24–3.

Umpires: R. C. Isherwood and M. W. Johnson.

## †AUSTRALIA v INDIA

At Melbourne, March 3. India won by eight wickets. Australia had two chances of reaching the semi-finals of the competition, both of which required them to win this match. They had either to score 223 in 50 overs themselves or, having failed to do that, bowl India out for 160 or fewer. They came nowhere near to doing either. Put in by Gavaskar (Hogg tossed up for Australia, Border being temporarily unwell), Australia were soon 37 for five, owing to a succession of loose strokes. Phillips launched something of a recovery, but when India batted Srikkanth and Shastri made light work of securing their side's 100 per cent record in the group matches. This enabled them to avoid West Indies in the semi-finals.

*Man of the Match*: R. J. Shastri. *Attendance*: 23,282.

### Australia

| | |
|---|---|
| G. M. Wood b Binny | 1 |
| R. B. Kerr b Kapil Dev | 4 |
| K. C. Wessels c Madan Lal b Kapil Dev | 6 |
| *A. R. Border b Binny | 4 |
| D. M. Jones c Viswanath b Amarnath | 12 |
| †W. B. Phillips c Amarnath b Sivaramakrishnan | 60 |
| S. P. O'Donnell c Amarnath b Shastri | 17 |
| G. F. Lawson c and b Sivaramakrishnan | 0 |
| R. M. Hogg run out | 22 |
| R. J. McCurdy not out | 13 |
| T. M. Alderman b Binny | 6 |
| B 2, l-b 9, w 5, n-b 2 | 18 |
| 1/5 2/5 3/17 4/17 5/37 6/85 7/85 8/134 9/147 (49.3 overs) | 163 |

Bowling: Kapil Dev 10–2–25–2; Binny 7.3–0–27–3; Madan Lal 5–0–18–0; Amarnath 7–1–16–1; Sivaramakrishnan 10–0–32–2; Shastri 10–1–34–1.

### India

R. J. Shastri c Phillips b O'Donnell ... 51
K. Srikkanth not out ................. 93
M. Azharuddin lbw b Alderman ...... 0
D. B. Vengsarkar not out ............ 11
L-b 1, w 3, n-b 6 ........... 10

1/124 2/125 (2 wkts, 36.1 overs) 165

*S. M. Gavaskar, M. Amarnath, Kapil Dev, R. M. H. Binny, Madan Lal, †S. Viswanath and L. Sivaramakrishnan did not bat.

Bowling: Lawson 8–1–35–0; Hogg 6–2–16–0; McCurdy 7.1–0–30–0; Alderman 8–0–38–1; O'Donnell 7–0–45–1.

Umpires: A. R. Crafter and P. J. McConnell.

## FINAL TABLES

### Group A

| | *P* | *W* | *L* | *NR* | *Pts* | *Run-rate* |
|---|---|---|---|---|---|---|
| India ................. | 3 | 3 | 0 | 0 | 6 | 4.42 |
| Pakistan ............. | 3 | 2 | 1 | 0 | 4 | 4.39 |
| Australia ............ | 3 | 1 | 2 | 0 | 2 | 3.98 |
| England .............. | 3 | 0 | 3 | 0 | 0 | 3.41 |

### Group B

| | *P* | *W* | *L* | *NR* | *Pts* | *Run-rate* |
|---|---|---|---|---|---|---|
| West Indies ........... | 2 | 1 | 0 | 1 | 3 | 5.87 |
| New Zealand ......... | 2 | 1 | 0 | 1 | 3 | 4.07 |
| Sri Lanka ............ | 2 | 0 | 2 | 0 | 0 | 3.16 |

## SEMI-FINALS

### †INDIA v NEW ZEALAND

At Sydney, March 5 (day/night). India won by seven wickets with 6.3 overs to spare. Put in by Gavaskar on a very slow pitch, New Zealand, who lost Wright to the third ball of the match, made no concerted effort to take the initiative until Cairns and Smith came together at 151 for seven in the 43rd over. When Snedden was out to the last ball of the innings, New Zealand became the fourth successive side India had bowled out in the competition. Needing 207 to win India were so pinned down for a while that after 20 overs they were only 46 for one. Howarth then took off Snedden after he had bowled five overs for only 7 runs, whereupon India gradually took control, Kapil Dev eventually sharing a brilliant partnership with Vengsarkar. The decisive over was the 34th, in which Kapil hit Hadlee for four blistering 4s and survived a hard, low chance to mid-off.

*Man of the Match:* R. J. Shastri. *Attendance:* 16,612.

### New Zealand

J. G. Wright c Viswanath b Kapil Dev . 0
P. E. McEwan c Viswanath b Binny . . 9
J. F. Reid c Kapil Dev b Shastri . . . . . . 55
M. D. Crowe c Azharuddin b Madan Lal 9
*G. P. Howarth run out . . . . . . . . . . . . . 7
J. V. Coney b Shastri . . . . . . . . . . . . . . . 33
†I. D. S. Smith c Amarnath b Madan Lal 19
R. J. Hadlee c Madan Lal b Shastri . . . 3
B. L. Cairns c Srikkanth b Madan Lal . 39
M. C. Snedden c Azharuddin b Madan Lal . 7
E. J. Chatfield not out . . . . . . . . . . . . . . 0
L-b 21, w 1, n-b 3 . . . . . . . . . . 25

1/0 2/14 3/52 4/69 5/119 6/145 7/151 8/188 9/206 (50 overs) 206

Bowling: Kapil Dev 10–1–34–1; Binny 6–0–28–1; Madan Lal 8–1–37–4; Amarnath 7–0–24–0; Sivaramakrishnan 9–0–31–0; Shastri 10–1–31–3.

### India

R. J. Shastri c McEwan b Hadlee . . . . . 53
K. Srikkanth c Reid b Chatfield . . . . . . 9
M. Azharuddin c Coney b Cairns . . . . . 24
D. B. Vengsarkar not out . . . . . . . . . . . . 63
Kapil Dev not out . . . . . . . . . . . . . . . . . . 54
B 1, l-b 2, n-b 1 . . . . . . . . . . . . 4

1/28 2/73 3/102 (3 wkts, 43.3 overs) 207

*S. M. Gavaskar, M. Amarnath, R. M. H. Binny, Madan Lal, †S. Viswanath and L. Sivaramakrishnan did not bat.

Bowling: Cairns 9–0–35–1; Hadlee 8.3–3–50–1; Chatfield 10–0–38–1; Snedden 8–1–37–0; Coney 8–0–44–0.

Umpires: R. A. French and P. J. McConnell.

## †PAKISTAN v WEST INDIES

At Melbourne, March 6 (day/night). Pakistan won by seven wickets, a sweeping and unexpected victory after Lloyd, playing his last match for West Indies, had won the toss and chosen to bat. Other than a rain-affected match against New Zealand and a canter against Sri Lanka, West Indies had had an idle three weeks and this showed in their cricket. They also missed Gomes, absent through injury. As Lloyd said afterwards, West Indies simply batted badly. Wasim Raja, with ten good overs of leg-breaks, and his brother, Ramiz, with a dashing innings of 60; Mudassar and Tahir, with accurate medium pace; Qasim Omar, with a precocious 42 not out, and Mohsin with a dogged 23 in 36 overs were the main contributors to Pakistan's success. West Indies' best efforts came from Marshall and Holding, who frequently beat the bat.

*Man of the Match:* Ramiz Raja. *Attendance:* 11,433.

### West Indies

D. L. Haynes c Mudassar b Tahir . . . . . 18
R. B. Richardson b Tahir . . . . . . . . . . . . 13
†P. J. L. Dujon c Anil b Wasim Raja . . 22
I. V. A. Richards c Anil b Tahir . . . . . . 1
*C. H. Lloyd c Miandad b Mudassar . . 25
A. L. Logie c Omar b Mudassar . . . . . . 8
M. D. Marshall c Miandad b Mudassar 10
R. A. Harper not out . . . . . . . . . . . . . . . 25
M. A. Holding b Akram . . . . . . . . . . . . . 5
J. Garner c Wasim Raja b Mudassar . . 13
W. W. Davis c Miandad b Mudassar . . 3
B 4, l-b 7, w 4, n-b 1 . . . . . . . . 16

1/29 2/44 3/45 4/61 5/75 6/96 7/103 8/122 9/152 (44.3 overs) 159

Bowling: Imran 9–1–39–0; Akram 10–2–26–1; Tahir 8–3–23–3; Wasim Raja 10–0–32–1; Mudassar 7.3–0–28–5.

### Pakistan

Mudassar Nazar c Logie b Marshall . . . 6
Mohsin Khan c Dujon b Garner . . . . . . 23
Ramiz Raja c and b Harper . . . . . . . . . . 60
Qasim Omar not out . . . . . . . . . . . . . . . . 42
*Javed Miandad not out . . . . . . . . . . . . . 10
B 3, l-b 7, w 6, n-b 3 . . . . . . . . 19

1/8 2/97 3/116 (3 wkts, 46 overs) 160

Imran Khan, Salim Malik, Tahir Naqqash, †Anil Dalpat, Wasim Raja and Wasim Akram did not bat.

Bowling: Marshall 9–2–25–1; Garner 8–3–19–1; Holding 8–3–19–0; Davis 7–0–35–0; Harper 10–1–38–1; Richards 4–0–14–0.

Umpires: R. C. Isherwood and S. G. Randell.

## PLATE FINAL

### †NEW ZEALAND v WEST INDIES

At Sydney, March 9. West Indies won by six wickets. Lloyd having returned home, Richards launched his career as West Indies' captain by leading them to an easy victory. After being put in, New Zealand could make little progress against the West Indian bowling and fielding on a slow pitch and turgid outfield. When West Indies batted Hadlee removed Haynes and Richardson in his first six overs, and Payne, getting a rare opportunity, and Logie had to take their time; but Richards made runs at will. West Indies won £8,500 and New Zealand £4,250.
*Man of the Match*: I. V. A. Richards. *Attendance*: 12,491.

#### New Zealand

| | | | |
|---|---|---|---|
| *G. P. Howarth lbw b Garner | 11 | R. J. Hadlee b Marshall | 11 |
| J. G. Wright c Logie b Garner | 5 | J. G. Bracewell not out | 11 |
| J. F. Reid c Dujon b Davis | 18 | E. J. Chatfield not out | 2 |
| M. D. Crowe c Harper b Holding | 8 | B 1, l-b 8, w 2, n-b 5 | 16 |
| J. J. Crowe b Harper | 1 | | |
| J. V. Coney c Payne b Garner | 35 | 1/14 2/24 3/45 (9 wkts, 50 overs) | 138 |
| †I. D. S. Smith c Payne b Harper | 15 | 4/51 5/52 6/78 | |
| B. L. Cairns b Holding | 5 | 7/83 8/116 9/127 | |

Bowling: Garner 10–2–29–3; Marshall 10–1–32–1; Davis 10–0–23–1; Holding 10–1–23–2; Harper 10–1–22–2.

#### West Indies

| | | | |
|---|---|---|---|
| D. L. Haynes c Coney b Hadlee | 1 | †P. J. L. Dujon not out | 9 |
| R. B. Richardson c Smith b Hadlee | 8 | L-b 3, w 2, n-b 3 | 8 |
| T. R. O. Payne b Chatfield | 28 | | |
| A. L. Logie not out | 34 | 1/4 2/24 3/54 (4 wkts, 37.2 overs) | 139 |
| *I. V. A. Richards b Hadlee | 51 | 4/126 | |

M. D. Marshall, R. A. Harper, M. A. Holding, J. Garner and W. W. Davis did not bat.

Bowling: Hadlee 10–4–23–3; Bracewell 8–2–42–0; Chatfield 9–0–25–1; Cairns 8–0–39–0; Coney 2.2–0–7–0.

Umpires: R. A. French and M. W. Johnson.

## FINAL

### †INDIA v PAKISTAN

At Melbourne, March 10 (day/night). India won by eight wickets. Showing the same qualities as in their previous matches – astute captaincy, steady bowling, with spin complementing medium pace, keen fielding and sensible batting – India became popular and confident winners of the tournament. Pakistan were never really in the game once Kapil Dev and Chetan Sharma (Binny was unfit to play because of a virus) had reduced them to 33 for four in the twelfth over, although Imran and Miandad did stage something of a recovery. In the end only a last-wicket partnership of 31 left India with as many as 177 to make. For India's first wicket Shastri and Srikkanth made 103, the watchful Shastri making an ideal foil to the dashing Srikkanth. Azharuddin contributed an attractive 25 off 26 balls and India went on to win with a comfortable 2.5 overs to spare. As they drove round the ground on a lap of honour aboard a car won by Shastri, for being chosen as "champion of champions", they were given a generous reception by a sizeable crowd. India's prize for winning was £22,500, Pakistan's £11,500 for finishing as runners-up.

*Man of the Match:* K. Srikkanth. *Attendance:* 35,296.

## Pakistan

| | |
|---|---|
| Mudassar Nazar c Viswanath b Kapil Dev | 14 |
| Mohsin Khan c Azharuddin b Kapil Dev | 5 |
| Ramiz Raja c Srikkanth b Chetan | 4 |
| Qasim Omar b Kapil Dev | 0 |
| *Javed Miandad st Viswanath b Sivaramakrishnan | 48 |
| Imran Khan run out | 35 |
| Salim Malik c Chetan b Sivaramakrishnan | 14 |
| Wasim Raja not out | 21 |
| Tahir Naqqash c Viswanath b Shastri | 10 |
| †Anil Dalpat c Shastri b Sivaramakrishnan | 0 |
| Azeem Hafeez not out | 7 |
| B 7, l-b 8, w 1, n-b 2 | 18 |
| 1/17 2/29 3/29 4/33 5/101 6/131 7/131 8/142 9/145 (9 wkts, 50 overs) | 176 |

Bowling: Kapil Dev 9–1–23–3; Chetan 7–1–17–1; Madan Lal 6–1–15–0; Amarnath 9–0–27–0; Shastri 10–0–44–1; Sivaramakrishnan 9–0–35–3.

## India

| | |
|---|---|
| K. Srikkanth c Wasim Raja b Imran | 67 |
| R. J. Shastri not out | 63 |
| M. Azharuddin b Tahir | 25 |
| D. B. Vengsarkar not out | 18 |
| L-b 2, w 2 | 4 |
| 1/103 2/142 (2 wkts, 47.1 overs) | 177 |

Kapil Dev, *S. M. Gavaskar, M. Amarnath, Madan Lal, Chetan Sharma, †S. Viswanath and L. Sivaramakrishnan did not bat.

Bowling: Imran 10–3–28–1; Azeem 10–1–29–0; Tahir 10–2–35–1; Wasim Raja 7.1–0–42–0; Mudassar 8–0–26–0; Salim 2–0–15–0.

Umpires: A. R. Crafter and R. C. Isherwood.

---

# WHITBREAD SCHOLARSHIPS

Whitbread Brewery Scholarships were awarded between 1976-77 and 1983-84 to help young cricketers further their experience by playing for a season in Australia. The following awards were made:

**1976-77:** C. W. J. Athey (Yorkshire), I. T. Botham (Somerset), M. W. Gatting (Middlesex), G. B. Stevenson (Yorkshire).
**1977-78:** C. S. Cowdrey (Kent), J. E. Emburey (Middlesex), J. A. Hopkins (Glamorgan), J. D. Love (Yorkshire).
**1978-79:** J. P. Agnew (Leicestershire), M. W. Gatting (Middlesex), W. Larkins (Northamptonshire), C. J. Tavaré (Kent).
**1979-80:** K. J. Barnett (Derbyshire), D. N. Patel (Worcestershire), A. C. S. Pigott (Sussex), R. G. Williams (Northamptonshire).
**1980-81:** N. G. B. Cook (Leicestershire), W. Hogg (Lancashire), D. M. Smith (Surrey).
**1981-82:** M. R. Benson (Kent), N. A. Foster (Essex), P. G. Newman (Derbyshire).
**1982-83:** D. J. Capel (Northamptonshire), R. K. Illingworth (Worcestershire), C. Penn (Kent), D. J. Thomas (Surrey).
**1983-84:** D. G. Aslett (Kent), D. B. D'Oliveira (Worcestershire).

# ROTHMANS TROPHY IN SHARJAH, 1984-85

By TONY LEWIS

A four-nations tournament of one-day matches, played in Sharjah at the end of March, was won by India. They took the Rothmans Trophy. Australia were runners-up and Pakistan beat England in the play-off for third place.

Although cricket in Sharjah began in 1981 and has been enthusiastically supported by many of the 700,000 Indians and Pakistanis who live in the United Arab Emirates, this was the first time that the Test match Boards of Control had chosen the sides and attended the competition. The representatives were delighted with what they saw – a well-organised contest, a new stadium for 12,000 spectators set like a mirage in the desert just outside the town, a field of real soil which had been hauled hundreds of miles by lorry before being heaped into a gaping hole in the sands, and a pitch on which the ball turned a lot, but which was level and fair.

The introduction of cricket to this particular part of the Emirates was the inspiration of the Arab businessman, Mr Abdulrahman Bukhatir. He grew to love cricket when he was a student in Pakistan and raised £2 million to build the stadium. His cricket manager is Asif Iqbal, the former Pakistan and Kent all-rounder. They organise matches without profit in mind, except to make contributions to the benefits of players past or present. This time the beneficiaries were Wasim Bari, Syed Kirmani, Eknath Solkar and Gul Mohammad.

India first beat Pakistan in an astonishing match. Imran Khan took six wickets for 14 runs when India were put in, yet still ended up on the losing side. There was a capacity crowd, live television coverage in Dubai, and recorded highlights made for India and Pakistan. It was a day of noisy partisanship. The batsmen were undone by an over-damp pitch in the morning which then turned sharply as soon as spin was applied. Quite easily the most talented innings was the 47 by Mohammad Azharuddin. Next, Australia beat England by two wickets off the last ball of the match. The only country not to take a full first team to the competition, England were led by Norman Gifford.

Few batsmen played the spin bowling well, or settled to the extremely slow surface. The only exceptions, in any of the matches, were Sunil Gavaskar, Javed Miandad, Allan Border, the new Australian captain, and, by way of a pleasant surprise for England followers, Robert Bailey, the young Northamptonshire batsman. Bailey showed an ability to adapt to the conditions by letting the ball come on to the bat.

By the time of the final, India were firm favourites and played like it. They bowled out Australia for 139 in 42.3 overs and then hit off the runs in 39.2 overs. Gavaskar played a skilful innings and was judged Man of the Series, partly for his useful batting and, more conspicuously, for five brilliant catches, three of them diving efforts at slip.

Another feature of Sharjah cricket is their practice of employing neutral umpires. This defused those situations near the bat where an appeal can lead to petulance and gamesmanship, not to say straightforward cheating. The umpires were H. D. Bird (England), M. W. Johnson (Australia), Swaroop Kishen (India) and Khizar Hayat (Pakistan).

Members of the four Boards of Control were satisfied that Sharjah is a worthy venue for international cricket. They saw the merit of international players parading in front of an eager public which is normally starved of top-class cricket. Sensibly, they have resolved not to treat it as a pirate organisation, but rather to embrace it. There might, otherwise, be a danger of a breakaway. The high prizemoney is alluring and at the moment out of proportion to the other rewards put up in world cricket, but if those in Sharjah follow the advice of the Boards of Control, there is no reason why cricket should not thrive in the unlikely setting of the Great Arabian Desert.

## SEMI-FINALS

## INDIA v PAKISTAN

At Sharjah, March 22. India won by 38 runs. Toss won by Pakistan.
*Man of the Match:* Imran Khan.

### India

| | |
|---|---|
| R. J. Shastri lbw b Imran | 0 |
| K. Srikkanth c Salim b Imran | 6 |
| M. Azharuddin b Tauseef | 47 |
| D. B. Vengsarkar c Ashraf b Imran | 1 |
| *S. M. Gavaskar c Ashraf b Imran | 2 |
| M. Amarnath b Imran | 5 |
| Kapil Dev b Tauseef | 30 |
| R. M. H. Binny c Miandad b Mudassar | 8 |
| Madan Lal c Ashraf b Imran | 11 |
| †S. Viswanath not out | 3 |
| L. Sivaramakrishnan c Salim b Akram | 1 |
| B 5, l-b 4, w 2 | 11 |
| 1/0 2/12 3/20 4/28 5/34 6/80 7/95 8/113 9/121 (42.4 overs) | 125 |

Bowling: Imran 10–2–14–6; Akram 7.4–0–27–1; Tahir 5–0–12–0; Mudassar 10–1–36–1; Tauseef 10–0–27–2.

### Pakistan

| | |
|---|---|
| Mudassar Nazar c Gavaskar b Binny | 18 |
| Mohsin Khan run out | 10 |
| Ramiz Raja c Gavaskar b Kapil Dev | 29 |
| *Javed Miandad c Gavaskar b Shastri | 0 |
| †Ashraf Ali c Vengsarkar b Sivaramakrishnan | 0 |
| Imran Khan st Viswanath b Sivaramakrishnan | 0 |
| Salim Malik c Gavaskar b Shastri | 17 |
| Manzoor Elahi c and b Madan Lal | 9 |
| Tahir Naqqash c Viswanath b Kapil Dev | 1 |
| Tauseef Ahmed b Kapil Dev | 0 |
| Wasim Akram not out | 0 |
| L-b 1, w 1, n-b 1 | 3 |
| 1/13 2/35 3/40 4/41 5/41 6/74 7/85 8/87 9/87 (32.5 overs) | 87 |

Bowling: Kapil Dev 6.5–1–17–3; Binny 3–0–24–1; Sivaramakrishnan 7–2–16–2; Shastri 10–5–17–2; Madan Lal 6–2–12–1.

Umpires: H. D. Bird and M. W. Johnson.

## AUSTRALIA v ENGLAND

At Sharjah, March 24. Australia won by two wickets. Toss won by Australia.
*Man of the Match:* G. R. J. Matthews.

### England

| | |
|---|---|
| G. Fowler c Hughes b Alderman | 26 |
| R. T. Robinson c Rixon b Matthews | 37 |
| M. D. Moxon lbw b O'Donnell | 0 |
| D. W. Randall st Rixon b Bennett | 19 |
| C. M. Wells lbw b Bennett | 17 |
| D. R. Pringle st Rixon b Border | 4 |
| P. H. Edmonds not out | 15 |
| †B. N. French c Rixon b Border | 4 |
| R. M. Ellison c Wessels b Border | 24 |
| N. A. Foster not out | 5 |
| B 9, l-b 5, w 6, n-b 6 | 26 |
| 1/47 2/53 3/95 4/109 5/123 6/128 7/134 8/169 (8 wkts, 50 overs) | 177 |

*N. Gifford did not bat.

Bowling: Alderman 7–1–36–1; McCurdy 5–0–23–0; O'Donnell 8–2–26–1; Bennett 10–2–27–2; Matthews 10–3–15–1; Border 7–0–21–3; Wessels 3–0–15–0.

## Australia

K. C. Wessels b Edmonds ........... 16
G. M. Wood c French b Pringle ...... 35
D. M. Jones c Moxon b Edmonds ..... 27
*A. R. Border c and b Pringle ........ 9
K. J. Hughes c French b Foster ...... 14
G. R. J. Matthews c Foster b Ellison .. 24
S. P. O'Donnell c Moxon b Ellison .... 19
†S. J. Rixon not out ................ 11
M. J. Bennett run out ............... 0
R. J. McCurdy not out .............. 6
L-b 9, w 8 .................. 17

1/54 2/64 3/82 4/100 5/120 6/151 7/168 8/168 (8 wkts, 50 overs) 178

T. M. Alderman did not bat.

Bowling: Foster 10–1–34–1; Ellison 10–1–28–2; Pringle 10–0–49–2; Edmonds 10–2–31–2; Gifford 10–1–27–0.

Umpires: Khizar Hayat and Swaroop Kishen.

## ENGLAND v PAKISTAN

At Sharjah, March 26. Pakistan won by 43 runs. Toss won by England. *Man of the Match:* Javed Miandad.

## Pakistan

Mudassar Nazar c French b Gifford ... 36
Mohsin Khan c Robinson b Pringle ... 13
Ramiz Raja c Robinson b Pringle ..... 16
*Javed Miandad c Gifford b Edmonds . 71
Salim Malik lbw b Gifford ........... 2
Imran Khan c Pringle b Gifford ...... 0
Shoaib Mohammad st French b Gifford 3
†Ashraf Ali not out .................. 19
Tahir Naqqash not out .............. 2
B 1, l-b 9, w 2, n-b 1 ........ 13

1/24 2/43 3/107 4/113 5/113 6/125 7/172 (7 wkts, 50 overs) 175

Tauseef Ahmed and Wasim Akram did not bat.

Bowling: Ellison 7–1–18–0; Pringle 7–1–32–2; Edmonds 10–0–47–1; Pocock 10–1–20–0; Gifford 10–0–23–4; Bailey 6–0–25–0.

## England

G. Fowler c Miandad b Tauseef ...... 19
R. T. Robinson b Tahir ............. 9
M. D. Moxon b Shoaib .............. 11
C. M. Wells b Shoaib ............... 5
R. J. Bailey not out ................ 41
D. R. Pringle b Akram .............. 13
P. H. Edmonds c and b Shoaib ....... 3
R. M. Ellison b Akram .............. 3
†B. N. French c Shoaib b Tahir ...... 7
*N. Gifford c Miandad b Imran ...... 0
P. I. Pocock run out ................ 4
B 1, l-b 12, n-b 4 .......... 17

1/19 2/35 3/48 4/49 5/76 6/89 7/98 8/117 9/132 (48.2 overs) 132

Bowling: Imran 9–2–26–1; Akram 10–0–28–2; Tahir 9.2–1–20–2; Tauseef 10–1–25–1; Shoaib 10–1–20–3.

Umpires: M. W. Johnson and Swaroop Kishen.

## FINAL

## AUSTRALIA v INDIA

At Sharjah, March 29. India won by three wickets. Toss won by India.
*Man of the Match:* M. Amarnath. *Man of the Series:* S. M. Gavaskar.

### Australia

G. M. Wood run out . . . . . . . . . . . . . . . . 27
K. C. Wessels c Gavaskar b Madan Lal 30
D. M. Jones c Viswanath b Madan Lal. 8
*A. R. Border c and b Amarnath . . . . . 27
K. J. Hughes c and b Amarnath . . . . . . 11
G. R. J. Matthews lbw b Kapil Dev . . . 11
S. P. O'Donnell run out . . . . . . . . . . . . . 3
†S. J. Rixon run out . . . . . . . . . . . . . . . . 4
M. J. Bennett lbw b Shastri . . . . . . . . . . 0
R. J. McCurdy c Vengsarkar b Shastri . 0
C. J. McDermott not out . . . . . . . . . . . . 0
L-b 13, w 5 . . . . . . . . . . . . . . . . 18

1/60 2/71 3/78 4/114 (42.3 overs) 139
5/115 6/131 7/138
8/139 9/139

Bowling: Kapil Dev 6–3–9–1; Binny 5–0–25–0; Madan Lal 7–0–30–2; Sivaramakrishnan 8–1–29–0; Shastri 9.3–1–14–2; Amarnath 7–1–19–2.

### India

R. J. Shastri c Rixon b O'Donnell . . . . . 9
K. Srikkanth lbw b McDermott . . . . . . . 0
M. Azharuddin c Jones b McDermott . 22
D. B. Vengsarkar b McDermott . . . . . . 35
S. M. Gavaskar run out . . . . . . . . . . . . . 20
M. Amarnath not out . . . . . . . . . . . . . . . 24
*Kapil Dev b Matthews . . . . . . . . . . . . . 1
R. M. H. Binny b Matthews . . . . . . . . . 2
Madan Lal not out . . . . . . . . . . . . . . . . . 7

L-b 9, w 7, n-b 4 . . . . . . . . . . . 20

1/2 2/37 3/41 4/98 (7 wkts, 39.2 overs) 140
5/103 6/117 7/120

†S. Viswanath and L. Sivaramakrishnan did not bat.

Bowling: McDermott 10–0–36–3; McCurdy 4–1–10–0; O'Donnell 4–1–11–1; Bennett 10–0–35–0; Matthews 10–1–33–2; Border 1.2–0–6–0.

Umpires: H. D. Bird and Khizar Hayat.

# ENGLAND YOUNG CRICKETERS IN WEST INDIES, 1984-85

The National Cricket Association experienced unforeseen administrative difficulties before the fourth England Young Cricketers team to tour the West Indies were able to leave for the Caribbean. The party, managed by Bob Willis, the former England captain, left on January 9, a week later than originally scheduled, the West Indies Board of Control having had to amend the itinerary agreed at the time of their invitation and reduce the tour to three venues – Barbados, St Lucia and Jamaica. This was because Antigua, Trinidad and Guyana, where matches were to have been played, refused to admit four of the players, Addison, Andrew, Burns and Palmer, who had played cricket in South Africa.

Subsequently most of the middle leg in St Lucia was washed out. The tourists, therefore, found it difficult to gain any real momentum, and this, allied to the fact that West Indies Young Cricketers were particularly strong, especially in fast bowling, meant that in cricketing terms the tour was not a great success. However, the English players returned as wiser cricketers.

The tour party was: R. G. D. Willis (*manager*), R. M. H. Cottam (*assistant manager/coach*), N. J. Lenham (*captain*) (Sussex), J. P. Addison (Leicestershire), S. J. W. Andrew (Hampshire), R. J. Blakey (Yorkshire), P. A. Booth (Yorkshire), N. D. Burns (Essex), P. A. J. De Freitas (Leicestershire), D. S. Hoffman (Warwickshire), C. S. Mays (Sussex), G. V. Palmer (Somerset), D. Ripley (Northamptonshire), M. A. Roseberry (Middlesex), I. Smith (Glamorgan), J. F. Sykes (Middlesex) and P. C. R. Tufnell (Middlesex).

## RESULTS

*Matches 13: Won 5, Lost 5, Drawn 3.*

*Note:* None of the matches played was first-class.

v Barbados Young Cricketers: at Cable and Wireless Ground, Barbados, January 12, 13, 14. England Young Cricketers won by five wickets. Barbados Young Cricketers 100 (P. C. R. Tufnell five for 32) and 172 (J. Butcher 61; P. A. J. De Freitas four for 46, P. C. R. Tufnell four for 47); England Young Cricketers 221 (G. V. Palmer 46, J. P. Addison 44; W. Coppin five for 54) and 53 for five (W. Coppin four for 28).

v Barbados Young Cricketers: at Cable and Wireless Ground, Barbados, January 14. The three-day fixture having finished early on the third day, a 45-overs match was arranged. England Young Cricketers won by 39 runs. England Young Cricketers 170 for seven (45 overs) (R. J. Blakey 46; R. Bedford four for 43); Barbados Young Cricketers 131 (38.3 overs) D. Braithwaite 55 not out; G. V. Palmer five for 18).

v Barbados Young Cricketers: at Kensington Oval, Bridgetown, January 16. Barbados Young Cricketers won by three wickets. England Young Cricketers 234 (49 overs) (N. J. Lenham 53, I. Smith 42); Barbados Young Cricketers 238 for seven (45 overs) (R. Holder 113 not out, M. Matthews 49).

## WEST INDIES YOUNG CRICKETERS v ENGLAND YOUNG CRICKETERS

### First "Test" Match

At Kensington Oval, Bridgetown, January 18, 19, 20. West Indies Young Cricketers won by four wickets. With the dismissal of Lenham and Blakey, England failed to capitalise on their sound start, allowing the spinners to dominate. West Indies, in reply, took a useful first-innings lead, despite good fast bowling from Andrew and De Freitas, and England fared even worse in their second innings. Only a tenth-wicket partnership of 35 between Sykes and Tufnell gave their total a vestige of respectability. However, they showed more spirit on the last day, removing six West Indian batsmen before the modest target of 65 was reached.

## England Young Cricketers

| First innings | | Second innings | |
|---|---|---|---|
| *N. J. Lenham lbw b Adams | 37 | c Mohammed b Manswell | 13 |
| R. J. Blakey b Hooper | 47 | c Gayle b Dixon | 38 |
| M. A. Roseberry lbw b Adams | 0 | lbw b Manswell | 2 |
| J. P. Addison c Coppin b Hooper | 7 | c Adams b Hooper | 7 |
| †N. D. Burns c Bishop b Adams | 0 | c Mohammed b Hooper | 0 |
| G. V. Palmer c and b Hooper | 8 | c Adams b Dixon | 10 |
| I. Smith b Coppin | 23 | c Hooper b Dixon | 8 |
| J. F. Sykes run out | 4 | not out | 23 |
| P. A. J. De Freitas b Dixon | 21 | c and b Dixon | 0 |
| S. J. W. Andrew not out | 1 | b Dixon | 7 |
| P. C. R. Tufnell b Dixon | 0 | c Barthley b Dixon | 13 |
| B 5, l-b 3, w 3, n-b 5 | 16 | L-b 2, w 2, n-b 11 | 15 |
| 1/75 2/75 3/89 4/91 5/102 6/130 7/134 8/146 9/164 | 164 | 1/23 2/31 3/46 4/50 5/70 6/81 7/85 8/85 9/101 | 136 |

Bowling: *First Innings*—Coppin 15–4–43–1; Manswell 8–3–10–0; Dixon 7.4–1–22–2; Hooper 27–10–59–3; Adams 20–10–22–3. *Second Innings*—Coppin 10–0–35–0; Manswell 8–3–21–2; Hooper 12–1–29–2; Adams 9–7–7–0; Dixon 6.5–0–42–6.

## West Indies Young Cricketers

| First innings | | Second innings | |
|---|---|---|---|
| *Z. Barthley c Burns b De Freitas | 0 | lbw b Andrew | 25 |
| D. Joseph c Burns b Andrew | 37 | c Burns b Andrew | 1 |
| R. Bishop b Andrew | 11 | st Burns b Tufnell | 14 |
| R. Holder b Andrew | 8 | lbw b Palmer | 4 |
| D. Mohammed b Andrew | 0 | b Palmer | 9 |
| J. Adams c Blakey b Palmer | 17 | not out | 0 |
| D. Dixon c Burns b De Freitas | 36 | | |
| C. Hooper c Lenham b Sykes | 58 | not out | 4 |
| †P. Gayle run out | 10 | | |
| W. Coppin c Addison b Palmer | 24 | c Burns b Andrew | 7 |
| S. Manswell not out | 1 | | |
| B 2, l-b 11, w 1, n-b 20 | 34 | L-b 3 | 3 |
| 1/1 2/27 3/44 4/44 5/89 6/114 7/141 8/124 9/230 | 236 | 1/5 2/17 3/38 4/51 5/63 6/63 | (6 wkts) 67 |

Bowling: *First Innings*—De Freitas 12–0–49–2; Andrew 20–2–77–4; Tufnell 5–0–33–0; Palmer 14–1–54–2; Sykes 9.1–5–10–1. *Second Innings*—Andrew 10–2–20–3; Palmer 8–3–23–2; Tufnell 8–3–21–1.

v West Indies Young Cricketers: at Kensington Oval, Bridgetown, January 21 (First One-day "International"). West Indies Young Cricketers won by 100 runs. West Indies Young Cricketers 271 for nine (50 overs) (C. Hooper 119 not out); England Young Cricketers 171 (45.5 overs) (N. D. Burns 58).

v West Indies Young Cricketers: at Kensington Oval, Bridgetown, January 23 (Second One-day "International"). England Young Cricketers won on faster scoring-rate. West Indies Young Cricketers 245 for six (48.4 overs) (V. Smith 70, Z. Barthley 61); England Young Cricketers 116 for eight (23 overs).

v Windward Islands Youth: at Mindoo Phillip Park, St Lucia, January 26, 27, 28. Drawn. England Young Cricketers 282 for nine dec. (J. F. Sykes 56, M. A. Roseberry 52; W. Edwards five for 50) and 86 for three dec.; Windward Islands Youth 95 (P. A. Booth six for 22) and 163 for four (F. Edmunds 72 not out, A. Scotland 43).

v Windward Islands Youth: at Mindoo Phillip Park, St Lucia, January 30. England Young Cricketers won by two wickets. Windward Islands Youth 148 (47 overs) (A. Scotland 50 not out); England Young Cricketers 149 for eight (48.5 overs).

## WEST INDIES YOUNG CRICKETERS v ENGLAND YOUNG CRICKETERS

### Second "Test" Match

At Mindoo Phillip Park, St Lucia, February 1, 2, 3. Drawn. Rain permitted only 31 overs. Barthley retired needing three stitches above his right eye following a blow from De Freitas.

### West Indies Young Cricketers

| | |
|---|---|
| *Z. Barthley retired hurt | 2 |
| D. Joseph c Ripley b Andrew | 8 |
| R. Bishop not out | 24 |
| R. Holder not out | 44 |
| L-b 2, w 4, n-b 5 | 11 |
| 1/35 (1 wkt) | 89 |

V. Smith, J. Adams, D. Dixon, M. Boodoe, W. Coppin, †P. Gayle and S. Manswell did not bat.

Bowling: Andrew 11–1–30–1; De Freitas 11–3–27–0; Palmer 5–1–14–0; Booth 4–0–16–0.

### England Young Cricketers

*N. J. Lenham, R. J. Blakey, M. A. Roseberry, J. P. Addison, †D. Ripley, C. S. Mays, G. V. Palmer, J. F. Sykes, P. A. J. De Freitas, P. A. Booth and S. J. W. Andrew.

v West Indies Young Cricketers: at Mindoo Phillip Park, St Lucia, February 5 (Third One-day "International"). West Indies Young Cricketers won by three wickets. England Young Cricketers 129 (46.4 overs) (W. Coppin four for 17); West Indies Young Cricketers 131 for seven (37 overs).

v Jamaica Young Cricketers: at Alcan Kirkvine Ground, Jamaica, February 7. England Young Cricketers won by five wickets. Jamaica Young Cricketers 56 (33 overs) (P. C. R. Tufnell five for 20); England Young Cricketers 57 for five (32 overs) (D. Wright four for 20).

v Jamaica Young Cricketers: at Alpart Sports Club, Jamaica, February 9, 10, 11. Drawn. Jamaica Young Cricketers 214 (D. S. Hoffman four for 24) and 181 (P. Gayle 62; P. A. Booth five for 41); England Young Cricketers 273 for four dec. (C. S. Mays 67 not out, N. J. Lenham 58, R. J. Blakey 56) and 72 for two.

v Jamaica Young Cricketers: at Sabina Park, Kingston, February 13. Jamaica Young Cricketers won on faster scoring-rate. England Young Cricketers 194 for seven (50 overs) (J. P. Addison 44); Jamaica Young Cricketers 134 for nine (34 overs).

## WEST INDIES YOUNG CRICKETERS v ENGLAND YOUNG CRICKETERS

### Third "Test" Match

At Sabina Park, Kingston, February 15, 16, 17. West Indies Young Cricketers won by an innings and 120 runs. A satisfactory performance by England in the field on the first day was spoilt on the second when an easy chance from Adams was dropped, letting him add 185 for the seventh wicket with Boodoe as West Indies compiled a daunting total. England had no answer to the pace of Coppin and ended the day in disarray at 72 for seven. The run-out of Booth set the tone for the third day, when Dixon took over from the absent Coppin as the main destroyer.

## West Indies Young Cricketers

| | |
|---|---|
| *Z. Barthley c Sykes b Palmer | 4 |
| D. Joseph lbw b Sykes | 52 |
| R. Bishop c Blakey b Booth | 34 |
| R. Holder st Ripley b Sykes | 29 |
| V. Smith lbw b Palmer | 20 |
| J. Adams c Blakey b De Freitas | 105 |
| D. Dixon c Ripley b Palmer | 8 |
| M. Boodoe c Palmer b Hoffman | 82 |
| W. Coppin c Smith b De Freitas | 10 |
| †P. Gayle not out | 1 |
| S. Manswell b Hoffman | 0 |
| B 24, l-b 2, w 4, n-b 4 | 34 |
| 1/31 2/71 3/117 4/123 5/164 6/179 7/364 8/368 9/378 | 379 |

Bowling: De Freitas 19–2–60–2; Palmer 26–5–76–3; Hoffman 15.3–3–57–2; Booth 35–9–81–1; Sykes 34–6–79–2.

## England Young Cricketers

| First innings | | Second innings | |
|---|---|---|---|
| M. A. Roseberry c Smith b Coppin | 11 | c Holder b Dixon | 2 |
| R. J. Blakey c Barthley b Coppin | 0 | c Gayle b Dixon | 62 |
| †D. Ripley c Holder b Adams | 19 | b Dixon | 16 |
| *N. J. Lenham b Coppin | 5 | b Boodoe | 24 |
| C. S. Mays b Coppin | 0 | c Gayle b Boodoe | 0 |
| G. V. Palmer c Barthley b Dixon | 23 | b Dixon | 3 |
| I. Smith c Bishop b Boodoe | 3 | b Coppin | 7 |
| J. F. Sykes b Coppin | 8 | c Holder b Dixon | 25 |
| P. A. Booth run out | 5 | c and b Dixon | 12 |
| P. A. J. De Freitas not out | 0 | not out | 4 |
| D. S. Hoffman b Coppin | 0 | b Dixon | 2 |
| W 5, n-b 6 | 11 | B 10, l-b 3, w 1, n-b 3 | 17 |
| 1/8 2/17 3/27 4/27 5/56 6/59 7/72 8/81 9/85 | 85 | 1/10 2/61 3/110 4/112 5/116 6/126 7/143 8/161 9/172 | 174 |

Bowling: *First Innings*—Coppin 15.3–3–36–6; Manswell 5–1–14–0; Dixon 13–4–25–1; Boodoe 8–6–2–1; Adams 5–4–8–1. *Second Innings*—Coppin 12–3–47–1; Dixon 24–8–50–7; Bishop 5–1–9–0; Adams 20–10–30–0; Boodoe 26–13–22–2; Barthley 1–0–3–0.

# CRICKET IN AUSTRALIA, 1984-85

By JOHN MACKINNON

The 3,000 spectators at the Sydney Cricket Ground on March 19 saw the most exciting finish to a Sheffield Shield final since its introduction to the competition in 1983. The match delighted supporters of four- and five-day cricket and provided a happy conclusion to the season after a surfeit of one-day internationals had exhausted both players and spectators alike.

The Shield routine was adjusted to the extent that a day's cricket was lengthened to six and a half hours and a minimum of 105 overs. However, the extra two hours added to each game had no significant effect on the number of outright results, there being only one more than in the previous season. The attitude of the captains was more important in this respect and it was no coincidence that two of the more negative sides, Victoria and Tasmania, occupied the bottom two places on the ladder.

The points system, twelve for an outright win in addition to four for a first-innings win, came in for criticism, as all systems have in previous years. In its defence, there was no disputing that New South Wales and Queensland were the two best sides in the competition, and David Hookes's enterprising captaincy was rewarded when South Australia finished third. In winning both the Shield and the McDonald's Cup, New South Wales were indebted to their captain, Dirk Wellham, as well as their astute coaches, R. B. Simpson and Bill Anderson. But their critics were quick to point out that the pitches at the Sydney Cricket Ground generally favoured spin bowling. Bob Holland, Murray Bennett and Greg Matthews enjoyed splendid seasons, all three being rewarded with Test selection. Even so, the pitch for the Shield final, played in Sydney, satisfied even the most ardent Queenslander, and in that game the faster bowlers were as effective as the spinners. The New South Wales attack held the key to the team's success with the Pakistan Test player, Imran Khan, making an outstanding contribution. Dave Gilbert's improvement was also recognised by the national selectors. With Geoff Lawson absent for most of the season, Gilbert gave the bowling an incisive edge. The winners' batting was workmanlike. John Dyson scored a half-century in every match he played. Peter Clifford confirmed the promise of his first season; Wellham was consistent at No. 3, and the middle order was dependably manned by Matthews, Steve Rixon and latterly by Stephen Waugh, who in his first year showed high promise. The fielding was disciplined and sometimes brilliant with Steve Smith emerging as one of the best outfielders in the country.

Fielding their full team, Queensland gained outright points from four of their first five matches and at that stage topped the table by some distance. International duties then deprived them of key players and the team faltered dramatically. The loss to South Australia in Adelaide was the last straw, a result which led to them playing the final away from home. Without Allan Border, Kepler Wessels and Greg Ritchie, the batting was brittle, though Andrew Courtice and Trevor Barsby showed considerable promise. The bowling relied almost exclusively on pace, Craig McDermott being particularly hostile and Jeff Thomson, John Maguire and Carl Rackemann all having their days. Ray Phillips was the most successful wicket-keeper in the country, without having much chance to prove himself with the spinners.

South Australia did not score a point until their fifth game, but ultimately came close to qualifying for the final. With Hookes having a moderate year with the bat, it was as well that Andrew Hilditch found his best form. The batting was further improved when Mike Haysman, Glen Bishop and Don O'Connor got going, and the reserve wicket-keeper, David Kelly, played some useful innings. The bowling was heavily dependent on Rod McCurdy and John Inverarity. McCurdy arrived from Victoria in exchange for Rodney Hogg and proved at times to be a fiery competitor. In contrast, the seemingly benign left-arm spin of Inverarity lured many a batsman to his doom. The West Australian announced his retirement at the end of the season.

Western Australia had the unenviable task of finding replacements for Dennis Lillee, Rodney Marsh and Bruce Laird, who had all retired. The batting for the most part measured up, even though Graeme Wood was often on Test duty, and Kim Hughes, after his traumatic departure from the Test scene, was out of sorts. Greg Shipperd topped the national averages in his dour, combative style, and of the younger players, Mark McPhee, Mike Veletta and Geoff Marsh all played big innings. The bowling, however, lacked depth. Terry Alderman was the most effective.

Victoria have been building a team for a number of years with no obvious improvement in performance. Their loss to New South Wales in Sydney, when victory beckoned, exemplified a negative attitude, which reflected poorly on the senior players. Mick Taylor had another splendid year with the bat, the ever-confident Dean Jones played some brilliant innings and Simon O'Donnell improved more than anyone. Wickets were often hard to come by. Bright, a cautious captain, bowled 515 overs for 40 wickets; Simon Davis toiled away manfully, but the rest of the bowling was, at best, steady. Michael Dimattina, in his first year, kept wicket well.

Tasmania's fortunes ran parallel to their weather, which was often dreadful. There were some splendid batting performances from David Boon, Roger Woolley and Gary Goodman, and Keith Bradshaw showed promise. Brian Davison was out for much of the season owing to a blow on the arm from Queensland's McDermott. But Tasmania's bowling was their main worry. Patrick Patterson was brought in to provide some West Indian fire, but problems with no-balls and altercations with his captain undermined his value. For Woolley it was a tough season. Although his batting flourished, his wicket-keeping was erratic and his captaincy was inhibited by a lack of confidence in his team.

The future of the Sheffield Shield must still cause concern to the Australian Cricket Board. The heavy programme of international matches made great demands on state teams' resources and public interest in cricket at all levels dwindled as the season advanced. The value of importing overseas players to bolster state sides was also questioned. Tasmania have been doing so for some time, and although Patterson took 32 wickets in the Shield he was not quite the answer. Imran Khan, on the other hand, was good value for New South Wales. West Indian fast bowlers are often sought, but the best of them, already much committed, demand a high wage. There has, also, been an ever-increasing flow of English county cricketers spending their winters in Australia. One of them, John Emburey, did well in club cricket in Melbourne and was denied a place in the struggling Victorian side only because of their refusal to include overseas players. An encouraging feature of the season was the re-emergence of spin, despite all the one-day cricket. A restoration of spinning skills is overdue; maybe the Sydney curator holds the key.

# FIRST-CLASS AVERAGES, 1984-85

## BATTING

(Qualification: 300 runs)

| | *M* | *I* | *NO* | *R* | *HI* | *100s* | *Avge* |
|---|---|---|---|---|---|---|---|
| G. Shipperd (*WA*) | 11 | 18 | 6 | 823 | 139 | 3 | 68.58 |
| D. M. Jones (*Vic*) | 7 | 11 | 1 | 681 | 243 | 2 | 68.10 |
| S. P. O'Donnell (*Vic*) | 6 | 8 | 1 | 398 | 129* | 1 | 56.85 |
| K. C. Wessels (*Qld*) | 11 | 19 | 0 | 1,020 | 173 | 3 | 53.68 |
| T. J. Barsby (*Qld*) | 5 | 9 | 0 | 461 | 137 | 2 | 51.22 |
| R. D. Woolley (*Tas*) | 11 | 16 | 2 | 717 | 144 | 1 | 51.21 |
| P. S. Clifford (*NSW*) | 12 | 21 | 3 | 919 | 143 | 3 | 51.05 |
| A. M. J. Hilditch (*SA*) | 11 | 19 | 0 | 960 | 184 | 2 | 50.53 |
| M. D. Taylor (*Vic*) | 11 | 18 | 2 | 801 | 234* | 2 | 50.06 |
| R. B. Kerr (*Qld*) | 10 | 18 | 4 | 623 | 201* | 2 | 44.50 |
| M. D. Haysman (*SA*) | 10 | 19 | 2 | 744 | 172 | 2 | 43.76 |
| G. M. Ritchie (*Qld*) | 11 | 15 | 0 | 639 | 136 | 1 | 42.60 |
| K. Bradshaw (*Tas*) | 7 | 12 | 2 | 419 | 121 | 1 | 41.90 |
| B. A. Courtice (*Qld*) | 7 | 13 | 0 | 540 | 135 | 1 | 41.53 |
| D. C. Boon (*Tas*) | 10 | 18 | 2 | 664 | 147 | 3 | 41.50 |
| D. M. Wellham (*NSW*) | 12 | 21 | 1 | 829 | 115 | 2 | 41.45 |
| J. Dyson (*NSW*) | 12 | 22 | 0 | 897 | 98 | 0 | 40.77 |
| D. F. G. O'Connor (*SA*) | 11 | 21 | 2 | 773 | 118 | 1 | 40.68 |
| A. R. Border (*Qld*) | 11 | 19 | 3 | 645 | 144* | 1 | 40.31 |
| M. W. McPhee (*WA*) | 8 | 13 | 0 | 513 | 135 | 1 | 39.46 |
| M. R. J. Veletta (*WA*) | 11 | 19 | 2 | 665 | 143 | 2 | 39.11 |
| G. W. Goodman (*Tas*) | 10 | 18 | 1 | 659 | 123 | 1 | 38.76 |
| G. M. Wood (*WA*) | 8 | 15 | 0 | 565 | 141 | 1 | 37.66 |
| G. N. Yallop (*Vic*) | 7 | 14 | 1 | 472 | 147 | 2 | 36.30 |
| G. R. J. Matthews (*NSW*) | 13 | 21 | 2 | 664 | 103 | 1 | 34.94 |
| G. R. Marsh (*WA*) | 12 | 20 | 3 | 592 | 143* | 1 | 34.82 |
| D. J. Kelly (*SA*) | 7 | 11 | 2 | 310 | 100* | 1 | 34.44 |
| D. W. Hookes (*SA*) | 11 | 20 | 0 | 664 | 151 | 1 | 33.20 |
| R. B. Phillips (*Qld*) | 12 | 18 | 3 | 491 | 59 | 0 | 32.73 |
| G. A. Bishop (*SA*) | 11 | 21 | 0 | 685 | 170 | 1 | 32.61 |
| G. S. Trimble (*Qld*) | 10 | 16 | 2 | 445 | 90 | 0 | 31.78 |
| K. J. Hughes (*WA*) | 10 | 19 | 2 | 537 | 183 | 2 | 31.58 |
| T. V. Hohns (*Qld*) | 12 | 18 | 1 | 536 | 103 | 2 | 31.52 |
| M. Ray (*Tas*) | 11 | 20 | 1 | 576 | 82 | 0 | 30.31 |
| R. J. Bennett (*Tas*) | 8 | 14 | 2 | 357 | 89 | 0 | 29.75 |
| P. I. Faulkner (*Tas*) | 8 | 12 | 1 | 326 | 100 | 1 | 29.63 |
| R. J. Bright (*Vic*) | 11 | 15 | 2 | 384 | 84 | 0 | 29.53 |
| D. J. Buckingham (*Tas*) | 8 | 14 | 1 | 382 | 78 | 0 | 29.38 |
| S. C. Clements (*WA*) | 8 | 13 | 1 | 317 | 60 | 0 | 26.41 |
| R. J. Inverarity (*SA*) | 10 | 16 | 2 | 363 | 69 | 0 | 25.92 |
| S. B. Smith (*NSW*) | 9 | 17 | 1 | 407 | 76 | 0 | 25.43 |
| S. J. Rixon (*NSW*) | 12 | 21 | 1 | 507 | 115* | 1 | 25.35 |
| S. L. Saunders (*Tas*) | 10 | 15 | 1 | 318 | 107 | 1 | 22.71 |

**Signifies not out.*

## BOWLING

(Qualification: 15 wickets)

| | *O* | *M* | *R* | *W* | *Avge* |
|---|---|---|---|---|---|
| Imran Khan (*NSW*) | 265.5 | 78 | 536 | 28 | 19.14 |
| M. J. Bennett (*NSW*) | 338.5 | 111 | 677 | 33 | 20.51 |
| G. F. Lawson (*NSW*) | 307.2 | 75 | 785 | 37 | 21.21 |

| | *O* | *M* | *R* | *W* | *Avge* |
|---|---|---|---|---|---|
| C. J. McDermott (*Qld*) ... | 243.3 | 55 | 779 | 35 | 22.25 |
| R. J. Inverarity (*SA*) ..... | 405.4 | 104 | 1,016 | 43 | 23.62 |
| R. G. Holland (*NSW*) .... | 620.3 | 181 | 1,522 | 59 | 25.79 |
| J. N. Maguire (*Qld*) ...... | 461.1 | 104 | 1,273 | 46 | 27.67 |
| K. H. MacLeay (*WA*) .... | 214.3 | 52 | 589 | 21 | 28.04 |
| T. M. Alderman (*WA*) .... | 421 | 112 | 1,247 | 44 | 28.34 |
| C. G. Rackemann (*Qld*) ... | 436 | 99 | 1,201 | 42 | 28.59 |
| J. R. Thomson (*Qld*) ..... | 326 | 65 | 1,135 | 38 | 29.86 |
| R. J. Bright (*Vic*) ........ | 515.3 | 163 | 1,218 | 40 | 30.45 |
| R. J. McCurdy (*SA*) ...... | 358 | 74 | 1,175 | 38 | 30.92 |
| W. M. Clark (*WA*) ....... | 287.5 | 77 | 712 | 21 | 33.90 |
| S. P. Davis (*Vic*) ......... | 389.1 | 68 | 1,089 | 32 | 34.03 |
| P. M. Clough (*WA*) ...... | 214.1 | 46 | 648 | 19 | 34.10 |
| B. Reid (*WA*) ........... | 226.4 | 65 | 581 | 17 | 34.17 |
| B. P. Patterson (*Tas*) ..... | 377 | 51 | 1,359 | 37 | 36.72 |
| G. R. J. Matthews (*NSW*) . | 378.2 | 121 | 924 | 25 | 36.96 |
| R. L. Brown (*Tas*) ....... | 255.4 | 41 | 1,083 | 29 | 37.34 |
| D. R. Gilbert (*NSW*) ..... | 403.1 | 89 | 1,136 | 30 | 37.86 |
| T. B. A. May (*SA*) ....... | 253.5 | 71 | 711 | 18 | 39.50 |
| T. V. Hohns (*Qld*) ....... | 336.4 | 89 | 845 | 20 | 42.25 |
| R. M. Hogg (*Vic*) ........ | 212.1 | 34 | 653 | 15 | 43.53 |
| I. R. Carmichael (*SA*) .... | 431.5 | 114 | 1,307 | 27 | 48.40 |
| T. G. Hogan (*WA*) ....... | 504.5 | 124 | 1,333 | 26 | 51.26 |
| P. I. Faulkner (*Tas*) ...... | 336.3 | 80 | 917 | 17 | 53.94 |
| S. L. Saunders (*Tas*) ...... | 271 | 48 | 878 | 15 | 58.53 |

## WICKET-KEEPING

R. B. Phillips (*Qld*) 56 (55ct, 1st); S. J. Rixon (*NSW*) 34 (27ct, 7st); M. G. Dimattina (*Vic*) 30 (24ct, 6st); R. D. Woolley (*Tas*) 28 (26ct, 2st); T. J. Zoehrer (*WA*) 27 (25ct, 2st); D. Kelly (*SA*) 24 (22ct, 2st); W. B. Phillips (*SA*) 15 (14ct, 1st).

## SHEFFIELD SHIELD, 1984-85

| | *Played* | *Won* | *Drawn* | *Lost* | *1st Inns Lead* | *Pts* |
|---|---|---|---|---|---|---|
| New South Wales .......... | 10 | 4 | 6 | 0 | 8 | 80 |
| Queensland ............... | 10 | 4 | 3 | 3 | 7 | 76 |
| South Australia ............ | 10 | 4 | 2 | 4 | 3 | 60 |
| Western Australia .......... | 10 | 2 | 7 | 1 | 4 | 42* |
| Victoria .................. | 10 | 0 | 6 | 4 | 4 | 18* |
| Tasmania ................. | 10 | 0 | 8 | 2 | 3 | 12 |

*Points: Outright win = 12; lead on first innings = 4.*

* *First-innings points shared.*

## WESTERN AUSTRALIA v TASMANIA

At Perth, October 19, 20, 21, 22. Drawn. Western Australia 4 pts. Western Australia's bid for outright victory was foiled by bad light which ended play with 11.3 overs remaining. Davison and Woolley had given Tasmania, chasing 316, a chance with a dashing fifth-wicket stand of

128 in 110 minutes, but once MacLeay broke through only Davison stood between them and defeat. The brilliant strokes of Hughes, whose chanceless innings occupied less than five hours, dominated Western Australia's first innings, but Tasmania's new pace attack fell apart when Brown hurt his side and Patterson bowled seventeen no-balls. At 176 for six Tasmania looked likely to have to follow-on, but Hughes dropped Woolley at mid-on, a mistake that proved costly as Woolley went on to make his highest first-class score.

## Western Australia

| First innings | | Second innings | |
|---|---|---|---|
| G. M. Wood run out | 94 | c Ray b Faulkner | 46 |
| M. R. J. Veletta b Faulkner | 21 | retired hurt | 16 |
| G. Shipperd run out | 46 | | |
| *K. J. Hughes c Ray b Saunders | 183 | (3) not out | 67 |
| G. R. Marsh b Hyatt | 6 | c Boon b Saunders | 30 |
| S. C. Clements c Woolley b Patterson | 51 | (4) run out | 0 |
| K. H. MacLeay c and b Saunders | 27 | (6) run out | 6 |
| †W. D. Hill c Boon b Saunders | 9 | | |
| T. G. Hogan run out | 11 | | |
| W. M. Clark b Patterson | 13 | | |
| T. M. Alderman not out | 9 | | |
| B 5, l-b 4, w 1, n-b 24 | 34 | B 2, l-b 1, n-b 2 | 5 |
| 1/52 2/163 3/217 4/234 5/356 6/421 7/466 8/481 9/485 | 504 | 1/63 2/70 3/146 4/170 (4 wkts dec.) | 170 |

Bowling: *First Innings*—Patterson 33.4–1–146–2; Brown 3–1–15–0; Faulkner 41–11–121–1; Saunders 33–6–105–3; Hyatt 18–3–46–1; Ray 21–2–62–0. *Second Innings*—Patterson 16–0–75–0; Faulkner 20.4–7–49–1; Saunders 11–2–43–1.

## Tasmania

| First innings | | Second innings | |
|---|---|---|---|
| M. Ray lbw b Alderman | 13 | c Clark b Alderman | 8 |
| G. W. Goodman c Alderman b Hogan | 57 | lbw b MacLeay | 10 |
| D. C. Boon lbw b Clark | 1 | b MacLeay | 2 |
| K. Bradshaw c Veletta b Clark | 16 | (5) c Alderman b MacLeay | 4 |
| B. F. Davison c Hill b Hogan | 29 | (4) not out | 98 |
| *†R. D. Woolley c Marsh b Alderman | 144 | c Hill b MacLeay | 61 |
| S. L. Saunders c Veletta b Clark | 1 | c Hogan b MacLeay | 1 |
| P. I. Faulkner c Hill b Alderman | 30 | b Hogan | 12 |
| R. S. Hyatt c Alderman b MacLeay | 16 | not out | 3 |
| B. P. Patterson c MacLeay b Clark | 12 | | |
| R. L. Brown not out | 11 | | |
| B 7, l-b 9, n-b 13 | 29 | B 1, l-b 9, n-b 3 | 13 |
| 1/25 2/36 3/99 4/100 5/161 6/176 7/251 8/279 9/328 | 359 | 1/13 2/18 3/41 4/47 5/175 6/179 7/201 (7 wkts) | 212 |

Bowling: *First Innings*—Alderman 29.1–2–110–3; Clark 37–14–70–4; Hogan 46–13–104–2; MacLeay 26–9–59–1. *Second Innings*—Alderman 16–1–66–1; Clark 6–0–31–0; Hogan 14–0–51–1; MacLeay 21.3–5–54–5.

Umpires: T. A. Prue and W. M. Powell.

## SOUTH AUSTRALIA v NEW SOUTH WALES

At Adelaide, October 19, 20, 21, 22. New South Wales won by 134 runs. New South Wales 16 pts. Dyson and Wellham consolidated a flying start by Smith, and then Clifford and Matthews accelerated the scoring for a lunchtime declaration on the second day. South Australia's fielding was poor, with Clifford enjoying four lives and McCurdy especially suffering from his fielders' errors. The South Australian innings consisted almost entirely of an eight-hour vigil by Hilditch. Smith fell to the first ball of New South Wales's second innings and McCurdy, who bowled very fast, went on to record his best-ever return. Only Geise resisted the onslaught, mixing watchful defence with some powerful strokeplay. South Australia's target of 279 in five and a half hours seemed attainable, but Lawson and Holland broke the back of their innings.

## New South Wales

| | | | |
|---|---|---|---|
| S. B. Smith c Haysman b Parkinson | 27 | c Bishop b McCurdy | 0 |
| J. Dyson c Hookes b Inverarity | 70 | lbw b McCurdy | 18 |
| *D. M. Wellham c Inverarity b Hookes | 80 | c Phillips b McCurdy | 3 |
| P. S. Clifford c McCurdy b Inverarity | 125 | (8) run out | 5 |
| G. G. Geise c Phillips b Inverarity | 1 | (4) c Hookes b McCurdy | 84 |
| G. R. J. Matthews c Carmichael b Inverarity | 86 | (5) c Haysman b Inverarity | 17 |
| †S. J. Rixon c May b Inverarity | 24 | (6) c Hookes b May | 3 |
| P. H. Marks not out | 18 | (7) lbw b McCurdy | 12 |
| G. F. Lawson not out | 4 | lbw b McCurdy | 0 |
| R. G. Holland (did not bat) | – | c Bishop b McCurdy | 0 |
| D. R. Gilbert (did not bat) | – | not out | 0 |
| L-b 5, w 6, n-b 1 | 12 | L-b 1, w 1 | 2 |
| 1/32 2/142 3/193 4/208 5/392 6/412 7/443 (7 wkts dec.) | 447 | 1/0 2/8 3/37 4/78 5/90 6/118 7/131 8/131 9/135 | 144 |

Bowling: *First Innings*—McCurdy 28–4–107–0; Parkinson 21–9–66–1; Carmichael 24–9–48–0; May 34–6–95–0; Inverarity 34–8–94–5; Hookes 7–0–32–1. *Second Innings*—McCurdy 17.4–2–55–7; Parkinson 5–3–12–0; Carmichael 9–3–27–0; May 16–8–36–1; Inverarity 10–4–13–1.

## South Australia

| | | | |
|---|---|---|---|
| A. M. J. Hilditch c and b Holland | 184 | b Holland | 56 |
| D. F. G. O'Connor c Wellham b Marks | 10 | lbw b Lawson | 0 |
| M. D. Haysman b Holland | 21 | c Geise b Lawson | 2 |
| *D. W. Hookes c Matthews b Marks | 1 | c Dyson b Marks | 12 |
| †W. B. Phillips b Holland | 26 | b Holland | 9 |
| G. A. Bishop c Marks b Lawson | 15 | lbw b Lawson | 6 |
| R. J. Inverarity lbw b Gilbert | 10 | c sub b Gilbert | 24 |
| T. B. A. May b Lawson | 26 | c Dyson b Holland | 1 |
| R. J. McCurdy c Smith b Holland | 4 | st Rixon b Holland | 13 |
| S. D. H. Parkinson not out | 0 | c Holland b Gilbert | 14 |
| I. R. Carmichael not out | 1 | not out | 0 |
| B 5, l-b 7, w 1, n-b 2 | 15 | B 4, l-b 3 | 7 |
| 1/40 2/94 3/95 4/178 5/215 6/245 7/306 8/312 9/312 (9 wkts dec.) | 313 | 1/1 2/15 3/65 4/74 5/89 6/95 7/100 8/124 9/144 | 144 |

Bowling: *First Innings*—Lawson 28.4–7–42–2; Gilbert 23–3–73–1; Marks 19–3–43–2; Holland 37–9–86–4; Matthews 19–1–57–0. *Second Innings*—Lawson 13–3–37–3; Gilbert 8–1–24–2; Marks 7–3–19–1; Holland 14.2–3–48–4; Matthews 3–1–9–0.

Umpires: A. R. Crafter and B. E. Martin.

## QUEENSLAND v VICTORIA

At Brisbane, October 26, 27, 28, 29. Queensland won by nine wickets. Queensland 16 pts. Put in to bat on a blameless pitch, Victoria capitulated to the Queensland pace attack. In contrast, the Queensland batsmen, having withstood an early assault by Hogg, took full control. Kerr, given an early life in the gully, provided solid support for Wessels and Ritchie in a stay of nearly five hours, but it was Ritchie who caught the eye in an innings lasting three and a half hours. The 21-year-old Trimble came near to his maiden first-class hundred. Victoria showed more resolve in their second innings, but poor running cost them dearly. For Queensland, Phillips showed good form behind the wicket, taking eight catches and not conceding a bye.

## Victoria

| | | | |
|---|---|---|---|
| P. A. Hibbert c Border b Rackemann | 15 | – b McDermott | 42 |
| M. B. Quinn c Phillips b Thomson | 0 | – run out | 54 |
| G. N. Yallop c Kerr b Rackemann | 0 | – run out | 2 |
| D. M. Jones c Phillips b McDermott | 26 | – c Ritchie b Hohns | 34 |
| M. D. Taylor c Kerr b McDermott | 57 | – c Ritchie b Rackemann | 15 |
| S. P. O'Donnell b McDermott | 5 | – run out | 54 |
| A. I. C. Dodemaide lbw b Maguire | 36 | – c Phillips b Maguire | 74 |
| †P. A. Hyde c Phillips b Maguire | 7 | – c Trimble b McDermott | 10 |
| *R. J. Bright c Phillips b Rackemann | 6 | – c Phillips b Rackemann | 19 |
| R. M. Hogg c Phillips b McDermott | 28 | – not out | 0 |
| S. P. Davis not out | 0 | – c Phillips b Rackemann | 0 |
| L-b 8, n-b 13 | 21 | L-b 8, w 1, n-b 6 | 15 |
| 1/1 2/8 3/21 4/104 5/107 6/121 7/132 8/150 9/189 | 201 | 1/74 2/77 3/132 4/150 5/150 6/253 7/271 8/319 9/319 | 319 |

Bowling: *First Innings*—Thomson 12–2–48–1; Rackemann 16–5–28–3; Maguire 14.1–6–31–2; McDermott 19–6–55–4; Hohns 24–13–31–0. *Second Innings*—Thomson 17–3–53–0; Rackemann 25.4–7–66–3; Maguire 16–4–56–1; McDermott 23–6–52–2; Hohns 40–16–81–1; Border 3–2–3–0.

## Queensland

| | | | |
|---|---|---|---|
| R. B. Kerr lbw b Bright | 106 | – not out | 19 |
| K. C. Wessels c Yallop b O'Donnell | 60 | – c Hyde b O'Donnell | 28 |
| *A. R. Border b O'Donnell | 0 | – not out | 8 |
| G. M. Ritchie c Jones b Davis | 136 | | |
| G. S. Trimble c Quinn b Bright | 90 | | |
| T. V. Hohns c Dodemaide b Bright | 25 | | |
| †R. B. Phillips c Hyde b O'Donnell | 0 | | |
| C. J. McDermott c Hibbert b Hogg | 14 | | |
| J. N. Maguire c Hyde b Hogg | 1 | | |
| C. G. Rackemann not out | 11 | | |
| J. R. Thomson b Dodemaide | 6 | | |
| B 3, l-b 10, n-b 5 | 18 | L-b 1 | 1 |
| 1/91 2/95 3/276 4/336 5/393 6/397 7/424 8/434 9/456 | 467 | 1/37 | (1 wkt) 56 |

Bowling: *First Innings*—Hogg 32–5–94–2; Davis 30–7–80–1; O'Donnell 22–3–84–3; Bright 31–2–133–3; Dodemaide 19.2–3–63–1. *Second Innings*—Davis 6.3–0–35–0; O'Donnell 6–0–20–1.

Umpires: M. W. Johnson and C. D. Timmins.

## NEW SOUTH WALES v WESTERN AUSTRALIA

At Canberra, October 26, 27, 28, 29. Drawn. Western Australia 4 pts. The first Sheffield Shield match at Canberra's Manuka Oval was a dismal affair, owing to an indifferent pitch and bad weather which reduced the playing time by seven and a half hours. Bowlers of both sides revelled in the conditions, although Wood and Veletta enjoyed a period of ascendancy in Western Australia's first innings. Lawson and Gilbert just failed to gain first-innings points for New South Wales. In the second innings, Dyson showed his best form in a forceful display, and Matthews played sensibly, but by the time Wellham could make a token declaration a draw was inevitable.

## New South Wales

| Batsman | First innings | | Second innings | |
|---|---|---|---|---|
| J. Dyson c Clements b MacLeay | 5 | – | lbw b Clark | 76 |
| S. B. Smith c Clements b MacLeay | 19 | – | lbw b Alderman | 3 |
| *D. M. Wellham c Hogan b MacLeay | 0 | – | lbw b Alderman | 23 |
| P. S. Clifford lbw b Alderman | 15 | – | lbw b Hogan | 22 |
| G. G. Geise lbw b Hogan | 0 | – | lbw b Alderman | 11 |
| G. R. J. Matthews c Hill b Clark | 33 | – | not out | 49 |
| †S. J. Rixon lbw b Hogan | 23 | – | c Shipperd b Clark | 7 |
| M. J. Bennett run out | 10 | – | lbw b Clark | 12 |
| G. F. Lawson c Clark b Alderman | 30 | – | b Alderman | 1 |
| R. G. Holland c Hill b Clark | 12 | – | b Clark | 1 |
| D. R. Gilbert not out | 0 | – | not out | 3 |
| B 1, l-b 4, n-b 4 | 9 | | B 2, l-b 6, n-b 2 | 10 |
| 1/24 2/24 3/27 4/32 5/49 6/80 7/104 8/126 9/154 | 156 | | 1/9 2/83 3/128 4/131 5/147 6/160 7/185 8/186 9/189 (9 wkts dec.) | 218 |

Bowling: *First Innings*—Alderman 14.4–2–46–2; MacLeay 28–8–49–3; Hogan 18–5–29–2; Clark 13–1–27–2. *Second Innings*—Alderman 36–9–62–4; MacLeay 9–3–15–0; Hogan 27–4–58–1; Clark 40–10–75–4.

## Western Australia

| Batsman | First innings | | Second innings | |
|---|---|---|---|---|
| G. M. Wood lbw b Holland | 61 | – | c Rixon b Gilbert | 3 |
| M. R. J. Veletta c Bennett b Gilbert | 49 | – | not out | 15 |
| G. Shipperd c Clifford b Lawson | 7 | – | not out | 6 |
| *K. J. Hughes not out | 18 | | | |
| G. R. Marsh c Holland b Lawson | 4 | | | |
| S. C. Clements lbw b Gilbert | 3 | | | |
| K. H. MacLeay c Rixon b Lawson | 0 | | | |
| †W. D. Hill lbw b Gilbert | 2 | | | |
| T. G. Hogan lbw b Lawson | 7 | | | |
| T. M. Alderman b Holland | 4 | | | |
| W. M. Clark run out | 0 | | | |
| B 6, l-b 6, w 2, n-b 2 | 16 | | L-b 1, n-b 1 | 2 |
| 1/112 2/127 3/132 4/138 5/141 6/142 7/149 8/162 9/169 | 171 | | 1/3 (1 wkt) | 26 |

Bowling: *First Innings*—Lawson 25–10–42–4; Gilbert 27–5–69–3; Geise 1–0–7–0; Bennett 7–1–19–0; Holland 10–3–22–2. *Second Innings*—Lawson 4–2–6–0; Gilbert 8–3–15–1; Geise 4–2–4–0.

Umpires: R. A. French and A. G. Marshall.

## VICTORIA v WESTERN AUSTRALIA

At Melbourne, November 9, 10, 11, 12. Drawn. Victoria 2 pts, Western Australia 2 pts. This game, played at Princes Park, Carlton, so that the Melbourne Cricket Ground could be saved for the heavy international programme, for the most part matched the drab weather, a final deluge saving Victoria when Western Australia were poised to take first-innings points. In Western Australia's innings Veletta hit his maiden century, and McPhee, for the visitors, and Dimattina, Victoria's wicket-keeper, made good impressions on their début. Bright, Victoria's captain, was critical of the covers provided by the Carlton authorities.

### Western Australia

| | | | |
|---|---|---|---|
| S. C. Clements c Dimattina b Hughes | 58 | T. G. Hogan c sub b Bright | 2 |
| M. R. J. Veletta c Dimattina b Davis | 100 | †W. D. Hill b Dodemaide | 8 |
| *G. Shipperd c Dimattina b Davis | 17 | W. M. Clark not out | 19 |
| G. R. Marsh c O'Donnell b Hughes | 20 | | |
| M. W. McPhee c Dimattina b Hughes | 85 | B 5, l-b 5 | 10 |
| P. M. Clough c Hibbert b Dodemaide | 9 | | — |
| K. H. MacLeay c Dodemaide b Bright | 52 | 1/112 2/170 3/177 4/266 | 389 |
| R. W. Gartrell c sub b Davis | 9 | 5/283 6/305 7/352 8/361 9/364 | |

Bowling: Hughes 32–6–84–3; O'Donnell 12–1–31–0; Dodemaide 28.2–5–70–2; Bright 43–15–113–2; Davis 26–2–69–3; Whiteside 7–1–12–0.

### Victoria

| | | | |
|---|---|---|---|
| P. A. Hibbert c Hill b MacLeay | 61 | †M. G. Dimattina not out | 8 |
| G. W. Richardson b Clark | 80 | M. G. Hughes b Clough | 13 |
| D. M. Jones b Clark | 33 | S. P. Davis not out | 1 |
| M. D. Taylor c Clements b Clark | 14 | | |
| W. G. Whiteside c Veletta b Hogan | 24 | B 3, l-b 13, n-b 3 | 19 |
| S. P. O'Donnell b Clough | 10 | | — |
| A. I. C. Dodemaide b Clark | 13 | 1/116 2/165 3/195 4/200 | (9 wkts) 310 |
| *R. J. Bright c Veletta b Clough | 34 | 5/216 6/249 7/267 8/292 9/308 | |

Bowling: Clough 32–6–78–3; MacLeay 24–5–48–1; Clark 43–17–89–4; Hogan 47.5–16–78–1; Gartrell 1–0–1–0.

Umpires: R. C. Bailhache and R. C. Isherwood.

## TASMANIA v NEW SOUTH WALES

At Launceston, November 9, 10, 11, 12. Drawn. New South Wales 4 pts. Heavy rain caused the match to be abandoned after a challenging declaration by Wellham had set Tasmania to make 283 in 90 overs. After the New South Wales first innings had been saved by a surprising last-wicket stand of 98 between Marks and Gilbert, Chappell's medium pace had Tasmania in trouble until Boon and Woolley produced the best batting of the match, adding 126 in under two hours. When Woolley was out, Gilbert's fiery bowling gave New South Wales the advantage. Boon was forced to retire at 132, hit on the head by a bouncer from Gilbert, and could add only 6 more runs when he resumed after a night's rest. A fourth-wicket stand of 171 in four hours by Wellham and Matthews set up New South Wales's challenge, only for the elements to intervene.

### New South Wales

| | | | |
|---|---|---|---|
| T. M. Chappell c Woolley b Patterson | 26 | – c Woolley b Faulkner | 2 |
| S. B. Smith c Saunders b Patterson | 54 | – c Woolley b Patterson | 12 |
| *D. M. Wellham c Davison b Faulkner | 9 | – c and b Ray | 115 |
| P. S. Clifford c Davison b Kirkman | 27 | – c Woolley b Patterson | 12 |
| G. R. J. Matthews c Woolley b Kirkman | 6 | – c Ray b Patterson | 66 |
| G. G. Geise c Ray b Hyatt | 39 | – not out | 15 |
| †S. J. Rixon c Bradshaw b Saunders | 33 | – run out | 19 |
| P. H. Marks c Ray b Patterson | 75 | – b Patterson | 2 |
| M. J. Bennett c Goodman b Hyatt | 2 | | |
| R. G. Holland lbw b Hyatt | 0 | | |
| D. R. Gilbert not out | 38 | | |
| L-b 14, w 2, n-b 8 | 24 | B 5, l-b 9, n-b 5 | 19 |
| | — | | — |
| 1/71 2/97 3/103 4/120 5/155 6/209 7/213 8/221 9/235 | 333 | 1/18 2/22 3/41 4/212 5/222 6/254 7/262 | (7 wkts dec.) 262 |

Bowling: *First Innings*—Patterson 26.2–4–102–3; Faulkner 35–8–94–1; Kirkman 17–4–63–2; Saunders 14–5–30–1; Hyatt 12–4–30–3. *Second Innings*—Patterson 22.3–3–68–4; Faulkner 30–7–51–1; Kirkman 10–3–29–0; Saunders 14–0–39–0; Hyatt 13–4–30–0; Ray 11–2–31–1.

**Tasmania**

| | | | |
|---|---|---|---|
| G. W. Goodman c Rixon b Chappell | 16 | – lbw b Gilbert | 53 |
| M. Ray c Bennett b Chappell | 10 | – not out | 38 |
| D. C. Boon lbw b Gilbert | 138 | – not out | 0 |
| K. Bradshaw b Marks | 0 | | |
| B. F. Davison c Smith b Chappell | 34 | | |
| *†R. D. Woolley c Chappell b Bennett | 55 | | |
| S. L. Saunders b Bennett | 10 | | |
| P. I. Faulkner c Rixon b Gilbert | 13 | | |
| R. S. Hyatt run out | 22 | | |
| W. S. Kirkman b Gilbert | 2 | | |
| B. P. Patterson not out | 7 | | |
| L-b 3, n-b 3 | 6 | B 1, l-b 1 | 2 |
| 1/26 2/38 3/41 4/91 5/217 6/241 7/277 8/281 9/287 | 313 | 1/89 | (1 wkt) 93 |

Bowling: *First Innings*—Gilbert 27.2–7–80–3; Marks 22–3–65–1; Chappell 19–5–55–3; Holland 15–4–46–0; Bennett 21–8–34–2; Matthews 14–2–30–0. *Second Innings*—Gilbert 8.2–1–36–1; Marks 4–1–6–0; Chappell 4–3–3–0; Holland 6–1–17–0; Bennett 8–0–21–0; Matthews 1–0–8–0.

Umpires: J. T. Hinds and S. G. Randell.

## VICTORIA v TASMANIA

At Melbourne, November 15, 16, 17, 18. Drawn. Victoria 4 pts. Early interference by rain made this match no more than a struggle for first-innings points. Tasmania, missing the attacking flair of Davison, batted through to stumps on the second day, Boon's hundred being his second in consecutive matches. If anything, Victoria's batsmen enjoyed better conditions, the pitch having dried out, and their early batsmen gave them a steady start, after which their grasp was never challenged.

**Tasmania**

| | | | |
|---|---|---|---|
| G. W. Goodman c Dimattina b O'Donnell | 7 | – lbw b Hogg | 0 |
| M. Ray c Dimattina b O'Donnell | 60 | – c O'Donnell b Davis | 8 |
| D. C. Boon b Bright | 104 | | |
| D. J. Buckingham c O'Donnell b Dodemaide | 71 | – b Dodemaide | 17 |
| R. J. Bennett c Dimattina b Hogg | 14 | – (3) not out | 14 |
| *†R. D. Woolley c Dimattina b Dodemaide | 10 | | |
| S. L. Saunders c Dimattina b Dodemaide | 6 | – (5) not out | 2 |
| P. I. Faulkner lbw b Whiteside | 27 | | |
| R. S. Hyatt c Davis b Whiteside | 36 | | |
| R. L. Brown c Davis b Bright | 20 | | |
| B. P. Patterson not out | 2 | | |
| B 1, l-b 6, w 1, n-b 3 | 11 | B 2 | 2 |
| 1/12 2/133 3/197 4/225 5/267 6/270 7/279 8/338 9/351 | 368 | 1/0 2/13 3/35 | (3 wkts) 43 |

Bowling: *First Innings*—Hogg 26–6–67–1; O'Donnell 29–10–72–2; Dodemaide 35–4–90–3; Davis 20–3–45–0; Bright 34.4–8–60–2; Whiteside 9–1–25–2; Jones 1–0–2–0. *Second Innings*—Hogg 7–0–18–1; Dodemaide 2–0–10–1; Davis 5–1–12–1; Hibbert 1–0–1–0.

### Victoria

| | |
|---|---|
| P. A. Hibbert lbw b Saunders | 39 |
| G. W. Richardson lbw b Faulkner | 87 |
| D. M. Jones c Woolley b Brown | 67 |
| M. D. Taylor c Ray b Boon | 118 |
| †M. G. Dimattina b Faulkner | 10 |
| W. G. Whiteside st Woolley b Hyatt | 7 |
| A. I. C. Dodemaide c Boon b Saunders | 12 |
| S. P. O'Donnell c and b Saunders | 42 |
| *R. J. Bright b Patterson | 42 |
| R. M. Hogg c and b Hyatt | 17 |
| S. P. Davis not out | 15 |
| B 14, l-b 13, n-b 8 | 35 |
| 1/95 2/158 3/243 4/295 5/334 6/366 7/412 8/413 9/430 | 491 |

Bowling: Patterson 34.3–7–107–1; Brown 25–2–101–1; Faulkner 37–10–68–2; Saunders 40–10–89–3; Hyatt 37–11–84–2; Ray 2–1–2–0; Boon 3–1–12–1; Buckingham 1–0–1–0; Woolley 1–1–0–0.

Umpires: R. C. Bailhache and R. C. Isherwood.

## QUEENSLAND v SOUTH AUSTRALIA

At Brisbane, November 16, 17, 18, 19. Queensland won by five wickets. Queensland 16 pts. When Border invited South Australia to take first innings, he could hardly have expected that Queensland would be chasing 370 on the fourth day to win. Yet his faster bowlers failed to make use of the early damp in the pitch. Aggressive strokeplay from Wessels and Ritchie put Queensland in control, and although McCurdy undermined their middle order they secured first-innings points. With Hookes and Haysman showing the way in their second innings, South Australia were able to set Queensland an imposing target. But a hamstring injury prevented McCurdy from bowling more than five overs; Wessels batted superbly for 205 minutes; and Queensland won with ten overs to spare.

### South Australia

| | | | |
|---|---|---|---|
| A. M. J. Hilditch run out | 7 | – c Phillips b McDermott | 41 |
| †W. B. Phillips c Rackemann b Thomson | 32 | – c Hohns b McDermott | 0 |
| *D. W. Hookes c Phillips b Rackemann | 5 | – (5) c Phillips b Maguire | 79 |
| G. A. Bishop lbw b McDermott | 87 | – b Border | 43 |
| D. F. G. O'Connor c Maguire b Thomson | 53 | – (3) c Ritchie b Hohns | 55 |
| M. D. Haysman c and b Hohns | 0 | – c Thomson b Border | 72 |
| J. J. Benton c Border b Hohns | 0 | – c Phillips b Rackemann | 21 |
| T. B. A. May c Phillips b Hohns | 18 | – b Border | 10 |
| R. J. McCurdy b Hohns | 34 | – b Wessels | 13 |
| S. D. H. Parkinson c Ritchie b Hohns | 15 | – not out | 8 |
| I. R. Carmichael not out | 1 | | |
| L-b 3, n-b 22 | 25 | L-b 10, n-b 23 | 33 |
| 1/8 2/22 3/84 4/154 5/163 6/163 7/197 8/230 9/270 | 277 | 1/5 2/63 3/139 4/219 5/263 6/306 7/346 8/365 9/375 (9 wkts dec.) | 375 |

Bowling: *First Innings*—Rackemann 14–2–43–1; McDermott 13–2–59–1; Maguire 17–2–64–0; Thomson 10–3–52–2; Hohns 25.1–9–56–5. *Second Innings*—Rackemann 21–2–63–1; McDermott 26–9–36–2; Maguire 19–4–59–1; Thomson 17–6–68–0; Hohns 23–3–90–1; Border 7–2–24–3; Wessels 5–0–25–1.

### Queensland

| | | | |
|---|---|---|---|
| R. B. Kerr c Bishop b May | 40 | – b McCurdy | 2 |
| K. C. Wessels c and b Hookes | 64 | – c and b Carmichael | 144 |
| *A. R. Border b Carmichael | 32 | – c Benton b Hookes | 41 |
| G. M. Ritchie c O'Connor b Parkinson | 84 | – c May b Carmichael | 37 |
| G. S. Trimble c Bishop b Carmichael | 0 | – not out | 67 |
| T. V. Hohns c Hilditch b McCurdy | 15 | – c Phillips b May | 3 |
| †R. B. Phillips lbw b McCurdy | 16 | – not out | 56 |
| C. J. McDermott c Phillips b McCurdy | 0 | | |
| J. N. Maguire not out | 10 | | |
| C. G. Rackemann not out | 4 | | |
| L-b 8, n-b 10 | 18 | B 1, l-b 10, n-b 9 | 20 |
| 1/104 2/125 3/198 4/208 5/238 6/259 7/259 8/267 | (8 wkts dec.) 283 | 1/6 2/108 3/207 4/236 5/255 | (5 wkts) 370 |

J. R. Thomson did not bat.

Bowling: *First Innings*—McCurdy 21–5–80–3; Parkinson 17–3–56–1; May 10–2–36–1; Carmichael 24–6–83–2; Hookes 1–0–10–1; Benton 1–0–10–0. *Second Innings*—McCurdy 5–1–18–1; Parkinson 10.1–1–41–0; May 32–8–113–1; Carmichael 31–6–111–2; Hookes 6–2–31–1; Haysman 2–0–4–0; O'Connor 1–0–4–0; Benton 10–1–37–0.

Umpires: C. D. Timmins and M. J. King.

## SOUTH AUSTRALIA v TASMANIA

At Adelaide, November 22, 23, 24, 25. Drawn. Tasmania 4 pts. Put in, Tasmania were a long time making their runs, and this may have cost them outright points. Goodman and Davison were forced to retire at various stages, and the wisdom of Goodman's return, after he had been to hospital with a head injury, was questioned, the score already being past 400. A typically aggressive innings by Hookes, who hammered six 6s in three and three-quarter hours' batting, failed to prevent the follow-on as accurate bowling by Brown caused the last five South Australian wickets to fall for only 6 runs. In their second innings Hilditch fought hard before Bishop combined watchful defence with some splendid hitting in a five-hour stay. His innings included seven 6s and fourteen 4s. Harms gave him courageous support for nearly three hours, although both players gave chances to Woolley at the wicket.

### Tasmania

| | |
|---|---|
| M. Ray c Harms b McCurdy | 49 |
| G. W. Goodman not out | 30 |
| R. J. Bennett c Kelly b McCurdy | 89 |
| D. J. Buckingham c and b Carmichael | 20 |
| B. F. Davison c sub b McCurdy | 66 |
| *†R. D. Woolley c Harms b Inverarity | 51 |
| S. L. Saunders st Kelly b Harms | 53 |
| P. I. Faulkner c Bishop b Inverarity | 40 |
| R. S. Hyatt not out | 56 |
| R. L. Brown c McCurdy b Zesers | 9 |
| B 5, l-b 5, n-b 14 | 24 |
| 1/80 2/129 3/201 4/271 5/334 6/388 7/388 8/401 | (8 wkts dec.) 487 |

B. P. Patterson did not bat.

Bowling: Carmichael 40–15–80–1; McCurdy 40–10–120–3; Zesers 34–9–85–1; Harms 30–10–49–1; Inverarity 44–12–113–2; Hookes 3–0–22–0; Haysman 3–0–8–0.

## South Australia

| First Innings | | Second Innings | |
|---|---|---|---|
| R. J. Inverarity run out | 25 | c sub b Patterson | 1 |
| A. M. J. Hilditch c Brown b Patterson | 16 | c Davison b Brown | 86 |
| D. F. G. O'Connor c Woolley b Patterson | 0 | hit wkt b Patterson | 16 |
| G. A. Bishop c Saunders b Brown | 10 | c and b Ray | 170 |
| *D. W. Hookes c Bennett b Brown | 151 | c sub b Brown | 4 |
| M. D. Haysman b Faulkner | 53 | c Hyatt b Saunders | 12 |
| †D. Kelly run out | 8 | c Brown b Hyatt | 17 |
| C. L. Harms b Brown | 0 | c Davison b Ray | 33 |
| A. K. Zesers lbw b Brown | 1 | b Ray | 17 |
| R. J. McCurdy c Woolley b Faulkner | 0 | c Brown b Bennett | 8 |
| I. R. Carmichael not out | 3 | not out | 6 |
| B 2, l-b 6, n-b 14 | 22 | B 4, l-b 1, n-b 8 | 13 |
| 1/33 2/34 3/50 4/63 5/237 6/283 7/284 8/285 9/285 | 289 | 1/12 2/74 3/138 4/143 5/160 6/207 7/344 8/351 9/362 | 383 |

Bowling: *First Innings*—Patterson 17–2–58–2; Faulkner 22–6–53–2; Brown 15–6–46–4; Saunders 9–1–72–0; Hyatt 13–3–52–0. *Second Innings*—Patterson 19–3–62–2; Faulkner 18–3–60–0; Brown 30–6–101–2; Saunders 23–4–74–1; Hyatt 22–3–51–1; Ray 11.5–4–28–3; Bennett 1–0–2–1.

Umpires: M. G. O'Connell and P. M. Cronin.

## WESTERN AUSTRALIA v NEW SOUTH WALES

At Perth, November 23, 24, 25, 26. Drawn. Western Australia 4 pts. The contest for first-innings points occupied three days with Clark and Clough, the last Western Australian batsmen, batting for nearly two hours and surviving some hostile bowling by Gilbert to clinch the issue. The earlier Western Australian batsmen had surrendered the initiative to the spinners, Matthews and O'Neill, with Matthews taking his first wickets of the season. The New South Wales batsmen had shown more urgency, particularly after Wellham and Clifford had batted defiantly, and their last four wickets added 169. When they used the last day for batting practice, Clifford enlivened an otherwise dreary period, his innings occupying three and a half hours and including fifteen 4s. Chappell batted for over five hours for his 65.

## New South Wales

| First Innings | | Second Innings | |
|---|---|---|---|
| T. M. Chappell c Zoehrer b Clough | 10 | c and b MacLeay | 65 |
| S. B. Smith b MacLeay | 27 | c and b MacLeay | 43 |
| *D. M. Wellham c Marsh b Clark | 86 | b MacLeay | 3 |
| P. S. Clifford c Zoehrer b Matthews | 51 | not out | 102 |
| G. R. J. Matthews c Veletta b Matthews | 11 | not out | 20 |
| G. G. Geise b Matthews | 1 | | |
| Imran Khan b Clough | 70 | | |
| M. D. O'Neill lbw b Clough | 8 | | |
| †S. J. Rixon c Marsh b MacLeay | 28 | | |
| P. H. Marks b Hogan | 51 | | |
| D. R. Gilbert not out | 21 | | |
| L-b 6, n-b 16 | 22 | B 2, l-b 8, n-b 2 | 12 |
| 1/42 2/42 3/154 4/176 5/178 6/217 7/268 8/295 9/341 | 386 | 1/70 2/78 3/189 | (3 wkts) 245 |

Bowling: *First Innings*—Matthews 27–7–92–3; MacLeay 26–6–90–2; Clough 24–6–67–3; Clark 28–8–74–1; Hogan 18–3–57–1. *Second Innings*—Matthews 3–0–6–0; MacLeay 27–10–66–3; Clough 18–4–64–0; Clements 6–2–19–0; Hogan 30–8–77–0; McPhee 2–1–2–0; Shipperd 1–0–1–0.

### Western Australia

S. C. Clements c Rixon b Imran .......... 40
M. R. J. Veletta c Geise b Gilbert .... 35
*G. Shipperd c Rixon b Matthews .... 61
G. R. Marsh run out .................. 73
M. W. McPhee c Smith b Imran ...... 25
K. H. MacLeay c Wellham b Matthews 17
†T. J. Zoehrer c Rixon b Matthews ... 50
T. G. Hogan b Matthews ............ 11
C. Matthews c Imran b O'Neill ....... 6
W. M. Clark not out ................ 46
P. M. Clough not out ............... 11
B 2, l-b 9, w 1 ........... 12

1/70 2/93 3/168 (9 wkts dec.) 387
4/221 5/253 6/299 7/321
8/324 9/340

Bowling: Gilbert 46–11–116–1; Imran 24–8–51–2; Marks 13–2–33–0; Matthews 43–14–92–4; Chappell 4–2–5–0; O'Neill 37–15–62–1; Geise 16–9–17–0.

Umpires: R. J. Evans and P. J. McConnell.

## TASMANIA v QUEENSLAND

At Launceston, November 30, December 1, 2. Queensland won by an innings and 105 runs. Queensland 16 pts. Although Queensland were splendidly served by their batsmen, especially Border, despite his being forced to retire temporarily after making 29, their star was McDermott. His speed and aggression quite overwhelmed Tasmania's first innings; and in their second he made short work of Ray and Boon, and then struck Buckingham and Davison, forcing both to retire hurt, the latter with a broken arm. In contrast most of the Queensland batsmen enjoyed themselves, Hohns equalling his highest Shield score in a stay of three hours.

### Tasmania

M. Ray c Border b Thomson ................ 28 – lbw b McDermott ............ 5
R. J. Bennett c Kerr b McDermott ........... 41 – b Thomson .................. 40
D. C. Boon b McDermott .................. 12 – c Phillips b McDermott ....... 1
D. J. Buckingham lbw b McDermott ......... 34 – b Thomson .................. 16
B. F. Davison c Border b Maguire ........... 30 – retired hurt ................. 11
*†R. D. Woolley c Phillips b Rackemann ..... 1 – (7) c Phillips b Hohns ......... 93
S. L. Saunders lbw b McDermott ............ 28 – (6) b Rackemann ............. 24
P. I. Faulkner lbw b McDermott ............. 0 – c Phillips b Rackemann ....... 26
R. S. Hyatt c Phillips b Maguire ............ 3 – not out ...................... 6
R. L. Brown not out ...................... 2 – c Ritchie b Hohns ............ 0
B. P. Patterson b McDermott ............... 0 – b Thomson .................. 0
B 1, l-b 4, w 3, n-b 13 .............. 21 B 8, n-b 7 ............ 15

1/52 2/86 3/96 4/139 5/148 200 1/9 2/13 3/79 4/97 5/214 237
6/173 7/173 8/187 9/200 6/214 7/236 8/237 9/237

Bowling: *First Innings*—Rackemann 13–1–60–1; McDermott 17–7–45–6; Thomson 4–0–27–1; Maguire 19–5–63–2. *Second Innings*—Rackemann 15–2–60–2; McDermott 11–0–44–2; Thomson 11–2–47–3; Maguire 12–3–40–0; Hohns 9–0–38–2.

### Queensland

R. B. Kerr c Woolley b Brown ....... 27
K. C. Wessels c Buckingham b Brown . 4
*A. R. Border not out ...............144
G. M. Ritchie c Bennett b Patterson .. 59
G. S. Trimble c Woolley b Brown ..... 36
T. V. Hohns c Boon b Saunders ...... 90
†R. B. Phillips c Woolley b Saunders .. 39
C. J. McDermott lbw b Patterson ..... 18
J. N. Maguire lbw b Ray ............ 61
C. G. Rackemann b Patterson ........ 17
J. R. Thomson b Faulkner ........... 25
B 9, l-b 7, w 2, n-b 4 ........ 22

1/11 2/57 3/136 4/171 5/264 542
6/301 7/321 8/432 9/483

Bowling: Patterson 40–5–141–3; Brown 21–2–112–3; Faulkner 33.5–8–107–1; Hyatt 13–1–51–0; Saunders 18–2–56–2; Davison 7–2–25–0; Ray 7–0–34–1.

Umpires: A. G. Jones and S. G. Randell.

## NEW SOUTH WALES v SOUTH AUSTRALIA

At Sydney, November 30, December 1, 2, 3. New South Wales won by 112 runs. New South Wales 16 pts. With the pitch tipped to favour spin, both sides selected three specialist slow bowlers. Holland was the most successful of them, being unlucky to miss getting all ten wickets in South Australia's second innings. Rixon was the New South Wales batting star, with a lively 58 in their first innings and a devastating century in the second, when he replaced the injured Smith as Dyson's opening partner. Their stand of 173 in even time enabled Wellham to make a challenging declaration late on the third day. For South Australia, Hilditch and O'Connor batted well and a close contest for first-innings points seemed likely until Lawson and Imran destroyed the middle of the order. Only a sturdy innings by Inverarity saved the follow-on. South Australia's hopes were further upset when Phillips dislocated a finger in the New South Wales second innings. Hookes kept wicket in his place and Inverarity partnered Hilditch as substitute opener, their stand of 87 being South Australia's best of the match.

### New South Wales

| | | | |
|---|---|---|---|
| S. B. Smith b McCurdy | 7 | | |
| J. Dyson c McCurdy b Inverarity | 16 | – b Inverarity | 72 |
| *D. M. Wellham b Harms | 89 | – b Carmichael | 1 |
| P. S. Clifford c Phillips b McCurdy | 64 | – c Haysman b Inverarity | 2 |
| G. R. J. Matthews c Haysman b Inverarity | 42 | – c Bishop b Inverarity | 0 |
| Imran Khan c Hookes b McCurdy | 43 | – not out | 23 |
| †S. J. Rixon b McCurdy | 58 | – (1) not out | 115 |
| M. J. Bennett lbw b McCurdy | 19 | | |
| G. F. Lawson c Harms b Inverarity | 17 | | |
| R. G. Holland c Bishop b Harms | 0 | | |
| D. L. Gilbert not out | 0 | | |
| B 2, l-b 10, n-b 3 | 15 | B 4, l-b 6 | 10 |
| 1/14 2/63 3/185 4/191 5/268 6/288 7/352 8/357 9/370 | 370 | 1/173 2/178 3/183 4/187 (4 wkts dec.) | 223 |

Bowling: *First Innings*—McCurdy 36–7–109–5; Carmichael 23–6–63–0; Inverarity 31.3–5–76–3; May 16–3–35–0; Harms 21–2–75–2. *Second Innings*—McCurdy 18–3–55–0; Carmichael 23–2–73–1; Inverarity 16–4–50–3; May 2–0–14–0; Hilditch 5–0–21–0.

### South Australia

| | | | |
|---|---|---|---|
| A. M. J. Hilditch c Dyson b Holland | 80 | – c Dyson b Holland | 47 |
| †W. B. Phillips run out | 20 | – (7) c Dyson b Holland | 13 |
| D. F. G. O'Connor b Lawson | 42 | – b Holland | 19 |
| G. A. Bishop c Rixon b Lawson | 29 | – c Gilbert b Holland | 11 |
| *D. W. Hookes c Rixon b Imran | 1 | – (6) c Imran b Holland | 15 |
| M. D. Haysman b Imran | 0 | – (5) c Dyson b Holland | 15 |
| R. J. Inverarity not out | 43 | – (2) b Holland | 36 |
| C. L. Harms b Lawson | 1 | – c Clifford b Holland | 1 |
| T. B. A. May c Clifford b Gilbert | 14 | – lbw b Lawson | 19 |
| R. J. McCurdy lbw b Lawson | 1 | – not out | 11 |
| I. R. Carmichael c Dyson b Holland | 11 | – b Holland | 24 |
| B 3, l-b 14, w 1 | 18 | B 7, l-b 3 | 10 |
| 1/60 2/138 3/174 4/177 5/179 6/179 7/182 8/230 9/231 | 260 | 1/87 2/100 3/120 4/128 5/145 6/150 7/151 8/180 9/186 | 221 |

Bowling: *First Innings*—Lawson 23–8–30–4; Imran 17–6–32–2; Gilbert 19–1–70–1; Holland 27.5–10–50–2; Bennett 9–1–31–0; Matthews 8–1–30–0. *Second Innings*—Lawson 19–6–39–1; Imran 9–4–14–0; Gilbert 4–0–10–0; Holland 38.5–12–83–9; Bennett 19–5–30–0; Matthews 10–2–35–0.

Umpires: R. A. French and R. G. Harris.

## QUEENSLAND v NEW SOUTH WALES

At Brisbane, December 7, 8, 9, 10. Drawn. New South Wales 4 pts. New South Wales became the first side during the season to take any points off Queensland, whose innings subsided against Imran, bowling at medium pace, and the off-spin of Matthews. McDermott had upset the early New South Wales batting, but after seven overs he left the field suffering from 'flu, whereupon Clifford and Matthews took control with some powerful hitting. Clifford was finally caught at deep third man, 2 short of his third hundred of the season. Matthews just missed his first-ever century when Phillips took a splendid one-handed catch behind the wicket. The match was badly affected by rain and poor light.

### New South Wales

| | | | |
|---|---|---|---|
| T. M. Chappell c Phillips b Maguire | 12 | – not out | 0 |
| S. B. Smith c Ritchie b McDermott | 0 | – not out | 15 |
| *D. M. Wellham c Hohns b McDermott | 9 | | |
| P. S. Clifford c Courtice b Thomson | 98 | | |
| G. R. J. Matthews c Phillips b McDermott | 97 | | |
| R. J. Bower c Trimble b Thomson | 7 | | |
| Imran Khan c Smart b Maguire | 17 | | |
| M. D. O'Neill not out | 13 | | |
| S. R. Waugh c Courtice b Thomson | 31 | | |
| †G. C. Dyer c Hohns b Rackemann | 39 | | |
| D. R. Gilbert c Ritchie b McDermott | 0 | | |
| B 9, l-b 9, n-b 16 | 34 | L-b 1 | 1 |
| 1/1 2/15 3/59 4/190 5/199 6/218 7/284 8/328 9/328 | 357 | | (no wkt) 16 |

Bowling: *First Innings*—McDermott 20–8–78–4; Maguire 24–7–42–2; Rackemann 31.5–5–96–1; Thomson 16–2–73–3; Hohns 14–2–50–0. *Second Innings*—McDermott 2.2–1–7–0; Maguire 2–0–8–0.

### Queensland

| | |
|---|---|
| R. B. Kerr c Smith b Gilbert | 6 |
| B. A. Courtice st Dyer b Matthews | 64 |
| C. B. Smart run out | 54 |
| G. M. Ritchie c Dyer b Gilbert | 71 |
| †R. B. Phillips b Matthews | 56 |
| G. S. Trimble lbw b Imran | 29 |
| T. V. Hohns c Dyer b Imran | 12 |
| C. J. McDermott not out | 4 |
| J. N. Maguire c and b Matthews | 3 |
| C. G. Rackemann c and b Matthews | 2 |
| *J. R. Thomson c Dyer b Imran | 0 |
| B 7, l-b 4, w 2, n-b 1 | 14 |
| 1/31 2/123 3/153 4/216 5/280 6/294 7/305 8/312 9/314 | 315 |

Bowling: Gilbert 31–8–105–2; Imran 40–19–47–3; Matthews 40–13–81–4; Waugh 23–12–34–0; Chappell 6–1–8–0; Bower 9–1–29–0.

Umpires: M. J. King and C. D. Timmins.

## QUEENSLAND v WESTERN AUSTRALIA

At Brisbane, December 14, 15, 16, 17. Queensland won by ten wickets. Queensland 16 pts. Thomson's bowling was decisive in a match which Queensland controlled from the start. Bowling with control rather than great pace, he achieved his best-ever figures in Western Australia's first innings and also did the hat-trick, bowling Marsh, then Clark and finally winning a protracted lbw decision against Alderman. Although much of the first day was lost to the weather, Wessels, whose innings of four hours included thirteen 4s and one 6, got Queensland away to an excellent start. Border's declaration on the second evening enabled Thomson to take two quick wickets before the close and Queensland claimed a further twelve on the third day to set up their fourth outright win in five matches.

## Queensland

| | | | |
|---|---|---|---|
| K. C. Wessels b Alderman | 137 | | |
| R. B. Kerr c Alderman b Clark | 22 | (1) not out | 14 |
| *A. R. Border b Clough | 42 | | |
| G. M. Ritchie c sub b Clark | 65 | | |
| G. S. Trimble lbw b Alderman | 0 | (2) not out | 0 |
| T. V. Hohns lbw b Hogan | 23 | | |
| †R. B. Phillips c Clements b Alderman | 5 | | |
| C. J. McDermott c Marsh b Clough | 30 | | |
| J. N. Maguire b Clark | 21 | | |
| C. G. Rackemann not out | 0 | | |
| B 7, l-b 8, n-b 6 | 21 | L-b 1 | 1 |
| 1/51 2/142 3/255 4/255 5/295 6/313 7/315 8/366 9/366 | (9 wkts dec.) 366 | | (no wkt) 15 |

J. R. Thomson did not bat.

Bowling: *First Innings*—Alderman 28–8–76–3; Clough 20.1–3–57–2; Clark 34–5–84–3; MacLeay 19–2–48–0; Hogan 31–5–86–1. *Second Innings*—MacLeay 2–0–3–0; Hogan 1–0–3–0; Shipperd 1–0–8–0.

## Western Australia

| | | | |
|---|---|---|---|
| S. C. Clements lbw b Thomson | 12 | c Ritchie b Maguire | 33 |
| M. R. J. Veletta c Phillips b Thomson | 58 | c Phillips b Rackemann | 59 |
| P. M. Clough b Thomson | 0 | (6) c Phillips b Rackemann | 21 |
| G. Shipperd b Thomson | 6 | (3) c Phillips b Thomson | 8 |
| *K. J. Hughes run out | 1 | (4) c McDermott b Thomson | 14 |
| G. R. Marsh b Thomson | 55 | (5) c Border b McDermott | 19 |
| K. H. MacLeay b McDermott | 1 | c McDermott b Hohns | 3 |
| †T. J. Zoehrer c Kerr b Rackemann | 1 | b Rackemann | 31 |
| T. G. Hogan not out | 8 | c McDermott b Rackemann | 10 |
| W. M. Clark b Thomson | 0 | st Phillips b Hohns | 11 |
| T. M. Alderman lbw b Thomson | 0 | not out | 0 |
| L-b 5, n-b 9 | 14 | B 8, n-b 7 | 15 |
| 1/20 2/20 3/41 4/44 5/116 6/124 7/133 8/156 9/156 | 156 | 1/95 2/97 3/121 4/124 5/159 6/168 7/194 8/206 9/220 | 224 |

Bowling: *First Innings*—McDermott 15–3–35–1; Thomson 14.5–5–27–7; Rackemann 12–1–39–1; Maguire 8–1–25–0; Hohns 12–4–25–0. *Second Innings*—McDermott 14–2–57–1; Thomson 13–1–37–2; Rackemann 16.3–4–57–4; Maguire 11–5–28–1; Hohns 14–3–37–2.

Umpires: C. D. Timmins and M. W. Johnson.

## VICTORIA v SOUTH AUSTRALIA

At Melbourne, December 14, 15, 16, 17. South Australia won by 167 runs. South Australia 12 pts, Victoria 4 pts. Heavy rain caused the loss of the first day. Hookes then revealed his intentions with an early declaration on the second, to which Bright responded in kind, but not before Victoria had taken four points for a first-innings lead. Zadow and Hilditch set up the South Australian second innings with a century opening stand in 90 minutes and Hookes finally set a target of 378 at something more than 4 runs an over. He provided a further surprise by himself sharing the new ball with McCurdy and removing Jones. Thereafter Victoria struggled for survival, and at 178 for eight all seemed lost. Bright and Hughes, however, defended stubbornly and South Australia got home with nine balls to spare. It had taken them five matches to secure their first points of the season.

### South Australia

| | | | |
|---|---|---|---|
| A. M. J. Hilditch b Davis | 47 | – c Dimattina b Bright | 88 |
| R. J. Zadow c Dimattina b Hughes | 0 | – c Dimattina b O'Donnell | 55 |
| D. F. G. O'Connor not out | 59 | – c and b Whiteside | 50 |
| G. A. Bishop c Richardson b Davis | 2 | – c Robinson b Bright | 10 |
| *D. W. Hookes c Robinson b Davis | 9 | – run out | 62 |
| W. M. Darling not out | 25 | – not out | 58 |
| †D. J. Kelly (did not bat) | | – not out | 36 |
| L-b 1, n-b 3 | 4 | B 6, l b 6, n-b 7 | 19 |
| 1/12 2/82 3/84 4/97 (4 wkts dec.) | 146 | 1/105 2/199 3/203 (5 wkts dec.) 4/235 5/316 | 378 |

R. J. Inverarity, A. K. Zesers, I. R. Carmichael and R. J. McCurdy did not bat.

Bowling: *First Innings*—Hughes 13.2–4–32–1; Dodemaide 12–3–43–0; Davis 17–2–55–3; Bright 10–4–15–0. *Second Innings*—Hughes 17–2–52–0; Dodemaide 9–0–48–0; Davis 15–1–62–0; Bright 32–8–100–2; O'Donnell 10–0–52–1; Whiteside 10–1–23–1; Robinson 4–0–29–0.

### Victoria

| | | | |
|---|---|---|---|
| D. B. Robinson c Kelly b McCurdy | 10 | – c and b O'Connor | 34 |
| G. W. Richardson c Kelly b Inverarity | 35 | – c Hookes b McCurdy | 9 |
| D. M. Jones not out | 58 | – c Bishop b Hookes | 5 |
| M. D. Taylor not out | 37 | – lbw b Inverarity | 28 |
| W. G. Whiteside (did not bat) | | – c Kelly b Hookes | 16 |
| S. P. O'Donnell (did not bat) | | – lbw b McCurdy | 38 |
| A. I. C. Dodemaide (did not bat) | | – b Zesers | 6 |
| *R. J. Bright (did not bat) | | – c Kelly b Carmichael | 33 |
| †M. G. Dimattina (did not bat) | | – c Kelly b Zesers | 1 |
| M. G. Hughes (did not bat) | | – not out | 9 |
| S. P. Davis (did not bat) | | – b Carmichael | 0 |
| W 1, n-b 6 | 7 | B 16, l-b 5, n-b 10 | 31 |
| 1/26 2/54 (2 wkts dec.) | 147 | 1/10 2/21 3/76 4/84 5/123 6/142 7/163 8/178 9/209 | 210 |

Bowling: *First Innings*—Zesers 8–0–50–0; McCurdy 15–3–44–1; Hookes 2–1–2–0; Carmichael 5–0–23–0; Inverarity 11–3–28–1. *Second Innings*—McCurdy 24–5–67–2; Hookes 14–5–38–2; Zesers 13–7–17–2; Carmichael 9.3–3–31–2; Inverarity 23–9–34–1; O'Connor 2–0–2–1.

Umpires: D. W. Holt and L. J. King.

## WESTERN AUSTRALIA v VICTORIA

At Perth, December 20, 21, 22, 23. Drawn. Victoria 4 pts. A target of 357 at approximately 4.25 runs per over was attractive enough for Marsh to thrash his way to a century in three and a quarter hours, but in the final hour it needed obdurate defence by the Western Australian batsmen to foil Victoria's bid for outright points. Jones dominated the first day, plundering the four-man Western Australian attack for seven and a quarter hours in all and hitting 33 4s and two 6s. Western Australia's first innings was held together by Shipperd, who batted for over seven hours. If their batting was pedestrian, it was in stark contrast to Clough's second-innings bowling effort which reduced Victoria to 47 for five. But a dashing innings by O'Donnell gave Bright his chance to make a challenging declaration.

### Victoria

| | | | |
|---|---|---|---|
| D. B. Robinson run out | 3 | c Zoehrer b Clark | 8 |
| W. G. Whiteside b Alderman | 0 | c Zoehrer b Clough | 25 |
| D. M. Jones lbw b Clough | 243 | b Clough | 8 |
| M. D. Taylor c Veletta b Hogan | 34 | lbw b Clough | 0 |
| G. W. Richardson c Clark b Clough | 28 | c Zoehrer b Clough | 0 |
| S. P. O'Donnell c Gartrell b Hogan | 42 | not out | 129 |
| A. I. C. Dodemaide c Alderman b Hogan | 22 | b Hogan | 35 |
| *R. J. Bright c Veletta b Hogan | 18 | not out | 10 |
| M. G. Hughes not out | 3 | | |
| †M. G. Dimattina lbw b Hogan | 0 | | |
| S. P. Davis c Zoehrer b Clark | 0 | | |
| B 1, l-b 4, w 1, n-b 6 | 12 | B 7, l-b 7, w 1, n-b 1 | 16 |
| 1/3 2/10 3/107 4/209 5/278 6/369 7/393 8/404 9/404 | 405 | 1/38 2/38 3/38 4/42 5/47 6/205 | (6 wkts dec.) 231 |

Bowling: *First Innings*—Alderman 30–9–106–1; Clough 30–4–101–2; Clark 34.5–6–87–1; Hogan 31–7–106–5. *Second Innings*—Clark 18–6–40–1; Alderman 19–4–55–0; Clough 17–6–59–4; Hogan 23–8–61–1; Gartrell 2–0–2–0.

### Western Australia

| | | | |
|---|---|---|---|
| *G. Shipperd not out | 131 | (6) c Hughes b Bright | 24 |
| M. R. J. Veletta lbw b O'Donnell | 8 | lbw b O'Donnell | 8 |
| M. W. McPhee c Dimattina b Hughes | 23 | c and b Davis | 25 |
| G. R. Marsh c Dimattina b Dodemaide | 0 | not out | 143 |
| R. W. Gartrell st Dimattina b Bright | 41 | c sub b Davis | 13 |
| S. C. Clements c Dimattina b Bright | 11 | (1) b Hughes | 12 |
| †T. J. Zoehrer c Richardson b Bright | 3 | c Richardson b Hughes | 4 |
| T. G. Hogan c Jones b Bright | 22 | c Bright b Hughes | 0 |
| W. M. Clark b Hughes | 9 | b Bright | 1 |
| T. M. Alderman b Davis | 15 | c Taylor b Bright | 4 |
| P. M. Clough c Dimattina b Davis | 2 | not out | 0 |
| B 4, l-b 2, w 1, n-b 8 | 15 | B 2, l-b 6, n-b 3 | 11 |
| 1/21 2/63 3/63 4/141 5/155 6/159 7/218 8/227 9/266 | 280 | 1/20 2/20 3/77 4/103 5/190 6/210 7/216 8/222 9/243 | (9 wkts) 245 |

Bowling: *First Innings*—O'Donnell 12–2–38–1; Hughes 26–11–69–2; Dodemaide 21–2–65–1; Davis 20.2–4–38–2; Bright 29–9–62–4; Whiteside 1–0–2–0. *Second Innings*—O'Donnell 12–3–46–1; Hughes 20–3–63–3; Dodemaide 11–3–32–0; Davis 12–2–39–2; Bright 26–9–56–3; Robinson 1–0–1–0.

Umpires: T. A. Prue and R. J. Evans.

## TASMANIA v SOUTH AUSTRALIA

At Hobart, December 20, 21, 22, 23. South Australia won by two wickets. South Australia 16 pts. After the loss of the first day to rain, Woolley declared Tasmania's first innings early, after Ray's effort to score a maiden Shield century had failed. In South Australia's reply, Bishop underlined his liking for Tasmania's bowling and O'Connor and Haysman batted enterprisingly. When Tasmania were all out in their second innings for 193, with much of the last day left, South Australia's task seemed easy enough, particularly when they reached 107 for one with Bishop and O'Connor seemingly well in command. Patterson then produced a devastating spell of four wickets for 2 runs in sixteen balls and South Australia slumped to 133 for seven. Hookes came in late, nursing a bruised thumb, and scored 35 in 28 balls. His dismissal at 171 still left Tasmania with a chance, but two lusty hits by McCurdy settled the match.

### Tasmania

| First innings | | Second innings | |
|---|---|---|---|
| G. W. Goodman c Kelly b McCurdy | 14 | hit wkt b McCurdy | 10 |
| M. Ray c sub b Inverarity | 82 | b McCurdy | 8 |
| R. J. Bennett c and b Inverarity | 60 | c McCurdy b Inverarity | 6 |
| D. J. Buckingham not out | 18 | c O'Connor b Hookes | 32 |
| K. Bradshaw not out | 0 | c Kelly b Zesers | 42 |
| *†R. D. Woolley (did not bat) | | c Bishop b Inverarity | 15 |
| R. S. Hyatt (did not bat) | | c Kelly b Carmichael | 50 |
| W. S. Kirkman (did not bat) | | run out | 6 |
| M. P. Tame (did not bat) | | not out | 7 |
| R. L. Brown (did not bat) | | c Kelly b Carmichael | 4 |
| B. P. Patterson (did not bat) | | b Carmichael | 0 |
| N-b 14 | 14 | B 2, l-b 3, w 1, n-b 7 | 13 |
| 1/27 2/157 3/182 (3 wkts dec.) | 188 | 1/9 2/20 3/53 4/60 5/83 6/155 7/177 8/185 9/189 | 193 |

Bowling: *First Innings*—McCurdy 15–3–57–1; Carmichael 16–1–49–0; Hookes 3–2–1–0; Zesers 18–6–60–0; Inverarity 12–2–21–2. *Second Innings*—McCurdy 17–5–38–2; Carmichael 14.1–3–32–3; Hookes 13–2–49–1; Zesers 12–5–28–1; Inverarity 23–12–29–2; O'Connor 3–0–11–0; Haysman 2–1–1–0.

### South Australia

| First innings | | Second innings | |
|---|---|---|---|
| R. J. Zadow lbw b Patterson | 2 | lbw b Kirkman | 31 |
| G. A. Bishop c Goodman b Tame | 88 | c Brown b Patterson | 60 |
| D. F. G. O'Connor not out | 72 | c Ray b Patterson | 24 |
| M. D. Haysman not out | 33 | lbw b Tame | 0 |
| W. M. Darling (did not bat) | | c Buckingham b Patterson | 5 |
| R. J. Inverarity (did not bat) | | b Patterson | 0 |
| †D. J. Kelly (did not bat) | | c Buckingham b Patterson | 2 |
| *D. W. Hookes (did not bat) | | c and b Brown | 35 |
| A. K. Zesers (did not bat) | | not out | 10 |
| R. J. McCurdy (did not bat) | | not out | 8 |
| L-b 9, n-b 1 | 10 | L-b 4, n-b 1 | 5 |
| 1/2 2/128 (2 wkts dec.) | 205 | 1/59 2/107 3/118 4/120 5/126 6/133 7/133 8/171 (8 wkts) | 180 |

I. R. Carmichael did not bat.

Bowling: *First Innings*—Patterson 15–2–50–1; Brown 13–2–54–0; Tame 11–0–58–1; Kirkman 10–3–34–0. *Second Innings*—Patterson 18.3–3–67–5; Brown 8–1–42–1; Tame 9–2–35–1; Kirkman 7–0–29–1; Hyatt 2–0–3–0.

Umpires: J. T. Hinds and A. G. Jones.

## WESTERN AUSTRALIA v SOUTH AUSTRALIA

At Perth, January 10, 11, 12, 13. Western Australia won by 21 runs. Western Australia 16 pts. South Australia were narrowly denied both first-innings and outright points. The first day belonged to McPhee and Shipperd. McPhee, only twenty and in his first season of first-class cricket, played with unfettered enthusiasm, scoring his runs out of 189 in three and three-quarter hours and hitting eighteen 4s and one 6. He was dropped three times in the 90s, each time by McCurdy on the leg side. South Australia were rescued in their first innings by Haysman and Inverarity, who added 214 for the sixth wicket. With only 1 run separating the first-innings scores, a draw seemed the most likely result. However, both captains went on the attack, and while Hughes made a fine century McCurdy's sustained hostility gave South Australia a chance of outright victory, their target being 243 at three and a half runs an over. At 164 for three, with O'Connor and Hookes going well, South Australia looked set for victory. But in the last 90 minutes they lost seven wickets for 57, owing to some excellent bowling by the nineteen-year-old Spalding.

### Western Australia

| | First innings | | Second innings | |
|---|---|---|---|---|
| M. R. J. Veletta | c Zadow b Zesers | 6 | lbw b McCurdy | 40 |
| M. W. McPhee | c McCurdy b Hookes | 135 | b McCurdy | 0 |
| G. Shipperd | c Carmichael b Hookes | 139 | c Haysman b Carmichael | 11 |
| *K. J. Hughes | c Haysman b Inverarity | 21 | c Haysman b Zesers | 111 |
| G. R. Marsh | c Kelly b Carmichael | 25 | c O'Connor b Carmichael | 14 |
| P. Gonnella | not out | 46 | c sub b Zesers | 12 |
| T. G. Hogan | c Zesers b McCurdy | 6 | (8) c Bishop b McCurdy | 14 |
| T. M. Alderman | c Kelly b Inverarity | 16 | (9) c O'Connor b Zesers | 5 |
| †T. J. Zoehrer | b McCurdy | 1 | (7) c Haysman b McCurdy | 23 |
| B. A. Reid | (did not bat) | – | not out | 2 |
| E. G. Spalding | (did not bat) | – | lbw b McCurdy | 0 |
| | L-b 8, n-b 6 | 14 | B 3, l-b 3, n-b 3 | 9 |
| | 1/56 2/189 3/244 4/318 5/349 6/379 7/380 8/409 (8 wkts dec.) | 409 | 1/0 2/19 3/98 4/139 5/179 6/212 7/230 8/237 9/241 | 241 |

Bowling: *First Innings*—McCurdy 23–2–84–2; Hookes 12–1–49–2; Carmichael 19–4–72–1; Zesers 30–6–85–1; Inverarity 28–5–83–2; Haysman 8–1–28–0. *Second Innings*—McCurdy 24–2–109–5; Hookes 1–0–1–0; Carmichael 17–3–72–2; Zesers 12–1–33–3; Bishop 3.3–0–20–0.

### South Australia

| | First innings | | Second innings | |
|---|---|---|---|---|
| G. A. Bishop | lbw b Alderman | 4 | lbw b Hogan | 25 |
| R. J. Zadow | b Alderman | 47 | b Hogan | 41 |
| D. F. G. O'Connor | b Hogan | 23 | c Veletta b Spalding | 52 |
| M. D. Haysman | c Alderman b Reid | 172 | c Hughes b Hogan | 2 |
| *D. W. Hookes | c Zoehrer b Alderman | 0 | c Zoehrer b Spalding | 73 |
| W. M. Darling | c Reid b Hogan | 19 | run out | 6 |
| R. J. Inverarity | c Hughes b Reid | 69 | (8) run out | 0 |
| †D. J. Kelly | c Gonnella b Alderman | 3 | (7) b Spalding | 0 |
| R. J. McCurdy | c Zoehrer b Alderman | 4 | (10) b Spalding | 13 |
| A. K. Zesers | c Hogan b Alderman | 22 | (9) b Alderman | 2 |
| I. R. Carmichael | not out | 8 | not out | 0 |
| | B 3, l-b 16, n-b 18 | 37 | L-b 4, n-b 3 | 7 |
| | 1/5 2/65 3/93 4/93 5/134 6/348 7/371 8/375 9/381 | 408 | 1/31 2/83 3/87 4/164 5/185 6/195 7/204 8/205 9/221 | 221 |

Bowling: *First Innings*—Alderman 43.4–14–109–6; Reid 45–14–106–2; Spalding 20–3–41–0; Hogan 39–10–112–2; Gonnella 8–2–21–0. *Second Innings*—Alderman 17.1–4–50–1; Reid 14–3–38–0; Spalding 13–1–37–4; Hogan 25–6–92–3.

Umpires: R. J. Evans and W. M. Powell.

## VICTORIA v QUEENSLAND

At Melbourne, January 11, 12, 13, 14. Drawn. Queensland 4 pts. Victoria asked Queensland to bat first on an unusually green Melbourne pitch, but Queensland's pace attack of Rackemann, Maguire and Thomson proved so much the stronger of the two that they still led by 200 runs on the first innings. Surprisingly Thomson did not enforce the follow-on, and Queensland's batsmen showed little urgency in their second innings. When the fourth day started, Queensland needed to take nine wickets to win outright, and when Victoria were 98 for three, with Hibbert suffering from a broken finger, their prospects were bright enough. But their bowlers wilted in great heat, and when Hohns dropped Jones off Rackemann, with the Victorian on 43, their chance was gone. Jones battled away for five and three-quarter hours in spite of various bouts of heat exhaustion.

### Queensland

| First innings | | Second innings | |
|---|---|---|---|
| R. B. Kerr c King b Graf | 3 | b Davis | 41 |
| B. A. Courtice c Jones b Davis | 69 | c sub b Bright | 70 |
| C. B. Smart b King | 38 | c Whiteside b Bright | 50 |
| G. S. Trimble b King | 15 | b Graf | 20 |
| T. J. Barsby b Davis | 49 | b Graf | 0 |
| A. B. Henschell c Hibbert b King | 16 | c Jones b Bright | 12 |
| T. V. Hohns c Dimattina b Graf | 32 | c Jones b Davis | 23 |
| †R. B. Phillips run out | 26 | not out | 28 |
| J. N. Maguire c Hibbert b Davis | 11 | not out | 8 |
| C. G. Rackemann not out | 18 | | |
| *J. R. Thomson b Davis | 10 | | |
| L-b 7, w 5, n-b 2 | 14 | L-b 5, w 1, n-b 2 | 8 |
| 1/12 2/67 3/87 4/177 5/190 6/211 7/256 8/269 9/284 | 301 | 1/85 2/139 3/186 4/186 5/189 6/203 7/244 (7 wkts dec.) | 260 |

Bowling: *First Innings*—Graf 22–7–51–2; Davis 30.3–4–106–4; King 20–5–61–3; Bright 25–11–49–0; Whiteside 11–4–27–0. *Second Innings*—Graf 16–3–40–2; Davis 27–4–79–2; King 20–1–64–0; Bright 35–13–60–3; Whiteside 5–1–12–0.

### Victoria

| First innings | | Second innings | |
|---|---|---|---|
| M. B. Quinn c Phillips b Rackemann | 16 | run out | 26 |
| P. A. Hibbert not out | 6 | | |
| D. M. Jones c Smart b Rackemann | 0 | c Phillips b Rackemann | 136 |
| G. N. Yallop c Courtice b Maguire | 21 | b Rackemann | 0 |
| M. D. Taylor c Phillips b Thomson | 3 | c Trimble b Hohns | 47 |
| W. G. Whiteside c Smart b Thomson | 0 | (2) c Phillips b Rackemann | 10 |
| S. F. Graf c Smart b Thomson | 0 | (6) b Hohns | 49 |
| *R. J. Bright c Phillips b Maguire | 19 | (7) not out | 40 |
| P. D. King b Maguire | 16 | (8) b Maguire | 37 |
| †M. G. Dimattina c Phillips b Rackemann | 7 | not out | 10 |
| S. P. Davis c Courtice b Maguire | 0 | | |
| B 4, l-b 4, n-b 5 | 13 | B 1, l-b 13, w 8, n-b 6 | 28 |
| 1/6 2/38 3/42 4/42 5/42 6/59 7/92 8/93 9/93 | 101 | 1/21 2/93 3/98 4/187 5/266 6/291 7/352 (7 wkts) | 383 |

Bowling: *First Innings*—Rackemann 12.5–4–28–3; Maguire 15–6–36–4; Thomson 11–4–29–3. *Second Innings*—Rackemann 36–8–98–3; Maguire 35–6–98–1; Thomson 18–3–57–0; Hohns 30–8–78–2; Henschell 7–1–38–0.

Umpires: R. C. Bailhache and D. E. Holden.

## NEW SOUTH WALES v TASMANIA

At Newcastle, January 17, 18, 19, 20. Drawn. New South Wales 4 pts. Wellham's decision to put Tasmania in appeared to be justified at lunch on the first day when they were 96 for four. However, Saunders, Bradshaw and the later batsmen made the most of an excellent pitch. Tasmania's decision to drop Patterson, after an altercation with Woolley, left their attack short-handed as first Dyson and Wellham, then Rixon and Clifford enabled New South Wales to race past the Tasmanian total. A grand burst of pace bowling by Imran after tea on the fourth day caused a late-order collapse in the Tasmanian second innings and New South Wales needed 212 off a minimum of 21 overs for outright points. Some spectacular hitting by Imran and Smith had 63 on the board after six overs, but the later batsmen could not sustain the effort.

## Tasmania

| | | | |
|---|---|---|---|
| G. W. Goodman c Rixon b Holland | 50 | – b Marks | 39 |
| M. Ray c Rixon b Marks | 15 | – c Smith b Imran | 5 |
| R. J. Bennett c and b Matthews | 18 | – c Smith b Imran | 3 |
| D. J. Buckingham st Rixon b Holland | 8 | – lbw b Holland | 78 |
| K. Bradshaw c Waugh b Imran | 78 | – lbw b Waugh | 63 |
| *†R. D. Woolley c sub b Marks | 30 | – (8) run out | 37 |
| S. L. Saunders b Marks | 107 | – (9) c sub b Imran | 0 |
| P. I. Faulkner c Dyson b Marks | 25 | – (7) b Matthews | 30 |
| R. S. Hyatt not out | 26 | – (6) c and b Matthews | 28 |
| M. P. Tame not out | 35 | – not out | 12 |
| R. L. Brown (did not bat) | | – b Imran | 4 |
| B 4, l-b 11, w 1, n-b 1 | 17 | B 6, l-b 12, w 4 | 22 |
| 1/30 2/66 3/89 4/96 5/155 6/246 7/326 8/349 (8 wkts dec.) | 409 | 1/12 2/159 3/169 4/212 5/250 6/304 7/305 8/305 9/305 | 321 |

Bowling: *First Innings*—Gilbert 16–3–52–0; Marks 25–4–83–4; Imran 33–11–78–1; Holland 50–17–102–2; Matthews 21–10–68–1; Waugh 6–2–11–0. *Second Innings*—Gilbert 9–1–36–0; Marks 11–2–38–1; Imran 28–10–44–4; Holland 20–5–52–1; Matthews 32–10–86–2; Waugh 11–1–47–1.

## New South Wales

| | | | |
|---|---|---|---|
| S. B. Smith c Woolley b Brown | 14 | – (2) b Brown | 62 |
| J. Dyson st Woolley b Ray | 87 | – (5) b Faulkner | 5 |
| *D. M. Wellham lbw b Ray | 113 | – (8) not out | 7 |
| †S. J. Rixon c Woolley b Saunders | 94 | – (3) b Faulkner | 33 |
| P. S. Clifford c Hyatt b Faulkner | 143 | – (4) run out | 0 |
| G. R. J. Matthews c Woolley b Tame | 8 | | |
| Imran Khan c Ray b Tame | 5 | – (1) b Brown | 30 |
| S. R. Waugh b Tame | 4 | – (6) c Woolley b Brown | 2 |
| P. H. Marks c Ray b Tame | 3 | – (7) c Ray b Goodman | 8 |
| R. G. Holland b Tame | 24 | | |
| D. R. Gilbert not out | 0 | | |
| B 1, l-b 17, n-b 6 | 24 | L-b 5 | 5 |
| 1/26 2/201 3/250 4/382 5/417 6/430 7/456 8/476 9/515 | 519 | 1/54 2/123 3/127 4/127 5/132 6/136 7/152 (7 wkts) | 152 |

Bowling: *First Innings*—Brown 25–2–112–1; Faulkner 37–5–103–1; Tame 25.3–3–74–5; Saunders 29–3–99–1; Ray 27–5–76–2; Hyatt 15–2–37–0. *Second Innings*—Brown 10–0–68–3; Faulkner 10–2–73–2; Goodman 1–0–6–1.

Umpires: R. A. Emerson and A. G. Marshall.

## WESTERN AUSTRALIA v QUEENSLAND

At Perth, January 17, 18, 19, 20. Western Australia won by two wickets. Western Australia 12 pts, Queensland 4 pts. On his 21st birthday and in only his second Shield match, Barsby saved Queensland with a splendid five-hour innings. Maguire then showed great stamina with the ball as he worked his way through the Western Australian batting, but any joy Queensland may have had from their first-innings lead was short-lived, Alderman taking four for 0 in seventeen balls at the start of their second innings. Hohns came to the rescue with his first century after twelve seasons of Shield cricket. It took him over five hours but Alderman's persistence still ensured a reasonably simple fourth-innings task for Western Australia. Queensland's bowlers, however, fought all the way and Shipperd, having batted for four and a quarter hours, made the winning hit with four overs remaining.

## Queensland

| Batsman | First innings | | Second innings | |
|---|---|---|---|---|
| B. A. Courtice c Zoehrer b Spalding | 14 | – | c Zoehrer b Alderman | 2 |
| R. B. Kerr lbw b Alderman | 35 | – | b Alderman | 11 |
| C. B. Smart b Hogan | 7 | – | lbw b Alderman | 0 |
| G. S. Trimble c Hogan b Alderman | 8 | – | lbw b Alderman | 0 |
| T. J. Barsby c Zoehrer b Reid | 133 | – | b Reid | 11 |
| T. V. Hohns c Zoehrer b Reid | 10 | – | b Reid | 103 |
| †R. B. Phillips c Zoehrer b Alderman | 10 | – | run out | 22 |
| J. N. Maguire c Hughes b Alderman | 34 | – | c Reid b Spalding | 1 |
| H. Frei b Reid | 26 | – | c Zoehrer b Alderman | 9 |
| C. G. Rackemann not out | 8 | – | b Alderman | 4 |
| *J. R. Thomson b Reid | 5 | – | not out | 0 |
| L-b 9, w 1, n-b 10 | 20 | | L-b 2, n-b 6 | 8 |
| 1/38 2/59 3/63 4/81 5/114 6/135 7/233 8/284 9/301 | 310 | | 1/7 2/7 3/7 4/18 5/30 6/95 7/113 8/133 9/169 | 171 |

Bowling: *First Innings*—Alderman 34–10–102–4; Spalding 14–6–35–1; Hogan 31–9–72–1; Reid 33.3–10–88–4; Gonnella 2–0–4–0. *Second Innings*—Alderman 27.2–10–42–6; Spalding 13–3–23–1; Hogan 23–6–44–0; Reid 27–10–60–2.

## Western Australia

| Batsman | First innings | | Second innings | |
|---|---|---|---|---|
| M. R. J. Veletta lbw b Maguire | 19 | – | run out | 22 |
| M. W. McPhee c Phillips b Maguire | 67 | – | lbw b Maguire | 16 |
| G. Shipperd run out | 15 | – | not out | 69 |
| *K. J. Hughes c Phillips b Maguire | 15 | – | b Frei | 1 |
| G. R. Marsh b Rackemann | 23 | – | c Phillips b Maguire | 10 |
| P. Gonnella c Kerr b Rackemann | 12 | – | c Courtice b Maguire | 28 |
| †T. J. Zoehrer lbw b Maguire | 58 | – | c Phillips b Thomson | 7 |
| T. G. Hogan c Phillips b Maguire | 14 | – | c Courtice b Rackemann | 27 |
| T. M. Alderman c Barsby b Rackemann | 18 | – | c Trimble b Rackemann | 1 |
| B. A. Reid c Kerr b Maguire | 6 | – | not out | 2 |
| E. G. Spalding not out | 0 | | | |
| L-b 7, n-b 27 | 34 | | B 8, l-b 1, n-b 9 | 18 |
| 1/98 2/101 3/130 4/136 5/172 6/176 7/215 8/241 9/274 | 281 | | 1/39 2/42 3/49 4/85 5/131 6/150 7/194 8/195 | (8 wkts) 201 |

Bowling: *First Innings*—Rackemann 26–9–62–3; Frei 16–4–44–0; Thomson 25–5–84–0; Maguire 34.3–7–84–6. *Second Innings*—Rackemann 13.5–2–30–2; Frei 21–8–53–1; Thomson 8–1–27–1; Maguire 25–3–79–3; Hohns 1–0–3–0.

Umpires: R. J. Evans and W. M. Powell.

## SOUTH AUSTRALIA v VICTORIA

At Adelaide, January 17, 18, 19, 20. South Australia won by an innings and 94 runs. South Australia 16 pts. Victoria's batting on a blameless pitch let them down. In their first innings, the seventeen-year-old Zesers, bowling at medium pace off ten paces, had his best return. He then helped O'Connor in an eighth-wicket partnership of 174, a Shield record for South Australia. Zesers also achieved the unlikely feat of being dropped by three fieldsmen from one ball which passed through the hands of Wiener, Richardson and Siddons in the slips before hitting the ground. O'Connor batted patiently for more than five hours in making his first century. Hookes gave the new ball to Inverarity in Victoria's second innings, and McCurdy also enjoyed himself at the expense of his former colleagues. The match was over before lunch on the final day.

## Victoria

| | | | |
|---|---|---|---|
| M. B. Quinn b Zesers | 16 | – c Haysman b McCurdy | 10 |
| J. M. Wiener c Haysman b Carmichael | 31 | – c Hilditch b Inverarity | 16 |
| G. N. Yallop c Kelly b Zesers | 34 | – c Hookes b McCurdy | 1 |
| M. D. Taylor c Kelly b Inverarity | 38 | – c Hookes b McCurdy | 17 |
| J. D. Siddons c Inverarity b Zesers | 15 | – c Kelly b Zesers | 46 |
| G. W. Richardson c Kelly b Zesers | 12 | – b Carmichael | 19 |
| *R. J. Bright run out | 15 | – c Hilditch b Inverarity | 7 |
| P. D. King c Kelly b Zesers | 11 | – (9) c Bishop b Inverarity | 20 |
| †M. G. Dimattina c Kelly b Inverarity | 0 | – (8) c Hilditch b Inverarity | 8 |
| C. K. Smith not out | 13 | – c Hilditch b McCurdy | 1 |
| S. P. Davis c Hilditch b Carmichael | 4 | – not out | 1 |
| B 1, l-b 6, n-b 1 | 8 | B 1, l-b 3 | 4 |
| 1/40 2/73 3/107 4/135 5/150 6/152 7/175 8/176 9/179 | 197 | 1/16 2/17 3/37 4/56 5/110 6/112 7/120 8/135 9/140 | 150 |

Bowling: *First Innings*—McCurdy 25–4–66–0; Carmichael 16–3–46–2; Zesers 35–18–51–5; Inverarity 13–3–22–2; Hilditch 4–2–5–0. *Second Innings*—Inverarity 24.3–6–63–4; McCurdy 22–10–52–4; Carmichael 5–3–6–1; Zesers 12–4–25–1.

## South Australia

| | |
|---|---|
| A. M. J. Hilditch c Siddons b Smith | 16 |
| R. J. Zadow c Taylor b Davis | 42 |
| †D. J. Kelly c Bright b Davis | 72 |
| G. A. Bishop st Dimattina b Bright | 0 |
| M. D. Haysman b King | 34 |
| *D. W. Hookes c Richardson b King | 25 |
| D. F. G. O'Connor st Dimattina b Bright | 118 |
| R. J. Inverarity run out | 13 |
| A. K. Zesers c Davis b Bright | 85 |
| R. J. McCurdy c Siddons b Smith | 19 |
| I. R. Carmichael not out | 1 |
| B 6, l-b 7, w 1, n-b 2 | 16 |
| 1/19 2/124 3/126 4/138 5/189 6/206 7/237 8/411 9/427 | 441 |

Bowling: Davis 36–10–103–2; Smith 20–3–69–2; Bright 59–20–99–3; King 29–2–90–2; Wiener 18–6–41–0; Siddons 8–0–26–0.

Umpires: A. R. Crafter and G. W. Pellen.

## VICTORIA v NEW SOUTH WALES

At Melbourne, January 25, 26, 27, 28. Drawn. New South Wales 4 pts. New South Wales made hard work of taking first-innings points after Victoria, who were put in to bat, had shown much-improved form. For New South Wales, the 23-year-old Seabrook, making his début, hit the ball through and over the field with great gusto, and in their opening partnership of 265 he and Dyson seemed to assure their side of a comfortable lead. However, when Seabrook left at 283, having hit 26 4s, the batting declined, and at 390 for eight New South Wales were struggling even for four points; but O'Neill found an unexpected partner in Holland. Victoria used the final five hours for batting practice, while Yallop scored his first century of the season.

### Victoria

| | | |
|---|---|---|
| J. M. Wiener c and b Matthews | 19 | – b Gilbert 9 |
| D. F. Whatmore st Rixon b Holland | 63 | – c Matthews b Imran 11 |
| G. N. Yallop c Wellham b Imran | 58 | – not out 125 |
| M. D. Taylor b Imran | 77 | – c Imran b Holland 2 |
| J. D. Siddons c Rixon b Gilbert | 17 | – c Rixon b Holland 68 |
| P. W. Young c Clifford b Marks | 55 | – not out 12 |
| *R. J. Bright c Rixon b Imran | 84 | |
| P. D. King st Rixon b Holland | 19 | |
| †M. G. Dimattina lbw b Holland | 12 | |
| M. G. Hughes b Holland | 8 | |
| S. P. Davis not out | 5 | |
| B 1, l-b 12, w 1, n-b 7 | 21 | L-b 9 9 |
| 1/43 2/115 3/179 4/215 5/283 6/303 7/344 8/364 9/380 | 438 | 1/17 2/25 3/33 4/200 (4 wkts) 236 |

Bowling: *First Innings*—Imran 38.2–10–106–3; Gilbert 30–13–61–1; Holland 50–17–111–4; Matthews 39–12–91–1; O'Neill 9–2–35–0; Marks 9–3–21–1. *Second Innings*—Imran 11–5–16–1; Gilbert 13–4–44–1; Holland 18–7–38–2; Matthews 15–3–46–0; O'Neill 4–0–16–0; Marks 17–5–47–0; Dyson 5–0–15–0; Clifford 2–1–4–0; Seabrook 1–0–1–0.

### New South Wales

| | |
|---|---|
| J. Dyson c and b Bright | 97 |
| W. J. S. Seabrook c Taylor b Bright | 165 |
| *D. M. Wellham c Dimattina b Davis | 30 |
| P. S. Clifford b Hughes | 25 |
| G. R. J. Matthews c Davis b Bright | 11 |
| Imran Khan c Dimattina b Davis | 15 |
| M. D. O'Neill not out | 45 |
| †S. J. Rixon c Siddons b Bright | 0 |
| P. H. Marks c Dimattina b Davis | 0 |
| R. G. Holland st Dimattina b Bright | 31 |
| D. R. Gilbert not out | 1 |
| B 4, l-b 9, w 4, n-b 5 | 22 |
| 1/265 2/283 3/332 4/333 5/349 6/381 7/381 8/390 9/435 | (9 wkts dec.) 442 |

Bowling: Hughes 31–8–78–1; Davis 48–14–108–3; King 12–1–66–0; Bright 47–13–139–5; Siddons 11–0–27–0; Wiener 6–1–11–0.

Umpires: D. W. Holt and L. J. King.

## QUEENSLAND v TASMANIA

At Brisbane, January 25, 26, 27, 28. Drawn. Tasmania 4 pts. Barsby's second century in consecutive matches, after he was missed three times before reaching 50, helped Queensland reach a respectable first-innings total. Kerr also showed his best form for some time in face of some hostile bowling by Patterson. When Tasmania batted Thomson took his 300th Shield wicket upon having Ray caught behind. Only C. V. Grimmett (512), A. A. Mallett (344), D. K. Lillee (323) and G. A. R. Lock (302) had previously achieved this feat. But in a consistent batting performance, Tasmania achieved their highest Shield score. The 22-year-old Bradshaw spent seven hours over his first century, while Faulkner reached a similar goal in cavalier style, hitting seven 6s and taking 24 off an over from Whyte. Woolley's declaration late on the third day left Queensland with little other option than to play out time. Kerr took the chance to make his highest first-class score and share a massive opening partnership with Courtice.

## Queensland

| | | | |
|---|---|---|---|
| R. B. Kerr c Woolley b Faulkner | 60 | – not out | 201 |
| B. A. Courtice c Ray b Goodman | 34 | – c Saunders b Hyatt | 135 |
| C. B. Smart c Ray b Brown | 50 | – not out | 21 |
| G. M. Ritchie c Woolley b Patterson | 2 | | |
| T. J. Barsby c Woolley b Patterson | 137 | | |
| T. V. Hohns c Woolley b Faulkner | 3 | | |
| †R. B. Phillips c Woolley b Patterson | 59 | | |
| G. K. Whyte c Buckingham b Patterson | 4 | | |
| J. N. Maguire b Brown | 10 | | |
| H. Frei c Buckingham b Patterson | 6 | | |
| *J. R. Thomson not out | 2 | | |
| B 7, l-b 2, n-b 8 | 17 | B 3, l-b 3, n-b 6 | 12 |
| 1/91 2/107 3/110 4/247 5/277 6/314 7/319 8/350 9/377 | 384 | 1/331 | (1 wkt) 369 |

Bowling: *First Innings*—Patterson 31.1–6–93–5; Brown 31–7–105–2; Faulkner 24–7–63–2; Saunders 13–1–39–0; Goodman 15–6–42–1; Ray 9–1–33–0. *Second Innings*—Patterson 21–4–44–0; Brown 15–3–74–0; Faulkner 11–1–33–0; Saunders 19–2–84–0; Goodman 1–0–1–0; Ray 17–2–37–0; Hyatt 29–6–73–1; Bradshaw 5–0–17–0.

## Tasmania

| | |
|---|---|
| G. W. Goodman c Smart b Maguire | 88 |
| M. Ray c Phillips b Thomson | 14 |
| R. J. Bennett c Smart b Thomson | 41 |
| D. J. Buckingham c Phillips b Maguire | 37 |
| K. Bradshaw b Maguire | 121 |
| *†R. D. Woolley c Frei b Hohns | 67 |
| S. L. Saunders c Courtice b Hohns | 4 |
| P. I. Faulkner c Maguire b Hohns | 100 |
| R. S. Hyatt not out | 6 |
| R. L. Brown b Hohns | 5 |
| L-b 7, w 2, n-b 15 | 24 |
| 1/22 2/113 3/189 4/192 5/311 6/319 7/488 8/502 9/507 | (9 wkts dec.) 507 |

B. P. Patterson did not bat.

Bowling: Thomson 32–8–105–2; Frei 29–10–67–0; Maguire 43–8–111–3; Hohns 40.3–6–129–4; Whyte 31–11–88–0.

Umpires: C. D. Timmins and M. J. King.

## SOUTH AUSTRALIA v WESTERN AUSTRALIA

At Adelaide, February 22, 23, 24, 25. Drawn. South Australia 4 pts. Needing full points to stay in contention for the Shield final, South Australia looked like gaining them after two days. Then a record second-wicket partnership of 248 in four and a half hours between Veletta and Shipperd swung the initiative towards Western Australia, and by the end of the game it was they who were nearer to winning. South Australia's first innings was flamboyantly launched by Hookes and held together by Haysman, both batsmen being especially severe on Hogan. In the light of their second-innings performance, Western Australia's first-innings collapse, after McPhee and Veletta had given them a splendid start, was inexplicable. Hookes's decision to enforce the follow-on looked to have been optimistic when Veletta and Shipperd were in command on the final day, but the four-man South Australian attack persisted well enough to leave their batsmen a target of 247 in a minimum of 41 overs. An early flurry of wickets ensured that South Australia concentrated their further efforts on survival.

## South Australia

| | | | |
|---|---|---|---|
| A. M. J. Hilditch c Marsh b Clough | 0 | | |
| G. A. Bishop c McPhee b Reid | 37 | c Marsh b Clough | 14 |
| R. J. Zadow run out | 14 | (1) c Bush b Clough | 6 |
| M. D. Haysman run out | 157 | not out | 30 |
| *D. W. Hookes c Zoehrer b Reid | 83 | b Reid | 6 |
| D. F. G. O'Connor run out | 35 | (5) c Zoehrer b Reid | 2 |
| R. J. Inverarity c Zoehrer b Reid | 9 | c McPhee b Hogan | 17 |
| †D. J. Kelly st Zoehrer b Hogan | 24 | (6) st Zoehrer b Hogan | 22 |
| T. B. A. May b Bush | 14 | (8) not out | 1 |
| I. R. Carmichael b Bush | 11 | | |
| W. Prior not out | 0 | | |
| L-b 10, w 2, n-b 8 | 20 | L-b 3, n-b 2 | 5 |
| 1/0 2/30 3/64 4/202 5/292 6/321 7/368 8/379 9/403 | 404 | 1/9 2/21 3/27 4/30 5/78 6/101 | (6 wkts) 103 |

Bowling: *First Innings*—Clough 31–7–100–1; Reid 35–6–90–3; Bush 33.1–9–88–2; Hogan 28–5–107–1; Gonella 2–0–9–0. *Second Innings*—Clough 11–2–20–2; Reid 10–1–37–2; Bush 10–3–30–0; Hogan 10–6–13–2.

## Western Australia

| | | | |
|---|---|---|---|
| M. R. J. Veletta run out | 36 | c Kelly b Carmichael | 143 |
| M. W. McPhee c Zadow b May | 60 | c Kelly b Prior | 0 |
| *G. Shipperd c Hilditch b Carmichael | 3 | lbw b Prior | 129 |
| G. R. Marsh lbw b Inverarity | 4 | b Carmichael | 67 |
| G. J. Ireland c Kelly b Carmichael | 0 | lbw b Prior | 22 |
| P. Gonnella not out | 45 | b May | 24 |
| †T. J. Zoehrer b Inverarity | 9 | lbw b Carmichael | 14 |
| T. G. Hogan run out | 19 | lbw b Inverarity | 11 |
| G. E. Bush c Hookes b May | 0 | c Haysman b May | 0 |
| P. M. Clough b May | 0 | not out | 12 |
| B. A. Reid b Carmichael | 8 | c Bishop b Inverarity | 23 |
| B 2, l-b 4, n-b 1 | 7 | B 3, l-b 11 | 14 |
| 1/82 2/97 3/101 4/105 5/105 6/126 7/170 8/170 9/170 | 191 | 1/0 2/248 3/336 4/372 5/382 6/406 7/412 8/412 9/424 | 459 |

Bowling: *First Innings*—Prior 12–5–24–0; Carmichael 24.4–13–41–3; Hookes 4–1–7–0; May 24–8–57–3; Inverarity 24–9–56–2. *Second Innings*—Prior 34–6–112–3; Carmichael 42–15–117–3; Hookes 2–0–13–0; May 52–22–95–2; Inverarity 33.5–12–75–2; Hilditch 1–1–0–0; Haysman 5–0–18–0; O'Connor 3–0–15–0.

Umpires: A. R. Crafter and G. W. Pellen.

## NEW SOUTH WALES v QUEENSLAND

At Sydney, February 22, 23, 24, 25. New South Wales won by an innings and 61 runs. New South Wales 16 pts. From the moment that Holland found the edge of Barsby's bat with his second ball, Queensland batted as though doomed on a pitch well suited to the New South Wales spinning trio. In the event Holland, Bennett and Matthews shared nine of Queensland's first-innings wickets; but it was the young fast bowler, Gilbert, who did the early damage in their second innings before Matthews achieved his best analysis. The two Queensland spinners,

Whyte and Hohns, were unable to instil the same doubts among the New South Wales batsmen. Dyson provided a solid foundation to the New South Wales innings. He shared useful partnerships with Wellham and Clifford; and then Matthews, in a disciplined display, guided New South Wales to a substantial lead. Queensland badly missed their Test representatives.

## Queensland

| | | | |
|---|---|---|---|
| B. A. Courtice c Dyer b Holland | 10 | – c Dyer b Matthews | 50 |
| T. J. Barsby c Dyer b Holland | 14 | – st Dyer b Holland | 30 |
| C. B. Smart lbw b Bennett | 20 | – c Wellham b Gilbert | 3 |
| G. M. Ritchie c Dyer b Matthews | 59 | – c Marks b Gilbert | 38 |
| A. B. Henschell c Clifford b Bennett | 4 | – c Marks b Matthews | 0 |
| T. V. Hohns c Dyer b Matthews | 1 | – (7) c Dyson b Gilbert | 6 |
| †R. B. Phillips b Matthews | 1 | – (8) b Gilbert | 4 |
| G. K. Whyte c Wellham b Bennett | 2 | – (9) c Waugh b Matthews | 11 |
| J. N. Maguire c and b Holland | 5 | – (10) c Dyson b Matthews | 0 |
| C. G. Rackemann not out | 25 | – (6) b Matthews | 0 |
| *J. R. Thomson run out | 4 | – not out | 0 |
| B 2, l-b 8, w 1 | 11 | B 5, l-b 4 | 9 |
| 1/21 2/38 3/62 4/66 5/69 6/77 7/88 8/110 9/146 | 156 | 1/44 2/63 3/126 4/126 5/130 6/130 7/140 8/149 9/151 | 151 |

Bowling: *First Innings*—Gilbert 12–3–28–0; Marks 4–1–8–0; Holland 25–9–49–3; Bennett 27–13–39–3; Matthews 16.5–8–22–3. *Second Innings*—Gilbert 16–5–42–4; Marks 6–0–15–0; Holland 21–12–39–1; Bennett 20–12–14–0; Matthews 26–13–32–5.

## New South Wales

| | |
|---|---|
| J. Dyson c Courtice b Maguire | 93 |
| W. J. S. Seabrook run out | 11 |
| *D. M. Wellham c Courtice b Hohns | 27 |
| P. S. Clifford c Phillips b Whyte | 45 |
| G. R. J. Matthews c Ritchie b Thomson | 87 |
| S. R. Waugh c Phillips b Maguire | 0 |
| P. H. Marks b Whyte | 3 |
| †G. C. Dyer c Phillips b Thomson | 43 |
| M. J. Bennett c Phillips b Rackemann | 22 |
| R. G. Holland c Henschell b Maguire | 27 |
| D. R. Gilbert not out | 1 |
| L-b 2, w 2, n-b 5 | 9 |
| 1/24 2/100 3/167 4/185 5/185 6/188 7/255 8/299 9/357 | 368 |

Bowling: Rackemann 22–2–70–1; Thomson 15–3–51–2; Whyte 33–10–77–2; Maguire 35–6–88–3; Hohns 20–2–50–1; Henschell 10–1–30–0.

Umpires: R. A. Emerson and R. A. French.

## TASMANIA v VICTORIA

At Devonport, February 22, 23, 24, 25. Drawn. Victoria 4 pts. Required to score 140 in twelve overs to win a rain-affected match, Victoria found it beyond them, the captains agreeing to halt proceedings five overs before the scheduled close. Whatmore and Yallop got Victoria's first innings off to an enterprising start with a second-wicket stand of 108 in 100 minutes. Several useful contributions followed. Flighting the ball in the breeze, Bright then bemused the Tasmanian batsmen, and although Ray put up some resistance in a three and a half hour innings, Tasmania never seemed likely to avoid the follow-on. Led by Boon they did better in their second innings, but when he, Bradshaw and Davison fell to McCarthy early on the fourth day, a Victorian victory seemed inevitable. Goodman and Saunders prevented it.

## Victoria

| First innings | | Second innings | |
|---|---|---|---|
| D. F. Whatmore c Woolley b Tame | 64 | c Patterson b Brown | 26 |
| P. W. Young c Woolley b Tame | 10 | (4) b Brown | 5 |
| G. N. Yallop lbw b Tame | 51 | (2) lbw b Patterson | 22 |
| M. D. Taylor c Boon b Saunders | 67 | | |
| J. D. Siddons lbw b Brown | 12 | (3) b Patterson | 0 |
| †M. G. Dimattina c Woolley b Tame | 8 | | |
| G. L. Jordan c Buckingham b Saunders | 29 | (6) not out | 1 |
| *R. J. Bright b Patterson | 30 | | |
| P. D. King c Buckingham b Brown | 65 | (5) not out | 2 |
| R. C. A. M. McCarthy c Goodman b Patterson | 36 | | |
| S. P. Davis not out | 0 | | |
| L-b 7, w 1, n-b 10 | 18 | B 1, n-b 1 | 2 |
| 1/20 2/128 3/131 4/164 5/205 6/238 7/257 8/307 9/357 | 390 | 1/36 2/38 3/49 4/57 | (4 wkts) 58 |

Bowling: *First Innings*—Patterson 30–3–123–2; Brown 22.4–2–94–2; Tame 38–7–138–4; Saunders 10–3–22–2; Goodman 2–0–4–0; Ray 2–1–2–0. *Second Innings*—Patterson 4–0–35–2; Brown 3–0–22–2.

## Tasmania

| First innings | | Second innings | |
|---|---|---|---|
| G. W. Goodman c and b Bright | 45 | lbw b King | 89 |
| M. Ray c Yallop b McCarthy | 65 | c Dimattina b Davis | 23 |
| D. C. Boon c Jordan b Bright | 7 | c King b McCarthy | 78 |
| D. J. Buckingham st Dimattina b Bright | 0 | c Whatmore b Davis | 2 |
| K. Bradshaw c Siddons b King | 20 | c Dimattina b McCarthy | 27 |
| *†R. D. Woolley b Bright | 22 | (7) c Whatmore b McCarthy | 32 |
| B. F. Davison c Davis b King | 5 | (6) b McCarthy | 0 |
| S. L. Saunders c Whatmore b Davis | 0 | b Bright | 69 |
| M. P. Tame c Siddons b Bright | 19 | lbw b Davis | 4 |
| R. L. Brown not out | 6 | not out | 1 |
| B. P. Patterson b Davis | 2 | b Davis | 0 |
| B 1, l-b 1, n-b 3 | 5 | B 3, l-b 1, w 3, n-b 1 | 8 |
| 1/75 2/99 3/99 4/131 5/153 6/165 7/167 8/176 9/193 | 196 | 1/38 2/40 3/142 4/143 5/143 6/187 7/318 8/332 9/332 | 333 |

Bowling: *First Innings*—McCarthy 22–6–75–1; King 10–4–27–2; Davis 21–3–50–2; Bright 21–10–41–5; Siddons 1–0–1–0. *Second Innings*—McCarthy 22–1–80–4; King 23–3–78–1; Davis 30.5–6–101–4; Bright 26–11–29–1; Siddons 6–1–16–0; Yallop 8–1–25–0.

Umpires: W. Elliott and I. Batt.

## NEW SOUTH WALES v VICTORIA

At Sydney, March 1, 2, 3, 4. New South Wales won by 25 runs. New South Wales 16 pts. Wellham set Victoria to make 269 to win in seven hours on a pitch which gave the spinners some encouragement. With twenty overs left they had reached 230 for six and victory seemed a formality. But Bright, the captain, and Emerson then added only 5 in nine overs, and when Bright was out Bennett had little difficulty in prizing out the remaining batsmen, who by now were intent on drawing the game. With seven balls left they lost it, humiliatingly. It was due to Matthews and the nineteen-year-old Waugh that New South Wales had made over 300 in their first innings. Matthews spent five hours over his first century, while Waugh played some fine cuts and drives. Victoria's first innings was notable for a five and a half hour century by Yallop and a hat-trick by Gilbert, consisting of Yallop, caught at slip, Bright and McCarthy.

### New South Wales

| Batsman | First innings | | Second innings | |
|---|---|---|---|---|
| W. J. S. Seabrook b Davis | 14 | – | c Siddons b McCarthy | 6 |
| J. Dyson c Whatmore b Bright | 28 | – | c Yallop b King | 54 |
| *D. M. Wellham c Taylor b Bright | 18 | – | run out | 81 |
| P. S. Clifford c Dimattina b Bright | 19 | – | not out | 38 |
| G. R. J. Matthews st Dimattina b Bright | 103 | – | not out | 14 |
| S. R. Waugh c Whatmore b McCarthy | 94 | | | |
| †G. C. Dyer c Dimattina b McCarthy | 2 | | | |
| P. H. Marks c Taylor b Davis | 15 | | | |
| M. J. Bennett c Emerson b Bright | 19 | | | |
| R. G. Holland c McCarthy b Davis | 10 | | | |
| D. R. Gilbert not out | 0 | | | |
| B 1, l-b 2, w 1 | 4 | | B 8 | 8 |
| 1/27 2/61 3/79 4/91 5/269 6/277 7/294 8/296 9/323 | 326 | | 1/12 2/137 3/159 (3 wkts dec.) | 201 |

Bowling: *First Innings*—Davis 29–4–75–3; McCarthy 18–6–66–2; Bright 39.5–12–112–5; Emerson 23–5–60–0; Siddons 3–1–10–0. *Second Innings*—Davis 15–1–32–0; McCarthy 10–3–26–1; Bright 17–7–52–0; Emerson 14–1–31–0; King 15–5–52–1.

### Victoria

| Batsman | First innings | | Second innings | |
|---|---|---|---|---|
| D. F. Whatmore b Waugh | 30 | – | b Holland | 34 |
| P. W. Young lbw b Gilbert | 17 | – | c Waugh b Bennett | 35 |
| G. N. Yallop c Waugh b Gilbert | 147 | – | c Matthews b Bennett | 8 |
| M. D. Taylor c Matthews b Bennett | 13 | – | c Waugh b Holland | 0 |
| J. D. Siddons c Dyson b Matthews | 12 | – | c Holland b Matthews | 75 |
| P. D. King c Marks b Gilbert | 5 | – | c Waugh b Matthews | 25 |
| D. L. Emerson b Bennett | 16 | – | (8) c Gilbert b Bennett | 32 |
| *R. J. Bright b Gilbert | 0 | – | (7) lbw b Bennett | 27 |
| R. C. A. M. McCarthy b Gilbert | 0 | – | (10) c Clifford b Bennett | 2 |
| †M. G. Dimattina not out | 9 | – | (9) not out | 2 |
| S. P. Davis lbw b Bennett | 1 | – | c Dyson b Bennett | 0 |
| B 1, l-b 4, w 1, n-b 3 | 9 | | L-b 2, n-b 1 | 3 |
| 1/44 2/71 3/100 4/135 5/161 6/249 7/249 8/249 9/249 | 259 | | 1/66 2/76 3/76 4/78 5/144 6/191 7/235 8/238 9/240 | 243 |

Bowling: *First Innings*—Gilbert 26–4–70–5; Marks 10–2–31–0; Waugh 9–2–15–1; Holland 25–12–44–0; Matthews 17–6–47–1; Bennett 25.4–11–47–3. *Second Innings*—Gilbert 16–3–44–0; Marks 5–1–12–0; Waugh 5–1–13–0; Holland 26–7–62–2; Matthews 26–12–53–2; Bennett 39.5–17–57–6.

Umpires: R. A. French and R. Emerson.

## SOUTH AUSTRALIA v QUEENSLAND

At Adelaide, March 1, 2, 3, 4. South Australia won by 12 runs. South Australia 12 pts, Queensland 4 pts. Outright victory would have guaranteed Queensland top place in the Shield table and home advantage in the final, and when by stumps on the third day South Australia held a lead of only 73 with three second-innings wickets left their hopes were justifiably buoyant. Even when Kelly, the South Australian wicket-keeper, scored a defiant hundred, his first in Shield cricket, Queensland's final target was still only 196 at 3 runs an over. However, their batting never came to terms with the task and the off-spinner, May, profiting from some reckless strokes, achieved his best analysis. Inverarity made his farewell appearance one to remember, resisting the Queensland bowlers almost single-handedly in South Australia's first innings and achieving the best bowling return of his 23-year career in Queensland's first. To cap a splendid match, he took a fine catch at deep mid-wicket to dismiss the last Queensland batsman.

## South Australia

| First Innings | | Second Innings | |
|---|---|---|---|
| A. M. J. Hilditch c Henschell b Maguire | 22 | run out | 34 |
| G. A. Bishop c Trimble b Maguire | 25 | c Phillips b Maguire | 2 |
| R. J. Zadow c Courtice b Maguire | 13 | c and b Maguire | 37 |
| M. D. Haysman c Henschell b Rackemann | 5 | c Maguire b Hohns | 42 |
| *D. W. Hookes c Barsby b Maguire | 18 | c Courtice b Thomson | 34 |
| D. F. G. O'Connor c Phillips b Rackemann | 2 | c Hohns b Rackemann | 57 |
| R. J. Inverarity c Rackemann b Maguire | 55 | lbw b Thomson | 4 |
| †D. J. Kelly c Smart b Rackemann | 26 | not out | 100 |
| T. B. A. May c Trimble b Thomson | 23 | c Courtice b Maguire | 10 |
| I. R. Carmichael c Hohns b Thomson | 4 | b Hohns | 19 |
| W. Prior not out | 0 | run out | 1 |
| B 2, l-b 6, w 2, n-b 7 | 17 | L-b 12, n-b 11 | 23 |
| 1/49 2/60 3/67 4/86 5/93 6/96 7/150 8/192 9/200 | 210 | 1/16 2/40 3/92 4/146 5/164 6/194 7/251 8/283 9/349 | 363 |

Bowling: *First Innings*—Thomson 20–2–71–2; Rackemann 26–13–46–3; Maguire 29.3–13–62–5; Hohns 10–3–19–0; Courtice 2–1–4–0. *Second Innings*—Thomson 20–5–67–2; Rackemann 38–11–77–1; Maguire 40–9–134–3; Hohns 30–9–65–2; Henschell 4–1–8–0.

## Queensland

| First Innings | | Second Innings | |
|---|---|---|---|
| B. A. Courtice c Kelly b Inverarity | 42 | c Hookes b Carmichael | 45 |
| T. J. Barsby c Hilditch b May | 72 | c O'Connor b Prior | 15 |
| C. B. Smart lbw b Inverarity | 0 | st Kelly b Inverarity | 54 |
| G. M. Ritchie c Haysman b Inverarity | 4 | c O'Connor b May | 11 |
| G. S. Trimble b Inverarity | 76 | b May | 8 |
| A. B. Henschell lbw b Inverarity | 73 | c Inverarity b May | 19 |
| T. V. Hohns not out | 72 | (9) c Inverarity b May | 7 |
| †R. B. Phillips c Bishop b Inverarity | 15 | (7) b May | 16 |
| J. N. Maguire b Inverarity | 0 | (8) b May | 0 |
| C. G. Rackemann not out | 15 | b Inverarity | 0 |
| *J. R. Thomson (did not bat) | | not out | 5 |
| B 1, l-b 5, w 1, n-b 2 | 9 | B 1, l-b 2 | 3 |
| 1/111 2/111 3/117 4/119 5/216 6/304 7/342 8/343 | (8 wkts dec.) 378 | 1/21 2/99 3/121 4/133 5/143 6/169 7/169 8/170 9/175 | 183 |

Bowling: *First Innings*—Prior 7–1–25–0; Hookes 9–1–32–0; Carmichael 32–9–117–0; Inverarity 33–8–86–7; May 32–10–98–1; Hilditch 8–1–14–0. *Second Innings*—Prior 11–2–36–1; Hookes 3–1–11–0; Carmichael 19–1–59–1; Inverarity 16–2–50–2; May 10.5–1–24–6.

Umpires: B. E. Martin and M. G. O'Connell.

## TASMANIA v WESTERN AUSTRALIA

At Hobart, March 1, 2, 3, 4. Drawn. Tasmania 4 pts. Rain prevented any play on the second and fourth days. Shipperd's declaration when Western Australia trailed by 149 in their first innings was aimed at making up lost time, but it was to no avail. The statistical highlight of the game was Boon's 147, his third century of the season and the ninth of his career.

### Tasmania

| | | |
|---|---|---|
| M. Ray c Marsh b Hogan | 53 – c Zoehrer b Spalding | 22 |
| G. W. Goodman b Clough | 6 – b Reid | 0 |
| D. C. Boon c and b Reid | 147 – c Shipperd b Clough | 9 |
| R. J. Bennett c Ireland b Reid | 1 – not out | 26 |
| K. Bradshaw not out | 41 – b Hogan | 7 |
| B. F. Davison c Veletta b Spalding | 5 – not out | 17 |
| *†R. D. Woolley not out | 42 | |
| B 2, l-b 5, w 2, n-b 3 | 12 L-b 2 | 2 |
| 1/27 2/106 3/113 4/234 5/252 (5 wkts dec.) | 307 1/0 2/27 3/40 4/58 (4 wkts) | 83 |

S. L. Saunders, B. P. Patterson, R. L. Brown and M. P. Tame did not bat.

Bowling: *First Innings*—Reid 29–12–77–2; Clough 21–5–71–1; Spalding 13–0–65–1; Hogan 31–5–79–1; Gonella 3–1–8–0. *Second Innings*—Reid 11–5–12–1; Clough 10–3–31–1; Spalding 7–3–6–1; Hogan 16–6–32–1.

### Western Australia

| | |
|---|---|
| M. W. McPhee c and b Tame | 52 |
| M. R. J. Veletta c Davison b Brown | 21 |
| *G. Shipperd not out | 27 |
| G. R. Marsh not out | 51 |
| B 3, n-b 4 | 7 |
| 1/65 2/75 (2 wkts dec.) | 158 |

G. J. Ireland, P. Gonnella, †T. J. Zoehrer, B. A. Reid, T. G. Hogan, E. G. Spalding and P. M. Clough did not bat.

Bowling: Patterson 10–3–47–0; Brown 11–1–36–1; Tame 18–3–48–1; Saunders 17–7–20–0; Ray 3–2–4–0.

Umpires: S. G. Randell and A. G. Jones.

## SHEFFIELD SHIELD FINAL

## NEW SOUTH WALES v QUEENSLAND

At Sydney, March 15, 16, 17, 18, 19. New South Wales won by one wicket. Queensland had Hohns to thank – he made his second century of the season – for reaching a satisfactory first-innings total. Imran was New South Wales's best bowler, Holland's leg-spin being ineffective. When New South Wales batted, Smith hit out well, but in spite of a marathon effort by Dyson they were in trouble at 226 for seven. Waugh then showed his attacking flair in taking his side to within 56 of Queensland. In their second innings Queensland collapsed first to the pace of Imran, then to the spin of Bennett, their last five wickets falling for 20 runs as the pitch showed signs of wear. Needing 220 to win New South Wales looked on the verge of defeat, and Queensland of their first-ever Sheffield Shield, at 175 for eight. But Clifford, dropped when 37, kept his head, and first Holland, then Gilbert, helped him take New South Wales to a thrilling victory, a cover drive by Gilbert producing the winning runs. The aggregate attendance was 24,000 and Queensland's fears of a pitch heavily weighted in favour of the spinners proved groundless.

## Queensland

| | | | |
|---|---|---|---|
| R. B. Kerr b Imran | 9 | – (2) lbw b Imran | 3 |
| B. A. Courtice b Gilbert | 5 | – (1) b Imran | 0 |
| K. C. Wessels c Dyson b Gilbert | 49 | – c Dyson b Holland | 22 |
| *A. R. Border c Dyson b Bennett | 64 | – (5) c Dyson b Imran | 45 |
| G. M. Ritchie c Waugh b Imran | 20 | – (6) c and b Bennett | 12 |
| G. S. Trimble c Wellham b Bennett | 38 | – (7) c Waugh b Bennett | 16 |
| T. V. Hohns st Rixon b Holland | 103 | – (8) c Clifford b Bennett | 2 |
| †R. B. Phillips c Smith b Waugh | 53 | – (4) c Wellham b Imran | 47 |
| J. N. Maguire b Imran | 19 | – b Imran | 4 |
| C. G. Rackemann b Imran | 1 | – c Imran b Bennett | 3 |
| J. R. Thomson not out | 0 | – not out | 1 |
| B 3, l-b 5, n-b 5 | 13 | B 3, l-b 2, w 1, n-b 2 | 8 |
| 1/12 2/18 3/99 4/141 5/159 6/224 7/321 8/370 9/374 | 374 | 1/0 2/3 3/41 4/116 5/129 6/143 7/154 8/154 9/160 | 163 |

Bowling: *First Innings*—Imran 27.3–6–66–4; Gilbert 27–6–67–2; Matthews 27–10–53–0; Waugh 12–6–15–1; Bennett 34–16–54–2; Holland 43–12–111–1. *Second Innings*—Imran 19–6–34–5; Gilbert 15–5–24–0; Bennett 20–4–32–4; Waugh 6–1–21–0; Holland 15–5–39–1; Matthews 2–0–8–0.

## New South Wales

| | | | |
|---|---|---|---|
| J. Dyson c Ritchie b Rackemann | 66 | – c Phillips b Thomson | 19 |
| S. B. Smith c Phillips b Maguire | 76 | – hit wkt b Rackemann | 7 |
| †S. J. Rixon c Phillips b Maguire | 0 | – (4) c and b Thomson | 2 |
| *D. M. Wellham lbw b Thomson | 31 | – (3) b Thomson | 39 |
| P. S. Clifford c Phillips b Thomson | 13 | – not out | 83 |
| G. R. J. Matthews lbw b Maguire | 16 | – c Phillips b Rackemann | 8 |
| Imran Khan c Phillips b Rackemann | 7 | – c Border b Rackemann | 18 |
| S. R. Waugh c Maguire b Thomson | 71 | – c Phillips b Rackemann | 21 |
| M. J. Bennett c Phillips b Border | 10 | – c Border b Rackemann | 1 |
| R. G. Holland c Trimble b Border | 0 | – c Kerr b Rackemann | 10 |
| D. R. Gilbert not out | 8 | – not out | 8 |
| L-b 1, n-b 19 | 20 | B 3, l-b 2, n-b 2 | 7 |
| 1/98 2/98 3/167 4/185 5/219 6/223 7/226 8/281 9/283 | 318 | 1/13 2/53 3/59 4/76 5/100 6/140 7/173 8/175 9/209 | (9 wkts) 223 |

Bowling: *First Innings*—Thomson 27.3–6–83–3; Rackemann 30–9–80–2; Maguire 33–6–90–3; Border 7–2–27–2; Waugh 24–7–37–0. *Second Innings*—Rackemann 30.2–8–54–6; Thomson 20–4–81–3; Maguire 14–2–27–0; Hohns 20–4–56–0.

Umpires: M. W. Johnson and R. A. French.

## SHEFFIELD SHIELD WINNERS

| | | | |
|---|---|---|---|
| 1892-93 | Victoria | 1906-07 | New South Wales |
| 1893-94 | South Australia | 1907-08 | Victoria |
| 1894-95 | Victoria | 1908-09 | New South Wales |
| 1895-96 | New South Wales | 1909-10 | South Australia |
| 1896-97 | New South Wales | 1910-11 | New South Wales |
| 1897-98 | Victoria | 1911-12 | New South Wales |
| 1898-99 | Victoria | 1912-13 | South Australia |
| 1899-1900 | New South Wales | 1913-14 | New South Wales |
| 1900-01 | Victoria | 1914-15 | Victoria |
| 1901-02 | New South Wales | 1915-19 | No competition |
| 1902-03 | New South Wales | 1919-20 | New South Wales |
| 1903-04 | New South Wales | 1920-21 | New South Wales |
| 1904-05 | New South Wales | 1921-22 | Victoria |
| 1905-06 | New South Wales | 1922-23 | New South Wales |

| | |
|---|---|
| 1923-24 | Victoria |
| 1924-25 | Victoria |
| 1925-26 | New South Wales |
| 1926-27 | South Australia |
| 1927-28 | Victoria |
| 1928-29 | New South Wales |
| 1929-30 | Victoria |
| 1930-31 | Victoria |
| 1931-32 | New South Wales |
| 1932-33 | New South Wales |
| 1933-34 | Victoria |
| 1934-35 | Victoria |
| 1935-36 | South Australia |
| 1936-37 | Victoria |
| 1937-38 | New South Wales |
| 1938-39 | South Australia |
| 1939-40 | New South Wales |
| 1940-46 | No competition |
| 1946-47 | Victoria |
| 1947-48 | Western Australia |
| 1948-49 | New South Wales |
| 1949-50 | New South Wales |
| 1950-51 | Victoria |
| 1951-52 | New South Wales |
| 1952-53 | South Australia |
| 1953-54 | New South Wales |
| 1954-55 | New South Wales |
| 1955-56 | New South Wales |
| 1956-57 | New South Wales |
| 1957-58 | New South Wales |
| 1958-59 | New South Wales |
| 1959-60 | New South Wales |
| 1960-61 | New South Wales |
| 1961-62 | New South Wales |
| 1962-63 | Victoria |
| 1963-64 | South Australia |
| 1964-65 | New South Wales |
| 1965-66 | New South Wales |
| 1966-67 | Victoria |
| 1967-68 | Western Australia |
| 1968-69 | South Australia |
| 1969-70 | Victoria |
| 1970-71 | South Australia |
| 1971-72 | Western Australia |
| 1972-73 | Western Australia |
| 1973-74 | Victoria |
| 1974-75 | Western Australia |
| 1975-76 | South Australia |
| 1976-77 | Western Australia |
| 1977-78 | Western Australia |
| 1978-79 | Victoria |
| 1979-80 | Victoria |
| 1980-81 | Western Australia |
| 1981-82 | South Australia |
| 1982-83 | New South Wales |
| 1983-84 | Western Australia |
| 1984-85 | New South Wales |

New South Wales have won the Shield 38 times, Victoria 24, South Australia 12, Western Australia 9, Queensland 0, Tasmania 0.

## †McDONALD'S CUP, 1984-85

At Brisbane, October 13. Queensland won by seven wickets. Victoria 202 (D. M. Jones 61, A. I. C. Dodemaide 40; K. C. Wessels four for 24); Queensland 203 for three (R. B. Kerr 92 not out; K. C. Wessels 73).

At Perth, October 13. Western Australia won by 46 runs. Western Australia 218 for five (G. R. Marsh 104 not out); Tasmania 172 (D. C. Boon 50, M. Ray 45; K. H. MacLeay five for 30).

At Brisbane, October 14. South Australia won by six wickets. Queensland 219 for five (G. M. Ritchie 65 not out, R. B. Kerr 50, K. C. Wessels 42); South Australia 223 for four (A. M. J. Hilditch 92 not out, M. D. Haysman 87 not out).

At Perth, October 14. New South Wales won by 14 runs. New South Wales 203 (S. B. Smith 73, D. M. Wellham 54); Western Australia 189 (T. M. Chappell four for 41).

At Devonport, November 3. New South Wales won by 90 runs. New South Wales 170 (D. M. Wellham 58, S. J. Rixon 52; B. P. Patterson four for 23); Tasmania 80.

At Adelaide, November 4. Victoria won by six wickets. South Australia 206 for six (D. W. Hookes 78; Victoria 209 for four (P. A. Hibbert 56, M. D. Taylor 54 not out, S. P. O'Donnell 45 not out).

### Semi-Finals

At Melbourne, December 29. New South Wales won by seven wickets. Victoria 181 for seven; New South Wales 185 for three (J. Dyson 84 not out, Imran Khan 73 not out).

At Adelaide January 5. South Australia won by 123 runs. South Australia 296 for six (D. W. Hookes 101, M. D. Haysman 100 not out, G. A. Bishop 41); Western Australia 173 (G. R. Marsh 48; R. J. McCurdy five for 23).

## FINAL

## †NEW SOUTH WALES v SOUTH AUSTRALIA

At Sydney, February 16. New South Wales won by 88 runs. New South Wales won the toss and batted first.

*Man of the Match*: D. M. Wellham.

### New South Wales

| | |
|---|---|
| J. Dyson c Kelly b Hilditch | 79 |
| W. J. S. Seabrook c Kelly b Carmichael | 5 |
| *D. M. Wellham c Kelly b Prior | 51 |
| P. S. Clifford b Carmichael | 69 |
| Imran Khan c Hookes b Prior | 36 |
| G. R. J. Matthews run out | 10 |
| †G. C. Dyer c O'Connor b Prior | 4 |
| T. M. Chappell not out | 8 |
| P. H. Marks not out | 7 |
| L-b 6, w 2, n-b 1 | 9 |
| 1/12 2/75 3/205 4/220 5/234 6/248 7/264 (7 wkts, 50 overs) | 278 |

M. J. Bennett and D. R. Gilbert did not bat.

Bowling: Brinsley 3–0–15–0; Carmichael 10–0–57–2; Hookes 3–0–23–0; Hilditch 10–0–51–1; Prior 10–0–53–3; Johnston 10–1–47–0; Wundke 4–0–26–0.

### South Australia

| | |
|---|---|
| A. M. J. Hilditch b Matthews | 33 |
| G. A. Bishop c Dyer b Gilbert | 10 |
| *D. W. Hookes c Clifford b Chappell | 16 |
| M. D. Haysman b Gilbert | 44 |
| D. F. G. O'Connor c Marks b Matthews | 3 |
| S. C. Wundke c Marks b Imran | 31 |
| P. Brinsley st Dyer b Matthews | 1 |
| †D. J. Kelly c Clifford b Marks | 30 |
| D. A. Johnston run out | 1 |
| I. R. Carmichael not out | 6 |
| W. Prior b Marks | 0 |
| B 5, l-b 6, w 4 | 15 |
| 1/20 2/45 3/74 4/80 5/135 6/140 7/166 8/167 9/189 (45.5 overs) | 190 |

Bowling: Imran 7–0–20–1; Gilbert 8–0–34–2; Marks 7.5–1–30–2; Chappell 6–0–28–1; Matthews 9–1–29–3; Bennett 8–0–38–0.

Umpires: A. G. Marshall and R. A. French.

## KNOCKOUT COMPETITION WINNERS

**Australasian Knockout:** 1969-70 New Zealand; 1970-71 Western Australia; 1971-72 Victoria; 1972-73 New Zealand.

**Gillette Cup:** 1973-74 Western Australia; 1974-75 New Zealand; 1975-76 Queensland; 1976-77 Western Australia; 1977-78 Western Australia; 1978-79 Tasmania.

**McDonald's Cup:** 1979-80 Victoria; 1980-81 Queensland; 1981-82 Queensland; 1982-83 Western Australia; 1983-84 South Australia; 1984-85 New South Wales.

---

## BAN ON AUSTRALIAN PLAYERS

Sixteen Australians who signed contracts to tour South Africa in 1985-86 and 1986-87 were forthwith banned from Test cricket for three years and from Sheffield Shield cricket for two for having done so. The players were: K. J. Hughes (*captain*), T. M. Alderman, J. Dyson, P. I. Faulkner, M. D. Haysman, T. G. Hogan, R. M. Hogg, T. V. Hohns, J. N. Maguire, R. J. McCurdy, C. G. Rackemann, S. J. Rixon, G. Shipperd, S. B. Smith, M. D. Taylor and G. N. Yallop. *Manager:* B. C. Francis.

# THE ASHES

"In affectionate remembrance of English cricket which died at The Oval, 29th August, 1882. Deeply lamented by a large circle of sorrowing friends and acquaintances, R.I.P. N.B. The body will be cremated and the Ashes taken to Australia."

Australia's first victory on English soil over the full strength of England, on August 29, 1882, inspired a young London journalist, Reginald Shirley Brooks, to write this mock "obituary". It appeared in the *Sporting Times*.

Before England's defeat at The Oval, by 7 runs, arrangements had already been made for the Hon. Ivo Bligh, afterwards Lord Darnley, to lead a team to Australia. Three weeks later they set out, now with the popular objective of recovering the Ashes. In the event, Australia won the first Test by nine wickets, but with England winning the next two it became generally accepted that they brought back the Ashes.

It was long accepted that the real Ashes – a small urn believed to contain the ashes of a bail used in the third match – were presented to Bligh by a group of Melbourne women. At the time of the 1982 centenary of The Oval Test match, however, evidence was produced which suggested that these ashes were the remains of a ball and that they were given to the England captain by Sir William Clarke, the presentation taking place before the Test matches in Australia in 1883. The certain origin of the Ashes, therefore, is the subject of some dispute.

After Lord Darnley's death in 1927, the urn was given to MCC by Lord Darnley's Australian-born widow, Florence. It can be seen in the cricket museum at Lord's, together with a red and gold velvet bag, made specially for it, and the scorecard of the 1882 match.

# FUTURE TOURS

**1986**
Australians to New Zealand
Pakistanis to Sri Lanka
Indians to England
New Zealanders to England
West Indians to Pakistan
Sri Lankans to India
New Zealanders to India and Sri Lanka*
Pakistanis to Australia*

**1986-87**
England and West Indians to Australia
One-day Tournament in Perth, Western Australia*
West Indians to New Zealand
New Zealanders to India and Sri Lanka*

**1987**
Pakistanis to England
Sri Lankans to England
World Cup in India and Pakistan
West Indians to India*

**1987-88**
England to Pakistan and New Zealand
England to Australia*
New Zealanders to Australia

**1988**
Australians to West Indies
West Indians to England
Sri Lankans to England
Australians to Pakistan

**1988-89**
England to India and Sri Lanka
West Indians and Pakistanis to Australia
Pakistanis to New Zealand

**1989**
Indians to West Indies
Australians to England

**1990**
England to West Indies*
Indians to New Zealand

* *Signifies unconfirmed.*

# CRICKET IN SOUTH AFRICA, 1984-85

By PETER SICHEL

Not unexpectedly, Transvaal again demonstrated their overwhelming superiority in the Currie Cup competition, and in so doing laid claim to being one of the outstanding provincial combinations in world cricket. They have proved repeatedly, in both the three-day and the one-day game, that they are not only adaptable but also capable of rising to an occasion. There were times when they appeared vulnerable, notably against Northern Transvaal at the Wanderers and again at Newlands against Western Province, but in each case a first-innings deficit was turned into victory, albeit by narrow margins. Individually, each man produced at least one outstanding performance during the season, but it was as a team that they were so convincing. Special mention, however, is due to Hugh Page, a right-arm fast-medium out-swinger of high potential. His height enabled him to obtain bounce and movement, which repeatedly had the best batsmen in trouble. Supported by the menacing Barbadian, Sylvester Clarke, and the guile of Alan Kourie, Transvaal boasted a three-pronged attack which was rarely, if ever, mastered.

If Transvaal were the team of the year, their northern neighbour surely produced the surprises. Northern Transvaal were a model side, expertly led by Lee Barnard and inspired by the former New Zealand captain, John Reid, now resident there. They were a happy side and a credit to their union, who supported them to the hilt. Often dubbed the Cinderellas of South African cricket, Northern Transvaal confounded the critics. Through dedication and positive cricket, they were rewarded with a place in the final of the Currie Cup in Pretoria. Eric Simons, a right-arm fast-medium bowler, emerged with exceptional credit, and was deservedly named one of South Africa's Cricketers of the Year. Mandy Yachad and Noel Day performed with distinction, the latter being regarded as the best wicket-keeper-batsman in the country. It was only a pity that the Northern Transvaal authorities saw fit to produce a green pitch for the Currie Cup final against Transvaal: the decision misfired badly, the home side being beaten by an innings in two days. This was a disappointing end to an otherwise splendid season.

Western Province had one of their worst seasons in recent years. Much needs to be done to restore them as one of the leading teams. After a good start in November, they went down to Eastern Province by an innings in Port Elizabeth, yet at Newlands, in the next round, they played well enough to restrict Transvaal to a 15-run victory; and later outplayed Northern Transvaal. Thereafter, apart from one or two instances, they could do nothing right. Natal found themselves in a similar situation, often promising much but achieving little. However, there is so much talent in both these sides that they can expect to do better in the future.

Eastern Province again struggled to keep up, and apart from an innings victory over Western Province they disappointed. They were handicapped by the loss of Ken Watson through injury, but their batting gave rise to concern. However, there are several young players of great potential in the province. It was announced that Border and Orange Free State would both be joining the top five teams in the premier competition in 1985-86.

The Castle Bowl again produced an extremely close finish, Transvaal B, as if to underline the strength and depth of cricket in that province, managing to edge out Orange Free State by a single point. Well led by Graham Johnson of Kent they produced a polished all-round performance. Eastern Province B, thanks to the emergence of some young players of great potential, showed a marked improvement, but Western Province B and Natal B, like their senior counterparts, were disappointing. Griqualand West, thanks largely to overseas imports, played well on occasions, but again failed to win a match.

The potential shown by Mark Rushmere of Eastern Province was an encouraging aspect of the South African season. Another to show consistency was Corrie van Zyl of the Orange Free State, who succeeded in capturing 50 wickets at 13.52, achieving ten wickets in a match twice and five in an innings on no fewer than five occasions. There were several other notable performances, including a hundred in each innings by Terry Reid of Eastern Province and a career-best nine for 72 by Gordon Parsons, the Leicestershire professional, playing for Boland. For Orange Free State, Alvin Kallicharran scored 623 runs at just under 70, failing only twice in ten innings.

Of other overseas professionals, both Laurie Potter and Paul Romaines batted well for Griqualand West, and Greg Thomas bowled fast and effectively on occasions. Peter Willey had a season he would probably want to forget, averaging only 10.81 with the bat and slightly more than 36 with the ball.

Transvaal again won the Nissan Shield, but it was Border who caused the stir by defeating Eastern Province in the first round at East London and then restricting Transvaal to a four-wicket win in the first leg of the semi-final. Western Province reached the final, which coincided with their bad slump and they were comprehensively defeated by nine wickets.

The impact of non-white players in the Currie Cup and Castle Bowl was illustrated by the fact that five of them turned out for Boland during the season, while Ronnie Engelbrecht was again a regular member of the Griqualand West team. There were also two in the representative South African Schools team, chosen after the Nuffield Week, namely Craig Marais and Shukri Conrad. Thanks not least to the John Passmore Cricket Week for African schools, there should soon be more Africans emerging on the scene.

## FIRST-CLASS AVERAGES, 1984-85

### BATTING

(Qualification: 5 innings, 400 runs, average 30.00)

| | *M* | *I* | *NO* | *R* | *HI* | *100s* | *Avge* |
|---|---|---|---|---|---|---|---|
| M. W. Rushmere (*E. Province B*) | 5 | 7 | 2 | 449 | 119* | 2 | 89.80 |
| A. I. Kallicharran (*OFS*) | 6 | 11 | 2 | 623 | 110 | 1 | 69.22 |
| C. E. B. Rice (*Transvaal*) | 10 | 15 | 2 | 629 | 126 | 3 | 48.38 |
| A. G. Elgar (*W. Province B*) | 5 | 10 | 0 | 475 | 97 | 0 | 47.50 |
| S. J. Cook (*Transvaal*) | 10 | 15 | 0 | 706 | 140 | 2 | 47.06 |
| L. Potter (*Griqualand W.*) | 6 | 12 | 2 | 462 | 165* | 1 | 46.20 |
| P. N. Kirsten (*W. Province*) | 8 | 14 | 2 | 511 | 133 | 2 | 42.58 |
| P. W. Romaines (*Griqualand W.*) | 6 | 12 | 1 | 462 | 170* | 1 | 42.00 |
| D. Bestall (*Natal*) | 9 | 15 | 3 | 468 | 134* | 1 | 39.00 |
| D. P. le Roux (*Boland*) | 6 | 11 | 0 | 425 | 71 | 0 | 38.63 |
| R. G. Pollock (*Transvaal*) | 10 | 15 | 0 | 567 | 114 | 1 | 37.80 |
| M. Yachad (*N. Transvaal*) | 10 | 20 | 0 | 751 | 124 | 2 | 37.55 |
| I. M. Wingreen (*W. Province B*) | 6 | 11 | 0 | 405 | 83 | 0 | 36.81 |
| H. R. Fotheringham (*Transvaal*) | 10 | 15 | 0 | 549 | 184 | 2 | 36.60 |
| B. J. Whitfield (*Natal*) | 9 | 16 | 2 | 465 | 96* | 0 | 33.21 |
| T. R. Madsen (*Natal*) | 9 | 14 | 1 | 415 | 111 | 1 | 31.92 |
| A. P. Kuiper (*W. Province*) | 9 | 15 | 0 | 477 | 87 | 0 | 31.80 |
| L. Seeff (*W. Province*) | 9 | 17 | 1 | 505 | 76 | 0 | 31.56 |
| P. H. Rayner (*W. Province*) | 9 | 17 | 2 | 457 | 69* | 0 | 30.46 |

* *Signifies not out.*

## BOWLING

(Qualification: 25 wickets, average 25.00)

| | *R* | *W* | *BB* | *Avge* |
|---|---|---|---|---|
| S. T. Clarke (*Transvaal*) | 738 | 58 | 5-8 | 12.72 |
| G. J. Parsons (*Boland*) | 515 | 39 | 9-72 | 13.20 |
| C. J. P. G. van Zyl (*OFS*) | 676 | 50 | 8-84 | 13.52 |
| E. O. Simons (*N. Transvaal*) | 727 | 51 | 6-26 | 14.25 |
| H. A. Page (*Transvaal/Transvaal B*) | 620 | 41 | 6-26 | 15.12 |
| E. A. Moseley (*E. Province*) | 557 | 34 | 5-48 | 16.38 |
| J. J. Hooper (*Transvaal B*) | 460 | 28 | 5-29 | 16.42 |
| G. L. Ackermann (*N. Transvaal/N. Transvaal B*) | 482 | 27 | 7-69 | 17.85 |
| C. D. Mitchley (*Transvaal/Transvaal B*) | 558 | 31 | 5-50 | 18.00 |
| A. J. Kourie (*Transvaal*) | 1,009 | 50 | 7-94 | 20.18 |
| G. S. le Roux (*W. Province*) | 624 | 27 | 4-46 | 23.11 |
| A. M. Ferreira (*N. Transvaal*) | 724 | 29 | 6-23 | 24.96 |

*Note:* Runs debited to these bowlers do not include wides and no-balls.

## CASTLE CURRIE CUP, 1984-85

| | | | | | *Bonus Points* | | *Total* |
|---|---|---|---|---|---|---|---|
| | *Played* | *Won* | *Lost* | *Drawn* | *Batting* | *Bowling* | *Points* |
| Transvaal | 8 | 7 | 0 | 1 | 34 | 40 | 144 |
| Northern Transvaal | 8 | 3 | 4 | 1 | 11 | 31 | 72 |
| Western Province | 8 | 2 | 3 | 3 | 21 | 30 | 71 |
| Natal | 8 | 1 | 3 | 4 | 19 | 27 | 56 |
| Eastern Province | 8 | 1 | 4 | 3 | 9 | 23 | 42 |

***Semi-finals:*** *Transvaal beat Natal by an innings and 4 runs. Northern Transvaal beat Western Province by eight wickets.*
***Final:*** *Transvaal beat Northern Transvaal by an innings and 5 runs.*

## NORTHERN TRANSVAAL v TRANSVAAL

At Berea Park, Pretoria, November 9, 10, 12. Transvaal won by five wickets. Transvaal 20 pts, Northern Transvaal 5 pts.

### Transvaal

| | | | |
|---|---|---|---|
| S. J. Cook c Day b Barnard | 52 | – c Day b Ferreira | 19 |
| H. R. Fotheringham c Day b Ackermann | 39 | – c Geringer b Simons | 0 |
| M. S. Venter c Day b Ferreira | 22 | – c Day b Simons | 23 |
| R. G. Pollock c Day b Weideman | 114 | – run out | 6 |
| *C. E. B. Rice not out | 102 | – b Simons | 9 |
| K. A. McKenzie c Simons b Ackermann | 10 | – not out | 6 |
| A. J. Kourie lbw b Geringer | 26 | – not out | 0 |
| †R. V. Jennings b Geringer | 0 | | |
| C. D. Mitchley c Ackermann b Ferreira | 21 | | |
| S. T. Clarke not out | 4 | | |
| B 4, l-b 7, n-b 7 | 18 | W 1, n-b 3 | 4 |
| 1/97 2/106 3/202 4/254 5/277 6/354 7/354 8/391 | (8 wkts dec.) 408 | 1/7 2/41 3/47 4/51 5/63 | (5 wkts) 67 |

N. V. Radford did not bat.

Bowling: *First Innings*—Weideman 30–7–82–1; Simons 14–2–87–0; Ferreira 36–7–128–2; Ackermann 8–0–32–2; Barnard 22–8–42–1; Geringer 5–1–19–2. *Second Innings*—Weideman 4–0–16–0; Simons 7–0–38–3; Ferreira 3.1–2–9–1.

### Northern Transvaal

| | | | |
|---|---|---|---|
| M. Yachad lbw b Kourie | 124 | – c McKenzie b Clarke | 4 |
| V. F. du Preez c Rice b Clarke | 12 | – c Jennings b Radford | 10 |
| K. D. Verdoorn c Rice b Kourie | 21 | – c Jennings b Mitchley | 1 |
| †N. T. Day c Jennings b Kourie | 15 | – c Clarke b Radford | 12 |
| *L. J. Barnard c Fotheringham b Clarke | 6 | – c Cook b Kourie | 21 |
| A. M. Ferreira b Kourie | 8 | – c Jennings b Radford | 30 |
| P. J. A. Visagie c and b Kourie | 13 | – c Venter b Clarke | 38 |
| A. Geringer c Jennings b Kourie | 14 | – c Jennings b Mitchley | 70 |
| I. F. N. Weideman c Kourie b Mitchley | 5 | – c Jennings b Clarke | 5 |
| G. L. Ackermann b Kourie | 0 | – c and b Kourie | 2 |
| E. O. Simons not out | 3 | – not out | 41 |
| L-b 8, w 1, n-b 2 | 11 | B 2, l-b 3, n-b 2 | 7 |
| 1/33 2/110 3/148 4/165 5/193 6/195 7/223 8/224 9/224 | 232 | 1/4 2/11 3/26 4/31 5/79 6/83 7/151 8/159 9/174 | 241 |

Bowling: *First Innings*—Clarke 16–3–37–2; Mitchley 5.2–1–35–1; Kourie 33–6–94–7; Radford 16–2–55–0. *Second Innings*—Clarke 14–4–64–3; Mitchley 12.2–5–40–2; Kourie 27–7–67–2; Radford 12–1–63–3.

Umpires: G. Baker and D. A. Sansom.

*Wides and no-balls not debited to bowlers' analyses.*

## WESTERN PROVINCE v EASTERN PROVINCE

At Newlands, Cape Town, November 16, 17. Western Province won by five wickets. Western Province 21 pts, Eastern Province 4 pts.

### Western Province

| | | | |
|---|---|---|---|
| L. Seeff c Richardson b Moseley | 30 | – c Willey b Watson | 0 |
| S. F. A. Bacchus c Willey b Brickett | 18 | – c Howell b Moseley | 25 |
| C. M. Wells c Willey b Moseley | 0 | – not out | 3 |
| P. H. Rayner c Shaw b Brickett | 64 | – c Richardson b Moseley | 7 |
| R. F. Pienaar c Richardson b Moseley | 32 | – c Richardson b Moseley | 5 |
| *A. P. Kuiper c Howell b Shaw | 87 | – c Daniell b Moseley | 0 |
| G. S. le Roux c Armitage b Shaw | 21 | – not out | 4 |
| S. T. Jefferies c Shaw b Brickett | 31 | | |
| †R. J. Ryall c Richardson b Moseley | 7 | | |
| D. Norman not out | 3 | | |
| L-b 8, w 1, n-b 11 | 20 | W 1 | 1 |
| 1/49 2/53 3/53 4/127 5/199 6/260 7/298 8/310 9/313 | (9 wkts dec.) 313 | 1/1 2/33 3/38 4/38 5/40 | (5 wkts) 45 |

D. L. Hobson did not bat.

Bowling: *First Innings*—Moseley 20.4–8–33–4; Watson 19–1–79–0; Brickett 17–2–63–3; Cowley 5–0–33–0; Shaw 11–3–36–2; Willey 14–2–49–0. *Second Innings*—Moseley 7–3–13–4; Watson 6.4–0–31–1.

### Eastern Province

| | | | |
|---|---|---|---|
| †D. J. Richardson c Ryall b le Roux | 37 | – c Ryall b le Roux | 13 |
| R. L. S. Armitage c Ryall b Jefferies | 5 | – c Seeff b Hobson | 18 |
| D. H. Howell b Jefferies | 10 | – b Jefferies | 2 |
| T. G. Shaw c Ryall b le Roux | 2 | – b Norman | 26 |

| | | | |
|---|---|---|---|
| P. Willey c Bacchus b le Roux | 2 | c Ryall b Wells | 2 |
| D. J. Callaghan b Hobson | 23 | c Bacchus b le Roux | 25 |
| I. K. Daniell lbw b Jefferies | 1 | c Rayner b Jefferies | 13 |
| *G. S. Cowley lbw b Hobson | 15 | hit wkt b le Roux | 56 |
| E. A. Moseley c Norman b Hobson | 8 | c Jefferies b le Roux | 17 |
| D. J. Brickett lbw b Norman | 11 | run out | 26 |
| W. K. Watson not out | 7 | not out | 5 |
| L-b 4, w 1, n-b 7 | 12 | B 1, l-b 11, w 2, n-b 4 | 18 |
| 1/19 2/37 3/47 4/55 5/67 6/68 7/96 8/110 9/118 | 133 | 1/17 2/22 3/30 4/33 5/60 6/108 7/140 8/157 9/203 | 221 |

Bowling: *First Innings*—le Roux 11–2–30–3; Jefferies 12–4–25–3; Hobson 12–1–39–3; Norman 5.3–0–9–1; Kuiper 6–0–18–0. *Second Innings*—le Roux 16–3–49–4; Jefferies 12–0–33–2; Hobson 17–3–74–1; Norman 5–2–15–1; Kuiper 5–1–13–0; Wells 5–0–19–1.

Umpires: E. Eveleigh and O. R. Schoof.

*Wides and no-balls not debited to bowlers' analyses.*

## NORTHERN TRANSVAAL v NATAL

At Berea Park, Pretoria, November 23, 24, 26. Northern Transvaal won by six wickets. Northern Transvaal 20 pts, Natal 5 pts.

### Natal

| | | | |
|---|---|---|---|
| B. J. Whitfield c Morris b Grobler | 15 | c Yachad b Grobler | 1 |
| M. B. Logan c Day b Ferreira | 27 | c Simons b Weideman | 13 |
| R. M. Bentley c Day b Grobler | 2 | c Day b Weideman | 4 |
| R. A. Smith c Day b Simons | 21 | c Day b Simons | 44 |
| C. L. King c Visagie b Grobler | 0 | b Grobler | 21 |
| †T. R. Madsen c Morris b Grobler | 43 | c Day b Grobler | 17 |
| D. Bestall c Day b Simons | 16 | not out | 96 |
| *P. B. Clift c Yachad b Simons | 30 | run out | 1 |
| K. R. Cooper lbw b Ferreira | 6 | c Day b Weideman | 5 |
| H. L. Alleyne c Day b Simons | 3 | b Grobler | 9 |
| I. Ebrahim not out | 0 | c Verdoorn b Grobler | 4 |
| L-b 4, w 1, n-b 2 | 7 | B 15, l-b 15 | 30 |
| 1/43 2/43 3/45 4/49 5/81 6/110 7/144 8/159 9/170 | 170 | 1/17 2/34 3/116 4/168 5/190 6/191 7/200 8/207 9/225 | 245 |

Bowling: *First Innings*—Weideman 15–7–30–0; Simons 17.2–3–43–4; Ferreira 16–4–58–2; Grobler 16–5–32–4. *Second Innings*—Weideman 16–1–58–3; Simons 11–2–33–1; Ferreira 8–1–30–0; Grobler 20.1–0–65–5; Morris 13–6–29–0.

### Northern Transvaal

| | | | |
|---|---|---|---|
| M. Yachad c Madsen b Cooper | 97 | c King b Alleyne | 12 |
| P. J. A. Visagie c Madsen b Cooper | 26 | c Cooper b Alleyne | 11 |
| K. D. Verdoorn lbw b Alleyne | 7 | c Logan b Alleyne | 6 |
| †N. T. Day b Bentley | 69 | not out | 34 |
| E. O. Simons c Bentley b Cooper | 1 | | |
| *L. J. Barnard c Madsen b Clift | 11 | c King b Clift | 20 |
| A. M. Ferreira b Clift | 4 | not out | 31 |
| A. Geringer c Madsen b Cooper | 38 | | |
| W. F. Morris b Bentley | 9 | | |
| I. F. N. Weideman c sub b Cooper | 4 | | |
| G. Grobler not out | 10 | | |
| B 7, l-b 4, n-b 6 | 17 | B 2, l-b 4, w 4, n-b 2 | 12 |
| 1/41 2/75 3/171 4/183 5/214 6/222 7/228 8/243 9/256 | 293 | 1/18 2/30 3/30 4/76 | (4 wkts) 126 |

Bowling: *First Innings*—Clift 25–4–74–2; Alleyne 9–0–42–1; Cooper 26.3–2–80–5; King 4–0–21–0; Ebrahim 11–2–40–0; Bentley 8–1–19–2. *Second Innings*—Clift 7–1–29–1; Alleyne 13.4–2–42–3; Cooper 14–2–32–0; King 2–0–11–0.

Umpires: J. W. Peacock and P. Smit.

*Wides and no-balls not debited to bowlers' analyses.*

## TRANSVAAL v EASTERN PROVINCE

At Wanderers, Johannesburg, November 24, 25, 26. Transvaal won by an innings and 143 runs. Transvaal 22 pts, Eastern Province 3 pts.

### Eastern Province

| | | | |
|---|---|---|---|
| I. K. Daniell c Venter b Kourie | 60 | – b Rice | 29 |
| †D. J. Richardson c Rice b Clarke | 8 | – c Jennings b Clarke | 0 |
| D. H. Howell b Kourie | 4 | – c Pollock b Hanley | 1 |
| P. Willey c Kourie b Hanley | 0 | – c Jennings b Hanley | 2 |
| T. B. Reid lbw b Kourie | 16 | – c Rice b Page | 22 |
| D. J. Callaghan c Venter b Clarke | 12 | – b Rice | 0 |
| *G. S. Cowley not out | 12 | – retired hurt | 10 |
| T. G. Shaw c Pollock b Clarke | 0 | – c Jennings b Page | 3 |
| D. J. Brickett b Clarke | 0 | – hit wkt b Hanley | 35 |
| E. A. Moseley b Clarke | 0 | – b Clarke | 16 |
| M. K. van Vuuren b Kourie | 0 | – not out | 0 |
| L-b 5, w 3, n-b 4 | 12 | B 4, l-b 5, w 5, n-b 4 | 18 |
| 1/47 2/77 3/78 4/78 5/112 6/112 7/113 8/123 9/123 | 124 | 1/3 2/21 3/31 4/64 5/64 6/64 7/77 8/136 9/136 | 136 |

Bowling: *First Innings*—Clarke 14–5–29–5; Hanley 9–2–28–1; Page 7–1–21–0; Kourie 17–7–34–4. *Second Innings*—Clarke 8.1–1–25–2; Hanley 12–4–19–3; Page 10–3–44–2; Kourie 2–1–12–0; Rice 8–4–18–2.

### Transvaal

| | |
|---|---|
| S. J. Cook c Richardson b Moseley | 107 |
| H. R. Fotheringham c Brickett b van Vuuren | 5 |
| M. S. Venter lbw b Moseley | 3 |
| R. G. Pollock c Howell b Willey | 26 |
| *C. E. B. Rice c van Vuuren b Shaw | 121 |
| K. A. McKenzie b van Vuuren | 0 |
| A. J. Kourie run out | 78 |
| H. A. Page c Cowley b van Vuuren | 9 |
| †R. V. Jennings not out | 9 |
| S. T. Clarke b Cowley | 6 |
| B 4, l-b 18, w 13, n-b 4 | 39 |
| 1/34 2/52 3/102 4/215 5/216 6/330 7/382 8/397 9/403 (9 wkts dec.) | 403 |

R. W. Hanley did not bat.

Bowling: Moseley 23–2–76–2; van Vuuren 24–2–85–3; Cowley 14.4–1–67–1; Willey 16–4–44–1; Brickett 14–1–49–0; Shaw 11–1–43–1.

Umpires: S. G. Moore and D. H. Bezuidenhout.

*Wides and no-balls not debited to bowlers' analyses.*

## EASTERN PROVINCE v NATAL

At St George's Park, Port Elizabeth, December 14, 15, 17. Drawn. Eastern Province 6 pts, Natal 4 pts.

## Eastern Province

| First innings | | Second innings | |
|---|---|---|---|
| I. K. Daniell b Clift | 40 | c Madsen b Lever | 12 |
| P. Willey c Bestall b Wulfsohn | 56 | lbw b Clift | 1 |
| R. L. S. Armitage c Madsen b Wulfsohn | 27 | | |
| M. Michau c Wulfsohn b Bentley | 71 | lbw b Lever | 103 |
| †D. J. Richardson c Bentley b Wulfsohn | 40 | lbw b Clift | 0 |
| D. J. Callaghan c Smith b Clift | 16 | c Daniels b Lever | 0 |
| *G. S. Cowley not out | 16 | hit wkt b Clift | 40 |
| M. W. Rushmere c Madsen b Clift | 1 | lbw b Clift | 0 |
| E. A. Moseley b Clift | 10 | not out | 3 |
| T. G. Shaw not out | 1 | c Robinson b Lever | 10 |
| M. K. van Vuuren (did not bat) | | not out | 1 |
| L-b 7, w 10, n-b 4 | 21 | L-b 7, w 1, n-b 6 | 14 |
| 1/88 2/135 3/142 4/242 5/264 6/280 7/281 8/297 | (8 wkts dec.) 299 | 1/11 2/11 3/27 4/34 5/114 6/114 7/180 8/184 | (8 wkts dec.) 184 |

Bowling: *First Innings*—Lever 22-5-64-0; Packer 9-3-32-0; Wulfsohn 19-4-67-3; Clift 25-6-52-4; Bentley 16-7-31-1; Daniels 7-3-26-0; Robinson 1-0-6-0. *Second Innings*—Lever 22-5-58-4; Packer 6-1-21-0; Wulfsohn 5-0-32-0; Clift 24-7-46-4; Bentley 2-0-13-0.

## Natal

| First innings | | Second innings | |
|---|---|---|---|
| B. J. Whitfield c van Vuuren b Shaw | 24 | c Daniell b van Vuuren | 5 |
| R. A. Smith st Richardson b Shaw | 69 | b van Vuuren | 8 |
| R. M. Bentley b Willey | 19 | not out | 61 |
| D. Bestall lbw b Cowley | 34 | c Rushmere b Willey | 6 |
| †T. R. Madsen c Cowley b Shaw | 23 | c Richardson b van Vuuren | 10 |
| N. P. Daniels c Richardson b Shaw | 2 | b Moseley | 31 |
| *P. B. Clift lbw b Cowley | 32 | b Moseley | 0 |
| C. Wulfsohn c Daniell b Shaw | 0 | b van Vuuren | 0 |
| K. Robinson b Moseley | 8 | | |
| T. J. Packer st Richardson b Shaw | 2 | | |
| J. K. Lever not out | 1 | not out | 0 |
| B 2, l-b 21, w 8, n-b 12 | 43 | B 1, l-b 6, w 3 | 10 |
| 1/87 2/147 3/175 4/188 5/194 6/245 7/245 8/249 9/255 | 257 | 1/12 2/21 3/35 4/62 5/128 6/128 7/131 | (7 wkts) 131 |

Bowling: *First Innings*—Moseley 25.5-12-26-1; van Vuuren 17-4-36-0; Cowley 17-2-40-2; Armitage 6-1-15-0; Shaw 20-5-42-6; Willey 17-4-43-1; Callaghan 3-1-12-0. *Second Innings*—Moseley 15.4-4-27-2; van Vuuren 20-8-45-4; Shaw 11-3-19-0; Willey 16-5-30-1.

Umpires: S. G. Moore and L. Rautenbach.

*Wides and no-balls not debited to bowlers' analyses.*

## TRANSVAAL v NORTHERN TRANSVAAL

At Wanderers, Johannesburg, December 14, 15, 16. Transvaal won by 55 runs. Transvaal 15 pts, Northern Transvaal 5 pts.

## Transvaal

| First innings | | Second innings | |
|---|---|---|---|
| S. J. Cook c Day b Ferreira | 80 | c Day b Simons | 1 |
| H. R. Fotheringham b Simons | 1 | c Geringer b Grobler | 20 |
| C. R. Norris c Geringer b Simons | 9 | lbw b Simons | 0 |
| R. G. Pollock b Grobler | 3 | c du Preez b Grobler | 9 |
| *C. E. B. Rice c Day b Simons | 4 | c Visagie b Grobler | 17 |

| | | | |
|---|---|---|---|
| K. A. McKenzie lbw b Ferreira | 16 | – lbw b Weideman | 32 |
| A. J. Kourie c Barnard b Ferreira | 10 | – b Weideman | 43 |
| H. A. Page c Day b Weideman | 0 | – lbw b Grobler | 35 |
| †R. V. Jennings c Verdoorn b Ferreira | 5 | – c Day b Simons | 8 |
| N. V. Radford lbw b Simons | 3 | – not out | 10 |
| S. T. Clarke not out | 7 | – c Grobler b Ferreira | 12 |
| L-b 15, w 1 | 16 | B 7, l-b 11, n-b 5 | 23 |
| 1/6 2/46 3/51 4/58 5/96 6/117 7/120 8/143 9/146 | 154 | 1/3 2/3 3/25 4/50 5/55 6/121 7/142 8/168 9/182 | 210 |

Bowling: *First Innings*—Weideman 13–1–53–1; Simons 14–3–34–4; Grobler 10–1–25–1; Ferreira 14.5–6–26–4. *Second Innings*—Weideman 18–6–32–2; Simons 16–4–42–3; Grobler 19.5–6–70–4; Ferreira 13–3–43–1.

### Northern Transvaal

| | | | |
|---|---|---|---|
| M. Yachad b Clarke | 5 | – lbw b Radford | 2 |
| V. F. du Preez c Kourie b Clarke | 33 | – c Jennings b Clarke | 1 |
| K. D. Verdoorn lbw b Norris | 23 | – lbw b Clarke | 0 |
| †N. T. Day lbw b Radford | 7 | – lbw b Clarke | 55 |
| *L. J. Barnard c Jennings b Page | 16 | – c Kourie b Clarke | 11 |
| A. Geringer c Kourie b Radford | 4 | – b Radford | 7 |
| A. M. Ferreira c Jennings b Clarke | 19 | – c Clarke b Norris | 11 |
| P. J. A. Visagie b Radford | 25 | – c Pollock b Norris | 4 |
| I. F. N. Weideman c Jennings b Clarke | 0 | – c McKenzie b Page | 16 |
| E. O. Simons c Jennings b Clarke | 12 | – not out | 27 |
| G. Grobler not out | 3 | – c Kourie b Clarke | 3 |
| B 1, l-b 8, n-b 5 | 14 | L-b 9, n-b 2 | 11 |
| 1/12 2/59 3/74 4/86 5/94 6/106 7/127 8/133 9/155 | 161 | 1/3 2/3 3/7 4/27 5/38 6/54 7/66 8/85 9/140 | 148 |

Bowling: *First Innings*—Clarke 18–4–38–5; Page 12–2–30–1; Radford 12.2–4–37–3; Norris 7–0–26–1; Kourie 4–1–16–0. *Second Innings*—Clarke 18–4–45–5; Page 6–1–24–1; Radford 16–5–44–2; Norris 7–0–24–2.

Umpires: D. D. Schoof and F. E. Wood.

*Wides and no-balls not debited to bowlers' analyses.*

## EASTERN PROVINCE v WESTERN PROVINCE

At St George's Park, Port Elizabeth, December 26, 27, 28. Eastern Province won by an innings and 3 runs. Eastern Province 17 pts, Western Province 1 pt.

### Western Province

| | | | |
|---|---|---|---|
| L. Seeff c Richardson b van Vuuren | 10 | – lbw b Moseley | 0 |
| S. F. A. Bacchus c Michau b Moseley | 12 | – b Moseley | 1 |
| P. N. Kirsten c Richardson b Moseley | 4 | – lbw b Moseley | 0 |
| P. H. Rayner c Richardson b Moseley | 0 | – c Daniell b Shaw | 69 |
| R. F. Pienaar c Richardson b Moseley | 61 | – lbw b Bauermeister | 34 |
| *A. P. Kuiper b Shaw | 24 | – c Shaw b Moseley | 55 |
| S. T. Jefferies c Moseley b Willey | 19 | – c van Vuuren b Bauermeister | 71 |
| †R. J. Ryall c Richardson b Shaw | 5 | – c Cowley b Moseley | 0 |
| D. Norman c Daniell b Shaw | 2 | – c Richardson b Bauermeister | 7 |
| D. L. Hobson c Amm b Bauermeister | 21 | – c Armitage b Bauermeister | 4 |
| B. Matthews not out | 0 | – not out | 0 |
| B 3, l-b 5, n-b 1 | 9 | L-b 8, w 1 | 9 |
| 1/23 2/25 3/27 4/28 5/56 6/93 7/116 8/128 9/156 | 167 | 1/0 2/0 3/9 4/94 5/124 6/220 7/222 8/244 9/246 | 250 |

Bowling: *First Innings*—Moseley 20.2–6–48–4; van Vuuren 12–0–47–1; Shaw 15–5–44–3; Willey 5–3–8–1; Bauermeister 6–2–11–1. *Second Innings*—Moseley 29–13–48–5; van Vuuren 15–5–30–0; Shaw 23–11–55–1; Willey 20–9–34–0; Bauermeister 21–2–66–4; Armitage 2–1–2–0; Cowley 3–1–6–0.

## Eastern Province

| | |
|---|---|
| I. K. Daniell lbw b Kuiper | 95 |
| P. G. Amm lbw b Norman | 74 |
| R. L. S. Armitage not out | 100 |
| M. Michau b Jefferies | 18 |
| †D. J. Richardson c Kirsten b Matthews | 63 |
| P. Willey c Hobson b Jefferies | 15 |
| *G. S. Cowley not out | 28 |
| B 2, l-b 9, n-b 16 | 27 |
| 1/162 2/190 3/245 4/353 5/380 | (5 wkts dec.) 420 |

T. G. Shaw, K. G. Bauermeister, E. A. Moseley and M. K. van Vuuren did not bat.

Bowling: Jefferies 33–3–104–2; Matthews 20–3–61–1; Hobson 28–7–71–0; Kuiper 16–3–45–1; Kirsten 22–4–65–0; Norman 16–3–47–1.

Umpires: L. Rautenbach and D. D. Schoof.

*Wides and no-balls not debited to bowlers' analyses.*

# TRANSVAAL v NATAL

At Wanderers, Johannesburg, December 26, 27, 28. Transvaal won by six wickets. Transvaal 17 pts, Natal 8 pts.

## Natal

| | | | |
|---|---|---|---|
| B. J. Whitfield c Kourie b Radford | 44 | b Radford | 11 |
| R. A. Smith c Jennings b Radford | 53 | c Fotheringham b Page | 11 |
| R. M. Bentley b Kourie | 34 | b Clarke | 13 |
| D. Bestall c Clarke b Page | 10 | lbw b Kourie | 36 |
| C. L. King c Page b Radford | 2 | b Kourie | 34 |
| M. B. Logan c Jennings b Page | 66 | c Kourie b Clarke | 3 |
| †T. R. Madsen c Kourie b Clarke | 1 | c Clarke b Page | 39 |
| *P. B. Clift c Kourie b Clarke | 0 | b Kourie | 4 |
| C. Wulfsohn b Kourie | 0 | c Norris b Kourie | 5 |
| J. K. Lever c Cook b Clarke | 16 | b Kourie | 4 |
| T. J. Packer not out | 0 | not out | 0 |
| B 1, l-b 10, w 4 | 15 | B 1, l-b 7, w 2 | 10 |
| 1/98 2/114 3/119 4/120 5/126 6/126 7/195 8/199 9/241 | 241 | 1/22 2/25 3/45 4/104 5/107 6/113 7/142 8/152 9/170 | 170 |

Bowling: *First Innings*—Clarke 16.3–5–20–3; Radford 26–5–70–3; Kourie 19–5–53–2; Page 19–3–52–2; Norris 7–1–31–0. *Second Innings*—Clarke 17–8–24–2; Radford 14–5–32–1; Kourie 26.5–6–69–5; Page 14–3–35–2.

## Transvaal

| | | | |
|---|---|---|---|
| S. J. Cook c King b Clift | 25 | lbw b Clift | 76 |
| H. R. Fotheringham c Madsen b Clift | 12 | lbw b Lever | 6 |
| C. R. Norris lbw b Lever | 6 | c Bestall b Clift | 14 |
| R. G. Pollock c Madsen b Packer | 93 | c Madsen b Lever | 41 |
| *C. E. B. Rice c Madsen b Clift | 9 | not out | 46 |
| K. A. McKenzie c Madsen b Wulfsohn | 35 | not out | 13 |
| A. J. Kourie c Smith b Clift | 1 | | |

| | | | |
|---|---|---|---|
| H. A. Page lbw b Lever | 10 | | |
| †R. V. Jennings c Bentley b Lever | 0 | | |
| S. T. Clarke not out | 0 | | |
| N. V. Radford c Madsen b Packer | 0 | | |
| B 6, l-b 7, w 2, n-b 1 | 16 | L-b 4, w 2, n-b 3 | 9 |
| 1/38 2/53 3/59 4/83 5/151 6/170 7/205 8/205 9/207 | 207 | 1/36 2/66 3/135 4/175 | (4 wkts) 205 |

Bowling: *First Innings*—Lever 23–7–41–3; Packer 12.5–2–42–2; Clift 22–4–55–4; Wulfsohn 11–0–49–1; King 3–0–4–0. *Second Innings*—Lever 23–7–61–2; Packer 7–1–49–0; Clift 17–5–42–2; Wulfsohn 4–0–20–0; King 3–0–24–0.

Umpires: A. J. Norton and H. R. Martin.

*Wides and no-balls not debited to bowlers' analyses.*

## NATAL v NORTHERN TRANSVAAL

At Kingsmead, Durban, December 31, January 1, 2. Natal won by eight wickets. Natal 18 pts, Northern Transvaal 3 pts.

### Northern Transvaal

| | | | |
|---|---|---|---|
| M. Yachad c King b Packer | 4 | c Whitfield b Packer | 60 |
| V. F. du Preez lbw b Cooper | 12 | lbw b Packer | 0 |
| K. D. Verdoorn lbw b King | 34 | lbw b Packer | 4 |
| †N. T. Day c Madsen b Lever | 0 | lbw b Packer | 15 |
| *L. J. Barnard run out | 28 | b Lever | 55 |
| A. Geringer c King b Cooper | 14 | c Madsen b Lever | 13 |
| A. M. Ferreira b Packer | 52 | b Lever | 57 |
| P. J. A. Visagie c Cooper b Clift | 28 | c Scott b Packer | 23 |
| I. F. N. Weideman c Bentley b Clift | 6 | run out | 2 |
| E. O. Simons not out | 5 | not out | 30 |
| G. Grobler b Clift | 0 | b Clift | 8 |
| L-b 3, n-b 7 | 10 | B 4, l-b 15, w 3, n-b 6 | 28 |
| 1/5 2/18 3/23 4/71 5/97 6/120 7/181 8/182 9/193 | 193 | 1/0 2/6 3/65 4/132 5/160 6/171 7/229 8/232 9/265 | 295 |

Bowling: *First Innings*—Lever 16–5–49–1; Packer 14–1–42–2; Cooper 14–6–33–2; Clift 8.4–0–39–3; King 4–1–20–1. *Second Innings*—Lever 38–15–74–3; Packer 25–6–90–5; Cooper 6–0–28–0; Clift 25.2–9–38–1; King 1–0–9–0; Bentley 14–4–28–0.

### Natal

| | | | |
|---|---|---|---|
| B. J. Whitfield c Day b Simons | 76 | c Yachad b Simons | 18 |
| R. A. Smith b Simons | 7 | b Ferreira | 15 |
| R. M. Bentley b Simons | 10 | not out | 17 |
| D. Bestall run out | 46 | not out | 12 |
| C. L. King b Geringer | 75 | | |
| D. A. Scott b Ferreira | 29 | | |
| †T. R. Madsen lbw b Simons | 111 | | |
| *P. B. Clift lbw b Geringer | 15 | | |
| K. R. Cooper c Geringer b Barnard | 19 | | |
| J. K. Lever not out | 14 | | |
| B 3, l-b 12, n-b 3 | 18 | L-b 5, n-b 2 | 7 |
| 1/12 2/36 3/142 4/161 5/195 6/307 7/349 8/380 9/420 | (9 wkts dec.) 420 | 1/34 2/36 | (2 wkts) 69 |

T. J. Packer did not bat.

Bowling: *First Innings*—Weideman 18–3–82–0; Simons 27.2–8–74–4; Grobler 27–5–83–0; Ferreira 27–2–73–1; Barnard 18–4–54–1; Geringer 7–0–36–2. *Second Innings*—Simons 8–2–19–1; Grobler 5–0–20–0; Ferreira 7.1–1–21–1; Yachad 1–0–2–0.

Umpires: O. R. Schoof and D. H. Bezuidenhout.

*Wides and no-balls not debited to bowlers' analyses.*

## WESTERN PROVINCE v TRANSVAAL

At Newlands, Cape Town, January 1, 2, 3. Transvaal won by 15 runs. Transvaal 18 pts, Western Province 8 pts.

### Transvaal

| | | | |
|---|---|---|---|
| S. J. Cook c Ryall b Norman | 18 | c Ryall b Norman | 19 |
| C. R. Norris c Bacchus b Jefferies | 55 | c Ryall b Jefferies | 10 |
| H. R. Fotheringham c Ryall b Jefferies | 0 | c Ryall b Norman | 29 |
| R. G. Pollock lbw b Kuiper | 21 | c Ryall b Jefferies | 38 |
| *C. E. B. Rice c Bacchus b Norman | 62 | lbw b Kuiper | 57 |
| K. A. McKenzie c Bacchus b Norman | 13 | c Rayner b Kirsten | 55 |
| A. J. Kourie c Ryall b Hobson | 15 | not out | 31 |
| H. A. Page st Ryall b Hobson | 0 | not out | 6 |
| †R. V. Jennings st Ryall b Hobson | 14 | run out | 1 |
| S. T. Clarke c Bacchus b Norman | 10 | | |
| N. V. Radford not out | 0 | b Jefferies | 0 |
| B 2, l-b 6, w 2, n-b 9 | 19 | B 12, l-b 6, w 3, n-b 8 | 29 |
| 1/34 2/35 3/66 4/173 5/175 6/203 7/203 8/203 9/218 | 227 | 1/39 2/50 3/116 4/116 5/116 6/221 7/242 8/250 (8 wkts dec.) | 275 |

Bowling: *First Innings*—Jefferies 23–4–59–2; Kuiper 13–5–28–1; Norman 19–4–53–4; Kirsten 12–3–24–0; Hobson 10.4–4–44–3. *Second Innings*—Jefferies 29–4–84–3; Kuiper 11–2–39–1; Norman 21–7–46–2; Kirsten 11–3–23–1; Hobson 19–4–54–0.

### Western Province

| | | | |
|---|---|---|---|
| S. F. A. Bacchus c Kourie b Clarke | 59 | c and b Clarke | 5 |
| P. H. Rayner c Jennings b Clarke | 40 | c Jennings b Clarke | 38 |
| L. Seeff lbw b Page | 26 | c Jennings b Page | 30 |
| P. N. Kirsten hit wkt b Clarke | 43 | c Norris b Kourie | 80 |
| R. F. Pienaar c Cook b Norris | 1 | c Kourie b Page | 0 |
| *A. P. Kuiper c McKenzie b Norris | 0 | c McKenzie b Kourie | 68 |
| G. J. Turner c Jennings b Radford | 20 | c Norris b Clarke | 2 |
| S. T. Jefferies c Radford b Clarke | 0 | c Norris b Kourie | 21 |
| †R. J. Ryall c Rice b Clarke | 6 | not out | 1 |
| D. Norman lbw b Radford | 2 | st Jennings b Kourie | 2 |
| D. L. Hobson not out | 11 | b Clarke | 1 |
| B 5, l-b 8, w 4, n-b 7 | 24 | B 3, l-b 2, w 1, n-b 1 | 7 |
| 1/95 2/106 3/164 4/165 5/167 6/192 7/192 8/206 9/219 | 232 | 1/23 2/56 3/95 4/96 5/212 6/215 7/248 8/250 9/252 | 255 |

Bowling: *First Innings*—Clarke 25–5–41–5; Radford 17.1–3–47–2; Kourie 22–4–74–0; Page 10–2–33–1; Norris 8–2–13–2. *Second Innings*—Clarke 23.4–2–106–4; Radford 5–0–23–0; Kourie 20–4–62–4; Page 10–3–36–2; Norris 3–0–21–0.

Umpires: P. de Klerk and B. Glass.

*Wides and no-balls not debited to bowlers' analyses.*

## EASTERN PROVINCE v TRANSVAAL

At St George's Park, Port Elizabeth, January 11, 12, 13. Drawn. Eastern Province 6 pts, Transvaal 8 pts.

### Transvaal

| First innings | | Second innings | |
|---|---|---|---|
| S. J. Cook lbw b Willey | 77 | b Moseley | 20 |
| C. R. Norris c Richardson b Moseley | 14 | c Richardson b Moseley | 2 |
| H. R. Fotheringham c Richardson b Cowley | 184 | c Moseley b van Vuuren | 2 |
| R. G. Pollock c Shaw b Moseley | 15 | c Cowley b van Vuuren | 53 |
| *C. E. B. Rice c Richardson b Bauermeister | 3 | c van Vuuren b Moseley | 6 |
| K. A. McKenzie st Richardson b Shaw | 8 | not out | 39 |
| A. J. Kourie b Bauermeister | 10 | b Cowley | 29 |
| †R. V. Jennings b Cowley | 22 | not out | 9 |
| H. A. Page not out | 17 | | |
| S. T. Clarke c Cowley b van Vuuren | 17 | | |
| N. V. Radford c Willey b van Vuuren | 0 | | |
| L-b 7, w 2, n-b 3 | 12 | B 4, l-b 3, w 3, n-b 1 | 11 |
| 1/56 2/144 3/168 4/177 5/192 6/243 7/319 8/350 9/379 | 379 | 1/6 2/26 3/39 4/104 5/108 6/155 (6 wkts dec.) | 171 |

Bowling: *First Innings*—Moseley 20–3–62–2; van Vuuren 29.3–8–89–2; Bauermeister 18–3–79–2; Willey 24–5–68–1; Shaw 14–4–36–1; Cowley 8–1–33–2. *Second Innings*—Moseley 18–4–43–3; van Vuuren 18–8–41–2; Bauermeister 12–0–62–0; Cowley 4–0–14–1.

### Eastern Province

| First innings | | Second innings | |
|---|---|---|---|
| I. K. Daniell lbw b Radford | 1 | c Page b Radford | 12 |
| P. Willey c Jennings b Kourie | 19 | c Fotheringham b Page | 11 |
| R. L. S. Armitage b Clarke | 0 | c Pollock b Page | 6 |
| M. Michau c Jennings b Clarke | 3 | b Kourie | 0 |
| †D. J. Richardson c Jennings b Clarke | 37 | c Kourie b Radford | 4 |
| *G. S. Cowley lbw b Kourie | 0 | hit wkt b Page | 0 |
| P. G. Amm c McKenzie b Clarke | 53 | not out | 44 |
| T. G. Shaw b Kourie | 8 | c Jennings b Page | 3 |
| K. G. Bauermeister c and b Clarke | 13 | c and b Kourie | 13 |
| E. A. Moseley c Rice b Radford | 40 | not out | 6 |
| M. K. van Vuuren not out | 42 | | |
| B 5, l-b 6, w 2, n-b 5 | 18 | B 1, l-b 3, w 4, n-b 2 | 10 |
| 1/1 2/2 3/18 4/61 5/71 6/71 7/80 8/108 9/164 | 234 | 1/21 2/33 3/34 4/43 5/63 6/63 7/67 8/102 (8 wkts) | 109 |

Bowling: *First Innings*—Clarke 16.4–4–52–5; Radford 12–2–49–2; Page 9–3–12–0; Kourie 20–6–84–3; Norris 3–0–19–0. *Second Innings*—Clarke 15–3–38–0; Radford 13–2–47–2; Page 12–7–12–4; Kourie 9–7–2–2.

Umpires: H. R. Martin and C. M. P. Coetzee.

*Wides and no-balls not debited to bowlers' analyses.*

## WESTERN PROVINCE v NATAL

At Newlands, Cape Town, January 12, 13, 14. Drawn. Western Province 6 pts, Natal 10 pts.

### Western Province

| First innings | | Second innings | |
|---|---|---|---|
| S. F. A. Bacchus c King b Packer | 36 | c Bestall b Clift | 65 |
| P. H. Rayner c Madsen b Clift | 37 | not out | 69 |
| L. Seeff c Smith b Alleyne | 26 | c Packer b Bestall | 28 |
| P. N. Kirsten c Bestall b Bentley | 52 | not out | 29 |

| | | | |
|---|---|---|---|
| R. F. Pienaar c Madsen b Alleyne | 2 | | |
| *A. P. Kuiper b Alleyne | 6 | | |
| S. T. Jefferies c Madsen b Packer | 26 | | |
| G. S. le Roux not out | 48 | | |
| †R. J. Ryall c Madsen b Bentley | 26 | | |
| D. Norman lbw b Alleyne | 2 | | |
| D. L. Hobson c Clift b Alleyne | 12 | | |
| B 1, l-b 10, w 1, n-b 10 | 22 | L-b 4, n-b 3 | 7 |
| 1/50 2/89 3/125 4/141 5/150 6/196 7/196 8/247 9/260. | 295 | 1/102 2/146 (2 wkts) | 198 |

Bowling: *First Innings*—Alleyne 24.5–4–103–5; Packer 20–4–61–2; Cooper 6–0–29–0; Clift 20–6–49–1; King 2–0–17–0; Bentley 6–2–14–2. *Second Innings*—Alleyne 7–0–49–0; Packer 8–2–25–0; Clift 20–8–31–1; King 8–0–26–0; Bentley 16–5–20–0; Bestall 4–2–3–1; Smith 2–0–17–0; Logan 2–0–16–0; Madsen 1–0–4–0.

## Natal

| | |
|---|---|
| B. J. Whitfield c Ryall b Hobson | 57 |
| R. A. Smith b le Roux | 3 |
| R. M. Bentley c Kuiper b Norman | 50 |
| D. Bestall not out | 134 |
| C. L. King c Norman b le Roux | 94 |
| M. B. Logan c Ryall b Norman | 10 |
| †T. R. Madsen c Ryall b le Roux | 23 |
| *P. B. Clift c le Roux b Hobson | 6 |
| H. L. Alleyne st Ryall b Hobson | 1 |
| T. J. Packer b Hobson | 1 |
| K. R. Cooper st Ryall b Hobson | 0 |
| L-b 5, w 3, n-b 5 | 13 |
| 1/4 2/85 3/155 4/299 5/313 6/378 7/385 8/390 9/392 | 392 |

Bowling: le Roux 28–4–79–3; Jefferies 27–3–91–0; Kirsten 14–5–36–0; Norman 23–2–81–2; Hobson 27.4–4–92–5.

Umpires: G. Rossiter and A. J. Norton.

*Wides and no-balls not debited to bowlers' analyses.*

# WESTERN PROVINCE v NORTHERN TRANSVAAL

At Newlands, Cape Town, January 18, 19, 21. Western Province won by an innings and 20 runs. Western Province 19 pts, Northern Transvaal 2 pts.

## Northern Transvaal

| | | | |
|---|---|---|---|
| M. Yachad c Seeff b le Roux | 1 | c Rayner b Hobson | 37 |
| W. Kirsh b le Roux | 0 | c Norman b Kirsten | 21 |
| *L. J. Barnard lbw b Norman | 54 | b Jefferies | 44 |
| †N. T. Day b Hobson | 21 | c and b Kirsten | 0 |
| K. D. Verdoorn c Ryall b Jefferies | 8 | lbw b le Roux | 17 |
| A. Geringer c Ryall b Jefferies | 2 | c Ryall b Hobson | 30 |
| A. M. Ferreira c and b Hobson | 8 | not out | 42 |
| P. J. A. Visagie c Ryall b Jefferies | 9 | c Jefferies b Hobson | 0 |
| W. F. Morris b Jefferies | 23 | c Rayner b Jefferies | 0 |
| E. O. Simons lbw b Hobson | 21 | b Jefferies | 0 |
| G. Grobler not out | 0 | c Pienaar b Jefferies | 7 |
| B 5, l-b 6, w 3, n-b 8 | 22 | B 9, l-b 7, w 1, n-b 4 | 21 |
| 1/2 2/9 3/74 4/93 5/97 6/108 7/115 8/122 9/163 | 169 | 1/63 2/77 3/77 4/136 5/154 6/172 7/178 8/178 9/219 | 219 |

Bowling: *First Innings*—le Roux 14–1–39–2; Jefferies 16.4–4–39–4; Norman 12–3–25–1; Hobson 10–1–44–3. *Second Innings*—le Roux 10–2–28–1; Jefferies 19.2–3–61–4; Norman 4–0–18–0; Hobson 18–6–62–3; Kirsten 8–1–29–2.

### Western Province

| | |
|---|---|
| S. F. A. Bacchus c Day b Grobler | 1 |
| P. H. Rayner b Morris | 37 |
| L. Seeff lbw b Morris | 71 |
| P. N. Kirsten not out | 126 |
| R. F. Pienaar lbw b Grobler | 28 |
| *A. P. Kuiper c sub b Morris | 64 |
| S. T. Jefferies c Barnard b Simons | 14 |
| G. S. le Roux c Grobler b Barnard | 24 |
| †R. J. Ryall b Morris | 14 |
| B 4, l-b 10, n-b 15 | 29 |
| 1/7 2/90 3/124 4/177 5/239 6/290 7/342 8/408 | (8 wkts dec.) 408 |

D. Norman and D. L. Hobson did not bat.

Bowling: Simons 28–4–80–1; Grobler 24–4–100–2; Morris 37.4–11–97–4; Ferreira 27–7–67–0; Geringer 3–1–4–0; Barnard 14–3–31–1.

Umpires: D. H. Bezuidenhout and G. Rossiter.

*Wides and no-balls not debited to bowlers' analyses.*

## NATAL v TRANSVAAL

At Kingsmead, Durban, January 19, 20, 21. Transvaal won by an innings and 21 runs. Transvaal 23 pts, Natal 6 pts.

### Natal

| | | | |
|---|---|---|---|
| B. J. Whitfield c Kourie b Clarke | 4 | b Clarke | 4 |
| M. B. Logan c Jennings b Clarke | 48 | c Rice b Page | 24 |
| R. M. Bentley c Norris b Page | 1 | c Cook b Kourie | 75 |
| D. Bestall c Jennings b Radford | 22 | c Rice b Page | 11 |
| C. L. King c Pollock b Page | 37 | c and b Kourie | 10 |
| R. A. Smith b Norris | 30 | c Jennings b Radford | 4 |
| †T. R. Madsen b Radford | 37 | c McKenzie b Kourie | 0 |
| *P. B. Clift b Clarke | 20 | not out | 39 |
| H. L. Alleyne b Radford | 0 | st Jennings b Kourie | 2 |
| T. J. Packer b Page | 14 | b Clarke | 0 |
| P. E. Smith not out | 3 | st Jennings b Kourie | 0 |
| L-b 5, w 1, n-b 3 | 9 | L-b 3, n-b 3 | 6 |
| 1/14 2/20 3/64 4/79 5/122 6/183 7/183 8/183 9/211 | 225 | 1/13 2/48 3/68 4/82 5/96 6/103 7/154 8/158 9/169 | 175 |

Bowling: *First Innings*—Clarke 18.4–3–26–3; Radford 15–3–31–3; Kourie 27–5–103–0; Page 19–3–41–3; Norris 3–0–15–1. *Second Innings*—Clarke 22–5–51–2; Radford 12–1–34–1; Kourie 33.4–12–61–5; Page 8–3–23–2.

### Transvaal

| | |
|---|---|
| S. J. Cook b Packer | 9 |
| C. R. Norris c Logan b Alleyne | 13 |
| H. R. Fotheringham c R. A. Smith b P. E. Smith | 31 |
| R. G. Pollock c Bestall b Alleyne | 3 |
| *C. E. B. Rice c R. A. Smith b Clift | 126 |
| K. A. McKenzie st Madsen b Bentley | 115 |
| A. J. Kourie not out | 54 |
| †R. V. Jennings c Bestall b Bentley | 0 |
| H. A. Page c Madsen b Alleyne | 19 |
| S. T. Clarke c Bestall b Packer | 15 |
| N. V. Radford c Madsen b Packer | 10 |
| L-b 13, w 1, n-b 12 | 26 |
| 1/20 2/46 3/55 4/78 5/315 6/327 7/327 8/379 9/396 | 421 |

Bowling: Alleyne 25–0–113–3; Packer 23–3–86–3; P. E. Smith 13–2–81–1; Clift 24–3–62–1; King 1–0–9–0; Bentley 12–0–44–2.

Umpires: D. D. Schoof and K. E. Liebenberg.

*Wides and no-balls not debited to bowlers' analyses.*

## NORTHERN TRANSVAAL v EASTERN PROVINCE

At Berea Park, Pretoria, January 25, 26, 28. Northern Transvaal won by 226 runs. Northern Transvaal 16 pts, Eastern Province 4 pts.

### Northern Transvaal

| First innings | | Second innings | |
|---|---|---|---|
| M. Yachad c Michau b Shaw | 31 | c Armitage b Moseley | 90 |
| W. Kirsh c Richardson b Moseley | 17 | c Armitage b Bauermeister | 89 |
| *L. J. Barnard b Armitage | 24 | lbw b Bauermeister | 21 |
| †N. T. Day c Daniell b Shaw | 2 | not out | 8 |
| K. D. Verdoorn lbw b Moseley | 15 | c Richardson b Moseley | 2 |
| A. Geringer b van Vuuren | 42 | c van Vuuren b Bauermeister | 17 |
| A. M. Ferreira c Michau b Shaw | 3 | not out | 25 |
| W. F. Morris c Callaghan b van Vuuren | 14 | | |
| I. F. N. Weideman c Richardson b van Vuuren | 7 | | |
| E. O. Simons not out | 43 | | |
| G. Grobler c Cowley b Shaw | 10 | | |
| B 6, l-b 11, w 6, n-b 4 | 27 | B 2, l-b 4, w 4, n-b 3 | 13 |
| 1/33 2/79 3/84 4/94 5/121 6/130 7/154 8/164 9/194 | 235 | 1/157 2/201 3/214 4/239 5/248 (5 wkts dec.) | 265 |

Bowling: *First Innings*—Moseley 23–5–52–2; van Vuuren 20–3–58–3; Bauermeister 11–1–22–0; Cowley 4–0–6–0; Shaw 32.3–9–51–4; Armitage 10–3–19–1. *Second Innings*—Moseley 19–3–64–2; van Vuuren 13–1–50–0; Bauermeister 9–0–64–3; Cowley 7–0–25–0; Shaw 10–2–24–0; Armitage 8–1–25–0.

### Eastern Province

| First innings | | Second innings | |
|---|---|---|---|
| I. K. Daniell c Morris b Simons | 5 | c Day b Simons | 10 |
| P. G. Amm b Simons | 9 | c Verdoorn b Weideman | 6 |
| R. L. S. Armitage c Day b Weideman | 2 | c Day b Ferreira | 18 |
| M. Michau c Yachad b Weideman | 32 | c Day b Grobler | 6 |
| T. G. Shaw b Simons | 24 | lbw b Ferreira | 8 |
| †D. J. Richardson lbw b Grobler | 6 | c Geringer b Ferreira | 12 |
| D. J. Callaghan c Geringer b Simons | 18 | not out | 21 |
| *G. S. Cowley not out | 32 | lbw b Ferreira | 4 |
| E. A. Moseley c Day b Simons | 4 | lbw b Ferreira | 0 |
| K. G. Bauermeister b Morris | 8 | b Ferreira | 0 |
| M. K. van Vuuren b Simons | 0 | b Morris | 11 |
| B 6, l-b 9, w 4, n-b 2 | 21 | B 2, l-b 9, w 1, n-b 5 | 17 |
| 1/7 2/14 3/21 4/69 5/81 6/91 7/141 8/146 9/156 | 161 | 1/17 2/23 3/32 4/62 5/78 6/82 7/98 8/98 9/98 | 113 |

Bowling: *First Innings*—Weideman 14–2–43–2; Simons 16–6–26–6; Grobler 11–1–36–1; Ferreira 10–3–18–0; Morris 4–0–17–1. *Second Innings*—Weideman 7–3–11–1; Simons 9–2–16–1; Grobler 4–0–13–1; Ferreira 15–9–23–6; Morris 13.1–2–33–1.

Umpires: D. H. Bezuidenhout and G. Hawkins.

*Wides and no-balls not debited to bowlers' analyses.*

## NATAL v WESTERN PROVINCE

At Kingsmead, Durban, January 26, 27, 28. Drawn. Natal 5 pts, Western Province 8 pts.

### Natal

| Batsman | First Innings | | Second Innings | |
|---|---|---|---|---|
| B. J. Whitfield | lbw b le Roux | 5 | not out | 96 |
| M. B. Logan | c Bacchus b Hobson | 37 | c Ryall b Hobson | 48 |
| R. M. Bentley | lbw b Kuiper | 16 | run out | 12 |
| *D. Bestall | c Bacchus b Hobson | 35 | c Kirsten b Hobson | 0 |
| R. A. Smith | c Rayner b le Roux | 7 | c Ryall b Hobson | 8 |
| †T. R. Madsen | c Ryall b le Roux | 54 | lbw b Norman | 22 |
| M. D. Mellor | c Ryall b Kuiper | 6 | not out | 29 |
| D. A. Scott | c Ryall b le Roux | 17 | c Ryall b le Roux | 2 |
| J. K. Lever | st Ryall b Hobson | 15 | | |
| T. J. Packer | not out | 5 | | |
| H. L. Alleyne | st Ryall b Hobson | 3 | | |
| | B 2, l-b 13, w 2, n-b 11 | 28 | B 6, l-b 13, w 5, n-b 4 | 28 |
| | 1/11 2/49 3/101 4/118 5/132 6/144 7/174 8/214 9/220 | 228 | 1/87 2/102 3/145 4/163 5/163 6/168 | (6 wkts dec.) 245 |

Bowling: *First Innings*—le Roux 19–3–46–4; Jefferies 20–4–33–0; Kuiper 13–2–41–2; Norman 7–2–21–0; Hobson 24.4–3–54–4; Kirsten 2–1–5–0. *Second Innings*—le Roux 17–4–40–1; Kuiper 10–3–28–0; Norman 13–4–21–1; Hobson 37–14–70–3; Kirsten 15–3–58–0.

### Western Province

| Batsman | First Innings | | Second Innings | |
|---|---|---|---|---|
| S. F. A. Bacchus | b Packer | 15 | c Logan b Alleyne | 8 |
| P. H. Rayner | lbw b Alleyne | 1 | not out | 20 |
| L. Seeff | c Madsen b Packer | 5 | not out | 11 |
| P. N. Kirsten | c Bestall b Alleyne | 133 | | |
| R. F. Pienaar | c Madsen b Packer | 42 | | |
| *A. P. Kuiper | c Bentley b Alleyne | 45 | | |
| S. T. Jefferies | b Lever | 19 | | |
| G. S. le Roux | c Madsen b Alleyne | 2 | | |
| †R. J. Ryall | run out | 1 | | |
| D. Norman | c Madsen b Packer | 6 | | |
| D. L. Hobson | not out | 3 | | |
| | L-b 3, w 1, n-b 4 | 8 | L-b 4, n-b 3 | 7 |
| | 1/5 2/13 3/31 4/154 5/237 6/252 7/258 8/271 9/271 | 280 | 1/22 | (1 wkt) 46 |

Bowling: *First Innings*—Alleyne 28–6–83–4; Lever 32–7–81–1; Packer 27.4–7–75–4; Mellor 1–0–5–0; Bentley 11–4–28–0. *Second Innings*—Alleyne 6–1–13–1; Lever 3–1–4–0; Packer 4–0–13–0; Mellor 3–1–4–0; Bentley 2–0–5–0.

Umpires: B. C. Smith and D. A. Sansom.

*Wides and no-balls not debited to bowlers' analyses.*

## NATAL v EASTERN PROVINCE

At Kingsmead, Durban, February 9, 10, 11. Drawn. Play restricted to the third day only because of rain.

### Eastern Province

| | | | |
|---|---|---|---|
| †D. J. Richardson c Madsen b Makin | 45 | M. W. Rushmere not out | 21 |
| P. G. Amm c Smith b Makin | 26 | B 2, l-b 2, n-b 3 | 7 |
| T. B. Reid c Mellor b Makin | 56 | | |
| M. Michau not out | 36 | 1/54 2/108 (4 wkts dec.) | 213 |
| D. J. Callaghan c Alleyne b Makin | 22 | 3/137 4/178 | |

P. Willey, *G. S. Cowley, E. A. Moseley, K. G. Bauermeister and M. K. van Vuuren did not bat.

Bowling: Alleyne 5–2–11–0; Packer 6–1–15–0; King 6–2–24–0; Makin 35–9–81–4; Mellor 20–7–56–0; Bentley 11–2–19–0.

### Natal

| | |
|---|---|
| B. J. Whitfield not out | 3 |
| M. B. Logan not out | 2 |
| (no wkt) | 5 |

R. M. Bentley, *D. Bestall, C. L. King, R. A. Smith, †T. R. Madsen, M. D. Mellor, M. D. Makin, H. L. Alleyne and T. J. Packer did not bat.

Bowling: Moseley 3–2–3–0; van Vuuren 2–1–2–0.

Umpires: H. R. Martin and B. C. Smith.

*No-balls not debited to bowlers' analyses.*

## NORTHERN TRANSVAAL v WESTERN PROVINCE

At Berea Park, Pretoria, February 8, 9, 11. Drawn. Northern Transvaal 5 pts, Western Province 5 pts.

### Northern Transvaal

| | | | |
|---|---|---|---|
| M. Yachad c Ryall b Norman | 6 | – c Elgar b le Roux | 8 |
| W. Kirsh c Elgar b le Roux | 5 | – retired hurt | 22 |
| *L. J. Barnard c Kuiper b Norman | 0 | – b Kuiper | 65 |
| †N. T. Day c Kuiper b Richardson | 51 | – c Rayner b Kuiper | 2 |
| C. P. L. de Lange c Ryall b Norman | 8 | – c Bacchus b Norman | 36 |
| A. Geringer c Richardson b le Roux | 11 | – c Ryall b Kuiper | 1 |
| A. M. Ferreira c Norman b Richardson | 8 | – c Ryall b Kuiper | 23 |
| W. F. Morris c Kuiper b Richardson | 0 | – not out | 10 |
| E. O. Simons c Seeff b Norman | 27 | – c Richardson b le Roux | 23 |
| I. F. N. Weideman c Elgar b Norman | 5 | | |
| G. Grobler not out | 3 | | |
| L-b 4, w 12 | 16 | B 4, l-b 6, w 4, n-b 1 | 15 |
| 1/13 2/13 3/22 4/40 5/62 6/81 7/81 8/107 9/131 | 140 | 1/8 2/65 3/131 4/135 5/150 6/178 7/205 (7 wkts dec.) | 205 |

Bowling: *First Innings*—le Roux 18–5–28–2; Norman 13–2–38–5; Richardson 10–3–23–3; Hobson 16–4–35–0. *Second Innings*—le Roux 16.2–2–59–2; Norman 13–2–36–1; Richardson 7–0–23–0; Hobson 3–0–17–0; Kuiper 19–1–55–4.

### Western Province

| First innings | | Second innings | |
|---|---|---|---|
| P. H. Rayner c Morris b Ferreira | 25 | c sub b Simons | 5 |
| A. G. Elgar c Yachad b Simons | 6 | c Simons b Weideman | 5 |
| L. Seeff run out | 6 | c Geringer b Simons | 52 |
| P. N. Kirsten c Day b Ferreira | 1 | c de Lange b Simons | 3 |
| S. F. A. Bacchus c Day b Grobler | 13 | lbw b Grobler | 5 |
| *A. P. Kuiper c Day b Ferreira | 13 | c Weideman b Ferreira | 12 |
| G. S. le Roux c Day b Ferreira | 8 | not out | 2 |
| †R. J. Ryall c Day b Simons | 8 | not out | 0 |
| R. Richardson not out | 3 | | |
| D. Norman b Simons | 0 | | |
| D. L. Hobson b Simons | 4 | | |
| L-b 2, w 8, n-b 7 | 17 | B 3, l-b 3, w 3 | 9 |
| 1/10 2/26 3/35 4/59 5/65 6/83 7/84 8/100 9/100 | 104 | 1/10 2/19 3/33 4/53 5/88 6/92 | (6 wkts) 93 |

Bowling: *First Innings*—Simons 14.3–2–26–4; Weideman 8–2–10–0; Ferreira 13–3–32–4; Grobler 7–0–19–1. *Second Innings*—Simons 11.4–1–20–3; Weideman 6–1–30–1; Ferreira 11–8–14–1; Grobler 6–1–20–1.

Umpires: S. G. Moore and P. Smit.

*Wides and no-balls not debited to bowlers' analyses.*

## EASTERN PROVINCE v NORTHERN TRANSVAAL

At St George's Park, Port Elizabeth, February 15, 16, 17. Northern Transvaal won by three wickets. Northern Transvaal 16 pts, Eastern Province 2 pts.

### Northern Transvaal

| First innings | | Second innings | |
|---|---|---|---|
| M. Yachad c Richardson b Shaw | 24 | lbw b Shaw | 53 |
| K. D. Verdoorn c Reid b Moseley | 9 | lbw b Shaw | 6 |
| *L. J. Barnard b Willey | 52 | c Michau b Willey | 5 |
| †N. T. Day b Shaw | 84 | run out | 7 |
| C. P. L. de Lange c Michau b Bauermeister | 23 | lbw b Willey | 1 |
| A. Geringer lbw b Willey | 5 | c and b Shaw | 2 |
| A. M. Ferreira lbw b Moseley | 7 | c Michau b Willey | 0 |
| E. O. Simons c Richardson b Moseley | 0 | not out | 1 |
| W. F. Morris c Amm b van Vuuren | 4 | not out | 2 |
| I. F. N. Weideman lbw b van Vuuren | 0 | | |
| G. Grobler not out | 14 | | |
| B 1, l-b 9, w 4, n-b 3 | 17 | B 3, l-b 3, n-b 1 | 7 |
| 1/24 2/50 3/111 4/163 5/170 6/185 7/185 8/203 9/203 | 239 | 1/21 2/36 3/56 4/57 5/77 6/78 7/82 | (7 wkts) 84 |

Bowling: *First Innings*—Moseley 22–10–44–3; van Vuuren 13–4–19–2; Bauermeister 10–2–33–1; Willey 35–12–62–2; Shaw 30.1–11–64–2. *Second Innings*—Moseley 10–3–18–0; van Vuuren 2–1–2–0; Willey 17–9–25–3; Shaw 25–11–32–3.

### Eastern Province

| First innings | | Second innings | |
|---|---|---|---|
| †D. J. Richardson lbw b Simons | 4 | b Morris | 35 |
| P. G. Amm lbw b Weideman | 0 | run out | 0 |
| T. B. Reid c Day b Weideman | 23 | c and b Simons | 4 |
| M. Michau lbw b Simons | 5 | c Day b Morris | 44 |
| P. Willey b Weideman | 0 | lbw b Ferreira | 11 |
| D. J. Callaghan c Day b Weideman | 1 | b Morris | 6 |

| | | | |
|---|---|---|---|
| *G. S. Cowley lbw b Morris | 14 | – c Grobler b Barnard | 87 |
| T. G. Shaw c Day b Weideman | 0 | – c and b Grobler | 18 |
| K. G. Bauermeister not out | 12 | – c Geringer b Morris | 4 |
| E. A. Moseley b Weideman | 6 | – c Geringer b Morris | 5 |
| M. K. van Vuuren lbw b Morris | 8 | – not out | 17 |
| B 6, l-b 2, n-b 2 | 10 | B 2, l-b 3, w 1, n-b 2 | 8 |
| 1/4 2/6 3/29 4/30 5/38 6/43 7/47 8/63 9/70 | 83 | 1/1 2/12 3/55 4/94 5/96 6/102 7/170 8/175 9/205 | 239 |

Bowling: *First Innings*—Simons 11–3–20–2; Weideman 14–2–43–6; Morris 6.5–4–10–2; Barnard 2–2–0–0. *Second Innings*—Simons 4–1–19–1; Weideman 7–1–20–0; Morris 35–12–83–5; Barnard 11.2–3–29–1; Grobler 12–2–48–1; Ferreira 18–7–32–1.

Umpires: S. G. Moore and C. M. P. Coetzee.

*Wides and no-balls not debited to bowlers' analyses.*

## TRANSVAAL v WESTERN PROVINCE

At Wanderers, Johannesburg, February 15, 16, 17. Transvaal won by an innings and 71 runs. Transvaal 21 pts, Western Province 3 pts.

### Western Province

| | | | |
|---|---|---|---|
| P. H. Rayner c Rice b Page | 9 | – c Jennings b Page | 26 |
| A. G. Elgar b Clarke | 0 | – c Rice b Kourie | 10 |
| L. Seeff c Venter b Clarke | 73 | – c Radford b Kourie | 40 |
| P. N. Kirsten lbw b Page | 8 | – c Page b Clarke | 25 |
| S. F. A. Bacchus c Pollock b Radford | 0 | – c Jennings b Page | 1 |
| *A. P. Kuiper c Jennings b Radford | 3 | – c Jennings b Page | 10 |
| R. F. Pienaar c Venter b Clarke | 11 | – run out | 0 |
| G. S. le Roux not out | 21 | – c Kourie b Page | 0 |
| †R. J. Ryall c Pollock b Radford | 5 | – not out | 9 |
| D. Norman c McKenzie b Kourie | 6 | – b Kourie | 5 |
| D. L. Hobson lbw b Page | 9 | – st Jennings b Kourie | 15 |
| B 1, l-b 3, n-b 1 | 5 | L-b 7 | 7 |
| 1/3 2/41 3/55 4/71 5/75 6/105 7/110 8/123 9/138 | 150 | 1/34 2/54 3/94 4/95 5/117 6/117 7/117 8/121 9/130 | 148 |

Bowling: *First Innings*—Clarke 17–12–14–3; Radford 19–7–32–3; Page 18.4–3–58–3; Kourie 22–3–41–1. *Second Innings*—Clarke 19–4–28–1; Radford 14–7–17–0; Page 19–4–56–4; Kourie 17.2–4–40–4.

### Transvaal

| | | | |
|---|---|---|---|
| S. J. Cook c Bacchus b Norman | 37 | A. J. Kourie not out | 41 |
| H. R. Fotheringham b le Roux | 80 | †R. V. Jennings not out | 41 |
| M. S. Venter c Bacchus b le Roux | 37 | B 1, l-b 3 | 4 |
| R. G. Pollock c Hobson b Kuiper | 52 | | |
| *C. E. B. Rice c Ryall b Norman | 67 | 1/64 2/151 3/162 4/235 5/280 6/292 | (6 wkts dec.) 369 |
| K. A. McKenzie c Ryall b Hobson | 10 | | |

H. A. Page, S. T. Clarke and N. V. Radford did not bat.

Bowling: le Roux 24–3–80–2; Kuiper 19–2–55–1; Hobson 32–4–136–1; Norman 18–6–60–2; Elgar 6–0–34–0.

Umpires: A. J. Norton and O. R. Schoof.

*Wides and no-balls not debited to bowlers' analyses.*

## SEMI-FINALS

## NORTHERN TRANSVAAL v WESTERN PROVINCE

At Berea Park, Pretoria, February 22, 23, 25, 26. Northern Transvaal won by eight wickets.

### Western Province

| First Innings | | Second Innings | |
|---|---|---|---|
| S. F. A. Bacchus c Day b Simons | 58 | c Barnard b Simons | 2 |
| P. H. Rayner c Day b Simons | 6 | c Day b Weideman | 4 |
| L. Seeff c Yachad b Ferreira | 76 | c Geringer b Simons | 21 |
| P. N. Kirsten c Day b Morris | 1 | c Weideman b Simons | 6 |
| C. M. Wells c Day b Morris | 11 | c Day b Ferreira | 29 |
| *A. P. Kuiper run out | 86 | b Weideman | 4 |
| G. J. Turner b Simons | 36 | c Day b Grobler | 40 |
| G. S. le Roux c Yachad b Weideman | 10 | c Morris b Ferreira | 7 |
| D. L. Hobson run out | 7 | c Day b Ferreira | 3 |
| †R. J. Ryall not out | 2 | c Yachad b Morris | 13 |
| D. Norman c Ferreira b Simons | 0 | not out | 16 |
| L-b 24, w 5, n-b 3 | 32 | L-b 3, w 8, n-b 4 | 15 |
| 1/19 2/103 3/106 4/135 5/191 6/295 7/308 8/319 9/325 | 325 | 1/7 2/7 3/15 4/70 5/76 6/86 7/101 8/130 9/157 | 160 |

Bowling: *First Innings*—Simons 20–5–62–4; Weideman 22–4–71–1; Ferreira 24–4–79–1; Grobler 15–2–36–0; Morris 18–5–45–2. *Second Innings*—Simons 20–6–31–3; Weideman 14–3–36–2; Ferreira 16.2–4–26–3; Grobler 9–2–20–1; Morris 10–2–32–1.

### Northern Transvaal

| First Innings | | Second Innings | |
|---|---|---|---|
| M. Yachad c Norman b le Roux | 120 | c Turner b Bacchus | 62 |
| W. Kirsh lbw b Norman | 31 | c Turner b Kuiper | 20 |
| *L. J. Barnard c and b Kirsten | 51 | not out | 33 |
| †N. T. Day c Ryall b le Roux | 0 | not out | 3 |
| A. Geringer b le Roux | 56 | | |
| C. P. L. de Lange lbw b Kirsten | 9 | | |
| A. M. Ferreira c Ryall b Wells | 8 | | |
| E. O. Simons c Kirsten b Norman | 58 | | |
| W. F. Morris b Hobson | 4 | | |
| I. F. N. Weideman not out | 15 | | |
| G. Grobler run out | 0 | | |
| B 5, l-b 9, n-b 5 | 19 | L-b 2 | 2 |
| 1/74 2/194 3/214 4/214 5/243 6/256 7/302 8/309 9/368 | 371 | 1/46 2/97 | (2 wkts) 120 |

Bowling: *First Innings*—le Roux 25.3–4–104–3; Kuiper 7–1–26–0; Wells 9–3–26–1; Hobson 20–0–84–1; Norman 15–3–34–2; Kirsten 24–3–78–2. *Second Innings*—le Roux 6–0–26–0; Kuiper 4–0–13–1; Hobson 7–1–40–0; Norman 5–1–19–0; Kirsten 2–0–12–0; Bacchus 1–0–2–1; Seeff 1.1–0–6–0.

Umpires: S. G. Moore and P. de Klerk.

*Wides and no-balls not debited to bowlers' analyses.*

## TRANSVAAL v NATAL

At Wanderers, Johannesburg, February 23, 24, 25. Transvaal won by an innings and 4 runs.

### Natal

| | First Innings | | Second Innings | |
|---|---|---|---|---|
| B. J. Whitfield c Venter b Kourie | 90 | – c Kourie b Page | 12 |
| M. B. Logan c Jennings b Page | 81 | – c Kourie b Clarke | 22 |
| R. M. Bentley c Rice b Clarke | 34 | – c Clarke b Page | 2 |
| C. L. King b Kourie | 47 | – b Page | 41 |
| †T. R. Madsen b Kourie | 12 | – not out | 23 |
| D. Bestall c and b Radford | 0 | – c Fotheringham b Page | 10 |
| R. A. Smith c Pollock b Radford | 0 | – c Jennings b Page | 0 |
| *P. B. Clift st Jennings b Kourie | 5 | – c McKenzie b Kourie | 2 |
| M. D. Makin run out | 8 | – c Fotheringham b Kourie | 2 |
| T. J. Packer not out | 1 | – b Kourie | 2 |
| H. L. Alleyne not out | 8 | – st Jennings b Kourie | 11 |
| L-b 11, w 4, n-b 7 | 22 | L-b 3, w 1, n-b 8 | 12 |
| 1/158 2/210 3/226 4/245 5/246 6/248 7/265 8/288 9/299 (9 wkts dec.) | 308 | 1/39 2/42 3/48 4/48 5/69 6/106 7/115 8/119 9/125 | 139 |

Bowling: *First Innings*—Clarke 17–6–40–1; Radford 27–3–100–2; Kourie 44–8–115–4; Page 12–3–31–1. *Second Innings*—Clarke 11–2–18–1; Radford 5–0–25–0; Kourie 13.4–1–53–4; Page 13–2–31–5.

### Transvaal

| | | | |
|---|---|---|---|
| S. J. Cook lbw b Makin | 140 | A. J. Kourie run out | 13 |
| H. R. Fotheringham c Bestall b Makin | 100 | †R. V. Jennings not out | 12 |
| M. S. Venter b Alleyne | 53 | B 5, l-b 10, w 1, n-b 2 | 18 |
| R. G. Pollock b Clift | 84 | | |
| *C. E. B. Rice b Alleyne | 0 | 1/232 2/276 3/384 (6 wkts dec.) | 451 |
| K. A. McKenzie not out | 31 | 4/384 5/396 6/428 | |

H. A. Page, S. T. Clarke and N. V. Radford did not bat.

Bowling: Alleyne 17–1–73–2; Packer 9–0–34–0; Clift 16–0–101–1; King 12–1–35–0; Makin 32–3–121–2; Bentley 13–0–64–0; Bestall 1–0–5–0.

Umpires: D. D. Schoof and D. A. Sansom.

*Wides and no-balls not debited to bowlers' analyses.*

## FINAL

## NORTHERN TRANSVAAL v TRANSVAAL

At Berea Park, Pretoria, February 8, 9. Transvaal won by an innings and 5 runs.

### Transvaal

| | | | |
|---|---|---|---|
| S. J. Cook lbw b Ferreira | 26 | H. A. Page b Simons | 26 |
| H. R. Fotheringham c Morris b Weideman | 40 | S. T. Clarke c Day b Simons | 11 |
| M. S. Venter c Geringer b Simons | 23 | N. V. Radford not out | 1 |
| R. G. Pollock b Weideman | 9 | L-b 7, w 3, n-b 7 | 17 |
| *C. E. B. Rice b Simons | 0 | | |
| K. A. McKenzie c Day b Simons | 1 | 1/55 2/96 3/101 | 232 |
| A. J. Kourie lbw b Simons | 28 | 4/101 5/109 6/109 7/178 | |
| †R. V. Jennings run out | 50 | 8/215 9/219 | |

Bowling: Simons 24.5–6–57–6; Weideman 28–8–71–2; Ferreira 19–6–31–1; Ackermann 12–2–36–0; Morris 7–2–20–0.

## Northern Transvaal

| | | | |
|---|---|---|---|
| M. Yachad c Page b Clarke | 4 | – lbw b Rice | 7 |
| W. Kirsh b Clarke | 24 | – c Fotheringham b Page | 20 |
| *L. J. Barnard b Page | 0 | – c Jennings b Page | 0 |
| †N. T. Day b Clarke | 0 | – c Pollock b Clarke | 30 |
| C. P. L. de Lange c Jennings b Clarke | 10 | – lbw b Page | 0 |
| A. Geringer b Clarke | 1 | – c Jennings b Kourie | 23 |
| A. M. Ferreira b Rice | 8 | – b Kourie | 37 |
| E. O. Simons c Jennings b Page | 0 | – c Jennings b Kourie | 6 |
| W. F. Morris c Venter b Page | 4 | – c Jennings b Page | 0 |
| I. F. N. Weideman not out | 0 | – lbw b Rice | 37 |
| G. L. Ackermann lbw b Page | 0 | – not out | 0 |
| L-b 6, w 3, n-b 1 | 10 | B 1, l-b 3, w 1, n-b 1 | 6 |
| 1/10 2/16 3/18 4/31 5/40 6/49 7/49 8/61 9/61 | 61 | 1/31 2/31 3/31 4/31 5/79 6/118 7/127 8/128 9/130 | 166 |

Bowling: *First Innings*—Clarke 11–5–8–5; Page 7.4–1–14–4; Radford 6–0–21–0; Rice 3–2–8–1. *Second Innings*—Clarke 12–3–34–1; Page 18–4–67–4; Radford 8–2–20–0; Rice 6.2–4–10–2; Kourie 8–2–29–3.

Umpires: D. A. Sansom and D. H. Bezuidenhout.

*Wides and no-balls not debited to bowlers' analyses.*

## CURRIE CUP WINNERS

| | | | |
|---|---|---|---|
| 1889-90 | Transvaal | 1952-53 | Western Province |
| 1890-91 | Griqualand West | 1954-55 | Natal |
| 1892-93 | Western Province | 1955-56 | Western Province |
| 1893-94 | Western Province | 1958-59 | Transvaal |
| 1894-95 | Transvaal | 1959-60 | Natal |
| 1896-97 | Western Province | 1960-61 | Natal |
| 1897-98 | Western Province | 1962-63 | Natal |
| 1902-03 | Transvaal | 1963-64 | Natal |
| 1903-04 | Transvaal | 1965-66 | Natal/Transvaal (Tied) |
| 1904-05 | Transvaal | 1966-67 | Natal |
| 1906-07 | Transvaal | 1967-68 | Natal |
| 1908-09 | Western Province | 1968-69 | Transvaal |
| 1910-11 | Natal | 1969-70 | Transvaal/W. Province (Tied) |
| 1912-13 | Natal | 1970-71 | Transvaal |
| 1920-21 | Western Province | 1971-72 | Transvaal |
| 1921-22 | Transvaal/Natal/W. Prov. (Tied) | 1972-73 | Transvaal |
| 1923-24 | Transvaal | 1973-74 | Natal |
| 1925-26 | Transvaal | 1974-75 | Western Province |
| 1926-27 | Transvaal | 1975-76 | Natal |
| 1929-30 | Transvaal | 1976-77 | Natal |
| 1931-32 | Western Province | 1977-78 | Western Province |
| 1933-34 | Natal | 1978-79 | Transvaal |
| 1934-35 | Transvaal | 1979-80 | Transvaal |
| 1936-37 | Natal | 1980-81 | Natal |
| 1937-38 | Natal/Transvaal (Tied) | 1981-82 | Western Province |
| 1946-47 | Natal | 1982-83 | Transvaal |
| 1947-48 | Natal | 1983-84 | Transvaal |
| 1950-51 | Transvaal | 1984-85 | Transvaal |
| 1951-52 | Natal | | |

## SAB CASTLE BOWL, 1984-85

| | Played | Won | Lost | Drawn | Bonus Points Batting | Bonus Points Bowling | Total |
|---|---|---|---|---|---|---|---|
| Transvaal B | 6 | 5 | 1 | 0 | 16 | 30 | 96 |
| Orange Free State | 6 | 4 | 1 | 1 | 22 | 25 | 87 |
| Border | 6 | 3 | 2 | 1 | 12 | 26 | 68 |
| Eastern Province B | 6 | 2 | 1 | 3 | 18 | 23 | 61 |
| Boland | 6 | 3 | 2 | 1 | 8 | 20 | 58 |
| Northern Transvaal B | 6 | 2 | 2 | 2 | 9 | 26 | 55 |
| Western Province B | 6 | 1 | 4 | 1 | 14 | 17 | 41 |
| Natal B | 6 | 0 | 3 | 3 | 15 | 23 | 38 |
| Griqualand West | 6 | 0 | 4 | 2 | 11 | 20 | 31 |

At Wanderers, Johannesburg, November 9, 10, 11. Transvaal B won by four wickets. Northern Transvaal B 155 (C. R. Norris five for 48) and 189 (P. A. Robinson 43, C. R. Norris four for 15); Transvaal B 240 (H. A. Page 57; G. Grobler four for 80) and 105 for six (G. Grobler four for 58). *Transvaal B 17 pts, Northern Transvaal B 4 pts.*

At Jan Smuts Ground, East London, November 17, 18, 19. Border won by seven wickets. Eastern Province B 185 (M. W. Rushmere 42; I. Foulkes five for 50) and 244 (M. W. Rushmere 83, M. Michau 42; R. C. Ontong four for 71); Border 283 (D. J. Cullinan 70, R. C. Ontong 55, G. L. Hayes 55; M. K. van Vuuren four for 59) and 147 for three (D. J. Cullinan 60 not out). *Border 19 pts, Eastern Province B 3 pts.*

At De Beers Stadium, Kimberley, November 17, 18, 19. Drawn. Griqualand West 302 (M. J. P. Ford 77, M. N. Kellow 76) and 251 (G. P. van Rensburg 64, M. J. D. Doherty 48, A. P. Beukes 40); Natal B 294 (D. A. Scott 72, M. J. Pearse 51, G. N. Lister-James 50; G. P. van Rensburg four for 46) and 32 for one. *Griqualand West 6 pts, Natal B 5 pts.*

At Ramblers, Bloemfontein, November 21, 22, 23. Orange Free State won by 54 runs. Orange Free State 327 (C. J. van Heerden 74, A. I. Kallicharran 69, C. J. P. G. van Zyl 49; M. D. Makin six for 36) and 239 (R. J. East 49, A. M. Green 41; M. D. Makin six for 99); Natal B 280 (D. A. Scott 67, A. C. Hudson 50, G. N. Lister-James 50; C. J. P. G. van Zyl four for 76) and 232 (P. H. Williams 89, C. J. P. G. van Zyl five for 56). *Orange Free State 16 pts, Natal B 7 pts.*

At Newlands, Cape Town, November 22, 23, 24. Western Province B won by 95 runs. Western Province B 175 (D. B. Rundle 41; G. J. Parsons four for 65) and 297 (T. A. Clarke 82, I. M. Wingreen 72, P. D. Swart 61; G. J. Parsons five for 106); Boland 173 (H. Joubert 45; J. During four for 37) and 204 (G. J. Parsons 76; K. J. Barnett 46). *Western Province B 16 pts, Boland 6 pts.*

At Uitenhage CC Ground, Uitenhage, November 23, 24, 25. Drawn. Northern Transvaal B 274 (W. Kirsh 119, C. P. L. de Lange 58, K. G. Bauermeister five for 40) and 214 for two (V. F. du Preez 117); Eastern Province B 433 (M. W. Rushmere 114, D. G. Emslie 84, A. V. Birrell 55, M. B. Billson 54; G. L. Ackermann six for 137). *Eastern Province B 6 pts, Northern Transvaal B 5 pts.*

At Ramblers, Bloemfontein, December 14, 15, 17. Orange Free State won by 155 runs. Orange Free State 166 (A. I. Kallicharran 90; C. D. Mitchley four for 55) and 372 (J. J. Strydom 88, B. M. Osborne 58; A. M. Green 57, A. I. Kallicharran 53); Transvaal B 189 (B. Roberts 63, M. S. Venter 40; C. J. P. G. van Zyl five for 38) and 194 (K. J. Rule 40, C. J. P. G. van Zyl seven for 71). *Orange Free State 15 pts, Transvaal B 6 pts.*

At Kingsmead, Durban, December 13, 14, 15. Drawn. Border 308 for seven dec. (I. Foulkes 132 not out, R. C. Ontong 60) and 258 for eight dec. (D. J. Cullinan 100, I. L. Howell 40); Natal B 276 for seven dec. (P. H. Williams 79, D. A. Scott 49, A. C. Hudson 46) and 152 for five (M. D. Mellor 46, A. C. Hudson 42). *Natal B 8 pts, Border 7 pts.*

At Oude Libertas, Stellenbosch, December 14, 15, 17. Boland won by seven wickets. Griqualand West 305 (P. W. Romaines 85, K. C. Dugmore 67, L. Potter 65; O. Henry four for 92) and 148 (O. Henry four for 41, G. J. Parsons four for 46); Boland 284 for eight dec. (S. A. Jones 87, N. M. Lambrechts 43; L. Potter four for 63) and 171 for three (J. B. Munnik 82 not out, D. P. le Roux 65). *Boland 13 pts, Griqualand West 6 pts.*

At Jan Smuts Oval, Pietermaritzburg, December 26, 27, 28. Transvaal B won by 119 runs. Transvaal B 223 (B. M. McMillan 65, P. L. Selsick 46, C. D. Mitchley 45; K. D. Robinson four for 19, P. E. Smith four for 50); and 161 (N. R. Boonzaaier 52; P. E. Smith four for 51); Natal B 135 (M. J. Pearse 51; C. D. Mitchley five for 50) and 130. *Transvaal B 17 pts, Natal B 5 pts.*

At Jan Smuts Ground, East London, December 26, 27, 28. Border won by seven wickets. Western Province B 176 (G. J. Turner 51; E. N. Trotman five for 30) and 237 (G. D. Tullis 56, A. G. Elgar 49; J. G. Thomas five for 68); Border 305 (I. L. Howell 64, E. N. Trotman 59, I. Foulkes 45; M. B. Minnaar five for 92) and 109 for three (I. Foulkes 42 not out). *Border 17 pts, Western Province B 3 pts.*

At Berea Park, Pretoria, December 31, January 1, 2. Northern Transvaal B won by ten wickets. Border 139 (P. A. Robinson four for 31) and 194 (G. C. G. Fraser 78 not out; J. C. van Duyker four for 40); Northern Transvaal B 257 (W. Kirsh 64, G. W. Jones 51, P. A. Robinson 43) and 77 for no wkt (M. Bacher 47 not out). *Northern Transvaal B 19 pts, Border 5 pts.*

At Wanderers, Johannesburg, January 12, 13, 14. Transvaal B won by two wickets. Boland 168 (C. D. Mitchley four for 46) and 198 (G. J. Parsons 51; B. M. McMillan four for 53); Transvaal B 183 (B. Roberts 55, C. D. Mitchley 46; G. J. Parsons nine for 72) and 184 for eight (B. Roberts 41, M. S. Venter 40). *Transvaal B 16 pts, Boland 5 pts.*

At De Beers Country Club, Kimberley, January 10, 11, 12. Orange Free State won by seven wickets. Griqualand West 209 (W. M. van der Merwe five for 54) and 233 (L. M. Phillip 82 not out, L. Potter 49); Orange Free State 242 (A. I. Kallicharran 110, R. A. le Roux 66; G. P. van Rensburg six for 91) and 201 for three (R. A. le Roux 89, A. I. Kallicharran 81 not out). *Orange Free State 18 pts, Griqualand West 7 pts.*

At Jan Smuts Oval, Pietermaritzburg, January 12, 13, 14. Drawn. Natal B 234 (M. J. Pearse 55; J. Havenga four for 60) and 275 for four dec. (M. D. Mellor 124 not out, M. J. Pearse 40); Eastern Province B 148 (D. H. Howell 59; C. M. Lister-James four for 55) and 173 for four (D. H. Howell 52, T. B. Reid 47). *Natal B 8 pts, Eastern Province B 5 pts.*

At Wanderers, Johannesburg, January 18, 19, 20. Transvaal B won by ten wickets. Transvaal B 374 for seven dec. (B. Roberts 90, K. J. Rule 68, N. R. Boonzaaier 52 not out, G. W. Johnson 50, P. L. Selsick 41; B. A. Matthews four for 58) and 53 for no wkt. Western Province B 222 (I. M. Wingreen 62, A. G. Elgar 41; C. D. Mitchley four for 40, J. J. Hooper four for 65) and 203 (I. M. Wingreen 83, A. G. Elgar 62; K. J. Kerr five for 36). *Transvaal B 18 pts, Western Province B 3 pts.*

At Pietersburg CC Ground, Pietersburg, January 17, 18, 19. Drawn. Boland 121 (P. A. Robinson five for 61, I. F. N. Weideman four for 52) and 193 for four (N. M. Lambrechts 58, D. P. le Roux 46, K. J. Barnett 42); Northern Transvaal B 269 (V. F. du Preez 74). *Northern Transvaal B 7 pts, Boland 3 pts.*

At Welkom Rovers Ground, Welkom, January 24, 25. Orange Free State won by an innings and 10 runs. Northern Transvaal B 118 and 172 (S. Vercueil 59 not out; C. J. P. G. van Zyl eight for 84); Orange Free State 300 (W. M. van der Merwe 96, A. I. Kallicharran 62). *Orange Free State 21 pts, Northern Transvaal B 5 pts.*

At R. J. E. Burt Oval, Constantia, January 25, 26, 27. Eastern Province B won by six wickets. Western Province B 335 (D. B. Rundle 110, A. G. Elgar 97, I. M. Wingreen 42; J. Havenga five for 88) and 263 for nine dec. (G. J. Turner 41, D. B. Rundle 40); Eastern Province B 275 for four dec. (T. B. Reid 120 not out, A. V. Birrell 82) and 326 for four (M. W. Rushmere 119 not out, T. B. Reid 111, D. H. Howell 42). *Eastern Province B 19 pts, Western Province B 7 pts.*

At Jan Smuts Ground, East London, January 26, 27, 28. Border won by five wickets. Griqualand West 232 (P. W. Romaines 55, L. M. Phillips 48, M. J. D. Doherty 41) and 288 for six dec. (L. Potter 165 not out, M. N. Kellow 50); Border 227 for eight dec. (E. N. Trotman 65, D. J. Cullinan 46, G. C. G. Fraser 42 not out; A. P. Beukes four for 50) and 296 for five (E. N. Trotman 102, D. J. Cullinan 71, R. C. Ontong 49 not out). *Border 15 pts, Griqualand West 5 pts.*

At Union CC Ground, Port Elizabeth, February 7, 8, 9. Eastern Province B won by seven wickets. Eastern Province B 346 for eight dec. (I. K. Daniell 101, M. B. Billson 94, P. A. Tullis 45; C. J. P. G. van Zyl four for 74) and 113 for three (D. H. Howell 44); Orange Free State 184 (A. M. Green 64, B. T. Player 42; D. J. Ferrant four for 35, R. L. S. Armitage four for 50) and 273 (A. I. Kallicharran 63, B. M. Osborne 61, W. M. van der Merwe 58). *Eastern Province B 20 pts, Orange Free State 4 pts.*

At Oude Libertas, Stellenbosch, February 8, 9, 11. Boland won by 76 runs. Boland 275 for eight dec. (D. P. le Roux 70, O. Henry 50) and 216 for seven dec. (D. P. le Roux 71, K. J. Barnett 59); Natal B 194 (D. A. Scott 44) and 221 (D. K. Pearse 58, B. D. C. Logan 49; O. Henry four for 64). *Boland 19 pts, Natal B 5 pts.*

At De Beers Country Club, Kimberley, February 15, 16, 17. Transvaal B won by an innings and 3 runs. Transvaal B 328 for eight dec. (P. L. Selsick 183, C. R. Norris 74; L. Potter four for 88); Griqualand West 120 (P. W. Romaines 53; J. J. Hooper five for 29) and 205 (A. P. Beukes 48; K. J. Kerr five for 35). *Transvaal B 22 pts, Griqualand West 4 pts.*

At Berea Park, Pretoria, February 14, 15, 16. Northern Transvaal B won by 8 runs. Northern Transvaal B 156 (P. L. Symcox 63; P. A. Koen four for 31, R. R. Lawrenson four for 32) and 163 (P. L. Symcox 43; D. B. Rundle four for 37); Western Province B 131 (G. L. Ackermann five for 42) and 180 (R. J. Knowles 44; G. L. Ackermann seven for 69). *Northern Transvaal B 15 pts, Western Province B 5 pts.*

At Oude Libertas, Stellenbosch, March 1, 2, 4. Boland won by 241 runs. Boland 201 (D. P. le Roux 57, N. M. Lambrechts 44; I. L. Howell six for 60) and 111 for three dec. (D. P. le Roux 64); Border 4 for no wkt dec. and 67. *Boland 12 pts, Border 5 pts.*

At Standard CC Ground, Cradock, March 1, 2, 3. Drawn. Griqualand West 176 (F. W. Swarbrook 49 not out) and 294 for two (P. W. Romaines 170 not out, L. Potter 62 not out); Eastern Province B 436 for seven dec. (M. B. Billson 91, M. W. Rushmere 82, R. L. S. Armitage 76, D. G. Emslie 70, M. K. van Vuuren 60). *Eastern Province B 8 pts, Griqualand West 3 pts.*

At Newlands, Cape Town, February 28, March 1, 2. Drawn. Orange Free State 471 (R. J. East 163 not out, A. M. Green 84, A. I. Kallicharran 79, W. M. van der Merwe 48; B. A. Matthews four for 109) and 54 for four; Western Province B 280 (A. G. Elgar 94; W. M. van der Merwe four for 41, C. J. P. G. van Zyl four for 62) and 310 (I. M. Wingreen 62, R. P. Richardson 52 not out; C. J. P. G. van Zyl five for 82). *Orange Free State 13 pts, Western Province B 7 pts.*

## OTHER FIRST-CLASS MATCHES

At Wanderers, Johannesburg, December 8, 10, 11. Transvaal won by five wickets. South African Universities 269 (G. J. Turner 66, R. F. Pienaar 54, P. H. Rayner 44) and 150 (P. G. Amm 75); Transvaal 221 (S. J. Cook 76; C. J. van Heerden four for 62) and 200 for five (M. S. Venter 64 not out, R. V. Jennings 46).

At UPE Ground, Port Elizabeth, October 4, 5, 6. Drawn. Eastern Province 287 for five dec. (D. J. Callaghan 171, P. G. Amm 53) and 305 for six (G. S. Cowley 145 not out, D. J. Callaghan 55); South African Defence Force 534 for 6 dec. (M. B. Logan 172, J. B. Commins 116 not out, S. Koch 67, D. J. Richardson 67, M. Bowman 45).

## †NISSAN SHIELD, 1984-85

### FIRST ROUND

At Kimberley, October 20. Northern Transvaal won by 52 runs. Northern Transvaal 222 (P. J. A. Visagie 55); Griqualand West 170 (R. D. Engelbrecht 47).

At Bloemfontein, October 20. Natal won by nine wickets. Orange Free State 251 for eight (C. J. van Heerden 96); Natal 257 for one (B. J. Whitfield 109 not out, R. M. Bentley 109 not out).

At East London, October 20. Border won by six wickets. Eastern Province 122; Border 128 for four (R. C. Ontong 56 not out).

## SECOND ROUND

At Cape Town, November 3. Western Province won by seven wickets. Western Province B 138 (A. P. Kuiper four for 14); Western Province 139 for three (L. Seeff 49).

At Johannesburg, November 3. Transvaal won by six wickets. Natal 246 for seven (C. L. King 76, P. B. Clift 47 not out); Transvaal 249 for four (S. J. Cook 88, H. R. Fotheringham 51, R. G. Pollock 47, C. E. B. Rice 42 not out).

At Stellenbosch, November 3. Northern Transvaal won by 105 runs. Northern Transvaal 230 for four (N. T. Day 93 not out, K. D. Verdoorn 86); Boland 125 (K. J. Barnett 49, D. P. le Roux 42; E. O. Simons six for 36).

At Johannesburg, November 18. Transvaal won by 76 runs. Transvaal 250 for five (R. G. Pollock 74, K. A. McKenzie 67); Natal 174 (B. J. Whitfield 72 not out; A. J. Kourie four for 45).

## SEMI-FINALS – FIRST LEG

At Pretoria, December 1. Western Province won by 69 runs. Western Province 246 for seven (P. N. Kirsten 105, R. F. Pienaar 50, P. H. Rayner 46); Northern Transvaal 177 (N. T. Day 43).

At East London, December 1. Transvaal won by four wickets. Border 199 (N. P. Minnaar 60, R. C. Ontong 60; H. A. Page four for 35); Transvaal 203 for six (K. A. McKenzie 77 not out, C. E. B. Rice 44).

## SEMI-FINALS – SECOND LEG

At Cape Town, January 5. Western Province won by 7 runs. Western Province 218 (L. Seeff 52, P. H. Rayner 45, S. F. A. Bacchus 42; A. Geringer five for 38); Northern Transvaal 211 (A. Geringer 67, W. F. Morris 44; S. T. Jefferies four for 26).

At Johannesburg, January 5. Transvaal won by 52 runs. Transvaal 258 for five (C. E. B. Rice 95, S. J. Cook 86); Border 206 for nine (R. C. Ontong 72; H. A. Page four for 17).

## FINAL

At Wanderers, Johannesburg, February 2. Transvaal won by nine wickets.

### Western Province

| | |
|---|---|
| S. F. A. Bacchus c Jennings b Page | 3 |
| P. H. Rayner c Jennings b Page | 11 |
| L. Seeff c Pollock b Mitchley | 67 |
| P. N. Kirsten c Jennings b Page | 11 |
| R. F. Pienaar lbw b Kourie | 17 |
| S. T. Jefferies c Clark b Kourie | 18 |
| *A. P. Kuiper c Jennings b Mitchley | 11 |
| A. G. Elgar c Pollock b Clarke | 18 |
| G. S. le Roux not out | 24 |
| †R. J. Ryall not out | 2 |
| L-b 5, w 7, n-b 6 | 18 |
| 1/21 2/25 3/44 4/86 5/118 6/144 7/170 8/173 (8 wkts, 55 overs) | 200 |

D. Norman did not bat.

Bowling: Clarke 11–3–18–1; Radford 11–0–40–0; Page 11–2–42–3; Mitchley 11–0–38–2; Kourie 11–1–44–2.

### Transvaal

| | |
|---|---|
| S. J. Cook c Ryall b le Roux | 85 |
| H. R. Fotheringham not out | 103 |
| *C. E. B. Rice not out | 3 |
| B 7, l-b 2, w 2 | 11 |
| 1/171 (1 wkt, 46 overs) | 202 |

R. G. Pollock, K. A. McKenzie, A. J. Kourie, †R. V. Jennings, H. A. Page, C. D. Mitchley, S. T. Clarke and N. V. Radford did not bat.

Bowling: le Roux 11–2–47–1; Jefferies 1–0–4–0; Kuiper 9–0–46–0; Kirsten 9–2–28–0; Norman 11–0–50–0; Pienaar 2–0–4–0; Elgar 3–0–12–0.

Umpires: D. H. Bezuidenhout and O. R. Schoof.

## CRICKET IN DENMARK, 1985

In January the International Women's Cricket Council admitted the Danish Cricket Association into its ranks. Shortly after this, Søren Henriksen followed his former clubmate, Ole Mortensen, into county cricket. In July the senior national team played a number of matches in Derbyshire and South Wales, to gain more experience on turf wickets with the 1986 ICC Trophy competition in mind. The national under-nineteen side also took part in the International Youth Cricket Tournament in Bermuda. Though unable to repeat the triumph of the 1983 side at The Hague, the junior side beat the Netherlands and Canada.

Two pioneer tours to England were undertaken. The first was by a national under-fourteen boys' team, which won all but one of its matches against school sides of similar age in Surrey. The other tour was made by the national women's team, which concluded a week of matches in the Home Counties with a victory over Kent.

On the home scene, new champions emerged in Esbjerg, a young side whose success owed much to the coaching of a former Sussex and England player, D. V. Smith. The Danish women's championship, meanwhile, remained in the hands of AB for the fourth year in a row. – *Peter S. Hargreaves.*

---

## OVERS BOWLED AND RUNS SCORED IN BRITANNIC ASSURANCE CHAMPIONSHIP, 1985

| | *Over-rate per hour* | | | *Run-rate per 100 balls* | | |
|---|---|---|---|---|---|---|
| | *1st half* | *2nd half* | *Total* | *1st half* | *2nd half* | *Total* |
| Derbyshire (13) | 18.47* | 17.86† | 18.21 | 47.99 | 45.17 | 46.64 |
| Essex (4) | 18.66 | 18.72 | 18.70 | 54.45 | 56.02 | 55.26 |
| Glamorgan (12) | 18.75 | 19.19 | 18.94 | 50.10 | 52.51 | 50.95 |
| Gloucestershire (3) | 17.10‡ | 17.05‡ | 17.08 | 51.10 | 50.95 | 51.45 |
| Hampshire (2) | 18.51 | 18.72 | 18.60 | 55.05 | 54.57 | 54.83 |
| Kent (9) | 17.14‡ | 18.09* | 17.61 | 51.75 | 52.67 | 52.25 |
| Lancashire (14) | 18.58 | 18.21* | 18.42 | 47.24 | 46.83 | 47.04 |
| Leicestershire (16) | 18.75 | 18.60 | 18.68 | 50.48 | 47.87 | 49.12 |
| Middlesex (1) | 18.57 | 17.84† | 18.25 | 53.25 | 51.56 | 52.43 |
| Northamptonshire (10) | 18.75 | 18.62 | 18.69 | 51.84 | 53.30 | 52.52 |
| Nottinghamshire (8) | 18.71 | 18.79 | 18.75 | 55.23 | 56.24 | 55.70 |
| Somerset (17) | 19.32 | 18.71 | 19.04 | 58.82 | 54.70 | 56.81 |
| Surrey (6) | 18.53 | 18.31* | 18.43 | 58.21 | 60.48 | 59.26 |
| Sussex (7) | 18.23* | 17.60† | 17.90 | 53.58 | 54.97 | 54.25 |
| Warwickshire (15) | 18.59 | 18.64 | 18.62 | 53.92 | 55.49 | 54.56 |
| Worcestershire (5) | 18.65 | 18.57 | 18.61 | 52.87 | 54.28 | 53.53 |
| Yorkshire (11) | 18.78 | 18.79 | 18.78 | 50.12 | 47.55 | 48.90 |
| 1985 average rate | | | 18.43 | | | 52.61 |
| 1984 average rate | | | 16.88 | | | 51.82 |
| 1983 average rate | | | 18.96 | | | 50.68 |
| 1982 average rate | | | 19.06 | | | 51.38 |
| 1981 average rate | | | 18.62 | | | 50.86 |
| 1980 average rate | | | 18.95 | | | 50.47 |
| 1979 average rate | | | 19.36 | | | 48.37 |
| 1978 average rate | | | 19.45 | | | 47.53 |

*1985 Championship positions are shown in brackets.*
* *£2,000 fine.* † *£3,000 fine.* ‡ *£4,000 fine.*

*Note:* In 1984, no financial penalty was incurred for failure to achieve a required over-rate, and the figures for 1984 do not make any allowance for the fall of wickets, which the figures for earlier years do.

# CRICKET IN WEST INDIES, 1984-85

By TONY COZIER

For the second successive year, the domestic season in West Indies was completed while the leading players were still on tour in Australia. This affected the overall standard and, just as understandably, upset the sponsors. Trinidad & Tobago won the Shell Shield outright for the first time since their heady days of 1969-70 and 1970-71, because they possessed the best balanced team, defeating Jamaica, Windward Islands and, finally, to their immense satisfaction, Barbados, their arch-rivals and the 1984 champions, by an innings.

Generally it was an undistinguished tournament, dominated by the bowlers with no outstanding batsmen but with worrying standards of out-cricket from most teams. The former Test captain, Rohan Kanhai, estimated that Jamaica, whom he coached, dropped as many as 50 catches in their five matches. There were only two totals in excess of 400, yet thirteen of under 200. Only two batsmen, Carlisle Best of Barbados (437 at 54.62) and Luther Kelly of Leeward Islands (403 at 40.30), both openers, topped 400 runs, and there were numerous inconsistencies in performance.

Trinidad & Tobago, a team traditionally strong in spin, were beaten by Guyana on a spinner's pitch in Georgetown. Jamaica were good enough to beat Barbados by an innings, yet lost three other matches and finished bottom of the table, their totals varying from 545 for eight declared against Barbados to 135 against Windward Islands and 131 against Leewards. Barbados's previously high standards dropped so dramatically that they lost by an innings for the first time in nineteen years of Shield competition – and did so twice.

Several established players did well. Best and Kelly had both been in the Shield for some time. The 36-year-old Jamaican captain, Basil Williams, scored 380 runs at 47.50 an innings; the experienced Leewards' batsman, Enoch Lewis, had 361 at 40.11, the left-handed Guyanese, Timur Mohamed, 310 at 38.75 in his ninth Shield season, and the tall Trinidad & Tobago opener, Philip Simmons, continued his development with 390 runs at 48.75.

The two leading bowlers were spinners with imposing Shield records: Clyde Butts had 32 wickets for Guyana at just under 20 each, enough to earn him inclusion in the Test team against New Zealand as the off-spinner, while a leg-spinner, Ganesh Mahabir, was just behind him with 30 even cheaper wickets. Yet, with so many leading players away, the opportunity again presented itself for newer, younger players to advance their reputations, and none did so more forcibly than Carl Hooper, an all-rounder from Guyana, aged eighteen, and two fast bowlers, Anthony Gray of Trinidad & Tobago and Anthony Merrick of Leewards.

Hooper left the youth series against England Young Cricketers with a century in the first "one-day international" to start his first-class career with a century against Barbados in his first innings. He batted with style and authority and bowled his off-breaks effectively, later taking five for 35 for the Under-23 XI against the New Zealanders. In his second season, Gray, 6 feet 7 inches tall, added a new dimension to Trinidad & Tobago's attack with a pace and hostility that earned him 23 wickets at just under 20 runs each. Merrick, strong and powerfully built, a graduate from the West Indies youth team that toured England in 1982, also had 23 wickets. Aged 21, both could anticipate bright futures.

One remarkable individual performance deserves recording. Trinidad & Tobago, set 294 to beat Windward Islands at Guaracara Park, Pointe-á-Pierre, were 171 for five on the final day when Kelvin Williams, their powerfully built all-rounder, with a reputation as a thunderous hitter, struck an undefeated 84 from 51 balls with nine 6s and three 4s, ending the match with four consecutive 6s off the Windwards' captain, Norbert Phillip. It was the stuff of which cricket legends are made and would have pleased one of Williams's predecessors in the Trinidad & Tobago team, the late Lord Learie Constantine.

The limited-overs tournament for the Geddes Grant-Harrison Line Trophy was comfortably won by Guyana, who won all three of their matches. With new sponsorship from the Canadian group, Northern Telecom, the annual youth championship was held in Barbados in August 1984 and reverted to its previous format with each team playing against the other. The title was retained by Barbados, who followed their three outright victories of 1983 with five more on this occasion. Performances in the tournament formed the basis for selection for the West Indies Young Cricketers team in the series against England in the Caribbean early in 1985.

## FIRST-CLASS AVERAGES, 1984-85

### BATTING

(Qualification: 200 runs, average 35)

| | *M* | *I* | *NO* | *R* | *HI* | *100s* | *Avge* |
|---|---|---|---|---|---|---|---|
| R. Seeram (*Guyana*) | 3 | 4 | 1 | 223 | 100* | 1 | 74.33 |
| C. A. Best (*Barbados*) | 5 | 9 | 1 | 437 | 147 | 2 | 54.62 |
| M. C. Worrell (*Barbados*) | 5 | 8 | 4 | 215 | 105 | 1 | 53.75 |
| P. V. Simmons (*T & T*) | 5 | 8 | 0 | 390 | 118 | 1 | 48.75 |
| A. B. Williams (*Jamaica*) | 5 | 8 | 0 | 380 | 102 | 1 | 47.50 |
| C. A. Davidson (*Jamaica*) | 3 | 5 | 0 | 214 | 98 | 0 | 42.80 |
| L. C. Sebastien (*Windward I*) | 5 | 8 | 2 | 242 | 60* | 0 | 40.33 |
| A. L. Kelly (*Leeward I*) | 5 | 10 | 0 | 403 | 88 | 0 | 40.30 |
| E. E. Lewis (*Leeward I*) | 5 | 9 | 0 | 361 | 103 | 1 | 40.11 |
| T. Mohamed (*Guyana*) | 5 | 9 | 1 | 310 | 80 | 0 | 38.75 |
| C. L. Hooper (*Guyana*) | 5 | 7 | 0 | 267 | 126 | 1 | 38.14 |
| W. W. Lewis (*Jamaica*) | 5 | 9 | 0 | 341 | 127 | 2 | 37.88 |
| G. Powell (*Jamaica*) | 4 | 7 | 0 | 261 | 110 | 1 | 37.28 |
| K. C. Williams (*T & T*) | 5 | 8 | 1 | 255 | 84* | 0 | 36.42 |
| M. A. Harper (*Guyana*) | 4 | 7 | 1 | 215 | 81 | 0 | 35.83 |

**Signifies not out.*

## BOWLING

(Qualification: 15 wickets)

| | *O* | *M* | *R* | *W* | *BB* | *Avge* |
|---|---|---|---|---|---|---|
| G. Mahabir (*T & T*) | 188.2 | 36 | 462 | 30 | 6-62 | 15.40 |
| T. Z. Kentish (*Windward I*) | 167 | 46 | 342 | 20 | 5-88 | 17.10 |
| C. G. Butts (*Guyana*) | 299.2 | 81 | 614 | 32 | 7-107 | 19.18 |
| A. H. Gray (*T & T*) | 125 | 15 | 458 | 23 | 6-78 | 19.91 |
| R. Nanan (*T & T*) | 161.5 | 40 | 302 | 15 | 3-38 | 20.13 |
| W. W. Daniel (*Barbados*) | 148 | 25 | 458 | 22 | 7-33 | 20.81 |
| A. G. Daley (*Jamaica*) | 195.4 | 24 | 638 | 29 | 5-64 | 22.00 |
| A. T. Merrick (*Leeward I*) | 146.2 | 21 | 530 | 23 | 5-101 | 23.04 |
| N. C. Guishard (*Leeward I*) | 187.5 | 44 | 403 | 17 | 5-49 | 23.70 |
| R. O. Estwick (*Barbados*) | 142 | 20 | 495 | 20 | 5-83 | 24.75 |

## SHELL SHIELD, 1984-85

| | *Won* | *Lost* | *Drawn* | *1st inns lead in drawn match* | *Pts* |
|---|---|---|---|---|---|
| Trinidad & Tobago | 3 | 1 | 1 | 1 | 56 |
| Leeward Islands | 2 | 1 | 2 | 1 | 44 |
| Guyana | 1 | 1 | 3 | 2 | 36 |
| Windward Islands | 1 | 1* | 3 | 0 | 33 |
| Barbados | 1 | 2 | 2 | 1 | 28 |
| Jamaica | 1 | 3 | 1 | 0 | 20 |

* 1st innings lead in match lost outright.

*Win = 16 pts; Draw = 4 pts; 1st innings lead in match lost outright = 5 pts; 1st innings lead in drawn match = 4 pts.*

## JAMAICA v TRINIDAD & TOBAGO

At Sabina Park, Kingston, January 24, 25, 26, 27. Trinidad & Tobago won by 77 runs. Trinidad & Tobago 16 pts.

### Trinidad & Tobago

| | | | |
|---|---|---|---|
| K. R. Bainey b Brown | 7 | c Francis b Brown | 17 |
| P. V. Simmons c and b Brown | 64 | c Thompson b Neita | 70 |
| R. A. Glasgow b Haynes | 17 | b Haynes | 7 |
| A. Rajah c Peters b Haynes | 11 | lbw b Daley | 38 |
| P. Moosai b Daley | 41 | (6) c Francis b Daley | 32 |
| *R. Nanan b Brown | 12 | (7) lbw b McLeod | 23 |
| K. C. Williams b Daley | 2 | (8) b Daley | 62 |
| †D. Williams run out | 20 | (5) c Francis b Daley | 14 |
| A. H. Gray c Francis b Neita | 0 | b Thompson | 8 |
| G. S. Antoine c Daley b Brown | 8 | c Peters b Haynes | 4 |
| G. Mahabir not out | 0 | not out | 0 |
| B 11, l-b 1, w 1, n-b 9 | 22 | B 16, l-b 9, w 2, n-b 15 | 42 |
| 1/67 2/96 3/109 4/120 5/147 6/154 7/188 8/188 9/200 | 204 | 1/60 2/87 3/130 4/151 5/162 6/206 7/247 8/278 9/317 | 317 |

Bowling: *First Innings*—McLeod 11–4–27–0; Daley 17.5–1–51–2; Thompson 4–0–17–0; Brown 29–14–44–4; Haynes 15–4–40–2; Neita 6–1–13–1. *Second Innings*—McLeod 10–2–35–1; Daley 24.4–4–69–4; Thompson 17–5–46–1; Brown 30–6–73–1; Haynes 21–3–64–2; Neita 3–1–5–1.

## Jamaica

| | | | |
|---|---|---|---|
| *A. B. Williams b Gray | 0 | – c Rajah b Gray | 102 |
| W. W. Lewis lbw b K. C. Williams | 24 | – c D. Williams b Nanan | 26 |
| O. W. Peters c D. Williams b Gray | 5 | – lbw b Nanan | 8 |
| †P. A. Francis c D. Williams b Gray | 1 | – (9) lbw b Mahabir | 16 |
| M. C. Neita not out | 75 | – (4) lbw b Gray | 34 |
| M. Williams c Simmons b Gray | 3 | – (5) lbw b Gray | 0 |
| R. C. Haynes c Mahabir b Antoine | 25 | – (6) c D. Williams b Gray | 5 |
| A. G. Daley b Nanan | 9 | – (7) c Bainey b Gray | 14 |
| E. E. Brown c D. Williams b Nanan | 1 | – (8) st D. Williams b Mahabir | 27 |
| K. W. McLeod run out | 0 | – c D. Williams b Gray | 0 |
| C. U. Thompson c Antoine b Mahabir | 21 | – not out | 8 |
| B 9, l-b 3, n-b 4 | 16 | B 7, l-b 15, n-b 2 | 24 |
| 1/3 2/27 3/31 4/52 5/59 6/107 7/133 8/134 9/137 | 180 | 1/85 2/107 3/172 4/174 5/184 6/202 7/215 8/241 9/242 | 264 |

Bowling: *First Innings*—Antoine 9–0–33–1; Gray 17–1–51–4; K. C. Williams 10–1–34–1; Nanan 12–1–30–2; Mahabir 2.5–0–6–1; Simmons 2–0–14–0. *Second Innings*—Antoine 3–0–16–0; Gray 23–2–78–6; K. C. Williams 3–0–13–0; Nanan 36–7–62–2; Mahabir 34.3–8–73–2.

Umpires: A. Gaynor and S. E. Parris.

## JAMAICA v WINDWARD ISLANDS

At Sabina Park, Kingston, January 31, February 1, 2, 3. Windward Islands won by seven wickets. Windward Islands 16 pts.

### Jamaica

| | | | |
|---|---|---|---|
| W. W. Lewis c Cadette b Phillip | 0 | – (2) b Etienne | 59 |
| *A. B. Williams c Cadette b Sebastien | 28 | – (5) c Charles b Phillip | 91 |
| O. W. Peters b Collymore | 1 | – (1) c Sebastien b Etienne | 72 |
| M. C. Neita b Phillip | 23 | – c and b Phillip | 6 |
| G. Powell c Collymore b Sebastien | 23 | – (3) c Sebastien b Phillip | 20 |
| R. C. Haynes c Maurice b Phillip | 15 | – c Collymore b Phillip | 1 |
| E. E. Brown run out | 16 | – lbw b Phillip | 2 |
| A. G. Daley c Kentish b Collymore | 2 | – not out | 45 |
| †P. A. Francis c and b Sebastien | 0 | – lbw b Phillip | 0 |
| E. L. Wilson c Cadette b Sebastien | 8 | – lbw b Collymore | 3 |
| B. McKenzie not out | 6 | – b Collymore | 3 |
| B 4, l-b 1, w 2, n-b 6 | 13 | B 2, l-b 6, n-b 10 | 18 |
| 1/0 2/1 3/57 4/59 5/84 6/111 7/115 8/116 9/120 | 135 | 1/109 2/141 3/149 4/165 5/180 6/188 7/292 8/292 9/311 | 320 |

Bowling: *First Innings*—Phillip 14–3–31–3; Collymore 14–1–50–2; Sebastien 13.1–1–49–4. *Second Innings*—Phillip 28–5–90–6; Collymore 26.2–4–81–2; Sebastien 4–1–28–0; Kentish 7–3–8–0; Etienne 36–12–69–2; Hinds 12–1–36–0.

### Windward Islands

| | | | |
|---|---|---|---|
| L. C. Sebastien b Wilson | 28 | – c Peters b Daley | 15 |
| L. D. John lbw b Daley | 137 | – c Neita b Daley | 1 |
| †I. Cadette c Francis b McKenzie | 56 | – b Daley | 0 |
| L. A. Lewis c Daley b McKenzie | 0 | | |
| F. X. Maurice c Daley b Wilson | 17 | – (4) not out | 20 |
| J. D. Charles c and b Haynes | 6 | – (5) not out | 5 |
| *N. Phillip b Daley | 22 | | |

| | | | |
|---|---|---|---|
| D. J. Collymore c Lewis b Haynes | 24 | | |
| S. J. Hinds b Daley | 72 | | |
| T. Z. Kentish not out | 29 | | |
| J. T. Etienne b Daley | 0 | | |
| B 3, l-b 8, n-b 3 | 14 | B 6, l-b 1, n-b 3 | 10 |
| 1/50 2/167 3/167 4/219 5/238 6/270 7/277 8/331 9/401 | 405 | 1/6 2/7 3/44 (3 wkts) | 51 |

Bowling: *First Innings*—Daley 29–3–108–4; McKenzie 30–7–67–2; Wilson 45–17–98–2; Haynes 29–3–74–2; Brown 17–4–32–0; Neita 4–1–15–0. *Second Innings*—Daley 8–0–25–3; McKenzie 3–0–9–0; Wilson 5.2–1–10–0.

Umpires: C. E. Cumberbatch and J. R. Gayle.

## BARBADOS v GUYANA

At Kensington Oval, Bridgetown, February 1, 2, 3, 4. Drawn. Barbados 8 pts, Guyana 4 pts.

### Barbados

| | | | |
|---|---|---|---|
| *C. A. Best c Harper b Butts | 67 | not out | 114 |
| A. S. Gilkes c Pydanna b Charles | 16 | b Butts | 40 |
| T. A. Hunte b Butts | 1 | c Pydanna b Charles | 53 |
| L. N. Reifer c Pydanna b Charles | 8 | | |
| S. R. Greaves st Pydanna b Butts | 44 | | |
| R. L. Skeete c Hooper b Kallicharran | 38 | | |
| N. A. Phillips c Charles b Butts | 0 | (4) not out | 2 |
| D. A. Cumberbatch c Lambert b Butts | 45 | | |
| †M. C. Worrell c Lambert b Butts | 105 | | |
| W. W. Daniel lbw b Butts | 5 | | |
| R. O. Estwick not out | 34 | | |
| B 7, l-b 6, w 2, n-b 6 | 21 | B 3, l-b 6, n-b 9 | 18 |
| 1/43 2/45 3/62 4/116 5/181 6/181 7/187 8/282 9/294 | 384 | 1/99 2/221 (2 wkts dec.) | 227 |

Bowling: *First Innings*—Joseph 9–0–50–0; Charles 18–2–66–2; Butts 55.4–17–107–7; Kallicharran 29–2–92–1; Hooper 14–0–56–0. *Second Innings*—Joseph 11–0–65–0; Charles 19–1–71–1; Butts 25–6–58–1; Kallicharran 6–0–24–0.

### Guyana

| | | | |
|---|---|---|---|
| A. A. Lyght b Estwick | 7 | lbw b Daniel | 10 |
| C. B. Lambert c Worrell b Estwick | 2 | c and b Estwick | 3 |
| A. F. D. Jackman c Best b Estwick | 24 | b Phillips | 8 |
| T. Mohamed c Cumberbatch b Daniel | 15 | lbw b Estwick | 61 |
| M. A. Harper lbw b Cumberbatch | 32 | (6) lbw b Best | 81 |
| C. L. Hooper run out | 126 | (5) c Worrell b Phillips | 0 |
| D. I. Kallicharran c Cumberbatch b Estwick | 34 | c Best b Estwick | 0 |
| G. E. Charles lbw b Estwick | 0 | (9) not out | 15 |
| *†M. R. Pydanna c Estwick b Daniel | 14 | (8) not out | 28 |
| C. G. Butts b Daniel | 6 | | |
| R. F. Joseph not out | 0 | | |
| B 1, l-b 1, w 1, n-b 8 | 11 | L-b 6, w 4, n-b 4 | 14 |
| 1/6 2/10 3/44 4/51 5/119 6/173 7/178 8/228 9/238 | 271 | 1/3 2/15 3/50 4/50 5/157 6/158 7/187 (7 wkts) | 220 |

Bowling: *First Innings*—Daniel 16–1–65–3; Estwick 17–1–83–5; Greaves 10–0–41–0; Phillips 8–2–25–0; Cumberbatch 11.1–0–55–1. *Second Innings*—Daniel 18–2–37–1; Estwick 16–2–77–3; Greaves 5–0–26–0; Phillips 13–1–42–2; Cumberbatch 6–1–25–0; Best 2–0–7–1; Skeete 1–1–0–0.

Umpires: A. Gaynor and N. Harrison.

## TRINIDAD & TOBAGO v LEEWARD ISLANDS

At Queen's Park Oval, Port-of-Spain, February 1, 2, 3, 4. Drawn. Trinidad & Tobago 8 pts, Leeward Islands 4 pts.

### Leeward Islands

| | | | |
|---|---|---|---|
| A. L. Kelly c D. Williams b Gray | 7 | – c Rajah b Mahabir | 55 |
| L. L. Lawrence st D. Williams b Mahabir | 31 | – c D. Williams b Antoine | 93 |
| E. E. Lewis c Rajah b Antoine | 12 | – b Mahabir | 1 |
| R. M. Otto c Simmons b K. C. Williams | 110 | – lbw b Mahabir | 34 |
| V. A. Eddy lbw b Nanan | 3 | – c D. Williams b Antoine | 11 |
| †S. I. Williams c Simmons b Gray | 18 | – not out | 31 |
| N. C. Guishard st D. Williams b Mahabir | 4 | | |
| C. E. I. Bartlette c Simmons b Nanan | 2 | | |
| T. A. Merrick c Gray b Nanan | 3 | | |
| *E. T. Willett b Mahabir | 1 | | |
| J. D. Thompson not out | 3 | | |
| B 1, l-b 4, w 2, n-b 3 | 10 | B 8, l-b 5, w 1, n-b 7 | 21 |
| 1/11 2/35 3/67 4/70 5/119 6/142 7/149 8/163 9/179 | 204 | 1/88 2/94 3/171 4/190 5/246 | (5 wkts) 246 |

Bowling: *First Innings*—Gray 15–4–36–2; K. C. Williams 18.3–5–38–1; Antoine 6–0–31–1; Nanan 24–8–40–3; Mahabir 28–7–54–3. *Second Innings*—Gray 15–1–57–0; K. C. Williams 12–1–34–0; Antoine 12.4–1–60–2; Nanan 20–8–29–0; Mahabir 28–5–53–3.

### Trinidad & Tobago

| | |
|---|---|
| K. R. Bainey c Williams b Willett | 19 |
| P. V. Simmons c Williams b Bartlette | 118 |
| R. S. Gabriel c Williams b Merrick | 22 |
| A. Rajah run out | 55 |
| P. Moosai c Otto b Bartlette | 13 |
| *R. Nanan c Otto b Bartlette | 46 |
| K. C. Williams lbw b Bartlette | 0 |
| †D. Williams c Guishard b Merrick | 13 |
| A. H. Gray st Williams b Guishard | 14 |
| G. S. Antoine not out | 12 |
| G. Mahabir c Kelly b Merrick | 7 |
| B 9, l-b 4, w 1, n-b 3 | 17 |
| 1/50 2/115 3/199 4/233 5/272 6/272 7/301 8/301 9/317 | 336 |

Bowling: Merrick 27.2–1–99–3; Bartlette 19–1–69–4; Willett 32–10–59–1; Thompson 17–5–49–0; Guishard 19–3–47–1.

Umpires: L. H. Barker and S. Mohammed.

## TRINIDAD & TOBAGO v WINDWARD ISLANDS

At Guaracara Park, Pointe-á-Pierre, February 8, 9, 10. Trinidad & Tobago won by four wickets. Trinidad & Tobago 16 pts, Windward Islands 5 pts.

### Windward Islands

| | | | |
|---|---|---|---|
| L. C. Sebastien c sub b Gray | 12 | – (6) not out | 31 |
| L. D. John c Simmons b K. C. Williams | 50 | – c D. Williams b Antoine | 43 |
| F. X. Maurice c D. Williams b Gray | 7 | – (4) c Rajah b Gray | 5 |
| L. A. Lewis c Mahabir b Gray | 37 | – (1) c Simmons b Gray | 6 |
| J. D. Charles run out | 49 | – b Mahabir | 21 |
| *N. Phillip c Rajah b Gray | 81 | – (7) c Furlonge b Mahabir | 4 |

| | | | |
|---|---|---|---|
| †I. Cadette c K. C. Williams b Gray | 0 | (3) c D. Williams b K. C. Williams | 2 |
| D. J. Collymore lbw b Mahabir | 1 | c Nanan b Antoine | 2 |
| S. J. Hinds c Rajah b Mahabir | 3 | b Antoine | 6 |
| T. Z. Kentish not out | 0 | c Moosai b Mahabir | 20 |
| J. T. Etienne b Mahabir | 0 | lbw b Mahabir | 0 |
| B 5, l-b 4, n-b 10 | 19 | L-b 2, n-b 4 | 6 |
| 1/25 2/82 3/124 4/215 5/218 6/236 7/252 8/259 9/259 | 259 | 1/13 2/25 3/32 4/78 5/82 6/96 7/106 8/115 9/146 | 146 |

Bowling: *First Innings*—Gray 21–3–86–5; K. C. Williams 15–4–30–1; Antoine 9–0–60–0; Simmons 1–0–5–0; Nanan 15–3–24–0; Mahabir 18.2–3–45–3. *Second Innings*—Gray 11–1–44–2; K. C. Williams 7–0–30–1; Antoine 11–2–33–3; Mahabir 12.3–1–37–4.

## Trinidad & Tobago

| | | | |
|---|---|---|---|
| P. V. Simmons run out | 5 | c Cadette b Kentish | 78 |
| R. S. Gabriel b Collymore | 14 | lbw b Phillip | 60 |
| D. C. Furlonge c Etienne b Collymore | 11 | (5) lbw b Kentish | 0 |
| A. Rajah c Kentish b Collymore | 13 | lbw b Kentish | 30 |
| P. Moosai st Cadette b Kentish | 14 | (3) c sub b Kentish | 7 |
| *R. Nanan c Charles b Kentish | 1 | c Sebastien b Kentish | 6 |
| K. C. Williams c Collymore b Phillip | 5 | not out | 84 |
| †D. Williams c and b Kentish | 16 | not out | 9 |
| A. H. Gray c Phillip b Kentish | 18 | | |
| G. S. Antoine not out | 1 | | |
| G. Mahabir c Charles b Hinds | 0 | | |
| B 1, l-b 4, n-b 9 | 14 | B 2, l-b 7, n-b 12 | 21 |
| 1/7 2/20 3/46 4/49 5/50 6/72 7/80 8/104 9/111 | 112 | 1/146 2/148 3/159 4/159 5/171 6/251 | (6 wkts) 295 |

Bowling: *First Innings*—Phillip 13–1–35–1; Collymore 16.5–4–45–3; Kentish 13–4–20–4; Etienne 1–0–7–0; Hinds 0.1–0–0–1. *Second Innings*—Phillip 21–3–87–1; Collymore 0–0–1–0; Kentish 33–5–88–5; Etienne 9–2–40–0; Hinds 12–1–61–0; Sebastien 1–0–9–0.

*Note:* Collymore, in the second innings, was injured after bowling 1 no-ball.

Umpires: C. E. Cumberbatch and M. Baksh.

## JAMAICA v BARBADOS

At Sabina Park, Kingston, February 8, 9, 10, 11. Jamaica won by an innings and 45 runs. Jamaica 16 pts.

## Barbados

| | | | |
|---|---|---|---|
| *C. A. Best lbw b Dixon | 30 | st Francis b Wilson | 147 |
| A. S. Gilkes c Davidson b Dixon | 5 | lbw b Daley | 3 |
| T. A. Hunte b Daley | 37 | lbw b Daley | 0 |
| L. N. Reifer c Davidson b Dixon | 0 | lbw b Adams | 21 |
| S. R. Greaves lbw b Wilson | 67 | c Francis b Daley | 18 |
| R. L. Skeete run out | 18 | b Dixon | 13 |
| †M. C. Worrell not out | 53 | c Francis b Dixon | 1 |
| D. A. Cumberbatch lbw b Daley | 11 | c Lewis b Wilson | 19 |
| R. O. Estwick lbw b Daley | 0 | lbw b Dixon | 11 |
| W. W. Daniel b Daley | 3 | not out | 7 |
| M. A. Small lbw b Daley | 0 | run out | 0 |
| B 2, l-b 7, w 1, n-b 6 | 16 | B 5, l-b 8, n-b 7 | 20 |
| 1/8 2/61 3/65 4/77 5/135 6/198 7/226 8/226 9/240 | 240 | 1/29 2/29 3/69 4/108 5/127 6/130 7/170 8/215 9/259 | 260 |

Bowling: *First Innings*—Daley 18.5–1–64–5; Dixon 20–1–81–3; Wilson 21–9–48–1; Neita 1–0–8–0; Adams 12–1–30–0. *Second Innings*—Daley 31–8–103–3; Dixon 26.5–3–80–3; Wilson 24–5–45–2; Adams 18–7–19–1.

## Jamaica

| | |
|---|---|
| O. W. Peters lbw b Daniel | 3 |
| W. W. Lewis lbw b Daniel | 3 |
| G. Powell c Daniel b Best | 110 |
| M. C. Neita c Worrell b Small | 49 |
| *A. B. Williams c Worrell b Cumberbatch | 59 |
| C. A. Davidson c Cumberbatch b Small | 98 |
| J. Adams c Worrell b Daniel | 40 |
| D. Dixon b Small | 75 |
| A. G. Daley not out | 50 |
| †P. A. Francis not out | 16 |
| B 17, l-b 10, w 7, n-b 8 | 42 |
| 1/7 2/8 3/122 4/218 5/271 6/369 7/438 8/496 (8 wkts dec.) | 545 |

E. L. Wilson did not bat.

Bowling: Estwick 20.2–4–60–0; Daniel 32–3–151–3; Small 33–3–147–3; Cumberbatch 27.4–2–98–1; Hunte 12.4–2–36–0; Best 11–2–26–1.

Umpires: J. R. Gayle and A. Weekes.

## LEEWARD ISLANDS v GUYANA

At Recreation Ground, St John's, Antigua, February 8, 9, 10, 11. Leeward Islands won by one wicket. Leeward Islands 16 pts.

### Guyana

| First innings | | Second innings | |
|---|---|---|---|
| A. A. Lyght lbw b U. V. C. Lawrence | 24 | lbw b Merrick | 23 |
| C. B. Lambert c and b Merrick | 53 | b Merrick | 16 |
| A. F. D. Jackman c Bartlette b Merrick | 18 | b Guishard | 21 |
| T. Mohamed c Eddy b Guishard | 27 | c Williams b Willett | 80 |
| M. A. Harper lbw b Merrick | 5 | c Otto b Merrick | 26 |
| C. L. Hooper c Kelly b Guishard | 9 | b Merrick | 10 |
| D. I. Kallicharran c Kelly b Merrick | 8 | b Willett | 16 |
| *†M. R. Pydanna c Merrick b Willett | 28 | c Bartlette b Guishard | 9 |
| C. G. Butts not out | 30 | run out | 3 |
| R. F. Joseph b Bartlette | 5 | not out | 1 |
| C. V. Solomon b Merrick | 0 | b Willett | 0 |
| B 1, l-b 1, n-b 5 | 7 | B 1, l-b 1, n-b 3 | 5 |
| 1/76 2/90 3/112 4/122 5/137 6/150 7/154 8/184 9/213 | 214 | 1/27 2/42 3/76 4/123 5/140 6/186 7/201 8/207 9/208 | 210 |

Bowling: *First Innings*—Merrick 22.3–2–101–5; Bartlette 7–0–28–1; U. V. C. Lawrence 15–4–36–1; Willett 9–4–16–1; Guishard 10–3–31–2. *Second Innings*—Merrick 19–4–76–4; Bartlette 11–1–47–0; U. V. C. Lawrence 3–1–7–0; Willett 17.1–1–40–3; Guishard 22–6–38–2.

### Leeward Islands

| First innings | | Second innings | |
|---|---|---|---|
| A. L. Kelly run out | 47 | b Butts | 54 |
| L. L. Lawrence b Butts | 36 | c Kallicharran b Solomon | 0 |
| E. E. Lewis c Joseph b Hooper | 70 | c Butts b Joseph | 0 |
| R. M. Otto c Lambert b Hooper | 17 | c Kallicharran b Joseph | 0 |
| V. A. Eddy c Lambert b Hooper | 3 | c Pydanna b Solomon | 8 |
| †S. I. Williams c Kallicharran b Butts | 31 | c Pydanna b Butts | 15 |
| U. V. C. Lawrence c Mohamed b Butts | 15 | b Butts | 21 |

| | | |
|---|---|---|
| N. C. Guishard c Harper b Butts | 32 – c Harper b Butts | 18 |
| T. A. Merrick c Pydanna b Joseph | 24 – c Lambert b Butts | 3 |
| C. E. I. Bartlette c Lambert b Butts | 0 – not out | 5 |
| *E. T. Willett not out | 7 – not out | 1 |
| B 1, l-b 4, n-b 6 | 11 L-b 2, n-b 5 | 7 |
| 1/89 2/93 3/153 4/163 5/191 6/207 7/253 8/266 9/266 | 293 1/1 2/11 3/11 4/24 5/64 6/101 7/108 8/124 9/131 | (9 wkts) 132 |

Bowling: *First Innings*—Joseph 4.5–0–27–1; Solomon 5–0–25–0; Butts 41–9–113–5; Hooper 21–3–79–3; Kallicharran 23–8–44–0. *Second Innings*—Joseph 5–0–15–2; Solomon 4–0–24–2; Butts 17.5–4–40–5; Hooper 3–0–13–0; Kallicharran 16–2–38–0.

Umpires: D. M. Archer and P. Whyte.

## BARBADOS v LEEWARD ISLANDS

At Kensington Oval, Bridgetown, February 16, 17, 18, 19. Barbados won by one wicket. Barbados 16 pts.

### Leeward Islands

| | | |
|---|---|---|
| A. L. Kelly b Daniel | 8 – c Best b Phillips | 58 |
| L. L. Lawrence c Hunte b Daniel | 12 – run out | 20 |
| E. A. Lewis c Phillips b Estwick | 10 – c Worrell b Phillips | 7 |
| R. M. Otto c Worrell b Daniel | 5 – c Estwick b Broomes | 14 |
| E. E. Lewis c Phillips b Estwick | 43 – c Worrell b Estwick | 103 |
| †S. I. Williams c Broomes b Daniel | 0 – b Daniel | 12 |
| N. C. Guishard c Gilkes b Estwick | 3 – c Worrell b Estwick | 40 |
| T. A. Merrick b Daniel | 0 – c Worrell b Estwick | 3 |
| C. E. I. Bartlette c Reifer b Daniel | 9 – c Worrell b Estwick | 0 |
| *E. T. Willett c Skeete b Daniel | 8 – not out | 1 |
| J. D. Thompson not out | 0 – c Worrell b Estwick | 0 |
| B 1, l-b 2, w 1, n-b 1 | 5 B 4, l-b 6, w 4, n-b 10 | 24 |
| 1/8 2/25 3/34 4/35 5/35 6/54 7/63 8/85 9/96 | 103 1/75 2/87 3/90 4/136 5/177 6/258 7/273 8/273 9/279 | 282 |

Bowling: *First Innings*—Daniel 13.4–4–33–7; Estwick 12–1–52–3; Phillips 5–0–14–0; Broomes 1–0–1–0. *Second Innings*—Daniel 22–7–65–1; Estwick 23.4–2–83–5; Phillips 17–3–47–2; Broomes 23–2–67–1; Reifer 4–1–10–0.

### Barbados

| | | |
|---|---|---|
| *C. A. Best c Kelly b Guishard | 26 – lbw b Thompson | 18 |
| A. S. Gilkes c Bartlette b Willett | 29 – b Guishard | 13 |
| N. Johnson c Kelly b Thompson | 29 – (6) c Williams b Merrick | 98 |
| G. N. Reifer c Otto b Guishard | 4 – c Otto b Guishard | 0 |
| R. L. Skeete c Williams b Guishard | 10 – c E. A. Lewis b Thompson | 12 |
| T. A. Hunte b Guishard | 1 – (3) c and b Thompson | 52 |
| N. A. Phillips c E. A. Lewis b Thompson | 0 – (8) not out | 21 |
| †M. C. Worrell not out | 22 – (7) c Otto b Guishard | 20 |
| R. O. Estwick c Willett b Guishard | 0 – lbw b Merrick | 0 |
| N. D. Broomes lbw b Thompson | 13 – run out | 0 |
| W. W. Daniel run out | 1 – not out | 6 |
| B 2, l-b 1, n-b 2 | 5 L-b 4, w 2, n-b 1 | 7 |
| 1/54 2/60 3/82 4/98 5/100 6/100 7/102 8/102 9/124 | 140 1/29 2/35 3/35 4/60 5/148 6/196 7/223 8/223 9/237 | (9 wkts) 247 |

Bowling: *First Innings*—Merrick 10–1–15–0; Bartlette 8–1–16–0; Willett 13–4–38–1; Guishard 23.5–3–49–5; Thompson 9–2–19–3. *Second Innings*—Merrick 9–3–24–2; Bartlette 3–1–13–0; Willett 19.4–2–44–0; Guishard 43–11–84–3; Thompson 40–9–78–3.

Umpires: N. Harrison and D. J. Narine.

## WINDWARD ISLANDS v GUYANA

At Arnos Vale, Kingstown, St Vincent, February 15, 16, 17, 18. Drawn. Windward Islands 4 pts, Guyana 8 pts.

### Guyana

| | | | |
|---|---|---|---|
| A. A. Lyght lbw b Phillip | 19 | – c Texeira b Thomas | 0 |
| C. B. Lambert c Thomas b Phillip | 5 | – b Murphy | 8 |
| A. F. D. Jackman lbw b Thomas | 16 | – run out | 33 |
| T. Mohamed c Phillip b Hinds | 58 | – c Hinds b Thomas | 16 |
| R. N. Seeram lbw b Murphy | 67 | – not out | 100 |
| M. A. Harper c Cadette b Kentish | 31 | – not out | 15 |
| C. L. Hooper b Thomas | 36 | | |
| D. I. Kallicharran c Cadette b Thomas | 88 | | |
| G. E. Charles lbw b Hinds | 3 | | |
| *†M. R. Pydanna c Cadette b Murphy | 46 | | |
| C. G. Butts not out | 3 | | |
| B 7, l-b 3, w 1, n-b 12 | 23 | B 2, l-b 2, n-b 10 | 14 |
| 1/9 2/34 3/62 4/125 5/139 6/240 7/267 8/276 9/384 | 395 | 1/3 2/11 3/48 4/108 (4 wkts) | 186 |

Bowling: *First Innings*—Phillip 21–3–74–2; Murphy 23–5–76–2; Thomas 19.5–0–73–3; Sebastien 6–1–10–0; Hinds 42–16–83–2; Kentish 35–11–55–1; Charles 6–1–14–0. *Second Innings*—Murphy 14–3–40–1; Thomas 22–3–59–2; Sebastien 12–2–43–0; Hinds 3–0–9–0; Kentish 6–2–12–0; Lewis 5–0–19–0.

### Windward Islands

| | |
|---|---|
| L. C. Sebastien b Charles | 57 |
| L. D. John b Charles | 1 |
| L. A. Lewis c and b Charles | 24 |
| J. D. Charles c Lambert b Butts | 11 |
| A. D. Texeira b Charles | 31 |
| *N. Phillip lbw b Butts | 80 |
| †I. Cadette b Charles | 5 |
| T. Z. Kentish c Mohamed b Charles | 40 |
| S. J. Hinds c Charles b Butts | 2 |
| W. Thomas not out | 9 |
| S. Murphy c Harper b Charles | 3 |
| B 9, l-b 3, w 1, n-b 5 | 18 |
| 1/3 2/67 3/89 4/131 5/132 6/162 7/257 8/261 9/273 | 281 |

Bowling: Charles 44.1–6–105–7; Harper 9–1–26–0; Butts 38–11–74–3; Kallicharran 19–6–40–0; Hooper 3–0–20–0, Lyght 2 0 4 0.

Umpires: L. H. Barker and M. Hippolyte.

## LEEWARD ISLANDS v JAMAICA

At Warner Park, Basseterre, St Kitts, February 22, 23, 24, 25. Leeward Islands won by eight wickets. Leeward Islands 16 pts.

### Leeward Islands

| | | | |
|---|---|---|---|
| A. L. Kelly lbw b Wilson | 35 | – run out | 22 |
| L. L. Lawrence lbw b Whittingham | 25 | – lbw b Daley | 5 |
| E. A. Lewis c Lewis b Adams | 30 | – not out | 29 |
| R. M. Otto c Adams b Whittingham | 7 | – not out | 14 |
| E. E. Lewis c Davidson b Daley | 92 | | |
| †S. I. Williams run out | 12 | | |

| | | | |
|---|---|---|---|
| E. A. E. Baptiste st Francis b Wilson | 24 | | |
| N. C. Guishard b Adams | 63 | | |
| T. A. Merrick lbw b Daley | 0 | | |
| *E. T. Willett b Wilson | 40 | | |
| J. D. Thompson not out | 23 | | |
| B 5, l-b 12, w 2, n-b 10 | 29 | L-b 1 | 1 |
| 1/47 2/81 3/92 4/116 5/139 6/219 7/248 8/248 9/343 | 380 | 1/23 2/31 (2 wkts) | 71 |

Bowling: *First Innings*—Daley 28–3–98–2; Dixon 24–6–73–0; Wilson 43–12–94–3; Whittingham 27–8–72–2; Adams 9–2–26–2. *Second Innings*—Daley 7–2–26–1; Dixon 2–0–13–0; Wilson 10.2–3–22–0; Adams 5–1–9–0.

### Jamaica

| | | | |
|---|---|---|---|
| W. W. Lewis b Merrick | 20 | – b Merrick | 48 |
| O. W. Peters lbw b Baptiste | 4 | – b Baptiste | 0 |
| G. Powell c Baptiste b Merrick | 7 | – c Guishard b Merrick | 55 |
| *A. B. Williams lbw b Baptiste | 1 | – (5) c Williams b Willett | 45 |
| C. A. Davidson b Merrick | 45 | – (6) c and b Merrick | 36 |
| J. Adams c Lawrence b Merrick | 0 | – (7) c Thompson b Merrick | 14 |
| E. Whittingham c and b Baptiste | 13 | – (4) c Merrick b Guishard | 54 |
| D. Dixon lbw b Willett | 17 | – c Otto b Merrick | 0 |
| A. G. Daley c Lawrence b Thompson | 10 | – b Baptiste | 13 |
| †P. A. Francis run out | 0 | – not out | 28 |
| E. L. Wilson not out | 7 | – c Otto b Willett | 1 |
| L-b 5, w 1, n-b 1 | 7 | B 1, l-b 9, w 2, n-b 13 | 25 |
| 1/12 2/35 3/36 4/50 5/54 6/75 7/100 8/117 9/117 | 131 | 1/1 2/111 3/121 4/218 5/218 6/251 7/253 8/277 9/283 | 319 |

Bowling: *First Innings*—Merrick 12.4–2–43–4; Baptiste 12–2–42–3; Thompson 12–3–24–1; Willett 12–3–17–1. *Second Innings*—Merrick 32–4–102–5; Baptiste 17–3–45–2; Thompson 14–1–44–0; Willett 30–14–45–2; Guishard 33–8–73–1.

Umpires: S. Mohammed and A. Weekes.

## WINDWARD ISLANDS v BARBADOS

At Windsor Park, Roseau, Dominica, February 22, 23, 24, 25. Drawn. Windward Islands 4 pts, Barbados 4 pts.

### Windward Islands

| | |
|---|---|
| L. C. Sebastien lbw b Daniel | 6 |
| L. D. John c Worrell b Estwick | 30 |
| L. A. Lewis lbw b Daniel | 76 |
| J. D. Charles st Worrell b Phillips | 29 |
| A. D. Texeira c Broomes b Phillips | 6 |
| R. Marshall c Worrell b Greaves | 7 |
| *N. Phillip c Hunte b Daniel | 0 |
| †I. Cadette c Worrell b Daniel | 7 |
| T. Z. Kentish c Johnson b Daniel | 14 |
| S. J. Hinds c Estwick b Greaves | 5 |
| W. Thomas not out | 0 |
| B 5, l-b 6, n-b 8 | 19 |
| 1/14 2/42 3/120 4/137 5/170 6/170 7/172 8/186 9/199 | 199 |

Bowling: Daniel 22.2–5–35–5; Estwick 23–5–49–1; Phillips 18–1–69–2; Greaves 12–1–27–2; Broomes 3–0–8–0.

### Barbados

| | | | |
|---|---|---|---|
| *C. A. Best c Lewis b Thomas | 11 | †M. C. Worrell not out | 8 |
| T. A. Hunte c Sebastien b Kentish | 6 | | |
| N. Johnson lbw b Kentish | 17 | L-b 1, n-b 3 | 4 |
| S. R. Greaves b Kentish | 12 | | |
| R. L. Skeete lbw b Marshall | 18 | 1/20 2/20 3/45 | (5 wkts) 83 |
| G. N. Reifer not out | 7 | 4/62 5/72 | |

N. A. Phillips, N. D. Broomes, R. O. Estwick and W. W. Daniel did not bat.

Bowling: Phillip 2–0–13–0; Thomas 4–0–14–1; Kentish 19–8–34–3; Hinds 7–2–8–0; Marshall 10–4–13–1.

Umpires: D. J. Narine and J. Simon.

## GUYANA v TRINIDAD & TOBAGO

At Bourda, Georgetown, February 22, 23, 24. Guyana won by ten wickets. Guyana 16 pts.

### Trinidad & Tobago

| | | | |
|---|---|---|---|
| R. S. Gabriel b Butts | 28 | – c Hooper b Hewitt | 16 |
| P. V. Simmons lbw b Charles | 24 | – c Hewitt b Butts | 22 |
| P. Moosai c Pydanna b Hewitt | 1 | – c Pydanna b Butts | 1 |
| A. Rajah c Pydanna b Charles | 11 | – c Mohamed b Hooper | 29 |
| D. I. Mohammed c Harper b Butts | 11 | – c Lambert b Kallicharran | 15 |
| *R. Nanan c Seeram b Kallicharran | 13 | – (7) c Charles b Hooper | 10 |
| R. C. Williams c Lambert b Butts | 23 | – (6) c Lambert b Hooper | 38 |
| †D. Williams c Lambert b Kallicharran | 3 | – b Butts | 11 |
| A. H. Gray st Pydanna b Kallicharran | 1 | – b Butts | 2 |
| G. S. Antoine not out | 2 | – not out | 5 |
| G. Mahabir c Seeram b Kallicharran | 4 | – c Lyght b Hooper | 0 |
| B 4, l-b 2 | 6 | B 1, l-b 11 | 12 |
| 1/31 2/32 3/53 4/71 5/76 6/108 7/113 8/120 9/123 | 127 | 1/42 2/42 3/48 4/73 5/122 6/139 7/141 8/147 9/158 | 161 |

Bowling: *First Innings*—Charles 10–1–43–2; Hewitt 11–3–39–1; Butts 17–8–14–3; Kallicharran 12.4–5–25–4. *Second Innings*—Charles 5–1–16–0; Hewitt 8–1–20–1; Butts 20–4–49–4; Kallicharran 9–2–37–1; Hooper 8.4–3–27–4.

### Guyana

| | | | |
|---|---|---|---|
| A. A. Lyght c D. Williams b Nanan | 46 | – not out | 29 |
| C. B. Lambert c Gabriel b Mahabir | 37 | – not out | 32 |
| T. Mohamed c and b Mahabir | 5 | | |
| M. A. Harper c Gabriel b Mahabir | 25 | | |
| R. N. Seeram c D. Williams b Antoine | 25 | | |
| C. L. Hooper c D. Williams b Nanan | 37 | | |
| D. I. Kallicharran c D. Williams b Mahabir | 20 | | |
| G. E. Charles b Nanan | 0 | | |
| *†M. R. Pydanna c Simmons b Mahabir | 0 | | |
| C. G. Butts not out | 7 | | |
| D. A. Hewitt b Mahabir | 13 | | |
| L-b 8, w 1, n-b 2 | 11 | L-b 1, w 1 | 2 |
| 1/80 2/85 3/100 4/139 5/148 6/202 7/202 8/206 9/206 | 226 | | (no wkt) 63 |

Bowling: *First Innings*—Gray 8–0–46–0; K. C. Williams 7–0–41–0; Nanan 21–6–38–3; Antoine 9–0–31–1; Mahabir 23.3–5–62–6. *Second Innings*—Nanan 6–0–28–0; Antoine 2–0–10–0; Mahabir 5.4–0–24–0.

Umpires: D. M. Archer and C. F. Vyfhuis.

## GUYANA v JAMAICA

At Hampton Court, Essequibo, Guyana, March 1, 2, 3, 4. Drawn. Guyana 8 pts, Jamaica 4 pts.

### Jamaica

| | | | |
|---|---|---|---|
| W. W. Lewis b Hooper | 34 | b Hooper | 127 |
| O. W. Peters lbw b Kallicharran | 28 | run out | 43 |
| G. Powell c and b Hooper | 1 | (4) c Hooper b Kallicharran | 45 |
| C. A. Davidson c Lambert b Kallicharran | 18 | (5) lbw b Hooper | 17 |
| *A. B. Williams c Pydanna b Kallicharran | 53 | absent injured | |
| T. A. Corke c Lambert b Hooper | 33 | (7) c Lambert b Butts | 7 |
| J. Adams not out | 19 | (6) c and b Kallicharran | 28 |
| D. Dixon b Kallicharran | 21 | c Kallicharran b Butts | 13 |
| A. G. Daley c Charles b Kallicharran | 9 | c Hooper b Kallicharran | 18 |
| †P. A. Francis c Hooper b Butts | 4 | (3) c Mohamed b Charles | 13 |
| E. L. Wilson b Butts | 0 | (10) not out | 14 |
| B 4, l-b 12, w 1 | 17 | B 5, l-b 10, w 1, n-b 1 | 17 |
| 1/53 2/57 3/76 4/91 5/175 6/199 7/209 8/228 9/237 | 237 | 1/117 2/156 3/228 4/254 5/260 6/273 7/294 8/314 9/342 | 342 |

Bowling: *First Innings*—Charles 6–1–13–0; Hewitt 6–1–22–0; Butts 36.5–8–68–2; Hooper 20–0–73–3; Kallicharran 23–6–45–5. *Second Innings*—Charles 16–0–62–1; Hewitt 8–2–12–0; Butts 49–14–92–2; Hooper 19–4–59–2; Kallicharran 37.5–4–102–3.

### Guyana

| | | | |
|---|---|---|---|
| A. A. Lyght c Francis b Daley | 39 | c Adams b Daley | 18 |
| C. B. Lambert c and b Wilson | 12 | not out | 24 |
| A. F. D. Jackman run out | 36 | | |
| T. Mohamed c Corke b Daley | 39 | (3) not out | 9 |
| R. N. Seeram c Lewis b Corke | 31 | | |
| C. L. Hooper lbw b Adams | 49 | | |
| D. I. Kallicharran c Corke b Daley | 10 | | |
| G. E. Charles c Peters b Adams | 25 | | |
| *†M. R. Pydanna not out | 25 | | |
| C. G. Butts b Dixon | 7 | | |
| D. A. Hewitt lbw b Daley | 14 | | |
| B 1, l-b 6, n-b 8 | 15 | L-b 2 | 2 |
| 1/34 2/72 3/115 4/152 5/180 6/195 7/252 8/254 9/266 | 302 | 1/30 | (1 wkt) 53 |

Bowling: *First Innings*—Daley 24.2–3–63–4; Dixon 16–2–48–1; Wilson 30–4–90–1; Adams 20–3–57–2; Corke 11–1–37–1. *Second Innings*—Daley 6–0–31–1; Dixon 5–1–20–0.

Umpires: L. H. Barker and D. J. Narine.

## LEEWARD ISLANDS v WINDWARD ISLANDS

At Grove Park, Charlestown, Nevis, March 1, 2, 3, 4. Drawn. Leeward Islands 8 pts, Windward Islands 4 pts.

### Leeward Islands

| | | | |
|---|---|---|---|
| A. L. Kelly b Kentish | 88 | b Thomas | 29 |
| L. L. Lawrence run out | 14 | lbw b Phillip | 6 |
| E. A. Lewis st Cadette b Kentish | 48 | c John b Thomas | 11 |
| N. C. Guishard c Charles b Kentish | 14 | (8) not out | 5 |
| R. M. Otto b Hinds | 1 | (4) run out | 20 |
| E. E. Lewis c Charles b Hinds | 8 | (5) b Kentish | 32 |

| | | | |
|---|---|---|---|
| †S. I. Williams b Kentish | 6 | (6) not out | 10 |
| E. A. E. Baptiste b Kentish | 38 | (7) c John b Kentish | 0 |
| T. A. Merrick not out | 48 | | |
| *E. T. Willett not out | 13 | | |
| B 4, l-b 8, w 1, n-b 1 | 14 | B 1, l-b 3, n-b 2 | 6 |
| 1/36 2/129 3/170 4/173 5/174 6/185 7/192 8/257 | (8 wkts dec.) 292 | 1/30 2/41 3/56 4/98 5/110 6/110 | (6 wkts dec.) 119 |

J. D. Thompson did not bat.

Bowling: *First Innings*—Phillip 9.2–0–27–0; Thomas 8–1–32–0; Kentish 45–13–98–5; Hinds 37–11–99–2; Marshall 11–3–24–0. *Second Innings*—Phillip 16–1–37–1; Thomas 12–2–44–2; Kentish 9–0–27–2; Hinds 4–1–7–0.

### Windward Islands

| | | | |
|---|---|---|---|
| L. C. Sebastien c Kelly b Guishard | 33 | not out | 60 |
| L. D. John b Baptiste | 4 | c and b Baptiste | 0 |
| L. A. Lewis c Williams b Willett | 13 | lbw b Baptiste | 5 |
| J. D. Charles lbw b Willett | 1 | (5) c Otto b Guishard | 34 |
| A. D. Texeira c E. A. Lewis b Baptiste | 36 | (4) c Kelly b Baptiste | 6 |
| R. Marshall b Willett | 14 | not out | 1 |
| *N. Phillip c and b Guishard | 3 | | |
| †I. Cadette run out | 34 | | |
| T. Z. Kentish b Baptiste | 4 | | |
| S. J. Hinds c Kelly b Willett | 14 | | |
| W. Thomas not out | 14 | | |
| L-b 2, w 1, n-b 4 | 7 | B 8, l-b 1, n-b 1 | 10 |
| 1/16 2/49 3/55 4/57 5/75 6/84 7/143 8/144 9/159 | 177 | 1/0 2/6 3/20 4/89 | (4 wkts) 116 |

Bowling: *First Innings*—Merrick 7–3–31–0; Baptiste 19–10–28–3; Guishard 26–5–59–2; Willett 20.3–3–46–4; Thompson 8–2–11–0. *Second Innings*—Merrick 7–1–39–0; Baptiste 7–1–23–3; Guishard 11–5–22–1; Willett 4–3–1–0; Thompson 7–1–22–0.

Umpires: D. M. Archer and A. Weekes.

## TRINIDAD & TOBAGO v BARBADOS

At Queen's Park Oval, Port-of-Spain, March 1, 2, 3. Trinidad & Tobago won by an innings and 54 runs. Trinidad & Tobago 16 pts.

### Barbados

| | | | |
|---|---|---|---|
| *C. A. Best c D. Williams b Gray | 2 | lbw b Mahabir | 22 |
| T. A. Hunte b Mahabir | 28 | (7) c K. C. Williams b Mahabir | 0 |
| N. Johnson c Simmons b Gray | 1 | c Nanan b K. C. Williams | 11 |
| S. R. Greaves lbw b Mahabir | 51 | c D. Williams b Gray | 0 |
| R. L. Skeete c Rajah b K. C. Williams | 48 | c Mohammed b Mahabir | 36 |
| G. N. Reifer c D. Williams b Nanan | 17 | run out | 0 |
| †M. C. Worrell lbw b Mahabir | 0 | (8) not out | 6 |
| N. A. Phillips c Simmons b Mahabir | 12 | (2) c Bodoe b Gray | 0 |
| E. Proverbs not out | 16 | st D. Williams b Mahabir | 8 |
| R. O. Estwick c Mohammed b Nanan | 0 | b Nanan | 8 |
| W. W. Daniel b Nanan | 5 | b Nanan | 3 |
| L-b 1, n-b 5 | 6 | B 3, l-b 7, n-b 4 | 14 |
| 1/2 2/4 3/39 4/136 5/136 6/136 7/154 8/178 9/178 | 186 | 1/1 2/16 3/17 4/78 5/78 6/78 7/79 8/87 9/102 | 108 |

Bowling: *First Innings*—Gray 8–3–30–2; K. C. Williams 13–1–36–1; Nanan 14.4–3–39–3; Mahabir 22–4–69–4; Bodoe 5–1–11–0. *Second Innings*—Gray 7–0–30–2; K. C. Williams 5–2–17–1; Nanan 11.5–5–12–2; Mahabir 13–3–39–4.

## Trinidad & Tobago

R. S. Gabriel lbw b Estwick ......... 4
P. V. Simmons lbw b Daniel ......... 9
A. Rajah c Best b Daniel ............ 57
P. Moosai c Best b Phillips ..........110
D. I. Mohammed lbw b Estwick ...... 2
M. Bodoe c Hunte b Greaves ........ 12
*R. Nanan c Reifer b Phillips ........ 4
K. C. Williams c Hunte b Phillips .... 41
†D. Williams not out ............... 49
A. H. Gray c Best b Greaves ......... 26
G. Mahabir c sub b Estwick ......... 0
L-b 5, w 1, n-b 28 .......... 34

1/15 2/16 3/147 4/151 5/184 6/193 7/262 8/291 9/343 — 348

Bowling: Daniel 27–4–72–2; Estwick 30–6–91–3; Greaves 24–3–91–2; Phillips 27–3–82–3; Proverbs 1–0–4–0; Reifer 1–0–3–0.

Umpires: C. E. Cumberbatch and P. White.

## SHELL SHIELD WINNERS

| | | | |
|---|---|---|---|
| 1965-66 | Barbados | 1976-77 | Barbados |
| 1966-67 | Barbados | 1977-78 | Barbados |
| 1968-69 | Jamaica | 1978-79 | Barbados |
| 1969-70 | Trinidad | 1979-80 | Barbados |
| 1970-71 | Trinidad | 1980-81 | Combined Islands |
| 1971-72 | Barbados | 1981-82 | Barbados |
| 1972-73 | Guyana | 1982-83 | Guyana |
| 1973-74 | Barbados | 1983-84 | Barbados |
| 1974-75 | Guyana | 1984-85 | Trinidad & Tobago |
| 1975-76 | Trinidad / Barbados | | |

## OTHER FIRST-CLASS MATCHES

## GUYSTAC TROPHY, 1984-85

### Formerly Jones Cup

## BERBICE v DEMERARA

At Albion Sports Complex, Berbice, November 9, 10, 11, 12. Demerara won by four wickets.

### Berbice

| | | | | |
|---|---|---|---|---|
| C. B. Lambert c Butts b Hooper | 104 | – | b Grenville | 13 |
| A. Sattaur c and b Charles | 28 | – | c Mohamed b Butts | 15 |
| L. Blackman b Butts | 18 | – | c Seeram b Grenville | 2 |
| H. Evans c Butts b Gomes | 18 | – | c Bamfield b Gomes | 42 |
| D. Persaud c Bamfield b Hooper | 13 | – | c Bamfield b Hooper | 55 |
| D. I. Kallicharran c White b Hooper | 37 | – | c Butts b Hooper | 26 |
| *†M. R. Pydanna c Seeram b Butts | 5 | – | c White b Butts | 25 |
| V. Benjamin c Seeram b Butts | 11 | – | b Hooper | 24 |
| H. Sackichand c and b Hooper | 21 | – | not out | 15 |
| R. F. Joseph not out | 8 | – | b Hooper | 2 |
| C. V. Solomon lbw b Hooper | 1 | – | c Lyght b Butts | 10 |
| B 1, l-b 1 | 2 | | B 7, l-b 1, w 1, n-b 4 | 13 |
| 1/70 2/106 3/148 4/177 5/185 6/192 7/214 8/253 9/258 | 266 | | 1/16 2/27 3/61 4/96 5/157 6/174 7/197 8/219 9/221 | 242 |

Bowling: *First Innings*—Grenville 5–0–23–0; Charles 10–0–59–1; Butts 34–10–80–3; Hooper 20.4–1–71–5; Gomes 7–0–31–1. *Second Innings*—Grenville 8–1–37–2; Charles 6–0–23–0; Butts 33.3–10–57–3; Hooper 27–5–71–4; Gomes 11–1–43–1; White 5–3–3–0.

## Demerara

| | | | |
|---|---|---|---|
| A. A. Lyght c Evans b Kallicharran | 104 | – run out | 34 |
| †S. Bamfield c Pydanna b Solomon | 21 | – lbw b Solomon | 19 |
| A. F. D. Jackman run out | 22 | – b Solomon | 39 |
| R. N. Seeram run out | 3 | – c Lambert b Solomon | 11 |
| *T. Mohamed c Sattaur b Benjamin | 8 | – run out | 48 |
| W. H. F. White c Benjamin b Sackichand | 44 | – not out | 22 |
| C. L. Hooper c and b Solomon | 32 | – lbw b Joseph | 5 |
| G. E. Charles c and b Kallicharran | 32 | – not out | 11 |
| C. G. Butts st Pydanna b Benjamin | 14 | | |
| M. Grenville b Solomon | 0 | | |
| G. Gomes not out | 0 | | |
| L-b 3, n-b 5 | 8 | B 10, l-b 17, w 1, n-b 5 | 33 |
| 1/48 2/95 3/107 4/125 5/209 6/213 7/246 8/288 9/288 | 288 | 1/47 2/62 3/84 4/155 5/181 6/193 (6 wkts) | 222 |

Bowling: *First Innings*—Joseph 8–0–67–0; Solomon 9–1–35–3; Benjamin 13.3–2–26–2; Sackichand 16–5–36–1; Kallicharran 29–3–94–2; Persaud 20–8–27–0. *Second Innings*—Joseph 10–2–45–1; Solomon 25.2–5–64–3; Benjamin 8–3–26–0; Sackichand 6–1–10–0; Kallicharran 17–4–31–0; Persaud 10–4–19–0.

Umpires: M. Baksh and D. J. Narine.

# BEAUMONT CUP, 1984-85

## SOUTH TRINIDAD v NORTH TRINIDAD

At Guaracara Park, Pointe-á-Pierre, January 3, 4, 5. North Trinidad won by an innings and 58 runs.

## South Trinidad

| | | | |
|---|---|---|---|
| K. R. Bainey lbw b Williams | 17 | – c Glasgow b Gray | 6 |
| M. Richardson c Glasgow b Williams | 15 | – lbw b Williams | 11 |
| R. Sampath c Rajah b Des Vignes | 22 | – c Williams b Gray | 14 |
| D. I. Mohammed b Williams | 0 | – st Glasgow b Joseph | 13 |
| T. Cuffy lbw b Joseph | 2 | – lbw b Mahabir | 71 |
| M. Bodoe b Mahabir | 26 | – lbw b Joseph | 1 |
| *R. Nanan c Gray b Mahabir | 42 | – lbw b Joseph | 3 |
| †D. Williams c Rajah b Joseph | 1 | – b Williams | 1 |
| L. Lagan run out | 8 | – c Glasgow b Mahabir | 7 |
| G. S. Antoine c and b Mahabir | 15 | – c Joseph b Mahabir | 6 |
| R. Sieuchand not out | 0 | – not out | 0 |
| B 3, l-b 3, w 3, n-b 3 | 12 | B 7, l-b 14 | 21 |
| 1/32 2/38 3/39 4/51 5/73 6/118 7/121 8/133 9/160 | 160 | 1/17 2/30 3/33 4/69 5/81 6/95 7/96 8/144 9/153 | 154 |

Bowling: *First Innings*—Williams 11–2–32–3; Gray 9–2–17–0; Joseph 21–5–44–2; Des Vignes 9–4–24–1; Mahabir 14–2–37–3. *Second Innings*—Williams 14–6–29–2; Gray 18–5–48–2; Joseph 11–4–19–3; Des Vignes 7–0–24–0; Mahabir 5.3–0–13–3.

## North Trinidad

| | |
|---|---|
| R. S. Gabriel c Richardson b Antoine | 0 |
| P. V. Simmons run out | 71 |
| †R. A. Glasgow st Williams b Sampath | 65 |
| A. Rajah c Williams b Sampath | 36 |
| *P. Moosai c Nanan b Sampath | 16 |
| D. C. Furlonge lbw b Nanan | 16 |
| A. H. Gray c Cuffy b Sampath | 9 |
| K. C. Williams c Cuffy b Nanan | 91 |
| H. J. Joseph b Nanan | 41 |
| G. Mahabir not out | 11 |
| M. Des Vignes lbw b Nanan | 0 |
| B 3, l-b 10, n-b 3 | 16 |
| 1/0 2/134 3/176 4/183 5/214 6/216 7/244 8/347 9/372 | 372 |

Bowling: Antoine 15–2–86–1; Sieuchand 16–1–67–0; Lagan 12–1–48–0; Nanan 24–5–67–4; Bodoe 25–6–49–0; Sampath 18–3–42–4.

Umpires: A. Lee King and Mohammed Hosein.

# †GEDDES GRANT-HARRISON LINE TROPHY, 1984-85

## Zone A

At Kensington Oval, Bridgetown, January 30. Guyana won by four wickets. Barbados 237 for eight (49 overs) (T. A. Hunte 114); Guyana 238 for six (44.4 overs) (A. A. Lyght 56, C. B. Lambert 54, A. F. D. Jackman 41).

At Sturge Park, Montserrat, February 6. Guyana won by 15 runs. Guyana 169 for eight (50 overs) (C. L. Hooper 58, G. E. Charles 49); Leeward Islands 154 (48.2 overs) (E. E. Lewis 48 not out; C. G. Butts four for 25).

At Kensington Oval, Bridgetown, February 14. Leeward Islands won by 1 run. Leeward Islands 289 for three (47 overs) (E. A. Lewis 145 not out, E. E. Lewis 55 not out, R. M. Otto 55); Barbados 288 (46.2 overs) (R. L. Skeete 68, N. Johnson 51, N. A. Phillips 47, T. A. Hunte 40; C. E. I. Bartlette five for 64).

## Zone B

At Sabina Park, Kingston, January 22. Jamaica won by 87 runs. Jamaica 220 for seven (46 overs) (O. W. Peters 69, A. B. Williams 43); Trinidad & Tobago 133 (40 overs) (M. C. Neita four for 48).

At Alcoa Sports Club, Jamaica, January 29. Windward Islands won by two wickets. Jamaica 143 (46 overs) (A. B. Williams 44); Windward Islands 144 for eight (45.4 overs) (D. Dixon four for 9).

At Shaw Park, Tobago, February 6. Trinidad & Tobago won by 48 runs in a match reduced by rain to twenty overs a side. Trinidad & Tobago 117 for nine (20 overs); Windward Islands 69 for four (20 overs).

## FINAL

## GUYANA v JAMAICA

At Bourda Oval, Georgetown. March 7. Guyana won by five wickets.

### Jamaica

| | |
|---|---|
| W. W. Lewis c Pydanna b Charles | 8 |
| O. W. Peters c White b Charles | 10 |
| G. Powell c Seeram b White | 29 |
| C. A. Davidson run out | 27 |
| E. Whittingham b White | 1 |
| J. Adams c Jackman b White | 9 |
| *T. Corke c Seeram b White | 2 |
| D. Dixon c Pydanna b Butts | 14 |
| A. G. Daley run out | 10 |
| †P. A. Francis not out | 8 |
| D. Meikle run out | 3 |
| B 4, l-b 7, w 3, n-b 4 | 18 |
| 1/15 2/31 3/66 4/70 5/88 6/99 7/101 8/118 9/131 (46.1 overs) | 139 |

Bowling: Hewitt 9.1–2–18–0; Charles 8–1–35–2; Butts 9–1–22–1; White 10–1–26–4; Hooper 10–0–27–0.

### Guyana

| | |
|---|---|
| A. A. Lyght c Francis b Dixon | 13 |
| R. N. Seeram c Powell b Daley | 0 |
| A. F. D. Jackman c Powell b Corke | 24 |
| T. Mohamed c Francis b Daley | 7 |
| M. A. Harper c Corke b Daley | 44 |
| C. L. Hooper not out | 22 |
| W. White not out | 14 |
| L-b 6, n-b 10 | 16 |
| 1/1 2/23 3/34 4/68 5/112 (5 wkts, 41 overs) | 140 |

*†M. R. Pydanna, G. E. Charles, C. G. Butts and D. A. Hewitt did not bat.

Bowling: Daley 10–1–22–3; Meikle 6–0–34–0; Dixon 9–1–29–1; Whittingham 6–0–35–0; Corke 10–1–14–1.

Umpires: D. J. Narine and L. H. Barker.

# CRICKET IN NEW ZEALAND, 1984-85

By C. R. BUTTERY

For the third time in the last four years Wellington won the Shell Trophy. Their captain, Robert Vance, thereby equalled the feat of his father, currently Chairman of the New Zealand Cricket Council, who led Wellington in the days when the Plunket Shield was the premier first-class competition. Wellington started the season badly with an outright loss to Canterbury when they came up against Richard Hadlee in top bowling form. However, they improved as time went on, and although able to record only two outright wins they accumulated enough points for leading on first innings to finish the season marginally ahead of Auckland and Canterbury. This was despite being without Jeremy Coney and Ewen Chatfield for five matches because of Test appearances against the visiting Pakistanis. Bruce Edgar and Vance scored consistently, while Evan Gray bowled well to collect 48 wickets in all matches. Gray was well supported by wicket-keeper Ervin McSweeney, who made eight stumpings and held seven catches from his bowling - including five in one innings against Northern Districts - while progressing towards a New Zealand wicket-keeping record of 42 dismissals for the season.

With a little more luck, Auckland could well have won the competition. At the start of their final game they were in second place, eight points behind Wellington and needing an outright win against Central Districts to win the series. After rain had washed out the first day, some excellent bowling by Gary Troup and Willie Watson saw Central Districts dismissed for 78 on the second; and Martin Snedden kept the game alive by declaring Auckland's first innings closed as soon as Central Districts' total was passed. Central Districts scored a more respectable 265 in their second innings, but Auckland's chase for victory faltered and the game ended with them narrowly avoiding defeat. Snedden did not allow the burdens of captaincy to affect his bowling and took 30 wickets during the season. He was supported by Troup and Watson, a newcomer to the side who bowled impressively. John Reid topped the country's averages, but his best performances were in the Tests. Trevor Franklin batted confidently throughout the season, scoring 522 runs at an average of 40.15.

The previous season's winners, Canterbury, finished in equal second place with Auckland. They were the only team to win three matches outright, but were led on first innings in six of their eight games. Paul McEwan had another season of prolific scoring and the batting was further strengthened by the return of John Wright after several years with Northern Districts. A milestone was reached by Richard Hadlee, who took his 1,000th first-class wicket during the season. When available, Hadlee bowled extremely well for Canterbury, but his batting was not up to his usual standard.

Otago won only one match. Their batting relied too much on Andrew Jones and Ken Rutherford, and if either failed the entire innings was in danger of collapsing. Jones was especially consistent. The nineteen-year-old Rutherford's solid 130 against Auckland helped him gain selection for New Zealand's tour to the West Indies. Otago's attack was fairly effective, Neil Mallender in particular recording some outstanding figures. He took seven for 27 against Auckland and six for 31 in the first innings against Northern Districts when, with John Cushen, he bowled Otago to their only win of the series.

Northern Districts were without Andy Roberts, who had retired, John Parker, who was unavailable, and Wright, now playing for Canterbury. The absence of these three experienced batsmen was reflected in the results, which saw Northern Districts lose four games. Their problems were compounded by Geoff Howarth being out of form.

Central Districts went from being runners-up in 1983-84 to finishing a poor last. Considering the strength of the batting, this was surprising. Ron Hart and Tony Blain were the country's leading run-scorers and Central Districts had two other reliable batsmen in Martin Crowe and Scott Briasco. Their problems lay with the bowling. Derek Stirling, who had bowled well during New Zealand's recent tour to Sri Lanka and Pakistan, failed to maintain his form and secured only ten wickets all season. His new-ball partner, Gary Robertson, obtained 21 at 35.10 each. The pace bowlers' lack of success forced the captain, Richard Hayward, to rely heavily on the slow left-arm spin of David O'Sullivan, who announced his retirement at the end of a season in which he took 38 wickets.

The lack of fast bowling support for, indeed of a successor to, Hadlee has been evident for some time, and with an eye to the future the New Zealand Cricket Council have organised a coaching school for young fast bowlers. Dennis Lillee and Frank Tyson have both visited New Zealand to provide coaching advice.

## FIRST-CLASS AVERAGES, 1984-85

### BATTING

(Qualification: 5 completed innings, average 35)

| | *I* | *NO* | *R* | *HI* | *Avge* |
|---|---|---|---|---|---|
| I. F. Reid (*Auckland*) | 9 | 1 | 465 | 158* | 58.12 |
| R. P. Jones (*Otago*) | 15 | 4 | 609 | 102* | 55.36 |
| M. D. Crowe (*Central Districts*) | 10 | 0 | 541 | 143 | 54.10 |
| T. E. Blain (*Central Districts*) | 15 | 1 | 678 | 129 | 48.42 |
| P. E. McEwan (*Canterbury*) | 11 | 1 | 482 | 105 | 48.20 |
| J. G. Wright (*Canterbury*) | 12 | 1 | 495 | 151* | 45.00 |
| R. T. Hart (*Central Districts*) | 15 | 0 | 665 | 111 | 44.33 |
| K. R. Rutherford (*Otago*) | 11 | 1 | 442 | 130 | 44.20 |
| B. L. Cairns (*Northern Districts*) | 7 | 1 | 252 | 89 | 42.00 |
| P. N. Webb (*Auckland*) | 9 | 3 | 245 | 76 | 40.83 |
| T. J. Franklin (*Auckland*) | 14 | 1 | 522 | 181 | 40.15 |
| C. J. Smith (*Central Districts*) | 12 | 3 | 352 | 103* | 39.11 |
| V. R. Brown (*Canterbury*) | 16 | 2 | 540 | 104 | 38.57 |
| R. H. Vance (*Wellington*) | 13 | 0 | 499 | 99 | 38.38 |
| J. V. Coney (*Wellington*) | 10 | 2 | 291 | 111* | 36.37 |
| B. A. Edgar (*Wellington*) | 12 | 1 | 390 | 82* | 35.45 |
| R. T. Latham (*Canterbury*) | 16 | 0 | 561 | 109 | 35.06 |

* *Signifies not out.*

## BOWLING

(Qualification: 25 wickets)

| | O | M | R | W | Avge |
|---|---|---|---|---|---|
| R. J. Hadlee (*Canterbury*) | 286.5 | 86 | 652 | 38 | 17.15 |
| M. C. Snedden (*Auckland*) | 253.3 | 82 | 533 | 30 | 17.76 |
| N. A. Mallender (*Otago*) | 259.5 | 73 | 637 | 35 | 18.20 |
| E. J. Gray (*Wellington*) | 432 | 148 | 1,024 | 48 | 21.33 |
| S. L. Boock (*Otago*) | 300 | 134 | 597 | 26 | 22.96 |
| J. A. Cushen (*Otago*) | 331.4 | 112 | 748 | 31 | 24.12 |
| D. R. O'Sullivan (*Central Districts*) | 425.3 | 124 | 1,042 | 38 | 27.42 |
| V. R. Brown (*Canterbury*) | 333 | 84 | 974 | 31 | 31.41 |

## SHELL TROPHY

| | | | | | Points | | |
|---|---|---|---|---|---|---|---|
| | Played | Won | Lost | Drawn | Outright win | 1st inns lead | Total |
| Wellington | 8 | 2 | 1 | 5 | 24 | 24 | 48 |
| Canterbury | 8 | 3 | 2 | 3 | 36 | 8 | 44 |
| Auckland | 8 | 2 | 0 | 6 | 24 | 20 | 44 |
| Otago | 8 | 1 | 2 | 5 | 12 | 24 | 33* |
| Northern Districts | 8 | 1 | 4 | 3 | 12 | 16 | 26* |
| Central Districts | 8 | 1 | 1 | 6 | 12 | 4 | 16 |

* *Otago were penalised 3 points and Northern Districts 2 points.*

## CANTERBURY v WELLINGTON

At Dudley Park, Rangiora, December 13, 14, 15. Canterbury won by 82 runs. Canterbury 12 pts, Wellington 4 pts.

### Canterbury

| First innings | | Second innings | |
|---|---|---|---|
| R. P. Jones c Vance b Cederwall | 5 | c Ormiston b Cederwall | 2 |
| A. P. Nathu c Ritchie b Cederwall | 23 | lbw b James | 1 |
| D. A. Dempsey c Vance b Maguiness | 13 | c McSweeney b Maguiness | 18 |
| *R. W. Fulton c Oakley b Maguiness | 0 | c McSweeney b Cederwall | 1 |
| R. T. Latham c Vance b Maguiness | 4 | c McSweeney b Larsen | 38 |
| V. R. Brown lbw b Larsen | 3 | c McSweeney b James | 104 |
| R. J. Hadlee lbw b Maguiness | 13 | c Vance b Larsen | 5 |
| G. K. MacDonald c Ritchie b Maguiness | 1 | c McSweeney b Maguiness | 15 |
| S. R. McNally c Oakley b Maguiness | 10 | c Vance b Maguiness | 8 |
| †A. W. Hart lbw b Maguiness | 4 | not out | 36 |
| C. H. Thiele not out | 3 | c Maguiness b Cederwall | 49 |
| L-b 7, w 1, n-b 1 | 9 | L-b 8, n-b 8 | 16 |
| 1/10 2/41 3/47 4/47 5/54 6/68 7/70 8/71 9/83 | 88 | 1/4 2/13 3/25 4/27 5/107 6/119 7/158 8/188 9/208 | 293 |

Bowling: *First Innings*—James 5–0–21–0; Cederwall 15–7–32–2; Maguiness 14.2–7–17–7; Larsen 4–1–11–1. *Second Innings*—James 29–8–95–2; Cederwall 26.4–4–65–3; Maguiness 31–7–82–3; Larsen 11–3–23–2; Pither 6–1–20–0.

### Wellington

| | | | |
|---|---|---|---|
| J. G. Boyle c Nathu b Thiele | 42 | – lbw b McNally | 0 |
| *R. H. Vance lbw b Hadlee | 30 | – c Latham b Hadlee | 1 |
| T. D. Ritchie c MacDonald b Brown | 3 | – lbw b McNally | 0 |
| R. W. Ormiston c McNally b Brown | 15 | – b Hadlee | 2 |
| D. F. Oakley lbw b Hadlee | 8 | – lbw b McNally | 1 |
| †F. B. McSweeney lbw b Hadlee | 24 | – c Hart b Hadlee | 41 |
| G. R. Larsen b Brown | 0 | – c Dempsey b Brown | 3 |
| G. N. Cederwall c Hart b Hadlee | 0 | – c Dempsey b Thiele | 5 |
| K. D. James c Dempsey b Brown | 0 | – run out | 22 |
| R. J. Pither not out | 8 | – not out | 19 |
| S. J. Maguiness c Hart b Hadlee | 43 | – c Hart b Hadlee | 4 |
| B 5, l-b 3, n-b 11 | 19 | L-b 5, n-b 4 | 9 |
| 1/68 2/78 3/105 4/108 5/138 6/141 7/141 8/141 9/141 | 192 | 1/0 2/0 3/4 4/5 5/5 6/16 7/33 8/71 9/94 | 107 |

Bowling: *First Innings*—Hadlee 30.1–13–46–5; Thiele 17–8–31–1; McNally 7–0–29–0; MacDonald 4–0–21–0; Brown 23–11–45–4; Dempsey 3–0–12–0. *Second Innings*—Hadlee 16.5–4–36–4; Thiele 6–1–11–1; McNally 11–4–22–3; MacDonald 1–1–0–0; Brown 10–3–33–1.

Umpires: T. J. Baines and F. R. Goodall.

## AUCKLAND v CANTERBURY

At Eden Park, Auckland, December 27, 28, 29. Auckland won by an innings and 36 runs. Auckland 16 pts.

### Auckland

| | |
|---|---|
| T. J. Franklin b Brown | 51 |
| P. A. Horne c Hart b Hadlee | 2 |
| J. F. Reid b Hadlee | 25 |
| J. J. Crowe c and b McNally | 14 |
| P. N. Webb lbw b Hadlee | 76 |
| A. J. Hunt c and b MacDonald | 16 |
| J. G. Bracewell c Hart b Thiele | 21 |
| *M. C. Snedden b Hadlee | 4 |
| †P. J. Kelly not out | 40 |
| G. B. Troup b Hadlee | 58 |
| S. R. Tracy b McNally | 6 |
| B 1, l-b 11, w 1, n-b 11 | 24 |
| 1/5 2/77 3/103 4/109 5/161 6/214 7/226 8/234 9/326 | 337 |

Bowling: Hadlee 35–14–74–5; Thiele 20–5–43–1; McNally 26–5–57–2; Latham 7–2–19–0; Brown 33–7–84–1; MacDonald 7–1–32–1; McEwan 4–1–16–0.

### Canterbury

| | | | |
|---|---|---|---|
| J. G. Wright c and b Troup | 8 | – c Reid b Troup | 4 |
| A. P. Nathu b Bracewell | 56 | – c Hunt b Troup | 25 |
| P. E. McEwan b Tracy | 2 | – c and b Snedden | 7 |
| R. T. Latham c Kelly b Troup | 8 | – c Kelly b Troup | 42 |
| V. R. Brown c Bracewell b Troup | 25 | – lbw b Troup | 4 |
| *R. W. Fulton c Kelly b Snedden | 0 | – c sub b Troup | 1 |
| R. J. Hadlee c Horne b Bracewell | 19 | – b Troup | 1 |
| G. K. MacDonald not out | 8 | – c Snedden b Bracewell | 14 |
| S. R. McNally b Tracy | 2 | – b Snedden | 15 |
| †A. W. Hart c Hunt b Tracy | 1 | – c Franklin b Bracewell | 9 |
| C. H. Thiele b Snedden | 2 | – not out | 7 |
| B 4, l-b 12, n-b 12 | 28 | L-b 6, n-b 7 | 13 |
| 1/16 2/20 3/35 4/94 5/96 6/137 7/146 8/151 9/153 | 159 | 1/20 2/31 3/64 4/77 5/86 6/93 7/94 8/114 9/128 | 142 |

Bowling: *First Innings*—Troup 15–4–37–3; Tracy 14–1–46–3; Snedden 18–3–37–2; Bracewell 14–6–23–2. *Second Innings*—Troup 17–1–53–6; Tracy 1–0–7–0; Snedden 16–4–24–2; Bracewell 16.4–6–48–2; Hunt 3–2–4–0.

Umpires: K. J. Barron and T. A. McCall.

## CENTRAL DISTRICTS v NORTHERN DISTRICTS

At Pukekura Park, New Plymouth, December 27, 28, 29. Central Districts won by five wickets. Central Districts 12 pts, Northern Districts 4 pts.

### Northern Districts

| | | | |
|---|---|---|---|
| L. M. Crocker b O'Sullivan | 26 | b Crowe | 51 |
| R. D. Broughton c Hart b O'Sullivan | 67 | b Crowe | 26 |
| W. P. Fowler c Briasco b Stirling | 24 | c Briasco b Crowe | 6 |
| B. G. Cooper c Smith b Visser | 91 | b Crowe | 8 |
| *G. P. Howarth c Smith b O'Sullivan | 39 | c Stirling b Robertson | 38 |
| B. R. Blair run out | 5 | c Blain b Crowe | 8 |
| C. M. Kuggeleijn c Smith b Robertson | 15 | c Briasco b O'Sullivan | 6 |
| †B. A. Young c Smith b Robertson | 7 | lbw b Visser | 18 |
| C. M. Presland c Smith b Robertson | 0 | c Blain b Robertson | 22 |
| B. P. Bracewell not out | 41 | c Visser b Robertson | 9 |
| S. M. Carrington c Briasco b Crowe | 0 | not out | 3 |
| L-b 8, w 1, n-b 7 | 16 | B 2, l-b 9, w 2, n-b 4 | 17 |
| 1/80 2/113 3/125 4/235 5/253 6/274 7/278 8/280 9/307 | 331 | 1/72 2/80 3/89 4/100 5/110 6/125 7/161 8/200 9/201 | 212 |

Bowling: *First Innings*—Stirling 21–8–57–1; Robertson 19–3–65–3; Crowe 15.2–5–54–1; Visser 15–3–51–1; O'Sullivan 28–7–96–3. *Second Innings*—Stirling 10–2–31–0; Robertson 12.5–0–54–3; Crowe 20–6–51–5; Visser 9–4–11–1; O'Sullivan 25–7–54–1.

### Central Districts

| | | | |
|---|---|---|---|
| R. T. Hart b Carrington | 0 | run out | 84 |
| T. E. Blain lbw b Bracewell | 15 | c Fowler b Presland | 25 |
| D. A. Stirling b Presland | 37 | | |
| P. S. Briasco c Young b Bracewell | 21 | b Bracewell | 8 |
| M. D. Crowe b Carrington | 20 | c Blair b Carrington | 143 |
| *R. E. Hayward lbw b Presland | 1 | not out | 48 |
| R. A. Pierce c and b Fowler | 21 | c Kuggeleijn b Fowler | 13 |
| †I. D. S. Smith c Bracewell b Blair | 51 | not out | 9 |
| G. K. Robertson b Carrington | 2 | | |
| D. R. O'Sullivan not out | 9 | | |
| P. J. Visser b Carrington | 0 | | |
| B 4, l-b 8, n-b 15 | 27 | L-b 3, w 1, n-b 7 | 11 |
| 1/7 2/57 3/62 4/98 5/99 6/114 7/175 8/181 9/203 | 204 | 1/46 2/55 3/222 4/305 5/328 | (5 wkts) 341 |

Bowling: *First Innings*—Carrington 16.5–6–39–4; Bracewell 17–3–59–2; Presland 12–1–67–2; Fowler 5–2–6–1; Blair 4–0–21–1. *Second Innings*—Carrington 16–1–61–1; Bracewell 16–1–75–1; Presland 10–1–65–1; Fowler 15.5–1–61–1; Blair 4–0–20–0; Kuggeleijn 10–0–38–0; Cooper 2–0–18–0.

Umpires: D. A. Kinsella and K. Thomson.

## OTAGO v WELLINGTON

At Molyneux Park, Alexandra, December 28, 29, 30. Wellington won by 26 runs. Wellington 16 pts.

### Wellington

| | | | |
|---|---|---|---|
| J. G. Boyle b Johnson | 9 | c Dawson b Cushen | 6 |
| B. A. Edgar run out | 39 | lbw b Mallender | 6 |
| *R. H. Vance lbw b Cushen | 24 | c Dawson b Mallender | 47 |
| J. V. Coney c and b Boock | 6 | c Walker b Boock | 32 |
| R. W. Ormiston c Lees b Mallender | 1 | lbw b Mallender | 11 |
| E. J. Gray lbw b Cushen | 6 | not out | 38 |
| †E. B. McSweeney c Facoory b Mallender | 5 | b Johnson | 6 |
| T. D. Ritchie c Lees b Cushen | 12 | lbw b Boock | 3 |
| G. N. Cederwall not out | 1 | b Cushen | 21 |
| S. J. Maguiness lbw b Boock | 3 | lbw b Cushen | 8 |
| E. J. Chatfield c Facoory b Boock | 8 | run out | 8 |
| L-b 5, w 1, n-b 4 | 10 | B 3, l-b 5, n-b 1 | 9 |
| 1/27 2/61 3/72 4/89 5/95 6/108 7/113 8/116 9/116 | 124 | 1/14 2/14 3/79 4/107 5/116 6/136 7/145 8/173 9/181 | 195 |

Bowling: *First Innings*—Mallender 19–7–29–2; Cushen 18–7–27–3; Johnson 7–2–13–1; Boock 26–11–50–3. *Second Innings*—Mallender 19.1–9–32–3; Cushen 24–11–31–3; Johnson 10–2–36–1; Boock 30–14–64–2; Walker 15–6–24–0.

### Otago

| | | | |
|---|---|---|---|
| P. R. Facoory c Maguiness b Cederwall | 2 | c Coney b Chatfield | 19 |
| S. J. McCullum c Ormiston b Maguiness | 11 | lbw b Chatfield | 42 |
| R. N. Hoskin st McSweeney b Gray | 17 | lbw b Chatfield | 2 |
| G. J. Dawson c Boyle b Maguiness | 7 | c and b Gray | 27 |
| A. H. Jones c McSweeney b Gray | 16 | c McSweeney b Cederwall | 31 |
| D. J. Walker run out | 14 | c Vance b Gray | 1 |
| *†W. K. Lees lbw b Chatfield | 22 | b Gray | 10 |
| N. A. Mallender c McSweeney b Maguiness | 6 | lbw b Gray | 17 |
| V. A. Johnson c McSweeney b Maguiness | 7 | c McSweeney b Gray | 11 |
| S. L. Boock c McSweeney b Chatfield | 0 | not out | 4 |
| J. A. Cushen not out | 1 | lbw b Chatfield | 1 |
| B 1, l-b 6, w 1 | 8 | B 4, l-b 12, n-b 1 | 17 |
| 1/2 2/17 3/27 4/53 5/64 6/88 7/95 8/107 9/108 | 111 | 1/24 2/25 3/27 4/101 5/114 6/123 7/135 8/156 9/169 | 182 |

Bowling: *First Innings*—Cederwall 4–1–7–1; Chatfield 22.5–6–37–2; Maguiness 20–9–29–4; Gray 12–2–31–2. *Second Innings*—Cederwall 10–1–34–1; Chatfield 28–9–56–4; Maguiness 19–5–33–0; Gray 36.5–14–43–5.

Umpires: W. C. Garrick and G. C. Morris.

## NORTHERN DISTRICTS v CANTERBURY

At Smallbone Park, Rotorua, January 1, 2, 3. Drawn. Canterbury 4 pts.

### Northern Districts

| | |
|---|---|
| R. D. Broughton lbw b McNally | 9 |
| L. M. Crocker c Wright b Hadlee | 12 |
| W. P. Fowler c Hart b Brown | 51 |
| B. G. Cooper b MacDonald | 9 |
| *G. P. Howarth c Brown b Hadlee | 9 |
| B. R. Blair lbw b Hadlee | 3 |
| C. M. Kuggeleijn st Hart b MacDonald | 50 |
| †B. A. Young st Hart b MacDonald | 9 |
| B. L. Cairns st Hart b McNally | 85 |
| B. P. Bracewell c MacDonald b Brown | 9 |
| S. M. Carrington not out | 18 |
| B 6, l-b 4, n-b 8 | 18 |
| 1/24 2/24 3/53 4/79 5/93 6/99 7/126 8/244 9/250 | 282 |

Bowling: Hadlee 35–14–53–3; McNally 30–14–54–2; Bateman 24–7–55–0; MacDonald 29–7–58–3; Brown 16–4–52–2.

### Canterbury

| | |
|---|---|
| J. G. Wright c Blair b Bracewell | 12 |
| A. P. Nathu b Cairns | 40 |
| *R. W. Fulton c Cairns b Cooper | 24 |
| R. T. Latham c Carrington b Cairns | 0 |
| V. R. Brown b Blair | 74 |
| P. E. McEwan lbw b Blair | 88 |
| R. J. Hadlee not out | 14 |
| G. K. MacDonald not out | 3 |
| B 7, l-b 12, n-b 10 | 29 |
| 1/12 2/80 3/80 4/99 5/246 6/280 | (6 wkts) 284 |

S. R. McNally, †A. W. Hart and G. C. Bateman did not bat.

Bowling: Bracewell 20–3–51–1; Carrington 14–5–36–0; Cairns 42–15–69–2; Fowler 15–4–37–0; Cooper 12–4–26–1; Kuggeleijn 13–5–30–0; Blair 13–4–16–2.

Umpires: G. I. J. Cowan and J. G. Reardon.

## WELLINGTON v AUCKLAND

At Basin Reserve, Wellington, January 1, 2, 3. Drawn. Auckland 4 pts.

### Auckland

| | | | |
|---|---|---|---|
| T. J. Franklin c Coney b Cederwall | 0 | c McSweeney b Maguiness | 32 |
| P. A. Horne c McSweeney b Cederwall | 13 | c sub b Gray | 31 |
| J. F. Reid c McSweeney b Coney | 82 | b Gray | 6 |
| J. J. Crowe c and b Cederwall | 21 | c Gray b Coney | 54 |
| P. N. Webb c Edgar b Coney | 14 | not out | 40 |
| A. J. Hunt b Gray | 24 | not out | 26 |
| J. G. Bracewell c McSweeney b Cederwall | 7 | | |
| *M. C. Snedden c Coney b Maguiness | 26 | | |
| †N. A. Scott lbw b Gray | 8 | | |
| S. R. Tracy c Maguiness b Gray | 33 | | |
| W. Watson not out | 4 | | |
| B 1, l-b 8, w 1 | 10 | B 1, l-b 5 | 6 |
| 1/5 2/79 3/135 4/136 5/147 6/169 7/169 8/205 9/225 | 242 | 1/60 2/65 3/79 4/150 | (4 wkts dec.) 195 |

Bowling: *First Innings*—Chatfield 34–11–76–0; Cederwall 24–9–54–4; Maguiness 18–5–53–1; Gray 21.4–9–30–3; Coney 10–2–20–2. *Second Innings*—Chatfield 15–3–36–0; Cederwall 4–0–21–0; Maguiness 20–8–29–1; Gray 20–5–61–2; Coney 11–2–42–1.

### Wellington

| | | | |
|---|---|---|---|
| J. G. Boyle c and b Bracewell | 18 | c Scott b Tracy | 35 |
| B. A. Edgar c Crowe b Snedden | 22 | c Bracewell b Snedden | 25 |
| *R. H. Vance b Bracewell | 13 | | |
| J. V. Coney c Hunt b Bracewell | 0 | c Scott b Tracy | 7 |
| R. W. Ormiston lbw b Snedden | 11 | b Tracy | 2 |
| E. J. Gray c and b Bracewell | 2 | c Scott b Bracewell | 19 |
| †E. B. McSweeney b Bracewell | 0 | c Watson b Bracewell | 28 |
| T. D. Ritchie not out | 52 | not out | 27 |
| G. N. Cederwall c Bracewell b Watson | 44 | not out | 24 |
| S. J. Maguiness c and b Bracewell | 1 | | |
| E. J. Chatfield c Franklin b Snedden | 8 | | |
| B 5, l-b 3, n-b 1 | 9 | B 2, l-b 2 | 4 |
| 1/38 2/46 3/46 4/63 5/69 6/69 7/69 8/134 9/137 | 180 | 1/34 2/48 3/54 4/93 5/107 6/137 | (6 wkts) 171 |

Bowling: *First Innings*—Tracy 11–4–40–0; Watson 15–6–29–1; Snedden 28–14–35–3; Bracewell 37–17–68–6. *Second Innings*—Tracy 13–3–48–3; Watson 7–3–27–0; Snedden 8–2–18–1; Bracewell 21–5–59–2; Hunt 3–1–7–0; Reid 2–0–8–0.

Umpires: M. M. Spring and S. J. Woodward.

## OTAGO v CENTRAL DISTRICTS

At Centennial Park, Oamaru, January 2, 3, 4. Drawn. Otago 4 pts.

### Otago

| First innings | | Second innings | |
|---|---|---|---|
| S. J. McCullum run out | 45 | c Robertson b O'Sullivan | 27 |
| P. R. Facoory lbw b O'Sullivan | 38 | c Briasco b O'Sullivan | 18 |
| R. N. Hoskin lbw b Crowe | 23 | c Hayward b Pierce | 24 |
| D. J. Walker b O'Sullivan | 9 | b O'Sullivan | 5 |
| A. H. Jones c Briasco b O'Sullivan | 53 | b Blain | 12 |
| G. J. Dawson c Hart b O'Sullivan | 7 | not out | 30 |
| *†W. K. Lees lbw b Robertson | 91 | not out | 20 |
| N. A. Mallender c Pierce b O'Sullivan | 88 | | |
| J. A. Cushen c Blain b O'Sullivan | 44 | b Stirling | 10 |
| P. S. Neutze c and b Pierce | 1 | | |
| S. L. Boock not out | 3 | | |
| B 5, l-b 20, n-b 3 | 28 | B 5, l-b 5, n-b 2 | 12 |
| 1/65 2/111 3/112 4/126 5/142 6/230 7/318 8/397 9/408 | 430 | 1/28 2/69 3/69 4/78 5/111 6/127 (6 wkts dec.) | 158 |

Bowling: *First Innings*—Stirling 18–3–74–0; Robertson 26–7–97–1; Gill 10–0–47–0; O'Sullivan 55–18–103–6; Crowe 14–4–40–1; Pierce 11–2–44–1. *Second Innings*—Stirling 5–0–10–1; Gill 3–0–3–0; O'Sullivan 32–15–39–3; Pierce 13–5–16–1; Briasco 15–3–40–0; Smith 6–2–15–0; Hayward 6–2–13–0; Hart 4–4–0–0; Blain 6–4–12–1.

### Central Districts

|  |  |
|---|---|
| T. E. Blain st Lees b Neutze | 129 |
| R. T. Hart c Walker b Boock | 59 |
| P. S. Briasco c Mallender b Neutze | 45 |
| M. D. Crowe st Lees b Neutze | 38 |
| *R. E. Hayward c Dawson b Neutze | 0 |
| D. A. Stirling c Dawson b Cushen | 14 |
| R. A. Pierce run out | 10 |
| †I. D. S. Smith c Lees b Cushen | 27 |
| S. J. Gill b Mallender | 17 |
| G. K. Robertson not out | 40 |
| D. R. O'Sullivan c Dawson b Neutze | 20 |
| L-b 2, n-b 8 | 10 |
| 1/137 2/215 3/264 4/277 5/286 6/301 7/302 8/338 9/352 | 409 |

Bowling: Mallender 21–2–88–1; Cushen 44–13–106–2; Boock 31–12–73–1; Neutze 26.2–1–109–5; Walker 11–3–31–0.

Umpires: G. C. Morris and N. A. Tapper.

## CENTRAL DISTRICTS v AUCKLAND

At Fitzherbert Park, Palmerston North, January 7, 8, 9. Drawn. Auckland 4 pts.

### Central Districts

| First innings | | Second innings | |
|---|---|---|---|
| R. T. Hart b Tracy | 27 | b Hellaby | 26 |
| T. E. Blain st Scott b Bracewell | 100 | lbw b Hellaby | 96 |
| P. S. Briasco c Franklin b Tracy | 0 | not out | 104 |
| *R. E. Hayward c Bracewell b Hellaby | 2 | c and b Webb | 65 |
| C. J. Smith c Scott b Watson | 7 | not out | 24 |
| R. A. Pierce c Scott b Tracy | 2 | | |
| †I. D. S. Smith c Scott b Watson | 46 | | |

| | | | |
|---|---|---|---|
| S. J. Gill c and b Bracewell | 39 | | |
| G. K. Robertson c Hunt b Watson | 73 | | |
| D. A. Stirling c Hunt b Tracy | 18 | | |
| D. R. O'Sullivan not out | 15 | | |
| B 4, l-b 4, n-b 8 | 16 | L-b 2, n-b 5 | 7 |
| 1/54 2/58 3/63 4/74 5/84 6/147 7/195 8/285 9/317 | 345 | 1/74 2/145 3/268 (3 wkts dec.) | 322 |

Bowling: *First Innings*—Tracy 19.4–6–91–4; Watson 25–7–88–3; Snedden 6–2–25–0; Bracewell 30–8–88–2; Hellaby 12–2–37–1; Hunt 4–0–8–0. *Second Innings*—Tracy 13–2–57–0; Watson 7–1–14–0; Snedden 20–5–40–0; Bracewell 8–2–24–0; Hellaby 13–1–39–2; Hunt 15–2–35–0; Webb 30–6–86–1; Crowe 10–6–20–0; Franklin 3–1–5–0.

## Auckland

| | |
|---|---|
| T. J. Franklin lbw b Robertson | 40 |
| J. G. Bracewell c I. D. S. Smith b Robertson | 54 |
| J. J. Crowe c Briasco b Pierce | 86 |
| M. J. Greatbatch c Stirling b Pierce | 29 |
| P. N. Webb not out | 44 |
| A. J. Hunt not out | 78 |
| B 1, l-b 5, w 2, n-b 9 | 17 |
| 1/95 2/107 3/207 4/221 (4 wkts dec.) | 348 |

*M. C. Snedden, †N. A. Scott, A. T. R. Hellaby, S. R. Tracy and W. Watson did not bat.

Bowling: Stirling 23–4–82–0; Gill 27–9–55–0; Robertson 22–2–58–2; O'Sullivan 47–10–116–0; Briasco 5–2–7–0; Pierce 10–4–23–2; Blain 1–0–1–0.

Umpires: J. G. Reardon and K. Thomson.

# NORTHERN DISTRICTS v OTAGO

At Harry Barker Reserve, Gisborne, January 7, 8, 9. Northern Districts won by 158 runs. Northern Districts 16 pts.

## Northern Districts

| | | | |
|---|---|---|---|
| L. M. Crocker c Jones b Cushen | 95 | c Facoory b Mallender | 10 |
| R. D. Broughton c McCullum b Boock | 21 | c Boock b Cushen | 28 |
| W. P. Fowler b Boock | 0 | c Lees b Mallender | 7 |
| B. G. Cooper c and b Cushen | 51 | c Lees b Boock | 60 |
| *G. P. Howarth lbw b Cushen | 12 | st Lees b Boock | 24 |
| B. R. Blair run out | 41 | c McCullum b Cushen | 3 |
| †B. A. Young c Mallender b Jones | 13 | not out | 26 |
| B. L. Cairns c Lees b Cushen | 89 | c Mallender b Boock | 13 |
| B. P. Bracewell c and b Mallender | 0 | not out | 14 |
| C. W. Dickeson b Mallender | 3 | | |
| S. M. Carrington not out | 0 | | |
| B 8, l-b 17, w 1, n-b 2 | 28 | L-b 2, n-b 1 | 3 |
| 1/43 2/43 3/148 4/175 5/186 6/229 7/293 8/316 9/351 | 353 | 1/25 2/35 3/64 4/124 5/128 6/136 7/165 (7 wkts dec.) | 188 |

Bowling: *First Innings*—Mallender 20–2–65–2; Cushen 31–10–109–4; Boock 46–22–85–2; Neutze 7–0–35–0; Jones 13–5–34–1. *Second Innings*—Mallender 9–0–18–2; Cushen 15–2–51–2; Boock 19–5–54–3; Neutze 12–0–63–0.

## Otago

| | | | |
|---|---|---|---|
| K. R. Rutherford c Crocker b Dickeson | 41 | c Blair b Dickeson | 9 |
| S. J. McCullum c Blair b Dickeson | 66 | c Young b Cairns | 17 |
| P. R. Facoory c Crocker b Cairns | 39 | c Fowler b Bracewell | 9 |
| R. N. Hoskin c Young b Carrington | 16 | c Young b Bracewell | 0 |
| A. H. Jones c Young b Bracewell | 45 | b Carrington | 25 |
| G. J. Dawson c Dickeson b Cairns | 9 | c Cooper b Dickeson | 12 |

| | | | |
|---|---|---|---|
| *†W. K. Lees lbw b Cairns | 1 | – lbw b Cairns | 21 |
| N. A. Mallender not out | 24 | – c Fowler b Carrington | 5 |
| J. A. Cushen b Cairns | 2 | – b Fowler | 8 |
| S. L. Boock not out | 10 | – lbw b Fowler | 7 |
| P. S. Neutze (did not bat) | | – not out | 0 |
| L-b 5, w 1, n-b 3 | 9 | B 2, l-b 3, w 1, n-b 2 | 8 |
| 1/108 2/123 3/144 4/177 5/221 6/223 7/223 8/234 | (8 wkts dec.) 262 | 1/20 2/36 3/37 4/41 5/58 6/93 7/99 8/114 9/118 | 121 |

Bowling: *First Innings*—Bracewell 21–6–55–1; Carrington 15–0–63–1; Cairns 25–7–39–4; Dickeson 25–7–54–2; Cooper 10–1–23–0; Blair 4–0–15–0; Fowler 7–2–8–0. *Second Innings*—Bracewell 8–1–32–2; Carrington 8–1–39–2; Cairns 10–3–20–2; Dickeson 12–1–21–2; Fowler 3.3–2–4–2.

Umpires: G. I. J. Cowan and T. A. McCall.

## CANTERBURY v CENTRAL DISTRICTS

At Lancaster Park, Christchurch, January 13, 14, 15. Canterbury won by 122 runs. Canterbury 16 pts.

### Canterbury

| | | | |
|---|---|---|---|
| A. P. Nathu c Briasco b Robertson | 49 | – st Hart b O'Sullivan | 9 |
| P. J. Rattray c Toynbee b Stirling | 9 | – c Blain b O'Sullivan | 20 |
| R. M. Carter c Briasco b Robertson | 11 | – lbw b Robertson | 36 |
| V. R. Brown c Hart b Robertson | 7 | – st Hart b Toynbee | 61 |
| R. T. Latham c Briasco b O'Sullivan | 95 | – c Briasco b O'Sullivan | 109 |
| *R. W. Fulton c Stirling b O'Sullivan | 35 | – c Hart b O'Sullivan | 5 |
| M. W. Priest lbw b O'Sullivan | 10 | – lbw b O'Sullivan | 4 |
| S. N. Bateman lbw b O'Sullivan | 2 | – run out | 12 |
| †A. W. Hart b Toynbee | 6 | – c Briasco b Toynbee | 2 |
| G. K. MacDonald c Robertson b O'Sullivan | 0 | – c Robertson b Toynbee | 5 |
| C. H. Thiele not out | 9 | – not out | 2 |
| B 2, l-b 7, w 2, n-b 2 | 13 | B 7, l-b 6, w 2 | 15 |
| 1/18 2/38 3/50 4/120 5/203 6/220 7/229 8/230 9/230 | 246 | 1/45 2/65 3/177 4/182 5/196 6/224 7/261 8/273 9/278 | 280 |

Bowling: *First Innings*—Stirling 12–5–25–1; Robertson 20–5–51–3; Visser 14–3–35–0; O'Sullivan 28–7–75–5; Toynbee 15.3–0–51–1. *Second Innings*—Stirling 6–0–28–0; Robertson 7–1–24–1; Visser 3–0–14–0; O'Sullivan 37–8–101–5; Toynbee 24.5–4–90–3; Gill 4–2–10–0.

### Central Districts

| | | | |
|---|---|---|---|
| T. E. Blain c Hart b Thiele | 6 | – st Hart b Thiele | 70 |
| †R. T. Hart c Brown b Thiele | 34 | – b Brown | 47 |
| P. S. Briasco c Rattray b MacDonald | 23 | – c Latham b Brown | 11 |
| D. A. Stirling c Latham b MacDonald | 0 | – b Brown | 42 |
| *R. E. Hayward b Thiele | 21 | – c Latham b MacDonald | 4 |
| C. J. Smith c Carter b Brown | 22 | – not out | 55 |
| M. H. Toynbee lbw b Bateman | 15 | – c MacDonald b Thiele | 0 |
| S. J. Gill lbw b Brown | 10 | – c Rattray b MacDonald | 6 |
| G. K. Robertson c Hart b Bateman | 5 | – b Thiele | 0 |
| D. R. O'Sullivan not out | 5 | – c Rattray b Brown | 3 |
| P. J. Visser c Hart b Thiele | 0 | – lbw b Thiele | 0 |
| L-b 3, n-b 6 | 9 | B 1, l-b 10, n-b 5 | 16 |
| 1/6 2/43 3/43 4/88 5/100 6/123 7/130 8/145 9/145 | 150 | 1/74 2/103 3/118 4/156 5/156 6/163 7/167 8/250 9/254 | 254 |

Bowling: *First Innings*—Thiele 11–3–45–4; Bateman 13–6–35–2; Brown 18–7–31–2; MacDonald 17–6–36–2. *Second Innings*—Thiele 14.5–4–35–4; Bateman 8–0–33–0; Brown 29–6–88–4; MacDonald 12–1–58–2; Priest 6–1–29–0.

Umpires: B. F. Aldridge and R. L. McHarg.

## WELLINGTON v NORTHERN DISTRICTS

At Basin Reserve, Wellington, January 13, 14, 15. Drawn. Wellington 4 pts.

### Wellington

| | | | |
|---|---|---|---|
| B. A. Edgar c Young b Bracewell | 81 | run out | 32 |
| J. G. Boyle c Young b Bracewell | 71 | c and b Cooper | 39 |
| *R. H. Vance c Fowler b Carrington | 54 | | |
| E. J. Gray c Cooper b Dickeson | 32 | | |
| †E. B. McSweeney c Young b Fowler | 6 | | |
| R. W. Ormiston b Bracewell | 28 | | |
| T. D. Ritchie c Young b Carrington | 32 | c Fowler b Kuggeleijn | 10 |
| G. R. Larsen not out | 26 | | |
| G. N. Cederwall lbw b Bracewell | 5 | c Bracewell b Dickeson | 29 |
| K. D. James lbw b Child | 11 | | |
| S. J. Maguiness b Child | 5 | not out | 2 |
| B 4, l-b 14, n-b 9 | 27 | B 1, l-b 4, n-b 1 | 6 |
| 1/161 2/165 3/209 4/221 5/262 6/324 7/332 8/337 9/372 | 378 | 1/63 2/78 3/105 4/118 (4 wkts dec.) | 118 |

Bowling: *First Innings*—Bracewell 37–3–114–4; Carrington 30–7–88–2; Child 11–3–28–2; Dickeson 44–18–82–1; Blair 5–1–14–0; Fowler 16–9–34–1. *Second Innings*—Dickeson 1.5–0–12–1; Kuggeleijn 20–5–48–1; Cooper 18–4–53–1.

### Northern Districts

| | | | |
|---|---|---|---|
| L. M. Crocker b Gray | 25 | st McSweeney b Gray | 57 |
| R. D. Broughton b Larsen | 35 | st McSweeney b Gray | 5 |
| *C. M. Kuggeleijn c McSweeney b Cederwall | 43 | c McSweeney b Gray | 2 |
| B. G. Cooper c Cederwall b James | 55 | st McSweeney b Gray | 3 |
| B. R. Blair c Ormiston b James | 4 | c Vance b Maguiness | 63 |
| W. P. Fowler lbw b Gray | 12 | lbw b Maguiness | 4 |
| †B. A. Young c McSweeney b Gray | 32 | st McSweeney b Gray | 5 |
| M. J. Child c Vance b Gray | 10 | not out | 8 |
| B. P. Bracewell c McSweeney b Gray | 27 | lbw b Maguiness | 8 |
| C. W. Dickeson run out | 0 | not out | 0 |
| S. M. Carrington not out | 8 | | |
| L-b 12, n-b 4 | 16 | B 4, l-b 8, n-b 6 | 18 |
| 1/40 2/77 3/168 4/170 5/176 6/200 7/222 8/249 9/249 | 267 | 1/31 2/131 3/139 4/139 5/150 6/154 7/163 8/167 (8 wkts) | 173 |

Bowling: *First Innings*—James 22–4–67–2; Cederwall 16–4–43–1; Gray 45.3–18–87–5; Maguiness 22–11–38–0; Larsen 12–7–16–1; Vance 3–2–4–0. *Second Innings*—James 7–3–13–0; Cederwall 6–0–23–0; Gray 19–5–61–5; Maguiness 9–0–39–3; Ormiston 4–0–25–0.

Umpires: S. C. Cowman and M. M. Spring.

## AUCKLAND v OTAGO

At Eden Park, Auckland, January 13, 14, 15. Drawn. Otago 4 pts.

### Auckland

| Batsman | First innings | | Second innings | |
|---|---|---|---|---|
| T. J. Franklin | c and b Johnson | 18 | c Lees b Mallender | 8 |
| P. A. Horne | c Hoskin b Johnson | 58 | c Lees b Mallender | 4 |
| M. Pringle | c McCullum b Walker | 72 | c McCallum b Mallender | 3 |
| A. J. Hunt | c Boock b Cushen | 24 | b Mallender | 2 |
| P. N. Webb | lbw b Mallender | 11 | lbw b Mallender | 4 |
| S. D. Adams | lbw b Boock | 5 | c Hoskin b Boock | 1 |
| *A. T. R. Hellaby | c Rutherford b Cushen | 29 | c Rutherford b Mallender | 2 |
| S. R. Gillespie | lbw b Cushen | 60 | c Walker b Boock | 13 |
| †N. A. Scott | not out | 10 | lbw b Mallender | 6 |
| R. J. Hunter | not out | 4 | not out | 4 |
| W. Watson | (did not bat) | | not out | 0 |
| | B 2, l-b 6, n-b 6 | 14 | B 2, l-b 1 | 3 |
| | 1/41 2/105 3/177 4/185 5/197 6/197 7/272 8/298 | (8 wkts dec.) 305 | 1/5 2/14 3/16 4/17 5/22 6/24 7/32 8/40 9/50 | (9 wkts) 50 |

Bowling: *First Innings*—Mallender 30–6–87–1; Cushen 39–16–92–3; Johnson 18–4–52–2; Boock 29–11–57–1; Jones 1–1–0–0; Walker 6–3–9–1. *Second Innings*—Mallender 22–13–27–7; Cushen 4–0–7–0; Boock 17–12–13–2.

### Otago

|  | | |
|---|---|---|
| K. R. Rutherford | c Adams b Watson | 130 |
| R. N. Hoskin | c Gillespie b Watson | 29 |
| G. J. Dawson | c Hellaby b Hunter | 33 |
| D. J. Walker | lbw b Hunt | 1 |
| A. H. Jones | c Scott b Watson | 28 |
| S. J. McCullum | c Scott b Gillespie | 28 |
| N. A. Mallender | lbw b Watson | 6 |
| *†W. K. Lees | not out | 54 |
| J. A. Cushen | c Franklin b Hunter | 17 |
| V. A. Johnson | lbw b Hellaby | 16 |
| S. L. Boock | b Hellaby | 0 |
| | B 16, l-b 11, w 1, n-b 7 | 35 |
| | 1/39 2/120 3/149 4/221 5/241 6/265 7/280 8/328 9/377 | 377 |

Bowling: Watson 39–7–96–4; Gillespie 23–13–43–1; Hunter 58–17–117–2; Hellaby 32.3–10–54–2; Hunt 20–4–40–1.

Umpires: K. J. Barron and K. Thomson.

## NORTHERN DISTRICTS v AUCKLAND

At Seddon Park, Hamilton, January 17, 18, 19. Auckland won by six wickets. Auckland 16 pts.

### Northern Districts

| Batsman | First innings | | Second innings | |
|---|---|---|---|---|
| L. M. Crocker | c Kelly b Watson | 13 | b Troup | 27 |
| R. D. Broughton | b Snedden | 26 | c Hunter b Snedden | 5 |
| *C. M. Kuggeleijn | c Hunt b Watson | 0 | c Horne b Hunter | 7 |
| B. G. Cooper | c Hunt b Troup | 16 | lbw b Troup | 2 |
| B. R. Blair | c Watson b Hunter | 53 | c Kelly b Snedden | 17 |
| W. P. Fowler | b Watson | 37 | c Hunt b Snedden | 4 |
| †B. A. Young | lbw b Watson | 26 | b Troup | 38 |
| M. J. Child | c Hunter b Snedden | 10 | c Horne b Hunter | 27 |
| B. P. Bracewell | lbw b Snedden | 21 | lbw b Snedden | 0 |
| C. W. Dickeson | lbw b Snedden | 9 | not out | 10 |
| S. M. Carrington | not out | 0 | c Pringle b Troup | 12 |
| | L-b 6, w 1, n-b 9 | 16 | L-b 6, n-b 2 | 8 |
| | 1/21 2/21 3/51 4/61 5/112 6/162 7/177 8/198 9/219 | 227 | 1/20 2/30 3/36 4/40 5/50 6/64 7/71 8/118 9/138 | 157 |

Bowling: *First Innings*—Troup 12–1–73–1; Watson 20–8–40–4; Snedden 23.5–9–78–4; Hellaby 3–0–10–0; Hunter 8–2–20–1. *Second Innings*—Troup 21–7–57–4; Watson 5–2–6–0; Snedden 17–9–21–4; Hellaby 2–0–11–0; Hunter 20–8–56–2.

## Auckland

| | | | |
|---|---|---|---|
| T. J. Franklin c Kuggeleijn b Bracewell | 181 | – b Carrington | 3 |
| P. A. Horne c Young b Bracewell | 3 | – c Kuggeleijn b Bracewell | 6 |
| M. Pringle c Blair b Dickeson | 11 | – lbw b Child | 17 |
| M. J. Greatbatch c and b Child | 22 | – not out | 32 |
| A. J. Hunt c Young b Dickeson | 18 | – lbw b Dickeson | 2 |
| A. T. R. Hellaby lbw b Blair | 16 | – not out | 5 |
| *M. C. Snedden c Child b Blair | 3 | | |
| †P. J. Kelly not out | 36 | | |
| G. B. Troup b Dickeson | 5 | | |
| B 1, l-b 9, n-b 9 | 19 | L-b 5, n-b 4 | 9 |
| 1/9 2/30 3/89 4/146 5/208 6/217 7/298 8/314 (8 wkts dec.) | 314 | 1/4 2/14 3/52 4/55 (4 wkts) | 74 |

R. J. Hunter and W. Watson did not bat.

Bowling: *First Innings*—Bracewell 36–5–67–2; Carrington 20–3–52–0; Dickeson 38.3–13–83–3; Child 21–8–35–1; Fowler 16–6–33–0; Blair 11–2–34–2. *Second Innings*—Bracewell 7–1–19–1; Carrington 7–2–10–1; Dickeson 11–3–30–1; Child 5–2–6–1; Crocker 0.2–0–4–0.

Umpires: J. G. Reardon and M. M. Spring.

# CANTERBURY v OTAGO

At Lancaster Park, Christchurch, January 17, 18, 19. Drawn. Otago 4 pts.

## Otago

| | | | |
|---|---|---|---|
| K. R. Rutherford b Thiele | 22 | – b Thiele | 29 |
| S. J. McCullum b Brown | 38 | – c Nathu b Brown | 28 |
| G. J. Dawson c Fulton b MacDonald | 79 | – c Brown b Thiele | 0 |
| R. N. Hoskin c Brown b MacDonald | 60 | – c Latham b Brown | 24 |
| A. H. Jones c MacDonald b Thiele | 62 | – not out | 43 |
| T. J. Wilson c Hart b Thiele | 52 | – c Carter b Brown | 7 |
| *†W. K. Lees c Nathu b Thiele | 20 | – st Hart b Brown | 15 |
| N. A. Mallender c Hart b McNally | 10 | – c Brown b MacDonald | 0 |
| J. A. Cushen c McEwan b Brown | 7 | – not out | 4 |
| V. A. Johnson b MacDonald | 17 | | |
| P. S. Neutze not out | 3 | | |
| B 6, l-b 4, n-b 3 | 13 | B 6, l-b 6 | 12 |
| 1/55 2/69 3/170 4/232 5/287 6/319 7/346 8/356 9/374 | 383 | 1/56 2/56 3/74 4/99 5/119 6/149 7/150 (7 wkts) | 162 |

Bowling: *First Innings*—Thiele 26–4–112–4; McNally 14–1–56–1; Brown 39–13–108–2; Hartshorn 13–3–40–0; MacDonald 22–7–57–3. *Second Innings*—Thiele 7–0–40–2; McNally 5–1–27–0; Brown 17–0–68–4; MacDonald 6–0–15–1.

## Canterbury

| | | | |
|---|---|---|---|
| A. P. Nathu c Lees b Johnson | 23 | – c Wilson b Johnson | 147 |
| R. M. Carter lbw b Johnson | 23 | – c Jones b Mallender | 0 |
| P. E. McEwan c Dawson b Johnson | 17 | – c Lees b Mallender | 13 |
| V. R. Brown lbw b Jones | 16 | – c Jones b Wilson | 71 |
| R. T. Latham c Lees b Johnson | 20 | – c Lees b Cushen | 44 |
| *R. W. Fulton c and b Jones | 5 | – c McCullum b Jones | 16 |
| D. J. Hartshorn lbw b Wilson | 48 | – not out | 14 |

| | | | |
|---|---|---|---|
| †A. W. Hart c Dawson b Jones | 33 | – c McCullum b Jones | 4 |
| S. R. McNally c Mallender b Cushen | 1 | – b Mallender | 11 |
| G. K. MacDonald c Hoskin b Jones | 0 | – not out | 25 |
| C. H. Thiele not out | 3 | | |
| B 4, l-b 5, n-b 5 | 14 | B 6, l-b 8, n-b 7 | 21 |
| 1/33 2/59 3/66 4/89 5/103 6/114 7/187 8/190 9/196 | 203 | 1/0 2/20 3/171 4/257 5/294 6/305 7/311 8/328 (8 wkts dec.) | 366 |

Bowling: *First Innings*—Mallender 14–4–37–0; Cushen 20–6–39–1; Johnson 18–5–59–4; Neutze 5–0–31–0; Jones 13.5–6–28–4; Wilson 2–2–0–1. *Second Innings*—Mallender 15–2–51–3; Cushen 29–8–79–1; Johnson 12–3–49–1; Neutze 20–4–74–0; Jones 23–8–50–2; Wilson 23–10–49–1.

Umpires: T. J. Baines and N. F. Tapper.

## CENTRAL DISTRICTS v WELLINGTON

At Horton Park, Blenheim, January 17, 18, 19. Drawn. Wellington 4 pts.

### Wellington

| | | | |
|---|---|---|---|
| B. A. Edgar c Visser b Stirling | 18 | – not out | 82 |
| J. G. Boyle c Hayward b Robertson | 46 | – c Blain b Robertson | 26 |
| *R. H. Vance c Blain b Robertson | 66 | – st Blain b O'Sullivan | 9 |
| R. W. Ormiston c Blain b Gill | 16 | | |
| E. J. Gray lbw b Robertson | 17 | | |
| †E. B. McSweeney c Blain b Gill | 95 | – c Visser b Pierce | 2 |
| T. D. Ritchie not out | 105 | – lbw b Visser | 0 |
| G. R. Larsen c Hart b Stirling | 14 | | |
| G. N. Cederwall not out | 3 | – b Pierce | 26 |
| S. J. Maguiness (did not bat) | | – st Blain b O'Sullivan | 7 |
| B 4, l-b 12, w 2, n-b 4 | 22 | B 7, l-b 1, n-b 1 | 9 |
| 1/31 2/96 3/124 4/173 5/176 6/330 7/393 (7 wkts dec.) | 402 | 1/45 2/97 3/98 4/110 5/152 6/161 (6 wkts dec.) | 161 |

K. D. James did not bat.

Bowling: *First Innings*—Stirling 24–1–80–2; Robertson 35–1–123–3; Visser 16–5–43–0; O'Sullivan 25–9–61–0; Gill 22–4–71–2; Pierce 4–1–8–0. *Second Innings*—Stirling 5–0–25–0; Robertson 8–1–29–1; Visser 15–3–38–1; O'Sullivan 13.3–3–35–2; Pierce 5–0–26–2.

### Central Districts

| | | | |
|---|---|---|---|
| C. J. Smith c McSweeney b Cederwall | 19 | – c McSweeney b Cederwall | 7 |
| R. T. Hart c Edgar b Gray | 108 | – st McSweeney b Gray | 38 |
| R. A. Pierce c McSweeney b Cederwall | 2 | – lbw b James | 15 |
| †T. E. Blain lbw b Maguiness | 22 | – c and b Cederwall | 4 |
| P. S. Briasco b Maguiness | 3 | – not out | 36 |
| *R. E. Hayward c Maguiness b Gray | 21 | – not out | 16 |
| S. J. Gill not out | 35 | | |
| G. K. Robertson c McSweeney b Cederwall | 7 | | |
| D. A. Stirling not out | 21 | | |
| L-b 2, w 2, n-b 11 | 15 | W 1, n-b 6 | 7 |
| 1/48 2/72 3/130 4/134 5/175 6/182 7/207 (7 wkts dec.) | 253 | 1/11 2/27 3/46 4/95 (4 wkts) | 123 |

D. R. O'Sullivan and P. J. Visser did not bat.

Bowling: *First Innings*—James 22–7–65–0; Cederwall 23–7–62–3; Maguiness 28–11–48–2; Gray 25–14–53–2; Larsen 11–4–23–0. *Second Innings*—James 8–4–16–1; Cederwall 10–2–33–2; Maguiness 3–2–4–0; Gray 9–5–14–1; Larsen 4–1–16–0; Edgar 2–1–1–0; Ritchie 2–1–4–0; Ormiston 4–1–27–0; McSweeney 1–0–8–0.

Umpires: B. F. Aldridge and S. C. Cowman.

## OTAGO v AUCKLAND

At Carisbrook, Dunedin, January 25, 26, 27. Drawn. Otago 4 pts.

### Otago

| First innings | | Second innings | |
|---|---|---|---|
| K. R. Rutherford not out | 89 | c Greatbatch b Hellaby | 61 |
| S. J. McCullum b Watson | 18 | run out | 22 |
| G. J. Dawson c and b Watson | 5 | lbw b Hellaby | 1 |
| R. N. Hoskin c Hunter b Watson | 5 | c sub b Hellaby | 3 |
| A. H. Jones c Hunter b Troup | 4 | not out | 58 |
| S. J. Richards c Hellaby b Snedden | 19 | | |
| *†W. K. Lees lbw b Hellaby | 12 | | |
| T. J. Wilson c Kelly b Snedden | 55 | b Hellaby | 33 |
| N. A. Mallender c Kelly b Watson | 9 | | |
| P. W. Hills c Kelly b Snedden | 0 | | |
| J. A. Cushen lbw b Snedden | 0 | | |
| B 3, l-b 17, n-b 5 | 25 | B 4, l-b 2 | 6 |
| 1/26 2/32 3/41 4/52 5/97 6/119 7/214 8/238 9/239 | 241 | 1/35 2/48 3/60 4/121 5/184 (5 wkts dec.) | 184 |

Bowling: *First Innings*—Troup 23–9–57–1; Watson 19–4–41–4; Snedden 28.2–6–74–4; Hunter 10–3–30–0; Hellaby 11–2–19–1. *Second Innings*—Troup 6–2–21–0; Watson 21–5–53–0; Snedden 9–2–20–0; Hellaby 24.5–6–84–4.

### Auckland

| First innings | | Second innings | |
|---|---|---|---|
| T. J. Franklin b Hills | 4 | b Wilson | 65 |
| P. A. Horne c Richards b Hills | 28 | c Jones b Wilson | 29 |
| M. Pringle c Lees b Hills | 10 | b Mallender | 38 |
| M. J. Greatbatch c Lees b Cushen | 13 | c Lees b Wilson | 55 |
| A. J. Hunt b Mallender | 51 | c Lees b Wilson | 2 |
| A. T. R. Hellaby lbw b Cushen | 6 | c and b Wilson | 17 |
| *M. C. Snedden lbw b Cushen | 5 | c Jones b Cushen | 7 |
| †P. J. Kelly lbw b Wilson | 20 | not out | 0 |
| G. B. Troup c Dawson b Mallender | 1 | b Wilson | 1 |
| R. J. Hunter not out | 28 | not out | 5 |
| W. Watson b Mallender | 0 | b Wilson | 0 |
| B 6, l-b 7, w 1, n-b 5 | 19 | B 8, l-b 8, n-b 2 | 18 |
| 1/20 2/51 3/58 4/77 5/96 6/119 7/138 8/144 9/171 | 185 | 1/59 2/120 3/152 4/180 5/189 6/208 7/222 8/237 9/237 (9 wkts) | 237 |

Bowling: *First Innings*—Mallender 27.4–9–48–3; Hills 17–2–55–3; Cushen 34–11–56–3; Wilson 8–4–13–1. *Second Innings*—Mallender 14–2–51–1; Hills 9–0–41–0; Cushen 22–7–72–1; Wilson 16–2–57–7.

Umpires: W. C. Garrick and R. L. McHarg.

## WELLINGTON v CANTERBURY

At Basin Reserve, Wellington, January 25, 26, 27. Wellington won by five wickets. Wellington 16 pts.

## Canterbury

| | | | |
|---|---|---|---|
| P. J. Rattray lbw b James | 0 | b Cederwall | 5 |
| A. P. Nathu c McSweeney b Cederwall | 6 | c Maguiness b Gray | 16 |
| P. E. McEwan c Ritchie b Griffiths | 56 | c Maguiness b Gray | 105 |
| V. R. Brown st McSweeney b Gray | 35 | c and b Gray | 16 |
| R. T. Latham c Cederwall b Griffiths | 28 | c Maguiness b Gray | 0 |
| *R. W. Fulton c Griffiths b Gray | 22 | b Gray | 34 |
| D. J. Hartshorn b Gray | 5 | not out | 17 |
| †A. W. Hart not out | 70 | b Griffiths | 0 |
| W. L. Eddington c and b Griffiths | 1 | not out | 49 |
| S. R. McNally c Vance b Gray | 3 | | |
| C. H. Thiele lbw b James | 28 | | |
| B 9, l-b 4, w 2, n-b 4 | 19 | B 3, l-b 12, w 1, n-b 5 | 21 |
| 1/0 2/10 3/62 4/124 5/131 6/161 7/166 8/171 9/193 | 273 | 1/9 2/72 3/108 4/112 5/154 6/185 7/188 (7 wkts dec.) | 263 |

Bowling: *First Innings*—James 14.1–4–23–2; Cederwall 13–2–37–1; Gray 29–6–107–4; Maguiness 16–5–44–0; Griffiths 18–5–49–3. *Second Innings*—James 5–0–30–0; Cederwall 7–0–28–1; Gray 45–14–115–5; Maguiness 22–10–40–0; Griffiths 18–7–35–1.

## Wellington

| | | | |
|---|---|---|---|
| B. A. Edgar c Hart b Thiele | 0 | c McEwan b Brown | 1 |
| J. G. Boyle c McEwan b Brown | 31 | c Rattray b Brown | 89 |
| *R. H. Vance lbw b Eddington | 99 | st Hart b Hartshorn | 31 |
| R. W. Ormiston c Latham b Thiele | 4 | b McEwan | 28 |
| E. J. Gray c Hart b Thiele | 33 | | |
| †E. B. McSweeney c Hartshorn b Brown | 32 | c Hart b Thiele | 21 |
| T. D. Ritchie c Hartshorn b Brown | 6 | not out | 20 |
| G. N. Cederwall not out | 57 | not out | 24 |
| K. D. James lbw b McEwan | 14 | | |
| S. J. Maguiness b Brown | 0 | | |
| A. Griffiths not out | 15 | | |
| B 17, l-b 3, w 2, n-b 1 | 23 | B 5, l-b 3, w 1 | 9 |
| 1/1 2/89 3/102 4/156 5/210 6/226 7/226 8/254 9/255 (9 wkts dec.) | 314 | 1/7 2/68 3/151 4/167 5/186 (5 wkts) | 223 |

Bowling: *First Innings*—Thiele 26–4–75–3; McNally 15–0–70–0; Eddington 10–3–39–1; Brown 34–8–83–4; Latham 5–0–19–0; McEwan 4–0–8–1. *Second Innings*—Thiele 9–0–46–1; McNally 2–1–9–0; Brown 19–3–84–2; McEwan 11–2–48–1; Hartshorn 8.2–2–28–1.

Umpires: K. Thomson and M. M. Spring.

# NORTHERN DISTRICTS v CENTRAL DISTRICTS

At Seddon Park, Hamilton, February 1, 2, 3. Drawn. Northern Districts 4 pts.

## Central Districts

| | | | |
|---|---|---|---|
| R. T. Hart run out | 60 | c Young b Bracewell | 6 |
| C. J. Smith c Kuggeleijn b Carrington | 18 | b Dickeson | 18 |
| P. S. Briasco c Dickeson b Bracewell | 10 | c Carrington b Dickeson | 76 |
| †T. E. Blain c Young b Bracewell | 20 | c Bracewell b Kuggeleijn | 72 |
| M. H. Toynbee run out | 24 | lbw b Dickeson | 34 |
| *R. E. Hayward c Kuggeleijn b Blair | 36 | not out | 35 |
| I. D. S. Smith b Dickeson | 12 | c Child b Dickeson | 20 |

| | | | |
|---|---|---|---|
| G. K. Robertson c Child b Bracewell | 39 | c Child b Dickeson | 16 |
| D. A. Stirling c Carrington b Dickeson | 0 | not out | 20 |
| D. R. O'Sullivan lbw b Child | 19 | | |
| K. W. Martin not out | 0 | | |
| B 1, l-b 6, w 2, n-b 7 | 16 | B 6, l-b 3, n-b 6 | 15 |
| 1/43 2/69 3/117 4/120 5/181 6/183 7/201 8/201 9/252 | 254 | 1/9 2/47 3/139 4/221 5/222 6/245 7/274 | (7 wkts dec.) 312 |

Bowling: *First Innings*—Bracewell 15–3–34–3; Carrington 16–2–62–1; Dickeson 30–10–44–2; Child 20.4–6–50–1; Blair 15–7–41–1; Kuggeleijn 3–0–16–0. *Second Innings*—Bracewell 10–4–18–1; Carrington 5–3–4–0; Dickeson 47–12–139–5; Child 1–1–0–0; Blair 13–3–29–0; Kuggeleijn 24–5–81–1; Cooper 7–0–32–0.

## Northern Districts

| | | | |
|---|---|---|---|
| L. M. Crocker lbw b Robertson | 15 | c Briasco b O'Sullivan | 36 |
| R. D. Broughton c I. D. S. Smith b Stirling | 15 | run out | 51 |
| *G. P. Howarth c Toynbee b Stirling | 12 | c and b Martin | 6 |
| B. P. Bracewell c I. D. S. Smith b Martin | 29 | not out | 4 |
| B. G. Cooper c Toynbee b O'Sullivan | 65 | run out | 25 |
| B. R. Blair c Blain b Martin | 19 | st Blain b O'Sullivan | 19 |
| C. M. Kuggeleijn b O'Sullivan | 31 | b O'Sullivan | 1 |
| †B. A. Young not out | 53 | not out | 4 |
| M. J. Child lbw b Robertson | 33 | b Toynbee | 10 |
| C. W. Dickeson b O'Sullivan | 5 | | |
| S. M. Carrington not out | 34 | | |
| B 2, l-b 7, w 2 | 11 | L-b 9 | 9 |
| 1/17 2/30 3/74 4/74 5/106 6/163 7/210 8/260 9/267 | (9 wkts dec.) 322 | 1/93 2/96 3/129 4/137 5/150 6/152 7/159 | (7 wkts) 165 |

Bowling: *First Innings*—Stirling 14–2–50–2; Robertson 21–4–99–2; O'Sullivan 37–14–80–3; Toynbee 11–4–31–0; Martin 27–9–53–2. *Second Innings*—Stirling 5–0–19–0; Robertson 7–0–28–0; O'Sullivan 20–5–64–3; Toynbee 5–2–9–1; Martin 10–0–32–1; I. D. S. Smith 1–0–4–0.

Umpires: M. M. Spring and S. C. Cowman.

# AUCKLAND v WELLINGTON

At Eden Park, Auckland, February 25, 26, 27. Drawn. Wellington 4 pts.

## Auckland

| | | | |
|---|---|---|---|
| T. J. Franklin c Ormiston b Chatfield | 12 | c Coney b Chatfield | 4 |
| P. A. Horne run out | 72 | c Vance b Gray | 70 |
| J. J. Crowe c McSweeney b Chatfield | 61 | c Maguiness b Gray | 41 |
| M. J. Greatbatch lbw b James | 67 | st McSweeney b Coney | 10 |
| P. N. Webb run out | 5 | not out | 51 |
| A. J. Hunt c McSweeney b Chatfield | 11 | c Vance b Gray | 6 |
| *M. C. Snedden c McSweeney b James | 18 | not out | 18 |
| J. G. Bracewell c Boyle b Maguiness | 1 | | |
| G. B. Troup c McSweeney b Maguiness | 26 | | |
| †N. A. Scott c McSweeney b Maguiness | 15 | | |
| W. Watson not out | 6 | | |
| B 4, l-b 10, w 1, n-b 2 | 17 | B 5, l-b 4, w 1, n-b 1 | 11 |
| 1/35 2/126 3/191 4/200 5/220 6/260 7/263 8/264 9/302 | 311 | 1/4 2/80 3/102 4/161 5/175 | (5 wkts) 211 |

Bowling: *First Innings*—Chatfield 40–15–85–3; James 20–5–51–2; Maguiness 36.3–9–72–3; Gray 19–7–70–0; Coney 10–5–19–0. *Second Innings*—Chatfield 5–1–16–1; James 6–1–22–0; Maguiness 4–0–7–0; Gray 18–2–70–3; Coney 15–4–44–1; Ormiston 2–0–15–0; Edgar 5–1–15–0; Vance 1–0–6–0; Boyle 1–0–5–0; Ritchie 1–0–2–0.

## Wellington

| | |
|---|---|
| J. G. Boyle lbw b Snedden | 5 |
| B. A. Edgar c Troup b Watson | 37 |
| *R. H. Vance c Scott b Troup | 59 |
| J. V. Coney c Greatbatch b Snedden | 20 |
| E. J. Gray c Scott b Troup | 49 |
| †E. B. McSweeney lbw b Bracewell | 41 |
| T. D. Ritchie lbw b Snedden | 19 |
| R. W. Ormiston not out | 27 |
| K. D. James lbw b Snedden | 36 |
| S. J. Maguiness c Scott b Hunt | 20 |
| E. J. Chatfield run out | 21 |
| B 4, l-b 13, n-b 9 | 26 |
| 1/8 2/89 3/128 4/136 5/189 6/239 7/243 8/306 9/337 | 360 |

Bowling: Troup 28–7–68–2; Watson 24–6–75–1; Snedden 40.2–13–89–4; Bracewell 38–10–84–1; Hunt 9–4–26–1; Horne 1–0–1–0.

Umpires: T. A. McCall and S. C. Cowman.

## CENTRAL DISTRICTS v CANTERBURY

At McLean Park, Napier, February 25, 26, 27. Drawn. Central Districts 4 pts.

### Central Districts

| | | | |
|---|---|---|---|
| R. T. Hart c Fulton b Hartshorn | 111 | – b Bateman | 7 |
| C. J. Smith run out | 2 | – not out | 103 |
| P. S. Briasco lbw b McNally | 2 | – c Hart b McNally | 75 |
| †T. E. Blain lbw b Thiele | 60 | – not out | 49 |
| G. N. Edwards c Fulton b Thiele | 4 | | |
| *R. E. Hayward c Latham b MacDonald | 44 | | |
| M. H. Toynbee not out | 40 | | |
| G. K. Robertson lbw b McNally | 40 | | |
| D. A. Stirling not out | 2 | | |
| B 2, l-b 8, n-b 3 | 13 | B 3, l-b 7, w 1 | 11 |
| 1/2 2/10 3/118 4/122 5/210 6/247 7/311 (7 wkts dec.) | 318 | 1/15 2/161 (2 wkts dec.) | 245 |

D. R. O'Sullivan and K. W. Martin did not bat.

Bowling: *First Innings*—Thiele 15–7–23–2; McNally 19–2–53–2; Bateman 11–3–37–0; Hartshorn 28–4–103–1; Brown 17–7–42–0; MacDonald 16–3–50–1. *Second Innings*—Thiele 1–0–5–0; McNally 23–5–93–1; Bateman 18–4–63–1; Hartshorn 10–1–38–0; Brown 9–4–24–0; MacDonald 3–0–12–0.

### Canterbury

| | | | |
|---|---|---|---|
| *R. W. Fulton b Martin | 21 | – c Blain b O'Sullivan | 33 |
| A. P. Nathu c Stirling b O'Sullivan | 39 | – b Toynbee | 51 |
| V. R. Brown lbw b Stirling | 0 | – not out | 61 |
| R. T. Latham c Blain b Stirling | 21 | – c Hart b Toynbee | 15 |
| D. J. Boyle b Martin | 17 | – st Blain b O'Sullivan | 0 |
| D. J. Hartshorn c Blain b Stirling | 103 | – lbw b Toynbee | 4 |
| †A. W. Hart st Blain b O'Sullivan | 18 | | |

| | | | |
|---|---|---|---|
| S. N. Bateman c Blain b Toynbee | 18 | not out | 10 |
| S. R. McNally b Robertson | 16 | c Smith b O'Sullivan | 2 |
| G. K. MacDonald not out | 12 | | |
| C. H. Thiele run out | 0 | | |
| B 13, l-b 11, w 1, n-b 2 | 27 | B 2, l-b 5, w 1 | 8 |
| 1/41 2/42 3/84 4/101 5/139 6/188 7/213 8/252 9/289 | 292 | 1/66 2/98 3/125 4/127 5/154 6/157 | (6 wkts) 184 |

Bowling: *First Innings*—Robertson 24–4–46–1; O'Sullivan 34–13–72–2; Stirling 11–0–39–3; Briasco 1–1–0–0; Toynbee 11–2–33–1; Martin 34–13–78–2. *Second Innings*—Robertson 7–2–27–0; O'Sullivan 17–1–65–3; Stirling 5–0–18–0; Toynbee 12–1–45–3; Martin 9–1–22–0.

Umpires: D. A. Kinsella and J. G. Reardon.

## OTAGO v NORTHERN DISTRICTS

At Carisbrook, Dunedin, February 25, 26, 27. Otago won by 58 runs. Otago 16 pts.

### Otago

| | | | |
|---|---|---|---|
| K. R. Rutherford c Dickeson b Carrington | 30 | c Broughton b Treiber | 0 |
| S. J. McCullum c Crocker b Treiber | 19 | c Broughton b Dickeson | 37 |
| S. J. Richards c and b Child | 0 | c Young b Treiber | 12 |
| *†W. K. Lees b Dickeson | 23 | c Blair b Carrington | 3 |
| A. H. Jones not out | 59 | lbw b Blair | 30 |
| S. Robinson c Young b Treiber | 2 | run out | 19 |
| T. J. Wilson c Young b Treiber | 4 | b Blair | 0 |
| N. A. Mallender c Young b Treiber | 1 | c Young b Blair | 0 |
| J. A. Cushen b Carrington | 1 | c Blair b Carrington | 14 |
| V. A. Johnson lbw b Blair | 5 | c Young b Treiber | 2 |
| S. L. Boock b Carrington | 6 | not out | 9 |
| B 3, l-b 10, w 1, n-b 1 | 15 | B 4, l-b 7 | 11 |
| 1/37 2/42 3/73 4/99 5/102 6/116 7/118 8/147 9/152 | 165 | 1/3 2/15 3/37 4/82 5/92 6/92 7/92 8/117 9/120 | 137 |

Bowling: *First Innings*—Carrington 16.2–4–37–3; Treiber 19–3–61–4; Child 8–2–21–1; Blair 8–2–20–1; Dickeson 11–5–13–1. *Second Innings*—Carrington 13.4–5–36–2; Treiber 18–8–44–3; Child 17–9–26–0; Blair 9–4–10–3; Dickeson 4–2–10–1.

### Northern Districts

| | | | |
|---|---|---|---|
| L. M. Crocker b Mallender | 0 | c Wilson b Mallender | 13 |
| R. D. Broughton c Lees b Cushen | 4 | lbw b Johnson | 4 |
| *C. M. Kuggeleijn b Mallender | 23 | c Lees b Cushen | 27 |
| B. G. Cooper c McCullum b Mallender | 1 | c Boock b Johnson | 19 |
| B. R. Blair c Jones b Johnson | 13 | c Lees b Cushen | 45 |
| W. P. Fowler c Lees b Mallender | 13 | b Johnson | 11 |
| †B. A. Young lbw b Cushen | 4 | c Lees b Mallender | 1 |
| M. J. Child lbw b Mallender | 5 | not out | 11 |
| S. M. Carrington c Lees b Cushen | 7 | b Cushen | 4 |
| C. W. Dickeson not out | 4 | c Lees b Cushen | 1 |
| K. Treiber b Mallender | 1 | b Cushen | 2 |
| B 2, l-b 5, n-b 1 | 8 | B 11, l-b 6, w 2, n-b 4 | 23 |
| 1/10 2/20 3/23 4/40 5/54 6/61 7/70 8/78 9/82 | 83 | 1/10 2/33 3/64 4/98 5/131 6/131 7/141 8/151 9/155 | 161 |

Bowling: *First Innings*—Mallender 16.1–9–31–6; Cushen 18–5–27–3; Johnson 10–4–18–1. *Second Innings*—Mallender 21–7–39–2; Cushen 25.4–12–37–5; Johnson 25–8–53–3; Boock 6–3–10–0; Wilson 4–2–5–0.

Umpires: W. C. Garrick and N. A. Tapper.

## CANTERBURY v NORTHERN DISTRICTS

At Lancaster Park, Christchurch, March 1, 2, 3. Canterbury won by eight wickets. Canterbury 12 pts, Northern Districts 4 pts.

### Northern Districts

| | | | |
|---|---|---|---|
| L. M. Crocker c Latham b Brown | 57 | – run out | 12 |
| R. D. Broughton c McEwan b McNally | 12 | – b Hadlee | 10 |
| *G. P. Howarth c Latham b McNally | 0 | – c Brown b Latham | 24 |
| B. G. Cooper c McNally b Masefield | 36 | – c sub b Latham | 9 |
| B. R. Blair c MacDonald b Brown | 42 | – run out | 66 |
| C. M. Kuggeleijn lbw b Hadlee | 3 | – lbw b Latham | 34 |
| †B. A. Young b MacDonald | 24 | – not out | 65 |
| M. J. Child lbw b McNally | 28 | – not out | 0 |
| B. P. Bracewell b McNally | 46 | | |
| C. W. Dickeson c Hart b Hadlee | 11 | | |
| K. Treiber not out | 0 | | |
| B 5, l-b 6, n-b 4 | 15 | B 7, l-b 8 | 15 |
| 1/26 2/26 3/85 4/128 5/132 6/182 7/189 8/241 9/270 | 274 | 1/14 2/35 3/58 4/81 5/119 6/232 (6 wkts dec.) | 235 |

Bowling: *First Innings*—Hadlee 19–5–43–2; McNally 24.4–7–77–4; McEwan 3–0–15–0; Masefield 16–1–59–1; Brown 18–3–45–2; MacDonald 12–1–24–1. *Second Innings*—Hadlee 12–5–16–1; McNally 15–6–37–0; Masefield 6–1–23–0; Brown 18–7–60–0; MacDonald 3–1–9–0; Latham 31–12–75–3.

### Canterbury

| | | | |
|---|---|---|---|
| J. G. Wright run out | 36 | – not out | 151 |
| A. P. Nathu c Young b Treiber | 14 | – lbw b Child | 4 |
| *R. W. Fulton c Broughton b Bracewell | 30 | | |
| V. R. Brown run out | 0 | – not out | 61 |
| R. T. Latham lbw b Treiber | 0 | | |
| R. J. Hadlee c Blair b Treiber | 8 | | |
| P. E. McEwan c Crocker b Dickeson | 39 | – run out | 69 |
| †A. W. Hart c Young b Blair | 23 | | |
| R. V. Masefield lbw b Bracewell | 8 | | |
| G. K. MacDonald not out | 8 | | |
| S. R. McNally b Child | 21 | | |
| B 2, l-b 6, n-b 15 | 23 | L-b 10, n-b 5 | 15 |
| 1/38 2/72 3/72 4/74 5/90 6/108 7/157 8/174 9/185 | 210 | 1/8 2/131 (2 wkts) | 300 |

Bowling: *First Innings*—Bracewell 15–1–67–2; Treiber 13–2–42–3; Child 11–3–34–1; Dickeson 18–8–38–1; Blair 8–2–21–1. *Second Innings*—Bracewell 6–2–22–0, Child 21–3–81–1; Dickeson 31–9–69–0; Blair 7–0–35–0; Kuggeleijn 6–0–31–0; Howarth 8–1–33–0; Cooper 4–1–15–0; Broughton 0.3–0–4–0.

Umpires: T. J. Baines and R. L. McHarg.

## WELLINGTON v OTAGO

At Basin Reserve, Wellington, March 1, 2, 3. Drawn. Otago 4 pts.

### Otago

| | | | |
|---|---|---|---|
| G. A. W. Blakely lbw b Gray | 28 | – b Cederwall | 6 |
| S. J. McCullum b Gray | 66 | – c Vance b James | 5 |
| K. R. Rutherford c Maguiness b Gray | 0 | – run out | 31 |
| K. J. Burns b Gray | 20 | – not out | 111 |

| | | | |
|---|---|---|---|
| A. H. Jones c and b Gray | 41 | – not out | 102 |
| R. N. Hoskin lbw b Griffiths | 6 | | |
| *†W. K. Lees b Cederwall | 26 | | |
| T. J. Wilson c Vance b James | 6 | | |
| N. A. Mallender c McSweeney b Gray | 40 | | |
| J. A. Cushen not out | 9 | | |
| S. L. Boock c Boyle b Cederwall | 10 | | |
| B 2, l-b 12, w 1, n-b 8 | 23 | B 12, l-b 2, n-b 4 | 18 |
| 1/86 2/86 3/121 4/131 5/139 6/179 7/202 8/231 9/262 | 275 | 1/11 2/11 3/61 (3 wkts) | 273 |

Bowling: *First Innings*—James 14–5–39–1; Cederwall 12.4–2–40–2; Maguiness 16–10–17–0; Gray 52–22–89–6; Griffiths 35–5–75–1; Vance 3–2–1–0. *Second Innings*—James 7–3–14–1; Cederwall 12–2–41–1; Maguiness 17–11–11–0; Gray 51–17–125–0; Griffiths 17–3–54–0; Vance 1–0–4–0; Ormiston 3–1–10–0.

## Wellington

| | |
|---|---|
| B. A. Edgar lbw b Boock | 47 |
| J. G. Boyle b Boock | 11 |
| *R. H. Vance c Mallender b Boock | 0 |
| R. W. Ormiston b Boock | 1 |
| †E. B. McSweeney c Rutherford b Boock | 0 |
| E. J. Gray b Jones | 10 |
| T. D. Ritchie lbw b Mallender | 60 |
| G. N. Cederwall b Jones | 7 |
| K. D. James c Lees b Mallender | 34 |
| S. J. Maguiness c McCullum b Boock | 14 |
| A. Griffiths not out | 4 |
| B 6, l-b 5, n-b 5 | 16 |
| 1/27 2/27 3/40 4/40 5/73 6/81 7/92 8/177 9/192 | 204 |

Bowling: Mallender 11.5–1–34–2; Boock 47–24–64–6; Cushen 8–4–15–0; Wilson 3–0–15–0; Jones 26–10–65–2.

Umpires: B. F. Aldridge and S. J. Woodward.

# AUCKLAND v CENTRAL DISTRICTS

At Eden Park, Auckland, March 1, 2, 3. Drawn. Auckland 4 pts.

## Central Districts

| | | | |
|---|---|---|---|
| R. T. Hart c Crowe b Bracewell | 13 | – c Webb b Watson | 45 |
| C. J. Smith c Webb b Watson | 10 | – c Bracewell b Snedden | 67 |
| P. S. Briasco lbw b Watson | 0 | – b Watson | 37 |
| *M. D. Crowe c Watson b Troup | 11 | – lbw b Snedden | 34 |
| T. E. Blain c Crowe b Troup | 1 | – c Crowe b Snedden | 9 |
| M. H. Toynbee b Troup | 4 | – c and b Snedden | 10 |
| †I. D. S. Smith c and b Watson | 11 | – c Crowe b Snedden | 20 |
| D. A. Stirling not out | 10 | – lbw b Bracewell | 7 |
| D. R. O'Sullivan c Horne b Troup | 4 | – c Reid b Bracewell | 6 |
| K. W. Martin c Snedden b Watson | 8 | – not out | 0 |
| G. K. Robertson c Webb b Watson | 0 | – c Crowe b Snedden | 0 |
| N-b 6 | 6 | B 17, l-b 6, w 1, n-b 6 | 30 |
| 1/18 2/18 3/31 4/33 5/37 6/48 7/48 8/59 9/66 | 78 | 1/87 2/150 3/199 4/206 5/219 6/241 7/242 8/249 9/263 | 265 |

Bowling: *First Innings*—Troup 14–4–28–4; Watson 14.1–5–36–5; Snedden 10–4–9–0; Bracewell 2–0–5–1. *Second Innings*—Troup 15–3–38–0; Watson 12–1–39–2; Snedden 29–9–63–6; Bracewell 38–9–98–2; Hunt 1–0–4–0.

## Auckland

| | | | |
|---|---|---|---|
| T. J. Franklin not out | 23 | – lbw b Martin | 81 |
| P. A. Horne not out | 55 | – c Martin b Robertson | 15 |
| J. F. Reid (did not bat) | | – c Toynbee b Martin | 19 |
| J. J. Crowe (did not bat) | | – b Briasco | 1 |
| M. J. Greatbatch (did not bat) | | – c Blain b Briasco | 6 |
| †P. N. Webb (did not bat) | | – c Martin b O'Sullivan | 0 |
| A. J. Hunt (did not bat) | | – b Martin | 39 |
| *M. C. Snedden (did not bat) | | – c Stirling b Martin | 1 |
| J. G. Bracewell (did not bat) | | – not out | 14 |
| G. B. Troup (did not bat) | | – c Crowe b O'Sullivan | 6 |
| B 2 | 2 | L-b 7, w 1 | 8 |
| (no wkt dec.) | 80 | 1/24 2/47 3/48 4/88 5/91 6/160 7/166 8/175 9/190 (9 wkts) | 190 |

W. Watson did not bat.

Bowling: *First Innings*—Stirling 5.4–0–18–0; Robertson 5–0–21–0; Martin 4–0–7–0; O'Sullivan 5–2–20–0; Toynbee 3–0–12–0. *Second Innings*—Stirling 3–0–13–0; Robertson 3–0–15–1; Martin 19–2–59–4; O'Sullivan 22–5–61–2; Toynbee 4–0–16–0; Briasco 17–9–19–2.

Umpires: D. A. Kinsella and T. A. McCall.

# CRICKET IN INDIA, 1984-85

By P. N. SUNDARESAN

The dominant features of the season were the efficient manner in which David Gower's England team shook off the effects of a defeat in the opening Test at Bombay and the luminous emergence of Mohammed Azharuddin, the 22-year-old Hyderabad batsman, with a world record of three successive Test centuries, starting from his début in Calcutta.

After a half-century in an Irani Trophy match against Bombay at the start of the season and another for the Board President's team against the England XI, Azharuddin scored 151 for the Under-25 team against the visiting side and then recorded the feat of a century in each innings – 121 and 105 not out – for Hyderabad in a South Zone Ranji Trophy tie against Andhra before gathering 110 on his Test début. That meant four hundreds in a row, and after a minor lapse when he scored 18 and 52 for South Zone against the Englishmen, Azharuddin followed up with centuries in the Madras and Kanpur Tests. In fourteen innings during the season Azharuddin hit six hundreds and four half-centuries. Another aspect of the youngster's performance was that he was involved in seven three-figure partnerships – every time he scored a hundred and once, in the first innings of the Madras Test, when he was out for 48.

The other personal performance of note was that of Ravi Shastri, who, in scoring 200 not out for Bombay against Baroda in the West Zone of the Ranji Trophy, hit six 6s in one over from the Baroda left-arm slow bowler, Tilakraj, to equal the world record of G. S. Sobers. That gave him twelve 6s in his innings, an Indian record, and he hit one more to join C. S. Greenidge, G. W. Humpage and Majid Khan on thirteen. Only the former New Zealand captain, J. R. Reid, with fifteen, has hit more. Shastri's double-hundred was also a world record, coming in 113 minutes off 123 balls.

Bombay repeated their performance of the previous season by defeating Delhi in the final to win the Ranji Trophy Championship for the 30th time. But their superiority in the West Zone league and the knockout was not as clear-cut as in some years. Only in their fourth and final match, against Saurashtra, in the West Zone did they emerge at the top of the table. This was the only match in the zone to provide an outright decision.

In the quarter-final against Haryana, Bombay conceded a first-innings lead, but recovered strongly to win by eight wickets. Tamil Nadu put them under pressure in the semi-final with an opening stand of 182 between V. Sivaramakrishnan (117) and C. S. Sureshkumar (106), but once this was broken they reasserted themselves, acting-skipper Sandip Patil piloting them to a tall score of 548, with a hard-hit 165, to ensure a first-innings lead.

The final against Delhi at the Wankhede Stadium was a close match with Delhi having an early edge but Ravi Shastri putting the issue beyond doubt for Bombay with accurate left-arm spin bowling which fetched him eight for 91 in Delhi's second innings and match figures of twelve for 182. Delhi, who were led by Madan Lal in the final, were weaker for the loss of Mohinder Amarnath, who had switched to Baroda, and Rajesh Shukla, who now played for Bihar. Maninder Singh, the left-arm spinner rejected by the Indian selectors, bowled with great heart in the final and was outstanding in the knockout stages of the Championship when he gathered 24 of his 31 wickets. Maninder was chiefly responsible for Delhi's triumph over Karnataka in the semi-final with a match haul of eleven for 148.

While the qualifiers for the knockout stages from the West, South and North Zones were as expected, there were surprises in the Central and East Zones. The failure of Rajasthan, Madhya Pradesh and Vidarbha to win a single tie in the Central Zone considerably helped Railways, who had a victory over Vidarbha in their final match to gain second place and an entry into the knockout. Bengal lost their traditional hold in the East Zone. Their match at Nowgong against Assam, the weakest side in the zone, was spoiled by weather, with some seven hours lost to rain and bad light, and ended in a draw. As Orissa and Bihar both beat Assam, they scored over Bengal and took the first two places.

Ghulam Parkar of Bombay had the best aggregate (660 runs) in the Championship, while S. S. Khandkar of Uttar Pradesh recorded the best individual score – 261 not out against Railways. Rajinder Goel, the veteran left-arm spinner, was persuaded to return from retirement to assist Haryana and he responded by bagging 39 wickets at 16.71 each: this was the best tally in the Championship. Against Jammu and Kashmir, Goel took seven wickets in each innings, for 36 and 38 respectively. An interesting bowling effort came from Uttar Pradesh's Rajinder Singh Hans, a left-arm spinner, and off-spinner Gopal Sharma when they shared all twenty wickets against Saurashtra in the preliminary knockout round.

Rest of India won the Irani Trophy, defeating Bombay, the 1983-84 Ranji Trophy champions, by four wickets. The final of the Duleep Trophy was played in February after the completion of the series against England, three months after the earlier rounds, and the match provoked little interest. South Zone, who were led by Syed Kirmani, bagged the trophy.

The committee set up by the Board of Control for Cricket in India, to suggest measures for tightening the format of Indian cricket, recommended that the Duleep Trophy competition be played on a league basis.

## FIRST-CLASS AVERAGES, 1984-85

### BATTING

(Qualification: 500 runs)

| | *I* | *NO* | *R* | *HI* | *100s* | *Avge* |
|---|---|---|---|---|---|---|
| M. Azharuddin (*Hyderabad*) | 14 | 4 | 991 | 151 | 6 | 99.10 |
| P Shastri (*Rajasthan*) | 12 | 2 | 711 | 159 | 2 | 71.10 |
| R. J. Shastri (*Bombay*) | 14 | 3 | 761 | 200* | 3 | 69.18 |
| M. Amarnath (*Baroda*) | 13 | 3 | 687 | 95 | 0 | 68.70 |
| K. Bhaskar Pillai (*Delhi*) | 11 | 2 | 576 | 149* | 2 | 64.00 |
| A. Malhotra (*Haryana*) | 12 | 2 | 542 | 132 | 2 | 54.20 |
| G. A. Parkar (*Bombay*) | 15 | 1 | 748 | 170* | 1 | 53.42 |
| V. Sivaramakrishnan (*Tamil Nadu*) | 14 | 2 | 639 | 117 | 3 | 53.25 |
| K. Srikkanth (*Tamil Nadu*) | 14 | 1 | 674 | 101 | 1 | 51.84 |
| R. Madhavan (*Tamil Nadu*) | 17 | 3 | 719 | 153* | 3 | 51.35 |
| D. B. Vengsarkar (*Bombay*) | 12 | 2 | 509 | 200* | 2 | 50.90 |
| A. Jabbar (*Tamil Nadu*) | 13 | 1 | 581 | 143 | 1 | 48.41 |

| | *I* | *NO* | *R* | *HI* | *100s* | *Avge* |
|---|---|---|---|---|---|---|
| S. M. H. Kirmani (*Karnataka*) ..... | 13 | 2 | 502 | 102 | 1 | 45.63 |
| C. P. S. Chauhan (*Delhi*) .......... | 16 | 2 | 629 | 115 | 1 | 44.92 |
| C. S. Pandit (*Bombay*) ............ | 16 | 2 | 610 | 126 | 2 | 43.57 |
| S. M. Patil (*Bombay*) ............. | 18 | 2 | 682 | 165 | 1 | 42.62 |
| L. S. Rajput (*Bombay*) ............ | 18 | 0 | 737 | 136 | 2 | 40.94 |
| R. Khanvilkar (*Karnataka*) ........ | 14 | 1 | 526 | 156 | 2 | 40.46 |
| S. M. Gavaskar (*Bombay*) .......... | 17 | 3 | 566 | 106 | 1 | 40.42 |
| S. S. Khandkar (*Uttar Pradesh*) ..... | 15 | 1 | 557 | 261* | 1 | 39.78 |
| Gursharan Singh (*Delhi*) ........... | 19 | 1 | 501 | 68 | 0 | 27.83 |

**Signifies not out.*

## BOWLING

(Qualification: 25 wickets)

| | *O* | *M* | *R* | *W* | *Avge* |
|---|---|---|---|---|---|
| Madan Lal (*Delhi*) ................ | 145 | 42 | 318 | 27 | 11.77 |
| R. S. Hans (*Uttar Pradesh*) ......... | 320.4 | 96 | 617 | 42 | 14.69 |
| R. Goel (*Haryana*) ................ | 388 | 133 | 652 | 39 | 16.71 |
| Maninder Singh (*Delhi*) ............ | 390.3 | 118 | 889 | 46 | 19.32 |
| A. Raghuram Bhat (*Karnataka*) ..... | 363.2 | 85 | 952 | 47 | 20.25 |
| R. S. Ghai (*Punjab*) ............... | 151.4 | 26 | 534 | 26 | 20.53 |
| S. Venkataraghavan (*Tamil Nadu*) ... | 260.5 | 54 | 632 | 30 | 21.06 |
| R. P. Singh (*Uttar Pradesh*) ........ | 203 | 31 | 735 | 30 | 24.50 |
| A. Patel (*Saurashtra*) .............. | 276.5 | 50 | 829 | 32 | 25.90 |
| R. J. Shastri (*Bombay*) ............ | 347.4 | 107 | 746 | 28 | 26.64 |
| S. Talwar (*Haryana*) .............. | 256.1 | 39 | 776 | 29 | 26.75 |
| G. Sharma (*Uttar Pradesh*) ......... | 357 | 80 | 906 | 33 | 27.45 |
| L. Sivaramakrishnan (*Tamil Nadu*) .. | 362.3 | 81 | 998 | 34 | 29.35 |
| K. D. Mokashi (*Bombay*) .......... | 262 | 52 | 786 | 26 | 30.23 |
| N. S. Yadav (*Hyderabad*) .......... | 293.2 | 61 | 882 | 29 | 30.41 |
| B. S. Sandhu (*Bombay*) ............ | 224.2 | 43 | 771 | 25 | 30.84 |
| R. R. Kulkarni (*Bombay*) .......... | 272.3 | 32 | 1,050 | 30 | 35.00 |

*Note: Matches taken into account are Ranji Trophy, Duleep Trophy, Irani Trophy and those against the England touring team in India.*

## RANJI TROPHY, 1984-85

*In the following scores, (M) indicates that the match was played on coir matting, (T) that it was played on turf, and * by the name of the team indicates that they won the toss.*

### Central Zone

At Nagpur (T), December 15, 16, 17. Uttar Pradesh won by three wickets. Vidarbha 207 (M. Kaore 56; R. S. Hans six for 38) and 262 (M. Kaore 70; R. S. Hans four for 59); Uttar Pradesh* 349 (A. Bambi 78, S. Chaturvedi 62, Yusuf Ali Khan 61; H. Wasu seven for 102) and 121 for seven. *Uttar Pradesh 26 pts, Vidarbha 11 pts.*

At Bhilai (T), December 15, 16, 17. Drawn. Madhya Pradesh* 392 for five dec. (M. Hassan 116 not out, R. Talwar 93, A. Laghate 61, S. Ansari 43) and 153 for five (M. Hassan 45 not out); Rajasthan 344 (P. Shastri 93, A. Asawa 89 not out, Dalbir Singh 46; N. Hirwani five for 101). *Madhya Pradesh 8 pts, Rajasthan 5 pts.*

At Akola (M), December 20, 21, 22. Drawn. Vidarbha* 299 (R. Pankule 69, P. Shetty 48; P. Sunderam four for 108) and 233 for nine dec. (S. Hedaoo 66 not out, P. Shetty 58; A. Mathur four for 39); Rajasthan 277 for seven dec. (P. Sharma 94, P. Shastri 87, A. Mudkavi 46; H. Wasu four for 82) and 104 for three. *Rajasthan 10 pts, Vidarbha 9 pts.*

At Jhansi (M), December 21, 22, 23. Drawn. Railways* 274 for eight dec. (P. Bhatnagar 75, S. Mehra 49) and 323 (P. Karkera 81, H. Mathur 68, N. Churi 57, A. Nandy 40; Gulrez Ali five for 94); Madhya Pradesh 286 (S. Ansari 87, Sanjeeva Rao 58, A. Laghate 50; S. Khan four for 85) and 129 for three (S. Ansari 55). *Railways 11 pts, Madhya Pradesh 10 pts.*

At Kanpur (T), December 26, 27, 28. Uttar Pradesh won by six wickets. Uttar Pradesh* 396 (R. Sapru 114, K. B. Kala 88, S. Mehrotra 40; Gopal Rao four for 75) and 89 for four; Madhya Pradesh 125 (R. S. Hans four for 7, A. Mathur four for 34) and 359 (S. Ansari 200; R. S. Hans five for 73, G. Sharma four for 107). *Uttar Pradesh 24 pts, Madhya Pradesh 8 pts.*

At Kota (T), December 27, 28, 29. Drawn. Rajasthan* 349 for seven dec. (P. Shastri 159, A. Asawa 75) and 183 for four dec. (P. Shastri 101 not out); Railways 266 (N. Churi 85, P. Karkera 41; S. Mudkavi eight for 60) and 23 for five. *Rajasthan 7 pts, Railways 6 pts.*

At Moradabad (M), January 11, 12, 13. Uttar Pradesh won by an innings and 68 runs. Uttar Pradesh* 497 for three dec. (S. S. Khandkar 261 not out, Yusuf Ali Khan 122, S. Chaturvedi 50); Railways 147 (R. P. Singh seven for 67) and 282 (S. Mehra 50, N. Churi 46; R. P. Singh four for 79). *Uttar Pradesh 30 pts, Railways 4 pts.*

At Sehore (T), January 11, 12, 13. Drawn. Vidarbha* 376 (V. Gawate 68, R. Pankule 49, S. Hedaoo 47; Asad Khan four for 99) and 253 (V. Shesh 77, S. Takle 40; A. Sabnis four for 70); Madhya Pradesh 293 for six dec. (R. Talwar 85, Sanjeeva Rao 56, A. Laghate 45) and 248 for eight (Asad Khan 41 not out, M. Satokar 41; S. Phadkar four for 56). *Madhya Pradesh 13 pts, Vidarbha 10 pts.*

At Jaipur (T), February 8, 9, 10. Drawn. Uttar Pradesh* 467 for seven dec. (S. Chaturvedi 182, R. Sapru 120) and 173 for three (Yusuf Ali Khan 83 not out, S. Chaturvedi 62); Rajasthan 328 (P. Shastri 79, A. Asawa 63 not out, S. Mudkavi 51; R. S. Hans four for 43). *Uttar Pradesh 10 pts, Rajasthan 6 pts.*

At Nagpur (T), February 4, 5, 6. Railways won by seven wickets. Vidarbha 283 for nine dec. (S. Hedaoo 64, P. Sahasrabudhe 47; A. Sharma four for 66) and 184; Railways* 324 for nine dec. (Hyder Ali 121, R. Jadhav 79) and 144 for three (R. Vats 69, N. Churi 40). *Railways 27 pts, Vidarbha 9 pts.*

Uttar Pradesh 90 pts, Railways 48 pts, Madhya Pradesh 39 pts, Vidarbha 39 pts, Rajasthan 28 pts. Uttar Pradesh and Railways qualified for the knockout stage.

## East Zone

At Nowgong (T), November 24, 25, 26. Drawn. Assam* 139 (K. Das 66) and 93 (D. R. Doshi four for 35); Bengal 112 (S. Uzir five for 29) and 11 for no wicket. *Bengal 6 pts, Assam 4 pts.*

At Ranchi (T), November 24, 25, 26. Drawn. Bihar* 307 for six dec. (B. S. Gossein 84, H. Gidwani 78, D. Augustus 73 not out; H. Praharaj four for 100) and 293 (Utpal Das 73, S. Das 45; H. Praharaj six for 86); Orissa 304 for six dec. (A. Jayaprakash 102 not out, S. Sahu 71 not out) and 59 for one. *Bihar 9 pts, Orissa 9 pts.*

At Calcutta (T), December 1, 2, 3. Drawn. Bengal* 301 for six dec. (Arun Lal 157 not out, R. C. Shukla 81) and 156 for nine dec. (Arun Lal 54); Bihar 172 (V. Venkatram 49 not out, Satish Singh 42) and 157 for four (H. Gidwani 84, R. Deora 55). *Bengal 11 pts, Bihar 9 pts.*

At Nowgong (T), December 1, 2, 3. Orissa won by an innings and 115 runs. Assam* 145 (A. Jayaprakash six for 66) and 123 (N. Konwar 43); Orissa 383 for seven dec. (H. Praharaj 197, A. Jayaprakash 88; H. Barua five for 52). *Orissa 31 pts, Assam 3 pts.*

At Nowgong (T), December 6, 7, 8. Bihar won by 81 runs. Bihar 247 (D. Augustus 49; N. Konwar six for 64) and 179 for three dec. (R. Deora 52); Assam* 114 (A. Kumar six for 27) and 231 (A. Das 85 not out, A. Kalita 40; A. Kumar six for 72). *Bihar 28 pts, Assam 7 pts.*

At Calcutta (T), December 8, 9, 10. Drawn. Orissa 206 (K. Dubey 60, S. Mitra 56; B. Burman four for 47) and 307 for seven dec. (K. Dubey 127, A. Bharadwaj 125 not out; D. R. Doshi four for 79); Bengal* 169 (Arun Lal 45, K. Dhab 43; L. K. Mahapatra four for 18) and 114 for two (P. Roy 60 not out). *Bengal 8 pts, Orissa 8 pts.*

Orissa 48 pts, Bihar 46 pts, Bengal 25 pts, Assam 14 pts. Orissa and Bihar qualified for the knockout stage.

## North Zone

At Delhi (T), November 25, 26, 27. Services won by an innings and 9 runs. Jammu and Kashmir 274 (S. Choudhry 67, P. Kaiser 55) and 225 (S. Choudhry 66, R. Pandit 51); Services* 508 for five dec. (A. K. Seth 130 not out, N. Gadkari 116 not out, Srikant 80, Ratan Das 77). *Services 29 pts, Jammu and Kashmir 7 pts.*

At Rohtak (T), November 29, 30, December 1. Haryana won by an innings and 71 runs. Jammu and Kashmir 101 (R. Goel seven for 36) and 152 (P. Kaiser 44; R. Goel seven for 38); Haryana* 324 for nine dec. (R. Chadda 53, Aman Kumar 47 not out, A. Malhotra 47; N. Khanday four for 59). *Haryana 30 pts, Jammu and Kashmir 3 pts.*

At Delhi (T), November 30, December 1, 2. Drawn. Delhi 335 (S. C. Khanna 114, C. P. S. Chauhan 57, K. Bhaskar Pillai 41; D. Chopra four for 92) and 137 for six dec. (Madan Lal 46 not out); Punjab* 228 (Yograj Singh 49 not out; K. Azad five for 80, Madan Lal four for 37) and 54 for five. *Delhi 11 pts, Punjab 8 pts.*

At Delhi (T), December 4, 5, 6. Delhi won by an innings and 45 runs. Jammu and Kashmir 88 (S. Valson four for 34) and 111 (Madan Lal nine for 50); Delhi* 244 (Gursharan Singh 64, Maninder Singh 61 not out; Ravi Pandit four for 46). *Delhi 30 pts, Jammu and Kashmir 5 pts.*

At Delhi (T), December 4, 5, 6. Drawn. Punjab* 464 for four dec. (K. P. Amarjeet 167, D. Chopra 120 not out, Balkar Singh 63, Navjot Singh 61) and 81 for five; Services 504 (B. Ghosh 151 not out, A. S. Bajwa 132, Sudhakar Rao 71, Ratan Das 54, A. K. Seth 45). *Services 6 pts, Punjab 5 pts.*

At Chandigarh (T), December 8, 9, 10. Punjab won by an innings and 169 runs. Jammu and Kashmir* 83 and 70 (D. Chopra four for 14); Punjab 322 (Satish Kumar 108, A. Sharma 62 not out; N. Khanday four for 97). *Punjab 31 pts, Jammu and Kashmir 2 pts.*

At Delhi (T), December 11, 12, 13. Haryana won by an innings and 24 runs. Services* 189 (Sudhakar Rao 52, A. S. Bajwa 42; S. Talwar six for 68) and 227 (B. Ghosh 90, Srikant 48, Ratan Das 41; R. Goel five for 75); Haryana 440 (A. Malhotra 132, R. Jolly 86, Aman Kumar 47, Deepak Sharma 43; A. Jha six for 179). *Haryana 29 pts, Services 4 pts.*

At Rohtak (T), December 15, 16, 17. Drawn. Delhi* 459 for five dec. (K. Bhaskar Pillai 149, C. P. S. Chauhan 115, S. C. Khanna 58, Madan Lal 43) and 175 for three (Gursharan Singh 57, C. P. S. Chauhan 53); Haryana 337 (R. Chadda 83, Aman Kumar 55). *Delhi 10 pts, Haryana 5 pts.*

At Delhi (T), December 21, 22, 23. Delhi won by nine wickets. Services* 191 (B. Ghosh 69) and 81 (S. Srivastava five for 21); Delhi 233 (K. Bhaskar Pillai 135; A. Jha five for 80) and 40 for one. *Delhi 25 pts, Services 5 pts.*

At Patiala (T), December 21, 22, 23. Drawn. Haryana* 299 (Chetan Sharma 53, Salim Ahmed 49; D. Chopra four for 79) and 190 for six (Aman Kumar 41); Punjab 264 for nine dec. (Navjot Singh 124; S. Talwar five for 129). *Punjab 6 pts, Haryana 4 pts.*

Delhi 76 pts, Haryana 68 pts, Punjab 50 pts, Services 44 pts, Jammu and Kashmir 17 pts. Delhi and Haryana qualified for the knockout stage.

## South Zone

At Secunderabad (T), November 13, 14, 15. Drawn. Tamil Nadu 421 (A. Jabbar 143, R. Madhavan 103; N. S. Yadav six for 166) and 191 for nine dec. (V. Sivaramakrishnan 47; Arhsad Ayub four for 63); Hyderabad* 258 for eight dec. (M. V. Narasimha Rao 72; T. A. P. Sekar four for 81) and 30 for one. *Tamil Nadu 9 pts, Hyderabad 7 pts.*

At Bangalore (T), November 18, 19, 20. Karnataka won by 167 runs. Karnataka 245 (R. M. H. Binny 87, R. Sudhakar Rao 57; J. K. Ghiya five for 66) and 210 for seven dec. (B. P. Patel 50); Andhra* 151 (G. A. Pratapkumar 40; A. Raghuram Bhat five for 72) and 137 (A. Raghuram Bhat four for 41). *Karnataka 29 pts, Andhra 9 pts.*

At Trivandrum (T), December 1, 2, 3. Karnataka won by 223 runs. Karnataka* 354 for two dec. (M. R. Srinivasaprasad 166 not out, G. R. Viswanath 129, R. M. H. Binny 40 not out) and 223 for two (M. R. Srinivasaprasad 79, S. Viswanath 60, G. R. Viswanath 45 not out); Kerala 207 (K. Jayaraman 75, S. Santosh 54; R. M. H. Binny five for 74) and 147 (L. Rajan 43; A. Raghuram Bhat four for 34). *Karnataka 31 pts, Kerala 5 pts.*

At Tellicherry (M), December 15, 16, 17. Tamil Nadu won by 165 runs. Tamil Nadu 281 (K. Srikkanth 50, V. Sivaramakrishnan 49, A. Jabbar 43; T. S. Mahadevan five for 81) and 263 for eight dec. (V. Sivaramakrishnan 100 not out); Kerala* 235 (K. Jayaraman 58; K. Arunkumar five for 59) and 144 (T. A. P. Sekar five for 65, K. Arunkumar four for 44). *Tamil Nadu 31 pts, Kerala 11 pts.*

At Salem (T), December 21, 22, 23. Karnataka won by four wickets. Tamil Nadu* 154 (K. Srikkanth 49; P. Rathod four for 38, A. Raghuram Bhat four for 59) and 194 (A. Jabbar 77, K. Srikkanth 43; A. Raghuram Bhat seven for 82); Karnataka 186 (S. Viswanath 69, G. R. Viswanath 41; S. Venkataraghavan seven for 69) and 163 for six (R. Khanvilkar 74) *Karnataka 24 pts, Tamil Nadu 8 pts.*

At Machilipatnam (M), December 22, 23, 24. Hyderabad won by eight wickets. Andhra* 289 (K. B. Ramamurthy 67) and 243 (K. V. S. D. Kamaraju 81; R. Yadav seven for 64); Hyderabad 305 for three dec. (M. Azharuddin 121, Abdul Azeem 81, K. A. Qayyum 59 not out) and 228 for two (M. Azharuddin 105 not out, Abdul Azeem 68). *Hyderabad 32 pts, Andhra 9 pts.*

At Secunderabad (T), December 30, 31, January 1. Drawn. Kerala 178 (K. Jayaraman 56; R. Yadav six for 55) and 243 for six (K. Jayaraman 71, S. Santosh 61); Hyderabad* 511 for six dec. (M. V. Narasimha Rao 160 not out, Abdul Azeem 103, Arshad Ayub 62, K. A. Qayyum 61, P. Jyotiprasad 44 not out). *Hyderabad 9 pts, Kerala 4 pts.*

At Vijayawada (T), January 4, 5, 6. Andhra won by an innings and 50 runs. Andhra 262 (J. K. Ghiya 61 not out, G. A. Pratapkumar 57; Ajay Verma four for 65); Kerala* 95 (S. Ramesh 40; J. K. Ghiya four for 27) and 117 (K. B. Ramamurthy six for 4). *Andhra 29 pts, Kerala 4 pts.*

At Madras (T), February 2, 3, 4. Tamil Nadu won by 150 runs. Tamil Nadu 331 for six dec. (R. Madhavan 153 not out) and 178 for two dec. (V. Sivaramakrishnan 99, S. Srinivasan 59 not out); Andhra* 136 (T. A. P. Sekar five for 36) and 223 (S. Venkataraghavan five for 81). *Tamil Nadu 30 pts, Andhra 5 pts.*

At Hassan (M), February 2, 3, 4. Drawn. Karnataka* 208 (G. R. Viswanath 46, S. Viswanath 45; N. S. Yadav five for 84) and 436 for seven (B. P. Patel 130 not out, J. Abhiram 81, R. M. H. Binny 61, P. Rathod 42); Hyderabad 305 (Arshad Ayub 71, Ehtesham-ud-Din 67 not out, K. A. Qayyum 48; P. Rathod four for 74). *Hyderabad 9 pts, Karnataka 7 pts.*

Karnataka 91 pts, Tamil Nadu 78 pts, Hyderabad 57 pts, Andhra 52 pts, Kerala 24 pts. Karnataka and Tamil Nadu qualified for the knockout stage.

## West Zone

At Pune (T), December 7, 8, 9. Drawn. Bombay* 310 for six dec. (L. S. Rajput 94, S. S. Hattangadi 72, C. S. Pandit 46; S. Jadhav four for 47) and 330 for nine dec. (B. S. Sandhu 83, S. M. Gavaskar 73 not out, S. S. Hattangadi 51; S. Gudge four for 93); Maharashtra 318 for eight dec. (R. Poonawala 65, S. Kalyani 55, R. B. Bhalekar 44, S. Jadhav 40; S. V. Nayak four for 83) and 212 for six (S. Gudge 59, M. D. Gunjal 51 not out, R. Poonawala 46). *Bombay 14 pts, Maharashtra 13 pts.*

At Ahmedabad (T), December 7, 8, 9. Drawn. Saurashtra* 335 for nine dec. (A. Pandya 113, K. Chauhan 60, K. D. Ghavri 59, R. Badiyani 42) and 219 for eight dec. (A. Pandya 44; B. Mistry four for 43); Gujarat 325 (S. Talati 82, A. Saheba 60, B. Mistry 56, P. Desai 47) and 113 for five (B. Mistry 66). *Saurashtra 12 pts, Gujarat 9 pts.*

At Baroda (T), December 20, 21, 22. Drawn. Maharashtra* 305 for eight dec. (S. Jadhav 123 not out, P. Pradhan 78, S. Kalyani 69) and 238 for five dec. (R. Poonawala 84, S. Jadhav 67 not out M. Dixit 40); Baroda 340 for nine dec. (A. D. Gaekwad 108, M. Amarnath 73 not out, R. Y. Deshmukh 50) and 45 for no wicket. *Baroda 9 pts, Maharashtra 8 pts.*

At Bombay (T), December 21, 22, 23. Drawn. Bombay 309 for four dec. (L. S. Rajput 110, G. A. Parkar 67, S. S. Hattangadi 46 not out) and 266 for three dec. (C. S. Pandit 106 not out, S. M. Gavaskar 62 not out, G. A. Parkar 51, L. S. Rajput 45); Gujarat* 297 (B. Mistry 70, S. Talati 55) and 139 for eight (B. Mistry 49; B. S. Sandhu four for 60). *Bombay 15 pts, Gujarat 7 pts.*

At Jamnagar (T), January 8, 9, 10. Drawn. Saurashtra 335 for eight dec. (B. Pujara 93, A. Pandya 76, A. Patel 67; S. Oak four for 54) and 158 (A. Pandya 51; S. Oak six for 55); Maharashtra* 301 for seven dec. (S. Kalyani 103, M. D. Gunjal 82, P. Pradhan 44) and 143 for four (S. Kalyani 64 not out; R. Jadeja four for 57). *Maharashtra 13 pts, Saurashtra 10 pts.*

At Bombay (T), January 8, 9, 10. Drawn. Bombay* 371 for four dec. (G. A. Parkar 170 retired hurt, S. S. Hattangadi 83, L. S. Rajput 66) and 457 for five dec. (R. J. Shastri 200 not out, L. S. Rajput 136, S. M. Gavaskar 49); Baroda 330 for eight dec. (S. Keshwala 100 not out, M. Amarnath 88, G. Tilakraj 55) and 81 for seven (B. S. Sandhu four for 43). *Bombay 14 pts, Baroda 6 pts. R. J. Shastri reached 200 in 113 minutes off 123 balls to record the fastest-ever double-century and in doing so he hit six 6s in one over from G. Tilakraj, equalling the record of G. S. Sobers. In all, Shastri hit thirteen 6s.*

At Baroda (T), January 27, 28, 29. Drawn. Saurashtra* 344 for nine dec. (K. Chauhan 122, R. Jadeja 42; D. V. Pardeshi seven for 76) and 219 (K. D. Ghavri 56, S. Pujara 54; D. V. Pardeshi six for 84); Baroda 307 (M. Amarnath 70, R. Y. Deshmukh 45, G. Tilakraj 41; B. Quereshi six for 87) and 169 for six (R. Parikh 43, A. D. Gaekwad 42). *Saurashtra 13 pts, Baroda 12 pts.*

At Pune (T), January 27, 28, 29. Drawn. Gujarat* 183 (B. Mistry 75; Azim Khan four for 34) and 373 (P. Desai 112, S. Pathak 74, J. Saigal 49, A. Saheba 40; S. Gudge five for 101); Maharashtra 290 (R. B. Bhalekar 78, S. Kalyani 51, S. Gudge 46) and 153 for six (M. D. Gunjal 40). *Maharashtra 11 pts, Gujarat 10 pts.*

At Surat (M), February 9, 10, 11. Drawn. Gujarat 370 for seven dec. (J. Saigal 85, S. Talati 83, A. Saheba 74, P. Desai 44) and 278 for eight dec. (B. Patel 70; S. Keshwala five for 89); Baroda* 288 (R. Y. Deshmukh 91, A. D. Gaekwad 40; B. Mistry four for 44, N. Patel four for 69) and 189 for three (A. D. Gaekwad 103, R. Parikh 72). *Baroda 12 pts, Gujarat 11 pts.*

At Gandhidham (M), February 9, 10, 11. Bombay won by six wickets. Saurashtra* 302 (B. Jadeja 56, A. Patel 49, B. Quereshi 40; R. R. Kulkarni five for 96) and 239 (B. Jadeja 71); Bombay 339 for nine dec. (G. A. Parkar 90, S. M. Patil 90, B. S. Sandhu 56 not out) and 204 for four (S. Mandle 76 not out, S. S. Hattangadi 53). *Bombay 31 pts, Saurashtra 14 pts.*

Bombay 74 pts, Saurashtra 49 pts, Maharashtra 45 pts, Baroda 39 pts, Gujarat 37 pts. Bombay and Saurashtra qualified for the knockout stage.

## KNOCKOUT STAGE

## RAILWAYS v HARYANA

At Delhi (T), February 22, 23, 24, 25. Drawn. Haryana declared winners by virtue of their first-innings lead. Toss won by Haryana.

### Haryana

| | | | |
|---|---|---|---|
| Ashwani Kumar b Sharma | 8 | c Vedraj b Sharma | 9 |
| Deepak Sharma lbw b Banerjee | 12 | lbw b Vats | 10 |
| R. Dogra c Vedraj b Sharma | 23 | c Jadhav b Rathod | 83 |
| Aman Kumar c Vedraj b Banerjee | 100 | lbw b Rathod | 18 |
| *R. Chadda c Dastane b Hyder Ali | 19 | lbw b Banerjee | 71 |
| M. Arya b Banerjee | 23 | b Banerjee | 1 |
| Satyadev st Vedraj b Dastane | 72 | b Mehra | 69 |
| †Salim Ahmed c and b Rathod | 38 | lbw b Dastane | 21 |
| R. Jolly c Vedraj b Dastane | 12 | c Banerjee b Mehra | 36 |
| S. Talwar retired hurt | 12 | | |
| R. Goel not out | 0 | not out | 0 |
| L-b 8, w 2, n-b 12 | 22 | B 2, l-b 4, n-b 11 | 17 |
| 1/10 2/49 3/49 4/100 5/197 6/205 7/295 8/319 9/341 | 341 | 1/9 2/26 3/61 4/181 5/191 6/218 7/284 8/332 9/335 | (9 wkts dec.) 335 |

Bowling: *First Innings*—Banerjee 28–3–111–3; Sharma 20–0–88–2; Vats 1–0–7–0; Dastane 31–12–61–2; Hyder Ali 29–16–32–1; Rathod 18.3–9–28–1; Jadhav 1–0–6–0. *Second Innings*—Banerjee 15–0–68–2; Sharma 10–2–46–1; Vats 4–1–10–1; Dastane 15–1–82–1; Hyder Ali 23–7–40–0; Rathod 47–25–73–2; Mehra 2.1–0–10–2.

### Railways

| First innings | | Second innings | |
|---|---|---|---|
| R. Vats c sub b Jolly | 19 | | |
| P. Karkera c and b Goel | 57 | not out | 75 |
| N. Churi c Satyadev b Goel | 35 | c Salim b Arya | 27 |
| U. Dastane b Goel | 28 | not out | 26 |
| S. Mehra c Arya b Goel | 6 | c Deepak b Jolly | 19 |
| R. Jadhav run out | 22 | | |
| †P. Vedraj lbw b Deepak | 20 | | |
| *Hyder Ali run out | 0 | | |
| P. Banerjee not out | 14 | | |
| G. L. Rathod c Arya b Deepak | 3 | | |
| A. Sharma c Goel b Deepak | 0 | | |
| B 3, l-b 4, w 1, n-b 1 | 9 | B 18, l-b 2, w 1 | 21 |
| 1/55 2/104 3/117 4/134 5/162 6/190 7/190 8/197 9/211 | 213 | 1/54 2/105 | (2 wkts) 168 |

Bowling: *First Innings*—Jolly 16–2–74–1; Chadda 2–0–4–0; Goel 48–16–71–4; Deepak 25–9–43–3; Satyadev 10–2–14–0. *Second Innings*—Jolly 14–0–52–1; Goel 16–8–18–0; Deepak 9–2–28–0; Arya 10–2–38–1; Ashwani Kumar 3–1–6–0; Aman Kumar 1–0–5–0; Salim 1–0–1–0.

Umpires: S. B. Kulkarni and A. L. Narasimhan.

## UTTAR PRADESH v SAURASHTRA

At Agra (T), February 22, 23, 24, 25. Uttar Pradesh won by 55 runs. Toss won by Uttar Pradesh.

### Uttar Pradesh

| First innings | | Second innings | |
|---|---|---|---|
| †S. Chaturvedi lbw b Rajesh Jadeja | 1 | c Pujara b Rajendra Jadeja | 0 |
| S. S. Khandkar b Patel | 54 | lbw b Quereshi | 5 |
| Yusuf Ali Khan c Ghavri b Rajesh Jadeja | 13 | c Chauhan b Patel | 25 |
| R. Sapru b Patel | 32 | b Quereshi | 19 |
| K. B. Kala c Chauhan b Patel | 31 | c B. Jadeja b Patel | 30 |
| A. Bambi b Patel | 0 | c Chauhan b Patel | 15 |
| A. G. Mathur b Patel | 9 | c B. Jadeja b Parsana | 7 |
| G. Sharma c Pujara b Parsana | 1 | c B. Jadeja b Quereshi | 21 |
| R. P. Singh b Parsana | 6 | run out | 17 |
| *R. S. Hans c Badiyani b Patel | 1 | not out | 15 |
| K. Bhattacharya not out | 0 | c Pandya b Quereshi | 5 |
| L-b 3, n-b 6 | 9 | B 10, l-b 3, n-b 4 | 17 |
| 1/3 2/23 3/103 4/112 5/112 6/149 7/150 8/150 9/153 | 157 | 1/4 2/10 3/46 4/56 5/82 6/95 7/119 8/135 9/163 | 176 |

Bowling: *First Innings*—Rajesh Jadeja 6–0–44–2; Rajendra Jadeja 10–2–31–0; Parsana 14.5–8–25–2; Quereshi 10–2–22–0; Patel 17–6–32–6. *Second Innings*—Rajesh Jadeja 3–1–4–0; Rajendra Jadeja 2–1–3–1; Parsana 7–0–28–1; Quereshi 25.2–7–51–4; Patel 24–4–65–3; Ghavri 5–1–12–0.

### Saurashtra

| First innings | | Second innings | |
|---|---|---|---|
| K. Chauhan lbw b Sharma | 12 | b Sharma | 20 |
| R. Badiyani c Yusuf Ali Khan b Hans | 8 | c Yusuf Ali Khan b Hans | 20 |
| B. Jadeja lbw b Hans | 31 | c Yusuf Ali Khan b Hans | 16 |
| †B. Pujara b Hans | 12 | lbw b Sharma | 3 |
| A. Pandya c Khandkar b Sharma | 41 | c Khandkar b Hans | 1 |
| Rajendra Jadeja c Mathur b Hans | 60 | lbw b Sharma | 1 |

| | | | |
|---|---|---|---|
| A. Patel st Chaturvedi b Hans | 0 | – c Sapru b Hans | 1 |
| *K. D. Ghavri c Singh b Sharma | 6 | – b Sharma | 4 |
| N. Parsana c Mathur b Sharma | 1 | – c Kala b Sharma | 4 |
| Rajesh Jadeja not out | 0 | – not out | 14 |
| B. Quereshi b Sharma | 0 | – c Sapru b Sharma | 5 |
| L-b 5 | 5 | B 4, l-b 9 | 13 |
| 1/16 2/20 3/43 4/72 5/159 6/166 7/173 8/175 9/175 | 176 | 1/40 2/40 3/47 4/59 5/64 6/65 7/70 8/74 9/81 | 102 |

Bowling: *First Innings*—Singh 2–0–10–0; Mathur 3–0–8–0; Sharma 25.5–6–60–5; Hans 29–10–63–5; Bhattacharya 4–0–30–0. *Second Innings*—Singh 2–0–12–0; Mathur 1–0–6–0; Sharma 15.4–6–26–6; Hans 16–4–45–4.

Umpires: S. Banerjee and B. R. Keshavamurthy.

## QUARTER-FINALS

## DELHI v UTTAR PRADESH

At Ferosha Kotla Ground, Delhi (T), March 7, 8, 9, 10. Delhi won by an innings and 101 runs. Toss won by Uttar Pradesh.

### Uttar Pradesh

| | | | |
|---|---|---|---|
| S. S. Khandkar c Khanna b Valson | 4 | – c Srivastava b Valson | 22 |
| †S. Chaturvedi c Khanna b Jain | 2 | – lbw b Valson | 9 |
| Yusuf Ali Khan c and b Jain | 7 | – c Maninder b Valson | 28 |
| R. Sapru b Jain | 0 | – run out | 9 |
| K. B. Kala b Jain | 4 | – c Valson b Maninder | 52 |
| A. Bambi c and b Maninder | 36 | – c sub b Maninder | 13 |
| A. Mathur c Khanna b Valson | 4 | – c Lamba b Srivastava | 14 |
| G. Sharma c Sharma b Maninder | 25 | – c Chauhan b Maninder | 9 |
| R. P. Singh lbw b Srivastava | 11 | – not out | 3 |
| *R. S. Hans c Bhaskar Pillai b Azad | 26 | – c and b Maninder | 0 |
| M. A. Ansari not out | 1 | – c Azad b Sharma | 13 |
| B 1, l-b 2, w 1 | 4 | L-b 4, n-b 3 | 7 |
| 1/6 2/6 3/12 4/16 5/17 6/22 7/80 8/85 9/115 | 124 | 1/27 2/48 3/71 4/72 5/103 6/154 7/154 8/164 9/164 | 179 |

Bowling: *First Innings*—Valson 14–1–38–2; Jain 16–4–35–4; Maninder 18–7–30–2; Azad 9.3–4–7–1; Srivastava 3–1–11–1. *Second Innings*—Valson 12–2–37–3; Jain 4–0–32–0; Maninder 26–7–54–4; Azad 8–3–13–0; Srivastava 10–0–28–1; Lamba 4–0–11–0; Sharma 0.5–0–0–1.

### Delhi

| | |
|---|---|
| C. P. S. Chauhan c Chaturvedi b Mathur | 13 |
| †S. C. Khanna lbw b Kala | 20 |
| Gursharan Singh b Sharma | 46 |
| *K. Azad c Khandkar b Singh | 69 |
| K. Bhaskar Pillai lbw b Mathur | 26 |
| R. Lamba lbw b Singh | 84 |
| A. Sharma c Sharma b Singh | 64 |
| Maninder Singh lbw b Ansari | 11 |
| D. K. Jain b Singh | 0 |
| S. Srivastava not out | 13 |
| S. Valson lbw b Sharma | 15 |
| B 17, l-b 21, w 4, n-b 1 | 43 |
| 1/32 2/48 3/136 4/187 5/215 6/338 7/375 8/375 9/379 | 404 |

Bowling: Mathur 17–2–63–2; Kala 7–3–17–1; Sharma 36.2–7–100–2; Hans 41–9–77–0; Ansari 23–6–34–1; Singh 21–3–75–4.

Umpires: V. K. Ramaswamy and N. C. Sen.

## TAMIL NADU v BIHAR

At Chidambaram Stadium, Madras (T), March 7, 8, 9 10. Tamil Nadu won by ten wickets. Toss won by Bihar.

### Bihar

| First innings | | Second innings | |
|---|---|---|---|
| †R. Deora c Reddy b Vasudevan | 44 | c Venkataraghavan b Vasudevan | 26 |
| S. Roy c Jabbar b Venkataraghavan | 49 | not out | 23 |
| H. Gidwani b Arunkumar | 40 | c and b Vasudevan | 32 |
| B. D. Gossein run out | 21 | run out | 42 |
| D. Augustus hit wkt b Venkataraghavan | 27 | c Reddy b Vasudevan | 6 |
| Satish Singh c and b Venkataraghavan | 7 | b Venkataraghavan | 14 |
| T. J. S. Lamba c R. Madhavan b Venkataraghavan | 0 | c Jabbar b Vasudevan | 35 |
| *V. Venkatram not out | 50 | c Jabbar b Arunkumar | 27 |
| Akhilesh Sinha run out | 7 | c Reddy b Venkataraghavan | 0 |
| Randhir Singh lbw b Venkataraghavan | 7 | c sub b Venkataraghavan | 20 |
| Avinash Kumar c Vasudevan b Venkataraghavan | 39 | not out | 23 |
| L-b 4, n-b 2 | 6 | B 6, l-b 7 | 13 |
| 1/57 2/116 3/154 4/162 5/182 6/186 7/195 8/208 9/223 | 297 | 1/63 2/70 3/113 4/131 5/158 6/169 7/176 8/200 9/232 | 261 |

Bowling: *First Innings*—Sekar 13–1–40–0; Arunkumar 25–2–89–1; Venkataraghavan 52–14–90–6; Vasudevan 36–10–74–1. *Second Innings*—Sekar 5–0–15–0; Arunkumar 11–0–42–1; Venkataraghavan 32–2–93–3; Vasudevan 28–4–90–4; R. Madhavan 1–0–5–0; Jabbar 2–0–3–0.

### Tamil Nadu

| First innings | | Second innings | |
|---|---|---|---|
| V. Sivaramakrishnan c Lamba b Randhir | 15 | not out | 108 |
| C. S. Sureshkumar lbw b Venkatram | 42 | not out | 76 |
| S. Srinivasan c Roy b Venkatram | 56 | | |
| R. Madhavan c Deora b Venkatram | 33 | | |
| A. Jabbar st Deora b Venkatram | 72 | | |
| N. P. Madhavan c Augustus b Venkatram | 5 | | |
| S. Vasudevan b Venkatram | 10 | | |
| *†B. Reddy c Satish b Gidwani | 31 | | |
| S. Venkataraghavan c Gidwani b Venkatram | 9 | | |
| K. Arunkumar c Gidwani b Venkatram | 33 | | |
| T. A. P. Sekar not out | 38 | | |
| B 9, l-b 3, w 4, n-b 2 | 18 | B 8, l-b 1, w 4 | 13 |
| 1/25 2/110 3/145 4/164 5/172 6/189 7/260 8/278 9/291 | 362 | (no wkt) | 197 |

Bowling: *First Innings*—Randhir 24–6–54–1; Sinha 11–3–38–0; Gidwani 8–2–23–1; Avinash Kumar 31–2–105–0; Venkatram 38.4–6–130–8. *Second Innings*—Randhir 4–1–8–0; Sinha 2–0–10–0; Gidwani 4–0–14–0; Avinash Kumar 23–0–64–0; Venkatram 22–1–74–0; Gossein 1–0–10–0; Augustus 0.2–0–8–0.

Umpires: R. B. Gupta and R. R. Kadam.

## KARNATAKA v ORISSA

At Chinnaswamy Stadium, Bangalore (T), March 7, 8, 9, 10. Karnataka won by 243 runs. Toss won by Karnataka.

### Karnataka

| First innings | | Second innings | |
|---|---|---|---|
| M. R. Srinivasaprasad c Bharadwaj b Praharaj | 14 | c Bose b Praharaj | 11 |
| C. Saldana c and b Mahapatra | 63 | not out | 118 |
| R. Khanvilkar c Dubey b Mahapatra | 30 | not out | 125 |
| *G. R. Viswanath c Sahu b Mahapatra | 31 | | |

| | | | |
|---|---|---|---|
| B. P. Patel c Bose b Sahu | 159 | | |
| J. Abhiram b Mahapatra | 2 | | |
| †S. M. H. Kirmani c Bose b Praharaj | 61 | | |
| A. K. Raghu c Bharadwaj b Praharaj | 13 | | |
| P. Rathod lbw b Praharaj | 1 | | |
| A. Raghuram Bhat not out | 29 | | |
| Sharad Rao c sub b Mahapatra | 40 | | |
| B 9, l-b 4, w 4, n-b 13 | 30 | W 2, n-b 5 | 7 |
| | 473 | (1 wkt dec.) | 261 |
| Penalty for 4 overs short | 16 | | |
| 1/17 2/66 3/126 4/200 5/203 6/348 7/384 8/388 9/402 | 489 | 1/21 | |

Bowling: *First Innings*—Praharaj 33–2–140–4; Sahu 22–3–101–1; Mahapatra 28–1–123–5; Mitra 17–1–75–0; Bharadwaj 3–0–21–0. *Second Innings*—Praharaj 14–1–59–1; Sahu 5–0–27–0; Mahapatra 15–0–80–0; Mitra 18–0–65–0; Bharadwaj 3–0–11–0; Jayaprakash 3–0–17–0; Panda 1–1–0–0, Mahalik 1–0–2–0.

## Orissa

| | | | |
|---|---|---|---|
| K. Dubey c Kirmani b Bhat | 53 | – lbw b Rathod | 60 |
| R. Panda lbw b Khanvilkar | 21 | – c and b Saldana | 22 |
| L. K. Mahalik c and b Rathod | 30 | – absent ill | |
| A. Bharadwaj c Bhat b Rathod | 1 | – b Srinivasaprasad | 6 |
| A. Jayaprakash b Rathod | 0 | – st sub b Bhat | 63 |
| D. Mahanty c Saldana b Bhat | 51 | – lbw b Srinivasaprasad | 5 |
| H. Praharaj b Khanvilkar | 34 | – c Sharad Rao b Srinivasaprasad | 8 |
| *S. Sahu run out | 52 | – absent ill | |
| S. Mitra b Bhat | 16 | – not out | 54 |
| †P. Bose not out | 4 | – c Raghu b Rathod | 5 |
| L. K. Mahapatra b Rathod | 1 | – c Khanvilkar b Bhat | 4 |
| B 2, l-b 3, n-b 8 | 13 | B 2, l-b 2 | 4 |
| 1/40 2/105 3/111 4/111 5/111 6/167 7/240 8/268 9/275 | 276 | 1/39 2/122 3/143 4/159 5/159 6/181 7/194 8/231 | 231 |

Bowling: *First Innings*—Khanvilkar 20–2–86–2; Sharad Rao 10–2–32–0; Bhat 35–13–55–3; Abhiram 12–2–39–0; Rathod 27.1–10–44–4; Srinivasaprasad 6–2–15–0. *Second Innings*—Sharad Rao 5–2–19–0; Bhat 21–4–65–2; Abhiram 10–0–24–0; Rathod 24–7–59–2; Srinivasaprasad 13–2–46–3; Saldana 4–2–7–1; Viswanath 1–0–7–0.

Umpires: R. Mehra and R. S. Rathore.

# HARYANA v BOMBAY

At Faridabad (T), March 7, 8, 9, 10. Bombay won by eight wickets. Toss won by Haryana.

## Haryana

| | | | |
|---|---|---|---|
| Ashwani Kumar c Rajput b Kulkarni | 56 | – lbw b Kulkarni | 4 |
| Deepak Sharma c Hattangadi b Mokashi | 10 | – c Nayak b Patil | 23 |
| R. Dogra c Pandit b Nayak | 0 | – c Pandit b Thakkar | 8 |
| Aman Kumar c Hattangadi b Mokashi | 22 | – c sub b Thakkar | 0 |
| *R. Chadda lbw b Patil | 23 | – c Rajput b Thakkar | 0 |
| M. Arya c and b Rajput | 14 | – c Hattangadi b Thakkar | 3 |
| Satyadev st Pandit b Mokashi | 50 | – b Kulkarni | 17 |

†Salim Ahmed c Parkar b Mokashi .......... 18 – b Patil .......................... 33
R. Jolly c Sandhu b Mokashi .................. 7 – not out .......................... 24
S. Talwar c Patil b Mokashi .................. 5 – b Patil .......................... 0
R. Goel not out ................................ 2 – lbw b Patil .................. 6
B 7, l-b 5, n-b 4 .................... 16 B 20, l-b 5, n-b 5 ....... 30

1/32 2/33 3/97 4/123 5/123 223 1/10 2/38 3/46 4/46 5/46 148
6/173 7/195 8/211 9/216 6/46 7/95 8/123 9/123

Bowling: *First Innings*—Sandhu 5-2-11-0; Kulkarni 12-0 40-1; Nayak 17-4-33-1; Mokashi 27-8-66-6; Thakkar 11-3-23-0; Patil 17-3-33-1; Rajput 4-0-5-1. *Second Innings*—Sandhu 6-3-6-0; Kulkarni 11-1-22-2; Nayak 5-1-18-0; Mokashi 6-0-10-0; Thakkar 18-6-32-4; Patil 16-4-31-4; Rajput 2-0-4-0.

### Bombay

L. S. Rajput b Talwar .......................... 9 – c Chadda b Goel .............. 43
G. A. Parkar b Talwar .......................... 11 – c Deepak b Talwar ............ 36
S. S. Hattangadi b Goel ........................ 27 – not out .......................... 13
*S. M. Patil c Chadda b Talwar ............. 6 – not out .......................... 59
S. V. Manjrekar c Ashwani b Goel ........... 57
†C. S. Pandit b Talwar ......................... 39
S. V. Nayak c and b Talwar ................. 16
B. S. Sandhu c Dogra b Talwar ............... 4
R. R. Kulkarni c Talwar b Goel ............. 11
R. Thakkar lbw b Talwar ........................ 0
K. D. Mokashi not out ........................... 0
B 11, l-b 4 .......................... 15 B 17, l-b 8, n-b 1 ....... 26

1/20 2/27 3/39 4/86 5/152 195 1/94 2/94 (2 wkts) 177
6/174 7/184 8/184 9/193

Bowling: *First Innings*—Jolly 3-1-2-0; Goel 38.4-13-59-3; Talwar 36-2-107-7; Deepak Sharma 2-0-12-0. *Second Innings*—Jolly 8-1-23-0; Goel 23-6-44-1; Talwar 16-1-63-1; Deepak Sharma 1.3-0-3-0; Arya 7-0-17-0; Satyadev 1-0-2-0.

Umpires: S. Das and S. R. Ramachandra Rao.

## SEMI-FINALS

## BOMBAY v TAMIL NADU

At Wankhede Stadium, Bombay (T), March 23, 24, 25, 26. Drawn. Bombay declared winners by virtue of their first-innings lead. Toss won by Tamil Nadu.

### Tamil Nadu

V. Sivaramakrishnan c Hattangadi b Mokashi . .117 – b Mokashi .................. 6
C. S. Sureshkumar c Z. Parkar b Sippy .......106 – c Z. Parkar b Kulkarni ........ 2
R. Madhavan c Z. Parkar b Sandhu ........... 29 – st Z. Parkar b Rajput ......... 73
B. Arun c G. A. Parkar b Kulkarni ........... 83 – st Z. Parkar b Mankad ........ 8
S. Srinivasan c Z. Parkar b Kulkarni ......... 11 – c and b Mankad .............. 27
A. Jabbar c Z. Parkar b Mokashi ............ 0 – not out .......................... 31
N. P. Madhavan c Sippy b Kulkarni ......... 4 – c G. A. Parkar b Kulkarni .....104

| | | | |
|---|---|---|---|
| *†B. Reddy b Mokashi | 6 | – c Sippy b Mankad | 5 |
| W. V. Raman run out | 16 | – lbw b Mokashi | 7 |
| S. Venkataraghavan c Hattangadi b Rajput | 0 | | |
| T. A. P. Sekar not out | 4 | | |
| B 5, l-b 2, w 2 | 9 | B 1, l-b 5, w 5, n-b 2 | 13 |
| | 385 | (8 wkts dec.) | 276 |
| Penalty for 6 overs short | 24 | | |
| 1/182 2/247 3/274 4/206 5/311 6/316 7/333 8/368 9/373 | 409 | 1/24 2/102 3/174 4/190 5/205 6/230 7/262 8/276 | |

Bowling: *First Innings*—Sandhu 24–7–72–1; Kulkarni 24.5–6–71–3; Patil 11–1–38–0; Mokashi 34–8–91–3; Rajput 20–4–45–1; Mankad 14–0–28–0; Manjrekar 4–0–22–0; Sippy 4–0–11–1. *Second Innings*—Kulkarni 10–1–59–2; Patil 3–0–12–0; Mokashi 30–7–66–2; Rajput 6–0–14–1; Mankad 22.2–2–86–3; Manjrekar 1–1–0–0; Sippy 8–1–32–0; G. A. Parkar 1–0–1–0.

## Bombay

| | |
|---|---|
| L. S. Rajput lbw b Arun | 0 |
| G. A.Parkar c R. Madhavan b Raman | 91 |
| S. S. Hattangadi c Arun b Sekar | 61 |
| R. V. Mankad c Reddy b Arun | 0 |
| *S. M. Patil st Reddy b R. Madhavan | 165 |
| S. V. Manjrekar run out | 3 |
| A. Sippy st Reddy b R. Madhavan | 50 |
| B. S. Sandhu c Reddy b Arun | 98 |
| †Z. Parkar c sub b Arun | 12 |
| R. R. Kulkarni c sub b Raman | 15 |
| K. D. Mokashi not out | 0 |
| L-b 21, n-b 8 | 29 |
| | 524 |
| Penalty for 6 overs short | 24 |
| 1/2 2/43 3/250 4/306 5/311 6/341 7/444 8/505 9/516 | 548 |

Bowling: Sekar 31–5–119–1; Arun 27–0–123–4; Venkataraghavan 27–4–73–0; Raman 32.4–4–139–2; R. Madhavan 11–0–42–2; Sureshkumar 1–0–7–0.

# KARNATAKA v DELHI

At Chinnaswamy Stadium, Bangalore (T), March 23, 24, 25, 26. Drawn. Delhi declared winners by virtue of their first-innings lead. Toss won by Karnataka.

## Karnataka

| | | | |
|---|---|---|---|
| C. Saldana c Chauhan b Maninder | 24 | – c Azad b Maninder | 9 |
| M. R. Srinivasaprasad b Prabhakar | 19 | – c Lamba b Prabhakar | 34 |
| R. Khanvilkar c Sharma b Maninder | 45 | – b Prabhakar | 2 |
| *G. R. Viswanath c Chauhan b Azad | 6 | – not out | 136 |
| B. P. Patel c Lamba b Srivastava | 55 | – c Chauhan b Maninder | 19 |
| J. Abhiram b Maninder | 5 | – lbw b Sharma | 36 |
| A. K. Raghu c Bhaskar Pillai b Maninder | 17 | – c and b Maninder | 34 |
| †Nandan c Sharma b Maninder | 2 | – c Chauhan b Maninder | 11 |
| P. Rathod c Sharma b Maninder | 0 | – st sub b Maninder | 4 |
| A. Raghuram Bhat b Srivastava | 6 | | |
| H. Surendra not out | 0 | – not out | 0 |
| L-b 5, n-b 5 | 10 | B 6, l-b 7, n-b 9 | 22 |
| 1/37 2/56 3/65 4/159 5/159 6/166 7/178 8/178 9/189 | 189 | 1/48 2/57 3/57 4/136 5/185 6/261 7/277 8/303 (8 wkts) | 307 |

Bowling: *First Innings*—Valson 7–0–24–0; Prabhakar 10–4–11–1; Lamba 4–3–2–0; Maninder 27–8–62–6; Azad 14–0–61–1; Srivastava 8.1–2–24–2. *Second Innings*—Valson 4–0–16–0; Prabhakar 13–1–42–2; Maninder 41–9–86–5; Azad 12–2–41–0; Srivastava 7–1–30–0; Sharma 13–3–34–1; Chauhan 14–1–34–0; Bhaskar Pillai 1–0–11–0; Gursharan 1–1–0–0.

## Delhi

| | |
|---|---|
| C. P. S. Chauhan c Nandan b Surendra | 20 |
| R. Lamba c Viswanath b Abhiram | 15 |
| Gursharan Singh b Surendra | 27 |
| †S. C. Khanna c Nandan b Bhat | 37 |
| K. Bhaskar Pillai c Nandan b Abhiram | 91 |
| *K. Azad c Raghu b Bhat | 13 |
| M. Prabhakar c Saldana b Khanvilkar | 87 |
| A. Sharma c Saldana b Surendra | 50 |
| Maninder Singh not out | 28 |
| S. Srivastava c sub b Surendra | 0 |
| S. Valson st Nandan b Surendra | 2 |
| B 1, l-b 4, n-b 1 | 6 |
| 1/22 2/59 3/74 4/108 5/128 6/291 7/299 8/367 9/367 | 376 |

Bowling: Khanvilkar 13–1–54–1; Abhiram 12–3–36–2; Bhat 44–14–101–2; Rathod 18–3–48–0; Surendra 32.2–4–126–5; Srinivasaprasad 1–0–6–0.

Umpires: M. Y. Gupte and N. N. Patwardhan.

## FINAL

## BOMBAY v DELHI

At Wankhede Stadium, Bombay (T), April 1, 2, 3, 5, 6. Bombay won by 90 runs. Toss won by Bombay.

### Bombay

| | First innings | | Second innings | |
|---|---|---|---|---|
| L. S. Rajput c Chauhan b Prabhakar | 0 | – | st Khanna b Maninder | 63 |
| G. A. Parkar c Khanna b Madan Lal | 23 | – | b Madan Lal | 14 |
| S. S. Hattangadi c Khanna b Valson | 7 | – | c Sharma b Madan Lal | 5 |
| S. M. Patil c Bhaskar Pillai b Maninder | 54 | – | c Azad b Maninder | 57 |
| *S. M. Gavaskar b Madan Lal | 106 | – | b Maninder | 64 |
| R. J. Shastri b Maninder | 29 | – | c Prabhakar b Maninder | 76 |
| †C. S. Pandit lbw b Prabhakar | 49 | – | c Maninder b Azad | 44 |
| A. Sippy c Sharma b Madan Lal | 16 | | | |
| K. D. Mokashi b Maninder | 14 | | | |
| R. R. Kulkarni c Srivastava b Madan Lal | 15 | – | not out | 17 |
| R. V. Kulkarni not out | 2 | | | |
| L-b 2, w 1, n-b 7 | 10 | | B 7, l-b 6, w 1, n-b 2 | 16 |
| | 325 | | (7 wkts dec.) | 356 |
| Penalty for 2 overs short | 8 | | Penalty for 2 overs short | 8 |
| 1/1 2/27 3/42 4/142 5/194 6/274 7/276 8/300 9/318 | 333 | | 1/13 2/31 3/129 4/160 5/275 6/306 7/356 (7 wkts dec.) | 364 |

Bowling: *First Innings*—Madan Lal 25–8–42–4; Prabhakar 17–3–69–2; Valson 12–0–50–1; Maninder 29.5–7–75–3; Srivastava 9–0–37–0; Azad 6–0–35–0; Sharma 4–1–15–0. *Second Innings*—Madan Lal 19–3–57–2; Prabhakar 10–3–39–0; Valson 2–0–33–0; Maninder 34–6–132–4; Srivastava 8–1–28–0; Azad 18.3–1–54–1.

### Delhi

| | First innings | | Second innings | |
|---|---|---|---|---|
| C. P. S. Chauhan c Hattangadi b Shastri | 98 | – | c Pandit b Shastri | 54 |
| †S. C. Khanna lbw b R. R. Kulkarni | 13 | – | st Pandit b Shastri | 27 |
| Gursharan Singh b R. R. Kulkarni | 10 | – | lbw b Mokashi | 2 |
| K. Azad c Pandit b R. R. Kulkarni | 9 | – | b Shastri | 0 |
| K. Bhaskar Pillai c Pandit b R. R. Kulkarni | 0 | – | c sub b Shastri | 60 |
| M. Prabhakar c R. R. Kulkarni b Shastri | 21 | – | c Rajput b Shastri | 44 |

| | | | |
|---|---|---|---|
| *Madan Lal c Pandit b Shastri | 78 | – run out | 6 |
| A. Sharma c Hattangadi b Mokashi | 131 | – b Shastri | 10 |
| Maninder Singh lbw b R. R. Kulkarni | 3 | – lbw b Shastri | 0 |
| S. Srivastava c Hattangadi b Shastri | 7 | – b Shastri | 3 |
| S. Valson not out | 21 | – not out | 0 |
| L-b 7 | 7 | B 1, l-b 2 | 3 |
| 1/27 2/41 3/52 4/65 5/87 6/191 7/268 8/311 9/330 | 398 | 1/95 2/100 3/100 4/122 5/171 6/187 7/198 8/198 9/206 | 209 |

Bowling: *First Innings*—R. R. Kulkarni 32–4–106–5; R. V. Kulkarni 21–4–55–0; Shastri 48–8–91–4; Sippy 3–0–20–0; Mokashi 16–3–63–1; Rajput 15–2–40–0; Patil 2–0–9–0; Gavaskar 1–0–7–0. *Second Innings*—R. R. Kulkarni 7–0–28–0; R. V. Kulkarni 4–0–15–0; Shastri 39.5–17–91–8; Mokashi 32–10–63–1; Rajput 3–0–9–0.

Umpires: B. Ganguli and V. K. Ramaswamy.

## IRANI TROPHY, 1984-85

## RANJI TROPHY CHAMPIONS (BOMBAY) v REST OF INDIA

At Ferosha Kotla Ground, Delhi (T), September 7, 8, 9, 11. Rest of India won by four wickets. Toss won by Rest of India.

### Bombay

| | | | |
|---|---|---|---|
| G. A. Parkar c Kapil Dev b Maninder | 33 | – b Maninder | 55 |
| L. S. Rajput c Khanna b Chetan | 5 | – b Chetan | 1 |
| D. B. Vengsarkar c Kapil Dev b Maninder | 23 | – lbw b Kapil Dev | 1 |
| S. M. Patil c Kapil Dev b Azad | 32 | – c and b Kapil Dev | 2 |
| *S. M. Gavaskar c Azharuddin b Prabhakar | 13 | – b Maninder | 14 |
| R. J. Shastri lbw b Kapil Dev | 58 | – c and b Maninder | 15 |
| †C. S. Pandit c and b Binny | 37 | – b Kapil Dev | 12 |
| R. Baindoor c Gaekwad b Kapil Dev | 0 | – c Azharuddin b Maninder | 6 |
| S. V. Nayak b Chetan | 0 | – not out | 24 |
| B. S. Sandhu not out | 4 | – run out | 6 |
| R. R. Kulkarni lbw b Chetan | 0 | – b Chetan | 7 |
| B 19, l-b 8, n-b 4 | 31 | B 8, l-b 4, w 1, n-b 7 | 20 |
| 1/6 2/53 3/80 4/106 5/157 6/225 7/225 8/229 9/236 | 236 | 1/10 2/12 3/24 4/70 5/98 6/99 7/120 8/129 9/141 | 163 |

Bowling: *First Innings*—Chetan 17.4–4–48–3; Kapil Dev 17–5–26–2; Binny 7–3–23–1; Prabhakar 16–3–41–1; Maninder 28–10–54–2; Azad 10–3–17–1. *Second Innings*—Chetan 12.4–1–47–2; Kapil Dev 11–3–17–3; Prabhakar 5–2–7–0; Binny 7–3–26–0; Maninder 22–9–34–4; Azad 6–2–20–0.

### Rest of India

| | | | |
|---|---|---|---|
| A. D. Gaekwad c sub b Sandhu | 14 | | |
| †S. C. Khanna c Parkar b Sandhu | 34 | – c Pandit b Sandhu | 23 |
| M. Azharuddin b Sandhu | 0 | – not out | 51 |
| A. Malhotra c Pandit b Shastri | 34 | – c and b Shastri | 16 |
| Yashpal Sharma c Pandit b Nayak | 25 | – st Pandit b Shastri | 1 |
| K. Azad b Baindoor | 30 | – lbw b Sandhu | 1 |
| R. M. H. Binny c Pandit b Rajput | 30 | – lbw b Sandhu | 0 |

| | | | |
|---|---|---|---|
| *Kapil Dev c Parkar b Nayak | 48 | – not out | 2 |
| M. Prabhakar lbw b Kulkarni | 18 | – c Rajput b Sandhu | 4 |
| Chetan Sharma not out | 24 | | |
| Maninder Singh c Pandit b Kulkarni | 7 | | |
| B 8, l-b 8, w 1, n-b 8 | 25 | L-b 5, n-b 4 | 9 |
| | 289 | | (6 wkts) 107 |
| Penalty for 1 over short | 4 | | |
| 1/45 2/45 3/67 4/115 5/123 6/167 7/197 8/240 9/274 | 293 | 1/28 2/33 3/93 4/99 5/104 6/104 | |

Bowling: *First Innings*—Kulkarni 19.2–2–97–2; Sandhu 18–1–75–3; Nayak 20–8–23–2; Shastri 18–5–41–1; Baindoor 11–0–34–1; Rajput 2–0–3–1. *Second Innings*—Kulkarni 5–0–32–0; Sandhu 13–3–41–4; Nayak 4–0–15–0; Shastri 8.5–3–14–2.

Umpires: P. G. Pandit and V. K. Ramaswamy.

## DULEEP TROPHY, 1984-85

### EAST ZONE v CENTRAL ZONE

At Brabourne Stadium, Bombay (T), October 20, 21, 22, 23. Central Zone won by nine wickets. Toss won by East Zone.

#### East Zone

| | | | |
|---|---|---|---|
| K. Dubey c Chaturvedi b Sunderam | 0 | – b R. P. Singh | 5 |
| Subroto Das b R. P. Singh | 3 | – c Chaturvedi b Sunderam | 17 |
| Arun Lal b Vivek Bhan Singh | 11 | – b Sharma | 44 |
| A. Mitra b Mudkavi | 115 | – c and b Sunderam | 8 |
| A. Jayaprakash b Hans | 33 | – lbw b Vivek Bhan Singh | 0 |
| R. C. Shukla lbw b Hans | 1 | – b Hans | 33 |
| A. Bhattacharjee c R. P. Singh b Hans | 13 | – not out | 24 |
| †S. Banerjee not out | 38 | – b Hans | 1 |
| S. Sahu c R. P. Singh b Sunderam | 4 | – c Sunderam b Hans | 17 |
| Randhir Singh c R. P. Singh b Hans | 21 | – c and b Mudkavi | 0 |
| *D. R. Doshi lbw b Hans | 1 | – absent injured | |
| B 5, l-b 11 | 16 | B 3 | 3 |
| 1/0 2/8 3/32 4/126 5/132 6/177 7/185 8/206 9/254 | 256 | 1/15 2/31 3/49 4/62 5/95 6/100 7/111 8/149 9/152 | 152 |

Bowling: *First Innings*—Sunderam 22–2–72–2; R. P. Singh 21–5–53–1; Vivek Bhan Singh 8–1–25–1; Hans 27.5–6–28–5; Sharma 19–4–33–0; Mudkavi 13–3–29–1. *Second Innings*—Sunderam 10–2–33–2; R. P. Singh 7–0–37–1; Vivek Bhan Singh 5–0–20–1; Hans 17–2–27–3; Sharma 12–2–27–1; Mudkavi 3–0–5–1.

#### Central Zone

| | | | |
|---|---|---|---|
| S. S. Khandkar b Randhir | 1 | – c Banerjee b Bhattacharjee | 10 |
| P. Shastri c Arun Lal b Bhattacharjee | 44 | – not out | 27 |
| †S. Chaturvedi c Arun Lal b Sahu | 6 | – not out | 15 |
| *Sanjeeva Rao lbw b Randhir | 2 | | |
| S. Mudkavi c Sahu b Bhattacharjee | 184 | | |
| S. Phadkar b Shukla | 8 | | |
| Vivek Bhan Singh run out | 7 | | |

| | | | |
|---|---|---|---|
| G. Sharma c Banerjee b Sahu | 24 | | |
| R. P. Singh c Mitra b Shukla | 20 | | |
| R. S. Hans c and b Shukla | 37 | | |
| P. Sunderam not out | 1 | | |
| B 3, l-b 7, w 2, n-b 6 | 18 | B 4, n-b 1 | 5 |
| 1/3 2/12 3/17 4/99 5/112 6/158 7/217 8/265 9/349 | 352 | 1/28 | (1 wkt) 57 |

Bowling: *First Innings*—Randhir 29–2–101–2; Sahu 16–6–36–2; Doshi 3.5–1–6–0; Shukla 44.1–7–95–3; Bhattacharjee 35.1–6–85–2; Jayaprakash 2–0–12–0; Arun Lal 3–0–7–0. *Second Innings*—Randhir 3–1–3–0; Sahu 2–0–6–0; Shukla 5–1–15–0; Bhattacharjee 6–0–26–1; Jayaprakash 1–0–3–0.

Umpires: B. Nagaraj Rao and A. K. Nayudu.

## SOUTH ZONE v WEST ZONE

At Wankhede Stadium, Bombay (T), October 27, 28, 29, 30. Drawn. South Zone declared winners by virtue of their first-innings lead. Toss won by West Zone.

### West Zone

| | | | |
|---|---|---|---|
| L. S. Rajput b Sekar | 0 | b Sivaramakrishnan | 51 |
| R. Poonawalla b Khanvilkar | 0 | c and b Sivaramakrishnan | 56 |
| C. S. Pandit c Jabbar b Ayub | 31 | c Khanvilkar b Ayub | 126 |
| *R. B. Bhalekar c Jabbar b Ayub | 75 | b Sivaramakrishnan | 28 |
| M. D. Gunjal lbw b Ayub | 0 | not out | 117 |
| †K. S. More c Jabbar b Sivaramakrishnan | 1 | c Khanvilkar b Ayub | 34 |
| S. Keshwala c Khanvilkar b Sivaramakrishnan | 49 | not out | 50 |
| N. Y. Satham b Bhat | 11 | | |
| A. Patel b Bhat | 3 | | |
| R. R. Kulkarni run out | 40 | | |
| R. C. Thakkar not out | 2 | c Srikkanth b Bhat | 14 |
| B 2, l-b 9, n-b 5 | 16 | B 4, l-b 6, w 1, n-b 4 | 15 |
| 1/0 2/0 3/62 4/62 5/77 6/145 7/166 8/182 9/196 | 228 | 1/111 2/124 3/201 4/269 5/307 6/373 | (6 wkts) 491 |

Bowling: *First Innings*—Sekar 12.2–2–36–1; Khanvilkar 6–0–30–1; Bhat 21–7–42–2; Ayub 24–7–48–3; Sivaramakrishnan 19–1–61–2. *Second Innings*—Sekar 6–2–18–0; Khanvilkar 3–0–14–0; Srikkanth 7–1–30–0; Ayub 46–7–179–2; Bhat 26–2–90–1; Sivaramakrishnan 24–2–98–3; Madhavan 2–0–9–0; Jabbar 14–4–43–0.

### South Zone

| | |
|---|---|
| †S. Viswanath b Patel | 74 |
| *K. Srikkanth st More b Patel | 101 |
| R. Madhavan c Thakkar b Kulkarni | 95 |
| R. Khanvilkar c More b Thakkar | 156 |
| A. Jabbar c and b Patel | 32 |
| K. A. Qayyum not out | 61 |
| L. Sivaramakrishnan c More b Thakkar | 10 |
| Arshad Ayub c More b Patel | 19 |
| T. A. P. Sekar st More b Thakkar | 5 |
| A. Raghuram Bhat c Pandit b Thakkar | 3 |
| M. Azharuddin absent injured | |
| B 12, l-b 4, w 2, n-b 7 | 25 |
| | 581 |
| Penalty for 3 overs short | 12 |
| 1/156 2/191 3/383 4/445 5/517 6/533 7/560 8/569 9/581 | 593 |

Bowling: Kulkarni 27–2–97–1; Keshwala 15–3–40–0; Patel 47–5–163–4; Thakkar 38.1–1–158–4; Satham 7–0–42–0; Bhalekar 3–0–14–0; Rajput 13–1–37–0; Gunjal 3–0–14–0.

Umpires: R. B. Gupta and R. S. Rathore.

## NORTH ZONE v CENTRAL ZONE

At Pune (T), October 27, 28, 29. North Zone won by ten wickets. Toss won by Central Zone.

### Central Zone

| | | | |
|---|---|---|---|
| S. S. Khandkar c Chauhan b Prabhakar | 20 | – b Valson | 80 |
| P. Shastri b Prabhakar | 20 | – c Navjot b Prabhakar | 60 |
| †S. Chaturvedi c Gursharan b Ghai | 2 | – not out | 66 |
| *Sanjeeva Rao c Malhotra b Prabhakar | 1 | – lbw b Azad | 10 |
| S. Mudkavi c Gursharan b Ghai | 12 | – b Valson | 3 |
| N. Churi c Arun b Prabhakar | 6 | – b Valson | 0 |
| Yusuf Ali Khan b Prabhakar | 0 | – c Gursharan b Valson | 0 |
| G. Sharma c Yashpal b Ghai | 2 | – b Chauhan | 46 |
| R. P. Singh c Valson b Ghai | 7 | – run out | 12 |
| R. S. Hans c Arun b Ghai | 4 | – b Prabhakar | 4 |
| P. Sunderam not out | 4 | – c Azad b Prabhakar | 1 |
| B 4, l-b 3, n-b 3 | 10 | B 1, l-b 4, n-b 15 | 20 |
| | 88 | | 302 |
| Penalty for 3 overs short | 12 | Penalty for 6 overs short | 24 |
| 1/38 2/43 3/44 4/51 5/69 6/69 7/69 8/75 9/83 | 100 | 1/137 2/159 3/159 4/163 5/165 6/194 7/266 8/295 9/300 | 326 |

Bowling: *First Innings*—Valson 5–1–19–0; Prabhakar 19–7–28–5; Ghai 13.4–4–33–5; Jha 1–0–1–0. *Second Innings*—Valson 23–0–84–4; Prabhakar 14.5–2–56–3; Ghai 16–2–67–0; Jha 4–0–21–0; Azad 17–5–44–1; Chauhan 6–0–19–1; Yashpal 2–0–6–0.

### North Zone

| | | | |
|---|---|---|---|
| C. P. S. Chauhan lbw b Sunderam | 98 | – not out | 19 |
| Navjot Singh c Mudkavi b Singh | 35 | | |
| A. Jha lbw b Singh | 0 | | |
| Gursharan Singh c and b Mudkavi | 63 | | |
| A. Malhotra st Chaturvedi b Mudkavi | 18 | | |
| Yashpal Sharma c Yusuf Ali Khan b Sharma | 100 | | |
| *K. Azad c sub b Singh | 13 | | |
| M. Prabhakar b Sharma | 54 | | |
| †Arun Sharma c Singh b Sharma | 0 | – not out | 1 |
| R. S. Ghai c Singh b Sunderam | 18 | | |
| S. Valson not out | 1 | | |
| B 1, l-b 6 | 7 | | |
| 1/95 2/95 3/160 4/213 5/216 6/252 7/340 8/345 9/401 | 407 | (no wkt) | 20 |

Bowling: *First Innings*—Sunderam 33.3–9–83–2; Singh 24–3–96–3; Hans 40–15–91–0; Sharma 36–8–83–3; Mudkavi 14–2–41–2; Shastri 1–0–6–0. *Second Innings*—Sunderam 2–0–7–0; Singh 1–0–8–0; Khandkar 0.5–0–5–0.

Umpires: R. R. Kadam and R. Mrutyunjayan.

## FINAL

## SOUTH ZONE v NORTH ZONE

At Ferosha Kotla Ground, Delhi (T), February 9, 10, 11, 12. South Zone won by 73 runs. Toss won by North Zone.

### South Zone

| | | | |
|---|---|---|---|
| V. Sivaramakrishnan c Khanna b Ghai | 26 | – c sub b Jha | 19 |
| M. R. Srinivasaprasad c Khanna b Valson | 0 | – c sub b Maninder | 0 |
| R. Madhavan c Khanna b Valson | 0 | – c Yashpal b Maninder | 14 |
| R. Khanvilkar c Khanna b Jha | 9 | – c Yashpal b Maninder | 4 |

| | | | |
|---|---|---|---|
| A. Jabbar c Yashpal b Ghai | 17 | c Azad b Ghai | 68 |
| *†S. M. H. Kirmani c Navjot b Maninder | 82 | c Azad b Jha | 50 |
| K. A. Qayyum lbw b Ghai | 0 | c and b Maninder | 19 |
| Arshad Ayub c Ghai b Jha | 20 | c Azad b Jha | 30 |
| N. S. Yadav c and b Maninder | 15 | lbw b Jha | 15 |
| A. Raghuram Bhat b Maninder | 5 | not out | 0 |
| B. Arun not out | 1 | b Jha | 1 |
| B 4, l-b 6, n-b 7 | 17 | B 2, l-b 6, w 5, n-b 3 | 16 |
| | 192 | | 236 |
| Penalty for 5 overs short | 20 | | |
| 1/1 2/12 3/38 4/44 5/79 6/79 7/128 8/173 9/184 | 212 | 1/5 2/22 3/54 4/96 5/102 6/102 7/154 8/205 9/233 | |

Bowling: *First Innings*—Ghai 20–4–72–3; Valson 10–1–47–2; Jha 12–2–41–2; Maninder 6.5–1–22–3; Azad 1–1–0–0. *Second Innings*—Maninder 28–7–95–4; Ghai 16–2–35–1; Jha 25.1–1–76–5; Valson 5–1–13–0; Azad 1–0–9–0.

## North Zone

| | | | |
|---|---|---|---|
| C. P. S. Chauhan c Jabbar b Khanvilkar | 17 | b Arun | 23 |
| Navjot Singh lbw b Khanvilkar | 1 | absent injured | |
| Gursharan Singh lbw b Khanvilkar | 68 | b Bhat | 15 |
| K. Bhaskar Pillai c Madhavan b Khanvilkar | 11 | c Madhavan b Yadav | 47 |
| Yashpal Sharma c Bhat b Arun | 32 | lbw b Arun | 0 |
| †S. C. Khanna c Madhavan b Bhat | 12 | lbw b Arun | 20 |
| *K. Azad lbw b Arun | 9 | b Bhat | 4 |
| R. S. Ghai c sub b Bhat | 1 | b Khanvilkar | 54 |
| A. Jha not out | 1 | lbw b Arun | 23 |
| Maninder Singh lbw b Bhat | 3 | not out | 2 |
| S. Valson b Bhat | 0 | lbw b Arun | 0 |
| L-b 4, n-b 1 | 5 | B 12, l-b 6, n-b 1 | 19 |
| | 160 | | 207 |
| Penalty for 1 over short | 4 | Penalty for 1 over short | 4 |
| 1/16 2/39 3/71 4/124 5/137 6/154 7/155 8/155 9/160 | 164 | 1/36 2/72 3/72 4/76 5/76 6/161 7/187 8/207 9/207 | 211 |

Bowling: *First Innings*—Khanvilkar 26–5–73–4; Arun 10–0–41–2; Bhat 23–8–42–4; Yadav 1–1–0–0. *Second Innings*—Khanvilkar 11–1–40–1; Arun 19.5–2–84–5; Bhat 19–5–51–2; Yadav 3–1–14–1.

Umpires: R. R. Kadam and R. S. Rathore.

---

## A FINE TRIBUTE

"I can't think of any group with whom my husband would rather have spent his last hours." Mrs Percy Norris, widow of the British Deputy High Commissioner, speaking after the assassination in Bombay of her husband a few hours after he had hosted a reception to the England cricket team in November 1984.

# CRICKET IN PAKISTAN, 1984-85

By QAMAR AHMED

The season was graced by visits from India and New Zealand. News of the assassination of India's Prime Minister, Mrs Indira Gandhi, resulted in the Indian tour being called off before the third and final Test in Karachi and the last of the one-day internationals in Peshawar. In the absence of such experienced players as Geoff Howarth and Richard Hadlee, New Zealand lost the first two of their three Test matches and were also beaten in the one-day series.

Three first-class competitions were played – the Patron's Trophy, the Quaid-e-Azam Trophy and the PACO Cup. The Patron's Trophy was won again by a Karachi team. Seventeen zonal teams, divided into four groups, contested it. In Group A, Karachi Whites, the eventual winners, had a smooth sailing, winning all their matches. In Group B, four of the six games ended without result. Karachi Blues led this group on points, with Bahawalpur not far behind. Lahore City Whites and Multan were no match for the other two teams. In Group C, in which five teams fought for the honours, Sargodha topped the list with 59 points from four matches, Lahore City Blues closely following. In Group D, Rawalpindi humbled Peshawar, Hazara and Dera Ismail Khan. Karachi Whites, Karachi Blues, Sargodha and Rawalpindi were the semi-finalists. The final proved to be a one-sided affair, Karachi Whites defeating Rawalpindi by ten wickets within two days.

Immediately afterwards, the premier tournament, the Quaid-e-Azam, was played and won by United Bank, who by virtue of their first-innings lead against Railways regained the Trophy which they had lost to National Bank the previous year. The championship was played then between ten teams. In 1984-85 there were twelve, divided into two groups. Karachi and Lahore were the new entries to what is basically a tournament of departmental and commercial organisations.

In Group A, HBFC and Allied Bank finished with the same number of points, but HBFC topped the group because of their faster run-rate. The tournament was not without controversy. The umpires reported that the match between HBFC and Allied Bank was "fixed", so as to enable Allied Bank to reach the semi-finals. The resulting enquiry confirmed the allegation. No fewer than 1,180 runs were scored in the match in 886 minutes, and both teams, by gaining maximum bonus points, were able to qualify for the semi-finals. They were then barred, however, from playing first-class cricket until the end of the 1985-86 season. Following this ban, Habib Bank and PACO replaced them in the PACO Cup; but the ban was lifted by the BCCP before the 1984-85 season had ended.

In Group B, only one of the fifteen matches ended in a draw. Railways won all their five matches and finished ahead of United Bank, Habib Bank, Lahore, MCB and a new entry, Water and Power Development Authority (WAPDA). United Bank beat HBFC by 244 runs in the first semi-final. Railways reached the final by virtue of a first-innings lead against Allied Bank. The Test batsman, Rizwan-uz-Zaman, was the most prolific scorer of the contest, making 556 runs at an average of 69.62 which included three centuries. Mohammad Nazir bagged 42 wickets at 14.40 apiece.

The PACO Cup Pentangular Championship, which had not been played in 1983-84, was also won by United Bank, who achieved just one less than maximum points. Habib Bank finished second, followed by Karachi, Railways and PACO. Ali Zia of United Bank topped the batting averages in the tournament by scoring 434 runs in four matches, averaging 62.00. Tauseef Ahmed, the Test off-spinner, took 41 wickets at 12.53 each. The leading batsmen of the first-class domestic season were Rizwan-uz-Zaman of PIA and Arshad Pervez of Habib Bank. They both crossed the 1,000 runs mark, Rizwan-uz-Zaman making 1,101 in nine matches at an average of 78.64, including five centuries. Arshad Pervez scored 1,253 runs in fourteen matches and also hit five centuries. The leading bowler was Tauseef Ahmed of United Bank, whose off-breaks brought him 83 wickets at 15.85 each. The leading wicket-keeper was Zulqarnain of Railways, who had 49 victims to his credit and Arshad Pervez of Sargodha and Habib Bank was the leading fielder with 24 catches. The Wills one-day tournament was not played.

## FIRST-CLASS AVERAGES, 1984-85

### BATTING

(Qualification: 600 runs, average 35)

| | *M* | *I* | *NO* | *R* | *HI* | *100s* | *Avge* |
|---|---|---|---|---|---|---|---|
| Rizwan-uz-Zaman (*Karachi/PIA*) | 9 | 17 | 3 | 1,101 | 166 | 5 | 78.64 |
| Arshad Pervez (*Sargodha/Habib Bank*) | 14 | 27 | 5 | 1,253 | 152* | 5 | 56.95 |
| Shahid Anwar (*Lahore City/Lahore*) | 8 | 15 | 1 | 746 | 153* | 4 | 53.28 |
| Mohammad Aslam (*Karachi*) | 9 | 15 | 2 | 637 | 164 | 2 | 49.00 |
| Shaukat Mirza (*PACO*) | 12 | 22 | 3 | 894 | 132 | 2 | 47.05 |
| Ijaz Ahmed (*Gujranwala/PACO*) | 12 | 23 | 2 | 983 | 201* | 2 | 46.80 |
| Ijaz Ahmed (*Multan/HBFC*) | 9 | 17 | 1 | 710 | 117 | 2 | 44.37 |
| Naved Anjum (*United Bank*) | 10 | 17 | 3 | 617 | 159 | 1 | 44.07 |
| Shafiq Ahmed (*United Bank*) | 11 | 21 | 4 | 742 | 118 | 2 | 43.64 |
| Saadat Ali (*United Bank*) | 11 | 20 | 1 | 817 | 169 | 3 | 43.00 |
| Nasir Shah (*Karachi*) | 9 | 17 | 2 | 639 | 120 | 1 | 42.60 |
| Asif Mujtaba (*Karachi*) | 13 | 22 | 2 | 842 | 94 | 0 | 42.10 |
| Moin-ul-Atiq (*Karachi*) | 13 | 24 | 2 | 919 | 140 | 3 | 41.77 |
| Ali Zia (*United Bank*) | 11 | 20 | 2 | 750 | 176 | 3 | 41.66 |
| Mansoor Akhtar (*United Bank*) | 11 | 21 | 0 | 857 | 180 | 2 | 40.80 |
| Tahir Shah (*Railways*) | 11 | 18 | 1 | 666 | 88 | 0 | 39.17 |
| Parvez Mir (*Lahore City/Lahore*) | 9 | 17 | 1 | 619 | 74 | 0 | 38.68 |
| Zafar Ali (*Karachi*) | 11 | 19 | 3 | 617 | 139* | 2 | 38.56 |
| Mohammad Ashraf (*Faisalabad/WAPDA*) | 9 | 18 | 1 | 647 | 140 | 3 | 38.05 |
| Saeed Azad (*Karachi*) | 12 | 19 | 0 | 678 | 120 | 1 | 35.68 |
| Ameer Akbar (*Railways*) | 11 | 19 | 2 | 602 | 107 | 2 | 35.41 |

**Signifies not out.*

### BOWLING

(Qualification: 30 wickets)

| | *O* | *M* | *R* | *W* | *BB* | *Avge* |
|---|---|---|---|---|---|---|
| Iqbal Qasim (*Karachi*) | 304.3 | 108 | 606 | 48 | 5-6 | 12.62 |
| Ijaz Faqih (*Karachi/MCB*) | 227.2 | 63 | 525 | 38 | 6-35 | 13.81 |
| Mohammad Nazir (*Railways*) | 546.2 | 169 | 947 | 66 | 7-62 | 14.34 |
| Aziz-ur-Rehman (*Sargodha*) | 203.3 | 42 | 522 | 34 | 7-45 | 15.35 |
| Tauseef Ahmed (*United Bank*) | 546.2 | 125 | 1,316 | 83 | 8-52 | 15.85 |
| Abdul Qadir (*Lahore City/Habib Bank*) | 471.5 | 106 | 1,349 | 72 | 9-59 | 18.73 |
| Nadeem Ghauri (*Railways*) | 385.3 | 83 | 956 | 50 | 8-68 | 19.12 |

| | *O* | *M* | *R* | *W* | *BB* | *Avge* |
|---|---|---|---|---|---|---|
| Farrukh Zaman (*Peshawar/MCB*) | 255.3 | 63 | 731 | 34 | 6-42 | 21.50 |
| Kazim Mehdi (*HBFC*) | 270.3 | 64 | 747 | 34 | 6-79 | 21.97 |
| Abdul Raqeeb (*Habib Bank*) | 339.4 | 75 | 913 | 41 | 5-61 | 22.26 |
| Jalal-ud-Din (*Allied Bank*) | 245.2 | 48 | 766 | 33 | 6-66 | 23.21 |
| Masood Anwar (*Multan/PACO*) | 413.4 | 86 | 1,141 | 47 | 6-94 | 24.27 |
| Tanvir Ali (*Karachi*) | 618.4 | 131 | 1,771 | 72 | 8-83 | 24.59 |
| Shahid Mahboob (*PACO*) | 321.4 | 50 | 1,028 | 39 | 5-68 | 26.35 |
| Saleem Jaffer (*Karachi*) | 387 | 59 | 1,251 | 35 | 3-41 | 35.74 |

## WICKET-KEEPING

Zulqarnain (*Railways*) 49 (40 ct, 9 st); Ashraf Ali (*United Bank*) 35 (30 ct, 5 st); Pervez-ul-Hasan (*Karachi*) 26 (22 ct, 4 st); Mohammad Ashraf (*Faisalabad/WAPDA*) 24 (20 ct, 4 st); Salim Yousuf (*Allied Bank*) 22 (17 ct, 5 st); Anil Dalpat (*Pakistan*) 16 (15 ct, 1 st); Masood Iqbal (*Lahore City/Habib Bank*) 16 (12 ct, 4 st); Nasir Jasra (*Sargodha*) 16 (14 ct, 2 st); Suleman Khwaja (*Lahore*) 16 (10 ct, 6 st); Wasim Arif (*HBFC*) 12 (6 ct, 6 st); Javed Qayyum (*Lahore*) 11 (5 ct, 6 st); Sanaullah (*PACO*) 11 (9 ct, 2 st); Zaheer Ahmed (*Habib Bank*) 11 (9 ct, 2 st); Maqsood Kundi (*Peshawar*) 10 (5 ct, 5 st); Nadeem Ahsan (*Gujranwala*) 10 (8 ct, 2 st); Sajid Abbasi (*Muslim Commercial Bank*) 10 (all ct); Taslim Arif (*National Bank*) 10 (all ct).

*Note: Matches taken into account are the Patron's Trophy, the Quaid-e-Azam Trophy, PACO Cup, two Test trial matches and those matches against the Indian and New Zealand touring teams in Pakistan.*

## BCCP PATRON'S TROPHY, 1984-85

*Note:* First innings closed at 75 overs.

### Group A

At Race Course Ground, Quetta, October 1, 2, 3. Sukkur conceded a walkover to Quetta. *Quetta 14 pts.*

At Bakhtiari Youth Centre "A" Ground, Karachi, October 8, 9. Karachi Whites won by an innings and 214 runs. Karachi Whites 328 for two (Mohammad Aslam 142 not out, Ijaz Faqih 125 not out); Sukkur 61 (Iqbal Qasim five for 6) and 53 (Ijaz Faqih five for 29). *Karachi Whites 18 pts, Sukkur 1 pt.*

At Niaz Stadium, Hyderabad, October 12, 13, 14. Drawn. Sukkur 213 (Aftab Soomro 54; Ghulam Hussain five for 56) and 302 for eight (Niamatullah 85, Arshad Ali 69; Ghulam Hussain seven for 128); Hyderabad 267 for five (Mir Hyder 96, Zulfiqar Ali 69, Taj Mohammad 40). *Hyderabad 10 pts, Sukkur 5 pts.*

At Bakhtiari Youth Centre "A" Ground, Karachi, October 16, 17, 18. Hyderabad were awarded a walk-over against Quetta, who failed to turn up for the match. *Hyderabad 14 pts.*

At Bakhtiari Youth Centre "A" Ground, Karachi, October 20, 21. Karachi Whites won by an innings and 228 runs. Karachi Whites 369 for six (Ijaz Faqih 124 not out, Sajad Ali 101, Saeed Azad 57); Quetta 66 and 75 (Iqbal Qasim five for 26, Ijaz Faqih four for 26). *Karachi Whites 18 pts, Quetta 3 pts.*

At Bakhtiari Youth Centre "A" Ground, Karachi, October 29, 30, 31. Karachi Whites, who did not enforce the follow-on, won by 370 runs. Karachi Whites 351 for five (Mohammad Aslam 164, Moin-ul-Atiq 112) and 243 for three dec. (Haaris A. Khan 139 not out, Tehsin Ahmed 46, Azeem Ahmed 45); Hyderabad 117 (Anwar Iqbal 47; Haaris A. Khan four for 14) and 107 (Taj Mohammad 47; Iqbal Qasim five for 25). *Karachi Whites 18 pts, Hyderabad 3 pts.*

Karachi Whites 54 pts, Hyderabad 27 pts, Quetta 17 pts, Sukkur 6 pts. Karachi Whites qualified for the semi-finals.

### Group B

At Bahawal Stadium, Bahawalpur, October 8, 9, 10. Bahawalpur won by eight wickets. Bahawalpur 287 for six (Farooq Shera 93, Qasim Shera 72, Azhar Abbas 67) and 93 for two;

Lahore City Whites 91 (Mohammad Altaf five for 26, Qasim Shera four for 26) and 285 (Shahid Anwar 109, Maqsood Raza 58; Mohammad Altaf five for 80, Abdul Rahim four for 112). *Bahawalpur 18 pts, Lahore City Whites 3 pts.*

At Sahiwal Stadium, Sahiwal, October 8, 9, 10. Drawn. Multan 243 for nine (Ijaz Ahmed 76, Javed Ilyas 45) and 311 for nine dec. (Humayun Muzammil 53, Mohammad Javed 47; Zahid Ahmad five for 94); Karachi Blues 280 for five (Asif Mujtaba 94, Aftab Baloch 68, Rizwan-uz-Zaman 59) and 168 for five (Rizwan-uz-Zaman 100 not out). *Karachi Blues 10 pts, Multan 6 pts.*

At Sahiwal Stadium, Sahiwal, October 12, 13, 14. Karachi Blues won by 164 runs. Karachi Blues 232 (Asif Mujtaba 66, Rizwan-uz-Zaman 64; Nasir J. Charlie six for 64) and 332 (Rizwan-uz-Zaman 166, Asif Mujtaba 55, Haseeb-ul-Hasan 50; Zulfiqar Butt five for 110); Lahore City Whites 225 for nine (Nadeem Ahmed 77, Shahid Anwar 60; Rizwan-uz-Zaman four for 29) and 175 (Javed Qayyum 70, Akhlaq Quereshi 50; Tanvir Ali five for 66). *Karachi Blues 17 pts, Lahore City Whites 7 pts.*

At Bahawal Stadium, Bahawalpur, October 12, 13, 14. Drawn. Multan 192 (Ijaz Ahmed 100 not out; Akram Chaudhri five for 37) and 273 (Humayun Muzammil 90 not out, Masood Anwar 72); Bahawalpur 265 for nine (Farooq Shera 101 not out, Azhar Abbas 61; Masood Anwar four for 81) and 65 for no wkt. *Bahawalpur 10 pts, Multan 5 pts.*

At Bahawal Stadium, Bahawalpur, October 16, 17, 18. Drawn. Bahawalpur 244 for seven (Farooq Shera 112 not out, Azhar Abbas 52) and 188 for nine (Mohammad Altaf 52 not out; Aqeel Qureshi five for 87); Karachi Blues 258 for five (Rizwan-uz-Zaman 157, Asif Mujtaba 58, Aftab Baloch 52 not out). *Karachi Blues 10 pts, Bahawalpur 6 pts.*

At MCC Ground, Multan, October 16, 17, 18. Drawn. Multan 309 for nine (Ijaz Ahmed 117, Naved Mushtaq 55) and 239 for eight dec. (Zakir Hussain 80, Islam-ul-Haq 65; Azhar Saeed four for 70); Lahore City Whites 223 (Nadeem Ahmed 78; Masood Anwar six for 94) and 255 for seven (Shahid Anwar 69, Maqsood Raza 65 not out, Ashfaq Ahmed 51; Masood Anwar five for 107). *Multan 10 pts, Lahore City Whites 6 pts.*

Karachi Blues 37 pts, Bahawalpur 34 pts, Multan 21 pts, Lahore City Whites 16 pts. Karachi Blues qualified for the semi-finals.

## Group C

At Sargodha Stadium, Sargodha, October 1, 2, 3. Sargodha won by 142 runs. Sargodha 258 for seven (Arshad Pervez 116 not out, Saleem Cheema 50; Akhtar Hussain four for 88) and 183 for eight (Azhar Sultan 50); Faisalabad 156 (Tahir Rasheed 46; Ghulam Abbas four for 44, Shakeel Cheema four for 57) and 143 (Wasim Hyder 51 not out; Aziz-ur-Rehman seven for 45). *Sargodha 18 pts, Faisalabad 5 pts.*

At Jinnah Park, Sialkot, October 1, 2, 3. Gujranwala won by 138 runs. Gujranwala 259 for eight (Tahir Mahmood 55, Sajid Bashir 43; Shahid Tanvir four for 75) and 178 for four dec. (Mansoor Khan 70, Tahir Mahmood 55); Lahore Division 200 for seven (Ashraf Ali 94, Tariq Mahmood 49) and 99 (Sajid Bashir four for 15). *Gujranwala 18 pts, Lahore Division 6 pts.*

At LCCA Ground, Lahore, October 8, 9, 10. Lahore City Blues won by seven wickets. Lahore Division 199 (Shahid Tanvir 95; Asim Butt four for 35 including a hat-trick) and 176 (Waqar Ali 57; Asim Butt five for 53, Aamer Malik four for 46); Lahore City Blues 195 (Akram Raza 47, Wasim Raja 40) and 181 for three (Mohsin Riaz 76 not out, Aamer Malik 72). *Lahore City Blues 15 pts, Lahore Division 5 pts.*

At Bagh-e-Jinnah Ground, Faisalabad, October 8, 9, 10. Faisalabad won by five wickets. Gujranwala 197 (Ijaz Ahmed 83; Tanvir Afzal six for 80) and 206 (Tahir Mahmood 56; Tanvir Afzal five for 86, Humayun Farkhan four for 74); Faisalabad 301 for seven (Mohammad Ashraf 140) and 104 for five (Shakir Ali 60 not out). *Faisalabad 18 pts, Gujranwala 5 pts.*

At LCCA Ground, Lahore, October 12, 13, 14. Lahore City Blues won by three wickets. Faisalabad 282 for four (Shuja-ud-Din 114, Mohammad Ashraf 101 not out) and 132 (Mohammad Ashraf 44; Arshad Butt four for 35); Lahore City Blues 194 (Wasim Raja 78; Tanvir Afzal four for 66) and 221 for seven (Mohsin Riaz 80, Parvez Mir 54; Tanvir Afzal five for 111). *Lahore City Blues 13 pts, Faisalabad 8 pts.*

At Sargodha Stadium, Sargodha, October 12, 13, 14. Sargodha won by 19 runs. Sargodha 312 (Mohammad Aslam 167, Qazi Waqar 40; Ijaz Ahmed four for 50) and 228 for nine dec.

(Mohammad Aslam 88, Saleem Cheema 65; Ijaz Ahmed four for 73); Gujranwala 188 (Aziz-ur-Rehman six for 70) and 333 (Tahir Mahmood 108, Yahya Khan 56 not out, Mansoor Khan 42, Mohammad Imtiaz 40; Aziz-ur-Rehman five for 74). *Sargodha 18 pts, Gujranwala 5 pts.*

At Sargodha Stadium, Sargodha, October 16, 17. Sargodha won by an innings and 44 runs. Lahore Division 152 (Sarfraz Azeem 62; Aziz-ur-Rehman four for 34) and 162 (Shahid Tanvir 97; Ghulam Abbas seven for 66); Sargodha 358 for three (Tasnim Abidi 131, Arshad Pervez 76 not out, Saleem Cheema 67, Azhar Sultan 41 not out). *Sargodha 18 pts, Lahore Division 3 pts.*

At Jinnah Park, Sialkot, October 20, 21, 22. Faisalabad won by 115 runs. Faisalabad 209 (Mohammad Ashraf 100; Gauhar Butt five for 30) and 193 (Bilal Ahmed 54); Lahore Division 177 (Tanvir Afzal four for 68, Humayun Farkhan four for 78) and 110 (Humayun Farkhan four for 25). *Faisalabad 16 pts, Lahore Division 5 pts.*

At LCCA Ground, Lahore, October 30, 31, November 1. Drawn. Gujranwala 257 (Ijaz Ahmed 74, Sajid Bashir 55; Akram Raza six for 97, Mazhar Hussain four for 24) and 325 (Ijaz Ahmed 75, Yahya Khan 63, Tahir Mahmood 61, Farhat Masood 41); Lahore City Blues 298 for nine (Mohsin Riaz 78, Parvez Mir 74, Suleman Khwaja 40) and 75 for four. *Lahore City Blues 10 pts, Gujranwala 8 pts.*

At LCCA Ground, Lahore, November 3, 4, 5. Lahore City Blues won by 108 runs. Lahore City Blues 226 for nine (Parvez Mir 50, Mohsin Riaz 42; Aziz-ur-Rehman four for 71, Ghulam Abbas four for 79) and 188 (Abdul Qadir 72, Parvez Mir 69 not out); Sargodha 174 (Mohammad Aslam 75; Asim Butt four for 38, Abdul Qadir four for 62) and 132 (Azhar Sultan 46, Mohammad Aslam 45; Abdul Qadir nine for 59). *Lahore City Blues 17 pts, Sargodha 5 pts.*

Sargodha 59 pts, Lahore City Blues 55 pts, Faisalabad 47 pts, Gujranwala 36 pts, Lahore Division 19 pts. Sargodha qualified for the semi-finals.

## Group D

At Pakistan Ordnance Factories Oval, Wah Cantt, October 1, 2. Rawalpindi won by an innings and 104 runs. Dera Ismail Khan 90 (Naeem Ahmed five for 12, Nasim Piracha four for 44) and 57 (Naeem Ahmed five for 12, Aziz Ahmed four for 20); Rawalpindi 251 for four dec. (Masood Anwar 86, Majid Khan 78 not out, Raja Afaq 41 not out). *Rawalpindi 18 pts, Dera Ismail Khan 2 pts.*

At Peshawar University Hostel No. 2 Ground, Peshawar, October 1, 2. Peshawar won by an innings and 1 run. Hazara 138 (Ijaz Butt 69; Farrukh Zaman four for 56) and 131 (Wasim Fazal 50; Aamer Mirza six for 29); Peshawar 270 for eight (Nasim Fazal 71, Wahid Khan 44 not out). *Peshawar 18 pts, Hazara 4 pts.*

At CMT & SD Ground, Rawalpindi, October 8, 9. Rawalpindi won by an innings and 53 runs. Rawalpindi 345 for five (Masood Anwar 186 including a century before lunch, Tariq Javed 73, Sabih Azhar 52 not out); Hazara 150 (Arshad Khattak 48) and 142 (Farrukh Ahmed 57; Raja Afaq five for 52). *Rawalpindi 18 pts, Hazara 4 pts.*

At Peshawar University Hostel No. 2 Ground, Peshawar, October 8, 9. Peshawar won by an innings and 25 runs. Dera Ismail Khan 69 (Farrukh Zaman four for 8) and 101 (Farrukh Zaman four for 26); Peshawar 195 (Qazi Shafiq 52, Abdur Rahim 41; Jamal A. Nasir four for 64). *Peshawar 15 pts, Dera Ismail Khan 4 pts.*

At University Ground, Peshawar, October 12, 13. Hazara won by 17 runs. Hazara 115 (Mohammad Junaid 42) and 124 (Jamal A. Nasir four for 45); Dera Ismail Khan 124 (Asif Aslam four for 47) and 98 (Imran Khaliq six for 28). *Hazara 14 pts, Dera Ismail Khan 4 pts.*

At Pakistan Ordnance Factories Oval, Wah Cantt, October 16, 17, 18. Rawalpindi won by 249 runs. Rawalpindi 225 for six dec. (Masood Anwar 88, Tariq Javed 84; Iqbal Butt five for 98) and 226 for five dec. (Tariq Javed 100); Peshawar 97 (Mohammad Riaz five for 10) and 105 (Mohammad Riaz four for 41). *Rawalpindi 17 pts, Peshawar 3 pts.*

Rawalpindi 53 pts, Peshawar 36 pts, Hazara 22 pts, Dera Ismail Khan 10 pts. Rawalpindi qualified for the semi-finals.

## Semi-finals

At Bagh-e-Jinnah Ground, Lahore, November 7, 8, 9, 10. Rawalpindi won by 32 runs. Rawalpindi 277 (Mujahid H. Mir 51 not out, Nasim Piracha 47, Shahid Gulraiz 42, Tariq Javed 41; Aziz-ur-Rehman four for 60) and 222 (Raja Afaq 60); Sargodha 214 (Arshad Pervez 115; Aziz Ahmed six for 62) and 253 (Arshad Pervez 110, Tasnim Abidi 43N Raja Afaq six for 68). *Rawalpindi qualified for the final.*

At National Stadium, Karachi, November 11, 12, 13, 14. Karachi Whites won by 204 runs. Karachi Whites 300 for nine (Moin-ul-Atiq 101) and 254 (Mohammad Aslam 87, Rashid Khan 48; Tanvir Ali six for 85); Karachi Blues 251 for eight (Rizwan-uz-Zaman 59; Iqbal Qasim four for 88) and 99 (Ijaz Faqih six for 44, Iqbal Qasim four for 18). *Karachi Whites qualified for the final.*

## Final

At National Stadium, Karachi, November 17, 18. Karachi Whites won by ten wickets with three days to spare. Rawalpindi 126 (Ijaz Faqih six for 35) and 132 (Zahid Ahmed six for 45); Karachi Whites 243 (Mohammad Aslam 75, Zafar Ali 48; Sabih Azhar four for 20) and 17 for no wkt.

# QUAID-E-AZAM TROPHY, 1984-85

*Note:* First innings closed at 85 overs.

## Group A

At Niaz Stadium, Hyderabad, December 6, 7, 8, 9. HBFC won by 140 runs. HBFC 243 (Sagheer Abbas 76, Tariq Alam 75 not out) and 367 (Tariq Alam 89, Ijaz Ahmed 83, Munir-ul-Haq 66 not out, Raees Ahmed 62; Wasim Raja four for 125); National Bank 281 (Asad Rauf 85, Shahid Tanvir 48, Mohammad Jamil 46; Kazim Mehdi four for 87) and 189 (Raees Ahmed five for 59). *HBFC 17 pts, National Bank 8 pts.*

At Bahawal Stadium, Bahawalpur, December 11, 12, 13, 14. Drawn. PACO 194 (Shaukat Mirza 96 not out; Tariq Wahab four for 40) and 266 (Shaukat Mirza 116 not out, Ijaz Ahmed 54, Quaisar Hussain 42; Kasim Mehdi six for 79); HBFC 212 (Ijaz Ahmed 61, Noor-ul-Qamar 50, Raees Ahmed 50; Arshad Nawaz five for 45) and 170 for four (Raees Ahmed 64, Tariq Alam 56 not out). *HBFC 8 pts, PACO 5 pts.*

At National Stadium, Karachi, December 23, 24, 25, 26. Drawn. PACO 215 (Umar Rasheed 53, Ijaz Ahmed 44, Shahid Mahboob 43; Tanvir Ali eight for 83) and 355 for two dec. (Ijaz Ahmed 201 not out, Shaukat Mirza 132); Karachi 234 for six (Moin-ul-Atiq 80) and 303 for four (Zafar Ali 111, Mohammad Aslam 71, Asif Mujtaba 61 not out, Moin-ul-Atiq 41). *Karachi 9 pts, PACO 5 pts.*

At Bahawal Stadium, Bahawalpur, December 23, 24, 25, 26. HBFC won by seven wickets. PIA 181 (Rizwan-uz-Zaman 50; Raees Ahmed four for 58) and 272 (Hasan Jamil 92, Aftab Baloch 66, Naeem Ahmed 46; Kazim Mehdi five for 62); HBFC 234 (Munir-ul-Haq 104 not out; Zahid Ahmad seven for 68) and 223 for three (Munir-ul-Haq 120 not out, Raees Ahmed 50). *HBFC 17 pts, PIA 5 pts.*

At Bahawal Stadium, Bahawalpur, December 29, 30, 31, January 1. PACO won by two wickets. PIA 86 (Mian Fayyaz five for 27) and 228 (Iqbal Sikandar 49 not out; Mian Fayyaz six for 101); PACO 149 (Moin Mumtaz 44) and 166 for eight (Moin Mumtaz 48; Rashid Khan five for 49). *PACO 14 pts, PIA 4 pts.*

At National Stadium, Karachi, December 30, 31, January 1, 3. Drawn. Allied Bank 315 for four (Athar A. Khan 154 not out, Iqtidar Ali 68) and 231 (Feroze Najamuddin 62, Zafar Ahmed 50, Talat Masood 45); Karachi 265 for nine (Asif Mujtaba 71, Tanvir Ali 51, Haaris A. Khan 40; Jalal-ud-Din four for 61) and 227 for nine (Saeed Ahmed 82; Jalal-ud-Din four for 43). *Karachi 6 pts, Allied Bank 10 pts.*

At National Stadium, Karachi, January 4, 5, 6, 7. Karachi won by eight wickets. National Bank 225 (Mohammad Jamil 47, Taslim Arif 41; Tanvir Ali four for 61) and 276 (Shahid Tanvir

60, Asad Rauf 44; Tanvir Ali four for 77); Karachi 323 for eight (Nasir Shah 88, Asif Mujtaba 57, Haseeb-ul-Hasan 54) and 182 for two (Sajid Khan 76). *Karachi 18 pts, National Bank 7 pts.*

At Bahawal Stadium, Bahawalpur, January 5, 6, 7, 8. Drawn. Allied Bank 276 for eight (Shoaib Habib 84 not out, Iqtidar Ali 76) and 276 (Iqtidar Ali 69, Shoaib Habib 50, Iqbal Sikandar five for 82); PIA 213 for nine (Hasan Jamil 56 not out, Rizwan-uz-Zaman 44, Naeem Ahmed 42) and 222 for three (Feroze Mehdi 104 not out, Aftab Baloch 48 not out). *PIA 6 pts, Allied Bank 10 pts.*

At National Stadium, Karachi, January 10, 11, 12, 13. Drawn. HBFC 301 for nine (Munir-ul-Haq 67, Rafat Alam 60, Wasim Arif 53, Raees Ahmed 41; Tanvir Ali six for 122) and 282 (Munir-ul-Haq 66, Rafat Alam 54, Raees Ahmed 49; Tanvir Ali eight for 93); Karachi 256 for eight (Nasir Shah 76 not out, Moin-ul-Atiq 43, Asif Mujtaba 43) and 139 for three (Saeed Azad 60, Haseeb-ul-Hasan 52 not out). *Karachi 8 pts, HBFC 10 pts.*

At Bahawal Stadium, Bahawalpur, January 10, 11, 12, 13. PACO won by 66 runs. PACO 185 for seven (Shoaib Habib four for 63) and 185 (Shaukat Mirza 74; Amin Lakhani six for 73); Allied Bank 127 (Mian Fayyaz four for 38) and 177. *PACO 15 pts, Allied Bank 4 pts.*

At Ibn-e-Qasim Bagh Stadium, Multan, January 16, 17, 18. Allied Bank won by two wickets. HBFC 263 (Sagheer Abbas 73, Rafat Alam 60, Tariq Alam 51; Jalal-ud-Din six for 66, Amin Lakhani four for 68) and 326 (Noor-ul-Qamar 101, Wasim Arif 60, Ijaz Ahmed 56; Jalal-ud-Din five for 63); Allied Bank 326 (Salim Yousuf 67, Zafar Ahmed 55, Feroze Najamuddin 54, Athar A. Khan 53, Talat Masood 45; Kazim Mehdi four for 52) and 265 for eight (Iqtidar Ali 77, Shoaib Habib 67; Kazim Mehdi four for 52). *Allied Bank 18 pts, HBFC 8 pts.*

At Bahawal Stadium, Bahawalpur, January 16, 17, 18, 19. PACO won by nine wickets. National Bank 143 (Shahid Mahboob four for 25, Mian Fayyaz four for 61) and 265 (Saleem Pervez 112; Masood Anwar five for 101); PACO 306 for seven (Moin Mumtaz 135 not out, Shaukat Mirza 46) and 103 for one (Ijaz Ahmed 50). *PACO 18 pts, National Bank 4 pts.*

At National Stadium, Karachi, January 16, 17, 18, 19. Drawn. Karachi 299 (Nasir Shah 62, Asif Mujtaba 59, Haseeb-ul-Hasan 57, Moin-ul-Atiq 52) and 350 for six dec. (Nasir Shah 120, Asif Mujtaba 54, Moin-ul-Atiq 45, Saeed Azad 45); PIA 286 for seven (Aftab Baloch 60 not out, Shahid Mohammad 49, Rashid Khan 43, Naeem Ahmed 41; Tanvir Ali five for 78) and 180 for three (Rizwan-uz-Zaman 104 not out). *Karachi 10 pts, PIA 8 pts.*

At National Stadium, Karachi, January 22, 23, 24. Allied Bank won by seven wickets. National Bank 257 (Sajid Ali 73, Mohammad Jamil 43, Saleem Pervez 41; Shoaib Habib five for 63) and 165 (Jalal-ud-Din four for 68); Allied Bank 296 for nine (Talat Masood 117; Iqbal Butt four for 81) and 130 for three (Athar A. Khan 45). *Allied Bank 18 pts, National Bank 8 pts.*

At National Stadium, Karachi, February 2, 3, 4, 5. Drawn. PIA 273 for seven (Rizwan-uz-Zaman 119, Shahid Mahmood 42) and 245 for three dec. (Rizwan-uz-Zaman 121 not out, Asif Mohammad 116 not out); National Bank 260 for eight (Saleem Anwar 125 not out, Saleem Pervez 47) and 158 for three (Sajid Ali 95, Saleem Anwar 51). *PIA 10 pts, National Bank 8 pts.*

HBFC 60 pts, Allied Bank 60 pts, PACO 57 pts, Karachi 51 pts, National Bank 35 pts, PIA 33 pts. Allied Bank and HBFC qualified for the semi-finals.

## Group B

At LCCA Ground, Lahore, November 29, 30, December 1. United Bank won by eight wickets. Lahore 230 (Shahid Anwar 115, Mazhar Hussain 83 not out) and 126 (Tauseef Ahmed five for 63, Shahid Butt four for 38); United Bank 299 for eight (Saadat Ali 116, Mansoor Akhtar 95; Parvez Mir five for 84) and 59 for two. *United Bank 18 pts, Lahore 7 pts.*

At Gaddafi Stadium, Lahore, November 29, 30, December 1. Railways won by an innings and 57 runs. Railways 313 for five (Ameer Akbar 103, Talat Mirza 63, Pervez Shah 51 not out, Tahir Shah 43); Habib Bank 114 and 142 (Sultan Rana 40; Shahid Pervez five for 27). *Railways 18 pts, Habib Bank 3 pts.*

At Gaddafi Stadium, Lahore, December 5, 6, 7, 8. United Bank won by eight wickets. Muslim Commercial Bank 226 for nine (Anwar-ul-Haq 113; Kamal Merchant five for 54) and 263 (Asif Ali 81 not out, Tariq Khan 41; Ehtesham-ud-Din nine for 124); United Bank 370 for six (Ali Zia 100, Mansoor Akhtar 65, Ashraf Ali 48 not out, Haroon Rashid 47, Sadiq Mohammad 43) and 121 for two (Shafiq Ahmed 62 not out). *United Bank 18 pts. Muslim Commercial Bank 6 pts.*

At Iqbal Stadium, Faisalabad, December 11, 12, 13, 14. Railways won by 71 runs. Railways 135 (Talat Mirza 40; Farrukh Zaman six for 42) and 275 (Shahid Saeed 69, Pervez Shah 46); Muslim Commercial Bank 200 (Babar Basharat 41; Mohammad Nazir six for 77) and 139 (Mohammad Nazir four for 35). *Railways 14 pts, Muslim Commercial Bank 6 pts.*

At LCCA Ground, Lahore, December 23, 24, 25, 26. Lahore won by five wickets. WAPDA 322 for seven (Akram Raza 101 not out, Tanvir Razzaq 98, Farrukh Raza 58; Parvez Mir four for 109) and 332 for six dec. (Tanvir Razzaq 90, Mohammad Ashraf 81, Akram Raza 51 not out); Lahore 250 (Mohammad Ishaq 86, Parvez Mir 54) and 406 for five (Shahid Anwar 137, Mohammad Ishaq 112, Aamer Sohail 57 not out, Parvez Mir 45). *Lahore 18 pts, WAPDA 8 pts.*

At Pindi Club Ground, Rawalpindi, December 23, 24, 25, 26. Habib Bank won by 173 runs. Habib Bank 321 for two (Anwar Miandad 118 not out, Arshad Pervez 88, Azhar Khan 68 not out) and 267 for eight dec. (Zaheer Ahmed 112 not out, Noman Shabbir 77; Asif Ali four for 71); Muslim Commercial Bank 263 for nine (Anwar-ul-Haq 79, Babar Basharat 42, Asif Ali 40; Azhar Khan four for 70) and 152 (Anwar-ul-Haq 76; Abdul Raqeeb five for 67). *Habib Bank 18 pts, Muslim Commercial Bank 5 pts.*

At LCCA Ground, Lahore, December 29, 30, 31, January 1. Drawn. No play being possible from nine minutes after tea on the first day, the match was abandoned, the ten points for an outright win being shared equally between the two sides. Lahore 310 for five (Shahid Anwar 153, Mohammad Ishaq 68) v Muslim Commercial Bank. *Lahore 9 pts, Muslim Commercial Bank 8 pts.*

At Pindi Club Ground, Rawalpindi, December 29, 30, 31, January 1. Habib Bank won by ten wickets. WADPA 148 (Sajjad Akbar 43; Liaqat Ali five for 59) and 248 (Shahid Pervez 65, Farrukh Raza 49, Haafiz Shahid 45; Abdul Raqeeb five for 61); Habib Bank 346 for six dec. (Azhar Khan 103, Sultan Rana 77, Tehsin Javed 55 not out, Zaheer Ahmed 47) and 54 for no wkt. *Habib Bank 18 pts, WAPDA 3 pts.*

At LCCA Ground, Lahore, January 4, 5. Railways won by an innings and 21 runs. Lahore 157 (Parvez Mir 50; Mohammad Nazir five for 52) and 69 (Nadeem Ghauri five for 24); Railways 247 (Ameer Akbar 107, Tahir Shah 60; Parvez Mir six for 65). *Railways 17 pts, Lahore 5 pts.*

At Gaddafi Stadium, Lahore, January 4, 5, 6, 7. United Bank won by two wickets. WAPDA 216 (Sajjad Akbar 84, Haafiz Shahid 64; Naved Anjum five for 58) and 168 (Sajjad Akbar 76 not out, Afzal Butt 46; Naved Anjum four for 41); United Bank 237 (Shafiq Ahmed 118, Naved Anjum 44; Imran Ali six for 80, Haafiz Shahid four for 77) and 151 for eight (Naved Anjum 43 not out; Haafiz Shahid seven for 59). *United Bank 17 pts, WAPDA 6 pts.*

At Gaddafi Stadium, Lahore, January 10, 11, 12, 13. Railways won by 14 runs. Railways 199 (Tauseef Ahmed eight for 83) and 150 (Shahid Saeed 50; Tauseef Ahmed seven for 65); United Bank 203 for six (Ashraf Ali 80 not out, Shafiq Ahmed 52 not out; Shahid Pervez four for 54) and 132 (Mohammad Nazir four for 34). *Railways 14 pts, United Bank 6 pts.*

At LCCA Ground, Lahore, January 10, 11, 12, 13. Habib Bank won by 53 runs. Habib Bank 280 (Azhar Khan 115; Parvez Mir five for 79) and 274 (Arshad Pervez 152, Agha Zahid 73); Lahore 292 (Mohsin Riaz 71, Khalid Javed 59 not out; Abdul Raqeeb four for 107, Abdul Qadir four for 115) and 209 (Parvez Mir 74, Khalid Javed 60; Abdul Qadir five for 97). *Habib Bank 18 pts, Lahore 8 pts.*

At Gujranwala Stadium, Gujranwala, January 10, 11, 12, 13. Muslim Commercial Bank won by five wickets. WAPDA 135 (Azmat Suleman 42; Farrukh Zaman six for 48) and 307 (Ashfaq Ahmed 58, Haafiz Shahid 56, Tanvir Razzaq 49, Mohammad Ashraf 40); Muslim Commercial Bank 217 (Nadeem Yousuf 61 not out, Mohiuddin Khan 40; Haafiz Shahid four for 54) and 229 for five (Babar Basharat 68 not out, Anwar-ul-Haq 44). *Muslin Commercial Bank 16 pts, WAPDA 4 pts.*

At LCCA Ground, Lahore, January 16, 17, 18. Railways won by an innings and 53 runs. Railways 267 for eight (Abdul Sami 63); WAPDA 96 (Tanvir Razzaq 44; Nadeem Ghauri four for 44) and 118 (Mohammad Nazir six for 44, Nadeem Ghauri four for 54). *Railways 18 pts, WAPDA 4 pts.*

At Gaddafi Stadium, Lahore, January 16, 17, 18. United Bank won by an innings and 7 runs. Habib Bank 152 (Arshad Pervez 84; Tauseef Ahmed five for 37) and 173 (Agha Zahid 49; Ehtesham-ud-Din seven for 77); United Bank 332 for nine (Saadat Ali 169, Shafiq Ahmed 52; Liaqat Ali six for 110). *United Bank 18 pts, Habib Bank 5 pts.*

Railways 81 pts, United Bank 77 pts, Habib Bank 62 pts, Lahore 47 pts, Muslim Commercial Bank 41 pts, WAPDA 25 pts. Railways and United Bank qualified for the semi-finals.

## Semi-finals

At National Stadium, Karachi, January 28, 29, 30, 31. United Bank won by 244 runs. United Bank 340 for seven (Mansoor Akhtar 101, Mahmood Rasheed 81, Kamal Merchant 40 not out; Izhar Ahmed four for 102) and 272 (Kamal Merchant 72, Mansoor Akhtar 45; Raees Ahmed four for 100); HBFC 164 (Sikander Bakht four for 51) and 204 (Ijaz Ahmed 88; Shahid Aziz six for 106). *United Bank qualified for the final.*

At Gaddafi Stadium, Lahore, January 28, 29, 30, 31. Drawn. Allied Bank 232 (Zafar Ahmed 73 not out, Iqtidar Ali 57; Mohammad Nazir four for 47) and 324 for seven dec. (Zafar Mehdi 94, Iqtidar Ali 62, Athar A. Khan 59); Railways 353 for nine (Manzoor Elahi 78 not out, Tahir Shah 76, Pervez Shah 57; Jalal-ud-Din four for 133) and 104 for two (Shahid Saeed 53 not out). *Railways qualified for the final by virtue of their first-innings lead.*

## Final

At Gaddafi Stadium, Lahore, February 3, 4, 5, 6, 7. Drawn. United Bank 214 (Shafiq Ahmed 43; Mohammad Nazir six for 70) and 568 for six dec. (Naved Anjum 159, Shafiq Ahmed 115, Mansoor Akhtar 87, Ali Zia 81, Ashraf Ali 58 not out); Railways 161 (Abdul Sami 51; Tauseef Ahmed seven for 61) and 115 for two (Ameer Akbar 52 not out, Talat Mirza 43). *United Bank won the Trophy by virtue of their first-innings lead.*

## QUAID-E-AZAM TROPHY WINNERS

| | | | |
|---|---|---|---|
| 1953-54 | Bahawalpur | 1972-73 | Railways |
| 1954-55 | Karachi | 1973-74 | Railways |
| 1956-57 | Punjab | 1974-75 | Punjab A |
| 1957-58 | Bahawalpur | 1975-76 | National Bank |
| 1958-59 | Karachi | 1976-77 | United Bank |
| 1959-60 | Karachi | 1977-78 | Habib Bank |
| 1961-62 | Karachi B | 1978-79 | National Bank |
| 1962-63 | Karachi A | 1979-80 | PIA |
| 1963-64 | Karachi Blues | 1980-81 | United Bank |
| 1964-65 | Karachi Blues | 1981-82 | National Bank |
| 1966-67 | Karachi | 1982-83 | United Bank |
| 1968-69 | Lahore | 1983-84 | National Bank |
| 1969-70 | PIA | 1984-85 | United Bank |
| 1970-71 | Karachi Blues | | |

## PACO CUP, 1984-85

| | *Played* | *Won* | *Lost* | *Drawn* | *Points* |
|---|---|---|---|---|---|
| United Bank | 4 | 4 | 0 | 0 | 71 |
| Habib Bank | 4 | 3 | 1 | 0 | 58 |
| Karachi | 4 | 1 | 2 | 1 | 42 |
| Railways | 4 | 1 | 2 | 1 | 38 |
| PACO | 4 | 0 | 4 | 0 | 20 |

*Note:* First innings closed at 85 overs.

## RAILWAYS v KARACHI

At Gaddafi Stadium, Lahore, February 9, 10, 11, 12. Drawn. Railways 10 pts, Karachi 8 pts.

### Railways

| | | | |
|---|---|---|---|
| Talat Mirza c Haaris b Asif | 61 | – c Pervez b Saleem | 2 |
| Shahid Saeed lbw b Saleem | 33 | – (6) lbw b Tanvir | 20 |
| Ameer Akbar c Pervez b Saleem | 32 | – (2) c Pervez b Saleem | 6 |
| Munawwar Javed c Pervez b Asif | 11 | – (3) c and b Tanvir | 51 |
| Tahir Shah c sub b Saleem | 75 | – (4) c Asif b Haaris | 88 |
| Pervez Shah c Pervez b Haaris | 18 | – (7) not out | 35 |
| Manzoor Elahi c and b Asif | 25 | – (5) lbw b Haaris | 0 |
| Musleh-ud-Din not out | 21 | – not out | 11 |
| *Mohammad Nazir not out | 9 | | |
| B 2, l-b 7, w 11, n-b 5 | 25 | B 4, l-b 7, w 1, n-b 3 | 15 |
| 1/69 2/111 3/138 4/165 5/208 6/259 7/291 | (7 wkts) 310 | 1/6 2/10 3/154 4/154 5/157 6/212 | (6 wkts dec.) 228 |

†Zulqarnain and Nadeem Ghauri did not bat.

Bowling: *First Innings*—Saleem 22–4–70–3; Haseeb 2–0–19–0; Tanvir 25–7–86–0; Haaris 17–2–58–1; Asif 18–2–62–3; Nasir 1–0–6–0. *Second Innings*—Saleem 15–2–55–2; Haseeb 7–1–24–0; Tanvir 17–3–58–2; Haaris 15–6–36–2; Asif 4.1–0–25–0; Nasir 0.5–0–6–0; Sajid 6–0–13–0.

### Karachi

| | | | |
|---|---|---|---|
| Mohammad Aslam c Talat b Manzoor | 12 | – c Zulqarnain b Manzoor | 11 |
| Moin-ul-Atiq c Nadeem b Manzoor | 31 | – c Zulqarnain b Pervez | 14 |
| Saeed Azad c Zulqarnain b Nadeem | 15 | – c Talat b Munawwar | 91 |
| *Nasir Shah lbw b Nazir | 86 | – c Tahir b Nazir | 19 |
| Asif Mujtaba b Nadeem | 20 | – run out | 24 |
| Sajid Khan b Nazir | 25 | – c Zulqarnain b Munawwar | 13 |
| Haseeb-ul-Hasan c Zulqarnain b Pervez | 7 | – b Nazir | 11 |
| Tanvir Ali c Pervez b Nadeem | 12 | – c Zulqarnain b Nadeem | 0 |
| Haaris A. Khan not out | 9 | – not out | 3 |
| Saleem Jaffer c Tahir b Nazir | 5 | – lbw b Nazir | 1 |
| †Pervez-ul-Hasan not out | 5 | – not out | 0 |
| B 17, l-b 4, w 1, n-b 4 | 26 | B 5, l-b 9, w 2 | 16 |
| 1/25 2/52 3/89 4/126 5/169 6/184 7/231 8/235 9/243 | (9 wkts) 253 | 1/27 2/27 3/77 4/162 5/180 6/193 7/195 8/195 9/202 | (9 wkts) 203 |

Bowling: *First Innings*—Manzoor 10–4–22–2; Musleh 6–0–38–0; Pervez 12–3–33–1; Nazir 33–5–73–3; Nadeem 24–4–66–3. *Second Innings*—Manzoor 7–3–30–1; Musleh 3–0–19–0; Pervez 6–2–28–1; Nazir 33–17–42–3; Nadeem 14–3–34–1; Munawwar 14–3–36–2.

Umpires: Shakeel Khan and Mian Mohammad Aslam.

## PACO v KARACHI

At Gaddafi Stadium, Lahore, February 14, 15, 16, 17. Karachi won by four wickets. Karachi 18 pts, PACO 4 pts.

### PACO

| | | | |
|---|---|---|---|
| Umar Rasheed b Haseeb | 2 | – run out | 18 |
| Junaid Alvi lbw b Saleem | 9 | – lbw b Tanvir | 6 |
| Ijaz Ahmed c Sajid b Haseeb | 13 | – c Asif b Saleem | 6 |
| Shaukat Mirza b Nadeem | 97 | – lbw b Saleem | 48 |

| | | | |
|---|---|---|---|
| Moin Mumtaz c Nasir b Tanvir | 26 | – c Pervez b Saleem | 0 |
| *Shahid Mahboob b Tanvir | 29 | – c Asif b Nadeem | 25 |
| Yahya Toor b Nadeem | 14 | – lbw b Nadeem | 21 |
| Arshad Nawaz lbw b Saleem | 3 | – c Moin b Nadeem | 15 |
| Masood Anwar run out | 3 | – (10) not out | 72 |
| Mian Fayyaz st Pervez b Nadeem | 0 | – (11) lbw b Moin | 13 |
| †Sanaullah not out | 0 | – (9) c Asif b Nadeem | 1 |
| B 1, l-b 6, w 1, n-b 1 | 9 | B 1, l-b 8, n-b 6 | 15 |
| 1/5 2/25 3/25 4/71 5/130 6/169 7/182 8/184 9/205 | 205 | 1/25 2/35 3/37 4/38 5/93 6/134 7/134 8/140 9/169 | 240 |

Bowling: *First Innings*—Saleem 28–2–75–2; Haseeb 6–0–16–2; Sajid 1–0–10–0; Tanvir 23–5–55–2; Asif 1–0–5–0; Nadeem 18.4–4–37–3. *Second Innings*—Saleem 26–7–73–3; Haseeb 2–0–17–0; Tanvir 29–10–69–1; Nadeem 22–6–50–4; Zafar 4–2–10–0; Nasir 3–1–8–0; Moin 1.5–0–4–1.

### Karachi

| | | | |
|---|---|---|---|
| Moin-ul-Atiq c Sanaullah b Shahid | 19 | – not out | 70 |
| Zafar Ali c Junaid b Shahid | 60 | – b Shahid | 20 |
| Saeed Azad b Yahya | 120 | – c Ijaz b Shahid | 8 |
| *Nazir Shah lbw b Yahya | 58 | – c Umar b Shahid | 1 |
| Haseeb-ul-Hasan not out | 9 | – (8) not out | 14 |
| Nadeem Moosa not out | 14 | – (7) c Sanaullah b Yahya | 16 |
| Asif Mujtaba (did not bat) | | – (5) c Yahya b Shahid | 18 |
| Sajid Khan (did not bat) | | – (6) c Moin b Shahid | 6 |
| B 1, l-b 5, n-b 2 | 8 | B 6, l-b 2 | 8 |
| 1/37 2/110 3/224 4/273 | (4 wkts) 288 | 1/57 2/71 3/72 4/108 5/118 6/139 | (6 wkts) 161 |

Tanvir Ali, Saleem Jaffer and †Pervez-ul-Hasan did not bat.

Bowling: *First Innings*—Shahid 25–1–103–2; Moin 7–1–21–0; Fayyaz 22–7–62–0; Arshad 21–4–62–0; Masood 5–1–14–0; Yahya 5–0–20–2. *Second Innings*—Shahid 20–1–68–5; Fayyaz 11–3–16–0; Arshad 7–3–20–0; Masood 24.1–10–31–0; Yahya 9–3–18–1.

Umpires: Shakoor Rana and Khizar Hayat.

## HABIB BANK v RAILWAYS

At LCCA Ground, Lahore, February 14, 15, 16, 17. Habib Bank won by 40 runs. Habib Bank 18 pts, Railways 6 pts.

### Habib Bank

| | | | |
|---|---|---|---|
| Agha Zahid b Nadeem | 45 | – (4) b Nadeem | 19 |
| Arshad Pervez c Munawwar b Nadeem | 123 | – st Zulqarnain b Nadeem | 48 |
| Zaheer Ahmed c Manzoor b Nadeem | 25 | – (6) c Tahir b Nadeem | 10 |
| Anwar Miandad c Zulqarnain b Nadeem | 27 | – (3) c Zulqarnain b Nadeem | 7 |
| Sultan Rana not out | 15 | – c Shahid b Hafeez | 5 |
| †Masood Iqbal not out | 10 | – (8) c Tahir b Nadeem | 3 |
| Tehsin Javed (did not bat) | | – (1) b Manzoor | 14 |
| Noman Shabbir (did not bat) | | – (7) not out | 66 |
| *Abdul Raqeeb (did not bat) | | – c Sami b Nadeem | 0 |
| Atiq-ur-Rehman (did not bat) | | – c and b Nadeem | 15 |
| Liaqat Ali (did not bat) | | – c and b Nadeem | 10 |
| B 2, l-b 6, n-b 2 | 10 | B 4, l-b 6 | 10 |
| 1/83 2/139 3/199 4/243 | (4 wkts) 255 | 1/32 2/51 3/85 4/94 5/94 6/119 7/125 8/125 9/173 | 207 |

Bowling: *First Innings*—Manzoor 10–3–26–0; Pervez 8–3–23–0; Nadeem 34–7–95–4; Hafeez 30–4–93–0; Sami 3–0–10–0. *Second Innings*—Manzoor 13–2–44–1; Pervez 6–1–13–0; Nadeem 32.5–8–68–8; Hafeez 16–2–33–1; Sami 6–0–21–0; Munawwar 1–0–2–0; Tahir 3–0–16–0.

## Railways

| | | | |
|---|---|---|---|
| Talat Mirza lbw b Raqeeb | 15 | c Sultan b Atiq | 4 |
| Shahid Saeed c Sultan b Raqeeb | 87 | b Anwar | 26 |
| Ameer Akbar c Noman b Anwar | 63 | lbw b Raqeeb | 22 |
| *Abdul Sami b Zahid | 47 | c and b Raqeeb | 8 |
| Manzoor Elahi st Masood b Raqeeb | 9 | (7) c Noman b Raqeeb | 6 |
| Pervez Shah c Arshad b Raqeeb | 24 | (8) c Tehsin b Anwar | 14 |
| Tahir Shah run out | 18 | (5) c Arshad b Raqeeb | 0 |
| Munawwar Javed not out | 13 | (6) not out | 30 |
| †Zulqarnain c Zahid b Raqeeb | 0 | (10) c Tehsin b Anwar | 0 |
| Nadeem Ghauri not out | 6 | (11) c Sultan b Atiq | 6 |
| Hafeez-ur-Rehman (did not bat) | | (9) run out | 4 |
| B 1, l-b 7, n-b 3 | 11 | B 4, l-b 1, n-b 4 | 9 |
| 1/25 2/125 3/209 4/220 5/241 6/268 7/274 8/274 | (8 wkts) 293 | 1/5 2/54 3/66 4/66 5/66 6/73 7/99 8/105 9/106 | 129 |

Bowling: *First Innings*—Liaqat 2–0–15–0; Atiq 9–0–35–0; Raqeeb 29–5–108–5; Noman 5–0–21–0; Anwar 12–2–36–1; Zahid 28–6–70–1. *Second Innings*—Liaqat 4–2–12–0; Atiq 5.2–2–16–2; Raqeeb 19–3–47–4; Noman 3–0–11–0; Anwar 12–2–28–3; Zahid 3–0–10–0.

Umpires: Mahboob Shah and Shakeel Khan.

# HABIB BANK v PACO

At LCCA Ground, Lahore, February 19, 20, 21. Habib Bank won by six wickets. Habib Bank 18 pts, PACO 8 pts.

## PACO

| | | | |
|---|---|---|---|
| Umar Rasheed c Atiq b Raqeeb | 31 | c Azhar b Qadir | 21 |
| Junaid Alvi lbw b Raqeeb | 16 | lbw b Qadir | 13 |
| Ijaz Ahmed b Qadir | 7 | c Masood b Atiq | 28 |
| Shaukat Mirza b Qadir | 11 | c Azhar b Qadir | 10 |
| Moin Mumtaz c and b Qadir | 103 | b Atiq | 28 |
| *Shahid Mahboob c Sultan b Qadir | 5 | c Raqeeb b Qadir | 27 |
| Yahya Toor not out | 76 | c Raqeeb b Qadir | 5 |
| Masood Anwar run out | 15 | (9) c Masood b Atiq | 17 |
| Arshad Nawaz c Arshad b Qadir | 5 | (8) lbw b Atiq | 6 |
| †Sanaullah b Qadir | 0 | not out | 2 |
| Mian Fayyaz not out | 6 | lbw b Atiq | 0 |
| L-b 6, n-b 1 | 7 | B 11, l-b 2, n-b 2 | 15 |
| 1/47 2/56 3/56 4/89 5/95 6/216 7/238 8/255 9/261 | (9 wkts) 282 | 1/33 2/48 3/76 4/76 5/125 6/137 7/141 8/166 9/172 | 172 |

Bowling: *First Innings*—Atiq 6–1–18–0; Sultan 2–0–3–0; Qadir 40–8–136–6; Raqeeb 23–3–70–2; Anwar 6–0–21–0; Azhar 8–0–28–0. *Second Innings*—Atiq 15.4–1–60–5; Qadir 23–6–69–5; Raqeeb 7–1–23–0; Anwar 1–0–7–0.

## Habib Bank

| | | | |
|---|---|---|---|
| Zaheer Ahmed c and b Masood | 39 | c Junaid b Shahid | 15 |
| Arshad Pervez b Shahid | 73 | c sub b Masood | 19 |
| Sultan Rana c Sanaullah b Masood | 12 | b Shahid | 27 |
| Azhar Khan b Arshad | 37 | b Arshad | 58 |
| Anwar Miandad c Yahya b Shahid | 14 | not out | 49 |

| | | | |
|---|---|---|---|
| Tehsin Javed b Shahid | 7 | not out | 23 |
| Noman Shabbir b Shahid | 41 | | |
| Abdul Qadir run out | 13 | | |
| Atiq-ur-Rehman b Arshad | 6 | | |
| †Masood Iqbal not out | 3 | | |
| *Abdul Raqeeb not out | 2 | | |
| B 5, l-b 11, w 1 | 17 | L-b 1 | 1 |
| 1/70 2/102 3/174 4/178 5/196 6/225 7/243 8/256 9/262 | (9 wkts) 264 | 1/18 2/48 3/75 4/137 | (4 wkts) 192 |

Bowling: *First Innings*—Shahid 28–3–88–4; Umar 2–0–9–0; Masood 13–2–33–2; Arshad 23–2–71–2; Fayyaz 15–3–31–0; Yahya 4–0–16–0. *Second Innings*—Shahid 22–4–70–2; Masood 19–5–53–1; Arshad 18–6–35–1; Yahya 3–0–19–0; Ijaz 1–0–1–0; Shaukat 1–0–9–0; Junaid 0.1–0–4–0.

Umpires: Mahboob Shah and M. Siddiq Khan.

## UNITED BANK v KARACHI

At Gaddafi Stadium, Lahore, February 19, 20, 21, 22. United Bank won by 234 runs. United Bank 18 pts, Karachi 8 pts.

### United Bank

| | | | |
|---|---|---|---|
| Mansoor Akhtar b Nadeem | 180 | run out | 9 |
| Saadat Ali b Nadeem | 75 | c Haseeb b Haaris | 134 |
| *Shafiq Ahmed b Nadeem | 40 | b Haaris | 61 |
| Ali Zia run out | 19 | lbw b Haaris | 31 |
| Mahmood Rasheed c Nadeem b Tanvir | 3 | c Zafar b Saleem | 7 |
| Naved Anjum c and b Nadeem | 14 | (7) not out | 24 |
| †Ashraf Ali run out | 25 | | |
| Sikander Bakht b Saleem | 1 | | |
| Tauseef Ahmed not out | 8 | | |
| Nasir Valika not out | 1 | (6) not out | 18 |
| L-b 4, w 2, n-b 1 | 7 | B 7, l-b 16, w 5 | 28 |
| 1/134 2/227 3/269 4/279 5/323 6/340 7/345 8/370 | (8 wkts) 373 | 1/21 2/167 3/228 4/250 5/274 | (5 wkts dec.) 312 |

Ehtesham-ud-Din did not bat.

Bowling: *First Innings*—Saleem 15–0–91–1; Haseeb 3–0–17–0; Haaris 7–1–22–0; Tanvir 21–2–93–1; Nadeem 32–2–118–4; Asif 5–0–17–0; Nasir 2–0–11–0. *Second Innings*—Saleem 18–0–76–1; Haseeb 9–0–42–0; Haaris 22–1–106–3; Tanvir 5–0–26–0; Nadeem 8–0–39–0.

### Karachi

| | | | |
|---|---|---|---|
| Zafar Ali c Saadat b Tauseef | 21 | (2) lbw b Ali Zia | 24 |
| Moin-ul-Atiq b Tauseef | 140 | (1) c Ali Zia b Tauseef | 27 |
| Saeed Azad c Mahmood b Ehtesham | 17 | lbw b Ali Zia | 11 |
| *Nasir Shah run out | 13 | c Mansoor b Tauseef | 27 |
| Asif Mujtaba b Tauseef | 45 | c Nasir b Tauseef | 1 |
| Nadeem Moosa run out | 18 | c Nasir b Tauseef | 8 |
| Haseeb-ul-Hasan not out | 24 | c Mansoor b Tauseef | 4 |
| Tanvir Ali lbw b Shafiq | 0 | b Shafiq | 8 |
| Haaris A. Khan run out | 9 | b Ali Zia | 17 |
| Saleem Jaffer (did not bat) | | lbw b Ali Zia | 9 |
| †Pervez-ul-Hasan (did not bat) | | not out | 4 |
| B 10, l-b 7, w 1, n-b 1 | 19 | B 2, l-b 2, n-b 1 | 5 |
| 1/67 2/98 3/123 4/226 5/257 6/272 7/278 8/306 | (8 wkts) 306 | 1/49 2/59 3/66 4/67 5/87 6/95 7/108 8/119 9/139 | 145 |

Bowling: *First Innings*—Ehtesham 13–3–35–1; Sikander 10–3–24–0; Ali Zia 22–4–72–0; Tauseef 32–4–107–3; Mansoor 2–0–19–0; Shafiq 6–0–32–1. *Second Innings*—Ehtesham 8–2–22–0; Sikander 5–0–12–0; Ali Zia 15.5–5–37–4; Tauseef 26–7–43–5; Shafiq 6–1–15–1; Naved 2–0–12–0.

Umpires: Amanullah Khan and Javed Akhtar.

## RAILWAYS v UNITED BANK

At Gaddafi Stadium, Lahore, February 24, 26, 27. United Bank won by 27 runs. United Bank 17 pts, Railways 4 pts.

### United Bank

| | | | |
|---|---|---|---|
| Mansoor Akhtar c Shahid Saeed b Shahid Pervez | 22 | b Nazir | 30 |
| Saadat Ali b Shahid Pervez | 27 | c Tahir b Pervez | 26 |
| *Shafiq Ahmed c Zulqarnain b Shahid Pervez | 10 | lbw b Nazir | 21 |
| Ali Zia run out | 9 | b Nadeem | 0 |
| Naved Anjum st Zulqarnain b Nadeem | 29 | st Zulqarnain b Nadeem | 7 |
| Nasir Valika c Zulqarnain b Shahid Pervez | 7 | c Manzoor b Nadeem | 0 |
| Waheed Mirza lbw b Nazir | 21 | (8) c and b Nadeem | 2 |
| †Ashraf Ali c Shahid Saeed b Nazir | 54 | (7) lbw b Nadeem | 9 |
| Tauseef Ahmed run out | 26 | c Ameer b Nazir | 3 |
| Sikander Bakht c Sami b Nazir | 15 | c Pervez b Nadeem | 0 |
| Shahid Butt not out | 0 | not out | 2 |
| B 7, l-b 9, n-b 1 | 17 | B 2, l-b 1, w 1 | 4 |
| 1/52 2/55 3/73 4/73 5/89 6/122 7/134 8/207 9/233 | 237 | 1/29 2/72 3/73 4/83 5/83 6/97 7/97 8/102 9/102 | 104 |

Bowling: *First Innings*—Manzoor 7–0–28–0; Pervez 5–1–13–0; Shahid Pervez 22–5–71–4; Nazir 35.3–10–56–3; Nadeem 15–1–53–1. *Second Innings*—Manzoor 4–0–30–0; Pervez 6–1–17–1; Shahid Pervez 5–1–9–0; Nazir 18.5–7–20–3; Nadeem 21–8–25–6.

### Railways

| | | | |
|---|---|---|---|
| Abdul Sami lbw b Tauseef | 23 | c Waheed b Sikander | 0 |
| Shahid Saeed lbw b Shahid | 27 | lbw b Shahid | 28 |
| Ameer Akbar c Ali Zia b Shahid | 6 | b Shahid | 38 |
| Munawwar Javed c Saadat b Shahid | 5 | c Ashraf b Shahid | 2 |
| Tahir Shah b Shahid | 31 | lbw b Tauseef | 31 |
| Pervez Shah b Shahid | 4 | st Ashraf b Shahid | 20 |
| Manzoor Elahi b Tauseef | 3 | c Ashraf b Tauseef | 5 |
| *Mohammad Nazir not out | 18 | b Tauseef | 10 |
| Shahid Pervez c Shahid b Tauseef | 1 | run out | 29 |
| †Zulqarnain lbw b Tauseef | 0 | c Saadat b Shahid | 5 |
| Nadeem Ghauri c Ashraf b Tauseef | 1 | not out | 2 |
| B 5, l-b 7, n-b 8 | 20 | B 2, l-b 3 | 5 |
| 1/58 2/60 3/68 4/85 5/95 6/104 7/120 8/127 9/131 | 139 | 1/0 2/48 3/54 4/87 5/113 6/129 7/131 8/155 9/173 | 175 |

Bowling: *First Innings*—Sikander 9–2–25–0; Naved 2–0–7–0; Shahid 25–12–33–5; Waheed 2–0–9–0; Tauseef 21.2–6–52–5; Ali Zia 1–0–1–0. *Second Innings*—Sikander 2–0–12–1; Naved 1–0–5–0; Shahid 26.1–5–73–5; Tauseef 27–2–80–3.

Umpires: Javed Akhtar and Feroze Butt.

## HABIB BANK v KARACHI

At LCCA Ground, Lahore, February 24, 26, 27, March 1. Habib Bank won by six wickets. Habib Bank 17 pts, Karachi 8 pts.

### Karachi

| First innings | | Second innings | |
|---|---|---|---|
| Moin-ul-Atiq c Masood b Raqeeb | 44 | (2) c Raqeeb b Qadir | 4 |
| Zafar Ali b Qadir | 29 | (1) c Sultan b Qadir | 2 |
| Saeed Azad b Qadir | 55 | c Tehsin b Qadir | 24 |
| *Nasir Shah c Arshad b Qadir | 13 | lbw b Azhar | 12 |
| Asif Mujtaba run out | 27 | c Anwar b Qadir | 7 |
| Nadeem Moosa lbw b Qadir | 11 | c and b Qadir | 45 |
| Haseeb-ul-Hasan b Zahid | 1 | lbw b Qadir | 10 |
| Tanvir Ali lbw b Zahid | 0 | lbw b Qadir | 34 |
| Haaris A. Khan lbw b Qadir | 5 | c Raqeeb b Qadir | 4 |
| Saleem Jaffer not out | 31 | not out | 2 |
| †Pervez-ul-Hasan not out | 23 | lbw b Raqeeb | 1 |
| B 4, l-b 14, n-b 1 | 19 | B 18, l-b 6, w 1, n-b 2 | 27 |
| 1/65 2/84 3/120 4/175 5/187 6/188 7/188 8/195 9/195 | (9 wkts) 258 | 1/4 2/30 3/52 4/58 5/91 6/136 7/145 8/159 9/160 | 172 |

Bowling: *First Innings*—Atiq 15–3–52–0; Zahid 13–3–31–2; Qadir 40–10–126–5; Raqeeb 17–3–31–1. *Second Innings*—Atiq 10–1–28–0; Qadir 36–14–67–8; Raqeeb 14.3–2–30–1; Noman 2–0–6–0; Azhar 10–5–17–1.

### Habib Bank

| First innings | | Second innings | |
|---|---|---|---|
| Agha Zahid b Saleem | 3 | c Pervez b Haseeb | 20 |
| Arshad Pervez b Tanvir | 42 | not out | 32 |
| Sultan Rana c Pervez b Tanvir | 28 | run out | 49 |
| Azhar Khan b Tanvir | 34 | b Tanvir | 17 |
| Anwar Miandad lbw b Tanvir | 3 | c Haaris b Asif | 64 |
| Tehsin Javed c Pervez b Tanvir | 11 | | |
| Noman Shabbir c Tanvir b Asif | 12 | | |
| Abdul Qadir b Tanvir | 39 | | |
| †Masood Iqbal c Haseeb b Tanvir | 2 | (6) not out | 9 |
| Atiq-ur-Rehman not out | 26 | | |
| *Abdul Raqeeb c Zafar b Tanvir | 10 | | |
| B 2, l-b 8, w 2, n-b 3 | 15 | B 1, l-b 11, n-b 6 | 18 |
| 1/16 2/79 3/86 4/104 5/125 6/130 7/180 8/180 9/186 | 225 | 1/49 2/72 3/122 4/195 | (4 wkts) 209 |

Bowling: *First Innings*—Saleem 22–3–58–1; Haseeb 10–2–25–0; Tanvir 32.2–6–87–8; Haaris 9–1–28–0; Nadeem 4–0–10–0; Asif 7–3–7–1. *Second Innings*—Saleem 9–1–33–0; Haseeb 10–0–28–1; Tanvir 22–6–70–1; Haaris 10–2–40–0; Nadeem 3–1–9–0; Asif 5–0–13–1; Saeed 0.1–0–4–0.

Umpires: Mian Mohammad Aslam and Athar Zaidi.

## HABIB BANK v UNITED BANK

At LCCA Ground, Lahore, March 3, 4, 5. United Bank won by 122 runs. United Bank 18 pts, Habib Bank 5 pts.

### United Bank

| First innings | | Second innings | |
|---|---|---|---|
| Mansoor Akhtar c Qadir b Atiq | 24 | c Raqeeb b Qadir | 45 |
| Saadat Ali c Sultan b Qadir | 43 | c Arshad b Qadir | 17 |
| *Shafiq Ahmed c Sultan b Raqeeb | 26 | lbw b Raqeeb | 3 |
| Ali Zia st Masood b Raqeeb | 96 | (5) b Raqeeb | 1 |
| Naved Anjum lbw b Azhar | 38 | (6) c Masood b Qadir | 24 |
| Mahmood Rasheed b Qadir | 6 | (7) c Azhar b Raqeeb | 0 |
| †Ashraf Ali c Anwar b Qadir | 12 | (8) c Sultan b Anwar | 9 |

| | | |
|---|---|---|
| Kamal Merchant c Raqeeb b Qadir | 6 – (9) not out | 1 |
| Tauseef Ahmed not out | 41 – (10) lbw b Qadir | 0 |
| Sikander Bakht b Qadir | 5 – (4) lbw b Qadir | 8 |
| Shahid Butt not out | 10 – run out | 0 |
| B 1, l-b 2, w 3, n-b 5 | 11 B 2, l-b 4, w 2, n-b 2 | 10 |
| 1/55 2/85 3/130 4/228 5/241 6/245 7/252 8/267 9/287 | (9 wkts) 318 1/39 2/52 3/78 4/79 5/93 6/94 7/117 8/117 9/117 | 118 |

Bowling: *First Innings*—Atiq 9–0–50–1; Zahid 12–0–29–0; Qadir 36–4–143–5; Raqeeb 18–1–66–2; Azhar 10–1–27–1. *Second Innings*—Atiq 3–1–15–0; Zahid 1–0–1–0; Qadir 20–6–64–5; Raqeeb 14–5–26–3; Anwar 2.2–0–6–1.

### Habib Bank

| | | |
|---|---|---|
| Agha Zahid c Mahmood b Tauseef | 8 – c Mahmood b Tauseef | 18 |
| Arshad Pervez c Mahmood b Sikander | 16 – lbw b Sikander | 0 |
| Sultan Rana c Saadat b Tauseef | 42 – c Shafiq b Tauseef | 43 |
| Azhar Khan b Tauseef | 9 – c Shafiq b Shahid | 57 |
| Anwar Miandad b Tauseef | 17 – c Shafiq b Shahid | 10 |
| Tehsin Javed c and b Tauseef | 10 – st Ashraf b Shahid | 2 |
| Noman Shabbir b Tauseef | 16 – c Mahmood b Tauseef | 3 |
| Abdul Qadir c Kamal b Tauseef | 34 – c Ashraf b Shahid | 0 |
| †Masood Iqbal b Tauseef | 4 – c Ashraf b Shahid | 2 |
| Atiq-ur-Rehman c Tauseef b Shahid | 3 – lbw b Shahid | 0 |
| *Abdul Raqeeb not out | 2 – not out | 0 |
| N-b 6 | 6 B 7, l-b 4, n-b 1 | 12 |
| 1/21 2/49 3/73 4/84 5/106 6/107 7/154 8/158 9/163 | 167 1/1 2/56 3/75 4/96 5/128 6/139 7/139 8/143 9/147 | 147 |

Bowling: *First Innings*—Sikander 11–2–34–1; Kamil 11–3–11–0; Shahid 24.3–5–70–1; Tauseef 24–6–52–8. *Second Innings*—Sikander 6–2–16–1; Kamil 5–3–6–0; Shahid 28.2–11–53–6; Tauseef 29–6–61–3.

Umpires: Khizar Hayat and Rab Nawaz.

## RAILWAYS v PACO

At Gaddafi Stadium, Lahore, March 3, 4, 5, 6. Railways won by 112 runs. Railways 18 pts, PACO 5 pts.

### Railways

| | | |
|---|---|---|
| Talat Mirza c Ijaz b Umar | 13 – (7) b G. M. Ahmed | 22 |
| Shahid Saeed c Shahid b Umar | 0 – (4) b G. M. Ahmed | 38 |
| Abdul Sami c Shahzad b Arshad | 54 – (1) b Umar | 49 |
| Ameer Akbar lbw b Arshad | 43 – (3) lbw b Shahid | 14 |
| Tahir Shah c Shaukat b Shahid | 80 – c Yahya b G. M. Ahmed | 42 |
| Musleh-ud-Din run out | 1 – (8) c and b G. M. Ahmed | 11 |
| Manzoor Elahi c and b Shahid | 3 – (6) c Yahya b G. M. Ahmed | 42 |
| *Mohammad Nazir b Arshad | 4 | |
| Shahid Pervez not out | 37 – not out | 19 |
| †Zulqarnain not out | 30 – (2) lbw b Shahid | 8 |
| L-b 13, w 3 | 16 B 2, l-b 4, w 1, n-b 2 | 9 |
| 1/5 2/15 3/94 4/150 5/153 6/171 7/188 8/218 | (8 wkts) 281 1/24 2/68 3/93 4/143 5/196 6/206 7/233 8/254 | (8 wkts dec.) 254 |

Nadeem Ghauri did not bat.

Bowling: *First Innings*—Shahid 27–5–98–2; Umar 9–1–27–2; Arshad 36–13–87–3; G. M. Ahmed 5–0–22–0; Masood 8–2–34–0. *Second Innings*—Shahid 25–3–57–2; Umar 12–1–41–1; Arshad 4–2–10–0; G. M. Ahmed 24.3–6–82–5; Masood 6–2–19–0; Moin 2–1–11–0; Yahya 22–9–28–0.

## PACO

| | | | |
|---|---|---|---|
| †Shahzad Bashir lbw b Nazir | 37 | – c Manzoor b Nadeem | 16 |
| Adnan Sabri c and b Nazir | 9 | – (3) c Tahir b Nadeem | 8 |
| Umar Rasheed b Nazir | 0 | – (6) st Zulqarnain b Nazir | 0 |
| Ijaz Ahmed c Zulqarnain b Nadeem | 16 | – (2) c Tahir b Nadeem | 107 |
| Shaukat Mirza c Shahid Saeed b Nadeem | 37 | – (4) c Tahir b Nazir | 1 |
| Moin Mumtaz c sub b Nazir | 15 | – (5) lbw b Nazir | 22 |
| *Shahid Mahboob lbw b Nazir | 0 | – c Shahid Saeed b Nazir | 4 |
| Yahya Toor c Zulqarnain b Nadeem | 12 | – c sub b Nadeem | 63 |
| Masood Anwar c Shahid Saeed b Nazir | 23 | – c and b Nadeem | 12 |
| Arshad Nawaz b Nazir | 7 | – b Nazir | 11 |
| G. M. Ahmed not out | 0 | – not out | 5 |
| B 6, l-b 2 | 8 | B 2, l-b 6, n-b 2 | 10 |
| 1/27 2/27 3/58 4/76 5/98 6/98 7/124 8/137 9/163 | 164 | 1/31 2/71 3/74 4/118 5/120 6/132 7/188 8/210 9/231 | 259 |

Bowling: *First Innings*—Manzoor 2–0–12–0; Musleh 1–0–8–0; Nadeem 31–9–62–3; Nazir 33.1–10–62–7; Shahid Pervez 3–0–12–0. *Second Innings*—Manzoor 3–0–13–0; Musleh 2–0–15–0; Nadeem 44.1–9–134–5; Nazir 44–11–89–5.

Umpires: Amanullah Khan and Ikram Rabbani.

# UNITED BANK v PACO

At Gaddafi Stadium, Lahore, March 7, 8, 9. United Bank won by 252 runs. United Bank 18 pts, PACO 3 pts.

## United Bank

| | | | |
|---|---|---|---|
| Mansoor Akhtar b Shahid Mahboob | 33 | – c Shahzad b Masood | 24 |
| Saadat Ali c and b Shahid Mahboob | 11 | – c Masood b Shahid Mahboob | 7 |
| *Shafiq Ahmed run out | 69 | – c Shahzad b Shahid Mahboob | 0 |
| Ali Zia c Yahya b Arshad | 176 | – not out | 102 |
| Naved Anjum not out | 15 | – (6) c sub b Yahya | 42 |
| Mahmood Rasheed not out | 0 | – (7) not out | 9 |
| Nasir Valika (did not bat) | | – (5) b Masood | 20 |
| B 8, l-b 11, w 3 | 22 | L-b 5, n-b 1 | 6 |
| 1/23 2/59 3/218 4/326 | (4 wkts dec.) 326 | 1/26 2/26 3/40 4/90 5/182 | (5 wkts dec.) 210 |

†Ashraf Ali, Kamal Merchant, Tauseef Ahmed and Shahid Butt did not bat.

Bowling: *First Innings*—Shahid Mahboob 30–4–118–2; Shahid Pervez 11–2–53–0; Umar 6–1–8–0; Masood 13–3–36–0; Arshad 9–3–31–1; Ahmed 11–1–38–0; Yahya 4–0–23–0. *Second Innings*—Shahid Mahboob 16–4–69–2; Shahid Pervez 2–0–15–0; Masood 18–4–63–2; Arshad 0.3–0–2–0; Ahmed 9.4–1–39–0; Yahya 4.3–0–17–1.

## PACO

| | | | |
|---|---|---|---|
| †Shahzad Bashir run out | 7 | – (2) c Nasir b Tauseef | 27 |
| Ijaz Ahmed b Shahid | 33 | – absent ill | |
| Umar Rasheed c Shafiq b Tauseef | 2 | – (1) c Mahmood b Tauseef | 0 |
| Shaukat Mirza c Shafiq b Tauseef | 0 | – (3) c Mansoor b Tauseef | 24 |
| Moin Mumtaz c Saadat b Ali Zia | 44 | – (4) run out | 23 |
| Yahya Toor c Ashraf b Tauseef | 0 | – c Mahmood b Tauseef | 13 |
| *Shahid Mahboob b Tauseef | 46 | – (5) lbw b Tauseef | 0 |

| | | | |
|---|---|---|---|
| Masood Anwar c Saadat b Tauseef | 10 | – (7) b Tauseef | 5 |
| Arshad Nawaz not out | 11 | – absent ill | |
| G. M. Ahmed c Mahmood b Tauseef | 0 | – (8) b Tauseef | 11 |
| Shahid Pervez b Tauseef | 6 | – (9) not out | 11 |
| B 4, l-b 2 | 6 | L-b 5 | 5 |
| 1/11 2/20 3/30 4/46 5/53 6/131 7/139 8/151 9/151 | 165 | 1/10 2/49 3/62 4/62 5/86 6/92 7/101 8/119 | 119 |

Bowling: *First Innings*—Kamal 4–2–2–0; Shafiq 2–1–1–0; Ali Zia 6–0–24–1; Shahid 19–4–65–1; Tauseef 22.4–2–67–7. *Second Innings*—Kamal 2–1–4–0; Shafiq 1–0–2–0; Shahid 15–1–51–0; Tauseef 17–6–52–7; Mansoor 2–0–5–0.

Umpires: Shakoor Rana and Saleem Khan.

## OTHER FIRST-CLASS MATCHES

### SIND GOVERNOR'S XI v PUNJAB GOVERNOR'S XI

At National Stadium, Karachi, September 1, 2, 3. Sind Governor's XI won by an innings and 104 runs. Punjab Governor's XI 157 (Naved Anjum 59, Masood Anwar 51; Shahid Mahboob four for 49, Azeem Hafeez four for 50) and 118 (Naved Anjum 55; Azeem Hafeez four for 24); Sind Governor's XI 379 for nine dec. (Sagheer Abbas 94, Sajid Ali 83, Shaukat Mirza 81; Tahir Naqqash four for 119).

### PUNJAB GOVERNOR'S XI v SIND GOVERNOR'S XI

At Gaddafi Stadium, Lahore, September 12, 13, 14, 15. Drawn. Sind Governor's XI 276 (Iqbal Sikandar 65, Shoaib Mohammad 64, Anwar Miandad 42; Tahir Naqqash six for 72) and 121 for five (Tahir Naqqash four for 35); Punjab Governor's XI 376 for nine dec. (Ramiz Raja 172; Rashid Khan six for 110).

---

## WORLD CUP, 1987

The 1987 World Cup, to be staged in India and Pakistan, will begin on October 9. It will be played as a series of two-day, single-innings, limited-overs matches, with the final in Calcutta on November 7 and 8. The eight countries will be divided into two groups: England, Pakistan, Sri Lanka and West Indies will comprise one; Australia, India, New Zealand and the winners of this year's ICC Trophy the other.

# CRICKET IN SRI LANKA, 1984-85

By GERRY VAIDYASEKERA

A strong Pakistan Under-23 team, containing six Test players, played seven matches in Sri Lanka, winning three, losing two and drawing two. Their three victories all came in one-day games. The Pakistani captain, Salim Malik, started the tour with scores of 113 not out, 56 and 140 not out. So far as the future of Sri Lankan cricket is concerned, the most creditable performances came from Roshan Jurangpathy, Asanka Gurusinghe, Roshan Mahanama and Hashan Tillekeratne. Jurangpathy, a seventeen-year-old schoolboy of Royal College, made 203 runs against the visitors, including an innings of 102, and with his off-breaks captured seventeen wickets at an average of 19.94.

The Australian Schoolboys (Under 19) also made a ten-day tour of the island in March 1985, playing two one-day games and a four-day "Test". The Australians had difficulty adapting to the slow, turning pitches and lost the four-day game by eight wickets. For the Sri Lankan schoolboys, Don Anurasiri (orthodox left-arm spin), Sanjeeva Weerasinghe (leg-breaks) and Jurangpathy all bowled effectively, so that cricket fans, disappointed by the failure of their Test players in the one-day series in Australia, were able to hold out bright hopes for the future.

Colombo Cricket Club, led by Roger Wijesuriya, retained the Lakspray Trophy. The runners-up in this, Sinhalese Sports Club, won the Donovan Andree Trophy from the Bloomfield Cricket and Athletic Club. Colombo Cricket Club and Moors Sports Club were declared joint winners of the Pure Beverages Trophy, the final ending without a result. The season started with the Bristol Under-25 Tournament, which was retained by the Bloomfield Cricket and Athletic Club with Sinhalese Sports Club as runners-up. Gampaha District won the inaugural National Cricket Tournament and took the J. R. Jayawardene Trophy when they beat Matara-Hambantota District on first innings. Gampaha had won their semi-final on the toss of a coin.

Several records were established by the Sinhalese Sports Club in their match against the Sebastianites at Maitland Place. SSC scored 530 for four declared in their first innings and 413 for one in their second, the first instance of totals of over 400 in each innings in senior cricket in Sri Lanka. Kapila Jayasooriya, going in first, scored 209 not out in the first innings, and his opening partner, Dhammika Ranatunga, 231 not out in the second. Stefan Anthonisz (132) and Ranatunga added 318 in 242 minutes for the first wicket and SSC gained a first innings lead of 319.

Three batsmen aggregated over 1,000 runs in the season – Ashley de Silva of Tamil Union headed the batting averages with 1,163 runs at 50.56 and four centuries. Susil Fernando of the Air Force scored 1,204 runs, average 50.16, and Sumithra Warnakulasuriya of SSC scored 1,044 runs.

For the first time in club cricket two bowlers claimed over 100 wickets in a season – Jayananda Warnaweera of Galle, who took 121 at an average of 12.57, and Jayantha Amerasinghe of Nomads with 105 at 12.11 apiece. Guy de Alwis of SSC led the wicket-keeping list with 57 victims (53 ct, 4 st). In one match he held eleven catches. Nalin de Alwis of the Air Force had 50 victims (44 ct, 6 st).

Tamil Union Cricket and Athletic Club, led by S. Skanda Kumar, toured Malaysia for the Silver Jubilee Tournament and became league and knockout champions, winning all their five matches.

Two first-class umpires, Herbie Felsinger and Errol Senevira, visited England to officiate in matches there. Ranjit Fernando, holder of the

Advanced Coaching Certificate of the NCA in England, was appointed executive secretary of the Sri Lankan Cricket Foundation, the main object of which is the development and expansion of the game in the island.

## PAKISTAN UNDER-23 IN SRI LANKA

†At Maitland Place, Colombo, May 9, 10. Drawn. Sri Lanka Board President's Colts XI 212 for six dec. (Roshan Mahanama 97 not out); Pakistan Under-23 301 for seven (Salim Malik 113 not out, Ramiz Raja 56).

†At Saravanamuttu Stadium, Colombo, May 11. Pakistan Under-23 won by four wickets. Sri Lanka Under-23 191 for nine (45 overs) (S. Warnakulasuriya 82 not out); Pakistan Under-23 193 for six (44 overs) (Salim Malik 56, Manzoor Elahi 42 not out).

## SRI LANKA UNDER-23 v PAKISTAN UNDER-23

At Asgiriya Stadium, Kandy, May 13, 14, 15, 16. Drawn.

### Pakistan Under-23

| | | | |
|---|---|---|---|
| Ijaz Ahmed c Vonhagt b Ranatunga | 28 | – hit wkt b Ratnayake | 24 |
| Shahid Anwar c Weerasinghe b Ratnayake | 8 | – b Ranatunga | 3 |
| Ramiz Raja lbw b Jurangpathy | 48 | | |
| Manzoor Elahi c Gurusinghe b Jurangpathy | 58 | – not out | 0 |
| *Salim Malik not out | 140 | | |
| Ghaffar Kazmi c sub b Ratnayake | 12 | – (3) not out | 11 |
| Akram Raza c Ranatunga b Ratnayake | 9 | | |
| †Zulqarnain lbw b Ratnayake | 1 | | |
| Azeem Hafeez lbw b Ratnayake | 1 | | |
| Wasim Akram not out | 12 | | |
| B 6, l-b 5, n-b 3 | 14 | B 3, l-b 3, w 1 | 7 |
| 1/38 2/46 3/115 4/175 5/213 6/229 7/234 8/246 (8 wkts dec.) | 331 | 1/28 2/45 (2 wkts) | 45 |

Mohsin Kamal did not bat.

Bowling: *First Innings*—Ratnayake 28–3–121–5; Vonhagt 2–0–11–0; Ranatunga 10–1–35–1; Weerasinghe 15–5–38–0; Wijemanne 13–4–34–0; Jurangpathy 20–2–78–2. *Second Innings*—Ratnayake 2.3–0–11–1; Ranatunga 4–1–20–1; Weerasinghe 2–0–7–0.

### Sri Lanka Under-23

| | |
|---|---|
| D. M. Vonhagt c Ghaffar b Kamal | 6 |
| †G. Wickramasinghe b Azeem | 4 |
| S. Warnakulasuriya c Ramiz b Azeem | 0 |
| A. P. Gurusinghe c sub b Raza | 19 |
| P. A. de Silva c Zulquarnain b Ghaffar | 92 |
| *A. Ranatunga c Zulquarnain b Wasim | 45 |
| R. S. Mahanama c Zulquarnain b Raza | 25 |
| B. R. Jurangpathy c Ghaffar b Kamal | 102 |
| R. J. Ratnayake c Anwar b Ijaz | 36 |
| C. D. U. S. Weerasinghe not out | 2 |
| B 5, l-b 6, w 4 | 15 |
| 1/7 2/7 3/24 4/48 5/155 6/191 7/225 8/326 9/346 (9 wkts dec.) | 346 |

S. Wijemanne did not bat.

Bowling: Azeem 19–4–70–2; Wasim 9–3–21–1; Kamal 27.4–5–80–2; Manzoor 8–3–24–0; Raza 27–9–69–2; Ghaffar 14–4–40–1; Malik 5–0–23–0; Ijaz 3–0–4–1.

Umpires: A. C. Felsinger and K. T. Ponnambalam.

*Wides and no-balls not debited to bowlers' analyses.*

## SRI LANKA UNDER-23 v PAKISTAN UNDER-23

At Saravanamuttu Stadium, Colombo, May 19, 20, 21, 22. Abandoned without a ball bowled owing to rain. A one-day game was scheduled for May 22.

†At Saravanamuttu Stadium, Colombo, May 22. Sri Lanka Under 23 won by four wickets. Pakistan Under-23 159 (43.4 overs) (Zulquarnain 41); Sri Lanka Under-23 163 for six (39.5 overs) (A. Gurusinghe 42 not out).

†At Maitland Place, Colombo, May 25. Pakistan Under-23 won by nine wickets. Sri Lanka Under-23 99 (24.4 overs); Pakistan Under-23 103 for one (17.1 overs) (Ijaz Ahmed 79 not out).

†At Maitland Place, Colombo, May 26. Pakistan Under-23 won by 2 runs. Pakistan Under-23 161 (27 overs) (Ramiz Raja 47; A. Ranatunga four for 25); Sri Lanka Under-23 159 (26.5 overs).

## SRI LANKA UNDER-23 v PAKISTAN UNDER-23

At Saravanamuttu Stadium, Colombo, May 28, 29, 30, 31. Sri Lanka Under-23 won by an innings and 14 runs. The match, originally scheduled to be played at Galle, was moved to Colombo following heavy rain.

### Sri Lanka Under-23

| | |
|---|---|
| †A. M. de Silva c Manzoor b Kamal | 7 |
| D. Ranatunga b Haafiz | 11 |
| R. S. Mahanama c Salim b Tanvir | 9 |
| *A. Ranatunga c Ghaffar b Haafiz | 0 |
| P. A. de Silva c Ijaz b Ghaffar | 66 |
| H. P. Tillekeratne b Kamal | 67 |
| A. P. Gurusinghe st Zulquarnain b Tanvir | 106 |
| B. R. Jurangpathy b Salim | 28 |
| R. J. Ratnayake c Kamal b Tanvir | 24 |
| R. P. W. Guneratne not out | 0 |
| S. D. Anurasiri lbw b Tanvir | 0 |
| B 13, l-b 4, w 4, n-b 5 | 26 |
| 1/16 2/27 3/27 4/45 5/142 6/219 7/294 8/344 9/344 | 344 |

Bowling: Azeem 10–3–30–0; Kamal 16–2–37–2; Haafiz 15–5–20–2; Tanvir 44.5–12–98–4; Ghaffar 29–3–76–1; Salim 20–3–47–1; Ramiz 1–0–8–0; Manzoor 2–0–2–0.

### Pakistan Under-23

| First innings | | Second innings | |
|---|---|---|---|
| Ijaz Ahmed lbw b Ratnayake | 6 | lbw b A. Ranatunga | 4 |
| Shahid Anwar c A. M. de Silva b Ratnayake | 44 | c D. Ranatunga b A. Ranatunga | 0 |
| Ramiz Raja c Guneratne b Jurangpathy | 35 | c Anurasiri b Jurangpathy | 7 |
| †Zulquarnain b Ratnayake | 7 | c A. Ranatunga b Anurasiri | 11 |
| *Salim Malik lbw b Jurangpathy | 3 | c sub b Ratnayake | 31 |
| Manzoor Elahi c sub b Jurangpathy | 7 | c P. A. de Silva b Jurangpathy | 57 |
| Ghaffar Kazmi lbw b Ratnayake | 6 | lbw b Jurangpathy | 5 |
| Tanvir Ali c Tillekeratne b Jurangpathy | 0 | c Ratnayake b Jurangpathy | 3 |
| Haafiz Shahid c A. M. de Silva b Ratnayake | 3 | not out | 27 |
| Mohsin Kamal not out | 10 | b Ratnayake | 0 |
| Azeem Hafeez b Ratnayake | 12 | b Ratnayake | 28 |
| B 3, l-b 4, w 3, n-b 4 | 14 | B 3, l-b 1, w 1, n-b 5 | 10 |
| 1/18 2/77 3/89 4/100 5/110 6/112 7/112 8/120 9/126 | 147 | 1/0 2/7 3/11 4/77 5/91 6/123 7/124 8/132 9/136 | 183 |

Bowling: *First Innings*—Ratnayake 22.4–7–60–6; A. Ranatunga 2–1–1–0; Jurangpathy 26–9–44–4; Anurasiri 7–2–10–0; Guneratne 2–0–17–0. *Second Innings*—Ratnayake 24–2–70–3; A. Ranatunga 11–3–15–2; Jurangpathy 21–6–59–4; Anurasiri 11–3–16–1; Guneratne 2–0–13–0.

Umpires: C. Perera and S. Ponnadurai.

*Wides and no-balls not debited to bowlers' analyses.*

## AUSTRALIAN SCHOOLBOYS (UNDER 19) IN SRI LANKA

†At Tyronne Fernando Stadium, Moratuwa, March 24. Australian Schoolboys won by six wickets. Sri Lankan Under-19 208 for seven (45 overs) (A. Gurusinghe 108, H. Tillekeratne 53 retired hurt); Australian Schoolboys 209 for four (40.3 overs) (T. Moody 83, J. Pyke 46, D. Reynolds 40).

†At Maitland Place, Colombo, March 25. Sri Lankan Under-19 won by five wickets. Australian Schoolboys 130 (40.1 overs) (G. Parker 40; K. Dandeniya four for 24); Sri Lankan Under-19 134 for five (41.1 overs) (H. Tillekeratne 40 not out; A. Zeaers four for 30).

†At Maitland Crescent, Colombo, March 27, 28, 29, 30. Sri Lankan Under-19 won by eight wickets. Australian Schoolboys 157 (S. Weerasinghe four for 16) and 237 (J. Pyke 72, G. Parker 44 not out; S. D. Anurasiri four for 91); Sri Lankan Under-19 312 (P. Rodrigo 86, G. Wickremasinghe 77, J. Jayaratne 64; G. Robertson four for 92) and 83 for two.

# CRICKET IN ZIMBABWE, 1984-85

By ALWYN PICHANICK

Zimbabwe entertained a young New Zealand team and a team of English county cricketers in the season under review. The New Zealand team, containing six Test players and captained by Jeff Crowe, proved to be highly professional and a competitive tour resulted. Four three-day matches were played against Zimbabwe, three of which were drawn, with the tourists obtaining the only win in the series in the second encounter.

For Zimbabwe, Andrew Pycroft, the captain, David Houghton, Robin Brown and Graeme Hick all batted well. Hick's performances showed great maturity for an eighteen-year-old. Among the bowlers, Kevin Duers made a highly successful début by taking wickets regularly, including eight wickets in an innings in the last three-day game of the tour. Four one-day matches were also played between the two sides, an exciting series being drawn with each side winning twice.

Towards the end of the season an English Counties side, organised and managed by M. D. Vockins, the secretary of Worcestershire, visited Zimbabwe. The team was well led by Mark Nicholas and contained four Test players, Chris Broad, Paul Terry, Andy Lloyd and Nick Cook. A number of games were played against the Zimbabwe B team, including a three-day match in Bulawayo. In addition, the tourists played two first-class matches against Zimbabwe, both in Harare. As a result of Nicholas's positive captaincy there were two exciting finishes with the tourists winning the first match and Zimbabwe coming from behind to win the second encounter in the last over after a chase against the clock.

In the five one-day matches played between the English tourists and Zimbabwe for the "Astra" series, the home team played outstandingly to win all five. The visitors, as experienced practitioners in this type of game, were full of praise for the way in which the Zimbabwean team played limited-overs cricket.

During the English summer of 1985 Zimbabwe embarked on a seven-week tour of England which was bedevilled by bad weather. Details of this can be found on page 309.

## YOUNG NEW ZEALANDERS IN ZIMBABWE

†At Harare South, October 3. Young New Zealanders won by 38 runs. Young New Zealanders 234 for five (50 overs) (T. J. Franklin 56); Zimbabwe Country Districts 196 (48 overs) (G. A. Hick 56).

## ZIMBABWE v YOUNG NEW ZEALANDERS

At Harare, October 5, 6, 8. Drawn.

## Young New Zealanders

| | |
|---|---|
| T. J. Franklin not out | 153 |
| B. A. Edgar c Brown b Duers | 2 |
| K. R. Rutherford c Brown b Rawson | 1 |
| *J. J. Crowe c Houghton b Duers | 5 |
| V. R. Brown c Paterson b Duers | 1 |
| P. E. McEwan c Pycroft b Duers | 0 |
| †E. B. McSweeney c Butchart b Traicos | 29 |
| M. C. Snedden c Butchart b Hick | 47 |
| J. G. Bracewell c Houghton b Rawson | 27 |
| D. A. Stirling c and b Traicos | 32 |
| S. R. Tracy c Butchart b Fletcher | 1 |
| B 4, l-b 7, n-b 2 | 13 |
| 1/8 2/9 3/18 4/20 5/20 6/79 7/161 8/227 9/308 | 311 |

Bowling: Rawson 32–8–87–2; Duers 25–5–82–4; Butchart 4–0–25–0; Traicos 32–10–70–2; Hick 15–6–23–1; Fletcher 5.2–1–13–1.

## Zimbabwe

| | | | |
|---|---|---|---|
| R. D. Brown c sub b Snedden | 45 | c McEwan b Brown | 6 |
| K. G. Walton c McSweeney b Snedden | 3 | lbw b Snedden | 37 |
| G. A. Hick c and b Snedden | 8 | c sub b Brown | 23 |
| *A. J. Pycroft c Bracewell b Stirling | 21 | b Tracy | 88 |
| †D. L. Houghton c McSweeney b Snedden | 21 | c Rutherford b Brown | 84 |
| D. A. G. Fletcher c McEwan b Snedden | 5 | not out | 32 |
| G. A. Paterson c McSweeney b Snedden | 0 | b Tracy | 0 |
| I. P. Butchart c McSweeney b Snedden | 18 | not out | 22 |
| P. W. E. Rawson c McSweeney b Snedden | 5 | | |
| A. J. Traicos c sub b Bracewell | 3 | | |
| K. G. Duers not out | 4 | | |
| L-b 1, n-b 8 | 9 | B 1, l-b 6, n-b 5 | 12 |
| 1/33 2/45 3/74 4/90 5/99 6/99 7/114 8/127 9/138 | 142 | 1/20 2/61 3/86 4/240 5/273 6/273 | (6 wkts) 304 |

Bowling: *First Innings*—Stirling 8–0–32–1; Tracy 2–1–4–0; Snedden 21.2–2–73–8; Bracewell 16–4–32–1. *Second Innings*—Stirling 15–4–61–0; Tracy 14–5–33–2; Snedden 17–5–50–1; Bracewell 24–5–83–0; Brown 20–8–43–3; Rutherford 2–0–27–0.

Umpires: D. B. Arnott and B. MacLachlan.

†At Harare, October 7. Zimbabwe won by virtue of losing fewer wickets, with the scores level. Zimbabwe 175 for nine (50 overs); Young New Zealanders 175 (50 overs).

†At Kwekwe, October 10. Young Zimbabwe won by three wickets. Young New Zealanders 188 (48 overs) (K. R. Rutherford 48); Young Zimbabwe 189 for seven (46.1 overs).

## ZIMBABWE v YOUNG NEW ZEALANDERS

At Bulawayo, October 12, 13, 15. Young New Zealanders won by eight wickets.

### Zimbabwe

| First innings | | Second innings | |
|---|---|---|---|
| G. A. Paterson c McSweeney b Snedden | 17 | c Rutherford b Stirling | 0 |
| K. G. Walton c Crowe b Tracy | 7 | c Rutherford b Stirling | 33 |
| R. D. Brown c Rutherford b Tracy | 3 | b Stirling | 0 |
| *A. J. Pycroft c and b Snedden | 74 | lbw b Snedden | 56 |
| †D. L. Houghton c Snedden b Brown | 54 | c Snedden b Stirling | 20 |
| G. A. Hick c Bracewell b Brown | 0 | run out | 30 |
| D. A. G. Fletcher c Rutherford b Bracewell | 93 | c McSweeney b Snedden | 2 |
| I. P. Butchart c Rutherford b Bracewell | 29 | c Franklin b Snedden | 14 |
| P. W. E. Rawson b Bracewell | 10 | b Brown | 1 |
| A. J. Traicos not out | 12 | c McEwan b Snedden | 2 |
| K. G. Duers (did not bat) | | not out | 4 |
| L-b 7, n-b 11 | 18 | B 2, l-b 1, n-b 2 | 5 |
| 1/27 2/30 3/35 4/153 5/165 6/167 7/251 8/277 9/317 | (9 wkts dec.) 317 | 1/0 2/2 3/72 4/99 5/143 6/143 7/146 8/149 9/158 | 167 |

Bowling: *First Innings*—Stirling 14–4–43–0; Tracy 11–0–42–2; Snedden 23–3–70–2; Brown 18–2–75–2; McEwan 1–0–5–0; Bracewell 16.5–2–75–3. *Second Innings*—Stirling 13–3–66–4; Tracy 5–1–14–0; Snedden 16–9–26–4; Brown 13–4–28–1; Bracewell 10–2–30–0.

### Young New Zealanders

| First innings | | Second innings | |
|---|---|---|---|
| T. J. Franklin c Traicos b Duers | 13 | run out | 5 |
| B. A. Edgar b Butchart | 203 | b Fletcher | 3 |
| K. R. Rutherford c Houghton b Duers | 27 | | |
| P. E. McEwan c Pycroft b Butchart | 69 | (3) not out | 35 |
| *J. J. Crowe c Houghton b Duers | 33 | (4) not out | 9 |
| V. R. Brown not out | 67 | | |
| J. G. Bracewell c Walton b Duers | 6 | | |
| D. A. Stirling b Duers | 1 | | |
| L-b 9, w 1 | 10 | L-b 4 | 4 |
| 1/33 2/69 3/203 4/290 5/411 6/426 7/429 | (7 wkts dec.) 429 | 1/6 2/36 | (2 wkts) 56 |

†E. B. McSweeney, M. C. Snedden and S. R. Tracy did not bat.

Bowling: *First Innings*—Rawson 32–6–112–0; Duers 34.1–6–108–5; Fletcher 11–3–29–0; Traicos 26–3–92–0; Butchart 16–0–47–2; Hick 7–0–32–0. *Second Innings*—Rawson 1.1–0–9–0; Fletcher 3–0–25–1; Butchart 2.2–0–18–0.

Umpires: D. B. Arnott and K. Kanjee.

†At Bulawayo, October 14. Young New Zealanders won by 100 runs. Young New Zealanders 195 for eight (40 overs) (J. J. Crowe 53); Zimbabwe 95 (34.4 overs).

†At Hwange, October 17. Young New Zealanders won by one wicket. Young Zimbabwe 208 (48.5 overs) (C. A. T. Hodgson 60); Young New Zealanders 209 for nine (48 overs).

## ZIMBABWE v YOUNG NEW ZEALANDERS

At Harare, October 19, 20, 22. Drawn.

### Young New Zealanders

| | |
|---|---|
| B. A. Edgar c Rawson b Curran | 41 |
| T. J. Franklin c Houghton b Duers | 9 |
| P. S. Briasco c Traicos b Hick | 89 |
| P. E. McEwan c Hick b Rawson | 153 |
| *J. J. Crowe b Fletcher | 2 |
| V. R. Brown not out | 85 |
| †E. B. McSweeney c Duers b Curran | 34 |
| J. G. Bracewell c Brown b Curran | 10 |
| M. C. Snedden lbw b Traicos | 6 |
| G. K. Robertson c Shah b Hick | 21 |
| D. A. Stirling st Houghton b Traicos | 33 |
| L-b 8, w 2, n-b 6 | 16 |
| 1/22 2/65 3/256 4/277 5/316 6/378 7/395 8/416 9/455 | 499 |

Bowling: Rawson 23-2-105-1; Duers 18-4-62-1; Curran 19-6-82-3; Traicos 28.5-9-80-2; Shah 8-2-30-0; Fletcher 16-5-43-1; Hick 22-2-89-2.

### Zimbabwe

| | | | |
|---|---|---|---|
| K. G. Walton c McSweeney b Robertson | 23 | lbw b Robertson | 2 |
| A. H. Shah c McSweeney b Robertson | 0 | b Snedden | 33 |
| R. D. Brown c McSweeney b Stirling | 0 | not out | 124 |
| †D. L. Houghton c McEwan b Bracewell | 33 | (5) lbw b Snedden | 2 |
| G. A. Hick lbw b Bracewell | 95 | (6) lbw b Brown | 22 |
| D. A. G. Fletcher c and b Bracewell | 10 | (7) not out | 47 |
| K. M. Curran c Crowe b Bracewell | 0 | | |
| P. W. E. Rawson c Crowe b Bracewell | 14 | | |
| A. J. Traicos c Crowe b Bracewell | 5 | | |
| K. G. Duers not out | 1 | | |
| *A. J. Pycroft absent ill | | (4) c Bracewell b Brown | 24 |
| B 2, l-b 12, n-b 7 | 21 | B 1, l-b 9, n-b 7 | 17 |
| 1/4 2/5 3/58 4/66 5/88 6/99 7/171 8/191 9/202 | 202 | 1/5 2/65 3/121 4/131 5/196 (5 wkts) | 271 |

Bowling: *First Innings*—Stirling 9-2-46-1; Robertson 12-2-47-2; Snedden 8-0-23-0; Bracewell 15.1-5-48-6; Brown 3-0-24-0. *Second Innings*—Stirling 7.1-1-20-0; Robertson 10-0-40-1; Snedden 19-3-58-2; Bracewell 27-4-72-0; Brown 25-6-71-2.

Umpires: D. B. Arnott and I. D. Robinson.
(B. MacLachlan stood in place of D. B. Arnott on the second and third days.)

†At Harare, October 21. Zimbabwe won by 138 runs. Zimbabwe 279 for four (50 overs) (D. L. Houghton 119 not out, G. A. Hick 61); Young New Zealanders 141 (38 overs) (J. G. Bracewell 59; I. P. Butchart five for 41).

†At Mutare, October 24. Young New Zealanders won by eight wickets. Zimbabwe 165 (48.4 overs) (K. G. Walton 50); Young New Zealanders 169 for two (42.2 overs) (T. J. Franklin 71, K. R. Rutherford 55 not out).

## ZIMBABWE v YOUNG NEW ZEALANDERS

At Harare, October 26, 27, 28. Drawn.

### Zimbabwe

| | First innings | | Second innings | |
|---|---|---|---|---|
| K. G. Walton c Hoskin b Robertson | 10 | – | c McSweeney b Stirling | 14 |
| A. H. Shah run out | 42 | – | c Briasco b Stirling | 0 |
| R. D. Brown c Hoskin b Bracewell | 73 | – | (7) not out | 16 |
| *A. J. Pycroft c McSweeney b Robertson | 31 | – | (5) lbw b Snedden | 2 |
| †D. L. Houghton c Bracewell b Snedden | 53 | – | (4) c McEwan b Snedden | 0 |
| G. A. Hick c McSweeney b Robertson | 88 | – | (3) not out | 38 |
| D. A. G. Fletcher c Hoskin b Bracewell | 23 | | | |
| I. P. Butchart c Crowe b Snedden | 71 | – | (6) lbw b Stirling | 0 |
| A. J. Traicos not out | 37 | | | |
| P. W. E. Rawson c sub b Bracewell | 13 | | | |
| B 8, l-b 6, w 2, n-b 22 | 38 | | B 5, n-b 6 | 11 |
| 1/38 2/84 3/140 4/220 5/238 6/305 7/357 8/452 9/479 (9 wkts dec.) | 479 | | 1/3 2/45 3/46 4/48 5/56 (5 wkts dec.) | 81 |

K. G. Duers did not bat.

*In the first innings, I. P. Butchart retired hurt at 321 for six and resumed at 357 for seven.*

Bowling: *First Innings*—Stirling 23–2–78–0; Robertson 20–1–113–3; Snedden 41–12–102–2; Bracewell 39–6–172–3. *Second Innings*—Stirling 12–2–40–3; Robertson 3–0–20–0; Snedden 9–2–16–2.

### Young New Zealanders

| | First innings | | Second innings | |
|---|---|---|---|---|
| *J. J. Crowe lbw b Duers | 88 | | | |
| B. A. Edgar c Houghton b Duers | 17 | | | |
| P. S. Briasco c Fletcher b Duers | 0 | | | |
| P. E. McEwan b Hick | 90 | – | (5) not out | 17 |
| R. N. Hoskin b Duers | 5 | – | (6) not out | 2 |
| V. R. Brown c Rawson b Duers | 17 | | | |
| †E. B. McSweeney c Houghton b Duers | 9 | – | (4) c Pycroft b Traicos | 0 |
| J. G. Bracewell c Houghton b Duers | 75 | | | |
| M. C. Snedden c Duers b Hick | 28 | – | (3) c Brown b Traicos | 12 |
| D. A. Stirling not out | 26 | – | (2) c and b Hick | 45 |
| G. K. Robertson c Rawson b Duers | 0 | – | (1) c Brown b Rawson | 14 |
| L-b 2, w 4, n-b 3 | 9 | | L-b 9 | 9 |
| 1/35 2/43 3/176 4/195 5/206 6/233 7/236 8/297 9/364 | 364 | | 1/26 2/59 3/69 4/95 (4 wkts) | 99 |

Bowling: *First Innings*—Rawson 17–3–71–0; Duers 25.5–4–102–8; Fletcher 4–1–19–0; Butchart 9–2–41–0; Traicos 15–2–43–0; Hick 17–0–86–2. *Second Innings*—Rawson 6–0–29–1; Duers 4–0–30–0; Traicos 4–0–18–2; Hick 2–0–13–1.

Umpires: B. MacLachlan and I. D. Robinson.

## ENGLISH COUNTIES XI IN ZIMBABWE

†At Harare South, February 13. English Counties XI won by 49 runs. English Counties XI 211 for six (50 overs) (B. C. Broad 111 not out); Zimbabwe Country Districts XI 162 (47.3 overs) (G. A. Hick 53).

## ZIMBABWE v ENGLISH COUNTIES XI

At Harare, February 15, 16, 18. English Counties XI won by 118 runs.

### English Counties XI

| | | | |
|---|---|---|---|
| B. C. Broad c Pycroft b Streak | 64 | (6) not out | 26 |
| T. A. Lloyd b Duers | 7 | (1) c Pycroft b Streak | 50 |
| *M. C. J. Nicholas c Butchart b Rawson | 6 | b Traicos | 0 |
| V. P. Terry lbw b Butchart | 15 | (2) not out | 80 |
| R. G. Williams b Rawson | 38 | (4) c Hick b Streak | 0 |
| P. Bainbridge c and b Rawson | 46 | (5) b Butchart | 17 |
| T. M. Tremlett c Houghton b Hick | 22 | | |
| N. F. Williams not out | 62 | | |
| †R. J. Parks c Houghton b Butchart | 8 | | |
| P. G. Newman c Rawson b Traicos | 8 | | |
| N. G. B. Cook c Streak b Rawson | 10 | | |
| B 1, l-b 5, w 1, n-b 2 | 9 | L-b 2, w 1, n-b 2 | 5 |
| 1/10 2/39 3/65 4/139 5/149 6/201 7/206 8/249 9/270 | 295 | 1/86 2/89 3/90 4/129 (4 wkts dec.) | 178 |

Bowling: *First Innings*—Rawson 29.3–5–92–4; Duers 20–1–67–1; Butchart 20–4–50–2; Traicos 27–8–50–1; Hick 9–2–18–1; Streak 5–0–12–1. *Second Innings*—Rawson 9–2–32–0; Duers 8–2–21–0; Traicos 12–1–49–1; Streak 14–3–29–2; Hick 6–2–27–0; Butchart 3–0–18–1.

### Zimbabwe

| | | | |
|---|---|---|---|
| R. D. Brown c Parks b N. F. Williams | 28 | c R. G. Williams b Cook | 15 |
| G. A. Paterson c sub b Tremlett | 14 | b Cook | 27 |
| G. A. Hick c Parks b Newman | 42 | lbw b Cook | 6 |
| *A. J. Pycroft c sub b Cook | 0 | (5) lbw b Cook | 0 |
| †D. L. Houghton b Newman | 11 | (4) c Bainbridge b R. G. Williams | 55 |
| A. C. Waller not out | 60 | st Parks b R. G. Williams | 0 |
| I. P. Butchart c Tremlett b Cook | 33 | c Nicholas b R. G. Williams | 23 |
| P. W. E. Rawson c Newman b Tremlett | 20 | lbw b Cook | 4 |
| D. H. Streak (did not bat) | – | c Cook b N. F. Williams | 2 |
| A. J. Traicos (did not bat) | – | c Parks b N. F. Williams | 0 |
| K. G. Duers (did not bat) | – | not out | 0 |
| L-b 5, n-b 6 | 11 | L-b 2, n-b 3 | 5 |
| 1/30 2/67 3/68 4/96 5/103 6/156 7/219 (7 wkts dec.) | 219 | 1/34 2/47 3/54 4/54 5/59 6/114 7/119 8/135 9/135 | 137 |

Bowling: *First Innings*—N. F. Williams 20–7–54–1; Newman 9–2–30–2; Tremlett 14.1–1–51–2; Cook 30–8–48–2; Bainbridge 5–0–31–0. *Second Innings*—Newman 4–0–17–0; N. F. Williams 9–3–28–2; Cook 21–8–41–5; R. G. Williams 14.4–2–39–3; Tremlett 3–1–10–0.

†At Harare, February 17. Zimbabwe won by 56 runs. Zimbabwe 232 for eight (50 overs) (D. L. Houghton 47, G. A. Hick 41); English Counties XI 176 for eight (50 overs) (B. C. Broad 52; I. P. Butchart five for 31).

†At Kwekwe, February 20. English Counties XI won by 37 runs. English Counties XI 214 for six (50 overs) (B. C. Broad 78); Zimbabwe B 177 (48.3 overs) (E. A. Brandes 47).

†At Bulawayo, February 22, 23, 25. English Counties XI won by 129 runs. English Counties XI 338 (P. Bainbridge 147 not out, M. C. J. Nicholas 91) and 260 for five dec. (V. P. Terry 135 not out, D. B. D'Oliveira 50); Zimbabwe B 331 (M. P. Jarvis 58, E. A. Brandes 56, K. G. Walton 54, A. H. Shah 50; R. G. Williams four for 86) and 138 (R. G. Williams seven for 49).

†At Bulawayo, February 24. Zimbabwe won by four wickets. English Counties XI 252 for seven (50 overs) (V. P. Terry 77, M. C. J. Nicholas 73); Zimbabwe 258 for six (48.5 overs) (R. D. Brown 80, A. C. Waller 56).

†At Hwange, February 27. English Counties XI won by seven wickets. Zimbabwe B 184 for eight (50 overs) (C. Robertson 41; G. Monkhouse five for 44); English Counties XI 186 for three (B. C. Broad 115).

## ZIMBABWE v ENGLISH COUNTIES XI

At Harare, March 1, 2, 4. Zimbabwe won by three wickets.

### English Counties XI

| | | | |
|---|---|---|---|
| B. C. Broad c Houghton b Duers | 59 | lbw b Rawson | 0 |
| V. P. Terry run out | 129 | b Rawson | 53 |
| *M. C. J. Nicholas c Hick b Traicos | 38 | c Houghton b Rawson | 95 |
| D. B. D'Oliveira lbw b Rawson | 22 | (5) lbw b Rawson | 6 |
| P. Bainbridge c Rawson b Traicos | 0 | (4) st Houghton b Traicos | 9 |
| R. G. Williams b Duers | 15 | not out | 8 |
| N. F. Williams not out | 13 | | |
| G. Monkhouse c Houghton b Duers | 0 | | |
| †R. J. Parks c Houghton b Rawson | 0 | | |
| P. G. Newman c Hick b Duers | 1 | | |
| N. G. B. Cook c Houghton b Rawson | 0 | | |
| B 2, l-b 2, w 4, n-b 3 | 11 | L-b 1, n-b 2 | 3 |
| 1/130 2/207 3/249 4/249 5/273 6/273 7/273 8/284 9/287 | 288 | 1/0 2/103 3/118 4/142 5/174 | (5 wkts dec.) 174 |

Bowling: *First Innings*—Rawson 27–7–80–3; Duers 19–5–49–4; Butchart 14–2–48–0; Traicos 30–8–64–2; Streak 6–1–19–0; Hick 4–0–24–0. *Second Innings*—Rawson 23.4–2–70–4; Duers 7–0–34–0; Traicos 23–5–48–1; Butchart 11–2–19–0; Streak 2–1–2–0.

### Zimbabwe

| | | | |
|---|---|---|---|
| R. D. Brown c Parks b N. F. Williams | 11 | lbw b N. F. Williams | 4 |
| G. A. Paterson lbw b Cook | 76 | b Newman | 12 |
| G. A. Hick st Parks b Cook | 14 | c and b N. F. Williams | 23 |
| *A. J. Pycroft c Bainbridge b N. F. Williams | 12 | c Parks b N. F. Williams | 4 |
| †D. L. Houghton not out | 26 | c Parks b Monkhouse | 84 |
| A. C. Waller c Terry b N. F. Williams | 0 | b Cook | 75 |
| I. P. Butchart c Terry b N. F. Williams | 0 | not out | 49 |
| P. W. E. Rawson c Parks b Monkhouse | 17 | c Cook b Monkhouse | 0 |
| D. H. Streak b N. F. Williams | 2 | not out | 21 |
| A. J. Traicos c Parks b N. F. Williams | 0 | | |
| K. G. Duers b N. F. Williams | 0 | | |
| L-b 1, n-b 19 | 20 | B 3, l-b 6, n-b 7 | 16 |
| 1/40 2/85 3/123 4/132 5/132 6/132 7/171 8/178 9/178 | 178 | 1/16 2/20 3/45 4/50 5/213 6/213 7/214 | (7 wkts) 288 |

Bowling: *First Innings*—N. F. Williams 18–3–55–7; Newman 9–0–37–0; Monkhouse 13–4–33–1; Cook 16–4–34–2; R. G. Williams 6–2–18–0. *Second Innings*—N. F. Williams 13–0–64–3; Newman 5–0–36–1; Cook 23.3–6–76–1; Monkhouse 10–0–60–2; R. G. Williams 6–0–34–0; Nicholas 2–0–9–0.

†At Harare, March 3. Zimbabwe won by seven wickets. English Counties XI 149 for eight (50 overs) (D. B. D'Oliveira 63; P. W. E. Rawson five for 33); Zimbabwe 150 for three (45.2 overs) (R. D. Brown 75).

†At Mutare, March 6. English Counties XI won by 71 runs. English Counties XI 255 for nine (50 overs) (B. C. Broad 76, M. C. J. Nicholas 56); Zimbabwe B 184 (C. A. P. Hodgson 68, D. L. Houghton 41).

†At Harare, March 9. Zimbabwe won by 29 runs. Zimbabwe 202 for six (50 overs) (G. A. Hick 61, R. D. Brown 49); English Counties XI 173 for nine (50 overs) (V. P. Terry 48).

†At Harare, March 10. Zimbabwe won by 76 runs. Zimbabwe 243 for nine (D. L. Houghton 76, A. J. Pycroft 53, A. H. Shah 40); English Counties XI 167 (47.4 overs) (M. C. J. Nicholas 42; G. A. Hick four for 32).

# CRICKET IN CANADA, 1985

By KENNETH R. BULLOCK

The 1985 season was the busiest in the history of Canadian cricket at the senior level. It opened early with the first Atlantic Triangular Tournament, hosted by Bermuda on May 24, 25, 26, with Bermuda, Canada and the United States participating. Play was restricted to 50 overs a side. Canada defeated the USA by 56 runs (224 for nine to 168 all out) in the first match. The second match, between Bermuda and the USA, was rained off when Bermuda had made 25 for one in reply to the USA's 202 for seven. In the final match Canada surprised a crowd of 1,500 by making 201 off 50 overs, recovering from 66 for five, and then bowling Bermuda out for 113. Thus Canada won the Sir Henry Tucker Trophy, emblematic of a new regional competition for Associate Members of the International Cricket Conference.

In July, Bermuda hosted the sixth International Youth Festival, for the first time, with the usual participants – Bermuda, Canada, Denmark, England North, England South, the Netherlands and Ireland. The tournament was won for the second time by Bermuda. Canada completed its first competition without a win, although the side played better than the results indicated and the tournament provided the best competition available at the under-nineteen level.

In August a national senior event was held in North York, Ontario, with all matches being played at the relatively new site of Ross Lord Park. The event was designed to bring the best 52 players in the country together for a week of training and competition. They were divided into four sides – Canada West (seven from British Columbia and six from Alberta), Canada East (seven from Quebec and six from Manitoba), Ontario West (eleven from Ontario and two from Saskatchewan), and Ontario East (eleven from Ontario and two from Nova Scotia). Ontario East and Ontario West each won twice and lost once in the round-robin phase before facing each other in the final, which was won by Ontario East. Farooq Kirmani, Canada's captain, won the batting title and F. Waithe the bowling title. The final three days of the week were taken up with the 63rd match in the series between the USA and Canada, which resulted in a draw, Canada thus retaining the K. Auty Trophy. The USA scored 242 for seven declared and 165 for eight, thereby only narrowly avoiding an innings defeat, in reply to Canada's record score of 437 for eight declared.

In September MCC visited Canada for the first time since 1967, their tour lasting from September 9 to September 30, beginning in Victoria and ending in Toronto. Altogether, they played twelve matches, won eight, drew four and lost none. One of the four drawn matches was rained off after six overs. Only British Columbia CA, Ottawa Valley-Quebec, and Toronto and District CA of the provincial or league sides gave MCC much trouble. In the match between Canada and MCC, records galore were accumulated, attractive cricket was enjoyed by the crowds, and in the end Canada attained an honourable draw. In three days 1,142 runs were scored while only fifteen wickets fell. Three centuries and two fifties were scored for MCC, and five fifties for Canada. It was good to have MCC back and it is everyone's hope that the next tour will be not too far off.

The Canadian Cricket Association held its semi-annual meeting in Toronto in April and its Annual General Meeting in Vancouver in November. Jack Kyle was re-elected President for his eighth term. Umpiring certification continued to be a most successful programme with the number of certified umpires reaching 450. Junior cricket continued to receive high priority, new programmes being initiated, most significantly in Ontario.

## CANADA v USA

At North York, Ontario, August 9, 10, 11. Drawn. Canada retained the K. Auty Trophy which they have held since 1979. USA won the toss and chose to bat on a placid pitch of matting on fine shale at Ross Lord Park, a relatively new public park in the city of North York, a borough of metropolitan Toronto. From the outset the visitors batted with caution before declaring at 242 for seven and leaving Canada seventeen minutes batting, in which Jack and Bagot put on 10 runs. The second day saw Canada reach 106 for no wicket by lunch. USA's total was passed by Budhoo and Kirmani with only four wickets down and Canada ended the day at 356 for six. Somewhat surprisingly, they elected to continue batting on the last day, adding 81 in an hour before closing their innings at a record score of 437 for eight, 195 runs ahead. By mid-afternoon Canada appeared set for an innings victory, USA being 99 for five with the spinners, Waithe and Etwaroo, in control. However, USA batted out time to finish at 165 for eight, still 30 runs behind. Canada's batting seemed to augur well for the future.

### USA

| | | | |
|---|---|---|---|
| J. Cummings c Abraham b Etwaroo | 25 | c Bagot b Abraham | 24 |
| N. Lashkari c M. Prashad b Waithe | 19 | run out | 3 |
| O. Durity not out | 87 | c M. Prashad b Waithe | 17 |
| K. Khan c Etwaroo b Neblett | 39 | (5) c Abraham b Neblett | 25 |
| †S. Smith c Jack b Etwaroo | 23 | (4) c Budhoo b Etwaroo | 17 |
| *H. Gordon c Waithe b Etwaroo | 0 | (9) not out | 11 |
| R. Ramlall c P. Prashad b Waithe | 5 | (6) c Waithe b Neblett | 10 |
| G. Foster b Abraham | 19 | (7) c Budhoo b Abraham | 26 |
| R. Mennon not out | 12 | | |
| T. Mills (did not bat) | | (8) b Waithe | 21 |
| B 6, w 3, n-b 4 | 13 | B 3, w 5, n-b 3 | 11 |
| 1/39 2/53 3/133 4/161 5/162 6/174 7/224 | (7 wkts dec.) 242 | 1/17 2/33 3/53 4/81 5/99 6/109 7/139 8/155 | (8 wkts) 165 |

K. Lorrick did not bat.

Bowling: *First Innings*—Clarkson 8–2–38–0; Abraham 14–3–45–1; Etwaroo 25–3–71–3; Waithe 28–7–53–2; Neblett 6–1–19–1; M. Prashad 4–0–10–0. *Second Innings*—Abraham 14–2–24–2; Neblett 8–0–34–2; Clarkson 10–1–28–0; Waithe 20–8–30–2; Etwaroo 16–3–46–1.

### Canada

| | |
|---|---|
| E. Jack c Mills b Khan | 57 |
| †D. Bagot b Khan | 57 |
| P. Prashad c Durity b Mennon | 28 |
| M. Prashad c Mennon b Khan | 10 |
| G. Budhoo c and b Khan | 79 |
| *F. Kirmani c Smith b Lorrick | 51 |
| C. Neblett not out | 86 |
| D. Etwaroo c Lashkari b Khan | 21 |
| M. Clarkson c Mennon b Mills | 13 |
| D. Abraham not out | 1 |
| B 3, l-b 11, w 3, n-b 17 | 34 |
| 1/130 2/151 3/151 4/219 5/275 6/342 7/407 8/429 | (8 wkts dec.) 437 |

F. Waithe did not bat.

Bowling: Mennon 18–3–54–1; Lorrick 19–4–51–1; Gordon 14–5–37–0; Foster 15–1–47–0; Mills 14–3–64–1; Ramlall 9–0–37–0; Khan 38–10–133–5.

## MCC IN CANADA, 1985

For the sixth time this century, MCC sent a team to Canada in September, 1985. The previous tour had been in 1967. The side, which was managed by Lt-Col. J. R. Stephenson, consisted of: N. E. J. Pocock (*captain*), R. W. Tolchard (*vice-captain*), J. Cumbes, F. L. Q. Handley, S. P. Henderson, T. J. Hopper, N. J. Kemp, P. J. Kippax, R. J. Lanchbury, P. J. Lewington, R. V. Lewis, W. G. Merry and D. Wilson.

In nineteen days 3,000 miles were covered and twelve matches played, including one of three days against Canada. Eight of the matches were won and four drawn. The steady bowling of the three experienced spinners – Kippax, Lewington and Wilson – was a feature of the tour. Henderson, who played in all the matches, headed the batting averages, though the outstanding innings was played by Lanchbury, whose 160 not out was the highest score ever made by an Englishman against Canada.

At Victoria, September 11. MCC won by 109 runs. MCC 219 for five dec. (R. V. Lewis 103, R. J. Lanchbury 61); Victoria & District XI 110 (P. J. Kippax five for 23).

At Vancouver, September 13. MCC won by 98 runs. MCC 204 for two dec. (F. L. Q. Handley 121, R. W. Tolchard 52 not out); British Columbia Mainland League 106 (D. Wilson five for 14).

At Vancouver, September 14. Drawn. MCC 124 (N. J. Kemp 59); British Columbia Cricket Association 123 for nine.

At Calgary, September 15. MCC won by eight wickets. Calgary & District XI 124; MCC 125 for two (R. V. Lewis 60).

At Edmonton, September 17. MCC won by 105 runs. MCC 241 (R. J. Lanchbury 100, S. P. Henderson 52; J. Hussein five for 38); Edmonton & District XI 136 (D. Wailoo 40; P. J. Lewington five for 50).

At Winnipeg, September 18. MCC won by 107 runs. MCC 271 for six (40 overs) (N. J. Kemp 115, S. P. Henderson 81, R. W. Tolchard 40 not out); Manitoba Cricket League 164 for nine (40 overs) (G. Boodoo 66, O. Dipchand 53).

At Toronto, September 20, 21, 22. Drawn. MCC 336 for two dec. (R. V. Lewis 131 not out, S. P. Henderson 100 not out, R. J. Lanchbury 59) and 300 for three dec. (R. J. Lanchbury 160, R. V. Lewis 64, F. L. Q. Handley 42); Canada 337 for six dec. (E. Jack 86, R. S. A. Jayasekera 65, D. Bagot 59, B. Singh 54) and 169 for four (F. Kirmani 93 not out).

At Ottawa, September 24. Drawn. MCC 156 (C. Henry five for 42); Quebec & Ottawa 73 for nine (P. J. Kippax four for 8).

At Toronto, September 26. Drawn when the match was abandoned owing to rain. MCC 24 for no wkt v Toronto CC.

At Toronto, September 27. MCC won by 43 runs. MCC 175 for eight (35 overs) (S. P. Henderson 65); Ontario Under-25 XI 132 for seven (35 overs) (P. Prashad 48).

At Cambridge, Ontario, September 28. MCC won by nine wickets. Hamilton & District XI 74 (D. Wilson four for 9); MCC 75 for one (F. L. Q. Handley 46 not out).

At Toronto, September 29. MCC won by 40 runs. MCC 230 for six (45 overs) (N. J. Kemp 59, F. L. Q. Handley 45); Toronto & District XI 190 for nine (45 overs) (C. Neblett 58).

---

## CANCELLED TOUR

Suspicions that sabotage was the cause of the crash of an Air India plane off Ireland in June 1985, with the loss of over 300 lives, prompted an Indian team, led by S. M. Gavaskar, to cancel a proposed tour of Canada. The ill-fated aircraft had been on a flight from Canada to India.

# WOMEN'S CRICKET, 1985

By NETTA RHEINBERG

The 1985 season was much interrupted by the weather, which badly affected most of the major fixtures, the county programme, and also the annual Cricket Week at Colwall, which nevertheless still attracted many players, young and old, from far and wide.

As with other sports organisations, volunteers to fill top administration positions in the Women's Cricket Association are hard to find, though the membership does not lack able and efficient personnel. Again helped by sponsorship, much attention has been given to junior cricket, and some of the youngsters coming along are, to quote an authoritative source, "frighteningly good". This bodes well for the future, especially after the disappointment of a lost Test series in Australia.

There has been a general move among other countries where women play the game to forge closer links with men's cricket. However, this is being regarded with caution in England where, as far as administration is concerned, women's cricket has always been controlled by women, although it has not been forgotten that, in many other aspects of the game, our men colleagues have given us a great deal of help and encouragement. After 60 years of existence, the WCA still has its problems, the main two being sponsorship and the media. How can women cricketers obtain sufficient publicity of the right kind, and how can sponsors be attracted? These are questions for which the administrators of women's cricket in England need to find an answer.

## ENGLAND WOMEN IN AUSTRALIA, 1984-85

The Margaret Peden Memorial Test Series, named after one of the renowned founder members of the Australian Women's Cricket Council, marked the 50th year of Test matches between the two countries and was commemorated by two special functions – an inaugural dinner at Perth and, at the end of the tour, a Golden Jubilee Dinner held in the Members' Dining-Room of the Melbourne Cricket Club.

England's performance, losing the rubber for only the second time in nine Test series, was a disappointment considering that the team contained much promise and talent. However, Australia, two-one victors in the five-Test series, proved to be the better side, bowling more consistently and not suffering, as England did, from a middle-order batting weakness. Nevertheless, the batting of both teams appeared over-cautious, an attitude that may have been induced by the lengthening of Test matches from three to four days' duration. Much of England's bowling lacked aggression, and a fast bowler was much needed. Furthermore, owing to the pressurised nature of the tour, coupled with the heat, England's players showed signs of tiredness halfway through the series. This showed in their defeat in all three limited-overs internationals.

Janette Brittin was named Player of the Series with a Test average of 42.90 in ten innings, closely followed by Jill Kennare of Australia, with 38.55 in nine innings. To commemorate the fifth Test at Bendigo, Kennare, named the Player of the Match, was presented with a gold nugget pendant, a suitable gesture following the award of gold pieces to all players in the first-ever women's cricket match played in Australia on this ground in 1874.

Jan Southgate, England's captain, aged 30, and Raelee Thompson, Australia's captain in place of the injured Sharon Tredrea, have both since announced their retirement.

## AUSTRALIA v ENGLAND

### First Test Match

At Perth, December 13, 14, 15, 16. Drawn. England, after winning the toss, were in trouble shortly after lunch at 93 for three, but Court came to the rescue with effective if unorthodox batting. At 263 for six England's position, helped by three dropped catches, looked good, but on the second day Fullston removed the tailenders cheaply. Australia began solidly and proved difficult to dislodge, both Kennare and Emerson showing considerable ability. England, with a lead of 39, set about consolidating, though Brittin, whose maiden Test century took her 135 minutes, might have hoped for more help from her colleagues. England's declaration set Australia a target of 281 but hopes of a victory were foiled by Kennare, whose 103, scored in 167 minutes, made her the sixth Australian to score a century in 50 years of England-Australia Test cricket.

### England

| First innings | | Second innings | |
|---|---|---|---|
| M. Lear b Tredrea | 5 | b Thompson | 23 |
| C. Hodges c Matthews b Wilson | 34 | c Dawson b Wilson | 6 |
| J. Brittin c Kennare b Fullston | 44 | b Thompson | 112 |
| *J. Southgate c Verco b Thompson | 22 | b Martin | 38 |
| J. Court c Jacobs b Wilson | 90 | c Price b Thompson | 12 |
| C. Watmough c Matthews b Thompson | 46 | c Tredrea b Thompson | 8 |
| †J. Edney c Verco b Fullston | 24 | c Verco b Wilson | 0 |
| J. Aspinall c Thompson b Fullston | 11 | not out | 30 |
| H. Stother c Verco b Fullston | 3 | c Matthews b Wilson | 0 |
| G. McConway b Martin | 0 | run out | 2 |
| A. Starling not out | 0 | not out | 4 |
| B 5, l-b 4, w 1, n-b 1 | 11 | B 4, l-b 2, n-b 1 | 7 |
| 1/9 2/81 3/93 4/148 5/226 6/263 7/282 8/287 9/288 | 290 | 1/22 2/65 3/171 4/188 5/204 6/205 7/209 8/215 9/218 (9 wkts dec.) | 242 |

Bowling: *First Innings*—Wilson 23–1–90–2; Tredrea 19–4–44–1; Martin 21–9–34–1; Thompson 27–9–50–2; Fullston 40.1–16–61–4; Verco 1–0–2–0. *Second Innings*—Wilson 20–12–25–3; Martin 17–10–28–1; Thompson 20–6–47–4; Jacobs 4–1–18–0; Verco 12–3–27–0; Fullston 32–5–91–0.

### Australia

| First innings | | Second innings | |
|---|---|---|---|
| P. Verco run out | 36 | run out | 9 |
| D. Emerson b Court | 84 | run out | 20 |
| J. Kennare c McConway b Aspinall | 56 | c Brittin b Stother | 103 |
| T. Dawson c Lear b McConway | 3 | run out | 20 |
| J. Jacobs lbw b Aspinall | 5 | c Edney b Stother | 11 |
| L. Fullston c Court b Starling | 21 | c Hodges b Starling | 3 |
| *S. Tredrea c Lear b Stother | 14 | c Edney b Starling | 27 |
| R. Thompson c Edney b Stother | 5 | not out | 4 |
| †C. Matthews b Starling | 12 | c Hodges b McConway | 3 |
| D. Wilson b Starling | 5 | | |
| D. Martin not out | 0 | not out | 0 |
| B 2, l-b 2, n-b 6 | 10 | B 1, l-b 2, n-b 6 | 9 |
| 1/97 2/157 3/160 4/174 5/200 6/217 7/228 8/242 9/247 | 251 | 1/28 2/38 3/51 4/79 5/91 6/195 7/198 8/201 (8 wkts) | 209 |

Bowling: *First Innings*—Aspinall 17–6–48–2; Starling 32–18–40–3; McConway 25–10–41–1; Stother 14.3–3–43–2; Hodges 13–4–24–0; Brittin 10–5–23–0; Court 7–0–28–1. *Second Innings*—Aspinall 4–1–10–0; Starling 21–10–47–2; McConway 20–8–34–1; Stother 13–3–44–2; Hodges 17–4–42–0; Brittin 3–0–20–0; Court 2–0–9–0.

Umpires: P. J. McConnell and D. G. Weser.

## AUSTRALIA v ENGLAND

### Second Test Match

At Adelaide, December 21, 22, 23, 24. England won by 5 runs. England again won the toss and batted, but a fine spell of bowling by Price, replacing Australia's injured captain, Tredrea, led to the innings folding in just over three hours. Watmough batted for 68 minutes without scoring. By the close Australia were within 7 of England's total with only one wicket down, Emerson, sister of T. M. Alderman, hitting an unbeaten 53. On the second day, she went on to 121 and, despite steady bowling by the left-arm spinner, McConway, Australia built a lead of 171. Solid scoring by England saw them to 279 for eight by the close of the third day, but they added only 17 on the fourth day, leaving Australia to score 126 to win. Contrary to all expectations Australia collapsed spectacularly, losing five wickets for 6 runs in three-quarters of an hour, and Price's half-century could not prevent England's victory in an exciting finish.

### England

| | | | |
|---|---|---|---|
| M. Lear lbw b Price | 7 | lbw b Price | 26 |
| C. Hodges b Price | 13 | c Verco b Fullston | 44 |
| J. Brittin c Fullston b Thompson | 22 | c and b Fullston | 15 |
| *J. Southgate c and b Fullston | 4 | lbw b Thompson | 25 |
| J. Court b Thompson | 6 | c Matthews b Thompson | 28 |
| C. Watmough c Emerson b Jacobs | 0 | c and b Wilson | 70 |
| †J. Edney c Thompson b Wilson | 4 | c Matthews b Fullston | 50 |
| J. Aspinall c Fellows b Price | 13 | c Price b Wilson | 20 |
| H. Stother lbw b Price | 0 | b Fullston | 2 |
| G. McConway not out | 3 | b Wilson | 8 |
| A. Starling b Jacobs | 6 | not out | 3 |
| B 2, w 1 | 3 | B 3, l-b 1, w 1 | 5 |
| 1/20 2/37 3/47 4/53 5/53 6/57 7/70 8/70 9/70 | 91 | 1/61 2/84 3/87 4/135 5/150 6/233 7/273 8/279 9/293 | 296 |

Bowling: *First Innings*—Wilson 15–4–32–1; Price 17–7–22–4; Thompson 10–4–16–2; Fullston 15–7–13–1; Jacobs 10.4–5–6–2. *Second Innings*—Wilson 27.1–10–45–3; Thompson 21–9–19–2; Jacobs 20–4–63–0; Fullston 54–21–96–4; Verco 8–3–13–0; Price 41.1–21–46–1.

### Australia

| | | | |
|---|---|---|---|
| P. Verco c Edney b McConway | 29 | lbw b Starling | 2 |
| D. Emerson c Brittin b Starling | 121 | c Hodges b Starling | 1 |
| L. Fullston c Hodges b Brittin | 29 | lbw b Aspinall | 28 |
| J. Kennare lbw b Brittin | 0 | b McConway | 0 |
| T. Dawson c Southgate b McConway | 0 | lbw b Brittin | 4 |
| J. Jacobs c and b Hodges | 11 | c Southgate b Starling | 0 |
| A. Fellows c McConway b Stother | 25 | c Hodges b McConway | 0 |
| K. Price b Stother | 39 | c Hodges b Starling | 51 |
| *R. Thompson st Edney b McConway | 0 | c Lear b McConway | 13 |
| †C. Matthews b McConway | 0 | c Edney b Starling | 9 |
| D. Wilson not out | 0 | not out | 1 |
| B 1, l-b 6, w 1 | 8 | B 4, l-b 3, n-b 4 | 11 |
| 1/80 2/147 3/147 4/148 5/164 6/214 7/233 8/242 9/250 | 262 | 1/2 2/4 3/4 4/4 5/6 6/73 7/96 8/96 9/110 | 120 |

Bowling: *First Innings*—Aspinall 12–1–39–0; Starling 20–4–48–1; McConway 27–12–32–4; Hodges 16–5–26–1; Court 17–3–52–0; Stother 12–4–43–2; Brittin 15–7–15–2. *Second Innings*—Starling 16.5–6–36–5; McConway 21–10–35–3; Stother 5–3–7–0; Hodges 8–3–12–0; Aspinall 7–2–11–1; Brittin 8–2–12–1.

Umpires: P. J. McConnell and A. R. Crafter.

## AUSTRALIA v ENGLAND

### Third Test Match

At Brisbane, January 1, 2, 3, 4. Drawn. England, winning the toss for the third time, again batted and were criticised for their cautious approach, their 275 taking nearly eight hours. However, following a torrential downpour 24 hours before the start of play, batting was not easy. Australia declared late on the third day, and on the fourth England plodded on to 204 for seven, Hodges taking 242 minutes over her 95. Larson, a leg-spinner and one of Australia's three changes, bowled consistently for her six wickets in the match.

### England

| | | | |
|---|---|---|---|
| J. Brittin b Verco | 36 | c Larson b Wilson | 39 |
| M. Lear b Wilson | 22 | b Thompson | 0 |
| C. Hodges run out | 32 | b Larson | 95 |
| *J. Southgate c Larson b Reeler | 74 | lbw b Verco | 39 |
| J. Court c Emerson b Larson | 6 | | |
| C. Watmough c and b Reeler | 17 | c Reeler b Larson | 1 |
| †J. Edney b Larson | 47 | not out | 16 |
| J. Aspinall b Wilson | 18 | b Thompson | 8 |
| H. Stother b Larson | 10 | c Emerson b Verco | 3 |
| G. McConway not out | 5 | not out | 2 |
| A. Starling hit wkt b Larson | 3 | | |
| B 4, l-b 1 | 5 | B 1 | 1 |
| 1/53 2/62 3/126 4/134 5/166 6/205 7/249 8/265 9/267 | 275 | 1/2 2/17 3/94 4/179 5/181 6/190 7/200 | (7 wkts) 204 |

Bowling: *First Innings*—Wilson 28–9–55–2; Price 23–9–42–0; Thompson 15–7–39–0; Verco 26–10–35–1; Keeler 15–8–27–2; Fullston 24–8–39–0; Larson 21–9–33–4. *Second Innings*—Price 5–1–8–0; Thompson 15–6–25–2; Verco 20–9–32–2; Fullston 23–9–36–0; Wilson 12–3–32–1; Larson 29–16–40–2; Reeler 6–2–18–0; Kennare 10–5–12–0.

### Australia

| | |
|---|---|
| P. Verco c Lear b Starling | 42 |
| D. Emerson b Stother | 84 |
| J. Kennare lbw b Stother | 17 |
| L. Reeler b McConway | 59 |
| W. Napier c Lear b Starling | 9 |
| L. Larson c Hodges b Starling | 52 |
| L. Fullston c Starling b Hodges | 13 |
| K. Price c Brittin b Starling | 18 |
| *R. Thompson lbw b Stother | 2 |
| †C. Matthews not out | 8 |
| D. Wilson not out | 7 |
| B 6, l-b 5, n-b 4 | 15 |
| 1/69 2/133 3/152 4/178 5/250 6/281 7/295 8/308 9/313 | (9 wkts dec.) 326 |

Bowling: Aspinall 16–3–38–0; Starling 36–18–50–4; Stother 33–11–58–3; Hodges 30–8–73–1; McConway 35–12–63–1; Brittin 16–3–33–0.

Umpires: J. King and C. D. Timmins.

## AUSTRALIA v ENGLAND

### Fourth Test Match

At Gosford, January 12, 13, 14, 15. Australia won by 117 runs. England won the toss for the fourth time and in perfect conditions put Australia in, hoping that in this coastal town the ball would move about early on. Their strategy failed and Australia, batting cautiously, scored 232 for eight by the close. Emerson and Verco established an Australian first-wicket Test record of 114. England struggled against the left-arm seam bowling of Martin, replacing Price who was injured, and despite Brittin's determined effort, Australia were batting again soon after tea. It took them until tea on the third day to reach 153 for nine, whereupon Thompson's declaration set England 246 to win in a little over seven hours. Once again, though, Australia's bowlers dictated the innings, and the match finished in mid-afternoon on the fourth day after England's last seven wickets had fallen for 26 runs.

### Australia

| | | | |
|---|---|---|---|
| P. Verco c Edney b Hodges | 48 | – lbw b Starling | 24 |
| D. Emerson c and b Hodges | 58 | – st Edney b McConway | 19 |
| J. Kennare c Court b McConway | 25 | – run out | 0 |
| L. Reeler lbw b Starling | 34 | – c Hodges b Starling | 7 |
| W. Napier c Edney b Aspinall | 3 | – c Hodges b Aspinall | 9 |
| L. Larson not out | 28 | – lbw b Stother | 10 |
| *R. Thompson lbw b Court | 9 | – not out | 24 |
| †C. Matthews lbw b McConway | 6 | – b Starling | 19 |
| D. Martin b McConway | 8 | – b Stother | 17 |
| L. Fullston (did not bat) | | – c Court b Starling | 8 |
| D. Wilson (did not bat) | | – not out | 12 |
| B 3, l-b 2, w 3, n-b 5 | 13 | B 1, l-b 1, n-b 2 | 4 |
| 1/114 2/117 3/149 4/170 5/185 6/202 7/220 8/232 | (8 wkts dec.) 232 | 1/35 2/37 3/51 4/60 5/61 6/80 7/99 8/99 9/129 | (9 wkts dec.) 153 |

Bowling: *First Innings*—Aspinall 12–5–25–1; Starling 29–12–43–1; Stother 11–5–29–0; McConway 26–10–39–3; Court 16–1–61–1; Hodges 8–1–20–2; Brittin 8–2–10–0. *Second Innings*—McConway 27–16–27–1; Starling 26–10–57–4; Hodges 16–5–33–0; Stother 17–9–24–2; Aspinall 9–6–10–1.

### England

| | | | |
|---|---|---|---|
| J. Brittin lbw b Verco | 45 | – b Martin | 65 |
| M. Lear b Wilson | 20 | – c Verco b Wilson | 2 |
| C. Hodges b Verco | 1 | – b Martin | 5 |
| *J. Southgate b Martin | 7 | – c Thompson b Fullston | 12 |
| J. Court b Wilson | 8 | – st Matthews b Fullston | 27 |
| C. Watmough c and b Fullston | 16 | – c Fullston b Thompson | 0 |
| †J. Edney b Martin | 3 | – b Verco | 0 |
| J. Aspinall not out | 28 | – c Martin b Wilson | 4 |
| H. Stother lbw b Martin | 0 | – c Matthews b Fullston | 4 |
| G. McConway b Martin | 0 | – st Matthews b Fullston | 3 |
| A. Starling c Reeler b Fullston | 9 | – not out | 1 |
| L-b 2, n-b 1 | 3 | B 4, l-b 1 | 5 |
| 1/66 2/66 3/67 4/76 5/93 6/103 7/103 8/103 9/103 | 140 | 1/7 2/19 3/48 4/102 5/107 6/108 7/114 8/120 9/127 | 128 |

Bowling: *First Innings*—Wilson 15–5–32–2; Martin 19–8–24–4; Thompson 11–7–9–0; Larson 7–2–20–0; Fullston 15.1–6–30–2; Verco 14–8–23–2. *Second Innings*—Wilson 22–9–29–2; Martin 26–20–12–2; Thompson 16–9–17–1; Fullston 25–8–53–4; Verco 17–9–12–1.

Umpires: A. Gray and A. Debnam.

## AUSTRALIA v ENGLAND

### Fifth Test Match

At Bendigo, January 25, 26, 27, 28. Australia won by seven wickets. England gave a tired performance in a match played in hot and exhausting conditions. Batting first on an easy wicket after again winning the toss, they began confidently, but Thompson, the Australian captain, bowling medium fast, produced her best Test performance and at the end of the day England were all out for 196. On the second day Australia celebrated National Day by scoring 228 for four, and they declared with a lead of 89 at 285 for eight on the third, when Kennare completed her second century of the series. This same day brought further troubles for England when Brittin and Hodges both went to unnecessary run-outs. England's slow scoring in the second innings caused heckling from the spectators, and a total of 204 was not enough to challenge the Australians, who were left to score 116 to win in 59 overs. Three Australian and two English players, as well as one of the umpires, suffered from stomach upsets on the fourth day, and the Australians fielded three substitutes, while a substitute umpire officiated.

### England

| | | | |
|---|---|---|---|
| J. Brittin c Reeler b Thompson | 16 | – run out | 35 |
| M. Lear lbw b Martin | 28 | – b Verco | 18 |
| C. Hodges b Martin | 39 | – run out | 0 |
| *J. Southgate c and b Thompson | 59 | – b Wilson | 26 |
| J. Court c Larson b Thompson | 5 | – b Wilson | 41 |
| J. Powell b Fullston | 13 | – c Wilson b Fullston | 27 |
| †J. Edney b Thompson | 19 | – c Martin b Verco | 17 |
| J. Aspinall b Thompson | 0 | – b Wilson | 0 |
| H. Stother b Larson | 5 | – lbw b Fullston | 20 |
| G. McConway c and b Fullston | 4 | – not out | 8 |
| A. Starling not out | 0 | – b Verco | 4 |
| B 5, l-b 2, w 1 | 8 | B 6, l-b 2 | 8 |
| 1/28 2/71 3/88 4/98 5/139 6/182 7/184 8/187 9/196 | 196 | 1/48 2/54 3/66 4/93 5/131 6/158 7/158 8/190 9/192 | 204 |

Bowling: *First Innings*—Wilson 16–1–44–0; Martin 23–9–37–2; Thompson 28–12–33–5; Fullston 24.1–12–31–2; Larson 10–0–29–1; Verco 8–1–15–0. *Second Innings*—Wilson 20–9–40–3; Martin 24–14–24–0; Thompson 25–17–28–0; Fullston 38–17–57–2; Verco 24.4–12–30–3; Larson 6–3–8–0; Reeler 1–0–7–0; Kennare 3–1–2–0.

### Australia

| | | | |
|---|---|---|---|
| P. Verco c Starling b Hodges | 40 | – b Brittin | 40 |
| D. Emerson lbw b Stother | 43 | – b Stother | 23 |
| J. Kennare run out | 104 | – run out | 42 |
| L. Reeler c Edney b Aspinall | 17 | – not out | 4 |
| K. Read c Edney b Starling | 21 | – not out | 5 |
| L. Larson lbw b McConway | 25 | | |
| *R. Thompson run out | 0 | | |
| L. Fullston c Hodges b McConway | 15 | | |
| †C. Matthews not out | 0 | | |
| B 11, l-b 2, w 2, n-b 5 | 20 | W 1, n-b 3 | 4 |
| 1/90 2/90 3/116 4/181 5/263 6/263 7/284 8/285 | (8 wkts dec.) 285 | 1/47 2/108 3/108 | (3 wkts) 118 |

D. Martin and D. Wilson did not bat.

Bowling: *First Innings*—Aspinall 17–7–39–1; Starling 23–7–70–1; McConway 28.1–13–52–2; Stother 25–6–63–1; Hodges 22–9–36–1; Brittin 7–2–12–0. *Second Innings*—McConway 20–8–30–0; Starling 14–3–40–0; Stother 11–2–22–1; Hodges 2–0–15–0; Brittin 3–1–11–1.

Umpires: M. Gandy and A. Nicosia
(Mr Daykin stood on the fourth day as A. Nicosia was unwell).

## AUSTRALIA v ENGLAND

### First One-day International

At South Melbourne, January 31. Australia won by 6 runs. Australia 169 for six (60 overs) (D. Emerson 70); England 163 (59.2 overs) (J. Brittin 73, C. Hodges 49).

### Second One-day International

At Aberfeldie Park, Melbourne, February 2. Australia won by 138 runs. Australia 253 (59 overs) (J. Kennare 122, D. Emerson 84; J. Aspinall four for 48); England 115 (47.1 overs).

### Third One-day International

At Melbourne, February 3. Australia won by nine wickets. England 157 (60 overs) (J. Court 45); Australia 158 for one (45.5 overs) (J. Kennare 100 not out, D. Emerson 84).

---

## ADDRESSES OF REPRESENTATIVE BODIES

INTERNATIONAL CRICKET CONFERENCE: J. A. Bailey, Lord's Ground, London NW8 8QN.

ENGLAND: Cricket Council, D. B. Carr, Lord's Ground, London NW8 8QN.

AUSTRALIA: Australian Cricket Board, D. L. Richards, 70 Jolimont Street, Jolimont, Victoria 3002.

WEST INDIES: West Indies Cricket Board of Control, G. S. Camacho, 8B Caledonia Avenue, Kingston 5, Jamaica.

INDIA: Board of Control for Cricket in India, R. S. Mahendra, Vijay Nagar Colony, Bhiwani 125021.

NEW ZEALAND: New Zealand Cricket Council, G. T. Dowling, PO Box 958, Christchurch.

PAKISTAN: Board of Control for Cricket in Pakistan, Lt-Col. Rafi Nasim, Gaddafi Stadium, Lahore.

SRI LANKA: Board of Control for Cricket in Sri Lanka, Nuski Mohamed, 35 Maitland Place, Colombo 7.

SOUTH AFRICA: South African Cricket Union, Dennis Carlstein, PO Box 55009, Northlands 2116, Transvaal.
South African Cricket Board, A. I. Mangera, PO Box 54059, Vrededorp 2141, Transvaal.

ARGENTINA: Argentine Cricket Association, R. H. Gooding, c/o The English Club, 25 de Mayo 586, 1002 Buenos Aires.

BANGLADESH: Bangladesh Cricket Control Board, Syed Ashraful Huq, The Stadium, Dacca.

BERMUDA: Bermuda Cricket Board of Control, C. W. Butterfield, PO Box 992, Hamilton.

CANADA: Canadian Cricket Association, K. R. Bullock, PO Box 1364, Brockville, Ontario, Canada K6V 5Y6.

DENMARK: Danish Cricket Association, Lars Kruse, Vedelsgade 12, PO Box 13, DK-4180 Soroe.

EAST AFRICA: East African Cricket Conference, S. Patel, PO Box 71712, Ndola, Zambia.

FIJI: Fiji Cricket Association, P. I. Knight, PO Box 300, Suva.

GIBRALTAR: Gibraltar Cricket Association, T. J. Finlayson, 21 Sandpits House, Withams Road.

HONG KONG: Hong Kong Cricket Association, S. K. Sipahimalani, Centre for Media Resources, University of Hong Kong, Knowles Bldg, Pokfulam Road.

ISRAEL: Israel Cricket Association, G. Kandeli, 35/7 Minz Street, Petach Tiqua.

KENYA: Kenya Cricket Association, K. G. Purohit, PO Box 46480, Nairobi.

MALAYSIA: Malaysian Cricket Association, K. Sivanesan, c/o Perbadanan Kemajuan, Negeri Selangor, Persiaran, P. Jaya, Selangor.

NETHERLANDS: Royal Netherlands Cricket Association, Hon. Secretary, Willem de Zwijgerlaan 96A, The Hague.

PAPUA NEW GUINEA: Papua New Guinea Cricket Board of Control, N. R. Agonia, PO Box 812, Port Moresby.

SINGAPORE: Singapore Cricket Association, R. Sivasubramaniam, 5000-D Marine Parade Road 22-16, Laguna Park, Singapore 1544.

USA: United States Cricket Association, Naseeruddin Khan, 2361 Hickory Road, Plymouth Meeting, Pennsylvania 19462.

WEST AFRICA: West Africa Cricket Conference, Lt-Col. W. A. Jibunoh, c/o Cricket Secretariat, National Sports Commission, PO Box 145, Lagos, Nigeria.

ZIMBABWE: Zimbabwe Cricket Union, A. L. A. Pichanick, PO Box 452, Harare.

BRITISH UNIVERSITIES SPORTS FEDERATION: 28 Woburn Square, London WC1.

CLUB CRICKET CONFERENCE: D. J. Annetts, 353 West Barnes Lane, New Malden, Surrey, KT3 6JF.

ENGLAND SCHOOLS' CRICKET ASSOCIATION: C. J. Cooper, 68 Hatherley Road, Winchester, Hampshire SO22 6RR.

IRISH CRICKET UNION: D. Scott, 45 Foxrock Park, Foxrock, Dublin 18, Ireland.

MINOR COUNTIES CRICKET ASSOCIATION: D. J. M. Armstrong, Thorpe Cottage, Mill Common, Ridlington, North Walsham, NR28 9TY.

NATIONAL CRICKET ASSOCIATION. B. J. Aspital, Lord's Ground, London NW8 8QN.

SCARBOROUGH CRICKET FESTIVAL: Lt Cdr H. C. Wood, MBE, North Marine Road, Scarborough, North Yorkshire, YO12 7TJ.

SCOTTISH CRICKET UNION: R. W. Barclay, Admin. Office, 18 Ainslie Place, Edinburgh, EH3 6AU.

COMBINED SERVICES: Colonel R. M. Brennan, c/o ASCB, Clayton Barracks, Aldershot, Hampshire.

THE SPORTS COUNCIL: John Wheatley, Director-General, 16 Upper Woburn Place, London WC1 0QP.

ASSOCIATION OF CRICKET UMPIRES: L. J. Cheeseman, 16 Ruden Way, Epsom Downs, Surrey, KT17 3LN.

WOMEN'S CRICKET ASSOCIATION: 16 Upper Woburn Place, London WC1 0QP.

*The addresses of MCC, the First-Class Counties, and Minor Counties are given at the head of each separate section.*

# BIRTHS AND DEATHS OF CRICKETERS

The qualifications are as follows:

1. All players who have appeared in a Test match.

2. Players who have appeared in 50 or more first-class matches during their careers and, if dead, were still living ten years ago.

3. Players who appeared in fifteen or more first-class matches in the 1985 English season.

4. English county captains, county caps and captains of Oxford and Cambridge Universities who, if dead, were still living ten years ago.

5. Oxford and Cambridge Blues of the last ten years. Earlier Blues may be found in previous *Wisdens*.

6. All players chosen as *Wisden* Cricketers of the Year, including the Public Schoolboys chosen for the 1918 and 1919 Almanacks. Cricketers of the Year are identified by the italic notation *CY* and year of appearance.

7. Players or personalities not otherwise qualified who are thought to be of sufficient interest to merit inclusion.

## Key to abbreviations and symbols

CUCC – Cambridge University, OUCC – Oxford University.

*Australian states*: NSW – New South Wales, Qld – Queensland, S. Aust. – South Australia, Tas. – Tasmania, Vic. – Victoria, W. Aust. – Western Australia.

*Indian teams*: Guj. – Gujarat, H'bad – Hyderabad, Ind. Rlwys – Indian Railways, Ind. Serv. – Indian Services, J/K – Jammu and Kashmir, Karn. – Karnataka (Mysore to 1972-73), M. Pradesh – Madhya Pradesh (Central India [C. Ind.] to 1939-40, Holkar to 1954-55, Madhya Bharat to 1956-57), M'tra – Maharashtra, Naw. – Nawanagar, Raja. – Rajasthan, S'tra – Saurashtra (West India [W. Ind.] to 1945-46, Kathiawar to 1949-50), S. Punjab – Southern Punjab (Patiala to 1958-59, Punjab since 1968-69), TC – Travancore-Colchin (Kerala since 1956-57), TN – Tamil Nadu (Madras to 1959-60), U. Pradesh – Uttar Pradesh (United Provinces [U. Prov.] to 1948-49), Vidarbha (CP & Berar to 1949-50, Madhya Pradesh to 1956-57).

*New Zealand provinces*: Auck. – Auckland, Cant. – Canterbury, C. Dist. – Central Districts, N. Dist. – Northern Districts, Wgtn – Wellington.

*Pakistani teams*: B'pur – Bahawalpur, HBL – Habib Bank Ltd, HBFC – House Building Finance Corporation, IDBP – Industrial Development Bank of Pakistan, Kar. – Karachi, MCB – Muslim Commercial Bank, NBP – National Bank of Pakistan, NWFP – North-West Frontier Province, PIA – Pakistan International Airlines, Pak. Us – Pakistan Universities, Pak. Rlwys – Pakistan Railways, PWD – Public Works Department, R'pindi – Rawalpindi, UBL – United Bank Ltd.

*South African provinces*: E. Prov. – Eastern Province, Griq. W. – Griqualand West, N. Tvl – Northern Transvaal, NE Tvl – North-Eastern Transvaal, OFS – Orange Free State, Rhod. – Rhodesia, Tvl – Transvaal, W. Prov. – Western Province. *Note:* SA XI denotes Springbok cap awarded for representative matches played by South Africa in 1982-84.

*West Indies islands*: B'dos – Barbados, BG – British Guiana (Guyana since 1966), Jam. – Jamaica, T/T – Trinidad and Tobago, Comb. Is. – Combined Islands.

* *Denotes Test player.* ** *Denotes appeared for two countries. There is a list of Test players country by country from page 85.*
† *Denotes also played for team under its previous name.*

Aamer Hameed (Pak. Us, Lahore, Punjab & OUCC) b Oct. 18, 1954
Abberley, R. N. (Warwicks.) b April 22, 1944
*A'Beckett, E. L. (Vic.) b Aug. 11, 1907
*Abdul Kadir (Kar. & NBP) b May 5, 1944
*Abdul Qadir (HBL, Lahore & Punjab) b Sept. 15, 1955
*Abel, R. (Surrey; *CY 1890*) b Nov. 30, 1857, d Dec. 10, 1936
Abell, Sir G. E. B. (OUCC, Worcs. & N. Ind.) b June 22, 1904
Aberdare, 3rd Lord (*see* Bruce, Hon. C. N.)
*Abid Ali, S. (H'bad) b Sept. 9, 1941
Abrahams, J. (Lancs.) b July 21, 1952
*Absolom, C. A. (CUCC & Kent) b June 7, 1846, d July 30, 1889
Acfield D. L. (CUCC & Essex) b July 24, 1947
*Achong, E. (T/T) b Feb. 16, 1904
Ackerman, H. M. (Border, NE Tvl, Northants, Natal & W. Prov.) b April 28, 1947
A'Court, D. G. (Glos.) b July 27, 1937
Adam, Sir Ronald, 2nd Bt (Pres. MCC 1946-47) b Oct. 30, 1885, d Dec. 26, 1982
Adams, P. W. (Cheltenham & Sussex; *CY 1919*) b 1900, d Feb. 28, 1962
*Adcock, N. A. T. (Tvl & Natal; *CY 1961*) b March 8, 1931
*Adhikari, H. R. (Guj., Baroda & Ind. Serv.) b July 31, 1919
*Afaq Hussain (Kar., Pak. Us, PIA & PWD) b Dec. 31, 1939
*Aftab Baloch (PWD, Kar., Sind, NBP & PIA) b April 1, 1953
*Aftab Gul (Punjab U., Pak. Us & Lahore) b March 31, 1946
*Agha Saadat Ali (Pak. Us, Punjab, B'pur & Lahore) b June 21, 1929
*Agha Zahid (Pak. Us, Punjab, Lahore & HBL) b Jan. 7, 1953
*Agnew, J. P. (Leics.) b April 4, 1960
Ainsworth, Lt-Cdr M. L. Y. (Worcs.) b May 13, 1922, d Aug. 28, 1978
Aird, R. (CUCC & Hants; Sec. MCC 1953-62, Pres. MCC 1968-69) b May 4, 1902
Aitchison, Rev. J. K. (Scotland) b May 26, 1920
Alabaster, G. D. (Cant., N. Dist. & Otago) b Dec. 10, 1933
*Alabaster, J. C. (Otago) b July 11, 1930
Alcock, C. W. (Sec. Surrey CCC 1872-1907, Editor *Cricket* 1882-1907) b Dec. 2, 1842, d Feb. 26, 1907
Alderman, A. E. (Derbys.) b Oct. 30, 1907
*Alderman, T. M. (W. Aust. & Kent; *CY 1982*) b June 12, 1956
Aldridge, K. J. (Worcs & Tas.) b March 13, 1935
Alexander of Tunis, 1st Lord (Pres. MCC 1955-56) b Dec. 10, 1891, d June 16, 1969
*Alexander, F. C. M. (CUCC & Jam.) b Nov. 2, 1928
*Alexander, G. (Vic.) b April 22, 1851, d Nov. 6, 1930
*Alexander, H. H. (Vic.) b June 9, 1905
*Alim-ud-Din (Rajputna, Guj., Sind, B'pur, Kar. & PWD) b Dec. 15, 1930
*Allan, D. W. (B'dos) b Nov. 5, 1937
*Allan, F. E. (Vic.) b Dec. 2, 1849, d Feb. 9, 1917
Allan, J. M. (OUCC, Kent, Warwicks. & Scotland) b April 2, 1932
*Allan, P. J. (Qld) b Dec. 31, 1935
Allbrook, M. E. (CUCC, Kent & Notts.) b Nov. 15, 1954
*Allcott, C. F. W. (Auck.) b Oct. 7, 1896, d Nov. 21, 1973
Allen, A. W. (CUCC & Northants) b Dec. 22, 1912
Allen, B. O. (CUCC & Glos.) b Oct. 13, 1911, d May 1, 1981
*Allen, D. A. (Glos.) b Oct. 29, 1935
*Allen, G. O. (CUCC & Middx; Pres. MCC 1963-64) b July 31, 1902
Allen, J. C. (Leewards) b Aug. 18, 1951
Allen, M. H. J. (Northants & Derbys.) b Jan. 7, 1933
*Allen, R. C. (NSW) b July 2, 1858, d May 2, 1952
Alletson, E. B. (Notts.) b March 6, 1884, d July 5, 1963
Alley, W. E. (NSW & Som.; *CY 1962*) b Feb. 3, 1919
Alleyne, H. L. (B'dos & Worcs.) b Feb. 28, 1957
*Allom, M. J. C. (CUCC & Surrey; Pres. MCC 1969-70) b March 23, 1906
*Allott, P. J. W. (Lancs.) b Sept. 14, 1956
Altham, H. S. (OUCC, Surrey & Hants; Pres. MCC 1959-60) b Nov. 30, 1888, d March 11, 1965
*Amarnath, Lala (N. Ind., S. Punjab, Guj., Patiala, U. Pradesh & Ind. Rlwys) b Sept. 11, 1911
*Amarnath, M. (Punjab & Delhi; *CY 1984*) b Sept. 24, 1950
*Amarnath, S. (Punjab & Delhi) b Dec. 30, 1948
*Amar Singh, L. (Patiala, W. Ind. & Naw.) b Dec. 4, 1910, d May 20, 1940
*Amerasinghe, A. M. J. G. (SL) b Feb. 2, 1954
*Ames, L. E. G. (Kent; *CY 1929*) b Dec. 3, 1905
**Amir Elahi (Baroda, N. Ind., S. Punjab & B'pur) b Sept. 1, 1908, d Dec. 28, 1980
*Amiss, D. L. (Warwicks.; *CY 1975*) b April 7, 1943
Anderson, I. S. (Derbys. & Boland) b April 24, 1960
*Anderson, J. H. (W. Prov.) b April 26, 1874, d March 11, 1926

*Anderson, R. W. (Cant., N. Dist., Otago & C. Dist.) b Oct. 2, 1948
*Anderson, W. McD. (Otago, C. Dist. & Cant.) b Oct. 8, 1919, d Dec. 21, 1979
Andrew, C. R. (CUCC) b Feb. 18, 1963
*Andrew, K. V. (Northants) b Dec. 15, 1929
*Andrews, B. (Cant., C. Dist. & Otago) b April 4, 1945
*Andrews, T. J. E. (NSW) b Aug. 26, 1890, d Jan. 28, 1970
Andrews, W. H. R. (Som.) b April 14, 1908
*Anil Dalpat (Kar. & PIA) b Sept. 20, 1963
Angell, F. L. (Som.) b June 29, 1922
*Anwar Hussain (N. Ind., Bombay, Sind & Kar.) b July 16, 1920
*Anwar Khan (Kar., Sind & NBP) b Dec. 24, 1955
*Appleyard, R. (Yorks.; *CY 1952*) b June 27, 1924
*Apte, A. L. (Ind. Us, Bombay & Raja.) b Oct. 24, 1934
*Apte, M. L. (Bombay & Bengal) b Oct. 5, 1932
*Archer, A. G. (Worcs.) b Dec. 6, 1871, d July 15, 1935
*Archer, K. A. (Qld) b Jan. 17, 1928
*Archer, R. G. (Qld) b Oct. 25, 1933
*Arif Butt (Lahore & Pak. Rlwys) b May 17, 1944
Arlott, John, (Writer & Broadcaster) b Feb. 25, 1914
Armitage, R. L. S. (E. Prov. & N. Tvl) b July 9, 1955
*Armitage, T. (Yorks.) b April 25, 1848, d Sept. 21, 1922
Armstrong, N. F. (Leics.) b Dec. 22, 1892
Armstrong, T. R. (Derbys.) b Oct. 13, 1909
*Armstrong, W. W. (Vic.; *CY 1903*) b May 22, 1879, d July 13, 1947
*Arnold, E. G. (Worcs.) b Nov. 7, 1876, d Oct. 25, 1942
*Arnold, G. G. (Surrey & Sussex; *CY 1972*) b Sept. 3, 1944
*Arnold, J. (Hants) b Nov. 30, 1907, d April 4, 1984
Arnold, P. (Cant. & Northants) b Oct. 16, 1926
*Arun Lal, J. (Delhi & Bengal) b Aug. 1, 1955
*Asgarali, N. (T/T) b Dec. 28, 1920
Ashdown, W. H. (Kent) b Dec. 27, 1898, d Sept. 15, 1979
*Ashley, W. H. (W. Prov.) b Feb. 10, 1862, d July 14, 1930
*Ashraf Ali (Lahore, Income Tax, Pak Us, Pak Rlwys & UBL) b April 22, 1958
Ashton, C. T. (CUCC & Essex) b Feb. 19, 1901, d Oct. 31, 1942
Ashton, G. (CUCC & Worcs.) b Sept. 27, 1896, d Feb. 6, 1981
Ashton, Sir H. (CUCC & Essex; *CY 1922*; Pres. MCC 1960-61) b Feb. 13, 1898, d June 17,1979
Asif Din, M. (Warwicks.) b Sept. 21, 1960
*Asif Iqbal (H'bad, Kar., Kent, PIA & NBP; *CY 1968*) b June 6, 1943
*Asif Masood (Lahore, Punjab U. & PIA) b Jan. 23, 1946
Aslett, D. G. (Kent) b Feb. 12, 1958
Aspinall, R. (Yorks.) b Nov. 27, 1918
*Astill, W. E. (Leics.; *CY 1933*) b March 1, 1888, d Feb. 10, 1948
*Athey, C. W. J. (Yorks. & Glos.) b Sept. 27, 1957
Atkinson, C. R. M. (Som.) b July 23, 1931
*Atkinson, D. St E. (B'dos & T/T) b Aug. 9, 1926
*Atkinson, E. St E. (B'dos) b Nov. 6, 1927
Atkinson, G. (Som. & Lancs.) b March 29, 1938
Atkinson, T. (Notts.) b Sept. 27, 1930
Attenborough, G. R. (S. Aust.) b Jan. 17, 1951
*Attewell, W. (Notts.; *CY 1892*) b June 12, 1861, d June 11, 1927
Austin, Sir H. B. G. (B'dos) b July 15, 1877, d July 27, 1943
*Austin, R. A. (Jam.) b Sept. 5, 1954
Avery, A. V. (Essex) b Dec. 19, 1914
Aworth, C. J. (CUCC & Surrey) b Feb. 19, 1953
Aylward, J. (Hants & All-England) b 1741, d Dec. 27, 1827
*Azad, K. (Delhi) b Jan. 2, 1959
*Azeem Hafeez (Kar. & Allied Bank) b July 29, 1963
*Azhar Khan (Lahore, Punjab, Pak. Us., PIA & HBL) b Sept. 7, 1955
*Azharuddin, M. (H'bad) b Feb. 8, 1963
*Azmat Rana (B'pur, PIA, Punjab, Lahore & MCB) b Nov. 3, 1951

*Bacchus, S. F. A. F. (Guyana & W. Prov.) b Jan. 31, 1954
*Bacher, Dr A. (Tvl) b May 24, 1942
*Badcock, C. L. (Tas. & S. Aust.) b April 10, 1914, d Dec. 13, 1982
*Badcock, F. T. (Wgtn & Otago) b Aug. 9, 1895, d Sept. 19, 1982
*Baichan, L. (Guyana) b May 12, 1946
*Baig, A. A. (H'bad, OUCC & Som.) b March 19, 1939
Bailey, Sir D. T. L. (Glos.) b Aug. 5, 1918
Bailey, J. (Hants) b April 6, 1908
Bailey, J. A. (Essex & OUCC; Sec. MCC 1974- ) b June 22, 1930
Bailey, R. J. (Northants) b Oct. 28, 1963
*Bailey, T. E. (Essex & CUCC; *CY 1950*) b Dec. 3, 1923
Bainbridge, P. (Glos.; *CY 1986*) b April 16, 1958
*Bairstow, D. L. (Yorks. & Griq. W.) b Sept. 1, 1951
Baker, C. S. (Warwicks.) b Jan. 5, 1883, d Dec. 16, 1976

Baker, R. P. (Surrey) b April 9, 1954
*Bakewell, A. H. (Northants; *CY 1934*) b Nov. 2, 1908, d Jan. 23, 1983
*Balaskas, X. C. (Griq. W., Border, W. Prov., Tvl & NE Tvl) b Oct. 15, 1910
*Balderstone, J. C. (Yorks. & Leics.) b Nov. 16, 1940
Baldry, D. O. (Middx & Hants) b Dec. 26, 1931
Baldwin, H. G. (Surrey; Umpire) b March 16, 1893, d March 7, 1969
*Banerjee, S. A. (Bengal & Bihar) b Nov. 1, 1919
*Banerjee, S. N. (Bengal, Naw., Bihar & M. Pradesh) b Oct. 3, 1911, d Oct. 14, 1980
*Bannerman, A. C. (NSW) b March 21, 1854, d Sept. 19, 1924
*Bannerman, Charles (NSW) b July 23, 1851, d Aug. 20, 1930
Bannister, C. S. (CUCC) b May 22, 1956
Bannister, J. D. (Warwicks.) b Aug. 23, 1930
*Baptiste, E. A. E. (Kent & Leewards) b March 12, 1960
Barber, A. T. (OUCC & Yorks.) b June 17, 1905, d March 10, 1985
*Barber, R. T. (Wgtn & C. Dist.) b June 23, 1925
*Barber, R. W. (Lancs., CUCC & Warwicks; *CY 1967*) b Sept. 26, 1935
*Barber, W. (Yorks.) b April 18, 1901, d Sept. 10, 1968
Barclay, J. R. T. (Sussex & OFS) b Jan. 22, 1954
*Bardsley, W. (NSW; *CY 1910*) b Dec. 7, 1882, d Jan. 20, 1954
Baring, A. E. G. (Hants) b Jan. 21, 1910
Barker, G. (Essex) b July 6, 1931
Barling, T. H. (Surrey) b Sept. 1, 1906
Barlow, A. (Lancs.) b Aug. 31, 1915, d May 9, 1983
Barlow, E. A. (OUCC & Lancs.) b Feb. 24, 1912, d June 27, 1980
*Barlow, E. J. (Tvl, E. Prov., W. Prov., Derbys. & Boland) b Aug. 12, 1940
*Barlow, G. D. (Middx) b March 26, 1950
*Barlow, R. G. (Lancs.) b May 28, 1851, d July 31, 1919
Barnard, H. M. (Hants) b July 18, 1933
Barnard, L. J. (Tvl & N. Tvl) b Jan. 5, 1956
Barnes, A. R. (Sec. Aust. Cricket Board 1960-81) b Sept. 12, 1916
*Barnes, S. F. (Warwicks. & Lancs.; *CY 1910*) b April 19, 1873, d Dec. 26, 1967
*Barnes, S. G. (NSW) b June 5, 1916, d Dec. 16, 1973
*Barnes, W. (Notts.; *CY 1890*) b May 27, 1852, d March 24, 1899
*Barnett, B. A. (Vic.) b March 23, 1908, d June 29, 1979
*Barnett, C. J. (Glos.; *CY 1937*) b July 3, 1910
Barnett, K. J. (Derbys. & Boland) b July 17, 1960
Barnwell, C. J. P. (Som.) b June 23, 1914
Baroda, Maharaja of (Manager, Ind. in Eng., 1959) b April 2, 1930
*Barratt, F. (Notts.) b April 12, 1894, d Jan. 29, 1947
Barratt, R. J. (Leics.) b May 3, 1942
*Barrett, A. G. (Jam.) b April 5, 1942
*Barrett, J. E. (Vic.) b Oct. 15, 1866, d Feb. 9, 1916
Barrick, D. W. (Northants) b April 28, 1926
*Barrington, K. F. (Surrey; *CY 1960*) b Nov. 24, 1930, d March 14, 1981
Barrington, W. E. J. (CUCC) b Jan. 4, 1960
Barron, W. (Lancs. & Northants) b Oct. 26, 1917
Barrow, A. (Natal) b Jan. 23, 1955
*Barrow, I. (Jam.) b Jan. 6, 1911, d April 2, 1979
Bartholomew, P. C. S. (T/T) b Oct. 9, 1939
*Bartlett, E. L. (B'dos) b March 18, 1906, d Dec. 21, 1976
*Bartlett, G. A. (C. Dist. & Cant.) b Feb. 3, 1941
Bartlett, H. T. (CUCC, Surrey & Sussex; *CY 1939*) b Oct. 7, 1914
Bartley, T. J. (Umpire) b March 19, 1908, d April 2, 1964
Barton, M. R. (OUCC & Surrey) b Oct. 14, 1914
*Barton, P. T. (Wgtn) b Oct. 9, 1935
*Barton, V. A. (Kent & Hants) b Oct. 6, 1867, d March 23, 1906
Barwick, S. R. (Glam.) b Sept. 6, 1960
Bates, D. L. (Sussex) b May 10, 1933
*Bates, W. (Yorks.) b Nov. 19, 1855, d Jan. 8, 1900
Bath, B. F. (Tvl) b Jan. 16, 1947
*Baumgartner, H. V. (OFS & Tvl) b Nov. 17, 1883, d April 8, 1938
Baxter, A. D. (Devon, Lancs., Middx & Scotland) b Jan. 20, 1910
*Bean, G. (Notts & Sussex) b March 7, 1864, d March 16, 1923
Bear, M. J. (Essex & Cant.) b Feb. 23, 1934
*Beard, D. D. (C. Dist. & N. Dist.) b Jan. 14, 1920, d July 15, 1982
*Beard, G. R. (NSW) b Aug. 19, 1950
Beauclerk, Lord Frederick (Middx, Surrey & MCC) b May 8, 1773, d April 22, 1850
Beaufort, 10th Duke of (Pres. MCC 1952-53) b April 4, 1900, d Feb. 5, 1984
Beaumont, D. J. (CUCC) b Sept. 1, 1944
*Beaumont, R. (Tvl) b Feb. 4, 1884, d May 25, 1958
*Beck, J. E. F. (Wgtn) b Aug. 1, 1934
Becker, G. C. (W. Aust.) b March 13, 1936
Bedford, P. I. (Middx) b Feb. 11, 1930, d Sept. 18, 1966
*Bedi, B. S. (N. Punjab, Delhi & Northants) b Sept. 25, 1946
*Bedser, A. V. (Surrey; *CY 1947*) b July 4, 1918

Bedser, E. A. (Surrey) b July 4, 1918
Beet, G. (Derbys.; Umpire) b April 24, 1886, d Dec. 13, 1946
*Begbie, D. W. (Tvl) b Dec. 12, 1914
Beldham, W. (Hambledon & Surrey) b Feb. 5, 1766, d Feb. 20, 1862
*Bell, A. J. (W. Prov. & Rhod.) b April 15, 1906, d Aug. 2, 1985
Bell, R. V. (Middx & Sussex) b Jan. 7, 1931
*Bell, W. (Cant.) b Sept. 5, 1931
Bellamy, B. W. (Northants) b April 22, 1891, d Dec. 20, 1985
*Benaud, J. (NSW) b May 11, 1944
*Benaud, R. (NSW; *CY 1962*) b Oct. 6, 1930
Bennett, B. W. P. (CUCC) b Feb. 6, 1955
Bennett, C. T. (CUCC, Surrey & Middx) b Aug. 10, 1902, d Feb. 3, 1978
Bennett, D. (Middx) b Dec. 18, 1933
Bennett, G. M. (Som.) b Dec. 17, 1909, d July 26, 1982
*Bennett, M. J. (NSW) b Oct. 16, 1956
Bennett, N. H. (Surrey) b Sept. 23, 1912
Bennett, R. (Lancs.) b June 16, 1940
Benson, M. R. (Kent) b July 6, 1958
Bensted, E. C. (Qld) b Feb. 11, 1901, d Jan. 21, 1980
Bentley, R. M. (Rhod., Zimb. & Natal) b Nov. 3, 1958
Bernard, J. R. (CUCC & Glos.) b Dec. 7, 1938
Berry, L. G. (Leics.) b April 28, 1906, d Feb. 5, 1985
*Berry, R. (Lancs., Worcs. & Derbys.) b Jan. 29, 1926
Beslee, G. P. (Kent) b March 27, 1904, d Nov. 3, 1975
Bessant, J. G. (Glos.) b Nov. 11, 1892, d Jan. 18, 1982
Bestall, D. (N. Tvl, Natal & E. Prov.) b May 28, 1952
*Betancourt, N. (T/T) b June 4, 1887, d Oct. 12, 1947
Beukes, A. P. (Griq. W.) b May 24, 1953
Bezuidenhout, S. J. (E. Prov.) b July 11, 1946
Bhalekar, R. B. (M'tra) b Feb. 17, 1952
*Bhandari, P. (Delhi & Bengal) b Nov. 27, 1935
*Bhat, R. (Karn.) b April 16, 1958
Bick, D. A. (Middx) b Feb. 22, 1936
Bickmore, A. F. (OUCC & Kent) b May 19, 1899, d March 18, 1979
Biddulph, K. D. (Som.) b May 29, 1932
Biggs, A. L. (E. Prov.) b April 26, 1946
*Bilby, G. P. (Wgtn) b May 7, 1941
*Binks, J. G. (Yorks.; *CY 1969*) b Oct. 5, 1935
*Binny, R. M. H. (Karn.) b July 19, 1955
*Binns, A. P. (Jam.) b July 24, 1929
Birch, J. D. (Notts.) b June 18, 1955
Bird, H. D. (Yorks. & Leics.; Umpire) b April 19, 1933
*Bird, M. C. (Lancs. & Surrey) b March 25, 1888, d Dec. 9, 1933
Bird, R. E. (Worcs.) b April 4, 1915, d Feb. 20, 1985
*Birkenshaw, J. (Yorks., Leics. & Worcs.) b Nov. 13, 1940
*Birkett, L. S. (B'dos, BG & T/T) b April 14, 1904
Birrell, H. B. (E. Prov., Rhod. & OUCC) b Dec. 1, 1927
*Bisset, Sir Murray (W. Prov.) b April 14, 1876, d Oct. 24, 1931
*Bissett, G. F. (Griq. W., W. Prov. & Tvl) b Nov. 5, 1905, d Nov. 14, 1965
Bissex, M. (Glos.) b Sept. 28, 1944
*Blackham, J. McC. (Vic.; *CY 1891*) b May 11, 1854, d Dec. 28, 1932
*Blackie, D. D. (Vic.) b April 5, 1882, d April 18, 1955
Blackledge, J. F. (Lancs.) b April 15, 1928
Blair, B. R. (Otago) b Dec. 27, 1957
*Blair, R. W. (Wgtn & C. Dist.) b June 23, 1932
Blair, W. L. (Otago) b May 11, 1948
Blake, D. E. (Hants) b April 27, 1925
Blake, Rev. P. D. S. (OUCC & Sussex) b May 23, 1927
*Blanckenberg, J. M. (W. Prov. & Natal) b Dec. 31, 1893, 'presumed dead'
*Bland, K. C. (Rhod., E. Prov. & OFS; *CY 1966*) b April 5, 1938
Blenkiron, W. (Warwicks.) b July 21, 1942
Bligh, Hon. Ivo (*see* 8th Earl of Darnley)
Block, S. A. (CUCC & Surrey) b July 15, 1908, d Oct. 7, 1979
Blofeld, H. C. (CUCC) b Sept. 23, 1939
Blundell, Sir E. D. (CUCC & NZ) b May 29, 1907, d Sept. 24, 1984
*Blunt, R. C. (Cant. & Otago; *CY 1928*) b Nov. 3, 1900, d June 22, 1966
*Blythe, C. (Kent; *CY 1904*) b May 30, 1879, d Nov. 8, 1917
*Board, J. H. (Glos.) b Feb. 23, 1867, d April 16, 1924
*Bock, E. G. (Griq. W., Tvl & W. Prov.) b Sept. 17, 1908, d Sept. 5, 1961
Boddington, R. A. (Lancs.) b June 30, 1892, d Aug. 5, 1977
Bodkin, P. E. (CUCC) b Sept. 15, 1924
*Bolton, B. A. (Cant. & Wgtn) b May 31, 1935
*Bolus, J. B. (Yorks., Notts. & Derbys.) b Jan. 31, 1934
*Bond, G. E. (W. Prov.) b April 5, 1909, d Aug. 27, 1965
Bond, J. D. (Lancs. & Notts.; *CY 1971*) b May 6, 1932
*Bonnor, G. J. (Vic. & NSW) b Feb. 25, 1855, d June 27, 1912
*Boock, S. L. (Otago & Cant.) b Sept. 20, 1951
*Boon, D. C. (Tas.) b Dec. 29, 1960
Boon, T. J. (Leics.) b Nov. 1, 1961
*Booth, B. C. (NSW) b Oct. 19, 1933

Booth, B. J. (Lancs. & Leics.) b Dec. 3, 1935
Booth, F. S. (Lancs.) b Feb. 12, 1907, d Jan. 21, 1980
*Booth, M. W. (Yorks.; *CY 1914*) b Dec. 10, 1886, d July 1, 1916
Booth, P. (Leics.) b Nov. 2, 1952
Booth, R. (Yorks. & Worcs.) b Oct. 1, 1926
*Borde, C. G. (Baroda & M'tra) b July 21, 1934
*Border, A. R. (NSW, Glos. & Qld; *CY 1982*) b July 27, 1955
Bore, M. K. (Yorks. & Notts.) b June 2, 1947
Borrington, A. J. (Derbys.) b Dec. 8, 1948
*Bosanquet, B. J. T. (OUCC & Middx; *CY 1905*) b Oct. 13, 1877, d Oct. 12, 1936
Boshier, B. S. (Leics.) b March 6, 1932
*Botham, I. T. (Som.; *CY 1978*) b Nov. 24, 1955
*Botten, J. T. (NE Tvl & N. Tvl) b June 21, 1938
Boucher, J. C. (Ireland) b Dec. 22, 1910
Bourne, W. A. (B'dos & Warwicks.) b Nov. 15, 1952
*Bowden, M. P. (Surrey & Tvl) b Nov. 1, 1865, d Feb. 19, 1892
Bowditch, M. H. (W. Prov.) b Aug. 30, 1945
*Bowes, W. E. (Yorks.; *CY 1932*) b July 25, 1908
*Bowley, E. H. (Sussex & Auck.; *CY 1930*) b June 6, 1890, d July 9, 1974
Bowley, F. L. (Worcs.) b Nov. 9, 1873, d May 31, 1943
Bowman, R. (OUCC & Lancs.) b Jan. 26, 1934
Box, T. (Sussex) b Feb. 7, 1808, d July 12, 1876
*Boyce, K. D. (B'dos & Essex; *CY 1974*) b Oct. 11, 1943
*Boycott, G. (Yorks. & N. Tvl; *CY 1965*) b Oct. 21, 1940
Boyd-Moss, R. J. (CUCC & Northants) b Dec. 16, 1959
Boyes, G. S. (Hants) b March 31, 1899, d Feb. 11, 1973
*Boyle, H. F. (Vic.) b Dec. 10, 1847, d Nov. 21, 1907
*Bracewell, B. P. (C. Dist., Otago & N. Dist.) b Sept. 14, 1959
*Bracewell, J. G. (Otago & Auck.) b April 15, 1958
*Bradburn, W. P. (N. Dist.) b Nov. 24, 1938
*Bradley, W. M. (Kent) b Jan. 2, 1875, d June 19, 1944
*Bradman, Sir D. G. (NSW & S. Aust.; *CY 1931*) b Aug. 27, 1908
Bradshaw, J. C. (Leics.) b Jan. 25, 1902, d Nov. 8, 1984
Brain, B. M. (Worcs. & Glos.) b Sept. 13, 1940
*Brann, W. H. (E. Prov.) b April 4, 1899, d Sept. 22, 1953
Brassington, A. J. (Glos.) b Aug. 9, 1954
Bratchford, J. D. (Qld) b Feb. 2, 1929
*Braund, L. C. (Surrey & Som.; *CY 1902*) b Oct. 18, 1875, d Dec. 22, 1955
Bray, C. (Essex) b April 6, 1898
Brayshaw, I. J. (W. Aust.) b Jan. 14, 1942
Brazier, A. F. (Surrey & Kent) b Dec. 7, 1924
Breakwell, D. (Northants & Som.) b July 2, 1948
*Brearley, J. M. (CUCC & Middx; *CY 1977*) b April 28, 1942
*Brearley, W. (Lancs.; *CY 1909*) b March 11, 1876, d Jan. 30, 1937
Breddy, M. N. (CUCC) b Sept. 23, 1961
*Brennan, D. V. (Yorks.) b Feb. 10, 1920, d Jan. 9, 1985
Brettell, D. N. (OUCC) b March 10, 1956
Brickett, D. J. (E. Prov.) b Dec. 9, 1950
Bridge, W. B. (Warwicks.) b May 29, 1938
Bridger, Rev. J. R. (Hants) b April 8, 1920
Brierley, T. L. (Glam. & Lancs.) b June 15, 1910
Briers, N. E. (Leics.) b Jan. 15, 1955
*Briggs, John (Lancs.; *CY 1889*) b Oct. 3, 1862, d Jan. 11, 1902
*Bright, R. J. (Vic.) b July 13, 1954
*Briscoe, A. W. (Tvl) b Feb. 6, 1911, d April 22, 1941
Bristowe, W. R. (OUCC) b Nov. 17, 1963
*Broad, B. C. (Glos. & Notts.) b Sept. 29, 1957
Broadbent, R. G. (Worcs.) b June 21, 1924
Brocklehurst, B. G. (Som.) b Feb. 18, 1922
*Brockwell, W. (Kimberley & Surrey; *CY 1895*) b Jan. 21, 1865, d July 1, 1935
Broderick, V. (Northants) b Aug. 17, 1920
Brodhurst, A. H. (CUCC & Glos.) b July 21, 1916
*Bromfield, H. D. (W. Prov.) b June 26, 1932
*Bromley, E. H. (W. Aust. & Vic.) b Sept. 2, 1912, d Feb. 1, 1967
*Bromley-Davenport, H. R. (CUCC, Bombay Eur. & Middx) b Aug. 18, 1870, d May 23, 1954
Brooker, M. E. W. (CUCC) b March 24, 1954
*Brookes, D. (Northants; *CY 1957*) b Oct. 29, 1915
Brookes, W. H. (Editor of *Wisden* 1936-39) b Dec. 5, 1894, d May 28, 1955
Brooks, E. W. J. (Surrey) b July 6, 1898, d Feb. 10, 1960
Brooks, R. A. (OUCC & Som.) b June 14, 1943
*Brown, A. (Kent) b Oct. 17, 1935
Brown, A. S. (Glos.) b June 24, 1936
*Brown, D. J. (Warwicks.) b Jan. 30, 1942
Brown, D. W. J. (Glos.) b Feb. 26, 1942
Brown, E. (Warwicks.) b Nov. 27, 1911
*Brown, F. R. (CUCC, Surrey & Northants; *CY 1933*; Pres. MCC 1971-72) b Dec. 16, 1910

*Brown, G. (Hants) b Oct. 6, 1887, d Dec. 3, 1964
Brown, J. (Scotland) b Sept. 24, 1931
*Brown, J. T. (Yorks.; *CY 1895*) b Aug. 20, 1869, d Nov. 4, 1904
*Brown, L. S. (Tvl, NE Tvl & Rhod.) b Nov. 24, 1910, d Sept. 1, 1983
Brown, S. M. (Middx) b Dec. 8, 1917
Brown, V. R. (Cant.) b Nov. 3, 1959
*Brown, W. A. (NSW & Qld; *CY 1939*) b July 31, 1912
Brown, W. C. (Northants) b Nov. 13, 1900
*Browne, C. R. (B'dos & BG) b Oct. 8, 1890, d Jan. 12, 1964
Bruce, Hon. C. N. (3rd Lord Aberdare) (OUCC & Middx) b Aug. 2, 1885, d Oct. 4, 1957
Bruce, S. D. (W. Prov. & OFS) b Jan. 11, 1954
*Bruce, W. (Vic.) b May 22, 1864, d Aug. 3, 1925
Bruyns, A. (W. Prov. & Natal) b Sept. 19, 1946
Bryan, G. J. (Kent) b Dec. 29, 1902
Bryan, J. L. (CUCC & Kent; *CY 1922*) b May 26, 1896, d April 23, 1985
Bryan, R. T. (Kent) b July 30, 1898, d July 27, 1970
*Buckenham, C. P. (Essex) b Jan. 16, 1876, d Feb. 23, 1937
Buckingham, J. (Warwicks.) b Jan. 21, 1903
Budd, E. H. (Middx & All-England) b Feb. 23, 1785, d March 29, 1875
Budd, W. L. (Hants) b Oct. 25, 1913
Buggins, B. L. (W. Aust.) b Jan. 29, 1935
Bull, C. L. (Cant.) b Aug. 19, 1946
Bull, D. F. E. (Qld) b Aug. 13, 1935
Bull, F. G. (Essex; *CY 1898*) b April 2, 1875, d Sept. 16, 1910
Buller, J. S. (Yorks. & Worcs.) b Aug. 23, 1909, d Aug. 7, 1970
Burden, M. D. (Hants) b Oct. 4, 1930
*Burge, P. J. (Qld; *CY 1965*) b May 17, 1932
*Burger, C. G. de V. (Natal) b July 12, 1935
Burgess, G. I. (Som.) b May 5, 1943
*Burgess, M. G. (Auck.) b July 17, 1944
*Burke, C. (Auck.) b March 22, 1914
*Burke, J. W. (NSW; *CY 1957*) b June 12, 1930, d Feb. 2, 1979
*Burke, S. F. (NE Tvl & OFS) b March 11, 1934
*Burki, Javed (Pak. Us, OUCC, Punjab, Lahore, Kar., R'pindi & NWFP) b May 8, 1938
*Burn, K. E. (Tas.) b Sept. 17, 1892, d July 20, 1956
Burnet, J. R. (Yorks.) b Oct. 11, 1918
Burnley, I. D. (CUCC) b March 11, 1963
Burnup, C. J. (CUCC & Kent; *CY 1903*) b Nov. 21, 1875, d April 5, 1960
Burrough, H. D. (Som.) b Feb. 6, 1909
Burrow, B. W. (Griq. W.) b Feb. 8, 1940
Burton, D. C. F. (CUCC & Yorks.) b Sept. 13, 1887, d Sept. 24, 1971
*Burton, F. J. (Vic. & NSW) b 1866, d Aug. 25, 1929
Burtt, J. W. (C. Dist.) b June 11, 1944
*Burtt, T. B. (Cant.) b Jan. 22, 1915
Bury, T. E. O. (OUCC) b May 14, 1958
Buse, H. T. F. (Som.) b Aug. 5, 1910
Bushby, M. H. (CUCC) b July 29, 1931
Buss, A. (Sussex) b Sept. 1, 1939
Buss, M. A. (Sussex & OFS) b Jan. 24, 1944
Buswell, J. E. (Northants) b July 3, 1909
*Butcher, A. R. (Surrey) b Jan. 7, 1954
*Butcher, B. F. (Guyana; *CY 1970*) b Sept. 3, 1933
Butcher, I. P. (Leics.) b July 1, 1962
*Butcher, R. O. (Middx, B'dos & Tas.) b Oct. 14, 1953
*Butler, H. J. (Notts.) b March 12, 1913
Butler, L. C. (Wgtn) b Sept. 2, 1934
*Butler, L. S. (T/T) b Feb. 9, 1929
*Butt, H. R. (Sussex) b Dec. 27, 1865, d Dec. 21, 1928
*Butts, C. G. (Guyana) b July 8, 1957
Butterfield, L. A. (Cant.) b Aug. 29, 1913
Buxton, I. R. (Derbys.) b April 17, 1938
*Buys, I. D. (W. Prov.) b Feb. 3, 1895, dead
*Bynoe, M. R. (B'dos) b Feb. 23, 1941

Caccia, Lord (Pres. MCC 1973-74) b Dec. 21, 1905
Caesar, Julius (Surrey & All-England) b March 25, 1830, d March 6, 1878
Caffyn, W. (Surrey & NSW) b Feb. 2, 1828, d Aug. 28, 1919
Caine, C. Stewart (Editor of *Wisden* 1926-33) b Oct. 28, 1861, d April 15, 1933
*Cairns, B. L. (C. Dist., Otago & N. Dist.) b Oct. 10, 1949
Calder, H. L. (Cranleigh; *CY 1918*) b 1900
*Callaway, S. T. (NSW & Cant.) b Feb. 6, 1868, d Nov. 25, 1923
*Callen, I. W. (Vic.) b May 2, 1955
*Calthorpe, Hon. F. S. Gough- (CUCC, Sussex & Warwicks.) b May 27, 1892, d Nov. 19, 1935
*Camacho, G. S. (Guyana) b Oct. 15, 1945
*Cameron, F. J. (Jam.) b June 22, 1923
*Cameron, F. J. (Otago) b June 1, 1932
*Cameron, H. B. (Tvl, E. Prov. & W. Prov.; *CY 1936*) b July 5, 1905, d Nov. 2, 1935
*Cameron, J. H. (CUCC, Jam. & Som.) b April 8, 1914
Campbell, K. O. (Otago) b March 20, 1943
*Campbell, T. (Tvl) b Feb. 9, 1882, d Oct. 5, 1924
Cannings, V. H. D. (Warwicks. & Hants) b April 3, 1919
Capel, D. J. (Northants) b Feb. 6, 1963
Caple, R. G. (Middx & Hants) b Dec. 8, 1939

Cardus, Sir Neville (Cricket Writer) b April 3, 1888, d Feb. 27, 1975
*Carew, G. McD. (B'dos) b June 4, 1910, d Dec. 9, 1974
*Carew, M. C. (T/T) b Sept. 15, 1937
*Carkeek, W. (Vic.) b Oct. 17, 1878, d Feb. 20, 1937
*Carlson, P. H. (Qld) b Aug. 8, 1951
*Carlstein, P. R. (OFS, Tvl, Natal & Rhod.) b Oct. 28, 1938
Carmody, D. K. (NSW & W. Aust.) b Feb. 16, 1919, d Oct. 21, 1977
Carpenter, D. (Glos.) b Sept. 12, 1935
Carpenter, R. (Cambs. & Utd England XI) b Nov. 18, 1830, d July 13, 1901
*Carr, A. W. (Notts.; *CY 1923*) b May 21, 1893, d Feb. 7, 1963
*Carr, D. B. (OUCC & Derbys.; *CY 1960*; Sec. TCCB 1974- ) b Dec. 28, 1926
*Carr, D. W. (Kent; *CY 1910*) b March 17, 1872, d March 23, 1950
Carr, J. D. (OUCC & Middx) b June 15, 1963
Carrick, P. (Yorks. & E. Prov.) b July 16, 1952
Carrigan, A. H. (Qld) b Aug. 26, 1917
Carrington, E. (Derbys.) b March 25, 1914
*Carter, C. P. (Natal & Tvl) b April 23, 1881, d Nov. 8, 1952
*Carter, H. (NSW) b Halifax, Yorks. March 15, 1878, d June 8, 1948
Carter, R. G. (Warwicks.) b April 14, 1933
Carter, R. G. M. (Worcs.) b July 11, 1937
Carter, R. M. (Northants & Cant.) b May 25, 1960
Cartwright, H. (Derbys.) b May 12, 1951
*Cartwright, T. W. (Warwicks., Som. & Glam.) b July 22, 1935
Carty, R. A. (Hants) b July 28, 1922
Cass, G. R. (Essex, Worcs. & Tas.) b April 23, 1940
Castell, A. T. (Hants) b Aug. 6, 1943
Castle, F. (Som.) b April 9, 1909
Catt, A. W. (Kent & W. Prov.) b Oct. 2, 1933
*Catterall, R. H. (Tvl, Rhod., Natal & OFS; *CY 1925*) b July 10, 1900, d Jan. 2, 1961
Causby, J. P. (S. Aust.) b Oct. 27, 1942
*Cave, H. B. (Wgtn & C. Dist.) b Oct. 10, 1922
Cederwall, B. W. (Wgtn) b Feb. 24, 1952
Chadwick, D. (W. Aust.) b March 29, 1941
Chalk, F. G. H. (OUCC & Kent) b Sept. 7, 1910, d Feb. 20, 1943
*Challenor, G. (B'dos) b June 28, 1888, d July 30, 1947
*Chandrasekhar, B. S. (†Karn.; *CY 1972*) b May 17, 1945
*Chang, H. S. (Jam.) b July 22, 1952
*Chapman, A. P. F. (Uppingham, OUCC & Kent; *CY 1919*) b Sept. 3, 1900, d Sept. 16, 1961
*Chapman, H. W. (Natal) b June 30, 1890, d Dec. 1, 1941
Chapman, T. A. (Leics. & Rhod.) b May 14, 1919, d Feb. 19, 1979
*Chappell, G. S. (S. Aust., Som. & Qld; *CY 1973*) b Aug. 7, 1948
*Chappell, I. M. (S. Aust. & Lancs.; *CY 1976*) b Sept. 26, 1943
*Chappell, T. M. (S. Aust., W. Aust. & NSW) b Oct. 21, 1952
*Chapple, M. E. (Cant. & C. Dist.) b July 25, 1930, d July 31, 1985
*Charlton, P. C. (NSW) b April 9, 1867, d Sept. 30, 1954
*Charlwood, H. R. J. (Sussex) b Dec. 19, 1846, d June 6, 1888
*Chatfield, E. J. (Wgtn) b July 3, 1950
*Chatterton, W. (Derbys.) b Dec. 27, 1861, d March 19, 1913
*Chauhan, C. P. S. (M'tra & Delhi) b July 21, 1947
Cheatle, R. G. L. (Sussex & Surrey) b July 31, 1953
*Cheetham, J. E. (W. Prov.) b May 26, 1920, d Aug. 21, 1980
Chester, F. (Worcs.; Umpire) b Jan. 20, 1895, d April 8, 1957
Chesterton, G. H. (OUCC & Worcs.) b July 15, 1922
*Chevalier, G. A. (W. Prov.) b March 9, 1937
Childs, J. H. (Glos. & Essex) b Aug. 15, 1951
Childs-Clarke, A. W. (Middx & Northants) b May 13, 1905, d Feb. 19, 1980
*Chipperfield, A. G. (NSW) b Nov. 17, 1905
Chisholm, R. H. E. (Scotland) b May 22, 1927
*Chowdhury, N. R. (Bihar & Bengal) b May 23, 1923, d Dec. 14, 1979
*Christiani, C. M. (BG) b Oct. 28, 1913, d April 4, 1938
*Christiani, R. J. (BG) b July 19, 1920
*Christopherson, S. (Kent; Pres. MCC 1939-45) b Nov. 11, 1861, d April 6, 1949
*Christy, J. A. J. (Tvl & Qld) b Dec. 12, 1904, d Feb. 1, 1971
*Chubb, G. W. A. (Border & Tvl) b April 12, 1911, d Aug. 28, 1982
Clark, D. G. (Kent; Pres. MCC 1977-78) b Jan. 27, 1919
Clark, E. A. (Middx) b April 15, 1937
*Clark, E. W. (Northants) b Aug. 9, 1902, d April 28, 1982
Clark, L. S. (Essex) b March 6, 1914
Clark, T. H. (Surrey) b Oct. 4, 1924, d June 15, 1981
*Clark, W. M. (W. Aust.) b Sept. 19, 1953
Clarke, Dr C. B. (B'dos, Northants & Essex) b April 7, 1918
Clarke, R. W. (Northants) b April 22, 1924, d Aug. 3, 1981
*Clarke, S. T. (B'dos, Surrey & Tvl) b Dec. 11, 1954

Clarke, William (Notts.; founded All-England XI & Trent Bridge ground) b Dec. 24, 1798, d Aug. 25, 1856
Clarkson, A. (Yorks. & Som.) b Sept. 5, 1939
Claughton, J. A. (OUCC & Warwicks.) b Sept. 17, 1956
*Clay, J. C. (Glam.) b March 18, 1898, d Aug. 12, 1973
Clay, J. D. (Notts.) b Oct. 15, 1924
Clayton, G. (Lancs. & Som.) b Feb. 3, 1938
Clements, S. M. (OUCC) b April 19, 1956
*Cleverley, D. C. (Auck.) b Dec. 23, 1909
Clift, Patrick B. (Rhod., Leics. & Natal) b July 14, 1953
Clift, Philip B. (Glam.) b Sept. 3, 1918
Clinton, G. S. (Kent, Surrey & Zimb.-Rhod.) b May 5, 1953
*Close, D. B. (Yorks. & Som.; *CY 1964*) b Feb. 24, 1931
Cobb, R. A. (Leics.) b May 18, 1961
Cobden, F. C. (CUCC) b Oct. 14, 1849, d Dec. 7, 1932
Cobham, 10th Visct (Hon. C. J. Lyttelton) (Worcs.; Pres. MCC 1954) b Aug. 8, 1909, d March 20, 1977
*Cochrane, J. A. K. (Tvl & Griq. W.) b July 15, 1909
*Coen, S. K. (OFS, W. Prov., Tvl & Border) b Oct. 14, 1902, d Jan. 28, 1967
*Colah, S. M. H. (Bombay, W. Ind. & Naw.) b Sept. 22, 1902, d Sept. 11, 1950
Colchin, Robert ("Long Robin") (Kent & All-England) b Nov. 1713, d April 1750
*Coldwell, L. J. (Worcs.) b Jan. 10, 1933
Coleman, C. A. R. (Leics.) b July 7, 1906, d June 14, 1978
*Colley, D. J. (NSW) b March 15, 1947
Collin, T. (Warwicks.) b April 7, 1911
*Collinge, R. O. (C. Dist., Wgtn & N. Dist.) b April 2, 1946
*Collins, H. L. (NSW) b Jan. 21, 1889, d May 28, 1959
Collins, R. (Lancs.) b March 10, 1934
*Colquhoun, I. A. (C. Dist.) b June 8, 1924
Comber, J. T. H. (CUCC) b Feb. 26, 1911, d May 3, 1976
*Commaille, J. M. M. (W. Prov., Natal, OFS & Griq. W.) b Feb. 21, 1883, d July 27, 1956
*Compton, D. C. S. (Middx & Holkar; *CY 1939*) b May 23, 1918
Compton, L. H. (Middx) b Sept. 12, 1912, d Dec. 27, 1984
*Coney, J. V. (Wgtn; *CY 1984*) b June 21, 1952
*Congdon, B. E. (C. Dist., Wgtn, Otago & Cant.; *CY 1974*) b Feb. 11, 1938
*Coningham, A. (NSW & Qld) b July 14, 1863, d June 13, 1939
*Connolly, A. N. (Vic. & Middx) b June 29, 1939
Connor, C. A. (Hants) b March 24, 1961
Constable, B. (Surrey) b Feb. 19, 1921
Constant, D. J. (Kent & Leics.; Umpire) b Nov. 9, 1941
*Constantine, Lord L. N. (T/T & B'dos; *CY 1940*) b Sept. 21, 1902, d July 1, 1971
Constantine, L. S. (T/T) b May 25, 1874, d Jan. 5, 1942
*Contractor, N. J. (Guj. & Ind. Rlwys) b March 7, 1934
*Conyngham, D. P. (Natal, Tvl & W. Prov.) b May 10, 1897
*Cook, C. (Glos.) b Aug. 23, 1921
*Cook, F. J. (E. Prov.) b 1870, dead
*Cook, G. (Northants & E. Prov.) b Oct. 9, 1951
Cook, G. G. (Qld) b June 29, 1910, d Sept. 12, 1982
*Cook, N. G. B. (Leics.) b June 17, 1956
Cook, S. J. (Tvl & SA XI) b July 31, 1953
Cook, T. E. (Sussex) b Feb. 5, 1901, d Jan. 15, 1950
*Cooper, A. H. C. (Tvl) b Sept 2, 1893, d July 18, 1963
*Cooper, B. B. (Middx, Kent & Vic.) b March 15, 1844, d Aug. 7, 1914
Cooper, F. S. Ashley- (Cricket Historian) b March 17, 1877, d Jan. 31, 1932
Cooper, G. C. (Sussex) b Sept. 2, 1936
Cooper, H. P. (Yorks. & N. Tvl) b April 17, 1949
Cooper, K. E. (Notts.) b Dec. 27, 1957
Cooper, K. R. (Natal) b April 1, 1954
Cooper, N. H. C. (Glos. & CUCC) b Oct. 14, 1953
*Cooper, W. H. (Vic.) b Sept. 11, 1849, d April 5, 1939
*Cope, G. A. (Yorks.) b Feb. 23, 1947
*Copson, W. H. (Derbys.; *CY 1937*) b April 27, 1908, d Sept. 14, 1971
Cordle, A. E. (Glam.) b Sept. 21, 1940
*Corling, G. E. (NSW) b July 13, 1941
Cornford, J. H. (Sussex) b Dec. 9, 1911, d June 17, 1985
*Cornford, W. L. (Sussex) b Dec. 25, 1900, d Feb. 6, 1964
Cornwallis, Capt. Hon. W. S. (2nd Lord Cornwallis) (Kent) b March 14, 1892, d Jan. 4, 1982
Corrall, P. (Leics.) b July 16, 1906
Corran, A. J. (OUCC & Notts.) b Nov. 25, 1936
Cosh, N. J. (CUCC & Surrey) b Aug. 6, 1946
*Cosier, G. J. (Vic., S. Aust. & Qld) b April 25,1953
*Cottam, J. T. (NSW) b Sept. 5, 1867, d Jan. 30, 1897
*Cottam, R. M. H. (Hants & Northants) b Oct. 16, 1944
*Cotter, A. (NSW) b Dec. 3, 1884, d Oct. 31, 1917
Cotterell, T. A. (CUCC) b May 12, 1963
Cotton, J. (Notts. & Leics.) b Nov. 7, 1940

Cottrell, G. A. (CUCC) b March 23, 1945
Cottrell, P. R. (CUCC) b May 22, 1957
Coulson, S. S. (Leics.) b Oct. 17, 1898, d Oct. 3, 1981
*Coulthard, G. (Vic.) b Aug. 1, 1856, d Oct. 22, 1883
*Coventry, Hon. C. J. (Worcs.) b Feb. 26, 1867, d June 2, 1929
Coverdale, S. P. (CUCC & Yorks.) b Nov. 20, 1954
Cowan, M. J. (Yorks.) b June 10, 1933
Cowan, R. S. (OUCC & Sussex) b March 30, 1960
*Cowans, N. G. (Middx) b April 17, 1961
*Cowdrey, C. S. (Kent) b Oct. 20, 1957
*Cowdrey, M. C. (OUCC & Kent; *CY 1956*) b Dec. 24, 1932
*Cowie, J. (Auck.) b March 30, 1912
Cowley, G. S. (E. Prov.) b March 1, 1953
Cowley, N. G. (Hants) b March 1, 1953
*Cowper, R. M. (Vic. & W. Aust.) b Oct. 5, 1940
Cox, A. L. (Northants) b July 22, 1907
Cox, G., jun. (Sussex) b Aug. 23, 1911, d March 30, 1985
Cox, G. R. (Sussex) b Nov. 29, 1873, d March 24, 1949
*Cox, J. L. (Natal) b June 28, 1886, d July 4, 1971
*Coxon, A. (Yorks.) b Jan. 18, 1916
Crabtree, H. P. (Essex) b April 30, 1906, d May 28, 1982
Craig, E. J. (CUCC & Lancs.) b March 26, 1942
*Craig, I. D. (NSW) b June 12, 1935
Cranfield, L. M. (Glos.) b Aug. 29, 1909
Cranmer, P. (Warwicks.) b Sept. 10, 1914
*Cranston, J. (Glos.) b Jan. 9, 1859, d Dec. 10, 1904
*Cranston, K. (Lancs.) b Oct. 20, 1917
*Crapp, J. F. (Glos.) b Oct. 14, 1912, d Feb. 15, 1981
*Crawford, J. N. (Surrey, S. Aust., Wgtn & Otago; *CY 1907*) b Dec. 1, 1886, d May 2, 1963
Crawford, N. C. (CUCC) b Nov. 26, 1958
*Crawford, P. (NSW) b Aug. 3, 1933
Crawley, A. M. (OUCC & Kent; Pres. MCC 1972-73) b April 10, 1908
Crawley, L. G. (CUCC, Worcs. & Essex) b July 26, 1903, d July 9, 1981
Cray, S. J. (Essex) b May 29, 1921
*Cresswell, G. F. (Wgtn & C. Dist.) b March 22, 1915, d Jan. 10, 1966
*Cripps, G. (W. Prov.) b Oct. 19, 1865, d July 27, 1943
*Crisp, R. J. (Rhod., W. Prov. & Worcs.) b May 28, 1911
*Croft, C. E. H. (Guyana & Lancs.) b March 15, 1953
*Cromb, I. B. (Cant.) b June 25, 1905, d March 6, 1984
Crookes, N. S. (Natal) b Nov. 15, 1935
Cross, G. F. (Leics.) b Nov. 15, 1943
*Crowe, J. J. (S. Aust. & Auck.) b Sept. 14, 1958
*Crowe, M. D. (Auck., C. Dist. & Som.; *CY 1985*) b Sept. 22, 1962
Crump, B. S. (Northants) b April 25, 1938
Crush, E. (Kent) b April 25, 1917
Cuffy, T (T/T) b Nov. 9, 1949
Cullinan, M. R. (SA Us & OUCC) b April 3, 1957
Cumbes, J. (Lancs., Surrey, Worcs. & Warwicks.) b May 4, 1944
*Cunis, R. S. (Auck. & N. Dist.) b Jan. 5, 1941
Cunningham, K. G. (S. Aust.) b July 26, 1939
*Curnow, S. H. (Tvl) b Dec. 16, 1907
Curran, K. M. (Glos. & Zimb.) b Sept. 7, 1959
Curtis, I. J. (OUCC & Surrey) b May 13, 1959
Curtis, T. S. (Worcs. & CUCC) b Jan. 15, 1960
Cuthbertson, G. B. (Middx, Sussex & Northants) b March 28, 1901
Cutmore, J. A. (Essex) b Dec. 28, 1898, d Nov. 30, 1985
*Cuttell, W. R. (Lancs.; *CY 1898*) b Sept. 13, 1864, d Dec. 9, 1929

*Da Costa, O. C. (Jam.) b Sept. 11, 1907, d Oct. 1, 1936
Dacre, C. C. (Auck. & Glos.) b May 15, 1899, d Nov. 2, 1975
Daer, A. G. (Essex) b Nov. 22, 1906
Daft, Richard (Notts. & All-England) b Nov. 2, 1835, d July 18, 1900
Dakin, G. F. (E. Prov.) b Aug. 13, 1935
Dalmeny, Lord (6th Earl of Rosebery) (Middx & Surrey) b Jan. 8, 1882, d May 30, 1974
*Dalton, E. L. (Natal) b Dec. 2, 1906, d June 3, 1981
*Dani, H. T. (M'tra & Ind. Serv.) b May 24, 1933
*Daniel, W. W. (B'dos, Middx & W. Aust.) b Jan. 16, 1956
Dansie, N. (S. Aust.) b July 2, 1928
*D'Arcy, J. W. (Cant., Wgtn & Otago) b April 23, 1936
Dare, R. (Hants) b Nov. 26, 1921
*Darling, J. (S. Aust.; *CY 1900*) b Nov. 21, 1870, d Jan. 2, 1946
*Darling, L. S. (Vic.) b Aug. 14, 1909
*Darling, W. M. (S. Aust.) b May 1, 1957
*Darnley, 8th Earl of (Hon. Ivo Bligh) (CUCC & Kent; Pres. MCC 1900) b March 13, 1859, d April 10, 1927
Davey, J. (Glos.) b Sept. 4, 1944
*Davidson, A. K. (NSW; *CY 1962*) b June 14, 1929
Davidson, J. E. (CUCC) b Oct. 23, 1964

Davies, A. G. (CUCC) b May 5, 1962
Davies, Dai (Glam.) b Aug. 26, 1896, d July 16, 1976
Davies, Emrys (Glam.) b June 27, 1904, d Nov. 10, 1975
*Davies, E. Q. (E. Prov., Tvl & NE Tvl) b Aug. 26, 1909, d Nov. 11, 1976
Davies, G. R. (NSW) b July 22, 1946
Davies, H. D. (Glam.) b July 23, 1932
Davies, H. G. (Glam.) b April 23, 1913
Davies, J. G. W. (CUCC & Kent; Pres. MCC 1985-86) b Sept. 10, 1911
Davies, T. (Glam.) b Oct. 25, 1960
*Davis, B. A. (T/T & Glam.) b May 2, 1940
*Davis, C. A. (T/T) b Jan. 1, 1944
Davis, E. (Northants) b March 8, 1922
*Davis, I. C. (NSW & Qld) b June 25, 1953
Davis, M. R. (Som.) b Feb. 26, 1962
Davis, P. C. (Northants) b May 24, 1915
Davis, R. C. (Glam.) b Jan. 1, 1946
*Davis, W. W. (Windwards & Glam.) b Sept. 18, 1958
Davison, B. F. (Rhod., Leics, Tas. & Glos.) b Dec. 21, 1946
Davison, I. (Notts.) b Oct. 4, 1937
Dawkes, G. O. (Leics. & Derbys.) b July 19, 1920
*Dawson, E. W. (CUCC & Leics.) b Feb. 13, 1904, d June 4, 1979
*Dawson, O. C. (Natal & Border) b Sept. 1, 1919
Day, A. P. (Kent; *CY 1910*) b April 10, 1885, d Jan. 22, 1969
Day, N. T. (Tvl) b Dec. 31, 1953
*de Alwis, R. G. (SL) b Feb. 15, 1959
*Dean, H. (Lancs.) b Aug. 13, 1884, d March 12, 1957
*Deane, H. G. (Natal & Tvl) b July 21, 1895, d Oct. 21, 1939
*De Caires, F. I. (BG) b May 12, 1909, d Feb. 2, 1959
*De Courcy, J. H. (NSW) b April 18, 1927
Deed, J. A. (Kent) b Sept. 12, 1901, d Oct. 19, 1980
Delisle, G. P. S. (Middx & OUCC) b Dec. 25, 1934
*Dell, A. R. (Qld) b Aug. 6, 1947
*de Mel, A. L. F. (SL) b May 9, 1959
*Dempster, C. S. (Wgtn, Leics., Scotland & Warwicks.; *CY 1932*) b Nov. 15, 1903, d Feb. 14, 1974
*Dempster, E. W. (Wgtn) b Jan. 25, 1925
*Denness, M. H. (Scotland, Kent & Essex; *CY 1975*) b Dec. 1, 1940
Dennett, E. G. (Glos.) b April 27, 1880, d Sept. 14, 1937
Denning, P. W. (Som.) b Dec. 16, 1949
Dennis, F. (Yorks.) b June 11, 1907
*Denton, D. (Yorks.; *CY 1906*) b July 4, 1874, d Feb. 16, 1950
Denton, W. H. (Northants) b Nov. 2, 1890, d April 23, 1979
Deodhar, D. B. (M'tra; oldest living Ranji Trophy player) b Jan. 14, 1892
*Depeiza, C. C. (B'dos) b Oct. 10, 1927
Derrick, J. (Glam.) b Jan. 15, 1963
*Desai, R. B. (Bombay) b June 20, 1939
De Saram, F. C. (OUCC & Ceylon) b Sept. 5, 1912, d April 11, 1983
de Schmidt, R. (W. Prov.; oldest surviving Currie Cup player) b Nov. 24, 1883
*de Silva, D. S. (SL) b June 11, 1942
*de Silva, G. R. A. (SL) b Dec. 12, 1952
*de Silva, P. A. (SL) b Oct. 17, 1965
De Vaal, P. D. (Tvl) b Dec. 3, 1945
Devereux, L. N. (Middx, Worcs. & Glam.) b Oct. 20, 1931
*Dewdney, C. T. (Jam.) b Oct. 23, 1933
Dewes, A. R. (CUCC) b June 2, 1957
*Dewes, J. G. (CUCC & Middx) b Oct. 11, 1926
Dews, G. (Worcs.) b June 5, 1921
*Dexter, E. R. (CUCC & Sussex; *CY 1961*) b May 15, 1935
*Dias, R. L. (SL) b Oct. 18, 1952
Dibbs, A. H. A. (Pres. MCC 1983-84) b Dec. 9, 1918, d Nov. 28, 1985
*Dick, A. E. (Otago & Wgtn) b Oct. 10, 1936
Dickeson, C. W. (N. Dist.) b March 26, 1955
*Dickinson, G. R. (Otago) b March 11, 1903, d March 17, 1978
*Dilley, G. R. (Kent) b May 18, 1959
Diment, R. A. (Glos. & Leics.) b Feb. 9, 1927
*Dipper, A. E. (Glos.) b Nov. 9, 1885, d Nov. 7, 1945
Divecha, R. V. (Bombay, OUCC, Northants, Vidarbha & S'tra) b Oct. 18, 1927
Diver, A. J. D. (Cambs., Middx, Notts. & All-England) b June 6, 1824, d March 25, 1876
Dixon, A. L. (Kent) b Nov. 27, 1933
*Dixon, C. D. (Tvl) b Feb. 12, 1891, d Sept. 9, 1969
Dodds, T. C. (Essex) b May 29, 1919
Doggart, A. G. (CUCC, Durham & Middx) b June 2, 1897, d June 7, 1963
*Doggart, G. H. G. (CUCC & Sussex; Pres. MCC 1981-82) b July 18, 1925
Doggart, S. J. G. (CUCC) b Feb. 8, 1961
Doherty, M. J. D. (Griq. W.) b March 14, 1947
*D'Oliveira, B. L. (Worcs.; *CY 1967*) b Oct. 4, 1931
D'Oliveira, D. B. (Worcs.) b Oct. 19, 1960
*Dollery, H. E. (Warwicks. & Wgtn; *CY 1952*) b Oct. 14, 1914
Dollery, K. R. (Qld, Auck., Tas. & Warwicks.) b Dec. 9, 1924
*Dolphin, A. (Yorks.) b Dec. 24, 1885, d Oct. 23, 1942
*Donnan, H. (NSW) b Nov. 12, 1864, d Aug. 13, 1956

*Donnelly, M. P. (Wgtn, Cant., Middx, Warwicks. & OUCC; *CY 1948*) b Oct. 17, 1917
*Dooland, B. (S. Aust. & Notts.; *CY 1955*) b Nov. 1, 1923, d Sept. 8, 1980
Dorrinton, W. (Kent & All-England) b April 29, 1809, d Nov. 8, 1848
Dorset, 3rd Duke of (Kent) b March 24, 1745, d July 19, 1799
*Doshi, D. R. (Bengal, Notts. & Warwicks.) b Dec. 22, 1947
*Douglas, J. W. H. T. (Essex; *CY 1915*) b Sept. 3, 1882, d Dec. 19, 1930
Dowding, A. L. (OUCC) b April 4, 1929
*Dowe, U. G. (Jam.) b March 29, 1949
*Dower, R. R. (E. Prov.) b June 4, 1876, d Sept. 15, 1964
Dowling, D. F. (Border, NE Tvl & Natal) b July 25, 1914
*Dowling, G. T. (Cant.) b March 4, 1937
*Downton, P. R. (Kent & Middx) b April 4, 1957
Draper, E. J. (E. Prov. & Griq. W.) b Sept. 27, 1934
*Draper, R. G. (E. Prov. & Griq. W.) b Dec. 24, 1926
Dredge, C. H. (Som.) b Aug. 4, 1954
*Druce, N. F. (CUCC & Surrey; *CY 1898*) b Jan. 1, 1875, d Oct. 27, 1954
Drybrough, C. D. (OUCC & Middx) b Aug. 31, 1938
*D'Souza, A. (Kar., Peshawar & PIA) b Jan. 1, 1938
*Ducat, A. (Surrey; *CY 1920*) b Feb. 16, 1886, d July 23, 1942
*Duckworth, C. A. R. (Natal & Rhod.) b March 22, 1933
*Duckworth, G. (Lancs.; *CY 1929*) b May 9, 1901, d Jan. 5, 1966
Dudleston, B. (Leics., Glos. & Rhod.) b July 16, 1945
*Duff, R. A. (NSW) b Aug. 17, 1878, d Dec. 13, 1911
*Dujon, P. J. (Jam.) b May 28, 1956
*Duleepsinhji, K. S. (CUCC & Sussex; *CY 1930*) b June 13, 1905, d Dec. 5, 1959
*Dumbrill, R. (Natal & Tvl) b Nov. 19, 1938
*Duminy, J. P. (OUCC, W. Prov. & Tvl) b Dec. 16, 1897, d Jan. 31, 1980
*Duncan, J. R. F. (Qld & Vic.) b March 25, 1944
*Dunell, O. R. (E. Prov.) b July 15, 1856, d Oct. 21, 1929
Dunning, B. (N. Dist.) b March 20, 1940
*Dunning, J. A. (Otago & OUCC) b Feb. 6, 1903, d June 24, 1971
*Du Preez, J. H. (Rhod. & Zimb.) b Nov. 14, 1942
*Durani, S. A. (S'tra, Guj. & Raja.) b Dec. 11, 1934
Durose, A. J. (Northants) b Oct. 10, 1944
*Durston, F. J. (Middx) b July 11, 1893, d April 8, 1965
*Du Toit, J. F. (SA) b April 5, 1868, d July 10, 1909
Dye, J. C. J. (Kent, Northants & E. Prov.) b July 24, 1942
Dyer, D. D. (Natal & Tvl) b Dec. 3, 1946
*Dyer, D. V. (Natal) b May 2, 1914
Dyer, R. I. H. B. (Warwicks.) b Dec. 22, 1958
*Dymock, G. (Qld) b July 21, 1946
Dyson, A. H. (Glam.) b July 10, 1905, d June 7, 1978
Dyson, J. (Lancs.) b July 8, 1934
*Dyson, John (NSW) b June 11, 1954

*Eady, C. J. (Tas.) b Oct. 29, 1870, d Dec. 20, 1945
Eagar, E. D. R. (OUCC, Glos. & Hants) b Dec. 8, 1917, d Sept. 13, 1977
Eagar, M. A. (OUCC & Glos.) b March 20, 1934
Eaglestone, J. T. (Middx & Glam.) b July 24, 1923
Ealham, A. G. E. (Kent) b Aug. 30, 1944
East, D. E. (Essex) b July 27, 1959
East, R. E. (Essex) b June 20, 1947
East, R. J. (OFS) b March 31, 1953
Eastman, G. F. (Essex) b April 7, 1903
Eastman, L. C. (Essex & Otago) b June 3, 1897, d April 17, 1941
*Eastwood, K. H. (Vic.) b Nov. 23, 1935
*Ebeling, H. I. (Vic.) b Jan. 1, 1905, d Jan. 12, 1980
Eckersley, P. T. (Lancs.) b July 2, 1904, d Aug. 13, 1940
Edbrooke, R. M. (OUCC) b Dec. 30, 1960
Eddy, V. A. (Leewards) b Feb. 14, 1955
*Edgar, B. A. (Wgtn) b Nov. 23, 1956
Edinburgh, HRH Duke of (Pres. MCC 1948-49, 1974-75) b June 10, 1921
Edmeades, B. E. A. (Essex) b Sept. 17, 1941
*Edmonds, P. H. (CUCC, Middx & E. Prov.) b March 8, 1951
Edmonds, R. B. (Warwicks.) b March 2, 1941
Edrich, B. R. (Kent & Glam.) b Aug. 18, 1922
Edrich, E. H. (Lancs.) b March 27, 1914
Edrich, G. A. (Lancs.) b July 13, 1918
*Edrich, J. H. (Surrey; *CY 1966*) b June 21, 1937
*Edrich, W. J. (Middx; *CY 1940*) b March 26, 1916
*Edwards, G. N. (C. Dist.) b May 27, 1955
*Edwards, J. D. (Vic.) b June 12, 1862, d July 31, 1911
Edwards, M. J. (CUCC & Surrey) b March 1, 1940
*Edwards, R. (W. Aust. & Vic.) b Dec. 1, 1942
*Edwards, R. M. (B'dos) b June 3, 1940

Edwards, T. D. W. (CUCC) b Dec. 6, 1958
*Edwards, W. J. (W. Aust.) b Dec. 23, 1949
Eele, P. J. (Som.) b Jan. 27, 1935
Eggar, J. D. (OUCC, Hants & Derbys.) b Dec. 1, 1916, d May 3, 1983
*Ehtesham-ud-Din (Lahore, Punjab, PIA, NBP & UBL) b Sept. 4, 1950
*Elgie, M. K. (Natal) b March 6, 1933
Elliott, C. S. (Derbys.) b April 24, 1912
*Elliott, H. (Derbys.) b Nov. 2, 1891, d Feb. 2, 1976
Elliott, Harold (Lancs.; Umpire) b June 15, 1904, d April 15, 1969
Ellis, G. P. (Glam.) b May 24, 1950
Ellis, J. L. (Vic.) b May 9, 1890, d July 26, 1974
Ellis, R. G. P. (OUCC & Middx) b Oct. 20 1960
Ellison, C. C. (CUCC) b Feb. 11, 1962
*Ellison, R. M. (Kent; *CY 1986*) b Sept. 21, 1959
Elms, R. B. (Kent & Hants) b April 5, 1949
*Emburey, J. E. (Middx & W. Prov.; *CY 1984*) b Aug. 20, 1952
*Emery, R. W. G. (Auck. & Cant.) b March 28, 1915, d Dec. 18, 1982
*Emery, S. H. (NSW) b Oct. 16, 1885, d Jan. 7, 1967
*Emmett, G. M. (Glos.) b Dec. 2, 1912, d Dec. 18, 1976
*Emmett, T. (Yorks.) b Sept. 3, 1841, d June 30, 1904
*Endean, W. R. (Tvl) b May 31, 1924
*Engineer, F. M. (Bombay & Lancs.) b Feb. 25, 1938
Enthoven, H. J. (CUCC & Middx) b June 4, 1903, d June 29, 1975
*Evans, A. J. (OUCC, Hants & Kent) b May 1, 1889, d Sept. 18, 1960
Evans, D. G. L. (Glam.; Umpire) b July 27, 1933
*Evans, E. (NSW) b March 6, 1849, d July 2, 1921
Evans, G. (OUCC, Glam. & Leics.) b Aug. 13, 1915
Evans, J. B. (Glam.) b Nov. 9, 1936
*Evans, T. G. (Kent; *CY 1951*) b Aug. 18, 1920
Every, T. (Glam.) b Dec. 19, 1909
Eyre, T. J. P. (Derbys.) b Oct. 17, 1939
Ezekowitz, R. A. B. (OUCC) b Jan. 19, 1954

Faber, M. J. J. (OUCC & Sussex) b Aug. 15, 1950
*Fagg, A. E. (Kent) b June 18, 1915, d Sept. 13, 1977
Fairbairn, A. (Middx) b Jan. 25, 1923
Fairbrother, N. H. (Lancs.) b Sept. 9, 1963
*Fairfax, A. G. (NSW) b June 16, 1906, d May 17, 1955
Fairservice, C. (Kent & Middx) b Aug. 21, 1909
Fairservice, W. J. (Kent) b May 16, 1881, d June 26, 1971
Falcon, M. (CUCC) b July 21, 1888, d Feb. 27, 1976
Fallows, J. A. (Lancs.) b July 25, 1907, d Jan. 20, 1974
*Fane, F. L. (OUCC & Essex) b April 27, 1875, d Nov. 27, 1960
Fantham, W. E. (Warwicks.) b May 14, 1918
*Farnes, K. (CUCC & Essex; *CY 1939*) b July 8, 1911, d Oct. 20, 1941
*Farooq Hamid (Lahore & PIA) b March 3, 1945
*Farrer, W. S. (Border) b Dec. 8, 1936
*Farrimond, W. (Lancs.) b May 23, 1903, d Nov. 14, 1979
*Farrukh Zaman (Peshawar, NWFP, Punjab & MCB) b April 2, 1956
*Faulkner, G. A. (Tvl) b Dec. 17, 1881, d Sept. 10, 1930
*Favell, L. E. (S. Aust.) b Oct. 6, 1929
*Fazal Mahmood (N. Ind., Punjab & Lahore; *CY 1955*) b Feb. 18, 1927
Fearnley, C. D. (Worcs.) b April 12, 1940
Featherstone, N. G. (Tvl, N. Tvl, Middx & Glam.) b Aug. 20, 1949
'Felix', N. (Wanostrocht) (Kent, Surrey & All-England) b Oct. 4, 1804, d Sept. 3, 1876
Fell, D. J. (CUCC) b Oct. 27, 1964
*Fellows-Smith, J. P. (OUCC, Tvl & Northants) b Feb. 3, 1932
Felton, N. A. (Som.) b Oct. 24, 1960
*Fender, P. G. H. (Sussex & Surrey; *CY 1915*) b Aug. 22, 1892, d June 15, 1985
Fenner, D. (Border) b March 27, 1929
*Ferguson, W. (T/T) b Dec. 14, 1917, d Feb. 23, 1961
*Fernandes, M. P. (BG) b Aug. 12, 1897, d May 8, 1981
*Fernando, E. R. N. S. (SL) b Dec. 19, 1955
Ferrandi, J. H. (W. Prov.) b April 3, 1930
Ferreira, A. M. (N. Tvl & Warwicks.) b April 13, 1955
**Ferris, J. J. (NSW, Glos. & S. Aust.; *CY 1889*) b May 21, 1867, d Nov. 21, 1900
*Fichardt, C. G. (OFS) b March 20, 1870, d May 30, 1923
Fiddian-Green, C. A. F. (CUCC, Warwicks. & Worcs.) b Dec. 22, 1898, d Sept. 5, 1976
Fiddling, K. (Yorks. & Northants) b Oct. 13, 1917
*Fielder, A. (Kent; *CY 1907*) b July 19, 1877, d Aug. 30, 1949
*Findlay, T. M. (Comb. Is. & Windwards) b Oct. 19, 1943
Findlay, W. (OUCC & Lancs.; Sec. Surrey CCC, Sec. MCC 1926-36) b June 22, 1880, d June 19, 1953
*Fingleton, J. H. (NSW) b April 28, 1908, d Nov. 22, 1981

*Finlason, C. E. (Tvl & Griq. W.) b Feb. 19, 1860, d July 31, 1917
Finney, R. J. (Derbys.) b Aug. 2, 1960
Firth, J. (Yorks. & Leics.) b June 27, 1918, d Sept. 6, 1981
Firth, Rev. Canon J. D'E. E. (Winchester, OUCC & Notts.; *CY 1918*) b Jan. 21, 1900, d Sept. 21, 1957
Fisher, B. (Qld) b Jan. 20, 1934, d April 6, 1980
*Fisher, F. E. (Wgtn & C. Dist.) b July 28, 1924
Fisher, P. B. (OUCC, Middx & Worcs.) b Dec. 19, 1954
*Fishlock, L. B. (Surrey; *CY 1947*) b Jan. 2, 1907
Fitzroy-Newdegate, Cdr. Hon. J. M. (Northants) b March 20, 1897, d May 7, 1976
Flanagan, J. P. D. (Tvl) b Sept. 20, 1947
*Flavell, J. A. (Worcs.; *CY 1965*) b May 15, 1929
*Fleetwood-Smith, L. O'B. (Vic.) b March 30, 1910, d March 16, 1971
Fletcher, D. A. G. (Rhod. & Zimb.) b Sept. 27, 1948
Fletcher, D. G. W. (Surrey) b July 6, 1924
*Fletcher, K. W. R. (Essex; *CY 1974*) b May 20, 1944
*Floquet, C. E. (Tvl) b Nov. 3, 1884, d Nov. 22, 1963
*Flowers, W. (Notts.) b Dec. 7, 1856, d Nov. 1, 1926
Foat, J. C. (Glos.) b Nov. 21, 1952
*Foley, H. (Wgtn) b Jan. 28, 1906, d Oct. 16, 1948
Folley, I. (Lancs.) b Jan. 9, 1963
Foord, C. W. (Yorks.) b June 11, 1924
Forbes, C. (Notts.) b Aug. 9, 1936
Ford, D. A. (NSW) b Dec. 12, 1930
*Ford, F. G. J. (CUCC & Middx) b Dec. 14, 1866, d Feb. 7, 1940
Ford, N. M. (OUCC, Derbys. & Middx) b Nov. 18, 1906
Ford, R. G. (Glos.) b March 3, 1907, d Oct. 1981
Foreman, D. J. (W. Prov. & Sussex) b Feb. 1, 1933
Fosh, M. K. (CUCC & Essex) b Sept. 26, 1957
Foster, D. G. (Warwicks.) b March 19, 1907, d Oct. 13, 1980
*Foster, F. R. (Warwicks.; *CY 1912*) b Jan. 31, 1889, d May 3, 1958
Foster, G. N. (OUCC, Worcs. & Kent) b Oct. 16, 1884, d Aug. 11, 1971
Foster, H. K. (OUCC & Worcs.; *CY 1911*) b Oct. 30, 1873, d June 23, 1950
Foster, M. K. (Worcs.) b Jan. 1, 1889, d Dec. 3, 1940
*Foster, M. L. C. (Jam.) b May 9, 1943
*Foster, N. A. (Essex) b May 6, 1962
Foster, P. G. (Kent) b Oct. 9, 1916
*Foster, R. E. (OUCC & Worcs.; *CY 1901*) b April 16, 1878, d May 13, 1914
*Fothergill, A. J. (Som.) b Aug. 26, 1854, d Aug. 1, 1932
Fotheringham, H. R. (Natal, Tvl & SA XI) b April 4, 1953
Foulkes, I. (Border & OFS) b Feb. 22, 1955
Fowler, A. J. B. (Middx) b April 1, 1891, d May 7, 1977
*Fowler, G. (Lancs.) b April 20, 1957
Fowler, W. P. (Derbys., N. Dist. & Auck.) b March 13, 1959
*Francis, B. C. (NSW & Essex) b Feb. 18, 1948
Francis, D. A. (Glam.) b Nov. 29, 1953
*Francis, G. N. (B'dos) b Dec. 7, 1897, d Jan. 12, 1942
*Francis, H. H. (Glos. & W. Prov.) b May 26, 1868, d Jan. 7, 1936
Francke, F. M. (SL & Qld) b March 29, 1941
*Francois, C. M. (Griq. W.) b June 20, 1897, d May 26, 1944
*Frank, C. N. (Tvl) b Jan. 27, 1891, d Dec. 26, 1961
*Frank, W. H. B. (SA) b Nov. 23, 1872, d Feb. 16, 1945
Franklin, H. W. F. (OUCC, Surrey & Essex) b June 30, 1901, d May 25, 1985
*Franklin, T. J. (Auck.) b March 18, 1962
Franks, J. G. (OUCC) b Sept. 23, 1962
*Frederick, M. C. (B'dos, Derbys. & Jam.) b May 6, 1927
*Fredericks, R. C. (†Guyana & Glam.; *CY 1974*) b Nov. 11, 1942
*Freeman, A. P. (Kent; *CY 1923*) b May 17, 1888, d Jan. 28, 1965
*Freeman, D. L. (Wgtn) b Sept. 8, 1914
*Freeman, E. W. (S. Aust.) b July 13, 1944
*Freer, F. W. (Vic.) b Dec. 4, 1915
French, B. N. (Notts.) b Aug. 13, 1959
Frost, G. (Notts.) b Jan. 15, 1947
Fry, C. A. (OUCC, Hants & Northants) b Jan. 14, 1940
*Fry, C. B. (OUCC, Sussex & Hants; *CY 1895*) b April 25, 1872, d Sept. 7, 1956
*Fuller, E. R. H. (W. Prov.) b Aug. 2, 1931
*Fuller, R. L. (Jam.) b Jan. 30, 1913
*Fullerton, G. M. (Tvl) b Dec. 8, 1922
Funston, G. K. (NE Tvl & Griq. W.) b Nov. 21, 1948
*Funston, K. J. (NE Tvl, OFS & Tvl) b Dec. 3, 1925
*Furlonge, H. A. (T/T) b June 19, 1934

Gabriel, R. S. (T/T) b June 5, 1952
*Gadkari, C. V. (M'tra & Ind. Serv.) b Feb. 3, 1928
*Gaekwad, A. D. (Baroda) b Sept. 23, 1952
*Gaekwad, D. K. (Baroda) b Oct. 27, 1928
*Gaekwad, H. G. (†M. Pradesh) b Aug. 29, 1923
Gale, R. A. (Middx) b Dec. 10, 1933

*Gallichan, N. (Wgtn) b June 3, 1906, d March 25, 1969
*Gamsy, D. (Natal) b Feb. 17, 1940
*Gandotra, A. (Delhi & Bengal) b Nov. 24, 1948
*Gannon, J. B. (W. Aust.) b Feb. 8, 1947
*Ganteaume, A. G. (T/T) b Jan. 22, 1921
Gard, T. (Som.) b June 2, 1957
Gardiner, H. A. B. (Rhod.) b Jan. 3, 1944
Gardiner, S. J. C. (CUCC) b March 19, 1947
Gardner, F. C. (Warwicks.) b June 4, 1922, d Jan. 13, 1979
Gardner, L. R. (Leics.) b Feb. 23, 1934
Garland-Wells, H. M. (OUCC & Surrey) b Nov. 14, 1907
Garlick, P. L. (CUCC) b Aug. 2, 1964
Garlick, R. G. (Lancs. & Northants) b April 11, 1917
*Garner, J. (B'dos, Som. & S. Aust.; *CY 1980*) b Dec. 16, 1952
Garnham, M. A. (Glos. & Leics.) b Aug. 20, 1960
*Garrett, T. W. (NSW) b July 26, 1858, d Aug. 6, 1943
*Gaskin, B. M. (BG) b March 21, 1908, d May 2, 1979
*Gatting, M. W. (Middx; *CY 1984*) b June 6, 1957
*Gaunt, R. A. (W. Aust. & Vic.) b Feb. 26, 1934
*Gavaskar, S. M. (Bombay & Som.; *CY 1980*) b July 10, 1949
*Gay, L. H. (CUCC, Hants & Som.) b March 24, 1871, d Nov. 1, 1949
Geary, A. C. T. (Surrey) b Sept. 11, 1900
*Geary, G. (Leics.; *CY 1927*) b July 9, 1893, d March 6, 1981
*Gedye, S. G. (Auck.) b May 2, 1929
*Gehrs, D. R. A. (S. Aust.) b Nov. 29, 1880, d June 25, 1953
*Ghavri, K. D. (S'tra & Bombay) b Feb. 28, 1951
*Ghazali, M. E. Z. (M'tra & Pak. Serv.) b June 15, 1924
*Ghorpade, J. M. (Baroda) b Oct. 2, 1930, d March 29, 1978
*Ghulam Abbas (Kar., NBP & PIA) b May 1, 1947
*Ghulam Ahmed (H'bad) b July 4, 1922
*Gibb, P. A. (OUCC, Scotland, Yorks. & Essex) b July 11, 1913, d Dec. 7, 1977
Gibbons, H. H. (Worcs.) b Oct. 10, 1904, d Feb. 16, 1973
*Gibbs, G. L. (BG) b Dec. 27, 1925, d Feb. 21, 1979
*Gibbs, L. R. (†Guyana, S. Aust. & Warwicks.; *CY 1972*) b Sept. 29, 1934
Gibbs, P. J. K. (OUCC & Derbys.) b Aug. 17, 1944
Gibson, C. H. (Eton, CUCC & Sussex; *CY 1918*) b Aug. 23, 1900, d Dec. 31, 1976
Gibson, D. (Surrey) b May 1, 1936
Gibson, J. G. (N. Dist. & Auck.) b Nov. 12, 1948
*Giffen, G. (S. Aust.; *CY 1894*) b March 27, 1859, d Nov. 29, 1927
*Giffen, W. F. (S. Aust.) b Sept. 20, 1861, d June 29, 1949
*Gifford, N. (Worcs. & Warwicks.; *CY 1975*) b March 30, 1940
*Gilbert, D. R. (NSW) b Dec. 19, 1960
*Gilchrist, R. (Jam. & H'bad) b June 28, 1934
Giles, R. J. (Notts.) b Oct. 17, 1919
Gill, A. (Notts.) b Aug. 4, 1940
Gill, L. L. (Tas. & Qld; oldest surviving Sheffield Shield player) b Nov. 19, 1891
Gilhouley, K. (Yorks. & Notts.) b Aug. 8, 1934
Gilliat, R. M. C. (OUCC & Hants) b May 20, 1944
*Gilligan, A. E. R. (CUCC, Surrey & Sussex; *CY 1924*; Pres. MCC 1967-68) b Dec. 23, 1894, d Sept. 5, 1976
*Gilligan, A. H. H. (Sussex) b June 29, 1896, d May 5, 1978
Gilligan, F. W. (OUCC & Essex) b Sept. 20, 1893, d May 4, 1960
*Gilmour, G. J. (NSW) b June 26, 1951
*Gimblett, H. (Som.; *CY 1953*) b Oct. 19, 1914, d March 30, 1978
Gladstone, G. (*see* Marais, G. G.)
Gladwin, Chris (Essex) b May 10, 1962
*Gladwin, Cliff (Derbys.) b April 3, 1916
*Gleeson, J. W. (NSW & E. Prov.) b March 14, 1938
*Gleeson, R. A. (E. Prov.) b Dec. 6, 1873, d Sept. 27, 1919
*Glover, G. K. (Kimberley & Griq. W.) b May 13, 1870, d Nov. 15, 1938
Glover, T. R. (OUCC) b Nov. 26, 1951
Goddard, G. F. (Scotland) b May 19, 1938
*Goddard, J. D. C. (B'dos) b April 21, 1919
*Goddard, T. L. (Natal & NE Tvl) b Aug. 1, 1931
*Goddard, T. W. (Glos.; *CY 1938*) b Oct. 1, 1900, d May 22, 1966
Goel, R. (Patiala & Haryana) b Sept. 29, 1942
Goldie, C. F. E. (CUCC & Hants) b Nov. 20, 1960
Goldstein, F. S. (OUCC, Northants, Tvl & W. Prov.) b Oct. 14, 1944
*Gomes, H. A. (T/T & Middx; *CY 1985*) b July 13, 1953
Gomes, S. A. (T/T) b Oct. 18, 1950
*Gomez, G. E. (T/T) b Oct. 10, 1919
*Gooch, G. A. (Essex & W. Prov.; *CY 1980*) b July 23, 1953
Goodway, C. C. (Warwicks.) b July 10, 1909
Goodwin, K. (Lancs.) b June 25, 1938
Goodwin, T. J. (Leics.) b Jan. 22, 1929
*Goonatillake, H. M. (SL) b Aug. 16, 1952
Goonesena, G. (Ceylon, Notts., CUCC & NSW) b Feb. 16, 1931
*Gopalan, M. J. (Madras) b June 6, 1909
*Gopinath, C. D. (Madras) b March 1, 1930
*Gordon, N. (Tvl) b Aug. 6, 1911

Gore, A. C. (Eton & Army; *CY 1919*) b May 14, 1900
Gorman, S. R. (CUCC) b April 28, 1965
Gothard, E. J. (Derbys.) b Oct. 1, 1904, d Jan. 17, 1979
Gould, I. J. (Middx, Auck. & Sussex) b Aug. 19, 1957
*Gover, A. R. (Surrey; *CY 1937*) b Feb. 29, 1908
*Gower, D. I. (Leics.; *CY 1979*) b April 1, 1957
Gowrie, 1st Lord (Pres. MCC 1948-49) b July 6, 1872, d May 2, 1955
Grace, Dr Alfred b May 17, 1840, d May 24, 1916
Grace, Dr Alfred H. (Glos.) b March 10, 1866, d Sept. 16, 1929
Grace, C. B. (Clifton) b March 1882, d June 6, 1938
*Grace, Dr E. M. (Glos.) b Nov. 28, 1841, d May 20, 1911
Grace, Dr Edgar M. (MCC) (son of E. M. Grace) b Oct. 6, 1886, d Nov. 24, 1974
*Grace, G. F. (Glos.) b Dec. 13, 1850, d Sept. 22, 1880
Grace, Dr Henry (Glos.) b Jan. 31, 1833, d Nov. 15, 1895
Grace, Dr H. M. (father of W. G., E. M. and G. F.) b Feb. 21, 1808, d Dec. 23, 1871
Grace, Mrs H. M. (mother of W. G., E. M. and G. F.) b July 18, 1812, d July 25, 1884
*Grace, Dr W. G. (Glos.; *CY 1896*) b July 18, 1848, d Oct. 23, 1915
Grace, W. G., jun. (CUCC & Glos.) b July 6, 1874, d March 2, 1905
*Graham, H. (Vic. & Otago) b Nov. 29, 1870, d Feb. 7, 1911
Graham, J. N. (Kent) b May 8, 1943
*Graham, R. (W. Prov.) b Sept. 16, 1877, d April 21, 1946
*Grant, G. C. (CUCC, T/T & Rhod.) b May 9, 1907, d Oct. 26, 1978
*Grant, R. S. (CUCC & T/T) b Dec. 15, 1909, d Oct. 18, 1977
Graveney, D. A. (Glos.) b Jan. 21, 1953
Graveney, J. K. (Glos.) b Dec. 16, 1924
*Graveney, T. W. (Glos., Worcs. & Qld; *CY 1953*) b June 16, 1927
Graves, P. J. (Sussex & OFS) b May 19, 1946
Gray, A. H. (T/T & Surrey) b May 23, 1963
*Gray, E. J. (Wgtn) b Nov. 18, 1954
Gray, J. R. (Hants) b May 19, 1926
Gray, L. H. (Middx) b Dec. 16, 1915, d Jan. 3, 1983
Greasley, D. G. (Northants) b Jan. 20, 1926
Green, A. M. (Sussex & OFS) b May 28, 1960
Green, D. J. (Derbys. & CUCC) b Dec. 18, 1935
Green, D. M. (OUCC, Lancs. & Glos.; *CY 1969*) b Nov. 10, 1939
Green, Brig. M. A. (Glos. & Essex) b Oct. 3, 1891, d Dec. 28, 1971
*Greenhough, T. (Lancs.) b Nov. 9, 1931
*Greenidge, A. E. (B'dos) b Aug. 20, 1956
*Greenidge, C. G. (Hants & B'dos; *CY 1977*) b May 1, 1951
*Greenidge, G. A. (B'dos & Sussex) b May 26, 1948
Greensmith, W. T. (Essex) b Aug. 16, 1930
*Greenwood, A. (Yorks.) b Aug. 20, 1847, d Feb. 12, 1889
Greenwood, H. W. (Sussex & Northants) b Sept. 4, 1909, d March 24, 1979
Greenwood, P. (Lancs.) b Sept. 11, 1924
Greetham, C. (Som.). b Aug. 28, 1936
*Gregory, David W. (NSW; first Australian captain) b April 15, 1845, d Aug. 4, 1919
*Gregory, E. J. (NSW) b May 29, 1839, d April 22, 1899
*Gregory, J. M. (NSW; *CY 1922*) b Aug. 14, 1895, d Aug. 7, 1973
*Gregory, R. G. (Vic.) b Feb. 26, 1916, d June 10, 1942
*Gregory, S. E. (NSW; *CY 1897*) b April 14, 1870, d August 1, 1929
*Greig, A. W. (Border, E. Prov. & Sussex; *CY 1975*) b Oct. 6, 1946
*Greig, I. A. (CUCC, Border & Sussex) b Dec. 8, 1955
*Grell, M. G. (T/T) b Dec. 18, 1899, d Jan. 11, 1976
*Grieve, B. A. F. (Eng.) b May 28, 1864, d Nov. 19, 1917
Grieves, K. J. (NSW & Lancs.) b Aug. 27, 1925
*Grieveson, R. E. (Tvl) b Aug. 24, 1909
*Griffin, G. M. (Natal & Rhod.) b June 12, 1939
*Griffith, C. C. (B'dos; *CY 1964*) b Dec. 14, 1938
Griffith, G. ("Ben") (Surrey & Utd England XI) b Dec. 20, 1833, d May 3, 1879
*Griffith, H. C. (B'dos) b Dec. 1, 1893, d March 18, 1980
Griffith, K. (Worcs.) b Jan. 17, 1950
Griffith, M. G. (CUCC & Sussex) b Nov. 25, 1943
*Griffith, S. C. (CUCC, Surrey & Sussex; Sec. MCC 1962-74; Pres. MCC 1979-80) b June 16, 1914
Griffiths, B. J. (Northants) b June 13, 1949
Griffiths, Sir W. H. (CUCC & Glam.) b Sept. 26, 1923
Grimes, A. D. H. (CUCC) b Jan. 8, 1965
Grimmett, C. V. (Wgtn, Vic. & S. Aust.; *CY 1931*) b Dec. 25, 1891, d May 2, 1980
Grimshaw, N. (Northants) b May 5, 1911
Gripper, R. A. (Rhod.) b July 7, 1938
*Groube, T. U. (Vic.) b Sept. 2, 1857, d Aug. 5, 1927
*Grout, A. T. W. (Qld) b March 30, 1927, d Nov. 9, 1968
Grove, C. W. (Warwicks. & Worcs.) b Dec. 16, 1912, d Feb. 15, 1982
Grover, J. N. (OUCC) b Oct. 15, 1915
Groves, B. S. (Border & Natal) b March 1, 1947

Groves, M. G. M. (OUCC, Som. & W. Prov.) b Jan. 14, 1943
Grundy, J. (Notts. & Utd England XI) b March 5, 1824, d Nov. 24, 1873
*Guard, G. M. (Bombay & Guj.) b Dec. 12, 1925, d March 13, 1978
*Guest, C. E. J. (Vic. & W. Aust.) b Oct. 7, 1937
*Guha, S. (Bengal) b Jan. 31, 1946
**Guillen, S. C. (T/T & Cant.) b Sept. 24, 1924
Guise, J. L. (OUCC & Middx) b Nov. 25, 1903
*Gunasekera, Y. (SL) b Nov. 8, 1957
**Gul Mahomed (N. Ind., Baroda, H'bad, Punjab & Lahore) b Oct. 15, 1921
*Guneratne, R. P. W. (SL) b Jan. 26, 1962
*Gunn, G. (Notts.; *CY 1914*) b June 13, 1879, d June 28, 1958
Gunn, G. V. (Notts.) b June 21, 1905, d Oct. 14, 1957
*Gunn, J. (Notts.; *CY 1904*) b July 19, 1876, d Aug. 21, 1963
Gunn, T. (Sussex) b Sept. 27, 1935
*Gunn, William (Notts.; *CY 1890*) b Dec. 4, 1858, d Jan. 29, 1921
*Gupte, B. P. (Bombay, Bengal & Ind. Rlwys) b Aug. 30, 1934
*Gupte, S. P. (Bombay, Bengal, Raja. & T/T) b Dec. 11, 1929
Gurr, D. R. (OUCC & Som.) b March 27, 1956
*Guy, J. W. (C. Dist., Wgtn, Northants, Cant., Otago & N. Dist.) b Aug. 29, 1934

Hacker, P. J. (Notts., Derbys. & OFS) b July 16, 1952
Hadlee, B. G. (Cant.) b Dec. 14, 1941
*Hadlee, D. R. (Cant.) b Jan. 6, 1948
*Hadlee, R. J. (Cant., Notts. & Tas.; *CY 1982*) b July 3, 1951
*Hadlee, W. A. (Cant. & Otago) b June 4, 1915
Hafeez, A. (*see* Kardar)
*Haig, N. E. (Middx) b Dec. 12, 1887, d Oct. 27, 1966
*Haigh, S. (Yorks.; *CY 1901*) b March 19, 1871, d Feb. 27, 1921
Halfyard, D. J. (Kent & Notts.) b April 3, 1931
*Hall, A. E. (Tvl & Lancs.) b Jan. 23, 1896, d Jan. 1, 1964
*Hall, G. G. (NE Tvl & E. Prov.) b May 24, 1938
Hall, I. W. (Derbys.) b Dec. 27, 1939
Hall, Louis (Yorks.; *CY 1890*) b Nov. 1, 1852, d Nov. 19, 1915
Hall, T. A. (Derbys. & Som.) b Aug. 19, 1930, d April 21, 1984
*Hall, W. W. (B'dos, T/T & Qld) b Sept. 12, 1937
Hallam, A. W. (Lancs. & Notts.; *CY 1908*) b Nov. 12, 1869, d July 24, 1940
Hallam, M. R. (Leics.) b Sept. 10, 1931
Halliday, S. J. (OUCC) b July 13, 1960
*Halliwell, E. A. (Tvl & Middx; *CY 1905*) b Sept. 7, 1864, d Oct. 2, 1919
*Hallows, C. (Lancs.; *CY 1928*) b April 4, 1895, d Nov. 10, 1972
Hallows, J. (Lancs.; *CY 1905*) b Nov. 14, 1873, d May 20, 1910
*Halse, C. G. (Natal) b Feb. 28, 1935
*Hamence, R. A. (S. Aust.) b Nov. 25, 1915
Hamer, A. (Yorks. & Derbys.) b Dec. 8, 1916
Hammond, H. E. (Sussex) b Nov. 7, 1907, d June 16, 1985
*Hammond, J. R. (S. Aust.) b April 19, 1950
*Hammond, W. R. (Glos.; *CY 1928*) b June 19, 1903, d July 1, 1965
*Hampshire, J. H. (Yorks., Derbys. & Tas.) b Feb. 10, 1941
*Hands, P. A. M. (W. Prov.) b March 18, 1890, d April 27, 1951
*Hands, R. H. M. (W. Prov.) b July 26, 1888, d April 20, 1918
*Hanif Mohammad (B'pur, Kar. & PIA; *CY 1968*) b Dec. 21, 1934
*Hanley, M. A. (Border & W. Prov.) b Nov. 10, 1918
Hanley, R. W. (E. Prov., OFS, Tvl, SA XI & Northants) b Jan. 29, 1952
*Hanumant Singh (M. Pradesh & Raja.) b March 29, 1939
Hardie, B. R. (Scotland & Essex) b Jan. 14, 1950
*Hardikar, M. S. (Bombay) b Feb. 8, 1936
*Hardinge, H. T. W. (Kent; *CY 1915*) b Feb. 25, 1886, d May 8, 1965
*Hardstaff, J. (Notts.) b Nov. 9, 1882, d April 2, 1947
*Hardstaff, J., jun. (Notts. & Auck.; *CY 1938*) b July 3, 1911
Hardy, J. J. E. (Hants) b Oct. 10, 1960
Harfield, L. (Hants) b Aug. 16, 1905
*Harford, N. S. (C. Dist. & Auck.) b Aug. 30, 1930, d March 30, 1981
*Harford, R. I. (Auck.) b May 30, 1936
Harman, R. (Surrey) b Dec. 28, 1941
*Haroon Rashid (Kar., Sind, NBP, PIA & UBL) b March 25, 1953
*Harper, R. A. (Guyana & Northants) b March 17, 1963
*Harris, 4th Lord (OUCC & Kent; Pres. MCC 1895) b Feb. 3, 1851, d March 24, 1932
Harris, David (Hants & All-England) b 1755, d May 19, 1803
Harris, M. J. (Middx, Notts., E. Prov. & Wgtn) b May 25, 1944
*Harris, P. G. Z. (Cant.) b July 18, 1927
*Harris, R. M. (Auck.) b July 27, 1933
*Harris, T. A. (Griq. W. & Tvl) b Aug. 27, 1916
Harrison, L. (Hants) b June 8, 1922
*Harry, J. (Vic.) b Aug. 1, 1857, d Oct. 27, 1919

Hart, G. E. (Middx) b Jan. 13, 1902
*Hartigan, G. P. D. (Border) b Dec. 30, 1884, d Jan. 7, 1955
*Hartigan, R. J. (NSW & Qld) b Dec. 12, 1879, d June 7, 1958
*Hartkopf, A. E. V. (Vic.) b Dec. 28, 1889, d May 20, 1968
Hartley, A. (Lancs.; *CY 1911*) b April 11, 1879, d Oct. 1918
*Hartley, J. C. (OUCC & Sussex) b Nov. 15, 1874, d March 8, 1963
Hartley, S. N. (Yorks. & OFS) b March 18, 1956
Harty, I. D. (Border) b May 7, 1941
Harvey, J. F. (Derbys.) b Sept. 27, 1939
*Harvey, M. R. (Vic.) b April 29, 1918
Harvey, P. F. (Notts.) b Jan. 15, 1923
*Harvey, R. L. (Natal) b Sept. 14, 1911
*Harvey, R. N. (Vic. & NSW; *CY 1954*) b Oct. 8, 1928
Harvey-Walker, A. J. (Derbys.) b July 21, 1944
*Haseeb Ahsan (Peshawar, Pak. Us, Kar. & PIA) b July 15, 1939
Hassan, B. (Notts.) b March 24, 1944
*Hassett, A. L. (Vic.; *CY 1949*) b Aug. 28, 1913
*Hastings, B. F. (Wgtn, C. Dist. & Cant.) b March 23, 1940
*Hathorn, C. M. H. (Tvl) b April 7, 1878, d May 17, 1920
*Hawke, 7th Lord (CUCC & Yorks.; *CY 1909*; Pres. MCC 1914-18) b Aug. 16, 1860, d Oct. 10, 1938
*Hawke, N. J. N. (W. Aust., S. Aust. & Tas.) b June 27, 1939
Hawker, Sir Cyril (Essex; Pres. MCC 1970-71) b July 21, 1900
Hawkins, D. G. (Glos.) b May 18, 1935
*Hayes, E. G. (Surrey & Leics.; *CY 1907*) b Nov. 6, 1876, d Dec. 2, 1953
*Hayes, F. C. (Lancs.) b Dec. 6, 1946
*Hayes, J. A. (Auck. & Cant.) b Jan. 11, 1927
Hayes, K. A. (OUCC & Lancs.) b Sept. 26, 1962
Hayes, P. J. (CUCC) b May 20, 1954
Haygarth, A. (Sussex; Historian) b Aug. 4, 1825, d May 1, 1903
*Haynes, D. L. (B'dos) b Feb. 15, 1956
Haynes, R. W. (Glos.) b Aug. 27, 1913, d Oct. 16, 1976
Hayward, T. (Cambs. & All-England) b March 21, 1835, d July 21, 1876
*Hayward, T. W. (Surrey; *CY 1895*) b March 29, 1871, d July 19, 1939
Haywood, P. R. (Leics.) b March 30, 1947
*Hazare, V. S. (M'tra, C. Ind. & Baroda) b March 11, 1915
Hazell, H. L. (Som.) b Sept. 30, 1909
Hazlerigg, Lord, formerly Hon. A. G. (CUCC & Leics.) b Feb. 24, 1910
*Hazlitt, G. R. (Vic. & NSW) b Sept. 4, 1888, d Oct. 30, 1915
*Headley, G. A. (Jam.; *CY 1934*) b May 30, 1909, d Nov. 30, 1983
*Headley, R. G. A. (Worcs. & Jam.) b June 29, 1939
Heane, G. F. H. (Notts.) b Jan. 2, 1904, d Oct. 24, 1969
Hearn, P. (Kent) b Nov. 18, 1925
*Hearne, Alec (Kent; *CY 1894*) b July 22, 1863, d May 16, 1952
**Hearne, Frank (Kent & W. Prov.) b Nov. 23, 1858, d July 14, 1949
*Hearne, G. A. L. (W. Prov.) b March 27, 1888, d Nov. 13, 1978
*Hearne, George G. (Kent) b July 7, 1856, d Feb. 13, 1932
*Hearne, J. T. (Middx; *CY 1892*) b May 3, 1867, d April 17, 1944
*Hearne, J. W. (Middx; *CY 1912*) b Feb. 11, 1891, d Sept. 13, 1965
Hearne, Thos. (Middx) b Sept. 4, 1826, d May 13, 1900
Hearne, Thos., jun. (Lord's Ground Superintendent) b Dec. 29, 1849, d Jan. 29, 1910
Heath, G. E. M. (Hants) b Feb. 20, 1913
Heath, M. (Hants) b March 9, 1934
Hedges, B. (Glam.) b Nov. 10, 1927
Hedges, L. P. (Tonbridge, OUCC, Kent & Glos.; *CY 1919*) b July 13, 1900, d Jan. 12, 1933
*Heine, P. S. (NE Tvl, OFS & Tvl) b June 28, 1928
*Hemmings, E. E. (Warwicks. & Notts.) b Feb. 20, 1949
Hemsley, E. J. O. (Worcs.) b Sept. 1, 1943
*Henderson, M. (Wgtn) b Aug. 2, 1895, d June 17, 1970
Henderson, R. (Surrey; *CY 1890*) b March 30, 1865, d Jan. 29, 1931
Henderson, S. P. (CUCC, Worcs. & Glam.) b Sept. 24, 1958
*Hendren, E. H. (Middx; *CY 1920*) b Feb. 5, 1889, d Oct. 4, 1962
*Hendrick, M. (Derbys. & Notts.; *CY 1978*) b Oct. 22, 1948
*Hendriks, J. L. (Jam.) b Dec. 21, 1933
*Hendry, H. L. (NSW & Vic.) b May 24, 1895
Henry, O. (W. Prov. & Scotland) b Jan. 23, 1952
Henwood, P. P. (OFS & Natal) b May 22, 1946
Herman, O. W. (Hants) b Sept. 18, 1907
Herman, R. S. (Middx, Border, Griq. W. & Hants) b Nov. 30, 1946
Heron, J. G. (Zimb.) b Nov. 8, 1948
*Heseltine, C. (Hants) b Nov. 26, 1869, d June 13, 1944
Heseltine, P. J. (OUCC) b June 21, 1960
Hever, N. G. (Middx & Glam.) b Dec. 17, 1924
Hewetson, E. P. (OUCC & Warwicks.) b May 27, 1902, d Dec. 26, 1977
Hewett, H. T. (OUCC & Som.; *CY 1893*) b May 25, 1864, d March 4, 1921

Hewitt, S. G. P. (CUCC) b April 6, 1963
*Hibbert, P. A. (Vic.) b July 23, 1952
Hick, G. A. (Worcs. & Zimb.) b May 23, 1966
Higgins, H. L. (Worcs.) b Feb. 24, 1894, d Sept. 15, 1979
*Higgs, J. D. (Vic.) b July 11, 1950
*Higgs, K. (Lancs. & Leics.; *CY 1968*) b Jan. 14, 1937
Hignell, A. J. (CUCC & Glos.) b Sept. 4, 1955
*Hilditch, A. M. J. (NSW) b May 20, 1956
Hill, Alan (Derbys. & OFS) b June 29, 1950
*Hill, Allen (Yorks.) b Nov. 14, 1843, d Aug. 29, 1910
*Hill, A. J. L. (CUCC & Hants) b July 26, 1871, d Sept. 6, 1950
*Hill, C. (S. Aust.; *CY 1900*) b March 18, 1877, d Sept. 5, 1945
Hill, E. (Som.) b July 9, 1923
Hill, G. (Hants) b April 15, 1913
*Hill, J. C. (Vic.) b June 25, 1923, d Aug. 11, 1974
Hill, L. W. (Glam.) b April 14, 1942
Hill, M. (Notts., Derbys & Som.) b Sept. 14, 1935
Hill, N. W. (Notts.) b Aug. 22, 1935
Hill, W. A. (Warwicks.) b April 27, 1910
Hills, J. J. (Glam.; Umpire) b Oct. 14, 1897, d Oct. 1969
Hills, R. W. (Kent) b Jan. 8, 1951
Hill-Wood, C. K. (OUCC & Derbys.) b June 5, 1907
Hill-Wood, Sir W. W. (CUCC & Derbys.) b Sept. 8, 1901, d Oct. 10, 1980
Hilton, C. (Lancs. & Essex) b Sept. 26, 1937
Hilton, J. (Lancs. & Som.) b Dec. 29, 1930
*Hilton, M. J. (Lancs.; *CY 1957*) b Aug. 2, 1928
*Hime, C. F. W. (Natal) b Oct. 24, 1869, d Dec. 6, 1940
*Hindlekar, D. D. (Bombay) b Jan. 1, 1909, d March 30, 1949
Hinks, S. G. (Kent) b Oct. 12, 1960
*Hirst, G. H. (Yorks.; *CY 1901*) b Sept. 7, 1871, d May 10, 1954
*Hitch, J. W. (Surrey; *CY 1914*) b May 7, 1886, d July 7, 1965
Hitchcock, R. E. (Cant. & Warwicks.) b Nov. 28, 1929
*Hoad, E. L. G. (B'dos) b Jan. 29, 1896
*Hoare, D. E. (W. Aust.) b Oct. 19, 1934
*Hobbs, Sir J. B. (Surrey; *CY 1909, special portrait 1926*) b Dec. 16, 1882, d Dec. 21, 1963
*Hobbs, R. N. S. (Essex & Glam.) b May 8, 1942
Hobson, D. L. (E. Prov., W. Prov. & SA XI) b Sept. 3, 1951
*Hodges, J. H. (Vic.) b July 31, 1856, d Jan. 17, 1933
Hodgkinson, G. F. (Derbys.) b Feb. 19, 1914
Hodgson, A. (Northants) b Oct. 27, 1951
Hodgson, K. I. (CUCC) b Feb. 24, 1960
Hoffman, D. S. (Warwicks.) b Jan. 13, 1966
Hofmeyr, M. B. (OUCC & NE Tvl) b Dec. 9, 1925
*Hogan, T. G. (Vic.) b Sept. 23, 1956
*Hogg, R. M. (S. Aust.) b March 5, 1951
Hogg, W. (Lancs. & Warwicks.) b July 12, 1955
Hohns, T. V. (Qld) b Jan. 23, 1954
*Holder, V. A. (B'dos & Worcs.) b Oct. 8, 1945
*Holding, M. A. (Jam., Lancs., Derbys. & Tas.; *CY 1977*) b Feb. 16, 1954
Holdsworth, R. L. (OUCC, Warwicks. & Sussex) b Feb. 25, 1899, d June 20, 1976
*Hole, G. B. (NSW & S. Aust.) b Jan. 6, 1931
*Holford, D. A. J. (B'dos & T/T) b April 16, 1940
*Holland, R. G. (NSW) b Oct. 19, 1946
Holliday, D. C. (CUCC) b Dec. 20, 1958
*Hollies, W. E. (Warwicks.; *CY 1955*) b June 5, 1912, d April 16, 1981
Hollingdale, R. A. (Sussex) b March 6, 1906
Holmes, Gp Capt. A. J. (Sussex) b June 30, 1899, d May 21, 1950
*Holmes, E. R. T. (OUCC & Surrey; *CY 1936*) b Aug. 21, 1905, d Aug. 16, 1960
Holmes, G. C. (Glam.) b Sept. 16, 1958
*Holmes, P. (Yorks.; *CY 1920*) b Nov. 25, 1886, d Sept. 3, 1971
Holt, A. G. (Hants) b April 8, 1911
*Holt, J. K., jun. (Jam.) b Aug. 12, 1923
Home of the Hirsel, Lord (Middx; Pres. MCC 1966-67) b July 2, 1903
Hone, Sir B. W. (S. Aust. & OUCC) b July 1, 1907, d May 28, 1978
*Hone, L. (MCC) b Jan. 30, 1853, d Dec. 31, 1896
Hooker, J. E. H. (NSW) b March 6, 1898, d Feb. 12, 1982
Hooker, R. W. (Middx) b Feb. 22, 1935
*Hookes, D. W. (S. Aust.) b May 3, 1955
*Hopkins, A. J. Y. (NSW) b May 4, 1874, d April 25, 1931
Hopkins, J. A. (Glam.) b June 16, 1953
Hopkins, V. (Glos.) b Jan. 21, 1911, d Aug. 6, 1984
*Hopwood, J. L. (Lancs.) b Oct. 30, 1903, d June 15, 1985
*Horan, T. P. (Vic.) b March 8, 1854, d April 16, 1916
*Hordern, H. V. (NSW & Philadelphians) b Feb. 10, 1883, d June 17, 1938
*Hornby, A. N. (Lancs.) b Feb. 10, 1847, d Dec. 17, 1925
Horner, N. F. (Yorks. & Warwicks.) b May 10, 1926
*Hornibrook, P. M. (Qld) b July 27, 1899, d Aug. 25, 1976
Horsfall, R. (Essex & Glam.) b June 26, 1920, d Aug. 25, 1981
Horsley, J. (Notts. & Derbys.) b Jan. 4, 1890, d Feb. 13, 1976
Horton, H. (Worcs. & Hants) b April 18, 1923

Horton, J. (Worcs.) b Aug. 12, 1916
*Horton, M. J. (Worcs. & N. Dist.) b April 21, 1934
Hossell, J. J. (Warwicks.) b May 25, 1914
*Hough, K. W. (Auck.) b Oct. 24, 1928
*Howard, A. B. (B'dos) b Aug. 27, 1946
Howard, A. H. (Glam.) b Dec. 11, 1910
Howard, B. J. (Lancs.) b May 21, 1926
Howard, K. (Lancs.) b June 29, 1941
*Howard, N. D. (Lancs.) b May 18, 1925, d May 31, 1979
Howard, Major R. (Lancs.; MCC Team Manager) b April 17, 1890, d Sept. 10, 1967
*Howarth, G. P. (Auck., Surrey & N. Dist.) b March 29, 1951
*Howarth, H. J. (Auck.) b Dec. 25, 1943
Howat, M. G. (CUCC) b March 2, 1958
*Howell, H. (Warwicks.) b Nov. 29, 1890, d July 9, 1932
Howell, M. (OUCC & Surrey) b Sept. 9, 1893, d Feb. 23, 1976
*Howell, W. P. (NSW) b Dec. 29, 1869, d July 14, 1940
Howland, C. B. (CUCC, Sussex & Kent) b Feb. 6, 1936
*Howorth, R. (Worcs.) b April 26, 1909, d April 2, 1980
Hughes, D. P. (Lancs. & Tas.) b May 13, 1947
*Hughes, K. J. (W. Aust.; *CY 1981*) b Jan. 26, 1954
Hughes, S. P. (Middx & N. Tvl) b Dec. 20, 1959
Huish, F. H. (Kent) b Nov. 15, 1869, d March 16, 1957
Hulme, J. H. A. (Middx) b Aug. 26, 1904
Human, J. H. (CUCC & Middx) b Jan. 13, 1912
Humpage, G. W. (Warwicks. & OFS; *CY 1985*) b April 24, 1954
Humphries, D. J. (Leics. & Worcs.) b Aug. 6, 1953
*Humphries, J. (Derbys.) b May 19, 1876, d May 8, 1946
Hunt, A. V. (Scotland & Bermuda) b Oct. 1, 1910
*Hunt, W. A. (NSW) b Aug. 26, 1908, d Dec. 31, 1983
*Hunte, C. C. (B'dos; *CY 1964*) b May 9, 1932
*Hunte, E. A. C. (T/T) b Oct. 3, 1905, d June 26, 1967
Hunter, David (Yorks.) b Feb. 23, 1860, d Jan. 11, 1927
*Hunter, Joseph (Yorks.) b Aug. 3, 1855, d Jan. 4, 1891
Hurd, A. (CUCC & Essex) b Sept. 7, 1937
*Hurst, A. G. (Vic.) b July 15, 1950
Hurst, R. J. (Middx) b Dec. 29, 1933
*Hurwood, A. (Qld) b June 17, 1902, d Sept. 26, 1982
*Hussain, M. Dilawar (C. Ind. & U. Prov.) b March 19, 1907, d Aug. 26, 1967
*Hutchings, K. L. (Kent; *CY 1907*) b Dec. 7, 1882, d Sept. 3, 1916
Hutchinson, J. M. (Derbys.) b Nov. 29, 1896
*Hutchinson, P. (SA) b Jan. 26, 1862, d Sept. 30, 1925
*Hutton, Sir Leonard (Yorks.; *CY 1938*) b June 23, 1916
*Hutton, R. A. (CUCC, Yorks. & Tvl) b Sept. 6, 1942
Huxford, P. N. (OUCC) b Feb. 17, 1960
Huxter, R. J. A. (CUCC) b Oct. 29, 1959
*Hylton, L. G. (Jam.) b March 29, 1905, d May 17, 1955

*Ibadulla, K. (Punjab, Warwicks., Tas. & Otago) b Dec. 20, 1935
*Ibrahim, K. C. (Bombay) b Jan. 26, 1919
*Iddon, J. (Lancs.) b Jan. 8, 1902, d April 17, 1946
*Ijaz Butt (Pak. Us, Punjab, Lahore, R'pindi & Multan) b March 10, 1938
*Ijaz Faqih (Kar., Sind, PWD & MCB) b March 24, 1956
*Ikin, J. T. (Lancs.) b March 7, 1918, d Sept. 15, 1984
*Illingworth, R. (Yorks. & Leics.; *CY 1960*) b June 8, 1932
Illingworth, R. K. (Worcs.) b Aug. 23, 1963
*Imran Khan (Lahore, Worcs., OUCC, PIA & Sussex; *CY 1983*) b Nov. 25, 1952
*Imtiaz Ahmed (N. Ind., Comb. Us, NWFP, Pak. Serv., Peshawar & PAF) b Jan. 5, 1928
*Imtiaz Ali (T/T) b July 28, 1954
Inchmore, J. D. (Worcs. & N. Tvl) b Feb. 22, 1949
*Indrajitsinhji, K. S. (S'tra & Delhi) b June 15, 1937
Ingle, R. A. (Som.) b Nov. 5, 1903
Ingleby-Mackenzie, A. C. D. (Hants) b Sept. 15, 1933
Inman C. C. (Ceylon & Leics.) b Jan. 29, 1936
Innes, G. A. S. (W. Prov. & Tvl) b Nov. 16, 1931, d July 19, 1982
*Inshan Ali (T/T) b Sept. 25, 1949
*Insole, D. J. (CUCC & Essex; *CY 1956*) b April 18, 1926
*Intikhab Alam (Kar., PIA, Surrey, PWD, Sind & Punjab) b Dec. 28, 1941
*Inverarity, R. J. (W. Aust. & S. Aust.) b Jan. 31, 1944
*Iqbal Qasim (Kar., Sind & NBP) b Aug. 6, 1953
*Irani, J. K. (Sind) b Aug. 18, 1923, dead
*Iredale, F. A. (NSW) b June 19, 1867, d April 15, 1926
Iremonger, J. (Notts.; *CY 1903*) b March 5, 1876, d March 25, 1956
*Ironmonger, H. (Qld & Vic.) b April 7, 1882, d June 1, 1971
*Ironside, D. E. J. (Tvl) b May 2, 1925

*Irvine, B. L. (W. Prov., Natal, Essex & Tvl) b March 9, 1944
*Israr Ali (S. Punjab, B'pur & Multan) b May 1, 1927
*Iverson, J. B. (Vic.) b July 27, 1915, d Oct. 24, 1973

*Jackman, R. D. (Surrey, W. Prov. & Rhod.; *CY 1981*) b Aug. 13, 1945
*Jackson, A. A. (NSW) b Sept. 5, 1909, d Feb. 16, 1933
Jackson, A. B. (Derbys.) b Aug. 21, 1933
Jackson, Sir A. H. M. (Derbys.) b Nov. 9, 1899, d Oct. 11, 1983
Jackson, E. J. W. (CUCC) b March 26, 1955
*Jackson, Rt Hon. Sir F. S. (CUCC & Yorks.; *CY 1894*; Pres. MCC 1921) b Nov. 21, 1870, d March 9, 1947
Jackson, G. R. (Derbys.) b June 23, 1896, d Feb. 21, 1966
*Jackson, H. L. (Derbys.; *CY 1959*) b April 5, 1921
Jackson, John (Notts. & All-England) b May 21, 1833, d Nov. 4, 1901
Jackson, P. F. (Worcs.) b May 11, 1911
Jacques, T. A. (Yorks.) b Feb. 19, 1905
*Jahangir Khan (N. Ind. & CUCC) b Feb. 1, 1910
*Jai, L. P. (Bombay) b April 1, 1902, d Jan. 29, 1968
*Jaisimha, M. L. (H'bad) b March 3, 1939
Jakeman, F. (Yorks. & Northants) b Jan. 10, 1920
*Jalal-ud-Din (PWD, Kar., IDBP & Allied Bank) b June 12, 1959
James, A. E. (Sussex) b Aug. 7, 1924
*James, K. C. (Wgtn & Northants) b March 12, 1904, d Aug. 21, 1976
James, R. M. (CUCC & Wgtn) b Oct. 2, 1934
*Jameson, J. A. (Warwicks.) b June 30, 1941
*Jamshedji, R. J. D. (Bombay) b Nov. 18, 1892, d April 5, 1976
*Jardine, D. R. (OUCC & Surrey; *CY 1928*) b Oct. 23, 1900, d June 18, 1958
Jardine, M. R. (OUCC & Middx) b June 8, 1869, d Jan. 16, 1947
*Jarman, B. N. (S. Aust.) b Feb. 17, 1936
Jarrett, D. W. (OUCC & CUCC) b April 19, 1952
*Jarvis, A. H. (S. Aust.) b Oct. 19, 1860, d Nov. 15, 1933
Jarvis, K. B. S. (Kent) b April 23, 1953
Jarvis, P. W. (Yorks.) b June 29, 1965
*Jarvis, T. W. (Auck. & Cant.) b July 29, 1944
*Javed Akhtar (R'pindi & Pak. Serv.) b Nov. 21, 1940
*Javed Miandad (Kar., Sind, Sussex, HBL, Glam. & H'bad; *CY 1982*) b June 12, 1957
*Jayantilal, K. (H'bad) b Jan. 13, 1948
*Jayasekera, R. S. A. (SL) b Dec. 7, 1957
Jayasinghe, S. (Ceylon & Leics.) b Jan. 19, 1931
Jefferies, S. T. (W. Prov., Derbys., Lancs. & SA XI) b Dec. 8, 1959
Jefferson, R. I. (CUCC & Surrey) b Aug. 15, 1941
*Jeganathan, S. (SL) b July 11, 1951
*Jenkins, R. O. (Worcs.; *CY 1950*) b Nov. 24, 1918
Jenkins, V. G. J. (OUCC & Glam.) b Nov. 2, 1911
*Jenner, T. J. (W. Aust. & S. Aust.) b Sept. 8, 1944
*Jennings, C. B. (S. Aust.) b June 5, 1884, d June 20, 1950
Jennings, K. F. (Som.) b Oct. 5, 1953
Jennings, R. V. (Tvl & SA XI) b Aug. 9, 1954
Jepson, A. (Notts.) b July 12, 1915
*Jessop, G. L. (CUCC & Glos.; *CY 1898*) b May 19, 1874, d May 11, 1955
Jesty, T. E. (Hants., Border, Griq. W., Cant. & Surrey; *CY 1983*) b June 2, 1948
Jewell, Major M. F. S. (Sussex & Worcs.) b Sept. 15, 1885, d May 28, 1978
*Jilani, M. Baga (N. Ind.) b July 20, 1911, d July 2, 1941
*John, V. B. (SL) b May 27, 1960
Johnson, C. (Yorks.) b Sept. 5, 1947
*Johnson, C. L. (Tvl) b 1871, d May 31, 1908
Johnson, G. W. (Kent & Tvl) b Nov. 8, 1946
*Johnson, H. H. H. (Jam.) b July 17, 1910
Johnson, H. L. (Derbys.) b Nov. 8, 1927
*Johnson, I. W. (Vic.) b Dec. 8, 1918
Johnson, L. A. (Northants) b Aug. 12, 1936
*Johnson, L. J. (Qld) b March 18, 1919, d April 20, 1977
Johnson, P. (Notts.) b April 24, 1965
Johnson, P. D. (CUCC & Notts.) b Nov. 12, 1949
*Johnson, T. F. (T/T) b Jan. 10, 1917, d April 5, 1985
Johnston, B. A. (Broadcaster) b June 24, 1912
*Johnston, W. A. (Vic.; *CY 1949*) b Feb. 26, 1922
Jones, A. (Glam., W. Aust., N. Tvl & Natal; *CY 1978*) b Nov. 4, 1938
Jones, A. A. (Sussex, Som., Middx, Glam., N. Tvl & OFS) b Dec. 9, 1947
Jones, A. L. (Glam.) b June 1, 1957
*Jones, A. O. (Notts. & CUCC; *CY 1900*) b Aug. 16, 1872, d Dec. 21, 1914
Jones, B. J. R. (Worcs.) b Nov. 2, 1955
*Jones, C. M. (C. E. L.) (BG) b Nov. 3, 1902, d Dec. 10, 1959
*Jones, D. M. (Vic.) b March 24, 1961
*Jones, Ernest (S. Aust. & W. Aust.) b Sept. 30, 1869, d Nov. 23, 1943
Jones, E. C. (Glam.) b Dec. 14, 1912
Jones, E. W. (Glam.) b June 25, 1942
*Jones, I. J. (Glam.) b Dec. 10, 1941
Jones, K. V. (Middx) b March 28, 1942
*Jones, P. E. (T/T) b June 6, 1917
Jones, P. H. (Kent) b June 19, 1935

Jones, S. A. (W. Prov. & Boland) b April 14, 1955
*Jones, S. P. (NSW, Qld & Auck.) b Aug. 1, 1861, d July 14. 1951
Jones, W. E. (Glam.) b Oct. 31, 1916
Jordaan, A. H. (N. Tvl) b July 22, 1947
Jordan, A. B. (C. Dist.) b Sept. 5, 1949
Jordan, J. M. (Lancs.) b Feb. 7, 1932
Jorden, A. M. (CUCC & Essex) b Jan. 28, 1947
Jordon, R. C. (Vic.) b Feb. 17, 1937
*Joshi, P. G. (M'tra) b Oct. 27, 1926
Joshi, U. C. (S'tra, Ind. Rlwys, Guj. & Sussex) b Dec. 23, 1944
*Joslin, L. R. (Vic.) b Dec. 13, 1947
Jowett, D. C. P. R. (OUCC) b June 24, 1931
Judd, A. K. (CUCC & Hants) b Jan. 1, 1904
Judge, P. F. (Middx, Glam. & Bengal) b May 23, 1916
Julian, R. (Leics.) b Aug. 23, 1936
*Julien, B. D. (T/T & Kent) b March 13, 1950
*Jumadeen, R. R. (T/T) b April 12, 1948
*Jupp, H. (Surrey) b Nov. 19, 1841, d April 8, 1889
*Jupp, V. W. C. (Sussex & Northants; *CY 1928*) b March 27, 1891, d July 9, 1960

*Kallicharran, A. I. (Guyana, Warwicks., Qld, Tvl & OFS; *CY 1983*) b March 21, 1949
*Kaluperuma, L. W. (SL) b May 25, 1949
*Kaluperuma, S. M. S. (SL) b Oct. 22, 1961
*Kanhai, R. B. (†Guyana, T/T, W. Aust., Warwicks. & Tas.; *CY 1964*) b Dec. 26, 1935
*Kanitkar, H. S. (M'tra) b Dec. 8, 1942
*Kapil Dev (Haryana, Northants & Worcs.; *CY 1983*) b Jan. 6, 1959
Kaplan, C. J. (OFS) b Jan. 26, 1909
**Kardar, A. H. (formerly Abdul Hafeez) (N. Ind., OUCC, Warwicks. & Pak. Serv.) b Jan. 17, 1925
Katz, G. A. (Natal) b Feb. 9, 1947
Kayum, D. A. (OUCC) b Oct. 13, 1955
*Keeton, W. W. (Notts.; *CY 1940*) b April 30, 1905, d Oct. 10, 1980
Keighley, W. G. (OUCC & Yorks.) b Jan. 10, 1925
*Keith, H. J. (Natal) b Oct. 25, 1927
Kelleher, H. R. A. (Surrey & Northants) b March 3, 1929
*Kelleway, C. (NSW) b April 25, 1886, d Nov. 16, 1944
Kelly, J. (Notts.) b Sept. 15, 1930
*Kelly, J. J. (NSW; *CY 1903*) b May 10, 1867, d Aug. 14, 1938
Kelly, J. M. (Lancs. & Derbys.) b March 19, 1922, d Nov. 13, 1979
*Kelly, T. J. D. (Vic.) b May 3, 1844, d July 20, 1893
*Kempis, G. A. (Natal) b Aug. 4, 1865, d May 19, 1890
*Kendall, T. (Vic. & Tas.) b Aug. 24, 1851, d Aug. 17, 1924
Kennedy, A. (Lancs.) b Nov. 4, 1949
*Kennedy, A. S. (Hants; *CY 1933*) b Jan. 24, 1891, d Nov. 15, 1959
*Kenny, R. B. (Bombay & Bengal) b Sept. 29, 1930
*Kent, M. F. (Qld) b Nov. 23, 1953
*Kentish, E. S. M. (Jam. & OUCC) b Nov. 21, 1916
*Kenyon, D. (Worcs.; *CY 1963*) b May 15, 1924
*Kerr, J. L. (Cant.) b Dec. 28, 1910
Kerslake, R. C. (CUCC & Som.) b Dec. 26, 1942
Kettle, M. K. (Northants) b March 18, 1944
*Khalid Hassan (Punjab & Lahore) b July 14, 1937
*Khalid Wazir (Pak.) b April 27, 1936
*Khan Mohammad (N. Ind., Pak. Us, Som., B'pur, Sind, Kar. & Lahore) b Jan. 1, 1928
Kidd, E. L. (CUCC & Middx) b Oct. 18, 1889, d July 2, 1984
*Killick, Rev. E. T. (CUCC & Middx) b May 9, 1907, d May 18, 1953
Kilner, Norman (Yorks. & Warwicks.) b July 21, 1895, d April 28, 1979
*Kilner, Roy (Yorks.; *CY 1924*) b Oct. 17, 1890, d April 5, 1928
Kimpton, R. C. M. (OUCC & Worcs.) b Sept. 21, 1916
*King, C. L. (B'dos, Glam., Worcs. & Natal) b June 11, 1951
*King, F. McD. (B'dos) b Dec. 14, 1926
King, I. M. (Warwicks. & Essex) b Nov. 10, 1931
King, J. B. (Philadelphia) b Oct. 19, 1873, d Oct. 17, 1965
*King, J. H. (Leics.) b April 16, 1871, d Nov. 18, 1946
*King, L. A. (Jam. & Bengal) b Feb. 27, 1939
Kingsley, Sir P.G.T. (OUCC) b May 26, 1908
*Kinneir, S. P. (Warwicks.; *CY 1912*) b May 13, 1871, d Oct. 16, 1928
*Kippax, A. F. (NSW) b May 25, 1897, d Sept. 4, 1972
Kirby, D. (CUCC & Leics.) b Jan. 18, 1939
*Kirmani, S. M. H. (†Karn.) b Dec. 29, 1949
Kirsten, P. N. (W. Prov., Sussex, Derbys. & SA XI) b May 14, 1955
Kirton, K. N. (Border & E. Prov.) b Feb. 24, 1928
*Kischenchand, G. (W. Ind., Guj. & Baroda) b April 14, 1925
Kitchen, M. J. (Som.) b Aug. 1, 1940
*Kline, L. F. (Vic.) b Sept. 29, 1934
*Knight, A. E. (Leics.; *CY 1904*) b Oct. 8, 1872, d April 25, 1946
*Knight, B. R. (Essex & Leics.) b Feb. 18, 1938
*Knight, D. J. (OUCC & Surrey; *CY 1915*) b May 12, 1894, d Jan. 5, 1960
Knight, J. M. (OUCC) b March 16, 1958

Knight, R. D. V. (CUCC, Surrey, Glos. & Sussex) b Sept. 6, 1946
Knight, W. H. (Editor of *Wisden* 1870-79) b Nov. 29, 1812, d Aug. 16, 1879
*Knott, A. P. E. (Kent & Tas.; *CY 1970*) b April 9, 1946
Knott, C. H. (OUCC & Kent) b March 20, 1901
Knott, C. J. (Hants) b Nov. 26, 1914
Knowles, J. (Notts.) b March 25, 1910
Knox, G. K. (Lancs.) b April 22, 1937
*Knox, N. A. (Surrey; *CY 1907*) b Oct. 10, 1884, d March 3, 1935
Kortright, C. J. (Essex) b Jan. 9, 1871, d Dec. 12, 1952
*Kotze, J. J. (Tvl & W. Prov.) b Aug. 7, 1879, d July 7, 1931
Kourie, A. J. (Tvl & SA XI) b July 30, 1951
*Kripal Singh, A. G. (Madras & H'bad) b Aug. 6, 1933
*Krishnamurthy, P. (H'bad) b July 12, 1947
Kuiper, A. P. (W. Prov. & SA XI) b Aug. 24, 1959
*Kulkarni, U. N. (Bombay) b March 7, 1942
*Kumar, V. V. (†TN) b June 22, 1935
*Kunderan, B. K. (Ind. Rlwys & Mysore) b Oct. 2, 1939
*Kuys, F. (W. Prov.) b March 21, 1870, d Sept. 12, 1953

Lacey, Sir F. E. (CUCC & Hants; Sec MCC 1898-1926) b Oct. 19, 1859, d May 26, 1946
*Laird, B. M. (W. Aust.) b Nov. 21, 1950
*Laker, J. C. (Surrey, Auck. & Essex; *CY 1952*) b Feb. 9, 1922
*Lall Singh (S. Punjab) b Dec. 12, 1909, d Nov. 1985
*Lamb, A. J. (W. Prov. & Northants; *CY 1981*) b June 20, 1954
Lamb, T. M. (OUCC, Middx & Northants) b March 24, 1953
Lambert, G. E. (Glos. & Som.) b May 11, 1919
Lambert, R. H. (Ireland) b July 18, 1874, d March 24, 1956
Lambert, Wm (Surrey) b 1779, d April 19, 1851
Lampard, A. W. (Vic. & AIF) b July 3, 1885, d Jan. 11, 1984
*Lance, H. R. (NE Tvl & Tvl) b June 6, 1940
Langdale, G. R. (Derbys. & Som.) b March 11, 1916
Langford, B. A. (Som.) b Dec. 17, 1935
*Langley, G. R. (S. Aust.; *CY 1957*) b Sept. 14, 1919
*Langridge, James (Sussex; *CY 1932*) b July 10, 1906, d Sept. 10, 1966
Langridge, J. G. (John) (Sussex; *CY 1950*) b Feb. 10, 1910
Langridge, R. J. (Sussex) b April 13, 1939
*Langton, A. B. C. (Tvl) b March 2, 1912, d Nov. 27, 1942
*Larkins, W. (Northants & E. Prov.) b Nov. 22, 1953
*Larter, J. D. F. (Northants) b April 24, 1940
*Larwood, H. (Notts.; *CY 1927*) b Nov. 14, 1904
*Lashley, P. D. (B'dos) b Feb. 11, 1937
Latchman, A. H. (Middx & Notts.) b July 26, 1943
*Laughlin, T. J. (Vic.) b Jan. 30, 1951
*Laver, F. (Vic.) b Dec. 7, 1869, d Sept. 24, 1919
Lawrence, D. V. (Glos.) b Jan. 28, 1964
*Lawrence, G. B. (Rhod. & Natal) b March 31, 1932
Lawrence, J. (Som.) b March 29, 1914
Lawrence, M. P. (OUCC) b May 6, 1962
*Lawry, W. M. (Vic.; *CY 1962*) b Feb. 11, 1937
*Lawson, G. F. (NSW & Lancs.) b Dec. 7, 1957
Leadbeater, B. (Yorks.) b Aug. 14, 1943
*Leadbeater, E. (Yorks. & Warwicks.) b Aug. 15, 1927
Leary, S. E. (Kent) b April 30, 1933
Lea, A. E. (CUCC) b Sept. 29, 1962
Lee, C. (Yorks. & Derbys.) b March 17, 1924
Lee, F. S. (Middx & Som.) b July 24, 1905, d March 30, 1982
Lee, G. M. (Notts. & Derbys.) b June 7, 1887, d Feb. 29, 1976
*Lee, H. W. (Middx) b Oct. 26, 1890, d April 21, 1981
Lee, I. S. (Vic.) b March 24, 1914
Lee, J. W. (Middx & Som.) b Feb. 1, 1904, d June 20, 1944
Lee, P. G. (Northants & Lancs.; *CY 1976*) b Aug. 27, 1945
*Lee, P. K. (S. Aust.) b Sept. 15, 1904, d Aug. 9, 1980
*Lees, W. K. (Otago) b March 19, 1952
*Lees, W. S. (Surrey; *CY 1906*) b Dec. 25, 1875, d Sept. 10, 1924
Leese, Sir Oliver, Bt (Pres. MCC 1965-66) b Oct. 27, 1894, d Jan. 20, 1978
*Legall, R. A. (B'dos & T/T) b Dec. 1, 1925
Legard, E. (Warwicks.) b Aug. 23, 1935
*Leggat, I. B. (C. Dist.) b June 7, 1930
*Leggat, J. G. (Cant.) b May 27, 1926, d March 8, 1973
*Legge, G. B. (OUCC & Kent) b Jan. 26, 1903, d Nov. 21, 1940
Lenham, L. J. (Sussex) b May 24, 1936
*le Roux, F. L. (Tvl & E. Prov.) b Feb. 5, 1882, d Sept. 22, 1963
le Roux, G. S. (W. Prov., Sussex & SA XI) b Sept. 4, 1955
le Roux, R. A. (OFS) b May 27, 1950
*Leslie, C. F. H. (OUCC & Middx) b Dec. 8, 1861, d Feb. 12, 1921
Lester, E. (Yorks.) b Feb. 18, 1923
Lester, G. (Leics.) b Dec. 27, 1915
Lester, Dr J. A. (Philadelphia) b Aug. 1, 1871, d Sept. 3, 1969
L'Estrange, M. G. (OUCC) b Oct. 12, 1952

Lethbridge, C. (Warwicks.) b June 23, 1961
*Lever, J. K. (Essex & Natal; *CY 1979*) b Feb. 24, 1949
*Lever, P. (Lancs. & Tas.) b Sept. 17, 1940
*Leveson Gower, Sir H. D. G. (OUCC & Surrey) b May 8, 1873, d Feb. 1, 1954
*Levett, W. H. V. (Kent) b Jan. 25, 1908
Lewington, P. J. (Warwicks.) b Jan. 30, 1950
*Lewis, A. R. (CUCC & Glam.) b July 6, 1938
Lewis, C. (Kent) b July 27, 1908
Lewis, D. J. (OUCC & Rhod.) b July 27, 1927
*Lewis, D. M. (Jam.) b Feb. 21, 1946
Lewis, E. B. (Warwicks.) b Jan. 5, 1918, d Oct. 19, 1983
Lewis, E. J. (Glam. & Sussex) b Jan. 31, 1942
*Lewis, P. T. (W. Prov.) b Oct. 2, 1884, d Jan. 30, 1976
Lewis, R. V. (Hants) b Aug. 6, 1947
*Leyland, M. (Yorks.; *CY 1929*) b July 20, 1900, d Jan. 1, 1967
*Liaqat Ali (Kar., Sind, HBL & PIA) b May 21, 1955
Liddicutt, A. E. (Vic.) b Oct. 17, 1891, d April 8, 1983
Lightfoot, A. (Northants) b Jan. 8, 1936
Lill, J. C. (S. Aust.) b Dec. 7, 1933
*Lillee, D. K. (W. Aust.; *CY 1973*) b July 18, 1949
*Lilley, A. A. (Warwicks.; *CY 1897*) b Nov. 28, 1866, d Nov. 17, 1929
Lilley, A. W. (Essex) b May 8, 1959
Lilley, B. (Notts.) b Feb. 11, 1895, d Aug. 4, 1950
Lillywhite, Fred (Sussex; Editor of *Lillywhite's Guide to Cricketers*) b July 23, 1829, d Sept. 15, 1866
Lillywhite, F. W. ("William") (Sussex) b June 13, 1792, d Aug. 21, 1854
*Lillywhite, James, jun. (Sussex) b Feb. 23, 1842, d Oct. 25, 1929
*Lindsay, D. T. (NE Tvl, N. Tvl & Tvl) b Sept 4, 1939
*Lindsay, J. D. (Tvl & NE Tvl) b Sept. 8, 1909
*Lindsay, N. V. (Tvl & OFS) b July 30, 1886, d Feb. 2, 1976
*Lindwall, R. R. (NSW & Qld; *CY 1949*) b Oct. 3, 1921
*Ling, W. V. S. (Griq. W. & E. Prov.) b Oct. 3, 1891, d Sept. 26, 1960
*Lissette, A. F. (Auck. & N. Dist.) b Nov. 6, 1919, d Jan. 24, 1973
Lister, J. (Yorks. & Worcs.) b May 14, 1930
Lister, W. H. L. (Lancs.) b Oct. 7, 1911
Littlewood, D. J. (CUCC) b Oct. 28, 1955
Livingston, L. (NSW & Northants) b May 3, 1920
Livingstone, D. A. (Hants) b Sept. 21, 1933
Livsey, W. H. (Hants) b Sept. 23, 1893, d Sept. 12, 1978
*Llewellyn, C. B. (Natal & Hants; *CY 1911*) b Sept. 26, 1876, d June 7, 1964
Llewellyn, M. J. (Glam.) b Nov. 27, 1953
Lloyd, B. J. (Glam.) b Sept. 6, 1953
*Lloyd, C. H. (†Guyana & Lancs.; *CY 1971*) b Aug. 31, 1944
*Lloyd, D. (Lancs.) b March 18, 1947
*Lloyd, T. A. (Warwicks. & OFS) b Nov. 5, 1956
Lloyds, J. W. (Som., OFS & Glos.) b Nov. 17, 1954
*Loader, P. J. (Surrey and W. Aust.; *CY 1958*) b Oct. 25, 1929
Lobb, B. (Warwicks. & Som.) b Jan. 11, 1931
*Lock, G. A. R. (Surrey, Leics. & W. Aust.; *CY 1954*) b July 5, 1929
Lock, H. C. (Surrey) b May 8, 1903, d May 18, 1978
Lockwood, Ephraim (Yorks.) b April 4, 1845, d Dec. 19, 1921
*Lockwood, W. H. (Notts. & Surrey; *CY 1899*) b March 25, 1868, d April 26, 1932
Lockyer, T. (Surrey & All-England) b Nov. 1, 1826, d Dec. 22, 1869
*Logan, J. D. (SA) b June 24, 1880, d Jan. 3, 1960
*Logie, A. L. (T/T) b Sept. 28, 1960
*Lohmann, G. A. (Surrey, W. Prov. & Tvl; *CY 1889*) b June 2, 1865, d Dec. 1, 1901
Lomax, J. G. (Lancs. & Som.) b May 5, 1925
Long, A. (Surrey & Sussex) b Dec. 18, 1940
Longfield, T. C. (CUCC & Kent) b May 12, 1906, d Dec. 21, 1981
Longrigg, E. F. (CUCC & Som.) b April 16, 1906, d July 23, 1974
Lord, Thomas (Middx; founder of Lord's) b Nov. 23, 1755, d Jan. 13, 1832
*Love, H. S. B. (NSW & Vic.) b Aug. 10, 1895, d July 22, 1969
Love, J. D. (Yorks.) b April 22, 1955
Lowndes, W. G. L. F. (OUCC & Hants) b Jan. 24, 1898, d May 23, 1982
*Lowry, T. C. (Wgtn, CUCC & Som.) b Feb. 17, 1898, d July 20, 1976
*Lowson, F. A. (Yorks.) b July 1, 1925, d Sept. 8, 1984
*Loxton, S. J. E. (Vic.) b March 29, 1921
*Lucas, A. P. (CUCC, Surrey, Middx & Essex) b Feb. 20, 1857, d Oct. 12, 1923
Luckes, W. T. (Som.) b Jan. 1, 1901, d Oct. 27, 1982
*Luckhurst, B. W. (Kent; *CY 1971*) b Feb. 5, 1939
Luddington, R. S. (OUCC) b April 8, 1960
Lumb, R. G. (Yorks.) b Feb. 27, 1950
*Lundie, E. B. (E. Prov., W. Prov. & Tvl) b March 15, 1888, d Sept. 12, 1917
Lynch, M. A. (Surrey & Guyana) b May 21, 1958
Lyon, B. H. (OUCC & Glos.; *CY 1931*) b Jan. 19, 1902, d June 22, 1970
Lyon, J. (Lancs.) b May 17, 1951

Lyon, M. D. (CUCC & Som.) b April 22, 1898, d Feb. 17, 1964
*Lyons, J. J. (S. Aust.) b May 21, 1863, d July 21, 1927
Lyons, K. J. (Glam.) b Dec. 18, 1946
*Lyttelton, Rt Hon. Alfred (CUCC & Middx; Pres. MCC 1898) b Feb. 7, 1857, d July 5, 1913
Lyttelton, Rev. Hon. C. F. (CUCC & Worcs.) b Jan. 26, 1887, d Oct. 3, 1931
Lyttelton, Hon. C. J. (*see* 10th Visct Cobham)
Lyttelton, Hon. R. H. (Eton) b Jan. 18, 1854, d Nov. 7, 1939

*McAlister, P. A. (Vic.) b July 11, 1869, d May 10, 1938
*Macartney, C. G. (NSW & Otago; *CY 1922*) b June 27, 1886, d Sept. 9, 1958
*Macaulay, G. G. (Yorks.; *CY 1924*) b Dec. 7, 1897, d Dec. 14, 1940
*Macaulay, M. J. (Tvl, W. Prov., OFS, NE Tvl & E. Prov.) b April 19, 1939
*MacBryan, J. C. W. (CUCC & Som.; *CY 1925*) b July 22, 1892, d July 15, 1983
*McCabe, S. J. (NSW; *CY 1935*) b July 16, 1910, d Aug. 25, 1968
McCanlis, M. A. (OUCC, Surrey & Glos.) b June 17, 1906
*McCarthy, C. N. (Natal & CUCC) b March 24, 1929
*McConnon, J. E. (Glam.) b June 21, 1922
*McCool, C. L. (NSW, Qld & Som.) b Dec. 9, 1915
McCorkell, N. T. (Hants) b March 23, 1912
*McCormick, E. L. (Vic.) b May 16, 1906
*McCosker, R. B. (NSW; *CY 1976*) b Dec. 11, 1946
*McDermott, C. J. (Qld; *CY 1986*) b April 14, 1965
*McDonald, C. C. (Vic.) b Nov. 17, 1928
*McDonald, E. A. (Tas., Vic. & Lancs.; *CY 1922*) b Jan. 6, 1891, d July 22, 1937
*McDonnell, P. S. (Vic., NSW & Qld) b Nov. 13, 1858, d Sept. 24, 1896
McEvoy, M. S. A. (Essex & Worcs.) b Jan. 25, 1956
McEwan, K. S. (E. Prov., W. Prov., Essex, W. Aust. & SA XI; *CY 1978*) b July 16, 1952
*McEwan, P. E. (Cant.) b Dec. 19, 1953
McFarlane, L. L. (Northants, Lancs. & Glam.) b Aug. 19, 1952
*McGahey, C. P. (Essex; *CY 1902*) b Feb. 12, 1871, d Jan. 10, 1935
*MacGibbon, A. R. (Cant.) b Aug. 28, 1924
*McGirr, H. M. (Wgtn) b Nov. 5, 1891, d April 14, 1964
*McGlew, D. J. (Natal; *CY 1956*) b March 11, 1929
*MacGregor, G. (CUCC & Middx; *CY 1891*) b Aug. 31, 1869, d Aug. 20, 1919
*McGregor, S. N. (Otago) b Dec. 18, 1931
McHugh, F. P. (Yorks. & Glos.) b Nov. 15, 1925
*McIlwraith, J. (Vic.) b Sept. 7, 1857, d July 5, 1938
Macindoe, D. H. (OUCC) b Sept. 1, 1917
*McIntyre, A. J. (Surrey; *CY 1958*) b May 14, 1918
McIntyre, J. M. (Auck. & Cant.) b July 4, 1944
*Mackay, K. D. (Qld) b Oct. 24, 1925, d June 13, 1982
McKay-Coghill, D. (Tvl) b Nov. 4, 1941
*McKenzie, G. D. (W. Aust. & Leics.; *CY 1965*) b June 24, 1941
McKenzie, K. A. (NE Tvl, Tvl & SA XI) b July 16, 1948
*McKibbin, T. R. (NSW) b Dec. 10, 1870, d Dec. 15, 1939
*McKinnon, A. H. (E. Prov. & Tvl) b Aug. 20, 1932, d Dec. 2, 1983
*MacKinnon, F. A. (CUCC & Kent) b April 9, 1848, d Feb. 27, 1947
McLachlan, I. M. (CUCC & S. Aust.) b Oct. 2, 1936
*MacLaren, A. C. (Lancs.; *CY 1895*) b Dec. 1, 1871, d Nov. 17, 1944
*McLaren, J. W. (Qld) b Dec. 24, 1887, d Nov. 17, 1921
MacLarnon, P. G. (OUCC) b Sept. 24, 1963
McLaughlin, J. J. (Qld) b Feb. 18, 1930
*Maclean, J. A. (Qld) b April 27, 1946
*McLean, R. A. (Natal; *CY 1961*) b July 9, 1930
*McLeod, C. E. (Vic.) b Oct. 24, 1869, d Nov. 26, 1918
*McLeod, E. G. (Auck. & Wgtn) b Oct. 14, 1900
*McLeod, R. W. (Vic.) b Jan. 19, 1868, d June 15, 1907
McMahon, J. W. (Surrey & Som.) b Dec. 28, 1919
*McMahon, T. G. (Wgtn) b Nov. 8, 1929
*McMaster, J. E. P. (Eng.) b March 16, 1861, d June 7, 1929
*McMillan, Q. (Tvl) b June 23, 1904, d July 3, 1948
*McMorris, E. D. A. (Jam.) b April 4, 1935
McNally, J. P. (Griq. W.) b Nov. 27, 1907
*McRae, D. A. N. (Cant.) b Dec. 25, 1912
*McShane, P. G. (Vic.) b 1857, d Dec. 11, 1903
McVicker, N. M. (Warwicks. & Leics.) b Nov. 4, 1940
*McWatt, C. A. (BG) b Feb. 1, 1922
*Madan Lal (Punjab & Delhi) b March 20, 1951
*Maddocks, L. V. (Vic. & Tas.) b May 24, 1926
*Madray, I. S. (BG) b July 2, 1934
Madson, M. B. (Natal) b Sept. 29, 1949
*Madugalle, R. S. (SL) b April 22, 1959
*Maguire, J. N. (Qld) b Sept. 15, 1956
*Mahmood Hussain (Pak. Us, Punjab, Kar., E. Pak. & NTB) b April 2, 1932

*Mailey, A. A. (NSW) b Jan. 3, 1886, d Dec. 31, 1967
*Majid J. Khan (Lahore, Pak. Us, CUCC, Glam., PIA, Qld & Punjab; *CY 1970*) b Sept. 28, 1946
*Maka, E. S. (Bombay) b March 5, 1922
*Makepeace, H. (Lancs.) b Aug. 22, 1881, d Dec. 19, 1952
Makinson, D. J. (Lancs.) b Jan. 12, 1961
*Malhotra, A. (Haryana) b Jan. 26, 1957
Mallender, N. A. (Northants & Otago) b Aug. 13, 1961
*Mallett, A. A. (S. Aust.) b July 13, 1945
Mallett, A. W. H. (OUCC & Kent) b Aug. 29, 1924
Mallett, N. V. H. (OUCC) b Oct. 30, 1956
*Malone, M. F. (W. Aust. & Lancs.) b Oct. 9, 1950
Malone, S. J. (Essex, Hants & Glam.) b Oct. 19, 1953
*Maninder Singh (Delhi) b June 13, 1963
*Manjrekar, V. L. (Bombay, Bengal, Andhra, U. Pradesh, Raja. & M'tra) b Sept. 26, 1931, d Oct. 18, 1983
*Mankad, A. V. (Bombay) b Oct. 12, 1946
*Mankad, V. (M. H.) (W. Ind., Naw., M'tra, Guj., Bengal, Bombay & Raja.; *CY 1947*) b April 12, 1917, d Aug. 21, 1978
*Mann, A. L. (W. Aust.) b Nov. 8, 1945
*Mann, F. G. (CUCC & Middx; Pres. MCC 1984-85) b Sept. 6, 1917
*Mann, F. T. (CUCC & Middx) b March 3, 1888, d Oct. 6, 1964
Mann, J. P. (Middx) b June 13, 1919
*Mann, N. B. F. (Natal & E. Prov.) b Dec. 28, 1920, d July 31, 1952
Manning, J. S. (S. Aust. & Northants) b June 11, 1924
*Mansell, P. N. F. (Rhod.) b March 16, 1920
*Mansoor Akhtar (Kar., UBL & Sind) b Dec. 25, 1956
*Mantri, M. K. (Bombay & M'tra) b Sept. 1, 1921
*Manzoor Elahi (Multan & Pak. Rlwys) b April 15, 1963
*Maqsood Ahmed (S. Punjab, R'pindi & Kar.) b March 26, 1925
*Marais, G. G. ("G. Gladstone") (Jam.) b Jan. 14, 1901, d May 19, 1978
Marie, G. V. (OUCC) b Feb. 17, 1945
*Markham, L. A. (Natal) b Sept. 12, 1924
*Marks, V. J. (OUCC & Som.) b June 25, 1955
Marlar, R. G. (CUCC & Sussex) b Jan. 2, 1931
Marner, P. T. (Lancs. & Leics.) b March 31, 1936
*Marr, A. P. (NSW) b March 28, 1862, d March 15, 1940
*Marriott, C. S. (CUCC, Lancs. & Kent) b Sept. 14, 1895, d Oct. 13, 1966
Marsden, R. (OUCC) b April 2, 1959
Marsden, Tom (Eng.) b 1805, d Feb. 27, 1843
Marsh, F. E. (Derbys.) b July 7, 1920
*Marsh, R. W. (W. Aust.; *CY 1982*) b Nov. 11, 1947
Marshal, Alan (Qld & Surrey; *CY 1909*) b June 12, 1883, d July 23, 1915
Marshall, J. M. A. (Warwicks.) b Oct. 26, 1916
*Marshall, M. D. (B'dos & Hants; *CY 1983*) b April 18, 1958
*Marshall, N. E. (B'dos & T/T) b Feb. 27, 1924
*Marshall, R. E. (B'dos & Hants; *CY 1959*) b April 25, 1930
Martin, E. J. (Notts.) b Aug. 17, 1925
*Martin, F. (Kent; *CY 1892*) b Oct. 12, 1861, d Dec. 13, 1921
*Martin, F. R. (Jam.) b Oct. 12, 1893, d Nov. 23, 1967
Martin, J. D. (OUCC & Som.) b Dec. 23, 1941
*Martin, J. W. (NSW & S. Aust.) b July 28, 1931
*Martin, J. W. (Kent) b Feb. 16, 1917
Martin, S. H. (Worcs., Natal & Rhod.) b Jan. 11, 1909
*Martindale, E. A. (B'dos) b Nov. 25, 1909, d March 17, 1972
Maru, R. J. (Middx & Hants) b Oct. 28, 1962
*Marx, W. F. E. (Tvl) b July 4, 1895, d June 2, 1974
*Mason, J. R. (Kent; *CY 1898*) b March 26, 1874, d Oct. 15, 1958
*Massie, H. H. (NSW) b April 11, 1854, d Oct. 12, 1938
*Massie, R. A. L. (W. Aust.; *CY 1973*) b April 14, 1947
*Matheson, A. M. (Auck.) b Feb. 27, 1906
*Mathias, Wallis (Sind, Kar. & NBP) b Feb. 4, 1935
*Matthews, A. D. G. (Northants & Glam.) b May 3, 1904, d July 29, 1977
Matthews, C. S. (Notts.) b Oct. 17, 1929
*Matthews, G. R. J. (NSW) b Dec. 15, 1959
*Matthews, T. J. (Vic.) b April 3, 1884, d Oct. 14, 1943
*Mattis, E. H. (Jam.) b April 11, 1957
Maudsley, R. H. (OUCC & Warwicks.) b April 8, 1918, d Sept. 29, 1981
*May, P. B. H. (CUCC & Surrey; *CY 1952*; Pres. MCC 1980-81) b Dec. 31, 1929
Mayer, J. H. (Warwicks.) b March 2, 1902, d Sept. 6, 1981
Mayes, R. (Kent) b Oct. 7, 1921
Maynard, C. (Warwicks. & Lancs.) b April 8, 1958
*Mayne, E. R. (S. Aust. & Vic.) b July 2, 1882, d Oct. 26, 1961
*Mayne, L. C. (W. Aust.) b Jan. 23, 1942
*Mead, C. P. (Hants; *CY 1912*) b March 9, 1887, d March 26, 1958
*Mead, W. (Essex; *CY 1904*) b March 25, 1868, d March 18, 1954
Meads, E. A. (Notts.) b Aug. 17, 1916
*Meale, T. (Wgtn) b Nov. 11, 1928

*Meckiff, I. (Vic.) b Jan. 6, 1935
*Meher-Homji, K. R. (W. Ind. & Bombay) b Aug. 9, 1911, d Feb. 10, 1982
*Mehra, V. L. (E. Punjab, Ind. Rlwys & Delhi) b March 12, 1938
*Meintjes, D. J. (Tvl) b June 9, 1890, d July 17, 1979
*Melle, M. G. (Tvl & W. Prov.) b June 3, 1930
Melluish, M. E. L. (CUCC & Middx) b June 13, 1932
*Melville, A. (OUCC, Sussex, Natal & Tvl; *CY 1948*) b May 19, 1910, d April 18, 1983
Mence, M. D. (Warwicks. & Glos.) b April 30, 1944
Mendis, G. D. (Sussex) b April 20, 1955
*Mendis, L. R. D. (SL) b Aug. 25, 1952
*Mendonca, I. L. (BG) b July 13, 1934
Mercer, J. (Sussex, Glam. & Northants; *CY 1927*) b April 22, 1895
*Merchant, V. M. (Bombay; *CY 1937*) b Oct. 12, 1911
*Merritt, W. E. (Cant. & Northants) b Aug. 18, 1908, d June 9, 1977
*Merry, C. A. (T/T) b Jan. 20, 1911, d April 19, 1964
*Meuleman, K. D. (Vic. & W. Aust.) b Sept. 5, 1923
*Meuli, E. M. (C. Dist.) b Feb. 20, 1926
Meyer, B. J. (Glos.) b Aug. 21, 1932
Meyer, R. J. O. (CUCC, Som. & W. Ind.) b March 15, 1905
Mian Mohammad Saaed (N. Ind. Patiala & S. Punjab; Pak.'s first captain) b Aug. 31, 1910, d Aug. 23, 1979
*Middleton, J. (W. Prov.) b Sept. 30, 1865, d Dec. 23, 1913
**Midwinter, W. E. (Vic. & Glos.) b June 19, 1851, d Dec. 3, 1890
*Milburn, B. D. (Otago) b Nov. 24, 1943
*Milburn, C. (Northants & W. Aust.; *CY 1967*) b Oct. 23, 1941
*Milkha Singh, A. G. (Madras) b Dec. 31, 1941
Miller, A. J. T. (OUCC & Middx) b May 30, 1963
*Miller, A. M. (Eng.) b Oct. 19, 1869, d June 26, 1959
*Miller, G. (Derbys. & Natal) b Sept 8, 1952
*Miller, K. R. (Vic., NSW & Notts.; *CY 1954*) b Nov. 28, 1919
*Miller, L. S. M. (C. Dist. & Wgtn) b March 31, 1923
Miller, R. (Warwicks.) b Jan. 6, 1941
*Miller, R. C. (Jam.) b Dec. 24, 1924
*Milligan, F. W. (Yorks.) b March 19, 1870, d March 31, 1900
*Millman, G. (Notts.) b Oct. 2, 1934
*Mills, C. H. (Surrey, Kimberley & W. Prov.) b Nov. 26, 1867, d July 26, 1948
Mills, G. H. (Otago) b Aug. 1, 1916
*Mills, J. E. (Auck.) b Sept. 3, 1905, d Dec. 11, 1972
Mills, J. M. (CUCC & Warwicks.) b July 27, 1921
Mills, J. P. C. (CUCC & Northants) b Dec. 6, 1958
Milner, J. (Essex) b Aug. 22, 1937
*Milton, C. A. (Glos.; *CY 1959*) b March 10, 1928
*Milton, W. H. (W. Prov.) b Dec. 3, 1854, d March 6, 1930
*Minnett, R. B. (NSW) b June 13, 1888, d Oct. 21, 1955
"Minshull", John (scorer of first recorded century) b *circa* 1741, d Oct. 1793
*Miran Bux, (Pak. Serv., Punjab & R'pindi) b April 20, 1907
*Misson, F. M. (NSW) b Nov. 19, 1938
*Mitchell, A. (Yorks.) b Sept. 13, 1902, d Dec. 25, 1976
*Mitchell, B. (Tvl; *CY 1936*) b Jan. 8, 1909
Mitchell, C. G. (Som.) b Jan. 27, 1929
**Mitchell, F. (CUCC, Yorks. & Tvl; *CY 1902*) b Aug. 13, 1872, d Oct. 11, 1935
*Mitchell, T. B. (Derbys.) b Sept. 4, 1902
*Mitchell-Innes, N. S. (OUCC & Som.) b Sept. 7, 1914
Mobey, G. S. (Surrey) b March 5, 1904
*Modi, R. S. (Bombay) b Nov. 11, 1924
*Mohammad Aslam (N. Ind. & Pak. Rlwys) b Jan. 5, 1920
*Mohammad Farooq (Kar.) b April 8, 1938
*Mohammad Ilyas (Lahore & PIA) b March 19, 1946
*Mohammad Munaf (Sind, E. Pak., Kar. & PIA) b Nov. 2, 1935
*Mohammad Nazir (Pak. Rlwys) b March 8, 1946
*Mohsin Kamal (Lahore & Allied Bank) b June 16, 1963
*Mohsin Khan (Pak. Rlwys, Kar., Sind., Pak. Us & HBL) b March 15, 1955
*Moir, A. McK. (Otago) b July 17, 1919
Moir, D. G. (Derbys. & Scotland) b April 13, 1957
*Mold, A. W. (Lancs.; *CY 1892*) b May 27, 1863, d April 29, 1921
*Moloney, D. A. R. (Wgtn, Otago & Cant.) b Aug. 11, 1910, d July 15, 1942
Monckton of Brenchley, 1st Lord (Pres. MCC 1956-57) b Jan. 17, 1891, d Jan. 9, 1965
Monkhouse, G. (Surrey) b April 26, 1954
*Moodie, G. H. (Jam.) b Nov. 25, 1915
*Moon, L. J. (CUCC & Middx) b Feb. 9, 1878, d Nov. 23, 1916
*Mooney, F. L. H. (Wgtn) b May 26, 1921
Moore, D. N. (OUCC & Glos.) b Sept. 26, 1910
Moore, H. I. (Notts.) b Feb. 28, 1941
Moore, R. H. (Hants) b Nov. 14, 1913
Morgan, D. C. (Derbys.) b Feb. 26, 1929
Morgan, J. T. (CUCC & Glam.) b May 7, 1907, d Dec. 18, 1976
Morgan, M. (Notts.) b May 21, 1936
*Morgan, R. W. (Auck.) b Feb. 12, 1941

*Morkel, D. P. B. (W. Prov.) b Jan. 25, 1906, d Oct. 6, 1980
*Morley, F. (Notts.) b Dec. 16, 1850, d Sept. 28, 1884
Morley, J. D. (Sussex) b Oct. 20, 1950
*Moroney, J. (NSW) b July 24, 1917
Morrill, N. D. (OUCC) b Dec. 9, 1957
*Morris, A. R. (NSW; *CY 1949*) b Jan. 19, 1922
Morris, H. (Glam.) b Oct. 5, 1963
Morris, H. M. (CUCC & Essex) b April 16, 1898
Morris, J. E. (Derbys.) b April 1, 1964
Morris, R. E. T. (W. Prov.) b Jan. 28, 1947
*Morris, S. (Vic.) b June 22, 1855, d Sept. 20, 1931
Morrisby, R. O. G. (Tas.) b Jan. 12, 1915
*Morrison, B. D. (Wgtn) b Dec. 17, 1933
*Morrison, J. F. M. (C. Dist. & Wgtn) b Aug. 27, 1947
Mortensen, O. H. (Denmark & Derbys.) b Jan. 29, 1958
*Mortimore, J. B. (Glos.) b May 14, 1933
Mortlock, W. (Surrey & Utd Eng. XI) b July 18, 1832, d Jan. 23, 1884
Moseley, H. R. (B'dos & Som.) b May 28, 1948
*Moses, H. (NSW) b Feb. 13, 1858, d Dec. 7, 1938
*Moss, A. E. (Middx) b Nov. 14, 1930
*Moss, J. K. (Vic.) b June 29, 1947
*Motz, R. C. (Cant.; *CY 1966*) b Jan. 12, 1940
Moulding, R. P. (OUCC & Middx) b Jan. 3, 1958
*Moule, W. H. (Vic.) b Jan. 31, 1858, d Aug. 24, 1939
Moxon, M. D. (Yorks. & Griq. W.) b May 4, 1960
Moylan, A. C. D. (CUCC) b June 26, 1955
Mubarak, A. M. (CUCC) b July 4, 1951
*Mudassar Nazar (Lahore, Punjab, Pak. Us, HBL, PIA & UBL) b April 6, 1956
*Muddiah, V. M. (Mysore & Ind. Serv.) b June 8, 1929
*Mufasir-ul-Haq (Kar., Dacca, PWD, E. Pak. & NBP) b Aug. 16, 1944, d July 27, 1983
Muncer, B. L. (Middx & Glam.) b Oct. 23, 1913, d Jan. 18, 1982
Munden, V. S. (Leics.) b Jan. 2, 1928
*Munir Malik (Punjab, R'pindi, Pak. Serv. & Kar.) b July 10, 1934
**Murdoch, W. L. (NSW & Sussex) b Oct. 18, 1854, d Feb. 18, 1911
*Murray, A. R. A. (E. Prov.) b April 30, 1922
*Murray, B. A. G. (Wgtn) b Sept. 18, 1940
*Murray, D. A. (B'dos) b Sept. 29, 1950
*Murray, D. L. (T/T, CUCC, Notts. & Warwicks.) b May 20, 1943
*Murray, J. T. (Middx; *CY 1967*) b April 1, 1935
Murray-Willis, P. E. (Worcs. & Northants) b July 14, 1910
Murray-Wood, W. (OUCC & Kent) b June 30, 1917, d Dec. 21, 1968
Murrell, H. R. (Kent & Middx) b Nov. 19, 1879, d Aug. 15, 1952
Murrills, T. J. (CUCC) b Dec. 22, 1953
*Musgrove, H. (Vic.) b Nov. 27, 1860, d Nov. 2, 1931
*Mushtaq Ali, S. (C. Ind., Guj., †M. Pradesh & U. Pradesh) b Dec. 17, 1914
*Mushtaq Mohammad (Kar., Northants & PIA; *CY 1963*) b Nov. 22, 1943
Muzzell, R. K. (W. Prov., Tvl and E. Prov.) b Dec. 23, 1945
Mynn, Alfred (Kent & All-Eng.) b Jan. 19, 1807, d Oct. 31, 1861

*Nadkarni, R. G. (M'tra & Bombay) b April 4, 1932
*Nagel, L. E. (Vic.) b March 6, 1905, d Nov. 23, 1971
*Naik, S. S. (Bombay) b Feb. 21, 1945
*Nanan, R. (T/T) b May 29, 1953
*Naoomal Jaoomal, M. (N. Ind. & Sind) b April 17, 1904, d July 18, 1980
*Narasimha Rao, M. V. (H'bad) b Aug. 11, 1954
Nash, J. E. (S. Aust.) b April 16, 1950
*Nash, L. J. (Tas. & Vic.) b May 2, 1910
Nash, M. A. (Glam.) b May 9, 1945
*Nasim-ul-Ghani (Kar., Pak. Us, Dacca, E. Pak., PWD & NBP) b May 14, 1941
*Naushad Ali (Kar., E. Pak., R'pindi, Peshawar, NWFP, Punjab & Pak. Serv.) b Oct. 1, 1943
*Navjot Singh (Punjab) b Oct. 20, 1963
*Navle, J. G. (Rajputna, C. Ind., Holkar & Gwalior) b Dec. 7, 1902, d Sept. 7, 1979
*Nayak, S. V. (Bombay) b Oct. 20, 1954
*Nayudu, Col. C. K. (C. Ind., Andhra, U. Pradesh & Holkar; *CY 1933*) b Oct. 31, 1895, d Nov. 14, 1967
*Nayudu, C. S. (C. Ind., Holkar, Baroda, Bengal, Andhra & U. Pradesh) b April 18, 1914
*Nazar Mohammad (N. Ind. & Punjab) b Aug. 5, 1921
*Nazir Ali, S. (S. Punjab & Sussex) b June 8, 1906, d Feb. 18, 1975
Neale, P. A. (Worcs.) b June 5, 1954
*Neblett, J. M. (B'dos & BG) b Nov. 13, 1901, d March 28, 1959
Needham, A. (Surrey) b March 23, 1957
Neilson, D. R. (Tvl) b Dec. 17, 1948
*Nel, J. D. (W. Prov.) b July 10, 1928
Nelson, G. W. (Border) b Nov. 14, 1941
Nevell, W. T. (Middx, Surrey & Northants) b June 13, 1916
*Newberry, C. (Tvl) b 1889, d Aug. 1, 1916
Newdick, G. A. (Wgtn) b Jan. 11, 1949
*Newham, W. (Sussex) b Dec 12, 1860, d June 26, 1944
Newland, Richard (Sussex) b *circa* 1718, d May 29, 1791

Newman, G. C. (OUCC & Middx) b April 26, 1904, d Oct. 13, 1982
*Newman, J. (Wgtn & Cant.) b July 3, 1902
Newman, J. A. (Hants & Cant.) b Nov. 12, 1884, d Dec. 21, 1973
Newman, P. G. (Derbys.) b Jan. 10, 1959
Newport, P. J. (Worcs.) b Oct. 11, 1962
*Newsom, E. S. (Tvl & Rhod.) b Dec. 2, 1910
Newstead, J. T. (Yorks.; *CY 1909*) b Sept. 8, 1877, d March 25, 1952
*Niaz Ahmed (Dacca, PWD, E. Pak. & Pak. Rlwys) b Nov. 11, 1945
Nicholas, M. C. J. (Hants) b Sept. 29, 1957
Nicholls, D. (Kent) b Dec. 8, 1943
Nicholls, R. B. (Glos.) b Dec. 4, 1933
*Nichols, M. S. (Essex; *CY 1934*) b Oct. 6, 1900, d Jan. 26, 1961
Nicholson, A. G. (Yorks.) b June 25, 1938, d Nov. 4, 1985
*Nicholson, F. (OFS) b Sept. 17, 1909, d July 30, 1982
*Nicolson, J. F. W. (Natal & OUCC) b July 19, 1899, d Dec. 13, 1935
*Nissar, Mahomed (Patiala, S. Punjab & U. Pradesh) b Aug. 1, 1910, d March 11, 1963
*Nitschke, H. C. (S. Aust.) b April 14, 1905, d Sept. 29, 1982
*Noble, M. A. (NSW; *CY 1900*) b Jan. 28, 1873, d June 21, 1940
*Noblet, G. (S. Aust.) b Sept. 14, 1916
*Noreiga, J. M. (T/T) b April 15, 1936
Norfolk, 16th Duke of (Pres. MCC 1957-58) b May 30, 1908, d Jan. 31, 1975
Norman, M. E. J. C. (Northants & Leics.) b Jan. 19, 1933
*Norton, N. O. (W. Prov. & Border) b May 11, 1881, d June 27, 1968
*Nothling, O. E. (NSW & Qld) b Aug. 1, 1900, d Sept. 26, 1965
*Nourse, A. D. ("Dudley") (Natal; *CY 1948*) b Nov. 12, 1910, d Aug. 14, 1981
*Nourse, A. W. ("Dave") (Natal, Tvl & W. Prov.) b Jan. 26, 1878, d July 8, 1948
Nugent, 1st Lord (Pres. MCC 1962-63) b Aug. 11, 1895, d April 27, 1973
*Nunes, R. K. (Jam.) b June 7, 1894, d July 22, 1958
*Nupen, E. P. (Tvl) b Jan. 1, 1902, d Jan. 29, 1977
*Nurse, S. M. (B'dos; *CY 1967*) b Nov. 10, 1933
Nutter, A. E. (Lancs. & Northants) b June 28, 1913
*Nyalchand, S. (W. Ind., Kathiawar, Guj. & S'tra) b Sept. 14, 1919
Nye, J. K. (Sussex) b May 23, 1914
Nyren, John (Hants) b Dec. 15, 1764, d June 28, 1837
Nyren, Richard (Hants & Sussex) b 1734, d April 25, 1797

Oakes, C. (Sussex) b Aug. 10, 1912
Oakes, J. (Sussex) b March 3, 1916
*Oakman, A. S. M. (Sussex) b April 20, 1930
Oates, T. W. (Notts.) b Aug. 9, 1875, d June 18, 1949
Oates, W. F. (Yorks. & Derbys.) b June 11, 1929
O'Brien, F. P. (Cant. & Northants) b Feb. 11, 1911
*O'Brien, L. P. (Vic.) b July 2, 1907
*O'Brien, Sir T. C. (OUCC & Middx) b Nov. 5, 1861, d Dec. 9, 1948
*Ochse, A. E. (Tvl) b March 11, 1870, d April 11, 1918
*Ochse, A. L. (E. Prov.) b Oct. 11, 1899, d May 6, 1949
*O'Connor, J. (Essex) b Nov. 6, 1897, d Feb. 22, 1977
*O'Connor, J. D. A. (NSW & S. Aust.) b Sept. 9, 1875, d Aug. 23, 1941
Odendaal, A. (CUCC & Boland) b May 4, 1954
*O'Donnell, S. P. (Vic.) b June 26, 1963
*Ogilvie, A. D. (Qld) b June 3, 1951
*O'Keeffe, K. J. (NSW & Som.) b Nov. 25, 1949
*Old, C. M. (Yorks., Warwicks. & N. Tvl; *CY 1979*) b Dec. 22, 1948
*Oldfield, N. (Lancs. & Northants) b May 5, 1911
*Oldfield, W. A. (NSW; *CY 1927*) b Sept. 9, 1894, d Aug. 10, 1976
Oldham, S. (Yorks. & Derbys.) b July 26, 1948
Oldroyd, E. (Yorks.) b Oct. 1, 1888, d Dec. 27, 1964
*O'Linn, S. (Kent, W. Prov. & Tvl) b May 5, 1927
Oliver, P. R. (Warwicks.) b May 9, 1956
Ollis, R. L. (Som.) b Jan. 14, 1961
*O'Neill, N. C. (NSW; *CY 1962*) b Feb. 19, 1937
Ontong, R. C. (Border, Tvl, N. Tvl & Glam.) b Sept. 9, 1955
Ord, J. S. (Warwicks.) b July 12, 1912
Orders, J. O. D. (OUCC) b Aug. 12, 1957
*O'Reilly, W. J. (NSW; *CY 1935*) b Dec. 20, 1905
O'Riordan, A. J. (Ireland) b July 20, 1940
Ormrod, J. A. (Worcs. & Lancs.) b Dec. 22, 1942
O'Shaughnessy, S. J. (Lancs.) b Sept. 9, 1961
Oslear, D. O. (Umpire) b March 3, 1929
*O'Sullivan, D. R. (C. Dist. & Hants) b Nov. 16, 1944
Outschoorn, L. (Worcs.) b Sept. 26, 1918
*Overton, G. W. F. (Otago) b June 8, 1919
*Owen-Smith, H. G. O. (W. Prov., OUCC & Middx; *CY 1930*) b Feb. 18, 1909
Owen-Thomas, D. R. (CUCC & Surrey) b Sept. 20, 1948
*Oxenham, R. K. (Qld) b July 28, 1891, d Aug. 16, 1939

Packe, M. St J. (Leics.) b Aug. 21, 1916, d Dec. 20, 1978

*Padgett, D. E. V. (Yorks.) b July 20, 1934
*Padmore, A. L. (B'dos) b Dec. 17, 1946
Page, J. C. T. (Kent) b May 20, 1930
Page, M. H. (Derbys.) b June 17, 1941
*Page, M. L. (Cant.) b May 8, 1902
*Pai, A. M. (Bombay) b April 28, 1945
*Paine, G. A. E. (Middx & Warwicks.; *CY 1935*) b June 11, 1908, d March 30, 1978
*Pairaudeau, B. H. (BG & N. Dist.) b April 14, 1931
*Palairet, L. C. H. (OUCC & Som.; *CY 1893*) b May 27, 1870, d March 27, 1933
Palairet, R. C. N. (OUCC & Som.; Joint-Manager MCC in Australia 1932-33) b June 25, 1871, d Feb. 11, 1955
Palia, P. E. (Madras, U. Prov., Bombay, Mysore & Bengal) b Sept. 5, 1910, d Sept. 9, 1981
*Palm, A. W. (W. Prov.) b June 8, 1901, d Aug. 17, 1966
*Palmer, C. H. (Worcs. & Leics.; Pres. MCC 1978-79) b May 15, 1919
*Palmer, G. E. (Vic. & Tas.) b Feb. 22, 1860, d Aug. 22, 1910
*Palmer, K. E. (Som.) b April 22, 1937
Palmer, R. (Som.) b July 12, 1942
Palmer, R. W. M. (CUCC) b June 4, 1960
Pardon, Charles Frederick (Editor of *Wisden* 1887-90) b March 28, 1850, d April 18, 1890
Pardon, Sydney H. (Editor of *Wisden* 1891-1925) b Sept. 23, 1855, d Nov. 20, 1925
*Parfitt, P. H. (Middx; *CY 1963*) b Dec. 8, 1936
Paris, C. G. A. (Hants; Pres. MCC 1975-76) b Aug. 20, 1911
Parish, R. J. (Aust. Administrator) b May 7, 1916
*Park, R. L. (Vic.) b July 30, 1892, d Jan. 23, 1947
*Parkar, G. A. (Bombay) b Oct. 24, 1955
*Parkar, R. D. (Bombay) b Oct. 31, 1946
Parkar, Z. (Bombay) b Nov. 22, 1957
*Parker, C. W. L. (Glos.; *CY 1923*) b Oct. 14, 1882, d July 11, 1959
Parker, E. F. (Rhod. & Griq. W.) b April 26, 1939
*Parker, G. M. (SA) b May 27, 1899, d May 1, 1969
Parker, G. W. (CUCC & Glos.) b Feb. 11, 1912
Parker, J. F. (Surrey) b April 23, 1913, d Jan. 27, 1983
*Parker, J. M. (N. Dist. & Worcs.) b Feb. 21, 1951
Parker, J. P. (Hants) b Nov. 29, 1902, d Aug. 9, 1984
*Parker, N. M. (Otago & Cant.) b Aug. 28, 1948
*Parker, P. W. G. (CUCC, Sussex & Natal) b Jan. 15, 1956
*Parkhouse, W. G. A. (Glam.) b Oct. 12, 1925
*Parkin, C. H. (Yorks. & Lancs.; *CY 1924*) b Feb. 18, 1886, d June 15, 1943
*Parkin, D. C. (E. Prov., Tvl & Griq. W.) b Feb. 18, 1870, d March 20, 1936
Parks, H. W. (Sussex) b July 18, 1906, d May 7, 1984
*Parks, J. H. (Sussex & Cant.; *CY 1938*) b May 12, 1903, d Nov. 21, 1980
*Parks, J. M. (Sussex & Som.; *CY 1968*) b Oct. 21, 1931
Parks, R. J. (Hants) b June 15, 1959
Parr, F. D. (Lancs.) b June 1, 1928
Parr, George (Notts. & All-England) b May 22, 1826, d June 23, 1891
*Parry, D. R. (Comb. Is. & Leewards) b Dec. 22, 1954
*Parsana, D. D. (S'tra, Ind. Rlwys & Guj.) b Dec. 2, 1947
Parsons, A. B. D. (CUCC & Surrey) b Sept. 20, 1933
Parsons, A. E. W. (Auck. & Sussex) b Jan. 9, 1949
Parsons, G. J. (Leics. & Boland) b Oct. 17, 1959
Parsons, Canon J. H. (Warwicks.) b May 30, 1890, d Feb. 2, 1981
*Partridge, J. T. (Rhod.) b Dec. 9, 1932
Partridge, N. E. (Malvern, CUCC & Warwicks.; *CY 1919*) b Aug. 10, 1900, d March 10, 1982
Partridge, R. J. (Northants) b Feb. 11, 1912
*Pascoe, L. S. (NSW) b Feb. 13, 1950
*Passailaigue, C. C. (Jam.) b Aug. 1902, d Jan. 7, 1972
*Patankar, C. T. (Bombay) b Nov. 24, 1930
**Pataudi, Iftikhar Ali, Nawab of (OUCC, Worcs., Patiala, N. Ind. & S. Punjab; *CY 1932*) b March 16, 1910, d Jan. 5, 1952
*Pataudi, Mansur Ali, Nawab of (Sussex, OUCC, Delhi & H'bad; *CY 1968*) b Jan. 5, 1941
*Patel, B. P. (Karn.) b Nov. 24, 1952
Patel, D. N. (Worcs.) b Oct. 25, 1958
*Patel, J. M. (Guj.) b Nov. 26, 1924
Paterson, R. F. T. (Essex) b Sept. 8, 1916, d May 29, 1980
Pathmanathan, G. (OUCC, CUCC & SL) b Jan. 23, 1954
*Patiala, Maharaja of (N. Ind., Patiala & S. Punjab) b Jan. 17, 1913, d June 17, 1974
*Patil, S. M. (Bombay) b Aug. 18, 1956
*Patil, S. R. (M'tra) b Oct. 10, 1933
Patterson, B. P. (Jam., Tas. & Lancs.) b Sept. 15, 1961
Pauline, D. B. (Surrey) b Dec. 15, 1960
Paulsen, R. G. (Qld & W. Aust.) b Oct. 18, 1947
Pawson, A. G. (OUCC & Worcs.; oldest living Blue) b May 30, 1888
Pawson, H. A. (OUCC & Kent) b Aug. 22, 1921
Payn, L. W. (Natal) b May 6, 1915
Payne, T. R. O. (B'dos) b Feb. 13, 1957

*Paynter, E. (Lancs.; *CY 1938*) b Nov. 5, 1901, d Feb. 5, 1979
Payton, D. H. (C. Dist.) b Feb. 19, 1945
Payton, W. R. D. (Notts.) b Feb. 13, 1882, d May 2, 1943
Pearce, G. (Sussex) b Oct. 27, 1908
Pearce, J. P. (OUCC) b April 18, 1957
Pearce, T. A. (Kent) b Dec. 18, 1910, d Aug. 11, 1982
Pearce, T. N. (Essex) b Nov. 3, 1905
*Pearse, C. O. C. (Natal) b Oct. 10, 1884, d May 7, 1953
Pearse, D. K. (Natal) b May 1, 1958
Pearson, D. B. (Worcs.) b March 29, 1937
*Peate, E. (Yorks.) b March 2, 1856, d March 11, 1900
Peck, I. G. (CUCC & Northants) b Oct. 18, 1957
*Peebles, I. A. R. (OUCC, Middx & Scotland; *CY 1931*) b Jan. 20, 1908, d Feb. 28, 1980
*Peel, R. (Yorks.; *CY 1889*) b Feb. 12, 1857, d Aug. 12, 1941
*Pegler, S. J. (Tvl) b July 28, 1888, d Sept. 10, 1972
*Pellew, C. E. (S. Aust.) b Sept. 21, 1893, d May 9, 1981
*Penn, F. (Kent) b March 7, 1851, d Dec. 26, 1916
Pepper, C. G. (NSW and Aust. Serv.; Umpire) b Sept. 15, 1918
Perkins, C. G. (Northants) b June 4, 1911
*Perks, R. T. D. (Worcs.) b Oct. 4, 1911, d Nov. 22, 1977
Perrin, P. A. (Essex; *CY 1905*) b May 26, 1876, d Nov. 20, 1945
Perryman, S. P. (Warwicks. & Worcs.) b Oct. 22, 1955
*Pervez Sajjad (Lahore, PIA & Kar.) b Aug. 30, 1942
Petchey, M. D. (OUCC) b Dec. 16, 1958
*Petherick, P. J. (Otago & Wgtn) b Sept. 25, 1942
*Petrie, E. C. (Auck. & N. Dist.) b May 22, 1927
Pfuhl, G. P. (W. Prov.) b Aug. 27, 1947
*Phadkar, D. G. (M'tra, Bombay, Bengal & Ind. Rlwys) b Dec. 10, 1925, d March 17, 1985
Phebey, A. H. (Kent) b Oct. 1, 1924
Phelan, P. J. (Essex) b Feb. 9, 1938
*Philipson, H. (OUCC & Middx) b June 8, 1866, d Dec. 4, 1935
*Phillip, N. (Comb. Is., Windwards & Essex) b June 12, 1948
Phillipps, J. H. (NZ Manager) b Jan. 1, 1898, d June 8, 1977
Phillips, R. B. (NSW & Qld) b May 23, 1954
*Phillips, W. B. (S. Aust.) b March 1, 1958
Phillipson, C. P. (Sussex) b Feb. 10, 1952
Phillipson, W. E. (Lancs.) b Dec. 3, 1910
*Philpott, P. I. (NSW) b Nov. 21, 1934
Piachaud, J. D. (OUCC, Hants & Ceylon) b March 1, 1937
Pickles, L. (Som.) b Sept. 17, 1932
Pienaar, R. F. (Tvl & W. Prov.) b July 17, 1961
*Pierre, L. R. (T/T) b June 5, 1921
*Pigott, A. C. S. (Sussex & Wgtn) b June 4, 1958
Pilch, Fuller (Norfolk & Kent) b March 17, 1804, d May 1, 1870
Pilling, H. (Lancs.) b Feb. 23, 1943
*Pilling, R. (Lancs.; *CY 1891*) b July 5, 1855, d March 28, 1891
Pinch, C. J. (NSW & S. Aust.) b June 23, 1921
*Pithey, A. J. (Rhod. & W. Prov.) b July 17, 1933
*Pithey, D. B. (Rhod., OUCC, Northants, W. Prov., Natal & Tvl) b Oct. 10, 1936
Pitman, R. W. C. (Hants) b Feb. 21, 1933
*Place, W. (Lancs.) b Dec 7, 1914
Platt, R. K. (Yorks. & Northants) b Dec. 21, 1932
*Playle, W. R. (Auck. & W. Aust.) b Dec. 1, 1938
Pleass, J. E. (Glam.) b May 21, 1923
*Plimsoll, J. B. (W. Prov. & Natal) b Oct. 27, 1917
Pocock, N. E. J. (Hants) b Dec. 15, 1951
*Pocock, P. I. (Surrey & N. Tvl) b Sept. 24, 1946
*Pollard, R. (Lancs.) b June 19, 1912, d Dec. 16, 1985
*Pollard, V. (C. Dist. & Cant.) b Burnley Sept. 7, 1945
Pollock, A. J. (CUCC) b April 19, 1962
*Pollock, P. M. (E. Prov.; *CY 1966*) b June 30, 1941
*Pollock, R. G. (E. Prov., Tvl & SA XI; *CY 1966*) b Feb. 27, 1944
*Ponsford, W. H. (Vic.; *CY 1935*) b Oct. 19, 1900
Pont, K. R. (Essex) b Jan. 16, 1953
*Poole, C. J. (Notts.) b March 13, 1921
Pooley, E. (Surrey & first England tour) b Feb. 13, 1838, d July 18, 1907
*Poore, M. B. (Cant.) b June 1, 1930
*Poore, Brig-Gen. R. M. (Hants & SA; *CY 1900*) b March 20, 1866, d July 14, 1938
Pope, A. V. (Derbys.) b Aug. 15, 1909
*Pope, G. H. (Derbys.) b Jan. 27, 1911
*Pope, R. J. (NSW) b Feb. 18, 1864, d July 27, 1952
Popplewell, N. F. M. (CUCC & Som.) b Aug. 8, 1957
Portal of Hungerford, 1st Lord (Pres. MCC 1958-59) b May 21, 1893, d April 22, 1971
Porter, A. (Glam.) b March 25, 1914
Pothecary, E. A. (Hants) b March 1, 1906
*Pothecary, J. E. (W. Prov.) b Dec. 6, 1933
Potter, G. (Sussex) b Oct. 26, 1931
Potter, J. (Vic.) b April 13, 1938
Potter, L. (Kent & Griq. W.) b Nov. 7, 1962
*Pougher, A. D. (Leics.) b April 19, 1865, d May 20, 1926
Pountain, F. R. (Sussex) b April 23, 1941

Powell, A. G. (CUCC & Essex) b Aug. 17, 1912, d June 7, 1982
*Powell, A. W. (Griq. W.) b July 18, 1873, d Sept. 11, 1948
*Prabhakar, M. (Delhi) b April 15, 1963
*Prasanna, E. A. S. (†Karn.) b May 22, 1940
Pratt, R. C. E. (Surrey) b May 5, 1928, d June 7, 1977
Pratt, R. L. (Leics.) b Nov. 15, 1938
Preece, C. R. (Worcs.) b Dec. 15, 1888, d Feb. 5, 1976
Prentice, F. T. (Leics.) b April 22, 1912, d July 10, 1978
Pressdee, J. S. (Glam. & NE Tvl) b June 19, 1933
Preston, Hubert (Editor of *Wisden* 1944-51) b Dec. 16, 1868, d Aug. 6, 1960
Preston, K. C. (Essex) b Aug. 22, 1925
Preston, Norman (Editor of *Wisden* 1951-80) b March 18, 1903, d March 6, 1980
Pretlove, J. F. (CUCC & Kent) b Nov. 23, 1932
Price, D. G. (CUCC) b Feb. 7, 1965
Price, E. J. (Lancs. & Essex) b Oct. 27, 1918
*Price, J. S. E. (Middx) b July 22, 1937
Price, M. R. (Glam.) b April 20, 1960
*Price, W. F. (Middx) b April 25, 1902, d Jan. 13, 1969
Prichard, P. J. (Essex) b Nov. 7, 1962
*Prideaux, R. M. (CUCC, Kent, Northants, Sussex & OFS) b July 13, 1939
Pridgeon, A. P. (Worcs.) b Feb. 22, 1954
*Prince, C. F. H. (W. Prov., Border & E. Prov.) b Sept. 11, 1874, d March 5, 1948
*Pringle, D. R. (CUCC & Essex) b Sept. 18, 1958
Pritchard, T. L. (Wgtn, Warwicks. & Kent) b March 10, 1917
*Procter, M. J. (Glos., Natal, W. Prov., Rhod. & SA XI; *CY 1970*) b Sept. 15, 1946
Prodger, J. M. (Kent) b Sept. 1, 1935
*Promnitz, H. L. E. (Border, Griq. W. & OFS) b Feb. 23, 1904, d Sept. 7, 1983
Prouton, R. O. (Hants) b March 1, 1926
Puckett, C. W. (W. Aust.) b Feb. 21, 1911
Pugh, C. T. M. (Glos.) b March 13, 1937
Pullan, D. A. (Notts.) b May 1, 1944
*Pullar, G. (Lancs. & Glos.; *CY 1960*) b Aug. 1, 1935
Pullinger, G. R. (Essex) b March 14, 1920, d Aug. 4, 1982
*Puna, N. (N. Dist.) b Oct. 28, 1929
*Punjabi, P. H. (Sind & Guj.) b Sept. 20, 1921
Pydanna, M. (Guyana) b Jan. 27, 1950

*Qasim Omar (Kar. & MCB) b Feb. 9, 1957
Quaife, B. W. (Warwicks. & Worcs.) b Nov. 24, 1899, d Nov. 28, 1984
*Quaife, William ("W. G.") (Warwicks. & Griq. W.; *CY 1902*) b March 17, 1872, d Oct. 13, 1951
Quick, I. W. (Vic.) b Nov. 5, 1933
Quinlan, J. D. (OUCC) b April 18, 1965
*Quinn, N. A. (Griq. W. & Tvl) b Feb. 21, 1908, d Aug. 5, 1934

*Rabone, G. O. (Wgtn & Auck.) b Nov. 6, 1921
*Rackemann, C. G. (Qld) b June 3, 1960
Radford, N. V. (Lancs., Tvl & Worcs.; *CY 1986*) b June 7, 1957
*Radley, C. T. (Middx; *CY 1979*) b May 13, 1944
*Rae, A. F. (Jam.) b Sept. 30, 1922
*Rai Singh, K. (S. Punjab & Ind. Serv.) b Feb. 24, 1922
Rait Kerr, Col. R. S. (Sec. MCC 1936-52) b April 13, 1891, d April 2, 1961
*Rajindernath, V. (N. Ind., U. Prov., S. Punjab, Bihar & E. Punjab) b Jan. 7, 1928
*Rajinder Pal (Delhi, S. Punjab & Punjab) b Nov. 18, 1937
Ralph, L. H. R. (Essex) b May 22, 1920
*Ramadhin, S. (T/T & Lancs.; *CY 1951*) b May 1, 1929
*Ramaswami, C. (Madras) b June 18, 1896
*Ramchand, G. S. (Sind, Bombay & Raja.) b July 26, 1927
*Ramiz Raja (Lahore & Allied Bank) b July 14, 1962
*Ramji, L. (W. Ind.) b 1900, d Dec. 20, 1948
Ramsamooj, D. (T/T & Northants) b July 5, 1932
*Ranasinghe, A. N. (SL) b Oct. 13, 1956
*Ranatunga, A. (SL) b Dec. 1, 1963
*Randall, D. W. (Notts.; *CY 1980*) b Feb. 24, 1951
Randhir Singh (Orissa & Bihar) b Aug. 16, 1957
*Rangachari, C. R. (Madras) b April 14, 1916
*Rangnekar, K. M. (M'tra, Bombay & †M. Pradesh) b June 27, 1917, d Oct. 11, 1984
*Ranjane, V. B. (M'tra & Ind. Rlwys) b July 22, 1937
*Ranjitsinhji, K. S., afterwards H. H. the Jam Saheb of Nawanagar (CUCC & Sussex; *CY 1897*) b Sept. 10, 1872, d April 2, 1933
*Ransford, V. S. (Vic.; *CY 1910*) b March 20, 1885, d March 19, 1958
Ransom, V. J. (Hants & Surrey) b March 17, 1918
*Rashid Khan (PWD, Kar. & PIA) b Dec. 15, 1959
Ratcliffe, R. M. (Lancs.) b Nov. 29, 1951
*Ratnayake, R. J. (SL) b Jan. 2, 1964
*Ratnayeke, J. R. (SL) b May 2, 1960
Rawlinson, H. T. (OUCC) b Jan. 21, 1963
Rayment, A. W. H. (Hants) b May 29, 1928
Raymer, V. N. (Qld) b May 4, 1918
*Read, H. D. (Surrey & Essex) b Jan. 28, 1910
*Read, J. M. (Surrey; *CY 1890*) b Feb. 9, 1859, d Feb. 17, 1929
*Read, W. W. (Surrey; *CY 1893*) b Nov. 23, 1855, d Jan. 6, 1907

Reddick, T. B. (Middx, Notts. & W. Prov.) b Feb. 17, 1912, d June 1, 1982
*Reddy, B. (TN) b Nov. 12, 1954
Redman, J. (Som.) b March 1, 1926, d Sept. 19, 1981
*Redmond, R. E. (Wgtn & Auck.) b Dec. 29, 1944
*Redpath, I. R. (Vic.) b May 11, 1941
Reed, B. L. (Hants) b Sept. 9, 1937
*Reedman, J. C. (S. Aust.) b Oct. 9, 1865, d March 25, 1924
Rees, A. (Glam.) b Feb. 17, 1938
Reeve, D. A. (Sussex) b April 2, 1963
Reeves, W. (Essex; Umpire) b Jan. 22, 1875, d March 22, 1944
*Rege, M. R. (M'tra) b March 18, 1924
*Rehman, S. F. (Punjab, Pak. Us & Lahore) b June 11, 1935
*Reid, J. F. (Auck.) b March 3, 1956
*Reid, J. R. (Wgtn & Otago; *CY 1959*) b June 3, 1928
Reid, K. P. (E. Prov. & Northants) b July 24, 1951
*Reid, N. (W. Prov.) b Dec 26, 1890, d June 10, 1947
Reidy, B. W. (Lancs.) b Sept. 18, 1953
*Relf, A. E. (Sussex & Auck.; *CY 1914*) b June 26, 1874, d March 26, 1937
*Renneburg, D. A. (NSW) b Sept. 23, 1942
Revill, A. C. (Derbys. & Leics.) b March 27, 1923
Reynolds, B. L. (Northants) b June 10, 1932
Reynolds, G. R. (Qld) b Aug. 24, 1936
Rhodes, A. E. G. (Derbys.) b Oct. 10, 1916, d Oct. 18, 1983
*Rhodes, H. J. (Derbys.) b July 22, 1936
Rhodes, S. D. (Notts.) b March 24, 1910
Rhodes, S. J. (Yorks. & Worcs.) b June 17, 1964
*Rhodes, W. (Yorks.; *CY 1899*) b Oct. 29, 1877, d July 8, 1973
Rice, C. E. B. (Tvl, Notts. & SA XI; *CY 1981*) b July 23, 1949
Rice, J. M. (Hants) b Oct. 23, 1949
*Richards, A. R. (W. Prov.) b 1868, d Jan. 9, 1904
*Richards, B. A. (Natal, Glos., Hants, S. Aust. & SA XI; *CY 1969*) b July 21, 1945
Richards, C. J. (Surrey & OFS) b Aug. 10, 1958
Richards, G. (Glam.) b Nov. 29, 1951
*Richards, I. V. A. (Comb. Is., Leewards, Som. & Qld; *CY 1977*) b March 7, 1952
*Richards, W. H. M. (SA) b Aug. 1862, d Jan. 4, 1903
*Richardson, A. J. (S. Aust.) b July 24, 1888, d Dec. 23, 1973
Richardson, A. W. (Derbys.) b March 4, 1907, d July 29, 1983
Richardson, D. J. (E. Prov., N. Tvl & SA XI) b Sept. 16, 1959
*Richardson, D. W. (Worcs.) b Nov. 3, 1934
Richardson, G. W. (Derbys.) b April 26, 1938
*Richardson, P. E. (Worcs. & Kent; *CY 1957*) b July 4, 1931
*Richardson, R. B. (Leewards) b Jan. 12, 1962
*Richardson, T. (Surrey & Som.; *CY 1897*) b Aug. 11, 1870, d July 2, 1912
*Richardson, V. Y. (S. Aust.) b Sept. 7, 1894, d Oct. 29, 1969
*Richmond, T. L. (Notts.) b June 23, 1890, d Dec. 29, 1957
Rickards, K. R. (Jam. & Essex) b Aug. 23, 1923
Riddington, A. (Leics.) b Dec. 22, 1911
Ridge, S. P. (OUCC) b Nov. 23, 1961
*Ridgway, F. (Kent) b Aug. 10, 1923
Ridings, P. L. (S. Aust.) b Oct. 2, 1917
*Rigg, K. E. (Vic.) b May 21, 1906
Riley, H. (Leics.) b Oct. 3, 1902
*Ring, D. T. (Vic.) b Oct. 14, 1918
Rist, F. H. (Essex) b March 30, 1914
Ritchie, G. G. (Tvl) b Sept. 16, 1933
*Ritchie, G. M. (Qld) b Jan. 23, 1960
*Rixon, S. J. (NSW) b Feb. 25, 1954
*Rizwan-uz-Zaman (Kar. & PIA) b Sept. 4, 1962
*Roach, C. A. (T/T) b March 13, 1904
*Roberts, A. D. G. (N. Dist.) b May 6, 1947
*Roberts, A. M. E. (Comb. Is., Leewards, Hants, NSW & Leics.; *CY 1975*) b Jan. 29, 1951
*Roberts, A. T. (Windwards) b Sept. 18, 1937
*Roberts, A. W. (Cant. & Otago) b Aug. 20, 1909, d May 13, 1978
Roberts, B. (Tvl & Derbys.) b May 30, 1962
Roberts, Pascal (T/T) b Dec 15, 1937
Roberts, W. B. (Lancs. & Victory Tests) b Sept. 27, 1914, d Aug. 24, 1951
*Robertson, J. B. (W. Prov.) b June 5, 1906
*Robertson, J. D. (Middx; *CY 1948*) b Feb. 22, 1917
Robertson, S. D. (Rhod.) b May 1, 1947
*Robertson, W. R. (Vic.) b Oct. 6, 1861, d June 24, 1938
Robertson-Glasgow, R. C. (OUCC & Som.) b July 15, 1901, d March 4, 1965
Robins, D. H. (Warwicks.) b June 26, 1914
Robins, R. V. C. (Middx) b March 13, 1935
*Robins, R. W. V. (CUCC & Middx; *CY 1930*) b June 3, 1906, d Dec. 12, 1968
Robinson, A. L. (Yorks.) b Aug. 17, 1946
Robinson, Emmott (Yorks.) b Nov. 16, 1883, d Nov. 17, 1969
Robinson, Ellis P. (Yorks. & Som.) b Aug. 10, 1911
Robinson, H. B. (OUCC & Canada) b March 3, 1919
Robinson, M. (Glam., Warwicks., H'bad & Madras) b July 16, 1921
Robinson, P. E. (Yorks.) b Aug. 3, 1963
Robinson, P. J. (Worcs. & Som.) b Feb. 9, 1943
Robinson, Ray (Writer) b July 8, 1908, d July 6, 1982
*Robinson, R. D. (Vic.) b June 8, 1946

*Robinson, R. H. (NSW, S. Aust. & Otago) b March 26, 1914, d Aug. 10, 1965
*Robinson, R. T. (Notts.; *CY 1986*) b Nov. 21, 1958
Robson, E. (Som.) b May 1, 1870, d May 23, 1924
Rochford, P. (Glos.) b Aug. 27, 1928
*Rodriguez, W. V. (T/T) b June 25, 1934
Roe, B. (Som.) b Jan. 27, 1939
Roebuck, P. G. P. (CUCC & Glos.) b Oct. 13, 1963
Roebuck, P. M. (CUCC & Som.) b March 6, 1956
Rogers, J. J. (OUCC) b Aug. 20, 1958
Rogers, N. H. (Hants) b March 9, 1918
Rogers, R. E. (Qld) b Aug. 24, 1916
Romaines, P. W. (Northants, Glos. & Griq. W.) b Dec. 25, 1955
*Roope, G. R. J. (Surrey & Griq. W.) b July 12, 1946
*Root, C. F. (Derbys. & Worcs.) b April 16, 1890, d Jan. 20, 1954
*Rorke, G. F. (NSW) b June 27, 1938
*Rose, B. C. (Som.; *CY 1980*) b June 4, 1950
Rosebery, 6th Earl of (*see* Dalmeny, Lord)
*Rose-Innes, A. (Kimberley & Tvl) b Feb. 16, 1868, d Nov. 22, 1946
Rosendorff, N. (OFS) b Jan. 22, 1945
Ross, C. J. (Wgtn & OUCC) b June 24, 1954
Rotherham, G. A. (Rugby, CUCC, Warwicks. & Wgtn; *CY 1918*) b May 28, 1899, d Jan. 31, 1985
Rouse, S. J. (Warwicks.) b Jan. 20, 1949
Routledge, R. (Middx) b July 7, 1920
*Routledge, T. W. (W. Prov. & Tvl) b April 18, 1867, d May 9, 1927
*Rowan, A. M. B. (Tvl) b Feb. 7, 1921
*Rowan, E. A. B. (Tvl; *CY 1952*) b July 20, 1909
*Rowe, C. G. (Wgtn & C. Dist.) b June 30, 1915
Rowe, C. J. C. (Kent & Glam.) b May 5, 1953
Rowe, E. J. (Notts.) b July 21, 1920
*Rowe, G. A. (W. Prov.) b June 15, 1874, d Jan. 8, 1950
*Rowe, L. G. (Jam. & Derbys.) b Jan. 8, 1949
*Roy, A. (Bengal) b June 5, 1945
*Roy, Pankaj (Bengal) b May 31, 1928
*Roy, Pranab (Bengal) b Feb. 10, 1957
*Royle, Rev. V. P. F. A. (OUCC & Lancs.) b Jan. 29, 1854, d May 21, 1929
*Rumsey, F. E. (Worcs., Som. & Derbys.) b Dec. 4, 1935
*Russell, A. C. [C. A. G.] (Essex; *CY 1923*) b Oct. 7, 1887, d March 23, 1961
Russell, P. E. (Derbys.) b May 9, 1944
Russell, R. C. (Glos.) b Aug. 15, 1963
Russell, S. E. (Middx & Glos.) b Oct. 4, 1937
*Russell, W. E. (Middx) b July 3, 1936
Russom, N. (CUCC & Som.) b Dec. 3, 1958
Rutherford, I. A. (Worcs. & Otago) b June 30, 1957
*Rutherford, J. W. (W. Aust.) b Sept. 25, 1929
*Rutherford, K. R. (Otago) b Oct. 26, 1965
Rutnagur, R. S. (OUCC) b Aug. 9, 1964
Ryan, M. (Yorks.) b June 23, 1933
Ryan, M. L. (Cant.) b June 7, 1943
*Ryder, J. (Vic.) b Aug. 8, 1889, d April 3, 1977

*Sadiq Mohammad (Kar., PIA, Tas., Essex, Glos. & UBP) b May 3, 1945
Sadler, W. C. H. (Surrey) b Sept. 24, 1896, d Feb. 12, 1981
*Saeed Ahmed (Punjab, Pak. Us, Lahore, PIA, Kar., PWD & Sind) b Oct. 1, 1937
*Saggers, R. A. (NSW) b May 15, 1917
Sainsbury, G. E. (Essex & Glos.) b Jan. 17, 1958
Sainsbury, P. J. (Hants; *CY 1974*) b June 13, 1934
*St Hill, E. L. (T/T) b March 9, 1904, d May 21, 1957
*St Hill, W. H. (T/T) b July 6, 1893, d 1957
*Salah-ud-Din (Kar., PIA & Pak. Us) b Feb. 14, 1947
Sale, R. (OUCC & Derbys.) b June 21, 1889, d Sept. 7, 1970
Sale, R., jun. (OUCC, Warwicks. & Derbys.) b Oct. 4, 1919
*Saleem Altaf (Lahore & PIA) b April 19, 1944
*Salim Malik (Lahore & HBL) b April 16, 1963
*Salim Yousuf (Sind, Kar., IDBP & Allied Bank) b Dec. 7, 1959
Sampson, H. (Yorks. & All-England) b March 13, 1813, d March 29, 1885
*Samuelson, S. V. (Natal) b Nov. 21, 1883, d Nov. 18, 1958
Sanderson, J. F. W. (OUCC) b Sept. 10, 1954
*Sandham, A. (Surrey; *CY 1923*) b July 6, 1890, d April 20, 1982
*Sandhu, B. S. (Bombay) b March 1, 1956
Sandman, D. McK. (Cant.) b Nov. 3, 1889, d Jan. 29, 1973
*Sardesai, D. N. (Bombay) b Aug. 8, 1940
*Sarfraz Nawaz (Lahore, Punjab, Northants, Pak. Rlwys & UBL) b Dec. 1, 1948
*Sarwate, C. T. (CP & B, M'tra, Bombay & †M. Pradesh) b June 22, 1920
*Saunders, J. V. (Vic. & Wgtn) b Feb. 3, 1876, d Dec. 21, 1927
Savage, J. S. (Leics. & Lancs.) b March 3, 1929
Savage, R. Le Q. (OUCC & Warwicks.) b Dec. 10, 1955
Savill, L. A. (Essex) b June 30, 1935
Saville, G. J. (Essex) b Feb. 5, 1944
Saxelby, K. (Notts.) b Feb. 23, 1959
*Saxena, R. C. (Delhi & Bihar) b Sept. 20, 1944

Sayer, D. M. (OUCC & Kent) b Sept. 19, 1936
*Scarlett, R. O. (Jam.) b Aug. 15, 1934
Schmidt, E. (E. Prov. & OFS) b Sept. 21, 1950
Schofield, R. M. (C. Dist.) b Nov. 6, 1939
Scholes, W. J. (Vic.) b Feb. 5, 1950
Schonegevel, D. J. (OFS & Griq. W.) b Oct. 9, 1934
*Schultz, S. S. (CUCC & Lancs.) b Aug. 29, 1857, d Dec. 18, 1937
*Schwarz, R. O. (Middx & Natal; *CY 1908*) b May 4, 1875, d Nov. 18, 1918
Scott, A. M. G. (CUCC) b March 31, 1966
*Scott, A. P. H. (Jam.) b July 29, 1934
Scott, Christopher J. (Lancs.) b Sept. 16, 1959
Scott, Colin J. (Glos.) b May 1, 1919
*Scott, H. J. H. (Vic.) b Dec. 26, 1858, d Sept. 23, 1910
Scott, M. E. (Northants) b May 8, 1936
*Scott, O. C. (Jam.) b Aug. 25, 1893, d June 16, 1961
*Scott, R. H. (Cant.) b March 6, 1917
Scott, S. W. (Middx; *CY 1893*) b March 24, 1854, d Dec. 8, 1933
*Scott, V. J. (Auck.) b July 31, 1916, d Aug. 2, 1980
*Scotton, W. H. (Notts.) b Jan. 15, 1856, d July 9, 1893
Seabrook, F. J. (CUCC & Glos.) b Jan. 9, 1899, d Aug. 7, 1979
*Sealey, B. J. (T/T) b Aug. 12, 1899, d Sept. 12, 1963
*Sealy, J. E. D. (B'dos & T/T) b Sept. 11, 1912, d Jan. 3, 1982
Seamer, J. W. (Som. & OUCC) b June 23, 1913
Sebastian, L. C. (Windwards) b Oct. 31, 1955
*Seccull, A. W. (Kimberley, W. Prov. & Tvl) b Sept. 14, 1868, d July 20, 1945
Seeff, L. J. (W. Prov. & SA XI) b May 1, 1959
*Sekar, T. A. P. (TN) b March 28, 1955
*Selby, J. (Notts.) b July 1, 1849, d March 11, 1894
Sellers, A. B. (Yorks.; *CY 1940*) b March 5, 1907, d Feb. 20, 1981
*Sellers, R. H. D. (S. Aust.) b Aug. 20, 1940
*Selvey, M. W. W. (CUCC, Surrey, Middx, Glam. & OFS) b April 25, 1948
*Sen, P. (Bengal) b May 31, 1926, d Jan. 27, 1970
*Sen Gupta, A. K. (Ind. Serv.) b Aug. 3, 1939
*Serjeant, C. S. (W. Aust.) b Nov. 1, 1951
Seymour, James (Kent) b Oct. 25, 1879, d Sept. 30, 1930
*Seymour, M. A. (W. Prov.) b June 5, 1936
*Shackleton, D. (Hants.; *CY 1959*) b Aug. 12, 1924
*Shafiq Ahmed (Lahore, Punjab, NBP & UBL) b March 28, 1949
*Shafqat Rana (Lahore & PIA) b Aug. 10, 1943
*Shahid Israr (Kar. & Sind) b March 1, 1950
*Shahid Mahmoud (Kar., Pak. Us & PWD) b March 17, 1939
*Shalders, W. A. (Griq. W. & Tvl) b Feb. 12, 1880, d March 18, 1917
*Sharma, C. (Haryana) b Jan. 3, 1966
*Sharma, G. (U. Pradesh) b Aug. 3, 1960
*Sharma, P. (Raja.) b Jan. 5, 1948
Sharp, G. (Northants) b March 12, 1950
Sharp, H. P. (Middx) b Oct. 6, 1917
*Sharp, J. (Lancs.) b Feb. 15, 1878, d Jan. 28, 1938
Sharp, K. (Yorks. & Griq. W.) b April 6, 1959
*Sharpe, D. (Punjab, Pak. Rlwys, Lahore & S. Aust.) b Aug. 3, 1937
*Sharpe, J. W. (Surrey & Notts.; *CY 1892*) b Dec. 9, 1866, d June 19, 1936
*Sharpe, P. J. (Yorks. & Derbys.; *CY 1963*) b Dec. 27, 1936
*Shastri, R. J. (Bombay) b May 27, 1962
*Shaw, Alfred (Notts. & Sussex) b Aug. 29, 1842, d Jan. 16, 1907
Shaw, C. (Yorks.) b Feb. 17, 1964
Shaw, J. H. (Vic.) b Oct. 18, 1932
*Sheahan, A. P. (Vic.) b Sept. 30, 1946
Sheffield, J. R. (Essex & Wgtn) b Nov. 19, 1906
*Shepherd, B. K. (W. Aust.) b April 23, 1937
Shepherd, D. J. (Glam.; *CY 1970*) b Aug. 12, 1927
Shepherd, D. R. (Glos.) b Dec. 27, 1940
*Shepherd, J. N. (B'dos, Kent, Rhod. & Glos.; *CY 1979*) b Nov. 9, 1943
Shepherd, T. F. (Surrey) b Dec. 5, 1889, d Feb. 13, 1957
*Sheppard, Rt Rev. D. S. (Bishop of Liverpool) (CUCC & Sussex; *CY 1953*) b March 6, 1929
*Shepstone, G. H. (Tvl) b April 8, 1876, d July 3, 1940
*Sherwell, P. W. (Tvl) b Aug. 17, 1880, d April 17, 1948
*Sherwin, M. (Notts.; *CY 1891*) b Feb. 26, 1851, d July 3, 1910
*Shillingford, G. C. (Comb. Is. & Windwards) b Sept. 25, 1944
*Shillingford, I. T. (Comb. Is. & Windwards) b April 18, 1944
*Shinde, S. G. (Baroda, M'tra & Bombay) b Aug. 18, 1923, d June 22, 1955
Shipman, A. W. (Leics.) b March 7, 1901, d Dec. 12, 1979
Shipperd, G. (W. Aust.) b Nov. 11, 1956
Shirreff, A. C. (CUCC, Hants, Kent & Som.) b Feb. 12, 1919
*Shivnarine, S. (Guyana) b May 13, 1952
*Shoaib Mohammad (Kar. & PIA) b Jan. 8, 1962
*Shodhan, R. H. (Guj. & Baroda) b Oct. 18, 1928
Short, A. M. (Natal) b Sept. 27, 1947

*Shrewsbury, Arthur (Notts.; *CY 1890*) b April 11, 1856, d May 19, 1903
*Shrimpton, M. J. F. (C. Dist. & N. Dist.) b June 23, 1940
*Shuja-ud-Din, Col. (N. Ind., Pak. Us, Pak. Serv., B'pur & R'pindi) b April 10, 1930
*Shukla, R. C. (Bihar & Delhi) b Feb. 4, 1948
*Shuter, J. (Kent & Surrey) b Feb. 9, 1855, d July 5, 1920
*Shuttleworth, K. (Lancs. & Leics.) b Nov. 13, 1944
*Sidebottom, A. (Yorks. & OFS) b April 1, 1954
Sidhu, N. S. (*see* Navjot Singh)
*Siedle, I. J. (Natal) b Jan. 11, 1903, d Aug. 24, 1982
*Sievers, M. W. (Vic.) b April 13, 1912, d May 10, 1968
*Sikander Bakht (PWD, PIA, Sind, Kar. & UBL) b Aug. 25, 1957
Silk, D. R. W. (CUCC & Som.) b Oct. 8, 1931
*Silva, S. A. R. (SL) b Dec. 12, 1960
Sime, W. A. (Notts.) b Feb. 8, 1909, d May 5, 1982
Simmons, J. (Lancs. & Tas.; *CY 1985*) b March 28, 1941
*Simpson, R. B. (NSW & W. Aust.; *CY 1965*) b Feb. 3, 1936
*Simpson, R. T. (Notts. & Sind; *CY 1950*) b Feb. 27, 1920
*Simpson-Hayward, G. H. (Worcs.) b June 7, 1875, d Oct. 2, 1936
Sims, Sir Arthur (Cant.) b July 22, 1877, d April 27, 1969
*Sims, J. M. (Middx) b May 13, 1903, d April 27, 1973
*Sinclair, B. W. (Wgtn) b Oct. 23, 1936
*Sinclair, I. McK. (Cant.) b June 1, 1933
*Sinclair, J. H. (Tvl) b Oct. 16, 1876, d Feb. 23, 1913
*Sincock, D. J. (S. Aust.) b Feb. 1, 1942
*Sinfield, R. A. (Glos.) b Dec. 24, 1900
*Singh, Charan K. (T/T) b 1938
Singh, Swaranjit (CUCC, Warwicks., E. Punjab & Bengal) b July 18, 1931
Singleton, A. P. (OUCC, Worcs. & Rhod.) b Aug. 5, 1914
*Sivaramakrishnan, L. (TN) b Dec. 31, 1965
Siviter, K. (OUCC) b Dec. 10, 1953
Skeet, C. H. L. (OUCC & Middx) b Aug. 17, 1895, d April 20, 1978
Skelding, Alec (Leics.) b Sept. 5, 1886, d April 17, 1960
Skinner, A. F. (Derbys. & Northants) b April 22, 1913, d Feb. 28, 1982
Skinner, D. A. (Derbys.) b March 22, 1920
Skinner, L. E. (Surrey & Guyana) b Sept. 7, 1950
Slack, W. N. (Middx & Windwards) b Dec. 12, 1954
Slade, D. N. F. (Worcs.) b Aug. 24, 1940
Slade, W. D. (Glam.) b Sept. 27, 1941
*Slater, K. N. (W. Aust.) b March 12, 1935
*Sleep, P. R. (S. Aust.) b May 4, 1957
*Slight, J. (Vic.) b Oct. 20, 1855, d Dec. 9, 1930
Slocombe, P. A. (Som.) b Sept. 6, 1954
*Smailes, T. F. (Yorks.) b March 27, 1910, d Dec. 1, 1970
Smales, K. (Yorks. & Notts.) b Sept. 15, 1927
Small, G. C. (Warwicks.) b Oct. 18, 1961
Small, John, sen. (Hants & All-England) b April 19, 1737, d Dec. 31, 1826
*Small, J. A. (T/T) b Nov. 3, 1892, d April 26, 1958
*Small, M. A. (B'dos) b Feb. 12, 1964
Smart, C. C. (Warwicks. & Glam.) b July 23, 1898, d May 21, 1975
Smart, J. A. (Warwicks.) b April 12, 1891, d Oct. 3, 1979
Smedley, M. J. (Notts.) b Oct. 28, 1941
*Smith, A. C. (OUCC & Warwicks.) b Oct. 25, 1936
Smith, A. J. S. (Natal) b Feb. 8, 1951
*Smith, Sir C. Aubrey (CUCC, Sussex & Tvl) b July 21, 1863, d Dec. 20, 1948
*Smith, C. I. J. (Middx; *CY 1935*) b Aug. 25, 1906, d Feb. 9, 1979
*Smith, C. J. E. (Tvl) b Dec. 25, 1872, d March 27, 1947
*Smith, C. L. (Natal, Glam. & Hants; *CY 1984*) b Oct. 15, 1958
Smith, C. S. (CUCC & Lancs.) b Oct. 1, 1932
*Smith, C. W. (B'dos) b July 29, 1933
*Smith, Denis (Derbys.; *CY 1936*) b Jan. 24, 1907, d Sept. 12, 1979
*Smith, D. B. M. (Vic.) b Sept. 14, 1884, d July 29, 1963
Smith, D. H. K. (Derbys. & OFS) b June 29, 1940
Smith, D. M. (Surrey & Worcs.) b Jan. 9, 1956
*Smith, D. R. (Glos.) b Oct. 5, 1934
*Smith, D. V. (Sussex) b June 14, 1923
Smith, Edwin (Derbys.) b Jan. 2, 1934
*Smith, E. J. (Warwicks.) b Feb. 6, 1886, d Aug. 31, 1979
*Smith, F. B. (Cant.) b March 13, 1922
*Smith, F. W. (Tvl) No details of birth or death known
Smith, G. (Kent) b Nov. 30, 1925
Smith, G. J. (Essex) b April 2, 1935
*Smith, Harry (Glos.) b May 21, 1890, d Nov. 12, 1937
*Smith, H. D. (Otago) b Jan. 8, 1913
*Smith, I. D. S. (C. Dist.) b Feb. 28, 1957
Smith, K. D. (Warwicks.) b July 9, 1956
Smith, L. D. (Otago) b Dec. 23, 1914, d Nov. 1, 1978
Smith, M. J. (Middx) b Jan. 4, 1942
*Smith, M. J. K. (OUCC, Leics. & Warwicks.; *CY 1960*) b June 30, 1933
Smith, N. (Yorks. & Essex) b April 1, 1949
*Smith, O. G. (Jam.; *CY 1958*) b May 5, 1933, d Sept. 9, 1959

Smith, P. A. (Warwicks.) b April 5, 1964
Smith, Ray (Essex) b Aug. 10, 1914
Smith, Roy (Som.) b April 14, 1930
Smith, R. A. (Natal & Hants) b Sept. 13, 1963
Smith, R. C. (Leics.) b Aug. 3, 1935
*Smith, S. B. (NSW) b Oct. 18, 1961
Smith, S. G. (T/T, Northants & Auck.; *CY 1915*) b Jan. 15, 1881, d Oct. 25, 1963
*Smith, T. P. B. (Essex; *CY 1947*) b Oct. 30, 1908, d Aug. 4, 1967
*Smith, V. I. (Natal) b Feb. 23, 1925
Smith, W. A. (Surrey) b Sept. 15, 1937
Smith, W. C. (Surrey; *CY 1911*) b Oct. 4, 1877, d July 16, 1946
*Smithson, G. A. (Yorks. & Leics.) b Nov. 1, 1926, d Sept. 6, 1970
*Snedden, C. A. (Auck.) b Jan. 7, 1918
*Snedden, M. C. (Auck.) b Nov. 23, 1958
Snellgrove, K. L. (Lancs.) b Nov. 12, 1941
*Snooke, S. D. (W. Prov. & Tvl) b Nov. 11, 1878, d April 4, 1959
*Snooke, S. J. (Border, W. Prov. & Tvl) b Feb. 1, 1881, d Aug. 14, 1966
*Snow, J. A. (Sussex; *CY 1973*) b Oct. 13, 1941
Snowden, A. W. (Northants) b Aug. 15, 1913, d May 7, 1981
Snowden, W. (CUCC) b Sept. 27, 1952
*Sobers, Sir G. S. (B'dos, S. Aust. & Notts.; *CY 1964*) b July 28, 1936
*Sohoni, S. W. (M'tra, Baroda & Bombay) b March 5, 1918
Solanky, J. W. (E. Africa & Glam.) b June 30, 1942
Solkar, E. D. (Bombay & Sussex) b March 18, 1948
*Solomon, J. S. (BG) b Aug. 26, 1930
*Solomon, W. R. T. (Tvl & E. Prov.) b April 23, 1872, d July 12, 1964
*Sood, M. M. (Delhi) b July 6, 1939
Southern, J. W. (Hants) b Sept. 2, 1952
*Southerton, James (Surrey, Hants & Sussex) b Nov. 16, 1827, d June 16, 1880
Southerton, S. J. (Editor of *Wisden* 1934-35) b July 7, 1874, d March 12, 1935
*Sparling, J. T. (Auck.) b July 24, 1938
Spencer, C. T. (Leics.) b Aug. 18, 1931
Spencer, J. (CUCC & Sussex) b Oct. 6, 1949
Spencer, T. W. (Kent) b March 22, 1914
Sperry, J. (Leics.) b March 19, 1910
*Spofforth, F. R. (NSW & Vic.) b Sept. 9, 1853, d June 4, 1926
*Spooner, R. H. (Lancs.; *CY 1905*) b Oct. 21, 1880, d Oct. 2, 1961
*Spooner, R. T. (Warwicks.) b Dec. 30, 1919
Springall, J. D. (Notts.) b Sept. 19, 1932
*Srikkanth, K. (TN) b Dec. 21, 1959
*Srinivasan, T. E. (TN) b Oct. 26, 1950
*Stackpole, K. R. (Vic.; *CY 1973*) b July 10, 1940
Standen, J. A. (Worcs.) b May 30, 1935
*Stanyforth, Lt-Col. R. T. (Yorks.) b May 30, 1892, d Feb. 20, 1964
*Staples, S. J. (Notts.; *CY 1929*) b Sept. 18, 1892, d June 4, 1950
Starkie, S. (Northants) b April 4, 1926
*Statham, J. B. (Lancs.; *CY 1955*) b June 16, 1930
*Stayers, S. C. (†Guyana & Bombay) b June 9, 1937
Stead, B. (Yorks., Essex, Notts. & N. Tvl) b June 21, 1939, d April 15, 1980
Stead, D. W. (Cant.) b May 26, 1947
*Steel, A. G. (CUCC & Lancs.; Pres. MCC 1902) b Sept. 24, 1858, d June 15, 1914
*Steele, D. S. (Northants & Derbys.; *CY 1976*) b Sept. 29, 1941
Steele, J. F. (Leics., Natal & Glam.) b July 23, 1946
Stephens, E. J. (Glos.) b March 23, 1910
Stephenson, G. R. (Derbys. & Hants) b Nov. 19, 1942
Stephenson, H. H. (Surrey & All-England) b May 3, 1832, d Dec. 17, 1896
Stephenson, H. W. (Som.) b July 18, 1920
Stephenson, Lt-Col. J. W. A. (Essex & Worcs.) b Aug. 1, 1907, d May 20, 1982
Stevens, Edward ("Lumpy") (Hants) b *circa* 1735, d Sept. 7, 1819
*Stevens, G. B. (S. Aust.) b Feb. 29, 1932
*Stevens, G. T. S. (UCS, OUCC & Middx; *CY 1918*) b Jan. 7, 1901, d Sept. 19, 1970
*Stevenson, G. B. (Yorks.) b Dec. 16, 1955
Stevenson, K. (Derbys. & Hants) b Oct. 6, 1950
Stevenson, M. H. (CUCC & Derbys.) b June 13, 1927
Stewart, A. J. (Surrey) b April 8, 1963
*Stewart, M. J. (Surrey; *CY 1958*) b Sept. 16, 1932
*Stewart, R. B. (SA) b Sept. 3, 1856, d Sept. 12, 1913
Stewart, R. W. (Glos. & Middx) b Feb. 28, 1945
Stewart, W. J. (Warwicks. & Northants) b Aug. 31, 1934
*Stirling, D. A. (C. Dist.) b Oct. 5, 1961
Stocks, F. W. (Notts.) b Nov. 6, 1917
*Stoddart, A. E. (Middx; *CY 1893*) b March 11, 1863, d April 4, 1915
*Stollmeyer, J. B. (T/T) b April 11, 1921
*Stollmeyer, V. H. (T/T) b Jan. 24, 1916
*Storer, W. (Derbys.; *CY 1899*) b Jan. 25, 1867, d Feb. 28, 1912
Storey, S. J. (Surrey & Sussex) b Jan. 6, 1941
Stott, L. W. (Auck.) b Dec. 8, 1946
Stott, W. B. (Yorks.) b July 18, 1934
Stovold, A. W. (Glos. & OFS) b March 19, 1953
*Street, G. B. (Sussex) b Dec. 6, 1889, d April 24, 1924
*Stricker, L. A. (Tvl) b May 26, 1884, d Feb. 5, 1960
Stringer, P. M. (Yorks. & Leics.) b Feb. 23, 1943
*Strudwick, H. (Surrey; *CY 1912*) b Jan. 28, 1880, d Feb. 13, 1970

Strydom, W. T. (OFS) b March 21, 1942
*Studd, C. T. (CUCC & Middx) b Dec. 2, 1860, d July 16, 1931
*Studd, G. B. (CUCC & Middx) b Oct. 20, 1859, d Feb. 13, 1945
Studd, Sir Peter M. (CUCC) b Sept. 15, 1916
Sturt, M. O. C. (Middx) b Sept. 12, 1940
*Subba Row, R. (CUCC, Surrey & Northants; *CY 1961*) b Jan. 29, 1932
*Subramanya, V. (Mysore) b July 16, 1936
Such, P. M. (Notts.) b June 12, 1964
Sudhakar Rao, R. (Karn.) b Aug. 8, 1952
Sueter, T. (Hants & Surrey) b *circa* 1749, d Feb. 17, 1827
*Sugg, F. H. (Yorks., Derbys. & Lancs.; *CY 1890*) b Jan. 11, 1862, d May 29, 1933
Sullivan, J. (Lancs.) b Feb. 5, 1945
Sully, H. (Som. & Northants) b Nov. 1, 1939
*Sunderram, G. R. (Bombay & Raja.) b March 29, 1930
Sunnucks, P. R. (Kent) b June 22, 1916
*Surendranath, R. (Ind. Serv.) b Jan. 4, 1937
Surridge, D. (CUCC & Glos.) b Jan. 6, 1956
Surridge, W. S. (Surrey; *CY 1953*) b Sept. 3, 1917
*Surti, R. F. (Guj., Raja. & Qld) b May 25, 1936
*Susskind, M. J. (CUCC, Middx & Tvl) b June 8, 1891, d July 9, 1957
*Sutcliffe, B. (Auck., Otago & N. Dist.; *CY 1950*) b Nov. 17, 1923
*Sutcliffe, H. (Yorks.; *CY 1920*) b Nov. 24, 1894, d Jan. 22, 1978
Sutcliffe, S. P. (OUCC & Warwicks.) b May 22, 1960
Sutcliffe, W. H. H. (Yorks.) b Oct. 10, 1926
Suttle, K. G. (Sussex) b Aug. 25, 1928
Sutton, R. E. (Auck.) b May 30, 1940
*Swamy, V. N. (Ind. Serv.) b May 23, 1924, d May 1, 1983
Swanton, E. W. (Middx; Writer) b Feb. 11, 1907
Swarbrook, F. W. (Derbys., Griq. W. & OFS) b Dec. 17, 1950
Swart, P. D. (Rhod., W. Prov., Glam. & Boland) b April 27, 1946
*Swetman, R. (Surrey, Notts & Glos.) b Oct. 25, 1933
Sydenham, D. A. D. (Surrey) b April 6, 1934
Symington, S. J. (Leics.) b Sept. 16, 1926

*Taber, H. B. (NSW) b April 29, 1940
*Taberer, H. M. (OUCC & Natal) b Oct. 7, 1870, d June 5, 1932
*Tahir Naqqash (Servis Ind., MCB, Punjab & Lahore) b June 28, 1959
Tait, A. (Northants & Glos.) b Dec. 27, 1953
*Talat Ali (Lahore, PIA & UBL) b May 29, 1950
Talbot, R. O. (Cant. & Otago) b Nov. 26, 1903, d Jan. 5, 1983
*Tallon, D. (Qld; *CY 1949*) b Feb. 17, 1916, d Sept. 7, 1984
*Tamhane, N. S. (Bombay) b Aug. 4, 1931
*Tancred, A. B. (Kimberley, Griq. W. & Tvl) b Aug. 20, 1865, d Nov. 23, 1911
*Tancred, L. J. (Tvl) b Oct. 7, 1876, d July 28, 1934
*Tancred, V. M. (Tvl) b 1875, d June 3, 1904
*Tapscott, G. L. (Griq. W.) b Nov. 7, 1889, d Dec. 13, 1940
*Tapscott, L. E. (Griq. W.) b March 18, 1894, d July 7, 1934
*Tarapore, K. K. (Bombay) b Dec. 17, 1910
Tarbox, C. V. (Worcs.) b July 2, 1891, d June 15, 1978
Tarrant, F. A. (Vic., Middx & Patiala; *CY 1908*) b Dec. 11, 1880, d Jan. 29, 1951
Tarrant, George F. (Cambs. & All-England) b Dec. 7, 1838, d July 2, 1870
*Taslim Arif (Kar., Sind & NBP) b May 1, 1954
*Tate, F. W. (Sussex) b July 24, 1867, d Feb. 24, 1943
*Tate, M. W. (Sussex; *CY 1924*) b May 30, 1895, d May 18, 1956
*Tattersall, R. (Lancs.) b Aug. 17, 1922
*Tauseef Ahmed (PWD & UBL) b May 10, 1958
*Tavaré, C. J. (OUCC & Kent) b Oct. 27, 1954
Tayfield, A. (Natal, Tvl & NE Tvl) b June 21, 1931
*Tayfield, H. J. (Natal, Rhod. & Tvl; *CY 1956*) b Jan. 30, 1929
*Taylor, A. I. (Tvl) b July 25, 1925
Taylor, B. (Essex; *CY 1972*) b June 19, 1932
*Taylor, B. R. (Cant. & Wgtn) b July 12, 1943
*Taylor, Daniel (Natal) b Jan. 9, 1887, d Jan. 24, 1957
*Taylor, D. D. (Auck. & Warwicks.) b March 2, 1923, d Dec. 5, 1980
Taylor, D. J. S. (Surrey, Som. & Griq. W.) b Nov. 12, 1942
Taylor, G. R. (Hants) b Nov. 25, 1909
*Taylor, H. W. (Natal, Tvl & W. Prov.; *CY 1925*) b May 5, 1889, d Feb. 8, 1973
*Taylor, J. M. (NSW) b Oct. 10, 1895, d May 12, 1971
*Taylor, J. O. (T/T) b Jan. 3, 1932
*Taylor, K. (Yorks. & Auck.) b Aug. 21, 1935
Taylor, K. A. (Warwicks.) b Sept. 29, 1916
*Taylor, L. B. (Leics. & Natal) b Oct. 25, 1953
Taylor, M. L. (Lancs.) b July 16, 1904, d March 14, 1978
Taylor, M. N. S. (Notts. & Hants) b Nov. 12, 1942
Taylor, N. R. (Kent) b July 21, 1959
Taylor, R. M. (Essex) b Nov. 30, 1909, d Jan. 1984
*Taylor, R. W. (Derbys.; *CY 1977*) b July 17, 1941
Taylor, T. J. (OUCC & Lancs.) b March 28, 1961
Taylor, T. L. (CUCC & Yorks.; *CY 1901*) b May 25, 1878, d March 16, 1960
Taylor, W. (Notts.) b Jan. 24, 1947

Tennekoon, A. P. B. (SL) b Oct. 29, 1946
*Tennyson, 3rd Lord (Hon. L. H.) (Hants; *CY 1914*) b Nov. 7, 1889, d June 6, 1951
*Terry, V. P. (Hants) b Jan. 14, 1959
*Theunissen, N. H. (W. Prov.) b May 4, 1867, d Nov. 9, 1929
Thomas, D. J. (Surrey & N. Tvl) b June 30, 1959
*Thomas, G. (NSW) b March 21, 1938
Thomas, J. G. (Glam. & Border) b Aug. 12, 1960
Thompson, A. W. (Middx) b April 17, 1916
*Thompson, G. J. (Northants; *CY 1906*) b Oct. 27, 1877, d March 3, 1943
Thompson, J. R. (CUCC & Warwicks.) b May 10, 1918
*Thompson, Nathaniel (NSW) b April 21, 1838, d Sept. 2, 1896
Thompson, P. M. (OFS & W. Prov.) b April 25, 1948
Thompson, R. G. (Warwicks.) b Sept. 26, 1932
*Thoms, G. R. (Vic.) b March 22, 1927
*Thomson, A. L. (Vic.) b Dec. 2, 1945
*Thomson, J. R. (NSW, Qld & Middx) b Aug. 16, 1950
*Thomson, K. (Cant.) b Feb. 26, 1941
*Thomson, N. I. (Sussex) b Jan. 23, 1929
Thorne, D. A. (Warwicks & OUCC) b Dec. 12, 1964
Thornton, C. I. (CUCC, Kent & Middx) b March 20, 1850, d Dec. 10, 1929
*Thornton, P. G. (Yorks., Middx & SA) b Dec. 24, 1867, d Jan. 31, 1939
*Thurlow, H. M. (Qld) b Jan. 10, 1902, d Dec. 3, 1975
Tilly, H. W. (Middx) b May 25, 1932
Timms, B. S. V. (Hants & Warwicks.) b Dec. 17, 1940
Timms, J. E. (Northants) b Nov. 3, 1906, d May 18, 1980
Timms, W. W. (Northants) b Sept. 28, 1902
Tindall, M. (CUCC & Middx) b March 31, 1914
Tindall, R. A. E. (Surrey) b Sept. 23, 1935
*Tindill, E. W. T. (Wgtn) b Dec. 18, 1910
*Titmus, F. J. (Middx, Surrey & OFS; *CY 1963*) b Nov. 24, 1932
Todd, L. J. (Kent) b June 19, 1907, d Aug. 20, 1967
Todd, P. A. (Notts.) b March 12, 1953
Tolchard, J. G. (Leics.) b March 17, 1944
*Tolchard, R. W. (Leics.) b June 15, 1946
Tomlins, K. P. (Middx) b Oct. 23, 1957
*Tomlinson, D. S. (Rhod. & Border) b Sept. 4, 1910
Tompkin, M. (Leics.) b Feb. 17, 1919, d Sept. 27, 1956
Toogood, G. J. (OUCC) b Nov. 19, 1961
*Toohey, P. M. (NSW) b April 20, 1954
Tooley, C. D. M. (OUCC) b April 19, 1964
Topham, R. D. N. (OUCC) b July 17, 1952
Tordoff, G. G. (CUCC & Som.) b Dec. 6, 1929
*Toshack, E. R. H. (NSW) b Dec. 15, 1914
Townsend, A. (Warwicks.) b Aug. 26, 1921
Townsend, A. F. (Derbys.) b March 29, 1912
*Townsend, C. L. (Glos.; *CY 1899*) b Nov. 7, 1876, d Oct. 17, 1958
*Townsend, D. C. H. (OUCC) b April 20, 1912
*Townsend, L. F. (Derbys. & Auck.; *CY 1934*) b June 8, 1903
Toynbee, M. H. (C. Dist.) b Nov. 29, 1956
*Traicos, A. J. (Rhod. & Zimb.) b May 17, 1947
*Travers, J. P. F. (S. Aust.) b Jan. 10, 1871, d Sept. 15, 1942
*Tremlett, M. F. (Som. & C. Dist.) b July 5, 1923, d July 30, 1984
Tremlett, T. M. (Hants) b July 26, 1956
*Tribe, G. E. (Vic. & Northants; *CY 1955*) b Oct. 4, 1920
*Trim, J. (BG) b Jan. 24, 1915, d Nov. 12, 1960
Trimble, S. C. (Qld) b Aug. 16, 1934
*Trimborn, P. H. J. (Natal) b May 18, 1940
**Trott, A. E. (Vic., Middx & Hawkes Bay; *CY 1899*) b Feb. 6, 1873, d July 30, 1914
*Trott, G. H. S. (Vic.; *CY 1894*) b Aug. 5, 1866, d Nov. 10, 1917
*Troup, G. B. (Auck.) b Oct. 3, 1952
*Trueman, F. S. (Yorks.; *CY 1953*) b Feb. 6, 1931
*Trumble, H. (Vic.; *CY 1897*) b May 12, 1867, d Aug. 14, 1938
*Trumble, J. W. (Vic.) b Sept. 16, 1863, d Aug. 17, 1944
*Trumper, V. T. (NSW; *CY 1903*) b Nov. 2, 1877, d June 28, 1915
*Truscott, P. B. (Wgtn) b Aug. 14, 1941
*Tuckett, L. (OFS) b Feb. 6, 1919
*Tuckett, L. R. (Natal & OFS) b April 19, 1885, d April 8, 1963
*Tufnell, N. C. (CUCC & Surrey) b June 13, 1887, d Aug. 3, 1951
Tuke, Sir Anthony (Pres. MCC 1982-83) b Aug. 22, 1920
Tunnicliffe, C. J. (Derbys.) b Aug. 11, 1951
Tunnicliffe, H. T. (Notts.) b March 4, 1950
Tunnicliffe, J. (Yorks.; *CY 1901*) b Aug. 26, 1866, d July 11, 1948
*Turnbull, M. J. (CUCC & Glam.; *CY 1931*) b March 16, 1906, d Aug. 5, 1944
*Turner, A. (NSW) b July 23, 1950
*Turner, C. T. B. (NSW; *CY 1889*) b Nov. 16, 1862, d Jan. 1, 1944
Turner, D. R. (Hants & W. Prov.) b Feb. 5, 1949
Turner, F. M. (Leics.) b Aug. 8, 1934
*Turner, G. M. (Otago, N. Dist. & Worcs.; *CY 1971*) b May 26, 1947
Turner, S. (Essex & Natal) b July 18, 1943
*Twentyman-Jones, P. S. (W. Prov.) b Sept. 13, 1876, d March 8, 1954
Twining, R. H. (OUCC & Middx; Pres. MCC 1964-65) b Nov. 3, 1889, d Jan. 3, 1979

*Tyldesley, E. (Lancs.; *CY 1920*) b Feb. 5, 1889, d May 5, 1962
*Tyldesley, J. T. (Lancs.; *CY 1902*) b Nov. 22, 1873, d Nov. 27, 1930
*Tyldesley, R. K. (Lancs.; *CY 1925*) b March 11, 1897, d Sept. 17, 1943
*Tylecote, E. F. S. (OUCC & Kent) b June 23, 1849, d March 15, 1938
*Tyler, E. J. (Som.) b Oct. 13, 1864, d Jan. 21, 1917
*Tyson, F. H. (Northants; *CY 1956*) b June 6, 1930

Ufton, D. G. (Kent) b May 31, 1928
*Ulyett, G. (Yorks.) b Oct. 21, 1851, d June 18, 1898
*Umrigar, P. R. (Bombay & Guj.) b March 28, 1926
*Underwood, D. L. (Kent; *CY 1969*) b June 8, 1945
Unwin, F. St G. (Essex) b April 23, 1911

*Valentine, A. L. (Jam.; *CY 1951*) b April 29, 1930
*Valentine, B. H. (CUCC & Kent) b Jan. 17, 1908, d Feb. 2, 1983
*Valentine, V. A. (Jam.) b April 4, 1908, d July 6, 1972
Vance, R. H. (Wgtn) b March 31, 1955
*van der Bijl, P. G. (W. Prov. & OUCC) b Oct. 21, 1907, d Feb. 16, 1973
*van der Bijl, V. A. P. (Natal, Middx, Tvl & SA XI; *CY 1981*) b March 19, 1948
Van der Gucht, P. I. (Glos. & Bengal) b Nov. 2, 1911
*Van der Merwe, E. A. (Tvl) b Nov. 9, 1904, d Feb. 28, 1971
*Van der Merwe, P. L. (W. Prov. & E. Prov.) b March 14, 1937
van Geloven, J. (Yorks. & Leics.) b Jan. 4, 1934
*Van Ryneveld, C. B. (W. Prov. & OUCC) b March 19, 1928
van Vuuren, M. K. (E. Prov.) b Aug. 20, 1958
Varachia, R. (First Pres. SA Cricket Union) b Oct. 12, 1915, d Dec. 11, 1981
Varey, D. W. (CUCC & Lancs.) b Oct. 15, 1961
Varey, J. G. (OUCC) b Oct. 15, 1961
*Varnals, G. D. (E. Prov., Tvl & Natal) b July 24, 1935
Vaulkhard, P. (Notts. & Derbys.) b Sept. 15, 1911
*Vengsarkar, D. B. (Bombay) b April 6, 1956
*Veivers, T. R. (Qld) b April 6, 1937
*Venkataraghavan, S. (†TN & Derbys.) b April 21, 1946
Verdoorn, K. D. (N. Tvl) b July 24, 1955
*Verity, H. (Yorks.; *CY 1932*) b May 18, 1905, d July 31, 1943
*Vernon, G. F. (Middx) b June 20, 1856, d Aug. 10, 1902
Vernon, M. T. (W. Aust.) b Feb. 9, 1937

Vigar, F. H. (Essex) b July 7, 1917
*Viljoen, K. G. (Griq. W., OFS & Tvl) b May 14, 1910, d Jan. 21, 1974
*Vincent, C. L. (Tvl) b Feb. 16, 1902, d Aug. 24, 1968
*Vine, J. (Sussex; *CY 1906*) b May 15, 1875, d April 25, 1946
*Vintcent, C. H. (Tvl & Griq. W.) b Sept. 2, 1866, d Sept. 28, 1943
Virgin, R. T. (Som., Northants & W. Prov.; *CY 1971*) b Aug. 26, 1939
*Viswanath, G. R. (†Karn.) b Feb. 12, 1949
*Vivian, G. E. (Auck.) b Feb. 28, 1946
*Vivian, H. G. (Auck.) b Nov. 4, 1912, d Aug. 12, 1983
*Voce, W. (Notts.; *CY 1933*) b Aug. 8, 1909, d June 6, 1984
*Vogler, A. E. E. (Middx, Natal, Tvl & E. Prov.; *CY 1908*) b Nov. 28, 1876, d Aug. 9, 1946
*Vizianagram, Maharaj Kumar Sir Vijaya of (U. Prov.) b Dec. 28, 1905, d Dec. 2, 1965

*Waddington, A. (Yorks.) b Feb. 4, 1893, d Oct. 28, 1959
Waddington, J. E. (Griq. W.) b Dec. 30, 1918
*Wade, H. F. (Natal) b Sept. 14, 1905, d Nov. 22, 1980
Wade, T. H. (Essex) b Nov. 24, 1910
*Wade, W. W. (Natal) b June 18, 1914
*Wadekar, A. L. (Bombay) b April 1, 1941
*Wadsworth, K. J. (C. Dist. & Cant.) b Nov. 30, 1946, d Aug. 19, 1976
*Wainwright, E. (Yorks.; *CY 1894*) b April 8, 1865, d Oct. 28, 1919
*Waite, J. H. B. (E. Prov. & Tvl) b Jan. 19, 1930
*Waite, M. G. (S. Aust.) b Jan. 7, 1911
*Walcott, C. L. (B'dos & BG; *CY 1958*) b Jan. 17, 1926
*Walcott, L. A. (B'dos) b Jan. 18, 1894, d Feb. 28, 1984
Walden, F. I. (Northants; Umpire) b March 1, 1888, d May 3, 1949
Walford, M. M. (OUCC & Som.) b Nov. 27, 1915
Walker, A. K. (NSW & Notts.) b Oct. 4, 1925
Walker, C. (Yorks. & Hants) b June 27, 1920
Walker, C. W. (S. Aust.) b Feb. 19, 1909, d Dec. 21, 1942
Walker, I. D. (Middx) b Jan. 8, 1844, d July 6, 1898
*Walker, M. H. N. (Vic.) b Sept. 12, 1948
*Walker, P. M. (Glam., Tvl & W. Prov.) b Feb. 17, 1936
Walker, W. (Notts.; oldest living County Champ. player) b Nov. 24, 1892
*Wall, T. W. (S. Aust.) b May 13, 1904, d March 25, 1981
*Wallace, W. M. (Auck.) b Dec. 19, 1916
Waller, C. E. (Surrey & Sussex) b Oct. 3, 1948

*Walsh, C. A. (Jam. & Glos.) b Oct. 30, 1962
Walsh, J. E. (NSW & Leics.) b Dec. 4, 1912, d May 20, 1980
*Walter, K. A. (Tvl) b Nov. 5, 1939
*Walters, C. F. (Glam. & Worcs.; *CY 1934*) b Aug. 28, 1905
*Walters, F. H. (Vic. & NSW) b Feb. 9, 1860, d June 1, 1922
Walters, J. (Derbys.) b Aug. 7, 1949
*Walters, K. D. (NSW) b Dec. 21, 1945
Walton, A. C. (OUCC & Middx) b Sept. 26, 1933
*Waqar Hassan (Pak. Us, Punjab, Pak. Serv. & Kar.) b Sept. 12, 1932
*Ward, Alan (Derbys., Leics. & Border) b Aug. 10, 1947
*Ward, Albert (Yorks. & Lancs.; *CY 1890*) b Nov. 21, 1865, d Jan. 6, 1939
Ward, B. (Essex) b Feb. 28, 1944
Ward, D. (Glam.) b Aug. 30, 1934
*Ward, F. A. (S. Aust.) b Feb. 23, 1909, d March 25, 1974
*Ward, J. T. (Cant.) b March 11, 1937
*Ward, T. A. (Tvl) b Aug. 2, 1887, d Feb. 16, 1936
Ward, William (MCC & Hants) b July 24, 1787, d June 30, 1849
*Wardle, J. H. (Yorks.; *CY 1954*) b Jan. 8, 1923, d July 23, 1985
*Warnapura, B. (SL) b March 1, 1953
Warne, F. B. (Worcs., Vic. & Tvl) b Oct. 3, 1906
Warner, A. E. (Worcs. & Derbys.) b May 12, 1959
*Warner, Sir Pelham (OUCC & Middx; *CY 1904, special portrait 1921*) b Oct. 2, 1873, d Jan. 30, 1963
*Warr, J. J. (CUCC & Middx) b July 16, 1927
*Warren, A. R. (Derbys.) b April 2, 1875, d Sept. 3, 1951
*Washbrook, C. (Lancs.; *CY 1947*) b Dec. 6, 1914
*Wasim Akram (Lahore & PACO) b Sept. 7, 1966
*Wasim Bari (Kar., PIA & Sind) b March 23, 1948
*Wasim Raja (Lahore, Sargodha, Pak. Us, PIA, Punjab & NBP) b July 3, 1952
Wass, T. G. (Notts.; *CY 1908*) b Dec. 26, 1873, d Oct. 27, 1953
Wassell, A. (Hants) b April 15, 1940
*Watkins, A. J. (Glam.) b April 21, 1922
*Watkins, J. C. (Natal) b April 10, 1923
*Watkins, J. R. (NSW) b April 16, 1943
Watkinson, M. (Lancs.) b Aug. 1, 1961
*Watson, C. (Jam. & Delhi) b July 1, 1938
Watson, F. B. (Lancs.) b Sept. 17, 1898, d Feb. 1, 1976
*Watson, G. D. (Vic., W. Aust. & NSW) b March 8, 1945
Watson, G. G. (NSW, W. Aust. & Worcs.) b Jan. 29, 1955
*Watson, W. (Yorks. & Leics.; *CY 1954*) b March 7, 1920
*Watson, W. (NSW) b Jan. 31, 1931
Watson, W. K. (Border, N. Tvl, E. Prov., Notts. & SA XI) b May 21, 1955
*Watt, L. (Otago) b Sept. 17, 1924
Watts, E. A. (Surrey) b Aug. 1, 1911, d May 2, 1982
Watts, H. E. (CUCC & Som.) b March 4, 1922
Watts, P. D. (Northants & Notts.) b March 31, 1938
Watts, P. J. (Northants) b June 16, 1940
*Wazir Ali, S. (C. Ind., S. Punjab & Patiala) b Sept. 15, 1903, d June 17, 1950
*Wazir Mohammad (B'pur & Kar.) b Dec. 22, 1929
*Webb, M. G. (Otago & Cant.) b June 22, 1947
*Webb, P. N. (Auck.) b July 14, 1957
Webb, R. T. (Sussex) b July 11, 1922
Webb, S. G. (Manager Australians in England 1961) b Jan. 31, 1900, d Aug. 5, 1976
*Webbe, A. J. (OUCC & Middx) b Jan. 16, 1855, d Feb. 19, 1941
Webster, J. (CUCC & Northants) b Oct. 28, 1917
Webster, Dr R. V. (Warwicks. & Otago) b June 10, 1939
Webster, W. H. (CUCC & Middx; Pres. MCC 1976-77) b Feb. 22, 1910
*Weekes, E. D. (B'dos; *CY 1951*) b Feb. 26, 1925
*Weekes, K. H. (Jam.) b Jan. 24, 1912
Weeks, R. T. (Warwicks.) b April 30, 1930
*Weir, G. L. (Auck.) b June 2, 1908
*Wellard, A. W. (Som.; *CY 1936*) b April 8, 1902, d Dec. 31, 1980
*Wellham, D. M. (NSW) b March 13, 1959
Wellings, E. M. (OUCC & Surrey) b April 6, 1909
Wells, A. P. (Sussex) b Oct. 2, 1961
Wells, B. D. (Glos. & Notts.) b July 27, 1930
Wells, C. M. (Sussex, Border & W. Prov.) b March 3, 1960
Wenman, E. G. (Kent & England) b Aug. 18, 1803, d Dec. 31, 1879
Wensley, A. F. (Sussex) b May 23, 1898, d June 17, 1970
*Wesley, C. (Natal) b Sept. 5, 1937
*Wessels, K. C. (OFS, W. Prov., N. Tvl, Sussex & Qld) b Sept. 14, 1957
West, G. H. (Editor of *Wisden* 1880-86) b 1851, d Oct. 6, 1896
*Westcott, R. J. (W. Prov.) b Sept. 19, 1927
Weston, M. J. (Worcs.) b April 8, 1959
*Wettimuny, M. D. (SL) b June 11, 1951
*Wettimuny, S. (SL; *CY 1985*) b Aug. 12, 1956
*Wharton, A. (Lancs. & Leics.) b April 30, 1923
*Whatmore, D. F. (Vic.) b March 16, 1954
Wheatley, K. J. (Hants) b Jan. 20, 1946
Wheatley, O. S. (CUCC, Warwicks. & Glam.; *CY 1969*) b May 28, 1935

Whitaker, Haddon (Editor of *Wisden* 1940-43) b Aug. 30, 1908, d Jan. 5, 1982
Whitaker, J. J. (Leics.) b May 5, 1962
Whitcombe, P. A. (OUCC & Middx) b April 23, 1923
White, A. F. T. (CUCC, Warwicks. & Worcs.) b Sept. 5, 1915
*White, D. W. (Hants & Glam.) b Dec. 14, 1935
White, E. C. S. (NSW) b July 14, 1913
*White, G. C. (Tvl) b Feb. 5, 1882, d Oct. 17, 1918
*White, J. C. (Som.; *CY 1929*) b Feb. 19, 1891, d May 2, 1961
White, Hon. L. R. (5th Lord Annaly) (Middx & Victory Test) b March 15, 1927
White, R. A. (Middx & Notts.) b Oct. 6, 1936
White, R. C. (CUCC, Glos. & Tvl) b Jan. 29, 1941
*White, W. A. (B'dos) b Nov. 20, 1938
Whitehead, J. P. (Yorks. & Worcs.) b Sept. 3, 1925
Whitehouse, J. (Warwicks.) b April 8, 1949
*Whitelaw, P. E. (Auck.) b Feb. 10, 1910
Whitfield, B. J. (Natal) b March 14, 1959
Whitfield, E. W. (Surrey & Northants) b May 31, 1911
Whiting, N. H. (Worcs.) b Oct. 2, 1920
Whitington, R. S. (S. Aust. & Victory Tests; Writer) b June 30, 1912, d March 13, 1984
*Whitney, M. R. (NSW & Glos.) b Feb. 24, 1959
Whittaker, G. J. (Surrey) b May 29, 1916
Whittingham, N. B. (Notts.) b Oct. 22, 1940
*Whitty, W. J. (S. Aust.) b Aug. 15, 1886, d Jan. 30, 1974
*Whysall, W. W. (Notts.; *CY 1925*) b Oct. 31, 1887, d Nov. 11, 1930
*Wiener, J. M. (Vic.) b May 1, 1955
*Wight, C. V. (BG) b July 28, 1902, d Oct. 4, 1969
*Wight, G. L. (BG) b May 28, 1929
Wight, P. B. (BG, Som., & Cant.) b June 25, 1930
*Wijesuriya, R. G. C. E. (SL) b Feb. 18, 1960
Wilcox, D. R. (CUCC & Essex) b June 4, 1910, d Feb. 6, 1953
Wild, D. J. (Northants) b Nov. 28, 1962
*Wiles, C. A. (B'dos & T/T) b Aug. 11, 1892, d Nov. 4, 1957
Wilkins, A. H. (Glam., Glos. & N. Tvl) b Aug. 22, 1953
Wilkins, C. P. (Derbys., Border, E. Prov. & Natal) b July 31, 1944
*Wilkinson, L. L. (Lancs.) b Nov. 5, 1916
Wilkinson, P. A. (Notts.) b Aug. 23, 1951
Wilkinson, Col. W. A. C. (OUCC) b Dec. 6, 1892, d Sept. 19, 1983
Willatt, G. L. (CUCC, Notts. & Derbys.) b May 7, 1918
*Willett, E. T. (Comb. Is. & Leewards) b May 1, 1953
Willett, M. D. (Surrey) b April 21, 1933
*Willey, P. (Northants, E. Prov. & Leics.) b Dec. 6, 1949
*Williams, A. B. (Jam.) b Nov. 21, 1949
Williams, C. B. (B'dos) b March 8, 1926
Williams, C. C. P. (OUCC & Essex) b Feb. 9, 1933
Williams, D. L. (Glam.) b Nov. 20, 1946
*Williams, E. A. V. (B'dos) b April 10, 1914
Williams, N. F. (Middx, Windwards & Tas.) b July 2, 1962
Williams, R. G. (Northants) b Aug. 10, 1957
*Williams, R. J. (Natal) b April 12, 1912, d May 14, 1984
Williamson, J. G. (Northants) b April 4, 1936
*Willis, R. G. D. (Surrey, Warwicks. & N. Tvl; *CY 1978*) b May 30, 1949
*Willoughby, J. T. (SA) b Nov. 7, 1874, d *circa* 1955
Willsher, E. (Kent & All-England) b Nov. 22, 1828, d Oct. 7, 1885
Wilmot, A. L. (E. Prov.) b June 1, 1943
Wilmot, K. (Warwicks.) b April 3, 1911
Wilson, A. (Lancs.) b April 24, 1921
Wilson, A. E. (Middx & Glos.) b May 18, 1912
*Wilson, Rev. C. E. M. (CUCC & Yorks.) b May 15, 1875, d Feb. 8, 1944
*Wilson, D. (Yorks. & MCC) b Aug. 7, 1937
Wilson, E. F. (Surrey) b June 24, 1907, d March 3, 1981
*Wilson, E. R. (CUCC & Yorks.) b March 25, 1879 d July 21, 1957
Wilson, J. V. (Yorks.; *CY 1961*) b Jan. 17, 1921
*Wilson, J. W. (Vic. & S. Aust.) b Aug. 20, 1921, d Oct. 13, 1985
Wilson, P. H. L. (Surrey, Som. & N. Tvl) b Aug. 17, 1958
Wilson, R. C. (Kent) b Feb. 18, 1928
Wiltshire, J. R. (Auck. & C. Dist.) b Jan. 20, 1952
*Wimble, C. S. (Tvl) b Jan. 9, 1864, d Jan. 28, 1930
Windows, A. R. (Glos. & CUCC) b Sept. 25, 1942
Winfield, H. M. (Notts.) b June 13, 1933
Wingfield Digby, A. R. (OUCC) b July 25, 1950
Winn, C. E. (OUCC & Sussex) b Nov. 13, 1926
Winslow, P. L. (Sussex, Tvl & Rhod.) b May 21, 1929
Wisden, John (Sussex; founder John Wisden and Co. and *Wisden's Cricketers' Almanack*) b Sept. 5, 1826, d April 5, 1884
*Wishart, K. L. (BG) b Nov. 28, 1908, d Oct. 18, 1972
Wolton, A. V. G. (Warwicks.) b June 12, 1919
*Wood, A. (Yorks.; *CY 1939*) b Aug. 25, 1898, d April 1, 1973

*Wood, B. (Yorks., Lancs., Derbys. & E. Prov.) b Dec. 26, 1942
Wood, C. J. B. (Leics.) b Nov. 21, 1875, d June 5, 1960
Wood, D. J. (Sussex) b May 19, 1914
*Wood, G. E. C. (CUCC & Kent) b Aug. 22, 1893, d March 18, 1971
*Wood, G. M. (W. Aust.) b Nov. 6, 1956
*Wood, H. (Kent & Surrey; *CY 1891*) b Dec. 14, 1854, d April 30, 1919
*Wood, R. (Lancs. & Vic.) b March 7, 1860, d Jan. 6, 1915
*Woodcock, A. J. (S. Aust.) b Feb. 27, 1948
*Woodfull, W. M. (Vic.; *CY 1927*) b Aug. 22, 1897, d Aug. 11, 1965
Woodhead, F. G. (Notts.) b Oct. 30, 1912
Woodhouse, G. E. S. (Som.) b Feb. 15, 1924
**Woods, S. M. J. (CUCC & Som.; *CY 1889*) b April 14, 1867, d April 30, 1931
Wookey, S. M. (CUCC & OUCC) b Sept. 2, 1954
Wooler, C. R. D. (Leics. & Rhod.) b June 30, 1930
Wooller, W. (CUCC & Glam.) b Nov. 20, 1912
Woolley, C. N. (Glos. & Northants) b May 5, 1886, d Nov. 3, 1962
*Woolley, F. E. (Kent; *CY 1911*) b May 27, 1887, d Oct. 18, 1978
*Woolley, R. D. (Tas.) b Sept. 16, 1954
*Woolmer, R. A. (Kent, Natal & W. Prov.; *CY 1976*) b May 14, 1948
*Worrall, J. (Vic.) b May 12, 1863, d Nov. 17, 1937
*Worrell, Sir F. M. M. (B'dos & Jam.; *CY 1951*) b Aug. 1, 1924, d March 13, 1967
Worsley, D. R. (OUCC & Lancs.) b July 18, 1941
Worsley, Sir W. A. 4th Bt. (Yorks.; Pres. MCC 1961-62) b April 5, 1890, d Dec. 4, 1973
*Worthington, T. S. (Derbys.; *CY 1937*) b Aug. 21, 1905, d Aug. 31, 1973
Wright, A. (Warwicks.) b Aug. 25, 1941
Wright, A. J. (Glos.) b July 27, 1962
*Wright, C. W. (CUCC & Notts.) b May 27, 1863, d Jan. 10, 1936
*Wright, D. V. P. (Kent; *CY 1940*) b Aug. 21, 1914
*Wright, J. G. (N. Dist. & Derbys.) b July 5, 1954
*Wright, K. J. (W. Aust. & S. Aust.) b Dec. 27, 1953
Wright, L. G. (Derbys.; *CY 1906*) b June 15, 1862, d Jan. 11, 1953
Wright, M. J. E. (N. Dist.) b Jan. 17, 1950
Wyatt, J. G. (Som.) b June 19, 1963
*Wyatt, R. E. S. (Warwicks. & Worcs.; *CY 1930*) b May 2, 1901
*Wynne, O. E. (Tvl & W. Prov.) b June 1, 1919, d July 13, 1975
*Wynyard, E. G. (Hants) b April 1, 1861, d Oct. 30, 1936

Yachad, M. (N. Tvl, Tvl & SA XI) b Nov. 17, 1960
*Yadav, N. S. (H'bad) b Jan. 26, 1957
*Yajurvindra Singh (M'tra & S'tra) b Aug. 1, 1952
*Yallop, G. N. (Vic.) b Oct. 7, 1952
*Yardley, B. (W. Aust.) b Sept. 7, 1947
*Yardley, N. W. D. (CUCC & Yorks.; *CY 1948*) b March 19, 1915
Yardley, T. J. (Worcs. & Northants) b Oct. 27, 1946
Yarnold, H. (Worcs.) b July 6, 1917, d Aug. 13, 1974
*Yashpal Sharma (Punjab) b Aug. 11, 1954
Yawar Saeed (Som. & Punjab) b Jan. 22, 1935
*Yograj Singh (Haryana & Punjab) b March 25, 1958
Young, D. M. (Worcs. & Glos.) b April 15, 1924
*Young, H. I. (Essex) b Feb. 5, 1876, d Dec. 12, 1964
*Young, J. A. (Middx) b Oct. 14, 1912
*Young, R. A. (CUCC & Sussex) b Sept. 16, 1885, d July 1, 1968
*Younis Ahmed (Lahore, Kar., Surrey, PIA, S. Aust., Worcs. & Glam.) b Oct. 20, 1947
*Yuile, B. W. (C. Dist.) b Oct. 29, 1941

*Zaheer Abbas (Kar., Glos., PWD, Dawood Indust., Sind & PIA; *CY 1972*) b July 24, 1947
*Zulch, J. W. (Tvl) b Jan. 2, 1886, d May 19, 1924
*Zulfiqar Ahmed (B'pur & PIA) b Nov. 22, 1926

## THE CRICKETERS' ASSOCIATION

The Cricketers' Association was formed in 1968, to work with the Test and County Cricket Board for the overall good of first-class cricket and its players. Membership is not compulsory, though the large majority of registered first-class cricketers are members. Players' views are communicated to the TCCB through representation on the Registration, Cricket and Discipline sub-committees.

### Officers, 1985-86

*President:* J. Arlott.

*Chairman:* G. Cook (Northamptonshire).

*Treasurer:* D. A. Graveney (Gloucestershire).

*Secretary:* J. D. Bannister
1a Pargeter Street, Walsall,
Staffordshire W5 8RP
(Telephone: 0922-27164/27669)

The eighteenth Annual General Meeting of the Association was held at Edgbaston on April 10, 1985. In addition to routine annual items, including minimum wage scales (an increase from £6,600 to £7,250 for a capped player), the 131 attending members gave qualified approval to the TCCB's proposed introduction of random drug tests.

Assured by committee officers that the Association would be fully involved in procedural arrangements, the members asked for a public announcement to be made, stating that the Association did not believe there was a problem in cricket but would cooperate, other sports having done so. It should be asked that a list of permitted medicines, such as aspirins, cold cures and pain-killers, be drawn up.

---

## THE CRICKETER CUP WINNERS, 1967-1985

*Sponsored by The Cricketer*

| | | |
|---|---|---|
| 1967 | REPTON PILGRIMS | beat Radley Rangers by 96 runs. |

*Final Sponsored by Champagne Mercier*

| | | |
|---|---|---|
| 1968 | OLD MALVERNIANS | beat Harrow Wanderers by five wickets. |
| 1969 | OLD BRIGHTONIANS | beat Stowe Templars by 156 runs. |
| 1970 | OLD WYKEHAMISTS | beat Old Tonbridgians by 94 runs. |

*Final Sponsored by Moët & Chandon*

| | | |
|---|---|---|
| 1971 | OLD TONBRIDGIANS | beat Charterhouse Friars on faster scoring-rate. |
| 1972 | OLD TONBRIDGIANS | beat Old Malvernians by 114 runs. |
| 1973 | RUGBY METEORS | beat Old Tonbridgians by five wickets. |
| 1974 | OLD WYKEHAMISTS | beat Old Alleynians on faster scoring-rate. |
| 1975 | OLD MALVERNIANS | beat Harrow Wanderers by 97 runs. |
| 1976 | OLD TONBRIDGIANS | beat Old Blundellians by 170 runs. |
| 1977 | SHREWSBURY SARACENS | beat Oundle Rovers by nine wickets. |
| 1978 | CHARTERHOUSE FRIARS | beat Oundle Rovers by nine wickets. |
| 1979 | OLD TONBRIDGIANS | beat Uppingham Rovers by 5 runs. |
| 1980 | MARLBOROUGH BLUES | beat Old Wellingtonians by 31 runs. |
| 1981 | CHARTERHOUSE FRIARS | beat Old Wykehamists by nine wickets. |
| 1982 | OLD WYKEHAMISTS | beat Old Malvernians on faster scoring-rate. |
| 1983 | REPTON PILGRIMS | beat Haileybury Hermits by seven wickets. |
| 1984 | OLD TONBRIDGIANS | beat Old Malvernians by seven wickets. |
| 1985 | OUNDLE ROVERS | beat Repton Pilgrims by three wickets. |

*From 1967 to 1983 the final was played at Burton Court, Chelsea. In 1984 and 1985 it was played at Vincent Square, Westminster.*

# OBITUARIES

ANSTRUTHER-GOUGH-CALTHORPE, SIR RICHARD HAMILTON, BT, who died at Elvetham, Hampshire, on February 7, 1985, aged 76, was in the Harrow XI in 1927 and headed the batting averages. A fine rackets player, who later won the Army Singles Championship six times, he was a typical rackets player type of bat, a good hitter of the ball with attractive strokes but radically unsound. He was President of the Warwickshire County Cricket Club from 1976 to 1980.

BARBER, ALAN THEODORE, who died at his home at Wokingham on March 10, 1985, at the age of 79, after several years of crippling illness, will be remembered by his contemporaries as a very good captain of Yorkshire and a gifted and versatile games-player. In all his games he was a fine competitor: the more critical the situation the better he played, and it was this determination, combined with a wonderful vitality and zest for life, which enabled him to instil into a side of tough Yorkshire professionals a discipline which had been lacking under some of his recent predecessors and yet to win at the same time not only their respect, but also their affection.

He captained Oxford at both cricket and soccer and in his last year won a place in the golf side – a tribute rather to his reputation as a fighter than to his technical skill. He was a prominent Corinthian footballer, twice won the Kinnaird Cup, the championship of Eton Fives, and was for years President of the Eton Fives Association. He had also been President of the Oxford Harlequins and was long an important member of the Old Salopians golf team in the Halford Hewitt.

Coming up to Oxford from Shrewsbury in 1926 after a two-year struggle with the examiners, he made a century in the Freshmen's match but had to wait till the tour before he got a game for the 'Varsity. Primarily a defensive and on-side player, he lacked the fluent strokes which were then regarded as the hallmark of an Oxford batsman. An innings of 54 in a crisis at Chelmsford won him his Blue and fortunate it was for Oxford that it did so. Left at Lord's to get 379 to beat Cambridge, they had two wickets down for 0 and Barber himself had been missed when his captain, E. R. T. Holmes, came in to join him. Together they added 183 in two hours, thirty-five minutes and, as long as they were together, Oxford still had a distinct chance. However, Holmes was out having made a glorious hundred, Barber followed shortly afterwards for 62, and the innings folded. After retaining his place in 1928 and helping in an opening stand of 66 at Lord's, he was appointed captain for 1929, in breach of the tradition by which the captain was normally the previous year's secretary. He proved an excellent choice and in the course of the season made the highest score of his first-class career, 119 against Nottinghamshire in The Parks, which took him only two and three-quarter hours, a sign that he was acquiring more ways of scoring. Later he played for Yorkshire, and against a strong England XI at Sheffield, after Percy Holmes had been out for 0, made 100 and with Oldroyd put on 204 for the second wicket.

In 1930 came the captaincy of Yorkshire. He was perhaps the first captain since Lord Hawke was in his prime some 30 years before who was worth his place as a player. Though he was not a heavy scorer, his defence was useful at a crisis and in the field he was fully up to the county's high standard. In his two years in the side he scored 1,050 runs with an average of 20.58. At the end of the season he had to choose between a long-term job captaining and administering Yorkshire and a career as a preparatory school master. Happily for the boys who were under his care at Ludgrove School, Wokingham, in the next 43 years, he chose the latter.

Herbert Sutcliffe's autobiography, *For England and Yorkshire*, contained the following tribute: "A. T. Barber, who captained Yorkshire for one season – 1930 – was a young man with a natural aptitude for leadership .... I shall always have the keenest admiration for the manner in which he tackled his job .... When he was compelled to leave county cricket he was sorry, but his regret was no greater than that of the members of the Yorkshire side, for they knew they had lost a first-class captain .... Barber had method in every move he made, he had personality, he earned the respect and comradeship of every member of the side." In 70 first-class matches, 42 of them for Yorkshire, he scored 2,261 runs at an average of 23.30.

BEESTON, NORMAN CHARLES, who died in Brisbane in February 1985, aged 84, was a regular member of the Queensland side in 1926-27, their first season of Sheffield Shield cricket. In seven matches he scored 187 runs.

BELL, ALEXANDER JOHN ("SANDY"), who played sixteen times for South Africa between 1929 and 1935, died in Cape Town on August 2, 1985, aged 79. In all but two of his Tests he opened the bowling, sometimes working up a good pace, bringing the ball down from a considerable height and capable of late in-swing. He toured England twice, in 1929 and 1935, and took 23 wickets in five Tests in Australia in 1931-32, claiming five wickets in an innings in successive Test matches at Sydney, Melbourne and Adelaide. He had his best Test figures in his first Test match, at Lord's, when he took the last six wickets in England's first innings and finished with six for 99. In the same series he shared what remains the record tenth-wicket partnership for South Africa in Test cricket – 103 with H. G. Owen-Smith at Headingley. Though no batsman himself, Bell's share was 26. Altogether he took 48 Test wickets (32.65) and 228 first-class wickets (23.29). At Cape Town in 1929-30 he took thirteen for 61 for Western Province against Eastern Province.

BERGIN, BERNARD FRANCIS, who died in Dublin on June 17, 1985, aged 71, was a right-hand opening bat who played twice for Ireland against New Zealand in 1937, one of fifteen instances of a first-class match being begun and finished in a day. His scores of 12 and 4 were the second highest in each Irish innings. He was the brother of S. F. Bergin, one of Ireland's best-known cricketers, who died in 1969.

BERRY, LESLIE GEORGE (he was in fact christened George Leslie) died at Leicester on February 5, 1985, aged 78. An ideal example of what is meant by a "good county cricketer", in 21 years of regular first-class cricket he took part in 610 matches, 606 of them for Leicestershire. He scored more runs for the county than any other player in its history, 30,143 with an average of 30.32, and made 45 centuries. He had a full range of strokes, the off drive and the pull being perhaps the most prominent, and a sound defence and for much of his career he opened the innings. Moreover his fielding could not be faulted: in his younger days he was usually on the boundary, later usually at mid-off, but he could in fact field anywhere. His admirers sometimes suggest that he was unlucky never to be picked for England or at least for the Players, and no-one will deny that, had he been so picked, he might well have made runs. The answer lies of course in the standard of English batting during his prime. Only twice did he average over 40 for a season: his successful competitors were scoring more heavily than that. In his best year, 1937, he scored 2,446 runs with an average of 52.04, and it is worth looking at the batting order for the Players at Lord's that year – Hutton, Barnett, Hardstaff, Hammond, Paynter, Compton, Ames, with James Langridge and Wellard to follow. Moreover Leyland, who was injured, was not playing. So Berry had to remain with the honourable record of being a great servant of Leicestershire.

Born at Dorking, but moving to Market Harborough when he was eight, he first appeared in 1924, but, though he immediately showed promise and got his 1,000 runs in his second season, it was not till 1928 that he made his first hundred, a magnificent 207 in three and a half hours against Worcestershire at Ashby de la Zouch. Two years later came the highest score of his career, 232 against Sussex at Leicester. His best years really commenced in 1932, when he scored 1,774 runs with an average of 38.56, and continued until after the war. He himself always remembered with particular pleasure the match with Nottinghamshire at Leicester in 1932, in which he made 72 and 75 not out against Larwood and Voce at their fastest. In the last innings Leicestershire needed 176 to win. Berry went in first and was still there when Corrall, the last man, came in with 22 wanted. Corrall defended magnificently and made 3 while Berry got the rest. He captained the county from 1946 to 1948 and in 1947, for the only time in his career, scored a hundred in each innings of a match, 165 and 111 not out against Essex at Clacton. As far on as 1949, when he was 43, he had one of the best seasons of his career, 1,853 runs with an average of 43.09. He finally retired at the end of 1951 and went to coach at Uppingham School, where he was such a success that he remained till 1979, when he was 73. He was also for many years a director of a sports shop in Leicester.

BHAGWATSINHJI, HH THE MAHARANA OF MEHAR, who died in Udaipur on November 3, 1984, aged 57, captained Rajputana for five seasons. He made 797 runs in the Ranji Trophy with an average of 17.07 and a top score of 78 against Baroda in 1957-58.

BIRD, RONALD ERNEST, who died at Feckenham, near Redditch, on February 20, 1985, aged 69, played for Worcestershire from 1946 to 1954, captaining them in the last three seasons. Getting a regular place in his first year at the age of 31, he showed distinct promise, playing many useful innings, and next year, when he was available for only half the matches, made his first century, 105 against Sussex, which enabled his side to win in face of a total of 301. In 1948 he hardly played, but after that appeared regularly until his retirement. In 1949 he got his 1,000 runs and, while temporarily acting as captain, he played a notable innings of 116 in rather over four hours, which had much to do with Worcestershire beating Yorkshire for the first time since 1939. By far his best season was 1952, his first year as captain: he scored 1,591 runs with an average of 37 and made three hundreds, including the highest innings of his career, 158 not out in four and a half hours against Somerset at Taunton. A middle-order batsman, usually at number four, he was a determined player, capable of aggression or defence as the situation demanded. He was also a courageous fieldsman close to the wicket, usually at short leg, where he held some fine catches. In his whole career he scored 7,700 runs with an average of 26.53 and made seven centuries. After retiring from cricket he played squash and lawn tennis for the county.

BLUNDEN, SIR WILLIAM, 6TH BT, died at Castle Blunden on October 20, 1985, aged 66. He was not in the XI at Repton, but in 1971 revived Nor Shuler, the Irish I Zingari, which was flourishing in the 1930s but had lain dormant since the war.

BOSWELL, CECIL STANLEY REGINALD, died in a nursing home near Norwich on August 15, 1985, aged 74. He played for Essex from 1932 to 1937 and showed some promise as a slow right-arm spinner, but failed to fulfil expectations. He was also a useful bat; against Gloucestershire at Gloucester in 1934 he made 69 and helped Nichols to put on 134 for the eighth wicket. After leaving Essex he played from 1939 to 1955 for Norfolk, for whom he did valuable work.

BRENNAN, DONALD VINCENT, who died after a long illness on January 9, 1985, aged 64, played for Yorkshire from 1947 to 1953 and throughout that time was their regular wicket-keeper. So highly was he rated that in 1951 he was preferred to Evans, who was perfectly fit and well, for the last two Test matches against South Africa. Granted that Evans had been temporarily below his best, that is an astonishing tribute, especially as in batting Evans was much the better of the two. Evans was potentially a fine batsman, who needed the challenge of a Test to bring out his best form: Brennan, whose average for his career was 10.49 and who never reached 50 in a county match, could do little more than stay in doggedly in a crisis. In fact, in his first Test he did just that: he stayed in three-quarters of an hour for 16, helping Bailey, who was playing a fighting innings, to put on 32, but the runs were less important than the time and, had Brennan been out quickly, England's position would have been precarious.

Apart from these matches, his representative cricket was confined to the MCC tour of India in 1951-52. He was particularly expert at standing up to the spinners: in the Yorkshire sides at that time he had plenty of opportunities with Wardle, Appleyard and Leadbeater, and he seldom missed a chance of stumping. In his first-class career he caught 316 batsmen and stumped 115. Originally in the XI at Downside, he graduated to the county side through the Bradford League, and after the claims of the family textile business had forced him to retire early, he did valuable work on the Yorkshire committee, feeling as deeply as anyone the disputes which came so constantly as to unsettle the well-being of the county.

BROCKWAY, WALTER CHARLES, died in Harare, Zimbabwe, on June 15, 1985, aged 78. Born at Blandford, he played for Dorset before the war and, after a spell on the Hampshire staff, for Berkshire after it, being then groundsman and coach to the Reading Cricket Club. Emigrating to South Africa, he made one appearance for Eastern Province in 1951 and then moved to Rhodesia, where he did invaluable work for the rest of his life, especially in coaching African schoolboys.

BRYAN, JOHN LINDSAY, who died at Eastbourne after a few days' illness on April 23, 1985, aged 88, was the oldest living Kent cricketer and the sole survivor both of the famous Cambridge XI of 1921 and of the MCC side to Australia in 1924-25. He was the eldest of three brothers who played with success for Kent, all three appearing on one occasion in the same match: all were left-handed bats and right-arm bowlers. A fourth brother played for Kent II.

Jack Bryan was captain of Rugby in 1914 and in August appeared for Kent II. In August 1919, after more than four years on active service, he played for the county in their last three matches. Going up to Cambridge, he made 83 in the Freshmen's match in 1920 and followed it with 97 for Perambulators against Etceteras, but so fierce was the competition that even after this he did not get a single game for the University. However, playing pretty regularly for Kent after term, he came third in their batting averages and made his first hundred for them, 125 against Worcestershire. In 1921 he scored 126 in the Seniors' match and throughout the season was one of the University's opening pair, finishing with the notable record of 935 runs and an average of 55. His highest score was 231 against Surrey at The Oval and his 62 against Oxford at Lord's was described by Sir Pelham Warner as the finest innings in the match. For Kent in the vacation he scored 920 runs with an average of 48. This was his only full season's first-class cricket: becoming a schoolmaster, he was never, after that, available for more than an occasional match before the end of July. However, he continued to appear for Kent in the holidays until 1932 and so highly was he regarded that he was thrice picked for the Gentlemen at Lord's before his first-class season had started, nor had it started in 1924 when he was picked for Australia. That tour was something of a disappointment for him. When he got a chance, he batted well enough and the Australians formed a high opinion of him, but with Hobbs and Sutcliffe to open, and Sandham and Whysall also in the side, there was no chance for him at numbers one or two and he was never in the running for a Test place.

He was, in fact, a model opening bat. Less vulnerable outside the off stump than most left-handers, he watched the ball carefully and regarded it as his first object to lay a good foundation to the innings: once this was safely achieved, he could score as fast as most people. Against Hampshire at Canterbury in 1923 Kent soon after the start were 20 for three. Bryan was naturally and properly cautious and took two hours to reach 50: when he was out he had made 236 out of 345 in four and three-quarter hours. One tremendous drive swerved round the right-hand end of the screen, through an open window into the pavilion dining-room, struck the edge of the table, flew up into the picture of Canterbury Week 1877, which still bears the scar, and was retrieved with a piece of glass embedded in it. It was his second 200 in consecutive matches: earlier that week he had scored 216 for the Butterflies against the Royal Artillery at Woolwich.

So sound was his method that he seemed to need little practice to be at his best. In 1925 his first match was against Nottinghamshire at Trent Bridge: Kent needed 327 to win and made them in four and a half hours, Bryan's share being 172 not out. He was a particularly fierce punisher of anything over-pitched on the leg or middle-and-leg, and equally severe on anything short of a length. On the off he relied mainly on a drive, usually played square and often going to third man. He never cut. Apart from his batting, he was a beautiful field, especially in the covers and the outfield, and bowled slow leg-breaks and googlies which, if their length was uncertain, spun so sharply that they might always get a needed wicket. In his one 'Varsity match, given three overs, he dismissed two good batsmen, L. P. Hedges and W. G. Lowndes, both with full pitches. Against Middlesex at Canterbury in 1923, he and his brother, G. J., opened together in Kent's second innings and put on 96 in a sensational match which Kent lost after a first innings of 445. Going on to Weston-super-Mare, they both made 0 in the first innings and so were deliberately sent in to "bustle" in the second: their partnership produced 60. Though both were accredited openers, the story suggests a light-hearted approach.

Jack Bryan's friends will remember him as a potentially great cricketer and a great schoolmaster. He gave some 60 years to St Andrew's School, Eastbourne, continuing to work actively on its behalf long after his official retirement. In all first-class cricket he scored 8,702 runs with an average of 36.25 and made seventeen centuries.

CHAPPLE, MURRAY ERNEST, who died at Hamilton on July 31, 1985, aged 55, had already been appointed to manage the New Zealand team to England in 1986. A burly cricketer and able administrator, he possessed a sharp sense of humour and warm personality, and his death was an untimely blow to New Zealand cricket. Making his début for Canterbury when he was nineteen, as a right-hand batsman and left-arm swing bowler, he went on to play fourteen times for New Zealand between 1952-53 and 1965-66, first as an opening batsman and then lower in the order, scoring 497 Test runs at an average of 19.11 with a top score of 76 against South Africa at Cape Town in 1953-54. After a season (1950-51) with Central Districts he forced his way into New Zealand's Test side by making an aggressive 165 for Canterbury against the touring South Africans at Christchurch in 1952-53, followed by 88 in the second innings. Of his fourteen Tests, eleven were in fact against South Africa, a country which he toured twice, the second time, in 1961-62, as vice-captain to John Reid. He was a member of the first New Zealand side to win a Test match, against West Indies at Auckland in 1955-56, and in his last Test match, against England at Christchurch in 1965-66, he was New Zealand's captain. Injury then precipitated his retirement, whereupon he became a New Zealand selector until 1970. He also managed the New Zealanders in West Indies in 1971-72 and in India and Pakistan in 1976-77. In first-class cricket he scored 5,344 runs (28.88) and hit four centuries. Switching from seam to orthodox left-arm spin, he also took 142 wickets, one of them in a Test match.

CORNFORD, JAMES HENRY (JIM), died in Harare, Zimbabwe, on June 17, 1985, aged 73. Born at Crowborough, he had a few trials for Sussex without success in 1931 and 1932, but in

1933 he jumped right to the front with 88 wickets at 19.77. With an action clearly modelled on Tate's, he bowled fast-medium, swinging the ball away, while at times making it come back very quickly off the pitch, and in his early seasons he was regarded as possibly a future England bowler. But he had neither the exceptional physique nor the exceptional talents of Tate. Moreover, with Tate's retirement the Sussex bowling was much weakened, and Cornford, always a whole-hearted trier, was sadly overbowled and was besides troubled by injuries. He never achieved the position that had been hoped and was often expensive, but he remained an invaluable county bowler. As far on as 1949, when he was 37, he had one of his best seasons, taking 89 wickets at 25.52. At Rushden that year he went to bed on Saturday night, having taken all the nine Northamptonshire wickets to have fallen: on the Monday morning George Cox had the tenth caught at the wicket. At the end of 1952 he retired to coach in Southern Rhodesia. He was a poor bat, whose highest score for Sussex was only 34, but by sheer perseverance he made himself into an adequate field. In his career of sixteen seasons he took 1,019 wickets at 26.49 and modern bowlers may note, with envy and, perhaps, with some feeling of guilt, that in all that time he is reputed not to have bowled a single no-ball.

COX, GEORGE, who died at Burgess Hill on March 30, 1985, aged 73, was a player who will be remembered with affection long after some who occupy a bigger space in the records have been forgotten. Though cricket was his profession, to him it was always a game, a game to be won certainly and, if not won, at least saved, but it was a game to be enjoyed: he enjoyed it himself and he did his best to make it enjoyable for the other players and the spectators. As a consequence, despite all the runs he scored he was more liable to bad patches than less adventurous batsmen and never achieved quite the aggregates and averages of those from whom England sides are usually selected. But to a county not lacking in solid batting he was invaluable. No match was ever lost until he was out in the second innings. Against Glamorgan at Hove in 1947 Sussex, set to get 376, were 40 for three: Cox made 205 not out and they won by five wickets. At Hove in 1938 Yorkshire seemed set to win by an innings: Cox, coming in at 82 for four, reached 50 in 28 minutes and 100 out of 114 in an hour, failing by three minutes to make the fastest hundred of the season. He finally reached 142 and Yorkshire, left to get 70, had some anxious moments before winning by four wickets. Again in 1949, when Sussex went in at Headingley 339 down on the first innings, he and John Langridge added 326 unfinished for the fourth wicket and averted a disaster. Indeed, nothing shows better the quality of his batting than his constant success against Yorkshire – six of his 50 hundreds were made against them, including, besides the instances quoted, a glorious 198 in 200 minutes at Hove in 1939 in the last match before the war: and those were the days when D. R. Jardine, hearing a good batsman discussed, always asked, "What is his record against Yorkshire?" It entirely disposes of any notion that Cox was just a fine hitter of poor bowling.

In style he batted like an old-fashioned amateur, scoring largely in front of the wicket, and he was an especially fine off-driver. It took an Oxford freshman, who had been told by his friends that Cox was vulnerable to the half-volley, less than an over to realise that his leg had been pulled. He was beautifully built (he was also a centre-forward, for Arsenal, Luton and Fulham) and was a glorious field at cover, with a weakness, which he shared with some other fine fields, for dropping now and then the simplest of chances. Though in the pre-war Sussex side he was not often allowed to bowl his slow "floaters", as he deprecatingly called them, after the war, when the county's bowling was weaker than for 50 years, he became almost a regular bowler. His figures, as one would expect, do not suggest that he much alarmed the opposition, but at least he kept matters reasonably in hand and the decencies were observed.

His father, also George, had played for Sussex from 1895 to 1928 and was later for many years the county's coach. "Young George" played from 1931 to 1960, was coach from 1960 to 1964, playing for and frequently captaining the Second XI, and after that not only served on the committee but was active until the last in helping and encouraging young players. The only break in his involvement with Sussex was when, for four seasons after retiring from regular first-class cricket, he was professional at Winchester, and even then he would play the odd match for the county in the holidays. The playing careers of father and son thus covered (with a break of two years) 65 years, and their connection with the county's cricket was 90 years unbroken.

At the outset of young George's career he was a bit slow to fulfil his obvious promise: his first hundred did not come until 1935 and it was 1937 before he got a regular place. Even then he struck such a bad patch in 1938 that he had to be relegated to the Second XI, but he regained his place and finished in a blaze of glory. From then on his position was never in doubt. In 1939 he scored 414 runs in two days. At Kettering, where Sussex scored 428 for five to beat Northamptonshire, he made 232, putting on 219 with John Langridge in two hours. Next day against Lancashire at Hove he made 182 and added 266 with James Langridge. After the war he batted as well as ever: indeed he had become a trifle sounder in defence, and the best season of his career was 1950 when, at 39, he scored 2,369 runs with an average of 49.35. His benefit in 1951 brought him £6,620, at that time a Sussex record. In his first-class career he scored 22,912 runs with an average of 32.96, his highest score being 234 not out against the Indians at Hove in 1946. A man of much charm and humour, he was in great demand as a speaker and was indeed widely loved.

CRAIG, REGINALD JACK, who died on April 17, 1985, aged 68, opened the batting for South Australia immediately after the Second World War, making 1,667 runs at an average of 30.49. Included in his four centuries was one against Hammond's MCC team in 1946-47 (111) and another of 100 against the Indians in the following year. He became a successful coach in Adelaide, and was instrumental in both Sobers and Barry Richards playing Sheffield Shield cricket for South Australia.

CROSS, ERIC PERCIVAL, who died at Birmingham on February 27, 1985, aged 88, kept wicket for Warwickshire in six matches in 1921 and one in 1923. He created a favourable impression, but, with "Tiger" Smith available, his opportunities were naturally limited. Between 1928 and 1934 he played frequently for Staffordshire. He had been in the XI at Denstone in 1912 and 1913.

CROTHERS, GEORGE MARCUS, who died at Lisburn, Co. Antrim, on February 6, 1982, was one of the best Irish wicket-keepers, representing his country nineteen times between 1931 and 1948, catching twelve and stumping ten. Educated at Royal Belfast Academical Institution, and unrelated to the more recent Irish bat, J. G. Crothers, he captained Ireland in his last match (against Yorkshire in Belfast) and later served two terms as a selector.

CULLEN, LEONARD, who died in South Africa on September 15, 1984, aged 69, was born in Johannesburg and was coached at St Andrew's College, Bloemfontein, by Len Bates of Warwickshire, who recommended him to Northamptonshire. A good natural all-round games-player, quick on his feet, he might have made the grade as a batsman had he concentrated on cricket, but his energies were too much divided: he was a particularly good swimmer. In eighteen matches for the county in 1934 and 1935 he made only 253 runs and his five wickets cost 59.09 runs each. His highest score was 40 against Worcestershire in 1934. His career was virtually ended by an extraordinary accident. Playing against Glamorgan at Llanelli in 1935, he fell out of a window in his hotel while walking in his sleep. Even this did not wake him, and when he came to he was some way from the hotel and had to ask his way back. His injuries kept him out of the side for some weeks and after one more appearance he returned to South Africa.

CUNNINGHAM, WILLIAM HENRY RANGER, who died in Christchurch on November 29, 1984, aged 84, was a survivor of the first New Zealand side to tour England, in 1927, two and a half years before New Zealand played their first official Test match. A bowler of fast-medium pace, he took 72 wickets for Canterbury and 22 for New Zealand before they were granted Test status. Most of the latter were on a tour to Australia in 1925-26. His best bowling figures were six for 33 for Canterbury against Auckland in 1924-25. He was also a good rugby league player. His enthusiasm for cricket never wavered, even after his sight had gone.

CUTMORE, JAMES ALBERT, who died at Brentwood on November 30, 1985, aged 86, was to be numbered among the stalwarts at the core of county cricket from 1925 to 1935, although the game's highest honours did not come his way. He first played for Essex in 1924 and established himself the next season, when he began what became an annual habit of making 1,000 runs a year. This ended only when he suddenly lost his form in 1936 and retired. By then he had made 15,937 runs with an average of 28.61 and hit fifteen centuries. His highest score was 238 not out against Gloucestershire at Bristol in 1927, when he batted for seven and a quarter hours and hit 32 4s, mostly off drives and strokes through the covers. His name was most closely linked with that of Dudley Pope, who was his opening partner for five seasons until he died in a road accident at the end of the 1934 season. Pope was the quieter of the pair, Cutmore emphatically the number one, anxious to master the bowling, though when necessary he could, and not infrequently did, fulfil a more stubborn role. The last season of his partnership with Pope was also Cutmore's best: he made 1,791 runs at an average of 41.65. Though he played only eight Championship matches in 1936 with poor results, he contributed largely to an Essex win against the touring Indian side. As the number seven batsman he scored 137, sharing an eighth-wicket partnership of 214 with Peter Smith. Away from cricket Cutmore was well known as a singer.

DIBBS, ARTHUR HENRY ALEXANDER, who died on November 28, 1985, aged 66, was President of MCC in 1983-84, having previously been on the Finance Committee of the club. An enthusiastic school and club cricketer, he captained Whitgift Middle School in 1935 and, for some years, the Westminster Bank XI, for whom he played from 1936 to 1958, military service intervening. He was Deputy Chairman of the National Westminster Bank from 1971 to 1982 and joint Deputy Chairman of British Airways from 1981 to 1985.

DRUMMOND, DUNCAN WEIR, who died at Greenock on May 17, 1985, aged 62, played regularly for Scotland between 1951 and 1961 as an all-rounder. He had a top score of 33 v MCC at Greenock in 1961 and his four for 73 against Worcestershire at Worcester in 1952 was his best analysis in a first-class match.

FENDER, PERCY GEORGE HERBERT, who died at Exeter on June 15, 1985, aged 92, was the last survivor of those who had played county cricket regularly before the Great War: more important, he was one of the most colourful figures in the cricket world for many years after it and was widely regarded as the shrewdest county captain of his generation. In a career of 26 years he scored 19,034 runs with an average of 26.66, took 1,894 wickets at 25.05, made 21 hundreds and caught 599 catches. Six times he did the double. But he was not a cricketer who could be judged on figures. *Wisden* has never been a slave to statistics and, when in 1915 he appeared as one of the Five Cricketers of the Year, it was after a season in which both his bowling and batting averages had been approximately 23 and he had not scored 1,000 runs nor taken 100 wickets. Yet the honour was fully deserved. Surrey had won the Championship and Tom Hayward had said that Fender was the making of their XI. In a crucial match, for instance, against Kent, the reigning champions, at Lord's in August (The Oval was occupied by the military), going in on a pitch made for Blythe, who took nine for 97, with a scoreboard reading 147 for four, he made 48 in twenty minutes, thus securing Surrey a lead of 94: he also took in the match five for 43 and thus played a big part in his side's victory. But besides his batting and bowling, Surrey that year owed much to his superb slip fielding. Their bowling, not strong for a champion county, depended largely on Hitch, who was fast, and Rushby, who was fast-medium, and on the perfect Oval pitches a dropped slip catch could easily mean a lost match.

Throughout his career Fender's policy was to hit fiercely, regardless of the state of the pitch, even of the quality of the bowling. He was a tremendous driver and also delighted in the pull, and he cut or slashed ferociously outside the off stump: he once slashed the ball over cover out of The Oval. It was difficult to set a field for him. His century in 35 minutes against Northamptonshire in 1920 remains a record, though it was equalled in farcical circumstances in 1983. His highest score, 185 against Hampshire in 1922, took 130 minutes and against Kent later that season he made 137 in an hour and a half, 52 of them off fourteen consecutive balls. It was not to be expected that one batting on these principles would be as consistent as a more sedate player, but in the very strong Surrey batting sides of those days another solid bat would have been neither here nor there: Fender the hitter was invaluable.

His attitude to bowling was the same. His object was to get the batsman out, and the tactics fostered by the modern one-day game would never have suited him. He had at his command a great variety of pace, spin and swing and all were fully employed. Inevitably his length sometimes suffered. Yet it was unwise to assume that because a batsman was out to a full toss it was a lucky wicket: almost as likely as not it was bowled for that very purpose. Probably he was least expensive when he concentrated on leg-breaks and googlies. Whatever he was bowling he had a wonderfully sharp eye for a batsman's weak points. There can be no doubt that his best role was as the fourth or fifth bowler in a strong bowling side. Unluckily this was a part he was seldom able to play, and for much of his time in the Surrey team he had to do the work of a stock bowler. As such he did wonders, but to borrow a phrase used by W.G. in a different context, he "never hadn't ought to have been put to it". His most spectacular bowling performance was against Middlesex at Lord's in 1927, when his analysis read 5.3–2–10–7; eleven balls produced six wickets for 1 run.

Born at Balham, he was educated at St George's, Weybridge, and St Paul's, where he was three years in the XI, heading the batting averages in each of them and in the second representing the Public Schools at Lord's. His family was living in Sussex and it was for them that he first appeared in county cricket in 1910, his last year at school, but neither then nor in 1911 did he do much. It was a brilliant 133 not out against Oxford University at Horsham in 1912 that showed his possibilities and won him a prolonged trial. In 1913 he got his 1,000 runs and was picked for the Gentlemen at both Lord's and The Oval, but the next year he switched his allegiance to Surrey, for whom he continued to appear until 1935. In 1919, having served in the Royal Flying Corps during the war, he was kept out of cricket by a broken leg, but in 1920 he did well enough to gain a place in the MCC team to Australia. There he headed the bowling averages for the Tests and twice in the course of them took five wickets in an innings, but the Australians did not think he had enough spin to be formidable on their pitches. In fact he proved only marginally a Test match player and this may have saved the selectors, who were thought never to favour him as a captain of England, an embarrassing problem. In only one series, in South Africa in 1922-23, did he keep his place throughout and South African cricket was then at a low ebb. In thirteen appearances for England between 1920 and 1929 he made 380 runs with an average of 19 and took 29 wickets at 40.86. Meanwhile in 1921 he had succeeded C. T. A. Wilkinson as captain of Surrey, a position which he held until he handed over to D. R. Jardine after 1931, and it was generally recognised that it was his captaincy more than anything else that kept a side so deficient in bowling so high in the table: twice they were second and only in his last three seasons did they fall below fifth.

After his retirement he continued for many years to play in less important cricket and many young players can testify to the encouragement he gave them and how much they were helped by his advice. He was a very kind man and would have been an excellent coach. He also made a considerable contribution to cricket literature, including four books on Test series, 1920-21, 1928-29, 1930 and 1934, which are among the best of their kind. *An ABC of Cricket* contains a fascinating account of his progress from prep school to county cricket, besides some admirable technical advice. At the same time his outspoken articles in newspapers did not always endear him to the authorities.

FRANKLIN, HENRY WILLIAM FERNEHOUGH, died in hospital on May 25, 1985, aged 83. Going up to Oxford after five years in the Christ's Hospital XI, he made 43 in the Freshmen's match in 1921 and took five for 16 in the second innings, but, though he had several games for the University and scored 53 against Middlesex, the champion county, he failed to get a Blue that year and in the next two years had only two games in all. Meanwhile in 1921 he had played for Surrey against Oxford at The Oval and later in that season had appeared regularly for Essex: but a batting average of 9 and a bowling average of 150 suggest that it must have been his beautiful and tireless fielding which kept him his place in a team several of whom were old enough to be his father. It was not until 1923 that he really did anything to justify the county's faith in him: then, going in tenth against Middlesex at Leyton, he made 106 and with his captain, J. W. H. T. Douglas, put on 160 in a little over two hours, which not only saved the follow-on but secured an honourable draw. In 1924 he at last got his Blue, though his record was undistinguished. However, against Cambridge at Lord's his 29 not out was the second-highest score in an innings of 133. He continued to play for Essex until 1931: being a schoolmaster, he was available only in the holidays, but, as so often happens, with years and experience he became an altogether sounder and more consistent batsman, who was constantly making useful scores besides picking up the odd wicket with some mild leg-breaks and enormously enlivening the fielding. Sometimes in these later years he captained the side. His outstanding performance was an innings of 104 against Somerset at Knowle in 1928, described by no less a judge than R. C. Robertson-Glasgow, who was playing, as "one of the finest attacking innings I ever saw". It included a 6 and seventeen 4s and even J. C. White, then in his prime, could not keep him quiet. A stylist, Franklin was quick on his feet and an especially good off-driver. He had in fact the gifts of the outstanding natural games-player. Though he had to wait for his rugger Blue until his fourth year, he played so well in the 'Varsity match that some critics rated him the best Oxford fullback since the legendary Strand-Jones more than twenty years earlier, and he later reached the final English trial, though he never got an international. A hockey Blue he missed only through illness. Apart from his games he was a good scholar, a talented actor and musician, and a man of wit and humour. From 1940 to 1962 he was Headmaster of Epsom College, having taught previously at Rugby and Radley. In all first-class cricket he made 2,212 runs with an average of 19.23 and took 46 wickets at 43.98.

GENDERS, WILLIAM ROY, who died at Worthing on September 28, 1985, aged 72, played three times for Derbyshire in 1946, five times for Worcestershire over the next two seasons, and twice for Somerset in 1949. His top score of 55 not out was made for Worcestershire against Derbyshire at Chesterfield. He wrote a short history of the Worcestershire County Cricket Club and another entitled *League Cricket in England*.

GRAHAM, LEONARD, who died on December 21, 1962, aged 61, played three times for Essex in 1926. He was one of three cricketers to have played football for Millwall, the others being A. S. Moule and C. P. McGahey. A stylish left-half, he was capped for England against Scotland and Wales in 1925.

HALES, LLOYD ARCHIBALD, died on September 12, 1984, aged 63. A good bat and useful medium-paced bowler, he was a prominent member of the Leicester Cricket Club and in 1947 appeared twice for the county. In his second match, against Warwickshire at Leicester, he played a valuable innings of 62: he and Chapman, coming together when six wickets were down for 143, added 126 and so had a big part in their side's victory.

HAMMOND, HERBERT EDWARD (JIM), died at his home at Brighton on June 16, 1985, aged 77. He first appeared for Sussex in 1928, but the team was strong at that time and it was not till 1934 that he secured anything approaching a regular place, though in 1930 he had a good trial and no less judges than A. C. MacLaren and Ranji, who saw him bowling at Eastbourne, were impressed by his possibilities. In 1934 he made 609 runs with an average of 24.36 and took 43 wickets at 28.51: more important, on a fast pitch against Surrey at The Oval he took eight for 76, perhaps the best performance of his career. In 1936 he made his only century, 103 not out at Edgbaston in a match ruined by rain: he and Jim Parks engaged in an unfinished opening stand of 214. His wickets, too, were less expensive that year (he had been unable to play until June): helped by an analysis of seven for 40 against Oxford, 59 wickets cost him only 20.77 each. By contrast, in 1937 when, with 91 wickets, he was the side's leading bowler, they cost 26.10. He continued as a fairly regular player until the war, though he sometimes missed matches through injury or had to stand down to make room for an occasional amateur. He retired after 1946.

Never in the top flight, he was none the less a useful county player, an imperturbable batsman, who often acted as an opener with some success if no-one better was available, a fast-medium bowler who did not perhaps attack the batsman as much as he might have done, but did valuable service at a time when the bowling resources were limited, and a reliable slip. Above all, whether batting, bowling or fielding, he put his whole heart into it and was always doing his best. From 1947 to 1961 he coached at Cheltenham College and then, after three seasons on the first-class umpires' list, went as professional to Brighton College, where he continued to umpire school matches even after his retirement. He was a well-known footballer: after getting an amateur international cap while playing for Lewes, he played for many years as a professional for Fulham. In all matches for Sussex he scored 4,251 runs with an average of 18.72 and took 428 wickets at 28.73.

HILL, BARRINGTON JULIAN WARREN, died at Sandwich on August 7, 1985, after a long illness, aged 70. A medium-pace right-arm bowler and a useful bat, he was captain of the XI at St Lawrence College and went up to Christ Church, where he had several trials for the University but did not get a Blue. Between 1935 and the war he did valuable work for Kent II. He was author of a short history of cricket and collaborated with R. L. Arrowsmith in *The History of I Zingari.* He was for many years a master at Eton.

HOPKINS, VICTOR, who died at his native place, Dumbleton, Gloucestershire, on August 6, 1984, aged 73, came straight from village cricket to keep wicket for the county in May 1934. At first he was an astonishing success and raised expectations that were not to be fulfilled. As the season went on he began to lose his confidence and in August was replaced by Dacre. In 1935 he kept in the early matches, but by then Harry Smith, who had been out of the side for three seasons owing to illness, was well enough to resume his place. At the end of the season Smith finally retired and in 1936 Hopkins again became the regular 'keeper. Part way through 1937 he broke a finger and, when he was fit to play again, did so as a batsman. It was virtually the end of his wicket-keeping. In 1938 E. A. Wilson of Middlesex had become qualified and thenceforward Hopkins had to rely purely on his batting. He could not secure a regular place, but played many useful innings and was at times employed to open. His highest score, 83 not out against Sussex at Worthing in 1939, turned an apparently certain defeat into a victory. After the war he played mainly for the Second XI, though his last appearance in the county side was not until 1948. Altogether he scored 2,608 runs with an average of 14.82, caught 138 batsmen and stumped 44.

HOPWOOD, JOHN LEONARD, who died at Denton on June 15, 1985, aged 81, was a utilitarian cricketer. One cannot imagine any spectator, reading of his death, looking back across 50 years and exclaiming nostalgically, "What fun he was to watch!" Indeed Lancashire supporters of his day, though much of the county's batting since the Great War had been far from scintillating, found themselves going back to Barlow in the 1880s for a parallel, and then they did at least admit that they would sooner watch Hopwood: but with a backlift like Woodfull's he could never be graceful. Again, as a slow left-arm bowler (he was a right-hand bat), though his figures clearly show how dangerous he could be when the pitch helped him, he is perhaps best remembered bowling by the hour, over the wicket, with six men on the leg, thus helping to conceal from the opposition the relative poverty of the Lancashire bowling, which was nothing like as strong as ten years earlier. These indeed were the tactics he employed at Old Trafford in 1934 against Australia in the first of his two Tests, and his figures show how skilfully he did so. In the first innings, against a side which included Bradman, Ponsford and McCabe, his figures read 38–20–46–0. After this it is a bit harsh to say, as critics tend to, that he was a disappointment in his Tests. Granted that he failed as a bat, it was not an easy assignment for an opener to go in eight, and no sane judge could have expected him to get many wickets except in the most favourable conditions – and then Verity would, as at Lord's, have done all that was required. Verity's analysis for the same innings at Old Trafford was 53–24–78–4.

To his county Hopwood was invaluable, and it is safe to say that in this same season, 1934, they could never have won the Championship without him. In county matches he headed the bowling with 110 wickets at 17.89 and was third in the batting with 1,583 runs and an average of 41.65. Against Gloucestershire at Bristol he scored 220, adding 316 with Ernest Tyldesley for the second wicket, and against Glamorgan at Liverpool he took seven for 13. Moreover he was a thoroughly reliable field near the wicket.

He had been slow to reach the top. After some unsuccessful trials in 1923, he first showed his possibilities by scoring 105 not out against the South Africans in 1924: however, in 21 innings in county matches that year he could average only 15. There was little advance in 1925, and in 1926 and 1927 he did not appear. So far he had been regarded solely as a bat, but in 1928 he showed that he was a potential bowler as well, taking 43 wickets at 22.14, besides making a couple of hundreds and averaging 32 with the bat. In 1929 he gained a regular place, which he retained until the war. In 1930 he made 1,000 runs and took 81 wickets and in 1934 and 1935 he did the double, the first Lancashire player to do so since James Hallows in 1904 and still the only one to perform the feat twice. In the last three seasons before the war there was a marked decline in his batting and he moved down the order, though he continued to be useful: however, he almost entirely lost his bowling. Ill health prevented him from resuming his career after the war. In all first-class cricket he scored 15,548 runs with an average of 32.84 and made 24 centuries: he took 671 wickets at 22.47. President of the Lancashire County Cricket Club in 1982, he was the first professional ever to hold the office.

HUGHES-HALLETT, LT-COL. NORTON MONTRESOR, who died on March 26, 1985, aged 89, was a tall, upstanding, attacking batsman who headed the Haileybury averages in 1913 and made 93 in 100 minutes against Cheltenham at Lord's. Later that summer he played three matches for Derbyshire with little success, but, playing three times for them again the next August, he scored 67 against Hampshire and 53 against Leicestershire. Unfortunately a severe wound in the Great War stopped him from appearing again for the county, though he did play a little first-class cricket in India.

HUNT, HUBERT, who died at Pill, near Bristol, on November 25, 1985, played for Somerset as an amateur in 1936. He was an off-break bowler who took seven for 49 against Derbyshire at Ilkeston, but in those days Wellard was beginning to switch from pace to spin when the need arose. Hunt had eleven matches for the county, unlike his brother, George, who made 233 appearances as a professional. He was a successful and popular club cricketer who took many wickets for Lodway. He also played for Cornwall

ISMAIL, MOHAMMAD KASIM, who died in Colombo in his early seventies, was Secretary and Treasurer of the Ceylon Cricket Association from 1943 to 1947 and the first Secretary of the Board of Control for Cricket in Sri Lanka. He was also, at different times, chairman of the selectors for Ceylon and Sri Lanka, and manager of teams to South India, Pakistan and Malaysia.

JOHNSON, TYRELL FRANCIS, who died in Trinidad on April 5, 1985, at the age of 68, played one Test match for West Indies, against England at The Oval in 1939, when with his first ball he caused Keeton to play on. He had also taken a wicket with his first ball of the tour, at Worcester. Very tall and thin, he bowled left-arm at a brisk medium pace and with appreciable in-swing. Of the sixteen first-class wickets he took on his one tour, those of Hutton and Oldfield also came in The Oval Test.

LAMBERT, HERBERT NORMAN, who died in New Plymouth on July 19, 1984, aged 84, made his first-class début for Wellington against Canterbury when he was only seventeen and soon established himself as a valuable member of the Wellington side as a right-hand batsman and off-break bowler. In 1922-23 he made a good impression on A. C. MacLaren's MCC side, scoring 66 and 63 against them at Wanganui and playing in the last two of the three representative matches. His one first-class century (107 in 149 minutes) was for Wellington against Otago at Dunedin in 1931-32, a match which Wellington needed to win, and did so, to take the Plunket Shield for the first time.

LAURIE, LT-COL. LAURENCE ERNEST, CBE, who died on August 21, 1985, aged 68, was a good natural games-player, who represented Northumberland from 1947 to 1958, making 3,909 runs with an average of 26.77. In his best season, 1953, his aggregate was 559 and his average 46.58. He captained the county from 1948 to 1958 and also captained the Minor Counties against the New Zealanders in 1958. A tall man and up-standing hitter, he had also played for the Army and been Chairman of the Scottish Sports Council.

LUSH, JOHN GRANTLEY (GINTY), who died in Sydney on August 22, 1985, played for New South Wales as a forcing batsman and lively bowler from 1933 to 1947, coming close to Test selection when he had match figures of thirteen for 115 for the state against G. O. Allen's MCC side at Sydney in 1936-37. "The MCC collapse against the fast-medium bowling of Lush was as complete as it was startling", said *Wisden.* He also played for Sir Julien Cahn's XI.

MACDONAGH, WILFRED, who died in Bangor, Co. Down, in 1983, aged 84, was for many years a mainstay of the Armagh club. A wicket-keeper and right-hand bat, he played twice for Ireland, in 1930, scoring 48 against Scotland, his only first-class match. Contrary to what has appeared in some recent record books, he was not an Irish hockey international.

MALIK, SARDAR HARDIT SINGH, CIE, OBE, died at Delhi in October, 1985, aged 90. Educated in England from the age of eight, he headed the batting averages at Eastbourne College and, going up to Balliol, attracted attention in the Freshmen's match in 1913 and in the Seniors' match in 1914 but did not have a game for the University. However, playing five matches for Sussex in August, 1914, he scored 71 against Leicestershire and 49 against Middlesex and showed himself fully up to first-class form. He was in fact playing for Sussex in the Canterbury Week when war was declared on August 4, and at the time of his death he was the last survivor of the Week before 1919. After gallant service in the Royal Flying Corps during the war, in which he was shot down and wounded, he returned to Oxford for a year in 1920, played a second time in the 'Varsity golf match and had a trial in the cricket side without success. For Sussex, however, in the Horsham Week he played a brilliant innings of 106 against Leicestershire: he and Albert Relf put on 175 for the seventh wicket "at a tremendous pace". He played no county cricket after 1921, but his turbaned figure was for many years a familiar sight on English golf courses when the demands of a distinguished career in the Indian diplomatic service, where he was his country's first High Commissioner to Canada and later their Ambassador in Paris, allowed. A man of great charm, he was widely loved.

MANN, JAMES E. F., who died in Victoria on June 25, 1984, aged 80, went to Cambridge from Geelong Grammar School and won his Blue in 1924, when he came third in the University's batting averages with a top score of 114 against Sussex at Hove.

MARSHALL, JOHN NORMAN, who died at Worthing on March 24, 1985, aged 80, was author of the standard history of Sussex cricket, a book which is rich in anecdote, much of which will not be found elsewhere, and is one of the most readable of county histories: indeed it deserves to be better known than it is. Another book, *The Duke who was Cricket*, a life of the second Duke of Richmond, is valuable for the use made of hitherto unpublished papers at Goodwood, which throw much light on early Sussex cricket. Besides these he wrote histories of Lord's, Headingley and Old Trafford. A journalist by profession and for a time editor of the *Evening News*, he made no claims to have been more than a humble player himself, but he was a great enthusiast.

MERCHANT, UDAYKANT MADHAVJI, who died in Bombay on February 7, 1985, following a stroke, aged 68, was the younger brother of Vijay Merchant, by whom he was somewhat overshadowed. He was, however, a considerable batsman in his own right, as is shown by a career batting average in first-class cricket of 55.78. He played in one unofficial "Test", against a Commonwealth team in 1949-50. In the Ranji Trophy, for Bombay, he scored 1,651 runs (average 63.50), including five centuries, two of them (143 and 156) in the same match against Maharashtra in 1948-49. His highest score was 217 for Bombay against

Hyderabad in 1947-48, when he and M. N. Raiji added 360 for the fifth wicket. For the Cricket Club of India in 1948-49 he scored 134 against the touring West Indians, and in his last year, 1946, he scored 132 in the Bombay Pentangular, for the Hindus against the Europeans.

MORGAN, AUBREY NIEL, CMG, died at his home in Washington, USA, where he had lived for over 50 years, on September 14, 1985, aged 81. A tearaway fast bowler, very fast for a schoolboy, he was in the Charterhouse XI in 1922 and played a few times for Glamorgan and for Wales in 1928 and 1929, captaining the county in at least one match. He was an elder brother of J. T. Morgan: they were not related to any other Morgans who have played for Glamorgan. Aubrey Morgan was decorated as Personal Adviser to Lord Franks when British Ambassador in Washington.

NASH, EDWARD MONTAGUE, who died on May 9, 1985, aged 83, was for many years between the wars the regular Wiltshire wicket-keeper and also a pretty useful hard-hitting bat. In 1936 and 1937 he kept for the Minor Counties against Oxford University. He also kept goal for Swindon Town and for Brentford.

NICHOLSON, ANTHONY GEORGE, who died on November 4, 1985, aged 47, was a medium-paced bowler who played a big part in Yorkshire's five Championship-winning seasons in the 1960s. When they won in 1962, Nicholson played in only five matches, but a year later he took 65 wickets, and when they became champions again, in 1966, at the start of a three-year run, he took 113 wickets at 15.50 apiece. This was his best season. He swung the ball, had excellent control and was often found to be sharper in pace than the batsman expected. He played for Yorkshire from 1962 to 1975, having previously been a policeman in Rhodesia, and took 876 first-class wickets at 19.74 each.

More than once Nicholson was close to playing for England. He was picked for the 1964-65 tour of South Africa but had to drop out through injury. Later, when he was a still better bowler, there were more good bowlers of his type available, and being a modest batsman with a build which made him less than agile in the field, he did not have the all-round qualifications of others. After retiring from first-class cricket he became a brewery representative. He played league cricket for some years and at the time of his death was the captain of the Ripon City Golf Club.

O'CONNOR, LEO PATRICK DEVEREAUX, who died on January 16, 1985, aged 94, played successfully for Queensland in the years leading up to their admission to the Sheffield Shield in 1926-27. In their first match, against New South Wales at Brisbane, he made 196 towards Queensland's winning target of 400. They were bowled out for 391. In the return match at Sydney a fortnight later O'Connor scored 103 and 143 not out and helped his side to a brilliant victory. There were four other hundreds in the same match – by Macartney, Jackson, Kippax and Oxenham. At 38, however, O'Connor was considered too old for the Australian team.

O'DONNELL, JOHN ALAN, died in Co. Wicklow on September 29, 1984, aged 89, being at the time the oldest Irish international. His two matches for Ireland in 1928 and 1930 were not first-class and brought him no success, but he scored well for the Merrion club in senior cricket.

PHADKAR, DATTATREYA GAJANAN (DATTU), who died in Madras, following heart surgery, on March 17, 1985, aged 59, was a right-arm medium-paced bowler and a forcing batsman, and, as such, one of India's best all-rounders in the years after the Second World War. He played in 31 Tests between 1947 and 1959, the first of them at Sydney, where he began with an innings of 51 and had bowling figures in Australia's one innings of three for 14 in ten overs. He scored another half-century in his next Test at Melbourne, the first of his two Test centuries (123) in his third at Adelaide, and 56 not out in his fourth, also at Melbourne. After making 115 against England at Calcutta in 1951-52, a match in which he also took four wickets, he had the misfortune to make his one tour of England in 1952, a wet summer when Bedser was at his best and Trueman was an emerging force. Phadkar's best score in that series was 64 in India's second innings at Headingley, after their first four wickets had gone down for no run. Besides England and Australia, Phadkar also toured West Indies (1952-53) and Pakistan (1954-55).

In the Ranji Trophy he played for Maharashtra, Bombay, Railways and Bengal, captaining Bombay for whom he had an especially successful season in 1948-49 with a batting average of 114. The highest of his eight first-class centuries was 217 for Bombay against Maharashtra in 1950-51; his best bowling was seven for 26 against T. N. Pearce's XI at Scarborough in 1952, and his best Test bowling seven for 159 against West Indies at Madras in 1948-49. All told he scored 5,554 runs in first-class cricket (average 38.83) and took 465 wickets (average 22.09). He scored 1,229 runs in Tests (average 32.34) and took 62 wickets (average 36.85). He served at different times as an Indian Test selector and was made an Honorary Life Member of MCC in 1969. Two months before he died he came to the Press Box at Eden Gardens, Calcutta, to inform the Editor of *Wisden* that he had been born not on December 12, 1925, as in the Almanack, but two days earlier.

POLLARD, RICHARD, who died on December 16, 1985, aged 73, first played for Lancashire Second XI in 1933. By 1938, when he took 149 wickets, he had established himself in first-class cricket as a fast-medium bowler and was bowling well for the Players at Lord's. The war took away what should have been his best years as a bowler, but in 1946, though 34 and still in the Army, he made an immediate impression. He had retained his ability to move the ball in the air and off the pitch. He was invariably accurate. His heavy build made him no great asset in the field, but he had the strength and enthusiasm to bowl long spells if required. Having taken nine for 53 on a damp pitch for the Players at Lord's, he was chosen for his first Test, in which he took five Indian wickets for 24 in the first innings at Old Trafford. In Australia in 1946-47 he began promisingly, having Bradman caught in the slips in MCC's match against South Australia, but Voce or Edrich was preferred as Bedser's partner with the new ball in the Test matches and Pollard's only Test was against New Zealand. In 1948, against Australia, he played in the last two of his four Tests. His dismissal of Bradman at Old Trafford, lbw for 7, made a stir in the prevailing climate of Australian dominance, and he also bowled Bradman for 33 at Headingley before toiling unavailingly in the second innings while Australia made their historic 404 for three. As a rugged number eleven batsman, he is mainly remembered perhaps for the violent pull in the Test match against Australia at Old Trafford in 1948 which had Barnes at short-leg carried off on a stretcher with damaged ribs. In his four Tests he took fifteen wickets at 25.20.

Dick Pollard retired after the 1950 season, having taken 1,122 first-class wickets at 22.56 apiece. His reputation as a great trier commended him to the Lancashire public so warmly that his benefit in 1949 produced £8,000, a figure surpassed only twice previously in England.

PRITTIE, THE HON. TERENCE CORNELIUS FARMER, MBE, who died in London on May 28, 1985, aged 71, was cricket correspondent of the *Manchester Guardian* in 1946 and author of several books on the game, *Mainly Middlesex*, written when he was a prisoner-of-war in Germany, *Lancashire Hot-Pot*, *Cricket North and South* and a history of Middlesex cricket. He also wrote, with John Kay, *Second Innings*.

PULLINGER, GEORGE RICHARD, who died on August 4, 1982, aged 62, was an amateur from Grays, who filled the gap in the Essex side caused by the absence of Preston in 1949. Available only in the first half of the season, he opened the bowling with Bailey and did useful, steady work, for which he received his county cap. His best performance was to take five for 54 against Somerset at Bath. After a few matches in 1950 he dropped out of first-class cricket. Altogether he took 41 wickets for Essex at 39.97 each.

PUNCH, AUSTIN THOMAS EUGENE, who died in Sydney in August, 1985, aged 91, represented New South Wales from 1919-20 until 1928-29 and also played once for Tasmania in 1927-28. A tall and forceful batsman, particularly strong on the front foot, he hit his highest score of 176, and only first-class century, for New South Wales against Otago when the state side toured New Zealand in 1923-24. For New South Wales against J. W. H. T. Douglas's MCC side in 1920-21 he scored 59 and 63 not out. In all first-class cricket he made 1,717 runs (35.04) and took 35 wickets with his occasional leg-breaks at 29.82 apiece. He scored heavily for North Sydney in first-grade cricket.

RICHARDSON, JOHN ALLAN, who died in hospital at Scarborough on April 2, 1985, aged 76, after a long illness, was a batsman who, if he could have spared the time from a busy life as an auctioneer and farmer, might well have been invaluable to Yorkshire even in their great sides under Brian Sellers. As it was, he could spare the time only for seven matches between 1936 and 1947, but in these he scored 308 runs with an average of 30.80. In 1937, in consecutive matches, he made 54 not out against Sussex at Sheffield and then against Gloucestershire at Headingley, facing Goddard on a turning pitch, got 38 and 41 and had much to do with a Yorkshire victory. His highest score for the county was 61 against MCC at Scarborough in 1947. Curiously enough, his début in first-class cricket was not for Yorkshire, but for the Gentlemen against the Players at Scarborough in 1934, when he made 35 not out against an attack which included Bowes, Nichols, Townsend and Verity. An upright, attacking batsman, who once drove McDonald for 6 in the first over of a club match, he was for years a very heavy scorer for Scarborough, once making six consecutive centuries for them.

ROSS, GORDON JOHN, who died at Lord's on April 27, 1985, aged 67, was closely connected with numerous cricket publications. He edited the *Playfair Cricket Monthly* throughout its thirteen years of existence, and at the time of his death he was editor of the *Playfair Cricket Annual*, as he had been since 1954, and also of *The Cricketer Quarterly Facts and Figures*. From 1978-80 he was Associate Editor, under Norman Preston, of *Wisden Cricketers' Almanack*, for whom he reviewed books (1979 to 1980) and wrote articles. For 30 years he had invariably been at work either on one of these publications, or on football and cricket brochures or on a book of some kind. His brochures covered football of both codes (he edited the *Playfair Rugby Annual* for many years), and his books included one on the University Boat Race as well as a short history of the game and other histories of Surrey (*The Surrey Story*), West Indian cricket and the Gillette Cup. He worked regularly for the sports' pages of the *Sunday Times*, besides writing for *The Times*, *The Scotsman* and the *Sunday Telegraph*. As a consultant to Gillette and then NatWest, he had been directly involved with one-day county cricket since its inception in 1963. A well-known and popular figure round the county grounds, always dapper and seldom to be seen without a red carnation in his button hole, he had just been watching a day's cricket when, having reached his car, he died. He was a vice-president of the Lancashire County Cricket Club.

ROTHERAM, GERARD ALEXANDER, died at Bakewell on January 31, 1985, aged 85. A member of a well-known Warwickshire cricket family, he headed the Rugby batting and bowling averages in 1917 with good figures, but it was his bowling which gained him a place among the five Public Schools' Cricketers of the Year in the 1918 *Wisden*. At Cambridge he got a Blue in 1919: his wickets were expensive, but, though he went in low, he had a batting average of 39.66, the result largely of valuable innings played at a crisis. When he made 84 not out, his highest score in first-class cricket, against the AIF, he and J. H. Naumann, coming together with nine wickets down for 148, added 145, and against Oxford he and G. A. Fairbairn put on 65 badly needed runs for the ninth wicket. Next year his bowling figures were much improved and he did admirable all-round work, so there was considerable criticism when he was unexpectedly left out at Lord's in favour of G. P. Brooke-Taylor, a batsman pure and simple.

Meanwhile Rotheram had been playing regularly for Warwickshire after term both in 1919 and 1920, and in 1921, being down from Cambridge, he was available for the whole season, though in fact he missed three weeks in June with a damaged arm. His batting was disappointing, but he took 88 wickets and, though his bowling average was 26.36, he made a big difference to a side which otherwise relied almost solely on Howell for its quicker bowling. This was the end of his first-class cricket in this country: he went out to New Zealand, where he spent many years and played a few times for Wellington. A fast-medium bowler with a good action, plenty of life and an effective slower ball, he just lacked the necessary accuracy to be in the top class. As a batsman he might be described as practical rather than a stylist and he was a fine fieldsman. In all first-class cricket he made 1,801 runs with an average of 18.76 and took 180 wickets at 28.36.

SHERWOOD, DAVE, who died on March 12, 1985, aged 73, was scorer for New South Wales for 50 years and made seven tours of England as the official Australian scorer. On both sides of the world he was as popular as he was helpful. His body was recovered from the sea near Sydney.

SPEAKMAN, FREDERICK SAMUEL, who died on August 14, 1985, reported Northamptonshire cricket for 40 years, representing *Wisden*, the national news agencies and countless papers; for more than 30 years he did not miss a day the county played at home. He was an old-fashioned sports reporter, with few literary flourishes but perfect shorthand and an unrivalled knowledge of Northampton goings-on; his rumpled, kindly presence was a County Ground landmark and will be much missed.

TANG CHOON, RUPERT P., who died on September 5, 1985, aged 71, played for Trinidad from 1934 to 1955 as a popular all-rounder. He came near to being chosen to tour England with the 1939 West Indian side as a stroke-making batsman, agile fielder and leg-break bowler. After the war he scored 103 for Trinidad against G. O. Allen's MCC side, adding 244 in three and a half hours with Gomez. "A neat, lithe batsman, Tang Choon gave a truly brilliant display", said *Wisden*. In 1934-35 he had also played against MCC, captained then by R. E. S. Wyatt. In 52 first-class matches Tang Choon scored 2,653 runs, including three centuries, and took 60 wickets.

WARDLE, JOHN HENRY, died at Hatfield, near Doncaster, on July 23, 1985, after a long illness, aged 62. For some ten years he was one of England's leading bowlers: he played in 28 Tests and would have played in many more had he not been a contemporary of Lock. Both were slow left-armers and in England the orthodox methods of Lock were usually preferred: abroad Wardle's ability to bowl chinamen and googlies made him the more dangerous of the two. He was in fact the first top-class English slow left-arm bowler to employ this style, if one excepts an occasional chinaman from Roy Kilner: otherwise it had been confined to change bowlers like Leyland and Compton. Wardle was equally at home in both styles.

Working as a fitter in a coal mine during the war, he had made a big reputation in league cricket, but in 1946, though he played a match or two for Yorkshire, Arthur Booth was preferred as Verity's successor in the county side. Wardle enjoyed a profitable season in the Second XI. In 1947 Booth was stricken with arthritis and in the early part of the season Yorkshire found themselves for the first time in nearly 70 years without a slow left-armer. It was not till mid-June that they turned to Wardle. In his first innings he took five for 41 against Somerset, and this was followed a few weeks later by seven for 66 against Middlesex and then six for 28 against Surrey. At the end of the season he had taken 86 wickets at 25.46 and secured a place in G. O. Allen's highly experimental MCC side to the West Indies. Not surprisingly, with so little experience behind him, he was a failure on the tour, but he was quite undaunted and how much he profited was shown when in 1948 he headed the Yorkshire averages with 129 wickets at 17.62.

Thenceforward he never looked back. Each year he took his 100 wickets and in Tests his record was 102 wickets at 20.39 and 653 runs with an average of 19.78. In England his chief bowling performance in these matches was seven for 56 against Pakistan at The Oval in 1954, but in 1953 at Old Trafford Australia in their second innings were 35 for eight when the match ended and of these Wardle had taken four for 7. Against South Africa in 1955 he headed the Test match bowling averages with fifteen wickets at 18.20. In Australia in 1954-55 he was a qualified success, most of the damage being done by the fast bowlers, but in 1956-57 in South Africa he enjoyed a triumph, heading the averages in first-class matches with 90 wickets at 12.25 (in all matches he took 105 wickets) and, though kept out of one Test by injury, taking in the other four 26 wickets at 13.80: in the second Test he took twelve for 89 in a memorable piece of bowling. He was also a fine, fearless left-handed hitter in the lower part of the order, never deterred by any bowler's reputation from hitting him hard, high and often, and frequently suggesting by his success that some of the earlier batsmen might have done better had they adopted more aggressive tactics.

His first-class career came to an unhappy end in 1958. On July 27 he received the expected invitation to go with MCC to Australia, but three days later the Yorkshire committee announced that they would not be employing him after the end of the year. Thereupon Wardle requested that he should stand down from the team for the Bank Holiday match with Lancashire because of comments he intended to make about his colleagues in a newspaper article to be published while the match was in progress. His request was granted and the article appeared in the *Daily Mail*. At this point MCC felt they were bound to consider the question and said that they intended to do so at a committee meeting on August 19. Meanwhile the Yorkshire committee, meeting on August 11 after reading the articles, terminated Wardle's engagement immediately. They explained that their original decision, which was unanimous, had been taken because on several occasions in the past he had been warned that "his general behaviour on the field and in the dressing-rooms left much to be desired" and he had paid no attention whatever. Now, by writing the articles without obtaining permission, he had in addition broken his contract. On August 19 the MCC committee, having interviewed him, withdrew the invitation for the Australian tour. It was no coincidence that Peter May's side suffered a heavy defeat. Wardle was still a beautiful bowler and he was an incalculable loss.

His further career may be briefly sketched. He bowled with great success in the Lancashire League (for Nelson and then for Rishton) and from 1963 to 1969 represented Cambridgeshire, taking in all 316 wickets at 14.14 and doing much to win them the Minor Counties' Championship in 1963. For the majority of batsmen at that level he was far too good. In 1970 Yorkshire elected him an Honorary Life Member and recently they had appointed him bowling consultant to the county. He was also elected an Honorary Member of MCC. In all first-class cricket he made 7,318 runs with an average of 16.11 and took 1,842 wickets at 18.95.

WATERS, ALBERT EDWARD, who died at Bristol in June 1985, aged 83, played for Gloucestershire as an amateur between 1923 and 1925, making his highest score of 42 in the first of his sixteen first-class matches, against Glamorgan at Cheltenham. In the same match he dismissed T. R. Morgan with the first ball he delivered for the county. He played later for Wiltshire, for whom, in 1928, also in his first match, he scored 131 against Surrey II at The Oval. His first-class record was 270 runs (12.85) and five wickets (75.40).

WEAVER, SAMUEL, died on April 15, 1985, aged 76. Better known as a soccer international left-half (while at Newcastle United), he had two games for Somerset in 1939 as a left-arm opening bowler but met with no success. In his second match, against Worcestershire at Kidderminster, Hazell joined him as the last man in with 6 needed to win but was out to the fourth ball of the last over and the game ended in a tie.

WILLSMORE, HURTLE BINKS, who died in Adelaide on September 17, 1985, aged 95, was one of the oldest surviving Sheffield Shield cricketers, having first played for South Australia in 1913-14. In all he scored 271 runs in first-class cricket at an average of 16.94 and took sixteen wickets at 32.88 apiece.

WILSON, JOHN WILLIAM, who died in Melbourne on October 13, 1985, aged 64, played once for Australia, against India at Bombay in 1956-57. A slow, orthodox left-arm bowler – a somewhat jerky action accounted for the nickname "Chuck" – he represented his native state of Victoria in 1949-50 before moving to Adelaide and playing for South Australia from 1950-51 until 1957-58. It was on the way home from the Australian tour of England in 1956 that he won his only cap. His figures in India's second innings were 21–11–25–1, Ramchand providing him with his one Test wicket. His outstanding performance in England had been against Gloucestershire on a difficult pitch at Bristol, when the county were bowled out for 44 and 124 and Wilson returned match figures of 37.1–21–61–12. Short and quite rotund, he took life as it came. In all first-class cricket he finished with 230 wickets at 30.52 apiece from 78 matches. He was not a batsman.

# THE LAWS OF CRICKET

## (1980 CODE)



## INDEX TO THE LAWS

Law 1. The Players ... 1223
Law 2. Substitutes and Runners: Batsman or Fieldsman Leaving the Field: Batsman Retiring: Batsman Commencing Innings ... 1223
Law 3. The Umpires ... 1224
Law 4. The Scorers ... 1226
Law 5. The Ball ... 1227
Law 6. The Bat ... 1227
Law 7. The Pitch ... 1227
Law 8. The Wickets ... 1228
Law 9. The Bowling, Popping and Return Creases ... 1228
Law 10. Rolling, Sweeping, Mowing, Watering the Pitch and Re-marking of Creases ... 1229
Law 11. Covering the Pitch ... 1230
Law 12. Innings ... 1230
Law 13. The Follow-on ... 1231
Law 14. Declarations ... 1231
Law 15. Start of Play ... 1231
Law 16. Intervals ... 1232
Law 17. Cessation of Play ... 1233
Law 18. Scoring ... 1234
Law 19. Boundaries ... 1235
Law 20. Lost Ball ... 1236
Law 21. The Result ... 1236
Law 22. The Over ... 1237
Law 23. Dead Ball ... 1238
Law 24. No-ball ... 1239
Law 25. Wide-ball ... 1240
Law 26. Bye and Leg-bye ... 1241
Law 27. Appeals ... 1241
Law 28. The Wicket is Down ... 1242
Law 29. Batsman Out of His Ground ... 1242
Law 30. Bowled ... 1242
Law 31. Timed Out ... 1243
Law 32. Caught ... 1243
Law 33. Handled the Ball ... 1244
Law 34. Hit the Ball Twice ... 1244
Law 35. Hit Wicket ... 1244
Law 36. Leg Before Wicket ... 1245
Law 37. Obstructing the Field ... 1245
Law 38. Run Out ... 1246
Law 39. Stumped ... 1246
Law 40. The Wicket-keeper ... 1246
Law 41. The Fieldsman ... 1247
Law 42. Unfair Play ... 1247
42.1. Responsibilities of Captains ... 1247
42.2. Responsibilities of Umpires ... 1247
42.3. Intervention by the Umpire ... 1247
42.4. Lifting the Seam ... 1248
42.5. Changing the Condition of the Ball ... 1248
42.6. Incommoding the Striker ... 1248

42.7. Obstruction of a Batsman in Running ........ 1248
42.8. The Bowling of Fast Short-pitched Balls ........ 1248
42.9. The Bowling of Fast High Full Pitches ........ 1248
42.10. Time Wasting ........ 1249
42.11. Players Damaging the Pitch ........ 1249
42.12. Batsman Unfairly Stealing a Run ........ 1249
42.13. Player's Conduct ........ 1249

## LAW 1. THE PLAYERS

### 1. Number of Players and Captain

A match is played between two sides each of eleven players, one of whom shall be captain. In the event of the captain not being available at any time, a deputy shall act for him.

### 2. Nomination of Players

Before the toss for innings, the captain shall nominate his players, who may not thereafter be changed without the consent of the opposing captain.

*Note*

**(a) More or Less than Eleven Players a Side**

A match may be played by agreement between sides of more or less than eleven players, but not more than eleven players may field.

## LAW 2. SUBSTITUTES AND RUNNERS: BATSMAN OR FIELDSMAN LEAVING THE FIELD: BATSMAN RETIRING: BATSMAN COMMENCING INNINGS

### 1. Substitutes

Substitutes shall be allowed by right to field for any player who, during the match, is incapacitated by illness or injury. The consent of the opposing captain must be obtained for the use of a substitute if any player is prevented from fielding for any other reason.

*Experimental Law: In normal circumstances, a substitute shall be allowed to field only for a player who satisfies the umpire that he had been injured or become ill during the match. However, in very exceptional circumstances, the umpires may use their discretion to allow a substitute for a player who had to leave the field or does not take the field for other wholly acceptable reasons, subject to consent being given by the opposing captain. If a player wished to change his shirt, boots etc., he may leave the field to do so (no changing on the field), but no substitute will be allowed.*

### 2. Objection to Substitutes

The opposing captain shall have no right of objection to any player acting as substitute in the field, nor as to where he shall field, although he may object to the substitute acting as wicket-keeper.

### 3. Substitute not to Bat or Bowl

A substitute shall not be allowed to bat or bowl.

### 4. A Player for whom a Substitute has Acted

A player may bat, bowl or field even though a substitute has acted for him.

### 5. Runner

A runner shall be allowed for a batsman who, during the match, is incapacitated by illness or injury. The person acting as runner shall be a member of the batting side and shall, if possible, have already batted in that innings.

### 6. Runner's Equipment

The person acting as runner for an injured batsman shall wear batting gloves and pads if the injured batsman is so equipped.

*Experimental Law: The player acting as runner for an injured batsman shall wear the same external clothing and external protective equipment as the injured batsman. (Subject to the approval of MCC, this experimental law will be officially adopted in May 1986.)*

### 7. Transgression of the Laws by an Injured Batsman or Runner

An injured batsman may be out should his runner break any one of Laws 33 (Handled the Ball), 37 (Obstructing the Field) or 38 (Run Out). As striker he remains himself subject to the Laws. Furthermore, should he be out of his ground for any purpose and the wicket at the wicket-keeper's end be put down he shall be out under Law 38 (Run Out) or Law 39 (Stumped), irrespective of the position of the other batsman or the runner, and no runs shall be scored.

When not the striker, the injured batsman is out of the game and shall stand where he does not interfere with the play. Should he bring himself into the game in any way, then he shall suffer the penalties that any transgression of the Laws demands.

### 8. Fieldsman Leaving the Field

No fieldsman shall leave the field or return during a session of play without the consent of the umpire at the bowler's end. The umpire's consent is also necessary if a substitute is required for a fieldsman, when his side returns to the field after an interval. If a member of the fielding side leaves the field or fails to return after an interval and is absent from the field for longer than fifteen minutes, he shall not be permitted to bowl after his return until he has been on the field for at least that length of playing time for which he was absent. This restriction shall not apply at the start of a new day's play.

### 9. Batsman Leaving the Field or Retiring

A batsman may leave the field or retire at any time owing to illness, injury or other unavoidable cause, having previously notified the umpire at the bowler's end. He may resume his innings at the fall of a wicket, which for the purposes of this Law shall include the retirement of another batsman.

If he leaves the field or retires for any other reason he may resume his innings only with the consent of the opposing captain.

When a batsman has left the field or retired and is unable to return owing to illness, injury or other unavoidable cause, his innings is to be recorded as "retired, not out". Otherwise it is to be recorded as "retired, out".

### 10. Commencement of a Batsman's Innings

A batsman shall be considered to have commenced his innings once he has stepped on to the field of play.

*Note*

**(a) Substitutes and Runners**
For the purpose of these Laws, allowable illnesses or injuries are those which occur at any time after the nomination by the captains of their teams.

## LAW 3. THE UMPIRES

### 1. Appointment

Before the toss for innings, two umpires shall be appointed, one for each end, to control the game with absolute impartiality as required by the Laws.

## 2. Change of Umpires

No umpire shall be changed during a match without the consent of both captains.

## 3. Special Conditions

Before the toss for innings, the umpires shall agree with both captains on any special conditions affecting the conduct of the match.

## 4. The Wickets

The umpires shall satisfy themselves before the start of the match that the wickets are properly pitched.

## 5. Clock or Watch

The umpires shall agree between themselves and inform both captains before the start of the match on the watch or clock to be followed during the match.

## 6. Conduct and Implements

Before and during a match the umpires shall ensure that the conduct of the game and the implements used are strictly in accordance with the Laws.

## 7. Fair and Unfair Play

The umpires shall be the sole judges of fair and unfair play.

## 8. Fitness of Ground, Weather and Light

(a) The umpires shall be the sole judges of the fitness of the ground, weather and light for play.

(i) However, before deciding to suspend play, or not to start play, or not to resume play after an interval or stoppage, the umpires shall establish whether both captains (the batsmen at the wicket may deputise for their captain) wish to commence or to continue in the prevailing conditions; if so, their wishes shall be met.

(ii) In addition, if during play the umpires decide that the light is unfit, only the batting side shall have the option of continuing play. After agreeing to continue to play in unfit light conditions, the captain of the batting side (or a batsman at the wicket) may appeal against the light to the umpires, who shall uphold the appeal only if, in their opinion, the light has deteriorated since the agreement to continue was made.

(b) After any suspension of play, the umpires, unaccompanied by any of the players or officials, shall, on their own initiative, carry out an inspection immediately the conditions improve and shall continue to inspect at intervals. Immediately the umpires decide that play is possible they shall call upon the players to resume the game.

## 9. Exceptional Circumstances

In exceptional circumstances, other than those of weather, ground or light, the umpires may decide to suspend or abandon play. Before making such a decision the umpires shall establish, if the circumstances allow, whether both captains (the batsmen at the wicket may deputise for their captain) wish to continue in the prevailing conditions; if so, their wishes shall be met.

## 10. Position of Umpires

The umpires shall stand where they can best see any act upon which their decision may be required.

Subject to this over-riding consideration, the umpire at the bowler's end shall stand where he does not interfere with either the bowler's run-up or the striker's view.

The umpire at the striker's end may elect to stand on the off instead of the leg side of the pitch, provided he informs the captain of the fielding side and the striker of his intention to do so.

## 11. Umpires Changing Ends

The umpires shall change ends after each side has had one innings.

## 12. Disputes

All disputes shall be determined by the umpires, and if they disagree the actual state of things shall continue.

## 13. Signals

The following code of signals shall be used by umpires who will wait until a signal has been answered by a scorer before allowing the game to proceed.

| | |
|---|---|
| Boundary | – by waving the arm from side to side. |
| Boundary 6 | – by raising both arms above the head. |
| Bye | – by raising an open hand above the head. |
| Dead Ball | – by crossing and re-crossing the wrists below the waist. |
| Leg-bye | – by touching a raised knee with the hand. |
| No-ball | – by extending one arm horizontally. |
| Out | – by raising the index finger above the head. If not out, the umpire shall call "not out". |
| Short run | – by bending the arm upwards and by touching the nearer shoulder with the tips of the fingers. |
| Wide | – by extending both arms horizontally. |

## 14. Correctness of Scores

The umpires shall be responsible for satisfying themselves on the correctness of the scores throughout and at the conclusion of the match. See Law 21.6 (Correctness of Result).

*Notes*

**(a) Attendance of Umpires**
The umpires should be present on the ground and report to the ground executive or the equivalent at least thirty minutes before the start of a day's play.

**(b) Consultation between Umpires and Scorers**
Consultation between umpires and scorers over doubtful points is essential.

**(c) Fitness of Ground**
The umpires shall consider the ground as unfit for play when it is so wet or slippery as to deprive the bowlers of a reasonable foothold, the fieldsmen, other than the deep-fielders, of the power of free movement, or the batsmen of the ability to play their strokes or to run between the wickets. Play should not be suspended merely because the grass and the ball are wet and slippery.

**(d) Fitness of Weather and Light**
The umpires should suspend play only when they consider that the conditions are so bad that it is unreasonable or dangerous to continue.

# LAW 4. THE SCORERS

## 1. Recording Runs

All runs scored shall be recorded by scorers appointed for the purpose. Where there are two scorers they shall frequently check to ensure that the score sheets agree.

## 2. Acknowledging Signals

The scorers shall accept and immediately acknowledge all instructions and signals given to them by the umpires.

## LAW 5. THE BALL

### 1. Weight and Size

The ball, when new, shall weigh not less than $5\frac{1}{2}$ ounces/155.9g, nor more than $5\frac{3}{4}$ ounces/163g; and shall measure not less than $8\frac{13}{16}$ inches/22.4cm, nor more than 9 inches/22.9cm in circumference.

### 2. Approval of Balls

All balls used in matches shall be approved by the umpires and captains before the start of the match.

### 3. New Ball

Subject to agreement to the contrary, having been made before the toss, either captain may demand a new ball at the start of each innings.

### 4. New Ball in Match of Three or More Days' Duration

In a match of three or more days' duration, the captain of the fielding side may demand a new ball after the prescribed number of overs has been bowled with the old one. The governing body for cricket in the country concerned shall decide the number of overs applicable in that country, which shall be not less than 75 six-ball overs (55 eight-ball overs).

### 5. Ball Lost or Becoming Unfit for Play

In the event of a ball during play being lost or, in the opinion of the umpires, becoming unfit for play, the umpires shall allow it to be replaced by one that in their opinion has had a similar amount of wear. If a ball is to be replaced, the umpires shall inform the batsman.

*Note*

**(a) Specifications**
The specifications, as described in 1 above, shall apply to top-grade balls only. The following degrees of tolerance will be acceptable for other grades of ball.

(i) *Men's Grades 2–4*
Weight: $5\frac{5}{16}$ ounces/150g to $5\frac{13}{16}$ ounces/165g.
Size: $8\frac{11}{16}$ inches/22.0cm to $9\frac{1}{16}$ inches/23.0cm.

(ii) *Women's*
Weight: $4\frac{15}{16}$ ounces/140g to $5\frac{5}{16}$ ounces/150g.
Size: $8\frac{1}{4}$ inches/21.0cm to $8\frac{7}{8}$ inches/22.5cm.

(iii) *Junior*
Weight: $4\frac{5}{16}$ ounces/133g to $5\frac{1}{16}$ ounces/143g.
Size: $8\frac{1}{16}$ inches/20.5cm to $8\frac{11}{16}$ inches/22.0cm.

## LAW 6. THE BAT

### 1. Width and Length

The bat overall shall not be more than 38 inches/96.5cm in length; the blade of the bat shall be made of wood and shall not exceed $4\frac{1}{4}$ inches/10.8cm at the widest part.

*Note*

(a) The blade of the bat may be covered with material for protection, strengthening or repair. Such material shall not exceed $\frac{1}{16}$ inch/1.56mm in thickness.

## LAW 7. THE PITCH

### 1. Area of Pitch

The pitch is the area between the bowling creases – see Law 9 (The Bowling and Popping Creases). It shall measure 5ft/1.52m in width on either side of a line joining the centre of the middle stumps of the wickets – see Law 8 (The Wickets).

### 2. Selection and Preparation

Before the toss for innings, the executive of the ground shall be responsible for the selection and preparation of the pitch; thereafter the umpires shall control its use and maintenance.

### 3. Changing Pitch

The pitch shall not be changed during a match unless it becomes unfit for play, and then only with the consent of both captains.

### 4. Non-Turf Pitches

In the event of a non-turf pitch being used, the following shall apply:

(a) Length: That of the playing surface to a minimum of 58ft/17.68m.

(b) Width: That of the playing surface to a minimum of 6ft/1.83m.

See Law 10 (Rolling, Sweeping, Mowing, Watering the Pitch and Re-marking of Creases) Note (a).

## LAW 8. THE WICKETS

### 1. Width and Pitching

Two sets of wickets, each 9 inches/22.86cm wide, and consisting of three wooden stumps with two wooden bails upon the top, shall be pitched opposite and parallel to each other at a distance of 22 yards/20.12m between the centres of the two middle stumps.

### 2. Size of Stumps

The stumps shall be of equal and sufficient size to prevent the ball from passing between them. Their tops shall be 28 inches/71.1cm above the ground, and shall be dome-shaped except for the bail grooves.

### 3. Size of Bails

The bails shall be each $4\frac{3}{8}$ inches/11.1cm in length and when in position on the top of the stumps shall not project more than $\frac{1}{2}$ inch/1.3cm above them.

*Notes*

**(a) Dispensing with Bails**

In a high wind the umpires may decide to dispense with the use of bails.

**(b) Junior Cricket**

For junior cricket, as defined by the local governing body, the following measurements for the wickets shall apply:

Width – 8 inches/20.32cm.
Pitched – 21 yards/19.20m.
Height – 27 inches/68.58cm.
Bails – each $3\frac{7}{8}$ inches/9.84cm in length and should not project more than $\frac{1}{2}$ inch/1.3cm above the stumps.

## LAW 9. THE BOWLING, POPPING AND RETURN CREASES

### 1. The Bowling Crease

The bowling crease shall be marked in line with the stumps at each end and shall be 8 feet 8 inches/2.64m in length, with the stumps in the centre.

### 2. The Popping Crease

The popping crease, which is the back edge of the crease marking, shall be in front of and parallel with the bowling crease. It shall have the back edge of the crease marking 4 feet/1.22m from the centre of the stumps and shall extend to a minimum of 6 feet/1.83m on either side of the line of the wicket.

The popping crease shall be considered to be unlimited in length.

### 3. The Return Crease

The return crease marking, of which the inside edge is the crease, shall be at each end of the bowling crease and at right angles to it. The return crease shall be marked to a minimum of 4 feet/1.22m behind the wicket and shall be considered to be unlimited in length. A forward extension shall be marked to the popping crease.

## LAW 10. ROLLING, SWEEPING, MOWING, WATERING THE PITCH AND RE-MARKING OF CREASES

### 1. Rolling

During the match the pitch may be rolled at the request of the captain of the batting side, for a period of not more than seven minutes before the start of each innings, other than the first innings of the match, and before the start of each day's play. In addition, if, after the toss and before the first innings of the match, the start is delayed, the captain of the batting side shall have the right to have the pitch rolled for not more than seven minutes.

The pitch shall not otherwise be rolled during the match.

The seven minutes' rolling permitted before the start of a day's play shall take place not earlier than half an hour before the start of play and the captain of the batting side may delay such rolling until ten minutes before the start of play should he so desire.

If a captain declares an innings closed less than fifteen minutes before the resumption of play, and the other captain is thereby prevented from exercising his option of seven minutes' rolling or if he is so prevented for any other reason, the time for rolling shall be taken out of the normal playing time.

### 2. Sweeping

Such sweeping of the pitch as is necessary during the match shall be done so that the seven minutes allowed for rolling the pitch, provided for in 1 above, is not affected.

### 3. Mowing

**(a) Responsibilities of Ground Authority and of Umpires**

All mowings which are carried out before the toss for innings shall be the responsibility of the ground authority; thereafter they shall be carried out under the supervision of the umpires. See Law 7.2 (Selection and Preparation).

**(b) Initial Mowing**

The pitch shall be mown before play begins on the day the match is scheduled to start, or in the case of a delayed start on the day the match is expected to start. See 3(a) above (Responsibilities of Ground Authority and of Umpires).

**(c) Subsequent Mowings in a Match of Two or More Days' Duration**

In a match of two or more days' duration, the pitch shall be mown daily before play begins. Should this mowing not take place because of weather conditions, rest days or other reasons, the pitch shall be mown on the first day on which the match is resumed.

**(d) Mowing of the Outfield in a Match of Two or More Days' Duration**

In order to ensure that conditions are as similar as possible for both sides, the outfield shall normally be mown before the commencement of play on each day of the match, if ground and weather conditions allow. See Note (b) to this Law.

### 4. Watering

The pitch shall not be watered during a match.

### 5. Re-marking Creases

Whenever possible the creases shall be re-marked.

### 6. Maintenance of Foot-holes

In wet weather, the umpires shall ensure that the holes made by the bowlers and batsmen are cleaned out and dried whenever necessary to facilitate play. In matches of two or more days' duration, the umpires shall allow, if necessary, the re-turfing of foot-holes made by the bowler in his delivery stride, or the use of quick-setting fillings for the same purpose, before the start of each day's play.

### 7. Securing of Footholds and Maintenance of Pitch

During play, the umpires shall allow either batsman to beat the pitch with his bat and players to secure their footholds by the use of sawdust, provided that no damage to the pitch is so caused, and Law 42 (Unfair Play) is not contravened.

*Notes*

**(a) Non-turf Pitches**
The above Law 10 applies to turf pitches.

The game is played on non-turf pitches in many countries at various levels. Whilst the conduct of the game on these surfaces should always be in accordance with the Laws of Cricket, it is recognised that it may sometimes be necessary for governing bodies to lay down special playing conditions to suit the type of non-turf pitch used in their country.

In matches played against touring teams, any special playing conditions should be agreed in advance by both parties.

**(b) Mowing of the Outfield in a Match of Two or More Days' Duration**
If, for reasons other than ground and weather conditions, daily and complete mowing is not possible, the ground authority shall notify the captains and umpires, before the toss for innings, of the procedure to be adopted for such mowing during the match.

**(c) Choice of Roller**
If there is more than one roller available, the captain of the batting side shall have a choice.

## LAW 11. COVERING THE PITCH

### 1. Before the Start of a Match

Before the start of a match, complete covering of the pitch shall be allowed.

### 2. During a Match

The pitch shall not be completely covered during a match unless prior arrangement or regulations so provide.

### 3. Covering Bowlers' Run-up

Whenever possible, the bowlers' run-up shall be covered, but the covers so used shall not extend further than 4 feet/1.22m in front of the popping crease.

*Note*

**(a) Removal of Covers**
The covers should be removed as promptly as possible whenever the weather permits.

## LAW 12. INNINGS

### 1. Number of Innings

A match shall be of one or two innings of each side according to agreement reached before the start of play.

### 2. Alternate Innings

In a two-innings match each side shall take their innings alternately except in the case provided for in Law 13 (The Follow-on).

### 3. The Toss

The captains shall toss for the choice of innings on the field of play not later than fifteen minutes before the time scheduled for the match to start, or before the time agreed upon for play to start.

### 4. Choice of Innings

The winner of the toss shall notify his decision to bat or to field to the opposing captain not later than ten minutes before the time scheduled for the match to start, or before the time agreed upon for play to start. The decision shall not thereafter be altered.

### 5. Continuation after One Innings of Each Side

Despite the terms of 1 above, in a one-innings match, when a result has been reached on the first innings, the captains may agree to the continuation of play if, in their opinion, there is a prospect of carrying the game to a further issue in the time left. See Law 21 (Result).

*Notes*

**(a) Limited Innings – One-innings Match**
In a one-innings match, each innings may, by agreement, be limited by a number of overs or by a period of time.

**(b) Limited Innings – Two-innings Match**
In a two-innings match, the first innings of each side may, by agreement, be limited to a number of overs or by a period of time.

## LAW 13. THE FOLLOW-ON

### 1. Lead on First Innings

In a two-innings match the side which bats first and leads by 200 runs in a match of five days or more, by 150 runs in a three-day or four-day match, by 100 runs in a two-day match, or by 75 runs in a one-day match, shall have the option of requiring the other side to follow their innings.

### 2. Day's Play Lost

If no play takes place on the first day of a match of two or more days' duration, 1 above shall apply in accordance with the number of days' play remaining from the actual start of the match.

## LAW 14. DECLARATIONS

### 1. Time of Declaration

The captain of the batting side may declare an innings closed at any time during a match, irrespective of its duration.

### 2. Forfeiture of Second Innings

A captain may forfeit his second innings, provided his decision to do so is notified to the opposing captain and umpires in sufficient time to allow seven minutes' rolling of the pitch. See Law 10 (Rolling, Sweeping, Mowing, Watering the Pitch and Re-marking of Creases). The normal ten-minute interval between innings shall be applied.

## LAW 15. START OF PLAY

### 1. Call of Play

At the start of each innings and of each day's play, and on the resumption of play after any interval or interruption, the umpire at the bowler's end shall call "play".

### 2. Practice on the Field

At no time on any day of the match shall there be any bowling or batting practice on the pitch.

No practice may take place on the field if, in the opinion of the umpires, it could result in a waste of time.

### 3. Trial Run-up

No bowler shall have a trial run-up after "play" has been called in any session of play, except at the fall of a wicket when an umpire may allow such a trial run-up if he is satisfied that it will not cause any waste of time.

## LAW 16. INTERVALS

### 1. Length

The umpire shall allow such intervals as have been agreed upon for meals, and ten minutes between each innings.

### 2. Luncheon Interval – Innings Ending or Stoppage within Ten Minutes of Interval

If an innings ends or there is a stoppage caused by weather or bad light within ten minutes of the agreed time for the luncheon interval, the interval shall be taken immediately.

The time remaining in the session of play shall be added to the agreed length of the interval but no extra allowance shall be made for the ten-minute interval between innings.

### 3. Tea Interval – Innings Ending or Stoppage within Thirty Minutes of Interval

If an innings ends or there is a stoppage caused by weather or bad light within thirty minutes of the agreed time for the tea interval, the interval shall be taken immediately.

The interval shall be of the agreed length and, if applicable, shall include the ten-minute interval between innings.

### 4. Tea Interval – Continuation of Play

If, at the agreed time for the tea interval, nine wickets are down, play shall continue for a period not exceeding thirty minutes or until the innings is concluded.

### 5. Tea Interval – Agreement to Forgo

At any time during the match, the captains may agree to forgo a tea interval.

### 6. Intervals for Drinks

If both captains agree before the start of a match that intervals for drinks may be taken, the option to take such intervals shall be available to either side. These intervals shall be restricted to one per session, shall be kept as short as possible, shall not be taken in the last hour of the match, and in any case shall not exceed five minutes.

The agreed times for these intervals shall be strictly adhered to, except that if a wicket falls within five minutes of the agreed time then drinks shall be taken out immediately.

If an innings ends or there is a stoppage caused by weather or bad light within thirty minutes of the agreed time for a drinks interval, there will be no interval for drinks in that session.

At any time during the match the captains may agree to forgo any such drinks interval.

*Notes*

**(a) Tea Interval – One-day Match**

In a one-day match, a specific time for the tea interval need not necessarily be arranged, and it may be agreed to take this interval between the innings of a one-innings match.

**(b) Changing the Agreed Time of Intervals**

In the event of the ground, weather or light conditions causing a suspension of play, the umpires, after consultation with the captains, may decide in the interests of time-saving to bring forward the time of the luncheon or tea interval.

## LAW 17. CESSATION OF PLAY

### 1. Call of Time

The umpire at the bowler's end shall call "time" on the cessation of play before any interval or interruption of play, at the end of each day's play, and at the conclusion of the match. See Law 27 (Appeals).

### 2. Removal of Bails

After the call of "time", the umpires shall remove the bails from both wickets.

### 3. Starting a Last Over

The last over before an interval or the close of play shall be started provided the umpire, after walking at his normal pace, has arrived at his position behind the stumps at the bowler's end before time has been reached.

### 4. Completion of the Last Over of a Session

The last over before an interval or the close of play shall be completed unless a batsman is out or retires during that over within two minutes of the interval or the close of play or unless the players have occasion to leave the field.

### 5. Completion of the Last Over of a Match

An over in progress at the close of play on the final day of a match shall be completed at the request of either captain, even if a wicket falls after time has been reached.

If, during the last over, the players have occasion to leave the field, the umpires shall call "time" and there shall be no resumption of play and the match shall be at an end.

### 6. Last Hour of Match – Number of Overs

The umpires shall indicate when one hour of playing time of the match remains according to the agreed hours of play. The next over after that moment shall be the first of a minimum of 20 six-ball overs (15 eight-ball overs), provided a result is not reached earlier or there is no interval or interruption of play.

### 7. Last Hour of Match – Intervals between Innings and Interruptions of Play

If, at the commencement of the last hour of the match, an interval or interruption of play is in progress or if, during the last hour, there is an interval between innings or an interruption of play, the minimum number of overs to be bowled on the resumption of play shall be reduced in proportion to the duration, within the last hour of the match, of any such interval or interruption.

The minimum number of overs to be bowled after the resumption of play shall be calculated as follows:

(a) In the case of an interval or interruption of play being in progress at the commencement of the last hour of the match, or in the case of a first interval or interruption, a deduction shall be made from the minimum of 20 six-ball overs (or 15 eight-ball overs).

(b) If there is a later interval or interruption, a further deduction shall be made from the minimum number of overs which should have been bowled following the last resumption of play.

(c) These deductions shall be based on the following factors:

- (i) The number of overs already bowled in the last hour of the match or, in the case of a later interval or interruption, in the last session of play.
- (ii) The number of overs lost as a result of the interval or interruption allowing one six-ball over for every full three minutes (or one eight-ball over for every full four minutes) of interval or interruption.
- (iii) Any over left uncompleted at the end of an innings to be excluded from these calculations.

(iv) Any over left uncompleted at the start of an interruption of play to be completed when play is resumed and to count as one over bowled.

(v) An interval to start with the end of an innings and to end ten minutes later; an interruption to start on the call of "time" and to end on the call of "play".

(d) In the event of an innings being completed and a new innings commencing during the last hour of the match, the number of overs to be bowled in the new innings shall be calculated on the basis of one six-ball over for every three minutes or part thereof remaining for play (or one eight-ball over for every four minutes or part thereof remaining for play); or alternatively on the basis that sufficient overs be bowled to enable the full minimum quota of overs to be completed under circumstances governed by (a), (b) and (c) above. In all such cases the alternative which allows the greater number of overs shall be employed.

### 8. Bowler Unable to Complete an Over during Last Hour of the Match

If, for any reason, a bowler is unable to complete an over during the period of play referred to in 6 above, Law 22.7 (Bowler Incapacitated or Suspended during an Over) shall apply.

## LAW 18. SCORING

### 1. A Run

The score shall be reckoned by runs. A run is scored:

(a) So often as the batsmen, after a hit or at any time while the ball is in play, shall have crossed and made good their ground from end to end.

(b) When a boundary is scored. See Law 19 (Boundaries).

(c) When penalty runs are awarded. See 6 below.

### 2. Short Runs

(a) If either batsman runs a short run, the umpire shall call and signal "one short" as soon as the ball becomes dead and that run shall not be scored. A run is short if a batsman fails to make good his ground on turning for a further run.

(b) Although a short run shortens the succeeding one, the latter, if completed, shall count.

(c) If either or both batsmen deliberately run short the umpire shall, as soon as he sees that the fielding side have no chance of dismissing either batsman, call and signal "dead ball" and disallow any runs attempted or previously scored. The batsmen shall return to their original ends.

(d) If both batsmen run short in one and the same run, only one run shall be deducted.

(e) Only if 3 or more runs are attempted can more than one be short and then, subject to (c) and (d) above, all runs so called shall be disallowed. If there has been more than one short run the umpires shall instruct the scorers as to the number of runs disallowed.

### 3. Striker Caught

If the striker is caught, no run shall be scored.

### 4. Batsman Run Out

If a batsman is run out, only that run which was being attempted shall not be scored. If, however, an injured striker himself is run out, no runs shall be scored. See Law 2.7 (Transgression of the Laws by an Injured Batsman or Runner).

### 5. Batsman Obstructing the Field

If a batsman is out Obstructing the Field, any runs completed before the obstruction occurs shall be scored unless such obstruction prevents a catch being made, in which case no runs shall be scored.

### 6. Runs Scored for Penalties

Runs shall be scored for penalties under Laws 20 (Lost Ball), 24 (No-ball), 25 (Wide-ball), 41.1 (Fielding the Ball) and for boundary allowances under Law 19 (Boundaries).

## 7. Batsman Returning to Wicket he has Left

If, while the ball is in play, the batsmen have crossed in running, neither shall return to the wicket he has left, even though a short run has been called or no run has been scored as in the case of a catch. Batsmen, however, shall return to the wickets they originally left in the cases of a boundary and of any disallowance of runs and of an injured batsman being, himself, run out. See Law 2.7 (Transgression by an Injured Batsman or Runner).

*Note*

**(a) Short Run**

A striker taking stance in front of his popping crease may run from that point without penalty.

# LAW 19. BOUNDARIES

## 1. The Boundary of the Playing Area

Before the toss for innings, the umpires shall agree with both captains on the boundary of the playing area. The boundary shall, if possible, be marked by a white line, a rope laid on the ground, or a fence. If flags or posts only are used to mark a boundary, the imaginary line joining such points shall be regarded as the boundary. An obstacle, or person, within the playing area shall not be regarded as a boundary unless so decided by the umpires before the toss for innings. Sightscreens within, or partially within, the playing area shall be regarded as the boundary and when the ball strikes or passes within or under or directly over any part of the screen, a boundary shall be scored.

## 2. Runs Scored for Boundaries

Before the toss for innings, the umpires shall agree with both captains the runs to be allowed for boundaries, and in deciding the allowance for them, the umpires and captains shall be guided by the prevailing custom of the ground. The allowance for a boundary shall normally be 4 runs, and 6 runs for all hits pitching over and clear of the boundary line or fence, even though the ball has been previously touched by a fieldsman. 6 runs shall also be scored if a fieldsman, after catching a ball, carries it over the boundary. See Law 32 (Caught) Note (a). 6 runs shall not be scored when a ball struck by the striker hits a sightscreen full pitch if the screen is within, or partially within, the playing area, but if the ball is struck directly over a sightscreen so situated, 6 runs shall be scored.

## 3. A Boundary

A boundary shall be scored and signalled by the umpire at the bowler's end whenever, in his opinion:

(a) A ball in play touches or crosses the boundary, however marked.

(b) A fieldsman with ball in hand touches or grounds any part of his person on or over a boundary line.

(c) A fieldsman with ball in hand grounds any part of his person over a boundary fence or board. This allows the fieldsman to touch or lean on or over a boundary fence or board in preventing a boundary.

## 4. Runs Exceeding Boundary Allowance

The runs completed at the instant the ball reaches the boundary shall count if they exceed the boundary allowance.

## 5. Overthrows or Wilful Act of a Fieldsman

If the boundary results from an overthrow or from the wilful act of a fieldsman, any runs already completed and the allowance shall be added to the score. The run in progress shall count provided that the batsmen have crossed at the instant of the throw or act.

*Note*

**(a) Position of Sightscreens**

Sightscreens should, if possible, be positioned wholly outside the playing area, as near as possible to the boundary line.

## LAW 20. LOST BALL

### 1. Runs Scored

If a ball in play cannot be found or recovered, any fieldsman may call "lost ball" when 6 runs shall be added to the score; but if more than 6 have been run before "lost ball" is called, as many runs as have been completed shall be scored. The run in progress shall count provided that the batsmen have crossed at the instant of the call of "lost ball".

### 2. How Scored

The runs shall be added to the score of the striker if the ball has been struck, but otherwise to the score of byes, leg-byes, no-balls or wides as the case may be.

## LAW 21. THE RESULT

### 1. A Win – Two-innings Matches

The side which has scored a total of runs in excess of that scored by the opposing side in its two completed innings shall be the winners.

### 2. A Win–One-innings Matches

(a) One-innings matches, unless played out as in 1 above, shall be decided on the first innings, but see Law 12.5 (Continuation after One Innings of Each Side).

(b) If the captains agree to continue play after the completion of one innings of each side in accordance with Law 12.5 (Continuation after One Innings of Each Side) and a result is not achieved on the second innings, the first innings result shall stand.

### 3. Umpires Awarding a Match

(a) A match shall be lost by a side which, during the match, (i) refuses to play, or (ii) concedes defeat, and the umpires shall award the match to the other side.

(b) Should both batsmen at the wickets or the fielding side leave the field at any time without the agreement of the umpires, this shall constitute a refusal to play and, on appeal, the umpires shall award the match to the other side in accordance with (a) above.

### 4. A Tie

The result of a match shall be a tie when the scores are equal at the conclusion of play, but only if the side batting last has completed its innings.

If the scores of the completed first innings of a one-day match are equal, it shall be a tie but only if the match has not been played out to a further conclusion.

### 5. A Draw

A match not determined in any of the ways as in 1, 2, 3 and 4 above shall count as a draw.

### 6. Correctness of Result

Any decision as to the correctness of the scores shall be the responsibility of the umpires. See Law 3.14 (Correctness of Scores).

If, after the umpires and players have left the field in the belief that the match has been concluded, the umpires decide that a mistake in scoring has occurred, which affects the result, and provided time has not been reached, they shall order play to resume and to continue until the agreed finishing time unless a result is reached earlier.

If the umpires decide that a mistake has occurred and time has been reached, the umpires shall immediately inform both captains of the necessary corrections to the scores and, if applicable, to the result.

## 7. Acceptance of Result

In accepting the scores as notified by the scorers and agreed by the umpires, the captains of both sides thereby accept the result.

*Notes*

**(a) Statement of Results**

The result of a finished match is stated as a win by runs, except in the case of a win by the side batting last when it is by the number of wickets still then to fall.

**(b) Winning Hit or Extras**

As soon as the side has won, see 1 and 2 above, the umpire shall call "time", the match is finished, and nothing that happens thereafter other than as a result of a mistake in scoring (see 6 above) shall be regarded as part of the match.

However, if a boundary constitutes the winning hit–or extras–and the boundary allowance exceeds the number of runs required to win the match, such runs scored shall be credited to the side's total and, in the case of a hit, to the striker's score.

# LAW 22. THE OVER

## 1. Number of Balls

The ball shall be bowled from each wicket alternately in overs of either six or eight balls according to agreement before the match.

## 2. Call of "Over"

When the agreed number of balls has been bowled, and as the ball becomes dead or when it becomes clear to the umpire at the bowler's end that both the fielding side and the batsmen at the wicket have ceased to regard the ball as in play, the umpire shall call "over" before leaving the wicket.

## 3. No-ball or Wide-ball

Neither a no-ball nor a wide-ball shall be reckoned as one of the over.

## 4. Umpire Miscounting

If an umpire miscounts the number of balls, the over as counted by the umpire shall stand.

## 5. Bowler Changing Ends

A bowler shall be allowed to change ends as often as desired, provided only that he does not bowl two overs consecutively in an innings.

## 6. The Bowler Finishing an Over

A bowler shall finish an over in progress unless he be incapacitated or be suspended under Law 42.8 (The Bowling of Fast Short-pitched Balls), 9 (The Bowling of Fast High Full Pitches), 10 (Time Wasting) and 11 (Players Damaging the Pitch). If an over is left incomplete for any reason at the start of an interval or interruption of play, it shall be finished on the resumption of play.

## 7. Bowler Incapacitated or Suspended during an Over

If, for any reason, a bowler is incapacitated while running up to bowl the first ball of an over, or is incapacitated or suspended during an over, the umpire shall call and signal "dead ball" and another bowler shall be allowed to bowl or complete the over from the same end, provided only that he shall not bowl two overs, or part thereof, consecutively in one innings.

## 8. Position of Non-striker

The batsman at the bowler's end shall normally stand on the opposite side of the wicket to that from which the ball is being delivered, unless a request to do otherwise is granted by the umpire.

# LAW 23. DEAD BALL

## 1. The Ball Becomes Dead

When:

(a) It is finally settled in the hands of the wicket-keeper or the bowler.

(b) It reaches or pitches over the boundary.

(c) A batsman is out.

(d) Whether played or not, it lodges in the clothing or equipment of a batsman or the clothing of an umpire.

(e) A ball lodges in a protective helmet worn by a member of the fielding side.

(f) A penalty is awarded under Law 20 (Lost Ball) or Law 41.1 (Fielding the Ball).

(g) The umpire calls "over" or "time".

## 2. Either Umpire Shall Call and Signal "Dead Ball"

When:

(a) He intervenes in a case of unfair play.

(b) A serious injury to a player or umpire occurs.

(c) He is satisfied that, for an adequate reason, the striker is not ready to receive the ball and makes no attempt to play it.

(d) The bowler drops the ball accidentally before delivery, or the ball does not leave his hand for any reason.

(e) One or both bails fall from the striker's wicket before he receives delivery.

(f) He leaves his normal position for consultation.

(g) He is required to do so under Law 26.3 (Disallowance of Leg-byes).

## 3. The Ball Ceases to be Dead

When:

(a) The bowler starts his run-up or bowling action.

## 4. The Ball is Not Dead

When:

(a) It strikes an umpire (unless it lodges in his dress).

(b) The wicket is broken or struck down (unless a batsman is out thereby).

(c) A unsuccessful appeal is made.

(d) The wicket is broken accidentally either by the bowler during his delivery or by a batsman in running.

(e) The umpire has called "no-ball" or "wide".

*Notes*

**(a) Ball Finally Settled**

Whether the ball is finally settled or not–see 1(a) above–must be a question for the umpires alone to decide.

**(b) Action on Call of "Dead Ball"**

(i) If "dead ball" is called prior to the striker receiving a delivery, the bowler shall be allowed an additional ball.

(ii) If "dead ball" is called after the striker receives a delivery, the bowler shall not be allowed an additional ball, unless a "no-ball" or "wide" has been called.

## LAW 24. NO-BALL

### 1. Mode of Delivery

The umpire shall indicate to the striker whether the bowler intends to bowl over or round the wicket, overarm or underarm, right- or left-handed. Failure on the part of the bowler to indicate in advance a change in his mode of delivery is unfair and the umpire shall call and signal "no-ball".

### 2. Fair Delivery–The Arm

For a delivery to be fair the ball must be bowled, not thrown–see Note (a) below. If either umpire is not entirely satisfied with the absolute fairness of a delivery in this respect he shall call and signal "no-ball" instantly upon delivery.

### 3. Fair Delivery–The Feet

The umpire at the bowler's wicket shall call and signal "no-ball" if he is not satisfied that in the delivery stride:

(a) The bowler's back foot has landed within and not touching the return crease or its forward extension; or

(b) Some part of the front foot whether grounded or raised was behind the popping crease.

### 4. Bowler Throwing at Striker's Wicket before Delivery

If the bowler, before delivering the ball, throws it at the striker's wicket in an attempt to run him out, the umpire shall call and signal "no-ball". See Law 42.12 (Batsman Unfairly Stealing a Run) and Law 38 (Run Out).

### 5. Bowler Attempting to Run Out Non-striker before Delivery

If the bowler, before delivering the ball, attempts to run out the non-striker, any runs which result shall be allowed and shall be scored as no-balls. Such an attempt shall not count as a ball in the over. The umpire shall not call "no-ball". See Law 42.12 (Batsman Unfairly Stealing a Run).

### 6. Infringement of Laws by a Wicket-keeper or a Fieldsman

The umpire shall call and signal "no-ball" in the event of the wicket-keeper infringing Law 40.1 (Position of Wicket-keeper) or a fieldsman infringing Law 41.2 (Limitation of On-side Fieldsmen) or Law 41.3 (Position of Fieldsmen).

### 7. Revoking a Call

An umpire shall revoke the call "no-ball" if the ball does not leave the bowler's hand for any reason. See Law 23.2 (Either Umpire Shall Call and Signal "Dead Ball").

### 8. Penalty

A penalty of 1 run for a no-ball shall be scored if no runs are made otherwise.

### 9. Runs from a No-ball

The striker may hit a no-ball and whatever runs result shall be added to his score. Runs made otherwise from a no-ball shall be scored no-balls.

### 10. Out from a No-ball

The striker shall be out from a no-ball if he breaks Law 34 (Hit the Ball Twice) and either batsman may be run out or shall be given out if either breaks Law 33 (Handled the Ball) or Law 37 (Obstructing the Field).

### 11. Batsman Given Out off a No-ball

Should a batsman be given out off a no-ball the penalty for bowling it shall stand unless runs are otherwise scored.

*Notes*

(a) **Definition of a Throw**
A ball shall be deemed to have been thrown if, in the opinion of either umpire, the process of straightening the bowling arm, whether it be partial or complete, takes place during that part of the delivery swing which directly precedes the ball leaving the hand. This definition shall not debar a bowler from the use of the wrist in the delivery swing.

**(b) No-ball Not Counting in Over**
A no-ball shall not be reckoned as one of the over. See Law 22.3 (No-ball or Wide-ball).

# LAW 25. WIDE-BALL

## 1. Judging a Wide

If the bowler bowls the ball so high over or so wide of the wicket that, in the opinion of the umpire, it passes out of the reach of the striker, standing in a normal guard position, the umpire shall call and signal "wide-ball" as soon as it has passed the line of the striker's wicket.

The umpire shall not adjudge a ball as being wide if:

(a) The striker, by moving from his guard position, causes the ball to pass out of his reach.

(b) The striker moves and thus brings the ball within his reach.

## 2. Penalty

A penalty of 1 run for a wide shall be scored if no runs are made otherwise.

## 3. Ball Coming to Rest in Front of the Striker

If a ball which the umpire considers to have been delivered comes to rest in front of the line of the striker's wicket, "wide" shall not be called. The striker has a right, without interference from the fielding side, to make one attempt to hit the ball. If the fielding side interfere, the umpire shall replace the ball where it came to rest and shall order the fieldsmen to resume the places they occupied in the field before the ball was delivered.

The umpire shall call and signal "dead ball" as soon as it is clear that the striker does not intend to hit the ball, or after the striker has made an unsuccessful attempt to hit the ball.

## 4. Revoking a Call

The umpire shall revoke the call if the striker hits a ball which has been called "wide".

## 5. Ball Not Dead

The ball does not become dead on the call of "wide-ball"–see Law 23.4 (The Ball is Not Dead).

## 6. Runs Resulting from a Wide

All runs which are run or result from a wide-ball which is not a no-ball shall be scored wide-balls, or if no runs are made 1 shall be scored.

## 7. Out from a Wide

The striker shall be out from a wide-ball if he breaks Law 35 (Hit Wicket), or Law 39 (Stumped). Either batsman may be run out and shall be out if he breaks Law 33 (Handled the Ball), or Law 37 (Obstructing the Field).

## 8. Batsman Given Out off a Wide

Should a batsman be given out off a wide, the penalty for bowling it shall stand unless runs are otherwise made.

*Note*

**(a) Wide-ball Not Counting in Over**
A wide-ball shall not be reckoned as one of the over–see Law 22.3 (No-ball or Wide-ball).

## LAW 26. BYE AND LEG-BYE

### 1. Byes

If the ball, not having been called "wide" or "no-ball", passes the striker without touching his bat or person, and any runs are obtained, the umpire shall signal "bye" and the run or runs shall be credited as such to the batting side.

### 2. Leg-byes

If the ball, not having been called "wide" or "no-ball", is unintentionally deflected by the striker's dress or person, except a hand holding the bat, and any runs are obtained the umpire shall signal "leg-bye" and the run or runs so scored shall be credited as such to the batting side.

Such leg-byes shall be scored only if, in the opinion of the umpire, the striker has:

(a) Attempted to play the ball with his bat; or

(b) Tried to avoid being hit by the ball.

### 3. Disallowance of Leg-byes

In the case of a deflection by the striker's person, other than in 2(a) and (b) above, the umpire shall call and signal "dead ball" as soon as 1 run has been completed or when it is clear that a run is not being attempted, or the ball has reached the boundary.

On the call and signal of "dead ball" the batsmen shall return to their original ends and no runs shall be allowed.

## LAW 27. APPEALS

### 1. Time of Appeals

The umpires shall not give a batsman out unless appealed to by the other side which shall be done prior to the bowler beginning his run-up or bowling action to deliver the next ball. Under Law 23.1 (f) (The Ball Becomes Dead), the ball is dead on "over" being called; this does not, however, invalidate an appeal made prior to the first ball of the following over provided "time" has not been called–see Law 17.1 (Call of Time).

### 2. An Appeal "How's That?"

An appeal "How's That?" shall cover all ways of being out.

### 3. Answering Appeals

The umpire at the bowler's wicket shall answer appeals before the other umpire in all cases except those arising out of Law 35 (Hit Wicket) or Law 39 (Stumped) or Law 38 (Run Out) when this occurs at the striker's wicket.

When either umpire has given a batsman not out, the other umpire shall, within his jurisdiction, answer the appeal or a further appeal, provided it is made in time in accordance with 1 above (Time of Appeals).

### 4. Consultation by Umpires

An umpire may consult with the other umpire on a point of fact which the latter may have been in a better position to see and shall then give his decision. If, after consultation, there is still doubt remaining the decision shall be in favour of the batsman.

### 5. Batsman Leaving his Wicket under a Misapprehension

The umpires shall intervene if satisfied that a batsman, not having been given out, has left his wicket under a misapprehension that he has been dismissed.

### 6. Umpire's Decision

The umpire's decision is final. He may alter his decision, provided that such alteration is made promptly.

### 7. Withdrawal of an Appeal

In exceptional circumstances the captain of the fielding side may seek permission of the umpire to withdraw an appeal provided the outgoing batsman has not left the playing area. If this is allowed, the umpire shall cancel his decision.

## LAW 28. THE WICKET IS DOWN

### 1. Wicket Down

The wicket is down if:

(a) Either the ball or the striker's bat or person completely removes either bail from the top of the stumps. A disturbance of a bail, whether temporary or not, shall not constitute a complete removal, but the wicket is down if a bail in falling lodges between two of the stumps.

(b) Any player completely removes with his hand or arm a bail from the top of the stumps, provided that the ball is held in that hand or in the hand of the arm so used.

(c) When both bails are off, a stump is struck out of the ground by the ball, or a player strikes or pulls a stump out of the ground, provided that the ball is held in the hand(s) or in the hand of the arm so used.

### 2. One Bail Off

If one bail is off, it shall be sufficient for the purpose of putting the wicket down to remove the remaining bail, or to strike or pull any of the three stumps out of the ground in any of the ways stated in 1 above.

### 3. All the Stumps Out of the Ground

If all the stumps are out of the ground, the fielding side shall be allowed to put back one or more stumps in order to have an opportunity of putting the wicket down.

### 4. Dispensing with Bails

If owing to the strength of the wind, it has been agreed to dispense with the bails in accordance with Law 8, Note (a) (Dispensing with Bails), the decision as to when the wicket is down is one for the umpires to decide on the facts before them. In such circumstances and if the umpires so decide, the wicket shall be held to be down even though a stump has not been struck out of the ground.

*Note*

**(a) Remaking the Wicket**
If the wicket is broken while the ball is in play, it is not the umpire's duty to remake the wicket until the ball has become dead–see Law 23 (Dead Ball). A member of the fielding side, however, may remake the wicket in such circumstances.

## LAW 29. BATSMAN OUT OF HIS GROUND

### 1. When out of his Ground

A batsman shall be considered to be out of his ground unless some part of his bat in his hand or of his person is grounded behind the line of the popping crease.

## LAW 30. BOWLED

### 1. Out Bowled

The striker shall be out *Bowled* if:

(a) His wicket is bowled down, even if the ball first touches his bat or person.

(b) He breaks his wicket by hitting or kicking the ball on to it before the completion of a stroke, or as a result of attempting to guard his wicket. See Law 34.1 (Out Hit the Ball Twice).

*Note*

**(a) Out Bowled–Not lbw**
The striker is out bowled if the ball is deflected on to his wicket even though a decision against him would be justified under Law 36 (lbw).

## LAW 31. TIMED OUT

### 1. Out Timed Out

An incoming batsman shall be out *Timed Out* if he wilfully takes more than two minutes to come in–the two minutes being timed from the moment a wicket falls until the new batsman steps on to the field of play.

If this is not complied with and if the umpire is satisfied that the delay was wilful and if an appeal is made, the new batsman shall be given out by the umpire at the bowler's end.

### 2. Time to be Added

The time taken by the umpires to investigate the cause of the delay shall be added at the normal close of play.

*Notes*

**(a) Entry in Scorebook**
The correct entry in the scorebook when a batsman is given out under this Law is "timed out", and the bowler does not get credit for the wicket.

**(b) Batsmen Crossing on the Field of Play**
It is an essential duty of the captains to ensure that the in-going batsman passes the out-going one before the latter leaves the field of play.

## LAW 32. CAUGHT

### 1. Out Caught

The striker shall be out *Caught* if the ball touches his bat or if it touches below the wrist his hand or glove, holding the bat, and is subsequently held by a fieldsman before it touches the ground.

### 2. A Fair Catch

A catch shall be considered to have been fairly made if:

(a) The fieldsman is within the field of play throughout the act of making the catch.

(i) The act of making the catch shall start from the time when the fieldsman first handles the ball and shall end when he both retains complete control over the further disposal of the ball and remains within the field of play.

(ii) In order to be within the field of play, the fieldsman may not touch or ground any part of his person on or over a boundary line. When the boundary is marked by a fence or board the fieldsman may not ground any part of his person over the boundary fence or board, but may touch or lean over the boundary fence or board in completing the catch.

(b) The ball is hugged to the body of the catcher or accidentally lodges in his dress or, in the case of the wicket-keeper, in his pads. However, a striker may not be caught if a ball lodges in a protective helmet worn by a fieldsman, in which case the umpire shall call and signal "dead ball". See Law 23 (Dead Ball).

(c) The ball does not touch the ground even though a hand holding it does so in effecting the catch.

(d) A fieldsman catches the ball, after it has been lawfully played a second time by the striker, but only if the ball has not touched the ground since being first struck.

(e) A fieldsman catches the ball after it has touched an umpire, another fieldsman or the other batsman. However, a striker may not be caught if a ball has touched a protective helmet worn by a fieldsman.

(f) The ball is caught off an obstruction within the boundary provided it has not previously been agreed to regard the obstruction as a boundary.

### 3. Scoring of Runs

If a striker is caught, no run shall be scored.

*Notes*

**(a) Scoring from an Attempted Catch**
When a fieldsman carrying the ball touches or grounds any part of his person on or over a boundary marked by a line, 6 runs shall be scored.

**(b) Ball Still in Play**
If a fieldsman releases the ball before he crosses the boundary, the ball will be considered to be still in play and it may be caught by another fieldsman. However, if the original fieldsman returns to the field of play and handles the ball, a catch may not be made.

## LAW 33. HANDLED THE BALL

### 1. Out Handled the Ball

Either batsman on appeal shall be out *Handled the Ball* if he wilfully touches the ball while in play with the hand not holding the bat unless he does so with the consent of the opposite side.

*Note*

**(a) Entry in Scorebook**
The correct entry in the scorebook when a batsman is given out under this Law is "handled the ball', and the bowler does not get credit for the wicket.

## LAW 34. HIT THE BALL TWICE

### 1. Out Hit the Ball Twice

The striker, on appeal, shall be out *Hit the Ball Twice* if, after the ball is struck or is stopped by any part of his person, he wilfully strikes it again with his bat or person except for the sole purpose of guarding his wicket: this he may do with his bat or any part of his person other than his hands, but see Law 37.2 (Obstructing a Ball From Being Caught).

For the purpose of this Law, a hand holding the bat shall be regarded as part of the bat.

### 2. Returning the Ball to a Fieldsman

The striker, on appeal, shall be out under this Law if, without the consent of the opposite side, he uses his bat or person to return the ball to any of the fielding side.

### 3. Runs from Ball Lawfully Struck Twice

No runs except those which result from an overthrow or penalty – see Law 41 (The Fieldsman) – shall be scored from a ball lawfully struck twice.

*Notes*

**(a) Entry in Scorebook**
The correct entry in the scorebook when the striker is given out under this Law is "hit the ball twice", and the bowler does not get credit for the wicket.

**(b) Runs Credited to the Batsman**
Any runs awarded under 3 above as a result of an overthrow or penalty shall be credited to the striker, provided the ball in the first instance has touched the bat, or, if otherwise, as extras.

## LAW 35. HIT WICKET

### 1. Out Hit Wicket

The striker shall be out *Hit Wicket* if, while the ball is in play:

(a) His wicket is broken with any part of his person, dress, or equipment as a result of any action taken by him in preparing to receive or in receiving a delivery, or in setting off for his first run, immediately after playing, or playing at, the ball.

(b) He hits down his wicket whilst lawfully making a second stroke for the purpose of guarding his wicket within the provisions of Law 34.1 (Out Hit the Ball Twice).

*Notes*

**(a) Not Out Hit Wicket**

A batsman is not out under this Law should his wicket be broken in any of the ways referred to in 1(a) above if:

(i) It occurs while he is in the act of running, other than in setting off for his first run immediately after playing at the ball, or while he is avoiding being run out or stumped.

(ii) The bowler after starting his run-up or bowling action does not deliver the ball; in which case the umpire shall immediately call and signal "dead ball".

(iii) It occurs whilst he is avoiding a throw-in at any time.

## LAW 36. LEG BEFORE WICKET

### 1. Out lbw

The striker shall be out *lbw* in the circumstances set out below:

**(a) Striker Attempting to Play the Ball**

The striker shall be out lbw if he first intercepts with any part of his person, dress or equipment a fair ball which would have hit the wicket and which has not previously touched his bat or a hand holding the bat, provided that:

(i) The ball pitched in a straight line between wicket and wicket or on the off side of the striker's wicket, or in the case of a ball intercepted full pitch would have pitched in a straight line between wicket and wicket; and

(ii) The point of impact is in a straight line between wicket and wicket, even if above the level of the bails.

**(b) Striker Making No Attempt to Play the Ball**

The striker shall be out lbw even if the ball is intercepted outside the line of the off stump if, in the opinion of the umpire, he has made no genuine attempt to play the ball with his bat, but has intercepted the ball with some part of his person and if the circumstances set out in (a) above apply.

## LAW 37. OBSTRUCTING THE FIELD

### 1. Wilful Obstruction

Either batsman, on appeal, shall be out *Obstructing the Field* if he wilfully obstructs the opposite side by word or action.

### 2. Obstructing a Ball From Being Caught

The striker, on appeal, shall be out should wilful obstruction by either batsman prevent a catch being made.

This shall apply even though the striker causes the obstruction in lawfully guarding his wicket under the provisions of Law 34. See Law 34.1 (Out Hit the Ball Twice).

*Notes*

**(a) Accidental Obstruction**

The umpires must decide whether the obstruction was wilful or not. The accidental interception of a throw-in by a batsman while running does not break this Law.

**(b) Entry in Scorebook**

The correct entry in the scorebook when a batsman is given out under this Law is "obstructing the field", and the bowler does not get credit for the wicket.

## LAW 38. RUN OUT

### 1. Out Run Out

Either batsman shall be out *Run Out* if in running or at any time while the ball is in play – except in the circumstances described in Law 39 (Stumped) – he is out of his ground and his wicket is put down by the opposite side. If, however, a batsman in running makes good his ground he shall not be out run out if he subsequently leaves his ground, in order to avoid injury, and the wicket is put down.

### 2. "No-ball" Called

If a no-ball has been called, the striker shall not be given run out unless he attempts to run.

### 3. Which Batsman Is Out

If the batsmen have crossed in running, he who runs for the wicket which is put down shall be out; if they have not crossed, he who has left the wicket which is put down shall be out. If a batsman remains in his ground or returns to his ground and the other batsman joins him there, the latter shall be out if his wicket is put down.

### 4. Scoring of Runs

If a batsman is run out, only that run which is being attempted shall not be scored. If, however, an injured striker himself is run out, no runs shall be scored. See Law 2.7 (Transgression of the Laws by an Injured Batsman or Runner).

*Notes*

**(a) Ball Played on to Opposite Wicket**
If the ball is played on to the opposite wicket, neither batsman is liable to be run out unless the ball has been touched by a fieldsman before the wicket is broken.

**(b) Entry in Scorebook**
The correct entry in the scorebook when a batsman is given out under this Law is "run out", and the bowler does not get credit for the wicket.

## LAW 39. STUMPED

### 1. Out Stumped

The striker shall be out *Stumped* if, in receiving the ball, not being a no-ball, he is out of his ground otherwise than in attempting a run and the wicket is put down by the wicket-keeper without the intervention of another fieldsman.

### 2. Action by the Wicket-keeper

The wicket-keeper may take the ball in front of the wicket in an attempt to stump the striker only if the ball has touched the bat or person of the striker.

*Note*

**(a) Ball Rebounding from Wicket-keeper's Person**
The striker may be out stumped if, in the circumstances stated in 1 above, the wicket is broken by a ball rebounding from the wicket-keeper's person or equipment or is kicked or thrown by the wicket-keeper on to the wicket.

## LAW 40. THE WICKET-KEEPER

### 1. Position of Wicket-keeper

The wicket-keeper shall remain wholly behind the wicket until a ball delivered by the bowler touches the bat or person of the striker, or passes the wicket, or until the striker attempts a run.

In the event of the wicket-keeper contravening this Law, the umpire at the striker's end shall call and signal "no ball" at the instant of delivery or as soon as possible thereafter.

### 2. Restriction on Actions of the Wicket-keeper

If the wicket-keeper interferes with the striker's right to play the ball and to guard his wicket, the striker shall not be out except under Laws 33 (Handled the Ball), 34 (Hit the Ball Twice), 37 (Obstructing the Field), 38 (Run Out).

### 3. Interference with the Wicket-keeper by the Striker

If in the legitimate defence of his wicket, the striker interferes with the wicket-keeper, he shall not be out, except as provided for in Law 37.2 (Obstructing a Ball From Being Caught).

## LAW 41. THE FIELDSMAN

### 1. Fielding the Ball

The fieldsman may stop the ball with any part of his person, but if he wilfully stops it otherwise, 5 runs shall be added to the run or runs already scored; if no run has been scored 5 penalty runs shall be awarded. The run in progress shall count provided that the batsmen have crossed at the instant of the act. If the ball has been struck, the penalty shall be added to the score of the striker, but otherwise to the scores of byes, leg-byes, no-balls or wides as the case may be.

### 2. Limitation of On-side Fieldsmen

The number of on-side fieldsmen behind the popping crease at the instant of the bowler's delivery shall not exceed two. In the event of infringement by the fielding side the umpire at the striker's end shall call and signal "no-ball" at the instant of delivery or as soon as possible thereafter.

### 3. Position of Fieldsmen

Whilst the ball is in play and until the ball has made contact with the bat or the striker's person or has passed his bat, no fieldsman, other than the bowler, may stand on or have any part of his person extended over the pitch (measuring 22 yards/20.12m × 10 feet/3.05m). In the event of a fieldsman contravening this Law, the umpire at the bowler's end shall call and signal "no-ball" at the instant of delivery or as soon as possible thereafter. See Law 40.1 (Position of Wicket-keeper).

### *Experimental Law: Fieldsmen's Protective Helmets*

*Protective helmets, when not in use by members of the fielding side, shall be placed, if above the surface, only on the ground behind the wicket-keeper. In the event of the ball striking the helmet whilst in this position, whether played or not, 5 penalty runs shall be awarded as laid down in Law 41.1 and Note (a). (This Experimental Law is currently in operation and subject to the approval of MCC will be officially adopted in May 1986.)*

*Note*

**(a) Batsmen Changing Ends**
The 5 runs referred to in 1 above (and the Experimental Law) are a penalty and the batsmen do not change ends solely by reason of this penalty.

## LAW 42. UNFAIR PLAY

### 1. Responsibility of Captains

The captains are responsible at all times for ensuring that play is conducted within the spirit of the game as well as within the Laws.

### 2. Responsibility of Umpires

The umpires are the sole judges of fair and unfair play.

### 3. Intervention by the Umpire

The umpires shall intervene without appeal by calling and signalling "dead ball" in the case of unfair play, but should not otherwise interfere with the progress of the game except as required to do so by the Laws.

## 4. Lifting the Seam

A player shall not lift the seam of the ball for any reason. Should this be done, the umpires shall change the ball for one of similar condition to that in use prior to the contravention. See Note (a).

## 5. Changing the Condition of the Ball

Any member of the fielding side may polish the ball provided that such polishing wastes no time and that no artificial substance is used. No-one shall rub the ball on the ground or use any artificial substance or take any other action to alter the condition of the ball.

In the event of a contravention of this Law, the umpires, after consultation, shall change the ball for one of similar condition to that in use prior to the contravention.

This Law does not prevent a member of the fielding side from drying a wet ball, or removing mud from the ball. See Note (b).

## 6. Incommoding the Striker

An umpire is justified in intervening under this Law and shall call and signal "dead ball" if, in his opinion, any player of the fielding side incommodes the striker by any noise or action while he is receiving the ball.

## 7. Obstruction of a Batsman in Running

It shall be considered unfair if any fieldsman wilfully obstructs a batsman in running. In these circumstances the umpire shall call and signal "dead ball" and allow any completed runs and the run in progress, or alternatively any boundary scored.

## 8. The Bowling of Fast Short-pitched Balls

The bowling of fast short-pitched balls is unfair if, in the opinion of the umpire at the bowler's end, it constitutes an attempt to intimidate the striker. See Note (d).

Umpires shall consider intimidation to be the deliberate bowling of fast short-pitched balls which by their length, height and direction are intended or likely to inflict physical injury on the striker. The relative skill of the striker shall also be taken into consideration.

In the event of such unfair bowling, the umpire at the bowler's end shall adopt the following procedure:

(a) In the first instance the umpire shall call and signal "no-ball", caution the bowler and inform the other umpire, the captain of the fielding side and the batsmen of what has occurred.

(b) If this caution is ineffective, he shall repeat the above procedure and indicate to the bowler that this is a final warning.

(c) Both the above caution and final warning shall continue to apply even though the bowler may later change ends.

(d) Should the above warnings prove ineffective the umpire at the bowler's end shall:

- (i) At the first repetition call and signal "no-ball" and when the ball is dead direct the captain to take the bowler off forthwith and to complete the over with another bowler, provided that the bowler does not bowl two overs or part thereof consecutively. See Law 22.7 (Bowler Incapacitated or Suspended during an Over).
- (ii) Not allow the bowler, thus taken off, to bowl again in the same innings.
- (iii) Report the occurrence to the captain of the batting side as soon as the players leave the field for an interval.
- (iv) Report the occurrence to the executive of the fielding side and to any governing body responsible for the match, who shall take any further action which is considered to be appropriate against the bowler concerned.

## 9. The Bowling of Fast High Full Pitches

The bowling of fast high full pitches is unfair. See Note (e).

In the event of such unfair bowling the umpire at the bowler's end shall adopt the procedures of caution, final warnings, action against the bowler and reporting as set out in 8 above.

## 10. Time Wasting

Any form of time wasting is unfair.

(a) In the event of the captain of the fielding side wasting time or allowing any member of his side to waste time, the umpire at the bowler's end shall adopt the following procedure:

(i) In the first instance he shall caution the captain of the fielding side and inform the other umpire of what has occurred.

(ii) If this caution is ineffective he shall repeat the above procedure and indicate to the captain that this is a final warning.

(iii) The umpire shall report the occurrence to the captain of the batting side as soon as the players leave the field for an interval.

(iv) Should the above procedure prove ineffective the umpire shall report the occurrence to the executive of the fielding side and to any governing body responsible for that match, who shall take appropriate action against the captain and the players concerned.

(b) In the event of a bowler taking unnecessarily long to bowl an over the umpire at the bowler's end shall adopt the procedures, other than the calling of "no-ball", of caution, final warning, action against the bowler and reporting.

(c) In the event of a batsman wasting time (See Note (f)) other than in the manner described in Law 31 (Timed Out), the umpire at the bowler's end shall adopt the following procedure:

(i) In the first instance he shall caution the batsman and inform the other umpire at once, and the captain of the batting side, as soon as the players leave the field for an interval, of what has occurred.

(ii) If this proves ineffective, he shall repeat the caution, indicate to the batsman that this is a final warning and inform the other umpire.

(iii) The umpire shall report the occurrence to both captains as soon as the players leave the field for an interval.

(iv) Should the above procedure prove ineffective, the umpire shall report the occurrence to the executive of the batting side and to any governing body responsible for that match, who shall take appropriate action against the player concerned.

## 11. Players Damaging the Pitch

The umpires shall intervene and prevent players from causing damage to the pitch which may assist the bowlers of either side. See Note (c).

(a) In the event of any member of the fielding side damaging the pitch, the umpire shall follow the procedure of caution, final warning, and reporting as set out in 10(a) above.

(b) In the event of a bowler contravening this Law by running down the pitch after delivering the ball, the umpire at the bowler's end shall first caution the bowler. If this caution is ineffective the umpire shall adopt the procedures, as set out in 8 above other than the calling and signalling of "no-ball".

(c) In the event of a batsman damaging the pitch the umpire at the bowler's end shall follow the procedures of caution, final warning and reporting as set out in 10(c) above.

## 12. Batsman Unfairly Stealing a Run

Any attempt by the batsman to steal a run during the bowler's run-up is unfair. Unless the bowler attempts to run out either batsman – see Law 24.4 (Bowler Throwing at Striker's Wicket before Delivery) and Law 24.5 (Bowler Attempting to Run Out Non-striker before Delivery) – the umpire shall call and signal "dead ball" as soon as the batsmen cross in any such attempt to run. The batsmen shall then return to their original wickets.

## 13. Player's Conduct

In the event of a player failing to comply with the instructions of an umpire, criticising his decisions by word or action, or showing dissent, or generally behaving in a manner which might bring the game into disrepute, the umpire concerned shall, in the first place, report the matter to the other umpire and to the player's captain requesting the latter to take action. If this proves ineffective, the umpire shall report the incident as soon as possible to the executive of the player's team and to any governing body responsible for the match, who shall take any further action which is considered appropriate against the player or players concerned.

*Notes*

**(a) The Condition of the Ball**
Umpires shall make frequent and irregular inspections of the condition of the ball.

**(b) Drying of a Wet Ball**
A wet ball may be dried on a towel or with sawdust.

**(c) Danger Area**
The danger area on the pitch, which must be protected from damage by a bowler, shall be regarded by the umpires as the area contained by an imaginary line 4 feet/1.22m from the popping crease, and parallel to it, and within two imaginary and parallel lines drawn down the pitch from points on that line 1 foot/30.48cm on either side of the middle stump.

**(d) Fast Short-pitched Balls**
As a guide, a fast short-pitched ball is one which pitches short and passes, or would have passed, above the shoulder height of the striker standing in a normal batting stance at the crease.

**(e) The Bowling of Fast Full Pitches**
The bowling of one fast, high full pitch shall be considered to be unfair if, in the opinion of the umpire, it is deliberate, bowled at the striker, and if it passes or would have passed above the shoulder height of the striker when standing in a normal batting stance at the crease.

**(f) Time Wasting by Batsmen**
Other than in exceptional circumstances, the batsman should always be ready to take strike when the bowler is ready to start his run-up.

## INTERNATIONAL CRICKET CONFERENCE

On June 15, 1909, representatives of cricket in England, Australia and South Africa met at Lord's and founded the Imperial Cricket Conference. Membership was confined to the governing bodies of cricket in countries within the British Commonwealth where Test cricket was played. India, New Zealand and West Indies were elected as members on May 31, 1926, Pakistan on July 21, 1953, and Sri Lanka on July 21, 1981. South Africa ceased to be a member of the ICC on leaving the British Commonwealth in May, 1961.

On July 15, 1965, the Conference was renamed the International Cricket Conference and new rules were adopted to permit the election of countries from outside the British Commonwealth.

## CONSTITUTION

**Chairman:** The President of MCC for the time being or his nominee.
**Secretary:** The Secretary of MCC.
**Foundation members:** United Kingdom and Australia.
**Full members:** India, New Zealand, West Indies, Pakistan and Sri Lanka.
**Associate members*:** Argentina (1974), Bangladesh (1977), Bermuda (1966), Canada (1968), Denmark (1966), East Africa (1966), Fiji (1965), Gibraltar (1969), Hong Kong (1969), Israel (1974), Kenya (1981), Malaysia (1967), Netherlands (1966), Papua New Guinea (1973), Singapore (1974), USA (1965), West Africa (1976) and Zimbabwe (1981).
**Affiliate members*:** Italy (1984), Switzerland (1985).

* *Year of election shown in parentheses.*

## MEMBERSHIP

The following governing bodies for cricket shall be eligible for election.

**Foundation Members:** The governing bodies for cricket in the United Kingdom and Australia are known as Foundation Members, and while being Full Members of the Conference such governing bodies have certain additional rights as set out in the rules of the Conference.

**Full Members:** The governing body for cricket recognised by the Conference of a country, or countries associated for cricket purposes, of which the representative teams are accepted as qualified to play official Test matches.

**Associate Members:** The governing body for cricket recognised by the Conference of a country, or countries associated for cricket purposes, not qualifying as Full Members but where cricket is firmly established and organised.

*Chairman:* P. A. Snow (Fiji). *Deputy Chairman:* J. Buzaglo (Gibraltar). *Hon. Treasurer:* G. Davis (Israel).

## TEST MATCHES

### 1. Duration of Test Matches

Within a maximum of 30 hours' playing time, the duration of Test matches shall be a matter for negotiation and agreement between the two countries in any particular series of Test matches.

When agreeing the Playing Conditions prior to the commencement of a Test series, the participating countries may:

(a) Extend the playing hours of the last Test beyond the limit of 30 hours, in a series in which, at the conclusion of the penultimate match, one side does not hold a lead of more than one match.

(b) Allow an extension of play by one hour on any of the first four days of a Test match, in the event of play being suspended for one hour or more on that day, owing to weather interference.

(c) Play on the rest day, conditions and circumstances permitting, should a full day's play be lost on either the second or third scheduled days of play.

(d) Make up time lost in excess of five minutes in each day's play owing to circumstances outside the game, other than acts of God.

*Note.* The umpires shall determine when such time shall be made up. This could, if conditions and circumstances permit, include the following day.

### 2. Qualification Rules

A cricketer is qualified to play in a Test match either by birth or residence.

(a) Qualification by birth. A cricketer, unless debarred by the Conference, is always eligible to play for the country of his birth.

(b) Qualification by residence. A cricketer, unless debarred by the Conference, shall be eligible to play for any country in which he is residing and has been residing during the four immediately preceding years, provided that he has not played for the country of his birth during that period.

*Note.* Notwithstanding anything hereinbefore contained, any player who has once played in a Test match for any country shall not afterwards be eligible to play in a Test match against that country, without the consent of its governing body.

## FIRST-CLASS MATCHES

### 1. Definitions

(a) A match of three or more days' duration between two sides of eleven players officially adjudged first-class shall be regarded as a first-class fixture.

(b) In the following Rules the term "governing body" is restricted to Foundation Members, Full Members and Associate Members of the conference.

## 2. Rules

(a) Foundation and Full Members of the ICC shall decide the status of matches of three or more days' duration played in their countries.

(b) In matches of three or more days' duration played in countries which are not Foundation Members or Full Members of the ICC:

- (i) If the visiting team comes from a country which is a Foundation or Full Member of the ICC, that country shall decide the status of matches.
- (ii) If the visiting team does not come from a country which is a Foundation or Full Member of the ICC, or is a Commonwealth team composed of players from different countries, the ICC shall decide the status of matches.

*Notes*

(a) Governing bodies agree that the interest of first-class cricket will be served by ensuring that first-class status is *not* accorded to any match in which one or other of the teams taking part cannot on a strict interpretation of the definition be adjudged first-class.

(b) In case of any disputes arising from these Rules, the Secretary of the ICC shall refer the matter for decision to the Conference, failing unanimous agreement by postal communication being reached.

## 3. First-class Status

The following matches shall be regarded as first-class, subject to the provisions of Definitions (a) being completely complied with:

(a) In the British Isles and Eire
The following matches of three or more days' duration shall automatically be considered first-class:

- (i) County Championship matches.
- (ii) Official representative tourist matches from Full Member countries unless specifically excluded.
- (iii) MCC v any first-class county.
- (iv) Oxford v Cambridge and either University against first-class counties.
- (v) Scotland v Ireland.

(b) In Australia

- (i) Sheffield Shield matches.
- (ii) Matches played by teams representing states of the Commonwealth of Australia between each other or against opponents adjudged first-class.

(c) In India

- (i) Ranji Trophy matches.
- (ii) Duleep Trophy matches.
- (iii) Irani Trophy matches.
- (iv) Matches played by teams representing state or regional associations affiliated to the Board of Control between each other or against opponents adjudged first-class.
- (v) All three-day matches played against representative visiting sides.

(d) In New Zealand

- (i) Shell Trophy matches.
- (ii) Matches played by teams representing major associations of the North and South Islands against opponents adjudged first-class.

(e) In Pakistan

- (i) Matches played by teams representing divisional associations affiliated to the Board of Control, between each other or against teams adjudged first-class.
- (ii) Matches between the divisional associations and the Universities past and present XI.
- (iii) Quaid-e-Azam Trophy matches.

(iv) BCCP Trophy Tournament matches.
(v) Pentangular Trophy Tournament matches.

(f) In Sri Lanka

(i) Matches of three days or more against touring sides adjudged first-class.
At the time of going to press details of domestic competitions with first-class status were not available.

(g) In West Indies

(i) Matches played by teams representing Barbados, Guyana, Jamaica, Trinidad, the Windward Islands and the Leeward Islands, either for the Shell Shield or against other opponents adjudged first-class.
(ii) The final of the inter-county tournament for the Jones Cup in Guyana between Berbice, Demerara and Essequibo.
(iii) The Beaumont Cup match in Trinidad & Tobago.

(h) In all Foundation (including South Africa) and Full Member countries represented on the Conference

(i) Test matches and matches against teams adjudged first-class played by official touring teams.
(ii) Official Test Trial matches.
(iii) Special matches between teams adjudged first-class by the governing body or bodies concerned.

# MAIN RULES AND PLAYING CONDITIONS OF LIMITED-OVERS COMPETITIONS

The following rules, playing conditions and variations of the Laws of Cricket are common to all three county competitions – the Benson and Hedges Cup (55 overs a side), the NatWest Bank Trophy (60 overs) and the John Player League (40 overs):

*Status of Matches*

Matches shall not be considered first-class.

*Declarations*

No declarations may be made at any time.

*Restriction on Placement of Fieldsmen*

At the instant of delivery a minimum of four fieldsmen (plus the bowler and wicket-keeper) must be within an area bounded by two semi-circles centred on each middle stump (each with a radius of 30 yards) and joined by a parallel line on each side of the pitch. In the event of an infringement, the square-leg umpire shall call "No-ball". The fielding circle should be marked by painted white "dots" at five-yard intervals.

*Fieldsman Leaving the Field*

In addition to Law 2.8, a player who suffers an injury caused by an external blow (e.g. not a pulled muscle) and has to leave the field for medical attention may bowl immediately on his return.

*Mode of Delivery*

No bowler may deliver the ball under-arm.

*Limitation of Overs by Any One Bowler*

No bowler may deliver more than one fifth of the allocated overs.

*Wide-ball – Judging a Wide*

Umpires are instructed to apply a very strict and consistent interpretation in regard to the Law in order to prevent negative bowling wide of the wicket or over the batsman's head.

The following criteria should be adopted as a guide to umpires:

1. If the ball passes either side of the wicket sufficiently wide to make it virtually impossible for the striker to play a "normal cricket stroke" both from where he is standing and from where he should normally be standing at the crease, the umpire shall call and signal "Wide".

2. If the ball passes over head-height of the striker standing upright at the crease, the umpire shall call and signal "Wide".

*Note*: The above provisions do not apply if the striker makes contact with the ball.

## RULES COMMON TO THE BENSON AND HEDGES CUP AND THE NATWEST BANK TROPHY

*The Result*

1. *A Tie.*

In the event of a tie, the following shall apply:

(i) The side taking the greater number of wickets shall be the winner.

(ii) If both sides are all out, the side with the higher overall scoring-rate shall be the winner.

(iii) If the result cannot be decided by either of the first two methods, the winner shall be the side with the higher rate after 30 overs or, if still equal, after twenty or, if still equal, after ten.

2. *Unfinished Match*

If a match remains unfinished after the allocated number of days, the winner shall be the side which has scored the faster in runs per over throughout the innings, provided that at least twenty overs have been bowled at the side batting second. If the scoring-rate is the same, the side losing fewer wickets in the first twenty overs of each innings shall be the winner.

If, however, at any time on the last day the umpires are satisfied that there is insufficient time remaining to achieve a definite result or, where applicable, for the side batting second to complete its 60 overs, they shall order a new match to be started, allowing an equal number of overs per side (minimum ten overs per side) bearing in mind the time remaining for play until scheduled close of play. In this event, team selection for the new match will be restricted to the eleven players and twelfth man originally chosen, unless authorised otherwise in advance by the Secretary of the Board.

In the event of no result being obtained within this rule, and the captains being unable to reach agreement on an alternative method of achieving a result, other than re-arranging the match, it shall be decided by the toss of a coin, except in a Benson and Hedges zonal match which shall be declared to have "No Result".

## RULES AND PLAYING CONDITIONS APPLYING ONLY TO THE BENSON AND HEDGES CUP

*Duration of Play*

The matches, of 55 overs per side, will be completed in one day, if possible, but two days will be allocated for zonal league matches and three days for knockout matches in case of weather interference. Matches started on Saturday but not completed may only be continued on Sunday with the approval of the Board.

Normal hours will be 11 a.m. to 7.30 p.m. (start at 2 p.m. on Sundays). The umpires may order extra time if they consider a finish can be obtained on any day, or in order to give the team batting second an opportunity to complete twenty overs.

*Intervals*

Lunch 1.15-1.55. The tea interval in an uninterrupted match will be taken at 4.30 or after 25 overs of the innings of the side batting second, whichever is the later. In a match which has had a delayed start or which is unlikely to be finished in a day, the tea interval will be at 4.30.

*Qualification of Players*

The University qualification will take precedence in respect of those players who are also qualified for county clubs and no cricketer may play for more than one team in the same year's competition.

*Scoring System*

In the zonal league matches the winning team scores two points. In a "no result" match each side scores one point.

If two or more teams in any zone finish with an equal number of points, their position in the table shall be based on the faster rate of taking wickets in all zonal league matches. This is calculated by total balls bowled, divided by wickets taken.

## RULES AND PLAYING CONDITIONS APPLYING ONLY TO THE NATWEST BANK TROPHY

*Duration and hours of play*

The matches, of 60 overs per side, will be completed in one day, if possible, but three days (four days, if Sunday play is scheduled) will be allocated in case of weather interference.

Cup Final only: If the match starts not less than half an hour late, owing to weather or the state of the ground, and not more than one and a half hours late, each innings shall be limited to 50 overs. If, however, the start is delayed for more than one and a half hours, the 60-over limit shall apply.

Normal hours will be 10.30-7.30. The umpires may order extra time if, in their opinion, a finish can be obtained on any day or in order to give the team batting second an opportunity to complete twenty overs.

The captains of the teams in the final shall be warned that heavy shadows may move across the pitch towards the end of the day and that no appeal against the light will be considered in such circumstances.

## RULES AND PLAYING CONDITIONS APPLYING ONLY TO THE JOHN PLAYER LEAGUE

*Hours of play*

All matches shall commence at 2 p.m. with a tea interval of fifteen minutes at the end of the over in progress at 4.15, or between innings, whichever is the earlier. The duration and time of the tea interval can be varied in the case of an interrupted match. Close of play shall normally be at 6.45 p.m. but play may continue after that time if, in the opinion of the umpires, the overs remaining can be completed by 7 p.m.

*Length of Innings*

(i) In an uninterrupted match:

(a) Each side shall bat for 40 overs unless all out earlier.

(b) If the side fielding first fails to bowl 40 overs by 4.15 p.m., the over shall be completed and the side batting second shall receive the same number of overs as their opponents.

(c) If the team batting first is all out within two minutes of the scheduled time for the tea interval, the innings of the side batting second shall be limited to the same number of overs as their opponents have received, the over in which the last wicket falls to count as a complete over.

(ii) In matches where the start is delayed or play is suspended:

(a) The object shall be to rearrange the number of overs so that both teams may receive the same number of overs (minimum ten each). The calculation of the overs to be bowled shall be based on an average rate of eighteen overs per hour (one over per $3\frac{1}{3}$ minutes or part thereof) in the time remaining before 6.45 p.m.

(b) If the start is delayed by not more than an hour and the match is thereby reduced to no fewer than 31 overs a side, the time of the close of the first innings shall be fixed allowing $3\frac{1}{3}$ minutes for each over.

(c) Where play is suspended after the match has started on the basis of each team batting for more than twenty overs, the number of overs should be rearranged so that both teams may bat for the same number of overs (minimum of 20 each); the calculation as above.

(d) If, owing to a suspension of play during the innings of the team batting second, it is not possible for that team to have the opportunity of batting for the same number of overs (minimum 20 overs) as their opponents, they will bat for a number of overs to be calculated as above. The team batting second shall not bat for a greater number of overs than their opponents unless the latter have been all out in fewer than the agreed number of overs.

(e) If there is insufficient time to provide for a match as above (20 overs minimum), that match shall be void and, conditions permitting, a new match of ten overs each side shall be played provided play begins no later than 5.30 p.m. If there is any suspension of play during the ten-overs match, it will be abandoned as a "No result".

*The Result*

(i) Where both sides have had the opportunity to bat for the same number of overs and the scores are level, the result is a tie, no account being taken of the number of wickets which have fallen.

(ii) If, owing to suspension of play, the number of overs in the innings of the side batting second has to be revised, their target score, which they must exceed to win the match, shall be calculated by multiplying the revised number of overs by the average runs per over scored by the side batting first. If the target score involves a fraction, the final scores cannot be equal and the result cannot be a tie.

(iii) If a match is abandoned before the side batting second has received its allotted number of overs, the result shall be decided on the average run-rate throughout both innings, provided the team batting second has received not less than twenty overs.

(iv) If a result cannot be achieved as above, the match shall be declared "No result".

(v) If the team batting first has been all out without using its full quota of overs, the calculation of the run-rate shall be based on the full quota of overs to which it was entitled.

*Scoring of points*

(i) The team winning a match to score four points.

(ii) In a "tie" each team to score two points.

(iii) In a "No Result" match each team to score two points.

(iv) If two or more teams finish with an equal number of points for any of the first four places, their final positions will be decided by:

(a) The most wins or, if still equal

(b) The most away wins or, if still equal

(c) The higher run-rate throughout the season.

# UMPIRES FOR 1986

## TEST MATCH UMPIRES

J. Birkenshaw, who played for Yorkshire, Leicestershire and Worcestershire between 1958 and 1981 and won five England caps, joins the panel of Test umpires for 1986. He replaces D. G. L. Evans, who was taken ill during the 1985 season, shortly after standing in the Lord's Test match, and underwent heart surgery in September. Evans retains his place on the first-class county list. The full Test panel is: H. D. Bird, J. Birkenshaw, D. J. Constant, K. E. Palmer, D. R. Shepherd, B. J. Meyer and A. G. T. Whitehead.

They will be reinforced by N. T. Plews, a former policeman, for the two Texaco Trophy series.

## FIRST-CLASS UMPIRES

For the first time for some years the overall first-class list shows no changes. Among the five reserves appointed are three former England players – M. Hendrick, D. Lloyd and H. J. Rhodes. The full list is: H. D. Bird, J. Birkenshaw, D. J. Constant, C. Cook, B. Dudleston, D. G. L. Evans, J. H. Hampshire, J. H. Harris, J. W. Holder, J. A. Jameson, A. A. Jones, R. Julian, M. J. Kitchen, B. Leadbeater, K. J. Lyons, B. J. Meyer, D. O. Oslear, K. E. Palmer, R. Palmer, N. T. Plews, D. R. Shepherd, R. A. White, A. G. T. Whitehead and P. B. Wight. *Reserves:* M. J. Harris, M. Hendrick, D. Lloyd, H. J. Rhodes and D. S. Thompsett.

## MINOR COUNTIES UMPIRES

N. P. Atkins, F. Bingley, K. Bray, C. J. Chapman, Dr D. Fawkner-Corbett, D. J. Dennis, R. H. Duckett, D. J. A. Edwards, P. J. Eele, W. H. Gillingham, D. J. Halfyard, D. B. Harrison, B. Knight, S. Levison, T. Lynan, G. I. McLean, T. G. A. Morley, D. Norton, M. K. Reed, K. S. Shenton, C. Smith, C. T. Spencer, G. A. Stickley, D. S. Thompsett, J. van Geloven, T. V. Wilkins, R. T. Wilson, T. G. Wilson. *Reserves:* H. J. Arnold, F. Elmore, R. G. Evans, S. T. Lamb, D. R. O'Neill, J. B. Seward, J. Stobart, A. R. Tayler, R. C. Tolchard, R. Walker, J. Wilson.

---

# HONOURS' LIST

In 1985, the following were decorated for services to cricket:

*New Year's Honours:* K. W. R. Fletcher (England) OBE; J. Garner (West Indies) MBE; C. G. Greenidge (West Indies) MBE; B. Sutcliffe (New Zealand) MBE.

*Queen's Birthday Honours:* A. M. E. Roberts (West Indies) CBE; D. B. Carr (England) OBE; T. M. Findlay (West Indies) MBE.

---

# SILK CUT CHALLENGE, 1985

The 1985 Silk Cut Challenge, a single-wicket competition played at Arundel on September 20 and 21, was won, like the inaugural event in 1984, by the South African, C. E. B. Rice. The runner-up was Imran Khan. Rice, who won £7,000, lost his wicket on neither day. The other challengers were R. J. Hadlee (third), I. V. A. Richards (fourth), I. T. Botham (fifth), S. P. O'Donnell (sixth) and G. A. Gooch (seventh).

# MEETINGS IN 1985

## TCCB SPRING MEETING

The Spring Meeting of the TCCB was held at Lord's on March 7, when the subject of over-rates and concern over off-the-field behaviour predominated. The Board's Executive Committee were to be asked to look in depth at such matters as hooliganism on county grounds with a view to limiting licensing hours at Sunday matches. They would also be considering the possibility of random drug tests in county cricket. There was a general wish to support the Sports Council in its campaign against drug-taking, though it was not thought to be a problem within the game. Although it had been hoped to reach an agreement with Australia that a minimum of 96 overs should be bowled in a day's play in the forthcoming Test matches, a figure of 90 seemed more likely. For the first time fines for falling behind the over-rate would be imposed in the one-day knockout competitions. These would be based on a minimum requirement of sixteen overs an hour. Fines were also to be restored for slow over-rates in the Britannic Assurance County Championship, the season to be divided into two halves for the purposes of assessment. In a ballot to elect the England selectors the existing committee of P. B. H. May (chairman), A. V. Bedser, P. J. Sharpe and A. C. Smith was reappointed, the unsuccessful candidates being R. Booth (Worcestershire) and F. J. Titmus (Middlesex). It was announced that an England B team would be selected to visit Sri Lanka, Zimbabwe and possibly Bangladesh early in 1986.

## TCCB EXECUTIVE COMMITTEE

The Executive Committee of the TCCB, meeting at Lord's on March 14, recommended that no action should be taken against I. T. Botham following his conviction in February of possessing 2.19 grammes of cannabis. The Board warned that in future any player involved in drug offences would be subject to harsh penalties. The TCCB had already agreed to support the Sports Council in its campaign against drug-taking.

## TCCB SPECIAL MEETING

At a Special Meeting of the full board of the TCCB, held at Lord's on June 6, changes were agreed in the disciplinary regulations which could result in the suspension of eligibility for selection for England of any registered player who is found guilty of using or possessing illegal drugs. A list of permitted medicines and banned substances had been drawn up and agreed, following consultation between the medical advisors of the TCCB and the Sports Council and with the co-operation of the Cricketers' Association. The choice of fixtures in which random dope tests might be carried out would be decided by the TCCB, with the technical analysis being conducted by the Drugs Control and Teaching Centre at Chelsea College.

## INTERNATIONAL CRICKET CONFERENCE

At its Annual Meeting, held at Lord's on July 17 and 18, the majority of members of the International Cricket Conference agreed that in the best interests of the game at Test match level, play should be based on a minimum of overs, and that the number of overs should be based on fifteen an hour as a minimum requirement. Countries agreed to keep a vigilant eye on umpiring standards, England indicating that in conjunction with a team of scientists they were working on the possibility of electronic aids being introduced to assist umpires, but that this was still very much at the experimental stage. The member countries agreed to a new interpretation for recording maiden overs. If any runs were registered against a bowler, whether or not off the bat, this would mean that a maiden over could not be recorded.

An itinerary for the 1987 World Cup in India and Pakistan was agreed, with the competition to be played between October 6 and November 10, 1987. The draw for the competition was confirmed, with India, Australia, New Zealand and the qualifying associate member to constitute Group A, and Pakistan, West Indies, Sri Lanka and England Group B. It was agreed that each full member country should supply at least one umpire and that India and Pakistan should each supply two. Any additional umpires should come from England. The Conference also gave its support for MCC's Bicentenary plans in 1987. Australia advised that they would be celebrating the America's Cup, an international yachting event, in Perth in January 1987 with a quadrangular tournament, and their Bicentenary in 1988 with a match between England and Australia.

Australia also agreed to produce a new draft law for consideration at the 1986 Conference, relating to the bowling of fast short-pitched balls – Law 42 (8). In the meantime, all countries agreed to instruct umpires to take a strong line on short-pitched fast bowling. A draft paper submitted by England was approved in principle by the Conference, updating existing conditions on commercial advertising. Consultations would be taking place with manufacturers with a view to approving a final policy in 1986.

Switzerland were elected to Affiliate Membership of the Conference.

## TCCB WINTER MEETING

At its Winter Meeting, held at Lord's on December 12, the TCCB introduced a system of instant fines, to be imposed in the event of misconduct by England players during home Test matches. The extent of any fine, up to a maximum of £500, would be decided by the Chairman of Selectors (or his nominee) and the captain, and the player would have the right of appeal. In 1986 India and New Zealand would be asked to agree to a minimum of 96 overs a day in the Test matches. Any time, up to an hour, lost to bad weather could be made up on the day, though play would have to end by 7.00 p.m. In the Britannic Assurance County Championship the minimum number of overs to be bowled in a day, which was 117 in 1984 and 112 in 1985, was further reduced to 110 (based on an average of seventeen an hour), this figure to remain unchanged for two years. The clause stating that "the risk of physical injury to batsmen" must be taken into account by umpires when ruling on the fitness of the light for play, which had been introduced in 1985, was to be removed at the request of the umpires. John Player Sunday League matches would revert to a 2.00 p.m. start except for the televised match or matches, which would continue to start at 1.30 p.m.

With counties continuing to look for loopholes in the rules of qualification, it was decided that residents of member countries of the European Economic Community would no longer be entitled to direct entry into county cricket without satisfying the requirements of the Registration Regulations as they apply to the qualifications for playing for England.

In future, Benson and Hedges Cup and NatWest Bank Trophy matches, in which no play had been possible because of the weather, would be decided not on the toss of a coin but by a competition between the sides based on bowling at pitched stumps. It was said that consideration was being given to the feasibility of universities besides Oxford and Cambridge making up the Combined Universities side in the Benson and Hedges Cup, as from 1987. The findings of the Working Party, set up at the end of 1984 to consider the general state of the English game, were expected to be made known early in 1986.

## I ZINGARI RESULTS, 1985

*Matches – 26: Won 5, Lost 1, Tied 1, Drawn 16, Abandoned 3.*

| | | |
|---|---|---|
| May 4 | Charterhouse School | Drawn |
| May 11 | Honourable Artillery Company | Drawn |
| May 12 | Sandhurst Wanderers | Won by 96 runs |
| May 19 | Staff College, Camberley | Won by 228 runs |
| May 25 | Eton Ramblers | Drawn |
| June 8 | Hurlingham CC | Abandoned |
| June 9 | Lord Porchester's XI | Abandoned |
| June 15 | Eton College | Drawn |
| June 18 | Winchester College | Lost by five wickets |
| June 22 | Guards CC | Drawn |
| June 23 | Lavinia, Duchess of Norfolk's XI | Drawn |
| June 29 | Harrow School | Tied |
| July 6 | Earl of Bessborough's XI | Drawn |
| July 7 | Hagley CC | Drawn |
| July 13 | Green Jackets Club (Centenary match) | Drawn |
| July 14 | Captain R. H. Hawkins's XI | Won by two wickets |
| July 20 | Bradfield Waifs | Won by six wickets |
| July 20 | Leicestershire Gentlemen | Drawn |
| July 21 | Sir John Starkey's XI | Drawn |
| July 28 | Royal Armoured Corps | Drawn |
| August 3 | Band of Brothers | Drawn |
| August 4 | R. Leigh-Pemberton's XI | Abandoned |
| August 10, 11 | South Wales Hunts XI | Drawn |
| August 18 | J. H. Pawle's XI | Won by six wickets |
| August 31 | Hampshire Hogs | Drawn |
| September 8 | Rickling Green CC | Drawn |

---

## INTER-SERVICES TOURNAMENT

### ROYAL NAVY v ARMY

At Aldershot, August 12. Army won by 4 runs. Army 124 for eight (35 overs) (CPO K. Brooks three for 33); Royal Navy 120 for eight (35 overs) (Capt. C. W. P. Hobson 39 not out).

### ROYAL NAVY v ROYAL AIR FORCE

At Aldershot, August 13. Royal Air Force won by 16 runs. Royal Air Force 92 (43.2 overs) (SAC J. Doherty 49; CPO K. Brooks four for 19, MEM A. Chester three for 19); Royal Navy 76 (48 overs) (Lt D. Wells 38; Flt Lt A. Spiller five for 17, SAC M. Ings four for 12).

### ARMY v ROYAL AIR FORCE

At Aldershot, August 14. Army won by 88 runs. Army 149 for seven (40 overs) (Capt. B. W. P. Bennett 69; Flt Lt A. Lamond four for 28); Royal Air Force 61 (32.5 overs) (Cpl S. C. Durston four for 6, Cpl A. Taylor four for 16).

# CRICKET BOOKS, 1985

By JOHN ARLOTT

Nearly 100 books and periodicals have been sent for inclusion in this notice. There are included some quite authoritative works, several original and illuminating titles, and some diverting pieces of writing.

In several ways the most important is *The Collins Who's Who of English First-Class Cricket 1945-1984* (Collins Willow; £25) by Robert Brooke, a founder of the Association of Cricket Statisticians. It includes everyone who played so much as a single match in that period; and, where they played in earlier years, gives their entire career records. Two further volumes will cover the scene back to 1744. The important, indeed, the essential quality of this book is that, so far as can be ascertained, it is *accurate*. Mr Brooke, as John Woodcock, editor of *Wisden*, points out in his Foreword, is no longer to be counted among those statisticians "whose obsession has as much to do with dogmatism as accuracy". That is the issue which separates this book from the ambitious volume which appeared a year earlier: and which contained crucial statistical inaccuracies apparent even to readers not overly concerned with statistics; and which, on subsequent consideration, prompted anxiety as to how many other items of dogmatic alteration in the accepted records of the game may have been made in it. This new volume demands respectful attention. It contains little more information than the previous work but it does include best performances; and the career statistics are well laid out.

*The Wisden Book of Test Cricket* (Macdonald/Queen Anne Press; £29.50), compiled and edited by Bill Frindall, contains full scores, bowling analyses, falls of wickets and notes on outstanding achievements in the 994 Test matches played down to August 28, 1984, plus details of the three abandoned and one cancelled in that period. That shows an addition of 70 since the earlier edition which ended at May 1978. There are appendices to cover a summary of results; details of the 58 grounds on which Tests have been played; players' career records, register and index. It is thus as thorough a reference as could be hoped within the covers of a single volume; it remains to be seen how long that physical containment remains conveniently possible.

We all plunge further into the debt of Margaret Hughes. Here, now, is a sixth posthumous Cardus title – *Cardus For All Seasons* (Souvenir Press; £8.95) edited by Sir Neville's faithful literary executor. These 45 essays from 1920 to 1969 come from a variety of sources – *The Guardian*, *The Nation*, *Illustrated Sporting and Dramatic News*, *The Field*, and *World Sports*. Wherever and whenever Neville Cardus wrote, he wrote at his best; he had style, the gift of delineating character, of the anecdote, of communicating both interest and pleasure, and, all through his career, there was a felicity about his work not excelled by any other cricket writer; nor, indeed, any other writer on sport; in fact by very few in other fields. He enjoyed himself with such ideas as this, of 1934 – a new one, to most, surely – "Colonel Watson, who used to hit the first ball he received, cry, 'Come three!' and get caught at the wicket racing for the fourth run." This is another delight; and now we await more. Or is that too much to ask?

*1000 Tests* (Strata Publications, 81 Christie Street, St Leonards, NSW, 2065, Australia; \$A5.95: £2.99), by Kersi Meher-Homji, a research scientist, is a generously colour-illustrated 80-page quarto issued to mark the occasion of the 1,000th Test match which – delayed by Mrs Gandhi's assassination – proved to be that between Pakistan and New Zealand at Hyderabad which began on November 25, 1984. It is a pleasantly entertaining souvenir-type publication with a foreword by Sunil Gavaskar.

*An Index to Wisden Cricketers' Almanack 1864-1984* (Macdonald/Queen Anne Press; £17.50), compiled by Derek Barnard, is of course larger – by 645 pages to 101 – than the Pogson volume (1864-1943), though less concentrated (single as against double-column and more widely spaced). It does, however, offer a valuable guide – for those professionally or studiously interested – to the major work of cricket reference.

Similarly, *The Dictionary of Cricket* (Allen & Unwin; £12.95), by Michael Rundell, succeeds W. J. Lewis's *The Language of Cricket* (OUP, 1934). Mr Rundell is an experienced dictionary editor and he has worked on up-to-date references. The scholar of the subject, however, will want both his book and the Lewis.

*Next Man In* (Pelham; £9.95) – subtitled "A Survey of Cricket Laws and Customs" – by Gerald Brodribb is a substantially rewritten version of the original edition of 1952. Compiled by one of the game's most patient and conscientious archivists, it is a most valuable work of historic reference. Nothing else quite like it exists, and thus it becomes another of the game's essential works.

Despite its title, *'Ave a Go Yer Mug* (Collins; $A14.95), by Richard Cashman, is an unusually scholarly work of social and cricket history. Mr Cashman is a cricket enthusiast, player and student; most significantly, however, he holds MA and PhD degrees from American universities and is a senior lecturer in history at the University of New South Wales. Here, he has written a study of Australian cricket crowds; their development – if that is the word – from the first inter-colonial larrikins to the "ockers" and super-hype of the 1980s. He writes shrewdly, informedly and penetratively, not without humour, readably and, above all, accurately. The illustrations and the quotations illuminate. This must, surely, become the classic work on its socially not inconsiderable subject.

Another well-observed and argued study is *Is it Cricket?* (Queen Anne Press; £8.95), by Michael Down, which is subtitled "Power, Money and Politics in Cricket since 1945". It can hardly fail to disturb the idealistic and peaceful thinking of those who have retained the feelings and nostalgias of which those of 1947 probably are the most euphoric of all. Mr Down is an Englishman who now lives and works in Pittsburgh. His biography of Archie MacLaren was a traditional cricket biography; this, though, looks on beyond those "carefree days" to a recognition that "the Americanization of the game is well in hand". It is a perceptive study which deserves attention and will certainly command the attention of everyone who even starts to read it; a salutary and clear piece of writing.

The name of Ken Kelly probably is not so familiar to cricket followers as his work, for he has been a major press photographer of the game since 1938, and a fierce enthusiast for it for even longer. His book *Cricket Reflections; Five Decades of Cricket Photographs* (David & Charles; £14.95) credits its text to David Lemmon but, clearly, he based it on Ken Kelly's memories and opinions. Fittingly it was a fellow Yorkshireman, Sir Leonard Hutton, who wrote the foreword. This is a highly expert survey, illustrated chiefly with Ken Kelly photographs, though, for the sake of historical perspective, he includes some far earlier work of others. Of his own photographs, most of the first were taken on one of the old, home-made, "Long Toms". For those taken since 1965 he has employed a new Japanese technique which he helped to pioneer in this country. He is characteristically generous about his fellow practitioners but this splendid, and often nostalgic, collection of cricket photographs is a fine example of the technique which has won him a number of awards.

*Double Century* (Collins Willow; £17.50), edited by Marcus Williams, is simply enough – though not a simple exercise – 200 years of cricket in *The*

*Times*. It is a huge, 621-page compilation. Its earliest entry, dated June 22, 1785, which in the old tradition was anonymous, concerns "the Lordling Cricketters who amuse themselves in White Conduit Fields"; the last, filed by John Woodcock, the paper's present cricket correspondent, in Madras on January 16, 1985, deals with England's score of 611 for five in the fourth Test against India. In between there is much distinguished writing; some describing historic cricketing events; some important obituaries, felicitous essays, and those fourth leaders which were such a joy. The roll of authors, too, is most impressive: Dudley Carew, Colin Cowdrey, R. H. Lyttelton, A. A. Thomson, P. G. H. Fender, P. F. Warner, Neville Cardus, R. C. Robertson-Glasgow, Sir Arthur Conan Doyle, Sir Donald Bradman, Alan Gibson . . . . Here, indeed, is a bedside book for the cricketer – but he will be wise not to hurry through it; it will take another two centuries to replace it.

A most unusual and attractive cricket book is *Cricket's Golden Summer* (Pavilion/Michael Joseph; £9.95) which consists of reproductions of some 40 paintings of eminent cricketers of the 1890-1914 period by Gerry Wright, accompanied by David Frith's commentary on them and their background. Mr Wright has established an extremely personal style; his cricketers are characters of their period, their stripes, badges and boater-bands are authentic, and he sets them in English gardens of the time. Mr Frith captures them in their true setting. It is all very pleasant.

*The Art of Nicholas Felix* (J. W. McKenzie, 12 Stoneleigh Park Road, Ewell, Epsom, Surrey, KT19 0QT; £16), by Gerald Brodribb, is published in a limited and signed edition of 220 copies. A 90-page octavo with six illustrations, it contains a brief life of "Felix" (Nicholas Wanostrocht; 1804-1876), observations on him as an artist, the most complete annotated catalogue ever – or ever likely to be – made of his paintings, drawings and engravings; a note on his writings and another on his relationship with G. F. Watts, who provided some (the best) of the lithographs for *Felix on the Bat* and the two quite outstanding studies of "The Batsman" (Fuller Pilch) and "The Bowler" (Alfred Mynn), both published by Wanostrocht. A most worthy piece of cricket scholarship.

*Ranji Trophy: Golden Years 1934-35 to 1983-84* (Board of Control for Cricket in India; no price given), by P. N. Sundaresan, was published to mark the golden jubilee of that competition. It is a 369-page octavo by the editor of the Board's Annual and a regular contributor to *Wisden*. It consists of essays on some 60 phases of the history of the Ranji Trophy with relevant statistics. A thorough review.

*100 Years at Southampton* (Hampshire County Cricket Club, Northlands Road, Southampton; £3, including cassette) is a 76-page quarto, both imaginatively and generously illustrated, and compiled – with an enthusiasm and driving power equal to that of his predecessor, Desmond Eagar – by the present captain, Mark Nicholas. It was devised to celebrate the centenary of the Hampshire headquarters and to raise funds for the club; it emerges as a pleasant read. With preface by the Duke of Edinburgh and introduction by the club's president, Cecil Paris, it has a range of contributors as varied as Sir Donald Bradman, E. W. Swanton, Dennis Lillee, Lloyd Budd, Tony Middleton, Colin Ingleby-Mackenzie, John Woodcock, Colin Cowdrey, Arthur Holt, Jim Bailey, Mike Brearley, Barry Richards, Jackie McGlew, Henry Blofeld, Tony Mitchener, "Lofty" Herman, Michael Parkinson, Dick Moore, Matthew Engel, Alan Lee, Brian Johnston, Jimmy Gray, Steve White, Ronny Aird, Brian Widlake, Richard Gilliat, Vic Isaacs, C. J. Knott; the county's admirable poetic voice, Imogen Grosberg, and photographs by Patrick Eagar.

*The Cricket Grounds of Worcestershire* (Association of Cricket Statisticians, Haughton Mill, Retford, Nottinghamshire) is the second in the Association's series planned to cover all the counties. It deals with all the ten grounds – not all actually or legally in Worcestershire – where the county has played first-class cricket; and has notes on the further nine which have housed Second XI fixtures. The full series will be a unique and worthwhile chronicle.

*Tilford Cricket Club 1885-1985* (obtainable from Colin Cooper, 19 Lavender Lane, Rowledge, Farnham, Surrey; £1.30), by Graham Collyer, is the history of the club that plays on the ground where "Silver Billy" Beldham himself played in the dim past. It is assumed that there was an earlier club, but of this one solid evidence of its centenary exists and it is contained here.

The 120th anniversary of Sydney University Cricket Club (believed to be the oldest existing and continuous club in Australia) has been marked by the issue of the appropriate *Annual Report* (a 64-page folio) and *A Souvenir of the Anniversary Celebration* (a four-page quarto). No price given for either, but the Honorary Secretary is Stephen Quartermain.

It is difficult to categorise *One Test After Another* (Stanley Paul; £8.95) by Henry Blofeld; he sub-titles it "Life in International Cricket" and looks at the Test scene since Packer and the establishment "buried the hatchet in each other's heads in 1979", with special reference to the Australian seasons of 1983-84 and 1984-85. It is important in evaluating any cricket work by Henry Blofeld to recognise that he is a genuine lover of cricket and has a broad mind with a sense of humour. So his book is probably as sound a survey as we are likely to get of this somewhat confused and controversial scene.

*An Australian Summer, The Recovery of The Ashes 1985* (The Kingswood Press; £9.95), by Patrick Eagar, with commentary by Alan Ross, is a survey of the Australian series of 1985, the recovery of the Ashes, and the Texaco one-day internationals. It was an interesting summer and, for English followers, an extremely satisfactory Test series. Patrick Eagar catches, as he has done now infallibly over many cricket seasons, the evocative moments; he has brought an impressive degree of understanding and instant reaction to cricket photography. Alan Ross provides a characteristically sympathetic commentary.

*The Bicentenary of Cricket in Scotland* (Clackmannan County Cricket Club, Paul C. M. Roberts, 2 Mount Hope, Bridge of Allan, FK9 4RL; £2), by Paul C. M. Roberts, is a 36-page octavo with a double-page colour reproduction of David Allan's painting of the Cathcart family 1785, and a 1935 scorecard tipped in. It marks the fact that the first recorded cricket match in Scotland was played at Alloa in Clackmannanshire on September 3, 1785.

*Corfu and Cricket* (Anglo-Corfiot Cricket Association, 15 St Peter's Square, London, W6 9AB; £2), a 48-page octavo edited by Ivo Tennant, marks the 150th anniversary of the first cricket match played between Greek teams on that island in 1835. There was play on the Esplanade Parade Ground between officers of the 32nd Foot as early as 1823, but two Corfiot clubs were formed in 1835. This study traces the development of a quite unique cricketing community (complete with unusual vocabulary) which is becoming increasingly attractive to visitors.

*A Chain of Spin Wizards* (Kennedy Bros., Goulbourne Street, Keighley, West Yorkshire, BD21 1PZ; £5.75), by Alan Hill, is a well-photo-illustrated 146-page large octavo account of the great Yorkshire tradition of slow left-arm spin bowlers, though, inevitably, the author, for all his loyalty and enthusiastic idealism, must end on the county's tribulations of today.

*Cricket Contrasts – from Crease to Commentary Box* (Stanley Paul; £7.95), by Jim Laker, is only partly autobiographical. Its importance – quite apart from some duly perceptive humour – lies in his observations and clearly thought-out opinions. He takes three famous matches and analyses them to illustrate the

changes in the game during the past three decades. He has had an unusual range of experience for, as player and commentator, he has been able widely to observe the range of top-class cricket since 1947, and those sharp eyes and shrewd brain have missed little: a sage view of the game.

*Cricket on the Air* (British Broadcasting Corporation; £8.50), by David Rayvern Allen, is a selection from 50 years of radio broadcasts on the game from before the days of commentary to the present. Mr Allen was an admirable choice for he combines not only the highways and byways of the BBC, but of broadcasting throughout the world, and has a scholarly and always interested knowledge of cricket. He has produced some classics and some absolute discoveries from the most unexpected places – such as the South Seas, Pitcairn Island, St Vincent and China, as well as the village green. Readable and often quite surprising.

*New South Wales versus Western Australia:* A Statistical Survey (available in the UK from E. K. Brown, Oughs Folly, Castle Lane, Liskeard, Cornwall, PL14 3AH) is the third volume of those state match histories by John King. It is a 32-page cyclostyled foolscap, with Mr King's invariably faithful statistics. Yet another of his immaculate and patient match histories is *South Australia versus Western Australia 1892-3 to 1984-5*, a 36-page cyclostyled folio with all the relevant facts and figures.

The booklet entitled *Alderbury Cricket Club 1885-1985* (Alderbury CC, Secretary, R. B. Weeks, Pinehurst, Firs Road, Alderbury, Salisbury, Wiltshire; no price given) is a 32-page octavo with photo illustrations. It describes itself as "a selective history and a few amusing reminiscences", and it marks the centenary of that Wiltshire village club. In it, county, minor county and village cricketers rub shoulders easily. The anonymous compiler, after his researches, decided "pitch, pavilion and privies seem to be recurrent themes through the old minute books – but I don't think it worth bothering about the details." It gives neither itself, its players nor the writer any airs, but they will relish it about the pavilion and the players' homes until the bi-centenary comes round.

*The History of Darfield Cricket Club* (from the author, I. M. Randerson, The Pavilion, School Street, Darfield, Barnsley, South Yorkshire; £3, including p & p) is a neatly produced 169-page soft backed octavo. The club name, of course, will be familiar to all who, reading through Yorkshire accounts or scores of the 1890s, came upon the distinction between J. T. Brown (Darfield) and J. T. Brown (Driffield). The Darfield J. T. was one of the fastest bowlers of his time whose career ended when he dislocated his shoulder. His brother, William, also played for the club and for Yorkshire; as did Ambrose Williams – nine for 29 versus Hampshire at Dewsbury in 1919 and dropped two matches later! Nothing in this history, though, is more interesting than the passage about Bob Needham, who literally was called up from the pit to play his only match for Yorkshire (v Essex in 1893 before the latter were recognised as first-class).

*The Book of Cricket Lists* (Futura; £2.50), edited by Norman Giller and introduced by Tom Graveney, is a 224-page octavo paperback in the now familiar "List" form. It bristles with famous names, "Greatest", "Heroes", "Finest", "Best of the Rest" and ends with "Top Ten Tables". A host of people pick their bests; there are lists of cricketers under their stars, the bespectacled, teams of captains; think of a list and it is there, all lightly readable.

*A Cricket Hotch-Potch* (Kennedy Bros., Goulbourne Street, Keighley, West Yorkshire, BD21 1PZ; £4.75), by Tom Naylor, with an introduction by Bill Bowes, is a 262-page octavo. The author writes cricket commentaries for the *Halifax Evening Courier* and his collection is described as "written as an appreciation to cricket and all connected with the game, especially Yorkshire members and players from 1928 onwards". The intention is to "make a donation to the British Diabetic Association".

*Test Match Special 3* (Queen Anne Press; £9.95), edited by Peter Baxter, is the mixture as before. As such, friendly, gossipy "shop" about – if sometimes characteristically obliquely so – the radio commentaries broadcast under that title. There, too, are all the familiar names – Tony L., Blowers, Johnners, Fred, C.M.-J. the Bearded Wonder, the Alderman, and all the visitors and supernumeraries – with Peter Baxter to whip them all in. Friendly; some of the jokes are hell, but there is nothing like it anywhere else in the cricket world; and it even has its devotees.

*Cricket Capers* (Michael Joseph; £4.95), edited by P.J.M., is a 48-page, pocket-sized collection of poetry, prose and pictures. The word for it is charming; easy and pleasing to read, look at and handle. It will find a place in many cricketers' Christmas stockings over the years; will prompt many "look at this" or "listen to this"; and deservedly so.

*The Punch Book of Cricket* (Granada; £7.95), edited by David Rayvern Allen, is a remarkable collection. Mr Allen has gone through every copy of *Punch* since the first, in 1841. Once more he has come up with some splendid finds. There is some wise and penetrative comment for this is not simply a funny, but a witty book: it is a marriage of two British institutions. Among the contributors, Neville Cardus, Mike Brearley, Michael Parkinson, A. P. Herbert, Basil Boothroyd, Stanley Reynolds, Ian Peebles, Bernard Hollowood, Frank Keating, Robert Morley, Compton Mackenzie, Ernest Shepherd, E. V. Knox, Roy Hattersley and Peter Tinniswood.

*Marks Out of XI* (Allen & Unwin; £8.95), by Vic Marks, is that cricketer's account of England's tour of India and Australia in the (English) winter of 1984-85. Unexpectedly it involves an excursion into Sri Lanka after Mrs Gandhi was assassinated; then England returned to take the series after being one Test down. Vic Marks relates the story – including Mrs Gandhi's funeral – with his characteristic neat observation and somewhat wry humour. He knows his cricket as well as anyone in the game; writes about it shrewdly and readably; and ends with a Latin quotation and the comment, "I assume my readership needs no translation".

There is little doubt – indeed, no argument – that Mike Brearley was among the best of cricket captains; so it is fitting that his book *The Art of Captaincy* (Hodder & Stoughton; £12.95) should be so clearly the best study of the subject. It is not simply the most profound and thorough work we have seen: it is most clearly laid out, illustrated with example, salted with humour and, above all, complete and practical. It does not go woollily round its subject, but keeps to the point. His training in classics and psychology has made Mike Brearley a most lucid expositor – and here he is at his best. Neither is it an arrogant book: avoiding faulting others, he is happy enough to admit his own errors and certainly does not gloss over the deficiencies of his batting. Essentially, he has laid out the benefit of his experience as a captain – not simply technically but personally, in striving to understand players, to motivate, to think, in fact, on various different levels at the same time in a way others can follow. But will they?

*Bodyline* (Collins Willow; £9.95), by Philip Derriman, is yet another attempt – as Douglas Jardine once put it – to change the result of the 1932-33 series by writing about it and, above all, by spectacularly misunderstanding Jardine. So many of his Australian critics, who must run into tens, if not hundreds of thousands, observe his sharpness of brain and clear sense of purpose; but they miss the sense of humour which was the key to the man. There are no fresh facts here; certainly no new, acceptable opinions; but the price is reasonable and the illustrations are extremely good.

*Long Days, Late Nights* (Robson; £7.50), by Frank Keating, is a collection of his essays – many, but not all, about cricket – written in his invariable vein of pleasure. The term "appreciation" is often used of essays, but here it is fully justified. Like Cardus, in standpoint though not in style, Frank Keating determinedly enjoys the sports he watches. Like Cardus, too, he nostalgically builds up his heroes, whether of the past, like Frank Woolley, or more recently, like Clive Lloyd, Greg Chappell or, which may surprise some, Geoffrey Boycott. As they pleased him, so he seeks, faithfully, and certainly not without humour, to convey that pleasure. He is indeed, as he seeks to be, a good – appreciative – read.

*Dublin University Cricket Club 1835-1985* (DUCC, no price given) is a 26-page cyclostyled quarto to mark, as its president points out, the sesquicentennial year with an informal and anecdotal look at the club through the eyes of some of the players who have passed through over the last 50 years. The club is fortunate to have been able to call on at least one representative in each of the last six decades. The result is a companionable and readable booklet.

*A Collection of Cricket Memories* (The Mike Turner Testimonial Fund, Grace Road, Leicester; no price given) is a handsomely produced, 112-page horizontal octavo which the Leicestershire secretary, characteristically, set out to make "different from the usual style of benefit publication". He succeeded with recollections from 40 cricketers and cricket-writers from across the country. The choice was wide, the result eminently readable.

*The Berkshire Schools Cricket Association Tour of Sri Lanka December 1984-1985* (from the Secretary, BSCA, 53 Hatherley Road, Reading; £1) is a 40-page octavo, probably unique in being devoted to a tour which never took place. Less than a fortnight before the scheduled departure, the Sri Lankan authorities cancelled it on security grounds because of political unrest there. The book is well made; with celebrity contributions and interviews. Happily the tour was provisionally rearranged for Easter 1986.

*Bishop's Stortford College Sri Lanka Cricket Tour 1985/6* (from Bishop's Stortford College, 10 Maze Green Road, Bishop's Stortford, Herts, CM23 2QZ; no price given) is a 32-page quarto celebrating a tour which was due to start on December 18, 1985, play fourteen matches in 25 days, to visit the "cultural triangle" and return on January 12, 1986. It, too, contains goodwill messages and celebrity contributions.

*Weston Creek Cricket Club Tour of England 1985* (from the Secretary, WCCC, PO Box 47, Weston Creek, ACT 2611, Australia; $A2.50) is a 32-page octavo, compiled and edited by the club's General Secretary, Percy Samara-Wickrama, to mark the first-ever tour of England by a grade club from Canberra. There is a welcome from Colin Cowdrey, "Recollections" from Brian Booth, who was coach of the club's first cricket school, and a message from Lancashire's John Abrahams, who is also the captain of Weston Creek. The line-up of players is enhanced by the presence of Cathy Phelan, a high school student who has been the scorer for the club's first-grade team for three seasons.

*Bill Frindall's XI Tour of New Zealand and Australia* (Newmans Tours Ltd, no price given) is a 36-page quarto devoted to a highly ambitious 27-day tour by a useful-looking party of twelve players, scorer and supporters (two females, of course) through those two countries. The text is interesting; often amusing and well decorated.

*Ashes '85* (Pelham Books; £10.95), by Matthew Engel, was the first account to appear of the England-Australia series of 1985, and is his first book. It is compiled largely from his reports to *The Guardian*. "Most readers will be well aware what happens in the end; the writer at the time had not got a clue. It was awfully tempting to try and do something about this when I was putting the book together, to amend the rushed judgements imposed by a newspaper deadline with the luxuries of hindsight. I have resisted with a fair amount of nobility." Memory confirms that. He regrets that there was no play – and no *Guardian* report – on the fourth day of the Lord's Test; but he was there. "Botham came out to join Gatting. The precedent in older minds was Lord's 1953 when Bailey and Watson engineered one of England's most famous Dunkirks. But you know Botham. His policy at Dunkirk would have been to try and march on Berlin." It is all done thoroughly and accurately, but lightly in tone, with an acceptable degree of humour. He is no chauvinist, but he cannot resist joining in the general atmosphere of English self-congratulation at the end. "There has been, to nick the title from Mike Brearley's account of the 1981 series, a phoenix from these Ashes too: it is David Gower."

*Shaw and Shrewsbury's Team in Australia 1884-5* (J. W. McKenzie, 12 Stoneleigh Park Road, Ewell, Epsom, Surrey, KT19 0QT; £24) was originally published by Alfred Shaw and Arthur Shrewsbury. Although it was not the first, it is by far the most expansive of the early tour books and, here, it is issued in a facsimile edition of 200 copies. It is something more than a mere period piece. If the match accounts are dated in style, they are still useful, and the background information is revealing indeed. It runs altogether to 181 pages of small-type text, and a few of the advertisements are also illuminating.

*Cricket Heroes* (Queen Anne Press; £9.95), edited by David Lemmon, is the second compilation of that name – the first was issued in 1958 – by members of the Cricket Writers Club. Their choice is almost as varied as the contributions; from living and dead, from four different nations – batsmen, bowlers, fast and slow, and a wicket-keeper. The glow of hero worship, for some of these heroes were obviously those of childhood or close friendship, adds a romantic quality to much of the writing. Indeed, it would make a fine bedside book.

*The Trent Bridge Battery* (Collins Willow in association with Gunn & Moore; £12), by Basil Haynes and John Lucas, is a study of that remarkable Nottingham cricketing family, the Gunns. It is difficult to imagine four more different characters; the shrewd, strict William; his sons, the dogged but humorous John, the delightfully whimsical George; and George's son, G. V. – the unlucky "Young George". Messrs Haynes and Lucas are both dons – Basil Haynes at Nottingham University, John Lucas at Loughborough – and for many years played for the same club. Their study is sensitive, well researched, accurate and neatly arranged; and with a spice of non-malicious humour. It will be read with pleasure; and the survivors of the Gunn family will be proud of it.

David Foot has applied himself both enthusiastically and diligently to the cricket of the West Country, and two of the characters in his *Cricket's Unholy Trinity* (Stanley Paul; £8.95) are from that part. In fact the label of "unholy trinity" is a little harsh on these men whom he presents sympathetically out of patient and personal research as men in the round. The three are Charlie Parker, the great slow – in fact, not so slow – left-arm bowler of Gloucestershire and – once – England; the right-arm bowler of infinite variety, Cecil Parkin of Yorkshire (once), Lancashire and, ten times in two years, England; and Jack MacBryan, the batsman of Cambridge University, Somerset and – once only when he did not bat – England. Through close investigation, going back to first-hand evidence through interviews with people who knew them well, Mr Foot has built up sensitive portraits of these men whom this reviewer met, without knowing well, for whom the author builds up a true sympathy.

*Gubby Allen; Man of Cricket* (Hutchinson/Stanley Paul; £12.95), by E. W. Swanton, has a Foreword by Lord Home of the Hirsel. Heavens! What a trinity of authority. It is, too, an authoritative biography; and "Gubby" is, indeed, a man of cricket. After Eton, he played first-class cricket, primarily for

Middlesex, Cambridge University, Free Foresters and England, from 1921 to 1954. That is a prodigious span, though he never played a full season and in latter years he took part in only a few games each year. Still, less than three months before his 51st birthday he scored 143 not out and took one (good) wicket for 5 runs against his old university. He captained Middlesex; played in 25 Tests for England and captained them in eleven. In 1931, against New Zealand at Lord's, he shared with Leslie Ames in the record Test partnership for the eighth wicket, which is also the record for all cricket at Lord's; where his ten for 40 (v Lancashire, 1929) remains the best innings bowling return. He has been both a member and chairman of selectors; committee member, chairman, treasurer, and president of MCC, and has been awarded the CBE. This is a record of amazing success and here it is quite immaculately recorded, with admiration but not fulsomely.

*That's Out!* (Arthur Barker; £8.50), by Dickie Bird, acknowledges the help of many people, but it is unmistakable and authentic autobiography. It is personal, full of the author's character, his stories, ideas, theories and pleasures, and it is readable. It has, which may surprise some people, a Foreword by Dennis Lillee, who finds the author a "great official and great man". It has, too, an inescapable feeling of Yorkshire loyalty.

*Boycott* (Methuen; £9.95), by Don Mosey, is in some ways as striking a cricket biography as has appeared for many years. The author's deep, careful and loyal study of his subject over many years has been succeeded by an "objective biography" written "in the face of active disapproval"; it reflects many facets of Geoffrey Boycott. In fact it has more conflicting ideas about him than any other book yet published. It is also, because it could not avoid it, an account of those many years of schism in Yorkshire county cricket which at times outstripped – at least in headline space – the news of the county's actual cricket. It is a book which will arouse heat, controversy and, in some cases, humour. The evidence is many-sided, though some may come to a straightforward conclusion so far as the book and its subject are concerned.

The amazing fact about *His Own Man: the Life of Neville Cardus* (Methuen; £12.95), by Christopher Brookes, is that it is the first biography of Neville Cardus to be written. Of course, he himself had written the towering *Autobiography* and followed it with *Second Innings* and *Full Score*; Dr Brookes is fully appreciative of the man who described himself as "the uneducated boy who became comfortably off without once consciously working to make money". This is a most thorough study, not least because of its close identification with its subject. "Once we, the readers, have entered into his perspective, we are obliged to look at the world through his eyes." He feels for, and with, Cardus; recognises his willingness, almost laughingly, and even in autobiography to hack facts to fit his story; and to "kill off" characters. He recognises too his inconsistencies; but all that lies in sympathy. Sir Neville would have been pleased with it – perhaps even a little flattered – for it is understanding.

*Percy Chapman: a Biography* (Queen Anne Press; £9.95), by David Lemmon, is a life of A. P. F. Chapman, the gloriously athletic cricketer who played for Oakham, Uppingham, Cambridge University, Kent and England, as a most splendid, even spectacular, left-hand batsman and exciting fieldsman; convivial and inspiring, if not tactically outstanding captain, social, and happily married man. That story is much to be relished and Mr Lemmon is both kind – and, surely, wise – to deal only briefly with the later, quite tragic decline of such a likeable and generous man.

Alan Gibson specifically disclaims *Growing Up with Cricket* (Allen & Unwin; £8.95) as being an autobiography. However, he says, to quote him, "Cricket has played a large part in my life; though it has remained separate

The Cricket Society
40th
ANNIVERSARY
1945 - 1985

from most of the rest of it. Some years ago I wrote an autobiography about the things which seemed to me most important, and cricket did not come into it much. Yet I knew that cricket was important to me. . . ." Of course he was, and is, right. Cricket can only be a minor aspect of a full life. Alan Gibson, who took a first in history at Oxford, was President of the Union, thinking Christian, a sensitive, all-round broadcaster and a student of hymn-writing, is hardly likely to find his life filled by a sport. It has, though, been one of the aspects he has, in these words, grown up with. He broadcasts imaginatively about it; and writes wittily about it in *The Times*; and here he is at his best; positive, then discursive; grave then light in touch; personal and objective. This is an intimate but not profound record; not profound because he recognises that cricket, although it can be serious, is not a profound matter; but an excellently witty book, with plenty of good stories and ideas even for those who do not agree with his major premise.

Everyone with the least knowledge of modern cricket knows that, after he went on the unofficial tour of South Africa in 1982, Graham Gooch was among the players banned from Test cricket for three years. In *Out of the Wilderness* (Collins Willow; £8.95) Graham Gooch, with the assistance of the experienced journalist, Alan Lee, tells the story of that tour, his own reactions, his successes with Essex, and, with his suspension over, his view of the future. He writes with pleasure on his "South African summers", with sympathy for Keith Fletcher who "said no to £45,000" to make that same South African tour; and declares that the thing he likes best is batting for England.

*At the Double* (Stanley Paul; £7.95), by Richard Hadlee, with Tony Francis, is an extremely happy collaboration; and perhaps one should add to it Hadlee's "Guru", Grahame Felton. It is the story of Richard Hadlee's splendid twelve months from August 1983 to August 1984 when he was a major influence in the rise of New Zealand and then performed the first double – 1,000 runs and 100 wickets – to be achieved in an English season since the change of the first-class fixture list in 1969. Hadlee himself makes his points uninhibitedly, often amusingly, strongly and forthrightly. Tony Francis, the Century Television sports presenter, has done an extremely entertaining editorial job on it and in an obviously agreed format, he interpolates, comments and observes on that splendid year.

*It's Knott Cricket, The Autobiography of Alan Knott* (Macmillan; £8.95). Although most would regard Alan Knott as a single-minded cricketer – and, without doubt, his concern with fitness, technique and playing standards is considerable – he is much concerned, as this book shows, with other matters. His religion ("I tried never to swear again after I became a Christian"), his involvement with Packer, his tour to South Africa, and his deep concern about the disruptive effect of cricket tours on domestic life are all to him serious matters, which he deals with gravely and responsibly. It is an unusually thought-provoking book by the normal levels of cricket literature and it demands respect.

In *Lamb's Tales* (Allen & Unwin; £8.95) Allan Lamb, with Peter Smith, recounts mainly his cricket career after leaving South Africa to make a living in England. He played successfully with Northamptonshire and established a worthy place in the England side. This is an interesting view of English – and world – cricket through the eyes of a modern-day South African career cricketer. Lamb is keenly observant, too, of technical and social developments within the game. Of English pace bowlers – "I blame the wickets as the greatest single factor in holding back players."

*A Classical Youth* (Blond; £12.95) is by Michael Longson, for many years senior classics master at Edinburgh Academy. He has now retired to concentrate on his hobbies of music, poetry and cricket. Indeed, throughout this autobiography, cricket keeps coming happily in; notably through his process of thinking himself into becoming a wicket-keeper; and he quotes imaginatively, in his poetry section, E. E. Bowen's neglected poem, "Lord's, 1878".

In *Playing Days* (Stanley Paul; £9.95), Tony Lewis is at his most evocative. Perhaps he would like to call it autobiography, but that must seem a pedestrian description for a book which captures so much of a man's emotional life. Here he is, Welshman, cricketer, rugby player, violinist, commentator, talker at his most happily conversational. It is hard not to read him too fast for he is, like the stories he tells, great fun.

Trevor McDonald's *Clive Lloyd* (Granada; £8.95), "The Authorised Biography", is an outstanding study of an outstanding cricketer. Lloyd has a fine record as a left-hand batsman of great punishing powers but capable at his side's need of a sound defensive game. He was one of the greatest cover points the game has known and, subsequently after injury, a fine slip field. As a captain, though, his record is not simply unequalled but unapproached and crucial in the development of West Indian cricket. Mr McDonald traces his development and places it within not only the cricket history but the social history of the West Indies, where cricket is toweringly important and the captaincy assumes great importance. His book is not simply a cricket book but an important section of Caribbean history, most sensitively understood, examined, explained and logically laid out.

*Ken McEwan* (Allen & Unwin; £8.95), by David Lemmon, is an understanding life of that player of Eastern Province, Western Province, South Africa, Sussex, Northamptonshire Second XI for a matter of a few hours, Western Australia and Essex. He is a quiet and unassuming young man who took time to mature as a batsman, though his keenness and certainty in the field always commended him, but Brian Taylor detected his promise at a single Second XI sight. It was that sighting which took him to Essex, where he played for twelve years with considerable success. Well liked there for his loyalty and enthusiasm, he emerged as a capable batsman, sound and with attractive attacking strokes. South African born, he returned there regularly and was perfectly frank about the fact that, unlike some of his countrymen, he had no wish to play for any other country. At the end of the 1985 season he did as he had always intended, and returned to the family farm in South Africa. This is a good and faithful record.

The title of Peter May's autobiography "with Michael Melford" is *A Game Enjoyed* (Stanley Paul; £9.95), and it is a story of almost unbroken success with Charterhouse, Cambridge University, Surrey – they twice won the County Championship under his captaincy – and England; indeed as England captain in a record number of 41 Tests. The appendix of statistics shows that in all cricket he scored 27,592 runs at an average of 51; in Tests, 4,537 at 46.77. He went on, of course, to be President of Surrey and an unusually young President of MCC, chairman of selectors, and a successful insurance broker. If it was not unbroken success, he can write "I sometimes see the 1958-59 tour of Australia referred to as the greatest failure of my career as England captain. I myself often think that it may have been one of my greatest successes. At the end of it, England and Australia were still speaking." Not everyone will agree with his opinion of South African affairs. The cricket historian of the future will find here all the essential facts of the career of a great batsman and his triumphs.

Don Mosey, following only by the accident of alphabetical order of biographical subject, in *The Best Job in the World* (Pelham Books; £9.95) is full of the enthusiasm its title argues. His career has been mainly in cricket, for newspapers and the BBC, and anyone who has listened to his broadcasts must have recognised beyond question his bursting enthusiasms. He has never played for England, but few who have could recount the experience with this amount of gusto. No-one could possibly agree with him all the time – he would be furious if anyone pretended to do so – but here he pours out his stories and feelings of cricket reporting and commentary, not only in England but New Zealand, India, Pakistan, West Indies and Sri Lanka. He covered the first Tests played in Colombo, Napier and St John's, Antigua; but he is not concerned to quote records; only to enjoy it all, crow about it, and share his pleasure.

*Standing Up, Standing Back* (Collins Willow; £8.95), by Bob Taylor with Patrick Murphy, is enthusiastic in a somewhat, but not completely, different fashion. Mr Murphy has most faithfully reflected the idealist and perfectionist character of Bob Taylor, one of the best of wicket-keepers. He captures, too, his unfailingly percipient reading – psychological as well as technical – of a cricket match. His judgement of events and his humane but clear-minded assessment of players is such as could persuade many writers about the game to go to his book for its judgements. Bob Taylor comes through it all as the man he is; never more revealingly than about his resignation from the Derbyshire captaincy. "After a time, I began to get depressed. I seemed to be telling someone off all the time; the rollickings were well deserved and I believe the players concerned respected me and accepted my complaints, but it seemed as if I was always getting at someone. I realised that, temperamentally, I'm not a captain – I'm a number two, a foreman who gets people moving on the pitch when we are fielding, a back-up to the captain." After the anxiety of that phase comes "1981" when all came right: his first century and recall to the England side; a world record for number of catches; and Derbyshire won the NatWest (their first trophy for 45 years); he was awarded the MBE, and had a county record benefit of £54,000. No wonder he heads the chapter "Life Begins at 40". Now he has become captain of the Derbyshire Second XI, "but I shall bat at number eleven and stay away from the wicket-keeper's gloves. . . . That will give a younger man a chance and me the opportunity to try to solve one of English cricket's biggest problems: the attitude of the young players. I shall try very hard not to be a bore about the old days, but they will have to realise that certain values are unchanging over the years." And his last word: "It's people like me, who have had a marvellous life out of the game, who will try to arrest the slump."

Bob Willis's autobiography, *Lasting the Pace* (Collins Willow; £9.95) could not be more aptly titled. Throughout his career critics were prepared to write him off; yet he came back again and again. Nothing in the entire book more nearly captures its spirit than Patrick Eagar's photograph of Willis moving into the delivery stride; he has captioned it "Not the most elegant of actions but one that served me, with a few modifications, for more than 48,000 first-class deliveries". In some ways this is a study in aggression, injuries and other setbacks, one of which almost caused him to quit early on. Yet that very aggression, the competitive streak, needed reinforcement. Bob Willis has always been a man of his own opinions, he has had his brushes with authority, and he heads one chapter "Malice and Mischief in the Media"; but he made his way through to play in 90 Tests, overcoming injuries that would have put many men out of the game, become captain of England ("the ultimate honour – I was flabbergasted") and to take 325 Test wickets, 128 against Australia – both England records.

*R. E. S. Wyatt – fighting cricketer* (Allen & Unwin; £12.95), by Gerald Pawle, is an extremely sound biography of the all-rounder who played first for Warwickshire and then Worcestershire between 1923 and 1951 (though he played his last first-class match – for the Free Foresters – in 1957 when he was 56). He captained both those counties, as well as England in sixteen of

his 40 Test matches. He scored 39,405 runs (with 85 centuries) at 40.05 and, as a bowler (out-swingers) took 901 wickets. This study, for which Mr Pawle travelled much to interview his subject's contemporaries, and which owes much, too, to his memory and opinions, shows him as a much greater cricketing figure than his modesty often allowed him to appear. The fact is that Bob Wyatt, as well as being a considerable competitor, quite unflinching against the fastest bowling, was also a deep thinker about the game. In truth he lived in it and for it; and it could well be argued that he was the most astute cricket brain of his time. One contemporary described him as the first amateur professional. Let it not be thought, though, that he is as solemn as he sometimes looked: he is a fine raconteur with a dry sense of humour. He suffered two broken ribs and twice a broken thumb; in the West Indies, Martindale broke his jaw in four places; and later his arm was broken in Australia. But as Cyril Walters recalled: "He never flinched. He used to stand there like a solid rock. He was very strong. And there was a stubborn streak in him." Certainly he played cricket to win, but by the highest standards. He was later a Test selector, an honorary member of MCC, and, in the best sense, an all-rounder.

Cricket humour has never been easy and has often been unfunny. In *W. G. Grace's Last Case* (Methuen; £3.95), by William Rushton, though, it succeeds. W. G. Grace on an American tour investigates the murder of the wicked bowler, Castor Vilebastard (pronounced "Villibart"). The humour is crazy but it is, nevertheless, extremely funny, and when such as Raffles, Pinkerton, Oscar Wilde, Sherlock Holmes and Dr Jekyll wander in it becomes even funnier. The author's drawings add to the mad delight.

*The Final Test* (Victor Gollancz; £5.95), by Gareth Owen, is a children's book with some sensitive touches and a half-happy ending in this world.

*Cricketdotes* (Richard Miller, 16 Greendykes Road, Dundee, DD4 7NA; £1.25), by W. F. Dyson, describes itself as "A collection of whimsical anecdotes, oddities and similies [*sic*] about cricket". It has some interesting oddities dredged from the record books.

*The Cricket Diary 1985* (John Dixon, 18 Ashley Avenue, Lower Weston, Bath, Avon, BA1 3DS; £3.50 plus 25p p & p) is a pleasant pocket diary with facing pages, apart from an apt quotation apiece, left blank for notes.

*The Tea Ladies Calendar 1985* (Rosalind S. Scott, 3 Herdus Road, Mirehouse, Whitehaven, CA28 8BY; no price given) describes itself as "An alternative view from the cricket pavilion". It has twelve comic drawings and a calendar.

*Playfair Cricket Annual 1985* (Queen Anne Press; £1.75) was the last issue edited by the late Gordon Ross, whose pride it was. This is the 38th edition of this pocket-sized reference book. As usual there are useful brief biographies, Test scores and statistics of the first-class game.

*Cricket '85* (Test and County Cricket Board, Lord's Ground, London, NW8 8QN; £1) is a 40-page quarto; as usual, most excellently produced, with attractive colour plates, feature articles by David Gower, Frank Tyson and Jack Bannister, and biographical notes on the touring Australian team.

*Indian Cricket 1985* (Kasturi & Sons Ltd, Madras; obtainable in the UK from Appleby Books, 5 St John's Street, Keswick; £5.75 post free), compiled by S. Thyagarajan, is the 39th edition. As voluminous as ever, it runs to 696 pages. It has every conceivable Indian statistic: a workmanlike index; feature articles by Asif Iqbal, R. Mohan and N. S. Ramaswami. The four cricketers of the year, all pictured in colour, are M. W. Gatting, G. Fowler, Mohammad Azharuddin and L. Sivaramakrishnan.

*DB Cricket Annual 1985* (Moa Publications, Auckland, New Zealand; \$NZ29.95; available in the UK from Appleby Books, 5 St John's Street, Keswick; £10.95 plus postage), edited by Don Neely, is the fourteenth edition.

It is a sturdy 245-page quarto. It covers three tours by New Zealand; one in New Zealand; the Shell Series; provincial reviews; the Cyclone Hawke Cup, the Prudential Under-22 Tournament and women's cricket in New Zealand and on tour in the UK, India and Australia. As well as first-class averages, there are substantial reviews by Dick Brittenden and statistics by Ian Smith. The illustration is generous and some plates, in full colour, are quite handsome.

*Irish Cricket Annual* (41 Londonbridge Road, Sandymount, Dublin 4; £2) is a 62-page quarto, well made and printed, with some good photographs and plenty of background to cricket in that country.

*Essex County Cricket Club 1985 Handbook* (Essex County Cricket Club, New Writtle Street, Chelmsford, CM2 0PG; £3) is generously spiced with feature articles and news of Graham Gooch's benefit season with Essex.

*Hampshire Handbook 1985* (Hampshire CCC, County Ground, Southampton, SO9 2TY; £1.50) is again edited by Peter Marshall with enthusiasm unabated. This year he has contributions by Paul Terry, Christopher Weeks, Tony Baker, Tony Mitchener, Mike Neasom and the scorer, Vic Isaacs.

*Kent County Cricket Club Annual 1985* (Kent CCC, St Lawrence Ground, Canterbury, Kent; £1.50) has a good county Who's Who and is generously illustrated with photographs.

*Yorkshire County Cricket Club Yearbook 1985* (Yorkshire County Cricket Club, Headingley Cricket Ground, Leeds, LS6 3BU) is a departure from the norm in this, its 87th edition. The illustrations should prove attractive to casual readers, and there are features by Bill Bowes, Sir Leonard Hutton, Norman Yardley, John Callaghan, Derek Hodgson, Martin Searby, David Warner and Tony Woodhouse, as well as the usual contributions.

*New Forest Club Cricket Association* (Victor Loveless, "Pipers", Pear Tree Drive, Landford, Wiltshire; no price given) is, as usual, fully informative about that competition, has a useful map, and some pleasing photographs.

Editorship of *The Cricketer Quarterly* (The Cricketer, Beech Hanger, Ashurst, Tunbridge Wells, Kent, TN3 9ST; £1.30) was taken over by Bill Frindall in summer 1985 (Vol. 13, No. 1.) after the death of Gordon Ross, and that issue opened with Mr Frindall's address at the memorial service to Mr Ross in June. The Quarterly, of course, has always been a book of facts and figures, and Mr Frindall makes his point flatly and plainly: "Priority must go to those contributions which are not published elsewhere". Hence an absence of the usual team photos and their replacement by portraits of English cricket newcomers. His commitment to the aim is plain and firm.

*Cricketer International* (The Cricketer, Beech Hanger, Ashurst, Tunbridge Wells, Kent, TN3 9ST; 95p monthly), edited by Christopher Martin-Jenkins, has now completed its 65th year and 66th volume; an historic record of cricket since Sir Pelham Warner founded it in 1921. Its contributors include the editor, E. W. Swanton, Tom Graveney, Peter Roebuck, Gerry Gomez, Alan Lee, Peter Walker, Robert Brooke and Phil Wilkins.

*Wisden Cricket Monthly* (Editorial, 6 Beech Lane, Guildown, Guildford, Surrey, GU2 5ES; subscription Wisden Cricket Monthly, Watling Street, Bletchley, Milton Keynes, MK2 2BW; 90p monthly), edited by David Frith, has run for six years and volumes and has proved a healthy growth. The two magazines have now become so distinctly separate in approach, style and contributors that there seems ample room for both it and *Cricketer International*. The chief contributors to *Wisden Cricket Monthly* are the editor, Bob Willis, David Gower, Peter Wynne-Thomas, Jim Laker and, with county notes, David Foot, Neil Hallam and Doug Ibbotson. (The reviewer also contributes regularly.)

*Cricketer* (Newspress Pty, 603-611 Little Lonsdale Street, Melbourne 3000, Australia; \$A2.40), the main Australian cricket magazine, edited by Ken

Piesse, numbers among its regular writers Max Walker, Frank Tyson, Bill Lawry, Ian Brayshaw, Richard Cashman, Alan McGilvray, Phil Wilkins and Kersi Meher-Homji. There are surveys of cricket in each state and a continuing pictorial bias with a central colour poster in each issue.

*Australian Cricket* (Federal Publishing Co., 140 Joynton Avenue, Waterloo, NSW, 2017, Australia; $A2.25 per monthly issue) is a newsprint-style publication 28cm by 43cm, with 32 pages, sixteen of them illustrated in colour. The approach is lively, with contributions by John Benaud, Tony Greig, David Hookes, Ken Casellas, Peter Hook, Rod Nicholson and Peter Philpott.

In the issue for May 1985 (Vol. 5, No. 4) *Cathedral End* announced that "this is the last edition of *Cathedral End* in its current style. A new national Journal for the Australian Cricket Society will be published as from next September. With the title 'Australian Cricket Journal' we will move into a new size and print format. The name 'Cathedral End' will be retained for the local news bulletins." Its successor, which is also edited by Chris Harte, is *Australian Cricket Journal* (details of subscription from GPO Box 696, Adelaide, South Australia, 5001). It is a 46-page quarto in better than usual cyclostyle and well laid out, with a few – though, as the editor explains – not necessarily relevant illustrations. It aims high: "The need for a cricket publication in Australia which deals with the less frivolous matters of our summer game has been obvious for some time". They have a contribution by Richard Cashman, a sympathetic obituary of P. G. H. Fender, a pro-South African piece by the editor, and some observations of Australian cricket by Gerald Howat, plus a piece on "Channel Nine Cricket" by Brian Matthews. The second issue is also interesting and well written. It will be most interesting to observe and, hopefully, enjoy its progress.

The new appearance among cricket magazines is the monthly *Cricketstar – Pakistan's National Cricket Magazine* (10 Fane Road, Lahore; Rs12.00). Edited by Gul Hameed Bhatti, it is a 102-page quarto with generous illustration, some of it in colour. It affords the closest view of Pakistan cricket we have yet seen.

*The New Zealand Cricket Player* (PO Box 28-280, Remuera, Auckland, New Zealand; $NZ1.75 per issue), edited by Richard Becht, appears in eight issues a year, September to April inclusive. It continues to give sound coverage to the increasingly important cricket of New Zealand. Dave Crowe, Bob Monteith, Don Neely and Don Cameron are familiar figures in the editorial pages.

*Irish Cricket Magazine* (41 Londonbridge Road, Sandymount, Dublin 4; £1) is edited by Gerard Siggins. It deals specifically with the cricket scene in Eire and with side glimpses outside. Reviews, some research – like the bibliography of Irish cricket club brochures – which must be unique, and personal profiles and obituaries.

Nico Craven's annual offering this year is called *Summer and Sunshine* (from the author, The Coach House, Ponsonby, Seascale, Cumbria, CA20 1BX; £2.25). He still continues to delight in his native Gloucestershire, but here he picks up cricket at Millom, Eskdale, Canon Frome and Worcester, and he finishes the season thinking about Gloucestershire's drive for the Championship.

☆ ☆ ☆ ☆ ☆

*Botham* (The Kingswood Press; £9.95), by Patrick Eagar, though primarily a picture book (what brilliant pictures, too!) also contains a long, generous and perceptive essay on England's great all-rounder by John Arlott and some good writing by Graeme Wright in eight shorter chapters introducing the various phases of Botham's first-class career. An illustrated biography of exceptional quality.

Five years after his retirement comes *Another Word from Arlott* (Pelham Books; £12.95); a further collection of John Arlott's broadcasts, cricket commentaries and writings selected by David Rayvern Allen. It was the same after reading Mr Allen's earlier Arlott anthology: the reader is left with the impression that almost wherever John Arlott were to find himself he would be the most articulate and encyclopaedically knowledgeable person present. That his spoken word transfers so effortlessly on to paper suggests that he could just as easily have ad-libbed a leading article on the Churches of Bournemouth as Laker's nineteen wickets against Australia at Old Trafford. There must be plenty more material in the archives yet for Mr Allen to complete a splendid hat-trick.

# FIXTURES, 1986

** Indicates Sunday play.* *† Not first-class.*

**Saturday, April 19**

The Parks — Oxford U. v Somerset
Fenner's — Cambridge U. v Leics.

**Wednesday, April 23**

Lord's — MCC v Middx
The Parks — Oxford U. v Glos.
Fenner's — Cambridge U. v Essex

**Saturday, April 26**

Bristol* — Glos. v Glam.
Leicester* — Leics. v Kent
Lord's — Middx v Derbys.
Trent Bridge* — Notts. v Hants
Taunton* — Somerset v Yorks.
Hove* — Sussex v Lancs.
Edgbaston* — Warwicks. v Essex
Worcester* — Worcs. v Surrey
Fenner's — Cambridge U. v Northants

**Wednesday, April 30**

Chesterfield — Derbys. v Somerset
Southampton — Hants v Glam.
Canterbury — Kent v Northants
Old Trafford — Lancs. v Leics.
The Oval — Surrey v Notts.
The Parks — Oxford U. v Middx
Fenner's — Cambridge U. v Warwicks.

**Saturday, May 3**

**†Benson and Hedges Cup** (1 day)

Chesterfield — Derbys. v Leics.
Bristol — Glos. v Somerset
Old Trafford — Lancs. v Yorks.
Lord's — Middx v Surrey
Hove — Sussex v Essex
Slough‡ — Minor Counties v Northants
The Parks — Oxford & Cam. U. v Hants
Glasgow (Titwood) — Scotland v Worcs.

‡ *To continue on Sunday if necessary.*

**Sunday, May 4**

Arundel — †Lavinia, Duchess of Norfolk's XI v Indians (1 day)

**Tuesday, May 6**

Worcester — Worcs. v Indians

**Wednesday, May 7**

Chelmsford — Essex v Kent
Old Trafford — Lancs. v Hants
Lord's — Middx v Leics.
Northampton — Northants v Glos.
Taunton — Somerset v Glam.
The Oval — Surrey v Warwicks.
Headingley — Yorks. v Sussex
The Parks — Oxford U. v Notts.

**Saturday, May 10**

Cheltenham Town CC* — Glos. v Indians

**†Benson and Hedges Cup** (1 day)

Swansea — Glam. v Sussex
Southampton — Hants v Middx
Canterbury — Kent v Surrey
Leicester — Leics. v Warwicks.
Northampton — Northants v Derbys.
Trent Bridge — Notts. v Yorks.
Taunton — Somerset v Essex
Perth (North Inch) — Scotland v Lancs.

**Tuesday, May 13**

**†Benson and Hedges Cup** (1 day)

Chelmsford — Essex v Glos.
Northampton — Northants v Leics.
Trent Bridge — Notts. v Scotland
Taunton — Somerset v Glam.
The Oval — Surrey v Hants
Worcester — Worcs. v Lancs.
Walsall — Minor Counties v Warwicks.
Fenner's — Oxford & Cam. U. v Kent

**Thursday, May 15**

The Oval — †Surrey v Indians (1 day)

**†Benson and Hedges Cup** (1 day)

Derby — Derbys. v Minor Counties
Chelmsford — Essex v Glam.
Bristol — Glos. v Sussex
Southampton — Hants v Kent
Lord's — Middx v Oxford & Cam. U.
Edgbaston — Warwicks. v Northants
Worcester — Worcs. v Notts.
Headingley — Yorks. v Scotland

**Saturday, May 17**

Southampton* Hants v Indians
Northampton Northants v Essex

**†Benson and Hedges Cup** (1 day)

Swansea Glam. v Glos.
Canterbury Kent v Middx
Liverpool Lancs. v Notts.
Leicester Leics. v Minor Counties
The Oval Surrey v Oxford and Cam. U.
Hove Sussex v Somerset
Edgbaston Warwicks. v Derbys.
Headingley Yorks. v Worcs.

**Wednesday, May 21**

Canterbury Kent v Indians
Chelmsford Essex v Yorks.
Lord's Middx v Glam.
Trent Bridge Notts. v Leics.
Taunton Somerset v Glos.
Hove Sussex v Surrey
Edgbaston Warwicks. v Northants
Worcester Worcs. v Lancs.
Fenner's Cambridge U. v Hants

**Saturday, May 24**

The Oval †ENGLAND v INDIA (1st 1-day Texaco Trophy)
Derby* Derbys. v Notts.
Cardiff Glam. v Somerset
Bournemouth Hants v Glos.
Lord's Middx v Sussex
Northampton Northants v Leics.
Edgbaston Warwicks. v Worcs.
Headingley Yorks. v Lancs.

**Monday, May 26**

Old Trafford †ENGLAND v INDIA (2nd 1-day Texaco Trophy)

**Thursday, May 29**

Belfast †Ireland v Indians (1 day)

**Benson and Hedges Cup – Quarter-Finals** (1 day)

**Saturday, May 31**

Northampton* Northants v Indians
Derby Derbys. v Essex
Southampton Hants v Notts.
Tunbridge Wells Kent v Worcs.
Old Trafford Lancs. v Warwicks.
Leicester Leics. v Glos.
The Oval Surrey v Middx
Horsham Sussex v Somerset

**Wednesday, June 4**

Swansea Glam. v Essex
Bristol Glos. v Warwicks.
Tunbridge Wells Kent v Sussex
Hinckley Leics. v Surrey
Trent Bridge Notts. v Somerset
Worcester Worcs. v Middx
Sheffield Yorks. v Derbys.
The Parks Oxford U. v Lancs.

**Thursday, June 5**

Lord's ENGLAND v INDIA (1st Cornhill Test, 5 days)

**Friday, June 6**

Northampton †Northants v Zimbabweans (1 day)

**Saturday, June 7**

Chelmsford Essex v Notts.
Bournemouth* Hants v Somerset
Old Trafford Lancs. v Middx
Northampton Northants v Worcs.
The Oval Surrey v Derbys.
Hove Sussex v Leics.
Edgbaston Warwicks. v Glam.
Harrogate Yorks. v Glos.
The Parks Oxford U. v Kent

**Wednesday, June 11**

**†Benson and Hedges Cup – Semi-Finals** (1 day)

**†ICC Trophy – First Round** (1 day)

Harrogate †Tilcon Trophy (3 days)
Coleraine †Ireland v Wales

**Thursday, June 12**

The Parks †Oxford & Cam. U. v Indians (2 days)

**Friday, June 13**

**†ICC Trophy – Second Round** (1 day)

**Saturday, June 14**

Leicester* Leics. v Indians
Ilford Essex v Hants
Gloucester Glos. v Derbys.
Old Trafford Lancs. v Worcs.
Lord's Middx v Yorks.
Northampton Northants v Warwicks.
Trent Bridge Notts. v Surrey
Bath Somerset v Kent
The Parks Oxford U. v Glam.
Hove* Sussex v Cambridge U.

**Monday, June 16**

†**ICC Trophy – Third Round** (1 day)

**Wednesday, June 18**

†**ICC Trophy – Fourth Round** (1 day)

| | |
|---|---|
| Ilford | Essex v Sussex |
| Swansea | Glam. v Warwicks. |
| Gloucester | Glos. v Kent |
| Basingstoke | Hants v Surrey |
| Trent Bridge | Notts. v Middx |
| Bath | Somerset v Northants |
| Worcester | Worcs. v Yorks. |

**Thursday, June 19**

| | |
|---|---|
| Headingley | ENGLAND v INDIA (2nd Cornhill Test, 5 days) |

**Friday, June 20**

†**ICC Trophy – Fifth Round** (1 day)

**Saturday, June 21**

| | |
|---|---|
| Chesterfield* | Derbys. v Glos. |
| Swansea | Glam. v Lancs. |
| Southampton | Hants v Kent |
| Lord's | Middx v Essex |
| Luton | Northants v Yorks. |
| Edgbaston | Warwicks. v Leics. |
| Worcester | Worcs. v Sussex |
| Fenner's | Cambridge U. v Surrey |

**Sunday, June 22**

| | |
|---|---|
| Arundel | †Lavinia, Duchess of Norfolk's XI v New Zealanders (1 day) |

**Monday, June 23**

†**ICC Trophy – Sixth Round** (1 day)

**Wednesday, June 25**

†**ICC Trophy – Seventh Round** (1 day)

| | |
|---|---|
| Fenner's | Oxford & Cam. U. v New Zealanders |

†**NatWest Bank Trophy – First Round** (1 day)

| | |
|---|---|
| Reading (Courage) | Berks. v Glos. |
| Birkenhead (Oxton CC) | Cheshire v Surrey |
| Derby | Derbys. v Cornwall |
| Exmouth | Devon v Notts. |
| Southampton | Hants v Herts. |
| Old Trafford | Lancs. v Cumb. |
| Leicester | Leics. v Ireland |
| Northampton | Northants v Middx |
| Jesmond | Northumb. v Essex |
| Edinburgh (Myreside) | Scotland v Kent |
| Taunton | Somerset v Dorset |
| Stone | Staffs. v Glam. |
| Hove | Sussex v Suffolk |
| Edgbaston | Warwicks. v Durham |
| Worcester | Worcs. v Oxon. |
| Headingley | Yorks. v Cambs. |

**Thursday, June 26**

| | |
|---|---|
| Chester-le-Street | †League Cricket Conference v Indians (1 day) |

**Friday, June 27**

†**ICC Trophy – Eighth Round** (1 day)

**Saturday, June 28**

| | |
|---|---|
| Lord's* | Middx v New Zealanders |
| Taunton* | Somerset v Indians |
| Bristol | Glos. v Surrey |
| Maidstone | Kent v Glam. |
| Liverpool | Lancs. v Derbys. |
| Leicester | Leics. v Notts. |
| Hastings | Sussex v Northants |
| Worcester | Worcs. v Hants |
| Bradford* | Yorks. v Warwicks. |

**Monday, June 30**

†**ICC Trophy – Ninth Round** (1 day)

**Wednesday, July 2**

†**ICC Trophy – Semi-Finals** (1 day)

| | |
|---|---|
| Chelmsford | Essex v New Zealanders |
| Derby | Derbys. v Worcs. |
| Cardiff | Glam. v Sussex |
| Bristol | Glos. v Yorks. |
| Maidstone | Kent v Somerset |
| Leicester | Leics. v Hants |
| Uxbridge | Middx v Surrey |
| Trent Bridge | Notts. v Warwicks. |
| Lord's | Oxford U. v Cambridge U. |

**Thursday, July 3**

| | |
|---|---|
| Edgbaston | ENGLAND v INDIA (3rd Cornhill Test, 5 days) |

**Friday, July 4**

†**ICC Trophy – Third-Place Play-off** (1 day)

**Saturday, July 5**

| | |
|---|---|
| Hove* | Sussex v New Zealanders |
| Derby | Derbys. v Kent |
| Cardiff | Glam. v Glos. |
| Old Trafford | Lancs. v Essex |
| Uxbridge | Middx v Warwicks. |
| Taunton | Somerset v Hants |
| The Oval | Surrey v Northants |
| Worcester | Worcs. v Notts. |
| Middlesbrough | Yorks. v Leics. |
| Lord's | †Eton v Harrow (1 day) |

**Monday, July 7**

| | |
|---|---|
| Lord's | †ICC TROPHY FINAL (1 day) |

**Wednesday, July 9**

| | |
|---|---|
| Norwich (Lakenham) | Minor Counties v New Zealanders |

**†NatWest Bank Trophy – Second Round**

| | |
|---|---|
| Southampton or St Albans | Hants or Herts. v Worcs. or Oxon. |
| Taunton or Bournemouth | Somerset or Dorset v Lancs. or Cumb. |
| Reading (Courage) or Bristol | Berks. or Glos. v Leics. or Ireland |
| Exmouth or Trent Bridge | Devon or Notts. v Scotland or Kent |
| Hove or Bury St Edmunds | Sussex or Suffolk v Staffs. or Glam. |
| Edgbaston or Darlington | Warwicks. or Durham v Northumb. or Essex |
| Derby or Truro | Derbys. or Cornwall v Cheshire or Surrey |
| Headingley or Wisbech | Yorks. or Cambs. v Northants or Middx |

**Saturday, July 12**

| | |
|---|---|
| Lord's | BENSON AND HEDGES CUP FINAL (1 day) |
| Scarborough* | Yorks. v Indians |
| Edgbaston (or Old Trafford) | Warwicks. v New Zealanders (or Lancs. if Warwicks. in B & H Cup Final) |

**Wednesday, July 16**

| | |
|---|---|
| Headingley | †ENGLAND v NEW ZEALAND (1st 1-day Texaco Trophy) |
| outhend | Essex v Leics. |
| ath | Glam. v Worcs. |
| tol | Glos. v Sussex |
| Lord's | Middx v Somerset |
| Northampton | Northants v Lancs. |
| Worksop | Notts. v Yorks. |
| The Oval | Surrey v Kent |
| Edgbaston | Warwicks. v Derbys. |

**Friday, July 18**

| | |
|---|---|
| Old Trafford | †ENGLAND v NEW ZEALAND (2nd 1-day Texaco Trophy) |

**Saturday, July 19**

| | |
|---|---|
| Trent Bridge* | Notts. v New Zealanders |
| Derby | Derbys. v Middx |
| Southend | Essex v Worcs. |
| Swansea | Glam. v Northants |
| Bristol | Glos. v Somerset |
| Portsmouth | Hants v Warwicks. |
| Canterbury | Kent v Lancs. |
| Leicester | Leics. v Sussex |
| Headingley* | Yorks. v Surrey |
| Dublin (Castle Avenue) | †Ireland v MCC |

**Wednesday, July 23**

| | |
|---|---|
| Portsmouth | Hants v Derbys. |
| Southport | Lancs. v Notts. |
| Leicester | Leics. v Glam. |
| The Oval | Surrey v Essex |
| Hove | Sussex v Worcs. |
| Scarborough | Yorks. v Kent |

**Thursday, 24 July**

| | |
|---|---|
| Lord's | ENGLAND v NEW ZEALAND (1st Cornhill Test, 5 days) |

**Saturday, 26 July**

| | |
|---|---|
| Abergavenny | Glam. v Derbys. |
| Northampton | Northants v Middx |
| Guildford | Surrey v Sussex |
| Edgbaston | Warwicks. v Lancs. |
| Worcester | Worcs. v Glos. |
| Sheffield | Yorks. v Notts. |

**Wednesday, July 30**

**†NatWest Bank Trophy – Quarter-Finals (1 day)**

**Thursday, July 31**

| | |
|---|---|
| Jesmond | †An England XI v Rest of the World XI (1 day) |

**Friday, August 1**

Jesmond †An England XI v Rest of the World XI (1 day)

**Saturday, August 2**

Derby* Derbys. v New Zealanders
Cheltenham Glos. v Hants
Canterbury Kent v Leics.
Old Trafford Lancs. v Yorks.
Lord's Middx v Northants
Weston-super-Mare Somerset v Worcs.
Eastbourne Sussex v Essex
Headingley* †England Young Cricketers v Sri Lanka Young Cricketers (1st "Test", 4 days)

**Wednesday, August 6**

Chelmsford Essex v Middx
Cheltenham Glos. v Notts.
Canterbury Kent v Hants
Leicester Leics. v Yorks.
Northampton Northants v Glam.
Weston-super-Mare Somerset v Warwicks.
The Oval Surrey v Lancs.
Eastbourne Sussex v Derbys.
Lord's †MCC Schools v NAYC (2 days)

**Thursday, August 7**

Trent Bridge ENGLAND v NEW ZEALAND (2nd Cornhill Test, 5 days)

**Friday, August 8**

Lord's †NCA Young Cricketers v Combined Services (1 day)

**Saturday, August 9**

Buxton Derbys. v Lancs.
Cheltenham Glos. v Middx
Southampton Hants v Sussex
Leicester Leics. v Essex
Wellingborough School Northants v Somerset
The Oval Surrey v Worcs.
Edgbaston Warwicks. v Kent
Bradford Yorks. v Glam.
Chelmsford* †England Young Cricketers v Sri Lanka Young Cricketers (1st 1-day "International")

**Monday, August 11**

Lord's †England Young Cricketers v Sri Lanka Young Cricketers (2nd 1-day "International")

**Wednesday, August 13**

Old Trafford (or Edgbaston) Lancs. v New Zealanders (or Warwicks. if Lancs. in NatWest Bank Semi-Final)

**†NatWest Bank Trophy – Semi-Finals**
(1 day)

**Saturday, August 16**

Swansea* Glam. v New Zealanders
Chesterfield Derbys. v Yorks.
Colchester Essex v Northants
Lord's Middx v Hants
Trent Bridge Notts. v Lancs.
Taunton Somerset v Surrey
Hove Sussex v Kent
Nuneaton (Griff & Coton) Warwicks. v Glos.
Worcester Worcs. v Leics.
Glasgow Scotland v Ireland
Bristol* †England Young Cricketers v Sri Lanka Young Cricketers (2nd "Test", 4 days)

**Wednesday, August 20**

Chesterfield Derbys. v Leics.
Colchester Essex v Glos.
Bournemouth Hants v Worcs.
Dartford Kent v Surrey
Lytham Lancs. v Glam.
Northampton Northants v Notts.
Taunton Somerset v Sussex
Headingley Yorks. v Middx

**Thursday, August 21**

The Oval ENGLAND v NEW ZEALAND (3rd Cornhill Test, 5 days)

**Saturday, August 23**

Chelmsford Essex v Surrey
Cardiff Glam. v Kent
Bournemouth Hants v Yorks.
Old Trafford Lancs. v Glos.
Leicester Leics. v Northants
Trent Bridge Notts. v Derbys.
Hove Sussex v Middx
Worcester Worcs. v Warwicks.

| | |
|---|---|
| Lord's | †National Club Cricket Championship Final (1 day) |

**Sunday, August 24**

| | |
|---|---|
| Lord's | †National Village Cricket Championship Final (1 day) |

**Wednesday, August 27**

| | |
|---|---|
| Swansea | Glam. v Surrey |
| Leicester | Leics. v Derbys. |
| Lord's | Middx v Lancs. |
| Northampton | Northants v Hants |
| Trent Bridge | Notts. v Kent |
| Taunton | Somerset v Essex |
| Edgbaston | Warwicks. v Yorks. |

**Saturday, August 30**

| | |
|---|---|
| Derby | Derbys. v Hants |
| Folkestone | Kent v Essex |
| Leicester | Leics. v Somerset |
| Hove* | Sussex v Notts. |
| Edgbaston | Warwicks. v Middx |
| Trent Bridge* | †England Young Cricketers v Sri Lanka Young Cricketers (3rd "Test", 4 days) |

**Sunday, August 31**

| | |
|---|---|
| Edgbaston | †Warwick Under-25 Final (1 day) |
| Scarborough | D. B. Close's XI v New Zealanders |

**Wednesday, September 3**

| | |
|---|---|
| Derby | Derbys. v Northants |
| Cardiff | Glam. v Notts. |
| Folkestone | Kent v Warwicks. |
| The Oval | Surrey v Glos. |
| Worcester | Worcs. v Somerset |
| Scarborough | †Essex v Lancs. (1 day, Asda Cricket Challenge) |

**Thursday, September 4**

| | |
|---|---|
| Scarborough | †Hants v Yorks. (1 day, Asda Cricket Challenge) |

**Friday, September 5**

| | |
|---|---|
| Scarborough | †Asda Cricket Challenge Final (1 day) |

**Saturday, September 6**

| | |
|---|---|
| Lord's | †NATWEST BANK TROPHY FINAL (1 day) |

**Wednesday, September 10**

| | |
|---|---|
| Old Trafford | Lancs. v Somerset |
| Trent Bridge | Notts. v Essex |
| Hove | Sussex v Hants |
| Worcester | Worcs. v Glam. |
| Scarborough | Yorks. v Northants |

**Saturday, September 13**

| | |
|---|---|
| Chelmsford | Essex v Glam. |
| Bristol | Glos. v Worcs. |
| Southampton | Hants v Lancs. |
| Canterbury | Kent v Middx |
| Trent Bridge | Notts. v Northants |
| Taunton | Somerset v Derbys. |
| The Oval | Surrey v Leics. |
| Edgbaston | Warwicks. v Sussex |

## INDIAN TOUR, 1986

**MAY**

| | |
|---|---|
| 4 Arundel | †v Lavinia, Duchess of Norfolk's XI (1 day) |
| 6 Worcester | v Worcs. |
| 10 Cheltenham Town CC* | v Glos. |
| 15 The Oval | †v Surrey (1 day) |
| 17 Southampton* | v Hants |
| 21 Canterbury | v Kent |
| 24 The Oval | †v ENGLAND (1st 1-day Texaco Trophy) |
| 26 Old Trafford | †v ENGLAND (2nd 1-day Texaco Trophy) |
| Belfast | †v Ireland (1 day) |
| Northampton* | v Northants |

**JUNE**

| | |
|---|---|
| 5 Lord's | v ENGLAND (1st Cornhill Test, 5 days) |
| 12 The Parks | †v Oxford & Cam. U. (2 days) |
| 14 Leicester* | v Leics. |
| 19 Headingley | v ENGLAND (2nd Cornhill Test, 5 days) |
| 26 Chester-le-Street | †v League Cricket Conference (1 day) |
| 28 Taunton* | v Somerset |

**JULY**

| | |
|---|---|
| 3 Edgbaston | v ENGLAND (3rd Cornhill Test, 5 days) |
| 12 Scarborough* | v Yorks. |

## NEW ZEALAND TOUR, 1986

**JUNE**

22 Arundel †v Lavinia, Duchess of Norfolk's XI (1 day)
25 Fenner's v Oxford & Cam. U.
28 Lord's* v Middx

**JULY**

2 Chelmsford v Essex
5 Hove* v Sussex
9 Norwich (Lakenham) v Minor Counties
12 Edgbaston (or Old Trafford) v Warwicks. (or Lancs. if Warwicks in B & H Cup Final)
16 Headingley †v ENGLAND (1st 1-day Texaco Trophy)
18 Old Trafford †v ENGLAND (2nd 1-day Texaco Trophy)
19 Trent Bridge* v Notts.
24 Lord's v ENGLAND (1st Cornhill Test (5 days)

**AUGUST**

2 Derby* v Derbys.
7 Trent Bridge v ENGLAND (2nd Cornhill Test, 5 days)
13 Old Trafford (or Edgbaston) v Lancs. (or Warwicks. if Lancs. in NatWest Bank Semi-Final)
16 Swansea* v Glam.
21 The Oval v ENGLAND (3rd Cornhill Test, 5 days)
31 Scarborough v D. B. Close's XI

## †ICC TROPHY, 1986

**Group A**

Argentina, Bangladesh, Denmark, East Africa, Kenya, Malaysia, Singapore, West Africa and Zimbabwe.

**Group B**

Bermuda, Canada, Fiji, Gibraltar, Hong Kong, Israel, The Netherlands, Papua New Guinea and USA.

**Wednesday, June 11**

Zimbabawe v Bangladesh (Moseley CC); West Africa v Kenya (Banbury XX CC); Argentina v Denmark (Kenilworth CC); Malaysia v East Africa (Burton CC); USA v Canada (Hinckley CC); Papua NG v The Netherlands (Wolverhampton CC); Bermuda v Fiji (Wellington CC); Hong Kong v Gibraltar (Bridgnorth CC).

**Friday, June 13**

Zimbabwe v West Africa (Water Orton CC); Bangladesh v Kenya (Wednesbury CC); Argentina v Malaysia (Studley CC); Denmark v Singapore (Bedworth CC); USA v Papua NG (Market Harborough CC); Canada v The Netherlands (Cheltenham CC); Bermuda v Hong Kong (Griff & Coton CC); Fiji v Israel Birmingham Municipal CC).

**Monday, June 16**

Zimbabwe v Kenya (Sutton Coldfield CC); Bangladesh v West Africa (Bromsgrove CC); Argentina v Singapore (Wombourne CC); Denmark v East Africa (Old Edwardians CC); USA v The Netherlands (Solihull CC); Canada v Papua NG (Walsall CC); Bermuda v Israel (Aldridge CC); Fiji v Gibraltar (Banbury CC).

**Wednesday, June 18**

Zimbabwe v Argentina (Fordhouses CC); Bangladesh v Malaysia (Moseley Ashfield CC); West Africa v East Africa (Brewood CC); Kenya v Singapore (Stafford CC); Canada v Hong Kong (Halesowen CC); Papua NG v Gibraltar (Cannock & Rugeley CC); The Netherlands v Israel (Old Silhillians CC); USA v Bermuda (Stratford-upon-Avon CC).

**Friday, June 20**

Zimbabwe v Denmark (Kidderminster CC); Bangladesh v East Africa (Coventry & North Warwick CC); West Africa v Singapore (Wightwick CC); Kenya v Malaysia (Allied Breweries CC); USA v Fiji (Blossomfield CC); Canada v Gibraltar (Swindon [Wilts.] CC); Papua NG v Israel (Worcester City CC); The Netherlands v Hong Kong (Wroxeter & Uppington CC).

**Monday, June 23**

Zimbabwe v Malaysia (Egerton Park CC); Bangladesh v Singapore (Lichfield CC); Denmark v West Africa (Alvechurch CC); Argentina v East Africa (Stourbridge CC); USA v Hong Kong (Leamington CC); Canada v Israel (Shrewsbury CC); Papua NG v Fiji (Old Hill CC); Bermuda v Gibraltar (Aston Unity CC).

**Wednesday, June 25**

Zimbabwe v East Africa (Nantwich CC); Bangladesh v Argentina (Hereford CC); Kenya v Denmark (Kenilworth Wardens CC); Malaysia v Singapore (Harborne CC); USA v Gibraltar (Aston Manor CC); Canada v Bermuda (Bournville CC); The Netherlands v Fiji (Gloucester City CC); Hong Kong v Israel (Barnt Green CC).

**Friday, June 27**

Zimbabwe v Singapore (Northampton Saints CC); West Africa v Argentina (Pickwick CC); Kenya v East Africa (Tamworth CC); Denmark v Malaysia (Bewdley CC); USA v Israel (Solihull Municipal CC); Papua NG v Bermuda (Nuneaton CC); The Netherlands v Gibraltar (Wellesbourne CC); Fiji v Hong Kong (Knowle & Dorridge CC).

**Monday, June 30**

Bangladesh v Denmark (Colwall CC); West Africa v Malaysia (Wishaw CC); Kenya v Argentina (Walmley CC); East Africa v Singapore (Streetly CC); Canada v Fiji (Kings Heath CC); Papua NG v Hong Kong (Olton & West Warwicks CC); The Netherlands v Bermuda (Smethwick CC); Gibraltar v Israel (Warwick CC).

**Wednesday, July 2**

**Semi-Finals:** at West Bromwich Dartmouth CC and Mitchells & Butlers CC.

**Friday, July 4**

**Third place play-off:** at Halesowen CC.

**Monday, July 7**

**Final:** at Lord's.

## †JOHN PLAYER SUNDAY LEAGUE, 1986

**MAY**

**4**–Essex v Warwicks. (Chelmsford); Glam. v Hants (Cardiff); Kent v Glos. (Canterbury); Lancs. v Sussex (Old Trafford); Leics. v Derbys. (Leicester); Middx v Notts. (Lord's); Yorks. v Somerset (Bradford).

**11**–Derbys. v Sussex (Derby); Glam. v Leics. (Swansea); Hants. v Northants (Southampton); Notts. v Warwicks. (Trent Bridge); Somerset v Middx (Taunton); Surrey v Yorks. (The Oval); Worcs. v Kent (Worcester).

**18**–Derbys. v Warwicks. (Leek CC); Glos. v Essex (Swindon); Leics. v Lancs. (Leicester); Middx v Kent (Lord's); Notts. v Sussex (Trent Bridge); Surrey v Glam. (The Oval); Yorks. v Worcs. (Headingley).

**25**–Glam. v Somerset (Cardiff); Kent v Surrey (Canterbury); Northants v Leics. (Northampton); Sussex v Glos. (Hove); Warwicks. v Worcs. (Edgbaston); Yorks. v Essex (Sheffield).

**JUNE**

**1**–Derbys. v Essex (Derby); Hants v Notts. (Southampton); Lancs. v Warwicks. (Old Trafford); Leics. v Glos. (Leicester); Surrey v Middx (The Oval); Sussex v Somerset (Horsham).

**8**–Essex v Notts. (Chelmsford); Lancs. v Middx (Old Trafford); Northants v Worcs. (Northampton); Surrey v Derbys. (The Oval); Warwicks. v Glam. (Edgbaston); Yorks. v Glos. (Headingley).

**15**–Essex v Hants (Ilford); Glos. v Derbys. (Gloucester); Lancs. v Worcs. (Old Trafford); Middx v Yorks. (Lord's); Northants v Warwicks. (Northampton); Notts. v Surrey (Trent Bridge); Somerset v Kent (Bath).

**22**–Glam. v Lancs. (Swansea); Hants v Kent (Basingstoke); Middx v Essex (Lord's); Northants v Yorks. (Luton); Somerset v Notts. (Bath); Warwicks. v Leics. (Edgbaston); Worcs. v Sussex (Worcester).

**29**–Glos. v Surrey (Bristol); Kent v Glam. (Maidstone); Leics. v Notts. (Leicester); Sussex v Northants (Hastings); Worcs. v Hants (Worcester).

**JULY**

**6**–Derbys. v Kent (Derby); Glam. v Glos. (Cardiff); Lancs. v Essex (Old Trafford); Middx v Warwicks. (Lord's); Northants v Surrey (Tring); Somerset v Hants (Taunton); Worcs. v Notts. (Worcester); Yorks. v Leics. (Middlesbrough).

**13**–Essex v Somerset (Chelmsford); Leics. v Middx (Leicester); Northants v Derbys. (Finedon); Notts. v Glos. (Trent Bridge); Sussex v Glam. (Hove).

**20**–Derbys. v Middx (Derby); Essex v Worcs. (Southend); Glam. v Northants (Neath); Glos. v Somerset (Bristol); Hants v Warwicks. (Portsmouth); Kent v Lancs. (Canterbury); Leics. v Sussex (Leicester).

**27**–Glam. v Derbys. (Ebbw Vale); Hants v Leics. (Southampton); Northants v Kent (Northampton); Somerset v Lancs. (Taunton); Surrey v Sussex (Guildford); Worcs. v Glos. (Hereford); Yorks. v Notts. (Hull or Scarborough).

**AUGUST**

**3**–Glos. v Hants (Cheltenham); Kent v Leics. (Canterbury); Lancs. v Yorks. (Old Trafford); Middx v Northants (Lord's); Notts. v Glam. (Trent Bridge); Somerset v Worcs. (Weston-super-Mare; Sussex v Essex (Eastbourne); Warwicks. v Surrey (Edgbaston).

**10**–Derbys. v Lancs. (Buxton); Glos. v Middx (Cheltenham); Hants. v Sussex (Bournemouth); Leics. v Essex (Leicester); Northants v Somerset (Wellingborough School); Surrey v Worcs. (The Oval); Warwicks. v Kent (Edgbaston); Yorks. v Glam. (Scarborough).

**17**–Derbys. v Yorks. (Chesterfield); Essex v Northants (Colchester); Middx v Hants (Lord's); Notts. v Lancs. (Trent Bridge); Somerset v Surrey (Taunton); Sussex v Kent (Hove); Warwicks. v Glos. (Edgbaston); Worcs. v Leics. (Worcester).

**24**–Essex v Surrey (Chelmsford); Hants v Yorks. (Bournemouth); Lancs. v Northants (Old Trafford); Notts. v Derbys. (Trent Bridge); Sussex v Middx (Hove); Warwicks. v Somerset (Edgbaston); Worcs. v Glam. (Worcester).

**31**–Derbys. v Hants (Heanor); Glos. v Northants (Moreton in Marsh); Kent v Essex (Folkestone); Lancs. v Surrey (Old Trafford); Leics. v Somerset (Leicester); Middx v Worcs. (Lord's); Yorks. v Warwicks. (Headingley).

**SEPTEMBER**

**7**–Glam. v Middx (Cardiff); Glos. v Lancs. (Bristol); Kent v Notts. (Canterbury); Surrey v Hants (The Oval); Sussex v Yorks. (Hove); Worcs. v Derbys. (Worcester).

**14**–Essex v Glam. (Chelmsford); Hants v Lancs. (Southampton); Kent v Yorks. (Canterbury); Notts. v Northants (Trent Bridge); Somerset v Derbys. (Taunton); Surrey v Leics. (The Oval); Warwicks. v Sussex (Edgbaston).

## †MINOR COUNTIES' CHAMPIONSHIP, 1986

*All matches are of two days' duration.*

**MAY**

**25**–Lincs. v Beds. (Sleaford); Northumb. v Herts. (Jesmond).

**26**–Berks. v Bucks. (Falkland CC, Newbury); Dorset v Wilts. (Sherborne School).

**27**–Cumb. v Herts. (Netherfield, Kendal); Durham v Beds. (Hartlepool); Northumb. v Suffolk (Jesmond).

**29**–Cumb. v Suffolk (Carlisle); Staffs. v Herts. (Burton upon Trent).

**JUNE**

**1**–Cheshire v Salop. (Nantwich).

**4**–Cambs. v Staffs. (Wisbech).

**9**–Durham v Lincs. (Stockton).

**15**–Beds. v Cumb. (Henlow); Herts. v Norfolk (Watford); Oxon. v Wilts. (Morris Motors).

**16**–Cornwall v Cheshire (Truro); Devon v Salop. (Bovey Tracey); Northumb. v Staffs. (Jesmond).

**17**–Beds. v Norfolk (Dunstable); Cambs. v Cumb. (Peterborough).

**18**–Cornwall v Salop. (Falmouth); Devon v Cheshire (Sidmouth); Durham v Staffs. (Darlington).

**29**–Dorset v Berks. (Sherborne School); Durham v Cumb. (Chester-le-Street); Herts. v Lincs. (St Albans); Salop. v Bucks. (Bridgnorth); Somerset II v Wilts. (Frome CC).

**JULY**

**1**–Cheshire v Bucks. (Oxton, Birkenhead).

**6**–Berks. v Oxon. (Bradfield College); Cornwall v Somerset II (St Austell); Lincs. v Cambs. (Burghley Park).

**13**–Beds. v Herts (Southill Park); Bucks. v Somerset II (Bletchley Town); Cheshire v Berks. (Bowdon); Oxon. v Cornwall (St Edward's School); Staffs. v Norfolk (Leek).

**15**–Beds. v Cambs. (Wardown Park); Cumb. v Norfolk (Kendal); Salop. v Berks. (Wellington); Wilts. v Cornwall (Devizes).

**16**–Devon v Somerset II (Exmouth).

**17**–Cambs. v Suffolk (Fenner's).

**20**–Lincs. v Staffs. (Lincoln Lindum); Oxon. v Somerset II (Banbury XX).

**21**–Bucks. v Cornwall (High Wycombe); Dorset v Devon (Dorchester); Herts. v Suffolk (Bishop's Stortford).

**23**–Berks. v Cornwall (Finchampstead).

**24**–Bucks. v Dorset (Slough); Suffolk v Norfolk (Ipswich School).

**[illegible]7**–Berks. v Somerset II (Kidmore End); Dorset v Cheshire (Sherborne School); [illegible]ncs. v Northumb. (Ross, Grimsby); [illegible]fs. v Cumb. (Stone).

**29**–Norfolk v Northumb. (Lakenham); Oxon. v Devon (Christ Church); Somerset II v Cheshire (Victoria Club, Street), Wilts. v Berks. (Swindon).

**31**–Norfolk v Cambs. (Lakenham); Wilts. v Devon (Trowbridge).

**AUGUST**

**3**–Staffs. v Beds. (Knypersley).

**4**–Norfolk v Lincs. (Lakenham); Somerset II v Salop. (Taunton); Suffolk v Durham (Mildenhall).

**6**–Cambs. v Herts. (Fenner's); Dorset v Salop. (Dean Park); Norfolk v Durham (Lakenham).

**10**–Beds. v Northumb. (Goldington Bury, Bedford); Cheshire v Oxon. (Boughton Hall, Chester); Cornwall v Dorset (Wadebridge); Cumb. v Lincs. (Barrow).

**11**–Bucks. v Devon (Marlow).

**12**–Cambs. v Northumb. (March); Salop. v Oxon. (Shrewsbury).

**13**–Berks. v Devon (Reading CC); Staffs. v Suffolk (Brewood); Wilts. v Bucks. (Chippenham).

**17**–Cheshire v Wilts. (Toft); Cumb. v Northumb. (Millom); Oxon. v Dorset (Christ Church).

**18**–Durham v Cambs. (Gateshead Fell); Suffolk v Lincs. (Bury St Edmunds).

**19**–Salop. v Wilts. (Newport).

**20**–Devon v Cornwall (Torquay).

**21**–Herts. v Durham (Letchworth).

**24**–Bucks. v Oxon. (Amersham); Suffolk v Beds. (Ransome's, Ipswich).

**25**–Somerset II v Dorset (Taunton).

**26**–Northumb. v Durham (Jesmond).

**SEPTEMBER**

**13**–Final Play-off (1 day) (Worcester). The composition of the Eastern and Western Divisions may be found on page 783.

# †MINOR COUNTIES' KNOCKOUT COMPETITION, 1986

*All matches are of one day's duration.*

### Qualifying Round

**May 25** Cambs. v Norfolk (Trinity, Cambridge); Cumb. v Cheshire (Penrith); Staffs. v Bucks. (Longton).

### First Round

**June 8** Berks. v Staffs. or Bucks. (Bracknell); Cambs. or Norfolk v Suffolk (Trinity, Cambridge or Horsford); Cumb. or Cheshire v Durham (Workington or Warrington); Devon v Cornwall (Bovey Tracey); Dorset v Wilts. (Sherborne School); Herts. v Beds. (Potters Bar); Northumb. v Lincs (Jesmond); Oxon. v Salop. (Christ Church).

**Quarter-finals** to be played on June 22.

**Semi-finals** to be played on July 6.

**Final** to be played on July 20.

# †SECOND ELEVEN CHAMPIONSHIP, 1986

*All matches are of three days' duration.*

### APRIL

**30**–Kent v Lancs. (Cheriton Rd, Folkestone); Yorks. v Glam. (Headingley).

### MAY

**7**–Derbys. v Northants (Ilkeston); Glos. v Somerset (Bristol); Warwicks. v Lancs. (Edgbaston).

**14**–Essex v Surrey (Chalkwell Park, Westcliff); Glam. v Somerset (Cardiff); Hants v Glos. (Bournemouth); Kent v Sussex (Maidstone); Leics. v Lancs. (Lutterworth); Notts. v Yorks. (Shireoaks).

**21**–Derbys. v Lancs. (Chesterfield); Glam. v Warwicks. (Swansea); Hants v Surrey (Southampton); Middx v Kent (Watford Town CC); Sussex v Notts. (Eastbourne); Yorks. v Northants (Bradford).

**28**–Derbys. v Worcs. (Bass, Burton upon Trent); Glam. v Glos. (Cardiff); Kent v Essex (Bowaters, Sittingbourne); Lancs. v Notts. (Ramsbottom CC); Middx v Northants (Harefield); Surrey v Hants (Guildford); Yorks. v Warwicks. (Hull).

### JUNE

**4**–Derbys. v Yorks. (Chesterfield); Essex v Northants (Valentine's Park, Ilford); Kent v Hants (Canterbury); Lancs. v Warwicks. (Preston); Notts. v Leics. (Worksop); Surrey v Glam. (The Oval); Worcs. v Somerset (Kidderminster).

**11**–Lancs. v Yorks. (Northern CC, Crosby); Northants v Middx (Old Northamptonians CC); Notts. v Derbys. (Collingham); Somerset v Glos. (Weston-super-Mare); Sussex v Essex (Eastbourne); Surrey v Kent (Guildford); Warwicks. v Leics. (Knowle & Dorridge CC).

**18**–Derbys. v Notts. (Derby); Kent v Yorks. (Canterbury); Lancs. v Leics. (Old Trafford); Northants v Essex (Overstone Park CC); Somerset v Worcs. (Taunton); Surrey v Middx (The Oval); Sussex v Hants (Arundel); Warwicks. v Glam. (Leamington CC).

**25**–Glos. v Glam. (Lydney); Hants v Kent (Bournemouth); Notts. v Lancs. (Worthington Simpson); Leics. v Northants (Lutterworth); Sussex v Middx (Horsham); Warwicks. v Worcs. (Griff & Coton, Nuneaton); Yorks. v Surrey (Elland).

### JULY

**2**–Kent v Middx (Canterbury); Lancs. v Somerset (Old Trafford); Northants v Derbys. (Woughton or Milton Keynes); Surrey v Essex (The Oval); Worcs. v Glos. (Kidderminster); Yorks. v Notts. (York).

**9**–Essex v Sussex (Chelmsford); Lancs. v Glam. (Old Trafford); Leics. v Notts. (Leicester); Middx v Hants (Lensbury CC); Northants v Yorks. (Northampton); Warwicks. v Somerset (Studley CC); Worcs. v Derbys. (Worcester).

**16**–Hants v Essex (Southampton); Northants v Leics. (Wellingborough School); Notts. v Glam. (Caythorpe); Sussex v Kent (Hastings); Surrey v Lancs. (Purley CC); Warwicks. v Glos. (Olton CC); Yorks. v Derbys. (Barnsley).

**23**–Derbys. v Glos. (Shipley CC); Essex v Notts. (Romford); Kent v Surrey (Canterbury); Middx v Warwicks. (South Hampstead CC); Northants v Lancs. (Overstone Park CC); Somerset v Hants (Yeovil).

**30**–Essex v Kent (Southchurch Park, Southend); Glam. v Yorks. (Swansea); Glos. v Warwicks. (Bristol); Lancs. v Derbys. (Heywood); Middx v Sussex (Harrow CC); Northants v Notts. (Peterborough); Surrey v Leics. (Banstead CC).

### AUGUST

**6**–Derbys. v Leics. (Derby); Glos. v Hants (Bristol); Middx v Surrey (Enfield CC); Notts. v Northants (Worthington Simpson, Newark); Somerset v Glam. (Bristol Imperial Athletic Ground); Sussex v Surrey (Hastings); Worcs. v Warwicks. (Worcester); Yorks. v Kent (Harrogate).

**13**–Sussex v Surrey (Hastings); Warwicks. v Middx (Moseley CC); Yorks. v Lancs. (Marske).

**20**–Glam. v Kent (Ebbw Vale); Glos. v Worcs. (Bristol); Hants v Sussex (Southampton); Leics. v Derbys. (Hinckley); Lancs. v Northants (Middleton CC); Middx v Essex (Harefield); Notts. v Warwicks. (Steetley); Surrey v Yorks. (Banstead CC).

**27**–Essex v Glos. (Chelmsford); Glam. v Notts. (Cardiff); Hants v Middx (Southampton); Lancs. v Surrey (Old Trafford); Sussex v Warwicks. (Eastbourne).

### SEPTEMBER

**3**–Essex v Middx (Chelmsford); Glos. v Derbys. (Bristol); Hants v Somerset (Southampton); Lancs. v Kent (Old Trafford); Warwicks. v Yorks. (Edgbaston).

**10**–Surrey v Sussex (The Oval).

## †WARWICK UNDER-25 COMPETITION, 1986

*All matches are of one day's duration.*

### APRIL

**30**–Somerset v Warwicks. (Taunton).

### MAY

**1**–Warwicks. v Somerset (Edgbaston).

**5**–Warwicks. v Worcs. (Edgbaston).

**12**–Warwicks. v Glos. (Edgbaston).

**13**–Kent v Hants (Maidstone).

**19**–Glos. v Somerset (Bristol); Middx v Northants (St Albans CC); Surrey v Hants (Purley CC); Worcs. v Warwicks. (Worcester).

**20**–Essex v Leics. (Wanstead CC); Glos. v Warwicks. (Bristol).

**27**–Essex v Middx (Metropolitan Police, Chigwell); Leics. v Northants (Leicester).

### JUNE

**2**–Somerset v Glos. (Taunton).

**9**–Leics. v Essex (Leicester); Sussex v Surrey (Arundel).

**10**–Glam. v Warwicks. (Tba).

**16**–Essex v Northants (Chelmsford); Worcs. v Somerset (Worcester); Yorks. v Derbys. (Huddersfield).

**17**–Hants v Surrey (Southampton); Leics. v Middx (Leicester); Notts. v Yorks. (Worksop College); Warwicks. v Glam. (Edgbaston).

**23**–Northants v Leics. (Great Oakley, Corby); Sussex v Hants (Arundel).

**24**–Hants v Kent (Bournemouth); Notts. v Derbys. (Trent Bridge).

**30**–Lancs. v Notts. (Old Trafford); Northants v Essex (Uppingham School); Surrey v Sussex (The Oval).

**JULY**

**1**–Kent v Surrey (Canterbury); Lancs. v Derbys. (Old Trafford); Northants v Middx (Northampton).

**7**–Derbys. v Yorks. (Heanor); Hants v Sussex (Southampton); Middx v Leics. (Ealing); Notts. v Lancs. (Trent Bridge).

**8**–Derbys. v Notts. (Heanor); Kent v Sussex (Tonbridge School); Yorks. v Lancs. (Doncaster).

**14**–Sussex v Kent (Hove).

**15**–Derbys. v Lancs. (Heanor).

**18**–Somerset v Worcs. (Taunton).

**21**–Lancs. v Yorks. (Old Trafford); Surrey v Kent (The Oval).

**22**–Middx v Essex (Winchmore Hill); Yorks. v Notts. (Bradford).

**AUGUST**

**31**–FINAL (Edgbaston).

## †BAIN DAWES 55-OVER COMPETITION

*All matches are of one day's duration.*

**MAY**

**2**–Warwicks. v Somerset (Edgbaston).

**5**–Leics. v Northants (Leicester).

**6**–Notts. v Leics. (Trent Bridge).

**13**–Leics. v Lancs. (Leicester).

**19**–Sussex v Kent (Hastings).

**20**–Derbys. v Lancs. (Chesterfield).

**26**–Surrey v Sussex (The Oval).

**27**–Lancs. v Notts. (Haslingden CC).

**JUNE**

**2**–Essex v Sussex (Chelmsford); Middx v Kent (Ealing).

**3**–Kent v Hants (Canterbury); Notts. v Yorks. (Thoresby Park); Sussex v Middx (Hove).

**9**–Derbys. v Northants (Derby); Lancs. v Yorks. (Aigburth, Liverpool); Somerset v Glam. (Taunton); Worcs. v Warwicks. (Worcester).

**10**–Glos. v Worcs. (Bristol).

**16**–Kent v Surrey (Bowaters, Sittingbourne); Glam. v Glos. (Gorseinon).

**23**–Kent v Essex (Bowaters, Sittingbourne); Glos. v Somerset (Bristol); Yorks. v Derbys. (Elland).

**24**–Northants v Lancs. (Uppingham School).

**30**–Yorks. v Leics. (Sheffield).

**JULY**

**1**–Hants v Sussex (Southampton).

**8**–Essex v Surrey (Metropolitan Police, Chigwell).

**14**–Derbys. v Leics. (Heanor); Notts. v Northants (Thoresby Park); Surrey v Middx (The Oval).

**15**–Hants v Essex (Southampton); Northants v Yorks. (Northampton).

**21**–Middx v Hants (Harefield); Warwicks. v Glam. (Usk CC).

**22**–Warwicks. v Glos. (Edgbaston).

**28**–Hants v Surrey (Bournemouth).

**29**–Middx v Essex (Enfield); Notts. v Derbys. (Caythorpe).

**SEPTEMBER**

**8**–FINAL.

## LORDS AND COMMONS CRICKET, 1985

With twelve of their fourteen fixtures completed, the Lords and Commons were luckier with the weather than many. They won three matches, drew two and lost seven. Despite the perennial problem caused by the electors' seeming unwillingness to send bowlers to Parliament, many of the defeats were close ones. There were two highlights of the season – a rare victory over Eton Ramblers (although it has to be admitted that the result of the toss had to be overruled at the whim of the Whips) and the first century by an MP (Lt Col. Michael Mates, the Conservative member for Petersfield).

ACAS 84; Lords and Commons 86 for five.
Lords and Commons 177; St Paul's School 181 for three.
Birkbeck College 211 for four; Lords and Commons 89 for eight.
Conservative Agents 227 for eight; Lords and Commons 230 for eight.
BBC 177 for two; Lords and Commons 86.
Guards CC 206 for four; Lords and Commons 189 for nine.
Dutch Parliament 217 for nine; Lords and Commons 215.
MCC 241 for six; Lords and Commons 209.
Eton Ramblers 150; Lords and Commons 151 for nine.
Old Westminsters 203; Lords and Commons 157.
Lords and Commons 127; Law Society 128 for seven.
Lords and Commons 133; Harrow Wanderers 134 for two.

---

## ERRATA IN WISDEN, 1983

Page 70 Cyril and Robert Christiani did not play for the Port Mourant club as stated. They both played for the British Guyana Cricket Club in Georgetown.
Robert Wight (not White), a nephew of C. V. Wight, bought Alvin Kallicharran his kit and provided him with work.

## WISDEN, 1984

Page 80 In the summary of Zaheer Abbas's 100 hundreds, 55 (not 54) were scored in England and seven (not eight) in Australia.

Page 401 In the match Gloucestershire v Nottinghamshire, K. E. Cooper was not out 18 (not retired hurt).

Page 741 In the match Middlesex v Leicestershire, N. G. B. Cook was caught by Radley (not Briers).

## WISDEN, 1985

Page 255 In the entry for 1876, W. G. Grace scored 177 (not 127) v Nottinghamshire.

Page 466 In the match Leicestershire v Sussex, P. B. Clift was caught by Gould (not Barclay) in Leicestershire's second innings.

Page 488 I. J. Gould 68 (not 67) dismissals – 62 ct, 6 st. J. R. T. Barclay 21 (not 22) catches.

Page 713 In the match Derbyshire v Sussex, K. J. Barnett was caught by Reeve (not Barclay).

Page 844 G. E. Edwards of Alleyn's School returned five for 1 v Royal Russell (not Wilson's).

Page 1137 A correspondent writes: "Whilst perusing the 1985 *Wisden*, I saw the quotation you have included, made by Robert Mugabe, whom you call the president of Zimbabwe. It is an excellent quotation, but unfortunately (for whom, I know not) Mr Mugabe is the prime minister. The president is a man called Canaan Banana, a man not taken by our summer game, but by association football. I am sure Mr Banana is used to people slipping up on Zimbabwe's unAfrican role of the president."